The Human Evolution Source Book

RUSSELL L. CIOCHON

The University of Iowa

JOHN G. FLEAGLE

State University of New York, Stony Brook

Advances in Human Evolution Series

Prentice Hall
Englewood Cliffs, New Jersey, 07632

Library of Congress Cataloging-in-Publication Data

The Human evolution source book / [edited by] Russell L. Ciochon, John G. Fleagle
    p.   cm. —(Advances in human evolution series)
   Included bibliographical references.
   ISBN 0-13-446097-9
   1. Human evolution. I. Ciochon, Russell L. II. Fleagle, John G. III. Series.
GN281.H8475   1993
573.2—dc20

                                              91–45200
                                              CIP

Acquisition Editor: Nancy Roberts
Editorial Assistant: Pat Naturale
Prepress Buyer: Kelly Behr
Manufacturing Buyer: Marianne Gloriande
Cover Designer: Marianne Frasco
Cover Photograph Courtesy of Milford Wolpoff
Production Editor: Patrick Walsh

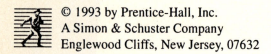
Printed in the United States of America

10 9 8 7 6 5 4 3

ISBN 0-13-446097-9

Prentice-Hall International, (UK) Limited, *London*
Prentice-Hall of Australia Pty. Limited, *Sydney*
Prentice-Hall Canada, Inc., *Toronto*
Prentice-Hall Hispanoamericana, S.A., *Mexico*
Prentice-Hall of India Private Limited, *New Delhi*
Prentice-Hall of Japan, Inc., *Tokyo*
Simon & Schuster Asia Pte. Ltd., *Singapore*
Editora Prentice-Hall do Brasil, Ltda., *Rio de Janeiro*

Contents

Part IV   Origins of the Genus *Homo* and the Emergence of Culture   289

Part V   Evolution of *Homo erectus*   348

Part VI   Evolution of *Homo sapiens*   423

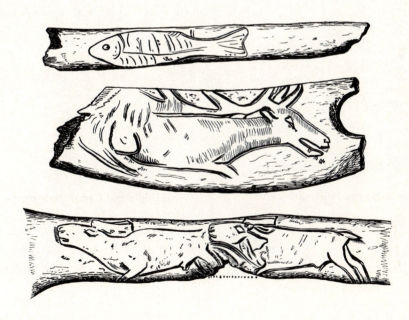

About the Authors

RUSSELL L. CIOCHON is Associate Professor of Anthropology and Pediatric Dentistry at the University of Iowa. He is the author of numerous research papers and four books, among them *New Interpretations of Ape and Human Ancestry* (edited jointly with Robert Corruccini) and *OTHER ORIGINS: The Search for the Giant Ape in Human Prehistory* (with John Olsen and Jamie James). Prof. Ciochon has also organized paleoanthropological field projects to Burma, India, China, Cambodia and Vietnam.

He is editor of **Advances in Human Evolution**, a new series of texts and monographs from Prentice Hall.

JOHN G. FLEAGLE is Professor of Anatomical Sciences and Anthropology at the State University of New York, Stony Brook. He has published nearly one hundred research papers on many aspects of primate evolution and comparative anatomy and four books, including *Primate Evolution and Human Origins* (edited jointly with Russell Ciochon) and *Primate Adaptation and Evolution*. Prof. Fleagle has organized numerous primatological field projects in Asia, Africa and South America. He is a member of the Sciences and Grants Committee of the L. S. B. Leakey Foundation, a Guggenheim Fellow and a MacArthur Fellow.

Reconstruction of the early Miocene site of Rusinga Island, Kenya, showing the diversity of fossil apes.

Preface

The fossil record of human evolution continues to grow at a steady pace. As new fossils are described and interpreted, new theoretical frameworks often emerge to explain the course of human evolution. This has been the basis for our understanding of human ancestry since the first discovery of fossil hominids in the middle 19th Century. Recently, new breakthroughs in interpreting evolution at the biomolecular level along with the development of more precise dating techniques of the fossils themselves has greatly contributed to our comprehension of the human career.

To provide a basis for understanding the recent development of human evolutionary thought we have assembled a collection of articles taken from the past 40 years of paleo-anthropological research (1952–1992). This collection is designed for use by students in anthropology, paleontology and evolutionary biology. *The Human Evolution Source Book* brings together the major ideas and publications on human evolution from the past four decades to provide the reader with an opportunity to examine the original articles which have shaped the development of this exciting and often controversial field.

The Human Evolution Source Book is divided into eight parts that survey the entire scope of human evolutionary inquiry with particular emphasis on the fossil record including several key archaeological studies. In each of the eight parts we present articles that highlight the major interpretations of the human paleontological record that have been influential over the last four decades. These articles are often ordered chronologically within each section to show how the debates and opinions on human evolution emerged. Each part is preceded by an editorial introduction to assist the reader in focusing on the major issues being debated and their changes through time. The articles selected range from short notes to relatively longer review papers with both scientific merit and readibility being major criteria for selection. A total of 60 chapters have been included in *The Human Evolution Source Book* along with a detailed glossary of key terms used throughout the text.

Part I, Biomolecular, Anatomical and Geological Background, presents the biomolecular, comparative anatomical and chronometric basis for interpreting the position of the human lineage within the hominoid family tree and for understanding the order of development of the anatomical features which distinguish humans from all living primates. **Part II, *Australopithecus* and Hominid Origins**, documents the early record of fossil hominids, their adaptive diversity, and phylogenetic relationships. **Part III, Theoretical Perspectives of Hominid Origins**, discusses the theoretical underpinnings of the hominid narrative framework. **Part IV, Origin of the Genus *Homo* and the Emergence Of Culture**, summarizes the earliest evidence of the genus *Homo* and the first appearance of stone tools in the fossil record. **Part V, Evolution of *Homo erectus***, provides an overview of our direct progenitor, *Homo erectus*, from its first discovery to the recent recovery of the earliest and most complete remains of the species. **Part VI, Evolution of *Homo sapiens***, opens with the controversial issue of how to decipher species in the fossil record and follows with a survey of various models for the evolution of anatomically modern *Homo sapiens*. **Part VII, The Neandertal Question and the Emergence of Modern Humans**, presents an historical review on the placement of neandertals in human evolution from anatomical, archaeological and cultural perspectives. **Part VIII, Concepts of Race and the Development of Modern Peoples**, reviews the changing concepts in our understanding of race in modern human populations and deals with the issue of the origin of modern human groups and the first evidence for the development of symbolic thought in humans.

This volume represents many thousands of hours of preparation since all of the text was scanned and formatted on personal computers at the University of Iowa and at SUNY Stony Brook. Numerous students and staff members helped along the way. We can acknowledge only a few here especially Maria Cole, Laurel Davies, Nhan Le, Julie McCarty, Elizabeth Ramsey, Kaye Reed, Stacey Hoff, Brigitte Holt, Erica Van Ostrand, and Shana Vong. At Prentice-Hall we thank our editor Nancy Roberts for giving us the latitude to produce a comprehensive reader/text on human evolution that is much longer than any of us expected. Nature artist Luci Betti at SUNY Stony Brook drew the frontis maps and many vignettes. For financial support during the preparation of this volume we acknowledge the L. S. B. Leakey Foundation, the National Geographic Society, the NIH Biomedical Research Support Grant program, the UI Faculty Scholar Program, the Carver Scientific Research Initiative Grants Program, and the MacArthur Foundation. We also thank all of our paleoanthropological colleagues for allowing us to generously reprint their research in this volume. We hope we have faithfully represented their views. Finally, we wish to note that the order of names on the title page and preface of this work was determined alphabetically.

Russell L. Ciochon
John G. Fleagle

HUMAN EVOLUTION TIME SCALE

Time M Yrs ago	Epochs	Paleomagnetic Chronology	
		Chrons	Events
1	PLEISTOCENE	BRUNHES (normal)	
		MATUYAMA (reversed)	Jaramillo
2			Olduvai
			Reunion
3	PLIOCENE	GAUSS (normal)	Kaena
			Mammoth
4		GILBERT (reversed)	Cochiti
			Nunivak
			Sidufjall
5			Thvera
5	Miocene	Hominoid Radiation	
25	Oligocene	Early Anthropoids	
50	Eocene	Prosimian Radiation	
	Paleocene	Plesiadapiform Radiation	

Glaciation Sequence		Time K Yrs ago	Temp. cold — warm	Oxygen Isotope Stages
Alpine	New			
Holocene	Present Interglaciation	10		1
Wurm IV		20		2
Wurm III/IV				
Wurm III		30		
Wurm II/III	Last Glaciation	40		3
		50		
Wurm II		60		
		70		4
Wurm I/II	Last Interglaciation	80		5a
				5b
Wurm I		90		5c
				5d
Riss/Wurm		100		5e
Riss	Penultimate Glaciation	200		6
Mindel-Riss		300		
Mindel		400		
Gunz-Mindel				
Gunz		500		

Australopithecine Sites

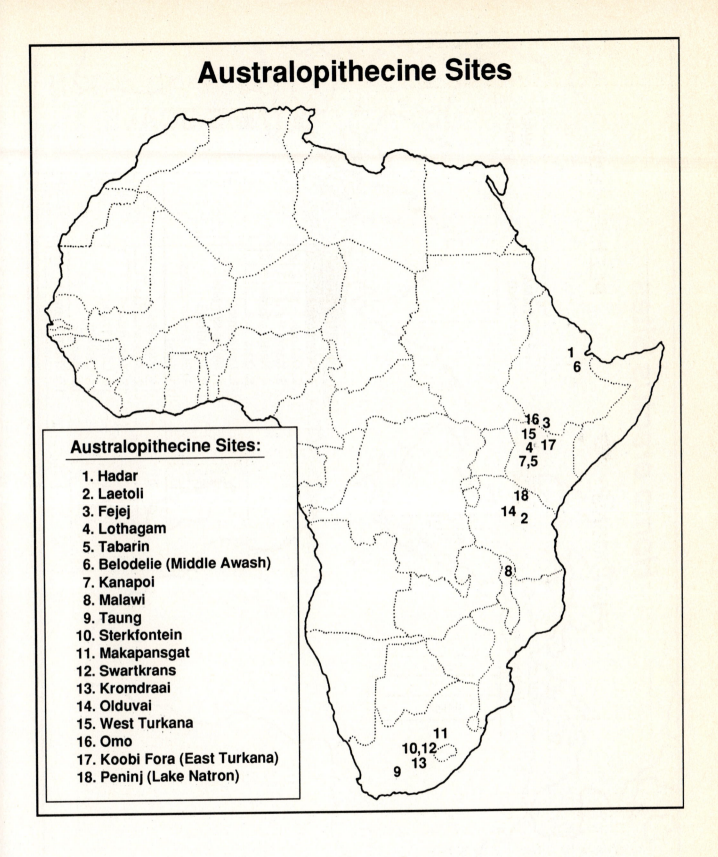

Australopithecine Sites:

1. Hadar
2. Laetoli
3. Fejej
4. Lothagam
5. Tabarin
6. Belodelie (Middle Awash)
7. Kanapoi
8. Malawi
9. Taung
10. Sterkfontein
11. Makapansgat
12. Swartkrans
13. Kromdraai
14. Olduvai
15. West Turkana
16. Omo
17. Koobi Fora (East Turkana)
18. Peninj (Lake Natron)

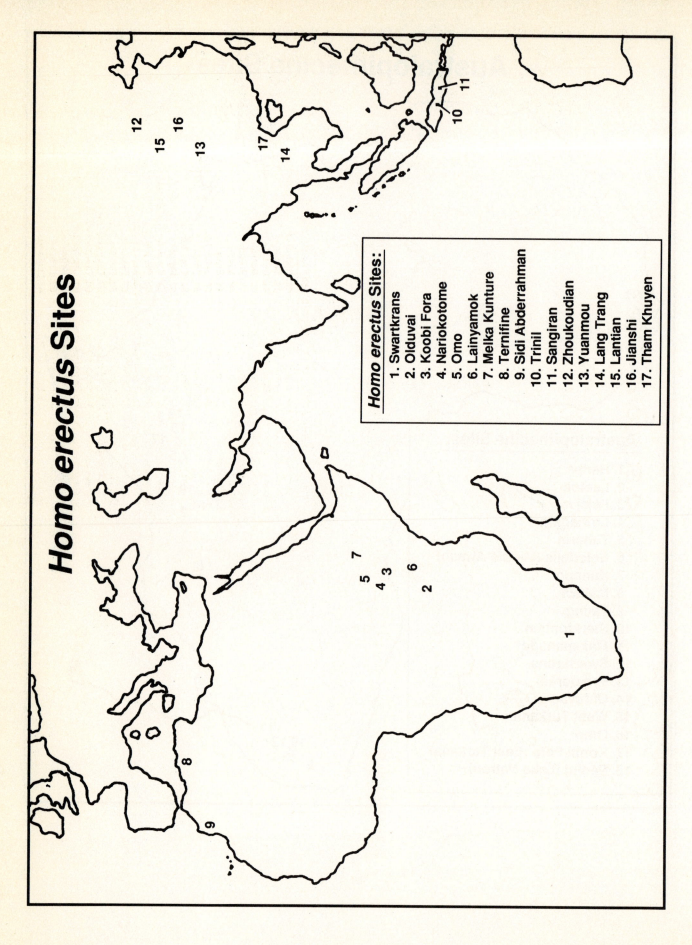

Homo erectus Sites

Homo erectus Sites:
1. Swartkrans
2. Olduvai
3. Koobi Fora
4. Nariokotome
5. Omo
6. Lainyamok
7. Melka Kunture
8. Ternifine
9. Sidi Abderrahman
10. Trinil
11. Sangiran
12. Zhoukoudian
13. Yuanmou
14. Lang Trang
15. Lantian
16. Jianshi
17. Tham Khuyen

Homo sapiens Sites

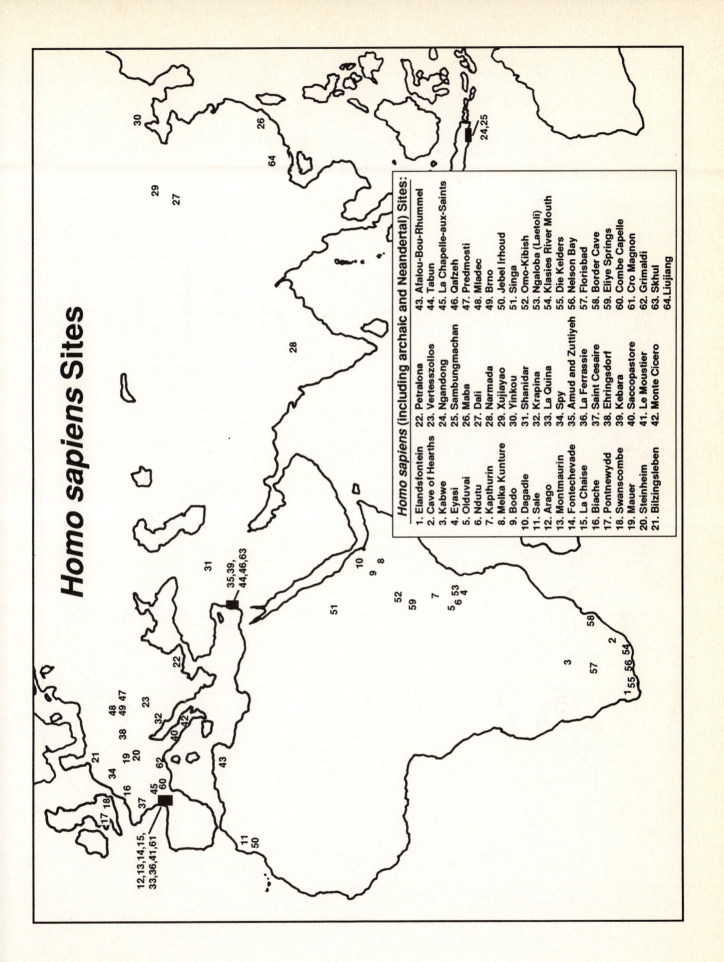

Homo sapiens (including archaic and Neandertal) Sites:

1. Elandsfontein
2. Cave of Hearths
3. Kabwe
4. Eyasi
5. Olduvai
6. Ndutu
7. Kapthurin
8. Melka Kunture
9. Bodo
10. Dagadle
11. Sale
12. Arago
13. Montmaurin
14. Fontechevade
15. La Chaise
16. Biache
17. Pontnewydd
18. Swanscombe
19. Mauer
20. Steinheim
21. Bilzingsleben
22. Petralona
23. Vertesszollos
24. Ngandong
25. Sambungmachan
26. Maba
27. Dali
28. Narmada
29. Xujiayao
30. Yinkou
31. Shanidar
32. Krapina
33. La Quina
34. Spy
35. Amud and Zuttiyeh
36. La Ferrassie
37. Saint Cesaire
38. Ehringsdorf
39. Kebara
40. Saccopastore
41. Le Moustier
42. Monte Cicero
43. Afalou-Bou-Rhummel
44. Tabun
45. La Chapelle-aux-Saints
46. Qafzeh
47. Predmosti
48. Mladec
49. Brno
50. Jebel Irhoud
51. Singa
52. Omo-Kibish
53. Ngaloba (Laetoli)
54. Klasies River Mouth
55. Die Kelders
56. Nelson Bay
57. Florisbad
58. Border Cave
59. Eliye Springs
60. Combe Capelle
61. Cro Magnon
62. Grimaldi
63. Skhul
64. Liujiang

Part I
Biomolecular, Anatomical and Geological Background

Paleoanthropology is a multidisciplinary field that draws on the methods and techniques of many fields of science, including vertebrate paleontology, molecular biology, comparative anatomy, and geology to address the many facets of human evolution. This first part consists of a collection of papers designed to provide background information in many of these fields and thus to set the stage for later chapters which deal more specifically with particular groups of hominids and specific issues in human evolution.

One of the major developments in evolutionary biology over the past 25 years has been the development of molecular biology in the study of phylogeny and systematics (see Gibbons 1991). Much of the pioneering research on biomolecular phylogeny has addressed the issue of the relationships among hominoid primates and the timing of the divergence between apes and humans beginning with the earliest studies by Goodman (1963) and Sarich and Wilson (e.g., 1967). The first four chapters review the results of the most recent biomolecular studies concerning human origins and hominoid phylogeny.

In Chapter 1, "Fossil Evidence on Human Origins and Dispersal," Peter Andrews provides a brief review of the fossil record of ape evolution and the dates for the branching of gibbons, orangutans, African apes, and hominids. He compares the estimated branching times from the fossil record with estimates for the same events derived from studies of DNA sequencing and DNA hybridization. He finds the two are generally compatible.

Chapter 2, "The Phylogeny of the Hominoid Primates as Indicated by DNA-DNA Hybridization" by Charles Sibley and Jon Ahlquist, reports the results of an extensive study of ape and human phylogeny that address both the phyletic relationships among hominoid genera and species as well as providing estimates of the dates of these divergences using a DNA clock. They conclude that humans share a much more recent common ancestry with chimpanzees than with gorillas, with the branches giving rise to orangutans and gibbons being even more distant. When the DNA-DNA hybridization data are calibrated using an orangutan-human divergence of 13–16 m.y.a., the estimated dates for the divergence of human and chimpanzees are 6.3–7.7 m.y.a., for humans and gorillas 8–10 m.y.a., for human and gibbons 18–22 m.y.a., and for hominoids and Old World monkeys 27–33 m.y.a. (These authors reported further results

of their work, with similar conclusions, several years later, see Sibley and Ahlquist 1987).

Chapter 3, "Molecular Insights into the Nature and Timing of Ancient Speciation Events: Correlates with Palaeoclimate and Palaeogeography," by John Cronin compares the molecular studies of hominoid phylogeny based on immunology and DNA sequencing with those based on DNA hybridization. The results from immunology and DNA sequencing yield younger dates for the divergence of hominoid lineages than those reported by Sibley and Ahlquist (Chapter 2). Cronin argues that these data do not support a closer relationship between humans and chimpanzees compared with gorillas. Rather they suggest a three-way splitting among the African apes and hominids between 4 and 6 m.y.a. He note that this correlates with a major climatic change approximately 5 m.y.a. and suggests that the evolutionary divergence of African hominoids may be related to retreat of Central African rainforests in the early Pliocene.

Chapter 4, "DNA Hybridization as a Guide to Phylogeny: Relations of the Hominoidea," by Jon Marks, Carl Schmid and Vince Sarich, reevaluates some of the DNA-DNA hybridization data of Sibley and Ahlquist and questions some of their results and interpretations. The authors provide a review of the methods used in this technique and likely sources of error. They reanalyze a set of raw data provided to them by Sibley and Ahlquist and argue that these data do not support a closer phyletic relationship between chimps and humans than that between humans and gorillas and argue that in evaluating DNA hybridization conclusions, particular attention must be paid to the nature of the results of the original experiments.

Although molecular and genetic studies have generally emphasized the striking similarities between humans and African apes, modern humans are nevertheless characterized by a number of distinctive anatomical specializations that separate us from other hominoids. Many of the articles dealing with the fossil record of human evolution in subsequent chapters are concerned with how, when, and why our distinctive anatomical characteristics appear in the course of hominid phylogeny (see McHenry 1975 for an insightful discussion of this topic). The next four chapters review four of the most unique aspects of human anatomy, illustrating the differences between humans and other primates.

In Chapter 5, "The Evolution of the Human Hand," John Napier reviews the way in which humans and other primates use their hands. He describes and illustrates hand movements and their relationship to the underlying structure of muscles and bone. He then discusses the evolution of hand function throughout primate evolution and how hand function is related to the manufacture and use of stone tools in early humans. Many of the basic principles of hand function and the evaluation of fossil hominid hands that are presented by Napier receive further discussion in subsequent chapters (see Chapters 14, 18, and 29).

Chapter 6, "The Antiquity of Human Walking," is also by John Napier. With extensive illustrations he describes the kinematics and physiology of human walking and relates the mechanical requirements of human bipedalism to the characteristic features of the human hip and foot. He compares the lower limb anatomy of bipedal humans with that of quadrupedal apes and reviews the evolution of locomotor abilities throughout primate evolution. He then presents his views on the ecological and behavioral parameters associated with the evolution of human bipedalism and compares them with the views of other authorities. More recent fossil discoveries have demonstrated that bipedalism was probably critical to the initial separation of hominids from our ape ancestors, and many of the anatomical observations made by Napier on the locomotor differences between apes and humans and their behavioral significance are discussed at length in later chapters (see Chapters 17, 18, 20, 21, 22, 24, 25, 29, and 30).

In Chapter 6, "The Anatomy of Human Speech," Jeffrey Laitman reviews the anatomy of the oral cavity and throat in humans and apes and relates the shape of this region to capabilities of speech production. He then discusses the reconstruction of speech potential in fossil hominids based on the anatomy of the skull base. The relative role of neurological and anatomical differences in accounting for the striking contrasts in ape and human language abilities is a longstanding topic of interest and debate in human evolution.

Chapter 8, "Hominid Paleoneurology" by Dean Falk reviews the fossil evidence of brain evolution in human evolution and what it can tell us about the evolution of human neural function, including speech, over the past 3 million years. She reviews controversies and difficulties in the interpretation of surface features on hominid endocasts. There seems to be clear evidence of cortical asymmetries, associated with handedness and with speech production as early as 2 m.y.a. She presents evidence for a gradual increase in hominid brain size over the past 3 million years, in contrast with others who have argues for punctuated changes. Finally, she reviews theories concerning the causal factors underlying hominid brain evolution and argues that language has been the prime mover.

Chapter 9, "Human Evolution: The Geological Framework" by Basil Cooke provides a broad overview of the geological context of the hominid fossil record. Cooke begins with a brief review of taphonomy, the various processes, life habits, climate, predator habits, sedimentology, etc., that determine whether or not an organism becomes part of the fossil record. He then provides a comparative calibration of fossil hominid sites from all over the world, and reviews the methods used to provide absolute and relative dates for fossil bearing deposits. The numerous time scales, diagrams, and maps he provides are valuable references for later chapters discussing the actual fossil evidence.

REFERENCES

Gibbons, A. 1991. Systematics goes molecular. *Science* 251:872-874.

Goodman, M. 1963. Serological analysis of the systematics of recent hominoids. *Human Biol.* 35:377-436.

McHenry, H. 1975. Fossils and the mosaic nature of human evolution. *Science* 190:425-431.

Sarich, V. M., and A. C. Wilson 1967. Immunological time scale for hominid evolution. *Science* 158:1200-1204.

Sibley, C. G., and J. E. Ahlquist 1987. DNA hybridization evidence of hominoid phylogeny: Results from an expanded data set. *J. Molec. Evol.* 26:99-121.

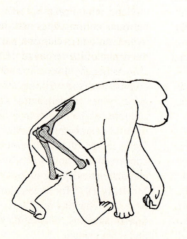
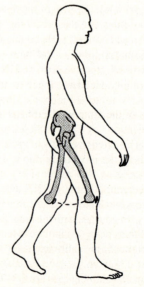

1

Fossil Evidence on Human Origins and Dispersal

P. Andrews

The close relationship of humans with apes has been recognized for many years. Darwin (1871) was very specific in his inferences about the common ancestor between humans and apes. He recognized the subdivision of the Catarrhini from other primates, and divided it into the monkeys and the anthropomorphous apes, with humans part of the latter group; and he further states that as "chimpanzees and gorillas . . . are now man's nearest allies, it is somewhat more probable that our early progenitors lived on the African continent than elsewhere." Darwin also had some more speculative things to say about early human ancestors, for instance, inferring that they had frugivorous diets (based on analogy of morphological form of teeth), that they were restricted to hot climates (loss of hair), and that they had diverged from the apes by the middle Miocene (because of the known existence of the fossil ape *Dryopithecus* in the middle Miocene deposits in Europe).

The evidence on which Darwin based the above conclusions was a mixture of comparative and fossil evidence, with the former predominating because of the extreme shortage of any fossil evidence. His comparative evidence, and that of Huxley (1863), provided a sound basis on which the mounting fossil evidence could subsequently be examined, and it is a tragedy of scientific misdirection that during the middle part of this century the evidence from fossils gained an ascendancy over the comparative method in interpreting hominoid phylogeny. It has taken an entirely new source of comparative data to redress the balance, that from molecular studies of proteins and DNA, but there is a danger now that in correcting and redirecting work on hominoid phylogeny some workers would like to eliminate fossils altogether. I think both sources of evidence have much to offer, however, and what is important is not to see them as competing with each other but as complementary disciplines that have much to offer each other.

The nature of fossil evidence is very different from that provided by comparative data. In the 1950 Cold Spring Harbor Symposium, Simpson stressed that the evidence of relationship provided by the comparative morphology of living animals gives only the end results of clearly historical processes, but tells us nothing of the processes themselves. This is true equally of gross morphology and of molecular similarity, and to translate the similarity-based sets of relationships into phylogenies requires an additional set of inferences about how phylogenetic change is presumed to

have occurred. These inferences are sometimes integrated into the similarity matrices in a way that blurs the distinction between the observable fact; for instance, similarity based on shared characters, and inference about evolutionary processes.

By contrast, fossils provide first-hand historical data (Simpson 1951), but the problem here is the incompleteness of the fossil record. The fossil remains are incomplete themselves, succession through time is broken by many gaps, and the spatial distribution of fossil faunas is incomplete, so that all we have to work on is isolated fragments of evidence. This greatly reduces the historical value of the fossil record. Simpson's view in 1950, as that of the majority of paleontologists of that period, was that despite these deficiencies the fossil record was still the primary source of historical data. This may be true of some groups of animals, but in my view the fossil evidence for hominoid evolution is too incomplete to base any general statement of hominoid phylogeny on it alone.

For the purposes of this paper I will accept the possibility of two sets of relationships for the Hominoidea (Fig. 1). These are identical except for the relationship between humans, chimpanzees, and gorillas: One set puts humans and chimpanzees more closely related, and this is based on the evidence from DNA-DNA hybridization (Sibley and Ahlquist 1984) and also supported by some evidence from DNA sequencing (Ferris *et al.* 1981a, b; Bishop and Friday 1985; Hasegawa *et al.* 1985), amino acid sequencing (Goodman *et al.* 1983, 1984; Koop *et al.* 1986), and some chromosomal evidence (Yunis and Prakash 1982). The other set of relationships groups chimpanzees and gorillas together in an African ape clade to which humans are related, and this is supported by morphological evidence (Andrews 1986b), some DNA sequencing (Brown *et al.* 1982; Templeton 1983, 1985), and some chromosomal evidence (Marks 1983). These references are not exhaustive (see Andrews 1986a, b for a full list of references), but they illustrate the lack of uniformity of the evidence and its interpretation. Any resolution of this discordance must await additional data, but in the meantime in this paper the fossil evidence for hominoid evolution will be discussed with these two possible sets of relationships in mind.

Three things have to be considered when using fossil evidence for dating evolutionary events. One is that any branch-

Reprinted with permission from *Cold Spring Harbor Symposia of Quantitative Biology*, Vol. 51, pp. 419-428. Copyright © 1986 by Cold Spring Harbor Laboratory.

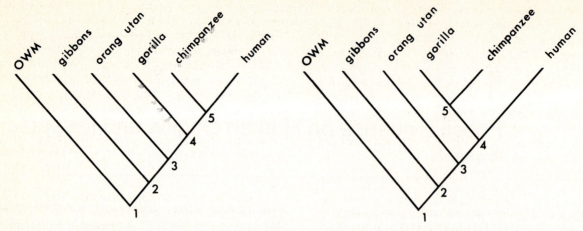

Figure 1. *Relationships of the Hominoidea. On the left is shown one possibility with the chimpanzee most closely related to humans, and on the right is shown the alternative of chimpanzees and gorillas more closely related.*

ing point always has two sets of descendants, and evidence for the timing of the branching point may come from either. For example, the divergence of the catarrhine primates into monkeys and apes (Cercopithecoidea and Hominoidea) could be dated by the first appearance of either in the fossil record, so that the date of origin of the hominoids could be indicated by the first appearance of cercopithecoids, if that were earlier than the earliest hominoid fossils. Stemming from this is the second point, that fossils only provide a minimum date of divergence, never a maximum, so that they indicate a time by which a lineage has originated, not the actual time. Finally, the way by which fossil taxa are identified is important, and in this paper the assignment of a fossil is only accepted when the presence of synapomorphies with particular lineages can be demonstrated.

HOMINOID DIVERSITY

The hominoids have traditionally been divided into the lesser apes and the great apes and humans. The lesser apes include the six species of gibbon and siamang; and the great apes include the orangutan from Borneo and Sumatra (recognized as two very distinct subspecies or perhaps two species), two species of chimpanzees from west and central Africa, and one species of gorilla with three relatively distinct subspecies having more limited distribution than chimpanzees.

The six species of gibbon and siamang have allopatric distributions and morphological variations indicative of recent speciation. The African great apes, on the other hand, have sympatric distributions and contracting ranges suggestive of earlier speciation and present relic status. The orangutan range is also apparently contracting, being formerly known from the mainland of southeast Asia, and its distribution is also suggestive of relic status.

Rates of divergence in the mitochondrial DNA molecule within and between species adds an interesting perspective to these general statements about extant apes. Within any one of the hominoid species the greatest percentage divergence in the mtDNA molecule is seen in the orangutan (Wilson *et al*

1985). The sequence divergence within this species is 3.65%, compared with a slightly greater figure for the divergence of the two species of chimpanzee and much lower figures within any of the other hominoid species (0.36-1.33%). The human figure is the lowest within the hominoids, and this will be commented on below, but all of the hominoids except the orangutan appear, on this evidence, to have had comparatively recent origins.

The fossil evidence for the separate lineages leading to extant hominoids will be discussed below, but there is some fossil evidence for the present relic status of most or all of the extant hominoids. Hominoids are first known from the fossil record about 22 million years ago (Myr), and between then and about 18 Myr they reach the highest diversity ever achieved, when 10 species are known within a very restricted area of east Africa (Andrews 1981; updated by including recent fossil discoveries). Between 15 and 18 Myr the number of fossil ape species falls to seven, but fewer sites are known from this time

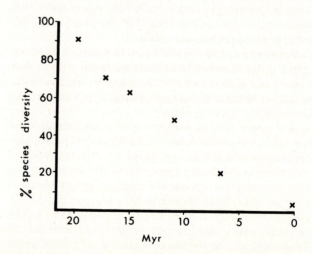

Figure 2. *Hominoid species diversity.* (Vertical axis) *Species diversity of hominoids as a percentage of catarrhines in Africa;* (horizontal axis) *time in millions of years.*

period, and so this fall may not be real. By the late Miocene, however, only two fossil ape species are known from Africa, so that within this continent, and between 22 and 8 Myr, there has been a dramatic fall in the diversity of fossil hominoids. This is shown in Figure 2 compared with total catarrhine diversity in the same area of east and north Africa. By calculating the regression of species numbers against time, it has been shown that the projected decline in numbers of hominoid species during the Miocene could have led to their extinction in Africa about 3 Myr (Andrews 1981). The number of species actually present at 3 Myr could not have been less than three (proto-chimpanzee, -gorilla, and -human), and probably it was no more than four, and these species may well have been represented by populations no larger than those of extant African ape species.

The fossil evidence for decrease in hominoid diversity, to the extent that they can be considered to have been bordering on extinction 3 Myr, is entirely consistent with their present relic distributions. The relatively high sequence divergence of mtDNA within the small populations of living great apes suggests they are remnants of formerly larger populations (Ferris et al. 1981b). They may have become subdivided into many populations in the past, and with contraction of their ranges the high mtDNA divergence resulting from their former variability could have been retained in the smaller relic population.

HOMINOID ORIGINS

In the preceding section, attention on hominoid diversity changes was focused on Africa, because the early evolutionary history of hominoids is entirely restricted to Africa, covering a period of approximately 9 Myr. The earliest known fossil that can be identified as hominoid is from 22 Myr deposits in Kenya (Andrews et al. 1981), and it is not until approximately 13 Myr that hominoids are known outside Africa (Andrews and Tobien 1977; Raza et al. 1983; Barry et al. 1985).

Two consequences of importance emerge from this observation. One is that the probable place of origin of the Hominoidea is somewhere in Africa. There is no shortage of fossil localities in Europe and Asia during the early part of the Miocene and late Oligocene, the periods covering the 15- to 30-Myr time interval, and the total absence of hominoids from these faunas can be considered significant in view of their number and range of habitats sampled.

The other consequence of the early hominoid fossil record in Africa is that the origin of the group can be put at earlier than 22 Myr. How much earlier it is difficult to be sure, but it has been shown in the preceding section that it was close to the beginning of this time that the hominoids reached their greatest species diversity, and this suggests that they were already well established by then and must have originated several million years prior to 22 Myr. There is no fossil record in Africa for the period 22-30 Myr, and therefore no direct evidence, but on the basis of the nature and extent of the early hominoid radiation the origin of the group probably occurred at least 3-5 Myr earlier than this, in other words between 25 and 28 Myr.

The sister group of the Hominoidea is the Cercopithecoidea, the Old World monkeys (Fig. 1). Fossil evidence for this group might also be expected to provide some information on the time and place of origin of the hominoids, but in fact little additional evidence is available. The earliest fossil

monkey is from early Miocene deposits in Africa which also yield early hominoids. The monkeys during the first half of the Miocene are rather rare (Delson 1975), and the great radiation leading to the many species living today did not take place until late in the Miocene when hominoid diversity was dropping quickly. It has been suggested that the two events may be causally linked (Andrews 1981). Like the hominoids, the early fossil record of monkeys is restricted to Africa, and in this case they are not found in Eurasian fossil deposits until late in the Miocene about 8 Myr ago. Therefore, the fossil evidence for monkeys gives added support to Africa as the center for catarrhine diversification but little additional information about the time of origin of either group.

For the timing of hominoid origins there is evidence available from comparative biology through the various estimates from molecular clocks. There are a number of problems with the interpretation of molecular clocks, many of which have been reviewed elsewhere (Read and Lestrel 1970; Read 1975; Corruccini et al. 1980; Goodman et al. 1983; Gingerich 1984; Wilson et al. 1985; Andrews 1986a, b; Koop et al. 1986). These have demonstrated fluctuations in rates of molecular change both within and between lineages that make the extrapolation of constant rates doubtful in many cases. One exception to this is the averaged rate demonstrated by Sibley and Ahlquist (1984), who were able to minimize the effects of homoplasy and functional constraints. Constant rates of change assume that all change is divergent and nonfunctional, and if either of these is incorrect the rates of change can be expected to fall over longer periods of time. By analyzing the whole of the DNA molecule, and restricting similarity to multiple units of DNA rather than to single-base changes (see below), the effects of function have been minimized and the probability of homoplasy greatly reduced by the hybridization process.

The molecular clocks provide a relative time scale that has to be calibrated by some independent means, usually the fossil record. This unfortunately introduces an element of circularity into the timing of evolutionary events. In the case of DNA-DNA hybridization, the calibration point used was the divergence of the orangutan (see below) from the other apes, assuming a divergence date of 13-16 Myr from the fossil record. On the basis of this the divergence of hominoids and cercopithecoids was calculated to be between 27 and 33 Myr. This calibration from the orangutan is probably accurate, and my results suggest further that orangutan divergence was closer to 13 than to 16 Myr, so that the more likely range of dates for the divergence of the hominoids is between the lower estimate, 27 Myr and about 30 Myr. This calibration will be discussed in more detail in the section on orangutan divergence, but it can be noted here that the range of dates provided by DNA-DNA hybridization of 27-30 Myr and the suggested minimum dates from the fossils of 25-28 Myr (Fig. 3) overlap to a certain extent.

Work on nuclear DNA sequencing used as calibration places the Anthropoidea divergence at 35-45 Myr (Koop et al. 1986). By this is probably meant the divergence of New World monkeys (Platyrrhines) and Old World monkeys and apes (Catarrhines). Again, this seems to be a reasonable calibration [Gingerich (1984) gives a date of 40 Myr for this event], and based on this Koop et al. (1986) obtain an age range of 22-28 Myr for the divergence of cercopithecoids and hominoids. This also overlaps with the fossil evidence, and, since the younger

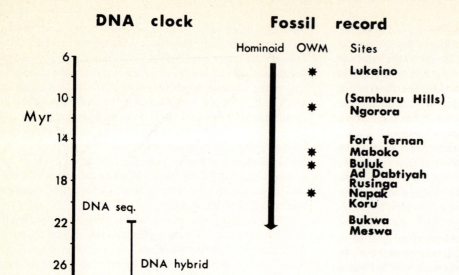

Figure 3. *Time ranges for hominoid origins provided by the molecular clock on the left and fossil evidence on the right. The hominoid fossil record extends back to just over 22 Myr, while that of cercopithecoids (OWM) extends to 19 Myr.*

dates can be shown to be less likely by fossil evidence, it seems possible to conclude that a realistic date is between 25 and 28 Myr for the separation of cercopithecoids and hominoids (Fig. 3).

GIBBON DIVERGENCE

There is little information from the fossil record about the time and place of gibbon origins. No fossil species that are clearly part of the gibbon clade have yet been recognized, and all we have to go on are fragmentary fossil hominoids from Kenya and Saudi Arabia that are considered to belong to the great ape and human clade, that is the sister group to the gibbons (Andrews *et al.* 1978). One specimen is from a locality called Ad Dabtiyah in Saudi Arabia, and it is dated by its faunal remains to about 16-17 Myr. Saudi Arabia geologically is on the African plate and so must be counted as part of Africa during the early part of the Miocene. The other specimens are from Buluk in northern Kenya (Leakey and Walker 1985), and have been radiometrically dated to older than 17 Myr. Both hominoids appear to be related to the later fossil genus *Kenyapithecus*, and, on the basis of this relationship and the characters they share with later and more complete hominoids, it can be concluded that both belong to the great ape and human clade, after, that is, the divergence of the gibbons. The gibbons, therefore, must have already been separate by this time, even if totally unknown as fossils, so this gives a minimum age of 17 Myr for gibbon origins.

There are several dates for gibbon divergence provided by molecular clocks. The DNA-DNA hybridization data give an age range of 18-22 Myr based on the calibration range accepted for orangutans of 13-16 Myr (Sibley and Ahlquist 1984). It was indicated in the previous section that the younger of these two dates is likely to be more realistic for the orangutan (see below), and in consequence the time of gibbon divergence is probably closer to 18 than to 22 Myr. Divergence data in nuclear DNA sequences are unfortunately not provided for the gibbon branching point (Koop *et al.* 1986), but extrapolating between the two adjacent branching points it would clearly have a similar if slightly younger age.

Sequencing of mtDNA has also been used to calculate divergence dates for the gibbons (Hasegawa *et al.* 1985). This is calibrated by assuming divergence of primates and ungulates at 65 Myr. This is a reasonable estimate based on available fossil evidence, but it appears likely that it is a branching point too remote from the hominoid branching points being considered here, so that with only a moderate amount of slowing down of sequence change the dates obtained would all be too young. The first date given for the gibbon branching point is 13.3 ± 1.5 Myr, and this is considerably younger than dates from other sources; succeeding branching points diverge still more from other sources. These workers now acknowledge (M. Hasegawa, pers. comm.) that their dates are in fact too young.

The dating of the gibbon branching point by the two nuclear DNA clocks gives a range of around 17-22 Myr for this event. By narrowing down the calibration range from the fossil record (based on other branching points), it is possible to give a more precise estimate at 17-20 Myr. This corresponds with the published evidence so far available from the fossil record, which indicates an age of greater than 17 Myr for the gibbon branching point.

ORANGUTAN DIVERGENCE

A recent spate of papers have documented previously unrecognized members of the orangutan clade in the fossil record (Andrews and Tekkaya 1980; Andrews and Cronin 1982; Pilbeam 1982; Ward and Pilbeam 1983; Andrews 1986b). These group the fossil genera *Sivapithecus* and *Ramapithecus* in the orangutan clade on the basis of a number of shared derived characters of the palate and face (Andrews and Cronin 1982). All of the fossil specimens that can be attributed to these genera with any degree of certainty (that is based on the shared presence of derived characters with the orangutan) come from the Miocene deposits in India, Pakistan, and Turkey. They have an age range of 8-11.8 Myr in Pakistan, a similar age in India, and an age of approximately 11 Myr in Turkey (Andrews and Tekkaya 1980; Raza *et al.* 1983; Barry *et al.* 1985). The earliest secure date is the one for the Chinji Formation in Pakistan at

11.8 Myr, and this indicates an age of at least 12 Myr or more for the branching point of the orangutan.

A number of other fossil discoveries have been attributed to *Sivapithecus* and *Ramapithecus*, and these must be examined briefly here. A number of discoveries from China, Greece, and Hungary extend the range of these genera, if correctly identified, but add little more information, for instance, in terms of dating. The discovery of large numbers of hominoid teeth at Pasalar in Turkey, some of which have been described by Andrews and Tobien (1977), appears to confirm the presence of *Sivapithecus* in these middle Miocene deposits, which are dated faunally to between 13 and 14 Myr. This may extend the temporal range of this genus to 14 Myr, and hence also the branching point of the orangutan. The Pasalar hominoids are very incomplete, however, and do not preserve most of the relevant body parts to identify orangutan synapomorphies, but their incisor proportions and the conformation of the enamel dentine junction (Martin 1985) of their molars are shared with later specimens of *Sivapithecus* and the orangutan. It is considered possible, therefore, that they should be referred to *Sivapithecus* and considered members of the orangutan clade. If this is correct, the time of divergence of the orangutan is placed at or before 14 Myr; if it is incorrect, the earliest date is about 12 Myr.

Historically, a number of specimens from Africa have been attributed to *Ramapithecus* and *Sivapithecus*. This was based on the shared presence of thick molar tooth enamel in these genera, but since this has been shown to be an ancestral great ape and human character (Martin 1985), and since the postcranial distinctions of the African material have been clarified (Harrison 1982), it has become evident that these African specimens from the sites of Fort Ternan and Maboko Island are cladistically distinct. They have therefore been returned to the genus originally described for them by Louis Leakey (1962), *Kenyapithecus*. This would be placed between nodes 2 and 3 of Figure 1, in contrast to *Sivapithecus* which is placed within node 3.

Finally, one additional discovery, also from Africa, must be commented on briefly. This is the hominoid from Buluk in northern Kenya, consisting of extremely fragmentary remains attributed to *Sivapithecus* by Brown *et al.* (1985). There are some similarities with this genus to be seen in the Buluk specimens, but the character of thick molar enamel, which is now being used to define the great ape and human clade including *Sivapithecus*, (Fig. 4), and which is also present in *Kenyapithecus*, appears not to be present in the Buluk material. Lacking this and other derived characters of *Kenyapithecus* and *Sivapithecus*, the Buluk material appears to represent a more primitive, perhaps unnamed, genus.

The conclusion from the fossils, therefore, is that the branching point of the orangutan took place at least 12 Myr and perhaps more than 14 Myr. All of the fossil discoveries that can be linked with the orangutan with any degree of certainty come from European and Asian deposits, and in fact the fossils from Pasalar appear to represent the earliest hominoid of any type yet known from outside Africa. It is likely that the *Sivapithecus* remains from the 13 to 14 Myr deposits at Pasalar represent the earliest emigration of hominoids out of Africa, and, although other types of hominoid are known from later deposits, the orangutan lineage was established in Eurasia by this time.

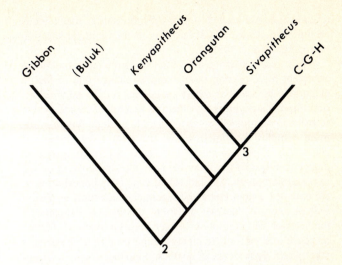

Figure 4. *Cladogram showing the relationships of* Sivapithecus, Kenyapithecus, *and the new Buluk fossil hominoids. C-G-H signifies chimpanzees, gorillas, and humans.*

The early branching of the orangutan lineage and its formerly more widespread distribution are consistent with the results from comparative biology. In this instance, the DNA-DNA hybridization results cannot be used to date the branching point, because this was the one used to calibrate the DNA clock in the first place. The nuclear DNA sequencing results give a date of 12.7-16.4 Myr for this branching point (Koop *et al.* 1986), which is compatible with the fossil record (Andrews and Cronin 1982), but the mtDNA clock of Hasegawa *et al.* (1985) gives a younger date of 9.7-12.1 Myr. As mentioned earlier, this date is probably too young.

It can be concluded that a combination of fossil and molecular dating is consistent in indicating an age of about 13-14 Myr for the branching point of the orangutan. The lineage is likely to have had an African origin, but this is unknown at present.

AFRICAN APE AND HUMAN DIVERGENCE

On this subject, full of uncertainties, there is little that I can add to my recent review (Andrews 1986b). The problem has already been laid out in the introduction and Figure 1, and as the fossil record provides no help in this instance I will just contrast two of the extremes of evidence and interpretation from comparative biology.

One of the strengths claimed for DNA-DNA hybridization (Sibley and Ahlquist 1984) is that reassociation of the DNA strands to form hybrid pairs depends not just on single-base equivalence of the DNA chains but on identity of multiple groups of bases. Sibley argues that whereas single-base changes could be duplicated by homoplasy, and hence distort the significance of DNA similarity, the multiple groups are complex and unlikely to be duplicated independently and so must be homologous. This is the basis for his claim that what is being measured by the hybridization technique is only, or at least mainly, homology, and it appears to be a convincing argument. This provides strong evidence in support of the relationship of humans and chimpanzees, with gorillas as the outgroup. This relationship is also supported by at least two uniquely shared nuclear DNA substitutions at the *n* locus (Koop *et al.* 1986) and at least one amino acid substitution (Goodman *et al.* 1983).

In a recent paper I have tried to formulate a functional argument for assessing morphological change that in fact is essentially the same as Sibley's argument for DNA hybridization. Simply stated this says that if a number of characters are functionally correlated so as to relate to a single function, the more complex the function, and the greater the number of characters relating to it, the less likely it is to be achieved independently and the more likely is the similarity to be the result of homology. The individual characters contributing to the complex cannot be treated separately but simply as part of a single multiple character, and for homology to be indicated all the parts of this multiple character must be identical. Shared presence of even a single highly complex multiple character is taken as strong evidence of homology and therefore of relationship. Two such complexes were provided linking chimpanzees and gorillas (Andrews 1986b), namely the characters of shoulder, elbow, wrist, and hand (all related to knuckle-walking); and the enamel prism morphology, developmental type, proportions, and growth rate (all relating to molar enamel thickness). These provide evidence for relationship between chimpanzees and gorillas that is at least as strong as that linking humans and chimpanzees.

One fossil that may be relevant to this branching point is the recently described upper jaw from the Samburu Hills in the Kenya rift valley (Ishida *et al.* 1984). This is faunally dated at between 7 and 9 Myr, and it is of particular interest because it is probably part of the African ape and human clade. Which part, however, is difficult to tell on the evidence available. It has the expanded premolar crowns with reduced sectoriality characteristic of the clade. It appears to have thick enamel that is considered primitive for the clade. In its molar proportions, however, with a particularly elongated third molar, and in the discrete nature of the molar cusps, lacking well-defined ridges connecting the cusps, there are similarities with the gorilla that are otherwise unique to this great ape. With only one specimen to go on, it is not possible to be sure of the significance of these characters, but it is possible that they are gorilla synapomorphies and that this fossil represents an early member of the gorilla lineage. Its date of 7-9 Myr is interesting in this respect, but it does not resolve the issue about order of splitting within the clade, although perhaps it lends some circumstantial support for the initial divergence of the gorilla.

This single fossil from the Samburu Hills in Kenya also provides some support for an African origin for the African ape and human clade (node 4 of Fig. 1). This is likely anyway on a vicariance model, with Africa the only continent common to all three living members of the clade, and it is further supported by the early human fossil record. It will be shown in the next section that the early history of the human lineage is confined to Africa so that while now the human species has a world-wide distribution it was originally an African group with a distribution probably very like that of the extant African apes.

The dates provided by the DNA clocks for the African ape and human branching point vary considerably (Fig. 5). The results from DNA-DNA hybridization give dates 8-10 Myr for gorilla divergence and 6.3-7.7 Myr for chimpanzee divergence (Sibley and Ahlquist 1984). The combined threeway split dated by Koop *et al.* (1986) is put at 6.3-8.1 Myr for nuclear DNA sequencing; and very young dates of 2.7-3.7 Myr are provided by Hasegawa *et al.* (1985) from mtDNA sequencing, dates that are acknowledged to be too young now by Hasegawa (pers. comm.). These dates are compatible with that from the Samburu Hills hominoid, but lack of additional fossils relating to this most interesting of branching points makes it difficult to say more at this stage.

HUMAN ORIGINS

The last stage of human evolution for which there is both fossil evidence and evidence for comparative biology is the emergence of modern humans, *Homo sapiens*. In addition, a number of intermediate stages are documented only by the fossil record covering evolution before the emergence of modern humans.

The earliest record of human fossils is in Africa at between 4 and 5 Myr. The remains are too fragmentary to do more than to document their existence at this time (Patterson *et al.* 1970; Hill 1985), but between 3 and 4 Myr much more complete fossil remains are known (White 1977; Johanson *et al.* 1982). These are all generally attributed to *Australopithecus*, and together with later australopithecines from South and East Africa (Howell 1978) they appear to form a clade, including both gracile and robust species (Rak 1983). Species belonging to this clade appear to be limited to Africa, as is the earliest known species attributed to the genus *Homo*, *H. habilis*. There is thus every indication from the fossil record that for at least 3 Myr of

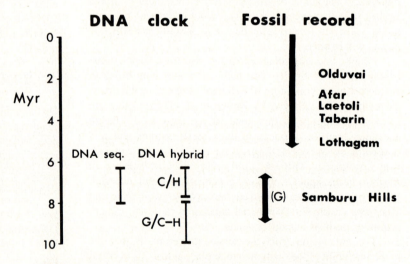

Figure 5. *Time ranges for divisions within the chimpanzee, gorilla, and human clade, from the molecular clock on the left and fossil evidence on the right. The data from DNA sequencing is for the three-way split between them, while DNA-DNA hybridization provides two dates, one for the initial divergence of gorillas from humans and chimpanzees, and a second for the divergence of the two latter species (see Fig. 1). The fossil record shows the time range of human fossils back to 5 Myr and the probable time range of the fossil from the Samburu Hills that may be related to the gorilla.*

recorded history the human lineage was confined to Africa, that there were at least two major subdivisions of the human lineage, and that the genus *Homo* also originated in Africa.

Early members of the genus *Homo* are well documented in East African deposits at Olduvai and Koobi Fora (Leakey and Walker 1976; Howell 1978; Leakey and Leakey 1978; Walker and Leakey 1978). They range from relatively small-brained *H. habilis* to larger-brained individuals, which have been referred to *H. erectus* but which may belong to the species named by Groves and Mazak (1975), *H. ergaster*. As originally defined, the species *H. erectus* was based on material with southeast Asia and China, and examination of these fossils and comparison with the African specimens attributed to the same species shows that the type material has a considerable number of derived characters not present in the African specimens or in later specimens of the genus *Homo*, including *H. sapiens* (Andrews 1984; Stringer 1984; Wood 1984). This raises the possibility that the Asian material, which probably dates to within the last million years, and which represents a derived version of the African fossils, was an emigrant offshoot from Africa that evolved in isolation in eastern Asia and did not contribute to the ancestry of modern humans.

The same contention would hold even if the African early Pleistocene fossils were referred to *Homo erectus*. There are taxonomic difficulties with such an arrangement, however, for there are no characters that define the species without making part of the species more closely related to *H. sapiens* than to the rest of *H. erectus*. This is clearly an unstable taxonomic arrangement, and it seems more reasonable to recognize the Asian material as an isolated emigrant population from an earlier African population and to distinguish them with different specific names.

Whatever taxonomic scheme is preferred, the major issue in question here is the nature of the transition from the early Middle Pleistocene species of *Homo* to *Homo sapiens*. I cannot review this complex subject adequately here, but some comment can be made on the collections of fossil remains from the three geographical regions relevant to the discussion.

THE FAR EAST

Specimens of *Homo erectus* come from deposits spanning in excess of half a million years, and the latest middle Pleistocene specimens of this species are contemporary with more advanced forms both in the same localities and elsewhere in the world. The undescribed Yingkou partial skeleton has clear affinities with modern humans, lacking the *H. erectus* synapomorphies but including many *H. sapiens* ones (Wu Ru-Kang, pers. comm.). Since this skeleton apparently occurs at levels contemporary with *H. erectus*, the strong possibility must be raised that it represents part of an immigrant population rather than having evolved in place in the Far East. Similarly, the Dali and Maba crania show modern human characters not present in *H. erectus* and could be later derivatives of this immigrant population.

EUROPE AND THE MIDDLE EAST

Between 300 and 35 thousand years ago (Kyr) the Neanderthals emerged in this area (Cook *et al.* 1982; Hublin 1982; Stringer 1985, 1989; Vandermeersch 1985). These authors identify pre-

Neanderthal characters (synapomorphies with later classic Neanderthals) in such early fossils as Petralona and Arago, which probably date back to between 300 and 400 Kyr. Additional Neanderthal synapomorphies are developed on later fossils, for instance in the sequence Swanscombe, Steinheim, Biache-Saint-Vaast, Saccopastore, Ehringsdorf, Krapina. These span approximately 200 Kyr, culminating in the classic Neanderthals of the last glaciation.

This evidence indicates the existence of a Neanderthal clade becoming progressively more differentiated through time (Vandermeersch 1985). It is replaced relatively abruptly at about 30-35 Kyr by modern humans in Western Europe, although evidence from Eastern Europe is claimed to show intermediate stages between Neanderthals and modern humans.

AFRICA

The two early human populations from the Far East and Europe, which are represented by the Yingkow and Dali specimens in the former and the Neanderthal lineage in the latter, are often collectively known as archaic *Homo sapiens*. This is essentially a grade concept meaning large-brained humans retaining many primitive characters. The same grade is also seen in Africa where it is exemplified by such specimens as those from Broken Hill and Saldanha. The dating of these sites is problematic, but they appear to be older than 200 Kyr (Stringer 1986). Similar aged and older fossils from North Africa take the fossil record back approximately 500 Kyr (e.g., at Ternifine), but the relationships of these fragmentary fossils with both earlier and later human fossils taxa are uncertain, so that no connection can presently be traced between the early Pleistocene so-called *Homo erectus* (= *Homo ergaster*?; Groves and Mazak 1975) from East Africa and these later forms.

After about 200 Kyr, a group of specimens is recognized spanning Africa from north to south. These show a mixture of archaic retentions with some modern human synapomorphies, as seen in, for instance, Florisbad, Djebel Irhoud 1, Ngaloba, and Omo 2. Later still, between 50 and 100 Kyr, is seen a population with modern human characteristics, and again it is pan-African. This includes such skulls as those from Omo 1, Dar-es-Soltan, Djebel Irhoud 2, and Klasies (and perhaps Border Cave). The earliest of these is a single specimen from Klasies, which is immediately above a raised beach with a date of 116-127 Kyr, and below a bed with two uranium series dates of 98 and 110 Kyr. This single specimen has uncertain affinities, and most of the specimens from Klasies River Mouth that have modern morphology are above this bed. These are older than 70 Kyr and may be as much as 100 Kyr or slightly younger. These, then, are the oldest recorded fossil of *Homo sapiens*, and they occur as part of a well-documented sequence going back in time to 200 Kyr or more. In Africa, therefore, the transition to *Homo sapiens* occurred at or before 100 Kyr and later than 200 Myr.

INTERREGIONAL MIGRATIONS

Combining the fossil evidence from these three regions shows that for at least four stages of human evolution the pattern has been: first appearance in Africa, sometimes followed by subsequent appearance and further development in other parts of the world. These four stages can be summarized as follows:

1. The human fossil record is limited to Africa for the first 3 Myr of recorded history.

2. The first appearance of *Homo* is also African, and at least two species are known, *H. habilis*, and a more advanced species that has been called either *H. erectus* or *H. ergaster*; these are dated at 1.6-2 Myr, and they are followed by the later appearance of the first non-African fossil humans in eastern Asia with the type and referred material of *H. erectus*. These are fairly clearly descended from the earlier African species.

3. The first appearance of what is generally called "archaic *Homo sapiens*" also takes place in Africa at about half a million years ago, and again there are later derivatives of this in Europe about 100 Kyr later and in China about 200 Kyr later. The Mauer jaw from Germany may be as old as the earliest African specimens, although its affinities are uncertain. In this case, therefore, the inference that this form evolved in Africa first is less well supported.

The taxonomic classification of these archaic humans is uncertain, but in view of their distinctiveness from *Homo sapiens*, itself a markedly polytypic species, it would seem better not to classify them together. There is less agreement about this interpretation in the literature, and some authorities suggest that these earliest representatives of *H. sapiens* evolved independently from separate populations of *H. erectus* in Europe, Asia, and Africa. This would imply the branching point for the human species at least 500 Kyr ago.

4. The earliest appearance of humans morphologically indistinguishable from modern humans occurs also in Africa at about 100 Kyr. This is followed by records in Europe and Asia between 30 and 40 Kyr. Again the inference is that modern humans evolved in Africa and subsequently dispersed into the rest of the world.

BIOCHEMICAL EVIDENCE

Several papers have recently put forward evidence for recent origin and population bottlenecks in the evolution of modern humans. Since this evidence is being discussed elsewhere in this volume, I will only mention some of the results here. Brown (1980) described low mtDNA sequence diversity for a small number of human samples, and he interpreted that as indicating a severe bottleneck in human evolution 180-360 Kyr ago. Avise

et al. (1984) challenged this view with a model showing the possibility of stochastic extinction of mtDNA lineages in non-expanding populations. Nei (1982) used 62 protein and 23 blood group loci to calculate proportions of polymorphic loci and average heterozygosity per locus for three races of humans, and he found that 90% of genetic diversity occurred within rather than between the populations, and that the negroid population was more distinct from the mongoloid and caucasoid groups than either was from the other. On the basis of protein evidence alone, he suggested dates of 26-56 Kyr for the separation of the caucasoid and mongoloid populations, and 79-150 Kyr for the separation of the negroids from them.

The evidence indicating an initial split between African populations and the rest (Nei 1982) has been greatly augmented by recent DNA sequencing. Five linked polymorphic restriction enzyme sites in the β-globin gene cluster have been examined for eight diverse human populations (Wainscoat *et al.* 1986) and these show a basic split between African and non-African populations, with the non-African populations losing the distinctive African haplotype through founder effect. No date is given for either the initial branching or for the bottleneck, but the higher genetic diversity of African populations may indicate a greater age for them.

A date is given by Cann *et al.* (1987) when they demonstrate similar results from mtDNA sequencing. They give a date of 140-290 Kyr for the origin of *Homo sapiens* based on 134 types of mtDNA and a mean rate of DNA divergence of 2-4% per million years. The initial split is again between African and non-African populations. The oldest cluster of human samples with no African members has an age range of 90-180 Kyr, and the inference here is that the ancestor must have left Africa by then (or left no African descendants). These dates from protein and DNA, and the evidence of African origin for the species, are entirely consistent with the model based on fossil evidence just presented and are strongly at variance with other interpretations of fossil evidence which take the origin of *Homo sapiens* back to 500 Kyr or more.

ACKNOWLEDGMENTS

I benefited greatly from discussion with Allan Wilson and Chris Stringer while preparing this paper, and I am also grateful to Chris Stringer and Lawrence Martin for comments on the manuscript.

REFERENCES

Andrews, P. 1981. Species diversity and diet in monkeys and apes during the Miocene, in: *Aspects of Human Evolution* (C. B. Stringer, Ed.), p. 25, Taylor and Francis, London.

Andrews, P. 1984. An alternative interpretation of the characters used to define *Homo erectus. Cour. Forschungsinst. Senckenb.* 69:167.

Andrews, P. 1986a. Molecular evidence for catarrhine evolution, in: *Major Topics in Primate and Human Evolution* (B. Wood *et al.*, Eds.), p. 107, Cambridge University Press, Cambridge, England.

Andrews, P. 1986b. Aspects of hominoid phylogeny, in: *Molecules and Morphology in Evolution—Conflict or Compromise* (C. Patterson, Ed.), Cambridge University Press, Cambridge, England.

Andrews, P., and Cronin, J. 1982. The relationships of *Sivapithecus* and *Ramapithecus* and the evolution of the orangutan. *Nature* 297:541.

Andrews, P., Hamilton, W. R., and Whybrow, R. J. 1978. Drypithecines from the Miocene of Saudi Arabia. *Nature* 274:249.

Andrews, P., Harrison, T., Martin, L., and Pickford, M. 1981. Hominoid primates from a new Miocene locality named Meswa Bridge in Kenya. *J. Hum. Evol.* 19:123.

Andrews, P., and Tekkaya, I. 1980. A revision of the Turkish Miocene hominoid *Sivapithecus meteai. Palaeontology* 23:85.

Andrews, P., and Tobien, H. 1977. New Miocene locality in Turkey with evidence on the origins of *Ramapithecus* and *Sivapithecus. Nature* 268:699.

Avise, J. C., Neigle, J. E., and Arnold, J. 1984. Demographic influences on mtDNA lineage survivorship in animal populations. *J. Mol. Evol.* 20:99.

Barry, J. C., Johnson, N. M., Raza, S. M., and Jacobs, L. 1985. Neogene mammalian faunal change in southern Asia: Correlations with climatic, tectonic and eustatic events. *Geology* 13:637.

Bishop, M. J., and Friday, A. E. 1985. Molecular sequences and hominoid phylogeny, in: *Major Topics in Primate and Human Evolution* (B. Wood *et al.*, Eds.), p. 150, Cambridge University Press, Cambridge, England.

Brown, F., Harris, J., Leakey, R. E., and Walker, A. C. 1985. Early *Homo erectus* skeleton from west Lake Turkana, Kenya. *Nature* 316:788.

Brown, W. M. 1980. Polymorphism in mtDNA of humans revealed by restriction endonuclease analysis. *Proc. Natl. Acad. Sci.* 77:3605.

Brown, W. M., Prager, E. M., Wang, A., and Wilson, A. C. 1982. Mitochondrial DNA sequences of primates: Tempo and mode of evolution. *J. Mol. Evol.* 18:225.

Cann, R. L., Stoneking, M., and Wilson, A. C. 1987. Mitochondrial DNA and human evolution. *Nature* 325:31.

Cook, J., Stringer, C. B., Currant, A. P., Schwarcz, H. P., and Wintle, A. G. 1982. A review of the chronology of the European Middle Pleistocene hominid record. *Yearb. Phys. Anthropol.* 25:19.

Corruccini, R. S., Baba, M., Goodman, M., Ciochon, R., and Cronin, J. E. 1980. Non-linear macromolecular evolution and the molecular clock. *Evolution* 34:1216.

Darwin, C. 1871. *The Descent of Man and Selection in Relation to Sex*, Murray, London.

Delson, E. 1975. Evolutionary history of the Cercopithecidae, in: *Approaches to Primate Paleobiology* (F. S. Szalay, Ed.), p. 167, Karger, Basel.

Ferris, S. D., Wilson, A. C., and Brown, W. M. 1981a. Evolutionary tree for apes and humans based on cleavage maps of mtDNA. *Proc. Natl. Acad. Sci.* 78:2432.

Ferris, S. D., Brown, W. M., Davidson, W. S., and Wilson, A. C. 1981b. Extensive polymorphism in the mtDNA of apes. *Proc. Natl. Acad. Sci.* 78:6319.

Gingerich, P. D. 1984. Primate evolution: Evidence from the fossil record, comparative morphology and molecular biology. *Yearb. Phys. Anthropol.* 27:57.

Goodman, M., Braunitzer, G., Stangl, A., and Schrank, B. 1983. Evidence on human origins from haemoglobins of African apes. *Nature* 303:546.

Goodman, M., Koop, B. F., Czelusniak, J., Weiss, M. L., and Slightom, J. L. 1984. The η globin gene, its long evolutionary history in the beta globin gene family of mammals. *J. Mol. Evol.* 180:803.

Groves, C. P., and Mazak, V. 1975. An approach to the taxonomy of the Hominidae: Gracile Villafranchian hominids of Africa. *Cas. Min. Geol.* 20:225.

Harrison, T. 1982. *Small Bodied Apes from the Miocene of East Africa*, Ph.D. thesis, University College, London.

Hasegawa, M., Krishino, H., and Yano, T. 1985. Dating of the human-ape splitting by a molecular clock of DNA. *J. Mol. Evol.* 22:160.

Hill, A. 1985. Early hominid from Baringo, Kenya. *Nature* 315:222.

Howell, F. C. 1978. Hominidae, in: *Evolution of African mammals* (V. C. Maglio and H. B. S. Cooke, Eds.), p. 154, Harvard University Press, Cambridge, Mass.

Hublin, J. J. 1982. Les Anteneandertaliens: Presapiens ou preneandertaliens. *Geobios Mem. Spec.* 6:345.

Huxley, T. H. 1863. *Evidence as to Man's Place in Nature*, Williams and Norgate, London.

Ishida, H., Pickford, M., Nakaya, H., and Nakaya, Y. 1984. Fossil anthropoids from Nachola and Samburu Hills, Samburu District, Kenya. *Afr. Study Monogr.* 2:73

Johanson, D. C., Taieb, M., and Coppens, Y. 1982. Pliocene hominids from the Hadar Formation, Ethiopia. *Am. J. Phys. Anthropol.* 57:373

Koop, B. F., Goodman, M., Xu, P., Chan, K., and Slightom, J. L. 1986. Primate η-globin DNA sequences and man's place among the great apes. *Nature* 319:234.

Leakey, L. S. B. 1962. A new lower Pliocene fossil primate from Kenya. *Ann. Mag. Nat. Hist.* 4:689.

Leakey, M. G., and Leakey, R. E. 1978. *The Koobi Fora Research Project: The Fossil Hominids and an Introduction to Their Context, 1968-1974*, Oxford University Press, Oxford.

Leakey, R. E., and Walker, A. C. 1976. *Australopithecus, Homo erectus* and the single species hypothesis. *Nature* 261:572.

Leakey, R. E., and Walker, A. C. 1985. New higher primates from the early Miocene of Buluk, Kenya. *Nature* 318:173.

Marks, J. 1983. Hominoid cytogenetics and evolution. *Yearb. Phys. Anthropol.* 26:131.

Martin, L. 1985. Significance of enamel thickness in hominoid evolution. *Nature* 314:260.

Nei, M. 1982. Evolution of human races at the gene level, in: *Human Genetics, Part A: The unfolding Genome* (B. Bonne-Tamis *et al.*, Eds.), p. 167, A. R. Liss, New York.

Patterson, B., Behrensmeyer, A. K., and Gill, W. D. 1970. Geology and fauna of a new Pliocene locality in Northwestern Kenya. *Nature* 226:918.

Pilbeam, D. R. 1982. New hominoid skull material from the Miocene of Pakistan. *Nature* 295:232.

Rak, Y. 1983. *The Australopithecine Face*, Academic Press, New York.

Raza, S. M., Barry, J. C., Pilbeam, D. R., Rose, M. D., Shah, S. M. I., and Ward, S. 1983. New hominoid primates from the middle Miocene Chinji Formation, Potwar Plateau, Pakistan. *Nature* 306:52.

Read, D. W. 1975. Primate phylogeny, neutral mutations and "molecular clocks." *Syst. Zool.* 24:209.

Read, D. W., and Lestrel, P. E. 1970. Hominid phylogeny and immunology: A critical appraisal. *Science* 168:578.

Sibley, C. G., and Ahlquist, J. E. 1984. The phylogeny of the hominoid primates, as indicated by DNA-DNA hybridzation. *J. Mol. Evol.* 20:2.

Simpson, G. G. 1951. Some principles of historical biology bearing on human origins. *Cold Spring Harbor Symp. Quant. Biol.* 15:55.

Stringer, C. B. 1984. The definition of *Homo erectus* and the existence of the species in Africa and Europe. *Cour. Forschungsinst. Senckenb.* 69:131.

Stringer, C. B. 1985. Middle Pleistocene variability and the origin of late Pleistocene humans, in: *Ancestors: The Hard Evidence* (E. Delson, Ed.), p. 289, A. R. Liss, New York.

Stringer, C. B. 1989. Documenting the origin of modern humans, in: *The Emergence of Modern Humans* (E. Trinkaus, Ed.), p. 67, Cambridge University Press, Cambridge, England.

Templeton, A. R. 1983. Phylogenetic inference from restriction endonuclease cleavage site maps with particular reference to the evolution of humans and apes. *Evolution* 37:221.

Templeton, A. R. 1985. The phylogeny of the hominoid primates: A statistical analysis of the DNA-DNA hybridization data. *Mol. Biol. Evol.* 2:420.

Vandermeersch, B. 1985. The origin of the Neanderthals, in: *Ancestors: The Hard Evidence* (E. Delson, Ed.), p. 306, A. R. Liss, New York.

Wainscoat, J. S., Hill, A. V. S., Boyce, A. L., Flint, J., Hernandez, M., Theim, S. L., Old, J. M., Lynch, J. R., Falusi, A. G., Weatherall, D. J., and Clegg, J. B. 1986. Evolutionary relationships of human populations from an analysis of nuclear DNA polymorphisms. *Nature* 319:491.

Walker, A. C., and Leakey, R. E. 1978. The hominids of East Turkana. *Sci. Am.* 239:44.

Ward, S., and Pilbeam, D. R. 1983. Maxillofacial morphology of Miocene hominoids from Africa and Indo-Pakistan, in: *New Interpretations of Ape and Human Ancestry* (R. L. Ciochon and R. S. Corruccini, Eds.), p. 211, Plenum Press, New York.

White, T. D. 1977. New fossil hominids from Laetolil, Tanzania. *Am. J. Phys. Anthropol.* 46:197.

Wilson, A. C., Cann, R. L., Carr, S. M., George, M., Gyllensten, U. B., Helm-Bychowsky, K. M., Higuchi, R. G., Palumbi, S. R., Prager, E. M., Sage, R. D., and Stoneking, M. 1985. Mitochondrial DNA and two perspectives on evolutionary genetics. *Biol. J. Linn. Soc.* 26:375.

Wood, B. A. 1984. The origin of *Homo erectus*. *Cour. Forschungsinst. Senckenb.* 69:99.

Yunis, J. J., and Prakash, O. 1982. The origin of man: A chromosomal pictorial legacy. *Science* 215:1525.

2

The Phylogeny of the Hominoid Primates, as Indicated by DNA-DNA Hybridization

C. G. Sibley and J. E. Ahlquist

INTRODUCTION

It is generally agreed that the living members of the primate superfamily Hominoidea are Man (*Homo sapiens*), the Common Chimpanzee (*Pan troglodytes*), the Pygmy Chimpanzee or Bonobo (*Pan paniscus*), the Gorilla (*Gorilla gorilla*), the Orangutan (*Pongo pygmaeus*), and the nine species of gibbons (*Hylobates*). The sister group of the Hominoidea is the Cercopithecoidea (Old World monkeys: baboons, macaques, colobines, etc.) (Honacki *et al.* 1982).

The boundaries of these groups are not in question, but the branching sequence of the lineages and the datings of the divergence nodes are still being debated. Within the past few years at least five possible branching patterns (cladograms) have received support from one or more sources. These five patterns are diagrammed in Figure 1.

The literature on the primates is large and we will not attempt to review or evaluate the evidence of hominoid relationships based on morphology, fossils, or behavior. We will consider the "molecular" evidence for the reconstruction of the hominoid phylogeny and present our DNA-DNA hybridization data, which support cladogram 1 in Figure 1. We will also discuss the dating in absolute time of the divergence nodes in the hominoid phylogeny.

METHODS

Our procedures are based primarily on those of Britten and Kohne (1968), Kohne (1970), Kohne and Britten (1971), and Britten *et al.* (1974). Descriptions of our methods have been published previously (Sibley and Ahlquist 1981a-c, 1982a-e, i, 1983, 1984a, b, 1985a, b, Sibley *et al.* 1982). (The 1981a and 1983 articles provide the most detailed discussions.) The following is a synopsis of the description in the 1983 article by Sibley and Ahlquist (pp 246-270):

DNAs were obtained from the nuclei of tissue cells, purified according to the procedures of Marmur (1961) and Shields and Straus (1975), and sheared by sonication into fragments with an average length of 0.5 kilobases (kb). The single-stranded fragments of the species to be used as "tracers" were allowed to reassociate to a C_0t of 1000 at 50°C in 0.48 M sodium phosphate buffer. This permitted most of the rapidly reassociating repeated sequences to form double-stranded molecules, while the slowly reassociating single-copy sequences remained single-stranded. The latter were recovered by chromatography on a hydroxyapatite (HAP) column. This process produced a single-copy DNA preparation consisting of one copy per genome of each original single-copy sequence plus *at least* one copy per genome of each repeated sequence that was kinetically different under these conditions. The single-copy DNA of the tracer species was labeled with radioiodine (^{125}I) according to the procedures of Commorford (1971), Prensky (1976), and Chan *et al.* (1976). DNA-DNA hybrids were formed from a mixture composed of one part (200 ng) of the tracer DNA and 1000 parts (200 ug) of sheared, whole DNA of the "driver" species. The

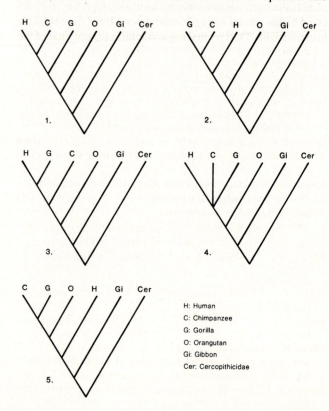

H: Human
C: Chimpanzee
G: Gorilla
O: Orangutan
Gi: Gibbon
Cer: Cercopithicidae

Figure 1. *Five cladograms proposed in recent studies of hominoid phylogeny.*

Reprinted with permission from the *Journal of Molecular Evolution*, Vol. 20, pp. 2-15. Copyright © 1984 by Springer-Verlag, New York.

hybrid combinations were heated to $100^{\circ}C$ for 10 min. to dissociate the double-stranded molecules into single strands, then incubated for 120 h (C_0t 16,000) at $60^{\circ}C$ in 0.48 M sodium phosphate buffer to permit the single strands to form hybrid duplexes. After incubation the buffer was diluted to 0.12 M and the hybrids were bound to HAP columns immersed in a temperature-controlled water bath at $55^{\circ}C$. The temperature was then raised in $2.5^{\circ}C$ increments from $55^{\circ}C$ to $95^{\circ}C$. At each of 17 temperatures the single-stranded fragments produced by the melting of duplexes were eluted in 20 ml 0.12 M sodium phosphate buffer. The radioactivity in each sample was counted and the values were used to calculate the $T_{50}H$ values.

We use the $T_{50}H$ statistic as a measure of the genealogical distance between the two taxa composing a DNA-DNA hybrid. $T_{50}H$ (or $T_{50}R$) is the temperature in degrees Celsius in an ideal, normalized, cumulative frequency distribution function at which 50% of all single-copy DNA sequences are in the hybrid form and 50% have dissociated. The $T_{50}H$ statistic was first suggested to Kohne (1970) and has been used by Bonner et al. (1981) and in most of our own publications. In calculation of $T_{50}H$ it is assumed that all of the single-copy sequences in the genomes of the two species being compared have homologs in the other species, that all single-copy sequences can hybridize with their homologs, and that all degrees of divergence can be detected. For homologous hybrids the $T_{50}H$ and T_m values derived from normalized cumulative distributions are equal. For hybrids between more divergent taxa the percentage of hybridization declines and the thermal stability curve is progressively truncated by the effects of experimental conditions. It is possible to estimate the $T_{50}H$ by making a graphic extrapolation of the most nearly linear portion of the sigmoid curve. A better procedure is to calculate the best-fitting linear regression to the part of the curve having the most constant slope and to find the temperature corresponding to its intercept with the 50% hybridization level. The most objective procedure is to fit a cumulative distribution function to the data and find its intercept with the temperature axis at the 50% hybridization level. Because $T_{50}H$ incorporates the percentage of hybridization it is more nearly linear with the true genealogical distance, and with absolute time, than either delta mode or delta T_m values. These advantages recommend it over the mode and T_m for phylogenetic comparisons.

To convert the delta $T_{50}H$ values into a phylogeny requires a procedure to obtain a hierarchical clustering of taxa. We use the "average linkage" procedure, which begins by clustering the closest pairs of taxa. The next step links the taxa having the smallest average distance to any existing cluster. This procedure continues until all the taxa are linked. The underlying rationale is that the only reason for "closeness" is true homology of characters, whereas "distance" may result from the failure to identify existing homologies. The DNA hybridization data are especially compatible with this view because there is no known reason other than nucleotide sequence homology for the thermal stabilities of DNA-DNA hybrids.

We measured the experimental error in our data and found that a single delta $T_{50}H$ value should be assumed to have a possible error of +/- 1.0 (Sibley and Ahlquist 1983). The delta values may be corrected for some sources of error (e.g., varia-

tion in fragment size) but we have found it possible to compensate for all sources of error by using five or more species and/or replicates for each pairwise comparison so that an average delta $T_{50}H$ value, its standard error (SE), and standard deviation (SD) can be calculated. Because of the incremental summation of values in the average linkage procedure, the older nodes in our phylogenies are often the averages of 10, 20, or more delta $T_{50}H$ measurements (see Table 2 and Fig. 5).

THE UNIFORM AVERAGE RATE OF DNA EVOLUTION

The time values calculated from the DNA hybridization data derive from the fact that the same average rate of DNA sequence evolution occurs in all lineages. We know this to be true for birds and we assume that it is also true for mammals, and probably for other eukaryotes. This seems reasonable because the uniform average rate (UAR) is nothing more (or less) than the inevitable statistical result of averaging over billions of nucleotides and millions of years. Different sequences evolve at different rates and homologous sequences in different species evolve at different rates. The rate of evolution of an individual sequence differs at different times and in different places in the same species, and so on. But the average rate is uniform in all lineages because the genome is extremely large compared with the range in the rates of individual sequences. We found evidence for the UAR in all of our more than 900 experimental sets involving ca. 18,000 DNA-DNA hybrids. The data in Table 1 of this paper also reveal the UAR, and they are but a small percentage of our total evidence. Thus the DNA "clock" is real and keeps excellent time.

It is useful to distinguish between the "protein clocks" (often called the "molecular clock") and the DNA clock. Each protein evolves at its own rate, and the rates for different proteins vary as much as those for individual genes (i.e., sequences), for obvious reasons. The protein clocks are bound to be more erratic and "sloppy" (Fitch 1976) than the DNA clock, which is averaged across the entire genome. Goodman et al. (1982a, b) have shown that individual proteins are "very poor evolutionary clocks because they evolve at markedly non-uniform rates." Avise and Aquadro (1982) reviewed the literature on "genetic distances" in vertebrates based on electrophoretic analyses of proteins, and found at least a 20-fold variation among different protein clock calibrations. Thus the existence of the UAR of DNA evolution does not dispute the existence of variable rates for individual genes, proteins, or morphological characters, which can evolve at many different rates. If one could obtain average rate values for a large enough sample of proteins, individual DNA sequences, or morphological characters, they too should exhibit a uniform average rate of change.

THE CALIBRATION PROBLEM

Although we are confident of the existence of the UAR in birds, and think it highly probable in mammals, we cannot yet be certain that the same average rate occurs in all vertebrates or in other organisms. We plan to carry out experiments to determine the degree of universality of the UAR, but for now we will assume that we are dealing with a UAR only in birds and mammals, and that because of the UAR the delta $T_{50}H$ values

Table 1 Delta $T_{50}H$ distance values for the DNA-DNA hybridization comparisons among the hominoids, and between them and several cercopithecids. The single-copy DNA of the first taxon in each combination was the radiolabeled tracer.

Pan paniscus × *Pan troglodytes*	0.4, 0.5, 0.9, 1.0, 1.1
Pan troglodytes × *Pan paniscus*	0.5
Homo sapiens × *Pan paniscus*	1.3, 1.7, 2.3
Pan paniscus × *Homo sapiens*	1.6, 1.9, 2.1, 2.1
Homo sapiens × *Pan troglodytes*	1.5, 1.7, 1.7, 1.9, 2.0, 2.0, 2.0
Pan troglodytes × *Homo sapiens*	1.6, 1.7, 1.7, 1.8, 1.8
Gorilla gorilla × *Pan paniscus*	2.0
Pan paniscus × *G. gorilla*	2.1, 2.3, 2.3, 2.4, 2.8
G. gorilla × *Pan troglodytes*	1.9, 2.1, 2.1, 2.3, 2.3
Pan troglodytes × *G. gorilla*	1.7, 2.1, 2.1, 2.2, 2.5
G. gorilla × *Homo sapiens*	2.1, 2.1, 2.2, 2.4, 2.4
Homo sapiens × *G. gorilla*	2.4, 2.5, 2.6, 2.6, 2.6
Pongo pygmaeus × *G. gorilla*	3.5, 3.6, 3.8, 3.8, 3.8
G. gorilla × *Pongo pygmaeus*	3.6, 3.8, 4.0, 4.0, 4.1
Pongo pygmaeus × *Homo sapiens*	3.1, 3.1, 3.5, 4.1, 4.2
Homo sapiens × *Pongo pygmaeus*	3.3, 3.5, 3.7, 3.8, 3.8, 3.9
Pongo pygmaeus × *Pan paniscus*	3.4, 3.4, 3.6, 3.6, 3.6, 3.7
Pan paniscus × *Pongo pygmaeus*	3.7, 3.9, 4.0
Pongo pygmaeus × *Pan troglodytes*	3.5, 3.6, 3.7, 3.9, 3.9
Pan troglodytes × *Pongo pygmaeus*	3.2, 3.5, 3.7, 3.8, 3.8
Homo sapiens × *Hylobates lar*	4.8, 4.9, 5.3, 5.4
Hylobates lar × *Homo sapiens*	5.1, 5.1, 5.4, 5.4, 5.4
Homo sapiens × *Hylobates syndactylus*	4.8
Hylobates lar × *H. syndactylus*	1.9, 2.1, 2.1, 2.5
Hylobates lar × *Pan paniscus*	5.9
Pan paniscus × *Hylobates lar*	5.1, 5.1, 6.0, 6.1
Hylobates lar × *Pan troglodytes*	4.8, 5.1, 5.2, 5.3, 5.4
Pan troglodytes × *Hylobates lar*	4.6, 4.7, 4.8, 5.3, 5.5
Hylobates lar × *G. gorilla*	4.7, 5.0, 5.3, 5.5, 5.6, 5.6
G. gorilla × *Hylobates lar*	5.0, 5.3, 5.5, 5.6, 5.6, 5.6
Hylobates lar × *Pongo pygmaeus*	4.6, 4.7, 4.9, 5.2, 5.5
Pongo pygmaeus × *Hylobates lar*	5.1, 5.4, 5.5
Pongo pygmaeus × *H. syndactylus*	4.8, 5.0, 5.0, 5.1, 5.1, 5.1, 5.5
Homo × *Allenopithecus nigroviridis*	7.1
Homo × *Papio hamadryas*	7.3, 7.9, 8.1, 8.2
Homo × *Macaca mulatta*	7.5, 7.7, 8.0
Homo × *Pygathrix nemaeus*	7.7
Pan troglodytes × *Papio hamadryas*	7.1, 7.2, 7.4, 7.7
Pan troglodytes × *Macaca mulatta*	8.1, 8.2, 8.3
Pan troglodytes × *Cercopithecus aethiops*	8.0
Pan troglodytes × *Pygathrix nemaeus*	7.8
Pan paniscus × *Papio hamadryas*	7.3, 7.5
Pan paniscus × *Cercopithecus aethiops*	8.3
Pan paniscus × *Macaca mulatta*	7.7, 8.6, 8.6
G. gorilla × *Papio hamadryas*	6.9, 7.0
G. gorilla × *Macaca mulatta*	7.5, 7.9, 8.0
Pongo pygmaeus × *Allenopithecus nigroviridis*	7.3, 7.5, 7.8, 7.8
Hylobates lar × *Pygathrix nemaeus*	7.1
Hylobates lar × *Macaca mulatta*	7.3, 7.8

are measures of *relative* time. They may, therefore, be used to reconstruct the branching pattern of a phylogeny. To convert the delta values into *absolute* time it is necessary to calibrate them against an external dating source, viz., fossils or geological events that have caused phyletic dichotomies. In a study of the ratite birds we used the opening of the Atlantic Ocean in the Cretaceous as a dating baseline by assuming that the common ancestor of the Ostrich (*Struthio camelus*) and the Common Rhea (*Rhea americana*) was separated into African and South American populations ca. 80 million years ago (MYA). This indicated that delta $T_{50}H$ value of 1.0 = 5.0 MY, which we have since recalculated as 4.5 MY (Sibley and Ahlquist 1981a, 1983). We now estimate that delta $T_{50}H$ 1.0 = 4-4.5 MY. Pilbeam (1982) has suggested that the Orangutan clade branched between 13 and 16 MYA, and he favors the 16 MYA divergence date. As we will show, this gives a calibration of delta $T_{50}H$ 1.0 = 4.32 MY, in excellent agreement with the ratite data and with two other avian datings noted in Sibley and Ahlquist (1983). It is possible that the regression between delta $T_{50}H$ and absolute time is slightly curvilinear, but the evidence is fragile and for the present we will assume linearity. This calibration is obviously subject to correction as more and better calibrating points become available.

GENERATION TIME

It has been proposed that the rate of genetic evolution is affected by the number of generations (Kohne 1970; Kohne *et al.* 1972). Others have presented evidence against this proposal (e.g., Sarich and Wilson 1973; Sarich and Cronin 1977). To test the hypothesis that the number of generations per unit of time affects the rate of DNA evolution we compared the DNAs of closely related species of procellariiform birds, which have greatly different generation lengths, against those of outside taxa in a "relative rate test" (Wilson and Sarich 1969). The results were clear; although albatrosses breed only six or seven times in 20 years, and storm petrels breed ca. 18 times in 20 years, their genealogical distances from outside taxa, a plover and a heron, were equal. We concluded that generation time has no effect on the average rate of DNA evolution (Sibley and Ahlquist 1983). Wilson *et al.* (1977) have reviewed this topic.

THE HOMINOID BRANCHING PATTERN

"We do not think it overstates the case to argue that until we have the cladistics we . . . really have nothing at all" (Sarich and Cronin 1976).

We agree with Sarich and Cronin. The branching pattern is one of the three components of a phylogeny, the others being the delineation of monophyletic clusters and the dating of the divergence nodes. But until the cladistic pattern is known, the phylogeny cannot be reconstructed. The five arrangements of the hominoid clades depicted in Figure 1 will be referred to by their numbers, 1 to 5, in the following discussion.

Cladogram 5 was supported by Kluge (1983) on the basis of a cladistic analysis of morphological and other characters, including molecular and chromosomal data.

Cladogram 4 includes the trichotomy among *Homo*, *Pan*, and *Gorilla*. It has proved difficult to break this trichotomy because these three lineages branched closely together in time, and the resolving power of most techniques cannot separate the nodes. The trichotomy has been proposed by Goodman (1975), Benveniste and Todaro (1976), Sarich and Cronin (1976), Romero-Herrera *et al.* (1978), Bruce and Ayala (1979), Ferris *et al.* (1981), Goodman *et al.* (1982a, b), and Brown (1983).

Cladogram 3 was suggested by Miller (1977) on the basis of chromosome banding patterns, but recent technical advances in karyology make this and other early chromosome banding studies obsolete, as shown by the work of Yunis and Prakash (1982).

Cladogram 2 has received considerable support. It is the pattern most often suggested by morphological studies (e.g., Delson *et al.* 1977; Oxnard 1981; Hoffstetter 1982), and Dene *et al.* (1976) interpreted their extensive immunodiffusion data as favoring a closer relationship between *Pan* and *Gorilla* than between *Pan* and *Homo*. In 1979 Dutrillaux favored number 2 over number 1, but in 1980 he was equivocal about this question.

Restriction endonuclease cleavage maps and partial sequences of the mitochondrial DNA (mtDNA) genome have been the subject of several studies, and the results have been interpreted as favoring number 4 (e.g., Ferris *et al.* 1981; Brown 1983; Goodman *et al.* 1983) or number 2 (Brown *et al.* 1982; Templeton 1983). However, none of these studies were able to rule out alternative branching patterns.

Ferris *et al.* (1981) used the maximum parsimony procedure to analyze their data from comparisons of restriction enzyme cleavage maps of primate mtDNAs. They concluded that they could not resolve the branching order among *Homo*, *Pan*, and *Gorilla* and "that at least ten times more genetic information will be required to resolve the branching order for the gorilla, chimpanzee, and human lineages definitively."

Brown *et al.* (1982) sequenced an 896-base pair (bp) segment of DNA from human, chimpanzee, Gorilla, Orangutan, and gibbon mitochondria. Among their conclusions was that

the present study has confirmed the phylogenetic conclusion drawn in an earlier study (Ferris *et al.* 1981) based on cleavage map comparisons of the whole mitochondrial genome. The parsimony method of tree construction, when applied to the 896 bp sequences, favors the branching order . . . which associates chimpanzee and gorilla most closely . . . but some alternative branching orders . . . cannot be ruled out by the present data.

The alternatives not ruled out are cladograms 1, 3, and 4 in Figure 1.

Brown (1983) reviewed the mtDNA studies made by himself and his colleagues and noted that "although parsimony analysis of mtDNA data suggests a closer association between chimpanzee and gorilla than between either of these and human

. . . the difference is so small that the branching of these three species is depicted as an unresolved trichotomy."

Templeton (1983) made an extensive analysis of the data produced by restriction endonuclease cleavage of the mtDNA genome. His principal interest was to develop "an algorithm of phylogenetic inference that deals more directly with the problem of convergent evolution and statistical inhomogeneity between different restriction enzymes." Templeton analyzed the data of Ferris *et al.* (1981) and concluded that cladogram 2 in Figure 1 was best supported by this analysis.

Thus Brown (1983 and personal communication) could not break the *Gorilla-Pan-Homo* trichotomy using mtDNA sequence data for at least 896 bases, while Templeton (1983) believed that he had sorted "out the genetic relationships of man *vs.* the chimps and gorillas" from the cleavage map data of Ferris *et al.* (1981).

Adams and Rothman (1982) suggested the mtDNA cleavage sites are distributed nonrandomly and cautioned that "these results constitute *prima facie* evidence for the action of natural selection and suggest that estimates of phylogenetic relationship, based on a phenetic approach using restriction enzyme data, will be biased." Templeton (1983) noted that he designed his procedure to avoid this problem. Avise and Lansman (1983) concluded that "attempts to infer phylogeny from mtDNA genotypes could be compromised if homoplasy (the evolutionary convergence or reversal of restriction sites) were common."

Goodman *et al.* (1983) used the maximum parsimony method to analyze "the available nucleotide sequence data of mammalian mtDNAs to investigate hominoid phylogeny." They used the mtDNA data for the "mouse and the ox as outgroups of the five hominoids" and calculated the "nucleotide replacement length . . . for each of the 105 possible branching orders among the five hominoid lineages." They found "two lowest length trees, each at 750 NRs (nucleotide replacements): one subdivides Homininae into a *Pan-Homo* branch and a *Gorilla* branch, and other . . . into a *Pan-Gorilla* branch and a *Homo* branch. For only 4 NRs more, i.e., a tree at 754 NRs, the third arrangement is obtained: a *Gorilla-Homo* branch joining *Pan*." They concluded that "the question still remains of whether the correct dichotomous branching order . . . can be resolved or whether the *Pan*, *Homo*, *Gorilla* trichotomy will continue indefinitely to describe the phylogenetic evidence."

Cladogram 1 in Figure 1 is supported by evidence from several sources. Seven years ago Goodman (1976) noted that "in general, the molecular data do not clearly show which two of these three hominines share the most recent common ancestor. However, the data on single-copy DNA and *a*-hemoglobin sequences, along with chromosome data . . . suggest that *Homo* and *Pan* share the most recent common ancestor." At the time Goodman wrote this statement the *a*-hemoglobin sequences were known, or partly known, for *Homo*, *Pan*, and *Gorilla*. The *Homo* and *Pan* *a*-hemoglobins were thought to be identical and the *Gorilla* *a*-hemoglobin was thought to differ from them by one amino acid replacement. However, alternative topologies were possible because complete sequences were not then available for some taxa. Today the complete *a*- and *B*-hemoglobin sequences are known for *Homo*, both species of *Pan*, and *Gorilla*. *Homo* and the two chimpanzees have identical *a*- and *B*-hemoglobin sequences from which *Gorilla* differs by one residue in each chain (Goodman *et al.* 1983). "At position *a*-23, gorilla has aspartic acid instead of glutamic acid. At *B*-104, gorilla has lysine instead of arginine." The *a*-23 aspartic acid residue in *Gorilla* hemoglobin is also found in Orangutan, the gibbons, and the cebids, indicating that it is the primitive condition and that glutamic acid is the shared, derived condition in *Pan* and *Homo*.

> Amino acid sequences of *Y*-haemoglobin chains also point to a *Homo-Pan* clade distinct from gorilla. There are two non-allelic chains in the hominines, $^G Y$ characterized by glycine at position 136 and $^A Y$ with alanine at this position. The two sequences in chimpanzee as inferred from amino acid composition data are identical to their human counterparts. In contrasts, gorilla $^A Y$... has arginine at position 104 whereas human and chimpanzee $^A Y$ chains have lysine. The presence of arginine at position 104 in Old World monkey . . . *Y*-haemoglobin chains raises the possibility that human and chimpanzee $^A Y$ have the derived rather than the primitive residue. (Goodman *et al.* 1983)

Goodman *et al.* concluded that the hominid radiation "as deduced from maximum parsimony trees of *a*- and *B*-haemoglobin sequences" was as depicted by cladogram 1 in Figure 1.

Goodman *et al.* (1982a, b) and Baba *et al.* (1982) have constructed a maximum parsimony tree of the primates based on the "tandem alignment" of the sequences of seven proteins: *a*- and *B*-hemoglobins, myoglobin, lens *a*-crystallin A, fibrinopeptides A and B, and cytochrome *c*. This analysis also produced cladogram 1, in which "the two most closely related genera are *Homo* and *Pan*."

Recent improvements in the techniques for producing banding patterns in chromosomes have made it possible to obtain detailed comparisons among primate karyotypes. Seuanez (1982) reported that "a comparison of the banded karyotypes of man, the chimpanzee, and the gorilla shows that we can derive the human karyotype from that of the chimpanzee with fewer rearrangements than from man to gorilla." However, Seuanez discounted his own observations because he thought that the DNA hybridization evidence "had shown that these three species are phylogenetically equidistant from one another" and that, therefore, the karyotype similarities are "irrelevant in terms of phyletic relationships between man, the chimpanzee, and the gorilla." But his faith in the trichotomy was misplaced and, as we will show, the karyotype evidence is congruent with our DNA hybridization evidence, and also with the earlier DNA-DNA comparisons.

The extensive comparisons of high-resolution banding patterns of chromosomes of *Homo*, *Pan*, *Gorilla*, and *Pongo* by Yunis and Prakash (1982) also supported cladogram 1. They concluded that their "detailed comparative analysis of high resolution chromosomes . . . provides evidence in favor of the existence of three ancestors to the great apes and man from which first the orang-utan, then the gorilla, and finally chimpanzee and man diverged." This impressive study demonstrated how an improvement in technique may yield a huge increase in information. The authors were able to prepare reconstructions on ancestoral karyotypes, as well as reconstruct the branching pattern of the lineages. Earlier techniques produced up to 500 bands per haploid set, but with the G-banding technique 1000 bands were resolved. By comparing the chromosomes of

"humans, apes, and some Old World monkeys" Yunis and Prakash were

> able to work backward in evolution to suggest likely karyotypes for three presumed common ancestors of apes and man. This study was based on the remarkable similarity of the chromosomes of man, chimpanzee, gorilla, and orangutan, the few changes needed to explain their differences, and the use ancestral chromosomal patterns to derive the general sequence of events that might have taken place in primate evolution prior to man's emergence. Such an approach suggests (i) the existence of a precursor to orangutan and a hominoid ancestor of gorilla, chimpanzee, and man; (ii) the emergence of the hominoid ancestor; and (iii) the existence of a progenitor of chimpanzee and man after the divergence of the gorilla.

DNA-DNA HYBRIDIZATION EVIDENCE

In 1976, when Goodman noted that "the data on single-copy DNA . . . suggest that *Homo* and *Pan* share the most recent common ancestor," the DNA-DNA hybridization evidence consisted primarily of the papers by Kohne *et al.* (1972) and Hoyer *et al.* (1972). Neither study presented a complete matrix of comparisons, and only one DNA-DNA hybrid was used for each comparison. The Kohne *et al.* study did not include *Gorilla* or *Pongo*, and thus contributed nothing toward the resolution of the *Homo-Pan-Gorilla* trichotomy problem. However, it did give the most commonly accepted branching pattern for the groups represented by the taxa they did compare, namely, *Homo*, *Pan*, *Hylobates*, *Cercopithecus*, *Macaca*, *Cebus*, and *Galago*.

The study by Hoyer *et al.* (1972) used *Homo* and *Pongo* single-copy DNAs as tracers and compared them with the DNAs of *Homo*, *Pan*, *Gorilla*, *Pongo*, *Hylobates*, and *Cercopithecus*. Only one comparison was made between the tracer DNAs of *Homo* and *Pongo* and the DNAs of each of the six genera. There was a poor reciprocal between *Homo* and *Pongo* (1.9-2.9), which they noted was "difficult to rationalize and emphasizes the need for more determinations of DNA homologies among the hominoids." (Indeed!) What the reciprocal discrepancy indicated was that experimental errors existed and that instead of obtaining only the two values, which, ideally, should have been identical, they should have obtained five or more values and averaged them to obtain the nodal value for the *Homo-Pongo* divergence. Instead, the authors concluded that

> The present DNA data do not tell us whether the chimpanzee and gorilla are closer cladistically to each other than to Man or whether one of these African apes might be closer cladistically to Man. The latter possibility is suggested by the closer distance between Man and chimpanzee than between Man and gorilla on using [^{3}H] human unique DNA sequences as the indicator of relatedness.

These statements indicate that the authors did not realize that their data quite clearly showed that *Homo* and *Pan* are closer than *Pan* and *Gorilla* or *Homo* and *Gorilla*. The *Homo-Pan* distance was "0.7 delta Te$_{50}$" units and the *Homo-Gorilla* was 1.4. These values indicate that *Homo-Pan* was the closest pair. The confusion was caused by the reciprocal discrepancy in the *Homo-Pongo* comparisons. From the vantage point of our larger data base it is now apparent that the distances between

Pongo and *Gorilla* (2.3) and *Pongo* and *Pan* (1.8) describe the same node, and thus the *Pongo* lineage divergence node was actually measured by four Te$_{50}$ values: 1.8, 1.9, 2.3, 2.9. The first three cluster quite closely together and average 2.0; the last stands out as the most discrepant. Because of the UAR we now know that all values in such a set should be equal and that departures from equality are due to experimental errors. The lower values in such a set are likely to be closer to the true value, because they presumably result from more accurate base pairing, whereas the larger values are probably caused by greater experimental error. With the advantage of hindsight, including the certainty that the *Pongo* divergence occurred before those of the African apes and man, we can "trim" the 2.9 value and use the 2.0 average of the other three values for the *Pongo* node.

If Hoyer *et al.* (1972) had completed the matrix and used at least five hybrids for each pairwise combination, it is virtually certain that their results would have been unequivocal, even with some poor reciprocals. This is suggested by the fact that the branching pattern becomes clear when their data for each node based on more than one measurement are averaged and a cladogram is constructed from the results, as in Figure 2.

The study by Benveniste and Todaro (1976) was also based on an incomplete matrix, but they labeled three genera: *Homo*, *Pan*, and *Gorilla*. However, they too made only one DNA-DNA hybrid for each pairwise comparison and their data did not resolve the *Homo-Pan-Gorilla* trichotomy. The *Homo-Pan* node for the reciprocal pair of values (2.3, 2.4) averaged 2.35 and the *Homo + Pan* x *Gorilla* node with four measurements

(2.4, 2.4, 2.6, 2.6) averaged 2.50. In this case the reciprocals were in excellent agreement, but the difference between the averages of the two subsets was only 0.15, and the values appeared to form a continuum from 2.3 to 2.6. This offered no basis for a separation between nodes, even if one were certain of the actual branching order. That the *Homo-Pan-Gorilla* divergence "emerges ... as a trichotomy" was the only possible conclusion from their data. The rest of their primate phylogeny was in agreement with those obtained from other sources of evidence, including ours.

RESULTS

In our DNA-DNA hybridization study of the hominoids we prepared single-copy, radioiodine-labeled tracers of *Homo*, *Pan troglodytes*, *Pan paniscus*, *Gorilla*, *Pongo*, and *Hylobates lar*. The whole, unlabeled DNAs of these taxa, plus those of *Hylobates syndactylus* and five species of cercopithecids, were used to form DNA-DNA hybrids. A complete matrix of the tracer species was produced, with multiple replicates for each combination. We had only small amounts of the DNAs of *P. paniscus* and *H. syndactylus*, so there were fewer comparisons for them than for the others.

Table 1 lists the delta T$_{50}$H values for the comparisons among the hominoids and between them and the cercopithecids. Table 2 is the reduced and folded matrix summarizing the 183 delta T$_{50}$H measurements. Inspection of the delta values will show that most reciprocals are nearly equal and that discrepancies are well within the known range of experimental error. The average reciprocal discrepancy is 0.18 for the 12 largest sets, and the discrepancies range from 0.02 to 0.35. The averages, standard errors (SE), and standard deviations (SD) provide evidence for the UAR of DNA evolution.

Figure 3 provides diagrams of the ranges, averages, SEs and SDs of the delta values. Figure 4 is a "distance Wagner" tree based on the data in Table 1. The distance Wagner procedure was described by Farris (1972).

It is obvious from these various ways of presenting the data that (1) the data fit the branching pattern of cladogram 1 of Figure 1, and (2) the only two sets that overlap are those for the *Gorilla* node and for the *Pan-Homo* node. These two overlap by a value of 0.6, which is more than 50% of the total ranges of each of the sets (1.0, 1.1), and the two averages are only delta T$_{50}$H 0.5 apart. (It is easy to see why Benveniste and Todaro [1976] were unable to separate the nodes with only four comparisons in the overlap zone.)

Although the delta T$_{50}$H values overlap due to experimental error, the 0.5 difference between the means is statistically significant. A comparison of the data sets using Student's *t*-test gave a value of P 0.001 for either 18 or 25 df. Thus the data show that *Homo* and *Pan* are more closely related to one another than either is to *Gorilla*.

TIME AND THE DNA "CLOCK"

The third element in the reconstruction of a phylogeny is time: the dating of the speciation events that initiated the divergent lineages described by the branching pattern. It is clear that for a distance measure to be an index to time it must be "clocklike," and therefore it must satisfy the "triangle inequality" defined by Farris (1981) as: " ... for any three taxa, *i, j, k, d(i,j) d(j,k)* +

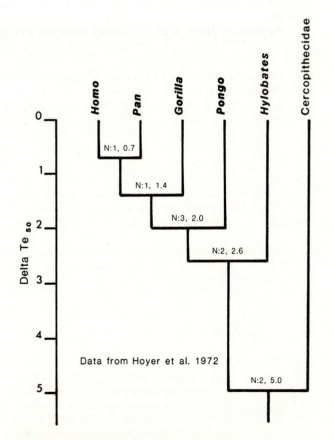

Figure 2. *Branching pattern of the hominoid phylogeny based on the data of Hoyer* et al. *(1972).*

Table 2. Matrix of average delta $T_{50}H$ distance values, standard error (SE), standard deviation (SD), and number (N) of DNA-DNA hybrids for each pairwise set of comparisons.

	Homo	Pan paniscus	Pan troglodytes	Gorilla gorilla	Pongo pygmaeus	Hylobates lar	Cerco- pithecids
Homo sapiens							
Pan paniscus	Δ1.9 0.1 SE 0.3 SD N = 7						
Pan troglodytes	Δ1.8 0.05 SE 0.2 SD N = 12	Δ0.7 0.1 SE 0.3 SD N = 6					
Gorilla gorilla	Δ2.4 0.1 SE 0.2 SD N = 10	Δ2.3 0.1 SE 0.3 SD N = 6	Δ2.1 0.1 SE 0.2 SD N = 10				
Pongo pygmaeus	Δ3.6 0.1 SE 0.4 SD N = 11	Δ3.7 0.1 SE 0.2 SD N = 9	Δ3.7 0.1 SE 0.2 SD N = 10	Δ3.8 0.1 SE 0.2 SD N= 10			
Hylobates lar	Δ5.2 0.1 SE 0.2 SD N = 10	Δ5.6 0.2 SE 0.5 SD N = 5	Δ5.1 0.1 SE 0.3 SD N = 10	Δ5.4 0.1 SE 0.3 SD N = 12	Δ5.1 0.1 SE 0.3 SD N = 15		
Cercopithecids	Δ7.7 0.1 SE 0.4 SD N = 9	Δ8.0 0.2 SE 0.6 SD N = 6	Δ7.7 0.1 SE 0.4 SD N = 9	Δ7.5 0.2 SE 0.5 SD N = 5	Δ7.6 0.1 SE 0.2 SD N = 4	Δ7.4 0.2 SE 0.4 SD N = 3	

$d(i,k)$. Distance measures satisfying this condition are called *metric*." We have never encountered a violation of the triangle inequality in our DNA-DNA data and we therefore consider them to be metric. Farris continues:

A distance measure that violates the triangle inequality cannot logically show clocklike behavior . . . metricity is required in order that distances be interpretable as amounts of evolutionary change. To . . . see why a nonmetric distance

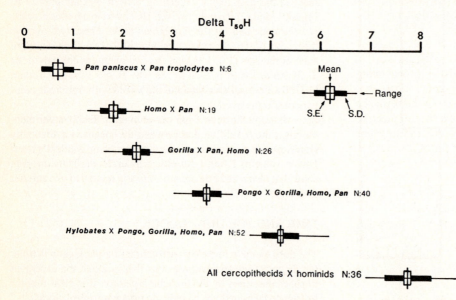

Figure 3. *Diagrams of the ranges, means, standard errors of the means, and standard deviations of the delta $T_{50}H$ values for the DNA-DNA hybridization comparisons among the hominoids, and between the hominoids and the cercopithecids.*

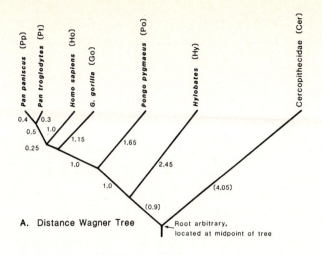

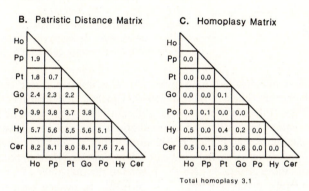

B. Patristic Distance Matrix

	Ho	Pp	Pt	Go	Po	Hy	Cer
Ho							
Pp	1.9						
Pt	1.8	0.7					
Go	2.4	2.3	2.2				
Po	3.9	3.8	3.7	3.8			
Hy	5.7	5.6	5.5	5.6	5.1		
Cer	8.2	8.1	8.0	8.1	7.6	7.4	
	Ho	Pp	Pt	Go	Po	Hy	Cer

C. Homoplasy Matrix

	Ho	Pp	Pt	Go	Po	Hy	Cer
Ho							
Pp	0.0						
Pt	0.0	0.0					
Go	0.0	0.0	0.1				
Po	0.3	0.1	0.0	0.0			
Hy	0.5	0.0	0.4	0.2	0.0		
Cer	0.5	0.1	0.3	0.6	0.0	0.0	
	Ho	Pp	Pt	Go	Po	Hy	Cer

Total homoplasy 3.1

Figure 4. *Distance Wagner tree based on the data in Table 1.*

cannot be fully clocklike, suppose that a distance measure d shows a constant rate of divergence. Given three taxa, i, j, k, two, say i and j, will be genealogically most closely related, and so will have an ancestor common to them but not to k. Since i and j diverged more recently from each other than either did from k, $d(i,j)$ $d(i,k)$, $d((j,k)$. Further, i and j diverged from k at the same time, inasmuch as at that time they were the same species. Then if d accurately reflects time, $d(i,k) = d(j,k)$. It is readily seen from these relations that if d is clocklike, then for any three taxa $d(i,j)$ max($d[i,k]$, $d[j,k]$). This condition is called the ultrametric inequality. . . . Since for positive d, the maximum of any two d values is no greater than their sum, it is seen that any ultrametric distance is also metric. Conversely, any distance that violates the triangle inequality must also be nonultrametric, and so cannot show a constant rate of divergence. Indeed, since ultrametrics are contained within the set of metrics, a distance showing strong departures from metricity cannot even be closer to ultrametric.

These definitions are satisfied by our DNA hybridization data, all 18,000+ hybrids in more than 900 experimental sets, without exception. It is possible that excessive experimental error might produce data that seem to violate the triangle inequality, but even the limited set of Benveniste and Todaro (1976) seemed "close to ultrametric-clocklike" to Farris (1981).

The "Relative Rate Test" (Sarich and Wilson 1967a, b) is another way of stating the triangle inequality. It describes the same pathways and provides a method to test for the uniformity of average rates of evolution along those pathways. Our DNA hybridization studies of birds contain literally hundreds of Relative Rate Tests and all the data obey the rules defined by Farris. The primate data also satisfy the conditions of the Relative Rate Test and Farris's definitions

The evidence for and the consistency of the DNA clock have been demonstrated repeatedly by our data and we entertain no doubts about the competence of the DNA hybridization technique for measuring genealogical distances and for providing accurate relative times for divergence nodes. We believe that this technique is probably the best method for the reconstruction of the phylogenies of living taxa and that it is effective for events as long ago as 150 MYA. We also find that it is misunderstood and unappreciated by some systematists. For example, Thorpe (1982) wrote that "DNA annealing studies provide little basis for a molecular clock..." and "while alternative techniques using certain specific components may provide some taxonomic information from DNA, reannealing results are unreliable and uninformative, and systematic conclusions from past studies using the whole genome must be treated with caution." Fortunately, Thorpe's comments are erroneous; however they are, in part, justified, for it is true that "past studies...must be treated with caution," but only because they were too limited in scope, used too few comparisons, and based conclusions on incomplete matrices. (We have examined three examples above.) Thorpe also suggested that DNA sequences ("specific components") may provide some taxonomic information. However, we can see no reason to expect data derived from base sequences to improve on those from amino acid sequences, which have produced contradictory results because different proteins evolve at different rates and represent but minute percentages of the genome. As Friday (1981) noted, "phylogenetic conclusions derived from a study of nucleotide sequences will be subject to the same suspicions as those derived from amino acid sequences." If Thorpe were correct in his comments, it would be inconceivable for us to have obtained the internally consistent phylogeny that we have reconstructed for the avian order Passeriformes, a group of ca. 5000 species (Sibley and Ahlquist 1980, 1981a, b, 1982a-i, Sibley et al. 1982). We realize that Thorpe did not know of these studies when he wrote his negative comments about DNA hybridization, but we have felt compelled to place our rebuttal on record.

DATING THE DIVERGENCE MODES

Figure 5 shows the regression between delta $T_{50}H$ values and absolute time based on Pilbeam's (1983) estimate that the *Pongo* clade branched ca. 16 MYA. Figure 6 is the phylogram of the hominoids based on the branching pattern indicated by the DNA hybridization data and on the datings of the divergences based on the regression shown in Figure 5. Table 3 contains estimates of branching times based on fossil, protein, and DNA hybridization data, illustrating the wide range in the dates that have been proposed.

"The dating of points of dichotomy on a cladogram using the evidence of the fossil record supposes the ability to make accurate decisions about the cladistic affinities of fossil species. It is well known that, in practice, this task can be difficult, especially in the vicinity of the split itself" (Friday 1981). The dating of divergence nodes from fossils is certain-

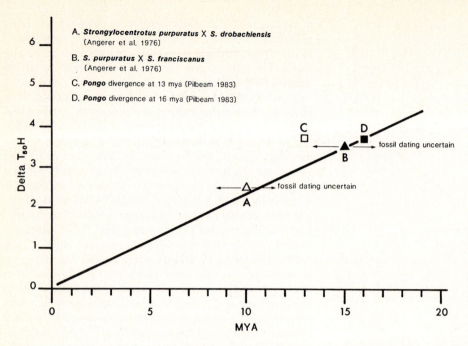

A. *Strongylocentrotus purpuratus* X *S. drobachiensis* (Angerer et al. 1976)

B. *S. purpuratus* X *S. franciscanus* (Angerer et al. 1976)

C. *Pongo* divergence at 13 mya (Pilbeam 1983)

D. *Pongo* divergence at 16 mya (Pilbeam 1983)

fossil dating uncertain

fossil dating uncertain

Figure 5. *Regression between time and delta $T_{50}H$ values. The slope is based on a proportionality constant of delta $T_{50}H$ 1.0 = 4.3 million years, which was derived from Pilbeam's (1983) estimate of the divergence time of the orangutan lineage as 16 MYA.*

ly difficult, but divergence times based on molecular evidence must agree to the extent that well-established fossil identities and dates will fit the lineages so defined. As long as the ramapithecines were believed to be ancestral to hominines the dating discrepancies between the fossils and the molecules could not be reconciled. Since ca. 1980 many paleontologists have accepted the evidence of recently discovered fossils from Pakistan and China indicating that *Sivapithecus* and

Ramapithecus were members of the pongine, not the hominine, clade (Andrews 1982; Ciochon and Corruccini 1982; Pilbeam 1982, 1983). Pilbeam (1983) has reviewed hominoid evolution and hominid origins, including the fossil and molecular evidence. He now thinks it "unlikely that *Ramapithecus* is a hominid; nor is *Sivapithecus*," but that both of "these genera . . . are . . . related to the orangutans." The pongine divergence time "can plausibly be pushed back to around 16 million years," or "to at least 13 million years and likely to 16 million years." This removes one of the main obstacles to agreement between the fossil and the molecular evidence.

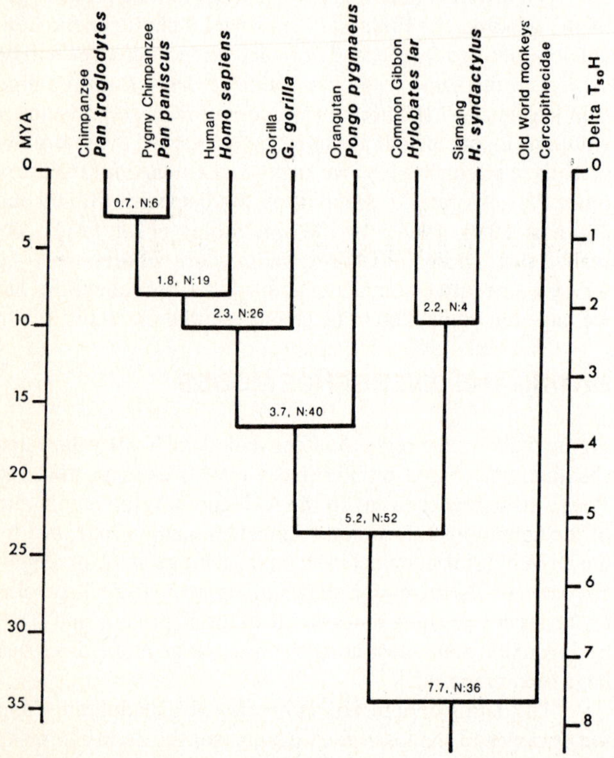

Ciochon and Corruccini (1982) have proposed a ". . . reconceptualization of Miocene Hominoidea . . . brought about by . . . five factors."

1. . . .increased doubt about the hominid affinities of *Ramapithecus*.
2. . . .discovery of many . . . new Miocene hominoid specimens. . . .
3. . . .reinterpretations regarding the postcranial data in Miocene hominoid evolution. . . .
4. The increasing acceptance or influence of biomolecular data for understanding the timing and relationships of hominoid cladogenesis.
5. The incredible discovery of . . . 3-4 million-year old hominids from Eastern Africa that have unexpectedly chimpanzee-like characteristics (see Johanson and White 1979).

The Pliocene australopithecines from Hadar, Ethiopia, and Laetoli, Tanzania have been dated between 2.6 and 3.8 MYA (Johanson and White 1979; White *et al.* 1981). Thus they fit easily within the *Homo* lineage indicated by the DNA hybridization data.

The delta $T_{50}H$ value for the *Pongo* divergence is 3.7. If we use Pilbeam's (1983) 16 MYA date for this node, delta $T_{50}H$ 1.0 = 4.3 MY, and if we use 13 MYA for the pongine divergence

Figure 6. *Phylogram of the hominoids and cercopithecids. The divergence dates are based on a proportionality constant of delta $T_{50}H$ 1.0 = 4.3 MY (see Fig. 5).*

Table 3. Proposed divergence dates of the anthropoid lineages [numbers = millions of years ago (MYA)]

Reference and data used

Divergence nodes	Patterson et al. (1970) "Lothagam Jaw"	Walker (1976) Fossil datings	Simons (1976) Fossil datings	Sarich and Cronin (1976) Albumin + transferrin	Jones (1976) 28S Ribosomal genes [Dates based on Simons (1964)]	Benveniste and Todaro (1976) DNA-DNA hybridization data "Corrected" for generation time	Andrews (1982) Based on ramapithecines on the Pongo lineage	Goodman et al. (1983) Amino acid sequences Eutherian node = 90 MYA	Goodman et al. (1983) Amino acid sequences Anthropoid node = 35 MYA	Sibley and Ahlquist DNA × DNA Pongo node = 13 MYA [Pilbeam (1983)] Delta T50H 1.0 = 3.5 MY	Sibley and Ahlquist DNA × DNA Pongo node = 13 MYA [Pilbeam (1983)] Delta T50H 1.0 = 3.5 MY
Pan troglodytes × *Pan paniscus*										2.4	3.0
Pan branch		3-4	18-19	4.4	30	12	6-7			6.3	7.7
Homo branch	3.7-8.3	15+	18-19	4.4	30	12	6-7	1.3	2.2	6.3	7.7
Gorilla branch		3-4	18-19	4.4		12	6-7	1.8	3.1	8.0	9.9
Pongo branch		15+		10±		18	10 ± 3			13	16
Hylobates branch		25+	27+	10±		26	12 ± 3			18.2	22.4
Hylobates lar × *Hylobates syndactylus*		2				7				7.7	9.5
Cercopithecid branch			33 ± 6	20	60	30		13.4	23	27	33

date, delta $T_{50}H$ 1.0 = 3.5 MY. If we use these two calibrations to calculate the probable ranges of the hominoid divergence nodes we obtain the following: *Pan troglodytes-Pan paniscus*, 2.4-3.0 MYA; *Homo*, 6.3-7.7 MYA; *Gorilla*, 8.0-9.9 MYA; *Pongo*, 13-16 MYA; *Hylobates*, 18.2-22.4 MYA; *H. lar-H. syndactylus*, 7.7-9.5 MYA; Cercopithecoidea, 27-33 MYA.

The delta $T_{50}H$ 1.0 = 4.3 MY calibration based on Pilbeam's 16-MYA date for the orangutan lineage divergence is in excellent agreement with three calibration points based on our avian data. The Ostrich-Rhea delta $T_{50}H$ value is 17.4; we estimated the divergence time to be 80 MYA, when the Atlantic Ocean was surely an effective barrier between the African and South American populations of their last common ancestor. This yields a calibration of delta $T_{50}H$ 1.0 = 4.6 MY. Similarly, we obtained a delta $T_{50}H$ value of 17.0 for the split between the Old World and New World suboscine passerine birds and estimated a 75-MYA divergence time for these volant groups, so delta $T_{50}H$ 1.0 = 4.4 MY (Sibley and Ahlquist 1984a, b). For the divergence between the New Zealand wrens (Oligomyodi: Acanthisittides) and the other suboscines the delta $T_{50}H$ value is 17.7, and the opening of the Tasman Sea is dated at ca. 80 MYA, giving a calibration of delta $T_{50}H$ 1.0 = 4.5 MY (Sibley *et al.* 1982). We thus have four calibration points giving delta $T_{50}H$ 1.0 = 4.3-4.6 MY. The range of dates considered from 16 to 80 MYA suggests that the regression is linear, and since the birds and the primates lie on the same regression line, it appears that the same average rate of DNA evolution occurs in both groups.

Thus we may be close to the correct calibration, but not as close as the available techniques permit. Furthermore, there are uncertainties in all of the fossil and geological datings, and additional calibration points should be obtained before concluding that the dating problem is solved. We agree with Pilbeam (1983) that "DNA hybridization, coupled with appropriate fossil-based calibration points, should give the best estimates for branching times. This proposition . . . needs thorough testing in groups such as rodents, bovids, and carnivores which have (unlike primates) an adequate fossil record for independent estimates of divergence dates." Jacobs and Pilbeam (1980) urged that

> a systematic analysis of such mammals begin...so that discussions of molecular evolution can be conducted within a more secure temporal framework, and so that molecular dates may be used to indicate possible weaknesses in inferred phylogenies. If it can be demonstrated that . . . the "clock" keeps reasonable time, it could then be used with confidence to help sort out the fossil record of less well documented or more controversial groups, such as the Hominoidea.

To the fossil-based calibration points we would add the geological datings of the intercontinental splits that occurred when Gondwanaland broke apart in the Cretaceous. Comparisons between vicariant taxon pairs that began their divergences when the southern continents drifted apart will also contribute to the solution of the calibration problem.

It has not escaped our attention that the divergence between the two species of *Hylobates* (ca. 9.5 MYA) occurred at virtually the same time as that of the *Gorilla* branch (ca. 9.9 MYA). If we apply the principle of categorical equivalence (Sibley and Ahlquist 1982d, 1983) substantial changes result in the classification of the hominoids. We prefer to defer consideration of this problem until the datings of the major nodes in the phylogeny of the primates are more certain.

ADDED NOTES

The recent discovery by Richard Leakey and Alan Walker of a fossil "sivapithecine" from Buluk, Kenya provides additional evidence and raises new questions. The material has been dated at ca. 17 MYA and Walker (personal communication) suggests at least two possible interpretations: (1) The new fossil from Kenya represents the African ancestor of the Orangutan clade; or (2) it represents the ancestor of all of the great apes, thus giving a "minimum great ape/gibbon split."

If we accept interpretation (1) above, the new fossil falls close to the regression line in Figure 5 and yields a proportionality constant of delta $T_{50}H$ 1.0 = 4.6 MY, in excellent agreement with our avian values and with the constant based on Pilbeam's (1983) estimate of the Orangutan divergence node as occurring 16 MYA.

If interpretation (2) is correct and the gibbon clade branched ca. 17 MYA, we obtain a proportionality constant of 3.3 MY and the following divergence dates: *Pan-Homo*, 5.9 MYA; *Gorilla*, 7.5 MYA; *Pongo*, 12.1 MYA; *Hylobates*, 17 MYA; and Cercopithecidae, 25.2 MYA.

Most of these divergence dates would be acceptable, given our present state of knowledge. However, the 12.1 MYA date for the Orangutan divergence may be questioned in view of the 13-MY-old sivapithecine fossils from Pakistan (Pilbeam 1982, 1983).

Thus, the significance of the Buluk fossils is not yet clear, but they are obviously an important addition to the evidence concerning hominoid phylogeny.

ACKNOWLEDGEMENTS

We thank L. Wallace, R. Gatter, E. Nowicki, and F. C. Sibley for laboratory assistance. Purified DNAs of several species were generously provided by O. A. Ryder (San Diego Zoo), and autopsy tissues were received from J. L. Palotay (Oregon Regional Primate Research Center), J. Johnson (Washington Regional Primate Research Center), G. B. Baskin (Delta Regional Primate Research Center), N. W. King, Jr. (New England Regional Primate Research Center), E. L. Simons and M. Stuart (Duke University Primate Center), A. G. Hendrickx (California Primate Research Center), R. E. Benveniste (NIH Frederick Cancer Research Center), E. Lockwood (Yerkes Primate Research Center), and J. Ogden and J. Seashore (Yale-New Haven Medical Center). National Science Foundation grant BNS 82-05774 supported the laboratory work.

REFERENCES

Adams, J., and Rothman, E. D. 1982. Estimation of phylogenetic relationships from DNA restriction patterns and selection of endonuclease cleavage sites. *Proc. Natl. Acad. Sci. USA* 79:3560-3564.

Andrews, P. 1982. Hominoid evolution. *Nature* 295:185-186.

Angerer, R. C., Davidson, E. H., and Britten, R. J. 1976. Single-copy DNA and structural gene sequence relationships among four sea urchin species. *Chromosoma* 56:213-216.

Avise, J. C., and Aquadro, C. F. 1982. A comparative summary of genetic distances in the vertebrates. *Evol. Biol.* 15:151-185.

Avise, J. C., and Lansman, R. A. 1983. Polymorphism of mitochondrial DNA in populations of higher animals, in: *Evolution of Genes and Proteins* (M. Nei and R. K. Koehn, Eds.), pp. 147-164, Sinauer Associates, Sunderland, Massachusetts.

Baba, M. L., Darga, L. L., and Goodman, M. 1982. Recent advances in molecular evolution of the primates, in: *Advanced Views in Primate Biology* (A. B. Chiarelli and R. S. Corruccini, Eds.), pp. 6-27, Springer-Verlag, Berlin.

Benveniste, R. E., and Todaro, G. J. 1976. Evolution of type C viral genes: Evidence for an Asian origin of man. *Nature* 261:101-108.

Bonner, T. I., Heinemann, R., and Todaro, G. J. 1981. A geographic factor involved in the evolution of the single-copy DNA sequences of primates, in: *Evolution Today, Proceedings of the 2nd International Congress on Systematic and Evolutionary Biology* (G. G. E. Scudder, and J. L. Reveal, Eds.), pp. 293-300, Hunt Institute of Botanic Documentation, Pittsburgh.

Britten R. J, Kohne D. E 1968. Repeated sequences in DNA. *Science* 161:529-540.

Britten, R. J., Graham, D. E., and Neufeld, B. R. 1974. Analysis of repeating DNA sequences by reassociation. *Methods Enzymol.* 29:363-418.

Brown, W. M. 1983. Evolution of animal mitochondrial DNA, in: *Evolution of Genes and Proteins* (M. Nei and R. K. Koehn, Eds.), pp. 62-88, Sinauer Associates, Sunderland, Mass.

Brown, W. M., Prager, E. M., Wang, A., and Wilson, A. C. 1982. Mitochondrial DNA sequences of primates: Tempo and mode of evolution. *J. Mol. Evol.* 18:225-239.

Bruce, E. J., and Ayala, F. J. 1979. Phylogenetic relationships between man and the apes: Electrophoretic evidence. *Evolution* 33:1040-1056.

Chan, H.-C., Ruyechan, W. T., and Wetmur, J. G. 1976. *In vitro* iodination of low complexity nucleic acids without chain scission. *Biochemistry* 15:5487-5490.

Ciochon, R. L., and Corruccini, R. S. 1982. Miocene hominoids and new interpretations of ape and human ancestry, in: *Advanced Views in Primate Biology* (A. B. Chiarelli and R. S. Corruccini, Eds.), pp. 149-159, Springer-Verlag, Berlin.

Commorford, S. L. 1971. Iodination of nucleic acids *in vitro*. *Biochemistry* 10:1993-2000.

Delson, E., Eldredge, N., and Tattersall, I. 1977. Reconstruction of hominid phylogeny: A testable framework based on cladistic analysis. *J. Hum. Evol.* 6:263-278.

Dene, H. T., Goodman, M., and Prychodko, W. 1976. Immunodiffusion evidence on the phylogeny of the primates, in: *Molecular Anthropology* (M. Goodman and R. E. Tashian, Eds.), pp. 171-196, Plenum Press, New York.

Dutrillaux, B. 1979. Chromosomal evolution in primates: Tentative phylogeny from *Microcebus murinus* (prosimian) to man. *Hum. Genet.* 48:251-314.

Dutrillaux, B. 1980. Chromosomal evolution of the great apes and man. *J. Reprod. Fertil.* (Suppl.) 28:105-111.

Farris, J. S. 1972. Estimating phylogenetic trees from distance matrices. *Am. Nat.* 106:645-668.

Farris, J. S. 1981. Distance data in phylogenetic analysis, in: *Advances in Cladistics* (V. A. Funk and D. R. Brooks, Eds.), pp. 3-23, New York Botanical Garden, New York.

Ferris, S. D., Wilson, A. C., and Brown, W. M. 1981. Evolutionary tree for apes and humans based on cleavage maps of mitochondrial DNA. *Proc. Natl. Acad. Sci. USA* 78:2432-2436.

Fitch, W. M. 1976. Molecular evolutionary clocks, in: *Molecular Evolution* (F. J. Ayala, Ed.), pp. 160-178, Sinauer Associates, Sunderland, Mass.

Friday, A. E. 1981. Hominoid evolution: the nature of biochemical evidence. *Symp. Soc. Study Hum. Biol.* 21:1-23.

Goodman, M. 1975. Protein sequence and immunological specificity: Their role in phylogenetic studies of primates, in: *Phylogeny of the Primates* (W. P. Luckett and F. S. Szalay, Eds.), pp. 219-248, Plenum Press, New York.

Goodman, M. 1976. Toward a genealogical description of the primates, in: *Molecular Anthropology* (M. Goodman and R. E. Tashian, Eds.), pp. 321-353, Plenum Press, New York.

Goodman, M., Olson, C. B., Beeber, J. E., and Czelusniak, J. 1982a. New perspectives in the molecular biological analysis of mammalian phylogeny. *Acta. Zool. Fennica.* 169:19-35.

Goodman, M., Weiss, M. L., and Czelusniak, J. 1982b. Molecular evolution above the species level: Branching pattern, rates, and mechanisms. *Syst. Zool.* 31:376-399.

Goodman, M., Braunitzer, G., Stangl, A., and Shrank, B. 1983. Evidence on human origins from haemoglobins of African apes. *Nature* 303:546-548.

Hoffstetter, R. 1982. Les primates Simiiformes. *Ann. Paleontol.* 68:241-290.

Honacki, J. H., Kinman, K. E., and Koeppl, J. W. (Eds). 1982. *Mammal Species of the World*, Association of Systematic Collections, Museum of Natural History, University of Kansas, Lawrence, Kansas.

Hoyer, B. H., van de Velde, N. W., Goodman, M., and Roberts, R. B. 1972. Examination of hominoid evolution by DNA sequence homology. *J. Hum. Evol.* 1:645-649.

Jacobs, L. L., and Pilbeam, D. 1980. Of mice and men: Fossil-based divergence dates and molecular "clocks." *J. Hum. Evol.* 9:551-555.

Johanson, D. C., and White, T. D. 1979. A systematic assessment of early African hominoids. *Science* 230:321-330.

Jones, K. W. 1976. Comparative aspects of DNA in higher primates, in: *Molecular Anthropology* (M. Goodman and R. E. Tashian, Eds.), pp. 357-368, Plenum Press, New York.

Kluge, A. G. 1983. Cladistics and the classification of the great apes, in: *New Interpretations of Ape and Human Ancestry* (R. L. Ciochon and R. S. Corruccini, Eds.), pp. 151-177, Plenum Press, New York.

Kohne, D. E. 1970. Evolution of higher-organism DNA. *Q. Rev. Biophys.* 33:327-375.

Kohne, D. E., and Britten, R. J. 1971. Hydroxyapatite techniques for nucleic acid reassociation. *Procedures Nucleic Acid Res.* 2:500-512.

Kohne, D. E., Chiscon, J. A., and Hoyer, B. H. 1972. Evolution of primate DNA sequences. *J. Hum. Evol.* 1:627-644.

Marmur, J. 1961. A procedure for the isolation of deoxyribonucleic acid from micro-organisms. *J. Mol. Bio.* 3:585-596.

Miller, D. A. 1977. Evolution of primate chromosomes. *Science* 198:1116-1124.

Oxnard, C. E. 1981. The place of man among the primates: Anatomical, molecular and morphometric evidence. *Homo.* 32:149-176.

Patterson, B., Behrensmeyer, A. K., and Sill, W. D. 1970. Geology and fauna of new Pliocene locality in north-western Kenya. *Nature* 226:918-921.

Pilbeam, D. 1982. New hominoid skull material from the Miocene of Pakistan. *Nature* 295:232-234.

Pilbeam, D. 1983. Hominoid evolution and hominoid origins, in: *Recent Advances in the Evolution of the Primates* (C. Chagas, Ed.), pp. 43-61, Pontificae Academiae Scientiarum Scripta Varia 50, Vatican, Rome.

Prensky, W. 1976. The radioiodination of RNA and DNA to high specific activities. *Methods Cell. Biol.* 13:121-152.

Romero-Herrera, A. E., Lehmann, H., Joysey, K. A., and Friday, A. E. 1978. On the evolution of myoglobin. *Philos. Trans. R. Soc. Lond.* 283:61-163.

Sarich, V. M., and Cronin, J. E. 1976. Molecular systematics of the primates, in: *Molecular Anthropology* (M. Goodman and R. E. Tashian, Eds.), pp. 141-170, Plenum Press, New York.

Sarich, V. M., and Cronin, J. E. 1977. Generation length and rates of hominoid molecular evolution. *Nature* 269:354-355.

Sarich, V. M., and Wilson, A. C. 1967a. Rates of albumin evolution in primates. *Proc. Natl. Acad. Sci. USA* 58:142-148.

Sarich, V. M., and Wilson, A. C. 1967b. Immunological time scale for hominid evolution. *Science* 158:1200-1204.

Sarich, V. M., and Wilson, A. C. 1973. Generation time and genomic evolution in primates. *Science* 179:1144-1147.

Seuanez, H. N. 1982. Chromosome banding and primate phylogeny, in: *Advanced Views in Primate Biology* (A. B. Chiarelli and R. S. Corruchini, Eds.), pp. 224-235, Springer-Verlag, Berlin.

Shields, G. F., and Straus, N. A. 1975. DNA-DNA hybridization studies of birds. *Evolution* 29:159-166.

Sibley, C. G., and Ahlquist, J. E. 1980. The relationships of the "primate insect eaters" as indicated by DNA-DNA hybridization, in: *Proceedings of the 17th International Ornithological Congress* (R. Nohring, Ed.), pp. 1215-1220, Deutsche Ornith Gesellsch, Berlin.

Sibley, C. G., and Ahlquist, J. E. 1981a. The phylogeny and relationships of the ratite birds as indicated by DNA-DNA hybridization, in: *Proceedings of the 2nd International Congress of Systematic and Evolutionary Biology* (G. G. E. Scudder and J. L. Reveal, Eds.), pp. 301-335, Hunt Institute of Botanic Documentation, Pittsburgh.

Sibley, C. G., and Ahlquist, J. E. 1981b. The relationships of the accentors (*Prunella*) as indicated by DNA-DNA hybridization. *J. Ornithol* 122:369-378.

Sibley, C. G., and Ahlquist, J. E. 1981c. The relationships of the wagtails and pipits (Motacillidae) as indicated by DNA-DNA hybridization. *L'Oiseau et RFO* 51:189-199.

Sibley, C. G., and Ahlquist, J. E. 1982a. The relationships of the Hawaiian honeycreepers (Drepaninini) as indicated by DNA-DNA hybridization. *Auk* 99:130-140.

Sibley, C. G., and Ahlquist, J. E. 1982b. The relationships of the Wrentit (*Chamaea fasciata*) as indicated by DNA-DNA hybridization. *Condor* 84:40-44.

Sibley, C. G., and Ahlquist, J. E. 1982c. The relationships of the vireos (Vireoninae) as indicated by DNA-DNA hybridization. *Wilson Bull.* 94:114-128.

Sibley, C. G., and Ahlquist, J. E. 1982d. The relationships of the Yellow-breasted Chat (*Icteria virens*), and the alleged "slow down" in the rate of macromolecular evolution in birds. *Postilla* 187:1-19.

Sibley, C. G., and Ahlquist, J. E. 1982e. The relationships of the Australo-Papuan scrub-robins (*Drymodes*) as indicated by DNA-DNA hybridization. *Emu* 82:101-105.

Sibley, C. G., and Ahlquist, J. E. 1982f. The relationships of the Australo-Papuan sittellas (*Daphoenositta*) as indicated by DNA-DNA hybridization. *Emu* 82:173-176.

Sibley, C. G., and Ahlquist, J. E. 1982g. The relationships of the Australasian whistlers (*Pachycephala*) as indicated by DNA-DNA hybridization. *Emu* 82:199-202.

Sibley, C. G., and Ahlquist, J. E. 1982h. The relationships of the Australo-Papuan fairy-wrens *Malurus* as indicated by DNA-DNA hybridization. *Emu* 82:251-255.

Sibley, C. G., and Ahlquist, J. E. 1982i. The relationships of the swallows (Hirundinidae). *J. Yamashina Inst. Ornithol.* 14:122-130.

Sibley, C. G., and Ahlquist, J. E. 1983. Phylogeny and classification of birds based on the data of DNA-DNA hybridization, in: *Current Ornithology* Vol. 1. (R. F. Johnston, Ed.), pp. 245-292, Plenum Press, New York.

Sibley, C. G., and Ahlquist, J. E. 1984. The relationship of the starlings (Sturnidae: Sturnini) and the mockingbirds (Sturnidae: Mimini) *Auk* 101:230-243.

Sibley, C. G., and Ahlquist, J. E. 1984b. The relationship of the Papuan genus (*Peltops*). *Emu* 84:181-183.

Sibley, C. G., and Ahlquist, J. E. 1985a. The phylogeny and classifications of the New World suboscine passerine birds (Passeriformes: Oligomyodi: Tyrannides), in: *Neotropical Ornithology* (P. Buckley, M. Foster, E. Morton, R. Ridgely, and N. Smith, Eds.), pp. 396-410. American Ornithologists' Union Monographs, Washington, D.C.

Sibley, C. G., and Ahlquist, J. E. 1985b. The phylogeny and classification of the Australo-Papuan passerine birds. *Emu* 85(1):1-14.

Sibley, C. G., Williams, G. R., and Ahlquist, J. E. 1982. The relationships of the New Zealand wrens (Acanthisittidae) as indicated by DNA-DNA hybridization. *Notornis* 29:113-130.

Sibley, C. G., Lanyon, S. M., and Ahlquist, J. E. 1984. The relationships of the Sharpbill (*Oxyruncus cristatus*). *Condor* 86:48-52.

Sibley, C. G., Schodde, R., and Ahlquist, J. E. 1984. The relationships of the Australo-Papuan treecreepers (Climacteridae) as indicated by DNA-DNA hybridization. *Emu* 84:236-241.

Simons, E. L. 1964. The early ancestors of man. *Sci. Am.* 211:50.

Simons, E. L. 1976. The fossil record of primate phylogeny, in: *Molecular Anthropology* (M. Goodman and R. E. Tashian, Eds.), pp. 35-62, Plenum Press, New York.

Templeton, A. R. 1983. Phylogenetic inference from restriction endonuclease site maps with particular reference to the evolution of humans and apes. *Evolution* 37:221-244.

Thorpe, J. P. 1982. The molecular clock hypothesis: Biochemical evolution, genetic differentiation and systematics. *Ann. Rev. Ecol. Systemat.* 13:139-168.

Walker, A. 1976. Splitting times among hominoids deduced from the fossil record, in: Molecular Anthropology (M. Goodman and R. E. Tashian, Eds.), pp. 63-77, Plenum Press, New York.

White, T. D., Johanson, D. C., and Kimbel, W. H. 1981. *Australopithecus africanus*: its phyletic position reconsidered. *S. Afr. J. Sci.* 77:445-470.

Wilson, A. C., and Sarich, V. M. 1969. A molecular time scale for human evolution. *Proc. Natl. Acad. Sci. USA* 63:1088-1093.

Wilson, A. C., Carlson, S. S., and White, T. J. 1977. Biochemical evolution. *Ann. Rev. Biochem.* 46:573-639.

Yunis, J. J., and Prakash, O. 1982. The origin of man: A chromosomal pictorial legacy. *Science* 215:1525-1530.

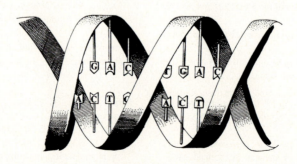

3

Molecular Insights into the Nature and Timing of Ancient Speciation Events: Correlates with Palaeoclimate and Palaeobiogeography

J. E. Cronin

The Miocene and Pleistocene witnessed the origin, radiation and evolution of the modern and extinct hominoid primates. The affinities of both the fossil and living forms in this group of primates are controversial. Substantial advances have recently been made in linking a specific fossil hominoid (*Sivapithecus meteai*) to the living orang-utan and thus, by inference, removing a putative ancestral hominid (*S. "Ramapithecus" punjabicus*) from consideration as a human ancestor (Andrews and Cronin 1982). Apart from recent Pleistocene forms, which are obviously related to the living orang-utan and gibbons and the Plio-Pleistocene hominids, no other fossil Miocene hominoid can be directly associated with any extant equivalent.

An important means of delineating the phylogeny of the living apes has been the study of macromolecules. Molecular comparisons have provided new insight into both the branching order, or cladistic relationships, of the living apes, as well as the timing of the origin of these lineages, through the molecular-clock hypothesis. Biomolecular dates, generated as long ago as 1967, are consistent both with recently acquired data and with a reanalysis of the molecular data as presented in this paper. These dates of the origins of lineages serve as markers to test environmental or biographic correlates of speciation. And the molecularly derived cladistics serve as a framework around which other forms of data can be organized in an evolutionary sequence. Such data are of importance in delineating and defining the history of any group under study. Once phylogenies have been constructed—and we are close to achieving this for the hominoids—the interpretation of correlated bodies of information is greatly facilitated. Specifically, palaeoclimatic and palaeobiogeographic evidence can be integrated with the molecular data to increase our understanding of hominoid evolution.

The molecular data have been critical to the resolution of many controversies regarding phyletic linkage over a wide taxonomic range. Data from immunodiffusion, microcomplement fixation, radioimmunoassay, amino acid sequence, electrophoresis, nucleic acid hybridization, nucleotide sequencing, restriction endonuclease mapping and cytogenetics have shown a fairly consistent pattern of branching sequences, or cladistics, among the hominoids, (Andrews and Cronin, 1982; Cronin, 1983), contrary to some interpretations of the molecular evidence (Schwartz 1984).

The biomolecular evidence argues for three major cladistic events in hominoid evolution (Fig. 1). First, the separation of the gibbon lineage from one leading to the great apes and man; second, the subsequent divergence of the orang-utan from the branch linking that African ape and man; and third, evidence from molecular comparisons that *Homo*, *Pan* and *Gorilla* shared a substantial lineage before their divergence. Evidence

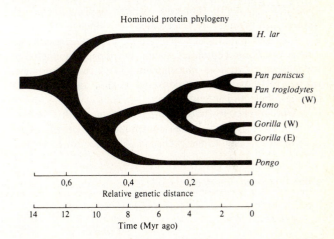

Hominoid protein phylogeny

Figure 1. *A protein phylogeny of the Hominoidea based on (Andrews and Cronin 1982; Cronin 1983; Sarich and Cronin 1976). The branching sequences are discussed in the text. The dates of divergence reflect the protein immunological and DNA hybridization data. Key points are the approximately 5.0 MYR ago date of divergence of* Homo-Pan *and* Gorilla, *and the approximately 2.0 MYR date of separation of* P. paniscus *and* P. troglodytes *and the separation at this time of* Gorilla *populations. The dates of origin of these lineages appear to correlate closely with ecological and climatic changes during the Plio-Pleistocene, as mentioned in the text. The speciation events, as detected by molecular studies, appear to be penecontemporaneous with recorded palaeontological and geological changes.*

Reprinted with permission from the *South African Journal of Science*, Vol. 82, pp. 83-85. Copyright © 1986 by South African Association for the Advancement of Science, Johannesburg.

as to which of the two extinct lineages shared a period of common ancestry to the exclusion of the third is equivocal. There is evidence in favour of the pairing of *Pan-Homo*, *Pan-Gorilla*, and *Homo-Gorilla* (in order of greatest likelihood). The difficulty in determining the sequence of divergence is primarily a result of the, temporally, extremely short lineages, and of the experimental error inherent in the techniques. No data have yet unequivocally demonstrated the actual phylogenetic linkage (Cronin 1983).

MOLECULAR CLOCK ESTIMATES OF HOMINOID DIVERGENCE

The molecular data argue for a monophyletic clustering of hominoids, with a separation from the cercopithecoids some 20 ± 2 Myr ago. The lineage leading to the gibbon is the first divergence detected in the evolution of living hominoids. This lineage, in my best estimate, would have separated some 12 ± 3 Myr ago, from that leading to the common *Pongo*-African ape and human line (Cronin 1983).

The second critical, and most controversial, point is the sequence of events leading to the origin of the modern orang-utan. This debate concerns the cladistic affinities of *Homo vis-a-vis* the living great apes. Some claim that the living great apes are a monophyletic cluster, with *Homo* being a sister taxon (Schwartz 1984). In my opinion this conclusion is incorrect. Molecular data indicate the existence of a common lineage leading to the African apes and Homo (Andrews and Cronin 1982; Cronin 1983). Numerous derived molecular changes have occurred which are shared along this lineage. These include derived amino acid changes in the proteins albumin and transferrin, fibrinopeptides, carbonic anhydrase, haemoglobin, myoglobin, changes in mitochondrial DNA restriction sites, nuclear DNA base substitutions and at least one locus with changes of electrophoretic charge.

With respect to the clustering of *Homo* with *Pan* and *Gorilla*, changes in molecular constitution support the existence of this lineage to the exclusion of *Pongo*. No molecular data favour the reversal of the positions of *Homo* and *Pongo*, although some results appear more reliable than others. This indicates that, in so far as the molecular evidence reveals phylogenetic relationships, the orang-utan is not associated with the African apes and is the sister taxon to the clade comprising the African apes and man (Andrews and Cronin 1982; Cronin 1983).

The divergence event described above resulted in the lineage leading to *Pongo* separating from that leading to humans and African ape some 10-13 Myr ago. Calculations based on rates of evolution of nucleic acids and serum proteins give dates ranging from 8.5 to 14 Myr for the origin of the orang-utan lineage (x = 9.9 ± 1.3). Including two standard deviations on each side of the mean gives us a range of 7 to 13 Myr. Four standard deviations, encompassing much more than 95% of the probabilities, would extend the range for this divergence back to 16 Myr. Similar analysis of the separation of the gibbons yields age estimates upwards of 16-17 Myr. Thus an estimate of 10 ± 3 Myr for the divergence of *Pongo* from humans and African apes is in order, given the approximate nature of the molecular clock. Such an estimate is in close agreement with the origin of the *Sivapithecus-Pongo* clade some 10-12 Myr ago (Andrews and Cronin 1982). This lineage, although probably originating in Africa, migrated soon afterwards to Eurasia. Subsequent evolution in this group of species probably occurred there rather than in Africa. The morphology of the *Sivapithecus* cluster of species suggests that the ancestral form did not require continuous dense tropical forest to permit emigration from Africa.

The lineage leading to hominids and African apes existed for 5-8 Myr before radiating into the three forms we see today, some 4-6 Myr ago (Table 1). The molecular data indicate the separation of hominids and African apes from 4.6 ± 0.7 Myr ago (Cronin and Meikle 1982), with a range of estimates from 3.0 to 6.7 Myr. The protein data yield estimates at the lower part of this range, whereas the DNA comparisons yield values at the upper end. The addition of two standard deviations gives an estimated range of 2.0-7.5 Myr for this divergence (Cronin and

Table 1. Molecular clock estimates of divergence times in millions of years.

	Sarich & Cronin [1]	Andrews & Cronin [2]	Sibley & Ahlquist [3]	Recalculated Sibley & Ahlquist [4]	Cronin [5]
Pan troglodytes vs. *P. paniscus*	2.0	—	2.4 – 3.0	1.8	2.0
Gorilla gorilla gorilla vs. *G. g. beringei*	2.0	—	—	—	2.0
Homo vs. *Pan*	4.0 – 5.0	5.0 ± 1.5	6.3 – 7.7	4.7	4.6 ± 0.7
Homo vs. *Gorilla*	4.5 – 5.0	5.0 ± 1.5	8.0 – 9.9	6.2	4.6 ± 0.7
Pan vs. *Gorilla*	4.0 – 5.0	5.0 ± 1.5	8.0 – 9.9	6.2	4.6 ± 0.7
African ape/human vs. *Pongo*	10.0 ± 2.0	10.0 ± 3.0	13 – 16	9.6	9.9 ± 1.3
Homo, Pan, Gorilla, Pongo vs. *Hylobates*	10.0 ± 2.0	12.0 ± 3.0	18.2 – 22.4	13.7	12.0 ± 3.0
Hominoid vs. cercopithecoid	20 ± 2	—	27 – 33	20.0	20 ± 2.0

[1] As estimated in Sarich and Cronin (1976).

[2] As estimated in Andrews and Cronin (1982).

[3] As estimated in Sibley and Ahlquist (1984).

[4] As discussed in text, revised from Sibley and Ahlquist (1984), in this article (ΔTH 1.0 = 2.6 MYR).

[5] As estimated given data in Andrews and Cronin (1982), Cronin (1983), Sibley and Ahlquist (1984), and in text.

Meikle, 1982). One must remember that the date of the first undoubted hominoid in the fossil record is less than two standard deviations from the mean time of divergence, as estimated from these data. Older specimens than this are fragmentary or of otherwise uncertain status.

The recent work of Sibley and Ahlquist (1984) has suggested that humans and chimpanzees may be the closest sister taxon, with *Gorilla* constituting an outgroup. They have estimated a divergence time of some 7.7 Myr. While the cladistic association of these two may be acceptable, I feel less comfortable with this date of divergence. Their analysis of the molecular clock estimate of ΔTH 1.0 units of DNA per 4.3 MYR is based on two divergence points as calibrated on estimates from the fossil record. The first is the origin of the orang-utan lineage in the first fossil sivapithecine of some 16 Myr ago. As is discussed in Andrews and Cronin (1982), this point is somewhat dubious. First, these forms may not be "true" sivapithecines (i.e. related to *Pongo* uniquely) in cladistic terms; secondly, the dating may not be secure; and thirdly, it is just such a lineage divergence that we are attempting to date using molecular criteria. It is not valid to use this estimate to set the molecular clock within the subset of data which the hypothesis is designed to test.

The second calibration chosen for this estimate is that of the divergence of ratite birds, based on separation of African and South American forms across the Altantic Ocean. We do not, as yet, know if DNA evolves in birds at the same rate as in mammals. This hypothesis is open to test, and I am not yet confident that this rate of evolution can be applied to mammalian DNA. It cannot yet be assumed as a basis for calculation dates of divergence within mammals.

Bearing in mind my unease with these calibration points, I have analyzed Sibley and Ahlquist's data for dates of divergence between hominoid primate lineages (Table 1). Since we do not, at this juncture, have New World monkey or prosimian DNA distances against which to test the hominoid DNA data, I have calibrated the newer DNA values by using our estimate of the Old World monkey-hominoid date of separation of 20 Myr ago. If this date is used, what dates of divergence can be calculated from the DNA distances? Or, stated differently, how well do the different molecular dates agree using this calibration point, which has emerged repeatedly from our own studies? Because the absolute distances are so highly correlated, the dates would also agree if another set point was chosen to calibrate the molecular clock. But until other DNA distances are published, I am satisfied with the close agreement of the times of divergence generated using this calibration point. No amount of manipulation will change the ratio of the different genetic distances between the lineages. Only with a total recalibration of the molecular clock (which is unlikely) will divergence dates among the hominoids differ markedly from those which we have published previously. The high correlation between genetic distances derived from different sources instills confidence in a clock model, independent of individual rates of evolution of specific molecules.

As is shown in Table 1, the Sibley/Ahlquist calibration appears to be too large by approximately 50%. Readjustment of ΔTH of 1.0-2.6 Myr (as opposed to 4.3 Myr) gives a date for the separation of the orang-utan lineage of some 9.6 Myr, and for the *Homo-Pan* separation of 4.7 Myr. This is in close agreement with our previously published estimates.

There is thus ever-increasing evidence for an entirely African origin for the common ancestral hominite lineage, followed by a radiation, within Africa, into the three living lineages of African apes and hominids. This three-fold separation, some 5.0 Myr ago, is remarkably close to the Messinian event and associated global ecological changes. It should not be forgotten that molecular research has predicted this date of divergence for more than 15 years; in fact, the molecular biologists deserve credit for drawing attention to this period as a crucial one for an understanding of human origins.

Similar types of molecular analysis among *Pan* species and *Gorilla* populations reveal a coincidence between divergences which may possibly relate to past climatic events. Separation within the *Pan* lineage between *P. paniscus* and *P. troglodytes* appears to have occurred around 2.0 Myr in conformity with results obtained for Eastern and Western populations of *Gorilla*. This is strikingly close to the first appearances of *Homo* and *A. robustus* in the fossil record, which may, in fact, be close to their true time of separation as discussed in Cronin *et al.* (1981). Great ecological changes at this time have been noted on the basis of analyses of the Omo basin deposits, among others, by Howell and his co-workers.

It is likely that retreat of the Central African rain forests may have promoted geographic separation of ancestral populations of these species, with subsequent divergent evolution. Speciation may be relatively slow when ecological restrictions on exploitable habitats lead to disjunct population distributions. In contrast, sympatric speciation or allopatric speciation in small populations may occur rapidly. These latter types of speciation may be promoted by small inbred populations as a result of changes at the genomic level. Such changes include pericentric inversion, or genome reorganization of gene order, or directional selection coupled with chromosomal and/or single genic changes. In view of the postulated nature of ancestral hominid and panid populations, it is not unlikely that speciation occurred rapidly within a restricted area characterized by a disjunct population distribution. The record of ecological changes at 5.0 and 2.0 Myr ago provides a ready, although as yet unproven, explanation for molecularly detectable penecontemporaneous speciations.

SUMMARY AND CONCLUSION

Molecular data constrain us in our interpretation of hominoid evolution. Ecological and palaeoclimatic data can be interpreted in light of the molecularly derived phylogenetic frameworks. Within the hominoids, there is evidence for an African origin for the ancestral gibbon lineage, some 13-15 Myr ago. The *Sivapithecus-Pongo* lineage seems also to have originated in Africa some 10-13 Myr ago, with at least some forms leaving Africa via an open woodland ecotome. A third lineage probably originated in Africa, resulting in the common hominid-panid clade approximately 9-10 Myr ago. Subsequent evolution is entirely African in distribution, with divergence of later lineages during worldwide climatic changes of which the Messinian event is a manifestation. Subsequent major ecological changes about 2.0 Myr ago are penecontemporaneous with hominid speciation and panid (including *Gorilla*) speciation or subspeciation. Molecular data have, over the last 15 years, been pointing to these critical periods; in particular, molecular results have focused attention on the hominid-panid split of some 5.0

Myr ago. New molecular data, particularly those from DNA hybridization studies, reinforce previous conclusions, as well as improving our ability to discriminate between alternative hypotheses at the trichotomous node where the ancestral species of *Homo, Pan* and *Gorilla* originate. Such pulses in evolution should be apparent in other lineages if speciation and ecological changes are interlinked. The patterns of speciation found at these times will help resolve questions concerning both the modes and the genetics of speciation, as well as contributing to the continuing debate on punctuational and gradual evolutionary models.

REFERENCES

Andrews, P., and Cronin, J. E. 1982. The relationship of *Sivapithecus* and *Ramapithecus* and the evolution of the orang-utan. *Nature* 297:541-546.

Cronin, J. E. 1983. Apes, humans and molecular clocks: a reappraisal, in: *New Interpretations of Ape and Human Ancestry* (R. L. Ciochon and R. S. Corruccini, Eds), pp. 115-150, Plenum Press, New York.

Cronin, J. E., and Meikle, E. 1982. Hominid and Gelada baboon evolution: agreement between molecular and fossil time scale. *Int. J. Primatol.* 3:469-482.

Cronin, J. E., Boas, N. T. Stringer, C. B., Rak, Y. 1981. Tempo and mode in hominid evolution. *Nature* 292:113-122.

Sarich, V. M., and Cronin, J. E. 1976. Molecular systematics of the primates in: *Molecular Anthropology* (M. Goodman and R. E. Tashian, Eds.), pp. 141-170, Plenum, New York.

Schwartz, J. 1984. The evolutionary relationships of man and orang-utans. *Nature* 308:501-505.

Sibley, C. G., and Ahlquist, J. E. 1984. The phylogeny of the hominoid primates, as indicated by DNA-DNA hybridization. *J. Molec. Evol.* 20:2-15.

4

DNA Hybridization as a Guide to Phylogeny: Relations of the Hominoidea

J. Marks, C. W. Schmid, and V. M. Sarich

INTRODUCTION

It was shown in the 1950's and 1960's that genetic, molecular, or biochemical methods can provide a powerful battery of procedures useful in the elucidation of phylogenetic branching patterns. These methods include immunology, protein sequencing, protein electrophoresis, chromosome banding, DNA mapping, DNA sequencing, and DNA hybridization. While each has its technical and theoretical assets and liabilities, all have pointed to common conclusions: that genetic distances among humans, chimpanzees, and gorillas are (1) very small, and (2) so similar that it is extremely difficult to determine which two taxa among the three are most closely related.

A recent study of the genetic affinities among the Hominoidea used the technique of DNA hybridization and denaturation (Sibley and Ahlquist 1984, 1987). One conclusion, that the sister taxon of the chimpanzees is *Homo*, not *Gorilla*, has been controversial (Andrews 1985, 1986; Lewin 1984, 1987). Its acceptance requires the re-interpretation of many anatomical features (Pilbeam 1986) and is difficult to reconcile as well with the least ambiguous cytogenetic features (Stanyon and Chiarelli 1982; Marks 1983). Any study claiming to have the power to resolve this long-standing molecular trichotomy will naturally be expected to stand up to the highest levels of analysis and critical scrutiny. Statistical examinations so far

published have appeared to bear out the original interpretation of the Sibley-Ahlquist conclusions (Templeton 1985, 1986; Saitou 1986; Ruvulo and Smith 1985; Fitch 1986; Felsenstein 1987).

In this paper we examine the methodology of DNA hybridization/denaturation used in the Sibley-Ahlquist study, and discuss the nature of these data and the possible sources of error which should be considered in evaluating the accuracy of phylogenetic conclusions based upon such studies. A major problem involves the unavailability of primary data and controls which would permit critical evaluation of the robusticity of Sibley and Ahlquist's conclusions. We present here an independent analysis of a subset of the Sibley-Ahlquist data, identify several unexpected features of these data, and conclude that if these data are representative of the complete Sibley-Ahlquist set, then they raise questions about the ability to resolve the genetic trichotomy of human-chimpanzee-gorilla.

GENERAL METHODOLOGY

DNA is a double-stranded molecule whose hereditary information is encoded in a sequence of nucleotide pairs. A nucleotide pair is held together by hydrogen bonds, two linking the A-T pair and three linking the G-C pair. The two strands of the DNA molecule can be split from one another by heating, which breaks

Reprinted with permission from the *Journal of Human Evolution*, Vol. 17, pp. 769-786. Copyright © 1988 by Academic Press Limited, London.

these hydrogen bonds. The DNA duplex is thus said to be denatured. The thermal stability of duplex DNA is proportional to the integrity of the base-pairing, such that poorly paired DNA strands will dissociate at a lower temperature than well-paired DNA strands. If the process of evolution can be reduced to the progressive accumulation of point mutations in DNA, then the melting temperature of DNA composed of two strands from different species will be an indication of the amount of genetic difference which has accumulated between those two species.

For a typical hybridization experiment (Sibley and Ahlquist 1983, 1984), the DNA from a single individual is first sheared to an approximate mean of 500 bp (base-pairs). Tracer DNA is prepared using only the least redundant portion of the genome, by denaturing the DNA and allowing it to renature to Cot [1] 1000. This DNA is passed through hydroxyapatite (HAP), which binds double-stranded DNA and allows single-stranded DNA to pass at 0.12 M phosphate concentration. The single-stranded DNA is retained as the "tracer."

This tracer DNA is then labeled radioactively, denatured, and allowed to hybridize to a 1000-fold excess of single-stranded driver DNA. If the tracer and driver are derived from the same species, homologous hybrids or homoduplex DNA is formed; if they are from different species, heterologous hybrids or heteroduplex DNA is formed (Sibley and Ahlquist 1983, p. 256). This hybridization is taken to a high Cot (16000) to ensure the adequate binding of tracer and driver, which takes about five days. This hybrid DNA is then loaded on to a HAP column, and the temperature is raised at regular intervals of 2.5 degrees. At each temperature, buffer is added and a fraction collected from the column. The radioactivity in the sample reflects the amount of denaturing of the tracer-driver hybrid between temperature steps.

A graph of radioactive counts versus temperature yields a bell-shaped curve; and to correct for any variation in intensity of labeling, this curve can be given as percentage of total counts eluted versus temperature. At lower temperatures, the DNA is double-stranded and remains bound to the HAP, and at the higher temperatures progressively more of the DNA denatures to single strands and "melts" off the columns. The melt itself occurs over a temperature range which may span 20 degrees Celsius (75°-95°). Examination of this curve is vital to the evaluation of a DNA hybridization experiment. A narrow, tall curve will have a smaller degree of experimental error associated with it than a wide, short curve. Sibley and Ahlquist (1984, 1987) have not previously presented such curves; we present such a curve, from their data, in Figure 1(a). It is evident that a considerable loss of information accompanies the reduction of a melting curve to a single "melting temperature."

A standard transformation from "amount of single-strand DNA" to "cumulative percentage of single-strand DNA" turns the approximately normal curve into a sigmoid curve. This graph is shown in Figure 1(b). The melting temperature is usually determined as the median value—the point at which 50% of the DNA is single-stranded, and 50% is double-stranded.

METHODOLOGICAL QUESTIONS

There are several questions which could legitimately be raised concerning the Sibley-Ahlquist study and which raise the possibility that a crude comparison of heteroduplex melting

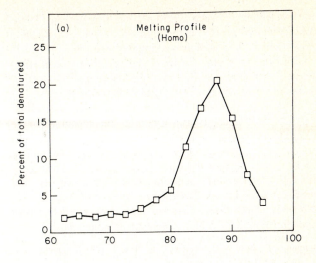

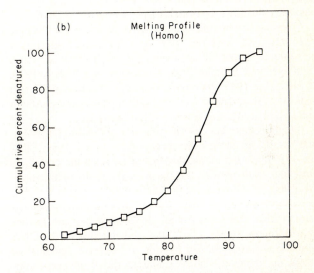

Figure 1. *A typical melting profile, for homoduplex DNA (human-human), the control for run 1151-1 of the Sibley-Ahlquist series.*

(a) The amount of single-stranded (i.e., denatured) DNA, given as a percentage of the total tracer DNA which elutes from the HAP column at a particular temperature, is plotted against temperature. A bell-curve, with a transition spanning approximately 15°C is generated.

(b) The same data are transformed into a cumulative sigmoid curve. The median, or 50% value, is usually taken to be the "melting temperature."

temperatures is not sufficiently sensitive *a priori* to resolve a close phylogenetic split.

First, the interval size at which Sibley and Ahlquist obtained data points is five times larger than the 0.5 degree difference which separates *Pan* and *Gorilla*.

Second, the melting transition is affected by factors other than base-pair mismatch, such as heterogeneity in base composition (Vizard *et al.* 1977), as A-T is held together by two hydrogen bonds and G-C by three. Additionally, the binding of double-stranded DNA to HAP affects the DNA melting temperature (Fox *et al.* 1980; Martinson 1973).

Third, Sibley and Ahlquist labelled the tracer DNA with ^{125}I, which is specific for cytosine, and which involves highly invasive techniques, such as acid pH, which depurinates DNA. Orosz and Wetmur (1974) found that the extent of iodination proportionally decreases the melting temperature.

Fourth, the length to which the DNA is sheared will affect the melting temperature, by virtue of a "stacking effect"—DNA is easier to denature at the ends than in the middles.

Fifth, the interspersion pattern of repetitive and single-copy DNA will affect its behavior during the preparation of the tracer DNA (Schmid and Deininger 1975). Repetitive DNA can denature at low temperatures, and Davidson *et al.* (1973) found a 5-10% contamination of *Xenopus* single-copy DNA by repetitive DNA after a single renaturation/HAP fractionation. The presence of human-ape DNA heteroduplexes melting at relatively low temperatures [*vide infra*, Fig. 2(c)] suggests just such contamination in the Sibley-Ahlquist hominoid data.

Sixth, duplex DNA may thermally elute from the HAP column without undergoing denaturation into single strands (Fox *et al.* 1980; Martinson 1973). This is a further source of possible contamination of tracer DNA by repetitive DNA.

Seventh, other studies cite a range of 0.9 to 2.4°C as the reduction in melting between human-chimpanzee heteroduplexes and human homoduplexes (Hoyer *et al.* 1972; Deininger and Schmid 1976; Benveniste and Todaro 1976; O'Brien *et al.* 1985). Indeed, the dendrogram drawn by O'Brien *et al.* (1985) based on DNA hybridization experiments clustered human and gorilla, not human and chimpanzee.

Eighth, there are several measures of "melting temperature" available. Some researchers (e.g., Brownell 1983; Bledsoe 1987), use the mode (the highest point on the graph), as most adequately representing the thermal stability of the tracer-driver hybrids. Others (e.g., Sheldon 1987; Caccone *et al.* 1988) use the median or 50% point (T_{50} or T_m) of the DNA which did form hybrids. Sibley and Ahlquist have based their conclusions on a different statistic: $T_{50}H$, the median value of the DNA which *could have* formed hybrids. As we will demonstrate below, the choice of statistic can affect the phylogenetic conclusions drawn, and $T_{50}H$ may detect artificial differences. These data are consequently vital for the proper interpretation of the Sibley-Ahlquist experiments, but have not been made available.

We reiterate that there exists a strong potential for generating well-supported conclusions about phylogeny from DNA hybridization, provided that the data and method of analysis are made available and clear. Like any other analytical technique, this method has limits of resolution, which are set largely by the factors we have just discussed. These eight possible sources of experimental and analytical error may simply constitute a moot point, if the data are of high precision and the distances among taxa are highly consistent and replicable. Alternatively, these reasons may explain a failure of this DNA hybridization technique to distinguish phylogenetic relations. It depends upon a close examination of the data. Whether this technique has indeed broken the apparent trichotomy among humans, chimpanzees, and gorillas is therefore an empirical question. It is a question that cannot be addressed or answered, however, until the actual data and methods of analysis have been made available and clear. We have analyzed a subset of the Sibley-Ahlquist data, and present the results of this analysis here. These data had been given to Roy Britten by Sibley and Ahlquist and were sent by Britten, with permission of Sibley, to J. M. on 2 December 1987.

ANALYSIS OF THE SIBLEY-AHLQUIST DATA SUBSET

Our analysis of the human-chimpanzee-gorilla split covers Sibley and Ahlquist's experiment 1151 (10 *Homo-Pan troglodytes*, 12 *Homo-Gorilla*), their experiment 1165 (3 *Homo-Pan troglodytes*, 1 *Homo-Pan paniscus*, 8 *Homo-Gorilla*), and their experiment 843 (1 *Pan paniscus-Homo*). There are thus 15 melts comparing humans and chimpanzees, and 20 melts comparing humans and gorillas.

The experiments were performed in runs of 25: using a tracer DNA sample, and hybridizing/melting it simultaneously to a sequence of 25 drivers, beginning with at least one homologous (control) DNA sample. With regard to the primates, we have all the available melts in experiments 1151 and 1165 (*Homo* tracer), 1200 (*Papio* tracer), and the first seven melts in experiment 843 (*Pan paniscus* tracer).

We begin this analysis by noting some difficulties with the $T_{50}H$ statistic. When the hybrid mixture is loaded onto the HAP column, some tracer DNA fails to hybridize. This DNA thus fails to bind to the HAP and elutes immediately at the start of the melting experiment, and permits an estimate of the percentage of hybridization relative to the homoduplex. As the temperature is raised, the DNA which has formed duplex structures begins to denature. When the median value is calculated, one therefore has the choice between taking 50% of the tracer DNA actually melting out of double-stranded structures (T_m), or 50% of the tracer DNA originating in both double-stranded and single-stranded structures ($T_{50}H$).

The $T_{50}H$ statistic assumes that all the DNA which did not hybridize was too divergent to do so. It thus assumes that all the *unhybridized* DNA is *unhybridizable* DNA. For closely related primate taxa, however, this equation is unwarranted: variation in the extent of hybridization is likely due not to extreme divergence, but rather to experimental error. Thus Sheldon (1987, p. 64) writes that "[f]or an unknown reason, [percent hybridization] among closely related organisms often has an unusually large variance." We believe that the incorporation of *unhybridized* DNA into the calculation of the median, by assuming it is *unhybridizable* DNA, introduces an incorrect assumption and a substantial amount of experimental error into the calculation of the median value.

$T_{50}H$ therefore measures not simply the thermal stability of the heteroduplexes, but the extent to which hybridization actually occurred as well—the initial conditions of the DNA melting experiment. A small difference in the extent of hybridization between tracer and driver will cause a difference in the $T_{50}H$ which is not related to the relative thermal stability of the hybrid DNA's. The percent hybridization incorporated into $T_{50}H$ can indeed affect the phylogenetic results, as noted by Templeton (1986).

In Figure 2, we compare the DNA melts of 1165-2 (human-chimp) and 1165-13 (human-gorilla). Figure 2(a) shows the $T_{50}H$ curve: at 50%, several degrees separate the two melts. However, because about 12% more of the human tracer DNA hybridized to the chimp than to the gorilla, the curves begin at different points. (The difference in percent hybridization actually arises *before* the graphs begin: it is based upon the amount of tracer DNA eluted at 55, 57.5 and 60 degrees. Thus in a cumulative graph, a weaker hybridization reaction starts at 62.5 degrees with a larger percentage of DNA single-stranded.)

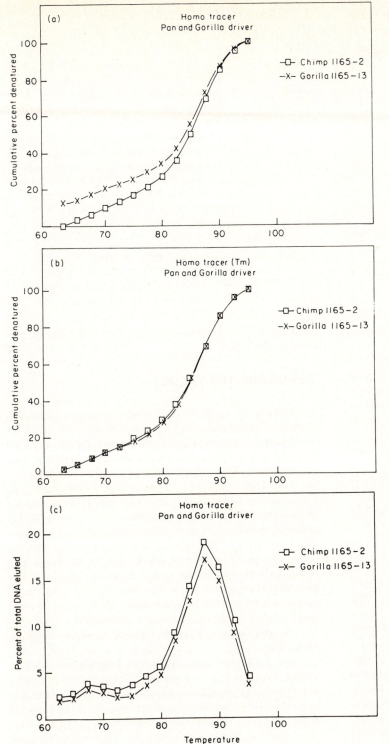

Figure 2. *Effect of normalized percent hybridization on melting temperature.*

(a) A cumulative sigmoid curve of two DNA melts (1165-2, human-chimp; and 1165-13, human-gorilla). The first point, at 62.5 degrees, reflects the fact that 10% of the human tracer DNA failed to form hybrids with the gorilla DNA, and came off the column before the graph actually begins. The 50% point here gives T50H; there is an obvious difference between this value for the human-chimp melt and the human-gorilla melt.

(b) The same data, in which the percent hybridization is not taken into consideration. The 50% point here gives T_m; the two curves are now virtually identical.

(c) The same data, shown in their "raw" or bell-shaped form. The two melts trace the same profile and peak at the same place; the only significant difference between them is absolutely more DNA at every point in the human-chimpanzee melt. The $T_{50}H$ value, consequently, indicated a difference in the thermal stability of the two heteroduplexes that did not actually exist.

Figure 2(b) shows the cumulative melts without the initial percent hybridization (T_m)—they are now nearly identical. This is corroborated by Figure 2(c), the raw melts: the curves actually possess the same shape and peak at the same point. The only difference of significance is that at every temperature there is more human tracer DNA in the human-chimp melt than in the human-gorilla melt. Therefore the difference in $T_{50}H$ between these two melts is attributable to the percent hybridization, at the bottom of the curves in Figure 2(a)—in other words, to the initial conditions of the melting experiment.

Should the DNA melts in Figure 2 be recorded as being very different or very similar? We feel that the difference in $T_{50}H$ values for these DNA melts does not accurately reflect the relationship between these two heteroduplex melts, which is in fact virtual identity. They are nearly equally thermally stable, though differing in the extent of hybridization. The apparent

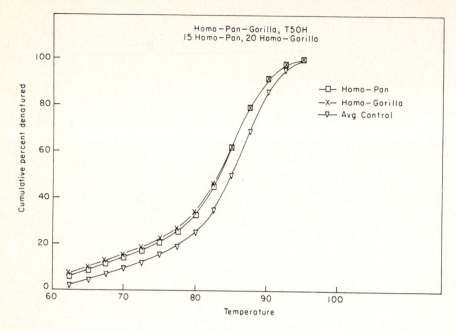

Figure 3. *T50H plot of the average of 15 human-chimp melts and 20 human-gorilla melts. The human-chimp melts are 1151-2,3,4,5,6,7,8,9,11,13; 1165-2,3,4,5; and 843-6. The human-gorilla melts are 1151-14, 15, 16, 17, 18, 19, 20, 21, 22, 23, 24, 25; and 1165-6, 7, 8, 9, 10, 11, 12, 13. This represents the entire sample of inter-generic comparisons for human-chimp-gorilla to which we have had access. At 50%, the T50H for human-chimp is slightly greater than that for human-gorilla.*

difference in thermal stability which would be perceived by $T_{50}H$ is artifactual.

If we take the mean value for percent single strand DNA eluted at each temperature, we are able to generate a mean human-chimp melting profile and a mean human-gorilla melting profile, for the data made available to us. As is evident from Figure 3, the human-gorilla curve is slightly to the left of the human-chimp curve at the 50% point, indicating a slightly greater $\Delta T_{50}H$ for human-gorilla, as per Sibley and Ahlquist [2].

Note, however, that the lowest point on the graph for human-gorilla is slightly higher than that for human-chimp. This is due to the fact that the mean percent hybridization for human-chimp is 96.1% and that for human-gorilla is only 95.2%.

The percent hybridization is highly variable, ranging from 90.7% to 102.3% in human-chimp and from 90.2% to 97.9% in human-gorilla. Since percent hybridization of heteroduplexes is normalized to the homoduplex control, a value over 100% indicates greater hybridization of *Homo-Pan* than *Homo-Homo*. The mean value of 96.1% for human-chimp has a standard deviation of 2.4, and the mean value of 95.2 for human-gorilla has an associated standard deviation of 1.6. This variable is subject to an intolerably large amount of experimental error in this case and obviously does not discriminate among these taxa. It is therefore unjustified to include it in the calculation of the melting temperature as part of the $T_{50}H$. If we remove the percent hybridization from the calculation, and measure only the median of the actual denaturation, we generate Figure 4(a).

At 50% denatured (or T_m), there is no difference whatsoever between the average human-chimp and the average human-gorilla melts. The virtual identity of these curves is reinforced by an examination of the modes (Figure 4[b]). The difference between them was entirely attributable to the difference in percent hybridization, to the initial conditions of the melt. It was consequently an artifact of the statistic used, and of a probably random fluctuation in normalized percent hybridization, which is probably measuring experimental error (un-hybridized DNA), not a phylogenetically relevant variable (unhybridizable DNA).

REPORTING THE VALUES

In their second paper on hominoid phylogeny, Sibley and Ahlquist (1987) listed their experiment numbers alongside the $T_{50}H$ values in their subsequent calculations. The data provided to us allow a comparison of the $\Delta T_{50}H$ values we obtain with those reported. This information is summarized in Table 1.

Our determination of $\Delta T_{50}H$ is highly concordant with theirs (Sibley and Ahlquist 1987) for run 1151, the results differing by only ±0.2 degrees, attributable to rounding-off. For run 843, we possess only six experiments. The *Pan paniscus-Pan troglodytes* temperatures are again highly concordant, but where we obtain a value of 2.6 degrees for the single *Pan paniscus-Homo sapiens* experiment, the reported values of four experiments comparing these same taxa, numbered 843, range only from 1.6 to 1.9 (Sibley and Ahlquist 1987). It may be noted that the value we obtain is above the reported mean for *Homo-Gorilla*, and outside the entire reported range of values for *Homo-Pan*.

Run 1165 raises other difficulties. Experiment 1165-2 involved a heterologous comparison (*Homo-Pan*) which had a higher percent hybridization than the homologous control. Experiment 1165-3 actually has a negative deviation from the control (Fig. 5). The *Homo-Pan* experiments in this run yield values ranging from -0.1 to 0.6 degrees. These values are again outside the entire reported ranges for *Homo-Pan* (Sibley and Ahlquist 1987). The $\Delta T_{50}H$ values for these four human-chimp melts are reported, however, as ranging from 1.2 to 1.7. The *Homo-Gorilla* melts in this run are similarly reported to be approximately 1.1 degrees higher than the values we obtained.

More difficult to interpret are the *Homo-Pongo* and *Homo-Hylobates* melts, experiments 1165-14 and 1165-15. The two melts are extremely similar in shape (Fig. 6), and indeed *Hylobates* actually appears to be slightly, though insignificantly, more similar to *Homo* than is *Pongo*. The published values (Sibley and Ahlquist 1987), however, give the $\Delta T_{50}H$ of the

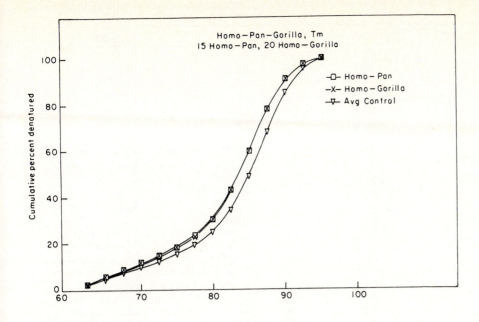

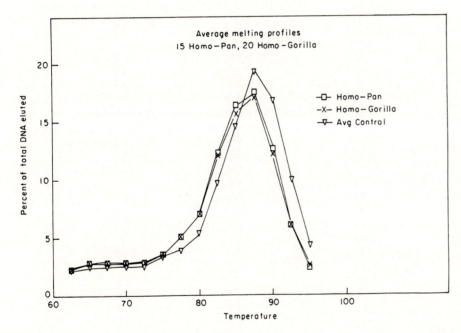

Figure 4. *Average melts of human-chimp and human-gorilla.*
(a) T_m plot of the average of 15 human-chimp melts and 20 human-gorilla melts. Only the average thermal stability of heteroduplexes is being considered, not the average amount of hybrid DNA formed. At 50% the T_m for human-chimp is identical to that for human-gorilla.
(b) "Raw" average plots for the same experiments. The two average heteroduplex curves peak at the same temperature.

single *Homo-Pongo* experiment in run 1165 to be *lower* than that of the single *Homo-Hylobates* experiment in run 1165, and differing from it by 0.9 degrees. This does not appear to be justified from the experimental data we have analyzed.

Finally, of the three *Papio-Homo* melts in run 1200, the range we obtain (2.4 degrees) is considerably greater than the range reported (0.9 degrees; Sibley and Ahlquist 1987). Other $\Delta T_{50}H$ values in this run are reported as either lower or higher than our calculated values. In this run the first four melts were homologous hybrids (*Papio*), of which 1200-2 was used for subsequent calculations. This raises, however, an interesting problem: for not only is the homolog used in subtraction to obtain the ΔT, but as well in calculating the normalized percent hybridization of the heterologous hybrids. If we take experiment 1200-15 (*Papio-Homo*), for example, we find 80.1%

hybridization when normalized against homolog 1200-2. But when normalized against homolog 1200-1 we calculate 88.9% hybridization; against homolog 1200-3, 79.5% hybridization; and against homolog 1200-4, 102.6% hybridization. Any of these other values will change the recorded $T_{50}H$ of the heterologous melts. Since in most experiments only one homologous melt was performed, the variability in $\Delta T_{50}H$ was automatically curtailed, as there was no variability possible in normalized percent hybridization. We feel that it would be sound to include multiple homologous controls in the same run.

In Table 2, we summarize the results of our analysis of the $\Delta T_{50}H$ values for the human-chimp-gorilla data subset, and contrast them with Sibley and Ahlquist's analysis of the same experiments. Where we find the mean difference in $\Delta T_{50}H$ for human-chimp and human-gorilla to be less than 0.2 degrees (and

Table 1. Calculated temperatures and deviations based upon Sibley and Ahlquist's data, compared with deviations reported in Sibley and Ahlquist (1987).

Run	Comparison	$T_{50}H$	ΔT	S & A ΔT
1151-1	Homo-Homo	84.6	—	
-9	Homo-Pan trog	82.9	1.7	1.7
-2	Homo-Pan trog	82.9	1.7	1.7
-5	Homo-Pan trog	82.8	1.8	1.7
-3	Homo-Pan trog	82.7	1.9	1.8
-4	Homo-Pan trog	82.6	2.0	1.8
-8	Homo-Pan trog	82.6	2.0	1.9
-6	Homo-Pan trog	82.5	2.1	2.0
-7	Homo-Pan trog	82.5	2.1	2.0
-11	Homo-Pan trog	82.5	2.1	2.1
-13	Homo-Pan trog	82.5	2.1	2.1
-16	Homo-Gorilla	82.7	1.9	2.0
-18	Homo-Gorilla	82.6	2.0	2.0
-15	Homo-Gorilla	82.5	2.1	2.1
-17	Homo-Gorilla	82.5	2.1	2.1
-20	Homo-Gorilla	82.5	2.1	2.1
-14	Homo-Gorilla	82.5	2.1	2.2
-19	Homo-Gorilla	82.4	2.2	2.2
-22	Homo-Gorilla	82.4	2.2	2.2
-23	Homo-Gorilla	82.4	2.2	2.2
-21	Homo-Gorilla	82.2	2.4	2.4
-24	Homo-Gorilla	82.2	2.4	2.4
-25	Homo-Gorilla	82.2	2.4	2.4
843-1	Pan pan-Pan pan	85.3	—	
-2	Pan pan-Pan trog	84.8	0.5	0.5
-3	Pan pan-Pan trog	84.4	0.9	0.8
-5	Pan pan-Pan trog	84.4	0.9	0.9
-4	Pan pan-Pan trog	84.3	1.0	1.0
-6	Pan pan-Homo	82.7	2.6	1.6-1.9
1165-1	Homo-Homo	85.4	—	
-3	Homo-Pan trog	85.5	−0.1	1.2
-4	Homo-Pan trog	85.3	0.1	1.5
-2	Homo-Pan trog	85.0	0.4	1.5
-5	Homo-Pan pan	84.8	0.6	1.7
-11	Homo-Gorilla	84.8	0.6	1.7
-9	Homo-Gorilla	84.7	0.7	1.8
-6	Homo-Gorilla	84.6	0.8	1.9
-12	Homo-Gorilla	84.6	0.8	2.0
-8	Homo-Gorilla	84.5	0.9	2.0
-13	Homo-Gorilla	84.3	1.1	2.2
-7	Homo-Gorilla	84.2	1.2	2.3
-10	Homo-Gorilla	84.1	1.3	2.3
-14	Homo-Pongo	82.3	3.1	3.1
-15	Homo-Hylobates	82.4	3.0	4.0
-17	Homo-Macaca	79.0	6.4	7.5
-16	Homo-Cercopithecus	78.8	6.6	7.1
-18	Homo-Papio	78.8	6.6	6.7
1200-2	Papio-Papio	86.6	—	
-17	Papio-Homo	79.6	7.0	7.0
-15	Papio-Homo	78.8	7.8	7.3
-16	Papio-Homo	77.2	9.4	7.9
-18	Papio-Pan trog	79.4	7.2	7.2
-19	Papio-Pan trog	78.7	7.9	7.9
-21	Papio-Gorilla	78.7	7.9	7.3
-20	Papio-Gorilla	78.6	8.0	7.5
-22	Papio-Pongo	78.0	8.6	7.6
-23	Papio-Pongo	78.4	8.2	8.2

"Run" refers to the experiment number given by Sibley and Ahlquist. "Comparison" refers to the genera being compared, except where species distinctions are noted. "$T_{50}H$" is the statistic we calculated from Sibley and Ahlquist's data. There are several ways to calculate the median value (Sibley and Ahlquist 1984, p. 3). We have obtained the highest concordance with the numbers in Sibley and Ahlquist (1987) by taking the most nearly vertical interval in the cumulative graph and extending it linearly to the 50% point; those are the numbers given here. "ΔT" is the deviation of the heterologous $T_{50}H$ from the homologous control. "S & A ΔT" is the value given in Sibley and Ahlquist (1987) for the experiment. Within a given run, they do not give the precise experiment number, but list the ΔT values for a given species pair in a given experiment in increasing order; we have done the same.

For run 843, we have only 843-6 comparing *Pan paniscus* to *Homo*; Sibley and Ahlquist (1987) list 4 values for this particular comparison in this experiment and we give the range of those values. Run 1200 includes 4 controls; we obtained maximum concordance using 1200-2.

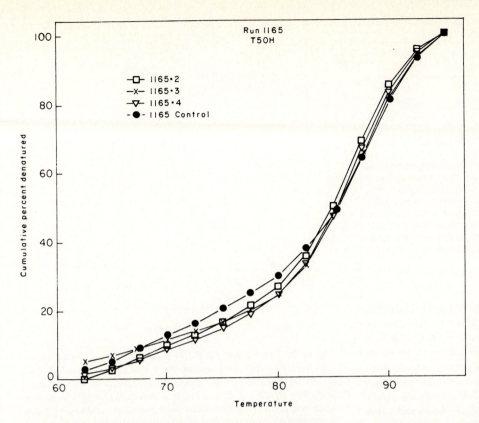

Figure 5. *The three human-common chimp melts from run 1165, with the control from the same experiment. Although the ΔT₅₀Hs are reported by Sibley and Ahlquist (1987) to be 1.2, 1.5, 1.5, the values we calculated are -0.1, 0.1 and 0.4.*

fully attributable, as indicated above, to the small difference in the mean initial conditions of the melting experiment), Sibley and Ahlquist's reported values for the same experiments give a mean difference of 0.37 degrees. The standard errors of these means, by our calculation, are approximately three times greater than those calculable from their reported values for these experiments (Table 2). The means and standard errors based on Sibley and Ahlquist (1987) for these 35 inter-generic comparisons are in close agreement with the means and standard errors they reported for all 226 inter-generic comparisons.

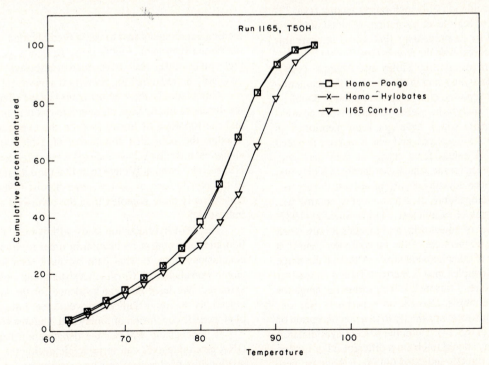

Figure 6. *The single human-orang and human-gibbon melts from run 1165, with the control from the same experiment. Although the ΔT₅₀Hs are reported by Sibley and Ahlquist (1987) to be 3.1 and 4.0, the values we calculate are 3.1 and 3.0.*

Table 2. Statistical comparison of the data reported by Sibley and Ahlquist (1987) and our analysis of the same data.

	This Study	S & A Values	S & A Total
Human-Chimp mean	1.54	1.76	1.63
Human-Chimp S. E.	0.21	0.06	0.03
Human-Gorilla mean	1.68	2.13	2.27
Human-Gorilla S. E.	0.14	0.04	0.03

"This Study" refers to our calculations based on the $\Delta T_{50}Hs$ given in Table 1. "S & A values" refers to the $\Delta T_{50}H$ values for the same experiments as reported in Sibley and Ahlquist (1987), Table 1. "S & A total" refers to the $\Delta T_{50}H$ values given for the entire sample in Sibley and Ahlquist (1987), Table 6. "S.E." is the standard error of the mean. Since the value for 843-6 (*Pan paniscus-Homo*) actually utilized by Sibley and Ahlquist is unknown, we have taken 1.75, the mean of 1.6 and 1.9, in calculating "S & A values." Sibley and Ahlquist give a mean of 1.64 and a standard error of 0.05 for 11 trials of *Homo-Pan paniscus*, and a mean of 1.63 and a standard error of 0.03 for 64 trials of *Homo-Pan troglodytes*.

We are therefore unable to replicate the $\Delta T_{50}H$ calculations of Sibley and Ahlquist for nearly 40% of the experiments for which numerical replication is possible, and we generally find the range and standard errors of $\Delta T50H$ values to be much greater than they have reported. This only covers a small fraction of their data; however, the possibility that the complete data set may be subject to the same sorts of discrepancies would render precise statistical analyses based on those published values, such as those of Felsenstein (1987), meaningless.

DISCUSSION

DNA hybridization is a powerful tool to assist primate biologists in the elucidation of branch-points among taxa. Yet in spite of claims for high-level resolution, no documentation has been presented by its proponents that would indicate this technique has in fact resolved the *Homo-Pan-Gorilla* split. We believe that the data reported by Sibley and Ahlquist (1987) have been faultily analyzed, and in the absence of documentation, we believe the reported conclusions are open to doubt.

The methods of analysis have also included several post-experimental adjustments which have not been mentioned in Sibley and Ahlquist's publications, and which we have deduced by comparing $\Delta T_{50}H$ values for a subset of their data with published $\Delta T_{50}H$ values for the same experiments in Sibley and Ahlquist (1987). These adjustments are of at least three sorts. First, the melting temperature of a homoduplex control was altered to adjust a bank of experiments (1165). Sheldon (1987) discusses this manner of adjustment, and invokes it only when the median melting temperature of the homoduplex control is discordant from that of other homoduplexes. Although the shape of the raw 1165 homoduplex melt is aberrant, Table 1 shows that the median temperature of this melt is well within the range for other homoduplex controls. Second, an experiment was exempted from this adjustment apparently to fit a preconception of the branching order (1165-14). Third, the percent hybridization of an experiment was altered to obtain a different $\Delta T_{50}H$ value than the experiment directly indicated (843-6; J. Ahlquist, personal communication to J. M., 21 March 1988). Other sorts of adjustments, the specific natures of which we cannot identify, were apparently made to the 1200 series. A comparison of

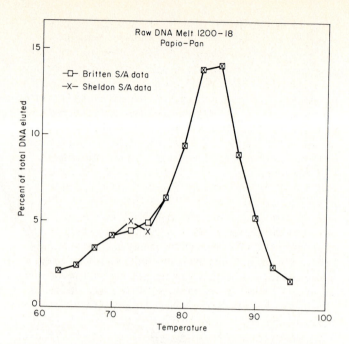

Figure 7. *Experiment 1200-18, a comparison of* Papio *(Cercopithecoidea) and* Pan *(Hominoidea). The data communicated to us by Fred Sheldon reveal a bimodal plot; compared with the data from Roy Britten, it appears that a transposition of values has occurred, converting the smaller peak into simply a shoulder. Such a transposition exists in five of the nine DNA melts in experiment 1200 reported in Sibley and Ahlquist (1987). The effect of this adjustment is more extreme with taxa more distantly related. We do not know the extent to which this type of adjustment was utilized, nor how often such a transposition exists within the data subset (besides experiment 1200) sent to us by Britten.*

melting experiments sent to us by Fred Sheldon with data from the same experiments sent to us by Britten (Figure 7) suggests that some values may have been transposed, converting an originally bimodal melting curve into a unimodal curve.

Cumulatively, these adjustments had the effect of changing the distances among taxa, the standard errors of those distances, and the topology of trees based on the experimental results. Though the published summaries of Sibley and Ahlquist's analytical techniques have recently been defended by Diamond (1988), it is abundantly clear to us that the data analysis leading to the conclusions of Sibley and Ahlquist (1984, 1987) was considerably more complex than the published accounts have indicated.

The DNA hybridization study will require full documentation and independent replication in order to draw any reliable conclusions from it; what data we have seen indicate that a *Homo-Pan* clade with *Gorilla* as a sister group cannot readily be extracted. We have not seen evidence for the high degree of objectivity and replicability that would merit acceptance of the phylogenetic conclusion of Sibley and Ahlquist (1984, 1987).

It is debatable whether the denaturation temperatures of DNA heteroduplexes can in principle decide the phylogenetic relationships of closely related taxa such as human, chimpanzee, and gorilla (Cracraft 1987). The possibility of representing the similarity between two highly complicated genomes adequately with a single statistic is probably no greater than the possibility of representing "intelligence" or "anatomical similarity" with a single statistic, despite the claims of some psychologists in the 1920s and some taxonomists in the 1960s. This does not, however, reflect unfavorably upon the use of ΔT simply as another distance metric, or upon the value of genetic distances generally.

In the future, greater care needs to be given to the scrutiny and presentation of DNA hybridization-based phylogenies, and particularly to the rudiments of data analysis. The low temperature end of a raw melting curve is produced by the thermal elution of unhybridized DNA, divergent unhybridizable DNA, low-temperature peaks and shoulders (as in Fig. 2 [c]), poorly hybridized DNA, and AT-rich DNA. The high temperature end represents well-paired and GC-rich DNA. A $T_{50}H$ median temperature simply reflects the relative sizes of these heterogeneous classes. A modal value (highest point) gives the temperature at which the greatest quantity of DNA melted. We believe that the modal temperature is the statistic of greatest biological and biochemical significance, and is therefore the statistic of choice for representing the relations of species' unique sequence genomes by a scalar quantity (Brownell, 1983; Bledsoe, 1987; Sarich *et al.* 1989).

If one eliminates the effects of base composition differences, genomic complexity, paralogous pairing, and low-temperature peaks, then the simple median (T_m or T_{50}) can be highly concordant with the mode, and closely correlated with overall base-pair mismatch, as Caccone *et al.* (1988) have shown. Therefore, where it can be shown that there are no low-temperature peaks, or anomalies in the shape of the raw data curve, the simple median (T_m or T_{50}) may be acceptable. The $T_{50}H$ statistic is unacceptable.

Finally, we wish to raise an issue about the "trichotomy" and about "breaking" it. By trichotomy, we mean the existence of a very short internodal distance on a dendrogram (outside the limits of technical resolution and leading in this case to human-chimp), relative to another, longer internodal distance (leading to human-chimp-gorilla). Most molecular studies show the latter node to be about 5 times larger than the former (Dene *et al.* 1976; Sarich and Cronin 1976; Ferris *et al.* 1981; Hixson *et al.* 1986; Koop *et al.* 1987; Maeda *et al.* 1988). Yet Sibley and Ahlquist reported a difference of less than two-fold (and in the unpublished, but already cited work of Caccone and Powell [1988; Diamond 1988] they are even more similar). To "break" the trichotomy, the nodes must be measured precisely *and the relative branch lengths must be retained*, if the evolutionary rates are similar across lineages, which appears to hold for DNA hybridization. If the internodal distance to human-chimp is *not* relatively short, then the gorilla split is not a very close one, although a considerable body of data suggests that it should be. In other words, one must identify a close split before resolving it. This is not merely a semantic point, but one of considerable gravity for a phenetic analysis, where

phylogenetic inferences are to be based on distances, not character states. The failure to find a close split creates a major discordance between this DNA hybridization work and other phenetic studies of the hominoid primates.

CONCLUSIONS

In our analysis of a subset of Sibley and Ahlquist's data, we find that an apparent linkage of human-chimpanzee is an artifact of the T50H statistic, reflecting slightly greater average hybridization of human-chimpanzee than human-gorilla, but not a difference in the thermal stability of duplexes formed. Further, these data were subjected to a battery of unreported manipulations in Sibley and Ahlquist (1984, 1987), which had the principal effect of converting outlier values into inlier values. The variability we find in delta-T50H values for any pair of species is much greater than that reported in Sibley and Ahlquist (1984, 1987).

We feel the DNA hybridization data are ambiguous with respect to the amount of difference between the single-copy sequences of human and chimpanzee. The DNA hybridization techniques afford a good, but rough, estimate of genomic similarity, and the data we have been permitted to examine merit a conservative conclusion: that humans, chimpanzees, and gorillas are exceedingly similar in their genetic makeup (Goodman, 1963; Sarich and Wilson, 1967).

ACKNOWLEDGMENTS

We gratefully acknowledge the helpful comments of Patrick Foley, Randy Skelton, and John Gillespie on an early draft, Lawrence Martin, Fred Sheldon, and Tony Bledsoe on a late draft, and many anonymous reviewers. We thank as well Eric Delson, Maryellen Ruvolo, and Peter Andrews for their patience, assistance, and input; and Charles Sibley, Jon Ahlquist, Roy Britten, and Emile Zuckerkandl for the opportunity and permission to examine some of the data.

NOTES

[1] Cot: DNA concentration x time allowed for the annealing reaction to proceed. Repetitive DNA anneals at low Cots (i.e., rapidly or in dilute concentrations); unique sequence DNA anneals at high Cots.

[2] It is not clear that the data from different experiments can be easily pooled. We have taken a simple average at each temperature across all experiments, which assumes in harmony with Sibley and Ahlquist's (1984, 1987) analysis that each value is independent of the others. These data will be published elsewhere (V. Sarich *et al.* 1989), so that others may subject them to more rigorous analyses.

REFERENCES

Andrews, P. 1985. Improved timing of hominoid evolution with a DNA clock. *Nature* 314:498-499.

Andrews, P. 1986. Molecular evidence for catarrhine evolution, in: *Major Topics in Primate and Human Evolution* (B. Wood, L. Martin, and P. Andrews, Eds.), pp. 107-129, Cambridge University Press, New York.

Benveniste, R. E., and Todaro, G. J. 1976. Evolution of type C viral genes: Evidence for Asian origin of man. *Nature* 261:101-108.

Bledsoe, A. H. 1987. DNA evolutionary rates in nine-primaried passerine birds. *Mol. Biol. Evol.* 4:559-571.

Brownell, E. 1983. DNA/DNA hybridization studies of muroid rodents: Symmetry and rates of molecular evolution. *Evolution* 37:1043-1051.

Caccone, A., DeSalle, R., and Powell, J. R. 1988. Calibration of the change in thermal stability of DNA duplexes and degree of base pair mismatch. *J. Mol. Evol.* 27:212-216.

Caccone, A., and Powell, J. R. 1988. A re-evaluation of higher primate phylogeny based on scnDNA. Paper presented at meeting of the Society for the Study of Evolution, June 1988.

Cantor, C., and Schimmel, P. 1980. *Biophysical Chemistry*. W.H. Freeman, San Francisco.

Cracraft, J. 1987. DNA hybridization and avian phylogenetics, in: *Evolutionary Biology* Vol. 21, (M. K. Hecht, B. Wallace, and G. T. Prance, Eds.), pp. 47-96, Plenum Press, New York.

Davidson, E. H., Hough, B. R., Amenson, C. S., and Britten, R. J. 1973. General interspersion of repetitive with non-repetitive sequence elements in the DNA of *Xenopus*. J. *Mol. Biol.* 77:1-23.

Deininger, P. L., and Schmid, C. W. 1976. Thermal stability of human DNA and chimpanzee DNA heteroduplexes. *Science* 194:846-848.

Dene, H. T., Goodman, M., and Prychodko, W. 1976. Immunodiffusion evidence on the phylogeny of the primates, in: *Molecular Anthropology* (M. Goodman and R. E. Tashian, Eds.), pp. 171-196, Plenum Press, New York.

Diamond, J. 1988. Relationships of humans to chimps and gorillas. *Nature* 334:656.

Felsenstein, J. 1987. Estimation of hominoid phylogeny from a DNA hybridization data set. *J. Mol. Evol.* 26:123-131.

Ferris, S. D., Brown, W. M., Davidson, W. S. and Wilson, A. C. 1981a. Extensive polymorphism in the mitochondrial DNA of apes. *Proc. Natl. Acad. Sci., USA*, 78:6319-6323.

Ferris, S. D., Wilson, A. C., and Brown, W. M. 1981b. Evolutionary tree for apes and humans based on cleavage maps of mitochondrial DNA. *Proc. Natl. Acad. Sci., USA*, 78:2432-2436.

Fitch, W. M. 1986. Commentary. *Mol. Biol. Evol.* 3:296-298.

Fox, G. M., Umeda, J., Lee, R. K.-Y., and Schmid, C. W. 1980. A phase diagram of the binding of mismatched duplex DNAs to hydroxyapatite. *Biochim. Biophys. Acta* 609:364-371.

Goodman, M. 1963. Serological analysis of the systematics of recent hominoids. *Hum. Biol.* 35:377-436.

Hixson, J. E., and Brown, W. M. 1986. A comparison of the small ribosomal DNA genes from the mitochondrial DNA of the great apes and humans: Structure, evolution, and phylogenetic implications. *Mol. Biol. Evol.* 3:1-18.

Hoyer, B. H., Van de Velde, N. W., Goodman, M., and Roberts, R. B. 1972. Examination of hominoid evolution by DNA sequence homology. *J. Hum. Evol.* 1:645-649.

Koop, B. F., Goodman, M., Xu, P., Chan, K., and Slightom, J. 1986. Primate eta-globin DNA sequences and man's place among the great apes. *Nature* 319:234-238.

Lewin, R. 1984. DNA reveals surprises in human family tree. *Science* 226:1179-1182.

Lewin, R. 1987. My close cousin the chimpanzee. *Science* 238:273-275.

Maeda, N., Wu, C.-I., Bliska, J., and Reneke, J. 1988. Molecular evolution of intergenic DNA in higher primates: Pattern of DNA changes, molecular clock, and evolution of repetitive sequences. *Mol. Biol. Evol.* 5:1-20.

Marks, J. 1983. Hominoid cytogenetics and evolution. *Phys. Anthrop. Yrbk.* 25:125-153.

Martinson, H. G. 1973. The nucleic acid-hydroxylapatite interaction. II. Phase transitions in the deoxyribonucleic acid-hydroxylapatite system. *Biochemistry* 12:145-150.

O'Brien, S. J., Nash, W. G., Wildt, D. E., Bush, M. E., and Benveniste, R. E. 1985. A molecular solution to the riddle of the giant panda's phylogeny. *Nature* 317:140-144.

Pilbeam, D. 1986. Hominoid evolution and hominoid origins. *Am. Anthrop.* 88:295-312.

Ruvolo, M., and Smith, T. F. 1985. Phylogeny and DNA-DNA hybridization. *Mol. Biol. Evol.* 3:285-289.

Saitou, N. 1986. On the delta-Q test of Templeton. *Mol. Biol. Evol.* 3:282-284.

Sarich, V. M., and Cronin, J. E. 1976. Molecular systematics of the primates, in: *Molecular Anthropology* (M. Goodman and R. E. Tashian, Eds.), pp. 141-170, Plenum Press, New York.

Sarich, V. M., Schmid, C. W., and Marks, J. 1989. DNA hybridization as a guide to phylogenies: A critical analysis. *Cladistics* 5:3–32.

Sarich, V. M., and Wilson, A. C. 1967. Immunological time scale for hominid evolution. *Science* 158:1200-1204.

Schmid, C. W., and Deininger, P. L. 1975. Sequence organization of the human genome. *Cell* 6:435-358.

Sheldon, F. 1987. Rates of single-copy DNA evolution in herons. *Mol. Biol. Evol.* 4:56-69.

Sibley, C. G., and Ahlquist, J. E. 1983. Phylogeny and classification of birds based on the data of DNA-DNA hybridization, in: *Current Ornithology*, Vol. 1 (R. F. Johnston, Ed.), pp. 245-292, Plenum Press, New York.

Sibley, C. G., and Ahlquist, J. E. 1984. The phylogeny of the hominoid primates, as indicated by DNA-DNA hybridization. *J. Mol. Evol.* 20: 2-15.

Sibley, C. G., and Ahlquist, J. E. 1987. DNA hybridization evidence of hominoid phylogeny: Results from an expanded data set. *J. Mol. Evol.* 26:99-121.

Stanyon, R., and Chiarelli, B. 1982. Phylogeny of the Hominoidea: The chromosome evidence. *J. Hum. Evol.* 11:493-504.

Templeton, A. R. 1985. The phylogeny of the hominoid primates: A statistical analysis of the DNA-DNA hybridization data. *Mol. Biol. Evol.* 2:420-433.

Templeton, A. R. 1986. Further comments on the statistical analysis of DNA-DNA hybridization data. *Mol. Biol. Evol.* 3:290-295.

Vizard, D. L., Rinehart, F. P., Rubin, C. M., and Schmid, C. W. 1977. Intramolecular base composition heterogeneity of human DNA. *Nucl. Acids Res.* 4:3753-3768.

5

The Evolution of the Hand

J. Napier

At Olduvai Gorge in Tanganyika two years ago L. S. B. Leakey and his wife Mary unearthed 15 bones from the hand of an early hominid. They found the bones on a well-defined living floor a few feet below the site at which in the summer of 1959 they had excavated the skull of a million-year-old man-ape to which they gave the name *Zinjanthropus*. The discovery of *Zinjanthropus* has necessitated a complete revision of previous views about the cultural and biological evolution of man. The skull was found in association with stone tools and waste flakes, indicating that at this ancient horizon toolmakers were already in existence. The floor on which the hand bones were discovered has also yielded stone tools and a genuine bone "lissoir," or leather working tool. Hence this even older living site carries the origins of toolmaking still further back, both in time and evolution, and it is now possible for the first time to reconstruct the hand of the earliest toolmakers.

Research and speculation on the course of human evolution have hitherto paid scant attention to the part played by the hand. Only last year I wrote: "It is a matter of considerable surprise to many to learn that the human hand, which can achieve so much in the field of creative art, communicate such subtle shades of meaning, and upon which the pre-eminence of *Homo sapiens* in the world of animals so largely depends, should constitute, in a structural sense, one of the most primitive and generalized parts of the human body." The implication of this statement, which expresses an almost traditional view, is that the primate forebears of man were equipped with a hand of essentially human form long before the cerebral capacity necessary to exploit its potential had appeared (Fig. 1). The corollary to this view is that the difference between the human hand and the monkey hand, as the late Frederic Wood Jones of the Royal College of Surgeons used to insist, is largely one of function

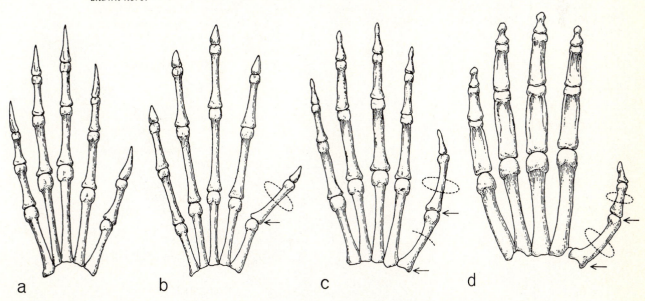

Figure 1. *Hands of living primates, all drawn same size, show evolutionary changes in structure related to increasing manual dexterity. Tree shrew (a) shows beginnings of unique primate possession, specialized thumb (digit at right). In tarsier (b) thumb is distinct and can rotate around joint between digit and palm. In capuchin monkey (c), a typical New World species, angle between thumb and fingers is wider and movement can be initiated at joint at base of palm. Gorilla (d), like other Old World species, has saddle joint at base of palm. This allows full rotation of thumb, which is set at a wide angle. Only palm and hand bones are shown here.*

a   b   c   d

rather than structure. Although broadly speaking it is true that the human hand has an extraordinarily generalized structure, the discovery of the Olduvai hand indicates that in a number of minor but nevertheless highly significant features the hand is more specialized than we had supposed.

Tool-using—in the sense of improvisation with naturally occurring objects such as sticks and stones—by the higher apes has often been observed both in the laboratory and in the wild and has even been reported in monkeys. The making of tools, on

the other hand, has been regarded as the major breakthrough in human evolution, a sort of status symbol that could be employed to distinguish the genus Homo from the rest of the primates. Prior to the discovery of *Zinjanthropus*, the South African man-apes (Australopithecines) had been associated at least indirectly with fabricated tools. Observers were reluctant to credit the man-apes with being toolmakers, however, on the ground that they lacked an adequate cranial capacity. Now that hands as well as skulls have been found at the same site with undoubted tools, one can

Figure 2. *Hand of modern man, drawn here actual size, is capable of precise movements available to no other species. Breadth of terminal phalanges (end bones of digits) guarantees secure thumb-to-finger grip. Thumb is long in proportion to index finger and is set a very wide angle. Strong muscles (*adductor pollicis *and* abductor pollicis*) implement movement of thumb toward and away from palm. Saddle joint at articulation of thumb metacarpal (a bone of the palm) and trapezium (a bone of the carpus, or wrist) enables thumb to rotate through 45 degrees around its own longitudinal axis and so be placed in opposition to all the other digits.*

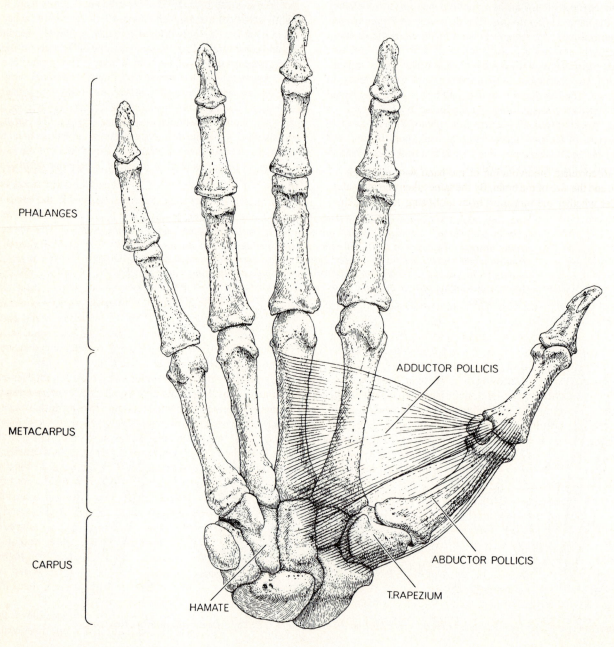

PHALANGES

METACARPUS

CARPUS

ADDUCTOR POLLICIS

ABDUCTOR POLLICIS

T.RAPEZIUM

HAMATE

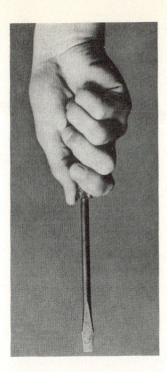

Figure 3. *POWER GRIP is one of two basic working postures of human hand. Used when strength is needed, it involves holding object between flexed fingers and palm while the thumb applies counterpressure.*

Figure 4. *PRECISION GRIP is second basic working posture and is used when accuracy and delicacy of touch are required. Object is held between tips of one or more fingers and the fully opposed thumb.*

begin to correlate the evolution of the hand with the stage of culture and the size of the brain. By the same token one must also consider whether the transition from tool-using to toolmaking and the subsequent improvement in toolmaking techniques can be explained purely in terms of cerebral expansion and the refinement of peripheral neuromuscular mechanisms, or whether a peripheral factor—the changing form of the hand—has played an equally important part in the evolution of the human species. And to understand the significance of the specializations of the human hand, it must be compared in action—as well as in dissection—with the hands of lower primates.

In the hand at rest—with the fingers slightly curled, the thumb lying in the plane of the index finger, the poise of the whole reflecting the balanced tension of opposing groups of muscles—one can see something of its potential capacity (Fig. 2). From the position of rest, with a minimum of physical effort, the hand can assume either of its two prehensile working postures. The two postures are demonstrated in sequence by the employment of a screw driver to remove a screw solidly embedded in a block of wood (Fig. 3, 4). The hand first grips the tool between the flexed fingers and the palm with the thumb reinforcing the pressure of the fingers; this is the "power grip." As the screw comes loose, the hand grasps the tool between one or more fingers and the thumb, with the pulps, or inner surfaces, of the finger and thumb tips fully opposed to one another; this is the "precision grip." Invariably it is the nature of the task to be performed, and not the shape of the tool or object grasped, that dictates which posture is employed. The power grip is the grip of choice when the full strength of the hand must be applied and the need for precision is subordinate; the precision grip comes into play when the need for power is secondary to the demand for fine control.

The significance of this analysis becomes apparent when the two activities are correlated with anatomical structure. The presence or absence of these structural features in the hands of a lower primate or early hominid can then be taken to indicate, within limits, the capabilities of those hands in the cultural realm of tool-using and toolmaking. In the case of the hand, at least, evolution has been incremental. Although the precision grip represents the ultimate refinement in prehensility, this does not mean that more primitive capacities have been lost. The human hand remains capable of the postures and movements of the primate foot-hand and even of the paw of the fully quadrupedal mammal, and it retains many of the anatomical structures that go with them. From one stage in evolution to the next the later capability is added to the earlier.

The study of primate evolution is facilitated by the fact that the primates now living constitute a graded series representative of some of its principal chapters. It is possible, at least, to accept a study series composed of tree shrews, tarsiers, New World monkeys, Old World monkeys and man as conforming to the evolutionary sequence. In comparing the hands of these animals with one another and with man's, considerable care must be taken to recognize specializations of structure that do not form part of the sequence. Thus the extremely specialized form of the hand in the anthropoid apes can in no way be regarded as a stage in the sequence from tree shrew to man. The same objection does not apply, however, to certain fossil apes. The hand of the Miocene ancestral ape *Proconsul africanus* does not, for example, show the hand specializations of living apes and can legitimately be brought into the morphological sequence that branches off on the man-ape line toward man.

In the lowliest of the living primates—the tree shrew that inhabits the rain forests of the East Indies and the Malay

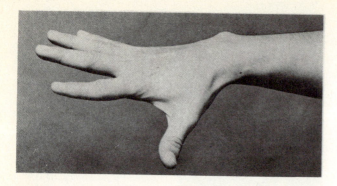

Figure 5. *DIVERGENCE, generally associated with weight-bearing function of hand, is achieved by extension at the metacarpophalangeal joints. All mammalian paws are capable of this action.*

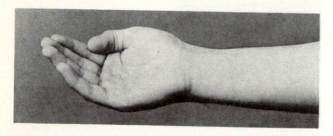

Figure 6. *CONVERGENCE is achieved by flexion at metacarpophalangeal joints. Two convergent paws equal one prehensile hand; many mammals hold food in two convergent paws to eat.*

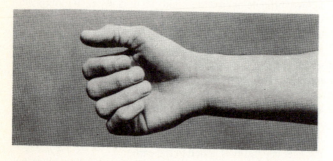

Figure 7. *PREHENSILITY, the ability to wrap the fingers around an object, is a special primate characteristic, related to the emergence of the specialized thumb during evolutionary process.*

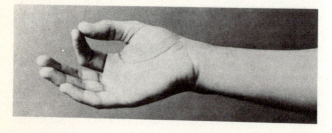

Figure 8. *OPPOSABILITY is ability to sweep thumb across palm while rotating it around its longitudinal axis. Many primates can do this, but underlying structures are best developed in man.*

Archipelago—the hand is little more than a paw. It exhibits in a primate sense only the most rudimentary manual capability. This is the movement of convergence that brings the tips of the digits together by a flexion of the paw at the metacarpophalangeal joints, which correspond in man to the knuckles at the juncture of the fingers and the rest of the hand. The opposite movement—divergence—fans the digits outward and is related to the pedal, or weightbearing, function of the paw (Fig. 5, 6). With its paws thus limited the tree shrew is compelled to grasp objects, for example its insect prey, in two-handed fashion, two convergent paws being the functional equivalent of a prehensile hand. For purposes of locomotion in its arboreal habitat, this animal does not require prehensility (Fig. 7) because, like the squirrel, it is small, it has claws on the tips of its digits and is a tree runner rather than a climber. Even in the tree shrew, however, the specialized thumb of the primate family has begun to take form in the specialized anatomy of this digit and its musculature. Occasionally tree shrews have been observed feeding with one hand.

The hand of the tarsier, another denizen of the rain forests of the East Indies, exhibits a more advanced degree of prehensility in being able to grasp objects by bending the digits toward the palm. The thumb digit also exhibits a degree of opposability (Fig. 8) to the other digits. This is a pseudo opposability in that the movement is restricted entirely to the metacarpophalangeal joint and is therefore distinct from the true opposability of man's thumb. The movement is facilitated by the well-developed abductor and adductor muscles that persist in the hands of the higher primates (See Fig. 2). With this equipment the tarsier is able to support its body weight on vertical stems and to grasp small objects with one hand.

The tropical rain forests in which these animals live today are probably not very different from the closed-canopy forests of the Paleocene epoch of some 70 million years ago, during which the first primates appeared. In the wide variety of habitats that these forests provide, ecologists distinguish five major strata, superimposed like a block of apartments. From the top down these are the upper, middle and lower stories (the last being the main closed canopy), the shrub layer and the herb layer on the ground. To these can be added a sixth deck: the subterrain. In the emergence of prehensility in the primate line the three-dimensional arrangement of this system of habitats played a profound role. Prehensility is an adaptation to arboreal life and is related to climbing. In animals that are of small size with respect to the branches on which they live and travel, such as the tree shrew, mobility is not hampered by lack of prehensility. They can live at any level in the forest, from the forest floor to the tops of the tallest trees, their stability assured by the grip of sharp claws and the elaboration of visual and cerebellar mechanisms.

The tree-climbing as opposed to the tree-running phase of primate evolution may not have begun until the middle of the Eocene, perhaps 55 million years ago. What environmental pressure brought about this adaptation can only be guessed at. Thomas F. Barth of the University of Chicago has suggested that the advent of the widely successful order of rodents in the early Eocene may have led to the displacement of the primates from the shrub strata to the upper three strata of the forest canopy. In any case little is known about the form of the primates that made this transition.

In *Proconsul*, of the early to middle Miocene of 20 million years ago, the fossil record discloses a fully developed tree-climbing primate. His hand was clearly prehensile. His thumb, however, was imperfectly opposable. Functionally this hand is comparable to that of some of the living New World monkeys.

True opposability appears for the first time among the living primates in the Old World monkeys. In these animals the carpometacarpal joint shows a well-developed saddle configuration comparable to that in the corresponding joint of the human hand. This allows rotation of the thumb from its wrist articulation. Turning about its longitudinal axis through an angle of about 45 degrees, the thumb can be swept across the palm, and the pulp of the thumb can be directly opposed to the pulp surfaces of one of or all the other digits. This movement is not so expertly performed by the monkeys as by man. At the same time, again as in man, a fair range of movement is retained at the metacarpophalangeal joint, the site of pseudo opposability in the tarsier.

The hands of anthropoid apes display many of these anatomical structures but do not have the same degree of functional capability. This is because of certain specializations that arise from the fact that these apes swing from trees by their hands. Such specializations would seem to exclude the apes from the evolutionary sequence that leads to man. In comparing the hand of monkeys with the hand of man one must bear in mind an obvious fact that is all too often overlooked: monkeys are largely quadrupedal, whereas man is fully bipedal. Variations in the form of the hand from one species of monkey to the next are related to differences in their mode of locomotion. The typical monkey hand is rather long and narrow; the metacarpal, or "palm," bones are short compared with the digits (except in baboons); the terminal phalanges, or finger-tip bones, are slender and the tips of the fingers are consequently narrow from side to side. These are only the most obvious differences between the foot-hand of the Old World monkey and that of man. They serve nonetheless to show how too rigid an application of Frederic Wood Jones's criterion of morphological similarity can mislead one into assuming that the only important difference between the hands of men and monkeys lies in the elaboration of the central nervous system.

It seems likely that the terrestrial phase of human evolution followed on the heels of *Proconsul*. At that time, it is well known, the world's grasslands expanded enormously at the expense of the forests. By the end of the Miocene, 15 million years ago, most of the prototypes of the modern plains-living forms had appeared. During this period, apparently, the hominids also deserted their original forest habitats to take up life on the savanna, where the horizons were figuratively limitless. Bipedal locomotion, a process initiated by life in the trees and the ultimate mechanism for emancipation of the hands, rapidly followed the adoption of terrestrial life. The use of the hands for carrying infants, food and even weapons and tools could not have lagged far behind. As Sherwood L. Washburn of the University of California has suggested on the basis of observations of living higher primates, tool-using must have appeared at an early stage in hominid evolution. It is a very short step from tool-using to tool-modifying, in the sense of stripping twigs and leaves from a branch in order to improve its effectiveness as a tool or weapon. It is an equally short further step to

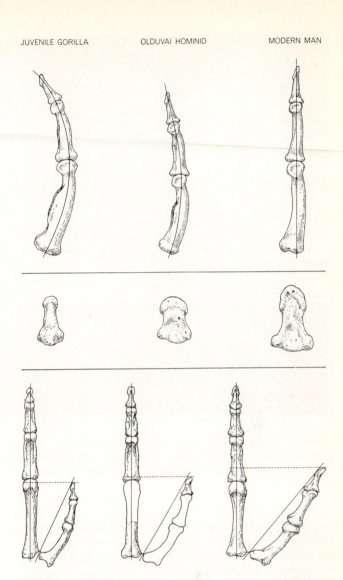

JUVENILE GORILLA   OLDUVAI HOMINID   MODERN MAN

Figure 9. *Hand Bones of juvenile gorilla, Olduvai hominid and modern man are compared. Phalanges (top row) decrease in curvature from juvenile gorilla to modern man. Terminal thumb phalanx (middle row) increases in breadth and proportional length. Third row shows increase in length of thumb and angle between thumb and index finger. Olduvai bones in outline in third row are reconstructed from other evidence; they were not found.*

toolmaking, which at its most primitive is simply the application of the principle of modification to a stick, a stone or a bone. Animal bones are a convenient source of tools; Raymond A. Dart of the University of Witwatersrand in South Africa has advanced the hypothesis that such tools were used by early man-apes as part of an "osteodontokeratic" (bone-tooth-hair) culture.

The tools from the pre-*Zinjanthropus* stratum at Olduvai Gorge are little more than pebbles modified in the simplest way by striking off one or more flakes to produce a chopping edge (Fig. 10). This technology could not have required either a particularly large brain or a hand of modern human proportions. The hand bones of the pre-*Zinjanthropus* individuals uncovered by the Leakeys in their more recent excavation of Olduvai Gorge are quite unlike those of modern *Homo sapiens*. But there seems to be no reason, on either geological or anthropological

Figure 10. *Stone tools to left of center are similar to those found at Olduvai Gorge, Tanganyika, in conjunction with the hand bones of an early hominid. Such crude tools can be made by using the power grip, of which the Olduvai hand was capable. Finely flaked Old Stone Age tools at right can be made only by using the precision grip, which may not have been well developed in Olduvai hand.*

grounds, for doubting that the tools found with them are coeval. Modern man must recover from his surprise at the discovery that hands other than his own were capable of shaping tools.

At this point it may be useful to return to the analysis of the manual capability of modern man that distinguishes the power and the precision grip. When compared with the hand of modern man, the Olduvai hand appears to have been capable of a tremendously strong power grip. Although it was a smaller hand, the relative lengths of the metacarpals and phalanges indicate that the proportion of digits and palm was much the same as it is in man. In addition, the tips of the terminal bones of all the Olduvai fingers are quite wide and the finger tips themselves must therefore have been broad—an essential feature of the human grip for both mechanical and neurological reasons. The curvature of the

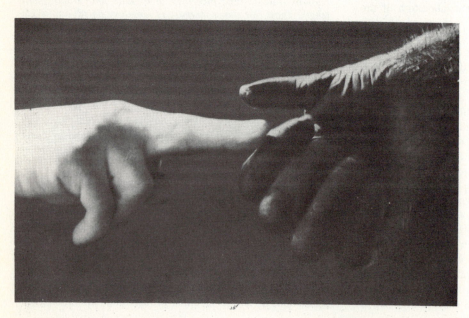

Figure 11. *Chimpanzee, attempting to grasp experimenter's finger, uses an inefficient precision grip. Because animal's thumb is so short in proportion to the digits, it is compelled to bend the digits forward and grasp the object between the sides of index finger and thumb.*

metacarpals and phalanges indicates that the fingers were somewhat curved throughout their length and were normally held in semiflexion. Unfortunately no hamate bone was found among the Olduvai remains. This wristbone, which articulates with the fifth metacarpal, meets at a saddle joint in modern man and lends great stability to his power grip.

It seems unlikely that the Olduvai hand was capable of the precision grip in its fullest expression. No thumb metacarpal was found in the Olduvai deposit; hence any inference as to the length of the thumb in relation to the other fingers must be derived from the evidence of the position of the wristbone with which the thumb articulates. This evidence suggests that the Olduvai thumb, like the thumb of the gorilla, was set at a narrower angle and was somewhat shorter than the thumb of modern man, reaching only a little beyond the metacarpophalangeal joint of the index finger (Fig. 9). Thus, although the thumb was opposable, it can be deduced that the Olduvai hand could not perform actions as precise as those that can be undertaken by the hand of modern man (See Fig.11).

Nonetheless, the Olduvai hand activated by a brain and a neuromuscular mechanism of commensurate development would have had little difficulty in making the tools that were found with it. I myself have made such pebble tools employing only the power grip to hold and strike two stones together.

The inception of toolmaking has hitherto been regarded as the milestone that marked the emergence of the genus *Homo*. It has been assumed that this development was a sudden event, happening as it were almost overnight, and that its appearance was coincidental with the structural evolution of a hominid of essentially modern human form and proportions. It is now becoming clear that this important cultural phase in evolution had its inception at a much earlier stage in the biological evolution of man, that it existed for a much longer period of time and that it was set in motion by a much less advanced hominid and a much less specialized hand than has previously been believed.

For full understanding of the subsequent improvement in toolmaking over the next few hundred thousand years of the Paleolithic, it is necessary to document the transformation of the hand as well as of the brain. Attention can now also be directed toward evidence of the functional capabilities of the hands of early man that is provided by the tools they made. These studies may help to account for the radical changes in technique and direction that characterize the evolution of stone implements during the middle and late Pleistocene epoch. The present evidence suggests that the stone implements of early man were as good (or as bad) as the hands that made them.

REFERENCES

Le Gros Clark, W. E. 1959. *The Antecedants of Man: An Introductoin to the Evolution of the Primates.* Edinburgh University Press, Edinburg.

Napier, J. R. 1956. The prehensile movements of the human hand. *Journal of Bone and Joint Surgery* 38B(4):902-913.

Napier, J. R. 1961. Prehensility and opposability in the hands of primates. *Symposia of the Zoological Society of London*, no. 5:115-132.

Oakley, K. P. 1950. *Man the Tool-Maker.* British Museum of Natural History, London.

Richards, P. W. 1957. *The Tropical Rain Forest.* Cambridge University Press, Cambridge.

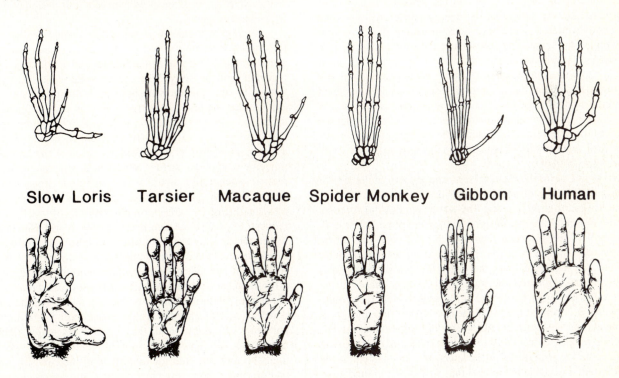

Slow Loris   Tarsier   Macaque   Spider Monkey   Gibbon   Human

6

The Antiquity of Human Walking

J. Napier

Human walking is a unique activity during which the body, step by step, teeters on the edge of catastrophe. The fact that man has used this form of locomotion for more than a million years has only recently been demonstrated by fossil evidence. The antiquity of this human trait is particularly noteworthy because walking with a striding gait is probably the most significant of the many evolved capacities that separate men from more primitive hominids. The fossil evidence—the terminal bone of a right big toe discovered in 1961 in Olduvai Gorge in Tanzania—sets up a new signpost that not only clarifies the course of human evolution but also helps to guide those who speculate on the forces that converted predominantly quadrupedal animals into habitual bipeds.

Man's bipedal mode of walking seems potentially catastrophic because only the rhythmic forward movement of first one leg and then the other keeps him from falling flat on his face. Consider the sequence of events whenever a man sets out in pursuit of his center of gravity. A stride begins when the muscles of the calf relax and the walker's body sways forward (gravity supplying the energy needed to overcome the body's inertia). The sway places the center of body weight in front of the supporting pedestal normally formed by the two feet. As a result one or the other of the walker's legs must swing forward so that when his foot makes contact with the ground, the area of the supporting pedestal has been widened and the center of body weight once again rests safely within it. The pelvis plays an important role in this action: its degree of rotation determines the distance the swinging leg can move forward, and its muscles help to keep the body balanced while the leg is swinging.

At this point the "stance" leg—the leg still to the rear of the body's center of gravity—provides the propulsive force that drives the body forward. The walker applies this force by using muscular energy, pushing against the ground first with the ball of his foot and then with his big toe. The action constitutes the "push-off," which terminates the stance phase of the walking cycle. Once the stance foot leaves the ground, the walker's leg enters the starting, or "swing," phase of the cycle. As the leg swings forward it is able to clear the ground because it is bent at the hip, knee and ankle. This high-stepping action substantially reduces the leg's moment of inertia. Before making contact with the ground and ending the swing phase the leg straightens at the knee but remains bent at the ankle. As a result it is the heel that strikes the ground first. The "heel strike" concludes the swing phase; as the body

continues to move forward the leg once again enters the stance phase, during which the point of contact between foot and ground moves progressively nearer the toes. At the extreme end of the stance phase, as before, all the walker's propulsive thrust is delivered by the robust terminal bone of his big toe (Fig. 1).

A complete walking cycle is considered to extend from the heel strike of one leg to the next heel strike of the same leg; it consists of the stance phase followed by the swing phase. The relative duration of the two phases depends on the cadence or speed of the walk. During normal walking the stance phase constitutes about 60 percent of the cycle and the swing phase 40 percent. Although the action of only one leg has been described in this account, the opposite leg obviously moves in a reciprocal fashion; when one leg is moving in the swing phase, the other leg is in its stance phase and keeps the body poised. Actually, during normal walking the two phases overlap, so that both feet are on the ground at the same time for about 25 percent of the cycle. As walking speed increases, this period of double leg support shortens.

Anyone who has watched other people walking and reflected a little on the process has noticed that the human stride demands both an up-and-down and a side-to-side displacement of the body. When two people walk side by side but out of step, the alternate bobbing of their heads makes it evident that the bodies undergo a vertical displacement with each stride. When two people walk in step but with opposite feet leading, they will sway first toward each other and then away in an equally graphic demonstration of the lateral displacement at each stride. When both displacements are plotted sequentially, a pair of low-amplitude sinusoidal curves appear, one in the vertical plane and the other in the horizontal (Fig. 2, 3). General observations of this kind were reduced to precise measurements during World War II when a group at the University of California at Berkeley led by H.D. Eberhart conducted a fundamental investigation of human walking in connection with requirements for the design of artificial legs. Eberhart and his colleagues found that a number of functional determinants interacted to move the human body's center of gravity through space with a minimum expenditure of energy. In all they isolated six major elements related to hip, knee and foot movement that, working together, reduced both the amplitude of the two sine curves and the abruptness with which vertical and lateral changes in direction took place. If any one of these six elements was

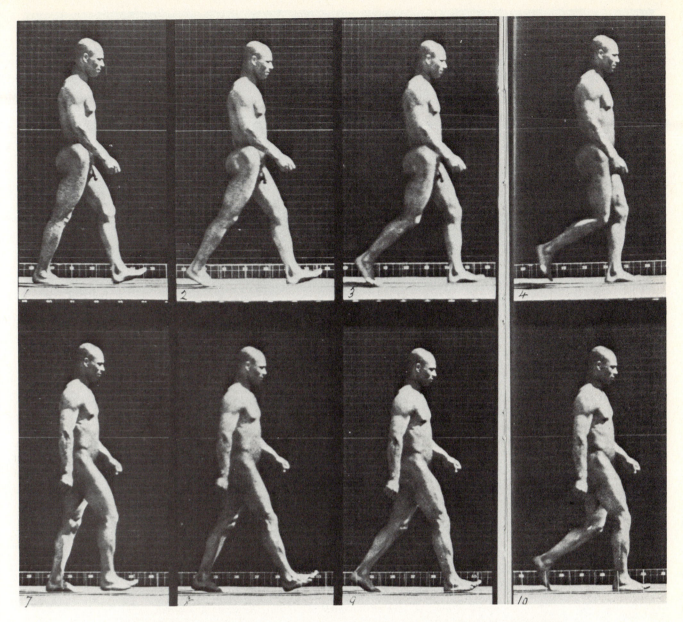

Figure 1. *WALKING MAN, photographed by Eadweard Muybridge in 1884 during his studies of human and animal motion, exhibits the characteristic striding gait of the modern human. The free foot strikes the ground heel first and the body's weight is gradually transferred from heel to ball of foot as the opposite leg lifts and swings forward. Finally the heel of the stance foot rises and the leg's last contact with the ground is made with the big toe.*

disturbed, an irregularity was injected into the normally smooth, undulating flow of walking, thereby producing a limp. What is more important, the irregularity brought about a measurable increase in the body's energy output during each step.

THE EVIDENCE OF THE BONES

What I have described in general and Eberhart's group studied in detail is the form of walking known as striding. It is characterized by the heel strike at the start of the stance phase and the push-off at its conclusion. Not all human walking is striding; when a man moves about slowly or walks on a slippery surface,

he may take short steps in which both push-off and heel strike are absent. The foot is simply lifted from the ground at the end of the stance phase and set down flat at the end of the swing phase. The stride, however, is the essence of human bipedalism and the criterion by which the evolutionary status of a hominid walker must be judged. This being the case, it is illuminating to consider how the act of striding leaves its distinctive marks on the bones of the strider.

To take the pelvis first, there is a well-known clinical manifestation called Trendelenburg's sign that is regarded as evidence of hip disease in children. When a normal child stands on one leg, two muscles connecting that leg and the pelvis—the gluteus medius and the gluteus minimus—con-

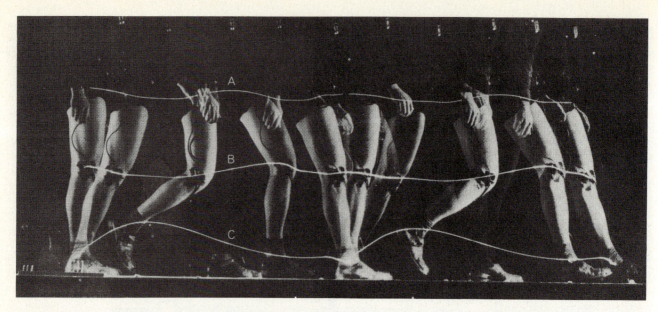

Figure 2. *WALKING CYCLE extends from the heel strike of one leg to the next heel strike by the same leg. In the photograph, made by Gjon Mili in the course of a study aimed at improvement of artificial legs that he conducted for the U.S. Army, multiple exposures trace the progress of the right leg in the course of two strides. The ribbons of light allow analysis of the movement.*

tract; this contraction, pulling on the pelvis, tilts it and holds it poised over the stance leg. When the hip is diseased, this mechanism fails to operate and the child shows a positive Trendelenburg's sign: the body tends to fall toward the unsupported side.

The same mechanism operates in walking, although not to the same degree. During the stance phase of the walking cycle, the same two gluteal muscles on the stance side brace the pelvis by cantilever action. Although actual tilting toward the stance side does not occur in normal walking, the action of the muscles

in stabilizing the walker's hip is an essential component of the striding gait. Without this action the stride would become a slow, ungainly shuffle.

At the same time that the pelvis is stabilized in relation to the stance leg it also rotates to the unsupported side. This rotation, although small, has the effect of increasing the length of the stride. A familiar feature of the way women walk arises from this bit of anatomical mechanics. The difference in the proportions of the male and the female pelvis has the effect of slightly diminishing the range through which the female hip can

Figure 3. *SINE CURVE described by the hip of a walking man was recorded on film by means of the experimental system (See Fig. 2). An interrupter blade, passing in front of the camera lens at constant speed, broke the light from lamps attached to the walker into the three rows of dots. The speed of hip (A), knee (B) or ankle (C) during the stride is determined by measuring between the dots.*

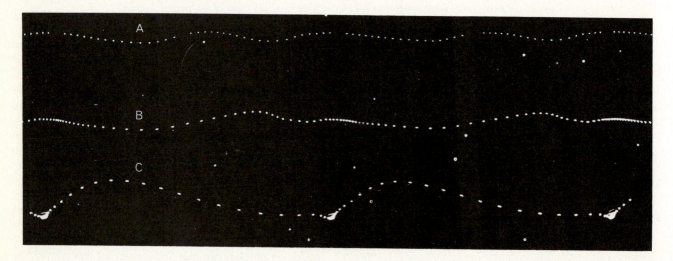

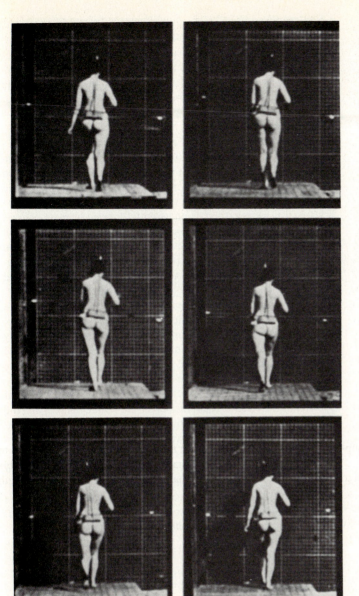

Figure 4. *PELVIC ROTATION of the human female is exaggerated compared to that of a male taking a stride of equal length because the two sexes differ in pelvic anatomy. Muybridge noted the phenomenon, using a pole with whitened ends to record the pelvic oscillations.*

forces acting on each part of the foot while it is in contact with the ground during the stance phase of the walking cycle. Many devices have been built for this purpose; one of them is the plastic pedograph. When the subject walks across the surface of the pedograph, a motion-picture camera simultaneously records the exact position of the foot in profile and the pattern of pressures on the surface. Pedograph analyses show that the initial contact between the striding leg and the ground is the heel strike. Because the foot is normally turned out slightly at the end of the swing phase of the walking cycle, the outer side of the back of the heel takes the brunt of the initial contact (Fig. 5). The outer side of the foot continues to support most of the pressure of the stance until a point about three-fifths of the way along the sole is reached. The weight of the body is then transferred to the ball of the foot and then to the big toe. In the penultimate stage of push-off the brunt of the pressure is under the toes, particularly the big toe. Finally, at the end of the stance phase, only the big toe is involved; it progressively loses contact with the ground and the final push-off is applied through its broad terminal bone.

The use of pedographs and similar apparatus provides precise evidence about the function of the foot in walking, but every physician knows that much the same information is recorded on the soles of everyone's shoes. Assuming that the shoes fit, their pattern of wear is a true record of the individual's habitual gait. The wear pattern will reveal a limp that one man is trying to hide, or unmask one that another man is trying to feign, perhaps to provide evidence for an insurance claim. In any case, just as the form of the pelvis and the femur can disclose the presence or absence of a striding gait, so can the form of the foot bones, particularly the form and proportions of the big-toe bones.

THE ORIGINS OF PRIMATE BIPEDALISM

Almost all primates can stand on their hind limbs, and many occasionally walk in this way. But our primate relatives are all, in a manner of speaking, amateurs; only man has taken up the business of bipedialism intensively. This raises two major questions. First, how did the basic postural adaptations that permit walking—occasional or habitual—arise among the primates? Second, what advantages did habitual bipedalism bestow on early man?

With regard to the first question, I have been concerned for some time with the anatomical proportions of all primates, not only man and the apes but also the monkeys and lower primate forms. Such consideration makes it possible to place the primates in natural groups according to their mode of locomotion. Not long ago I suggested a new group, and it is the only one that will concern us here. The group comprises primates with very long hind limbs and very short forelimbs. At about the same time my colleague Alan C. Walker, now at Makerere University College in Uganda, had begun a special study of the locomotion of living and fossil lemurs. Lemurs are among the most primitive offshoots of the basic primate stock. Early in Walker's studies he was struck by the frequency with which a posture best described as "vertical clinging" appeared in the day-to-day behavior of living lemurs. All the

move forward and back (Fig. 4). Thus for a given length of stride women are obliged to rotate the pelvis through a greater angle than men do. This secondary sexual characteristic has not lacked exploitation; at least in our culture female pelvic rotation has considerable erotogenic significance. What is more to the point in terms of human evolution is that both the rotation and the balancing of the pelvis leave unmistakable signs on the pelvic bone and on the femur: the leg bone that is joined to it. It is by a study of such signs that the walking capability of a fossil hominid can be judged.

Similar considerations apply to the foot. One way the role of the foot in walking can be studied is to record the vertical

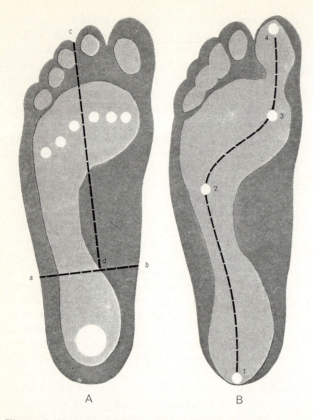

Figure 5. *DISTRIBUTION OF WEIGHT in the human foot alters radically as action takes the place of rest. When motionless (A), the foot divides its static load (half of the body's total weight) between its heel and its ball along the axis a-b. The load on the ball of the foot is further divided equally on each side of the axis c-d. When striding (B), the load (all of the body's weight during part of each stride) is distributed dynamically from the first point of contact (1, heel strike) in a smooth flow via the first and fifth metatarsal bones (2, 3) that ends with a propulsive thrust (4, push-off) delivered by the terminal bone of the big toe.*

animals whose propensity for vertical clinging had been observed by Walker showed the same proportions—that is, long hind limbs and short forelimbs—I had proposed as forming a distinct locomotor group.

When Walker and I compared notes, we decided to define a hitherto unrecognized locomotor category among the primates that we named "vertical clinging and leaping," a term that includes both the animal's typical resting posture and the essential leaping component in its locomotion. Since proposing this category a most interesting and important extension of the hypothesis has become apparent to us. Some of the earliest primate fossils known, preserved in sediments laid down during the Eocene times and therefore as much as 50 million years old, are represented not only by skulls and jaws but also by a few limb bones. In their proportions and details most of these limb bones show the same characteristics that are displayed by the living members of our vertical-clinging-and-leaping group today. Not long ago Elwyn L. Simons of Yale University presented a reconstruction of the lemur-like North American Eocene primate *Smilodectes* walking along a tree branch in a quadrupedal position in an earlier *Scientific American* article. Walker and I would prefer to see

Smilodectes portrayed in the vertical clinging posture its anatomy unequivocally indicates. The fossil evidence, as far as it goes, suggests to us that vertical clinging and leaping was a major primate locomotor adaptation that took place some 50 million years ago. It may even have been the initial dynamic adaptation to tree life from which the subsequent locomotor patterns of all the living primates, including man, have stemmed.

Walker and I are not alone in this view. In 1962 W. L. Straus, Jr., of Johns Hopkins University declared: "It can safely be assumed that primates early developed the mechanisms permitting maintenance of the trunk in the upright position....Indeed, this tendency toward truncal erectness can be regarded as an essentially basic primate character." The central adaptations for erectness of the body, which have been retained in the majority of living primates, seem to have provided the necessary anatomical basis for the occasional bipedal behavior exhibited by today's monkeys and apes.

What we are concerned with here is the transition from a distant, hypothetical vertical-clinging ancestor to modern, bipedal man. The transition was almost certainly marked by an intermediate quadrupedal stage. Possibly such Miocene fossil forms as *Proconsul*, a chimpanzee-like early primate from East Africa, represent such a stage. The structural adaptations necessary to convert a quadrupedal ape into a bipedal hominid are centered on the pelvis, the femur, the foot and the musculature associated with these bones. Among the non-human primates living today the pelvis and femur are adapted for four-footed walking; the functional relations between hip-bones and thigh muscles are such that, when the animal attempts to assume a bipedal stance, the hip joint is subjected to a stress and the hip must be bent. To compensate for the resulting forward shift of the center of gravity, the knees must also be bent. In order to alter a bent-hip, bent-knee gait into man's erect, striding walk, a number of anatomical changes must occur (Fig. 6). These include an elongation of the hind limbs with respect to the forelimbs, a shortening and broadening of the pelvis, adjustments of the musculature of the hip (in order to stabilize the trunk during the act of walking upright), a straightening of both hip and knee and considerable reshaping of the foot.

Which of these changes can be considered to be primary and which secondary is still a matter that needs elucidation. Sherwood L. Washburn of the University of California at Berkeley has expressed the view that the change from four-footed to two-footed posture was initiated by a modification in the form and function of the gluteus maximus, a thigh muscle that is powerfully developed in man but weakly developed in monkeys and apes (Fig. 7, 8). In a quadrupedal primate the principal extensors of the trunk are the "hamstring" muscles and the two upper-leg muscles I have already mentioned: the gluteus medius and gluteus minimus. In man these two muscles bear a different relation to the pelvis, in terms of both position and function. In technical terms they have become abductor muscles of the trunk rather than extensor muscles of the leg. It is this that enables them to play a critical part in stabilizing the pelvis in the course of striding. In man the extensor function of these two gluteal muscles has been taken over by a third, the gluteus maximus. This muscle,

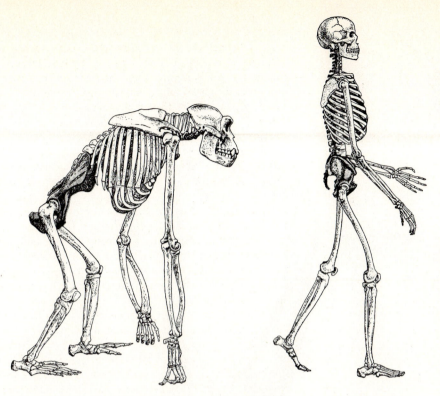

Figure 6. *SHAPE AND ORIENTATION of the pelvis in the gorilla and in man reflect the postural differences between quadrupedal and bipedal locomotion. The ischium in the gorilla is long, the ilium extends to the side and the whole pelvis is tilted toward the horizontal (See Fig. 11). In man the ischium is much shorter, the broad ilium extends forward and the pelvis is vertical.*

insignificant in other primates, plays a surprisingly unimportant role in man's ability to stand, or even to walk on a level surface. In standing, for example, the principal stabilizing and extending agents are the muscles of the hamstring group. In walking on the level the gluteus maximus is so little involved that even when it is paralyzed a man's stride is virtually unimpaired. The gluteus maximus comes into its own in man when power is needed to give the hip joint more play for such activities as running, walking up a steep slope or climbing stairs (Fig. 9). Its chief function in these circumstances is to correct any tendency for the human trunk to jackknife on the legs.

Because the gluteus maximus has such a specialized role I believe, in contrast to Washburn's view, that it did not assume its present form until late in the evolution of the striding gait. Rather than being the initial adaptation, this muscle's enlargement and present function appear to me far more likely to have been one of the ultimate refinements of human walking. I am in agreement with Washburn, however, when he states that changes in the ilium or upper pelvis, would have preceded changes in the ischium, or lower pelvis. The primary adaptation would probably have involved a forward curvature of the vertebral column in the lumbar region. Accompanying this change would have been a broadening and a forward rotation of the iliac portions of the pelvis. Together these early adaptations provide the structural basis for improving the posture of the trunk.

Assuming that we have now given at least a tentative answer to the question of how man's bipedal posture evolved, there remains to be answered the question of why. What were the advantages of habitual bipedalism? Noting the comparative energy demands of various gaits, Washburn points out that human walking is primarily an adaptation for covering long distances economically. To go a long way with a minimum of effort is an asset to a hunter; it seems plausible that evolutionary selection for hunting behavior in man was responsible for the rapid development of striding anatomy. Gordon W. Hewes of the University of Colorado suggests a possible incentive that, acting as an agent of natural selection, could have prompted the quadrupedal ancestors of man to adopt a two-footed gait. In Hewes's view the principal advantage of bipedalism over quadrupedalism would be the freeing of the hands, so that food could be carried readily from one place to another for later consumption. To assess the significance of such factors as survival mechanisms it behooves us to review briefly the ecological situation in which our prehuman ancestors found themselves in Miocene times, between 15 and 25 million years ago (Fig. 10).

THE MIOCENE ENVIRONMENT

During the Miocene epoch the worldwide mountain-building activity of middle Tertiary times was in full swing. Many parts of the earth, including the region of East Africa where primates of the genus *Proconsul* were living, were being faulted and uplifted to form such mountain zones as the Alps, the Himalayas, the Andes and the Rockies. Massive faulting in Africa gave rise to one of the earth's major geological features: the Rift Valley, which extends 5,000 miles from Tanzania across East Africa to Israel and the Dead Sea. A string of lakes lies along the floor of the Rift Valley like giant stepping-stones. On their shores in Miocene times lived a fantastically rich fauna, inhabitants of the forest and of a new ecological niche—the grassy savanna.

These grasslands of the Miocene were the domain of new forms of vegetation that in many parts of the world had taken

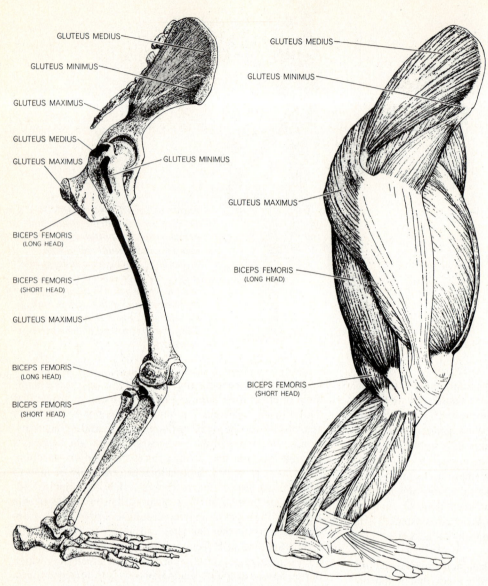

GLUTEUS MEDIUS

GLUTEUS MINIMUS

GLUTEUS MAXIMUS

GLUTEUS MEDIUS

GLUTEUS MAXIMUS — GLUTEUS MINIMUS

BICEPS FEMORIS
(LONG HEAD)

BICEPS FEMORIS
(SHORT HEAD)

GLUTEUS MAXIMUS

BICEPS FEMORIS
(LONG HEAD)

BICEPS FEMORIS
(SHORT HEAD)

GLUTEUS MEDIUS

GLUTEUS MINIMUS

GLUTEUS MAXIMUS

BICEPS FEMORIS
(LONG HEAD)

BICEPS FEMORIS
(SHORT HEAD)

Figure 7. *QUADRUPEDAL POS-TURE needs two sets of muscles to act as the principal extensors of the hip. These are the gluteal group (the gluteus medius and minimus in particular), which connects the pelvis to the upper part of the femur, and the hamstring group, which connects the femur and the lower leg bones. Of these only the biceps femoris is shown in the gorilla musculature at right. The skeletal regions to which these muscles attach are shown at left. In most primates the gluteus maximus is quite small.*

the place of rain forest, the dominant form of vegetation in the Eocene and the Oligocene. The savanna offered new evolutionary opportunities to a variety of mammals, including the expanding population of primates in the rapidly shrinking forest. A few primates—the ancestors of man and probably also the ancestors of the living baboons—evidently reacted to the challenge of the new environment.

The savanna, however, was no Eldorado. The problems facing the early hominids in the open grassland were immense. The forest foods to which they were accustomed were hard to come by; the danger of attack by predators was immeasurably increased. If, on top of everything else, the ancestral hominids of Miocene times were in the process of converting from quadrupedalism to bipedalism, it is difficult to conceive of any advantage in bipedalism that could have compensated for the added hazards of life in the open grassland. Consideration of the drawbacks of savanna living has led me to a conclusion contrary to the one generally accepted: I doubt that the advent

of bipedalism took place in this environment. An environment neglected by scholars but one far better suited for the origin of man is the woodland-savanna, which is neither high forest nor open grassland. Today this half-way-house niche is occupied by many primates, for example the vervet monkey and some chimpanzees. It has enough trees to provide forest foods and ready escape from predators. At the same time its open grassy spaces are arenas in which new locomotor adaptations can be practiced and new foods can be sampled. In short, the woodland-savanna provides an ideal nursery for evolving hominids, combining the challenge and incentive of the open grassland with much of the security of the forest. It was probably in this transitional environment that man's ancestors learned to walk on two legs. In all likelihood, however, they only learned to stride when they later moved into the open savanna.

Moving forward many millions of years from Miocene to Pleistocene times, we come to man's most immediate hominid precursor: *Australopithecus*. A large consortium of

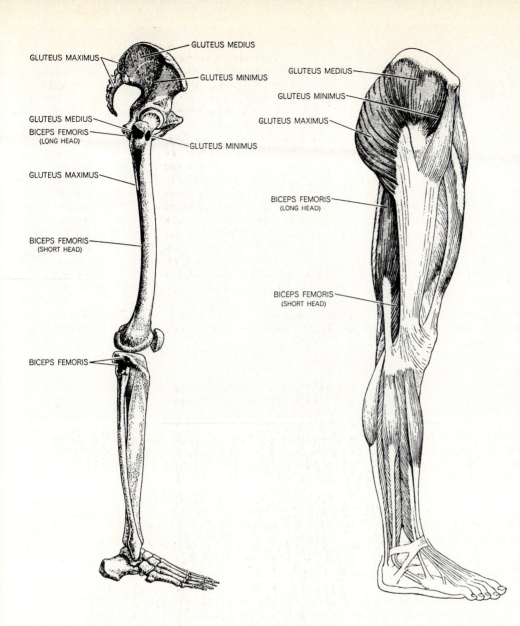

GLUTEUS MEDIUS

GLUTEUS MAXIMUS

GLUTEUS MINIMUS

GLUTEUS MEDIUS
BICEPS FEMORIS
(LONG HEAD)

GLUTEUS MINIMUS

GLUTEUS MAXIMUS

BICEPS FEMORIS
(SHORT HEAD)

BICEPS FEMORIS

GLUTEUS MEDIUS

GLUTEUS MINIMUS

GLUTEUS MAXIMUS

BICEPS FEMORIS
(LONG HEAD)

BICEPS FEMORIS
(SHORT HEAD)

Figure 8. *BIPEDAL POS-TURE brings a reversal in the roles played by the same pelvic and femoral muscles. Gluteus medius and gluteus minimus have changed from extensors to abductors and the function of extending the trunk, required when a biped runs or climbs, has been assumed by the gluteus maximus. The hamstring muscles, in turn, now act mainly as stabilizers and extensors of the hip. At right are the muscles as they appear in man; the skeletal regions to which their upper and lower ends attach are shown at left.*

authorities agrees that the shape of the pelvis in *Australopithecus* fossils indicates that these hominids were habitually bipedal, although not to the degree of perfection exhibited by modern man. A few anatomists, fighting a rearguard action, contend that on the contrary the pelvis of *Australopithecus* shows that these hominids were predominantly quadrupedal. I belong to the first school but, as I have been at some pains to emphasize in the past, the kind of upright walking practiced by *Australopithecus* should not be equated with man's heel-and-toe, striding gait.

FROM BIPEDALIST TO STRIDER

The stride, although it was not necessarily habitual among the earliest true men, is nevertheless the quintessence of the human locomotor achievement. Among other things, striding involves extension of the leg to a position behind the vertical axis of the spinal column. The degree of extension needed can only be achieved if the ischium of the pelvis is short. But the ischium of *Australopithecus* is long, almost as long as the ischium of an

ape (Fig. 11). Moreover, it has been shown that in man the gluteus medius and the gluteus minimus are prime movers in stabilizing the pelvis during each stride; in *Australopithecus* this stabilizing mechanism is imperfectly evolved. The combination of both deficiencies almost entirely precludes the possibility that these hominids possessed a striding gait. For *Australopithecus* walking was something of a jog trot. These hominids must have covered the ground with quick, rather short steps, with their knees and hips slightly bent; the prolonged stance phase of the fully human gait must surely have been absent.

Compared with man's stride, therefore, the gait of *Australopithecus* is physiologically inefficient. It calls for a disproportionately high output of energy; indeed, *Australopithecus* probably found long-distance bipedal travel impossible. A natural question arises in this connection. Could the greater energy requirement have led these early representatives of the human family to alter their diet in the direction of an increased reliance on high-energy foodstuffs, such as the flesh of other animals?

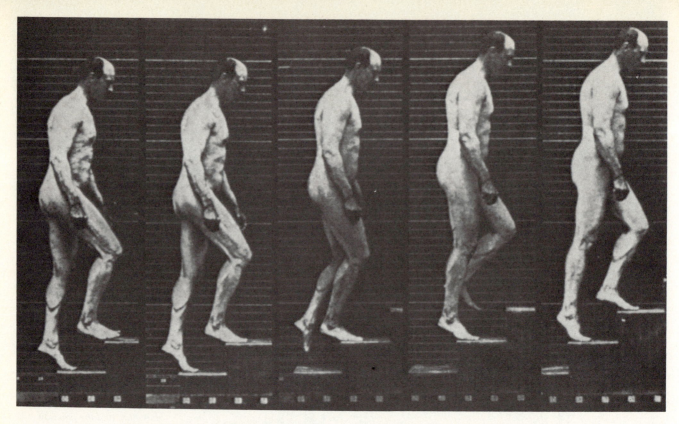

Figure 9. *STAIR-CLIMBING, like running, is a movement that brings the human gluteus maximus into play. Acting as an extensor of the trunk, the muscle counteracts any tendency for the body to jackknife over the legs. Photographs are from Muybridge's collection.*

The pelvis of *Australopithecus* bears evidence that this hominid walker could scarcely have been a strider. Let us now turn to the foot of what many of us believe is a more advanced hominid. In 1960 L. S. B. Leakey and his wife Mary unearthed most of the bones of this foot in the lower strata at Olduvai Gorge known collectively as Bed I, which are about 1.75 million years old. The bones formed part of a fossil assemblage that has been designated by the Leakeys, by Philip

Figure 10. *ECOLOGICAL PATHWAY to man's eventual mastery of all environments begins (left) with a quadrupedal primate ancestor living in tropical forest more than 20 million years ago. During Miocene times mountain-building produced new environments. One, a transition zone between forest and grassland, has been exploited by three groups of primates. Some, for example the chimpanzees, have only recently entered this woodland savanna. Both the newly bipedal hominids and some ground-living quadrupedal monkeys, however, moved beyond the transition zone into open grassland. The quadrupeds, for example the baboons, remained there. On the other hand, the forces of natural selection in the new setting favored the bipedal hominid hunters' adaptation of the striding gait typical of man. Once this adaptation developed, man went on to conquer most of the earth's environments.*

TROPICAL FOREST WOODLAND SAVANNA OPEN GRASSLAND

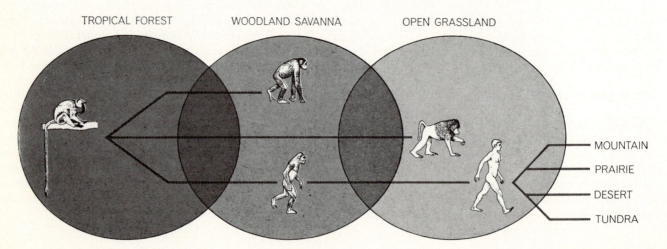

MOUNTAIN

PRAIRIE

DESERT

TUNDRA

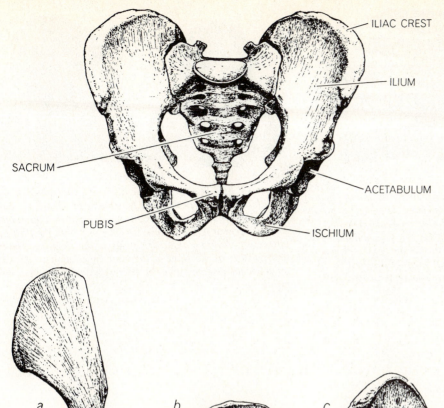

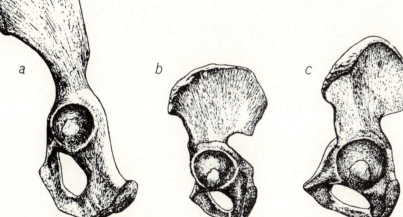

Figure 11. *COMPONENTS OF THE PELVIS are identified at top; the bones are those of the human pelvis. Below, ilium and ischium of a gorilla (a), of* Australopithecus *(b) and of modern man (c) are seen from the side (the front is to the left in each instance). The ischium of* Australopithecus *is longer than man's; this almost certainly kept the early hominid from striding in the manner of* Homo sapiens. *Instead the gait was probably a kind of jog trot.*

Tobias of the University of the Witwatersrand and by me as possibly the earliest-known species of man: *Homo habilis*. The foot was complete except for the back of the heel and the terminal bones of the toes; its surviving components were assembled and studied by me and Michael Day, one of my colleagues at the Unit of Primatology and Human Evolution of the Royal Free Hospital School of Medicine in London. On the basis of functional analysis the resemblance to the foot of modern man is close, although differing in a few minor particulars. Perhaps the most significant point of resemblance is that the stout basal bone of the big toe lies alongside the other toes (Fig. 12). This is an essentially human characteristic; in apes and monkeys the big toe is not exceptionally robust and diverges widely from the other toes. The foot bones, therefore, give evidence that this early hominid species was habitually bipedal. In the absence of the terminal bones of the toes, however, there was no certainty that *Homo habilis* walked with a striding gait.

Then in 1961 in a somewhat higher stratum at Olduvai Gorge (and thus in a slightly younger geological formation), a single bone came to light in an area otherwise barren of human bones. This fossil is the big-toe bone I mentioned at the beginning of this article (Fig. 13). Its head is both tilted and twisted with respect to its shaft, characteristics that are found only in modern man and that can with assurance be correlated with a striding gait. Day has recently completed a dimensional analysis of the bone, using a multivariate statistical technique. He is able to show that the fossil is unquestionably human in form.

There is no evidence to link the big-toe bone specifically to either of the two recognized hominids whose fossil remains have been recovered from Bed I at Olduvai: *Homo habilis* and *Zinjanthropus boisei*. Thus the owner of the toe remains unknown, at least for the present. Nonetheless, one thing is made certain by the discovery. We now know that in East Africa more than a million years ago there existed a creature whose mode of locomotion was essentially human.

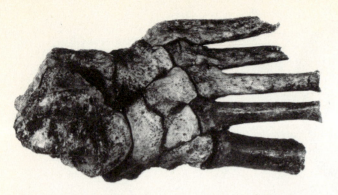

Figure 12. *PRIMITIVE FOOT, complete except for the back of the heel and the tips of the toes, was unearthed from the lower level at Olduvai Gorge in Tanzania. Attributed to a very early hominid,* Homo habilis, *by its discoverer, L. S. B. Leakey, it is about 1.75 million years old. Its appearance suggests that the possessor was a habitual biped. Absence of the terminal bones of the toes, however, leaves open the question of whether the possessor walked with a stride.*

Figure 13. *BIG-TOE BONE, also discovered at Olduvai Gorge, is considerably younger than the foot bones in Figure 12, but still probably more than a million years old. It is the toe's terminal bone (bottom view at left, top view at right) and bore the thrust of its possessor's push-off with each swing of the right leg. The tilting and twisting of the head of the bone in relation to the shaft is unequivocal evidence that its possessor walked with a modern stride.*

7

The Anatomy of Human Speech

J. Laitman

The question of when our ancestors were first able to produce articulate speech has long puzzled scientists. Anthropologists who trace the development of complex behavior in the archeological record, as well as linguists concerned with the definition of language, have offered many reasoned accounts about how prehistoric humans crossed some "vocal threshold," abandoning apelike grunts for the mellifluous tones of an Olivier. During the last century, paleoneurologists, who reconstruct the brains of human ancestors from fossil remains, have added their thoughts about the evolution of speech. These scientists use endocasts—natural casts formed within braincases—and the impressions left on the inside of fossil skulls to estimate the size and location of specific areas of the brain. While offering valuable information, paleoneurology has not been able to tell us much about the inner workings of the brain and, as a result, can offer only limited evidence about when speech may have evolved.

Within the last decade, however, a number of researchers have begun exploring a new approach to solve this old mystery. The technique, which, for lack of an easier term, may be called paleolaryngology, looks to both comparative anatomy and the fossil record in order to reconstruct the components of our ancestors' vocal tract—the larynx, pharynx, tongue, and associated structures. Unlike scientists who have sought to explain language origins, those of us who trace the evolution of the vocal tract have focused our attention on more specific questions: What was the anatomy of our ancestors' vocal tract, what were its functions, and how did it compare with that of present-day humans? Findings from both my own studies and those of other researchers, including anatomist Edmund Crelin of Yale University School of Medicine and linguist Philip Lieberman of Brown University, are providing clues toward answering these questions.

My interest in tracing the origins of speech arose from my investigation of developmental change in the upper respiratory tract of mammals in general and human infants in particular. Eight years ago, I joined with Edmund Crelin, an expert in the anatomy of human newborns, to begin studying the similarities and differences in the upper respiratory tracts of humans and other mammals. In our research, we examined mammals ranging from dolphins to apes, using a variety of techniques, from classic post-mortem dissections to sophisticated cineradiographic (X-ray movie) monitoring.

We found that the position of the larynx, or voice box, in the neck is of paramount importance in determining the way an animal breathes, swallows, and vocalizes. Two general anatomical patterns appear to exist, each with its own functional consequences. The first we might call the "basic" mammalian

Reprinted with permission from *Natural History*, Vol. 92, No. 8, pp. 20-27. Copyright © 1984 by American Museum of Natural History, New York.

Figure 1. *Based on fossil remains of an australopithecine, the earliest known ancestral human, these drawings depict the head, neck, and vocal tract during normal respiration. As in most mammals, air travels in a direct pathway from the nasal cavity to the lungs.*

pattern. In almost all mammals, at all stages of development, the larynx is found high in the neck, lying roughly opposite the first to third cervical vertebrae. This high position enables the larynx to lock into the nasopharynx--the air space near the "back door" of the nasal cavity. In this position, the larynx provides a direct passageway for air between the nose and the lungs. While an animal is breathing, liquid can flow around either side of the interlocked larynx and nasopharynx, through channels known as the piriform sinuses, and then to the

esophagus and stomach. Thanks to these separate pathways for food and air, a cow, cat, or monkey can simultaneously swallow liquids and breathe.

While the basic mammalian pattern allows simultaneous breathing and swallowing, it severely limits the array of sounds an animal can produce. Above the larynx is the pharynx, an air cavity surrounded by membranes and musculature that is part of the food pathway and can also modify sound. In most mammals the high position of the larynx leaves room for only

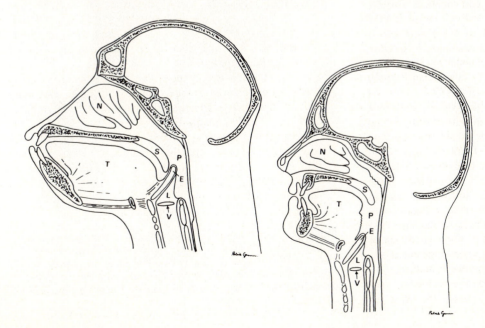

Figure 2. *Cross sections of the head of the adult chimpanzee, left, and adult human, right, show the positions of vocal tract structures during respiration. The human larynx is lower in the neck, increasing the size of the pharynx--the space between the larynx and the back of the nasal cavity.. N = Nasal cavity, S = Soft palate, T = Tongue, P = Pharynx, L = Larynx, E = Epiglottis, V = Vocal fold.*

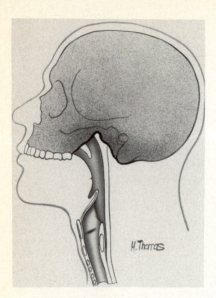
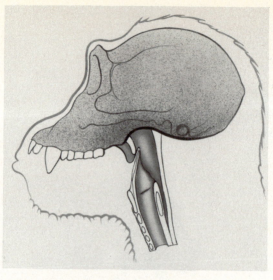

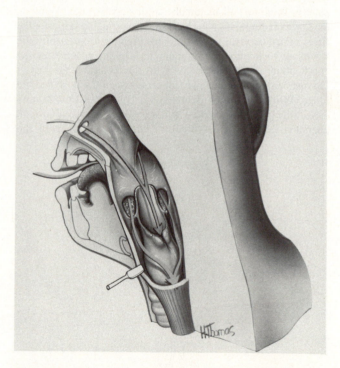

Figure 3. *The base of the chimpanzee skull, left, is relatively nonflexed, or flat, and the larynx is high in the neck. In contrast, the base of the adult human skull, right, is flexed, or arched, and corresponds to a larynx positioned much lower.*

a small pharyngeal cavity, which has a minimal capacity to modify the initial, or fundamental, sounds generated at the vocal folds (vocal cords). As a result, most mammals depend largely on altering the shape of the oral cavity and lips to modify laryngeal sounds. While some animals can approximate some of the sounds of human speech, they are anatomically incapable of producing the range of sounds necessary for complete, articulate speech.

Standing in contrast to the basic mammalian pattern is the human one. Our studies revealed a significant change that occurs during the development of human infants. Until the age of approximately one and one-half to two years, the position of the larynx in human infants is high in the neck, much like that of any other mammal. Our cineradiographic studies showed that newborns breathe, swallow, and vocalize in much the same fashion as monkeys and apes. With respect to the upper respiratory tract, we might say that baby humans have the functional anatomy of monkeys. Sometime around the second year of life, however, the larynx of the human infant begins to descend into the neck, dramatically altering the way the child breathes, swallows, and vocalizes. Exactly how and when this descent occurs are still mysteries. But the end result is that the larynx moves to a position that is different from that known in any other mammal. In an adult human, the position of the larynx corresponds to the fourth to almost the seventh cervical vertebrae, considerably lower than in other species.

In this unique anatomical pattern, the larynx cannot lock into the back of the nasal cavity to separate the breathing and swallowing pathways. After infancy, the human respiratory and digestive tracts cross above the larynx. This crossing can, and often does, have unfortunate drawbacks. One is that a bolus, or chewed mass, of food can easily lodge in the entrance of the larynx, blocking the airway and causing suffocation. In addition, adult humans cannot drink and breathe simultaneously without choking. As compensation, however, the descent of the larynx into the neck has produced an anatomical feature of enormous value: a greatly expanded pharyngeal chamber above the vocal folds. Consequently, sounds emitted from the larynx can be modified to a greater degree than is possible for newborns and any nonhuman mammal. In essence, the expanded

pharynx is the key to our ability to produce fully articulate speech.

During the course of our investigations, my colleagues and I noticed that the shape of the bottom of the skull, or basicranium, is related to the position of the larynx. This is not surprising, since the basicranium serves as the roof of the upper respiratory tract. To define differences in shape objectively, we solicited the help of our longtime co-worker Raymond Heimbuch, formerly of Yale and now manager of statistical programming at Ortho Pharmaceutical. Together

Figure 4. *A view inside the head and neck of a chimpanzee shows how the high position of the larynx enables the animal to breathe and to swallow liquids simultaneously. The upper arrow indicates the flow of air and the lower arrow shows the pathway that liquid can take around the larynx to the esophagus. The two pathways do not cross.*

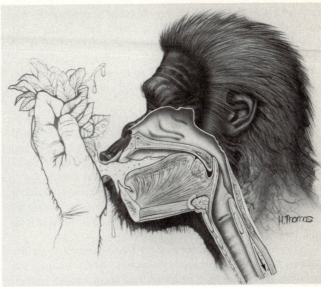

Figure 5. These are reconstructions of an australopithecine drinking water from leaves. As with the chimpanzee (see above), the high position of the larynx would have allowed this early hominid to swallow and breathe simultaneously, an ability lost in modern adult humans.

we performed detailed statistical analyses of the shape of the basicranium for many species of mammals. Using these results, we came to the conclusion that two basic skull/larynx configurations exist. In one, the basicranium is fairly flat and is related to a larynx positioned high in the neck. This is the pattern found consistently in all mammals we studied except for older humans. In the second configuration, the basicranium is markedly arched, or flexed, and the corresponding larynx is low in the neck. This pattern is found only in humans after the age of about two years.

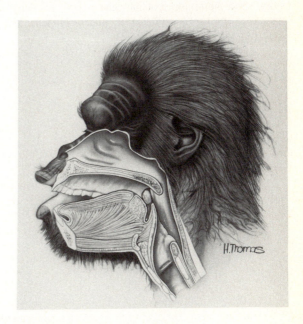

Figure 6. As shown in this reconstruction of an australopithecine vocalizing, the volume of the throat above the larynx was much smaller than in modern adult humans. This limited pharyngeal space could not modify sounds produced at the vocal folds to the extent achieved by Homo sapiens.

The discovery of these two distinct configurations in living mammals has given us the tool we need to reconstruct the approximate level of the larynx and associated structures in fossil species, including early hominids (ancestral humans). If, for example, a skull has an essentially flat, or nonflexed, basicranium—like that of a living chimpanzee or monkey—we can reconstruct the position of the larynx high in the neck. Conversely, fossil crania exhibiting the marked flexion of modern adult humans can be reconstructed with a vocal tract like our own. Once the position of the larynx is determined in this manner, we can infer a fossil hominid's breathing, swallowing, and vocalizing patterns.

Using the statistical methods developed on living mammals, I have evaluated the basicrania of the original fossil hominid remains housed in collections throughout Africa and Europe, and used this information to reconstruct their vocal tracts. This process was not always as easy as it sounds: fossil skulls dated at 2 to 3 million years before the present are seldom in the best condition. Fortunately, a large enough sample of skulls, with intact basicrania remain to give us a valuable look into the past.

Our research in recent months has concentrated on the earliest hominids, the australopithecines, which roamed the savannas of southern and eastern Africa about 4 to 1.5 million years ago. We know from their skeletal anatomy that they were erect bipeds whose brains were only slightly larger than those of modern apes. Our analysis of many specimens has revealed that their basicrania were essentially nonflexed, much like those of chimpanzees. By the methods outlined above, we have reconstructed these hominids with a larynx positioned high in the neck. In sum, we find that the australopithecines probably had vocal tracts much like those of living monkeys or apes. Consequently, they would have also had the ability to swallow liquids and breathe simultaneously. More important to our story, these hominids probably had a very restricted vocal repertoire compared with that of modern humans. The high position of their larynges would have made it impossible for them to produce some of the universal vowel sounds found in human speech patterns. These early hominids undoubtedly had some sort of communication system, probably slightly more advanced than that of the living apes, but they could not speak the way we do today

If the australopithecines had vocal tracts that were essentially apelike, when did the modern human evolve? This is the question we are now trying to answer. While we have not yet come to a definite conclusion, our preliminary data on the skulls of *Homo erectus*, hominids that lived some 1.6 million to 300,000 or 400,000 years ago, are providing some intriguing clues. Members of this group have been found in locations as diverse as Lake Turkana in Kenya, Sangiran in Java, and the Choukoutian caves (home of the famous Peking man) in China. It is among some specimens of this species that we have found the first examples of incipient basicranial flexion away from the nonflexed apelike condition of the australopithecines and toward that shown by modern humans. This indicates to us that the larynx in *Homo erectus* may have begun to descend into the neck, increasing the area available to modify sounds.

The crucial changes in the restructuring of our ancestors' vocal tract may thus have begun more than one and one-half million years ago. The anatomical Rubicon had been crossed: the basic mammalian pattern, retained by our australopithecine ancestors, was now altered as the larynx became lower in the neck. Did these ancestral humans have the ability to speak exactly as we can today? Probably not; although change had begun, their vocal abilities were probably somewhat intermediate between those of the australopithecines and modern humans. Our fossil data suggest that the first examples of full basicranial flexion—comparable to that found among humans today—did not appear until the arrival of *Homo sapiens* some 300,000 to 400,000 years ago. It may have been then that a modern vocal tract appeared and our ancestors began to produce fully articulate speech.

8

Hominid Paleoneurology

D. Falk

INTRODUCTION

Chimpanzees are our closest living cousins. They resemble us anatomically, and molecular evolutionists have determined that humans and chimpanzees may have diverged from a common ancestor as recently as five million years ago (MYR BP) (Sarich 1971). Some workers even entertain the possibility of a viable hybrid because the two taxa share at least 98% of their non-repeated DNA (Lovejoy 1981). I find this notion surprising because, no matter how similar we appear to chimpanzees anatomically, genetically, or socially, we do not think like chimpanzees. Although sign-language experiments with great apes are fascinating, it is doubtful that any ape anywhere will ever sign an utterance on the order of "Hey there, wanna play a friendly game of chess?" Our conscious thought processes differ profoundly from those of other primates. Exploring why this is true is the domain of paleoneurology.

Hominid paleoneurology is the study of brain evolution based on direct examination of the fossil record of humans and their closest hominid relatives. Paleoneurologists analyze endocranial casts (endocasts) that reproduce details of the external morphology of brains that have been imprinted on the internal surfaces of skulls. An endocast may be formed naturally when a skull fills up with sediment that solidifies and fossilizes; or one may prepare an endocast in the laboratory by casting the interior of the braincase with latex (see Falk 1978 for details). For reasons that are not entirely clear (Falk 1980a), earlier small-brained hominids produce more detailed endocasts than do later larger-brained hominids. Because cranial capacities (i.e. braincase volume) approximate brain size, paleoneurologists collect them enthusiastically, although often by primitive means such as filling skulls with mustard seed and then measuring total seed volume in a graduated cylinder. In fact, the study of change in cranial capacity over time is a major theme in hominid paleoneurology.

Paleoneurology must be viewed within the wider context of hominid evolution, a field that has changed dramatically since an earlier review (Falk 1980b). Since then, the theory of punctuated equilibria (Gould and Eldredge 1977) has had an impact on hominid paleontology, as has the question of whether or not *A. afarensis* constitutes one or more species of early hominid (Falk 1986a; Falk and Conroy 1983; Olson 1981; Olson 1985; Zihlman 1985). Furthermore, in the past six years, serious questions have been raised about what if any role brain evolution had in the origin and adaptive radiation of the first

hominids (Lovejoy 1981). The details of brain lateralization in primates have been further explored (Falk 1987). These developments have influenced recent paleoneurological research on (a) specific fossils or species of early hominids, (b) interpretations of changes in brain size over time, and (c) proposed scenarios that account for hominid brain evolution.

ENDOCASTS

Australopithecines

Interpretations of sulcal patterns reproduced on australopithecine endocasts remain controversial. In 1983(a), Holloway described an endocast prepared from *Australopithecus afarensis* AL 162-28, one of the oldest known hominids, dated to over three MYR BP. The volume of this endocast is estimated to be between 350 and 400 cm^3 (Falk 1985b; Holloway 1983a), which represents the smallest adult brain according to Holloway in the hominid fossil record to date. Despite this small brain size, the sulcal pattern indicates that "some degree of cerebral organization had occurred almost 3-4 MYR ago towards a more human pattern."

I analyzed an endocast from the same specimen in 1985 (Falk 1985b) and, contrary to Holloway, concluded that the entire sulcal pattern is ape-like and that there is no evidence for expansion or reorganization in the parietal/occipital region. Our different interpretations hinge on a particular feature that I identify as the lunate sulcus but that Holloway views as a depression caused by lipping at the lambdoid suture. We also disagree about the proper orientation of the specimen (Falk 1986c; Holloway and Kimbel 1986).

The different interpretations of AL 162-28 by Holloway and myself are consistent with our earlier analyses (and differences) over endocasts that represent other australopithecine species. This debate originated in 1979 when Radinsky opened the question of whether the lunate sulcus is in a pongid-like or human-like position on the Taung endocast. In 1980, I showed that sulcal patterns on seven australopithecine natural endocasts appear to be ape-like rather than human-like (Falk 1980a). The Taung (holotype for *Australopithecus africanus*) endocast was a focal point of this article, and Holloway (1981b) questioned my interpretation of that specimen, particularly the identification of a possible medial end of the lunate sulcus. He concluded that "the Taung endocast *does not* show a pongid pattern."

What followed was an exchange of four more papers between 1983 and 1985 (Falk 1983b, 1985a; Holloway 1984, 1985) in which each of us bolstered his/her original interpretation. These papers again focus on the Taung endocast and lunate sulcus, and they provide critical analyses of (a) the use of stereoplotting to transfer sulci between differently shaped endocasts (Falk 1983b), (b) measurement of indexes from photographs rather than directly from specimens (Holloway 1984), and (c) confounding of measurements taken directly from specimens and those taken from photographs (Falk 1985a).

The lunate sulcus is a crescent-shaped sulcus that approximates the anterior boundary of the visual cortex in anthropoids. Because of expansion of the parietal association cortex located in front of the lunate sulcus, this sulcus has been "pushed" towards the occipital pole during human evolution. That is, the lunate sulcus is located farther back in human than in ape (and monkey) brains.

The lunate sulcus usually does not reproduce well on hominoid endocasts, and it is unfortunate that the wider discussion regarding cortical organization of australopithecines has been focused on *one dimple* reproduced on the Taung endocast! I continue to believe that this feature probably represents the medial end of the lunate sulcus (Falk 1985a). However, it should again (Falk 1980a) be noted that no matter what the dimple in question represents on the Taung endocast, all of the numerous other sulci on all of the australopithecine endocasts are consistent with an ape-like sulcal pattern. Holloway does not agree with this interpretation (Holloway 1985) and, since neither of us is changing his/her opinion, it is time that other workers examine the evidence (Falk 1985a).

The Transition to *Homo*

The undue emphasis on the lunate sulcus is all the more surprising because, as early as 1950, Connolly showed that the lateral edge of the frontal lobe is the best area of the cerebral cortex for distinguishing human from ape sulcal patterns. An endocast of KNM-ER 1805 from Kenya, dated to approximately 16 MYR BP, reproduces ape-like fronto-orbital sulci at the lateral borders of the frontal lobes (Falk 1983a), an observation that is disputed by Holloway (1983b). Because of its pongid-like sulcal pattern, I attribute this enigmatic specimen to the genus *Australopithecus*.

Another specimen from Kenya, KNM-ER 1470, is approximately 2 MYR old and one of the earliest known *Homo habilis* specimens. The endocast from this specimen reproduces a sulcal pattern in the left frontal lobe that is associated with Broca's speech area in living people, a finding that has led to the conclusion that *H. habilis* may have been capable of speech (Falk 1983a; Tobias 1981). This conclusion is in keeping with Holloway's (1983b) observation of a pronounced left-occipital-right-frontal petalia pattern in the endocast of ER 1470 that may indicate functional cortical asymmetry. Surprising corroborative evidence has also been provided recently by Toth's (1985) analyses of stone flakes, which indicate that hominids were predominantly right-handed by 2 MYR BP. (The speech organs and the right hand are controlled by adjacent areas in the left frontal lobe.)

An early emergence of cortical lateralization in hominids is also supported by Holloway's studies of cortical asymmetries

in *Homo erectus* and Neandertal endocasts (Holloway 1981d, 1981e). LeMay (Galaburda *et al.* 1978; LeMay 1976, 1977) has shown that right-handedness in humans is correlated with right frontal and left occipital lobes that are wider and project further than do their counterparts (i.e. right frontal and left occipital "petalias"). According to Holloway (1981d, p. 520), "While asymmetries in pongids are not unusual, particularly in the anterior-posterior dimension, the combination of left-occipital, right-frontal, in *both* A-P *and* lateral dimensions is particularly (and significantly so) strong in both fossil hominids and modern *Homo sapiens....*"

Specifically, Holloway has shown that the petalia patterns associated with right-handedness appear in endocasts representing *H. erectus* (Holloway 1981d) and Neandertals (Holloway 1981e), and "that this pattern does extend back to the Australopithecines." An analysis of hominid petalia patterns by sex would be interesting since it has been reported that extant males show greater degrees of frontal and occipital petalias than do females, and that reversals of these asymmetries are more common in females (Bear *et al.* 1986).

Venous Sinuses

During the past six years, the field of paleoneurology has make a surprising contribution to the ongoing discussions concerning early hominid systematics. As early as 1967, Tobias documented an unusual enlarged occipital/marginal (O/M) venous sinus system for draining blood from the cranium that distinguishes skulls of robust australopithecines from those of other hominids. This sinus system is reproduced on the posterior underneath portion of endocasts. I believe that Holloway was the first to observe that two of the Hadar *A. afarensis* specimens also have clear impressions of the O/M sinus, and that "although named *A. afarensis*, the morphology to this author's mind is more reminiscent of a smaller robust Australopithecine" (Holloway 1981c).

Unlike any other group of hominids, 100% of scorable *A. afarensis* specimens (n=5) and 100% of scorable robust australopithecines (n=7) exhibit this unusual sinus system (Falk 1986a; Falk and Conroy 1983). A systematic implication of this finding is that robust australopithecines are descendants of *A. afarensis*, as Olson (1981) first suggested, rather than of *A. africanus* (Johanson and White 1979; Kimbel 1984). Furthermore, two separate studies of early hominid postcrania (Senut and Tardieu 1985; Zihlman 1985) and one of footprints (Tuttle 1985) suggest that so-called *A. afarensis* may have included more than one species. In other words, it now seems possible that robust and gracile australopithecines coexisted during the earliest part of the current hominid fossil record. The recent discovery of WT 17000 (Walker *et al.* 1986), a robust australopithecine from Kenya dated to 2.5 Myr BP, lends exciting support to the systematic conclusions deduced, at least in part, from endocasts.

Methodological Notes

One of the most serious problems for paleoneurologists is to obtain reliable information other than cranial capacity from endocasts (Falk 1982, 1986d; Galaburda and Pandya 1982; Holloway 1981a). Holloway (1981a) uses a stereoplotter and discriminant analysis to quantify taxa-specific shape differences from the dorsal surface of hominoid endocasts. Radial distances are measured from a central point within the endocast to specific points on its surface, and these data are recorded in a polar coordinate system. Using stereoplotting, Holloway has shown that endocasts from various hominoids differ most in the lower parietal lobule, anterior occipital zone, and dorsoanterior region of the frontal lobe. The goal of quantifying brain or endocast shape differences between hominoid taxa with a highly accurate stereoplotter is exciting. However, stereoplotting should not be used to "transfer" a feature on one endocast to another, differently shaped endocast, for reasons that are delineated elsewhere (Falk 1983b).

Three recent papers have dealt with the issue of how best to estimate cranial capacity from *Homo habilis*-type specimen OH 7, which consists of two partial parietal bones (Holloway 1983c; Vaisnys *et al.* 1984; Wolpoff 1981). These discussions concern problems in the reconstruction of the bones themselves as well as reconstruction of cranial capacity from fragmentary skull specimens. Regression techniques are analyzed for estimating cranial capacity from external bony measurements as well as from partial endocasts. Wolpoff (1981) estimates the capacity of this specimen to be approximately 600 cm^3 using multiple regression techniques on external parietal dimensions.

Holloway (1983c) questioned Wolpoff's reconstruction of the hominid parietals and estimated approximately 700 cm^3 for the cranial capacity of OH 7. A more formal analysis between chords measured from exteriors of skulls and cranial capacities resulted in an estimate of 690 cm^3, but with a wide uncertainty range (538-868 cm^3). As Vaisnys *et al.* (1984) point out, Wolpoff's and Holloway's estimates differ "by amounts less than the uncertainty associated with the estimates."

The most recent methodological step in paleoneurology is the use of advanced computer graphics technology, developed by M. Vannier and G. Conroy of Washington University School of Medicine, to image and analyze the surface morphology of endocasts in three dimensions (Falk *et al.* 1986; Vannier *et al.* 1985). Surface coordinates are measured using an electromagnetic digitizer that allows an operator to identify significant landmarks interactively and encode them in a machine-readable form. The x, y, and z coordinates are entered into a Unigraphics Computer Aided Design (CAD) system that provides many critical facilities for analyzing the data. For example, information such as sulcal length, cortical asymmetries, and volume enclosed within a three-dimensional surface are easily obtained. A collaborative effort is under way (Falk *et al.* 1986) to use these techniques to investigate hundreds of endocasts from rhesus monkey skulls.

BRAIN SIZE

The interior of the skull contains the brain and the fluids and meninges that cover it. Consequently, the endocranial volume, or cranial capacity, is slightly larger than brain size, so that cranial capacity (cm^3) = 1.05 x brain size (Hofman 1983). In light of the close correspondence between endocranial volume and brain size, it is not surprising that the field of paleoneurology is dominated by investigations of cranial capacity. What is surprising is how little agreement there is about the evolution of such an apparently straightforward parameter.

Paleoneurologists agree that brain size relative to body size ("relative cranial capacity") is perhaps more meaningful than brain size alone. However, since it is difficult to identify the species associated with postcranial bones such as femora that are often used to estimate body weight, determining relative cranial capacities for fossil hominids remains problematical. Taxonomic assignment is also uncertain for certain "intermediary" skulls. For example, are ER 1805 and ER 1813 representatives of the genus *Australopithecus* or the genus *Homo*? Such questions are not trivial for paleoneurological studies because their answers will have significant impact on the determination of rates of brain enlargement that characterize various lineages.

Another problem concerns current controversies in early hominid evolution and systematics. Was there really stasis in brain size before 2 MYR BP, and was the earliest part of the record therefore characterized by "mosaic evolution" in which bipedalism preceded brain enlargement (Lovejoy 1981)? How many species of early hominids were there at any given time, and what implications does the answer to this question have for our views of brain evolution?

Rethinking Early Hominid Brain Size

Three new developments make it imperative that cranial capacity be reanalyzed for the genus *Australopithecus*: (a) A newly discovered robust australopithecine skull, WT 17000, has been described as having a 410-cm^3 cranial capacity and a very early date of 2.55 MYR BP (Walker *et al.* 1986). (b) Other new evidence suggests that so-called *A. afarensis* contains both gracile and robust australopithecines (Falk 1986a; Falk and Conroy 1983; Olson 1981, 1985; Senut and Tardieu 1985; Tuttle 1985; Zihlman 1985), as is the case for that genus subsequent to 2.55 MYR BP. (c) Recent microscopic examinations of tooth enamel (Bromage 1985; Bromage and Dean 1985) and dental development (Smith 1986) in fossil hominids suggest that estimates of adult cranial capacities must be revised for juvenile australopithecines. These lines of evidence are taken into account in the model presented below.

Table 1 provides estimates of cranial capacities and dates for certain fossil hominids. With the exception of the first three (Hadar) specimens, most of the capacities for the African hominids were estimated from fairly complete specimens. Fragmentary specimens such as STS 19/58 were excluded. In a few cases where more than one worker has estimated capacity, such as for OH 7, estimates determined from fragmentary specimens were averaged and included.

I have provided new adult estimates for two juvenile specimens, AL 333-105 and Taung, in this study. The age at death of Taung has recently been revised from an estimate of six years to 2.7-3.7 years, on the basis of incremental lines in tooth enamel (Bromage 1985). Using this younger dental age, an estimate of 404 cm^3 for the juvenile (Holloway 1983a), and Passingham's curve for brain development in chimpanzees (Passingham 1975), I estimate an adult capacity for Taung ranging from 404-420 cm^3, with a mean of 412 cm^3. Application of Passingham's curve for brain development in *Pan* is preferable to that for humans because (a) brain size of early hominids approximates that of chimpanzees, and (b) the curves for brain volume relative to body weight are essentially parallel in pongids and australopithecines, leading Hofman to conclude (Hofman 1983, p. 107) that "as with pongids, the australopithecines probably differed only in size, but not in

Table 1. Cranial capacities of hominids.

Specimen	Type[a]	cm³	Capacity Reference	Date (MYR)	Date Reference
African					
AL 333-45	r	493	50	2.90–3.20	7
AL 162-28	?	375	23, 50	2.90–3.20	7
AL 333-105	r	343	50, t.s.[b]	2.90–3.20	7
		X = 404			
MLD 37/38	g	435	50	-2.80	81
STS 60	g	428	50	2.40-2.80	89
STS 5	g	485	50	2.40-2.80	89
		X = 449			
WT 17000	r	410	90	2.55	90
ER 1470	Hh	752	50	2.00	14
OH 7	Hh	675	50, 83, 86, t.s.[b]	1.90	14
OH 13	H	655	50, 83, t.s.[b]	1.90	
		X = 665			
OH 5	r	530	80	1.80	14
ER 1813	g	510	50	1.80	14
ER 407	r	508	31, 50	1.64-1.88	11, 59
ER 732	r	500	50	1.64-1.88	11, 59
ER 406	r	510	50	1.64-1.88	60
		X = 506			
ER 3733	He	848	50	1.64-1.88	60
SK 1585	r	530	50	1.60-1.80	89
ER 1805	g	582	50	1.64	11, 59
Taung	g	412	9, 50, t.s.[b]	1.00-2.00	63
OH 9	He	1067	50	1.30	14
Non-African					
He javanicus	4	958 (815-1059)	50	1.60-.60	41
He pekinensis	5	1043 (915-1225)	93	0.70-.50	41
He soloensis	5	1151 (1013-1250)	50	0.80-.46	41
		1097			
H euro pre-Wurm		1314 (1170-1460)	41	0.30-.10	41
H neand euro		1487 (1300-1641)	41	0.07-.04	41
Hs euro Wurm		1460 (1293-1748)	41	0.04	41
Hs recens		1465 (1156-1775)	41	0	

[a] g, gracile australopithecine; r, robust australopithecine; H, *Homo*; h, *habilis*; e, *erectus*; s, *sapiens*

[b] This study.

design. Increases in body size within this taxon as well as in brain size took place without significant changes in degree of encephalization." If Taung was as old as 3.7 years, Passingham's curve suggests that its adult cranial capacity had already been achieved!

An exciting new study of dental development by Smith (Smith 1986) confirms that dental ages for *A. africanus* and *A.*

afarensis are best estimated by using pongid rather than human standards. Although Smith (personal communication) has not had the opportunity to study the dentition of AL 333-105, this specimen is reported to have an unerupted, upper, permanent first molar crown (Kimbel *et al.* 1982). Therefore, on the basis of Smith's dental development chart for pongids, this specimen would be approximately 2.5 years old. I estimate an adult

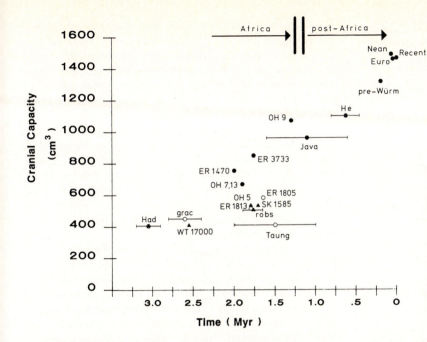

Figure 1. *Mean cranial capacity plotted against time for entries from Table 1.* ▲, *robust australopithecines;* ○, *gracile australopithecines;* ●, Homo. *Had, Hadar specimens (first three entries in table 1); grac, gracile australopithecines MLD 37/38, STS 60, STS5; robs, robust australopithecines ER 407, 732, 406; other abbreviations, see Table 1. Horizontal bars indicate time ranges.*

cranial capacity of 343 cm³ for AL 333-105 using an age of 2.5 years and Passingham's (1975) chimpanzee brain development curve.

Researchers frequently present double logarithmic graphs of cranial capacity versus time (Hofman *et al.* 1986). These can be misleading and inappropriate (Godfrey and Jacobs 1981), so for the purposes of this paper, untransformed data from Table 1 are graphed in Figure 1. A number of conclusions may be drawn from Figure 1: (a) The plots for robust and gracile australopithecines overlap and show only slight increase in cranial capacity over time as compared to the plots for *Homo.* (b) Rather than being surprisingly small (Walker *et al.* 1986), the "new" WT 17000 falls among the plots for other australopithecines. The South African robust specimen, SK 1585, clumps with the East African robust australopithecines, OH 5, ER 406, ER 407, and ER 732. (c) Controversial specimens ER 1805 and ER 1813 from Kenya cluster with *Australopithecus* and not with *Homo,* a fact that provides evidence in addition to the morphology of the cerebral cortex (Falk 1983a) for including them in the former rather than the latter genus. Furthermore, removing these specimens from the graph would not alter point (a). Nevertheless, these East African specimens share some characteristics with *Homo* (Cronin *et al.* 1981), which is perhaps best explained by a common gracile australopithecine ancestor.

Interesting conclusions may also be drawn regarding the genus *Homo.* (a) The plots for the genus *Homo* in Africa are well above, and their course shows a steeper increase than, those for australopithecines. Although the earliest plots for *Homo* outside of Africa apparently fall below those for Africa, the course of the non-African plots also increases dramatically, at least until fairly recent times. (b) There are no capacities for the genus *Homo* prior to ER 1470, and *we do not know from whence that specimen originated.* However, since ER 1470 shares a number of features with gracile australopithecines, it is a good bet that it descended from a gracile australopithecine species as Cronin *et al.* suggest (1981). In sum, I agree with Godfrey and Jacobs that (1981, p. 255) "it is clear that hominid

brain size has increased dramatically in the past several million years and that little of this increase can be explained as an allometric effect of the concomitant (but far less dramatic) increase in body weight. . . ."

Rates of Increase: Gradual or Punctuated?

Gould and Eldredge's (1977) theory of punctuated equilibria has had a significant impact on paleoneurology. Since 1981 at least five papers (Blumenberg 1983; Cronin *et al.* 1981; Godfrey and Jacobs 1981; Grusser and Weiss 1985; Hofman 1983) have addressed the question of whether the evolution of brain size was cumulative and gradual ("phyletic gradualism") or whether it was characterized by long periods of stasis punctuated by rapid increases in brain size ("punctuated equilibria"). Although these papers analyze much the same data base for brain size and time, one author believes that hominid brain evolution is an example of punctuated evolutionary change (Hofman 1983); others refute this conclusion (Cronin *et al.* 1981; Grusser and Weiss 1985); and still another holds that either model could be true (Blumenberg 1983). To add to the confusion, Godfrey and Jacobs (1981) claim the data are compatible with either a punctuational or an autocatalytic model, the later suggested by a curvilinear pattern "that is *not* inconsistent with a strict gradualist interpretation. . . ."

In order to explore the evolutionary rates at which hominid brains enlarged during the past 3 MYR, the data in Table 1 were used to calculate units of evolutionary rate, described and termed darwins by Haldane (1949), that measure an increase (or decrease) in size by a factor of *e* per million years. According to Haldane:

$$1 \text{ darwin} = \frac{\log_e x_2 - \log_e x_1}{t},$$

where t = time, X_2 = the value of the characteristic at t_2, X_1 = the value at t_1. Table 2 provides the absolute and percentage changes in cranial capacity between different groups of

Table 2. Changes in cranial capacity during hominid evolution.

Hominids	cm^3	Percentage	Millidarwins[b]
A. afarensis—A. africanus[a]	45	11	235
A. Africanus[a]—ER 1805, ER 1813	97	22	222
A. afarensis—WT 17000	6	1	30
WT 17000—robust australopiths	106	26	291
A. africanus[a]—H. habilis	245	55	670
H. habilis—H. erectus, Af.	264	38	768
H. erectus, Af.—H. e. Java	0	0	0
H. e. Java—H. e., Solo and Pek.	139	15	288
H. e., Solo and Pek.—pre-Würm	217	20	420
pre-Würm—Neandertal	173	13	853
Neandertal—Recent	−22	−1	−271

[a] Because of problems with dating, Taung is excluded from this analysis.

[b] The rate of evolutionary change is expressed as millidarwins per million years. See the text for the formula.

hominids, as well as the evolutionary rates in millidarwins for the changes in mean cranial capacity.

Figure 2 presents graphs of the data from Table 2. The rates plotted for both South African australopithecines and WT 17000 were determined with *A. afarensis* (the first three entries in Table 1) as a starting point, since I believe this "species" contains both gracile and robust australopithecines (Falk 1986b), and since the plots for both groups overlap in Figure 1. The earliest robust australopithecine from Kenya, WT 17000, weighs in with a rate of 30 millidarwins, which is a perfectly respectable rate of increase for a mammalian feature. Haldane found the median rate of increase for certain horse tooth measurements to be 40 millidarwins (Haldane 1949), for example. Interestingly, the rate of change in cranial capacity appears to increase in robust australopithecines but not in the gracile lineage, although again the two plots overlap.

As noted above, it is not known where ER 1470 originated, and it may well have evolved from gracile australopithecine

stock at a much earlier date. Therefore, although the rate plotted for *Homo habilis* was determined by using South African australopithecines, the line connecting the two is dashed to indicate uncertainty. If *H. habilis* did stem from a population similar to the South African australopithecines, then the rates of increase in brain size are extremely high (Haldane 1949) for African specimens representing the genus *Homo*.

The only stasis apparent in Figure 2 is represented by the drop to zero millidarwins between *H. erectus* in Africa and *H. erectus* in Java. Because brain size averages 958 cm² in both groups, the rate of increase is zero. It should be noted however, that sample sizes for all of these fossil hominids are tiny and that this apparent example of stasis could change with changed dates for some of the *H. erectus* specimens or with the addition of just a few specimens.

The situation for the non-African specimens is clearer. Sample sizes are larger and Figure 2 shows a dramatic increase in the rates of brain enlargement up through Neandertals (see Grusser and Weiss 1985; Henneberg 1986 for discussions of recent and future trends). Thus, brain evolution both in and out of Africa appears to have been *autocatalytic*, whereby "the tempo of rising encephalization accelerated as cranial capacity itself increased" (Godfrey and Jacobs 1981).

So what does it all mean? Contrary to Hofman (1983) and Godfrey and Jacobs (1981), and in keeping with Grusser and Weiss (1985) and Cronin *et al.* (1981), I believe these data fail to support a model of long periods of stasis characterized by very slow change in cranial capacity for the genus *Homo*. Most of the time, cranial capacity increased, and at an accelerated pace. The apparent stasis between African and non-African hominids is interesting. As mentioned above, it could be an artifact; or it could imply that while brain evolution accelerated in other parts of the world, it lagged behind (below) the curve for Africa. Only additional *H. erectus* fossils from both Africa and Asia will permit us to assess the situation more fully. Nevertheless, the only part of the record where *prolonged* stasis could have occurred for *Homo* is prior to *H. habilis*. What is needed (paradoxically?) to demonstrate stasis at that time is discovery of an early ancestor of *H. habilis* with a brain as large as that of its descendant.

In sum, brain enlargement in *Homo* appears to be autocatalytic—i.e. the present data support a souped-up version of the gradualists' model. Despite the break between Africa and Asia illustrated in Figure 2, the best refuge for punctuated

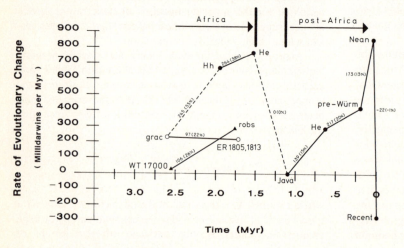

Figure 2. *Rate of evolutionary change in cranial capacity (millidarwins) plotted against time. Data from Table 2; abbreviations as in Figure 1; see text for formula and discussion. Each line is labeled with the absolute change in cranial capacity (cm³) as well as the frequency it represents. Dashed lines indicate uncertainty about ancestral relationships. The only stasis represented occurs between* H. erectus *in Africa and Java. The rates for* Homo *are extremely high and suggest that brain evolution in this genus was autocatalytic.*

equilibriumists is in the early, presently unknown, part of the fossil record. There they must look for the required prolonged stasis in brain size, as well as for the dramatic "burst" that led, hypothetically, to our genus.

Mechanisms Underlying the Increase in Brain Size

What accounts for the dramatic increase in brain size that occurred during human evolution? Several workers have attempted to identify areas of the brain that may have been favored by natural selection, but their findings remain controversial. Hofman (1983) claims that marked expansion of the cerebral cortex, a neurologic component associated with higher brain functions, characterized hominid brain evolution. Passingham (1985), on the other hand, points out that the percentage of neocortex in human brains is only slightly higher than that in chimpanzee brains, and that the rate of growth of human neocortex would be expected for a nonhuman primate with as large a brain. He adds that "in this as in other respects . . . our brain declares us to be a member of the order of the Primates." Other papers focus on specific thalamic nuclei as well as the limbic system in general (Armstrong 1980a, b, 1981, 1982, 1986; MacLean 1985; Passingham 1987; Vilensky *et al.* 1981). Although a discussion of comparative neurology is beyond the scope of this review, these papers open the question of the relative importance of subcortical structures for hominid brain evolution.

An important paper in theoretical neurobiology by Lumsden (1983) proposes a mechanistic model that links the evolution of brain size with developing intellectual capacity. This theory is based on the premise that humans are born with innate biases such as a preference for sweet and an aversion to bitter tastes, or the ability to discriminate phonemes. The neurological basis for these "epigenetic rules" are "neuronal groups," each of which responds as a unit to a specific signal from the environment. Novelties in the environment that confer selective advantages (e.g. language) result in selection for additional neuronal groups capable of processing these new stimuli. Since neuronal groups consist of space-filling assemblages of neuronal circuits, "selectional hominid brains" enlarged over time.

Passingham (1985) has shown that the human brain achieves its size by lengthening the time of growth rather than by growing at an unusual rate. In keeping with this, Hofman (1984), claims that brain size coevolved with longevity in hominids. He speculates that longevity was a prerequisite for the prolonged brain growth, learning and delayed sexual development that characterizes humans. It is not difficult to imagine a causal relationship between increased life span and reproductive fitness. If longer lives correlate with bigger brains, could part of the increase in brain size during hominid evolution be explained as a mechanistic side effect of direct selection for longevity? Whatever the answer to this question, shifts in lengths of developmental phases during ontogeny may have been a key factor in hominid brain evolution.

CONCLUSION

Why Did Hominid Brains Evolve?

In 1980, I reviewed "prime movers" that had been postulated (independently) as the main impetus for hominid brain evolu-

tion. I concluded that prime mover scenarios were interesting but extremely speculative (Falk 1980b). Although current scenarios are still speculative, I believe that the field of theoretical neurobiology is coalescing towards a better understanding of the factors responsible for hominid brain evolution. Extant hominid brains are lateralized, big, and capable of language. Furthermore, it appears that hominids were fully bipedal, right-handed (Toth 1985), and language bearing (Falk 1983a; Tobias 1981) by 2 MYR BP. Below, I try to account for these facts by piecing together the best findings in the current paleoneurological literature.

Lateralization in *Homo sapiens* may be viewed as a manifestation of a general rule that emerges from observations of animals as diverse as rats and birds (Flor-Henry 1980). In rodents, direction of circling behavior is associated with fighting and sexual display (Glick *et al.* 1977). Left lateralized control of male bird song is associated with territoriality and mate attraction (Nottebohm 1977). Therefore neural asymmetry may increase the efficiency of spatial analysis involved in mate attraction and territoriality (Flor-Henry 1980; Webster 1977). Thus, the evolutionary history of basic neurological asymmetry appears to be ancient, and ongoing research suggests that nonhuman primates, although they lack language, are characterized by lateralized brains (see Falk 1987 for review; Falk 1980c; Holloway and De La Coste-Lareymondie 1982). If so, hominid brains would already have been fundamentally asymmetrical at the time of their origin, and the extreme lateralization associated with language and handedness in extant humans would represent elaborations based on this substrate.

The importance of left-hemisphere "sequencers" in hominid evolution has emerged as a dominant theme in paleoneurology (Bradshaw and Nettleton 1982; Calvin 1982; Passingham 1981). The left hemisphere is responsible for sequencing time-dependent, serial, segmental processes. Broca's area regulates the sequence of sounds produced in speech, whereas an area of premotor cortex above Broca's area is responsible for sequencing movements of the right hand (Passingham 1981). In conjunction with the recognition of the importance of sequencers, another question has arisen that concerns the order in which tool use, right-handedness, and speech arose in hominid evolution.

Bradshaw and Nettleton (1982) believe that tool use preceded right-handedness which preceded fine motor coordination of speech articulators. Calvin (1982) believes that throwing was the prime mover of early hominid brain evolution and that handedness and language may have had a common origin in the neurological sequencing circuits that resulted from selection for throwing.

For a number of reasons, I continue to believe that language is the best candidate for a prime mover of hominid brain evolution (Falk 1980b). Passingham (1981) cogently argues that central organs such as vocal cords are bilaterally innervated, and that it is therefore most efficient for a single hemisphere to dominate for functions where complex sequences of movement must be programmed, such as speech (see also Ojemann 1983). Throwing (Calvin 1982), tap dancing (D. Falk, *Braindance*, in preparation), and speech (Ojemann 1983) all depend on left-hemisphere sequencers, but it is much easier to imagine that language processes produced a catalytic effect on brain evolution than that either throwing or tap dancing did. The first leads to conscious thought, whereas the others result merely in downed rabbits or simple joy. (This observation is not meant to detract from Calvin's throwing theory [Calvin 1982], which is both interesting and provocative.)

It is frequently stated that bipedality appeared long before the advanced hominid brain (Blumenberg 1983; Lovejoy 1981). While it is true that brain enlargement appears less remarkable in australopithecines than in *Homo* (Fig. 1), the earliest specimens do have the smallest cranial capacities in the hominid record to date. Without a fossil record of the presumed first bipeds (5 MYR BP?) we have no basis for understanding the relationship between the earliest morphological modifications for habitual bipedalism (Richards 1986) and cranial capacity, let alone brain evolution. More to the point, the earliest record of an "advanced" hominid brain is from ER 1470 (*H. habilis*) at 2 MYR BP. Since we do not know whence ER 1470 came, only one assertion can be made about the relationship between bipedalism and brain evolution: It is highly un-

likely that a dramatic shift in locomotor pattern occurred without corresponding evolutionary changes in the nervous system, as Washburn suggested some time ago (Washburn 1960, 1968). (Washburn has recently clarified his earlier views [see Washburn 1982].) Whether or not these earliest changes were reflected in brain size, or were graduated or punctuated, remains to be seen.

ACKNOWLEDGEMENTS

I thank Jack Harris for helpful discussion regarding the most probable dates of hominids from Kenya and Holly Smith for her thoughts on the dentition of AL 333-105. Criss Helmkamp prepared Figures 1 and 2. This research was supported by Public Health Service grant number 1 RO1 NS24904-01 and National Science Foundation grant BNS-8796195.

REFERENCES

Armstrong, E. 1980a. A quantitative comparison of the hominoid thalamus. II. Limbic nuclei anterior principalis and lateralis dorsalis. *Am. J. Phys. Anthropol.* 52:43-54.

Armstrong, E. 1980b. A quantitative comparison of the hominoid thalamus. III. A motor substrate—the ventrolateral complex. *Am. J. Phys. Anthropol.* 52:405-419.

Armstrong, E. 1981. A quantitative comparison of the hominoid thalamus. IV. Posterior association nuclei—the pulvinar and lateral posterior nucleus. *Am. J. Phys. Anthropol.* 55:369-383.

Armstrong, E. 1982. Mosaic evolution in the primate brain: Differences and similarities in the hominoid thalamus, in: *Primate Brain Evolution: Methods and Concepts* (E. Armstrong and D. Falk, Eds.), pp. 131-161, Plenum, New York.

Armstrong, E. 1986. Enlarged limbic structures in the human brain: The anterior thalamus and medial mamillary body. *Brain Res.* 362:394-397.

Bear, D., Schiff, D., Saver, J., Greenberg, M., and Freeman, R. 1986. Quantitative analysis of cerebral asymmetries. *Arch. Neurol.* 43:598-603.

Blumenberg, B. 1983. The evolution of the advanced hominid brain. *Curr. Anthropol.* 24:589-623.

Boaz, N. T., Howell, F. C., and McCrossin, M. L. 1982. Faunal age of the Usno, Shungura B and Hadar Formations, Ethiopia. *Nature* 300:633-635.

Bradshaw, J. L., and Nettleton, N. C. 1982. Language lateralization to the dominant hemisphere: Tool use, gesture and language in hominid evolution. *Curr. Psychol. Rev.* 2:171-192.

Bromage, T. G. 1985. Taung facial remodeling: A growth and development study, in: *Hominid Evolution: Past, Present, and Future* (P. V. Tobias, Ed.), pp. 239-245, Liss, New York.

Bromage, T. G., and Dean, M. C. 1985. Re-evaluation of the age at death of immature fossil hominids. *Nature* 317:525-527.

Brown, F. H., McDougall, I., Davies, T., and Maier, R. 1985. An integrated Plio-Pleistocene chronology for the Turkana Basin, in: *Ancestors. The Hard Evidence* (E. Delson, Ed.), pp. 82-90, Liss, New York.

Calvin, W. H. 1982. Did throwing stones shape hominid brain evolution? *Ethiol. Sociobiol.* 3:115-124.

Connolly, C. J. 1950. *External Morphology of the Primate Brain*. Thomas, Springfield, Ill.

Cronin, J. E., Boaz, N. T., Stringer, C. B., and Rak, Y. 1981. Tempo and mode in hominid evolution. *Nature* 292:113-122.

Falk, D. 1978. External neuroanatomy of Old World monkeys. *Contrib. Primatol.* 15:1-95.

Falk, D. 1980a. A reanalysis of the South African australopithecine natural endocasts. *Am. J. Phys. Anthropol.* 53:525-539.

Falk, D. 1980b. Hominid brain evolution: The approach from paleoneurology. *Yearb. Phys. Anthropol.* 23:93-107.

Falk, D. 1980c. Language, handedness, and primate brains: Did the australopithecines sign? *Am. Anthropol.* 82:72-78.

Falk, D. 1982. Mapping fossil endocasts, in: *Primate Brain Evolution: Methods and Concepts* (E. Armstrong and D. Falk, Eds.), pp. 217-226, Plenum, New York.

Falk, D. 1983a. Cerebral cortices of East African early hominids. *Science* 221:1072-1074.

Falk, D. 1983b. The Taung endocast: A reply to Holloway. *Am. J. Phys. Anthropol.* 60:479-489.

Falk, D. 1985a. Apples, oranges, and the lunate sulcus. *Am. J. Phys. Anthropol.* 67:313-315.

Falk, D. 1985b. Hadar AL 162-28 endocast as evidence that brain enlargement preceded cortical reorganization in hominid evolution. *Nature* 313:45-47.

Falk, D. 1986a. Evolution of cranial blood drainage in hominids: Enlarged occipital/marginal sinuses and emissary foramina. *Am. J. Phys. Anthropol.* 70:311-324.

Falk, D. 1986b. Hominid evolution. *Science* 234:11.

Falk, D. 1986c. Reply to Holloway and Kimbel: Endocast morphology of Hadar hominid AL 162-28. *Nature* 321:536-537.

Falk, D. 1986d. Endocranial casts and their significance for primate brain evolution, in: *Comparative Primate Biology*, Vol. 1: *Systematics, Evolution and Anatomy* (D. R. Swindler, Ed.), pp. 477-490, Liss, New York.

Falk, D. 1987. Brain lateralization in primates and its evolution in hominids. *Yearb. Phys. Anthropol.* 30:107-125.

Falk, D., Cheverud, J., Vannier, M. W., and Conroy, G. C. 1986. Advanced computer graphics technology reveals cortical asymmetry in endocasts of rhesus monkeys. *Fol. Primatol.* 46:98-103.

Falk, D., and Conroy, G. 1983. The cranial venous sinus system in *Australopithecus afarensis*. *Nature* 306:779-781.

Falk, D., and Kasinga, S. 1983. Cranial capacity of a female robust australopithecine (KNM-ER 407) from Kenya. *Am. J. Phys. Anthropol.* 12:515-518.

Flor-Henry, P. 1980. Evolutionary and clinical aspects of lateralized sex differences. *Behav. Brain Sci.* 3:235-236.

Galaburda, A .M., LeMay, M., Kemper, T. L., and Geschwind, N. 1978. Right-left asymmetries in the brain. *Science* 199:852-856.

Galaburda, A. M., and Pandya, D. N. 1982. Role of architectonics and connections, in: *Primate Brain Evolution: Methods and Concepts* (E. Armstrong and D. Falk, Eds.), pp. 203-216, Plenum, New York.

Glick, S. D., Zimmerberg, B., and Jerussi, T. P. 1977. Adaptive significance of laterality in the rodent. *Ann. NY Acad. Sci.* 299:180-185.

Godfrey, L., and Jacobs, K. H. 1981. Gradual, autocatalytic and punctuational models of hominid brain evolution: A cautionary tale. *J. Hum. Evol.* 10:255-272.

Gould, S. J., and Eldredge, N. 1977. Punctuated equilibria: Tempo and mode of evolution reconsidered. *Paleobiology* 3:115-151.

Grusser, O. J., and Weiss, L. R. 1985. Quantitative models on phylogenetic growth of the hominid brain, in: *Hominid Evolution: Past, Present and Future* (P. V. Tobias, Ed.), pp. 457-464, Liss, New York.

Haldane, J. B. S. 1949. Suggestions as to quantitative measurement of rates of evolution. *Evolution* 3:51-56.

Henneberg, M. 1986. Human cranial capacity decrease in Holocene: A result of generalized structural reduction. *Am. J. Phys. Anthropol.* 69:213-214.

Hofman, M. A. 1983. Encephalization in hominids: Evidence for the model of punctuationalism. *Brain Behav. Evol.* 22:102-117.

Hofman, M. A. 1984. On the presumed coevolution of brain size and longevity in hominids. *J. Hum. Evol.* 13:371-376.

Hofman, M. A., Laan, A. C., and Uylings, B. M. 1986. Bivariate linear models in neurobiology: Problems of concept and methodology. *J. Neurosci. Methods* 18:103-114.

Holloway, R. L. 1981a. Exploring the dorsal surface of hominoid brain endocasts by stereoplotter and discriminant analysis. *Philos. Trans. R. Soc. London Ser. B* 292:155-166.

Holloway, R. L. 1981b. Revisiting the South African Taung australopithecine endocast: The position of the lunate sulcus as determined by the stereoplotting technique. *Am. J. Phys. Anthropol.* 56:43-58.

Holloway, R. L. 1981c. The endocast of the Omo L338y-6 juvenile hominid: Gracile or robust *Australopithecus? Am. J. Phys. Anthropol.* 54:109-118.

Holloway, R. L. 1981d. The Indonesian *Homo erectus* brain endocasts revisited. *Am. J. Phys. Anthropol.* 55:503-521.

Holloway, R. L. 1981e. Volumetric and asymmetry determinations on recent hominid endocasts: Spy I and II, Djebel Ihroud I, and the Sale *Homo erectus* specimens, with some notes on Neandertal brain size. *Am. J. Phys. Anthropol.* 55:385-393.

Holloway, R. L. 1983a. Cerebral brain endocast pattern of *Australopithecus afarensis* hominid. *Nature* 303:420-422.

Holloway, R. L. 1983b. Human paleontological evidence relevant to language behavior. *Hum. Neurobiol.* 2:105-114.

Holloway, R. L. 1983c. The O.H. 7 (Olduvai Gorge, Tanzania) parietal fragments and their reconstruction: A reply to Wolpoff. *Am. J. Phys. Anthropol.* 60:505-516.

Holloway, R. L. 1984. The Taung endocast and the lunate sulcus: A rejection of the hypothesis of its anterior position. *Am. J. Phys. Anthropol.* 64:285-287.

Holloway, R. L. 1985. The past, present, and future significance of the lunate sulcus in early hominid evolution, in: *Hominid Evolution: Past, Present and Future* (P. V. Tobias, Ed.), pp. 47-62, Liss, New York.

Holloway, R. L., and De La Coste-Lareymondie, M. C. 1982. Brain endocast asymmetry in pongids and hominids: Some preliminary findings on the paleontology of cerebral dominance. *Am. J. Phys. Anthropol.* 58:101-110.

Holloway, R. L., and Kimbel, W. H. 1986. Endocast morphology of Hadar hominid AL 162-28. *Nature* 321:536.

Johanson, D. C., and White, T. D. 1979. A systematic assessment of early African hominids. *Science* 203:321-330.

Kimbel, W. H. 1984. Variation in the pattern of cranial venous sinuses and hominid phylogeny. *Am J. Phys. Anthropol.* 63:243-263.

Kimbel, W. H., Johanson, D. C., and Coppens, Y. 1982. Pliocene hominid cranial remains from the Hadar Formation, Ethiopia. *Am J. Phys. Anthropol.* 57: 453-500.

Leakey, M. G., and Leakey, R. E. 1978. *Koobi Fora Research Project*, Vol. I, *The Fossil Hominids and an Introduction to Their Context* 1968-1974. Clarendon Press, Oxford.

Leakey, R. E. F., and Walker, A. C. 1976. *Australopithecus, Homo erectus* and the single species hypothesis. *Nature* 261:572-574.

LeMay, M. 1976. Morphological cerebral asymmetries of modern man, fossil man, and non-human primates. *Ann. NY Acad. Sci.* 280:349-360.

LeMay, M. 1977. Asymmetries of the skull and handedness. *J. Neurol. Sci.* 32:213-225.

Lewin, R. 1985. Surprise findings in the Taung child's face. *Science* 228:42-44.

Lovejoy, C. O. 1981. The origin of man. *Science* 211:341-350.

Lumsden, C. J. 1983. Neuronal group selection and the evolution of hominid cranial capacity. *J. Hum. Evol.* 12:169-184.

MacLean, M. D. 1985. Brain evolution relating to family, play, and separation call. *Arch. Gen. Psychiatry* 42:405-417.

Nottebohm, F. 1977. Asymmetries in neural control of vocalization in the canary, in: *Lateralization in the Nervous System* (S. Harnad, R. Doty, L. Golstein, J. Jaynes and G. Krauthamer, Eds.), pp. 23-44, Academic, New York.

Ojemann, G. A. 1983. Brain organization for language from the perspective of electrical stimulation mapping. *Behav. Brain Sci.* 6:189-230.

Olson, T. R. 1981. Basicranial morphology of the extant hominoids and Pliocene hominids: The new material from the Hadar Formation, Ethiopia, and its significance in early human evolution and taxonomy, in: *Aspects of Human Evolution* (C. B. Stringer, Ed.), Taylor and Francis, London.

Olson, T. R. 1985. Cranial morphology and systematics of the Hadar Formation hominids and *"Australopithecus" africanus*, in: *Ancestors: The Hard Evidence* (E. Delson, Ed.), pp. 102-119, Liss, New York.

Passingham, R. E. 1975. What's so special about man's brain? *New Sci.* 68:510-511.

Passingham, R. E. 1981. Broca's area and the origins of human vocal skill. *Philos. Trans. R. Soc. London Ser. B* 292:167-175.

Passingham, R. E. 1985. Rates of brain development in mammals including man. *Brain Behav. Evol.* 26:167-175.

Passingham, R. E. 1986. Reorganization in the human brain as illustrated by the thalamus. *Brain Behav. Evol.* 29:68-76.

Radinsky, L. B. 1979. *The fossil record of primate brain evolution*, 49th James Arthur Lect., Am. Mus. Nat. Hist., New York.

Richards, G. 1986. Freed hands or enslaved feet? A note on the behavioural implications of ground-dwelling bipedalism. *J. Hum. Evol.* 15:143-150.

Sarich, V. 1971. A molecular approach to the question of human origins, in: *Background for Man* (V. Sarich and P. Dolhinow, Eds.), pp. 60-81, Little, Brown, Boston.

Senut, B., and Tardieu, C. 1985. Functional aspects of Plio-Pleistocene hominid limb bones: Implications for taxonomy and phylogeny, in: *Ancestors. The Hard Evidence* (E. Delson, Ed.), pp. 193-201, Liss, New York.

Smith, H. 1986. Dental development in *Australopithecus* and early *Homo. Nature* 323:327-330.

Tobias, P. V. 1967. *Olduvai Gorge*, Vol II. *The Cranium and Maxillary Dentition of Australopithecus (Zinjanthropus) boisei*, Cambridge Univ. Press, Cambridge.

Tobias, P. V. 1980. "*Australopithecus afarensis*" and *A. africanus*: Critique and an alternative hypothesis. *Palaeontol. Afr.* 23:1-17.

Tobias, P. V. 1981. The emergence of man in Africa and beyond. *Philos. Trans. R. Soc. London Ser. B* 292:43-56.

Tobias, P. V. 1985. Single characters and the total morphological pattern redefined: The sorting effected by a selection of morphological features of the early hominids, in: *Ancestors. The Hard Evidence* (E. Delson, Ed.), pp. 94-101, Liss, New York.

Toth, N. 1985. Archeological evidence for preferential right-handedness in the lower and middle Pleistocene, and its possible implications. *J. Hum. Evol.* 14:607-614.

Tuttle, R. H. 1985. Ape footprints and Laetoli impressions: A response to the SUNY claims, in: *Hominid Evolution: Past, Present and Future* (P. V. Tobias, Ed.), pp. 129-133, Liss, New York.

Vaisnys, J. R., Lieberman, D., and Pilbeam, D. 1984. An alternative method of estimating the cranial capacity of Olduvai hominid 7. *Am. J. Phys. Anthropol.* 65:71-81.

Vannier, M. W., Conroy, G. C., Krieg, J., and Falk, D. 1985. Three-dimensional imaging for primate biology. *Proc. Natl. Comput. Graphics Assoc.*, Dallas 3:156-160.

Vilensky, J. A., Van Hoesen, G. W., and Damasio, A.R. 1981. The limbic system in human evolution. *Am. J. Phys. Anthropol.* 54:286.

Vrba, E. S. 1985. Early hominids in Southern Africa: Updated observations on chronological and ecological background, in: *Hominid Evolution: Past, Present and Future* (P. V. Tobias, Ed.), pp. 195-200, Liss, New York.

Walker, A., Leakey, R. E., Harris, J. M., and Brown, F. H. 1986. 2.5-MYR *Australopithecus boisei* from west of Lake Turkana, Kenya. *Nature* 322:517-522.

Washburn, S. L. 1960. Tools and human evolution. *Sci. Am.* 203:63-75.

Washburn, S. L. 1968. *The Study of Human Evolution.* Oregon State Syst. Higher Educ. Condon Lect, Eugene.

Washburn, S. L. 1982. Human evolution. *Perspect. Biol. Med.* 25:583-602.

Webster, W. G. 1977. Territoriality and the evolution of brain asymmetry. *Ann. NY Acad. Sci.* 299:213-221.

Weidenreich, F. 1943. The skull of *Sinanthropus pekinensis. Palaeont. Sin.* 127:1-486.

Wolpoff, M. H. 1981. Cranial capacity estimates for Olduvai hominid 7. *Am. J. Phys. Anthropol.* 56:297-304.

Zihlman, A. L. 1985. *Australopithecus afarensis*: Two sexes or two species? in: *Hominid Evolution: Past, Present and Future* (P. V. Tobias, Ed.), pp. 213-218, Liss, New York.

9

Human Evolution: The Geological Framework

H. B. S. Cooke

INTRODUCTION

We humans seem to have a built-in curiosity about our ancestry that extends beyond the limits of our personal genealogical trees to a thirst for knowledge of the origins of man himself [1]. Indeed this curiosity has led to the development of many fascinating myths and legends that are reflected in the traditions of peoples in all parts of our planet, sometimes so deeply ingrained in their beliefs that alternative hypotheses were deemed unacceptable. It is a mere twelve decades since the revolution in thought that followed publication of Thomas Huxley's *Man's Place in Nature* (1863) and only eleven since the appearance of Charles Darwin's *The Descent of Man* (1871). At that time, although some remains had been found at a few sites in Europe, the only significant human fossils known were the skullcap and skeletal fragments from the Neander valley in Germany (1856) and the remarkable skulls and associated skeletons of five individuals from the Cro-Magnon cave in the south of France (1868). Today these remains are generally recognized as representing two varieties of our own species—Neanderthal Man or *Homo sapiens neanderthalensis* and Cro-Magnon Man, *Homo sapiens sapiens*, both of whom lived during the last glacial stage of the Pleistocene Period or "Great Ice Age."

The study of the actual skeletal remains of early man is the task of the physical anthropologist, who must obviously be well versed in human anatomy and familiar with the ranges of variability that are encountered in living populations of man. However, he must also be knowledgeable about the anatomy of the great apes and other primates with which man shares many anatomical, physiological and behavioural resemblances. Thus, evaluation of the characteristics of the fossil remains themselves is essentially a zoological problem. Yet any particular specimen represents only an instant in geological time and if we are to make meaningful comparisons between specimens it is essential that we place each find as accurately as possible into a common time frame, for only then are we entitled to formulate sound theories about the evolutionary pathways that may have been followed. Dating of the sediments is not solely the task of the geologist but calls also for the skills of the paleontologist, geophysicist, geochemist, palynologist and others. Nor is dating the only product of a multidisciplinary attack, for the deposits can yield much information about the environmental setting and even about the way of life of our remote relatives. Thus the bones themselves tell only part of the story.

PRESERVATION OF HOMINID FOSSILS

Fossil remains of man are rare and it would seem that the farther back in time we go, the rarer the discoveries become. There are probably several reasons for this. When a land animal dies in the open its remains are soon attacked by scavengers which scatter the bones and may even destroy them. What survives the scavengers is bleached by the sun and rotted by the rain. So if the bones are to have a reasonable chance of survival they must be protected in some way, more especially through rapid burial by sediment. This is most readily accomplished in low-lying basins, where lakes are fed by streams carrying sediment in suspension or in the flood plain areas adjoining meandering streams. Animals sometimes become trapped in the boggy borders of lakes and the bones of their skeletons may then remain associated to provide paleontological treasure, but man was probably too intelligent to be trapped in this manner so associated skeletons are extremely rare until deliberate burial of the dead became customary. Very commonly, the remains that we find buried in riverine or lacustrine deposits were transported by flowing water for some distance and they may thus be broken or show signs of damage. Even after burial in such an "open site," the bones may still be destroyed by percolating ground water, especially in areas where the water is rendered acid by forest debris. Indeed, the forest environment is an exceptionally poor one for preservation of bone and the fossil record is distorted by under-representation of forest dwellers. On the other hand, the presence of alkalis or lime in the soil helps to prevent solution of buried bone and one useful source of alkaline material can be volcanic dust, thus favouring preservation in volcanic regions provided, of course, that the volcanic activity does not destroy the deposits!

Another type of environment favourable for the preservation of animal bones is to be found in caves and fissures, especially in limestone regions. Caverns are formed by solution of the limestone in the upper part of the saturated zone, or groundwater. As regional erosion slowly lowers the landscape and deepens the valleys, the groundwater table sinks and the caverns are drained, but dripstones (such as stalactites and stalagmites) are deposited on the walls of the cavern by percolating water. Rainwater passing downwards from the surface dissolves the limestone along planes of weakness so that chimneys, or "avens," develop and eventually open to the surface. At this stage soil and surface debris begin to wash into the fissures and build up deposits on the cavern floor, often to be subsequently cemented into a hard "breccia" by percolating lime-charged water. The fissures are commonly concealed by bushes, or even trees, and unwary animals fall into the natural trap so that their bones accumulate on the cave floor, entombed by further falls of debris. Sometimes the head of the aven may provide a rock shelter or den for animals and their bones and the bones of their prey ultimately find their way into the deeper cavern. Erosion of the surface continues and at different stages more avens open, or the existing ones enlarge, and the roof of the original cavern becomes thinner and thinner until it is gone and the cave deposits themselves are exposed on the surface.

Apart from such deep caves, which fortunately preserve material of considerable antiquity for us to examine, surface caves of all kinds provide convenient shelters that have been used as dens, not only by animals but also by man. The cave floor is continuously covered with dust and dirt carried in by wind, water and the occupants, leaving a layered sequence in which we search eagerly for the ancient garbage that helped to build up the deposits. Such shallow caves are eventually destroyed by erosion so that few of the ones known today are of antiquity comparable to those of the deeper caverns, but they are very valuable sources of material and information.

Thus we see that the geological environments suitable for the preservation of remains of early man are very limited. The best conditions are probably represented by the "closed" environments offered by rock shelters, surface caves and subsurface caverns, although in the latter case the depositional mechanisms may lead to complex stratigraphic situations that can be difficult to interpret. Each individual cave deposit represents a discrete and isolated entity, usually covering a rather limited span of geological time—sometimes even a single catastrophic event—so that correlation between different caves and the determination of relative ages are difficult. By way of compensation for these difficulties, the fossils themselves are normally very well preserved.

The "open" sites are usually associated with fluviatile, lacustrine or volcanic environments, or occasionally with delta or lagoonal marine settings. Individual sites may be of very limited extent, leading to the same problems of correlation that we find with caves, but quite often the fossil-bearing areas occur as parts of a laterally extensive deposit and within a stratigraphic succession that represents a significant span of geological time. Such spatially and temporally extensive deposits are particularly valuable in establishing successive changes in the faunas and also in providing a reference framework for correlation. When such stratal sequences also include volcanic ash or lava horizons that can be used for radiometric dating, the situation is almost ideal but, alas, is also rare.

Although human fossils do occasionally occur in splendid isolation, they are normally associated in some way with animal fossils that can be identified and employed as an aid in correlation between scattered sites, or in the construction of a "synthetic" sequence by interweaving the data from many sites with overlapping faunas and ages. However, the associated fossils are also of considerable interest in providing information both about the conditions of deposition of the deposit itself and about the ecological environment prevailing at the time. The study of death assemblages—now known as "taphonomy"—is a fresh and expanding field that is beginning to explain some former puzzles. It is also proving very useful in directing field geologists into seeking out the particular depositional facies that appear to be most promising for yielding fossils; indeed "prospecting" for particularly suitable sedimentary environments is already productive. Taphonomic studies also provide a basis for trying to evaluate what components of the total spectrum of animals normally inhabiting an area actually find their way into the fossil assemblages. This is an important element in attempts to evaluate the paleoecology and paleoenvironment and may provide clues to the dietary preferences and habits of early man (see, for example, Behrensmeyer and Hill 1980, Brain 1981). Environmental interpretation in turn, is assisted by the collection and evaluation of fossil pollens, beetles or other invertebrates, coprolites, chemical studies of fossil soils, and so on. Thus very careful geological fieldwork is now an essential part of the search for early man and a fossil divorced from its context loses a great deal of its potential value for complete interpretation.

GEOLOGICAL TIME

The point in time where the line leading to man separated from that leading to the great apes is still a mystery and, although studies of biochemical and cellular factors suggest that the branching took place only 6 to 8 MYA, it is to the fossil record that we must look for definitive evidence of what actually occurred. It is very important that each relevant fossil should be carefully dated. The problem has been well analyzed and discussed by Oakley (1953, 1966), who recognized two main classes of dating, namely "Relative Dating" and "Chronometric Dating." Relative dating places an event with reference to some other event in a time sequence and represents the stratigraphical age of a specimen or of a geological formation. Oakley suggested a hierarchy of relative datings, R.1 being the age relation between the specimen and its containing deposit or associated fossils, R.2 the stage in the local or regional stratigraphic sequence to which the fossil-bearing horizon can be referred, R.3 the inferred position of that stage in terms of wide scale, or world, stratigraphy, and R.4 the geological age of a specimen inferred indirectly from the morphology. The R.1 dating is fundamental if we are to avoid being misled by intrusive burial or by derivation through erosion of an earlier horizon. It was R.1 dating that unmasked the Piltdown fraud. In the earlier days of paleoanthropology, before so much attention was paid to proper dating, R.4 type arguments were used to recognize "primitive" characters as "early" and "advanced" characters as "late," which is not necessarily true. However, R.4 dating can be used with some precision for correlation in cases where fossil mammals are abundant and were changing rapidly through time and where the changes can be calibrated or controlled from a thick sequence of well-dated strata. The South African australopithecine cave deposits are largely dated in this way by comparison with the excellent sequences now known from East Africa.

Chronometric dating (sometimes called "Absolute" dating) relies on actual assessment or measurement of the age in years and again Oakley (1953, 1966) has suggested a useful hierarchy. A.1 involves direct dating of the specimen, for example by measuring the carbon 14-radioactivity of the bone itself. A relatively new technique is the estimation of the degree of racemization of amino acids in organic tissue, but the accuracy of the method is dependent on assumptions about the thermal history of the deposit and the results are not always reliable. A.2 dating is derived from direct determination by physical measurements of the age of the sediments containing the fossil. The most important techniques are the radioactivity of carbon-14 in charcoal or shell for deposits younger than 50,000 years or, for older beds, the radioactive decay of potassium to produce argon in minerals that crystallize in lavas or are ejected as volcanic ash falls (tuffs). Other methods, such as fission track dating of zircons, or other suitable grains occurring in ash falls are sometimes valuable and there are also other methods such as uranium series dating, the hydration of obsidian, or the thermoluminescence of quartz grains, that have limited applications. A.3 dating involves correlation of the fossil-bearing horizon with another deposit whose actual age has been determined by A.1 or A.2 methods. Geochemical characteristics of volcanic ash layers are proving increasingly important for confirming or amending age determinations in some areas. A.4 dating involves making estimates of age on the basis of some theoretical consideration, such as the matching of climatic fluctuations observed in the strata with astronomically derived curves for effective solar radiation, or matching terrestrial glacial/interglacial episodes with the marine paleotemperature or oxygen isotope record.

A relatively new technique of particular importance for the last few million years of geological time is paleomagnetic stratigraphy (Fig. 1). As molten lavas cool and crystallize, magnetizable minerals in them acquire and retain a direction of polarity parallel to the lines of force of the Earth's magnetic field at that time. By measuring the polarity in lavas from many parts of the world, especially in areas like Iceland and Hawaii, and by dating the lavas by the K/Ar method, it is possible to study the behaviour of the Earth's magnetic field through time. It is found that the direction of polarity remains stable for long periods and then, quite suddenly, reverses itself and again remains stable in the new direction. The ages at which the geomagnetic inversions occur can be defined quite narrowly from the K/Ar ages and a reversal time scale can be constructed to fit all the data. When the field was directed towards the north rotational pole of the Earth, as at present, the field is said to be "normal," and when it is directed towards the south pole it is "reversed." Figure 1 shows the geomagnetic polarity time scale for the past 5 million years, using the revised determinations of Mankinen and Dalrymple (1979). The longer periods of general stability are called "Polarity Epochs" or "Chrons" but within them are shorter episodes, termed "Polarity Events" or "Subchrons" (Cox, Doell and Dalrymple 1964). The net result is a

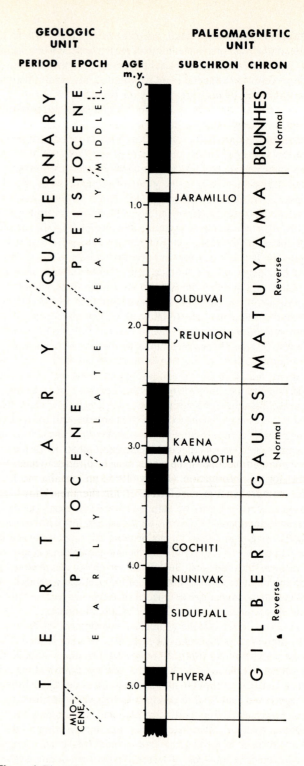

Figure 1. *The paleomagnetic time scale for the past 5 million years. The ages for the boundaries are those of Mankinen and Dalrymple (1979).*

sequence of normal and reversed episodes that is unique and forms a "fingerprint" with which the sequence of changes in other sections can be compared. As the process is a global one, the reversal episodes are synchronous in all parts of the Earth.

Fortunately, sediments can also acquire the appropriate magnetic imprint and use of the polarity time scale has revolutionized the interpretation of ocean floor cores, where sedimentation is usually more or less continuous so that the sequence can be traced back through time and the epoch and event boundaries identified with a high degree of probability. In terrestrial sequences, continuous deposition is very unusual and unfortunately there is no identifying characteristic in the magnetic signals themselves that differentiates one reversal episode from another; it is only the pattern presented by a succession of reversals that makes the "fingerprint" matching possible. Accordingly, in terrestrial sequences it is necessary to obtain at least one approximate date somewhere within the span of the magnetic measurements in order to facilitate proper matching with the paleomagnetic time scale. Even then some ambiguity may remain. However, where good matching can be achieved, the reversal boundaries carry with them a very accurate date and this makes possible reliable age determination even in the absence of radioactive isotopes or other sources of A.1 or A.2 chronometric dating. So, while inherently an A.3 or A.4 method, it can achieve A.2 quality results in favourable circumstances. The geomagnetic polarity time scale is now commonly shown along with a radiometric age scale in charts of Pliocene-Pleistocene events, although this does not always mean that paleomagnetic data have been used in the allocation of stratigraphic units to their places in the time scale.

STRATIGRAPHY AND CHRONOLOGY OF HOMINID SITES

It is impossible in less space than a major volume to attempt to evaluate the geological setting and age estimates of all the known hominid specimens; the reader must be directed to other sources for this information. Oakley (1966) presented a most useful comprehensive tabulation of all the then-known specimens, together with their date of discovery, an estimate of the stratigraphic age, the chronometric age (if any), and categorization of the status of the age determination on his "A" scale. Day (1977) has provided a short summary of the geological setting and dating estimates for the most important fossil hominids, including useful references for additional data. The whole problem of dating hominid remains is discussed in a volume edited by Bishop and Miller (1972) in which Isaac has included a valuable critical appraisal of localities and dates associated with archaeological occurrences. This volume also includes an appendix with charts showing the rather limited chronometric dating controls for fossil hominids known at that time, which were exclusively African. A comprehensive volume focused on the middle part of the Pleistocene, edited by Butzer and Isaac (1975) also includes an appendix setting out in tabular form the estimated ages for most of the major hominid fossils of the past 2 million years, drawing particular attention to the range of uncertainty regarding those age estimates. It is not proposed here to attempt to repeat these data, but it seems worthwhile to offer some general observations on the broad features of the geological framework in the major areas from which human fossils have come.

Europe

Although the existence of a former more extensive ice cover in Switzerland was realized in the 1820's and in other parts of Europe shortly thereafter, it was not until more than 25 years later that the existence of evidence for multiple glaciations was recognized. In 1909 Penck and Brückner established the classical sequence of four glacial periods in the Alps, naming them, from youngest to oldest, Würm, Riss, Mindel and Günz, to which were subsequently added two earlier and lesser glacial episodes named the Donau (Eberl 1930) and Biber (Schaefer 1956). North Germany was glaciated by a Scandinavian-centred ice sheet, and four glacial stages were named Weichsel (youngest), Warthe, Saale and Elster, but they do not match directly with the four main Alpine glaciations as the Warthe appears to be coupled closely with the Saale and the two together are regarded as representing phases of the Riss Glaciation of the Alps; the Günz equivalent is not recognized in the glaciated Scandinavian North German region. Further study has led to the recognition of breaks (interstadials) within the major glaciations, thus dividing the glacial units into two or more stages, and it is now realized that the actual situation is much more complex than would be inferred from the simple "four glacial" concept. It is in some ways unfortunate that the Alpine terms of Penck and Brückner have been used very widely—even outside Europe—as if they had some magical global application. Indeed, intercorrelation between different parts of Europe is still far from settled and correlation with the four North American glaciations is a matter of debate.

The thick sedimentary sequence in the Netherlands is slowly becoming the standard reference section for European Pleistocene stratigraphy. The succession has been probed by large numbers of boreholes and twenty-four lithostratigraphic formations with proper stratotypes are recognized for the later Tertiary and Quaternary (Zagwijn and van Staalduinen 1975). Actual glacial deposits are rare in the Netherlands basin, although both the Elster and the Saale are represented. However, abundant pollens make it possible to estimate the prevailing climatic conditions and to construct a curve showing the changes through the almost unbroken sequence. No radiometric dates are available, but there are sufficient paleomagnetic data to provide good control. Figure 2 shows the results in simplified form (following Zagwijn 1975a, b). It is clear that the sequence is complex and that there is potential difficulty in distinguishing interglacials from interstadials. Other work, principally in eastern Europe, has shown that deposits of the silt material called *loess*, which is derived by wind deflation from unvegetated outwash plains or newly exposed till, can be divided into depositional units that are separated by soil-forming warmer intervals; there are nine such units within the 700,000 year time span of the Brunhes normal polarity epoch (Kukla 1970, 1975, 1977). This complexity of the climatic changes is borne out by the record from deep-sea cores, both from fluctuations in the ratios of warm and cold loving organisms (see Ruddiman and McIntyre 1973, 1976) and by the oxygen isotope record (Shackleton and Opdyke 1973, 1976).

There is not yet agreement on how the glaciation chronology, the loess stratigraphy and the deep sea record are to be reconciled. There is evidence that at least the Eemian interglacial was short (25-30,000 years) and some authorities consider the other interglacials also to be short, leading to the rather widely accepted chronology shown in Figure 3b. However, there is also some evidence to suggest that in certain regions, interstadials have been confused with interglacials—for example a so-called "Eemian" in some areas between the Warthe and Saale phases of the Saale Glaciation. Zagwijn (1975a, b) compresses the later glacials and gives the "Cromerian" Complex a substantial range in time (Figs. 2, 3a) whereas other

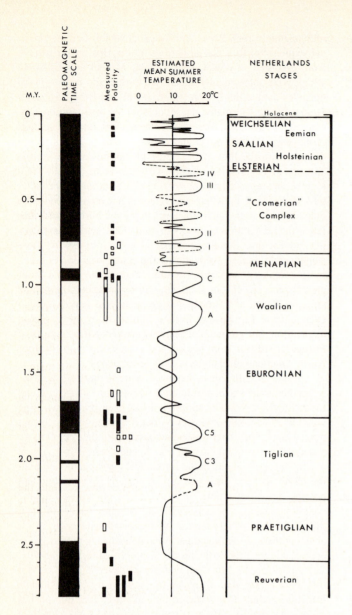

Figure 2. *Climato-stratigraphic subdivision of the Quaternary in the Netherlands, showing the application of paleomagnetic data for age control of the sequence. The curve shows fluctuations in the mean summer temperature as deduced from pollen data. (Slightly modified from Zagwijn 1975a, b.) The names of the cold stages are indicated in CAPITALS and warm, or interglacial, stages in lower case.*

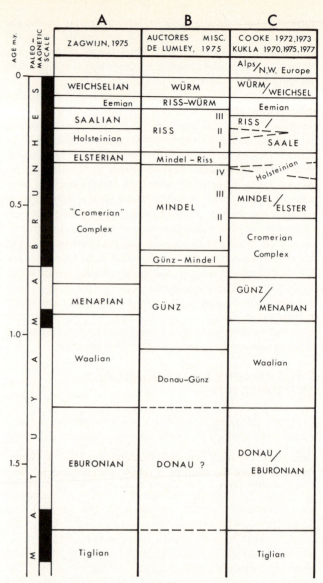

Figure 3. *Three different interpretations of the climato-stratigraphic subdivision of the Quaternary sequence in Europe. (A) follows Zagwijn (1975b), with great compression of the post-Cromerian. (B) represents the most widely used scheme of many European workers. (C) is an interpretation that takes more account of the loess stratigraphy but also suggests that there has been some confusion of interglacial and interstadial environments.*

authorities would restrict it. A compromise time scale is shown in Figure 3c. It may be expected that these different interpretations would affect the "absolute" ages assigned to the European fossil hominids but in fact it is only the earlier ones that are significantly affected, as will be seen in Table 1. Of course, other chronologies would give different results but the dates given in Table 1 probably reflect reasonable limiting ages.

Africa

North Africa has yielded a fine jaw from Ternifine, Algeria, a partial cranium from Salé and both cranial and mandibular remains from Sidi Abderrahman in Morocco; all of these have

Homo erectus affinities but are poorly dated, though probably belonging to the later part of the Middle Pleistocene. A few Neanderthal-like specimens have also come from Morocco and Libya and more modern forms from other localities. There is also a curious specimen from Yayo, Chad that may be attributed to *Homo*, perhaps *H. erectus*; its age is uncertain.

Sub-Saharan Africa has furnished a few skulls of neanderthaloid character, notably the skull and other fragments from Broken Hill (or Kabwe) in Zambia which some authorities separate from the neanderthals proper as an African race, *Homo sapiens rhodesiensis*. To this form are also ascribed the Saldanha (or Hopefield, or Elandsfontein) cranium and mandibular fragments from the southwestern tip of the continent, the Cave

Table 1. Comparison of age estimates of European hominids according to different chronologies.

FOSSIL	STRATIGRAPHIC AGE	ESTIMATED CHRONOMETRIC AGE		
		A	B	C
Cro-magnon	Last glaciation	<50,000	<50,000	<50,000
Neanderthal	Last glaciation	<75,000	<75,000	<75,000
Krapina	Late Eemian	c85,000	c85,000	c85,000
Fontéchevade	Eemian	c100,000	c100,000	c100,000
Steinheim	Eemian	c100,000	c100,000	c100,000
Arago	Early Riss	c180,000	c250,000	c250,000
Swanscombe	Late Holsteinian	c210,000	c300,000	c300,000
Mauer	Mindel Interstadial	c230,000	c480,000	c480,000
Vértesszöllös*	Mindel Interstadial	c280,000	c480,000	c480,000

* There is a thorium/uranium determination of >300,000 years (Cherdyntsev *et al.* 1965) but is not generally considered reliable.

of Hearths mandible from the Transvaal, and from East Africa the two crania from Lake Eyassi, Tanzania. There are also a number of interesting remains apparently ancestral to the modern African races of man. Most of these specimens are of Upper Pleistocene age, but the Saldanha skull is probably Middle Pleistocene.

The more ancient hominid remains occur in two widely different settings, the South African cave breccias and the East African rift valley deposits. The latter are all essentially similar in origin, comprising sequences of fluviolacustrine sediments with occasional horizons of volcanic tuffs that may be dated radiometrically or by fission-track dating of zircons or of volcanic glass. The most famous is the deposit at Olduvai Gorge, Tanzania, where the skull of a robust australopithecine was found in 1959 (Olduvai Hominid 5) and a radiometric age of 1.75 million years (Leakey, Evernden and Curtis 1961) provided the first concrete evidence for the antiquity of the australopithecines. A number of other important discoveries of hominids have been made at various levels. The 100 m thick deposit ranges in time from 2.1 million years at the base of Bed I to 0.8-0.6 million years for Bed IV. Paleomagnetic observations support the radiometric dates and this is the type location for the "Olduvai Event" of the magnetic polarity time scale. The geology has been described in detail by Hay (1976). Immediately south of Olduvai there is an older deposit, the Laetoli (or Laetolil) beds, consisting largely of fine volcanic tuffs that yielded important hominid fossils dated at close to 3.6 million years (M. D. Leakey *et al.* 1976) as well as well-preserved footprints of the hominids of this remote time (M. D. Leakey and Hay 1979, M. D. Leakey 1981).

Other important sequences are those of the Omo area of southwestern Ethiopia, where the 750-m thick Shungura Formation is divided into alphabetically labelled members by volcanic tuff horizons, most of which have been well dated. Detailed paleomagnetic studies have led to slight adjustments of some of the dates with the result that it now provides an unusually well controlled sequence. The Basal unit has an age close to 3.5 million years and unit L is approximately 0.8 million years old. Hominid remains occur throughout, and the succession forms a valuable reference frame for correlation of other deposits. The Omo river delta discharges into the north end of Lake Turkana (formerly Lake Rudolf) and on the east side of the lake, over an area 40 to 50 km in radius around Koobi

Fora, similar fluviolacustrine deposits have yielded numerous hominid fossils. Two major units were recognized, but recent revision of the stratigraphy (Brown and Cerling 1982) suggests that it should all be included under the name of the Koobi Fora Formation. The East Turkana sediments were about 475 m thick and cover a time range similar to that of the Omo, but there is an erosional gap in the middle of the sequence so that the equivalents of Shungura Members D, E and F seem to be generally missing (Harris and White 1979, Cerling and Brown 1982). To the south of Lake Turkana, two restricted areas at Kanapoi and Lothagam have yielded fragmentary hominid fossils. Kanapoi is dated as close to 4 million years and Lothagam is estimated to be about 5.5-6.0 million years old.

In Ethiopia the Awash River drains northwards into the Afar depression. Exposed in the middle reaches of the valley is a thick sequence of deposits that covers a time range from the upper Miocene to the Upper Pleistocene and has yielded vertebrate fossils throughout, including some hominids (Taieb 1974, Kalb *et al.* 1982a, b). Although work is proceeding on other portions of this very promising area, the most intensively studied section is that near Hadar, where the Hadar Formation has yielded a superb fauna, including valuable hominid material (Johanson *et al.* 1982). The Hadar sequence is stated to range from about 4.0 to 2.7 million years (Johanson *et al.* 1982) but there are problems with some of the data and the paleomagnetic records would accord better with a range nearer 3.5 million years at the base and a corrected radiometric age closer to 3.1 million years for the Kadada Moumou Basalt (Aronson *et al.* 1977). In the upper part of the Middle Awash sequence, the Bodo Member of the Wehaieta Formation has yielded an archaic *Homo* cranium of probably Middle Pleistocene age. Tentative correlations are shown in Figure 4.

In South Africa the important australopithecine deposits are cave breccias resulting from the slumping of surface debris into ancient underground caverns, as was described above. Subsequent to their primary filling, the deposits have been subjected to erosion and new channels, fissures or cavities were sometimes developed within the earlier breccias so that breccias of different ages may be in contact (see Brain 1981). Erosion has generally removed most or all of the original roof so that the pinkish-brown breccias are exposed at the surface. Each site samples a different time span and correlation between the deposits relies on the faunal material.

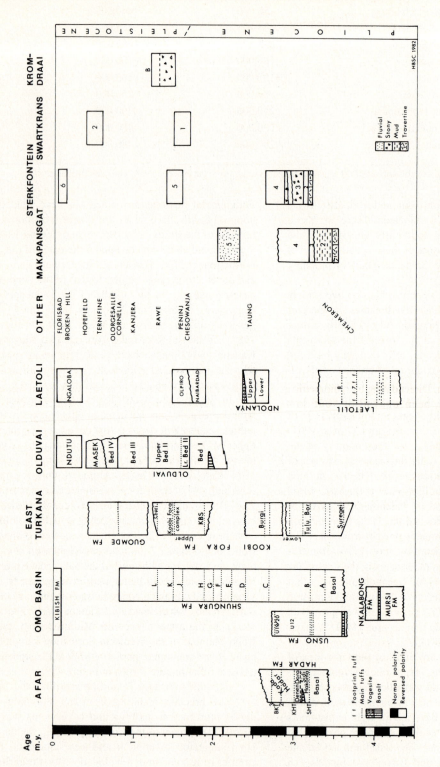

Figure 4. *Tentative correlation of the main hominid-bearing stratigraphic units in Africa. The East African sequences are generally controlled by some radiometric dates and paleomagnetic records. The South African sites have no radiometric ages and are correlated mainly on faunal grounds by comparison with the East African sequence; there is some confirmatory paleomagnetic information but it can be ambiguous.*

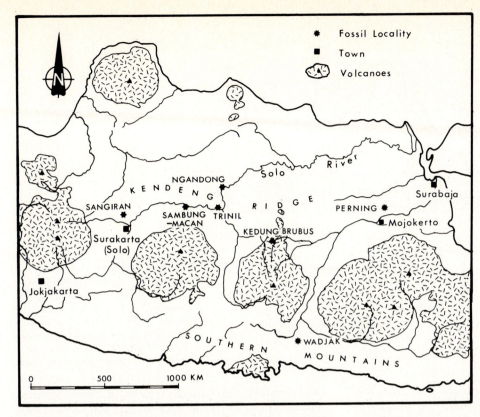

Figure 5. *Simplified map of part of eastern Java to show the location of the principal hominid fossil sites.*

Comparison with the faunal sequence in East Africa suggests that the deposits of the Makapansgat Limeworks are probably close to 3.0 million years old while the Lower Breccia at Sterkfontein is slightly younger. Direct dating by radiometric or geochemical methods have been unavailing, but some paleomagnetic observations support the 3 million year age implied by the fauna (McFadden *et al.* 1979). On similar faunal grounds, the Sterkfontein Extension site (Member 5) with its stone tools, is estimated to be only half as old. At Swartkrans there are two breccias with different faunas, Member 1 with a faunally estimated age of about 1.7 million years and Member 2 as perhaps only about 0.5 million years. At Kromdraai, the australopithecine breccia ("B") is estimated faunally to be about 1.5 million years old. The deposit at Taung, which furnished the type specimen of *Australopithecus africanus*, is poorly dated but may lie somewhere between the ages of Sterkfontein and Swartkrans 1, probably close to 2.0-2.5 million years.

Indonesia

The discovery of the "Java Ape-Man" at Trinil 90 years ago was a landmark in paleoanthropology and has been followed by further important finds of *Homo erectus* near Sangiran and also by the recovery of other material at Ngandong, generally termed "Solo Man." All these localities lie in the drainage basin of the Solo River in eastern Java (Djava) between Surakarta and Surabaya, while an isolated site at Perning, near Mojokerto, lies some distance from the Solo River about 40 kilometers west of Surabaya. Isolated finds have been made at Sambungmacan, 20 kilometers west of Trinil, and at Kedung Brubus, 100 kilometers east of Surakarta (Fig. 5). A list of discoveries, in chronological order, has been given by Jacob (1975).

Java is part of an island arc system extending through Sumatra (Sumatera) and Timor, bordered on the south side by the deep Java Trench. It is a tectonically active belt and is marked by a line of young volcanoes. The geology has been described in some detail by Van Bemmelen (1949). The Southern Mountains of Java are built of volcanic rocks with interbedded marine sediments of Miocene age, injected by granitic intrusives. These rocks were uparched in the later Tertiary to form a chain of islands, while the area to the north (now the area of the Solo River drainage system) was a shallow platform in which Pliocene deposits were laid down. The Pliocene Kalibeng Formation consists of marls, clays and silts, with occasional horizons of volcanic tuff, and the uppermost part includes marine limestones. Increased volcanic activity is apparent at the base of the overlying Pucangan Formation as volcanic mudflow breccias (lahars) occur in some areas. The "typical" sediments of the Pucangan Formation are freshwater "black clays" suggesting deposition in a ponded lake, but there are localized fluviatile sections with vertebrate fossils and also some marine horizons suggesting that there were occasional short-lived connections with the sea; farther to the east the Pucangan Formation is represented largely by a marine facies. The relatively quiet deposition of the Pucangan Formation was succeeded by an influx of coarser debris so that the Kabuh Formation has some conglomerates but is largely made up of crossbedded sandstones and tuffaceous sandstones with plant remains and vertebrate fossils, although clays and silts also occur. The Kabuh Formation has furnished the bulk of the hominid remains. Rapid growth of the volcanoes, perhaps accompanied by regional uplift, is reflected in the Notopuro Formation, in which lahar flows and explosive volcanic breccias are prominent and mammalian fossils are only rarely preserved. The age of the Notopuro Formation is uncertain but it is generally believed to be Middle to Upper Pleistocene.

Fossil vertebrates occur sporadically in the Pliocene Beds in Western Java, where uplift seems to have begun earlier than

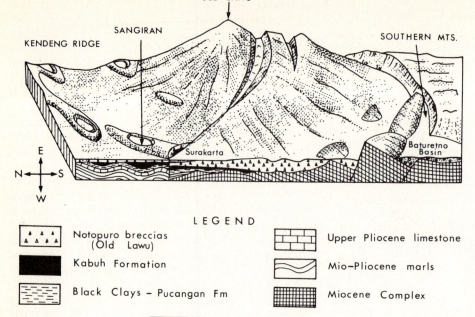

LEGEND

Notopuro breccias (Old Lawu)	Upper Pliocene limestone
Kabuh Formation	Mio-Pliocene marls
Black Clays - Pucangan Fm	Miocene Complex
Alluvial deposits	

Figure 6. *Schematic diagram to show the development of the Sangiran dome at the end of the Notopuro period, leading to exposure of the Kabuh and earlier deposits that are normally concealed by a blanket of Notopuro breccias (modified after van Bemmelen 1949).*

in the eastern part of the country. Here two faunal units were distinguished, an earlier Tjidjulang Fauna and a later Kali Glagah Fauna, but they are virtually unknown in the Solo River basin. Both faunas have a Siva-Malayan aspect. In eastern Java, the Pucangan Formation contains a rich and varied fauna with some Siva-Malayan elements but with others showing a connection with the faunas of southern China. First recognized in the area around Mojokerto, it is distinguished at the Jetis (or Djetis) Fauna and has been recorded from the type area westwards as far as Surakarta. Fossils do not occur in the Pucangan beds at Trinil but there the Kabuh Formation contains a slightly different assemblage known as the Trinil Fauna, which has affinities with the *Stegodon-Ailuropoda* fauna of southern China. Von Koeningswald (1949) regarded the Jetis and Trinil faunas as distinct, placing the former as Early and the latter as Middle Pleistocene, but Hooijer (1951, 1962) denied the distinction and considered that both are probably Middle Pleistocene. Sartono *et al.* (1981) report the discovery of some elements of the Trinil fauna in the upper volcanic facies of the Pucangan Formation, suggesting that the two faunas overlap and that there is need for re-investigation and possible revision. In any case, lateral facies changes probably diminish the value of the equation of the Formations to the faunal units.

The Formations described above underlie the upper reaches of the Solo River, which cuts into them, but successive phases of incision—probably controlled by tectonic events rather than by climate—have led to the development of river terraces on the flanks of the river. Only three were formally recognized and named the Ngandong, Low and Flood terraces respectively. More recent work has disclosed the existence of three earlier terraces, although they are rather obscured (Sartono 1976). The most important is the Ngandong terrace, about 20 m above the present river bed and, in the type area, only some 50 m above sea level. This terrace is the source of the fossil hominids collectively called "Solo Man." An abundant mammalian fauna occurs and constitutes the Ngandong Fauna of Von

Koeningswald (1951), usually regarded as Upper Pleistocene but quite possibly ranging back into the Middle Pleistocene; some elements of this fauna have been found in the Notopuro beds. The hominid remains show clear evidence of river transport and it has been suggested by Santa Luca (1980) that they could have been derived by erosion from an earlier deposit and may not be contemporary with the mammalian fauna; this is an R.1 dating problem that should be capable of testing by chemical or other means but is at present unresolved.

At Trinil the type material of *Homo erectus* came from the Kabuh beds exposed on the flanks of the river and not from the terrace gravels. The most important hominid site is the Sangiran area, north of Surakarta, where the fossiliferous deposits that are normally concealed beneath a blanket of Notopuro beds are well exposed as a result of tectonic upwarping to form the Sangiran Dome (Fig. 6), A schematic cross-section in the northwestern part of the Sangiran dome, showing only the major facies, is shown in Figure 7A, following Semah *et al.* (1981). The term "grenzbank" has been applied to a calcified conglomerate that forms a convenient marker horizon for the boundary between the Pucangan Formation and the Kabuh Formation. The relative positions of the hominid fossils from Sangiran are shown diagrammatically in Figure 7B, from Jacob (1980) but the thicknesses do not appear to be to scale.

A cranium of *Homo erectus* and some stone artifacts were found at Sambungmacan, near the Solo River some twenty-five km west of Trinil, but the stratigraphy of the site is not clear (Sartono 1979). Jacob *et al.* (1978) placed the fossil near the boundary between the Pucangan and Kabuh beds and suggested that the normal magnetic polarity might indicate an age of about 900,000 years and represent the Jaramillo Event. Sartono (1979), on the other hand, considers that both the Kabuh and the Pucangan are missing from the area and that the fossil-bearing deposit most likely represents the Ngandong Formation; this would place the paleomagnetic signal as within the Brunhes normal epoch.

Dating of the Pucangan-Kabuh succession is still unsatis-

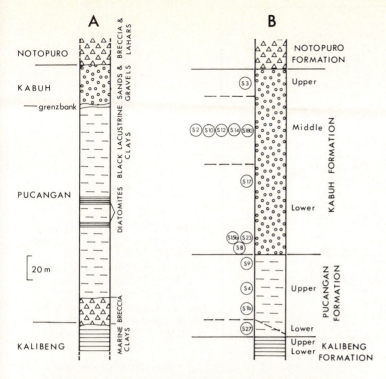

Figure 7. *(A) Schematic cross-section in the northwestern part of the Sangiran dome, showing the relative thickness of the major facies (after Semah* et al. *1981). (B) Relative positions of the hominid fossils from the Sangiran area, not to scale (from Jacob 1980). The specimen numbers are shown in the circles.*

et al. (1981) consider belongs to the Kabuh Formation rather than the Pucangan, but the problem is far from resolved and the age of these specimens must await further field studies. On balance it seems likely that the Pucangan Formation may range from about 1.9 MY to perhaps 0.9 MY, while the Kabuh Formation covers a rather short time span from 0.9-0.7 MY. More detailed studies of the paleomagnetic record and the ages of the interbedded tuffs are required.

China

China has approximately the same area as Canada but covers a range of latitude equivalent to that from Jamaica to Hudson Bay, thus having a tropical climate in the south and an arctic one in the north. More than half of the total area is part of the vast plateau system of Inner Asia, culminating in the high tableland of Tibet (Xizang), most of which is over 3500 metres above sea level and includes the highest point on earth, Mt. Everest (Jolmo Lungma— 8848m). The Tibetan ranges are continued southwards in the Hingduan and Daxne mountains of the Yunnan and western provinces, although at lesser elevations, and these ranges merge into an extensive highland area that occupies the southeastern part of the country. The two great rivers of China, the Yellow River (Huang) and the Yangtze (Chang) originate in the Tibetan highlands and are flanked by extensive lowlands in their lower reaches. The only other extensive lowland area is the Manchurian Plain (or Northeast Plain) lying between the Korean highlands in the east and the Da Hinggan range on the west. The Qin Ling range lies on the south side of the Yellow River and forms a convenient line of separation between the well watered and forested southeastern part of the country and the semi-desert and desert of the Mongolian plateau and the Gobi desert to the north and the Taklimakan desert of the Tarim basin to the west. The northwestern desert region includes the Turpan depression, 154 metres below sea level in strong contrast to the elevated Tibetan Plateau.

The complex mountain and basin structure is the consequence of the geologically recent (Miocene) collision of the Indian Plate and the Asian Plate and the whole region is still tectonically and seismically active. The several scattered and isolated basins were receptacles for Cenozoic sediments, often coarse grained at the base and becoming finer in the upper part, when lacustrine conditions prevailed. Widespread uplift and tectonic activity in the Miocene was followed by another cycle of deposition but through much of China erosion has been a dominant feature. The pioneer work of Lee (1939) and the classic syntheses of Teilhard de Chardin (1941) and Movius (1948) led to recognition in the Yellow River basin of a succession of sedimentary cycles, separated by erosion intervals and the following scheme was developed:

Young alluvium
    Panchiao erosion
Malan Loess
    Chingshui erosion
Upper Sanmenian-Choukoutienian Reddish Clay
    Huangshui erosion

factory. A pumice from Sangiran sites 10 and 12 is reported to have a radiometric age of 830,000 years and tektites from the top of the Kabuh beds at Sangiran were dated at 710,000 years (Jacob 1975). Basalts from the Muriah volcanic complex some 80 km north of Trinil have been dated as close to 500,000 years (Von Koeningswald 1962, Evernden and Curtis 1965) and are said to be from volcanic breccias that contain a typical Trinil vertebrate fauna. There is thus quite a scatter in age estimates. Preliminary results of a paleomagnetic study are not definitive (Semah *et al.* 1981) but give weak indications of a reversed polarity field through most of the Pucangan Formation, with a strong reversed signal in and near the diatomite zone (see Fig. 7A). In contrast, the Kabuh beds show normal polarity, with the reversal not far from the contact with the Pucangan. While it is possible that this change is at the base of the Jaramillo event, it is equally likely that it represents the Brunhes/Matayuma transition with an age of 0.73 million years. The rather uncertain normal magnetization at the bottom of the Pucangan and top of the upper Kalibeng Formation might possibly represent the Olduvai event. This is not incompatible with the analysis by Siesser and Orchiston (1978) of forminifera in claystone attached to a mandible from the lower Pucangan beds, which they considered to be Pliocene with a minimum age of 1.6 million years.

The juvenile mandible from Kedung Brubus, found in 1890, and the child skull discovered in 1936 at Perning, near Mojokerto, although widely separated in space, have both been regarded as about 1.9 million years old on the basis of age determinations on pumice from Mojokerto and on andesite from Kedung Brubus (Jacob 1975). Doubt has been cast on the stratigraphic assignment of the Mojokerto skull, which Sartono

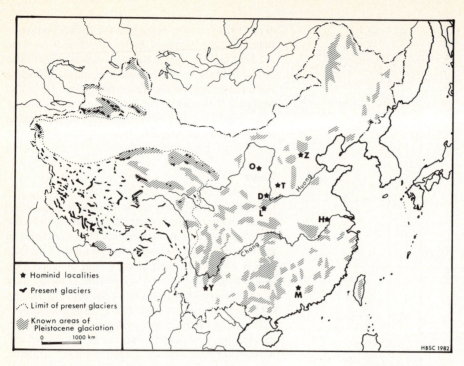

Figure 8. *Sketch map showing the distribution of existing glaciers in China and the main areas affected by glaciers in the Pleistocene (after Sun et al. 1981). The major hominid localities are shown by stars as follows: Y—Yuanmou; L—Lantian; Z—Zhoukoudian; H—Hexian; D—Dali; M—Maba; T—Dingcun; O—Ordos.*

Lower Sanmenian Red Clay (Nihowan Beds)
    Fenho erosion
Pliocene Beds (including Red Clays with Hipparion)

The Nihowan fauna includes *Proboscihipparion, Equus sanmeniensis* and *Elephas planifrons* and is regarded as of Villafranchian age. The Upper Sanmenian fauna contains the same *Equus* species, lacks *Proboscihipparion* and has a more advanced elephant, *Elephas hysudricus*, regarded as Middle Pleistocene. The Malan loess is late Pleistocene, associated with *Equus hemionus* and *Elephas namadicus*. The classic areas are generally north of the Qin Ling range and correlation with the area to the south is complicated by the fact that North China and South China are different zoogeographic provinces (Pei 1957). In the south, the place of *Elephas* is generally taken by *Stegodon*, although *Elephas* may also occur, and *Ailuropoda*—the so-called "giant panda"—is often present, thus providing a link with Java and other parts of the Siva-Malayan geographic region. Li (1981) suggests that four sub-divisions may be recognized and other groupings of local faunas have been proposed (Ji 1982; Wang and Ouyang 1982). A stratigraphic scheme of classification proposed by Liu *et al.* (1964) provides the general framework now being followed by many Chinese workers and Liu's tables have been translated in a valuable survey by Chang (1977). Aigner (1972) has suggested faunal and climatic correlations with the European sequence. Useful data on recent views are also presented by Howells and Tsuchitani (1977).

Glaciers are found at present in the high Tibetan Plateau and in the Tian Shan mountains on the north side of the Tarim basin. During the Pleistocene these glaciers were more extensive but eastern Tibet and the adjoining highlands of Sichuan and northern Yunnan (much of which is over 4,000 metres above sea level) also harboured major glaciers and there is good evidence for glaciation in other highland areas (see Fig. 8). In some valleys the ice descended as low as 3,000 metres and is

even reported as extending below this level into the lower reaches of the Yangtze River. A number of separate glacial stages can be distinguished in eastern China and each is apparently associated with its own distinctive till deposits. Five glacial stages have been named the Hongya (oldest), Poyang, Taku, Lushan and Tali glaciations and there is also a phase of periglacial activity, called the Dongcheng, between the Hongya and the Poyang (see Sun *et al.* 1981).

One of the effects of glacial activity is the production of large quantities of finely ground rock or mineral particles, often called "rock flour," and this material is carried away from the edge of the ice by meltwater. The finest fraction is removed by streams but the silty material is left on the outwash plains and is readily carried away by the wind to be deposited eventually somewhere downwind of the source as loess. Similar material can also be derived from desert areas where, as in the outwash plains of glaciated regions, there is no vegetation to bind the surface. China has received dust from both sources and loess covers more than three quarters of a million square kilometres, commonly 50 m thick and in places reaching as much as 500 m. The major area is in the basin of the Yellow River (Huang), which derives its name from the discolouration caused by the constant load of yellow loess that it carries. The Chinese loess is fully described by Liu and Chang (1962) and has been reviewed briefly by Brown (1977). The northern limit of the loess coincides remarkably well with the Great Wall and the southern margin is formed by the Qin Ling range. The "Loess Plateau" of eastern Gansu, central and northern Shaanxi and Shanxi is very fertile, as are also the loess areas of Henan and the redeposited loessic alluvial plains of the Yellow River basin. Three major phases of loess deposition are recognized, the Wucheng, Lishi, and Malan. The Wucheng loess is associated with the Nihowan fauna. Paleomagnetism has furnished dating control for the loess sequences (Heller and Liu 1982). A much simplified outline is presented here in Figure 9 to show the relative ages assigned to the glacial and loess stages and the relative positions of the principal hominid fossil remains.

The oldest hominid so far found consists of two incisors

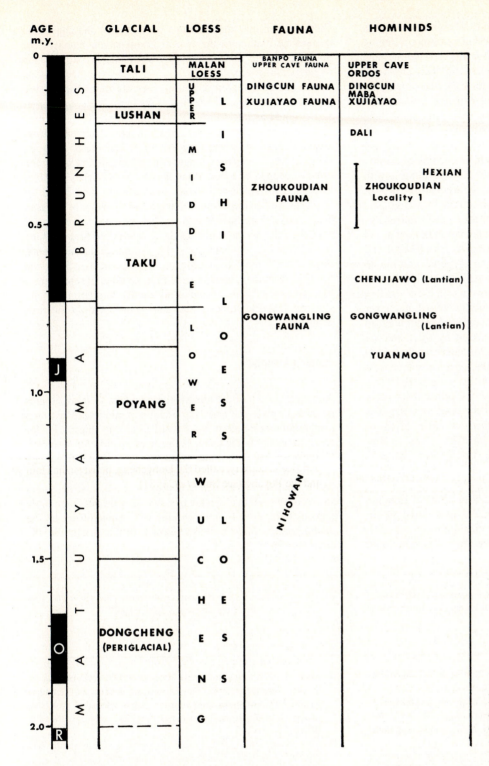

AGE m.y.	GLACIAL	LOESS	FAUNA	HOMINIDS

Figure 9. *Simplified climato-stratigraphic scheme for China to show the relative positions of the main hominid occurrences.*

recovered in red clays at Yuanmou, 100 km northwest of Kunming in Yunnan Province, southwest China. The 650 m thick Yuanmou Formation is divided into four members and has a good mammalian fauna. There has been some disagreement about the environmental interpretation but Ji and Li (1979) have reinterpreted the fauna as representing a subtropical assemblage of early Pleistocene age. Paleomagnetic study of the Yuanmou Formation led to placement of the hominid fossils at 1.7 million years (see Atlas 1980). However, this assessment has been revised recently and the fossils are now placed at the Jaramillo

Event with an estimated age of around 900,000 years BP (Wu Rukang, personal communication).

A skull cap from red clays at Gongwangling ("Lantian Man") near Xi'an in southern Shaanxi, has been placed by paleomagnetic dating between the Jaramillo Event and the base of the Brunhes (Ma *et al.* 1978). The Lantian jawbone came from similar deposits near Chinjiawo village, about 30 km from the skull site and is assigned to the lower part of the Brunhes Normal paleomagnetic epoch. Faunal comparisons have been made by Ji (1980).

The most famous area for hominid fossils is near the village of Zhoukoudian (Choukoutien), some 45 km southwest of Beijing (Peking), where the Western Hills rise from the great North China Plain. The Ordovician limestones here contain many caves and fissure fillings and twenty-two localities have been found, although only a few have yielded hominid remains or artifacts. The most extensive is Locality 1 or the "Lower Cave," in Dragon Bone Hill, where the filling of a former cave measures 140 m in length (east-west) and 40 m in breadth at its widest part. The original cave roof collapsed into the deposits from time to time as erosion thinned it and the present site is essentially only the filling, as with the South African sites. The thickness of the accumulated deposit is more than 40 m and it has been divided into 13 stratigraphic units, numbered from top to bottom. The basal gravel and reddish silt includes glacially worn pebbles and pollens indicating a cold environment, most probably the terminal part of the Taku Glacial stage. The first stone tools are found just above the unit but no hominid remains occur with them. A sandy layer follows and is rich in hyena bones and coprolites, above which occur the first hominid fossils, which continue sporadically through the upper part of the breccia. Ash layers, burned seeds and bones attest to the use of fire. Climatic changes indicated by the fauna are discussed by Xu and Ouyang (1982), who deduce an alternation of colder and warmer stages through the sequence and suggest correlation with Kukla's (1975, 1977) loess cycles D, E, F. This is in agreement with the faunal correlations. Some of the other localities in the vicinity cover parts of the same time range as Locality 1 (Localities 2, 3, 13) but others are older (12,18) or younger (15, 22, 4, the latter connected to "New Cave" or Xindong Cave). Very much younger is the "Upper Cave," which is late Pleistocene and has yielded some fine hominid material as well as a radiocarbon date of 18,500 years BP.

An important discovery was made in 1980 in Longtan (Dragon-Pool) Cave at Hexian, Anhui Province, some 60 km southwest of Nanjing (Nanking). The cranium is almost complete and was the first *Homo erectus* skull to be found in South China. A rich mammalian fauna is distinctive and appears to correspond neither to the typical Zhoukoudian fauna of the north nor to the *Ailuropoda-Stegodon* fauna of South China (Huang *et al.* 1982).

A nearly complete cranium, recently described by Wu (1981) as Dali Man is regarded as the earliest *Homo sapiens* and is dated as late Middle Pleistocene (circa 0.15-0.2 m.y. BP). Maba Man is represented by an incomplete cranium from a cave deposit in Guangdong Province. The site of Dingcun (Ting-ts'un) comprises a lengthy stretch of alluvial sands and gravels, capped by loess, along the east bank of the Fen River in Shanxi Province and it has yielded more than 2,000 artifacts as well as three hominid teeth and a portion of parietal. The Ordos site in Inner Mongolia also consists of river terrace deposits and was the source of the first hominid find in China in 1922 (an incisor) but later yielded some cranial fragments, three limb bones and some stone implements. Like the material from the Upper Cave at Zhoukoudian, it represents a modern type of man, although not totally Mongoloid. Many sites of late Pleistocene age also occur, mainly in cave deposits.

CONCLUSION

Although in each of the regions discussed above it now seems possible to place the more important hominid fossils within a local relative chronology, there is still a considerable margin for error; for example the changes in age estimation for Yuanmou Man from 1.7 to 0.9 million years. The existence of this range of uncertainty must be recognized in the formulation of theories on the pathways of human evolution on a global scale. Great strides have been made in the past two decades but much work remains to be done by inter-disciplinary teams to firm-up the dating framework, as well as to provide further insight into the environments of the past.

NOTES

1. It is hoped that no offence will be taken by women at this conventional use of the masculine form which is employed for simplicity but is intended to embrace human males and females alike; who, after all, is interested in the ancestry of "personkind"?

REFERENCES

Aigner, J. S. 1972. Relative dating of North Chinese faunal and cultural complexes. *Arctic Anthropology* 9(2):36-79.

Aronson, J. L., Schmitt, T. J., Walter, R. C., Taieb, M., Tiercelin, J. J., Johanson, D. C., Naeser, C. W., and Nairn, A. E. M. 1977. New geochronologic and paleomagnetic data for the hominid-bearing Hadar Formation of Ethiopia. *Nature* 267:323-327.

Atlas of Primitive Man in China. 1980. Compiled by Institute of Vertebrate Paleontology and Paleoanthropology, Chinese Academy of Sciences, distributed by Van Nostrand Reinhold, New York, and Beijing: Science Press.

Behrensmeyer, A. K., and Hill, A. P. (Eds.). 1980. *Fossils in the Making,* University of Chicago Press, Chicago.

Bemmelen, R. W. Van. 1949. *The Geology of Indonesia.* Vol. 1A, Martinus Nijhoff, the Hague.

Bishop, W. A., and Miller, J. A. (Eds.). 1972. *Calibration of Hominid Evolution,* Scottish Academic Press, Edinburgh.

Brain, C. K. 1981. *The Hunters or the Hunted?* University of Chicago Press, Chicago.

Brown, F. H. 1977. Notes on Chinese Loess, in: *Paleoanthropology in the People's Republic of China,* National Academy of Sciences, Committee on Scholarly Communication with the People's Republic of China, Report No. 4, (W. W. Howells and P. J. Tsuchitani, Eds.), pp. 168-178, Washington, D.C.

Brown, F. H., and Cerling, C. E. 1982. Stratigraphic significance of the Tulu Bor Tuff of the Koobi Fora Formation. *Nature* 299:212-215.

Butzer, K. W., and Isaac, G. Ll. (Eds.). 1975. *After the Australopithecines,* Mouton, the Hague.

Cerling, T. E., and Brown, F. H. 1982. Tuffaceous marker horizons in the Koobi Fora region and the lower Omo valley. *Nature* 299:216-221.

Chang, K. C. 1977. Chinese paleoanthropology. *Ann. Rev. Anthropol.* 6:137-159.

Conroy, C. C., Jolly, C. J., Cramer, D., and Kalb, J. E. 1978. Newly discovered fossil hominid skull from the Afar depression, Ethiopia. *Nature* 276:67-70.

Cox, A., Doell, R. R., and Dalrymple, G. B. 1964. Geomagnetic polarity epochs. *Science* 143:351-352.

Day, M. H. 1977. *Guide to Fossil Man*, 3rd Ed., University of Chicago Press, Chicago.

Eberl, B. 1930. *Die Eiszietenvolge im nördlichen Alpenvorlander*, Benno Filser, Augsbrug.

Evernden, J. F. and Curtis, G. H. 1965. The potassium-argon dating of late Cenozoic rocks in East Africa and Italy. *Curr. Anthropol.* 6:343-385.

Harris, J. M., and White, T. D. 1979. Evolution of the Plio-Pleistocene African Suidae. *Trans. Am. Phil. Soc.* 69:128 pp.

Hay, R. L. 1976. *Geology of the Olduvai Gorge*, University of California Press, Berkeley.

Heller, F., and Liu, T-s. 1982. Magnetostratigraphic dating of loess deposits in China. *Nature* 300:431-433.

Hooijer, D. A. 1951. The geological age of *Pithecanthropus, Meganthropus* and *Gigantopithecus. Am. J. Phys. Anthropol.* 9:265-281.

Hooijer, D. A. 1962. The Middle Pleistocene fauna of Java, in: *Evolution und Hominisation* (G. Kurth, Ed.), pp. 108-111, Gustav Fischer, Stuttgart.

Howells, W. W., and Tsuchitani, P. J., (Eds.) 1977. *Paleoanthropology in the People's Republic of China*, National Academy of Sciences, Committee on Scholarly Communication with the People's Republic of China, Report No. 4, Washington. D.C.

Huang, W., Fang, D. and, Ye, X. 1982. Preliminary study on the fossil hominid skull and fauna of Hexian, Anhui. *Verte. PalAsiatica* 20(3):248-254 (in Chinese; English summary pp. 255-256).

Isaac, G. Ll. 1972. Chronology and the tempo of cultural change during Pleistocene, in: *Calibration of Hominid Evolution* (W. W. Bishop and J. A. Miller, Eds.), pp. 381-430, Scottish Academic Press, Edinburgh.

Jacob, T. 1975. Morphology and paleoecology of early man in Java, in: *Paleoanthropology, Morphology and Paleoecology* (R. H. Tuttle, Ed.), pp.311-325, Mouton, The Hauge.

Jacob, T. 1980. The *Pithecanthropus* of Indonesia: Phenotype, genetics and ecology, in: *Current Argument on Early Man* (L. K. Königsson, Ed.), pp. 170-179, Pergamon Press (for the Royal Swedish Academy of Sciences), Oxford.

Jacob, T. 1981. Solo Man and Peking Man, in: Homo erectus: *Papers in Honour of Davidson Black* (B. A. Sigmon and J. S. Cybulski, Eds.), pp. 87-104, University of Toronto Press, Toronto.

Jacob, T., Soejono, R. P., Freeman, L. G., and Brown, F. H. 1978. Stone tools from Mid-Pleistocene sediments in Java. *Science* 202:885-887.

Ji, H-x. 1980. The subdivision of Quaternary mammalian faunas of Lantian district, Shaanxi. *Verte. PalAsiatica* 18(3):220-227 (in Chinese; English summary pp.227-228).

Ji, H-x. 1982. The living environment of the Quaternary mammalian faunas in South China. *Verte. PalAsiatica* 20(2):148-154 (in Chinese; English summary p. 154).

Ji, H-x., and Li, Y-x. 1979. Note on the living environment of Youanmou Man. *Verte. PalAsiatica* 17(4):318-324 (in Chinese; English summary pp.324-326).

Johanson, D. C., Taieb, M., and Coppens, Y. 1982. Pliocene hominids from the Hadar Formation, Ethiopia (1973-1977): Stratigraphic, chronologic, and paleoenvironmental contexts, with notes on hominid morphology and systematics. *Am. J. Phys. Anthropol.* 57(4):373-402.

Kalb, J. E., Oswald, E. B., Tebedge, S., Mebrate, A., Tola, E., and Peak, D. 1982a. Geology and stratigraphy of Neogene deposits, Middle Awash Valley, Ethiopia. *Nature* 298:17-25.

Kalb, J. E., Jolly, C. J., Tebedge, S., Mebrate, A., Smart, C. Oswald, E. R., Whitehead, P. E., Wood, C. B., Adefris, T. and Rawn-Schatzinger, V. 1982b. Vertebrate faunas from the Awash Group, Middle Awash Valley, Afar, Ethiopia. *J. Verte. Paleont.* 2(2):237-258.

Kalb, J. E., Wood, C. B, Smart, C., Oswald, E. B,. Mebrate, A., Tebedge, S., and Whitehead, P. E. 1980. Preliminary geology and paleontology of the Bodo D'Ar hominid site, Afar, Ethiopia. *Palaeogeo. Palaeoclim. Palaeoecol.* 30:107-120.

Koenigswald, G. H. R. von. 1949. The discovery of early man in Java and southern China, in: *Early Man in the Far East: Studies in Physical Anthropology* (W. W. Howells, Ed.), pp. 83-98, Philadelphia.

Koenigswald, G. H. R. von. 1951. Geology and paleontology, in: *Morphology of Solo Man* (F. R. Weidenreich, Ed.), pp. 219-221, American Museum of Natural History, Anthropological Papers.

Koenigswald, G. H. R. von. 1962. Das absolute Alter des *pithecanthropus erectus* Dubois, in: *Evolution und Hominisation* (G. Kurth, Ed.), pp. 112-119, Gustav Fischer, Stuttgart.

Kukla, G. J. 1970. Correlation between loesses and deep sea sediments. *Geologiska Föreningen i Stockholm Förhandlingar* 92:148-180.

Kukla, G. J. 1975. Loess stratigraphy of Central Europe, in: *After the Australopithecines* (K. W. Butzer and G. Ll. Isaac, Eds.), pp. 99-188, Mouton, the Hague.

Kukla, G. J. 1977. Pleistocene land-sea correlation, 1: Europe. *Earth Science Reviews* 13:307-374.

Leakey, L. S. B., Evernden, J. H., and Curtis, G. H. 1961. The age of Bed 1, Olduvai Gorge, Tanganyika. *Nature* 191:478-479.

Leakey, M. D. 1981. Tracks and tools. *Phil. Trans. R. Soc. Lond. B* 292:95-102.

Leakey, M. D., and Hay, R. L. 1979. Pliocene footprints in the Laetoli Beds at Laetolil, N. Tanzania. *Nature* 278:317-323.

Leakey, M. D., Hay, R. L., Curtis, G. H., Drake, R. E., Jackes, M. K., and White, T. D. 1976. Fossil hominids from the Laetolil Beds, Tanzania. *Nature* 262:460-466.

Lee, J. S. 1939. *The Geology of China*, Murby, London.

Li, Y. 1981. On the subdivisions and evolution of the Quaternary mammalian faunas of South China. *Verte. PalAsiatica* 19(1):67-75 (in Chinese; English summary pp. 75-76).

Liu, T. S., and Chang, C. Y. 1962. The Loess of China. *Acta Geologica Sinica* 42 (in Chinese).

Liu, T. S., Liu, M. H., Wu, T. J., and Cheng, C. H. 1964. On the stratigraphic division of the Chinese Quaternary, in: *Problems of the Geology of the Quaternary*, pp. 45-64 , Compiled by Institute of Geology, Academia Sinica (in Chinese).

Ma, X., Qian, F., Li, P., and Ju, S. 1978. Paleomagnetic dating of Lantian Man. *Verte. PalAsiatica* 16(4):238-243 (in Chinese).

McFadden, P. L., Brock, A., and Partridge, T. C. 1979. Palaeomagnetism and the age of the Makapansgat hominid site. *Earth and Planetary Science Letters* 44:373-382.

Mankinen, E. A. and Dalrymple, G. B. 1979. Revised geomagnetic polarity time scale for the interval 0-5 m.y.B.P. *Jour. Geophys. Res.* 84:615-626.

Movius, H. L. 1948. The Lower Paleolithic cultures of southern and eastern Asia. *Trans. Am. Phil. Soc. n.s.* 38(4):329-420.

Oakley, K. P. 1953. Dating fossil human remains, in: *Anthropology Today* (A. L. Kroeber, Ed.), pp. 43-56, University of Chicago Press, Chicago.

Oakley, K. P. 1966. *Frameworks for Dating Early Man*, Aldine, Chicago.

Pei, W-c. 1957. The zoogeographical divisions of Quaternary mammalian faunas in China. *Verte. PalAsiatica* 1(1):9-24.

Penck, A., and Brückner, E. 1909. *Die Alpen im Eiszeitalter*, Tauchnitz, Leipzig.

Ruddiman, W. F., and McIntyre, A. 1973. Time-transgressive deglacial retreat of polar water from the North Atlantic. *Quaternary Research* 3:117-130.

Ruddiman, W. F., and McIntyre, A. 1976. Northeast Atlantic paleoclimatic changes over the past 600,000 years, in: *Investigation of Late Quaternary Paleoceanography and Paleoclimatology* (R. M. Cline and R. D. Hays, Eds.), pp. 111-146, Geological Society of America, Memoir 145.

Santa Luca, A. P. 1980. *The Ngandong Fossil Hominids: A Comparative Study of a Far Eastern* Homo Erectus *Group, Yale University Publications in Anthropology* 78.

Sartono, S. 1976. Genesis of the Solo terraces. *Modern Quaternary Research in S.E. Asia* 2:1-21.

Sartono, S. 1979. The stratigraphy of the Sambungmacan site, Central Java. *Modern Quaternary Research in S.E. Asia* 5:83-88.

Sartono, S., Semah, F., Astadiredja, K. A. S., Sukendarmono, M., and Djubiantono, T. 1981. The age of *Homo modjokertentis. Modern Quaternary Research in S.E. Asia* 6:91-102.

Schaefer, I. 1956. Sur la division du Quaternaire dans l'avantpays des Alpes en Allemagne. *IV INQUA Congress Actes* II:910.

Semah, F., Sartono, S., Ziam, Y., and Djubiantono, T. 1981. A paleomagnetic study of the Plio-Pleistocene sediments from Sangiran and Simo (Central Java): Initial results. *Modern Quaternary Research in S.E. Asia* 6:103-110.

Shackleton, N. J., and Opdyke, N. D. 1973. Oxygen isotope and paleomagnetic stratigraphy of equatorial Pacific core V28-238: Oxygen isotope temperatures and ice volumes on a 105 and 106 year scale. *Quaternary Research* 3:39-55.

Shackleton, N. J., and Opdyke, N. D. 1976. Oxygen isotope and paleomagnetic stratigraphy of Pacific core V28-239, late Pliocene to latest Pleistocene, in: *Investigations of late Quaternary Paleoceanography and Paleoclimatology* (R. M. Cline and R. D. Hays, Eds.), pp. 449-464, Geological Society of America, Memoir 145.

Siesser, W. G., and Orchiston, D. W. 1978. Micropaleontological re-assessment of the age of *Pithecanthropus* mandible C from Sangiran, Indonesia. *Modern Quaternary Research in S.E. Asia* 4:25-30.

Sun, D-g., Chou, M-l., and Wu, X-h. 1981. Brief notes on Quaternary glaciations in China, in: *Quaternary glaciations in the Northern Hemisphere. Report No. 6* (V. Sibrava and F. W. Shotton, Eds.), pp. 244-262, Geological Survey for INQUA, Prague.

Taieb, M. 1974. Evolution Quaternaire du bassin de l'Awash, Ph.D. dissertation, l'Université de Paris VI, 390 pp. (unpublished).

Teilhard de Chardin, P. 1941. *Early Man in China*, Institute de Géo-Bioloie, Pekin.

Wang, L., and Ouyang, L. 1982. Subdivision of *Ailuropoda-Stegodon* fauna by applying cluster analysis. *Verte. PalAsiatica* 20(3):257-263 (in Chinese; English summary p. 263).

Wu, X. 1981. A well-preserved cranium of an archaic type of *Homo sapiens* from Dali, China. *Scientia Sinica* 24(5):530-641.

Xu, Q., and Ouyang, L. 1982. Climatic change during Peking Man's time. *Acta Anthropologica Sinica* 1(1):80-88 (in Chinese, English summary pp. 89-90).

Zagwijn, W. H. l975a. Chronostratigrafie en biostratigrafie: Indeling van het Kwartair op grond van veranderingen in vegetatie en klimaat, in: *Toelichting bij geologische overzichtskaarten van Nederland* (W. H. Zagwijn en C. J. van Staalduinen, Eds.), pp. 109-114, Rijks Geologische Dienst, Haarlem.

Zagwijn, W. H. 1975b. Variations in climate as shown by pollen analysis, especially in the Lower Pleistocene of Europe, in: *Ice Ages: Ancient and Modern* (A. E. Wright and F. Mosley, Eds.), pp. 137-152, Steel House Press, Liverpool.

Zagwijn, W. H., and Staalduinen, C. J. van. 1975. *Toelichting bij geologische overzichtskaarten van Nederland,* Rijks Geologische Dienst, Haarlem.

Reconstruction of *Australopithecus afarensis* from the early Pliocene of East Africa. Illustration from *Primate Adaptation and Evolution*, Academic Press, 1988.

Part II
Australopithecus and Hominid Origins

This part deals with the earliest hominids, the australopithecines. This is one of the true glamour areas of human evolution as these fossils document the initial divergence of the human lineage from that of our ape ancestors (see Part III for theoretical discussions of human origins). The articles in this part cover a wide range of topics, including systematics, phylogeny, locomotion, diet, and paleoenvironments. Although the first australopithecine was found in 1924, and many more were recovered in the succeeding two decades (see Chapter 19), new information added about this group of hominids has exploded in the last twenty years. As a result, the chapters of this part are all relatively recent, and the final chapter was prepared specifically for this volume. The articles in this section have been chosen to present something of a revisionist history of the discipline. That is, they reflect a diversity of issues that, in our view, are very much alive today rather than other issues that have waxed and waned over the years.

"The Origin and Adaptive Radiation of the Australopithecines" by John T. Robinson provides an overview of this group when they were known primarily from South Africa and the finds from Olduvai Gorge in East Africa were just being announced. In contrast with many authorities of the time, and later decades as well, Robinson emphasized the diversity rather than the uniformity of early hominids. In his view, the gracile *Australopithecus africanus* and robust *Paranthropus robustus*, both from South Africa, are representative of two distinct lineages with major differences in dietary adaptation (see also Chapter 15). *Paranthropus* was a plant eater, while *Australopithecus* had a dentition more similar to later hominines and "included a more carnivorous element" (p. 90). He also notes that the sites yielding the different taxa indicate a wet environment for *Australopithecus* and a drier one for *Paranthropus* (see also Chapter 16). Robinson emphasizes that bipedal locomotion is the major adaptive feature that separated the australopithecines from ancestral apes (see Chapters 17, 18). He notes that since many primates, as well as other animals, use tools, it would not be unexpected that both *Australopithecus* and *Paranthropus* used some type of tools (see also Chapter 14), but suggests that the evidence put forth for this is weak.

"A Systematic Assessment of Early African Hominids" by Donald C. Johanson and Tim. D. White has been the point of departure for studies of early hominid evolution over the past decade. This paper provided the first thorough description of the earliest hominid *Australopithecus afarensis* from early Pliocene deposits at Hadar, Ethiopia and Laetoli, Tanzania, and a broader reassessment of the phylogeny of hominid evolution.

Johanson and White argue that there is but a single fossil hominid species from Hadar and Laetoli and this taxon represents the common ancestor of all later hominids. In their view, *A. afarensis* shares primitive cranial and dental features with extant great apes and Miocene hominids, but shows pelvic and hindlimb features indicative of well-developed adaptation to bipedal walking. In their view, *A. afarensis* gave rise to two distinct lineages of later hominids—a robust lineage consisting of *A. africanus*, *A. robustus*, and *A. boisei* and a gracile lineage, *Homo habilis*, *H. erectus*, and *H. sapiens*. The initial publication of this paper met with considerable dispute over both the allocation of Hadar and Laetoli fossils to a single taxon and the hypothesized phylogeny. As noted in other chapters of this part, both issues remain alive and are debated today.

"Phylogenetic Analysis of Early Hominids," by Randall Skelton, Henry M. McHenry, and Gerald Drawhorn, is one of the first and most thorough attempts to analyze early hominid phylogeny using the techniques of quantitative phylogenetic (cladistic) analysis. Their analysis is based on 69 traits which they discuss in terms of 12 complexes arranged according to the way they are distributed among the four taxa being considered—*A. afarensis*, *A. africanus*, *A. robustus/boisei*, and *Homo habilis*. In addition to this character analysis, the authors discuss several of the resulting phylogenies and compare their results with other proposed phylogenies. They find that in the most parsimonious phylogeny *A. afarensis* gives rise to *A. africanus*, and *A. africanus*, in turn, gives rise to *A. robustus* and *H. habilis*, these last two taxa sharing a common ancestor since *A. africanus* (see Chapter 19 for further discussion and comparison of these alternate phylogenies).

Chapter 13, "2.5 myr *Australopithecus boisei* from West of Lake Turkana, Kenya" by Alan Walker, Richard E. Leakey, John M. Harris, and Frank H. Brown, describes the "black skull," an early robust australopithecine that led to considerable rethinking of many of the phylogenies discussed in earlier chapters. This skull showed the unexpected combination of very primitive basicranial anatomy as in *A. afarensis* with the presumably derived large dentition and broad face of *A. robustus* and *A. boisei*. As discussed in Chapter 19, there are several ways to reinterpret early hominid phylogeny in light of this new information.

Chapter 14, "Hand of *Paranthropus robustus* from Member 1, Swartkrans: Fossil Evidence for Tool Behavior" by Randall L. Susman, argues that *P. robustus* had a hand morphology consistent with tool manufacture. In Susman's view, the making of tools cannot be advanced as a unique characteristic of the genus *Homo* nor can the lack of such abilities in *Paranthropus* have caused their extinction through competition. Susman's allocation of the hand bones is based on the overwhelming abundance of cranial remains of *P. robustus* in these deposits and on their difference from hand remains attributed to *Homo erectus* in the same cave (see also Chapter 10, Trinkaus and Long 1990; Susman 1991 a,b).

In Chapter 15, "The Diet of South African Australopithecines Based on a Study of Dental Microwear," Frederick Grine demonstrates differences in occlusal wear on the deciduous and permanent molar teeth of *Australopithecus* and *Paranthropus* from South Africa. *Paranthropus* shows greater heterogeneity of wear and more pits than *Australopithecus*, suggesting a diet of substantially harder objects (see also Grine 1991; Ungar and Grine 1981).

In Chapter 16, "Ecological and Adaptive Changes Associated with Early Hominid Evolution," Elisabeth Vrba relates major events in early hominid phylogeny to ecological changes in Africa as reflected in antelope evolution. She argues that the origin of the taxa *Australopithecus*, *Paranthropus*, and *Homo* as well as the extinction of the robust lineage are probably coincident with major climatic changes in Africa and in turn to global climatic events (see also Vrba 1988).

As noted by Robinson in Chapter 10, one of the major issues in early hominid evolution is the locomotor abilities of *Australopithecus* and the origin of bipedal walking. In Chapter 17, "Biomechanical Perspectives on the Lower Limb of Early Hominids," C. Owen Lovejoy argues that australopithecines show the same biomechanical pattern as modern humans, ex-

cept in one respect in which *Australopithecus* is better adapted for bipedalism. He finds no evidence for intermediate adaptation in *Australopithecus*. This article was written before the discovery of the very complete skeletal remains from Hadar (Johanson *et al.* 1982) but in Lovejoy's view (see Chapter 10, Chapter 22; Lovejoy 1988; Johanson and Edey 1981) the remains of *A. afarensis* support the earlier argument of a complete adaptation to modern bipedalism in the earliest hominids.

Chapter 18, "Arboreality and Bipedality in the Hadar Hominids" by Randall Susman, Jack T. Stern, Jr. and William L. Jungers, offers a very different perspective of the locomotor habits of *A. afarensis* from that put forth by Lovejoy. While these authors agree with Lovejoy that *A. afarensis* was a biped, they argue that the nature of its bipedal behavior, as reflected in many aspects of the foot and pelvis, was different from that of later hominids. Moreover, they argue that this early hominid retained many primitive adaptations in its forelimb and foot that indicate that arboreal climbing was a significant aspect of its behavioral repertoire (see also Stern and Susman 1983, 1991; Susman and Stern 1991).

Chapter 19, "Australopithecine Taxonomy and Phylogeny: Historical Background and Recent Interpretation," is an up-to-date review of this active and contentious area of human evolution. It summarizes recent finds and interpretations and places them in a historical perspective. As Grine's chapter emphasizes, each new fossil discovery seems to force an expansion of alternatives and a reanalysis of earlier views. Clearly our appreciation of the evolutionary and adaptive events in this aspect of human evolution is itself only in the incipient stages.

REFERENCES

Grine, F. E. 1981. Trophic differences between 'gracile' and 'robust' australopithecines: A scanning electron microscope analysis of occlusal event. *S. Afr. J. Sci.* 77:203-230.

Johanson, D. C. and Edey, M. 1981. *Lucy: The Beginnings of Humankind.* Simon & Schuster, New York.

Johanson, D. C. *et al.* 1982. Pliocene hominid fossils from Hadar, Ethiopia. *Am. J. Phys. Anthropol.* 57:373-719.

Lovejoy, C. O. 1988. Evolution of human walking. *Sci. Amer.* 259:118-125.

Stern, J. T. Jr. and Susman, R. L. 1983. The locomotor anatomy of *Australopithecus afarensis. Am. J. Phys. Anthropol.* 60:279-317.

Stern, J. T. Jr. and Susman, R. L. 1991. "Total morphological pattern" versus the "magic trait": Conflicting approaches to the study of early hominid bipedalism. *Origine(s) de la bipedie chez les hominides.* (Cahiers de Paleoanthropologie) (Y. Coppens and B. Senut, Eds.), pp. 99-111, Editions du CNRS, Paris.

Susman, R. L. 1991a. Species attribution of the Swartkrans thumb metacarpals: Reply to Drs. Trinkaus and Long. *Am. J. Phys. Anthropol.* 86:549-552.

Susman, R. L. 1991b. Who made the Oldowan tools? Fossil evidence for tool behavior in Plio-Pleistocene hominids. *J. Anthropological Res.* 47(2):129-151.

Susman, R. L. and Stern, J. T. Jr. 1991. Locomotor behavior of early hominids: Epistemology and fossil evidence. *Origine(s) de la bipedie chez les hominides.* (Cahiers de Paleoanthropologie) (Y. Coppens and B. Senut, Eds.), pp. 121-131, Editions du CNRS, Paris.

Trinkaus, E. and Long, J. C. 1990. Species attribution of the Swartkrans Member 1 first metacarpals: SK 84 and SKX 5020. *Am. J. Phys. Anthropol.* 83:419-424.

Ungar, P. S. and Grine, F. E. 1991. Incisor size and wear in *Australopithecus africanus* and *Paranthropus robustus. J. Hum. Evol.* 20: 313-340.

Vrba, E. S. 1988. Late Pliocene climatic events and hominid evolution, in: *Evolutionary History of the "Robust" Australopithecines* (F. E. Grine, Ed.), pp. 405-426, Aldine de Gruyter, Hawthorne, New York.

AUSTRALOPITHECUS

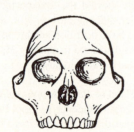

PARANTHROPUS

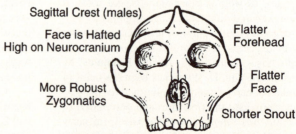

10

The Origin and Adaptive Radiation
of the Australopithecines

J. T. Robinson

INTRODUCTION

Understanding of the australopithecines has advanced enormously since the first paper concerning them was published in 1925. At first material of this group was known from South Africa only and scientific opinion was strongly inclined to discount the views of the local workers. This situation has changed greatly: it is now generally agreed that the australopithecines are hominids, not pongids. While by far the greater proportion of the considerable number of specimens now known are South African, there are very encouraging signs that other areas will contribute significantly to our knowledge. It is greatly to be hoped that these promises are to he fulfilled since, in my opinion at least, australopithecines were spread across the Old World from South Africa to the Far East and it would be very valuable to have specimens from widely separated localities.

The chief purpose of the present paper is to speculate about the nature of the forces which operated to bring the australopithecine group into existence and which controlled its evolution.

AUSTRALOPITHECINE TAXONOMY

Any consideration of the evolution of the australopithecines must first take notice of the taxonomy of this group. This has been dealt with in a number of publications (e.g. Robinson 1954a, 1954b, 1956 and 1961) but will briefly be referred to here again. The reason for this is that without recognition of taxonomic differentiation within the group, it is futile to consider adaptive radiation within it. Furthermore, it would appear that many authors tend to think of the group as being essentially taxonomically uniform and make statements purporting to refer to all the known australopithecines when this is not the case. As an example may be quoted the statement "...the whole canine-premolar complex is reduced in the australopithecines..." (Washburn and Howell 1960). This hardly does justice to the fact that the whole complex, as listed by these authors, differs very considerably in *Australopithecus* and *Paranthropus*. Furthermore, these differences have far-reaching implications. Or again the same authors in referring to the australopithecine discovery at site FLK in the Olduvai Gorge state, "It affords clear-cut evidence that these primitive hominids (i.e. the australopithecines) were to some extent carnivorous and predaceous...". Now quite apart from the fact that the interpretation here given is one of several which may be drawn from the actual evidence and is therefore not clear-cut proof the evidence concerned refers to one type of australopithecine only. In view of the fact that the dental specialisations of the two main types of australopithecine differ appreciably, it surely is unsafe to generalise from a small amount of information at one site which at the time had yielded only one type of australopithecine. Similarly, discussions about a possible osteodontokeratic culture of australopithecines (in the paper here referred to as well as in the rest of the literature) proceed as though the evidence being debated concerns australopithecines in general. In actual fact most of the evidence so far employed comes from a single site, with some additional information from two others—but all are *Australopithecus* sites. *Paranthropus* may or may not have had such a culture, but whether it did or not cannot be determined from sites which have yielded only *Australopithecus*.

The above point has been dealt with at some length, not in order to attempt to refute the views of the authors concerned, but to stress the need to remember when discussing the australopithecines that at least two types are known which differ considerably in their morphology and apparently also in their ecology and behaviour. If this fact is ignored, discussions are as likely to lead to obfuscation as to clarification of the issues involved.

SOUTH AFRICAN AUSTRALOPITHECINES

The two types of South African australopithecine are *Australopithecus africanus* DART and *Paranthropus robustus* Broom (Robinson 1954a). Previous to the latter analysis the only taxonomic analysis was that of Broom (1950) who placed the known forms in 5 species of 3 genera—but who thought that a fourth genus should be erected for the Makapan form. Several other schemes have been suggested without being legitimate taxonomic analyses lending legality to the suggested classifications. One may note here in passing that palaeo-anthropologists in general seem to pay very scant, or no, attention to the International Rules governing nomenclature. Mayr (1950) suggested placing the australopithecines and all true men together

Reprinted with permission from *Evolution und Hominization*, edited by G. Kurth, pp. 150-175, Verlag, Stuttgart. Copyright © 1962 by Stuttgarter Verlagskontor Gmbh, Stuttgart.

in the genus *Homo* so that the family Hominidae would contain the one genus alone. Washburn and Patterson (1951) suggested putting all the hominids in two genera, *Australopithecus* and *Homo*. Howell (1959) seems to agree with the latter view except that he would split the genus *Australopithecus* into two sub-genera: *A. (Australopithecus)* and *A. (Paranthropus)*.

The practising taxonomist is in the first place primarily concerned with identification and therefore looks for what are generally referred to as good diagnostic characters which enable him to distinguish as easily as possible between closely related forms. The characters adopted are arrived at empirically: that is to say, if observation shows that a particular feature, *taking its range of variation into account*, characterises the group concerned and no others, then it is a good taxonomic character. In some cases it will be found that a single character is so clearly diagnostic that it is not necessary to use others in order to identify accurately the form concerned. Usually however it is necessary to use a group of characters in order to achieve certainty of identification. Where a new form is being dealt with it is always necessary to use a constellation of characters in order to determine its relationships. The level at which a character is useful is again determined by observation. For example, in arthropods the number of bristles on a particular segment of a limb may vary from one species to another but remain constant within any one species. Such a character would be useful only at the species level. But the number of limbs or of wings, for example, are constant over far larger groups than the species and are therefore useless for distinguishing species but are invaluable as characters defining much larger taxonomic groups. Limb number, for instance, is a diagnostic arthropod character at the class level.

In this practical, workaday taxonomic sense, the characters which distinguish *Australopithecus* and *Paranthropus* are legion since the two can be distinguished by means of almost any bits of skeleton now known in both forms. This in itself is an instructive fact since at low levels of taxonomic distinction general similarity is so great that good diagnostic characters are not common. In general, it may be said that taxonomic experience in mammalogy shows that if two forms are readily distinguishable by means of almost any part of the skeleton, then it is highly unlikely that the taxonomic difference between them will be of less than generic magnitude. It does not follow, however, that generically distinct forms will necessarily differ markedly in all skeletal characters. It should be emphasised that this statement is not a theoretical one suggested as a standard for taxonomists, but is a generalisation based on what is found by experience to be the case in mammalian systematics.

There are a number of very good taxonomic characters which distinguish *Australopithecus* and *Paranthropus* according to the known material. For example the first lower deciduous molar not only allows instantaneous recognition (even when very considerably worn) of which group is being dealt with, but serves to distinguish *Paranthropus* from all other hominids in which the tooth is known (Fig. 1). Furthermore, this tooth is of the same type in *Australopithecus* as it is in all fossil and living hominines in which its nature is known. Fortunately the deciduous first lower molar is known in Pekin man and also Neanderthal man. Consequently the morphology of dm₁ serves not only to emphasize the distinction between *Paranthropus* and *Australopithecus*, but at the same time underlines the similarity between the latter and hominines. The permanent

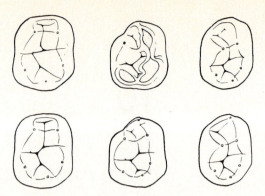

Figure 1. *Upper row: examples of the deciduous first lower molar in* Paranthropus, Australopithecus *and* Homo *(modern Bushman). Lower row: diagrammatic representations the cusp and fissure patterns of the teeth in upper row. Twice natural size.*

lower canine is another good diagnostic feature. The two australopithecines can be separated at a glance by means of this tooth, which is relatively large and highly asymmetric in crown structure in *Australopithecus* while in *Paranthropus* the crown is small and more symmetrical with little relief on the lingual surface though the root is substantial (Fig. 2). The large difference in size between the post-canine teeth and the anterior teeth is also a good diagnostic feature. In *Australopithecus* the canines and incisors are fairly large for a hominid and the postcanine teeth are of proportionate size. In *Paranthropus*, on the other hand, the canines and incisors are appreciably smaller while the post-canine teeth are larger than those of *Australopithecus*. The *Australopithecus* condition fits very well with that found in the hominines, whereas that of *Paranthropus* is quite aberrant and unlike that seen in any other known hominid.

These are some of the most striking diagnostic features distinguishing the two forms, and there are many others: the nasal cavity floor and its relation to the subnasal maxillary surface, the nature and shape of the palate, the shape and structure of the face and of the braincase, etc. However lack of space prohibits detailed discussion of them here.

In contrast to this view, which I have described as the practical, workaday taxonomic approach, there is a larger and more satisfying view which sees the animal not as a series of taxonomic characters, but as an individual which is part of a population in its natural environment. In such a view the isolated characters of the other approach or aspect of systematics are seen as part of an integrated pattern. According to this viewpoint the difference between the two types of australopithecine is even more obvious.

In *Paranthropus* it seems clear that the architecture of the skull and head in general is strongly related to specialisations of the dentition (Fig. 3). The small anterior teeth, in the maxilla set in relatively lightly-constructed bone and in the mandible in a more or less vertical symphysial region with no trace of chin, results in a relatively orthognathous face. The massive postcanine teeth with strongly developed root systems are set in massive bone. The areas of support and the channels of dissipation of the forces generated by chewing are well developed. Examples of these are the thickened columns up either side of the nasal aperture, the enormously thickened palate anteriorly (over a centimetre thick in one adolescent

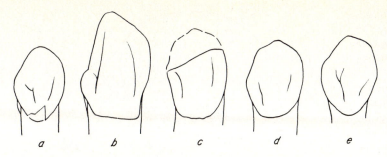

Figure 2. *Mandibular canines of (a)* Paranthropus, *(b)* Australopithecus, *(c) and (d)* Homo *(Pekin man) and (e)* Homo *(modern Bantu). It will he recalled that (a) is from a very robust form while (b) is from a small and lightly built form. (c) and (d) after Weidenreich. Twice natural size.*

where it can be measured opposite M^1), the pterygo-palatine complex and the zygomatic process of the maxilla. The strongly developed musculature required to operate this massive postcanine dental battery has also affected the architecture of the skull in an obvious manner. The temporalis and masseter muscles were manifestly very large. The former was so large as to cover a large portion of the calvaria and more than reach the midline, since all known adults of both sexes with this portion of the skull preserved have a sagittal crest. The origin of the masseter, especially the superficial portion, is very clearly marked and extensive. Similarly the insertion is extensive on the broad and high ramus. The masseter must thus have been large and powerful. The pterygoid muscles were evidently large also as evidenced, for example, by the relatively great development of the lateral pterygoid plate.

The relatively poor development of the anterior teeth reduces maxillary prognathism. The support needed for the relatively massive post-canine dentition has resulted in a strongly stressed, hence completely nasal area. The massive chewing muscles go with a strongly developed zygomatic region—among other things. These factors result in the typically wide, massive, but either flat or actually dished face of *Paranthropus*. The total lack of a true forehead and the relatively great postorbital constriction make the brow ridges seem massive and projecting; though in actual fact they are not especially strongly developed. The well developed postorbital constriction—which is in part at least associated with the great development of the temporalis muscle, the sagittal crest—which is directly due to the relatively great size of the temporalis as compared to the size of the braincase and the absence of a true forehead result in a braincase shape quite distinct from that seen in all other known hominids (see Fig. 3). The robust jugal arch and the attachment requirements of massive nuchal muscles result in a mastoid region which projects laterally significantly more than does the braincase above this region.

It is therefore apparent that the effect of the dental specialisations on skull architecture has been far-reaching in *Paranthropus* more so even than here indicated since only the more obvious features have been mentioned. The result is a skull which bears a considerable superficial resemblance to that of some pongids. However, another important factor has affected skull architecture in the former: erect posture. This has resulted in a very significant lowering of the relative height of the occiput which is quite differently oriented in the erectly

bipedal hominids compared to the condition in the quadrupedal pongids or all other terrestrial vertebrates. This clearly distinguishes the skulls of both types of australopithecine from those of pongids, though not from each other, as has been shown by the use of Le Gros Clark's nuchal-area height index (Le Gros Clark 1950; 1955; Ashton and Zuckerman 1951, and Robinson 1958).

In *Australopithecus* the dental picture is quite different from that in *Paranthropus*. The anterior teeth are relatively larger and the posterior teeth relatively smaller than in the latter—a condition which very closely resembles that found in early hominines. Because of the large anterior teeth, the face is more prognathous. Owing to the smaller post-canine dentition the chewing forces were weaker and the musculature less strongly developed. This is shown by such things as the much weaker root systems of the postcanine dentition, less robust bone in which the teeth are set, more slender zygomatic bone and zygomatic processes of maxilla and temporal, as well as lateral pterygoid plate. Furthermore the attachments for muscles are far less obvious than in *Paranthropus*. Besides these points there is normally no trace of sagittal crest since the temporalis muscles do not normally approach the dorsal midline of the calvaria at all closely. However, while the evidence listed above indicates clearly that the temporal muscle was smaller in *Australopithecus* than in *Paranthropus*, the lack of sagittal crest is not entirely due to this fact since another factor is also operative in this case: the braincase is relatively higher. The index devised by Le Gros Clark and called by him the supraorbital height index, shows clearly (Robinson 1961) that calvaria height above the superior margin of the orbits is very

Figure 3. *Facial views of skulls of (a)* Australopithecus *and (b)* Paranthropus. *Top views of skulls of (c)* Australopithecus *and (d)* Paranthropus. *Both skulls are of females.*

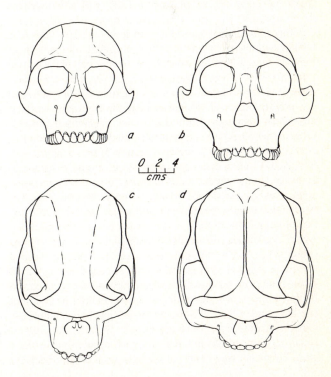

near the hominine condition in *Australopithecus* but of approximately average pongid condition in *Paranthropus*. The usual absence of a sagittal crest in the former is thus due both to reduced temporalis muscle size and increase in relative height of the braincase (see also Robinson, 1958).

Both types of australopithecine are hominids, hence the basic similarity of their skulls inherited from a common ancestor. Since both were also erectly bipedal, the modifications of the occiput resulting from this locomotor specialisation are also found in both. Beyond this the two skull types differ sharply (Fig. 4). The differences, as I have tried to show, appear to belong in each case to a pattern controlled chiefly by the specialisations of the dentition. Within the context of hominid affinity and morphology, it is very difficult to see how these differences of dental specialisation can be due to anything other than dietary specialisation. The dental specialisations thus at once reflect also ecological and behavioural features of the creatures. As has been argued elsewhere (Robinson 1954, 1956 and 1961), it seems clear that *Paranthropus* was a plant eater. The evidence for the presence of grit in the diet suggests that the plant food included roots and bulbs. On the other hand, the very great similarity in the dental and skull morphology of *Australopithecus* and early hominines leads one to suppose that their dietary habits were similar and included a substantial carnivorous element. Circumstantial support for this view comes from the climatic data which indicates that the vegetarian was present in the Sterkfontein valley in the wetter climatic periods, not the drier ones. One may note that the term "vegetarian" is used here in the spirit of the Oxford Dictionary definition which is not concerned with what type of plant tissue is eaten but rather with the fact that flesh does not feature in the diet.

If these conclusions are correct—and the morphological differences do not make sense to me if they are not—then they concern a matter of considerable importance since an anatomically specialised vegetarian is far from typical of hominids as we know them. As has already been demonstrated, the morphology of *Australopithecus* links it very closely with hominines the differences between the latter and it being just the sort of differences normally found between more and less advanced members of a single phyletic sequence. But the morphology of *Paranthropus* is aberrant, no matter with what part of the known *Australopithecus* hominine sequence one compares it. Furthermore, it is aberrant not only in such major adaptive features as the modified size and proportion along the tooth row—reflecting dietary adaptation—but also in such relatively minor features as the modified crown pattern of dm$_1$. It is difficult to conceive of the latter as being a feature of real adaptive significance. Consequently both the ecological and behavioural evidence, on the one hand and the morphological on the other, agree precisely in demonstrating an adaptive difference between the *Paranthropus* phyletic line and the *Australopithecus*-hominine one. In effect *Paranthropus* a pongid-like hominid. Again circumstantial evidence is available which supports this conclusion. At Swartkrans remains of *Paranthropus* and a hominine were found at the same level scattered amongst each other. It must be accepted, therefore, that both forms occurred in the Sterkfontein valley at the same time. In Java the Sangiran site has yielded both "Pithecanthropus" and "Meganthropus" remains. According to Von Koenigswald "Pithecanthropus" IV and the type mandible of "Meganthropus" came from the black clay (Putjangan beds) and not far from each other. The 1952

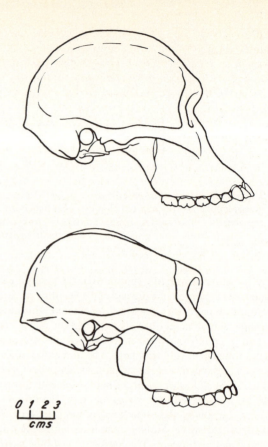

Figure 4. *Side views of female skulls of* Australopithecus *(above) and* Paranthropus.

mandible of "Meganthropus" came from the later Kabuh conglomerate of the Sangiran dome, as did "Pithecanthropus" II and III. Evidently, therefore, these two creatures were not merely contemporaneous in this region, but remained so over a substantial period of time. As indicated elsewhere (Robinson 1953, 1955) and later in this paper, "Meganthropus" is fairly clearly a *Paranthropus*. The evidence therefore indicates that an early hominine and *Paranthropus* co-existed in two different places separated by many thousands of miles. This is hardly likely to have occurred if the ecological requirements of the two were virtually identical, but is readily understood if the requirements and behaviour of the two lines were as different as the present analysis indicates. A final point of significance is that all of the australopithecine material so far discovered falls readily into one or other of the two groups—whether found in the far East, East Africa or the Sterkfontein valley—and are as different when both occur in the same valley as when occurring far apart. This suggests that the two groups are clear-cut and stable, rather than being merely minor modifications of the same thing.

NON-SOUTH AFRICAN AUSTRALOPITHECINES

Australopithecines are at present known from two areas outside of South Africa: Java and East Africa. The Javanese form was first designated *Meganthropus palaeojavanicus* (Weidenreich 1945), but detailed analysis of the available information resulted in this form being placed in the genus *Paranthropus* (Robinson 1953, 1955). The reason for this is that, with only trivial exceptions, the features of the known specimens fall within the observed range of the known *Paranthropus* material. Among these features are the massive mandible and the combination of small canines and incisors with enormously robust postcanine teeth. Although no incisor crowns are known, roots of both are present in the 1952 mandible and, along with the roots of the canine and other teeth, reflect the characteristic *Paranthropus* condition.

The conclusion that "Meganthropus" is a *Paranthropus* has been contested by Von Koenigswald who has, however, produced no cogent evidence to refute it. A few points from the evidence which has been advanced will here be considered briefly to show that in almost every case the disagreement stems from not taking into account the observed variation in the known material.

It is stated that the anterior fovea of P_2 in "Meganthropus" is "broad" while that in australopithecines is "pit like". The observed range of variation in both sorts of australopithecine actually includes a range from pit-like to broader than that of the Javanese form. The latter form is stated to differ from australopithecines in that the lower permanent molars and dm_3 have uninterrupted connection between protoconid and metaconid, while in the australopithecines this is absent. However, both types of australopithecine have both conditions; i.e. both presence in various degrees, or absence, of a trigonid crest connecting protoconid and metaconid. Such a crest appears to be normal on dm_2 and common on M_1 in *Paranthropus*. Great stress is placed on the observation that the Javanese form has P_3 larger than P_4 (crown) and that the reverse is true of australopithecines. This is a matter of proportion, not absolute size, and can thus be checked on a good cast since shrinkage will not have been strongly differential between two adjacent crowns of similar shape and size on the same cast. Employing the same measuring technique as that used in the monographic study of the australopithecine dentition, it appears that in the 1941 mandible the two teeth are virtually identical in size with P_4 actually slightly the larger. The roots of these teeth in the 1952 mandible suggest that P_4 may have been relatively even larger in that specimen. In which case it would be fair to say that on available evidence the Javan form has P_3 either subequal to P_4 or larger. The proportion between these two teeth actually varies appreciably in the australopithecines, ranging from virtual identity in size to P_4 being considerably larger than P_3. The Javan form is said to differ from the australopithecines in that P_4 is single-rooted in the former and double-rooted in the latter. The 1941 specimen from Java certainly has the buccal face of the root of P_4 single but the lingual aspect is so much broader that it seems that a lingual cleft is present. That is, like the root of P_3 of that specimen, the root is partially divided. On the other hand the 1952 specimen manifestly had a double-rooted P_4 on the left side. The crown of this is tooth is gone and two roots with two pulp cavities are clearly visible on the cast kindly made available to me by Dr. Marks. Here again the australopithecines exhibit both of these conditions and both can be demonstrated in *Paranthropus* alone.

From these remarks it will be evident that in each case the characters of the Javanese "Meganthropus" fall within the observed range of the corresponding features in the far more extensive collections of australopithecine material. Not only is there no valid evidence differentiating "Meganthropus" from the australopithecines, but the former exhibits some features which are diagnostic of *Paranthropus*. It is therefore reasonable to regard "Meganthropus" as a member of the genus *Paranthropus*.

Leakey (1959) has reported the discovery of a good skull of a late adolescent australopithecine from Olduvai. He regards this form as being new and has named it *Zinjanthropus boisei*. It has, however, been shown (Robinson 1960) that the skull and dental characters, and their pattern of specialisation, are typically those of *Paranthropus*. As in the case of "Meganthropus", the morphological differences which are held to validate generic distinction from *Paranthropus* either disappear or become very slight if the *observed* range of variation of these features is taken into account. Hence the proposal that this form be placed in the genus *Paranthropus*.

In 1939 Kohl-Larsen discovered in the Laetolil beds near Lake Eyassi in East Africa, a fragment of maxilla containing P_3 and P_4 as well as an isolated upper molar. These were named *Praanthropus* (a *nomen nudum* since no species name was given) by Hennig (1948) and *Meganthropus africanus* by Weinert (1950, 1951)—a conclusion supported by Remane (1951). This matter has been considered at some length (Robinson 1953, 1955) and the conclusion drawn that (1) since one form is known only by mandibular and the other only by maxillary material, no evidence exists for placing them in the same genus; (2) since the East African specimen exhibits characters which fall within the observed range of the corresponding features of *Australopithecus*, the logical course is to refer the material to the latter genus. This is also the opinion of Von Koenigswald (1957).

Very recently Leakey (1961) has announced the discovery of further material at Olduvai, including a juvenile mandible from the bottom of Bed I. The mandible appears to have the characteristics of *Australopithecus*, though perhaps not the parietals.

We may conclude, therefore, that:—

(1) *Paranthropus* is a very well defined genus which includes a somewhat aberrant type of hominid whose morphological, ecological and behavioural adaptations are quite distinct from those of all other known hominids;

(2) *Paranthropus* is known from South Africa, East Africa and Java;

(3) *Paranthropus* occurs synchronously at the same site, both in Java and South Africa, with an early hominine;

(4) *Australopithecus* differs clearly in morphological, ecological, and behavioural adaptations from *Paranthropus*, but exhibits very considerable similarity in these respects with hominines;

(5) *Australopithecus*, like *Paranthropus*, is known from both South Africa and East Africa, but not from the Far East—on currently available evidence.

CULTURAL STATUS OF THE AUSTRALOPITHECINES

The cultural status achieved by the australopithecines is also related to the subject of this paper. Since the relationship between the australopithecines and the stone industries found with them in the Sterkfontein valley and at Olduvai has been discussed elsewhere recently (Robinson 1958, 1960), the argument will not be repeated here. The conclusion was reached that, despite commonly held opinion to the contrary, there is as yet no proof that either form of australopithecine possessed a settled stone culture.

The evidence in fact favours the conclusion that the australopithecines were primarily no more than tool users, employing whatever came conveniently to hand in the form of sticks, stones, bones, etc. This aspect of *Australopithecus* behaviour has been dealt with at considerable length by Dart (e.g. 1957a, 1957b, 1958, 1960). In my opinion the evidence provided is enough to establish that this form was a tool user, though this is disputed by some other authors. For example Mason (1961) holds that since a bone culture (due presumably to *Homo sapiens*) has been found in a Middle Stone Age (end-Pleistocene) deposit and since early hominines were already in existence in australopithecine times, therefore the Makapan Limeworks bone culture should attributed to a hominine who preyed on *Australopithecus* there. Washburn (1957) has argued against *Australopithecus* having had a bone culture. His argument turns on whether the bones associated with this form represent bone accumulation by the latter or by carnivorous animals such as hyaenids. Washburn and Howell (1960) accept the bone associated with the Olduvai *Paranthropus* as food remains of this vegetarian form and therefore as proof of predatory activity. However, in the same paragraph they state: "It is very unlikely that the earlier and small-bodied australopithecines (i. e. *Australopithecus*) did much killing,..." without explaining why associated faunal remains are accepted as food remains of an australopithecine in the one case but not in the other. The logic of this is not clear, especially as the form for which predation is accepted is a specialised vegetarian while the other is not, and both of these authors believe both forms of australopithecine to have had a stone culture.

Tool using is by no means confined to primates, as is very well known. It must be deemed highly probable that primates of the degree of development of the australopithecines and which were erectly bipedal, hence having emancipated front limbs, used tools sometimes. Since later hominines are known to have used bone tools—indeed some still do—the australopithecine cannot be held to be too advanced to use bone. But since many authors believe the australopithecines to have *made* stone tools, these authors at least cannot hold them to have been too primitive to have *used* tools. As much bone is associated with *Australopithecus* as a rule, and as some of it appears to have been altered in a manner suggesting use, it seems entirely reasonable to conclude that *Australopithecus* was a tool user. This is supported, but not proved, by the fact that the two main accumulations of *Australopithecus* remains are older than the first definite evidence of the presence of a more advanced hominid in that general geographic region. However, it would seem that the osteodontokeratic prowess of *Australopithecus* has been over-rated. On general grounds it seems probable that *Paranthropus* also used tools, though such activity may have been much more poorly developed in this vegetarian.

THE ORIGIN OF THE AUSTRALOPITHECINAE

The Subfamily Homininae includes form broadly distinguished morphologically by having erect bipedal posture and a large brain, and behaviourally by relatively complex cultural activity.

The latter feature is largely dependent on the large brain since it appears that intelligence of the hominine calibre is not associated with brains smaller than an ill-defined lower limit in volume of the general order of about 800 cm^3.

The Subfamily Australopithecinae includes forms which have the erect posture, but not the large brain, of the hominines. Erect posture is more than adequately proven by the morphology of one virtually complete pelvis with most of the spinal column and a proximal portion of femur; three other adult innominate bones and two juvenile specimens; two proximal ends of femora and two distal ends, as well as a number of skulls showing the structure and orientation of the occiput. The pelvic morphology is very closely similar to that of hominines. There is a short broad innominate with expanded posterior part of the ilium, consequently a well developed, deep, greater sciatic notch, and an iliac crest in the form of a sinusoidal curve when seen from the top; a broad sacrum; distinct lumbar lordosis and femur with a strong lateral lean of the shaft from the vertical when the distal articular surfaces are placed on a flat horizontal surface with the shaft as nearly vertical as possible. The occiput has the near-horizontal disposition found in erect bipeds. Functionally the locomotor mechanism appears to be that of an erect biped. For example the arrangement of the origin and insertion of *gluteus maximus* are such that this muscle must have acted as an extensor of the thigh. *Gluteus medius* must have been an abductor. A well developed anterior inferior iliac spine suggests a powerful *rectus femoris*—and therefore probably quadriceps as a whole. This is a very important muscle in erect bipedal locomotion and unsupported standing. A well defined attachment area just below that for the direct head of *rectus femoris*, and a pronounced femoral tubercle, indicate a powerful ilio-femoral ligament strengthened and functioning in the manner of that in hominines and there is even evidence for locking of the knee joint with the leg straight. In function and morphology the locomotor mechanism of australopithecines differed in relatively minor points only from that of hominines.

The Subfamily Australopithecinae must have originated from some more primitive primate group. It is not our aim here to enquire closely into what that group might be. The ancestral form may have been a member of the same early hominid stock to which *Proconsul* belongs, as is commonly believed, or it may have been part of an independent line already quite distinct at the time the early Miocene East African pongids lived. *Amphipithecus* and *Oreopithecus* suggest that the hominids may have resulted from a line, slow-rate during most of its history, which has been independent since the prosimian stage.

The Australopithecinae would appear to differ from pongids primarily in having erect bipedal posture, a primitive culture and in the nature of the dentition. The main differences between pongid and australopithecine dentitions occur in the anterior teeth, especially in the canines, the incisors and P3. The reduction in canine size, as was suggested already by Charles Darwin, probably resulted from the use of tools. Effective tool using could only have become possible after erect posture had been acquired. The altered character of the incisors and canines in early hominids may therefore have been a consequence chiefly of changed posture and locomotion. The differences between the pongid and hominid types of P3 cannot primarily have been due to these changes, however, as is clearly shown by the evidence.

The key feature, then, in the origin of the australopithecines is the change to erect bipedal posture and locomotion. This represents a major adaptive shift which opened up entirely new evolutionary possibilities in this primate line as compared to all known previous ones.

The manner of origin of erect posture is, however, not clear. A critical part of the change centers around the shift in function of *gluteus maximus* from being primarily an abductor of the thigh to an extensor. The power provided by this muscle, especially in the second half of a stride, is largely responsible for the efficacy of upright locomotion; without it the inefficient, shuffling gait seen in pongids walking upright is the best that is possible. Naturally this statement is an oversimplification; but whereas the rest of the pelvic and thigh musculature of pongids and hominids is very similar in function, *gluteus maximus* functions very differently in the two groups and this difference is of great importance in locomotion. It is readily apparent that a short, broad innominate—with most of the breadth increase being in the posterior part of the ilium—is a major cause of the change in function of *gluteus maximus*, since these changes place the origin of the muscle well behind the acetabulum. This, and the fact that the thigh is normally in at least a fairly extended position in erect bipeds, places the main line of action of the muscle behind the hip joint; hence contraction causes extension of the thigh, not abduction.

Higher primates are much given to rearing up on their hind limbs under various circumstances normal to their way or life. This probably occurs mainly for purposes of getting food, improving visibility or play—though the gibbon often does this in the trees as part of locomotion. It seems reasonable to suppose that members of a population in which the point has been reached where in the erect position *gluteus maximus* functions chiefly as an extensor, would find it easier to use this posture or mode of locomotion and would therefore use it more frequently. This is especially the case if, as seems likely, the population was ground-dwelling and living in broken forest and grass country and avoidance of becoming food for other animals depended chiefly on vision and alertness, rather than on speed, large canine teeth, horns etc.

If erect posture and locomotion came to be used frequently under such circumstances, the nature of selection on the locomotor apparatus would alter considerably. Relatively minor changes only would at that stage be required to adapt fully to erect posture as the normal habit. Rapid adaptation to erect posture could be expected. The other important part of this same change, which would make selection favour the new adaptive shift and increase its rate is of course the advantage conferred by having freed hands. It is now well recognised that even a small advantage is sufficient to allow selection to operate effectively and in this case the advantage would certainly not be small. Consequently it is very easy to see how natural selection would bring about a rapid re-adaptation of the group in respect of posture and locomotion once the innominate became sufficiently broad and short for the change of function of *gluteus maximus* to occur.

The difficulty—at least for me—is explaining the process which led to the changes in the innominate. Starting from the general sort of pelvis found in the prosimians and arboreal monkeys, it is difficult to see what manner of locomotory specialisation could have brought about the required pelvic changes. Forms specialising in the direction of brachiating seem to acquire a pelvis which is long and narrow. This is the case in the pongids as well as in *Ateles*, which is a New World monkey which brachiates to an appreciable extent. The innominate of the gorilla has a broadened ilium and it could thus be argued that since the gorilla has reached a size too large for it to be a successful brachiator and has become largely a ground-dweller this could be the answer. That is to say, a brachiator which came down out of the trees would have a broadened innominate, which could have been the starting point for the changes culminating in the hominid pelvis. However, this is clearly not the case since the increase in ilium breadth is entirely in the anterior portion of the bone an related to the stoutness of trunk in this animal. There is no shortening of the pelvis and no expansion of the posterior portion of the ilium. Brachiators, whether modified for ground dwelling or not, do not appear to offer any suggestion of tendencies in the required direction. Postulating that an arboreal form without brachiating specialisations descended to the ground does not appear to help either. The chacma baboon can be taken as an example. Here again there is no evidence of a tendency for the pelvis to become short and broad in the required manner. The known non-hominid primate locomotory specialisations therefore do not appear to afford any help in explaining how an arboreal primate pelvis could have become modified to the point where changed muscular function could provide a basis for altered selection pressures causing adaptation to erect posture.

Probably the pelvic modifications were associated with changes which were not primarily concerned with locomotion but which rendered the pelvis preadaptive for erect posture though it is not clear what these could have been.

Whatever the reason for the pelvic changes it is a fact that they did occur and once they had, a new adaptive trend came into being. It would seem that the process occurred in two phases: the first during which it is difficult to see how selection for erect posture as such could have been operating, can in retrospect be regarded as the preadaptive phase; followed by the adaptive phase during which selection pressures were directly concerned with erect posture. This is, of course, typical of instances where a sharp adaptive shift occurs. In this instance the threshold involves the changed function of *gluteus maximus*. Before this, changes in the pelvis represent a prospective adaptation; after the threshold was crossed, adaptation to the new adaptive zone was rapid under the direct control of selection.

In this connection it is of great significance that, according to Schultz (1960), *Oreopithecus* had a somewhat shortened innominate with a relatively broad ilium. Not only this, but the increased breadth is primarily posteriad in the region of the sacro-iliac articulation, judging from an illustration published by Schultz. No other modern fossil pelvis of which I am aware exhibits a clear tendency toward modification in the direction of that of hominids; but that of *Oreopithecus* unmistakably does, judging by Schultz's paper. Since *Oreopithecus* apparently dates from the very early Pliocene (Hurzeler 1958), it would appear to have occurred at an appropriate time to have been an early, pre-bipedal, australopithecine ancestor or a member of a group which provided such an ancestor. This evidence would appear to be very strong support for the opinion of Hurzeler that *Oreopithecus* is related to the known hominids more closely than to pongids or cercopithecoids. What is known of the skull and dental morphology appears to be entirely consistent with such a view. The short face, relatively small canines (still substantial in males), compact tooth row with little or no diastemata, occlusal pattern of the upper molars and vertical chin region, all fit in with the suggested early hominid affinity but do not appear to constitute powerful evidence of such a view. Also the occlusal pattern of the lower molars is not clearly of the *dryopithecus* pattern type found in hominids, but this feature is not a serious difficulty with regard to hominid affinity. The strongly bicuspid P3 does not in any way fit with what is known of either cercopithecoid or pongid dentitions but does suggest hominid affinity.

Apart from *Oreopithecus*, hominids are the only known higher primates which are characterised by having a fully bicuspid P3 This feature, along with the innominate which shows a tendency to shorten and for the ilium to expand posteriorly, appears to me to suggest a very real possibility that *Oreopithecus* is part of the hominid stream of evolution, though not necessarily a hominid.

In any event, by whatever route and for whatever reason it may have occurred, the adaptive shift in the locomotor apparatus did occur and so gave rise to an erectly bipedal primate. This was first hominid and the ancestor of the known australopithecines. Since vegetarianism in its broadest sense is characteristic of non-hominid higher primates, it is probable that the stock in which this change occurred was also primarily vegetarian. There is no reason to suppose that diet could have been an important factor in the locomotory changes. Furthermore, if hominine carnivorousness had had a very long history, then one could expect to find some clear evidence of dental specialisation for carnivorousness in the later forms. This is not the case. We may assume, therefore, that the first product of the adaptive shift centering around emerging erect posture - that is to say, the first australopithecine - was a predominantly bipedal vegetarian.

Since the conclusion has already been reached that *Paranthropus* is a vegetarian, it is worth enquiring into the possibility that this form could be a little-modified descendant of the early type of australopithecine. As has been seen, erect posture is likely to have led to tool-using and this probably in turn, would lead to reduction of canine teeth. One might expect, however, that reduction of canines would proceed more rapidly in a vegetarian tool-user. Until the use of tools had been appreciably refined, substantial canines would be advantageous to a meat eater. *Paranthropus* has much reduced canines and incisors, but large postcanine teeth and thus agrees with expectation. But the skull in some respects is primitive for a hominid. There is no true forehead, the brow ridges are rendered prominent by a well developed postorbital constriction and the vertex rises very little above the level of the supraorbital ridges. This latter point is well demonstrated by the supraorbital height index of Le Gros Clark (1950). The value of this index for *Australopithecus* (Sts. 5) is 61 (68 according to Le Gros Clark, 74 according to Ashton and Zuckerman [1951]). This approaches the figure for modern hominines which, according to Ashton and Zuckerman averages about 70 and ranges from about 63 to about 77. The value for several specimens of Pekin man, determined from illustrations, appears to range from about 63 to 67. On the other hand the three great apes have mean values for this index which range from 49 for the orang to 54

for the gorilla according to Ashton and Zuckerman. The figure obtained for *Paranthropus* from Swartkrans is 50 and that for *Paranthropus* from Olduvai, determined from photographs, appears to be just over 50. It will therefore be seen that this feature (which reflects some aspects of cranial, and presumably also brain, morphology) presents a typically pongid appearance in *Paranthropus* but closely approximates the early—and even modern—hominine condition in *Australopithecus*. If the conclusion that *Australopithecus* was carnivorous to a significant degree is sound, then this is yet a further feature in which this genus is more advanced in the hominine direction than was *Paranthropus*.

The fact that a characteristic feature of the hominine skull—relatively high-domed calvaria—had not yet started to appear in *Paranthropus* but was already well advanced in *Australopithecus*, and the vegetarian specialisation of the former, indicate that it is the more primitive of the two australopithecine types. It would therefore seem probable that *Paranthropus* is a descendant of the earliest australopithecines which retains the same basic adaptational features of that early stock.

If *Paranthropus* represents basically the original australopithecine stock and *Australopithecus* represents an adaptively different line evolving in a different direction, how did the latter line arise?

It seems unlikely that the earliest australopithecines can have been as recent in age as the Pleistocene since the two forms were already well differentiated early in that period. On the other hand it seems logical to suppose that tool-using, tool-making and increased brain size are virtually inevitable consequences of erect posture and that they will have followed the origin of the latter fairly rapidly in terms of the geological time scale. It is therefore likely that australopithecines will have originated in the latter half of the Tertiary; probably in the Pliocene, possibly in the Miocene.

There is reason to believe that most of the Miocene was a period of expanding forests in Africa, but that the late Miocene and Pliocene was a time of desiccation and shrinking forests. The Kalahari sands of central and southern Africa throw some light on this matter. The original Kalahari sands overlie unconformably the Kalahari Limestone plain which resulted from the African erosion cycle of early to mid-Tertiary times. However they pre-date the cutting of the Kalahari rivers into the limestone in the Lower Pleistocene. It would therefore seem that between the wetter period of the earlier Miocene and that of the early Pleistocene, considerable desiccation occurred, during which the extensive deposits of Kalahari sand were formed. These extend from fairly far south in South Africa right up into the Congo basin. The studies of botanists and of entomologists studying humicolous faunas support these conclusions in demonstrating marked forest expansion in the Miocene with equally marked recession in the Pliocene, leaving residual forests in a ring round the central Congo basin and in East Africa, and with a certain amount of expansion again in the Pleistocene. (See for example, Mabbutt 1955, 1957; Cahen and Lepersonne 1952. Also private communication from Leleup on humicolous faunas.)

One may conclude from this that suitable habitats for the vegetarian, original australopithecine (*Paranthropus*) line will have become increasingly scarce through the late Tertiary. This will have been as true for other forms requiring forest or broken forest habitat and reasonably moist conditions, hence it could be expected that competition for such environments may have been more severe than usual. On the other hand grass savannah and other more arid environments will have expanded at this time and so provided increased opportunity for animals adapted to, or capable of adapting to, such conditions.

The climatic changes will not have been sudden. Australopithecines living in areas which subsequently became semiarid or arid, will have found that the dry season of the year gradually became longer and drier. Finding food will thus have become more difficult in these times and it is reasonable to suppose that insects, reptiles, small mammals, birds' eggs and nestlings, etc; will have been eaten to supplement their diet. It is known that purely vegetarian primates will eat meat readily in captivity and that baboons, for example, will upon occasion do so in the wild. Taking to a semi-carnivorous diet under environmental pressure could therefore occur fairly easily. As desiccation proceeded such a deme will have found that it had to rely on the seasonal supplement to its normal diet more frequently and to a greater degree. Under these circumstances it could be expected that the population density will have dropped—to vanishing point in some areas. But it is not inconceivable that in at least some areas the creatures will have adapted reasonably well to the altering circumstances and adopted a certain amount of carnivorousness as a normal part of their way of life.

However, with such modifications in their environment, selection pressures will have altered. What may have been at that stage no more than a fairly elementary level of tool-using will have had obvious advantages in the changing food situation. Improved tool-using will have been favoured by selection and any improvements will have made the creatures better adapted to carnivorousness. Similarly, improved intelligence will have had obvious benefits under the circumstances and will therefore certainly have been favoured by selection. Since there appears to be some relationship between intelligence and brain volume with regard to that portion of the range of primate brains between the brain size of the larger pongids and that of the early hominines, it is probable that this part of the process of selection for improved intelligence will have been accompanied by increase in brain volume. Improved intelligence will have led, in turn, to improved tool-using ability and this to even better adaptation to partially carnivorous diet and general adaptation to a more arid environment.

The changed environmental circumstances resulting from the known desiccation of a substantial part of Africa during the later Tertiary could therefore very easily have led to a second adaptive shift and the establishment of a second phyletic line in the australopithecines in which carnivorousness and an enhanced level of cultural activity were important features (Fig. 5). *Australopithecus* is evidently just such a line and it is of interest that this form is present in the Sterkfontein valley in the more arid periods, while *Paranthropus* is present only in the wetter periods (for climatic data see Brain, 1958). The canines of *Australopithecus* are appreciably less reduced than those of *Paranthropus*; suggesting that the former genus arose from the *Paranthropus* line well before the reduction of the anterior teeth in the latter had reached the stage found in the known forms. The increase in adaptation to arid or semi-arid conditions and carnivorousness will have kept the canines as large as they originally were or even increased their size slightly.

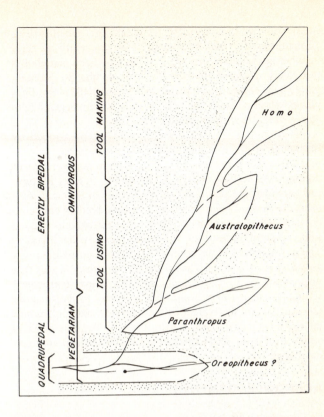

Figure 5. *Diagrammatic representation of the more important adaptive zones occupied by the hominid evolutionary stream. The threshold between the quadrupedal and bipedal stages is a major one between essentially discontinuous zones. The second and third thresholds—change to omnivorous diet and tool manufacture—are of great importance but did not involve clearly discontinuous zones. It should be emphasised that this is not a family tree but an adaptive grid.*

Naturally, once the line adapting to drier conditions had become established, producing *Australopithecus* as we know it, its evolution would not stop there. The selection pressures operating—and entirely different from those controlling the direction of the *Paranthropus* line—would not cease to operate and therefore it is virtually inevitable that adaptation would be carried well past the *Australopithecus* stage. By this stage it would appear that the cultural situation would be the vital factor. The need for tool-using in successfully adapting to the different way of life would, as indicated, place a high premium on intelligence. As this improved, presumably by an increase in size of the cerebral cortex so as to provide increased correlation and association areas, cultural facility also improved. When the modification of the brain had proceeded to the point where hominine levels of intellectual ability began to appear—apparently when the brain volume reached the order of 750-1000 cm^3—facility with tools reached a point where a characteristically hominine phenomenon appeared: the deliberate manufacture of tools for particular purposes. This provided still further scope for development and it appears that increase in brain size now occurred rapidly to approximately the modern volume. At this point it seems that correlation between brain size and intelligence is not especially close. Cultural activity did not improve as rapidly at first, but subsequently the improved use of the cultural capacity occurred with rapidly increasing momentum. "Telanthropus", from Swartkrans, was apparently an early member of this hominine stage. It has now been included in the genus *Homo* (Robinson 1961). From the Sterkfontein valley have come, therefore, members of both the major lines of australopithecine evolution as well as members of both stages of the *Australopithecus-Homo* stream.

It seems to me that the adaptive shift occasioned by increasing aridity and the necessity to use meat as a normal part of the diet was a second critical point in the evolution of hominines. The first was the adaptive shift to erect posture; this provided the possibility of becoming an efficient tool-user. The second point was that of being forced by changing environmental conditions to take to meat-eating, thus placing a heavy premium on tool-using and improved intelligence. The development of the hominine grade of organization was a natural consequence. The third point or threshold was that where simple cultural activity and increasing intelligence reached a stage where tool-using gave way to tool-making (see Fig. 5) and the typical cultural activity and approach to environmental challenges of man appeared. The potentialities which then came into existence are still being explored and developed.

ACKNOWLEDGEMENTS

It is a pleasure to record here my indebtedness to Dr. J. A. J. Meester, mammalogist at the Transvaal Museum, for valuable discussions and for reading this paper in manuscript; to Mrs. O. Cook for bibliographic assistance and to Mrs. D. Durrant for preparation of this manuscript for publication.

APPENDIX

The genera *Australopithecus* and *Paranthropus* were defined (Robinson 1954a) in terms of the information then available. At present only three genera are recognised by me in the Family Hominidae; the above two and *Homo* (Robinson 1961). These three are defined below. It is recognised that not all of the characters mentioned are independent: in such definitions it is not easy to indicate overall patterns.

Genus *Paranthropus*

This genus includes vegetarian hominids with an endocranial volume of the order of 450-550 cm^3. Forehead completely absent; supraorbital height index about 50 (about the average for pongids). Bony face either quite flat or actually dished. Distinction between floor of nasal cavity and subnasal maxillary surface totally absent. Zygomatic arch strongly developed; temporal fossa large. Palate appreciably deeper posteriorly than anteriorly. Lateral pterygoid plate strongly developed and large. Sagittal crest normally present in both sexes. Internal mandibular arch contour V-shaped. Ascending ramus vertical and high. Tooth row compact, without diastemata. Anterior teeth very small compared to post-canine teeth. Canine small and wears down from tip. virtually completely molarised dm$_1$ with anterior fovea centrally situated and with complete margin. Maxillary canine and incisor sockets in almost straight line across front of palate. Cultural development relatively poor.

Genus *Australopithecus*

This genus includes omnivorous hominids with an endocranial volume of the order of 450-550 cm^3. Distinct forehead, but never markedly developed; supraorbital height index about 60. Bony face moderately—not completely—flat. Distinction between floor of nasal cavity and subnasal maxillary surface present but poor. Zygomatic arch moderately developed; temporal fossa of medium size. Palate of more or less even depth. Lateral pterygoid plate relatively small. Sagittal crest normally absent—may occur in extreme cases. Internal mandibular arch contour V-shaped. Ascending ramus usually sloping backward and of moderate height. Tooth row compact, no diastemata. Anterior and postcanine teeth harmoniously proportioned. Canine wears down from tip, moderately large in all known cases. Incompletely molarised dm$_1$, anterior fovea displaced lingualward and open to that side. Maxillary incisor and canine sockets in parabolic curve. Cultural development relatively poor.

Genus *Homo*

This genus includes omnivorous hominids with an endocranial volume in excess of 750 cm^3 and with considerable variability. Distinct forehead always present—may be markedly developed; supraorbital height index above 60. Bony face aquiline to moderately flat. Distinction between floor of nasal cavity and subnasal maxillary surface always sharp. Zygomatic arch moderately to poorly developed; temporal fossa medium to small. Palate of more or less even depth. Lateral pterygoid plate relatively small. Sagittal crest never present. Internal mandibular arch contour U-shaped. Ascending ramus usually sloping and of moderate height but rather variable. Tooth row normally compact and without diastemata—latter present in some early individuals. Anterior and postcanine teeth harmoniously proportioned. Canines wear down from tip; moderately large in early members to small in later forms. Incompletely molarised dm$_2$, anterior fovea displaced lingualward and usually open to that side. Maxillary incisor and canine sockets in parabolic curve. Cultural development moderate to very strong.

ADDENDUM

The *Australopithecus*-like form from Bed I, Olduvai, referred to in the above paper has now been included with additional material in a new taxon, *Homo "habilis"* (Leakey, Tobias and Napier 1964). This step met with considerable, resistance from workers who do not regard it as representing a taxon distinct from ones already known (e. g. Campbell 1964; Le Gros Clark 1964; Oakley and Campbell 1964; Robinson 1965a and b, 1966a and b).

As originally defined the taxon includes material from chiefly the lower levels of Bed I and also from the lower half of Bed II. At the present time Leakey uses the name approximately as it was originally defined; Tobias, however, uses it as applying only to the non-*Paranthropus* hominid material from Bed I.

The nomenclatural validity of this taxon is at best dubious since the original taxonomic description contained a statement to the effect that further investigation might show that it and

"Telanthropus" from Swartkrans represent the same taxon. This constitutes conditional proposal of the new taxon as the implication is clear that the new taxon would be valid only if further investigation showed that it was not the same as "Telanthropus". According to the International Code of Zoological Nomenclature, Article 15, names conditionally proposed after 1960 are not valid and available for use.

As I have attempted to show (in papers quoted above, especially 1967), there are quite other reasons for regarding this taxon as invalid as a new species of hominid. Firstly, the Bed I and Bed II specimens do not appear to have exactly the same characteristics; the Bed I material seems to be very similar to the South African material of Australopithecus (sensu stricto) in its morphology, while the Bed II material appears to represent, as does "Telanthropus" from Swartkrans, an early phase of Homo erectus. The taxon, as originally proposed, thus does not appear to include one single, well-defined form of hominid.

Secondly, the morphological grounds for distinguishing H. 'habilis' appear to be unacceptable in some cases and at best very slender and insecure in others. As an example, a feature which has been stressed as a distinguishing character is the relative narrowness of the post-canine teeth, especially in the mandible. However, it can readily be shown that the ability to distinguish H. 'habilis' from Australopithecus (sensu stricto) in this respect depends on using the observed range of variation only of the very small samples involved. If estimated standard population ranges of variation (three times the standard deviation on either side of the mean) are used instead, there is extensive overlap. Indeed, study of this character demonstrates beyond question that it completely fails as a diagnostic criterion, both at the species and at the genus levels in hominids and cannot, therefore, be used for distinguishing H. 'habilis' taxonomically. This example is representative of the most secure type of distinguishing evidence which has been advanced—and it has been demonstrated to be invalid. Another category of evidence is simply not helpful; such as the structure of the foot or hand. The former is regarded as being of so advanced nature as to suggest Homo affinities. However, this evidence does not assist in distinguishing H. 'habilis' from Australopithecus (sensu stricto) since neither the hand nor the foot is known in the latter. It has been suggested also that a single estimated value of 680 cm^3 for the endocranial capacity of a Bed I individual supports taxonomic distinction from Australopithecus (sensu stricto), which appears to have a somewhat smaller endocranial volume. This evidence seems to me be insecure for three quite distinct reasons. Assuming that the estimate is correct, which is not self-evident since it is based on two incomplete and disarticulated parietals, then one must first take note of the fact that it is a single value, hence its relation to the range of variation in the original population is unknown. Clearly it would make an appreciable difference to a taxonomic assessment if this value is near the lower end of the range of variation or near the upper end. Secondly, there are grounds for believing that the hominine brain expansion had already started in Australopithecus, as is indicated by the relatively high-domed brain case referred to in the main body of this paper, whereas in Paranthropus this had not begun. If the brain of Australopithecus was undergoing expansion, then different demes at about the same time level could differ to

some extent with respect to average brain size and it would be very probable that appreciable differences would exist between samples of the lineage taken at different time levels. Thirdly, it seems clear that variation in brain size in modern man and also the African great apes is such that the observed upper limits exceed appreciable especially in man, the traditional limit set by three times the standard deviation above the mean calculated from samples of substantial size. If this was true also of Australopithecus (sensu stricto), then the difference between the single value for H. 'habilis' and the small series for Australopithecus, need not be significant.

There is yet another difficulty with respect to the arguments used to establish H. 'habilis'; the taxonomic viewpoint seems to have involved some confusion. This is shown, for example, by the fact that the species description in the original taxonomic account is much concerned with distinguishing between the new taxon and taxa believed to be in different genera. This demonstrates an insufficiently clear conception of the species as distinct from the genus and the relation between the two. This is a confusion which is not confined to the present case, however, but is characteristic of the whole field of human palaeontology. It seems to me (Robinson 1967) that part of the reason for this type of confusion is an insufficiently clear appreciation in practice of the fact that taxa within a single phyletic sequence, which thus has genetic continuity throughout, differ in nature from taxa which are each part of different phyletic sequences and which therefore were parts of genetic streams which were isolated from each other. Careful analysis from this point of view is therefore required in assessing the taxonomic status of a group of fossils. This becomes especially important in cases, such as the present one, where the new material is not completely isolated in space and time from all the known closely related material.

It would seem that there is a reasonable case to be made out for the view that the Bed I material attributed to H. 'habilis' represents an advanced level of Australopithecus (sensu stricto) which was already making primitive stone artefacts of an early Oldowan type. Following an appreciable time gap, the Bed II material attributed to H. 'habilis' in the original taxonomic description represents this same phyletic sequence but now at a stage where it is manufacturing developed Oldowan artefacts, the general tooth size has reduced, the average massiveness of the corpus mandibulae has reduced and the space between the two halves of the mandible has become relatively wider and more U-shaped rather than having the more primitive V-shape and the braincase has become larger. This seems, in fact, to be an early H. erectus stage, which is followed in that area at the level of the top of Bed II by what seems to be a fully developed H. erectus in the form of Hominid 9 from LLK II. It is consequently possible that the Olduvai specimens reflect the transformation of Australopithecus (sensu stricto) into H. erectus and that the material which has been named H. 'habilis' is simply a part of this sequence.

A point of considerable interest, which seems to me to be clear from the Oldowan and Peninj material, is that both Paranthropus and Australopithecus existed in the same region and seem to have done so over a very long period of time—more than a million years, if present dating evidence is even approximately correct. This is consistent with the view that these two forms were not only different in morphology but also in behaviour and ecology and that *Paranthropus* represents a stable adaptation. For example the skull from the lower half of Bed I has all of the diagnostic features of the *Paranthropus* skull as known from South Africa, while the Peninj mandible, which is evidently much later and from upper Bed II time, also agrees very closely indeed with the South African specimens. If the view is correct that the other material from Olduvai represents a single, second lineage, then it was changing steadily through all of the time during which the *Paranthropus* line appears to have been stable. Finally, since fully developed *H. erectus* was already present at about the time the still purely *Paranthropus* Peninj specimen occurs, it would seem very improbable that *Paranthropus* could have been directly in the line of descent of *H. sapiens*. This agrees with the previously known evidence from Swartkrans and Sangiran, in both of which *Paranthropus* and *H. erectus* are coeval. The new material from Olduvai thus is of very great interest when taken in conjunction with the much more extensive collections from South Africa.

There is another point which should be raised here; I now disagree with much of what I wrote in the main paper on the subject of erect posture. This change of view has resulted chiefly from dissections I have since made on chimpanzee and human cadavers. Further study on a wider range of primate material is being carried out by Mrs. B. Sigmon Storck at this university.

Following Washburn (1950) I accepted the view that *Gluteus Maximus* is an important postural muscle in man that its function is and quite different in man as contrasted with pongids and other quadrupeds and that the origin of bipedality could easily be explained in terms of this change in function. However, it would appear that these views are not consonant with the facts.

Gluteus Maximus is rather differently arranged in pongids as compared to man but its function appears to be essentially the same in the two. It arises mainly, in the pongids, from the distal end of the sacrum—not from the posterior end of the iliac blade, from the sacro-tuberous ligament, and has a very powerful origin, at least in the African great apes, from the ischial tuberosity. The upper portion of the muscle is weakly developed and arises from the gluteal aponeurosis over the powerfully developed *Gluteus Maximus*. This portion of the muscle is thus not powerful and its chief function is abduction of the thigh upon the trunk. However, the lower portion of the muscle, especially the very powerful portion arising from the ischial tuberosity, functions virtually as another hamstring as far as the hip joint is concerned, being a very powerful extensor of the thigh on the trunk. It is clear that extension is by far the predominant function of the muscle. Since this is also true for man, there does not seem to be any possibility of postulating a change in function of this muscle from the ape grade of organisation to the hominid grade which could thereafter have been the basis for a different pattern of selection.

Furthermore, there seems to be real doubt about *Gluteus Maximus* being an important muscle in normal bipedal walking in man. According to the work of Joseph (1960) and Basmajian (1962), this muscle is electrically silent during normal bipedal walking or standing at ease. Its main function

appears to be to assist the hamstrings, as a reserve supply of power, when extra power is needed in moving the trunk against gravity—as in climbing up stairs, standing up from a crouched position or lifting or lowering the trunk from the hips. The improved efficiency of human bipedality as compared to that of pongids appears to be a consequence of differences in the skeletal architecture of the pelvis and thigh, especially the length of the hamstring moment arm, the length of the femur and the spatial relationship between the two, as well as the angle of the ischium to the horizontal. By the time the femur shaft of a pongid reaches the vertical during extension of the lower limb on the trunk in bipedal walking, the hamstrings and *Gluteus Maximus* have run out of power. In man, because the moment arm is appreciably shorter and is arranged in a slightly more nearly horizontal position and because the femur shaft is much longer, the hamstrings have not run out of power at that point but can pull the femur a little further back. This, along with the spring action of the foot, give the human stride its power in the closing phases. In the African pongids hamstrings and *Gluteus Maximus* function in the same manner as is true of man but they, especially the hamstrings, are relatively powerful and are more specialised for power than for speed. In the case of man, the hamstrings are not especially powerfully developed and their normal action emphasises speed more than power-speed of action, that is, rather than speed over the ground.

The interpretation which has been included in the main body of this paper and others (e. g. Robinson 1962, 1963 and 1964), based on Washburn, was educative and had some quite elegant aspects such as the change in selection pattern which followed on change of function. But, alas! for the slaying of a beautiful theory by some ugly facts! The situation is different and much more subtle than that—and much more interesting as well. However, this matter and its implications for the early hominids will be discussed at length elsewhere.

Finally, I no longer believe that it is meaningful to distinguish a genus *Australopithecus* (sensu stricto) from *Homo*. This matter has been discussed at some length in Robinson 1967, to which the reader is referred for details. As is apparent in main body of this paper, the evidence seems to point to the conclusion that the difference between *Australopithecus* and *Homo* is of a quite different sort to that between either of these and *Paranthropus*. The Olduvai evidence makes this even more clear than it already was on the basis of the South African evidence. Consequently it seems to me that *Australopithecus* represents merely the earlier stages of the establishment of the adaptive pattern characteristic of *Homo* and therefore does not merit generic distinction if the genus is to be regarded as a monophyletic category reflecting a single distinct and distinctive adaptive zone or pattern. This seems especially the case since it appears that stone tool making was actually already in progress at Olduvai at a time when the brains of the makers were still within the pongid size range, so that one of the more obvious reasons advanced for retaining a generic distinction appears to have been demolished. Species distinction thus seems the most that is here called for—though, as I have noted elsewhere, distinction between successional taxa in the same lineage is so completely arbitrary in nature that it makes little difference what classification is adopted in such cases as long as an author explains his usage if it differs from a commonly accepted one.

REFERENCES

Ashton, E. H., and Zuckerman, S. 1951. Some cranial indices of *Plesianthropus* and other primates. *Amer. J. phys. Anthrop.* 9:283-296.

Barthomelew, G. A., and Birdsell, J. B. 1953. Ecology and the proto-hominids. *Amer. Anthrop.* 55:481-498.

Basmajian, J. 1962. *Muscles Alive. Their Functions Revealed by Electromyography*, Williams and Wilkins Co., Baltimore.

Brain, C. K. 1958. The Transvaal ape-man-bearing cave deposits. *Transv. Mus. Mem.* 11.

Broom, R. 1950. The genera and species of the South African fossil ape-men. *Amer. J. phys. Anthrop.* 8:l-14.

Cahen, L., and Lepersonne, J. 1952. Equivalence entre le Systeme du Kalahari du Congo Belge et les Kalahari Beds d'Afrique Australe. *Mem. Soc. belge Geol.*, Sec. 8, 4:1-64.

Campbell, B. 1964. Just another "man-ape"? *Discovery* 25:37-38.

Dart, R. A. 1957a. The Osteodontokeratic Culture of Australopithecines. *Transv. Mus. Mem.* 10.

Dart, R. A. 1957b. The Makapansgat australopithecine osteodontokeratic culture, in: *Proc. 3rd. Pan-Afr. Congress on Prehistory*, pp. 161-171, Livingstone, 1955.

Dart, R. A. 1958. Bone tools and porcupine gnawing. *Amer. Anthrop.* 60:715-724.

Dart, R. A. 1960. The bone-tool manufacturing ability of *Australopithecus prometheus. Amer. Anthrop.* 62:134-143.

Heberer, G. 1952. Fortschritte in der Erforschung der Phylogenie der Hominoidea. *Erg. Anat. Entw. Gesch.* 34:499-637.

Heberer, G. 1956. Die Fossilgeschichte der Hominoidea. *Primatologia* 1, pp. 379-560. Basel.

Heberer, G. 1958a. L'Hominisation: Selection, adaptation ou orthogenese, in: *Coll. Internat.: Les Processus de l'Hominisation*, p. 179, Paris.

Heberer, G. 1958b. Das Tier-Mensch-Ubergangsfeld. *Stud. gen.* 11:341.

Heberer, G. 1959. The descent of man and the present fossil record. *Cold Spr. Harb. Symp. Quant. Biol.* 24:235-244.

Heberer, G. 1960. Darwins Urteil uber die abstammungsgeschichtliche Herkunft des Menschen und die heutige palaanthropologische Forschung. *Hundert Jahre Evolutionsforschung* 397. Stuttgart.

Hennig, E. 1948. Quartarfaunen und Urgeschichte Ostafrikas. *Naturw. Rdsch. Jahrg.* 1, Heft 5, pp. 212-230.

Howell, F. C. 1959. The Villafranchian and human origins. *Science* 130:831.

Hurzeler, J. 1958. *Oreopithecus bambolii* Gervais. *Verh. naturf. Ges. Basel* 69:l-48.

Joseph, J. 1960. Man's Posture, in: *Electromyographic Studies*, pp. 111-124, Thomas, Springfield, Ill.

Leakey, L. S. B. 1959. A new fossil skull from Olduvai. *Nature* 184:491-493.

Leakey, L. S. B. 1961. New finds at Olduvai George. *Nature* 189:649-650.

Leakey, L. S. B., Tobias, P. V., and Napier, J. R. 1964. A new species of the genus *Homo* from Olduvai Gorge. *Nature* 202:7-9.

Le Gros Clark, W. E. 1964. Letter to Editor. *Discovery* 25:49.

Le Gros Clark, W. E. 1950. New palaeontological evidence bearing on the evolution of the Hominoidea. *Quart. J. geol. Soc. London* 105:225-264.

Le Gros Clark, W. E. 1955. *The Fossil Evidence for Human Evolution*, University of Chicago Press, Chicago.

Mabbutt, J. A. 1955. Erosion surfaces in Namaqualand and the ages of surface deposits in the south-western Kalahari. *Trans. geol. Soc. S. Afr.* 58:13-30.

Mabbutt, J. A. 1957. Physiographic evidence for the age of the Kalahari sands of the south-western Kalahari, in: *Proc. 3rd. Pan-Af. Congress on Prehistory*, pp. 123-126, Livingstone, 1955.

Mason, R. J. 1961. The earliest tool-makers in South Africa. *S. Afr. J. Sci.* 57:13-16.

Mayr, E. 1950. Taxonomic categories in fossil hominids. *Cold Spr. Harb. Symp. Quant. Biol.* 15:109-118.

Oakley, K. P., and Campbell, B. 1964. Newly described Olduvai hominid. *Nature* 202:732.

Remane, A. 1951. Die Zahne des *Meganthropus africanus. Z. Morph. Anthr.* 42:311-329.

Robinson, J. T. 1953. *Meganthropus*, australopithecines and hominids. *Amer. J. phys. Anthrop.* 11:l-38.

Robinson, J. T. 1954a. The genera and species of the Australopithecinae. *Amer. J. phys. Anthrop.* 12:181-200.

Robinson, J. T. 1954b. Prehominid dentition and hominid evolution. *Evolution* 8:324-334.

Robinson, J. T. 1955. Further remarks on the relationship between *Meganthropus* and Australopithecines. *Amer. J. phys. Anthrop.* 13:429-445.

Robinson, J. T. 1956. The Dentition of the Australopithecinae. *Trans. Mus. Mem.* 99.

Robinson, J. T. 1958. Cranial cresting patterns and their significance in the Hominoidea. *Amer. J. phys. Anthrop.* 16:397-428.

Robinson, J. T. 1960. The affinities of the new Olduvai Austrlopithecine. *Nature* 186:456-458.

Robinson, J. T. 1961. The australopithecines and their bearing on the origin of man and of stone tool-making. *S. Afr. J. Sci.* 57:3-13.

Robinson, J. T. 1962. The origin and adaptive radiation of the australopithecines, in: *Evolution und Hominisation* (G. Kurth, Ed.), pp. 120-140, Gustav Fischer Verlag, Stuttgart.

Robinson, J. T. 1963. Adaptive radiation in the Australopithecines and the origin of man, in: *African Ecology and Human Evolution* (F. C. Howell and F. Bourliere, Eds.), p. 385-416, Aldine Publishing Co., Chicago.

Robinson, J. T. 1964. Some critical phases in the evolution of man. *S. Afr. Archeol. Bull* 29:3-21.

Robinson, J. T. 1965a. *Homo "habilis"* and the Australopithecines. *Nature* 205:121-124.

Robinson, J. T. 1965b. CA comment on 'New discoveries in Tanganyika: their bearing on hominid evolution' by P. V. Tobias. *Current Anthropology* 6:403-404.

Robinson, J. T. 1966. The distinctiveness of *Homo habilis. Nature* 209:957-960.

Robinson, J. T. 1967. Variation and the taxonomy of the early hominids, in: *Evolutionary Biology* (Th. Dobzhansky, M. Hecht, and T. Steere, Eds.), pp. 69-99, Appleton-Century-Crofts, New York.

Schultz, A. H. 1960. Einige Beobachtungen und MaB am Skelett von *Oreopithecus. Z. Morph. Anthr.* 50:136-149.

Von Koenigswald, G. H. R. 1957. *Meganthropus* and the Australopithecinae, in: *Proc. 3rd. Pan-Afr. Congress on Prehistory*, pp. 158-160, Livingstone, 1955..

Washburn, S. L. 1950. The analysis of primate evolution, with particular reference to the origin of man. *Cold Spring Harbor Symp. Quant. Biol* 15:67-78.

Washburn, S. L. 1957. Australopithecines: the hunters or the hunted? *Amer. Anthrop.* 59:612-614.

Washburn, S. L., and Howell, F. C. 1960. Human evolution and culture, in: *Evolution after Darwin*, Vol. 2 (S. Tax, Ed.), pp. 33-48, University of Chicago Press, Chicago.

Washburn, S. L., and Patterson, B. 1951. Evolutionary importance of the South African man-apes. *Nature* 167:650-651.

Weidenreich, F. 1945. Giant early man from Java and south China. *Anthrop. Pap. Amer. Mus.* 40:l-182.

Weinert, H. 1950. Uber die neuen Vor- und Fruhmenschenfunde aus Africa, Java, China und Frankreieh. *Z. Morph. Anthr.* 42:113-148.

Weinert, H. 1951. Uber die Vielgestaltigkeit der Summoprimaten vor der Menschwerdung. *Z. Morph. Anthr.* 43:73-103.

11

A Systematic Assessment of Early African Hominids

D. C. Johanson and T. D. White

Paleoanthropological research in eastern and southern Africa has provided an extensive fossil record documenting human evolution over the last 2.5 million years. The accumulated fossil remains from sites such as Koobi Fora, Olduvai Gorge, Omo, Sterkfontein, and Swartkrans (Fig. 1) have been studied, described, and afforded diverse phylogenetic and taxonomic interpretations (Walker and Leakey 1978; Coppens et al., Eds. 1976; Jolly, Ed. 1978; Tobias 1973a; Howell 1978; Robinson 1972).

The sites of Laetolil in Tanzania and Hadar in Ethiopia (Fig. 1) have yielded abundant remains of human ancestors that have been dated firmly between 3 and 4 million years ago. These new hominid fossils, recovered since 1973, constitute the earliest definitive evidence of the family Hominidae [1]. The morphology and attributes of these remains are demonstrably more primitive than those of hominid specimens from other sites. Because of their great age, abundance, state of preservation, and distinctive morphology, the Laetolil and Hadar fossils provide a new perspective on human phylogeny during Pliocene and Pleistocene times.

It is not our aim in this article to review the extensive literature that deals with hominid origins, phylogeny, and taxonomy. Our first intention is to describe some of the most salient morphological features of the newly recovered Pliocene hominids from Laetolil and Hadar. We will then assess the phylogenetic position of the new specimens within the Hominidae in light of their distinctive skeletal anatomy. Finally, we will express the implications of these findings in a taxonomic evaluation.

BACKGROUND

The major hominid collections from Laetolil were made by Mary D. Leakey's expedition. Laetolil lies about 50 kilometers (30 miles) south of Olduvai Gorge in northern Tanzania (Fig. 1). The ongoing fieldwork was initiated at Laetolil in 1974, and the geology, paleontology, and history of the site have been described by M. D. Leakey et al. (1976). The fossil hominids consist primarily of dental and gnathic remains derived from the Laetolil Beds and are radiometrically placed between 3.6 and 3.8 million years ago (M. D. Leakey et al. 1976). Laetolil hominids (L. H.) 1 through 14 have been described (White 1977b) and nine additional specimens have been recovered.

Hadar is located in the Afar triangle of Ethiopia (Fig. 1). Intensive paleoanthropological fieldwork was conducted at the site between 1972 and 1977 by the International Afar Research Expedition (Taieb et al. 1976; Aronson et al. 1977; Johanson and Taieb 1976; Johanson, Gray, and Coppens 1978). Abundant, diverse, well-preserved fossils were recovered from the Hadar Formation. On the basis of geochronologic and biostratigraphic evidence, this formation has been dated between 2.6 and 3.3 million years ago (Aronson et al. 1977). A remarkable collection of hominid specimens representing a minimum of 35 and a maximum of more than 65 individuals was recovered. Preservation is outstanding and some Hadar specimens are exceptionally complete. In several cases there are associated skeletal parts of the same individual (Fig. 5; Johanson and Taieb 1976; Johanson et al. 1978; Taieb et al. 1978). Nearly all anatomical regions of the body are represented in the collections from Hadar. This situation is unprecedented for the earlier portion of the fossil hominid record. For example, we have nearly 40 percent of a skeleton known as "Lucy" from Afar Locality (A.L.) 288 and more than 200 specimens representing an absolute minimum of 13 individuals from A.L. 333 and 333w. Some of the material has been presented (Johanson and Taieb 1976; Johanson, Gray, and Coppens 1978; Taieb et al. 1978; Johanson, Taieb, Coppens, and Roche 1978; Johanson and Coppens 1976; Taieb 1975; Johanson 1976; Taieb et al. 1974; Taieb, Johanson, and Coppens 1975; Taieb, Johanson, Coppens, and Bonnefille 1975), but a large portion of the sample is currently under investigation and will be fully described in the near future.

\A comparative study of the Hadar and Laetolil hominids has clarified the relationship between the two collections. The strong morphological and chronological continuity seen between the Hadar and Laetolil fossil hominid samples strongly suggests that these collections are most conveniently and effectively considered together in the following systematic assessment.

ANATOMICAL EVIDENCE

The Laetolil and Hadar fossil hominid remains have a distinctive suite of primitive cranial and postcranial characteristics. Some of these have been mentioned in earlier publications but this is the first report on the combined sample as of September

Figure 1. *Geographic location of the major fossil hominid sites discussed in the text: 1, Hadar; 2, Omo; 3, Koobi Fora; 4, Olduvai Gorge; 5, Laetolil; 6, Makapansgat; 7, Sterkfontein, Swartkrans, and Kromdraai, and 8, Taung.*

1978. It is not possible in an article of this length to describe them in detail; instead, some of the major anatomical features of the material are outlined below.

Dentition

As with other paleontological materials from these sites, the dental elements comprise the largest portion of the Pliocene hominid sample from Hadar and Laetolil.

Incisors: The upper centrals are characterized by their great mesiodistal dimension, which contrasts with the diminutive mesiodistal diameter of the lateral incisors (A.L. 200-la; L.H.-3).

Canines: The large, asymmetric, pointed lowers project slightly above the tooth row and usually have a pronounced lingual ridge (A.L. 400-la, 128-23; L.H.-3). The uppers also are large and project slightly. When worn, they often bear an exposed strip of dentine along the distal occlusal edge (A.L. 200-la; L.H.-5). Apical wear is often present as well. Both upper and lower canine roots are massive and long.

Premolars: The lower third premolars (P3) are characterized by a dominant, elongate buccal cusp. The extensive buccal face often shows vertical wear striae produced by occlusion with the overlapping upper canine. A smaller lingual cusp is usually present, but some specimens (A.L. 288-1, 128-23) display only an inflated lingual ridge. The P3 often possesses two distinct roots with the anterior one angulated mesiobucally (A.L. 333w-60; L.H.-4). In occlusal view, P3 crown shape is normally an elongated oval, the long axis of which is oriented mesiobuccal to distolingual at 45 to 60 to the mediodistal axis of the tooth row. The upper third premolar (P^3) is sometimes three-rooted, with a pointed buccal cusp and an extensive, asymmetric buccal face (A.L. 200-la: L.H.-6). The buccal cervicoenamel line projects toward the mesiobuccal root, and in occlusal view the mesial placement of the lingual cusp gives the crown an asymmetric appearance. The P^3 tends to be slightly larger than the upper fourth premolar (P^4), and the

latter does not show mesiodistal elongation of the buccal crown portion.

Molars: The lower molars, particularly the first and second, tend to be square in outline. The cusps are usually arranged in a simple Y-5 pattern, surrounding wide occlusal foveae. The third molars are generally larger and their distal outlines are rounded. The molar side sequence is normally $M_3 > M_2 > M_1$. The upper molars usually follow the same size sequence, their occlusal foveae are wide, and their hypocones are fully developed.

Deciduous dentition: The deciduous canines are morphologically similar to their adult counterparts in relative size, morphology, and occlusal projection (A.L. 333-99, 104; L.H.-2). The deciduous first molars conform to the molarized human pattern and show deep buccal grooves (A.L. 333-43, -86; L.H.-2).

Overall, the adult and deciduous dentitions are variably intermediate between Hominidae and Pongidae in most of the features enumerated by Le Gros Clark (1950b). Neither metric data (Table 1) [2] nor morphological considerations [3] suggest to us that more than one evolving hominid lineage is represented in the dental samples from Hadar and Laetolil.

Cranium

Portions of several adult and juvenile faces are available from Hadar and Laetolil. The adults show strong alveolar prognathism associated with somewhat procumbent incisors, the curved roots of which promote a convex clivus. The lower margin of the pyriform aperture is marked laterally by a raised border (A.L. 200-la, 333-1). The large canine roots are reflected in strong canine jugae, which contribute to the formation of pillars lateral to the pyriform aperture. These pillars act to set this region apart from the zygomatic processes of the maxillae. The anterior margins of these large processes are located above the junction of P^4 and M^1 and are oriented nearly perpendicular to the tooth rows. The inferior margins of the zygomatic arches are flared anteriorly and laterally. The palates are shallow anteriorly and their lateral margins tend to converge posteriorly, (Fig. 2). The dental arcades are long, narrow, and straight-sided instead of parabolic. The tooth row is sometimes interrupted by diastemata between the lateral incisors and canines (A.L. 200-la).

Preserved portions of the adult crania A.L. 333-45 (Fig. 3) and A.L. 288-1 show a host of primitive features. There are strong muscle markings including a compound temporal-nuchal crest on both sides of A.L. 333-45. The temporal lines converge anteriorly and closely approximate the midline. An anteriorly placed sagittal crest is possible, but the relevant portions are not preserved. The smaller specimen, A.L. 288-1, is less robust but is morphologically similar in its preserved portions [4]. Specimen A.L. 333-45 is heavily pneumatized in lateral portions of the cranial base. The nuchal plane is concave and is longer than the occipital plane. The mastoid region is flattened posteriorly and the mastoid tips point anteroinferiorly. The external auditory meatus takes on a tubular appearance when viewed basally, strongly resembling the pongid condition. The mandibular fossae are broad, have little relief, and are placed only partially beneath the braincase. There is a strong

Table 1. Combined metric data for the Laetolil and Hadar hominid dentitions. Only measurements on intact teeth are provided. The measurement technique is described elsewhere (White 1977b). Mesiodistal diameters for postcanine teeth are corrected for interproximal attrition except in cases where that was impossible. For anterior teeth, (w) indicates worn teeth representing range values. Other abbreviations: MD, mediodistal; BL, buccolingual; N, number; R, range; X, mean; and S.D., standard deviation.

Dentition	Lower		Upper	
	MD	BL	MD	BL
Permanent				
First incisor (I1)				
N	1	3	4	5
R		7.3-7.7	90w-11.8	7.1-8.6
X̄	5.6w	7.50	10.36	8.16
S.D.		0.20	1.17	0.60
Second incisor (I2)				
N	4	3	6	8
R	5.7w-7.1w	6.7-7.8	6.7w-8.2	6.2-8.1
X̄	6.28	7.37	7.65	7.18
S.D.	0.59	0.59	0.59	0.65
Canine (C)				
N	5	9	10	10
R	7.9-11.7	8.8-12.0	8.9-11.6	9.3-12.5
X̄	9.16	10.17	9.92	10.94
S.D.	1.54	1.15	0.74	1.11
Third premolar (P3)				
N	14	14	8	7
R	8.2-12.6	9.5-12.6	7.2-9.3	9.8-13.4
X̄	9.51	10.60	8.50	12.03
S.D.	1.09	0.98	0.74	1.19
Fourth premolar (P4)				
N	13	12	8	5
R	7.7-10.9	9.8-12.8	7.6-9.7	11.1-12.6
X̄	9.58	10.93	8.95	12.00
S.D.	0.95	0.92	0.68	0.60
First molar (M1)				
N	18	16	9	9
R	10.1-14.6	11.0-13.9	10.8-13.7	11.2-15.0
X̄	12.85	12.62	12.22	13.23
S.D.	1.05	0.90	0.92	1.24
Second molar (M2)				
N	17	17	3	3
R	12.1-15.4	12.1-15.2	12.1-13.5	13.4-15.0
X̄	14.02	13.44	12.83	14.40
S.D.	1.08	1.06	0.70	0.87
Third molar (M3)				
N	11	12	5	5
R	13.3-16.3	11.7-14.9	11.4-14.3	13.1-15.5
X̄	14.55	13.23	12.54	14.22
S.D.	0.8	1.02	1.32	1.05

crania, although preliminary observations suggest that it is small, probably within the known range of other *Australopithecus* species (*sensu stricto*). Studies of the cranial remains from Hadar and Laetolil have shown the distinctiveness of this anatomical region and promise to provide additional information concerning the ontogeny and functional anatomy of these early hominids [5].

Mandible

A combined sample of at least 25 adult and juvenile individuals represented by mandibular remains is available from Hadar and Laetolil. The mandibles from the two sites are strikingly similar (Fig. 4). Some major parts of the complex of features distinguishing this collection from other fossil hominid mandibles are described here.

Although ascending rami are poorly represented, available adult mandible specimens (A.L 333-108) indicate large but not necessarily high mandibular rami. The condyles (A.L. 333w-le, 16) are large and concordant with the broad articular surfaces of the preserved crania. The A.L. 288-1 mandibular ramus slopes somewhat posteriorly. The ramus usually joins the corpus at a high position, defining a narrow, restricted extramolar sulcus (A.L. 266-1; L.H.-4).

The mandibular corpora are variable in size, and larger specimens are relatively deep in their anterior portions. The lateral contours in the region of the mental foramen are usually hollowed (A.L. 333w-60; L.H.-4). The mental foramina tend to occupy positions low on the corpus and open anterosuperiorly (A.L. 277-1, 288-1; L.H.-4). The mandibular canal passes immediately below the distal root of the third lower molar (M3). The base of the corpus is everted, and the anterior portion of the corpus is rounded and bulbous. The symphyseal section usually shows a moderate superior transverse torus. The inferior transverse torus is low and rounded rather than shelf-like. There is strong posterior angulation of the symphyseal axis (A.L. 400-la: L.H.-4). In occlusal aspect, the molars and premolars form straight rows and the anterior portion of the dental arcade tends to be narrow, especially in the smaller specimens. Some specimens show slight postcanine diastemata (A.L. 266-1; L.H.-4). The dramatic size differences seen between such morphologically similar mandibular specimens as A.L. 333w-60 and A.L. 333w-l2 suggest a high level of sexual dimorphism within a single hominid lineage [6]

Postcranium

Comparison of the Hadar and Laetolil postcranial material with other Plio-Pleistocene remains is hampered at this time by difficulties in associating cranial and postcranial material found at other sites. In addition, a number of skeletal elements found at Hadar (particularly some of the hand and foot bones) are either absent or poorly represented at other sites, which makes meaningful comparisons impossible. However,

entoglenoid process. A very weak articular eminence results in a mandibular fossa that is open anteriorly. The preserved occipital condyle is located below the external auditory meatus in lateral view and bears a strong angulation across its articular surface. It has not yet been possible to make satisfactory estimates of cranial capacity on the basis of preserved portions of

Table 1. (cont.)

Dentition	Lower		Upper	
	MD	BL	MD	BL
	Deciduous			
First deciduous incisor (di1)				
N	1	1		
R				
X̄	4.2	3.6		
S.D.				
Second deciduous incisor (di2)				
N	2	3	1	1
R	4.8-5.7	4.2-5.0		
X̄	5.25	4.63	5.7	4.5
S.D.		0.40		
Deciduous canine (dc)				
N	3	2	3	4
R	6.2-6.6	5.8	6.8-7.7	5.3-6.5
X̄	6.43	5.8	7.37	5.95
S.D.	0.21		0.49	0.49
First deciduous molar (dm1)				
N	4	4	4	3
R	8.5-9.6	7.6-8.4	8.1-9.4	8.9-9.3
X̄	9.15	7.93	8.68	9.17
S.D.	0.48	0.36	0.54	0.23
Second deciduous molar (dm2)				
N	2	2	4	4
R	11.6-12.6	9.7-10.6	9.9-10.8	10.5-12.6
X̄	12.1	10.15	10.23	11.20
S.D.			0.40	0.95

some anatomical features of the postcranium are already obvious and deserve mention.

The postcranial skeleton is well represented, and all analyses so far indicate that the hominids were adapted to bipedal locomotion. This is especially evident from the analysis of the knee joint anatomy (Johanson *et al.* 1976).

The most complete adult skeleton is that of A.L. 288-1 ("Lucy," Fig. 5). The small body size of this evidently female individual (about 3.5 to 4.0 feet in height) is matched by some other postcranial remains (A.L. 128, 129) and these smaller specimens can be contrasted with other larger but morphologically identical individuals from Hadar (A.L. 333 and 333w, Fig. 6). We consider that much of this body size difference reflects sexual dimorphism [7]. All of the postcranial elements indicate high levels of skeletal robustness with regard to muscular and tendinous insertions.

The humerofemoral index (ratio of the length of the humerus to the length of the femur) of the A.L. 288-1 specimen is approximately 83.9 (Johanson and Taieb 1976). This value is high relative to modern humans. The hand bones from Hadar also differ from those of modern humans—for instance, in the "wasted appearance of the capitate (A.L. 288-1, 333-40), the lack of a styloid process on the third metacarpal (A.L.333-l6, -65), and the longitudinal curvature of the phalanges (A.L. 333-19, -63). A cervical vertebra with a long spinous process (A.L. 333-106) is quite distinct. Two pedal navicular bones (A.L. 333-47, -36) exhibit extensive cuboideonavicular facets and the pedal phalanges are highly curved. One of the potentially most significant bones, the A.L. 288-1 innominate, is currently being reconstructed. Its morphology is commensurate with a bipedal mode of locomotion. The specimen displays a straight anterior margin between the anterior superior and inferior spines, lending a heightened appearance to the ilium. These and additional postcranial features will be elucidated by biomechanical and anatomical studies [8].

In summary. the Hadar and Laetolil remains seem to represent a distinctive early hominid form characterized by substantial sexual dimorphism and a host of primitive dental and cranial characteristics. We interpret this material as representing a single hominid lineage [9]. An alternative interpretation would be that some smaller individuals, particularly the partial "Lucy" skeleton, represent a distinct lineage contemporary with the majority of the Hadar and Laetolil fossil hominids (Leakey 1976; Leakey and Lewin 1977, 1978). For the reasons discussed above, we consider that the available evidence cannot be used to convincingly argue for the presence of two distinct hominid species at either site. The Hadar and Laetolil hominids are most parsimoniously interpreted as representing one sexually dimorphic hominid taxon.

PHYLOGENETIC CONSIDERATIONS

The overview of the Laetolil and Hadar remains presented above indicates that these forms represent the most primitive group of demonstrable hominids yet recovered from the fossil record. Although clearly hominid in their dentition, mandibles, cranium, and postcranium, these forms retain hints of a still poorly known Miocene ancestor.

Figure 2. *Comparison of the (A) A.L. 200-la and (B) A.L. 199-1 palates found at Hadar. The palate in (B) consists of a right half, but the intact midline permits photographic mirror-imaging. Note the morphological identity but different size of the specimens.*

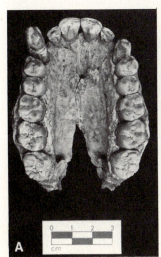
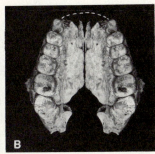

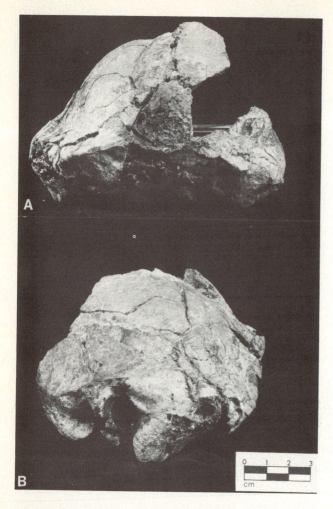

Figure 3. *(A) Occipital and (B) left lateral views of the A.L. 333-45 partial cranium from Hadar. The specimen suffered postmortem distortion, but many important anatomical details are discernible.*

The Laetolil and Hadar fossil hominids are important primarily because of their bearing on questions of early hominid phylogeny. They allow a perception of human evolution that was hitherto impossible. However, before we deal specifically with hominid phylogeny, it is necessary to view hominoid evolution in broader perspective.

Figure 4. *Occlusal views of the mandibles from (A) Hadar (A.L. 400-la) and (B) Laetolil (L.H.-4). Note the similarities in dentition, dental arcade shape, and mandibular morphology.*

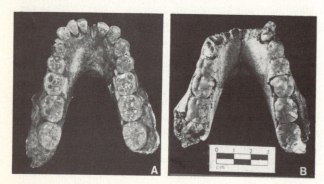

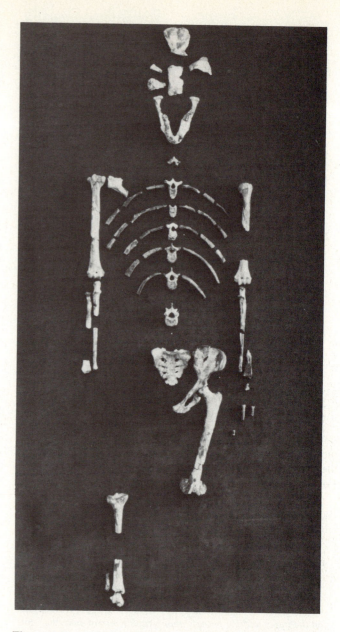

Figure 5. *Partial skeleton of "Lucy" (A.L. 288-1). This specimen is the most complete Pliocene hominid thus far discovered. The total length of the femur is 28 cm.*

Miocene relations

The ancestry of the Laetolil and Hadar hominids is not well understood. It must lie within the Miocene hominoid radiation of Africa and Eurasia, and *Ramapithecus* is the candidate most often considered to fulfill this role (Simons 1977). Pilbeam *et al*. (1977a) suggested that characters typical of extant Pongidae are not necessarily useful in understanding or classifying Miocene hominoid radiation. They proposed instead that the more advanced members of this radiation be divided into two families, the Dryopithecidae and the Ramapithecidae. We concur with the observation that *Ramapithecus* shares numerous adaptive similarities in its dental and gnathic composition with other Miocene forms such as *Sivapithecus* and *Gigantopithecus*. Many of these

Figure 6. *Comparison of large (A.L. 333-4) and small (A.L. 129-1a) distal femora from Hadar. Note the size difference but morphological identity.*

features were once thought to be distinctive of the family Hominidae (Simons 1976c).

Some interpretations of the postcranial anatomy (Washburn 1971; Lewis 1973) and biochemical affinities (Sarich 1971; Sarich and Wilson 1967) of modern humans and extant African apes suggest that the pongid-hominid divergence was late in time. Some paleontologists, anatomists, and biochemists, however, place the divergence earlier in the middle Miocene or even the Oligocene (Simons 1977; Straus 1949; Lovejoy and Meindl 1973). Of course, genetic divergence (lineage separation) does not necessarily coincide with morphological divergence. The lack of a consistent definition of *Ramapithecus* and its detailed similarity to other Miocene hominoid genera combine with the primitive appearance of the Laetolil and Hadar material to suggest that a late divergence must remain a possibility. Ultimate resolution of the question will come only with the collection and analysis of further hominoid remains dating between 5 and 15 million years ago. Critical to this resolution will be the recovery of specimens representing lineages of the extant pongids.

Plio-Pleistocene Relations

Bipedalism appears to have been the dominant form of terrestrial locomotion employed by the Hadar and the Laetolil hominids. Morphological features associated with this locomotor mode are clearly manifested in these hominids, and for this reason the Laetolil and Hadar hominoid remains are unequivocally assigned to the family Hominidae. Representing, as they do, the earliest well-known hominids, what are their relationships with previously discovered Plio-Pleistocene hominids dating later in time? Our interpretations of hominid phylogeny during this period are given in Fig. 7, which indicates some of the more important sites and specimens along with their chronological placement.

The interpretation of hominid phylogeny presented in Figure 7 relies heavily on the remains recovered since 1960 in eastern Africa. To fully appreciate this new resolution of early hominid phylogeny, it is necessary to consider the historical

framework of fossil hominid discoveries. This is particularly true because the recent discoveries from eastern Africa have usually been interpreted in terms of a framework formulated on the basis of the South African discoveries.

South African Discoveries

The description and naming of the Taung skull from South Africa as the holotype of *Australopithecus africanus* by Dart (1925) represented a milestone in human evolutionary studies. Until the discovery of the Olduvai Hominid 5 (O.H. 5) cranium in 1959 (Leakey 1959), Plio-Pleistocene hominids from the South African cave breccias at Taung, Sterkfontein, Makapansgat, Kromdraai, and Swartkrans dominated thinking on the earlier phases of human evolution. The distinctive character of the Kromdraai find led Broom (1938), to propose a different type of hominid, which he called *Paranthropus robustus*. Additional discoveries at Swartkrans reinforced Broom's recognition of a distinct, robust hominid lineage. However, hints of a second hominid type in the deposit at Swartkrans prompted Broom and Robinson (1949) to name the species *Telanthropus capensis*, which they considered to be ancestral to later forms of humans. Differences between fossil hominids from Taung, the Sterkfontein Type Site, and Makapansgat (collectively known as gracile australopithecines) and those from Kromdraai and Swartkrans (collectively known as robust australopithecines, with the exception of *Telanthropus*) were detailed by Broom (1950) and Robinson (1972). Doubts concerning the dating of these hominids have obscured their phylogenetic relationships, and some authors have suggested that the gracile and robust hominids represent nothing more than large and small forms of the same hominid species (Mayr 1950).

East African Discoveries

The 1959 discovery of a very large and robust cranium at Olduvai Gorge demonstrated the presence of the robust hominid form in East Africa and focused attention on this part of the world. Soon thereafter, a smaller-toothed and apparently larger-brained hominid (O.H. 7) was recovered from equivalent levels and named *Homo habilis* (Leakey *et al.* 1964). Debate concerning the differences between *H. habilis* and the gracile australopithecines from South Africa ensued (Robinson 1965, 1966; Leakey 1966; Tobias 1966; Brace *et al.* 1973). The debate illustrates the difficulties encountered when interpreting the East African collections in a framework devised for the South African fossil hominids. While taxonomic considerations received paramount attention, phylogenetic aspects tended to be obscured. More recently, Brace (1973) and Wolpoff (1974) have claimed that only one lineage of Plio-Pleistocene hominid could be demonstrated in southern or eastern Africa at any point in the past.

In 1975, fieldwork at Koobi Fora in northern Kenya resulted in the demonstration of contemporaneity between KNM-ER 3733, an unequivocal *Homo erectus* cranium, and KNM-ER 406, an obvious robust australopithecine (Leakey and Walker 1976) [1O]. This was dramatic confirmation of earlier interpretations that had suggested the existence of two distinct hominid lineages in the African early Pleistocene. One lineage, commonly referred to as robust australopithecine, is represented by specimens exhibiting craniofacial and dental features that apparently reflect an adaptation involving a very heavily masticated diet [11]. Members of this lineage have been recovered from both eastern and southern African deposits. Important derived characteristics that differentiate more evolved members of this lineage have been recognized by numerous authors (Robinson 1972; Broom and Robinson 1949; Broom 1950; Robinson 1956; Howell 1972; Tobias 1967). These include extremely molarized deciduous and adult premolars, a relatively expanded postcanine dentition, and development of mandibular and cranial features related to a large masticatory apparatus. The latter are seen especially well in such specimens as O.H. 5 and KNM-ER 406, which have large, anteriorly placed zygomatics, large temporal fossae, and anteriorly placed sagittal crests. The mandibles have broad, deep rami and heavy buttressing of the corpus. Most if not all of these anatomical specializations are related to a craniofacial adaptation that maximizes vertical occlusal force and spreads this force across an enlarged postcanine dentition (White 1977b). This lineage displays no substantial tendency to expand cranial capacity.

Members of the second lineage are characterized by a contrasting suite of dental and cranial features and have been referred to the genus *Homo*. This lineage lacks the specializations related to a heavily masticated diet, but exhibits a definite tendency toward expansion of the brain. Among hominid populations comprising this second lineage there were undoubtedly substantial ranges of variation in cranial capacity, and to sort single specimens into either lineage solely on the basis of this criterion could be misleading. Mandibles, dentitions, and other cranial characteristics, aside from overall cranial capacity, serve to distinguish this from the other, more specialized lineage. Ultimately, the tendencies for brain expansion and gracilization of the masticatory apparatus characteristic of the earliest portions of this lineage culminated in the species *Homo sapiens* [12] (Lovejoy 1974; Walker 1973). Some investigators (Walker and Leakey 1978; Leakey 1976; Leakey and Lewin 1977, 1978) have alluded to the existence of a third lineage in eastern Africa between 1 and 2 million years ago. The evidence for this third species, usually regarded as northern gracile *Australopithecus*, consists of three or four fragmentary crania. The morphology and dimensions of these specimens suggest to us that they are better considered as representatives of a variable, sexually dimorphic *Homo* lineage sampled through time.

Gracile Australopithecine Affinities

With the demonstration of two evolving lineages in the early Pleistocene (1.5 million years ago) of eastern Africa, it is necessary to reassess the phylogenetic affinities of the South African fossil hominids. Many students of early hominid evolution consider the gracile australopithecines to most closely approximate the ancestral hominid stock (Tobias 1967). Both robust australopithecines and the earliest representatives of the genus *Homo* are thought to have arisen either from the gracile species represented at Taung, the Sterkfontein Type Site, and Makapansgat or from a closely related form. Before the recovery and analysis of the Pliocene fossils from Hadar and Laetolil, such an evolutionary model best fit the available evidence. We presently enjoy a unique perspective afforded by the Hadar and Laetolil material. Study of these new fossils has

prompted us to reexamine earlier hypotheses concerning affinities of the South African gracile australopithecines.

Of primary consideration in the phylogenetic interpretation of the South African gracile australopithecines is their chronological placement. The South African cave breccias have not been radiometrically dated. Consideration of the fauna from these sites relative to dated fauna in eastern Africa leads to the placement indicated in Figure 7 (White and Harris 1977; Vrba 1975). It should be noted that fauna data place the Sterkfontein Type Site and Makapansgat deposits earlier than Bed I Olduvai, and postdating the Hadar and Laetolil remains. The third site yielding a gracile australopithecine, in fact the holotype of *A. africanus* (Dart 1925), is Taung. Despite the recent claims of Partridge (1973) and Butzer (1974), Taung must be considered undated (Bishop 1978).

It is significant that some of the gracile australopithecine specimens from Makapansgat have been considered robust by various workers (Aguirre 1970; Wallace 1975). Even 48 years after its description, the Taung specimen was hypothesized to represent a late surviving *A. robustus* (Tobias 1973a). Many workers have pointed out the similarities between gracile and robust australopithecines from South Africa in dietary adaptation (Wolpoff 1974; Tobias 1967; Wallace 1975) as well as locomotion (Lovejoy 1974; Walker 1973). Others have consistently maintained a generic distinction between the forms (Robinson 1956, 1972; Clark 1978). Our own examination of the relevant fossils suggests an alternative to these opposing interpretations.

Detailed morphological analysis of the gracile australopithecine sample from South Africa indicates an evolutionary status consistent with its relative chronological placement. The sample differs from the Hadar and Laetolil material in the direction of robust australopithecines. The South African gracile australopithecine group lacks elements in the suite of primitive characteristics described above for the Hadar and

Figure 7. *Hominid phylogeny in the Pliocene and early Pleistocene based on the available fossil record. Some of the more important fossil samples and specimens are shown in their approximate chronological positions. The dark portions indicated periods from which hominid fossils are well known.*

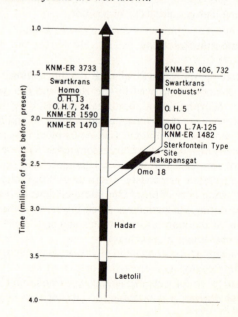

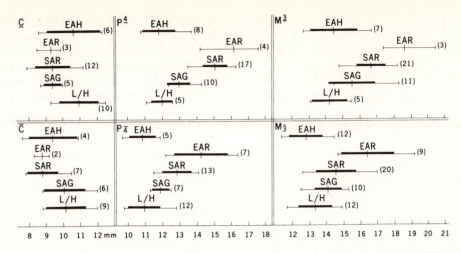

Figure 8. *Buccolingual tooth crown dimensions for the fossil hominids discussed in the text. The observed sample ranges are indicated by light horizontal lines, the arithmetic means by light vertical lines and 1 standard deviation from the mean by darker horizontal bars. The number of specimens is shown in parentheses. Mesiodistal crown lengths and crown areas show the same tendencies, but buccolingual dimensions are used in this graphic treatment because they are not affected by interproximal attrition during the life of an individual. Only tooth crowns that are complete or that can be estimated within 0.2 mm are included. All specimens were measured and assigned to a sample set by one of the authors. Abbreviations: L/H, Laetolil and Hadar; SAG, South African gracile (Taung, Makapansgat, Sterkfontein Type Site); SAR, South African robust (Kromdraai, Swartkrans non-Homo); EAR, East African robust (Olduvai Beds I and II, East Turkana Lower and Upper Members, Natron, Chesowanja); and EAH, East African Homo (Olduvai Beds I and II, East Turkana Lower and Upper Members). Note the relative placement of the gracile australopithecine sample between the earlier Laetolil and Hadar sample and the later robust australopithecines of South Africa. Only C, P4, and M3 are displayed graphically, but the mesiodistal and buccolingual means of the SAG sample are intermediate between the means for the L/H and SAR samples for every postcanine tooth, upper and lower (except the P3 buccolingual dimension, which is larger in SAG than in SAR). These diagrams lend graphic support to morphological considerations described in the text. They are presented merely as supplementary evidence for the arguments presented there.*

Laetolil hominids. It seems to share several distinctive, derived characters with later robust australopithecines. These include stronger molarization of the premolars, increased relative size of the postcanine dentition, increased buttressing of the mandibular corpus in the symphyseal region, and increased robustness of the corpus itself. Dental metrics reinforce the hypothesis that the Sterkfontein Type Site and Makapansgat gracile australopithecines represent a link between the basal, undifferentiated hominids at Hadar and Laetolil and the later robust australopithecines (Fig. 8).

Of course, morphological and metrical comparisons should not be expected to unerringly place every single individual along an evolving lineage. Our interpretation of the South African gracile australopithecines is based on a consideration of the available sample characteristics for the fossil hominids. We are fully aware that individual traits and even single specimens can be matched in samples that we consider to represent different evolutionary entities and ultimately taxa. For example, the matching of individual specimens and demonstration of overlap between the samples from Sterkfontein and Swartkrans serve to point out the general similarities of these groups, but at the same time conceal real and biologically meaningful differences which we consider to have phylogenetic significance.

Likewise, it is possible to emphasize the similarities between the Laetolil and Hadar fossils and the gracile australopithecines from South Africa. To include the more archaic material from eastern Africa in an already established gracile australopithecine phylogenetic or taxonomic category would obscure the evolutionary relationships and significance of the new material. We propose below a taxonomy consistent with these observations.

TAXONOMIC CONSIDERATIONS

The ultimate goal of human evolutionary studies is to understand phylogenetic relationships and adaptive patterns among the hominids. Such understanding has sometimes been hampered by an emphasis on naming the hominid specimens. We recognize the usefulness of classifying fossil materials, and we agree with Simpson (1963) that "classification is not intended to be an adequate expression of phylogeny but only to be consistent with conclusions as to evolutionary affinities. The evolutionary affinities of the Hadar and Laetolil material are discussed above. Our interpretation of hominid phylogeny during the Pliocene and Pleistocene is presented in figure 7.

Taxonomic debate often stems from the inability of Linnean nomenclature to cope with an evolutionary progression of paleontological remains. This becomes particularly evident when the members of an evolving lineage are represented by a fairly complete fossil record. To us, this to be the case for

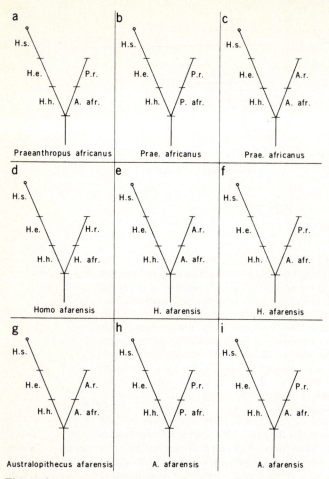

Figure 9. *Alternative taxonomic schemes available for representing Plio-Pleistocene human evolution. Abbreviations: H.,* Homo; *A.,* Australopithecus; *Prae.,* Praeanthropus; *P.,* Paranthropus; *s.,* sapiens; *e.,* erectus; *h.,* habilis; *r.,* robustus; *and afr.,* africanus. Australopithecus boisei *is considered conspecific with* A. robustus.

Plio-Pleistocene hominids, and this situation is not unique among vertebrates (White and Harris 1977; Maglio 1973).

Several alternative taxonomic schemes may be generated on the basis of our phylogenetic reconstruction (Fig. 7). A number of examples are shown in Figure 9. Alternatives a to c would adopt generic distinction for the new material based on Senyurek's study (1955) of the original Garusi maxillary fragment recovered from Laetolil in 1939. He used the genus *Praeanthropus* of Henning (1948) and the species named *africanus* suggested by Weinert (1950), producing the binomen *Praeanthropus africanus*. Among other problems, adoption of such a distinction would imply that the Hadar and Laetolil fossil hominids were significantly different in their adaptation from later hominids. Our examination of the material suggests that such distinction is inconsistent with its observed phylogenetic and adaptive affinities.

A scheme that places the Laetolil and Hadar remains in the genus *Homo* (Fig. 9, d to f) will undoubtedly be favored by some. Such a scheme, as shown in figure 9d, follows Mayr's (1951) suggestion that all hominid fossils be placed in species of the genus *Homo*. He later withdrew this suggestion (Mayr 1963), stating that "The extraordinary brain evolution between

Australopithecus and *Homo* justifies the generic separation of the two taxa, no matter how similar they might be in many other morphological characters. We concur with this contention that the unique adaptive and evolutionary trends seen in the lineage leading to *H. sapiens* merit generic distinction. This trend is not yet evident in the Laetolil and Hadar hominids. For this reason, we favor the schemes shown in figure 9, g to i.

The alternatives shown in figure 9, h and i, would tend to obscure phylogenetic continuity by unnecessary generic splitting. The taxonomic scheme we consider most useful in expressing our phylogenetic findings is shown in figure 9g. We follow Mayr (1950) in his perception of the genus *Homo* as being characterized by progressive brain enlargement associated with increasing cultural elaboration. The first species for which these trends can be discerned is *Homo habilis* (Leakey *et al.* 1964).

The juvenile status of the Taung holotype specimen of *A. africanus* precludes its precise phylogenetic placement. We agree with the traditional and widely accepted approach in which the specimen is considered to be indistinguishable from the Sterkfontein Type Site fossils (Tobias 1965, 1967, 1973a; Robinson 1956, 1972; Le Gros Clark 1950b; Mayr 1951; Howell 1972: Wallace 1975; Pilbeam 1972). Since the later sample is significantly less primitive than the Hadar and Laetolil material, a new species of the genus *Australopithecus* has been created (Johanson, White and Coppens 1978). This most primitive *Australopithecus* species is *A. afarensis* and is based on the holotype specimen L.H.-4 as well as a series of paratypes from both Laetolil and Hadar. It obtains its name from the Afar region of Ethiopia, which has produced the most abundant evidence.

DISCUSSION

We have presented the phylogenetic hypothesis that most parsimoniously accommodates the new fossil hominids from Laetolil and Hadar (Fig. 10). The recovery of the well-dated Hadar and Laetolil hominids extends our understanding of human origins well into the Pliocene. The implications of the new material for understanding the mode and tempo of hominid evolution are great. The apparent lack of morphological differences between fossils separated by at least 0.5 million years at Laetolil and Hadar suggests relative stasis in the earliest documented portions of hominid evolution. The dramatic morphological changes initiated between 2 and 3 million years ago suggest that this relative stasis was upset. Although the precise reasons for the phyletic divergence that led to *A. robustus* through the earlier, intermediate *A. africanus* are not well understood, a South African origin for this stock is plausible. Whatever the case, the clear niche divergence between *H. erectus* and *A. robustus* about 1.5 million years ago indicated by the eastern African fossil record indicates that an increased evolutionary rate for the period between 2 and 3 million years ago may ultimately be shown by larger fossil samples.

Another implication of the new fossil hominid material concerns sexual dimorphism. The extent of size and morphological variation in the Pliocene hominids from Hadar and Laetolil comes as no surprise, since later portions of the hominid fossil record also show greater sexual dimorphism than exists among modern humans (Brace 1973; Weidenreich 1943; de Lumley and de Lumley 1974). However, although the Laetolil and Hadar fossil hominids show marked body size

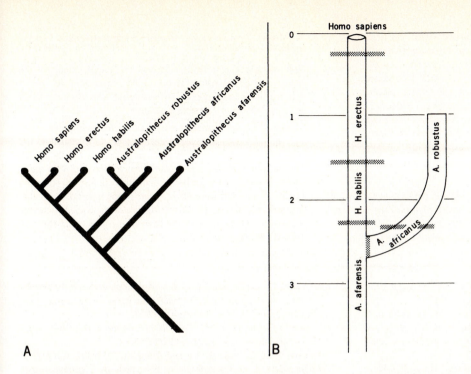

Figure 10. *(A) Cladogram of the family Hominidae. (B) Phylogenetic tree of the family Hominidae. See text for a discussion of the views represented by these diagrams.*

A

B

dimorphism, the metric and morphological dimorphism of the canine teeth is not as pronounced as in most other extant, ground-dwelling primates. This implies a functional pattern different from that seen in other primates and may have significant behavioral implications.

In this article we have avoided placing emphasis on taxonomic problems inherent in paleontological material. Instead, we have tried to provide a phylogenetic framework for the early Hominidae that will allow anatomical, biomechanical, and behavioral studies of fossil humans to proceed constructively.

ACKNOWLEDGMENTS

We express our appreciation to the Provisional Military Government of Socialist Ethiopia and the United Republic of Tanzania for providing encouragement and cooperation during fieldwork at Hadar and Laetolil. We thank the following for financial support: National Science Foundation, National Geographic Society, L. S. B. Leakey Foundation, Wenner-Gren Foundation, Cleveland Museum of Natural History and Centre National de la Recherche Scientifique (CNRS). M. D. Leakey kindly made the Laetolil fossil available for our study. Thanks are due F. C. Howell for critically reviewing the manuscript. Y. Rak, O. Lovejoy, and G. Eck provided helpful comments and observations. Dr. Lovejoy kindly provided the Libben Amerindian data. Special gratitude is expressed to W. O. Kimbel, who contributed valuable assistance and comments during the preparation of this article. This study was based on hominid specimens from Hadar and Laetolil listed in Johanson, White and Coppens (1978).

NOTES

[1] We are aware of the hominid specimens from Lothogam (5.5 million years), and Kanapoi (about 4.0 million years). However, these remains are so fragmentary that accurate assessment of their taxonomic affinities is difficult.

[2] Figure 8 clearly indicates that the observed ranges of buccolingual tooth diameters in the *A. afarensis* teeth are no larger than in the other fossil hominid samples. The coefficients of variation of the buccolingual diameters for the lower molars of *A. afarensis* are as follows: M_1, 7.1 ($N = 16$), M_2, 7.9 ($N = 17$) M_3, 7.7 ($N = 12$). Comparable figures for *Pan troglodytes* (Johanson 1974a) are: M_1, 5.2 ($N = 409$), M_2, 5.8 ($N = 333$), M_3, 6.0 ($N = 252$); for *Pan paniscus* (Johanson 1974b): M_1, 6.8 ($N = 91$), M_2, 6.6 ($N = 50$), M_3, 5.9 ($N = 28$); *Gorilla gorilla* (Mahler 1973): M_1, 6.4 ($N = 374$), M_2, 7.0 ($N = 370$), M_3, 7.9 ($N = 335$); *Pongo Pygmaeus* (Mahler 1973): M_1, 8.1 ($N = 129$), M_2, 9.6 ($N = 133$), M_3, 9.6 ($N = 110$); *Homo sapiens* (Wolpoff 1971a): M_1, 7.2 ($N = 558$), M_2, 8.7 ($N = 529$), M_3, 10.5 ($N = 448$). Hence, the coefficients of variation for the *A afarensis* molars are well within the ranges derived for extant hominoids.

[3] The lack of a distinct lower P3 metaconid in some Hadar specimens may be interpreted by some as taxonomically diagnostic. However, our own investigation of the variability in this feature in both extant and extinct hominoids suggests that the presence or absence of a lower P3 metaconid has minimal phyletic valence.

[4] Not enough of the A.L. 288-1 cranium is preserved to provide meaningful metric comparisons between it and the A.L. 333-45 specimen. However, differences in vault thickness, temporal line expression and nuchal crest development are indicative of a degree of sexual dimorphism similar to that found in the common chimpanzee.

[5] W.O. Kimbel of the Cleveland Museum of Natural History, together with the authors, is currently undertaking an in-depth study of the cranial remains from Hadar.

[6] The variation in Hadar and Laetolil adult mandible height and breadth measurements at the junction of lower M1 and M2 is large ($N = 12$, coefficient of variation (CV) for height = 11.40; CV for breadth = 11.19), but not excessive when compared to the variation observed in samples of modern *Homo sapiens* ($N = 20$; CV for height = 8.85; CV for breadth 11.59), *Pan troglodytes* ($N = 21$; CV for height = 10.79; CV for breadth = 9.42), and *Gorilla gorilla* ($N = 22$; CV for height = 11.07; CV for breadth = 7.54). The high degree of variation in mandibular breadth among hominids reflects the forward position of the corpus-ramus junction.

[7] Using an average of biepicondylar breadth and medal and lateral condylar height measurements, we find that the difference between the largest (A.L. 333-4) and smallest [A.L. 129-la] Hadar femora is 80.8 percent. Comparable figures for Libben Amerindians ($\overline{X}$, 89.6 percent; maximum, 73.5 percent, N = 50), *Pan troglodytes* ($\overline{X}$, 95.1 percent; maximum, 80.6 percent, N = 20), and *Gorilla gorilla* ($\overline{X}$, 76.0 percent; maximum, 61.9 percent, N = 30) indicate that the percentage difference between Hadar femora does not exceed ranges for other hominoids.

[8] C.O. Lovejoy of Kent State University, together with the authors, is currently engaged in intensive descriptive and analytical study of the Hadar postcranial remains.

[9] Some of our previously published interpretations of the Laetolil and Hadar fossil hominids differ from those presented here. This is because a more thorough study of the material has prompted us to elaborate and clarify some of these earlier preliminary statements.

[10] KNM-ER is Kenya National Museum's designation for East Turkana fossils.

[11] Robinson (1956 and 1972) pioneered the interpretation that the cranial and dental specializations of the robust hominid species reflect a diet demanding extensive mastication. This diet was thought to consist almost of vegetable materials.

[12] The emphasis on distinctive cranial and dental anatomy of members of these two lineages is not intended to overshadow the possibility that differences in postcranial anatomy may be found. No essential differences in basic locomotor mode of Plio-Pleistocene hominids have yet been convincingly delineated [Lovejoy (1974) versus Robinson (1972)], but minor morphological differences may ultimately allow distinctions to be made between or within the two lineages on the basis of the postcranial skeleton (Walker 1973).

REFERENCES

Aguirre, E. 1970. Identification de "Paranthropus" nen Makapansgat. *Cron. XIth Congr. Nac. Arguel., Madrid*, p. 98-124.

Aronson, J. L., Schmitt, T. J., Walter, R. C., Taieb, M., Tiercelin, J. J., Johanson, D. C., Naeser, C. W., and Nairn, A. E. M. 1977. New geochronologic and paleomagnetic data for the hominid-bearing Hadar Formation, Ethiopia. *Nature* 267:323-327.

Bishop, W. W. 1978. Geochronological framework for African Plio-Pleistocene Hominidae: as Cerberus sees it, in: *Early Hominids of Africa* (C.J. Jolly, Ed.), pp. 255-265, St. Martins, New York.

Brace, C. L. 1973. Sexual dimorphism in human evolution. *Yrbk. Phys. Anthro.* 16:31-49.

Brace, C. L., Mahler, P. E., and Rosen, R. B. 1973. Tooth measurements and the rejection of the taxon *"Homo habilis"*. *Yrbk. Phys. Anthro.* 16:50-68.

Broom, R. 1938. The Pleistocene anthropoid apes of South Africa. *Nature (Lond.)* 142:377-379.

Broom, R. 1950. The genera and species of the South African fossil ape-men. *Amer. J. Phys. Anthro.* 8:1-13.

Broom, R., and Robinson, J. T. 1949. A new type of fossil man. *Nature (Lond.)* 164:322.

Butzer, K. W. 1974. Paleoecology of South African Australopithecines: Taung revisited. *Curr. Anthro.* 15:367-382.

Clarke, R. J. 1978. *The Cranium of the Swartkrans Hominid, SK 847 and its Relevance to Human Origins*, Doctoral Thesis, University of Witwatersrand.

Coppens, Y., Howell, F. C., Isaac, G. L., and Leakey, R. E. F., Eds. 1976. *Earliest Man and Environments in the Lake Rudolf Basin*, Univeristy of Chicago Press, Chicago.

Dart, R. A. 1925. *Australopithecus africanus*: The man-ape of South Africa. *Nature (Lond.)* 155:195-199.

De Lumley, H., and De Lumley, M. A. 1974. Pre-Neanderthal human remains from Arago cave in Southeast France. *Yrbk. Phys. Anthro.* 17:162-168.

Hennig, E. 1948. Quartarfaunen und Urgeschichte Ostafrikas. *Naturwiss. Rundsch.* 1(5):212-217

Howell, F. C. 1972. Recent advances in human evolutionary studies, in: *Perspectives on Human Evolution* (S. L. Washburn and P. Dolhinow, Eds.), pp. 51-128, Holt, Rinehart and Winston, New York.

Howell, F. C. 1978. Hominidae, in: *Evolution of African Mammals* (V. J. Maglio and H.B.S. Cooke, Eds.), pp. 154-248, Harvard University Press, Cambridge.

Johanson, D. C. 1974. *An Odontological Study of the Chimpanzee with some Implications for Hominoid Evolution*. Ph.D. Thesis, University of Chicago.

Johanson, D. C. 1974. Some metric aspects of the permanent and deciduous dentition of the pygmy chimpanzee (*Pan paniscus*), *Am. J. Phys. Anthro.* 41:39-48.

Johanson, D. C. 1976. Ethiopia yields first "family" of early man. *Natl. Geogr.* 150:790-811.

Johanson, D. C., and Coppens, Y. 1976. A preliminary anatomical diagnosis of the first Plio-Pleistocene hominid discoveries in the central Afar, Ethiopia. *Amer. J. Phys. Anthro.* 45:217-234.

Johanson, D. C., and Taieb, M. 1976. Plio-Pleistocene hominid discoveries in Hadar, Ethiopia. *Nature (Lond.)* 260:293-297.

Johanson, D. C., Gray, B. T., and Coppens, Y. 1978. Geological framework of the Pliocene Hadar Formation (Afar, Ethopia) with notes on Paleontology, including hominids, in: *Geological Background to Fossil Man* (W. W. Bishop, Ed.), pp.549-564, Scottish Academic Press, Edinburgh.

Johanson, D. C., Lovejoy, C. O., Burstein, A. H., and Heiple, K. G. 1976. Functional implications of the Afar knee joint. *Amer. J. Phys. Anthro.* 44:188. (Abstract)

Johanson, D. C., Taieb, M., Coppens, Y. and Roche, H. 1978. Expedition internationale de l'Afar Ethiopie (4 eme et 5 eme campagne 1975-1977): Nouvelles decouvertes d'hominides et de couvertes d'industries lithiques pliocene a Hadar. *C. R. Acad. Sci., Paris, Ser. D.* 287:237-240.

Johanson, D. C., White, T. D., and Coppens, Y. 1978. A new species of the genus *Australopithecus* (Primates:Hominidae) from the Pliocene of Eastern Africa. *Kirtlandia* 28:1-14.

Jolly, C. J., Ed. 1978. *Early Hominids of Africa*, St. Martin's, New York.

Leakey, L. S. B. 1959. A new fossil skull from Olduvai. *Nature (Lond.)* 184:491-493.

Leakey, L. S. B. 1966. *Homo habilis*, *Homo erectus* and the australopithecines. *Nature (Lond.)* 209:1279-1281.

Leakey, L. S. B., Tobias, P. V., and Napier, J. R. 1964. A new species of the genus *Homo* from Olduvai Gorge. *Nature (Lond.)* 202:7-9.

Leakey, M. D., Hay, R. L., Curtis, G. H., Drake, R. E., Jackes, M. K., and White, T. D. 1976. Fossil hominids from the Laetolil Beds, Tanzania. *Nature (Lond.)* 262:460-466.

Leakey, R. E. F. 1974. Further evidence of Lower Pleistocene hominids from East Rudolf, North Kenya 1973. Nature 248:653-656.

Leakey, R. E. F. 1976. Hominids in Africa. *Amer. Sci.* 64:174-178.

Leakey, R. E. F., and Lewin, R. 1977. *Origins*, Dutton, New York.

Leakey, R. E. F., and Lewin, R. 1978. *People of the Lake*, Doubleday, Garden City, New York.

Leakey, R. E. F., and Walker, A. C. 1976. *Australopithecus*, *Homo erectus*, and the single species hypothesis. *Nature (Lond.)* 261:572-574.

Le Gros Clark, W. E. 1950. Hominid characteristics of the australopithecine dentition. *J. R. Anthro. Inst.* 80(1,2):37-54.

Lewis, O. J. 1973. The hominoid os capitum, with special reference to the fossil bones from Sterkfontein and Olduvai Gorge. *J. Hum. Evol.* 2:1-11.

Lovejoy, C. O. 1974. The gait of australopithecines. *Yrbk. Phys. Anthro.* 17:147-161.

Lovejoy, C. O., and Meindl, R. S. 1973. Eukaryote mutation and the protein clock. *Yrbk. Phys. Anthro.* 16:18-30.

Maglio, V. 1973. Origin and evolution of the Elephantidae. *Trans. Amer. Phil. Soc.*, n.s. 63(3):5-149.

Mahler, P. E. 1973. *Metric Variation in the Pongid Dentition*, Ph.D. Thesis, University of Michigan.

Mayr, E. 1950. Taxonomic categories in fossil hominids. *Cold Spring Harbor Symp. Quant. Biol.* 15:108-118.

Mayr, E. 1963. The taxonomic evaluation of fossil hominids, in: *Classification and Human Evolution* (S.L. Washburn, Ed.). pp. 332-346, Aldine, Chicago.

Partridge, T. C. 1973. Geomorphological dating of cave openings at Makapansgat, Sterkfontein, Swartkrans and Taung. *Nature (Lond.)* 240:75-79.

Pilbeam, D. R. 1972. *The Ascent of Man*, MacMillan, New York.

Pilbeam, D. R., Meyer, G. E., Badgley, C. Rose, M. D., Pickford, M. H. L., Behrensmeyer, A. K., and Ibrahim Shah, S. M. 1977. New hominoid primates from the Siwaliks of Pakistan and their bearing on hominoid evolution. *Nature (Lond.)* 270:689-695.

Robinson, J. T. 1956. The dentition of the Australopithecinae. *Transvaal Mus. Mem.* No. 9.

Robinson, J. T. 1965. *Homo 'habilis'* and the Australopithecines. *Nature (Lond.)* 205:121-124.

Robinson, J. T. 1966. The distinctiveness of *Homo habilis. Nature (Lond.)* 209:957-960.

Robinson, J. T. 1972. *Early Hominid Posture and Locomotion*, University of Chicago Press, Chicago.

Sarich, V. M. 1971. A molecular approach to the question of human origins, in: *Background for Man* (P. Dolhinow and V.M. Sarich, Eds.), pp. 60-81, Little, Brown, Boston.

Sarich, V. M., and Wilson, A. C. 1967. Immunological time scale for hominid evolution. *Science* 158:1220-1203.

Senyurek, M. 1955. A note on the teeth of *Meganthropus africanus* from Tanganyika Territory. *Belleten (Ankara)* 19:1-55.

Simons, E. L. 1976c. The nature of the transition in the dental mechanism from pongids to hominids. *J. Human Evol.* 5:511-528.

Simons, E. L. 1977. *Ramapithecus. Sci. Amer.* 236:35-38.

Simpson, G. G. 1963. The meaning of taxonomic statements, in: *Classification and Human Evolution* (S. L. Washburn, Ed.), pp. 1-31, Aldine, Chicago.

Straus, W. L., Jr. 1949. The riddle of man's ancestry. *Quart. Rev. Biol.* 24:200-223.

Taieb, M. 1975. La decouverte de restes d'hominides vieux de plus trois millions d'annes en Ethiopie. *Bull. Mem. Soc. Anthropol., Paris, Ser. 2* 13:87-89.

Taieb, M., Johanson, D. C., and Coppens, Y. 1975. Expedition internationale de l'Afar, Ethiopie (3e campagne 1974): Decouverte d'hominides plio-pleistocenes a Hadar. *C. R. Acad. Sci., Paris, Ser. D.* 281:1297-1300.

Taieb, M., Johanson, D .C., Coppens, Y., and Aronson, J. L. 1976. Geological and paleontological background of Hadar hominid site, Afar, Ethiopia. *Nature (Lond.)* 260:289-293.

Taieb, M., Johanson, D. C., Coppens, Y., and Bonnefille, R. 1975. Hominides de l'Afar central, Ethiopie. *Bull. Mem. Soc. Anthropol., Paris, Ser. 2* 13:117-124.

Taieb, M., Johanson, D. C., Coppens, Y., Bonnefille, R. and Kalb, J. 1974. Decouverte d'Hominides dans les series plio-pleistocenes d'Hadar (Bassin de l'Awash; Afar, Ethiopie). *C. R. Acad. Sci., Paris, Ser. D.* 279:735-738.

Taieb, M., Johanson, D. C., Coppens, Y., and Tiercelin, J. J. 1978. Expedition internationale de l'Afar, Ethiopie (4 eme et 5 eme Campagne 1975-1977): Chronostratigraphie des gisements a hominides pliocene de l'Hadar et correlations avec les sites prehistoriques du Kada Gona. *C. R. Acad. Sci., Paris, Ser.D.* 287:459-461.

Tobias, P. V. 1965. Cranial capacity of *Zinjanthropus* and other Australopithecines. *Curr. Anthro.* 6(4):414-417.

Tobias, P. V. 1966. The distinctiveness of *Homo habilis. Nature (Lond.)* 209:953-953.

Tobias, P. V. 1967. *Olduvai Gorge, Vol. 2, The Cranium and Maxillary Dentition of* Australopithecus (Zinjanthropus) boisei, Cambridge University Press.

Tobias, P. V. 1973a. Implications of the new age estimates of the early South African hominids. *Nature (Lond.)* 246:79-83.

Tobias, P. V. 1973b. New developments in hominid paleontology in South and East Africa. *Ann. Rev. Anthro.* 2:311-334.

Vrba, E. S. 1975. Some evidence of chronology and paleoecology of Sterkfontein, Swartkrans, and Kromdraai from the fossil Bovidae. *Nature (Lond.)* 254:301-304.

Walker, A. 1973. New *Australopithecus* femora from East Rudolph, Kenya. *J. Hum. Evol.* 2:545-555.

Walker, A., and Leakey, R. E. F. 1978. The hominids of East Turkana. *Sci. Amer.* 239(2):54-66.

Wallace, J. A. 1975. Dietary adaptations of *Australopithecus* and early *Homo*, in: *Paleoanthropology, Morphology and Paleoecology* (R.H. Tuttle, Ed.), pp. 203-223, Mouton, The Hague.

Washburn, S. L. 1971. The study of human evolution, in: *Background for Man* (P. Dolhinow and V. Sarich, Eds.), pp. 82-121, Little, Brown and Co., Boston.

Weidenreich, F. 1943. The skull of *Sinanthropus pekinensis*: a comparative study on a primitive hominid skull. *Palaeontologica Sinica* 10:1-484.

Weinert, H. 1950. Uber die Neuen vor- und Fruhmenschenfunde aus Africa, Java, China und Frankreich. *Z. Morph. Anthro.* 42:113-148.

White, T. D. 1977a. New fossil hominids from Laetolil, Tanzania. *Amer. J. Phys. Anthro.* 46:197-230.

White, T. D. 1977b. *The Anterior Mandibular Corpus of Early African Hominidae: Functional Significance of Shape and Size*, Ph.D. Thesis, University of Michigan.

White, T. D., and Harris, J. M. 1977. Suid evolution and correlation of African hominid localities. *Science* 198:13-21.

Wolpoff, M. H. 1971. Metric trends in hominid dental evolution. *Case West. Reserve Univ. Stud. Anthropol.* 2:1-244.

Wolpoff, M. H. 1974. The evidence for two australopithecine lineages in South Africa. *Yrbk. Phys. Anthro.* 17:113-139.

12

Phylogenetic Analysis of Early Hominids

R. R. Skelton, H. M. McHenry, and G. M. Drawhorn

Most researchers in the field of hominid evolution are in agreement that the living human genus, *Homo*, evolved from some species of the near human genus *Australopithecus*. Until recently, there was also widespread agreement that *Homo* was derived from the species *A. africanus* (e.g., Delson 1978; Tattersall and Eldredge 1977; Wallace 1978; Wolpoff 1982a). It was generally thought that *A. africanus* was primitive in almost every respect in relation to later hominids such as *H. habilis* and the "robust" australopithecine lineage (Eldredge and Tattersall 1975). During the past few years, the proposal of a new species, *A. afarensis*, that is more primitive than *A. africanus* in many respects (Johanson, White, and Coppens 1978) has forced many researchers to reformulate their ideas on this subject and resulted in a multiplicity of hypotheses about evolutionary relationships within the Hominidae. Most of the current hypotheses agree that the course of evolution from the earliest species of the genus *Homo*, *H. habilis*, through *H. erectus* to *H. sapiens* was essentially linear. The major point of contention is which species was the last ancestor of *H. habilis*. Species that have recently been considered for this role include *A. afarensis* (e.g., White, Johanson, and Kimbel 1981), *A. africanus* (e.g., Tobias 1980a), and various as yet undiscovered species of *Australopithecus, Homo*, or some other genus (e.g., Boaz 1983; Leakey 1981; Olson 1981). We shall use phylogenetic analysis to develop a new perspective on this subject.

SPECIES AND SPECIMENS

There are four species of interest here. Specimens of *A. afarensis* (Johanson, White, and Coppens 1978) have been recovered from Hadar, Ethiopia, dating from 2.9 to at least 3.2 million years B.P. (Boaz, Howell, and McCrossin 1982; Brown 1982) and perhaps as early as 3.75 million years B.P. (Aronson and Taieb 1981); from Laetoli Tanzania, dating from 3.65 to 3.75 million years B.P.; and possibly from the older strata at Omo and other locations (Day, Leakey, and Olson 1980; Howell 1978, 1982; Howell and Coppens 1976; Johanson 1980; Johanson and Edey 1981; Johanson and Taieb 1976; Johanson, Taieb, and Coppens 1982; Johanson and White 1979; Johanson, White, and Coppens 1978, 1982; Johanson *et al.* 1982; Kimbel, Johanson, and Coppens 1982; Kimbel, White, and Johanson 1984; Leakey *et al.* 1976; Leakey and Walker 1980; McHenry and Corruccini 1980; Ward, Johanson, and Coppens 1982; White 1977a, b, 1980a, b; White and Johanson 1982; White, Johanson, and Kimbel 1981) [1].

Specimens that have been assigned unambiguously to *A. africanus* (Dart 1925) have been recovered from Sterkfontein and Makapansgat, South Africa. The age of these sites is not known with accuracy, but both are probably in the range of 2.3 to 3.2 million years B.P. (Boaz, Howell, and McCrossin 1982; Grine 1981; Tobias 1978, 1980a, b; Vrba 1975).

H. habilis [2] (Leakey, Tobias, and Napier 1964) and *A. robustus/boisei* [3] are found contemporaneously at a number of sites dating to less than 2.0 million years B.P., including Olduvai, Tanzania; Omo, Ethiopia; East Turkana (Koobi Fora), Kenya; and Swartkrans, South Africa (Boaz and Howell 1977; Clarke 1977; Howell 1976, 1978, 1982; Leakey 1976; Olson 1978; Vrba 1981).

PHYLOGENETIC ANALYSIS

The method of phylogenetic analysis (often called cladistic analysis) [4] was formulated by Hennig (1966) and has been applied to primate and hominid evolution by several workers (e.g., Ciochon 1983; Delson 1975a, b, 1978; Delson, Eldredge, and Tattersall 1977; Luckett and Szalay 1978; Rosenberger and Szalay 1980; Schwartz and Krishtalka 1977; Szalay 1975a, 1977a, b, 1981; Szalay and Delson 1979; Szalay and Drawhorn 1980; Tattersall and Eldredge 1977; Vrba 1979a). Herein we attempt to synthesize several approaches to phylogenetic analysis, but we do not intend this to be a thorough review of the method.

Despite the confusion that has grown up around phylogenetic analysis and the diversity of viewpoints and terminology seen in the literature (Holmes 1980), its application is quite straightforward. The analysis of relationships between fossil species relies most heavily on the comparative anatomy of the fossils themselves. Since every species (living or fossil) exhibits many hundreds or thousands of traits, not all of which are equally useful for reconstructing evolutionary relationships, the investigator must be very selective in his choice of traits to use. Phylogenetic analysis is basically a set of criteria for selecting appropriate traits and a methodology for using them to assess evolutionary relationships.

In selecting traits for analysis, three classes of homologous traits [5] must be distinguished: those that are unique and derived (i.e., transformed relative to some primitive condition), those that are shared and primitive (i.e., inherited more or less without modification from a remote ancestor), and those that are shared and derived [6]. The only traits useful for

Reprinted with permission from *Current Anthropology*, Vol. 27, pp. 21-35. Copyright © 1986 by the Wenner-Gren Foundation for Anthropological Research.

reconstructing evolutionary relationships are those that are both shared and derived [7]. The importance of such traits is that if two or more species (living or fossil) share one or more derived traits relative to other species, then they must have shared a more recent common ancestor and must be more closely related to each other than either is to any other species.

Phylogenetic analysis proceeds by a series of logical steps: establishing a morphocline, determining the direction of change in the morphocline, constructing a cladogram, deriving a phylogeny, and postulating a scenario. (Tattersall and Eldredge [1977] discuss all of these steps, but they do not make clear in what sequence to apply them; Cracraft [1981] also discusses most of these steps.)

Morphoclines

A morphocline is a serial arrangement of the conditions of a trait such that each condition is logically derivable from its neighbors in the sequence. This sequence should be as linear as possible, but branches are allowed if the data clearly indicate their necessity [8].

Once a morphocline is constructed, the direction of the change represented within it must be determined (Maslin 1952) [9]. In the absence of any information other than the conditions of the traits it is impossible to do this. The direction of change can only be determined from information extraneous to the morphocline itself (Schaeffer, Hecht, and Eldredge 1972).

The most straightforward method of determining the direction of change in a morphocline is to assume that the conditions of traits that appear earlier in the fossil record are the more primitive. The direction of change will then be from the oldest to the youngest (Szalay and Drawhorn 1980, Tattersall and Eldredge 1977). This approach has been criticized (Cracraft 1974, Nelson 1978), but we agree with Bretsky (1975:114) that "the fossil record does not give us the revealed truth about evolution, but neither do rules about determining the direction of evolutionary change without recourse to stratigraphic data." It is difficult to imagine how the direction of change in morphoclines concerning extinct species could be determined without consulting the fossil record.

The direction of change in a morphocline may also be determined by several other methods, including (1) examining other species that are known to be more distantly related, often called outgroups, and assuming that the outgroup exhibits the primitive condition (Cracraft 1981, Watrous and Wheeler 1981); (2) examining the embryological and postnatal development of the trait, often called ontogeny, and assuming that the condition found earliest in development is most primitive (Cracraft 1981, Tattersall and Eldredge 1977); and (3) examining the distribution of the trait in closely related species, assuming that the most common traits are primitive (Schaeffer, Hecht, and Eldredge 1972; Tattersall and Eldredge 1977, but see the critique of this method by Watrous and Wheeler 1981). Ideally, more than one of these methods should be used to determine the direction of change. In our analysis we rely heavily on the fossil record and on the outgroup method, using the African apes (chimpanzee and gorilla) and the orangutan as outgroups.

It is often possible to reduce a large number of traits to a smaller number of complexes of covarying traits (Eldredge and Tattersall 1975). It is generally not advisable to consider traits that appear to be evolving in tandem as separate. since

this tends to inflate the importance of what may actually be only one phenomenon. Traits that follow the same or very similar morphoclines and that are not known to be functionally independent should be reduced to a single complex. Here the discretion of the investigator comes into play in determining how much weight a complex should be given in relation to a single trait. Even though a complex may represent a single phenomenon, if it is well developed it must be given more weight than a single trait. Although complexes should be weighted roughly equally, those that include more traits should logically be considered more "important" than those that include fewer traits.

Ideally, the traits within a complex should be functionally related (Kimbel 1984). It is, however, very difficult in most cases to demonstrate such functional relationships or their absence. Where we suggest functional meanings for our complexes or parts thereof, we do not intend these to be rigorous statements of the functions of the traits involved. We feel that the conservative approach is to place all traits that follow a single morphocline in a single complex, even if this groups together traits that are not functionally related. Similarly, not separating traits that follow different morphoclines simply because they might be functionally related results in loss of information. Therefore, our sole criterion for grouping traits into complexes is that they all follow the same morphocline.

We begin our phylogenetic analysis by developing polarized morphoclines for 69 traits. Most of these traits are taken from White, Johanson, and Kimbel (1981) and Kimbel, White, and Johanson (1984). Many of them are illustrated in Johanson and Edey (1981), White, Johanson, and Kimbel (1981), or Rak (1983). Some of these traits were recognized as important over 30 years ago by Clark (1947a, b, 1950), among others. We distinguish 12 complexes of traits, ordered and ranked, as far as possible, in a sequence of decreasing numbers of traits included within them.

Complex 1 (Table 1) includes the greatest number of traits (17). It distinguishes *A. afarensis* from the other three species. *A. africanus*, *A. robustus/boisei*, and *H. habilis* share 17 derived traits for which *A. afarensis* exhibits the primitive condition. This demonstrates that the former three species are more closely related to each other than any of the three is to *A. afarensis* and that *A. afarensis* is distinctly more primitive.

Wolpoff (1982a) lists additional derived traits that are shared by *A. africanus*, *A. robustus/boisei*, and *H. habilis*. These include loss of the triangular shape of the occlusal surface of the lower third molars, the appearance of a symmetrical shape of the occlusal surface of the upper first premolars, reduction in height of the buccal cusps of the permanent upper molars, location of the inferior transverse torus of the mandible higher and more forward, and a more posterior orientation of the roots of the lower first premolars. It is likely that some or all of these traits would fit into Complex 1, but the exact conditions of the traits in each species are not described in enough detail for us to confirm that they follow the defining morphocline of this complex.

Traits 1-10 seem to be functionally related to the size and shape of the incisors, canines, and premolars. Some of these are concerned with the upper canine/lower-first-premolar shearing complex that is present in *A. afarensis* but not in the other three species. White, Johanson, and Kimbel (1981:452) consider the primitiveness of the anterior dentition especially diagnostic of

Table 1. Complex 1.   A. afarensis → { A. africanus, A. robustus/bosei, H. habilis

	Species			
Trait	A. afarensis	A. africanus	A. robustus/ boisei	H. habilis
1. Postion of I_2 roots relativie to margins of nasal aperture	partly lateral	medial	medial	medial
2. Maxillary posterior tooth row convergence/ divergence	converge	diverge	diverge	diverge
3. Deciduoud canine shape	tall/narrow/ pointed	low/wide/ blunt	low/wide/ blunt	low/wide/ blunt
4. Projection of upper canine	projecting	not projecting	not projecting	not projecting
5. Mesial contact facet on upper canine	present	absent	absent	absent
6. Distal contact facet on upper canine	present	absent	absent	absent
7. Mesial occlusal edge shape of lower canine	steep/straight/ elongated	horizontal/ curved/shorter	horizontal/ curved/shorter	horizonal/ curved/shorter
8. P^3 occlusal crown outline	long/narrow/oval	round	round	round
9. P^3 metaconid development	absent to weak	strong	strong	strong
10. P^3 occlusal wear relative to other postcanine teeth	limited	equal	equal	equal
11. Divergence of temporal lines relative to lambda	below	above	above	above
12. Transverse concave curvature of nuchal plane	often present	absent	absent	absent
13. Depth of mandibular fossa	shallow	deep	deep	deep
14. Pneumatization of temporal squama	extensive	reduced	reduced	reduced
15. M_3 distal accessory cusps	absent	present	present	present
16. Breadth of M^2 talonid relative to trigonid	talonid wider	equal	equal	equal
17. Flat shallow palate	present	absent	absent	absent

Table 2. Complex 2.   A. afarensis → A. africanus → { A. robustus/boisei, H. habilis

	Species			
Trait	A. afarensis	A. africanus	A. robustus/boisei	H. habilis
18. Subnasal prognathism	pronounced	intermediate	reduced	reduced
19. Mandibular symphysis inclination	receding	intermediate	vertical	vertical
20. Orientation of tympanic plate	less vertical	more vertical	nearly vertical	nearly vertical
21. Flexion of cranial base	weak	moderate	strong	strong
22. Size of posterior relative to anterior part of temporalis muscle	large	intermediate	small	small
23. Position of widest part of extramolar sulcus	at M^2	intermediate	at M^3	at M^3
24. Position of postglenoid process relative to tympanic plate	completely anterior	variable	merge superiorly	merge superiorly
25. Tubular tympanic	yes	variable	no	no
26. Articular eminence of manidbular fossa	weak	intermediate	strong/cylindrical	strong/cylindrical
27. Position/orientation of foramen magnum	posterior/angled	intermediate	forward/horizontal	forward/horizontal
28. Coronally oriented petrous bones	no	variable	yes	yes
29. Distance between M_3 and temporomandibular joint	long	variable	short	short
30. Lingual ridge on lower canine	prominent	intermediate	absent	absent
31. Lower canine distal occlusal edge length	long	intermediate	short	short
32. Basin-like canine fossa	present	variable	absent	absent
33. Number of lower-incisor mammelons	7	5	3	3

Table 3. Complex 3. _A. afarensis_ → $\begin{Bmatrix} A.\ africanus \\ H.\ habilis \end{Bmatrix}$ → _A. robustus/bosei_

	Species			
Trait	_A. afarensis_	_A. africanus_	_H. habilis_	_A. robustus/ boisei_
34. I$_1$ incisal edge	long	intermediate	intermediate	short
35. P^3 talonid height	low	intermediate	intermediate	high
36. Upper premolar occlusal outline	asymmetric	intermediate	intermediate	oval
37. Approximation of P$_4$ cusp apices	widely separated	intermediate	intermediate	close
38. Wear disparity between buccal and lingual molar cusps	strong	intermediate	intermediate	weak
39. Degree of lower molar cusp swelling	weak	intermediate	intermediate	strong
40. Position of mental foramen	always below mid-corpus	variable	variable	always above mid-corpus
41. Mandibular diastema	frequent	rare	rare	absent
42. Transverse buttress from canine juga to zygomatic arch	present	absent	absent	variable

A. afarensis, and we concur on the basis of this complex. Traits 11-14 are concerned with the shape of the base and posterior part of the skull, while Traits 15 and 16 (and possibly 17) are concerned with molar shape.

Complex 2 (Table 2) includes 16 traits. The morphocline for this complex shows the primitive condition in _A. afarensis_ evolving into an intermediate condition in _A. africanus_ that in turn evolves into the condition seen in _A. robustus/boisei_ and _H. habilis_. _A. robustus/boisei_ and _H. habilis_ share 16 derived traits relative to _A. africanus_, which also displays a derived condition of these same 16 traits relative to _A. afarensis_.

Traits 18-29 can plausibly be related to a progressive trend toward reduction of prognathism in the hominid lineage. Through time the hominid upper and lower jaws retracted, eventually coming to lie almost completely under the rest of the face in _A. robustus/boisei_ and _H. habilis_. Rak (1983), Kimbel, White, and Johanson (1984), and Kimbel and Rak (1985) argue that the reduction of prognathism in _A. robustus/boisei_ and _H. habilis_ is a parallelism [10] and that, in fact, different mechanisms were responsible for it in the two species. The close similarity of these species in Traits 18-29, which are probably related to reduction of prognathism, makes it quite

unlikely that they evolved similar conditions independently. (This problem of possible parallelism is discussed in more detail below.) Traits 30-32 are related to the shape of the canines. The function of Trait 33 (the number of lower-incisor mammelons) is unknown.

Complex 3 (Table 3) includes nine traits. Again, _A. afarensis_ exhibits the primitive condition. Here an intermediate condition is seen in _A. africanus_ and _H. habilis_ and the most extreme form of the derived condition in _A. robustus/boisei_. Most of the traits in Complex 3 seem to have something to do with heavy mastication.

Complex 4 (Table 4) includes eight traits. This complex is very important to the full understanding of the course of hominid evolution, because it contradicts the clear picture presented by Complexes 1, 2, and 3. _A. afarensis_ exhibits the primitive condition for these eight traits, while successive forms of the derived condition are seen in _H. habilis, A. africanus,_ and _A. robustus/boisei_. This complex suggests that _H. habilis_ is more primitive than _A. africanus_ and that the condition of these eight traits in _A. africanus_ is derived from the condition seen in _H. habilis_. The functional relatedness of these traits is not immediately obvious, but some of them are iden-

Table 4. Complex 4. _A. afarensis_ → _H. habilis_ → _A. africanus_ → _A. robustus/bosei_

	Species			
Trait	_A. afarensis_	_H. habilis_	_A. africanus_	_A. robustus/ boisei_
43. Relative size of upper canine	very large	large	medium	small
44. Separation of vomer and anterior nasal spine	wide	variable	narrow	absent
45. Nasoalveolar clivus convexity	convex	variable	straight	concave
46. Width of mandibular extramolar sulcus	narrow	narrow	variable/wide	wide
47. Anterior projection of zygomatic bone	absent	weak/absent	intermediate	strong
48. Hollowing above and behind mental foramen	prominent	moderate	reduced	absent
49. Mental foramen opens laterally	rarely	often	usually	always
50. Height of masseter origin	lowest	low	intermediate	high

Table 5. Complex 5. $\left\{\begin{array}{l}A.\ afarensis\\ H.\ habilis\end{array}\right\} \rightarrow A.\ africanus \rightarrow A.\ robustus/bosei$

Trait	Species			
	A. afarensis	H. habilis	A. africanus	A. robustus/ boisei
51. Deciduous M^1 distal crown profile	tapering/narrow	tapering/narrow	square	square/bulbous
52. Height of mandibular ramus relative to breadth	low	low	intermediate	high
53. Upper canine jugum independent of margin of nasal aperture	yes	yes	variable	no
54. Eversion of basal contour of manidbular corpus	frequent	frequent	infrequent	rare
55. Distinct subnasal and intranasal components of nasoalveolar clivus	yes	yes	intermediate	no

Table 6. Complex 6. $H.\ habilis \rightarrow A.\ afarensis \rightarrow A.\ africanus \rightarrow A.robustus/bosei$

Trait	Species			
	H. habilis	A. afarensis	A. africanus	A. robustus/ boisei
56. Relative size of postcanine teeth	smallest	moderate	large	very large
57. Robusticity of zygomatic arches	weak	moderate	strong	very strong
58. Height of mandibular ramus origin on corpus	high	less high	intermediate	low
59. Most common site of anterior origin of zygomatic arch	M^1	M^1/P^4	P^4	P^3

Table 7. Complex 7. $A.\ afarensis \rightarrow H.\ habilis \rightarrow \left\{\begin{array}{l}A.\ africanus\\ A.\ robustus/bosei\end{array}\right.$

Trait	Species			
	A. afarensis	H. habilis	A. africanus	A. robustus/ boisei
60. Margins of piriform aperture	sharp/discontinuous	veriable	rounded/continuous	rounded/continuous
61. Degree of mesial appression of M$_1$ and M$_2$ hypoconulids	strong	intermediate	weak	weak
62. Distinct nasocanine and nasoalveolar contours	yes	variable	no	no

tified by Rak (1983) as responses to increasingly heavy chewing.

Complex 5 (Table 5) includes five traits and is similar to Complex 4. The primitive condition of these traits seen in *A. afarensis* and *H. habilis* evolved into an intermediate derived condition in *A. africanus* and then into the derived condition seen in *A. robustus/boisei*. As with Complex 4, this complex implies that for these traits *H. habilis* is more primitive than *A. africanus*. These traits can also plausibly be explained as a result of the trend toward heavy chewing.

Complex 6 (Table 6) includes four traits. The morphocline upon which this complex is based contradicts the patterns of all five of the previous complexes. For these four traits the most primitive condition is exhibited by *H. habilis* and successive forms of the derived condition by *A. afarensis, A. africanus,* and *A. robustus/boisei*. This complex suggests that *H. habilis* is more primitive than even *A. afarensis*. Traits 56 and 57 are clearly related to a trend toward enlargement of the teeth and the masticatory musculature (including the bony supports) in the hominid lineage. Traits 58 and 59 may also reflect this trend.

Complex 7 (Table 7) includes three traits and is similar to Complexes 4 and 5. The primitive condition of these traits seen in *A. afarensis* evolved into an intermediate derived condition in *H. habilis* and then into the derived condition seen in *A. africanus* and *A. robustus/boisei*. Trait 60 is identified by Rak (1983) as being a result of the trend toward heavy chewing, and Traits 61 and 62 can plausibly be related to this same trend.

Complex 8 (Table 8) is composed of two traits of unrelated function. This complex is compatible with Complexes 1-3 but not with Complexes 4-7. In these two traits *A. afarensis* is most

Table 8. Complex 8. A. afarensis → A. africanus → A. robustus/boisei → H. habilis

	Species			
Trait	A. afarensis	A. africanus	A. robustus/ boisei	H. habilis
63. C/P$_3$ juga	prominent	pronounced/variable	reduced/variable	very reduced
64. Inclination of nuchal plane	steep	less steep	variable	fairly horizontal

Table 9. Complex 9. A. afarensis → A. robustus/bosei → { A. africanus / H. habilis }

	Species			
Trait	A. afarensis	A. robustus/ boisei	A. africanus	H. habilis
65. Compound temporal/nuchal crest	present	males only	absent	absent
66. Flaring of parietal mastoid angles to form asterionic notch	present	weak	absent	absent

Table 10. Complex 10. A. afarensis → { A. africanus / A. robustus/bosei } → H.habilis

	Species			
Trait	A. afarensis	A. africanus	A. robustus/ boisei	H. habilis
67. Inflection of mastoids beneath cranial base	strong	reduced	reduced	weak

Table 11. Complex 11. A. afarensis → H.habilis → A. robustus/boisei → A. africanus

	Species			
Trait	A. afarensis	H. habilis	A. robustus/ boisei	A. africanus
68. Anterior pillars	absent	rare	variable	present

Table 12. Complex 12. { A. afarensis / A. robustus/boisei } → A. africanus → H.habilis

	Species			
Trait	A. afarensis	A. robustus/ boisei	A. africanus	H. habilis
69. Length of nuchal plane relative to occipital plane	long	long	intermediate	short

primitive and *A. africanus, A. robustus/boisei,* and *H. habilis* show successive degrees of the derived condition.

Complex 9 (Table 9) is also composed of two traits. It presents a completely different picture from that of any previous complex. The primitive condition in *A. afarensis* evolved into the intermediate derived condition seen in *A. robustus/boisei,* which in turn evolved into the derived condition seen in *A. africanus* and *H. habilis.* This complex suggests that *A. robustus/boisei* is more primitive than both *A. africanus* and *H. habilis.* The function of these two traits is not obvious.

Complexes 10-12 (Tables 10-12) include only one trait each. Complex 10 is compatible with Complexes 1, 2, 3, and 8. Complex 11 is similar to Complex 4. Complex 12 is similar to Complex 9.

Cladograms

The next step in a phylogenetic analysis is to construct a cladogram from the polarized morphocline. A cladogram is a construct that indicates the order in which the species diverged. It shows which species are more closely related to each other and nothing more. A cladogram is usually presented in the form of a tree with the species under investigation at the tips of the branches (Farris 1976; Hull 1979). A cladogram is derived in a straightforward manner from a polarized morphocline by placing species that share a derived trait or set of traits on the same branch, indicating that they are more closely related to each other than to species that do not share that derived trait or set of traits.

When, as often happens, different morphoclines suggest different branching orders, the investigator must choose between them. Often, some cladograms will be compatible in that the pattern of relationships depicted in one cladogram will be simply a refinement of the relationships shown in another. Using this idea, the number of cladograms for consideration may be reduced to a few. These few incompatible cladograms show relationships between the species that are contradictory and conflicting. This conflict is resolved by applying the principle of maximum parsimony. Maximum parsimony is achieved by the cladogram that requires the fewest evolutionary events—acquisitions, losses, or modifications of traits—to produce a tenable hypothesis for the evolutionary relationships between the species involved (Engelmann and Wiley 1977). The principle of maximum parsimony penalizes hypotheses that require evolutionary reversals or convergences, [11] since each of these counts as two events rather than one.

The cladograms derived from the morphoclines for the 12 complexes are shown in Figure 1. By combining compatible cladograms, these may be reduced to four. The most parsimonious of these is shown in Figure 2. It is compatible with Complexes 1, 2, 3, 8, and 10 and is identical to Cladograms 2

and 8. Of the original 69 traits, 45 (65%) are consistent with this cladogram. It implies that *H. habilis* and *A. robutus/boisei* are more closely related to each other then either is to *A. africanus* and that *A. africanus* is more closely related to the former species than it is to *A. afarensis*.

The next most parsimonious cladogram is shown in Figure 3a. It is compatible with Complexes 1, 3, 4, 5, 7, and 11 and identical to Cladograms 4, 7, and 11. Of the 69 traits, 44 (64%) are consistent with this cladogram. It implies that *A. africanus* and *A. robustus/boisei* are more closely related to each other than either is to *H. habilis* and that *H. habilis* is more closely related to *A. africanus* and *A. robustus/boisei* than it is to *A. afarensis*.

The third most parsimonious cladogram is shown in Figure 3b. It is compatible with Complexes 1, 9, 10, and 12 and identical to Cladograms 9 and 12. Of the 69 traits, 21 (30%) are consistent with it. This cladogram implies that *A. africanus* and *H. habilis* are more closely related to each other than either is to *A. robustus/boisei* and that *A. robustus/boisei* is more closely related to the former two species than it is to *A. afarensis*.

The least parsimonious cladogram is shown in Figure 3c. It is compatible with Complexes 5 and 6 and identical to Cladogram 6. Of the 69 traits, 9 (13%) are consistent with it. It implies that *A. africanus* and *A. robustus/boisei* are more closely related to each other than either is to *A. afarensis* and that *A. afarensis* is more closely related to *A. africanus* and *A. robustus/boisei* than to *H. habilis*.

Other cladograms are possible, but these four represent the minimum set to which the cladograms based on the 12 complexes can be reduced without compromising any traits.

Figure 1. *Cladograms for Complexes 1-12.*

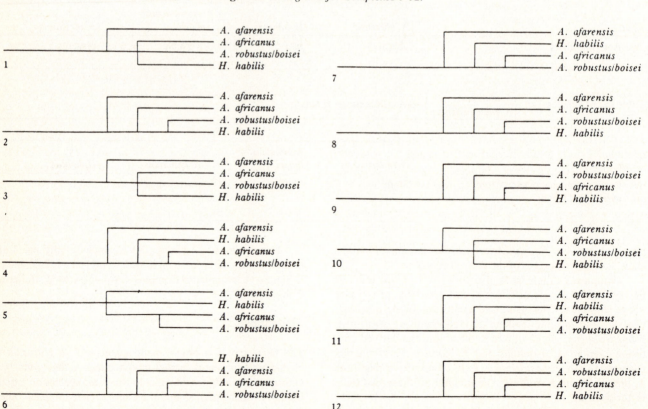

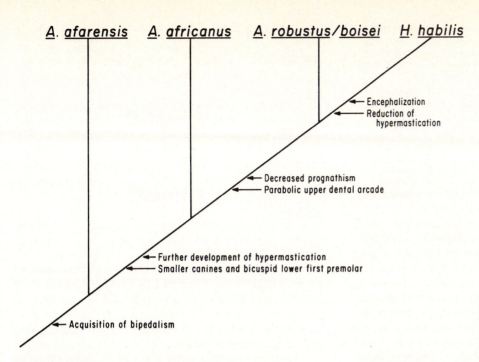

A. _afarensis_   A. _africanus_   A. _robustus/boisei_   H. _habilis_

← Encephalization
← Reduction of hypermastication

← Decreased prognathism
← Parabolic upper dental arcade

← Further development of hypermastication
← Smaller canines and bicuspid lower first premolar

← Acquisition of bipedalism

Figure 2. _Most parsimonious cladogram, based on 45 of the 69 traits, and the derived conditions characterizing each branch._

Phylogenies

The next step in phylogenetic analysis is to derive a phylogeny from the cladogram. A phylogeny incorporates information not contained in the cladogram, such as the chronological and geographic distributions of the species involved. A phylogeny differs from a cladogram in involving inferences concerning the ancestor-descendant relationships between the species (Szalay 1982; Tattersall and Eldredge 1977). More than one phylogeny may be developed from a single cladogram (Platnick 1977; Wiley 1979). Each phylogeny, with its specific assignment of ancestry, must be considered a hypothesis. Ancestry can never be proven, but the hypothesis that one species is ancestral to another may be falsified by demonstrating that the proposed ancestor does not match the hypothetical ancestral morphology reconstructed from the morphologies of the proposed descendants [12] (Delson 1977) or by finding a condition of at least one trait in the proposed ancestor from which it is impossible or unlikely for the condition of the trait found in the proposed descendant to have been derived (Engelmann and Wiley 1977).

Harper (1976) discusses additional criteria for choosing the best phylogeny. The principle of minimum stratigraphic gaps assigns a penalty to any phylogeny that postulates a lineage or species existing through a period of time from which no specimens of that lineage or species have yet been recovered. The principle of minimum anatomical gaps makes the best phylogeny the one that requires the least anatomical change between ancestor and descendant species. The principle of maximum utilization of available information requires that the best phylogeny be the one that accounts for the most of the available anatomical, paleontological, neontological, stratigraphic, and geological information. Thus, a phylogeny based on many traits is better than one based on just a few, and a phylogeny that incorporates nonanatomical information is better than one that does not. It is virtually impossible to design a phylogeny that accounts in a satisfactory manner for every known detail of every specimen, but it is unfortunately quite common to use a restricted set of anatomical traits while ignoring a larger set of traits or other types of information.

The conclusion to be drawn from our most parsimonious cladogram (Fig. 2) is that the last common ancestor of _A. robustus/boisei_ and _H. habilis_ was derived relative to _A. africanus_. This result is primarily due to the 16 traits of Complex 2. We are not the first to recognize the possibility that the last common ancestor of _A. robustus/boisei_ and _H. habilis_ postdated _A. africanus_ (see, e.g., Yaroch and Vitzthum 1984), and others have noted close resemblances between _A. robustus/boisei_ and _H. habilis_ in basicranial morphology (Dean and Wood 1981), canine size (Wolpoff 1978), canine crown morphology, and lack of prognathism (Wood 1981). We feel, however, that a population of hominids resembling _A. africanus_ in all respects except for having the _robustus/boisei-habilis_ condition of the 16 traits in Complex 2 would still fit comfortably within the definition of _A. africanus_. The existing specimens of _A. africanus_ were all recovered from a small geographic area and perhaps a relatively small time span as well. Therefore, it is probable that a population of _A. africanus_ existed at some time and place not yet sampled which had the derived condition for the traits represented in Complex 2.

We suggest, therefore, a phylogeny wherein _A. afarensis_ was ancestral to _A. africanus_, which was in turn ancestral to both _A. robustus/boisei_ and _H. habilis_ (Fig. 4). It is derived from the most parsimonious cladogram and satisfies all the criteria for the best phylogeny. First, there is little evidence suggesting that _A. afarensis_ was not ancestral to _A. africanus_ or that _A. africanus_ could not have been ancestral to _A. robustus/boisei_ and _H. habilis_. Delson, Eldredge, and Tattersall (1977; Delson 1978) reconstruct the morphology of the common ancestor of _A. africanus, A. robustus/boisei,_ and _Homo_ and conclude that _A. africanus_ matches this morphology and lacks any traits that would exclude it from this ancestral position. Tattersall and Eldredge (1977:208) consider _A. africanus_ a "perfect ancestor" for _H. habilis_ and _A. robustus/boisei._ In a separate analysis, we (McHenry and Skelton 1985) reconstruct the last common ancestor of _H. habilis_ and _A. robus-_

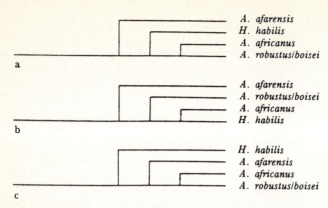

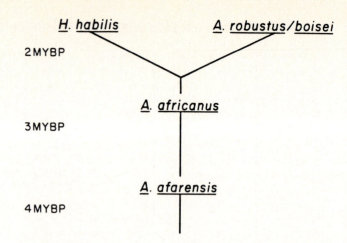

Figure 3. a, *second most parsimonious cladogram, based on 44 of the 69 traits; b, third most parsimonious cladogram, based on 21 of the 69 traits; c, least parsimonious cladogram, based on 9 of the 69 traits.*

Figure 4. *Phylogeny for the four early hominid species that preserves the evolutionary relationships between them shown in the cladogram of Figure 2.*

tus/boisei as being most similar to *A. africanus*. Second, there are no significant spans of time for which the phylogeny requires the existence of a species that has not been recovered from that period. Third, only a minimum of change is required between any ancestral species and its descendant. Fourth, the phylogeny incorporates and explains most of the available pertinent evidence.

The most obvious phylogeny that can be derived from the second most parsimonious cladogram (Fig. 3a) is one in which *A. afarensis* is ancestral to *H. habilis*, which is in turn ancestral to both *A. africanus* and *A. robustus/boisei*. We know of no published phylogeny that supports the idea that *H. habilis* was ancestral to *A. africanus*; its degree of encephalization, if nothing else, is generally recognized to exclude it from this position. Perhaps the most reasonable phylogeny that could be derived from the cladogram of Figure 3a would be one similar to our phylogeny of Figure 4, with *H. habilis* and *A. robustus/boisei* diverging directly from *A. africanus*. This rearrangement would imply a reinterpretation of the conditions of 17 traits (Complexes 4, 5, 7, and 11) of *H. habilis* as unique and derived rather than primitive. Another phylogeny compatible with this cladogram would show *A. afarensis* as the common ancestor of a lineage leading to *H. habilis* and a lineage leading to *A. africanus* and *A. robustus/boisei*. This rearrangement would require reinterpreting the conditions of 38 traits (Complexes 1, 3, 4, 7, and 11) as convergences or parallelisms between the Homo lineage and the lineage including *A. africanus* and *A. robustus/boisei*.

The most obvious phylogeny to be derived from the cladogram of Figure 3b is one in which *A. afarensis* is ancestral to *A. robustus/boisei,* which is ancestral to *A. africanus* and *H. habilis*. Since it is quite unlikely (because of the size of its molars) that *A. robustus/boisei* was ancestral to *A. africanus* and *H. habilis*, the best phylogeny that could be derived from this cladogram would place *A. africanus* in the pivotal ancestral position. This would result in a phylogeny identical to the one just described as the best phylogeny derivable from the cladogram of Figure 3a. With this rearrangement the conditions of three traits (Complexes 9 and 12) in *A. robustus/boisei* would have to be considered unique and derived rather than primitive. Another phylogeny derivable from this cladogram is one in which *A. afarensis* is ancestral to two lineages, one leading to *A. africanus* and *H. habilis* and the other to *A. robustus/boisei*. With this rearrangement, all the 21 traits upon which the cladogram is based have to be reinterpreted as convergences

between the *A. robustus/boisei* lineage and the lineage leading to *A. africanus* and *H. habilis*.

The most obvious phylogeny that can be derived from the cladogram of Figure 3c is one in which *H. habilis* is ancestral to *A. afarensis*, which is in turn ancestral to *A. africanus* and *A. robustus/boisei*. As discussed above, however, *H. habilis* cannot have been ancestral to *A. afarensis*. Leakey's (1981) phylogeny, recognizing this, replaces *H. habilis* in the ancestral position by an unknown species and treats it as independently derived from this ancestor. This requires no reinterpretation of traits. Another phylogeny that may be derived from this cladogram is one in which *A. afarensis* is ancestral to two lineages. one leading to *H. habilis* and one leading to *A. africanus* and *A. robustus/boisei*. This requires reinterpreting the conditions of four traits (Complex 6) of *H. habilis* as unique and derived. This arrangement is the phylogeny advocated by Johanson and White (1979).

Scenario

The logical conclusion to a phylogenetic analysis is to postulate a scenario. A scenario is a story, based in part on the phylogeny, that purports to explain how evolution proceeded. It usually includes statements about the adaptation and ecology of the species involved (Tattersall and Eldredge 1977). The hominid fossil record is not sufficiently well known that a scenario for hominid evolution may be proposed with a high degree of confidence, but we summarize some current ideas and outline a tentative scenario below.

Sometime prior to 4 million years B. P., the genus *Australopithecus* diverged from some hominoid ancestor. Although it is unlikely that the morphology of this ancestor was exactly like that of any living species, the gibbon (Tuttle 1974), the pygmy chimpanzee (Zihlman *et al.* 1978; Zihlman and Lowenstein 1983), and the common chimpanzee (Keith 1934) have all been proposed as approximate models. This ancestor is reconstructed in detail by Ciochon (1983) and would have been fairly generalized, showing similarities to all of the modern hominoids just listed. It seems likely on biogeographic and morphological grounds that the hominid lineage diverged in Africa from a distinctly African hominoid (Bernor 1983; Kay and Simons 1983; Ward and Kimbel 1983). Comparative immunological, DNA similarity, and chromosomal studies demonstrate that the closest living relatives of modern *H. sapiens* are the living African apes (Cronin 1983; de Grouchy, Turleau, and Finaz 1978; Goodman, Baba, and Darga 1983; Sarich 1968, 1983; Sarich and Wilson 1967; Yunis and Prakash 1982; Yunis, Sawyer, and Dunham 1980).

Hominid divergence was accompanied by the development of bipedalism, which distinguishes the hominid lineage from the rest of the Hominoidea (McHenry 1975). The earliest known hominid species is *A. afarensis*, which existed with relatively little change from about 3.75 to about 2.8 million years B. P. The earliest specimens of *A. afarensis* for which we have reliable information on the locomotor anatomy show that this species is undoubtedly bipedal (Lovejoy 1979; McHenry 1982; McHenry and Temerin 1979; White 1980a, b; Wolpoff 1982a) and shares a distinctive pattern of bipedalism with *A. africanus* and *A. robustus/boisei*. There is, however, a difference between the pelvic morphology of *Australopithecus* and that of *Homo* that seems to be at least partly due to an interaction with the trend toward encephalization in *Homo* (Lovejoy 1979); *H. habilis* seems to have a more modern style of bipedalism (Kennedy 1983; McHenry 1982; Tattersall and Eldredge 1977). The upper limb of *Australopithecus*, and to a certain extent that of *H. habilis* as well, retains many primitive features not seen in more modern members of the genus *Homo* (Stern and Susman 1983; Susman and Stern 1982; Vallois 1977; Vrba 1979b). This may reflect a life-style for these species that included more climbing than is typical of *H. sapiens*. The exact stimulus leading to the development of bipedalism is unknown and has been the subject of much speculation (e. g., Jolly 1970; Lovejoy 1981; Robinson 1972; Rodman and McHenry 1980; Washburn 1960).

The development of the trend toward an increased emphasis on heavy chewing may have begun with the initial divergence of the hominid lineage (de Bonis 1983; Kay and Simons 1983; Pickford 1982, 1983) or earlier, with the common ancestor of the African and Asian large-bodied hominoids (Boaz 1983; Greenfield 1980, 1983; Lapson and Pilbeam 1982; Wolpoff 1982b, 1983). *A. afarensis* is megadont, with postcanine teeth much larger relative to a scaled measure of body size than is expected for a hominoid (McHenry 1983a, 1984). Since megadontia is a primary indicator of heavy chewing, we must conclude that the trend toward heavy chewing began with, or prior to, *A. afarensis*. There is much disagreement as to what dietary substances were responsible for this trend. Some possibilities include small objects and seeds (Jolly 1970), grains and roots with some protein (Wolpoff 1973), meat and bone (Szalay 1975b), vegetable material (Pilbeam and Gould 1974), and small, hard-shelled fruits (Walker 1981). There is also evidence that the diet of early hominids was quite broad and diverse (Peters and O'Brien 1981).

Although correlations between past environmental changes and evolutionary events must remain tentative, it is possible that the changes seen in the earliest known hominids were a response to a more open (less forested) habitat associated with a colder, drier climate (Brain 1981; Ciochon 1983). Periods of cold/dry climate occurred at 6.5 million years B.P. (Ciochon 1983), 5.0-4.5 million years B.P. (Brain 1981; Hayes and Frakes 1975; Shackleton and Kennett 1975), and 3.9-3.4 million years B.P. (Ciesielski 1975).

Sometime between 3.0 and 2.5 million years B.P., *A. afarensis* evolved into *A. africanus* via a major rearrangement in certain anatomical complexes, including the size and shape of the canines and premolars and the shape of the posterior part of the skull. There was also further modification of the masticatory anatomy in response to a further development of the trend toward heavy chewing, as described by Rak (1983). *A. africanus* is known unambiguously only from two sites with uncertain dating but appears to have existed for some time at around 2.5 million years B.P. The dental differences between *A. afarensis* and *A. africanus* are presumably due to an intensification of the dietary specializations that accompanied the original divergence of the hominid lineage. One of the major changes was reduction in the size of the canines, the cause of which has historically been the topic of much speculation (e.g., Jungers 1978; Kay 1981; McHenry 1982; Washburn 1960; Washburn and Ciochon 1974; Wolpoff 1978; Wood 1979) and remains unknown. These changes may have occurred in association with a cold/dry climatic episode that occurred at about 3.2-3.0 million years B.P. (Keigwin and Thunell 1979; Shackleton and Kennett 1975).

Between 2.5 and 2.0 million years B.P., some population of *A. africanus* evolved the derived condition for several traits that in our currently known fossil sample are shared exclusively by *A. robustus/boisei* and *H. habilis*. These changes include especially the reduction of prognathism and further change in the shape of the lower canines and probably represent a further development of the distinctive hominid specialization. A cold/dry episode has been identified in the period 2.6-2.3 million years B.P. (Bonnefille 1983; Shackleton and Kennett 1975) and may be involved in these changes.

Also within the time span of 2.5-2.0 million years B.P., the hominid lineage divided into two branches, one leading to *A. robustus/boisei* and the other leading to *H. habilis*. The major change leading to *A. robustus/boisei* was a significant decrease in the size of the incisors (Wood and Stack 1980). Although there are some traits unique to the *A. robustus/boisei* lineage (Delson, Eldredge, and Tattersall 1977; Tobias 1972; Rak 1983), many of the changes seen in this lineage are probably dependent upon increasing body size (allometry). The unique traits in this lineage that are not a straightforward result of increased body size are probably due primarily to an increased emphasis on heavy chewing (Rak 1983). The extreme morphology of this lineage might also be a result of character displacement in response to competition from *Homo* (Summers and Neville 1978). These changes and the divergence of *Homo* may be correlated with a cold/dry climatic episode that occurred at about 2.0-1.8 million years B.P. (Cerling, Hay, and O'Neil 1977).

Two major changes led to the *Homo* lineage: significant encephalization and an apparent reversal of the trend toward heavy chewing. These two changes constitute a trend that characterized the *Homo* lineage up to the appearance of *H. sapiens* (McHenry 1982; Wolpoff 1971). Isaac (1978a, b, 1981) makes a convincing argument that an adaptation emphasizing extrasomatic (cultural) means of responding to the environment accompanied the divergence of the *Homo* lineage. *H. habilis* used stone tools, possibly for processing the meat that was definitely a component of its diet (Bunn 1981; Isaac and Crader 1981; Speth and Davis 1976).

The more controversial of these two major changes and the one that is more important to the present study is the apparent reversal of the trend toward heavy chewing. In many traits related to heavy chewing (see especially Complexes 4-7) *A. afarensis* has a condition that is not as developed as that seen in *A. africanus* and *A. robustus/boisei*. If *H. habilis* is descended from *A. africanus*, then it might be expected to exhibit the more developed condition of these traits. The conditions of these traits in *H. habilis*, however, often appear as undeveloped as those of *A. afarensis*. Some researchers interpret this to mean that *A. afarensis* and *H. habilis* share the primitive conditions for these traits (e. g., White 1977a; White, Johanson, and Kimbel 1981; Rak 1983). However, if *A. africanus* is the immediate ancestor of *Homo*, as our analysis suggests, then it is more likely that the reduced masticatory apparatus of *H. habilis* is unique and derived rather than primitive. It has been widely acknowledged since Weidenreich (1936) that reduction in the size of the dentition characterizes the *Homo* lineage (e. g., Delson 1978; Isaac 1982; Johanson 1980; McHenry 1982, 1983a, 1984; White, Johanson, and Kimbel 1981; McHenry and Skelton 1985). It does not seem unreasonable to postulate that this same well-documented trend may have also characterized the transition between *Australopithecus* and *Homo* (see, e.g., McHenry 1984; Pilbeam and Gould 1974; Smith 1982. Wolpoff 1971). In this view, the resemblances between *A. afarensis* and *H. habilis* in traits related to mastication are not shared primitive conditions but independently acquired states that resulted from dental reduction in the transition from *A. africanus* to *H. habilis*. This dental reduction affected an entire complex of interrelated traits, including those of the face (Rak 1983, 1985; Ward and Kimbel 1983) and the molars (Corruccini and McHenry 1980), that superficially align *A. afarensis* and *H. habilis*. Many of the similarities between *A. afarensis* and *H. habilis* are simply due to similar size, and when the detailed morphology of that region is examined the two species are usually found to be quite different.

This scenario summarizes the present state of our understanding of early hominid evolution. Like all scenarios, it is entirely testable, as are the conclusions drawn at the lower levels of the phylogenetic analysis. It may be useful to indicate what sorts of information at the various levels could falsify our hypothesis:

1. Demonstration that our data were substantially inaccurate.
2. Substantial reinterpretation of the morphoclines for the functional complexes.
3. Demonstration, through the use of new and different data that gave a different series of morphoclines from those considered (Delson, Eldredge, and Tattersall 1977), that our cladogram was not the most parsimonious.
4. Demonstration that *A. afarensis* could not have been ancestral to *A. africanus* or that *A. africanus* could not have been ancestral to *A. robustus/boisei* and/or *H. habilis*, either morphologically or in terms of time. (Correcting for this on the criteria already discussed would require putting *A. afarensis* or *A. africanus* or both on separate side branches. This would not falsify the cladogram, and the close evolutionary relationship between *A. africanus*, *A. robustus/boisei*, and *H. habilis* would be maintained.)

5. Discovery of specimens of any of the four species at times substantially outside the ranges given or substantial reinterpretation of the timing and/or nature of important events. (This would falsify the scenario but not necessarily the phylogeny.)

OTHER HYPOTHESES

Several phylogenies incorporating the four hominid species have recently been proposed. We shall treat five of the best-known of these as critiques of our own. Phylogeny A (Fig. 5) is that of Tobias (1980a); Phylogeny B that of White, Johanson, and Kimbel (1981); Phylogeny C that of Olson (1981); Phylogeny D our interpretation of the hypothesis of Leakey (1976, 1981; Walker and Leakey 1978), an interpretation similar to that of Cronin et al. (1981); Phylogeny E that of Boaz (1983); and Phylogeny F our own (McHenry and Skelton 1985 and Fig. 4).

Tobias (1980a, 1981) proposes a phylogeny very similar to ours, the only significant difference being that he includes the *A. afarensis* specimens within the species *A. africanus*, with the Hadar and Laetoli samples each being assigned to a different subspecies within *A. africanus*. We prefer to retain the taxon *A. afarensis* and agree with Ciochon (1983:822) that "White et al. [1981] demonstrate beyond any reasonable doubt that *A. afarensis* is a species distinct from *A. africanus*...." *A. afarensis* and *A. africanus* are certainly similar in many respects but differ in important ways that are not emphasized by Tobias. Generally speaking, *A. afarensis* retains many primitive features that are absent in *A. africanus* (Johanson and White 1979).

White, Johanson, and Kimbel

White, Johanson, and Kimbel's (1981) phylogeny is distinctive in that *A. africanus* is removed from the lineage leading to *H. habilis* and placed in a lineage leading only to *A. robustus/boisei*. These researchers use phylogenetic analysis [13] and identify a formidable list of traits as being shared by *A. africanus* and *A. robustus/boisei* but not by *A. afarensis* (see also Johanson and White 1979; Kimbel, White, and Johanson 1984). In many cases, however, the condition of these traits in *H. habilis* is not given. This is an unfortunate omission, because, as is pointed out by Wolpoff (1982a:116), "in a good number of these the resemblance is to later hominids recognized to be in the genus *Homo* by the authors (*Homo habilis*, *Homo erectus*)." Unless the reader is thoroughly familiar with the morphology of the *H. habilis* specimens, he may mistakenly assume that the majority of these traits are not also shared by *Homo*. When the traits for which *Homo* shares the extreme form of the derived condition are removed from the list, the vast majority of those remaining are related to heavy chewing (most of them belonging to our Complexes 4-7 and 11). When the traits for which the condition in *Homo* is derived in the direction of *A. africanus* and *A. robustus/boisei* are removed, there are very few traits left indeed (most of which are included in our Complexes 5 and 6—9 traits in all).

The major difference between our hypothesis and that of White, Johanson, and Kimbel (1981) is that while we view the similarities between *H. habilis* and *A. robustus/boisei* as shared derived traits and the similarities between *H. habilis* and *A. afarensis* as due to unique and derived conditions in *H. habilis*

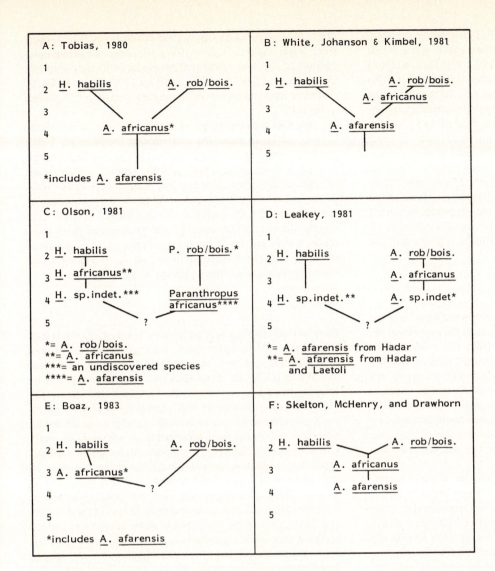

Figure 5. *Six current phylogenies for the four early hominid species.*

that are convergent on the primitive conditions of *A. afarensis*, they view the similarities between *H. habilis* and *A. robustus/boisei* as the result of convergent or parallel evolution and the similarities between *H. habilis* and *A. afarensis* as shared primitive traits. On this basis, according to their view, the morphology of *A. africanus* precludes its having been ancestral to *Homo*. Therefore, they derive *Homo* directly from *A. afarensis*.

The methodology of phylogenetic analysis is clear on the point that similarities in derived traits between two species should be considered evidence for their sharing derived traits unless parallelism or convergence can be demonstrated (e.g., Harper 1976). Rak (1983), Kimbel, White, and Johanson (1984), and Kimbel and Rak (1985) attempt to demonstrate parallelism in the traits shared by *H. habilis* and *A. robustus/boisei*. Their hypothesis is that the conditions of the traits in question (see especially our Complex 2) in *A. robustus/boisei* are the result of retraction of the palate, while a similar morphology was obtained in *H. habilis* through shortening of the palate. Their argument includes only one measured specimen of *H. habilis,* however, not enough for a convincing argument.

From the point of view of White, Johanson, and Kimbel, our phylogeny might be seen as calling for the reversal of too

many traits to be viable. As we have said, however, there are good reasons for accepting the apparent reversal in the *Homo* lineage of many traits related to heavy chewing. Our analysis also shows that there are more traits for which *A. afarensis* is too primitive to have been the most recent ancestor of *H. habilis* and for which *A. africanus* exhibits the appropriate derived condition. To exclude *A. africanus* from the ancestry of *Homo* would require the independent evolution of more traits (48) than would have to be reversed (21) if *A. africanus* is accepted as the most recent ancestor of *Homo*. We agree with Wolpoff (1982a:124) that

> the very case that establishes *Australopithecus afarensis* as a distinctly more primitive australopithecine species also reveals *Australopithecus africanus* to possess a suite of derived features shared with early members of the lineage leading to *Homo sapiens*. That some of these are also shared with the other Pleistocene hominid lineage (a few of them uniquely so) is best explained by the contention that *Australopithecus africanus* is the latest common ancestor.

Another drawback to the phylogeny of White, Johanson, and Kimbel is that it violates the principle of minimum stratigraphic gaps in postulating a time span of at least .6 million years (from 2.6 to 2.0 million years B.P.) during which members of the *Homo* lineage existed but from which not a single specimen has been recovered (Boaz 1979, 1983). Delson (1981) suggests that the specimens from Omo that Howell (1978) assigns to *A. afarensis* may help fill this gap, but the specimens in question are so fragmentary that any definite species assignment must remain tentative. In fact, Howell and Coppens (1976:524) originally concluded that at least some of these specimens "cannot be separated on the basis of size, proportions, and crown morphology from *Australopithecus africanus* samples from Sterkfontein and Makapansgat limeworks." Hunt and Vitzthum (1984) examined these fragmentary fossils from Omo metrically and determined that the specimens recovered from the relevant time span at Omo actually resemble *A. africanus* more than *A. afarensis* in those features that are diagnostic.

Olson

Olson's (1981) phylogenetic analysis uses some features of the cranium, especially the shape of the base of the cranium in the occipitomastoid region, to reconstruct the evolutionary relationships between the four hominid species. In his phylogeny *A. afarensis* and *A. robustus/boisei* belong to one lineage, which he calls the "*Paranthropus*" lineage, while *A. africanus* and *H. habilis* belong to a second, which he calls the "*Homo*" lineage. (This is essentially the taxonomy proposed by Robinson [1967].) He sees the common ancestor of these two lineages as an unnamed species that has not yet been discovered.

We disagree with Olson's phylogeny for several reasons. First, the relevant anatomy of some of the specimens he uses is damaged or ambiguous, and alternative reconstructions are possible (Kimbel 1984). Second, although Olson makes a convincing case that for most living species the traits he uses are stable over the lifetime of an individual, we feel that there is evidence that young specimens of *A. robustus/boisei* may exhibit a different and more *Homo*-like morphology from fully adult members of that species. Third, we feel that he has misclassified the species of some of his specimens. For example, he designates SK-47 as a member of "*Homo*" on the basis of its basicranial morphology rather than as a specimen of *A. robustus* on the basis of its dental morphology as is suggested by Clarke (1977) and Grine (1981). Fourth, his list of traits is rather limited, and we point out the many traits that clearly link *A. robustus/boisei* to *A. africanus* and *H. habilis*. Finally, his phylogeny violates the principle of minimum stratigraphic gaps by necessitating several long periods of time in which certain species existed but from which no specimens of those species have been recovered. The most prominent of these stratigraphic gaps is between *A. afarensis* and *A. robustus/boisei* and represents at least 1 million years.

Leakey

Leakey's (1981) phylogeny implies that *Homo* diverged before the evolution of the genus *Australopithecus*. He feels that the range of variation found in the Hadar sample is too large for a single species and that two species are represented there. He assigns the larger specimens to an unnamed species of the genus *Homo* and the smaller specimens to an unnamed species of the genus *Australopithecus*. This hypothesis receives some support from Tuttle (cited in Herbert 1982), who concludes from comparison of the foot remains from Hadar with the footprints discovered at Laetoli (Leakey and Hay 1979; White 1980a, b) that more than one species of hominid existed prior to 3 million years B.P.

We feel that the range of variation found in the Hadar sample, which is about the same as that found in the living gorilla (White, Johanson, and Kimbel 1981), is not large enough to warrant dividing the sample into two species. We also point out that any hypothesis that does not recognize the close evolutionary relationship between *A. robustus/boisei* and *H. habilis* must account for the presence of many shared derived traits linking the two species and that the presence of these traits makes it unlikely that *Homo* diverged prior to the evolution of *A. africanus*. There is, furthermore, no fossil evidence that *Homo* predates *A. africanus* (Tobias 1978).

Boaz

Boaz's (1983) phylogeny, like Tobias's, lumps *A. afarensis* with *A. africanus* in the latter taxon, although Boaz (1979) does recognize that specimens assigned to *A. afarensis* by Johanson and White (1979) are more primitive. We do not agree with lumping these two species for the reasons stated above. The most distinctive feature of this phylogeny is that *A. robustus/boisei* is hypothesized to have diverged prior to the evolution of *A. africanus* (and presumably *A. afarensis* as well). Earlier work by Delson (1978) supports this idea. These authors apparently regard *A. robustus/boisei* as being unique and derived in such a way that it cannot be closely related to *H. habilis*. Delson, Eldredge, and Tattersall (1977) identify its unique and derived traits to be primarily factors of the dentition and bony crests of the skull. While many unique and derived traits are undoubtedly present in *A. robustus/boisei*, they do not conflict with the pattern of relationships between the species based on shared derived traits. We agree with Wood (1981) that the extreme morphology of *A. robustus/boisei* may divert attention from the derived traits it shares with *H. habilis* and *A. africanus*. The large number of shared derived traits linking *A. africanus*, *A. robustus/boisei*, and *H. habilis*, especially those that are shared only by *A. robustus/ boisei* and *H. habilis*, make it extremely unlikely that *A. robustus/boisei* diverged prior to the evolution of *A. africanus*. Finally, Boaz's phylogeny, like that of Olson, violates the principle of minimum stratigraphic gaps by necessitating a long period during which the *A. robustus/boisei* lineage must have existed but from which no specimens have been recovered.

CONCLUSIONS

The presence of a number of derived traits that are shared by *A. africanus*, *A. robustus/boisei*, and *H. habilis* indicates that these three species are closely related and form an evolutionary group distinct from *A. afarensis* and any earlier species. Furthermore, the presence of derived traits that are shared only by *A. robustus/boisei* and *H. habilis* indicates that a population of hominids of the genus *Australopithecus* that closely resembled *A. africanus* but was even less primitive was probably the last common ancestor of the two. It can be regarded as unlikely that any species more ancient and/or primitive than *A. africanus* was the last ancestor of either the *Homo* lineage or the *A. robustus/boisei* lineage.

The differences between our hypothesis and that of Tobias (1980a) are mainly a matter of taxonomy. The hypothesis of White, Johanson, and Kimbel (1981) postulates the divergence of *Homo* from *A. afarensis* and cannot account for the shared derived traits that link *H. habilis* with *A. africanus* and *A. robustus/boisei*. Leakey's (1981) hypothesis postulates the divergence of *Homo* at an even earlier date and similarly fails to account for the aforementioned shared derived traits linking the later hominids. The hypotheses of Olson (1981) and Boaz (1983) derive *A. robustus/boisei* from *A. afarensis* or some even more ancient species and cannot account for the shared derived traits linking *A. robustus/boisei* with *A. africanus* and *H. habilis*. Taken together, these six phylogenies represent almost every logical way of arranging these species. The fact that rigorous use of the methodology of phylogenetic analysis allows one of these to be unambiguously chosen as the best phylogeny illustrates the utility of the method for paleoanthropology.

COMMENTS

Alan Bilsborough, *Department of Anthropology, University of Durham, England.*

Skelton, McHenry, and Drawhorn have made a timely and stimulating contribution to the debate about the phyletic relationships of early hominid species. Their paper has prompted me to think carefully—although whether sufficiently so remains to be determined—about interpretations of australopithecine diversity, in particular about the distribution and significance of character variation between taxa. I find the authors' emphasis on the similarities between the robust australopithecines and early Homo a valuable counter to my own too-ready tendency to stress the contrasts between those groups. I am in general agreement with their phyletic conclusions and have elsewhere argued along broadly similar lines, particularly in relation to *A. afarensis* and *A. africanus*, although on the basis of (mainly) different evidence and alternative approaches to phyletic inference. The following comments are accordingly directed principally to the authors' methods and the underlying logic thereof rather than to their results.

Although making reference to sites, the authors do not list the hominid specimens upon which the character analysis is based. While this is understandable in terms of limitation of space, it is nonetheless regrettable, since the included specimens and their groupings will critically determine the morphoclines derived and their polarities. The composition of the *A. boisei* sample (does it, for example, include specimens such as KNM-ER 407 and 732?) and its lumping with *A. robustus* is a case in point—amalgamation should surely follow the character analysis, not precede it. The composition of the *H. habilis* sample is another; are the South African specimens SK 847 and Stw 53 included? Skelton *et al.* note the possibility that the sample may, in fact, be heterogeneous and contain individuals from more than one species; resolution of that issue will certainly affect the parameters of *H. habilis*. I am surprised by the authors' inclusion of KNM-ER 1470 among the "undisputed members of *H. habilis*." So far as I am aware, this specimen has been formally assigned only generically; it certainly differs in several respects from the Olduvai hypodigm of *H. habilis*.

The authors mention but, again doubtless because of space limitation, do not discuss in detail the relationship between individual characters and structural/functional complexes. They note that "it is generally not advisable to consider traits that appear to be evolving in tandem as separate, since this tends to inflate the importance of what may actually be only one phenomenon." However, they also state that complexes containing more traits should be considered as more important than those that include fewer, and their preferred cladograms and consequent phyletic arguments accord with this principle. In such cases it is especially important that highly correlated characters be eliminated, since their inclusion means that repeatedly sampled single traits are, in effect, biasing the outcome. Various morphometric techniques, as well as careful character selection, can assist in this respect; in the present study several characters appear to be logically and/or functionally strongly correlated, e.g 4, 5, 6, 41, 43; 8, 9; 44, 45, 55.

Given the mosaic nature of morphological change, it is not surprising that different structural/functional complexes produce different morphocline polarities and thus different cladograms. What appears potentially especially interesting in this study is that certain characters, apparently forming part of a single structural/functional complex (e.g., the canines or the subnasal region), indicate differing polarities, especially among the later hominid groups; I suspect that they would repay further study, but without more details and some indication of their intragroup variability and sample sizes, it is impossible to assess their significance.

The authors, quite rightly in my view, favour the cladogram that is consistent with the maximum number of characters; in so doing they not only follow the principle of maximum parsimony but also, despite their advocacy of cladistic principles, adopt an essentially phenetic approach to phyletic reconstruction. Their prior lumping of *A. robustus/boisei* on the basis of "very similar adaptations" further illustrates this. While they might argue that emphasis upon shared derived characters distinguishes cladistics, character selection is not the sole preserve of cladists; contrary to what is sometimes stated, phenetics does not obviate the need for judicious character selection and definition. Here I am not quarreling with the authors' approach, and I broadly agree with what McHenry has written elsewhere on the relationship between phenetic and cladistically based enquiries—but I think the phenetic component to the present analysis should be recognised and acknowledged.

Cladistic techniques necessarily reduce to bald qualitative statements what are, in fact, quantitative differences—e.g., when does a mandibular fossa (13) cease to be shallow and become deep? As a corollary, the approach suppresses within-group variability and emphasises between-group differences even when there is significant overlap. The *A. africanus* sample exhibits considerable variability, with some specimens possessing character states that are otherwise considered diagnostic of *A. afarensis*; Tobias (1980a) has forcefully drawn attention to some of these, and there are undoubtedly others.

Similarly, the *A. afarensis* sample, judging from casts, photographs, and published descriptions, also shows marked diversity, with some specimens failing to conform to the character states summarised in this article. The extent and significance of such intragroup variation needs to be assessed and its significance evaluated as a necessary part of any analysis of between-group differences. Character states need to be rigorously defined and carefully expressed. For example, how is robusticity of zygomatic arch (57) estimated? Again, to what are the sizes of canine (43) and postcanine teeth (56) relative? If to each other, then they are, of course, logically correlated.

The cladistic approach to hominid phylogeny, with its exclusive emphasis on shared derived characters and the use of pongid outgroup comparators without any detailed rationale to justify their selection as opposed to that of any other groups, assumes that the phylogeny, at least in its broad outlines, is already known. Such a priori phyletic knowledge appears to be based upon assessments of overall similarity, and cladistic studies thus embody at worst an element of tautology, at best an often unacknowledged foundation in phenetics. Given such ambiguity and the continuing controversy over, for example, the use of outgroup comparators, ontogenetic data, and the validity of palaeontological and stratigraphic information, the claimed objectivity of cladistics appears less than firmly grounded.

In short, I find Skelton et al.'s paper a valuable one, particularly for its stress on the patterns of australopithecine between-group differences, and I do not contest its general phyletic conclusions. However, given the phenetic thread to their study, I am less convinced than are the authors that those conclusions provide a vindication of the cladistic approach or of the general utility of that approach for reconstructing hominid phylogeny.

A. T. Chamberlain and B. A. Wood, *Department of Anatomy, University of Liverpool, England*
We are pleased to comment on a study which brings a relatively rigorous analytical technique to bear on the study of hominid relationships. Tattersall and Eldredge (1977) distinguished between three classes of phylogenetic hypothesis, in order of increasing complexity (1) the hypothesis of relationships (i.e., a cladogram), (2) the phylogenetic tree, and (3) the scenario. The first is based on the distribution of shared derived character states between taxa; hypotheses of ancestry (phylogenies) and evolutionary history (scenarios) augment the synapomorphy data of the cladogram by the progressive inclusion of autapomorphic, geological, ecological, and other information.

Skelton et al. suggest that their interest is in hypotheses of ancestry by way of their declaration that "the major point of contention is which species was the last ancestor of *H. habilis*." Determining the correct cladogram for the Hominidae does not uniquely identify such an ancestor, but it may help to exclude taxa from consideration. For example, while Skelton et al.'s "best" cladogram (Fig. 2) permits any species of *Australopithecus* to be ancestral to *Homo*, their next most parsimonious cladogram (Fig. 3a) allows only *A. afarensis* to occupy this position.

We are, however, skeptical whether their data allow them to rank the cladograms so confidently. They base their hierarchy of cladograms on the principle of maximum parsimony, interpreting it to favour the cladogram requiring the minimum number of character state changes. Nonetheless, their "second-best" cladogram is supported by no fewer than 44 characters, compared with the 45 characters supporting the "best" cladogram. The former is also identical to the

cladogram of three trait "complexes" (whereas the "best" cladogram is identical to that of two) and compatible with the pattern of six trait "complexes" (whereas the "best" cladogram is compatible with five). Indeed, since it is difficult to demonstrate that Skelton et al.'s characters are not functionally interrelated, it is arguable that the evidence of the trait "complex" patterns should outweigh that of the characters taken individually, in which case the "second-best" cladogram would be the preferred one.

In addition to these observations on the results, we would like to offer comments on the underlying assumptions and the methodology of the study. First, while we agree with the authors that the only traits useful for a cladistic analysis are those that are both shared and derived, we are not so sanguine about the assumption that the apparent sharing of even one such trait by two taxa *must* (our emphasis) indicate a more recent common ancestor and thus a uniquely close relationship. This would be the case if it were "known" that there was no convergence in the evolution of higher primates. There is no evidence that we know of to suggest that early hominids are categorically free of convergence, and indeed our experience (Wood and Chamberlain 1986) suggests that it is more common than has been supposed. This suggests that the proper approach is a more probabilistic one, with the most likely pattern of relationships being supported by a significant majority of uncorrelated characters. Secondly, we are concerned that the choice of characters may itself lead to the incorporation of one or more sets of unintentional biases. We would be happier if the protocol of character selection were made explicit or, if such a protocol is absent, would wish to read the authors' observations about the possibility of bias. Characters gleaned from other studies inevitably reflect the preoccupations of those studies and may not represent a suitable sample of characters with which to assess relationships.

Thirdly, we are unhappy about the logical basis and the practice of their treatment of morphoclines. The use of stratigraphy to determine polarity has been heavily criticised (e.g., Schaeffer et al. 1972, Bonde 1977). Yet it is apparent that Skelton et al. have, in nearly all instances, accepted the character state of *A. afarensis* (the earliest currently known hominid) as the primitive condition, to the extent that *A. afarensis* possesses a derived condition in only four traits. Furthermore, in every one of their 69 morphoclines the primitive character state is at one pole of the morphocline. This is surprising, for the plesiomorphous condition need not be at the end of a morphocline and may occupy any position on it. For example, Bonde (1977) points out that the number of tetrapod digits runs from eight in ichthyosaurs to zero in snakes, yet the plesiomorphous condition is five. We cannot agree with their acceptance of the dictum of Bretsky (1975), and we believe that their sentence which follows its statement is both untrue (for hypothetical forms can be postulated) and a non sequitur.

Fourthly, we are troubled by their use of the term "complex" as they apply it to the constellation of characters which support a particular cladogram. Others have given the same term a more functional connotation, in the sense that they have applied it to a group of characters which are prescriptive of the same pattern of relationships because they are functionally linked, for example, by mastication or locomotion. We believe that the term "complex" should be used in this context and that it will be confusing if it is given the wider connotation Skelton *et al.* have done. The term "clique," used by Estabrook, Strauch, and Fiala (1977) to refer to a collection of compatible cladistic characters, might be more appropriate here.

Lastly, we are puzzled by Skelton *et al.*'s claim that scenarios are "entirely testable" when they state elsewhere that "correlations between past environmental changes and evolutionary events must remain tentative." The classes of information which they claim will "test" the scenarios will, in fact, only serve to falsify the lowest-order hypothesis, that of relationships. The phylogenetic tree and scenario overlie the cladogram and are dependent on it. If the cladogram fails, the others must fail too, much as a house of cards will tumble when its base is disturbed.

Vaclav Vancata, *Laboratory of Evolutionary Biology, Czechoslovak Academy of Sciences, Czechoslovakia*
This study of hominid phylogeny indicates the real possibility of a late divergence of the australopithecine grade, i.e., the derivation of *Homo habilis* as late as in the *Australopithecus africanus* phase (*contra* Johanson and White 1979). The phylogenetic position of *A. africanus* remains uncertain, however, and the analysis has a number of shortcomings and inconsistencies.

It would be far beyond the scope of my comment to discuss phylogenetic systematics (for such discussion, see, e.g., Cracraft 1981, Gingerich 1979, Simpson 1975, Wiley 1981). The main problem of a phylogenetic analysis is, however, not the scarcity or imprecision of data but the method itself, which is unable "to reflect all the various aspects of evolution" (Wiley 1981:242). It does not matter that evolutionary systematics also has many shortcomings in this respect (cf. Wiley 1981), because phylogenetic analysis is inherently incapable of reflecting them (e.g., Gingerich 1979; Simpson 1975) while the evolutionary approach offers real possibilities for solving this problem (Mlikovsky 1983, Mlikovsky, Belka, and Zemek 1985).

Skelton *et al.*'s paper itself supports this view in that its results originate in the examination of a paraphyletic group of fossil hominids using recent hominoids as an outgroup, which in fact accords with the evolutionary approach (*sensu* Wiley 1981). Although I prefer evolutionary systematics, I shall attempt to support and explain my standpoint from a strictly cladistic point of view.

A very important question of phylogenetic analysis is the monophyly of the group examined, including the criteria for its testing (cf. Cracraft 1981; Wiley 1981). The results presented by the authors show the group to be a paraphyletic one (*sensu* Wiley 1981:259) because *A. afarensis* is ancestral to *A. africanus* only. Consequently, the morphoclines should be reexamined within the framework of a monophyletic group (i.e., *A. africanus*, *A. robustus/boisei*, and *H. habilis*).

Similarly, the use of recent pongids as the outgroup is incorrect in a strictly cladistic sense because "fossils should be treated separately" (Wiley 1981:217) and consequently Upper Miocene hominoids (ramapithecids?) should be the outgroup.

The authors state that their "sole criterion for grouping traits into complexes is that they all follow the same morphoclines." Several questions arise with regard to the complexes of characters: Are they comparable, and how are we to understand and compare the characters in a given complex, which are quite different in genetic and epigenetic (and adaptive) nature? In my opinion, a tuberculum on the tooth crown is scarcely comparable to a major structural character of the mandible. Similarly, if the complexes originated from the analysis, they should be understood as complex system characters with approximately equal weight; if not, additional data should be examined, if possible, and "noise" characters should be excluded. Is there any sense in creating and comparing ad hoc morphoclines with little or no functional meaning, the only criterion being "the more the better"? This criterion would be acceptable only if a representative set of characters (i.e., representative from both systematic and adaptive points of view; cf. Cracraft 1981) grouped in balanced complexes "really" existed.

It could hardly have been achieved in this study, because all the characters come from the skull. Furthermore, 27 characters describe teeth, 28 characters concern jaws or the masticatory apparatus as a whole, and only 14 characters are not in direct connection with the masticatory apparatus. At first glance, the set of characters has limited information value (cf. Sigmon 1985) and does not secure the analysis against misinterpretation of derived or ancestral features. The smaller the region or the more limited the functional system, the greater the danger of incorrect differentiation between homologous and analogous features (from the cladistic point of view; cf. Wiley 1981) and between apomorphic and plesiomorphic and between synapomorphic and symplesiomorphic characters. Thus parallelisms and convergences may be understood as synapomorphies or symplesiomorphies, in direct contradiction to the principles of phylogenetic analysis.

If the limits of the given set of characters are demonstrated by reexamination of the morphoclines in the framework of a strictly monophyletic group (i.e., without *A. afarensis*), quite different results are obtained. Only Complexes 2 and 8 (19 characters) support the authors' hypothesis, while Complexes 3, 4, 5, 6, and 7 (29 characters) might be interpreted as supporting the hypothesis of Johanson and White (1979) and Complexes 1, 9, 11, and 12 (21 characters) have no sound systematic interpretation. Similar results might be obtained if we were to accept the lumping of *A. africanus* and *A. afarensis* (*sensu* Tobias 1980a) and consider that group *ad definitio* monophyletic. Such results could be interpreted in any clear-cut cladogram. They show the necessity for a reevaluation of the set of characters and a search for other systematically representative characters. There are distinctive systematic features on other parts of the australopithecine skeleton: the brain (e.g., Falk 1983, 1985), the cranial venous system (Falk and Conroy 1983), and the postcranial skeleton (e.g., Stern and Susman 1983; Susman, Stern, and Jungers 1984; Vancata 1981, 1983, 1985a, b). Analysis of a broader and more various system of characters should help us to avoid the danger of one-sided interpretation.

What, then, is the position of *A. afarensis* and *A. africanus* from the evolutionary point of view? In strictly systematic terms, the question cannot be answered with certainty. *A. afarensis* is most probably ancestral to *A. africanus*, but either of them could be ancestral to *H. habilis*.

A. africanus seems the more probable ancestor to *H. habilis* (as is shown by the authors), but the known finds are geographically limited and appear in some respects too derived to be directly ancestral to *Homo* (cf. Johanson and White 1979; Blumenberg and Lloyd 1983; Tobias 1980a; White, Johanson, and Kimbel 1981). *A. afarensis*, on the other hand, is, according to the known fossil finds, too primitive for the direct derivation of the genus *Homo* from its morphology (see, e.g., Falk 1985; Stern and Susman 1983; Susman, Stern, and Jungers 1984; Vancata 1985a). We must keep in mind that all these issues are matters of taxonomic classification of fossil finds. Different classifications of *A. afarensis* (cf. Susman, Stern, and Jungers 1984; Tardieu 1979; Tobias 1980a) make possible quite different interpretations of hominid phylogeny.

Considering the major evolutionary grades in australopithecine evolution, however, *A. afarensis* can be definitively taken as the ancestral grade to *A. africanus,* and the *A. africanus* grade should be ancestral to *H. habilis* and *A. robustus/boisei.* Although the overall metric characters of the teeth of *A. afarensis* appear to be more similar to those of *H. habilis* than to those of more advanced australopithecine species (Blumenberg and Lloyd 1983), other characters of the skull and jaws (Boaz 1983, Dean and Wood 1981), the brain (e.g., Falk 1983, 1985), and the postcranial skeleton (Stern and Susman 1983; Susman, Stern, and Jungers 1984; Vancata 1984, 1985a, b) strongly support the pattern of evolution that results from Skelton *et al.*'s phylogenetic study. Therefore their hypothesis seems more conclusive than the others.

The authors have shown not only the necessity and usefulness of a precise, consistent analysis of evolutionary patterns but also the many drawbacks and shortcomings of phylogenetic analysis, which "is impractical and unacceptable for its ostensible purpose, application to classification" (Simpson 1975:13).

Reply

R. R. Skelton, H. M. McHenry, and G. M. Drawhorn, *Department of Anthropology, University of California, Davis, Calif., U.S.A.*
We are grateful to these scholars who have taken the time to comment on our analysis. Their comments are uniformly thoughtful and informative. Many of the points raised are ones about which we ourselves have debated.

Bilsborough and Vancata agree in general with our conclusions regarding ancestry but raise similar questions about our methodology. Chamberlain and Wood do not take a position on our conclusions but are even more critical of our methodology. Although we do not consider ourselves "formulators" or "theorists" of phylogenetic (cladistic) analysis, we do fit into the categories of "users" and "proponents" of this approach. As such we will attempt to answer some of the more important questions raised.

All the commentators raise questions about our choice of specimens and traits. Bilsborough in particular would have appreciated a complete list of specimens used but correctly concludes that space limitations prevented us from providing one. The problem is even greater than it first seems, since different fragmentary specimens have different anatomical parts represented. In order to document our traits fully we would have had to construct a separate list of specimens used for each trait. Such a treatment was part of an early draft, but its inclusion nearly doubled the length of the paper.

Because of the questions raised, a brief description of how traits were selected is in order. First, we extracted a list of traits from the most complete comparative analysis of the early hominids to date, that of White, Johanson, and Kimbel (1981). Second, we refined this list using information from Tobias

(1980) and several other sources. Third, we attempted to confirm these traits independently in all species and specimens of interest. In many cases one of us (H.M.M.) has examined the original specimens. In other cases we relied on examination of casts and published descriptions. Fourth, we gathered and verified traits from other sources and included them when appropriate. Where the condition of a trait was ambiguous for any reason, we eliminated the trait from our list. In a few cases, the trait was unambiguous but variable and is described as such in our data tables. Our fundamental criterion for inclusion of a trait on our list was that we were able to verify its condition in the species of interest. Since most of our traits came originally from White *et al.* (1981), any bias present due to trait selection should favor their hypotheses. To answer some of Bilsborough's specific questions: KNM-ER 407 and 732 are included in our *A. robustus/boisei* series (possible females); SK 847 and Stw 53 are included in our *H. habilis* series.

All the commentators correctly point to our ambivalence concerning the weight that complexes of traits should be given relative to single traits. In our opinion this is an insoluble problem given the current level of theory and borders on paradox. Our solution is that while complexes of traits should be weighted equally, those including greater numbers of traits are more likely to be real phenomena and less likely to be random "noise." They are, therefore, more important, but perhaps we should use the word "reliable" rather than "important." Vancata advocates eliminating the "noise" traits from the analysis, but this comes dangerously close to the all too common practice of ignoring traits that do not fit one's conclusions. We prefer to include these traits but to give complexes that include them less weight in our analysis (especially if the complex includes only that one trait). Chamberlain and Wood object to our use of the word "complex." We agree that "clique" would be an acceptable, even preferable, substitute, but we are surprised by their repeated implication that functional relatedness can be either proven or disproven unambiguously.

Bilsborough and Chamberlain and Wood additionally question our use of maximum parsimony in choosing the "best" cladogram, given our prior use of complexes of traits. Although other valid approaches can be imagined, we use complexes of traits as a utilitarian device at the level of the morphocline only. In this context, it serves to reduce the number of data elements from several discrete traits to a few complexes of traits, resulting in a reduction in the complexity of the analysis. At the level of the cladogram the standard practice is to choose the cladogram that explains the greatest number of discrete traits— not the greatest number of trait complexes. Given lack of precedence and demonstrated reliability of other criteria, we are reluctant to advocate any other than the accepted one of maximum parsimony.

Vancata points out that our traits are limited to the cranium and especially to the teeth. However, existing evidence suggests that *A. afarensis* and *A. africanus* are extremely similar postcranially (McHenry 1983b). Although differences in the lower limb and foot may exist between some of the species, these are not documented well enough in all the species for us to use them in this analysis. Some investigators use *H. sapiens* specimens in lieu of *H. habilis* specimens when the latter do not exist, but we feel that this practice may give misleading results because of continuing evolution of traits in the intervening time-span between these two species.

Both Bilsborough and Vancata have reservations about our use of the great apes as outgroups, Bilsborough because it assumes a priori knowledge of phylogeny and Vancata because Wiley (1981) suggests that only other fossil species should be used as outgroups. We feel that we have used the outgroup method correctly, and since we also use time as a polarizing criterion we feel that the correct polarity has been obtained. We did start with the a priori assumption that the great apes are more distantly related based on the molecular evidence cited in the scenario section of our paper. We did not use Miocene apes as outgroups because we do not reliably know how they are related phylogenetically to the Hominidae, but we agree that the Ramapithecidae would make an ideal outgroup if it could be demonstrated that this group is not derived in the direction of the orangutan.

Chamberlain and Wood are "unhappy" with our use of time as a polarizing criterion and seem to imply that this gives us misleading results. However, we feel that the primitiveness of *A. afarensis* is not an artifact of our methodology but a reflection of its ancestral status. Their criticism of this method, combined with the reservations Bilsborough and Vancata have about the outgroup method, suggests that there is no universally accepted method for polarizing morphoclines. It was for this reason that we used both methods in our analysis.

Bilsborough and Vancata both raise questions about our taxonomy. We stress that this is not a taxonomic paper, and we agree with Vancata that phylogenetic analysis is impractical for classification. We are not prepared to debate the details of the taxonomy of the specimens here, but a further clarification of how we are using the taxonomy in this analysis is in order. It could probably be almost universally agreed upon that there are three broad groups of early hominids: a "gracile australopithecine" group, a "robust australopithecine" group, and an "early *Homo*" group. We use this basic division with slight modifications. We assign members of the "early *Homo*" group to *H. habilis*, even though there may be more than one species represented and many of the specimens (e.g., KNM-ER 1470) have not been formally assigned to this species. We use the name "*A. robustus/boisei*" to refer to the "robust australopithecine" group. We divide the "gracile australopithecine" group into two categories for the purposes of this study, an earlier *A. afarensis* group and a later *A. africanus* group. Alternative taxonomies are possible, but changing the names or subdividing the categories would not change our conclusion that the most recent ancestor of *H. habilis* was *A. africanus* (one may use these taxonomic names in as broad or as narrow a sense as desired). Bilsborough's observation that lumping species suppresses within-group variability is accurate, but in this analysis we are more interested in the pattern of variation between groups.

In response to Bilsborough's reference to a "phenetic thread" in our study due to the use of maximum parsimony and lumping of species, we reply that we are not opposed to phenetic analyses as long as shared derived traits are used exclusively. We agree with Bilsborough that cladistics is not completely objective, but we do feel that its results are more reproducible than those of alternative types of methodology.

To answer another of Bilsborough's specific questions, anterior and posterior tooth size is expressed relative to our best estimates of body weight with allometry taken into account.

We disagree with Vancata's assertion that the Hominidae is a paraphyletic group. We believe that the family is monophyletic and that all hominids are descended from a single recent common ancestor.

Although we discuss the meanings of the complexes and cladograms derived from them in the phylogenies section of our paper, Vancata's reinterpretation of which phylogenies are supported by each complex prompts us to be more specific. Complexes 1, 3, and 10 are compatible with the phylogeny advocated by Tobias (Fig. 5a) and with ours (Fig. 5f). Complexes 2 and 8 are compatible only with our phylogeny. Complexes 4, 7, 9, and 11 are not compatible with any of the six phylogenies of Figure 5, but with reinterpretation of traits these could be made to fit Tobias's phylogeny, White *et al.*'s phylogeny (Fig. 5b), or even our own. Complex 5 is compatible with the phylogeny proposed by White *et al.* (Fig. 5b) or with Leakey's (fig. 5d). Complex 6 is compatible only with Leakey's phylogeny. Complex 12 is compatible with either Olson's phylogeny (Fig. 5c) or Boaz's (Fig. 5e).

We are unable to see how our "best" cladogram (Fig. 2) allows any australopithecine species to be ancestral to *Homo* as suggested by Chamberlain and Wood, unless they mean "ancestral" in the broad sense. This cladogram effectively excludes *A. afarensis* and *A. africanus* from being the last direct ancestor of *Homo*, leaving only *A. robustus/boisei* as a candidate. As we explained, we reject *A. robustus/boisei* as being too derived to have been ancestral to *Homo* and are forced to postulate a hypothetical ancestral species very similar to *A. africanus* in morphology. The problem with Chamberlain and Wood's interpretation of our "second-best" cladogram (Fig. 3a) is that if *A. afarensis* is ancestral to *H. habilis,* then *H. habilis* must be ancestral to *A. africanus* and *A. robustus/boisei*—a hypothesis that can be rejected for reasons given in our paper.

We are puzzled by Chamberlain and Wood's assertion that we do not consider possible convergence (or parallelism). In fact we extensively discuss this possibility. Occam's razor suggests that shared traits are probably shared due to common ancestry, but the possibility of convergence is always present. This leads to our position that shared traits should be considered to be shared through common ancestry unless convergence can be demonstrated. Simple assertion of the possibility of convergence does not demonstrate its reality.

We urge the reader to examine the comments of these respondents as carefully as our own paper. These scholars have forced us to clarify much of our thinking about the methodology we use. This will serve as a special reminder that the philosophical bases of phylogenetic analysis are not universally agreed upon and that although we consider the cladistic method superior there are many thoughtful and precise scholars who do not agree with us. In the future we expect to see a synthesis of the best features of all approaches to determining the evolutionary relationships between species. We are especially gratified that Bilsborough and Vancata agree with our conclusions even though they have reservations about our methodology.

We agree that if a cladogram can be falsified, then any phylogeny or scenario based upon it is also likely to be falsified. However, the reverse is not true. Falsification of a phylogeny does not result in falsification of the underlying cladogram. Some classes of data, for example, temporal and geographical ranges of species, could be used to falsify a scenario but not a cladogram.

[1] For giving one of us (H. M. M.) permission to examine the original fossil material and for other kindnesses, we thank C. K. Brain, E. Vrba, and the staff of the Transvaal Museum, Pretoria; P. V. Tobias, A. Hughes, and the staff of the Department of Anatomy, University of Witwatersrand, Johannesburg; R. E. Leakey, M. D. Leakey, the late L. S. B. Leakey, L. Jacobs, and the staff of the National Museums of Kenya, Nairobi; D. C. Johanson and the staff of the Cleveland Museum of Natural History; and Tadesse Terfa, Mammo Tessema, Woldesenbet Abomssa, and the staff of the National Museum of Ethiopia, Addis Ababa. Partial funding for this research was provided by the Committee on Research, University of California, Davis (H. M. M.), the Regents of the University of California (G. M. D. and R. R. S.), and National Science Foundation grant No. BNS-7918340 (R. R. S. and H. M. M.).

[2] Some authorities, notably Leakey (1976, 1981), consider what we call H. habilis to comprise two species, *H. habilis* and another as yet unnamed. This idea is supported by Falk's (1983) study of endocasts, which showed that KNM-ER-1813 has an endocranial morphology different from that of undisputed members of *H. habilis* such as KNM-ER-1470. If a second species is represented (and only one of us [R. R. S.] thinks this is likely), it differs from *H. habilis* only in the degree of encephalization. We feel justified, therefore, in lumping these specimens with *H. habilis* for the purpose of this analysis.

[3] Although Rak (1983) makes a convincing case that *A. robustus* (Broom 1938) and *A. boisei* (Leakey 1959) are different species and have different facial morphologies, we lump them for present purposes on the basis of their very similar adaptations (Cachel 1975).

[4] Cladistic analysis is more properly defined as the analysis of branching. With this approach, the reconstruction of phylogenies is of secondary or no importance (Nelson 1979). Because it is very difficult to do for extinct species (Van Valen 1978), we are not attempting cladistic classification.

[5] Homologous traits are traits that have approximately the same form because of inheritance from a common ancestor. Thus, the wings of birds and bats are homologous as forelimbs, having been inherited from some common reptilian ancestor, but are analogous, not homologous, as wings because their common ancestor was not winged.

[6] Alternative terms are "autapomorphies" for unique derived traits, "symplesiomorphies" for shared primitive traits, and "synapomorphies" for shared derived traits (Hennig 1966).

[7] An example of a primitive trait for Mammalia is the presence of a furry coat. Both dogs and apes have furry coats, whereas humans have the unique derived trait of lacking a furry coat. Apes are not more closely related to dogs than to humans because they have a furry coat, and humans' lack of a furry coat gives no information as to which furry-coated species are their closest relatives.

[8] For example, given three species, one with 30 teeth, one with 28 teeth, and one with 20 teeth, a morphocline incorporating them would be of the form 30↔ 28↔20. The double-headed arrows imply that the direction of the change has not yet been determined. At this point, the condition of having 30 teeth is equally likely to be primitive as the condition of having 20 teeth.

[9] The direction of change in a morphocline is usually called its "polarity."

[10] A parallelism is the situation in which two closely related species independently evolve identical conditions of a trait. It differs from a convergence (see n. 11) only in the closeness of the relationship between the species.

[11] An evolutionary reversal is obtained when an evolutionary event is followed by another event that results in a condition similar to the original one. An evolutionary convergence is obtained when evolutionary events occurring independently in separate lineages lead to similar morphologies that are not due to common descent.

[12] This hypothetical reconstructed ancestral morphology is usually called a "morphotype."

[13] Despite their careful and detailed treatment of the morphology, there is a problem with their phylogenetic analysis. Their phylogeny can be derived only with difficulty from the cladogram presented, which implies some suite of shared derived traits that link all members of the genus Australopithecus and distinguish them from *Homo*. Although the phylogeny in question can be derived from this cladogram by reinterpreting the traits of *H. habilis* as being unique and derived, their cladogram actually is more compatible with the phylogeny of Leakey (1981). A better cladogram would take the form of a trichotomy with separate branches leading to *A. afarensis*, *H. habilis*, and *A. africanus* and then to *A. robustus/boisei* from a common node, as in the cladogram for our Complex 5. Some investigators object to the use of trichotomous cladograms, but in this case one of this form is clearly warranted (Delson, Eldredge, and Tattersall 1977; Nelson and Platnick 1980). Furthermore, the cladogram presented by White, Johanson, and Kimbel (1981) is a "corrected" cladogram. The original cladogram published by Johanson and White (1979) is also inappropriate and actually is the same as our Figure 2.

REFERENCES

Aronson, J. L., and Taieb, M. 1981. Geology and paleogeography of the Hadar hominid site, in: *Hominid sites: Their geologic settings* (G. Rapp, Jr., and C. F. Vondra, Eds.), Westview Press, Boulder.

Bernor, R. L. 1983. Geochronology and zoogeographic relationships of Miocene Hominoidea, in: *New interpretations of ape and human ancestry* (R. L. Ciochon, and R. S. Corruccini, Eds.), pp. 21-64, Plenum Press, New York.

Blumenberg, B., and Lloyd, A. T. 1983. *Australopithecus* and the origin of the genus *Homo*: Aspects of biometry and systematics with accompanying catalog of tooth metric data. *Bio Systems* 16:127-67.

Boaz, N. T. 1979. Hominid evolution in eastern Africa during the Pliocene and early Pleistocene. *Annual Review of Anthropology* 8:71-85.

Boaz, N. T. 1983. Morphological trends and phylogenetic relationships from Middle Miocene hominoids to Late Pliocene hominids, in: *New interpretations of ape and human ancestry* (R. L. Ciochon and R. S. Corruccini, Eds.), pp. 705-20, Plenum Press, New York.

Boaz, N. T., and Howell, F. C. 1977. A gracile hominid cranium from Upper Member G of the Shungura Formation, Ethiopia. *Amer. J. Phys. Anthro.* 46:93-108.

Boaz, N. T., Howell, F. C., and McCrossin, M. L.. 1982. Faunal age of the Usno, Shungura B, and Hadar Formations, Ethiopia. *Nature* 300:633-35.

Bonde, N. 1977. Cladistic classification as applied to vertebrates, in: *Major patterns in vertebrate evolution* (M. K. Hecht, P. C. Goody, and B. M. Hecht, Eds.), pp. 741-804, Plenum Press, New York.

Bonnefille, R. 1983. Evidence for a cooler and drier climate in the Ethiopian uplands towards 2.5 Myr ago. *Nature* 303:487-91.

Brain, C. K. 1981. Hominid evolution and climatic changes. *South African Journal of Science* 77:104-5.

Bretsky, S. S. 1975. Allopatry and ancestors: A response to Cracraft. *Systematic Zoology* 24:113-19.

Broom, R. 1938. The Pleistocene anthropoid apes of South Africa. *Nature* 142:377-79.

Brown, F. H. 1982. Tulu Bor Tuff at Koobi Fora correlated with the Sidi Hakoma Tuff at Hadar. *Nature* 300:631-33.

Bunn, H. T. 1981. Archaeological evidence for meat-eating by Plio-Pleistocene hominids from Koobi Fora and Olduvai Gorge. *Nature* 291:574-77.

Cachel, S. 1975. A new view of speciation in *Australopithecus*, in: *Paleoanthropology, morphology, and paleoecology* (R. H. Tuttle, Ed.), pp. 183-201, Mouton, The Hague.

Cerling, T. E., Hay, R. L., and O'Neil, J. R. 1977. Isotopic evidence for dramatic climatic changes in East Africa during the Pleistocene. *Nature* 267:137-38.

Ciesielski, P. F. 1975. Biostratigraphy and paleoecology of Neogene and Oligocene silicoflagellates from cores recovered during Antarctic Leg 28, Deep Sea Drilling Project. *Initial Reports of the Deep Sea Drilling Project* 28:625-92.

Ciochon, R. L. 1983. Hominid cladistics and the ancestry of modern apes and humans: A summary statement, in: *New interpretations of ape and human ancestry* (R. L. Ciochon and R. S. Corruccini, Eds.), pp. 783-843, Plenum Press, New York.

Clark, W. E. LeGros. 1947a. Observations on the anatomy of the fossil Australopithecinae. *Journal of Anatomy* 81:300-333.

Clark, W. E. LeGros. 1947b. The importance of the fossil Australopithecinae in the study of human evolution. *Science Progress* 35:377-95.

Clark, W. E. LeGros. 1950. Hominid characters of the australopithecine dentition. *Journal of the Royal Anthropological Institute* 80:37-54.

Clarke, R. J. 1977. A juvenile cranium and some adult teeth of early *Homo* from Swartkrans, Transvaal. *South African Journal of Science* 73:46-49.

Corruccini, R. S., and McHenry, H. M. 1980. Cladometric analysis of Pliocene hominids. *Journal of Human Evolution* 9:209-21.

Cracraft, J. 1974. Phylogenetic models and classification. *Systematic Zoology* 23:71-90.

Cracraft, J. 1981. The use of functional and adaptive criteria in phylogenetic systematics. *American Zoologist* 21:324-45.

Cronin, J. E. 1983. Apes, humans, and molecular clocks: A reappraisal, in: *New interpretations of ape and human ancestry*. (R. L. Ciochon and R.S. Corruccini, Eds.), pp. 115-49. Plenum Press, New York.

Cronin, J. E., Boaz, N. T., Stringer, C. B., and Rak, Y. 1981. Tempo and mode in hominid evolution. *Nature* 292:113-22.

Dart, R. A. 1925. *Australopithecus africanus*: The man-ape of South Africa. *Nature* 115:195-99.

Day, M. H., Leakey, M. D., and Olson, T. R. 1980. On the status of *Australopithecus afarensis*. *Science* 207:1102-3.

Dean, M. C., and Wood, B. A. 1981. Metrical analysis of the basicranium of extant hominoids and *Australopithecus*. *Amer. J. Phys. Anthro.* 54:63-71.

De Bonis, L. 1983. Phyletic relationships of Miocene hominoids and higher primate classification, in: *New interpretations of ape and human ancestry*. (R. L. Ciochon and R. S. Corruccini, Eds.), pp. 625-50, Plenum Press, New York.

De Grouchy, J., Turleau, C., and Finaz, C. 1978. Chromosomal phylogeny of the primates. *Annual Review of Genetics 12:289-328.*

Delson, E. 1975a. Evolutionary history of the Cercopithecidae. *Contributions to Primatology* 5:167-217.

Delson, E. 1975b. Toward the origin of the Old World monkeys, *Problems actuels de paléontologie: Evolution des Vertebres (Colloque International, Centre National de la Recherche Scientifique no. 218)*, pp. 839-50.

Delson, E. 1977. Catarrhine phylogeny and classification: Principles, methods, and comments. *J. Hum. Evol.* 6:433-59.

Delson, E. 1978. Models of early hominid phylogeny, in: *Early hominids of Africa*. (C. J. Jolly, Ed.) pp. 517-41, Duckworth, London.

Delson, E. 1981. Paleoanthropology: Pliocene and Pleistocene human evolution. *Paleobiology* 7:298-305.

Delson, E., Eldredge, N., and Tattersall, I. 1977. Reconstruction of hominid phylogeny: A testable framework based on cladistic analysis. *J. Hum. Evol.* 6:433-59.

Eldredge, N. and Tattersall, I. 1975. Evolutionary models, phylogenetic reconstruction, and another look at hominid phylogeny. *Contributions to Primatology* 5:218-42.

Engelmann, G. F., and Wiley, E. O. 1977. The place of ancestor-descendant relationships in phylogeny reconstruction. *Systematic Zoology* 26:1-11.

Estabrook, G. F., Strauch, J. G., Jr., and Fiala, K. L. 1977. An application of compatibility analysis to the Blackiths' data on orthopteroid insects. *Systematic Zoology* 26:269-76.

Falk, D. 1983. Cerebral cortices of East African early hominids. *Science* 221:1072-74.

Falk, D. 1985. Hadar AL 162-28 endocast as evidence that brain enlargement preceded cortical reorganization in hominid evolution. *Nature* 313:45-47.

Falk, D., and Conroy, G. C. 1983. The cranial venous system in *Australopithecus afarensis*. *Nature* 306:779-81.

Farris, J. S. 1976. Phylogenetic classification of fossils with recent species. *Systematic Zoology* 25:271-83.

Gingerich, P. D. 1979. Paleontology, phylogeny, and classification: An example from the mammalian fossil record. *Systematic Zoology* 28:451-63.

Goodman, M., Baba, M. L., and Darga, L. L. 1983. The bearing of molecular data on the cladogenesis and times of divergence of hominoid lineages, in: *New interpretations of ape and human ancestry*. (R. L. Ciochon and R. S. Corruccini, Eds.), pp. 67-86, Plenum Press, New York.

Greenfield, L. O. 1980. A late divergence hypothesis. *Amer. J. Phys. Anthro.* 52:351-65.

Greenfield, L. O. 1983. Toward the resolution of discrepancies between phenetic and paleontological data bearing on the question of human origins, in: *New interpretations of ape and human ancestry* (R. L. Ciochon and R. S. Corruccini, Eds.), pp. 695-703, Plenum Press, New York.

Grine, F. E. 1981. Trophic differences between "gracile" and "robust" australopithecines: A scanning electron microscope analysis of occlusal events. *South African Journal of Science* 77:203-30.

Harper, C. 1976. Phylogenetic inference in paleontology. *Journal of Paleontology* 50:180-93.

Hayes, D. E., and Frakes, L. A. 1975. General synthesis, Deep Sea Drilling Project Leg 28. *Initial Reports of the Deep Sea Drilling Project* 28:919-42.

Hennig, W. 1966. *Phylogenetic systematics*. University of Illinois Press, Urbana.

Herbert, W. 1982. Was Lucy a climber? Dissenting views of ancient bones. *Science News* 122:116.

Holmes, E. B. 1980. Reconsideration of some systematic concepts and terms. *Evolutionary Theory* 5:35-87.

Howell F. C. 1976. An overview of the Pliocene and earlier Pleistocene of the Lower Omo Basin, southern Ethiopia, in: *Human origins: Louis Leakey and the East African evidence* (G. Ll. Isaac and E. K. McCown, Eds.), pp. 227-68, Benjamin, Menlo Park, Calif.

Howell, F. C. 1978. Hominidae, in: *Evolution of African mammals* (V. J. Maglio and H. B. S. Cooke, Eds.), pp. 154-248, Harvard University Press, Cambridge.

Howell, F. C. 1982. Origins and evolution of African Hominidae, in: *The Cambridge history of Africa*, vol. 1. (J. D. Clark, Ed.), Cambridge University Press, Cambridge.

Howell, F. C., and Coppens, Y. 1976. An overview of Hominidae from the Omo succession, Ethiopia, in: *Earliest man and environments in the Lake Rudolf Basin: Stratigraphy, paleoecology, and environments* (Y. Coppens, F. C. Howell, G. Ll. Isaac, and R. E. F. Leakey, Eds.), pp. 522-32, University of Chicago Press, Chicago.

Hull, D. L. 1979. The limits of cladism. *Systematic Zoology* 28:416-40.

Hunt, K. D., and Vitzthum, V. J. 1984. A dental metric assessment of the phylogenetic position of *Australopithecus africanus*. *Amer. J. Phys. Anthro.* 63:172.

Isaac, G. Ll. 1978a. The food-sharing behavior of protohuman hominids. *Scientific American* 238:90-108.

Isaac, G. Ll. 1978b. Food sharing and human evolution. *Journal of Anthropological Research* 34:311-25.

Isaac, G. Ll. 1981. The early development of protohuman socio-cultural behavior. *Quarterly Review of Archeology* 2:15-17.

Isaac, G. Ll. 1982. Aspects of human evolution, in: *Essays on evolution: A Darwin centenary volume* (D. S. Bendall, Ed.), Cambridge University Press, Cambridge.

Isaac, G. Ll., and Crader, D. C. 1981. To what extent were early hominids carnivorous? An archaeological perspective, in: *Omnivorous Primates* (R. S. O. Harding and G. Teleki, Eds.), pp. 37-103, Columbia University Press, New York.

Johanson, D. C. 1980. Early African hominid phylogenesis: A reevaluation, in: *Current arguments on early man*, (L.-K. Königsson, Ed.), pp. 31-69, Pergamon Press, Oxford.

Johanson, D. C., Lovejoy, C. O., Kimbel, W. H., White, T. D., Ward, S. C., Bush, M. E., Latimer, B. M., and Coppens, Y. 1982. Morphology of the Pliocene partial hominid skeleton (AL-288-1) from the Hadar Formation, Ethiopia. *Amer. J. Phys. Anthro.* 57:403-52.

Johanson, D. C., and Edey, M. A. 1981. *Lucy: The beginnings of humankind.* Simon and Schuster, New York.

Johanson, D. C., and Taieb, M. 1976. Plio-Pleistocene hominid discoveries in Hadar, Ethiopia. *Nature* 260:293-97.

Johanson, D. C., Taieb, M., and Coppens, Y. 1982. Pliocene hominids from the Hadar Formation, Ethiopia (1973-1977): Stratigraphic, chronologic, and paleoenvironmental contexts with notes on hominid morphology and systematics. *Amer. J. Phys. Anthro.* 57:373-402.

Johanson, D. C., and White, T. D. 1979. A systematic assessment of early African hominids. *Science* 203:321-30.

Johanson, D. C., White, T. D., and Coppens, Y. 1978. A new species of the genus *Australopithecus* (Primates: Hominidae) from the Pliocene of eastern Africa. *Kirtlandia* 28:1-14.

Johanson, D. C., White, T. D., and Coppens, Y. 1982. Dental remains from the Hadar Formation, Ethiopia: 1974-1977 collections. *Amer. J. Phys. Anthro.* 57:545-604.

Jolly, C. J. 1970. The seed eaters: A new model of hominid differentiation based on a baboon analogy. *Man* 5:5-27.

Jungers, W. L. 1978. On canine reduction in early hominids. *Current Anthropology* 19:155-56.

Kay, R. F. 1981. The nut-crackers: A new theory of the adaptations of the Ramapithecinae. *Amer. J. Phys. Anthro.* 55:141-51.

Kay, R. F., and Simons, E. L. 1983. A reassessment of the relationship between Later Miocene and subsequent Hominoidea, in: *New interpretations of ape and human ancestry* (R. L. Ciochon and R. S. Corruccini, Eds.), pp. 577-624, Plenum Press, New York.

Keigwin, L. D., Jr., and Thunell, R. C. 1979. Middle Pliocene climatic change in the western Mediterranean from faunal and oxygen isotopic trends. *Nature* 282:294-96.

Keith, A. 1934. *The construction of man's family tree.* Watts, London.

Kennedy, G. E. 1983. A morphometric and taxonomic assessment of a hominine femur from the Lower Member, Koobi Fora, Lake Turkana. *Amer. J. Phys. Anthro.* 61:429-36.

Kimbel, W. H. 1984. Variation in the pattern of cranial venous sinuses and hominid phylogeny. *Amer. J. Phys. Anthro.* 63:243-63.

Kimbel, W. H., Johanson, D. C., and Coppens, Y. 1982. Pliocene hominid cranial remains from the Hadar Formation, Ethiopia. *Amer. J. Phys. Anthro.* 57:453-500.

Kimbel, W. H., and Rak, Y. 1985. Functional morphology of the asterionic region in extant hominoids and fossil hominids. *Amer. J. Phys. Anthro.* 66:31-54.

Kimbel, W. H., White, T. D., and Johanson, D. C. 1984. Cranial morphology of *Australopithecus afarensis*: A comparative study based on a composite reconstruction of the adult skull. *Amer. J. Phys. Anthro.* 64:337-88.

Liapson, S. and Pilbeam, D. 1982. *Ramapithecus* and hominoid evolution. *J. Hum. Evol.* 11:515-18.

Leakey, L. S. B. 1959. A new fossil skull from Olduvai. *Nature* 184:491-93.

Leakey, L. S. B., Tobias, P. V., and Napier, J. 1964. A new species of the genus *Homo* from Olduvai Gorge. *Nature* 202:7-9.

Leakey, M. D., and Hay, R. L. 1979. Pliocene footprints in the Laetolil Beds at Laetoli, northern Tanzania. *Science* 278:317-23.

Leakey, M. D., Hay, R. L., Curtis, G. H., Drake, R. E., Jackes, M. K., and White, T. D. 1976. Fossil hominids from the Laetolil Beds. *Nature* 262:460-66.

Leakey, R. E. F. 1976. Hominids in Africa. *American Scientist* 64:174-78.

Leakey, R. E. F. 1981. *The making of mankind.* Dutton, New York.

Leakey, R. E. F., and Walker, A. 1980. On the status of *Australopithecus afarensis. Science* 207:1103.

Lovejoy, C. O. 1979. A reconstruction of the pelvis of AL288 (Hadar Formation, Ethiopia). Paper presented at the 48th annual meeting of the American Association of Physical Anthropologists. San Francisco, Calif.

Lovejoy, C. O. 1981. The origin of man. *Science* 211:341-50.

Luckett, W. P., and Szalay, F. S. 1978. Clades versus grades in primate phylogeny, in: *Recent advances in primatology*, vol. 3, *Evolution* (D. J. Chivers and K. A. Joysey, Eds.), pp. 227-37, Academic Press, London.

McHenry, H. M. 1975. Fossils and the mosaic nature of human evolution. *Science* 190:425-31.

McHenry, H. M. 1982. The pattern of human evolution: Studies on bipedalism, mastication, and encephalization. *Annual Review of Anthropology* 11:151-73.

McHenry, H. M. 1983a. Relative size of the cheek teeth in *Australopithecus*. Paper presented at the 52d meeting of the American Association of Physical Anthropologists, Indianapolis, Ind. *Amer. J. Phys. Anthro.* 60:224.

McHenry, H. M. 1983b. The capitate of *Australopithecus afarensis* and *A. africanus. Amer. J. Phys. Anthro.* 62:187-98.

McHenry, H. M. 1984. Relative cheek-tooth size in *Australopithecus. Amer. J. Phys. Anthro.* 64:297-306.

McHenry, H. M., and Corruccini, R. S. 1980. On the status of *Australopithecus afarensis. Science* 207:1103-4.

McHenry, H. M., and Skelton, R. R. 1985. Is *Australopithecus africanus* ancestral to *Homo*? in: *Hominid Evolution: The Past, Present, and Future* (P. V. Tobias, Ed.), pp. 221-226, Liss, New York.

McHenry, H. M., and Temerin, L. A. 1979. The evolution of hominid bipedalism: Evidence from the fossil record. *Yearbook of Physical Anthropology* 22:105-31.

Maslin, T. P. 1952. Morphological criteria of phyletic relationships. *Systematic Zoology* 1:49-70.

Mlikovsky, J. 1983. On the foundation of biological systematics: A historical approach, in: *General questions of evolution* (V. J. A. Novak and K. Zemek, Eds.), pp. 305-17, Czechoslovak Academy of Sciences, Praha.

Mlikovsky J., Belka, L. and Zemek, K. 1985. Morphogenesis and the problem of morphospecies, in: *Evolution and morphogenesis* (J. Mlikovsky and V. J. A. Novak, Eds.), pp. 201-11, Academia, Praha.

Nelson, G. J. 1978. Ontogeny, phylogeny, paleontology, and the biogenetic law. *Systematic Zoology* 27:324-45.

Nelson, G. J. 1979. Cladistic analysis and synthesis: Principles and definitions with a historical note on Adanson's *Familles des Plantes* (1763-1764). *Systematic Zoology* 28:1-21.

Nelson, G. J., and Platnick, N. I. 1980. *Cladistics and vicariance patterns in comparative biology.* Columbia University Press, New York.

Olson, T. R. 1978. Hominid phylogenetics and the existence of *Homo* in Member I of the Swartkrans Formation, South Africa. *J. Hum. Evol.* 7:159-78.

Olson, T. R. 1981. Basicranial morphology of the extant hominoids and Pliocene hominids: The new material from the Hadar Formation, Ethiopia, and its significance in early human evolution and taxonomy, in: *Aspects of human evolution* (C. B. Stringer, Ed.), pp. 99-128, Taylor and Francis, London.

Peters, C. R., and O'Brien, E. M. 1981. The early hominid plant food niche: Insights from an analysis of plant exploitation by *Homo, Pan*, and *Papio* in eastern and southern Africa. *Current Anthropology* 22:127-40.

Pickford, M. 1982. New higher primate fossils from the Middle Miocene deposits at Majiwa and Kaloma, western Kenya. *Amer. J. Phys. Anthro.* 58:1-19.

Pickford, M. 1983. Sequence and environments of the Lower and Middle Miocene hominoids of western Kenya, in: *New interpretations of ape and human ancestry* (R. L. Ciochon and R. S. Corruccini, Eds.), pp. 421-39, Plenum Press, New York.

Pilbeam, D., and Gould, S. J. 1974. Size and scaling in human evolution. *Science* 186:892-901.

Platnick, N. I. 1977. Cladograms, phylogenetic trees, and hypothesis testing. *Systematic Zoology* 26:438-42.

Rak, Y. 1983. *The australopithecine face.* Academic Press, New York.

Rak, Y. 1985. Australopithecine taxonomy and phylogeny in light of facial morphology. *Amer. J. Phys. Anthro.* 66:281-87.

Robinson, J. T. 1967. Variation and taxonomy of the early hominids, in: *Evolutionary biology*, vol. 1. (T. Dobzhansky, M. K. Hecht, and W. Steere, Eds.), pp. 64-99, Appleton-Century-Crofts, New York.

Robinson, J. T. 1972. *Early hominid posture and locomotion.* University of Chicago Press, Chicago.

Rodman, P. S., and McHenry, H. M. 1980. Bioenergetics and the origin of hominid bipedalism. *Amer. J. Phys. Anthro.* 52:103-6.

Rosenberger, A. L., and Szalay, F. S. 1980. On the tarsiiform origins of the Anthropoidea, in: *Evolutionary biology of the New World monkeys and continental drift* (R. L. Ciochon and A. B. Chiarelli, Eds.), pp. 139-57, Plenum Press, New York.

Sarich, V. M. 1968. The origin of the hominids: An immunological approach, in: *Perspectives in human evolution*, vol. 1. (S. L. Washburn and P. C. Jay, Eds.), pp. 94-121, Holt, Rinehart and Winston, New York.

Sarich, V. M. 1983. Appendix: Retrospective on hominoid macromolecular systematics, in: *New interpretations of ape and human ancestry* (R. L. Ciochon and R. S. Corruccini, Eds.), pp. 137-50, Plenum Press, New York.

Sarich, V. M., and Wilson, A. C. 1967. Immunological time scale for human evolution. *Science* 158:1200-1203.

Schaeffer, B., Hecht, M., and Eldredge, N. 1972. Phylogeny and paleontology, in: *Evolutionary biology*, vol. 6. (T. Dobzhansky, T. M. Hecht, and W. Steere, Eds.), pp. 31-46, Appleton-Century-Crofts, New York.

Schwartz, J., and Krishtalka, L. 1977. Revision of Picrodontidae (Primates, Plesiadapiformes): Dental homologies and relationships. *Annals of the Carnegie Museum* 46:55-70.

Shackleton, N. J., and Kennett, J. P. 1975. Late Cenozoic oxygen and carbon isotopic changes at DSDP site 284: Implications for glacial history of the Northern Hemisphere and Antarctic. *Initial Reports of the Deep Sea Drilling Project* 29:801-8.

Sigmon, B. 1985. The 'head' focus in human paleontology, in: *Evolution and morphogenesis* (J. Mlikovsky and V. J. A. Novak, Eds.), pp. 635-46, Academia, Praha.

Simpson, G. G. 1975. Recent advances in methods of phylogenetic inference, in: *Phylogeny of the Primates: A multidisciplinary approach* (W. P. Luckett and F. S. Szalay, Eds.), pp. 3-19, Plenum Press, New York.

Smith, P. 1982. Dental reduction: Selection or drift? in: *Teeth: Form, function, and evolution* (Bjorn Kurten, Ed.), pp. 366-79, Columbia University Press, New York.

Speth, J. D., and Davis, D. D. 1976. Seasonal variability in early hominid predation. *Science* 192:441-45.

Stern, J. T., Jr., and Susman, R. L. 1983. The locomotor anatomy of *Australopithecus afarensis. Amer. J. Phys. Anthro.* 60:279-317.

Summers, R. W., and Neville, M. K. 1978. On the sympatry of early hominids. *American Anthropologist* 80:657-60.

Susman, R. L., and Stern, J. T. 1982. Functional morphology of *Homo habilis. Science* 217:931-34.

Susman, R. L., Stern, J. T., and Jungers, W. L. 1984. Arboreality and bipedality in the Hadar hominids. *Folia Primatologica* 43:113-56.

Szalay, F. S. 1975a. Phylogeny of primate higher taxa: The basicranial evidence, in: *Phylogeny of the Primates* (W. P. Luckett and F. S. Szalay, Eds.), pp. 91-125, Plenum Press, New York.

Szalay, F. S. 1975b. Hunting-scavenging protohominids: A model for hominid origins. *Man* 10:420-29.

Szalay, F. S. 1977a. Constructing primate phylogenies: A search for testable hypotheses with maximum empirical content. *J. Hum. Evol.* 6:3-18.

Szalay, F. S. 1977b. Ancestors, descendants, sister groups, and testing of phylogenetic hypotheses. *Systematic Zoology* 26:12-18.

Szalay, F. S. 1981. Functional analysis and the practice of the phylogenetic method as reflected in some mammalian studies. *American Zoologist* 21:37-45.

Szalay, F. S. 1982. A new appraisal of marsupial phylogeny and classification, in: *Carnivorous marsupials* (M. Archer, Ed.), pp. 621-40, Royal Zoological Society of New South Wales, Sydney.

Szalay, F. S., and Delson, E. 1979. *Evolutionary history of the Primates.* Academic Press, New York.

Szalay, F. S., and Drawhorn, G. 1980. Evolution and diversification of the Archonta in an arboreal milieu, in: *Comparative biology and evolutionary biology of the tree shrews* (W. P. Luckett, Ed.), pp. 133-69, Plenum Press, New York.

Tardieu, C. 1981. Morpho-functional analysis of the articular surfaces of the knee-joint in primates, in: *Primate evolutionary biology* (B. Chiarelli and R. S. Corruccini, Eds.), pp. 68-80, Springer, Berlin.

Tattersall, I., and Eldredge, N. 1977. Fact, theory, and fantasy in human paleontology. *American Scientist* 65:204-11.

Tobias, P. V. 1972. "Dished faces," brain size, and early hominids. *Nature* 239:468-69.

Tobias, P. V. 1978. The place of *Australopithecus africanus* in hominid evolution, in: *Recent advances in primatology*, vol. 3, *Evolution* (D. J. Chivers and K. A. Joysey, Eds.), pp. 373-94, Academic Press, London.

Tobias, P. V. 1980a. *Australopithecus afarensis* and *A. africanus*: A critique and an alternative proposal. *Paleontologia Africana* 23:1-17.

Tobias, P. V. 1980b. A study and synthesis of the African hominids of the Late Tertiary and Early Quaternary Periods, in: *Current arguments on early man* (L.-K. Königsson, Ed.), pp. 86-113, Pergamon Press, Oxford.

Tobias, P. V. 1981. The emergence of man in Africa and beyond. *Philosophical Transactions of the Royal Society of London*, Series B, 292:43-56.

Tuttle, R. 1974. Darwin's apes, dental apes, and the descent of man: Normal science in evolutionary anthropology. *Current Anthropology* 15:389-426.

Vallois, H. V. 1977. Interpretation of the scapula of *Plesianthropus transvaalensis. J. Hum. Evol.* 6:675-79.

Vancata, V. 1981. Evolution of hominoid locomotor apparatus and locomotion: Origin and evolution of hominid bipedality (in Czech). CSc. (Ph.D.) diss., Department of Evolutionary Biology, MBU CSAV Praha.

Vancata, V. 1983. Comment on: The evolution of the advanced hominid brain, by Bennett Blumenberg. *Current Anthropology* 24:607-9.

Vancata, V. 1984. The rate and mode of evolution of the early hominid lower limb. *Anthropologia Contemporanea* 7:106.

Vancata, V. 1985a. Macroevolutionary trends in higher primate lower limb: Adaptive changes on femur and tibia and their functional and ecological meaning, in: *Evolution and morphogenesis.* (J. Mlikovsky and V. J. A. Novak, Eds.), pp. 573-80, Academia, Praha.

Vancata, V. 1985b. Origin of hominoid bipedality: Adaptive or non-adaptive process? *International Symposium "Biological Evolution,"* Abstracts, pp. 76-78, Adriatica Editrice, Bari.

Van Valen, L. 1978. Why not to be cladist. *Evolutionary Theory* 3:285-99.

Vrba, E. S. 1975. Some evidence of chronology and palaeoecology of Sterkfontein, Swartkrans, and Kromdraai from the fossil Bovidae. *Nature* 254:301-4.

Vrba, E. S. 1979a. Phylogenetic analysis and classification of fossil and recent Alcelaphini Mammalia: Bovidae. *Biological Journal of the Linnaean Society* 11:207-28.

Vrba, E. S. 1979b. A new study of the scapula of *Australopithecus africanus* from Sterkfontein. *Amer. J. Phys. Anthro.* 5:117-29.

Vrba, E. S. 1981. The Kromdraai australopithecine site revisited in 1980: Recent investigations and results. *Annals of the Transvaal Museum* 33:17-60.

Walker, A. 1981. Diet and teeth. *Philosophical Transactions of the Royal Society of London*, Series B, 272:57-64.

Walker, A., and Leakey, R. E. F. 1978. The hominids of East Turkana. *Scientific American* 239:54-66.

Wallace, J. 1978. Evolutionary trends in the early hominid dentition, in: *Early hominids of Africa* (C. J. Jolly, Ed.), pp. 285-310, Duckworth, London.

Ward, S. C., Johanson, D. C., and Coppens, Y. 1982. Subocclusal morphology and alveolar process relationships of hominid gnathic elements from the Hadar Formation: 1974-1977 collections. *Amer. J. Phys. Anthro.* 57:605-30.

Ward, S. C., and Kimbel, W. H. 1983. Subnasal alveolar morphology and the systematic position of *Sivapithecus. Amer. J. Phys. Anthro. 61:157-71.*

Washburn, S. L. 1960. Tools and human evolution. *Scientific American* 203:3-15.

Washburn, S. L., and Ciochon, R. L. 1974. Canine teeth: Notes on controversies in the study of human evolution. *American Anthropologist* 76:765-84.

Watrous, L. E., and Wheeler, Q. D. 1981. The outgroup comparison method of character analysis. *Systematic Zoology* 30:1-11.

Weidenreich, F. 1936. The mandibles of *Sinanthropus pekinensis. Palaeontologica Sinica*, Series D, no. 4(7):1-162.

White, T. D. 1977a. New fossil hominids from Laetoli, Tanzania. *Amer. J. Phys. Anthro.* 46:197-230.

White, T. D. 1977b. *The anterior mandibular corpus of early African Hominidae: Functional significance of shape and size.* Ph.D. Diss., University of Michigan, Ann Arbor, Mich.

White, T. D. 1980a. Evolutionary implications of Pliocene hominid footprints. *Science* 208:175-76.

White, T. D. 1980b. Additional fossil hominids from Laetoli, Tanzania: 1976-1979 specimens. *Amer. J. Phys. Anthro.* 53:487-504.

White, T. D., and Johanson, D. C. 1982. Pliocene hominid mandibles from the Hadar Formation, Ethiopia: 1974-1977 collections. *Amer. J. Phys. Anthro.* 57: 501-44.

White, T. D., Johanson, D. C., and Kimbel, W. H. 1981. *Australopithecus africanus:* Its phyletic position reconsidered. *South African Journal of Science* 77:445-70.

Wiley, E. O. 1979. Cladograms and phylogenetic trees. *Systematic Zoology* 28:88-92.

Wiley, E. O. 1981. *Phylogenetics: The theory and practice of phylogenetic systematics.* Wiley, New York.

Wolpoff, M. H. 1971. Metric trends in hominid dental evolution. *Studies in Anthropology, Case Western Reserve University* 2:1-244.

Wolpoff, M. H. 1973. Posterior tooth size, body size, and diet in South African gracile australopithecines. *Amer. J. Phys. Anthro.* 39:375-94.

Wolpoff, M. H. 1978. Some aspects of canine size in the australopithecines. *J. Hum. Evol.* 7:115-26.

Wolpoff, M. H. 1982a. Australopithecines: The unwanted ancestors, in: *Hominid origins* (K. J. Reichs, Ed.), pp. 109-26, University Press of America, Washington, D. C.

Wolpoff, M. H. 1982b. *Ramapithecus* and hominid origins. *Current Anthropology* 23:501-22.

Wolpoff, M. H. 1983. *Ramapithecus* and human origins: An anthropologist's perspective of changing interpretations, in: *New interpretations of ape and human ancestry* (R. L. Ciochon and R. S. Corruccini, Eds.), pp. 651-76, Plenum Press, New York.

Wood, B. A. 1979. Models for assessing relative canine size in fossil hominids. *J. Hum. Evol.* 8:493-5O2.

Wood, B. A. 1981. Human origins: Fossil evidence and current problems of analysis and interpretation, in: *Progress in anatomy*, vol. 1. (R. J. Harrison, Ed.), pp. 229-45, Cambridge University Press, Cambridge.

Wood, B. A., and Chamberlain, A. T. 1986. *Australopithecus:* Grade or clade? in: *Major topics in primate and human evolution* (B. A. Wood, P. Andrews, and L. Martin, Eds.), pp. 220-248. Cambridge University Press, Cambridge.

Wood, B. A., and Stack, C. G. 1980. Does allometry explain the differences between "gracile" and "robust" australopithecines? *Amer. J. Phys. Anthro.* 52:55-62.

Yaroch, L. A., and Vitzthum, V. J. 1984. Was *Australopithecus africanus* ancestral to the genus *Homo? Amer. J. Phys. Anthro.* 63:237.

Yunis, J. J., and Prakash, O. 1982. The origin of man: A chromosomal pictorial legacy. *Science* 215:1525-3O.

Yunis, J. J., Sawyer, J. R., and Dunham, K. 1980. The striking resemblances of high-resolution G-banded chromosomes of man and chimpanzee. *Science* 208:1145-48.

Zihlman, A. L., Cronin, J. E., Cramer, D. L., and Sarich, V. M. 1978. Pygmy chimpanzee as a possible prototype for the common ancestor of humans, chimpanzees, and gorillas. *Nature* 275:744-46.

Zihlman, A. L., and Lowenstein, J. M. 1983. *Ramapithecus* and *Pan paniscus:* Significance for human origins, in: *New interpretations of ape and human ancestry* (R. L. Ciochon and R. S. Corruccini, Eds.), pp. 677-94, Plenum Press, New York.

13

2.5 Myr *Australopithecus boisei* from West of Lake Turkana, Kenya

A. Walker, R. E. Leakey, J. M. Harris and F. H. Brown

The 'hyper-robust' hominid *Australopithecus boisei* is well known from several East African Plio-Pleistocene deposits dated between 2.2 and 1.2 Myr (Howell 1978, Coppens 1983). It has been thought of variously, as: the northern vicar of the equally well-known *A. robustus* (Tobias 1973); the extremely specialized end-member of the robust clade (Rak 1983, 1985); an already developed species which immigrated from another, unknown area (Boaz 1983); and as representing individuals at the large end of a single *Australopithecus* species that also encompasses *A. robustus* and *A. africanus* (Wolpoff 1980).

There is a growing consensus that the east and south African samples are different enough to allow them to be placed in separate species (Howell 1978; Coppens 1983; Tobias 1973; Rak 1983, 1985). The type specimen of *A. boisei* is Olduvai Hominid 5 (Leakey 1959; Tobias 1967).

These two robust species are placed in the genus *Paranthropus* by some authors (Robinson 1962, 1967). Although recognizing that the two known samples overlap in time, some have advocated an ancestor-descendant relationship with *A. robustus* giving rise to *A. boisei*. Perhaps the most compelling recent evidence for this last view is Rak's exemplary study of the structure and function of the australopithecine face (Rak 1983, 1985). He has followed an evolutionary scheme in which the origins of the robust clade are in *A. africanus*, which is thereby removed from consideration as a human ancestor (Johanson and White 1979). This scheme has not found universal acceptance (Tobias 1980; Olson 1981).

LOCALITIES

Prospecting was carried out in 1985 in Pliocene sediments to the west of Lake Turkana, Kenya. It led to the recovery of two *A. boisei* specimens. A cranium and a partial mandible were discovered at two separate localities: sediments in the Lomekwi and Kangatukuseo drainages (see Fig. 1) at approximately 3°45'N, 35°45'E.

The general dip of strata is to the east in the Lomekwi drainage, but the strata at Lomekwi I from which the cranium was derived are deformed into a syncline by drag along a fault that truncates the section about 50 m east of the site. Several small faults cut the section west of the site, but it has been possible to link the short sections together by analysis of volcanic ash layers in the sequence. The total thickness of section immediately surrounding the site is less than 15 m, and the volcanic ash layer which caps the section is compositionally indistinguishable from Tuff D of the Shungura Formation. Earlier (Harris and Brown 1985), this tuff was referred to the informally designated Upper Burgi Tuff of the Koobi Fora Formation. With more numerous analyses it is now clear that the Upper Burgi Tuff also correlates with Tuff D, and an additional correlation datum is provided between the Shungura Formation and the Koobi Fora Formation. Tuff D has been dated at 2.52 ± 0.05 Myr (Brown, McDougall, Davies, and Maier 1985). This age is an average computed from samples from the Shungura Formation in Ethiopia, and from the correlative unit at Kangatukuseo. The cranium derives from a level 3.8 m below Tuff D. Around 10 m below Tuff D there is a second ash layer. In the Lokalalei drainage, about 4 km northwest of the site, there are three ash layers exposed in sequence. The lowest correlates with a tuff in submember C9 of the Shungura Formation, and the upper two correlate with the two ash layers exposed at the site of the cranium. On this basis, the cranium is shown to lie within strata correlative with submember C9 of the Shungura Formation. Based on the K/Ar chronology of the Shungura Formation and scaling on the basis of constant sedimentation rates there, the cranium is estimated to be 2.55 Myr old. Using palaeomagnetic polarity boundaries as the basis of chronological placement, the age of the cranium would be ~2.45 Myr, as there is a slight discordance between the two chronologies (Hillhouse, Cerling, and Brown 1986). Therefore, we believe that the age of the cranium can be confidently stated as 2.50 ± 0.07 Myr, including all errors. The sediments from which the cranium derives are overbank deposits of a large perennial river, probably the ancestral Omo.

The mandible from Kangatukuseo III derives from a level about 19 m above Tuff D. Tuff E is not exposed in Kangatukuseo, but it is exposed in the northern part of the Lomekwi drainage, and in the southern Lokalalei drainage. There, sediments correlative with Member D of the Shungura Formation are at least 26 m thick. On this basis, the mandible is assigned to the central part of Member D of the Shungura Formation, the best age estimate for which is 2.45 ± 0.05 Myr. The section is faulted east of the mandible site, and older sediments are exposed along the drainage east of that point. In fact, the entire section exposed in Kangatukuseo lies within an interval from ~25 m above Tuff D to 5 m below that tuff. The mandible was

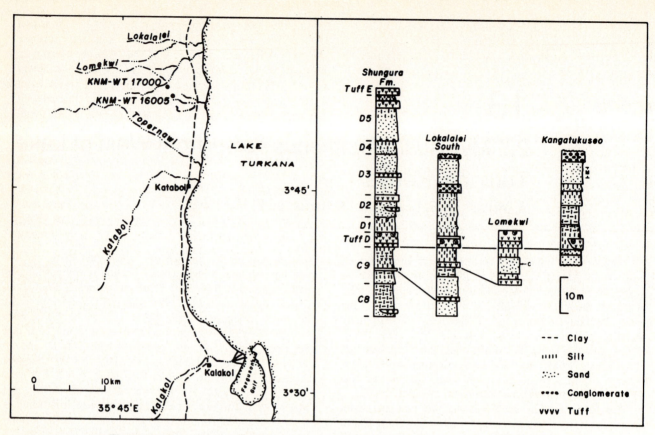

Figure 1. *Map and sections showing geographical and stratigraphic positions of KNM-WT 16005. C, cranium; M, mandible.*

collected from a sandstone layer ~6 m thick, deposited by a large river system. Thin basalt pebble conglomerates intercalated in this part of the section show that the site lay near the boundary between sediments deposited by this large river, and alluvial fan deposits derived from the west.

The interval of section from which the australopithecine specimens were collected has also yielded over 200 fossils representing more than 40 other mammalian species (Table 1), including the skeleton of a ground-dwelling colobine and a relatively complete camel mandible. Bovids are the most common elements of the fauna at this level and most represent species that are otherwise known from the lower portion of the Omo Shungura succession. But whereas alcelaphines and impalas predominate at lower horizons west of Lake Turkana, reduncine bovids are the commonest fossils at the australopithecine sites reported here and are taxonomically different from those recovered slightly higher in the sequence. *Elephas recki shungurensis* is the common elephant at the localities considered here while *Notochoerus scotti* and *Kolpochoerus limnetes* are the common suids. Although all three taxa have lengthy Pliocene distributions, the West Turkana specimens closely match samples of these species from Omo Shungura Members C and D—thus supporting the estimate of age derived from the tuff analyses. The age estimate is corroborated by the apparent absence of the elephantids *Loxodonta adaurora*, *Loxodonta exoptata* and *Elephas recki brumpti*, and of the suids *Nyanzachoerus kanamensis*, *Notochoerus euilus*, *Kolpochoerus afarensis* and *Potamochoerus* sp., all of which occur in older horizons in the upper reaches of the Laga Lomek-

Table 1. Fossil mammals from the new australopithecine localities west of Lake Turkana

Theropithecus brumpti	*Giraffa* sp.
T. cf. *brumpti*	*Aepyceros* sp.
Cercopithecidae large	*Connochaetes* sp.
Cercopithecidae medium	*Parmularius* cf. *braini*
Cercopithecidae small	Alcelaphini medium
Papionini medium/large	Alcelaphini small
Parapapio ado	*Menelikia* sp.
Paracolobus mutiwa	*Kobus sigmoidalis*
Australopithecus boisei	*Kobus* sp. A
Hyaena sp.	*Kobus* sp. B
Homotherium sp.	*Kobus* sp. C
Felidae	*Kobus* sp. D
Viverridae	*Kobus* sp. E
Carnivora indet.	*Kobus* sp. F
Deinotherium bozasi	Reduncini indet.
Elephas recki shungurensis	Reduncini large
Hipparion hasumensis	Reduncini medium
Ceratotherium sp.	Reduncini small
Diceros bicornis	*Tragelaphus nakuae*
Notochoerus scotti	*Tragelaphus* sp.
Kolpochoerus limnetes	Bovini
Hexaprotodon protamphibius	*Gazella* aff. *granti*
Hippopotamus imagunculus	*Antidorcas recki*
Camelus sp.	Antilopini
Sivatherium maurusium	

wi. Also missing from the australopithecine-bearing assemblage are the reduncine bovid *Menelikia lyrocera* and equids of the genus *Equus*, both of which occur higher in the sequence.

SPECIMENS

KNM-WT 17000 is an adult cranium with the following parts missing: all of the tooth crowns except a half molar and the right P^3; some facial bone fragments which have spalled off the infilled maxillary sinus; most of the frontal processes and temporal plates of the zygomatics; the zygomatic arches themselves; a large part of the frontal and parietals superiorly (but a piece of the sagittal crest on the anterior part of the parietal is preserved); parts of both pterygoid regions inferiorly and the posterior part of the maxilla and palate on the right side; and the inferior part of the nuchal region of the occipital. There is no bilateral asymmetry and all bony contacts are sharp. There is no evidence of any plastic deformation and the brain case has retained its spheroidal shape (Fig. 2).

It is a massively-built cranium with a very large facial skeleton, palate and large cranial base, but with a small brain case. The palate and cranial base are roughly the same size as in Olduvai Hominid (O.H.) 5. The cranial base is about the same size as, but the palate is slightly larger than in, KNM-ER 406 (Leakey, Mungai, and Walker 1971). The cranial capacity is 410

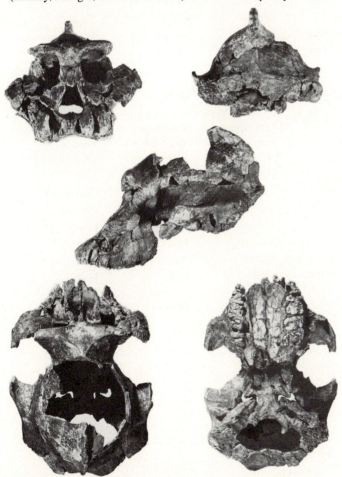

Figure 2. *Anterior, posterior, left lateral, superior and inferior views of cranium KNM-WT 17000. Scale in cm.*

ml (mean of five determinations by water displacement with a standard error of 4.32). This measurement is probably accurate since the orbital plates of the frontals, the cribiform plate region of the ethmoid, one anterior clinoid and both posterior clinoid processes are preserved together with the rest of the cranial base. The missing cranial vault fragments can be reconstructed with fair certainty by following the internal contours all around them. This is the smallest published cranial capacity for any adult fossil hominid, although A.L. 162-28 from Hadar (Kimbel, Johanson, and Coppens 1982) must have been smaller. Given the massive face and palate combined with a small brain case, it is not surprising that the sagittal crest is the largest ever in a hominid. Further, the sagittal crest joins completely to compound temporal-nuchal crests with no intervening bare area (Dart 1948). The foramen magnum position is far forward as in other robust *Australopithecus* specimens (Dean and Wood 1982).

The one complete tooth crown, right P^3, is 11.5 mesiodistally by 16.2 buccolingually. This is bigger mesiodistally (md) than O.H. 5 (10.9) and smaller buccolingually (bl) (17.0) (Leakey 1959; Tobias 1967). These dimensions are completely outside the recorded range for *A. robustus* (9.2-10.7 md, 11.6-15.2 bl) and at the high end of the range for *A. boisei* (9.5-11.8 md, 13.8-17.0 bl) (White, Johanson, and Kimbel 1981). Only the largest *A. boisei* mandibles found so far (for example, KNM-ER 729 and 3230 (Leakey and Leakey 1978) would fit this cranium. It is unfortunate that the region of the occipital which would show the grooves for the occipital and marginal sinuses is missing, but the small sigmoid sinuses appear to have no contribution from transverse ones. Thus we feel that enlarged occipital and a marginal sinuses may have been present.

Most of the previously recorded differences between *A. boisei* and *A. robustus* have involved greater robustness in the former. In fact for those parts preserved in KNM-WT 17000, the definitions originally given by Tobias (1967) include only two characters that cannot be simply attributed to this robustness. One is that the supraorbital torus is 'twisted' along its length. Subsequent discoveries of *A. boisei* specimens show that O.H. 5 is extreme in its supraorbital torus development and that others are not so 'twisted'. The other character is that *A. boisei* palates are deeper anteriorly than those of *A. robustus*, in which they tend to be shallow all along the length. Recently, Rak (1983, 1985) has undertaken a study of the australopithecine face and has documented structural differences between the faces of all four species. Skelton *et al.* (1986) have just made a cladistic analysis of early hominids; Table 2 lists some of the characteristics given as typical of *Australopithecus* species by these authors (see Skelton, McHenry, and Drawhorn 1986 and refs therein) as well as the condition found in KNM-WT 17000. For most features the new specimen resembles *A. boisei*.

There are some features of KNM-WT 17000 that differ from all other 'hyper-robust' specimens as well as from robust ones. The most obvious and important is the prognathic mid- and lower facial region. In superior view all other robust crania are so orthognathic that only a small part of the incisor region projects past the supraorbital tori. In KNM-WT 17000 the mid-face projects strongly past the tori and the anterior maxilla projects well forwards as a square muzzle. In summary, we regard this specimen as part of the *A. boisei* clade and view its differences from the younger sample as being either primitive,

Table 2. Compilation of features of *Australopithecus* species

Feature	A. afarensis	A. africanus	A. robustus	A. boisei	KNM-WT 17000
Position of I^2 roots relative to nasal aperture margins	Lateral	Medial	Medial	Medial	Medial
Divergence of temporal lines relative to lambda	Below	Above	Above	Above	Above
Lateral concavity of nuchal plane	Present	Absent	Absent	Absent	Probably present
Depth of mandibular fossa	Shallow	Deep	Deep	Deep	Shallow
Temporal squama pneumatization	Extensive	Weak	Weak	Weak	Extensive
Flat, shallow palate	Present	Absent	Absent	Absent	Present
Subnasal prognathism	Pronounced	Intermediate	Reduced	Reduced	Pronounced
Orientation of tympanic plate	Less vertical	Intermediate	Vertical	Vertical	Intermediate
Flexion of cranial base	Weak	Moderate	Strong	Strong	Weak
Relative sizes of posterior to anterior temporalis	Large	Intermediate	Small	Small	Large
Position of postglenoid process relative to tympanic	Completely anterior	Variable	Merge superiorly	Merge superiorly	Completely anterior
Tubular tympanic	Present	Intermediate	No	No	Intermediate
Articular eminence	Weak	Intermediate	Strong	Strong	Weak
Foramen magnum relative to tympanic tips	Anterior	Intermediate	Anterior	Anterior	Anterior
Coronally placed petrous temporals	No	Variable	Yes	Yes	Yes
Distance between M^1 and temporomandibular joint	Long	Variable	Short	Short	Long
P^3 outline	Asymmmetric	Intermediate	Oval	Oval	Oval
Relative size of C	Very Large	Medium	Small	Small	Small
Anterior projection of zygomatic	Absent	Intermediate	Strong	Very strong	Very Strong
Height of masseter origin	Lowest	Intermediate	High	High	High
Canine jugum separate from margin of pyriform aperture	Yes	Variable	No	No	No
Distinct subnasal and intranasal parts of clivus	Yes	Intermediate	No	No	No
Relative size of post-canine teeth	Moderate	Large	Very large	Very large	Very large
Robustness of zygomatic arches	Moderate	Strong	Very strong	Very strong	Very strong
Common origin of zygomatic archs	M^1/P^4	P^4	P^4	P^3	P^3
C jugum	Prominent	Pronounced	Reduced	Lost	Lost
Inclination of nuchal plane	Steep	Less steep	—	Variable	Less steep
Compound of temporonuchal crest	Present	Absent	Males only	Males only	Present
Posterionic notch	Present	Absent	Absent	Absent	Probably present
Medial inflection of mastoids	Strong	Reduced	Reduced	Reduced	Reduced
Anterior facial pillars	Absent	Present	Present	Absent	Absent
Length of nuchal plane relative to occipital	Long	Intermediate	Long	Long	Long
Braincase relative to face	—	High	Low	Low	Low
Nasals wide above frontonasal suture	—	No	Yes	Yes	Yes
Nasoalveolar gutter presnt	No	No	Yes	Yes	Yes
Infraorbital foramen high	Yes	Yes	No	No	No
Maxillary fossula present	No	Yes	Yes	No	No
Inferior orbital margins soft laterally	—	No	Yes	No	Yes
Greatest orbital height	—	Middle	Middle	Medial	Middle
Foramen magnum heart-shaped	—	No	No	Yes	Yes

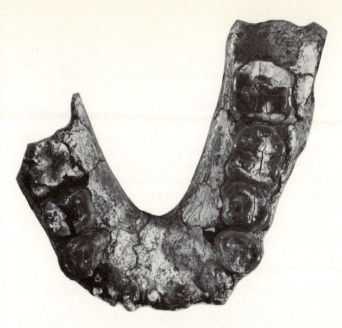

Figure 3. *Occlusal view of mandible KNM-WT 16005. Scale in cm.*

or part of normal intraspecific variation that has not been documented before, or both.

Mandible KNM-WT 16005 has the body preserved to the M$_3$ alveoli on the left and the M$_2$ alveoli on the right. The base is missing. The incisors and canines are, as judged from their roots, relatively very small and the post-canine teeth relatively very large. In its size, shape and proportions, KNM-WT 16005 is very similar to the Peninj mandible (Leakey and Leakey 1964), except that the P$_4$ and M$_1$, of the latter are a little larger and the M$_2$ a little smaller than this specimen. KNM-WT 16005 is smaller than the mandible which KNM-WT 17000 possessed. Tooth measurements are given in Table 3, and the specimen is shown in Fig. 3.

Although future finds may show that KNM-WT 17000 is well within the range of variation of *A. boisei*, it is also possible that the differences will prove sufficient to warrant specific distinction. If the latter proves to be the case we suggest that some specimens from the same time period and from the same sedimentary basin (for example, Omo 1967-18 from the Shungura Formation) will be included in the same species. Omo 1967-18 is the type specimen of *Paraustralopithecus aethiopicus* Arambourg and Coppens (Arambourg and Coppens 1967). In our view, the appropriate name then would be *Australopithecus aethiopicus*.

CONCLUSIONS

The new specimens show that the *A. boisei* lineage was established at least 2.5 Myr ago and further that, in robustness and tooth size, at least some members of the early population were

Table 3. Tooth measurements of KNM-WT 16005 (mm)

	Mesiodistal	*Buccolingual*
Left P$_3$	10.7	13.8
P$_4$	(12.0)	(15.0)
M$_1$	15.7	14.3
M$_2$	(17.0)	16.7

as large as any later ones. Although one authority suggested that the robust australopithecines became smaller in skull and tooth size with time (Robinson 1972), most have pointed out that the available sample showed the opposite, that within *A. boisei* there has been an increase in size and robustness of the skull and jaws. This was apparently an artifact of sampling and is no longer correct.

Although recognizing that at least some populations of *A. robustus* and *A. boisei* overlapped in their time ranges, Rak (1983, 1985) hypothesized that the former was ancestral to *A. boisei*. This is no longer tenable. *A. robustus* shares with younger examples of *A. boisei* several features which are clearly derived from the condition seen in KNM-WT 17000. These include the cresting pattern—with the emphasis on the anterior and middle parts of the temporalis muscle—the orthognathism and the deep temporomandibular joint with strong eminence. At the same time KNM-WT 17000 is clearly a member of the *A. boisei* lineage, as demonstrated by the massive size, extremely large palate and teeth, the build of the infraorbital and nasal areas and the anterior position and low take-off of the zygomatic root.

Therefore, this new specimen shows that *A. robustus* is a related, smaller species that was either derived from ancestral forms earlier than 2.5 Myr and/or has evolved independently in southern Africa, perhaps from *A. africanus*. It has been suggested before that *A. robustus* was derived from *A. africanus* (Rak 1983, 1985), but by those who believed *A. robustus* then gave rise to *A. boisei*—an interpretation that is now unlikely.

The idea that *A. africanus* was the earliest species of a lineage in which *A. robustus* led to *A. boisei* is challenged by the new evidence. KNM-WT 17000 shows that all known *A. africanus* share features which are derived relative to it. Many of these same features were cited by White *et al.* (1981) in arguing that *A. afarensis* is more primitive than *A. africanus*. Features showing KNM-WT 17000 to be more primitive than *A. africanus* that were also used to distinguish the primitiveness of *A. afarensis* are: a very flat, shallow palate; pronounced subnasal prognathism; compound temporal/nuchal crests; sagittal crest with emphasis on posterior fibres of the temporalis muscle; an extensively pneumatized squamous temporal, which in KNM-WT 17000 is 11.5 thick just above the supraglenoid gutter; small occipital relative to nuchal plane; pneumatization of lateral cranial base to produce strongly flared parietal mastoid angles; shallow and mediolaterally broad mandibular fossae; tympanics completely posterior to the postglenoid process. In KNM-WT 17000, the asterionic region is poorly preserved, but an asterionic notch was probably present, which is an additional feature also cited to demonstrate the primitiveness of *A. afarensis*.

Other primitive features found in KNM-WT 17000, but not known or much discussed for *A. afarensis*, are: very small cranial capacity; low posterior profile of the calvaria; nasals extended far above the frontomaxillary suture and well onto an uninflated glabella; low calvaria with receding frontal squama; and extremely convex inferolateral margins of the orbits such as found in some gorillas. Thus there are many features in which KNM-WT 17000 is more primitive than *A. africanus* and similar to *A. afarensis* yet KNM-WT 17000 is clearly a member of the *A. boisei* clade. Further, although the dating of the South African sites is admittedly still imprecise and populations of ancestral species may survive a speciation event, the time sequence of the fossils is becoming increasingly less supportive of the idea of an *africanus-robustus-boisei* lineage.

Finally, it is striking that many of the features of this cranium shared by *A. afarensis* are primitive and not found in *A. robustus* or later specimens of *A. boisei*. These primitive features shared by KNM-WT 17000 and *A. afarensis* are almost exclusively confined to the calvaria, despite the largely complete face of KNM-WT 17000 and the existence of several partial facial specimens at Hadar. However, not one individual adult specimen of *A. afarensis* preserves a facial skeleton attached to a calvaria. This observation raises two alternatives: first, that these features are primitive to the Hominidae and therefore not of great taxonomic value in determining relationships among hominids; second, that, as Olson (1985) has suggested, the specimens identified as *A. afarensis* include two species, one of which gives rise directly to *A. boisei*. Whatever the final answer, these new specimens suggest that early hominid phylogeny has not yet been finally established and that it will prove to be more complex than has been stated.

ACKNOWLEDGEMENT

We thank the Government of Kenya and the Governors of the National Museums of Kenya. This research is funded by the National Geographic Society, Washington, D.C., the Garland Foundation and the National Museums of Kenya. F. H. B. was funded for analyses by NSF grant BNS 8406737. We thank Bw. Kamoya Kimeu and his team for invaluable help. Many colleagues, but especially M. G. Leakey and P. Shipman, helped in various ways.

REFERENCES

Arambourg, C., and Coppens, Y. 1967. Notes des Membres et Correspondants et Notes Presentées ou Transmisées par Leur Soins. *C. R. Hebd. Seanc. Acad. Sci., Paris* 265:599-590.

Boaz, N. T. 1983. Morphological Trends and Phylogenetic Relationships from Middle Miocene Hominids to Late Pliocene Hominids, in: *New Interpretations of Ape and Human Ancestry* (R. L. Ciochon and R. S. Corruccini, Eds.), pp. 705-720, Plenum Press, New York.

Brown, F. H., McDougall, I., Davies, T., and Maier, R. 1985. An Integrated Plio-Pleistocene Chronology for the Turkana Basin, in: *Ancestors: The Hard Evidence* (E. Delson, Ed.), pp. 82-90, Liss, New York.

Coppens, Y. 1981. Les Hominids du Pliocene et du Pleistocene d'Afrique Orientale et Leur Environment in: *Morphologie Evolutive—Morphogenese du Crane at Origine de l'Homme* (M. Sakka, Ed.), pp. 155-168, CRNS, Paris.

Coppens, Y. 1983. Systematique, Environment and Culture des Australopitheques, Hypotheses and systheses. *Bull. Mem. Soc. Anthrop. Paris* 10:273-284.

Dart, R. A. 1948. The Makapansgat Proto-Human *Australopithecus prometheus. Am. J. Phys. Anthrop.* 6:259-284.

Dean, M. C., and Wood, B. A. 1982. Basicranial Anatomy of Plio-Pleistocene Hominids from East and South Africa. *Am. J. Phys. Anthrop.* 59:157-174.

Harris, J. M., and Brown, F. H. 1985. New Hominid Locality West of Lake Turkana, Kenya. *National Geographic Res.* 1:289-297.

Hillhouse, J. J., Cerling, T. E., and Brown, F. H. 1986. Magnetostratigraphy of the Koobi Fora Formation, Lake Turkana, Kenya. *J. Geophys. Res.* 91(11): 581-595.

Howell, F. C. 1978. Hominidae, in: *Evolution of African Mammals* (V. J. Maglio and H. B. S. Cooke, Eds.), pp. 154-248, Harvard University Press, Cambridge.

Johanson, D. C., and White, T. D. 1979. A Systematic Assessment of Early African Hominids. *Science* 203:321-330.

Kimbel, W. H., Johanson, D. C., and Coppens. Y. 1982. Pliocene Hominid Cranial Remains from the Hadar Formation, Ethiopia. *Am. J. Phys. Anthrop.* 57:453-499.

Leakey, L. S. B. 1959. A New Fossil Skull from Olduvai. *Nature* 184:491-493.

Leakey, L. S. B., and Leakey, M. D. 1964. Recent Discoveries of Fossil Hominids in Tanganyika: at Olduvai and Near Lake Natron. *Nature* 202:5-7.

Leakey, M. D., and Leakey, R. E. 1978. *Koobi Fora Research Project*, The Hominid catalogue Vol. 1, Clarendon, Oxford.

Leakey, R. E. F., Mungai, J. M., and Walker, A. C. 1971. New Australopithecines from East Rudolf, Kenya. *Am. J. Phys. Anthrop.* 35:175-186.

Olson, T. R. 1981. Basicranial morphology of the extant hominoids and Pliocene hominids: The new material from the Hadar Formation and its significance in early human evolution and taxonomy, in: *Aspects of Human Evolution* (C. B. Stringer, Ed.), pp. 99-128, Taylor & Francis, London.

Olson, T. R. 1985. Cranial Morphology and Systematics of the Hadar Formation Hominids and *"Australopithecus" africanus*, in: *Ancestor: the Hard Evidence* (E. Delson, Ed.), pp. 102-119, Liss, New York.

Rak, Y. 1983. *The Australopithecine Face*, Academic, pp. 1-169, New York.

Rak, Y. 1985. Australopithecine Taxonomy and Phylogeny in Light of Facial Morphology. *Am. J. Phys. Anthrop.* 66:281-288.

Robinson, J. T. 1962. The origins and adaptive radiation of the Australopithecines, in: *Evolution und Hominisation* (G. Kurth, Ed.) pp. 120-140, Fischer, Stuttgart.

Robinson, J. T. 1967. Variation and the taxonomy of early hominids, in: *Evolutionary Biology* (T. Dobzhansky, M. K. Hecht, and W. Steere, Eds.) pp. 69-100, Appleton-Century Crofts, New York.

Robinson, J. T. 1972. *Early Hominid Posture and Locomotion*. University of Chicago Press, Chicago.

Skelton, R. R., McHenry, H., and Drawhorn, G. M. 1986 Phylogenetic Analysis of Early Hominids. *Curr. Anthrop.* 27:21-43.

Tobias, P. V. 1967. *Olduvai Gorge* Vol. 2, Cambridge University Press, Cambridge.

Tobias, P. V. 1973. New Developments in Hominid Paleontology in South and East Africa, in: *Annual Review of Anthropology*, Vol 2 (B.J. Siegel, A. R. Beals, and S. A. Tyler, Eds.), pp. 311-354, Annual Reviews, Palo Alto.

Tobias, P. V. 1980. *"Australopithecus afarensis"* and *A. africanus*: Critique and alternative hypothesis. *Palaeonto. Afr.* 23:1-17.

White, T. D., Johanson, D. C., and Kimbel, W. H. 1981. *Australopithecus africanus*: its Phynetic Position Reconsidered. *S. Afr. J. Sci.* 77:445-470.

Wolpoff, M. H. 1980. *Paleoanthropology*, Knopf, New York.

14

Hand of *Paranthropus Robustus* from Member 1, Swartkrans: Fossil Evidence for Tool Behavior

R. L. Susman

The genus *Paranthropus* generally has been assumed to consist of small-brained, large-toothed early hominids that subsisted on a vegetarian diet (Robinson 1954, 1962b; Wolpoff 1973; Du Brul 1977; Grine 1981). Stone artifacts found with *Paranthropus* have been attributed to their contemporaries of the genus *Homo* (Robinson 1953; Mason 1962; Tobias 1965). With a small brain and a vegetarian diet, it was thought that *Paranthropus* had neither the intellect nor the impetus to engage in tool behavior (Robinson 1962a, b). Further, the lack of tool behavior was thought to have contributed to the eventual extinction of *Paranthropus* in the early middle Pleistocene. Most inferences about *Paranthropus* have come from studies of cranio-dental remains (Broom and Robinson 1952; Tobias 1971; Rak 1983). Until now the only postcranial fossils referred to *Paranthropus* are seven bones from Swartkrans (Broom and Robinson 1949; Napier 1959; Robinson 1972; Rightmire 1972; Brain, Vrba, and Robinson 1974) and four from Kromdraai (Broom and Schepers 1946)[1].

There are 22 hand bones among 37 new hominid postcranials from Swartkrans (Susman 1989). These include one nearly complete pollical (=thumb) metacarpal, one complete pollical distal phalanx, three finger metacarpals, six proximal phalanges, eight middle phalanges, two distal phalanges, and a triquetral. Of the new hand fossils, eight are from Member 1. Member 1 [2], the earliest of five members, is dated at 1.8 million years (Vrba 1982). It has yielded remains of approximately 130 hominid individuals. The attribution of individual fossils to *Paranthropus* is complicated by the presence of a second hominid taxon (*Homo* cf. *erectus*) at Swartkrans. In Member 1, however, more than 95% of the cranio-dental remains are attributed to *Paranthropus*. This fact suggests that there is an overwhelming probability that any one specimen recovered from Member 1 samples *Paranthropus*. Equally important in this regard, morphological criteria can also be used to distinguish the two hominids at Swartkrans. For example, whereas SK 84 resembles a thumb metacarpal from East Africa that is clearly associated with a *Homo erectus* skeleton (WT 15000), both SK 84 and WT 15000 share a feature that is distinct to them (and presumably distinct to *Homo erectus*), and both differ from a new pollical metacarpal, SKX 5020. This suggests strongly that SKX 5020 ought to be assigned to *Paranthropus*. SKX 5016, a pollical distal phalanx, is consistent both metrically and morphologically with SKX 5020. SKX 5016 is incompatible in size with SK 84 [3].

These new fossils provide the first direct morphological evidence that bears on the question of whether or not *Paranthropus* had the capacity to make and use tools. When comparisons are made between *Paranthropus* and *Homo habilis* (from Bed I, Olduvai Gorge), the criteria used to infer the advent of a well-developed precision grip in *Homo habilis* (Napier 1962a, b; Leakey, Tobias and Napier 1964) are present in *Paranthropus*. The hand evidence no longer supports the idea that early *Homo* is distinguished from *Paranthropus* by morphological adaptations to precision grasp [4] and tool behavior (Robinson 1972).

Numerous comparative and functional studies of living primates have identified morphological correlates of precision and power grasping (Napier 1961, 1962b; Susman 1979; Marzke 1983; Marzke and Shackley 1986; Susman and Creel 1979). These and other studies have documented the advent of human-like precision grasping in early hominids (Napier 1961, 1962a, b; Susman 1979; Marzke 1983; Marzke and Shackley 1986; Susman and Creel 1979). The fossil record reveals that early hominids such as *Australopithecus afarensis*, dated at more than 3.0 million years old, did not possess a derived human-like thumb or fingers (Susman and Stern 1979; Bush 1980; Bush, Lovejoy, Johanson, and Coppens 1982). However, by approximately 1.8 million years ago (600,000 years after stone artifacts appear in the fossil record) hominid fossils show clear signs of a more human-like thumb and fingers.

The new Swartkrans fossils are direct evidence by which to assess the manual dexterity of *Paranthropus robustus* and thus to judge the potential for tool behavior in the "robust" australopithecines. The thumb is the most diagnostic element of the human hand in that the thumb is relatively long in comparison to the fingers (Midlo 1934; Napier and Napier 1967; Napier 1980), the intrinsic thumb muscles [5] are well differentiated and a specifically human muscle, the flexor pollicis longus, is present. The flexor pollicis longus inserts on a large area on the antero-basal surface of the distal phalanx, and since no monkey or ape possesses a flexor pollicis longus muscle, its bony counterpart on the distal phalanx is lacking also in monkeys and apes. The thumb of *Paranthropus* did possess a flexor pollicis longus muscle as judged by the well-defined area of insertion proximally on the volar aspect of SKX 5016 (Fig. 1a).

Another distinctly human feature of SKX 5016 is the broad, expanded apical tuft on the distal end of the phalanx. A

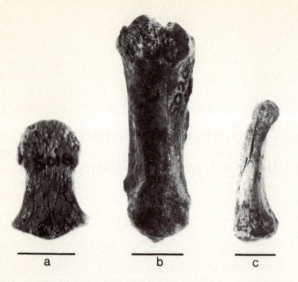

Figure 1. (a) *Volar surface of SKX 5016, pollical distal phalanx from Member 1. Note the broad apical tuft and large basal pit for insertion of an apparently well-developed, distinctly human-like flexor pollicis longus muscle.* (b) *SKX 5020; volar surface of first metacarpal from Member 1. This bone has a number of derived, human-like traits and is compatible in size with the SKX 5016 distal phalanx when the two are compared to an interspecific (African ape and human) regression of distal phalanx length on metacarpal length* [3]. (c) *Manual proximal phalanx SKX 5018 from Member 1 (lateral view). SKX 5018 has a human-like curvature (included angle) while retaining a primitive (pongid-like) overall morphology (see Fig. 3). All scales, 1 cm.*

broad apical tuft is found on all five human manual rays but, among extant primates, it reaches its acme in the human thumb. These tufts have the effect of broadening the bony support for the well-innervated and well-vascularized, fleshy fingertip. Neither apes nor monkeys have enlarged fleshy pads on their fingertips and neither do these primates have expanded bony tufts on their distal phalanges. The relative development of the apical tuft on the human thumb is shown in Figure 2. When breadth of the tuft is compared to the basal diameter of the distal phalanx, a dramatic size increase is seen in humans and especially *Paranthropus* and *Homo habilis* (Fig. 2). The interspecific regression, which is heavily weighted by the human sample, yields a positive slope (1.32). The African ape regression, with a slope of 0.998, reveals an isometric relation between tuft and phalangeal size in the apes. While apical tufting is pronounced in humans, it is even more so in *Paranthropus* (and *Homo habilis*). As judged by SKX 5016, the thumb of Paranthropus undoubtedly had a very pronounced fleshy tip.

The pollical metacarpal in humans is thick and has a very broad basal articular surface. SKX 5020, is a human-like, right first metacarpal with a thick shaft and a broad base. The saddle joint at the base of the thumb in Old World monkeys, apes, and humans allows concomitant flexion and axial rotation of the thumb so that its volar surface opposes those of the fingers. While Old World monkeys, apes, and humans all have a saddle joint at the base of the thumb, humans have an exceptionally broad basal joint. The increased surface area in the human thumb serves to reduce joint stress in the form of compressive forces that result from contraction of the powerful flexor pollicis longus and hypertrophic intrinsic thumb muscles. Joint compression forces in the carpometacarpal joint of humans average 12.0 kg during simple pinching; these forces reach 120

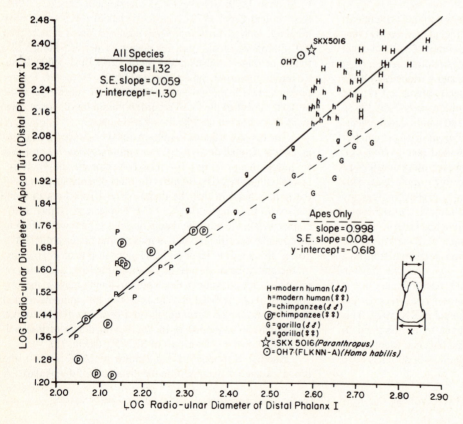

Figure 2. *Regression (least squares) of apex breadth on radio-ulnar breadth of the pollical distal phalanx. Humans display positive allometry of apical breadth (=expanded tuft) which reflects the broad, fleshy volar tip of the human thumb. Apes (dashed line) reveal an isometric relationship (slope, 0.998) of thumb tip to thumb base. Note the extreme breadth of the* Paranthropus *thumb which indicates an enhanced volar surface for precision grasping. OH7 from Bed I, Olduvai Gorge (roughly the same geologic age as Swartkrans Member 1), has a similar thumb morphology.*

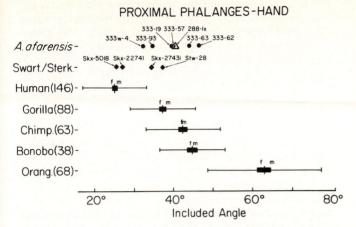

PROXIMAL PHALANGES-HAND

Figure 3. *Curvatures of manual proximal phalanges. Included angles are size-independent measures of longitudinal curvature. SKX 5018 is straight and essentially on the human mean whereas Stw-28, a presumptive gracile australopithecine from Member 4, Sterkfontein, and the geologically earlier* A. afarensis *phalanges fall within the African ape ranges. Vertical lines are group means, black bars are 95% limits of the population.* Australopithecus afarensis *from site AL 333=* ●; *A. afarensis ("Lucy")* = △. *Male and females means* = m *and* f.

kg during strong grasping (Cooney and Chao 1977). Finally, the human thumb has a well-developed opponens pollicis muscle that serves to rotate the thumb into opposition with the fingers. An indication of the strong development of this muscle is seen at its insertion site on the metacarpal shaft at which point in humans a crest or other indication is normally found. SKX 5020 displays a human-like crest on its lateral margin (Fig. 1b).

The finger bones (digits II through V) of *Paranthropus* also show signs of a well-developed precision grip and a lessened potential for power grasping. Evidence of a derived, human-like precision grip is suggested by the short, straight proximal phalanges of rays II through V. Whereas manual proximal phalanges II through V in earlier hominids such as *Australopithecus afarensis* (and *A. africanus*) possess ape-like curvatures and are relatively long (Stern and Susman 1983; Susman, Stern, and Jungers 1984), the proximal phalanges of *Paranthropus* lack primitive, ape-like curvatures (Fig. 3). SKX 5018, a complete proximal phalanx (Fig. 1c), has an included angle of 25.9°, essentially at the human mean of 24° and well outside of the 95% confidence limits of any ape mean. While this and other proximal phalanges from Swartkrans retain a some-

what primitive overall character (Susman, 1988), the reduced curvatures suggest a reduced emphasis on power grasping (compared to earlier hominids) and a diminished climbing ability.

Earlier assertions that *Paranthropus* was not a toolmaker or user (Robinson 1953, 1961; Mason 1962) were not based on anatomical evidence. Earlier morphological and comparative evidence (Tobias 1965) consisted mainly of assumptions about the relation between brain volume (and intelligence) and cultural capacity. There were no fossils and, thus, there could be no discussion of relevant, diagnostic fossil evidence. The new Member 1 hand fossils indicate that the hand of *Paranthropus* was indeed "hominized." The human-like first metacarpal, the human-like first distal phalanx with its broad apical tuft and flexor pollicis longus insertion, and the short, straight fingers indicate that the robust australopithecines had much the same morphological potential for refined precision grasping and for tool behavior as do modern humans (and as did *Homo habilis* [6]).

Not only is the morphology of the hand of *Paranthropus* suggestive of tool behavior, but numerous bone and stone artifacts are also found in Member 1 and throughout Swartkrans (Brain 1982). The bone artifacts are mostly shaft fragments that show signs of having been used for digging (Brain 1985). The stone artifacts range in size from 13 g to 1257 g and have a primitive character (Leakey 1970). Given the widespread notion that *Paranthropus* lived on an essentially vegetarian diet consisting of hard food items (Grine 1981, 1986), it might be that *Paranthropus* fashioned bone and stone implements and then used them for vegetable procurement and processing. If so, then perhaps *Paranthropus* invented or adapted tool behavior to vegetarian subsistence while the other early hominids applied their tools to a different dietary regime. In any case, the new evidence from Swartkrans demands a reassessment of traditional views of the robust australopithecines and long held notions that the advent of tool behavior and "culture" distinguished early *Homo* from other early hominids, that tools initiated the human career, and that, because of the lack of tool behavior (or the morphological potential for it), *Paranthropus* became extinct.

ACKNOWLEDGEMENTS

I thank C. K. Brain for the opportunity to study the Swartkrans fossils and for his invaluable insights into the paleobiology and geology of the Swartkrans site. I also thank F. Grine for sharing his insights on Plio-Pleistocene hominids with me and for his comments on this manuscript. Supported by NSF grants BNS 83-112906 and BNS 85-19747. Funds were also provided by a BRSG from the School of Medicine, SUNY, Stony Brook.

NOTES

[1]   There are other hominid postcranials described by Broom from Kromdraai. The TM 1517 hand bones are, in fact, those of a cercopithecoid monkey (personal observation; Day and Thornton 1986).

[2]   Member 1 is the earliest of five distinct members at Swartkrans. Member 1 corresponds to the former "orange" or "pink" breccia of Broom and Robinson. There is a minimum of 125 *Paranthropus* individuals represented by craniodental remains in Member 1. *Homo cf. erectus* is represented by only five individuals.

[3]   SKX 5016 compares favorably to the larger of the two metacarpals (SKX 5020) from Swartkrans. The slope of the line (logged) com-

paring length of chimpanzee and human thumb metacarpals and pollical distal phalanges is 1.34 (SE=0.126 and y-intercept -1.996). The line predicts a distal phalanx with a length of 20.9 mm when x = the length of SKX 5020. The actual length of SKX 5016 is 19.8 mm. SK 84, a first metacarpal from Swartkrans described earlier by Napier (1959) and most likely that of *Homo erectus*, predicts a distal phalanx with a length of only 15.7 mm (well outside the 95% confidence limits of the interspecific regression line).

[4]   These adaptations include expanded breadth of the distal (terminal) phalanges resulting in broad, fleshy fingertips; long thumb relative to the index and other fingers; a broad basal articular surface on the

first metacarpal; well-developed and well-differentiated intrinsic and extrinsic thumb muscles; and relatively short and straight fingers.

[5] The "intrinsic" thumb muscles are the adductor pollicis (oblique and transverse heads), the opponens pollicis, the abductor pollicis brevis, and the flexor pollicis brevis (superficial and deep heads). Occasionally in humans an additional muscle is found, the first volar interosseous muscle of Henle.

[6] It is possible that *Paranthropus* and other early hominids evolved human-like hands for precision grasping of something other than stone or bone artifacts. Arguing against this proposition is the fact that while primates such as baboons and geladas are adept at handling small food objects, and free-ranging chimpanzees manipulate food objects and handle stones and sticks, no monkey or ape displays human-like thumbs or fingers as did early hominids such as *Paranthropus* and *Homo habilis*.

REFERENCES

Brain, C. K. 1982. The Swartkrans site: stratigraphy of the fossil hominids and a reconstruction of the environment of early *Homo*, in: *Pretirage 1er Congres International Paleontologie Humaine* (H. DeLumley and M. A. DeLumley, Eds.), pp. 676-706, Centre National de la Recherche Scientifique, Nice.

Brain, C. K. 1985. Cultural and taphonomic comparisons of hominids from Swartkrans and Sterkfontein, in: *Ancestors: The Hard Evidence* (E. Delson, Ed.), pp. 72-75, Liss, New York.

Brain, C. K., Vrba, E. S., and Robinson, J. T. 1974. A new hominid innominate home from Swartkrans. *Ann. Trans. Mus.* 29:55-63.

Broom, R. and Robinson, J. T. 1949. Thumb of the Swartkrans Ape-Man. *Nature* 164:841-842.

Broom, R., and Robinson, J. T. 1952. Swartkrans Ape-Man, *Paranthropus crassidens*. *Trans. Mus. Mem.* 6:1-123.

Broom, R., and Schepers, G. W. H. 1946. The South African fossil ape-men, the Australopithecinae. *Trans. Mus. Mem.* 2:1-272.

Bush, M. E. 1980. The thumb of *Australopithecus afarensis*. *Amer. J. Phys. Anthro.* 52:210.

Bush, M. E., Lovejoy, C. O., Johanson, D. C., and Coppens, Y. 1982. Hominid carpal, metacarpal and phalangeal bones recovered from the Hadar Formation: 1974-1977 collections. *Amer. J. Phys. Anthro.* 57:651-677.

Cooney, W. P., and Chao, E. Y. S. 1977. Biomechanical analysis of static forces in the thumb during hand function. *J. Bone Jt. Surg.* 59A:27-36.

Day, M. H., and Thornton, G. M. B. 1986. The extremity bones of *Paranthropus robustus* from Kromdraai B, East Formation Member 3, Republic of South Africa—A reappraisal. *Anthropos.* 23:91-99.

Du Brul, E. L. 1977. Early hominid feeding mechanisms. *Amer. J. Phys. Anthro.* 47:305-320.

Grine, F. E. 1981. Tropic differences between "Gracile" and "Robust" *Australopithecus*: A scanning electron microscope analysis of occlusal events. *S. Afr. J. Sci.* 77:203-230.

Grine, F. E. 1986. Dental evidence for dietary differences in *Australopithecus* and *Paranthropus*: A quantitative analysis of perminant molar microwear. *J. Hum. Evol.* 15:783-822.

Leakey, L. S. B., Tobias, P. V., Napier, J. R. 1964. A new species of the genus homo from Olduvai Gorge, Tanzania. *Nature* 202:308-312.

Leakey, M. D. 1970. Stone artifacts from Swartkrans. *Nature* 225:13-16.

Marzke, M. W. 1983. Joint functions and grips of the *Australopithecus afarensis* hand, with special reference to the region of the capitate. *J. Hum. Evol.* 12:197-211.

Marzke, M. W., and Shackley, M. S. 1986. Hominid hand use in the Pliocene and Pleistocene: Evidence from experimental archaeology and comparative morphology. *J. Hum. Evol.* 15:439-460.

Mason, R. J. 1962. *Australopithecus* and artifacts at Sterkfontein. Part II. The Sterkfontein stone artifacts and their makers. *S. Afr. Archeol. Bull.* 17:109-125.

Midlo, C. 1934. Form of the hand and foot in primates. *Amer. J. Phys. Anthro.* 19:337-389.

Napier, J. R. 1956. The prehensile movements of the human hand. *J. Bone Jt. Surg.* 38B:902-913.

Napier, J. R. 1959. Fossil metacarpals from Swartkrans. *Br. Mus. Nat. Hist. Fossil Mamm. Afr.* 17:1-18.

Napier, J. R. 1961. Prehensility and opposability in the hands of primates. *Symp. Zool. Soc. London* 5:115-132.

Napier, J. R. 1962a. Fossil hand bones from Olduvai Gorge. *Nature* 196:409-411.

Napier, J. R. 1962b. The evolution of the hand. *Sci. Am.* 205:155-161.

Napier, J. R. 1980. *Hands*. Pantheon, New York.

Napier, J. R., and Napier, P. H. 1967. *Handbook of the Living Primates*. Academic Press, London.

Rak, Y. 1983. *The Australopithecine Face*. Academic Press, New York.

Rightmire, G. P. 1972. Mutivariate analysis of an early hominid metacarpal from Swartkrans. *Science* 176:159-161.

Robinson, J. T. 1953. *Telanthropus* and its phylogenetic significance. *Amer. J. Phys. Anthro.* 11:445-501.

Robinson, J. T. 1954. Prehominid dentition and hominid evolution. *Evolution* 8:324-334.

Robinson, J. T. 1961. The australopithecines and their bearing on the origin of man and of stone tool-making. *S. Afr. J. Sci.* 57:3-13.

Robinson, J. T. 1962a. *Australopithecus* and artifacts at Sterkfontein. Part I. Sterkfontein stratigraphy and the significance of the Extension Site. *S. Afr. Archeol. Bull.* 17:85-108.

Robinson, J. T. 1962b. The origins and adaptive radiation of the Australopithecines, in: *Evolution and Hominization* (G. Kurth, Ed.), pp. 120-140, Fischer, Stuttgart.

Robinson, J. T. 1972. *Early Hominid Posture and Locomotion*. University of Chicago Press, Chicago.

Stern, J. T., and Susman, R. L. 1983. The locomotor anatomy of *Australopithecus afarensis*. *Amer. J. Phys. Anthro.* 60:279-317.

Susman, R. L. 1979. Comparitive and functional morphology of hominid fingers. *Amer. J. Phys. Anthro.* 50:215-236.

Susman, R. L. 1988. New postcranial remains from Swartkrans and their bearing on the functional morphology and behavior of *Paranthropus robustus*, in: *Evolutionary History of the Robust Australopithecines* (F. E. Grine, Ed.), pp.149-172, Aldine de Gruyter, New York.

Susman, R. 1989. New hominid fossils from Swartkrans Formation (1979-1986 excavations): Postcranial specimens. *Amer. J. Phys. Anthro.* 79:451-474.

Susman, R. L., and Creel, N. 1979. Functional and morphological affinities of the subadult hand (O.H.7) from Olduvai Gorge. *Amer. J. Phys. Anthro.* 51:311-331.

Susman, R. L., and Stern, J. T. 1979. Telemetered electromyography of flexor digitorum profundus and flexor digitorum superficialis in *Pan troglodytes* and implications and interpretation of the O.H. 7 hand. *Amer. J. Phys. Anthro.* 50:565-574

Susman, R. L., Stern, J. T., and Jungers, W. L. 1984. Arboreality and bipedality in the Hadar hominids. *Folia Primatol.* 43:113-156.

Tobias, P. V. 1965. *Australopithecus, Homo habilis*, tool-using and tool-making. *S. Afr. Archeol. Bull.* 20:167-192.

Tobias, P. V. 1971. *The Brain in Hominid Evolution*. Columbia University Press, New York.

Vrba, E. S. 1982. Biostratigraphy and chronology, based particularly on Bovidae, of southern hominid-associated assemblages: Makapansgat, Sterkfontein, Taung, Kromdraai, Swartkrans: also Elandsfontein (Saldanha), Broken Hill (Now Kabwe) and the Cave of the Hearths, in: *Pretirage, 1er Congres International Paleontologie Humaine* (F. DeLumley and M. A. DeLumley, Eds.), pp. 707-752, Centre National de la Recherche Scientifique, Nice.

Wolpoff, M. A. 1973. Posterior tooth size, body size, and diet in the South African gracile australopithecines. *Amer. J. Phys. Anthro.* 39:375-394.

15

The Diet of South African Australopithecines
Based on a Study of Dental Microwear

F. E. Grine

INTRODUCTORY BACKGROUND

Because trophic factors bear directly upon the structures comprising the masticatory apparatus, as well as upon musculo-skeletal developments associated with food acquisition, diet represents a significant element in the interpretation of the Plio-Pleistocene hominid fossil record. For this reason, the dietary habits of the australopithecines have been the subject of vigorous study and debate since their remains were first discovered in the breccia cave deposits of South Africa some sixty years ago.

From his initial description of the juvenile australopithecine from the site of Taung, Dart (1925, 1949, 1957, 1958) championed the idea that *Australopithecus africanus* (the so-called 'gracile' form) was a predatory and carnivorous hominid. The so-called 'robust' australopithecines from the sites of Kromdraai and Swartkrans, attributed by Broom (1938, 1949) to the genus *Paranthropus*, were considered by Robinson (1954a, 1954b) to have subsisted on an essentially herbivorous diet. Thus, Robinson (1954b) proposed that the observable morphological differences between *Australopithecus* and *Paranthropus* were related primarily to their different feeding habits. According to Robinson (1954b; 1961), the herbivorous diet of *Paranthropus* was attested to by its larger postcanine teeth, its relatively smaller anterior teeth, the peculiar configuration of its facial skeleton, the larger inferred size of its masticatory musculature, and by the apparent presence of more antemortem enamel chipping than on the cheek teeth of *Australopithecus*. Robinson argued that the inferred trophic differences between *Australopithecus* and *Paranthropus* were related to their having occupied different 'adaptive zones' rather than different aspects of the same 'adaptive zone'.

Largely through the pioneering work of Brain (1981), the notion that *Australopithecus* was the hunter rather than the hunted, has been largely discounted. At the same time, Tobias (1967), Brace (1969) and Wolpoff (1974), amongst others, have argued that the differences between *Australopithecus* and *Paranthropus* which were noted by Robinson are minimal in number and importance, and that those that do exist are related to the allometric effects of estimated body size differences between these 'gracile' and 'robust' forms. Wolpoff (1974:128), for example, concluded that the morphological patterns displayed by both samples give 'the uniform interpretation of adaptation to a very heavily masticated herbivorous diet.' Many workers have come to regard *Paranthropus* as simply a 'robust' version of *Australopithecus*.

The questions raised about whether the morphological differences between *Australopithecus* and *Paranthropus* are not simply the scaling effects of concomitant body size differences, rather than evidence of distinct functional adaptations, have been the subject of debate for the past decade. The problem of sorting those features that are requisite consequences of allometric scaling from those that are related to ecologically significant functional differences is of fundamental importance in any attempt to interpret the course of early hominid evolution. Unfortunately, there are few *a priori* expectations about the relationship between morphology and size change (Jungers and Grine 1986). Indeed, highly correlated size related changes may themselves reflect major adaptive differences along a size gradient of individuals or taxa (Smith 1980; Jungers 1984; Fleagle 1985).

Much of the recent work on the problem of allometric scaling in early hominid evolution has focused on the relative sizes of the incisors, canines and cheek teeth (Pilbeam and Gould 1974; Kay 1975; Wood and Stack 1980), and upon the relationship between overall size and relative crown proportions in the mandibular molars of the australopithecines (Wood et al. 1983; Wood 1984; Jungers and Grine 1986).

Robinson (1954a, 1954b) considered the disparity in the sizes of the canines and cheek teeth in *Australopithecus* and *Paranthropus* to provide perhaps the most compelling evidence for their dietary, and thus generic, distinction. While both Brace (1967) and Wolpoff (1974) have expressed doubts that such a disparity exists, an overwhelming body of evidence suggests that in both the deciduous and permanent dentitions, the canines of *Paranthropus* are relatively smaller than those of *Australopithecus* (Tobias 1967; Wood and Stack 1980; Grine 1982). This comparative diminution in *Paranthropus* canine size represents a departure from the scale effects seen in other primates, and it may have been related to a functional shift from shearing to apical crushing activity (Wallace 1978; Grine 1981, 1984).

In addition to their relatively small canines, *Paranthropus* incisors are small in comparison to the sizes of their cheek teeth (Robinson 1954a; Tobias 1967; Grine 1982). Hylander (1975) has observed that relative incisor size tends to be highly correlated with diet in extant anthropoids. Species that feed on large food objects (e.g., large fruits) have relatively larger incisors than those that subsist on smaller foods. By analogy, the sizes of the primary dietary items may have differed between *Australopithecus* and *Paranthropus*. Alternatively, or perhaps concomitantly, incisal preparation and/or manipulation of food items may have differed between these Plio-Pleistocene hominids.

Postcanine tooth size in the early hominids has been considered to scale with positive allometry to estimates of body weight, where an *Australopithecus* to *Paranthropus* cheek tooth area slope of 0.71 has been noted as being very similar to the mammalian basal metabolic slope of 0.75 (Pilbeam and Gould 1974). This purported link has been taken to signify functional equivalence in *Australopithecus* and *Paranthropus* premolar and molar size (Pilbeam and Gould 1974; Wood and Stack 1980; Peters 1981). That is, it has been argued that *Paranthropus* required larger postcanine teeth simply to process more food per chewing cycle in order to maintain a larger body size, but the foods that were masticated would not necessarily have differed from those eaten by *Australopithecus*.

Contrary to these arguments of functional (i.e., metabolic) equivalence, however, tooth and body size regressions for a variety of mammals, including primates, are equivalent to or lower than the isometric slope of constant proportionality (Creighton 1980; Kay 1985; Gingerich and Smith 1985). Larger animals do not appear to require relatively larger teeth simply to process greater quantities of the same sorts of foods eaten by their smaller relatives in order to maintain functional equivalence. Postcanine tooth area in mammals does not appear to parallel basal metabolic rate, because tooth size is related to energy capacity, not energy rate. What must be of concern in attempts to relate tooth size to metabolic rate is the frequency, or rate of masticatory cycles by which foods of given caloric content are processed (Calder 1984). Moreover, with regard to the australopithecines, the rather incredibly wide range of body sizes estimates that have been provided for these early hominids makes attempts to provide accurate tooth-body size regressions extremely tenuous (Grine 1981).

It has also been argued that since the apparent lines of action of the masticatory muscles of the 'robust' australopithecines were similar to those of modern humans, the manner in which bite forces can be applied to foods are the same, and that because the postcanine occlusal area of the 'robust' australopithecines is some four to five times that of modern humans, *Paranthropus* would have had to have generated four to five times the bite force of modern humans just to maintain equivalent occlusal pressures (Walker 1981). This line of reasoning has been used to suggest that *Paranthropus* did not necessarily chew anything that could not have been masticated also by modern humans; rather, *Paranthropus* was simply processing greater quantities of these sorts of foods (Walker 1981). However, studies by Hylander (1985) have shown that the relationships between size and the scaling of trophic structures are difficult to predict, suggesting that occlusal areas are not geometrically related to the amount of bite force required to generate equivalent pressures. In a word, occlusal masticatory pressures are not necessarily (in fact, they are hardly ever) applied evenly across the entire occlusal area.

While analyses of cheek tooth size scaling and masticatory biomechanics have provided invaluable insights as to the pos-sible functional and adaptive significance of the trophic structures of the Plio-Pleistocene australopithecines, such extrapolations by analogy must be treated with circumspection. *Australopithecus* and *Paranthropus* were unique taxa in their own rights. Because no living mammal possesses the unique dental proportions and facial morphology displayed by *Paranthropus*, interpretations of the dietary habits and adaptations of the 'robust' australopithecines that are based upon the odontometrics of extant primate species will be of a rather *ad hoc* nature (Kay and Covert 1984).

The interpretations that result from such analyses, however, may be tested by examination of the tooth surfaces of these extinct taxa, for it is the tooth surfaces that made intimate contact with the food items comprising the diets of these hominids.

A number of recent studies have demonstrated the potential of examining dental microwear in the determination of the masticatory jaw movements and diets of extant as well as extinct species (Walker *et al.* 1978; Walker 1981; Gordon 1982; Peters 1982; Teaford and Walker 1984; Teaford 1985). Despite the potentially valuable information that may be gained through an examination of tooth wear, there have been surprisingly few attempts to apply observations of occlusal attrition in the reconstruction of early hominid diets.

Macroscopic Tooth Wear

The gross (i.e., macroscopic) patterns of wear displayed by early hominid teeth have been commented upon by Robinson (1961), Tobias (1967), Wolpoff (1973, 1975), Wallace (1973, 1975) and Grine (1981) amongst others, with conflicting interpretations. As noted above, Robinson (1961) opined that *Paranthropus* specimens displayed more antemortem enamel chipping on their cheek teeth than did specimens of *Australopithecus*, and this was held as evidence that the former consumed more grit-laden vegetables. Tobias (1967) and Wallace (1973), on the other hand, observed no appreciable differences between the 'gracile' and 'robust' fossils, and Wallace concluded that neither form had very much dust or grit associated with their dietary staples. At the same time, Robinson (1956), Wallace (1975) and Grine (1981) have noted that in both the deciduous and permanent cheek teeth, the buccal and lingual cusps tend to display more even rates of attrition in *Paranthropus* than in *Australopithecus*. Wolpoff (1973, 1975), on the other hand, has maintained that gross tooth wear patterns are extremely variable within the 'gracile' and 'robust' australopithecine samples, and that this variability seems to have no bearing upon the taxonomic attribution of the specimens.

Microscopic Tooth Wear

The first microscopical study of australopithecine tooth wear was that by Wallace (1972). Using a low-power, binocular light microscope, he found the enamel facets on the cheek teeth of both *Australopithecus* and *Paranthropus* to be comparably 'shiny' and 'polished'. Although Wallace was compelled to argue that the dentition of *Paranthropus* exhibited an increased efficiency over that of *Australopithecus* for crushing and grinding, no occlusal evidence of crushing and grinding events on the teeth of *Paranthropus* was observed by him. The microscopical techniques that were employed by Wallace (1972,

1975), however, are incapable of resolving details of occlusal wear that are readily visible with scanning electron microscopy, and which have been shown to be of potential value in the analysis of jaw movements and diet (Walker *et al.* 1978; Walker 1981; Gordon 1982; Teaford and Walker 1984; Teaford 1985, 1986). Despite the demonstrated utility of scanning electron microscopy in this area, there have been relatively few attempts to apply it in studies of early hominid tooth wear (Grine 1977, 1981, 1984; Ryan 1979; Walker 1980, 1981; Puech *et al.* 1983). Moreover, none of these studies has been of a quantitative nature.

The quantitative analysis of dental microwear, which was pioneered largely by Gordon (1982), has been shown to be useful in distinguishing between species with principally frugivorous or folivorous diets, and especially between taxa that masticate soft or hard food objects (Teaford and Walker 1984; Teaford 1985, 1986). These studies provide some useful baseline data against which the parameters gleaned from the teeth of extinct taxa can be compared.

DECIDUOUS MOLAR WEAR IN SOUTHERN AFRICAN AUSTRALOPITHECINES

The studies by Grine (1977, 1981, 1984), the first undertaken on fossil hominid specimens, were restricted to comparisons of the details of occlusal wear displayed by the deciduous molars of the southern African specimens of *Australopithecus* and *Paranthropus*. It was observed that in slightly and moderately worn teeth, the Phase I facets of Kay and Hiiemae (1974)—that is, the surfaces that move across one another as the lower molars are drawn upward and mesially into centric occlusion—were more highly angled to the horizontal occlusal plane in *Australopithecus* than in *Paranthropus*. Thus, the molars of *Australopithecus* would have followed a somewhat more vertical path into centric occlusion than those of *Paranthropus*, suggesting that Phase I movement in *Australopithecus* would have comprised more 'shearing' activity, whereas *Paranthropus* molars would have engaged in more crushing and 'grinding' activity on these surfaces. This is supported by the observation that the Phase I surfaces of *Australopithecus* crowns tend to be polished with elongate wear scratches, while these facets on *Paranthropus* teeth tend to be more heavily gouged and pitted (Grine 1981, 1984). The Phase II facets— those that approach one another as the molars move into centric occlusion—of both australopithecine taxa tend to be more heavily pitted than the Phase I surfaces, but the pits tend to be both larger and more numerous on *Paranthropus* specimens. Moreover, the increased reliance on crushing activity in *Paranthropus* is attested to also by the observation that the leading and trailing edges of dentine islands on the molar crowns tend to be stepped, whereas in *Australopithecus* only the trailing edges display this configuration (Grine 1977, 1981, 1984).

The observed differences in the patterns of wear displayed by the deciduous molars of these early hominid specimens were interpreted as evidence that the diets of *Australopithecus* and *Paranthropus* were qualitatively different, and that the so-called 'robust' australopithecines processed harder food items than did the 'gracile' *Australopithecus*.

In light of subsequent studies in which the quantitative analysis of microwear was introduced (Gordon 1982; Teaford

and Walker 1984; Teaford 1985, 1986), a quantitative assessment of the details of occlusal wear preserved on the permanent molars of southern African specimens of *Australopithecus* and *Paranthropus* was undertaken. This analysis was undertaken in order to compare the results obtained for these early hominids with the accumulated data for extant primate species of known dietary proclivities, and in order to test the conclusions reached in the earlier, qualitative studies on deciduous molar wear in *Australopithecus* and *Paranthropus*.

PERMANENT MOLAR WEAR IN SOUTHERN AFRICAN AUSTRALOPITHECINES

This study is based upon the scanning electron microscope (SEM) examination of occlusal wear features on the permanent upper second molars (M^2s) of southern African specimens of *Australopithecus* and *Paranthropus*. The M^2 was chosen for study because most of the available comparative data for extant primates have been recorded for this tooth (Gordon 1982; Teaford and Walker 1984; Teaford 1985, 1986). The *Australopithecus* sample comprises 10 molars (N = 10 individuals) from Member 4 of the Sterkfontein Formation, and the *Paranthropus* sample is made up of 9 molars (N = 9 individuals) from Member 1 of the Swartkrans Formation and Member 3 of the Kromdraai Formation.

The teeth chosen for examination were carefully cleaned, first with cotton wool soaked in acetone, and then with 95% ethanol; vigorous scrubbing was avoided. Molds of the cleaned teeth were made with 3M Regular Set Express impression material, and epoxy resin replicas were made with Araldite 502 hardened with Araldite HY 956, which catalyzes at room temperature. The replicas were sputter coated with approximately 200nm of gold and examined in an AMR 1400 at an accelerating voltage of 10 kV in the secondary electron mode. All micrographs were recorded using Polaroid Type 55 P/N film.

Phase I and Phase II protoconal facets were examined on each specimen, where the facet was orientated normal (or nearly normal) to the electron beam, and where micrographs were recorded at what was judged to be the center of the facet. In some instances, however, natural postmortem and/or preparation damage marred the center of the surface so that micrographs had to be recorded closer to the edge of the facet. In all cases, the entire facet was examined so as to ensure that the region micrographed was not unusual. Micrographs at 100x were recorded for use in counting the number of wear features displayed within that field, and micrographs at 200x were recorded for use in measuring the diameters of the wear features.

Three groups of variables considered in the present study are recorded here. These variables include: (i) the number of microwear features (i.e., scratches and pits) per mm^2, (ii) the orientation of the wear scratches, and (iii) the diameters of the microwear features. These parameters were recorded for two Phase I facets (numbers 5 and 6) and one Phase II facet (number 9) on each of the molars (Fig. 1).

Microwear Feature Incidences

Within both australopithecine samples, the densities of microwear features per mm^2 tend to be higher on Phase II than on Phase I facets, and features tend to be more numerous on

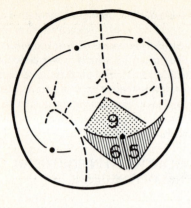

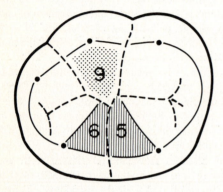

Figure 1. *Generalized maxillary right and mandibular left molars viewed occlusally to illustrate the reciprocal location of the Phase I (numbers 5 and 6) and Phase II (number 9) facets examined in this study. B, buccal; M, mesial; L, lingual; D, distal.*

both facet types on *Paranthropus* than on *Australopithecus* M^2s (Table 1). The *Paranthropus* sample incidences are significantly higher than the corresponding *Australopithecus* densities for Phase I facet 6 and for Phase II facet 9. Gordon (1982) has recorded average feature densities for *Pan troglodytes* M^2s, and the values obtained by her for Phase I facets (between 368 and 426 per mm^2) and for Phase II facets (between 679 and 793 per mm^2) are higher than the corresponding incidences of either australopithecine sample. Gordon's (1982) figures indicate that in *Pan*, as in *Australopithecus* and *Paranthropus*, Phase I sur-

Table 1. Total number of M^2 microwear features per mm^2.

Facet	Sample	$\overline{X}$	SD	"t"	P
9	*Australopithecus*	290.4	82.7	3.39	<0.005
	Paranthropus	437.6	106.2		
5	*Australopithecus*	251.6	78.1	1.73	
	Paranthropus	306.4	57.0		
6	*Australopithecus*	208.8	53.1	4.91	<0.001
	Paranthropus	341.2	64.5		

Table 2. Australopithecine M^2 scratch and pit frequencies.

PERCENTAGES FROM SAMPLE TOTALS					
Facet	Sample	Scratch	Pit	X^2	p
9	*Australopithecus*	68.9	31.3	7.92	<0.005
	Paranthropus	49.2	50.8		
5	*Australopithecus*	84.8	15.2	10.98	<0.001
	Paranthropus	64.4	35.6		
6	*Australopithecus*	87.5	12.5	19.41	<0.001
	Paranthropus	60.1	39.9		
AVERAGES OF INDIVIDUAL PERCENTAGES					
Facet	Sample	Scratch	Pit	X^2	p
9	*Australopithecus*	69.2	30.8	6.55	<0.02
	Paranthropus	51.5	48.5		
5	*Australopithecus*	85.5	14.4	10.91	<0.001
	Paranthropus	65.4	34.6		
6	*Australopithecus*	87.3	12.7	16.91	<0.001
	Paranthropus	62.0	38.0		

faces tend to exhibit fewer features per mm^2 than do Phase II facets.

Scratches and pits were scored independently by subjective determination following the method of Gordon (1982). Teaford and Walker (1984) employed a length to width ratio of 10:1 to define whether a feature was categorized as a scratch or a pit. The 'gouge' and 'striation' categories recognized by Gordon (1982) are subsumed here under the designation 'scratch', and subsequent measurements of the features on the australopithecine crowns revealed that most of the 'pits' recognized in the present study possessed length-width ratios that fell between about 1:1 and 4:1. Thus, the results obtained here are not directly comparable to those recorded by Teaford and Walker (1984), who recognized notably longer features as 'pits'.

The percentage frequencies of scratches and pits on the protoconal facets of *Australopithecus* and *Paranthropus* molars are recorded in Table 2. Percentage incidences derived from the total number of features recorded for each sample, as well as those calculated from the percentage values for individual specimens reveal that *Paranthropus* possesses significantly greater densities of pits on both facet types. Moreover, the differences between these taxa are notably greater for the Phase I than for the Phase II surfaces. Indeed, the Phase I facet pitting frequencies in the *Paranthropus* sample are higher even than the Phase II facet incidences in the *Australopithecus* sample (Fig. 2).

The occlusal pitting frequencies recorded by Gordon (1982) of between 13.1% and 23.6% for Phase I surfaces and of between 42.5% and 45.8% for Phase II surfaces of *Pan troglodytes* M^2s are higher than the incidences recorded here for the molars of *Australopithecus*, but lower than the corresponding frequencies for *Paranthropus*.

Occlusal Scratch Orientation

The angles at which the wear scratches on the three protoconal facets diverge from the principal buccolingual (BL) crown axis in the *Australopithecus* and *Paranthropus*

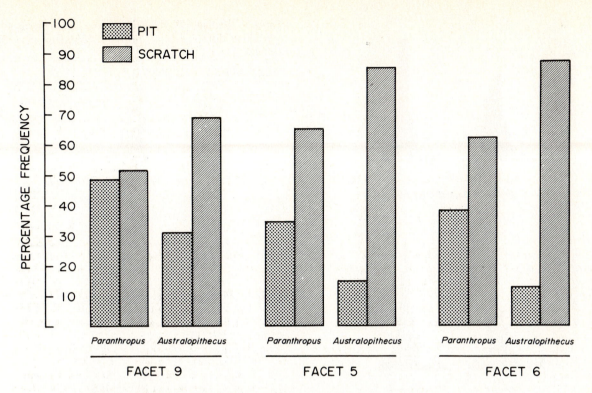

Figure 2. *Histograms of the relative frequencies of scratches and pits on facets 9 (Phase II), 5 and 6 (Phase I) of* Australopithecus *and* Paranthropus M^2s. *Frequencies from averages of individual percentages comprising each sample.*

samples are depicted graphically in Figure 3. It is evident that in both of these early hominid samples, the scratches are predominantly of a distobuccal-mesiolingual orientation. On average, somewhat less than 23% of included scratches in both taxa show a mesiobuccal-distolingual orientation, which supports earlier observations (Grine 1981) that the power stroke during active side mastication in australopithecines proceeded along a distobuccal-mesiolingual axis. Also, in both samples, the scratches on Phase II facet 9 display a greater degree of directional heterogeneity than those on the Phase I surfaces (Fig. 3).

Figure 3 also reveals that the scratches on *Australopithecus* crowns display a greater degree of directional similitude than those on *Paranthropus* homologues for all three facets. Bartlett's X^2 analyses indicate that the *Australopithecus* and *Paranthropus* sample distributions differ significantly for all three facets (Table 3), although the presence of cells without observations (Fig. 3) may render the results of a X^2 evaluation rather suspect. However, the nonparametric Kolmogorov-Smirnov test may be validly applied in the analysis of these distributions, its results being conservative for grouped data such as these. This test (Table 3) reveals that the *Australopithecus* and *Paranthropus* samples differ significantly for Phase II facet number 9 and for Phase I facet number 6.

The differences between the *Australopithecus* and *Paranthropus* sample distributions would seem to be related primarily to an increased amount of eccentricity of jaw movement during active side mastication in *Paranthropus*. Such a difference in the variability of scratch orientation is likely to be related to differences in the mechanical proper-

ties of the food items that were processed by these early hominidtaxa.

Microwear Feature Diameters

The average lengths and widths of the wear scratches and pits obtained for facets 5, 6 and 9 of *Australopithecus* and *Paranthropus* M^2s are recorded in Tables 4 and 5 respectively. Within both early hominid samples, the scratches tend to be longer on the Phase I than on the Phase II surfaces, while the scratches tend to be broader on the Phase II facets. At the same time, pits tend to be larger in both their length and width on the Phase II than on the Phase I facets.

Scratches on all three *Australopithecus* wear surfaces are significantly longer than those of *Paranthropus* (facet 5, "t" = 3.82, p < 0.002) (facet 6, "t" = 2.64, p < 0.02) (facet 9, "t" = 2.34, p < 0.05). Scratches on all three *Paranthropus* surfaces, however, are significantly broader than those of *Australopithecus* (facet 5, "t" = 9.19, p < 0.001) (facet 6, "t" = 6.43, p < 0.001) (facet 9, "t" = 5.93, p < 0.001). Moreover, the relative variability in measured scratch length and width, as represented by the CV values (Table 4), is greater in *Paranthropus* than in *Australopithecus* for each of the three facets.

Microwear pits on all three *Paranthropus* surfaces are significantly longer than those of *Australopithecus* (facet 5, "t" = 4.36, p < 0.001) (facet 6, "t" = 6.59, p < 0.001) (facet 9, "t" = 5.97, p < 0.001). Similarly, the pits on *Paranthropus* molars are significantly broader than those on *Australopithecus* homologues (facet 5, "t" = 5.12, p < 0.001) (facet 6, "t" = 8.69, p < 0.001) (facet 9, "t" = 5.61, p < 0.001).

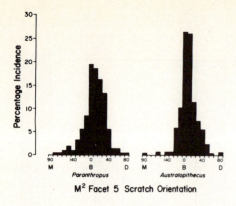

M² Facet 5 Scratch Orientation

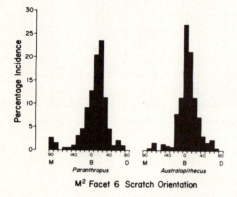

M² Facet 6 Scratch Orientation

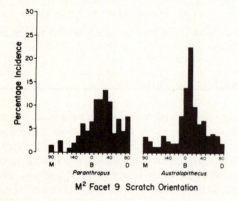

M² Facet 9 Scratch Orientation

Figure 3. *Histograms of occlusal scratch orientation on facets 5 and 6 (Phase I) and facet 9 (Phase II) of* Australopithecus *and* Paranthropus *M²s. M, mesial; B, buccolingual crown axis; D, distal.*

In contrast to the situation for scratch dimensions, the relative variability in measured pit length and width in the *Paranthropus* sample exceeds that of *Australopithecus* only for facet 5 (Table 5).

Thus, scratches tend to be longer but narrower on *Australopithecus* molars, while pits tend to be larger in both diameters on *Paranthropus* crowns. These conditions are realized by the length and width averages displayed by the pooled microwear features (i.e., scratches and pits) on the protoconal facets of *Australopithecus* and *Paranthropus* M²s (Table 6). These data reveal that in both samples, the wear features tend to be shorter and wider on Phase II than on Phase I surfaces (Fig. 4); the feature length means are significantly greater for all three facets in *Australopithecus*, while the feature width means are

Table 3. Bartlett's X^2 and Kolmogorov-Smirnov tests of scratch orientation distributions of *Australopithecus* and *Paranthropus* samples.

BARTLETT'S X^2 ANALYSIS

Comparison	X^2		p
facet 9	28.94		<0.05
facet 5	45.91		<0.005
facet 6	42.30		<0.005

KOLMOGOROV-SMIRNOV

Comparison	Observed D	Expected D	p
facet 9	0.234	0.132	<0.05
facet 5	0.108	0.124	
facet 6	0.168	0.126	<0.05

Table 4. Microwear scratch dimensions (μm).

Sample*	Facet	N	$\overline{X}$	SD	SE	CV
SCRATCH LENGTH						
Australopithecus	9	10	112.06	19.92	6.30	17.8
	5	10	167.59	26.42	8.35	15.8
	6	10	141.88	34.89	11.03	24.6
Paranthropus	9	9	81.67	35.38	11.79	43.3
	5	9	109.80	38.92	12.97	35.5
	6	9	9.97	1.44	11.30	33.9
SCRATCH WIDTH						
Australopithecus	9	10	1.04	0.16	0.05	15.4
	5	10	0.91	0.07	0.02	7.7
	6	10	0.93	0.13	0.04	14.0
Paranthropus	9	9	1.87	0.41	0.14	21.9
	5	9	1.89	0.33	0.11	17.5
	6	9	1.73	0.37	0.12	21.4

* Sample means computed from individual specimen averages.

Table 5. Microwear pit dimensions (μm).

Sample *	Facet	N	$\overline{X}$	SD	SE	CV
PIT LENGTH						
Australopithecus	9	10	7.95	1.54	0.49	19.4
	5	10	6.00	0.89	0.28	14.8
	6	10	6.15	1.08	0.34	17.6
Paranthropus	9	9	11.72	1.16	0.39	9.9
	5	9	10.22	2.92	0.97	28.6
	6	9	9.97	1.44	0.48	14.4
PIT WIDTH						
Australopithecus	9	10	5.04	1.13	0.36	22.4
	5	10	3.67	0.60	0.19	16.4
	6	10	3.70	0.79	0.25	21.4
Paranthropus	9	9	8.18	1.31	0.44	16.0
	5	9	7.07	2.01	0.67	28.4
	6	9	7.13	0.93	0.31	13.0

* Sample means computed from individual specimen averages.

Table 6. Dimension of pooled microwear features (µm).

Sample *	Facet	N	$\bar{X}$	SD	SE	CV
FEATURE LENGTH						
Australopithecus	9	10	73.33	17.45	5.52	23.8
	5	10	113.02	21.46	6.79	19.0
	6	10	93.80	26.62	8.42	28.4
Paranthropus	9	9	49.04	19.07	6.36	38.9
	5	9	81.71	30.85	10.28	37.8
	6	9	66.25	22.13	7.38	33.4
FEATURE WIDTH						
Australopithecus	9	10	2.61	0.88	0.28	33.7
	5	10	1.86	0.35	0.11	18.8
	6	10	1.91	0.26	0.08	13.6
Paranthropus	9	9	4.92	1.00	0.33	20.3
	5	9	3.58	0.95	0.32	26.5
	6	9	3.83	0.81	0.27	21.2

* Sample means computed from individual averages for combined scratch and pit diameters.

significantly larger for all three surfaces in the *Paranthropus* sample.

DISCUSSION

Since Robinson's (1954a) proposal that *Australopithecus* and *Paranthropus* possessed different trophic adaptations, the functional, taxonomic and paleoecological implications of the morphological differences between these so-called 'gracile' and 'robust' australopithecines have been the subject of vigorous debate.

Examination of the details of occlusal wear displayed by the deciduous and permanent molars of the southern African specimens of *Australopithecus* and *Paranthropus* has revealed several rather striking differences between them. Specifically, the qualitative observations made by Grine (1977, 1981, 1984) on the patterns of wear shown by the milk teeth are supported by quantitative assessments of the wear details possessed by the permanent molars of these early hominid taxa. That is, while

Figure 4. *Lengths and widths of pooled microwear features on M^2 protoconal facets in* Australopithecus *and* Paranthropus. *Data from Table 6. Bars = 1 SD on either side of means (circles).*

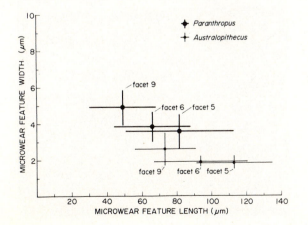

the Phase II surfaces tend to possess more occlusal pitting than the Phase I facets, and the pits tend to be larger on the Phase II than on the Phase I surfaces in both *Australopithecus* and *Paranthropus*, the molars of *Paranthropus* differ significantly from those of *Australopithecus* in that the latter tend to display fewer pits on both facet types. In addition, the pits tend to be significantly larger on *Paranthropus* molars, while scratches tend to be significantly longer but narrower on *Australopithecus* crowns. Wear scratches tend also to display noticeably greater homogeneity of orientation on *Australopithecus* teeth.

It is of considerable interest in terms of masticatory function that the differences in microwear between *Australopithecus* and *Paranthropus* tend to mirror the differences between the Phase I and Phase II facets within each of these taxa. Thus, the increased incidences of pitting, the shorter and broader scratches, the larger size of the pits, and the increased heterogeneity of scratch orientation shown by *Paranthropus* molars tend to resemble the conditions displayed by Phase II facets, whereas the traits of *Australopithecus* crowns are similar to those of Phase I surfaces.

During active side mastication, the Phase I facets move past one another in a shearing type of activity as the mandibular molars are drawn upward, forward and medially. At the same time, the Phase II facets approach one another, thus crushing or compressing food items. Following the attainment or approximation of centric occlusion, the Phase II facets move past one another as the mandibular molars are drawn downward. Thus, Phase II facets engage in more crushing and grinding activity during mastication, while the Phase I facets tend to engage in more shearing activity. The differences between these activities are reflected by the microwear details preserved by the Phase I and Phase II facets.

The fact that the differences between the *Australopithecus* and *Paranthropus* molars tend to correspond to the differences between the Phase I and Phase II facets within these taxa suggests that the molars of *Paranthropus* were used for more crushing and grinding than those of *Australopithecus*. The details of occlusal wear displayed by the deciduous and permanent teeth suggest that *Paranthropus* did not simply process greater amounts of the same foods that were masticated by *Australopithecus*.

Dietary Implications of Microwear

As noted elsewhere (Grine 1984), microwear patterns may not be indicative of diet *per se* because similar wear details can be produced by different agents. Enamel scratches, for example, may be engendered by intrinsic dietary items such as opaline phytoliths (Baker *et al.* 1959; Walker *et al.* 1978), or by extraneous material such as exogenous 'grit' (Covert and Kay 1981; Gordon and Walker 1983). Similar diets may also produce different wear patterns if the food preparation techniques employed by two species differ. For example, hard pericarps may be cracked extraorally or intraorally; in each case the seed itself may be masticated, but the latter type of behavior may result in microwear details that would not be apparent on the teeth of animals that use extensive manual (e.g., artifactual) preparation.

Nevertheless, there does seem to be a reasonable relationship between microwear and some broad dietary parameters in extant mammals, including primates (Walker *et al.* 1978; Gordon 1982; Teaford and Walker 1984; Teaford 1985, 1986). Thus, it appears possible to distinguish between browsing and grazing habits, and between taxa that feed on hard food objects and those that do not.

With regard to the australopithecines, it would seem reasonable, contrary evidence notwithstanding, to discount habitual and extensive extraoral food preparation as a confounding factor in the analysis of diet. Thus the microwear patterns displayed by the molars of 'gracile' and 'robust' australopithecines may be legitimately compared to those documented for living primates with different dietary habits.

The percentage incidence of occlusal pitting shown by *Paranthropus* molars is significantly higher than that displayed by *Australopithecus* crowns. The *Paranthropus* pitting frequency is higher than that recorded for *Pan troglodytes* by Gordon (1982), whereas the *Australopithecus* frequency is lower. Teaford and Walker (1984) have recorded Phase II facet pitting frequencies for seven species of living primates. They noted that the pitting incidences for *Cercocebus albigena*, *Cebus apella* and *Pongo pygmaeus*, the diets of which consist of hard food items such as the kernels and seeds of the date palm, palm nuts and bark (Chalmers 1968; Rodman 1977; Izawa and Mizuno 1977), are higher than the pitting frequencies on the molars of *Pan troglodytes*, the diet of which is comprised of between 56% to 71% of fruit and between 18% to 28% of young leaves and stems (Hladik 1977; Wrangham 1977). The pitting frequencies obtained by Teaford and Walker (1984) for *Colobus guereza*, which subsists mainly on a rather monotonous diet of young leaves (Oates 1977), *Alouatta*, one of the most intensely folivorous platyrrhine genera (Milton 1980), and *Gorilla*, the most exclusively folivorous great ape (Fossey and Harcourt 1977), are lower than the *Pan troglodytes* incidence.

Data for the widths of pooled microwear features on Phase II facets for a variety of living primates with known dietary habits have been recorded by Teaford and Walker (1984) and Teaford (1985, 1986). The australopithecine sample means, which are compared to the corresponding values for extant primates in Figure 5, suggest that the diet of *Paranthropus* consisted of comparatively hard objects. The *Australopithecus* mean, on the other hand, is comparable to the values shown by the more folivorous taxa examined by Teaford and Walker. It should be noted, however, that while the mean of the *Australopithecus* sample is comparable to those for folivorous taxa, this does not necessarily indicate that *Australopithecus* was an intense folivore. This is because no comparative data have been recorded for extant primate species whose diets consist principally of fruits without the inclusion of hard objects. Thus, while *Australopithecus* may have subsisted on a more intensely folivorous diet than *Paranthropus*, the diet of *Australopithecus* may also have been primarily frugivorous. It would seem obvious, however, that the diet of *Paranthropus* consisted of harder food items than the diet of *Australopithecus*.

The details of microwear preserved by the molars of these early hominids from southern Africa indicate that the diets of *Paranthropus* and *Australopithecus* were qualitatively dissimilar (Figs 6-8). The 'robust' australopithecines, therefore, do not appear to have been masticating greater quantities of the same foods that were chewed by *Australopithecus*. These apparent dietary differences, and the substantial differences in their trophic adaptations do not appear to be related solely to the estimated differences in their body sizes. There would seem

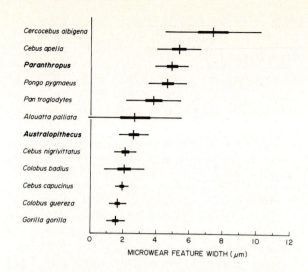

Figure 5. *Comparison of widths of pooled microwear features on M² facet 9 amongst extant primate taxa*, Australopithecus *and* Paranthropus. *Data for extant taxa from Teaford (1985, pers. comm.) and data for fossil taxa from Table 6. Vertical line = means; horizontal lines = 1 SD on either side of mean; horizontal bars = 1 SE on either side of mean.*

to be scant justification for regarding *Paranthropus* as simply a 'robust' version of *Australopithecus*.

Figure 6. *Scanning electron micrographs of Phase I facet 5 showing occlusal wear details displayed by specimens of* Australopithecus *and* Paranthropus. *Scale bar = 100 μm.*

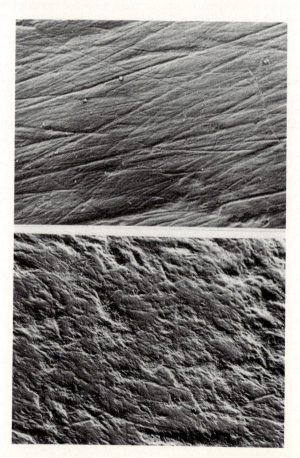

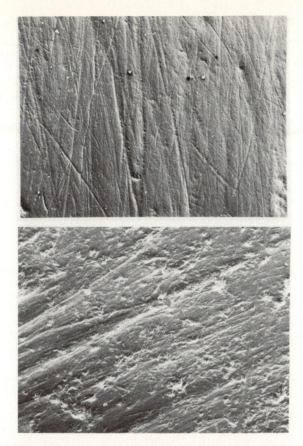

Figure 7. *Scanning electron micrographs of Phase I facet 6 showing occlusal wear details displayed by specimens of* Australopithecus *and* Paranthropus. *Scale bar = 100* μm.

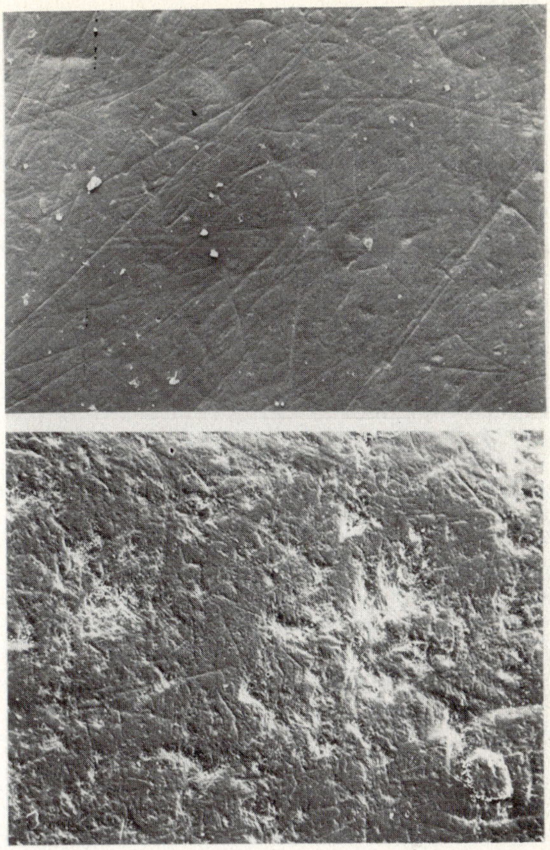

Figure 8. *Scanning and electron micrographs of Phase II facet 9 showing occlusal wear details displayed by specimens of* Australopithecus *and* Paranthropus. *Scale bar = 100* μm.

SUMMARY

Details of occlusal wear on the deciduous and permanent molars of southern African specimens of *Australopithecus* (the so-called 'gracile' australopithecine) and *Paranthropus* (the so-called 'robust' australopithecine) indicate that the diets of these Plio-Pleistocene hominid taxa were qualitatively dissimilar. The Phase I and Phase II facets of *Paranthropus* crowns display significantly greater numbers of microwear features, significantly higher incidences of occlusal pitting, significantly shorter but wider scratches and significantly larger pits than do *Australopithecus* teeth. Also, the scratches on *Paranthropus* molars display greater heterogeneity of orientation than those on *Australopithecus* crowns.

The differences in these parameters between *Australopithecus* and *Paranthropus* are comparable to the differences displayed between the Phase I and Phase II surfaces within each taxon. Thus, the wear patterns shown by Paranthropus indicate that its molars engaged in more crushing and grinding activities than the cheek teeth of *Australopithecus*. Moreover, the more numerous and larger pits on the Paranthropus crowns, as well as the greater heterogeneity of scratch orientation shown by these teeth strongly suggest that the foods that were processed by *Australopithecus* and *Paranthropus* differed in their mechanical properties.

Comparisons of the microwear details on the permanent second molars of the australopithecines with those recorded by Gordon (1982), Teaford and Walker (1984) and Teaford (1985, 1986) for extant primate species indicate that *Paranthropus* masticated substantially harder objects than were chewed by *Australopithecus*. These comparisons also suggest that *Australopithecus* may have been more folivorous than *Paranthropus*, although comparative data for primate species whose diets consist principally of fruits without the inclusion of hard objects are not yet fully available.

The inferred dietary differences, and the differences in the trophic adaptations of these Plio-Pleistocene hominids do not appear to be related solely to differences in their estimated body sizes. There would appear to be scant justification, therefore, for regarding *Paranthropus* as simply a 'robust' version of *Australopithecus*.

ACKNOWLEDGEMENTS

I thank C. K. Brain, E. S. Vrba, and P. V. Tobias for permission to examine the fossil hominid material in their care, and for the generous hospitality that they showed during my visits to their institutions. I am grateful to E. A. Peterson for her painstaking care and expertise in the manufacture of the casts. I thank J. G. Fleagle, W. L. Jungers, R. F. Kay, D. W. Krause, K. D. Gordon, and M. F. Teaford for many fruitful discussions about body size, trophic adaptations and tooth wear. This work was supported by a grant from the L. S. B. Leakey Foundation.

REFERENCES

Baker, G., Jones, L. H. P., and Wardrop, I. D. 1959. Cause of wear in sheep's teeth. *Nature* 184:1583-1584.

Brace, C. L. 1967. Environment, tooth form and size in the Pleistocene. *J. Dent. Res.* 46:809-816.

Brace, C. L. 1969. The australopithecine range of variation. *Amer. J. Phys. Anthro.* 31:255.

Brain, C. K. 1981. *The Hunters or the Hunted?* University of Chicago Press, Chicago.

Broom, R. 1938. The Pleistocene anthropoid apes of South Africa. *Nature* 142:377-379.

Broom, R. 1949. Another type of fossil ape-man *(Paranthropus crassidens). Nature* 163:57.

Calder, W. A. 1984. *Size, Function and Life History.* Harvard University Press, Cambridge, Mass.

Chalmers, N. R. 1968. Group composition, ecology and daily activities of free living mangabeys in Uganda. *Folia primatol.* 8:247-262.

Covert, H. H., and Kay, R. F. 1981. Dental microwear and diet: implications for determining the feeding behaviors of extinct primates, with a comment on the dietary pattern of *Sivapithecus. Amer. J. Phys. Anthro.* 55:331-336.

Creighton, G. K. 1980. Static allometry of mammalian teeth and the correlation of tooth size and body size in contemporary mammals. *J. Zool. (London)* 191:435-443.

Dart, R. A. 1925. *Australopithecus africanus:* the man-ape of South Africa. *Nature* 115:195-199.

Dart, R. A. 1949. The predatory implemental technique of *Australopithecus. Amer. J. Phys. Anthro.* 7:1-16.

Dart, R. A. 1957. The osteodontokeratic culture of *Australopithecus prometheus. Transvaal Museum Memoir* No. 10, pp. 1-105.

Dart, R. A. 1958. The minimal bone-breccia content of Makapansgat and the australopithecine predatory habit. *Amer. Anthropol.* 60:923-931.

Fleagle, J. G. 1985. Size and adaptation in Primates, in: *Size and Scaling in Primate Biology* (W.L. Jungers, Ed.), pp. 1-19, Plenum, New York.

Fossey, D., and Harcourt, A. H. 1977. Feeding ecology of the free-ranging mountain gorilla *(Gorilla gorilla beringei),* in: *Primate Ecology* (T. H. Clutton-Brock, Ed.), pp. 415-447, Academic, New York.

Gingerich, P. D., and Smith, B. H. 1985. Allometric scaling in the dentition of primates and insectivores, in: *Size and Scaling in Primate Biology,* (W. L. Jungers, Ed.), pp. 257-272, Plenum, New York.

Gordon, K. D. 1982. A study of microwear on chimpanzee molars: implications for dental microwear analysis. *Amer. J. Phys. Anthro.* 59:195-215.

Gordon, K. D., and Walker, A. C. 1983. Playing 'possum' a microwear experiment. *Amer. J. Phys. Anthro.* 60:109-112.

Grine, F. E. 1977. Analysis of early hominid deciduous molar wear by scanning electron microscopy: a preliminary report. *Proceeding of the Electron Microscopy Society of Southern Africa* 7:157-158.

Grine, F. E. 1981. Trophic differences between 'gracile' and 'robust' australopithecines: a scanning electron microscope analysis of occlusal events. *S. Afr. J. Sci.* 77:203-230.

Grine, F. E. 1982. A new juvenile hominid (Mammalia: Primates) from Member 3, Kromdraai Formation, Transvaal, South Africa. *Ann. Transvaal Mus.* 33:165-239.

Grine, F. E. 1984. Deciduous molar microwear of South African australopithecines, in: *Food Acquisition and Processing in Primates,* (D. J. Chivers, B. A. Wood, and A. Bilsborough, Eds.), pp. 525-534, Plenum, New York.

Hladik, C. M. 1977. Chimpanzees of Gabon and Chimpanzees of Gombe: some comparative data on the diet, in: *Primate Ecology,* (T. H. Clutton-Brock, Ed.), pp. 481-501, Academic, New York.

Hylander, W. L. 1975. Incisor size and diet in anthropoids with special reference to Cercopithecidae. *Science* 189:1095-1098.

Hylander, W. L. 1985. Mandibular function and biomechanical stress and scaling. *Amer. Zool.* 25:315-330.

Izawa, K. and Mizuno, A. 1977. Palm-fruit cracking behavior of wild black-capped capuchin *(Cebus apella). Primates* 18:773-792.

Jungers, W. L. 1984. Aspects of size and scaling in primate biology with special reference to the locomotor skeleton. *Yrbk. Phys. Anthro.* 27:73-97.

Jungers, W. L., and Grine, F. E. 1986. Dental trends in the australopithecines: the allometry of mandibular molar dimensions, in: *Major Topics in Primate and Human Evolution,* (B. A. Wood, L. B. Martin, and P. Andrews, Eds.), pp. 203-219, Cambridge University Press, Cambridge.

Kay, R. F. 1975. Allometry and early hominids. *Science* 189:63.

Kay, R. F. 1985. Dental evidence for the diet of *Australopithecus. Annual Rev. Anthro.* 14:315-341.

Kay, R. F., and Covert, H. H. 1984. Anatomy and behavior of extinct primates,. in: *Food Acquisition and Processing in Primates,* (D. J. Chivers, B. A. Wood, and A. Bilsborough, Eds.), pp. 467-508, Plenum, New York.

Kay, R. F., and Hiiemae, K. M. 1974. Jaw movement and tooth use in recent and fossil primates. *Amer. J. Phys. Anthro.* 40:227-256.

Milton, K. 1980. *The Foraging Strategy of Howler Monkeys.* Columbia University Press, New York.

Oates, J. F. 1977. The guereza and its food, in: *Primate Ecology,* (T. H. Clutton-Brock, Ed.), pp. 275-322, Academic, New York.

Peters, C. R. 1981. Robust vs. gracile early hominid masticatory capabilities: the advantages of the megadonts, in: *The Perception of Human Evolution,* (L. L. Mai, E. Shanklin, and R. W. Sussman, Eds.), pp.161-181, University of California Press, Los Angeles.

Peters, C. R. 1982. Electron-optical microscope study of incipient dental microdamage from experimental seed and bone crushing. *Amer. J. Phys. Anthro.* 57:283-301.

Pilbeam, D. R., and Gould, S. J. 1974. Size and scaling in human evolution. *Science* 186:892-901.

Puech, P. F., Albertini, H. and Serratrice, C. 1983. Tooth micro-wear and dietary patterns in early hominids from Laetoli, Hadar and Olduvai. *J. Hum. Evol.* 12:721-729.

Robinson, J. T. 1954a. The genera and species of the Australopithecinae. *Amer. J. Phys. Anthro.* 12:181-200.

Robinson, J. T. 1954b. Prehominid dentition and hominid evolution. *Evolution* 8:324-334.

Robinson, J. T. 1956. The Dentition of the Australopithecinae. *Transvaal Museum Memoir* No. 9.

Robinson, J. T. 1961. The australopithecines and their bearing on the origin of man and of stone tool making. *S. Afr. J. Sci.* 57:3-16.

Rodman, P. S. 1977. Feeding behaviour of orang-utans of the Kutai Nature Reserve, East Kalimantan, in: *Primate Ecology,* (T. H. Clutton-Brock, Ed.), pp. 383-413, Academic, New York.

Ryan, A. S. 1979. Scanning electron microscopy of tooth wear on the anterior teeth of *Australopithecus afarensis. Amer. J. Phys. Anthro.* 50:478.

Smith, R. J. 1980. Rethinking allometry. *Journal of Theoretical Biology* 87:97-111.

Teaford, M. F. 1985. Molar microwear and diet in the genus *Cebus. Amer. J. Phys. Anthro.* 66:363-370.

Teaford, M. F. 1986. Dental microwear and diet in two species of *Colobus,* in: *Primate Ecology and Conservation,* (J. G. Else and P. C. Lee, Eds.), Cambridge University Press, Cambridge.

Teaford, M. F., and Walker, A. C. 1984. Quantitative differences in dental microwear between primate species with different diets and a comment on the presumed diet of *Sivapithecus. Amer. J. Phys. Anthro.* 64:191-200.

Tobias, P. V. 1967. *The Cranium and Maxillary Dentition of Australopithecus (Zinjanthropus) boisei.* Cambridge University Press, Cambridge.

Walker, A. C. 1980. Functional anatomy and taphonomy, in: *Fossils in the Making* (A. K. Behrensmeyer and A. P. Hill, Eds.), pp. 182-196, University of Chicago Press, Chicago.

Walker, A. C. 1981. Dietary hypotheses and human evolution. *Phil. Trans. Royal Soc., London,* Series B, 292:57-64.

Walker, A. C., Hoeck, H. N., and Perez, L. 1978. Microwear of mammalian teeth as an indicator of diet. *Science* 201:808-810.

Wallace, J. A. 1972. *The Dentition of the South African Early Hominids: A Study of Form and Function.* Ph.D. Thesis, University of the Witwatersrand, Johannesburg, South Africa.

Wallace, J. A. 1973. Tooth chipping in the australopithecines. *Nature* 244:117-118.

Wallace, J. A. 1975. Dietary adaptations of *Australopithecus* and early *Homo*, in: *Paleoanthropology, Morphology and Paleoecology*, (R. Tuttle, Ed.), pp. 203-223, Mouton, The Hague.

Wallace, J. A. 1978. Evolutionary trends in the early hominid dentition, in: *Early Hominids of Africa*, (C. Jolly, Ed.), pp. 285-310, Duckworth, London.

Wolpoff, M. H. 1973. Posterior tooth size, body size and diet in South African gracile australopithecines. *Amer. J. Phys. Anthro.* 39:375-394.

Wolpoff, M. F. 1974. The evidence for two australopithecine lineages in South Africa. *Yrbk. Phys. Anthro.* 17:113-139.

Wolpoff, M. H. 1975. Some aspects of human mandibular evolution, in: *Determinants of Mandibular Form and Growth*, (J. A. McNamara, Ed.), pp. 1-64, Center for Human Growth and Development, Ann Arbor.

Wood, B. A. 1984. Interpreting the dental peculiarities of the 'robust' australopithecines, in: *Food Acquisition and Processing in Primates*, (D. J. Chivers, B. A. Wood, and A. Bilsborough, Eds.), pp. 535-544, Plenum, New York.

Wood, B. A., and Stack, K. C. G. 1980. Does allometry explain the differences between "gracile" and "robust" australopithecines? *Amer. J. Phys. Anthro.* 52:55-62.

Wood, B. A., Abbott, S. A., and Graham, S. H. 1983. Analysis of the dental morphology of Plio-Pleistocene hominids. II. Mandibular molars—study of cusp area, fissure pattern and cross-sectional shape of the crown. *J. Anat.* 137:287-314.

Wrangham, R. W. 1977. Feeding behaviour of chimpanzees in Gombe National Park, Tanzania, in: *Primate Ecology*, (T. H. Clutton-Brock, Ed.), pp. 503-538, Academic, New York.

16

Ecological and Adaptive Changes Associated with Early Hominid Evolution

E. S. Vrba

INTRODUCTION

The richest and most spectacular modern, large mammal fauna on earth inhabits the African savanna. There is evidence that the origin of the extensive savanna—today occupying some 65% of Africa and ranging from dense, moist woodlands and thickets through open shrublands to vast treeless grasslands (Huntley and Walker 1982)—dates to the end of the Miocene. Many of the typical monophyletic groups of savanna mammals are first recorded near the Miocene-Pliocene boundary, together with the Hominidae. The human family was among the "founder members" and for most of its history an endemic part of the African savanna biota.

What were the physical and biotic changes that caused hominid evolution? Which environmental variables were of major importance in the ecology of our early relatives, and how might hominids have been adapted to these variables? How did the nature and breadth of habitat preferences differ among hominid species? The few available hominid fossils on their own cannot take us very far towards answering these questions. Instead, the changes in man's family tree need to be studied as

an integral part of wider biotic, climatic, and geological evolutionary rhythms.

That is the approach I have taken. In particular, I have used data on antelopes (Bovidae) and on environmental variation in space and time to generate some, and test other, hypotheses of hominid paleobiology. Bovids are especially useful for such analyses: They are by far the most numerous large mammals in most African Miocene-Recent fossil assemblages. Using skull differentiation among extant species as a guide, fossil morphologies are usually readily identifiable to species level. Most clades have undergone a rapid turnover of species since the Miocene and are still in a phase of radiation. They are dominant in the modern large mammal fauna (some 70 species of African Bovidae comprise nearly 40% of hoofed mammals in the world), and their biology has been intensively studied. The vast majority of extant antelope species are narrowly habitat-specific. As a result, bovid data can contribute to the study of hominid chronology and paleoecology (Vrba 1974, 1975, 1980a, 1982).

Furthermore, early Hominidae were large-bodied, mobile, herbivorous (at least to a large extent), endemic, savanna mammals—all features shared with the abundant antelopes that evolved together with them. It is thus hardly surprising to find that hominid evolutionary pulses—in lineage splitting (speciation), phenotypic change, and extinction—have followed rhythms similar to those in several antelope phylogenies (Vrba 1984a). This evidence implies not only synchrony, but also in some cases broad ecological analogy, of evolutionary response to the same widespread oscillations in temperature, rainfall, and vegetation cover. I suggest that the evolutionary patterns of Bovidae and other mammal groups can be used to generate hypotheses on the causes of hominid evolution and on the nature of early hominid adaptations.

ANTELOPES AS PALEOECOLOGICAL INDICATORS

To assess which, if any, bovid taxa may be reliable habitat indicators in the Plio-Pleistocene, I first asked: Are extant African Bovidae, at the generic and tribal level, significantly associated with each other and with particular habitats? To answer this question I analyzed modern census data from 16 wildlife areas in subsaharan Africa. The nine tribes of Bovidae analyzed all originated either near the end of the Miocene or previously. There are morphological reasons for hypothesizing that most are monophyletic, *sensu stricto*. A multidimensional graphical technique called correspondence analysis was performed on these data (Vrba 1980a; Greenacre and Vrba 1984). It can be called an objective method of statistical analysis in the sense that it does not *a priori* presume any structure (or causative factor) underlying the data. Instead, it reveals any non-random structure *a posteriori*. In this particular case it primarily grouped bovid taxa with each other and with game areas. It secondarily showed associations between bovid taxa and independently-included ecological variables like vegetation cover, rainfall, altitude, soil nutrient status, etc. A remarkable and consistent association of Alcelaphini (the hartebeest-wildebeest-blesbuck group) and Antilopini (the gazelle-springbuck group) with open grassland was demonstrated. In areas with a combination of low altitude and low rainfall (0-400 mm mean annual) as well as those of high altitude with medium rainfall (400-800 mm mean annual) the resultant vegetational physiognomy is a low ratio of wood- to grass-cover. In such areas alcelaphines plus antilopines never account, in this data set, for less than 65% of the total antelope frequency; they never amount to more than 30% in predominantly bush-covered areas.

One remarkable result of the correspondence analysis is that it clearly pinpoints *gross vegetational physiognomy* (i.e., as defined by proportions of wood- versus grass-cover, not by plant species) as of primary importance (accounting for 40% of the variation) in determining tribal distribution of modern antelopes. In fact, the main result is that a particular tribe might be strongly associated with an overall physiognomy of characteristic wood-grass-cover, while in contrast it may range across diverse categories of soil nutrient status and primary productivity, geography, and even to some extent rainfall and altitude (Greenacre and Vrba 1984).

A second interesting result is that, with few exceptions, the associations with gross vegetational physiognomy are evident at the level of whole monophyletic groups, the tribes. The extant distribution suggests that, in spite of a high species turnover (individual clades may show up to 30 speciation events in 5 m.y.), speciation hardly ever results in entry into a significantly different habitat of grass-wood ratio. It seems that once an ancestral species of a clade is established as (for example) an open grassland grazer, its descendant species are highly unlikely to switch to a browsing, predominantly woodland existence. From a perusal of the literature, I suggest that such constraints on "switching" basic vegetational habitats are general for diverse mammal groups.

Was there such an association between Alcelaphini/Antilopini and open habitat, and between other groups and more woody environs, early on in the histories of these groups, or is it a recent phenomenon? A number of lines of evidence suggest that the habitat associations are ancient: 1) the phylogenetic distributions of extant habitat preferences mostly assort strictly according to monophyletic groups, and the latter had originated before the Early Pliocene; 2) the phylogenetic and temporal distribution of morphological characters strongly supports a notion of fidelity throughout the Plio-Pleistocene of modern tribal habitat associations; and 3) the Miocene-Recent speciation and extinction curves of Alcelaphini-plus-Antilopini are inverse to those of other tribes combined. 4) Furthermore, wherever the hypothesis has been tested so far in the fossil record it has been found supported. For instance, Kappelman (personal communication) reports that, in the lower Olduvai strata, high alcelaphine plus antilopine frequencies coincide with high frequencies of murids (Jaeger 1976) and pollen types (Bonnefille 1979) that indicate open habitat. Thus, I have concluded that the "Alcelaphini-plus-Antilopini criterion" is a reliable indicator of gross vegetation cover in the early hominid record.

ENVIRONMENTS OF HOMINID SUCCESSIONS IN THE TRANSVAAL AND EAST AFRICA

I applied the criterion of the proportions of alcelaphine plus antelopine individuals, out of all bovids present, to the various hominid-associated assemblages in South Africa. The percentages of Alcelaphini plus Antilopini from Makapansgat Member 3 and Sterkfontein Member 4 are very much lower than those of later assemblages, such as those from Swartkrans Member 1 and Sterkfontein Member 5. These results obtained for various Transvaal fossil assemblages, together with the associated hominid species, are represented in Figure 1. (The Kromdraai australopithecine stratum, KBE Member 3, is not included because very few bovid specimens are present in this assemblage; see Vrba 1981).

After careful and detailed consideration of taphonomic biases, I have concluded (Vrba 1980a) that this difference in representation of antelope taxa represents a real change in the vegetation and climatic conditions of the Plio-Pleistocene transition in the Transvaal. One important consideration is that the same change, across the same time interval, is evident in East African stratigraphic sequences. For instance, on the environments of the Omo Shungura Formation, Howell (1978, p. 228) notes:

> Vegetation in the earlier time range (2.5 m.y.) on pollen evidence (Bonnefille 1976), 'included closed and/or open woodland, tree/shrub grassland, grassland, and some shrub thicket and shrub steppe' (Carr 1976). By contrast, 0.5 m.y. later...total diversity of plant taxa is markedly reduced, species of mesic habitat affiliation decrease markedly, as does the percentage of pollen from woody plants, and the proportion of pollen with plains habitat affiliation increases markedly. These changes suggest 'more xerophytic plant community types of grassland, tree/shrub steppe' (Carr 1976). This rather profound environmental change is wholly corroborated by the

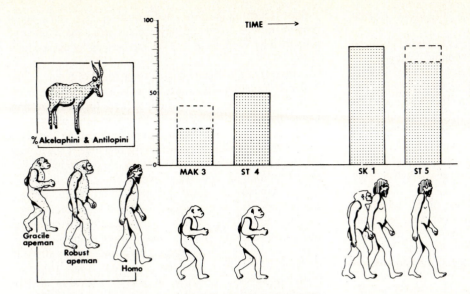

Figure 1. *Associations in four Transvaal limestone cave members from three cave formations. The members are arranged from left to right according to my estimate of chronological sequence. (MAK=Makapansgat Limeworks; ST=Sterkfontein; SK=Swartkrans; numbers refer to members.) Top: histograms of minimum numbers of bovid individuals of Alcelaphini plus Antilopini, calculated as percentages of the total bovid assemblages. Dotted lines denote uncertainty, due, for instance, to possible admixture from other members. Bottom: Hominid species. Recent work suggests ST 5 predates SK 1.*

microvertebrate fossil record (Jaeger and Wesselman 1976). A robust australopithecine (*A. boisei*) appears for the first time in the Omo succession at about the time of this environmental change, as does also an early species of genus *Homo*.

By the "2.5 to 2.0 m.y." interval Howell meant Shungura Members C to E, now re-dated to "earlier than 2.52 to about 2.4" (Brown *et al.* 1985). This time level falls between ST 4 and later Transvaal strata (Fig. 1). Thus, the East African change, both as regards environment and hominid evolution, parallels the southern evidence across the same time level.

It is important to recognize clearly the limits of what I am claiming here. The analysis of extant antelopes suggests that tribal distribution is *primarily* determined by gross height and spacing of bush and tree cover. The latter is secondarily related to combinations of temperature, rainfall, and other factors (Greenacre and Vrba 1984). If this is valid, then the bovid change in the Transvaal succession tells us that a gross vegetational change occurred, from proportionally more bush and tree cover somewhere near 3 m.y. ago to more dominant open grassland close to 2 m.y. ago. However, any conclusion from these data on how this change correlates with temperature and rainfall must be secondary and more speculative. There are lines of evidence that suggest that for any one area a change to more open habitat very probably correlates with reduced temperature, and *vice versa*, and less certainly with reduced rainfall (reviewed in Brain 1981; Vrba 1985). Secondly, precisely of what nature and magnitude was the alleged vegetation change? I have argued (Vrba 1985) that the change in the Transvaal before 2 m.y. ago was not of large scale, such as from dense woodland/forest to treeless grassland. Rather the change was probably more subtle, occurring somewhere along the vegetational sliding scale *within* the spectrum of moderately open to open savanna environments. The bovid data are not at variance with Butzer's (1971) conclusion that each of the breccias in question, including Sterkfontein Member 4, basically represents colluvial sediments compatible only with an incomplete mat of vegetation.

In sum, the southern African evidence indicates a more vegetationally open and probably more arid environment for the Swartkrans apeman and *Homo*, postdating a wetter and

more bush-covered period during which Sterkfontein *Australopithecus africanus* lived in the area. Butzer's (1974) suggestion of a relatively humid environment for the Taung *A. africanus* is in agreement with the Transvaal evidence. As pointed out above, East African data suggest a similar environmental change associated with the same phase in hominid evolution. What we know of the environments associated with *Australopithecus afarensis/africanus* in eastern Africa is not at variance with a notion that the pre-2.5 m.y. hominids lived in areas with a relatively higher wood-grass ratio and more mesic conditions than their descendant species (reviewed in Vrba 1985).

I conclude that we have a strong suggestion, of a broad and unprecise nature but nonetheless reasonably supported, of a difference in habitat specificity between early hominid species as a whole, not just between their local populations. I have argued elsewhere (Vrba 1980b) that significant evolutionary change is a direct function of environmental change. Thus I see the correlation between different habitats and different hominid species as likely to indicate causation: a widespread change in temperature, rainfall, and vegetation cover *caused* the evolution of the hominid phenotypes currently included in the species *Homo habilis*, *Australopithecus robustus*, and *A. boisei*.

A separate question is whether the postulated environmental change caused *the particular lineage splitting event* that led to *Homo* on the one hand and "robust" australopithecines on the other. One argument would disagree: White *et al.* (1981) see the Hadar and Laetoli hominids as belonging to the directly ancestral species of the crucial splitting event, with *A. africanus* already diverged from the ancestry of *Homo*. They argue that both Makapansgat and Sterkfontein *A. africanus* belong in the 2.0-2.5 m.y. time range, and place the branching that gave rise to *Homo* earlier (see Fig. 2). Other anthropologists, notably Tobias (e.g., 1985), place the split between 2.5 and 2.0 m.y. ago, with *A. africanus* as the direct ancestor. If the latter view is correct, then the widespread environmental change which I have discussed may have been the cause of the major branching event in hominid evolution: as woodland habitats shrank and fragmented, the preferred habitats of A. *africanus* did as well. Isolated populations and speciation in allopatry may have given rise to earliest *Homo* and to one or more robust australopithecine species.

I await with interest the further developments in the crucial debate between different arguments on hominid phylogeny. As one who has attempted to contribute to early hominid chronology (e.g., Vrba 1975, 1982) I can observe the following. The confidence that we can now feel regarding the current conflicting reports on the dating of Sterkfontein Member 4, Makapansgat Member 3, and Hadar leaves something to be desired. But in regard to the debate on hominid phylogeny I do not regret that: one can cite the cogent argument that what is crucial to phylogenetic analysis is character analysis and not the temporal placement of taxa.

I suggest that, whatever the outcome of the debate on hominid phylogeny, we have good evidence of a causal environmental influence on hominid evolution between the times represented by *A. africanus* finds on the one hand, and the Swartkrans Member 1 and Sterkfontein Member 5 hominids on the other.

MIOCENE—RECENT EVOLUTIONARY PULSES

Figure 2 compares a curve of first records for bovid species, from Late Miocene-Recent African strata south of the Sahara, with a phylogenetic tree of Hominidae following widespread consensus on the timing of speciation events. A number of taphonomic and chronologic biases are inherent in my procedures for scoring speciation frequencies of Bovidae (Vrba 1984). In Figure 3 a part of the hominid tree is compared with oxygen isotope curves from the deep sea record. I am assuming that these climatic data, especially those of Thunell and Williams (1983), represent global changes in temperature. Although most sources agree with the estimates in Figure 3 of

earliest records in the *Homo* and robust lineages, some would propose different hominid phylogenies (e.g., the alternative supported by White *et al.* [1981], represented by dashed lines in Fig. 2).

In spite of the uncertainties, a comparison of Figures 2 and 3, also with additional data on terminal Miocene cooling (review in Brain 1981), suggests certain hypotheses for further testing. During the end of the Miocene, when temperatures plunged to a low point unprecedented during the entire preceding Tertiary, a number of bovid tribes appeared for the first time. They include the essentially African tribes Alcelaphini, Aepycerotini, Reduncini, Hippotragini and Tragelaphini. Thus, global climatic change may have coincided with hominid origin (Brain 1981) and perhaps also with a spectacular bovid radiation into new "adaptive zones" (Fig. 2). Near 2.5 m.y. ago global temperatures again plunged to a low point. A peak in bovid origination seems to be synchronous with this cooling event and perhaps also with the hominid speciation event that gave rise to *Homo* and robust australopithecines (Figs. 2, 3). Intriguingly, a wave of antelope evolutionary activity may also coincide with the origin of *Homo sapiens* (Fig. 2), and the global mean "cooling step" at 0.9 m.y. could be synchronous with extinction of the robust australopithecines (Fig. 3). The fossil records of other mammals (e.g., Maglio and Cooke 1978) tentatively suggest that the evolutionary peaks in Figure 2 may be paralleled in other lineages. In fact the patterns point to the possibility of widespread climatic changes as major causes of evolutionary turnover.

I predict that we may find, as data that are more numerous and more chronologically secure become available, that evolution occurs in concerted pulses that involve many groups. Diverse lineages in the biota should respond by synchronous waves of speciation and extinction to global temperature extremes and attendant environmental changes.

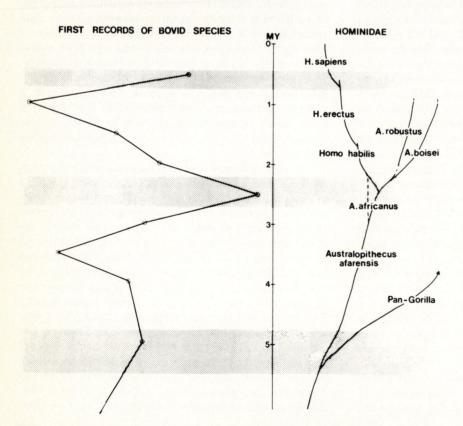

FIRST RECORDS OF BOVID SPECIES   MY   HOMINIDAE

H. sapiens

H. erectus

A. robustus

Homo habilis   A. boisei

A. africanus

Australopithecus
afarensis

Pan - Gorilla

Figure 2. *Rates of origination of all species of Bovidae known from sub-saharan Africa, Late Miocene-Recent, and a phylogenetic tree of Hominidae (dashed alternative for origin of* Homo *after White* et al. *1981; see text). Stippled bands represent approximate timing of major evolutionary events in bovid and hominid radiation. Chronology updated after Brown* et al. *(1985). my, Millions of years.*

EVOLUTION IN ECOLOGICAL CHARACTERS OF HOMINIDAE

It is likely that hominids at some point underwent a significant ecological "switch," in terms of vegetation cover and yearround availability of moisture; and it is possible that this switch coincided with a speciation event that led to *Homo* on the one hand and *A. robustus/boisei* on the other. If so, it was a remarkable and rare event in the context of Miocene-Recent mammal evolution (e.g., Vrba 1980a; Greenacre and Vrba 1984). An examination of similar events in other phylogenies suggests hypotheses of changes in adaptive characters that may have occurred in the hominids.

Resource Breadth

Extant survivors of lineages that entered more open, arid habitats typically are either more generalist in breadth of resource use than their more numerous, bush-loving relatives (i.e., they can subsist in the ancestral and in the new environments), or they are specialists on open habitats (see Vrba 1984 for some examples). The hominine lineage may have taken the first evolutionary route, the robust one the second.

There are of course numerous publications on diet and dietary breadth in early hominid species (reviewed in Grine 1981). One early "dietary hypothesis" is that of Robinson (1963): the cranial, mandibular, and dental differences between the Transvaal apemen reflect the fact that *A. africanus* was an omnivore living in drier, more open conditions, while the robust apemen were specialist, extreme herbivores living in a wetter and vegetationally more luxurious environment. Up to the early 1970s Robinson's conclusions were the dominant views on environment and trophic adaptation of Transvaal hominids. On the basis of alcelaphine and antelopine proportions, I wrote in 1975 (*contra* Robinson 1963) that we "should consider whether [the musculature of robust apemen] was so massive and the molars proportionally so large, because their 'vegetables' were of the tough grassland type." Since then there has been agreement with this suggestion from many different kinds of analyses. For instance, recently Grine (1981) reviewed many hypotheses of early hominid diet and ecology and added new data on the scanning electron microscopic details of occlusal wear of Transvaal hominid teeth. His findings suggest "that the 'robust' forms employed more crushing and puncture-crushing activity and relied more heavily upon Phase II activity than did the 'gracile' australopithecines...It is concluded that the 'robust' hominids habitually, or at least seasonally, triturated harder, more resistant and perhaps smaller food objects than were masticated by the 'gracile' australopithecines" (p. 203). He considers that robusts were adapted to xeric environments, where many of the available food staples are relatively tough. In principle, hypotheses of dietary breadth are testable via several kinds of analyses, such as Grine's (1981) on toothwear, and trace element and isotopic analyses of fossils.

An attendant prediction is that the geographic distributions of habitat specialists should be more restricted and more sus-

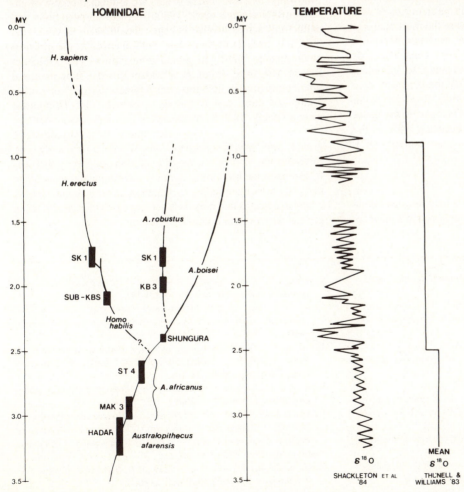

Figure 3. *A comparison, over the time range 3.5 m.y. to Recent, of the hominid tree with oxygen isotope data from the deep sea record. Solid rectangles represent chronological estimates (after Brown et al. 1985, for East Africa, and my biochronology for South Africa) for hominid occurrences from particular strata, including earliest records of the Homo and robust lineages. The climatic curve on the left is adapted from Shackleton et al. (1984, Figs. 3, 4). It refers to deep sea oxygen isotope data from a North Atlantic site. The curve on the right, adapted from Thunell and Williams (1983, Fig. 5), represents a schematic summary of mean oxygen isotope values from deep sea sites in the Pacific, Caribbean, Mediterranean, and off Northwest Africa. I am assuming that these oxygen isotope curves represent changes in temperature.*

ceptible to environmental fluctuations than those of generalists. Thus we may (or may not) find in one particular stratigraphic column that *A. robustus* (or *A. boisei*) was at different times absent and present in the area (as the geographic distribution shrank and expanded) in predictable synchrony with environmental changes as independently deduced, while *Homo* persisted through the oscillations.

Mobility

As Baker (1978) observed, most animals are "migratory" to some extent. But it is undeniable that those living in open, arid habitats, where resources tend to be patchy in space and/or time, invariably have a greater tendency to seasonal and more extensive movement (see also Wiens 1976). Did one or both of the hominid lineages that diverged during the Pliocene migrate seasonally across ecotonal margins? That hypothesis has been tested and found supported in species of hypsodont herbivores. At present I cannot think of any way to test it in early hominid species.

A related hypothesis is that apemen in the *A. afarensis/africanus* lineage (if really in habitats where trees were more prevalent and larger) were relatively more arboreal and less bipedal than their descendants (although each species both climbed and walked). There are of course several anatomical studies that have tried to test this. Among them, in a 1979 paper I noted on the basis of the STS 7 scapula of *A. africanus* that this Sterkfontein hominid, although apparently a biped, may have been more adapted to tree-climbing than later hominids. (Incidentally, Stern and Susman 1983, p. 280, group me among those who "view that the evidence is equivocal because the functional significance of morphologic differences between australopithecines and humans is moot." This is inaccurate. In fact, I concluded that "gracile australopithecines had a greater potential for climbing, hanging, reaching and arm-swinging than has modern man" Vrba 1979, p. 128). I await with interest the further developments in the debate on this issue, recently rekindled in regard to the Hadar hominids by workers such as Stern and Susman (1983, on the "arboreal side") and Lovejoy *et al.* (1982, on the "bipedal side").

Social Behavior

It is well-known that evolution towards life in more vegetationally open and arid environments is invariably accompanied by fundamental changes in social behaviour, whatever group of mammals one may be considering. Furthermore, the evolutionary responses tend to be similar from group to group (e.g., Krebs and Davies 1978; Estes, submitted). Thus I welcome a hypothesis like Lovejoy's (1981) (whether it may be found true in detail or not) that focuses on the role of reproductive and social behavior in hominid evolution. Can we perceive traces in the hominid record after 2.5 m.y. of features such as increased gregariousness, more emphasis on visual communication and reduced sexual dimorphism, etc.? Such features occur convergently in diverse mammal lineages—including primates—that evolved into open habitats.

CONCLUSION

Near 2.5 million years ago a particularly marked and widespread environmental change occurred in Africa. It involved an increase in open grasslands at the expense of wood and tree cover, probably resulting from a global reduction in temperature and associated changes in rainfall. The environmental changes caused the evolutionary changes in hominids that are observed in both eastern and southern Africa over the same time period. This suggestion was essentially put forward by Vrba (1974, 1975) and has since received empirical support from various new data.

Some prevalent models of evolution (such as allopatric speciation, and particularly punctuated equilibria) predict the following: 1) Evolutionary events are a direct function of environmental change (Vrba 1980b). 2) Thus, speciations and extinctions across diverse lineages should occur as concerted pulses in predictable synchrony with changes in the physical environment, chiefly in global temperature. The Miocene-Recent African record of the abundant Bovidae supports these predictions, and the literature suggests that data on diverse other faunal and floral groups may do so as well. Thus Hominidae were probably "founder members" of the biota of the extensive African savanna, together with many other phylogenetic groups. Similarly, the origin of *Homo* was not an isolated event. Instead it was part of a wave of evolutionary activity that was forced upon the biota by a common environmental cause. The perspective of mammalian evolution in general suggests some adaptive changes that may have accompanied the Late Pliocene ecological switch in hominid evolution.

REFERENCES

Baker, R. R. 1978. *The Evolutionary Ecology of Animal Migration*, Hadder and Stoughton, London.

Bonnefille, R. 1979. Méthode palynologique et reconstitutions paléoclimatiques au Cénozoique dans le Rift Est Africain. *Bull. Soc. géol. France sér.* (7)2:331-342.

Brain, C. K. 1981. The evolution of man in Africa: Was it a consequence of Cainozoic cooling? *Annex. Transv. Geol. Soc. S. Afr.* 84:1-19.

Brown, F. H., McDougall, I., Davies, T., and Maier, R. 1985. An integrated Plio-Pleistocene chronology for the Turkana Basin, in: *Ancestors: The Hard Evidence* (E. Delson, Ed.), pp. 82-90, Alan R. Liss, Inc., New York.

Butzer, K. W. 1971. Another look at the australopithecine cave breccias of the Transvaal. *Am. Anthrop.* 73:1197-1201.

Butzer, K. W. 1974. Paleoecology of South African australopithecines— Taung revisited. *Current Anthrop.* 15:367-388.

Greenacre, M. J., and Vrba, E. S. 1984. A correspondence analysis of biological census data. *Ecology* 65:984-997.

Grine, F. E. 1981. Trophic differences between "gracile" and "robust" australopithecines: A scanning electron microscope analysis of occlusal events. *S. Afr. J. Sci.* 77:203-230.

Howell, F. C. 1978. Hominidae, in: *Evolution of African Mammals* (V. J. Maglio and H. B. S. Cooke, Eds.), pp. 154-248, Harvard University Press, Cambridge, Massachusetts.

Huntley, B. J., and Walker, B. H. (Eds.) 1982. *Ecology of Tropical Savannas*. Springer-Verlag, New York.

Jaeger, J. J. 1976. Les rongeurs (Mammalia, Rodentia) du Pléistocéne Inférieur d'Olduvai Bed I (Tanzania). 1ere Partie: Les Muridés, in: *Fossil Vertebrates of Africa*, Vol. 4 (R. J. G. Savage and S. C. Coryndon, Eds.) Academic Press, London.

Krebs, J. R., and Davies, N. B. (Eds.) 1978. *Behavioral Ecology: An Evolutionary Approach*. Blackwell, London.

Lovejoy, C. O. 1981. The origin of man. *Science* 211:341-350.

Lovejoy, C. O., Johanson, D. C., and Coppens, Y. 1982. Hominid lower limb bones recovered from the Hadar formation: 1974-1977 collections. *Am. J. Phys. Anthropol.* 57:679-700.

Maglio, V. J., and Cooke, H. B. S. (Eds.) 1978. *Evolution of African Mammals*. Harvard University Press, Cambridge, Massachusetts.

Robinson, J. T. 1963. Adaptive radiation in the australopithecines and the origin of man, in: *African Ecology and Human Evolution* (F. C. Howell and F. Bourliere, Eds.), pp. 385-416, Aldine, Chicago.

Shackleton, N. J., Backman, J., Zimmerman, H., Kent, D. V., Hall, M. A., Roberts, D. G., Schnitker, D., Baldauf, J. G., Desprairies, A., Homrighausen, R., Huddlestun, P., Keene, J. B., Kaltenback, A. J., Krumsieck, K. A. O., Morton, A. C., Murray, J. W., and Westberg-Smith, J. 1984. Oxygen isotope calibration of the onset of ice-rafting and history of glaciation in the North Atlantic region. *Nature* 307:620-623.

Stern, J. T., and Susman, R. L. 1983. The locomotor anatomy of *Australopithecus afarensis*. *Am. J. Phys. Anthrop.* 60:279-317.

Thunell, R. C., and Williams, D. F. 1983. The stepwise development of Pliocene-Pleistocene paleoclimate and paleoceanographic conditions in the Mediterranean: Oxygen isotope studies of DSDP Sites 125 and 132, in: Reconstruction of Marine Paleoenvironments (J.E. Meulenkamp, Ed.), *Utrecht Micropal. Bull.* 30:111-127.

Tobias, P. V. 1985. Punctuational and phyletic evolution in the hominids, in: *Species and Speciation* (E. S. Vrba, Ed.), *Transvaal Museum Monographs*, Pretoria.

Vrba, E. S. 1974. Chronological and ecological implications of the fossil Bovidae at the Sterkfontein Australopithecine site. *Nature* 250:19-23.

Vrba, E. S. 1975. Some evidence of chronology and palaeoecology of Sterkfontein, Swartkrans and Kromdraai from the fossil Bovidae. *Nature* 254:301-304.

Vrba, E. S. 1979. A new study of the scapula of *Australopithecus africanus* from Sterkfontein. *Amer. J. Phys. Anthrop.* 51:117-129.

Vrba, E. S. 1980a. The significance of bovid remains as indicators of environment and predation patterns, in: *Fossils in the Making: Vertebrate Taphonomy and Paleoecology* (A. K. Behrensmeyer and A. P. Hill, Eds.), pp. 247-271, The University of Chicago Press, Chicago.

Vrba, E. S. 1980b. Evolution, species and fossils: How does life evolve? *S. Afr. J. Sci.* 76(2):61-84.

Vrba, E. S. 1981. The Kromdraai Australopithecine site revisited in 1980: Recent investigations and results. *Ann. Transv. Mus.* 33:18-60.

Vrba, E. S. 1982. Biostratigraphy and chronology, based particularly on Bovidae of southern African hominid-associated assemblages: Makapansgat, Sterkfontein, Taung, Kromdraai, Swartkrans; also Elandsfontein (Saldanha), Broken Hill (now Kabwe) and Cave of Hearths. *Prétirage, ler Cong. Internat. Paléontol. Hum.* CNRS, Nice, pp. 707-752.

Vrba, E. S. 1984. Evolutionary pattern and process in the sister-group Alcelaphini-Aepycerotini (Mammalia: Bovidae), in: *Living Fossils* (N. Eldredge and S. M. Stanley, Eds.), pp. 62-79, Springer-Verlag, New York.

Vrba, E. S. 1985. Palaeoecology of early Hominidae, with special reference to Sterkfontein, Swartkrans and Kromdraai, in: *l'Environnement des Hominidés* (Y. Coppens, Ed.), Singer-Polignac, Paris, pp. 345-369.

White, T. D., Johanson, D. C., and Kimbel, W. H. 1981. *Australopithecus africanus*: Its phyletic position reconsidered. *S. Afr. J. Sci.* 77:445-470.

Wiens, J. A. 1976. Population responses to patchy environments. *Ann. Rev. Ecol. Syst.* 7:81-120.

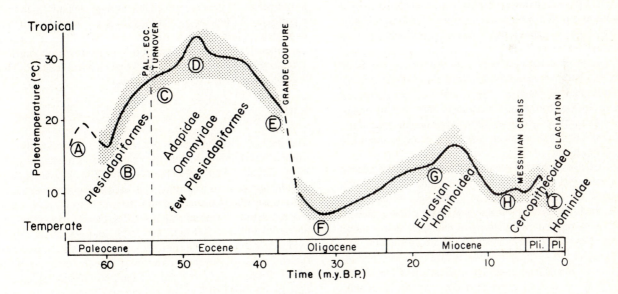

Climatic Change and the Major Radiations of the Primates (A to I) in the Cenozoic

17

Biomechanical Perspectives on the Lower Limb of Early Hominids

C. Owen Lovejoy

The characteristic locomotor pattern of *Homo sapiens* is made possible by a series of morphological features of his lower limb. These may be said to constitute its total morphological pattern (Le Gros Clark 1964). The individual features of this pattern are well known and include a number of distinctive characteristics of the ilium and femur. While significant alterations of the tibia, fibula, tarsus, ischium, and pubis are apparent, these are generally more conservative and thus retain more similarity with those of other higher primates.

In the interpretation of fossil limb samples (as with those of *Australopithecus*) an adherence to a strict morphological interpretation of individual features is usually unsatisfactory if the object of study is a reconstruction of locomotor pattern. A morphological alteration is not of itself an adaptation. Rather, it is the mechanical EFFECT of the anatomical change that constitutes the actual adaptation. Morphological changes can thus be direct or indirect; i.e. they may themselves cause a mechanical effect or they may be an alteration produced BY a mechanical alteration.

Each of the adaptations to bipedalism characteristic of the human lower limb has been the result either of natural selection or of the well-documented phenomenon of mammalian musculoskeletal plasticity. What must then be regarded as significant in the reconstruction of gait patterns is not fossil morphology but its resultant—something that we may call the total biomechanical pattern. That is, study of morphological change in limb segments must have as its objective the understanding of the effects of alterations of form upon the mechanics of function. The biomechanical pattern that emerges should be our primary objective.

Isolated morphological features vary significantly more than do the mechanical attributes that are their result. To state this in other terms, the total morphological pattern and its individual elements are distinctly more variable than the total biomechanical pattern. For example, occasionally a first metatarsal can be found that has no facet for articulation with the second metatarsal. The hallux of such an individual, however, is fully adducted, and his gait pattern is completely normal. The morphological feature (the articular facet) serves as an indication of the position of the hallux. It is the latter that is important to the gait pattern not the former. Both nonmetric and metric variations of the hominid postcranial skeleton are extensive and must be given full consideration in the reconstruction of locomotor patterns of extinct related species.

The first task in the reconstruction of locomotor patterns from fossil samples lies, then, in the assessment of the biomechanical significance of each of its morphological features—that is to say, in determining whether or not the feature IS of mechanical significance.

We shall review the morphological features of each of the limb segments of the australopithecine lower limb. We shall attempt to isolate those features that are of mechanical significance and, once these have been established, we shall compare them to their counterparts in *Homo sapiens*. Those differences that are revealed by using this approach can then serve as an indication of the mechanical differences in the limb skeletons of *Australopithecus* and *H. sapiens*. This will then allow an interpretation of the australopithecine locomotor pattern.

Most previous accounts of australopithecine postcranial material have been based primarily upon material from South Africa, as the East African material has only recently become available for analysis. Casts of some of these newer specimens have been made generally available through an ambitious casting program of the Kenya National Museum. Therefore, in this paper both South and East African material will be discussed. In general, specimens from both regions show marked similarity in both anatomical and biomechanical features. This will be given further discussion below.[1]

ILIUM

The general morphological pattern of the australopithecine ilium is clearly hominid, and the available specimens are strikingly similar to the modern human ilium. This includes a large and distinct posterior portion. This indicates that the origin of the gluteus maximus was equally favorable to its position in modern man for femoral extension. The clearly formed sciatic notch in STS-14, STS-65, TM-1517, and SK-50 is ample evidence of this point. The retroauricular part is also substantial, indicating a well-developed sacroiliac articular complex (Dart 1957), although the robusticity of the ilium in this region can only be observed in STS-14 and the two adolescent ilia from Makapan (MLD-7 and MLD-25). These specimens demonstrate only limited robusticity in this region, and Robinson believes the auricular surface of STS-14 to be small compared to *H. sapiens*. However, both of these factors are most

Reprinted with permission from *Primate Functional Mophology and Evolution*, edited by R. H. Tuttle, pp. 291-326, Mouton, The Hague. Copyright © 1975 by Mouton, The Hague. Reprinted by permission of Mouton de Gruyter, a Division of Walter de Gruyter, Berlin.

likely due to the relatively small body size of these specimens. When dealing with the surface areas of joints, linear normalization for body size is not justified, as body weight is of prime consideration. Robinson (1972) bases his opinion upon the breadth of the auricular surface of STS-14 (29.5 millimeters). The same measurement on a small sample of *H. sapiens* gave a mean value of 62 millimeters (Schultz 1930). Robinson's estimate for body size in females such as STS-14 is 40-60 pounds. Thus the static pressure on the auricular joint surface would be the same in STS-14 and *H. sapiens* if the specimens measured by Schultz had body weights of about 80-120 pounds. It seems as if a more detailed study might reveal that STS-14 had a BROADER auricular surface relative to the modern average. In general, with the exceptions of some of those particular features to be noted below, the consensus of most authors is that the ilium of *Australopithecus* is very similar to that of modern man (Dart 1949, 1957, 1958; Le Gros Clark 1967; Lovejoy, Heiple, and Burstein 1973; Lovejoy 1973; Robinson 1972).

Anterior Inferior Iliac Spine

A large anterior inferior iliac spine is clearly present in all adult australopithecine ilia (Lovejoy, Heiple, and Burstein 1973; Lovejoy 1973; Robinson 1972). Robinson points out that impressions for the iliofemoral ligament and the reflected head of the rectus femoris are both distinctly present.

Lateral Iliac Flare

A more pronounced lateral iliac flare among australopithecine specimens has been pointed out by a number of authors (Le Gros Clark 1967; Lovejoy, Heiple, and Burstein 1973; Lovejoy 1973; Robinson 1972; Zihlman 1969). The immediate mechanical import of this feature is an increased distance (along a horizontal through both acetabulae in an articulated pelvis) from the acetabulum to the lateralmost extent of the iliac crest. It is thus a feature fully commensurate with a long femoral neck, and its mechanical effects are the same as those mentioned below.

Anterior Superior Iliac Spine

An additional feature also noted by most authors is the distinctive anterior prolongation of the anterior superior iliac spine in australopithecine ilia. As Robinson (1972) points out, this prolongation is associated with a greater robusticity of the ilium in this region. Various interpretations have been suggested for this feature. It seems most likely that it is simply a secondary result of the greater iliac flare. Such flare places the anterior part of the ilium in a more posterior position than in *H. sapiens* (Lovejoy, Heiple, and Burstein 1973). The prolongation of the spine in *Australopithecus* compensates for this and results in a similar position (relative to the hip joint) of the inguinal ligament and sartorius (Lovejoy, Heiple, and Burstein 1973; Lovejoy 1973). Furthermore, as slight variations in the degree of lateral iliac flare would have substantial effects upon the position of these structures, greater variation in the projection of the anterior superior spine should be expected. That is, while the depth of the notch separating anterior superior and inferior spines is variable in *H. sapiens*, it must be expected to vary to a greater degree in australopithecines as a result of the greater lateral iliac flare in the latter (Figure 1).

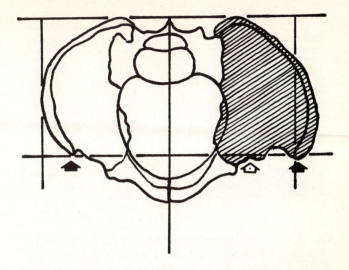

Figure 1. *Superior view of MLD-7 articulated with a Bushman pelvis of equivalent osteological age. Symmetrical coordinate lines have been included to demonstrate the relative spatial positions of various bony features. Note the more pronounced lateral flare in MLD-7, resulting in a more lateral position of the abductors relative to the hip joint. Note that the positions of the anterior superior iliac spines are equivalent in both ilia (solid arrows) despite the much deeper notch separating it from the anterior inferior spine in MLD-7. The well-developed iliopsoas groove in the australopithecine specimen is indicated with an open arrow. (Drawn from a photograph in Dart 1949)*

Iliac Pillar

Most authors now agree that a distinct iliac pillar is present in australopithecine ilia (Dart 1957; Day 1959; Lovejoy, Heiple, and Burstein 1973; Lovejoy 1973; Robinson 1972; Zihlman 1969). However, Robinson and Lovejoy, Heiple, and Burstein point out that it differs somewhat from that of sapiens, in that its position is more anterior than is usually the case in modern man. This feature can again be related to the greater lateral flare of australopithecine ilia as discussed above (Lovejoy, Heiple, and Burstein 1973; Lovejoy 1973; Robinson 1972) (Figure 1).

ISCHIUM

Although the earlier literature has consistently suggested *Australopithecus* to have a longer ischium than *H. sapiens*, more recently it has been pointed out that the metric used to assess ischial length was a non-functional one, having no bearing on the mechanical length of the ischium. That metric was taken between the border of the ischial tuberosity and the rim of the acetabulum (Washburn 1963). It thus bears no necessary relation to the length of the lever arm of the hamstrings (Lovejoy, Heiple, and Burstein 1973; Lovejoy 1973). Only two measurable ischia are available for *Australopithecus*, those of STS-14 and of SK-50. If ischial length is taken as the distance from the center of the acetabulum to the center of the ischial tuberosity (hamstring impression), and if this distance is normalized for body size by means of another dimension of the innominate, both these specimens have ischia well within the range of variation of *H. sapiens*. Schultz and Robinson utilize the ratio between functional ischial length and acetabulum diameter as an index of ischial length. Schultz found

Table 1. Relative ischial length in *Australopithecus* and *Homo sapiens*

Observer Metric	STS-14	SK-50	Number	Modern man mean	Standard Deviation
Schultz (1969) $\dfrac{\text{Acetabulum diameter}}{\text{Functional ischial length}} \times 10^2$	80	67	24	67.6	—
Robinson (1972) $\dfrac{\text{Acetabulum diameter}}{\text{Functional ischial length}} \times 10^2$	87	62	40	68.4	4.3
Lovejoy et al. (1973) $\dfrac{\text{Iliac height}}{\text{Functional ischial length}} \times 10^2$	47	—	25	48	3.4

that STS-14 had a relatively SHORT ischium and that SK-50 had an ischium/acetabulum ratio almost identical to modern man (Table 1). Lovejoy, Heiple, and Burstein reached a similar conclusion for STS-14 by comparing ischium length to ilium height. The ratio between these metrics in STS-14 was almost identical to the human mean, but the ilium height of SK-50 could not be measured. Robinson concluded that the ischial length of modern man was significantly shorter than that of SK-50. However, the data that he used do not justify his interpretation. He found that the mean value of the ischium/acetabulum ratio (multiplied by 100) was 68 in modern man (N = 40) with a standard population range of 56-81. His ratios for STS-14 and SK-50 were 87 and 62 respectively.[2] Thus, one can only conclude that the data of Robinson and Schultz show both australopithecine specimens to have ischia of similar length to those of modern man (although the ischium of STS-14 appears to be quite short).

Lovejoy, Heiple, and Burstein (1973) have suggested that the form of the ischial tuberosity of STS-14 differed from that of modern man. This statement can now be shown to be in error as a result of the recent description of the specimen by Robinson (1972). He points out that the actual surface of the ischial tuberosity was not fully preserved and thus no statements can be made of its form. The only specimen that can thus afford knowledge of the tuberosity is MLD-8. This specimen has an ischial tuberosity whose form is essentially identical to that of modern man (Lovejoy, Heiple, and Burstein 1973).

PUBIS

Although a portion of the pubic ramus was preserved in STS-65, only in STS-14 was the symphysis also preserved. Robinson notes no particular difference in this specimen and the pubis of modern man, save a relatively marked length (although the specimen is clearly within the range of variation of modern man).[3] While the length of the pubis is not critical to an interpretation of australopithecine locomotion, it is of some interest with respect to the dimensions of the birth canal in these early hominids and will be discussed further below.

FEMUR

Lesser Trochanter

The form and position of the lesser trochanter [4] are well within the range of variation of their position in *H. sapiens*. Some authors have stated that its position on the femoral shaft is more lateral

than in modern man (Broom, Robinson, and Schepers 1950; Day 1969; Le Gros Clark 1967; Napier 1964). However, a metric assessment of the position of the lesser trochanter with respect to the femoral shaft was made using a moderate sample of Amerindian femora. Both SK-82 and SK-97 were within one standard deviation of the mean of this modern sample (Lovejoy and Heiple 1972). Robinson (1972) states that the lesser trochanter of STS-14, while not fully preserved, can be located because the bone surface forming its base was preserved. He concludes that its position in this specimen is "slightly unusual" because it probably did not protrude beyond the medial border of the shaft, while in *Homo sapiens* "the lesser trochanter is so situated that when the femur is viewed directly from the back, the trochanter protrudes past the medial border of the shaft" (Robinson 1972: 130). This is only true in selected specimens. In the Amerindian population studied by Lovejoy and Heiple (1972), the modal position of this apophysis was one in which it failed to protrude by a significant distance. Variability is great, however, as can be seen by reference to Figure 2. Furthermore, the functional position of this feature varies with anteversion of the femoral neck (Lovejoy and Heiple 1972; Walker 1973). The newer East African material (cf. Figure 2) confirms that *Australopithecus* was equally as variable as modern man in this feature, and that australopithecine and modern femora do not differ significantly in this regard.

Greater Trochanter

The position of the greater trochanter in australopithecine femora appears to have been slightly different from its position in modern man, although an overlapping range of variation in the two species is clearly indicated. In *Australopithecus* the lateral flare of this apophysis from the shaft of the bone is somewhat less pronounced than in *H. sapiens*. We have elsewhere (Lovejoy and Heiple 1972) suggested that this is perhaps due to a more laterally situated femoral shaft than in sapiens. Walker (1973) has suggested that the condition might be related to the somewhat higher bicondylar angle of australopithecine femora. In Robinson's opinion (1972), the difference is due to a less prominent distal part and slightly more anterior position of the gluteus minimus attachment. But again, this is a highly variable feature in modern femora. In any case, the position of the greater trochanter with respect to the center of the hip joint is the critical dimension, because this directly determines the mechanical advantage of the anterior gluteals. Where the trochanter lies with respect to the femoral shaft does not affect this dimension. Thus this morphological difference between

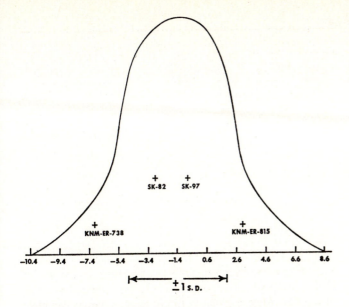

Figure 2. *Normal curve fitted to sample of ninety-six human femora (ninety-six individuals) measured for the position of the lesser trochanter relative to the femoral shaft (all measurements in millimeters). Identical measurements made on australopithecine specimens are 0 (SK-97); -3 (SK-82); -7 (KNM-ER-738); +3 (KNM-ER-815). The mean of the Amerindian sample was - 1.4 millimeters; S.D. = 3.6; range = +8 to -8.5; X^2 for fit data to normal distribution was P = .26*

modern and australopithecine femora is not one of immediate mechanical significance.

Although the STS-14 femur is damaged in this region, Robinson (1972) suggests that a somewhat greater flare may have been present in this specimen. In those East African femora in which the position of the greater trochanter can be observed, it appears to conform to the pattern described above (Walker 1973).

Additional minor morphological differences between the proximal surface anatomy of australopithecine and sapiens femora have been described, including the rather deep trochanteric fossa. None of these, however, would appear to have any significant effect upon gait pattern.

Intertrochanteric Line

Walker points out that of five specimens now available in which the development of the intertrochanteric line can be studied, none shows this feature to be well developed. Day has suggested that the development of the intertrochanteric line is related to its tension during life. This would appear not to be the case on the following grounds:

1. It is absent or only slightly developed in a significant proportion of modern femora (over 50 percent of a large Amerindian sample and over 25 percent of a Zulu sample (Lovejoy and Heiple 1972).
2. Specimens can be found in which the heaviest development of cortical bone is in that region of the ligament's insertion where it is most slackened (the medial synovial reflection).

3. Other, almost equally large ligamentous structures fail to produce rugosities similar to the intertrochanteric line.
4. The development of the intertrochanteric line is clearly age-related and is almost always absent in Amerindian femora prior to fusion of the femoral epiphyses.

The lack of an intertrochanteric rugosity in australopithecine femora is thus problematical, although no mechanical significance is apparently involved. The massive anterior inferior iliac spine is a clear indication that a well-developed Bigelow's ligament was present in *Australopithecus* (Lovejoy, Heiple, and Burstein 1973; Robinson 1972). We would venture to say that its clear association with age and its limited expression in five australopithecine specimens simply reflects a younger age of death in these specimens than in those usually found in dissection rooms. In any case, there appears to be no mechanical significance attributable to this feature.

Obturator Externus Groove

A distinct obturator externus groove is identifiable in at least several australopithecine specimens, including OH-20 (Day 1969) and SK-82 and SK-97 (Robinson 1972). It is variably developed in *H. sapiens* and again is a morphological feature of no immediate mechanical significance. However, its presence serves as an indication that the obturator externus tendon was closely applied to the posterior surface of the femoral neck, a situation only explicable by consistent full extension of the hip.

Collo-Diaphyseal Angle

The neck-shaft angles of several australopithecine specimens are given in Table 2. All are well within the range of variation of *H. sapiens*, although their mean value lies well below that of most sapiens populations. While Robinson attributes no significance to these lower values, Walker (1973) believes the low neck-shaft angle to be a populational characteristic of *Australopithecus*. From the number of specimens now available, it would appear that the population means of the two taxa do differ. On the other hand, the great range of variation in *H. sapiens* indicates that the angle is not critical to locomotor pattern. The net biomechanical effect of a lower collo-diaphyseal angle is an increase in the distance between the greater trochanter and femoral head, i.e. a greater effective neck length. This appears to have been the primary import of this feature in *Australopithecus* (see below).

Femoral Neck Length

Most students of australopithecine postcranial morphology have commented upon the unusually long neck of the femur (Campbell 1966; Day 1969; Le Gros Clark 1967; Napier 1964; Zihlman 1969). In Robinson's opinion, the necks of STS-14, SK-82, and SK-97 are relatively long, but as he points out, "such a statement is not easy to document even though it is an obvious impression from visual observation" (1972: 128). He further notes that a problem of definition is immediately apparent when australopithecine neck length is considered:

The point I wish to make is that there appear at first glance to be two differences between the *Paranthropus* and *H. sapiens*

Table 2. Metric parameters of australopithecine and modern human femora

	SK-97	SK-82	KNM-ER-815	KNM-ER-738	STS-14	OH-20
Neck-shaft angle	118	120	115	115	118	115
Maximum femoral length	—	—	—	—	—	—
Maximum diameter femoral head	37	34	—	34	31	—
Biomechanical neck length	67	64	—	54	53	78
$\dfrac{\text{Biomechanical neck length}}{\text{Maximum femoral length}} \times 10^3$	—	—	—	—	—	—
$\dfrac{\text{Maximum diameter femoral head}}{\text{Maximum femoral length}} \times 10^3$	—	—	—	—	—	—
$\dfrac{(\text{Maximum diameter femoral head})^2}{(\text{Maximum femoral length})^3} \times 10^3$	—	—	—	—	—	—

femora—smaller head and more tapering, longer neck in the former—but these are really two aspects of one difference. Both types of femur have much the same functional distance between the acetabulum and the shaft axis; since the head in *Paranthropus* occupies a smaller part of that functional distance, the neck occupies more (1972: 145).

A variety of metrics have been suggested for use in estimating the relative length of the femoral neck (see, for example, Napier 1964). However, most of these are unsatisfactory because they are dependent upon other morphological landmarks, which in turn vary independently of neck length (as Robinson points out). Using various metrics, Walker was able to demonstrate a statistically significant, longer neck length in his reconstruction (based primarily on specimens KNM-ER-993 and OH-20). Thus, MORPHOLOGICALLY, the neck length of the australopithecine femur can be considered greater than that of *H. sapiens*. This kind of measurement, however, fails to clarify the important question that Robinson posed.

Because our concern here is the reconstruction of gait pattern, our primary interest should lie in the mechanical significance of femoral neck length. While an increase in neck length results in a greater distance from origin to insertion of many of the muscles about the hip, it has relatively little effect upon their mechanical function, with two exceptions—gluteus medius and gluteus minimus. Their lever arm in effecting abduction is the normal from their line of action to the center of the hip joint. An increase in the length of the femoral neck increases this lever arm. We have elsewhere suggested the use of a metric that directly approximates this distance (from the femur alone) and is at the same time unaffected by morphological variations not immediately involved. This metric (biomechanical length of the femoral neck) is defined and illustrated in Figure 3. When this metric is normalized (for body mass and stature) by femoral length, it provides a direct measure of the relative length of the abductor lever arm. Unfortunately, most of the femoral specimens of *Australopithecus* are not sufficiently preserved for accurate estimate of their overall length, and this is a necessity for meaningful comparison with *H. sapiens* and other primate species. A sufficient amount of the STS-14 femur was preserved for a reasonable estimate of its length (Lovejoy and Heiple 1970; Robinson 1972). In addition, as Walker's reconstruction (1973)

of the East African femur is based upon an almost complete femoral shaft (KNM-ER-993) and a proximal portion (OH-20) of very similar size, robusticity, and morphology, it is also a reasonable one for use in estimating relative mechanical neck length. Values for normalized femoral neck length for these two specimens and a moderate sample of Amerindians are provided in Table 2. Both specimens have significantly longer femoral necks than the Amerindians, and it should be remembered that these values are INDEPENDENT OF FEMORAL HEAD SIZE. Thus, the impression obtained by most observers is confirmed, despite the reservations of Robinson. While relative femoral neck length in *Australopithecus* was probably not outside the range of modern sapiens, it appears that the populational means for this biomechanical characteristic are different.

Femoral Head Size

The size of the femoral head in *Australopithecus* has also been a topic of some discussion. It has usually been regarded as significantly smaller than that of *H. sapiens* and has thereby been considered evidence for incomplete bipedal adaptation in these early hominids. Normalization by femoral length, however, is even more necessary for femoral head diameter than for neck length, because the former is a metric whose value is directly proportional to a joint surface. It therefore requires consideration of the square-cube law; i.e. if an object is increased in size, its surface area increases in proportion to the square of a characteristic dimension, while its mass increases in proportion to the cube of that characteristic dimension. Thus, if the mass of an animal increases, its joint surface areas must increase at a much greater rate if articular cartilage is to be sufficient for the increased loads. Therefore, in order to determine whether or not the femoral head of australopithecine specimens is small, we must also know femoral length so that some relationship with body mass and stature can be included. This, again, is only possible for two specimens—STS-14 and the Walker reconstruction. When the head diameters of these specimens are normalized either partially (head diameter/femoral length) or completely (head diameter[2]/femoral length[3]), both fall well within the range of variation of modern femora (Table 2).

Table 2. *(cont'd.)*

| STS-14 Reconstruction | | KNM-ER-993/OH-20 Reconstruction | Amerindian | |
Lovejoy and Heiple	Robinson	Walker	Mean	Standard deviation
118	118	116	128	3.6
280	310	360	450	29
31	31	34	45	3.4
53	53	72	68	5.3
189	171	200	151	7.0
111	100	94	100	4.4
44	32	25	22	2.4

There remain, however, several additional australopithecine specimens for which head diameter is known but for which no reliable estimate of femoral length is possible. Robinson has normalized the South African specimens (STS-14, SK-82, and SK-97) by means of shaft diameters below the lesser trochanter. While the resulting ratios for STS-14 are similar to those for his sapiens sample, they are somewhat lower for SK-82 and SK-97, implying either a more robust shaft relative to femoral head diameter or a relatively small head. In Walker's opinion (1973) the former of these two possible interpretations is correct: "The femoral heads in *Australopithecus* do not seem, therefore, as writers have suggested, to be small for

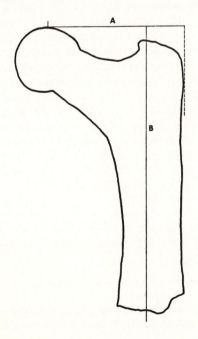

Figure 3. *Biomechanical length of the femoral neck (A). This metric may be defined as the length of a line from the most lateral point on the greater trochanter to its tangential point of intersection with the most cephalad point in the femoral head. It is taken perpendicular to the centroidal axis of the shaft (B). (See Lovejoy, Heiple, and Burstein 1973).*

the femur length, although since the femur is very robust the heads may be small relative to the shaft dimensions."

Walker's choice of these two interpretations appears to be quite reasonable and soundly based. The femoral shaft of KNM-ER-993 was complete from distal end to lesser trochanter. Thus, despite the fact that his femoral length is dependent upon reconstruction, any error will be minimal. When shaft diameters of the specimen are normalized by its length, the results are ratios that indicate a shaft robusticity somewhat greater than that of sapiens. Therefore, Robinson's use of shaft robusticity as a normalization factor for head diameter would appear to be the poorer choice. Such is not completely the case, however. Why there should be greater shaft robusticity in *Australopithecus* becomes a legitimate question. Possibly it was the result of somewhat greater muscularity in australopithecines and perhaps greater body weight relative to sapiens. This would then beg the question of femoral head size once more.

From the evidence presented thus far, it is our opinion that the populational means of femoral head diameter were possibly slightly lower than those of sapiens, although certainly not outside the modern range of variation. This is made clear not only by the above metrics but also by the acetabular study of Schultz. He concluded:

> From these observations it is evident that the acetabulum of *Australopithecus africanus* does not significantly differ from that of recent man, particularly, that its large proportionate size indicates the acquisition of the erect posture. . . . It seems most likely that *Australopithecus robustus* also has a relative acetabular diameter equalling that of recent man and surpassing the corresponding values of other recent primates (1969: 197).

Finally, we have elsewhere pointed out (Lovejoy, Heiple, and Burstein 1973; Lovejoy 1973) that the dimension that is critical to the interpretation of gait pattern is not femoral head size per se but the resultant pressure imposed upon the articular cartilage of the femoral head. This will be discussed further below.

Femoral Head Coverage

Recently, Jenkins (1972) made observations on the form of the femoral head in *Australopithecus*. He suggested that a prolongation of the articular surface of the femoral head onto the neck of the femur occurs anteriorly in modern man and posteriorly in the chimpanzee, and that the former is "related to a relatively deep and ventrally facing acetabulum" in man and a shallower and more laterad acetabulum in the chimpanzee. He then concludes that:

> The intermediate configuration of the femoral head margin in *A. robustus*. . . together with the relatively shallow acetabulum. . . is evidence that femoral excursion was of an intermediate pattern. . . . If the *A. robustus* femur were adducted as much as in man, a disproportionate area of articular surface would lie outside the bony acetabulum (1972: 879).

These conclusions are based upon conjectures that are not permissible and they are contrary to the evidence. The following points may be raised:

1. Jenkins's observations require a detailed knowledge of acetabular form. The specimen he used was SK-50, the acetabulum of which required extensive reconstruction. In his description of the original specimen Robinson points out that a 9-millimeter crack passing through the upper portion of the acetabulum has caused it to lie:

> in a quite unnatural position in relation to the other portion. The remainder of the acetabulum has been warped so that the pubic margin lies closer to the ischial margin than was originally the case and thereby the acetabular notch is reduced to approximately half of its original width (1972: 88).

2. Femoral head coverage depends upon the orientation of the innominate in space. The posterior part of the ilium of SK-50 is poorly preserved and there is no auricular surface. Nor is there a sacrum for this specimen.

3. The proximal femoral specimen used was that of SK-82, which is not the same individual represented by SK-50. Robinson's observations on the relation between SK-50 and the Swartkrans proximal femoral samples are particularly interesting with regard to Jenkins's reconstruction: "It is clear, however, that the head of SK-97 would fit this acetabulum [SK-50] more successfully than would SK-82—in fact, the former appears to be of exactly the right size for the acetabulum" (1972: 142). In any, case, slight differences in femoral head coverage cannot be demonstrated using specimens from different individuals.

4. The extension of the articular surface that occurs in the SK-82 specimen is not similar to that of the chimpanzee. It is a distinct localized projection onto the femoral neck which may be matched with some frequency in Amerindian femora. Its form shows it to be clearly unrelated to femoral head coverage. On the other hand, SK-97 shows a form of its articular surface which matches Jenkins's description of modern man perfectly (see Robinson 1972: Figure 82).

5. Orientation of the femoral fragment requires both a knowledge of anteversion and of the bicondylar angle (shaft obliquity). Both of these were unknown for SK-82.

6. The acetabula of modern man and chimpanzee are not different with regard to depth (as Jenkins suggested). Schultz, in his study of the STS-14 acetabulum (he rightly concluded that the SK-50 specimen was too distorted for study), found that its relative acetabular depth stood "well within the range of the same relation [depth/diameter] among recent genera, whose averages have been found to differ remarkably little" (1969: 194).

Linea Aspera

Robinson has recently concluded that the linea aspera of STS-14, while small in development relative to its usual condition in modern man, is of the *H. sapiens* type in principle and is well defined" (1972: 131). He points out that the Swartkrans specimens are too poorly preserved to make observations. Leakey, Mungai, and Walker (1972) report the presence of a linea aspera in the newer East African specimens, including KNM-ER-736 and KNM-ER-361.

Intercondylar Notch

We have elsewhere pointed out that the intercondylar notch of *Australopithecus* is similar to that of *H. sapiens* (Heiple and Lovejoy 1971). There appears to be no disagreement with this assessment in the recent literature (see Robinson 1972; Walker 1973). The greater depth of the intercondylar notch in hominids can be related to the more elliptical form of the femoral condyles (Heiple and Lovejoy 1971). The attachments for the anterior and posterior cruciate ligaments are like those in *H. sapiens* (Robinson 1972).

Lateral Condylar Projection

We have elsewhere pointed out that the form of the femoral condyles in STS-34 and TM-1513 is like that of *H. sapiens* and unlike that of quadrupedal primates. In hominids, both condyles show a distinct elliptical shape (Figure 4), indicating a specialization for maximum cartilage contact in the knee joint only during full extension of the lower limb. In quadrupeds, on the other hand, the condyles show no such specialization to one position, being essentially circular in cross-sectional outline. Walker (1973) reports a similar condition in KNM-ER-993.

Bicondylar Angle

The bicondylar angles of STS-34 and TM-1513 have been the topic of some discussion. Le Gros Clark (1947) originally reported TM-1513 to have an angle of AT LEAST 7°, and Kern and Straus (1949) incorrectly assumed this to mean exactly 7°. We have elsewhere pointed out that the methods usually employed in obtaining the obliquity of the shaft have been inadequate, because they employed specific morphological landmarks of no mechanical significance. We have used as a definition the angle between the condylar plane and the centroidal axis of the shaft. We found that using sharp shadow tracings, the bicondylar angle (so defined) could be obtained from only the distal portion of a femur (equal to the amount preserved in STS-34 and TM-1513) within ±1° of the actual value assessed from the complete femur (Lovejoy and Heiple 1971). Values obtained for STS-34 and TM-1513 were 14° and 15° respectively. Robinson gives values of 8° and 9° for these specimens but does not specify his methods. An additional specimen in which almost all of the shaft is preserved, KNM-ER-993, is now available. Walker reports the shaft obliquity as 15°.

Patellar Groove

We have elsewhere pointed out that a deep patellar groove and high lateral lip are present on the distal femur specimens STS-34 and

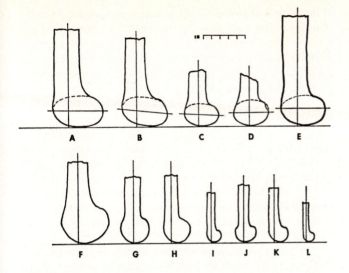

Figure 4. *Lateral condylar projections of a number of primates. Each is a tracing of a photograph of the lateral articular surface taken perpendicular to the bicondylar plane. Top row: A and B. Homo sapiens (Amerindian); C. TM-1513; D. STS-34 (reversed); E. KNM-ER-993-Walker reconstruction (reversed). Note that the long axis of the ellipse in B and C can be made parallel to the bicondylar plane by slight anterior bowing of the femur or by slight hyperextension of the knee. Bottom row: F. Pan gorilla (CMNH-B1431); G. Pan troglodytes (CMNH-B1769); H. Pongo (CMNH-B1055); I. Hylobates (CMNH-B161); J. Papio (CMNH-B1043); K. Pygathrix (CMNH-B1511): L. Macaca (KSU-12). (CMNH: Cleveland Museum of Natural History; KSU: Kent State University).*

TM-1513, indicating a clear adaptation to prevention of patellar dislocation in full femoral-tibial extension. This is an adaptation clearly absent in quadrupedal hominoids and one that is directly related to a valgus knee position produced by a high bicondylar angle (Heiple and Lovejoy 1971). Preuschoft (1971) also notes the importance of this adaptation in bipeds but concludes that it was incomplete in *Australopithecus*. His conclusion, however, is based upon only the TM-1513 sample, in which "a large flake of bone is missing from the lateral epicondylar area" (Walker 1973). When this defect is corrected by conservative reconstruction (based on the form of the complete lateral condyle of STS-34), the specimen is found to have a clearly elevated lateral lip similar to modern man (Heiple and Lovejoy 1971; Walker 1973). A similar condition exists in KNM-ER-993 (Walker 1973). Perhaps little more need be said but to quote Robinson's recent summary:

> These two specimens [STS-34 and TM-1513] are of very great interest since they give information about the whole of the distal end of the *H. africanus* femur and demonstrate that, with quite minor exceptions such as the slightly narrow intercondylar fossa of TM-1513, the anatomy is simply that of *H. sapiens* to an extraordinarily detailed extent (1972: 137).

TIBIA

The australopithecine tibia is now known to a limited extent from two specimens that have received preliminary description: OH-6 (Davis 1964) and KNM-ER-741 (Leakey, Mungai, and Walker 1972). The distal joint surface is known only from OH-6. As far as could be detected from this specimen, no significant differences exist with respect to *H. sapiens* (Davis 1964).

With respect to the proximal part of the bone, Davis has suggested three distinct differences from the typical human condition. These are a greater extent of the tibialis posterior relative to that of the flexor digitorum longus, a somewhat smaller soleus, and a large popliteus in which "the direction of muscle pull was nearly vertical" (Davis 1964: 968). Several comments seem necessary concerning this interpretation. First, the proximal end of the bone was not fully preserved. The extent of the areas of origin and insertion of the proximal musculature in the fossil therefore depend to some extent upon its reconstructed length (this is especially true of the popliteus). The estimate made by Davis was 277 ± 10 millimeters. It was "deduced from comparisons of the relative length of the shaft below the nutrient foramen in the fossil and in other higher primates" (Davis 1964: 947). The position of the nutrient foramen is highly variable in the human tibia and should not, therefore, be used as a basis for metrical analysis (Hrdlicka 1898; Lovejoy 1970). We mention this point because, in our opinion, the actual length of the fossil tibia was less than 277 millimeters.

The lowermost portion of the area of origin of the tibialis posterior is clearly defined on the posterolateral aspect of OH-6, the typical V-form of its most distal extent being clearly marked and similar to its sapiens position. The majority of its origin, however, is somewhat disturbed by damage to the shaft's posterolateral aspect (near the postmortem break with the missing proximal portion. While the large, posterior, vertical ridge is accentuated by this defect, it is nonetheless clearly a true morphological feature of the bone and thus very probably the soleal line. Here we are in disagreement with Davis, who notes the presence of this bony ridge but does not identify it. He suggests that below the area of the popliteus, there is "a strongly marked crest which continues into a short weakly marked soleal line which does not gain the lateral border of the bone" (1964: 968).

The interpretation of these two crests is clearly required for a complete understanding of the morphology of OH-6. The "strongly marked crest" of which Davis speaks is homologous to a well-developed UPPER part of the soleal line seen in some sapiens specimens in which this rugosity is divided into two distinct portions or in which its course is nearly vertical prior to its juncture with the area of origin of the flexor digitorum longus. This may be seen in OH-6 and in an Amerindian specimen. In both specimens the soleal line descends almost vertically along the proximal part of the shaft and then makes a well-defined medialward shift as it reaches the area of origin of the flexor digitorum longus. At the juncture of the shaft, a ridge continues as well on the posterolateral aspect of the bone, defining the medialmost extent of the tibialis posterior. The area enclosed by these two divisions is occupied by the flexor digitorum longus. As OH-6 is distinctly similar to this type of sapiens morphology, there is little reason to suggest that the relative development of the flexor digitorum longus and tibialis posterior were significantly different in OH-6. In fact, the relationships of these three muscles is so highly variable in both extent of origin and location that Davis's conjecture is not permissible. Vallois describes specimens in which

> . . . la ligne oblique fait defaut ou est à peine indiquée; dans d'autres, elle ne s'unit pas au bord interne de l'os et se continue directement avec la crête longitudinale qui, sur la face postérieure, sépare le jambier postérieure du fléchisseur commun des orteils (1938: 98).

Furthermore, if the present interpretation is correct, rather than displaying a weakly developed soleal line, OH-6 displays a soleal rugosity comparable to those most robustly developed in the Amerindian population used for comparison in this analysis. The most important aspect of the posterior morphology of OH-6 is thus the presence of the large soleal line on both tibia and fibula, because in the gorilla the origin of the soleus is usually restricted to the fibula, save a "rudimentary" origin from the popliteal line (Gregory 1950).

Finally, some comment seems in order concerning Davis' conclusions regarding the popliteus. He has remarked that the texture of the bone in the region of its origin "suggests that the direction of muscle pull was nearly vertical" (1964: 968). This seems highly improbable. First, the top one-half of the area of popliteal origin is missing in the fossil (if the length estimate of Davis is accepted, almost all of it is missing). Second, a vertically oriented tendon for the popliteus would be contrary to its condition in all other higher primates, where it is angled laterally about 45.

Evidence is now available concerning the above points from the newer specimen KNM-ER-741, in which most of the proximal joint surface is well preserved. This specimen is very similar to many Amerindian tibiae; in fact, the detailed description provided by Leakey, Mungai, and Walker (1972) serves as an accurate description of many Amerindian tibiae because of their great similarity to the fossil. Unfortunately, despite its greater size relative to OH-6, it is a quite gracile specimen and its regions of muscular origin are therefore only lightly marked. The following points can be made, however.

On the posterior-medial aspect of the shaft, a concave impression for the origin of the flexor digitorum longus is clearly present and identical to its condition in many modern tibiae. Although the area for origin of the tibialis posterior is not clearly marked, its anterior limit (i.e. the anterolateral limit of the posterior compartment) can be palpated. There is no evidence that the relative areas of origin of these two muscles are not similar to their condition in modern man. The soleal line is not prominent, but its course is similar to its path in numerous modern specimens. Although the lateral condyle is damaged, Leakey, Mungai, and Walker point out that a popliteus groove is detectable and in a position similar to modern tibiae.

In summary, combining the evidence from OH-6 and KNM-ER-741, one may conclude that both the proximal and distal joint surfaces and the shaft of the bone indicate that the australopithecine tibia approximates the modern human pattern with such fidelity that no locomotor or mechanical differences are implied by the morphology of these bones.

FIBULA

Davis (1964) concluded that the shaft of the OH-6 fibula "in many ways resembles that of *H. sapiens*; indeed, there are fibulae from modern human beings which resemble it almost perfectly" (1964: 968). His conclusions concerning the lateral malleolus were that it was essentially similar to the *H. sapiens* condition.

TARSUS

The foot of *Australopithecus* is partially known from two specimens, an incomplete talus from Kromdraai (TM-1517) and an almost entire foot from Olduvai (OH-8). The striking similarity of these specimens to those of modern man has been generally recognized. However, minor morphological variations of these specimens have been used to suggest that they are not indicative of a fully bipedal gait. As pointed out earlier, minor morphological variations are in themselves of such small significance as to make them dubious in reconstructing gait pattern.

Both the Olduvai and Kromdraai specimens display features clearly indicative of complete upright bipedalism. In fact, as far as we can detect, they do not differ from modern specimens in any detail, when the range of variation of modern man is given proper consideration. While our study of these specimens is based upon available casts and published measurements (the cast available for OH-8 is an articulated specimen so that joint surfaces cannot be completely studied), those differences that have been asserted to exist with modern specimens are primarily features of the talus, and an individual cast is available for this bone.

Of primary significance to most workers appears to be the "horizontal axis of the talar neck," the magnitude of which is said to lie outside the range of modern human variation (Day and Napier 1964; Day and Wood 1968; Robinson 1972). This angle is given by Day and Wood as 28° in OH-8 and 32° in TM-1517. Their sample of 128 human tali yielded a mean value of 19° with a standard deviation of 3.4°. Thus the Olduvai specimen would appear to lie just inside and the Kromdraai specimen just outside three standard deviations from the human mean. A primary problem, of course, lies with the adequacy of the modern sample. The average Amerindian talus appears to display considerably greater divergence of the talar neck than was the case in the sample used by Day and Wood. This could be related to footwear, substrate, posture, locomotor habits, etc. In any case, the divergence of the talar neck is as great in numerous Amerindian specimens as it is in the two australopithecine tali. The divergence of the neck is difficult to measure reliably (Barnett 1955). For this reason, we have not attempted to assess this feature quantitatively for the Amerindian population used in this study, but two samples from this population are included for comparison with the australopithecine specimens.

Many workers have assumed that a high angle of divergence of the talar neck is related to divergence of the hallux. This would appear doubtful for several reasons. First, three joint surfaces separate the talar neck from the hallux. Slight alterations in the form of these would have far greater effect upon hallucal divergence than would the deviation of the talar neck from the central axis of the trochlear surface. Second, Barnett measured this angle in a number of primates and found it to be about equal to the human value in a number of forms (rhesus, baboon, orangutan), all with fully divergent halluces (Barnett 1955). From his own study he concluded:

> Medial deviation of the neck within the foot is found in species with a wide foot, for example, those with a plantigrade gait or a fossorial habit, and in arboreal species in which the body weight is deviated within the foot towards the medial side (1955: 229).

Finally, it should also be pointed out that the angle of divergence of the talar neck in the adult foot is the result of a REDUCTION of its original angle of divergence in the infant, where it averages about 35° (Trotter 1966). The talar neck angle is thus probably higher in Amerindians (and australopithecines) than in some other modern human populations because of factors such as those mentioned above, and the high angles of divergence in TM-1517 and OH-8 do not indicate any differences in the gait patterns of australopithecines and modern man.

A second feature that has been suggested to differ in the modern and australopithecine foot is the metatarsal robusticity index. When the middle circumference of the bone is divided by its length, some indication of the "robusticity" of the metatarsal is obtained (roentgenographic determination would of course be more accurate). When the five metatarsals from a single individual are compared, the relative robusticity of the metatarsals shows distinctive patterns in hominids and pongids, although both show great variation. Archibald, Lovejoy, and Heiple (1972) studied the distribution of the metatarsal robusticity pattern in a modern sample of Amerindian feet. They found that the pattern that characterizes the OH-8 metatarsus was the second most frequently occurring pattern in the Amerindian population and that it differed substantially from the pongid pattern.

THE TOTAL BIOMECHANICAL PATTERN OF THE LOWER LIMB SKELETON OF *AUSTRALOPITHECUS*

For the most part it is apparent that most of the morphological features of the australopithecine lower limb are within the range of variation of *H. sapiens*. For some of these features there appears to be little or no difference between sapiens and australopithecine populations. For others, however, there is an apparent overlap between the two populations, but the average expressions or populational means appear to differ. A summary of morphological differences between *Australopithecus* and *H. sapiens* is presented in Table 3. The most immediate implications of this summary are that the total morphological patterns of *Australopithecus* and *H. sapiens* differ only slightly, and that a great wealth of features indicating a completely bipedal gait are present, although there are some consistent differences, especially with regard to the hip joint. In order to interpret the latter, it is first necessary to compare australopithecines and modern man with respect to those morphological features that have mechanical importance. Table 4, therefore, lists the mechanical differences that are important to gait pattern and that result from the morphological differences listed in Table 3.

Only one significant difference between *H. sapiens* and *Australopithecus* emerges from Table 4. This can be shown to be a difference in femoral head pressure (Lovejoy, Heiple, and Burstein 1973). That is, whereas the femoral head of *Australopithecus* is slightly smaller than that of *H. sapiens*, the lever arm of the abductors is at the same time greater than in *H. sapiens*. Lovejoy, Heiple, and Burstein (1973) calculated the resultant femoral head pressure in STS-14 (which includes a whole pelvis and much of a femur from the same individual) and a series of Amerindians. The effects of the greater length of the abductor lever arm were found to be quite substantial. Despite a slightly smaller femoral head in STS-14, the static pressure on the articular cartilage of the hip joint was found to be only HALF that of the Amerindian average. They concluded that the morphology of the australopithecine hip complex was equally or more favorably adapted to bipedal locomotion than that of *H. sapiens*. Those morphological changes that separate *Australopithecus* and *H. sapiens* were judged to result from an enlarged birth canal in the latter and not from any difference in gait pattern. This is illustrated in Figure 5. As the dimensions of the fetal cranium increased during the Pleistocene, changes were required in the dimensions of the hip complex. The posterior extension of the ilium and of the caudal portion of the sacrum were already present in *Australopithecus* (Robinson 1972). The increase in the size of the birth canal between *Australopithecus* and *H. sapiens* therefore took the form of an increase in interacetabular distance. This increase in the coronal diameter of the birth canal in turn caused a reduction in lateral iliac flare and a commensurate decrease in the lever arm of the abductors. Such a decrease would have resulted in femoral head pressures beyond physiological limits were the relative size of the femoral head not correspondingly increased as well.

As a wide birth canal is essentially required only in females, it might be expected that modern males would have a greater tendency to retain those abductor advantages seen in *Australopithecus*, i.e. they should demonstrate a greater lateral flare than females. A series of metrics were therefore taken from a sample of articulated Amerindian pelves, the purpose of which was to quantify the amount of lateral flaring of the iliac blades. These metrics are explained in Figure 6 and the results of the survey are given in Figure 7. As can be seen by reference to the latter figure, a bimodal distribution of lateral iliac flare resulted from this survey, with males having a greater average degree of flare. The distributions were significantly different (P<.001). It was also suggested above that greater lateral flare should result in greater relief of the anterior superior iliac spine. This feature was also assessed in the Amerindian sample by means of the methods described in Figure 8. Again males were found to express a more australopithecine-like condition than did females. The distribution was again bimodal, with males having generally more protuberant anterior superior spines. The difference between the two populations was significant at the .001 level.

STS-14 exhibits features that are both android and gynecoid in nature if compared with modern pelves. A visual impression of

Figure 5. *Schematic representation of pelvic evolution during the Pleistocene. While total pelvic breadth (relative to stature) remains substantially unchanged, the coronal diameter of the birth canal (pelvic outlet) increases in response to greater term fetal cranial capacity. This increases the torque developed about the hip joint during the stance phase of gait, and at the same time reduces the lever arm of the abductors. These changes required greater iliac robusticity and relative femoral head size in later Pleistocene hominids. The reduction of lateral iliac flare resulted in a less protuberant anterior superior spine, a more posterior position of the iliac pillar, a reduction in femoral neck length, etc. (see Lovejoy, Heiple, and Burstein 1973; Lovejoy 1973).*

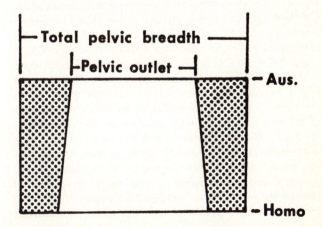

Table 3. Morphological differences in the lower limb skeleton of *Australopithecus* and *Homo sapiens*

Bone Morphological feature	Difference between *H. sapiens* and *Australopithecus*
Femur	
Neck-shaft angle	Somewhat lower populational mean (116 °) in *Australopithecus*
Femoral neck length	Somewhat greater in *Australopithecus* when normalized by femoral length
Bicondylar angle	Slightly higher in *Australopithecus*
Flare of greater trochanter	Somewhat less in *Australopithecus*
Intertrochanteric line	Average expression slightly less in *Australopithecus*?
Position of lessor trochanter	None
Intercondylar notch	None
Femoral head coverage	None on basis of present evidence
Linea aspera	None on basis of present evidence
Lateral condylar projection	None
Patellar groove	None
Ilium	
Size of auricular surface	None when normalized for body weight
Anterior inferior iliac spine	None
Lateral iliac flare	Greater in *Australopithecus* but populational overlap with *H. sapiens*
Iliac pillar	Position more anterior in *Australopithecus*
Anterior superior iliac spine	More protuberant in *Australopithecus*
Ischium	
Functional length	None
Morphology of ischial tuberosity	None on basis of present evidence
Pubis	
Length	Slightly lower in *Australopithecus* than in *H. sapiens* (but well with range of variation) on basis of one specimen
Tibia	
Proximal region and joint surface	None
Shaft	None
Distal region and joint surface	None
Fibula	None
General morphology	
Tarsus	
Horizontal angle at talar neck	Slightly greater in *Australopithecus* but well within range of variations of *H. sapiens*
Robusticity pattern of metatarsals	None

this relationship can be obtained by comparing STS-14 with modern pelves of fairly marked sexual dimorphism (Figure 9). The marked similarity of the australopithecine specimen with that of the male can be readily seen with respect to lateral flaring, while on the other hand, the subpubic angle of the former is obtuse, resembling that of the modern female. This is most likely a product of the relatively high interacetabular diameter of STS-14, which is in turn probably due to both the small stature of this particular specimen and to the fact that is almost certainly a female. Male australopithecine specimens (e.g. SK-50?) are likely to exhibit smaller interacetabular distances and therefore more lateral flaring and greater relief of the anterior superior iliac spine.

In summary, it must be pointed out that pelvic form is a highly variable and complex trait and that those factors enumerated above, while contributing significantly to the form of the adult pelvis, are most certainly not the only factors involved. This, in conjunction with the very limited sample available from which to reconstruct the australopithecine pelvis, means that a quantitative test of the hypothesis being presented here is not possible; yet when the factors of hip joint pressure and parturition are combined in the analysis of bipedal hominids, it would appear that what evidence is available at this point strongly favors the present explanation of pelvic differences in australopithecines and modern man.

If the iliac position and form in the modern male is more conservative than that of the modern female, it might also be expected that males would tend to be more conservative with regard to proximal femoral morphology as well. Although biomechanical neck length of the femur is not generally available in the literature, the angle between the shaft and neck is a frequently recorded metric for most skeletal populations. Interestingly, Walker points out that the neck-shaft angle does "demonstrate sexual dimorphism in man with females having higher angles than males by sometimes as much as 3 between the means of the sexes" (1973).

DIFFERENCES IN THE LOWER LIMB SKELETON OF THE SOUTH AFRICAN ALLOMORPHS

Some mention should be made of the taxonomic implications of the available lower limb samples of *Australopithecus*, especially with regard to the long-standing argument concerning taxonomic division of the South African australopithecines into two distinct taxa. This division has recently been strongly questioned by Wolpoff, but it is not our intent here to attempt any resolution of

Table 4. Biomechanical differences in the lower limb skeleton of *Australopithecus* and *Homo sapiens*

Bone Morphological feature	Difference between H. sapiens and Australopithecus
Femur	
Mechanical length of femoral neck	Greater in *Australopithecus* as a result of both a lower neck-angle and a greater morphological neck length
Femoral head size	Slightly greater in *H. Sapiens* relative to body weight
Position of knee joint in locomotion	None
Ilium	
Position of Abductors	More lateral in *Australopithecus*. Commensurate with longer femoral neck length. Causes protuberance of anterior superior spine and more anterior position of iliac pillar
Ischium	
No differences	
Pubis	
No differences	
Tibia	
No differences	
Fibula	
No differences	
Tarsus	
Angle of talar neck	Greater frequency of flatfoot in *Australopithecus*?

this argument. Rather, we wish only to discuss the lower limb in particular. The question may also arise as to differences between South and East African samples. These will also be discussed.

When the total evidence is considered, it would appear unlikely that any differences can be shown to exist between samples of the two alleged allomorphs of South Africa with regard to their lower limb skeletons. Rather, there appears to be a wealth of indications that no significant mechanical differences exist between these supposed taxa. Walker (1973) and Zihlman (1969) have reached similar conclusions.

This conclusion can be most easily demonstrated by briefly repeating what we have done through this paper, i.e. by comparing the mechanical features of the specimens of *Australopithecus* with those of *H. sapiens*. Taking, for example, proximal femoral anatomy, we find that STS-14 (attributed to the gracile form) and SK-97 and SK-82 (attributed to the robust form) share the same features that distinguish them from

modern man. All three specimens have a somewhat lower neck-shaft angle, a longer femoral neck, a similar position of the lesser trochanter, etc. Turning to the pelvis, we find the same conditions to hold true. Both SK-50 (robust) and STS-14 (gracile) have protuberant anterior superior spines, greater lateral flare, well-developed inferior spines, an anterior pillar position, etc. Robinson bases his distinction of the gracile and

Figure 7. *Results of the metrics taken on 34 female and 27 male articulated Amerindian pelves (as described in Figure 6) in order to measure differences in lateral flare. The male mean was about 31° and that of the females 28°. The populations are distinctly bimodal and differ significantly (P = .001; t test).*

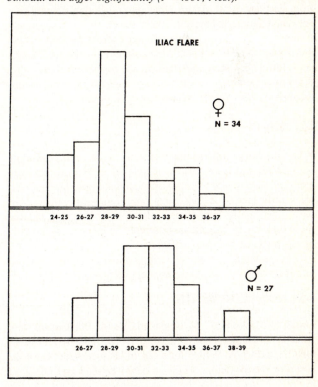

Figure 6. *Metrics used to determine the degree on iliac flare in an articulated pelvis. When the interacetabular distance (distance between the centers of the acetabula) (AD) is subtracted from maximum iliac breadth (IB) and divided by two times the iliac height, the result is the tangent of angle theta. Angle theta is defined for this study as the amount of lateral iliac flare.*

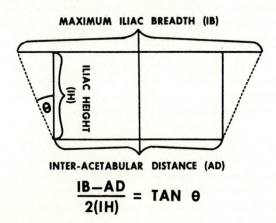

$$\frac{IB - AD}{2(IH)} = TAN\ \theta$$

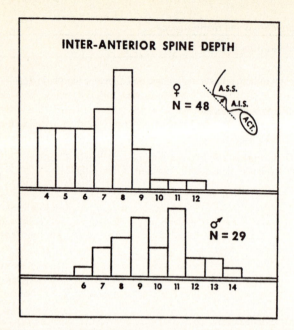

Figure 8. *Results of a series of metrics taken on forty-eight female and twenty-nine male Amerindian ilia in order to compare protuberance of the anterior superior spine. The metric taken is illustrated by the inset. It was defined as the maximum depth of the notch between the anterior superior and inferior spines taken perpendicular to a tangent to the most anterior extension of each spine. The populations are distinctly bimodal and differ significantly (P = .001; t test)*

robust forms primarily upon ischial length, which he believes to be significantly greater in the robust than in the gracile form. As pointed out above, however, both of these ischia have functional lengths well within the range of variation of modern man; they therefore cannot be used for taxonomic distinctions.

A similar situation would appear to hold true for specimens from East and South Africa, although to date only comparisons between femora can be made. Again, the East African specimens demonstrate the same kinds of differences from the modern condition as do those from South Africa: slightly smaller head, longer neck, lower neck-shaft angle, less greater trochanteric flare, and a distal femur similarly adapted as in *H. sapiens* (essentially indistinguishable save for the higher bicondylar angle).

SUMMARY

When the lower limb samples of *Australopithecus* (including both South and East African samples described to date) are analyzed with regard to morphological features of biomechanical significance, it is found that only minor differences exist with respect to the lower limb skeleton of modern man and that these differences indicate no difference in gait pattern but only one of response to encephalization.

For a number of years and throughout much of the literature there has been an a prior assumption that australopithecine

ACKNOWLEDGMENTS

I wish to thank Dr. K. G. Heiple and Dr. A. Burstein for their valuable discussions and criticisms; Dr. M. Day for a cast of OH-20; and Dr. A. Walker for a cast of his reconstruction of the australopithecine femur based on KNM-ER-933 and OH-20. I wish also to thank Dr. M. Wolpoff for measurements of australopithecine specimens and discussions of their morphology and condition, and Mr. B. Thorton and Mr. T. Calhoun for measurements of Amerindian pelves. The photographs are by Mr. L. Rubin.

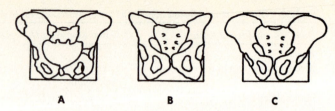

Figure 9. *Photographic tracings of three pelves in anterior view. Coordinate lines have been inserted over each to clarify its width in relation to its height. Specimen A (STS-14: Robinson reconstruction) is 47 percent broader than it is high. Specimen B (KSU-99902) (female) is 29 percent broader than it is high, while specimen C (KSU-02055B) (male) is 58 percent wider than it is high. Note the pronounced lateral flaring in specimen C compared to that of B, but the similarity in subpubic angle in B and A. Both Amerindian specimens are from the same skeletal population. For further discussion see text.*

locomotion and postcranial morphology were "intermediate" between quadrupedalism and the bipedalism of modern man. There is no basis for this assumption either in terms of Neo-Darwinian theory or, as pointed out above, in terms of the lower limb skeleton of *Australopithecus*. It is often claimed, principally on the basis of this a priori assumption, that morphological features shared by both modern man and *Australopithecus* do not necessarily indicate similar gait patterns (see, for example, Jenkins 1972). Although this might be true in terms of a single feature, it is demonstrably not true when the total mechanical pattern is considered. As we have seen, the only significant difference between the total biomechanical patterns of *Australopithecus* and *H. sapiens* is one that indicates that *Australopithecus* was at an advantage compared with modern man (femoral head pressure). This brings us to a second point.

There also appears in the literature a tendency to regard human bipedalism as a kind of locomotor pinnacle. Such is not the case. Human bipedalism is merely the combination of three simple elements (trunk progression, limb progression, control of pelvic tilt) (see Lovejoy 1973). Only the last of these is not part of the locomotor adaptation of any terrestrial mammal. No mysterious requirements need be satisfied for man to walk erect. He must simply obtain (by natural selection or by musculoskeletal plasticity) those basic adaptations of his joints and orientations of his muscles that are necessary to effect the above three requirements. All of these adaptations (a valgus knee position, a mechanism to prevent lateral patellar dislocation, an increased cartilage contact in the knee joint, a well-developed iliofemoral ligament, a long abductor lever, a posterior position of the gluteus maximus, etc.) are demonstrably present in *Australopithecus*.

In summary, the lower limb skeleton of *Australopithecus* points to a long history of bipedalism among hominids. If bipedalism was fully evolved during the basal Pleistocene, then the transition from quadrupedalism to bipedalism must lie in earlier strata. Just how old bipedalism is and under what conditions selection favored its adoption are important questions that can only be answered by further excavations of fossil strata that predate Pleistocene man.

NOTES

[1] All measurements reported in this paper were made on original specimens or taken from the literature.

[2] Robinson states (1972: 93) that the acetabulum diameter of SK-50 is 62 percent of its ischium length. I was unable to locate anywhere in his text (1972) the actual estimates for acetabulum diameter or functional ischium length. Robinson does give the distance from the acetabular rim to th nearest edge of the tuberosity (27 millimeters), but this is not an estimate of functional ischial lehgth, as Robinson points out. Lovejoy, Heiple, and Burstein (1973) estimated the functional ischial length in SK-50 as 60 millimeters, and this has subsequently been confirmed on the original specimen by Dr. Milford Wolpoff. Broom, Robinson, and Schepers (1950) and Schultz (1969) use 50 millimeters as an estimate for acetabluar diameter in SK-50. THIS GIVES A FUNCTIONAL ISCHIAL LENGTH RATIO OF 83 PERCENT, ALMOST IDENTICAL TO THAT OF STS-14, IN WHICH IT IS 87 PERCENT!. In order to obtain the 62 percent suggested by Robinson for SK-50 (using the Lovejoy, Heiple, and Burstein estimate of functional ischial length), an acetabulum diameter of 37 millimeters is required. This is clearly too small because the diameter of the femoral head of SK-97 (which Robinson has suggested to be a good fit for SK-50) is also 37 millimeters. Allowing a conservative 4-millimeter increase over femoral head size to acetabulum size for SK-50, functional ischial length would become 68 percent—IDENTICAL TO THE MEAN OF ROBINSON'S MODERN HUMAN SAMPLE! If the opinion stated in this paper is correct—that the femoral head (and acetabulum) diameters of australopithecines were probably somewhat smaller than those of modern man—this would imply that the functional ischial length of SK-50 is actually SHORTER than that of modern man.

[3] I have recently had the opportunity to study a complete cast of the STS-14 pelvis. In my opinion, the pubic bones have been reconstructed with too great a ventral deviation; that is, the pubic symphysis would appear to have been in a more dorsal position than is indicated by the reconstruction. This alteration would considerably shorten the pubic bones.

[4] The present discussion does not include the new femoral material recently recovered at East Rudolph. Comment on these specimens will be deferred until more detailed information is available.

REFERENCES

Archibald, J. D., Lovejoy, C. O., Heiple, K. G. 1972. Implications of relative robusticity in the Olduvai metatarsus. *American Journal of Physical Anthropology* 37:93-96.

Barnett, C. H. 1955. Some factors influencing angulation of the neck of the mammalian talus. *Journal of Anatomy* 89:225-23O.

Broom, R., Robinson, J. T., Schepers, G. W. H. 1950. Sterkfontein ape-man *Plesianthropus. Transvaal Museum Memoir* 4. Transvaal Museum, Pretoria.

Campbell, B. G. 1966. *Human Evolution*. Chicago: Aldine.

Dart, R. A. 1949. Innominate fragments of *Australopithecus prometheus. American Journal of Physical Anthropology* 7:301-334.

Dart, R. A. 1957. The second adolescent (female) ilium of *Australopithecus prometheus. Journal of the Palaeontology Society of India* 2:73-82.

Dart, R. A. 1958. A further adolescent ilium from Makapansgat. *American Journal of Physical Anthropology* 16:473-479.

Davis, P. R. 1964. Hominid fossils from Bed I, Olduvai Gorge, Tanganyika: a tibia and fibula. *Nature* 201:967-970.

Day, M. H. 1959. *Guide to Fossil Man*. London: Camelot Press.

Day, M. H. 1969. Femoral fragment of a robust australopithecine from Olduvai Gorge, Tanzania. *Nature* 221:230-233.

Day, M. H., Napier, J. R. 1964. Hominid fossils from Bed I, Olduvai Gorge, Tanganyika: fossil foot bones. *Nature* 201:967-970.

Day, M. H., Wood, B. A. 1968. Functional affinities of the Olduvai Hominid 8 talus. *Man* 3:440-455.

Gregory, W. K., editor 1950. *The Anatomy of the Gorilla*. Columbia University Press, New York.

Heiple, K. G., Lovejoy, C. O. 1971. The distal femoral anatomy of *Australopithecus. American Journal of Physical Anthropology* 35:75-84.

Hrdlicka, A. 1898. Study of the normal tibia. *American Anthropologist* 11 (old series): 307-312.

Jenkins, F. A., Jr. 1972. Chimpanzee bipedalism: cineradiographic analysis and implications for the evolution of gait. *Science* 178:877-879.

Kern, H. M., Straus, W. L., Jr. 1949. The femur of *Plesianthropus transvaalensis. American Journal of Physical Anthropology* 7:53-77.

Leakey, R. E. F., Mungai, J. M., Walker, A. C. 1972. New australopithecines from East Rudolf, Kenya (II). *American Journal of Physical Anthropology* 36:235-251.

Le Gros Clark, W. E. 1947. Observations on the anatomy of the fossil Australopithecinae. *Journal of Anatomy, London* 81:300-313.

Le Gros Clark, W. E. 1964. *The Fossil Evidence for Human Evolution* (second edition). University of Chicago Press, Chicago.

Le Gros Clark, W. E. 1967. *Man-Apes or Ape-men? The story of discoveries in Africa*. Holt, Rinehart and Winston, New York.

Lovejoy, C. O. 1970. *Biomechanical Methods for the Analysis of Skeletal Variation with an Application by Comparison of the Theoretical Diaphyseal Strength of Platycnemic and Euricnemic Tibias*. Doctoral dissertation, University of Massachusetts, Amherst.

Lovejoy, C. O. 1973. The biomechanics of stride and their bearing on the gait of *Australopithecus. Yearbook of Physical Anthropology* 17:147-161.

Lovejoy, C. O., Heiple, K. G. 1970. A reconstruction of the femur of *Australopithecus africanus. American Journal of Physical Anthropology* 32:33-40.

Lovejoy, C. O., Heiple, K. G. 1971. Femoral anatomy of *Australopithecus africanus* and *robustus* (abstract). *American Journal of Physical Anthropology* 35:286.

Lovejoy, C. O. Kingsburg, G., Heiple, K. G. 1972. Proximal femoral anatomy of *Australopithecus. Nature* 235:175-176.

Lovejoy, C. O., Heiple, K. G., Burstein, A. H. 1973. The gait of *Australopithecus. American Journal of Physical Anthropology* 38:757-779.

Napier, J. R. 1964. The evolution of bipedal walking in the hominids. *Archives de Biologie* (Liège) 75:673-708.

Preuschoft, H. 1971. Body posture and mode of locomotion in early Pleistocene hominids. *Folia Primatologica* 14:209-240.

Robinson, J. T. 1972. *Early Hominid posture and Locomotion*. University of Chicago Press, Chicago.

Schultz, A. H. 1930. The skeleton of the trunk and limbs of higher primates. *Human Biology* 2:303-438.

Schultz, A. H. 1969. Observations on the acetabulum of Primates. *Folia Primatologica* 11:181-199.

Trotter, M. 1966. "Osteology," in *Morris' Human Anatomy*. (B. J. Anson, Ed.), pp. 133-315, McGraw-Hill, New York.

Vallois, H. V. 1938. Les methodes de mensuration de la platycnemie: etude critique. *Bulletin et Memoires de la Societe d'Anthropologie, Paris, Serie* 89:97-108.

Walker, A. C. 1973. New *Australopithecus* femora from East Rudolf, a:love Kenya. *Journal of Human Evolution* 2:545-555.

Washburn, S. L. 1963. "Behavior and human evolution," in *Classification and Human Evolution*. (S. L. Washburn, Ed.), pp. 190-203, Aldine, Chicago.

Zihlman, A. L. 1969. *Human Locomotion: a Reappraisal of the Functional and Anatomical Evidence*. Doctoral dissertation, University of California, Berkeley.

Zihlman, A. L. 1971. The question of locomotor differences in *Australopithecus. Proceedings of the 3rd International Congress of Primatology*. S. Karger, Basel.

18

Arboreality and Bipedality in the Hadar Hominids

R. L. Susman, J. T. Stern, Jr., and W. L. Jungers

INTRODUCTION

Once upon a time there lived a species of ape that ventured down from the trees and discovered that it could walk on two legs as well as do you and I. From that moment on, this ape determined to find all its food and secure all its resting (or hiding) places on the ground. It forsook its old home among the branches and was henceforth a *terrestrial biped*.

Such a fairy tale seems hard to believe. Must not there have been a period of time when both the trees and the ground served as important areas for life's activities, as they do today for living great apes? Must not there have been a period of time when the human ancestor was neither as good at moving on two legs as it could become, nor as good at scrambling in the trees as it once had been? We expect that such a period of time did exist, and that the hominid fossils from the Hadar formation, Ethiopia were plucked from it.

As best we can determine, the origins of such a view are to be found in Senut's study of the forelimb (Senut 1978, 1980; Senut and LeFloch 1981), which prompted her to assert a "certain ability and possibly propensity on the part of these hominids to climb trees" (1980, p. 91). Shortly thereafter, Tardieu (1979, 1981, 1983) identified similarities between the knee-joint bones of the small specimens from Hadar and those of living apes, leading her to suggest that such specimens came from an animal that was far better adapted to arboreal movement and rather less adapted to bipedalism than are modern humans. Tuttle (1981) called attention to the curved proximal phalanges of the foot and hand, the rod-like pisiform and the robust hook of the hamate as indicating that the Hadar hominids "may have engaged in notable tree-climbing, perhaps for night rest" (1981, p. 92). Though noting certain differences between the Afar specimens and modern humans with regard to lateral flare and orientation of the iliac blades, Tuttle remained in doubt about whether "a human pelvic tilt mechanism or lateral flexion and rotation of the spine was predominant during their bipedal walking" (1981, p. 92). Jungers (1982) demonstrated that the high humerofemoral index of A.L. 288-1 was the result of a short lower limb relative to body size rather than the presence of a long upper limb. This combination of limb lengths endowed the fossil species with climbing abilities greater than in humans but diminished from those of apes. Jungers also showed that the cost of bipedal locomotion must have been higher in the

species represented by Lucy than it is in modern humans. An attempt to refute Jungers' arguments was made by Wolpoff (1983a, b), but further analyses by Jungers and Stern (1983) provided confirmation of the original conclusions. Marzke (1983, p. 198) remarked on certain anatomical features of the Hadar hand bones that "recall the bony apparatus which accommodates the well developed flexor musculature in living apes and positions it for efficient hook-like grip of the branches by the flexed fingers during arboreal climbing and feeding." Cook *et al.* (1983, p. 100) concluded from their study of vertebral pathology in A.L. 288-1 that the distribution and nature of the lesions are compatible with a view that, in the fossil species, "climbing and acrobatic activities may have been proportionately more important than they are in modern humans."

Stern and Susman (1983a) produced the first publication of a comprehensive functional analysis of the Hadar postcranial material.

> We discovered a substantial body of evidence indicating arboreal activities were so important to A. afarensis that morphologic adaptations permitting adept movement in the trees were maintained. This conclusion, in and of itself, does not ineluctably lead to a second deduction that the nature of terrestrial bipedality, when it was practiced, was different from modern humans. However, we do believe this second conclusion to be reasonable even though the evidence in its favor is much less compelling than that indicating a significant degree of arboreality.' (Stern and Susman 1983a, p.313)

Subsequent to these studies, Schmid (1983) published a consideration of several anatomical features of the Hadar postcranial material, with emphasis on the shape of the thorax in relation to pelvic structure. He concluded (p. 303) "dass wir *Australopithecus* sowohl mehrheitlich als eine arboreale wie auch als terrestrische Lebensform betrachten müssen." Finally, McHenry's (1983) analysis of australopithecine, pongid, and human capitates led him to state (p. 17), "The morphological differences between the capitate of *Australopithecus* and *H. sapiens* may relate to the retention of climbing ability and an absence of certain grip capabilities in these early hominids."

Arrayed against this rather extensive list of persons who found evidence that some or all of the individuals at Hadar were distinct from modern humans in their lifestyle and locomotion, are other researchers who espouse a very different view. Their analyses, to date, have indicated full bipedality functionally equivalent to the modern mode (Johanson *et al.* 1976, 1982a; Lovejoy 1979, 1981; Wolpoff 1980, 1983a, b; Johanson and Edey 1981). Neither do they see the distinct morphology of the foot as evidence for climbing (Lovejoy, quoted in R. E. F. Leakey 1981; Latimer, cited in Johanson and Edey 1981; Latimer 1983, 1984; Gomberg and Latimer 1984). Although a consideration of Lucy's (A.L. 288-1) relatively long arms led to the statement, "Logic suggests that she may have done a good deal of climbing to escape predators or to find food" (Lovejoy, cited in Johanson and Edey 1981, p. 348), the absence of long, ape-like fingers caused rejection of this conclusion. Wolpoff (1980) speculated that long arms gave these early hominids the advantage of being able to wield clubs at objects relatively far from the body, and thus to reduce risk of injury to themselves while hunting or defending from large animals.

In hopes of clarifying, and possible resolving, the controversy surrounding locomotor behavior in the Hadar hominids, a Symposium, sponsored by The Institute of Human Origins, was held in April of 1983 in Berkeley, California. This symposium allowed persons with differing views to challenge one another's interpretations of the fossil evidence. Many verbal criticisms of our work were offered at the Berkeley Symposium. To date, the abstracts by Latimer (1984) and Suwa (1984) represent the only published rejoinders to our studies. Nonetheless, the papers presented at the Berkeley Symposium are a matter of public record, and Dr. D. C. Johanson and The Institute of Human Origins were kind enough to provide us with a complete audiotape record of the public sessions. Additionally, Dr. T. White and Mr. G. Suwa generously sent a copy of their manuscript on the Laetoli footprints and the reconstruction of Lucy's foot, in which they challenge some of our interpretations. The following presents new data that extend our earlier work on the locomotor anatomy of *A. afarensis*, and in so doing constitutes a response to those criticisms of which we are aware.

ANATOMIC ADAPTATIONS TO ARBOREAL BEHAVIOR IN THE HADAR HOMINIDS

Interlimb Proportions

At a value of approximately 85, the humerofemoral index of Lucy (and presumably her male counterparts, because this index is not sexually dimorphic in hominoids) has been shown to be intermediate between the values that characterize humans of small stature (pygmies, $\overline{X} = 73.7$) and small-bodied African pongids (bonobos, $\overline{X} = 97.8$). It has also been demonstrated that this unique ratio of fore- to hindlimb bony elements is due to a relatively short hindlimb in A.L. 288-1, comparable to that seen in apes of similar body size (Jungers 1982; Jungers and Stern 1983). Although such proportions would not necessarily endow Lucy with a capability for climbing equivalent to living chimpanzees, such interlimb ratios would clearly facilitate climbing in comparison to modern humans. In other words, considerable competence in climbing can be preserved in a relatively large-bodied primate like *A. afarensis* even if relative forelimb length has been reduced to modern proportions, provided that hindlimb length remains relatively even shorter (Cartmill 1974; Jungers 1978, 1984a, b).

Upper Limb

Bush (1980) stated that the thumb bones of *A. afarensis* indicate beginning differentiation toward the modern hominid pattern. The relatively short length of this ray, and the gracility of its metacarpal, caused Bush to comment that "evolutionary changes of the thumb appear to lag behind other aspects of the postcranial skeleton" (1980, p. 210). Tuttle (1981) also observed that the pollical metacarpal was "rather chimpanzee-like", as was the pollical articular surface of the trapezium. However, he likened the proximal phalanx of the first ray to that of gracile humans. He suggested that the thumb of the Hadar species acted conspicuously in strong power grips.

Tuttle's comments on specimens of the remaining hand bones included reference to the ventral curvature and well-developed flexor-sheath ridges of the proximal phalanges, the general similarity of the metacarpals to human ones (except that the heads and bases are relatively narrow), the absence of a styloid process on the base of the 3rd metacarpal, the robust hook of the hamate, the rod-like (therefore, chimpanzee-like) pisiform, and well-developed finger tips. These observations led Tuttle (1981, p. 93) to conclude that Hadar hominids probably used their hands "primarily as manipulatory and climbing organs."

Bush *et al.* (1982) consideration of the finger bones (Johanson *et al.* 1982a, pp. 384-385) revealed only a 'mild to moderate' curvature of the proximal phalanges and a 'variable' development of the flexor-sheath ridges. He described the sites of insertion of the flexor digitorum superficialis onto the middle phalanges as 'well developed'. He disagreed with Tuttle by stating that the apical tufts of the terminal phalanges are not well developed. Acknowledging that the shape of the pisiform is similar to chimpanzees, Bush identified the dorsal trapezoid facet on the capitate and the lateral waisting of this bone as further resemblances to *Pan*. He pointed out only three similarities to humans: (1) a single concave facet on the capitate for the second metacarpal; (2) the absolute length of the metacarpals and phalanges, and (3) the lack of dorsal transverse ridges on metacarpal heads II-V. This last-mentioned trait may be viewed as no more than indicative of the absence of adaptation to knuckle-walking (Tuttle 1967); it has no bearing on use of the hand in suspensory behaviors.

Stern and Susman (1983a) offered comments that were in general confirmatory of previous worker's observations. The ape-like nature of the pisiform, capitate, and pollical metacarpophalangeal joint was emphasized, as was the attenuated appearance of the metacarpal and proximal phalanx of the thumb. Our study of the metacarpals of the fingers did not support Tuttle's contention that they are basically human-like. The large heads and bases of these bones, together with their parallel-sided and somewhat curved shafts create an appearance which differs from chimpanzees only in the absence of knuckle-walking features. We also found that Tuttle's description of the distal phalanges as indicating well-developed finger tips was not as accurate as Bush's statement that the apical tufts are not well developed. Rather than confining our comments to descriptive terms, we measured the radio-ulnar breadth of the apical tufts and found that in the fossils (A.L. 333w-11, -50) it is the same proportion (62%) of the radio-ulnar breadth of the base as it is in chimpanzees (see Susman and Creel 1979 for a detailed consideration of, and rationale for, these measurements). In

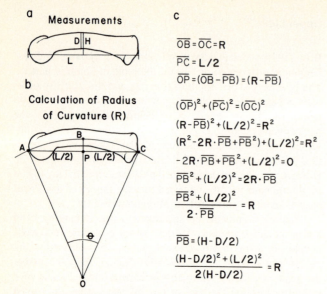

a

Measurements

D | H

L

b

**Calculation of Radius
of Curvature (R)**

A — B — C

(L/2) P (L/2)

Θ

O

c

$$\overline{OB} = \overline{OC} = R$$

$$\overline{PC} = L/2$$

$$\overline{OP} = (\overline{OB} - \overline{PB}) = (R - \overline{PB})$$

$$(\overline{OP})^2 + (\overline{PC})^2 = (\overline{OC})^2$$

$$(R - \overline{PB})^2 + (L/2)^2 = R^2$$

$$(R^2 - 2R \cdot \overline{PB} + \overline{PB}^2) + (L/2)^2 = R^2$$

$$-2R \cdot \overline{PB} + \overline{PB}^2 + (L/2)^2 = 0$$

$$\overline{PB}^2 + (L/2)^2 = 2R \cdot \overline{PB}$$

$$\frac{\overline{PB}^2 + (L/2)^2}{2 \cdot \overline{PB}} = R$$

$$\overline{PB} = (H - D/2)$$

$$\frac{(H - D/2)^2 + (L/2)^2}{2(H - D/2)} = R$$

Figure 1. *Measurement and calculation of radius of curvature of
a proximal phalanx. (a) Three measurements provided the basis for
calculating radius of curvature: L = length (maximum was used for
finger bones, interarticular for toe bones), D = dorsoplantar midshaft diameter, H = height of the dorsal surface of the bone (at its
midshaft) above a line connecting the centers of the proximal and
distal articular surfaces. (b) The radius of curvature (R = $\overline{OA}$ =
$\overline{OB}$ = $\overline{OC}$) can be calculated if one knows $\overline{PB}$ and $\overline{PC}$. Θ is the
included angle of the phalanx. (c) These formulae show how $\overline{PB}$
and $\overline{PC}$ may be determined from the measurements of L, D and H,
and how the radius of curvature (R) may then be calculated. Θ is
equal to 2*Arc-sin[L/2R].*

Table I. Values of the parameter 'H' (Fig. 1) for manual proximal
phalanges from Hadar.

Specimen	H, mm
A.L. 288-1x	5.5
A.L. 333-19	6.3
A.L. 333-57	6.0
A.L. 333-62	6.4
A.L. 333-63	6.9
A.L. 333-93	5.6
A.L. 333w-4	6.8

objects with radii of curvature near infinity. Our results
showed that the curvatures of the fossil manual proximal
phalanges were far in excess of human values and in most
cases even greater than the mean for bonobos. Such extreme
curvatures are surprising, but this is true because we failed to
consider the possibility that phalangeal curvature might be
influenced by length of the bone.

On the face of it, a consideration of the relationship between curvature and length ought not to dispel the surprise
inherent in our previous results. Preuschoft (1970, 1971) indicates that a theoretical analysis leads to the conclusion that
longer phalanges should be more curved in order to reduce
bending stresses. Thus, the short absolute length of the fossils
compared to great ape manual proximal phalanges would lead
us to predict a diminished rather than accentuated curvature in
the former. However, we have since discovered a relationship
between radius of curvature and length which is not compatible
with this theoretical prediction.

Figure 2 presents plots of radius of curvature against
phalangeal length for *Pan paniscus* and *Pongo pygmaeus*. Such
graphs are representative of those obtained for the other apes as
well. For apes, the correlation coefficients for regressions of
radius of curvature on maximum length ranged from 0.72 in
gorillas to 0.90 in bonobos. The value was only 0.48 for our
human sample of manual proximal phalanges. Figure 2 shows
that bones with greater lengths have larger radii of curvature,
thus are *straighter*. This is true when bones from the same ray
of different individuals are compared, or when comparison is
made between bones of different rays from the same individual.

Figure 3 presents a plot of the regression lines for radius of
curvature against length for each species of great ape (with male
and female gorillas illustrated separately) and humans. The
envelopes enclosing all the data points for humans (37 individuals, 146 phalanges), African apes (48 individuals, 189
phalanges), and orangutans (18 individuals, 68 phalanges) are
also drawn. Fossils from the A.L. 333 and A.L. 333w sites are
plotted as solid stars; Lucy's manual proximal phalanx appears
as an open star. 6 of the 7 Hadar specimens fall outside the
envelope for humans. The one specimen (A.L. 333w-4) that
falls within the human envelope is also contained within the
envelope for African apes and lies closer to the regression lines
for gorillas than to that for humans. Of the six fossils outside
the human envelope, three (A. L. 333-19, -57, -63) are within
the envelope for African apes, and three (A.L. 288-1x, A.L.
333-62, -93) lie along its lower left border. One could imagine
that if there existed African apes with somewhat smaller upper
limbs than possessed by extant forms, their phalanges would be
positioned as are these last three Hadar fossils.

humans the average proportion is 69%, a value that is statistically significantly different from that of chimpanzees (Susman
and Creel 1979). On lateral view, the distal phalanges from
Hadar also have a shape which resembles that of chimpanzees
more than humans.

Stern and Susman (1983a) went beyond a vague qualitative description of proximal phalangeal curvature by presenting a quantitative analysis of this trait. In that paper, details
on how this curvature was measured were not presented, so
we will do so at this time. Using standard calipers, the length
(L) [1] and dorsoplantar midshaft diameter (D) were
measured (Fig. 1a). Then, using a specially designed coordinates calipers (courtesy of W. W. Howells), the height (H)
of the dorsal surface of the phalanx (at its midshaft) above a
line connecting the centers of the proximal and distal articular
surfaces was measured (Fig. 1a). Parts b and c of Figure 1
illustrate how these three parameters can be used to derive the
radius of a circle that passes through the centers of the articular surfaces and the center of the shaft at its midpoint.
Values for L and B of the relevant fossils can be obtained from
Bush *et al.* (1982) and Johanson *et al.* (1982b). Table I
presents values of H measured on casts of these fossils. In
Stern and Susman (1983a), the reciprocal of the calculated
radius (multiplied by 10^4) was used as the measure of curvature. Reciprocation of the radius of curvature is standard
practice because it enables consideration of nearly straight

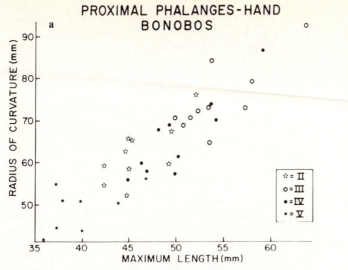

PROXIMAL PHALANGES-HAND
BONOBOS

☆ = II
o = III
• = IV
★ = V

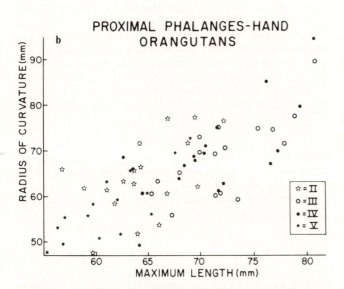

PROXIMAL PHALANGES-HAND
ORANGUTANS

☆ = II
o = III
• = IV
★ = V

Figure 2. *Radius of curvature plotted against maximum length for the manual proximal phalanges of bonobos and orangutans. For both bonobos (a) and orangutans (b), the box at the lower right indicates the symbols used to differentiate phalanges from different rays. Bones with greater lengths have larger radii of curvatures, thus are straighter, than bones of lesser length. This is true when phalanges from the same ray are compared or when comparison is made between bones from different rays. The two graphs shown are representative of those obtained for other apes.*

Another way of illustrating this same finding makes use of the fact that if a regression of radius of curvature against length had a y-intercept of 0, then the included angle (Θ = 2 Arcsin[L/2R], fig. 1b) should be independent of length. In other words, all manual proximal phalanges from a given species should be characterized by the same value of included angle regardless of the ray from which any phalanx was derived or the size of any individual. In fact, the y-intercepts for gibbons, siamangs, orangutans, male gorillas, female gorillas, and chimpanzees do not differ significantly from 0. Even in cases where the y-intercepts do differ significantly from 0 (bonobos and humans), the included angle varies remarkably little between rays. Figure 4 is a graph of included angle (indicating variation)

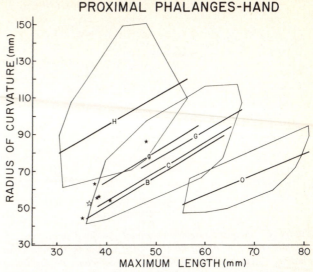

PROXIMAL PHALANGES-HAND

Figure 3. *Regression lines and envelopes for radius of curvature plotted against maximum length for manual proximal phalanges. Six regression lines are drawn. Each is interrupted by a letter indicating the position of the mean length, and predicted radius at this length, for the sample from which the regression line was generated: H = humans, G = male gorillas, g = female gorillas, C = chimpanzees, B = bonobos, O = orangutans. The envelope for the human sample encloses the data points for 146 phalanges from 37 individuals. The envelope for the African ape sample encloses the data points for 189 phalanges from 48 individuals. The envelope for the orangutan sample encloses the data points for 68 phalanges from 18 individuals. ☆ = A.L. 288- 1x; ★ = manual proximal phalanges from the A.L. 333 site (-19, -57, -62, -63, -93) and A.L. 333w-4. The latter specimen lies within both the human and African ape envelopes, but closest to the regression lines for gorillas. The remaining fossils lie in a position predicted for African apes with somewhat smaller upper limbs than possessed by extant species.*

of the manual proximal phalanges for each ape, humans, and the fossils. This figure clearly shows the similarity between the Hadar fossils and African apes, particularly the gorilla.

The analysis of curvature as a function of length reveals two important facts: (1) that curvature of manual proximal phalanges does not increase as does length, as predicted by some theories, but, in fact, decreases as the bones become longer, and (2) the curvature of the fossil hand bones from Hadar are most closely matched by slight extension of the pattern seen among African apes into a range of smaller absolute size.

The only other bone of the forelimb considered by Stern and Susman (1983a) was the scapula. It was demonstrated that the A.L. 288-11 scapular fragment has a glenoid surface that is oriented cranially relative to the axillary border (as indicated by the ventral stress-bearing bar). In this important feature Lucy's scapula was virtually identical to that of a great ape and had a probability of less than 0.001 of coming from the population represented by our modern human sample. Interestingly, the same cranially oriented glenoid is found in STS-7 (Oxnard 1968; Ciochon and Corruccini 1976; Vrba 1979). This is one of the facts adduced by McHenry (1983) to support an argument that *A. afarensis* and *A. africanus* are only trivially different postcranially.

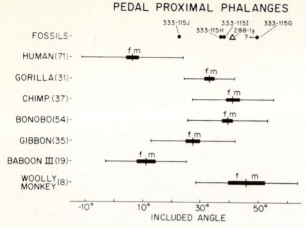

Figure 4. *Included angles of manual proximal phalanges. In parentheses following the name of each sample is the number of phalanges in that sample. The vertical bar indicates the position of the sample mean (the means for the different sexes are indicated by an 'm' for males and an 'f' for females). The solid black rectangle spans the 95% confidence limits for the mean; the horizontal line spans the 95% fiducial limits of the population. Fossils are labelled. As judged by the included angle, the curvatures of the Hadar phalanges are very closely allied to those of African apes, particularly the gorilla. The one fossil (A.L. 333-62) that falls outside the 95% fiducial limits for gorillas is distorted in such a way as to increase its apparent (and measured) curvature.*

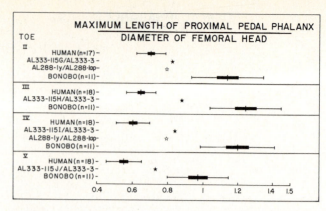

Figure 5. *Length of pedal proximal phalanges expressed as a proportion of femoral head diameter. For the human and bonobo samples (n = number of individuals), the vertical line indicates the mean, the solid black rectangle spans the 95% confidence limits of the mean, and the horizontal line spans the 95% fiducial limits of the population. For each phalanx from the A.L. 333-115 foot, the length has been divided by the diameter of the A.L. 333-3 femoral head. Lucy's phalanx is treated as either from the 2nd or 4th toe, and its length is expressed relative to the diameter of her femoral head. The relative lengths of the fossil pedal proximal phalanges are intermediate between those of bonobos and humans. The A.L. 333-115 foot differs from humans, and is allied to apes, in possessing a proximal phalanx from ray II that is shorter than the corresponding bones from rays III and IV.*

The possibility has been raised that, in humans, glenoid orientation is correlated with scapular size; Lucy might have had an orientation completely compatible with that of a very small human. In order to test this possibility we regressed bar-glenoid angle against the craniocaudal length of the glenoid cavity for a sample of 50 modern human scapulae. There occurred a slight trend for smaller scapulae to have more cranially directed glenoids, but the correlation coefficient was a mere 0.29. The predicted value of bar-glenoid angle for a modern human scapula of Lucy's size was 140 degrees (however, Lucy's glenoid length of 22.5 mm is outside the range, 27.0-36.6 mm, of our modern human sample). The value of 130 degrees for A.L. 288-11 is outside the 95% fiducial limits predicted for human specimens of her size. There is no basis for asserting that the cranially directed glenoid of Lucy is a mere reflection of her small size.

At the Berkeley Symposium, reference was made to the existence of a Libben Indian scapula with the same bar-glenoid angle as Lucy's scapula. We are confronted here with how much weight to attach to the existence of such a specimen when interpreting the fossil. We have no knowledge of that particular Indian's life-style (it has been suggested jocularly that he or she may have been the 'designated climber' for the tribe) or the normality of its upper limb use during life. The field of statistics has been developed precisely to enable probabilities to be assigned to comparative statements. Our approach and analysis is scientifically valid and any challenge to it must await estimates of mean glenoid orientation and variability within other human samples [2]. A second point to be made in this context is that it would not negate our conclusions even if a single trait characterizing the fossil were to be found with appreciable frequency within a large sample of modern humans. The true question is whether or not there exists a normal human in-

dividual who possesses the *set of features* characterizing the fossil species (in this case, a single Libben Indian with the combination of hand and scapular morphology described above for Lucy). More will be said on this point in our discussion of the fibulae from Hadar (see below).

Lower Limb

In order to interpret the evolutionary significance of the lower limb fossils from Hadar, Tuttle (1981) refers to his creation of a 'hypothetical hylobatian' ancestor that commonly stood and walked bipedally in the trees. This hypothetical ape, unlike any living ape, possessed hip bones that were not exceptionally long and had a wide sacrum. Like living African apes, it had wide and laterally projected iliac blades, a well-developed hallux, and curved pedal phalanges. Thus, Tuttle came to the following conclusion about the fossils from Ethiopia: "the curved pedal phalanges, robust hallux, strongly developed peroneal muscles, broad sacrum, and shortness and lateral orientation of the iliac blades are quite compatible with the idea that the Hadar hominids were derived rather recently from arboreal bipeds" (1981, p. 92). We cannot treat the notion of an "arboreal bipedal hylobatian ancestor" for the Hadar populations as more than speculation, but we do agree with Tuttle in calling attention to curved pedal phalanges, strong peroneal muscles and a laterally oriented iliac blade as characters indicating adaptation to movement in the trees. The correlation of these traits with arboreality was questioned by Latimer and Lovejoy (cited in Johanson and Edey 1981; and at the Berkeley Symposium).

Stern and Susman (1983a) compared A.L. 333-115 pedal phalanx length to A.L. 333-3 femoral head diameter in order to assess relative length of the toes in the Hadar species. The

Table II. Relative length of proximal pedal phalanx in modern humans and 'Lucy' (A.L. 288-1).

Ratio			Whites (pooled sexes)		Pygmies (pooled sexes)		A.L. 288-1
			ray II	ray IV	ray II	ray IV	
$\dfrac{\text{Phalanx length}}{\text{Femur length}}$ (× 100)		n	18	18	5	5	1
		x̄	6.54	5.59	6.62	5.88	8.07
		SD	0.41	0.42	0.38	0.35	—

————————— 3.73 SD units ————————→

←————————— 5.91 SD units —————————

————————— 3.82 SD units ————————→

←————————— 6.26 SD units —————————

results are presented in Figure 5, which shows the intermediate position of the fossils compared to bonobos and humans. In Stern and Susman (1983a), attention was also drawn to the fact that the 2nd proximal phalanx of the A.L. 333-115 foot is shorter than either the 3rd or 4th. To our knowledge this condition does not occur in humans (Martin and Saller 1959), but typifies apes. We neglected to include a consideration of the one pedal proximal phalanx (A.L. 288-1y) of Lucy in our previous study, but it has been entered into Figure 5 (as either from the 2nd or 4th ray). The length of A.L. 288-1y relative to femoral head diameter is nearly the same as in the A.L. 333 specimens. It is also possible to compare the A.L. 288-1y specimen directly to femoral length (Table II). Such a comparison confirms that, regardless of the ray to which this phalanx is assigned, its relative length is far outside the normal range of variation seen in modern humans, including pygmies. Finally, White and Suwa (1987) have reconstructed Lucy's foot with the result that the relative length of her toes (expressed as a proportion of the length of the foot from the calcaneal tuberosity to the tip of the 3rd metatarsal) is virtually halfway between those of gorillas and those of modern humans, and about 45% - 50% longer than the toes of a scaled-down human.

Although the toes of *A. afarensis* were long compared to modern humans, still they were short compared to living apes. The question arises as to whether or not the Hadar hominids could use them effectively in climbing. One answer may come from a comparison of their length to the fingers of young human children. Comparing the estimates of Lucy's toe length presented by White and Suwa (1987) with radiologic measurements of young children (Garn *et al.* 1972) demonstrates that the small individuals of the fossil species had toes about as long as the fingers of 2-year-old humans. The toes of the larger individuals from Hadar can be estimated to be more than 40% longer than those of Lucy (White and Suwa 1987). Thus, if there were no anatomical restrictions to toe flexion in *A. afarensis*, at the very least the small individuals should have been able to grab with their toes as well as 2-year-old children grab with their fingers. The large Hadar individuals probably could use their toes for simple grasping as effectively as considerably older human children use their fingers. If the pedal flexor musculature of the fossil species were highly developed (as indicated by the robust fibulae) the strength of toe grip may have well exceeded the strength of hand grip in young humans.

Even though the Hadar toe bones are relatively long, if they were also straight this would have to be considered an indication that the Hadar hominids did not use their toes in climbing. Thus,

as with the manual phalanges, we performed an analysis of pedal phalangeal curvature that sought to replace vague assertions with quantification (Stern and Susman 1983a). The method was the same as for finger bones (Fig. 1). We used our own measurements for L and B taken on the original fossils of the A.L. 333-115 foot (they are very close to those published by Latimer *et al.* [1982]). Table III presents the values of H for the relevant fossils. Using the reciprocal of the radius of curvature as our measure, we found that all but the 5th proximal phalanx (A.L. 333-115J) were more curved than in the average bonobo. But again, we neglected to consider a potential relationship between length and curvature. When this is done, the same phenomenon as previously described for the manual proximal phalanges occurs. For apes and woolly monkeys, radius of curvature increases (thus, the bones become straighter) as length increases. The correlations of the regressions of radius on length are lower for the pedal proximal phalanges (ranging from a mere 0.28 in *Pan troglodytes* to 0.70 in gorillas) than we found for manual proximal phalanges. (One cannot perform such a regression for humans since some bones are perfectly straight and thus have infinite radii of curvature.) We again found that the included angle (Θ Fig. 1b) was length-independent for the pedal proximal phalanges, and is the most informative way of comparing species. Figure 6 is a graph of included angle for pedal proximal phalanges from several species of nonhuman primates, humans and the Hadar fossils. This graph shows that chimpanzees and bonobos have pedal proximal phalanges of nearly identical curvature and have the most curved toe bones of any ape plotted in Figure 6. (However, to place matters in perspective, the single specimen of orangutan that we measured was characterized by an average included angle for the lateral 4 pedal proximal phalanges of 84.3 degrees.) Figure 6 also shows that gorilla proximal toe bones are significantly less curved than those of *Pan*, and that human pedal phalanges are nearly straight. The 95% fiducial limits for humans do not overlap those of the African apes. With the exception of the proximal phalanx of the 5th toe, the Hadar fossils lie far outside the human 95% fiducial limits and closest to the means for chimpanzees or bonobos. Stern and Susman (1983a) noted that the proximal phalanx of the 5th toe from Hadar is exceptionally straight, given the curvature of the other toe bones. Figure 6 shows that this particular proximal phalanx lies at the extreme end of the human 95% fiducial limits. Therefore, it does suggest the beginnings of evolution toward the human condition.

Figure 6 also includes data on the proximal pedal phalanx (A.L. 288-1y) from Lucy. Stern and Susman (1983a) neglected

Table III. Values of the parameter 'H' (Fig. 1) for pedal proximal phalanges from Hadar.

Specimen	H, mm
A.L. 288-1y	3.9
A.L. 333-115G	6.5
A.L. 333-115H	5.5
A.L. 333-115I	5.5
A.L. 333-115J	4.4

to analyze this bone, and comments were made at the Berkeley Symposium to the effect that Lucy's toe bone appears straight. In fact, it does not appear so to us (readers may judge for themselves by looking at Fig. 14G in Johanson *et al.* [1982b]), and quantitative analysis demonstrates that it is as curved as the A.L. 333-115 specimens.

Because baboons have proximal phalanges of approximately the same absolute length as those from the A.L. 333-115 foot, we thought a comparison of these highly terrestrial primates to the fossils might be revealing. Indeed, Figure 6 shows that the 3rd pedal proximal phalanges of baboons are relatively straight, and that the corresponding fossil (A.L. 333-115H) is far removed from the baboon distribution. This is not due to a peculiarity of Old World monkeys, since two proximal pedal phalanges from the 3rd ray of the highly arboreal genus *Nasalis* (Hornaday 1929; Davis 1962; Kern 1964; Kawabe and Mano 1972) were characterized by included angles of 32.8 and 35.8 degrees, well within the distributions of African apes.

A suggestion was also made by Latimer at the Berkeley Symposium that the relatively straight toe bones of gibbons

indicate that curvature is not correlated highly with arboreality. In a previous study, Tuttle (1972, p. 173) had said "The phalanges of pedal digits II-V, like those of the hand, are curved ventrally in the Hylobatidae..." Figure 6 shows that Tuttle's visual assessment is more accurate than Latimer's. The fact that the toe bones of *Hylobates* are the least curved of all the apes might suggest some influence of body weight on degree of curvature. On the other hand, woolly monkeys, which are comparable in size to gibbons, have toe bones considerably more curved that those of *Hylobates* (Fig. 6). It may be that during climbing gibbons use their feet in a manner different from other climbing primates, a possibility alluded to by Stern and Susman (1981). Regardless, the inclusion of data on gibbons confirms, not dispels, the link between curvature and arboreality indicated by all other data.

Not only are the Hadar pedal phalanges long and exceptionally curved, but there are other morphological criteria to support our contention that the foot of *A. afarensis* was unlike that of later hominids in both morphology and function. One such morphological feature of *afarensis* that sets it apart from humans is the lack of dorsoplantar expansion at the base of proximal phalanges II-V (A.L. 333-115G-J). Rather, the A.L. 333-115 phalanges reveal a basal morphology similar to that of the apes (Fig. 7). The functional significance of this similarity is appreciated by references to the work of Preuschoft (1970), who has suggested that the unique morphology of the plantar aspect of the base of human pedal proximal phalanges is related to the presence of a well-developed plantar aponeurosis in humans. Preuschoft notes that during the terminal phase of toe-off the 'windlass' of the human foot (Hicks 1953) is driven, tightening the plantar aponeurosis and increasing the dorsoplantar bending moments at the base of the proximal phalanges. Susman (1983) and others (eg. Loth 1908; Sokoloff 1971) have noted that great apes lack a well-developed plantar aponeurosis

Figure 6. *Included angles of pedal proximal phalanges. In parentheses following the name of each sample is the number of phalanges in that sample. The vertical bar indicates the position of the sample mean (the means for the different sexes are indicated by an 'm' for males and an 'f' for females). The solid black rectangle spans the 95% confidence limits for the mean; the horizontal line spans the 95% fiducial limits of the population. Fossils are labelled. The true position of the A.L. 333-115G phalanx is probably further to the left than is plotted, because the fossil has been distorted so as to increase its measured curvature. As judged by the included angle, the curvatures of the Hadar phalanges are most closely allied to those of chimpanzees or bonobos, and, except for A.L. 333-115J, are far removed from the human distribution.*

Figure 7. *Lateral view of proximal pedal phalanges from ray III. Similarities between A.L. 333-115H and the chimpanzee are seen in their curvatures and overall profiles. The pedal proximal phalanx of humans has a thick base relative to a thin distal moiety. A.L. 333-115H shares with humans an excavation of the dorsal aspect of the proximal articular surface.*

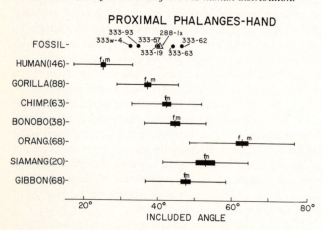

PROXIMAL PHALANGES-HAND

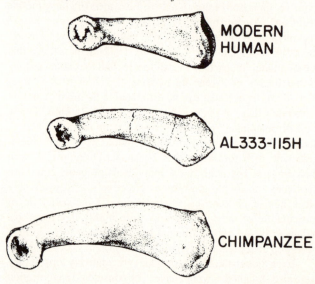

MODERN HUMAN

AL333-115H

CHIMPANZEE

and lack a toe-off mechanism such as occurs in humans. The implication is that the Hadar species had an incompletely developed toe-off mechanism.

A point to be emphasized, however, is that the bases of the A.L. 333-115 pedal proximal phalanges also display a human-like trait wherein they are excavated on their proximo-dorsal margins (seen best in lateral view, Fig. 7). Correlated with this trait is the presence of extended dorsal articular surfaces on the metatarsal heads. Latimer and we are in agreement that these aspects of the structure of the fossil metacarpophalangeal joints are to be interpreted as indicating an enhanced range of dorsiflexion compared to that of apes. We also agree that these traits are indicative of bipedality, since the acme of their expression is seen in human (versus pongid) feet and can be related to the expected dorsiflexion of the toes at the termination of stance phase during bipedal progression.

For Latimer, increased range of dorsiflexion at the metatarsophalangeal joints is inextricably linked to decreased range of plantarflexion. He took exception to our contention that the anatomy of the Hadar foot gives "no reason to deduce that the range of plantarflexion (at the metatarsophalangeal joint) was markedly limited or incompatible with hind-limb prehension" (Stern and Susman 1983a, p. 308). Latimer's consideration of arcs that he visually fit to the heads of the metatarsals, and his manipulation of the fossil metatarsophalangeal joints, led him to assert that flexion was reduced much below what occurs in apes, with the range of motion being the same in the fossil as in modern humans. We dispute the accuracy of Latimer's assessment. First, a similar method of analysis was tried (on a different set of bones) by Napier in 1959, but later abandoned because visually 'fitting' a curve to a joint surface is little more than another form of subjective 'eyeball' assessment. Our eyeball assessment is that the plantar extents of the articular surfaces on the lateral 4 fossil metatarsal heads do not display a reduction that would restrict the range of motion so as to preclude substantial toe flexion. At the present time there is no quantitative measure of toe flexion with which to compare A.L. 333-115, pongids and hominids. Pending the presentation of objective data, and given that inspection of the fossils mitigates against Latimer's assumption, we suggest that there is no particular reason for linking the enhancement of dorsiflexion to the diminution of plantarflexion.

One very important point regarding the determination of the range of dorsi- and plantarflexion at the metatarsophalangeal joints of A.L. 333-115 has been overlooked by Latimer. In animals in which the closed-packed position of a metatarso- or metacarpophalangeal joint is in *flexion*, the plantar aspect of the metatarsal or metacarpal head is wide (medio-lateral dimension) and there is an obvious narrowing of the head near its dorsal margin. This configuration characterizes fingers and toes of all the apes and humans with two notable exceptions: (1) the principal *weight-bearing* fingers of the African 'knuckle-walkers', in whom the metacarpal heads are widest on their dorsal aspect (Susman 1979) and (2) the heads of metatarsals I-IV in humans, which are also widened dorsally. The African apes load their fingers (principally rays III and IV) with the metacarpophalangeal joints in dorsiflexion—this is the closed-packed position—thus the articular surfaces are expanded medio-laterally on their dorsal aspects. Human metatarsal heads I-IV are also expanded dorsally (especially compared to those of apes, Fig. 8) indicating the enhancement of dor-

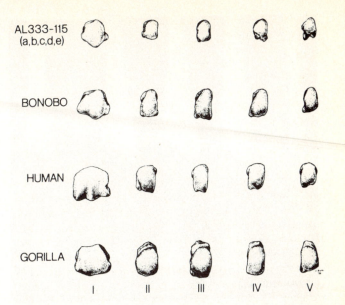

Figure 8. *Distal view of metatarsal heads I-V (from left to right) in A.L. 333-115, bonobo, modern human, and gorilla. Note the narrowing of the dorsal aspects of the metatarsal heads in the apes and in A.L. 333-115. The metatarsal heads in humans, on the other hand, remain medio-laterally broad on their dorsal aspects, a feature which accommodates the close-packing of the metatarsophalangeal joints (especially in rays I-IV) during toe-off.*

siflexion at toe-off and a reduced emphasis on toe flexion in human locomotion. The A.L. 333-115 metatarsals are *not* medio-laterally expanded on their dorsal aspects as are those of humans; rather, they resemble pongids with wide plantar expansions of the metatarsal heads [3] (Fig. 8). This indicates an emphasis on flexion of the toes exceeding that in humans.

Even though *afarensis* walked bipedally on the ground, there is little question that stability of its 1st - 4th (and perhaps 5th) metatarsophalangeal joints at toe-off was less than in later hominids and modern humans. The toes of *afarensis* were undoubtedly more mobile (especially medio-laterally) than those of modern humans, and this ancient hominid had not entirely sacrificed toe flexion, a capability which would have been maintained for arboreal activities.

Tuttle's (1981) assertion that the Hadar species had large peroneal muscles is based on the presence of wide peroneal grooves on the back of the fossil fibulae (Fig. 9; and [Johanson *et al.* 1978, 1982a]). It is not clear why Tuttle considered well-developed peroneal muscles to be a sign of arboreal adaptation since his only functional statement is that, "In apes, the peroneus longus muscle is a powerful flexor of the hallux; and in man, it is an everter of the foot" (1981, p. 91). In fact, we doubt the first part of this assertion. In the course of electromyographic studies of the peroneal muscles in chimpanzees, gibbons, and spider monkeys (Stern and Susman 1983a, b), we routinely stimulated these muscles through indwelling fine wires in order to verify electrode position. In all cases, stimulation of peroneus longus produced an *adduction* of the hallux at the tarsometatarsal joint. In no real sense can the muscle be considered to produce either flexion or opposition; nor is there any electromyographic evidence to indicate that peroneus longus is a flexor of the great toe. When it is active in powerful gripping it may be behaving in a manner analogous to

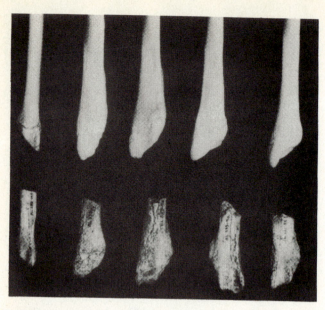

Figure 9. *Posterior view of distal fibulae illustrating the peroneal groove. The top row contains 1 distal fibula of* Pan paniscus *on the left, followed by 4 human fibulae. The human fibula on the right was selected from a sample of 185 as being relatively typical. The other 3 human fibulae were selected because they had the largest peroneal grooves. Although our human sample is comprised of specimens purchased from commercial suppliers (and, therefore, probably represents Indo-Pakistani peoples), we observed no greater development of the peroneal groove among specimens from the sub-Saharan African collection of the American Museum of Natural History. The bottom row contains casts of the Hadar fossils. From left to right they are A.L. 288-1at, A.L. 333w-37, A.L. 333-9b, A.L. 333-9a, and A.L. 333-85. Lucy's fibulae closely resembles that of the bonobo. The larger Hadar fibulae are more similar to modern humans in overall configuration. However, with the exception of A.L. 333w-37 which is damaged, the large fossil fibulae all show very wide peroneal grooves with particularly prominent medial lips.*

the action of the adductor pollicis during powerful gripping by the thumb. Furthermore, it should be pointed out that it is the tendon of the peroneus brevis, not peroneus longus, that actually lies in the groove of the fibula. Therefore, one cannot rule out the possibility that development of the peroneus brevis was as important (or more important) to the Hadar species as that of the peroneus longus. The significance of this point is moot, since our EMG studies on nonhuman primates and humans have revealed that the two muscles are recruited simultaneously during most behaviors.

The EMG studies conducted in our laboratory (Stern and Susman 1983a, b) demonstrated that in nonhuman primates the peroneal muscles were markedly recruited during locomotion on branches, but only sporadically used during locomotion on the ground. In humans, the peroneus brevis and longus are recruited most prominently when weight is transferred across the ball of the foot from the outside towards the inside. We interpret the primary function of these muscles in humans to be that of regulating (or, when necessary, preventing) supination of the forefoot. The peroneus longus does not function in maintenance of the longitudinal arch per se (Jones 1941; Gray 1969); neither is there evidence that flexor digitorum longus or

tibialis posterior, either of which is better suited for arch-support (Harris and Beath 1948; Inman and Mann 1978), are active for this purpose.

One is thus faced with the question of whether the large peroneal muscles of the Hadar species indicate an ape-like role during arboreal locomotion or an enhanced necessity to prevent supination of the forefoot during terrestrial activity. Gomberg and Latimer (1984) demonstrate that *A. afarensis* possessed a navicular and cuboid very similar in morphology to those of a chimpanzee, and conclude that the fossil species was characterized by a wide flat tarsus with more mobility at the transverse tarsal joint than occurs in modern humans. Nonetheless, these authors reject such traits as signs of arboreal adaptation, preferring to suggest (pers. comm.) that the foot was less stable during striding bipedality. Thus, it would seem that they would opt for the view that muscular effort was used to compensate for osseoligamentous inadequacy. At the moment, this question cannot be resolved. However, if the constant effort of large extrinsic muscles were required to control movement within the foot during bipedal walking, this manner of progression would certainly have been different from, and more costly (and possible more fatiguing), than in modern humans.

We agree with Tuttle (1981) that the iliac blades of the Hadar hominids were projected laterally. We attempted to gain some impression of just how laterally by articulating Lucy's innominate with her sacrum in a way that we thought was relatively unaffected by the damage to the bones. The result (Fig. 10) suggests a lateral projection of the iliac blades resembling that of the chimpanzee. Recently Schmid (1983) has reconstructed the A.L. 288-1 rib cage as being chimpanzee-like, and he noted that this is consistent with laterally oriented iliac blades.

We never put forward the orientation pictured in Figure 10 as anything more than approximate. At the Berkeley symposium our approximation was strongly criticized as failing to compensate correctly for the considerable distortion to the A.L. 288-1ao in-nominate. Lovejoy offered his 'restoration' of Lucy's pelvis as the only acceptable indicator of orientation of the iliac blades. A photograph of this reconstruction was published in *Science 81* (April) and has been reproduced (courtesy of D. Brill) as Figure 11. Our perception of this reconstruction is that it portrays the iliac blades of the Hadar species as intermediate in orientation between apes and humans.

Tuttle (1981) did not make it clear whether he believes that laterally projected iliac blades are associated with arboreal locomotion generally or arboreal bipedality specifically. Stern and Susman (1981) related the dorsally directed iliac surface characteristic of apes to the action of the lesser gluteal muscles as medial rotators. This action is called upon in chimpanzees, orangutans and gibbons during bipedalism on horizontal trunks or on the ground; it is also necessary during the propulsive phase of vertical climbing. Therefore, we are of the opinion that the orientation of the iliac blades in the Hadar species is well-suited for a part-time climber and part-time terrestrial biped.

In Stern and Susman (1983a) we identified several other aspects of lower limb structure that suggest adaptation to arboreal locomotion. These include: (1) relatively long maximum moment arm for extension of the hip by the hamstring muscles; (2) articular coverage of the femoral head in A.L. 288-lap similar to that of apes in a way that Jenkins (1972) has interpreted as signifying a greater range of abduction than occurs in

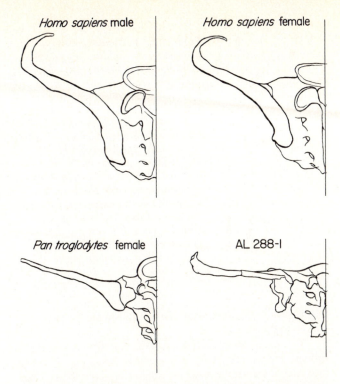

Figure 10. *Cranial view of the iliac crest in articulated pelves. This figure is reproduced from Stern and Susman (1983a). It illustrates the results of our efforts to determine iliac orientation in A.L. 288-1 (a fuller explanation is to be found in the original paper). There has been damage to the fossil and the orientation that is depicted was not claimed to be other than approximate. However, we did emphasize that the true orientation was more likely to have resembled a chimpanzee than a human. Our portrayal of iliac orientation in the fossil has been strongly criticized as failing to compensate adequately for damage to the specimens.*

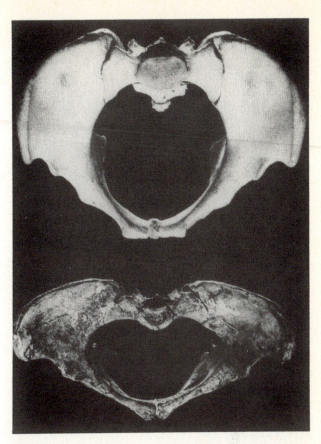

Figure 11. *'Restoration' of the A.L. 288-1 pelvis by Lovejoy, compared to a human pelvis. This figure (photo by D. Brill, copyright 1981) is reproduced from the April issue of Science 81. At the top of the picture is an articulated modern human pelvis. Below is Lovejoy's 'restoration' of the A.L. 288-1 pelvis. It appears to depict an iliac orientation for the fossil that is intermediate between those of humans and apes.*

humans; (3) articular relationships between talus, distal tibia and fibula that indicate an enhanced range of plantarflexion at the ankle joint; (4) a first tarsometatarsal joint exhibiting structural signs of some remaining ability to abduct the hallux. Additionally, we interpreted the absence of marked curvature of that portion of the ischial tuberosity giving origin to the sacrotuberous ligament, the minimal curvature of the sacrum, and the poorly marked upper lateral angles of the sacrum as indicating that the development of sacrotuberous and sacroiliac ligaments was no more than incipient. Criticisms have been leveled at our discussions dealing with some of these traits.

It has been said that had we seen the original specimen of Lucy's femoral head we would not have drawn the articular margin as we did. We interpreted a small smooth prominence at the anterosuperior corner of the femoral head (see Fig. 11c in [Johanson *et al.* 1982b]) as being nonarticular, whereas Lovejoy believes it is a proper part of the intracapsular articular surface. We hope to inspect the original fossils ourselves in order to resolve this difference of opinion.

Lovejoy proceeded to say that the position of the fovea capitis of the femur is a good indicator of motion at the hip, and that the fovea is medially directed in the Hadar fossils (A.L. 288-lap and A.L. 333-3), indicating permanent adduction of the thigh as in humans. To our eyes (Fig. 12), the fovea of the large A.L. 333-3 specimen does not seem so medially directed, but since neither Lovejoy nor we have done a quantitative study comparable to that of Jenkins and Camazine (1977), all such statements are of little persuasion. Such a study is presently being undertaken (Kapp, pers. commun.) and, among other things, confirms the visual impression (Fig. 12) that the fovea capitis of gorillas has a similar orientation in the coronal plane to that of humans. We begin to doubt that among primates there is a sufficiently close relationship between foveal position and range of movement to support Lovejoy's assertion that the Hadar hominids did not have a greater range of abduction at the hip than do modern humans.

We again have been challenged for attempting to judge the degree of plantarflexion at the ankle by considering the articular relationships between the talus and fibula. When a fibula with an obliquely disposed proximal border of the distal articular facet is articulated with a talus, one gains the impression that upon full plantar flexion the long axis of the fibula will be brought more into line with the foot than can occur in humans (Fig. 10 and 14 in [Stern and Susman 1983a]). Of course, we did note that the posterior inclination of distal articular surface

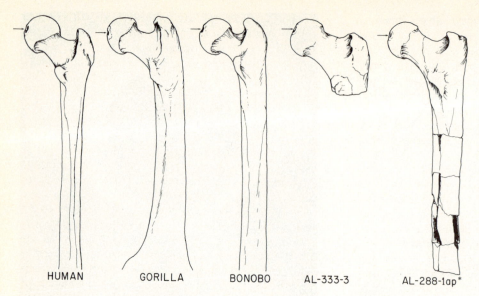

Figure 12. *Posterior view of proximal femora illustrating position of fovea capitis. The arrows point to the foveae capitis femoris. This pit faces more medially in humans than in bonobos (and most other nonhuman primates). The position of the A.L. 333-3 fovea compared to humans and apes is debatable. The fovea of A.L. 288-1ap faces relatively medially, but so does that of gorillas. The significance of foveal position for deducing mobility at the hip among primates is unclear. Further study will be required to quantify foveal position in primates and to assess what, if anything, it tells us about the range of thigh abduction in the Hadar species. * = reversed to facilitate comparison.*

HUMAN   GORILLA   BONOBO   AL-333-3   AL-288-1ap*

of Lucy's tibia also pointed to a plantarflexion 'set' at the ankle, and we admitted to misgivings about the fact that the large tibiae (A.L. 333-6, -7) seem to be giving a different message about this phenomenon than do the fibulae. This apparent contradiction would be partially resolved if the fibula in the large Hadar specimens was more obliquely disposed relative to the tibia (in a sagittal plane) than typifies modern humans. Such a condition would occur if as in apes, the Hadar tibia was relatively short and/or retroflexed.

At the Berkeley Symposium, Latimer claimed that not only is the talo-fibular articulation a poor choice to gauge range of motion at the ankle joint, but that articulation of the talus and tibia shows humans to have a slightly greater range of plantarflexion at the ankle than do African apes. Latimer also produced an X-ray of a human in full plantarflexion demonstrating the same angle between the long axis of the talus and that of the fibula as in our drawing of Lucy (Fig. 14 in Stern and Susman 1983a).

We do not in any way accept Latimer's arguments. First, when we articulate the talus and tibia of apes we are able to get a greater degree of plantarflexion than when the same two bones are articulated in humans. Second, we never stated, nor ever would state, that the maximum degree of plantarflexion obtained by articulating dry bones is equal in absolute value to that occurring in life. Our only contention was that differences between species as judged by dry bones ought to be in the same direction as those that occur in life. It is completely irrelevant to compare an X-ray of a living human to our drawing of Lucy's ankle. The only comparison that can have bearing on our conclusions is one between the maximally plantarflexed ankles of living humans and living apes. Thus, two of us (R.L.S. and J.T.S.) underwent cinefluography of our ankles during plantarflexion [4] and had conventional X-ray films taken of our ankles manipulated into maximum plantarflexion. The results were compared to X-rays of the ankle of a chimpanzee that had been anesthetized and manipulated into maximum plantarflexion. Figure 13 illustrates that the maximum amount of plantarflexion at the talocrural joint is considerably greater in a chimpanzee than in a human. We have not been able to locate a published X-ray of a human foot (even in ballet dancers or in the condition of pes equinus (Montagne *et al.* 1980) showing

the degree of talocrural plantarflexion illustrated for the chimpanzee in Figure 13.

We are not impressed by the claim that there exist Libben Indians characterized by a somewhat obliquely disposed proximal border of the distal articular facet of the fibula. Once again we emphasize that we do not base our functional assessment on any single trait but rather a set of functionally related features. As stated in Stern and Susman (1983a, p. 305): "For each of the four isolated traits we have considered, one of the

Figure 13. *Radiographs of the ankle in maximum plantarflexion. For both the human and chimpanzee, maximum plantarflexion was brought about by external manipulation of the foot. The talus of the chimpanzee could be brought into virtual alignment with the long axis of the tibia, whereas such a degree of plantarflexion was not possible in our 2 human subjects, nor have we been able to locate published X-rays of humans that show a range of plantarflexion comparable to that in the chimpanzee illustrated.*

MAXIMUM PLANTARFLEXION

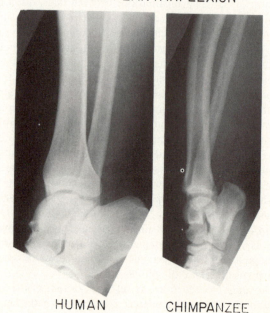

HUMAN   CHIMPANZEE

larger Hadar specimens may fall within the human range, or conversely, a particular human may fall within the Hadar range." However, our comparison of the fossils to a sample of 185 modern human fibulae led us to conclude: "the Hadar sample of fibulae almost certainly comes from a population that possessed a more obliquely disposed proximal border of the distal facet, a greater downward inclination of the same facet, a more anteriorly directed subcutaneous surface, and more powerful peroneal muscles than typify modern humans". This conclusion has not been challenged.

The issue of hallucial abduction in the Hadar hominids received its initial impetus from the description of the A.L. 333-28 medial cuneiform as possessing a "reniform facet for the first metatarsal [that] is markedly convex", (Latimer *et al.* 1982, p. 704). Since the only primates which possess a convex first tarsometatarsal joint are those with abductible great toes, this description by Latimer and co-workers leads ineluctably to the conclusion that *A. afarensis*, likewise, had a divergent great toe. Since this published description, Latimer has revised his appraisal of the shape of the *afarensis* hallucial tarsometatarsal joint, and it is most recently described (at the Berkeley Symposium) as 'very flat' and indicating no ability to abduct the hallux. To bolster his argument that the big toe was not abductible, Latimer claimed that the Hadar medial cuneiform shows a bump for a secondary insertion of peroneus longus. We do not dispute the presence of a tubercle on the plantar surface of this bone, but we do call attention to Sarrafian's (1983, p. 69) identification of this tubercle in humans as the site of attachment of an intertarsal ligament and not the insertion of peroneus longus.

If the hallucial tarsometatarsal joint of the Hadar species were 'very flat' it would then bear a morphological resemblance to later hominids (including Olduvai Hominid 8). The functional implication would also be clear, since a flat hallucial tarsometatarsal joint signals a more stable, plantigrade and 'bipedal' foot (for a fuller explanation see Susman 1983). Our judgement is that the curvature of the distal articular facet of A.L. 333-28 is intermediate in degree between that of a typical chimpanzee and a typical human, though within the human range. We draw attention to the fact that White and Suwa (1987) comment on the 'anteromedial' deviation of the big toe impression of the Laetoli footprints.

No universally agreed upon answer to the question of abductibility of the hallux in the Hadar species is forthcoming. However, Latimer's statement that an abductible big toe is needed in order to climb is unsupportable. Indeed, how incorrect is the assertion that a well-developed hallux is necessary for climbing has been known at least since the early nineteenth century from observations of both orangutans and their anatomy (Abel 1819). This quintessential arboreal great ape possesses a diminutive hallux (Midlo 1934). In Midlo's metric comparisons orangutans are characterized as having the shortest great toe among the Hominoidea. One might argue that the orangutan is a poor choice for comparison with *A. afarensis* due to the fact that orangutans use their long curved lateral toes for grasping branches, twigs and foliage while climbing. While *A. afarensis* had very curved toes, they were not either absolutely or relatively as long as the toes of orangutans. But we do not argue that *afarensis* climbed like an orangutan. Rather, we suggest that these early hominids climbed vertical trunks with their forefoot (and at times midfoot also) applied to the surface,

and that on the smaller supports, while they grasped with their toes, they emphasized use of their powerful hands. The sort of foot postures we envision for afarensis during vertical climbing are those common to all primates when they are on large trunks, viz. the foot is applied to the surface and the hallux is not necessarily opposed to the lateral toes. In the small branch setting the opposability of the great toe may be more crucial, but an abductible hallux is by no means a sine qua non of arboreality.

For further insight into this problem we can also look at arboreal primates which lack opposability of the thumb but are still adept in the trees. Ateline monkeys and African colobines are skillful climbers (of large trunks and small branches) while lacking opposable thumbs (Mittermeier and Fleagle 1976). Overall, while the overemphasis on any one living model in this regard is to be avoided, the above serves to illustrate that one need not possess either an opposable thumb or great toe to maintain skill as an arborealist. Moreover, the derived aspects of the hip and knee in the Hadar hominids and a number of derived features in the foot lead one to expect a mode and frequency of climbing and arborealism not precisely represented in extant pongids or other primates.

Other evidence on the morphology of the hallux comes from the A.L. 333-115 partial foot skeleton. In this specimen the hallux retains a primitive pongid-like metatarsophalangeal joint. The pongid-like character of the first metatarsal head in A.L. 333-115 is clearly seen in distal (Fig. 8) and dorsal (Fig. 14) views: the distal articular surface of A.L. 333-115A is convex mediolaterally. This is unlike the condition in humans wherein the metatarsal is flat on its distal surface and the hallucial metatarsophalangeal joint has an enlarged area of articulation, especially in dorsiflexion. Pongids, on the other hand, have a concavo-convex articulation and reduced stability in the hallucial metatarsophalangeal joint. This is the joint that in humans is intimately involved in toe-off, and the broad flat articular surfaces in humans reflect a joint that is very stable mediolaterally at the end of stance phase before toe-off. The same joint in A.L. 333-115 does not indicate a similar sort of stability but rather mimics the more mobile hallucial metatarsophalangeal joint in the African apes. Thus, here again, we see a morphology in A.L. 333-115 that is functionally nonhuman in terms of the kinematics of terminal stance and toe-off.

Criticism of our comments about the sacrotuberous and sacroiliac ligaments took the form of an assertion that Lucy's ischium shows a distinct rugosity for the sacrotuberous ligament. It was further stated that it would indeed be peculiar if Lucy did not have a well-developed sacrotuberous ligament since all great apes and humans do. The implication was that the existence of this ligament is a shared derived feature of the hominoid lineage. We take issue with all these remarks. First, we note that the 'rugosity' on Lucy's ischium (which we did not observe on the cast) was not considered significant enough to merit mention in the detailed description of the A.L. 288-1ao innominate presented by Johanson *et al.* (1982b). Second, Stern (1972) has shown that a well-developed sacrotuberous ligament is not characteristic of all great apes, such a structure being very weak, or even absent, in orangutans. Finally, there is not even justification on morphologic grounds for asserting that the sacrotuberous ligament in African apes is homologous to that in humans. That the sacrotuberous ligament of humans was newly acquired in our lineage subsequent to its divergence from

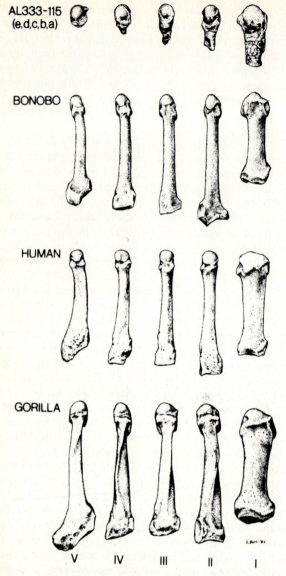

AL333-115
(e,d,c,b,a)

BONOBO

HUMAN

GORILLA

V   IV   III   II   I

Figure 14. *Dorsal view of metatarsal heads I-V (from right to left) in A.L. 333-115, bonobo, modern human, and gorilla. The metatarsal head of ray I in humans is unique among hominoids in having a relatively flat contour from side to side, while in apes and A.L. 333-115 the same surface is highly convex. The condition in apes reflects enhanced mobility of the great toe in arboreal primates; such mobility is inferred for A.L. 333-115.*

the African apes is as likely as any other evolutionary history for this structure (Stern 1971).

Conclusion

In the preceding paragraphs we have summarized the evidence presented previously by Jungers (1982), Stern and Susman (1983a), and Jungers and Stern (1983) on anatomic structures indicating adaptations for arboreal locomotion in the Hadar species. To this evidence must be added that provided by other researchers cited in the 'Introduction' (see above). Our subsequent analyses have strengthened the conclusion that the Hadar hominids spent significant time in the trees. None of the

criticisms that were verbalized at the symposium seem to us to be of great substance.

ANATOMIC TRAITS INDICATING A UNIQUE MANNER OF BIPEDAL PROGRESSION IN THE HADAR HOMINIDS

The relative length of Lucy's limbs, discussed above in the context of adaptations for arboreality, also has implications for the manner in which the Hadar hominids practiced bipedalism. Femur length in Lucy was absolutely and relatively shorter than in any modern human. Compared to extant hominoids of comparable body mass, hindlimb proportions in A.L. 288-1 are found to be most similar to those of bonobos (Jungers 1982; Jungers and Stern 1983). Employing *total pelvic height* (TPH) as a substitute variable for body mass (because it is highly correlated and isometric with body mass in *H. sapiens*), relative femur length in Lucy is found to be shorter than in any modern human, pygmy or otherwise (Table IV) [5]. A relatively short hindlimb probably also characterized the large Hadar individuals (assuming that they are conspecific with Lucy) and *A. africanus* (as judged by STS 14). Unless angular excursion of the hindlimb was greatly exaggerated in these ancient hominids (contrary to the evidence of reduced excursion discussed below), the short hindlimb implies a short stride length. This fact has several implications for the nature of bipedality practiced by the Hadar species. The short stride length "forces a higher cadence (steps per unit time) to reach the same velocity; a greater number of steps would be needed to move the same distance" (Jungers and Stern 1983, p. 681). This means that the muscles necessary to accelerate and decelerate the limbs and center of mass at each step would have been turned on and off more frequently at any given speed or over any given distance. Stride frequency, therefore, can be seen as one of the limiting factors in overall cost of terrestrial locomotion, i.e. cost increases in proportion to the number of strides taken (Heglund *et al.* 1974, 1982). Hindlimb elongation in later stages of human evolution could provide an energetic advantage to a full-time terrestrial biped (Rodman and McHenry 1980; Steudel and Myers 1984). A significant benefit of mass redistribution and hindlimb elongation might also accrue to a dedicated biped with respect to increased maximum speed of locomotion.

In 1973 Zuckerman *et al.* (1973) published a discriminant function analysis of the innominate of primates and the STS 14 hip bone representing S. African *Australopithecus africanus*. Finding that the fossil was similar to humans with regard to characters relating to transmission of weight from the trunk to the lower limbs, but that it approached non-human primates with regard to muscular disposition, the authors concluded (p. 72): "If *Australopithecus* had been habitually or occasionally bipedal, its weight would have been carried more efficiently than in any subhuman primate. But any bipedalism must, because of the almost certain lack of any powerful source of abduction at the hip, have been quite different from that typical of *Homo sapiens*." Our analysis of the geologically older Hadar lower limb bones, though using different methodology, gave virtually the same result.

In Stern and Susman (1983a) we explained how the reduced iliac height, posterior displacement of the sacral articular surface, anterior placement of the 'iliac pillar,' and valgus knee are traits that indicate some level of adaptation to terrestrial

Table IV. Relative length of humerus and femur in modern humans and 'Lucy' (A.L.288-1).

Ratio		Male whites	Female whites	Pygmies (pooled sexes)	A.L. 288-1
Humerus length	n	9	9	20	1
Total pelvic height	x̄	1.50	1.53	1.59	1.51
	SD	0.03	0.03	0.06	—
				←———— 0.33 SD units ————→	
			←———— 0.67 SD units ————→		
			←———— 1.33 SD units ————→		
Femur length	n	9	9	20	1
Total pelvic height	x̄	2.10	2.15	2.16	1.77
	SD	0.08	0.06	0.09	—
				←———— 4.13 SD units ————→	
			←———— 6.33 SD units ————→		
			←———— 4.33 SD units ————→		

bipedality, but not kinematic and kinetic identity to modern humans. The first three of these traits make it easier to balance the trunk upon the femoral heads. They are joined in promoting this goal by the reduction in size of the upper limb (Preuschoft 1978; Zihlman and Brunker 1979; Jungers and Stern 1983). The valgus knee enables placement of the foot more directly beneath the center of gravity of the body, permitting a longer time for executing the swing phase of the opposite limb.

Three traits that other authors have viewed as more specifically indicating a human-like gait are: (1) the presence of an iliopsoas groove; (2) osteologic signs of a well-developed iliofemoral ligament, and (3) an obturator externus groove. We found none of these in the A.L. 288-1 innominate or femur. The A.L. 333-3 femur has a clearly defined intertrochanteric line, presumably for attachment of the iliofemoral ligament, but Lovejoy's (1975) statement that such a marking is not related to tension in the ligament during life but is age-related, caused us to question its functional significance. At the Berkeley Symposium, Lovejoy presented his view that Lucy's ilium shows a distinct rugose area for origin of the iliofemoral ligament. This point remains in dispute. Regardless, the actual functional significance of an iliofemoral ligament for locomotion, as opposed to posture, is equally debatable.

In Stern and Susman (1983a) we argued that a deep femoral patellar groove with a prominent lateral lip need not be diagnostic of a fully extended knee, since the patella does not sit in this groove unless the knee is partly flexed. Additionally, we showed (as did Tardieu 1979, 1983) that femoral condylar shape in the Hadar fossils was not all that similar to modern humans. In the large specimens particularly, the lateral lip of the patellar groove is poorly developed. Although we analyzed shape of the patellar groove in several ways (Stern and Susman 1983a), one simple method of demonstrating the disparity between the large Hadar and Human knees is to compare condylar length ratios. Table V shows that in modern humans the lateral femoral condyle is longer than its medial counterpart. This is due primarily to development of the lateral lip of the patellar groove. The large A.L. 333-4 distal femur is far removed from the human condition by having a medial condyle that is longer than the lateral. With regard to condylar length ratio (and other measures of the patellar groove), the small A.L. 129-1a distal femur is more similar to that of modern humans than are the large Hadar specimens.

Our analysis of the femoral condyles was conducted in a manner compatible with guidelines laid down by Heiple and Lovejoy (1971), but this has been criticized as incorrect. Instead, Lovejoy now asserts that one should identify a line passing through the meniscal impressions on the distal surfaces of the medial and lateral femoral condyles, and then measure the heights of the patellar groove lips relative to this line. Having not heard a complete argument for acceptance of this new technique, nor having attempted to duplicate it on a series of extant and fossil primates, we will delay comment on its value. However, it does seem that if one makes the Hadar fossils more similar to humans with regard to height of patellar lips by virtue of using the intermeniscal line as a reference, then one must at the same time make the fossils more different from humans with regard to the lengths of those parts of the femoral condyles that actually articulate with the tibia. This would lead to the expectation of considerable conjunct rotation at the knee.

Like Zuckerman et al., (1973), we emphasized orientation of the iliac blades in attempting to determine the manner of terrestrial bipedalism. As mentioned above, Tuttle (1981) noted the lateral orientation of the iliac blades from Hadar, but he stated (p. 92) "whether a human pelvic tilt mechanism or lateral flexion and rotation of the spine was predominant during bipedal walking remains to be established". We concluded,

Table V. Condylar length ratio[1] of femur.

Specimens	Ratio
Human	
Authors' sample (n = 40)	1.062 (SD = 0.026)
Halaczek (1972) (n = 21)	1.077 (range = 1.03–1.18)
A.L. 129-1a	
Johanson and Coppens (1976)	1.005[2]
Authors' measurements	1.035 (on cast)
A.L. 333-4	
Lovejoy et al. (1982)	0.971[3] (reconstructed estimate)
Lovejoy et al. (1982)	0.947[3] (actual measurment)
Authors' measurements	0.954[3] (on cast)

[1]Ratio of anteroposterior length of lateral femoral condyle to anteroposterior length of medial femoral condyle.

[2]Significantly different from human, p<0.02 (one-tailed t-test).

[3]Significantly different from human, p<0.001 (one-tailed t-test).

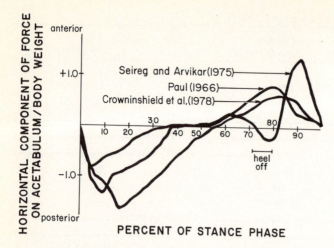

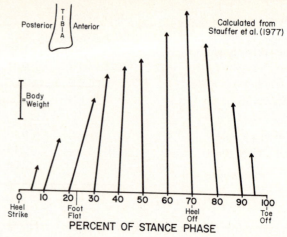

Figure 15. *Horizontal component of the hip-joint force during the stance phase of human walking. The data used to compose this graph were derived from 3 different sources, labelled on the figure. The abscissa represents the stance phase of human walking from heel-strike (0) to toe-off (100). A deviation of the plotted line above the abscissa represents a force on the acetabulum directed anteriorly. The magnitude of this force is expressed as a fraction of body weight (ordinate). Anteriorly directed forces of substantial magnitude occur at (or after) heel-off when the limb is extended behind the hip-joint. Although the vertical component of the hip-joint force (not plotted) is much larger than the horizontal component, the existence of a substantial anteriorly directed horizontal component near the termination of stance phase suggests to us that it is during this period of the human gait cycle that the ventral horn of the acetabulum is most stressed.*

Figure 16. *Force exerted on the tibia by the talus during the stance phase of human walking. The data used to compose this graph were derived from Stauffer et al. (1977). The abscissa represents the stance phase of human walking from heel-strike (0) to toe-off (100). The length of the vector indicates the magnitude (scaled to body weight) of the ankle joint reaction force. When the vector inclines upward and to the right, the force on the distal articular surface of the tibia is directed anterior to the shaft of the tibia. When the vector inclines upward and to the left, the force is directed posterior to the tibial shaft. An anterior inclination of the distal articular surface of the tibia is thought to be an indicator of the ability to resist forces directed posterior to the tibial shaft. Such forces arise in the latter part of stance phase, when the limb is extended behind the hip. The fact that Lucy's distal tibial articular surface does not incline anteriorly suggests to us that during bipedal walking her lower limb may not have extended behind the hip to the degree observed in humans.*

based on the results of an earlier EMG study (Stern and Susman 1981), that the orientation of the iliac blades in the Hadar species meant that the lesser gluteal muscles were better suited to balancing the trunk on the femoral heads by acting as medial rotators on a partly flexed thigh than by acting as abductors on a completely extended lower limb.

If the lower limb of the Hadar species were not as extended as the human lower limb during terrestrial bipedalism, then the forces transmitted through the joints of the lower limb ought to have different directions and magnitudes. For one thing, if the lower limb yields at the hip or knee upon the onset of stance phase, the force transmitted through the sacro-iliac articulation will be modulated. Such being the case, the need for sacro-iliac stabilization (see Weisl 1955) would be reduced, and ligaments that serve this function might be less developed than in modern humans. Evidence for less-developed sacrotuberous and sacro-iliac ligaments in Lucy has been summarized above.

The complete extension of the human limb at the end of stance phase of bipedalism is associated with a horizontal component of the hip joint force tending to push the femoral head against the anterior horn of the acetabular surface (Fig. 15). At the same time, the force transmitted by the talus to the tibia passes posterior to the long axis of the tibial shaft (Fig. 16) and is resisted by the anterior inclination of the distal articular surface of the tibia. In Stern and Susman (1983a) we demonstrated that the anterior horn of the acetabulum of Lucy is diminutive, causing her to have an acetabular shape that is 4.5 SD units away from the mean of a sample of 98 modern humans, and similar to what is found in male gorillas. We also

showed that the distal articular surface of Lucy's tibia (while resembling humans in that its lateral segment is inferiorly, rather than inferolaterally, directed) has a posterior inclination comparable to that of apes (Table VI) and is, therefore, poorly suited for transmission of forces that occur in human bipedalism. The issue is greatly complicated by the very great similarity of the larger tibiae from Hadar to those of modern humans (Tab. VI).

There are three calcaneal fragments from Hadar: A.L. 333-8, A.L. 333-37 and A.L. 333-55. Of the first, Latimer *et al.* (1982, p. 701) state: "The lateral process [of the tuberosity] is indistinct. In its place a bony ridge runs obliquely across the lateral surface of the calcaneal body, ending in the massive peroneal tubercle." Of the second they say (p. 702), "On the plantar surface... the lateral tuberosity is relatively indistinct. The lateral surface erosion has removed all evidence of the peroneal trochlea." Of the third calcaneal fragment, it is claimed (p. 702): "In lateral aspect the dominant feature is the massive peroneal trochlea... An inflated ridge of bone courses backward and inferiorly to the small lateral process of the calcaneal tuberosity." At the Berkeley Symposium, however, Latimer stated that "In fact close inspection of the Hadar calcanei will disclose a lateral plantar process as well as a large peroneal trochlea." The lateral plantar process was thus represented as

Table VI. Anteroposterior tilt of distal articular surface of tibia.

Specimens	Tilt[1] (degrees)
Human European (n = 50)	+7.9 (SD = 3.5)
Human Bushman (n = 8)	+7.8 (SD = 3.9)
Gorilla (n = 10)	-4.3 (SD = 1.4)
Chimpanzee (n = 12)	-2.2 (SD = 2.8)
Orangutan (n = 8)	-2.7 (SD = 0.9)
A.L. 288-1ar	-5[2]
A.L. 333-6	+5

[1] + = Anteriorly directed. - = posteriorly directed; data on extant genera from Davis (1964).

[2] Significantly different from human, p < 0.001 (one-tailed t-test)

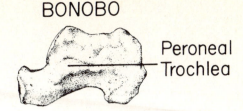

BONOBO — Peroneal Trochlea

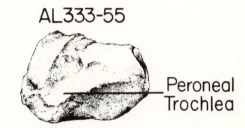

AL333-55 — Peroneal Trochlea

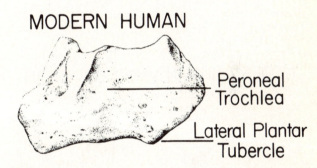

MODERN HUMAN — Peroneal Trochlea / Lateral Plantar Tubercle

Figure 17. *Lateral view of the calcaneus. Note the well-developed peroneal trochlea in the bonobo and in A.L. 333-55. Humans lack such a distinctive peroneal trochlea. Note also the lateral plantar tubercle in the human; in this view, what appear to be corresponding prominences in the ape and the fossil actually are the* medial *plantar tubercles.*

more well expressed than it was earlier (Latimer *et al.* 1982). This, as the original published description suggested, is not so. One thing is agreed by all on both sides of the question, the Hadar calcanei display a prominent peroneal trochlea—'massive' as described by Latimer and co-workers (Fig. 17).

We stated (Stern and Susman 1983a; and at the Berkeley Symposium) that the presence of a large peroneal trochlea and a diminutive lateral plantar tubercle were primitive traits reflecting the 'non-modern-human' aspect of the *A. afarensis* hindfoot. We noted that the large peroneal trochlea of *afarensis* was correlated with the large peroneal groove on the fibula, and that these indicated the existence of pongid-like peroneal muscles. Concomitantly, the small lateral plantar tubercle also imparts a primitive aspect to the Hadar calcanei. Humans, both fossil and living, possess well-developed lateral plantar tubercles; apes do not display a lateral plantar tubercle (Fig. 18). We made an additional point (Stern and Susman 1983a; and at the Berkeley Symposium) that there seemed to be an inverse relationship between the peroneal trochlea and the lateral plantar tubercle in all of the Hominoidea, and that this idea was not new, a similar suggestion having been proposed by Weidenreich (1940). At the Berkeley Symposium Latimer expressed the view that "It is curious and difficult to imagine how one bony prominence on the lateral side of the calcaneus associated with the musculature of the leg could migrate inferiorly and become associated with the plantar musculature of the foot." Thus, we were gratified to discover the recent article by Lewis (1983) who also postulated the origin of the lateral plantar tubercle of humans from the peroneal trochlea of an ancestral form, and pointed out that, in addition to Weidenreich (1940), Laidlaw (1904, 1905) had come to the same conclusion. The lateral plantar process (or external plantar tubercle as it was referred to by Laidlaw) is thought to come from the peroneal trochlea as the need in bipeds for a broader plantar base develops, concomitant with the elaboration of both the plantar aponeurosis and the abductor digiti minimi, and with the evolution of quadratus plantae into a two-part muscle.

For the purpose of additional clarification, we would like to point out that in humans there is a prominent fibrous bridge along the ridge that runs from the lateral plantar process to the peroneal trochlea. This is not simply a "diffuse fascial origin of abductor digiti minimi..." (Latimer, Berkeley Symposium). Moreover, the abductor digiti minimi does not shift its action from an abductor of the 5th toe in apes to a supporter of the arch

in humans as stated by Latimer (Berkeley Symposium). Our EMG data do not support the notion of the abductor digiti minimi as an arch supporter (Reeser *et al.* 1983), and neither is there any theoretical reason to expect a muscular tie for the arch on the lateral side of the foot where the arch is at its lowest point. The one candidate for arch support among the intrinsic foot muscles is abductor hallucis, which may provide some rheological support to the medial longitudinal arch (Reeser *et al.* 1983). This latter possibility can easily be demonstrated in dissecting room cadavers by transecting the abductor hallucis and noting the flattening effect on the medial longitudinal arch.

We mentioned above how the metatarsophalangeal joints of the A.L. 333-115 foot indicate less stability in dorsiflexion than is found in modern humans. The relatively long toes of the Hadar hominids also have implications for assessing their

BONOBO

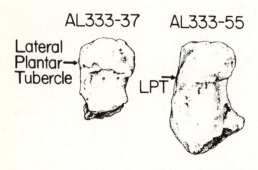

AL333-37   AL333-55

Lateral
Plantar →
Tubercle

LPT →

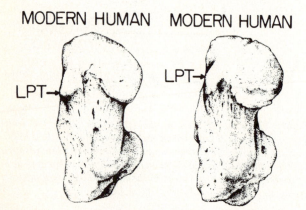

MODERN HUMAN   MODERN HUMAN

LPT →

LPT →

Figure 18. *Plantar view of the calcaneus. The fossil calcanei display broad bodies similar to humans and unlike the narrow body of the ape calcaneus. However, the fossils also display a poorly developed to nonexistent lateral plantar tubercle, and thus, in this regard, more closely resemble the condition seen in apes.*

precise manner of bipedality. It has been argued elsewhere (Jungers and Stern 1983) that *A. afarensis* was characterized by a relatively high ratio of total foot length to hindlimb length. Such proportions would affect both speed and kinematic details of walking. White and Suwa (1987; also see Suwa 1984) reconstructed total foot length in A.L. 288-1 to be 161 mm using a 'reduced' version of the O.H. 8 (*H. habilis*) tarsometatarsus. Based on the highly correlated relationship between 'subtalar length' (from heel to the most distal point on the head of metatarsal II, in this case) and talus length documented by these workers for all hominoids, we regard the 161 mm value to be too conservative. An adult female bonobo (AMNH 86857) with a talus the same length as A.L. 288-1 possesses a subtalar length of 127 mm, approximately 6.5 mm longer than the value

derived for Lucy from the O.H. 8 foot. Adding this 6.5 mm to the length reconstructed by White and Suwa, a better estimate of foot length in Lucy would be 167-168 mm. Other dimensions of the talus of AMNH 86857 are actually smaller than in Lucy (e.g. breadth of the trochlear surface, width of the talar head). Accordingly, a value of 168 mm may itself be too conservative an estimate for A.L. 288-1 total skeletal foot length. Regardless, using a value of 168 mm, the ratio of foot length to femur length for this fossil (0.60) would be outside the normal range of variation in modern humans.

Compared to modern humans of comparably small body size (i.e., pygmies), Lucy's foot is relatively very long. An *inter*populational regression of skeletal foot length on femur length for a sample of modern humans comprised of both pygmies and material derived from American cadavers (Cleveland Museum of Natural History) predicts a foot length for Lucy (based on her 280-mm-long femur) of 125 mm. Our reconstructed value of 168 mm is 34% *longer* than this prediction. Because the predicted value of 125 mm is based on extrapolation of the regression to femur lengths below that found in the original data base, it assumes that the vector slope and length are independent. To circumvent this problem, we can inquire about the femur length of Lucy compared to that of a human pygmy with an absolutely shorter foot. An Akka female (Flower 1888) with a skeletal foot length of 158 mm has a femur that is 334 mm long; Lucy's femur is 280 mm long. Foot-length to femur-length ratios are 0.47 and 0.60, respectively. In this respect, Lucy is more similar to human children (Anderson *et al.* 1956, 1964) than to human adults of small body size.

It is especially significant that the extra length of Lucy's foot seems to be concentrated in the *forefoot*, specifically the toes (White and Suwa 1987; Suwa 1984). Since the toes of children (and also adults) just clear the substrate during the swing phase of walking, longer forefeet result in larger vertical excursions, velocities and accelerations of the more proximal joints and limb segments (Foley *et al.* 1979). This gives the impression of a high-stepping gait described as a more jerky, less flowing' and 'less efficient' mode of walking (Foley *et al.* 1979). At the very least, even if all other aspects of Lucy's gait were essentially modern (and we strongly doubt that they were), one might expect this kinematic similarity to human children (Jungers and Stern 1983). In addition, the ratio of forefoot length to leg length has been isolated on independent biomechanical criteria as an important factor in determining the maximum speed of walking: the higher the ratio, the greater the effect on swing phase duration and the lower the maximum speed (Mochon and McMahon 1980). Again, compared to modern humans, especially those of similar size, the maximum velocity of gait in Lucy was probably lower and the overall energetic costs were substantially greater.

Finally, Stern and Susman (1983a) drew upon the evidence of the Laetoli footprints to support a view that, in walking, the duration and distribution of force on the medial part of the foot were different than in modern humans. M.D. Leakey (1981) had noted that the ball of the foot is not very prominent in the small prints comprising the G1 trail. None of the footprint contours illustrated by Day and Wickens (1980) (Fig. 19) show the medial 'swelling' at the base of the big toe which is so characteristic of all human footprints (both juvenile and adult) that we have observed [6]. Our own examination of the casts of the Laetoli footprints left us with the impression that they were not

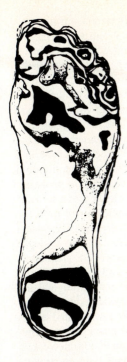

Figure 19. *Contour maps of the Laetoli footprints compared to a human footprint (from Day and Wickens 1980, except that the human footprint at the left and the Laetoli footprint at the right have been reversed for ease of comparison to the Laetoli footprint in the middle; used with permission of Macmillan Journals Limited). The figure shows that the Laetoli prints analyzed by Day and Wickens lack the characteristically human medial swelling produced by the ball of the foot at the level of the hallux. Although such a difference between the Laetoli footprints and those of humans indicates a corresponding difference in the mechanism of weight transfer during bipedalism, White and Suwa (1987) state that Day and Wickens may not have chosen the best preserved Laetoli prints for their analysis.*

markedly similar to footprints of humans. We even mentioned the possibility that the lateral toes may have been partly curled.

White and Suwa (in press) draw attention to the fact that many of the Laetoli footprints have been improperly excavated, and persons unfamiliar with the technique used for each print might easily be led astray by artifactual morphology. Such information is disconcerting because it greatly reduces the scientific value of many of the Laetoli prints as evidence for anything other than demonstrating that the animal which made them was walking bipedally at the time. We certainly have much reduced faith in our conclusions about these footprints, and are forced to rely more heavily on the evidence of the fossils from Hadar.

Conclusions

The A.L. 288-1 partial skeleton points in the direction of a manner of bipedality that involves less complete extension of the lower limb during terrestrial bipedalism than occurs in modern humans, and a more costly gait by virtue of the short stride length relative to body mass and the long forefoot relative to the rest of the lower limb. But we must state now, as we have done previously, that the greater similarity of the large proximal femur (A.L. 333-3) and large distal tibiae (A.L. 333-6, -7) to those of modern humans engender doubts about what seems so obvious from a consideration of Lucy's skeleton.

In Stern and Susman (1983a), we suggested three alternate possibilities for interpreting the different morphologies of the large and small specimens from Hadar. First, they may have come from different taxa, as has been suggested by Senut (1978) and Tardieu (1979, 1981, 1983). If such were the case, the small taxon would be significantly arboreal and practice a uniquely nonhuman manner of bipedalism. The large taxon would combine a primitive foot, knee, and hand with an 'advanced' hip and ankle to yield a partly arboreal being that might have been more similar to modern humans in manner of bipedal progression.

The second alternative was that the large and small specimens represent different sexes of the same taxon but that the marked sexual dimorphism in postcranial structure is not to be viewed as indicating any comparable difference in behavior. Thus, the males are structured the way large *A. afarensis* ought to be in order to do the same things that the females do. This single behavioral repertoire would include significant arboreality and a unique manner of bipedalism.

Finally, the alternative which we preferred is that there is extraordinary sexual dimorphism at Hadar, and that the sexes partitioned their time between the trees and ground differently. The heavy males spent less time in the trees than did females. Although Tardieu's (1979, 1983) assessment of terminal locking rotation in the knee, and our own observations on the proximal femur and ankle, might support a conclusion that the males walked bipedally in a manner more similar to humans than did the females, we held back from this specific suggestion because it was seemingly refuted by the structure of the patellar groove of the femur and the foot. We are not frightened by the idea that the sexes may have practiced bipedalism in ways which were not precisely identical. If the Hadar specimens are all of one taxon, the sexual dimorphism in postcranial structure is unparalleled among living primates; maybe the degree of difference between locomotion of the sexes is similarly unparalleled.

We still do not believe that the evidence from the postcranial skeleton is sufficient to choose between the alternatives outlined above with any great level of confidence. We will stand by our previous choice of sexual dimorphism coupled with sexual dinichism.

NON-ANATOMIC CONSIDERATIONS

One of the interesting sidelights of the Berkeley Symposium was the fact that several persons commented privately that they were impressed by the anatomic evidence we provided, but that they found it intuitively difficult to accept the existence of an animal that spent a significant amount of time in the trees without being as adept as an ape, and also lived on the ground without being as quick and agile on two legs as are humans. In the 'Introduction' to this paper we mentioned how it is equally difficult to conceive of such a stage having been averted by the human lineage. Rose (1984) has dealt with this issue, and presented a convincing argument that "If bipedalism is seen within the context of changing positional repertoires then far from having been abrupt and complete, its evolution can be seen as having taken place over a considerable time span and to have been closely linked with changing patterns of food acquisition behavior." The crucial question may reduce to whether or not this time span was considerable enough to be picked up in the fossil record.

We wonder why there is such reluctance to accept the idea that a behaviorally and structurally intermediate human ancestor could exist for a geologically significant period of time. Would the same resistance be offered to the suggestion that the fossil record might reveal a stage during which the ancestors of whales were neither as mobile on the ground as they had been, nor as adept in the water as they would become (Gingerich et al. 1983)? Furthermore, there exist such intermediately adapted animals today. The chimpanzee spends a great portion of its time in the trees, but is not as highly adapted for movement in this milieu as is the orangutan. The chimpanzee also spends a substantial portion of its time on the ground, as a quadruped, but its manner of quadrupedalism is more costly than that of almost any other ground-dwelling quadrupedal mammal (Taylor et al. 1982). Compromise to increase the range of habitat use seems to be the best explanation for this apparently 'stable' adaptation in chimpanzees.

It probably was not necessary for the earliest biped to have been as adept on two legs as are humans. There is compelling evidence that hunting of savanna game played no part in the subsistence pattern of the earliest hominids (Lovejoy 1981; Issac 1982, 1984; Potts 1985; Walker, cited by Lewin 1983). They may have walked on two legs for the purpose of passing between trees or clumps of trees (Rodman and McHenry 1980), or for brief ventures into the grassland to obtain food. Such bouts of bipedalism may not have been of longer duration than those of which some extant nonhuman primates are capable. But, even if they were, the Hadar hominids had undergone changes to enable the trunk to be more readily balanced on the femoral heads, and such changes alone would have been sufficient to increase the bipedal range of the animal well beyond that of extant nonhuman primates. There is no need to expect adaptations for especially low cost and high speed of bipedal progression in the earliest hominids.

The final point we wish to make regards non-morphological evidence for our suggestion that Australopithecus afarensis was a more skillful climber while at the same time a less adept biped than later hominids. This evidence we regard as ancillary, but it lends 'outside' support to the anatomic evidence and allows the possibility for falsifying our hypothesis with extra-morphological data.

The first issue is that of the ecological status of A. afarensis, viz. how might 30-kg hominids, such as 'Lucy' and her sisters, have survived in a completely terrestrial niche—one that occasioned 'full-blown bipedality'. We feel, based on the extensive literature on free-ranging primates, that creatures such as represented by A.L. 288-1 could not have survived full-time on the ground. Today, all primates from common chimpanzees (which range from 27 up to 70 kg), to vervet monkeys and baboons (which range from less than 3 to over 40 kg), are obliged at least to sleep in trees (or on rocky cliff-faces). They all feed in trees, and it has been noted by fieldworkers ever since the pioneering studies of Washburn and Devore (1961) that sleeping trees and food trees are principal factors limiting group ranges and ranging patterns. It should be pointed out that A. afarensis possessed neither the formidable canine teeth of baboons nor the body size and canines of chimpanzees. How could this ancient hominid have fared better on the ground than these extant primates, which must rely on the trees? The only way, it seems to us, if for afarensis to have made and used some sort of tools, or perhaps to have lived in highly organized social groups such as those of modern-day terrestrial primates. But the evidence of tool use is lacking from the time ranges in question at Hadar, and the model for the socioecology of A. afarensis presented by those most familiar with the paleontological and paleoecological evidence (Lovejoy 1981) claims that afarensis most probably lived as monogamous pair-bonded adults with their offspring. We are aware of the many counter arguments against this scenario, but, within such a framework, it is inconceivable to us that if the larger male A. afarensis were off foraging during the day, and leaving the diminutive females with their offspring to fend for themselves, that the latter would have survived without recourse to the trees. Indeed, no living primate does so. Even comparatively large female gorillas (85 kg) are highly dependent on the trees for sleeping. Thus, it seems that the only possibilities of survival, especially if the Hadar hominids were monogamous, would have rested in their being at least part-time arborealists.

Finally, we would like to consider briefly the issue of the habitats at Hadar and Laetoli. Of course it would weaken any suggestion of arboreality for afarensis if it could be shown that these sites, at the times in question, were devoid of trees. In fact this argument was raised both informally and during the Berkeley Symposium. Two things bear noting in this regard. First is the direct answer to the question of the environmental conditions at Hadar and Laetoli. It has been stated by a number of experts that at Hadar there was a mosaic of forest, woodland, and more open habitats. The forests in the vicinity of the Hadar localities were likely similar to forests of the Ethiopian highlands today and the Kakamega Forest of Kenya (F.C. Howell, Berkeley Symposium). This inference is based on microfauna and pollen analysis by experts who have worked at Hadar. Others tell us that there were colobine monkeys at Hadar and Laetoli (Delson, pers. comm.), and additional elements of the fauna that indicate forested conditions. Laetoli was, by numerous accounts, drier than Hadar (Delson, pers. comm.; White, Berkeley Symposium). But, even the driest reaches (including deserts) inhabited by primates today have at least some trees (e.g. Kummer 1968; McGrew et al. 1981). These may be along rivers or perennial water courses, or concentrated near water holes or ephemeral lakes. It may be that these areas, however small, were where the small-bodied hominids lived. It may have been these areas, shrinking through time in relative proportion to the overall habitat, that the hominids sought out for food and as a haven from predators. Secondly, it must be kept in mind that no matter what the sedimentology, palynology, macrobotanical, or faunal remains tell us about the paleoenvironment, they cannot place the hominids in any *one* component of a mosaic habitat (Oxnard 1983). All experts who commented at Berkeley (including Johanson, Howell, and White) noted that any number of habitats were available to the hominids at Hadar and Laetoli, and that hominids most probably ranged widely in both areas over a variety of habitats.

Bipedalism may have been a response to the need to travel to and among the ever shrinking forested areas. As time went on, increasing body size, tool use, and social cohesiveness would have eventually freed hominids from reliance on the trees. With *Homo erectus* we encounter hominids that are large, robust and with sufficiently sophisticated culture (including refined stone tools, fire, etc.) to allow for 'full-time' terrestriality [7]. We do not, however, feel that at the *afarensis* (or even *Homo habilis*) grade, hominids were of sufficient size or cultural capacity for full-time terrestrial life.

ACKNOWLEDGEMENTS

We are grateful to the following persons and institutions for allowing us ready access to paleontological and osteological specimens: (1) D. C. Johanson and The Institute of Human Origins; (2) W. H. Kimbel, B. M. Latimer, and the Cleveland Museum of Natural History; (3) I. Tattersall, G. Musser, and the American Museum of Natural History; (4) C. Stringer and the British Museum of Natural History; (5) B. Senut and the Musée de l'Homme, Paris; (6) R. E. F. Leakey, M. D. Leakey, and the Kenya National Museum, and (7) Section of Vertebrate Anatomy, Musée Royal de l'Afrique Centrale, Tervuren. Luci Betti deserves credit for the illustrations and Joan Kelly for typing the manuscript. This research was supported by NSF Research Grants BNS 81-19664, BNS 82-17635, BNS 83-11206, and BNS 83-18013.

NOTES

[1] Interarticular length is the preferred measurement, and it was used in calculating the curvature of toe bones. For manual phalanges, maximum length was substituted because it enabled us to increase greatly our sample sizes. Such a substitution increases somewhat the calculated values for radius of curvature, but will not affect the position of different species relative to one another, or the position of fossils relative to extant forms.

[2] We did compare our sample of humans to that of Ashton and Oxnard (1964), and found that theirs was characterized by an even less cranially oriented glenoid than our own.

[3] The measurement values for metatarsal heads II-V (A.L. 333-115 B, D, C, E) are B: dorsal medio-lateral breadth = 6.0 mm, plantar medio-lateral breadth = 10.5 mm; D: dorsal = 6.1 mm, plantar = 9.0 mm; C: dorsal = 8.7 mm, plantar = 9.3 mm; E: dorsal = 6.4 mm, plantar = 8.1 mm. Thus, it can be seen that the fossil metatarsal heads are relatively narrow on their dorsal surfaces, as are those of apes. Metatarsal head V is the most variable in modern humans and its reduced role in toe-off (as weight is shifted to the medial side of the foot) is reflected in this and other aspects of its morphology.

[4] Maximum plantarflexion was brought about first by voluntary contraction of the triceps surae with the foot bearing no weight, and then by the radiologist attempting to plantarflex manually the subject's ankle to the limit of movement. These two methods gave the same results, as one might expect by considering the tremendous strength of the triceps surae.

[5] Total pelvic height can be shown to be a homologous measurement in A.L. 288-1 and modern humans due to similarities in the intrinsic proportions of the os coxae. Ischial shank length as a percentage of iliac blade length (both measured from the center of the acetabulum) averages 54.6 (SD = 2.4) in a sample of 10 pygmies. The corresponding value is 54.9 in the fossil.

[6] The reader may be interested in viewing the pictures of human fetuses in England (1983) to be convinced that the medial swelling of the ball of the big toe is not a function of distortion to the foot caused by wearing shoes. Additionally, whereas some humans appear to have no, or a very indistinct medial swelling when the sole of the non-weight-bearing foot is viewed, the swelling always becomes prominent when weight is borne and the hallux dorsiflexed, as at the termination of stance phase in walking. The impression of this swelling in the ground is also more marked in persons who walk toed-out. Thus, its absence in the right footprints of the G-1 trail at Laetoli is all the more significant.

[7] We fully recognize that modern forest-dwelling tribal people climb trees to collect honey, fruit, insects and other foods, and occasionally to flee from danger.

REFERENCES

Abel, C. 1819. *Narrative of a Journey in the Interior of China: and a voyage to and from that country in the years 1816 and 1817*. Longmans, London.

Anderson, M., Blais, M., Green, W. T. 1956. Growth of the normal foot during childhood and adolescence. *Am. J. phys. Anthrop.* 14:287-308.

Anderson, M., Messner, M. B., Green, W. T. 1964. Distribution of lengths of the normal femur and tibia in children from one to eighteen years of age. *J. Bone Jt. Surg.* 46A:1197-1202.

Ashton, E. H., Oxnard, C. E. 1964. Functional adaptations in the primate shoulder girdle. *Proc. zool. Soc. Lond.* 142:49-66.

Bush, M. E., The thumb of *Australopithecus afarensis* (Abstract). *Am. J. phys. Anthrop.* 52:210.

Bush, M. E., Lovejoy, C. O., Johanson, D. C., Coppens, Y. 1982. Hominid carpal, metacarpal and phalangeal bones recovered from the Hadar formation: 1974-1977 collections. *Am. J. phys. Anthrop.* 57:651-667.

Cartmill, M. 1974. Pads and claws in arboreal locomotion, in: *Primate locomotion* (Jenkins, Ed.), pp. 45-83, Academic Press, New York.

Ciochon, R. L., Corruccini, R. S. 1976. Shoulder joint of Sterkfontein *Australopithecus*. *S. Afr. J. Sci.* 72:80-82.

Cook, D. C., Buikstra, J. E., DeRousseau, C. J., Johanson, D. C. 1983. Vertebral pathology in the Afar australopithecines. *Am. J. phys. Anthrop.* 60:83-102.

Crowninshield, R. D., Johnston, R. C., Andrews, J. G., Brand, R. A. 1978. A biomechanical investigation of the human hip. *J. biomech.* 11:75-85.

Davis, D. D. 1962. Mammals of the lowland rain forest of north Borneo. *Bull. natn. Mus. St. Singapore* 31:1-129.

Davis, P. R. 1964. Hominid fossils from bed I, Olduvai Gorge, Tanganyika. A tibia and fibula. *Nature* 201: 967-970.

Day, M. H., Wickens, E. H. 1980. Laetoli Pliocene hominid footprints and bipedalism. *Nature* 286: 385-387.

England, M. A. 1983. Color atlas of life before birth. *Normal Fetal Development*, Yearbook Medical Publ., Chicago.

Flower, W. H. 1888. Description of two skeletons of Akkas, a pygmy race from Central Africa. *J. R. anthrop. Inst.* 18:3-18.

Foley, C. D., Quanbury, A. O., Steinke, T. 1979. Kinematics of normal child locomotion—a statistical study based on TV data. *J. Biomech.* 12:1-8.

Garn, S. M., Hertzog, K. P., Poznanski, A. K., Nagy, J. M. 1972. Metacarpophalangeal length in the evaluation of skeletal malformation. *Radiology* 105:375-381.

Gingerich, P. D., Wells, N. A., Russell, D. E., Ibrahim Shah, S. M. 1983. Origin of whales in epicontinental remnant seas: new evidence from the Early Eocene of Pakistan. *Science* 220:403-406.

Gomberg, D. N., Latimer, B. 1984. Observations on the transverse tarsal joint of *A. afarensis*, and some comments on the interpretation of behaviour from morphology (Abstract). *Am. J. phys. Anthrop.* 63:164.

Gray, E. R. 1969. The role of leg muscles in variations of the arches in normal and flat feet. *J. Am. phys. Therapy Assoc.* 49:1084-1088.

Halaczek, B. 1972. Die Langknochen der Hinterextremität bei simischen Primaten. *Eine Vergleichend-Morphologische Untersuchung,* Diss. Anthropologisches Institut der Universität Zürich.

Harris, R. I., Beath, T. 1948. Hypermobile flat-foot with short Tendo Achilles. *J. Bone Jt Surg.* 30 A:116-138.

Heglund, N. C., Fedak, M. A., Taylor, C. R., Cavagna, G. A. 1982. Energetics and mechanics of terrestrial locomotion. IV. Total mechanical energy changes as a function of speed and body size in birds and mammals. *J. exp. Biol.* 97: 57-66.

Heglund, N. C., McMahon, T. A., Taylor, C. R. 1974. Scaling stride frequency and gait to animal size: mice to horses. *Science* 186:1112-1113.

Heiple, K. G., Lovejoy, C. O. 1971. The distal femoral anatomy of *Australopithecus. Am. J. phys. Anthrop.* 35:75-84.

Hicks, J. H. 1953. The mechanics of the foot. II. The plantar aponeurosis and the arch. *J. Anat.* 88:25-30.

Hornaday, W. T. 1929. *Two Years in the Jungle,* 10th ed., Scribner, New York.

Inman, V. T., Mann, R. A. 1978. Biomechanics of the foot and ankle, in: *DuVries' Surgery of the Foot,* 4th Ed. (Mann, Ed.), pp. 3-21, Mosby, St. Louis.

Issac, G. L. 1982. Aspects of human evolution, in: *Essays on Evolution: a Darwin Centenary Volume* (Bendall, Ed.), Cambridge University Press, Cambridge.

Issac, G. L., 1984. The archeology of human origins: studies of the Lower Pleistocene in East Africa: 1971-1981, in: *Advances in World Archeology,* vol. 3 (Wendorf, Ed.), Academic Press, New York.

Jenkins, F. A., Jr. 1972. Chimpanzee bipedalism: cineradiographic analysis and implications for the evolution of gait. *Science* 178:877-879.

Jenkins, F. A., Jr., Camazine, S. M. 1977. Hip structure and locomotion in ambulatory and cursorial carnivores. *J. Zool. Lond.* 181:351-370.

Johanson, D. C., Coppens, Y. 1976. A preliminary anatomical description of the first Plio/Pleistocene hominid discoveries in the Central Afar, Ethiopia. *Am. J. phys. Anthrop.* 45:217-234.

Johanson, D. C., Edey, M. 1981 *Lucy. The Beginnings of Humankind,* Simon and Schuster, New York.

Johanson, D. C., Lovejoy, C. O., Burstein, A. H., Heiple, K. G. 1976. Functional implications of the Afar knee joint (Abstract). *Am. J. phys. Anthrop.* 44:188.

Johanson, D. C., Taieb, M., Coppens, Y. 1982a. Pliocene hominids from the Hadar formation, Ethiopia (1973-1977): stratigraphic, chronologic and paleoenvironmental contexts, with notes on hominid morphology and systematics. *Am. J. phys. Anthrop.* 57:373-402.

Johanson, D. C., Lovejoy, C. O., Kimbel, W. H., White, T. D., Ward, S. C., Bush, M. E., Latimer, B. M., Coppens, Y. 1982b. Morphology of the Pliocene partial hominid skeleton (AL 288-1) from the Hadar formation, Ethiopia. *Am. J. phys. Anthrop.* 57:403-452.

Johanson, D. C., White, T. D. Coppens, Y. 1978. A new species of the genus *Australopithecus* (primates: Hominidae) from the Pliocene of Eastern Africa. *Kirtlandia,* No. 28, pp. 1-14.

Jones, R. L. 1941. The human foot. An experimental study of its mechanics, and the role of its muscles and ligaments in support of the arch. *Am. J. Anat.* 68: 1-39.

Jungers, W. L. 1978. The functional significance of skeletal allometry in *Megaladapis* in comparison to living prosimians. *Am. J. phys. Anthrop.* 19:303-314.

Jungers, W. L. 1982. Lucy's limbs: skeletal allometry and locomotion in *Australopithecus afarensis. Nature* 297:76-678.

Jungers, W. L. 1984a. Scaling of the hominoid locomotor skeleton with special reference to the lesser apes, in: *The Lesser Apes: Evolutionary and Behavioral Biology* (Chivers, Preuschoft, Brockelman, Creel, Eds.), pp. 146-169, Edinburgh University Press, Edinburgh.

Jungers, W. L. 1984b. Body size and scaling of limb proportions in primates, in: *Size and Scaling in Primate Biology* (Jungers, Ed.), pp. 345-381, Plenum Press, New York.

Jungers, W. L., Stern, J. T., Jr. 1983. Body proportions, skeletal allometry and locomotion in the Hadar hominids: a reply to Wolpoff. *J. hum. Evol.* 12:673-684.

Kawabe, M., Mano, T. 1972. Ecology and behavior of the wild proboscis monkey, *Nasalis larvatus* (Wurmb), in Sabah, Malaysia. *Primates* 13:213-228.

Kern, J. A. 1964. Observations on the habits on the proboscis monkey, *Nasalis larvatus* (Wurmb), made in the Brunei Bay area, Borneo. *Zoologica, N.Y.* 49:183-192.

Kummer, H. 1968. *Social Organization of Hamadryas Baboons. A field study,* University of Chicago Press, Chicago.

Laidlaw, B. A. 1904. The varieties of Os Calcis. *J. Anat.* 38:133-143.

Laidlaw, B. A. 1905. The Os Calcis. Part II. *J. Anat.* 39:161-177.

Latimer, B. M. 1983. The anterior foot skeleton of *Australopithecus afarensis* (Abstract). *Am. J. phys. Anthrop.* 60:217.

Latimer, B.M. 1984. The pedal skeleton of *Australopithecus afarensis* (Abstract). *Am. J. phys. Anthrop.* 63:182.

Latimer, B. M., Lovejoy, C. O., Johanson, D. C., Coppens, Y. 1982. Hominid tarsal, metatarsal and phalangeal bones recovered from the Hadar formation: 1974-1977 collections. *Am. J. phys. Anthrop.* 53:701-719.

Leakey, M. D. 1981. Tracks and tools. *Phil. Trans. R. Soc. B,* 292:95-102.

Leakey, R. E. F. 1981. *The Making of Mankind,* Dutton, New York, pp. 69-70.

Lewin, R. 1983. Studying humans as animals. *Science* 220:1141.

Lewis, 0. J. 1983. The evolutionary emergence of refinement of the mammalian pattern of foot architecture. *J. Anat.* 137:21-45.

Loth, E. 1908. Die Aponeurosis plantaris in dem Primatenreich. *Gegenbaurs morph. Jb.* 38:194-322.

Lovejoy, C. O. 1975. Biomechanical perspectives on the lower limb of early hominids, in: *Primate Functional Morphology and Evolution* (Tuttle, Ed.), pp. 291-326, Mouton, The Hague.

Lovejoy, C. O. 1979. A reconstruction of the pelvis of AL-288 (Hadar formation, Ethiopia) (Abstract). *Am. J. phys. Anthrop.* 50:460.

Lovejoy, C. O. 1981. The origin of man. *Science* 211:341-350.

Lovejoy, C. O., Johanson, D. C., Coppens, Y. 1982. Hominid lower limb bones recovered from the Hadar formation: 1974-1977 collections. *Am. J. phys. Anthrop.* 57:679-700.

Martin, R., Saller, K. 1959. *Lehrbuch der Anthropologie,* 3. Aufl., vol. II, Fischer, Stuttgart.

Marzke, M. W. 1983. Joint function and grips of the *Australopithecus afarensis* hand, with special reference to the region of the capitate. *J. hum. Evol.* 12:197-211.

McGrew, W. C., Baldwin, P. J., Tutin, C. E. G. 1981. Chimpanzees in a hot, dry and open habitat: Mt. Assirik, Senegal, West Africa. *J. hum. Evol.* 10:227-244.

McHenry, H. M. 1983. The capitate of *Australopithecus afarensis* and *A. africanus. Am. J. phys. Anthrop.* 62:187-198.

Midlo, C. 1934. Form of hand and foot in primates. *Am. J. phys. Anthrop.* 19:337-389.

Mittermeier, R .A., Fleagle, J. G. 1976. The locomotor and postural repertoires of *Ateles geoffroyi* and *Colobus quereza* and a reevaluation of the locomotor category semibrachiation. *Am. J. phys. Anthrop.* 45:235-256.

Mochon, S., McMahon, T. A. 1980. Ballistic walking. *J. Biomech., Tokyo* 13:49-57.

Montagne, J., Chevrot, A., Galmiche, J.-M. 1980. *Atlas de Radiologie du Pied,* Masson, Paris.

Napier, J. R. 1959. Fossil metacarpals from Swartkrans. *Fossil Mam. of Africa*, No. 17, British Museum Natural History, London.

Oxnard, C. E. 1968. A note on the fragmentary Sterkfontein scapula. *Am. J. phys. Anthrop.* 28:213-218.

Oxnard, C. E. 1983. *The Order of Man*, Hong Kong University Press, Hong Kong.

Paul, J. 1966. The biomechanics of the hip joint and its clinical relevance. *Proc. R. Soc. Med.* 59:943-947.

Potts, R., 1985. Hominid hunters? Problems of identifying the earliest hunter/gatherers, in: *Human Evolution and Community Ecology. Prehistoric human adaptation in biological perspective* (Foley, Ed.), Academic Press, New York.

Preuschoft, H. 1970. Functional anatomy of the lower extremity, in: *The chimpanzee*, vol. 3, Karger, Basel, pp. 221-294.

Preuschoft, H. 1971. Mode of locomotion in subfossil giant lemurids from Madagascar. *Proc. 3rd Int. Congr. Primat., Zurich 1970*, Karger, Basel, pp. 79-90.

Preuschoft, H. 1978. Recent results concerning the biomechanics of man's acquisition of bipedality, in: *Recent Advances in Primatology*, vol. 3. *Evolution* (Chivers, Joysey, Eds.), pp. 435-458, Academic Press, London.

Reeser, L. A., Susman, R. L., Stern, J. T., Jr. 1983. Electromyographic studies of the human foot: experimental approaches to hominid evolution. *Foot Ankle* 3:391-407.

Rodman, P. S., McHenry, H. M. 1980. Bioenergetics and the origin of hominid bipedalism. *Am. J. phys. Anthrop.* 52:103-106.

Rose, M. D. 1984. Food acquisition and the evolution of positional behavior: the case of bipedalism, in: *Food acquisition and processing in primates* (Chivers, Wood, Bilsborough, Eds.), pp. 509-524, Plenum Press, London.

Sarrafian, S. K. 1983. *Anatomy of the Foot and Ankle*, Lippincott, Philadelphia.

Schmid, P. 1983. Eine Rekonstruktion des Skelettes von A.L. 288-1 (Hadar) und deren Konsequenzen. *Folia primatol.* 40:283-306.

Seireg, A., Arvikar, R. J. 1975. The prediction of muscular load sharing and joint reaction forces in the lower extremities during walking. *J. Biomech., Tokyo* 8:89-102.

Senut, B. 1978. *Contribution a l'étude de l'humérus et de ses articulations chez les hominides du Plio-pléistocène*, Doctoral Thesis, Paris.

Senut, B. 1980. New data on the humerus and its joints in Plio-Pleistocene hominids. *Collegium Antropologicum* 4:87-93.

Senut, B., LeFloch, P. 1981. Divergence des piliers de la palette humérale chez les primates hominoides. *C.r. hebd. Seanc. Acad. Sci., Paris, Ser. II* 292:757-760.

Sokoloff, S. 1971. The muscular anatomy of the chimpanzee foot. *Gegenbaurs morph. Jb.* 119:86-125.

Stauffer, R. N., Chao, E. Y. S., Brewster, R. C. 1977. Force and motion analysis of the normal, diseased, and prosthetic ankle joint. *Clin. Orthop. Rel. Res.* 127:189-196.

Stern, J. T., Jr. 1971. Functional myology of the hip and thigh of Cebid monkeys and its implications for the evolution of erect posture. *Biblthca primatol.*, No. 14, Karger, Basel.

Stern, J. T., Jr. 1972. Anatomical and functional specializations of the human gluteus maximus. *Am. J. phys. Anthrop.* 36:315-340.

Stern, J. T., Jr., Susman, R. L. 1981. Electromyography of the gluteal muscles in *Hylobates, Pongo* and *Pan*: implications for the evolution of hominid bipedality. *Am. J. phys. Anthrop.* 55:153-166.

Stern, J. T., Jr., Susman, R. L. 1983a The locomotor anatomy of *Australopithecus afarensis*. *Am. J. phys. Anthrop.* 60:279-317.

Stern, J. T., Jr., Susman, R. L. 1983b Functions of peroneus longus and brevis during locomotion in apes and humans. *Am. J. phys. Anthrop.* 60:256-257 (Abstract).

Steudel, K., Myers, M. 1984. Can energetic cost of locomotion be an important constraint in primate limb design and structural evolution? (Abstract). *Am. J. phys. Anthrop.* 63:221.

Susman, R. L. 1979. Comparative and functional morphology of hominoid fingers. *Am. J. phys. Anthrop.* 50:215-236.

Susman, R. L. 1983. Evolution of the human foot: evidence from Plio-Pleistocene hominids. *Foot Ankle* 3:365-376.

Susman, R. L., Creel, N. 1979. Functional and morphological affinities of the subadult hand (O.H. 7) from Olduvai Gorge. *Am. J. phys. Anthrop.* 51:311-332.

Suwa, G. 1984. Could *Australopithecus afarensis* have made the Laetoli footprints? (Abstract). *Am. J. phys. Anthrop.* 63:224-225.

Tardieu, C. 1979. *Analyse morpho-fonctionnelle de l'articulation du genou chez les primates*. Application aux hominides fossiles; thesis Paris.

Tardieu, C. 1981. Morpho-functional analysis of the articular surfaces of the knee-joint in primates, in: *Primate Evolutionary Biology* (Chiarelli, Corrucini, Eds.), pp. 68-80, Springer, Berlin.

Tardieu, C. 1983. L'articulation du genou. Analyse morpho-fonctionnelle chez les primates. *Application aux Hominides Fossiles*, CNRS, Paris.

Taylor, C. R., Heglund, N. C., Maloiy, C. M. O. 1982. Energetics and mechanics of terrestrial locomotion. I. Metabolic energy consumption as a function of speed and body size in birds and mammals. *J. Exp. Biol.* 97:1-21.

Tuttle, R. H. 1967. Knuckle-walking and the evolution of hominoid hands. *Am. J. phys. Anthrop.* 26:171-206.

Tuttle, R. H. 1972. Functional and evolutionary biology of hylobatid hands, in: Gibbon and Siamang, vol. 1, pp. 136-206, Karger, Basel.

Tuttle, R. H. 1981. Evolution of hominid bipedalism and prehensile capabilities. *Phil. Trans. R. Soc.* 292:89-94.

Vrba, E. S. 1979. A new study of the scapula of *Australopithecus africanus* from Sterkfontein. *Am. J. phys. Anthrop.* 51:117-130.

Washburn, S. L., Devore, I. 1961. The social life of baboons. *Scient. Am.* 204:62-71.

Weidenreich, F. 1940. The external tubercle of the human tuber calcanei. *Am. J. phys. Anthrop.* 26:473-487.

Weisl, H. 1955. The movements of the sacro-iliac joint. *Acta anat.* 23:80-91.

White, T. D., Suwa, G., 1987. Hominid footprints at Laetoli: facts and interpretations. *Am. J. phys. Anthrop.* 72:485–514.

Wolpoff, M. H. 1980. *Paleoanthropology*, Knopf, New York.

Wolpoff M. H. 1983a. Lucy's lower limbs: long enough for Lucy to be fully bipedal? *Nature* 304:59-61.

Wolpoff, M. H. 1983b Lucy's little legs. *J. hum. Evol.* 12:443-453.

Zihlman, A. L., Brunker, L. 1979. Hominid bipedalism: then and now. *Yb. phys. Anthropol.* 22:132-162.

Zuckerman, S., Ashton, E. H., Flinn, R. M., Oxnard, C. E., Spence, T. F. 1973. Some locomotor features of the pelvic girdle in primates. *Symp. zool. Soc. Lond.* 33:71-165.

19

Australopithecine Taxonomy and Phylogeny: Historical Background and Recent Interpretation

F. E. Grine

The Pliocene and early Pleistocene witnessed the emergence and initial radiation of the Hominidae. Early hominid fossils are known only from African localities, and those that are not considered to belong to the genus *Homo* (*sensu stricto*) are generally referred to as "australopithecines." These specimens are commonly attributed to the genus *Australopithecus*, although a growing body of evidence indicates that a second genus, *Paranthropus*, should be recognized for the so-called "robust" australopithecines.

The purpose of this chapter is to provide a brief historical review together with a summary of recent work that has been undertaken in an attempt to understand more completely the early hominid fossil record.

HISTORICAL BACKGROUND

In 1924, Raymond A. Dart obtained the skull of a juvenile hominoid individual from the Buxton lime quarry at Taung in the northern Cape Province of South Africa. Dart (1925), who recognized that the fossil (Fig. 1) represented a novel taxon, designated it *Australopithecus africanus*. In his analysis of the Taung skull, Dart recognized several distinctly hominid, or "humanlike," features, such as the ventral position of the foramen magnum (which he interpreted as being indicative of bipedal locomotion) and the relatively small canines, together with more primitive, or "apelike" characters, such as a comparatively small brain size and a relatively large snout. Dart proposed that *Australopithecus* was a primitive human forebear whose small brain precluded it from being recognized as a member of the genus *Homo*, but whose hominid features excluded it from known great-ape genera. He proposed, instead, that *Australopithecus africanus* should be accorded separate "intermediate" familial rank between the Hominidae and the "Pongidae." Dart's claims for the evolutionary significance of *Australopithecus africanus* were hotly disputed by the leading paleoanthropologists of his day (e.g., Woodward 1925; Keith 1931), and despite studies by Broom (1925a, 1925b, 1929), Sollas (1926), Dart (1926, 1929, 1934), Romer (1930) and others, the hominid status of *Australopithecus* began to be more generally accepted only more than a decade after the discovery of the Taung skull. This acceptance resulted primarily from the work by Robert Broom.

In 1936 Broom, a vertebrate paleontologist, recovered fossils of an adult individual from the site of Sterkfontein in the Transvaal Province of South Africa (Fig. 2). He recognized that this extinct form was very similar to the Taung skull; thus, he (Broom 1936) initially attributed the Sterkfontein fossils to *Australopithecus*, albeit to a separate species, *A. transvaalensis*. Two years later, however, Broom (1938) proposed that the Sterkfontein hominids should be placed in a separate genus, *Plesianthropus* (whence the name "Mrs. Ples" for the STS 5 cranium from Sterkfontein), on the basis of a juvenile mandibular fragment that he compared to the symphysis of the Taung child. Following the Second World War, early hominid fossils were discovered at the site of Makapansgat in the northern Transvaal of South Africa (Fig. 2). These were described by Dart (1948), who recognized them as being morphologically similar to those from Taung and Sterkfontein; he attributed them to the genus *Australopithecus*, but to a separate species, *A. prometheus*. The species (i.e., trivial) name chosen by Dart reflected his belief that the black coloration exhibited by the fossil animal bones from Makapansgat resulted from their having been burnt in fires made by the early hominids. It is now recognized, however, that this coloration resulted from staining by manganese dioxide rather than from their having been exposed to fire. In addition to his interpretation of the Makapansgat animal bones as hominid food refuse, Dart (1957) considered that many of these elements bore the marks of having been used as tools by *Australopithecus*. The supposed bone tools from Makapansgat were referred by Dart (1957) to the "Osteodontokeratic Culture," and his provocative interpretations were largely responsible for the initiation and emergence of modern studies of taphonomy. It is perhaps ironic that such studies have revealed that the animal bones in question show no actual evidence of having been modified by hominids, and that they most likely were accumulated by carnivores and scavengers such as leopards and hyenas (Brain 1981). Rather than being a hunter, *Australopithecus* appears to have been one of the hunted!

The majority of paleoanthropologists currently recognize that the hominid fossils from Taung, Sterkfontein (Member 4), and Makapansgat (Members 3 and 4) represent a single species of *Australopithecus*, namely *A. africanus*. Broom (1950) recognized three species among the fossils from these three sites, and while others have attempted to divide the hypodigm in a variety

New contribution specially prepared for *The Human Evolution Source Book*. Copyright © 1993 by Frederick E. Grine.

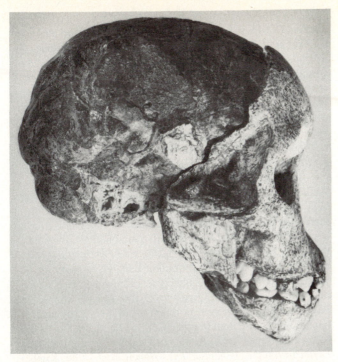

Figure 1. *Right lateral view of the child skull from the Buxton Quarry at Taung, South Africa. This is the type of* Australopithecus africanus *Dart, 1925.*

Figure 2. *Map of Africa showing the location of the principal australopithecine sites in Ethiopia, Kenya, Tanzania, and South Africa.*

of fashions dependent upon perceived differences in morphology and/or temporal distribution (e.g., Aguirre 1970; Tobias 1973, 1978, 1988; Clarke 1988), such schemes have not received any significant support.

The South African karst cave sites are not amenable to direct radiometric dating, and while there has been considerable controversy over their geochronological ages (Partridge 1973, 1982; Brock *et al.* 1977; Vogel 1985), the most reasonable interpretations are undoubtedly based upon faunal comparisons with dated eastern African sites (Vrba 1982; White *et al.* 1982; Cooke 1983; Delson 1988). These studies suggest that the Makapansgat fossils are between 3.0 and 2.5 Myr (million years) old, the Sterkfontein remains are about 2.5 Myr old, and the Taung fossil is probably somewhat younger at about 2.3 to 2.0 Myr.

In 1938 hominid fossils from the site of Kromdraai (Fig. 2) were described by Broom, who recognized than as being morphologically distinct from the Sterkfontein and Taung remains. Broom (1938) referred the Kromdraai fossils to a distinct genus and species, *Paranthropus robustus*. Ten years later, hominid fossils were discovered at the site of Swartkrans, and these were ascribed by Broom (1949) to a second species of *Paranthropus*, namely *P. crassidens*. Broom (1938, 1949, 1950) and his colleague John T. Robinson (1954) recognized that the Kromdraai and Swartkrans hominid specimens, which they attributed to *Paranthropus*, differed from those of *Australopithecus* in a number of morphological features including a flattened facial skeleton, a low forehead, and a notably enlarged postcanine dentition, among others. While Broom (1950) considered that the Kromdraai and Swartkrans *Paranthropus* specimens represented two species, Robinson (1954) was of the opinion that the differences between them were indicative of a subspecific distinction. The majority of

workers currently recognize the australopithecine fossils from Swartkrans and Kromdraai as representing a single species, although Howell (1978), Grine (1982, 1985a, 1988) and Jungers and Grine (1986) have argued that a species-specific distinction between these samples may, indeed, be warranted. Moreover, many workers hold that the southern African specimens of *Australopithecus* and *Paranthropus* may be accommodated comfortably within a single genus, *Australopithecus*.

The site of Swartkrans has yielded australopithecine fossils from Members 1, 2 and 3 (Brain *et al.* 1988; Grine 1988b, 1989), while the hominid fossils from Kromdraai probably all derive from a single lithostratigraphic unit (Member 3) (Vrba 1981). Faunal correlations with radiometrically dated eastern African sites suggest that the Swartkrans australopithecine fossils from Members 1 and 2 are between about 1.8 and 1.5 Myr old; the Member 3 remains may date to only 0.9 Myr, although there is no indication that the Member 3 fauna differs from that from Members 1 and 2 (Brain 1988; Brain *et al.* 1988; Delson 1988). The geochronological age of Kromdraai is difficult to determine precisely, but it is probably roughly similar to that of Swartkrans (Vrba 1981, 1982; Delson 1988).

In 1959, a cranium with extraordinarily large cheek teeth was discovered by Mary and Louis Leakey in Bed I of Olduvai Gorge, Tanzania (Fig. 2). This specimen was attributed by Louis Leakey (1959) to a novel taxon, *Zinjanthropus boisei*, although it was immediately recognized by Robinson (1960) as having very close affinities to the *Paranthropus* specimens from Swartkrans and Kromdraai. At present, most workers regard the Olduvai cranium as being representative of a distinct species of *Australopithecus*, *A. boisei*, or of *Paranthropus*, *P. boisei*. Following their 1959 discovery, the Leakeys found *P. boisei* fossils at other localities within Beds I and II of Olduvai Gorge and at the site of Peninj, near Lake Natron, Tanzania (Leakey and Leakey 1964; Leakey 1978). Between 1966 and 1974, teams led by F. Clark Howell and Y. Coppens recovered numerous jaws and teeth of *P. boisei* from the sediments of the Shungura

Formation along the Omo River in southern Ethiopia (Fig. 2). More particularly, fossils that have been referred to that species have been recovered from Members D, E, F, G and K of the Shungura Formation (Howell 1978; Grine 1985; White 1988), although the attribution of some of the specimens from below Tuff G to *P. boisei* now appears to be questionable. In 1970, a partial *P. boisei* cranium was found in the Chemoigut Formation near Chesowanja, Kenya (Carney *et al.* 1971). Work led by Richard Leakey from 1968 to the present time in the Koobi Fora Formation on the eastern side of Lake Turkana (Fig. 2) has resulted in the discovery of a large number of spectacular *P. boisei* fossils (Leakey *et al.* 1978; Leakey and Walker 1985, 1988), and exploration within the last several years on the western side of Lake Turkana has also provided fossils attributable to *P. boisei* (Leakey and Walker 1988).

Recent geological work at these various eastern African *P. boisei*-bearing localities, and especially the work by F. H. Brown and his colleagues in the Turkana Basin has revealed that *P. boisei* spans the period from about 2.4 Myr to about 1.4 or 1.2 Myr (Brown and Feibel 1988; Klein 1988; White 1988). The specific attribution of some of the geochronologically earlier fossils, such as those represented by isolated teeth from Members D and E of the Shungura Formation may be questionable, and the allocation of some specimens from Shungura Member C and its equivalent in the Nachukui Formation on the West side of Lake Turkana have been thrown into question by recent discoveries (Walker *et al.* 1986), but most workers would probably agree that *P. boisei* is undoubtedly represented in East Africa between 2.2 and 1.4 Myr.

In 1935, Louis and Mary Leakey discovered fossiliferous deposits at the site currently known as Laetoli, some 50 km south of Olduvai Gorge. Work there in the 1930's by L. Kohl-Larsen resulted in a handful of fossils, and during the 1970's, teams led by Mary Leakey explored these deposits further and found a number of early hominid fossils including a partial juvenile skeleton. In 1978-1979, volcanic-ash layers bearing hominid footprint trails were discovered at Laetoli (Leakey and Harris 1987). Between 1973 and 1977, teams led by Don Johanson recovered an abundance of Pliocene hominid fossils from the sediments of the Hadar Formation in Ethiopia (Fig. 2). Comparisons of the Laetoli and Hadar fossils led Johanson, White and Coppens (1978) to conclude that they represented a separate, distinctly primitive species, which they named *Australopithecus afarensis*.

The Laetoli hominids date to about 3.5 Myr, while those from the Hadar site date to between about 3.5 and 2.8 Myr (Brown 1982; Brown *et al.* 1985; Sarna-Wojcici *et al.* 1985). In addition to the fossils from Laetoli and Hadar, isolated specimens from several East African localities have been referred to *A. afarensis*. These fossils include: isolated hominid teeth from Fejej and the Usno Formation in the Omo Basin; partial mandibular corpora from the sites of Lothagam and Tabarin, near Lake Baringo, Kenya; a cranial fragment from the Tulu Bor Member of the Koobi Fora Formation; a proximal femur from Maka and a frontal fragment from Belohdelie, in the Middle Awash, Ethiopia (White 1984; Asfaw 1987; Ward and Hill 1987; Kimbel 1988; Fleagle *et al.* 1991). The Usno teeth and Tulu Bor cranial fragment date to just over 3.0 Myr, while the Belohdelie, Maka and Tabarin fossils are around 4.0 Myr old. Thus, specimens that have been attributed to *A. afarensis* span the period from about 4.0 to about 3.0 Myr.

The 1985 discovery by Alan Walker of a nearly complete cranium (KNM-WT 17000) on the West side of Lake Turkana (Walker *et al.* 1986) has led to the recognition by a number of workers of a fifth, distinct australopithecine species. The specimen combines a number of primitive features of the cranial base displayed also by *A. afarensis*, but not by other known hominid species, with a number of rather specialized, or derived features of the face shown by *P. robustus* and *P. boisei*, but not by *A. afarensis* or *A. africanus*. The cranium was found in the sediments of the Lomekwi Member of the Nachukui Formation, and is dated to about 2.5 Myr.

Because of its age and resemblance to later *P. boisei* crania, Walker and Leakey (Walker *et al.* 1986; Leakey and Walker 1988; Walker and Leakey 1988) have argued that the specimen represents an early member of that species. They also noted, however, that because of its primitive morphological features, the Lomekwi cranium might be attributed to a separate species from *P. boisei*. Such an attribution certainly appears to be warranted (Grine 1988a; Kimbel *et al.* 1988). It has been argued that the taxonomic designation for this species should be *Paranthropus aethiopicus*, in reference to a similarly ancient hominid mandible from Member C of the Shungura Formation that was attributed by C. Arambourg and Y. Coppens (1968) to *Paraustralopithecus aethiopicus* (Walker *et al.* 1986; Kimbel *et al.* 1988). It is possible that some of the isolated teeth from the earlier portion of the geological record in the Omo Basin that have been attributed previously to *P. boisei* should be referred to *P. aethiopicus*.

At present, then, at least five australopithecine species— *Australopithecus afarensis*, *A. africanus*, *Paranthropus robustus*, *P. boisei* and *P. aethiopicus*—are recognizable in the Plio-Pleistocene fossil record of Africa. The generally recognized *P. robustus* hypodigm from Kromdraai and Swartkrans may itself contain two taxa, *P. robustus* and *P. crassidens*, as argued by Howell (1978) and Grine (1982, 1985a). There has been considerable disagreement over the taxonomic status of the Hadar and Laetoli samples (e.g., Tobias 1980; Olson 1981; Ferguson 1983; Zihlman 1985), and the number of species represented in the Sterkfontein Member 4 deposits has been questioned recently (Clarke 1988; Kimbel and White 1988b). A detailed treatment of these taxonomic arguments is beyond the scope of this paper, and while some aspects will be discussed below, the five aforementioned species are recognized here as being clearly identifiable.

The question of the generic attribution of these five species—(are all attributable to a single genus, *Australopithecus*, or do the morphological specializations of the so-called "robust" species warrant their consideration as a separate genus, *Paranthropus*?)—has been resurrected recently by new discoveries and new phylogenetic analyses.

The name *Paranthropus*, which means literally "beside man" or "next to man" was coined by R. Broom (1938), when he described the hominid fossils from the site of Kromdraai as belonging to the taxon *Paranthropus robustus*. Subsequently discovered specimens from Swartkrans were also placed in the genus *Paranthropus* by Broom and Robinson, and Robinson also recognized that *Zinjanthropus* was a junior synonym of *Paranthropus*. Broom (1950) considered the Kromdraai and Swartkrans forms to be so distinctive that he proposed that they be placed in their own subfamily, the Paranthropinae, to distinguish them from the Australopithecinae. While Robinson did not support a suprageneric distinction between these forms, he (1954, 1972) argued that *Australopithecus* and *Paranthropus* represented separate phyletic lines of evolution, and that they occupied different adaptive zones rather than different aspects of the same adaptive zone.

Studies such as those of Tobias (1967) and Wolpoff (1974), in which all australopithecines were viewed as comprising a single evolutionary grade of organization, questioned the generic distinctiveness of *Paranthropus*. Such "grade"-orientated phenetic studies have influenced opinion such that at present most students of (and all textbooks on) hominid evolution regard *Paranthropus* as a junior synonym of *Australopithecus*. Indeed, some workers have even argued that all australopithecine fossils simply represent temporal and/or size variants within the range of variation of a single anagenetic lineage!

Despite the overwhelming influence of the "grade" paradigm, a strong body of evidence has accumulated which indicates that *Paranthropus* specimens exhibit a host of derived morphological specializations that probably reflect significant functional differences between them and other early hominid species. These characteristic craniodental features are almost certainly related to trophic (i.e., dietary) parameters, but because a number of workers have argued that these specializations were foreshadowed in the morphology of *Australopithecus africanus*, there has been a general reluctance to assign the "robust" and/or "hyper-robust" forms separate generic status. The question of the monophyletic nature of the "robust" australopithecines has been thrown into question by the recent discovery by Walker *et al.* (1986), who argued that the South African "robust" species (from Swartkrans and Kromdraai) likely evolved from *Australopithecus africanus*, while the East African "robust" form probably evolved from *A. afarensis*. This phylogenetic scheme, which assumes a tremendous amount of convergent evolution, would imply that not all "robust" species could be assigned to the genus *Paranthropus*. While the name *Paranthropus* could still be applied to the Swartkrans and Kromdraai australopithecines, this would mean that the name *Zinjanthropus* would have to be applied to the East African "robust" australopithecines. Alternatively, all australopithecine species could be accorded recognition under the genus *Australopithecus* according to such a diphyletic scheme.

The most parsimonious interpretation of the fossil record, however, indicates that the "robust" australopithecines form a monophyletic clade, and under this arrangement there can be little doubt about the validity (and the necessity) of the generic name *Paranthropus*. Indeed, Robinson (1972) has argued that since *Australopithecus africanus* was part of the human lineage, the genus name *Australopithecus* should be regarded as a junior synonym of *Homo* (see also Olson 1978, 1981). Increasing evidence suggests that the genus *Australopithecus*—even as constituted by only *A. afarensis* and *A. africanus*—may be paraphyletic. Thus, the continued use of the name *Australopithecus* may be questionable, especially if *A. africanus* is considered to be the most primitive member of the *Homo* line.

Despite these potential problems, the genus name *Australopithecus* is here recognized for the species *A. afarensis* and *A. africanus*, and the genus name *Paranthropus* is here recognized for the species *P. robustus, P. boisei* and *P.*

aethiopicus. The principal morphological features that serve to distinguish each of these species, together with aspects of their paleobiology, are outlined below.

AUSTRALOPITHECINE SPECIES

Australopithecus afarensis

The hypodigm of this species consists of specimens from the Hadar Formation, Fejej, Maka and Belohdelie, the Usno Formation, the Laetolil Beds, the Tulu Bor Member of the Koobi Fora Formation (e.g., KNM-ER 2602), and the site of Tabarin. Fossils of this eastern African species appear to span the period from about 4.0 to about 2.8 Myr.

This species (Fig. 3) is characterized primarily by a suite of primitive craniodental features, including strong facial prognathism, a flat (unflexed) cranial base, a relatively flat glenoid fossa without a discernible articular eminence, a postglenoid process that is situated anterior to the tympanic, a tubular tympanic, a strongly flared parietal mastoid angle with an asterionic notch, close approximation of lambda and inion, nasion that is coincident with a high glabella, an anteriorly flat (shallow) palate, a mediolaterally and supero-inferiorly convex nasoalveolar clivus that is demarcated from the floor of the nose by a horizontal sill, maxillary lateral incisor roots that are situated lateral to the lateral walls of the pyriform aperture, relatively large canines, and sectorial (unicuspid) to semisectorial (with a small metaconoid) lower anterior premolars. Endocranial capacity estimates range between about 310 cc and

Figure 3. *Left lateral view of a composite reconstruction of an adult male cranium of* Australopithecus afarensis. *The reconstruction incorporates some twelve individual skull fragments, including the AL 200-1a palate, and eleven cranial and mandibular pieces from Hadar site 333 (Kimbel* et al. *1984), together with the AL 58-22, AL 333-125 and BEL-VP-1/1 fragments as guides to the form and inclination of the frontal (Kimbel and White 1988). Courtesy of W.H. Kimbel.*

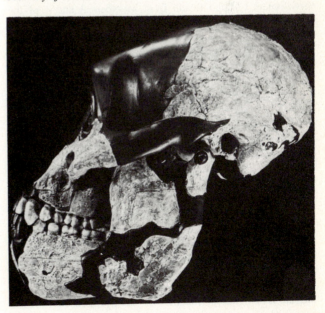

485 cc with an average of approximately 400 cc for three Hadar specimens (Holloway 1988).

The cranial and postcranial remains indicate a high degree of sexual dimorphism in body size, with differences between presumptive females and males being similar to those exhibited by extant gorillas and orangutans. Body sizes, as determined from measurements of the articular surfaces of the hindlimb elements, likely ranged between about 30.5 kg and 80.5 kg (Jungers 1988). Estimates by McHenry (1988) using diaphysis dimensions are very similar to those obtained by Jungers (1988).

The postcranial skeleton, together with the footprint trails preserved at Laetoli indicate that *A. afarensis* walked bipedally, but detailed analyses of the bones suggest that the type of gait employed was not exactly the same as that of modern humans (Jungers 1982; Stern and Susman 1983; Susman *et al.* 1984, 1985). Furthermore, a suite of postcranial features indicates that *A. afarensis* was adapted to arboreal climbing (Stern and Susman 1983; Susman *et al.* 1984, 1985). This earliest hominid likely spent a considerable amount of time (perhaps feeding and sleeping) in an arboreal milieu. Analysis of the knee joints from Hadar has suggested that the small (presumptive female) and large (presumptive male) specimens differed in a manner suggestive of differing degrees of arboreality (Senut and Tardieu 1985), such as is encountered today in orang-utans.

Paleoenvironmental reconstructions indicate diverse habitats from well-watered and wooded environments (e.g., Hadar) to more open conditions (e.g., Laetoli). Specimens of *A. afarensis* are found in a diversity of habitats, which indicates that this species had a fairly broad range of locomotor and dietary abilities. Compared to body size estimates, tooth size in *A. afarensis* is relatively large (McHenry 1988).

Australopithecus africanus

This is the type species of the genus *Australopithecus*. The holotype derives from the site of Taung, and the hypodigm of this species is comprised by specimens from Member 4 of the Sterkfontein Formation and from Members 3 and 4 of the Makapansgat Formation. The fossils from Makapansgat likely date to around 3.0 Myr; those from Sterkfontein date upward to perhaps 2.5 Myr, while the Taung specimen probably dates to between 2.3 and 2.0 Myr. Because of the nature of the karst caverns that have entrapped the bones, these dates are reliable only as "time capsules" between the time at which the first aven opened to the surface, to the complete filling of the cavity. Thus, *A. africanus* may have been present in southern Africa substantially earlier than the 3.0 Myr realized at Makapansgat, and although the Sterkfontein Member 4 fauna may be temporally mixed, it is unlikely that *A. africanus* persisted much after 2.0 Myr because its remains are not encountered in any of the karst sites that postdate 2.0 Myr.

This species (Fig. 4) is characterized principally by a more globular and less pneumatized cranium than that of *A. afarensis*, with a more pronounced forehead, a greater separation of lambda and inion, a high glabella that is separated from nasion, a prognathic but flattened nasoalveolar clivus, a anteriorly deep (shelved) palate, maxillary lateral incisor roots that are situated medial to the lateral margins of the pyriform aperture, a deepened glenoid fossa with a distinct articular eminence, a vertically steep tympanic plate, and bicuspid lower anterior

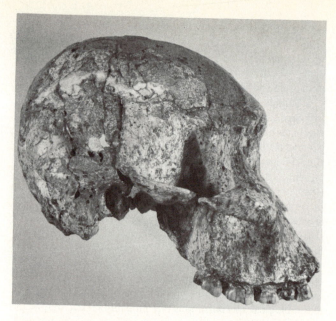

Figure 4. *Right lateral view of an adult cranium of* Australopithecus africanus *(STS 71). Courtesy of W.H. Kimbel.*

premolars. Endocranial capacity estimates range between some 428 cc and 510 cc, with an average of about 450 cc for seven specimens (Holloway 1988).

Dental and skeletal dimensions indicate that sexual dimorphism in *A. africanus* was also of considerable magnitude. Body weight estimates range between about 33.5 kg and 67.5 kg for presumptive female and male individuals (Jungers 1988). Postcranial elements are similar to those of *A. afarensis*, which suggests that *A. africanus* retained adaptations for arboreal climbing along with the adaptations for bipedal terrestrial locomotion (Robinson 1972; Vrba 1979; McHenry 1986), although several subtle differences between the postcranial elements of *A. afarensis* and *A. africanus* have been observed (McHenry 1986).

Paleoenvironmental reconstructions suggest fairly mesic (wet) conditions with notable bush and tree cover (Vrba 1985, 1988). The microscopic details of tooth wear indicate that the diet of *A. africanus* consisted principally of fruits and leaves (Grine 1986, 1987; Grine and Kay 1988; Kay and Grine 1988).

Paranthropus robustus

This is the type species of the genus *Paranthropus*. The holotype derives from the site of Kromdraai (TM 1517), and the hypodigm of this species is composed of a small number of specimens from that site, all of which probably derive from Member 3 (Vrba 1981), and by a large number of specimens from Swartkrans. The majority of the fossils from Swartkrans derive from Member 1 (both the "Hanging Remnant" and the "Lower Bank"); a number of specimens derive from Member 2 and a few derive from Member 3 (Brain *et al.* 1988). Howell (1978) and Grine (1982, 1985a) have argued that differences in detailed morphology between the Kromdraai and Swartkrans samples probably warrant their specific separation, but even if they are considered as separate species—*P. robustus* and *P. crassidens*, respectively—the differences between them are comparatively slight; thus, these specimens are regarded here

Figure 5. *Left lateral view of an adult cranium of* Paranthropus robustus *from Swartkrans Member 1 "Hanging Remnant" breccia. The specimen (SK 48) has been crushed in the posterior part of the brain case.*

under a single taxonomic category. The Swartkrans specimens probably date to between 1.8 and 1.5 Myr, although the Member 3 fossils may be substantially younger at about 1.0 Myr (Brain 1988); the Kromdraai fossils are probably similar in age to those from Swartkrans (Delson 1988).

This species (Fig. 5) is characterized by a number of craniodental features that are most likely related to the generation of powerful chewing forces. The cranium possesses a flattened, "dished" face with the cheeks situated anterior to the margins of the pyriform aperture, a facial skeleton that is hafted high on the calvaria, a low forehead with a concave frontal trigone, a prominent glabella that is situated below the level of the supraorbital margin, nasion that is nearly coincident with glabella, a maxillary trigone (a triangular depression on the front of the cheek bone), a flattened nasoalveolar clivus that grades imperceptibly into the floor of the nose, an anterior vomer insertion that is coincident with the anterior nasal spine, a medially thickened maxillary palatal process, an anteriorly shallow palate, a coronally inclined petrous pyramid (high petromedian angle), a deep glenoid fossa with a distinct articular eminence, a vertically deep tympanic plate, a bulbous mastoid region that is inflated beyond the supramastoid crest, canines that are situated in the same coronal plane as the incisors, absolutely and especially relatively small incisors and canines, and greatly enlarged premolars and molars. An endocranial capacity estimate of some 530 cc has been recorded for the single reliable specimen from Swartkrans (Holloway 1988).

The postcranial skeleton possesses certain features that are present also in *A. afarensis* and *A. africanus*, such as a relatively small femoral head together with a long and anteroposteriorly flattened femoral neck (Robinson 1972). The morphology of the proximal radius is like that seen in earlier australopithecine species and living great apes, suggestive of arboreal capabilities (Susman and Grine 1989). Foot and leg elements indicate the employment of bipedal terrestrial locomotion (Robinson 1972; Susman and Brain 1988), and recent studies of skeletal elements from Swartkrans suggest that the hand of *P. robustus* may have

been similar to that of modern humans (Susman 1988). However, specific attribution of some of the postcranial material from Swartkrans is made difficult by the presence of *Homo erectus* fossils in the same strata (Brain *et al.* 1988). Body size estimates for *P. robustus* range between about 42.5 and 65.5 kg (Jungers 1988), and these values suggest that *P. robustus* may not have been substantially larger than either *P. afarensis* or *A. africanus*.

Paleoenvironmental reconstructions suggest a prevalence of xeric (dry), open grassland conditions during the accumulation of the *P. robustus* fossils at Swartkrans (Vrba 1988), although recent work suggests the close proximity of a larger river at certain times (Brain *et al.* 1988). Dental microwear evidence suggests that the diet of *P. robustus* was composed of harder items (such as nuts) than were chewed by *A. africanus*; concomitantly, the dietary regimen of *P. robustus* may have included items with substantial amounts of extraneous grit, such as tubers (Grine 1986, 1987; Grine and Kay 1988; Kay and Grine 1988).

Paranthropus boisei

Specimens that have been attributed to this species derive from Members D, E, F, G and K of the Shungura Formation, Beds I and II of Olduvai Gorge, the Chemoigut and Humba Formations, the Kaitio and Lokalalei Members of the Nachukui Formation, and from the Burgi, KBS and Okote Members of the Koobi Fora Formation. These fossils date from some 2.4 to about 1.3 Myr. If the allocation of the earliest specimens to *P. boisei* is incorrect, this species range would span the period from at least 2.2 until 1.3 Myr.

Many of the craniodental features that characterize this taxon are possessed also by *P. robustus*, although many of the attributes that are associated with mastication appear to be even more exaggerated in *P. boisei* (Fig. 6). Thus, the cranium shows high hafting of the facial skeleton, a "dished" midface, a concave frontal trigone, depressed glabella that is nearly coincident

Figure 6. *Right lateral view of an adult male cranium of* Paranthropus boisei *(KNM-ER 406) discovered by R. E. F. Leakey in the Upper KBS Member of the Koobi Fora Formation. Courtesy of W. H. Kimbel.*

with nasion, a high petromedian angle, a high incidence of an occipital/marginal sinus rather than transverse sinuses, and absolutely and relatively small incisors and canines with large premolars and molars. Crania of *P. boisei* differ from those of *P. robustus*, however, in greater maxillary depth, an anteriorly deep (shelved) palate, the absence of a maxillary trigone, zygomatics that tend to be laterally bowed with a "visor"-like configuration of the cheek, a heart-shaped foramen magnum with a straight or posteriorly convex anterior margin, and temporoparietal overlap at asterion. The cheek teeth of *P. boisei* also tend to be larger than those of *P. robustus*; indeed, dimensions of *P. boisei* premolars and molars are the largest recorded for any hominid taxon. Endocranial capacity estimates range between about 500 and 530 cc with an average of approximately 515 cc for four specimens (Holloway 1988). Thus, as in *P. robustus*, the endocranial capacity of *P. boisei* tends to be greater than that of *A. afarensis* and *A. africanus* specimens.

Craniodental and postcranial elements reveal the presence of considerable sexual dimorphism in body size. Recent body weight estimates for three specimens from Koobi Fora range between about 52.0 kg and 60.0 kg, although other, less complete postcranial elements indicate a greater range (Jungers 1988; McHenry 1988). The few securely assigned *P. boisei* postcranial elements reveal a picture of a biped that retained adaptations to arboreal locomotion (e.g., relatively long arms such as displayed by *A. afarensis*, and ape-like proximal radius morphology that suggests a long lever arm of the biceps muscle as is found in *A. afarensis* and *A. africanus*) (Grausz *et al.* 1988). Paleoenvironmental reconstructions reveal a variety of potential habitats, with a possible preference for well-watered sites such as riverine gallery forests, although the preferred habitat of *P. boisei* remains a debated issue (Shipman and Harris 1988; Vrba 1988; White 1988). Microwear on *P. boisei* cheek teeth suggests the mastication of some hard items, although they may have played less of a role than in the dietary regimen of *P. robustus*; the diet of *P. boisei* may have entailed the prolonged chewing of tough or fibrous vegetable foods, perhaps with relatively little nutritional value (Walker 1981).

Paranthropus aethiopicus

At present, this taxon is known from only a single, nearly edentulous cranium (KNM-WT 17000) (Fig. 7), an incomplete and edentulous mandible (Omo 18-1967-18), and possibly some other fragmentary craniodental remains. These specimens derive from the Lomekwi Member of the Nachukui Formation, Member C of the Shungura Formation, and possibly from Member D and E of the Shungura Formation. At present, then, fossils that are attributable to *P. aethiopicus* date to about 2.6 to 2.3 Myr.

The cranium of *P. aethiopicus* differs from that of *P. boisei* and *P. robustus*, and it resembles that of *A. afarensis* in the presence of an elongate, unflexed base, marked alveolar prognathism, a shallow glenoid fossa without a clearly discernible articular eminence, a strongly flared parietal mastoid angle, and nasion that is coincident with a high glabella.

On the other hand, the *P. aethiopicus* cranium possesses a number of features shared by *P. robustus* and *P. boisei* specimens, including a "dished" midface with the cheeks located anterior to the level of the pyriform aperture, a nasoalveolar clivus that passes smoothly into the floor of the nose, a

Figure 7. *Left lateral view of the adult male cranium of* Paranthropus aethiopicus *(KNM-WT 17000) from the Lomekwi Member of the Nachukui Formation. Courtesy of R. E. F. Leakey and A. C. Walker.*

vertically deep and mediolaterally concave tympanic plate, a high petromedian angle, and a medially thickened palate. Like *P. robustus* specimens, it possesses a maxillary trigone and an anteriorly shallow palate, and like *P. boisei* specimens, it has a heart-shaped foramen magnum with a straight anterior margin. The single measurable premolar (a P3) associated with the Lomekwi cranium is similar in size to later *P. boisei* homologues, and the preserved roots of the other cheek teeth attest to their comparatively large sizes (Walker and Leakey 1988). The endocranial capacity of the single known (male) cranium is some 410 cc (Holloway 1988; Walker and Leakey 1988).

The Lomekwi cranium would have been associated with a mandible as large as some of the largest known *P. boisei* specimens from Koobi Fora and the Omo (e.g., KNM-ER 729). The mandible from Member C of the Shungura Formation, the type of *P. aethiopicus* (Omo 18-1967-18), is notably smaller. If the Omo mandible and the Lomekwi cranium are actually attributable to the same species, it would appear that *P. aethiopicus* exhibited considerable size dimorphism. Postcranial bones have not yet been assigned to *P. aethiopicus*, but it would seem safe to assume that they will exhibit the same characters as the other species, including (1) considerable differentiation in size, (2) morphological features associated with bipedal terrestrial locomotion, and (3) morphological features associated with a retained capability at arboreal climbing, such as relatively long arms and an ape-like proximal radius.

EVOLUTIONARY RELATIONSHIPS OF AUSTRALOPITHECINE SPECIES

There is considerable debate and controversy concerning the phylogenetic relationships among australopithecine species, and the evolutionary relationship of these taxa with *Homo*. Indeed, each phylogenetic hypothesis that has been put forward since the initial analysis of the Taung skull has been either falsified outright or at least altered in some manner by ongoing research and new discoveries. The recent discovery of the *P.*

aethiopicus cranium (KNM-WT 17000) has continued this scientific tradition. Despite the fact that these various hypotheses have been either rejected or altered substantially by recent discoveries and analyses, it is useful to review some of the more salient hypotheses because of the impact that they have had upon perceptions and subsequent interpretations of the course of early hominid evolution. Six such hypotheses will be reviewed here.

Hypothesis One   (Fig. 8). As advocated by P. V. Tobias (1980, 1988), the Hadar and Laetoli fossils represent geographically separate subspecies of *Australopithecus africanus*, which is the last common ancestor of the "robust" australopithecine and *Homo* lineages. More specifically, South African *A. africanus* (especially as represented by the Taung specimen) supposedly displays shared derived features with the "robust" australopithecines and early *Homo* (Tobias 1988), although the method by which he determined character polarity is highly questionable. Moreover, despite the fact that Tobias (1980) has argued that the Laetoli and Hadar fossils should not have been combined in the hypodigm of a single species by Johanson *et al.* (1978), he nevertheless places them together with fossils from South Africa, in *A. africanus*. This hypothesis does not adequately account for the overwhelming morphological evidence that separates *A. afarensis* from *A. africanus*; moreover, it has been effectively falsified by the cranial morphology displayed by *Paranthropus aethiopicus*. The KNM-WT 17000 cranium exhibits derived features in common with "robust" australopithecine taxa (*Paranthropus robustus* and *P. boisei*), while displaying primitive cranial characteristics such

Figure 8. *Phylogenetic scheme depicted by Hypothesis One.*

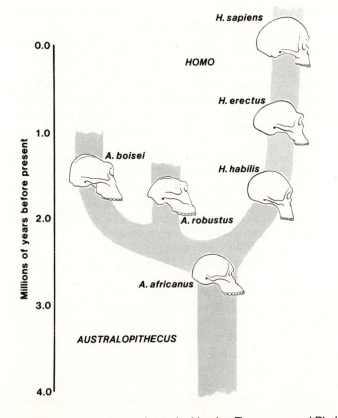

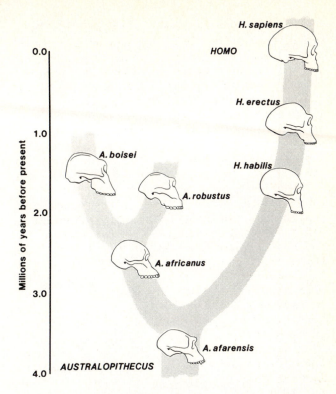

Figure 9. *Phylogenetic scheme depicted by Hypothesis Two.*

as those found in *A. afarensis*—this effectively removes *A. africanus* from an evolutionary relationship with the "robust" australopithecine lineage.

Hypothesis Two   (Fig. 9). Advanced by Johanson and White (1979), and advocated by them (White *et al.* 1981) and others (e.g., Rak 1983), *Australopithecus afarensis* represents the stem hominid from which both the *Homo* and "robust" australopithecine lineages diverged. According to this hypothesis, *A. africanus* is more closely related to the "robust" taxa *A. robustus* and *A. boisei* than to any other hominid taxon by virtue of shared craniodental specializations (e.g., morphoclines involving the anterior pillars, increased cheek-tooth size, etc.). *A. afarensis* was held to be the forebear of *Homo*, not because of linkage by any synapomorphy, but simply because the interpretation of "robust" characters in *A. africanus* removed it from this ancestral position. This hypothesis has been falsified by the discovery of the *P. aethiopicus* cranium for the same reasons that the KNM-WT 17000 cranium falsifies Hypothesis One.

Hypothesis Three   (Fig. 10). As formally advanced by Skelton *et al.* (1986), and as advocated until recently by others (e.g., Dean 1986), *A. afarensis* represents the stem hominid from which *A. africanus* evolved. *Homo* and "robust" australopithecine (i.e., *P. robustus* and *P. boisei*) species share several derived features in common (e.g., a high petromedian angle) that attest to their having shared a last common ancestor, and that role is filled by an *A. africanus*-like form. While *A. africanus* itself, as currently known, could not have been the actual last common ancestor because it lacks several features possessed in common by *Homo* and "robust" australopithecines

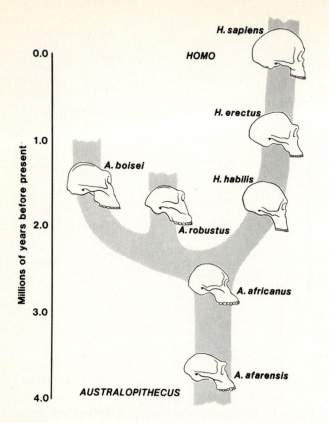

Figure 10. *Phylogenetic scheme depicted by Hypothesis Three.*

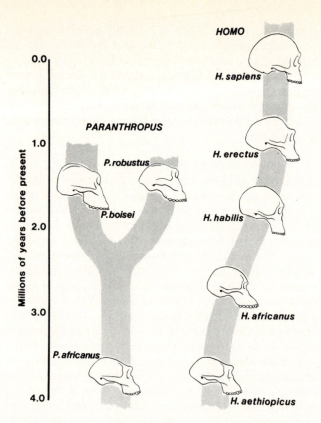

Figure 11. *Phylogenetic hypothesis depicted by Hypothesis Four.*

(e.g., a high petromedian angle), a form very similar to *A. africanus* would have been a likely candidate for ancestry. This hypothesis has been falsified by the cranial morphology displayed by *P. aethiopicus* for the reason that it removes *A. africanus* from close relationship with the "robust" australopithecine line.

Hypothesis Four (Fig. 11). As advanced originally by J. T. Robinson in the late 1960's and early 1970's (e.g., see 1972), this hypothesis was modified by Olson (1981), who incorporated the Hadar and Laetoli fossils in the interpretation of early hominid evolution. According to this hypothesis, the "robust" australopithecines (*Paranthropus*) comprise a distinct evolutionary lineage that diverged very early from the *Homo* line. Since *P. robustus* and *P. boisei* belong to a separate evolutionary clade, they should be accorded generic distinctiveness from the species that comprise the *Homo* line. Robinson argued that since *A. africanus* was part of the latter, there was no valid reason to recognize *Australopithecus* as a distinct genus: the specimens from Taung, Sterkfontein and Makapansgat would be recognized as belonging to the species *Homo africanus*.

This hypothesis, which was put forward prior to the discovery of the large Hadar and Laetoli samples, was altered slightly by Olson (1981), who argued that these samples contain the remains of two species: one was held to be part of the *Paranthropus* lineage, while the other was thought to represent an early member of the *Homo* line. Interestingly, while Robinson recognized the few "Garusi" fossils that were discovered in the 1930's to be part of the *Homo* line (*H. africanus*), Olson interpreted the Laetoli remains as being part of the

Paranthropus lineage (*P. africanus*). Olson (1981) also posited that a portion of the Hadar assemblage (especially the specimens from site 333) comprised part of the *Paranthropus* clade, while the other Hadar fossils represented an early species of *Homo*, namely *H. aethiopicus* [1].

While several authors (e.g., Tobias 1980; Olson 1981; Ferguson 1983; Zihlman 1985) have had difficulty in recognizing the validity of *Australopithecus afarensis*, no two individuals who have been opposed to this species have been able to agree on the correct attribution of the Hadar and Laetoli fossils. This, in itself, is quite suggestive of the fact that there is no clear dichotomy within the hypodigm proposed by Johanson *et al.* (1978).

There is a growing concensus concerning the validity of *A. afarensis*, as represented by the Hadar and Laetoli samples. Notwithstanding Olson's claim to be able to recognize two species in the *A. afarensis* hypodigm, the phylogenetic scheme depicted in Fig. 11 has been corroborated in large measure by the cranial morphology exhibited by *P. aethiopicus*. That is, the Lomekwi cranium bears testament to the derivation of the "robust" australopithecines from an *A. afarensis*-like ancestor.

Hypothesis Five (Fig. 12). As advocated by Walker *et al.* (1986), *A. afarensis* represents the common root from which evolved the eastern African "robust" lineage (*A. aethiopicus* and *A. boisei*) and a southern African lineage that led to the "robust" form *A. robustus* and to *Homo* through a common ancestor in *A. africanus*. This hypothesis states that the morphological resemblances between the *A. robustus* and *A. boisei* specimens are due to functional convergence. The large number

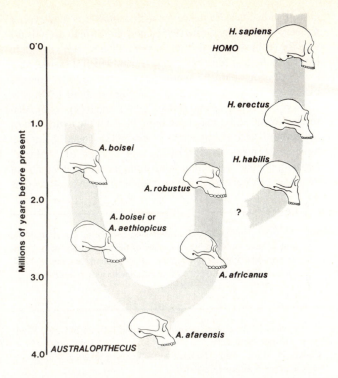

Figure 12. *Phylogenetic scheme depicted by Hypothesis Five.*

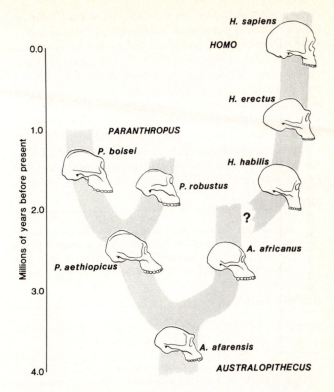

Figure 13. *Phylogenetic scheme depicted by Hypothesis Six.*

of detailed similarities between the southern and eastern African "robust" forms, some of which (e.g., the pattern of venous drainage from the endocranium; the pattern of middle meningeal vasculature, etc.) are difficult to ascribe to the masticatory apparatus, and the differences between these species in features that are part of the masticatory system (e.g., differences in glenoid morphology, palatal depth, zygomatic configuration, etc.) suggest that common ancestry rather than convergent evolution is at the root of their resemblances.

Hypothesis Six   (Fig. 13). As advanced by Grine (1988a, b) and, in part, by Kimbel *et al.* (1988), is similar to Hypothesis Four inasmuch as it recognizes the "robust" taxa from southern and eastern Africa—*P. robustus* and *P. boisei*, together with *P. aethiopicus*—as representing a monophyletic clade. It differs from Hypothesis Four, however, in the recognition of *A. afarensis* as represented by the Hadar and Laetoli fossils. According to this hypothesis, *A. afarensis* is the last common ancestor of a *Paranthropus* lineage and a line that led to *Homo* through a form similar in morphology to *A. africanus*. This last hypothesis stems from the interpretation of the evolutionary relationships of *P. aethiopicus*, as represented by the cranium (KNM-WT 17000) from the Lomekwi Member of the Nachukui Formation.

This specimen exhibits a number of primitive features in common with *Australopithecus afarensis*, and a number of evolutionarily derived features in common with *Paranthropus robustus* and *P. boisei*. This suggests very strongly that *Paranthropus aethiopicus* is phylogenetically intermediate between *A. afarensis*, on the one hand, and *P. robustus* and *P. boisei*, on the other. At the same time, *A. africanus* is unlikely to be closely related to the "robust" australopithecine lineage—the features that *A. africanus* has in common with the later "robust" australopithecines are most likely ascribable to parallelisms.

SUMMARY AND CONCLUSIONS

Current evidence indicates that the early hominids were considerably more diverse (speciose) than has been envisioned for the past three decades, with at least five australopithecine species existing from some 4.0 to about 1.3 Myr. While there is no doubt that at least one major cladogenetic event occurred—i.e., that between the "robust" australopithecine and human lines—there has been considerable debate as to exactly where and when this split took place. The australopithecine species that are currently recognized in the African fossil record show a considerable diversity in craniodental characters, but there are some similarities that appear to persist through all species.

All species of *Paranthropus* and *Australopithecus* were bipedal, and all appear to have retained morphological attributes that are likely associated with movement (e.g., climbing) in an arboreal mileau. There appear to be subtle differences, however, in the degree of arboreality displayed by the various taxa. All australopithecine species are megadont for their body sizes, but the species of *Paranthropus* evince inordinate expansion in the size of the premolars and molars, especially in relation to their somewhat reduced anterior teeth. There is evidence for considerable sexual dimorphism in all species; the degree approximates that shown by extant gorillas and orangutans.

The increase in endocranial capacity that is shown by members of the *Paranthropus* lineage appears to parallel the increase in brain size that characterized the evolutionary history of our own lineage, although the magnitude of interspecific increase in the former is clearly not as dramatic.

Undisputed stone (or bone) tools are not known to be associated with *Australopithecus* species or with specimens of

Paranthropus aethiopicus. While stone and/or bone tools are known from sites that contain *P. robustus* and *P. boisei* fossils, early members of the genus *Homo* are also known from these same localities or sites. Indeed, it has been suggested that *Paranthropus* species may have been driven to extinction through competition with *Homo erectus*, who might have possessed a distinct ecological advantage through the utilization of lithic technology in the procurement of food (Klein 1988). By the same token, if species of *Paranthropus* did interact through indirect ecological (i.e., trophic) competition with early *Homo*, it is quite possible that the early evolutionary course of our own genus was profoundly influenced by the "robust" australopithecines. Evidence for such competition, however, is not very convincing (Grine 1985b), and it is difficult to envisage why the "robust" australopithecines would have been driven to extinction by a species (*H. erectus*) with which they probably had been geographically sympatric for some 300 kyr. There is evidence of major global climatic changes at about 1.0 Myr or 900 kyr B.P. (Prentice and Denton 1988), and it is possible that these climatic shifts may have brought about the extinction of the "robust" australopithecines (Klein 1988). The problem that besets attempts to determine the causes of "robust" australopithecine extinction stems from the fact that we do not yet know precisely when they vanished from the fossil record.

NOTE

[1] Considerable confusion has arisen over the use of the nomen '*aethiopicus*' by Tobias (1980) as a subspecies designation for the entire Hadar fossil hominid collection (i.e., *A. africanus aethiopicus*), and by Olson (1981) as the trivial name for the earliest species of *Homo* (i.e., *H. aethiopicus*) comprising a portion of the Hadar sample, when priority usage of the name exists with Arambourg and Coppens (1968) in their description of the Omo 18-1967-18 mandible as the type of *Paraustralopithecus aethiopicus*.

REFERENCES

Aguirre, E. 1970. Identification de '*Paranthropus*' en Makapansgat. *Cronica XI Cong. Nac. Arquelogia, Merida* 1969:98-124.

Arambourg, C., and Coppens, Y. 1968. Decouverte d'un Australopithecien nouveau dans les gisements de l'Omo (Ethiopie). *S. Afr. J. Sci.* 64:58-59.

Asfaw, B. 1987. The Belohdelie frontal: new evidence of early hominid cranial morphology from the Afar of Ethiopia. *J. Hum. Evol.* 16:611-624.

Brain, C. K. 1981. *The Hunters or the Hunted? An Introduction to African Cave Taphonomy*. University of Chicago Press, Chicago.

Brain, C. K. 1988. New information from the Swartkrans cave of relevance to "robust" australopithecines, in: *Evolutionary History of the "Robust" Australopithecines* (F. E. Grine, Ed.), pp. 311-316, Aldine de Gruyter, New York.

Brain, C. K., Churcher, C. S., Clark, J. D., Grine, F. E., Shipman, P., Susman, R. L., Turner, A., and Watson, V. 1988. New evidence of early hominids, their culture and environment from the Swartkrans cave, South Africa. *S. Afr. J. Sci.* 84:828-835.

Brock, A., McFadden, P. L., and Partridge, T. C. 1977. Preliminary paleomagnetic results from Makapansgat and Swartkrans. *Nature* 255:249-250.

Broom, R. 1925a. Some notes on the Taung skull. *Nature* 155:569-571.

Broom, R. 1925b. On the newly discovered South African man-ape. *Nat. Hist.* 25:409-418.

Broom, R. 1929. Note on the milk dentition of *Australopithecus*. *Proc. Zool. Soc. Lond.* 1928:85-88.

Broom, R. 1936. A new fossil anthropoid skull from South Africa. *Nature* 138:486-488.

Broom, R. 1938. The Pleistocene anthropoid apes of South Africa. *Nature* 142:377-379.

Broom, R. 1949. Another new type of fossil ape-man. *Nature* 163:57.

Broom, R. 1950. The genera and species of the South African fossil ape-men. *Amer. J. Phys. Anthro.* 8:1-13.

Brown, F. H. 1982. Tulu Bor Tuff at Koobi Fora correlated with the Sidi Hakoma Tuff at Hadar. *Nature* 300:631-633.

Brown, F. H., and Feibel, C. S. 1988. "Robust" hominids and Plio-Pleistocene paleogeography of the Turkana Basin, Kenya and Ethiopia, in: *Evolutionary History of the "Robust" Australopithecines* (F. E. Grine, Ed.), pp. 325-341, Aldine de Gruyter, New York.

Brown, F. H., McDougall, I., Davies, T., and Maier, R. 1985. An integrated Plio/Pleistocene chronology of the Turkana Basin, in: *Ancestors: the Hard Evidence* (E. Delson, Ed.), pp. 82-90, Alan R. Liss, New York.

Carney, J., Hill, A., Miller, J. A., and Walker, A. C. 1971. Late australopithecine from Baringo. *Nature* 230:509-514.

Clarke, R. J. 1988. A new *Australopithecus* cranium from Sterkfontein and its bearing on the ancestry of *Paranthropus*, in: *Evolutionary History of the "Robust" Australopithecines* (F. E. Grine, Ed.), pp. 285-292, Aldine de Gruyter, New York.

Cooke, H. B. S. 1983. Human evolution: the geological framework. *Canadian J. Anthro.* 3:143-161.

Dart, R. A. 1925. *Australopithecus africanus*: the man-ape of South Africa. *Nature* 115:195-199.

Dart, R. A. 1926. Taungs and its significance. *Nat. Hist.* 26:315-327.

Dart, R. A. 1929. A note on the Taungs skull. *S. Afr. J. Sci.* 26:648-658.

Dart, R. A. 1934. The dentition of *Australopithecus africanus*. *Folia Anat. Japon.* 12:207-221.

Dart, R. A. 1948. The Makapansgat proto-human *Australopithecus prometheus*. *Amer. J. Phys. Anthro.* 6:259-284.

Dart, R. A. 1957. The osteodontokeratic culture of *Australopithecus prometheus*. *Mem. Transvaal Mus.* 10:1-105.

Dean, M. C. 1986. *Homo* and *Paranthropus*: similarities in the cranial base and developing dentition, in: *Major Topics in Primate and Human Evolution* (B. A. Wood, L. B. Martin and P. Andrews, Eds.), pp. 249-265, Cambridge University Press, Cambridge.

Delson, E. 1988, Chronology of South African australopith site units, in: *Evolutionary History of the "Robust" Australopithecines* (F. E. Grine, Ed.), pp. 317-324, Aldine de Gruyter, New York.

Ferguson, W. W. 1983. An alternative interpretation of *Australopithecus afarensis* fossil material. *Primates* 24:397-409.

Fleagle, J. G. *et al.* 1991. New hominid fossils from Fejej, southern Ethiopia. *J. Hum. Evol.* 21:145-152.

Grausz, H. M., Leakey, R. E. F., Walker, A. C., and Ward, C. V. 1988. Associated cranial and postcranial bones of *Australopithecus boisei*, in: *Evolutionary History of the "Robust" Australopithecines* (F. E. Grine, Ed.), pp. 127-132, Aldine de Gruyter, New York.

Grine, F. E., 1982. A new juvenile hominid (Mammalia; Primates) from Member 3, Kromdraai Formation, Transvaal, South Africa. *Ann. Transvaal Mus.* 33:165-239.

Grine, F. E. 1985a. Australopithecine evolution: the deciduous dental evidence, in: *Ancestors: the Hard Evidence* (E.Delson, Ed.), pp. 153-167, Alan R. Liss, New York.

Grine, F. E. 1985b. Was interspecific competition a motive force in early hominid evolution? in: *Species and Speciation* (E.S. Vrba, Ed.), pp. 143-152, Transvaal Museum Monographs, Pretoria.

Grine, F. E. 1986. Dental evidence for dietary differences in *Australopithecus* and *Paranthropus*: a quantitative analysis of permanent molar microwear. *J. Hum. Evol.* 15:783-822.

Grine, F.E. 1987. L'Alimentation des Australopitheques d'Africa du Sud, d'apres des microtraces d'usure sur les dents. *L'Anthropologie* 91:467-482.

Grine, F. E. 1988a. Evolutionary history of the "robust" australopithecines: a summary and historical perspective, in: *Evolutionary History of the "Robust" Australopithecines* (F. E. Grine, Ed.), pp. 509-519. Aldine de Gruyter, New York.

Grine, F. E. 1988b. New craniodental fossils of *Paranthropus* from the Swartkrans Formation and their significance in "robust" australopithecine evolution, in: *Evolutionary History of the "Robust" Australopithecines* (F. E. Grine, Ed.), pp. 223-244, Aldine de Gruyter, New York.

Grine, F. E. 1989. New hominid fossils from the Swartkrans Formation (1979-1986 excavations): craniodental remains. *Amer. J. Phys. Anthro.* 79:409-449.

Grine, F. E., and Kay, R. F. 1988. Early hominid diets from quantitative image analysis of dental microwear. *Nature* 333:765-768.

Howell, F. C. 1978. Hominidae, in: *Evolution of African Mammals* (V. J. Maglio and H. B. S. Cooke, Eds.), pp. 154-248, Harvard University Press, Cambridge, Mass.

Holloway, R. L. 1988. "Robust" australopithecine brain endocasts: some preliminary observations, in: *Evolutionary History of the "Robust" Australopithecines* (F. E. Grine, Ed.), pp. 97-106, Aldine de Gruyter, New York.

Johanson, D. C., White, T. D. 1979. A systematic assessment of early African hominids. *Science* 202:321–330.

Johanson, D. C., White, T. D., and Coppens, Y. 1978. A new species of the genus *Australopithecus* (Primates:Hominidae) from the Pliocene of eastern Africa. *Kirtlandia* 28:1-14.

Jungers, W. L. 1982. Lucy's limbs: skeletal allometry and locomotion in *Australopithecus afarensis*. *Nature* 297:678-679.

Jungers, W. L. 1988. New estimates of body size in australopithecines, in: *Evolutionary History of the "Robust" Australopithecines* (F. E. Grine, Ed.), pp. 115-126, Aldine de Gruyter, New York.

Jungers, W. L., and Grine, F. E. 1986. Dental trends in the australopithecines: the allometry of mandibular molar dimensions, in: *Major Topics in Primate and Human Evolution* (B. A. Wood, L. B. Martin and P. Andrews, Eds.), pp. 203-219, Cambridge University Press, Cambridge.

Kay, R. F., and Grine, F. E. 1988. Tooth morphology, wear and diet in *Australopithecus* and *Paranthropus* from southern Africa, in: *Evolutionary History of the "Robust" Australopithecines* (F. E. Grine, Ed.), pp. 427-448, Aldine de Gruyter, New York.

Keith, A. 1931. *New Discoveries Relating to the Antiquity of Man*. Williams and Norgate, London.

Kimbel, W. H. 1988. Identification of a partial cranium of *Australopithecus afarensis* from the Koobi Fora Formation, Kenya. *J. Hum. Evol.* 17:647-656.

Kimbel, W. H., and White, T. D. 1988a. A revised reconstruction of the adult skull of *Australopithecus afarensis*. *J. Hum. Evol.* 17:545-550.

Kimbel, W. H., and White, T. D. 1988b. Variation, sexual dimorphism and the taxonomy of *Australopithecus*, in: *Evolutionary History of the "Robust" Australopithecines* (F.E. Grine, Ed.), pp. 175-192, Aldine de Gruyter, New York.

Kimbel, W. H., White, T. D., and Johanson, D. C. 1984. Cranial morphology of *Australopithecus afarensis*: a comparative study based on a composite reconstruction of the adult skull. *Amer. J. Phys. Anthro.* 64:337-388.

Kimbel, W. H., White, T. D., and Johanson, D. C. 1988. Implications of KNM-WT 17000 for the evolution of "robust" *Australopithecus*, in: *Evolutionary History of the "Robust" Australopithecines* (F. E. Grine, Ed.), pp. 259-268, Aldine de Gruyter, New York.

Klein, R. G. 1988. The causes of "Robust" Australopithecine extinction, in: *Evolutionary History of the "Robust" Australopithecines* (F. E. Grine, Ed.), pp. 499-507, Aldine de Gruyter, New York.

Leakey, L. S. B. 1959. A new fossil skull from Olduvai. *Nature* 184:967-970.

Leakey, L. S. B., and Leakey, M. D. 1964. Recent discoveries of fossil hominids in Tanganyika at Olduvai and near Lake Natron. *Nature* 202:5-7.

Leaky, M. D. 1978. Olduvai fossil hominids: their stratigraphic positions and allocations, in: *Early Hominids of Africa* (C. Jolly, Ed.), pp. 3-16, Duckworth, London.

Leakey, M. D., and Harris, J. M. 1987. *Laetoli: a Pliocene Site in Northern Tanzania*. Oxford University Press, Oxford.

Leakey, R. E. F., and Walker, A. C. 1985. Further hominids form the Plio-Pleistocene of Koobi Fora, Kenya. *Amer. J. Phys. Anthro.* 67:135-163.

Leakey, R. E. F., and Walker, A. C. 1988. New *Australopithecus boisei* specimens from East and West Lake Turkana, Kenya. *Amer. J. Phys. Anthro.* 76:1-24.

Leakey, R. E. F., Leakey, M. G., and Behrensmeyer, A. K. 1978. The hominid catalogue, in: *Koobi Fora Research Project*, Vol 1, *The Fossil Hominids and an Introduction to their Context* (M. G. Leakey and R. E. F. Leakey, Eds.), pp. 86-187, Clarendon, Oxford.

McHenry, H. M. 1986. The first bipeds: a comparison of the *A. afarensis* and *A. africanus* postcranium and implications for the evolution of bipedalism. *J. Hum. Evol.* 15:177-191.

McHenry, H. M. 1988. New estimates of body weight in early hominids and their significance to encephalization and megadontia in "robust" australopithecines, in: *Evolutionary History of the "Robust" Australopithecines* (F. E. Grine, Ed.), pp. 133-148, Aldine de Gruyter, New York.

Olson, T. R. 1978. Hominid phylogenetics and the existence of *Homo* in Member I of the Swartkrans Formation, South Africa. *J. Hum. Evol.* 7:159-178.

Olson, T. R. 1981. Basicranial morphology of the extant hominids and Pliocene hominids: the new material from the Hadar Formation, Ethiopia, and its significance in early human evolution and taxonomy, in: *Aspects of Human Evolution* (C. B. Stringer, Ed.), pp. 99-128, Taylor and Francis, London.

Partridge, T. C. 1973. Geomorphological dating of cave openings at Makapansgat, Sterkfontein, Swartkrans and Taung. *Nature* 246:75-79.

Partridge, T. C. 1982. Dating of South African hominid sites. *S. Afr. J. Sci.* 78:300-301.

Prentice, M. L., and Denton, G. H. 1988. The deep-sea oxygen isotope record, the global ice sheet system and hominid evolution, in: *Evolutionary History of the "Robust" Australopithecines* (F. E. Grine, Ed.), pp. 383-404, Aldine de Gruyter, New York.

Rak, Y. 1983. *The Australopithecine Face*. Academic, New York.

Robinson, J. T. 1954. The genera and species of the Australopithecinae. *Amer. J. Phys. Anthro.* 12:181-200.

Robinson, J. T. 1960. The affinities of the new Olduvai australopithecine. *Nature* 186:456-458.

Robinson, J. T. 1972. *Early Hominid Posture and Locomotion*. University of Chicago Press, Chicago.

Romer, A. S. 1930. *Australopithecus* not a chimpanzee. *Science* 71:482-483.

Sarna-Wojcici, A. M., Meyer, C. E., Roth, P. H., and Brown, F. H. 1985. Ages of tuff beds at East African early hominid sites and sediments in the Gulf of Aden. *Nature* 313:306-308.

Senut, B., and Tardieu, C. 1985. Functional aspects of Plio-Pleistocene hominid limb bones: implications for taxonomy and phylogeny, in: *Ancestors: The Hard Evidence* (E. Delson, Ed.), pp. 193-201, Alan R. Liss, New York.

Shipman, P., and Harris, J. M. 1988. Habitat preference and paleoecology of *Australopithecus boisei* in eastern Africa, in: *Evolutionary History of the "Robust" Australopithecines* (F. E. Grine, Ed.), pp. 343-382, Aldine de Gruyter, New York.

Skelton, R. R., McHenry, H. M., and Drawhorn, G. M. 1986. Phylogenetic analysis of early hominids. *Current Anthropology* 27:21–35.

Sollas, W. J. 1926. A sagittal section of the skull of *Australopithecus africanus*. *Quart. J. Geol. Soc. Lond.* 82:1-11.

Stern, J. T., and Susman, R. L. 1983. The locomotor anatomy of *Australopithecus afarensis*. *Amer. J. Phys. Anthro.* 60:279-317.

Susman, R. L. 1988. New postcranial remains from Swartkrans and their bearing on the functional morphology and behavior of *Paranthropus robustus*, in: *Evolutionary History of the "Robust" Australopithecines* (F. E. Grine, Ed.), pp. 149-174, Aldine de Gruyter, New York.

Susman, R. L., and Brain, T. M. 1988. New first metatarsal (SKX 5017) from Swartkrans and the gait of *Paranthropus robustus*. *Amer. J. Phys. Anthro.* 77:7-15.

Susman, R. L., and Grine, F. E. 1989. New *Paranthropus robustus* radius from Member 1, Swartkrans Formation. *Amer. J. Phys. Anthro.* 78:311-312.

Susman, R. L., Stern, J. T., and Jungers, W. L. 1984. Arboreality and bipedality in the Hadar hominids. *Folia Primatol.* 43:113-156.

Susman, R. L., Stern, J. T., and Jungers, W. L. 1985. Locomotor adaptations in the Hadar hominids, in: *Ancestors: The Hard Evidence* (E. Delson, Ed.), pp. 184-192, Alan R. Liss, New York.

Tobias, P. V. 1967. *The Cranium and Maxillary Dentition of Australopithecus (Zinjanthropus) boisei.* Olduvai Gorge, Vol. 2. Cambridge University Press, Cambridge.

Tobias, P. V. 1973. Implications of the new age estimates of the early South African hominids. *Nature* 246:79-83.

Tobias, P. V. 1978. The South African australopithecines in time and hominid phylogeny, with special reference to the dating and affinities of the Taung skull, in: *Early Hominids of Africa* (C. Jolly, Ed.), pp. 45-84, Duckworth, London.

Tobias, P. V. 1980. "*Australopithecus afarensis*" and *A. africanus*: critique and an alternative hypothesis. *Palaeont. Afr.* 23:1-17.

Tobias, P. V. 1988. Numerous apparently synapomorphic features in *Australopithecus robustus*, *Australopithecus boisei* and *Homo habilis*: support for the Skelton-McHenry-Drawhorn hypothesis, in: *Evolutionary History of the "Robust" Australopithecines*, (F. E. Grine, Ed.), pp. 293-309, Aldine de Gruyter, New York.

Vogel, J. C. 1985. Further attempts at dating the Taung tufas, in: *Hominid Evolution: Past, Present and Future* (P. V. Tobias, Ed.), pp. 189-194, Alan R. Liss, New York.

Vrba, E. S. 1979. A new study of the scapula of *Australopithecus africanus* from Sterkfontein. *Amer. J. Phys. Anthro.* 51:117-129.

Vrba, E. S. 1981. The Kromdraai australopithecine site revisited in 1980: recent investigations and results. *Ann. Transvaal Mus.* 33:17-60.

Vrba, E. S. 1982. Biostratigraphy and chronology, based particularly on Bovidae, of southern African hominid-associated assemblages: Makapansgat, Sterkfontein, Taung, Kromdraai, Swartkrans; also Elandsfontein (Saldanha), Broken Hill (now Kabwe) and Cave of Hearths, in: *Pretirage 1er Cong. Internat. Paleont. Humaine*, Vol. II, pp. 707-752, Cent. Nat. Rech. Sci., Nice.

Vrba, E. S. 1985. Ecological and adaptive changes associated with early hominid evolution, in: *Ancestors: The Hard Evidence* (E. Delson, Ed.), pp. 63-71, Alan R. Liss, New York.

Vrba, E. S. 1988. Late Pliocene climatic events and hominid evolution, in: *Evolutionary History of the "Robust" Australopithecines* (F. E. Grine, Ed.), pp. 405-425, Aldine de Gruyter, New York.

Walker, A. C. 1981. Dietary hypotheses and human evolution. *Phil. Trans. Roy. Soc. Lond.*, B 292:57-64.

Walker, A. C., and Leakey, R. E. F. 1988. The evolution of *Australopithecus boisei*, in: *Evolutionary History of the "Robust" Australopithecines* (F. E. Grine, Ed.), pp. 247-258, Aldine de Gruyter, New York.

Walker, A. C., Leakey, R. E. F., Harris, J. M., and Brown, F. H. 1986. 2.5-Myr *Australopithecus boisei* from West of Lake Turkana, Kenya. *Nature* 322:517-522.

Ward, S., and Hill, A. 1987. Pliocene hominid partial mandible from Tabarin, Baringo, Kenya. *Amer. J. Phys. Anthro.* 72:21-38.

White, T. D. 1984. Pliocene hominids from the Middle Awash, Ethiopia. *Cour. Forsch. Inst. Senckenberg* 69:57-68.

White, T. D. 1988. The comparative biology of "robust" *Australopithecus*: clues from context, in: *Evolutionary History of the "Robust" Australopithecines* (F. E. Grine, Ed.), pp. 449-483, Aldine de Gruyter, New York.

White, T. D., Johanson, D. C., and Kimbel, W. D. 1981. *Australopithecus africanus*: its phyletic position reconsidered. *S. Afr. J. Sci.* 77:445–470.

White, T. D., Johanson, D. C., and Kimbel, W. H. 1982. Dating of South African hominid sites. *S. Afr. J. Sci.* 78:301-302.

Wolpoff, M. H. 1974. The evidence for two australopithecine lineages in South Africa. *Yrbk. Phys. Anthro.* 17:133-139.

Wood, B. A., and Chamberlain, A. T. 1986. *Australopithecus*: grade or clade? in: *Topics in Primate and Human Evolution* (B. A. Wood, L. B. Martin, and P. Andrews, Eds.), pp. 220-248, Cambridge University Press, Cambridge.

Woodward, A. S. 1925. The fossil anthropoid ape from Taungs. *Nature* 155:235-236.

Zihlman, A. L. 1985. *Australopithecus afarensis*: two sexes or two species? in: *Hominid Evolution: Past, Present and Future* (P. V. Tobias, Ed.), pp. 213-220, Alan R. Liss, New York.

Part III
Theoretical Perspectives of Hominid Origins

However exciting bones and stones (and molecules) may be, these materials do not speak for themselves to tell us about human evolution. In the absence of some theoretical context, fossils are little more than odd stones or relics. Their main interest lies in providing some empirical evidence to support or disprove various theories that have been developed to explain how and why humans came to be the way we are (e.g., Landau 1984, 1991; Cartmill *et al.* 1986; Kinzey 1987). The articles in this part are devoted to theoretical views of human evolution and interpreting the fossil remains discussed in earlier and later chapters. Some chapters are largely concerned with promoting one theory (those by Washburn and Lancaster, Zihlman and Tanner, Lovejoy, and Shipman) while those by Fedigan and Isaac provide a broader review. Although these articles all deal with aspects of early human evolution, they often address different phases of human evolution. Zihlman and Tanner (Chapter 21) and Lovejoy (Chapter 22) are specifically concerned with the initial divergence of humans from apes, while Lancaster and Washburn (Chapter 20) and Shipman (Chapter 25) address later phases of human evolution involving the use of stone tools. Theories are inherently speculative and consequently subject to debate. Most of the articles in this part are provocative and have generated considerable comment and criticism, both positive and negative. We could not possibly reprint all of the comments that the articles in this part have generated, but much of this follow-up debate is referenced in the two review articles by Fedigan and Isaac and others are included in the following paragraphs.

Chapter 20, "The Evolution of Hunting" by Sherwood Washburn and C.S. Lancaster, is reprinted from the volume, *Man the Hunter* (Lee and DeVore 1968). Noting that agriculture has been a common means of hominid subsistence for only a few thousands of years, the authors argue that hunting was the primary means of subsistence throughout most of hominid evolution. Consequently they suggest how most of the features that distinguish humans from other primates, both physically and mentally, have arisen in the context of a hunting way of life. The hunting theory of hominid origins has received considerable criticism on several fronts. Many have noted that it is inconsistent with paleontological and archaeological data (which indicate that tools postdate human origins by several million years, see Chapters 22-24). Moreover, ethnographic data show that hunting rarely accounts for a substantial portion of the foods consumed even by hunters and gatherers (see Chapters 21 and 23). Finally, many have objected that this theory largely ignores the role of females in hominid evolution. Nevertheless, it has been a conspicuous aspect in theoretical discussions of human evolution from Darwin (1871) through the present (see for example, Hawkes 1990), especially following the appearance of stone tools.

Chapter 21, "Gathering and the Hominid Adaptation" by Adrienne Zihlman and Nancy Tanner, specifically addresses many of the problems of the hunting theory. Since it is gathering, primarily by women, that provides most of the subsistence for living hunter–gather groups, and plant foods provide the subsistence for our closest relatives, chimpanzees, Zihlman and Tanner argue that hominid origins and the evolution of bipedality almost certainly took place in the context of an herbivorous or omnivorous diet. Such a model also accords best with the dentition of the earliest hominids and with the absence of any tools clearly related to hunting or butchering (see also Kappelman and Hatley 1980). Zihlman and Tanner's model of early hominid evolution has been widely acclaimed for redressing a longstanding male bias in human evolution by emphasizing the role of females (see also Chapter 23). It draws quite heavily on phylogenetic studies showing a close genetic relationship between humans and chimpanzees and ethological studies of great apes in, quite appropriately, reconstructing early hominids as slightly modified chimpanzees rather than little people.

Chapter 22, "The Origin of Man" by Owen Lovejoy, offers a view of early hominids that is similar to that of Zihlman and Tanner in seeing the bipedal gathering of plant foods as the major subsistence activity of early hominids. It differs in postulating very different daily activity patterns for males and females, with males as the sex primarily responsible for subsistence gathering, and in hypothesizing a major shift in reproductive success as the critical difference between early hominids and other hominoids. In contrast with most other theorists, Lovejoy sees hominid origins taking place in a mosaic environment of forests and savannah rather than in open savannah (see also Rodman and McHenry 1980; Susman 1987). Lovejoy's model is one of the most widely cited papers in recent decades [see *Lucy, The Beginnings of Humankind* by Johanson and Edey (1981) for a popular discussion of Lovejoy's theory] and accordingly has also been the subject of considerable criticism (see *Science*, vol. 217, pp. 295-306; and Chapter 23).

Chapter 23, "The Changing Role of Women in Models of Human Evolution" by Linda Fedigan, reviews models of human evolution, and specifically hominid origins, from Darwin (1871) to Washburn and Lancaster (Chapter 20), Zihlman and Tanner (Chapter 21) and Lovejoy (Chapter 22). Although her emphasis is on the role of women, she compares and contrasts many other aspects of the model and relates them to changes in the paleontological record, primatological studies, other social sciences, and contemporary society. She reviews in considerable detail the evidence available from primate studies concerning which aspects of behavior and ecology early hominids might be expected to retain from a hominoid ancestry (see also Wrangham 1987; Gighlieri 1987), the significance of sexual dimorphism in early hominids (see also McHenry 1991), and inferences concerning maturation rates in early hominids based on dental development (see also Beynon and Dean 1988).

Chapter 24, "Aspects of Human Evolution," is one of the last papers written by the late Glynn Isaac, an outstanding Paleolithic archaeologist who contributed much to our understanding of human evolution in East Africa and has produced many illustrious students. This paper provides another historical review of theories of human origins and early human evolution, this time from the perspective of an African archaeologist. Through diagrams and tables, Isaac provides excellent summaries of the history of paleontological discoveries, theories of hominoid phylogeny, morphological and technological change in human evolution. He reviews theories explaining the origin of hominid bipedalism and those designed to account for the later appearance of the brain-culture system, and discusses the need for setting up testable theories and then subjecting them to falsification.

Chapter 25, "Early Hominid Lifestyle: Hunting and Gathering or Foraging and Scavaging?" by Pat Shipman, presents another theory concerning the behavior of early tool-using hominids that has become particularly popular in recent years (see also Szalay 1975; Binford 1981; Blumenschine 1987, 1989; Potts 1988 for other reviews of the scavenging theory). She briefly critiques the theories of Lovejoy (Chapter 22) and Isaac (Chapter 24) and proposes ways of testing them through analysis of archaeological and faunal remains and information about the behavior of extant hunters and gatherers. Her results suggest a more opportunistic and less systematic use of carcasses by early hominids than that which characterizes active hunters. Instead, she suggests that early tool-using hominids were probably mainly foraging for plant foods and scavenging for meat. Much of current archaeological work on early hominid behavior is devoted to evaluating the alternative evidence for hunting or scavenging among early tool using hominids.

REFERENCES

Beynon, A.D. and Dean, M.C. 1988. Distinct dental development patterns in early fossil hominids. *Nature* 335:509-514.

Binford, L.R. 1981. *Bones: Ancient Men and Modern Myths*. Thames and Hudson, New York.

Blumenschine, R.J. 1987. Characteristics of an early hominid scavenging niche. *Current Anthropol.* 28:383-407.

Blumenschine, R.J. 1989. A landscape taphonomic model of the scale of prehistoric scavenging opportunities. *J. Hum. Evol.* 18:345-371.

Cartmill, M., Pilbeam, D., and Isaac, G. 1986. One hundred years of paleoanthropology. *Amer. Sci.* 74:410-420.

Darwin, C. 1871. *The Descent of Man and Selection in Relation to Sex*. John Murray, London.

Gighlieri, M. P. 1987. Sociobiology of the great apes and the hominid ancestor. *J. Hum. Evol.* 16:319-357.

Hawkes, K. 1990. Why do men hunt? Some benefits for risky strategies, in: *Risk and Uncertainty* (E. Cashdan, Ed.), pp. 145-166, Westview Press, Boulder, CO.

Johanson, D. C. and Edey, M. 1981. *Lucy: The Beginnings of Humankind*. Simon & Schuster, New York.

Kappelman, J. and Hatley, T. 1980. Bears, pigs, and Plio–Pleistocene hominids: A case for the exploitation of belowground food resources. *Human Ecology* 8:371-387.

Kinzey, W.G., Ed. 1987. *The Evolution of Human Behavior: Primate Models*. SUNY Press, Albany.

Landau, M. 1984. Human evolution as narrative. *Am. Sci.* 72:262-268.

Landau, M. 1991. *Narratives of Human Evolution*. Yale University Press, New Haven.

Lee, R.B. and DeVore, I., Eds. 1968. *Man the Hunter*. Aldine, Chicago.

McHenry, H.M. 1991. Sexual dimorphism in *Australopithecus afarensis*. *J. Hum. Evol.* 20:21-32.

Potts, R. 1988. *Early Hominid Activities at Olduvai*. Aldine de Gruyter, Hawthorne, NY.

Rodman, P.S. and McHenry, H.M. 1980. Bioenergetics and the origin of hominid bipedalism. *Am. J. Phys. Anthropol.* 52:103-106.

Susman, R.L. 1987. Chimpanzees: Pygmy chimpanzees and common chimpanzees: Models for the behavioral ecology of the earliest hominids, in: *The Evolution of Human Behavior: Primate Models* (W. G. Kinzey, Ed.), pp. 72-86, SUNY Press, Albany.

Szalay, F.S. 1975. Hunting-scavenging protohominids: A model for hominid origins. *Man* 10:420-429.

Wrangham, R.W. 1987. African Apes: The significance of African apes for reconstructing human social evolution, in: *The Evolution of Human Behavior: Primate Models* (W. G. Kinzey, Ed.), pp. 51-71, SUNY Press, Albany.

20

The Evolution of Hunting

S. L. Washburn and C. S. Lancaster

It is significant that the title of this symposium is Man the Hunter for, in contrast to carnivores, human hunting, if done by males, is based on a division of labor and is a social and technical adaptation quite different from that of other mammals. [1] Human hunting is made possible by tools, but it is far more than a technique or even a variety of techniques. It is a way of life, and the success of this adaptation (in its total social, technical, and psychological dimensions) has dominated the course of human evolution for hundreds of thousands of years. In a very real sense our intellect, interests, emotions, and basic social life—all are evolutionary products of the success of the hunting adaptation. When anthropologists speak of the unity of mankind, they are stating that the selection pressures of the hunting and gathering way of life were so similar and the result so successful that populations of *Homo sapiens* are still fundamentally the same everywhere. In this essay we are concerned with the general characteristics of man that we believe can be attributed to the hunting way of life.

Perhaps the importance of the hunting way of life in producing man is best shown by the length of time hunting has dominated human history. The genus *Homo* [2] has existed for some 600,000 years, and agriculture has been important only during the last few thousand years. Even 6,000 years ago large parts of the world's population were nonagricultural, and the entire evolution of man from the earliest populations of *Homo erectus* to the existing races took place during the period in which man was a hunter. The common factors that dominated human evolution and produced *Homo sapiens* were preagricultural. Agricultural ways of life have dominated less than 1 per cent of human history, and there is no evidence of major biological changes during that period of time. The kind of minor biological changes that occurred and which are used to characterize modern races were not common to *Homo sapiens*. The origin of all common characteristics must be sought in preagricultural times. Probably all experts would agree that hunting was a part of the social adaptation of all populations of the genus *Homo*, and many would regard *Australopithecus* [3] as a still earlier hominid who was already a hunter, although possibly much less efficient than the later forms. If this is true and if the Pleistocene period had a duration of three million years, then pre-*Homo erectus* human tool using and hunting lasted for at least four times as long as the duration of the genus *Homo*. No matter how the earlier times may ultimately be interpreted, the observation of more hunting among apes than was previously suspected (Goodall 1965) and increasing evidence for hunting by

Australopithecus strengthens the position that less than 1 per cent of human history has been dominated by agriculture. It is for this reason that the consideration of hunting is so important for the understanding of human evolution.

When hunting and the way of life of successive populations of the genus *Homo* are considered, it is important to remember that there must have been both technical and biological progress during this vast period of time. Although the locomotor system appears to have changed very little in the last 500,000 years, the brain did increase in size and the form of the face changed. But for present purposes it is particularly necessary to direct attention to the cultural changes that occurred in the last ten or fifteen thousand years before agriculture. There is no convenient term for this period of time, traditionally spoken of as the end of the Upper Paleolithic and the Mesolithic, but Binford and Binford (1966) have rightly emphasized its importance.

During most of human history, water must have been a major physical and psychological barrier and the inability to cope with water is shown in the archeological record by the absence of remains of fish, shellfish, or any object that required going deeply into water or using boats. There is no evidence that the resources of river and sea were utilized until this late preagricultural period, and since the consumption of shellfish in particular leaves huge middens, the negative evidence is impressive. It is likely that the basic problem in utilization of resources from sea or river was that man cannot swim naturally but to do so must learn a difficult skill. In monkeys the normal quadrupedal running motions serve to keep them afloat and moving quite rapidly. A macaque, for example, does not have to learn any new motor habit in order to swim. But the locomotor patterns of gibbons and apes will not keep them above the water surface, and even a narrow, shallow stream is a barrier for the gorilla (Schaller 1963). For early man, water was a barrier and a danger, not a resource. (Obviously water was important for drinking, for richer vegetation along rivers and lakeshores, and for concentrating animal life. Here we are referring to water as a barrier prior to swimmimg and boats, and we stress that, judging from the behavior of contemporary apes, even a small stream may be a major barrier.)

In addition to the conquest of water, there seems to have been great technical progress in this late preagricultural period. Along with a much wider variety of stone tools of earlier kinds, the archeological record shows bows and arrows, grinding stones, boats, houses of much more advanced types and even villages, sledges drawn by animal and used for transport, and the domestic dog. These facts have two special kinds of significance for this symposium. First, the technology of *all* the living hunters belongs to this late Mesolithic era at the earliest, and many have elements borrowed from agricultural and metal-using peoples. Second, the occasional high densities of hunters mentioned as problems and exceptions at the symposium are based on this very late and modified extension of the hunting and gathering way of life. For example, the way of life of the tribes of the Northwest Coast, with polished stone axes for woodworking, boats, and extensive reliance on products of the river and sea, should be seen as a very late adaptation. Goldschmidt's distinction (1959, pp.185-93) between nomadic and sedentary hunting and gathering societies makes this point in a slightly different way. He shows the social elaboration which comes with the settled groups with larger populations.

The presence of the dog (Zeuner 1963) is a good index of the late preagricultural period, and domestic dogs were used by hunters in Africa, Australia, and the Americas. Among the Eskimo, dogs were used in hunting, for transportation, as food in time of famine, and as watchdogs. With dogs, sleds, boats, metal, and complex technology, Eskimos may be a better example of the extremes to which human adaptation can go than an example of primitive hunting ways. Although hardly mentioned at the symposium, dogs were of great importance in hunting, for locating, tracking, bringing to bay, and even killing. Lee (1965, p. 131) reports that one Bushman with a trained pack of hunting dogs brought in 75 per cent of the meat of a camp. Six other resident hunters lacked hunting packs and accounted for only 25 per cent of the meat. Dogs may be important in hunting even very large animals; in the Amboseli Game Reserve in Kenya one of us saw two small dogs bring a rhinoceros to bay and dodge repeated charges.

With the acquisition of dogs, bows, and boats it is certain that hunting became much more complex in the last few thousand years before agriculture. The antiquity of traps, snares, and poisons is unknown, but it appears that for thousands of years man was able to kill large game close in with spear or axe. As Brues (1959) has shown, this limits the size of the hunters, and there are no very large or very small fossil men. Pygmoid hunters of large game are probably possible only if hunting is with bows, traps, and poison. It is remarkable that nearly all the estimated statures for fossil men fall between 5 feet 2 inches and 5 feet 10 inches. This suggests that strong selection pressures kept human stature within narrow limits for hundreds of thousands of years and that these pressures relaxed a few thousand years ago, allowing the evolution of a much wider range of statures.

Gathering and the preparation of food also seem to have become more complex during the last few thousand years before agriculture. Obviously gathering by nonhuman primates is limited to things that can be eaten immediately. In constrast, man gathers a wide range of items that he cannot digest without soaking, boiling, grinding, or other special preparation. Seeds may have been a particularly important addition to the human diet because they are abundant and can be stored easily. Since grinding stones appear before agriculture, grinding and boiling may have been the necessary preconditions to the discovery of agriculture. One can easily imagine that people who were grinding seeds would see repeated examples of seeds sprouting or being planted by accident. Grinding and boiling were certainly known to the preagricultural peoples, and this knowledge could spread along an Arctic route, setting the stage for a nearly simultaneous discovery of agriculture in both the New and Old Worlds. It was not necessary for agriculture itself to spread through the Arctic but only the seed-using technology, which could then lead to the discovery of seed planting. If this analysis is at all correct, then the hunting-gathering adaptation of the Indians of California, for example, should be seen as representing the possibilities of this late preagricultural gathering, making possible much higher population densities than would have been the case in pregrinding and preboiling economy.

Whatever the fate of these speculations, we think that the main conclusion, based on the archeological record, ecological considerations, and the ethnology of the surviving hunter-gatherings, will be sustained. In the last few thousand years before agriculture, both hunting and gathering became much more complex. This final adaptation, including the use of products of river and sea and the grinding and cooking of otherwise inedible seeds and nuts, was worldwide, laid the basis for the discovery of agriculture, and was much more effective and diversified than the previously existing hunting and gathering adaptations.

Hunting by members of the genus *Homo* throughout the 600,000 years that the genus has persisted has included the killing of large numbers of big animals. This implies the efficient use of tools, as Birdsell stressed at the symposium. The adaptive value of hunting large animals has been shown by Bourlière (1963), who demonstrated that 75 per cent of the meat available to human hunters in the eastern Congo was in elephant, buffalo, and hippopotamus. It is some measure of the success of human hunting that when these large species are protected in game reserves (as in the Murchison Falls or Queen Elizabeth Parks in Uganda), they multiply rapidly and destroy the vegetation. Elephants alone can destroy trees more rapidly than they are replaced naturally, as they do in the Masai Amboseli Reserve in Kenya. Since the predators are also protected in reserves, it appears that human hunters have been killing enough large game to maintain the balance of nature for many thousands of years. It is tempting to think that man replaced the saber-toothed tiger as the major predator of large game, both controlling the numbers of the game and causing the extinction of Old World saber-tooths. We think that hunting and butchering large animals put a maximum premium on cooperation among males, a behavior that is at an absolute minimum among the nonhuman primates. It is difficult to imagine the killing of creatures such as cave bears, mastodons, mammoths—or *Dinotherium* at a much earlier time—without highly coordinated, cooperative action among males. It may be that the origin of male-male associations lies in the necessities of cooperation in hunting, butchering, and war. Certainly butchering sites, such as described by F. Clark Howell in Spain, imply that the organization of the community for hunting large animals goes back for many, many thousands of years. From the biological point of view, the development of such organizations would have been paralleled by selection for an ability to plan and cooperate (or reduction of rage). Because females and juveniles may be involved in hunting small creatures, the social organization of big-game hunting would also lead to an intensification of a sexual division of labor.

It is important to stress, as noted before, that human hunting is a set of ways of life. It involves divisions of labor between male and female, sharing according to custom, cooperation among males, planning, knowledge of many species and large areas, and technical skill. Goldschmidt (1966, p. 87 ff.) has stressed the uniqueness and importance of human sharing, both in the family and in the wider society, and Lee (personal communication) emphasizes orderly sharing as fundamental to human hunting society. The importance of seeing human hunting as a whole social pattern is well illustrated by the old idea, recently revived, that the way of life of our ancestors was similar to that of wolves rather than that of apes or monkeys. But this completely misses the special nature of the human adaptation. Human females do not go out and hunt and then regurgitate to their young when they return. Human young do not stay in dens but are carried by mothers. Male wolves do not kill with tools, butcher, and share with females who have been gathering. In an evolutionary sense the whole human pattern is new, and it is the success of this particularly human way that dominated human evolution and determined the relation of biology and culture for thousands of years. Judging from the archeological record, it is probable that the major features of this human way, possibly even including the beginnings of language, had evolved by the time of *Homo erectus*. [4]

THE WORLD VIEW OF THE HUNTER

Lévi-Strauss urged that we study the world view of hunters, and, perhaps surprisingly, some of the major aspects of world view can be traced from the archeological record. We have already mentioned that boats and the entire complex of fishing, hunting sea mammals, and using shellfish was late. With this new orientation, wide rivers and seas changed from barriers to pathways and sources of food, and the human attitude toward water must have changed completely. But many hundreds of thousands of years earlier, perhaps with *Australopithecus*, the relation of the hunters to the land must also have changed from an earlier relationship which may be inferred from studies of contemporary monkeys and apes. Social groups of nonhuman primates occupy exceedingly small areas, and the vast majority of animals probably spend their entire lives within less than four or five square miles. Even though they have excellent vision and can see for many miles, especially from tops of trees, they make no effort to explore more than a tiny fraction of the area they see. Even for gorillas the range is only about fifteen square miles (Schaller 1963), and it is of the same order of magnitude for savanna baboons (DeVore and Hall 1965). When Hall tried to drive a troop of baboons beyond the end of their range, they refused to be driven and doubled back into familiar territory, although they were easy to drive within the range. The known area is a psychological reality, clear in the minds of the animals. Only a small part of even this limited range is used, and exploration is confined to the canopy, lower branches, and bushes, or ground, depending on the biology of the particular species. Napier (1962) has discussed this highly differential use of a single area by several species. In marked contrast, human hunters are familiar with very large areas. In the area studied by Lee (1965), eleven waterholes and 600 square miles supported 248 Bushmen, a figure less than the number of baboons supported by a single waterhole and a few square miles in the Amboseli Reserve in Kenya. The most minor hunting expedition covers an area larger than most nonhuman primates would cover in a lifetime. Interest in a large area is human. The small ranges of monkeys and apes restrict the opportunities for gathering, hunting, and meeting conspecifics, and limit the kind of predation and the number of diseases. In the wide area, hunters and gatherers can take advantage of seasonal foods, and only man among the primates can migrate long distances seasonally. In the small area, the population must be carried throughout the year on local

resources, and natural selection favors biology and behavior that efficiently utilize these limited opportunities. But in the wide area, natural selection favors the knowledge that enables a group to utilize seasonal and occasional food sources. Gathering over a wide and diversified area implies a greater knowledge of flora and fauna, knowledge of the annual cycle, and a different attitude toward group movements. Clearly one of the great advantages of slow maturation is that learning covers a series of years, and the meaning of events in these years become a part of the individual's knowledge. With rapid maturation and no language, the chances that any member of the group will know the appropriate behavior for rare events is greatly reduced.

Moving over long distances creates problems of carrying food and water. Lee (1965, p. 124) has pointed out that the sharing of food even in one locality implies that food is carried, and there is no use in gathering quantities of fruit or nuts unless they can be moved. If women are to gather while men hunt, the results of the labors of both sexes must be carried back to some agreed upon location. Meat can be carried away easily, but the development of some sort of receptacles for carrying vegetable products may have been one of the most fundamental advances in human evolution. Without a means of carrying, the advantages of a large area are greatly reduced, and sharing implies that a person carries much more than one can use. However that may be, the whole human pattern of gathering and hunting to share—indeed, the whole complex of economic reciprocity that dominates so much of human life—is unique to man. In its small range, a monkey gathers only what it itself needs to eat at that moment. Wherever archeological evidence can suggest the beginnings of movement over large ranges, cooperation, and sharing, it is dating the origin of some of the most fundamental aspects of human behavior—the human world view. We believe that hunting large animals may demand all these aspects of human behavior which separate man so sharply from the other primates. If this is so, then the human way appears to be as old as *Homo erectus*.

The price that man pays for his high mobility is well illustrated by the problems of living in the African savanna. Man is not adapted to this environment in the same sense that baboons or vervet monkeys are. Man needs much more water, and without preparation and cooking he can only eat a limited number of the foods on which the local primates thrive. Unless there have been major physiological changes, the diet of our ancestors must have been far more like that of chimpanzees than like that of a savanna-adapted species. Further, man cannot survive the diseases of the African savanna without lying down and being cared for. Even when sick, the locally adapted animals are usually able to keep moving with their troop; and the importance to their survival of a home base has been stressed elsewhere (DeVore and Washburn 1963). Also man becomes liable to new diseases and parasites by eating meat, and it is of interest that the products of the sea, which we believe were the last class of foods added to human diet, are widely regarded as indigestible and carry diseases to which man is particularly susceptible. Although many humans die of disease and injury, those who do not, almost without exception, owe their lives to others who cared for them when they were unable to hunt or gather, and this uniquely human caring is one of the patterns that builds social bonds in the group and permits the species to occupy almost every environment in the world.

A large territory not only provides a much wider range of possible foods but also a greater variety of potentially useful materials. With tool use this variety takes on meaning, and even the earliest pebble tools show selection in size, form, and material.

When wood ceases to be just something to climb on, hardness, texture, and form become important. Availability of materials is critical to the tool user, and early men must have had a very different interest in their environment from that of monkeys or apes. Thus, the presence of tools in the archeological record is not only an indication of technical progress but also an index of interest in inanimate objects and in a much larger part of the environment than is the case with nonhuman primates.

The tools of the hunters include the earliest beautiful manmade objects, the symmetrical bifaces, especially those of the Acheulian tradition. Just how they were used is still a matter of debate, but, as contemporary attempts to copy them show, their manufacture is technically difficult, taking much time and practice and a high degree of skill. The symmetry of these tools may indicate that they were swung with great speed and force, presumably attached to some sort of handle. A tool that is moved slowly does not have to be symmetrical, but balance becomes important when an object is swung rapidly or thrown with speed. Irregularities will lead to deviations in the course of the blow or the trajectory of flight. An axe or spear to be used with speed and power is subject to very different technical limitations from those of scrapers or digging sticks, and it may well be that it was the attempt to produce efficient high-speed weapons that first produced beautiful, symmetrical objects.

When the selective advantage of a finely worked point over an irregular one is considered, it must be remembered that a small difference might give a very large advantage. A population in which hunters hit the game 5 per cent more frequently, more accurately, or at greater distance would bring back much more meat. There must have been strong selection for greater skill in manufacture and use, and it is no accident that the bones of smallbrained men (*Australopithecus*) are never found with beautiful, symmetrical tools. If the brains of contemporary apes and men are compared, the areas associated with manual skills (both in cerebellum and cortex) are at least three times as large in man. Clearly, the success of tools has exerted a great influence on the evolution of the brain, and has created the skills that make art possible. The evolution of the capacity to appreciate the product must evolve along with the skills of manufacture and use, and the biological capacities that the individual inherits must be developed in play and practiced in games. In this way, the beautiful, symmetrical tool becomes a symbol of a level of human intellectual achievement, representing far more than just the tool itself.

In a small group like the hunting band, which is devoted to one or two major cooperative activities, the necessity for long practice in developing skills to a very high level restricts the number of useful arts, and social organization is relatively simple. Where there is little division of labor, all men learn the same activities, such as skill in the hunt or in war. In sports (like the decathlon) we take it for granted that no one individual can achieve record levels of performance in more than a limited set of skills. This kind of limitation is partially biological but it is also a matter of culture. In warfare, for example, a wide variety of weapons is useful only if there are enough men to permit a division of labor so that different groups can practice different skills. Handedness, a feature that separates man from ape, is a part of this biology of skill. To be ambidextrous might seem to be ideal, but in fact the highest level of skill is attained by concentrating both biological ability and practice primarily on one hand. The evolution of handedness reflects the importance of skill, rather than mere use.

Hunting changed man's relations to other animals and his view of what is natural. The human notion that it is normal for animals to flee, the whole concept of animals being wild, is the result of man's habit of hunting. In game reserves many different kinds of animals soon learn not to fear man, and they no longer flee. James Woodburn took a Hadza into the Nairobi Park, and the Hadza was amazed and excited, because although he had hunted all his life, he had never seen such a quantity and variety of animals close at hand. His previous view of animals was the result of his having been their enemy, and they had reacted to him as the most destructive carnivore. In the park the Hadza hunter saw for the first time the peace of the herbivorous world. Prior to hunting, the relations of our ancestors to other animals must have been very much like those of the other noncarnivores. They could have moved close among the other species, fed beside them, and shared the same waterholes. But with the origin of human hunting, the peaceful relationship was destroyed, and for at least half a million years man has been the enemy of even the largest mammals. In this way the whole human view of what is normal and natural in the relation of man to animals is a product of hunting, and the world of flight and fear is the result of the efficiency of the hunters.

Behind this human view that the flight of animals from man is natural lie some aspects of human psychology. Men enjoy hunting and killing, and these activities are continued as sports even when they are no longer economically necessary. If a behavior is important to the survival of a species (as hunting was for man throughout most of human history), then it must be both easily learned and pleasurable (Hamburg 1963). Part of the motivation for hunting is the immediate pleasure it gives the hunter, and the human killer can no more afford to be sorry for the game than a cat can for its intended victim. Evolution builds a relation between biology, psychology, and behavior, and, therefore, the evolutionary success of hunting exerted a profound effect on human psychology. Perhaps, this is most easily shown by the extent of the efforts devoted to maintain killing as a sport. In former times royalty and nobility maintained parks where they could enjoy the sport of killing, and today the United States government spends many millions of dollars to supply game for hunters. Many people dislike the notion that man is naturally aggressive and that he naturally enjoys the destruction of other creatures. Yet we all know people who use the lightest fishing tackle to prolong the fish's futile struggle, in order to maximize the personal sense of mastery and skill. And until recently war was viewed in much the same way as hunting. Other human beings were simply the most dangerous game. War has been far too important in human history for it to be other than pleasurable for the males involved. It is only recently, with the entire change in the nature and conditions of war, that this institution has been challenged, that the wisdom of war as a normal part of national policy or as an approved road to personal social glory has been questioned.

Human killing differs from killing by carnivorous mammals in that the victims are frequently of the same species as the killer. In carnivores there are submission gestures or sounds that normally stop a fatal attack (Lorenz 1966). But in man there are no effective submission gestures. It was the Roman emperor who might raise his thumb; the victim could make no sound or gesture that might restrain the victor or move the crowd to pity. The lack of biological controls over killing conspecifics is a character of human killing that separates this behavior sharply from that of other carnivorous mammals. This difference may be interpreted in a variety of ways. It may be that human hunting is so recent from an evolutionary point of view that there was not enough time for controls to evolve. Or it may be that killing other humans was a part of the adaptation from the beginning, and our sharp separation of war from hunting is due to the recent development of these institutions. Or it may be simply that in most human behavior stimulus and response are not tightly bound. Whatever the origin of this behavior, it has had profound effects on human evolution, and almost every human society has regarded killing members of certain other human societies as desirable (Freeman 1964). Certainly this has been a major factor in man's view of the world, and every folklore contains tales of culture heroes whose fame is based on the human enemies they destroyed.

The extent to which the biological bases for killing have been incorporated into human psychology may be measured by the ease with which boys can be interested in hunting, fishing, fighting, and games of war. It is not that these behaviors are inevitable, but they are easily learned, satisfying, and have been socially rewarded in most cultures. The skills for killing and the pleasures of killing are normally developed in play, and the patterns of play prepare the children for their adult roles. At the conference Woodburn's excellent motion pictures showed Hadza boys killing small mammals, and Laughlin described how Aleuts train boys from early childhood so that they would be able to throw harpoons with accuracy and power while seated in kayaks. The whole youth of the hunter is dominated by practice and appreciation of the skills of the adult males, and the pleasure of the games motivates the practice that is necessary to develop the skills of weaponry. Even in monkeys, rougher play and play fighting are largely the activities of the males, and the young females explore less and show a greater interest in infants at an early age. These basic biological differences are reinforced in man by a division of labor which makes adult sex roles differ far more in humans than they do in nonhuman primates. Again, hunting must be seen as a whole pattern of activities, a wide variety of ways of life, the psychobiological roots of which are reinforced by play and by a clear identification with adult roles. Hunting is more than a part of the economic system, and the animal bones in Choukoutien are evidence of the patterns of play and pleasure of our ancestors.

THE SOCIAL ORGANIZATION OF HUMAN HUNTING

The success of the human hunting and gathering way of life lay in its adaptability. It permitted a single species to occupy most of the earth with a minimum of biological adaptation to local conditions. The occupation of Australia and the New World was probably late, but even so there is no evidence that any other primate species occupied more than a fraction of the area of *Homo erectus*. Obviously, this adaptability makes any detailed reconstruction impossible, and we are not looking for stages in the traditional evolutionary sense. However, using both the knowledge of the contemporary primates and the archeological record, certain important general conditions of our evolution may be reconstructed. For example, the extent of the distribution of the species noted above is remarkable and gives the strongest sort of indirect evidence for the adaptability of the way of life, even half a million years ago. Likewise all evidence suggests that the local group was small. Twenty to fifty individuals is suggested by Goldschmidt (1959, p. 187). Such a group size is common in nonhuman primates and so we can say with some assurance that the number did not increase greatly until after agriculture. This means that the number of adult males who might cooperate in

hunting or war was very limited, and this sets limits to the kinds of social organizations that were possible. Probably one of the great adaptive advantages of language was that it permits the planning of cooperation between local groups, temporary division of groups, and the transmission of information over a much wider area than that occupied by any one group.

Within the group of the nonhuman primates, the mother and her young may form a subgroup that continues even after the young are fully grown (Sade 1965, 1966; Yamada 1963). This grouping affects dominance, grooming, and resting patterns, and, along with dominance, is one of the factors giving order to the social relations in the group. The group is not a horde in the nineteenth-century sense, but it is ordered by positive affectionate habits and by the strength of personal dominance. Both these principles continue into human society, and dominance based on personal achievement must have been particularly powerful in small groups living physically dangerous lives. The mother-young group certainly continued and the bonds must have been intensified by the prolongation of infancy. But in human society, economic reciprocity is added, and this created a wholly new set of interpersonal bonds.

When males hunt and females gather, the results are shared and given to the young, and the habitual sharing between a male, a female, and their offspring becomes the basis for the human family. According to this view, the human family is the result of the reciprocity of hunting, the addition of a male to the mother-plus-young social group of the monkeys and apes.

A clue to the adaptive advantage and evolutionary origin of our psychological taboo on incest is provided by this view of the family. Incest prohibitions are reported universally among humans and these always operate to limit sexual activity involving subadults within the nuclear family. Taking the nuclear family as the unit of account, incest prohibitions tend to keep the birth rate in line with economic productivity. If in creating what we call the family the addition of a male is important in economic terms, then the male who is added must be able to fulfill the role of a socially responsible provider. In the case of the hunter this necessitates a degree of skill in hunting and a social maturity that is attained some years after puberty. As a young man grows up, this necessary delay in his assumption of the role of provider for a female and her young is paralleled by a taboo which prevents him from prematurely adding unsupported members to the family. Brother-sister mating could result in an infant while the brother was still years away from effective social maturity. Father-daughter incest could also produce a baby without adding a productive male to the family. This would be quite different from the taking of a second wife which, if permitted, occurs only when the male has shown he is already able to provide for and maintain more than one female.

To see how radically hunting changed the economic situation, it is necessary to remember that in monkeys and apes an individual simply eats what it needs. After an infant is weaned, it is on its own economically and is not dependent on adults. This means that adult males never have economic responsibility for any other animal, and adult females do only when they are nursing. In such a system, there is no economic gain in delaying any kind of social relationship. But when hunting makes females and young dependent on the success of male skills, there is a great gain to the family members in establishing behaviors which prevent the addition of infants, unless these can be supported.

These considerations in no way alter the importance of the incest taboo as a deterrent to role conflict in the family and as the necessary precondition to all other rules of exogamy. A set of behaviors is more likely to persist and be widespread, if it serves many uses, and the rule of parsimony is completely wrong when applied to the explanation of social situations. However, these considerations do alter the emphasis and the conditions of the discussion of incest. In the first place, a mother-son sexual avoidance may be present in some species of monkeys (Sade 1966) and this extremely strong taboo among humans requires a different explanation than the one we have offered for brother-sister and father-daughter incest prohibitions. In this case, the role conflict argument may be paramount. Second, the central consideration is that incest produces pregnancies, and the most fundamental adaptive value of the taboo is the provision of situations in which infants are more likely to survive. In the reviews of the incest taboo by Aberle *et al.* (1963) and Mair (1965), the biological advantages of the taboo in controlling the production of infants are not adequately considered, and we find the treatment by Service (1962) closest to our own. In a society in which the majority of males die young, but a few live on past forty, the probability of incest is increased. By stressing the average length of life rather than the age of the surviving few, Slater (1959) underestimated the probability of mating between close relative. Vallois (1961, p. 222) has summarized the evidence on length of life in early man and shows that "few individuals passed forty years, and it is only quite exceptionally that any passed fifty."

That family organization may be attributed to the hunting way of life is supported by ethnography. Since the same economic and social problems as those under hunting continue under agriculture, the institution continued. The data on the behavior of contemporary monkeys and apes also show why this institution was not necessary in a society in which each individual gets its own food. [5] Obviously the origin of the custom cannot be dated, and we cannot prove *Homo erectus* had a family organized in the human way. But it can be shown that the conditions that make the family adaptive existed at the time of *Homo erectus*. The evidence of hunting is clear in the archeological record. A further suggestion that the human kind of family is old comes from physiology; the loss of estrus is essential to the human family organization, and it is unlikely that this physiology, which is universal in contemporary mankind, evolved recently.

If the local group is looked upon as a source of male-female pairs (an experienced hunter-provider and a female who gathers and who cares for the young), then it is apparent that a small group cannot produce pairs regularly, since chance determines whether a particular child is a male or female. If the number maturing in a given year or two is small, then there may be too many males or females (either males with no mates or females with no providers). The problem of excess females may not seem serious today or in agricultural societies, but among hunters it was recognized and was regarded as so severe that female infanticide was often practiced. How grave the problem of imbalance can become is shown by the following hypothetical example. In a society of approximately forty individuals there might be nine couples. With infants born at the rate of about one in three years, this would give three infants per year, but only approximately one of these three would survive to become fully adult. The net production in the example would be one child per year in a population of forty. And because the sex of the child is randomly determined, the odds that all the children would be male for a three-year period are 1 in 8. Likewise the odds for all surviving children being female for a three-year period are 1 in 8. In this example the chances of all

surviving children being of one sex are 1 in 4, and smaller departures from a 50/50 sex ratio would be very common.

In monkeys because the economic unit is the individual (not a pair), a surplus of females causes no problem. Surplus males may increase fighting in the group or males may migrate to other groups.

For humans, the problem of imbalance in sex ratios may be met by exogamy, which permits mates to be obtained from a much wider social field. The orderly pairing of hunter males with females requires a much larger group than can be supported locally by hunting and gathering, and this problem is solved by reciprocal relations among several local groups. It takes something on the order of 100 pairs to produce enough children so that the sex ratio is near enough to 50/50 for social life to proceed smoothly, and this requires a population of approximately 500 people. With smaller numbers there will be constant random fluctuations in the sex ratio large enough to cause social problems. This argument shows the importance of a sizable linguistic community, one large enough to cover an area in which many people may find suitable mates and make alliances of many kinds. It does not mean either that the large community or that exogamy does not have many other functions, as outlined by Mair (1965). As indicated earlier, the more factors that favor a custom, the more likely it is to be geographically widespread and long lasting. What the argument does stress is that the finding of mates and the production of babies under the particular conditions of human hunting and gathering favor both incest taboo and exogamy for basic demographic reasons.

Assumptions behind this argument are that social customs are adaptive, as Tax (1937) has argued, and that nothing is more crucial for evolutionary success than the orderly production of the number of infants that can be supported. This argument also presumes that, at least under extreme conditions, these necessities and reasons are obvious to the people involved, as infanticide attests. The impossibility of finding suitable mates must have been a common experience for hunters trying to exist in very small groups, and the initial advantages of exogamy, kinship, and alliance with other such groups may at first have amounted to no more than, as Whiting said at the conference, a mother suggesting to her son that he might find a suitable mate in the group where her brother was located.

If customs are adaptive and if humans are necessarily opportunistic, it might be expected that social rules would be particularly labile under the conditions of small hunting and gathering societies. At the conference, Murdock (1968) pointed out the high frequency of bilateral kinship systems among hunters, and the experts on Australia all seemed to believe that the Australian systems had been described in much too static terms. Under hunting conditions, systems that allow for exceptions and local adaptation make sense and surely political dominance and status must have been largely achieved.

CONCLUSION

While stressing the success of the hunting and gathering way of life with its great diversity of local forms and while emphasizing the way it influenced human evolution, we must also take into account its limitations. There is no indication that this way of life could support large communities of more than a few million people in the whole world. To call the hunters "affluent" is to give a very special definition to the word. During much of the year, many monkeys can obtain enough food in only three or four hours of gathering each day, and under normal conditions baboons have plenty of time to build the Taj Mahal. The restriction on population, however, is the lean season or the atypical year, and, as Sahlins recognized, building by the hunters and the accumulation of gains was limited by motivation and technical knowledge, not by time. Where monkeys are fed, population rises, and Koford (1966) estimates the rate of increase on an island at 16 per cent per year.

After agriculture, human populations increased dramatically in spite of disease, war, and slowly changing customs. Even with fully human (*Homo sapiens*) biology, language, technical sophistication, cooperation, art, the support of kinship, the control of custom and political power, and the solace of religion—in spite of this whole web of culture and biology—the local group in the Mesolithic was no larger than that of baboons. Regardless of statements made at the symposium on the ease with which hunters

obtain food some of the time, it is still true that food was the primary factor in limiting early human populations, as is shown by the events subsequent to agriculture.

The agricultural revolution, continuing into the industrial and scientific revolutions, is now freeing man from the conditions and restraints of 99 per cent of his history, but the biology of our species was created in that long gathering and hunting period. To assert the biological unity of mankind is to affirm the importance of the hunting way of life. It is to claim that, however much conditions and customs may have varied locally, the main selection pressures that forged the species were the same. The biology, psychology, and customs that separate us from the apes—all these we owe to the hunters of time past. And, although the record is incomplete and speculation looms larger than fact, for those who would understand the origin and nature of human behavior there is no choice but to try to understand "Man the Hunter."

NOTES

[1] This paper is part of a program on primate behavior, supported by the United States Public Health Service (Grant No. 8623) and aided by a Research Professorship in the Miller Institute for Basic Research in Science at the University of California at Berkeley. We wish to thank Dr. Phyllis C. Jay for her helpful criticism and suggestions about this paper.

[2] The term *Homo* includes Java, Pekin, Mauer, etc., and later forms.

[3] Using the term to include both the small *A. africanus* and large *A. robustus* forms. Simpson (1966) briefly and clearly discusses the taxonomy of these forms and of the fragments called *Homo habilis*.

[4] In speculations of this kind, it is well to keep the purpose of the speculation and the limitation of the evidence in mind. Our aim is to understand human evolution. What shaped the course of human evolution was a succession of successful adaptations, both biological and cultural. These may be inferred in part from the direct evidence of the archeological record. But the record is very incomplete. For example, Lee (personal communication) has described, for the Bushmen, how large game may be butchered where it falls and only meat brought back to camp. This kind of behavior means that analysis of bones around living sites is likely to underestimate both the amount and variety of game killed. If there is any evidence that large animals were killed, it is probable that far more were killed than the record shows. Just as the number of human bones gives no indication of the number of human beings, the number of animal bones, although it

provides clues to the existence of hunting, gives no direct evidence of how many animals were killed. The Pleistocene way of life can only be known by inference and speculation. Obviously, speculations are based on much surer ground when the last few thousand years are under consideration. Ethnographic information is then directly relevant and the culture bearers are of our own species. As we go farther back in time, there is less evidence and the biological and cultural difference becomes progressively greater. Yet it was in those remote times that the human way took shape, and it is only through speculation that we may gain some insights into what the life of our ancestors may have been.

[5] The advantage of considering both the social group and the facilitating biology is shown by considering the "family" in the gibbon. The social group consists of an adult male, an adult female, and their young. But this group is maintained by extreme territorial behavior in which no adult male tolerates another, by aggressive females with large canine teeth, and by very low sex drive in the males. The male-female group is the whole society (Carpenter 1941; Ellefson 1966). The gibbon group is based on a different biology from that of the human family and has none of its reciprocal economic functions. Although the kind of social life seen in chimpanzees lacks a family organization, to change it into that of a man would require far less evolution than would be required in the case of the gibbon.

REFERENCES

Aberle. D.F., Bronfenbrenner, U., Hess, E.H., Miller, D.R., Schneider, D.M., and Spuhler, J.M. 1963. The incest taboo and the mating patterns of animals. *American Anthropologist* 65:253-65.

Binford, L.R., and Binford, S.R. 1966. The predatory revolution: a consideration of the evidence for a new subsistence level. *American Anthropologist* 68(2):508-512.

Bourliere, F. 1963. Observations on the ecology of some large African mammals, in: *African Ecology and Human Evolution* (F.C. Howell and F. Bourliere, Eds.), Aldine, Chicago.

Brues, A. 1959. The spearman and the archer, an essay on selection in body build. *American Anthropologist* 61:457-69.

Carpenter, C.R. 1941. *A Field Study in Siam of the Behavior and Social Relations of the Gibbon (Hylobates lar)*, Johns Hopkins Press, Baltimore.

DeVore, I. and Hall, K.R.L. 1965. Baboon ecology, in: *Primate Behavior* (I. DeVore, Ed.), Holt, Rinehart, and Winston, New York.

DeVore, I. and Washburn, S.L. 1963. Baboon ecology and human evolution, in: *African Ecology and Human Evolution* (F.C. Howell and F. Bourliere, Eds.), Aldine, Chicago.

Ellefson, J.O. 1966. *A Natural History of Gibbons in the Malay Peninsula*, Unpublished doctoral dissertation, University of California, Berkeley.

Freeman, D. 1964. Human aggression in anthropological perspective, in: *The Natural History of Aggression* (J.D. Carthy and F.J. Ebling, Eds.), Academic Press, New York.

Goldschmidt, W.R. 1959. *Man's Way: a Preface to the Understanding of Human Society*, Henry Holt, New York.

Goldschmidt, W.R. 1966. *Comparative Functionalism: an Essay in Anthropological Theory*, University of California Press, Berkeley.

Goodall, J. and von Lawick, H. 1965. My life with wild chimpanzees (16mm film), National Geographic Society, Washington, D.C.

Hamburg, D.A. 1963. Emotions in the perspective of human evolution, in: *Expression of the Emotions in Man* (P.H. Knapp, Ed.), International Universities Press, New York.

Koford, C.B. 1966. Population changes in rhesus monkeys: Cayo Santiago, 1960-1964. *Tulane Studies in Zoology* 13:1-7.

Lee, R.B. 1963. The population ecology of man in the early Upper Pleistocene of southern Africa. *Proceedings of the Prehistoric Society* 29:235-57.

Lorenz, K.Z. 1966. *On Aggression*. Trans. by Marjorie K. Wilson, Harcourt, Brace, and World, New York.

Mair, L. 1965. *An Introduction to Social Anthropology*, Clarendon Press, Oxford.

Murdock, G.P. 1968. The current status of the world's hunting and gathering peoples, in: *Man the Hunter* (R.B. Lee and I. DeVore, Eds.), pp.13-20, Aldine, Chicago.

Napier, J.R. 1962. Monkeys and their habitats. *New Scientist* 15:88-92.

Sade, D.S. 1965. Some aspects of parent-offspirng and sibling relations in a group of rhesus monkeys, with a discussion of grooming. *Am. J. Phys. Anthropol.* 23(1):1-17.

Sade, D.S. 1966. *Ontogeny of Social Relations in a Group of Free Ranging Rhesus Monkeys* (*Macaca mulatta* Zimmerman). Unpublished doctoral dissertation, University of California, Berkeley.

Schaller, G.B. 1963. *The Mountain Gorilla: Ecology and Behavior*, Univ. of Chicago Press, Chicago.

Service, E.R. 1962. *Primitive Social Organization: an Evolutionary Perspective*, Random House, New York.

Simpson, G.G. 1966. The biological nature of man. *Science* 152(3721):472-78.

Slater, M.K. 1959. Ecological factors in the origin of incest. *American Anthropologist* 61:1042-59.

Tax, S. 1937. Some problems of social organization, in: *Social Anthropology of North American Tribes* (F. Eggan, Ed.), University of Chicago Press, Chicago.

Vallois, H.V. 1961. The social life of early man: the evidence of skeletons, in: *Social life of Early Man* (S.L. Washburn, Ed.), Aldine, Chicago.

Yamada, M. 1963. A study of blood-relationship in the natural society of the Japanese macaque. *Primates* 4:43-66.

Zeuner, F.E. 1963. *A History of Domesticated Animals*, Harper and Row, New York.

21

Gathering and the Hominid Adaptation

A. Zihlman and N. Tanner

INTRODUCTION

For most of human history, until the advent of domesticated plants and animals, a gathering-hunting way of life provided the economic base for human existence. Did gathering and hunting arise simultaneously, or one much earlier than the other? How have they been interrelated during various stages of hominid evolution, and what have been the implications for social life?

We believe that the divergence of early hominids from the apes was based on gathering plant foods on the African savannas: a new feeding pattern in a new environment that led to the invention of tools for obtaining, transporting, and preparing a range of foods that could potentially be shared with more than one individual. This adaptation combined two behavioral elements—bipedal locomotion and tool use—that made possible the search, collection, and transport of food over considerable distances for sharing. This pattern contrasts with that of apes in forest habitats, where each individual forages for food and eats it on the spot. Plant foods formed the bulk of early hominid diet and predatory behavior provided some meat. Hunting with tools, we believe, did not fully develop until the later part of the Pleistocene, perhaps as late as *Homo sapiens* (see Table 1).

Table 1. Major events in human evolution

Time scale (Years before present)	Events	Interpretation
10,000	Domestication of plants and animals in the Old World	Major changes in family and sex roles? Food concentrated; Permanent settlements
100,000	Spread of *Homo sapiens* throughout the Old World	Gathering-hunting well developed
	Humans in Europe and northern Asia	Beginning of hunting in temperate regions?
1,000,000	Human populations expand to Southeast Asia	Gathering successful in habitats outside Africa
2,000,000	Earliest stone tools; some in association with animal bones	Butchering large animals for meat; predation continues
3,000,000	Abundant hominid fossils in East and South Africa	Sharing food among kin; gathering and predation of small animals
4,000,000	Fossil evidence for human line in Africa	Moving into savanna; collecting dispersed food bipedally with organic tools; mothers sharing food with young
6,000,000	*Chimpanzee-gorilla-human divergence??*	

The social life of early hominids was necessarily interrelated with their subsistence pattern. If it is assumed that they were primarily hunters, and that meat procured by males made up a large portion of their caloric intake, there are different deductions to be made about mating patterns, social relations, economics, and sex roles (Washburn and Lancaster 1968; Isaac 1976), than if it is hypothesized that plants formed the primary food source and were gathered and shared mostly by females.

This paper presents a reconstruction of the way of life of *Australopithecus* [1], based on interpretations of new evidence and reinterpretation of the old. We challenge the assumption that hunting arose early in human evolution and that meat was a primary food source. In its stead, we propose that gathering of plant foods was the basic adaptation, and we interpret social organization, parental investment, and mating patterns within this framework.

QUESTIONING THE HUNTING HYPOTHESIS

The assumption that hunting was invented early pervades the literature on human evolution (Tiger 1969; Tiger and Fox 1971; Pfeiffer 1972; Washburn and Moore 1974; Cachel 1975; Suzuki 1975). Because the difference between hunting and predation is often glossed over when discussing early hominids, we define hunting as the catching, killing, and butchering of large and small animals with the help of tools, in contrast to simple predation, which is the capturing and killing by hand of relatively small animals.

It is usually further assumed that a male-female pair bond or nuclear family was essential to reduce competition among males for females and to insure that females and young were fed. While females, burdened with young, cared for them at the home base, man the hunter, tool-maker, and tool-user hunted in cooperative male groups and defended the helpless females and young.

Is hunting the inevitable interpretation? New data present a basis for challenging the presumption of an early hunting adaptation with meat the major food source. This information is derived from several sources: studies of gathering-hunting peoples, the fossil and archaeological records, primate behavior, and concepts in evolutionary biology.

The significance of gathering first became apparent at a conference on "hunting-gathering" peoples, organized by Richard Lee and Irven DeVore in 1966. There it was revealed that the majority of such groups in Africa, Asia, Australia, and North America subsists mainly on plant foods gathered by women, or on fish, and much less on hunting per se. In actuality, most such groups are "gatherer-hunters" (Lee and DeVore 1968a). Fluidity and flexibility appear as the most characteristic social structural features of modern gathering-hunting groups. Lee and DeVore (1968b) propose that vegetable foods were probably always available and that early women likely played an active role in subsistence. Linton (1971) further emphasized the role of women in gathering during evolution and reexamined the assumptions underlying the hunting hypothesis.

Recent studies of early hominid dentition reveal extensive wear and chipping, and suggest a diet that required a great deal of chewing or was quite gritty (Wallace 1972; Wolpoff 1973). These are not the teeth of a predominantly meat eating species. The masticatory apparatus itself of both ancient and modern humans is specialized for grinding tough foods, a parallel to conventional herbivores (Crompton and Hiiemäe 1969).

Recent studies on bone accumulations from hominid sites (Behrensmeyer 1975; Brain 1976) are beginning to distinguish among several possibilities: whether the animal bones are residues from hominid meals, tools used by hominids, or natural death assemblages. The studies indicate that bone breakage and concentration may be due more to carnivore activity and transportation by water before burial, and less to hominid activities, than previously supposed.

In primate field studies, predatory behavior and meat eating have been well documented in chimpanzees and baboons (Teleki 1973a; Harding 1973; Strum 1975; Hausfater 1976). Chimpanzees eat mostly fruit but occasionally kill small animals with their hands, consume the meat at leisure, and share with others. Contrary to previous assumptions, neither upright walking, weapons, nor possibly even the need for food are necessary for predation by baboons and chimpanzees, or by extension, for early hominid predation (Kitahara-Frisch 1975). This reduces the likelihood that predatory behavior and meat eating were the new elements in hominid origins; on the contrary, the omnivorous diet of humans probably represents the continuation of an ancient primate pattern (Harding 1975).

New theoretical concepts have been developed that focus on the evolution of social behavior and broaden out from a simply descriptive ethology. They have provided an impetus for looking at kinship and mating systems of primates and humans. These approaches combine genetic-evolutionary theory with observed social patterns and examine the selective advantages of various behaviors in terms of reproductive success. From this, models have been proposed to explain the evolution of altruistic behaviors through kin selection and of mating systems through parental investment and sexual selection (Hamilton 1964; Trivers 1972; Eberhard 1975; Wilson 1975).

The fossil and anatomical data, observations of living primates and information on contemporary gatherer-hunters, all lead us to question the view that early humans were hunters and primarily meat eaters from their first appearance on the savanna. These new data and sociobiological concepts provide a basis for proposing a different interpretation of early hominid behavior.

WHY CHIMPANZEES AS A MODEL FOR HOMINID ORIGINS?

Chimpanzees fascinate zoo-goers and behaviorists alike because of their "humanlike" intelligence, gestures, facial expressions, and ability to communicate. Their anatomical similarity to humans was noted a hundred years ago by Huxley and Darwin and detailed more recently by numerous others. On the assumption of phylogenetic continuity, chimpanzees are compared frequently with early human fossils to assess evolutionary change.

The biochemical evidence from studies on protein, DNA, and chromosomal similarity has demonstrated an even closer relationship than was previously suspected. Virtual identity of many human and chimpanzee proteins (Wilson and Sarich 1969; Cronin 1975; King and Wilson 1975) suggests that the two species are as close as sibling species with an evolutionary divergence about five or six million years ago (Sarich and Cronin 1976). Molecular studies provide a valuable perspective on phylogeny, especially because of the skimpy fossil record for hominids and African apes during the crucial period of divergence between five and ten million years ago.

Behavioral continuity between humans and chimpanzees is documented from observations in the field and laboratory (Goodall 1976). Particularly applicable to the study of human evolution are the findings that chimpanzees prepare and use tools, prey upon small mammals, occasionally walk bipedally, share plant and animal food (Teleki 1974, 1975), and communicate social and environmental information (Menzel 1973a; Menzel and Halperin 1975). Since similarities in behavior, anatomy, and genes in the two species are so extensive, it becomes extremely unlikely that all these shared traits are due to evolutionary convergence. In fact, all the elements appear to be present in chimpanzees that one might postulate necessary in an ancestral population giving rise to the australopithecines and, ultimately, modern humans.

The omnivorous and diverse chimpanzee diet includes a preponderance of fruits, supplemented by buds, insects, and animals weighing five to ten pounds. Plant and animal foods are occasionally shared among associated chimpanzees. Both females and males modify and use materials in a variety of ways—as sponges, probes, hammers, and levers (Goodall 1968a); they also wave objects during displays and sometimes throw stones or branches at other animals (Kortlandt 1967; Albrecht and Dunnett 1971).

Chimpanzee social organization is flexible and suited to ranging over many square miles in search of food. There is a stable regional population or "community" of 30 to 80 chimpanzees which occupies a similar home range; the smaller units, "bands," or subgroups change frequently in number and composition, depending on varying food supply, encounters with other subgroups, or personal choice (Itani and Suzuki 1967; Izawa 1970). There are enduring relationships between mothers and offspring, siblings, and friends of the same or opposite sex (Goodall 1971). Their extensive communicative repertoire permits varied and complex responses to different social situations (Goodall 1968b).

Chimpanzees have been found in a variety of habitats—humid tropical forests, gallery and montane rain forests, savanna woodlands with wet and dry seasons, and dry, sparsely wooded areas—over a broad geographical range covering much of equatorial Africa from Guinea in the west to Tanzania in the east (Jones and Sabater Pi 1971; Kano 1971). Size of home range varies with the habitat and presumably food availability, from only a few square miles in the Budongo Forest in Uganda, to about 80 square miles in the drier areas of Tanzania (Reynolds 1965; Suzuki 1969), to as much as 200 square miles in the Ugalla areas of Tanzania (Itani 1978). Certainly no greater flexibility and adaptability in ecological range than this is needed to serve as a useful model of early hominids venturing into the African savanna.

EVALUATING OTHER SPECIES AS MODELS

Because the savanna is the setting for hominid origins and early evolution, and because baboons and social carnivores number among savanna inhabitants, these species have often been proposed as models for hominid social behavior (Washburn and DeVore 1961; Schaller and Lowther 1969; Kummer 1971). The assumption here is that similar selective pressures operated on all three. We will briefly evaluate these models vis-à-vis the chimpanzee model.

Savanna and hamadryas baboons feed on the ground in open grasslands in eastern and southern Africa. Savanna baboons live in troops consisting of many males and females, with a central hierarchy formed by a few males. Males are twice the size of females, strong, and have large canine teeth; their fighting ability gives pause even to such predators as cheetahs and leopards. Since predator pressure is great, the troop always moves as a unit (Hall and DeVore 1965). There are no lone baboons, in contrast to occasional lone chimpanzees or lions. The closely related hamadryas baboons inhabit arid parts of Ethiopia, where food is scarce but predator pressure less. They forage on the sparse and scattered food resources during the day in one-male, multi-female units, and come together in the evening in large groups at the few available sleeping cliffs (Kummer 1968).

By analogy then, it is proposed that the early hominids, as they moved onto the savanna, adopted a social structure like that of baboons. A major difficulty with the baboon model, but paradoxically one reason it has been so favored, is the rigid social organization and male hierarchy. Their inflexibility makes it difficult to imagine how hominid gathering and later hunting could develop, with the essential frequent changes in group size and composition that are apparent in most gathering-hunting peoples today.

The carnivore model seems to originate primarily from that view of human evolution which focuses on the "hunting way of life." Carnivores and living gathering-hunting peoples at first glance seem similar in these features: they hunt cooperatively, share meat, and have a division of labor. These traits are assumed to have been equally characteristic of early hominids. But on closer examination, the analogy does not hold up.

Much has been made of meat sharing; however, this is highly variable among carnivores. Their young have a relatively long period of development and cannot provide for themselves. African hunting dogs and wolves, for example, regurgitate meat for the young and their male or female caretaker (Kühme 1965); lions, hyenas, and leopards lead the young to the kill, but lion cubs eat last and often die of starvation (Schaller 1972). Adult carnivores, such as hyenas, do not share meat, but merely tolerate other adults feeding alongside (Kruuk 1972). Sharing among chimpanzees and humans is a more give-and-take process. In contrast to the usual assumption about early humans, there is no division of labor among carnivores except for adults staying with the young while the others go after prey, and females do much of the killing and providing for the young.

Certain characteristics of predatory mammals—persistence, strategy, cognitive mapping, cooperation—have been described as forming "a behavioral substrate that fostered the evolution of human intelligence" (Peters and Mech 1975:280). But these behaviors are neither unique to predators nor equivalent to those of human groups. Chimpanzees map resources cognitively (Menzel 1973b) and demonstrate persistence and strategy in going after prey (Teleki 1973b), as do baboons (Harding and Strum 1976). "Cooperation" during the hunt in lions, hunting dogs, and hyenas involves several individuals engaging in the same activity at the same time; this behavior has been selected because it increases the success of capturing and killing prey. However, cooperation in this sense seems qualitatively different from human cooperation, which implies conscious choice and self-identification as a group member. In any case, several chimpanzees may also participate in a common activity, such as searching for food and going after small prey.

We are not minimizing the insights gained from other species in understanding human origins. But a species' adaptation is the result of interaction between potentialities inherent in its genetic makeup and the challenges of the environment. Ecological factors can influence but not determine social structure (Eisenberg, Muckenhirn, and Rudran 1972; Gartlan 1973; Altmann 1974). Models based on particular adaptations, such as living in a savanna habitat, cannot replace a more comprehensive model that includes not only ecological and behavioral factors, but a common, recent evolutionary history—as the chimpanzee model does.

AUSTRALOPITHECUS: DIRECT EVIDENCE OF THE PAST

Fossil hominids become abundant at the period referred to as the Plio-Pleistocene (about 3.5 million years ago), and by two million years ago there was a radiation of two or more species. The existing fossil record is not inconsistent with an estimated divergence of apes and humans some five or six million years ago. The earliest possible evidence of hominids consists of a fragmentary jaw from Lothagam and a piece of arm bone from Kanapoi, sites located west and southwest of Lake Turkana (formerly Lake Rudolf), Kenya. These fragments are about five million years old (Coppens *et al.* 1976). After this time, hominid remains are found in several areas: East Africa in the Omo Basin and Afar lowlands of Ethiopia, at Koobi Fora east of Lake Turkana, and in Tanzania at Olduvai Gorge and Laetolil; and South Africa at the cave sites Swartkrans, Sterkfontein, and Makapan. There is as yet no fossil record for chimpanzees and gorillas, presumably because their forested environment did not favor fossilization.

How might we reconstruct the adaptation of early hominids, given the fossil and archaeological evidence and a behavioral model of a chimpanzeelike ancestor? The data which provide a basis for interpretation include: 1) location and environmental setting of the hominid sites; 2) the bones and teeth of the hominids for clues on functional anatomy and conditions of transport and deposition; 3) and the context and association of animal bones and stones, which give some indication of hominid activities, possible predators, food sources, and animals coexisting with the hominids.

Hominid fossils are found at sites near water sources-streams, lakeshores, or karstic sinkholes—in the eastern and southern savannas, away from the tropical rainforests of central Africa which most monkeys and apes inhabit (Butzer 1978). The vegetation today in savannas varies from wooded areas along water courses to low shrub, woodlands, and open grassland areas; and, as is characteristic of tropical savannas, the plant life is dominated by the alternation of wet and dry seasons (Bourlière and Hadley 1970). There is evidence suggesting that this patchy character also existed during the Plio-Pleistocene. In the Omo Basin, for example, studies on fossil pollens confirm the mosaic nature of the vegetation between 2.5 and 2 million years ago (Bonnefille 1976); and the overlap of fossil pollen taxa with present day flora suggests that plant community types of closed and/or open woodland, grassland, tree-shrub grassland, shrub thicket, and shrub steppe characterized this area during the Plio-Pleistocene (Carr 1976).

Volcanic activity in eastern Africa left materials for absolute dating by potassium-argon, and ages of several sites have been calculated with the dates falling between five and one million years ago (Bishop and Miller 1972). Unfortunately, dating the South African sites has proved difficult, because

there was no volcanic activity there during the last five million years. Animal associations, however, have been used to estimate relative ages.

Overall, the anatomy of *Australopithecus* is quite well known. Remains of all parts of the skeleton exist: teeth; skulls and faces; and arm, hand, pelvic, leg, and foot bones (Tobias 1972). Teeth are the most numerous. The large molar and premolar teeth show extensive wear, and skull and jaw features indicate well-developed chewing muscles. The canine teeth in all specimens are small; in contrast with most other primates, hominid canine size does not differ markedly by sex. Skeletal remains suggest that the australopithecines were within the body weight range of chimpanzees, but with body mass proportioned differently. Anatomical features of the pelvic, leg, and foot bones indicate that effective bipedalism had already developed (Le Gros Clark 1967). The foot had a large nonopposable great toe for stability and support of body weight, and the pelvis was shaped for extensive attachment of muscles critical for bipedalism (Zihlman and Cramer 1976). Arm bones were very much like our own, and hand bones indicate a well-muscled thumb capable of power and hand skills. The brain was comparatively small by human standards, averaging about 500 cubic centimeters with a range of 435-650 cubic centimeters (Tobias 1975); but with its expanded cortex it was significantly larger than brains of living chimpanzees, when considered relative to body weight (Holloway 1972).

Hominid bones are often found in association with stones and animal bones; in East Africa this occurs in areas called "living floors"—sites undisturbed by water action where occupation remains (both stones and bones) were found *in situ* and were sealed by subsequent deposits. Shaped stones identifiable as worked tools have been found in both East and South African sites from two million years on (M. D. Leakey 1970a, 1970b, 1971; Merrick *et al.* 1973; Tobias 1965). Shaped cores (called choppers), flake tools, and material remaining from tool manufacture, as well as stone piles possibly used as bases for crude shelters- all provide evidence of hominid activity. In addition to tools, there are at these sites stone materials, not modified, shaped, or worn with use, that originate from sources some distance away. At this stage, tools were simply and crudely made and primarily multi-purpose.

The animal bones at the hominid sites include a variety of species and sizes: reptiles; fish; small animals; medium-sized mammals such as pigs, antelopes, baboons, and carnivores; and large ungulates such as giraffes, hippos, and elephants. Predators, such as hyenas, leopards, lions, and sabre-toothed cats were numerous at this time and posed a formidable danger to hominids (Cooke 1963). In the South African cave at Swartkrans, for example, there is convincing evidence that leopards killed and ate australopithecines (Brain 1970).

Early hominid sites have primary associations of animal bones, stone tools, rock debris, and foreign stones. The pattern of the animal bone concentrations varies from site to site and the association of the bones with stone tools may or may not be fortuitous. Although some of the animal bones may represent the remains of hominid meal taking and possibly butchering, natural processes other than hominid activity might have been significant factors in these depositions. Scavenging by carnivores, bone collecting by porcupines and hyenas, and sorting of bones by moving water may also have accounted for the associated animal bones at the hominid sites (Behrensmeyer 1976; Brain 1978). Plants do not fossilize as bones may under optimal circumstances, and information on ancient plant life through the study of fossil pollens is only beginning to accumulate at these early sites. So, although the paleontological and archaeological records provide some information on australopithecine economic activities, this evidence alone cannot be taken to represent the entire picture; biases of preservation in overrepresenting animal bones and underrepresenting plant remains must be taken into account.

Organic tools, such as wooden digging implements; containers made of skin, bark, bamboo, or vines; and vegetation used in constructing shelters are important to the way of life of many living peoples. In addition, plants and insects are often used as food. Yet campsite residues composed of only organic debris, such as that left by many modern gatherer-hunters, would leave little or no trace in an archaeological record (Lee 1968a). By analogy, the available record of early hominid activity has biases built in by the procedures used to locate and identify sites and in the differential preservation of animal bones contrasted with plant remains and in stone artifacts as opposed to organic implements. In interpreting early hominid behavior, we must account for the available fossil and archaeological material and also recognize that extremely important evidence may not have been preserved.

GATHERING AS THE ECONOMIC BASE OF EARLY HOMINID LIFE

We propose that the new pattern in hominid behavior and the basis of divergence from the ancestral apes was the bipedal gathering of plant food. The early hominids moved from the forest into the savanna, a mosaic of mixed and patchy vegetation. Potential plant as well as animal food was abundant, but so were predators. Sticks may have been used for digging up roots and knocking down nuts and fruits; crude containers would have made it possible to collect in quantity and return to a shaded, safe, and social place for eating and sharing with others. Gathering enough for more than one individual would have been especially important for females with dependent offspring (Tanner and Zihlman 1976).

Meat was likely not a major dietary component, although it was occasionally obtained in the manner of chimpanzees- by catching and killing small animals and pulling them apart with their bare hands. Predatory behavior no doubt occurred more frequently in the early forest-dwelling hominids because of the greater availability of young and small animals on the savanna [2]. Scavenging and the consumption of large dead animals found by chance were probably infrequent activities early in the hominid divergence, but after tools for cutting were invented, butchering large animal finds might have become fairly common. More regular protein sources probably included eggs, insects and other invertebrates, and small vertebrates. Gathering techniques could encompass these foods as well as seeds, fruits, roots, and other plants.

Gathering and Hominid Anatomy

The gathering hypothesis must be evaluated in terms of australopithecine anatomy: bipedal locomotion, large posterior teeth, small canines, skull morphology, and body size. We think that bipedal locomotion developed for covering long distances while carrying gathered food for sharing, digging sticks, objects for defense, and offspring. It has been proposed that this locomotor pattern developed to track animals and to carry tools for hunting and the meat back to camp. But endurance for long distance walking does not differ by sex. The large home range needed for obtaining widely dispersed resources on the savanna suggests both females and males travelled frequently and far. With hands and arms freed from locomotor functions, the effectiveness of capturing small prey with the hands might also increase.

The large, worn and chipped teeth suggest that gritty plant foods were a significant part of diet (Wallace 1975), and the markings on the skull and jaw indicate prominent attachments for large chewing muscles (Wolpoff 1974). Gritty and tough foods may have included fibrous vegetation, seeds, roots, and other food from the ground. Indeed, the molars and premolars provided a larger grinding surface, relative to body size, in all species of these early hominids than is present in either apes or later hominids (Pilbeam and Gould 1974). The reduced canines are incorporated into the incisor row and function as part of the overall biting and grinding mechanism (Pilbeam 1972).

Bipedalism, body size, and canines have implications for anti-predator behavior too. Canine and body size must have differed only slightly in australopithecines by sex (Zihlman 1976). When there are marked differences between the sexes, as in baboons, large male canine and body size may function as part of a species' defense (Leutenegger and Kelly 1977); but this kind of anatomical adaptation was not available to the early hominids. The scattered trees on the savanna could not have been a practical retreat for hominids with nongrasping feet, burdened with food, tools, and infants. Upright posture probably enhanced alternative defenses: an expanded field of vision for avoiding predators, and increased effectiveness of arm-waving displays, threats, and hurling objects.

With bipedalism came the loss of a grasping foot for young to cling to mothers, and a long time for walking skills to develop in the young. Hominid mothers, then, had to carry and care for their offspring for an extended period; even after the young could walk, they could not go far without occasionally being carried. Among Kalahari !Kung gatherer-hunters, children lack endurance to keep up with a gathering group and ask to be carried when tired (Draper and Cashdan 1974).

The minimal sexual dimorphism in body and canine size in *Australopithecus* has social implications. In primates, large canines are a visible threat, and larger-bodied individuals can dominate smaller ones. The small canines and not more than moderate body size differences in *Australopithecus* may reflect increased sociability among all group members—with minimal dominance of one sex over the other and alternatives for communicating other than physical appearance.

Gathering and Tools

Tool use as an essential part of hominid evolution interrelates with diet, bipedalism, and social behavior. The earliest human technological inventions were probably in the realm of gathering—pointed sticks and stones for digging, large leaves and nut shells as crude containers, and rocks to crack open nuts and scrape dirt from roots and tubers. They were often organic, perhaps reminiscent of some chimpanzee tools; or if stone, they were not used in a context or sufficiently modified to be recognizable to archaeologists. A sling-container invented early would have been an enormous advantage for mothers supporting infants who could no longer cling.

Worked stone tools appear in the archaeological record about two million years ago [3], almost two million years after the first fossil hominids. The functions of stone tools are not well known. But at three sites at Olduvai Gorge and Koobi Fora, Lake Turkana, flake tools occur in association with a dismembered elephant or hippo (M. D. Leakey 1971; Isaac, Leakey, and Behrensmeyer 1971) and presumably were used for butchering the large animals. Stone artifacts called "choppers" might be interpreted as digging tools or may have been used for making organic tools; others called "spheroids" perhaps were utilized to pound tough plant food prior to eating.

Tools have important implications for social behavior. When tool using and making are an integral part of food getting, a long period is necessary for the young to master the appropriate skills. For example, chimpanzees require four to five years before they are proficient at "termiting" (McGrew 1978). With tool using, as with bipedalism, the young must be cared for while learning. Containers are a means for the adults, especially mothers, to provide food for the younger members less able to gather effectively. The invention of cutting tools, such as those for butchering large animals, enhances the ease of sharing food. As with gathering, females were probably very involved in butchering to provide meat to share with offspring. The way of life of these early hominids thus relied upon tools made and used by both sexes.

Gathering and Social Behavior

How did australopithecine social behavior, especially mating patterns and the care and socialization of the young, interrelate with gathering? What was the role of males? This subject is further removed from economics and therefore more in the realm of speculation, but concepts of kin and parental investment provide a framework for our interpretations.

Among chimpanzees and other primates, maternal investment is high, and the young have strong ties which persist throughout life with their mothers and siblings. Hominid mothers probably carried and nursed their young for almost four years—the average time for chimpanzees and mothers in many gathering-hunting societies (Goodall 1967; Lee 1972). Even after weaning, it was several years before hominid young were independent in locomotion and in using tools to get food. Maternal investment increased in early hominids as the period of dependency lengthened. Hominid mothers probably gathered food frequently and intensively, because the survival of their offspring depended on it.

Because so much energy went into the care of the offspring to ensure survival to adulthood and because the period of development and dependency was long, selection would have also favored a social group where several individuals besides the mother assisted in the care, protection, and feeding of the young. The mother-offspring unit was the most likely core unit within the larger group structure, as it is in many monkeys and apes (Lancaster 1975). Strong sibling ties were probably the basis for extending this core. These small kin groups, perhaps three to eight individuals, shared food and helped protect each other and, particularly, the immature members. Such care not only would have increased the chances that young born in the group would reach adulthood and reproduce, but would have increased a mother's reproductive rate by allowing her to have another offspring before the first was entirely independent. Sisters and brothers of the mother or her older offspring well might have assisted in providing such nurturing. This type of behavior would have evolved through kin selection, an aspect of natural selection where an individual, by contributing to the survival of kin with whom he or she shares genes, passes on those common genes to the next generation (Hamilton 1964; Eberhard 1975). We suggest that australopithecine kin ties, especially among siblings, were increased over those of their primate ancestors. The relatively strong bond we envision between mothers and sons and between male and female siblings would serve to integrate male hominids into the kin group, where they contributed to the survival of their shared genes through kin investment.

Parental investment involves energy expenditure and caring for one offspring at the expense of investing in future offspring. Mating patterns in many vertebrate species have been shown to correlate with the relative amount of parental investment: the sex which invests most in each offspring selects mates from among several potential partners while the other sex "competes" for the limited partners (Trivers 1972). This process of sexual selection is one aspect of natural selection. The necessarily high maternal investment of early hominids suggests that females, rather than males, chose their mates.

What kinds of males might these females choose and how were the males competing? It seems plausible that females might have preferred the more sociable males, and that males therefore were "competing" in being sociable not only by their involvement in their own kin groups where they were sharing food, protecting, and carrying their siblings or sister's offspring, but also in friendly interaction with females and males at the campsites where members of several subgroups met and slept. Specific studies of mating patterns in monkeys and apes are few, but female choice of sexual partners has been observed in several species including chimpanzees, baboons, and macaques (Nishida 1968; Sugiyama 1969; McGinnis 1973; Lindburg 1975; Saayman 1975). There is evidence that females may avoid aggressive males as sexual partners and may choose sociable ones. McGinnis reports that chimpanzee females may run from males that approach to mate in a threatening manner. In a baboon troop, the male most preferred as a sexual partner was the least aggressive; he spent the most time near females and their offspring, frequently intervened on their behalf during antagonistic encounters, and was often groomed by females in all stages of the reproductive cycle (Saayman 1975).

The small australopithecine canines may be an anatomical expression of increased sociability among all group members [4]. Selection pressure for large canines was reduced, due to their integration into the changing masticatory apparatus and their replacement by tools in protective functions. But there may also have existed a positive selection pressure for small canines as a result of reduced intragroup aggression and dominance displays (Holloway 1967). Such behaviors, we believe, would have been highly advantageous to the australopithecine way of life.

The settings for early mating and social interactions were campsites along water sources, for which evidence exists as long ago as two million years (M. D. Leakey 1976). We do not know the length of time these sites were used nor the number of individuals who associated there, but these wooded areas may have provided protected places for eating, sleeping, and social interactions. The size of campsite groupings was probably variable. Within a regional community, subgroups or "bands," consisting primarily of kin groupings, may have been the smaller units. Two or more such small groups, perhaps somewhat related genetically, might have associated frequently, with still larger groups congregating anywhere food, water, and trees were abundant.

These larger groups would have made possible a wide choice of sexual partners. As with chimpanzees, the sexual act did not automatically imply aggression between males or long-term bonds between males and females (Sugiyama 1973). We hypothesize female choice operating among hominids, but with considerable variability and flexibility in mating patterns, especially in the length of time a mating pair stayed together. At this stage in evolution, we propose relatively distinct economic and sexual units; the economic units were the smaller kin groups that shared food and cared for young, whereas the sexual or reproductive units were the larger associations at campsites and abundant food sources.

Social behavior is a major part of subsistence and survival. We propose for the australopithecines a cooperative kin group where both sexes engaged in gathering, butchering, and defense, and where food was shared among close kin. Several adults in the group, particularly males unencumbered by infants, were advantageous for defense against predators; but several females, without a male present, could defend themselves and young adequately when necessary. We do not envision a rigid division of labor by sex, but doubtless the frequency of certain activities varied both by sex and age. Females carrying young could not travel as far in search of food and would likely concentrate on reliable sources, whereas males might gather less consistently and more frequently chase small animals and bring back meat to share.

Natural selection would have enhanced those processes adaptive for the gathering way of life: greater intelligence for cognitive mapping of food sources, for communicating this information to others, and for participating in complex social relations. Hominids needed to conceptualize, find, or make digging tools and containers, apply their use to widely scattered food resources, and pass on the techniques to subsequent generations. Selection would have favored young who readily learned the techniques and technology of gathering by observing and imitating the adults. Effective communication, still nonverbal, along with reduction of the threatening large canines, would have increased sociability.

Flexibility in behavior, organizational fluidity, and sociability were vital ingredients in hominid survival and success. They were essential for effectively exploiting savanna resources, for diminishing death by predation, and for increasing the chances of survival of the young. It is difficult to begin with a baboon social model or a pair bond model and end up with the flexibility that is characteristic of gathering-hunting peoples today (Bicchieri 1972), as well as the cultural variability in social organizations and ecological adaptations of peoples around the world, historically and at present. In *Australopithecus*, flexibility in behavior and social structure, plus the ability to learn and communicate effectively, were as much a part of the hominid potential as the ability to walk upright and to make and use tools: they provided the type of biological base from which later, culture-bearing humans evolved.

THE ORIGIN OF HUNTING

Hunting, as pointed out earlier, is rarely precisely defined; it may mean predation, scavenging, butchering, or taking prey-large or small, solitary or in herds. It may mean killing with teeth, bare hands, or tools. Not only is there no simple extension from chimpanzee predation to hunting, in the sense of killing with tools, but also the social implications of these modes of obtaining meat are very different. The comparison of carnivore with human hunting confuses rather than clarifies, because it is a mixture of behavioral, technical, and dietary analogies with no consistent evolutionary or genetic framework. Not to distinguish each factor involved in "hunting" is to ignore differences in technique that may have taken several million years to evolve.

Plants were almost certainly a major food source for early hominids (Bartholomew and Birdsell 1953; Washburn and Avis 1958; Isaac 1971). Meat consumption likely increased, first, by more frequent predation of small animals. Sharp implements began to be used to dress scavenged meat and butcher large animals trapped in swamps. Eventually, hominids developed to the point of killing animals at close range with various artifacts and, only much later, pursuing and killing them with specialized tools.

Hunting with tools is a high risk, low return activity that, to be reasonably effective, requires precise skills and refined tools. It seems logical to us that it could only have become common in this form after gathering was fully developed. Gathering then could have provided a secure nutritional and social base from which a few hunters could go forth and expend energy for uncertain success. Hunting perhaps had its technological base in the system of tool-aided gathering and its social base in the gathering kin group, where some individuals engaged in predatory activity, and both plant and animal food were regularly shared (Zihlman 1978).

In support of this hypothesis, the small flake tools apparently used to butcher the elephant and hippo at Olduvai and Koobi Fora may well have developed from artifacts originally used to divide, scrape, or otherwise process plant foods and to prepare organic tools. The three butchering sites are located along ancient lakeshores, probably swampy areas. There, big animals could have been trapped and killed, rather than being tracked and hunted down—a much more advanced social and technical development.

We believe that this style of hunting did not emerge until about half a million years ago. Meat may have become a critical food source when hominids expanded out of Africa into the temperate zones where plant availability is seasonal (Butzer 1971; Campbell 1972). Hominids entered Southeast Asia about a million years ago, but there were no large herd animals there, and no suggestive collections of tools and animal bones have been found from this period (Luchterhand 1974). There is evidence that hominids were in Europe by half a million years ago (Butzer and Isaac 1975), and there are associations of tools and dismembered elephant bones from the Middle Pleistocene in Spain, in what were ancient swamps.

Possibly the earliest undisputed evidence for hunting with weapons is found at Lehringen, northwestern Germany, a site from the Third Interglacial (about 0.1 million). Here was uncovered a fossil elephant with a wooden spear nearly eight feet long between its ribs (Movius 1950). The spear point had been sharpened with stone knives and hardened by fire. This was probably after the first appearance of *Homo sapiens*.

We have stressed gathering plant foods as the critical innovation in human evolution, one that logically emerged from ape behaviors, such as tool using and food sharing. The omnivorous diet of chimpanzees, with 98 percent of foods being plants, finds a parallel among living gatherer-hunters where gathered plant foods may account for 50 to 90 percent of their diet (Lee 1965, 1968b; Gale 1970). We believe that the picture of hunting emerging from the very beginning of human origins with meat as a major food source is no longer supported by the evidence.

It is all too easy to make generalizations about "human nature" based on contemporary societies, particularly our own culture, or look to animal behavior for "evidence" of these conceptions and project them back in time to human origins. It is more sound, we believe, to start with the primates genetically most closely related to our species and consider how, consistent with evolutionary principles, human society may have developed in stages of increasing technical and social complexity from the hominid divergence five or six million years ago to the modern age.

NOTES

[1] We have chosen to use the term *Australopithecus* to delineate the earliest hominids, undoubtedly more than one species, dated between about two and four million years ago. Taxonomically, two or more lines have been identified, and R. Leakey and others have given them two generic names (*Homo* and *Australopithecus*) However, we refer to them collectively as the genus *Australopithecus* because: 1) they shared a number of anatomical and behavioral characteristics as part of their adaptation to the African savanna during the Plio-Pleistocene; and 2) they are differentiated as a group from apes by bipedalism, large grinding teeth, small canines, and larger brains.

[2] The frequency and sophistication of predatory activity in one troop of baboons at Gilgil, Kenya increased rapidly as the antelope population increased (Harding and Strum 1976).

[3] Redating of the KBS tuff from 2.6 to 1.8-1.6 million years ago (Curtis *et al.* 1975) apparently changes the age of the archaeological sites at Koobi Fora, Lake Turkana (Isaac, Harris, and Crader 1976) to less than two million years old.

[4] Among nonhuman primates, minimal canine dimorphism indicates minimal social role differentiation between the sexes and less competition between males than in species where canines are dimorphic (Leutenegger and Kelly 1977).

REFERENCES

Albrecht, H., and Dunnett, S. C. 1971. *Chimpanzees in Western Africa*. R. Piper, Munich.

Altmann, S. A. 1974. Baboons, space, time and energy. *Am. Zool.* 14:221-248.

Bartholomew, G., and Birdsell, J. 1953. Ecology and the Protohominids. *Am. Anthrop.* 55:481-498.

Behrensmeyer, A. K. 1975. The taphonomy and paleoecology of Plio-Pleistocene vertebrate assemblages east of Lake Rudolf, Kenya. *Bull. Mus. Comp. Zool., Harvard* 146(10):473-578.

Behrensmeyer, A. K. 1976. Fossil assemblages in relation to sedimentary environments in the East Rudolf Succession. In *Earliest Man and Environments in the Lake Rudolf Basin: Stratigraphy, Paleoecology, and Evolution* (Y. Coppens, F. C. Howell, G. L. Isaac, and R. E. F. Leakey, Eds.) University of Chicago Press, Chicago.

Bicchieri, M. G., Ed. 1972. *Hunters and Gatherers Today: A Socioeconomic Study of Eleven Such Cultures in the Twentieth Century*. Holt, Rinehart and Winston, New York.

Bishop, W. W., and Miller, J. A., Eds. 1972. *Calibration of Hominoid Evolution*. University of Toronto Press, Toronto.

Bonnefille, R. 1976. Palynological evidence for an important change in the vegetation of the Omo Basin between 2.5 and 2 million years. In *Earliest Man and Environments in the Lake Rudolf Basin: Stratigraphy, Paleoecology and Evolution* (Y. Coppens, F. C. Howell, G. L. Isaac, and R. E. F. Leakey, Eds.) University of Chicago Press, Chicago.

Bourlière, F., and Hadley, M. 1970. The ecology of tropical savannas. *Annual Review of Ecology and Systematics* 1:125-152.

Brain, C. K. 1970. New finds at the Swartkrans Australopithecine site. *Nature* 225:1112-1119.

Brain, C. K. 1976. Some principles in the interpretation of bone accumulations associated with man. In *Human Origins: Louis Leakey and the East African Evidence* (G. L. Isaac and E. R. McCown, Eds.) W. A. Benjamin, Menlo Park, CA.

Brain, C. K. 1978. Some aspects of the South African Australopithecine sites and their bone accumulations. In *Early Hominids of Africa* (C. J. Jolly, Ed.) Duckworth, London.

Butzer, K. 1971. *Environment and Archaeology: An Ecological Approach to Prehistory*. Aldine, Chicago.

Butzer, K. 1978. Geo-ecological perspectives on early hominid evolution. In *Early Hominids of Africa* (C. J. Jolly, Ed.) Duckworth, London.

Butzer, K., and G. Isaac, Eds. 1975. *After the Australopithecines: Stratigraphy, Ecology and Culture Change in the Middle Pleistocene*. World Anthropology Series. Mouton, The Hague.

Cachel, S. 1975. A new view of speciation in *Australopithecus*. In *Socioecology and Psychology of Primates* (R. H. Tuttle, Ed.) World Anthropology Series. Mouton, The Hague.

Campbell, B. 1972. Man for all seasons. In *Sexual Selection and Descent of Man 1871-1971* (B. Campbell, Ed.) Aldine, Chicago.

Carr, C. J. 1976. Plant ecological variation and pattern in the Lower Omo Basin. In *Earliest Man and Environments in the Lake Rudolf Basin: Stratigraphy, Paleoecology, and Evolution* (Y. Coppens, F. C. Howell, G. L. Isaac, and R. E. F. Leakey, Eds.) University of Chicago Press, Chicago.

Cooke, H. B. S. 1963. Pleistocene mammal faunas of Africa, with particular reference to southern Africa. In *African Ecology and Human Evolution* (F. C. Howell and F. Bourlière, Eds.) Aldine, Chicago.

Coppens, Y., Howell, F. C., Isaac, G. L., and Leakey, R. E. F., Eds. 1976. *Earliest Man and Environments in the Lake Rudolf Basin: Stratigraphy, Paleoecology, and Evolution*. University of Chicago Press, Chicago.

Crompton, A. A., and Hiiemäe, K. 1969. How mammalian molar teeth work. *Discovery* 5(1):23-34.

Cronin, J. E. 1975. *Molecular Systematics of the Order Primates*. Ph.D dissertation in Genetics-Anthropology, University of California, Berkeley.

Curtis, G. H., Drake, R., Cerling, T., and Hampel, J. 1975. Age of KBS tuff in Koobi Fora formation, East Rudolf, Kenya. *Nature* 258:395-398.

Draper, P., and Cashdan, E. 1974. *The Impact of Sedentism on !Kung Socialization*. Paper presented at the American Anthropological Association Meeting, Mexico City.

Eberhard, M. J. W. 1975. The evolution of social behavior by kin selection. *Q. Rev. Biol.* 50(1):1-33.

Eisenberg, J. F., Muckenhirn, N. A., and Rudran, R. 1972. The relation between ecology and social structure in primates. *Science* 176:863-874.

Gale, F., Ed. 1970. *Woman's Role in Aboriginal Society*. Australian Aboriginal Studies, number 36. Social Anthropology Series 6. Australian Institute of Aboriginal Studies, Canberra.

Gartlan, J. S. 1973. Influences of phylogeny and ecology on variations in the group organization of primates. In *Precultural Primate Behavior. Symposia of the Fourth Congress of Primatology*, Volume 1 (E. W. Menzel, Jr., Ed.) S. Karger, Basel.

Goodall, J. (Van Lawick) 1967. Mother-offspring relationships in free-ranging chimpanzees. In *Primate Ethology* (D. Morris, Ed.) Weidenfeld and Nicolson, London.

Goodall, J. (Van Lawick) 1968a. The behavior of free-living chimpanzees in the Gombe Stream Reserve. *Anim. Behav. Monographs* 1:165-311.

Goodall, J. (Van Lawick) 1968b. Expressive movements and communication. In *Primates: Studies in Adaptation and Variability* (P. Jay, Ed.) Holt, Rinehart and Winston, New York.

Goodall, J. (Van Lawick) 1971. *In the Shadow of Man.* Houghton Mifflin, Boston.

Goodall, J. (Van Lawick) 1976. Continuities between chimpanzee and human behavior. In *Human Origins: Louis Leakey and the East African Evidence* (G. L. Isaac and E. R. McCown, Eds.) W. A. Benjamin, Menlo Park, CA.

Hall, K. R. L., and DeVore, I. 1965. Baboon social behavior. In *Primate Behavior: Studies of Monkeys and Apes* (I. DeVore, Ed.) Holt, Rinehart and Winston, New York.

Hamilton, W. D. 1964. The genetical evolution of social behavior. *J. Theor. Biol.* 7:1-52.

Harding, R. S. O. 1973. Predation by a troop of olive baboons (*Papio anubis*). *Am. J. Phys. Anthrop.* 38:587-591.

Harding, R. S. O. 1975. Meat-eating and hunting in baboons. In *Socioecology and Psychology of Primates* (R. H. Tuttle, Ed.) World Anthropology Series. Mouton, The Hague.

Harding, R. S. O., and Strum, S. C. 1976. Predatory baboons of Kekopey. *Nat. Hist.* 85(3):46-53.

Hausfater, G. 1976. Predatory behavior of yellow baboons. *Behaviour* 56(1-2):45-68.

Holloway, R. L., Jr. 1967. Tools and teeth: some speculations regarding canine reduction. *Am. Anthrop.* 69:63-67.

Holloway, R. L., Jr. 1972. Australopithecine endocasts, brain evolution in the hominoidea and a model of hominid evolution. In *The Functional and Evolutionary Biology of Primates* (R. H. Tuttle, Ed.) Aldine, Chicago.

Isaac, G. L. 1971. The diet of early man: aspects of archaeological evidence from lower and middle pleistocene sites in Africa. *World Archaeology* 2:277-299.

Isaac, G. L. 1976. The activities of early African hominids: review of archaeological evidence from the time span two and a half to one million years ago. In *Human Origins: Louis Leakey and the East African Evidence* (G. L. Isaac and E. R. McCown, Eds.) W. A. Benjamin, Menlo Park, CA.

Isaac, G. L, Harris, J. W. K., and Crader, D. 1976. Archaeological evidence from the Koobi Fora formation. In *Earliest Man and Environments in the Lake Rudolf Basin: Stratigraphy, Paleoecology, and Evolution* (Y. Coppens, F. C. Howell, G. L. Isaac, and R. E. F. Leakey, Eds.) University of Chicago Press, Chicago.

Isaac, G. L., Leakey, R. E. F., and Behrensmeyer, A. K. 1971. Archaeological traces of early hominid activities, east of Lake Rudolf, Kenya. *Science* 1973:1129-1134.

Itani, J. 1978. Distribution and adaptation of chimpanzees in an arid area (Ugalla Area, Western Tanzania). In *The Great Apes: Perspectives on Human Evolution* 5 (D. Hamburg and E. McCown, Eds.) W. A. Benjamin, Menlo Park, Ca.

Itani, J., and A. Suzuki. 1967. The social unit of chimpanzees. *Primates* 8:355-381.

Izawa, K. 1970. Unit groups of chimpanzees and their nomadism in the savanna woodland. *Primates* 11:1-46.

Jones, C., and Sabater Pi, J. 1971. Comparative ecology of *Gorilla gorilla* (Savage and Wyman) and *Pan troglodytes* (Blumenbach) in Rio Muni, West Africa. *Bibliotheca. Primatol.*, no. 13. S. Karger, Basel.

Kano, T. 1971. The chimpanzee of Filabanga, western Tanzania. *Primates* 12(3-4):229-246.

King, M., and Wilson, A. 1975. Evolution at two levels in humans and chimpanzees. *Science* 188:107-116.

Kitahara-Frisch, J. 1975. Book review of G. Teleki's *The Predatory Behavior of Wild Chimpanzees*. *Primates* 16(1):103-106.

Kortlandt, A. 1967. Experimentation with chimpanzees in the wild. In *Progress in Primatology* (D. Starck, R. Schneider, and H. J. Kuhn, Eds.) Gustav Fischer, Stuttgart.

Kruuk, H. 1972. *The Spotted Hyena: A Study of Predation and Social Behavior.* Wildlife, Behavior and Ecology Series. University of Chicago Press, Chicago.

Kühme, W. 1965. Communal food distribution and division of labor in African hunting dogs. *Nature* 205:443-444.

Kummer, H. 1968. *Social Organization of Hamadryas Baboons.* University of Chicago Press, Chicago.

Kummer, 1971. *Primate Societies: Group Techniques of Ecological Adaptation.* Aldine, Chicago.

Lancaster, J. 1975. *Primate Behavior and the Emergence of Human Culture.* Holt, Rinehart and Winston, New York.

Leakey, M. D. 1970a. Early artefacts from the Koobi Fora area. *Nature* 226:228-230.

Leakey, M. D. 1970b. Stone artefacts from Swartkrans. *Nature* 225:1222-1225.

Leakey, M. D. 1971. *Olduvai Gorge*, volume 3. Excavations in Beds I and II, 1960-1963. Cambridge University Press, Cambridge.

Leakey, M. D. 1976. A summary and discussion of the archaeological evidence from Bed I and Bed II, Olduvai Gorge, Tanzania. In *Human Origins: Louis Leakey and the East African Evidence* (G. L. Isaac and E. R. McCown, Eds.) W. A. Benjamin, Menlo Park, Ca.

Lee, R. B. 1965. *Subsistence Ecology of !Kung Bushmen.* Ph.D. dissertation, University of California, Berkeley.

Lee, R. B. 1968a. Comments. In *New Perspectives in Archaeology* (S. R. Binford and L. R. Binford, Eds.) Aldine, Chicago.

Lee, R. B. 1968b. What hunters do for a living, or how to make out on scarce resources. In *Man the Hunter* (R. B. Lee and I. DeVore, Eds.) Aldine, Chicago.

Lee, R. B. 1972. Population growth and the beginning of sedentary life among the !Kung Bushmen. In *Population Growth: Anthropological Implications* (B. Spooner, Ed.) MIT Press, Cambridge, Mass.

Lee, R. B., and DeVore, I., Eds. 1968a. *Man the Hunter.* Aldine, Chicago.

Lee, R. B., and DeVore, I. 1968b. Problems in the study of hunters and gatherers. In *Man the Hunter* (R. B. Lee and I. DeVore, Eds.) Aldine, Chicago.

Le Gros Clark, W. E. 1967. *Man-Apes or Ape-Men? The Story of Discoveries in Africa.* Holt, Rinehart and Winston, New York.

Leutenegger, W., and Kelly, J. T. 1977. Relationship of sexual dimorphism in canine size and body size to social, behavioral and ecological correlates in anthropoid primates. *Primates* 18(1): 117-136.

Lindburg, D. 1975. Mate selection in the Rhesus monkey, *Macaca mulatta*. *Am. J. Phys. Anthrop.* 42:315.

Linton, S. 1971. Woman the gatherer: male bias in anthropology. In *Women in Perspective: A Guide for Cross-Cultural Studies* (S. E. Jacobs, Ed.) University of Illinois Press, Urbana. Reprinted under Sally Slocum in *Toward an Anthropology of Women* (R. R. Reiter, Ed.) Monthly Review, New York.

Luchterhand, K. 1974. *Mid-Pleistocene Hominid Distribution and Adaptation in Eastern Asia.* Ph.D. dissertation, University of Chicago.

McGinnis, P. R. 1973. *Patterns of Sexual Behaviour in a Community of Free-living Chimpanzees.* Ph.D. dissertation, Cambridge University, Cambridge, England.

McGrew, W. C. 1978. Evolutionary implications of sex differences in chimpanzee predation and tool use. In *The Great Apes: Perspectives on Human Evolution* 5 (D. Hamburg and E. McCown, Eds.) W. A. Benjamin, Menlo Park, CA.

Menzel, E. W. 1973a. Leadership and communication in young chimpanzees. In *Precultural Primate Behavior* (E. W. Menzel, Ed.) S. Karger, Basel.

Menzel, E. W. 1973b. Chimpanzee spatial memory organization. *Science* 182:943-945.

Menzel, E. W., and Halperin, S. 1975. Purposive behavior as a basis for objective communication between chimpanzees. *Science* 189:652-654.

Merrick, H. V., DeHeinzelin, J., Halsaerts, P., and Howell, F.C. 1973. Archaeological occurrences of Early Pleistocene Age from the Shungura Formation, Lower Omo Valley, Ethiopia. *Nature* 242:572-575.

Movius, H. L., Jr. 1950. A wooden spear of Third Interglacial Age from Lower Saxony. *Southwest J. Anthrop.* 6:139-142.

Nishida, T. 1968. The social group of wild chimpanzees in the Mahali Mountains. *Primates* 9:167-224.

Peters, R., and Mech, L. D. 1975. Behavioral and intellectual adaptations of selected mammalian predators to the problem of hunting large animals. In *Sociobiology and Psychology of Primates* (R. H. Tuttle, Ed.) World Anthropology Series. Mouton, The Hague.

Pfeiffer, J. 1972. *The Emergence of Man* (second edition) Harper and Row, New York.

Pilbeam, D. 1972. Evolutionary changes in hominoid dentition through geological time. In *Calibration of Hominoid Evolution* (W. W. Bishop and J. A. Miller, Eds.) Scottish Academic, Edinburgh.

Pilbeam, D., and Gould, S. J. 1974. Size and scaling in human evolution. *Science* 186:892-901.

Reynolds, V. 1965. Some behavioral comparisons between the chimpanzee and the mountain gorilla in the wild. *Am. Anthrop.* 67:691-706.

Saayman, G. S. 1975. The influence of hormonal and ecological factors upon sexual behavior and social organization in Old World primates. In *Socioecology and Psychology of Primates* (R. H. Tuttle, Ed.) World Anthropology Series. Mouton, The Hague.

Sarich, V. M., and Cronin, J. E. 1976. Molecular systematics of the primates. In *Molecular Anthropology* (M. Goodman and R. E. Tashian, Eds.) Plenum, New York.

Schaller, G. 1972. *The Serengeti Lion.* University of Chicago Press, Chicago.

Schaller, G., and Lowther, G. 1969. The relevance of carnivore behavior to the study of early hominids. *Southwest. J. Anthrop.* 25(4):307-341.

Strum, S. C. 1975. Primate predation: interim report on the development of a tradition in a troop of olive baboons. *Science* 187:255-257.

Sugiyama, Y. 1969. Social behavior of chimpanzees in the Budongo Forest, Uganda. *Primates* 10:197-225.

Sugiyama, Y. 1973. The social structure of wild chimpanzees: a review of field studies. In *Comparative Ecology and Behavior of Primates* (R. Michael and J. Crook, Eds.) Academic, New York.

Suzuki, A. 1969. An ecological study of chimpanzees in a savanna woodland. *Primates* 10:103-148.

Suzuki, A. 1975. The origin of hominid hunting: a primatological perspective. In *Socioecology and Psychology of Primates* (R. H. Tuttle, Ed.) World Anthropology Series. Mouton, The Hague.

Tanner, N., and Zihlman, A. 1976. Women in evolution. Part I: Innovation and selection in human origins. *Signs: J. Women Cult. Soc.* 1(3, Part 1):585-608.

Teleki, G. 1973a. *The Predatory Behavior of Wild Chimpanzees.* Bucknell University Press, Lewisburg, PA.

Teleki, G. 1973b. The omnivorous chimpanzee. *Scient. Am.* 228(1):33-42.

Teleki, G. 1974. Chimpanzee subsistence technology: materials and skills. *J. Human Evol.* 3:575-594.

Teleki, G. 1975. Primate subsistence patterns: collector-predators and gatherer-hunters. *J. Human Evol.* 4:125-184.

Tiger, L. 1969. *Men in Groups.* Random House, New York.

Tiger, L., and R. Fox. 1971. *The Imperial Animal.* Holt, Rinehart and Winston, New York.

Tobias, P. V. 1965. *Australopithecus, Homo habilis,* Tool-using and tool-making. *S. Afr. Archaeol. Bull.* 20(80):167-192.

Tobias, P. V. 1972. Progress and problems in the study of early man in Sub-Saharan Africa. In *Functional and Evolutionary Biology of Primates* (R. H. Tuttle, Ed.) Aldine, Chicago.

Tobias, P. V. 1975. Brain evolution in the Hominoidea. In *Primate Functional Morphology and Evolution* (R. H. Tuttle, Ed.) World Anthropology Series. Mouton, The Hague.

Trivers, R. L. 1972. Parental investment and sexual selection. In *Sexual Selection and the Descent of Man 1871-1971* (B. Campbell, Ed.) Aldine, Chicago.

Wallace, J. A. 1972. Tooth chipping in the australopithecines. *Nature* 244:117-118.

Wallace, J. A. 1975. Dietary adaptation of *Australopithecus* and early *Homo.* In *Paleoanthropology, Morphology and Paleoecology* (R. H. Tuttle, Ed.) World Anthropology Series. Mouton, The Hague.

Washburn, S. L., and Avis, V. 1958. Evolution of human behavior. In *Behavior and Evolution* (A. Roe and G. G. Simpson, Eds.) Yale University Press, New Haven.

Washburn, S. L., and DeVore, I. 1961. Social behavior of baboons and early man. In *Social Life of Early Man* (S. L. Washburn, Ed.) Aldine, Chicago.

Washburn, S. L., and Lancaster, C. S. 1968. The evolution of hunting. In *Man the Hunter* (R. B. Lee and I. DeVore, Eds.) Aldine, Chicago.

Washburn, S. L., and Moore, R. 1974. *Ape into Man: A Study of Human Evolution.* Little, Brown and Co., Boston.

Wilson, A. C., and Sarich, V. M. 1969. A molecular time scale for human evolution. *Proc. Natl. Acad. Sci.* 63:1088-1093.

Wilson, E. O. 1975. *Sociobiology: The New Synthesis.* Harvard University Press, Cambridge, MA.

Wolpoff, M. H. 1973. Posterior tooth size, body size and diet in South African gracile australopithecines. *Am. J. Phys. Anthrop.* 39:375-394.

Wolpoff, M. H. 1974. Sagittal cresting in the South African australopithecines. *Am. J. Phys. Anthrop.* 40(3):397-408.

Zihlman, A. L. 1976. Sexual dimorphism and its behavioral implications in early hominids. Prepared for Colloque VI "Les plus anciens hominides." *Neuvieme Congrès International des Sciences Préhistoriques et Protohistoriques.* September 13-18, Nice, France.

Zihlman, A. L. 1978. Women in evolution, Part II: Subsistence and social organization in early hominids. *Signs: J. Women Cult. Soc.* 4(1, Part 2):4-20.

Zihlman, A. L., and Cramer, D. 1976. Human locomotion. *Nat. Hist.* 85(1):64-69.

22

The Origin of Man

C. O. Lovejoy

During the last quarter-century the study of human origins has proved remarkably successful. Crucial fossils and primate behavioral data are now available from which to reconstruct man's evolution during the last 15 million years. Equally important is the recognition of a close genetic relationship between man and the other extant hominoids (especially *Pan* and *Gorilla*) (Goodman 1976; King and Wilson 1975; Sarich 1968, 1971; Kohne 1972; Kohne *et al.* 1970; Lovejoy and Meindl 1972). Experiments on DNA hybridization indicate at least 98 percent identity in nonrepeated DNA in man and chimpanzee, sufficient similarity to suggest the possibility of a viable hybrid. These data confirm studies by comparative anatomists who have emphasized the striking anatomical similarities of apes and man (Huxley 1863; Gregory 1930; Keith 1923, 1929; Le Gros Clark 1962). As a consequence of this physical similarity, models of human origin must directly address the few primary differences separating humans from apes. Clearly, the rate of acquisition of these differences, the fossil evidence bearing on their first appearance, and their underlying selection are crucial to an understanding of human evolution.

MATERIAL CULTURE

The most commonly cited distinction between man and apes is the former's reliance on material culture. The belief that tools were pivotal to the divergence of hominids was initiated by Darwin (1871) and has remained the most popular view (Bartholomew and Birdsell 1953; Mann 1972; Washburn 1960, 1963, 1968; DeVore 1965; Tobias 1971; Washburn and Ciochon 1974). Darwin was impressed by the absence of large canines in man and attributed their reduction to tool use. As Holloway (1967) and Jolly (1970) have cogently argued, however, tool use is not an explanation of canine reduction since there is no behavioral contradiction in having both functional canines and tools. There is little doubt that material culture has played a role in the evolution of *Homo sapiens* and *H. erectus*, but this does not require it to have been a significant factor in the origin of hominids. In fact, the earliest recognizable tools are only about 2 million years old [1], but there is considerable evidence placing the phyletic origin of hominids in the middle to late Miocene (12 to 6 million years ago) (Simons 1972, 1978; Pilbeam 1972; Jolly 1978; Greenfield 1979). Although the earliest tools will have left no record because of the use of perishable materials, there is still the necessary presumption of

a 6- to 10-million-year period dominated by reliance on material culture—a view with numerous short comings.

The use of primitive tools by extant pongids (Kortlandt 1967; Goodall 1965; Wright 1978) supports the contention of comparable abilities in early hominids, but it also demonstrates that tool use is a general capacity of pongids, none of which exhibit the unique characters of hominids [2]. If tools were the primary determinant of early hominization, why should their first appearance be so late in the hominid record? More importantly, what activity requiring tools was critical to early hominid survival and phyletic origin [3]? It is now clear that hunting does not qualify as such an activity [4]. From the first recognizable tools to the industrial revolution required only 2 million years, whereas if tools played a part in the origin of hominids, they must have remained primitive and unchanged for at least 5 million years. It is likely that either the earliest hominids made no use of tools at all, or that such use was comparable to that in other extant hominoids and was not critical to their survival or pivotal to their origin.

EXPANSION OF THE NEOCORTEX

It is now clear that the marked expansion of the hominid cerebral cortex took place during the last 2 to 3 million years (Johanson and White 1979; Radinsky 1975). Detailed study of the Hadar crania from Ethiopia, recently attributed to *Australopithecus afarensis* (Johanson White and Coppens 1978), has revealed that they were strikingly primitive [5]. Preliminary estimates of cranial capacity indicate a brain size well within the range of extant pongids (Holloway, personal communication). The pelvis of the skeleton known as Lucy from Afar Locality (A.L.) 288 has been fully reconstructed (Lovejoy 1979). One of its most salient features is a birth canal whose shape and dimensions show little or no effects of selection for passage of enlarged fetal crania, adaptations that so clearly dominate the form of the modern human pelvis (Lovejoy *et al.* 1971; Lovejoy 1974, 1975).

BIPEDALITY

Bipedality is an unusual mode of mammalian locomotion. Contrary to the so called efficiency argument, energy expenditure for bipedal walking is probably not significantly different from that during quadrupedal locomotion (Lovejoy 1978; Taylor and Rowntree 1973; Cavagna *et al.* 1964). Yet the adoption of

Reprinted with permission from *Science*, Vol. 211, pp. 341-350. Copyright © 1981 by the American Association for the Advancement of Science.

non-saltatory bipedal progression is disadvantageous because both speed and agility are markedly reduced (Lovejoy 1974, 1975, 1978; Lovejoy *et al.* 1971) [6]. All present evidence, especially that made available by the postcranium of *A. afarensis*, confirms an essentially complete adaptation to bipedal locomotion by at least 4 million years ago (Lovejoy 1979; Johanson *et al.* 1976). This conclusion is provided unequivocal support by the hominid footprints discovered at Laetoli in Tanzania (Johanson and White 1980).

DENTITION

Additional distinctions between hominids and pongids are found in their respective jaws and teeth. In fact, these differences have allowed the identification of possible hominids in the Miocene—there are no distinctive postcranial or cranial remains of undoubted hominid affinities before about 4 million years ago. As a result of recent field work in Mio-Pliocene deposits (Johanson and Taieb 1976; Johanson and Coppens 1976; M.D. Leakey *et al.* 1976; White 1977; Coppens *et al.*, Eds. 1976; Tobias 1973; R.E. Leakey *et al.* 1971, 1972; Day and Leakey 1973, 1974; Leakey and Wood 1973; Day *et al.* 1974, 1976; Howell 1969; Howell and Wood 1974; Pilbeam *et al.* 1977), it is now possible to suggest a broad schedule of phases in the evolution of the hominoid dentition that can serve as an outline of hominoid phyletic events during the last 23 million years.

Phase I

This phase has a generalized dryopithecine dentition including a distinct Y-5 lower molar cusp pattern with bunodont crowns, thin enamel, and cheek teeth small relative to body size; incisors are broad with canine-premolar shear. This phase is associated with forest faunas and floras (Pilbeam 1969, 1976; Simons and Pilbeam 1965, 1972; Simons 1976) and is shared by all hominoids before 15 million years ago (range, 23 to 15 million years) (Pilbeam *et al.* 1977; Pilbeam 1969, 1976; Simons and Pilbeam 1965, 1972; Simons 1976; Tobias and Coppens, Eds. 1976).

Phase II

This phase shows a shift toward greater molar dominance. About, 14 million years ago, hominoids fall into two groups. The first retained phase I characters and may constitute ancestral populations of extant apes (*Proconsul*, "*Rangwapithecus*" and *Limnopithecus*, *Dryopithecus* (Pilbeam *et al.* 1977). A second group exhibits enamel thickening, increased molar wear gradient, and moderate anterior dental reduction or increased relative molar size, or both. Mandibles are more robust and prognathism is reduced. The shift toward greater molar dominance has partially been attributed to greater reliance on terrestrial food sources. This group includes genera (*Ramapithecus* and *Sivapithecus*) probably related to hominids, an extinct ape (*Gigantopithecus*), and possibly the modern orang-utan (range, 14 to 8 million years) (Greenfield 1979; Pilbeam *et al.* 1977; Pilbeam 1969, 1976; Simons and Pilbeam 1965, 1972; Simons 1976, Tobias and Coppens, Eds. 1976; Greenfield 1977) [7].

Phase III

This phase represents a conservative period. The dentition of *A. afarensis* appears only moderately changed in morphology and proportions from phase II; the features include comparatively large incisors, frequently a unicuspid lower first premolar, canines of moderate size, molars of moderate size (relative to body size and later hominids), and loss of canine-premolar shear (range, 7 to 2.5 million years) (Greenfield 1979; Johanson and White 1979).

Phase IV

This phase represents Plio-Pleistocene specialization. The sample in this time range is divisible into two clades or phyletic lines (Johanson and White 1979). The first was possibly restricted to savannah and grassland. It displays extreme anterior tooth reduction and excessive molar dominance and became extinct by mid-Pleistocene (*A. africanus*—*A. robustus*—"*A. boisei*"). A second clade, ancestral to *H. erectus*, retained a more generalized dentition in the early Pleistocene but underwent dentognathic reduction in the middle and upper Pleistocene as a consequence of reliance on material culture (for example, reduced dental manipulation and greater preoral food preparation [Brace and Montagu 1977]). My view is that this clade occupied more varied habitats. Both groups are probably directly descendant from *A. afarensis* (Johanson and White 1979).

MODELS OF HUMAN ORIGIN

A model of hominid origin proposed by Jolly (1970) uses analogy to anatomical and behavioral characters shared by *Theropithecus gelada* and some early hominids. He suggests that early hominid populations relied on small-object feeding, that this dietary specialization led to a suite of adaptations to the grassland savannah, and that bipedality developed in response to feeding posture. Yet geladas, which do rely on small-object feeding, are not bipedal and show no significant adaptations to bipedality. Bipedal locomotion is clearly not required for extensive small object feeding especially on grasslands where speed and agility are of great value in animals who also lack wide visual fields and sensitive olfaction [8]. Furthermore, the dental morphology of *A. afarensis* is considerably more generalized than that of later hominids. The dietary specialization seen in *A. robustus* is possibly accountable by Jolly's model, but the more generalized dentition of *A. afarensis* is not [9]. It is more likely that hominids venturing into open habitats were already bipedal and that their regular occupation of savannahs was not possible until intensified social behavior was well developed.

Other theorists have viewed hominization as the direct result of savannah occupation by prehominids. Proponents of this view believe that the selective pressures of life on grassland savannahs directly produced the human character complex. Bipedal locomotion is posited as sentinel behavior and as an adaptation allowing weapons to be used against predators. Intelligence is said to be favored because highly integrated troop behavior is necessary for predator repulsion. Differences in some behaviors of chimpanzee populations now living in woodland savannahs versus those inhabiting more forested areas are cited as evidence (Kortlandt 1962, 1972).

There are many problems with this view. Bipedality is useless for avoidance or escape from predators. Occasional bipedality, as seen in many primates, is sufficient for the use of weapons. Most importantly, brain expansion and cultural development remotely postdate hominid divergence.

Furthermore, Miocene ecology is inconsistent with the savannah selection theory. While cooling, aridity, and increased seasonality had pronounced effects on Old World floras, the predominant effect of these climate trends, in areas where hominids are known to have been present, appears to have been the development of diversified mosaics, rather than broad-scale forest reduction (Moreau 1951; Butzer 1977; Campbell 1972; Andrews and Van Couvering 1975) It would be more correct to say that hominids of the middle and late Miocene were presented with a greater variety of possible habitats than to view them as having suffered an imposed "terrestrialization." It is also clear that some Miocene sites at which possible hominids have been recovered had canopy forest conditions (Greenfield 1979; Kretzoi 1975; Kennedy 1978). While increased seasonality would have imposed a need for larger feeding ranges, occasional use of woodlands and edaphic grasslands would not necessarily impose elevated carnivore pressure. Nor, as was pointed out above, would early hominids be required to abandon quadrupedality in order to use more orthograde positional behavior during feeding. Quite the contrary, it would appear that late Miocene habitat mosaics would allow adoption of bipedality (in forests and transition mosaics) rather than directly select for it. All present evidence therefore indicates that hominid clade evolved in forest or mosaic conditions, or both [10], rather than only on grassland or savannahs, and that bipedal locomotion was not a response to feeding posture, material culture, or predator avoidance.

In summary, four major character complexes are usually cited as distinguishing hominids from pongids. Hominids have remarkable brain expansion, a complex material culture, anterior dental reduction and molar dominance, and bipedal locomotion. Only bipedal locomotion and partial dental modifications can be shown to have an antiquity even approximating the earliest appearance of unquestioned, developed hominids (*A. afarensis*).

DEMOGRAPHIC STRATEGY AND THE EVOLUTION OF HOMINIDS

The order Primates has long been recognized to display a *scala naturae* consisting of "intercalary types"—extant forms that represent earlier stages in the development of major adaptive trends. Figure 1 is a well-known diagram of the chronology of life phases in living primates. There is an obvious trend toward prolonged life-span, which has both physiological and demographic correlates bearing directly on the phyletic origin of hominids.

The physiological correlates (Fig. 1) include a longer period of infant dependency, prolonged gestation, single births, and successively greater periods between pregnancies. Cutler (1976) has demonstrated that such developmental parameters are "qualitatively and sequentially similar in different mammalian species" but proceed "at different characteristic rates

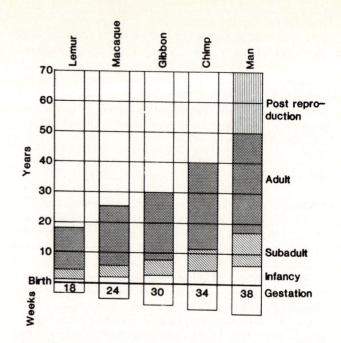

Figure 1. *Progressive prolongation of life phases and gestation in primates. Note the proportionality of the four indicated phases. The post-reproductive phase is restricted to man and is probably a recent development (Lovejoy* et al. *1977; after Schultz 1969).*

defined by the reciprocal of the MLP" (maximum life potential). The progressive slowing of life phases can in turn be accounted for by an increasingly K-type demographic strategy [11]. With each step in the *scala naturae*, populations devote a greater proportion of their reproductive energy to subadult care, with increased investment in the survival of fewer offspring. Among chimpanzee populations, this trend appears to have resulted in marginal demographic conditions. Field studies at Gombe in Tanzania show the average period between successful births to be 5.6 years (Teleki *et al.* 1976). This can be attributed in part to a greatly prolonged period of subadult dependency. Van Lawick-Goodall's (1976) description of the chimpanzee life phases is instructive:

> The infant does not start to walk until he is six months old, and he seldom ventures more than a few yards from his mother until he is over nine months old. He may ingest a few scraps of solid food when he is six months, but solids do not become a significant part of his diet until he is about two years of age and he continues to nurse until he is between four-and-a-half and six years old, Moreover, while he may travel short distances . . . when he is about four years old, he continues to make long journeys riding on his mothers back until he is five or six. . . .

This extreme degree of parental investment has profound demographic consequences. A chimpanzee female does not reach sexual maturity until she is about 10 years old. If she is to reproduce herself and her mate, that is maintain a stable population, she must survive to an age of 21 years [12]. Whereas in rhesus macaques, the age is only about 9 years [13].

Figure 2 shows a balance depicting the reciprocal relation between longevity and the primary demographic elements of parental investment. The two sides of this hypothetical balance are physiologically interdependent; as longevity is increased,

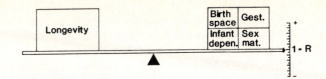

Figure 2. *Mechanical model of demographic variables in hominoids. The R is the intrinsic rate of population increase (1 = static population size). An increase in the lengths of the four periods on the bar to the right (birth space, gestation, infant dependency, and sexual maturity) is accompanied by a comparable shift of longevity to the left, but without realization of that longevity, prolonged maturation reduces R and leads to extinction or replacement by populations in which life phases are chronologically shorter. Of the four variables on the right, only birth space can be significantly shortened (shifted to the left) without alteration of primate aging physiology.*

each of the developmental stages is proportionately prolonged. The relationships between these variables, in fact, are not exactly linear, but they do have remarkably high correlations in most mammals (Cutler 1976). As the scale indicates, greater longevity is accompanied by a proportionate delay in reproductive rate and therefore requires a female to survive to an older age in order to maintain the same reproductive value (measured at birth) (Fisher 1930). Put another way, the total reproductive rate of a primate species can remain constant with progressive increases in longevity only if the crude mortality rate is correspondingly reduced. Actual mortality rate is dependent on both maximum life potential, a genetic factor, and environmental interaction. Deaths caused by predation, accident, parasitism, infection, failure of food supply, and so forth, are at least partially stochastic events beyond the complete control of the organism. Only if mechanisms are developed to increase an organism's resistance to such factors, can the effects of increased longevity be reproductively accommodated. Strong social bonds, high levels of intelligence, intense parenting, and long periods of learning are among factors used by higher primates to depress environmentally induced mortality. It is of some interest that such factors also require greater longevity (for brain development, learning, acquisition of social and parenting skills) and that they constitute reciprocal links leading to greater longevity. This positive feedback system, however, has an absolute limit; environmentally induced mortality can never be completely under organism control, no matter how effective the mechanisms developed to resist it.

Suppose that late Miocene hominoids were approaching the effective limit of this feedback system or at least were sufficiently near the limit not to thrive in novel environments [14]. Two demographic variables could be altered to improve reproductive success survivorship (the probability of surviving) and the time period between successive births (the birth space). All other factors are direct linear functions of mammalian developmental physiology and could not be altered. The argument is subject to the following simple quantification

$$RV = l(s) \int_s^{MLP} l(x)b(x)dx \qquad (1)$$

where RV is reproductive value of a cohort measured at birth, that is, the expected number of offspring produced by a unit radix; $b(x)$ is fertility at age x; $l(x)$ is survivorship at age x; s is

Table 1. Relative reproductive values of Old World Primates calculated from Eq.4 (see text) and multiplied by 10 for clarity.

Annual survivorship	Reproductive Values		
	Old World monkeys*	Chimpanzees†	Man‡
.90	17	4	2
.92	23	7	4
.94	31	13	9
.96	42	25	24
.98	58	50	64

*Maximum life potential = 20; sexual maturity = 4; birth space = 2 (Drickamer, 1974; Napier and Napier, 1967) [13]. †Maximum life potential = 40; sexual maturity = 10; birth space = 3 (Napier and Napier 1967; Teleki et al. 1976; Van Lawick-Goodall 1969) [16]. ‡Maximum life potential = 60; sexual maturity = 15; birth space = 2.5.

age at sexual maturation; and MLP = maximum life potential. Assuming that a female gives birth at age s years and subsequently every β (birth space) years until reaching MLP, her total offspring would be given by

$$\frac{MLP - s}{\beta} \qquad (2)$$

Fertility is then seen to be dependent on birth space β according to

$$\int_s^{MLP} b(x)dx = \frac{MLP - s}{\beta} \qquad (3)$$

A simple solution (but one which is fully acceptable because of the proportionate relation between MLP and s) is $b(x)$ $1/\beta$. The expression for RV then becomes

$$RV = \frac{1}{\beta} [l(s) \int_s^{MLP} l(x)dx] \qquad (4)$$

Because the term in brackets is independent of β, RV is inversely proportional to β, and RV is increased by a shorter birth space, by greater values of $l(x)$ for any age, or by both. Table 1 provides reproductive values for chimpanzees, Old World monkeys, and man from estimated values of β, s, and MLP under the simplifying assumption of $l(x) = l^x$. It can be seen from this table that both chimpanzees and humans have considerably lower reproductive values than Old World monkeys for low values of $l(x)$. As the values used for calculation are conservative, the existence of successful hominid clades in Pliocene mosaics suggests that both birth space reduction and elevation of survivorship had probably been accomplished. This is without explanation unless a major change in reproductive strategy accompanied occupation of novel environments by these hominids. Yet neither brain expansion nor significant material culture appear at this time level and were therefore not responsible for this shift.

A BEHAVIORAL MODEL FOR EARLY HOMINID EVOLUTION

Any behavioral change that increases reproductive rate, survivorship, or both, is under selection of maximum intensity. Higher primates rely on social behavioral mechanisms to promote survivorship during all phases of the life cycle, and one could cite numerous methods by which it theoretically could be increased. Avoidance of dietary toxins, use of more reliable food sources, and increased competence in arboreal locomotion are obvious examples. Yet these are among many that have remained under strong selection throughout much of the course of primate evolution, and it is therefore unlikely that early hominid adaptation was a product of intensified selection for adaptations almost universal to anthropoid primates. For early hominids we must look beyond such common variables to novel forms of behavioral change. The tendency has been to concentrate on singular, extraordinary traits of later human evolution such as intense technology, organized hunting, and the massive human brain. Yet these adaptations were not likely to have arisen de novo from elemental behaviors seen in extant nonhuman primates, such as the primitive tool using of the chimpanzee, in the absence of a broad selective milieu. It is more probable that significant preadaptations were present in early hominids that served as a behavioral base from which the "breakthrough" adaptations [15] of later hominids could progressively develop. We are therefore in search of a novel behavioral pattern in Miocene hominoids that could evolve from typical primate survival strategies, but that might also include important elements of other mammalian strategies, that is, a behavioral pattern that arose by recombination of common mammalian behavioral elements and that increased survivorship and birthrate.

In her essay on mother-infant relationships among chimpanzees, Van Lawick-Goodall (1969) [16] noted two primary causes of mortality among infants: "inadequacy" of the mother-infant relationship and "injuries caused by falling from the mother." An intensification of both the quality and quantity of parenting would unquestionably improve survivorship of the altricial chimpanzee infant. The feeding and reproductive strategies of higher primates, however, largely prevent such an advancement. The mother must both care for the infant and forage for herself. A common method of altricial infant care in other mammals is sequestration of offspring at locations of maximum safety. Nests, lodges, setts, warrens, dreys, dens, lairs, and burrows are examples of this strategy. A similar adaptation in primates is usually not possible, however, because the need to forage requires both mother and infant to remain mobile. The requirement of mother-infant mobility is a significant cause of mortality and is at the same time the most important restriction on primate birth spacing.

Many primates display significant sex differences in foraging. Diet composition, selection of food items, feeding time, and canopy levels and sites differ in some species (Clutton-Brock 1977). In at least *Pongo pygmaeus* and *Colobus badius*, males often feed at lower canopy levels than females (Clutton-Brock and Harvey 1977; Sussman, Ed. 1979) [17]. In the gelada baboon, all-male groups "tended not to exploit quite the same areas as the reproductive units thus reducing indirect competition for food" (Crook 1972). Clutton-Brock (1977) notes that an increased separation of males from female-offspring foraging sites is advantageous where (i) animals feed outward from a fixed base, (ii) the adult sex ratio is close to parity, and (iii) feeding rate is limited by search time rather than by handling time, which is the time spent both preparing and consuming food. Similar feeding differences by sex are found in birds and other mammals. (Selander 1966, 1972; Hutchinson 1965).

It is reasonable to assume that Miocene hominoids traveled between food sources on the ground and that these primates would be best characterized as omnivores (Greenfield 1979). These are ecologically sound assumptions. Increased seasonality coupled with already occurring local biotic variation (edaphic grasslands, savannah, woodland, forest) (Jolly 1970; Greenfield 1979; Moreau 1951; Butzer 1977; Campbell 1972; Andrews and Van Couvering 1975) would have presented variable and mosaic conditions. Occupation of heterogeneous ("patchy") environments and use of variable food sources favors a generalist strategy, whereas reliance on a homogeneous diet requires high food concentrations [18, 19]. The time spent searching for food is greatest among generalists who live in food-sparse environments (Pianka 1974). In short, Miocene ecological conditions support the view that feeding rate would have been more dependent on search time than handling time.

Greater seasonality and the need to increase both birthrate and survivorship would also favor at least partial separation of male and female day ranges since this strategy would increase carrying capacity and improve the protein and calorie supply of females and their offspring. Terrestriality, however, would require a centrifugal or linear displacement of males, as opposed to vertical in canopy feeding. Given the Miocene conditions described above, such separation could become marked especially in the dry season. If such separation were primarily due only to an increase in the male day range, moreover, the range of the female-offspring group could be proportionally reduced by progressive elimination of male competition for local resources. This separation would be under strong positive selection. Lowered mobility of females would reduce accident rate during travel, maximize familiarity with the core area, reduce exposure to predators, and allow intensification of parenting behavior, thus elevating survivorship [20]. Such a division of feeding areas, however, would not genetically favor males unless it specifically reduced competition with their own biological offspring and did not reduce their opportunities for consort relationships. Polygynous mating would not be favored by this adaptive strategy because the advantage of feeding divergence is reduced as the number of males is reduced. Conversely, a sex ratio close to parity would select for the proposed feeding strategy. Such a ratio would obtain if the mating pattern were monogamous pair bonding. In this case, males would avoid competition with their bonded mates and biological offspring (by using alternative feeding sites) and not be disadvantaged by physical separation, that is, there would be no loss of consort opportunity. In short, monogamous pair bonding would favor feeding divergence by "assuring" males of biological paternity and by reducing feeding competition with their own offspring and mates.

Such a system would increase survivorship and would also favor any increase in the reproductive rate of a monogamous pair so long as feeding strategy was sufficient to meet the increased load on the sources of protein and calories. One element of feeding among forest chimpanzees is the "food call" sometimes made by males upon discovery of a new food source (Reynolds and Reynolds 1965; Van Lawick-Goodall 1968; Sugiyama 1968, 1969) [21]. In the proposed system, however, selection would not favor this behavior; instead, selection would favor a behavior that would benefit only the male's own reproductive unit. The simple alternative to the food call would involve collecting the available food item or items and returning them to the mate and offspring. Contrary to the opinion that such behavior would be altruistic, it would not be so in the proposed system, because it would only benefit the biological offspring of the male carrying out the provisioning and thus would be under powerful, direct selection. If this behavior were to become a regular component of the male's behavioral repertoire, it would directly increase his reproductive rate by correspondingly improving the protein and calorie supply of the female who could then accommodate greater gestational and lactation loads and intensify parenting [22]. The behavior would thus achieve both an increase in survivorship and a reduction in birth space. It would allow a progressive increase in the number of dependent offspring because their nutritional and supervisory requirements could be met more adequately.

Behaviors associated with similar reproductive strategies are in fact present in other primates. In both the Callitrichidae and Aotinae, extensive paternal care of the young constitutes a critical part of reproductive strategy in some species (Mitchell and Brandt 1972; Kummer 1971; Hershkovitz 1977). Among callitrichids, the social unit is usually an adult male and female, plus one to several subadults. Maternal care is largely restricted to sucking and grooming, the male being responsible for subadults at all other times. The modal birth is dizygotic twins (Clutton-Brock 1977; Hershkovitz 1977). It is likely that this system is a partitioning of care in response to the high protein and calorie requirements of these small species. Male care during foraging tends to equilibrate the high caloric load imposed on females by lactation and gestation of two (and sometimes three) offspring the process of twinning being an obvious demographic adaptation of elevated birthrate. As Hershkovitz (1977) notes: "survival of a population [of callitrichids] in the wild depends on close synchronization between cyclical nutritional requirements for young and old and the seasonal changes in the quality and quantity of available food." This same statement could be as well applied to early hominids, especially given increased Miocene seasonality and the need for a decrease in birth spacing. The altricial infants of Miocene hominoids, however, would have required reduced mobility and therefore prevented a callitrichid strategy of male care, with the simplest solution being the male provisional model proposed above.

THE ORIGIN OF BIPEDALITY

Provisioning is, of course, the primary parental care strategy of most canids and birds (Grzimek, Ed. 1975; Lack 1968; Eisenberg 1966) [21]. Both groups exhibit direct male involvement similar to that described for callitrichids. Their offspring are normally immature at birth, immobile, and require constant provisioning and parenting. In some species, a sexual division of labor, like that posited here for early hominids, is observed. Female hornbills (Bucerotidae), for example, depend totally on male provisioning for their survival and that of their offspring. Monogamous pair bonding is characteristic of 90 percent of bird species (Lack 1968; Emlen and Oring 1977) [23] and is the most common mating system in provisioning canids (Grzimek, Ed. 1975). Both groups, as a fundamental feature of reproductive strategy, commonly sequester their offspring at home bases [24].

One critical difference separates provisioning in birds and canids from that suggested for early hominids. Birds and canids can carry in their mouths or regurgitate (or both) a significant proportion of their body weight. Oral carrying would have been inadequate for early hominids, however, and a strong selection for bipedality, which would allow provisions to be carried "by hand," would thus accompany provisioning behavior [25].

Chimpanzees are fully capable of short-range bipedal walking and a variety of hindlimb stances (Bauer 1977), but because they lack the pelvic and lower limb adaptations characteristic of hominids, bipedal walking leads to rapid fatigue (Lovejoy 1978). It appears likely that the skeletal alterations for bipedality would be under strong selection only by consistent, extended periods of upright walking and not by either occasional bipedality or upright posture. While primitive material culture does not impose this kind of selection, carrying behavior of the type suggested above, does. It is likely that the need to carry significant amounts of food was a strong selection factor in favor of primitive material culture (Leakey and Lewin 1978; Hewes 1961). Although it is not a significant shift from primitive tools of the type used by chimpanzees today, such as "termite sticks" and "leaf sponges," to simple and readily available natural articles that could be used to enhance carrying ability, it is a significant shift from such primitive and occasional tool use to the stone tools of the basal Pleistocene. Development of such tools is most likely to have followed an extended period of more primitive material culture, which was not critical to survival. It has been suggested frequently that the earliest tools were weapons. However, the progressive development of more advanced stone tools from rudimentary weapons is unlikely. A prolonged and extensive period of regular and habitual use of simple (primitive) carrying devices could eventually allow the coordination and pattern recognition necessary for a more advanced reliance on material culture.

The sequential evolution of behavior proposed in this article has a high probability of mirroring actual behavioral events during the Miocene. In most higher primates, male fitness is largely determined by consort success of one sort or another (Trivers 1972). Male enhancement of offspring is for the most part indirect and is expressed more in terms of demic or kin selection by general behaviors such as territory defense or predator recognition and repulsion (Hrdy 1976). Females are solely responsible for true parenting and their ability in this is under strong selection. However, progressive intensification of higher primate K strategy elevates parenting requirements and lowers reproductive rate. The most obvious, and perhaps only, additional mechanism available with which to meet this "demographic dilemma" is an increase in the direct and continuous participation by males in the reproductive process. Whatever the actual sequence of events, whether as posed above or by some alternative order, such additional investment would improve survivorship and favor a mating structure that intensified energy apportionment to the male's biological offspring. Two mating patterns satisfy this latter requirement: polygyny (one male and several females) or monogamy. The former, however, requires male energy to continue to be devoted to maintaining consorts, and a pool of competing males is ensured by polygynous structure itself, thereby directing it away from direct enhancement of survivorship.

In their synthesis of the evolution of mating systems, Emlen and Oring (1977) stress three factors common to polygynous mating structure, (i) One sex is predisposed to assume most, or all, of the parental care, (ii) Parental care requirements are minimal, (iii) A superabundant food resource enables a single parent to provide full parental care. As has been noted above, however, survivorship of offspring must have been critical to Miocene hominoids; further female parenting is negated by the mobile feeding strategy; hominoid males may be considered an "untapped" pool of reproductive energy; and Miocene ecological conditions required a generalist feeding strategy. Conditions were prime for the establishment of male parental investment and a monogamous mating structure. Finally, it should be pointed out that only among primates in which the male is clearly and directly involved in the parenting process should monogamy be found. This is exactly the case, as this mating structure is found only in gibbons, siamangs, and the New World taxa discussed above (Clutton-Brock 1977).

HUMAN SEXUAL BEHAVIOR AND ANATOMY

The highly unusual sexual behavior of man may now be brought into focus. Human females are continually sexually receptive [26] and have essentially no externally recognizable estrous cycle; male approach may be considered equally stable. Copulation shows little or no synchronization with ovulation (McChance et al. 1937) [27]. As was pointed out above, the selective emergence of a monogamous mating structure and male provisioning would require that males not be disadvantaged in obtaining consorts. Provisioning in birds and canids is normally made possible by highly restricted breeding seasons and discrete generations, the female normally is impregnable for only brief periods during which parental care is not required. The menstrual cycle of higher primates (Beach 1947; Chance 1962), however, requires regular male proximity for reproductive success. The progressive elimination of external manifestations of ovulation and the establishment of continual receptivity would require copulatory vigilance in both sexes in order to ensure fertilization. Moreover, copulation would increase pairbond adhesion and serve as a social display asserting that bond. Indeed, any sequestration of ovulation (J. Lancaster, personal communication) would seem to directly imply both regular copulatory behavior and monogamous mating structure. It establishes mathematical parity between males restricted to a single mate and those practicing complete promiscuity, and the balance of selection falls to the offspring of pair bonded males, since their energetic capacity for provisioning (and improved survivorship and reproductive rate) is maximized.

Man displays a greater elaboration of epigamic characters than any other primate (Jolly 1970; Crook 1972; Morris 1967; Beach 1978). Frequently, our sexual dimorphism is tacitly accepted as evidence for a polygynous mating structure because marked sexual dimorphism is most often a product of elaboration of characters of attraction, display, and agonistic behavior in males of polygynous species. Among primates, the degree of sexual dimorphism corresponds closely to the degree of male competition for mates (Clutton-Brock and Harvey 1977; Crook 1972; Morris 1967). Yet human sexual dimorphism is clearly not typical as is even made clear by the fossil record. In their discussion of A. afarensis, Johanson and White (1979) [28] note that although this species shows "marked body size dimorphism, the metric and morphological dimorphism of the canine teeth is not as pronounced as in other extant, ground-dwelling

primates. This implies a functional pattern different from that seen in other primates and may have significant behavioral implication." There can be no doubt that large male canines are part of the "whole anatomy of bluff, threat, and fighting" (Washburn and Ciochon 1974). The reduction and effective loss of canine dimorphism in early hominids therefore serves as primary evidence in favor of the proposed behavioral model [29]. But it is important to stress that while canine dimorphism was undergoing reduction, other forms of dimorphism were apparently being accentuated, as judged from their expression in modern man, who remains the most epigamically adorned primate.

Since man displays a highly unusual mating structure, it is perhaps not surprising that his epigamic, or perhaps parasexual, anatomy is equally unusual and fully explicable by that mating structure. If pair bonding was fundamental and crucial to early hominid reproductive strategy, the anatomical characters that could reinforce pair bonds would also be under strong positive selection. Thus the body and facial hair, distinctive somatotype, the conspicuous penis of human males, and the prominent and permanently enlarged mammae of human females are not surprising in light of Mayr's (1972) observation that in "monogamous species such as herons (egrets) in which the pair bond is continuously tested and strengthened by mutual displays, there has been a 'transference' of the display characters from the males to the females with the result that both sexes have elaborate display plumes." In man, however, marked epigamic dimorphism is achieved by elaboration of parasexual characters in both males and females, rather than in males alone. Their display value is clearly cross-sexual and not intrasexual as in other primates. It should be stressed that these epigamic characters are highly variable and can thus be viewed as a mechanism for establishing and displaying individual sexual uniqueness, and that such uniqueness would play a major role in the maintenance of pair bonds (Crook 1972). This is especially important when other epigamic features of man (pubic, axillary, and scalp hair), which have been elaborated in both sexes, are considered. Such characters may also contribute to individual sexual uniqueness [30]. Redolent individuality is clearly the most probable role of axillary and urogenital scent "organs" (eccrine and apocrine glands plus hair), which are unique among mammals (Montagna 1975). An objection that might be voiced in response to these suggestions is that such auxiliary pair-bond "enhancers" are eclipsed by the paramount role of culture in the mating practices of nontechnological societies. Quite the contrary, the more that culture can be shown to dominate the mating structure and process of recent man, the more ancient must be the anatomical-physiological mechanisms involved in the formation and maintenance of pair bonds [31].

HIGHER PRIMATE PALEOGEOGRAPHY

The present-day geographic distributions of Old World monkeys and apes are shown in Fig. 3. The great apes are markedly restricted and occupy only minor areas where minimal environmental changes have taken place since the early Miocene. Yet the fossil record shows that their lineal ancestors (dryopithecines, sensu lato) spread throughout the Old World following the establishment of a land bridge and forest corridor between Africa and Eurasia about 16 to 17 million years ago,

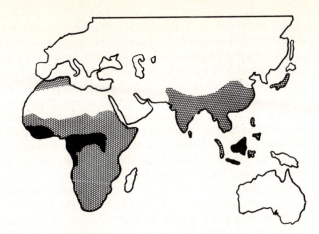

Figure 3 *Approximate distribution of extant Old World monkeys (hatched) and pongids (gorilla, chimpanzee, orang-utan) (solid) (Kortlandt 1972; Sussman Ed., 1979; Schultz 1969; Napier and Napier 1967).*

and that they enjoyed considerable success after their colonization of Europe and Asia (Andrews and Van Couvering 1975; Delson 1975). Old World monkeys, on the other hand, were much less abundant during this period (Delson and Andrews 1975). After the middle and late Miocene, however, a marked reduction in dryopithecine numbers occurred. While this cannot be deduced from the sparce fossil record of the late Miocene and early Pliocene, the distribution of extant descendants of the dryopithecines is ample evidence of their relict status. Today, Old World monkeys are clearly the dominant and successful group, having replaced the dryopithecines and their descendants during the last 12 million years (Delson 1975). One hominoid group did survive and remain relatively abundant— the Hominidae. It is probable that the hominoid trends of prolonged longevity and increased parental investment are the key to the replacement of most pongid taxa by Old World monkeys, which are reproductively more prosperous. If only a portion of Miocene hominoids made the adaptations described above, two distinct groups would subsequently result. One group might counter the "demographic dilemma" according to the model suggested in this article; a second group could survive by occupying habitats with minimal environmental hazards. Hominids, being more demographically resistant to environmentally induced mortality, would be more capable of expanding into novel and varied habitats, especially mosaics, and of competing with the radiating Old World monkeys. Conversely, the extant pongids are by implication descendant of populations progressively more restricted to highly favorable forest conditions, where minimal seasonality in food supply, low predation pressure, and limited size of the home range would be in effect. These differences in habitat preference would result in a more extensive fossil record for hominids than pongids, both by virtue of the geographic expansion of hominids and as a consequence of the occupation of habitats with more favorable conditions of fossilization. It is therefore quite possible that the sivapithecines (*sensu lato*) of the middle and late Miocene, which already evince dental modifications adumbrating those of late Pliocene hominids (Greenfield 1979), may have contained primitive emergent hominids, at least behaviorally, if not phylogenetically.

THE NUCLEAR FAMILY

Man's most unique character is without question his enormous intelligence, and its evolutionary pathway has fascinated all who have attempted to explain the human career. Hunting and tool-making are most frequently cited as "primal causes" for the Pleistocene acceleration in hominid brain development. Yet have these not figured so prominently because they leave ubiquitous evidence—the archeological record? Other human behaviors at least as critical to survival (especially reproductive behavior) are not "fossilized." It is now clear that man probably remained an omnivore throughout the Pleistocene and that hunting may have always been an auxiliary food source [32].

As Reynolds (1976) stressed, intense social behavior would seem the most likely single cause of the origin of human intelligence if one origin must be isolated. Tools are used to manipulate the environment and are thus a vehicle of intelligence, not necessarily a cause. Chimpanzees occasionally use tools (a behavior that has fascinated many early hominid theorists), but tools are not critical to their survival. Primates, which are the most intelligent mammals, have achieved evolutionary success primarily by their social and reproductive behavior, which is their most developed original character. It seems reasonable therefore to propose that a further elaboration of this adaptive strategy is the most likely "cause" of early hominid success and the further development of intelligence.

It is of interest to explore one further effect of the proposed model on early hominid social structure. The strong maternal and sibling ties of higher primates are now well documented (Van Lawick-Goodall 1976, 1969; Yamanda 1963; Koford 1963; Reynolds 1976; Kaufmann 1965). The matrifocal unit of chimpanzees continues throughout the life of the mother, as do sibling ties. In the proposed hominid reproductive strategy, the process of pair bonding would not only lead to the direct involvement of males in the survivorship of offspring, in primates as intelligent as extant hominoids, it would establish paternity, and thus lead to a gradual replacement of the matrifocal group by a "bifocal" one—the primitive nuclear family (Beach 1978) [33]. The effects of such a social unit on survivorship and species success could be profound. It could lead to a further shortening of birth space, which would accelerate the reproductive rate and amplify sibling bonds. Reduction of birth space would allow coincident protraction of the subadult (learning) period [34]. Behaviors that in other primates are common causes of infant death (for example, agonistic buffering) (Hrdy 1975) would be largely eliminated, while those that might improve survivorship (for example, adoption) (Teleki *et al.* 1976; Kummer 1967; Sade 1967) would be facilitated. The age until which an orphaned chimpanzee does not survive the death of its mother is "around 5 years of age, but may stretch another 3 to 4 in special circumstances" (Teleki *et al.* 1976). Survival of a second parent may have been a crucial reproductive advance in early hominids (Wolpoff 1979, cited in *Mosaic*). Primiparous females are much less adept than multiparous mothers. Drickamer (1974) found that in free-ranging *Macaca mulatta* "between 40 and 50% of the infants born first or second to a female did not survive their first year, but by the fourth infant born to the same female only 9% died during the first 12 months." Lancaster (1972) notes that: "Recent field and laboratory workers have shown that in many species of mammals, and especially in monkeys and apes, learning and experience play vital roles in the development of the behavior patterns used in mating and maternal care." The effect of intensified parenting, protracted learning, and enhanced sibling relationships would have a markedly beneficial effect upon survivorship. Such projections of the behavior of developing hominids are certainly not new, but they have not received their due emphasis. Can the nuclear family not be viewed as a prodigious adaptation central to the success of early hominids? It may certainly be considered as being within the behavior repertoire of hominoid primates, provided that the reproductive and feeding strategies commensurate to its development were themselves under strong selection. This brief review of the fossil record and some primate behavioral and ecological adaptations would seem to strongly favor the correctness of this view.

CONCLUSION

It is a truism to say that even late Pliocene hominids must have been unusual mammals, both behaviorally and anatomically. As was pointed out above, emphasis in models of human origin has traditionally been on singular, extraordinary traits of later human evolution. The model proposed in this article has placed greater emphasis on a fundamental behavioral base from which these unusual adaptations could be directionally selected.

The proposed model accounts for the early origin of bipedality as a locomotor behavior directly enhancing reproductive fitness, not as a behavior resulting from occasional upright feeding posture. It accounts for the origin of the home base in the same fashion as it has been acquired by numerous other mammals. It accounts for the human nuclear family, for the distinctive human sexual epigamic features, and the species' unique sexual behavior. It accounts for a functional, rudimentary material culture of long-standing, and it accounts for the

greater proportion of r-selected [11] characters in hominids relative to other hominoids. It accounts for these characters with simple behavioral changes common to both primates and other mammals and in relatively favorable environments, rather than by rapid or forced occupation of habitats for which early hominoids were clearly not adaptively or demographically equipped. It is fully consistent with primate paleogeography, present knowledge of higher primate behavior patterns (as well as those of other mammals), and the hominid fossil record.

If the model is correct, the conventional concept that material culture is pivotal to the differentiation and origin of the primary characters of the Hominidae is probably incorrect. Rather, both advanced material culture and the Pleistocene acceleration in brain development are sequelae to an already established hominid character system, which included intensified parenting and social relationships, monogamous pair bonding, specialized sexual reproductive behavior, and bipedality. It implies that the nuclear family and human sexual behavior may have their ultimate origin long before the dawn of the Pleistocene.

ACKNOWLEDGMENTS

I thank G. J. Armelagos, T. Barton, B. Campbell, T. Gray, F. C. Howell, K. Jacobs, D. C. Johanson, B. Kimbel, A. E. Mann, R. S. Meindl, R. P. Mensorth, M. H. Wolpoff, P. Shipman, A. C. Walker, T. D. White, and S. Ward, who read earlier versions of this paper and provided valuable comments. I thank D. C. Johanson, C. J. Jolly, J. Lancaster, R. S. Meindl, and T. D. White for valuable discussions about its content. I thank T. Barton for discussions and advice with respect to the quantitative approach used, L. don Carlos and R. P. Mensforth for research assistance, and R. S. Meindl for listening to endless anecdotes about the behavior of canids, rodents, and birds.

NOTES

[1] Artifacts have been found *in situ* in the Gona region of the Hadar formation by the International Afar Research Expedition. Stratification of the Gona region is at present under investigation and correlations with the KH member are as yet uncertain. At present the artifacts are thought to overlie deposits equivalent to BKT$_2$ tuff of the KH member, which has a potassium-argon age determination of about 2.6 million years. The artifacts may therefore be older than 2 million years (D. C. Johanson, personal communication).

[2] A convincing and more detailed argument is provided by Jolly (1970).

[3] Whether or not the early evolution of material culture did in fact proceed in a gradualistic manner is difficult to establish. A punctuated equilibrium model is equally applicable to the early artifact record, and it is not unlikely that material culture proceeded at variable rates.

[4] Contrary to popular opinion, there is no evidence whatsoever that early hominids hunted. Bipedality is probably the mode of locomotion least adapted to hunting, unless sophisticated technology is available (or unusually high levels of intelligence, or both). The evidence made available by *A. afarensis* is particularly striking. Further australopithecine evolution from that species is documented by a reduction of the anterior dentition and further enlargement of the grinding teeth. Artifacts do not appear until 7 million years ago, and when they do appear it is difficult to interpret them as hunting implements. In short, if the evidence made available by the fossil record is to be used in

reconstructing early hominid evolution, one of its clearest implications is that hunting was not a dietary significant behavior. See also Jolly (1973), Andrews and Van Couvering (1975), Mann (1981), Delson (1975) and Schultz (1969).

[5] Among the salient features of the *A. afarensis* cranium are a convex nasal clivis, a uniformly shallow palate anterior to the incisal foramen, an independent juga with individual sharp lateral margins of the nasal aperture, a true canine fossa, a rounded tympanic plate with an inferiorly directed surface, a compound temporal-nuchal crest in large and small individuals, an occipital plane that is short relative to the nuchal plane, and a relatively vertical nuchal plane and posterior positioned foramen magnum (W.H. Kimbel, personal communication). See also Johanson and White (1979).

[6] I have elsewhere pointed out that the resting lengths of the major propulsive muscles about the hip and knee in quadrupedal primates are so substantially altered by the adoption of erect posture that the regular effective use of both quadrupedal and bipedal locomotion is not possible. Thus the transition to bipedality as a habitual mode of locomotion must have been relatively rapid (Lovejoy [1978]; Lovejoy, Heiple, and Burstein [1973]).

[7] While there is general agreement as to those morphological features directly associated with molar dominance in the group of hominids referred to as phase II, there is some disagreement as to the distinctiveness of other dentognathic characters. See P. Andrews and I. Tekkaya (1976).

[8] This is especially true of *Erythrocebus patas* which is both a small-object feeder and the fastest ground living primate (Hall 1965).

[9] It should also be pointed out that changes in the masticatory apparatus of hominids are a reflection of changes in habitat and are not necessarily the initial cause of clade differentiation. Care must be taken not to view those characters that allow identification of early hominids as synonomous with actual forces of divergence.

[10] Greenfield (1979) concludes that "*Sivapithecus* utilized a broad range of zones including tropical rain forests (Chinji of India), subtropics (Rudabanya and Chinji-Nagri of India and Pakistan), and woodland and bush habitats (Late Nagri and Early Dhok Pathan of India and Pakistan, Fort Ternan)."

[11] The K and r are opposite ends of the continuum of reproductive strategy. In the r strategy, the number of offspring is maximized at the expense of parental care; at the K end (the effective limit of which is 1), parental care is maximized.

[12] A female chimpanzee reaches sexual maturity at about age 10 years. Using the average span of 5.6 years between successful births (Teleki, Hunt and Pfifferling 1976) gives a required life expectancy of about 21 years (a chimpanzee infant usually dies after his mother's death if it is not at least 4 years old). The authors (Teleki *et al.* 1976. p. 577) conclude similarly that "The mean generation span, or elapsed time between birth of a female and birth of her median offspring, is about 19.6 years for a sample of ten Gombe females with three or more recorded births." Their most realistic estimate at achieved reproduction is three to four "offspring that are successfully raised to sexual maturity" (Teleki *et al.* 1976).

[13] Demographic studies of Old World monkey populations are at present insufficient to provide accurate data for unprotected and undisturbed populations (D. S. Sade *et al.* 1976), but approximations can be made adequately from observations of protected or introduced populations. Ninety percent of adult females in the Chhatari population studied by Southwick and Siddiqi (1976) gave birth yearly during the 14-year study period. Infant mortality averaged 16.1 percent, and juvenile mortality was judged very low (the actual figure was 33 percent but most of this loss was attributed to trapping). A reasonable figure with this data is 7 to 9 years, from methods similar to those used in Teleki, Hunt and Pfifferling (1976). L. C. Drickamer (1974) found first birth to occur in females of 4 years on the average in free-ranging rhesus at La Parguera, Puerto Rico, and in animals of this age 68 to 77 percent produced infants each year. Although first year mortality was high for first and second born offspring (40 to 50 percent), it was only 9 percent for third born. These data support the above conclusion as do those of C. B. Koford (1965) on rhesus from Cayo Santiago.

[14] It is in fact more likely that they were not, or at least not in the extreme forms seen in extant hominoids. The hominid adaptations proposed in this article are more likely to have been developed to prevent the "demographic dilemma." Modern pongids probably represent terminal phases at extreme parental investment only because of long-term occupation of particularly favorable environments, hence their very restricted present-day distribution.

[15] By breakthrough adaption is meant that which allows or precedes an adaptive radiation. While the Old World monkeys replaced all other hominoids, the hominids were successful in many of the same environments occupied by monkeys, including the Pleistocene savannahs.

[16] It should also be pointed out that falls as a consequence of mother-infant travel would be a more critical selection factor in early hominids than other primates. Van Lawick-Goodall (1969, p. 474) points out that "in striking contrast to most other primate species, the small chimpanzee infant often appears unable to remain securely attached to its mother if she makes a sudden movement. For several months after birth of her infant the mother may have to support it, thus hindering her movements . . ." Mortality as a consequence of

falling may thus be viewed as one selection factor in favor of terrestrial care, but more importantly, the adoption of bipedality would mean the loss of most or all of the prehensibility of the infant foot, which is an important grasping organ in the chimpanzee infant. This, in turn, selects for a more secure infant carrying ability in the mother and thus bipedality. This form of selection can clearly not be viewed as the initial selective force for bipedal locomotion, but in conjunction with others, would certainly contribute to the total selective pattern.

[17] Clutton-Brock (1977) notes that "although sex differences in feeding behavior are common among primates there is little evidence to suggest that they have evolved to minimize feeding competition between the sexes." Yet for the two species just cited this may indeed be the case. *Colobus badius* uses a more generalist feeding strategy than its sympatric congenerics, has a larger number of adult males within the troop (T. T. Struhsaker and J. F. Oates, in Sussman [1979, pp. 165-1860]) and has the highest population density of any Old World monkey (T. H. Clutton-Brock, in Sussman [1979, pp. 503-512]). It is clearly true of the orang (Horr, in Sussman [1979]).

[18] This forms the basis for an additional criticism of the hominid model proposed by Jolly (1970). Gelada baboons are highly specialized feeders whose feeding rate is largely limited by handling time.

[19] "Although nutritional factors alone would not preclude the possibility that early hominids were dietarily quite specialized, (from) the available archaeological evidence and (from what is known of the dietary patterns of living gatherer-hunters and chimpanzees) it appears unlikely that all early hominids were almost exclusively carnivorous or herbivorous. It is more reasonable to suggest that the diet fell within the broad range of today's gatherer-hunter diets, but that within the wide spectrum of this adaptation, local environment resources and seasonal scarcity may have forced some individual populations to become more dependent on vegetable or animal tissue foods than others" (A. E. Mann, personal communication, 1981).

[20] D. A. Horr (in Sussman 1979, p. 320) comments with respect to the orang-utan: ". . . orang social organization might easily be explained as follows: In order not to overload the food supply, orangs disperse themselves in the jungles. Females carrying infants or tending young juveniles can best survive if they don't have to move far. Young orangs could also best learn the jungle in a restricted, familiar area. . . . Adult males are unencumbered by young and can move easily over wider areas. This means that they compete with females for food only for short periods of time, and thus do not overload her food supply and force her to move over wide areas."

[21] See R. W. Wrangham (1977) for other discussion on the possible functions of the "food call."

[22] Such loads can become intense (up to 1.5 times normal resting basal metabolic rate in females) (O. W. Portman 1970). The modern human preparation for lactation is an average accumulation of 9 pounds of subcutaneous fat (D. B. Jelliffe and E. F. P. Jelliffe 1978). A major birth interval limitation in hominoid primates may well be the lactational loads placed on the mother (in contradistinction to the needs of the infant) and any improvement in feeding strategy could "support" a reduction in birth space on this basis.

[23] Monogamy is especially characteristic of long-lived (K-selected) birds (Davis 1976; Mills 1973; Coulson 1966).

[24] Such sequestration is common among rodents as well with perhaps its most classic expression in castorids, which are comparatively K-selected (requiring 1 to 4 years to mature sexually) and live in stable family groups.

[25] A second, also important, element of food-handling behavior may have been premastication. Reduction of birth space would have required an earlier reinitiation of ovulation, which would in turn have required a reduction of mechanical stimuli to the mechanoreceptors of the nipple and areola and thereby a reduction in prolactin levels (R. C. Kolodny, L. S. Jacobs, W. H. Daughaday 1972); hence, an

earlier age of weaning. Parental premastication would have facilitated such behavior, at the same time enhancing parental bonds (see discussion of the nuclear family). This could have also increased the rate of dental wear and have been an auxiliary selection component of the dentognathic changes characteristics of early hominids.

[26]   D. C. Johanson, personal communication.

[27]   J. R. Udry and N. M. Morris (1968) did find such a relationship, but it is a moot point since with sequestration of ovulation and its external manifestations, copulation would require female initiation.

[28]   In other primates that are monogamous, there is little dimorphism. All of these, however, live in territorial family groups (Jolly 1972) and there is therefore no intragroup competition for mates. Strong sexual dimorphism is usually a consequence of either differential competition for mates or differential exploitation of resources (Clutton-Brock 1977; Selander 1972; Hutchinson 1965). In *A. afarensis*, according to the proposed model, dimorphism would be favored on the latter basis. Small female body size would reduce calorie-protein requirements, while large body size would increase male mobility and predator resistance.

[29]   This is not meant to imply that it was a cause of canine reduction, but only that the process could occur by a combination of relaxation of selection on large male canine size and a positive selective mechanism for reduced canines. The latter is most likely to be found in the concurrent dentognathic changes of greater molar dominance and general anterior tooth reduction (Jolly 1970; Johanson and White 1979).

[30]   Modern man displays a remarkable number of morphological traits that may be considered epigamic (hair color and type, lip size and form, corporal hair patterning, eyebrows, facial countenance, and so forth). Attempts have been made to correlate some of these with geographic variables, but they have been largely unsuccessful. An alternative explanation is that disruptive selection acts to maximize the variability of these features within populations, thereby enhancing the distinctiveness of potential and actual mates in establishing and maintaining pair bonds. The subsequent geographic isolation, whether partial or complete, of a population could then have resulted in a truncation of expression and apparent uniqueness of some features that maintained their epigamic significance in the population (for example, the epicanthic eye fold). The obvious polygenic basis of such traits and their reappearance in unrelated populations (Bushman, Lapps, infant Euroamericans) indicate that their expression is a consequence of elevated frequencies of genes that may be universal in *H. sapiens*, but below an expressive threshold in some populations.

[31]   Further evidence of the age of pair bonding is provided by the absence of strong canine dimorphism in *A. afarensis* (Johanson and White 1979). The only other Old World higher primates without canine dimorphism are the gibbon and siamang, which are monogamous (Washburn and Ciochon 1974).

[32]   The provisioning model proposed here effectively accounts for the origin of hunting by means of a progressive elaboration of provisioning behavior (that is, collecting—scavenging + collecting—hunting + scavenging + collecting) without the requirement that hunting be critical to human evolution at any point. The similarity in social behavior between canids and early humans has often been cited and attributed to hunting. It is more likely that such similarities take origin in reproductive strategy (pair bonding, intratroop cooperation, provisioning, male involvement in subadult care, and so forth) and that hunting merely represents one food procurement method that satisfies the economic requirements of the social system. There are numerous carnivores that do not display this form of reproductive strategy, and there are some rodents that do but, of course, do not hunt (see footnote [24]).

[33]   The term bifocal is preferable to nuclear family because the latter carries manifest connotations from its application to Western and non-Western modern human cultures, none of which are implied by its use here.

[34]   A. E. Mann's (1975) extensive studies of dental development and wear in australopithecines indicate a prolonged period of development was established by about 2.5 million years ago. K. R. McKinley's survivorship calculations based upon Mann's (1972) data led him to conclude that australopithecines show a hominid rather than a nonhuman primate "birth spacing pattern." While these calculations require a number of assumptions about the origin and nature of the death assemblages at Swartkrans and Sterkfontein, they are strong evidence that a major demographic shift was fully developed by 2.0 to 2.5 million years ago which included an extended period of subadult dependency.

REFERENCES

Andrews, P., and Tekkaya, I. 1976. *Ramapithecus* in Kenya and Turkey, in: *Les Plus Anciens Hominides* (P.V. Tobias and Y. Coppens, eds.), pp. 7-25, Union Internationale des Sciences Prehistoriques et Protohistoriques (IXth Congress).

Andrews, P., and Van Couvering, J.H. 1975. Paleoenvironments in the East African Miocene, in: *Approaches to Primate Paleobiology* (F.S. Szalay, ed.), pp. 62-103, Karger, Basel.

Bartholomew, G.A., and Birdsell, J.A. 1953. Ecology and the protohominids. *Am. Anthropol.* 55:481-498.

Bauer, H.R. 1977. Chimpanzee bipedal locomotion in the Gombe National Park, East Africa. *Primates* 18:913-921.

Beach, F.A. 1947. Evolutionary changes in the physiological control of mating behavior in mammals. *Psychol. Rev.* 54:297-315.

Beach, F.A. 1978. Human sexuality and evolution, in: *Human Evolution: Biosocial Perspectives* (S.L. Washburn and E.R. McCown, eds.), pp. 123-154, Benjamin-Cummings, Menlo Park.

Brace, C.L., and Montagu, A. 1977. *Human Evolution* (2nd ed), MacMillan, New York.

Butzer, K.W. 1977. Environment, culture and human evolution. *Amer. Sci.* 65:572-584.

Campbell, B.G. 1972. Man for all seasons, in: *Sexual Selection and the Descent of Man 1871-1971* (B.G. Campbell, ed.), pp. 40-58, Aldine, Chicago.

Cavagna, G.A., Saibene, F.P., and Margaria, R. 1964. Mechanical work in running. *J. Appl. Phys.* 19:249-256.

Chance, M.R.A. 1962. Social behavior and primate evolution, in: *Culture and the Evolution of Man* (M.F. Ashley-Montagu, ed.), pp. 84-130, Oxford University Press, New York.

Clutton-Brock, T.H. 1977. Some aspects as intraspecific variation in feeding and ranging behavior in primates, in: *Primate Ecology* (T.H. Clutton-Brock, ed.), pp. 539-556, Academic Press, New York.

Clutton-Brock, T.H. 1979. Primate social organization and ecology, in *Primate Ecology: Problem Oriented Field Studies* (R.W. Sussman, ed.), pp. 503-512, Wiley, New York.

Clutton-Brock, T.H., and Harvey, P.H. 1977. Primate ecology and social organization, *J. Zool., London* 183:1-39.

Coppens, Y., Howell, F.C. Isaac, G.L., and Leakey, R.E.F., Eds. 1976. *Earliest Man and the Environments in the Lake Rudolf Basin*, Univ. Chicago Press, Chicago.

Coulson, C. 1966. The influence of the pair-bond and age on the breeding biology of the kittiwake gull *Rissa tridactyla*. *J. Anim. Ecol.* 35:269-279.

Crook, J.H. 1972. Sexual selection, dimorphism and social organization in the primates, in: *Sexual Selection and the Descent of Man* (B.G. Campbell, ed.) pp. 231-281, Aldine, Chicago.

Cutler, R.G. 1976. Evolution of longevity in primates. *J. Hum. Evol.* 5:169-202.

Darwin, C. 1871. *The Descent of Man, and Selection in Relation to Sex*, Murray, London.

Davis, J.W.F. 1976. Breeding success and experience in the arctic skua, *Stercorarius parasiticus* (L.). *J. Anim. Ecol.* 45:351.

Day, M.H., and Leakey, R.E.F. 1973. New evidence for the genus *Homo* from East Rudolf, Kenya (I). *Amer. J. Phys. Anthro. 39:341-354.*

Day, M.H., and Leakey, R.E.F. 1974. New evidence if the genus *Homo* from East Rudolf, Kenya (III). *Amer. J. Phys. Anthro.* 41(3):367-380.

Day, M.H., Leakey, R.E.F., Walker, A.C., and Wood, B.A. 1974. New hominids from East Rudolf, Kenya (I). *Amer. J. Phys. Anthro.* 42:461-476.

Day, M.H., Leakey, R.E.F., Walker, A.C., Wood, B.A. 1976. New hominids from East Turkana, Kenya. *Amer. J. Phys. Anthro.* 45:369-436.

Delson, E. 1975. Evolutionary history of the Cercopithecidae, in: *Approaches to Primate Paleobiology* (F.S. Szalay, ed.), *Contrib. Primatol.* 5:167-217, Karger, Basel.

Delson, e., and Andrews P. 1975. Evolution and interrelationships of the catarrhine primates, in: *Phylogeny of the Primates* (W.P. Luckett and F.S. Szalay, eds.), pp. 405-446, Plenum Press, New York.

DeVore, I. 1965. Male dominance and mating behavior in baboons, in: *Sex and Behavior* (F. Beach, ed.), pp. 266-289, Wiley, New York.

Drickamer, L.C. 1974. A ten year summary of the population and reproductive data for the free ranging *Macaca mulatta* at La Parguera, Puerto Rico. *Folia Primatologica* 21:61-80.

Eisenberg, J.F. 1966. The social organization of mammals. *Handbk. Zool.* 10(7):1-92.

Emlen, S.T., and Oring, L.W. 1977. Ecology, sexual selection and the evolution of mating systems. *Science* 197:215.

Fisher, R.A. 1930. *Genetical Theory of Natural Selection*, Claredon, Oxford.

Goodall, J. 1965. Chimpanzees of the Gombe Stream Reserve, in: *Primate Behavior: Field Studies in Monkeys and Apes* (I. DeVore, ed.), pp. 425-473, Holt, Rinehart and Winston, New York.

Goodman, M. 1976. Toward a genealogical description of the primates, in: *Molecular Anthropology* (M. Goodman and R.E. Tashian, eds.), pp. 321-353. Plenum Press, New York.

Greenfield, L.O. 1977. *Ramapithecus and Early Hominid Origins*, Ph.D. Thesis, University Microfilms, University of Michigan.

Greenfield, L.O. 1979. On the adaptive pattern of *"Ramapithecus"*. *Amer. J. Phys. Anthro.* 50:527-548.

Gregory, W.K. 1930. The origin of man from a brachiating anthropoid stock. *Science* 71:645-650.

Grzimek, H.C.B., ed. 1975. *Animal Life Encyclopedia*, Van Nostrand Reinhold, New York.

Hall, K.R.L. 1965. Behavior and ecology of the wild Patas monkey, *Erythrocebus patas*, in Uganda. *J. Zool.* 148:15-87.

Hershkovitz, P. 1977. *Living New World Monkeys (Platyrrhini), with an Introduction to Primates, Vol. 1*, University of Chicago, Chicago.

Hewes, G.W. 1961. Food transport and the origin of hominid bipedalism. *Amer. Anthropol.* 63:687-710.

Holloway, R.L. 1967. Tools and teeth; some speculations regarding canine reduction. *Amer. Anthropol.* 69:63-67.

Horr, D.A. 1979. The Borneo Orang-utan, in: *Primate Ecology: Problem Oriented Field Studies* (R.W. Sussman, ed.), pp. 317-321, Wiley, New York.

Howell, F.C. 1969. Remains of Hominidae from Pliocene Pleistocene formations in the lower Omo basin, Ethiopia. *Nature (Lond.)* 223:1234-1239.

Howell, F.C., and Wood, B.A. 1974. Early hominid ulna from the Omo Basin, Ethiopia. *Nature (Lond.)* 249:174-176.

Hrdy, S.B. 1976. The care and exploitation of non-human primate infants by conspecifics other than the mother, in: *Advances in the Study of Behavior* (J.S. Rosenblatt, R.A. Hinde, E. Shaw, and C. Beers, eds.), pp. 101-158, Academic Press, New York.

Hutchinson, G.E. 1965. *The Ecological Theatre and the Evolutionary Play*, Yale University Press, New Haven.

Huxley, T.X. 1863. *Evidence as to Man's Place in Nature*, Williams and Norgate, London.

Jelliffe, D.B., and Jelliffe, E.F.P. 1978. *Human Milk in the Modern World*, Oxford University Press, Oxford.

Johanson, D.C., and Coppens. Y. 1976. A preliminary anatomical diagnosis of the first Plio-Pleistocene hominid discoveries in the central Afar, Ethiopia. *Am. J. Phys. Anthro.*45:217-234.

Johanson, D.C., and Taieb, M. 1976. Plio-Pleistocene hominid discoveries in Hadar, Ethiopia. *Nature (Lond.)* 260:293-297.

Johanson, D.C., and White, T.D. 1979. A systematic assessment of early African hominids. *Science 203: 321-330.*

Johanson, D.C., and White, T.D. 1980. On the status of *Australopithecus afarensis. Science* 207:1104-1105.

Johanson, D.C., White, T.D., and Coppens, Y. 1978. A new species of the genus *Australopithecus* (Primates Hominidae) from the Pliocene of Eastern Africa. *Kirtlandia* 28:1-14.

Johanson, D.C., Lovejoy, C.O., Burnstein, A.H., and Heiple, K.G. 1976. Functional implications of the Afar knee joint. *Am. J. Phys. Anthro.* 44:188. (Abstract)

Jolly, C.J. 1970. The seed-eaters: a new model of hominid differentiation based on a baboon analogy. *Man* 5:5-28.

Jolly, C.J. 1972. The classification and natural history of *Theropithecus (Simopithecus)* (Andrews, 1916), baboons of the African Plio-Pleistocene. *Bull. Brit. Nat. Hist. Geol.* 22:1-122.

Jolly, C.J. 1973. Changing views of hominid origins. *Yrbk. Phys. Anthro.* 16:1-17.

Jolly, C.J., Ed. 1978. *Early Hominids of Africa,* St. Martin's, New York.

Kaufman, J.H. 1965. A three year study of mating behavior in a free-ranging band of Rhesus monkeys. *Ecology* 46:500-512.

Keith, A. 1923. Man's posture: its evolution and disorders. *Brit. Med. J.* 1:451-454, 499-502, 545-548, 587-590, 624-626, 669-672.

Keith, A. 1929. *The Antiquity of Man, Vol. 1 and 2*, Williams and Norgate, London.

Kennedy, G. E. 1978. Hominoid habitat shifts in the Miocene. *Nature (Lond.)* 271:11.

King, M.C., and Wilson, A.C. 1975. Evolution at two levels in humans and chimpanzees. Science 188:107-116.

Koford, C.B. 1963. Rank of mothers and sons in bands of Rhesus monkeys. *Science 141:356.* (Abstract)

Koford, C.B. 1965. Population dynamics of Rhesus monkeys on Cayo Santiago, in: *Primates Behavior: Field Studies of Monkeys and Apes* (I. DeVore, ed.), pp. 160-174, Holt, Rinehart, and Winston, New York.

Kohne, D.E. 1972. Evolution of primate DNA: a summary, in: *Perspectives on Human Evolution*, Vol. 2 (S.L. Washburn and P. Dolhinow, eds.), pp. 166-168, Holt, Rinehart, and Winston, New York.

Kohne, D.E., Chiscon, J.A., and Hoyer, B.H. 1970. Nucleotide sequence change in nonrepeated DNA evolution. *Carnegie Inst., Washington Yrbk.* 69:488-501.

Kolodny, R.C., Jacobs, L.S., AND Daughaday, W.H. 1972. Mammary stimulation causes prolactin secretion in non-lactating women. *Nature (Lond)* 238:284-285.

Kortlandt, A. 1962. Chimpanzees in the wild. *Sci. Amer. 296:128-138.*

Kortlandt, A. 1967. Experimentation with chimpanzees in the wild. in: *Progress in Primatology* (D. Stark, et al., eds.), pp. 208-224, Gustav Fischer, Stuttgart.

Kortlandt, A. 1972. *New Perspectives on Ape and Human Evolution*, University of Amsterdam.

Kretzoi, M. 1975. New ramapithecines and *Pliopithecus* from the lower Pliocene of Rudabanya in north-eastern Hungary. *Nature (Lond.)* 257:578-581.

Kummer, H. 1967. Tripartite relations in Hamadryas baboons, in: *Social Communication Among Primates* (S. Altman, ed.), pp. 63-72, University of Chicago Press, Chicago.

Kummer, H. 1971. *Primate Societies*, Aldine, Chicago.

Lack, D. 1968. *Ecological Adaptions for Breeding in Birds*, Mentheun, London.

Lancaster, J.B. 1972. Play-mothering: The relations between juvenile females and young infants among free ranging vervet monkeys, in: *Primate Socialization* (F.E. Poirier, ed.), pp. 83-104, Random House, New York.

Leakey, M.D., Hay, R.L., Curtis, G.H., drake, R.E., Jackes, M.K., and White, T.D. 1976. Fossil hominids from the Laetolil beds, Tanzania. *Nature (Lond.)* 262:460-466.

Leakey, R.E.F., and Lewin, R. 1978. *People of the Lake*, Doubleday, New York.

Leakey, R.E.F., Mungai, J.M., and Walker, A.C. 1971. New Australopithecines from East Rudolf, Kenya (I). *Am. J. Phys. Anthro.* 35:175-186.

Leakey, R.E.F., Mungai, J.M., and Walker, A.C. 1972. New Australopithecines from East Rudolf, Kenya (II). *Am. J. Phys. Anthro.* 36:235-252.

Leakey, R.E.F., and Wood, B.A. 1973. New evidence for the genus *Homo* from East Rudolf, Kenya (II). *Am. J. Phys. Anthro.* 39:355-368.

Le Gros Clark, W.E. 1962. *The Antecedents of Man, Edinburgh University Press, Edinburgh.*

Lovejoy, C.O. 1974. The gait of autralopithecines. *Yrbk. Phys. Anthro.* 17:147-161.

Lovejoy, C.O. 1975. Biomechanical perspectives on the lower limb of early hominids, in: *Primate Functional Morphology and Evolution* (R.H. Tuttle, ed.), pp. 291-326, Mouton, The Hague.

Lovejoy, C.O. 1978. A biomechanical view of the locomotor diversity of early hominds, in: *Early Hominids of Africa* (C. Jolly, ed.), pp. 403-429, St. Martin's, New York.

Lovejoy, C.O. 1979. A reconstruction of the pelvis of A.L. 288 (Hadar Formation, Ethiopia). *Amer. J. Phys. Anthro.* 50:460. (Abstract)

Lovejoy, C.O. Heiple, K.G., and Burstein, A.H. 1973. The gait of *Australopithecus. Amer. J. Phys. Anthro.* 38:757-780.

Lovejoy, C.O. and Meindl, R.S. 1972. Eukaryote mutation and the protein clock. *Yearbk. Phys. Anthro.* 16:18-30.

Lovejoy, C.O., Meindl, R.S., Pryzbeck, T.R., Barton, T.S., Heiple, K.G., and Kotting, D. 1977. Paleodemography of the Libben site, Ottawa County, Ohio. *Science* 198:291-293.

McChance, R.A. Luff, M.C., and Widdowson. E.E. 1937. Physical and emotional periodicity in women. *J. Hygiene* 37:571-611.

McKinley, K.R. 1971. Survivorship in gracile and robust australopithecines: a demographic comparison and a proposed birth model, *Am. J. Phys. Anthro.* 34:417-426.

Mann, A.E. 1972. Hominid and cultural origins. *Man* 7:379-387.

Mann, A.E. 1975. Some paleodemographic aspects of the South African australpithecines. *Univ. Penn. Publ. Anthro.* 1.

Mann, A.E. 1981. The evolution of hominid dietary patterns, in: *Omnivorous Primates* (R.S.O. Harding and G. Teleki, eds.), pp. 10-36, Columbia Univ. Press, New York.

Mayr, E. 1972. Sexual selection and natural selection, in: *Sexual Selection and the Descent of Man 1871-1971* (B. Campbell, ed), pp. 87-104, Aldine, Chicago.

Mills, J.A. 1973. The influence of age and pairbond on the breeding biology of the Red-billed gull *Larus novaehollandiae scopulinus. J. Anim. Ecol.* 42:147-162.

Mitchell, G., and Brandt, E.M. 1972. Paternal behavior in primates, in: *Primates Socialization* (F.E. Poirier, ed.), pp. 173-206, Random House, New York.

Montagna, W. 1975. The skin of primates, in: *Biological Anthropology* (S.H. Katz, ed.), pp. 341-351, Freeman, San Francisco.

Moreau, R.E. 1951. Africa since the Mesozoic with particular reference to certain biological problems. *Proc. Zool. Soc. London* 121:869-913.

Morris, D. 1967. *The Naked Ape*, Cape, London.

Napier, J.R., and Napier, P.H. 1967. *A Handbook of Living Primates*, Academic Press, London.

Pianka, E.R. 1974. *Evolutionary Ecology*, Harper and Row, New York.

Pilbeam, D.R. 1969. Tertiary Pongidae of East Africa: evolutionary relationships and taxonomy. *Peabody Mus. Nat. Hist., Yale Univ. Bull.* 31:1-185.

Pilbeam, D.R. 1972. *The Ascent of Man*, MacMillan, New York.

Pilbeam, D.R. 1976. Neogene hominds of South Asia and the origins of Homindae, in: *Le Plus Anciens Hominides* (P.V. Tobias and Y. Coppens, eds.), pp. 39-59. C.N.R.S., Paris.

Pilbeam, D.R., Meyer, G.E., Badgley, C., Rose, M.D., Pickford, M.H.L., Behrensmeyer, A.K., and Ibrahim, Shah, S.M. 1977. New hominid primates from the Siwaliks of Pakistan and their bearing on hominoid evolution. *Nature (Lond)* 270:689-695.

Portman, O.W. 1970. Nutrition requirements (NCR) of nonhuman primates, in: *Feeding and Nutrition of Nonhuman Primates* (R.S. Harris, ed.), pp. 87-116. Academic Press, New York.

Radinsky, L.B. 1975. Primate brain evolution. *Amer. Sci.* 63(6):656-663.

Reynolds, V. 1976. *The Biology of Human Action*, Freeman, San Francisco.

Reynolds, V., and Reynolds, F. 1965. Chimpanzees in the Budongo Forest, in: *Primate Behavior: Field Studies of Monkeys and Apes* (I. DeVore, ed.), pp. 368-424, Holt, Rinehart, and Winston, New York.

Sade, D.S. 1967. Determinants of dominance in a group of free ranging Rhesus monkeys, in: *Social Communication Among the Primates* (S. Altman, ed.), pp. 99-115, University of Chicago Press, Chicago.

Sade, D.S., Cuching, K., Cuching, P., Dunaif, J., figueroa, A., Kaplan, J.R., Lauer, C., Rhodes, D., and Schneider, J. 1976. Population dynamics in relation to social structure in Cayo Santiago. *Yrbk. Phys. Anthro.* 20:253-262.

Sarich, V.M. 1968. The origin of the hominds: an immunological approach in: *Perspectives on Human Evolution* (S.L. Washburn and P.C. Jay, eds.), pp. 94-121, Holt, Rinehart, and Winston, New York.

Sarich, V.M. 1971. A molecular approach to the question of human origins, in: *Background for Man* (P. Dolhinow and V.M. Sarich, eds.), pp. 60-81, Little, Brown, Boston.

Schultz, A.H. 1969. *The Life of Primates*, Universe Books, New York.

Selander, R.K. 1966. Sexual dimorphism and differential niche utilization in birds. *Condor* 68:113-151.

Selander, R.K. 1972. Sexual selection and dimorphism in birds. in: *Sexual Selection and the Descent of Man* (B.G. Campbell, ed.), pp. 180-230, Aldine, Chicago.

Simons, E.L. 1972. *Primates Evolution, an Introduction to Man's Place in Nature*, MacMillan, New York.

Simons, E.L. 1976. Relationship between *Dryopithecus, Sivapithecus*, and *Ramapithecus* and their bearing on hominid origins, in: *Les Plus Anciens Hominides* (P.V. Tobias and Y. Coppens, eds.), pp. 60-67, C.N.R.S., Paris.

Simons, E.L. 1978. Diversity among early hominids: a vertebrate paleontologist's viewpoint, in: *Early Hominids of Africa* (C. Jolly, ed.), pp. 543-566, Duckworth, London.

Simons, E.L., and Pilbeam, D. 1965. Preliminary revisions on the Dryopithecianae (Pongidae, Anthropoidea). *Folia Primatologica 3:81-152.*

Simons, E.L., and Pilbeam, D.R. 1972. Hominoid paleoprimatology, in: *The Functional and Evolutionary Biology of Primates* (R. Tuttle, ed.), pp. 36-62, Aldine Atherton, Chicago.

Southwick, C.H., and Siddiqi, M.F. 1976. Demographic characteristics of semiprotected Rhesus groups in India. *Yrbk. Phys. Anthro.* 20:242-252.

Struhsaker, T.T., and Oates, J.F. 1979. Comparison of the behavior and ecology of Red Colobus and Black-and-White Colobus monkeys in Uganda: a summary, in: *Primate Ecology: Problem Oriented Field Studies* (R.W. Sussman, ed.), pp. 165-186, Wiley, New York.

Sugiyama, Y. 1968. Social organization of chimpanzees in the Budongo Forest, Uganda. *Primates* 9:225-258.

Sugiyama, Y. 1969. Social behavior of chimpanzees in the Budongo Forest, Uganda. *Primates* 10:197-225.

Sussman, R.W., Ed. 1979. *Primate Ecology: Problem Oriented Field Studies*, Wiley, New York.

Taylor, C.R., and Rowntree, V.J. 1973. Running on 2 or 4 legs: which consumes more energy? *Science* 179:186-187.

Teleki, G., Hunt, E., and Pfifferling, J.H. 1976. Demographic observations (1963-1973) on the chimpanzees of Gombe National Park, Tanzania. *J. Hum. Evol.* 5:559-598.

Tobias, P.V. 1971. *The Brain in Hominid Evolution*, Columbia University Press, New York.

Tobias, P.V. 1973. New developments in hominid paleotology in South and East Africa. *Ann. Rev. Anthro.* 2:311-334.

Tobias, P.V., and Coppens, Y., Eds. 1976. *Les Plus Anciens Hominides*, Union internationale des Sciences Prehistoriques et Protohistoriques (IXth Congress).

Trivers, R. 1972. Parental investment and sexual selection, in: *Sexual Selection and the Descent of Man: 1871-1971* (B. Campbell, ed.), pp. 136-179, Aldine, Chicago.

Udry, J.R., and Morris, N.M. 1968. Distribution of coitus in the menstrual cycle. *Nature (Lond.)* 220:593-596.

Van Lawick-Goodall, J. 1968. The behavior of free-living chimpanzees in the Gombe Stream area. *Anim. Behav. Monogr.* 1:161-311.

Van Lawick-Goodall, J. 1969. Mother off-spring relations in in free-ranging chimpanzees, in: Primate Ethology (D. Morris, ed.), pp. 287-346, Aldine, Chicago.

Van Lawick-Goodall, J. 1976. Continuities between chimpanzee and human behavior in:*Human Origins: Louis Leakey and the East African Evidence* (G.L. Isaac and E.R. McCown, eds.), pp. 81-95, Benjamin Cummings, Menlo Park.

Washburn, S.L. 1960. Tools and human evolution. *Sci. Amer.* 203:63-75.

Washburn, S.L., Ed. 1963. *Classification and Human Evolution*, Aldine, Chicago.

Washburn, S.L. 1968. *The Study of Human Evolution*, Condon Lecture Series, Oregon State System of Higher Education, Eugene.

Washburn, S.L., and Ciochon, R.L. 1974. Canine teeth: notes on controversies on the study of human evolution. *Amer. Anthropol.* 76:765-784.

White, T.D. 1977. New fossil hominids from Laetolil, Tanzania. *Amer. J. Phys. Anthro.* 46:197-230.

Wolpoff, M.H. 1979. cited in "Form and Function; The Anatomists View." *Mosaic* 10(2): 23-29.

Wrangham, R.W. 1977. Feeding behavior of chimpanzees in Gombe National Park, Tanzania, in: *Primate Ecology* (T.H. Clutton-Brock, ed.), pp. 504-538, Academic Press, New York.

Wright, R.V.S. 1978. Imitative learning of a flaked stone technology—the case of the orangutan, in: *Human Evolution: Biosocial Perspectives* (S.L. Washburn and E.R. McCown, Eds.), pp. 215-238, Benjamin Cummings, Menlo Park.

Yamada, M. 1963. A study of blood-relationship in the natural society of the Japanese macaque. *Primates* 4:43-65.

23

The Changing Role of Women in Models of Human Evolution

L. M. Fedigan

INTRODUCTION

Imagine three anthropologists:

A primatologist observes a female chimpanzee fashioning several crude tools from grass stems, which she will use to fish termites from an underground nest over many hours, in the presence of her sometimes intrigued, sometimes impatient offspring. An ethnographer lives with a group of human foragers at one of their campsites on the edge of a waterhole, recording in detail the daily patterns of adult women and men as they go about their lives, obtaining and preparing food, caring for their children, enjoying their leisure, interacting with their neighbors. An archaeologist and a team of bone hunters fan out across an escarpment slowly descending the years, squatting every now and then to peer and scratch carefully at the surface; they walk and look and listen for the call that will signal a "find."

Probably the primatologist and ethnographer would quite properly deny that the objective of their research was the reconstruction of the lives of our earliest human ancestors. The latter is there first and foremost to understand the lives of these contemporary human beings before their way of living disappears entirely, and the former works to explicate the animal species for itself, another life form in danger of disappearing before we can understand it. Nonetheless, the information obtained from all these studies will be gathered up, if not by the original researchers, then by others, and woven into a scientific story of the origins and evolution of early human behavior. For

we have a powerful urge to know our origins—scientists and public alike—allied to a strong cultural imperative to justify our present social arrangements through reference to historical precedents. And what more significant guide to comprehending the structure of our own underlying nature could we discover than the original blueprint for human society?

That is why the practice of modeling the life of early humans, although shunned by many anthropologists, is nevertheless a scientific game played with great determination; its reward is the right to propound a view of human nature. Some of these models are widely disseminated, in high school and college textbooks, in popularized scientific writings, in fiction, on film. And in a society which tends to believe that what is natural is good, or at least acceptable, "scientific" statements about the original nature of human society represent applications of data which even those who disapprove of such modeling can ill afford to ignore.

In this review, I take one aspect common to models of early hominid life, namely, the reconstruction of sex roles, examining in particular the part that women are seen to have played in human society and in the evolution of those characteristics that distinguish us from our primate relatives. The title of this review allows me to examine not only how the perceptions of women's roles in human evolution have changed, but also to describe how women lately have come to play a part in the very construction of models of their origins. As anthropologists, we might have expected that women, with their distinctive life experiences, would have origin stories to tell that would differ in significant ways from those of men.

This review begins with an historical overview of the more influential models, from Darwin's ideas in 1871 (Darwin 1936a) to those of Lovejoy in 1981. Then I attempt to dis-articulate the models for an examination of their significant parts by discussing separately the major sources of evidence and/or analogy for early human social life: the comparative data from studies of primate societies; the indirect data from contemporary human foraging societies; and the archaeological and paleontological evidence drawn from the material remains of our ancestors. Throughout these sections, I also make reference to the cultural assumptions about the appropriate behavior of men and women that inform our theories. The final section suggests how we may improve our ability to reconstruct an early human society that is more than a backward projection of current cultural beliefs and practices.

HISTORICAL CONTEXT

Although evolution as a concept was in use by social philosophers and natural historians long before Darwin's time, it was in scholarly treatises of the second half of the nineteenth century that the idea of gradual, adaptive change came to be widely applied to the place of humans and human societies in the natural world. Evolutionary models became something of a fashion among European and North American scholars, including those interested in explaining the social nature of humans, as well as those more concerned with the biological nature of humankind.

Biological Evolution in the Nineteenth Century

After publishing *The Origin of the Species* in 1859 (Darwin 1936b), which set out his theory of, and evidence for, natural selection, Darwin was left with several puzzles. Two of these were: the explanation of secondary sexual characteristics in a wide range of species, and the extent to which evolutionary theory could be applied to human behavior and biology. He set out to explore both of these topics in his 1871 book, *The Descent of Man and Selection in Relation to Sex* (Darwin 1936a). The book thus has two intertwining objectives: the development of a theory of sexual selection applicable to the entire animal kingdom, and the establishment of the human species as subject to the laws of both natural and sexual selection. In the process of demonstrating that the characteristic features of the human phenotype and the human way of thinking and living show rudimentary similarities with those of other animals, Darwin also provided sketches of his own view of early human life. Especially in the course of discussing the application of sexual selection theory to humans, he provided us with a clear picture of how he saw the roles and the interrelationships of men and women in human society. First let us look briefly at Darwin's conclusions on sexual selection and the human place in nature, the two platforms on which he was to build his scenario of early human social life.

Darwin's reasoning was that secondary sexual characteristics, which neither are directly necessary for reproduction nor for survival, were the result of two types of interactions involving the sexes: competition and choice. Competition, Darwin believed, generally occurred between males for access to female mates, and choice, he reasoned, was exercised by females from among the male mates available to them. Thus, certain traits in males which enhanced their ability to win in competitions and/or to be chosen by females were sexually selected. It seemed obvious to Darwin that sexual selection had occurred in humans, because he believed the human male to be more courageous, energetic, inventive, pugnacious, and sexually assertive than the female. The human male is also bigger than the human female, because, Darwin argued, in primitive times men fought to the death for access to women, and in modern times his size advantages are maintained because he has to work harder than woman for their joint subsistence. Women are more nurturant, more reclusive, and more altruistic than men, traits which occur because of the lack of selection for the assertive, selfish male traits listed above, and also because of an extension of "maternal instincts" toward other members of the group as well as toward infants.

Several authors (e.g. Fee 1976; Martin and Voorhies 1975; Tanner 1981) have pointed out that Darwin projected onto the large screen of nature his own images of appropriate role behavior for men and women, images which were clearly drawn from upper-class Victorian culture in Britain in the 1800s. Not so often pointed out (but see Zihlman 1978a, b) are certain inconsistencies in the conceptualization and application of sexual selection theory itself. For example, Darwin saw selection as operating almost entirely on males. Competition selected for male armaments (size, strength, weapons) and choice selected for male ornaments (colors, elaborate headdresses, beautiful voices). Females of the species were seen to be, as a general rule, similar in appearance and behavior to juveniles, their traits occurring in the absence of sexual selection. Darwin weakened his principle of female choice by equivocating about the actual power of females to exercise choice in determining which males would mate. At times he thought females had the selective power to bring about elaborate male features such as the peacock's tail. At other times he thought that females could do no more than accept the least distasteful male available, or accept the winner of a previous male-male competition, a lack of selective power which elsewhere I have likened to "Hobson's choice" (Fedigan 1982).

Having already equivocated about the power of female choice to bring about sexual selection in animals, Darwin then contradicted himself when applying the theory to humans. For Darwin believed that the human female was sexually selected by males. Since this is the opposite of his principle of female choice, it is odd that Darwin argued repeatedly that men in various societies around the world exercise choice among possible female mates on the basis of the latters' appearance and behavior. He did seem to believe that female choice had operated on human progenitors, but apparently at some point in human evolution he saw the process reversing. The human species appears to be the only one for which Darwin argued that males presently exercise both the mechanisms of competition and of choice, although nowhere does he discuss the matter of how or why the process of intersexual selection reversed, with choice as well as competition becoming the prerogative of the human male.

Darwin's second objective in *The Descent of Man* was to demonstrate that many human features, then thought to be unique, had simple analogs in other animal species. Thus, he spent two chapters discussing the evidence for rudimentary beginnings of higher mental powers in animals: faculties of mind such as reasoning, imagination, aesthetics, ability to produce material objects, and religious beliefs. He also argued that humans shared with many animal species the "social instincts": desire for company, sympathy for others in the social group, altruism, love of praise and fear of blame. However, the most important characteristic to distinguish early humans from animals was a sense of morality. Once humans had developed the "self-regarding virtues," which Darwin saw as self-control and awareness of good and evil, they began to develop societies based on higher mental faculties than those of other animals. He believed that early men developed their tool-making skills to produce weapons and to become efficient hunters. They also began to accumulate property which helped to bring about social stratification. To alleviate sexual jealousy and because of their ability to exercise self-control, marriage practices were instituted which would regulate sexual behavior, primarily of women. In some societies, powerful men could take more than one wife.

In sum, Darwin suggested that early humans lived in small hunting communities made up of monogamous or polygynous units. Before cultural practices such as infanticide were introduced, which he thought would counter the effects of natural and sexual selection, these biological processes selected for courageous, intelligent, tool-using men. In the absence of an understanding of how traits are biologically transmitted to the next generation, Darwin used a concept he called "equal transmission of characters" to explain how women were not left totally behind in the process of human evolution. In this way, Darwin helped to pioneer what I call the "coat-tails" theory of human evolution: traits are selected for in males and women evolve by clinging to the men's coat-tails. This model became, and remains, the predominant image of human evolution, though rarely so candidly stated as by Darwin:

> Thus man has ultimately become superior to woman. It is indeed fortunate that the law of equal transmission of characters to both sexes prevails with mammals. Otherwise it is probable that man would have become as superior in mental endowment to woman as the peacock is in ornamental plumage to the peahen (Darwin 1936a, p. 874).

Social Evolution in the Nineteenth Century

In the nineteenth century, the biological and social sciences were not the widely separate fields built on often incompatible paradigms that they are today. There was great overlap and cross-fertilization of ideas between those interested largely in human biological nature and those interested mainly in human social evolution. All of the writers discussed in this section were contemporaneous with Darwin, and most of their major works were published after The Origin of the Species but before The Descent of Man (e.g. Bachofen 1961; Lubbock 1873; Maine 1861; McLennan 1865; Morgan 1870). Thus, some of these scholars such as McLennan are widely quoted in the human behavior sections of The Descent of Man, and must have had an impact on Darwin's view of early human society, even though they did not share the same understanding of "evolution" (see below). On the other hand, a few of the writings discussed in this section (Engels 1972; Spencer 1873) appeared after Darwin's Descent of Man and were clearly influenced by the

latter. Perhaps it is because of such cross-fertilization of ideas that many of these multiple schemes of human social evolution seem to be variations on a single theme.

In essence, the theme of the nineteenth century social modelers was that all human societies pass through a series of stages which represent technological and social progression from an initial primitive aggregation to the final civilized state. Furthermore, most of these scholars believed that contemporary societies of the world are at various stages along the path toward their common goal of civilization, and therefore they could be used as representatives of landmarks along the way in a reconstruction of the human social journey. It is important to note at this point that such a view of the evolution of societies is different from Darwin's view of the evolution of species, and may in fact have little in common other than a concept of "change over time." Certainly the principles of natural and sexual selection are irrelevant to these models of social evolution, whereas *progressive* change (only episodically implicit in Darwin's works) is the leitmotif of nineteenth century social evolution theory.

Although there were variations, a common concern of the authors was the increasing regulation of human sexual behavior as societies progressed toward more complex technological, political, economic, and kinship systems. Since this concern with the regulation of sexuality directly reflected their definitions of male and female roles, it is upon this aspect of the models that I shall focus. All of these scholars, except Maine, believed that the original human societies were promiscuous. (Interestingly, Darwin, anticipating modern opinion, expressed doubt about this assumption because he believed that no known human society or nondomestic animal society is totally promiscuous, even if individuals mate with multiple partners.) This initial stage of promiscuity was followed by a universal matrilineal stage, which in turn was followed by the present patrilineal stage. During the matrilineal stage, the only kinship ties that were recognized were those of women to their children, so that what we would now call "matrifocal" units prevailed. It was because many of these scholars believed that group or "consanguineous marriages" were occurring in the matrilineal stage that they concluded the fathers' relationships to their offspring would not have been recognized.

There was considerable confusion in these works and in many subsequent interpretations of them between matrilineality, or reckoning of descent through the female line, and matriarchy, or rule by older women. Bachofen (1861) used ancient myths to argue that women had dominated society in its earliest stages and were later to lose power. Morgan (1870; 1877) used his extensive knowledge of the Iroquois to argue that women in the promiscuous and matrilineal stages were either equal to, or dominant over, men, and were in control of sexual relations, descent, and property. He believed that these forms of female power were lost as societies evolved toward civilization (see discussion in Martin and Voorhies 1975). However for the other modelers (Lubbock 1873; McLennan 1865; Spencer 1873) the story of social evolution was not one of the decline of female power during the evolution of societies, but rather of the rise of female prestige. In particular, they argued that when matrilineality was overthrown by patrilineality and the monogamous marriage, women were finally and rightfully protected and supported by individual men. Women were thus able to give up unseemly productive labor and overt sexuality in the public domain and retreat to their "natural," socially valued domestic functions.

Some years after the publication of these works and of Darwin's *Descent of Man*, Engels (Engels 1972) was to reinterpret Morgan's extensive work on the Iroquois in order to argue that early human and matrilineal societies did offer greater social power and prestige to women, that these earliest societies were in fact socially egalitarian, the opposite conclusion to that of McLennan, Lubbock, and Spencer. According to Engels, it was only with the invention of agriculture that the accumulation of property became important to men, and patrilineal descent systems were instituted to afford men greater control over the disposition of their property, of which their wives and children became a part.

Respective Fates of These Early Models

Darwin's views on the evolution of human behavior were reinterpreted by Herbert Spencer to support his views of appropriate political action in Britain in the late 1800s. A coverage of social Darwinism is beyond the scope of this review. However, it is fair to say that whereas Darwin's ideas on the biological mechanisms of evolution throughout the plant and animal kingdom were to have continual and increasing influence on the life sciences of the twentieth century, his ideas specifically on human social and racial evolution were largely dropped or forgotten. Even when aspects of his thoughts on early humans reappear in modern models, his work often is not cited and apparently not remembered.

The ideas of the social evolutionists suffered a more severe fate than mere neglect. In the first half of the twentieth century, the Boasian school of historical particularism took it as part of their mandate to discredit the methodology, the data, and the conclusions of the nineteenth century social evolutionists. The teleology and ethnocentrism of these models (that all societies are progressing toward one goal, represented by European civilizations) was particularly offensive to a discipline founded on cultural relativity. Furthermore, the nineteenth century modelers had worked largely in the absence of good ethnographic data. With the rise of extensive field research in the early twentieth century (much of it conducted on nonindustrial societies by Boas and his students), it became increasingly obvious that the earlier models had relied on incomplete and often incorrect data. Although there have continued to be some evolutionists among social anthropologists, the days of "modeling" early human societies from a social scientist's perspective largely ended at the turn of the century.

Engel's work had a somewhat different fate. Recall that he had drawn the opposite conclusion about female status from that of several of his contemporaries, namely that the amount of labor which women put into subsistence is directly correlated with their social power and prestige. Although his work has been largely ignored in Western anthropology, it has been taken up by Russian anthropologists, and by a few American women anthropologists such as Leacock (1972; 1978) and Reed (1975), who continue to theorize on the evolution of women's status in relation to productive labor and in the context of hypothesized evolution in social organizations.

Overview of Twentieth Century Models

For the first half of the twentieth century, sociocultural anthropologists labored mainly in an effort to collect vital information on nonindustrial societies before the latter transformed entirely under the impact of contact with colonizing or emergent nation-states. Various theories of sociocultural patterns such as functionalism and structuralism emerged, and social evolution remained very much out of favor. Physical anthropologists for their part, largely under the influence of Ales Hrdlicka, also occupied themselves greatly with data collection, primarily in the area of anthropometry. Although occasional sparks of interest in human social origins appeared throughout this time, it was not until the 1960s that a strong interest was rekindled among physical and some social anthropologists.

When models of human social evolution and origins began to reappear widely (Fox 1967; Lee and DeVore 1968a; Sahlins 1960; Service 1962; 1966; Tiger 1969; Washburn 1961; Washburn and Ciochon 1976; Washburn and DeVore 1961; Washburn and Lancaster 1968), they shared one powerful theme: "Man the Hunter." The lines of thought, drawn from the accumulating anthropological literature of the first half of the century, by mid-century seem to have converged into a strong focus on one distinguishing human trait: the pursuit, killing, and eating of animals with the use of tools. The most influential and widely quoted expression of this new model was undoubtably Washburn & Lancaster's 1968 paper on the "Evolution of Hunting" (see Lee and DeVore 1968a). In it they argued that hunting demands all those qualities of human behavior that separate man so sharply from the other primates. Thus, although the exact sequence of events varies in the different versions that were to follow (e.g. Ardrey 1976; Crook 1980; Isaac 1971; Pfeiffer 1972; Tiger 1969), the hunting model was premised on the idea that this means of procuring food was the catalyst for all of the technological, social, and intellectual achievements of human beings. Just a short list of traits believed to have resulted from hunting (which was said to be not simply a subsistence technique, but a way of life) would include: bipedalism, elaborate tool kits, development of language, appreciation of beauty, male aggressiveness and pleasure in killing, division of labor, the nuclear monogamous family, loss of female estrus, the invention of incest taboos, and bonding between males. Furthermore, Washburn and Lancaster argued that the killing of animals with tools dominated human history for such a long time that it became the shaping force of the human psyche for all time, even when men no longer hunt for a living. This argument was repeated in so many articles and introductory textbooks that it took on something akin to the status of a received truth.

Although the Washburn and Lancaster paper was later to be singled out for both emulation and criticism, it was by no means the most extreme statement of the hunting hypothesis. For example, it only traced human hunting patterns (by which the authors clearly meant big game hunting) back to the beginnings of *Homo erectus* (dated at 600,000 years B. P. when their article was written), whereas most others extended the hunting argument back to "99%" of the entire 2-3 million years of hominid evolution. The latter was in spite of the lack of any paleoanthropological evidence of hunting at these early dates. Indeed, if one takes the parsimonious view that hunting can be said to be a common activity only when an extensive hunting technology is found, which the Oldowan and Acheulian tool industries clearly were not, then we must wait until the Upper Paleolithic for the first incontrovertible evidence of hunting-based societies. Furthermore, Washburn and Lancaster recognized that "gathering" as a means of procuring food also set humans apart from other primates, and that "receptacles for carrying vegetable products may have been one of the most fundamental advances in human evolution" (Washburn and Lancaster 1968, p. 297). In contrast, Debetz (1961) denied the possibility of gathering having played any role in human evolution, and most authors of the two influential compendiums of the time, *Man the Hunter* (Lee and DeVore 1968a) and *The Social Life of Early Man* (Washburn 1961), simply failed to mention means of procuring food other than hunting.

The picture of human sex roles that emerges from the hunting models is altered in metaphor, but is little changed in essence from that drawn by Darwin a century earlier. Men are still seen as actively and aggressively engaged in procuring food and defending their families, whereas women are seen as dependents, who remain close to home to trade their sexual and reproductive capacities for protection and provisioning. Some authors such as Sahlins (1960) retained Darwin's concern over the control of human sexuality, which at least implied a consideration of two sexes. However, many of the human evolution models of the 1960s, premised as they were on the idea that "hunting is the master behavior pattern of the human species" (Hamburg 1968; Laughlin 1968), and assuming that women do not participate in hunting, effectively omitted the female half of the human species from any consideration whatsoever.

In retrospect, there are two significant peculiarities of the book *Man the Hunter*. Based on a symposium that gathered together ethnographers from around the world to exchange information and ideas on foraging societies, this volume stands as a landmark for studies of contemporary foraging peoples and as a sourcebook for Man the Hunter models. The first peculiarity is that the participants were unable to agree on a definition of hunting (see Deetz 1968, p. 281, Lee and DeVore 1968b, p. 4; Schneider 1968, p. 341), a failure which could not help but weaken any resultant theorizing, and which inevitably led to later disagreements over generalizations about the importance of hunting in human foraging patterns (e.g. Ember 1978). The second rather odd aspect of the book concerns its title and its ostensive promotion of the hunting model. For it was the very same ethnographic information collected on modern hunter-gatherers, and the interpretations made by the collectors for this volume, which were to turn the minds of many researchers away from hunting as a central humanizing activity and toward alternative explanations of human origins, that is, to the significance of human gathering, carrying, and sharing of mainly vegetable foods. For example, Lee (1968) argued in a paper entitled "What hunters do for a living," that plant and marine resources are far more important than game animals (i.e. "hunters" gather for a living); and Deetz (1968) cautioned of hunting that we must not let the label overdescribe the subject. From this perspective, the papers in *Man the Hunter*, championing as they did the explanatory power of hunting, also provided the insights and the data that were to lead to its undoing.

In 1971, Sally Linton published a paper entitled, "Woman the Gatherer" (Linton 1971), in which she pointed out various shortcomings and examples of androcentric bias in the Wash-

burn and Lancaster paper, and then drew on a variety of sources to develop a model of early hominid females gathering, carrying, and sharing foods with their young. It seemed to her that these three patterns exhibited by hominid females would have been a logical extension of the intense mother-infant bond found in all primates, and she suggested that the first cultural inventions were containers to hold the products of gathering and the infants. According to Linton, the hunting of large animals by males was a late development, after the matrifocal sharing-family was well established. She argued that the first hunters shared food not with sexual partners, but with their mothers and siblings who had shared with them. Such a scenario would obviously set human sex roles on a very different foundation from the "male as husband and provider/protector" model that has come down to us from Darwin. Men would still hunt and women would still gather, but sexual bonds and sexual exchange would not be the cornerstone of society, and the activities of women as autonomous individuals in society would play for almost the first time a significant part in the story of how we evolved those traits that make us uniquely human.

Linton's ideas, only generally sketched out in her essay, obviously struck a chord with a number of women anthropologists, because several of them (Dahlberg 1981a; 1981b; Gayle 1978; Lancaster 1975, 1976, 1978; Martin and Voorhies 1975; Tanner 1981; Tanner and Zihlman 1976) began to focus simultaneously on the question of what women did in early human societies.

Zihlman (Tanner and Zihlman 1976; Zihlman 1976, 1978a, 1978b, 1981, 1982, 1983, 1984, 1985, 1986; Zihlman *et al.* 1978; Zihlman and Tanner 1978) produced a series of elaborations on what came to be called the "Woman the Gatherer" model, in which she stressed that obtaining plant food with tools was the "new" or catalytic event in human evolution. She argued that bipedal locomotion and the invention of carrying devices first enabled women to walk long distances with babies in slings in order to exploit the resources of the more open savannah areas, and to carry these gathered plant foods back to safer familiar areas for shared consumption with their children. Plants and not meat were the focus of technological and social innovation for the emerging hominids three million years ago, and females, ever responsible for the nourishment of themselves and their young, were the providers and the inventors. It might be said by critics that males have now become the inconsequential sex in the story of our origins, because they may bring in meat, but these modelers see it as being of little importance, and it is shared with the matrifocal unit to which the males belong rather than with dependent female sexual partners. Indeed, in some early versions of the Woman the Gatherer model, the male's role was so little described that he might be said to have evolved clinging to the apron strings of the women. In more recent versions (Zihlman and Tanner 1978), called simply the "gathering model," the male's role is elaborated, but still considered to be secondary to the part played by women in unique human inventions.

In retrospect, it may seem discouraging that the choice had to be seen as either hunting *or* gathering, with either men *or* women inventing the cultural patterns that make us distinct. However, at the time, it must have seemed necessary to establish that a credible scientific origin story could be constructed in which women invented tools, chose mates, developed social systems, provided for themselves and their offspring, and generally participated in the evolution of significant human abilities.

Zihlman (1983) described four types of reaction to the gathering model: to accept it wholeheartedly; to reject it as sex-biased; to integrate its parts into existing models; or to ignore it even while taking its salient features. The latter two reactions are of most interest to this review, since they brought changes to the scenarios of human evolution.

The response of some of the proponents of the hunting model was to superimpose the new model on the older hunting scheme, and to emphasize a mixed economy in which early hominid men and women were mutually interdependent (e.g. Isaac 1980; Lancaster 1975, 1976, 1978; Leakey 1981; Lee 1974, 1979). In many respects this has been a gesture of conciliation and a genuine attempt to modify the models to accommodate new thinking. Many authors now emphasize the importance of *sharing* between gathering women and hunting or scavenging men as the key human invention, i.e. the sexual division of labor. Isaac (1978, 1980, 1982, 1984; Isaac and Crader 1981) has done the most to develop a model in which food sharing is the "central platform." He argued that the archaeological evidence from East Africa demonstrates that the earliest hominids carried food and tools to certain locations where we now find their remains. In his view, this is evidence that the unique human social and economic arrangement of sexual division of labor had already begun to take place, and the reason they carried food to consistent locations was in order to share it. He hypothesized that males and females ranged in separate groups, engaging in specialized activities, and brought food back to a home base to share, as do contemporary foragers.

Unfortunately for the sake of conciliation, and for what seems at first sight an anthropologically pleasing "holistic" approach, models are constructed on a foundation of assumptions about causal chains and about human sex roles. It may not be possible to simply superimpose one on the other like so many building blocks without resulting faults in the logic of the whole. Gould (1981), for example, has said that food-sharing models are really about meat sharing, and both Hayden (1981) and Isaac (1978, 1982) have stated that neither sharing nor social living would have been particularly advantageous to foragers living largely on vegetable foods. Indeed, Isaac in his later versions (1984) still tended to see meat eating, now scavenged rather than hunted, as the key factor in the development of human intelligence, language, and social patterns. And since he saw women as encumbered with children and handicapped in meat-obtaining activities (Isaac 1978), females still do not seem to be credited with full partnership in the "sharing" model. The recognition that simple choppers and hand axes would have facilitated scavenging, but not hunting, has been slow to find its expression and implications in the sharing model (e.g. Lee 1968). There has been no "scavenging model"; rather, scavenging has replaced or been added to hunting, without any concomitant changes to other aspects of the model or consideration of its implications for sex roles.

The fourth reaction described by Zihlman has been to ignore women's productive roles (and women anthropologists' models) altogether, while incorporating some of their undeniably salient points. The currently most quoted model of human social evolution contains such borrowings and could be said to illustrate this fourth response.

In 1981 Owen Lovejoy published a paper entitled "The Origin of Man" (Lovejoy 1981), in which the postulated sex roles and division of labor of early hominids were described precisely as Darwin had imagined them 100 years earlier; women remained around home bases to bear and rear children and were dependent on men to protect and provision them. The arguments as to why women had to remain dependent and sedentary were new, but otherwise the origin story remained familiar. Lovejoy's argument drew from several new and diverse sources (such as life history theory) and can be summarized as follows. The earliest hominids were able to become successful as a lineage, especially in comparison to their ape relatives, by facilitating higher fecundity and lower infant mortality rates than the present chimpanzee life history pattern of one infant every four years and only five live offspring in a female's lifetime. Hominids increased their reproductive success by reducing the mobility of lactating mothers and inventing the provisioning of the sedentary females by mobile, bipedal males. Lovejoy's scenario began with the assertion that hunting was not the crucial human technological invention, but rather that gathering was the key innovation. It did so without any reference to the published Woman the Gatherer models, which had accumulated the major body of evidence and arguments for gathering (and against hunting) as the "master behavior pattern."

Further, Lovejoy attributed the collecting of plant food items, and all the ramifications of gathering and sharing in hominid evolution, to the early hominid men. Since male anthropologists had shown no previous signs of wishing to associate their sex with gathering, and since all of the ethnographic evidence points to women as primary gatherers, this sudden enthusiasm for gathering has been seen as the co-opting of the gatherer model (Zihlman 1983). The core assumption of Lovejoy's scheme is that for hominoid females, successful rates of reproduction *and* productive activities are incompatible, and thus men produced the impetus for hominid success by inventing the provisioning of vegetable foods to sedentary, monogamous female mates.

No extended analyses of Lovejoy's model have yet appeared (but see Blanc 1983; Cann and Wilson 1982; Hill 1982; McHenry 1982; Nelson and Jurmain 1985; Zihlman 1985, and below); however, his view of early hominid sex roles is cited in many recent editions of physical anthropology textbooks and popular accounts. Appearing as it did in an invited article in the prestigious journal *Science*, Lovejoy's model could be said to represent the current orthodoxy about human evolution.

Another recent, but much less widely noted, model of human origins (Leibowitz 1983) began with a similar question to that of Lovejoy's (how were early humans able to survive and succeed?), but offered a very different, even opposing answer. Leibowitz argued that a sexual division of labor was a very late human invention, and that for much of hominid evolution both males and females engaged in the same sorts of productive activities (Zihlman 1981). Females simply combined productive activities with reproductive activities, as do many contemporary women. In Leibowitz's view, the key human invention was production, by which she means food-getting with tools, and which was initially unspecialized and undifferentiated by age or sex within the group. She drew an analogy to the manner in which every weaned member of a monkey or ape social group is an independent foraging unit.

Like Lovejoy, Leibowitz interpreted the material evidence to mean that early hominids were "hovering precariously on the edge of extinction" (Leibowitz 1983, p. 135), and argued that their major hedge against a marginal replacement rate was to invent the practice of accumulating surplus food through production. All individuals in the group participated in gathering surplus and in the resultant sharing or exchange. In her view, it was only with the invention of fire and projectile weaponry at the time of late *Homo erectus* that a sexual division of labor began to appear. The sexual division of labor also served as an instrument for stabilizing and extending both intragroup sharing and intergroup exchange. However, for most of human history, production alone (and not a specialization of roles by age and sex) was necessary and sufficient to create the characteristic human patterns.

Leibowitz's idea is noteworthy for two reasons: it shows again how the same data can be interpreted in quite different ways, and it is one of the very few attempts (see also Cucchiari 1981) to strip away the remaining assumption common to all models, that sex differences must have been significant in the earliest stages of human evolution. It seems that one of our own cultural patterns is to oppose male to female characteristics and to assume and emphasize sex and gender differences rather than similarities. That human technological and social success can be attributed to a specialization of tasks by sex is an often repeated assumption of anthropology, and some type of sexual division of labor seems to be universal in human societies today, although the importance accorded it is variable. Yet it can be very enlightening to think through what we have assumed to be the less probable solution. Could characteristic human societies have originated without a sexual division of labor beyond that directly related to insemination, gestation, and lactation? Could some behavioral invention, characteristic of neither males nor females and requiring equivalent participation, have been the catalytic event that set humans moving along their own distinctive evolutionary path? Given that primate females are able to combine foraging with infant care, and that women in most societies contribute at least as much as men to subsistence in addition to their reproductive activities, Leibowitz's scenario may be no more or less data-based and plausible than the many models that seek to give preeminence to one or the other sex in the story of human evolution.

In the following sections, I review these "data bases" or the sources of evidence from primatology, ethnography, and paleoanthropology for the models just described.

THE PRIMATE EVIDENCE

Primatologists who are trained as anthropologists not infrequently study their infrahuman subjects with an eye to casting some light on the behavior and evolution of our own species. It is reasoned that since humans are members of the order Primates, the study of our nearest animal relations can help us to understand both the ways in which we are similar to other species and the ways in which we are distinctive. Although many primatologists are uncomfortable with inferences drawn from animals to humans, and unhappy with what they regard to be facile analogies made in the past, there exists considerable pressure from colleagues and the public alike to make primate studies more directly relevant to the study of humans.

Such was the intent of one of the earliest and most widely publicized field studies of a nonhuman primate, the baboon. DeVore and Washburn (1963, Washurn and DeVore 1961) observed common baboons in East Africa in 1959-60 and constructed a model of early human life based on baboons. They argued that early hominids, like baboons, differentiated from other primates by exploiting the resources of the East African savannah. Like baboons, humans would have become both predators of savannah flora and fauna and the prey of the large savannah carnivores. In order to protect themselves, given their relatively ineffectual physical abilities as individuals, the model proposes that both humans and baboons came to rely upon a social system of defense. This social system was said to be based on the bonding and cooperation of mature males organized into a rigid dominance hierarchy and employing an "army-like" pattern of "troop" movement across the dangerous plains [e.g. "Baboons move in a carefully structured defense formation, guarding the nucleus of females and infants. Early humans may have traveled in similar formation" (Friedl and Pfeiffer 1977, p. 94)]. According to the model, and there are many versions of it (Ardrey 1961; Morris 1967; Pfeiffer 1972; Tiger 1969; Tiger and Fox 1971), human males distinguished themselves even further as exploiters of the savannah through the invention of weapons and thus hunting, which in turn led to unique human traits like language and the family. However, it was argued, this complex of distinct human characteristics initially was founded on a social system very like that which DeVore described for baboons.

Such a "baboonization" (Pfeiffer 1972) model of early human life experienced a popularity that may have surprised even its authors. Throughout the 1960s and 1970s, no textbook or course in introductory anthropology, and no concluding chapter on the human species in the animal behavior and evolutionary theory texts, seemed complete without reference to the baboon analogy for early humans. Even an elementary school social science curriculum, called "Man, A Course of Study" included extensive coverage of the baboon model.

Criticism of this depiction of baboon social life and of this model for early human life has come from many quarters, including primatologists, ecologists, and social anthropologists, and such critiques will not be covered in detail here (but see Fedigan 1982). For the purposes of this review, the portrayal of primeval sex roles in the baboon model can be said to have been traditional and consistent with contemporary role expectations for Western men and women (Maccoby and Jacklin 1974; Martin and Voorhies 1975): males were seen as aggressive, competitive, and protective; females were seen as nurturant, dependent, and submissive.

Today, with the extensive evidence available from anatomical, biochemical, paleontological, and behavioral studies, it is widely accepted that chimpanzees are the nonhuman primate most closely related to humans, and it may seem odd to have chosen any other species from which to draw analogies. However, at the time the baboon model was developed, this presumably was not so evident, and the ecological analogy between these two distantly related primates was widely accepted.

In the past decade, many reconstructions of early hominid life have drawn heavily from the accumulating data on the behavior of common chimpanzees (*Pan troglodytes*) and pygmy chimpanzees (*Pan paniscus*). Following a line of argument established by Darwin nearly a century ago, some of the recent models suggest that chimpanzees show rudimentary patterns of behavior that also might have been exhibited by our common ape forebears, and which were greatly elaborated by hominids as the latter differentiated from the other hominoids. Some of these patterns of behavior, it is argued, were ultimately to become the distinguishing characteristics of the human lineage. Even though chimpanzees have traveled their separate evolutionary route for the past 5 million years, it is believed that their traits can give us some clues to the general "ape-like" way of life of our hominoid ancestors, a way of life that was to set the stage for the human pattern. The rest of this section is organized around the behavioral characteristics of chimpanzees which modelers have isolated and suggested as possible antecedents for human patterns (see especially Goodall 1976, Mc-Grew 1981).

Social Bonds

The core of chimpanzee social life (indeed, almost all mammalian social life) is the enduring mother-offspring bond. In most primate species, the male emigrates at puberty whereas the female remains close to her mother for life. In chimpanzees, the reverse seems to be the case, with adolescent females leaving their mothers and communities at first estrus, but whether temporarily for mating, or permanently to live in a new community, is not yet well established. Nonetheless, a chimpanzee mother suckles each infant for around four years and remains physically close to her offspring until they reach sexual maturity at ten to twelve years of age. Since a female chimpanzee bears an infant approximately every four years, she may have two or more dependent offspring traveling with her at any one time, but usually only one that is suckling and being carried. Her mature sons, and less frequently her mature daughters, also travel with her on occasion. Some male-male bonds are formed (often between maternal brothers), and estrous females may travel and forage with male parties, but the enduring and primary social unit is matrifocal, that is, centered upon and articulated around the ties between a female and her offspring.

Most versions of the Woman the Gatherer model have used this aspect of chimpanzee social bonding (and primate social life in general) to argue that the matrifocal unit, and not the nuclear family, whether monogamous or polygynous, was the core of early hominid society. The intensive and extensive mother-offspring bond of the ape, it is argued, could only have become more elaborated in a lineage such as hominids, with their increasingly altricial infants. Following this argument, the initial social ties of adult males would have been to their maternal kin and not to their temporary sexual partners.

Chimpanzees are not as promiscuous as initially reported; still, sexual bonding is temporary. Individuals of both sexes avoid mating with close kin, and although males may occasionally act possessively or competitively in a mating context, most copulations are casual and opportunistic, with females exhibiting preferences for certain males over others. Much has been made of the "loss of estrus" in the human female as compared to other primates and its supposed causal relationship to permanent pair bonds. However, we now know that female pygmy chimpanzees in the wild copulate throughout their monthly cycles [Badrian and Badrian (1984)] but are not pair bonded to males, whereas monogamous nonhuman primate species all show pair bonding but no loss of estrus. Thus the hypothesized correlation between loss of estrus and monogamy is not supported by the primate data.

Social Dynamics

Chimpanzee social life is complex in that two levels have been identified: (a) a large community of individuals who recognize each other and are not mutually antagonistic when they meet, and (b) smaller parties of individuals who travel, sleep, and forage together. Their social life is fluid in that the composition of parties fluctuates frequently, with only the mother-dependent offspring unit remaining constant. Such a pattern has been referred to as a "fission-fusion" social organization.

Wrangham (1979) has conceptualized a chimpanzee community as a cooperative group of related males who overlap the individual ranges of individual female-offspring units and sometimes behave antagonistically toward members of neighboring communities. Foraging parties within the community are believed to fluctuate in size and composition in relation to the changing abundance and distribution of food resources. This complex, fluid, and environmentally responsive social system has been described by many modelers (e.g. McGrew 1981; Reynolds 1966; Zihlman 1978) as containing the essential ingredients for early hominid foragers to adapt their social groups to both the resources and the technological innovations important in the human way of life.

Feeding, Food Sharing, and Tool Use

Probably no aspect of chimpanzee behavior has interested anthropologists more than their dietary and technological habits. It is now widely known that chimpanzees learn to make a variety of simple tools which vary in structure and function from community to community. Tools are occasionally used in agonistic contexts, usually by males, but more commonly for food collecting and processing. Hammerstones are used to crack open hard fruits, and probes are used to collect insects from underground nests. The majority of tool making and tool use is done by females. This is because mature females consume many more social insects than do males and thus exhibit much more fishing for termites than their male counterparts. The pursuit and killing of small animals, primarily carried out by males, is done without the use of tools.

As exciting as the reports of tool use and "hunting" by chimpanzees were the initial descriptions of food sharing in these animals. Except for suckling infants, the basic primate rule of feeding seems to be each individual for itself. Although it is likely that social groups enhance the abilities of individuals to find and defend food sources, each nonhuman primate past the age of weaning, male or female, is in all other respects an economically independent foraging unit. Provisioning of dependents is not a characteristic of the primate order, and even minimal sharing of food [which Isaac (1978) dubbed as "tolerated scrounging"] is very rare.

The first descriptions of food sharing in the chimpanzee placed such behavior in the context of meat eating (Goodall 1968; Teleki 1973). It is mainly adult males that kill animals and eat meat, and mainly old, past-prime males who are the recipients of shared meat. However, close female kin of the meat possessor and estrous females also receive more than expected shares. These data seem ideally constituted to construct a model of how human hunting innovations would lead to male provisioning of a nuclear family with meat, and indeed they have been used to this end (Fisher 1982).

However, further field studies of both the common and pygmy chimpanzees and specific investigations of the nature of food sharing (Kuroda 1984; McGrew 1979; Silk 1978) have since demonstrated that a great deal of sharing also occurs with plant food, particularly large or hard-to-open fruits. More importantly, in common chimpanzees the vast majority of such sharing (McGrew reports 86%) occurs within the matrifocal family. And the provision of food by mothers to their offspring, either through cadging of scraps or through unsolicited donations, accounted for almost all cases of plant food sharing in McGrew's study.

Several authors (McGrew 1981; Tanner 1981; Zihlman 1982) have used the information on sex differences in chimpanzee tool use and food sharing to reconstruct how these patterns might have been further elaborated upon by transitional hominids. They argue that gathering, the catalytic innovation in hominid technology, was invented by females whose digging sticks and unmodified stone hammers were refinements on the female ape's tool kit of termite probes and pounding stones. Furthermore, gathering as a pattern of accumulating surplus vegetable food leads to carrying and sharing of foods. Primate females, with few exceptions, are adapted to the burden of carrying infants, and hominid females would have invented slings to carry their nonclinging infants and their food supplies. Extended human sharing of accumulated or surplus foods would have been founded primarily on the ape pattern of matrifocal sharing.

Chimpanzee females are also mobile and clearly capable of finding food for themselves and their dependent young, thus undermining Lovejoy's argument that a hominoid female could not combine successful reproduction with subsistence activities. Lovejoy's view of the chimpanzee life history pattern as leading to a marginal existence, hovering on the edge of extinction, has been criticized by several other researchers (Harley 1982; Isaac 1982; Wolfe et al. 1982; Wood 1982). They counterargued that chimpanzee females produce and rear offspring at about the same rate as the other great apes, and more importantly, at comparable rates to human females in foraging societies. At Gombe Stream Reserve, the chimpanzee females who have been followed over their lifetimes have each raised several offspring to maturity, a replacement rate that certainly would not lead a population to the brink of extinction if it were also maintained outside the protected park. It is clear that the low population of chimpanzees in Africa today is the result of historically recent human destruction of the animal and its habitat.

Still, there clearly exists enough complexity in chimpanzee behavior and enough diverse conclusions from the studies of these animals to give rise to many different scenarios. Specifically with reference to sex roles, some of the resultant models have tended to continue the emphasis on males as the main actors in the development of distinctive human abilities, using as a foundation the data on male chimpanzee aggressiveness or male ranging behavior or male hunting patterns (Reynolds 1966; Symons 1979; Teleki 1973). Whereas others, using the findings on the central significance of the female chimpanzee in social bonding and in food procurement patterns, have

proposed a radical or nontraditional view of human females as prime movers in the evolution of the essential hominid traits such as tool use and sharing (Dahlberg 1981; Linton 1971; Zihlman 1982). Finally, some authors have explored the manner in which sex differences in chimpanzee behavior might have set the stage for sexual division of labor in the first hominid societies (Galdikas and Teleki 1981; Hamburg and McCown 1979; Lancaster 1975; 1976; McGrew 1979).

THE ETHNOGRAPHIC EVIDENCE

Until the advent of agricultural practices based on the domestication of plants and animals no more than 12,000 years ago, peoples around the world must have lived as foragers. The archaeological evidence of lithic artifacts dating back some 2 million years indicates that human foragers have long acquired and/or processed their food with the assistance of tools. And the evidence appearing at various, mainly later Pleistocene dates of cut marks on animal bones, of homebases with remains of plant food collections, of the use of fire, and of increasingly sophisticated tools for food collecting and processing all point to a hunting and gathering subsistence pattern at least in late-middle and upper paleolithic peoples. Reserving for later the issue of whether the earliest hominids were already hunter-gatherers, or simply generalized foragers with tools, or perhaps even toolless primates who differed little from the ape forms except in being bipedal, the significant point for this section is that the vast majority of the cultural remains of paleolithic peoples have been interpreted as resulting from the technological system of hunting and gathering. And since there are obvious technological similarities between these archaeological remains and the material culture of contemporary hunter-gatherers, and in some cases ecological/environmental similarities, some researchers have turned to the study of modern hunter-gatherers to shed light on the reconstruction of the social patterns of prehistoric foragers. The logic is that social structures respond to environmental exigencies and correspond to technological systems. Thus, it is argued that the basic social forms widely found in contemporary hunter-gatherers, especially those dwelling in tropical zones, probably occurred as well in paleolithic hunter-gatherers.

A number of anthropologists have objected to the use of ethnographic evidence to reconstruct early human social life, and these objections will be described briefly since they do have a bearing on the assessment of the models themselves. Freeman (1968) has objected to analogies drawn between prehistoric and modern groups on both methodological and theoretical grounds. First, he argued that to force archaeological evidence into frames of reference developed for contemporary data inevitably distorts and obscures the prehistoric analysis. It also prevents the development of frameworks based directly on the prehistoric material. Secondly, he argued that like environmental stimuli do not necessarily produce like cultural responses, because sociocultural systems have tended to regional-and-resource specialization during the course of human history. More recently, in an extensive analysis of the relevance of contemporary hunter-gatherers to paleolithic societies, Testart (1978) also emphasized the particular nature of each society's history, the importance of regional events, climate, fauna, flora, and the 10,000 years of individual histories that separate today's hunter-gatherers from their paleolithic antecedents. Nonetheless, Testart's detailed analysis of the ethnographic evidence led him to conclude that at least some contemporary hunter-gatherers can provide insights into prehistoric patterns.

A second criticism of the ethnographic analogy rests on ideological grounds. Berndt (1981), for example, has objected to the implication that the study of modern Australian aborigines can help us to understand early human societies. She suggested that this view is harkening back to the nineteenth century social evolutionist and colonialist racist attitudes that aboriginal peoples are "primitives" or "survivals"; that they are lower on an evolutionary scale and thus inferior. Schrire (1980) has argued for the !Kung, on somewhat similar grounds to Berndt for the Australian aborigines, that we should not regard contemporary foraging peoples as "living fossil groups." This objection is also in part substantive; following Boas, most social anthropologists have argued that there are *no* modern representatives of past cultural stages. Therefore, many draw the conclusion that any attempt at reconstruction or analogy based on contemporary peoples is not only futile but also contrary to those tenets of anthropology based upon a non-hierarchical view of cultural variation.

Others (e.g. Lee 1974) reply that to suggest that similar economies and similar technologies may be associated with similar social structures, and to construct hypotheses on the basis of such similarities, is not to suggest social evolution in any pejorative sense. Similar reservations about the appropriateness of animal analogies to human behavior have been expressed. A discussion of the proper use of analogy in natural and social science might be useful in the context of human evolution theories, but it is beyond the terms of this review. Without presupposing the conclusions of such a discussion, it is nevertheless necessary here to accept the usage and to go on to the question of which, if any, of the modern hunting and gathering societies provide the most appropriate analogies.

The most systematic attempt to answer this question is by the French ethnographer Alain Testart (1978). In the process of considering the issue of why some hunting and gatherering societies persist in their subsistence system rather than adopting sedentary or pastoral lifeways, Testart drew up a classification of six types of hunter-gatherers. Of these six, only two categories, one largely comprised of North American Indian societies, the other containing notably the !Kung and Australian Aborigines, were found by Testart to have structural features that would make them good choices as models for earlier foraging societies. Testart then eliminated North American Indian societies because of their recency, geography, and specialization for a habitat unsuitable to agriculture, leaving as the group of choice such societies as the !Kung and the Australian Aborigines. At the end of his careful and well-reasoned analysis, Testart returned to the ideological question by noting that the choice of a contemporary society and its application by analogy to paleolithic peoples may be informed as much by subjective factors as by overt criteria.

Lee (1974, 1979; Lee and DeVore 1968b) has directly refuted several objections to the ethnographic analogy (see also Yellen 1976), arguing that the use of !Kung data to illuminate the past is not to regard these people as living fossils. The !Kung have a long history in southern Africa, over which time regional events would have had an impact on social forms, and they have not lived in isolation from nonforaging peoples and ways of life. Nonetheless, Lee believes that by proceeding cautiously with these caveats in mind, there is much to be learned about a hunter-gatherer way of life from studies of contemporary !Kung and other foragers. In his view, they have a core of features in common which "represents the basic human adaptation stripped of the accretions and complications brought about by agriculture, urbanization, advanced technology, and national and class conflict—all of the 'advances' of the last few thousand years" (Lee 1979, p. 3).

As a result of extracting these "core features," Lee characterized the basic or generalized hunter-gatherer society as a flexible, bilaterally organized, nonterritorial group, with a particular emphasis on the genealogical core as consisting of both related males and related females (Lee 1974). Earlier, Lee & DeVore (1968b) had defined several features generally characteristic of the hunting and gathering way of life: 1. groups are small and mobile, with fluctuating membership; 2. food surpluses are not prominent, and mobility places constraints on the accumulation of any type of surplus, thus the system is basically egalitarian; 3. groups are not strongly attached to any one area and do not ordinarily maintain exclusive rights to resources (i.e. they are nonterritorial); and 4. reciprocity and a division of labor lead to an emphasis on sharing resources.

Leacock (1972, 1978) has identified several of the same features in her analyses of present and past hunter-gatherers although she placed somewhat more emphasis on egalitarianism and the lack of specialization or hierarchies related to resources. Lee (1974) stated that his view of hunter-gatherers and thus early humans as living in flexible, bilaterally organized groups is a correction to the "patrilineal horde" model first developed by Radcliffe-Browne for Australian Aborigines (Radcliffe-Brown 1930) and then applied by others (e.g. Fox 1967; Service 1962, 1966) to the reconstruction of early human social life.

The Roles of Women in Hunter-Gatherer Society

The picture that was painted of the social role of women in much early ethnographic and ethnological work on hunter-gatherers was of a dependent, lesser, and even passive social category. Ethnographers, mainly men, studied social phenomena of greater interest to men and talked mainly to male informants. The emphasis on hunting, weapons, and warfare ignored the contributions of women to subsistence and to social dynamics. Theoretical models (e.g. Levi-Strauss 1949) viewed men as actors and women as objects of sexual exchange. However, in the last two decades, many new ethnographic studies employing female as well as male perspectives have been undertaken (see extensive review in Quinn 1977). Thus, a picture of women as active, competent, contributing, and even self-sufficient members of hunter-gatherer societies, with their own stories to tell, has begun to emerge from the shadows of early ethnographic scenarios.

In particular, Lee's (Lee 1968, 1980; Lee and DeVore 1976) continuing analysis of women's contribution to subsistence in contemporary hunter-gatherer societies has been an important starting point in a reassessment of the parts women might have played in early human society. In a survey of 58 foraging societies from around the world (Lee 1968), Lee concluded that on average hunted foods contributed only 35% of the diet and thus, contrary to popular conception, men provided less than half of the food of "hunting" peoples. Of the

58 societies he surveyed, 29 (slightly more than half) depend primarily on gathering, one third primarily on fishing, and only one-sixth primarily on hunting. Thus, he concluded that except in the Arctic, where meat is of primary importance, plant food, shell fish, and fish, collected primarily by women, form the bulk of the diet. Hence his argument that foraging women generally are capable of feeding themselves and are not dependent on men for subsistence.

These conclusions were taken up enthusiastically by the various modelers of Woman the Gatherer and are also occasionally mentioned in introductory textbooks, perhaps to temper the emphasis on males as providers in descriptions of hunter-gatherers. Hiatt (1978) extended Lee's analysis to demonstrate the economic importance of women in Australian Aborigine society in particular and in tropical hunter-gatherers in general. Martin and Voorhies (1975) and Whyte (1978) also extracted samples of foraging societies from Murdock's *Atlas* and concluded that women generally contribute substantially to subsistence. However, the different samples and definitions used in these studies render detailed comparisons impracticable. Ember (1978), for example, drew a different sample from the *Atlas*, using different definitions of hunting and came to differing conclusions from those of Lee, Hiatt, Martin & Voorhies, and Whyte.

There is a serious problem in any attempted generalizations from Murdock's *Ethnographic Atlas*. The foraging societies described in the *Atlas* are not a random sample, nor a representative sample, nor a complete compilation of all the hunter-gatherers societies that have existed, even in historical times. Worldwide surveys taken from the *Atlas* may well be biased toward those cultural zones which for many reasons have been more often studied, unless some form of corrective representative sampling is attempted. Furthermore, the quality of the data coded for the various societies is uneven and often unrefined, as noted by Hayden (1981), and ethnographers often have not collected the original data with Murdock's ultimate categories in mind.

Also taking a different view from that of Testart, Ember argued that North American foragers are more instructive about the past than those of the Old World. However, for the purpose of extrapolation to early human societies that existed in the African equatorial zones, it seems clear that one would not want a comparative sample composed predominantly of North American temperate and arctic zone dwellers. Tropical and subtropical zones offer a greater abundance and diversity of edible plants than do more northerly latitudes, and various researchers (Hiatt 1978; Martin and Voorhies 1975; Testart 1978) have demonstrated that in contemporary tropical and subtropical foragers, meat forms a small proportion of the diet, whereas vegetable foods provide a high percentage of the subsistence base. Testart found that the percentage of meat in the diet of hunter-gatherers correlated with latitude, going from a low of 10% near the equator to 90% in the Arctic.

Finally, the issues are further muddled by the fact that although women are primarily associated with gathering plant foods, they do also obtain small animals and occasionally hunt with weapons for larger ones (Estioko-Griffin and Griffin, 1981). Men, on the other hand, often help with gathering or feed themselves on plant matter while hunting. Dahlberg (1981) presented a short but cogent overview of the results of various surveys on male and female contributions to subsistence, using different samples and different definitions of hunting, gathering, and fishing.

The issue of differential contribution to subsistence has been dealt with at some length because it is important in assessing women's status in early foraging societies. Women's reproductive roles have never been in question (except the degree to which they are handicapping); it is their productive capabilities that are contentious. Anthropologists who have followed Engel's argument at its most basic (e.g. Leacock 1972, 1978) have long argued that those women who actively contribute to subsistence, and who are not economically dependent but interdependent with all the other producing members of the group, will have equivalent status to that of the men. Others (Friedl 1975) have modified this argument to add that women must not only contribute to subsistence but also have a measure of personal control over the disposition and distribution of the fruits of their labor in order to achieve power and prestige equivalent to that of the men. The ability to control production and distribution is more difficult to demonstrate, and possibly is less true of women than the ability to contribute to production. However, if the data continue to show that women are not economically dependent on men for provisioning in most hunter-gatherer societies, indeed that they often produce more than do the men, then the assumption of the nonproductive female, which has been a key element in most reconstructions of our earliest ancestors, must be seriously reexamined.

Implications for Recent Models

Since the ethnographic evidence on contemporary hunter-gatherers in tropical and subtropical zones supports the economic independence claimed in the Woman the Gatherer model, and since no ethnographic example exists of sedentary women in foraging societies being provisioned by their husbands with plant foods, it is not surprising that the male provisioning model makes no reference to ethnographic sources. Lovejoy's argument that early human females would not have been able to carry babies and burdens, and would have had to remain sedentary in order to reproduce successfully, is also contradicted by ethnographic evidence. It is clear that in most parts of the world foraging women are assigned the tasks of carrying heavy burdens: food, children, water, and firewood. Sedentary women simply do not exist in hunter-gatherer societies. Where quantitative data have been collected, it has been found that women are away from basecamp for equivalent amounts of time and walk equivalent distances, carrying infants and heavier burdens than do the men.

Finally, Lovejoy's argument that the earliest foragers would have differentiated from the apes by rapidly increased reproduction (becoming "*r*" selected) is not supported by any of the ethnographic (or paleolithic) evidence. Contemporary foraging women only produce one child that is raised every three to four years (a reproductive rate that is strikingly similar to the rate found in female apes), and may be assumed to arrange their reproductive lives around the demands of their productive activities (a unique skill in humans which, however, never seems to appear on the trait lists). The paleoanthropological record shows that the great population increase, indicating heightened fecundity and possibly concomitant sedentarization of women, which Lovejoy postulated as one of the first and necessary events in human evolution, actually does not occur until much later in human evolution, when humans radically altered their subsistence techniques to domesticate their food resources.

Although she did not use ethnographic sources, Leibowitz's model of an early human society in which every mature individual could feed itself and also contribute to the group without a sexual division of labor could have been supported by the example of one contemporary foraging group, the Tasaday (Fernandez and Lynch 1972). Although much controversy and too much publicity surrounded the contacting of this isolated foraging group in the Philippines in the 1960s, there are many noteworthy aspects to their lifeway. The Tasaday seem to have been isolated from all but two neighboring groups of people, similar to themselves, for at least 600 years, and they practiced a simple but successful way of living. The small band (24 people) practiced no sexual division of labor, and until first contacts with explorers, no hunting or trapping. However, they collected small animals from riverine areas, without the use of tools, to supplement their vegetable foods. The technology was very simple, food was easily gathered in a few hours, a short distance from the home base, and readily shared throughout the group. As Hayden (1981) noted in his worldwide survey of hunter-gatherer groups, an unmeasured but possibly large proportion of food is simply "snacked" in an ad hoc fashion as people move about collecting a surplus to be brought back to camp. In the Tasaday, all decisions were made by consensus, with no evidence of an authority structure or dominant sex. In these respects, the Tasaday would illustrate Leibowitz's model of an egalitarian, unspecialized, autonomous-yet-sharing, tool-using, foraging group.

THE MATERIAL EVIDENCE

Paleoanthropologists work with three types of material evidence about the early hominids: their osteological remains, the physical traces of their various activities, and the associated or contextual information on the environment in which they lived. The latter two will be discussed under "archaeological evidence" in a following section; here I will discuss briefly how these osteological remains are described and interpreted, focusing on those aspects that are relevant to sex role reconstruction.

Before describing the data, a few comments on the distinction between material evidence and inferred evidence would be useful. Bones and stones are a very fragmentary record of the past, and, like other empirical phenomena, cannot speak for themselves. Thus in some respects, inference and interpretation must occur in every description, at every level. However, to clarify the distinctions, Isaac and Crader (1981) have suggested three levels of interpretation in paleoanthropology: first, interpretation of the empirical evidence (the "finds"); second, interpretation of the processes that led to this material evidence; and third, the formulation of general models to explain the evidence. In terms of the earliest hominids, we can use the fossil material to draw some first-order, descriptive inferences about body size and shape, locomotor and dental patterns. At a second level, we can infer behavioral and environmental patterns and the selective pressures that might have led to these characteristic phenotypes. Finally, we can construct models that incorporate our various second-order inferences into a coherent framework of explanation. Although interpretation does occur even in seemingly straightforward descriptions of the fossil remains, which are fragmentary and often must be "reconstructed," still, as we move from descriptions of material remains to processes and then to models, our inferences are increasingly dependent upon assumptions to be tested by internal consistency and plausibility, and decreasingly by reference to empirical evidence.

Fossil Evidence for Early Hominid Sex Role

Descriptive Data In East Africa, approximately three million years ago, one or more species of hominid lived in a savannah-like habitat of grasslands interspersed with pockets of forested and riverine areas. Paleoanthropologists have classified these creatures as hominids because they were bipedal and had human-like dentition, but they have not yet agreed upon the number of species living contemporaneously. For the sake of simplicity, I will refer to the very earliest hominids collectively as australopithecines. These hominids were small in frame and short in stature, with brains no larger than those of contemporary chimpanzees. Their dentition was distinctive from that of the pongids, with characteristically small, incisiformed canines in both males and females and large thickly enameled molars. Relative dimensions of their limbs and aspects of their fingers and toes indicate that they continued to have some grasping ability and may still have spent some time moving around in the trees, but their lower limbs and the shape of the pelves indicate they walked on two legs on the ground. Beyond these rather minimal descriptive statements (and even they are not without contention and exceptions), we move quickly into the realms of either morphological detail or of second-order interpretations. Because this review focuses on the reconstruction of sex roles, comments on the processes that led to the general australopithecine phenotype will be limited to those aspects that seem most relevant to female and male patterns.

Diet Diet plays a major role in models of human evolution and thus many researchers have turned to an analysis of tooth shape, and more recently, tooth wear patterns, in order to infer what the earliest hominids might have eaten. One recent consensus appears to be that their tooth morphology indicates omnivory, with no clear specializations for meat-shearing or seed-grinding or bone-gnawing (e.g. Harding and Teleki 1981; Mann 1975, 1981). Studies of tooth wear, masticatory musculature, and "microscratches" on the surfaces of teeth indicate that although there is variation between species (especially between later robust and gracile australopithecines), these early hominids were eating a variety of foods, some of them soft fruits and others tough, fibrous, and hard to chew. There does not seem to be consensus on whether these foods were generally gritty, indicating that they were mainly tubers and roots dug from the earth, or clean, which might suggest that they were fruits and other products from trees (cf Isaac 1984; Zihlman 1985). More importantly for this review, it is not yet possible to determine from tooth wear or from chemical analysis of bones what proportions of plants and meat occurred in these early human diets.

One feature of human dentition that has long intrigued physical anthropologists is that canines are relatively small in males as well as in females. In most primate species, and in the fossil forms that are believed to be ancestral to the australopithecines, canines are larger in males than females. It is usually suggested that large male canines in primates are selected for, either as part of a male protective role against predators or as part of sexual selection, resulting from male-male competition. For hominids, the traditional explanation, which forms part of the hunting model, is that male canine size was reduced after the invention of weapons removed the need for canines as defensive tools (see Washburn and Ciochon 1976). This explanation has become dated with the growing recognition that the reduction in hominid canines began long before the appearance of tools in the paleontological record. On the other hand, following the principle of female choice, but contradicting Darwin's contention of male choice in humans, some versions of the gathering model (Zihlman 1978) have suggested that female proto-hominids may have selected males with smaller canines as preferred mates because the latter represented less of an aggressive threat to them and their offspring. Finally, it may simply be that smaller anterior teeth (incisors and canines) and larger, thicker posterior teeth (premolars and molars) were adaptations to produce flat, durable surfaces for chewing the fibrous foods that comprised the omnivorous diet of the earliest hominids.

Body Size And Sexual Dimorphism

A second aspect of the fossil record that would bear directly on models of sex roles concerns the degree of sexual dimorphism in the earliest hominids. Although degree of sexual dimorphism does not correlate perfectly with sex roles, dominance relations, or mating systems in the other primate or mammalian species (Ralls 1977), nonetheless monogamous primates tend to be monomorphic and behaviorally undifferentiated by sex, whereas highly dimorphic species tend to be polygynous and male-dominated.

Unfortunately, there is little agreement on whether or to what degree the earliest hominids were dimorphic. It is not a simple matter to sex fragmentary fossil hominids, especially when only a few individuals are known of a given "type" or species. The gracile and robust australopithecine material from South and East Africa was sometimes interpreted as representing the females (gracile) and males (robust) of one species (e.g. Brace 1973). However, most would now agree that separate gracile and robust species existed in South and East Africa, and it is not clear what the degree of sexual dimorphism would have been within these species.

The problem of distinguishing species differences from sex differences has now reemerged with the very earliest hominid material from Hadar, presently dated at 2.9 to 3.2 million years ago. The famous "Lucy" and "First Family" fossils are interpreted by finders Johanson and White (1979) as one highly variable, sexually dimorphic species, *Australopithecus afarensis*, whereas they are interpreted by some of the French members of the team (Senut and Tardieu 1981; Tardieu 1983) and by Zihlman as two separate species. All agree that there is a great deal of size variation in the fossil hominids from Hadar, so much so that Zihlman has argued from the limited published measurements that if these hominids do represent only one species, they would be more dimorphic than any known primate (Zihlman 1986). Other researchers, however, continue to discuss and analyze the Hadar material as one highly variable and dimorphic species (e.g. McHenry 1982; Stern and Susman 1983).

Birth, Growth, And Death

The evidence for relatively small brain size in the earliest hominids suggests that although the shape of the pelvis had altered to accommodate bipedal walking, the process of giving birth was not yet the problem for these females that it was to become for their large-brained descendents. However, the earliest hominid infants would have had feet adapted more for bipedal walking and less for grasping, and thus may have needed support from their mothers, a problem that pongid mothers do not have to accommodate. Even if their infants were more precocial than those of modern humans, and even if the long arms and stronger hands of an *afarensis* infant would have helped them to cling (especially if their mothers were hairy, something not recorded), it is probable that early hominid females would have had to find some way to support poorly grasping infants. Or perhaps mothers would have had to restrict their long-distance traveling. Mann's study of early hominid dental development (Mann 1975) indicates that at least some australopithecine children (perhaps only those of two million rather than 3-4 million years ago) matured over roughly comparable periods to human children today, and thus more slowly than modern apes. This would also have presented caretakers with an increased burden, and females would either have had to space birth intervals widely apart to accommodate dependent children as do modern hunter-gatherers, or they would have had to find some method to care for more than one dependent child at a time. Mann's analysis of dental indicators of age at death in australopithecines suggests that life spans were short, perhaps no more than 25 years. Again, this is the kind of first and second-order evidence that can be used to construct quite different models. For example, it can be used to support the arguments that Lovejoy and Leibowitz made for a highly stressed, even threatened, hominid population, or more conservatively, as simply evidence for a demographic pattern similar to that of most modern hunter-gatherer societies and thus not a significant feature.

Third-Order Interpretations: Modeling Sex Roles and Social Bonds from Fossil Material

Pilbeam (Landau *et al.* 1982; Pilbeam 1980) has said that despite their claim to be based on fossil evidence, most paleontological models of human evolution are relatively "fossil-free." This is perhaps best demonstrated through reference to the following list of the traits commonly focused upon by modelers of early hominid evolution.

Physical traits:	Upright posture and bipedal walking;
	Reduced anterior tooth size and enlarged cheek teeth;
	Increasing brain size;
	Increasing hand-eye and fine motor coordination.
Ecological traits:	Open-country, savannah habitat;
	Heavy predator pressure;
	Terrestrial diet.
Technological traits:	Tool use;
	Hunting and scavenging;
	Gathering;
	Homebases.

Cognitive traits: Language;
Intelligence;
Self-awareness.

Social dynamics: Food sharing;
Division of labor;
"Loss" of estrus in females;
The husband-father role;
Altricial infants and long
dependency periods.

Many theorists have drawn up attribute lists such as the one above, in which traits found in contemporary human beings, but not in modern apes, often are projected back along the hominid record to an assumed very early appearance at the time of the divergence between hominids and apes. However, it is important to recognize that fossil evidence for these traits, having occurred in the earliest hominids of 3-4 million years ago, only exists for the first two of the 19 attributes listed. In addition, we have archaeological evidence for tool use some two million years ago and for aspects of a scavenging/hunting and gathering subsistence pattern (homebases with hearths, projectiles) only much more recently, in the middle to upper Paleolithic. For the majority of these assumed early hominid traits (e.g. self-awareness, loss of estrus), it is unlikely that we will ever find material evidence, and thus, as Pilbeam has argued, most stories of human origins are "unconstrained" by the fossil data, which are used instead to support or embellish preexisting frameworks of explanation.

For example, the analyses of teeth of the earliest hominids indicate that they were omnivorous, but they do not make it possible to determine what proportions of plants and meat occurred in the diet. Therefore, a scavenging or a hunting or a gathering model could claim some support from tooth measurements and wear patterns, and theorists have offered widely different interpretations of the reduction in canine size. Likewise, until the question of sexual dimorphism versus species differences is resolved for the earliest australopithecines, it is possible to argue for any type of hominid mating system, unconstrained by the apparent relationship between phenotype and mating patterns in primates, that is between extreme dimorphism and polygyny or between monomorphism and monogamy. Indeed, Lovejoy appeared to accept the one, highly dimorphic species argument for *Australopithecus afarensis*, while arguing at the same time that they were monogamous. Finally, the evidence that early hominid infants had poorly grasping feet and possibly were dependent for long periods of time, which may have presented early hominid mothers with a special problem, can be interpreted in two opposing manners. First, as in the homebase model, it is possible to argue that the females became less mobile and more dependent upon males to provision and protect them, or second, as in the gathering model, we can argue that females resolved this problem themselves through technological inventions which in turn led to innovations with wider applicability.

Archaeological Evidence for Early Human Social Life

The assumption that the earliest hominids practiced a way of living that was somewhere along a direct line between the generalized lifeway of the chimpanzee and that of the contemporary hunter-gatherer is best exemplified by the earlier work of Glynn Isaac (1971, 1978, 1980; Isaac et al. 1981). Several of Isaac's papers began by listing the traits that distinguish modern humans, *Homo sapiens*, from the common chimpanzee, *Pan troglodytes*, and attempting to identify the time periods in the archaeological and paleontological record when these distinctively human traits first appeared. As Isaac himself acknowledged in his recent papers (e.g. Isaac 1984), there was a strong tendency to extrapolate the modern traits as far back into the record as possible. The earliest hominids were credited with complex social, intellectual, and technological abilities, not quite at the level of modern hunter-gatherers, but recognizably "human" nonetheless.

More recently, there has been a reassessment of the archaeological evidence for, and interpretations of, early hominid behavior (Binford 1981; Isaac 1984; Potts 1984; Shipman 1983; Zihlman 1983). Although the study of human evolution often has been characterized by heated debate, not all of it enlightening, these recent attempts to test fundamental archaeological assumptions and to develop alternative ways of explaining the material evidence have been, in Isaac's own words, "liberating" and an "exciting exercise of alternating leaps of imagination with rigorous testing" (Isaac 1980, p. 66). Most of these new problem-oriented studies and experimental investigations of the processes that produce archaeological remains are beyond the range of this review, but the recognition that early hominids may have been very different in lifeway from modern humans has also been liberating from the perspective of sex role reconstruction. And the most important aspect of this minor paradigmatic revolution for women's roles concerns the new interpretations of bone-and-artifact associations, or what were traditionally known as "home bases."

Isaac, it will be recalled, had developed a "sharing" model which was founded on the fact that in the early East African sites of around two million years ago, tools are found in dense patches in association with the bony remains of many animal species. Both stones and bones appear to have been transported to "central locations." Beginning with this one piece of material evidence, Isaac suggested that humans carried food and possessions to consistent locations as part of a social system involving home bases, division of labor, hunting and gathering, substantial meat eating, food sharing, and food preparation. As Potts (1984) has noted, Isaac's model could as appropriately have been entitled a "home base" model as a "sharing" model, since all the other social characteristics are constructed upon the initial interpretation that stone-bone associations are evidence of "social and industrial foci in the lives of the early hominid tool-makers to which food was brought for collective consumption" (Isaac 1984, p. 24).

Several researchers (e.g. Binford 1981; Potts 1984) have now challenged the home base interpretation. Binford (1981) analyzed some of the published evidence from Olduvai Gorge to argue that the "so-called" living sites or home bases were in fact the remains of carnivore activities. Isaac (1984) countered that the published data sets on which Binford worked were declared by their author (M. D. Leakey) to be incomplete and preliminary, and that Binford had not accounted for the fact that the bone assemblages come from patches in which thousands of humans artifacts (tools) also occur. Thus Potts's (1984) detailed, first-hand analysis of the Olduvai Gorge and Koobi Fora stone-bone concentrations was to be very influential.

Potts came to a different, but nonetheless startling, conclusion from both Binford and Isaac about the processes which formed the bone-stone tool assemblages. He argued that the animal bones at these sites were marked *both* by carnivore teeth and by stone tools, including tooth marks from gnawing and cutmarks made by slicing, scraping, and chopping with stone. Somehow, both early hominids and large carnivores were active at these locations, in some cases upon the same parts of the carcass, even the same bones. However, it is not whole carcasses of animals that are represented and the bones were not completely processed for meat and marrow, suggesting that hominids were abandoning considerable portions of the available food. Finally, the incredible density of bones at some of the sites and the patterns of weathering indicate bone accumulation spanning 5-10 years. All four factors according to Potts, argue against a home base interpretation of the sites. The presence of large carnivores would certainly have restricted the activities of early hominids at such locations, and surely campsites would never have been established in such unsafe places. Modern hunter-gatherers carry whole or nearly whole carcasses back to camp, not restricted portions, and they intensively modify the bones of animal food. Finally, hunter-gatherers rarely occupy a campsite for a long period of time, and seldom reoccupy an old site. Thus Potts concluded that it is not possible to assume that the behaviors associated with home bases (sharing, division of labor) occurred at the early sites in Olduvai.

How then can one explain the presence of hominids at these sites? Potts argued that the sites represent stone tool caches and meat-processing locations. Because animal carcasses attract many meat-eaters, the hominids were forced to transport parts of the animal away from the original location where it was obtained either by scavenging or hunting. These portions of meat were taken to the nearest stone tool cache in the foraging area, where raw stone, manufactured tools, and bones remained from previous visits. Even chimpanzees are known to take food, in this case vegetable food, to consistent locations where tools have been left for processing (Boesch and Boesch 1981). It is hypothesized that the hominids processed the meat quickly with the stone tools in the cache and abandoned the site before direct confrontation occurred with the carnivores who were attracted to the remains. Thus, over the years, many remains of partially processed, gnawed bones and large numbers of stone tools were accumulated in one location. Such sites could represent the antecedents of home bases, but Potts believes that until hominids gained the controlled use of fire to make home bases safe from carnivores, and the first evidence of controlled use of fire is much more recent in the record, they may well have continued to sleep in trees and to range widely during the day as do the other primate species.

One implication of this new understanding of bone-and-artifact associations for early hominid sex roles is clear: if there is not evidence for home bases where the sick and the dependent waited for the well and the productive, then perhaps we can finally free our minds of the image of dawn-age women and children waiting at campsites for the return of their provisioners. Even though the sharing model and many other anthropological scenarios appear to be about a division of labor in which women return to camp with vegetables and men with meat, it has almost always been assumed that women would have been more tied to the campsites. Women and homes have been inextricably linked in our cultural imagery, and thus the shaking loose from the home base focus for early hominid social life may allow our imaginations to turn to alternative scenarios.

CONCLUSION: HOW CAN WE IMPROVE OUR RECONSTRUCTIONS OF EARLY HUMAN SOCIAL BEHAVIOR?

Given the necessarily limited evidence of social life and the correspondingly large role played by speculation in the endeavor to reconstruct early hominid society, it seems appropriate to ask if it is worth doing at all. As I have pointed, out many primatologists and anthropologists oppose such modeling, often for different reasons than the one offered by Evans-Pritchard some years ago (Evans-Pritchard 1965), that it is a waste of time to speculate upon unanswerable questions. Yet origin myths exist in all societies, leading me to suspect that humans have "wasted their time" in just this manner ever since self-awareness became one of the hominid characteristics. Indeed, some scholars have argued that storytelling itself is a defining human trait (see Landau 1984); that "our need for chronological and causal connection defines and limits all of us—helps to make us what we are" (Scholes 1981, p. 207).

Furthermore, it is hard to imagine other sciences such as physics attempting to restrict themselves only to nonspeculative, empirically answerable questions. Pilbeam has argued that some unanswerable questions in paleoanthropology "still ought to be asked because they help to direct research efforts and channel thinking into fruitful pathways. The problem comes in knowing which unanswerable questions to ask" (Pilbeam 1980, p. 268). Elsewhere in the same article (and see Landau *et al.* 1982) Pilbeam made it clear that, in his opinion, reconstructions of early hominid behavior would be much improved through greater reference to the actual fossil and archaeological data. Because contemporary apes are not necessarily like fossil apes, and because the hominoid fossil record in any case is virtually nonexistent, Pilbeam has concluded that a comparative approach is not likely to yield fruitful theories. It should be added to Pilbeam's point about these models being "fossil-free" that few reconstructions, even ostensibly comparative ones, take complete or accurate account of the primate and ethnographic data that are available. Zihlman's most recent publications on the gathering model attempt to account for more of the data from all three sources than any other model I have seen, and yet her interpretation of early hominid life has received no more attention from the paleoanthropologists than other less "data-based" models.

Thus one answer that has been offered to the question of how theories of early hominid behavior can be improved is by giving them a firmer empirical foundation. However, it is clear that the data-bases of human evolution will always remain limited, and as Isaac has noted, the really important aspects of any model cannot be addressed "purely by recovering bones, stones, and pollen from layered prehistoric deposits" (Isaac 1984, p. 248). Isaac believed that there are two related routes to a fuller understanding of the dynamics of human evolution. The first is an emphasis on problem-oriented and experimental studies of the processes that might have led to characteristic archaeological remains by making use of analogous modern activities and environments. The second is that propositions should be expressed as a series of falsifiable, alternative hypotheses, and tests should involve attempts to overturn intuitively favored hypotheses. His suggestion was that reconstructions would be better served by each researcher providing a series of alternative models, rather than promoting and defending a single model.

Both Pilbeam's and Isaac's suggestions reflect the view that greater scientific rigor will solve, or help to solve, the problems of subjectivity in models of human evolution. But another analyst (Landau 1984) has suggested that it will probably be impossible to remove the subjective or "storytelling" element from evolutionary accounts. Landau argued that many scientific theories are essentially narratives, that is, the creative piecing together of an organized and plausible sequence of events by application of the imagination to standard forms. Particularly paleoanthropology with its description of the events of human evolution is, in her view, a form of storytelling, open to narrative analysis (see also Perper and Schrire 1977). Landau did not address the question of the part played by "fiction" in human evolution models which would be one implication of a literary analysis to which many scientists would object. But surely any modeler would agree that it takes creativity as well as data to create a plausible account of human evolution. And neither creative nor scientific minds function in a cultural vacuum. Landau's narrative analysis attempts to make some of the implicit structural guidelines of any human origins model explicit. I recount her approach here with the suggestion that the process of attempting to bring hidden assumptions and structures into the open will allow us, if not to eliminate or even agree upon them, at least to become critically aware of their potential presence and influence.

Landau took a structural approach that looks for common elements in the different versions of the human evolution story. For example, she identified four major events or episodes that are consistently emphasized by paleoanthropologists: a shift from trees to the ground (terrestriality); development of upright posture (bipedalism); the development of the brain, intelligence, and language (encephalization); and the development of technology, morals, and society (culture). She suggested that the question of which episode came first has been a major source of debate since Darwin, but in all versions the same episodes are recognized. She then argued that the diverse theories of what happened in human evolution actually follow a common narrative structure. This structure takes the form of a "hero story" in which the protagonist (= hominid) starts from humble origins on a journey in which he will be both *tested* by environmental stresses (savannah predators, etc) and by his own weaknesses (bipedalism, lack of biological armaments), and *gifted* by powerful agents (intelligence, technological inventions, social cooperation) until he is able to transform himself into a truly human hominid, the hero's final triumph which always ends the story.

Landau regards this approach to human evolution accounts not as a criticism but as a demonstration to scientists that they are interpreters of text as well as of nature, and as a potentially useful tool in comparing structural and conceptual differences between theories. If she is correct that human evolution theories follow a common narrative structure and adhere to a recognizable literary model (the hero's tale), which can be traced back through many centuries of European storytelling, this approach may give us some insight into why women generally play a subordinate role in these stories. For clearly the tale of the hero is about men and not heroines; women function in such stories either as secondary characters (mothers, sisters) related to the hero, or as potentially desirable sexual partners, often in need of rescue. If the contemporary Western raconteurs of human evolution had been raised in different narrative traditions, for example learning as children the enduring Chinese legend of the woman warrior, the female troubleslayer who rides into adventures carrying her infant in a sling inside her armor, then perhaps women would not have been so consistently restricted to the merely reproductive/domestic roles in our origin stories.

I have argued that one recurring theme in the human evolution accounts, from Darwin to Lovejoy, is that early men were the achievers, the producers, and technological innovators; whereas early women were limited by the reproductive demands of bearing and rearing children. Or as Sacks (1982) has put it: men make culture and women make babies, two mutually exclusive activities. Anthropologists have long applied sets of dichotomous attributes to the roles of men and women in human society: public/domestic, productive/reproductive, culture/nature. However, a number of women anthropologists (e.g. Leacock 1978; Sacks 1982) have begun to challenge these dichotomies as being largely a reflection of the Western cultural belief in the opposition of the sexes that has been mistakenly generalized into a universal and "natural" human principle. These dichotomies are also present as hidden assumptions in most models of human origins, and yet we do not know how generally they express the human condition today, much less in the past. For example, foraging societies do not have secluded family units or households within the band, nor are women confined to campsites. Thus a discussion of public/male versus domestic/female spheres has not been a particularly insightful approach to understanding the lives of these people. If Potts (1984) is correct that our early ancestors lived without home bases, the domestic, "housebound" vision of early women becomes singularly inappropriate.

A similar inapplicability may exist for the productive/reproductive dichotomy. Does a foraging woman or a foraging society functionally compartmentalize human lives and activities into these two supposedly opposing realms, or is this merely an abstract and possibly ethnocentric conceptualization of how lives should be arranged? Is it necessary to assume, as does Lovejoy for example, that the human female's energy is so limited that productive activities must necessarily be detrimental to reproduction, that the behaviors involved in subsistence and child rearing are incompatible and mutually exclusive? One of the peculiar human phenomena that anthropologists have identified is that it is possible for people to widely and passionately hold cultural beliefs that are in direct contradiction to their social actions. I suggest that this is the case with our own cultural belief that the people who are reproductively engaged cannot be productively active, a tenet clearly belied by the sexual makeup of the workforce in our society today. When Spencer first articulated this "ideal" in Victorian England (called by historians the "cult of female domesticity"), women of the working classes were widely employed in industry at the same time as they were reproducing at a rate alarming to the social Darwinists. Indeed, in all social systems except those based on intensive agriculture or some forms of pastoralism, the same women who bear and rear offspring always have contributed actively to subsistence, and in many societies they are even more responsible for production than the men. The assumption of female domesticity has functioned as a pillar in the construction of most theories of human social evolution, and yet its accuracy and applicability have never been openly debated.

Theories of human origins do function as symbolic statements about and indeed prescriptions for human nature. By making the assumptions of any theory more explicit, one can test or debate them rather than continuing to act as though differences between models reflect only varying descriptions of the material evidence. When the evidence changes, as when gathering replaces hunting in economic importance, but the implications for men and women are seen to remain fundamentally the same, as when Man the Hunter becomes Man the Provider, it is clear that powerful cultural sex role expectations inform these reconstructions even more strongly than does material evidence.

Some readers may find it hard to accept that cultural beliefs and narrative traditions play a significant role in scientific models of human evolution. However, I would argue that the theories reviewed in this paper do combine the realms of science and of storytelling. If this is so, we can begin the useful exercise of learning to analyze how the two realms interact and overlap in a given model and how we can evaluate the model according to the criteria appropriate to each realm. To paraphrase Kermode (1967), if we cannot free ourselves of subjectivity, then we must attempt to make sense of it. People will not stop wanting to hear origin stories and scientists will not cease to write scholarly tales. But we can become aware of the symbolic content of our stories, for much as our theories are not independent of our beliefs, so our behavior is not independent of our theories of human society. In these origin tales we try to coax the material evidence into telling us about the past, but the narrative we weave about the past also tells us about the present.

SUMMARY

1. Scientific models of early human social life are not simply plausible inferences from the material evidence, but also function as statements of human nature. Such models rely heavily upon speculation, which often is culturally informed. Some social and natural scientists doubt the value of such theorizing.

2. Darwin developed the theory of sexual selection to account for secondary sex differences. Applying it to human traits, he argued that men were selected for courage, intelligence, and technological abilities, whereas women were selected for generalized maternal attributes, only acquiring intelligence secondarily through males.

3. Nineteenth century social theorists believed all societies go through common stages: promiscuity, matrilineality, and patrilineality. However, they disagreed on whether or not women benefit from increasing social control of human sexuality. The rejection of social Darwinism and the collection of systematic ethnographic data led to the abandonment of theorizing about human social evolution in anthropology until the 1960s.

4. Man the Hunter, a model drawn from primate, ethnographic, and archaeological evidence, became the dominant theory of the 1960-1980 period. Although differing from Darwin's scenario in evidence and concepts, Man the Hunter represents a continuation of his belief that only male traits were selected and that women play an insignificant part in human evolution.

5. A reappraisal of the primate, ethnographic, and material data led some anthropologists, most of them women, to propose a "countermodel" called Woman the Gatherer, in which gathering, sharing, and tool use were described as female inventions, crucial to the evolution of humans. Both hunting models and gathering models appeal to similar sources of evidence, yet present opposing and mutually exclusive accounts of human social evolution and thus of human nature.

6. The most widely discussed current theory, Lovejoy's male provisioning model, makes male gathering and the provision of sedentary, highly fecund, and monogamous females the central adaptation in human evolution, and is premised upon the supposed failure of pongid reproductive life history patterns.

7. Appeals to theorists to tie their models more closely to empirical evidence and to account for more of the evidence led to modifications, especially to the gathering model and to some extent to the hunting model, where the importance of scavenging was recognized. However, the resulting models have received no more attention than more speculative ones.

8. Isaac advocated more testing of experimental models with multiple hypotheses to increase the rigor of the models and to reduce the advocacy of modelers. Yet it seems unlikely that increased scientific data, or rigor, would solve the problem of subjective interpretations. Most of the important features that define sex-role differentiation are intangible.

9. If theories of human evolution are seen as narratives as well as scientific discourse, the literary analysis of the structure of origin stories might allow us to distinguish the subjective from the empirical, the art from the science. Reconstructions of the past are in some respects also reflections of the present.

ACKNOWLEDGEMENTS

This paper was written with the help of a Release-Time Grant from the Faculty of Arts, University of Alberta, and with the research and editorial assistance of Larry Fedigan. I thank C. Lanigan and N. Collinge for help with the manuscript, and NSERC (#A7723) for continuing support of my research.

REFERENCES

Ardrey, R. 1961. *African Genesis*, Dell, New York.

Ardrey, R. 1976. *The Hunting Hypothesis*, Atheneum, New York.

Bachofen, J. 1861. *Das Mutterrecht*, Benno Schwabe, Basel.

Badrian, A., and Badrian, N. 1984. Social organization of *Pan paniscus* in the Lomako Forest, Zaire, in: *The Pygmy Chimpanzee: Evolutionary Biology and Behavior* (R. L. Susman, Ed.), pp. 325-345, Plenum, New York.

Berndt, C. H. 1981. Interpretations and "facts" in Aboriginal Australia, in: *Woman the Gatherer* (F. Dahlberg, Ed.), pp. 153–203, Yale University Press, New Haven.

Binford, L. R. 1981. *Bones, Ancient Men and Modern Myths*, Academic, New York.

Blanc, M. 1983. La bipedie, une affaire de sexe? *Recherche* 141:240–243.

Boesch, C., and Boesch, H. 1981. Sex differences in the use of natural hammers by wild chimpanzees. *J. Hum. Evol.* 10:585–593.

Brace, C. L. 1973. Sexual dimorphism in human evolution. *Yearb. Phys. Anthropol.* 16:31–49.

Cann, R. L., and Wilson, A. C. 1982. Models of human evolution. *Science* 211:303–304.

Crook, J. H. 1980. *The Evolution of Human Consciousness*, Clarendon, Oxford.

Cucchiari, S. 1981. The gender revolution and the transition from bisexual horde to patrilocal band, in: *Sexual Meanings. The Cultural Construction of Gender and Sexuality* (S. B. Ortner and H. Whitehead, Eds.), pp. 31–79, Cambridge University Press, Cambridge.

Dahlberg, F., Ed. 1981. *Woman the Gatherer*, Yale University Press, New Haven.

Dahlberg, F. 1981. Introduction, in: *Woman the Gatherer* (F. Dahlberg, Ed.), pp. 1–33, Yale University Press, New Haven.

Darwin, C. 1936a (orig. 1871). *The Descent of Man and Selection in Relation to Sex*, Modern Library, New York.

Darwin, C. 1936b (orig. 1859). *The Origin of Species*, Modern Library, New York.

Debetz, G. F. 1961. The social life of early paleolithic man as seen through the work of Soviet anthropologists, in: *Social Life of Early Man* (S. L. Washburn, Ed.), pp. 137–175, Aldine, Chicago.

Deetz, J. 1968. Hunters in archeological perspective, in: *Man the Hunter* (R. B. Lee and I. DeVore, Eds.), pp. 281–285, Aldine, New York.

DeVore, I., and Washburn, S. L. 1963. Baboon ecology and human evolution, in: *African Ecology and Human Evolution* (F. C. Howell and F. Bourliere, Eds.), pp. 335–367, Aldine, Chicago.

Ember, C. 1978. Myths about hunter-gatherers. *Ethnology* 17:439–448.

Engels, F. 1972 (orig. 1884). *The Origin of the Family, Private Property and the State. In the Light of the Researches of Lewis Henry Morgan*, Int. Publ., New York.

Estioko-Griffin, A., and Griffin, P. B. 1981. Woman the hunter: the Agta, in: *Woman the Gatherer* (F. Dahlberg, Ed.), pp. 121–151, Yale University Press, New Haven.

Evans-Pritchard, E. E. 1965. *Theories of Primitive Religion*, Clarendon, Oxford.

Fedigan, L. M. 1982. *Primate Paradigms. Sex Roles and Social Bonds*, Eden, Montreal.

Fee, E. 1976. Science and the woman problem: Historical perspectives, in: *Sex Differences, Social and Biological Perspectives* (M. S. Teutelbaum, ed.) pp. 175–223, Anchor, Garden City.

Fernandez, C. A., and Lynch, F. S. J. 1972. The Tasaday: Cave dwelling food gatherers of South Cotabato, Mindenao. *Philip. Soc. Rev.* 20:279–330.

Fisher, H. E. 1982. *The Sex Contract. The Evolution of Human Behavior*, Quill, New York.

Fox, J. R. 1967. *Kinship and Marriage*, Penguin, Baltimore.

Freeman, L., Jr. 1968. A theoretical framework for interpreting archeological materials, in: *Man the Hunter* (R. B. Lee and I. DeVore, Eds.), pp. 262–267, Aldine, New York.

Friedl, E. 1975. *Women and Men. An Anthropological View*, Holt, Rinehart and Winston, New York.

Friedl, J., and Pfeiffer, J. E. 1977. *Anthropology. The Study of People*, College Press, New York.

Galdikas, B. M. F., and Teleki, G. 1981. Variations in subsistence activities of female and male pongids: New perspectives on the origins of hominid labor division. *Curr. Anthropol.* 22:241–320.

Gayle, F., Ed. 1978. *Women's Role in Aboriginal Society*, Aust. Inst. Aboriginal Studies, Canberra.

Goodall, J. 1968. The behavior of freeliving chimpanzees of the Gombe Stream Reserve. *Anim. Behav. Monogr.* 1:161–311.

Goodall, J. 1976. Continuities between chimpanzee and human behavior, in: *Human Origins. Louis Leakey and the East African Evidence*, (G. Isaac and E. R. McCown, Eds.), pp. 81–95, Benjamin, Menlo Park, CA.

Gould, R. A. 1981. Comparative ecology of food-sharing in Australia and Northwest California, in: *Omnivorous Primates. Gathering and Hunting in Human Evolution* (R. S. O. Harding and G. Teleki, Eds.), pp. 422–454, Columbia University Press, New York.

Hamburg, D. A. 1968. Primate behavior and the evolution of aggression, in: *Man the Hunter* (R. B. Lee and I. DeVore, Eds.), pp. 339–341, Aldine, New York.

Hamburg, D. A., and McCown, E. R., Eds. 1979. *The Great Apes, Perspectives on Human Evolution*, Vol. 5, Cummings, Menlo Park, CA.

Harding, R. S. O., and Teleki, G., Eds. 1981. *Omnivorous Primates. Gathering and Hunting in Human Evolution*, Columbia University Press, New York.

Harley, D. 1982. Models of human evolution (letter). *Science* 211:296.

Hayden, B. 1981. Subsistence and ecological adaptations of modern hunter-gatherers, in: *Omnivorous Primates. Gathering and Hunting in Human Evolution* (R. S. O. Harding and G. Teleki, Eds.), pp. 344–421, Columbia University Press, New York.

Hiatt, B. 1978. Woman the Gatherer, in: *Women's Role in Aboriginal Society* (F. Gayle, Ed.), pp. 4–15, Aust. Inst. Aboriginal Studies, Canberra.

Hill, K. 1982. Hunting and human evolution. *J. Hum. Evol.* 11:521–544.

Isaac, G. 1971. The diet of early man: Aspects of archeological evidence from lower and middle Pleistocene sites in Africa. *World Archeol.* 2:278–299.

Isaac, G. 1978. The food-sharing behavior of protohuman hominids. *Sci. Am.* 238:90–106.

Isaac, G. 1980. Casting the net wide: A review of archeological evidence for early hominid land-use and ecological relations, in: *Current Argument on Early Man* (L. K. Konigsson, Ed.), pp. 226–251, Pergamon, Oxford.

Isaac, G. 1982. Models of human evolution (letter). *Science* 211:295.

Isaac, G. 1984. The archeology of human origins: Studies of the lower Pleistocene in East Africa 1971–1981, in: *Advances in World Archaeology* (F. Wendorf and A. E. Close, Eds.), pp. 1–87, Academic Press, Orlando.

Isaac, G., and Crader, D. 1981. To what extent were early hominids carnivorous? An archeological perspective, in: *Omnivorous Primates. Gathering and Hunting in Human Evolution* (R. S. O. Harding and G. Teleki, Eds.), pp. 37–103, Columbia University Press, New York.

Johanson, D. C., and White, T. D. 1979. A systematic assessment of early hominids. *Science* 203:321–330.

Kermode, F. 1967. *The Sense of an Ending*, Oxford University Press, Oxford.

Kuroda, S. 1984. Interaction over food among pygmy chimpanzees, in: *The Pygmy Chimpanzee: Evolutionary Biology and Behavior* (R. L. Susman Ed.), pp. 301–323, Plenum, New York.

Lancaster, J. B. 1975. *Primate Behavior and the Emergence of Human Culture*, Holt, Rinehart and Winston, New York.

Lancaster, J. B. 1976. Sex roles in primate societies, in: *Sex Differences, Social and Biological Perspectives* (M. S. Teutelbaum, Ed.), pp. 22–61, Anchor, Garden City.

Lancaster, J. B. 1978. Carrying and sharing in human evolution. *Hum. Nat.* 1:82–89.

Landau, M. 1984. Human evolution as narrative. *Am. Sci.* 72:262–268.

Landau, M., Pilbeam, D., and Richard, A. 1982. Human origins a century after Darwin. *Bioscience* 32:507–12.

Laughlin, W. S. 1968. Hunting. An integrating biobehavior system and its evolutionary importance, in: *Man the Hunter* (R. B. Lee and I. DeVore, Eds.), pp. 304–320, Aldine, New York.

Leacock, E. B. 1972. Introduction, in: *The Origin of the Family, Private Property and the State. In the Light of the Researches of Lewis Henry Morgan*, pp. 7–67, Int. Publ., New York.

Leacock, E. B. 1978. Women's status in egalitarian society: Implications for social evolution. *Curr. Anthropol.* 19:247–75.

Leakey, R. E. 1981. *The Making of Mankind*, Dutton, New York.

Lee, R. B. 1968. What hunters do for a living, or, how to make out on scarce resources, in: *Man the Hunter* (R. B. Lee and I. DeVore, Eds.), pp. 30–48, Aldine, New York.

Lee, R. B. 1974. Male-female residence arrangements and political power in human hunter-gatherers. *Arch. Sex Behav.* 3:167–173.

Lee, R. B. 1979. *The Dobe !Kung*, Holt, Rinehart and Winston, New York.

Lee, R. B. 1980. Lactation, ovulation and women's work, in: *Biosocial Mechanisms of Population Regulation* (M. N. Cohen, R. S. Malpass, and H. G. Klein, Eds.), pp. 321–348, Yale University Press, New Haven.

Lee, R. B., and DeVore, I., Eds. 1968a. *Man the Hunter*, Aldine, New York.

Lee, R. B., and DeVore, I. 1968b. Problems in the study of hunters and gatherers, in: *Man the Hunter* (R. B. Lee and I. DeVore, Eds.), pp. 3–12, Aldine, New York.

Lee, R. B., and DeVore, I. 1976. *Kalahari Hunter-Gatherers*, Harvard University Press, Cambridge.

Leibowitz, L. 1983. Origins of the sexual division of labor, in: *Women's Nature. Rationalization of Inequality* (M. Lowe, R. Hubbard, Eds.), pp. 123–147, Pergamon, New York.

Levi-Strauss, C. 1949. *The Elementary Structures of Kinship*, Beacon Press, Boston.

Linton, S. 1971. Women the gatherer: Male bias in anthropology. In *Women in Perspective—A guide for Cross-Cultural Studies* (S. E. Jacobs, Ed.), pp. 9–21, University of Illinois Press, Urbana.

Lovejoy, C. O. 1981. The origin of man. *Science* 211:341–50.

Lubbock, J. 1873 (orig. 1870). *The Origin of Civilization and the Primitive Condition of Man: Mental and Social Conditions of Savages*, New York, Appleton.

Maccoby, E. E., and Jacklin, C. N. 1974. *The Psychology of Sex Differences*, Stanford University Press, Stanford.

Maine, H. 1861. *Ancient Law*, Murray, London.

Mann, A. E. 1975. *Paleodemographic aspects of the South African Australopithecines*, University of Pennsylvania Publ. Anthropol. No. 1, Philadelphia.

Mann, A. E. 1981. Diet and human evolution, in: *Omnivorous Primates. Gathering and Hunting in Human Evolution* (R. S. O. Harding and G. Teleki, Eds.), pp. 10–36, Columbia University Press, New York.

Martin, M. K., and Voorhies, B. 1975. *Female of the Species*, Columbia University Press, New York.

McGrew, W. C. 1979. Evolutionary implications of sex differences in chimpanzee predation and tool use, in: *The Great Apes, Perspectives on Human Evolution, Vol. 5* (D. A. Hamburg and E. R. McCown, Eds.), pp. 441–463, Cummings, Menlo Park, CA.

McGrew, W. C. 1981. The female chimpanzee as a human evolutionary prototype, in: *Woman the Gatherer* (F. Dahlberg, Ed.), pp. 35–73, Yale University Press, New Haven.

McHenry, H. M. 1982. The pattern of human evolution: Studies on bipedalism, mastication, and encephalization. *Ann. Rev. Anthropol.* 11:151–173.

McLennan, J. 1865. *Primitive Marriage: An Inquiry into the Origin of the Form of Capture in Marriage Ceremonies*, Black, Edinburgh.

Morgan, L. H. 1870. *System of Consanguinity and Affinity of the Human Family*, GPO, Washington, D.C.

Morgan, L. H. 1877. *Ancient Society*, World Publ., New York.

Morris, D. 1967. *The Naked Ape*, Trinity, London.

Nelson, H., and Jurmain, R. 1985. *Introduction to Physical Anthropology*, 3rd Ed., West Publ., St. Paul.

Perper, T., and Schrire, C. 1977. The Nimrod connection: Myth and science in the hunting model, in: *The Chemical Senses and Nutrition* (M. K. Kare and O. Maller, Eds.), pp. 447–459, Academic, New York.

Pfeiffer, J. E. 1972. *The Emergence of Man*, Harper and Row, New York.

Pilbeam, D. 1980. Major trends in human evolution, in: *Current Argument on Early Man* (L. K. Konigsson, Ed.), pp. 261–285, Pergamon, Oxford.

Potts, R. 1984. Home bases and early hominids. *Am. Sci.* 72:338–347.

Quinn, N. 1977. Anthropological studies on women's status. *Ann. Rev. Anthropol.* 6:181–225.

Radcliffe-Brown, A. R. 1930. Social organization of Australian tribes. *Oceania Monogr.* No. 1.

Ralls, K. 1977. Sexual dimorphism in mammals: Avian models and unanswered questions. *Am. Nat.* 111:917–938.

Reed, E. 1975. *Woman's Evolution*, Pathfinder, New York.

Reynolds, V. 1966. Open groups in hominid evolution. *Man* 1(NS):441–452.

Sacks, K. 1982. *Sisters and Wives*, University of Chicago Press, Chicago.

Sahlins, M. D. 1960. The origin of society. *Sci. Am.* 203:76–86.

Schneider, D. M. 1968. Are the hunter-gatherers a cultural type? Discussions, in: *Man the Hunter* (R. B. Lee and I. DeVore, Eds.), pp. 341–342, Aldine, New York.

Scholes, R. 1981. Language, narrative and antinarrative, in: *On Narrative* (W. J. T. Mitchell, Ed.), pp. 200–208, University of Chicago Press, Chicago.

Schrire, C. 1980. An inquiry into the evolutionary status and apparent identity of San hunter-gatherers. *Hum. Ecol.* 8:9–32.

Senut, B., and Tardieu, C. 1981. Functional aspects of Plio-Pleistocene hominid limb bones: Implications for taxonomy and phylogeny, in: *Ancestors. The Hard Evidence* (E. Delson, Ed.), Liss, New York.

Service, E. R. 1962. *Primitive Social Organization. An Evolutionary Perspective*, Random House, New York.

Service, E. R. 1966. *The Hunters*, Prentice Hall, Englewood Cliffs.

Shipman, P. 1983. Early hominid lifestyle: Hunting and gathering or foraging and scavenging, in: *Animals and Archaeology*. 1st Ed. (J. Clutton-Brock and C. Grigson, Eds.), 31–49, British Archaeol. Rep., Oxford.

Silk, J. B. 1978. Patterns of food sharing among mother and infant chimpanzees at Gombe Stream National Park, Tanzania. *Folia Primatol.* 29:129–141.

Spencer, H. 1873. Psychology of the sexes. *Sci. Monthly* 4:31–32.

Stern, J., and Susman, R.L. 1983. The locomotor anatomy of *Australopithecus afarensis*. *Am. J. Phys. Anthropol.* 60:279–285.

Symons, D. 1979. *The Evolution of Human Sexuality*, Oxford University Press, Oxford.

Tanner, N. M. 1981. *On Becoming Human*, Cambridge University Press, Cambridge.

Tanner, N. M., and Zihlman, A. 1976. Women in evolution. Part I: Innovation and selection in human origins. *Signs* 1:585–608.

Tardieu, C. 1983. L'articulation de genou: Analyse morphogonctionnelle hez les primates et les hominides fossiles. *Cah. Paleoanthropol.* CNRS, Paris.

Teleki, G. 1973. *The Predatory Behavior of Wild Chimpanzees*, Bucknell University Press, Lewisburg, PA.

Testart, A. 1978. Les societes de chasseure-cueilleurs. *Pour la Sci.* 16:99–108.

Tiger, L. 1969. *Men in Groups*, Random House, New York.

Tiger, L., and Fox, R. 1971. *The Imperial Animal*, Dell, New York.

Washburn, S. L. 1961. *Social Life of Early Man*, Aldine, Chicago.

Washburn, S. L., and Ciochon, R. L. 1976. Canine teeth: Notes on controversies in the study of human evolution. *Am. Anthropol.* 76:765–784.

Washburn, S. L., and DeVore, I. 1961. Social behavior of baboons and early man, in: *Social Life of Early Man* (S. L. Washburn, Ed.), pp. 91–103, Aldine, Chicago.

Washburn, S. L., and Lancaster, C. S. 1968. The evolution of hunting, in: *Man the Hunter* (R. B. Lee and I. DeVore, Eds.), pp. 293–303, Aldine, New York.

Whyte, M. K. 1978. *The Status of Women in Preindustrial Societies*, Princeton University Press, Princeton, NJ.

Wolfe, L. D., Gray, J. P., Robinson, J. G., Lieberman, L. S., and Peter, E. H. 1982. Models of human evolution (letter). *Science* 217:302.

Wood, J. 1982. Models of human evolution (letter). *Science* 211:297–298.

Wrangham, R. W. 1979. Sex differences in chimpanzee dispersion, in: *The Great Apes, Perspectives on Human Evolution*, Vol. 5 (D. A. Hamburg and E. R. McCown, Eds.), pp. 481–489, Cummings, Menlo Park, CA.

Yellen, J. E. 1976. Settlement patterns of the !Kung An archeological perspective, in: *Kalahari Hunter-Gatherers* (R. B. Lee and I. DeVore, Eds.), pp. 48-72, Harvard University Press, Cambridge.

Zihlman, A. L. 1976. Sexual dimorphism and its behavioral implications in early hominids, in: *Les Plus Anciens Hominides* (P. V. Tobias and Y. Coppens, Eds.), 4:1-36, CNRS, Paris.

Zihlman, A. L. 1978a. Women in evolution, Part II: Subsistence and social organization among early hominids. *Signs* 4:4-20.

Zihlman, A. L. 1978b. Motherhood in transition from ape to human, in: *The First Child and Family Formation* (W. B. Miller and L. F. Newman, Eds.), pp. 35-50, Carolina Popul. Cent., Chapel Hill.

Zihlman, A. L. 1981. Women as shapers of human adaptation, in: *Woman the Gatherer* (F. Dahlberg, Ed.), pp. 75-120, Yale University Press, New Haven.

Zihlman, A. L. 1982. *What happened to Woman the Gatherer?* Presented at Am. Anthropol. Assoc. Meeting, Washington, DC.

Zihlman, A. L. 1983. A behavioral reconstruction of *Australopithecus*, in: *Hominid Origins. Inquiries Past and Present* (K. J. Reichs, Ed.), pp. 207-238, University Press of America, Washington, DC.

Zihlman, A. L. 1984. Pygmy chimps, people and the pundits. *New Sci.* 104:39-40.

Zihlman, A. L. 1985. Gathering stories for hunting human nature. *Feminist Studies* 11:364-377.

Zihlman, A. L. 1986. *Australopithecus afarensis*, two sexes or two species? in: *Hominid Evolution: The Past, Present, and Future* (P. V. Tobias, Ed.), Liss, New York.

Zihlman, A. L., Cronin, J. E., Cramer, D. L., and Sarich, V. M. 1978. Pygmy chimpanzee as a possible prototype for the common ancestor of humans, chimpanzees and gorillas. *Nature* 275:744-746.

Zihlman, A. L., and Tanner, N. 1978. Gathering and the hominid adaptation, in: *Female Hierarchies* (L. Tiger and H. T. Fowler, Eds.), pp. 163-194, Beresford, Chicago.

24

Aspects Of Human Evolution

G. Ll. Isaac

Understanding the literature on human evolution calls for the recognition of special problems that confront scientists who report on this topic. Regardless of how the scientists present them, accounts of human origins are read as replacement materials for genesis. They fulfill needs that are reflected in the fact that all societies have in their culture some form of origin beliefs, that is, some narrative or configurational notion of how the world and humanity began. Usually, these beliefs do more than cope with curiosity, they have allegorical content, and they convey values, ethics and attitudes. The Adam and Eve creation story of the Bible is simply one of a wide variety of such poetic formulations.

We are conscious of a great change in all this, starting in the eighteenth and nineteenth centuries. The scientific movement which culminated in Darwin's compelling formulation of evolution as a mode of origin, seemed to sweep away earlier beliefs and relegate them to the realm of myth and legend. Following on from this, it is often supposed that the myths have been replaced by something quite different, which we call 'science'. However, this is only partly true; scientific theories and information about human origins have been slotted into the same old places in our minds and our cultures that used to be occupied by the myths. The information component has then inevitably been expanded to fill the same needs. Our new origin beliefs are in fact surrogate myths, that are themselves part science, part myths.

It is also true that the study of human evolution is a meeting ground of science and humanism. We can and should seek to be rigorous in our testing of propositions and hypotheses so that we achieve an expanding corpus of secure information and orderly knowledge—but as I have already indicated, the meaning that people attach to these findings will surely be affected in subtle and complex ways by variations in individual experience of humanity and by the ethos of the times. Just as historians expect to have to rewrite continuously the comprehension of history, so will consumers of human evolution evidence want to re-evaluate the meaning of their 'facts'.

Clear examples of myth-making extensions of scientific information include the embellishment of the man-the-hunter theme. Archaeology does provide strong indications of early hominid involvement in the acquisition and consumption of meat from large animals. However, romantic and symbolic meanings that go far beyond the empirical information have commonly been attached to the evidence. In fact, themes that are common in folklore, mythology and the scriptures are unconsciously attached to the archaeological findings (cf. Morgan 1972; Perper and Schrire 1977). Similarly, in recent years, in order to redress the imbalances of years of unconscious male bias in versions of the story of human evolution, women writers have set forth female-gathering hypotheses as rivals. Various of these are perfectly plausible and deserve to be tested, but meanwhile they clearly have the same social function as legitimizing myths. Further evidence of the emotional charge that attaches to the form and content of interpretations of human evolution can be seen in the reception given to sociobiology. People clearly do want to be free to choose their evolutionary origin stories. Bear this in mind as you read this and other accounts of human evolution.

As a starting point, I am going to take a question: What has science learned about human evolution that was not known to Charles Darwin when in 1871 he wrote *The Descent of Man*? I shall then go on to look briefly at some points of current debate, and at lines of enquiry that are now getting under way.

In 1871 the Neanderthal and Gibraltar skulls were the only significant human fossils known. In his 1863 essay, *Man's Place in Nature*, Huxley had already shown that the Neanderthal form was effectively a variant of the human type rather than an evolutionary link, so that Darwin's concept of human evolution was of necessity 'fossil free' (cf. Pilbeam 1980). Darwin based his ideas on comparative anatomy plus what little was known of the natural history of apes, plus a general knowledge of human behaviour patterns (augmented by his own ethnographic observations during the voyage of the *Beagle*). Darwin's notions were configurational rather than fully narrative (Fig. 1). He envisaged a series of interconnected ingredients which promoted or had been promoted by natural selection to produce humanity. The key elements were non-arboreal habitat plus upright bipedal stance with the hands free. Darwin perceived this condition to be helpless and defenseless, and he envisaged two concurrent lines of evolutionary solution—the use of the hands to make and wield tools and weapons plus the development of '. . . social qualities which lead him to give and receive aid from his fellow men'. To this mix was added 'the natural selection arising from the competition of tribe with tribe . . . together with the inherited effects of habit, . . . which . . . would under favourable conditions have sufficed to raise man to his present high position in the organic scale'. Darwin wrote 'The small strength and speed of man, his want of natural weapons are more than counterbalanced . . . by his intellectual powers,

Reprinted from *Evolution from Molecules to Men*, edited by D. Bendall, pp. 509-543, Cambridge University Press, New York. Copyright © 1983 by Cambridge University Press, New York.

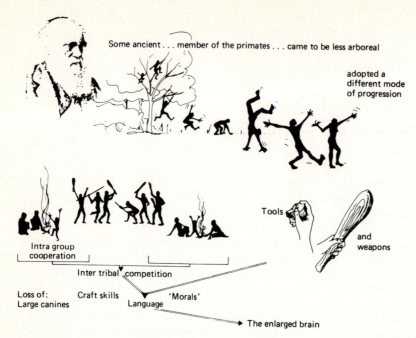

Some ancient . . . member of the primates . . . came to be less arboreal

adopted a different mode of progression

Intra group cooperation

Inter tribal competition

Loss of: Large canines

Craft skills

Language

'Morals'

Tools

and weapons

The enlarged brain

Figure 1. *Darwin's concept of human evolution involved an initial event, 'leaving the trees', followed by the adoption of a bipedal stance with hands free. Natural selection then acted on a system of adaptation that involved tools, weapons, social cooperation and tribal warfare . . . finally delivering an animal with an enlarged brain and a strong moral sense.*

through which he has formed for himself weapons, tools etc'. One can thus read Darwin's writing as arguing both that the brain led the way in evolutionary change and also that it followed. For this reason the elements are best viewed as a configuration rather than a narrative. However, there is one storyline, namely that the process began with leaving the trees and adopting an upright stance.

So, in *The Descent of Man*, there is a first approximation that brought a whole series of potentially important topics and issues up for consideration: habitat shifts, bipedalism, tool use and social systems involving reciprocal altruism...to say nothing of group selection. As I shall show, with the exception of group selection, these elements are still part of discourse; they contend for pride of place in explanation, they are all subjects of active investigation and we have by no means yet succeeded in evaluating their interaction, or their relative importance. It might well be asked, what in that case is new? In reply one can best respond that since Darwin, there have been surges of growth in several major fields of inquiry that relate closely to understanding human evolution:

(1) recovery of fossil hominoids and hominids;

(2) excavation of archaeological evidence covering two or three million years of co-evolution of brain and culture;

(3) field studies of primate behaviour and ecology;

(4) analytic studies of the ecology and social systems of human hunter-gatherers;

(5) effective inquiry into climatic and environmental changes over the past several million years;

(6) biochemical measurement of degrees of relatedness;

(7) the growth of explicit theory concerning evolutionary ecology and concerning relations between social systems, ecology and population genetics.

Several of these lines have developed only in the last 10 or 20 years and their eventual implications for our understanding of human evolution have not yet been fully worked out.

My own research is on archaeological evidence for early stages in the differentiation of human-like behaviour patterns, and because a short review cannot be comprehensive, I am going to focus on the study of the past, rather than on the implications of neontological studies.

BIOCHEMICAL EVIDENCE

The rise of biochemistry and molecular biology has led to the development of rigorous, quantitative information on degrees of relationship (Fig. 2). This in turn calls both for revisions to the family tree and for some careful thinking about interpretations of the fragmentary fossil record. There has been heated debate over both these issues, but rearguard actions apart, the battle now appears to be over, in favour of the biochemistry.

Figure 2 summarizes the evidence that the human lineage diverged from a common ancestor with African apes no more than four to six, or seven million years ago. Chimpanzees and gorillas emerge as sibling species with humans.

If rather than molecules, the physiology and behaviour of humans is compared with that of their close living relatives, then particularly important contrasts can be seen in three, or maybe four, systems.

(1) The *locomotor system* with modifications especially of the foot, pelvic complex, the back and the hands.

(2) The *socio-reproductive system*, with human females losing conspicuous oestrus and concealing ovulation, and with the males investing in the feeding of offspring and mates.

(3) The *brain-speech-technology-culture system*, involving an enlarged modified brain, prolonged infancy with an extended learning period, during which young humans must assimilate language, the making and using of tools and complex bodies of customs, rules and information.

(4) The *food choice-masticatory and digestive system*. Modern humans tend to eat a rather different diet from apes with strong biases towards including more animal tissue and

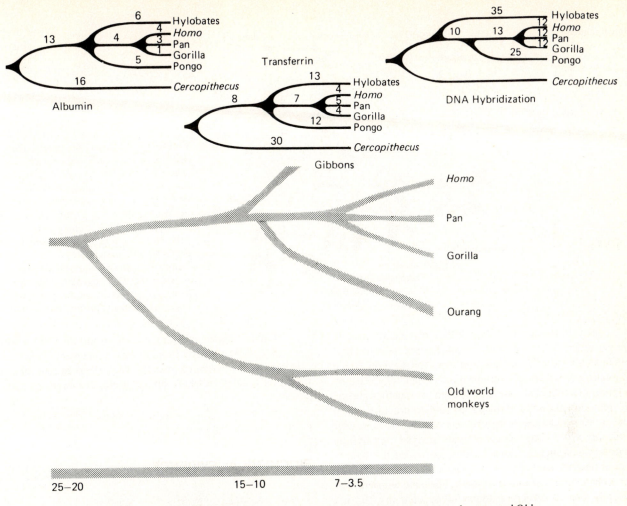

Figure 2. *Biochemical evidence concerning degrees of relatedness among the apes and Old World monkeys. Along the top are examples of a series of molecule types for which comparative matrices have been determined. From these matrices trees can be drawn showing branching sequence and quantitative estimates of differences attributed to each internode. Taken together, these and other biochemical determinations provide unambiguous evidence of the branching sequence shown below. Given strong evidence of stochastic consistency in the rates of cumulative change, estimates of divergence times can be offered. The time scale is a 'rubber ruler', which can be proportionately stretched or shrunk, but if this portion of the overall vertebrate phylogenetic tree were to be stretched beyond the limits shown, one would have great difficulty accommodating the estimates for divergence times in the rest of the Mammalia and Vertebrata. (Based on Sarich & Cronin 1976; see also Wilson, Carlson and White 1977 for a review).*

more starch. Relative to apes, humans have small front teeth and thick-enamelled back teeth. This was even more pronounced at an early stage in hominoid divergence.

Accepting these contrasts, students of human evolution are then confronted by a number of questions. What was the common ancestral condition? When did each of these systems start to become modified? Under what circumstances did change occur? What have been the selection patterns favouring these trends of change? We are thus facing a challenge first to determine the sequence of changes, which I shall term the *narrative* and second to inquire into the mechanisms, which can be called the *dynamics*. It is the first of these that has commanded most explicit attention during century since Darwin, and indeed this is often treated as being synonymous with the study of human evolution. However, in recent years, curiosity about

mechanisms has become steadily more conspicuous and in the last part of this chapter I shall argue that it is here that some of the most exciting growing points in research are to be discerned.

NARRATIVE

For the past 100 years, most of the specific effort devoted to this branch of science has been in pursuit of missing chapters in the story. I will attempt, with the aid of diagrams, to provide a simplified summary of the sequence of changes as they are now known. However, before doing so, it is fun to be able to draw attention to a recent analysis of what goes on when scientists deal with origins.

Misia Landau (1981) has done a careful analysis of a series of accounts of human evolution starting with Darwin's own writings. She points out two main things: (1) the same elements

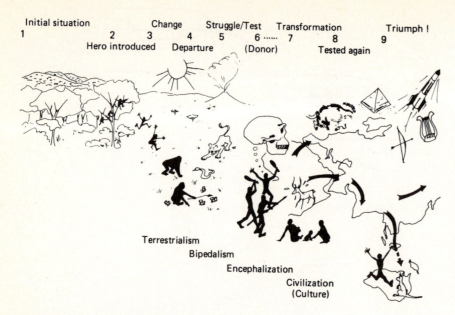

Initial situation Change Struggle/Test Transformation Triumph !
1 2 3 4 5 6 ······ 7 8 9
Hero introduced Departure (Donor) Tested again

Terrestrialism
Bipedalism
Encephalization
Civilization
(Culture)

Figure 3. *Accounts of human origins are almost invariably cast as narratives that follow the format of hero tales in folklore (Landau 1981). Here one common version is shown involving leaving the forest, struggling in the harsh savannah, being granted aid by a donor (natural selection) which promotes solutions in the form of brain enlargement, tools, hunting and social living. Final triumph takes the form of a spread across the globe and the development of art and civilization.*

tend to recur in the accounts though they may be arranged in different order. These elements or episodes are 'terrestriality' (coming to the ground), 'bipedalism', 'encephalization' (brain and intellect enlargement), 'civilization' (technology, custom, tradition, social morals, etc.); (2) although the specifics and the order may vary, the accounts tend to a common structure, which under scrutiny emerges as the structure of folkloric hero tales (cf. Propp 1968). One version of this analysis is playfully suggested in Figure 3. Misia Landau has called the literary genre of the narratives the 'anthropogenic'.

When I first read Landau's work, I became worried. Was there any way to present a sequential account that did not involve the hero-story structure? If not, did that disqualify study of the narrative of human evolution from being science?

I have got used to the idea now—and would counter-argue that provided the fit between the stories and empirical evidence is improvable through testing and falsification, then this is indeed science. (If any of the rest of the scientific community is inclined to snigger at the embarrassment of palaeoanthropologists over all this, pause and reflect. I bet that the same basic findings would apply to accounts of the origin of mammals, or of flowering plants, or of life . . . or even the big bang and the cosmos.)

One of the major developments since the time of Darwin has been the recovery of substantial numbers of hominoid and hominid fossils from all over the Old World. Our grasp of several phases of human evolution need no longer be fossil-free.

Figure 4 provides histograms that give some idea of the distribution of finds shown in relation to sequence of discovery and to time and geography. This summary chart deals with the romance of exploration and discovery as far as I intend to take it in this review. The legitimate excitement which scientists and lay folk alike feel over the finding of missing links, is thoroughly familiar from newspapers and magazines—as is the existence of still another involvement of palaeoanthropology with hero mythologies. (As an aside, it is also apparent from this popular literature that bits of old hominid bone arouse excitements quite beyond their information content. Our field has unwittingly got mixed up in latter-day sacred-ancestor fetishism!)

Figure 5 shows that for the last four million years a useful if still somewhat patchy fossil record of members of the family Hominidae has been recovered. We need more, but what we have is a handy start. A similar useful but patchy series of

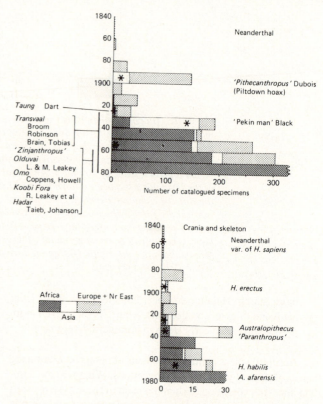

Figure 4. *The romance of discovery expressed as a histogram. Bars represent numbers of specimens recovered in each continent in each decade since 1840 (based on Oakley, Campbell & Mollison 1971-77). The upper frame shows all specimens, the lower shows only crania, maxillae, mandibles and ± whole skeletons. Major discoveries are indicated by place and person. The sequence is shown in which the various taxa were recovered. In general, the most human-like taxa were found first and this has affected interpretation (see Reader 1980). Records for 1970-80 are incomplete.*

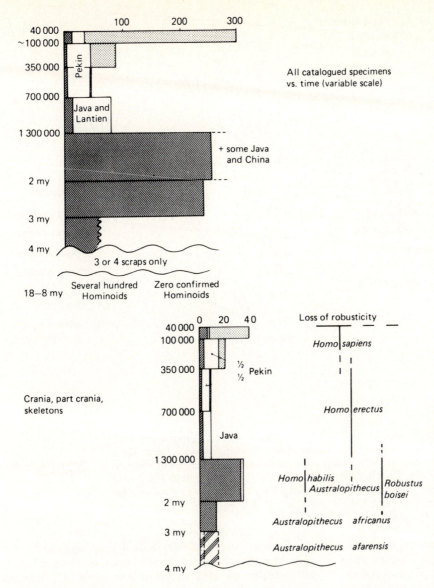

All catalogued specimens
vs. time (variable scale)

Pekin

Java and
Lantien

+ some Java
and China

3 or 4 scraps only

Several hundred Hominoids | Zero confirmed Hominoids

18–8 my

Crania, part crania,
skeletons

½ Pekin
½

Java

Loss of robusticity

Homo sapiens

Homo erectus

Homo habilis
Australopithecus   Robustus boisei

Australopithecus   africanus

Australopithecus   afarensis

Figure 5. *As for Fig. 4 but with specimen numbers shown relative to variable divisions of a chronometric time scale. The time ranges of taxa in common usage are also shown (bottom right). Note: Before about 1-2 mya all material comes from Africa while Europe dominates the Upper Pleistocene record because of the large number of caves which have been excavated there. These are mainly 'neanderthal' fossils.*

hominoid fossils has been recovered from the time range from about eighteen to eight million years ago. In spite of loudly enunciated early claims to the contrary, a consensus is now emerging that none of these earlier hominoids can be classified as members of the family Hominidae.

Between the Miocene and the Pliocene to Pleistocene fossil samples, there is a four to five million year gap, a period for which we have as yet virtually no hominoid fossils of any kind. This is the period during which the biochemical evidence would indicate that hominids, chimps and gorillas separated. Although we know more than Darwin did about the range of skeletal organization patterns that existed before divergence, our interpretation of the divergence itself is still obliged to be fossil free.

Perhaps 95% of the hominoid palaeontology literature deals directly or indirectly with taxonomy and naming. This is a necessary, but boring topic, and I propose to deal with it in diagrams (Fig. 6a, b). The genera represented here are clustered by Pilbeam into four families. Each of these can be thought of as a small-scale adaptive radiation. Drawing phyletic lines is much more speculative. Fig. 6b shows three schemes for deriv-

ing the later families (radiations) from the earlier ones. It should be noted that Scheme a, which has for a long time been confidently advocated by palaeontologists, is contradicted by the steadily strengthening corpus of biochemical evidence.

Note that while there is a four-million year record of fossil hominidae there is no record at all for the chimp or gorilla. Pilbeam (1980) has rightly pointed out that securing such a fossil record would be a major contribution to understanding human evolution.

Figure 7 presents a highly simplified summary of successive anatomical shifts that can be detected from the samples of hominid fossils which have so far been recovered. These span the time range four million years to the present. As I understand the record, it divides in two parts with the features of the first (4–2 mya) part being:

(1) The earliest known hominids were *fully bipedal* (although their feet, hands and shoulders may still have been more adapted for tree-climbing than are modern human limbs and extremities). All subsequent hominids were fully bipedal (Lovejoy 1978; McHenry and Temerin 1979).

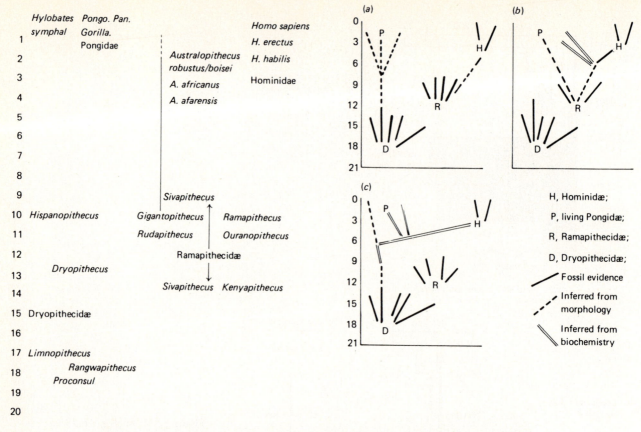

Figure 6. *Left: Described genera of fossil and living hominoids shown against a time scale with family groupings indicated (based on Pilbeam 1980 with modifications). Right: Three alternative phylogenetic schemes of which (a) is incompatible with the biochemical evidence. The hominid species are widely but not universally accepted (see Tobias 1980, White et al. 1981; Leakey 1981). Note: from biochemistry the living Pongidae emerge as a polyphyletic group.*

(2) The earliest hominids had *large cheek teeth with thick enamel* plus relatively small anterior teeth. Canines were reduced relative to both Dryopithecine apes and modern pongids, but in the very earliest sample series, *Australopithecus afarensis* these projected further than those of subsequent hominids (Wolpoff 1973, 1975, Johanson and White 1979, Wood 1981).

(3) The earliest hominids had brains the size of modern pongids in bodies that were probably a little smaller than modern ape bodies (Pilbeam and Gould 1974; Holloway 1981; Tobias 1981).

(4) Many workers feel that no known fossiliferous formation that dates to between 2.5 and 4 mya contains more than one sympatric species of hominid, though if this is true of the Hadar, then the early forms were as sexually dimorphic as gorillas. (For a contrary view see R. Leakey 1981, p. 70.)

At about two million years ago, the second part begins and the situation became more complex in interesting ways. Samples from all richly fossiliferous localities start to be differentiated into two (or perhaps more?) sympatric species. One of these forms shows a tendency to cheek tooth enlargement and to increase in body size (*Australopithecus robustus* in South Africa and *A. boisei* in East Africa). Others show some reduction in tooth size and a marked increase in cranial capacity (*Homo habilis*).

Between two and one million years ago in Africa, specimens of both species are often found in the same layers, but thereafter the ultra megadont form disappears from the record. The discovery of the existence of two species of hominid in the time range 2.2 to 1.2 mya is one of the exciting, original contributions of palaeontology. It could not have been predicted from any other class of evidence.

Dating from two million years to the present, fossil specimens have been found which are usually classified into three successive species of the genus *Homo*. If cranial capacities are plotted against time they show a tendency to increase until a levelling off occurs in the last few hundred thousand years. If cheek-tooth size is plotted in the same way, it shows a decrease until in the recent past a size range equivalent to that of both Dryopithecine and chimpanzee cheek teeth is reached.

A final anatomical shift occurs which is much less well known but which may be of fairly profound importance. Between about 50,000 or so and 30,000 years ago, with precise timing varying from region to region, all surviving human populations show a marked reduction in skeletal robusticity. Virtually all previous hominid fossils show a thickness of bone, plus muscular ridging that is outside the range that can be induced in modern humans even by extreme muscular training and stresses. There are also some subtle changes in skull architecture and pelvic form (Trinkaus and Howells 1979). These

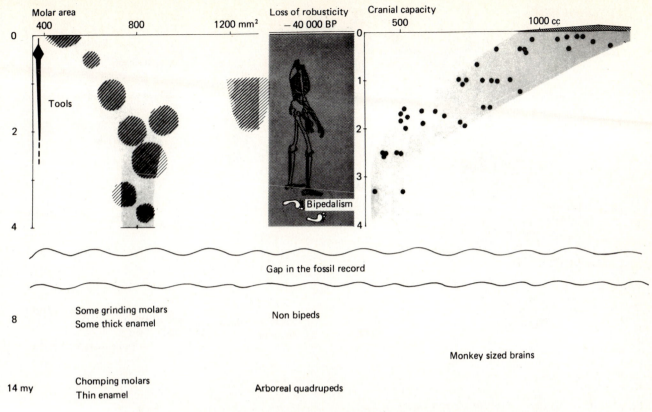

Figure 7. *A graphic* **summary** *of changes in anatomy of hominoid and hominid fossils shown in relation to the time scale. Left: teeth and jaws; center: post-cranial and locomotor pattern which has been essentially unchanging over the past 4 my; right: cranial capacity. (For details and sources, see Figs. 9, 10 and the text.)*

are the major contrasts separating modern humans from neanderthals, neanderthaloids and 'archaic *Homo sapiens*'. The biological meaning of this loss of robusticity is as yet poorly understood (J. D. Clark 1982).

One of the specific characteristics of the human evolutionary lineage has been the propensity to make tools—and to discard them. This has created a trail of litter that can be traced back some two to two and a half million years. Archaelogical study of this trail of refuse represents a major contribution to our knowledge of what has happened during the final two million years or so of the co-evolution of the brain and culture (Fig. 8).

Stone tools comprise the most widespread and persistent element of this record. The oldest known sets from sites such as Olduvai, Omo, Koobi Fora, Hadar, Melka Kunture and Swartkrans are all in East and South Africa. They are simple in terms of technology and design. Rocks were broken by conchoidal fracture so as to generate a varied set of sharp-edged forms. Experiment shows that these forms can be used effectively to cut off branches and to sharpen them as digging sticks or spears, or to cut up animal carcasses, ranging in size from gazelles to elephants. Newly developed techniques for determining use patterns from microscopically detectable polishes on the edges join other lines of evidence to show that some early examples were indeed used for cutting up carcasses, others for whittling wood and others for cutting plant tissue (Keeley and Toth 1981; Bunn 1981; Potts and Shipman 1981). Thus, we begin to see that in spite of their simplicity these early artifacts

had considerable importance in effecting novel adaptations. They are to be understood mainly as meat-cutting tools and as tools for making tools.

From the first appearance of stone artifacts, these occur both scattered over the landscape and in conspicuous localized concentrations which archaeologists call sites. These concentrations are often found to involve quantities of broken animal bones among the artifacts. This has led archaeologists to write into their narratives the early beginning of hunting (or at least, meat eating) and the early adoption of a socio-economic pattern involving 'camps' or 'home bases' and food sharing (e.g. Leakey 1971; Isaac 1978). The validity of these interpretations is currently subject to testing and debate (Binford 1981; Bunn *et al.* 1980; Isaac 1981) (see below).

In Fig. 8, notice that the antiquity of control over fire is currently highly uncertain. It goes back at least half a million years, but may go back to one and a half or two million years or more (Gowlett, Harris, Walton and Wood 1981). Notice also that many material culture attributes of humans appear only in the last 1% to 5% of the record. This wave of innovation occurs in the same time range as the loss of robusticity. This could be taken to mean that many of the familiar accoutrements of being human came only towards the very end of the narrative.

Hominoid fossils of the early and maybe the middle Miocene all come from some sort of tropical forest context. The late Miocene is more complex—some hominoids continued to live in forests, but others, including the ramapithecines which had somewhat hominid-like teeth, seem often to have lived in

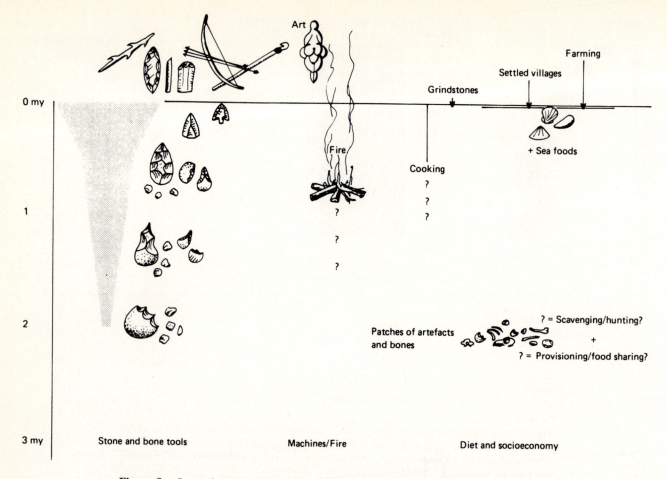

Figure 8. *Some elements of the archaeological record shown in relation to a time scale. Many familiar elements such as putting handles on tools, art, bows, spear throwers, villages, grindstones, etc. only appear very late in the known sequence. (See G. Clark 1977 for a summary, and Isaac 1972a for a discussion of the tempo of change.)*

more open, varied woodland habitats (see Behrensmeyer 1982 for review with references and Butzer 1976, 1977). This is interesting, but as we have seen it is quite uncertain whether or not this ramapithecine adaptive radiation is in any way ancestral to the Hominidae.

However this may be, faunal analysis and fossil pollen analyses combine to show that the earliest known fossil specimens of hominids between 4 and 2 mya all derive from strata that were laid down under non-forest conditions. The environments represented are very varied and range from open thorn-veldt grassland (Laetoli and some Transvaal layers) to complex mosaics of grassland, marsh, riverine gallery woods and lake margins (e.g. Hadar, Olduvai, Omo and Koobi Fora, see Jolly 1978; Bishop 1978).

This association of hominid fossils with relatively open country has commonly been taken as vindication of Darwin's narrative propositions that our early ancestors left the trees, an idea which has also become enshrined in our folk sense of human evolution. However, one of the surprising twists of discovery in recent years has been the recognition (1) that the hands, feet and shoulders of the early hominids may have been highly adapted for tree climbing (Susman and Creel 1979; Vrba 1979) and (2) that early archaeological sites commonly occur where groves of trees would have grown (Isaac 1972b, 1976). Perhaps

bipedalism is yet another example of changing so as to remain the same with the new locomotor pattern being extensively used initially to move between widely spaced patches of trees. Maybe we left the forest a while ago but the trees only much more recently (cf. Romer 1959; Rodman and McHenry 1980).

After two million years ago, available evidence allows us to believe in the kind of success story we clearly love for ourselves—expanding geographic distribution, and expanding range of habitats used. Notice though, that the occupation of really extreme environments such as unbroken forests, deserts or tundra can only be documented inside the last 100,000 years.

Whether it had any influence or not, the last two and a half million years of geologic time has witnessed global climatic oscillations of increasing amplitude. These involve the so-called ice ages. Following relatively stable, equable conditions in the Miocene and early Pliocene, there have been some 16 or 17 ice ages since the emergence of the genus *Homo* two million years ago (cf. Butzer 1976, Shackleton 1982).

DYNAMICS

Thus it can be seen that over the past decade the outlines of a four million year narrative of human evolution has emerged, and curiosity has begun to switch over to questions about the

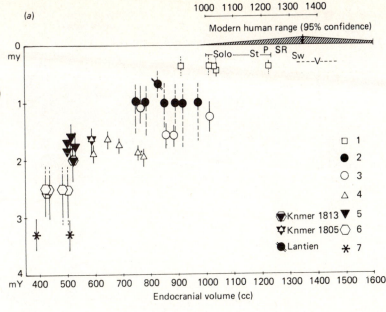

(a)

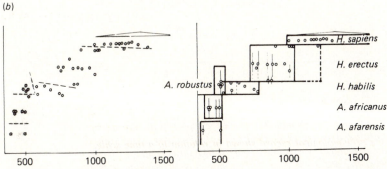

(b)

Figure 9. (a) *Endocranial volumes of hominid fossil skulls plotted against a time scale. The degree of uncertainty about age is indicated by the vertical bars. 7 = Australopithecus afarensis from Hadar; 6 = A. africanus; 5 = A. robustus and A. boisei; 4 = Homo habilis; 3 = H. erectus (E. Africa); 2 = H. erectus (Java and Lantien); 1 = H. erectus (Pekin). Early* H. sapiens *(the range for skulls) P = Petralona, St = Steinheim, S = Saldanha, R = Kabwe (Rhodesia man), Sw = Swanscombe, V = Vertesszöllös. (b) The same data (left) fitted to a phyletic gradualist model and (right) to a punctuated model. The species indicated at the right apply to both versions (sources: Holloway 1981; Day 1977; Howell 1978; Tobias 1981; Cronin* et al. *1981). For discussion of relation to body size see Pilbeam and Gould 1974.*

evolutionary mechanisms involved. Here, I can only touch hastily on aspects of a few selected topics.

One such is the question as to whether human evolution over the past several million years has proceeded by a process of cumulative genetic changes that pervaded populations over wide areas so that all went through evolutionary transformation, or whether successive species of hominids all exhibit stasis, with widespread change being accomplished by species replacement events (Gould and Eldredge 1977). It should be noted in advance that these alternative models do not seem to me to be entirely mutually exclusive.

Figures 9 and 10 show data for two relatively simple measurable attributes of hominid fossils plotted against time. Contrary to the view of Cronin *et al.* (1981), Fig. 9b suggests that both gradualist models and punctuated equilibrium models can equally well be fitted to the available data. The best case for stasis in the record is the taxon *Homo erectus*. It can be argued that the first appearance of this taxon looks like a punctuation event and the taxon lasts a million years. However, at its later end many investigators seem to be reporting mosaic patterns of transition into 'archaic *Homo sapiens*' and this would not be compatible with a clear-cut punctuation event.

Numbers of workers, myself included, have tended to think of the loss of robusticity transition of 30,000–50,000 years ago as a possible example of a punctuation/genetic replacement event. But this view would seem to be falsified

by the new mitochondrial DNA data (Ferris *et al.* 1981; Cann *et al.* 1982).

Figure 10 also illustrates a possible example within the hominid fossil record of the effects of the breakdown of barriers which had separated trivially differentiated allopatric species. According to one interpretation two species of *Australopithecus* came to have overlapping ranges, and responded by undergoing niche separation and character displacement (Schaffer 1968; Swedlund 1974) One of the resultant species or (species complex) is *Australopithecus robustus/boisei* which underwent selection for enlarged body size, and perhaps, following the Jarman-Bell principle, a coarsening of diet. The other became *Homo habilis* and retained moderate body size and took to higher quality foods perhaps acquired in part through the aid of tools. Maybe this is indeed a fairy story, but it is fun and it may turn out to be at least partly true.

The peculiarities of the early hominid megadont phase presumably relates to diet, but what this was continues to baffle us. Scanning electron microscope (SEM) studies of tooth wear by Alan Walker (1981) and others suggest that non-siliceous plant tissues were being consumed presumably fruits (*sensu lato*) or seeds. But what fruits or seeds? And why such large teeth? These questions call for studies of floristic communities and the feeding opportunities they offer as well as scrutiny of fossils.

A battery of new techniques for palaeodietary studies are being developed, including SEM studies and the analysis for the

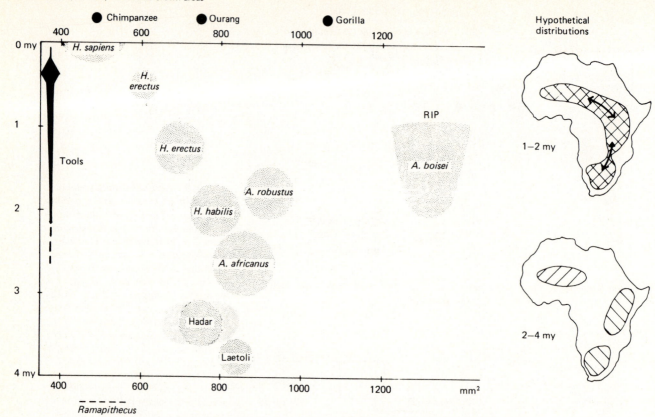

Cheek teeth (P3—M4)   Summed crown areas

● Chimpanzee   ● Ourang   ● Gorilla

Hypothetical distributions

Figure 10. *The size (total area in mm²) of mandibular cheek teeth plotted against a time scale with means for each taxon/sample shown schematically as a stippled zone. Mean values for the closest living relatives of man and for* Ramapithecus *are shown for comparison. If one bears in mind that hominids between 2 and 4 mya were smaller than H. sapiens and no bigger than chimpanzees, then it is apparent that they had proportionately large teeth (see Pilbeam and Gould 1974). A. boisei was certainly not as large as a gorilla and was ultra-megadont. The maps at right suggest a scenario of allopatric speciation followed by the breakdown of isolation, range overlap and perhaps character displacement. Some authorities (e.g. Leakey 1981) would split the Hadar sample between two taxa, others (Johanson and White 1979) regard it as one highly dimorphic taxon (Sources: Wolpoff 1975; Tobias 1981; White, Johanson and Coppens 1982.)*

strontium and ¹³C composition of old bones. A major onslaught on this fundamental problem seems to be getting underway (Walker 1981).

As the outlines of the narrative of human evolution have emerged, two particularly intriguing puzzles have emerged with it. *Under what selection pressures did, firstly, the two-legged gait and, secondly, the enlarged brain become adaptive?* The first of these can be rephrased as: Why did ancestral hominids become bipedal when all other primate species which have come to the ground have adopted some or other form of quadrupedal locomotion? Many thinkers on these topics, starting with Darwin, have tended to opt for an all-purpose explanation which might explain both bipedalism and brain enlargement, for instance, tool and weapon carrying. However, since specific evidence for the two evolutionary shifts are separated by at least two million years, it may be wise to uncouple the searches for explanations.

Figure 11 playfully indicates some of the competing explanations which have been or are being discussed in relation to bipedalism.

More fossils, more palaeoenvironmental, and palaeodietary data will certainly help to advance understanding on this question, but it should also be clear that intelligent neontological/ecological work is called for. For instance, do potential feeding niches really exist that would make bipedalism adaptive?

THE BRAIN-CULTURE SYSTEM

We all share in some degree the conviction that our words, our intellect, our consciousness, our aesthetic and moral sense, constitute the quintessential characteristics of being human. Further we associate these qualities directly with the evolutionary enlargement and reorganization of our brains. The issue can be put like this: 'The brain is the organ of culture, and culture is the function of the brain'. The term culture refers to the intricate body of language, craft skills, social custom, traditions and information which humans learn while growing up and living in any human society. (For a good

The Origin of Bipedalism: Rival Hypotheses

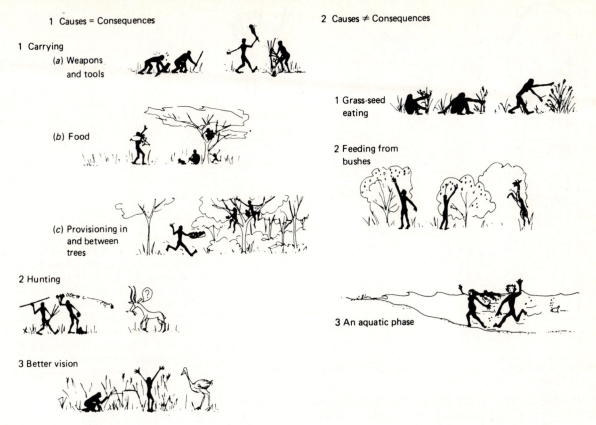

Figure 11. *Rival theories to account for the adoption of a bipedal gait. References: 1a, e.g. Darwin 1871; Washburn and Moore 1980; 1b, e.g. Hewes 1961; Lancaster 1978; 1c, e.g. Lovejoy 1981; 2, e.g. Washburn and Lancaster 1968; 3, various; 4, Jolly 1970; 5, Pilbeam 1980; 6, Hardy 1960; Morgan 1972, 1982. Note: Palaeoanthropologists in general judge the aquatic hypothesis to be highly improbable or impossible, but it cannot be formally eliminated yet, and it is fun to keep on the list meanwhile.*

discussion of this, see Geertz 1973.) Cultural complexity and flexibility of this kind is unknown in any other organism and would be impossible without the hypertrophied brain. It is also hard to make sense of the intricacy of the brain without supposing that the adaptive advantages that have brought it into existence have long involved culture of increasing complexity. However, to keep our topic from becoming dull and predeterministic perhaps we should allow for the possibility that the enlarged brain, like bipedalism, might have been a pre-adaptive development that was favoured by selection for reasons other than culture. This point notwithstanding, for the time being I shall treat the brain and the culture it sustains as likely to have evolved as a single adaptive complex, that is to say as a co-evolution (see Wilson 1983).

We are rightly impressed with the biological success that seems to have followed from the development of the brain through some critical thresholds, but it must be remembered that enlarged brains require prolonged infant dependency and high quality nutrition (Sacher and Staffeldt 1974; Martin in Lewin 1982). Both of these are expensive commodities in the economy of nature. No other lineage has experienced selection producing such an extreme development. The central puzzle to understanding our origins, therefore, remains the problem of figuring out under what novel selective circumstances this trend

was initiated, and under what conditions the selection was sustained.

Set out below is a list of some of the distinctive innovations which have been suggested and discussed as prime movers in the initiation of the trend towards elaboration of the brain-culture system.

(1) The use of tools and weapons (e.g. Darwin 1871; Washburn 1960; Tobias 1967, 1981);

(2) Hunting (e.g. Darwin 1871; Dart 1925, 1953; Ardrey 1961; Washburn and Lancaster 1968);

(3) Gathering (e.g. Zihlman and Tanner 1979; Tanner 1981);

(4) Generalized social cooperation with 'autocatalytic' feedback (e.g. Darwin 1871; Lovejoy 1981);

(5) Adoption by small-brained hominids of a socio-reproductive system involving food sharing, provisioning and central place foraging (e.g. Hewes 1961; Washburn 1965; Isaac 1978; Lancaster 1978).

It should be noted that these competing explanations are *not* mutually exclusive, and future research will have to involve subtle assessment of their relative importance at different stages rather than simple Popperian falsification.

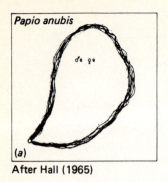

Papio anubis

(a)

After Hall (1965)

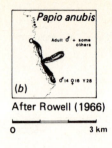

Papio anubis

Adult ♂ + some others

(b)

♂14 ♀16 Y26

After Rowell (1966)

0 ————— 3 km

Gorilla gorilla

♂5 ♀10 Y8

(c)

After Schaller (1964)
Fifteen days

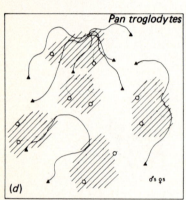

Pan troglodytes

(d)

♂5 ♀5

Invented from Wrangham

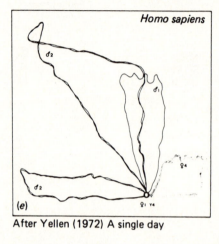

Homo sapiens

♂2

♂1

♀4

♂2

♀1 Y4

(e)

After Yellen (1972) A single day

Figure 12. *The contrast between human ranging patterns and those of a representative sample of non-human primates (see Isaac 1980 for sources and discussion).* Note: *Humans are represented by San hunter-gatherers, but the same basic pattern would be found if agriculturalists were represented, or modern city dwellers with offices and supermarkets as the endpoints of radiating movements.*

It should also be noted that the study of the fossil and archaeological record will not suffice by themselves to distinguish among hypotheses. It is all very well arguing that tool-use was a pivotal development that imposed novel selection pressure, but under what circumstances would tools be adaptive? As I argued in the paper *Casting the Net Wide* (Isaac 1980) answering this kind of question calls for problem-oriented quantitative field studies of feeding possibilities and foraging strategies.

Over the past 12 years my own research has been focused first on developing and then on testing the predictions of the so-called 'Food-sharing hypothesis' and its possible bearing on the initiation of selection for larger brain size. I shall briefly indulge myself by discussing aspects of this model and this work.

The first point to be made is that major changes have occurred in human ranging patterns and feeding behaviour (Fig. 12). These changes involve the collective acquisition of food, postponement of consumption, transport, and communal consumption at a home base or central place. These features are so basic in our lives that we take them for granted and very often they do not even appear on lists of contrasts between humans and non-human primates. However, if we could interview a chimpanzee about the behavioural differences separating us, this might well be the item that it found most impressive—'These humans get food and instead of eating it promptly like any sensible ape, they haul it off and share it with others.'

The food-sharing hypothesis should be renamed the central place foraging hypothesis. It incorporates tools and meat eating. It postulates that at some time before two million years ago, the behaviour of at least one kind of small-brained hominid was modified to include the elements shown in Figure 13, namely the use of tools, the acquisition of meat, perhaps preferentially

by males, the transport of portions of that meat to central places where it would be apt to be collectively consumed by members of a social group some of whom, especially females and young, had not participated in its acquisition. At the beginning or at some subsequent stage, female gathering was surely included in the system. Conscious motivation for 'sharing' need *not* have been involved. The model works provided that radiative ranging patterns developed with transport of some food back to the foci of social aggregation.

For me, the interest of the model is not that 'humans' existed 2 mya but that it promises to help explain how the non-human hominids of that time began to be modified into humans. Once food transport was initiated, novel selection pressures would come to bear on (1) ability to communicate about the past, future, and the spatially remote and (2) enhanced abilities to plan complex chains of eventualities and to play what one might call 'social chess' in one's mind. That is, the adoption of food-sharing would have favoured the development of language, social reciprocity and the intellect. Evolutionary strategy models should now be developed to explore the conditions under which food sharing might become an ESS (see Maynard Smith, 1983).

Clearly, part of the nutritional cost of brain enlargement and the costs of prolonged dependency during brain growth with extended learning would be taken care of by the provisioning/nurturing characteristics which in this scenario would already be part of the system.

The model arose as a post-hoc explanation of the existence of concentrated patches of discarded artifacts and of broken-up bones in layers between 1.5 and 2 mya. Having set it up, we have turned around and have been enjoying the sport of trying to knock it down, with the help of fierce critics (e.g. Binford 1981).

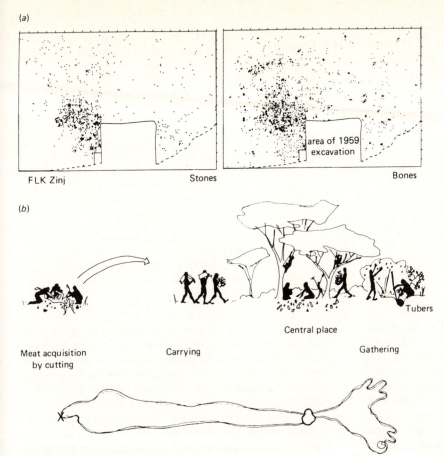

(a)

FLK Zinj   Stones

area of 1959 excavation

Bones

(b)

Meat acquisition by cutting

Carrying

Central place

Gathering

Tubers

Figure 13. *(a) Two plans of an excavation which appears to be a well preserved early central-place foraging base—the FLK Zinj site at Olduvai (Based on Leakey 1971). More than 2,400 stone artifacts and 40,000 bone fragments (right) occur within a radius of 10 m. Some 8% of the identifiable bones show the marks of sharp stone tools (Bunn 1982) and these include damage due to dismemberment marks and to meat removal. (See also Potts 1982 and Potts and Shipman 1981 for detailed information and a more conservative estimate of cut mark damage frequency.) (b) A hypothetical model of the processes involved in site formation. The transport of stones and bones (meat) is certain, the transport of plant foods is possible but unconfirmed. Whether sharing occurred at all is harder to judge—and whether it was incidental or 'deliberate' is impossible to tell.*

The technicalities of this debate and this research go beyond the scope of this review (see Isaac 1981, 1982; Bunn *et al.* 1980; Bunn 1981; Potts and Shipman 1981). Suffice it to say that in my view, we have obtained ample confirmation that hominids were indeed acquiring meat through the use of tools and were transporting this to favoured localities where the observed concentrated patches of bones and tools formed. Whether these places were 'home bases' or whether provisioning and/or active food sharing were going on, is harder to judge. My guess now is that in various ways, the behaviour system was less human than I originally envisaged, but that it did involve food transport and de facto, if not purposive, food sharing and provisioning.

The food-sharing model has been widely misunderstood as implying that by two million years ago there existed friendly, cuddly, cooperative human-like hominids. This need not be so. The attractiveness of this model is that it seems entirely feasible for such a behavioural system to come into existence among *non human* hominids that had brains no larger than those of living apes, and it is my strong suspicion that if we had these hominids alive today, we would have to put them in zoos, not in academies.

Clearly, this initial configuration can very readily be plugged into models involving kin-selection, and/or tit-for-tat selection patterns that would provide plausible, if hard-to-test models of the subsequent elaboration of brain-speech-culture-society systems (Fig. 14). Amongst other things, the provisioning and division of labour implied by the system would make bonded male-female reproductive modules highly adaptive, if they did not already exist at the outset.

IN CONCLUSION

No two people who undertook to review this topic would have tackled it in the same way. I have chosen to stress inquiries focussed on stratified evidence from the past, while other writers would equally legitimately have emphasized the contributions made by studies of biochemistry, ecological dynamics or by comparative behaviour and sociobiology.

Following the pioneer descriptive phases of primate studies, various workers have begun to search out generalizations among non-human primates concerning relationships between food choice, ranging patterns, reproductive strategies and social format (e.g. Clutton-Brock and Harvey 1977; Wrangham 1979, 1980; Milton 1981). The results have not yet been fully assimilated into thinking about human evolution, but already it emerges that humans have distinctive ecological relationships and social configurations that are outside the range of other primate patterns. My hunch would be that this will prove to be connected with the colonization of habitats where potential foods were more patchy and more widely dispersed than is normal for primates. This in turn involved altered diets which focus on two distinctive and quite different things: first on plant foods that yield large numbers of calories per item (e.g. tubers and nuts) and second, significant feeding on the meat of large animals and/or fish. Acquisition of all of these is facilitated by tool use. It is at present uncertain when and by what stages these shifts occurred. Finding out is one of the major challenges that confronts palaeoanthropology.

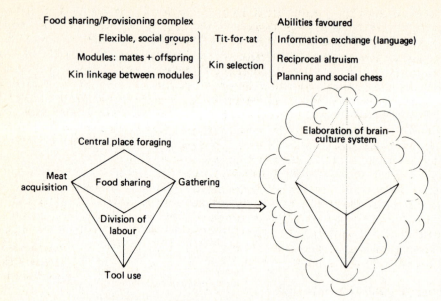

Food sharing/Provisioning complex

Flexible, social groups ⎫
Modules: mates + offspring ⎬ Tit-for-tat
Kin linkage between modules ⎭ Kin selection

Abilities favoured

Information exchange (language)
Reciprocal altruism
Planning and social chess

Central place foraging

Meat acquisition — Food sharing — Gathering

Division of labour

Tool use

Elaboration of brain—culture system

Figure 14. *The 'food sharing' or 'central-place-foraging' hypothesis suggests a socio-reproductive milieu in which 'mental and emotional proclivities' could be selected that started to transform non-human hominid systems into human type systems. Communication, reciprocal help and planning ahead would all be favoured (left). Novel behavioural ingredients form structural members in a non-human system. These same elements now enveloped as core-components within highly elaborated, flexible, variable cultural systems (right); see text; Isaac (1978); Maynard-Smith (1983) and E.O. Wilson (1983) for discussion of the issues and of the modes of selection that are indicated.*

Relative to other primates, humans have highly distinctive social patterns. In spite of tremendous variation this almost always includes reproductive units involving direct male investment in child rearing, and comprising one male and one or more females. These units are almost invariably integrated as modules into highly variable larger scale social entities. I can see no way of predicting the human pattern from the primate patterns without introducing some novel elements into the mix of variables. One candidate for an influential novelty may well be the significant incorporation of dietary components to which one sex rather than the other had preferential access. Clearly, meat is one such commodity, though it may not be the only one.

Lovejoy (1981) has argued that monogamous pair bonding and food transport preceded meat eating and the formation of bands. However, we need to retain as the alternative hypothesis that pair bonding occurred within multi-male, multi-female social groups and was associated with division of food acquisition labour. Recent examination of relations between mating system, body size and testis size in primates does not support a multi-male social group for *Homo* (Harcourt *et al.* 1981; Martin and May 1981). However, if early ancestral hominids already had mated pair modules within the troop this objection might not apply.

Relating studies of the present to studies of the past will require changes of emphasis. Much of the literature on the stratified record of human evolution is devoted to the taxonomy of individual fossils and to arguments about whether particular ones are on the line or not. The topic is in its own way important, but with major taxa reasonably clearly established the younger generation of scientists is becoming more and more involved in enquiring into relationships between shifts in anatomical configurations and shifts in modes of adaptation. This line of research can be pursued profitably even if we do not know which particular fossils are indeed on the line and which are off it. I would go on to predict that progress with this topic will involve much less narrow focus on fossils. Hominid palaeontologists and archaeologists will need to collaborate in assessing the adaptive significance of technology, subsistence patterns and socioeconomic arrangements. For this, the ar-

chaeologists will have to give up the artifact typology fixation that has been their equivalent of fossil-philia. Both archaeologists and hominid palaeontologists are also going to have to work closely with ecologists. This has started, e.g. Schaller and Lowther 1969, Peters and O'Brien 1981, and J. Sept and A. Vincent (personal communication).

In summary, improvements in knowledge about human evolution require the acquisition of richly diverse classes of information. This includes both stratified evidence from the past and the elucidation of the intricate features of living behavioural and ecological systems. As is normal in science, hypotheses regarding both narrative and mechanisms need to be restlessly formulated, tested and revised. However, as indicated in the introduction, and as amply illustrated in Darwin's own treatment of the topic, the meaning that each of us finds in the growing corpus of secure, tested information, nonetheless remains a humanistic abstraction.

ACKNOWLEDGEMENTS

My being in a position to undertake this review stems from an appointment in East Africa, given me in 1961 by the late Louis Leakey. Since then my wife and I have been part of a goodly company of researchers in East Africa during a period of exciting discoveries. Many of my ideas surely derive from this participation. I recognize particularly strong influence from discussions with S. L. Washburn, D. R. Pilbeam, J. D. Clark, Vince Sarich and A. C. Walker. Also from the team that has worked with Richard Leakey and me at Koobi Fora. My wife is a part of the talking, the fieldwork and the laboratory work, and she draws the figures. For this paper, Jeanne Sept has done the lighthearted sketches (Figs. 1, 3, 11, 13). Stanley Ambrose encouraged me to think about the material in Fig. 10 and he is preparing a paper on character displacement in hominids. I wish to pay tribute to three great scientists, recently deceased, who did much to foster the study of biological and cultural co-evolution—Kenneth Oakley, Francois Bordes and Charles McBurney. The last-named especially was my mentor during my student days and after.

FURTHER READING

Lancaster, J. 1975. *Primate Behaviour and the Emergence of Human Culture*. Holt, Rinehart and Winston, New York.

Leakey, R. 1981. *The Making of Mankind*. Michael Joseph, London.

Pfeiffer, J. 1978. *The Emergence of Man*. Harper & Row, New York.

Pilbeam, D. R. 1980. Major trends in human evolution. In *Current Argument on Early Man*, Ed. L-K. Konigsson, pp. 261-85. Pergamon Press, Oxford.

Reader, J. 1981. *Missing Links*. Little, Brown and Co., Boston.

Washburn, S. L., and Moore, R. 1980. *Ape into Human*. 2nd ed. Little, Brown and Co., Boston.

REFERENCES

Ardrey, R. 1961. *African Genesis*. Collins, London.

Behrensmeyer, A. K. 1982. The geological context of human evolution. *Annual Review of Earth and Planetary Sciences* 10:39-60.

Behrensmeyer, A. K., and Hill, A. 1981. *Fossils in the Making*. Chicago University Press, Chicago.

Binford, L. R. 1981. *Bones: ancient men and modern myths*. Academic Press, New York.

Bishop, W. W. 1978. *Geological Background to Fossil Man: recent research in the Gregory Rift Valley, East Africa*. Scottish Academic Press, Edinburgh.

Bunn, H. (1981). Archaeological evidence for meat-eating by Plio-Pleistocene hominids from Koobi Fora and Olduvai Gorge. *Nature* 291:574-7.

Bunn, H. 1982. Archaeological evidence for meat-eating by Plio-Pleistocene Koobi Fora, Kenya and Olduvai Gorge, Tanzania. In *Proceedings of the 4th International Congress on Archaeozoology, London*. British Archaeological Record, Oxford.

Bunn, H., Harris, J. W. K., Isaac, G. Ll., Kaufulu, Z., Kroll, E., Schick, K., Toth, N., and Behrensmeyer, A. K. 1980. FxJj50: an early Pleistocene site in northern Kenya. *World Archaeology* 12:109-36.

Butzer, K. W. 1976. Pleistocene climates. *Geoscience and Man* 13:27-44.

Butzer, K. W. 1977. Environment, culture and human evolution. *American Scientist* 65:572-84.

Cann, R., Brown, W. M., and Wilson, A. C. 1982. Evolution of human Mitochondrial DNA: molecular, genetic and anthropological implications. *Proceedings of the 6th International Congress of Human Genetics*, Jerusalem.

Clark, G. 1977. *World Prehistory*, 3rd ed. Cambridge University Press, Cambridge.

Clark, J. D. 1982. New men, strange faces, other minds: an archaeologist's perspective on recent discoveries relating to the origin and spread of modern man. *Proceedings of the British Academy*.

Clutton-Brock, T. H., and Harvey, P. H. 1977. Primate ecology and social organization. *Journal of Zoology* 183:1-39.

Cronin, J., Boaz, N., Stringer, C., and Rak, Y. 1981. Tempo and mode in hominid evolution. *Nature* 292:113-22.

Dart, R. 1925. *Australopithecus africanus*: the man-ape of Southern Africa. *Nature* 115:195-9.

Dart, R. 1953. The predatory transition from ape to man. *International Anthropological and Linguistic Review* 1:201-19.

Darwin, C. 1871. *The Descent of Man and Selection in Relation to Sex*. John Murray, London.

Day, M. 1977. *Guide of Fossil Man*. University of Chicago Press, Chicago.

Ferris, S. D., Wilson, A. C., and Brown, W. M. 1981. Evolutionary tree for apes and humans based on cleavage maps of mitochondrial DNA. *Proceedings of the National Academy of Sciences, USA* 78:2432-6.

Geertz, C. 1973. The growth of culture and the evolution of mind. In *The Interpretation of Cultures*, (C. Geertz, Ed.), pp. 55-83. Basic Books, New York.

Gould, S. J., and Eldredge, N. 1977. Punctuated equilibria: the tempo and mode of evolution reconsidered. *Paleobiology* 3:115-51.

Gowlett. A. J., Harris, J. W. K., Walton, D., and Wood, B. A. 1981. Early archaeological sites, hominid remains and traces of fire from Chesowanja, Kenya. *Nature* 294:125-9.

Hall, R. 1965. Behaviour and ecology of the wild Patas monkey, *Erythrocebus patas*, in Uganda. *Journal of Zoology* 148:15-87.

Hardy, A. 1960. Was man more aquatic in the past? *New Scientist* 7:642-5.

Harcourt, A. H., Harvey, P. H., Larson, S. G., and Short, R. V. 1981. Testis weight and breeding system in primates. *Nature* 293:55-7.

Hewes, G. 1961. Food transport and the origin of hominid bipedalism. *American Anthropologist* 63:687-710.

Holloway, R. L. 1981. Exploring the dorsal surface of hominoid brain endocasts by stereoplotter and discriminant analysis. *Philosophic Transactions of the Royal Society, London* B 292:155-66.

Howell, F. C. 1978. Hominidae. In *Evolution of African Mammals*, (V. J. Maglio and H. B. S. Cooke, Eds.), pp. 154-248. Academic Press, New York.

Huxley. T. H. 1863. *Evidence as to Man's Place in Nature*. Williams and Norgate, London.

Isaac, G. Ll. 1972a. Chronology and the tempo of cultural change during the Pleistocene. In *Calibration of Hominoid Evolution*, (W. W. Bishop and J. A. Miller, Eds.), pp. 381-430. Scottish Academic Press, Edinburgh.

Isaac, G. Ll. 1972b. Comparative studies of Pleistocene site locations in East Africa. In *Man, Settlement and Urbanism*, (P. J. Ucko and G. W. Dimbleby, Eds.), pp. 165-76. Duckworth and Co, London.

Isaac, G. Ll. 1976. The activities of early African hominids. In *Human Origins: Louis Leakey and the East African Evidence*, (G. Ll. Isaac and E. R. McCown, Eds.), pp. 483-514. W. A. Benjamin, Menlo Park, CA.

Isaac, G. Ll. 1978. Food sharing and human evolution: archaeological evidence from the Plio-Pleistocene of East Africa. *Journal of Anthropological Research* 34:311-25.

Isaac, G. Ll. 1980. Casting the net wide: a review of archaeological evidence for early hominid land-use and ecological relations. In *Current Argument on Early Man*, (L-K. Konigsson, Ed.), pp. 226-53. Pergamon Press, Oxford.

Isaac, G. Ll. 1981. Archaeological tests of alternative models of early hominid behaviour: excavation and experiments. *Philosophical Transactions of the Royal Society, London* B 292:177-88.

Isaac, G. Ll. 1982. Bones in contention. *Proceedings of the 4th International Congress on Archaeozoology, London*. British Archaeological Record, Oxford.

Johanson, D. C., and White, T. D. 1979. A systematic assessment of early African hominids. *Science* 202:321-30.

Jolly, C. 1970. The seed eaters: a new model of hominid differentiation based on a baboon analogy. *Man* 5:5-26.

Jolly, C. 1978. *Early Hominids of Africa*. Duckworth, London.

Keeley, L., and Toth, N. 1981. Microwear polishes on early stone tools from Koobi Fora, Kenya. *Nature* 293:464-5.

Lancaster, J. 1978. Carrying and sharing in human evolution. *Human Nature* 1:82-9.

Landau, M. 1981. *The Anthropogenic: Paleoanthropological Writing as a Genre of Literature*. Ph.D. Dissertation, Yale University.

Leakey, M. D. 1971. *Olduvai Gorge*, Vol. 3. Cambridge University Press, Cambridge.

Leakey, R. E. 1981. *The Making of Mankind*. Michael Joseph, London.

Lewin, R. 1982. How did humans evolve big brains? *Science* 216:840-1.

Lovejoy. O. 1978. A biomechanical review of the locomotor diversity of early hominids. In *Early Hominids of Africa*, (C. Jolly, Ed.), pp. 403-43. Duckworth, London.

Lovejoy, O. 1981. The origin of man. *Science* 211, 341:50.

McHenry, H., and Temerin, L. A. 1979. The evolution of hominid bipedalism: evidence from the fossil record. *Yearbook of Physical Anthropology* 22:105-31.

Martin, R., and May, R. 1981. Outward signs of breeding. *Nature* 293:8-9.

Maynard Smith, J. 1983. Game theory and the evolution of cooperation. In *Evolution from Molecules to Men*, (D.S. Bendall, Ed.), pp. 445-456. Cambridge University Press, Cambridge.

Milton, K. 1981. Distribution patterns of tropical plant foods as an evolutionary stimulus to primate mental development. *American Anthropologist* 83:534-48.

Morgan, E. 1972. *The Descent of Woman*. Souvenir Press, London.

Morgan, E. 1982. *The Aquatic Ape*. Souvenir Press, London.

Oakley. K. P., Campbell. B. C. and Molleson, T. I. (1971-1977). *Catalogue of Fossil Hominids*. British Museum (Natural History), London.

Perper, T., and Schrire, C. 1977. The Nimrod connection: myth and science in the hunting model. In *The Chemical Senses and Nutrition*, (M. R. Kare, Ed.), pp. 447-59. Academic Press, New York.

Peters, C. R., and O'Brien, E. M. 1981. The early hominid plant-food niche: insights from an analysis of human, chimpanzee, and baboon plant exploitation in eastern and southern Africa. *Current Anthropology* 22:127-40.

Pilbeam, D. R. 1980. Major trends in human evolution. In *Current Argument on Early Man*, (L-K. Konigsson. Ed.), pp. 261-85. Pergamon Press, Oxford.

Pilbeam, D. R., and Gould, S. J. 1974. Size and scaling in human evolution. *Science* 186:892-901.

Potts, R. 1982. *Lower Pleistocene Site Formation and Hominid Activities at Olduvai Gorge. Tanzania*. Ph.D. Thesis, Department of Anthropology. Yale University, New Haven.

Potts, R., and Shipman, P. 1981. Cutmarks made by stone tools on bones from Olduvai Gorge, Tanzania. *Nature* 291:577-80.

Propp, V. 1968. *Morphology of the Folktale*. University of Texas Press, Austin.

Reader, J. 1980. *Missing Links*. Little, Brown and Co., Boston.

Rodman, P., and McHenry, H. 1980. Bioenergetics and the origin of bipedalism. *American Journal of Physical Anthroplogy* 52:103-6.

Romer, A. 1959. *The Vertebrate Story*. 4th ed. University of Chicago Press, Chicago.

Rowell, T. 1966. Forest living baboons in Uganda. *Journal of Zoology* 149:344-64.

Sacher, G. A., and Staffeldt, E. F. 1974. Relations of gestation time to brain weight for placental mammals. *American Naturalist* 108:593-614.

Sarich, V., and Cronin, J. 1976. Molecular systematics of the Primates. In *Molecular Anthropology*, (M. Goodman, R. E. Tashian and J. H. Tashian, Eds.), pp. 141-170. Plenum Press, New York.

Schaffer, W. 1968. Character displacement and the evolution of the Hominidae. *The American Naturalist* 102:559-71.

Schaller, G. 1964. *The Mountain Gorilla: Ecology and Behaviour*. University of Chicago Press, Chicago.

Schaller, G., and Lowther, G. 1969. The relevance of carnivore behaviour to the study of early hominids. *Southwestern Journal of Anthropology* 25:307-41.

Shackleton, N. 1982. The deep-sea record of climate variability. *Progress in Oceanography* 11:199-218.

Simons, E. 1972. *Primate Evolution*. Macmillan, New York.

Susman, R., and Creel, N. 1979. Functional and morphological affinities of the subadult hand (OH 7) from Olduvai Gorge. *American Journal of Physical Anthropology* 51:311-31.

Swedlund, A. C. 1974. The use of ecological hypotheses in australopithecine taxonomy. *American Anthropologist* 76:515-29.

Tanner, N. 1981. *On Becoming Human*. Cambridge University Press, Cambridge.

Tobias, P. V. 1967. Cultural hominization among the earliest African Pleistocene hominids. *Proceedings of the Prehistoric Society* 33:367-76.

Tobias, P. V. 1980. *Australopithecus afarensis* and *A. africanus*: critique and alternative hypotheses. *Palaeontologia Africana* 23:1-17.

Tobias, P. V. 1981. The emergence of man in Africa and beyond. *Philosophical Transactions of the Royal Society, London* B 292:43-56.

Trinkaus, E., and Howells, W. W. 1979. The Neanderthals. *Scientific American* 241:118-133.

Vrba, E. 1979. A new study of the scapula of *Australopithecus africanus* from Sterkfontein. *American Journal of Physical Anthropology* 51:117-30.

Walker, A. 1981. Dietary hypotheses and human evolution. *Philosophical Transactions of the Royal Society, London* B 292:57-64.

Washburn, S. L. 1960. Tools and human evolution. *Scientific American* 203:62-75.

Washburn, S. L. 1965. An ape's eye view of human evolution. In *The Origins of Man*, (I. DeVore, Ed.), pp. 89-96. Wenner Gren Foundation, New York.

Washburn, S. L., and Lancaster, C. 1968. Hunting and human evolution. In *Man the Hunter*, (R. Lee and I. DeVore, Eds.), pp. 293-303. Aldine, Chicago.

Washburn, S. L., and Moore, R. 1980. *Ape into Human*, 2nd edn. Little, Brown and Co., Boston.

White, T. D., Johanson, D. C., and Coppens, Y. 1982. Dental remains from the Hadar Formation, Ethiopia: 1974-1977 collections. *American Journal of Physical Anthropology* 57:545-603.

White. T. D., Johanson, D. C., and Kimbel, W. H. 1981. *Australopithecus africanus*: its phyletic position reconsidered. *South African Journal of Science* 77:445-70.

Wilson, A., Carlson, S., and White, T. J. 1977. Biochemical evolution. *Annual Review of Biochemistry* 46:573-639.

Wilson, E.O. Sociobiology and the Darwinian approach to mind and culture. In *Evolution from Molecules to Men*, (D.S. Bendall, Ed.), pp. 545-553. Cambridge University Press, Cambridge.

Wolpoff, M. 1973 Posterior tooth size, body size and diet in South African gracile australopithecines. *American Journal of Physical Anthropology* 39:375-94.

Wolpoff, M. 1975. Some aspects of human mandibular evolution. In *Determinants of Mandibular Form and Growth*, (J. McNamara, Ed.), pp. 1-64. Center for Human Growth and Development, Ann Arbor.

Wood, B. A. 1981. Tooth size and shape and their relevance to studies of hominid evolution. *Philosophical Transactions of the Royal Society, London* B, 292:65-76.

Wrangham, R. 1979. On the evolution of ape social systems. *Social Science Information* 18:335-68.

Wrangham, R. 1980. An ecological model of female-bonded primate groups. *Behaviour* 75:262-300.

Yellen, J. 1972. Trip V. Itinerary May 24-June 9, 1968. Pilot Edition of Exploring Human Nature. Education Development Center Inc., Cambridge, Mass.

Zihlman, A., and Tanner, N. 1979. Gathering and the hominid adaptation. In *Female Hierarchies*. (L. Tiger and H.M. Fowler, Eds.), pp. 163-94. Beresford Book Service, Chicago.

25

Early Hominid Lifestyle: Hunting and Gathering or Foraging, and Scavenging?

P. Shipman

In the last few years, two new and provocative theories on the directions of early hominid evolution have been advanced by Isaac (1978) and Lovejoy (1981). At the risk of doing the authors an injustice by oversimplifying their theories, these can be summarized as follows:

Isaac's Food Sharing Hypothesis

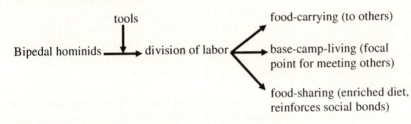

Lovejoy's Pair-Bonding Hypothesis

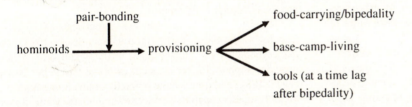

Despite differences in their ideas, Lovejoy and Isaac share a similar image of the social organization and food-procuring strategy of early hominids. For the purpose of this paper, it will be assumed that Isaac's food sharing is basically the same as Lovejoy's provisioning behavior.

In fact, two widespread and deeply entrenched notions, borrowed from the ethnographic literature by paleoanthropologists, account for the similarity in Isaac's and Lovejoy's reconstructions (among others). The first is that food-sharing, especially of meat obtained by hunting large game, is universal and is fundamentally human. Yet there are documented examples of peoples who do not share meat with their entire social group: the Dassenetch (Gifford 1977), the Maasai (Beckwith and Ole Saitoti, 1980), the Ik (Turnbull 1972), and on occasion, the Valley Bisa (Marks 1976). Even among genuine and habitual food-sharers, the reality deviates

from the paradigm. Although the ideal of food-sharing is heavily stressed among the San Bushmen (Marshall 1965), the actual distribution of meat is sufficiently unregulated to be a constant source of complaint and argument. Further, San hunters travelling in a very small group may choose not to inform the entire band of a successful hunt and may consume the meat a few kilometers away from the main camp (Yellen, pers. comm.).

The second widespread belief that colors thinking in paleoanthropology is that men hunt, while women and children gather, because women with children cannot hunt. Although this is unquestionably a common pattern, it is not a universal one. For example Turnbull (1965) reports that Pygmy women and children routinely participate in hunts in the Ituri Forest (see also McKennan 1959). Particular hunting techniques and perhaps particular ecological situations make it possible for all group members to participate in hunting.

The point here is not to argue that food-sharing or the division of labor along lines of age and sex do not occur. Both clearly do occur, frequently, and have obvious adaptive values. The point is that, since these patterns are not found among all living humans, it is unreasonable to assume that such patterns were present in early hominid groups. Rather, these are hypotheses worthy and capable of testing. I shall attempt to do just that in this paper.

I am basing my interpretations on an analysis of data collected with the help of Rick Potts (Potts and Shipman 1981). We replicated 85 marks on bones from Beds I and II, Olduvai, and identified the unknowns by comparison with a large sample of marks of known origin under the scanning electron microscope (SEM). Before discussing the use of these data in a test of Isaac's and Lovejoy's hypotheses, I shall first discuss their reliability.

Identification based on microscopic features was tested for reliability against other suggested criteria, using marks of known origin. Width of marks is used by Bunn (1981), who states that cutmarks at Olduvai are significantly narrower than

Table 1 Maximum and minimum widths of cutmarks and toothmarks of known origin

	Type of mark	N	Mean width (mm)	Range	Standard Deviation	Variance
MAXIMA	Cutmarks	166	.32	.05–3.0	.39	.15
	Toothmarks	103	.55	.05–3.0	.73	.54
MINIMA	Cutmarks	166	.27	.05–4.2	.37	.14
	Toothmarks	103	.48	.05–3.0	.68	.43

N.B. The cutmarks used here were all I produced during butchery experiments using stone tools; about half of the marks were made by colleagues rather than by myself. The toothmarks here were obtained from bones chewed by zoo or wild carnivores of families or genera represented at Olduvai Gorge in the fossil record: felids, canids, hyaenids.

Statistical analyses were performed treating maxima and minima as if they were separate data sets to indicate the magnitude of error resulting from different measurements of the same marks.

toothmarks. Since all of these marks are of unknown origin, Bunn demonstrates only that he consistently identifies narrower marks as cutmarks and wider ones as toothmarks.

To investigate the usefulness of the width criterion, I collected data on 166 marks created during butchering experiments and 103 toothmarks of known origin; some anatomical features and preparators'/excavators' marks were also included in the sample. All cutmarks were made with newly-manufactured stone tools of flint, chert, obsidian, lava, basalt, or quartzite. The tools had edge angles comparable to those of tools from Beds I and II, Olduvai (Potts, pers. comm.). Tooth-marked bones were chewed by wild or captive animals of taxa represented at Olduvai; they ranged in size from small (jackal) to large (spotted hyena). Because cutmarks and toothmarks vary in width along a single mark, decreasing by as much as 80% of maximum width, I measured both maximum and minimum widths using an ocular micrometer (Table 1).

These data show that the mean *maximum* width of cutmarks is not significantly different from that of carnivore tooth scratches (*contra* Bunn). Indeed, the range of maximum cutmark widths encompasses the entire range of maximum tooth scratch widths. In contrast, the mean *minimum* width of cutmarks is significantly narrower than that of tooth scratches (Student's t-test, $p < .001$, 371 degrees of freedom; Kolmogorov-Smirnov = 1.59, $p < .05$). However, because even the ranges of minimum widths of the different marks overlap extensively, this criterion is most useful in confirming prior identification of sets of marks. Butchery experiments revealed three factors that cause variations in cutmark width: 1) the angle at which the tool is used; 2) the amount of soft tissue interposed between the tool and the bone surface; 3) the load applied to the tool. Each of these factors may vary in a single mark or between different marks. Thus two marks made by a single tool—or even two parts of one mark appearing on different fragments of one bone—may be identified differently using the width criterion. Finally, previous work has ignored vascular grooves, bone laminae, and preparators'/excavators' marks, all of which show mean widths comparable to Bunn's and mine for cutmarks. The risk of inaccurate identification of unknown marks based on width seems unacceptably high.

Cross-sectional shape, suggested by Potts and Shipman (1981) and Bunn (1981) to be diagnostic, is also a poor criterion. Although slicing marks are described as V-shaped and tooth scratches as U-shaped in these works, reality is poorly reflected in these morphological ideals.

Replicas of known carnivore tooth scratches and slicing marks were made, sectioned, and inspected under a microscope.

Even a limited sample ($N = 30$) showed that the shapes of these marks are highly variable (Figure 1). Slicing marks and tooth scratches in my sample neither conformed to the previously published descriptions nor showed any consistent differences suitable for use as diagnostic criteria. This is, in part, confirmed by Walker and Long (1977), who observed much shape variability in the cutmarks they examined. Therefore, this criterion is judged of little value in assessing the cause of an unknown mark.

The microscopic criteria are substantially more reliable than width or cross-section; my control sample now exceeds 700 marks and the microscopic criteria are diagnostic in every case. However, the size of the analyzed sample is small: there are only 23 cutmarks of various types and 48 toothmarks. The remaining 14 marks are attributed to preparators and excavators or are too poorly preserved to be identified. I now have a much larger sample of replicas from early butchery sites at Olduvai, Torralba/Ambrona (Spain), and Gadeb (Ethiopia), but these have yet to be inspected under the SEM. For this reason, I emphasize that the conclusions presented here are preliminary and await further confirmation.

To date, there have been few direct tests of Isaac's or Lovejoy's hypotheses using rigorous data. Isaac (1978, 1981) has argued that the clustering of artifacts and broken bones provides support for the concept of home bases, but Binford (1977, 1981) and others have pointed out that hominids are not the only agents capable of concentrating bones. Binford favors as major alternative hypotheses the hydraulic concentration of remains and the creation of "sites" by carnivores.

Potts, Bunn, and I (Potts and Shipman 1981; Shipman 1981a, b; Bunn 1981) have shown that the stone tools and bones at some early sites (FxJj5O, Koobi Fora; various Bed I and II sites, Olduvai Gorge) are *causally*, not *casually*, associated. The main thrust of these papers has been to demonstrate the existence of cutmarks on various bones. Such evidence in part refutes Binford's claim that the sites were formed by carnivore or hydraulic activities, in that we know that at least some of the bones were acted upon by early hominids wielding stone tools. This evidence does not preclude the possibility of multiple agents of concentration; indeed, all of the works by Potts, Bunn and me discuss evidence of carnivore activity at the same sites and on some of the same bones that the hominids damaged. Experimental work on the effects of fluvial transport and abrasion on bones (Shipman and Rose 1983), shows that the microscopic features diagnostic of cutmarks are obliterated after as little as 5 hours of abrasion. Therefore, fluvial transport of bones with microscopically-identified cutmarks can be safely

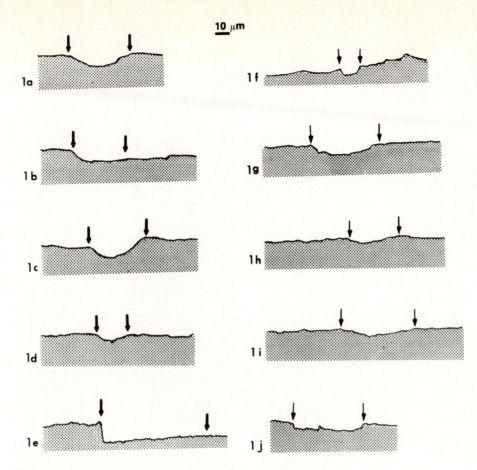

10 μm

1a 1f
1b 1g
1c 1h
1d 1i
1e 1j

Figure 1 *Camera lucida tracings (50x) of ten grooves of known origin reveal the variability in cross-sectional shapes of stone tool marks (1a-e) and carnivore teeth scratches (1f-j). The arrows indicate the margins of the marks. The same tool was used to make marks 1a and 1b.*

ruled out. This, although we have refuted the extreme of the alternative interpretation of these sites—that the bones and stones are accidentally associated—we have strongly supported a more moderate version of this interpretation: that hominids were not the only agents of damage and concentration at work on these sites. In essence, we are still left seeking ways to support or refute the Isaac and Lovejoy visions of early hominid life.

How can the Lovejoy and Isaac hypotheses be tested? Since both authors have drawn upon ethnographic analogies from recent hunter-gatherers to construct their theories, it is suitable to go to these same sources to seek testable predictions. In short, I have asked "What do recent hunter-gatherers do to carcasses that reflects food-carrying, food-sharing and base-camp-living?" Table 2 shows a set of correlates of different types of behavior important to Isaac's or Lovejoy's scenarios; the presence or absence of these correlates can thus be used to test whether or not these behaviors existed.

In each instance, it is important to ask if finding the predicted evidence constitutes proof of or merely support for the existence of the behavior. Is the evidence both necessary and sufficient, in the sense used in geometry, or is it merely necessary? Could more than one behavior result in the same correlate?

The last behavior, division of labor, is given support only by the recent work of Keeley and Toth (1981), who demonstrate convincingly that the stone tools from Koobi Fora were used on vegetable material and on soft tissues such as meat. Although their evidence is congruent with the idea that a division of labor for food procurement existed, it cannot be considered proof of

anything except the varied diet of early hominids because other species, including striped hyenas (Kruuk 1976) also leave evidence of mixed plant and animal diets in their refuse piles.

As discussed above, Potts, Bunn and I have all documented the presence of cutmarks on bones at sites from about 1.5 to nearly 2 m.y. ago. Although it is tempting to take this evidence as proof of meat-eating, it is prudent to exercise caution at this junction. First, the cutmarks demonstrate *only* that the hominids were using stone tools to remove tissues from carcasses; they do not tell us what the hominids did with the tissues afterwards. For direct proof of meat consumption, we must turn to comparative microwear studies (Walker 1981), or to evidence of ancient pathologies induced by meat-eating (Walker *et al.* 1982). Both these lines of evidence suggest a dietary shift from australopithecine frugivory to omnivory (probably including more meat) in *Homo erectus*. Second, the placement of the marks on the bones in the Olduvai

Table 2 Correlates of hominid behaviors, based on living hunter-gatherers

Behavior	Correlate
Meat-eating	Cutmarks on bones
Food-sharing	Disarticulation of carcasses
Food-carrying	Differential carcass utilization
Base-camp-living	Disarticulation of medium to large carcasses, defleshing of very large carcasses.
Division of labor	Combination of bony and plant remains at the base camp

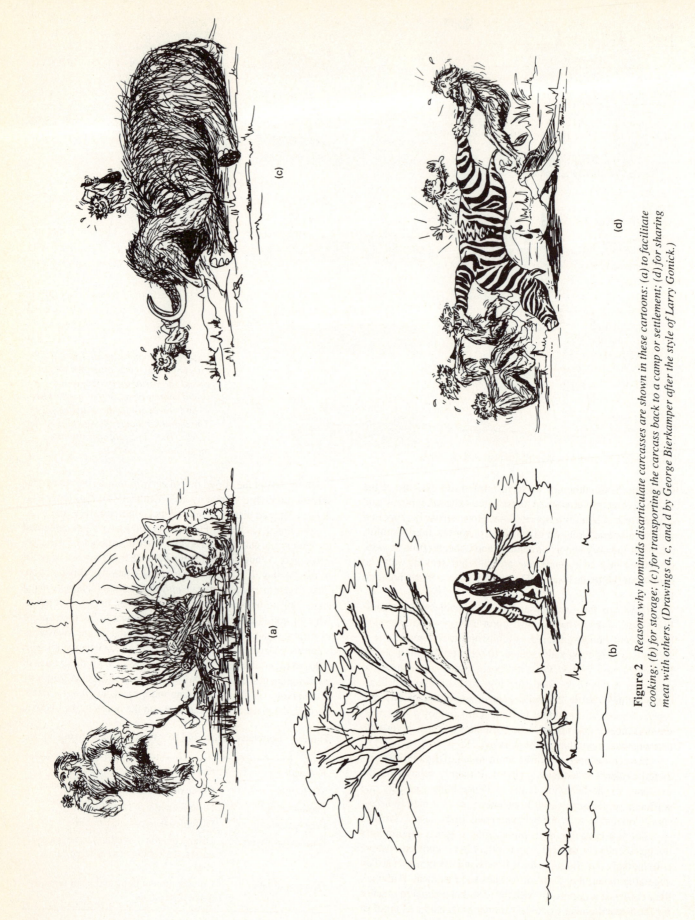

Figure 2 *Reasons why hominids disarticulate carcasses are shown in these cartoons: (a) to facilitate cooking; (b) for storage; (c) for transporting the carcass back to a camp or settlement; (d) for sharing meat with others. (Drawings a, c, and d by George Bierkamper after the style of Larry Gonick.)*

282

Table 3 Location of cutmarks and toothmarks on Olduvai bones relative to muscle masses

	Meat-bearing bones	Non-meat bearing bones
Cutmarks	9	10
Toothmarks	29	6

A chi-squared test of this distribution equals 5.39585, with one degree of freedom; p <.03, indicating a significant statistical difference.

sample is inconsistent with the idea that obtaining meat was the primary or sole objective of carcass-processing. As Table 3 shows (see also Potts and Shipman 1981; Shipman 1981a), the tooth scratches are most frequently located on meat-bearing areas, as might be expected if these are indeed caused by predators, whereas the cutmarks are nearly equally distributed in meat-bearing and non-meat-bearing areas. These data have led me to speculate elsewhere (Shipman 1981a) that many of these marks result from skinning or tendon removal rather than from meat production. Some possible uses of skin or tendon area as strips for binding or tying or as sacklike carrying containers, though many other uses can also be imagined. The real importance of this finding is that it raises the possibility that early hominids may have used carcasses as resources from which to obtain a variety of useful products, rather than simply as food sources.

The tests of food-sharing, food-carrying, and base-camp-living, can be conducted using the type of data Potts and I collected on the Olduvai bones. If these behaviors were being practiced, three main patterns ought to be discerned:

1) Differential carcass utilization based on size.

Carcasses of different sizes are treated differently. Using the San Bushman analogy so commonly enjoyed in scenarios of early hominid life, small animals are either eaten at the kill by the hunters or carried to the home base intact. Medium- to large-size animals are cut up and disarticulated at the kill site; some parts are eaten at the kill site by the hunters and the remainder is carried back to the camp to be further disarticulated and shared. Very large animals may be too heavy to be carried by the hunters even when disarticulated; more people may be summoned from the base camp or the carcass may be defleshed at the kill site and strips of meat carried to the camp (e.g., Lee 1968; Marshall 1965; Yellen 1977). Differential treatment of carcasses is also reported among many other hunting and gathering groups.

2) Transport and Disarticulation of Carcasses.

Animals larger than roughly 40 kilos are simply too heavy and cumbersome to be transported intact. Commonly, animals above this size are disarticulated at the kill site and carried back to the camp by members of the hunting party.

3) Food-sharing and disarticulation.

The butchery and subsequent distribution of meat among members of a social group very often proceeds along the lines of disarticulation. This is so common that reconstruction of butchery patterns routinely figure a complete skeleton with indications of the locations of frequently-found butchery marks (slicing, scraping, chopping, or sometimes fractures of various

types). Such marks show a great tendency to cluster around the major joints of the limbs, as distinct from skinning marks which often occur on ungulate metapodia or phalanges and/or on the lateral or medial surfaces of the mandibular corpus. (See Guilday et al. 1962 or Binford 1981, for example).

Before conducting a search for such patterning in the Olduvai remains, we must consider whether similar patterns of disarticulation and carcass utilization might arise from other causes. Why do hominids disarticulate carcasses? I have identified four major reasons (Figure 2a-e):

1. *cooking*—the carcass is too big to cook in one piece
2. *storage*—part of the carcass is set aside to be stored or protected from predators until later
3. *transport*—the carcass is too big to carry in one piece
4. *sharing*—the hunter has an obligation to share meat with other members of the group (division of labor, pair-bonding)

Reasons 1 and 2 are unlikely to apply to early hominids. Cooking almost certainly did not occur during Bed I Olduvai times since the earliest evidence of fire comes from Chesowanja at 1.4 m.y. (Gowlett et al. 1981, but see Isaac 1982); the next oldest evidence is at about .5 m.y. from Choukoutien (Clark 1970). Storage in the strict sense is also unlikely to have occurred, since modern hunter-gatherers characteristically have no means of meat storage at their disposal, with the exception of those in cold climates (Service 1979; Suttles 1968). Meat is sometimes dried in strips by hunter-gatherers, but these are apparently eaten within a few days (Marshall 1965; Woodburn 1968). The only intrinsic reason why dried meat could not be kept longer is the danger of attracting predators (Gould 1980), hardly a problem for the San, but possibly a great one for early hominids. In summary, the practice of carcass disarticulation, if shown to have occurred at Olduvai by a clustering of cutmarks at or near the major limb joints (Figure 3), would constitute major support of the food-sharing, food-carrying, base-camp-living scenario of early hominid life.

Figure 4 shows the location of the cutmarks and toothmarks in the Olduvai sample relative to major joints (N = 70, since not all marks occur on bones sufficiently identifiable for such distinctions to be made). For comparison, data on the location of nearly 300 cutmarks on bones from the Neolithic site, Prolonged Drift (Kenya), are also shown. These Neolithic marks almost certainly represent both disarticulation and skinning marks (Gifford et al. 1981); their patterning is strikingly reminiscent of those produced by recent peoples.

Both cutmarks *and* toothmarks from Olduvai show a pattern of distribution that is statistically different from that of the Neolithic cutmarks (chi-squared equals 99.34 and 100.78 respectively, with one degree of freedom in each case; p <0.001 in each case). On the other hand, there is no statistical difference between the distributions of Olduvai cutmarks and toothmarks. The conclusions must be that the Olduvai hominids are rarely if ever disarticulating carcasses. Thus both Isaac's and Lovejoy's hypotheses are refuted by these data; food-carrying and food-sharing (and, by implication, base-camp-living) did not occur at these sites.

The Olduvai sample is, unfortunately, too small for a meaningful test of differential carcass utilization to be conducted. However, since disarticulation has been demonstrated

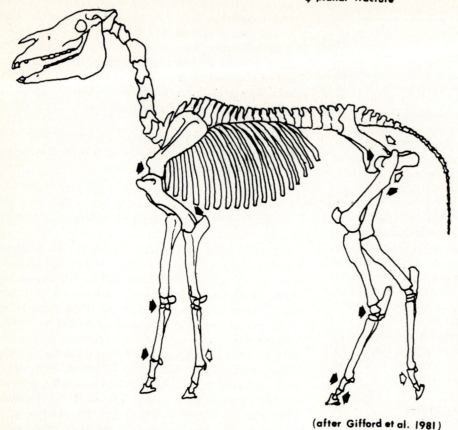

▶ cutmark

◊ planar fracture

(after Gifford et al. 1981)

Figure 3 *The arrows on this drawing of a zebra skeleton indicate the locations of the more common cutmarks or planar fractures found on nearly 300 bones from the Neolithic site of Prolonged Drift, Kenya (data from Gifford et al. 1981). Butchery and disarticulation marks were found in similar places on bovid bones from the same site.*

not to have occurred in Bed I times, whether or not differential carcass utilization occurred, we must recast our vision of early hominid life in new terms.

What evidence do we have that might bear on the question of early hominid behavior?

1. There are clusters of bones and tools, which we call "sites," but which we can demonstrate are often if not always the result of the actions of multiple taphonomic agents. This taphonomic overprinting is bound to confuse whatever patterning of remains was left by the hominids.

2. Early hominids used carcasses as resources for a variety of substances; in the process of procuring these substances, they damaged the bones with their stone tools.

3. Since disarticulation and systematic butchery (*sensu* Guilday *et al.* 1962) did not occur, little or no food-carrying or sharing occurred and it cannot be assumed that the hominids returned to a base camp and extended social group at frequent intervals.

4. Since systematic, regular patterns of carcass utilization and semi-permanent habitation are not supported, by implication these data suggest a more opportunistic use of animal resources and a more fluid, impermanent style of habitation.

5. Hominids at later sites apparently behaved differently with regard to carcasses from those at Olduvai about 2 m.y. years ago. Between .4 and .7 m.y. ago, at Olorgesailie, hominids carried out a systematic butchery and disarticu-

lation of giant gelada baboons (Shipman *et al.* 1981). Bones from a site at Gadeb, Ethiopia (Clark 1980; Clark and Kurashina 1979) that dates to between 1.5 and .7 m.y. show marks that may have resulted from butchery and disarticulation. (These marks form part of my larger sample of replicas that have yet to be examined under the SEM.) Therefore, sometime between 2 m.y. and about 1 m.y., hominids processing carcasses moved from a distinctly nonhuman to a distinctly human pattern. Brain (1981) documents a similar transition in South Africa, where australopithecines were predominantly preyed upon by carnivores but early *Homo* joined the ranks of predators.

What scenario or theory of early hominid evolution can be construed that fits these data?

First of all, let us consider how previous theories about early hominids have been constructed. Many of the seminal papers in paleoanthropology have used a procedure I call "triangulation." That is, the behavior of modern chimps or occasionally other mammals and that of modern hunter-gatherers (usually San Bushman) are reviewed and the behavior of early hominids is pictured as a hybrid of these. There are several reasons why triangulation is unlikely to be fruitful. First no scientist would claim that either chimps or hunter-gatherers stopped evolving and changing their behavior at or near the point of the pongid-hominid divergence. If we all agree that both species have probably changed considerably, why should we expect their behavior to tell us anything about that of early hominids? It

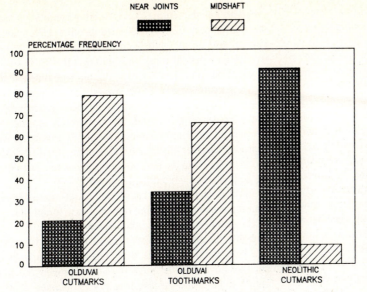

NEAR JOINTS   MIDSHAFT

Figure 4 *Locations of Olduvai cutmarks and toothmarks, relative to joints, are compared with the locations of butchery marks on bones from Prolonged Drift, Kenya, a Neolithic site. The pattern of distribution of Olduvai cutmarks or Olduvai toothmarks differs statistically from that of Neolithic butchery marks (chi-squared equals 99.34 and 100.78 respectively with one degree of freedom in each case; p <0.001 in each case). The two types of marks from Olduvai do not differ statistically from each other.*

might be argued that such an exercise will yield an assessment of the shared capabilities of each which might be presumed to also have been shared by early hominids. In this respect, triangulation is an approach borrowed from comparative anatomy. However, I think this approach is indefensible as a means of reconstructing complex behaviors such as foraging strategies and social organization unless such behaviors are genetically controlled, which I do not believe is the case. If there is an apparent trend in human evolution that can be identified, it is *towards* behavioral flexibility and adaptability and away from genetic specialization and canalization. The second problem with this approach, or even with using Bushman (or any other hunter-gatherer group) in a more limited analogy is that there are major, readily identifiable differences between modern hunter-gatherers and early hominids that almost certainly invalidate the analogy. Five major areas of difference come to mind:

1. The brains of modern hunter-gatherers are bigger and tremendously more complex than those of early hominids (Holloway 1974, 1981). Whatever these differences in organization and size of the brain mean in terms of mental capabilities, we can be sure that the San and other modern humans have far different capabilities than those of early hominids.

2. All modern hunter-gatherers have fire, but early hominids did not. The implications of possessing and controlling fire are enormous. One major benefit of possessing fire was surely the ability to keep predators away from the hominids and their food remains; another is that it can be used to cook or dry meat, thus forestalling spoilage. As others before me have observed (Gould 1980), taking large quantities of raw meat to the place one sleeps is a dangerous occupation unless predators can be repeatedly and successfully driven off.

3. Modern hunter-gatherers live nearly always in ecologically marginal areas that are different in many respects from the environments faced by early hominids (Laughlin 1968; Clark 1968). We have no means of assessing how the behaviors of modern hunter-gatherers might alter if their environments were less difficult.

However, if the literature on modern hunter-gatherers is accurate, their social behaviors are related to their environmental adaptations and thus can be expected to be unlike those of peoples inhabiting other environments (Howell 1968:287).

4. Modern hunter-gatherers, although generally considered to be non-technological peoples, possess tools, implements and weapons that far exceed those preserved from Bed I times in their complexity and sophistication. Even if we postulate the existence of many items for which we have no evidence (always a dangerous practice), the stone tools are pitiful compared to modern spears, guns, arrows, and knives.

5. Finally, because modern hunter-gatherers usually live in ecologically marginal areas, they are not faced with the intense competition from predators that early hominids in East or South Africa must have faced. It is amply documented that interference between predators in such areas as the Serengeti today has a marked effect on the social organization, feeding strategies, and life expectancies of the species involved. It is difficult to predict what alterations of behavior modern hunter-gatherers might adopt if faced with an array of predators more numerous and diverse than those extant today.

Others have frequently stressed the need to choose analogies with care (e.g. Yellen 1977). My point is that even carefully-chosen analogies may be misleading. Gould (1980:29) quotes a wonderful definition of analogy from the *Fontana Dictionary of Modern Thought*:

Likeness or similarity, usually with the implications that the likeness in question is systematic or structural. To argue by analogy is to infer from the fact that one thing is in some respects similar to another that the two things will also correspond in some other, as yet unexamined, respects ... (In logic) ... It is a form of reasoning that is peculiarly liable to yield false conclusions from true premises.

If chimps, Bushmen, and analogies are thrown to the wind, what is left?

The evidence at hand suggests a more opportunistic and less systematic use of carcasses than is seen in modern human behavior. This might indicate that early hominids were not particularly social animals, somewhat like orangs, or that they were not in full control of the carcasses. My prejudices incline me to place a higher probability on the latter alternative.

I propose as an alternative to the human-type hunter-gatherer models that early hominids were predominantly scavenging for meat and foraging for plant foods. Isaac (1978), Clark (1975) and others have raised this possibility before without subjecting it to testing. Predictions are difficult to generate since no recent human group known obtains most of its meat by scavenging. However, for reasons articulated above, recent humans may be a particularly poor choice of analogue anyway. Vrba (1980) generalizing from other mammals, suggests two criteria for recognizing scavenged assemblages: 1) a broad range of prey-animal sizes; 2) a low proportion of juveniles. I would add two more criteria to these: 3) a broad range of prey-species' habits; 4) a skew in the distribution of prey sizes towards the large end of the range. Because of the taphonomic overprinting known to have occurred at Olduvai, other possible criteria—such as body part of representation—are difficult to use here.

My criteria are formulated largely on the basis of logic rather than data. It seems logical to me that early hunters were more likely to have hit upon a strategy suitable for hunting a single type of animal rather than a more broadly applicable strategy. A similar behavior, called "targeting" by Meehan (1983), has been observed among living hunter-gatherers and other mammals. I also think smaller carcasses, whether juvenile or adult, are less likely to be available for scavenging than larger ones. Some support of this idea can be found in Kruuk's (1972) observation that he was often unable to identify smaller prey caught by hyenas because there was little left by the time he approached.

If these four criteria are applied only to those bones from Olduvai demonstrated to have been cut by hominids, all four criteria are met. The species range from small bovid to giraffid (a broad range) but nearly all are size class III or larger (see Brain 1981 for size classes and Potts and Shipman, 1981, for a species list). The species include bovids, equids, giraffids, which might be expected to show variability in habitats and habits. Very few juveniles are present but the sample is small and preservation is expected to favor adults. Based on this small sample of cut-marked bones, scavenging as a dominant mode of meat procurement seems highly probable. Perhaps the unusual distribution of cutmarks at Olduvai relative to the Neolithic site studied by Gifford et al, (1981) is a direct consequence of the opportunistic foraging-scavenging mode of life. Removing meat and other useful materials from a carcass as rapidly and efficiently as possible makes sense if the hominids were likely to be displaced or attacked by carnivores. Potts (1982) has reached a similar conclusion from other data and points out that this is a somewhat

cheetah-like adaptation. Cheetahs are generally subordinate to other carnivores (Kruuk 1972) and therefore have specialized in slicing meat off of carcasses rapidly (Ewer 1973). Disarticulating a leg or part of a leg and running off with it, hyena-style, involves much greater risk to a hominid who is unable to defend himself consistently from predators. Although the same predators might be equally attracted to a meat-carrying hominid and a leg-carrying hominid, the meat yields more calories per unit weight and can be eaten on the run if need be. (I would not contend, however, that disarticulation and food-transport never occur, simply that the data suggest they were less frequent than the behaviors I have outlined above.)

If this scenario is accurate and stands up to further proof, then the transition from the opportunistic foraging scavenging mode of life to recognizable human hunting and gathering probably occurred between 1 and 2 m.y. ago. I postulate that this behavioral shift was triggered by a change or a set of changes that directly affected and improved the hominids' ability to control a carcass once it was obtained. If we look to the fossil and archaeological record, three striking changes did occur during this time period:

1. *Homo erectus*, sporting a larger, more complex brain and a bigger body appeared;
2. the Acheulian tool-kit, with its greater variety and technological sophistication, developed;
3. fire apparently came under hominid control.

Any of these developments, or perhaps all in conjunction with others that remain as yet unrecognized, may account for the behavioral shift I postulate.

ACKNOWLEDGMENTS

This paper could not have been written, nor the work upon which it is based done, without the help of Jennie Rose. The work was supported by Boise Fund, by National Science Foundation Grants (BNS 80-1397 and BNS 802-1297), and by a National Institutes of Health Biomedical Research Program grant (5 S07RRO7041-13). I thank Richard and Mary Leakey, the governments of Tanzania and Kenya, and the paleontology staff of the National Museums of Kenya for their assistance in studying the Olduvai materials. Part of the work was performed on permit £OP. 13/001/6C70 issued by the President's Office of Kenya. Rick Potts, Alan Walker, Henry Bunn and Glynn Isaac all discussed these topics with me. My special thanks to George Bierkamper for drawing Figures 2a, c and d, and to Larry Gonick, upon whose work (*The Cartoon History of the Universe, vol. 2*) those drawings were based, for permission to produce them here.

REFERENCES

Beckwith, C., and Ole Saitoti, T. 1980. *Maasai*. Harry N. Abrams, New York.

Binford, L. R. 1977. Olorgesailie deserves more than the usual book review. *Journal of Anthropological Research* 33 4:493-502.

Binford, L. R. 1981. *Bones: Ancient Men and Modern Myths*. Academic Press, San Francisco.

Brain, C. K. 1981. *The Hunter or the Hunted? An Introduction to African Cave Taphonomy*. University of Chicago Press, Chicago.

Bunn, H. 1981. Archaeological evidence for meat-eating by Plio-Pleistocene hominids from Koobi Fora and Olduvai Gorge. *Nature (London)* 291:574-577.

Clark, J. D. 1968. Studies of hunter-gatherers as an aid to interpretation of prehistoric societies, in: *Man the Hunter* (R.B. Lee and I. DeVore, Eds.), pp. 276-280, Aldine Publishing Company, Chicago.

Clark, J. D. 1970. *Prehistory of Africa*. Praeger Publishers, New York.

Clark, J. D. 1975. A comparison of the Late Acheulian industries of Africa and the Middle East, in: *After the Australopithecines* (K. W. Butzer and G. Ll. Isaac, Eds.), pp. 605-660, Mouton, The Hague.

Clark, J. D. 1980. The Plio-Pleistocene environmental and cultural sequences at Gadeb, northern Bale, Ethiopia, in: *Proceedings of the 8th Pan African Congress of Prehistory and Quaternary Studies: Nairobi 1977* (R. E. Leakey and B.A. Ogot, Eds.), pp. 189-193, The International Louis Leakey Memorial Institute for African Prehistory.

Clark, J. D., and Kurashina, H. 1979. Hominid occupation of the East-Central highlands of Ethiopia in the Plio-Pleistocene. *Nature (London)* 282:33-39.

Ewer, R. F. 1973. *The Carnivores.* Cornell University Press, Ithaca.

Gifford, D. P. 1977. *Observations of Modern Human Settlements as an Aid to Archaeological Interpretation.* Ph.D. Thesis, University of California, Berkeley.

Gifford, D. P., Isaac, G. Ll., and Nelson, C. M. 1981. Evidence for predation and pastoralism at Prolonged Drift: A pastoral Neolithic Site in Kenya. *Azania* 15:57-108.

Gould, R. A. 1980. *Living Archaeology.* Cambridge University Press, Cambridge.

Gowlett, J. A., Harris, J. W. K., and Wood, B. A. 1981. Early archaeological sites, hominid remains and traces of fire from Chesowanja, Kenya. *Nature (London)* 294:125-129.

Guilday, J. E., Parmalee, P. W., and Tanner, D. P. 1962. Aboriginal butchering techniques at the Eschelman site (36LA12), Lancaster County, Pennsylvania. *Pennsylvania Archaeologist* 32:59-83.

Holloway, R. L. 1974. The casts of fossil hominid brains, in: *Human Ancestors: Readings from Scientific American* (R. E. Leakey and G. Ll. Isaac, Eds.), pp. 74-83, W. H. Freeman and Co., San Francisco.

Holloway, R. L. 1981. Exploring the dorsal surface of hominoid brain endocasts by stereoplotter and discriminant analysis. *Philosophical Transactions of the Royal Society of London*, Series B 292 (1057):155-166.

Howell, F. C. 1968. Discussion: The use of ethnography in reconstructing the past, in: *Man the Hunter* (R. B. Lee and I. DeVore, Eds.), pp. 287-288, Aldine Publishing Company, Chicago.

Isaac, G. Ll. 1978. The food-sharing behavior of proto-human hominids. *Scientific American* 238:90-108.

Isaac, G. Ll. 1981. Archaeological tests of alternative models of early hominid behavior: Excavation and experiment. *Philosophical Transactions of the Royal Society of London*, Series B 292 (1057):177-188.

Isaac, G. Ll. 1982. Early hominids and fire at Chesowanja, Kenya. *Nature (London)* 296:870.

Keeley, L.M., and Toth, N. 1981. Microwear polishes on early stone tools from Koobi Fora. *Nature (London)* 293:464-466.

Kruuk, H. 1972. *The Spotted Hyena: A Study of Predation and Social Behavior.* University of Chicago Press, Chicago.

Kruuk, H. 1976. Feeding and social behavior of the striped hyaena (*Hyaena vulgaris Desmarest*). *East African Wildlife Journal* 14(2):91-112.

Laughlin, W. S. 1968. Hunting: An integrating biobehavioral system and its evolutionary importance, in: *Man the Hunter* (R. B. Lee and I. DeVore, Eds.), pp. 304-320, Aldine Publishing Company, Chicago.

Lee, R. B. 1968. What hunters do for a living, or, how to make out on scarce resources, in: *Man the Hunter* (R. B. Lee and I. DeVore, Eds.), pp. 30-48, Aldine Publishing Company, Chicago.

Lovejoy, C. O. 1981. The origin of man. *Science* 211:341-350.

Marks, S. A. 1976. *Large Mammals and a Brave People.* Seattle and London: University of Washington Press.

Marshall, I. 1965. The !Kung Bushmen of the Kalahari Desert, in: *Peoples of Africa* (J. L. Gibbs, Ed.), pp. 241-278, Holt, Rinehart and Winston, New York.

McKennan, R. 1959. The Upper Tanana Indians. *Yale University Publications in Anthropology* 55:1-226.

Meehan, B. (1983). Contemporary and prehistoric shell gathering strategies. *Animals and Archaeology*, Vol. 2. Oxford: BAR.

Potts, R. 1982. *Lower Pleistocene Site Formation and Hominid Activities at Olduvai Gorge, Tanzania.* Ph. D. Thesis. Harvard University, Cambridge, MA.

Potts, R., and Shipman, P. 1981. Cutmarks made by stone tools on bones from Olduvai Gorge, Tanzania. *Nature (London)* 291:577-580.

Service, E. R. 1979. *The Hunters.* Prentice Hall, Englewood Cliffs, N.J.

Shipman, P. 1981a. Applications of scanning electron microscopy to taphonomic problems, in: *Annals of the New York Academy of Sciences* (A-M. Cantwell, J. B. Griffin and N. Rothschild, Eds.), 276:357-385.

Shipman, P. 1981b. *Life History of a Fossil: An Introduction to Vertebrate Taphonomy and Paleoecology.* Harvard University Press, Cambridge, MA.

Shipman, P., Bosler, W. and Davis, K. L. 1981. Butchering of giant geladas at an Acheulian site. *Current Anthropology* 22(33):257-268.

Shipman, P., and Rose, J. J. (1983). Bone tools: An experimental approach. In: *The Dutton and Selby Sites* (D. Stanford, Ed.), Smithsonian Institution Press, Washington D.C.

Suttles, W. 1968. Coping with abundance: Subsistence on the Northwest Coast, in: *Man the Hunter* (R. B. Lee and I. DeVore, Eds.), Aldine Publishing Company, Chicago.

Turnbull, C. 1965. The Mbuti Pygmies of the Congo, in: *Peoples of Africa* (J. L. Gibbs, Ed.), pp. 279-318, Holt, Rinehart and Winston, New York.

Turnbull, V. 1972. *The Mountain People.* Simon and Schuster, New York.

Vrba, E. S. 1980. The significance of bovid remains as indicators of environment and predation patterns, in: *Fossils in the Making* (A. K. Behrensmeyer and A. P. Hill, Eds.), pp. 247-272, University of Chicago Press, Chicago.

Walker, A. 1981. Dietary hypotheses and human evolution. *Philosophical Transactions of the Royal Society of London*, Series B 292(1057):57-64.

Walker, A., Zimmerman, M. R., and Leakey, R. E. F. 1982. A possible case of hypervitaminosis A in *Homo erectus*. *Nature (London)* 296:248-250.

Walker, P, and Long, J. C. 1977. An experimental approach to the morphological characteristics of tool marks. *American Antiquity* 42(4):605-618.

Woodburn, J. 1968. An introduction to Hadza ecology, in: *Man the Hunter* (R. B. Lee and I. DeVore, Eds.), pp 49-55, Aldine Publishing Company, Chicago.

Yellen, J. E. 1977. *Archaeological Approaches to the Present: Models for Reconstructing the Past.* Academic Press, New York.

Olduvai Gorge, Tanzania, the type locality of *Homo habilis* (photo courtesy of Curtis Marean).

Part IV
Origins of the Genus *Homo* and the Emergence of Culture

The chapters in this part address the first appearance and early evolution of our own genus, *Homo*. The earliest, and most primitive species of our genus, *Homo habilis*, has been a source of continuous controversy and confusion ever since its initial description (Chapter 26, see also Chapter 10 Addendum), and the identity and nature of this species is far from being resolved (see Tobias 1991; Wood 1991). The articles in this part discuss the criteria used to identify this species and distinguish it from species of *Australopithecus* or *Homo erectus*; the skeletal morphology and locomotor habits of *Homo habilis*, and finally the cultural remains usually associated with and attributed to this species (but see Chapter 14).

In Chapter 26, "A New Species of the Genus *Homo* From Olduvai Gorge" L.S.B. Leakey, P.V. Tobias, and J.R. Napier, provide the original description of *Homo habilis* based on associated remains of a juvenile individual, including a lower jaw, parietals and parts of a hand. They also describe numerous other dental and cranial remains, as well as a foot and a clavicle. Because *H. habilis* was more primitive than any later species of *Homo* in several features, the authors revised the definition of the genus to include the new species. Not surprisingly, description of this new taxon received very mixed responses (see Tobias 1965 and comments; also Chapter 10 Addendum, Chapter 31). Some questioned the reconstructed cranial capacity that distinguished *H. habilis* from *Australopithecus* and others suggested that this new species was perhaps a chimera composed of a mixture of older fossils of *Australopithecus* and younger ones of *Homo erectus*.

In Chapter 27, "Evidence for an Advanced Plio–Pleistocene Hominid from East Rudolph, Kenya" Richard Leakey, describes the famous skull of KNM-ER 1470. Although Leakey does not attribute this specimen to *Homo habilis*, the fossil clearly provided further evidence of a large-brained primitive hominid from the late Pliocene/early Pleistocene of East Africa that differed from *Australopithecus* and *Homo erectus* (see also Howell 1978). Subsequent revision of the stratigraphy and radiometric dating of the region has led to consensus that the age of these remains is approximately 1.8 m.y.a., rather than 2.9 m.y.a. as originally thought (e.g., Feibel *et al.* 1989).

Chapter 28, "The Koobi Fora Hominids and Their Bearing on the Origins of the Genus *Homo*" by Alan Walker, provides a broad overview and discussion of the Koobi Fora hominids and offers alternative ways of grouping the specimens and deciphering their phylogenetic relationships. He argues that "the greatest probability is that there were three contemporary species" from the Upper Member of the Koobi Fora Formation, *Australopithecus boisei*, *Australopithecus africanus*, and *Homo erectus*. The Lower Member contains one population that was antecedent to *Homo erectus* in the Upper Member, and similar to *Homo habilis*, as well as other specimens more similar to *Australopithecus africanus*.

Chapter 29, "Functional Morphology of *Homo habilis*" by Randall Susman and Jack Stern, reviews the hand, foot, tibia, and fibula from Olduvai Gorge that have been attributed to *Homo habilis*. They argue that all of these bones may have come from a single, juvenile individual. The hand bones demonstrate human-like features in the thumb and fingertips associated with manipulative skills while the proximal parts of the hand retain more primitive, ape-like features indicating suspensory behavior (see also Susman and Creel 1979). The leg and foot bones show derived bipedal adaptations as found in modern humans (see also Susman 1983), but lacking in *Australopithecus afarensis* (Chapter 18). The combination indicates the retention of climbing abilities in small Plio–Pleistocene hominids well after they became habitual bipeds.

Chapter 30, "New Partial Skeleton of *Homo habilis* from Olduvai Gorge, Tanzania" by Donald C. Johanson and colleagues, describes further remains of *Homo habilis* that elucidate aspects of body proportions in this species. They find that *Homo habilis* has a long, ape-like forelimb as in *Australopithecus afarensis*, supporting Susman and Stern's suggestion (Chapter 30) that this species retained climbing abilities. Similarly, they find that in tooth size to body size proportions, *Homo habilis* has large teeth, comparable to small individuals of *A. afarensis*. They suggest that the many primitive skeletal features in *Homo habilis* at ~1.8 m.y.a. contrasted with the more modern skeleton of *Homo erectus* at ~1.6 m.y.a. (Chapter 39) "may imply an abrupt transition between these taxa in eastern Africa."

Chapter 31, "Origin and Evolution of the Genus *Homo*" by Bernard Wood, is an up-to-date review of *Homo habilis* and its close relatives from the latest Pliocene and earliest Pleistocene of Africa. As others (Walker, Chapter 28; Stringer 1986) had suggested, Wood finds that the fossil hominids from this time period in East Africa are attributable to several taxa. He recognizes at least three different species in the genus *Homo*, *H.*

habilis, H. rudolfensis, and *H. ergaster* in early Pleistocene deposits of Kenya. He reviews the cranial, dental, and postcranial features of *Homo habilis* and its sister taxon, *Homo rudolfensis,* provides a redefinition of the genus *Homo,* and discusses the phylogenetic relationships among all early hominids.

Chapter 32, "Cutmarks Made by Stone Tools on Bones from Olduvai Gorge, Tanzania" by Rick Potts and Pat Shipman, discusses the function of the Oldowan tools commonly associated with the remains of *Homo habilis* and other Plio-Pleistocene hominids. Using scanning electron microscopy (SEM) they demonstrate that the cutmarks on bones from Olduvai Gorge have a characteristic pattern of grooves and scratches resulting from the action of stone tools (but see Andrews and Cook 1985; Behrensmeyer *et al.* 1986). This work provided the first clear evidence that bones associated with fossil hominids and stone tools had been processed by hominids, and the as-

sociation was not just the result of depositional agents. Moreover, they provide support for utilization of animal carcasses and bones by early hominids.

Chapter 33, "The Oldowan Reassessed: A Close Look at Early Stone Artifacts" by Nick Toth, discusses how Oldowan tools were probably made and used, and the significance of his results for interpreting the behavior of early hominids. On the basis of experimental studies replicating early hominid artifact types and using them for a variety of functions as well as careful study of Plio-Pleistocene artifacts and their materials, he argues that flake-tools were a very important part of the Oldowan technology and many of the core-tools may be simply by-products of flake production. He provides evidence that tools and cores for tool manufacture were transported from site to site, but questions the extent to which early hominids were dependent upon stone tools in their subsistence behavior.

REFERENCES

Andrews, P. and Cook, J. 1985. Natural modification to bones in a temperate setting. *Man* 20:675-691.

Behrensmeyer, A.K., Gordon, K. and Yangi, G. 1986. Trampling as a cause of bone damage and pseudo-cutmarks. *Nature* 319:768-771.

Feibel, C.S., Brown, F.H., and McDougall, I. 1989. Stratigraphic context of fossil hominids from the Omo Group deposits: Northern Turkana Basin, Kenya and Ethiopia. *Am. J. Phys. Anthropol.* 78:595-622.

Howell, F.C. 1978. Hominidae, in: *Evolution of African Mammals* (V. Maglio and B. Cooke, Eds.), pp. 154-248, Harvard University Press, Cambridge, MA.

Stringer, C. B. 1986. The credibility of *Homo habilis*, in: *Major Topics in Primate and Human Evolution* (B. Wood, L. Martin, and P. Andrews, Eds.), pp. 266-294, Cambridge University Press, Cambridge.

Susman, R. L. 1983. Evolution of the human foot: Evidence from Plio-Pleistocene hominids. *Foot & Ankle* 3:365-376.

Susman, R.L. and Creel, N. 1979. Functional and morphological affinities of the subadult hand (O.H. 7) from Olduvai Gorge. *Am. J. Phys. Anthropol.* 51:311-332.

Tobias, P.V. 1965. New discoveries in Tanganyika: Their bearing on hominid evolution. *Current Anthropol.* 6:391-411.

Tobias, P.V. 1991. *Olduvai Gorge, Volume IV. The Skulls, Endocasts and Teeth of* Homo habilis. Cambridge University Press, Cambridge.

Wood, B.A. 1991. *Koobi Fora Research Project Volume 4: Hominid Cranial Remains*. Clarendon Press, Oxford.

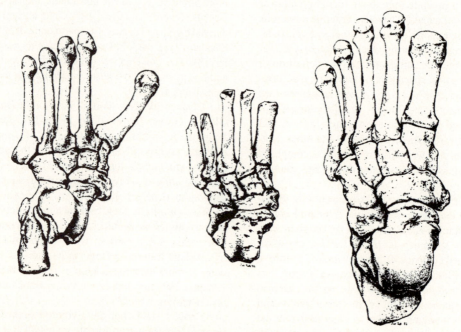

Tarsal and metatarsal structure of chimpanzee (left), *Homo habilis* (center) and a human (right). Illustration by Luci Betti (From Susman 1983).

26

A New Species of the Genus *Homo* from Olduvai Gorge

L. S. B. Leakey, P. V. Tobias and J. R. Napier

The recent discoveries of fossil hominid remains at Olduvai Gorge have strengthened the conclusions—which each of us had reached independently through our respective investigations—that the fossil hominid remains found in 1960 at site *F.L.K.N.N.* I, Olduvai, did not represent a creature belonging to the sub-family Australopithecinae [1].

We were preparing to publish the evidence for this conclusion and to give a scientific name to this new species of the genus *Homo*, when new discoveries described by L. S. B. and M. D. Leakey (1964) were made.

An examination of these finds has enabled us to broaden the basis of our diagnosis of the proposed new species and has fully confirmed the presence of the genus *Homo* in the lower part of the Olduvai geological sequence, earlier than, contemporary with, as well as later than, the *Zinjanthropus* skull, which is certainly an australopithecine.

For the purpose of our description here, we have accepted the diagnosis of the family Hominidae, as it was proposed by Sir Wilfrid Le Gros Clark in his book *The Fossil Evidence for Human Evolution* (1955, p. 110). Within this family we accept the genus *Australopithecus* with, for the moment, three subgenera (*Australopithecus*, *Paranthropus* and *Zinjanthropus*) and the genus *Homo*. We regard *Pithecanthropus* and possibly also *Atlanthropus* (if it is indeed distinct) as species of the genus *Homo*, although one of us (L.S.B.L.) would be prepared to accept sub-generic rank.

It has long been recognized that as more and more discoveries were made, it would become necessary to revise the diagnosis of the genus *Homo*. In particular, it has become clear that it is impossible to rely on only one or two characters, such as the cranial capacity or an erect posture, as the necessary criteria for membership of the genus. Instead, the total picture presented by the material available for investigation must be taken into account.

We have come to the conclusion that, apart from *Australopithecus* (*Zinjanthropus*), the specimens we are dealing with from Bed I and the lower part of Bed II at Olduvai represent a single species of the genus *Homo* and not an australopithecine. The species is, moreover, clearly distinct from the previously recognized species of the genus. But if we are to include the new material in the genus *Homo* (rather than set up a distinct genus for it, which we believe to be unwise), it becomes necessary to revise the diagnosis of this genus. Until now, the definition of *Homo* has usually centered about a "cerebral Rubicon" variably set at 700 c.c. (Weidenreich), 750 c.c. (Keith) and 800 c.c. (Vallois). The proposed new definition follows:

**Family   HOMINIDAE (as defined by Le Gros Clark 1955)
Genus *Homo* Linnaeus**

Revised Diagnosis of the Genus *Homo*

A genus of the Hominidae with the following characters: the structure of the pelvic girdle and of the hind limb skeleton is adapted to habitual erect posture and bipedal gait; the fore-limb is shorter than the hind-limb; the pollex is well developed and fully opposable and the hand is capable not only of a power grip but of, at the least, a simple and usually well developed precision grip [2]; the cranial capacity is very variable but is, on the average, larger than the range of capacities of members of the genus *Australopithecus*, although the lower part of the range of capacities in the genus *Homo* overlaps with the upper part of the range in *Australopithecus*; the capacity is (on the average) large relative to body-size and ranges from about 600 c.c. in earlier forms to more than 1,600 c.c.; the muscular ridges on the cranium range from very strongly marked to virtually imperceptible, but the temporal crests or lines never reach the midline; the frontal region of the cranium is without undue post-orbital constriction (such as is common in members of the genus *Australopithecus*); the supra-orbital region of the frontal bone is very variable, ranging from a massive and very salient supra-orbital torus to a complete lack of any supra-orbital projection and a smooth brow region; the facial skeleton varies from moderately prognathous to orthognathous, but it is not concave (or dished) as is common in members of the Australopithecinae; the anterior symphyseal contour varies from a marked retreat to a forward slope, while the bony chin may be entirely lacking, or may vary from a slight to a very strongly developed mental trigone; the dental arcade is evenly rounded with no diastema in most members of the genus; the first lower premolar is clearly bicuspid with a variably developed lingual cusp; the molar teeth are variable in size, but in general are small relative to the size of these teeth in the genus *Australopithecus*; the size of the last upper molar is highly variable, but it is generally smaller than the second upper molar and commonly also smaller than the first upper molar; the lower third molar is sometimes appreciably larger than the second; in relation to the position seen in the Hominoidea as a whole, the canines are small, with little or no overlapping after the initial stages of wear, but when compared with those of members of the genus *Australopithecus*, the incisors and canines are not very small relative to the molars and premolars; the teeth in general, and particularly the molars and premolars, are not enlarged bucco-lingually as they are in the genus *Australopithecus*; the first deciduous lower molar shows a variable degree of molarization.

Genus *Homo* **Linnaeus**
Species *habilis* **sp. nov.**

(NOTE: The specific name is taken from the Latin, meaning "able, handy, mentally skillful, vigorous." We are indebted to Prof. Raymond Dart for the suggestion that *habilis* would be a suitable name for the new species.)

A species of the genus *Homo* characterized by the following features:

A mean cranial capacity greater than that of members of the genus *Australopithecus*, but smaller than that of *Homo erectus*; muscular ridges on the cranium ranging from slight to strongly marked; chin region retreating, with slight or no development of the mental trigone; maxillae and mandibles smaller than those of *Australopithecus* and within the range for *Homo erectus* and *Homo sapiens*; dentition characterized by incisors which are relatively large in comparison with those of both *Australopithecus* and *Homo erectus*; canines which are proportionately large relative to the premolars; premolars which are narrower (in bucco-lingual breadth) than those of *Australopithecus*, but which fall within the range for *Homo erectus*; molars in which the absolute dimensions range between the lower part of the range in *Australopithecus* and the upper part of the range in *Homo erectus*; a marked tendency towards bucco-lingual narrowing and mesiodistal elongation of all the teeth, which is especially evident in the lower premolars (where it expresses itself as a marked elongation of the talonid) and in the lower molars (where it is accompanied by a rearrangement of the distal cusps); the sagittal curvature of the parietal bone varies from slight (within the hominine range) to moderate (within the australopithecine range); the external sagittal curvature of the occipital bone is slighter than in *Australopithecus* or in *Homo erectus*, and lies within the range of *Homo sapiens*; in curvature as well as in some other morphological traits, the clavicle resembles, but is not identical to, that of *Homo sapiens sapiens*; the hand bones differ from those of *Homo sapiens sapiens* in robustness, in the dorsal curvature of the shafts of the phalanges, in the distal attachment of *flexor digitorum superficialis*, in the strength of fibro-tendinous markings, in the orientation of trapezium in the carpus, in the form of the scaphoid and in the marked depth of the carpal tunnel; however, the hand bones resemble those of *Homo sapiens sapiens* in the presence of broad, stout, terminal phalanges on fingers and thumb, in the form of the distal articular surface of the capitate and the ellipsoidal form of the metacarpo-phalangeal joint surfaces; in many of their characters the foot bones lie within the range of variation of *Homo sapiens sapiens*; the hallux is stout, adducted and plantigrade; there are well-marked longitudinal and transverse arches; on the other hand, the 3rd metatarsal is relatively more robust than it is in modern man,

and there is no marked difference in the radii of curvature of the medial and lateral profiles of the trochlea of the talus.

Geological Horizon

Upper Villafranchian and Lower Middle Pleistocene.

Type

The mandible with dentition and the associated upper molar, parietals and hand bones, of a single juvenile individual from site *F.L.K.N.N.* I, Olduvai, Bed I.

This is catalogued as Olduvai Hominid 7.

Paratypes

(a) An incomplete cranium, comprising fragments of the frontal, parts of both parietals, the greater part of the occipital, and parts of both temporals, together with an associated mandible with canines, premolars and molars complete on either side but with the crowns of the incisors damaged, parts of both maxillae, having all the cheek teeth except the upper left fourth premolar. The condition of the teeth suggests an adolescent. This specimen, from site *M.N.K.* II, Olduvai, Bed II, is catalogued as Olduvai Hominid 13.

(b) The associated hand bones, foot bones and probably the clavicle, of an adult individual from site *F.L.K.N.N.* I, Olduvai, Bed I. This is catalogued as Olduvai Hominid 8.

(c) A lower premolar, an upper molar and cranial fragments from site *F.L.K.* I, Olduvai, Bed I (the site that yielded also the *Australopithecus* [*Zinjanthropus*] skull). This is catalogued as Olduvai Hominid 6. (It is possible that the tibia and fibula found at this site belong with *Homo habilis* rather than with *Australopithecus* (*Zinjanthropus*). These limb bones have been reported on by Dr. P. R. Davis (1964).

(d) A mandibular fragment with a molar in position and associated with a few fragments of other teeth from site *M.K.* I., Olduvai, Bed I. This specimen is catalogued as Olduvai Hominid 4.

Description of the Type

Preliminary descriptions of the specimens which have now been designated the type of *Homo habilis*, for example, the parts of the juvenile found at site *F.L.K.N.N.* I in 1960, have already been published in *Nature* by one of us (Leakey 1961a, b). A further detailed description and report on the parietals, the mandible and the teeth are in active preparation by one of us (P. V. T.), while his report on the cranial capacity (Tobias 1964) as well as a preliminary note on the hand by another of us (Napier 1962a) have been published. We do not propose, therefore, to give a more detailed description of the type here.

Description of the Paratypes

A preliminary note on the clavicle and on the foot of the adult, which represents paratype (b), was published in *Nature* (see Leakey 1960), and a further report on the foot by Dr. M. H. Day and Dr. J. R. Napier (1964) was published in *Nature* earlier this year.

The following additional preliminary notes on the other paratypes have been prepared by one of us (P. V. T.).

DESCRIPTION OF PARATYPES

(A) Olduvai Hominid 13 from *M.N.K.* II

An adolescent represented by a nearly complete mandible with complete, fully-erupted lower dentition, a right maxillary fragment including palate and all teeth from P^3 to M^3, the latter in process of erupting; the corresponding left maxillary fragment with M^1 to M^3, the latter likewise erupting, the isolated left P^3; parts of the vault of a small, adult cranium, comprising much of the occipital, including part of the posterior margin of *foramen magnum*, parts of both parietals, right and left temporosphenoid fragments, each including the mandibular fossa and foramen ovale. The distal half of a humeral shaft (excluding the distal extremity) may also belong to Olduvai Hominid 13. The *corpus mandibulae* is very small, both the height and thickness at M_1 falling below the australopithecine range and within the hominine range. All the teeth are small compared with those of Australopithecinae, most of the dimensions falling at or below the lower extreme of the australopithecine ranges. On the other hand, practically all the dental dimensions can be accommodated within the range of fossil Homininae. The Olduvai Hominid 13 teeth show the characteristic mesiodistal elongation and labiolingual narrowing, in some teeth the *L/B* index exceeding even those of the type Olduvai Hominid 7, and paratype Olduvai Hominid 6. The occipital bone has a relatively slight sagittal curvature, the Occipital Sagittal Index being outside the range for australopithecines and for *Homo erectus pekinensis* and within the range for *Homo sapiens*. On the other hand, the parietal sagittal curvature is more marked than in all but one australopithecine and in all the Peking fossils, the index falling at the top of the range of population means for modern man. Both parietal and occipital bones are very small in size, being exceeded in some dimensions by one or two australopithecine crania and falling short in all dimensions of the range for *Homo erectus pekinensis*. The form of the parietal—anteroposteriorly elongated and bilaterally narrow, with a fairly abrupt lateral descent in the plane of the parietal boss—reproduces closely these features in the somewhat larger parietal of the type specimen (Olduvai Hominid 7 from *F.L.K.N.N.* I).

(B) Olduvai Hominid 6 from *F.L.K.* I

An unworn lower left premolar, identified as P_3, an unworn, practically complete crown and partly developed roots of an upper molar, either M^1 or M^2, as well as a number of fragments of cranial vault. These remains were found at the *Zinjanthropus* site and level, some *in situ* and some on the surface. Both teeth are small for an australopithecine, especially in buccolingual breadth, but large for *Homo erectus*. The marked tendency to elongation and narrowing imparts to both teeth an *L/B* index outside the range for all known australopithecine homologues and even beyond the range for *Homo erectus pekinensis*. The elongating-narrowing tendency is more marked in this molar than in the upper molar belonging to the type specimen (Olduvai Hominid 7) from *F.L.K.N.N.* I.

(C) Olduvai Hominid 8 from *F.L.K.N.N.* I

Remains of an adult individual found on the same horizon as the type specimen, and represented by two complete proximal phalanges, a fragment of a rather heavily worn tooth (premolar or molar), and a set of foot-bones possessing most of the specializations associated with the plantigrade propulsive feet of modern man. Probably the clavicle found at this site belongs to this adult rather than to the juvenile-type specimen; it is characterized by clear overall similarities to the clavicle of *Homo sapiens sapiens*.

(D) Olduvai Hominid 4 from *M.K.* I

A fragment of the posterior part of the left *corpus mandibulae*, containing a well-preserved, fully erupted molar, either M_2 or M_3. The width of the mandible is 19.2 mm, level with the mesial half of the molar, but the maximum width must have been somewhat greater. The molar is 15.1 mm in mesiodistal length and 13.0 mm in buccolingual breadth; it is thus a small and narrow tooth by australopithecine standards, but large in comparison with *Homo erectus* molars. There are several other isolated dental fragments, including a moderately worn molar fragment. These are stratigraphically the oldest hominid remains yet discovered at Olduvai.

REFERRED MATERIAL

Olduvai Hominid 14 from *M.W.K.* II

(1) A juvenile represented by a fragment of the right parietal with clear, unfused sutural margins; two smaller vault fragments with sutural margins; a left and a right temporal fragment, each including the mandibular fossa.

(2) A fragmentary skull with parts of the upper and lower dentition of a young adult from site *F.L.K.* II, Maiko Gully, Olduvai, Bed II, is also provisionally referred to *Homo habilis*. This specimen is catalogued as Olduvai Hominid 16. It is represented by the complete upper right dentition, as well as some of the left maxillary teeth, together with some of the mandibular teeth. The skull fragments include parts of the frontal, with both the external orbital angles preserved, as well as the supra-orbital region, except for the glabella; parts of both parietals and the occipital are also represented.

IMPLICATIONS FOR HOMINID PHYLOGENY

In preparing our diagnosis of *Homo habilis,* we have not overlooked the fact that there are several other African (and perhaps Asian) fossil hominids whose status may now require re-examination in the light of the new discoveries and of the setting up of this new species. The specimens originally described by Broom and Robinson as *Telanthropus capensis* and which were later transferred by Robinson to *Homo erectus* may well prove, on closer comparative investigation, to belong to *Homo habilis*. The Kanam mandibular fragment, discovered by the expedition in 1932 by one of us (L. S. B. L.), and which has been shown to possess archaic features (Tobias 1960, p. 946), may well justify further investigation along these lines. The Lake Chad craniofacial fragment, provisionally described by M. Yves Coppens in 1962, as an australopithecine, is not, we are convinced, a member of this sub-family. We understand that the discoverer himself, following his investigation of the australopithecine originals from South Africa and Tanganyika, now shares our view in this respect. We believe that it is very probably a northern representative of *Homo habilis*.

Outside Africa, the possibility will have to be considered that the teeth and cranial fragments found at Ubeidiyah on the Jordan River in Israel may also belong to *Homo habilis* rather than to *Australopithecus*.

CULTURAL ASSOCIATION

When the skull of *Australopithecus* (*Zinjanthropus*) *boisei* was found on a living floor at *F.L.K.* I, no remains of any other type of hominid were known from the early part of the Olduvai sequence. It seemed reasonable, therefore, to assume that this skull represented the makers of the Oldowan culture. The subsequent discovery of remains of *Homo habilis* in association with the Oldowan culture at three other sites has considerably altered the position. While it is possible that *Zinjanthropus* and *Homo habilis* both made stone tools, it is probable that the latter was the more advanced tool maker and that the *Zinjanthropus* skull represents an intruder (or a victim) on a *Homo habilis* living site.

NOTES

[1] See Davis (1964), Day and Napier (1964), Tobias (1964) and Leakey and Leakey (1964).

The recent discovery of a rough circle of loosely piled stones on the living floor at site *D.K.* I, in the lower part of Bed I, is noteworthy. This site is geologically contemporary with *M.K.* I, less than one mile distant, where remains of *Homo habilis* have been found. It seems that the early hominids of this period were capable of making rough shelters or windbreaks and it is likely that *Homo habilis* may have been responsible.

RELATIONSHIP TO *AUSTRALOPITHECUS* (*ZINJANTHROPUS*)

The fossil human remains representing the new species *Homo habilis* have been found in Bed I and in the lower and middle part of Bed II. Two of the sites, *M.K.* I. and *F.L.K.N.N.* I, are geologically older than that which yielded the skull of the australopithecine *Zinjanthropus*. One site, *F.L.K.* I, has yielded both *Australopithecus* (*Zinjanthropus*) and remains of *Homo habilis*, while two sites are later, namely *M.N.K.* II and *F.L.K.* II Maiko gully. The new mandible of *Australopithecus* (*Zinjanthropus*) type from Lake Natron, reported by Leakey and Leakey (1964), was associated with a fauna of Bed II affinities.

It thus seems clear that two different branches of the Hominidae were evolving side by side in the Olduvai region during the Upper Villafranchian and the lower part of the Middle Pleistocene.

[2] For the definition of "power grip" and "precision grip," see Napier (1962b) which is reprinted in Chapter 5 of *The Human Evolution Source Book*. See also Napier (1956).

REFERENCES

Davis, P. R. 1964. Hominid fossils from Bed I, Olduvai Gorge, Tanganyika: A Tibia and Fibula. *Nature* 201:967-968.

Day, M. H. and Napier, J. R. 1964. Hominid fossils from Bed I, Olduvai Gorge, Tanganyika: Fossil Foot Bones. *Nature* 201:969-970.

Leakey, L. S. B. 1960. Recent discoveries at Olduvai Gorge. *Nature* 188:1050-1052.

Leakey, L. S. B. 1961a. New finds at Olduvai Gorge. *Nature* 189:649-650.

Leakey, L. S. B. 1961b. The juvenile mandible from Olduvai. *Nature* 191:417-418.

Leakey, L. S. B. and Leakey, M. D. 1964. Recent discoveries of fossil hominids in Tanganyika: At Olduvai and near Lake Natron. *Nature* 202:5-7.

Le Gros Clark, W. 1955. *The Fossil Evidence for Human Evolution*. University of Chicago Press, Chicago.

Napier, J. R. 1956. The prehensile movements of the human hand. *J. Bone Jt. Surg.* 38B:902-913.

Napier, J. R. 1962a. Fossil hand bones from Olduvai Gorge. *Nature* 196:409-411.

Napier, J. R. 1962b. The evolution of the human hand. *Scientific American* 207:56-62.

Tobias, P. V. 1960. The Kanam jaw. *Nature* 185:946-947.

Tobias, P. V. 1964. The Olduvai Bed I hominine with special reference to its cranial capacity. *Nature* 202:3-4.

27

Evidence for an Advanced Plio-Pleistocene Hominid from East Rudolf, Kenya

R. E. F. Leakey

Preliminary descriptions are presented of four specimens collected from East Rudolf during 1972. Most of the collection recovered during this field season has been reported recently in *Nature* (Leakey 1973); the specimens described here are sufficiently important to be considered separately and in more detail. The collections of fossil hominids recovered from East Rudolf during earlier field seasons and detailed descriptions of some of these specimens have been published previously (Leakey 1971, 1972; Leakey, Mungai, and Walker 1971, 1972).

The specimens described here are: (1) a cranium, KNM-ER 1470; (2) a right femur, KNM-ER 1472; (3) a proximal fragment of a second right femur, KNM-ER 1475; and (4) an associated left femur, distal and proximal fragments of a left tibia, and a distal left fibula, KNM-ER 1481. They were all recovered from area 131 (see Fig. 1) and from deposits below the KBS Tuff which has been securely dated at 2.6 m.y. (Fitch and Miller 1970).

Area 131 consists of approximately 30 km^2 of fluviatile and lacustrine sediments. The sediments are well exposed and show no evidence of significant tectonic disturbance; there is a slight westward dip of less than 3°. Several prominent marker horizons provide reference levels and have permitted physical correlation of stratigraphical units between area 131 and other areas in the East Rudolf locality.

Several tuffs occur in the vicinity of area 131. The lowest of these is the Tulu-Bor Tuff which is not exposed in the area itself but does outcrop nearby in several stream beds. Above this horizon, in a composite section, there is some 60 m of sediment capped by the prominent KBS Tuff. This latter tuff has been mapped into areas 108 and 105 (also shown in Fig. 1) from where samples have been obtained for K/Ar dates. An account of the geology is given by Vondra and Bowen (Vondra and Bowen 1973). A section showing the vertical position of these four hominids in relation to the KBS Tuff is given in Fig. 2.

At present, analysis of samples collected for dating from the KBS Tuff in area 131 has proved inconclusive because of the apparent alteration of the sanidine felspars. This was not seen in the 105/108 samples from the same horizon which provided the date of 2.61 m.y. and there is no reason to suspect the validity of that date (personal communication from J. A. Miller).

Detailed palaeomagnetic investigation of the sedimentary units is being undertaken by Dr A. Brock (University of Nairobi). Systematic sampling closely spaced in the section has identified both the Mammoth and Kaena events in area 105 between the

Tulu-Bor and KBS Tuffs, a result which supports the 2.61 m.y. date on the latter. The mapping of several horizons has established a physical correlation between areas 105 and 131. During the 1973 season, the area 131 succession will be sampled in detail in an attempt to confirm this correlation. Available evidence points to a probable date of 2.9 m.y. for the cranium KNM-ER 1470, and between 2.6 and 2.9 m.y. for the other specimens reported here.

Figure 1. *Map showing sites of discovery of fossil hominids KNM-ER 1470, 1472, 1475 and 1481 in the East Rudolf locality. Succession shown in Fig. 2 was taken from the position indicated by the dotted line.*

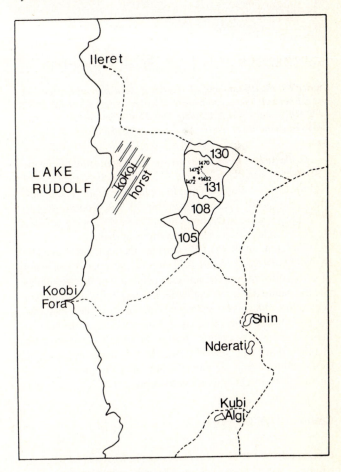

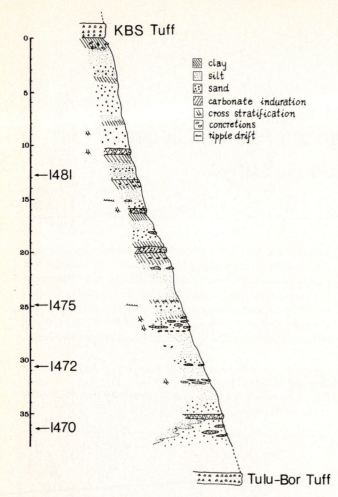

KBS Tuff

clay
silt
sand
carbonate induration
cross stratification
concretions
ripple drift

←1481

←1475

←1472

←1470

Tulu–Bor Tuff

Figure 2. *Stratigraphical succession of the sediments in area 131 and the vertical relationships of the fossil hominids KNM-ER 1470, 1472, 1475, and 1481 to the KBS Tuff. Dotted line shown in Fig. 1 marks the position at which the section was taken.*

Collections of vertebrate fossils recovered from below the KBS Tuff in areas 105, 108 and 131 all show the same stage of evolutionary development and this evidence supports the indicated age for this phase of deposition at East Rudolf. Maglio (1972) has discussed the fossil assemblages following detailed studies of field collections from various horizons.

The cranium (KNM-ER 1470) and the postcranial remains (KNM-ER 1472, 1475 and 1481) were all recovered as a result of surface discovery. The unrolled condition of the specimens and the nature of the sites rules out the possibility of secondary deposition—there is no doubt in the minds of the geologists that the provenance is as reported. All the specimens are heavily mineralized and the adhering matrix is similar to the matrix seen on other fossils from the same sites. In due course, microscopic examination of thin sections of matrix taken from the site and on the fossils might add further evidence.

Cranium KNM-ER 1470

Cranium KNM-ER 1470 was discovered by Mr. Bernard Ngeneo, a Kenyan, who noticed a large number of bone fragments washing down a steep slope on one side of a gully. Careful examination

showed that these fragments included pieces of a hominid cranium. An area of approximately 20 m x 20 m was subsequently screened and more than 150 fragments were recovered.

The skull is not fully reconstructed. Many small fragments remain to be included and it may be some time before the task is completed. At present the cranial vault is almost complete and there are good joins between the pieces. The face is less complete and although there are good contacts joining the maxilla through the face to the calvaria, many pieces are still missing. The orientation of the face is somewhat uncertain because of distortion of the frontal base by several small, matrix filled cracks. The basicranium shows the most damage and is the least complete region.

The cranium (see Fig. 3) shows many features of interest. The supraorbital tori are weakly developed with no continuous supratoral sulcus. The postorbital waisting is moderate and there is no evidence of either marked temporal lines or a temporal keel. The vault is domed with steeply sloping sides and parietal eminences. The glenoid fossae and external auditory meati are positioned well forward by comparison with *Australopithecus*. The occipital area is incomplete but there is no indication of a nuchal crest or other powerful muscle attachments.

In view of the completeness of the calvaria, it has been possible to prepare in modelling clay an endocranial impression which has been used to obtain minimum estimates for the endocranial volume. Six measurements of the endocast by water displacement were made by Dr. A. Walker (University of Nairobi), and gave a mean value of 810 cm^3. Further work on this will be undertaken but it seems certain that a volume of greater than 800 cm^3 for KNM-ER 1470 can be expected.

The palate is shallow, broad and short with a nearly straight labial border that is reminiscent of the large *Australopithecus*. The great width in relationship to the length of the palate does contrast markedly, however, with known australopithecine material. The molars and premolar crowns are not preserved, but the remaining roots and alveoli suggest some mesiodistal compression. The large alveoli of the anterior teeth suggest the presence of substantial canines and incisors.

Femur KNM-ER 1472

KNM-ER 1472, a right femur, was discovered as a number of fragments by Dr. J. Harris. It shows some features that are also seen in the better preserved left femur, KNM-ER 1481, but other features, such as the apparently very straight shaft and the bony process on the anterior aspect of the greater trochanter, require further evaluation.

Femoral Fragment KNM-ER 1475

The proximal fragment of femur, KNM-ER 1475, was discovered by Mr. Kamoya Kimeu. Its condition is such that a final taxonomic identification will be difficult and it is therefore included only tentatively in this report. This fragment shows some features such as a short, more nearly cylindrical neck, which are not seen in the femurs of *Australopithecus*.

Associated Skeleton KNM-ER 1481

A complete left femur, KNM-ER 1481, associated with both ends of a left tibia and the distal end of a left fibula were also discovered by Dr. J. Harris.

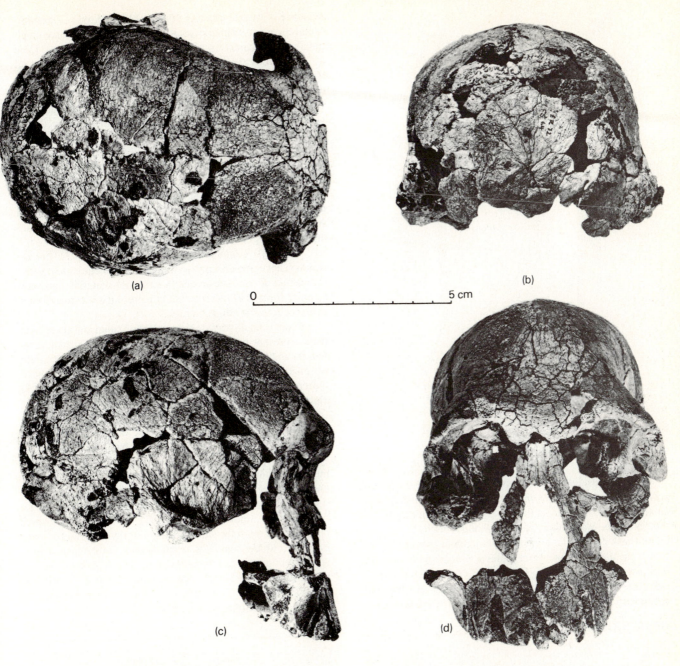

(a)

(b)

0 _____ 5 cm

(c)

(d)

Figure 3. *Cranium KNM-ER 1470.* (a) *Superior aspect;* (b) *posterior aspect;* (c) *lateral aspect;* (d) *facial aspect.*

The femur (see Fig. 4) is characterized by a very slender shaft with relatively large epiphyses. The head of the femur is large and set on a robust cylindrical neck which takes off from the shaft at a more obtuse angle than in known *Australopithecus* femurs. There is a marked insertion for gluteus maximus and the proximal region of the shaft is slightly flattened anteroposteriorly. The femoro-condylar angle is within the range of *Homo sapiens.* When the femur is compared with a restricted sample of modern African bones, there are marked similarities in those morphological features that are widely considered characteristic of modern *H. sapiens.* The fragments of tibia and fibula also resemble *H. sapiens* and no features call for specific comment at this preliminary stage of study.

Homo or Australopithecus?

The taxonomic status of the material is not absolutely clear, and detailed comparative studies which should help to clarify this problem have yet to be concluded. The endocranial capacity and the morphology of the calvaria of KNM-ER 1470 are characters that suggest inclusion within the genus *Homo*, but the maxilla and facial region are unlike those of any known form of hominid. Only the flat fronted wide palate is suggestive of *Australopithecus*, but its extreme shortening and its shallow nature cannot be matched in existing collections representing this genus. The postcranial elements cannot readily be distinguished from *H. sapiens* if one considers the range of variation known for this species.

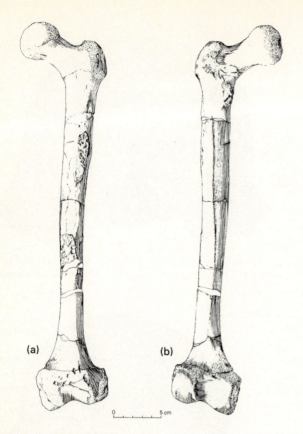

Figure 4. *Left femur KNM-ER 1481.* (a) *Anterior aspect;* (b) *posterior aspect.*

The East Rudolf area has provided evidence of the robust, specialized form of *Australopithecus* from levels which span close to 2 m.y. (2.8 m.y.-1.0 m.y.) (Leakey 1973); throughout this period the morphology of this hominid is distinctive in both cranial and postcranial elements. The cranial capacity of the robust australopithecine from Olduvai Gorge, *A. boisei*, has been estimated for OH 5 to be 530 cm^3 (Tobias 1971); this is the same value as that estimated by Holloway for the only specimen in South Africa of *A. robustus* which provides clear evidence of cranial capacity (Tobias 1971). Holloway has also found the mean cranial capacity of six specimens of the small gracile *A. africanus* from South Africa (Holloway 1970) to be 422 cm^3. Thus, to include the 1470 cranium from East Rudolf within the genus *Australopithecus* would require an extraordinary range of variation of endocranial volume for this genus. This seems unacceptable and also other morphological considerations argue strongly against such an attribution.

The Olduvai Gorge has produced evidence of an hominine, *H. habilis*; the estimated endocranial volumes for three specimens referred to this species are 633, 652 and 684 cm^3 (Holloway 1970). The Olduvai material is only known from deposits that are stratigraphically above a basalt dated at 1.96 m.y. (Curtis and Hay 1972). At present therefore there does not seem to be any compelling reason for attributing to this species the earlier, larger brained, cranium from East Rudolf.

The 1470 cranium is quite distinctive from *H. erectus* which is not certainly known from deposits of equivalent Pleistocene age. It could be argued that the new material represents an early form of *H. erectus*, but at present there is insufficient evidence to justify this assertion.

There is no direct association of the cranial and postcranial parts at present, and until such evidence becomes available, the femora and fragment of tibia and fibula are only provisionally assigned to the same species as the cranium, KNM-ER 1470. Differences from the distinctive *Australopithecus* postcranial elements seem to support this inferred association.

For the present, I propose that the specimens should be attributed to *Homo* sp. indet. rather than remain in total suspense. There does not seem to be any basis for attribution to *Australopithecus* and to consider a new genus would be, in my mind, both unnecessary and self defeating in the endeavour to understand the origins of man.

I should like to congratulate Mr. Ngeneo and Dr. Harris for finding these important discoveries. Dr. Bernard Wood spent many long hours at the site screening for fragments and assisted my wife, Meave, and Dr. Alan Walker in the painstaking reconstruction work. I thank them all. The support of the National Geographic Society, the National Science Foundation, the W. H. Donner Foundation and the National Museum of Kenya is gratefully acknowledged.

REFERENCES

Curtis, G. H., and Hay, R. L. 1972. Further geological studies and potassium-argon dating at Olduvai Gorge and Ngorongoro Crater, in *Calibration of Hominoid Evolution* (W. W. Bishop and J. A. Miller, Eds), pp. 289-301, Scottish Academic Press, Edinburgh.

Fitch, F. J., and Miller, J. A. 1970. Radioisotopic age determinations of Lake Rudolf artifact site. *Nature* 226:226-228.

Holloway, R. L. 1970. Australopithecine endocast (Taung specimen, 1924): A new volume determination. *Science* 168:966-968.

Leakey, R. E. F. 1971. Further evidence of Lower Pleistocene hominids from East Rudoph, North Kenya. *Nature* 231:241-245.

Leakey, R. E. F. 1972. Further evidence of Lower Pleistocene hominids from East Rudolph, North Kenya, 1971. *Nature* 237:264-269.

Leakey, R. E. F. 1973. Further evidence of Lower Pleistocene hominids from East Rudolph, North Kenya, 1972. *Nature* 242:170-173.

Leakey, R. E. F., Mungai, J. M., and Walker, A. C. 1971. New australopithecines from East Rudolf, Kenya. *Amer. J. Phys. Anthrop.* 35:175-186.

Leakey, R. E. F. Mungai, J. M., and Walker, A. C. 1972. New australopithecines from East Rudolf, Kenya (II). *Amer. J. Phys. Anthrop.* 36:235-252.

Maglio, V. J. 1972. Vertebrate faunas and chronology of hominid-bearing sediments east of Lake Rudolf, Kenya. *Nature* 239:379-385.

Tobias, P. V. 1971. *The Brain in Hominid Evolution*, Columbia University Press, New York and London.

Vondra, C., and Bowen, B. 1973. Stratigraphical relationships of the Plio-Pleistocene deposits, East Rudolf, Kenya. *Nature* 242:391-393.

28

The Koobi Fora Hominids and Their Bearing on the Origins of the Genus *Homo*

A. Walker

The sample of early hominid fossils from Africa has increased dramatically over the last decade. The Koobi Fora Research Project, under the leadership of Richard Leakey and Glynn Isaac, has been a major factor in creating collections, not only of hominids, but also of other animal groups. These new collections have been supported by a wealth of detailed studies on the geology, geochronology, and taphonomy and have their value enhanced by coming from the same depositional basin as a number of very important early archaeological sites.

The publication of the new fossils has been in two forms. First there are Richard Leakey's short notes and commentaries (Leakey 1970, 1971, 1972, 1973a, 1973b, 1974, 1976; Leakey and Walker 1976) and second there are fairly detailed descriptions by Leakey and his colleagues (Leakey *et al.* 1971, 1972; Day and Leakey 1973, 1974; Leakey and Walker 1973; Leakey and Wood 1974a, 1974b; Day *et al.*; 1975, 1976). The reasons for this manner of presentation are as follows. When it became clear that the Koobi Fora sediments were very rich in hominid fossils it was decided that as well as presenting the new material as quickly as possible in the form of announcements, we would be providing a service to other paleoanthropologists by delaying formal, monographic treatment in favor of detailed descriptions, photographs, and measurements. In this way we felt we could provide a source of data for those who did not have ready access to original specimens. Thus others would be able to contribute to discussions about the fossils, since they would not have to wait the many years it takes to produce a monographic, comparative account. Those of us involved in making these basic descriptive accounts did so knowing that the more discussion generated among other paleoanthropologists, the better would be our own final accounts when they came to be written. However, the initial warm response to this program has cooled somewhat; many of our colleagues now say that they would prefer more interpretative accounts. This is, in fact, more difficult than it would seem. Not only is it time consuming to compile a fully documented comparative account with interpretations, but there are many other new hominid fossils that have been found at other sites that would have to be considered.

In this paper I am going to deal first with the Koobi Fora hominids and then attempt an interpretation that takes into account fossils from elsewhere. A history of the Koobi Fora Research Project and an introduction to the hominid fossils and their context can be found in Leakey and Leakey (1978).

GEOLOGICAL SETTING

In order to use the hominid fossils in any evolutionary scheme (other than a purely cladistic one to establish relationships), their placement in time must be established. Many geological and geochronological studies have been carried out in the area to the east of Lake Turkana that enable us to place the fossils in their correct geological context (Behrensmeyer 1970; Vondra *et al.* 1971; Bowen and Vondra 1973; Johnson 1974; Vondra and Bowen 1976, 1978; Findlater 1976, 1978a, 1978b; Cerling 1976; Johnson and Raynolds 1976; Cerling *et al.* 1975). In addition, Behrensmeyer, Bowen, and Findlater have recorded microstratigraphic sections at nearly all of the hominid localities in order to determine the environment of sedimentary burial (Behrensmeyer 1975, 1976; Findlater 1978a, 1978b; Leakey *et al.* 1978). This task has been undertaken in an attempt to make generalizations about paleoenvironments from burial environments.

Potassium-argon age determinations have been made on some of the tuffs in the basin (Fitch and Miller 1970, 1976; Fitch *et al.* 1974, 1976, 1978; Curtis *et al.* 1975), and the results from one particular tuff have caused a celebrated minor controversy. Fission track dating of zircons from the same tuffs have been carried out by Hurford (1974) and Hurford *et al.* (1976). Paleomagnetic stratigraphic studies have also been used in an attempt to extend the isotopic age results into the main sediment body (Brock and Isaac 1974, 1976). Although the broad outlines of the geology are relatively simple, the wealth of information available on detailed problems is overwhelming. The account given here is necessarily simplified and incomplete.

About 800 km^2 of sediments are exposed in a wide coastal strip from the Ethiopian border in the north to south of Allia Bay (see Figure 1). The sediments are about 300 m in thickness and are draped over older volcanic rocks such that, on the whole, they dip away from both the Suregei escarpment in the east and the Kokoi volcanic horst that lies between the Ileret and Koobi Fora regions. The sediments vary from fluviatile to lacustrine,

Reprinted with permission from *Homo erectus: Papers in Honor of Davidson Black*, edited by B. A. Sigmon and J. S. Cybulski, pp. 193-215, University of Toronto Press, Toronto. Copyright © 1981 by University of Toronto Press, Canada.

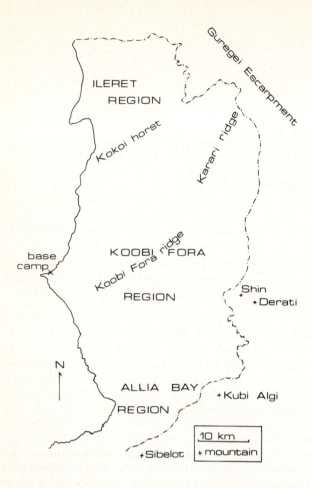

Figure 1. *Map of the Koobi Fora region showing the major geographical features. Lake Turkana is to the west of the coastline.*

with channel and floodplain deposits predominant inland and lacustrine deposits predominant to-wards the lake.

The whole sediment body is a complex interdigitating series of alternating fluviatile and lacustrine sediments brought about by alternating lake regressions and transgressions. There were periods when the land was being built out into the lake by delta and coastal plain incrementation and there were times when the lake transgressed and lacustrine deposition took place far to the east. These oscillations are long term and relatively gradual and are probably representative of times when the lake was externally drained and thus had a stable water level. Super-imposed on the oscillatory cycle are more sudden events where lake levels changed rapidly and erosion surfaces were either cut into the previously laid down sediments or suddenly inundated. These events probably took place when the lake level was low and the lake was internally drained, as it is today. Thus at any particular time the sedimentary environments from east to west were, in order, alluvial valley plain, alluvial valley coastal plain and/or delta plain, lacustrine high energy, and lacustrine low energy. However, at any particular time the boundaries of these environments would not necessarily be at the same place as at another. For instance, at the maximum of the transgression following the post-KBS tuff erosion surface, the shoreline in the Koobi Fora region was well inland towards the escarpment, whereas at Okote tuff times it was nearly where it is today. Put another way, if a core were taken from a drilling that went

vertically through the sediments, then alternate thicknesses of fluviatile and lacustrine sediments would be found, together with their intermediates. These would be cut across in places by erosion surfaces that were in turn filled by sediments deposited during the next lake transgression.

At infrequent intervals, the lakes that fed the area would become choked with volcanic ash from some as yet unknown source or sources. These ashes have been deposited in both river channels and/or floodplains. If they were not destroyed by subsequent erosion, they remain today as clear tuffaceous marker horizons for geological correlation and as the source of material for radiometric age determinations. They are isochronous horizons and as such are extremely important, for in the complexities of the rapid lateral facies changes that occur throughout the rest of the sediment body, such horizons are not easy to distinguish. Detailed stratigraphic sections which place the hominid fossils in their exact positions in a stratigraphic section for a particular area have been published (Leakey *et al.* 1978). It cannot be overemphasized that these sections will give only relative positions of the hominids within that particular section. An estimate of the temporal positions cannot be made from sediment thickness or position between dated tuffs.

The sediments are exposed in three clearly defined major regions: Ileret, to the north of the Kokoi horst; Koobi Fora, to the east of the base camp as far as the escarpment; and Allia Bay, to the south. Each region is divided into smaller areas for convenience of reference. The areas are bounded by natural features such as sand rivers, patches of vegetation, etc. The areas are shown in Figure 2. The major tuffs used for correlation both within and between areas are given in Figure 3. The most important correlations are those between the Ileret and Koobi Fora regions. The correlation between the Chari and Karari tuffs is considered to be satisfactory. The Ileret Lower and Middle tuffs, as a complex, are correlated with the Okote complex (that includes the Koobi Fora tuff). The KBS tuff, formally named in area 105, is satisfactorily correlated through the Karari region to Ileret, but is less safely correlated, it appears, towards Koobi Fora. White and Harris (1977) have questioned this together with the correlation of the underlying tuffs along the Koobi Fora ridge areas. Their doubts have arisen from their studies of suid evolution in Africa. However, the exact placement of the KBS tuff in these areas probably has bearing on only two hominid fossils, these being very fragmentary specimens.

Radioisotopic age determinations on feldspar crystals from the tuffs show that the Chari/Karari tuffs are about 1.2 million to 1.3 million years old. The overlying Guomde Formation is thought to be, on paleomagnetic grounds, about 700,000 years old. The Middle/Lower-Okote tuff complex is between 1.5 million and 1.6 million years old. The KBS tuff complex is either about 2.4 million years (Fitch *et al.* 1976) or between 1.6 million and 1.8 million years (Curtis *et al.* 1975). The Tulu Bor tuff is a little over 3 million years old.

The sediments between the KBS and Chari/Karari tuff complexes are known as the Upper Member of the Koobi Fora Formation (Bowen and Vondra 1973). Those below the KBS and above the Suregei tuff complex are the Lower Member of the Koobi Fora Formation. The Kubi Algi Formation lies below the Suregei tuff complex. For the purposes of dealing with the early hominid fossil record, the units to be considered are: the Guomde Formation (only at Ileret); the upper and lower parts of the Upper Member of the Koobi Fora Formation; and the upper part of the Lower Member of the Koobi Fora Formation.

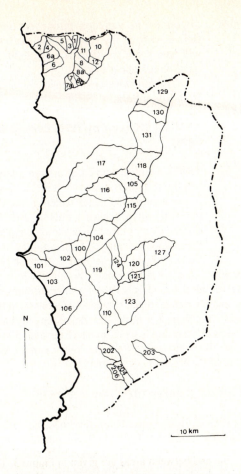

Figure 2. *Collection areas in the region.*

Only tooth fragments have been found in the lower part of the Lower Member of the Koobi Fora Formation. Basic and dating information is compiled in Figure 3.

What evidence can be brought to bear on the problem of the date of the KBS tuff? It is clear that both the Cambridge and Berkeley laboratories have been trying their best to resolve the issue. The two groups are using slightly different techniques and many of the arguments deal with complex geophysics and geochemistry. Whatever the real age of the KBS tuff may turn out to be, it must be remembered that the task of the geochronologist is to date the age of the rock (in this case the age of last heating of the feldspars). Then the age of the rock still has to be related to the sedimentary and biological events for which an age determination is needed. It is clear, then, that paleontologists have nothing to offer the geophysicists to help resolve what are basically geophysical and geochemical problems. Paleomagnetic stratigraphy studies (Brock and Isaac 1974) that seemed to corroborate the earlier dates are not as straightforward as had been thought (Brock and Isaac 1976), nor, apparently, is the polarity time-scale itself (Brown and Shuey 1976). Fission-track determinations give an age of about 2.4 million years (Hurford, Gleadow, and Naeser 1976) and thus support the older date. White and Harris (1977), in their study of pig evolution, suggest that the fossil pigs would support the younger age, that is, 1.6 million years to 1.8 million years. Dr P.G. Williamson of Bristol University is using the molluscs. His results may be of great help, since the sample sizes of invertebrate fossils can be large and the results, therefore, more reliable. As far as paleoanthropologists are concerned, then, we must wait for the solution.

THE HOMINID SAMPLE

Most of the hominids are surface finds. That is, they were found washing out of the sediments. The question of provenience must be raised in such cases, because direct evidence of stratigraphic level is lacking. In very nearly all the cases, the fossils can be shown to have come from a nearby horizon. The sediments are nearly horizontal and the elevations of the erosion gulleys in which the fossils are found are not great. The chances of a mistake being made in the stratigraphic level, then, are slight, and the limits of uncertainties are recorded. The Koobi Fora sample has suffered from many taphonomic biases (see Be-

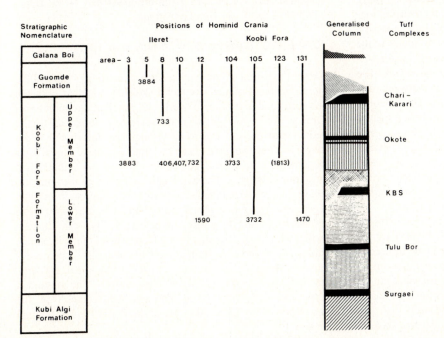

Figure 3. *Stratigraphic nomenclature and relative positions of the hominid fossils at East Turkana.*

Table 1 Representation of parts of the skeleton in the East Turkana hominids; postcranial parts are either complete or incomplete

Cranial and axial		Upper limb		Lower limb	
Crania with teeth	7	Scapulae	1	Pelvis	2
Crania without teeth	2	Humeri	9	Femora	23
Calvaria only	1	Radii	5	Tibiae	13
Mandibles with teeth	19	Ulnae	4	Fibulae	4
Mandibles without teeth	26	Metacarpals	2	Tarsals	4
Maxillae with teeth	2	Phalanges	2	Metatarsals	4
Maxillae without teeth	3			Phalanges	6
Cranial fragments	10				
Isolated teeth or groups of teeth	31				
Vertebrae	3				

hrensmeyer 1975), among them being differential preservation of body parts. Table 1 is a compilation of the Koobi Fora sample by body part. By far the greatest representation is teeth, followed by mandibles or mandibular fragments. This is the usual case in vertebrate fossil collections because the teeth and jaws are better able to resist carnivore and scavenger activity, as well as the destructive processes of sedimentary burial and exhumation. Postcranial elements are not common and there is a total lack of many parts. Associated cranial and postcranial material is rare and associated teeth, jaws, and postcranial elements are rarer.

To give some idea of the size of the Koobi Fora sample, we can ask the following questions. What fraction of the original hominid population is now represented in the collection? We can take a two-million-year period (about the span covered by the sediments) and use a generation length of twenty years. For hominids that had a population density as low as that of hunting dogs (*Lycaon pictus*) there would have been only eight per generation over the area (0.01 per km^3 [Kruuk 1972]). For hominids that had a population density as high as that of baboons (*Papio anubis*) there would have been 8000 per generation over the area (10 per km^2 [DeVore and Hall 1965]). Calculating for the 100,000 generations over the two-million-year period, the 150 individuals in the Koobi Fora collection represent only two ten-thousandths to two ten-millionths of the original population. We can further ask, what is the fraction represented by skulls, or at least good cranial specimens? The answer, following the same calculation, is between one hundred-thousandth and one hundred-millionth. This calculating has been carried out as though there were only one species of hominid. If we were to split the collections into several species, then the fractions would be much smaller. What this shows, regardless of how accurate the figures might be, is that the sample of past populations that we work with is miniscule. We might as well take as representative, in the worst instance, two individuals from the population of the United States.

I am not dealing here with fragmentary specimens or postcranial specimens, but only relatively complete crania. One of the examples, KNM-ER 1813, will demonstrate my reluctance at this stage to enter into taxonomic conjecture over fragments of mandibles, isolated teeth, or even whole mandibles with teeth. In dealing with the Koobi Fora cranial specimens I am going to claim that I can see three cranial variants (Leakey, Leakey, and Behrensmeyer 1978; Walker and Leakey 1978) and that there is

discontinuous variation throughout the sample. Before some of my readers close the book now, I will later agree that there is a possibility that I am quite wrong about this.

The following are the good cranial specimens from Koobi Fora.

KNM-ER 406 (Leakey 1970; Leakey *et al.* 1971)

This is a fine specimen of a large adult cranium lacking the tooth crowns and incisor roots, some of the bone of the facial skeleton, and the tips of the mastoid processes. This is clearly an individual very close in morphology and size to the hyper-robust, crested *Australopithecus* cranium from Olduvai Gorge Bed 1 (Tobias 1967). The zygomatic arches are more strongly built and wider altogether than OH 5, but this is mainly illusory, since the missing incisor region and the palate, when reasonably reconstructed, have an almost identical shape in both. The cranial capacity has not been calculated directly, but is likely to be a little over 500 cm^3. The specimen is from area 10 in the lower part of the Upper Member of the Koobi Fora Formation.

KNM-ER 407 (Leakey 1971; Day *et al.* 1976)

This is a cranium missing the facial skeleton including the supraorbital tori. The cranium is lightly built and globular, with marked postorbital constriction and well-developed *M. temporalis* gutters in the zygomatic processes of the temporals. The temporal lines can be followed and come as close to each other as 21 mm. The greatest width of the cranium is at the supramastoid crests, and the posterior profile is bell-shaped. The mastoids are well developed and extensively pneumatized. Details of some parts of the cranium are excellent, but crushing during fossilization had displaced many fragments that could not be returned to their original position. The cranial capacity is unknown, but likely to be close to 500 cm^3. The specimen comes from area 10 in the lower part of the Upper Member of the Koobi Fora Formation.

KNM-ER 732 (Leakey 1971; Leakey *et al.* 1972)

This is the partial cranium of an adult, consisting of most of the right and parts of the left facial skeleton, together with the frontoparietal part of the calvaria and the right temporal bone. Only half the second premolar crown remains together with the roots (or alveoli) of this tooth through the third molar and a single incisor. The midline can be found, and the temporal lines do not meet in a crest but come close to the midline just posterior to bregma. The zygomatic processes of the temporal are very large and guttered superiorly for the temporalis muscle. The cranium is globular and thinly built. The supraorbital tori are not strong and the postorbital constriction is great. The face is flat, with widely flaring zygomatic processes of the maxillae, and would have had a slight amount of subnasal alveolar prognathism (from reconstruction). The roots and alveoli are large and the half premolar is 9.0 mm mesiodistally. The mastoid is large and well pneumatized. The specimen comes from the lower part of the Upper Member of the Koobi Fora Formation in area 10.

KNM-ER 733 (Leakey 1971; Leakey and Walker 1973)

Although a fragmentary specimen, this partial skull has preserved the right mandibular body and third molar, part of the right parietal, much of the left maxilla, most of the left frontal, most of the right zygomatic, and many parts of the cranial vault. From the teeth and the alveoli in the maxilla, this specimen is one like KNM-ER 406, with large posterior teeth and smaller anterior teeth. The conformation of the frontal is also very like that of KNM-ER 406, with the frontal rising very slowly, and with no strong curvatures front the moderately sized supraorbital tori. The zygomatic is massive, and, if oriented to give a realistic orbital margin, was extremely wide and flaring. The temporal lines, though raised, do not meet in a crest on the preserved parts. The cranial capacity cannot be accurately estimated, The specimen comes from within the Okote tuff complex (Lower/Middle tuff complex of Ileret) of the upper part of the Upper Member of the Koobi Fora Formation in area 8.

KNM-ER 1470 (Leakey I973b; Day et al. 1975)

This is a partial adult cranium, missing most of the base, and parts of the facial skeleton. There are no tooth crowns, but the matrix-filled alveoli of the anterior teeth and the broken roots and alveoli of the rest of the teeth are present. The cranial capacity is between 770 and 775 cm^3, and the vault is thin and lightly built. The supraorbital tori are not salient. The greatest width of the cranium is at the supramastoid crest and the posterior profile is bell-shaped. Postorbital constriction is moderate. The facial skeleton is large, being some 95 mm from nasion to alveolare. The face is fairly flat, with the upper edges of the pyriform aperture everted. The alveoli and roots suggest large incisors and canines and moderately large posterior teeth. There is some distortion in the specimen. The midline relationships are not affected, but plastic deformation and/or rotation of some elements have made the left and right positions of porion very asymmetrical. Since porion position has been used to distinguish *Australopithecus* and *Homo* (Wood 1976), this is of some consequence (Walker 1976). Porion is relatively far posterior in *Australopithecus*. Figure 4 is an equal-angle stereographic projection of KNM-ER 1470 that shows the midline structures in correct alignment. The coronal and squamous structures have been plotted and the coronal is as nearly symmetrical as might be expected in an undistorted skull. The squamous suture has, however, been depressed on the right side so that the right temporal and porion have been carried downwards and forwards. The opposite movement, that of the left temporal moving upwards and backwards, can be rejected easily, since there is no overlapping or crushing at the squamous suture or elsewhere. On the right side, the squamous suture has slid open and there is a gap in the right side of the cranium. The forward movements of part of the right temporal can be seen in the plotted positions of other parts of it. Hence the position of porion in this cranium is close to the mean of *Australopithecus*. The specimen was collected from the upper part of the Lower Member of the Koobi Fora Formation in area 131.

KMN-ER 1590 (Leakey 1973a; Day et al. 1976)

This is a partial cranium of a juvenile with only the frontal and parietal bones, petrous, and some fragments of the calvaria.

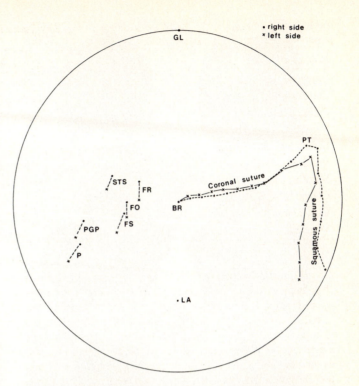

Figure 4. *Sterographic projection (equal angular) of features of KNM-ER 1470 in Norma verticalis. See Oyen and Walker (1977) for details of method. The coronal sutures are aligned, but the right temporal has been rotated, opening the squamous suture. Left and right sides have been plotted on one side for comparison. Points on the basal side of the temporals have been plotted on the other side of the plot. In all cases the right side has been moved forward. Abbreviations: GL, glabella; BR, bregma; LA, lambda; PT, pterion: STS, sphenotemporal suture; FR, foramen rotundum; FO, foramen ovale; FS, foramen spinosum; PGP, postglenoid process; P, porion.*

Several teeth and developing tooth crowns are preserved. The cranium was evidently large, since direct comparison with KNM-ER 1470 suggests that 1590 was bigger, even though it still had its second deciduous molar and deciduous canine in place and the central incisor was not quite in occlusion. The developing crowns of the anterior teeth are very large indeed, and those of the posterior teeth are also moderately large. The specimen is from area 12 in the upper part of the Lower Member of the Koobi Fora Formation.

KNM-ER 1805 (Leakey 1974; Day et al. 1976)

This is a nearly complete skull, missing only the rami of the mandible, most of the lower teeth and the supraorbital ridges and zygomatic bones. The elongated, ovoid braincase is small (cranial capacity about 580 cm^3) and has massive nuchal crests and a tiny, bifid sagittal crest well back on the parietal bones. The postorbital constriction is moderate. The facial skeleton has been crushed, so that the teeth and roots have been displaced in their alveoli and pieces of maxillary and palatal bone moved relative to each other. My colleague, Linda Perez, has undertaken the reconstruction of the facial fragment. This has been done, not on the original, but on a carefully painted plaster cast, using the original as a control. The various displaced parts were repositioned according to their edges and curvatures. The

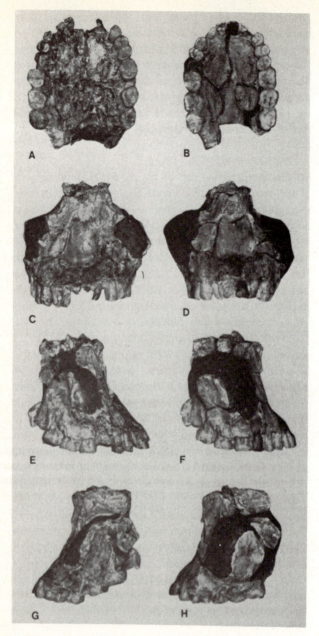

Figure 5. *Specimen KNM-ER 1805 before and after reconstruction.*

before and after photographs from this exercise are shown in Figure 5. The original palate was far too broad to occlude properly with its mandible. Ms. Perez has aligned the maxillary fragments using the undistorted mandible as a guide. The resulting arcade is a smooth parabolic one. The teeth are of moderate size. The face is broad in the nasal region. The facial fragment can be articulated using anatomical features of the orbit as a guide, and the result is shown in Figure 6. The specimen comes from area 130 in the lower part of the Upper Member of the Koobi Fora Formation.

KNM-ER 1813 (Leakey 1974; Day *et al.* 1976)

This is a nearly complete cranium, missing part of the left facial skeleton, some of the base, and part of the occipital. Nearly all

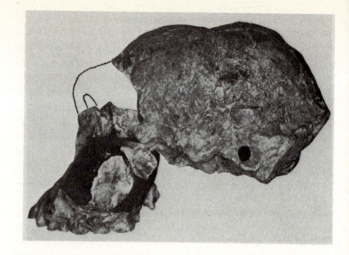

Figure 6. *Lateral view of reconstruction of KNM-ER 1805 cranium.*

teeth are represented, on either the left or right. The elongated ovoid cranium is small, with globular braincase of about 510 cm^3 in capacity. The vault is thin and in posterior profile has a bell shape. The widest part of the cranium is at the supramastoid crest. The postorbital constriction is moderate and the supraorbital tori are not particularly strong. The facial skeleton is large relative to the braincase. Despite the fact that the teeth are only of modest proportions for an early hominid, they are relatively large. The temporal lines do not come close to the midline. The gutters for the posterior fibers of *M. temporalis* are only moderately developed. The most striking resemblance is between this specimin and Olduvai Hominid 13 (Leakey and Leakey 1964; Tobias and von Koenigswald 1964). In practically every detail of size and shape of the teeth and all preserved parts, these two specimens are extremely close. Figure 7 shows the palate of both specimens. This is of great interest, because of all the specimens assigned to *Homo habilis*, Olduvai Hominid 13 is the only one that most authorities agree was in, or close to, the ancestry of *Homo erectus*. In fact, it has been reconstructed with an *erectus*-like vault (Brace 1973). Now we can see from comparison with 1813 that Olduvai Hominid 13 was probably not much like *Homo erectus*. Rather, it probably had a facial skeleton, palate, and teeth of the size of an *erectus* set on a very small calvaria. Even with a mandible containing

Figure 7. *Comparative palatal views of KNM-ER 1813 and Olduvai Hominid 13.*

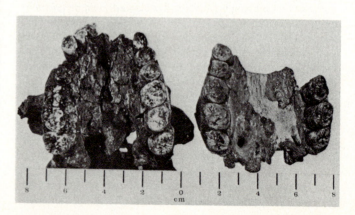

all its teeth, and much of the rest of the cranium, it seems that this is not enough to accurately determine the affinities of a particular hominid. The specimen comes from area 123 and its stratigraphic position is still not certainly known. Provisionally it is placed in the lower part of the Upper Member of the Koobi Fora Formation.

KNM-ER 3733 (Leakey and Walker 1976)

This is a nearly complete cranium, lacking parts of the lower facial skeleton and certain teeth. The cranium is large (cranial capacity about 850 cm^3) and very thick. The lateral profile is long and flattened, with a pronounced occipital projection and has a large part of the braincase behind the external auditory meatus. The supraorbital tori are projecting, but not particularly massive. There is a distinct postglabellar sulcus and the frontal rises steeply behind it to reach vertex at bregma. The facial skeleton is relatively small and tucked well under the braincase. The zygomatic portions are deep. The nasals are longitudinally concave and laterally convex and project over a wide, low pyriform aperture. The palate is roughly square in outline, with the incisor alveoli set in almost a straight line. The anterior teeth are moderately large, as judged by their alveoli, and the posterior teeth are of only moderate proportions. Although both third molars are missing, they were present in life, because the distal faces of the second molars bear contact facets.

No traces of third molar roots remain, so the chances are high that the crowns and roots were reduced in size. The specimen is very reminiscent of those from Peking (Weidenreich 1943) but it is more complete than any of the Chinese specimens. The cranium comes from area 104 and was in situ in the lower part of the Upper Member of the Koobi Fora Formation.

KNM-ER 3732 (Leakey 1976)

This is a partial cranium that has the supraorbital tori and much of the top of the cranial vault preserved, together with part of the left facial skeleton. In all preserved parts it closely resembles KNM-ER 1470. It comes from the upper part of the Lower Member of the Koobi Fora Formation in area 105.

KNM-ER 3883 (Walker and Leakey 1978)

This is a cranium that lacks the facial skeleton, except for parts around the nasals, the right orbit and right side of the pyriform aperture. In nearly all respects it is very similar to KNM-ER 3733. The supraorbital tori are a little more massive and, as a consequence, the postglabellar sulcus is shallow. The mastoid and preserved parts of the facial skeleton are also more robust than in KNM-ER 3733. The cranial capacity has not yet been recorded, but it is likely to be close to 850 cm^3. This specimen comes from the lower part of the Upper Member of the Koobi Fora Formation in area 3.

KNM-ER 3884 (Walker and Leakey 1978)

This is a crushed cranium, with all its teeth, from the Guomde Formation. It is of great interest because of its age—about 700,000 years. Preparation has begun, but no statements can be made at present about taxonomic affinities. This specimen comes from area 5.

This list includes all specimens that offer more than just fragmentary information about the cranium. What sense can be made of this sample? Taking first the sample from the Upper Member of the Koobi Fora Formation, that is, those dated between about 1.2 million years to either about 1.6 million years or about 2.4 million years, it appears that there are three forms present. These are: (1) hyper-robust crania with large facial skeletons and postcanine teeth, and small braincases; (2) crania with small braincases and smaller teeth and faces, that nonetheless still have large faces and teeth relative to the calvaria; (3) crania that show remarkable similarities to those from Java and China which have been called *Homo erectus*. These have larger, low braincases and relatively small facial skeletons and teeth.

Rather than trying to assign these specimens to known taxa, it is more instructive to see what are the possibilities of taxonomic arrangement. Figure 8 outlines the proposed scheme. There are 5 possibilities that can be considered:

1 They are all from one species, and the finding of three forms is just an artifact of sampling or pattern recognition. That is, in fact, the single species hypothesis (Brace 1967; Wolpoff 1971), which states that there has only ever been one hominid species. The idea is based on a series of assumptions about the adaptive nature of hominid morphology and on the principle of competitive exclusion (Gauss 1934). Bluntly put, adherents believe that the basic hominid characteristics of bipedal locomotion, reduced canines, delayed physical maturity, and so on have come about in response to more effective and greater dependence upon culture. The assumption of a basic hominid cultural adaptation, taken together with Gauss's principle, leads to

Figure 8. *The three forms of crania (a, b, c) found in the Upper Member of the Koobi Fora Formation, and the five possibilities of their groupings (see text for discussion).*

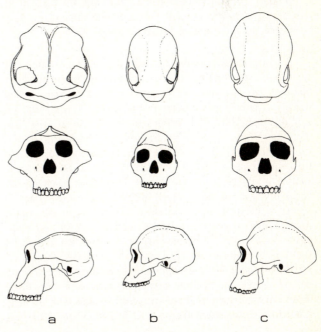

a   b   c

the conclusion that two hominid species would not be able to exist sympatrically.

2 They are all separate species. In this case, the hyper-robust crania would be placed in the taxon *Australopithecus* (or *Paranthropus*) *robustus* (or *boisei*). They have their greatest similarities with specimens from Olduvai (Olduvai Hominid 5), Chesowanja (Carney *et al.* 1971), Swartkrans (Broom and Robinson 1952), and Kromdraai (Broom and Schepers 1946). The fact that, on the whole, the East African specimens are larger could be explained by placing them in a separate species (*A. boisei*), or by claiming that they represent northern populations of *A. robustus* and that a geographic size cline exists. Faunal indications of ages of the South African sites would rule out the possibility of one group being ancestral to the other, since all of them are essentially contemporaneous (White and Harris 1977).

Possibilities 3, 4, and 5 group pairs of forms together within one species, leaving the other form as a separate species.

3 The robust crania and the small-brained, small-toothed forms are from one species and the *Homo erectus* are separate. Here the smaller individuals would be females of a sexually dimorphic species. This would mean accepting a normal amount of cranial capacity dimorphism, but an unusual amount of dimorphism in tooth proportions and size.

4 This possibility is that the robust crania and the large-brained crania would be from the same highly variable species, and that the small-toothed, small crania are in one, less variable species. This second species would probably be *Australopithecus africanus* and would have its affinities with specimens from Sterkfontein (Broom and Robinson 1950). In order to accept the other crania in a single species, we would have to accommodate both extremes of braincase variability and dental variability.

5 The last possibility is that the robust crania are in a separate species and the small-toothed forms are in their own, highly variable species. In this last case, the amount of dental variability is small, but the cranial variability is very great, not only in size, but also in shape.

Having decided that there are only these five possibilities (if we recognize the three forms) it remains to assign the probabilities that each case is correct. These need not be, at this stage, actual numerical probabilities. For the first possibility, it is my opinion that the probability of it being correct is close to zero. The demonstration of two fine *H. erectus* crania and robust *Australopithecus* in the same time period amounts to a rejection of the single species hypothesis. To place all these fossils in the same species would be to assign to past populations much greater variability than can be observed in any living hominid ones. It seems to me that the masticatory adaptations in the robust *Australopithecus* crania overshadow the braincase in a quite opposite way to the overshadowing of the dentition and facial skeletons by braincase seen in members of the genus *Homo*.

Possibility 2 has, in my opinion, the greatest chance of being correct, despite the fact that some specimens, especially those that are fragmentary, might be incorrectly placed. For instance, it is possible that the small crania, KNM-ER 732 and KNM-ER 407, could be female *A. robustus* as Leakey (1971) proposed (see also Robinson 1972). This would mean, however, that even more fragmentary specimens than these would be impossible to sort into types and thus, even if it has occurred, this error would be difficult to substantiate. The specimen, Sts 71, from Sterkfontein shows a number of features that are reminiscent of these two East Turkana crania, among them the wide zygomatic process of the temporal, the fairly flat frontal region, the mastoid inflation and the large zygomatic process of the maxilla.

Possibility 3 has a lesser chance of being correct, but the possibility must be faced that dimorphism within *Australopithecus* might have been greater than anything encountered today. The cranial capacity variability would be within the bounds of present-day values for humans and pongids. The dental variability would be greater than encountered today.

Possibility 4 has very little chance of being correct, for the very same reasons as number one. If skulls as different as robust *Australopithecus* and *Homo erectus* are from the same African populations, then where are the robust specimens at Peking and in Java? The *Meganthropus* specimens, so often brought forward as being Asian robust *Australopithecus*, are not convincing (see Tobias and von Koenigswald 1964).

The fifth possibility suffers from the same problem as the fourth. That is, although dentally the specimens could be accounted for in one very variable population, the cranial capacity dimorphism seems far too extreme. Besides this, the cranial construction of the *H. erectus* crania and the all-important features of the relationship between facial skeleton and braincase is clearly very different from that of the small-brained, small-toothed form. The same question can be asked here about the Asian sites. Where are the crania that look like KNM-ER 1813 in China and Java?

To summarize, it seems that the greatest probability is that there were three contemporary species during this time period. Taxonomically, these would be *Australopithecus boisei* (or *robustus*), *Australopithecus* cf. *africanus*, and *Homo erectus*. There is a lesser probability that the first two are really from one taxon, and there is hardly any probability that the other three possibilities are correct.

During the earlier time period, that is from the upper part of the Lower Member of the Koobi Fora Formation, the cranial sample is not large. The three crania that have been found below the KBS, or its lateral equivalents, are all of the form exemplified by KNM-ER 1470. They all have indications of a cranial capacity between 700 and 800 cm³. They all show an *Australopithecus*-like construction of the cranial vault. The facial skeleton of one, together with the teeth of another, show that the facial skeleton was extremely large relative to the braincase, as in *Australopithecus*. There is mandibular and dental evidence that at least the small *Australopithecus* was also present. It is the taxonomic status of these crania from below the upper part of the Lower Member that is important in understanding the origins of the genus *Homo*.

Some time ago I had the task of writing about the specimens belonging to *Australopithecus* from East Turkana (Walker 1976). I found that before I could do so I had to consider the factors that should be thought of when making a generic diagnosis. The points considered ranged from the trivial to the difficult, but my colleague Eric Delson chastized me gently for not paying enough attention to cladistic analysis. I have read those efforts that have been published concerning hominid evolution and have found myself confused (and sometimes dismayed), as have Kay and Cartmill (1977), at the inconsistencies in what is supposed to be a highly consistent exercise. At the heart of the trouble, I suspect, lie the problems of how to deal with great variability in a tiny sample, and the problems of deciding upon primitive characters. I will admit, however, that the recent rush of claims for early specimens of the genus *Homo* from both East and South Africa most likely stem from workers emphasizing primitive states. Those of the school of cladistics are, I feel, also deluding themselves that any particular phyletic relationship may be testable in any normal sense of testability [see Kuhn (1970), for instance, for a discussion of Karl Popper's views].

The only realistic way of dealing with the present tiny sample in a cladistic way that avoids the problems of variability, might be to deal with the single specimens, imperfect as they are, and construct cladograms for them. This would remove some difficulties, but the record is still very inadequate. I find the cladistic attempts to date excessively typological, yet I know how difficult it is to avoid thinking of, say, Sts 5 when dealing with Sterkfontein, since good specimens are so few. In fact, there are *no* complete crania or skulls of any early hominids. As for dealing with postcranial remains, we must continually remind ourselves that we have *no* specimen of any early hominid individual in which decent cranial and postcranial remains are associated. The Afar skeleton (Johanson and Taieb 1976) is the best by far, but there is not much of the skull in that magnificent specimen. There are *no* associated cranial and postcranial remains, from any site, of robust *Australopithecus*.

I find, on balance, that the crania from the Lower Member are best placed in the genus *Australopithecus*, their major differences from *A. africanus* being probably only of size. Nevertheless, I think that they represent the antecedent population to the *H. erectus* population that is sampled in the Upper Member, for to postulate an Asian or Eurasian origin for the later population is unnecessarily complicated. If indeed *H. erectus* evolved outside of Africa, it entered just when one part of the *Australopithecus* radiation had gained larger sizes (including brain size), and had already begun to litter the East African landscape with stone tools.

The species for these specimens would probably be *Homo habilis* (Leakey *et al.* 1964), but not in their sense entirely. Only Olduvai Hominids 7 and 16 fit into this category in my scheme, and since both are so very fragmentary, it is difficult to be dogmatic. Other specimens assigned to *H. habilis*, such as Olduvai Hominids 13 and 24 are, to my mind, part of the small-toothed small-brained species that I regard as an East African, late population of *A. africanus*.

Several other points are brought out by this assessment. The composite cranium, SK 847, from Swartkrans (Brain 1970) that has been an advanced hominid for some and an *Australopithecus* for others, seems to be a very fragmentary specimen of a very adult *H. erectus* (see Figure 9). The similarities to KNM-ER 3733 are striking, and I am no longer convinced that the midline relationships are any guide as to the

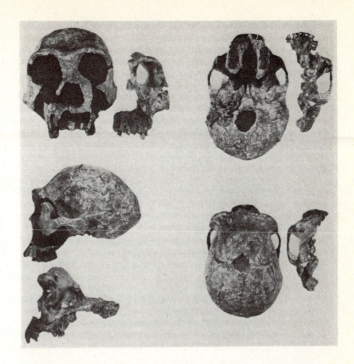

Figure 9. *Comparison of the more complete cranium KNM-ER 3733 and the composite cranium SK 847 from Swartkrans.*

real-life ones, especially since the specimen has suffered some postfossilization damage. As it happens, the faunal relationships show that SK 847 and KNM-ER 3733 are of approximately the same age (White and Harris 1977). Apart from showing that *H. erectus* was contemporary with a large robust *Australopithecus* at Swartkrans, as it was at East Turkana, this also shows that it is hardly worthwhile dealing with any fragmentary specimens if a new taxon is being recorded. As hominid specimens go, SK 847 is a reasonably complete one, yet it is not complete enough to satisfy skeptics. It takes, apparently, a specimen as good as 3733 for that, and 3733 is one of the most complete fossil hominid crania known.

The East Turkana fossils, although only a tiny sample of past populations, show us that the hominids underwent a minor radiation about two million years ago. One of the species, *H. habilis*, was a larger version of the species ancestral to all of them. This large species underwent changes that transformed it to *Homo erectus*. The time period required for the changes was either very short (on the order of about a few hundred thousand years), or quite long (about a million years). Resolution of the problem of the age of the KBS tuff will tell us whether our own genus arose rather suddenly or gradually (Eldredge and Gould 1972). This should be one of the most urgent tasks for our colleagues in the relevant disciplines. At a time when modes of evolution are beginning to be discussed in detail, the matter of our own origins should be of the highest priority.

REFERENCES

Behrensmeyer, A. K. 1970. Preliminary geological interpretation of a new hominid site in the Lake Rudolf basin. *Nature* 226:225-226.

Behrensmeyer, A. K. 1975. The taphonomy and paleoecology of Plio-Pleistocene vertebrate assemblages east of Lake Rudolf, Kenya. *Bulletin of the Museum of Comparative Zoology, Harvard* 146:473-578.

Behrensmeyer, A. K. 1976. Fossil assemblages in relation to sedimentary environments in the East Rudolf succession, in: *Earliest Man and Environments in the Lake Rudolf Basin: Stratigraphy, Paleoecology, and Evolution* (Y. Coppens, F. C. Howell, G. Ll. Isaac, and R. E. F. Leakey, Eds.), pp. 383-401. University of Chicago Press, Chicago and London.

Bowen, B. E., and Vondra, C. F. 1973. Stratigraphical relationships of the Pilo-Pleistocene deposits, East Rudolf, Kenya. *Nature* 242:391-393.

Brace, C. L. 1967. *The Stages of Human Evolution: Human and Cultural Origins*. Prentice Hall, Englewood Cliffs, N.J.

Brace, C. L. 1973. Sexual dimorphism in human evolution. *Yearbook of Phys. Anthro*. 16:31-49.

Brain, C. K. 1970. New finds at the Swartkrans australopithecine site. *Nature* 225:1112-1119.

Brock, A., and Isaac, G. Ll. 1974. Paleomagnetic stratigraphy and chronology of hominid-bearing sediments east of Lake Rudolf, Kenya. *Nature* 247:344-348.

Brock, A., and Isaac, G. Ll. 1976. Reversal stratigraphy and its application at East Rudolf, in: *Earliest Man and Environments in the Lake Rudolf Basin: Stratigraphy, Paleoecology, and Evolution* (Y. Coppens, F. C. Howell, G. Ll. Isaac, and R. E. F. Leakey, Eds.), pp. 148-162. University of Chicago Press, Chicago and London.

Broom, R., and Robinson, J. T. 1950. Sterkfontein ape-man, *Plesianthropus. Transvaal Museum Memoir* 4.

Broom, R., and Robinson, J. T. 1952. Swartkrans ape-man; *Paranthropus crassidens. Transvaal Museum Memoir* 6.

Broom, R., and Schepers, G. W. H. 1946. The South African fossil ape-men; the Aurstralopithecinae. *Transvaal Museum Memoir* 2.

Brown, F. H., and Shuey, R. T. 1976. Magnetostratigraphy of the Shungura and Usno formations, Lower Omo Valley, Ethiopia, in: *Earliest Man and Environments in the Lake Rudolf Basin: Stratigraphy, Paleoecology, and Evolution* (Y. Coppens, F. C. Howell, G. Ll. Isaac, and R. E. F. Leakey, Eds.), pp. 64-78. University of Chicago Press, Chicago and London.

Carney, J., Hill, A., Miller, J. A., and Walker, A. 1971. Late australopithecine from Baringo District, Kenya. *Nature* 230:509-514.

Cerling, T. E. 1976. Oxygen-isotope studies of the East Rudolf volcanoclastics, in: *Earliest Man and Environments in the Lake Rudolf Basin: Stratigraphy, Paleoecology, and Evolution* (Y. Coppens, F. C. Howell, G. Ll. Isaac, and R. E. F. Leakey, Eds.), pp. 105-114. University of Chicago Press, Chicago and London.

Cerling, T. E., Biggs, D. L., Vondra, C. F., and Sveck, H. 1975. Use of oxygen isotope ratios in correlation of tuffs, East Rudolf basin, northern Kenya. *Earth and Planetary Science Letters* 25:291-296.

Curtis, G. H., Drake, R., Cerling, T. F., and Hampel, J. H 1975. Age of KBS tuff in Koobi Fora formation, East Rudolf, Kenya. *Nature* 258:395-398.

Day, M. H., and Leakey, R. E. J. 1973. New evidence of the genus *Homo* from East Rudolf, Kenya (I). *Amer. J. Phys. Anthro*. 39:341-354.

Day, M. H. and Leakey, R. E. F. 1974. New evidence of the genus *Homo* from East Rudolf, Kenya (III). *Amer. J. Phys. Anthro*. 41:367-380.

Day, M. H., Leakey, R. E. F., Walker, A. C., and Wood, B. A. 1975. New hominids from East Rudolf, Kenya (I). *Amer. J. Phys. Anthro*. 42:461-476.

Day, M. H., Leakey, R. E. F., Walker, A. C., and Wood, B. A. 1976. New hominids from East Turkana, Kenya. *Amer. J. Phys. Anthro*. 45:369-436.

DeVore, I, and Hall, K. R. L. 1965. Baboon ecology, in: *Primate Behavior: Field Studies of Monkeys and Apes* (I. DeVore, Ed.), pp. 20-52. Holt, Rinehart and Winston, New York.

Eldredge, N., and Gould, S. J. 1972. Punctuated equilibria: an alternative to phyletic gradualism, in: *Models in Paleobiology* (J. J. M. Schopf, Ed.), pp. 82-115. Freeman and Co., San Francisco.

Findlater, I. C. 1976. Tuffs and the recognition of isochronous mapping units in the East Rudolf succession, in: *Earliest Man and Environments in the Lake Rudolf Basin: Stratigraphy, Paleoecology, and Evolution* (Y. Coppens, F. C. Howell, G. Ll. Isaac, and R. E. F. Leakey, Eds.), pp. 94-104. University of Chicago Press, Chicago and London.

Findlater, I. C. 1978a. Stratigraphy, in: *Koobi Fora Research Project. Vol. 1: The Fossil Hominids and an Introduction to Their Context 1968-1974* (M. Leakey and R. E. F. Leakey, Eds.). Oxford University Press, London.

Findlater, I. C. 1978b. Isochronous surfaces within the Plio-Pleistocene sediments east of Lake Turkana, in: *Geological Background to Fossil Man* (W. W. Bishop, Ed.), pp. 415-420. Scottish Academic Press, Edinburgh.

Fitch, F. J., Findlater, I. C., Watkins, R. T., and Miller, J. A. 1974. Dating of the rock succession contributing fossil hominids at East Rudolf, Kenya. *Nature* 252:213-215.

Fitch, F. J., Hooker, P. J., and Miller, J. A. 1976. ^{40}Ar/^{39}Ar dating of the KBS tuff in Koobi Fora formation, East Rudolf, Kenya. *Nature* 263:740-744.

Fitch, F. J., Hooker, P. J., and Miller, J. A. 1978. Geochronological problems and radioisotopic dating in the Gregory Rift Valley, in: *Geological Background to Fossil Man* (W. W. Bishop, Ed.), pp. 441-461. Scottish Academic Press, Edinburgh.

Fitch, F. J., and Miller, J. A. 1970. Radioisotopic age determinations of Lake Rudolf artefact site. *Nature* 226:226-228.

Fitch, J. J., and Miller, J. A. 1976. Conventional Potassium-Argon and Argon-40 / Argon-39 dating of volcanic rocks from East Rudolf, in: *Earliest Man and Environments in the Lake Rudolf Basin: Stratigraphy, Paleoecology, and Evolution* (Y. Coppens, F. C. Howell, G. Ll. Isaac, and R. E. F. Leakey, Eds.), pp. 123-147. University of Chicago Press, Chicago and London.

Gauss, G. F. 1934. *The Struggle for Existence*. Williams and Wilkins, Baltimore.

Hurford, A. J. 1974. Fission-track dating of a vitric tuff from East Rudolf, Kenya. *Nature* 249:236-237.

Hurford, A. J., Gleadow, A. J. W., and Naeser, C. W. 1976. Fission-track dating of pumice from the KBS tuff, East Rudolf, Kenya. *Nature* 263:738-740.

Johanson, D. C., and Taieb, M. 1976. Plio-Pleistocene hominid discoveries in Hadar, Ethiopia. *Nature* 260:293-297.

Johnson, G. D. 1974. Cainozoic lacustrine stromatolites from the hominid-bearing sediments east of Lake Rudolf, Kenya. *Nature* 247:520-523.

Johnson, G. D., and Raynolds, R. G. H. 1976. Late Cenozoic environments of the Koobi Fora formation: the Upper Member along the western Koobi Fora ridge, in: *Earliest Man and Environments in the Lake Rudolf Basin: Stratigraphy, Paleoecology, and Evolution* (Y. Coppens, F. C. Howell, G. Ll. Isaac, and R. E. F. Leakey, Eds.), pp. 115-122. University of Chicago Press, Chicago and London.

Kay, R. F., Cartmill, M. 1977. Cranial morphology and adaptations of *Palaechthon nacimienti* and other Paromomyidae (Plesiadapoidea, ?Primates), with a description of a new genus and species. *J. Hum. Evol*. 6:19-53.

Kruuk, H. 1972. *The Spotted Hyena; a Study of Predation and Social Behavior*. University of Chicago Press, Chicago.

Kuhn, R. S. 1970. *The Structure of Scientific Revolutions*. University of Chicago Press, Chicago and London.

Leakey, L. S. B., and Leakey, M. D. 1964. Recent discoveries of fossil hominids in Tanganyika at Olduvai and near Lake Natron. *Nature* 202:5-6.

Leakey, L. S. B., Tobias, P. V., and Napier, J. R. 1964. A new species of the genus *Homo* from Olduvai Gorge. *Nature* 202:7-9.

Leakey, M. G., and Leakey, R. E. F., Eds. 1978. *Koobi Fora Research Project. Vol. 1: The Fossil Hominids and an Introduction to Their Context 1968-1974*. Oxford University Press, London.

Leakey, R. E. F. 1970. Fauna and artefacts from a new Plio-Pleistocene locality near Lake Rudolf in Kenya. *Nature* 226:223-224.

Leakey, R. E. F. 1971. Further evidence of Lower Pleistocene hominids from East Rudolf, North Kenya. *Nature* 231:241-245.

Leakey, R. E. F. 1972. Further evidence of Lower Pleistocene hominids from East Rudolf, North Kenya, 1971. *Nature* 237:264-269.

Leakey, R. E. F. 1973a. Further evidence of Lower Pleistocene hominids from East Rudolf, North Kenya, 1972. *Nature* 242:170-173.

Leakey, R. E. F. 1973b. Evidence for an advanced Plio-Pleistocene hominid from East Rudolf, Kenya. *Nature* 242:447-450.

Leakey, R. E. F. 1974. Further evidence of Lower Pleistocene hominids from East Rudolf, North Kenya, 1973. *Nature* 248:653-656.

Leakey, R. E. F. 1976. New hominids fossils from the Koobi Fora formation in northern Kenya. *Nature* 262:574-576.

Leakey, R. E. F., Leakey, M. G., and Behrensmeyer, A. K. 1978. The hominid catalogue, in: *Koobi Fora Research Project. Vol. 1: The Fossil Hominids and an Introduction to Their Context 1968-1974* (M. G. Leakey and R. E. F. Leakey, Eds.), Oxford University Press, London.

Leakey, R. E. F., Mungai, J. M., and Walker, A. C. 1971. New australopithecines from East Rudolf, Kenya. *Amer. J. Phys. Anthro.* 35:175-186.

Leakey, R. E. F., Mungai, J. M., and Walker, A. C. 1972. New australopithecines from East Rudolf, Kenya (II). *Amer. J. Phys. Anthro.* 36:235-252.

Leakey, R. E. F., and Walker, A. C. 1973. New australopithecines from East Rudolf, Kenya (III). *Amer. J. Phys. Anthro.* 39:205-222.

Leakey, R. E. F. and Walker, A. C. 1976. *Australopithecus, Homo erectus* and the single-species hypothesis. *Nature* 261:572-574.

Leakey, R. E. F., Wood, B. A. 1974a. New Evidence of the genus *Homo* from East Rudolf, Kenya (IV). *Amer. J. Phys. Anthro.* 41:237-44.

Leakey, R. E. F., Wood, B. A. 1974b. A hominid mandible from East Rudolf, Kenya. *Amer. J. Phys. Anthro.* 41:245-50.

Oyen, O. J., Walker, A. C. 1977. Stereometric craniometry. *Amer. J. Phys. Anthro.* 46:177-82.

Robinson, J. T. 1972. The bearing of East Rudolf fossils on early hominid systematics. *Nature* 240:239-240.

Tobias, P. V. 1967. *Olduvai Gorge, Vol. 2: The Cranium and Maxillary Dentition of* Australopithecus (Zinjanthropus) boisei. Cambridge University Press, Cambridge.

Tobias, P. V., and von Koenigswald, G. H. R. 1964. A comparison between the Olduvai hominines and those of Java, and some implications for hominid phylogeny. *Nature* 204:515-518.

Vondra, C. F., and Bowen, B. E. 1976. Plio-Pleistocene deposits and environments, East Rudolf, Kenya, in: *Earliest Man and Environments in the Lake Rudolf Basin: Stratigraphy, Paleoecology, and Evolution* (Y. Coppens, F. C. Howell, G. Ll. Isaac, and R. E. F. Leakey, Eds.), pp. 79-93. University of Chicago Press, Chicago and London.

Vondra, C. G., Johnson, G. D., Bowen, B. E., and Behrensmeyer, A. K. 1971. Preliminary stratigraphical studies of the East Rudolf basin, Kenya. *Nature* 231:245-248.

Vondra, C. F. and Bowen, B. E. 1978. Stratigraphy, sedimentary facies and paleoenvironments, East Turkana, Kenya, in: *Geological Backround to Fossil Man* (W. W. Bishop, Ed.), pp. 395-414. Scottish Academic Press, Edinburgh.

Walker, A. 1976. Remains attributable to *Australopithecus* in the East Rudolf succession, in: *Earliest Man and Environments in the Lake Rudolf Basin: Stratigraphy, Paleoecology, and Evolution* (Y. Coppens, F. C. Howell, G. Ll. Isaac, and R. E. F. Leakey, Eds.), pp. 484-489. University of Chicago Press, Chicago and London.

Walker, A., and Leakey, R. E. F. 1978. The hominids of East Turkana. *Sci. Amer.* 239(2):54-66.

Weidenreich, F. 1943. The skull of *Sinanthropus pekinensis*: A comparative study of a primitive hominid skull. *Paleontol. Sin.* n. s. D., No. 10.

White, T. D., and Harris, J. M. 1977. Suid evolution and correlation of African hominid localities. *Science* 198:13-21.

Wolpoff, M. H. 1971. Competitive exclusion among Lower Pleistocene hominids: the single species hypothesis. *Man* 6:601-614.

Wood, B. A. 1976. Remains attributable to *Homo* in the East Rudolf succession, in: *Earliest Man and Environments in the Lake Rudolf Basin: Stratigraphy, Paleocology, and Evolution* (Y. Coppens, F. C. Howell, G. Ll. Isaac, and R. E. F. Leakey, Eds.), pp. 490-506. University of Chicago Press, Chicago and London.

29

Functional Morphology of *Homo habilis*

R. L. Susman and J. T. Stern

Olduvai Gorge in northern Tanzania has yielded a wealth of early human fossils and cultural remains over the last 23 years (Leakey 1971, Day 1977). None of the questions raised by the fossil finds has been more debated than whether or not an advanced hominid, early *Homo* (*Homo habilis*), existed contemporaneously with *Australopithecus boisei* (Leakey, Tobias, and Napier 1964; Brace 1972, 1975; Wolpoff 1970; Tobias 1965). As a result of corroborative evidence from East Turkana, Kenya (Leakey and Walker 1976, Howell 1978), and the Omo River Valley, Ethiopia, *Homo habilis* has been accepted as a valid taxon (Wolpoff 1981). Although the taxonomic controversy has abated, our understanding of the anatomy and functional morphology of *Homo habilis* is still obscure. This is in part because of conflicting functional conclusions regarding fossils assigned to *Homo habilis* (Lovejoy 1975; Day and Napier 1964; Davis 1964; Lewis 1980, 1981; Robinson 1972; Wood 1974a) and in part because of uncertainty over the associations of various parts of the postcranium with one taxon or another (Leakey, Tobias, and Napier 1964; Davis 1964; Day 1965, 1976, 1977, 1978; Howell 1965).

The most important relevant postcranial remains from Olduvai Gorge come from sites FLK (level 22) and FLK NN (level 3) (Leakey, Tobias, and Napier 1964; Day and Napier 1964; Davis 1964; Napier 1962; Leakey 1960, 1961a). In early 1960 a tibia and fibula (O.H. 35) were found at the former site. Not much later, and nearby, a hand, skull, and jaw (O.H. 7) and a foot (O.H. 8) were recovered from FLK NN (level 3). The juvenile hand, jaw, and skull fragments became the holotype of *Homo habilis* (Leakey, Tobias, and Napier 1964; Leakey and Leakey 1964); the foot, purported to be that of an elderly female [1], became part of the paratype. The FLK tibia and fibula (O.H. 15) were placed in taxonomic limbo (Leakey, Tobias, and Napier 1964; Day and Napier 1964; Davis 1964; Day 1965, 1978; Howell 1965). In the years that followed, O.H. 35 was assigned to *Australopithecus africanus* (Howell 1978), *A. robustus* (Wood 1974), and *Homo habilis* (Day 1977). Because one study of the O.H. 7 hand (Susman and Creel 1979) suggested that the taxonomic assessment and assignments of the Bed I material might be different from those originally reported, we undertook further study of the O.H. 7, 8, and 35 fossils in order to better understand the functional morphology and habitus of *Homo habilis*.

The O.H. 7 hand has 13 bones (Day 1976; Napier 1962; Susman and Creel 1979). The absence of epiphyses on the middle phalanges and the presence of fused basal epiphyses on the distal phalanges indicate that the individual was of a developmental stage equivalent to a modern human female of 13 years 6 months (Greulich and Pyle 1966). The morphology and length of the distal phalanges resemble those of living humans (Susman and Creel 1979; Susman 1979), but the fossil distal phalanges differ from humans principally in the greater diameter at mid-shaft. The middle phalanges differ from humans by being robust and curved, with well-marked flexor digitorum superficialis insertions that suggest powerful grasping potential, such as that of living apes (Susman and Creel 1979; Susman and Stern 1979). The broken proximal phalanges with their thick cortices and marked curvatures also suggest a powerful grasping hand similar in overall configuration to chimpanzees and female gorillas.

Two wrist bones, a scaphoid and a trapezium, shed light on the thumb of *Homo habilis*. The scaphoid tubercle (partially broken) and articular surface for the trapezium are pongid-like, but the pollical carpometacarpal joint is distinctively human-like. The broad, flattened metacarpal surface on the trapezium indicates a strong, stout thumb. This morphology correlates with that of the distal phalanges and suggests that changes in the human direction are well advanced in the thumb and finger-tips of *Homo habilis* but that power-grasping capabilities (Napier 1956, 1960) are retained in the more proximal segments of the fingers (Susman and Creel 1979).

The O.H. 8 foot, which has been extensively studied (Day and Napier 1964; Lewis 1981; Day and Wood 1968; Lisowski, Albrecht, Oxnard 1974, 1976; Oxnard 1975; Oxnard and Lisowski 1980; Wood 1974b; Wood and Henderson 1977), was judged to that of an adult [2] and was thought to represent a different individual from O.H. 7. Our analysis indicates that the foot is that of a subadult individual. We base this conclusion on the fact that metatarsals IV and V (and perhaps I also) have been broken by carnivore biting, whereas metatarsals II and III give the appearance of bones that are simply lacking their epiphyses (Susman and Creel 1979) (Fig. 1). That metatarsals II and III lack the heads can be adduced by two facts: the distal ends of the bones have been lost at the point where the epiphyseal plate is normally located (that is, at the epicondylar line), and radiographically the two bones retain trabeculae in their distal ends, indicating that they lack only the epiphysis. Metatarsals IV and V, broken-further proximally, have no cancellous network in their distal ends, and their medullary cavities are open at the break points. Furthermore, the age of O.H. 8, as judged from the fused basal epiphysis of metatarsal I, together with the unfused heads of metatarsals II and III, is 13.7 to 13.9 years [3]. This age for the foot concurs with the age estimate of 13.6 years for the O.H. 7 hand, which was found on the same surface and close by, and it thus appears that the hand and foot may be from the same individuals.

The foot has a metatarsal robusticity formula fully commensurate with a bipedal striding gait (Archibald et al. 1972) The plane of the first tarsometatarsal joint is human-like in that the articular surface of the medial cuneiform faces distally. Opposing tubercles for the attachments of the medial tarsometatarsal ligament prevent any significant abduction at that joint. This configuration is distinct from that in nonhuman primates where there is wide abduction of the halluces. The fossil hallux is stout, has proportions (relative to metatarsal II) that are within the human range and, as in humans, displays less axial torsion than that of apes. Metatarsal V, if its shape had not been distorted [2], shows a mediolateral flattening of its proximal portion similar to that of humans and distinct from apes. The calcaneus has an excavation on the inferomedial aspect of the distal surface. Into this excavation fits a projection of the cuboid which rotates into a close-packed position that prevents extreme

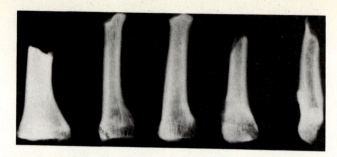

Figure 1. *Radiograph of O.H. 8 metatarsals I through V (left to right, lateral views). Although there is some postmortem erosion of the ends, epiphyseal lines can be seen on the distal ends of metatarsals II and III (which lack epiphyses). Metatarsals I, IV, and V have been broken, perhaps by carnivores.*

supination of the forefoot at the midtarsal joint. The same condition of the calcaneocuboid articulation is present in humans, but apes and monkeys retain a more generalized pivot joint permitting greater mobility. The cuboid is narrower and more rectangular (in dorsal view) than that of African apes, and the peroneal groove is also narrower in the fossil and in humans than in the apes. As in humans, the inferior aspect of the navicular is expanded in the area which serves as the attachment site for the cubonavicular and plantar calcaneonavicular ligaments. The tuberosity of the navicular is also human-like in its relative reduction, unlike the African apes. The surface for the medial cuneiform is flat to concave in humans and O.H. 8; it is convex in the apes (and monkeys). The lateral cuneiform assumes a rectangular, human-like appearance and departs from the square shape (in dorsal view) of African apes.

The O.H. 35 tibia and fibula also represent *Homo habilis*, as suspected by other workers (Leakey, Tobias, Napier 1964; Howell 1965). The bones articulate perfectly with the O.H. 8 foot (Fig. 2, A to C), and their state of preservation, weathering, and patina and the relative dimensions compared to the foot [4] lead us to wonder if the O.H. 8 foot and O.H. 35 leg might represent the same individual [5].

The O.H. 35 specimens were first studied by Davis (1964) who commented that the shaft of the fibula "in many ways resembles that of *H. sapiens*; indeed there are fibulae from modern human beings which resemble it almost exactly." Our observations on the O.H. 35 fibula indicate that, although certain traits found in the fossil are more typical of pongids than of modern humans (for example, the surface for the origin of the peroneus brevis is convex rather than concave, and there is a marked ridge between that region of the posterior surface devoted to origin of the flexor hallucis longus and the region of the medial surface devoted to the same muscle), Davis' statement is correct. Furthermore, the fossil has characteristics that are found in no ape [6]. Some of these traits do not lend themselves readily to functional interpretation, but those concerning the articular facet for the talus suggest that the extreme plantarflexion potential which characterizes the ape ankle was absent (Stern and Susman 1983).

Davis (1964) found the O.H. 35 tibia to be less modern in aspect than the fibula. He drew attention to the rounded anterior border, the extensive origin of the tibialis posterior, supposedly atypical markings for the popliteus, and the apparent failure of the soleal line to reach the lateral border of the shaft. Lovejoy (1975, 1978) asserted that the fossil is atypical only in the particularly marked development of the crest between the

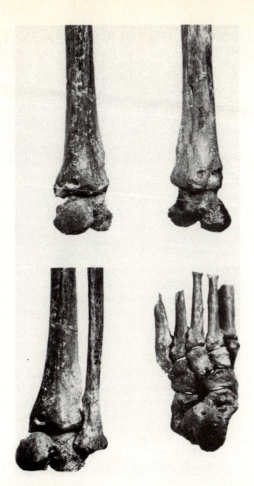

Figure 2. *(A) Anterior view of O.H. 8 talus and O.H. 35 tibia. (B) Posterior view of O.H. 8 talus and O.H. 35 tibia. (C) Anterolateral view of the O.H. 8 talus articulated with the O.H. 35 tibia and fibula. Note the congruent interosseous ridges at the location of the tibiofibular syndesmosis on the leg, and the fit of the fibular malleolus and talus. The patina on the bones is identical and the distal portion of the fibula and talus are eroded on their adjacent inferolateral surfaces. (D) The articulated O.H. 8 foot, dorsal view.*

origins of the tibialis posterior and flexor digitorum longus. Other traits of the O.H. 35 tibia that are less typical of modern tibiae are (i) the weak development of the interosseous ridge and (ii) the marked platycnemia associated with both a posterior pilaster between the subcutaneous surface and interosseous ridge at midshaft, and a laterally rather than posteriorly facing tibialis posterior origin. However, like Lovejoy (1975, 1978) we note that all the atypical traits of the O.H. 35 tibia can be matched in some modern humans with certain individuals possessing most, if not all, of them. Furthermore, there are characteristics of the fossil that are not seen among ape tibiae [7].

Thus our observations on the O.H. 35 tibia and fibula indicate that they have no features which cannot be readily found in a moderate sample of modern humans. The fossils have numerous features never observed in nonhuman primates. Some of these latter traits, particularly those relating to joint surfaces, are strong indicators of human-like bipedality (Stern and Susman 1983), and there is little doubt that the O.H. 35 leg was that of an habitual biped.

From a functional viewpoint the implications of the determination that the O.H. 7 hand, O.H. 8 foot, and O.H. 35 leg belong to the same taxon (and perhaps the same individual) are that *Homo habilis* possessed a derived, bipedal morphology of the leg and foot together with a hand that, although advanced in its thumb and fingertip morphology (Napier 1962; Leakey 1961; Susman and Creel 1979), still retained climbing potential (Susman and Stern 1979). Since *Homo habilis* was a small hominid, lacking large, projecting canines and with only rudimentary toolmaking skills (Leakey 1971), it is likely that a selective advantage would have derived from its ability to sleep (Susman and Stern 1979; Issac 1978; Young, Jope, and Oakley 1981; Gelder 1978), escape, and perhaps occasionally feed in trees. The phenotypic plasticity of bone suggests that the thick-walled, robust, and heavily muscled character of the O.H. 7 hand is not simply a vestige of a suspensory (hominid) heritage. Rather, certain features of the limbs of *Homo habilis* and other Pliocene-Pleistocene hominids (Stern and Susman 1982, 1983) suggest a significant component of climbing was present in the locomotor behavior of small Pliocene-Pleistocene hominids well beyond the point at which they became habitual bipeds.

ACKNOWLEDGMENTS

We thank M. Leakey, and R. E. F. Leakey for allowing us to study fossils from Olduvai Gorge and East Turkana. We also thank F. J. Muruka of Kenyatta National Hospital and the staff of the Louis Leakey Memorial Institute for their hospitality. Supported by the awards committee of the State University of New York and by NSF grants BNS 7924070, BNS 8119664 and BNS 7924162.

NOTES

[1] At first, however, Leakey (1961) considered the foot to be that of a child. He referred to it as the "pre-Zinjathropus child."

[2] The lateral tarsus and metatarsal bases display abnormal bony deposition (Fig. 1D). Originally thought to be a sign of age-related arthritis, the osteophytes on the lateral tarsus and metatarsals—at the joint margins rather than on the articular surface—are as likely the product of a traumatically induced pathology (Susman and Creel 1979). The injury and subsequent pathology may also explain the flattening of the lateral tarsus (C. E. Oxnard and F. P. Lisowski 1980).

[3] See Hoerr et al. 1962. The age of 13.7 to 13.9 years is based on the standard for human females. Day (1976) has indicated that the ages for the mandible and hand of O.H. 7 are similar, and Wolpoff (personal communication) estimated an age on the basis of dental eruption of 13.0 years for the O.H. 7 mandible. Tobias (1971) gives an age of "about 12 years" for this jaw.

[4] When an index of foot length to tibia length is computed the value for O.H. 8/35 is 25 to 27; for modern human, 26.8 ($N = 10$; standard deviation = 1.32); *Pan troglodytes*, 34.9 ($N = 10$; S.D. = 0.64); and for *Gorilla*, 35.9 ($N = 7$; S.D. = 4.22). Foot length was measured from the proximal edge of the navicular to the epicondyle of metatarsal II, and the ratio was computed from Davis' (1964) estimate of length for the O.H. 35 tibia and our own estimate. Lovejoy (1975) noted an error in Davis' estimate of tibial length. On the basis of extrapolation from the position of the nutrient foramen, Davis predicted a length of the O.H. 35 tibia of 277 ±10 mm. (By this same method we obtained a value of 274 mm.) But, the nutrient foramen of the fossil

is located along the soleal line proximal to its juncture with the crest between tibialis posterior and flexor digitorum longus, an unusually high position which, as Lovejoy stated, will give a falsely high value for tibial length. We have two modern tibiae with virtually the same location of the nutrient foramen. Using these as a basis for predicting the length of O.H. 35, we obtain estimates of 251 and 262 mm respectively. If one assumes that the break at the proximal end of the shaft occurred at the inferior limit of the tibial tuberosity (as observation suggests) we obtain a length estimate for the O.H. 35 tibia of 259 mm. None of these estimates can be considered precise, but we believe they clearly indicate that Davis' value is too high.

[5] One argument against this view is that the distal epiphysis of the O.H. 35 tibia is already fused. In human females the distal tibial epiphysis fuses at a mean age of 14.1 years, thus later than the metatarsal epiphyses. However, the standard deviation for fusion of the human distal tibial epiphysis is 1.1 years. A second argument against O.H. 35 and O.H. 8 coming from the same individual derives from stratigraphic considerations. The position of the FLK level 22 ("Zinj") floor from which O.H. 35 came is said to be 1 to 2 feet above the FLK NN level 3 occupation floor which yielded O.H. 7 and 8. However, the relevant levels at both sites are described as gray silty clays with nodular limestone inclusions and upper weathered com-

ponents (Leakey 1971). In the description of level 22 at FLK it has been pointed out that "both the nature of the clay and the mode of occurrence of the remains in the occupation floor bear a close resemblance to the conditions pertaining in level 3 at FLK NN" (Leakey 1971, p. 49). The two sites are separated by a considerable distance of around 200 m or more, but such a wide distribution of the bones may reflect carnivore or scavenger activity which scattered the bones at a presumptive muddy lakeshore.

[6] These traits include (i) an extreme anteroposterior slenderness of the neck; (ii) a marked buttress extending proximally from the area of origin of tibialis posterior; (iii) a prominent anterior expansion of the lateral malleolus associated with an acute angle between the articular facet for the talus and the subcutaneous surface, which acuteness causes the subcutaneous surface to face more laterally than anteriorly; (iv) the superior portion of the articular facet is directed medially rather than inferomedially; and (iv) the superior edge of the facet runs an anteroposterior course rather than on an oblique downward course.

[7] These traits include (i) the inferior rather than inferolateral direction of the lateral segment of the articular surface for the talus, (ii) the anterior inclination of this same surface, (iii) the lateral convexity of the upper shaft and (iv) the anterior concavity of the shaft.

REFERENCES

Archibald, J. D., Lovejoy, C. O., and Heiple, K. G. 1972. Implications of relative robusticity in the Olduvai metatarsus. *Amer. J. Phys. Anthrop.* 37:93-96.

Brace, C. L. 1967. *The Stages of Human Evolution.* Prentice Hall, Englewood Cliffs, NJ.

Brace, C. L. 1972. Sexual dimorphism in human evolution. *Yrbk. Phys. Anthrop.* 16:50-68.

Davis, P. R. 1964. Hominid fossils from Bed I, Olduvai Gorge, Tanganyika: A tibia and fibula. *Nature* 201:967-970.

Day, M. H. 1965. *The Guide to Fossil Man.* First edition. Meridian Books, New York.

Day, M. H. 1976. Hominid postcranial material from Bed I, Olduvai Gorge. in: *Human Origins* (G. L. Isaac and E. R. McGown, Eds.), pp. 363-374, W. A. Benjamin, Inc., Menlo Park, CA.

Day, M. H. 1977. *Guide to Fossil Man.* Third edition. University of Chicago Press, Chicago.

Day, M. H. 1978. Functional interpretation of the morphology of postcranial remains of early African hominids. in: *Earliest Hominids of Africa*, (C. J. Jolly, Ed.), pp. 311-345, St. Martin's Press, New York.

Day, M. H. and Napier, J. R. 1964. Hominid fossils from Bed I, Olduvai Gorge: Fossil foot bones. *Nature* 201:967-971.

Day, M. H. and Wood, B. A. 1968. Functional affinities of the Olduvai hominid 8 talus. *Man* 3:440-455.

Greulich, W. W. and Pyle, S. I. 1966. *Radiographic Atlas of Skeletal Development of the Hand and Wrist.* Second edition. Stanford University Press, Stanford, CA.

Hoerr, N. L., Pyle, S. I., and Francis, C. C. 1962. *Radiographic Atlas of Skeletal Development of the Foot and Ankle.* Thomas, Springfield, IL.

Howell, F. C. 1965. Comments on P. V. Tobias. New discoveries in Tanganyika: Their bearing on hominid evolution. *Curr. Anthropol.* 6:399-401.

Howell, F. C. 1978. Hominidae. in: *Evolution of African Mammals*, (V. J. Maglio and H. B. S. Cooke, Eds.), pp. 154-248, Harvard University Press, Cambridge, MA.

Isaac, G. L. 1978. The food-sharing behavior of protohuman hominids. *Sci. Amer.* 238:90-108.

Isaac, G. L. 1981. Archaeological tests of alternative models of early hominid behaviour: Excavation and experients. *Phil. Trans. Royal Soc. London* 292B:177-188.

Leakey, L. S. B. 1960. Recent discoveries at Olduvai Gorge. *Nature* 188:1050-1052.

Leakey, L. S. B. 1961a. New finds at Olduvai Gorge. *Nature* 189: 649-650.

Leakey, L. S. B. 1961b. New links in the chain of human evolution: Three major new discoveries from Olduvai Gorge, Tanganyika. *Illustrated London News* 238:346-348.

Leakey, L. S. B. 1963. Archeological excavations at Olduvai Gorge, Tanzania. *Annu. Res. Rep. Nat. Geogr. Soc., 1963,* pp. 179-182. Washington, D.C.

Leakey, L. S. B. and Leakey, M. D. 1964. Recent discoveries of fossil hominids in Tanganyika: At Olduvai and Lake Natron. *Nature* 202:5-7.

Leakey, L. S. B., Tobias, P. V., and Napier, J. R. 1964. A new species of the genus *Homo* from Olduvai Gorge. *Nature* 202:7-9.

Leakey, M. D. 1971. *Olduvai Gorge*, Volume 3. Cambridge University Press, Cambridge.

Leakey, R. E. F., and Walker, A. C. 1976. *Australopithecus, Homo erectus,* and the single species hypothesis. *Nature* 261:572-574.

Lewis, O. J. 1980. The joints of the evolving foot, part III. *J. Anat.* 131:275-298.

Lewis, O. J. 1981. Functional morphology of the joints of the evolving foot. *Symp. Zool. Soc. London* 46:169-188.

Lisowski, F. P., Albrecht, G. H., and Oxnard, C. E. 1974. The form of the talus in some higher primates: A multivariate study. *Amer. J. Phys. Anthrop.* 41:191-215.

Lisowski, F. P., Albrecht, G. H., and C. E. Oxnard. 1976. African fossil tali: Further multivariate morphometric studies. *Amer. J. Phys. Anthrop.* 45:5-18.

Lovejoy, C. O. 1975. Biomechanical perspectives on the lower limb of early hominids. in: *Primate Functional Morphology and Evolution* (R. H. Tuttle, Ed.), pp. 291-326, Mouton, The Hague.

Lovejoy, C. O. 1978. A biomechanical view of the locomotor diversity of early hominids. in: *Earliest Hominids of Africa* (C. L. Jolly, Ed.), pp. 403-429, St. Martin's Press, New York.

Napier, J. R. 1956. The prehensile movements of the human hand. *J. Bone Jt. Surg.* 38B:902-913.

Napier, J. R. 1960. Studies of the hands of living Primates. *Proc. Zool. Soc. London* 134:647-657.

Napier, J. R. 1962. Fossil hand bones from Olduvai Gorge. *Nature* 196:409-411.

Oxnard, C. E. 1975. *Uniqueness and Diversity in Human Evolution.* University of Chicago Press, Chicago.

Oxnard, C. E. and Lisowski, P. 1980. Functional articulation of some hominoid foot bones: Implications for the Olduvai (Hominid 8) foot. *Amer. J. Phys. Anthrop.* 52:107-117.

Robinson, J. T. 1972. *Early Hominid Posture and Locomotion.* Univesity of Chicago Press, Chicago.

Stern, J. T. and Susman, R. L. 1982. The locomotor behavior of *Australopithecus afarensis. Amer. J. Phys. Anthrop.* 57:232.

Stern, J. T. and Susman, R. L. 1983. The locomotor anatomy of *Australopithecus afarensis. Amer. J. Phys. Anthrop.* 60:279-317.

Susman, R. L. 1979. Comparative and functional morphology of hominid fingers. *Amer. J. Phys. Anthrop.* 50:215-236.

Susman, R. L. and Creel, N. 1979. Functional and morphological affinities of the subadult hand (O.H. 7) from Olduvai Gorge. *Amer. J. Phys. Anthrop.* 5:311-332.

Susman, R. L. and Stern, J. T. 1979. Telemetered electromyography of flexor digitorum profundus and flexor digitorum superficialis in *Pan troglodytes* and implications for interpretation of the O.H. 7 hand. *Amer. J. Phys. Anthrop.* 50:565-574.

Tobias, P. V. 1965. New discoveries in Tanganyika: Their bearing on hominid evolution. *Curr. Anthropol.* 6:391-399.

Tobias, P. V. 1971. *The Brain in Hominid Evolution.* Columbia University Press, New York.

Van Gelder, R. 1978. The voice of the missing link. in: *Earliest Hominids of Africa* (C. J. Jolly , Ed.), pp. 431-439, St. Martin's Press, New York.

Wolpoff, M. H. 1970. The evidence for multiple hominid taxa at Swartkrans. *Amer. Anthropol.* 72:576-607.

Wolpoff, M. H. 1973. The evidence for two australopithecine lineages in South Africa. *Yrbk. Phys. Anthrop.* 17:113-139.

Wolpoff, M. H. 1981. Cranial capacity estimates for Olduvai hominid 7. *Amer. J. Phys. Anthrop.* 56:297-304.

Wolpoff, M. H. and Brace, C. L. 1975. Allometry and early hominids. *Science* 189:61-63.

Wood, B. A. 1974a. Olduvai bed I postcranial fossils: A reassessment. *J. Hum. Evol.* 3:373-378.

Wood, B. A. 1974b. Evidence on the locomotor pattern of *Homo* from early Pleistocene of Kenya. *Nature* 251:135-136.

Wood, B. A. and Henderson, A. 1977. The functional anatomy of the Olduvai (O.H. 8) foot. *J. Anat.* 124:252.

30

New Partial Skeleton of *Homo habilis* from Olduvai Gorge, Tanzania

D. C. Johanson, F. T. Masao, G. G. Eck, T. D. White, R. C. Walter, W. H. Kimbel, B. Asfaw, P. Manega, P. Ndessokia, and G. Suwa

Olduvai Gorge in northern Tanzania has yielded important evidence bearing on human origins and evolution. Discoveries made from the 1950s to the 1970s have demonstrated the coexistence of two hominid taxa in late Pliocene and early Pleistocene strata at the site: *Australopithecus boisei* and *Homo habilis.* (Leakey 1959; Leakey, Tobias, and Napier 1964; Tobias 1967). Palaeoanthropological research at Olduvai has been carried out since 1985 by a team from the National Museums of Tanzania, the Tanzanian Department of Antiquities, the Institute of Human Origins and the University of California, Berkeley. We report here the discovery of a new hominid specimen from lower Bed I at Olduvai Gorge.

RECOVERY

On 21 July 1986, the third day of surface survey of the 1986 field season, one of us (T. D. W.) discovered a fragment of hominid ulna on the surface of Bed I sediments at FLK, near Geological Locality 45c (Hay 1976) and 25 m west of the road to FLK Zinj (Fig. 1a and b). A search and screening of the adjacent surface resulted in the recovery of maxillary, calvarial, mandibular, radial, humeral, femoral and tibial fragments of what appears to be a single hominid individual. This specimen is designated Olduvai Hominid (OH) 62.

STRATIGRAPHY AND GEOLOGICAL FRAMEWORK

The site at which OH 62 was found lies roughly 250 m southeast of the FLK (*Zinjanthropus*) locality (Fig. 1a). Hominid fragments were found on the surface and in a thin colluvial soil (Fig. 1b and c), over an area of about 40 m^2 on the north side of a small knoll, Dik Dik Hill (DDH).

Roughly 16 m of deposits are exposed in the gorge wall immediately south-west of the hominid discovery. These consist of Bed I and lower Bed II sediments unconformably capped by the Ndutu Beds. Lower Bed I lava forms the present-day valley floor. Roughly 2 m of beige tuffaceous silts and clays, which are subjacent to Tuffs IC and ID, overlie the lava.

The base of the section at the hominid site (Trench 2) consists of thinly laminated beige and brown clays (Unit 2-1), which are overlain by 30 cm of tuffaceous silts and silty clays containing large, altered pumice clasts (up to 3 cm) in the basal part (Unit 2-2) (Fig. 1b and c). This sequence is unconformably capped by a 0-50 cm colluvium containing large lithic clasts. All of the vertebrate (including hominid) fossils were on top of or within this colluvium.

The colluvium capping DDH (Unit 2-3, Fig. 1c) probably formed as a lag deposit after a section of the gorge wall collapsed

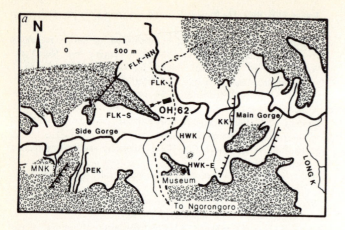

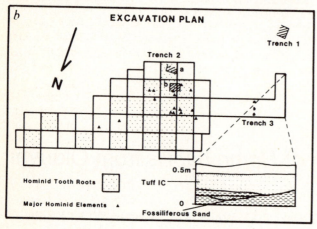

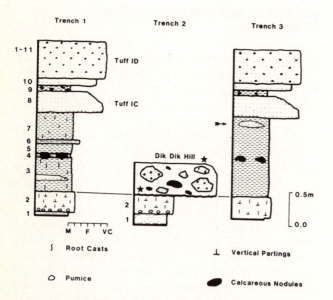

Figure 1. *a*, *Plan view of the junction of the Main and Side gorges, showing the location of the OH 62 hominid site. Patterned areas represent high grassy plains. Gorge sediments are depicted in white, adjacent to stream channels. Several major faults are shown, with hatchure marks indicating down-throw directions. Dashed lines represent roads. **b**, Excavation plan for OH 62 site, showing distribution pattern of hominid remains within the 2 m x 2 m grid system. Geological trenches discussed in the text are illustrated. The summit of Dik Dik Hill occurs between Trench 2a and 2b. The western-most edge of Trench 3 exposes a 0.5 m section of Tuff IC that is underlain by a dark discontinuous channel sand (inset). This sand contains vertebrate fossils with preservation features like those of OH 62. **c**, Detailed stratigraphy of the hominid site (Dik Dik Hill) and adjacent sediments, as discussed in the text. The hominid level is indicated by the stars, and the fossiliferous channel sand by the arrow. The lateral dimension of each unit refers to clast size according to the scale at the base of the diagram: mud (M), fine (F), very course (VC).*

The occurrence of OH 62 in colluvial soil on the flank of DDH and the surface distribution pattern of numerous associated fragments of one hominid individual indicate that OH 62 eroded from DDH. In addition, *in situ* nonhominid fossils were found in a dark, discontinuous laminated sand immediately below Tuff IC in Trench 3 (Fig. 1b). These remains are similar in preservation to OH 62. Thus, through several indirect yet highly congruent lines of evidence we conclude that OH 62 derives from lower Bed I deposits below Tuff ID, most probably from the sand lens below Tuff IC, roughly equivalent to the FLK (*Zinjanthropus*) level (Hay 1976). This implies an age for OH 62 of between 1.85 Myr, the age of Tuff 1B (Curtis and Hay 1972; using revised K–AR constants, Steiger and Jäger 1977), and 1.75 Myr, the inferred age of Tuff IF (Hay 1976). There are no firm isotopic ages for Tuffs IC or ID, although tuffs between ID and IC are dated to 1.80 Myr (±0.08, 1 S. D.)(Curtis and Hay 1972).

The hominid bones, including entire shafts, shattered as they eroded from the deposit and deflated as particles in a colluvial lag, or desert pavement. We estimate on geomorphological grounds that the process of exposure took centuries.

ASSOCIATIONS

Screening and excavation recovered nearly 18,000 fragments of fossil bone and tooth. The hominid fossils are highly lithified and dark grey to black in colour, distinguishing them from specimens derived from higher in the section. Most of the nonhominid fossils associated with OH 62 are small fragments of small to medium sized mammals and reptiles. These include: *Kobus sigmoidalis, cf.* Antelopini, cf. Alcelaphini, Giraffidae (cf. *Sivatherium*), Hippopotamidae, Suidae, Deinotheriidae, Carnivora (cf. large lutrine mustelid or viverrid), Cercopithecidae, Hystricidae, Cricetidae, Aves (cf. *Struthio*), Reptilia (Varanidae, *Crocodylus*, Serpentes, Chelonia), Amphibia (cf. Anura) and Pisces (*Clarius*).

Artefacts recovered on the surface and in the lag deposit are cores and flakes typical of the Oldowan industry, but whether they are contemporary with the hominid cannot be established. No stone tools were found in the outcrop of the laminated sand unit.

and deflated. Tuff ID forms a resistant ledge in the local topography, and there are numerous examples nearby where portions of this ledge have calved away from the gorge wall, leaving a lag similar to that observed at DDH. More than 95% of the lithic clasts in the colluvium (Trench 2) are positively correlated with deposits equivalent to and below Tuff ID (Trench 1).

Table 1. List of remains attributed to OH 62

A. Partial maxilla with R$\underline{C}$, partial RP^4, RM^1 mesiobuccal root fragment; partial L$\underline{C}$, L$\underline{P}^3$ root fragment, LP^4 root fragment, partial LM^2-LM^3 ($\overline{32}$ conjoined pieces)
B. Frontal process of left zygomatic
C. Posterior wall fragment of zygomatic process, right maxilla
D. Posterior wall fragment of zygomatic process, left maxilla
E. Maxillary and palatine fragments (15 pieces)
F. Fragment of greater wing of right sphenoid
G. Greater wing fragment of left sphenoid
H. Occipital fragment with superior sagittal sulcus
I. Cranial vault fragments (21 pieces)
J. Right mandibular condyle
K. Anteromedial wall of left mandibular corpus
L. Posteromedial fragment of left mandibular corpus
M. Basal fragment of right mandibular corpus
N. Mandible fragments (17 pieces)
O. Root and distal crown fragment of R$\overline{C}$
P. Root of L$\overline{C}$
Q. Root of LP$_4$
R. Lingual root of RP^3
S. Buccal fragment of RM^1
T. Labial fragment of I^1 (side indeterminate)
U. Dental crown and root fragments (position and side indeterminate) (161 pieces)
V. Right humerus shaft (5 conjoined pieces)
W. Right radius shaft (13 conjoined pieces)
X. Proximal, midshaft, and distal fragments of right ulna (4, 6 and 1 conjoined pieces)
Y. Proximal shaft and neck of left femur (10 conjoined pieces)
Z. Proximal fragment of right tibia
Total number of pieces = 302

PRELIMINARY DESCRIPTION OF THE SKELETON

After full conjoining of the recovered pieces it is evident that parts of the skull, right arm and both legs are represented (Table 1). There is no duplication of elements, which suggests the presence of only one individual. Preservation and colour of all fragments correspond and all elements are fully adult.

All limb bone articular ends are missing except for a portion of the proximal ulna. The bones show no evidence of rodent- or carnivore-induced damage and display no cutmarks or evidence of peri-mortem fracture. The bone surfaces are slightly weathered and suggest limited exposure before deposition.

SKULL

The skull of OH 62 is represented by portions of the palate, face, calvaria, mandible and dentition. The following descriptions focus only on features of taxonomic importance.

Palate (Fig. 2a). The palatal surface is preserved between the incisor alveoli and the M2/M3 level, but the alveolar processes are broken at most tooth positions. The palate is moderately deep posteriorly, and shelves inferiorly anterior to the large incisive fossa. As judged by estimates of internal breadth (~35 mm) and length (~41 mm, measured to mid-M^2 level), it is clear that the palate is relatively wide compared to *Australopithecus* (for example, A.L. 200-1a, Sts 5, Sts 52a, OH 5). In size and morphology, the OH 62 palate is similar to OH 24, and especially to Stw 53, a *Homo habilis* skull from the Sterkfontein (Member 5) Extension Site breccia in South Africa (Hughes and Tobias 1977; Tobias 1978).

Face. (Fig. 2b). Most of the region around the nasal cavity, including the right zygomatic process of the maxilla, is preserved. The maxilla is moderately prognathic. It is evident that the nasoalveolar clivus is flat, short and minimally projecting relative to the bicanine line. The eroded remnant of a small, but distinct, anterior nasal spine is present at the entrance to the nasal cavity. The spine is separated from the nasal orifice of the incisive canals, and hence from the inferred anterior insertion of the vomer, by a 6.0 mm long, horizontal intranasal platform. Laterally, the inferior nasal margin demarcates a fairly distinct change in contour between the clivus and the nasal cavity floor.

The anterolaterally facing nasal process of the maxilla shows that superiorly the lateral margin of the nasal aperture was sharp and everted. An 'anterior pillar' is not present, and there are no indications of a distinct canine fossa or 'maxillary furrow' intervening between the nasal and zygomatic processes. The zygomatic process arises low on the maxilla. Its root is positioned posteriorly, at the M1 level.

The isolated frontal processs of the left zygomatic is slender and bears a weak postmarginal process on its temporal face. The facial plate of the process, separated from the orbital plate by a sharp lateral orbital margin, faces distinctly laterally.

In almost all these characters, the OH 62 facial skeleton closely resembles specimens attributed to *Homo habilis* or *Homo sp.* (for example OH 24, KNM-ER 1470, 1813, SK 847, and especially Stw 53). Specializations defining *Australopithecus africanus, A. robustus* and *A. boisei* are notably absent in the new Olduvai face. (Clarke 1977; Rak 1983).

Calvaria. Very little of the cranial vault of OH 62 survives. Preserved fragments of the sphenoid, occipital, and other vault bones reveal no taxonomically valuable morphology.

Mandible. The preserved right condylar neck is gracile and the condyle is small compared to 'robust' *Australopithecus* specimens. A basal fragment evinces a degree of eversion similar to that seen in *H. habilis* mandible KNM-ER 1802, although the OH 62 mandible base was obviously less robust.

Dentition. Molar wear pattern and anterior/posterior dental proportions (as estimated from maxillary alveoli and preserved canine and molar crowns) indicate that OH 62 does not represent a 'robust' *Australopithecus*. Both P^3 and P^4 possess double buccal roots. These roots lack the massiveness of 'robust' *Australopithecus* homologues and are similar to the condition seen in Stw 53.

The right $\underline{C}$ measures 9.9 mm buccolingually. The buccolingual breadths of the left M^2 and M^3 are estimated to be ~16.0 mm and ~15.5 mm, respectively. These molar dimensions approximate those of OH 16 and Stw 53, and lie in the upper range of early *Homo* specimens. The canine/molar breadth ratio is therefore at the low end of the *Homo* range.

Other morphological features, such as a virtual lack of asymmetry in upper canine occlusal outline, a simple distal buccal groove on the lower canine lacking a 'V' configuration, and M^3 with a relatively short mesiodistal dimension lingually, suggest that OH 62 represents *Homo* rather than *A. africanus*.

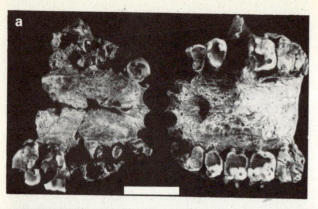
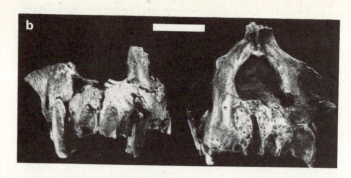
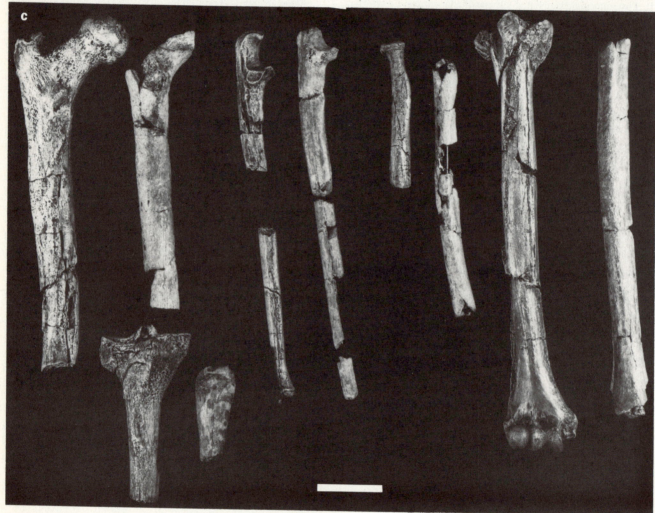

Figure 2. a, *Palatal views of OH 62 (left) and Stw. 53 (cast, right) maxillae. Bar, 2 cm.* b, *Facial views of OH 62 (left) and Stw. 53 (cast, right). Bar, 2 cm.* c, *Postcranial elements of OH 62 compared with those of* A. afarensis *specimen A.L. 288-1 ('Lucy'). The Olduvai fossils are to the right in each comparison. Bar, 4 cm.*

POSTCRANIUM

Description of the OH 62 postcranium will focus on comparisons with the A.L. 288-1 partial skeleton from Hadar ('Lucy'; Johanson *et al.* 1982) because of the size and anatomical similarities between these two hominid individuals (Fig. 2c).

Humerus. The OH 62 humeral shaft is essentially intact, with most of the bicipital groove present. The proximal shaft circumference closely approximates that recorded for A.L. 288-1, whereas the distal shaft of OH 62 is slightly thinner. We conservatively estimate the OH 62 humeral length at ~27 mm longer than that of A.L. 288-1. The total OH 62 upper arm was almost certainly longer than that of 'Lucy'.

Radius. Most of the radial tuberosity is intact and about two-thirds of the shaft below this point is preserved. The shaft exhibits moderate mediolateral bowing and a weak interosseous crest. The radial tuberosity is larger, more rounded and less divided than that of the A.L. 288-1 radius. Shaft circumference is greater than that measured for A.L. 288-1 and the radius of OH 62 is slightly more robust in comparable parts.

Ulna. The proximal ulna segment retains the inferior extension of the trochlear notch and a bit of eroded radial notch. The entire anatomy of the OH 62 proximal ulna is very similar to that recorded for A.L. 288-1. Mediolateral and anteroposterior measures of OH 62 and A.L. 288-1 at the level of the radial notch differ by less than 1 mm and shaft circumferences at the base of the brachialis insertion are the same. The distal OH 62 shaft fragment shows part of a pronator quadratus insertion. Shaft circumference at the distal end of this line (minimum shaft circumference) is 2 mm less than that measured on A.L. 288-1.

Femur. A visible obturator externus groove marks the posterior surface of the femur neck. The estimated neck/shaft angle of OH 62 is roughly the same as that documented for A.L. 288-1 (123°). The inferior half of the neck suggests the neck was flattened anteroposteriorly and was at least as long as that of A.L. 288-1. Anteroposterior and mediolateral shaft diameters at the base of the OH 62 lesser trochanter are both 21 mm, whereas homologous measures for the more anteroposteriorly compressed A.L. 288-1 shaft are 27 mm and 18 mm, respectively. Shaft circumference of the OH 62 specimen near midshaft is 9 mm less than that measured on A.L. 288-1. Even allowing for slight exfoliation of the OH 62 femur, visual comparison makes it obvious that this individual's femur was smaller and less robust than the A.L. 288-1 femur.

Tibia. Only the tibial tuberosity and the shaft immediately distal to it are preserved. The tuberosity is large and the surface lateral to it is deeply excavated as in A.L. 288-1. The tuberosity is well demarcated from the intracapsular area above by a marked transverse groove similar to that seen on the A.L. 288-1 and A.L. 129-1b proximal tibiae. Unlike these and other Hadar tibiae, however, OH 62 lacks any pit associated with the tibialis anterior muscle.

DISCUSSION

The new OH 62 partial skeleton from Bed I represents a significant addition to the hominid fossil record because of its bearing on several key issues concerning *Homo habilis*, a taxon originally created on the basis of fragmentary cranial and questionably associated postcranial elements from Olduvai Gorge (Leakey, Tobias and Napier 1964).

Several important conclusions about the OH 62 partial skeleton emerge from the first round of analysis. First, body size for this fully adult individual is estimated to be as small as or smaller than that of any known fossil hominid. Second, in addition to size, there are striking anatomical and proportional similarities between the OH 62 postcranial skeleton and small *Australopithecus* individuals (especially A.L. 288-1). Third, the strong morphological similarities of the OH 62 face, palate and dentition to *Homo habilis* (especially Stw 53) warrant attribution of the Olduvai individual to this taxon. This represents the

first time that limb elements have been securely assigned to *Homo habilis*.

Taxonomy

The original description of Bed I *Homo habilis* elicited assertions that species-level distinction from *Australopithecus africanus* was unwarranted (Robinson 1965; 1967; Brace, Mahler and Rosen 1973). More complete cranial material from Koobi Fora (KNM-ER 1470, 1590, 1813, 3732) and Sterkfontein (Stw 53) has shown that *Homo habilis* does indeed merit specific distinction from *A. africanus* (Hughes and Tobias 1977; Rak 1983; Wood 1978). However, this more complete material has led some investigators to divide the larger collection into *A. africanus* (such as KNM-ER 1813, OH 13), and *Homo* (such as KNM-ER 1470, 1590) sub-samples (Walker and Leakey 1978). Others have suggested a similar division but discern at least two "non-australopithecine" species in the sample (Wood 1985; Stringer 1986).

Many workers continue to follow Tobias (1983) in placing all of the late Pliocene-early Pleistocene, non-'robust' specimens that fall outside the range of *Homo erectus* into a variable, polymorphic species *Homo habilis* (Johanson and White 1979; Kimbel *et al*. 1984; Skelton *et al*. 1986; Howell 1978; Wolpoff 1980). This view holds that morphological differences between individuals such as KNM-ER 1470 and 1813 reflect sexual, geographical and chronological factors within a single species. Given the evidence currently available, we agree and therefore view OH 62 as an elderly member of *Homo habilis*. The similarity between comparable Stw 53 and OH 62 cranial and dental parts shows that this taxon was widespread in Africa.

Differentiation of *Australopithecus* and early *Homo* species at sites such as Olduvai, Omo and Koobi Fora has been accomplished exclusively on the basis of cranial, mandibular and dental characters. Taxonomic attribution of the wide variety of isolated postcranial elements found at these sites has been made only through speculation. Pilbeam's recent review reveals this when he states: "There are no clear associations between skulls of *Homo habilis* and the other bones of the species, but the limb bones that are assumed to represent it, unlike those of *Australopithecus*, resembles those of species of the genus *Homo* (with the exception of modern *Homo sapiens*)" (Pilbeam 1984).

On the contrary, the new OH 62 partial skeleton as well as the juvenile hand parts described as part of the holotype (OH 7; Susman and Stern 1982) show that *Homo habilis* had a postcranium similar in many ways to mid-Pliocene *A. afarensis*. Until now, late Pliocene-early Pleistocene postcrania have been sorted into *Homo* or 'robust' *Australopithecus* species on the basis of size and assumed limb proportions. This practice is seriously undermined by OH 62. Many previous taxonomic attributions based on postcrania should thus be regarded as highly tenuous.

Functional anatomy

Susman and Stern's assessment of the limited postcranial remains of *Homo habilis* led them to characterize members of this taxon as habitual bipeds who retained primitive characters in the hand but were "... less arboreal and more modern in their bipedality than the hominids of 3-4 million years ago." (Stern and Susman 1983). Allegedly primitive features of the Olduvai *H. habilis* foot (OH 8) have been noted by Wood (1974) and Lewis (1980). The discovery of long and powerful arms in *Homo habilis* and *Australopithecus*-like aspects of pelvic and proximal femoral anatomy in early *Homo erectus* (KNM-WT 15000; Brown *et al.* 1985) emphasize the mosaic pattern of evolution in the early hominid postcranial skeleton. However, the juxtaposition of an otherwise relatively derived *H. erectus* postcranium at ~1.6 Myr (KNM-WT 15000) and a postcranially primitive *H. habilis* at ~1.8 Myr (OH 62) may imply an abrupt transition between these taxa in eastern Africa.

We estimate the OH 62 humerus length at 264 mm, 27 mm longer than the A.L. 288-1 humerus (Johanson *et al.* 1982). If the length of the less robust OH 62 femur was no greater than that of A.L. 288-1 (280 mm), the Olduvai individual would have a humerofemoral index of close to 95%. Further work on this intriguing issue is in progress.

The new partial skeleton OH 62 offers additional evidence regarding the relative size of the postcanine denti- tion. McHenry has concluded that postcanine megadontia (relative to body size estimates) was reduced in *Homo habilis* compared to the *Australopithecus* condition (McHenry 1984). Our measurements indicate that the length of the postcanine tooth row relative to body size in OH 62 was at least as great as that of the comparably small A.L. 288-1 specimen of *Australopithecus afarensis*. Thus, the degree of megadontia in *Homo habilis* may, in fact, be little changed from the *Australopithecus* condition.

The very small body size of the OH 62 individual suggests that views of human evolution positing incremental body size increase through time may be rooted in gradualistic preconceptions rather than fact (Cronin *et al.* 1981). It is not possible to estimate cranial capacity for OH 62, but this skeleton and other available data on cranial capacity suggest the possibility that small individuals of *Australopithecus* and *Homo habilis* were differentiated by cranial capacity but not by body size. This reinforces the view that encephalization in the terminal Pliocene played a key role in hominid evolution (Tobias 1983; Holloway 1983).

ACKNOWLEDGMENTS

We thank the Tanzanian Government, including the National Scientific Research Council, the National Museums, the Department of Antiquities, and the Ngorongoro Conservation Area for encouragement, support and permission to conduct research at Olduvai and Laetoli. This new discovery emphasizes the need for continuing management of Tanzanian sites such as Olduvai Gorge. Special thanks are due to Professor Msangi and Professor Hirji, Dr Waane, and Mr Mturi. Support of the faculty and associates of the University of Dar es Salaam, including J. Karoma and P. Schmidt of the Archaeology Unit and Professor Aswathanaratana, and others is appreciated. Advice and field assistance was provided by Lew and Nancy Binford and George and June Frison. Field support and assistance was provided by Sandy Evans of Abercrombie and Kent, E. A. von Mutius, Peter Lauwo, Lucas Tarimo, Stanley Nderingo, James Shreeve, Jeremy Paul, Mzee Mrisho, Alberto Angela, and Hans Schneider. Thanks go to Owen Lovejoy for assistance with the postcranium, and to Mary Leakey for providing the specimen number for the new hominid. We are especially grateful to Gordon Getty, David Koch, and Ligabue Research and Study Center for their financial support.

REFERENCES

Brace, C. L., Mahler, P. E., and Rosen, R. B. 1973. Tooth measurements and the rejection of the taxon "*Homo habilis*." *Yearb. Phys. Anthrop.* 16:50-68.

Brown, F., Harris, J., Leakey, R., and Walker, A. 1985. Early *Homo erectus* skeleton from west Lake Turkana Kenya. *Nature* 316:788-792.

Clarke, R. J. 1977. *The Cranium of the Swartkrans hominid, SK 847, and its Relevance to Human Origins*. Ph.D. Thesis, University of Witwatersrand, Johannesburg.

Cronin, J. E., Boaz, N. T., Stringer, C. B., and Rak, Y. 1981. Tempo and mode in hominid evolution. *Nature* 292:113-122.

Curtis, G. H., and Hay, R. L. 1972. Further geological studies and potassium-argon dating at Olduvai Gorge and Ngorongoro Crater, in: *Calibration of Hominoid Evolution* (W. W. Bishop and J. A. Miller, Eds.), pp. 289-301. Scottish Academic, Edinburgh.

Hay, R. L. 1976. *Geology of the Olduvai Gorge*. University of California Press, Berkeley.

Holloway, R. L. 1983. Human paleontological evidence relevant to language behavior. *Hum. Neurobiol.* 2:105-114.

Howell, F. C. 1978. Hominidae, in: *Evolution of African Mammals* (V. M. Maglio and H. B. S. Cooke, Eds.), pp. 154-258. Harvard University Press, Cambridge, Mass.

Hughes, A. R., and Tobias, P. V. 1977. A fossil skull probably of the genus *Homo* from Sterkfontein Transvaal. *Nature* 265:310-312.

Johanson, D. C., *et al.* 1982. Morphology of the Pliocene partial hominid skeleton (A. L. 288-1) from the Hadar formation, Ethiopia. *Am. J. Phys. Anthrop.* 57:403-452.

Johanson, D. C., and White, T. D. 1979. A systematic assessment of early African hominids. *Science* 203:321-330.

Kimbel, W. H., White, T. D., and Johanson, D. C. 1984. Cranial morphology of *Australopithecus afarensis*: A comparative study based on a composite reconstruction of the adult skull. *Am. J. Phys. Anthrop.* 64:337-388.

Leakey, L. S. B. 1959. A new fossil skull from Olduvai. *Nature* 184:491-493.

Leakey, L. S. B., Tobias, P. V., and Napier, J. R. 1964. A new species of the Genus *Homo* from Olduvai Gorge. *Nature* 202:7-9.

Lewis, O. J. 1980. The joints of the evolving foot. Part III. The fossil evidence. *J. Anat.* 131:275-298.

McHenry, H. M. 1984. Relative cheek-tooth size in *Australopithecus*. *Am. J. phys. Anthrop.* 64:297-306.

Pilbeam, D. R. 1984. The descent of hominoids and hominids. *Sci. Am.* 250:84-97.

Rak, Y. 1983. *The Australopithecine Face*, Academic, New York.

Robinson, J. T. 1965. *Homo 'habilis'* and the Australopithecines. *Nature* 205:121-124.

Robinson, J. T. 1967. Variation and the taxonomy of the early hominids, in: *Evolutionary Biology*, Vol. 1 (T. Dobzhansky, M. K. Hecht, and W. C. Steere, Eds.), pp. 69-100. Appleton-Century-Crofts, New York.

Skelton, R. R., McHenry, H. M., and Drawhorn, G. M. 1986. Phylogenetic analysis of early hominids. *Curr. Anthrop.* 27:21-43.

Steiger, R. H., and Jäger, E. 1977. Subcommission of geochronology;

convention on the use of decay constants in geo- and cosmochronology. *Earth Planet. Sci. Lett.* 36:359-362.

Stern, J. T., and Susman, R. L. 1983. The locomotor anatomy of *Australopithecus afarensis. Am. J. Phys Anthrop.* 60:279-317.

Stringer, C. B. 1986. The credibility of *Homo habilis,* in: *Major Topics in Primate and Human Evolution* (B. A. Wood, L. Martin, and P. Andrews, Eds.), pp. 266-294. Cambridge University Press, Cambridge.

Susman, R. L., and Stern, J. T. 1982. Functional morphology of *Homo habilis. Science* 217:931-934.

Tobias, P. V. 1978. The earliest Transvaal members of the genus *Homo* with another look out same problems of hominid taxonomy and systematics. *Z. Morph. Anthrop.* 69:225-265.

Tobias, P. V. 1983. Hominid evolution in Africa. *Can. J. Anthrop.* 3:163-185.

Tobias, P. V. 1967. *The Cranium and Maxillary Dentition of Australopithecus (Zinjanthropus) boisei, Olduvai Gorge,* Volume 2. Cambridge University Press, Cambridge.

Walker, A. C., and Leakey, R. E. 1978. The hominids of East Turkana. *Sci. Am.* 239:54-66

Wolpoff, M. H. 1980. *Paleoanthropology,* Knopf, New York.

Wood, B. A. 1985. Early *Homo* in Kenya, and its systematic relationship, in: *Ancestors: The Hard Evidence* (E. Delson, Ed.), pp. 206-214. Liss, New York.

Wood, B. A. 1978. Classification and phylogeny of East African hominids, in: *Recent Advances in Primatology,* Vol. 3 (D. J. Chivers and K. A. Joysey, Eds.), pp. 351-372. Academic, London.

Wood, B. A. 1974. Olduvai Bed I post-cranial fossils: a reassessment. *J. Hum. Evol.* 3:373-378.

31

Origin and Evolution of the Genus *Homo*

B. Wood

Traditionally *Homo* has been associated with brain enlargement, the acquisition of culture, a reduction in emphasis on mastication as a means of food preparation and breakdown, and a bipedal gait. The australopithecines, on the other hand, are judged not to have advanced much beyond extant apes in relative brain size, to have been dependent on large postcanine teeth for processing food and to have mixed climbing with bipedalism. Any proposal claiming to have identified the earliest evidence for *Homo* needs to demonstrate a shift from the australopithecine to the hominine grade, but the closer to the cusp between the grades the greater the difficulty distinguishing them. This review draws upon recent developments in taxonomy and systematics and focuses on the evidence for, and the controversies about, the origin and subsequent evolution of *Homo*.

HOMO HABILIS: THE CASE FOR AN EARLY *HOMO* TAXON

A little over a quarter of a century ago, in a letter to *Nature*, Louis Leakey, Phillip Tobias and John Napier (Leakey *et al.* 1964) claimed to have identified a new, and probably the earliest, species of our own genus *Homo*. They proposed that the new taxon, *Homo habilis* from Olduvai Gorge, Tanzania, was distinct from contemporary australopithecines but acknowledged that with respect to brain and tooth size it was significantly more primitive than *Homo erectus*, hitherto the oldest recognized *Homo* species. The proposal attracted strong, but conflicting, criticism. While some colleagues expressed the reservation that *H. habilis* showed too few advanced features to merit generic separation from *Australopithecus* (Le Gros Clark 1964; Holloway 1965) others complained that part of the fossil evidence included within the new species was indistinguishable from *H. erectus* (Robinson 1965; Brace *et al.* 1972). Although both Leakey and Tobias subsequently modified their detailed perceptions

of *H. habilis* (Tobias 1965; Leakey 1966), the latter continues (Tobias 1991) to support its morphological integrity and distinctiveness. In the subsequent twenty-five years, additional fossil evidence from Olduvai (Leakey *et al.* 1971; Johanson *et al.* 1987) and from sites elsewhere (Fig. 1), particularly in East Africa (Leakey 1973; Boaz and Howell 1977; Coppens 1980), has confirmed the existence of a fossil hominid which is distinct from both *Australopithecus* and *Homo erectus* (Skelton *et al.* 1986; Chamberlain and Wood 1987).

Figure 1. *Location of sites where remains attributed to, or likened to,* Homo habilis *have been found.*

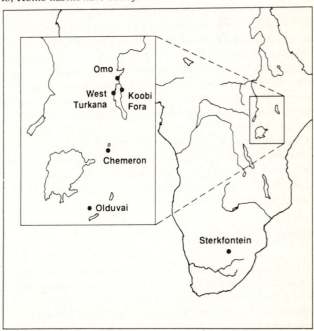

Table 1 Fossil hominid remains, by site, formally, or informally, allocated to, or declared to have affinities with, *Homo habilis* (better-preserved specimens are in bold type).

Sites	Skulls & Crania	Mandibles	Teeth	Postcranial
Olduvai (OH)	6, **7**, **13**, 14, **16**, **24**, 52, 62	**7**, **13**, 37, 62	4, 6, 15, **16**, 17, 21, 27, 31, 32, **39**, 40, 41, 42, 44, 45, 46, 47, 55, 56	**7**, **8**, 10, 35, 43, 48, 49, 50, 62
Koobi Fora (KNM-ER)	807, **1470**, 1478, **1590**, **1805**, **1813**, **3732**, 3735, 3891	819, **1482**, 1483, 1501, 1502, 1506, 1801, **1802**, **1805**, 3734	808, 809, 1462, 1480, 1508, 1814	**813**, **1472**, **1481**, **3228**, 3735
Omo	**L894-1**	**Omo 75-14, Omo 222-2744**	L26-1g; L28-30, 31; L398-573, 1699; Omo 29-43; Omo 33-740, 3282, 5496; Omo 47-47; Omo 74-18, Omo 75s-15, 16; Omo 123-5495; Omo 166-781; Omo 177-4525; Omo 195-1630; Omo K7-19; Omo SH1-17; P933-1	
West Turkana	Kangaki I site (no specimen no. given)	—	—	—
Chemeron	KNM-BC 1	—	—	—
Sterkfontien	**Stw 53**, SE 255, 1508, 1579, 1937, 2396; Sts 19	—	—	—

While it was correct to claim that "late in the 'seventies, the simple abandonment of the question marks, and the employment of italics, gently heralded the willingness of colleagues to use *H. habilis* without contempt or blushing" (Tobias 1989), this acceptance took place and continues in the absence of any consensus about the nature and relationships of the new species. Many palaeoanthropologists are content for the hypodigm (the list of fossils allocated to a species) of *H. habilis* to comprise all, or nearly all, of the material listed in Table 1 (Howell 1978; Tobias 1985); others opt for more restricted membership (Walker and Leakey 1978; Stringer 1986, 1987; Groves and Mazak 1975, Chamberlain 1989). Doubts have also been expressed about the apparently excessive range of morphological variation of the postcranial material which is attributed to *H. habilis* (Wood 1974a,b, 1987; Kennedy 1983a; Wood 1987, Lewis 1989). Several questions are addressed in this review. Does the fossil evidence for *H. habilis* subsume more than one species? If the main hypodigm *is* judged to be heterogeneous, what taxa are represented in the sample? Do they belong to *Homo*, or is one, or more, an australopithecine? What are the implications for the debate about the lack of 'taxonomic space' between *Australopithecus* and *Homo erectus* (Robinson 1965, 1972)? How have Leakey *et al*'s diagnosis of *H. habilis*, and their attempts, and those of others, to define the genus *Homo*, fared when matched with newer evidence about *H. habilis*? Does the definition of *Homo* need modification, and if so, how? Finally, have the results of systematic analyses of material allocated to *H. habilis* clarified its relationships with other early hominid taxa?

FOSSIL EVIDENCE

The initial description of *Homo habilis* referred to seven cranial and postcranial specimens (Box 1). Of the Olduvai fossils subsequently added to the hypodigm (Table 1) the cranium OH 24 and the partial skeleton OH 62 are the most important. Although OH 24 was found on the surface it was assigned to Lower Bed I, beneath Tuff 1B (Hay 1976). Its early date (Table 2) thus countered criticisms that *H. habilis* was a mistaken amalgamation of earlier, more

'*Australopithecus*-like' remains and later, '*erectus*-like,' and dentally more advanced remains from the middle strata of Bed II (Robinson 1965). The partial skeleton OH 62, recovered more recently by Johanson and his colleagues (Johanson *et al*. 1987) provides only meagre additional evidence about the cranium of *H. habilis*, but the postcranial material is a potentially rich, but controversial, source of information about detailed morphology and limb proportions (Box 2). A temporal fragment recovered from Chemeron, a locality in the Baringo Basin, which lies in the Gregory Rift Valley to the south of Lake Turkana, was not initially allocated, or referred to *H. habilis*, but a substantial number of its traits were listed as being compatible with those of *H. habilis* (Tobias 1967). A recent reassessment of this fragment cites two features that are apparently unique to *Homo* (Hill *et al*. 1992).

The largest contribution to the *H. habilis* hypodigm, in both numerical terms (Table 1) and with regard to the quality of the fossil evidence, comes from another site associated with the

Table 2 Best estimates of the geological age of some of the better-preserved East African fossil evidence for *H. habilis*.

Myr	Olduvai (OH)	Koobi Fora (KNM-ER)	Omo
1.6	13		
	16		
1.7			
1.8		3891	
	7, 8, 62		
		1805	
	24		
1.9		1470, 1802, 1813, 3732, 3735	L894-1
2.0			

BOX 1   First evidence of *Homo habilis*.

In addition to the type specimen, six specimens were assigned to *H. habilis* in the original description (Leakey *et al.* 1964).

Type: The juvenile skeleton (OH 7) was found in 1960 at site FLKNN in Bed I. It comprises parts of both parietals, much of the alveolar process and dentition, but little else, of a mandible and at least 13 hand bones.

Paratypes: These are remains resembling the type specimen and include skull fragments and teeth (OH 4 and 6), part of an adult foot (OH 8) and an incomplete skull of an adolescent (OH 13).

Referred specimens: A collection of juvenile cranial pieces (OH 14) and the fragmented cranial vault and dentition (OH 16) of a young adult.

Howell (1978) proposed that OH 6, 8 and 14 be excluded from *H. habilis*; Tobias includes OH 6 and 14 in his latest list (1991), but questions the allocation of OH 8.

DISTINGUISHING FEATURES

The authors of the original report listed the following features of *H. habilis* but they are not all distinctive:

Cranial and Mandibular

1. Maxilla and mandible smaller than in *Australopithecus*, but equivalent in size to *H. erectus* and *H. sapiens*.
2. Brain size greater than *Australopithecus*, but smaller than *H. erectus*.
3. Slight to strong muscular markings.

4. Parietal bone curvature in the sagittal plane varying from slight (i.e. hominine) to moderate (i.e. australopithecine).
5. Relatively open-angled external sagittal curvature to occipital.
6. Retreating chin, with a slight or absent mental trigone.

Dental

7. Incisors large with respect to those of *Australopithecus* and *H. erectus*.
8. Molar size overlaps the ranges for *Australopithecus* and *H. erectus*.
9. Canines large relative to premolars.
10. Premolars narrower than in *Australopithecus* and within the range of *H. erectus*.
11. All teeth relatively narrow buccolingually and elongated mesiodistally, especially the mandibular molars and premolars.

Postcranial

12. Clavicle resembles *H. sapiens*.
13. Hand bones have broad terminal phalanges, capitate and MCP articulations resembling *H. sapiens*, but differ in respect of the scaphoid and trapezium, attachments of the superficial flexor tendons and the robusticity and curvature of the phalanges.
14. Foot bones resemble *H. sapiens* in the stout and adducted big toe, and well-marked foot arches, but differ in the shape of the trochlea surface of the talus and the relatively robust third metatarsal.

Gregory Rift, Koobi Fora, which lies on the north-east shore of Lake Turkana; recent examinations of the homogeneity of the *H. habilis* hypodigm have focused on the crania KNM-ER 1470 and 1813 which just antedate the evidence from Olduvai (Table 2). Hominid remains recovered from the northern group of Turkana basin sediments, specifically from Members G and H of the Omo Shungura Formation, have also been likened to *H. habilis*. These include a fragmented cranium (Boaz and Howell 1977), two mandibles and some 20 isolated teeth, (Coppens 1979; Howell *et al.* 1987), (Table 1). A cranial fragment recovered from the Nachukui Formation, on the western shores of Lake Turkana, has also been referred to *H. habilis* (Harris *et al.* 1988). The first assessment of the hominid remains recovered from Hadar in Ethiopia and Laetoli in Tanzania suggested that an early *Homo* species may be represented (Leakey *et al.* 1976; Johanson and Taieb 1976), but these specimens have now all been accommodated within a single species, *Australopithecus afarensis* (Johanson *et al.* 1978).

A fragmentary skull, Stw 53, recovered from the southern African cave site of Sterkfontein, together with isolated teeth also recovered from Member 5 at Sterkfontein, have been said to resemble *H. habilis* (Hughes and Tobias 1977). Several authors have proposed that hominine material (Broom and Robinson 1950; Clarke 1977a) can also be identified within

Member 4 at Sterkfontein, a collection which is dominanted by remains attributed to *A. africanus* (Table 1). Attribution to *H. habilis* is also among the options which have been considered for both cranial, SK 847 and SK 27, and dental, SK 2635, remains from Member 1 at Swartkrans (Clarke and Howell 1972; Clarke 1977a; Howell 1978). Although several authors have linked SK 847 with *H. erectus*, recent studies have emphasised its affinites with Stw 53 (Chamberlain 1987; Grine *et al.* in press) and thus indirectly with *H. habilis*.

Proposals that *H. habilis* has been identified at sites beyond Africa, in the Near East and Asia, have not been sustained. The hominid fragments from Ubeidiyah in Israel were listed (Leakey *et al.* 1964) as possible members of the *H. habilis* hypodigm and it was tentatively suggested that remains from Indonesia assigned to *Meganthropus palaeojavanicus* may be synonymous with *H. habilis* (Tobias and von Koenigswald 1964). Both proposals have since been abandoned (Tobias 1991).

HOMO HABILIS—ONE SPECIES OR TWO?

From the outset, doubts have been expressed about the taxonomic homogeneity of the Olduvai hypodigm of *H. habilis* (Table 3). The initial criticisms, that there was a temporal basis for the taxonomic heterogeneity, (Robinson 1965) were effectively countered by the discovery of OH 24 (see above), but Louis Leakey still felt it necessary to invoke time to explain at least some of the range of morphology subsumed within *H. habilis*. He cast OH 7 and OH 13 as, respectively, the early and late representatives of a "*sapiens*-like" lineage, whose morphology he contrasted with the "protopithecanthropine" features of specimens such as OH 16 (Leakey 1966). A subsequent assessment also hinted that more than one species may be represented within the Olduvai hypodigm but sorted the specimens differently, concluding that the morphological differences between OH 13 and 24, on the one hand, and OH 16 and OH 7, on the other, probably "suggests the possibility of taxonomic variation" (Leakey *et al.* 1971:312).

The additions to the *H. habilis* hypodigm provided by the Koobi Fora remains apparently failed to clarify the situation. Several experienced observers (Howell 1978; Tobias 1985; White *et al.* 1981; Johanson 1989) continue to stress the taxonomic unity of the augmented hypodigm, while other authors have re-emphasised the australopithecine affinities of part of the enlarged hypodigm (Leakey 1974; Olson 1978; Leakey and Walker 1980). The theme of the morphological dichotomy between OH 13, 24 and OH 7, 16, suggested by Mary Leakey and her colleagues (Leakey *et al.* 1971) has been taken up by others (Leakey 1974; Leakey and Walker 1980) who suggest that *H. habilis* should be restricted to OH 7 and 16, that is the larger-toothed, bigger-brained, and presumably larger-bodied, component of the main hypodigm. In this scheme, specimens not showing such attributes, such as OH 13 and 24 and KNM-ER 1805 and 1813 from Koobi Fora, were judged to be "late-surviving small *Australopithecus* individuals that were contemporaneous first with *H. habilis*, then with *H. erectus*" (Leakey and Walker 1980:1103).

These latter proposals involve removing a substantial part of the *H. habilis* hypodigm from *Homo*, but other authors who have been ready to accept that *H. habilis* subsumed more than one fossil hominid species have been prepared to accommodate both subsets within the same genus. While some workers have subscribed to a split of the hypodigm based, among other considerations, on brain and tooth size (Stringer 1986, 1987; Wood 1985), others have suggested schemes which partition the remains geographically, with *H. habilis* being confined to Olduvai, and one, or more, new species of *Homo* being recognised at Koobi Fora (Groves and Mazak 1975; Chamberlain 1989; Groves 1989). Groves and Mazak designated one of these new species *Homo ergaster*, but others consider *H. ergaster* most probably synonymous with (Chamberlain 1989), or a subset of *H. erectus* (Wood 1991) (see below).

Recent research has explicitly compared variation within *H. habilis* with that observed within living primates in order to assess the probability that *H. habilis* samples a single species. The evidence and the methods differed as did the conclusions. While a study that concentrated on comparing two crania, KNM-ER 1470 and 1813 (Fig. 2), cast doubt on a single species solution (Lieberman *et al.* 1988) another, focusing on brain size, (Miller 1991) supported it. The former study concluded that the contrasts between KNM-ER 1470 and 1813 were greater in degree than the equivalent differences between male and female gorilla crania, whereas the latter investigation concluded that the endocranial volumes, 752 and 510 cm^3, of the two fossil crania did not imply a degree of intraspecific variation exceeding that observed in sexually dimorphic higher primate species. Considerations of intraspecific variability have recently become more sophisticated to the extent that separate attention has been paid to the pattern as well as to the degree of morphological variation (Wood *et al.* 1991). Variables are assessed as being 'good' or 'poor' taxonomic discriminators, with greater emphasis being placed on those variables which are known to vary more between rather than within species closely related to the early hominids.

The two most recent detailed studies of *H. habilis* (Tobias 1991; Wood 1991) differ in their emphasis but are partly consistent in their taxonomic conclusions. Tobias (1991) provides a magisterial review of the detailed morphology of the Olduvai remains attributed to *H. habilis*. He concludes that the features which were originally said to characterise *H. habilis* (Leakey *et al.* 1964) (Box 1) have stood the test of time. He has no hesitation in retaining all of the Olduvai hypodigm within *H. habilis* and he also includes the material from Koobi Fora that has been referred to *Homo habilis*; his is a single species interpretation of *Homo habilis*. My own approach was different in that I submitted the cranial remains attributed to *H. habilis* to examinations explicitly designed to test the null hypothesis of a single early *Homo* species. The degree of variation in the sample was compared to that in another synchronic hominid species, *Paranthropus boisei*, as well as to the degree of variation observed in *Homo erectus* and an extant *Gorilla* sample. Patterns of variation in early *Homo* were compared with that in *Homo sapiens* and *Pan troglodytes*, the two species most closely related to early hominids, and which we have shown share patterns of cranial variation (Wood *et al.* 1991). In the event there

Table 3. Multiple taxon solutions for crania and mandibles attributed to *H. Habilis*.

Authors	Specimens OH	KNM-ER	Taxon names	Comments
Robinson (1965)	7	—	*A.* aff. *A. africanus*	C/P$_3$ ratio; $\overline{\text{C}}$ morphology
	13	—	*H.* aff. *H. erectus*	U-shaped mandibular contour; gracile mandibular corpus
Leakey et al. (1971)	7, 16	—	*H. habilis*	*H. erectus*-type, evenly curved lambdoid suture
	13, 24	—	*H. habilis/Homo* sp.	*H. sapiens*-type, V-shaped lambdoid suture
Groves (1979)	7, 13, 16, 24	—	*H. habilis*	Narrow premolar; upper face>mid face
	—	1470, 1590, 1802	*H. rudolfensis*	Mid face>upper face; P$_4$ large relative to canine size
	—	730, 820, 992, 1805, 1813	*H. ergaster*	Broad premolars; P$_4$<P$_3$
Leakey et al. (1978)	7	1470, 1590, 1802	*H. habilis*	Enlarged anterior and cheek teeth; robust mandibles; cranial capacity >750cm^3
	13	992, 1813	*A.* aff. *A. Africanus*	Small molars and premolars; cranial capacity approx. 600 cm^3
Stringer (1986)	7, 24	1470, 1590, 1802, 3732	*H. habilis* (group 1)	Large cranial capacity approx. 750cm^3; flat lower face; large teeth and jaws
	13, 16	992, 1805, 1813	*H. habilis* (group 2) or *H. ergaster*	Small cranial capacity approx 510 cm^3; projecting lower face; small teeth and jaws
Chamberlain (1989)	7, 13, 16, 24, 37	—	*H. habilis sensu stricto*	Premolars and molars mesiodistally elongated; reduced jaw size relative to neurocranium
	—	992, 1470, 1483, 1802, 1805, 1813, 3734	*Homo* sp.	Mandibular premolar roots complex; shares traits with 'robust' australopithecines
Wood (1991)	7, 13, 16, 24, 37, and so on	1478, 1501, 1805, 1813, 3735, and so on	*H. habilis*	Small neurocranium approx. 500 cm^3; upper face>mid face; small buccolingually narrow P$_3$-M$_1$; M$_3$ reduction
	—	1470, 1482, 1590, 1802, 3732, and so on	*H. rudolfensis*	Large neurocranuim approx. 750 cm^3; orthognathic with mid face>upper face; large postcanine teeth; M$_3$>M$_2$

were few cases where the degree of variation in the main *H. habilis* hypodigm exceeded that in the comparators, but there were several examples (e.g. facial shape and premolar tooth morphology) where the pattern of cranial, mandibular and dental variation differed from that in the comparative samples. However, in each case the evidence for taxonomic heterogeneity came not from the Olduvai part of the hypodigm but from remains referred to *H. habilis* from the Koobi Fora site collection. This led me to agree with Tobias, and accept the Olduvai hypodigm of *H. habilis* as sound evidence for that species, but to suggest that the Koobi Fora hypodigm sampled two species of early *Homo*, one conspecific with *H. habilis* from Olduvai and the other a new species of early *Homo*, already dubbed *Homo rudolfensis* (Alexeev 1986) (Figure 3; Box 3). *Homo ergaster* (Groves and Mazak 1975) is not available as the name of the second species of early *Homo* for the type specimen KNM-ER 992 resembles, though is not necessarily conspecific with, *Homo erectus*. Thus, I have put forward *Homo ergaster* (Wood 1991) as the proper name for the probable African precursor of *Homo erectus*, a taxon which would also include the crania KNM-ER 3733 and 3883 and probably also the skeleton KNM-WT 15000, although formal assignment of that specimen must await its detailed description and analysis.

EVIDENCE FROM THE LIMBS

It is all too common for debates about early hominid taxonomy to dwell exclusively on the cranial evidence and to ignore the rest of the skeleton. This reflects the relative scarcity of postcranial remains (Table 1) as well as a tendency to regard the postcranial skeleton as primarily a source of functional rather than taxonomic evidence. In the event, morphological characterisation of the postcranial anatomy of *H. habilis*, together with the latter's functional interpretation, have proved to be topics every bit as controversial as those involving the cranial evidence.

The first integrated account of fossil evidence of the foot and leg of *H. habilis*, like that of the cranium, was based on the evidence from Olduvai, and emphasised the ways in which these remains resembled those of *Homo sapiens* (Napier 1964). However, functional conclusions based on more detailed descriptions of foot (OH 8, 10) and leg (OH 35) fossils, which most likely are from the same individual (Susman and Stern 1982), were generally more cautious. They stressed that the unique striding gait of *Homo sapiens* had not yet been achieved (Day and Napier 1964), and suggested that the knee joint may have been imperfectly adapted to bipedalism (Davis 1964). Despite these caveats the inferred

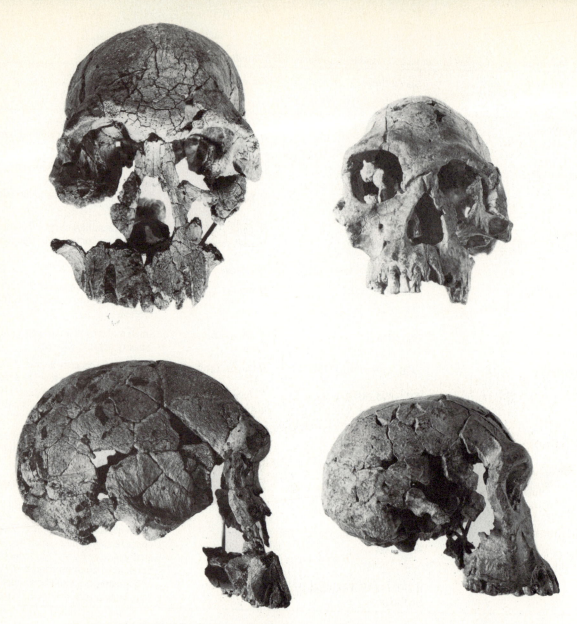

Figure 2. *Two views of the crania KNM-ER 1470 (left) and 1813 (right). These two crania, both dating from around 1.9 Myr, would need to be subsumed within a single early* Homo *species. While they share a similarly shaped neurocranium, differences in their facial anatomy are less easy to accommodate within a single species model.*

functional affinities between the fossils of *H. habilis* and *H. sapiens* continued to be emphasised, and a bipedal gait of the modern human type was widely claimed for the former species.

Subsequent reassessments of the anatomy of the OH 8 foot were to place more stress on its potential for climbing and on the extent to which that specimen had retained anatomical features also seen in living non-human anthropoid apes (Susman and Stern 1982; Lewis 1989). These observations were particularly pertinent, for while it was deduced that OH 8 apparently possessed the mechanism that transforms the foot into a rigid, close-packed, organ during the support phase of bipedal walking (Lewis 1989) it was concluded that it lacked at least some of the refinements (e.g. lateral deviation of the heel) which are present in *H. sapiens*. The same author was also struck by the lack of evidence for a propulsive role for the big toe, an important factor in the bipedal gait of modern humans (Lewis 1972).

A somewhat different and more complex interpretation of the hindlimb anatomy of early *Homo* has emerged from studies of the Koobi Fora evidence, although Tobias (1991) correctly cautions that the specimens providing much of the conflicting evidence (i.e. the femora KNM-ER 1472 and 1481A and the talus KNM-ER 813) may not belong to *H. habilis*, but to *H. erectus* or *H. ergaster*. However, the features which prompted some to assign KNM-ER 1472 and 1481A to *H. erectus* (Kennedy 1983b) may not be diagnostic of that species (Trinkaus 1984) and are likely to be derived features of all *Homo* species, including *H. habilis*. Others have demonstrated that the two Koobi Fora specimens are distinct from australopithecine femora (McHenry and Corruccini 1978) and have shown that a talus, KNM-ER 813, from a similar-aged horizon as the femora, resembles modern human tali much more closely than do australopithecine tali (Wood 1974b). Thus, there are at Koobi Fora leg fossils whose later *Homo*-like morphology contrasts with that of the more australopithecine-like morphology

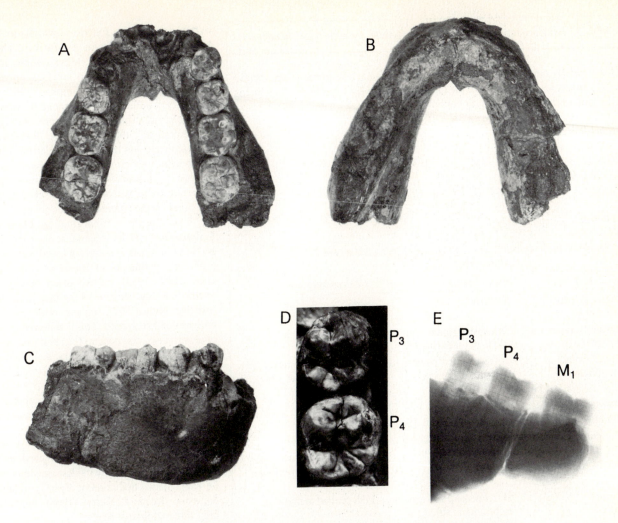

Figure 3. *The adult mandible KNM-ER 1802 has been assigned to* Homo rudolfensis. *Pertinent features include a sharp, everted, base (B) together with substantial premolar crowns incorporating molarised roots and a marked talonid (A, C-E). A. Occlusal; B. Basal; C. Right lateral; D. Occlusal details of right P3 and P4 (2X lifesize); E. Radiograph of left corpus (lifesize).*

of the Olduvai remains. These relatively derived remains from Koobi Fora are found alongside a specimen such as KNM-ER 3735, which is judged to resemble the more primitive OH 62 skeleton (Leakey *et al.* 1989).

An analysis of estimated stature/body weight relationships has also demonstrated that whereas predictions based on the two Koobi Fora femora are in line with modern human and archaic *H. sapiens* relationships, they are substantially different from predictions based on the australopithecine-like Olduvai *Homo habilis* remains which, instead conform to predictions based on the living African apes (Aiello 1992). This wide range of morphology has no apparent allometric basis, at least as far as the proximal femur is concerned (Wood and Wilson 1986), and thus provides additional evidence for taxonomic heterogeneity within early *Homo* (Wood 1987; 1991).

Evidence of the forelimb skeleton of Olduvai *H. habilis* is meagre, with the OH 7 hand providing the most pertinent information. Its fragmentary nature precludes comprehensive morphological and functional analysis, but it is generally interpreted as demonstrating a mosaic of an ape-like carpus with a

thumb which could have both been rotated within the hand to allow pulp-to-pulp opposition, as well as used to provide the kind of firm support which is essential for effective tool manufacture and manipulation (Susman and Stern 1982; Trinkaus 1989; Lewis 1989). Taken together with the evidence of the relatively primitive limb proportions of OH 62, (Johanson *et al.* 1987; Hartwig-Schrerer and Martin 1991) the architecture of the limbs of *H. habilis sensu stricto* emerges as being closer to that of the australopithecines than to later *Homo*.

DEFINING THE GENUS *HOMO*

The task of hominid palaeontologists would be greatly eased if agreement could be reached about criteria for including material into the genus *Homo*. However, a distinguished taxonomist, Ernst Mayr, has insisted that "there are no absolute generic characters" and continued that "it is impossible to define and delimit genera on a purely morphological basis" (Mayr 1950:117). The nearest he came to a definition of *Homo* was that it was characterised by "upright posture, with its shift to a terrestrial mode of living and the freeing of the anterior

Homo habilis sensu stricto and *Homo rudolfensis* have been suggested (Wood 1991) as species components of the larger *Homo habilis* hypodigm. Specimens allocated to the two taxa are set out below:

Homo habilis sensu stricto
Olduvai:
OH 4, 6, 8, 10, 13-16, 21, 24, 27, 35, 37, 39-45, 48-50, 52, 62.
Koobi Fora:
KNM-ER 1478, 1501, 1502, 1805, 1813, 3735.

Homo rudolfensis
Koobi Fora:
KNM-ER 813, 819, 1470, 1472, 1481-1483, 1590, 1801, 1802, 3732, 3891.

Skull and Teeth	*Homo habilis s.s.*	*Homo rudolfensis*
Absolute brain size (cm^3)	$\overline{X} = 610$	$\overline{X} = 751$
Overall cranial vault morphology	Enlarged occipital contribution to the sagittal arc*	Primitive condition
Endocranial morphology	Primitive sulcal pattern (Falk 1983; but see Holloway 1985)	Frontal lobe asymmetry (Falk 1983; Tobias 1987)
Suture pattern	Complex	Simple
Frontal	Incipient supraorbital torus	Torus absent
Parietal	Coronal > sagittal chord	Primitive condition
Face—overall	Upper face > midface breadth	Midface > upperface breadth: markedly orthognathic
Nose	Margins sharp and everted; evident nasal sill	Less everted margins; no nasal sill
Malar surface	Vertical, or near vertical	Anteriorly-inclined
Palate	Foreshortened	Large
Upper teeth	Probably two-rooted premolars	Premolars three-rooted; absolutely and relatively large anterior teeth
Mandibular fossa	Relatively deep	Shallow
Foramen magnum	Orientation variable	Anteriorly-inclined
Mandibular corpus	Moderate relief on external surface, Rounded base	Marked relief on external surface, Everted base
Lower teeth	Buccolingually-narrowed post-canine crowns	Broad postcanine crowns
	Reduced talonid on P$_4$ M$_3$ reduction	Relatively large P$_4$ talonid No M$_3$ reduction
	Mostly single-rooted mandibular premolars	Twin, plate-like, P$_4$ roots, and bifid, or even twin, plate-like P$_3$ roots

* but see Tobias (1991) for a contrary view

Postcranium		
Limb proportions	Ape-like	?
Forelimb robusticity	Ape-like	?
Hand	Mosaic of ape-like and modern human-like features	?
Hindfoot	Retains climbing	Later *Homo*-like adaptations
Femur	Australopithecine-like	Later *Homo*-like

extremity for new functions which, in turn, have stimulated brain evolution" (Mayr 1950:110). Thus defined, Mayr's genus *Homo* embraced the then known australopithecines, *H. erectus* and *H. sapiens*. Simpson (1961) subsequently warned, in the context of what he described as "the chaos of anthropological nomenclature," that genera are "necessarily more arbitrary and less precise in definition than the species," but suggested that a genus can be defined as "a group of species believed to be more closely related among themselves than to any other species placed in other genera."

The dictum adumbrated by Mayr and Simpson, that it is the species that make the genus and not *vice versa*, is borne out by critical inspection of the definitions of *Homo* provided by Le Gros Clark (1955) and Robinson (1968). The former is a concatenation of the features of what was then known of *H. sapiens*, *Homo neanderthalensis* and *H. erectus*. This is reflected in some of the proposed components (e.g. brain size with a range of 900-2000 cm^3), but the definition also includes references to morphological trends, e.g. a centrally-situated foramen magnum, reduced lingual cusp on the P$_3$, relative size reduction of the third molar, and follows Mayr to the extent that it specifies a "limb skeleton adapted for a fully erect posture and gait" (Le Gros Clark 1955:86). When announcing *H. habilis*, Louis Leakey and his colleagues (1964) made only modest amendments to Le Gros Clark's definition of *Homo*, and later in the same decade Robinson (1968) emphasized only three additional features, a nasal sill, "harmoniously proportioned" anterior and postcanine teeth and incompletely molarised dm$_1$ crowns.

Few explicit definitions of *Homo* have been offered in the recent literature, but the increasing use of cladistic methods within hominid palaeontology means that it is possible to deduce the character state changes which define the *Homo* clade. Cladistic analyses of early hominids are presently confined to cranial evidence, and surprisingly few of these analyses combine data from early hominids, later *Homo* and extant *H. sapiens*. We have investigated the distribution of 90 cranial, mandibular and dental characters across a range of hominid species and outgroups (Chamberlain and Wood 1987) and the resulting *Homo* clade was defined by 8 character state changes (Box 4). Others (Stringer 1987) have also emphasised reduced prognathism, dental reduction and brain enlargement as factors defining the *Homo* clade.

DIAGNOSTIC FEATURES OF *H. HABILIS*

The newly-announced *H. habilis* species (Leakey *et al.* 1964) was characterised by the features listed in Box 1. Of the eleven features which relate to the cranium, mandible and den-

Cladistic, or phylogenetic analysis, is a method of investigating the relationships between taxa. It makes the assumption that morphological evolution is parsimonious, i.e. similar morphological features, or characters, are more likely to be derived from a shared common ancestor than to have evolved independently. Each character has a hypothetical morphocline of states, from primitive to derived. The primitive condition is assumed to be that which is most widely distributed in related taxa and/or the condition which has the least complex developmental history. Character states uniquely defining a taxon are known as autapomorphies; their distribution does not help in establishing relationships. Character states distributed within part of the cladogram, i.e. defining a 'node' are called synapomorphies and states common to all the taxa in a cladogram are referred to as symplesiomorphies. Each character and the distribution of its states among the taxa to be assessed allows the generation of a cladogram. The cladogram, or pattern of relationships, supported by the majority of characters is assumed to be the most probable hypothesis of relationships.

The cladogram presented below is the most parsimonious generated from a set of 90 cranial, mandibular and dental characters (Chamberlain and Wood 1987; Wood 1991). The resulting *Homo* clade is defined by the following character state changes at Node A:

1. Increased cranial vault thickness.
2. Reduced postorbital constriction.
3. Increased contribution of the occipital bone to cranial sagittal arc length.
4. Increased cranial vault height.
5. More anteriorly-situated foramen magnum.
6. Reduced lower facial prognathism.
7. Narrower tooth crowns, particularly mandibular premolars.
8. Reduction in length of the molar tooth row.

The two species comprising the original *H. habilis* hypodigm, *H. habilis sensu stricto* and *H. rudolfensis* (Wood 1991) share a hypothetical ancestor with each other which neither shares with any other taxon. That sister group is defined by the five character state changes at Node B, namely:

1. Elongated anterior basicranium.
2. Higher cranial vault.
3&4. Mesiodistally-elongated M_1 and M_2.
5. Narrow mandibular fossa.

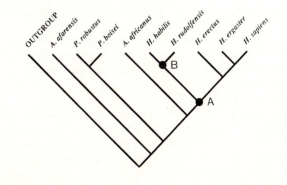

tition, four—the absolute size of the maxilla and mandible, brain size, the degree of parietal sagittal curvature and molar crown size—were said to be intermediate between the condition in the australopithecines and in the then oldest hominine taxon, *H. erectus*. In two characters, the hypodigm was specified as resembling existing taxa, i.e. occipital sagittal curvature (*H. sapiens*) and premolar width (*H. erectus*). The reference to a retreating chin, with no mental trigone, does not suggest a significant departure from the australopithecine condition, and another character, the degree of cranial muscular marking, is too non-specific to be helpful. The dental diagnostic features are relative incisor and canine size and the shape of the tooth crowns, with buccolingual narrowing of the mandibular premolars and molars being especially mentioned. However, it should be noted that several other workers have disputed the uniqueness, among Plio-Pleistocene hominids, of narrow premolars (Robinson 1965, 1966; White *et al.* 1981). As for the gait implications of the postcranial skeleton, while all the remains which have been entertained as belonging to the hypodigm of *H. habilis* have been interpreted as belonging to a bipedal hominid, the extent to which *H. habilis* had retained the potential for climbing is still debated (Prost 1990; Rose 1984).

A later paper (Vandebroek 1969) expanded on the 1964 definition, and emphasised peculiarities of the morphology of the mandibular canines and premolars of *H. habilis* (e.g. small anterior fovea and cusp asymmetry in the latter) and in a figure also drew attention to differences in the trend of mandibular premolar crown size between *H. habilis* and australopithecines. Tobias (1989) has cited additional "critical features of the morphology of *H. habilis*" (ibid., p. 143). These include the relative crown size of M_2 and M_3, vertically-thin brow ridges, minimal pneumatization of the cranium, a prognathous face, an anteriorly-situated foramen magnum, a short basicranium, coronally-orientated petrous bones and a "very robust" mandible with a slight chin. However, the author does not indicate whether any of these features are unique to *H. habilis*. In an encyclopaedic 'summary' of the features of *H. habilis*, the same author (Tobias 1991) makes reference to 344 cranial, mandibular and dental traits, but although their expression is meticulously recorded for *A. africanus*, *P. robustus*, *P. boisei* and *H. erectus*, their wider comparative context is not explored, and thus their taxonomic and phylogenetic utility have yet to be demonstrated.

Cladistic analyses have made little contribution to the search for distinctive features, or autapomorphies, of *H. habilis*. In an early study (Eldredge and Tattersall 1975), an endocranial volume of more than 600 cm³ was cited as a character distinguishing *A. habilis* (i.e. *H. habilis*) from *A. africanus*, but in a wider taxonomic context this cannot be regarded as anything other than a component of what has been called a 'combination' definition (Wood 1984). Others were more explicit stating "we have been able to identify no autapomorphic features of *H. habilis*." (Delson *et al.* 1977:273). This was also implicitly conceded in another analysis (Olson 1978) but the latter's utility is reduced because no distinction was made between 'gracile' australopithecines from southern Africa and the Olduvai hypodigm of *H. habilis*. A cladistic analysis based on quantitative cranial data (Wood and Chamberlain 1986) deduced only one *H. habilis* autapomorphy, a relatively narrow mid-face, but more recently, using an augmented data set (Chamberlain and Wood 1987), we have identified two further *H. habilis*

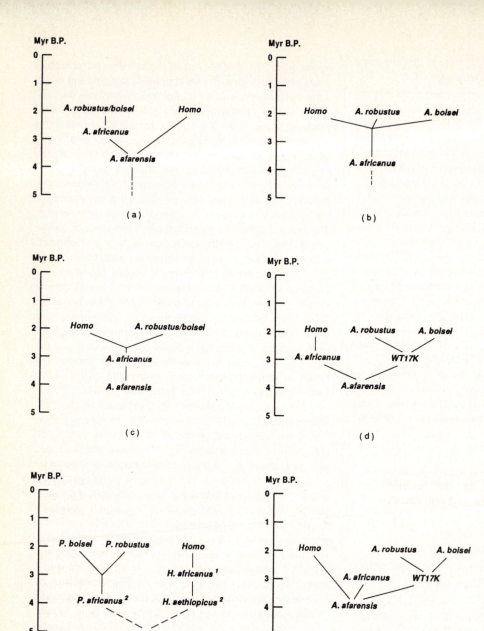

Figure 4. *Comparison of the relationships of the* Homo *lineage/clade within published early hominid phylogenetic schemes; a, Johanson and White 1979; b, Tobias 1980; c, Skelton* et al. *1986; d, Delson 1986; e, Olson 1978; f, Wood 1991.*

autapomorphies—an elongated anterior basicranium and a mesiodistally-elongated M^1 crown. When the two proposed species subdivisions of the early *Homo* hypodigm, *H. habilis sensu stricto* and *H. rudolfensis*, are included separately in a cladistic analysis, they are linked as sister taxa within a clade defined by five character states (Box 4).

PHYLOGENETIC RELATIONSHIPS OF *H. HABILIS*

Phylogenetic analyses which have included *H. habilis* as a separate and unified species have almost all resulted in the conclusion that it, along with *H. erectus* and *H. sapiens*, is part of a clade, or monophyletic group, corresponding to the genus *Homo*. Within such a clade, *H. habilis* is usually, but not universally, nominated as the sister taxon of *H. erectus* and *H. sapiens* (Skelton *et al.* 1986; Chamberlain and Wood 1987; Stringer 1987; White *et al.* 1981; Wood and Chamberlain 1986; Bonde 1977; Johanson and White 1979), species which are themselves clearly defined cladistically (Chamberlain and

Wood 1987; Stringer 1987). There is, however, substantially less consensus about the relationships of *H. habilis*, and the *Homo* clade, with australopithecine taxa (Fig. 4). The position of *A. africanus* is pivotal for these interpretations. While some writers have interpreted it as being exclusively ancestral to either the *Homo* (Fig. 4d,e) or the 'robust' australopithecine clades (Fig. 4a), others see *A. africanus* as the common ancestor of the two clades (Fig. 4b and c).

The results of two formal cladistic analyses of early hominids, (Skelton *et al.* 1986; Chamberlain and Wood 1987) although based on different cranial data sets, concur to the extent that both studies show that *A. africanus* is not strongly associated with either the *Homo* or the 'robust' australopithecine clades (Fig. 4f). This is not due to *A. africanus* lacking features of either of the two clades, but rather it is because it represents a mosaic of relatively primitive characters (e.g. the cranial base) and characters which are derived in either the direction of *Homo* (e.g. cranial vault), or of the 'robust' australopithecines (e.g. face and masticatory

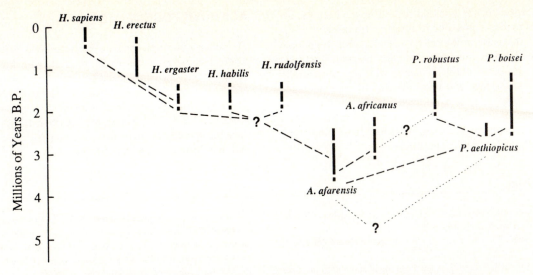

Figure 5 *A phylogenetic scheme for hominid evolution based on a recent analysis of hominid taxonomy and relationships. The horizontal axis corresponds to relative and absolute postcanine toothsize, so that forms with substantial tooth rows are to the right and species demonstrating premolar and molar reduction and simplification are to the left. The phylogeny represented by the bold broken lines assumes that the two best known 'robust' australopithecine speces,* P. robustus *and* P. boisei, *shared a common ancestor which was not unlike* P. aethiopicus *(i.e., like KNM-WT 17000). However, this monophyletic origin for* Paranthropus *is only marginally more parsomonius than deriving* P. robustus *from* A. africanus. *The similarities in facial form between* H. rudolfensis *and a probable* Paranthropus *clade are most parsimoniously interpreted as convergent features.*

apparatus). This suggests that *A. africanus* is too specialised to be ancestral to either the *Homo* or the 'robust' australopithecine clades, or for it to be the common ancestor of all later hominids (Fig. 4f).

CONCLUSIONS

There is little doubt that the larger *H. habilis* hypodigm subsumes remains which are more derived than either *A. afarensis* or *A. africanus*, yet are distinct from approximately contemporary remains which are usually attributed to African *H. erectus*, or by some, to *H. ergaster*. However, if its taxonomic integrity is retained, it is a species which manifestly embraces an unusually wide degree of variation in both the cranium (Stringer 1986; Wood 1985, 1991; Lieberman *et al.* 1988) and the postcranial skeleton (Wood 1987). Those who believe this range of variation to be unacceptably wide, and thus for whom *H. habilis* represents more than one species, are divided themselves about how the hypodigm should be apportioned.

The majority of authors, be they supporters of a single species, or a multiple species resolution of *H. habilis*, regard the Olduvai hypodigm as taxonomically homogenous, with only a minority dissenting from this view (Skelton *et al.* 1986; Walker and Leakey 1978; Stringer 1986) (Table 2). As for the Koobi Fora early *Homo* evidence, this is either regarded as belonging to a single species, but one distinct from *H. habilis sensu stricto*, (Chamberlain 1987) or the hypodigm is interpreted as being a taxonomically heterogenous one which samples *H. habilis sensu stricto* and at least one other *Homo* species (Wood 1991) for which *H. rudolfensis* has apparent priority as a species name (Groves 1989; Alexeev 1986). These two early *Homo* species are sufficiently distinct for them to have substantially different grounds for their inclusion in *Homo* (Box 3). Whereas *H. habilis sensu stricto* is hominine with respect to its masticatory com-

plex, it retains an essentially australopithecine postcranial skeleton. *Homo rudolfensis*, on the other hand, apparently combines a later *Homo*-like postcranial skeleton with a face and dentition which are adaptively analogous to those of the 'robust' australopithecines, especially *P. boisei*.

The earliest sound evidence for the larger *H. habilis sensu lato* hypodigm is dated to approximately 1.9 Myr BP (Table 2), but a series of isolated teeth from Members E, F and G of the Omo Shungura Formation and the evidence of the Chemeron temporal fragment may extend its known time range to well beyond 2.0 Myr BP (Hill *et al.* 1992; Wood 1991; Feibel *et al.* 1989). The former date, 1.9 Myr BP, is little different from the age of the earliest known evidence for *Homo ergaster*, the early African equivalent of *H. erectus*. If early *Homo* does subsume more than one species, the period prior to 2.0 Myr BP may have witnessed not merely the emergence of one hominid of the *Homo* grade, but a substantial radiation of early hominids, namely *Homo habilis sensu stricto*, *Homo rudolfensis* and *Homo ergaster* (Fig. 5), each demonstrating a significant and distinctive shift away from the australopithecine adaptive plateau.

The multiple species solution for the remains attributed to early *Homo* must now be tested. This will involve establishing sound criteria for confirming hypotheses of taxonomic heterogeneity, including refining the distinctions between the degree and pattern of variability, as well as confirming the suitability of comparative analogues for assessing within and between species variation. Other tests might also be explored, for instance, how realistic are the ranges of body weight estimated for each taxon? Do the proposed taxa imply either unacceptably large, or unreasonably small, levels of sexual dimorphism? Is there any evidence that they occupied the same, or different, parts of the palaeolandscape?

If the multiple species solution survives rigorous examination, other aspects of the hominid record, particularly the archaeological evidence, must be integrated with this new interpretation of the paleontological data. Only when functional morphological studies are integrated with the contextual, and particularly the behavioural, evidence will we substantially increase our knowledge and understanding of the emergence and early evolution of our own genus. However, taxonomic interpretations of the fossil record are the foundation upon which more complex hypotheses, including those embracing ecological principles, can be constructed.

ACKNOWLEDGEMENTS

The author's own researches on the evidence for early *Homo* from Koobi Fora were at the invitation of Richard Leakey and the co-operation of the Director and Trustees of the National Museums of Kenya is gratefully acknowledged. The Leverhulme Trust and The Royal Society have been generous in their support of this research. Andrew Chamberlain has contributed significantly to the ideas incorporated in this review, and Craig Engleman, Paula Guest and Bob Read helped with its production.

REFERENCES

Aiello, L.C. 1992. Allometry and the analysis of size and shape in human evolution. *J. Hum. Evol.* 22:127-147.

Alexeev, V.P. 1986. *The Origins of the Human Race.* Progress Publishers, Moscow.

Boaz, N.T. and Howell, F.C. 1977. A gracile hominid cranium from Upper Member G of the Shungura Formation, Ethiopia. *Am. J. Phys. Anthrop.* 46:93-108.

Bonde, N. 1977. Cladistic classification as applied to vertebrates, in: *Major Patterns in Vertebrate Evolution* (M.K. Hecht, P.C. Goody, and B.M. Hecht, Eds.), pp. 741-804, Plenum Press, New York.

Brace, C.L., Mahler, P.E., and Rosen, R.B. 1972. Tooth measurements and the rejection of the taxon "Homo habilis." *Yrbk. Phys. Anthrop.* 16:50-68.

Broom, R. and Robinson, J.T. 1950. Further evidence of the structure of the Sterkfontein ape-man, *Plesianthropus*, in: Broom, R., Robinson, J.T., and Schepers, G.W.H., Sterkfontein ape-man *Plesianthropus. Mem. Transv. Mus.* 4:1-117.

Chamberlain, A.T. 1987. *A Taxonomic Review and Phylogenetic Analysis of Homo habilis.* Ph.D. Thesis, University of Liverpool.

Chamberlain, A.T. 1989. Variation within *H. habilis*, in: *Hominidae: Proceedings of the 2nd International Congress of Human Paleontology* (G. Giacobini, Ed.), pp. 175-181, Jaca Books, Milan.

Chamberlain, A.T. and Wood, B.A. 1987. Early hominid phylogeny. *J. Hum. Evol.* 16:119-133.

Clarke, R.J. 1977a. *The Cranium of the Swartkrans Hominid SK 847 and its Relevance to Human Origins.* Ph.D. Thesis, University of the Witwatersrand.

Clarke, R.J. 1977b. A juvenile cranium and some adult teeth of early *Homo* from Swartkrans, Transvaal. *S. Afr. J. Sci.* 73:46-49.

Clarke, R.J. and Howell, F.C. 1972. Affinities of the Swartkrans 847 hominid cranium. *Am. J. Phys. Anthrop.* 37:319-336.

Coppens, Y. 1979. Les hominidés du Pliocène et du Pléistocène de la Rift Valley. *Bull. Soc. Géol. Fr.* 21:313-320.

Coppens, Y. 1980. The differences between *Australopithecus* and *Homo*; preliminary conclusions from the Omo Research Expedition's studies, in: *Current Argument on Early Man* (L- K. Königsson, Ed.), pp. 207-225, Pergamon Press, Oxford.

Davis, P.R. 1964. Hominid fossils from Bed I, Olduvai Gorge, Tanganyika. *Nature* 201:967.

Day, M.H. and Napier, J.R. 1964. Hominid fossils from Bed I, Olduvai Gorge, Tanganyika: fossil foot bones. *Nature* 201:969-970.

Delson, E. 1986. Human phylogeny revised again. *Nature* 322:496-497.

Delson, E., Eldredge, N., and Tattersall, I. 1977. Reconstruction of hominid phylogeny: a testable framework based on cladistic analysis. *J. Hum. Evol.* 6:263-278.

Eldredge, N. and Tattersall, I. 1975. Evolutionary models, phylogenetic reconstruction, and another look at hominid phylogeny, in: *Approaches to Primate Paleobiology* (F. Szalay, Ed.), pp. 218-242, S. Karger, Basel.

Falk, D. 1983. Cerebral cortices of East African early hominids. *Science* 221:1072-1074.

Feibel, C.S., Brown, F.H., and McDougall, I. 1989. Stratigraphic context of fossil hominids from the Omo Group deposits: Northern Turkana Basin, Kenya and Ethiopia. *Am. J. Phys. Anthrop.* 78:595-622.

Grine, F.E., Demes, B., Jungers, W.L., and Cole T.M. in press. Is the Sk 847 cranium from Swartkrans a *Homo erectus*? Maybe—maybe not. (Abstract submitted to the 4th International Senckenberg Conference: 100 Years of *Pithecanthropus*—The *Homo erectus* Problem).

Groves, C.P. 1989. *A Theory of Human and Primate Evolution.* Oxford University Press, Oxford.

Groves, C.P. and Mazak, V. 1975. An approach to the taxonomy of the Hominidae: Gracile Villafranchian hominids of Africa. *Cas. Miner. Geol.* 20:225-247.

Harris, J.M., Brown, F.H., Leakey, M.G., Walker, A.C., and Leakey, R.E.F. 1988. Pliocene and Pleistocene hominid-bearing sites from west of Lake Turkana, Kenya. *Science* 239:27-33.

Hartwig-Scherer, S. in press. *S. Cour. Forsch. Inst. Senckenberg.*

Hartwig-Scherer, S. and Martin, R.D. 1991. Was "Lucy" more human than her "child"? Observations on early hominid postcranial skeletons. *J. Hum. Evol.* 21:439-449.

Hay, R. 1976. *Geology of Olduvai Gorge.* University of California Press, Berkeley.

Hill, A., Ward, S., Deino, A., Curtis, G., and Drake, R. 1992. Earliest *Homo*. *Nature* 355:719-722.

Holloway, R.L. 1965. Cranial capacity of the hominine from Olduvai Bed I. *Nature* 208:205-206.

Holloway, R.L. 1985. The past, present, and future significance of the lunate sulcus in early hominid evolution, in: *Hominid Evolution: Past, Present, and Future* (P.V. Tobias, Ed.), pp. 47-62, Alan R. Liss, New York.

Howell, F.C. 1978. Hominidae, in: *Evolution of African Mammals* (V.J. Maglio and H.B.S. Cooke, Eds.), pp. 154-248, Harvard University Press, Cambridge.

Howell, F.C., Haesaerts, P., and de Heinzelin, J. 1987. Depositional environments, archeological occurrences and hominids from Member E and F of the Shungura Formation (Omo Basin, Ethiopia). *J. Hum. Evol.* 16:665-700.

Hughes, A.R. and Tobias, P.V. 1977. A fossil skull probably of the genus *Homo* from Sterkfontein, Transvaal. *Nature* 265:310-312.

Johanson, D.C. 1989. A partial *Homo habilis* skeleton from Olduvai Gorge, Tanzania: a summary of preliminary results, in: *Hominidae: Proceedings of the 2nd International Congress of Human Paleontology* (G. Giacobini, Ed.), pp. 155-166, Jaca Books, Milan.

Johanson, D.C., Masao, F.T., Eck, G.G., White, T.D., Walter, R.C., Kimbel, W.H., Asfaw, B., Manega, P., Ndessokia, P., and Suwa, G. 1987. New partial skeleton of *Homo habilis* from Olduvai Gorge, Tanzania. *Nature* 327:205-209.

Johanson, D.C. and Taieb, M. 1976. Plio-Pleistocene hominid discoveries in Hadar, Ethiopia. *Nature* 260:293-297.

Johanson, D.C. and White, T.D. 1979. A systematic assessment of early African hominids. *Science* 202:321-330.

Johanson, D.C., White, T.D., and Coppens, Y. 1978. A new species of the genus *Australopithecus* (Primates: Hominidae) from the Pliocene of East Africa. *Kirtlandia* 28:1-14.

Kennedy, G.E. 1983a. Some aspects of femoral morphology in *Homo erectus*. *J. Hum. Evol.* 12:587-616.

Kennedy, G.E. 1983b. A morphometric and taxonomic assessment of a hominine femur from the Lower Member, Koobi Fora, Lake Turkana. *Am. J. Phys. Anthrop.* 61:429-436.

Leakey, L.S.B. 1966. *Homo habilis, Homo erectus,* and the australopithecines. *Nature* 209:1279-1281.

Leakey, L.S.B., Tobias, P.V., and Napier, J.R. 1964. A new species of the genus *Homo* from Olduvai Gorge. *Nature* 202:7-9.

Leakey, M.D., Clarke, R.J., and Leakey, L.S.B. 1971. New hominid skull from Bed I, Olduvai Gorge, Tanzania. *Nature* 232:308-312.

Leakey, M.D., Hay, R.I., Curtis, G.H., Drake, R.E., Jackes, M.K., and White, T.D. 1976. Fossil hominids from the Laetoli Beds. *Nature* 262:460-466.

Leakey, R.E.F. 1973. Evidence for an advanced Plio-Pleistocene hominid from East Rudolf, Kenya. *Nature* 242:447-450.

Leakey, R.E.F. 1974. Further evidence of Lower Pleistocene hominids from East Rudolf, North Kenya, 1973. *Nature* 248:653-656.

Leakey, R.E.F., Leakey, M.G., and Behrensmeyer, A.K. 1978. The hominid catalogue, in: *Koobi Fora Research Project, Vol.1: The Fossil Hominids and an Introduction to Their Context, 1968-1974* (M.G. Leakey and R.E.F. Leakey, Eds.), pp. 86-182, Clarendon Press, Oxford.

Leakey, R.E.F. and Walker, A.C. 1980. On the status of *Australopithecus afarensis*. *Science* 207:1103.

Leakey, R.E.F, Walker, A.C., Ward, C.V., and Grausz, H.M. 1989. A partial skeleton of a gracile hominid from the Upper Burgi Member of the Koobi Fora Formation, East Lake Turkana, Kenya, in: *Hominidae: Proceedings of the 2nd International Congress of Human Paleontology* (G. Giacobini, Ed.), pp. 167-173, Jaca Books, Milan.

Le Gros Clark, W.E. 1955. *The Fossil Evidence for Human Evolution: An Introduction to the Study of Paleoanthropology,* 1st ed. University of Chicago Press, Chicago.

Le Gros Clark, W.E. 1964. Letter to the editor: The evolution of man. *Discovery* 25:49.

Lewis, O.J. 1972. The evolution of the hallucial tarsometatarsal joint in the Anthropoidea. *Am. J. Phys. Anthrop.* 37:13-34.

Lewis, O.J. 1989. *Functional Morphology of the Evolving Hand and Foot.* Oxford University Press, Oxford.

Lieberman, D.E., Pilbeam, D.R., and Wood, B.A. 1988. A probabilistic approach to the problem of sexual dimorphism in *Homo habilis*: a comparison of KNM-ER 1470 and KNM-ER 1813. *J. Hum. Evol.* 17:503-511.

Mayr, E. 1950. Taxonomic categories in fossil hominids. *Cold Spring Harbor Symp. Quant. Biol.* 15:109-118.

McHenry, H.H. and Corruccini, R.S. 1978. The femur in early human evolution. *Am. J. Phys. Anthrop.* 49:473-488.

Miller, J.A. 1991. Does brain size variability provide evidence of multiple species in *Homo habilis*? *Am. J. Phys. Anthrop.* 84:385-398.

Napier, J.R. 1964. The evolution of bipedal walking in the hominids. *Arch. Biol. (Liège)* 75: Suppl, 673-708.

Olson, T.R. 1978. Hominid phylogenetics and the existence of *Homo* in Member I of the Swartkrans Formation, South Africa. *J. Hum. Evol.* 7:159-178.

Prost, J.H. 1980. Origin of bipedalism. *Am. J. Phys. Anthrop.* 52:175-189.

Robinson, J.T. 1965. *Homo 'habilis'* and the australopithecines. *Nature* 205:121-124.

Robinson, J.T. 1966. The distinctiveness of *Homo habilis*. *Nature* 209:957-960.

Robinson, J.T. 1968. The origin and adaptive radiation of the australopithecines, in: *Evolution and Hominisation,* 2nd ed. (G. Kurth, Ed.), pp. 150-175, Fischer Verlag, Stuttgart.

Robinson, J.T. 1972. The bearing of East Rudolf fossils on early hominid systematics. *Nature* 240:239-240.

Rose, M.D. 1984. Food acquisition and the evolution of positional behaviour: the case of bipedalism, in: *Food Acquisition and Processing in Primates* (D.J. Chivers, B.A. Wood, and A. Bilsborough, Eds.), pp. 509-524, Plenum Press, New York.

Simpson, G.G. 1961. *Principles of Animal Taxonomy.* Columbia University Press, New York.

Skelton, R.R., McHenry, H.M., and Drawhorn, G.M. 1986. Phylogenetic analysis of early hominids. *Curr. Anthropol.* 27:21-43.

Stringer, C.B. 1986. The credibility of *Homo habilis*, in: *Major Topics in Primate and Human Evolution* (B. Wood, L. Martin, and P. Andrews, Eds.), pp. 266-294, Cambridge University Press, Cambridge.

Stringer, C.B. 1987. A numerical cladistic analysis for the genus *Homo*. *J. Hum. Evol.* 16:135-146.

Susman, R.L. and Stern, J.T. 1982. Functional morphology of *Homo habilis*. *Science* 217:931-934.

Tobias, P.V. 1965. New discoveries in Tanganyika: their bearing on hominid evolution. *Current Anthropology* 6:391-411.

Tobias, P.V. 1967. Pleistocene deposits and new fossil localities in Kenya, Part II: The Chemeron temporal. *Nature* 215:479-480.

Tobias, P.V. 1980. "*Australopithecus afarensis*" and *A. africanus*: Critique and an alternative hypothesis. *Paleont. Afr.* 23:1-17.

Tobias, P.V. 1985. Single characters and the total morphological pattern redefined: The sorting effected by a selection of morphological features of the early hominids, in: *Ancestors: The Hard Evidence* (E. Delson, Ed.), pp. 94-101, Alan R. Liss, New York.

Tobias, P.V. 1987. The brain of *Homo habilis*: a new level of organization in cerebral evolution. *J. Hum. Evol.* 16:741- 761.

Tobias, P.V. 1989. The status of *Homo habilis* in 1987 and some outstanding problems, in: *Hominidae: Proceedings of the 2nd International Congress of Human Paleontology* (G. Giacobini, Ed.), pp. 141-149, Jaca Books, Milan.

Tobias, P.V. 1991. *Olduvai Gorge, Volume IV. The Skulls, Endocasts, and Teeth of* Homo habilis. Cambridge University Press, Cambridge.

Tobias, P.V. and von Koenigswald, G.H.R. 1964. A comparison between the Olduvai hominids and those of Java and some implications for hominid phylogeny. *Nature* 204:515-518.

Trinkaus, E. 1984. Does KNM-ER 1481A establish *Homo erectus* at 2.0 myr B.P.? *Am. J. Phys. Anthrop.* 64:137-139.

Trinkaus, E. 1989. Olduvai Hominid 7 trapezial metacarpal I articular morphology: Contrasts with recent humans. *Am. J. Phys. Anthrop.* 80:411-416.

Vandebroek, G. 1969. L'homme et les préhumains, in: *Évolution des Vertébrés de Leur Origine à L'Homme,* pp. 450-518, Masson, Paris.

Walker, A. and Leakey, R.E.F. 1978. The hominids of East Turkana. *Sci. Am.* 239(2):44-56.

White, T.D., Johanson, D.C., and Kimbel, W.H. 1981. *Australopithecus africanus*: Its phyletic position reconsidered. *S. Afr. J. Sci.* 77:445-470.

Wood, B.A. 1974a. Olduvai Bed I post-cranial fossils: A reassessment. *J. Hum. Evol.* 3:373-378.

Wood, B.A. 1974b. Evidence on the locomotor pattern on *Homo* from early Pleistocene of Kenya. *Nature* 251:135-136.

Wood, B.A. 1984. The origin of *Homo erectus*. *Cour. Forsch. Inst. Senckenberg* 69:99-111.

Wood, B.A. 1985. Early *Homo* in Kenya and its systematic relationships, in: *Ancestors: The Hard Evidence* (E. Delson, Ed.), pp.206-214, Alan R. Liss, New York.

Wood, B.A. 1987. Who is the "real" *Homo habilis*? *Nature* 327:187-188.

Wood, B.A. 1991. *Koobi Fora Research Project IV: Hominid Cranial Remains from Koobi Fora.* Clarendon Press, Oxford.

Wood, B.A. and Chamberlain, A.T. 1986. *Australopithecus*: grade or clade? in: *Major Topics in Primate and Human Evolution* (B. Wood, L. Martin, and P. Andrews, Eds.), pp. 220-248, Cambridge University Press, Cambridge.

Wood, B.A., Li, Y., and Willoughby, C. 1991. Intraspecific variation and sexual dimorphism in cranial and dental variables among higher primates and their bearing on the hominid fossil record. *J. Anat.* 174:185-205.

Wood, B.A. and Wilson, G.B. 1986. Patterns of allometry in modern human femora, in: *Variation, Culture, and Evolution in African Populations* (R. Stringer and J.K. Lundy, Eds.), pp. 101-108, Witwatersrand University Press, Johannesburg.

32

Cutmarks Made by Stone Tools on Bones from Olduvai Gorge, Tanzania

R. Potts and P. Shipman

Fossils from Olduvai Gorge, Tanzania, show cutmarks which establish that hominids were using stone tools'on animal tissues during the Lower Pleistocene in Africa. We identified cutmarks by elimination of other likely causes of the marks on the bone surfaces, for example, gnawing or chewing by carnivores or rodents, and damage made by tools of excavators or preparators. This was achieved by comparing the marks on the fossils with those produced by known causes on modern bones, using scanning electron microscopy (SEM). Because the fossils occur as part of accumulations of animal remains in relatively undisturbed geological contexts, we conclude that there is a functional association between the stone artefacts and bones at these sites, rather than an accidental, postmortem association (Leakey 1971; Hay 1976).

The problem in identifying cutmarks produced by stone edges is that similar grooves and marks can be made on bone surfaces by a variety of processes. As part of a study (Shipman 1981) of the effects of various taphonomic processes on bones, the following types of mark were investigated: carnivore tooth scratches, incisal gnawing by rodents or carnivores, root etching, abrasion by windborne and waterborne sedimentary particles, and excavators' and preparators' marks. Each of these alterations to bone surfaces are macroscopically similar to cutmarks. Because the microscopic structure of a bone is a major determinant of its response to potentially destructive forces (Lanyon and Smith 1970; Evans 1973; Lakes and Saha 1979; Bonnichsen 1978; Sadek-Kooros 1972; Brain 1976), several hundred such marks, produced on modern bones by known events, were inspected by SEM to clarify the interaction between these forces and the microscopic structure of the bone. This study yielded morphological criteria by which cutmarks of various types could be distinguished from the similar marks produced by other events or by normal anatomical features (Fig. 1). Samples are too small at present to develop quantitative criteria.

The controls and a sample of similar marks on fossil bones were inspected on epoxy replicas of bone surfaces; these replicas (which are expected to have a resolution of 0.25 μm) were coated with 200 Å of gold palladium to enhance SEM image quality (Walker 1981). Despite the low magnifications used in some cases, the depth of field and image quality of the SEM offered a substantial advantage over a light microscope.

Several types of cutmark were defined for the control sample, on the basis of their mode of production and micro-scopic characteristics. The term 'cutmarks' is used here as a general term for marks made by stone tools; microscopically, these are elongated grooves with V-shaped cross-sections. Slicing marks are produced by drawing the edge of an artefact across a bone surface in a direction continuous with the long axis of the edge. This creates many fine, parallel striations, visible at a magnification of X30-X35 or less, within each main groove because the edges of artefacts are not perfectly straight; each small deviation of the edge to one side or the other leaves its own microscopic track. Chopping marks are produced by striking the bone surface with an artefact at a roughly perpendicular angle—these have V-shaped cross-sections and small fragments of bone crushed inwards at the bottom of the main groove. Chopping marks are often broader at the top than slicing marks and do not show fine parallel striations. Scraping marks are formed by drawing an edge across a bone surface in a direction roughly perpendicular to the long axis of the edge. This action results in multiple, fine, parallel striations across a broad area of bone rather than confined to a single, elongated main groove (Fig. 1a-c).

No process has yet been discovered which produces marks that mimic slicing, chopping or scraping marks on a microscopic level. Tooth scratches and gnawing of carnivores produce grooves with rounded or flat bases respectively; both lack the fine parallel striations of slicing or scraping marks. Very fine tooth scratches may be as narrow as cutmarks and usually require magnification of X20-X50 before they can be distinguished from cutmarks. Commonly, rodent gnawing marks are a series of short, very broad, parallel grooves which can be identified with the naked eye. Abrasion by windborne or waterborne sedimentary particles, or by collision of bones with rocks during hydraulic transport, removes external bone surfaces and opens up vascular canals originally lying below the surface, to give a grossly striated appearance. Microscopically, these canals differ from tooth scratches, in showing openings even smaller vascular canals, and from slicing marks in lacking striations. Scratches produced on fossils with metal tools used for excavation or preparation are not always V-shaped in cross section and do not show fine, parallel striations characteristic of cutmarks on fresh bones. The edges of such scratches or grooves are often much more irregular than tooth scratches or gnawing marks (Fig. 1d-g).

Numerous fossil bone specimens showing surface marks were found during a study of 12 excavated levels in Beds I and

Reprinted with permission from *Nature*, Vol. 291, pp 577–580. Copyright © 1981 by Macmillan Journals Ltd., London.

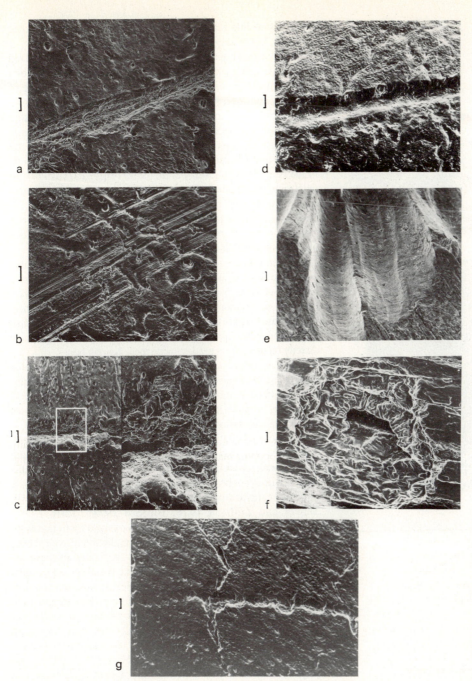

Figure 1. *Micrographs of various tooth and tool marks. The bar or bars to the left of each figure represent 100μm. a, A slicing mark on a modern bone, showing the fine parallel striations within the main groove. b, A scraping mark on a modern bone, showing fine striations across a broad area. c, A chopping mark on a modern bone, shown at two magnifications. Left, at low power; note the broad, V-shaped groove lacking fine striations. Right, at higher power; note the fragments of bone crushed inwards at the bottom of the groove. d, A carnivore tooth scratch on a modern bone. Although this is the functional equivalent of a slicing mark, there are no fine striations. e, A rodent gnawing mark on a modern bone. This is the functional equivalent of a scraping mark, but gnawing produces only broad, shallow grooves without fine striations. f, A puncture produced by a carnivore canine on a modern bone. Punctures are functionally equivalent to chopping marks and are similar in that fragments of bone are crushed inwards. However, punctures are typically rounded in outline, unlike chopping marks. g, A preparator's marks on a fossil bone, produced by an action similar to slicing. The lack of striations distinguish it from a slicing mark and the irregular edges of the groove distinguish it from a tooth scratch.*

II Olduvai Gorge (Potts 1982). A sample of 75 bone surfaces, some with several marks, was chosen and replicated from fossils at each level. A wide range of skeletal parts, taxa and types of surface damage were included to make the sample as representative as possible. The surface of the fossils was brushed for several minutes with solvents before replication—this was necessary because preservatives completely obscure the microscopic characteristics. The replicas were inspected and photographed at magnifications comparable with those used for the control sample of modern bones.

In the replicated Olduvai sample (*N*=85 marks on 75 bones), 24% of the specimens possessed marks which were considered to be cutmarks as they more closely resembled those produced by slicing, chopping or scraping than those produced by any other cause so far investigated. Isolated or multiple fine grooves, which

could have been confused with cutmarks from a macroscopic inspection, often resembled tooth scratches or narrow gnawing marks much more closely in terms of microscopic detail. Table 1 gives the numbers of fossils with each type of mark; Fig. 2a shows a series of slicing and scraping marks on a fossil.

Significantly, several bones had both slicing marks and tooth scratches, including three specimens which showed intersections between these types of mark (Fig. 2b,c). Thus it is clear that, at least in some cases, hominids and carnivores were able to use the same parts of carcasses in turn. Furthermore, slicing marks are present on at least one specimen from FLK NN, Level 2, although no stone tools are known from that site. One possible interpretation of this evidence is that carnivores scavenged this bone from a hominid campsite and removed it to another area. Another likely explanation is that hominids were the primary

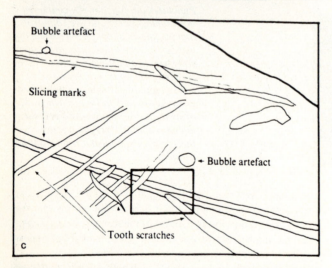

Bubble artefact

Slicing marks

Bubble artefact

Tooth scratches

c

Figure 2. *Marks on Olduvai fossils.* a, *A series of slicing and scraping marks run roughly horizontally across the micrograph. A slicing mark made later in time runs diagonally downwards across the earlier marks. The specimen is an indeterminate shaft fragment from DK I, Level 3.* b, *Two slicing marks run roughly horizontally across this micrograph. The lower one is overlaid by several tooth scratches which must have been made after the slicing marks. The box encloses the intersection of two of these tooth scratches with the slicing mark. The specimen is an equid tibia from FLK Zinj.* c, *A tracing of the micrograph in b, with various features labelled.*

agent responsible for accumulating and damaging the bones at FLK NN, Level 2, but did not discard stone tools there.

Cutmarks were commonly found on fragments of fossilized bone, particularly on pieces of limb bone shaft, which suggests that the marks occurred during defleshing or dismembering of carcasses with stone tools (Table 1). However, the cutmarks on bones identifiable to skeletal element and species are neither frequent enough nor do they have sufficient regularity of location to suggest a consistent butchery pattern such as can be reconstructed for various species' carcasses much later in time in the New World (Guilday *et al.* 1962; Frison 1971, 1974). To determine the number of cutmarks in a single taxon, all marks found on all postcrania (N=138) of one species, *Equus oldowayensis*, were examined; only 2.9% showed cutmarks. If one or more standard strategies for butchery of equids with stone tools existed, that sample is too small to reveal them.

Specimens from identified skeletal elements were divided into meat-bearing and non-meat-bearing bones. Table 2 shows a preferential occurrence of tooth marks on meat-bearing bones; cutmarks occur about equally on both kinds of bone. Evidently, hominid use of stone tools on bones was not directed solely towards meat acquisition. Carnivores and rodents, however, focused more directly on meat or on tissues inside meat-bearing bones.

Our evidence supports Leakey's (1971) conclusion that there is a direct causal association between the stone artefacts and fossilized bones at many Olduvai sites. This evidence is important because it comes from some of the oldest known excavated archaeological levels: for example, DK I, Level 3, is older than 1.79±0.03 Myr (Hay 1976). Furthermore, the cutmarks indicate that hominids processed carcasses to obtain animal material such as meat, ligament or bone. However, this evidence does not bear directly on questions about the frequency of meat-eating and hunting among early hominids (Isaac 1978; Tanner and Zihlman 1976; Binford 1978; Jolly 1970). Moreover, the occurrence of both cutmarks and tooth marks on the bones documents an overprinting of taphonomic events; both hominids and other animals modified the bones in these assemblages. Therefore we cannot attribute the observed patterns of faunal and skeletal representation solely to hominid activity.

This study establishes: (1) a technique for distinguishing cutmarks made with stone artefacts from similar marks not involving early hominid activities; (2) that cutmarks were produced by hominids using stone artefacts on animal tissues at these sites at least as early as 1.79 Mya; (3) that these assemblages were exposed to multiple agents of damage and accumulation and thus their composition cannot be taken as indicative solely of hominid behaviours; (4) that not all bones altered by hominids will be found in association with stone tools; and (5) that hominids and carnivores were in competition for carcasses or bones, perhaps to obtain different substances.

ACKNOWLEDGMENTS

We thank the governments of Kenya and Tanzania, Mary and Richard Leakey, and the National Museums of Kenya for permission to study fossils and bones in their care; and Alan Walker and Glynn Isaac for valuable comments. We also thank Linda Perez, Wendy Bosler and Karen Lee Davis for technical assistance. This work was funded by NSF grant BNS 78 19174 to R.P., the Boise Fund (to R.P. and P.S.) and a NIH biomedical research grant 5 S07RR07041-13 to P.S.

Table 1. Data on frequencies and locations of different types of marks on fossils from Beds I and II, Olduvai Gorge.

Type of mark	No. of specimen	Locations	Taxa	Sites
Slicing	13	Metatarsal shaft (2), radius shaft (2), limb shaft fragment, (2), humerus shaft, metacarpal shaft, proximal ulna, distal metacarpal, rib shaft, tibial crest, proximal radius	*Kobus sigmoidalis, Equus oldowayensis,* giraffid indeterminate, small bovid indeterminate, large bovid indeterminate, bovid indeterminate, medium/large mammal indeterminate	DK Levels 2 and 3, FLK NN Levels 2 and 3, FLK 'Zinj,' MNK Main
Scraping	5	Scapula blade, humerus shaft, radius shaft, metatarsal shaft, limb shaft fragment	*Kobus sigmoidalis, Equus oldowayensis,* giraffid indeterminate, medium mammal indeterminate, large mammal indeterminate	DK Level 3, FLK 'Zinj,' MNK Main
Chopping	5	Metacarpal shaft (2), metapodial shaft, prosimal phalanx shaft, limb shaft fragment	*Parmularius altidens, Equus oldowayensis,* bovid indeterminate, mammal indeterminate	DK Levels 2 and 3, FLK NN Level 2, MNK Main
Tooth/ gnawing	48	Limb shaft fragment (12), proximal rib (6), humerus shaft, (4), rib shaft (3), femur shaft (3), tibial crest (2), metacarpal shaft (2), proximal metacarpal (2), scapula glenoid, proximal ulna, radius shaft, radio-ulna shaft, mandibular corpus, hyoid, parietal vault, proximal femur, acetabulum, distal tibia, fibula shaft, metatarsal shaft, cuneiform, indeterminate fragment	*Kobus sigmoidalis, Megalotragus kattwinkeli, Elephas recki, Deinotherium* sp.; *Equus oldowayensis, Cercocebus, Homo habilis,* Tragelaphini indeterminate, Reduncini intermediate, Antilopini indeterminate, medium/large bovid indeterminate, medium/large mammal indeterminate, large mammal indeterminate, very large mammal indeterminate, mammal indeterminate	DK Levels 2 and 3, FLK NN Levels 2 and 3, FLN 'Zinj," FLK N Level 6, FLK N Deino. Level, MKN Main, TK Upper Floor
Preparation/ excavation	7	Scapula blade, cervical vertebra, rib shaft, astragalus, cuneiform limb shaft fragment, indeterminate fragment	*Elephas recki,* Alcelaphini indeterminate, medium bovid indeterminate, medium/large Carnivora indeterminate, mammal indeterminate	FLK 'Zinj,' FLK NN Level 6
Undetermined	7	Rib shaft, distal tibia, patella, metatarsal shaft, lateral cuneiform, limb shaft fragment, indeterminate fragment	*Equus oldowayensis,* small bovid indeterminate, very small mammal indeterminate, large mammal indeterminate	DK Level 3, FLK NN Level 2, FLK N Level 6, MNK Main

Seventy-five surfaces were examined; 10 of these possessed marks which classified into two different types. Numbers in parentheses after skeletal location signify the number of times different specimens showed a particular type of mark in that location.

REFERENCES

Binford, L. R. 1978. *Nunamuit Ethnoarchaeology.* Academic, New York.

Bonnichsen, R. 1978. *Pleistocene Bone Technology in the Beringium Refugium* Archaeological Surv. Canada. no. 89.

Brain, C. K. 1976. Some principles in the interpretation of bone accumulations associated with man, in: *Human Origins* (G. Ll. Isaac and E. McCown, Eds.), pp. 97-116. Benjamin, Menlo Park, CA.

Evans, F. G. 1973. *Mechanical Properties of Bone.* Thomas, Springfield, IL.

Frison, G. C. 1971. Shohonean antelope procurement in the Upper Green River Basin, Wyoming. *Plains Anthropologist* 16:258-284.

Frison, G. C. 1974. *The Casper Site.* Academic, New York.

Guilday, J. E., Parmalee, P. W., and Tanner. D. P. 1962. Aboriginal butchering techniques at the Eschelman Site (36 La 12) in Lancaster County, PA. *Penna. Archaeo.* 32:59-83.

Hay, R. L. 1976. *Geology of the Olduvai Gorge.* University of California Press, Berkeley, Los Angeles and London.

Isaac, G. Ll. 1978. The food-sharing behavior of protohuman hominids. *Scientific American* 238(4):90-108.

Jolly, C. J. 1970. The seed-eaters: a new model of hominid differention based on a baboon analogy. *Man* 5:5-20.

Lakes, R., and Saha, S. 1979. Cement line motion in bone. *Science* 208:501-503.

Lanyon, L. E., and Smith, R. N. 1970. Bone strain in the tibia during normal quadrupedal locomotion. *Acta Orthop. Scand.* 41:238-248.

Leakey, M. D. 1971. *Olduvai Gorge,* Vol.3. Cambridge University Press, London and New York.

Potts, R. B. 1982. *Lower Pleistocene Site Formation and Hominid Activities at Olduvai Gorge, Tanzania.* Ph. D. Dissertation, Harvard University.

Sadek-Kooros. H. 1972. Primitive bone fracturing: a method of research. *Am. Antiq.* 37:369-382.

Shipman, P. 1981. Applications of scanning electron microscopy to taphonomic problems. *Annals of the New York Academy of Sciences* 376:357-385.

Tanner, N., and Zihlman, A. 1976. Women in evolution. Part I: innovation and selection in human origins. *Signs* 3:585-608.

Walker, A. 1981. Diet and teeth: Dietary hypotheses and human evolution. *Philosoph. Trans. Roy. Soc. Lond.* B292:56-64.

Table 2. Occurrence of stone tool cutmarks and animal tooth marks on meat-bearing bones (major limb bones and axial elements) as opposed to non-meat-bearing bones (metapodials, podials, phalanges).

	Stone cutmark	Tooth mark
Meat-bearing bone	10	27
Non-meat-bearing bone	9	7

This sample consists of 53 fossil surfaces from Olduvai, identified to skeletal element. $x^2 = 4.15$, degrees of freedom = 1, $0.025 < P < 0.05$.

33

The Oldowan Reassessed: A Close Look at Early Stone Artifacts

N. Toth

INTRODUCTION

It seems certain that the development of technology, along with a suite of other behavioral and biological adaptations, was critical in the success of the genus *Homo* over the last 2 million years. Flaked stone artifacts are the earliest definite signs of modification of natural materials for use as tools, and suggest a much more complicated technological repertoire than has been observed in modern non-human primates. It is crucial to our understanding of early hominid origins that we explore the adaptive role these stone technologies played, and that we search for any other clues these lithic assemblages may yield concerning proto-human behavioral patterns.

This paper is concerned with very early stone artifact assemblages that first appear in the prehistoric record over 2 million years ago (Isaac 1982) and pre-date assemblages characterized by large bifacial forms ("picks," "hand-axes," "cleavers") considered to be the hallmark of the "Acheulean" techno-complex, which emerges in Africa approximately 1.5 million years ago (Isaac 1982). These earliest assemblages have been classified in various ways in different regions: terms such as "Oldowan" and "Developed Oldowan A" at Olduvai Gorge, Tanzania (Leakey 1971), and "KBS" and "Karari" at Koobi Fora, Kenya (Isaac and Harris 1978) have been applied to some local occurrences of pre-Acheulean industries in Africa. Often these pre-Acheulean industries are generically referred to as part of the "Oldowan Industrial Complex" (Isaac 1984), a convention which will be followed here. While there are certainly some technological and typological changes that occur through time as at Olduvai Gorge (Leakey 1971), all of these assemblages are usually characterized by simple cores, retouched flakes, unretouched flakes and flake fragments ("*debitage*"), and battered stones. Clark (1971) has referred to this technological stage as a "Mode I" industry.

Several sites believed to be over 1.5 million years old are generally regarded as a part of this technological mode.

East Africa: Gona (Hadar), Ethiopia (Corvinus 1976; Corvinus and Roche 1976, 1980; Roche and Tiercelin 1977, 1980; Harris 1983); Omo, Ethiopia (Clark and Kurashina 1979); Melka Kunture, Ethiopia (Merrick and Merrick 1976; Chevaillon 1976); Gadeb, Ethiopia (Chavaillon 1971; Chavaillon *et al.* 1979); Koobi Fora, Kenya (Isaac and Harris 1978); Chesowanja, Kenya (Harris and Bishop 1976; Gowlett *et al.* 1981);

Olduvai Gorge, Tanzania (Leakey 1971, 1975); Laetoli, Tanzania (Harris 1980).

North Africa: the Morrocan coastal sequence (STIC quarry, Sidi Abderaman quarry) (Biberson 1961); Ain Hanech, Tunisia (Biberson 1961).

South Africa: Sterkfontein and Swartkrans (Brain 1981).

Broadly contemporaneous hominids include robust australopithecines (usually designated *Australopithecus boisei* in East Africa and *Australopithecus robustus* in South Africa), *Homo habilis* and *Homo erectus*. The robust australopithecine lineage first appeared before 2 million years ago and seems to have become extinct by 1 million years ago (Howell 1978), while *Homo habilis* first appeared about 2 million years ago and probably evolved into *Homo erectus* about 1.5 million years ago (Howell 1978). It is generally assumed that fossil forms attributed to the genus *Homo* were the principal tool-makers responsible for archaeological sites. Archaeological sites that appear to pre-date the earliest known *Homo* fossils are relatively rare, and when tools first become fairly common in the record, fossils of larger-brained forms attributed to *Homo* generally occur at the same localities (e.g. Koobi Fora, Olduvai, Sterkfontein, Swartkrans). Whether the robust australopithecines contemporaneous with early forms of *Homo* made or used stone tools (perhaps emulating their larger-brained "cousins") is still unresolved.

The most widely used classificatory system for such assemblages was developed by Mary Leakey in her analysis of the early palaeolithic sites at Olduvai Gorge (Leakey 1971), and is based on the morphology of the cores and retouched flakes ("tools") found at these sites. Here categories include "choppers," "polyhedrons," "discoids," "heavy-duty scrapers," "subspheroids," "spheroids," "protobifaces," and a range of retouched forms such as "light-duty scrapers," "burins" (rare), and "awls" (rare). Some of these forms are shown in Figure 1.

This paper will assess the behavioral implications of such early stone technologies based on a long-term study of Plio-Pleistocene occurrences at Koobi Fora, Kenya (see Figure 2) (Isaac and Harris 1978). These sites have been radiometrically dated to between 1.9 and 1.5 million years ago (Figure 3). These assessments have been based upon an extensive experimental program of manufacturing and using early stone artifact forms, and analysis of excavated lithic assemblages in light of the experimental results.

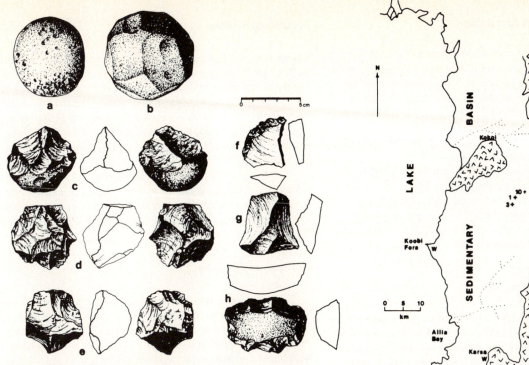

Figure 1. *A range of Oldowan forms and their traditional classificatory designations. (a) hammerstone, (b) subspheroid, (c) bifacial chopper, (d) polyhedron (e) discoid, (f) flake scraper, (g) fake, (h) core scraper. (Parts (c)-(h) after Barbara Isaac). Drawn by J. Ogden.*

METHODS

My study was designed as a holistic approach to early lithic technology, considering the acquisition of raw materials, curation and transport, artifact manufacture, use, possible rejuvenation, discard, and final incorporation of stone artifacts into the geological record. The principal goal of this study was to learn as much as possible about early hominid behavior from the stone artifacts that these proto-humans left behind.

Figure 2. *Map showing the Koobi Fora study area, with the location of the early archaeological sites that were analyzed. The sites were numbered in order of their discovery. Site FxJj 63 is an early Acheulean site of uncertain age, and is not included in this discussion. Experimental workshop locations are shown with the symbol "W."*

A more detailed exposition of the methodology and the basic data of this study is presented in Toth (1982). A summary of the analytical procedures employed followed.

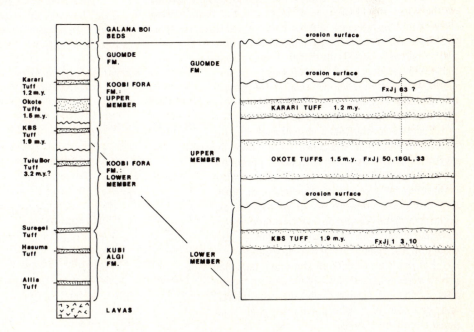

Figure 3. *Generalized stratigraphic section at Koobi Fora. The Oldowan occurrences (FxJj 1, 3, 10, 50, 18GL and 33) are found in the Lower and Upper Members of the Koobi Fora Formation.*

Studies of Raw Material Acquisition

Ancient river gravels at Koobi Fora contemporaneous with the early archaeological sites were analyzed to identify the types of raw materials available to hominids and how the palaeogeographic locations of the gravels related to archaeological occurrences. Quantitative information on cobble size and shape was compiled and analyzed. (The principal rock type at all Koobi Fora sites was basalt lava, though smaller amounts of ignimbrite, chert and quartz were also used).

Modern river gravels at Koobi Fora were also analyzed in terms of lithology, size, and shape, for comparison with fossil gravels. All of the rock types used in prehistoric times at Koobi Fora are available in modern channel beds today. Replicative and functional experiments (discussed below) were conducted to discern the mechanical properties and functional capabilities of the various rock types.

Studies of Artifact Manufacture

All stone artifacts from excavated Koobi Fora sites were examined for technological features in order to discern patterns of manufacture and reconstruct the reduction of lithic material. Conjoining studies by the Koobi Fora research team successfully refitted numerous stages of flaking from some sites, which provided additional technological information.

Several thousand experiments were conducted replicating characteristic Koobi Fora stone artifact forms to determine which techniques and methods were most effective and appropriate for producing the prehistoric forms. Observations were also made of novice stone-knappers with no formal training in lithic analysis or typological systems with special regard to their knapping strategies and resultant artifact forms.

Based upon the analysis of the Koobi Fora materials and the results of the experimental replicative program, 29 different ways of reducing cobbles and flakes into characteristic Koobi Fora cores and retouched flakes were identified (called "reduction modes") (Toth 1982). These reduction modes were defined on the basis of: (1) the type of blank ("initial form") being reduced (cobble, all cortical flake, half-cortical flake, non-cortical flake); (2) the flaking pattern (unifacial, bifacial, polyfacial); and (3) the extent of flaking (partial circumference, total circumference). Experiments were performed to determine what patterns of *débitage* (especially whole flakes) were produced by each reduction mode.

For each Koobi Fora archaeological site, the excavated cores and retouched pieces were assigned as closely as possible to their appropriate reduction mode. Comparisons were made between archaeological (excavated) populations of flakes and computer simulations of predicted (experimental flake populations which should be represented at each site if all of the stages of core reduction had taken place at the site location.

For one site, FxJj50, all cores and retouched pieces were replicated blow-by-blow to produce an almost identical facsimile, and the experimental and archaeological flake populations then compared (Bunn *et al.* 1980).

Functional Studies

A wide range of replicated Koobi Fora stone artifact forms (as well as tools of more perishable materials) were used for a wide variety of activities in order to gain a better understanding of which artifact forms were most appropriate for particular functions. Experiments included animal butchery (of goats, sheep, pigs, cows, wildebeest, horses, and elephants), bone-breaking, hide working, woodworking, grass cutting, digging, and nut-cracking.

Contextual information from archaeological sites was considered for direct evidence of tool use. Lines of evidence included micro-wear traces on stone artifacts (Keeley and Toth 1981) and patterns of bone modification from Koobi Fora sites (Bunn 1981, 1982).

Taphonomic Studies

Based on the experimental study of archaeological site formation by Schick (1984), computer simulations were conducted to see how assemblage composition at Early Stone Age sites would be affected by different hydrological forces before final burial and incorporation in the geological record.

The results of my study suggest a need to rethink some common assumptions about the nature of these early stone technologies. These conceptions (or misconceptions) about the earliest archaeological traces will be discussed below.

CORES AS STYLISTIC NORMS?

One prevalent assumption in studies of early stone tools is that the morphological forms called "types" were functionally significant norms that represent target forms or "mental templates" (as defined by Deetz 1967) of their hominid makers. In other words, an early hominid would, with premeditation, set out to make a "bifacial chopper" or "polyhedron" by selecting the proper piece of rock and reducing it in a predetermined manner.

Based on my experimental replication of thousands of Oldowan cores and retouched pieces, as well as observations of novice stone-knappers working cobbles (African assistants and Berkeley students), I would argue that much of the variety in

Figure 4. *Starting points (blanks or "initial forms") for producing a range of Oldowan and early Acheulean forms. The terms used to describe cobble stone are qualitative.*

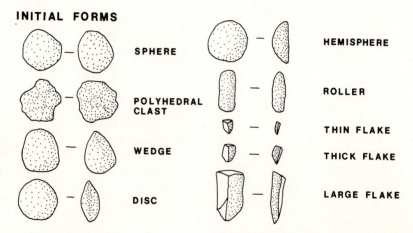

INITIAL FORMS

SPHERE

HEMISPHERE

POLYHEDRAL CLAST

ROLLER

WEDGE

THIN FLAKE

THICK FLAKE

DISC

LARGE FLAKE

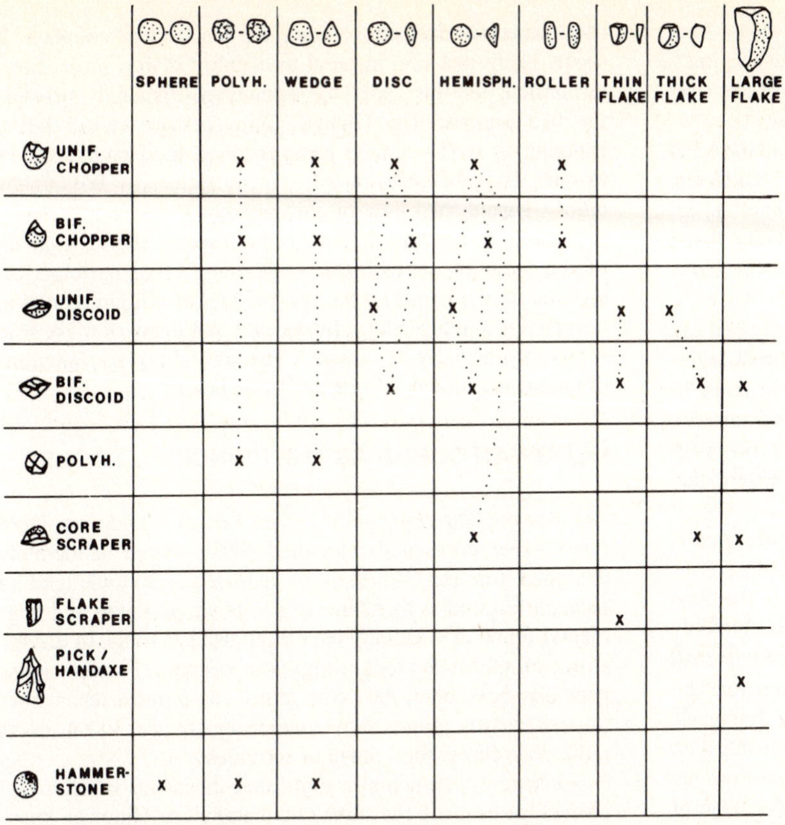

	SPHERE	POLYH.	WEDGE	DISC	HEMISPH.	ROLLER	THIN FLAKE	THICK FLAKE	LARGE FLAKE
UNIF. CHOPPER		X	X	X	X	X			
BIF. CHOPPER		X	X	X	X	X			
UNIF. DISCOID				X	X		X	X	
BIF. DISCOID				X	X		X	X	X
POLYH.		X	X						
CORE SCRAPER					X			X	X
FLAKE SCRAPER						X			
PICK / HANDAXE									X
HAMMERSTONE	X	X	X						

Figure 5. *Chart showing the relationships between the initial form and probable end products for Oldowan and early Acheulean forms. Many core forms, such "choppers," "discoids," "polyhedrons" and "core scrapers" can be produced without premeditation during the process of flake production, and in fact these forms can often grade into one another during reduction.*

form that one observes among Oldowan cores can be produced as by-products of flake production (or as technological "paths of least resistance") (Toth 1982: 147, 328).

Figure 4 shows a range of raw material forms used as blanks ("initial forms") for manufacturing Koobi Fora cores and retouched pieces. Depending on rock type, blank size, and blank shape, the knappers could produce a wide range of morphological end products, including most of the Oldowan core forms or "types" (Figure 5). Certain forms, such as retouched flakes ("light duty scrapers" or "flake scrapers") and some of the small "discoids" certainly do appear to have been made for use, since the tiny flakes removed would not have been very useful. But I have replicated many of the other Oldowan "core tool" forms, including "choppers," "polyhedrons," larger "discoids," and "heavy-duty scrapers" ("core scrapers") without premeditation during experimentations in the production of flakes from a variety of initial forms.

An interesting pattern emerges when one examines the relationship between artifact size and palaeogeographic location at Koobi Fora (Isaac 1976; Isaac and Harris 1978; Harris 1978; Harris and Isaac 1980; Toth 1982). Figure 6 shows the relationship between the maximum artifact size and maximum unflaked clast size at Koobi Fora sites and the distance between the sites and the margin of the sedimentary basin (where the artifact-bearing beds contact the volcanic highlands). There is a general decrease in the size of artifacts and unflaked material at sites as one moves away from the volcanics towards the proto-lake Turkana to the west. This is primarily because stream gradients and carrying capacity decreased away from the highlands. Sites FxJj 1, 3, and 10, in the Lower Member of the Koobi Fora Formation, and dated

Figure 6. *Diagram showing the relationship between artifact size and distance from the volcanic highlands (the basin margin or interface between the sedimentary basin and the volcanics). The maximum dimensions of the largest cores,(■——■), flakes (▼---▼), and unflaked clasts (●···●) from each site are plotted against the estimated distance of the sites from the basic margin. Note the general decrease in size of lithic material away from the basin margin, in the direction of the proto-Lake Turkana.*

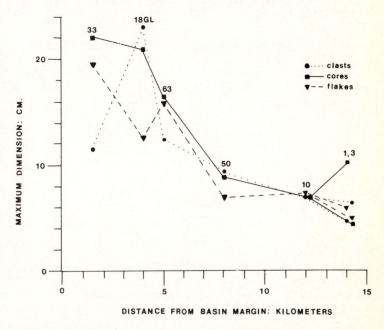

to approximately 1.9 million years ago, are further away from the volcanics, and are found in low-energy sedimentary regimes. At these sites, hominids must have transported artifacts over minimal distances of several kilometers (Isaac 1976).

This implies that sites nearer the volcanics would have had larger sizes of locally available lava clasts to flake, which can have technological and typological repercussions upon an artifact assemblages. My replication experiments indicate that a wider range of morphological core forms is to be expected if larger sizes of raw material are used (Toth 1982: 141–142). Larger cobbles can usually be flaked more intensively and can potentially produce a wider variety of final core morphologies ("types"). While other factors such as activity variation or sedimentary context may also have their effect upon intersite assemblage variability (Harris 1978), much of the observed range of variation in core forms could be, to a large extent, due to variation in the size of the available raw material.

The type of available raw material as well as the size is obviously going to have a great effect on the range of artifact forms possible. Two examples show this relationship well. In the Omo valley, southern Ethiopia (Merrick and Merrick 1976), the only apparent raw material available in many areas consisted of small quartz pebbles. As a result, the range of forms from relevant archaeological sites consist simply of sharp quartz fragments produced by flaking or smashing small quartz clast (probably with some sort of bipolar technique). The size and the non-isotropic nature of the quartz pebbles would severely limit the range of possible artifact forms produced. The second example concerns the presence of "subspheroids" or "spheroids" only at some Oldowan sites. At Koobi Fora the principal raw material is basalt lava, and there is an almost total lack of spheroids or subspheroids. At Olduvai, where larger pieces of quartz and quartzite were avail-

able, spheroids and subspheroids are much more common. It seems likely that raw material availability is to a great extent responsible for this aspect of assemblage variability between the two regions. The Olduvai forms perhaps reflect heavy battering as well—curated hammerstones, food processors, or (to me, less believably) missiles. Investigations by Willoughby (1981), should shed light on this problem.

Based on my experimental work, it seems likely that much of the variation in Oldowan technology often attributed to stylistic norms is in fact the end product of a lithic reduction designed to produce sharp flakes, and that many of these core forms may actually be "waste." The question of the functions of Oldowan artifacts will be discussed below.

OLDOWAN CORES AS THE PRINCIPAL TOOLS?

Another popular conception is that Leakey's Oldowan "tool types"—her cores and retouched pieces—were deliberately designed for use. While it is generally acknowledged in palaeolithic studies that some of the *débitage* (flakes and fragments) found at sites may have been used as tools, in discussions of Oldowan technology the primary emphasis has generally been upon the "core tools". Also, most reconstructions of early hominids show them using chopper-like artifacts rather than flakes for a range of activities.

I have experimentally replicated thousands of Oldowan artifact forms using the same raw materials as Oldowan knappers and have used these for a wide range of functional experiments (Toth 1982: 288–324). These experiments indicate that flakes are especially critical for butchering animal carcasses, since a sharp edge is essential for initial slitting of the skin. A flake or a sharp retouched flake edge is also best for meat

Figure 7. *Diagram summarizing the potential uses for Oldowan and Acheulean forms, based on feasibility experiments with replicated stone tools. Cob., cobble; h.s., hammerstone; ch., chopper; poly., polyhedron; disc., discoid; c.sc., core scraper; fl., flake; fl.sc., flake scraper; anv., anvilstone; h.a., handaxe; cl., cleaver (a), acute edge; (s), steep edge.*

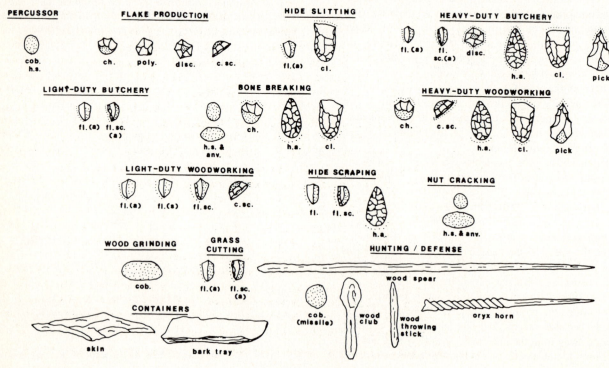

Table 1. Chart showing relative efficiency of certain artifact forms for a variety of functions, based on feasibility experiments.

	Stone flaking	Flake production	Hide slitting	Heavy-duty butchery	Light-duty butchery	Bone breaking	Heavy-duty woodwork	Light-duty woodwork	Hide scraping	Nut cracking	Grass cutting	Missiles	Weapons (hypothetical)	Total score
Steep chopper		xxx				xx	x						xx	8
Acute chopper		xxx	x	x		x	xxx	xx					xx	13
Polyhedron		xxx												3
Bifacial discoid		xxx	x	xx				x	x					8
Core scraper		xxx					xx	xx						7
Acute flake scraper			x	xxx	xx			xxx	xxx		xx			14
Steep flake scraper								xxx	xxx					6
Flake			xxx	xxx	xxx			xx	xx		xxx			16
Handaxe		x	x	xxx	x	xx	xx		x				xx	13
Cleaver (bit)			xxx	xxx	x		xxx						xx	12
Pick (steep edge)				xx			x						xx	5
Hammer-stone	xxx					xxx				xxx		xxx	xx	14
Anvil	x					xxx				xxx				7

X = Possible, but not usually efficient: XX = fair: XXX = good.

cutting (Acheulean handaxes and cleavers with sharp edges are also excellent meat cutting tools). As a result, I suggest that simple flakes and fragments were probably at least as important as Oldowan cores for use as tools, and are particularly suited for cutting tasks. Figure 7 and Table 1 summarize the results of my experimental studies of the functions of stone artifact forms.

However, this is not to say that Oldowan core forms were never used as tools. Experimentation has shown, for example, that heavy core forms with relatively sharp edges (less than 80°) are excellent wood chopping and adzing tools (Toth 1982: 301–305). Ethnographically, the Australian aborigines, among others, have been observed using simple chopper-like forms and other tools for woodworking (Hayden 1979).

Bone-breaking for marrow acquisition is another activity for which a relatively massive tool is best. Although experiments have shown that a simple unflaked cobble will serve, heavier cores, especially those with steeper edge angles, might also have been used to crack open bones.

Lewis Binford (1983 and pers. comm.) has suggested that most early stone technologies were directed towards the scavenging of animal carcasses by using core tools for breaking open bones for their marrow and for chopping dried, hardened, relict meat off bones scavenged from carnivore kills.

There are several lines of evidence which may help resolve these differences of opinion. These include (1) micro-wear analysis of stone artifacts, (2) studies of bone modification, and (3) differential use of raw materials.

At Koobi Fora archaeological sites, most of the artifacts are made of basalt, a material that at present is not known to produce identifiable use-polishes. A small percentage of the raw material from some of the Koobi Fora sites is fine-grained siliceous rock ("chert," "chalcedony"), that is amenable to the analytical techniques developed by Keeley (1980) for studying European flint artifacts. Nine of 56 artifacts so far examined exhibited wear patterns that could be interpreted along functional lines. All of these were unretouched flakes or flake fragments. The functions suggested for these artifacts were (1) animal butchery/meat cutting (four examples), (2) wood-working, including sawing and scraping (three examples), and (3) cutting of soft plant matter (two examples) (Keeley and Toth 1981). It is interesting that none of these used pieces would have been placed in the "tool" category typologically.

More recently I examined a "classic" bifacial chopper of chert from site FxJj50 at Koobi Fora (rare, since most cores are of lava) for use-wear traces. Although the specimen was very fresh, no polishes or other diagnostic features were observed.

A technology similar to that seen in the Oldowan can be observed in the Lower Paleolithic of Europe. Keeley (1980) examined artifacts from Middle Pleistocene sites in England, including Clacton-on-Sea. This assemblage is essentially a Mode I ("Clactonian") technology characterized by simple cores made on flint cobbles, as well as on flakes and retouched flakes. The majority of cores from Clacton did not have observable use-polishes; most of the used pieces were flakes and retouched flakes, interpreted mainly as wood-working, hide-working, and butchery tools. This study suggests that flake-tools were used at least as much as core-tools in some Mode I industries.

Bunn (1981, 1982), Potts and Shipman (1981) and Potts (1982) have found evidence of animal butchery at several early sites. Fine striations microscopically interpreted as cut-marks

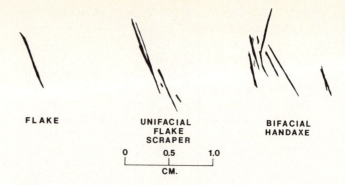

Figure 8. *Macroscopic patterns of bone striae produced by different artifact edges. With scanning electron microscopy, each groove actually consists of many parallel tracks.*

have been identified on the bones of a wide range of mammalian species, from small bovid to elephant sizes. Many of these marks occur macroscopically as single striae or intersecting multiple striae. Under a scanning electron microscope these marks consist of numerous fine parallel tracks. Experiments show that similar modifications can be made with sharp unretouched flakes (often producing the single striations) and unifacially or bifacially retouched flakes (producing the intersecting striations and irregularities in the working edge) (Figure 8).

The striations are found in anatomical areas that are consistent with skinning, dismembering, and removing meat from bones (Bunn 1982). This strongly suggests that early hominids butchered carcasses, acquired through hunting or scavenging, which had reasonable amounts of meat on them.

The presence of numerous cut-marks implies that sharp stone artifacts, especially flakes and retouched flakes, had been used at Olduvai and Koobi Fora sites. This does not, however, preclude the use of some Oldowan core forms as butchery tools, as Binford has suggested. Potts (1982: 117) has reported several signs of modification on Olduvai bones that appear to be chopmarks, perhaps signs of bone breaking, dismembering, or chopping off dried meat. Leakey (1971) has reported other evidence suggesting that some Oldowan cores may have been used as tools at Olduvai Gorge. There is a curious lack of lava *débitage* associated with most Oldowan/Developed Oldowan sites in Beds I and II, despite an abundance of lava cores ("choppers," "polyhedrons," etc.). It thus appears that flaked lava cores were transported to the sites. In contrast, *débitage* of quartz and quartzite is much more common, as are small retouched forms (light-duty scrapers, etc.) in these materials. Quartz and quartzite cores are not very common in Bed I, but predominate in Bed II. This apparent differential treatment of raw materials may imply different functions as well. For example, it is possible here that quartz and quartzite flakes and retouched pieces were frequently used, and, in the lower levels, commonly transported tools forms, while, in lava, cores rather than flakes may have been curated and transported as tools, or as highly curated, infrequently flaked cores.

To sum up, it seems likely that flake-tools were a very important part of Oldowan technology, and, in my estimation, probably were at least as important as the so-called "core-tools." Many of the Oldowan "core-tool" forms could have simply been by-products of flake manufacture.

OLDOWAN TECHNOLOGY AS INDICATION OF LOW COGNITIVE SKILLS?

To describe the Oldowan as a fairly simple, opportunistic industrial mode does not necessarily imply that early hominids had low cognitive skills. We must keep in mind that stone artifacts (and material culture in general) need not reflect cognitive ability. An interesting investigation of the possible reflection of cognitive abilities in evident technological skills was conducted by Wynn (1979), in which he applied principles proposed by the Swiss psychologist Piaget for judging developmental cognitive levels, to aspects of Lower Palaeolithic stone assemblages from East Africa.

In his study, Wynn examined early artifact forms for symmetry of planform, symmetry of cross-section, and evidence of the ability to create an arbitrary straight edge. He argued that these features can be seen in later Acheulean forms at Isimila, Tanzania, but not in the Oldowan forms from the lower beds of Olduvai Gorge. He infers rightly, I think, that later Acheulean hominids (presumably late *Homo erectus* or archaic *Homo sapiens*) had relatively sophisticated cognitive skills. He goes on to suggest that the makers of the Oldowan assemblages (presumably *Homo habilis* or early *Homo erectus*) did not have these skills. This may be true, but we must be cautious in making such statements, since lithic technology may not reflect true cognitive ability. Some late Pleistocene and Holocene assemblages from Southeast Asia, Australia, Tasmania, and the North American west coast, for example, are certainly the products of *Homo sapiens sapiens*, with modern cognitive abilities, but are still essentially Mode I technologies that would fail to meet Piaget's criteria for advanced cognition.

On the technological side, we must remember that most Oldowan artifacts were made from cobbles or chunks of raw material. It is much more difficult to shape a cobble or chunk into a symmetrical, straight-edged form by flaking than it is to shape a large flake. The knapping of large flake blanks is a hallmark of Acheulean technology after 1.5 million years ago, and often produced highly symmetrical artifacts. However, when Acheulean knappers flaked small cobbles, they normally produced Oldowan-like forms.

It is clear that early stone tool-making hominids did have a good sense of the mechanics of stone fracture and a fundamental sense of the geometry of core manipulation. Normally one needs an acute angle on the edge of a core to remove a flake by percussion. It is clear that Oldowan hominids were able to find these angles on cores and to strike the cores with the proper force, at the proper point of percussion. Modern beginning knappers usually do not exhibit this ability until they have several hours of flaking practice. The core forms modern beginners produce early on are characterized by steep edges, small flake scars, and large amounts of battering from the hammerstone.

THE OLDOWAN AS AN ESSENTIALLY EXPEDIENT TECHNOLOGY?

Binford (1979) makes a distinction between tools that are retained for future use (curated tools) and those that are made and used in response to an immediate need without much premeditation (expedient tools). He suggests that earlier technologies, such as the Mousterian, were essentially expedient ones, while others, such as Upper Palaeolithic industries of Western Europe, were curatorially organized.

Many prehistorians apparently feel that early stone technologies do not exhibit patterns that suggest much foresight and premeditation, and that these technologies are the product of very simple organizational systems.

While I certainly do not feel that Oldowan technologies were as premeditated and as carefully curated as many later technologies, there is evidence that Oldowan hominids habitually transported materials, presumably for future use. This evidence includes (1) direct evidence of raw material transport, (2) evidence that only some stages of flaking are represented at archaeological sites, and (3) evidence from refitting lithic materials from archaeological sites.

At Koobi Fora (Isaac 1976; Harris 1978; Harris and Isaac 1980) and at Olduvai (Leakey 1971; Hay 1976) there is good evidence for the transport of raw material and artifacts over several kilometers. I take this to indicate that early hominid technology sometimes was directed toward later use of tools, and should be regarded as curational behavior.

Interestingly, chimpanzees exhibit a more expedient technology. Studies of termite and ant fishing (McBeath and McGrew 1982; Nishida and Hiraiwa 1982) and of nut cracking with unflaked stone tools (Boesch and Boesch 1981; Sugiyama and Koman 1979), show that chimpanzees rarely transport raw materials or tools very far. Often transport distances are just a few meters, and apparently never more than several hundred meters (Boesch and Boesch 1981). In one study of chimpanzee ant-fishing (Nishida and Hiraiwa 1982), the maximum time between tool manufacture and use was only 17 min. While chimpanzees exhibit some premeditation, it appears to be of a much lower order than that of Oldowan hominids. It has even been argued (McBeath and McGrew 1982) that chimpanzees in Senegal do most of their termiting in one major habitat because it contained abundant *Grewia* plants, the source of the best termite probes.

Comparisons were also made between the actual flake populations at the Koobi Fora archaeological sites and my predictions of the hypothetical flake populations at these sites, assuming all of the *débitage* from the excavated cores and retouched pieces was represented (Toth 1982). A given core type produces a predictable set of flake types, and hence the manufacture of a given set of cores generates a predictable

FLAKE TYPES

I   II   III   IV   V   VI

Figure 9. *Flake type classification used in the analysis of Koobi Fora sites. Types I–III have cortical platforms, suggesting unifacial flaking of cobbles. Types IV–VI have non-cortical platforms. Within these two division, flakes are further classified by total, partial, and absence of cortex on the dorsal surface.*

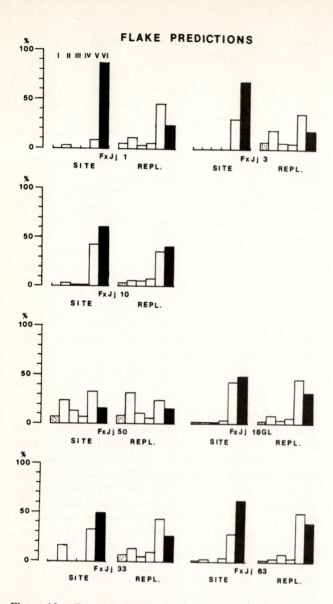

FLAKE PREDICTIONS

Figure 10. *Comparison of the excavated flake populations from Koobi Fora sites with computer-simulated predictions of flake populations. Note that later stages of flaking (represented by non-cortical, type VI flakes) occur in greater than expected proportions at most excavated sites.*

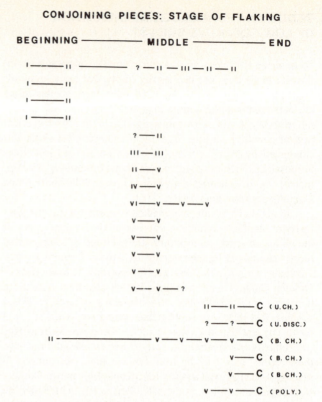

Figure 11. *Chart showing stages of flaking represented at site FxJj 50 based on conjoining pieces. The beginning stage of flaking was defined as a flake type I (cortical butt, total cortex dorsal surface) conjoining with at least one other flake. The end or terminal stage of flaking was defined as a core (C) with at least one conjoining flake. Roman numerals represent the six flake types. Note that complete reduction sequences are rarely represented in the excavated area.*

population of flakes types within an assemblage. A six-type system of classification of whole fakes was employed to document which stages of flaking were represented in flaking experiments and at archaeological sites (Toth 1982). This system was based on the presence, partial absence, or total absence of cortex on the dorsal surface of the flake, and on the presence or absence of cortex on the platform (butt) of the flake (see Figure 9). In general, percentages of completely non-cortical flakes (Type VI) tend to represent later stages of reduction of Oldowan cores. My study indicates that these later stages of flaking are disproportionately represented at these Koobi Fora sites (Figure 10, Table 2), indicating transport of partially-flaked cores to the site from another knapping location.

A third line of evidence suggesting hominid transport of artifactual materials is from refitting studies at Koobi Fora sites, especially site FxJj 50 (Bunn *et al.* 1980). Conjoining pieces at

this site were normally found very close together, suggesting that this site had not undergone serious fluvial disturbance. Though a large area was excavated, few of the artifacts from this site (about 15%) were conjoinable to others. Of 63 cores and retouched pieces, for example, only six had any conjoining *débitage* within the excavated area. From the model of flaking stages represented by the major refitted pieces (Figure 11) it is clear that the complete reduction sequences are rarely represented within the excavated areas.

The model I have proposed for early hominid tool use thus includes transport of a wide range of lithic raw materials around the landscape for future use (simple curation behavior) (Toth 1982). Some of this raw material "drops out" at concentrations that archaeologists call "sites." The model I envision is one of hominids testing out raw materials from stream gravel bars, and transporting the best pieces to activity areas. When sites are abandoned, the best lithic materials (large cores and flakes, a few hammerstones, etc.) will be carried off for future use. Perhaps many sites were re-occupied over time before final burial. New material may have been brought to these localities, and old material that had been discarded there might have been re-used and reduced further. Finally the sites were completely abandoned, perhaps sometimes as a direct result of floods that led to site burial.

Table 2. Comparison of the excavated flake populations from Koobi Fora sites with computer-simulated predictions of expected flake populations. Percentage of cores replicated denotes those that could be assigned to reduction modes.

		I	II	III	IV	V	VI	Total	Percentage cores simulated
FxJj 1	Site	0 (0-00)	1 (0-04)	0 (0-00)	0 (0-00)	2 (0-09)	20 (0-87)	23	
	Simulation	3 (0-06)	6 (0-12)	2 (0-04)	3 (0-06)	24 (0-47)	13 (0-25)	51	100%
FxJj 3	Site	0 (0-00)	0 (0-00)	0 (0-00)	0 (0-00)	4 (0-31)	9 (0-69)	13	
	Simulation	2 (0-08)	4 (0-20)	1 (0-07)	2 (0-07)	8 (0-37)	4 (0-20)	21	100%
FxJj 10	Site	0 (0-00)	2 (0-03)	1 (0-01)	1 (0-01)	23 (0-33)	42 (0-61)	69	
	Simulation	3 (0-03)	6 (0-06)	5 (0-05)	8 (0-08)	35 (0-36)	39 (0-41)	96	92%
FxJj 50	Site	24 (0-07)	85 (0-24)	45 (0-13)	25 (0-07)	118 (0-33)	56 (0-16)	353	
	Simulation	31 (0-09)	107 (0-32)	37 (0-11)	19 (0-06)	83 (0-25)	54 (0-16)	331	79%
FxJj 18GL	Site	8 (0-02)	9 (0-02)	3 (0-01)	21 (0-04)	220 (0-43)	252 (0-49)	513	
	Simulation	58 (0-03)	152 (0-09)	74 (0-04)	98 (0-06)	775 (0-46)	535 (0-32)	1692	83%
FxJj 33	Site	0 (0-00)	1 (0-17)	0 (0-00)	0 (0-00)	2 (0-33)	3 (0-50)	6	
	Simulation	39 (0-06)	93 (0-13)	31 (0-14)	60 (0-09)	295 (0-43)	174 (0-25)	692	85%
FxJj 63	Site	2 (0-01)	5 (0-03)	0 (0-00)	8 (0-04)	58 (0-29)	126 (0-63)	199	
	Simulation	3 (0-01)	6 (0-02)	24 (0-07)	10 (0-03)	174 (0-49)	140 (0-39)	357	88%

EARLY HOMINID DEPENDENCE UPON LITHIC TECHNOLOGY?

It is often assumed that as lithic technology progressed, early hominids became more and more dependent on stone tools for a wide range of activities. In the long run, this appears certain. But in the earlier periods of stone technology, there may have been much less dependence upon stone tools.

At Koobi Fora, especially in the Upper Member, there is a fascinating dichotomy in the distribution of hominid fossils and archaeological sites (Isaac and Harris 1978). Hominids, especially the more gracile forms generally attributed to the genus *Homo*, tend to be found in the vicinity of the proto-Lake Turkana (Behrensmeyer 1975), while archaeological sites tend to be found inland along stream courses in the alluvial valleys. There are some obvious reasons for this pattern. First, bones are more likely to be preserved in low-energy situations, such as in proximity to the lake, where stream gradients are low. Second, stone tools tend to be found upstream, nearer the sources of suitable raw materials for flaking.

The interesting pattern that emerges at Koobi Fora is that hominids appear to have transported raw materials a few kilometers from their gravel sources to form low-density archaeological sites, such as the Lower Member sites at Koobi Fora. These were near the lake at a time when its level was much higher, and the shore over 10 km inland from the present shoreline. Normally, however, the proto-humans did not carry and discard enough lithic material in lake margin environments to form many recognizable archaeological sites. This was especially true in Upper Member times, when the lakeshore was in approximately its present location (Findlater 1978). The fact that remains of large-brained, probable tool-making hominids occur relatively often in these lake margin areas suggests that foraging in these areas did not depend much on stone tools. Some cut-marked bones in these areas (Bunn 1981, 1982), suggest some lithic transport (or the transport of parts of butchered animal carcasses), but very few concentrations of artifacts have been found near the lake.

It is possible that early hominids made much use of relatively perishable or unmodified material such as bone, wood, horn, or shell. Brain (1982) has reported polished and striated bones interpreted as digging tools from early Pleistocene deposits at Swartkrans and Sterkfontein, South Africa. Perhaps shells were also used for cutting tools at Koobi Fora. Fractured shell edges can be very sharp (P. Williamson, pers. comm. and pers. obs.) and might even make cut-marks on animal bones.

CONCLUSIONS

Some of the major conclusions drawn from my study are that (1) many of the Oldowan core forms could simply be by-products of flake manufacture, and may not really represent deliberate stylistic norms, (2) unretouched flakes were probably at least as important as cores or retouched flakes as tools, especially for activities related to animal butchery, (3) stone technology is not necessarily a good criterion for judging cognitive abilities, (4) Oldowan technology can be considered as a simple curated technology, (5) early stone-tool making hominids were not necessarily dependent upon the use of stone tools in this early period.

These conclusions are principally drawn from analytical and experimental studies of the Koobi Fora archaeological occurrences in northern Kenya, dated to between 1.9 and 1.4 million years ago. But, as White has pointed out (in Rosenthal 1982), these early hominids were probably very opportunistic. Whether the behavioral patterns seen at one locality can be used as a model for all early hominid tool-using groups is doubtful. We might expect a wide range of variation in the behavioral, adaptive, and technological patterns depending upon local circumstances.

Future research should help clarify the range of these patterns as seen in the prehistoric record through diligent survey, careful excavation of the best-preserved sites, further actualistic studies, and new analytical approaches to the archaeological record.

ACKNOWLEDGEMENTS

The research outlined in this article was made possible by a grant from the National Science Foundation to the Koobi Fora Research Project, directed by Richard Leakey and Glynn Isaac. The archaeological research at Koobi Fora was directed by Glynn Isaac and John W. K. Harris, who provided advice and logistic support during the course of my study. Special thanks to Kathy Schick, Tim White, John Parkington, and John W. K. Harris for valuable suggestions regarding this paper, and to Judith Ogden for the drawings in Figure 1.

REFERENCES

Behrensmeyer, A. K. 1975. Taphonomy and palaeoecology in the hominid fossil record. *Yearbook of Physical Anthropology* 19:36-50.

Biberson, P. J. 1961. *Le Paléolithique Inférieur du Maroc Atlantique.* Rabat: Public Service des Antiquités du Maroc, 17.

Binford, L. 1979. Organization and formation processes: looking at curated technologies. *Journal of Anthropological Research* 35:255-273.

Binford, L. 1983. *In Pursuit of the Past.* Thames and Hudson, New York.

Boesch, C., and Boesch, H. 1981. Sex differences in the use of natural hammers by wild chimpanzees: a preliminary report. *Journal of Human Evolution* 10:585-593.

Brain, C. K. 1981. *The Hunters or the Hunted?* University of Chicago Press, Chicago.

Brain, C. K. 1982. The Swartkrans site: Stratigraphy of the fossil hominids and a reconstruction of the environment of early *Homo. Congrès International de Paléontologie Humaine, Premier Congrès, Prétirage, Tome 2*, pp. 676-706. Centre National de Recherche Scientifique, Nice, France.

Bunn, H. T. 1981. Archaeological evidence for meat-eating by Plio-Pleistocene hominids from Koobi Fora and Olduvai Gorge. *Nature* 291:574-577.

Bunn, H. T. 1982. *Meat Eating and Human Evolution: Studies of the Diet and Subsistence Patterns of Plio-Pleistocene Hominids in East Africa.* Ph.D. Dissertation, University of California, Berkeley.

Bunn, H., Harris, J. W. K., Isaac, G., Kafulu, Z., Kroll, E., Schick, K., Toth, N., and Behrensmeyer, A. K. 1980. FxJj 50: An early Pleistocene site in northern Kenya. *World Archaeology* 12:109-136.

Chavaillon, J. 1971. Les habitats Oldowayens de Melka-Kunturé. *Actes du VIIe Congrès Panafricain de Préhistoire et Quaternaire.* Addis Ababa.

Chavaillon, J. 1976. Evidence for the technical practices of Early Pleistocene hominids: Shungura Formation, Lower Omo Valley, Ethiopia, in: *Earliest Man and Environments in the Lake Rudolf Basin: Stratigraphy, Palaeoecology, and Evolution* (Y. Coppens, F. C. Howell, G. Ll. Isaac & R. E. Leakey, Eds.), pp. 565-573. University of Chicago Press, Chicago.

Chavaillon, J., Chavaillon, N., Hours, F., and Piperno, M. 1979. From the Oldowan to the Middle Stone Age at Melka-Kunturé (Ethiopia): Understanding cultural changes. *Quaternaria* 21:87-114.

Clark, J. D., Cole, G., Isaac, G. L., and Kleindeinst, M. 1966. Precision and definition in African archaeology. *South African Archaeological Bulletin* 21:114-121.

Clark, J. D., and Kurashina, H. 1979. Hominid occupation of the East Central Highland of Ethiopia in the Plio-Pleistocene. *Nature* 282:33-39.

Clark, J. D. G. 1971. *World Prehistory: a New Outline.* Cambridge University Press, Cambridge.

Corvinus, G. 1976. Prehistoric exploration at Hadar, Ethiopia. *Nature* 261:571-572.

Corvinus, G., and Roche, H. 1976. La préhistoire dans la région d'Hadar (Bassin de l'Awash, Afar, Ethiopie): premiers résultats. *L'Anthropologie* 80:315-324.

Corvinus, G., and Roche, H. 1980. Prehistoric exploration at Hadar in the Afar (Ethiopia) in 1973, 1974 and 1976, in: *Proceedings, VIIIth Panafrican Congress of Prehistory and Quaternary Studies,* Nairobi, Kenya, (R. E. F. Leakey and B. A. Ogot, Eds.), pp. 186-188.

Deetz, J. 1967. *Invitation to Archaeology.* Natural History Press, Garden City.

Findlater, I. 1978. Stratigraphy, in: *Koobi Fora Research Project,* Vol. I (R. E. F. Leakey and B. A. Ogot, Eds.), pp. 14-31. Clarendon Press, Oxford.

Gowlett, J. A., Harris, J. W. K., Walton, D., and Wood, B. A. 1981. Early archaeological sites, hominid remains and traces of fire from Chesowanja, Kenya. *Nature* 294:125-129.

Harris, J. W. K. 1978. *Karari Industry: Its Place in African Prehistory.* Ph.D. Dissertation, University of California, Berkeley.

Harris, J. W. K. 1980. Archaeological studies at Laetoli, Northern Tanzania. *L. S. B. Leakey Foundation News* 2:5.

Harris, J. W. K. 1983. Cultural beginnings: Plio-Pleistocene archaeological occurrences from the Afar, Ethiopia, in: *African Archaeological Review* (N. David, Ed.), 1:3-31. Cambridge University Press, Cambridge.

Harris, J. W. K., and Bishop, W. W. 1976. Sites and assemblages from the early Pleistocene beds of Karari and Chesowanja, in: *Les Plus Anciennes Industries en Afrique, Colloque 5, 9e Congrès internationale des sciences préhistoriques et protohistoriques, Nice* (J. D. Clark & G. Ll. Isaac, Eds.), pp. 70-117.

Harris, J. W. K., and Isaac, G. Ll. 1980. Early Pleistocene site locations at Koobi Fora, Kenya, in: *Proceedings, VIIIth Panafrican Congress of Prehistory and Quaternary Studies,* Nairobi, Kenya (R. E. F. Leakey and B. A. Ogot, Eds.), pp. 205-207.

Hay, R. L. 1976. *Geology of Olduvai Gorge.* University of California Press, Berkeley.

Hayden, B. 1979. *Palaeolithic Reflections: Lithic Technology and Ethnographic Excavation among the Australian Aborigines.* Humanities Press, New Jersey.

Howell, F. C. 1978. Hominidae. in: *Evolution of African Mammals.* (V. Maglio and H. B. Cooke, Eds.), pp. 154-248. Harvard University Press, Cambridge, MA.

Isaac, G. Ll. 1976. Plio-Pleistocene artifact assemblages from East Rudolf, Kenya, in: *Earliest Man and Environments in the Lake Rudolf Basin* (Y. Coppens, F. C. Howell, G. Ll. Isaac, and R. E. Leakey, Eds.), pp. 552-564. University of Chicago Press, Chicago.

Isaac, G. Ll. 1982. The earliest archaeological traces, in: *The Cambridge History of Africa, Vol. 1. From the Earliest Times to c. 500 B.C.* (J. D. Clark, Ed.), Cambridge University Press, Cambridge.

Isaac, G. Ll. 1984. The archaeology of human origins: studies of the Lower Pleistocene in East Africa. 1971–1981, in: *Advances in World Archaeology 3* (F. Wendorf and A. Close, Eds.), pp. 1-87. Academic Press, New York.

Isaac, G. Ll., and Harris, J. W. K. 1978. Archaeology, in: *Koobi Fora Research Project: Volume I* (M. G. Leakey and R. E. Leakey, Eds.), pp. 64-85. Clarendon Press, Oxford.

Isaac, G. Ll., and Isaac, B. 1977. *Olorgesailie; Archaeological Studies of a Middle Pleistocene Lake Basin in Kenya.* University of Chicago Press, Chicago.

Keeley, L. H. 1980. *Experimental Determination of Stone Tool Uses: A Microwear Analysis,* University of Chicago Press, Chicago.

Keeley, L. H., and Toth, N. 1981. Microwear polishes on early stone tools from Koobi Fora, Kenya. *Nature* 293:464-465.

Leakey, M. D. 1971. *Olduvai Gorge,* Vol. 3. Cambridge University Press, London.

Leakey, M. D. 1975. Cultural patterns in the Olduvai sequence, in: *After the Australopithecines* (K. Butzer and G. Ll. Isaac, Eds.), pp. 477-493. Mouton, The Hague.

McBeath, N., and McGrew, W. 1982. Tools used by wild chimpanzees to obtain termites at Mt. Assirik, Senegal: The influence of habitat. *Journal of Human Evolution* 11:65-72.

Merrick, H. V., and Merrick, J. P. S. 1976. Archaeological occurrences of earlier Pleistocene age from the Shungura Formation, in: *Earliest Man and Environments in the Lake Rudolf Basin* (Y. Coppens, F. C. Howell, G. Ll. Isaac and R. E. F. Leakey, Eds.), pp. 574-584. University of Chicago Press, Chicago.

Movius, H. 1949. The Lower Palaeolithic cultures of Southern and Eastern Asia. *Transactions of the American Philosophical Society* 38:329-420.

Nishida, T., and Hiraiwa, M. 1982. Natural history of a tool-using behavior by wild chimpanzees upon wood-boring ants. *Journal of Human Evolution* 11:73-99.

Potts, R. B. 1982. *Lower Pleistocene Site Formation and Hominid Activities at Olduvai Gorge, Tanzania.* Ph.D. Dissertation, Harvard University.

Potts, R. B., and Shipman, P. 1981. Cutmarks made by stone tools on bones from Olduvai Gorge, Tanzania. *Nature* 291:577-580.

Roche, H., and Tiercelin, J. J. 1977. Decouverte d'une industrie lithique ancienne *in situ* dans la formation d'Hadar, Afar central, Ethiopie. *Comptes Rendus Acad. Sci., Paris*, série D, 284:871-874.

Roche, H., and Tiercelin, J. J. 1980. Industries lithiques de la formation plio-pleistocène d'Hadar: Campagne 1976, in: *Proceedings, VIIIth Panafrican Congress of Prehistory and Quaternary Studies,* Nairobi, Kenya (R. E. F. Leakey and B. A. Ogot, Eds.), pp. 194-199.

Rosenthal, L. 1982. Lunch with Lucy. *Science 82*, September, p. 98.

Schick, K. D. 1984. *Processes of Palaeolithic Site Formation: An Experimental Study.* Ph.D. Dissertation, University of California, Berkeley.

Suqiyama, Y., and Koman, J. 1979. Tool-using behavior by wild chimpanzees upon wood-boring ants. *Journal of Human Evolution* 11:73-79.

Toth, N. 1982. *The Stone Technologies of Early Hominids at Koobi Fora, Kenya: An Experimental Approach.* Ph.D. Dissertation, University of California, Berkeley.

Willoughby, P. 1981. *Spheroids and Battered Stone: A Case Study in Technology and Adaptation in African Early and Middle Stone Age.* Unpublished manuscript.

Wynn, T. 1979. The intelligence of later Acheulean hominids. *Man* 14:371-391.

Part V

Evolution of *Homo erectus*

The discovery of *Homo erectus* fossils, on the Indonesian island of Java in 1891 by Eugene Dubois, marked the beginning of paleo-anthropology as a field science. It was the first instance of a student of human evolution recovering the remains of a hominid ancestor that was clearly human but undeniably more primitive than the modern species. Part V addresses a variety of topics on the history of recovery, diversity, tempo and mode of evolution, and the paleocultural attributes of *Homo erectus*. As one of the longest-lived and most geographically widespread hominid species, *Homo erectus* raises many issues of evolutionary change and biogeography.

In Chapter 34, "Davidson Black, Peking Man, and the Chinese Dragon," G.H.R. von Koenigswald provides a delight-ful summary of the events surrounding the discovery of the first fossils of *Homo erectus* from China. The first evidence of a fossil hominid in China (an isolated molar) was found in an apothecary shop in Peking about 1900, as a result of the ancient Chinese belief that fossil bones and teeth of extinct animals have strong curative powers. Von Koenigswald relates the story of the first recovery of *Homo erectus* (then called *Sinanthropus pekinensis*) at the cave site of Zhoukoudian by geologist Otto Zdansky and anatomist Davidson Black. The chapter closes with von Koenigswald describing his discovery at an apothecary in Hong Kong of the giant extinct ape *Gigan-topithecus*, which coexisted with *Homo erectus* in southern China and Southeast Asia (see also Ciochon 1991).

Chapter 35, "*Homo erectus*—Who, When and Where: A Survey" by William W. Howells, is a definitive overview of the new discoveries and interpretations of *Homo erectus* made be-tween 1960 and 1980. This was a period of intense fieldwork, which saw the world sample of *H. erectus* triple. With the new finds came a plethora of new taxonomic names, especially at the subspecies level. By tracing the development of these names, it is possible to visualize the strong emphasis placed on morphological transformation as an evolutionary mode during this period. Howells also discusses rates of evolution within *Homo erectus* and what he calls the zone of transition from *H. erectus* to *H. sapiens*. Many of Howells' views form the basis for our current understanding of *Homo erectus* (Rightmire 1990).

In Chapter 36, "Peking Man," Wu Rukang and Lin Shenglong review the well known *Homo erectus* cave site of Zhoukoudian, located about 30 miles southwest of Beijing. This large karst cave (140 meters in length) was occupied for a period of more than 200,000 years, beginning about 420,000 years ago. The site has yielded skulls and limb bones of more than 40 individuals and numerous artifacts. Wu and Li argue that *Homo erectus* was using

the cave at Zhoukoudian as a permanent base. There is evidence of controlled fires that were used for cooking, as well as animal remains which appear to have been butchered. Wu and Li advance the idea that a progressive lithic culture with increasing complexity developed at Zhoukoudian.

Chapter 37, "Patterns in the Evolution of *Homo erectus*" by G. Phillip Rightmire, is an attempt to determine the rate of evolu-tion within the *Homo erectus* lineage over the 1.3 m.y. range of the species. Rightmire uses cranial, dental, and mandibular measure-ments of all the specimens then assigned to *Homo erectus* in his search for evolutionary trends. His metrical analysis by mean least squares regression reveals no significant trends in the rate of morphological change in *Homo erectus* over more than one mil-lion years of its evolutionary history; in other words, *Homo erectus* is best viewed as a stable taxon at evolutionary stasis. From these results Rightmire speculates that the origin of *Homo sapiens* from *H. erectus* could have occurred by a rapid, short pulse of evolution late in the Middle Pleistocene, possibly supporting the punctuated equilibrium model of speciation.

Chapter 38, "Evolution in *Homo erectus*: The Question of Stasis" by Milford Wolpoff, is a direct rebuttal of Rightmire's analysis of evolutionary rates in *Homo erectus* (Chapter 37). Wolpoff concludes that Rightmire's statistical analysis was flawed, because least squares regression is an inappropriate technique for the analysis he attempted (see also comments by Levinton 1982). Wolpoff selected 92 specimens of *Homo erec-tus* (Rightmire used 65) and divided them into three temporal subsets (Rightmire used six groupings). Based on thirteen vari-ables (including cranial capacity), Wolpoff demonstrates sig-nificant evolutionary trends within *Homo erectus* and shows that the rate of change (calculated in "darwins") is at or above the average for other fossil vertebrate groups. Though *Homo erectus* is clearly not at evolutionary stasis, Wolpoff concludes that his data nonetheless cannot disprove a punctuated equi-librium model nor fully support a phyletic gradualism model for *H. erectus*. Wolpoff's demonstration that significant mor-phological change separates his early and late *erectus* samples foreshadows recent attempts to divide *Homo erectus* into several species (see Chapter 31).

In Chapter 39, "Early *Homo erectus* Skeleton from West Lake Turkana, Kenya," Frank Brown, John Harris, Richard Leakey and Alan Walker announce the discovery of the most complete early hominid skeleton ever recovered—a male *Homo erectus* judged to be about 12 years of age. This unique specimen, given the number WT 15000, was nicknamed the "strapping youth" because at 12 years of age it was already five feet four inches in height; its full adult stature would likely have approached six feet. The specimen is well dated by K/Ar at close to 1.6 m.y.a. Though Brown *et al.* note the strapping youth had limb proportions similar to modern humans, there were other unexpected differences in the shape of the thorax and in the pelvic region. A monographic treatment of this important specimen currently underway (Walker and Leakey, Eds. 1993) should yield significant information on the morphological configuration and adaptations of the earliest *Homo erectus*.

Chapter 40, "Paleobiology and Age of African *Homo erectus*" by Eric Delson, was published as a comment on the discovery of the West Turkana *Homo erectus*. Delson summarizes and expands on the interpretations of WT 15000 by Brown *et al.* through wide-ranging comparisons with other *Homo erectus* finds in Africa and Asia. Noting that the 1.6 m.y.-old WT 15000 and other early *H. erectus* specimens from East Turkana (ER 3733 and 3883) seem to form a unique grouping within *Homo erectus*, Delson speculates that these African specimens may belong to a separate species of early *Homo*, a view later formalized by Wood in Chapter 31 (see also discussion below).

Chapter 41, "The Lower Paleolithic: Current Evidence and Interpretations" by Arthur Jelinek, presents an overview of the stone tools that were probably made and used by *Homo erectus*. Though there is no established link between Lower Paleolithic industries and *Homo erectus*, it is this species of early hominid which was most common during the temporal range of the Lower Paleolithic. Throughout Africa, Europe and western Asia, the Acheulian stone tool industry is classically associated with *Homo erectus*, and in eastern Asia, the chopper/chopping tool industry of an equivalent age is linked to Asian *Homo erectus*. Jelinek summarizes and interprets all Lower Paleolithic industries, addressing the dual questions of what significance these artifacts had for the people who made them, and what relationship the industries recovered by archaeologists have to the original cultural systems in which they were manufactured.

Though new finds of *Homo erectus* from Asia and Africa have continued at a steady pace over the past one hundred years, only recently have anthropologists begun to question our conception of this taxon as a species (see Rightmire 1990, 1992). Today, the taxonomic identity of the fossils traditionally placed in *Homo erectus* is being challenged on two fronts. On the one hand, there is an increasing number of authorities who believe

that *Homo erectus* should be restricted to the Asian fossils, and that the African fossils placed in this taxon should be assigned to one or more separate species (e.g., Andrews 1984; Turner and Chamberlain 1989; Clarke 1990; Wood, Chapter 31). These researchers argue that the Asian specimens share derived features which distinguish them from the African remains and also preclude them from the ancestry of later species of *Homo*. These geographical distinctions have been questioned by other workers who point to variability within both the African and Asian samples that tends to negate separate taxonomic assignments (e.g., Bräuer and Mbua 1992; Rightmire 1990).

The second challenge to the specific identity of *Homo erectus* comes from the proponents of the multiregional model of modern human origins (Wolpoff and Thorne 1992; see also Chapters 44 and 48). They argue that because populations of early hominids normally attributed to *Homo erectus* evolved gradually into regional variants of early *Homo sapiens*, there was clearly reproductive continuity between the early and late populations. Thus *Homo erectus* should be abandoned as a separate taxon and all fossil hominids subsequent to *Homo habilis* should be placed in a single species—*Homo sapiens*. The continuity argument is fueled by the continual debate over the appropriate placement—either *Homo erectus* or early *Homo sapiens*—of many recently recovered Middle Pleistocene hominids. These include the Narmada skull from India (compare de Lumley and Sonakia 1985 with Kennedy *et al.* 1991) and the recently described hominid crania from Yunxian, Hubei Province, China (see photograph on page 408) assigned to *Homo erectus* by Li and Etler (1992; but see Gibbons 1992).

These striking differences of opinion over the taxonomy of *Homo erectus* have been brought about both by new discoveries that have expanded the morphological diversity of the fossil sample and also by profound differences in the way researchers approach the evolutionary process and its results. Is it more important to emphasize morphological transformation (descent with modification) as Darwin did, or is taxic diversification (the bushy nature of evolution and species diversity through time) the more important feature? These issues are far from being resolved; indeed, many of the critical arguments have yet to be published. In the chapters of Part V, *Homo erectus* is used in the conservative sense of earlier decades, but the distinct viewpoints of this ongoing debate are clearly present (see Chapters 37, 38, 40; also 42, 44, 48).

REFERENCES

Andrews, P. 1984. An alternative interpretation of the characters used to define *Homo erectus*. *Cour. Forsch. Inst. Senckenberg* 69:167-175.

Bräuer, G. and Mbua, E. 1992. *Homo erectus* features used in cladistics and their variability in Asian and African hominids. *J. Hum. Evol.* 22:79-108.

Ciochon, R. L. 1991. The ape that was. *Natural History* 11/91:54-63.

Clarke, R. J. 1990. The Ndutu cranium and the origin of *Homo sapiens*. *J. Hum. Evol.* 19:699-736.

de Lumley, M. A. and Sonakia, A. 1985. Premiere decouverte d'un *Homo erectus* sur le continent indien a Hathnora dans la Moyenne vallee de la Naramada. *L'Anthropologie* 89(1):13-61.

Gibbons, A. 1992. An about-face for modern human origins. *Science* 256:1521.

Kennedy, K. A. R., Sonakia, A. Chiment, J. and Verma, K. K. 1991. Is the Narmada hominid an Indian *Homo erectus*? *Amer. J. Phys. Anthropol.* 86:475-496.

Levinton, J. S. 1982. Estimating stasis: Can a null hypothesis be too null? *Paleobiology* 8:307.

Li Tianyuan and Etler, D. 1992. New middle Pleistocene hominid crania from Yunxian in China. *Nature* 357:404-407.

Rightmire, G. P. 1990. *The Evolution of Homo erectus: Comparative Anatomical Studies of an Extinct Human Species*. Cambridge University Press, Cambridge.

Rightmire, G. P. 1992. *Homo erectus*: Ancestor or evolutionary side branch? *Evolutionary Anthropology* 2:43-49.

Turner, A. and Chamberlain, A. 1989. Speciation, morphological change and the status of African *Homo erectus*. *J. Hum. Evol.* 18:115-130.

Walker, A. and Leakey, R. E., Eds. 1993. *The Nariokotome Homo erectus Skeleton*. Harvard University Press, Cambridge, MA (in press).

Wolpoff, M. and Thorne, A. G. 1992. One hundred years of *Pithecanthropus* is enough. *Amer. J. Phys. Anthropol.*, Supplement 13:175-176.

34

Davidson Black, Peking Man, and the Chinese Dragon

G. H. R. von Koenigswald

With the discovery of Peking Man, Davidson Black became world famous. For the first time, fossil skulls and jaws of a genuine primitive 'human' being had been found in China. However, these discoveries in the countryside of Peking were not completely unexpected. Around 1900, some 25 years before Davidson Black's identification of *Sinanthropus pekinensis*, a human tooth had already been obtained in a Peking drugstore. Although no one could be sure that this mysterious tooth came from Peking, the find serves to illustrate an important 'source' of fossil remains in China.

To the Chinese people, the dragon is real. It is real because they find 'dragon' bones and teeth in many places of their country. These fossils are frequently the remains of large animals, such as horses, rhinoceroses, and elephants, and the people have felt that the remains of such mighty animals must have great medical power. Thus, the peasants have collected these remains and have sold them to drugstores. Unfortunately for the paleontologist, the dragon teeth, 'lung tse,' are regarded as having greater medicinal value than the dragon bones, 'lung ku.' Therefore, skulls and jaws are generally broken to separate the teeth. Because the material is very expensive, sold according to weight, and used only in small quantities, whole teeth are often broken as well. The breaking serves another purpose for it results in exposing the pulp cavity which often shows small crystals of calcite due to fossilization, proof that the item is a genuine dragon tooth of first quality.

Many of the 'dragon' remains are of Pliocene fauna and occur in veritable 'bone beds,' the long teeth of *Hipparion* sometimes serving as their trademark. *Hipparion* is a three-toed horse and the index fossil of the Pliocene period. Its remains are common; over the years I have seen between 30,000 and 50,000 isolated teeth. They can be bought in practically every ordinary Chinese drugstore, even those in small Chinese communities outside the country. Under such circumstances, we have found dragon teeth all over Southeast Asia, from Bangkok to Singapore, across Indonesia, and up to the Philippines. We have seen the teeth in San Francisco, New York, and Honolulu, and even in Canada. There are several such drugstores in Toronto, not far from City Hall, and we have found one on Pender Street in Vancouver in the back of a modern shopping center.

Fossils from Chinese drugstores have been known for a long time. Dr K. A. Haberer, a German naturalist who had travelled in northern China between 1899 and 1901, was, however, the first to make a systematic collection of dragon teeth. He did so not to amass 'souvenirs,' as has been stated in one of the books about Davidson Black (Hood 1964), but on behalf of Professor von Zittel in Munich, his teacher and the first paleontologist to write a treatise of paleontology. Haberer's collection was described by Max Schlosser (1903) in a monumental publication containing 14 large plates. The bulk of the collection came from Pliocene deposits but also contained material from the Pleistocene epoch. The rich Pliocene fauna contained the teeth of bears, different hyaenas (one as large as a calf), otters, saber-toothed tigers, beavers, mastodons, different rhinoceroses (including a new species, *Rhinoceros habereri* Schlosser), *Hipparion* (more than 600 teeth), a large *Anchitherium* (another three-toed horse but with low-crowned teeth), pigs, a very large camel, giraffes, different species of deer, and antelopes.

From Haberer's collection many species were described for the first time and gave us an idea about the richness of the fossil Chinese fauna. But the prize specimen of this collection was the aforementioned human tooth from a drugstore in Peking (Figure 1). It is a small upper molar, very worn and with fused roots. Some red earth is still attached to the roots. Because this condition appears with *Hipparion* teeth, as well as with other Pliocene fossils, and the preservation is generally similar, Schlosser suggested that the human tooth might be of Pliocene age. But Schlosser was cautious; he referred to the tooth as '?Anthropoide g. et sp. indet?' However, the last sentence of his long discussion reads as follows: 'Der Zweck dieser Mitteilung ist, spätere Forscher, denen es vielleicht vergönnt ist, in China vielleicht Ausgrabungen vorzunehmen, darauf Aufmerksam zu machen, dass dort entweder ein neuer fossiler Anthropoide oder der Tertiärmensch oder doch ein Altpleistozäner Mensch zu

Figure 1. *'Haberer's tooth,' an human upper molar from a drugstore in Peking. Actual size. (After Schlosser 1903.)*

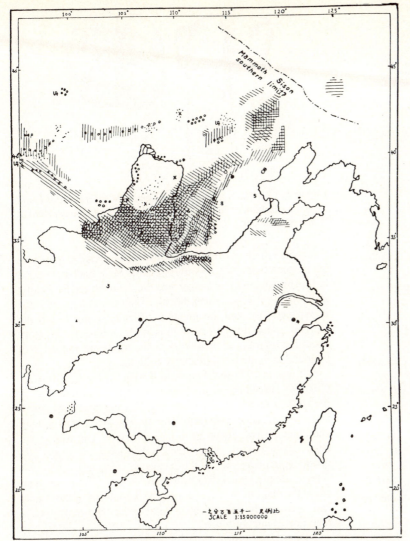

1. 益州(四川成都州北彭縣漢縣) Yi Chou (*Kuang Han Hsien, near Chengtu, Szechuan*) 2. 巴州(四川巴縣) Pa Chou (*Pa Hsien, Szechuan*)
3. 漑川(陝西南鄭縣) Liang Chou (*Nan Cheng Hsien, Shensi*) 4. 剡川(浙江天台縣附近) Yen Chou (*Near Tien Tai Hsien, Chekiang*)
5. 滄州(河北倉縣) Tsang Chou (*Tsang Hsien, Hopei*) 6. 太原(山西陽曲) Tai Yuan (*Yangchü, Shansi*) 7. 龍門(山西河津陝西韓城之間)
Lung Men (*Between Hochin Shansi & Hancheng, Shensi*) 8. 鎮州(河北正定諸縣) Chen Chou (*Chengting, Hopei*)

Distribution of DRAGON BONES in China,
Fossil fauna from the formations of,
Lower Pliocene ▦, Late Pliocene ▦.
⊕ Early Pleistocene ▨, Late Pleistocene ▨.
Compounded from ''Fossil Man in China'', by Davidson Black,
The numbered places refer to the Pen T'sao records.

Figure 2. *Davidson Black's distribution of fossil mammals according to the information of the old Chinese pharmacopoeia. (After Read 1934.)*

finden sein durfte' (Schlosser 1903:21). Thus Schlosser, already in 1903, expressed the hope that future scientists would find in China a new anthropoid, either a man of Tertiary age or a hominid from the Lower Pleistocene. This was almost a prophecy, for the hope was fulfilled 25 years later by Davidson Black.

Black must have been very much intrigued by the 'dragon bones.' He published a map of their locations according to the information of the *Pen T'sao*, the old Chinese pharmacopoeia. The last official edition of these writings is from 1597, but some

of the records on which they are based go back to the Wei Period, 7th century BC. I am here reproducing this unique map according to Read (1934) who has made a special study of Chinese drugs (Figure 2).

China and its antiquities generated much interest in Sweden following that country's dispatch of missionaries to China. As a result, the Swedish Academy sent a number of scientists to China in the 1920's to collect fossils. This began the fine collections now at the University of Uppsala. Shortly thereafter the Swedish match king, Ivar Kreuger, founded the *Palaeontologia Sinica* for the publication of paleontological and paleoanthropological papers resulting from Chinese studies. It was in this series, of course, that Black's and Franz Weidenreich's famous studies on Peking Man were published. At its inception Black's name appeared as one of the 'Honorary Research Associates' (Figure 3).

In connection with the Swedish research program, Otto Zdansky was first to dig in Chou Kou Tien in 1921 and 1923. He also found the first human teeth: a very worn upper molar, already recognized in the field, and a first premolar, recognized while the collection was in Sweden. Zdansky cautiously described the two teeth as '?*Homo* sp.' (Zdansky 1928:131). He found a second lower premolar in his collections in 1952 (Zdansky 1952). That human remains might be expected at Chou Kou Tien was first predicted by J. Gunnar Andersson. He suspected that strange sharp fragments of quartz, not infrequent at the site, might be primitive implements of early man.

After Zdansky had left, Davidson Black, with the help of the Rockefeller Foundation, continued work at Chou Kou Tien. His collaborator was Dr. Birger Bohlin, a young and enthusiastic Swedish paleontologist. On October 16, 1927, a large human molar (see Figure 4) was found by Bohlin, who hastened to bring his precious find directly to Peking to personally hand it over to Black. Black directly recognized that this remarkable tooth was unlike any other known human molar and described the find as *Sinanthropus pekinensis* (Black 1927). Peking Man was born! When later the skulls came to light it became evident that Black was right, as some scientists had doubted that just one tooth was enough to recognize a new type of early man. With the skulls he could demonstrate that Peking Man was closely related to the famous Java ape-man, *Pithecanthropus*. Eugene Dubois, a Dutch physician, had discovered in 1891 near Trinil in Central Java a flat skull cap with a heavy torus above the eyes. For many scientists the find was not enough to prove the human nature of this much disputed fossil. By Black's discovery the discussion had come to an end. *Pithecanthropus*, too, was undoubtedly a primitive hominid.

Enthusiastically, I published my first paper on Black's discovery (1931). But most disappointing for us, Dubois would never admit any relationship between Java Man and Peking

PALÆONTOLOGIA SINICA

中 國 古 生 物 誌

Palæontologists to the Geological Survey: Chief Palæontologist: A. W. Grabau:
Palæontologists: Y. C. Sun, C. Ping, T. C. Chow, Y. T. Chao (deceased).
C. C. Tien, C. C. Young, C. C. Yü, S. S. Yoh, K. H. Hsü, W. C Pei, T. K. Huang, Y. S. Chi.

EDITORS:
V. K. TING AND Y. C. SUN

FOUNDER

提 倡 人

Ivar Kreuger, Sweden

克魯格　瑞典

PATRON

贊 助 人

Sinyuan Daw King, Chekiang

金燕沁閣浙江吳興前清中書科中書

HONORARY RESEARCH ASSOCIATES

名 譽 研 究 員

Carl Wiman, Upsala

維曼　瑞典

T. G. Halle, Stockholm

赫勒　瑞典

J. S. Lee, Shanghai

李四光　上海

Davidson Black, Peiping.

步達生　　北平

Figure 3. *Davidson Black as "Honorary Research Associate" of the* Palaeontologia Sinica.

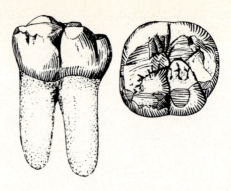

Figure 4. *The first tooth of Peking Man, a lower first molar found by Birger Bohlin. It is very long and broad, and also taurodont. Twice natural size.*

Man, and even went so far as to suddenly declare that 'his' *Pithecanthropus* was not human at all, but merely a giant gibbon as the find had been referred to by some of his adversaries. He had lost his ape-man monopoly after nearly 40 years, and this apparently was too much for him. A new skull, *Pithecanthropus* II, which we found in 1937 at Sangiran, Central Java, and more complete than his own find, he declared to be a fake.

Now, after World War II, all the precious remains of Peking Man have been lost. It is not necessary to repeat the sad story here. We also lost part of our fossil collections during the Japanese occupation in Java. Some boxes with fossils simply vanished. Nobody could really be interested in fossil teeth and bones, but they are gone nonetheless. It is the same with the Peking fossils, and I do not believe all the romantic stories about mysterious ladies and boxes filled with human bones (see Janus 1975). But one remark is in order. With the help of my wife and some Swedish and Swiss friends we were eventually able to save all our human fossil material from Java. After the war, at the American Museum of Natural History in New York, we divided our finds for study. Professor Franz Weidenreich took charge of the Solo skulls, also discovered in Java, while I studied my *Pithecanthropus* remains. One day we were visited by a Professor Watson of London. In Weidenreich's office Watson spotted the Solo skulls, and being a paleontologist he

recognized them as original specimens. He asked no questions but mistook them for the skulls of Peking Man. Back in London he told his students that he had seen Weidenreich and the Peking skulls in New York. When this bit of information got into the newspapers, we had the greatest difficulty trying to tell the journalists that this had been an error. Nevertheless, the story about Peking Man in New York came into being and can still be found in modern publications in China.

It was in 1937 that I came to Peking for the first time. C. C. Young, an old friend since my student days in Munich, took me to Chou Kou Tien. The roads were bad, but there was a small and uncomfortable local train. The site was a large quarry, long and quite narrow, about 20 m below surface. The walls were neatly painted with white lines, subdividing the place into quadrangles on account of the excavation. On a hill nearby was a small temple, which had been moved there from its original site at the place of the excavation. The inner walls of the temple had been newly painted by a local artist who had given a rendition of our activities.

During my visit I naturally learned a lot about Davidson Black. He had made many friends, had lived a very social life, and had spent many evenings in the Peking Hotel. But around midnight he used to disappear into his office, working until the early hours of the morning, then going home only to reappear around noon. In 1939 we spent five months in Peking, working together with Weidenreich on a comparative study of *Pithecanthropus* and *Sinanthropus*. But due to the war our results were not published, except for a short article in *Nature* (von Koenigswald and Weidenreich 1939). On March 15, the anniversary date of Davidson Black's death, the whole Department of Anatomy of the Rockefeller Medical Center—the Jüh Wang Fu—with Professor Weidenreich and all his assistants went out to the little clean European cemetery of Peking to decorate Black's grave with fresh flowers to commemorate the man who had contributed so much to the science of early man.

Because of the later Japanese occupation it was not possible to go out to Chou Kou Tien again, but we still kept contact with the people there. In 1973 we went to Peking on a most generous invitation of the Academia Sinica. We found Chou Kou Tien greatly changed. The road to the place had been paved and, being in good condition, we went by car. The site had been made a national monument with signs and explanations all over the place. There was an excellent little museum, exhibiting casts of the original skulls, and very good reconstructons by Wu Ju

Figure 5. *Selection of 'Dragon Teeth' from drugstores in Hong Kong and Canton. About two-thirds actual size. (Coll. v. Koenigswald; photo: Hoffman/Senckenberg.) Key: see Figure 6.*

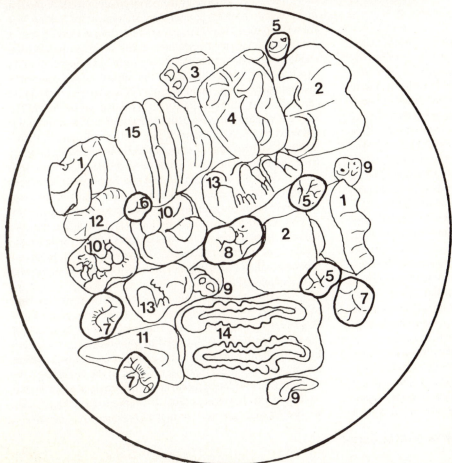

Figure 6. Key to Figure 5 *A Pleistocene assemblage:* 1, *deer;* 2, *rhinoceros;* 3, *mountain goat;* 4, *giant tapir;* 5, Sinanthropus 'officianalis'; 6, Homo sapiens ('Haberer' type); 7, *fossil giant orang;* 8, Gigantopithecus blacki *v.K.;* 9, *monkey* (Macaca robusta); 10, *giant panda;* 11, *tiger;* 12, *bear;* 13, *pig;* 14, *Stegodon;* 15, *elephant.*

Kang of Peking Man himself and, on a small scale, of his life and of the animals that had lived at the time. Many original fossils were on exhibit, from Chou Kou Tien and from other places, and there was even the fine cast of a large dinosaur. There were many visitors, including apparently whole schools of children who came here by bus to have a glimpse of China's earliest history.

My own search for dragon teeth began early in 1931 when I came to Java to serve as a paleontologist to the Geological Survey. I had finished my studies in Munich, had known old Professor Schlosser quite well, and was familiar with the Haberer Collection. In Java the Chinese community was large, and the people lived exactly as in China. There were even typical Chinese drugstores along Pasar Baru in Bandung, where we lived, but it took me sometime to discover what I was after. First I had asked for 'gigi binatang,' teeth of animals, until a friendly old Chinese told me that these were 'Dragon Teeth.' Once I had a prescription, I found them everywhere, as I have already told in the beginning.

This had been the first time that somebody had looked for this mysterious medicine outside of China. I had hoped to discover by this most romantic method a Pliocene Man, but while there was quite a lot of Pliocene material on the market, I never found a single tooth of a fossil primate in this assemblage, not even a common monkey.

But besides the Pliocene fossils there was a different kind of material on the market (Figures 5 and 6). It came, as we learned, via Hong Kong and Canton where Haberer had not collected. The original sites, as we were told, were caves and fissure fillings in the southern Chinese provinces of Guangxi and Guangdong. On Black's map this region is blank. In these provinces there are many limestone formations that show typically Karst weathering and dissection. The neighborhood of Kweiling is one of the most romantic landscapes in Asia and has inspired Chinese painters from the Han Period on.

The drugstore material from the south was different in age, preservation, and faunal content. The teeth were not as heavily fossilized as those from the Pliocene; it seems that they were regarded as a kind of 'Dragon Teeth—second quality' and were apparently younger. Teeth of elephants were proof of Pleistocene age. The preservation was most unusual in that all bony parts, including the roots, had been gnawed away by large porcupines who need the lime for their quills. They damaged as well our hope of ever getting complete jaws and skulls from these sites, or only as exceptional specimens. One site is known where the bones have been preserved, but this is in Szechuan.

Species for species, the composition of the fauna is different from the Pliocene assemblage. There is neither *Hipparion*, nor even modern horse. Many bears of modern type, dog and tiger, and teeth of the Giant Panda are not as rare but the Lesser Panda is practically absent. There are rhinoceroses, pigs, and deer. Also present are the teeth of *Stegodon* (a primitive elephant with low-crowned molars) and those of true elephants, but there are no mastodon remains. However, and most important, there are many teeth of various primates including Man!

There are, to begin with, two species of common monkeys, a larger form (*Macaca cf. robusta*) and a smaller one, the latter probably identical with the 'Golden Monkey' of China. There are a number of isolated teeth of the gibbon, certainly representing two species. Then, to our surprise, we found quite a

series of teeth of the orangutan (*Pongo*), still living in the south on the islands of Sumatra and Borneo. But most of the Chinese orangutan teeth are much bigger than those of the modern form, some of them even surpassing the large teeth of the gorilla, the most powerful of the living anthropoids. We collected more than 1,500 teeth, so this animal must have been quite common. Interestingly some of the teeth we found differed from the orangutan teeth in having less wrinkles and a double cusp on the middle of the upper molar. These teeth are so similar to certain ones of *Australopithecus* from Swartkrans in South Africa, that they most probably indicate an australopithecoid form in China, which we have called *Hemanthropus*. A few isolated teeth and no indication of the site is all we have at this moment. In Java we have similar problems with *Meganthropus*.

We also have a large selection of human teeth. Most of them are recent or subrecent. Some have, as x-ray pictures show, a very high pulp chamber. They are as taurodont as some of the famous Neanderthal teeth from Europe, especially those from the classical site of Krapina. Whether they indicate a kind of Neanderthal Man from China, we do not know. Other teeth are very small, like the first tooth obtained by Haberer in a drugstore in Peking. The same type of teeth are also to be found in a small fragment of a jaw with some red clay attached. Schlosser, just by means of the red clay on the Peking drugstore tooth, was inclined to discuss its Pliocene age. Father Teilhard de Chardin, who studied my collection, assured me that these teeth must come from Mesolithic layers, often present in Chinese caves. Hence, Haberer's tooth from Peking must belong to a Mesolithic *Homo sapiens*, and it was after all a modern tooth which touched off the hunt for Peking Man.

But there are other human teeth which are well fossilized. Among them are two first lower premolars of considerable size, more than twice as large as the corresponding teeth of modern man. Exactly such large premolars are typical for Peking Man from Chou Kou Tien. Thus in our collection, we have traces of Peking Man from southern China. There are in the molars some smaller differences from the classic form—no cingulum in the lower molars, Carabelli's pit in the upper—so we decided to preliminarily assign a new name, *Sinanthropus officinalis*, '*Sinanthropus* from the drugstores' (von Koenigswald 1952).

The greatest surprise in the collection is a last lower molar, obtained in 1935 in Hong Kong. This tooth, larger than a gorilla's and the larger orangutan teeth, is markedly different from the orangutan teeth of the same drugstore. The tooth is higher, there are no wrinkles, and the cusps must have been depressed but are rather high and swollen. This unusual type must have belonged to an as-yet-unknown higher primate. I was so convinced that this must be the very first indication of a completely new species that on the basis of this single tooth I created a new genus and species. I have called the find *Gigantopithecus blacki* v.K., in honor of the discoverer of Peking Man (von Koenigswald 1935).

Weidenreich and others would not believe me and first referred the tooth in question to a giant orangutan. Later, Weidenreich changed his mind and even went so far as regarding *Gigantopithecus* as ancestral to *Homo sapiens*! The reduction of the human dentition in the course of evolution is evident, so why couldn't there have been a giant in the beginning? But the teeth (later we found more) are too overspecialized to fit into the *Homo* line. It was not before 1956, more than 20 years after we had spotted that creature in the drugstores, that Dr. Woo, a

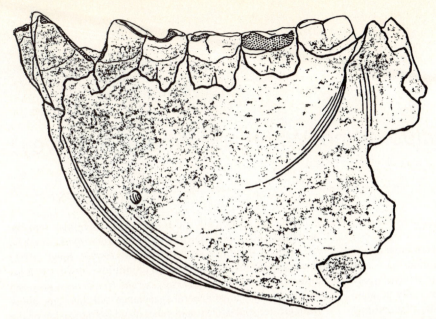

Figure 7. *Side view of the* Gigantopithecus blacki *mandible III. This is the largest mandible of a higher anthropoid ever found; from isolated teeth it must be deduced that there are still larger jaws. About three-quarters actual size. (After Woo 1962).*

member of the Chinese Geological Survey, found during excavations of caves in the Daxin and Liucheng Districts in Guangxi many isolated teeth and three enormous mandibles, firmly establishing and recognizing the existance of *Gigantopithecus blacki* (Woo 1962).

Gigantopithecus (Figure 7) was the largest higher primate that ever lived. The geological age is Lower to Middle Pleistocene. The skull is still unknown; according to our estimates (based on the size of the dentition) the brain capacity might have been as high as 700 cm^3 and, therefore, in a prehuman range. The position of this creature is still under dispute. For some it is an exceptional anthropoid (also my first impression, therefore the name *pithecus*), for others he might be an offshoot of the human line, an offshoot that acquired gigantic size. There is a Tertiary forerunner from the Indian Siwalik Hills, of Middle Pliocene age, and very recently a probably ancestral form of Lower Pliocene age has turned up in Europe (not yet described).

China is full of surprises, and so are the Chinese drugstores. In our experiences answers come straight from the Dragon's mouth.

REFERENCES

Black, D. 1927. On a lower molar hominid tooth from the Chou Kou Tien deposit. *Palaeontologia Sinica*, Series D, 7(1).

Black, D. 1931. On an adolescent skull of *Sinanthropus pekinensis* in comparison with an adult skull of the same species and with other hominid skulls, recent and fossil. *Palaeontologia Sinica*, Series D, 7(2).

Hood, D. 1964. *Davidson Black, A Biography.* University of Toronto Press, Toronto.

Janus, C. G. 1975. *The Search of Peking Man.* Macmillan, New York.

von Koenigswald, G. H. R. 1935. Eine fossile Saugetierfauna mit simia aus Sudchina. *Proceedings, Koninklijke Akademie van Wetenschappen, Amsterdam* 38:872-879.

von Koenigswald, G. H. R. 1952. *Gigantopithecus blacki* von Koenigswald, a giant fossil hominoid from the Pleistocene of southern China. *Anthropological Papers of the American Museum of Natural History* 43:295-325.

von Koenigswald, G. H. R., and Weidenreich, F. 1939. The relationship between *Pithecanthropus* and *Sinanthropus. Nature* 144:926-929.

Read, B. E. 1934. Chinese materia medica: dragons and snakes. *Peking Natural History Bulletin* 8(4):1-66.

Schlosser, M. 1903. Die fossielen saugetiere Chinas. *Abhandlungen der Bayerische Akademie der Wissenschaften* 22:1-221.

Woo, J. K. 1962. The mandibles and dentition of *Gigantopithecus. Palaeontologia Sinica*, New Series D, 11:1-94.

Zdansky, O. 1928. Die saugetiere der quartarfauna von Chou-K'ou-Tien. *Palaeontologia Sinica*, Series C, 5:1-146.

Zdansky, O. 1952. A new tooth of *Sinanthropus pekinensis* Black. *Acta Zoologica* 33:189-191.

Editor's Note: The correct spelling of the "Peking Man" locality, referred to by G. H. R. von Koenigswald in this chapter as Chou Kou Tien, is Zhoukoudian following the Chinese *pinyin* system of orthography.

35

Homo erectus—Who, When and Where: A Survey

W. W. Howells

INTRODUCTION

We should begin consideration of *Homo erectus* by considering *Homo sapiens*. This is the one good species, and the senior species, of Hominidae, and yet attempts to define it have largely been in abeyance since Linnaeus. This is not really strange, even though we know so much about the species that defining it is almost like trying to write out the unwritten British constitution. For the first half of this century there existed two parallel and totally unrelated trends in hominid taxonomy, if it can be so called. They are familiar enough.

In the first, starting with the closing years of the 19th century, there was a flood of proposed binomials (see Campbell 1965), running from *Pithecanthropus erectus*, which was justifiable, to *Homo novusmundus* for a post-Pleistocene American Indian, which was not. Such naming was only for reference (and for the greater glory of the fossil concerned), not for disciplined classification.

In the same period, following Huxley's lead, there were writings aimed at anatomically distinguishing man from other primates, especially the anthropoid apes. Risking the displeasure of modernist persons, I say "man," because that is the word those writers used (to mean humanity, not masculinity), but mainly because they were talking about man, not about *Homo sapiens* in a taxonomic sense. There is no point in giving examples. It may suffice simply to note that the 14th edition of the Encyclopaedia Britannica, published in 1928 in 23 volumes, makes a total of two passing references (not descriptions) to *H. sapiens* and *Homo rhodesiensis*, respectively.

Then, as the midpoint of the century approached, and perhaps enlightened by recognition of the australopithecines as true hominids, the anthropologists finally saw that they had a problem. Weidenreich (1943, 1946) was a great contributor, with his rigorous descriptions and his systematic attempt to reconstruct phylogeny; in 1940 he actually suggested reducing *Pithecanthropus* and *Sinanthropus* to subspecies of *Homo erectus* (Weidenreich 1940) [1]. Simpson proposed that all hominids above the australopithecines could be accommodated in two genera (*Homo* and *Pithecanthropus*) and noted that the Hominidae might well be excused from the conventions of normal zoological taxonomy, in view of the nature of this particular arena. Le Gros Clark (1955) pointed out various incongruities in practice, such as the unnecessary proliferation of taxonomic names and the confusion in previous writings between anatomical characters of "man," i.e., hominids in

general, and specifically of *Homo sapiens*. He also lent his weight to sinking *Sinanthropus* into *Pithecanthropus* (which he later agreed should be sunk in toto into *Homo*). Mayr (1951) formally proposed reducing all hominids above australopithecines to two species, *H. sapiens* and *H. erectus*, a proposal that promptly gained general acceptance. All this came about from greater sophistication in general and from focusing on the relatively abundant materials from the Far East, which could be subsumed under *H. erectus*. We shall consider shortly whether the impulse to baptize fossils, whatever their state and context, with formal names, is dead, or may rise like the phoenix once again. The virtues of vernacular names, as being non-committal, are something to remember.

We are faced now with definitions. As I suggested, it is only proper to define *Homo erectus* with reference to *H. sapiens*, not the other way. Definitions of the latter have been sketchy in the extreme (Le Gros Clark 1955), except for Howell's very recent work (1978). Without citing this, and with attention only to certain aspects, as a sort of *aide mémoire*, *H. sapiens* may be epitomized as follows.

The species is polytypic, especially in external traits of color, hair form and so on, to a degree which in other species allows subspecific distinctions. Such distinctions have been unsatisfactory in our own, however, due to a lack of good geographical separation of such subdivisions, to their intergrading, and to different levels of differentiation among them (see, e.g., Garn 1965). Nevertheless, the polytypy is important, and it is essential in considering evolution and phylogeny within *Homo*. The general degree of variation, however, is not exceptional, as Schultz (1963) has shown by comparison with chimpanzees, which have a far more limited habitat. Hence the seemingly wide limits of such variation, in some characters both external and skeletal, are acceptable as those of a good species and are not in themselves indicative of polyphyletic origins.

Body form and post-cranial skeleton are, neglecting details, those of a large animal with its own well-evolved mode of bipedality. Polytypy in these aspects, other than that of size, appears to be limited to modest differences in trunk and limb proportions that are evident during growth (Hiernaux 1965) and may thus result from some genetically fairly simple differences in ontogenetic processes.

Cranial shape differences, although more obvious, may have a similar nature: if population differences are extensions of those discernible in a single population (Howells 1973),

Reprinted with permission from the *Yearbook of Physical Anthropology*, Vol. 23, pp. 1–23. Copyright © 1980 by Alan R. Liss, Inc., New York.

deducible as multivariate characters and trends, they may be under a not too complicated polygenic control of growth patterns. They may also harmonize with such other influences as population differences in brain size, tooth size (e.g., Brace 1980) and tooth pattern (Turner 1979). This is the polytypic aspect: in general, the skull of *H. sapiens* is thin-walled, enclosing an internal volume of 1,300 cc or more on the average, with the vault developed vertically, in balance on the spine, so that the foramen magnum is inclined slightly forward and the nuchal musculature is small and has little effect on the shape of the occipital. The face is short and well retracted beneath the anterior cranium, leading to verticality, to a forward-facing of the malar-maxillary surfaces, and to an elevation of the nose relative to the face. The small dentition is integral to the pattern, being likewise retracted relative to the vault, and also to the body of the mandible, so that the alveolar border lies interior to the outline of the body of the mandible, which in turn leads to emergence of a bony chin and an incurvation between chin and teeth.

Larnach (1978) developed a set of specific traits, which, taken as a pattern and used to rate specimens, distinguished sharply between crania of modern *Homo sapiens* of all populations (the set was selected for particular application to aboriginal Australians) and all other hominids. The traits are: (1) juxta-mastoid ridge present (lateral to occipital groove), (2) postglenoid tubercle present, (3) petro-tympanic axis of temporal is not angled, but transverse, (4) supraorbital torus has at least some sign of separation of medial and lateral elements, (5) infraorbital fossa usually present, (6) malar tuberosity present, (7) a suprameatal tegmen, or ridge overhanging the meatus, is not present, (8) supraorbital torus lacks a lateral wing, projecting in the axis of the torus, (9) mastoid process is vertical. Obviously, these traits are noted largely with reference to structures seen in other hominids.

Homo erectus is the only other species that can be defined with any confidence and, compared to *Homo sapiens*, definition is necessarily limited. As a paleospecies, only skeletal and dental characters may be used; and the degree of polytypy associated with it is not known. An attempt to define the species after including in it all possible contemporary material would, it seems to me, be self-defeating. In fact, writers have, by general agreement, used the only adequate material, the Far Eastern fossils on which it was founded, including both the Javan and Chinese.

Weidenreich's definition (1943) consisted of the specification of a large number of cranial characters; it was meant actually as a description of the Peking fossils treated comparatively with the Ngandong series and other Javan material then known. Jacob (1976) gives a checklist of traits based on Trinil and Sangiran specimens that agrees well with Weidenreich's. Howell's description (1978) is also similar, if based on a broader group including Lan-t'ien and two African skulls. From all this, it is possible to distill a limited description as follows:

A cranial capacity greater than *Australopithecus*, averaging a little over 1,000 cc; a longer, thick-boned vault, though sharing with *Australopithecus* a marked postorbital constriction of the frontal region; and the greatest breadth lying at the base, coinciding with the auricular breadth.

A low frontal with a supraorbital torus which is straight across when seen both from in front and from above. The contained sinuses are variable (being small in the Chinese crania), as is the presence of a supratoral sulcus, or inflection, in the profile above the torus.

In the midvault, a parietal arc which is the smallest of the three bones contributing to the total sagittal arc. A sagittal keeling is present, often with parasagittal depressions and with a particular mounding up of bone at and around bregma along the coronal suture as well. The parietal bone approaches the rectangular, with a relatively long and straight temporo-parietal suture.

An occipital which is sharply angled in profile, with the upper plate relatively small. The occipital torus is a heavy mound, which may have a triangular eminence at the midline which also marks the point to which the greatest antero-posterior length of the vault is measured, and which may have a supratoral sulcus. The torus encloses a large area of nuchal attachment below, and continues laterally to merge with the supramastoid crest.

The face is short but heavily constructed, relatively wide, with frontally facing malar surfaces. The nasal bones are wide and low both above and below; the inferior margin of the nasal aperture is simple, without sill, groove or post-marginal drop in the floor.

In the temporal region, the robust zygomatic arch root continues into the supramastoid crest, creating a sulcus above it; both the mastoid and supramastoid crests are strong. A tegmen, or secondary roofing process, overhangs the auditory meatus. A post-glenoid process is absent. The internal wall of the glenoid fossa is formed by the plate of the temporal bone, not by an ento-mastoid process involving the sphenoid.

Not all of these or other characters distinguish East Asian *H. erectus* from modern *H. sapiens*, from other Pleistocene hominids, or from *Australopithecus*; they do, however, tend to bring the Chinese and Javanese specimens together and allow distinctions in detail from, for example, Broken Hill and, markedly, from Neanderthals as well as from moderns. By comparison, this description applies fairly fully to the Ngandong, the other Javanese, and the Chinese crania (as far as the state of material allows); and the differences that Weidenreich and others have been able to record among the three groups are minor. Let us note that Santa Luca, after a recent (1977) exhaustive comparison of details (though not by personal examination of the Sangiran specimens), is unwilling to recognize even subspecific differences after taking into account the time dimension (subspecies have a duration in time), and would assign all three groups to *H. erectus erectus*. Accepting a certain circularity of reasoning, this would reinforce a definition and description of *H. erectus* based on the collective sample involved.

In coming to the actual material in the light of the above definition, we shall consider only fossils contemporaneous with the East Asiatic samples or those having the same gross morphological characters as to heaviness and cranial capacities averaging 1,000 cc or above. Otherwise we invite too many problems for a coherent consideration of *H. erectus* as a species. Thus we accept all finds of the Middle Pleistocene plus those of the Lower Pleistocene that are not referred to *Homo habilis* or to australopithecine species. At the later end we exclude fossils except for purposes of discussion: it is not likely that any fossils now known to be of Upper Pleistocene derivation would be classed as *H. erectus*, either formally or informally.

For limits of the Middle Pleistocene, we may use the generally agreed dates (see Butzer and Isaac 1975) of the beginning of the last interglacial, about 125,000 years ago, as the termination, and the magnetic polarity reversal to the Brunhes normal, or about 700,000 years, as the beginning. We should take note, however, that the latter may eventually turn out to be somewhat unsuitable. Klein (1977), for example, with special reference to Southern Africa, would use a round one million years, and various gathering indications suggest that this limit might better include the span of dominance of *H. erectus*, as well as marking the disappearance of robust australopithecines in East Africa, whatever might be the merits of such a limit in geological or faunal terms. Writers are apt to allude to "late Lower or early Middle Pleistocene" rather indefinitely, and this interval of absolute time might, for the moment, be equated with that ambiguous zone until things become clearer, if they ever do. In any case, chronological placement of most of the fossils is still so uncertain that any date suggested here merely represents one or another current estimate, likely to be revised in the future as in the recent past; the allocations are (or the purposes of description and survey. The best that can be hoped for is some general idea of regional correlation and local chronological ordering.

RECENT DISCOVERIES

What is new, in the second half of the century, is (a) new finds, (b) a creeping re-expansion of formal taxonomy, and (c) a number of critical papers on general problems (as distinct from attempts purely at phylogenetic interpretation). We shall, of course, take account of all the material, with special attention to the newest, however the inventory that follows here is not meant to be absolutely complete, but rather suited to this survey and discussion. Details of enumeration and description may be found in the British Museum's "Catalogue of Fossil Hominids" and other special sources (e.g., Howell 1978, for Africa; Jacob 1975, for Indonesia).

The pattern of discovery to a degree continues that of the past. Java has gone on producing material at a familiar pace, while in Europe fossils have been sparse and fragmentary, with two spectacular exceptions (Petralona, Arago). India continues a blank; China has just begun to produce significant finds again. Africa has taken more of its rightful place. However, if one were to take Weidenreich or Boule as a standard, description has been rather slow, and even preparation, especially in the case of delicate specimens, has delayed full appreciation of some finds.

Indonesia

In spite of limited resources and manpower (compared, let us say, to East Africa), the Sangiran dome has continued as a source of fossils from both the Kabuh and Puchangan beds (with Trinil and Jetis fauna, respectively.) Through 1979, erosion sites in the various surrounding villages had produced this inventory as a probable count of individuals:

Calvarias or calottes (at least two with facial parts)	7
Fragmented skulls or parts	9
Mandibles, maxillae, and parts	6
Endocranial cast	1
Femoral fragments	2

These are in addition to the specimens assigned to *Meganthropus* and *Pithecanthropus dubius*. I owe all this and other information to the great kindness of Teuku Jacob (see Jacob 1975, and personal communication; also Oakley *et al.* 1975). We have, of course, the finds from outside Sangiran: Trinil 2 (the original calotte), Perning 1 (Modjokerto), and the important calvaria Sambungmachan 1 of 1973 (Jacob 1978b). Otherwise, localities outside the Sangiran dome have given nothing new, although two moderately fossilized femora, identifiable as *H. sapiens*, have been found at Trinil. Added to the four found by Dubois's collectors but only recognized in Leyden decades later, these would seem to support the doubts of Day and Molleson (1973) as to the actual contemporaneity of the first Trinil calotte and femur, and raise again the possibility of some redeposition at Trinil.

Stone implements, previously not known in association with any of the fossils (but see von Koenigswald and Ghosh 1972) were found near the Sambungmachan skull (Jacob *et al.* 1978) and also near one of the femora in the Sangiran area, in each case well down in the Kabuh beds, above the "Grenzbank" marking their lowest levels.

The Ngandong (Solo man) cranial and tibial fossils, found in the 1930s in the Notopuro beds above the Kabuh, were long believed (though on slight evidence) to be of very late date (Last Glacial). World War II upset all records of associations with the abundant faunal material; and the cultural material supposed to be that of the Solo people actually came from another site. After searches for other possible locations, a return to Ngandong (Jacob 1977) produced more animal fossils and parts of three more hominids (Ng 15-17) from the 24.5 meter terrace of the Solo River, but no cultural remains.

> The new cranial portions are entirely characteristic of the original sample. Morphologically the latter corresponds in general to *Homo erectus* defined for Chou-k'ou-tien, except for larger average size. Vault bones are wider and longer, but the sagittal profile is the same. The frontal is flatter, lacking a supratoral sulcus. The occipital crest is marked, with a triangular eminence at the midline.

Curtis has obtained a preliminary potassium-argon date (Lestrel 1976) of 310,000 ± 100% (no small range of possible error!), while allowing that the figure might quite well be greater, on the order of 500,000, so that the Ngandong group might eventually be placed well back in the Middle Pleistocene [2]. This would accord with Jacob's argument (1975, 1978c) for a continuity in the Javanese phylum: he believes that Sambungmachan and Sangiran 17 converge morphologically on the Ngandong sample and should be classed with it, eroding any distinction based on a time difference alone. This is a matter to take up later.

China

From 1928 until the disruption preceding World War II, Locality 1 at Chou-k'ou-tien produced remains of perhaps 48 individuals, represented by parts ranging from five moderately good calvarias down to single teeth, but in a good number of cases consisting of calvarial or mandibular parts of significance. Except for two teeth in Uppsala, the first recognized, all the material disappeared from view on December 8, 1941,

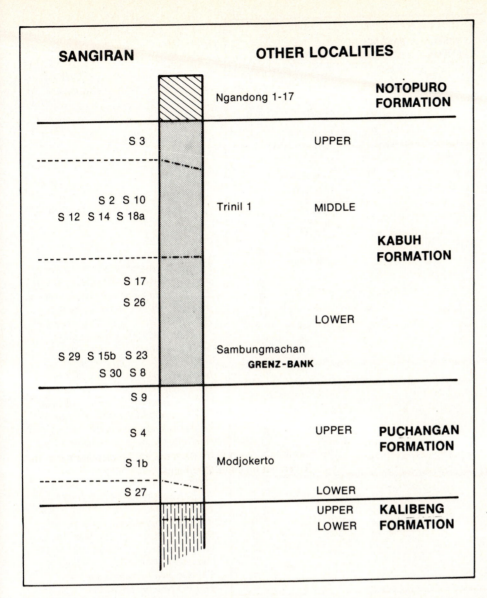

Figure 1. *Geological distribution of Javanese fossils, redrawn from Jacob (1978a). The original gives those found in the Sangiran area, a considerable part of the total number, but omits those recovered elsewhere. The Ngandong group is not meant to show a relative chronological position to scale.*

Within the figure:

SANGIRAN | **OTHER LOCALITIES**

Ngandong 1-17 — **NOTOPURO FORMATION**

S 3 — UPPER

S 2 S 10
S 12 S 14 S 18a — Trinil 1 — MIDDLE

KABUH FORMATION

S 17
S 26 — LOWER

S 29 S 15b S 23
S 30 S 8 — Sambungmachan — **GRENZ-BANK**

S 9

S 4 — UPPER — **PUCHANGAN FORMATION**

S 1b — Modjokerto

S 27 — LOWER

UPPER LOWER — **KALIBENG FORMATION**

as they were being removed from Peking by U.S. Marines in an attempt to forestall their capture by the Japanese.

These remains came from a number of different loci within Locality 1, the only locality out of some 15 in the lower cave complex, which has yet yielded human remains. Since resumption of intermittent work at Chou-k'ou-tien, the following parts have been found, also at different loci in the main deposit:

1949	three teeth from below Locus C.
1951-53	humeral and tibial diaphyses (not associated), two teeth.
1959	several parts of a mandible.
1966	most of a frontal; right half of an occipital (both this and the frontal part apparently having parietal parts attached); a premolar tooth.

The 1966 parts were mutually separated by distances of less than a meter, in a stratum identified as number 3 of the main deposit, though separated by a gap from Locus H of that deposit;

the stratum is believed to post-date the collapse of the cave roof here, and thus to be relatively late. Nevertheless, the parts proved to fit the left temporal-parietal-occipital, and the smaller temporal fragment, found by Weidenreich in Locus H and recorded by him as "Skull V." The whole is now known by this designation, and forms a respectable calvaria, with an estimated cranial capacity of 1,140 cc. The specimen is certainly large with, as restored, a glabello-occipital length of 213 mm and a biauricular breadth of 148.5 (Chiu *et al.* 1973).

The Chinese, using paleomagnetic methods, have placed the fossil-bearing levels of the deposit within the present Brunhes normal polarity phase, and thus aged less than 0.69 million years (Liu *et al.* 1977). Chinese scholars appear now to be using a date of 400,000 to 500,000 years. It should be remarked that all excavations to date at Locality 1 have removed not more than half of the main deposit, allowing hope of more hominid remains.

The finds from the Lan-t'ien localities are estimated by Ma *et al.* (1978) to be earlier. They consist of the 1963 mandible from Chen-chia-wo, dated at about 650,000, and the 1964 Gong-wang-ling cranium, at 750,000-800,000. The latter is

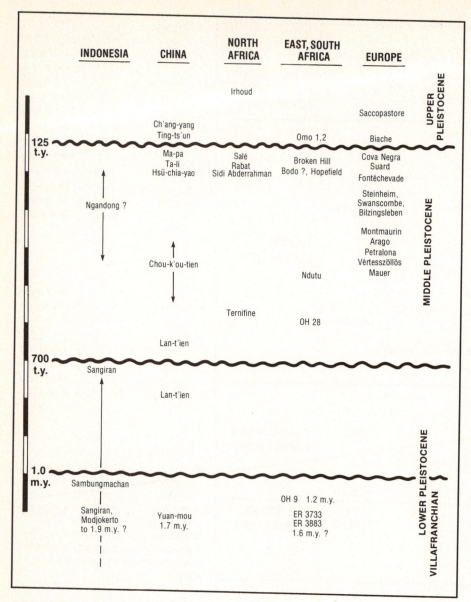

INDONESIA	CHINA	NORTH AFRICA	EAST, SOUTH AFRICA	EUROPE	
		Irhoud			UPPER PLEISTOCENE
				Saccopastore	
	Ch'ang-yang Ting-ts'un		Omo 1,2	Biache	
	Ma-pa Ta-li Hsü-chia-yao	Salé Rabat Sidi Abderrahman	Broken Hill Bodo ?, Hopefield	Cova Negra Suard Fontéchevade	
				Steinheim, Swanscombe, Bilzingsleben	MIDDLE PLEISTOCENE
Ngandong ?				Montmaurin Arago Petralona Vértesszöllös Mauer	
	Chou-k'ou-tien		Ndutu		
		Ternifine	OH 28		
	Lan-t'ien				
Sangiran					
	Lan-t'ien				
					LOWER PLEISTOCENE
Sambungmachan					
			OH 9 1.2 m.y.		VILLAFRANCHIAN
Sangiran, Modjokerto to 1.9 m.y. ?	Yuan-mou 1.7 m.y.		ER 3733 ER 3883 1.6 m.y. ?		

125 t.y.

700 t.y.

1.0 m.y.

Figure 2. *Approximate time chart of the major fossils mentioned in the text. This is meant for rough orientation for general reference (for example, to show the relative lateness of even the "early" Europeans), and is not intended to convey accurate dates. It cannot be too strongly emphasized how much uncertainty attaches to placement of all but a few of the fossils, absolutely or relatively, especially for the Middle Pleistocene. For example, Ndutu may be shown as considerably too early; Steinheim, Swanscombe and Bilzingsleben appear as a group, but their actual chronological order is not clear.*

The fossils of oldest date (more than 1.1 million years) are not shown in actual relative positions. Chinese names, as in the text, are uniformly in Wade-Giles orthography, not the current official one. For the current spelling of Chinese locality names, see the Editor's Note on page 370.

clearly more primitive in morphology than the Chou-k'ou-tien examples. The left upper incisors from Yuan-mou are considerably older, being placed by paleomagnetic dating at 1.7 million years (Li *et al.* 1977), an order of age equivalent to that of the oldest claimed for Java. The teeth are fairly robust, and thick labio-lingually at the base; shoveling is marked, and there is a slight central ridge on the lingual surface; wear is distinctly sloping in a labio-lingual direction, not edge-to-edge.

For later times, important new finds have now appeared in North China. A cranium found in 1978 near Ta-li, in the valley of the Lo River just west of the last bend of the Yellow River, in Shaanxi, is one of the best preserved hominid fossils, being damaged only by tooth loss and some upward compression of the maxilla. In preliminary descriptions (Wang *et al.* 1979) and in photos it presents a mosaic of archaic and progressive features, while conforming to the above definition of *Homo erectus* in almost none of them, The vault is very low, with bone thickness at least equal to the Peking sample and with an estimated capacity of 1,120 cc (sex is judged to be male); the sides are vertical, however, and there is no sagittal keeling. The

supraorbitals are heavy and slightly arched; viewed from above the contour is convex, with a slight notch at glabella.

The occiput is rounded in lateral profile, and such cresting as there may be appears to be low, with a downward-facing nuchal area. A projecting "bun" is conspicuously absent. The face is also incongruously progressive, being distinctly retracted under the vault and displaying a well-developed suborbital fossa. Breakage of the zygomata makes judgment of breadth difficult from photographs, but even with distortion allowed for, the face cannot have had a height comparable to Neanderthals or Broken Hill.

The find was made in level 3 of a formation of nine levels, suggesting a "warm and wet environment in the terminal part of the middle Pleistocene" (Wu and You 1979). Level 8 has given thermoluminenscence dates of 41,000 and 71,000; though this is well above the find level, precise age would seem to be indefinite. Another site, Hsü-chia-yao in Shaanxi, between Ta-li and Chou-k'ou-tien, is dated from fauna as late Middle Pleistocene, or late Rissian equivalent. Excavations in 1976 produced cranial parts of several individuals, differing in age and sex (Chia *et al.* 1979; Wei 1979). Morphology of the fragments would seem to represent the same population as the Ta-li cranium. The vault bones are very thick, but maximum breadth would have been placed higher than in the Peking fossils. The occipital torus was strongly developed in one specimen, but the occiput was less projecting (as in Ta-li). A juvenile maxilla is small and low, with reduced protrusion; again a resemblance to Ta-li. Teeth are large and robust, with wrinkled molar crowns; an isolated incisor is very strongly shovelled.

Chinese authorities interpret the fossils as transitional between Peking man and Neanderthals (or *Palaeanthropus*), also Ma-pa. From the apparent conformation, it is difficult to find likenesses elsewhere (see below): Ta-li contrasts radically with Neanderthals in the face, with Broken Hill in face and some aspects of vault, and with Ngandong in frontal and occiput. It is perhaps less unlike Petralona (although less projecting facially or occipitally) or Salé; however, all of this is preliminary only. One can, however, agree with the Chinese in taking account here of Ma-pa, which indeed suggests a gracile version of Ta-li, thinner and somewhat fuller in the vault with similarly arched supraorbitals and similar in transverse profile and vertical view. This South Chinese fossil has been placed as late Middle or early Upper Pleistocene (like those above) as has the Ch'ang-yang maxillary fragment. This last shows an orthognathous face and a well-developed nasal sill and definite nasal spine, also suggested in the Ta-li and Hsü-chia-yao specimens. Accordingly, all these fossils may be outlining a coherent population in China at the Middle-Upper Pleistocene boundary with a character of its own. At any rate, it seems unlikely that any one specimen could be morphologically removed from it.

Africa (Southern)

Broken Hill 1, found in 1921, was the first focus of attention, and latterly has been one of discussion as to whether it should be ranked as *Homo erectus* (Coon 1962) or as an African Neanderthal (e.g., Brose and Wolpoff 1971). Only since World War II has it been possible to suggest other Southern African finds as likely additions to this population (of course not forgetting the maxilla, Broken Hill 2, and the post-cranial bones). Such are the Cave of Hearths mandible (found in 1947) and the Hopefield calvaria (1953). The Bodo skull (1976) from the Awash Valley in Ethiopia probably extends the form well to the north and perhaps makes a better case for considering the Eyasi fragments of 1935-38 as candidates for inclusion.

From the nature of the material it is not easy to characterize the population with great confidence. The supraorbital torus is massive, convex forward in horizontal outline (unlike eastern *Homo erectus*), and the very large frontal sinuses extend well up into the frontal squama. The vault is relatively vertical-sided, with a sagittal elevation which is not a special formation as in *Homo erectus*. This describes Broken Hill 1; Hopefield seems to conform. The face of the former is high and projecting; but the Broken Hill 2 maxilla has a suborbital fossa, and is smaller altogether. The type skull has a pronounced occipital crest, again not as massive as in *H. erectus*, with the large nuchal area facing down and the smaller upper plate being vertical.

Long undated by any means, archaeological and faunal associations eventually led to estimating a late date for Broken Hill (45,000 to 35,000; see Oakley 1957) and to an Upper

Pleistocene assignment for Hopefield. Recent datings of the Middle Stone Age cultures, and of the Vaal-Cornelia faunal stage with which Hopefield is associated, have made it much more likely that both finds are later Middle Pleistocene, and possibly earlier still (Klein 1973). The associations for Bodo are "consistent with a Middle Pleistocene age" (Conroy *et al.* 1978). This new specimen is striking for its massiveness, with a heavy malar and a facial breadth (158 mm) comparable to that of the large, Ngandong-like Sangiran 17 ("*Pithecanthropus* VIII"). In other characters, such as the form, thickness, and breadth of the supraorbital torus, Bodo resembles Broken Hill, as it does in having a modest prominence of the nasalia. In the innocent days of forty years ago it was sometimes suggested that Broken Hill was a case of glandular aberration; the massive Bodo specimen puts that idea to rest.

Africa (Northwest)

Middle Pleistocene recoveries in Algerian and Moroccan coastal sites have been mostly mandibular, the exception being the Salé partial vault and lower face. They range in estimated age from late Middle Pleistocene back to the still uncertain age of the important Ternifine ("*Atlanthropus*") remains, which are associated with an Early Acheulian industry but of which the age can only be called relatively early in the Middle Pleistocene. The finds, with their years of discovery, and in probable order of increasing age, are as follows:

Salé (1971):	ca. 160,000 (Jaeger 1976) (or Anfatian? Jaeger 1975).
Rabat (1933):	mandible plus fragments. More than 200,000 m.y.a. Tensiftian, = Penultimate glacial phase, or Rissian equivalent.
Thomas Quarries mandible (1969) and cranial parts (1972):	Tensiftian.
Sidi Abderrahman (1955) mandibular parts:	Early Tensiftian.
Ternifine (1954-5): three mandibles plus parietal.	Amirian?

There is some agreement among workers (see Howell 1978) to regard all these as *H. erectus* in character ("pithecanthropoid" among French students), while also seeing the latest, especially Rabat and Salé, as showing some non-modern *sapiens* traits, although the low Salé vault is estimated to have a cranial volume of only 930 to 960 cc (Jaeger 1976). All this valuable but difficult and meager material has been reported by a number of authors, in some cases several times. Whether an intensive review by a single scholar would give a clearer picture remains to be seen.

East Africa

This region came into prominence only 20 years ago, with the establishment of the presence of *Australopithecus* (sensu lato)

as well as of hominids which represent the probable local emergence of *Homo* (as *H. habilis*?). These include fossils of *H. erectus* of both Middle and Lower Pleistocene date, regardless of how the limit between these time periods is set.

The Bodo cranium from Ethiopia, described above with the Southern African grouping used, has been presumed to be of later Middle Pleistocene age, but its associations are quite unclear and it may be older. A mandible from the Kapthurin beds, Baringo, Kenya, is also probably upper Middle Pleistocene, and appears to resemble the less evolved specimens from Morocco such as Sidi Abderrahman, according to Howell, who says "it reveals some important divergences from *Homo erectus.*"

The remaining material is distinctly earlier. The 1973 Ndutu cranium from Tanzania (Mturi 1976; Clark 1976), a fairly well-preserved specimen, is placed at between 400,000 and 600,000 years, being perhaps generally contemporaneous with the Peking population, to which it bears resemblances. The vault is thick, with apparently prominent supraorbitals (these are damaged) but with a rather vertical frontal, giving rise to a supratoral sulcus behind them. The occipital torus is also thick. On the other hand, there is less robusticity of muscle markings on the occiput, with less of an angle in profile, and without extension of the supramastoid crest over the auditory meatus. The sides of the vault are more vertical and no sagittal torus is evident. Somewhat older are the innominate bone and femoral shaft of OH 28 from upper Bed IV at Olduvai. These bones are massive, especially if, as the wide sciatic notch suggests, the individual was female. The innominate is thick, with a massive iliac pillar; it suggests a lack of some of the stress-resisting refinements reached in modern innominates.

Also from Bed IV, probably comparable in age to OH 28 (700,000 years or less?) is the incomplete and fragmentary cranium of OH 12. This and the good calotte of OH 9, from upper Bed II (at about 1.2 million years, well into the Lower Pleistocene), have recently been described by Rightmire (1979a). The latter has the robusticity and size of Asian *H. erectus*; the cranial capacity has been estimated by Holloway at 1,067 cc. While the character in general also resembles *H. erectus* as defined, there are differences. The supraorbital torus, though heavy, has an indentation and depression in the region of glabella. There is no frontal crest. The occipital torus is only moderately developed toward the midline and fades out laterally before the superior line joins a strong mastoid crest. A post-glenoid process, unlike the Chinese fossils, is well-developed, and there may be other differences in the temporal region.

Probably of the same age (Westphal *et al.* 1979) is the Melka Kontouré parietal bone from the Gomboré II site and level, on the Awash River, Ethiopia; it is considered by the finders (Chavaillon *et al.* 1974; Chavaillon and Coppens 1975) and by Howell (1978) to be *Homo erectus*, from its very limited curvature and simplicity of markings. [A robust distal humerus from Gomboré IB is much older, about 1.5 million years (Chavaillon *et al.* 1977). It is classed as *Homo*, possibly *erectus* according to Coppens (1978), though even having *H. sapiens sapiens* aspects, since it can be compared with the corresponding parts of humeri attributed to robust australopithecines. But we should not attempt to consider postcranial materials at this time level.]

The 1970s saw the appearance of rich material from Koobi Fora, Lake Turkana (East Rudolph), at the hands of Richard Leakey and co-workers—a real embarrassment of riches which at the moment defies simple interpretation. Since it represents more than one species or evolutionary stage, there is no consensus as to how it should be sorted out; however, allocation by date and site may be found in Walker and Leakey (1978), and judgment as to species (*H. habilis* versus *H. erectus*) is given in Howell (1978). The nub of the matter is the appearance of at least two convincing cranial specimens of *H. erectus*, ER 3733 and ER 3883 (along with much other material so assigned by Howell), of which ER 3733 is conservatively dated at 1.5 million years, and thus contemporaneous in East Africa not only with the robust australopithecine but perhaps with *H. habilis* as well. This skull has been diagnosed as *H. erectus* by Leakey and Walker (1976) because of its specific similarity of form to the Peking crania. It is smaller and less robust than OH 9 (having an estimated capacity of 830 cc). However, Rightmire (1979a) finds the two to be similar in many features, various of which constitute departures from the Peking type of *H. erectus*. These include the form of the supraorbital torus; details of the occipital, including lesser emphasis of a nuchal crest, lack of a frontal crest and a sagittal torus; features and form of the temporal region, etc. The points of similarity allow the suggestion of a persistence, with little change, of a population of *H. erectus* grade from about 1.5 million years up to, and apparently into, the Middle Pleistocene. If the Ndutu cranium reflects a progressive version of this form, as is possible, the continuity extends to contemporaneity with the population of Chou-k'ou-tien, over a total span of a million years.

Europe

This region stands in contrast to Africa in the lesser antiquity and number of its fossil finds. It remains poor in Middle Pleistocene specimens, and wanting in those from the Lower Pleistocene. The continent was, of course, subjected to climatic insults not experienced by Africa; nevertheless, there were long periods of climate warmer than today's, and there appear to be as many finds associated with colder phases as with warmer. Much of the dating remains indefinite or approximate and has lately been subject to some important revisions. The following list, comprising almost all but the most meager fragments, gives a probable temporal ordering as understood at present.

Penultimate Glacial phase:
  La Chaise, Suard Cave 1949-): various cranial, mandibular and post-cranial parts or fragments
  Le Lazaret (1964): parietal plus two teeth
  Cova Negra (1933): parietal
  Atapuerca (1976): two mandibles, other fragments
  Fontéchevade (1947): calotte, frontal fragment
Great Interglacial:
  Azykh (1968): mandible, Azerbaijan, USSR
  Steinheim (1933): cranium
  Swanscombe (1935-55): vault bones
  Bilzingsleben (1972-): cranial fragments

Antepenultimate Glacial phase:

    Montmaurin (1949): mandible

    Arago (1964-): anterior cranium plus parietal, mandibles, innominate

    Petralona (1960): cranium

    Vértesszöllös (1965): occipital, two teeth

Antepenultimate Interglacial:

    Mauer (1908): mandible

The outstanding specimens have been the Arago collection and the excellent Petralona skull, now cleaned of encrustation but not yet described in this state. Not included above are some individuals represented by teeth alone, or other fragments. Also omitted is the Prezletice molar fragment, evidently that of a bear (Vlcek 1978a).

Among the mandibles, M.-A. de Lumley (1976, 1978) finds a certain homogeneity in the group of Mauer, Arago, Atapuerca, Montmaurin and Azykh. The last, like Montmaurin, has a low but very robust body (Roginskij and Levin 1978). These authors cite H. de Lumley as also finding many features in the Azykh jaw shared with the Arago mandibles. These early specimens are separable from Neanderthals, lacking the postmolar gap before the ascending ramus, which in the Neanderthals reflects the projecting face and dentition. As to crania, Piveteau (1976) finds the Suard parts to be more progressive than those of the Peking population and, especially in specific details of the temporal and occipital, to be suggestive of the Neanderthals. They are not lacking, however, in *erectus*-like features as well, in the enlarged pyramid and reduced squama and mastoid. He and Mme. de Lumley (1969; M.-A. de Lumley 1978) place the Lazaret parietal as more advanced than the Ternifine specimen, though low in height but vertical-sided; it contrasts sharply with the parietals of Cova Negra and Fontéchevade, which exhibit a rounded transverse contour adumbrating the Neanderthal. In general, they and other French authors have dwelt on the morphological variety of later Middle Pleistocene fossils, to the point of entertaining the possibility (though evidently not with conviction) of different populations leading separately to Neanderthal and anatomically modern lines, respectively. This same feeling formerly attached to the more complete earlier, and longer known fossils: Fontéchevade, Steinheim and Swanscombe, which once were proposed as early "pre-sapiens" forms in the direct ancestry of modern man. Subsequent analysis (e.g., Stringer 1974; Trinkaus 1973) has placed these closer to "classic" Neanderthals, and thus as acceptable "pre-neanderthals." The important thing here is that these later Middle Pleistocene fossils cannot be fitted by any definition of *Homo erectus*. However, the apparently contemporaneous Bilzingsleben occipital and frontal parts appear much more primitive, and Vlcek (e.g. 1978b) feels that they correspond closely to the same parts of the OH 9 cranium from Olduvai. The supraorbital and frontal toral fragments are in fact persuasive in this respect. But see below.

The still earlier crania or parts thereof (Arago, according to the de Lumley's latest datings; Petralona; Vértesszöllös) are not at the moment interpreted in uniform fashion; however, all are taken to express a level of morphology more evolved than typical *H. erectus*. Arago has been seen by the de Lumleys as having some early Neanderthal traits, though the facial form

lacks the definite character of the group. Petralona has a massive face and brow ridges and lacks any distinctive Neanderthal (sensu stricto) traits; nonetheless, Stringer *et al.* (1979) find that it has affinities with Arago, Vértesszöllös and Bilzingsleben, and perhaps with Steinheim and Swanscombe, and in this way affording a population possibly ancestral to later European hominids and verging on a *Homo sapiens* grade. More succinctly, Petralona has been referred to as an advanced *H. erectus*, perhaps out of ambivalence. As to Vértesszöllös, Thoma from the beginning (1966) has classed it as borderline *H. sapiens*, partly from the inference of a large brain based on the relatively high squama of the occipital. There has ensued a running argument between Thoma and Wolpoff (1971 and later). The latter advocates assignment to *H. erectus* but also disputes the whole possibility of more than one lineage existing at the time in question, as a return to a "pre-sapiens" doctrine. The argument has broadened examination of the Vértesszöllös fossil, but it serves mainly as a good example of the difficulty of interpretation of intermediate forms, especially from incomplete pieces, and perhaps of the futility of aiming at a precise and simple nomenclatural and taxonomic framework, at least at present.

Going on from all the above, Howell (1981; idea first raised in 1960) and Stringer (1980) have concluded that in fact *Homo erectus* cannot be recognized in Europe at all. The three crania just discussed all suggest a beginning relative increase in cranial capacity; and all have some common aspects in spite of the size difference between Petralona and Arago. It is true that the younger Bilzingsleben specimen (now dated by thorium-uranium isotopes to 228,000 years by Harmon *et al.* 1980) is *erectus*-like in the parts recovered, but this is also true of these parts in Vértesszöllös and Petralona; and the latter in its other parts is distinctly less like basic *H. erectus*. Hence, Stringer holds, Bilzingsleben is perhaps not a good argument for a *Homo erectus* generally co-eval with Swanscombe and Steinheim. The mandibles likewise, Howell and Stringer believe, show common features from Mauer to Arago, which features Howell sees as distinctions from eastern *H. erectus*, Stringer apparently agreeing in essence. The upshot is their suggestion that the first hominid arrivals in Europe had already gone beyond a *Homo erectus* grade, and that if representatives of the latter are found in the future they will prove to be earlier in date.

Such might well be forthcoming. Possible crude tools from Chilhac in the Auvergne are estimated to be 1.8 million years old (Guth 1974), equivalent to the oldest in East Turkana or Olduvai by the latest dating (Butzer 1978), if a little younger than those from the Omo. Some other early industries are reported, as at Vallonet (0.95 million years?, H. de Lumley 1976), at La Roche Lambert, again in the Massif Central, where the fauna has a "middle Villafranchian aspect," and at El Aculadero in Spain (for these two, see Bordes and Thibault 1977).

Almost no useful postcranial parts have come to light. A late iliac piece from the Grotte du Prince, found in 1968, is Neanderthal-like (M.-A. de Lumley 1976). The 1978 innominate from Arago, though not of particularly large size, is remarkably thick, doubtless like *H. erectus* in this; the de Lumleys (1979) suggest that the slightly oval form of the acetabulum implies a degree of mobility somewhat limited compared to that in modern man.

In summary, the situation as to material of, or relating to, *H. erectus* is as follows. In Asia there have been three major samplings—little else—which in a detailed way exhibit a certain common character that can be defined and that can be used as a definition for *H. erectus*: dates are Lower and early Middle Pleistocene, except for the later (?) Ngandong. In Africa, dates are even more extensive in their range, with the fossils also more widely dispersed though at present not equally copious with the Far Eastern. In Europe the specimens are not only late but relatively scrappy; and the earliest, even including Mauer, may be later than the Chou-k'ou-tien population, which renders the conclusion of Howell and Stringer—absence from Europe of *H. erectus*—less surprising though not less interesting.

If this is the case, the next question relates to how comprehensive we may accept the species *Homo erectus* as having been, in time and space. We should remember that the Ngandong population can hardly be classed as other than *H. erectus* (past views to the contrary); and unless all estimates of its age are seriously in error, it continued into the late Middle Pleistocene as a contemporary of many of the populations of which specimens have been reviewed above. However, for the time range of one million to 500,000 years ago, we know at present of no hominids anywhere that were not of a grade represented by *H. erectus*, whether this means they were morphologically all one species or not.

RECENT INTERPRETATIONS

The recognition 30 years ago of two species only, *H. sapiens* and *H. erectus*, and the elimination of much previously existing nomenclature may have induced a sense of simple dichotomy among Middle and Upper Pleistocene hominids. This in turn may have been influencing the expression of ideas in subtle ways: phylogenetic interpretations and, especially, attempts at formal taxonomy. The latter may exercise its own influences on thinking and writing, especially among those not primarily engaged in problems of paleoanthropology (Howells 1981). I must emphasize that the main authors cited below are in the very forefront of work on the materials and are fully aware of the complexities involved. Their nomenclature may be in mutual disagreement, but for the correct purpose of expressing their individual ideas of phylogenetic arrangements.

Taxonomic nomenclature

Primarily by way of exemplification of taxonomic revision in deleting older genera and species, Campbell (1965) noted that the following would be appropriate nomina for subspecies of *Homo erectus*. The specimens, or the previous names, are in most cases self-evident.

Homo erectus erectus
Homo erectus modjokertensis
Homo erectus pekinensis
Homo erectus capensis [3]
Homo erectus habilis [3]
Homo erectus leakeyi
Homo erectus mauritanicus (Ternifine)

Homo erectus heidelbergensis

The following have also been nominated as subspecies:

Homo erectus ngandongensis (Sartono 1975)
Homo erectus yuanmouensis (Li *et al.* 1977)
Homo erectus bilzingslebenensis (Vlcek 1978b)
Homo erectus tautavelensis (de Lumley and de Lumley 1979)

There may be others besides these twelve; and it is obvious that further possible specimens or groups might have been given equal treatment. We need not dally with details. My point here is that, taken together, these taxa suggest to the unwary a kind of equality of status—a universality of the species *H. erectus* in time and space. In this way they may tend to inhibit examination of the major and minor differences or groupings among the fossils [4]. Of course, this has not happened in the minds of the workers themselves. Campbell, for example, immediately followed his 1965 list of appropriate names with a tabulation of geographical and chronological positions—i.e., of evolutionary grades among the various subspecies of a given region.

In meeting the dilemma of accommodating both time and geography, such grades have been the recourse of many recent writers, from Tobias and von Koenigswald (1964) to Stringer *et al.* (1979), particularly in the attempt to make bridges between *Homo erectus* and *H. sapiens*. This is doubtless the major problem of later Pleistocene hominids. In this vexatious matter, there is the clear disagreement between Howell and Stringer on the one hand, who would deny the presence of *H. erectus* in Europe (as known from present material) and, on the other hand, any investigator who would accept the three European subspecies of *H. erectus* listed above.

As to *Homo sapiens*, available definitions apply to anatomically modern man (usually designated *H. sapiens sapiens*), but definitions hardly exist in any case, except for the brief one given earlier and a detailed and explicit one by Howell (1978). Mention should be made of Coon (1962) who, although he discussed a number of cranial characters in terms of their modern variation, actually separated *H. sapiens* and *H. erectus* fossils by a few traits of vault form and tooth and brain size, which put the threshold well below anatomical moderns alone. Others have agreed that *H. sapiens* should indeed include a number of specimens or populations that were not anatomically modern but that for various reasons (brain size, loss of *erectus* occipital or temporal traits) could hardly be included in *H. erectus*. They are usually given the slightly evasive appellation of "archaic" *H. sapiens*, and in fact seem to be accepted as such simply on the basis of not being *H. erectus*. In formal nomenclature the subspecies [5] that have most commonly been named in recent years (e.g., Campbell 1963) are the following:

Homo sapiens sapiens
Homo sapiens neanderthalensis
Homo sapiens rhodesiensis
Homo sapiens soloensis

The last three populations have been muzzily called "Neanderthals" for some time, but this usage is rejected by leading students today. There are questions relating to each of the same three taxa, which will be noted later. This applies especially to *H. s. soloensis*, since it would remove the Ngandong fossils from *H. erectus*, which by common consent of the moment would be their proper assignment (e.g., Santa Luca 1977; Jacob 1978c). The problem with the other two is the built-in implication that all three descend from some common ancestral subspecies of *Homo sapiens*.

Phylogenetic problems

These were addressed in somewhat similar fashion and in authoritative detail twenty years ago by Howell (1960), in what seems like the distant past in view of the new finds. As ever, the several aspects of these problems are so interrelated that a tidy treatment is difficult. There has been considerable writing in the last few years addressed to pattern and theory: the pace and nature of differentiation across space and of change over time. Students on the whole have been chary of comprehensive, systematic schemes, such as Coons (1962) major effort in this direction for which, as with Howell, much important present information was then lacking.

Differentiation within *Homo erectus*

The successor forms named just above as subspecies of *H. sapiens* are seen today by those who have recently studied them closely as quite distinct from one another. This degree of differentiation has not been remarked for the populations of *H. erectus*, at least in a systematic way; comparison of one with another has been made as to common or different cranial traits, but not so as to suggest general regional patterns (again, it would hardly be a reliable exercise in view of the state of the material). Such regional differentiation should be expected a priori, given the presence of *Homo* in East Asia and Africa by 1.5 million years ago. (In fact, one of the most surprising things in the discovery of ER 3733 is similarity of its appearance to the Chou-k'ou-tien specimens, thousands of miles away and a million years younger). Also, archaeology lends some support to the presumption. Movius (1944) discerned a separation of two long-enduring traditions of stone-working techniques: the Acheulian handaxe/cleaver complex of Africa and Europe, and the chopper/chopping-tool complex of Asia east of India. This distinction is now seen to be less absolute, with the finding of bifacial tools in East Asia on material which is suitable; nevertheless, that region has not revealed the profusion of handaxes found in many African sites. Dealing with actual fossils, Stewart (1970) compared mandibles of east and west (Sangiran 1, or Mandible B of the Puchangan beds and a Peking jaw versus Mauer and Ternifine mandible III), finding contrasts in certain features expressing body breadth in the anterior portion. In the first pair breadth is less between the mental foramina and also at the base; the western pair is thought by Stewart to foreshadow Neanderthals in those respects. Howell, on the other hand, in his earlier review (1960), paying more attention to teeth, found Ternifine to be close to the Peking specimens, and thus distinguished between a European and an Afro-Asian lineage in the early Middle Pleistocene. Other attempts at interregion comparisons have been less systematic, consisting mainly of pointing out some distinctions, as those between early African crania and classic *H. erectus* (e.g., Rightmire 1979a).

Evolutionary change

In each region students have been gathering the fossils into possible groups showing an evolutionary succession. Those concerned with Java (Jacob 1975, 1979; von Koenigswald 1975; Sartono 1975) have no trouble pointing out such changes from Puchangan to Notopuro levels. Jacob believes the robust and primitive form represented by Sangiran 4 (*Pithecanthropus* IV of 1939) gave rise to two lines, the more gracile "Trinil" form and a contemporary and later line from Sambungmachan (and Sangiran 17, or *Pithecanthropus* VIII) to the Ngandong population. But there are no signs of this complex having led to *H. sapiens*, and Jacob (1976) points out the crucial nature of the gap between Ngandong and the first representative of anatomical moderns. At the moment, there is the appearance of an evolutionary dead end. Movius (1978) has also drawn attention to the apparent stagnation of the chopper-chopping tool complex until fairly recent times, which in this case would carry over into the period of occupation by recent man.

As to Locality 1 in China, the duration of occupation here is not known, but Chinese scholars feel that the newest cranial find, of 1966, which is also from a level high in the whole deposit, may be more progressive than the average of the other specimens (Howells 1977). It remains to be examined whether the new finds, perhaps 300,000 years younger, of Ta-li and Hsü-chia-yao, with which Ma-pa may be included, are actually to be viewed as lineal descendents of the Chou-k'ou-tien population. They are not at first look recognizable as such: progressive as to face and some other traits, they recall *Homo erectus*, in vault thickness, brain and tooth size, to a greater degree than their presumed contemporaries in Europe or Africa.

For Africa a principal recent student has been Rightmire, who in a series of papers has taken cognizance of materials from the early Turkana specimens of *H. erectus* to present populations. In his latest survey (1980) of Middle Pleistocene fossils, detailed comparison leads him to conclude that in spite of obvious differences, especially robustness, ER 3733 and OH 9 have common features disallowing their taxonomic separation. (The earliest North African specimens, which are actually much later, cannot usefully be compared, since they are mandibles and the East African are calvaria). Later skulls, Salé and Ndutu, are different, verging on *H. sapiens*. This species, at its archaic level, takes in Broken Hill, etc., together with Florisbad and the early Upper Pleistocene Omo skulls from the Kibish Formation. Thus he accepts two groups, one clearly *H. erectus*, and one *H. sapiens*, although he is not claiming that this grouping is established or obvious, only that it cannot be ruled out. The persisting features are such that, in Africa, a transition from *Homo erectus* to *Homo sapiens* should be accepted, taking place in a region not determined as yet. Elsewhere (1976) he suggests (as does Howell 1978) that these archaic specimens are properly included in *H. s. rhodesiensis*. This implies a specifically African evolutionary sequence, separate from those in other regions [6]. Others (e.g., Saban 1977) have proposed a further independent lineage for Northwest Africa, culminating in the Upper Pleistocene Jebel Irhoud crania. Howell, in fact, places the latter in *H. s. neanderthalensis* (1978); Piveteau (1967), however, questions any affiliation of them with European Neanderthals, and Hublin and Tillier (1981) find that the juvenile mandible will not allow for a Neanderthal facial projection.

Students of European remains (Stringer *et al.*, the de Lumleys, Piveteau) agree in perceiving evolutionary change, specifically in a direction toward the Neanderthals, whether or not they agree as to whether the early specimens should be *H. erectus* or *H. sapiens*. The French, in particular the de Lumleys, have in fact simply been using the term "ante-neanderthals" for the whole series, without even implying anything more than precedence in time. They also stress (M.-A. de Lumley 1978; Piveteau 1967) that great variation or polymorphism characterizes the morphology of these earlier populations, such that if the two Arago mandibles had been found at different levels they might have been assigned to two different human lines (comment of H. de Lumley-see Boné *et al.* 1978, p. 182). As we have seen, this reflects the earlier idea of two distinct populations, pre-sapiens and pre-neanderthal, although present opinion in the same quarters has relinquished that idea. In any event the variation, Piveteau has noted, contrasts with the homogeneity displayed by the Neanderthals later on. And toward the end of the Middle Pleistocene, Neanderthal characters appear in such specimens as Fontéchevade, Cova Negra and the Suard remains, becoming patent in the Biache skull (Vandermeersch 1978a), probably early in the Last Interglacial, and progressively more evident through that phase.

To look back for an instant to the question of regional differentiation, it seems clear that (unless the Ngandong series is still grossly misdated) a marked difference in general degree of evolutionary development existed between Java and western Europe toward the end of the Middle Pleistocene, while there are beginning to be signs of well-marked four-way morphological differences between Europe, Africa, China and Java.

Pace of change in *Homo erectus*

The above suggests that change was leisurely for most of the Middle Pleistocene, as it was earlier, when compared to late times. But this is a relative statement. It was clearly slow in the Far East. Africa is hard to evaluate in these terms. If European fossils first appear at a more advanced level of development (Howell, Stringer), subsequent change was not rapid there.

Rightmire has attempted (1981a) to make a gross quantitative statement by measuring the regression of certain characters on time. For a time span from over 1.5 million years (ER 3733, Puchangan fossils of Java) to the later Middle Pleistocene, he incorporated such specimens as could usefully be measured. He found definite trends toward increased brain volume (perhaps barely significant statistically) and toward decreased biauricular (i.e., basal) cranial breadth. Trends toward decreased lower first molar size and mandibular robusticity were barely discernible, and were fluctuating. He suggests that this indicates there was little systematic change over time in the *H. erectus* skull followed by a short pulse of evolution late in the Middle Pleistocene. If this later transition was indeed rapid, he points out, continuities between specific *H. erectus* populations and later ones will be obscured and difficult to identify, which is an important point in our present ignorance of such transitions.

Patterns of transition to *Homo sapiens*

This is the fundamental query, the disappearance of *H. erectus* by the end of the Middle Pleistocene, and the rise of "archaic *Homo sapiens.*" The many hypotheses offered fall into three general kinds of approach determined in part by data and theory available. They have not usually been rigorous in distinguishing between "archaic *H. sapiens*" and anatomically modern man; it is the former that must be considered here.

The first approach is a gradualist or uniformist interpretation, associated with the names of Weidenreich (1946) and Coon (1962). These scholars proposed an early differentiation among regional populations of *H. erectus*, essentially into subspecies that evolved locally and independently (Coon) into five daughter subspecies of *Homo sapiens*, leading to racial divisions of the present day. Other writers adhering to this school have interposed a "Neanderthal phase" (Hrdlicka 1927; see Howells 1976 for a review) to recognize what has been called archaic *H. sapiens* herein. This general view, that all major populations of *H. erectus* led eventually to the modern populations of the same region, is not now in high favor. It might seem that those writers who allow an evolution into *H. s. neanderthalensis* in Europe (e.g., Stringer, 1980) plus another into *H. s. rhodesiensis* in Africa (e.g., Rightmire 1976, 1981b) plus a possible third into the Irhoud population of Morocco, are likewise suggesting independent evolution of subspecies of *H. erectus* into subspecies of *H. sapiens*, the idea for which Coon was berated. I do not think so. The confusion is terminological only: what the writers are actually saying is that different populations of *H. erectus* had divergent Upper Pleistocene descendants, not that all eventuated in anatomically modern races.

A second approach even allows, as a logical possibility, that no population of *H. erectus* was ancestral to *H. sapiens*. This is the rigorous application of cladistic analysis (Tattersall and Eldredge 1977; Delson *et al.* 1977; Olson 1978), which imposes as one condition that a taxon with discernible derived or autapomorphic characters cannot be taken as ancestral to another in which they are not present. This would revive Leakey's (1966) hypothesis that *H. sapiens* arose directly from *H. habilis*, having the "primitive" character of a high round braincase, with the derived low and heavy braincase of *Homo erectus* putting that species on a side branch of the cladogram. This is only a suggestion, not an essential part of the approach, which is addressed to providing more testable models for phylogenetic schemes and which is likely to be more widely used in future.

The third approach is simply pragmatic, and shares more with the idea of "punctuated equilibria" (Eldredge and Gould 1972). Without understanding the processes by which the robust cranial character of *H. erectus* appeared (from a probable gracile australopithecine source) and then disintegrated in later hominids (Weidenreich 1941), it would accept that some, but not necessarily all, populations of *H. erectus* had Upper Pleistocene issue. It allows for different rates of evolution in different main populations, and for some competitive replacement of one by another as speeding the establishment of progressive forms (see Pilbeam 1975).

The Lesson of the Neanderthals

Perhaps a clearer feeling for the meaning of some of the above problems may be had by concentrating on a concrete event. This is the case of the Neanderthals, for whom the fossils are comparatively so ample. It is now clear that, from the Last Interglacial to their rather abrupt disappearance in the late Last Glacial, the Neanderthals exhibited a common physique and a unique cranial pattern (Trinkaus and Howells 1979), having in addition certain cranial details seen in all specimens examined and in no other hominids except sporadically in ante-neanderthals (Santa Luca 1978; Hublin 1978). This marks their presence in Western Europe, western Asia and the Near East, and not elsewhere: contemporary North Africans like Jebel Irhoud are excluded. This homogeneous and individual morphology had a period of stasis or equilibrium verging on 100,000 years. As noted above, its antecedents were apparently such forms as Mauer and Petralona, in whom some writers perceive Neanderthal-like traits, that continued through more evidently Neanderthal-like but highly varied specimens of somewhat later date. The pattern seems to have jelled in the beginning of the Upper Pleistocene, for reasons quite unknown (cold adaptation is an argument difficult to sustain in view of the interglacial date), and perhaps in Europe itself (Vandermeersch 1978b).

The meaning for *H. erectus* is as follows. We have this one fairly clear case of a *H. erectus* successor evolving in a major tract over several hundred millennia. It gives some evidence of the pace of evolution, and perhaps of the kind of "pulse" of rapid change suggested by Rightmire, leading to a more homogeneous and static form. Rightmire proposes (1981b) a similar event for emergence of the Rhodesian man population, which is reasonable in the light of the Neanderthals. The latter, from the weight of present evidence, are unlikely to have been directly ancestral to anatomically modern populations. (As Stringer et al. say, this ancestry would be ruled out if Neanderthals exhibit clearly autapomorphic traits—unique specializations—such as seem to have been identified in recent studies).

This gives us a window for viewing the much more meager remains of other latest Middle Pleistocene human populations. For the African one provisionally grouped around the Broken Hill fossils as *H. s. rhodesiensis*, the evidence scarcely allows us to make judgments. It might have been a source, or the source, of anatomical moderns. It does not appear to present clearly autapomorphic characters like those of the Neanderthals, but the sample size is so very small as to leave the matter in the balance. (If it should include Ndutu and the very robust Bodo specimen, things are still more difficult.)

The same can be said about the still more restricted sample of supposedly contemporary Chinese fossils. It has not so far been recognized as a subspecies of *H. sapiens*, but the situation appears parallel. With the above Africans it shares a similar level of archaism, clearly above that of *H. erectus*. Otherwise it differs from them in most of its main characters but at the same time exhibits, in preliminary publication, no autapomorphic features. We could not now say whether it might be an appropriate source for anatomical moderns. We must wait to see, as dates become ever firmer, whether such actual moderns as Omo 1 or the Border Cave individuals (Rightmire, 1981b) were not treading on the heels of the above two populations.

Matters Remaining

Progress during the 1970s has been very considerable, not as to finds alone but especially as to dating. If many dates are far from exact, at least some formerly baffling fixations have been relaxed, and enough satisfying estimates have been made to give greater coherence to general discussions. And as we have seen, both practical re-evaluation of materials and theoretical attempts to improve evolutionary models for hominids have had obvious effects. Major specific problems still face us. One is the relations between early *Homo* populations in Africa and Asia at

ages of over a million years. Another is the arrival of anatomically modern *H. sapiens*. This is not the subject of this review; nevertheless it does oblige us to consider again the derivation of the "archaics," remembering what this further implies as to evolution within *H. erectus*.

This inevitably brings up again the awkwardness of formal nomenclature as problems get precise. Careful naming is important in stating opinions as to morphology and phylogeny, but is it a good tool for opening up the broadest questions considered above? Or does it tend to blur what we are trying to think about?

Does it help, for example, to say that *H. sapiens* evolved from *H. erectus*? On its face this seems all too obvious [7], if it simply means that Upper Pleistocene men descended in some manner from those of the Middle Pleistocene—who else? Then perhaps we should say so. We should ask what is in the mind of a particular writer when he makes the first statement. An overall gradualism? or more local phenomena? Does he mean *Homo sapiens neanderthalensis* from *Homo erectus heidelbergensis*? For example, Stringer (1980) observes that Petralona gives evidence that *Homo sapiens* (including here Neanderthals) was derived from at least one geographic variant of the species *Homo erectus*. That is much more specific; and he also says that the importance of Petralona is not in its classification as *H. sapiens* or *H. erectus* but rather in its showing a mosaic of traits of the two. This would testify to a gradual local evolution between the two. Here we are back at a central point of this whole discussion: the familiar problem in anagenetic series, in which there is no clear line of division, and in which some forms are called "transitional" when they fall between previously perceived stages. This may or may not be just. In the hominid case it may be: there may turn out to be greater variation among the "transitional" or "archaic *H. sapiens*" forms of the late Middle Pleistocene than within the earlier, frankly *H. erectus* populations on the one hand or recent man on the other. The situation is getting so complex that it might be wise to suspend close concern with formal names in some phylogenetic discussions.

For example, in *Homo sapiens* three subspecies (at least, and neglecting the new Chinese finds) have currency: *H. sapiens sapiens*, *H. s. neanderthalensis*, and *H. s. rhodesiensis*. They appear to be constituting assertions about the late history of *H. erectus*, for which we now lack a basis. If all three of those named independently progressed beyond a *H. erectus* level, they are sister species, not subspecies of *H. sapiens*. If, however, *H. s. sapiens* and *H. s. neanderthalensis* had a common post-*erectus* ancestor in such a group as that once known as "pre-neanderthal" or "progressive" (perhaps as *H. s. steinheimensis*?) then all three named in this sentence are proper subspecies (Mayr 1951). But then what about *H. s. rhodesiensis* as a member of this set of subspecies? It can be, and is being, argued that the fossils under this name represent an independent African line of development out of *H. erectus*, in fact one for which at the present time there are fewer obstacles than for Europe as a direct ancestor for moderns. The same may come to be said for the new Chinese fossils from Ta-li and Hsü-chia-yao. Thus a European "pre-neanderthal" ancestor for all of *H. s. sapiens*, or for any, may be illusory, an accident of the history of fossil recovery.

So we might be wise to be continually careful in writing about *Homo erectus*, making clear whether one is referring to a population or taxon with a workable definition (such as might embrace all the Chou-k'ou-tien and Javanese fossils), or to a grade taken broadly, or to a time zone (Campbell 1972). The history of argument about the "Neanderthal phase" should show what the problems may be. As to subspecies of *H. erectus*, these are of course legitimate and what we should look for; we should expect their development and their survival over considerable periods. There is no reason to suppose that *H. erectus* as a species did not include all hominids for a long interval. But the bestowing of names, like having a child, carries responsibilities. To be too liberal with subspecific names, even awarding them to single specimens (e.g., *H. e. leakeyi*), rather than to recognizable populations, is both to injure their use and to confuse the search for real lineages.

ACKNOWLEDGEMENTS

I have been generously helped with information and comment by K. C. Chang, Eric Delson, Teuku Jacob, Richard Klein, Philip Rightmire, Christopher Stringer and Erik Trinkaus, who are of course blameless for anything said here.

This paper has been intended as a survey of the state of information, not as a compendium. Discussion is meant to be general, without attempting to evaluate or reconcile the opinions of others as to dates, morphology or taxonomic names. Another paper, dealing more broadly with problems, and complementary to this one, was presented at the Davidson Black Symposium in Toronto in 1976 (herein referenced as Howells 1981), and should appear in the publication this year. S. M. Stanley's *Macroevolution* (1979) makes the case for rapid local branching speciation (which produces major change but is hard to detect in the fossil record) as a major source of evolutionary change (see punctuated equilibria above). This should figure in future discussion.

NOTES

[1] He did not follow this up, and in fact declared his intentions of continuing to use the prevailing generic and other names simply as labels.

[2] To toy with morphological dating, Lestrel and Read (1973) computed regression estimates of brain size on time, getting in this way an estimate for the Ngandong group of 265,000 years; Lestrel later (1976) revised the regressions and got a Ngandong age of something between 463,000 and 790,000.

[3] Transferred as subspecies to *Australopithecus africanus* in Campbell (1972), who in this and other writings on phylogeny is more specific about his ideas as to the actual structure of *Homo erectus*.

[4] cf. Stringer *et al.* (1979), who also point out that subspecies terms are most appropriately used geographically, and advocate numbered grades within *Homo sapiens* as the least ambiguous approach to relationships within a region, in this case Europe.

[5] There have been others, e.g., *H. s. steinheimensis*, in addition of course to Linnaeus's varieties. Howell (1978), following Wells (1969), puts various early but anatomically modern African specimens into *Homo sapiens afer*, probably the only considered use of one of Linnaeus's subspecies in recent times. Howell also refers, without discussion, to *H. s. sapiens*. It might be well to mention a certain confusion in the use of *H. s. sapiens*. It is now quite generally applied to all living populations, but Campbell (e.g., 1963) indicates that, if more than one subspecies of living humanity is to be recognized, then *H. s. sapiens* properly refers, following Linnaeus, to Caucasoids although Linnaeus also designated these as *H. s. europaeus*). Thus "*H. s. sapiens*" might appear in two different sets of subspecies, one composed exclusively of different living subspecies, the other subsuming all of them as *H. s. sapiens* as against other, fossil subspecies.

[6] Such a view is certainly fortified by the freshly reported skull (L.H. 18) from the Ngaloba beds at Laetolil (Day, M. Leakey and Magori, 1980, who share this view). The date is estimated at 120,000 ± 30,000 years. The skull appears clearly to be a robust and archaic *H. sapiens sapiens*, somewhat like Omo 2 in presenting a mixture of modern and archaic traits. It is thick, with an estimated capacity of 1,200 cc. The supraorbital torus is large (by modern standards) but divided: the frontal is receding; the vault is vertical-sided with definite parietal bosses; the occipital is rounded, with a low inion; the face is vertical and generally modern, evidently quite broad, and with alveolar prognathism.

[7] Which is not necessarily so. LeGros Clark (1955, 1964) observed that, while reasonable and consistent with the evidence available, it was to be accepted as "not very much more than a working hypothesis." And Howell very recently (1978) does not go beyond "most, if not all, students consider it likely that *H. erectus* gave rise to *H. sapiens*."

REFERENCES

Boné, E., Coppens, Y., Genet-Varcin, E., Grassé, P. P., Heim, J.-L., Howells, W. W., Hürzeler, J., Krukoff, S., de Lumley, H., de Lumley, M.-A., Piveteau, J., Saban, R., Thoma, A., Tobias, P. V., and Vandermeersch, B. 1978. *Les Origines Humaines et les Époques de l'-Intelligence. Colloque International Organisé par la Fondation Singer-Polignac,* June 1977. Masson, Paris.

Brace, C. L. 1980. Australian tooth-size clines and the death of a stereotype. *Curr. Anthropol.* 21:141-164.

Bordes, F., and Thibault, C. 1977. Thoughts on the initial adaptation of hominids to European glacial conditions. *Q. Res.* 8:115-127.

Brose, D. S., and Wolpoff, M. H. 1971. Early upper Paleolithic man and late paleolithic tools. *Am. Anthropol.* 73:1156-1194.

Butzer, K. W. 1978. Climate patterns in an un-glaciated continent. *Geog. Mag.* (London) 51:201-208.

Butzer, K. W., and Isaac, G. Ll., Eds. 1975. *After the Australopithecines: Stratigraphy, Ecology, and Culture Change in the Middle Pleistocene.* Mouton, The Hague.

Campbell, B. 1963. Quantitative taxonomy and human evolution, in: *Classification and Human Evolution* (S. L. Washburn, Ed.), pp. 50-74, Aldine, Chicago.

Campbell, B. 1965. The nomenclature of the Hominidae including a definitive list of hominid taxa. *R. Anthropol. Inst.,* Occ. Paper No. 22.

Campbell, B. 1972. Conceptual progress in physical anthropology: Fossil man. *Annu. Rev. Anthropol.* 1:27-54.

Chavaillon, J., Brahimi, C., and Coppens, Y. 1974. Première découverte d'hominidé dans l'un des sites acheuléens de Melka Kunturé (Éthiopie). *C. R. Acad. Sci.* 278:3299-3302.

Chavaillon, J., Chavaillon, N., Coppens, Y., and Senut, B. 1977. Presence d'hominidé dans le site oldowayen de Gomboré I à Melka Kunturé, Éthiopie. *C. R. Acad. Sci.* 285:961-963.

Chavaillon, J., and Coppens, Y. 1975. Découverte d'hominidé dans un site acheuleen de Melka Kunture (Ethiopie). *Bull. Mem. Soc. Anthropol. Paris* 2:125-128.

Chia Lan-po, Wei Qi, and Li Chao-rong 1979. Report on the excavation of Hsuchiayao man site in 1976. *Vert. PalAs.* 17:277-293.

Chiu Chung-lang, Ku Yu-min, Chang Yin-yun, and Chang Sen-shui 1973. Peking man fossils and cultural remains newly discovered at Choukoutien. *Vert. PalAs.* 11/2:109-131.

Clark, R. H. 1976. New cranium of *Homo erectus* from Lake Ndutu, Tanzania. *Nature* 262:485-487.

Conroy, G. C., Jolly, C. J., Cramer, D. and Kalb, J. E. 1978. Newly discovered fossil hominid skull from the Afar depression, Ethiopia. *Nature* 276:67-70.

Coon, C. S. 1962. *The Origin of Races*. Knopf, New York.

Coppens, Y. 1978. Les hominidés de Pliocene et du Pléistocène d'Ethiopie: Chronologie, systématique, environment, in: *Les Origines Humaines et les Époques de l'Intelligence* (Boné, É., *et al.*, Eds.), pp. 79-106, Masson, Paris.

Day, M. H., and Molleson, T. I. 1973. The Trinil femora, in: *Human Evolution* (M. H. Day, Ed.), pp. 127-154, Taylor and Francis, London.

Day, M. H., Leakey, M. D., and Magori, C. 1980. A new hominid fossil skull (L. H. 18) from the Ngaloba beds, Laetoli, northern Tanzania. *Nature* 284:55-56.

Delson, E., Eldredge, N., and Tattersall, I. 1977. Reconstruction of hominid phylogeny: A testable framework based on cladistic analysis. *J. Hum. Evol.* 6:263-278.

Eldredge, N., and Gould, S. J. 1972. Punctuated equilibria: An alternative to phyletic gradualism, in: *Models in Paleobiology* (J. M. Schopf, Ed.), pp. 82-115, W. H. Freeman, San Francisco.

Garn, S. M. 1965. *Human Races*. 2nd ed. C. C. Thomas, Springfield, Illinois.

Guth, C. 1974. Découverte dans le Villafranchien d'Augergne de galets aménagés. *C. R. Acad. Sci.* 279:1071-1073.

Harmon, R. S., Glazek, J. and Nowak, K. 1980. 230$_{Th}$/234$_{U}$ dating of travertine from the Bilzingsleben archaeological site. *Nature* 284:132-135.

Hiernaux, J. 1965. Ontogénèse des différences interpopulationelles en proportions corporelles: quelques processus observés. *Bull. Mem. Soc. Anthropol. Paris*, XIe series, 7:451-459.

Howell, F. C. 1960. European and Northwest African Middle Pleistocene hominids. *Curr. Anthropol.* 1:195-232.

Howell, F. C. 1981. Some Views of *Homo erectus* with special reference to its occurrence in Europe, in: *Homo erectus: Papers in honor of Davidson Black* (B. A. Sigmon and J. S. Cybulski, Eds.), pp. 153-157, University of Toronto Press, Toronto.

Howell, F. C. 1978. Hominidae, in: *Evolution of African Mammals* (V. J. Maglio and H. S. B. Cooke, Eds.), pp. 154-248, Harvard University Press, Cambridge, MA.

Howells, W. W. 1973. *Cranial Variation in Man. A Study by Multivariate Analysis*. Peabody Museum Papers, Vol. 67. Peabody Museum, Cambridge, MA.

Howells, W. W. 1976. Explaining modern man: evolutionists versus migrationists. *J. Hum. Evol.* 5:477-495.

Howells, W. W. 1977. Hominid fossils, in: *Paleoanthropology in the People's Republic of China* (W. W. Howells and P. Tsuchitani, Eds.), National Academy of Sciences, CSCPRC Rpt. No. 4, Washington, D.C.

Howells, W. W. 1981. *Homo erectus* in human descent: ideas and problems, in: *Homo erectus: Papers in Honor of Davidson Black* (B. A. Sigmon and J. S. Cybulski, Eds.), pp. 153-157, University of Toronto Press, Toronto.

Hrdlicka A. 1927. The Neanderthal phase of man. *J. R. Anthropol. Inst.* 57:249-274.

Hublin, J.-J. 1978. Quelques caractères apomorphes du crâne néandertalien et leur interprétation phylogénique. *C. R. Acad. Sci.* 287:923-926.

Hublin, J. J., and Tillier, A. M. 1981. The Mousterian juvenile mandible from Irhoud (Morocco): A phylogenetic interpretation, in: *Aspects of Human Evolution* (C. B. Stringer, Ed.), pp. 167-185, Taylor and Francis, London.

Jacob, T. 1975. Morphology and paleoecology of early man in Java, in: *Paleoanthropology, Morphology and Paleoecology* (R. H. Tuttle, Ed.), pp. 311-326, Mouton, The Hague.

Jacob, T. 1976. Early populations in the Indonesian region, in: *The Origin of the Australians* (R. L. Kirk and A. G. Thorne, Eds.), pp. 81-93, Australian Institute of Aboriginal Studies, Canberra.

Jacob, T. 1977. *New Ngandong Finds from Java, Indonesia*, Paper presented at 48th ANZAAS Congress, Melbourne.

Jacob, T. 1978a. *Pithecanthropus* of Indonesia: The phenotype, genetics and ecology, in: *Current Argument on Early Man* (L. -K. Konigsson, Ed.), Proceedings of Nobel Symposium, 41, Karlskoga, Sweden, May, 1978.

Jacob, T. 1978b. The Fossil Skull Cap from Sambungmachan and Its Implications to Human Evolution. Paper presented at Xth International Congress of Anthropological and Ethnological Sciences, December, New Delhi.

Jacob, T. 1978c. The puzzle of Solo man. *Mod. Q. Res. Southeast Asia* 4:31-40.

Jacob, T. 1979. Hominine evolution in South East Asia. *Arch. Phys. Anthropol. Oceania* 14:1-10.

Jacob, T., Soejono, R. P., Freeman, L. G., and Brown, F. H. 1978. Stone tools from mid-Pleistocene sediments in Java. *Science* 202:885-887,

Jaeger, J. J. 1975. Découverte d'un crâne d'hominidé dans le Pléistocène moyen du Maroc, in: *Problemes actuels de Paléontologie—Evolution des Vertébrés*. International Symposium of C.N.R.S. No. 218, pp. 897-902.

Jaeger, J. J. 1976. *Les Hominidés d'Afrique du Nord*. Paper presented at IX International Congress of Prehistoric and Protohistoric Sciences, Nice, September, 1976.

Klein, R. G. 1973. Geological antiquity of Rhodesian man. *Nature* 244:311-312.

Klein, R. G. 1977. The ecology of early man in Southern Africa. *Science* 197:115-126.

von Koenigswald, G. H. R. 1975. Early man in Java: Catalogue and problems, in: *Paleoanthropology, Morphology and Paleoecology* (R.H. Tuttle, Ed.), pp. 303-310, Mouton, The Hague.

von Koenigswald, G. H. R., and Ghosh, A. K. 1972. Stone implements from the Trinil beds of Sangiran, Central Java. *Proc. Konink. Neder. Akad. Weten.*, Ser. B. 76:1-34.

Larnach, S. L. 1978. Australian aboriginal craniology. *Oceania Monogr.* No. 21. University of Sydney, Sydney.

Leakey, L. S. B. 1966. *Homo habilis, Homo erectus* and the australopithecines. *Nature* 209:1279-1281.

Leakey, R. E. F. and Walker, A. C. 1976. *Australopithecus, Homo erectus* and the single species hypothesis. *Nature* 261:572-574.

Le Gros Clark, W. E. 1955. *The Fossil Evidence for Human Evolution*. University of Chicago Press, Chicago. 1st Ed.

Le Gros Clark, W. E. 1964. *The Fossil Evidence for Human Evolution*. University of Chicago Press, Chicago. 2nd Ed.

Lestrel, P. E. 1976. Hominid brain size *versus* time: Revised regression estimates. *J. Hum. Evol.* 5:207-212.

Lestrel, P. E., and Read, D. W. 1973. Hominid cranial capacity *versus* time: A regression approach. *J. Hum. Evol.* 2:405-411.

Li Pu, Chien Fang, Ma Hsing-hua, Pu Ching-yu, Hsing Li-sheng, and Chu Shih-chiang. 1977. Preliminary study on the age of Yuanmou man by paleomagnetic technique. *Sci. Sinica* 20:645-664.

Liu Chun, Zhu Xiangyuan, and Ye Sujuan. 1977. A paleomagnetic study on the cave-deposits of Zhoukoudian (Choukoutien), the locality of *Sinanthropus*. *Sci. Geol. Sin.* 1:25-33 (in Chinese: English abstract).

de Lumley, H. 1976. Les premières industries humaines en Provence. *La Préhistoire Française*, Vol. l/2, pp. 765-776. Éditions du CNRS, Paris.

de Lumley, M.-A. 1976. Les Anténéandertaliens dans le sud. *La Préhistoire Française*, Vol. I/1, pp. 547-560. Éditions du CNRS, Paris.

de Lumley, M.-A. 1978. Les Anténéanderthaliens, in: *Les Origines Humaines et les Époques de l'Intelligence* (É. Boné, *et al.*, Eds.), pp. 159-182, Masson, Paris.

de Lumley, H., and de Lumley, M.-A. 1979. L'homme de Tautavel. *Doss. Arch.* 36:54-59.

de Lumley, M.-A., and Piveteau, J. 1969. Les restes humains de la grotte du Lazaret (Nice, Alpes-Maritimes). *Mem. Soc. Préhist. Franc.* 7:223-232.

Ma Xinghua, Qian Fang, Li Pu, and Ju Shiqiang 1978. Paleomagnetic dating of Lantian man. *Vert. PalAs.* 16:238-243 (In Chinese).

Mayr, E. 1951. Taxonomic categories in fossil hominids. *Cold Spring Harbor Symp. Quant. Biol.* 15:109-117.

Movius, H. L., Jr. 1944. Early man and Pleistocene stratigraphy in southern and eastern Asia. *Peabody Mus. Papers*, Vol. 29, No. 3.

Movius, H. L. Jr. 1978. Southern and eastern Asia: Conclusions, in: *Early Paleolithic in South and East Asia* (F. Ikawa-Smith, Ed.), pp. 351-355, Mouton, The Hague.

Mturi, A. A. 1976. New hominid from Lake Ndutu, Tanzania. *Nature* 262:484-485.

Oakley, K. P. 1957. The dating of the Broken Hill, Florisbad and Saldanha skulls. *Third Pan Afr. Cong. Prehist.* 1955:76-79.

Oakley, K. P., Campbell, B. G., and Molleson, T. I. 1975. *Catalogue of Fossil Hominids. Part III. Americas, Asia, Australia.* British Museum (Natural History), London.

Olson, T. R. 1978. Hominid phylogenetics and the existence of *Homo* in Member I of the Swartkrans formation, South Africa. *J. Hum. Evol.* 7:159-178.

Pilbeam, D. 1975. Middle Pleistocene hominids, in: *After the Australopithecines* (K. W. Butzer and G. Ll. Isaac, Eds.), pp. 809-856, Mouton, The Hague.

Piveteau, J. 1967. Un pariétal humain de la grotte du Lazaret (Alpes-Maritimes). *Ann. Paleontol.* 53:165-199.

Piveteau, J. 1976. Les anténéandertaliens du sud-ouest. *La Préhistoire Française*, Vol. I/1, pp. 561-566. Editions du CNRS, Paris.

Rightmire, G. P. 1976. Relationships of Middle and Upper Pleistocene hominids from sub-Saharan Africa. *Nature* 260:238-240.

Rightmire, G. P. 1979a. Cranial remains of *Homo erectus* from Beds II and IV, Olduvai Gorge, Tanzania. *Am. J. Phys. Anthropol.* 51:99-116.

Rightmire, G. P. 1979b. Implications of Border Cave skeletal remains for later Pleistocene human evolution. *Curr. Anthropol.* 20:23-35.

Rightmire, G. P. 1980. *Homo erectus* and human evolution in the African Middle Pleistocene. *Am. J. Phys. Anthropol.* 53:225-241.

Rightmire, G. P. 1981a. Patterns in the evolution of *Homo erectus*. *Paleobiology* 7:241-246.

Rightmire, G. P. 1981b. Later Pleistocene hominids of eastern and southern Africa. *Anthropologie* 19:15-26.

Roginskij, Ya Ya. and Levin, M. G. 1978. *Anthropology*. Vyasaha Shkola, Moscow (in Russian).

Saban, R. 1977. The place of Rabat man (Kébibat, Morocco) in human evolution. *Curr. Anthropol.* 18:518-524.

Santa Luca, A. P. 1977. *A Comparative Study of the Ngandong Fossil Hominids*. Doctoral Dissertation, Harvard University.

Santa Luca, A. P. 1978. A re-examination of presumed Neanderthal-like fossils. *J. Hum. Evol.* 7:619-636.

Sartono, S. 1975. Implications arising from *Pithecanthropus* VIII, in: *Paleoanthropology, Morphology and Paleoecology*. (R. H. Tuttle, Ed.), pp. 327-360, Mouton, The Hague.

Schultz, A. H. 1963. Age changes, sex differences, and variability as factors in the classification of Primates, in: *Classification and Human Evolution*, (S. L. Washburn, Ed.), pp. 85-115, Aldine, Chicago.

Stanley, S. M. 1979. *Macroevolution: Pattern and Process*. W. H. Freeman, San Francisco.

Stewart, T. D. 1970. The evolution of man in Asia as seen in the lower jaw. *Proc. 8th Int. Cong. Anthropol. Eth. Sci.* 1:263-266.

Stringer, C. B. 1974. Population relationships of later Pleistocene hominids: A multivariate study of available crania. *J. Archeol. Sci.* 1:317-342.

Stringer, C. B. 1980. The phylogenetic position of the Petralona cranium. *Anthropos.* 7:81-95.

Stringer, C. B., Howell, F. C., and Melentis, J. K. 1979. The significance of the fossil hominid skull from Petralona. Greece. *J. Archeol. Sci.* 6:235-253.

Tattersall, I. and Eldredge, N. 1977. Fact, theory, and fantasy in human paleontology. *Am Sci.* 65:204-211.

Thoma, A. 1966. L'occipital du l'homme mindélien de Vértesszöllös. *L'Anthropologie* 70:495-534.

Tobias, P. V., and von Koenigswald, G. H. R. 1964. A comparison between the Olduvai hominines and those of Java and some implications for hominid phylogeny. *Nature* 204:515-518.

Trinkaus, E. 1973. A reconsideration of the Fontéchevade fossils. *Am. J. Phys. Anthropol.* 39:25-35.

Trinkaus, E., and Howells, W. W. 1979. The Neanderthals. *Sci. Am.* 241:94-105.

Turner, C. G. II 1979. Sinodonty and sundadonty: a dental anthropological view of Mongoloid microevolution, origin, and dispersal into the Pacific Basin, Siberia and the Americas. Paper presented at XIV Pacific Science Congress, Khabarovsk, USSR, August, 1979.

Vandermeersch, B. 1978a. Le crâne pre-wurmien de Biache-Saint-Vaast (Pas de Calais), in: *Les Origines Humaines et les Époques du l'-Intelligence* (É. Boné, *et al.*, Eds.), pp. 153-157, Masson, Paris.

Vandermeersch, B. 1978b. Quelques aspects du problème de l'origine du l'homme moderne, in: *Les Origines Humaines et les Epoques du l'-Intelligence* (É. Boné, *et al*, Eds.), pp. 251-260, Masson, Paris.

Vlcek, E. 1978a. Diagnosis of a fragment of the "hominid molar" from Prezletice, Czechoslovakia. *Curr. Anthropol.* 19:145-146.

Vlcek, E. 1978b. A new discovery of *Homo erectus* in Central Europe. *J. Hum. Evol.* 7:239-251.

Walker, A., and Leakey, R. E. F. 1978. The hominids of East Turkana. *Sci. Am.* 239:54-66.

Wang Yung-shin, Hsëh Hsiang-hsi, Yüeh Lo-p'ing, Chao Chü-fa and Liu Shun-t'ang 1979. Discovery and preliminary study of the Dali man fossil from Shensi. *Sci. Bull.* (Ke-hsueh T'ung-pao), 1979:303-306 (in Chinese).

Wei Chi 1979. Ricerca dei discendenti dell'uomo di Pechino. *Min. Med.* 70:2723-2728.

Weidenreich, F. 1940. Some problems dealing with ancient man. *Am. Anthropol.* 42:375-383.

Weidenreich, F. 1941. The brain and its role in the phylogenetic transformation of the human skull. *Trans. Am. Phil. Soc.* 31:321-442.

Weidenreich, F. 1943. The skull of *Sinanthropus pekinensis*. *Palaeo. Sin.* n.s. D, no. 10, whole ser. no. 127. Peiping.

Weidenreich, F. 1946. *Apes, Giants and Man*. University of Chicago Press, Chicago.

Wells, L. H. 1969. *Homo sapiens afer*: content and earliest representatives. *S. Afr. Archaeol. Bull.* 24:172-173.

Westphal, M., Chavaillon, J., and Jaeger J.-J. 1979. Magnétostratigraphie des dépôts pléistocènes du Melka-Kunturé (Ethiopie): premieres donnes. *Bull. Soc. Geol. du France* 21:237-241.

Wolpoff, M. H. 1971. Vértesszöllös and the Presapiens theory. *Am. J. Phys. Anthropol.* 35:209-216.

Wu Xin-zhi, and Yu-zhu You. 1979. A preliminary observation of Dali man site. *Vert. PalAs.* 17:294-303.

Editor's Note: The correct spelling of the Chinese hominid localities in this chapter following the current *pinyin* system of orthography is as follows:

Ch'ang-yang = Changyang	Chen-chia-wo = Chenjiawo
Chou-k'ou-tien = Zhoukoudian	Gong-wang-ling = Gongwangling
Hsü-chia-yao = Xujiayao	Lan-t'ien = Lantian
Ma-pa = Maba	Ta-li = Dali
Ting-ts'un = Dincun	Yuan-mou = Yuanmou

These spellings also apply to the Chinese localities discussed in Chapter 37, pages 381-385, and in a few instances to subsequent chapters as well.

36

Peking Man

Wu Rukang and Lin Shenglong

One of the sites with the longest history of habitation by man or his ancestors is a cave near the railroad station in Zhoukoudian, a town some 50 kilometers southwest of Beijing. Whereas modern cities are generally no more than a few thousand years old, the cave at Zhoukoudian was occupied almost continuously for more than 200,000 years. The multiple layers of fossil-bearing deposits indicate that early men first took shelter in the cave 460,000 years ago, and the last of them did not abandon the site until 230,000 years ago, when they were forced out by the filling of the cave with rubble and sediment. The species of mankind that lived there is classified as *Homo erectus pekinensis* or Peking man. (The name became established before the customary English spelling of the city was changed to Beijing.)

The long record of habitation at Zhoukoudian offers an opportunity to trace the development of a single community over a period that spans a significant fraction of the evolution of the genus *Homo*. The period is long enough for progressive changes in the form of the fossils themselves to be discerned; one of the important changes in physical features is an increase in cranial capacity. Equally important, it is possible to reconstruct certain events in the cultural evolution of the species. There is evidence in the cave deposits that Peking man was able to control fire and that he employed it for cooking. The fossilized remains of animal bones indicate that the Zhoukoudian cave dwellers were effective hunters of both large and small game; fossilized seeds suggest another component of the diet. An abundance of flaked-stone implements provides information on toolmaking skills. From an analysis of the materials recovered from the cave it is even possible to speculate on the social organization of the community. For example, there is information to support conjectures about the sharing of food and the division of labor between the sexes.

In the past five years a comprehensive investigation of the Zhoukoudian site has been undertaken by more than 120 Chinese scientists, including us. The work is sponsored by the Institute of Vertebrate Paleontology and Paleoanthropology of the Chinese Academy of Sciences, and the contributors represent 17 universities and research institutions. Their fields of expertise range from early man and his artifacts to the study of ancient climate, caves and the terrains in which they form, ancient soils, pollen and the dating of archaeological materials. Here we shall present the salient findings of the group and attempt to sketch a portrait of Peking man in his native environment.

In the overall scheme of higher primate evolution Peking man and the other examples of *Homo erectus* are a compara-tively late development. The first hominoid, the ancestor of both man and the anthropoid apes, had branched off from the other primates by about 35 million years ago. It walked quad-rupedally and relied on seeds and fruits for its food. From 10 to eight million years ago the first hominid, the founder of a genetic lineage whose only living representative is modern man, diverged from the other hominoids such as the chimpan-zee and the gorilla. The most primitive hominids apparently had a small cranium, with a capacity of perhaps 350 cubic cen-timeters; they could walk on their hind limbs and may have been able to carry objects while walking. It was not until about four million years ago that an advanced hominid, classified in the genus *Australopithecus*, appeared. The earliest remains of australopithecines have been found in the middle Awash River valley of Ethiopia. The skeleton was evidently capable of sup-porting a fully bipedal gait and the brain case had a capacity close to 500 cubic centimeters.

In the past 100 years many fossils of manlike skulls and skeletal fragments more advanced than those of *Australopithecus* have been found in Europe, Asia and Africa. For a time almost every discovery gave rise to a new taxonomic division, but virtually all these later specimens have now been subsumed in the single species *Homo erectus*. On the basis of chronological studies of the geologic context in which the fossils were found it has been ascertained that the species emerged at least 1.5 million years ago. *Homo erectus* could walk upright, as the species name suggests, but his skull was still very primitive, with a cranial capacity ranging from 850 to 1,100 cubic centimeters. He was able to make more advanced stone implements than the pebble tools of earlier hominids. Some later specimens of *Homo erectus*, including Peking man, developed a quite elaborate culture characterized by the inhabit-ing of caves and the hunting of game. They were also able to make use of fire to cook food, although it is not yet clear whether they were actually able to kindle a fire.

The subsequent course of development from *Homo erectus* to modern man cannot be traced in detail. Suffice it to say that about 200,000 years ago there appeared a form of man with a less heavily built face and a larger brain case than those of *Homo erectus*. The members of this species, early representatives of *Homo sapiens*, came to flourish in Europe, Asia and Africa somewhat less than 100,000 years ago. They were capable of building shelters in the open air and of starting a fire, and they made highly refined stone tools. Because of the closeness of their morphology to that of modern man and the progressiveness of their culture, they are considered to be among the direct ancestors of the modern *Homo sapiens*.

THE CAVE OF ZHOUKOUDIAN

The cave in Zhoukoudian where the remains of Peking man have been found is in a limestone formation called Dragon-Bone Hill. Before it was known as a site of early man it had long been a favorite haunt of dragon-bone collectors. Dragons had an important place in traditional Chinese culture, and their bones (actually the fossils of various mammals) were thought to have great medicinal value. Indeed, it was the dragon-bone collectors who found the first evidence of Peking man, although they did not recognize its significance.

At the beginning of the 20th century a number of paleontologists and anthropologists visited Zhoukoudian in search of evidence of primitive man. Notable among them were J. G.

Anderson, a Swedish geologist, and Walter W. Granger, a paleontologist of the American Museum of Natural History. On a routine survey of Dragon-Bone Hill in 1921 Anderson, Granger and O. Zdansky, an Austrian paleontologist working as Anderson's assistant, were directed by local residents to a cave that was said to be "full of dragon bones." Nothing of interest was found, however, except some quartz fragments; because the fragments were far from their geologic context, Anderson considered them artifacts of early man.

Although survey excavations were undertaken in the cave, the progress of discovery was slow. In 1923 Zdansky found two anthropomorphic teeth. When a systematic excavation was started in 1927, Birger Böhlin, a Swedish paleontologist, discovered a well-preserved lower molar. Davidson Black, who was then professor of anatomy at Peking Union Medical College, assigned the fossil to the new species *Sinanthropus pekinensis*. From 1927 to 1937, when worked was stopped by the

Figure 1. *Limestone cave was inhabited by Peking man, a variety of* Homo erectus, *beginning 460,000 years ago and continuing until 230,000 years ago. The cave was discovered in the early 1920's. Excavations over the past 50 years and more have revealed evidence of the use of fire, an assemblage of 100,000 stone artifacts, fossilized bones and teeth of more than 40 individuals and fossil remains of animal and plant species that were presumably part of Peking man's diet. The photograph shows the east entry to the cave, which was the primary entrance in the first phase of Peking man's occupation. The entry was abandoned after a massive collapse of some 300,000 years ago.*

Japanese invasion of China, the cave was continuously excavated. Pei Wenzhong, who was in charge of the Zhoukoudian excavation from 1928 through 1935, found the first complete cranium in the winter of 1929, thereby providing a sound basis for scientific studies of Peking man.

Since the founding of the People's Republic of China in 1949 the excavation of the cave has been resumed by the Institute of Vertebrate Paleontology and Paleoanthropology. Up to 1966 fossils of more than 40 males and females of various ages had been found associated with tens of thousands of stone artifacts and evidence of fire use. In addition the fossils of two species of plants (and pollen of many more species) and 96 kinds of mammals were found. The abundance of the fossils and the thoroughness with which they have been studied make it possible to reconstruct elements of Peking man's 200,000-year history.

The cave, called formally Zhoukoudian Locality I, is a huge karst cave in a limestone structure formed in the Ordovician period, about half a billion years ago. Karst landscape, which takes its name from that of a region along the Dalmatian coast of Yugoslavia, is formed by the work of underground water on massive soluble limestones. The karst cave inhabited by Peking man is 140 meters long from east to west. The widest part, which measures 40 meters, is at the eastern end; the narrowest part, at the western end, is only a little more than two meters wide.

The original cave, however, was not like this, nor was it habitable at the outset for Peking man. The formation of the cavern inside the hill began in the Pliocene epoch, about five million years ago, when water percolating along both horizontal and vertical cracks dissolved the limestone and carried it away in solution. The horizontal erosion created a long cave with both ends narrower than the central part; the vertical erosion followed precipitous fissures, creating funnel-shaped gullies whose bottom was deep, rough and bumpy. The original cave was a hollow in Dragon-Bone Hill without openings to the surface. Owing to the continual scouring of the hill by the ancient Zhoukou River, however, a spur on the eastern slope of the hill was cut off early in the Pleistocene epoch, exposing the eastern wall of the cave to water erosion. As a result the eastern slope developed a diagonal fissure approximately at the present-day location of the small east entry to the cave. The fissure became progressively wider and in the end established a connection between the Zhoukou River and the cave. Sand and dirt carried by the river were washed into the cave, gradually leveling the uneven bottom and creating a spacious, flat floor. It was at this point that Peking man took up residence.

At first Peking man made his entrance from the east and lived mainly in the eastern section. About 350,000 years ago, however, there was a massive cave-in in the part of the eastern section now called the Dove Hall. An enormous amount of eroded rock fell from the roof, blocking the east entry completely. Peking man had to abandon what had been the most spacious part of the cave, but he was able to enter the cave again through

Figure 2. *Site of the cave is the small town of Zhoukoudian, some 50 kilometers southwest of Beijing* (right). *It is administratively subordinate to Fangshan, a suburban county of Beijing about 150 kilometers from the seacoast* (left) *In the northwestern part of the town is Dragon-Bone Hill, named for the mammalian fossils collected there by local residents, who thought they were dragon bones of great medicinal value. Zhoukoudian Locality I, which is one of four paleoanthropologic sites on the hill, is the cave that was inhabited by Peking man himself.*

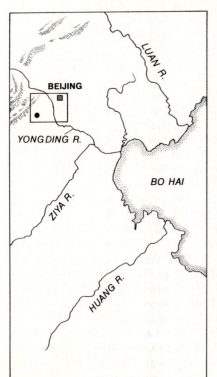

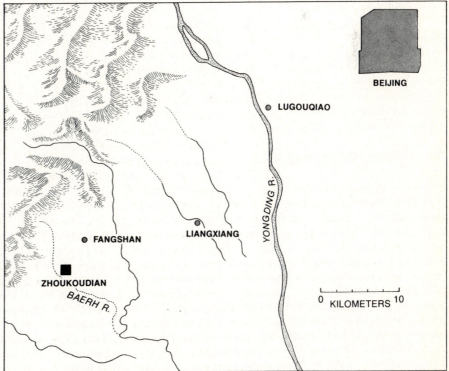

a fissure in the central section. He thereafter lived in the western section until 230,000 years ago, when the cave was completely filled with the detritus of human occupation and with eroded limestone.

The cave remained filled with these deposits until its excavation. The deposits that included remains of Peking man had a thickness of about 40 meters, which was divided into 10 layers by Pierre Teilhard de Chardin and Yang Zhongjian, a Chinese paleontologist, in 1929. The Chinese archaeologist Jia Lanpo analyzed the deposits below the 10th layer in 1951 and defined three more layers (11 through 13). The various investigators have agreed to identify the deposits as those of the Zhoukoudian period. Although the period was generally recognized as belonging to the Middle Pleistocene, about half a million years ago, until recently the chronology was so sweeping and lacking in detail that it gave no idea about the evolution of Peking man himself.

Dozens of workers in five institutions have recently finished a series of chronological investigations and so for the first time have given a comparatively exact age for each layer. The 10th layer was dated by counting the tracks left in crystalline minerals by the disintegration of nuclei of uranium 238, the most abundant isotope of uranium. The rate of such fission events is constant, and so the number of tracks is a measure of the time that has elapsed since the mineral formed. It was concluded that the 10th layer was laid down 460,000 years ago.

Workers at the Institute of Geology of the Chinese Academy of Sciences have ascertained by the dating technique called the uranium-series method that the ninth and eighth layers were deposited 420,000 years ago. In the uranium-series method what is measured are the relative abundances of uranium 234 and the product of its radioactive decay, thorium 230. The decay proceeds at a constant, known rate; the ratio of the two elements therefore indicates the time since the uranium-bearing mineral was formed.

Still another method was applied to the dating of the seventh layer, which turns out to be between 370,000 and 400,000 years old. The age was established by examining the natural remanent magnetism of minerals in the layer. When a magnetic mineral crystalizes, its magnetic axis becomes aligned with the direction of the earth's magnetic field. Periodic reversals of the earth's field thus leave a record in the rocks, which identifies their time of deposition. The uranium-series method has also been applied to the deposits in the three topmost layers. The results indicate an absolute age of 230,000 years.

THE FOSSILS OF PEKING MAN

The fossils of Peking man discovered over the past 50 years have been catalogued as follows: six complete or almost complete skulls and 12 other skull fragments, 15 pieces of mandibles, 157 teeth, three fragments of humerus (the bone of the upper arm), one clavicle (collarbone), seven fragments of femur (the thighbone), one fragment of tibia (shinbone) and one lunate bone (a wristbone shaped like a half moon). They were found at 15 widely scattered places in the cave. The fossils represent material from more than 40 male and female individuals, who died at various ages. From the fossil material it is possible to reconstruct the physical form and appearance of Peking man.

Like other examples of *Homo erectus* that emerged in the Middle Pleistocene, Peking man had a skeleton much like that of modern man. The main difference is that the limb bones had a thicker wall and a smaller marrow cavity. The skull of Peking man, however, differed substantially from the modern form. It was much thicker and flatter and had protruding brows and a marked angle at the rear. The brain case was larger than that of *Homo habilis*, a species that flourished 1.8 million years ago, and even larger than that of Java man, the somewhat older form of *Homo erectus*; the cranial capacity was still much smaller than that of modern man. The teeth were larger and more robust than those of *Homo sapiens* and had traces of an enamel collar, called a cingulum, around the crown. The cingulum is a primitive trait in prehistoric man.

All fossils of Peking man found so far have been analyzed by one of us (Wu Rukang) and Dong Xingren of the Institute of Vertebrate Paleontology and Paleoanthropology. We have given particular attention to the question of Peking man's cranial capacity. It should be stressed that brain size cannot be taken unconditionally as an indicator of human intelligence; a hominid with a bigger brain case is not necessarily smarter. Nevertheless, modern man, with an average cranial capacity of 1,450 cubic centimeters, must have evolved from an earlier form of man with a smaller cranium. The tendency is therefore for the human cranial capacity to increase, and the capacity of a given species or subspecies may provide some information about its place in human evolution.

It is generally accepted that the cranial capacity of man and his ancestors was stable at from 500 to 800 cubic centimeters in the interval from three to 1.5 million years ago. This is the cranial size measured in fossils of *Australopithecus* and *Homo habilis*. Java man, the form of *Homo erectus* that appeared about a million years ago, had a cranial capacity of some 900 cubic centimeters. When Peking man emerged, the average capacity had reached 1,054 centimeters.

It should be pointed out that this brain-case value for Peking man is an average based on the six relatively complete skulls found at Zhoukoudian. One of the six is the skull of a child who died at the age of eight or nine. A juvenile skull is obviously smaller than that of an adult; if it were not taken into account, the average cranial capacity of Peking man would be 1,088 cubic centimeters.

Because of the long time span covered by the fossils of Peking man, it may even be possible to trace changes in morphology, and in particular an increase in cranial capacity, over the history of the habitation of the site. The average capacity of four skulls found in the eighth and ninth layers (which are dated to more than 400,000 years ago) is 1,075 cubic centimeters. The one skull unearthed in the third layer (230,000 years old) has a capacity of 1,140 cubic centimeters. It seems that Peking man became more manlike in anatomy after 200,000 years of cave dwelling.

It is acknowledged in the anthropological community that the morphological evolution of early man was much slower and so less obvious than the transformation of behavior and lifestyle. Toolmaking techniques and the tools themselves are therefore an important measure of human evolution. In the case of Peking man a systematic study of the lithic culture was done three years ago by Pei Wenzhong and Zhang Shenshui of the Institute of Vertebrate Paleontology and Paleoanthropology. They came to believe Peking man's evolution is more clearly mirrored in his tools and toolmaking behavior than in his fossil remains.

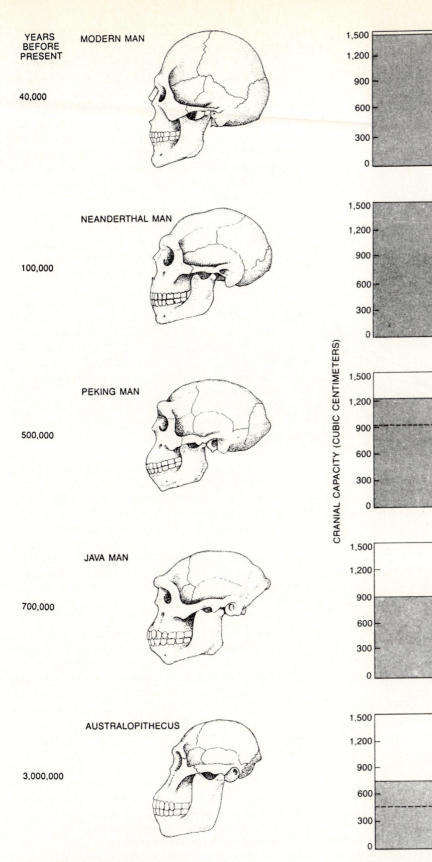

Figure 3. *Human evolution can be traced through morphological changes in the skull* (left) *and through an increase in cranial capacity* (right). *The early hominid* Australopithecus, *which appeared some four million years ago, had a flat skull with protruding jawbones and a small brain case (between 450 and 750 cubic centimeters). About 1.5 million years later came* Homo erectus. *Two examples of* Homo erectus, *Java man and Peking man, were comparatively advanced in their facial structure and cranial capacity, which ranged from 850 cubic centimeters to more than 1,000 cubic centimeters. They differed in their age, skull shape and brain size. Not until some 100,000 years ago did Neanderthal man, the first member of the species* Homo sapiens, *come into existence; by then the brain case was much larger and the jawbones were less protuberant. Modern man, the subspecies* Homo sapiens sapiens, *emerged about 40,000 years ago.*

THE TOOLS OF PEKING MAN

The stone industry of Peking man was an advanced one both in the selection of materials exploited and in the toolmaking techniques applied to them. The stone artifacts produced by Peking man are primarily made of vein quartz, rock crystal, flint and sandstone, suggesting that he did not rely exclusively on water-rounded pebbles for tool material. He often had to walk

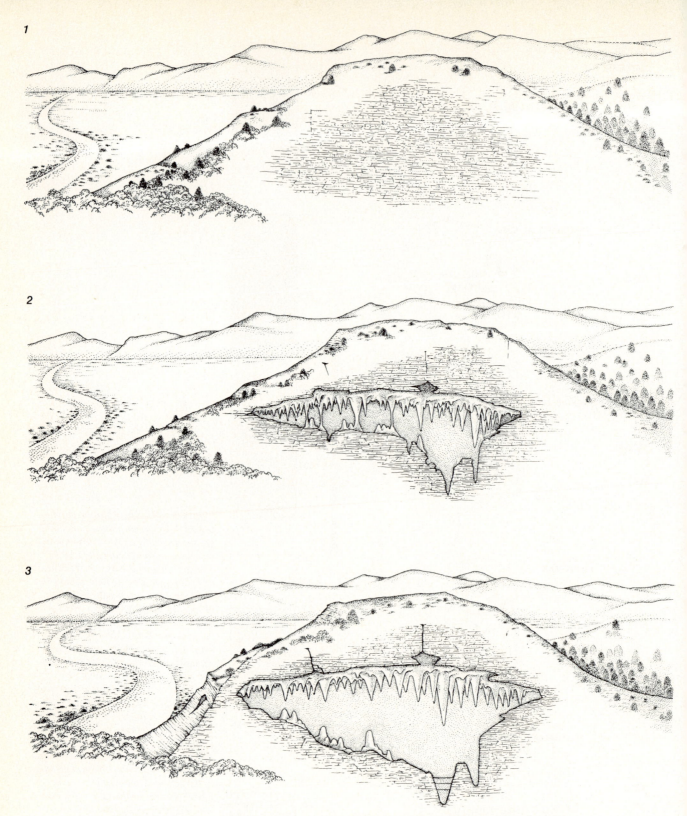

Figure 4. *Evolution of the cave at Zhoukoudian Locality 1 is schematized here in six stages. Dragon-Bone-Hill, in which the cave was created, is a limestone structure formed about 450 million years ago (1). As limestone was dissolved by underground water the cave began to form inside the hill about five million years ago (2). When the eastern spur of the hill was cut off by the scouring of the ancient Zhoukou River some three million years ago, a small entry to the cave appeared on the eastern slope and became progressively larger (3). Sand and dirt were carried by the river into the cave, leveling the gullies created by the erosion of the limestone. The resulting spacious shelter was adopted by Peking man about 460,000 years ago (4). The east entry and the eastern part of the cave were the main areas of habitation until the collapse of the roof 300,000 years ago forced a move to the western part, with access through a fissure in the central section (5). By the time Peking man left the cave 230,000 years ago it had been filled with fallen rock and the detritus of human occupation (6).*

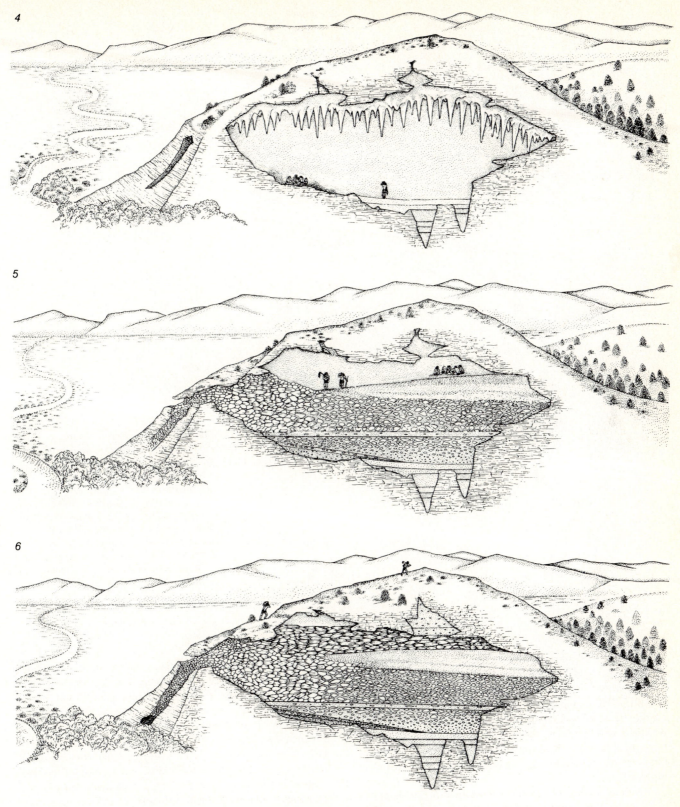

Figure 4. *(cont.)*

some distance to get vein quartz and rock crystal where they had been exposed by the weathering of granite formations.

Most of the tools are flakes of various sizes made in one of three ways. In the technique called anvil percussion a large flat stone (the anvil) was placed on the ground and forcefully struck with a piece of sandstone. Flakes chipped off the sandstone were gathered up, and those with a suitable shape and edge were selected either for direct use or for later

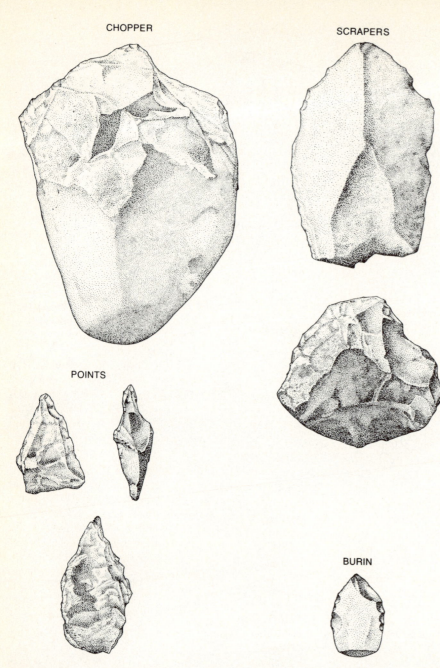

CHOPPER

SCRAPERS

POINTS

BURIN

Figure 5. *Stone tools made by Peking man are of four main types: the chopper* (upper left), *the scraper* (upper right), *the point* (lower left) *and the burin* (lower right). *They were formed out of vein quartz, rock crystal, flint and sandstone. Some of the flakes were put into service as tools without further trimming; others were retouched into more specialized tools such as points and burins. The stone industry was dominated by small tools with a length of less than 40 millimeters and a weight of less than 20 grams, although most of the early tools are larger.*

retouching. In another method, called direct percussion, the core flint was held in one hand and flakes were detached from it by striking it with a hammerstone held in the other hand. The third flaking method is called bipolar percussion. Again a large, flat anvil was set on the ground. A piece of vein quartz was then held upright on the anvil with one hand and crushed by vertical blows with a hammerstone grasped in the other. In this way flakes could be chipped off both ends; they are called bipolar flakes.

Although some of the flakes recovered at Zhoukoudian were used as they were, it is evident that some of them had been trimmed into more specialized tools such as scrapers, points, choppers, burins and awls. The retouching was done mainly by the direct-percussion process. Most of the tools were trimmed on their back surface rather than on the one that had been worked in the initial flaking operation. Sometimes both faces were retouched.

The evolution of Peking man's lithic culture was divided into three periods by Pei and Zhang. The division was made according to changes in tool size, in tool material and in tool-making technique. The stone tools found in the eighth through the 11th layers represent the earliest culture, which prevailed between 460,000 and 420,000 years ago. It is characterized by large tools weighing more than 50 grams and longer than 60 millimeters and by the indiscriminate application of the three toolmaking processes. At this stage tools made out of softer materials such as sandstone account for 15 to 20 percent of the artifacts. In the middle stage, from 370,000 to 350,000 years ago, the anvil-percussion process was practically abandoned and the bipolar-percussion process became the main method of flaking stone. As a result the proportion of the tools having a weight of less than 20 grams and a length of less than 40 millimeters increased to 68 percent. In contrast large tools diminished to 12 percent.

Figure 6. *Use of fire by Peking man, attested to by layers of ashes, can be traced to the beginning of his residence in the cave. Four layers of ashes have been identified in the cave deposits; the thickest layer is some six meters deep and the thinnest one is a little more than a meter deep.*

The last stage lasted from 300,000 to 230,000 years ago. It was clearly the most advanced: the tools had become smaller and the tool materials were of better quality. Among the stone tools excavated from layers one through five the small tools increased dramatically to 78 percent of the total, whereas the large tools decreased further to 5 percent. Although the tools of the third period were still made mainly out of quartz, fewer were made out of the coarse varieties of the stone, such as vein quartz, and the fraction of the tools made out of flint increased to as much as 30 percent in the uppermost layers. In the meantime sandstone tools had diminished to less than 1 percent of the total.

Another indication of the advanced state of Peking man's culture is his use of fire: evidently the art had already been mastered at the very beginning of his habitation of the cave. There are four large, thick layers of ashes deposited in periods ranging in age from 460,000 to 230,000 years. The thickest one, formed between 310,000 and 290,000 years ago, is six meters deep in certain places. Some of the ash deposits are in scattered piles, suggesting that Peking man had the ability to control fire and keep it burning for a long time.

How did Peking man make a fire and control it? A conclusive answer cannot be given, but an inference can be drawn. Peking man seems to have been too primitive to start a fire; instead he was probably dependent on natural fires outside the cave, generally started by lighting. Presumably the fire was captured by lighting a bunch of twigs or some other kindling and bringing it back to the cave. Given the rarity of natural fire, it must have been vitally important to avoid letting the fire go out. One way of maintaining a fire would have been to add wood to it continuously. Another would have been to cover burning charcoal with ash or soil to slow its burning. A new fire could then be made by blowing on the coals. Some charcoal found in the cave may be a remnant of the latter process.

What was the nature of the environment outside the cave at the time Peking man occupied the site? On the basis of a study of pollen at Zhoukoudian Locality I, Kong Zhaochen of the Institute of Botany of the Chinese Academy of Sciences and his colleagues have suggested that Peking man lived in the climate of an interglacial period; indeed, the climate of the period was not much different from that of northern China today. The vegetation consisted of temperate deciduous forests and steppes on the plains and in the valleys and coniferous forests on the mountains.

A temperate climate entails the rigors of a cold winter every year but also provides many kinds of edible plant products. The adoption of a cave as shelter and the use of fire may have been inspired directly by the need for surviving cold weather.

A variety of plants supplied not only firewood but also fruits and seeds. Among the deposits in the cave are quantities of charred seeds of the Chinese hackberry, which were obviously gathered and roasted by Peking man. Evidently the seeds served as food. The analysis of pollen in the deposits gives evidence of other plants, such as walnut, hazelnut, pine, elm and rambler rose. The fruits and seeds of those species must also be considered candidates for inclusion in Peking man's diet.

Hunting was a valuable adaptation to the environment since meat could supply more calories and protein than a vegetarian diet. Peking man was evidently able to compete successfully with large carnivores as a hunter. An abundance of fossil bones of mammals of various sizes found in the cave indicates that Peking man not only hunted small game but also was capable of killing large animals.

Among carnivores a natural relation generally exists between the size of the predator and that of its prey. A fox cannot kill a zebra, but the zebra is the favorite food of lions. Owing to his use of weapons, Peking man escaped the limitations of his size. In particular he became an efficient hunter of deer, some of which were larger and faster than he was. The large quantity of fossils belonging to a least 3,000 individual deer of two species, the thick-jawed deer (*Megaceros pachyosteus*) and the sika deer (*Pseudaxis grayi*), could be regarded as an indication that deer were the commonest prey of Peking man.

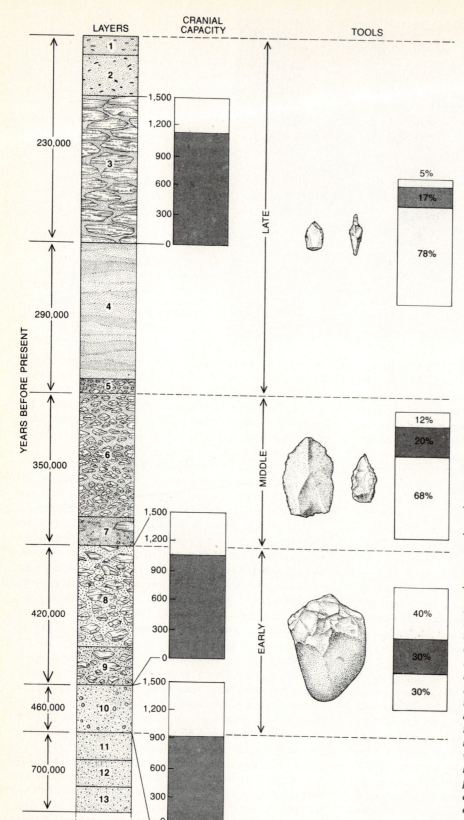

Figure 7. *Evolution of Peking man in the course of 230,000 years of cave dwelling is suggested by an increase in brain size (left) and the development of a more refined lithic culture (right). The cave deposits that include fossils of Peking man are divided into 13 layers. Skulls have been recovered from layer 10, from the boundary between layer 9 and layer 8 and from layer 3. The measured cranial capacities are 915 cubic centimeters for the earliest skull, an average of 1,075 cubic centimeters for four later skulls and 1,140 cubic centimeters for the most recent one. It seems that brain size increased by more than 100 cubic centimeters during the occupation of the cave. The cultural development of Peking man is broken down into three stages. In the earliest stage the artifacts were mainly choppers and scrapers; 40 percent were large tools (white), 30 percent were of intermediate size (gray) and 30 percent were small (white). In the latest stage more complex tools appeared. The proportion of large and medium tools decreased respectively to 5 and 17 percent, whereas the proportion of small ones increased to 78 percent.*

SOCIAL ADAPTATIONS

As we have shown, Peking man was a cave dweller, a fire user, a deer hunter, a seed gatherer and a maker of specialized tools. The fossil and artifactual evidence attest to his biological and technological adaptation. It is more difficult to trace his social adaptation since little evidence is available. Nevertheless, three hypotheses can be put forward on the basis of our studies.

Generally speaking, gathering is a simple labor that can be undertaken by single individuals. Hunting, in contrast, and particularly the hunting of large animals, is so complicated, difficult and hazardous that the cooperation of numerous individuals is needed. It can be inferred, therefore, that Peking man was more likely to have been living in a group than in solitude when he began to hunt deer. Furthermore, thousands of fossils of prey species found in the cave suggest that these primitive hunters may have preferred to bring prey back to the cave and share the meat with the others in the community rather than to consume it where it was killed.

Second, the hunting of large and fast-moving animals such as deer may have been difficult for women because of physiological limitations (such as pregnancy and child rearing). It is thus possible to speculate that the hunting behavior of

Peking man may have caused or contributed to the sexual division of labor within the group. The pattern of male hunters and female gatherers, which is common in hunting-and-gathering societies today, may have already been established.

Third, the existence of a consistently progressing lithic culture throughout a period lasting for 200,000 years or more suggests that the earliest practice of education may have taken place in Peking man's cave. It is out of the question that each generation could recapitulate the entire history of stone-tool development, from striking a pebble in order to make a crude tool to trimming a flake into a specialized scraper. Tool-making techniques, like modern science and technology, must have been conveyed from the old to the young.

REFERENCES

Black, D. 1927. On a lower molar hominid tooth from the Choukoutien deposit. *Palaeontologica Sinica*, Series D, 7(1):1-28.

Black, D. 1927. On an adolescent skull of *Sinanthropus pekinensis* in comparison with an adult skull of the same species and with other hominid skulls, recent and fossil. *Palaeontologica Sinica*, Series D, 7(2):1-144.

Chia Lan-po. 1975. *The Cave Home of Peking Man.* Foreign Language Press.

Pei, W. C. 1931. Notice of the discovery of quartz and other stone artifacts in the Lower Pleistocene hominid-bearing sediments of the Choukoutien Cave deposit. *Bulletin of the Geological Society of China* 1(2):109-139.

Weidenreich, F. 1935. The *Sinanthropus* population of Chou Kou Tien. *Bulletin of the Geological Society of China* 14(4): 427-461.

37

Patterns in the Evolution of *Homo erectus*

G. P. Rightmire

INTRODUCTION

A major problem in paleoanthropology is how earlier populations of the genus *Homo* evolved in different regions of the Old World over a long span of time, beginning 2.0 to 1.5 Myr ago. At present, there is no firm consensus as to the number of distinct species existing during this period. Some fossil material from East Africa has been referred to *Homo habilis* (L. S. B. Leakey *et al.* 1964), while other remains representing early *Homo* sp. are known from the Lower Member of the Koobi Fora formation and from the Omo (Howell 1978). Hominids from Putjangan deposits in Indonesia are attributed to another species (*Homo modjokertensis*) by von Koenigswald (1950, 1975). Some of the latter material is likely to be contemporary with *Homo erectus* recovered from the Upper Member of the Koobi Fora Formation at East Turkana (R. E. Leakey and Walker 1976). This picture is undeniably complex, and the origins of mid-Pleistocene *Homo* are not clear. However, many hominine fossils which are younger than 1.5 Myr and which predate the later Middle Pleistocene can be identified unequivocally as *Home erectus*. Important questions concern the tempo of evolution exhibited by this fossil species and also the mode by which speciation within this lineage has given rise to *Homo sapiens*. With present anatomical and stratigraphic information, it is

possible to ascertain whether change in Mid-Pleistocene populations has been regular and progressive or whether there is little evidence for morphological trends through time. One view is that *Homo erectus* has undergone steady phyletic evolution, and many workers see the fossils as making up a variable grade rather than as representative of a stable taxon. A recent statement is that of Bilsborough (1976) who has attempted to identify changes distinguishing *Homo* from *Australopithecus* and also major differences between "early" and "late" *Homo erectus* specimens. From dental and cranial measurements, Bilsborough concludes that *Homo erectus* exhibits rapid phyletic evolution, with the result that "later" fossils (e.g. Choukoutien) closely resemble *Homo sapiens*. Models of punctuated equilibrium have been contrasted with those of gradualism in the recent paleobiological literature, however, and there is now some feeling that long periods of stasis interupted by episodes of rapid evolution may be the rule for many species (Eldredge and Gould 1972; Gould and Eldredge 1977). In this report, I use cranial, dental and mandibular measurements to search for trends in the evolution of *Homo erectus*. Results indicate that little directional change has taken place during the duration of the species.

Attention is here restricted to a single species-level taxon, while other studies of evolutionary rates and trends in hominids

Reprinted with permission from *Paleobiology*, Vol. 7, pp. 241–246. Copyright © 1981 by The Paleontological Society.

Table 1. Dates assigned to *Homo erectus* remains included in regression analyses. Specimens are listed by locality, and numbering follows the convention current in the literature. Salé, Sidi Abderrahman, Ternifine and Thomas Quarry are in the Northwest African Maghreb, while Baringo, Koobi Fora and Ileret (ER designations) and Olduvai Gorge (O.H. designations) are in East Africa. The Asian hominids are known from sites in China (Choukoutien, and the two Lantian localities of Chenchiawo and Gongwangling) and in Indonesia (Ngandong, Sambungmachan, Sangiran and Trinil). All ages are necessarily approximate. Radiometric and/or paleomagnetic results of varying detail and reliability are available for some localities (Baringo, Ileret, Koobi Fora, Olduvai, Choukoutien, Lantian, Sangiran), but it would be more accurate to give age ranges in most cases. However, estimates of actual dates are needed for quantitative treatment.

Age (myr)	Africa		Europe		Asia	
	Crania	*Mandibles/teeth*	*Crania*	*Mandibles/teeth*	*Crania*	*Mandibles/teeth*
0.2	Salé	Baringo Sidi Abderraham Thomas Quarry 1	Petralona	Arago II, XIII Montmaurin	Ngandong I, V, VI, IX, X , XI	
0.4						
0.6	O.H. 12	Ternifine 1, 2, 3 O.H. 23		Mauer	Choukoutien II, III, V, X, XI, XII	Choukoutien (6 jaws plus isolated teeth), Chenchiawo
0.8		O.H. 22 O.H. 51 Swartkrans (SK 15)			Gongwangling Trinil 2 Sangiran 2, 3 10, 12, 17, Sambungmachan	
1.0						
1.2	O.H. 9				Sangiran 4	Sangiran B, Sangiran 5
1.4	O.H. 13 ER-3733 ER-3883	O.H. 13 ER-730, ER-992				
1.6						

have usually dealt with several species and with specimens assigned to *Australopithecus* as well as *Homo*. Reasons for choosing *Homo erectus* are several. Fossil remains are still somewhat scarce and fragmentary but are known from localities distributed widely over the Old World. Recent discoveries in East Africa (R.E. Leakey and Walker 1976) and Northwest Africa (Jaeger 1975) as well as new studies of Olduvai hominids (Rightmire 1979, 1980) have made available fresh anatomical information. Analyses of deep sea cores, continental sedimentary sequences and faunal assemblages have also contributed greatly to our understanding of mid-Pleistocene stratigraphy (Butzer and Isaac 1975; Bishop 1978). Some of the fossils can be placed satisfactorily in chronological frameworks, although gaps remain. Dating of the Indonesian hominids is uncertain, for example, and most European specimens can be located only broadly within earlier or later divisions of the Middle Pleistocene. Finally, there is relatively good agreement as to the identification of individual fossils, while considerable controversy surrounds the systematics of other extinct species of *Homo* and *Australopithecus*. Probably a majority of the remains allocated to *Homo erectus* by me would also be sorted this way by other workers. However, in order to increase numbers as much as possible, I have treated as *Homo erectus* some specimens which are frequently viewed differently, e.g., as archaic *Homo sapiens*. (Table 1).

MATERIALS AND METHODS

Characters selected for analysis are cranial capacity, breadth of the cranial base, width of the first lower molar, and mandibular robusticity. Many other traits can be examined, but these four

should provide preliminary indications of change or stasis in key regions of the skull and dentition. Endocranial volume and tooth size figure prominently in descriptions of *Homo erectus* (Le Gros Clark 1964; Howell 1978). Biauricular breadth is consistently important in multivariate statistical work on human crania. This measurement is highly correlated with the primary discriminant function computed by Howells (1973) in a study of 17 modern populations and should carry comparable weight in an analysis of more archaic skulls. Thickness of the mandibular corpus is related to development of a lateral prominence and its anterior extensions (superior or marginal tori) and to expression of the alveolar prominence. In a biomechanical study of early hominid mandibles, White (1977) notes that a swollen lateral prominence acts as an anchor for the ascending ramus and probably also functions in internal buttressing. This feature, while variably developed, is thus likely to have mechanical significance. A robusticity index (thickness/height) may not provide the most satisfactory guide to relative corpus width, but this ratio can be calculated easily from measurements available in the literature (see also Tobias 1971). Techniques for measuring these characters should be similar among different authors, although some variation in dental dimensions may be due to observer error. Sample sizes for the four analyses range from 23 to 33 for *Homo erectus* materials spanning more than 1.3 Myr before the onset of the Upper Pleistocene (Table 2).

RESULTS

Brain volume in *Homo erectus* is plotted against time in Fig. 1. For this purpose, the Ngandong crania with capacities measured recently by Holloway (1980) are treated provisionally as *Homo*

Table 2. Data on *Homo erectus* cranial capacity, biauricular breadth, first lower molar width, and mandibular robusticity from which regression relationships are calculated. For each time period, numbers of specimens (n), mean measurement values ($\bar{x}$), standard deviations (s) and ranges are listed.

Age of fossil assemblage (Myr)	Cranial capacity	Biauricular breadth	M₁ width	Mandibular robusticity
0.2	n = 1, $\bar{x}$ = 945	n = 1, $\bar{x}$ = 127		
0.3	n = 6, $\bar{x}$ = 1162.8 s = 93.3 range = 1013–1251	n = 5, $\bar{x}$ = 148.8 s = 9.9 range = 133–163	n = 5, $\bar{x}$ = 11.1 s = 1.4 range = 9.5–13.2	n = 6, $\bar{x}$ = 54.8 s = 7.9 range = 49.3–70.7
0.6	n = 7, $\bar{x}$ = 1011.7 s = 159.7 range = 727–1225	n = 5, $\bar{x}$ = 146.1 s = 4.1 range = 141–151	n = 20, $\bar{x}$ = 11.8 s = 0.8 range = 10.1–13.0	n = 12, $\bar{x}$ = 58.3 s = 5.7 range = 48.5–66.7
0.8	n = 8, $\bar{x}$ = 923.8 s = 104.4 range = 780–1059	n = 6, $\bar{x}$ = 128.8 s = 10.8 range = 115–145	n = 3, $\bar{x}$ = 12.1 s = 0.4 range = 11.8–12.6	n = 2, $\bar{x}$ = 66.6 s = 7.4 range = 61.4–71.9
1.2	n = 2, $\bar{x}$ = 983.5 s = 118.1 range = 900–1067	n = 2, $\bar{x}$ = 145.5 s = 14.8 range = 135–156	n = 2, $\bar{x}$ = 13.0	n = 2, $\bar{x}$ = 48.6 s = 2.0 range = 47.2–50.1
1.5	n = 3, $\bar{x}$ = 767.3 s = 103.9 range = 650–848	n = 2, $\bar{x}$ = 131.5 s = 0.7 range = 131–132	n = 3, $\bar{x}$ = 11.4 s = 0.4 range = 10.9–11.7	n = 3, $\bar{x}$ = 63.8 s = 4.8 range = 58.8–68.3

erectus (Santa Luca 1978, 1980) and assigned a late Middle Pleistocene age of 0.3 Myr (Jacob 1978). Here as elsewhere it is assumed that hominids from the Putjangan levels at Sangiran are roughly contemporary with upper Bed II at Olduvai, while the later Sangiran (Kabuh levels), Trinil and Sambungmachan fossils are lumped together at 0.8 Myr. The Gongwangling cranium is also assumed to be approximately 0.8 Myr old, on paleomagnetic evidence (Ma Xinghua *et al.* 1978). Means are calculated principally from volumes determined by Holloway (1975, 1976) for African and Indonesian crania and by Weidenreich (1943) for Choukoutien individuals. Least squares linear regression for cranial capacity (*Y*) on time (*X*) gives the relationship

$$Y = 1100.30 - 175.58X$$

There is a slight trend, and the negative slope shows volume to be increasing in individuals of more recent date at a rate of approximately 175 ml per 1.0 Myr. However, the standard error of this coefficient is 91.11, and .95 confidence limits are −175.58 ± 252.92, so there is no evidence that the regression differs significantly from zero. Indications of gradual change are even less clear when two of the more questionable crania are dropped from the analysis. Olduvai Hominid 13 is usually referred to *Homo habilis*, while the Petralona fossil, with an endocranial volume of about 1200 ml, is similar to *Homo erectus* in some respects but shares other features with early *Homo sapiens*. Stringer *et al.* (1979) argue that Petralona and other European specimens of the later Middle Pleistocene should be placed in a morphologically archaic grade of *Homo sapiens*. If these individuals are omitted, the curve is flatter, and the regression coefficient is again not distinguishable from zero.

Biauricular breadth measured on 23 crania including Petralona appears to fluctuate with time (Fig. 1). The regression relationship is

$$Y = 139.11 - 1.52X$$

but little of the variance in breadth is explained by differences in ages of the specimens. The hypothesis that the slope is equal to zero cannot be rejected (t = -0.16, P > .88). Width of M_1 increases slightly in the older fossils, although this tendency apparently does not continue at 1.5 Myr (Fig. 2). Linear regression of molar size on time takes the form

$$Y = 11.62 + 0.22X$$

and the .95 confidence interval calculated for this slope again includes zero. Neither here nor in the case of robusticity measured on 25 *Homo erectus* jaws, where the regression line is

$$Y = 56.77 + 1.90X$$

is there much indication of a real trend with time.

DISCUSSION

While some questions remain, this evidence suggests little systematic change either in cranial capacity or in other important aspects of *Homo erectus* skull and dental morphology. The fossils are admittedly sparse, especially in some of the Lower Pleistocene assemblages, and it is not possible to correct for the effects of sex dimorphism on the analysis. Individuals such as Olduvai Hominid 9 are likely to be male, while some of the smaller crania such as Olduvai Hominid 12 are probably female. Most of the fossils cannot be sexed with any accuracy, and there is no certainty that males and females are equally represented in the small samples drawn from any given time period. Differences in stature or overall body size not directly related to sex dimorphism may also influence the results, particularly in the case of cranial capacity. Brain volume is partly a function of body bulk, and it would be helpful if relative brain sizes could be determined for populations included in this study. However, stature or body weight estimates are difficult to obtain for *Homo erectus* individuals, and it is not possible, for example, to ascertain whether a slight trend toward increasing

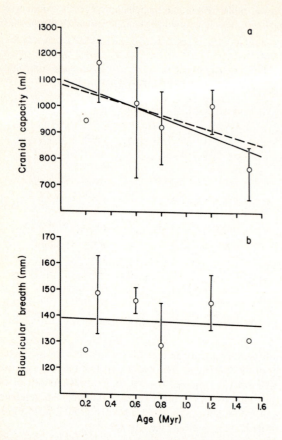

Figure 1. *Cranial capacity and biauricular breadth of* Homo erectus *skulls plotted against time. Means for each assemblage are indicated by (o) while the bars show observed ranges of variation. (a) Analysis of cranial volume is based on 27 individuals from Ngandong, Salé, Petralona, Choukoutien, Trinil, Sangiran, Sambungmachan, Gongwangling, Olduvai and East Turkana. Least squares linear regression for all skulls is given by the solid line. The second (dashed) regression line is constructed without Petralona and O.H. 13. This second line has the form Y = 1079.33 - 138.04X. Confidence intervals for the slope are - 138.04 ± 223.21 at a probability of .95 and the regression coefficient is not distinguishable from zero. (b) Analysis of cranial base breadth is based on the same individuals as (a), excluding Choukoutien II, Sangiran 3, Gongwangling, O.H. 12 and O.H. 13. The confidence interval for the regression coefficient is -1.52 ± 26.81 at a probability of .95.*

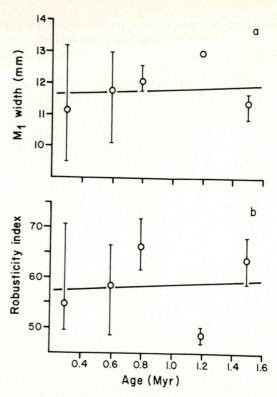

Figure 2. *M₁ width and mandibular robusticity for* Homo erectus *plotted against time. Means for each assemblage are indicated by (o) while bars show observed ranges of variation. (a) Regression analysis of bucco-lingual breadth is based on 33 molar teeth from Arago, Montmaurin, Mauer, Baringo, Thomas Quarry, Sidi Abderrahman, Ternifine, Choukoutien, Chenchiawo, Sangiran, Swartkrans, Olduvai and East Turkana. In specimens preserving dentition on both left and right sides, only one side was measured. The confidence interval for the regression slope is 0.229 ± 2.75 using a probability of .95. (b) Robusticity is defined as a thickness/height of the mandibular body, usually measured at the level of the first molar. Analysis is based on 25 jaws from Arago, Moutmaurin, Mauer, Baringo, Thomas Quarry, Sidi Abderrahman, Ternifine, Choukoutien, Chenchiawo, Sangiran, Olduvai and East Turkana. The confidence interval for the regression coefficient is 1.90 ± 27.46 using a probability of .95.*

brain volume may be related to changes in body size during the Middle Pleistocene. If this is the case, then an extended period of evolutionary stasis in (relative) brain size is implied.

In light of this comment on rates of morphological change in *Homo erectus*, it is tempting to conclude that the transition to *Homo sapiens* occurred relatively rapidly. After more than a million years of stasis, trends toward expansion of the brain and braincase and reduction in size of the jaws and dentition may have been established in early *Homo sapiens* populations during a short pulse of evolution, late in the Middle Pleistocene. Stanley (1978, 1979) has postulated this punctuational mode of speciation for many Cenozoic mammals, and humans may be no exception. Given this interpretation, it is not likely that hominids representing small, regionally restricted, transitional populations would actually be recovered as fossils, and because of this gap in the record, there

should be little difficulty in distinguishing *Homo erectus* from anatomically more modern *Homo sapiens*.

There are indications that this reading of the evidence is not entirely correct, however. A few human remains have been recovered, particularly in Africa but also from at least one European locality, which may in fact stem from populations intermediate in form. One is the partial cranium from Bodo in Ethiopia (Conroy *et al.* 1978). The low, slightly keeled and heavy browed Bodo frontal bone resembles that of Broken Hill (generally recognized as "archaic" *Homo sapiens*), while the face is very broad with deep and massively constructed zygomatic arches. Unfortunately most of the cranial base and occiput are missing. The hominid from Lake Ndutu, near Olduvai in northern Tanzania, has been described by Clarke (1976) as *Homo erectus*, though it is clear that there are also similarities to more modern humans. Much more complete is the important fossil from Petralona, discovered in 1960 but only recently cleaned of calcareous matrix. There seems to be no firm consensus as to which taxon this individual should be assigned, although the recent study of Stringer *et al.* (1979) suggests that the specimen should be viewed as "primitive" *Homo sapiens*. Derived features of the Petralona cranium said to ally it with later humans include slight reduction of the occipital torus, more horizontal positioning of the nuchal plane and relative lengthening of the upper scale of the occipital bone.

While none of these fossils is securely dated, each can be advanced to support an argument that (late) *Homo erectus* populations are not very different from (early) *Homo sapiens*, given the rather vague definitions presently accepted for each taxon. There is also a possibility that such "transitional" populations were spread over a large geographic range. Claims for local gradualism have usually been based on Pleistocene skeletal sequences from the northwest African Maghreb (e.g. Saban 1977) or from Indonesia (Jacob 1975; Sartono 1975), but in both instances there are problems relating to provenience and dating as well as disagreements about anatomical interpretation of the fossil record. In fact, it is still extremely difficult to detect continuity between individual *Homo erectus* assemblages and early *Homo sapiens* from the same geographic region.

The analysis presented here does not settle the question of how speciation progressed in the later *Homo* lineage, but a traditional gradualist view is not supported. *Homo erectus* was apparently a stable taxon, exhibiting little morphological change throughout most of its long history. It may be inferred that the tempo of human evolution quickened toward the close of the Middle Pleistocene, even if there was no very rapid replacement of *Homo erectus* by *Homo sapiens* as would be predicted by a punctuational model. Whether the transition to more modern humans occurred in Africa or elsewhere cannot be determined with present information.

ACKNOWLEDGEMENTS

I thank M. D. Leakey, R. E. Leakey, B. A. Ogot and M. A. de Lumley for access to fossil specimens. C. B. Stringer, A. C. Walker and K. Bell provided valuable assistance, and this work was supported by grants from the NSF (BNS 75-02679, BNS 80-04852) and the National Geographic Society.

REFERENCES

Bilsborough, A. 1976. Patterns of evolution in Middle Pleistocene hominids. *J. Hum. Evol.* 5:423-439.

Bishop, W. W., Ed. 1978. *Geological Background to Fossil Man.* 585 pp. Scottish Academic Press, Edinburgh.

Butzer, K. W., and Isaac, G. Ll., Eds. 1975. *After the Australopithecines.* Mouton, The Hague.

Clarke, R. J. 1976. New cranium of *Homo erectus* from Lake Ndutu, Tanzania. *Nature* 262:485-487.

Conroy, G. C., Jolly, C. J., Cramer, D., and Kalb., J. E. 1978. Newly discovered fossil hominid skull from the Afar Depression, Ethiopia. *Nature* 276:67-70.

Eldredge, N., and Gould, S. J. 1972. Punctuated equilibria: An alternative to phyletic gradualism, in: *Models in Paleobiology* (T. J. M. Schopf, Ed.), pp. 82-115. Freeman, Cooper, San Francisco.

Gould, S. J. and Eldredge, N. 1977. Punctuated equilibria: the tempo and mode of evolution reconsidered. *Paleobiology* 3:115-151.

Holloway, R. L. 1975. Early hominid endocasts: volumes, morphology and significance for hominid evolution, in: *Primate Functional Morphology and Evolution* (R. H. Tuttle, Ed.), pp. 393-415. Mouton, The Hague.

Holloway, R. L. 1976. Some problems of hominid brain endocast reconstruction, allometry and neural reorganization, in: *Les Plus Anciens Hominides* (P. V. Tobias and Y. Coppens, Eds.), pp. 69-119. CNRS, Paris

Holloway, R. L. 1980. Indonesian "Solo" (Ngandong) endocranial reconstructions: Preliminary observations and comparisons with Neanderthal and *Homo erectus* groups. *Am. J. Phys. Anthropol.* 53:285-295.

Howell, F. C. 1978. Hominidae, in: *Evolution of African Mammals* (V. J. Maglio and H. B. S. Cooke, Eds.), pp. 154-248. Harvard University Press, Cambridge, MA.

Howells, W. W. 1973. *Cranial Variation in Man.* Pap. Peabody Mus. 67. Harvard University, Cambridge, MA.

Jacob, T. 1975. Morphology and paleoecology of early man in Java, in: *Paleoanthropology, Morphology and Paleoecology* (R. H. Tuttle, Ed.), pp. 311-325. Mouton, The Hague.

Jacob, T. 1978. The puzzle of Solo man, in: *Modern Quaternary Research in Southeast Asia,* 4 (G. J. Barstra and W. A. Casparie, Eds.), pp. 31-40. Balkema, Rotterdam.

Jaeger, J. J. 1975. Découverte d'un crâne d'Hominidé dans le Pléistocène Moyen du Maroc. *Colloque Int. CNRS, Évol. Vert.* 218:897-902.

von Koenigswald, G. H. R. 1950. Fossil hominids of the Lower Pleistocene of Java. *18th Int. Geol. Cong.* 9:59-61.

von Koenigswald, G. H. R. 1975. Early man in Java: Catalogue and problems, in: *Paleoanthropology, Morphology and Paleoecology* (R. H. Tuttle, Ed.), pp. 303-309. Mouton, The Hague.

Leakey, L. S. B., Tobias, P. V., and Napier, J. R. 1964. A new species of the genus *Homo* from Olduvai Gorge. *Nature* 202:7-9.

Leakey, R. E., and Walker, A. C. 1976. *Australopithecus, Homo erectus* and the single species hypothesis. *Nature* 261:572-574.

Le Gros Clark, W. E. 1964. *The Fossil Evidence for Human Evolution.* University of Chicago Press, Chicago.

Ma Xinghua, Qian Fang, Li Pu, and Ju Shiqiang. 1978. Paleomagnetic dating of Lantian man. (In Chinese) *Vertebrata PalAsiatica* 16:238-243.

Rightmire, G. P. 1979. Cranial remains of *Homo erectus* from Beds II and IV, Olduvai Gorge, Tanzania. *Am. J. Phys. Anthropol.* 51:99-115.

Rightmire, G. P. 1980. Middle Pleistocene hominids from Olduvai Gorge, northern Tanzania. *Am. J. Phys. Anthropol.* 53:225-241.

Saban, R. 1977. The place of Rabat man (Kebibat, Morocco) in human evolution. *Curr. Anthropol.* 18:518-524.

Santa Luca, A. P. 1978. A re-examination of presumed Neanderthal-like fossils. *J. Hum. Evol.* 7:619-636.

Santa Luca, A. P. 1980. *The Ngandong Fossil Hominids.* Yale University Publ. Anthropol. 78. Yale University, New Haven.

Sartono, S. 1975. Implications arising from *Pithecanthropus* VIII, in: *Paleoanthropology, Morphology, and Paleoecology* (R. H. Tuttle Ed.), pp. 327-360. Mouton, The Hague.

Stanley, S. M. 1978. Chronospecies' longevities, the origin of genera and the punctuational model of evolution. *Paleobiology* 4:26-40.

Stanley, S. M. 1979. *Macroevolution: Patterns and Process.* Freeman, San Francisco.

Stringer, C. B., Howell, F. C. and Melentis, J. K. 1979. The significance of the fossil hominid skull from Petralona, Greece. *J. Archaeol. Sci.* 6:235-253.

Tobias, P. V. 1971. Human skeletal remains from the Cave of Hearths, Makapansgat, northern Transvaal. *Am. J. Phys. Anthropol.* 34:335-367.

Weidenreich, F. 1943. The skull of *Sinanthropus pekinensis. Palaeontol. Sin.,* New Ser. D 10:1-292.

White, T. D. 1977. *The Anterior Mandibular Corpus of Early African Hominidae: Functional Significance of Shape and Size.* Thesis, University of Michigan, Ann Arbor.

38

Evolution in *Homo erectus*: The Question of Stasis

M. H. Wolpoff

Of the two claims of punctuated equilibrium—geologically rapid origins and subsequent stasis—the first has received most attention, but Eldredge and I have repeatedly emphasized that we regard the second as more important. We have, and not facetiously, taken as our motto: stasis is data.

(S. J. Gould 1982, p. 85)

INTRODUCTION

Punctuational and gradualistic models of evolutionary change are not mutually exclusive, in the sense that each could account for some significant changes over the course of evolution. Thus, in ongoing discussions of these models, debate has centered on the issue of which of these processes has *predominated* over the course of biological evolution.

Perhaps because of our special interest in our own ancestors, the hominids are often brought into the discussion. In particular, the species directly ancestral to us, *Homo erectus*, has become a focus in several wide-ranging presentations supporting the punctuational model (Gould and Eldredge 1977; Stanley 1979, 1981; Eldredge and Tattersall 1982). The perception of *H. erectus* in these accounts is characterized by Stanley's statement (1981, p. 148): "there was no approach toward *Homo sapiens* in forehead development or, we may infer, in intellect ... as far as we can tell, throughout his existence *Homo erectus* did not vary greatly in form."

Paleoanthropological positions on the issue of evolution within *H. erectus* are diverse. Some paleoanthropologists argue that the species shows continuous (although not necessarily constant) evolution over the span of its existence (Mann 1971; Tobias 1971; Bilsborough 1976; Wolpoff 1980b; Cronin *et al.* 1981; Allen 1982). Others claim that the species is characterized by a long period of evolutionary stasis with a clearly delineated beginning and end (Howells 1980; Delson 1981; Rightmire 1981; Day 1982; Kennedy 1983).

Both Day and Kennedy based their conclusions on the assessment of a single postcranial bone, either later (Day) or earlier (Kennedy) than *H. erectus* is traditionally considered to extend in time. Each attributes the bone in question to *H. erectus* on the basis of morphological similarity and then claims to have shown stasis for *H. erectus* because of the morphological similarity between the (earlier or later) *H. erectus* sample and the bone in question. With regard to femur, even if this reasoning was appropriate (for a contrary argument, see Trinkaus 1984), it is far from clear that the data actually show stasis

(Bridges 1984), while the innominate sample is too small to support any interpretation. Only Bilsborough (1976) and Rightmire (1981) have published quantitative analyses comparing *H. erectus* samples to support their claims.

Bilsborough (1976) examined changes in *H. erectus* using both univariate techniques and a multivariate statistic, Generalized Distance (D^2) obtained by a Q-technique applied to a number of variables. *Homo erectus* was divided into an early and late sample for the analysis, which also included *Australopithecus africanus* and modern *H. sapiens*. It was concluded that *H. erectus* populations are characterized by rapid evolutionary change.

Rightmire (1981) reported Bilsborough's results, but subsequently ignored them in arguing that *H. erectus* is characterized by evolutionary stasis. Rightmire chose four variables and attempted a least mean squares regression for each of these against time (geological age). He divided his total sample of 65 individuals (16 of which may not be *H. erectus*) into six groups and regressed the average dimension for each group against the average age for the group. Thus, each of his regressions had six points and five degrees of freedom. None of the slopes calculated were significant, and Rightmire therefore concluded that the species shows evolutionary stasis.

There is reason to believe that Rightmire's results are an artifact of his procedure. Allen (1982), for instance, repeated the regression analysis for Rightmire's sample but used individual "best estimate" dates for each specimen instead of dividing the sample into six groups and using their averages. She showed that all of the resulting regression slopes were significant, and concluded that there were evolutionary trends within *H. erectus*.

In one way or another all of these analyses are flawed. a number of specimens have been discovered or made available for study since Bilsborough's work, and in fact neither Bilsborough nor Rightmire included all of the *H. erectus* specimens that were known when their studies were published. Rightmire divided the sample into few components to allow a regression analysis to show significance (there were only five degrees of freedom regardless of sample size) unless the slopes attained extraordinary magnitude (Rightmire 1982). Moreover, he included a number of specimens in his analysis that many paleoanthropologists feel do not represent *H. erectus*. This made his assertion of evolutionary stasis unexpected by any model. By including (what many regard as) late australopithecines and (what many regard as) archaic *H. sapiens*, the combined sample should have shown significant change by

Reprinted with permission from *Paleobiology*, Vol. 10, pp. 389–406. Copyright © 1984 by The Paleontological Society.

either a gradualistic or a punctuational model unless there was no evolutionary change from late australopithecines to early *H. sapiens*. In correcting for the problem of too few sample groups for a regression analysis, Allen's analysis becomes sensitive to the exact date estimates used for individual specimens. While some of these are established with accuracy, others have much larger error ranges (and others are little better than guesses within broad time spans). The effect of varying date estimates on the results of her regressions are unclear.

In sum, in an analysis of evolutionary change (or its absence, stasis) it is desirable to examine a sample of *H. erectus* that is more narrowly defined to minimize the possibility of spurious results. A regression approach is clearly inappropriate (Levinton 1982), and units of analysis are required that have no finer resolution than the accuracy of the dates for the fossils themselves allow. This work will focus on a conservatively and narrowly defined *H. erectus* sample, divide all of the known specimens attributable to this sample into three temporal subsets with low enough temporal resolution to be certain that the specimens can be placed accurately, and examine these subsets for evidence of evolutionary stasis.

THE HOMO ERECTUS SAMPLE

Home erectus remains were first discovered in Indonesia, with subsequent early discoveries also made in Indonesia and in China. Indeed, the majority of known *H. erectus* remains are still from these east Asian regions, in spite of additional discoveries in Europe and Africa. The taxon, as it is regarded today, is a meld of older genus names that were used to reflect geographic and in some cases also temporal variation; for instance, *Sinanthropus, Pithecanthropus, Atlanthropus,* etc.

As recently as the 1950s, *H. erectus* was distinctly delineated by clear temporal boundaries. At its "beginning," the only hominid samples known to be older were the south African australopithecines, and these were not even universally regarded as hominids at the time. At its "end," the oldest of the later remains were European specimens from Steinheim, Swanscombe, and Mauer (Broken Hill was then regarded as being very late), and these showed numerous distinctions from the youngest known *H. erectus* sample from Zhoukoudian (reviewed by Howell 1960). Thus, a clear definition of the taxon and broad agreement about its contents were developed, based initially on easily delineated morphological distinctions from earlier and later hominid samples.

In the following decades, these boundaries became increasingly blurred, and finally in the view of many paleoanthropologists indistinct (Hemmer 1967; Mann 1971; Bilsborough 1976; Wolpoff 1980b; Cronin *et al.* 1981; Jelínek 1981). The discovery of *H. erectus* remains from below the Okote Tuff at Lake Turkana provided an "origins" age of more than 1.7 Myr. Earlier in time, the late australopithecine sample (late *H. habilis*) is now known to include specimens such as ER 1813, OH 16, and OH 13 that vary markedly in the *H. erectus* direction (Tobias 1980; Wolpoff 1980b; Cronin *et al.* 1981). At the late end of the time range, a number of Middle Pleistocene specimens were discovered in Europe, beginning in the 1950s. Many of these are evidently males corresponding to previously discovered females (Wolpoff 1980a). These specimens, which are much more robust (and *erectus*-like), include Petralona, Vértesszöllös, Bilzingsleben, and the Arago males. Their dis-

covery resurrected the question of whether some or all early Europeans represent *H. erectus*, and dramatically blurred the boundary by the very inability to resolve the problem (Wolpoff 1980a; Cronin *et al.* 1981; Jelínek 1981; Stringer 1981). Even in east Asia, where *H. erectus* samples are the largest and most complete, the late end of the range is extremely difficult to delineate, as evidenced by the difficulties in agreeing on whether the Ngandong sample is *H. erectus* or *H. sapiens* (Weidenreich 1943; Jacob 1976; Santa Luca 1980; Wolpoff 1980a, 1980b; Holloway 1981; Wolpoff *et al.* 1984).

The purpose of this short history is to explain why paleoanthropologists do not agree on which particular specimens belong in *H. erectus, and* to justify the use of a conservative definition of the taxon in this examination of whether or not it was characterized by evolutionary stasis. The conservative definition of *H. erectus* is based on the historic precedence of features characterizing the taxon as originally defined, and a reasonable estimation of the expected observed ranges and increased combinatorial possibilities for these features, because attempts at a broader morphological definition have failed when applied on a worldwide basis (Wolpoff *et al.* 1984). However, in this case a historic definition seems in line with normal taxonomic usage. Simpson (1961, p. 165), in discussing the implications of phyletic evolution, argues that "the lineage must be chopped into segments for purposes of classification, and this must be done arbitrarily." In practice, however, phyletic species are rarely defined in a completely arbitrary way. This is because "in most fossil sequences there are convenient breaks between horizons to permit a nonarbitrary delimitation of species" (Mayr 1969, p. 35) because of accidents of discovery, and if "one or more species are found and defined before the more extensive lineage is at hand, those species should be preserved as far as possible" (Simpson 1961, p. 166). The history of *H. erectus* discoveries reflects such a process. While various paleoanthropologists have subsequently attempted to include a wider range of specimens in the taxon (Howells 1980; Santa Luca 1980; Rightmire 1981), this would expand its range both in morphological variation and in temporal span. Thus, adhering to a definition based on the features originally ascribed to the taxon, and reasonable variants of these features, weights this analysis in favor of stasis, since the conservative definition limits the number of specimens and the range of potential variability included. In this regard, the sample used here is more limited in its morphological variation than the sample used by Rightmire (1981) in his "demonstration" of stasis.

To minimize error due to absolute age determinations and to maximize the sizes of samples for comparison, the conservative *H. erectus* sample is divided into three time spans, as detailed below. The earliest sample is from the Lower Pleistocene. The late sample is from the traditional "endpoint" of the species, and the middle sample is from the earlier Middle Pleistocene, between these in age.

Specifically (see Table 1), the early sample includes the remains attributed or attributable to *H. erectus* from the Lower Pleistocene deposits at east Turkana [1], Olduvai Beds II and III, the Lower Pleistocene Beds at Laetoli, Omo Member J and above, and the Lower Pleistocene sites from east Asia including specimens from the Putjangan Formation near and at Sangiran in Indonesia and Chinese specimens from the Dragon Bone cave at Jian Shi and from the Badong District—36 individuals. The middle sample is comprised of specimens from Olduvai Bed IV and the Masek Beds, Chad, Ternifine, Thomas,

Table 1. Composition of the hominid samples, by specimen and measurement or measurements represented.

	Cranial Capacity	Bregma-inion length	Maximum cranial breadth	Biparietal breadth	Biasterionic breadth	Biauricular breadth	Auricular-bregma height	Midorbit supraorbital height	Central parietal thickness	Mandibular P_3—M_2 chord	Corpus breadth at M_1	Corpus height at M_1/M_2	Breadth of M_1
Lower Pleistocene													
H. erectus sample													
ER 727											X	X	
730										X	X	X	X
731												X	
806													X
820													X
992										X	X	X	X
1593									X			X	
1648									X				
1805	X	X	X	X	X	X	X		X	X	X	X	
1808								X	X	X	X	X	
1821									X				
3733	X	X	X	X	X	X	X	X	X				
3883	X	X	X	X	X	X	X	X					
OH 9	X		X	X	X	X	X	X	X				
EM 550									X				
EM 551									X				
51											X	X	
Laetoli 29B											X	X	
Omo K7–19													X
Modjokerto	X												
Sangiran 1										X	X	X	X
4	X	X	X	X	X	X	X		X				
5											X	X	
6											X	X	X
9										X	X	X	X
27								X					
P12													X
S14													X
S33													X
S51													X
S52													X
S53													X
S72													X
S98													X
Jian Shi PA 504													X
Badong District PA 507													X
Early Middle Pleistocene													
H. erectus sample													
OH 12	X				X			X	X				
22										X	X	X	X

Table 1. (cont.)

	Cranial Capacity	*Bregma-inion length*	*Maximum cranial breadth*	*Biparietal breadth*	*Biasterionic breadth*	*Biauricular breadth*	*Auricular-bregma height*	*Midorbit supraorbital height*	*Central parietal thickness*	*Mandibular P$_3$–M$_2$ chord*	*Corpus breadth at M$_1$*	*Corpus height at M$_1$/M$_2$*	*Breadth of M$_1$*
SK 15											X	X	X
Baringo										X	X	X	X
Gombde II									X				
Chad								X					
Ternifine 1										X	X	X	X
2										X	X	X	X
3										X	X	X	X
4				X					X				
Thomas 1								X			X	X	X
3								X					
Trinil 2	X	X		X	X			X					
Sangiran 2	X	X	X	X	X	X	X	X	X				
3	X	X		X	X				X				
10	X	X	X	X	X	X	X	X	X				
12	X	X	X	X	X	X	X		X				
13A									X				
17	X	X	X	X	X	X	X	X	X				
18A								X					
20									X				
22											X	X	X
Lantian PA 102										X	X	X	X
PA 105	X			X				X	X				
Longgudong PA 531													X
Later Middle Pleistocene													
***H. erectus* sample**													
Sambungmachan	X	X	X	X	X	X	X	X					X
CKT A1													X
A2										X	X		X
A3													X
B1													X
B2													X
B3													X
B4													X
C1													X
C3													X
D1	X	X	X	X	X	X	X	X	X				
E1	X	X	X	X	X	X	X	X	X				
F1													X
G1											X	X	X
G2									X				
H1										X	X	X	
H3	X	X	X	X	X	X	X	X					
H4											X		X

Table 1. (cont.)

	Cranial Capacity	Bregma-inion length	Maximum cranial breadth	Biparietal breadth	Biasterionic breadth	Biauricular breadth	Auricular-bregma height	Midorbit supraorbital height	Central parietal thickness	Mandibular P₃—M₂ chord	Corpus breadth at M₁	Corpus height at M₁/M₂	Breadth of M₁
CKT I1									X				
K1										X	X	X	X
L1	X	X	X	X	X	X	X	X	X				
L2	X	X	X	X	X	X	X	X	X				
L3	X	X	X	X	X	X	X	X	X				
L4													
M2													X
O2										X	X	X	
PA 86													X
PA 69/70										X	X	X	
Hexian PA 830	X		X	X	X	X	X	X					X
831											X		
834											X	X	X
S. officinalis 3													X
													X
Latest sample													
Ngandong 1	X	X	X	X	X	X	X	X	X				
3			X	X	X	X	X		X				
4			X	X				X	X				
5	X	X	X	X	X	X	X	X	X				
6	X	X	X	X	X	X	X	X					
8				X	X				X				
9	X	X	X	X	X		X	X	X				
10	X	X	X	X	X	X	X	X	X				
11	X	X	X	X	X	X	X	X	X				
15									X				
Petralona	X	X	X	X	X	X	X	X	X				
Arago 21	X		X	X			X	X	X				
Vértesszöllös	X				X								

Gomboré II, Baringo Kapthurian Formation, Swartkrans Member II, the Indonesian remains from Trinil and from the Kabuh Formation at Sangiran, and from China both Lantian specimens (Gongwangling and Chenchiawo) and the remains from and attributable to Longgudong—25 individuals. The late sample is from Zhoukoudian, Hexian, the isolated teeth from south China, and the Indonesian site of Sambungmachan—31 individuals. In all, 92 *H. erectus* individuals are represented in these samples. Dates and provenances for the individuals are reviewed by Curtis (1981), Howell (1978), Jacob (1976), Matsu'ura (1982), Sartono (1982), Sartono and Djubiantono (1983), Wolpoff *et al.* (1984), and Zhou *et al.* (1982).

These samples are similar to Bilsborough's (1976) and Rightmire's (1981), and had these authors divided *H. erectus* into three time spans, sample compositions would have been almost the same for the specimens that their analyses share with this one. This analysis includes more *H. erectus* specimens than either of the previous ones, but omits certain individuals Rightmire included because these do not fit the conservative definition of the taxon; in particular OH 13, Sidi Abderrahman, Salé, Petralona, Montmaurin, and the Arago and Ngandong samples.

While this exhausts the sample that can be attributed to *H. erectus*, as conservatively defined, a number of other specimens have also been included in the taxon by some paleoanthropologists. The Ngandong remains, Petralona, Vértesszöllös, Bilzingsleben, and the Arago sample are thought by some to represent *H. erectus*, although this is by no means a universal opinion and many paleoanthropologists regard some or all of these as *H. sapiens* (Weidenreich 1943; Stringer *et al.* 1979; Wolpoff 1980a; Stringer 1981). It would be a mistake to include these in the *H. erectus* sample analyzed here, because it could be argued that by including specimens that may be *H. sapiens*, analysis might appear to show a lack of stasis in the sample when there actually was stasis for *H. erectus* more accurately defined. If these is error in which specimens are included in *H. erectus*, it is better to err on the conservative side. Thus, as a matter of interest, a fourth "later sample" of 13 individuals was constructed of the above specimens. However, *no statements made about* H. erectus *refer to this sample*. It is not analyzed along with the *H. erectus* remains either for the presence of evolutionary change or for the determination of its rate.

METHODS

The three temporal spans within the *H. erectus* sample were compared for a number of measurements. The same comparisons were made between the late *H. erectus* sample and the even later hominid group described above. All of the linear measurements were taken by the author on original specimens, with the exception of those for the Hexian cranium which are from published sources (Wu and Dong 1982; Wu 1983). Cranial capacities have been reported by Weidenreich (1943, 1945), Chiu *et al.* (1973), Wolpoff (1977), Riscutia (1975), Holloway (1978, 1980, 1981, 1982, 1983), Stringer *et al.* (1979).

Measurements were chosen to reflect different parts of the cranium and mandible and, as far as possible, these represent metrics with the largest sample sizes. Moreover, the four measurements used by Rightmire (1981) are also included.

Cranial capacity is an absolutely critical measure, reflecting the size of an organ that changes more over the course of human evolution than does any other. It was also used by Rightmire (1981).

The cranial length measure chosen was the bregma to inion chord. The sample size for this measure is much larger that for the more traditional length measure from glabella to opisthocranion (which for this sample is the same as to bregma). For instance, in the middle sample there are only two specimens that allow the length from glabella to be taken, while the sample size for the length from inion is six.

Four cranial breadth measurements were used. The maximum cranial breadth and the biparietal (i.e., braincase) breadth describe somewhat different aspects of the cranium because of the marked basal pneumatization in *H. erectus*. Biasterionic breadth estimates the breadth of the nuchal plane, an area that expands dramatically with the appearance of *H. erectus* and markedly changes again in *H. sapiens* in response to the changing function of the nuchal musculature (Wolpoff 1980b). Biauricular breadth was included because Rightmire (1981) used it.

The only cranial height measure with sufficient sample sizes was the sagittal projection of the chord from the auricular point to bregma.

Two other structures that are independent of the gross size of the vault were included. The height (thickness) of the supraorbital torus over the middle of the orbit provided a measurement of brow ridge size. Thickness of the cranial vault walls was measured by the parietal thickness at its approximate center.

For the mandible three dimensions were used. The length of the tooth row between the most mesial point on the P_3 root where it enters the alveolus and the most distal point on the M_2 root where it enters the alveolus provides a measure of the room that the postcanine tooth row takes up. This particular measurement can be made on the alveolar rim of the mandibular corpus, whether or not the crowns of the teeth are preserved. The maximum breadth of the corpus at the M_1 position and the vertical height of the corpus between M_1 and M_2 were chosen to reflect the gross corpus dimensions.

Finally, the breadth of M_1 was reported to reflect the changes in posterior tooth size, one of the most dramatically changing features in human evolution. M_1 is used because its sample size is best, it has the highest heritability of the molars, and it was used by Rightmire (1981). The breadth dimension (rather than length or area) is reported because it is unaffected by interproximal attrition and thereby is independent of age at death.

Means and other summary statistics for these measurements are reported in Table 2, and frequency distributions for a number of them are shown in figures. The means are compared with a single-sided Student's *t*-test, with significance reported at the .05 level.

Comparisons are made between the temporally adjacent *H. erectus* samples, between the early and the late *erectus* samples, and between the late *erectus* sample and the sample of later hominids described above for all but the masticatory-related measurements—these have too small a sample size to report for the latest hominid sample and thus the last of the comparisons shown in Table 2 is not made for them (for details of dental variation during this time span, see Wolpoff 1982).

An average evolutionary rate, in darwins, was determined for the *H. erectus* sample, as conservatively defined, by comparing the means for the early and late *H. erectus* samples. In almost all cases the mean value for the middle *H. erectus* sample is between the earlier and the later sample means, and for the two exceptions the mean of the middle sample is virtually identical to the early (for biasterionic breadth) or the late (for central parietal thickness) sample means. Thus, comparing the early and late samples is a reasonable basis for an average estimate of rate. The duration for the rate calculation was determined by comparing the mean age of the crania in the late sample with the mean age for the early specimens. This was found to be almost exactly 1 Myr (1.4 Myr for the early sample average and 0.4 Myr for the late sample average). Fortunately, these mean dates could be determined with reasonable accuracy. It is mainly in the middle sample that many of the date determinations are less accurate and specimens can only be placed within a broad temporal span. It is likely that the probable error in the average rates does not exceed 10%.

RESULTS

With only a few exceptions, the differences between the early and late *H. erectus* samples are marked and significant (Table 2) [2]. In only two of the variables (midorbit supraorbital thickness and biasterionic breadth) does this comparison of means not attain significance. Between the adjacent temporal samples the magnitudes of the differences are somewhat less; the differences between the early and middle samples are significant in three cases (two of these are mandibular), and significance between the middle and late samples is only attained

Table 2. Comparison of sample statistics for *Homo erectus* divided into three time spans, and a sample of later hominids attributed to *H. erectus* by some authors, but to *H. sapiens* by others. The average rate of evolutionary change for the three *H. erectus* samples is given in darwins, and the significance of various comparisons of the means at the 0.05 level using a single sided student's *t*-test is indicated. The three possible comparisons are made within the *H. erectus* sample, and the late *erectus* group is compared with the sample of later hominids (L-LL). Details of the samples and of the measurements examined are in Table 1 and the text. Specific frequency distributions for most of the measurements are given in Figures 1-12.

	Homo erectus			Rate of change (darwins)	Homo erectus or sapiens	Significance at 5% level			
	Early	*Middle*	*Late*		*Latest*	*E–M*	*M–L*	*E–L*	*L–LL*
Cranial capacity	810	886	1,060	(.27)	1,155		X	X	X
n	6	8	8		9				
σ	175.9	112.5	93.6		75.5				
Bregma-inion length	123.2	132.0	139.1	(.12)	149.4			X	X
n	4	6	6		7				
σ	11.0	10.4	6.9		7.0				
Maximum cranial breadth	142.4	148.5	151.1	(.06)	151.9			X	
n	5	4	7		9				
σ	7.5	8.7	5.8		7.4				
Biparietal breadth	127.5	137.5	139.9	(.09)	144.3			X	X
n	5	8	8		11				
σ	13.3	8.5	5.1		4.7				
Biasterionic breadth	113.9	112.5	119.0	(.04)	125.2				X
n	5	7	8		11				
σ	13.3	9.4	11.1		4.6				
Biauricular breadth	135.4	137.0	145.0	(0.7)	143.2			X	
n	4	4	7		8				
σ	4.2	10.0	3.5		7.6				
Auricular-bregma height	86.2	91.8	96.8	(.12)	102.0			X	X
n	5	4	7		9				
σ	6.6	4.1	5.9		5.1				
Midorbit supraorbital height	13.8	13.8	13.3	(−.04)	13.3				
n	5	8	8		9				
σ	3.7	3.5	1.9		2.6				
Central parietal thickness	9.2	10.8	10.7	(.15)	9.6	X		X	
n	10	11	7		9				
σ	1.4	2.1	0.9		2.0				
Mandibular P_3–M_2 chord	43.6	42.8	38.9	(−.11)			X	X	
n	6	7	6						
σ	2.0	1.7	1.8						
Corpus breadth at M_1	20.4	17.5	17.3	(−.16)		X		X	
n	11	9	9						
σ	2.6	1.9	2.5						
Corpus height at M_1/M_2	34.2	30.6	29.8	(−.14)		X		X	
n	13	9	6						
σ	4.3	4.1	3.8						
Breadth of M_1	12.4	12.1	11.8	(−.05)				X	
n	18	10	20						
σ	1.0	0.7	0.8						

in the cranial capacity and the posterior dental chord length of the mandible.

In the comparison of the late *H. erectus* sample with the even later Middle Pleistocene specimens, significance is attained in 5 of the 7 cranial measures. *In almost every instance the change between late* erectus *and this latest sample is in the same direction as the change within* H. erectus.

One of the most dramatic changes is in cranial capacity (Fig. 1)[3]. Changes in the mean, mode, and range all reflect the continuous expansion of vault size within *H. erectus*, while the samples overlap in range, following a pattern one might expect under a model of shifting allele frequencies for this polygenic

feature. The magnitude of average change contradicts the assertion that if there is any gradual evolution in a chronospecies, it is of very low magnitude and "a typical chronospecies does not exhibit a great deal more total variability, from end to end, than is found among the living populations of a similar species" (Stanley 1981, p. 14). Late *H. erectus* cranial capacity is 31% greater than the early sample's mean. In contrast, the largest mean capacity for a living human population is barely 10% greater than the smallest populational mean, according to data reported by Tobias (1971). Thus, *H. erectus* provides a valid basis for rejecting the claim that "no gradualism has been detected within any hominid taxon... the trend to larger brains

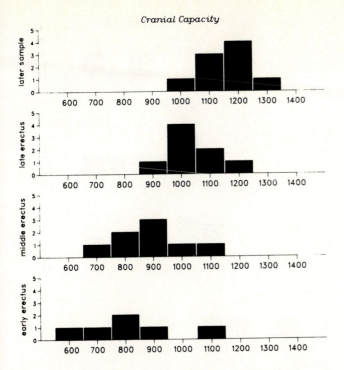

Figure 1. *Distribution of cranial capacity in cubic centimeters for three* Homo erectus *samples and a sample of later hominids. See Table 2 for the means and other statistics.*

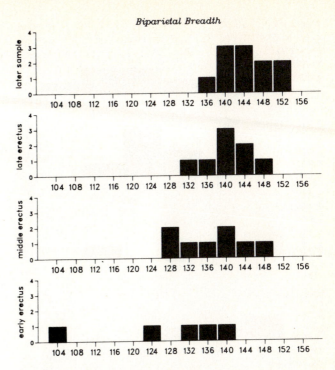

Figure 2. *Distribution of the biparietal breadth in millimeters for three* Homo erectus *samples and a sample of later hominids. See Table 2 for the means and other statistics.*

arises from differential success of essentially static taxa" (Gould and Eldredge 1977, p. 115).

With a significant trend in cranial capacity increase, as expected the linear dimensions of the vault also increase, in most cases significantly. Moreover, the *pattern* of dimensional increase for vault measurements is of some interest (apart from the *fact* of increase) because of the disproportionate rates of change, many of which continue through the Upper Pleistocene and in some cases continue through modern populations. For instance, within *H. erectus* the increase in biparietal breadth (Fig. 2) is of greater magnitude than the increase in maximum cranial breadth (Fig. 3), and the biparietal breadth increase attains significance for more comparisons within the sample. Moreover, the *rate* of maximum cranial breadth change decreases, the greatest difference in average maximum cranial breadths is between the early and middle samples. Throughout *H. erectus, even* in the latest *erectus* sample, the maximum cranial breadth remains much greater than the biparietal breadth, but by the Upper Pleistocene the continuation of these two trends results in the maximum cranial breadth *becoming* the biparietal breadth. What happens is a combination of continued parietal expansion (reflecting larger braincases) combined with a much lower rate of expansion (and ultimately a reduction) for the pneumatization of the cranial base. The altered relationship between these measures of breadth is only expressed in Upper Pleistocene hominids, but the evolutionary trends leading to this altered relationship are clearly evident within *H. erectus*.

The pattern of expansion in biasterionic and biauricular breadths is somewhat different. The expansion of biauricular (Fig. 4) breadth is almost as rapid as the biparietal expansion. Biasterionic expands more slowly within *H. erectus*; there is no significant change (actually a very slight decrease) between the early and middle samples, and the difference between the early

and late samples does not attain statistical significance. Interestingly, there is a jump in the expansion of biasterionic breadth between the late *H. erectus* sample and the sample of later hominids, and this difference is significant. Thus, biasterionic breadth begins its expansion only in the late *H. erectus* sample,

Figure 3. *Distribution of the maximum breadth of the cranium in millimeters for three* Homo erectus *samples and a sample of later hominids. See Table 2 for the means and other statistics.*

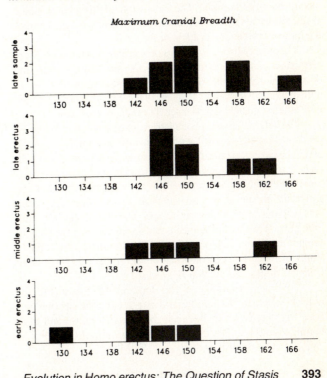

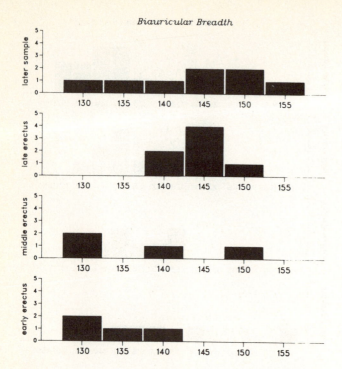

Figure 4. *Distribution of biauricular breadth in millimeters for three* Homo erectus *samples and a sample of later hominids. See Table 2 for the means and other statistics.*

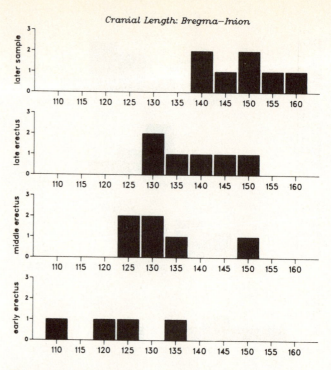

Figure 5. *Distribution of the bregma-inion length in millimeters for three* Homo erectus *samples and a sample of later hominids. See Table 2 for the means and other statistics.*

and this is a continuing trend in the later hominids. Biasterionic breadth is the only cranial dimension examined that responds significantly to something that can be independent of vault size; in this case, the width of the nuchal plane, which is a function of the size of the nuchal musculature. The hypothesis that the size of the nuchal musculature in hominids reflects the magnitude of anterior tooth loading suggests an explanation for this pattern of change because the hominid remains from the early Upper Pleistocene have the largest anterior teeth of any Pleistocene hominid sample. The expansion of the nuchal plane accelerates after *H. erectus*, coincidently with the expansion of the incisors in the Upper Pleistocene.

The other two measures of vault size, length as measured from bregma to inion (Fig. 5) and height as measured by the projection of the auricular-bregma distance into the sagittal plane (Fig. 6), both increase more rapidly than any of the breadth dimensions and both attain statistical significance for the *H. erectus* span.

The additional morphological features examined are independent of vault size, at least in principle. The thickness of the parietal bone at its center (Fig. 7) increases significantly within *H. erectus*, and at a much faster rate than the rate of change in darwins reported would suggest, since all of the increase is between the early and middle *H. erectus* samples. This thickness decreases between the late *H. erectus* sample and the sample of later hominids. While the difference is not significant, it is tempting to suggest that a continuation of this trend results in the much thinner vaults of modern populations. However, in this case there is no evidence of this trend within *H. erectus*.

Thickness (height) of the supraorbital torus (Fig. 8) reduces between the middle and late *H. erectus* samples but does not change at all between the late *H. erectus* and later hominid samples. The difference between middle and late *H. erectus* is not significant.

The measures of mandibular size show marked reduction, and this is surely related to posterior dental reduction. The breadth of the M_1 (Fig. 9) reduces significantly within *H. erectus*, a trend that continues through the whole span of the

Figure 6. *Distribution of the auricular-bregma height projected into the sagittal plane, in millimeters, for three* Homo erectus *samples and a sample of later hominids. See Table 2 for the means and other statistics.*

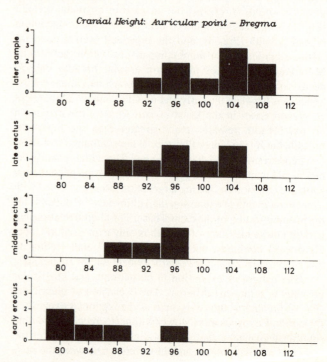

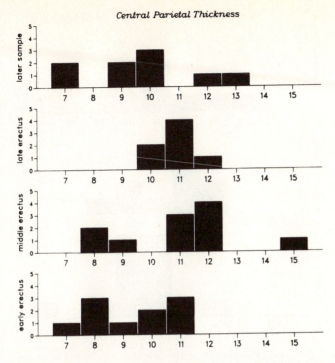

Figure 7. *Distribution of the thickness of the parietal at its center in millimeters for three* Homo erectus *samples and a sample of later hominids. See Table 2 for the means and other statistics.*

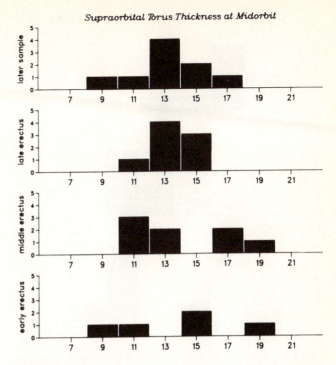

Figure 8. *Distribution of the height (thickness) of the supraorbital torus at the mid-orbit position, in millimeters, for three* Homo erectus *samples and a sample of later hominids. See Table 2 for the means and other statistics.*

Pleistocene. Similarly, the mandibular measure directly reflecting the size of the dentition, the alveolar length from P_3 to M_2 (Fig. 10) also reduces significantly. This reduction is of greater magnitude because it includes the size of two teeth which show even more reduction than M_1 within *H. erectus*, these are the M_2 and the P_4.

The mandibular corpus height (Fig. 11) and breadth (Fig. 12) dimensions change significantly and dramatically through the *H. erectus* span, at a much higher rate than the M_1 reduces, and indeed at a higher rate than the change in any of the cranial dimensions except for central parietal thickness. Moreover, the rate determination is an underestimate of the actual rate, since the bulk of the mandibular corpus reduction is between the early and middle *H. erectus* samples. Breadth of the corpus reduces more rapidly than height, reflecting a trend that results in the relatively thin mandibles of modern populations. It is possible that the posterior dental reduction is a consequence of the more rapid changes in the mandibular corpus dimensions, leading to crowding and insufficient room for the developing tooth crowns. The corpus dimensions may more directly reflect the decreasing use of the posterior dentition.

These reductions of masticatory structures contrast with the expanding cranial vault. If the expansion in brain size and in the vault dimensions related to it were "explained" by a hypothetical increase in body size alone, this would make the reducing masticatory structures even more significant. Similarly, an attempt to "explain" the reducing masticatory structures by a hypothetical decrease in body size would throw the increasing vault sizes into even greater contrast. Actually, what little evidence there is for body sizes within *H. erectus* indicates no significant change at all (Wolpoff 1980b). The minimal interpretation of these data, if the body

size information is discounted, is that at least one adaptive complex changes significantly within *H. erectus*. The likely interpretation is that both adaptive systems change significantly.

Figure 9. *Distribution of the transverse breadth of the* M_1 *in millimeters for three* Homo erectus *samples. See Table 2 for the means and other statistics.*

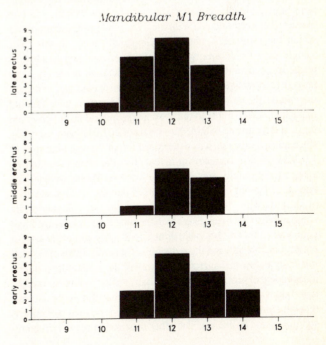

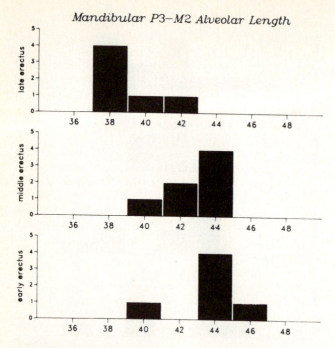

Figure 10. *Distribution of the alveolar distance on the mandible from the P₃ to the M₂, in millimeters, for three* Homo erectus *samples. See Table 2 for the means and other statistics.*

DISCUSSION

It would appear that there are significant evolutionary changes within a conservatively defined sample of *H. erectus*. Of course, all of the measurements examined do not change, but punctuationalism and stasis are contentions about the evolution of *lineages*, and not about individual measurements. The changes documented within *H. erectus* involve certainly one and most probably two adaptive systems, the two which change the most over the full course of Plio-Pleistocene hominid evolution.

The rate of change in these systems is of interest. The estimations of evolutionary rates are influenced by how well the group in question has been studied (Williams 1957) and by the duration over which the estimate is obtained (Gingerich 1983). In this case, sample sizes for *H. erectus* are hardly overwhelming (tending to result in an *under*estimation of rates), although evidently large enough to show significant differences within the sample. As to their magnitude, the rates calculated are for a 1-Myr span, which should make them comparable to the average (geometric mean) observed fossil vertebrate rate of 0.08 darwins reported by Gingerich (1983), since this average rate was determined for an average time span of 1.6 Myr. Such a comparison reveals that the changes within *H. erectus* are generally at or above the fossil vertebrate average. The rate of change for cranial capacity (0.09 darwins, the reported rate of 0.27 darwins divided by three to make the volumetric rate comparable to the linear rates) is more rapid than the average fossil vertebrate rate. Of the vault dimensions, only the expansion of biasterionic breadth and the reduction of supraorbital thickness fall markedly below this average, and both of these are at least in part independent of gross vault size. The rate of reduction for M₁ breadth falls below the fossil vertebrate average, but this is the slowest reducing of the posterior teeth and as detailed above its reduction is significant for *H. erectus*. The other mastication-related structures

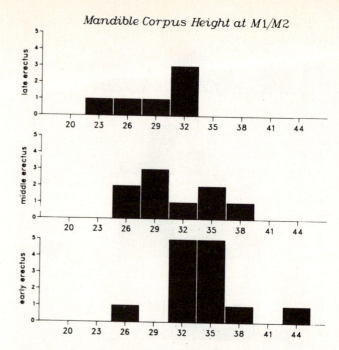

Figure 11. *Distribution of the height of the mandible in millimeters, taken between the first and second molar positions, for three* Homo erectus *samples. See Table 2 for the means and other statistics.*

of the mandible reduce at a rate markedly above the fossil vertebrate average. The average absolute rate of change for all the dimensions examined is 0.10 darwins [4].

Thus, one must conclude not only that there are significant evolutionary trends within *H. erectus* but also that the rate of change within the taxon is at or above the fossil vertebrate

Figure 12. *Distribution of the breadth of the mandible in millimeters, taken at the M₁ position, for three* Homo erectus *samples. See Table 2 for the means and other statistics.*

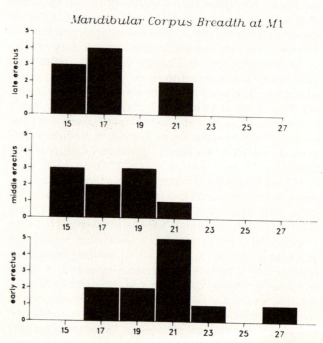

average. One could hardly regard these data as *supporting* the interpretation of evolutionary stasis!

However, supporting a model of evolutionary change is one thing and disproving it is another, and we may legitimately ask whether these data disprove the interpretation of stasis for *H. erectus*. Gould and Eldredge (1977, p. 133) have argued that even when a lineage *appears* to show gradual change it actually reflects stasis because the rates of change "are only sufficient to cast a superficial molding upon the pattern of evolutionary change." This argument presupposes that the rates of phyletic change are *constant* and that average rates for long durations apply to a species at all times and over all durations, an unlikely and unsupportable assumption (Charlesworth *et al.* 1982; Gingerich 1983). Moreover, there is something suspicious about a "superficial molding" interpretation for the changes within *H. erectus*. This is because the main patterns of change are bidirectional, *expansion* of the cranial vault and *reduction* of the masticatory apparatus, and are in exactly the directions revealed by comparing the preceding and subsequent species. Even the details of change (greater expansion of biparietal breadth than of maximum cranial breadth, greater reduction of mandibular corpus thickness than of corpus height) adhere to the macroevolutionary patterns revealed by comparing the three Pleistocene species of the genus *Homo*. Thus, most of the specific differences characterizing the comparison of *H. habilis* with *H. sapiens* are reflected in the progressive changes *within* the *H. erectus* sample. While serendipity undoubtedly plays a role in the evolutionary process, it is asking too much to invoke it as an explanation here. In this case the rates of change within *H. erectus* are neither an obvious reflection of stasis nor the "fundamental mystery" that Gould and Eldredge (1977, p. 134) suggest.

The fact is that the criteria required to adequately disprove gradual change in the fossil record are very difficult to meet (Levinton and Simon 1980; Charlesworth *et al.* 1982; Schopf and Hoffman 1983), as are the criteria required to validly reject the punctuated equilibrium interpretation (Gould and Eldredge 1977). Yet the ready acceptance of the *H. erectus* analysis published by Rightmire (1981) as a valid disproof of gradualism for the taxon suggests that the sample size and the geographic and temporal distribution of this species were considered sufficient to disprove gradualism and thereby to establish stasis validly. Unless more stringent criteria are required to disprove stasis, the present study meets or exceeds the same criteria of sample size and geographic range, and it should be concluded that stasis for *H. erectus* can be rejected.

There are two other reasons why the *H. erectus* sample does not fit the predictions of the punctuational model. One of these involves the late or continued survival of ancestral species (a prediction of the model). Gould (1976) raised this for *H. erectus* through his contention that early specimens overlapped in time with late surviving ancestral forms in east Africa. He may have (and Stanley, 1979, definitely has) derived this idea from publications by Leakey and Walker (1976, expanded in Walker and Leakey 1978, and argued more recently in Leakey and Walker 1980). Leakey and Walker based their argument for temporal overlap on ER 1805 and on ER 1813 as well as other specimens from area 123 which were then placed "provisionally" in the Upper Member of the Koobi Fora Formation at east Turkana. However, ER 1805 is not widely regarded as an australopithecine [1] (Howell 1978; Wolpoff 1980b; Thorne and Wolpoff 1981), and area 123 is now recognized to be in the Lower Member so that the specimens in it are earlier than the

known remains of *H. erectus* from east Turkana. Thus, at the moment *there are no sites where* H. erectus *remains are stratigraphically interdigitated with remains clearly attributed to (non-boisei) australopithecines*. While it has been argued that the comparison of radiometric or faunal dates for *different* sites shows (non-boisei) australopithecines at some sites to have the same age as *H. erectus* at others, all of these dates have probable error ranges that exceed the date differences between the sites. The fact that no evidence from a *single* site with both *H. erectus* and *H. habilis* shows these species overlapping in stratigraphic position indicates strongly that *H. habilis* and *H. erectus* are neither narrowly nor broadly contemporary.

The other reason concerns the boundaries of *H. erectus*. Here, too, predictions of the punctuational model are not clearly met. In punctuational theory, species are distinct entities with a "real" beginning and end (Gould and Eldredge 1977; Vrba 1980). However, as discussed above, for *H. erectus* these terminal boundaries seem to be indistinct (Mann 1971; Wolpoff 1980a; Cronin *et al.* 1981; Jelínek 1981; Wolpoff *et al.* 1984). Indeed, because the *erectus/sapiens* boundary is so difficult to delineate on morphological grounds alone, a number of authors have discussed whether *H. erectus* should be distinguished from *H sapiens* (Weidenreich 1943; Wolpoff *et al.* 1984), and some have suggested that *H. erectus* be formally sunk (Hemmer 1967; Jelínek 1981).

While this research provides some interesting and perhaps important information about *H. erectus*, it is *not* a general disproof of the punctuated equilibrium model. Indeed, this model has proven to be excruciatingly difficult to test in the fossil record (Levinton and Simon 1980; Schopf 1981, 1982; Charlesworth *et al.* 1982; Schopf and Hoffman 1983). Moreover, it is possible that nothing can totally disprove this model because there surely are *some* species that are characterized by periods of stasis followed by speciation with rapid change and subsequent species replacement. The issue addressed here is not whether the model is generally valid or invalid, but the often repeated claim that punctuated equilibrium is the most probable (common) source of evolutionary change. Analysis of a single species cannot resolve this either, but the fact is that *H. erectus* has been repeatedly promoted as one of the best examples of stasis in the fossil record, and the claim that stasis is common can only be addressed through specific analyses of the species that are said to show it (cf. Bookstein *et al.* 1978; Malmgren and Kennet 1981; Raup and Crick 1981). If "stasis is data," *H. erectus* is clearly one species providing evidence that stasis is less common than thought.

ACKNOWLEDGMENTS

I am sincerely grateful for the many scientists who allowed me access to the original materials in their care, and who treated me with kindness and courtesy during my stay. I thank C. Arambourg of the Musée d'Histoire Naturelle (Paris); C. K. Brain and E. Vrba of the Transvaal Museum (Pretoria); Y. Coppens and J.-L. Heim of the Musée de l'Homme (Paris); F. C. Howell of the University of California (Berkeley); J. Hublin of the University of Paris; T. Jacob of Universitas Gadjah Mada (Jogjakarta); D. Kadar of the Museum Geologi (Bandung); the late G. H. R. von Koenigswald of the Senckenberg Museum (Frankfurt); R. E. F. Leakey and M. Leakey of the National Museums of Kenya (Nairobi); H. and M.-A. de Lumley of the Laboratoire de

Préhistoire du Musée National d'Histoire Naturelle (Paris); D. Mania of the Landesmuseum für Vorgeschichte (Halle/Salle); J. Melentis of the University of Thessaloniki; C. B. Stringer of the British Museum of Natural History (London); I. Tattersall of the American Museum of Natural History (New York); Wu Rukang, Wu Xinzhi, Zhang Yinyun, and Dong Xingren of the Institute for Vertebrate Paleontology and Paleoanthropology (Beijing); and F. Fulep of the Magyar Nemzeti Museum (Budapest). This research was supported by NSF grants BNS 76-8279 and INT 81-17276 and grants from the National Academy of Sciences Eastern European Program. For their substantial help in preparing this manuscript I am indebted to D. Evon, P. Gingerich, G. P. Rightmire, M. D. Russell, and A. C. Walker. I also thank C. L. Brace, P. Bridges D. W. Frayer, and K. Rosenberg.

NOTES

[1] In the initial descriptions and subsequent summary of the east Turkana hominid discoveries (Leakey and Leakey 1978), species allocations for the specimens were not provided. The allocations used here are based on the author's experience with the original material and reflect the application of conservative criteria in the assessments. Thus, for instance, ER 1648 and 1821 are large cranial fragments (used only for cranial thickness measures) with a temporal line that marks a distinct angulation between the superior and lateral aspects of the vault. This is a morphology not found in any of the australopithecine species, but common in *Homo erectus*. Similarly, the isolated ER 806 dentition is found within the Okote tuff, where the only hominids that can be unambiguously identified are *H. erectus* and *Australopithecus boisei*. The teeth are far too small to possibly represent the megadont australopithecine species. Finally, including the east Turkana specimen ER 1805 (Day *et al.* 1976) in the *H. erectus* sample, instead of describing it as a "bizarre" australopithecine with a "pongid-like" morphology, as some have suggested, is a consequence of considering the morphological details that align it with *H. erectus* and distinguish it from any of the australopithecine species. The appearance of several functional complexes supports this contention. These include the emphasis on posterior temporalis as indicated by the posterior approach of the temporal lines, the expansion of the nuchal plane to incorporate the posterior aspect of the mastoid, the marked expansion of the anterior braincase reflected in the lack of significant postorbital constriction, and the broadening of the face that is indicated by the very wide interorbital area and the notable distance between the infraorbital foramina. Other details that support this diagnosis include the deep digastric grooves and the postbregmatic depression. It is the expansion of the posterior temporalis and of the nuchal musculature on a small vault that results in the sagittal and compound temporal/nuchal crests (with the associated shelving in the region of the parietal notch) that has confused the interpretation of this individual. The small postcanine dentition indicates that these muscular expansions reflect an increasing use of the anterior dentition in horizontal loading and do not result from the pattern of molar loading that causes muscular hypertrophy in the australopithecines.

[2] If ER 1805 were to be omitted from the analysis, some of the means for the early group would change. However, the only loss of significance, as indicated on Table 2, is the significance of the difference in cranial capacity between the early and middle *H. erectus* samples. *In all other cases, the significances indicated in Table 2 are retained,* and the relations of magnitudes of the means also remain the same. While the author does not believe that this specimen should be omitted from the sample, the fact is that analysis of evolutionary trends within an *H. erectus* sample not including ER 1805 has exactly the same results. Similarly, excluding the several cranial fragments from the analysis of cranial thickness (the only place they appear) does not significantly change the mean for the early sample. While larger samples would be desirable, the present sample sizes are large enough to shield the analysis from extreme sensitivity to single specimens. Thus, it must be concluded that an even more narrowly defined *H. erectus* sample also shows the same pattern of significant evolutionary change!

[3] The Modjokerto child is included in the cranial capacity analysis (this is the only comparison where this specimen appears). While widely regarded as an infant, or at the most 2-3 years in age (Grimm 1941; Boule and Valois 1957; Coon 1962), there are contradictions in its morphology that have always suggested that so young an age may be incorrect (Piveteau 1957; LeGros Clark 1964). The young age was thought to be indicated by an open bregmatic fontanelle (this is actually broken bone), the relatively high vault (actually the auricular-bregmatic height is the lowest of the Indonesian sample, and relative to the bregma-inion length it is at the sample's mean), and the elongated parietal relative to the other vault bones (the parietal/occipital length ratio is also at the Indonesian sample's mean, and, while the ratio with frontal length is long, this probably reflects the lack of glabellar swelling). What does suggest a young age is the thinness of the vault and of the supraorbital torus. On the other hand, several features indicate that the specimen is far from being an infant. These include the ossified tympanic region, the depth of the glenoid fossa, the development of the mastoid process (similar to Sangiran 2), the development of the nuchal torus with a distinct although not projecting triangular inion prominence below it, the postorbital constriction, the low frontal inclination, and the marked projection of the supraorbital region anterior to the frontal squama with the consequent supratoral sulcus. The lack of cranial remains for other *Homo erectus* children makes an exact age estimation difficult, but comparison of these features with those of the few other children known in the hominid fossil record indicates the specimen is almost certainly older than Taung and Gibraltar and younger than Teshik Tash. This would bracket it between 6 and 9 years in age, and indeed taking the differences in adult morphology into account the Modjokerto child most closely resembles La Quina 18 (about 7 years in age) in the development of the features enumerated above. At this age, it is unlikely that the adult capacity would be more than 8% greater if one assumes that a human growth curve was followed (Ashton and Spence 1958; Schultz 1965), and it would be less if the growth rate in *H. erectus* were more rapid.

As to the capacity of the specimen, the liquid capacity of the *outside* of the vault determined by Riscutia (1975) by immersing it in water and measuring the displacement was 673 cc, not markedly different from the endocranial capacity estimate suggested by Dubois (1936)—650 cc—and by Boule and Vallois (1957)—not more than 700 cc. Clearly, the brain size cannot be larger than this figure. However, Riscutia's estimate was for the outside of the vault. He then attempted to determine how much smaller the endocranial capacity actually was. Using a spherical model he determined the effects on the endocranial volume of average vault thicknesses of 1, 2, and 3 mm. These were, respectively, 637 cc, 601 cc, and 568 cc. From my measurements of vault thicknesses where the specimen is broken, 3 mm would be a *minimum* average for the braincase. If an actual endocranial estimate of 568 cc (or even 601 cc) follows from this work, the adult estimate of 650 cc that I used in the analysis is quite reasonable, if not an overestimate of the likely adult volume. Given the capacity estimates for OH 12 and ER 1805, this figure is not outside the known (or excluding ER 1805 the reasonably expected) range for *H. erectus*.

[4] Without ER 1805 the average rate of change is slightly less, 0.08 darwins.

REFERENCES

Allen, L. L. 1982. Stasis vs. evolutionary change in *Homo erectus*. *Am. J. Phys. Anthropol.* 57:166.

Ashton, E. H., and Spence, T. F. 1958. Age changes in the cranial capacity and foramen magnum of hominoids. *Proc. Zool. Soc. Lond.* 130:169-181.

Bilsborough, A. 1976. Patterns of evolution in Middle Pleistocene hominids. *J. Hum. Evol.* 5:423-439.

Bookstein, F. L., Gingerich, P. D., and Kluge, A. G. 1978. Hierarchical linear modeling of the tempo and mode of evolution. *Paleobiology* 4:120-134.

Boule, M., and Vallois, H. V. 1957. *Fossil Men*. Dryden, New York.

Bridges, P. S. 1984. *Homo erectus* femora: implications for gradualism. *Am. J. Phys. Anthropol.* 63:142.

Charlesworth, B., Lande, R., and Slatkin, M. 1982. A Neo-Darwinian commentary on macroevolution. *Evolution* 36:474-498.

Chiu Chunglang, Gu Yümin, Zhang Yinyun, and Chang Shenshui. 1973. Newly discovered *Sinanthropus* remains and stone artifacts at Choukoutien. *Vertebr. PalAsiat.* 11:109-131.

Coon, C. S. 1962. *The Origin of Races*. Knopf, New York.

Cronin, J. E., Boaz, N. T., Stringer, C. B., and Rak, Y. 1981. Tempo and mode in hominid evolution. *Nature* 292:113-122.

Curtis, G. H. 1981. Man's immediate forerunners: Establishing a relevant time scale in anthropological and archaeological research. *Phil. Trans. R. Soc. Lond.* 292, B:7-20.

Day, M. H. 1982. The *Homo erectus* pelvis: Punctuation or gradualism? in: *L'Homo erectus et la Place de l'Homme de Tautavel Parmi les Hominides Fossiles*, Vol. 1, pp. 411-421. Louis-Jean Scientific and Literary Publication, Nice.

Day, M. H., Leakey, R. E. F., Walker, A. C., and Wood, B. A. 1976. New hominids from east Turkana, Kenya. *Am. J. Phys. Anthropol.* 45:369-436.

Delson, E. 1981. Paleoanthropology: Pliocene and Pleistocene human evolution. *Paleobiology* 7:298-305.

Dubois, E. 1936. Racial identity of *Homo soloensis* Oppenoorth (including *H. modjokertensis* von Koenigswald) and *Sinanthropus pekinensis* Davidson Black. *Proc. Konink. Ned. Akad. Wetensch.* 39:1180-1185.

Eldredge, N., and Tattersall, I. 1982. *The Myths of Human Evolution*. Columbia, New York.

Gingerich, P. D. 1983. Rates of evolution: Effects of time and temporal scaling. *Science* 222:159-161.

Gould, S. J. 1976. Ladders, bushes, and human evolution. *Nat. Hist.* 85(4):24-31.

Gould, S. J. 1982. The meaning of punctuated equilibrium and its role in validating a hierarchical approach to macroevolution, in: *Perspectives on Evolution* (R. Milkman, Ed.), pp. 83-104. Sinauer, Sunderland, MA.

Gould, S. J., and Eldredge, N. 1977. Punctuated equilibria: The tempo and mode of evolution reconsidered. *Paleobiology* 3:115-151.

Grimm, H. 1941. Untersuchungen über den Fossilen Hominiden-schädel von Modjokerto auf Java. *Anthropol. Anz.* 17:254-265.

Hemmer, H. 1967. *Allometrie-Untersuchungen zur Evolution des menschlichen Schädels und seiner Rassentypen*. Fischer, Stuttgart.

Holloway, R. L. 1978. Problems in brain endocast interpretation and African hominid evolution, in: *Early Hominids of Africa* (C. J. Jolly, Ed.), pp. 379-402. Duckworth, London.

Holloway, R. L. 1980. Indonesian "Solo" (Ngandong) endocranial reconstructions: Preliminary observations and comparisons with Neandertal and *Homo erectus* groups. *Am. J. Phys. Anthropol.* 53:285-295.

Holloway, R. L. 1981. The Indonesian *Homo erectus* brain endocasts revisited. *Am. Phys. Anthropol.* 55:502-521.

Holloway, R. L. 1982. *Homo erectus* brain endocasts: Volumetric and morphological observations with some comments on cerebral asymmetries, in: *L'Homo erectus et la Place de L'Homme de Tautavel parmi les Hominides Fossiles*, Vol. 1, pp. 355-369. Louis-Jean Scientific and Literary Publications, Nice.

Holloway, R. L. 1983. Human paleontological evidence relevant to language behavior. *Human Neurobiol.* 2:105-114.

Howell, F. C. 1960. European and Northwest African middle Pleistocene hominids. *Cur. Anthropol.* 1:195-232.

Howell, F. C. 1978. Hominidae, in: *Evolution of African Mammals* (V. J. Maglio and H. B. S. Cooke, Eds.), pp. 154-248. Harvard, Cambridge, MA.

Howells, W. W. 1980. *Homo erectus*—who, when and where: a survey. *Yearb. Phys. Anthropol.* 23:1-23.

Jacob, T. 1976. Early populations in the Indonesian region, in: *The Origins of the Australians* (R. L. Kirk and A. G. Thorne, Eds.), pp. 81-93. Australian Institute of Aboriginal Studies, Canberra.

Jelínek, J. 1981. Was *Homo erectus* already *Homo sapiens*? Les Processus de L'Hominisation. *CNRS Int. Colloq.* No. 599:91-95.

Kennedy, G. E. 1983. A morphometric and taxonomic assessment of a hominine femur from the Lower Member, Koobi Fora, Lake Turkana. *Am. J. Phys. Anthropol.* 61:429-436.

Leakey, M. G., and Leakey, R. E. F., Eds. 1978. *Koobi Fora Research Project*. Vol. 1. *The Fossil Hominids and an Introduction to Their Context 1968–1974*. Clarendon, Oxford.

Leakey, R. E. F., and Walker, A. C. 1976. *Australopithecus*, *Homo erectus*, and the single species hypothesis. *Nature* 261:572-574.

Leakey, R. E. F., and Walker, A. C. 1980. On the status of *Australopithecus afarensis*. *Science* 207:1103.

LeGros Clark, W. E. 1964. *The Fossil Evidence for Human Evolution*, rev. ed. University of Chicago, Chicago.

Levinton, J. S. 1982. Estimating stasis: Can a null hypothesis be too null? *Paleobiology* 8:307.

Levinton, J. S, and Simon, C. M. 1980. A critique of the punctuated equilibria model and implications for the detection of speciation in the fossil record. *Syst. Zool.* 29:130-142.

Malmgren, B. A., and Kennett, J. P. 1981. Phyletic gradualism in a late Cenozoic planktonic foraminiferal lineage; DSDP Site 284, southwest Pacific. *Paleobiology* 7:230-240.

Mann, A. 1971. *Homo erectus*, in: *Background for Man* (P. Dolhinow and V. Sarich, Eds.), pp.166-177. Little, Brown, Boston.

Matsu'ura, S. 1982. A chronological framing of the Sangiran hominids. *Bul. Nat. Sci. Mus.*, Tokyo, Ser. D, 8:1-53.

Mayr, E. 1969. *Principles of Systematic Zoology*. McGraw-Hill, New York.

Piveteau, J. 1957. *Traité de Paléontologie*. Vol. 7, *Les Primates et l'-Homme*. Masson, Paris.

Raup, D. M., and Crick, R. E. 1981. Evolution of single characters in the Jurassic ammonite *Kosmoceras*. *Paleobiology* 7:200-215.

Rightmire, G. P. 1981. Patterns in the evolution of *Homo erectus*. *Paleobiology* 7:241-246.

Rightmire, G. P. 1982. Reply to Levinton. *Paleobiology*. 8:307-308.

Riscutia, C. 1975. A study on the Modjokerto infant calvarium, in: *Paleoanthropology: Morphology and Paleoecology* (R. H. Tuttle, Ed.), pp. 373-375. Mouton, The Hague.

Santa Luca, A. P. 1980. *The Ngandong Fossil Hominids*. Yale University Publications Anthropology, No. 78. Yale University, New Haven, Conn.

Sartono, S. 1982. Characteristics and chronology of early men in Java, in: *L'Homo erectus et la Place de L'Homme de Tautavel parmi les Hominides Fossiles*, Vol. 2, pp. 491-541. Louis-Jean Scientific and Literary Publications, Nice.

Sartono, S. and Djubiantono, T. 1983. Note on the paleomagnetic age of Homo modjokertensis, in: *L'Homo erectus et la Place de L'Homme de Tautavel parmi les Hominides Fossiles*, Vol. 2, pp. 534-541. Louis-Jean Scientific and Literary Publications, Nice.

Schopf, T. J. M. 1981. Punctuated equilibrium and evolutionary stasis. *Paleobiology* 7:156-166.

Schopf, T. J. M. 1982. A critical assessment of punctuated equilibria. I. Duration of taxa. *Evolution* 36:1144-1157.

Schopf, T. J. M., and Hoffman, A. 1983. Punctuated equilibrium and the fossil record. *Science* 219:438-439.

Schultz, A. H. 1965. The cranial capacity and orbital volume of hominoids according to age and sex, in: *Homenaje a Juan Comas en su 65 Anniversario*, Vol. 2. Libros de Mexico, Mexico City.

Simpson, G. G. 1961. *Principles of Animal Taxonomy*. Columbia University Press, New York.

Stanley, S. M. 1978. Chronospecies' longevities, the origin of genera, and the punctuational mode of evolution. *Paleobiology* 4:26-40.

Stanley, S. M. 1979. *Macroevolution: Patterns and Process*. W. H. Freeman, San Francisco.

Stanley, S. M. 1981. *The New Evolutionary Timetable*. Basic, New York.

Stringer, C. B. 1981. The dating of European Middle Pleistocene hominids and the existence of *Homo erectus* in Europe. *Anthropologie (Brno)* 19:3-14.

Stringer, C. B., Howell, F. C., and Melentis, J. 1979. The significance of the fossil hominid skull from Petralona, Greece. *J. Archaeol. Sci.* 6:235-253.

Thorne, A. G., and Wolpoff, M. H. 1981. Regional continuity in Australasian Pleistocene hominid evolution. *Am. J. Phys. Anthropol.* 55:337-349.

Tobias, P. V. 1971. *The Brain in Hominid Evolution*. Columbia University Press, New York.

Tobias, P. V. 1980. *Homo habilis* and *Homo erectus*: From the Oldowan men to the Acheulian practitioners. *Anthropologie (Brno)*. 18:115-119.

Trinkaus, E. 1984. Does KNM-ER 1481A establish *Homo erectus* at 2.0 myr. B.P.? *Am. J. Phys. Anthropol.* 64:1377-140.

Vrba, E. 1980. Evolution, species, and fossils: How does life evolve? *S. Afr. J. Sci.* 76:61-84.

Walker, A. C., and Leakey, R. E. F. 1978. The hominids of east Turkana. *Sci. Am.* 239(2):54-66.

Weidenreich, F. 1943. The skull of *Sinanthropus pekinensis*: A comparative study of a primitive hominid skull. *Paleontol. Sin.* n.s. D, No. 10.

Weidenreich, F. 1945. Giant early man from Java and south China. *Anthropol. Pap. Am. Mus. Nat. Hist.* 40:1-134.

Williams, A. 1957. Evolutionary rates of brachiopods. *Geol. Mag.* 94:201-211.

Wolpoff, M. H. 1977. Some notes on the Vértesszöllös occipital. *Am. J. Phys. Anthropol.* 47:357-364.

Wolpoff, M. H. 1980a. Cranial remains of Middle Pleistocene European hominids. *J. Hum. Evol.* 9:339-358.

Wolpoff, M. H. 1980b. *Paleoanthropology*. Knopf, New York.

Wolpoff, M. H. 1982. The Arago dental sample in the context of hominid dental evolution, in: *L'Homo erectus et la Place de l'Homme de Tautavel Parmi les Hominides Fossiles*, Vol. 1, pp. 389-410. Louis-Jean Scientific and Literary Publications, Nice.

Wolpoff, M. H., Wu Xinzhi, and Thorne, A. G. 1984. Modern *Homo sapiens* origins: A general theory of hominid evolution involving the fossil evidence from east Asia, in: *The Origins of Modern Humans* (F. H. Smith and F. Spencer, Eds.), pp. 411-483. Liss, New York.

Wu Maolin. 1983. *Homo erectus* from Hexian, Anhui, found in 1981. *Acta Anthropol. Sin.* 2:109-115.

Wu Rukang, and Dong Xingren. 1982. Preliminary study of *Homo erectus* remains from Hexian, Anhui. *Acta Anthropol. Sinica.* 1:2-13.

Zhou Mingzhen, Li Yanxian, and Wang Linghong. 1982. Chronology of the Chinese fossil hominids, in: *L'Homo erectus et la Place de l'Homme de Tautavel parmi les Hominides Fossiles*, Vol. 2, pp. 593-604. Louis-Jean Scientific and Literary Publications, Nice.

39

Early *Homo erectus* Skeleton From West Lake Turkana, Kenya

F. Brown, J. Harris, R. Leakey and A. Walker

During the course of palaeontological exploration on the west side of Lake Turkana, Bw. Kamoya Kimeu found a small fragment of hominid frontal bone exposed on the surface at the site of Nariokotome III, on the south bank of the Nariokotome River. The approximate latitude and longitude of the site are 4°08' N, 35°54' E (Fig. 1). Near the site the Plio-Pleistocene beds strike N 7° E and dip 5° to the west. Exposures are reasonably good along the south bank of the Nariokotome where a section was measured to establish the stratigraphic position of the hominid (Fig. 2). Several tuffs occur within this section that have been correlated with tuffs elsewhere in the Turkana Basin on the basis of their chemical composition. The hominid derives from a siltstone that immediately overlies a tuff identified as a component ash of the Okote Tuff complex of the Koobi Fora Formation. The age of this tuff is ~1.65 Myr (McDougall, Davies, Maier, and Rudowski 1985; Brown and

Feibel 1985). An ash that correlates with Tuff L of the Shungura Formation (Chari Tuff of the Koobi Fora Formation) dated at 1.39 Myr (McDougall 1985; Brown, McDougall, Davies, and Maier 1985) lies 34 m above the hominid level. An unnamed tuff dated at 1.33 Myr (Brown, McDougall, Davies, and Maier 1985) lies 46 m above the specimen. Thus, the hominid is probably very close to 1.6 Myr in age.

The strata consist predominantly of pale yellowish-brown sandstones and siltstones and very pale yellowish-brown to medium-brown siltstones. The sandstones and siltstones are either laminated or massive. The tuff that underlies the hominid fills cracks in an underlying sandy siltstone and contains small-to-medium-scale trough crossbeds truncated at their tops and overlain by siltstone. A small lens of fine tuffaceous sand that lies ~1 m above the hominid level contains abundant amphioxea and amphistrongyla of freshwater sponges. A tuff that lies 6.7 m

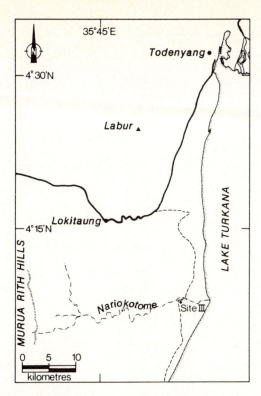

Figure 1. *Map of northern Kenya to show location of site Nariokotome III.*

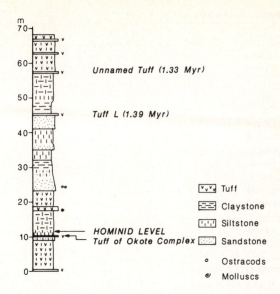

Figure 2. *Section at site Nariokotome III to show stratigraphic position of KNM-WT 15000.*

out from tuffaceous sediments. Excavation of an area ~5 x 6 m has led so far to the recovery of the mandible, several isolated teeth and much of the postcranial skeleton. A list of the parts

above the hominid level contains reworked molluscs at the base and a sandstone 13.8 m above the hominid is capped by an ostracod-rich layer 10 cm thick. Mammalian fossils are rare at this locality, the most abundant vertebrate fossils being parts of small and large fish. The depositional environment was evidently an alluvial plain of low relief, consistent with the fossil fauna in the section. It is likely that the plain was only slightly higher in elevation than a lake which existed nearby, such that with only minor changes in lake level, typical lacustrine forms (for example, ostracods, molluscs) could invade the area.

Twenty-five other vertebrate-bearing sites were located and collected during the 1984 season. Individual sites were labelled by the name of the ephemeral river draining their exposures and were further numbered sequentially in order of their discovery (Table 1). As at Koobi Fora, the Okote Tuff was used as a marker horizon in the subdivision of the fossiliferous succession. Fossil assemblages were retrieved from horizons a short depth below the Okote Tuff at five localities and slightly above it at eight localities (see Table 2). Appreciably fewer taxa are represented at these new localities than at equivalent places at Koobi Fora, but this may be an artifact of sample size. The distribution of identifiable species at sites on both sides of the lake, specifically the presence of *Deinotherium bozasi, Elephas recki ileretensis, Diceros bicornis, Metridiochoerus andrewsi* and *Gazella janenschi* only at horizons below the Okote tuff and *Metridiochoerus compactus* only at horizons above this tuff, provides a measure of correlative support for geochemical analyses of the tephra. *Tragelaphus scriptus* is the only species from this part of the section on the west side of the lake that is not represented yet at Koobi Fora.

Following the initial discovery, screening and washing of surface float and pebble lag led to the recovery of most of the hominid calvaria. The facial skeleton was found just eroding

Table 1. Fossiliferous sites west of Lake Turkana.

Locality	Abbreviation	Horizon
Kaitio I	KI I	Indet.
Kaitio II	KI II	Indet.
Kalachoro I	KL I	Below Chari Tuff
Kalachoro II	KL II	Below Chari Tuff
Kalachoro III	KL III	Below Okote Tuff
Kalachoro IV	KL IV	Indet.
Kalachoro V	KL V	Below Chari Tuff
Kalachoro VI	KL VI	Below Okote Tuff
Kalakodo	KK	Below KBS Tuff
Kangaki	KG I	Below KBS Tuff
Kangaki II	KG II	Below KBS Tuff
Loruth Kaado I	LK I	Below Tulu Bor Tuff
Loruth Kaado II	LK II	Below Tulu Bor Tuff
Loruth Kaado III	LK III	Below Chari Tuff
Loruth Kaado IV	LK IV	Below Okote Tuff
Nachakui I	NC I	Above Chari Tuff
Nachakui II	NC II	Above Chari Tuff
Nachakui III	NC III	Indet.
Nanyangakipi	NN	Just below/above Okote Tuff
Nariokotome I	NK I	Galana Boi Beds
Nariokotome II	NK II	Below Chari Tuff
Nariokotome III	NK III	Immediately above Okote Tuff
Nariokotome IV	NK IV	Below Chari Tuff
Natoo	NT	Below Okote Tuff
Nyaena Engol I	NY I	Below Okote Tuff
Nyaena Engol II	NY II	Indet.

Indet., indeterminate horizon.

Table 2. Faunal list.

Taxon	West Turkana		East Turkana	
	KLIII, KLIV, LKIV, NY, NN	NT, LKIII, KLI KLII, KLV, NKIII	Below Okote	Above Okote
Pisces	✓	✓	✓	✓
Crocodylus sp.		✓	✓	✓
Euthecodon brumpti	✓	✓	✓	
Trionyx sp.	✓	✓	✓	
Geochelone sp.		✓	✓	✓
Aves	✓	✓	✓	✓
Hystrix sp.		✓	✓	
Theropithecus oswaldi	✓	✓	✓	✓
Homo erectus		✓	✓	✓
Canis sp.	✓		✓	
Carnivora gen. indet.	✓			
Deinotherium bozasi	✓		✓	
Elephas recki ileretensis	✓		✓	
Elephas recki recki		✓		✓
Hipparion ethiopaeum		✓	×	×
Equus koobiforensis	✓	✓	✓	
Diceros bicornis	✓		✓	
Ceratotherium simum	✓		✓	
Metridiochoerus andrewsi	✓		✓	
Metridiochoerus modestus	✓		✓	✓
Metridiochoerus compactus		✓		✓
Kolpocheroerus limnetes		✓	✓	✓
Hexaprotodon karumensis	✓	✓	✓	✓
Hippopotamus gorgops	✓		✓	✓
Hippopotamus aethiopicus	✓	✓	✓	✓
Aepyceros sp.	✓	✓	✓	✓
Megalotragus sp.		✓	✓	✓
Connochaetes sp.	✓	×	✓	✓
Damaliscus sp.	✓	✓	✓	✓
Pelorovis sp.	✓	✓	✓	
Pelorovis olduwayensis		×	✓	✓
Syncerus caffer	×	×	×	
Tragelaphus strepsiceros	✓	✓	✓	✓
Tragelaphus scriptus	✓			
Menelikia lyrocera		✓	✓	✓
Kobus sigmoidalis	✓		✓	✓
Kobus kob		✓	✓	✓
Kobus leche		?	✓	✓
Antidorcas recki	✓		✓	✓
Gazella janenschi	✓		✓	
Gazella praethomsoni	✓		✓	✓
Gazella sp.		✓		

✓, Species present; ×, comparable species present; ?, stratigraphic position uncertain.

found so far is given in Table 3. The site plan of the excavation (Fig. 3) shows that the skeleton was dispersed before final sedimentary burial. The bones were found in a layer of tuffaceous silt of variable thickness deposited on a more indurated, flat-lying tuffaceous sand with orange root casts. The top of the fossiliferous horizon shows many signs of bioturbation and several of the bones were found broken or lying in positions suggesting that they had been trampled by large mammals. The general alignment of the long bones, separation of elements once in close articulation and the linear dispersal of the skeleton over at least 7 m, indicate minor water transport (see Fig. 3). Postmortem damage is seen and some parts of the bones are

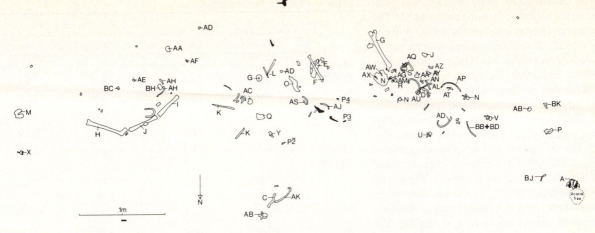

Figure 3. *Detail of site plan showing distribution of* H. erectus *bones. Major hominid parts are as lettered in Table 3. Non-hominid bones, mostly fish, are in solid.*

crushed, particularly where there is much cancellous tissue. There are no signs of carnivore or scavenger damage and the only pathology is a minor amount of alveolar resorption on the right mandibular body which took place before the right dm_2 was shed. The only other fauna found so far in the fossiliferous bed are many opercula of the swamp snail *Pila*, a few bones of the catfish *Synodontis* and two fragments of indeterminate large mammal bone, although equid and pygmy hippopotamus remains were found on the surface here.

The cranium has been assembled from about 70 pieces. The only main pieces missing are the nasals, ethmoid, lacrimals, central parts of the supraorbital tori, parts of the sphenoid and some parts of the vault, the two largest being bits of the right frontal near bregma and right parietal near lambda. The sutures

Table 3. Skeletal parts of KNM-WT 15000.

Cranium (A)	Right rib 4 (AI, BD, BE)
Mandible (B)	Right rib 5 fragment (BJ)
Cervical vertebra 7 (R)	Right rib 6 (AL)
Thoracic vertebra 1 (S)	Left rib 7 (AP)
Thoracic vertebra 2 (T)	Right rib 7 (AK)
Thoracic vertebra 3 (U)	Left rib 8 (AU)
Thoracic vertebra 6 or 7, spine and laminae (BI)	Right rib 8 (AM)
Thoracic vertebra 8 (V)	Left rib 9 (AO)
Thoracic vertebra 9 (W)	Right rib 9 (AS)
Thoracic vertebra 10 (X)	Right rib 10 (AJ)
Thoracic vertebra 11 (Y)	Left rib 11 (AN)
Lumbar vertebra 1, body and right lamina and inferior facet (AR, BA)	Left clavicle (C)
Lumbar vertebra 2 (AA, AV)	Right clavicle (D)
Lumbar vertebra 3, pedicle laminae and spine (Z)	Left scapula, spine and axillary border (BK, BL)
Lumbar vertebra 4 (AB)	Right scapula (E)
Lumbar vertebra 5 (AC)	Right humerus (F)
Sacral vertebra 1 (AD)	Left ilium (L, BF, BG)
Sacral vertebra 3, laminae and spine (BB)	Left ischium (Q)
Sacral vertebra, right half (BC)	Right ilium (O)
Sacral vertebra 5 (AE)	Right ischium (P)
Coccygeal vertebra 1 (AF)	Right pubic fragments (AW, AX)
Left rib 1 (AG)	Left femur (G)
Right rib 1 (AY, AZ)	Right femur (H, M)
Left rib 2 (AQ)	Left tibia (I)
Right rib 2 (AH)	Right tibia (J)
Left rib 3 (AT)	Left fibula (K, BH)
	Right fibula (L)

were all unfused. The facial skeleton was positioned on the braincase by using the mandible. The mandible is undistorted, but the calvaria has a slight overall plastic deformation with the upper part displaced to the left. Only a preliminary cranial reconstruction (Fig. 4) has been possible so far and the capacity has not been measured. Table 4 lists the teeth found so far and their measurements. They are all close to the mean size recorded for Homo erectus from Zhoukoudian (Weidenreich 1937). The M3 germs will have to be examined radiologically. Several of the teeth were excavated separately and returned to their alveoli. The alveoli for the deciduous upper canines are still visible lateral to the permanent canine alveoli, and the left upper canine was in the process of erupting. The degree of root development of the isolated teeth, the tooth wear stages and the eruption stage are equivalent to that in 12 ± 1-year-old modern human males (Garn, Lewis, Koski, and Polacheck 1958). The canines erupted later than the M2s, and although this is not usual, it is a known human condition (Garn and Koski 1957). The dental age is matched in the postcranial skeleton where all epiphyses are unfused and the incongruity between growth-plate surfaces suggests that much further growth would have been possible. The cranium does not show strong tori, temporal or nuchal lines because it was immature at death (see Fig. 4). Despite this, its tori are thicker, its palate broader and its facial skeleton bigger and more massive than those of the presumed female cranium KNM-ER 3733 (Leakey and Walker 1976), which is from a roughly equivalent time horizon in the same basin. We take this to mean that there was probably considerable sexual dimorphism in the crania of early *H. erectus*. It is conceivable that this individual, had it lived to maturity, might have developed as strong and robust a cranium as that of Olduvai Hominid 9 (Leakey 1959).

Previous *H. erectus* postcranial material has been either fragmentary, not definitely associated, disputed as to species or diseased. From Trinil, Indonesia (Dubois 1926), there are several fragmentary and one complete (but pathological) femora. Despite the fact that it was these specimens that led to the species name, there are doubts as to whether they are *H. erectus* (Day and Molleson 1973) with the most recent concensus being that they probably are not. Until recently the only *H. erectus* postcranial bones from China were from Zhoukoudian (Weidenreich 1941) and these were very fragmentary, with no complete lengths or articular surfaces. The reported clavicle is probably not even primate (Day 1977). Recent newspaper accounts report an *H. erectus* cranium, innominate, ulna, three vertebrae, a rib, some hand and foot bones, a patella and a partial innominate from Yingkou, Liaoning Province, China, which are said to be 200,000 yr old (Lu 1984; Wei 1984).

H. erectus postcrania have also been found at Olduvai Gorge, Tanzania, and East Turkana, Kenya. An associated fragmentary left innominate and femoral shaft (OH 28) from Bed IV Olduvai have been described as belonging to this species (Day 1971). Tibial and femoral shafts (OH 34) from Bed III Olduvai (Day and Molleson 1976) may belong, but are so badly eroded that their analytical value is slight. An undescribed ulna (OH 36) from Bed II Olduvai has also been attributed to this species (Day 1977). There are many postcranial bones from

Table 4. Tooth measurements (mm).

	Right		Left	
	Mesiodistal	*Buccolingual*	*Mesiodistal*	*Buccolingual*
Mandible				
C	8.8	9.0	8.6	9.4
P_3	9.0	10.1	8.5	10.1
P_4	—	—	9.0	9.5
M_1	11.9	11.1	12.2	10.9
M_2	12.4	11.4	12.2	11.5
Maxilla				
I^2	7.9	8.5	7.9	8.3
P^3	8.3	11.5	—	—
P^4	8.2	11.5	—	—
M^1	12.2	11.8	11.1	11.8
M^2	12.5	12.6	13.3	11.7

East Turkana (Day and Leakey 1974; Leakey and Walker 1985). Only one is definitely associated with complete enough cranial remains to be absolutely certain of attribution and, unfortunately, that individual had suffered from a disease which affected the postcranial skeleton (Leakey and Walker 1985; Walker, Zimmerman and Leakey 1982). The East Turkana specimens are mainly isolated and/or fragmentary.

The finding of KNM-WT 15000 will allow not only the study of the morphology and proportions of this individual, but also allow firmer attributions and enhance the analytical value of very many other isolated or fragmentary specimens. Recognizing that the excavation has yet to be completed and that this will probably result in the recovery of more parts, a complete assessment of this individual will not yet be attempted. There are, however, some points which can confidently be made. The stature of the individual has been estimated by using regression equations developed on modern human adult males (Trotter and Gleser 1952) to be 1.68 m (caucasian) or 1.64 m (blacks). This individual would not have been quite that tall, because the cranium does not have the great height of modern *Homo sapiens*. Despite the young age of the individual, the length of the long bones are very close to the means for white North American adult males given by Schultz in 1937 (Schultz 1937). We have examined casts and originals of other early *H. erectus* postcranial bones and find that all of them are large. Stini (1974) noted current secular trends of increase in body size in many human populations and wondered whether the trend was revealing a genetic potential left over from early hunter and gatherer ancestors. The new *H. erectus* data support this hypothesis.

The vertebrae show some interesting differences from those of modern humans. The spinous processes on all vertebrae recovered so far are relatively longer and less inclined inferiorly than their modern counterparts and the laminae are much less broad. This means that the marked imbrication of the laminae and spines of adjacent vertebrae (particularly the thoracic series) so typical of *H. sapiens* is much less marked. The vertebral foramen is smaller relative to vertebral body size in the lower cervical and thoracic series, unlike that of modern humans, but about the same in the lumbar series. The inferior articular facets of the fifth lumbar vertebra face almost directly anteriorly and are slightly concave, in contrast to the usual human condition in which the surfaces face laterally and are cylindrically convex (Cihak 1970).

Although we have yet to recover sufficient parts of the pubic bones to complete a full reconstruction, the innominates are very similar indeed to OH 28 and KNM-ER 3228 (Day 1971; Rose 1984), but the strong iliac pillar had not yet developed. The sacrum is represented by S1 and S5, the spine of S3 and half of S4. Although we can reasonably estimate the sacral width, precise alignment with the pelvis must wait for the recovery of S2. There was a remarkable degree of iliac flare (Lovejoy, Heiple, and Burstein 1973); this flare is concordant with the extremely long femoral necks, which are relatively as long as those of robust australopithecines (Lovejoy, Heiple, and Burstein 1973). The biomechanical advantage of the abductor mechanism (Lovejoy, Heiple, and Burstein 1973) was much enhanced relative to the condition in *H. sapiens*. The biomechanical neck length of 85 mm is well over 3 s.d. from the mean of a sample of *H. sapiens* (Lovejoy, Heiple, and Burstein 1973). As well as having a long femoral neck, the neck-shaft angle is very small at 110°, being 5 s.d.s from the mean of the same *H. sapiens* population. The femoral head diameter at 44.0 mm is almost exactly on an *H. sapiens* mean (Pearson and Bell 1919) and scales with femoral length in the same way as *H. sapiens* and *Australopithecus boisei* (Walker 1973).

Martin (1983), following a stimulating discussion of human and great ape brain growth, suggested that early *H. erectus* could have produced their adult brain sizes by modification of the rate and/or extent of fetal growth without any need for significant postnatal postponement of fetal growth patterns as found in humans. This is dependent, however, on *H. erectus* pelves having allowed the birth of an infant as large as those of *H. sapiens*. Modern human populations show little, if any, sexual dimorphism in the absolute width of the sacrum (Flander 1978), a major determinant of pelvic inlet size. The interacetabular distance in WT 15000 is very small and surely correlated both with the great iliac flare and long femoral necks. It seems likely to us that early *H. erectus* birth-canal diameters would have been significantly smaller than in *H. sapiens* and that passage of a modern-sized, full-term fetus would have been impossible. The continuation after birth of fetal growth rates, found only in humans, must have been part of the developmental mechanism of *H. erectus*. Already then, by 1.6 Myr ago, the secondarily altricial condition (which leads to increased infant dependency) must have been present.

This skeleton has already shown that our views of early *H. erectus* morphology must be modified. With the possibility of

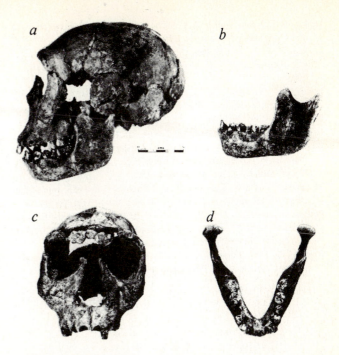

Figure 4. *KNM-WT 15000. a, Left lateral view of skull; b, left lateral view of mandible; c, frontal view of cranium; and d, occlusal view of mandible.*

finding more parts when the excavation is continued and with further analysis, KNM-WT 15000 will provide a firmer foundation for the identification and understanding of unassociated postcranial bones and early hominid growth patterns. Except for those representing the latest stages of our evolution, it is also the first fossil hominoid, let alone hominid, in which brain and body size can be measured accurately on the same individual. These two crucial variables, on which so much speculation about human origins and behaviour has been based, can now be determined for at least one individual early hominid.

We thank the Government of Kenya and the Governors of the National Museums of Kenya. This research is funded by the National Geographic Foundation, Washington DC, the Garland Foundation and the National Museums of Kenya. We thank Bw. Kamoya Kimeu and his prospecting team for their invaluable help. We also thank M. G. Leakey, M. D. Leakey and V. Morrell for assistance in the field and J. Mutaba, Z. Otieno, E. Mbua, P. Waterford-Trill, S. Kasinga and C. Kiarie for technical help.

REFERENCES

Brown, F. H., and Feibel, C. S. 1985. Stratigraphical notes the Okote Tuff Complex at Koobi Fora, Kenya. *Nature* 316:794-797.

Brown, F. H., McDougall, I., Davies, T., and Maier, R. 1985. An Integrated Plio-Pleistocene chronology for the Turkana basin, in: *Ancestors: The Hard Evidence*, (E. Delson, Ed.), pp. 82-90, Liss, New York.

Cihak, R. 1970. Variations of lumbosacral joints and their morphogenesis. *Acta Univ. Carol. Medica* 16:145-165.

Day, M. H. 1971. Postcranial remains of *Homo erectus* from Bed IV, Olduvai Gorge, Tanzania. *Nature* 232:383-387.

Day, M. H. 1977. *Guide to Fossil Man.* Cassell, London.

Day, H. H., and Leakey, R. E. F. 1974. New evidence of the genus *Homo* from East Rudolf, Kenya (III). *Am. J. Phys. Anthrop.* 41:367-380.

Day, M. H., and Molleson, T. I. 1973. The Trinil femora, in: *Human Evolution* (M. H. Day, Ed.), pp. 127-154, Taylor and Francis, London.

Day, M. H., and Molleson, T. I. 1976. The puzzle from JK2—a femur and a tibial fragment (O.H. 34) from Olduvai Gorge, Tanzania. *J. Hum. Evol.* 5:455-465.

Dubois, E. 1926. On the principle characters of the femur of *Pithecanthropus erectus*. *Proceedings, Koninklijke Nederlandse Akademie van Wetensschappen* 29:730-743.

Flander, L B. 1978. Univariate and multivariate methods for sexing the sacrum. *Am. J. Phys Anthrop.* 49:103-110.

Garn, S. M. and Koski, K. 1957. Tooth eruption sequence in fossil and recent man. *Nature* 190:442-443.

Garn, S. M., Lewis, A. B., Koski, K., and Polacheck, D. L. 1958. The sex difference in tooth calcification. *J. Dent. Res.* 37:561-657.

Leakey, L. S. B. 1959. A new fossil skull from Olduvai. *Nature* 184:491-493.

Leakey, R. E. F., and Walker, A. C. 1976. *Australopithecus, Homo erectus, and single species hypothesis. Nature* 261:572-574.

Leakey, R. E. F., and Walker, A. C. 1985. Further hominids from the Plio-Pleistocene of Koobi Fora, Kenya. *Am. J. Phys. Anthrop.* 67:135-163.

Lovejoy, C. O., Heiple, K. G., and Burstein, A. H. 1973. The gait of *Australopithecus. Am J. Phys. Anthrop.* 38:757-780.

Lu, Z. 1984. How *Homo erectus* was found. *China Daily*, November 30.

Martin, R. D. 1983. *52nd James Arthur Lecture*, Am. Mus. Nat Hist., New York.

McDougall, I. 1985. K-Ar and ^{40}Ar/^{39}Ar Dating of the hominid-bearing Pliocene-Pleistocene sequence at Koobi Fora, Lake Turkana, Northern Kenya. *Bull. Geol. Soc. Am.* 96:159-175.

McDougall, I., Davis, T., Maier, R., and Rudowski, R. 1985. Age of the Okote Tuff Complex at Koobi Fora, Kenya. *Nature* 316:792-794.

Pearson, K. and Bell, J. 1919. A study of the long bones of the English skeleton. Part I: The Femur. *Drapers Co. Res. Mem., Biometric Ser.* 10. Cambridge University Press, Cambridge.

Rose, M, D. 1984. A hominine hip bone, KNM-ER 3228, from East Lake Turkana, Kenya. *Am. J. Phys. Anthrop.* 63:371-378.

Schultz, A. H. 1937. Proportions, variability, and asymmetrics of the long bones of the limbs and clavicles in man and apes. *Hum. Biol.* 9:281-328.

Stini, W. A. 1974. Adaptive strategies of human populations under nutritional stress, in: *Biosocial Interrelations in Population Adaptation* (R. E. Johnston and E. S. Watts, Eds.), pp. 19-41. Mouton, The Hague.

Trotter, M., and Gleser, G. C. 1952. Estimation of stature from long bones of American whites and negroes. *Am. J. Phys. Anthrop.* 10:463-514.

Walker, A. 1973. New *Australopithecus* femora from East Rudolf, Kenya. *J. Hum. Evol.* 2:545-555.

Walker, A., Zimmerman, M. R., and Leakey, R. E. F. 1982. A possible case of hypervitaminosis in *Homo erectus. Nature* 296:248-250.

Wei, L. 1984. 200,000-year-old skeleton unearthed. *Beijing Rev.* 27:33-34, December 3.

Weidenreich, F. 1937. The dentition of *Sinanthropus pekinensis*: a comparative odontography of the hominids. *Palaeontol. Sin.* n.s. D, No. 1, pp. 1-180.

Weidenreich, F. 1941. The extremity bones of *Sinanthropus pekinensis. Palaeontol. Sin.* n.s. D, No. 5, pp. 1-150.

40

Palaeobiology and Age of African *Homo erectus*

E. Delson

Finds of ever-older human relatives and potential ancestors have caught the public's imagination in recent years. Kenyan fossils newly described by Brown *et al.* (1985) could help to swing the pendulum of public interest back toward younger fossils belonging to species of our own genus, *Homo*. Since 1969, Richard Leakey and his colleagues have recovered human and other fossils from deposits along the eastern shore of Lake Turkana in northern Kenya. Now, a group has crossed to the west side of the lake; early work has yielded a fossil already touted in the press as a "strapping youth" whose bones will shed yet more light on human ancestry (Joyce 1984).

The new fossil has been identified as a representative of *Homo erectus*, the extinct species first named *Pithecanthropus erectus* or "Java Man" by Dubois in 1894. Skulls of many individuals of this form are now known from Java and China, mainly estimated to date between 1.2 and .25 Myr old (Pope 1984; Wu 1985). It is widely accepted that populations similar to *H. erectus* were directly ancestral to the earliest members of the living species *H. sapiens*, although the exact timing, geography and mode of transformation are still controversial. Unfortunately, limb bones are scarce in the Asian sites, and some of the most complete have been questioned as to their specific identification (Day 1984).

That is the main value of the new Kenya fossil—it preserves almost all of the skeleton of a 1.6-Myr-old individual who can be sexed (as male, by pelvis shape) and aged (12 years, from tooth eruption timing). Fossils identified as *H. erectus* have been known in eastern Africa since 1960, when Louis Leakey reported a skull cap from Olduvai which matched those from Asia. Moreover, Olduvai and other sites have yielded partial limbs and pelves attributed to *H. erectus*, but none has been associated with a well-preserved cranium, always rendering precise taxonomic identification doubtful. The West Turkana fossil (catalogued as KNM-WT 15000) preserves most of the skull and lacks only the extremities and forelimbs (the right humerus remains). The team expects to find additional portions of the skeleton with further excavation, but this degree of preservation is otherwise unknown before the Neanderthals of 40,000-100,000 years ago. By comparison, 'Lucy,' the 3-Myr-old partial adult female skeleton of *Australopithecus afarensis* recovered by Johanson (Johanson and Edey 1981), has a lower jaw but only bits of the skull; many fewer ribs and vertebrae; the upper and lower leg bones of only one side of the body; but does preserve most of the two forearms and left humerus missing in WT 15000.

What will this new information tell us about how *H. erectus* lived? That is still hard to say, but one point much emphasized is the apparently great height of the individual: 1.6 m (5 ft 5 in) at death, perhaps 1.8 m (6 ft) if adult (Joyce 1984). Brown *et al.* (1985) have moderated this claim, especially because the skull of *H. erectus* was lower than that of the modern *H. sapiens* whose bones were used to develop the height regressions; the regression estimates should consequently be reduced.

Previous estimates for the height of *H. erectus* ranged between 1.55 and nearly 1.8 m (Clark 1978; Wolpoff 1980).

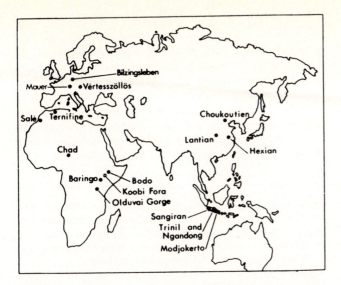

Figure 1. *Locations of major* Homo erectus *sites. There is controversy over whether the European and Baringo fossils should be allocated to* H. erectus *or* H. sapiens *(Brown and Feibel 1985).*

They were usually based only on the length of the femur (thigh bone) and did not consider skull height differences. Thus, the WT fossil might not have been especially large for this species to begin with. Moreover, additional cavils need to be evaluated. Modern humans show an adolescent growth spurt, especially in males. If such a spurt existed in *H. erectus*, it might have led to a height greater than the estimated 1.6 m, had the specimen lived longer.

Similarly, it is unclear that dental eruption timing then was the same as it is today; T. Bromage and C. Dean have questioned the equivalence of such timing in *Homo* and *Australopithecus* species based on counts of perikymata (developmental lines in tooth enamel) (Lewin 1985). On the other hand, if most *H. erectus* individuals were rather shorter than WT 15000 (which is less likely), it is possible that this individual was atypically tall or died young because selection acted against his continued growth.

Palaeoanthropologists will probably be more interested, however, in the insights that this fossil will provide into the patterns of growth and inter-individual differences among earlier humans. As evidenced by both dental eruption and epiphyseal fusion stages, WT 15000 was clearly juvenile. Yet Brown *et al.* (1985) note that the face is larger and more massive than that of an adult *H. erectus* skull from the east side of Lake Turkana they have just described (Leakey and Walker 1985). That skull, ER 3733, is widely accepted as female, so that its relative gracility campared with WT 15000 is not surprising (except for the age of the latter). It would be interesting to compare WT 15000 with ER 3883 (Leakey and Walker 1985). Some authors think the latter was a male (Wolpoff 1980) but I consider it another female and the large but stratigraphically younger Olduvai OH9 to be the male in this sexually dimorphic species.

This question leads inexorably to the two main recent foci of attention on *H. erectus*: does the species illustrate stasis or phyletic change through its 1.5 Myr span; and are the African forms really the same species as the Asian? One of the most important types of information that bear on both

these questions is accurate ages for the fossils. Although Pope (1984) and other workers have recently argued that the oldest Asian *H. erectus* are often significantly younger than previously thought (1-1.2 Myr at the most), careful re-analysis of several East African geological sequences has clarified the age of the earliest supposed members of the taxon there. McDougall *et al.* (1985) present new data on the age of one major Turkana Basin marker horizon, the Okote Tuff complex. They report that the basal levels of this 10–15-m-thick unit date to no more than 1.64 Myr. The pumice fragments dated have a composition different from that of the enclosing tuff, suggesting reworking upwards of older pumice into the slightly younger tuff. Brown and Feibel (1985) offer further local correlations and review other dates which indicate that it is not much younger (> 1.52, probably > 1.6 Myr). In addition, they determined that a tuff slightly below the horixon of WT 15000 is equivalent to one of two newly defined tuffs on either side of the Lower Okote, yielding the age of 1.55-1.65 Myr for the skeleton.

These dates and others in the Early Pleistocene (through to perhaps 1.0 Myr) make it simple to begin the study of temporal variation in *H. erectus*. But as noted by Pope (1984), dates in Asia are still highly uncertain and younger African fossils (especially in the Maghreb) are also of questionable age. Thus, although studies such as those of Howells (1980) and Rightmire (1981) have suggested that variation through time is not continuous or even directional in *H. erectus*, Wolpoff (1984) has recently argued strongly for a gradualistic view of temporal variation and change in this species. His comparisons of 13 cranial characters across specimens grouped into three time ranges are superficially persuasive but there are too many potential problems for his analysis to be convincing. Several individual fossils are of questionable identification, sexual variation is not considered and the raw data are not available to see the precise effects of these factors. Equivocal age determinations and the use of time bands rather than age estimates that would permit regression analysis also disturb me. As Wolpoff notes, it has been "excruciatingly difficult to test the punctuated equilibrium model in the fossil record," not least because of methodological disagreements among researchers.

An examination of Wolpoff's list of specimens reveals that whereas East African and Indonesian fossils dominated the 'early' and 'middle' *H. erectus* time groups, the sample from Zhoukoudian, China dominates the 'late.' Some authors have recently questioned whether such comparisons are as meaningful as we might like—are the African fossils indeed members of a palaeobiological species *H. erectus* as defined from the unique characteristics of the Asian specimens defining this taxon? Howell (1978) reviewed the concensus position of geographical identity some years ago, providing a detailed descriptive definition without specific regard for the derived versus the conservative nature of the characters discussed. Rightmire (1984, 1985) has been the most vocal recent proponent of the view, arguing that several uniquely derived characters define *H. erectus* in Asia and Africa without recourse to the arbitrary use of temporal gaps or rubicons.

On the other hand, Wood (1984) and Andrews (1984) argue strongly that African fossils assigned to *H. erectus* share only conservatively retained features with Asian members of that species, not any of their derived characters. Thus, they imply the need for recognition of a new species to receive African fossils possibly intermediate between *H. habilis* and *H. sapiens*. Stringer (1984) is more cautious, but agrees with the lack of shared derived features in specimens from the two regions; he notes further that if *H. erectus* were to be defined broadly enough to include all of these fossils, most derived conditions seen in the younger Asian specimens (especialy those found in China) would reject the concept of stasis in favor of definite change over time.

Palaeoanthropologists continually make the claim that more fossils will help answer pressing questions, and field workers who find them reap well-deserved rewards. If WT 15000 is any example of the quality of material to be expected in future years from the West Turkana sequence, there will certainly be much grist for our mills. But the milling process must include careful and probing analyses of all the available fossils, matched with a willingness to test both revisionist and entrenched hypotheses and to embrace new interpretations, if we are to take full advantage of the hard-won fossils.

REFERENCES

Andrews, P. J. 1984. An alternative interpretation of the characters used to define *Homo erectus*. *Cour. Forsch. Inst. Senckenberg* 69:167-175.

Brown, F. H., and Feibel, C. S. 1985. Stratigraphical notes on the Okote Tuff complex at Koobi Fora, Kenya. *Nature* 316:794-797.

Brown, F., Harris, J., Leakey, R., and Walker, A. 1985. Early *Homo erectus* skeleton from west Lake Turkana, Kenya. *Nature* 316:788-792.

Clark, W. E. Le Gros. 1978. *The Fossil Evidence for Human Evolution*, 3rd Ed. University of Chicago Press, Chicago.

Day, M. H. 1984. The postcranial remains of *Homo erectus* from Africa, Asia and possibly Europe. *Cour. Forsch. Inst. Senckenberg* 69:113-121.

Howell, F. C. 1978. Hominidae, in: *Evolution of African Mammals* (V. J. Maglio and H. B. S. Cooke, Eds.), pp. 154-248, Harvard University Press, Cambridge, MA.

Howells W. W. 1980. *Homo erectus*–Who, when and where: A survey. *Ybk. Phys. Anthrop.* 23:1-23.

Johanson, D. C., and Edey, M. 1981. *Lucy: the Beginnings of Humankind*. Simon and Schuster, New York.

Joyce, C. 1984. Now Pekin Man turns up in Kenya. *New Scient.* 104:8.

Leakey, R. E. F., and Walker, A. C. 1985. Further hominids from the Plio-Pleistocene of Koobi Fora, Kenya. *Am. J. Phys. Anthrop.* 67:135-163.

Lewin, R. 1985. Surprise findings in the Taung child's face. *Science* 228:42-44.

McDougall, I., Davies, T., Maier, R., and Rudowski, R. 1985. Age of the Okote Tuff complex at Koobi Fora, Kenya. *Nature* 316:792-794.

Pope, G. G. 1984. The antiquity and paleoenvironment of the Asian Hominidae, in: *The Evolution of The East Asian Environment* (R. O. Whyte, Ed.), pp. 822-847, University of Hong Kong.

Rightmire, G. P. 1981. Patterns in the evolution of *Homo erectus*. *Paleobiology* 7:241-246.

Rightmire, G. P. 1984. Comparisons of *Homo erectus* from Africa and Southeast Asia. *Cour. Forsch. Inst. Senckenberg* 69:83-98.

Rightmire, G. P. 1985. The tempo of change in the evolution of mid-Pleistocene *Homo*, in: *Ancestors: The Hard Evidence* (E. Delson, Ed.), pp. 255-264, Liss, New York.

Stringer, C. 1984. The definition of *Homo erectus* and the existence of the species in Africa and Europe. *Cour. Forsch. Inst. Senckenberg* 69:131-143.

Wolpoff, M. H. 1980. *Paleoanthropology*. Random House, New York.

Wolpoff, M. H. 1984. Evolution in *Homo erectus*: The question of stasis. *Paleobiology* 10:389-406.

Wood, B. A. 1984. The origin of *Homo erectus*. *Cour. Forsch. Inst. Senckenberg* 69:99-111.

Wu Rukang 1985. New Chinese *Homo erectus* and recent work at Zhoukoudian, in: *Ancestors: The Hard Evidence* (E. Delson, Ed.), pp. 245-248, Liss, New York.

Lateral and facial views of EV 9002, newly discovered *Homo erectus* cranium from Yunxian, Hubei, China (photos courtesy of Li Tianyuan).

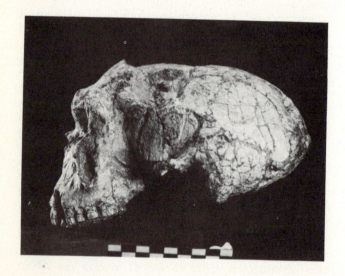

41

The Lower Paleolithic: Current Evidence and Interpretations

A. J. Jelinek

The earliest evidences of deliberate manufacture of tools by man's ancestors have been of deep interest to prehistorians since the general recognition of the significance of the collections of Boucher de Perthes in the mid-nineteenth century. Within these Lower Paleolithic collections of stone artifacts lies much of our evidence of the beginnings of the patterns of cultural behavior that distinguish man from other creatures.

The term "Lower Paleolithic" is to some degree an outmoded survival of late nineteenth century thinking based upon typological constructs drawn from a limited sample of artifacts, most of which had been found in northern and southwest France. It was first used by de Mortillet in 1872 (Mortillet 1872) to distinguish those chipped stone industries in which bone and antler tools were then unknown from an "Upper Paleolithic" in which such tools were associated with those of chipped stone. By the early twentieth century the term had been restricted to Acheulian and pre-Acheulian hand axe (biface) industries and the subsequent Mousterian. The Mousterian was eventually distinguished from the earlier industries as the "Middle Paleolithic," although the initial justification for this division now appears weak. It was based upon an apparently greater frequency of flake tools (predominantly scrapers) in the Middle Paleolithic, as opposed to core tools (predominantly hand axes) in the Lower Paleolithic, a difference which was largely the result of the collecting techniques of the nineteenth century. At that time the earlier Paleolithic of western Europe was known primarily from collections made by unskilled laborers from terrace gravels in northern France: the specimens collected tended to be restricted to symmetrical and easily recognizable bifaces. The appeal of symmetry and regular flake patterns on these specimens for the collectors employing the workmen was probably also a factor in determining what was saved as "representative" of these industries. In contrast, while hand axes were present in the Mousterian, it was known primarily from more objective samples of chipped stone implements, including a predominance of scrapers made on flakes, derived from rock shelter deposits in southwest France. Subsequent methodical excavation of earlier Paleolithic sites has shown that instances in which bifaces predominate over flake tools are rare and that in most sites where bifaces are present their ratio to flake tools is low. Thus the use of these kinds of ratios as a typological basis for distinguishing between a Lower and Middle Paleolithic is open to question. There is little doubt, however, that more refined typological studies initiated by Bordes (1950) have resulted in the isolation of Mousterian assemblages in the early phases of the Würm glaciation that are distinct from earlier assemblages and warrant the transitional status of "Middle" Paleolithic. The recognition of the particular Mousterian assemblages isolated by Bordes in western Europe becomes increasingly questionable with distance as technological and typological emphases appear which are not closely paralleled in the European industries. While they may not be identical to the Mousterian of western Europe, all of these assemblages seem to be a part of the same trends toward diversity of contemporary industries and diminishing emphasis on biface manufacture throughout the western Old World. This suggests a significant change in technological patterns at the end of the Middle Pleistocene (beginning of the Last Interglacial) in most areas in which chronological placement is possible and thus favors a termination for Lower Paleolithic industries at that time.

As a result of these more recent interpretations, de Mortilliet's term "Lower Paleolithic" is now generally accepted by prehistorians to include all evidence of cultural activity from the earliest appearance of chipped stone tools in the Lower Pleistocene up to the onset of the last interglacial episode (the beginning of the Upper Pleistocene). Even this usage, however, is not without some inconsistencies since it is evident that in some areas Acheulian hand axe industries or other patterns typical of the Lower Paleolithic persist well into the last interglacial. The inconsistencies are hardly surprising since the term refers to a cultural manifestation rather than a time period and thus exhibits the differing temporal persistence of characteristic Middle Pleistocene industries in each geographical region.

One question that emerges from an initial consideration of the archaeological evidence from the Lower and Middle Pleistocene is whether these data show patterns through time sufficiently similar to justify lumping them under a single label, or whether there exist internal differences of an order comparable to the distinctions between Middle and Upper Paleolithic. If the latter situation obtains, would it be desirable, in the interests of consistent usage, to subdivide the Lower Paleolithic into two or more units? This is not a novel proposition; similar classifications were proposed near the turn of the century to incorporate questionable artifacts underlying the hand axe industries into an "Eolithic," while as recently as 1961 Grahame Clark (Clark

1969) presented a quadrimodal division of Paleolithic industries in which the first two modes correspond to the Lower Paleolithic. The major basis for these proposed chronological subdivisions has been the absence of bifaces in an earlier phase as opposed to the presence of this form through the later portion of the sequence. Since the temporal priority of nonbiface industries has been well demonstrated in east and northwest Africa and seems indicated by recent discoveries in Europe (Bordes and Viguier 1971; Fridrich 1976; Radmilli 1976) and since, in a technological sense, the process of biface manufacture seems to imply a qualitative step in the preconception of tool form and character, it would appear that there is some real justification for proposing a "Basal Paleolithic" phase to precede the traditional Lower Paleolithic. Several complicating factors emerge, however, when such a division is proposed. Chief among them is the presence of nonbiface industries throughout the Middle Pleistocene in many areas of the Old World. In some instances these industries are clearly not simple extensions of the Lower Pleistocene chopper-tool complexes, such as the Oldowan, but have developed distinctive patterns of tool manufacture that differentiate them from both the earlier Oldowan and the contemporary hand axe industries. A well-known example of such a Middle Pleistocene nonbiface industry is the Clactonian (Fig. 1), which has recently been contrasted with the Acheulian by Collins (1969, p. 269). It is

clear on the basis of earlier descriptions (Breuil 1932; Warren 1951) as well as Collins's typological and technological comparisons, that this industry is not simply a nonbiface facies of the Acheulian, but includes high frequencies of tool types that are rare to absent in Acheulian collections, as well as basic techniques of flake manufacture that contrast with the Acheulian. Therefore, the single factor of the presence or absence of hand axes is not sufficient to distinguish a Basal Paleolithic (characterized by a Lower Pleistocene Oldowan industry) from the more evolved Lower Paleolithic industries of the Middle Pleistocene.

A major barrier to the comparison of Lower Paleolithic industries in widely separated areas of the Old World is the present state of descriptive terminology and typology applied to these industries. At present two major systems of description and typology are being used, as well as several less widely applied systems. This diversity can be traced to formal differences in industries in different time periods and different regions of the Old World and to the accidents of historical tradition in the development of different "schools" of prehistoric archaeology. The major descriptive/typological traditions are the French school, derived largely from the taxonomic concepts of Breuil and Peyrony and presently best exemplified in the work of Bordes (1961) and his students, and secondly, the British-African school whose influence can be seen in the work of M. D. Leakey (1971) and that of J. D. Clark and M. Kleindienst (1974). Classification based in the former tradition is widely employed in Europe, the Near East, and northwest Africa, while the influence of the latter school is chiefly seen in the description of material from sub-Saharan Africa.

These two traditions can be compared by examining the particular artifact typologies of the prehistorians just mentioned. Since Bordes' system is designed to include classification of both Lower and Middle Paleolithic collections and the Clark-Kleindienst classification spans the full range of the Paleolithic, this comparison will be restricted to only the categories of tools that occur in the Lower Paleolithic. Table 1 indicates the different basic emphases in taxonomic divisions in the three systems. It is clear that in each system there are types that span several typological categories in the other systems. In some cases, even basic terminological usage is inconsistent between systems, as in the complete absence of cores in Leakey's classification; all artifacts that would be classified as cores in the other systems are included in tools in this classification. In general, the Leakey system includes the fewest formal distinctions and the Bordes system the most detailed distinctions. Most tools classified in the Leakey system can be fully accommodated in either the Clark-Kleindienst or Bordes system, but full equivalence is lacking between the latter two systems, since each includes more detail in some categories than does the other. In general, it is easier to translate a classification from the two more elaborate systems to the simpler Leakey system, but even here full equivalence is not assured, and the absence of formal distinctions held to be significant by most Paleolithic scholars reduces the utility and interest of comparisons within this system. The Clark-Kleindienst system can be seen as a promising effort in the direction of uniformity. Here equivalent terms from the Bordes typology were listed for each type seen as most closely resembling one in the Bordes classification. Despite these preliminary efforts at standardization, it is clear that to a significant degree comparative

Figure 1 *Clactonian and Tayacian stone tools from England and France. Clactonian flint core (a) and flake tools (b,c) from Swanscombe, Kent; Flake tool (d) from Clacton-on-Sea, Essex; Acheulo-Clactonian scraper (e) from Suffolk; Proto-Mousterian flake tool (f) from Combe Capelle, Dordogne; Tayacian flake (g) from La Micoque, Tayac, Dordogne. Adapted from Oakley (1964).*

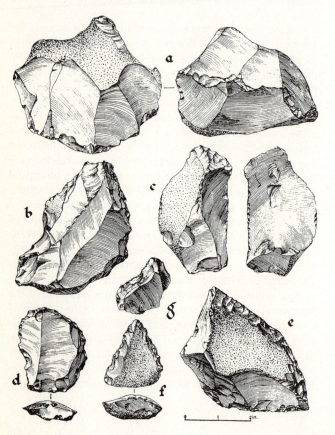

Table 1. Relationship of some Lower Paleolithic artifact types in three classifications[a]

Bordes	Clark-Kleindienst	M. D. Leakey
Chopping tools (bifacial) = Choppers (unifacial)	Choppers[c] (mostly bifacial) 5 categories (grade into cores) ←→ 3	Choppers (mostly bifacial) 5 categories
Bifaces Abbevillian Ficron Nucleiforme } ←?→	Some core-axes[c] ? ←?→	Proto bifaces
13 Shapes (outline + thickness) Partiels } ←→ =	Hand-axes[b] 8 shapes (outline) ←2→ Lanceolates[b] Some core-axes[c] ?	Bifaces { Irregular ovates Double pointed Flat butted } =
Hachereaux s. éats 6 categories ←?→ =	Cleavers[b], 4 shapes ←→ Chisels[c] ←?→	Cleavers =
Pics Some bifaces ? } =	Picks[c], 4 categories ←?→ Some core-axes[c] ?	Trihedrals Oblong picks Heavy duty picks } =
Bifaces a dos ←?→	Knives[b] ←?→	
Boules polyédriques ←?→	Some cores ? Spheroids[c] = ←?→	Polyhedrons Spheroids Subspheroids
Bifaces discoides ←?→	Some disc cores ? Discoids[d] ←?→	Discoids
Scrapers Racloir, 18 forms ←?→ Transversaux (3) ←→ = Grattoirs (2)	Scrapers; large[b], small[d] Side, indefinite number forms Side flake End, some nosed ? ←?→ =	Scrapers[e] Side, some hollow and discoidal End, some nosed ?
Notches ←?→	Some notched scrapers ? ←?→	Some hollow
Denticulates ←?→	Some denticulate scrapers ? ←?→	
Rabot ←?→	Some core scrapers ←?→	Discoidal Some peramital ?

[a]Key: [b] Large cutting tools, usually > 100 mm.
[c] Heavy duty tools > or < 100 mm.
[d] Light duty tools, usually < 100 mm.
[e] Divided into heavy duty (> 50 mm) and light duty (< 50 mm).

= ——→ Equivalent; fewer to more categories.
←——→ Equivalent.
←—?—→ Some question of equivalence.
←—3—→ Number of equivalent categories.
——→ ? No apparent equivalent.

research in the Lower Paleolithic continues to be hampered by the barriers of provincial taxonomic systems which must be standardized before fully effective communication between scholars can be established. The present dilemma of the students of these industries is roughly comparable to that of comparative anatomists attempting to communicate in the absence of a standard Latin-Greek anatomical taxonomy.

The emphasis placed on the classification and comparison of chipped stone tools in Lower Paleolithic studies is, of course, a reflection of the fact that such materials form the overwhelming bulk of our evidence of the activities of man in this period. Two basic questions that must be dealt with by archaeologists when they use these materials for their interpretation of the life ways of Lower Paleolithic man are: (a) what significance did these artifacts have for the people who made them; and (b) what relationship do the remains of these lithic industries that are accessible to the archaeologist have to the full cultural system in which they were manufactured?

In order to answer the first question we invariably make assumptions relating to the cognitive abilities of the hominids who produced the artifacts. Some of these assumptions can be based upon the uniformity of the industries over periods of hundreds of thousands of years. The absence of evidence of innovation and differentiation in the tool forms that can be observed over these prolonged intervals can be taken as evidence against the presence of the conceptual abilities relating to abstraction and synthesis that characterize modern *Homo*

sapiens. One important implication of this evidence relates to the role of verbal communication based upon these conceptual abilities. With regard to stone tools, the repetition of patterns and lack of innovation suggest that they may have been the product of complex forms of imitative behavior in a pattern no longer to be found among the Hominidae, and that verbal direction played a minimal role in the learning processes associated with tool manufacture. The learning abilities of the Pongidae suggest a propensity among man's ancestors for the development of complex imitative behavior. It is interesting in this regard that in the replication of chipped stone tools in experimental archaeology, demonstration and imitation play a far more significant role than description. In fact, difficulty in describing precisely the techniques employed in such manufacture is a common frustration among modern lithic technologists.

It seems evident that the most desirable qualities of chipped stone for Paleolithic man were sharp and durable edges for the cutting, piercing, and abrasion of softer materials. The extent to which Lower Paleolithic man manipulated and modified materials other than stone remains a matter of speculation due to the almost complete lack of preservation of most organic substances in Lower and Middle Pleistocene contexts. One clue in this regard is afforded by the relatively extensive preservation of bone, ivory, and enamel in some Lower Paleolithic sites. While these materials are amenable to shaping and modification by cutting, chiseling, and abrasion, there is virtually no evidence for the employment of these techniques on what must have been relatively abundant raw material. Instead, when bone is employed for tool manufacture, it appears to have been worked by the same techniques that we see employed in the shaping of stone, i.e. by chipping. Probably because deliberately chipped bones appear somewhat similar to bones smashed for marrow or otherwise broken in butchering, extensive studies of deliberately shaped bone in the Lower Paleolithic are rare. Nevertheless, some examples of Lower Paleolithic chipped bone have been reported from as widely scattered localities as central Spain (Biberson 1964) and Northern China (Breuil 1939), suggesting that bone may have been a more important item in the technology of these early hominids than has been appreciated by lithic-oriented prehistorians. But the restriction of shaping techniques to breaking and chipping suggests a limited awareness of the potential of this qualitatively distinct material in artifact manufacture. Earlier suggestions that the Australopithecines of South Africa had developed an industry of modified bone tools now seem refuted by studies of bone alteration by hyaenas (Shipman and Phillips 1976; Sutcliffe 1970). Beyond these infrequent reports of bone artifacts there is an almost complete absence of direct evidence of nonlithic tool manufacture in the Lower Paleolithic. Exceptions to this are the two well-known pointed wooden shafts from a Middle Pleistocene context in England (Warren 1922) and early Late Pleistocene Germany (Movius 1950), which are generally interpreted as deliberately shaped spears, and several wooden tools (not yet fully reported) from the Kalambo Falls site in southeast Africa (Howell and Clark 1963, p. 521). How extensively, and with what techniques for modification, wood, hide, and animal and vegetable fiber were employed in the technology of Lower Paleolithic man remains unknown. It is curious that if as has been supposed the wooden shafts mentioned above were shaped by shaving and scraping with stone tools, there is virtually no evidence of the employment of these useful techniques on ivory, antler, or bone. This suggests that the woodworking technology of Lower Paleolithic man may have been fairly rudimentary and confined to the removal of inconvenient branches and nodes by chopping, with fire employed to some degree for shaping and hardening.

The utility of chipped stone for Lower and Middle Pleistocene hominids and the significance of its employment for their evolution should not be underestimated. It seems unlikely that the omnivorous diet of the Australopithecines could have led to a successful utilization of large game without these supplementary teeth and claws of stone for butchering their kills. The extent to which tools were used in gaining access to otherwise unavailable vegetal resources and to small game and nonmammalian fauna is another aspect of technological development that awaits exploration.

Assuming that the above is a reasonable appraisal of the role of stone tools in the technology of Lower Paleolithic man, we can now examine the collections of these artifacts available to the archaeologist as indicators of the life-ways of the hominids that made them. One aspect of our interpretation is related to the kinds of planning and intelligence that we attribute to these hominids. Once these creatures became dependent upon the use of stone in the procurement and processing of food, it became necessary for them to integrate these variables in order to obtain food; sufficient anticipation was necessary to insure the presence of both meat and stone at the same place in order to utilize the protein effectively. Where game was abundant and useful stone infrequent, there must have been considerable selective advantage for those hominids who could best anticipate how to bring these resources together. It seems likely that the development of these kinds of abilities played a significant role in the development of the kind of conceptualization upon which much of the success of man's later cultural adaptation is based. There is little doubt that these abilities changed through the Lower Paleolithic and that Late Middle Pleistocene man was far more efficient in this regard than his early Lower Pleistocene antecedents. Thus in some respects it is difficult to generalize about the significance of stone tool collections and assemblages for the whole of the Lower Paleolithic.

One area in which some generalization is possible concerns the nature of these artifacts in relation to their place in a fully functioning technological system. It is evident that most of the artifacts in an archaeological site were deliberately abandoned. The chief exception to this would be material lost or misplaced before the termination of the occupation. Possible causes for the abandonment of artifacts may have been that they were seen as exhausted in terms of function in the technology; others may have been too bulky or heavy for the anticipated move. Depending upon the degree of anticipation of future activities that we attribute to the inhabitants of the site, it is possible that objects were abandoned because they would not be appropriate to subsequent activities, because sufficient

similar material would be available at future sites when it was needed, or more promising material was available en route. It is also possible, if return visits to the site were anticipated, as in a regular seasonal round, that the material left at the site was to some extent seen as a cache from which future implements could be made and was more conveniently left where it was until needed. It is from collections resulting from these problematical circumstances of deposition that prehistorians have reconstructed the activities and historical traditions of Lower Paleolithic man. The inability of the archaeologist to identify the circumstances under which the artifacts were abandoned inhibits his ability to interpret them. In the absence of some understanding of the environmental and social variables affecting the prehistoric men who left the artifact concentration it is difficult for the archaeologist to establish the significance of these artifacts to those extinct hominids.

To some degree, experimental studies of lithic technology and careful analysis of the context and character of later industries have contributed to our ability to interpret these most ancient artifacts. Here also our additional knowledge may raise more questions than it answers. As an example, we may consider the "spheroids" which occur frequently in the Lower and Middle Pleistocene industries of Africa (Fig. 2). Many workers interpret these chipped ball-like specimens as deliberately manufactured implements; in extreme instances they are seen as components of complex tools such as the bolas (M. D. Leakey 1971, p. 266). Occasionally they exhibit signs of abrasion as though they had been used for pounding or hammering on other stones. The lithic technologist's interpretation of these objects, however, may be quite different. By experimentation it can be established that the angles between the numerous flake scars that form the surface of the spheroid are too wide to serve as platforms from which further flakes can be struck, so that the spheroid can be viewed as an exhausted core from which every possible flake has been struck. It is reasonable to suppose that such symmetrical exhausted cores might have been used as convenient pounders, hammers, or even missiles, although this may not have been the original intent of their fabricators. This kind of interpretation leads to the very large question of the multiple use of artifacts and the implications of this multiple use for the final character of the assemblage that remains for the archaeologist.

There is a tendency on the part of prehistorians to compartmentalize the artifacts they recover into formal types and to use this classification in their interpretation in such a way as to view each artifact as a tool made for one particular purpose. In part this is probably at the least an unconscious extension of the specialized nature of tools in modern technology. Chipped stone tools, on the other hand, can be viewed as temporary stages in the reduction of pieces of raw material. Each specimen has the potential of assuming a succession of forms through modification dictated by convenience or a changing succession of tasks at hand. This tendency for a metamorphosis of tools through a succession of modifications has been referred to as the *Frison effect* in a previous paper (Jelinek 1976), following the clear demonstration by Frison (1968) of these patterns in a late prehistoric site in western North America. The dilemma introduced into archaeological interpretation by the Frison effect is that it is seldom possible to distinguish the full sequence of modifications (typological transitions) through which a particular piece of stone has passed. The form of the tool seen by

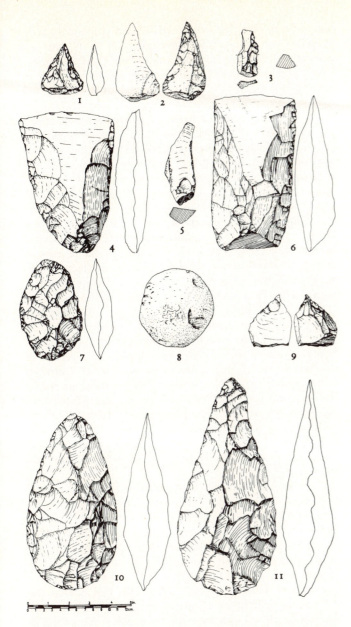

Figure 2 *Upper Acheulian tools from Kalambo Falls, Tanzania. (1) convergent scraper, (2) concave side-scraper, (3) denticulated side-scraper, (4) divergent edged cleaver, (5) flake knife with marginal retouch, (6) parallel edged scraper, (7) ovate handaxe, (8) spheroid, (9) awl, (10) elongated ovate handaxe, (11) lanceolate handaxe. Adapted from Clark (1970).*

the archaeologist is that of the last modification prior to its abandonment, and it may not be possible to identify previous uses of the specimen on the site—uses that represent different tool types. Thus the prehistorian probably seldom, if ever, sees a full and functional tool kit representing all or even most of the activities that have taken place on a site. Perhaps the best that we can hope for is that similar traditions of manufacture of tools for similar tasks will result in similar lithic refuse. Beyond these limitations we must also allow for the probable opportunistic behavior of prehistoric man. Ethnographic analogy (Gould, Koster, and Sontz 1971; White 1968) suggests that frequent use was made of otherwise unmodified simple flakes which under most circumstances would not be considered as tools at all by

the archaeologist. Thus the major body of artifactual materials upon which interpretations of the cultural activities of Lower Paleolithic man must be based can in most circumstances be expected to represent only a very incomplete picture of the employment of even this one substance (stone) in the technology, and much of even this limited aspect of the activities of these hominids seems inaccessible to us throughout the forseeable future.

There remains considerable disagreement among prehistorians regarding the significance of those patterns of artifact form that can be distinguished in the limited samples just described. The typological systems mentioned earlier for the classification of lithic artifacts are based on the recognition of repeated patterns of modification (e.g. the convex retouched edge of a flake paralleling the axis of flaking that signals "*racloir simple convexe*" to François Bordes.) All of the major typologies employed in the classification of Lower Paleolithic material at present are based on the intuitive recognition of attribute combinations related to manufacture or modification of the piece. The recognition of these patterns has resulted from the examination of large numbers of artifacts by the proponent of each typology. What kind of significance these classificatory units had for the manufacturers of the tools remains to be demonstrated. It seems likely on the basis of recent ethnographic work (Gould, Koster, and Sontz 1971) that our present classifications are overly elaborated in terms of the kinds of tools that would be recognized by the authors of these industries. In fact, we have yet to see a clear demonstration that most of the distinctions made in our classification are of utility in distinguishing the repeated patterns of related types that we interpret as traditionally (stylistically) or functionally significant cultural units.

The one class of Lower Paleolithic chipped stone material that has probably been subjected to most careful and objective examination and classification includes the bifaces (or hand axes) that are the hallmark of most Middle Pleistocene cultures in the western Old World (Fig. 2–Fig. 4). While such studies (Bordes 1961; Doran and Hodson 1975; Graham 1970; Roe 1968, 1970; Wymer 1968) suggest that some subclasses can be objectively defined in large populations of bifaces on the basis of attribute clusters, and that bifaces with certain attributes are largely restricted in time or space, prehistorians are still without firm evidence relating to the function of these first recognized and most elaborate of Lower Paleolithic stone tools. The wide variation in form of these tools suggests that a bifacial mode of manufacture was employed as a basic pattern into which variations for slicing, piercing, chopping, and abrading tools could be introduced; i.e. particular kinds of bifaces were produced for different functional purposes, or certain kinds of bifaces could have been reshaped by several successive modifications for a series of different tasks. The possibility that these bifaces were also ready sources (as specialized cores) for thin sharp flakes has been given little consideration in the literature. An additional complicating factor is the probability that some differences in the patterns of biface manufacture were primarily matters of stylistic preference and were largely irrelevant to function.

Thus the prehistorian is limited in the kinds of interpretations he can make of the Lower Paleolithic record by the nature of the artifactual evidence, which is largely confined to the stone tools, cores, flakes, and debris that were abandoned following the final occupation of a site by hominids whose ways

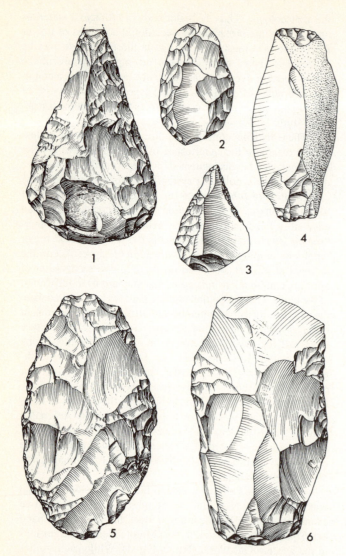

Figure 3 *Middle and Upper Acheulian tools from England and France. Handaxe (1) from Swanscombe, Kent; Side-scraper (2), point (3), and end-scraper (4) from Saint Acheul, Amiens; 'Limande' (5) from Cagny, near Amiens; Bifacial cleaver (6) from Bihorel near Rouen. Adapted from Bordes (1968).*

tion surfaces were, for some unknown period following their abandonment, subject to scavenging for tools and raw materials. Our sample is further limited by the fact that preservation of these early prehistoric remains was limited to those contexts that escaped the destructive forces of weathering and erosion. Chiefly represented are situations in topographic lows where water transport of sediments was responsible for covering and protecting occupation surfaces. In rare instances in Lower and Middle Pleistocene contexts we find artifacts in cave and rock shelter deposits; here the limitations on space and apparent frequent reutilization over long periods of time pose special problems in interpretation. It is a maxim in Paleolithic archaeology, as in paleontology, that we will never know what was going on on the hilltops (or even in the uplands in most instances). Conversely, coastal environments have also lost most of their Lower Paleolithic sites through marine erosion during periods of eustatic and tectonically caused fluctuation in sea level. In many areas coastal occupations of interglacial date remain submerged below 100 or more meters of ocean.

In a general sense, as we come up through time in prehistory we see an increasing abundance of preserved sites, although in the Lower Paleolithic random factors of destruction have removed all sites in many areas through great periods of time and we are left with isolated concentrations of remains in a few favored localities representing widely disparate spatial and temporal contexts. When we consider the limited time represented by any single occupation by the small bands of food collectors that were responsible for the Lower Paleolithic cultural record we can see just how limited our evidence is for the interpretation of this early phase of hominid behavior and cultural development.

Our knowledge of man's cultural activities in the 3 million or so years of the Lower Pleistocene is based largely on the excavation of just over a dozen sites in the restricted locality of Olduvai Gorge in northern Tanzania and about a dozen more throughout the rest of the Old World. The entire excavated area of occupation surfaces is well under the size of a modern football field. We are fortunate in that virtually all of these excavations have been conducted with full use of the meticulous techniques of spatial recording and ancillary analysis developed over the last three decades. We are not so fortunate in our knowledge of Middle Pleistocene prehistory, where a substantial portion of our knowledge is based upon earlier excavations and extensive surface collections in which controls and appreciation of nonartifactual materials varied considerably. This period of approximately half a million years is represented by excavations of perhaps four dozen in situ deposits of cultural material, less than half of which were conducted with modern techniques of recording and ancillary analysis. Also, large geographical areas known from scattered finds to have been inhabited are completely without excavated sites.

In addition to the internal chronological problems of length of time and number of occupations represented by each concentration of artifacts, there remains the major chronological challenge of relating these isolated sites to each other through the relatively enormous expanse of time included in the Lower and Middle Pleistocene. In a few restricted localities, such as Olduvai Gorge and Ubeidiya, these relationships can be determined by direct stratigraphic superposition in a well-controlled section. Here, however, major portions of the geologic structure

of thinking may have differed to a significant degree from our own. A further difficult and crucial problem in this interpretation relates to the question of obtaining evidence beyond the artifacts themselves—the context of the material and the implications of this context for the length of time the site was occupied and the environmental conditions at the time of occupation. In few Lower Paleolithic sites can we state with certainty that the accumulation of artifacts represents a single undisturbed short-term occupation—the kind of occupation that could be expected to result in the spatial segregation of functionally related artifacts that in turn might provide clues to the social patterns of the group that occupied the site. Instead there is every reason to believe that we are in most cases dealing with repeated brief utilization of environmentally favorable localities that resulted in the gradual accumulation of artifacts and reutilization of artifacts on the occupation surface and that repeatedly disturbed previous functionally related spatial relationships. At the least it may be assumed that these occupa-

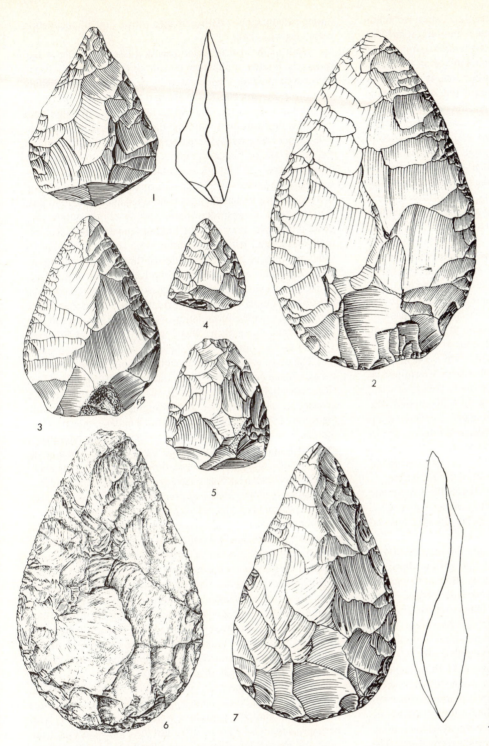

Figure 4 *Acheulian handaxes from France. (1) Late Acheulian, (2-3) Mousterian of Acheulian tradition, (4) Mousterian of late Acheulian tradition, (5) Mousterian of Acheulian tradition, (6) Middle Acheulian, (7) Middle or Upper Acheulian. Adapted from Bordes (1961).*

may reflect relatively short periods of deposition, leaving us with no knowledge of much of the time sequence represented by the interval between the lowest and highest sites in the sequence. At Olduvai, for instance, a recent estimate (Hay 1971) suggests that the whole deposition of Bed I took place over an interval of approximately 100,000 years, or less than 4% of the estimated time span of the Lower Pleistocene. Yet this particular section has provided us with 80% of the occurrences of Oldowan industries at the Gorge (M. D. Leakey 1975). Beyond these exceptional stratigraphic controls broader stratigraphic correlations have been employed in the East

Rudolf and Omo areas of northeast Africa. Here relative chronological position is based upon the position of sites with respect to major stratigraphic boundaries, resulting in more general and scattered relationships of equivalence and succession than is the case at Olduvai. When we look for correlations beyond those areas within which regional stratigraphic controls are possible we find ourselves on less firm ground. The two major methods of relating widely separated deposits to a common chronological sequence are: (*a*) the use of absolute dating techniques and (*b*) the placing of sites within a sequence of environmental and/or geological events of broad global extent.

The most extensively employed absolute dating technique for Lower Paleolithic remains is the potassium-argon radioactive decay series. While there have been instances of misleading results from the application of this technique, as in the recent dating of the KBS tuff in the East Rudolf area, it is generally accepted as reliable for Lower and Middle Pleistocene dating. Since its initial application to deposits at Olduvai Gorge in 1961 (Leakey, Evernden, and Curtis 1961), potassium-argon dating has revolutionized our conception of the length of the period of man's development by extending the age of the Pleistocene back beyond 3.5 million years. Unhappily the archaeological use of this technique depends upon the presence of volcanic extrusives from eruptions contemporary with or (less desirable stratigraphically) bracketing artifactual materials. It is therefore limited to relatively few of the situations in which Lower Paleolithic remains are found. We are, in fact, fortunate that so many of our Lower Pleistocene finds occur in areas of extensive vulcanism during that period in East Africa. Outside of this area, direct applications of the technique to the dating of archaeological remains have been few and in most instances somewhat unsatisfactory. Another technique which appears to promise wider application, though much more general time placement, is paleomagnetic dating, based upon periods of reversal in the polarity of the earth's magnetic field (Cox 1969). The absolute time scale for these magnetic episodes has been determined by potassium-argon dating of volcanic materials whose crystalization preserved the magnetic polarity at the time of eruption. The fact that heating to relatively low temperatures can cause magnetic realignment suggests that this technique ultimately can be applied on a worldwide scale to the study of sites where fire was in contact with magnetic minerals. The promise of this technique for widespread correlation has recently led to the eminently sensible proposal that the boundary between the Lower and Middle Pleistocene be taken as the point of change between the Matuyama Reversed Epoch and present-day Brunhes Normal Epoch, about 700,000 years ago (Butzer and Isaac 1975). The acceptance of such a proposal will require the reevaluation of faunally based sequences that previously provided the basis for major subdivisions within the Pleistocene. Olduvai Gorge can again furnish an example. Here earlier correlations based on the time of replacement of a Villafranchian fauna suggested that the Lower Pleistocene ended with the deposition of the lower portion of Bed II; the paleomagnetic correlations would place the Lower/Middle Pleistocene boundary between Beds III and IV. The advantage of taking the single event of a paleomagnetic transition rather than faunal changes as the chronological anchor for a major time boundary is that since faunal extinctions and appearances did not occur simultaneously throughout the world, this type of biostratigraphic evidence may be misleading when used as the basis for widespread time correlations. The difficulty with paleomagnetic dating in the correlation of Lower Paleolithic cultures is that the major periods of stable paleomagnetic polarity are too long to be of much use except in determining very general time placement (Lower vs Middle Pleistocene) and they are punctuated by brief periods of apparent short reversals called "events." While the probability of a site dating within one of these brief abnormal events is small, the possibility of a misleading paleomagnetic placement, in the absence of other dating evidence, must always be considered. It may, however, ultimately be possible, with the aid of supporting chronological evidence, to employ these events in more ac-

curate paleomagnetic dating of sites whose time of occupation coincides with them.

Both of the dating techniques discussed above have had relatively limited application outside of the northeast African area where they have been extensively employed in the study of Lower Pleistocene sites. By far the majority of Lower Paleolithic sites in the Old World have been correlated both relatively and absolutely through the use of biostratigraphic or paleoclimatically related sequences. The basic shortcoming of the broad use of biostratigraphic evidence for the relatively brief (in terms of biological evolution) spans of time represented by the Lower Paleolithic is the insupportable assumption of synchronous faunal changes mentioned above. Beyond this, the time span of most identifiable species allows only a very general time placement for the kind of faunal assemblage normally associated with a Paleolithic site. Thus a particular assemblage may be said to characterize the early or late Middle Pleistocene but is seldom diagnostic beyond that level of difference, and even here there is occasional disagreement. The use of paleoclimatically linked evidence for Lower Paleolithic correlation, since the formulation of the Alpine sequence of four major glaciations early in this century (Penck and Brückner 1909), has been dominated by the basic four-glacial concept.

The early attempts at paleoclimatic correlation now seem naive, with all of the Lower Paleolithic compressed into the Last (Riss-Würm) Interglacial (Osborn 1916, p. 108), but within a decade the careful work of such stratigraphers as Commont in the north of France had shown that the hand axe industries had their beginnings at least as early as the penultimate interglacial (Mindel-Riss). The subsequent extension of this chronology to areas outside of western Europe through the use of glacially related phenomena such as raised marine beaches and evidence of changes in temperature and precipitation have led to a common employment of Alpine Glacial chronological terms in areas well removed from continental Europe, as well as assumptions of equivalence for local terminology. A challenge to this four-glacial (later modified to six glacials) model of Pleistocene climatic change has emerged from extensive recent paleoclimatic studies based on temperature changes reflected in microorganisms and chemical changes in deep sea deposits. It is assumed that the closely correlated temperature fluctuations seen in widely distributed deep sea cores reflect synchronous global oscillations in climate, which recent studies tend to link to astrophysical mechanisms responsible for continental glaciation (Hayes, Imbrie, and Shackleton 1976).

In contrast to the four- or six-glacial mode for all of the Pleistocene, these cores suggest a prolonged sequence of alternately warm and cold periods of roughly equal intensity, with perhaps as many as eight over the last 700,000 years (since the onset of the Middle Pleistocene) (Emiliani and Shackleton 1974). Since the Late Pleistocene is defined as including only the last major glaciation and the preceding interglacial, which can be dated to correspond with the last of these eight major oscillations, it would appear that we may have as many as seven glacial events comparable to the Würm in the Middle Pleistocene. It is interesting that recent studies of cycles of loess deposition in central Europe appear to support the climate sequence seen in the deep sea cores (Kukla 1975, pp. 169-70). This new evidence suggests that the traditional model of climatic succession based on evidence of Alpine and continental glaciation is oversimplified (Kukla 1975, p. 178], and has resulted from the destruction of a substantial portion of continental sediments through glacial removal and erosion, and that the chronological arrangement of sites in the Middle Pleistocene, particularly in Europe and adjacent areas, will require serious reexamination. We can no longer with any confidence refer a site with an "early Middle Pleistocene" fauna and evidence of a cold environment to a Mindel Glacial time, sites with cold "late Middle Pleistocene" fauna to a Riss Glacial time, or all sites with a "warm Middle Pleistocene" fauna to a "Great Interglacial" or Mindel-Riss interglacial (or Hoxnian or Holstenian) time. Instead it appears that there may have been six warm interglacials and seven glacials in the Middle Pleistocene during the time span previously assigned to the two glacials and one interglacial in the traditional sequence.

The implications of this postulated sequence beyond the temperate areas are equally profound, since such factors as sea level and atmospheric circulation patterns can also be expected to have fluctuated many more times than had previously been suspected. It is likely, for example, that previous correlations of particular cool pluvial conditions in the Levant with the Mindel and Riss glaciations will need further examination, as will the correlation of Middle Pleistocene industries with the Mindel-Riss Interglacial on the basis of particular raised marine beaches.

In view of the relatively slow evolution of the fauna during the Middle Pleistocene, it appears that the most promising solution to the correlation of Middle Pleistocene sites lies in linking archaeological sites to more detailed local stratigraphic and climatological sequences and in the development and wider application of such absolute dating techniques as paleomagnetic and thermoluminescence dating. At present all we can say is that many of the correlations proposed in recent syntheses are probably incorrect (at least in a detailed sense) and their revision will require considerable new evidence. We are probably most secure in our Middle Pleistocene correlations at the upper end of the time scale, where effects of the penultimate glacial ("Riss") can, in many instances, be isolated from earlier cold periods. Prior to this last cold phase of the Middle Pleistocene we now have a much broader range of possible time positions for our cultural evidence. Yet within this time range lie many sites whose relative chronological positions have been the subject of recent controversy. In Europe, these sites and localities would include Swanscombe, Terra Amata, Torralba and Ambrona, Torre in Pietra, Clacton, Hoxne, Mauer, Vértesszöllös, and the Carpentier pit at Abbeville.

Granted the limitations mentioned in the preceding discussion of the nature of our evidence of Lower Paleolithic man, what *do* we know about man's early development as a tool-making creature? The earliest evidence for the manufacture of stone tools at the time of this writing is based on a find by J. Chavaillon dated to approximately 2.5 million years and derives from Member C of the Shungura Formation of the Lower Omo River valley in southern Ethiopia (Isaac 1976, p. 487). Earlier reports of stone tools of a similar age in the KBS industry from the east Rudolf area of Kenya have been revised and the age of this industry is now considered to be about 1.6–1.8 million years (Curtis, Drake, Cerling, and Hampel 1975). Thus, by shortly after two million years ago, we have firm evidence of the use of stone tools in a broad area of east Africa extending from Olduvai Gorge in northern Tanzania, through the east Rudolf area of Kenya, and into the Southern

Omo valley of Ethiopia. The evidence for these early cultures, associated hominids, and their geological and environmental setting have recently been treated in detail in two important volumes of collected papers (Coppens, Howell, Isaac, and Leakey 1976; Isaac and McCown 1976). In a provocative paper, Isaac (1976) attempts to reconstruct as much as possible of what the current evidence from the Koobi Fora formation in the east Rudolf area suggests about the life ways of the hominids responsible for the early archaeological sites. These are the more important points in his treatment:

(*a*) By that time there were already several well-defined formal categories of chipped stone tools. This may imply a significant period of development of tool use prior to the appearance of these industries.

(*b*) Artifact concentrations are suggestive of a "home base" which served as a focal point for cultural activities. Important here is the notion that at least some of the products of the food quest were brought back to the base camp to be divided among the band. It is certain that many if not all artifacts were transported here. The relatively small size of these concentrations (5 to 20 meters in diameter) suggests that relatively small populations were involved, and this is emphasized when we consider that we really have no way of distinguishing single from multiple occupations in these sites. Further evidence in this regard may be seen in the work of Merrick at the FtJi2 occurrence in the Omo area, where there is some evidence for two closely superimposed lenses of artifacts in a concentration with a maximum extent of 20 meters (Merrick 1976). It is tempting to speculate that these larger concentrations may reflect periodic re-use of a favorable locality in a restricted territory.

(*c*) The association of artifact concentrations with stream channel deposits suggests a preferred habitat relating to the exploitation of ecotonal environments in the vicinity of gallery forest and adjacent savannah. Here Isaac recognizes the selective nature of the depositional forces that have preserved his material, but he feels the evidence is sufficiently strong to warrant his interpretation of a culturally significant association. An additional relevant factor might be the probable preference by the hominids for sites near a water supply.

Within about half a million years of the appearance of these widespread early manifestations of tool use, the first evidences of the manufacture of bifaces are apparent in the Developed Oldowan industries at Olduvai (especially at site MNK and the Lower Floor at TK) (M. D. Leakey 1975, p. 484), and are probably associated with the Karari Industry in the east Rudolf area (Harris and Bishop 1976). In the Olduvai sequence their appearance is accompanied by an increase in spheroids and battered pieces. If they are associated with the Karari industry, it is possible to say that in both areas they coincide with a generally wider range of distinct tool forms, suggesting that they are part of an overall elaboration of the technological system. In view of a recent report of the discovery of a hominid provisionally classified as early *Homo erectus* (KNM-ER 3733) from the east Rudolf area in this time horizon (Leakey and Walker 1976), it may be that these more elaborate industries reflect the presence of more advanced hominids than those responsible for the earlier Oldowan industries.

The time of the earliest appearance of Lower Paleolithic industries in the rest of the Old World is still relatively unknown. There is increasing evidence for a middle Lower Pleistocene arrival of man in Europe; e.g. the Sandalja I Cave (Yugoslavia) human incisor and chopper associated with a Middle Villafranchian fauna (Malez 1976), and the recent finds of pebble tools near Cadiz, in a depositional context comparable to that in which similar material was reported by Biberson, from an apparently middle Lower Pleistocene context in Morocco (Bordes and Viguier 1971; F. Bordes, personal communication). Recent evidence from Iran suggests a Lower Pleistocene date for the appearance of man in Southwest Asia (Thibault 1976); however, no firm evidence has yet appeared to support a comparable date for early tool manufacture in other areas of Asia. Aside from these brief glimpses of Lower Pleistocene man beyond Africa, there is still so little evidence, despite extensive examination of many Lower Pleistocene localities, that we are forced to conclude that hominid populations were thinly scattered in Europe and Asia at that time. Probably they were confined to warmer southern regions of these continents, and perhaps then only preceding glaciation or during interglacial periods. In contrast, during the Middle Pleistocene there is fairly abundant evidence of Lower Paleolithic man from the temperate latitudes of north China to Great Britain.

There is little question that this successful adaptation to cooler environments is related to the control of fire. The full implications of the incorporation of fire into the technology of Middle Pleistocene man have yet to be understood. Most obviously it was used to modify the temperature of habitation areas and allow biological survival in environments otherwise untenable for an essentially tropical adapted hominid. Beyond this, however, the use of fire in shaping wood and the influence on utilization of wood resulting from continuing collection of fuel are important considerations. Probably of widest interest, and most likely to be accessible to present analytical techniques, are the effects of the deliberate employment of fire in hunting practices. That the use of fire in hunting may be a very ancient practice seems suggested by the perhaps unique evidence of burned wood preserved at Torralba (Howell, Butzer, and Aguirre 1962), although even here the possibility that the fire was accidental or simply a defense against the glacial climate cannot be eliminated. Whether Middle Pleistocene man ever consciously appreciated the advantages of improving the forage for the animals he hunted by deliberate burning is open to question, but with this force in his control the possibility for increased survival through the use of these techniques must be considered. Perhaps it is not too far-fetched to suggest that examination of the palynological record in favorable localities may reveal evidence of unexpectedly frequent environmental alteration attributable to fire in this period.

One aspect of the Lower Paleolithic in the Middle Pleistocene that has been the focus of considerable attention on the part of prehistorians is the diversity of lithic industries. By the 1940s a basic geographical division was recognized between the "hand axe" industries of the western Old World and Peninsular India and the "chopper/chopping-tool" industries of northern India and east Asia (Fig. 5, Fig. 6). More recently it has been recognized that bifaces similar or identical to western examples

Figure 5 *Chopper-Chopping tools from Choukoutien, China. (1) Cleaver-like tool from Locality 13; (2-4) Flakes with some secondary working from Locality 1; (5) Large chopper from Locality 1. Adapted from Movius (1949) and Wymer (1982).*

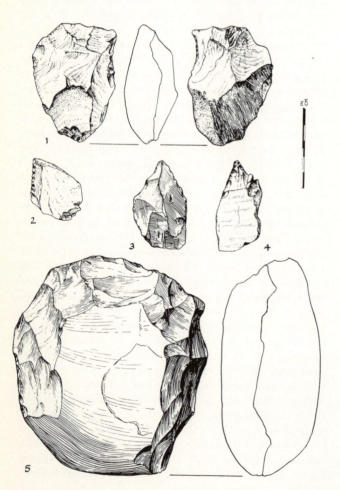

Figure 6 *Stone tools from Southeast Asia. (1) Anyathian chopper-core made from fossil wood, Burma; (2) Tampanian flake of quartzite from Kota Tampan, Perak, Malaysia; (3) Patjitanian flake with secondary working made from silicified limestone, South-central Java. Adapted from Movius (1949), Walker and Sieveking (1962) and Wymer (1982).*

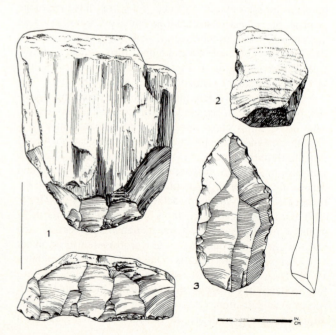

are present in the late Lower Paleolithic of Java (Bordes 1968) and, apparently in small numbers, in Middle Pleistocene industries in China (Fig. 5) (e.g. Laritchev). In the latter case especially, these kinds of tools appear to occur so infrequently that their significance is open to question. Certainly the interpretation of Laritchev (1976) that "Hand axes...are in the same extent characteristic for East and Southeast Asia as for South Asia (India), Near East, Africa and Europe" is a clear overstatement in the light of present evidence. The few widely scattered (in space and time) bifaces from China that he cites do not convey the impression of a thriving Acheulian industry. It seems likely that such tool forms may have resulted (though rarely) from the range of lithic manufacturing techniques employed in that area. Here the danger of using a single tool form as a diagnostic index fossil is particularly apparent. A study of the full industry, including frequencies of tool types, techniques of flake extraction, etc. would quickly serve to demonstrate the profound differences between the northern Chinese industries and the Acheulian of the western Old World.

It has long been obvious that the western Lower Paleolithic is not a uniform group of industries. Specifically, there appear to be several manifestations of nonbiface industries in Europe in circumstances that suggest that the two kinds of industries may be contemporaneous. A discussion incorporating several interpretations of the significance of these different industries was recently initiated by Collins (1969) and illustrates the divergence of opinions currently held by prehistorians on this question. Unfortunately, as Frenzel noted perceptively in his "Comment" (Frenzel 1969), this discussion suffers from a heavy reliance on the now questionable evidence for correlation based on the traditional interpretation of Middle Pleistocene glacial succession (see above). The same uncertainties affect the otherwise useful and very thorough discussion of many of these industries by Howell (1966). It is clear that most of the arguments raised in these discussions cannot be resolved until better agreement has been reached on the chronological relationships of the sites and industries. Even among the Acheulian biface industries of western Europe there appears to be some geographically consistent variability: occasional flake cleavers similar to those of the African Acheulian (see Fig. 2) are associated with high frequencies of relatively crude hand axes and little Levallois technique in Spain and the southwest of France; in contrast, there is general absence of flake cleavers, more frequent refined bifaces, and a greater use of Levallois technique in northern France and England (Bordes 1966, 1968, 1971). Whether this difference relates to an African influence via Gibraltar, as has been suggested (Alimen 1975; Bordes 1966), or whether the prevalence of more massive raw material sources (quartzites in Spain and Bergerac flint in southwest France) stimulated independent invention remains an open question. Certainly the presence of immense flat ovate flakes with the platform trimmed away in a bifacial "retouch of accommodation" in Locality 15 at Choukoutien (personal observation) suggests an independent development of a flake cleaver technique in northern China. The presence of African-style flake cleaver and biface industries at Jisr Banat Yaqub in the Levant (Stekelis 1960), where massive basalts were available, and in massive quartzite on the Indian Penninsula, both quite distant from similar industries in Africa, suggests that raw material resources may have been an important factor in the development of such industries. This raw material association

is particularly evident in the Levant, where other Acheulian industries (all made on nodular chert) show little evidence of these African techniques.

Variability in the African industries is best examined for the Lower Paleolithic in the well-controlled sequence at Olduvai Gorge. Here there is a relatively prolonged period of contemporaneity of two distinct industries: the Acheulian, characterized by hand axes and other tools made on large flat flakes, and the Developed Oldowan, in which such tools and flakes are absent and there is a prevalence of choppers and spheroids. M. D. Leakey (1975) refers these industries to distinct traditions, apparently related to independent populations of hominids. She also sees distinctive variability within the Acheulian; this suggests "that the artifacts from each site or level were made by a group of people who had their own tradition in tool making and standard tool kit from which they did not deviate to any appreciable extent" (Leakey 1975, p. 492). In the absence of any clear trend toward increasing refinement in biface manufacture (Leakey 1975), as had originally been proposed by L. S. B. Leakey (1951), the general picture that emerges is a period of perhaps a million years in which the only variability in the stone tool technology of Acheulian hominids seems to have been an apparently random fluctuation in the relative frequencies of particular artifact forms. Possibly more insight into this variability can be gained through a look at the somewhat later African Acheulian manifestations at Isimila or Olorgesailie. Here in two areally and temporally restricted sequences of late Acheulian industries we can see considerable variability in the tool forms produced.

At Isimila 3 types of industries were described (Kleindienst 1961) based on the relative frequencies of small tools, large sharp-edged tools, and large blunt-edged or "heavy duty" tools. While these industries would all be classified as Acheulian by M. D. Leakey on the basis of the presence of bifacial hand axes and cleavers, the kinds of differences that they exhibit are to some extent reminiscent of the Acheulian-Developed Oldowan variation. One interpretation of the Isimila evidence might be that each of the samples represents a point on a continuum of variability within a single basic industry, with each of the three variants showing a predominance of certain task-specific elements. Given the rather small sample size ($\overline{X} = 90$ for the nine cases) and the presence of some elements in each class in each sample, this does not seem to be an unreasonable assumption. If we examine the ratios of two sets of pairs of variables examined by Kleindienst for the stratigraphic sequence at Isimila and Olorgesailie (Kleindienst 1961) as shown in Table 2, it appears that: (a) a rather close correlation exists between the presence of shaped tools and larger implements on the one hand and waste and small implements on the other, and (b) at Olorgesailie there is a clear trend through time in the eleven strata from high ratios of waste and small tools to high ratios of shaped tools and large tools and then a gradual return to the original pattern. At Isimila there is a suggestion of a trend from more waste and small tools to more shaped tools and large tools, but it is not as clear as the trend at Olorgesailie. Such differences may indicate shifts in the kinds of tasks performed in a given locality as resources changed over time, the Olorgesailie evidence indicating a possible full cycle in this kind of change. Detailed environmental analysis might substantiate this hypothesis. It does seem likely on the basis of variation in styles of hand axe and cleaver manufacture between

Table 2. Ratios of some basic classes of lithic materials from two late Acheulian sites in East Africa.

Stratigraphy	Waste (%)	N1	Small tools (%)	N2
Isimila				
SST. 1a; up. J6–J7	42.7	233	9.5	95
SST. 1a; H9–J8	41.9	186	5.3	95
SST. 1a; K14	60.6	434	21.6	125
SST. 1b; lo. J6–J7	76.1	932	42.0	88
SST. 1b; K6	36.4	305	2.6	177
SST. 2; J12	68.2	148	7.5	40
SST. 3; lo. H15	77.4	328	12.2	41
SST. 3; lo. K18 TR2	84.8	1546	54.9	93
SST. 3; K19	74.6	528	23.4	90
Olorgesailie				
L.S. 13	72.7	278	100.0	17
L.S. 12	75.0	88	100.0	3
L.S. 11	70.0	434	81.3	59
L.S. 10	68.2	890	47.9	148
L.S. 9	40.9	215	6.0	99
L.S. 8	58.7	443	14.0	135
L.S. 7	40.5	205	8.1	112
L.S. 6	65.9	740	50.0	150
L.S. 3	61.5	465	73.5	87
L.S. 2	64.3	451	69.8	106
L.S. 1	74.5	428	98.2	70

[a]N1 = number of tools + waste; N2 = number of shaped tools. From Kleindienst (1961).

samples that many of these occupations may represent distinct limited traditions of implement manufacture within distinct social groups. Perhaps if similarly abundant samples in comparable restricted time periods and spatial loci were available in the million year sequence of Acheulian at Olduvai, similar trends or cyclical patterns might be evident there as well.

In terms of more specific interpretations of social patterns and way of life of Middle Pleistocene man we are limited to too few examples of in situ artifact distributions to make meaningful generalizations. The evidence of Lazaret (de Lumley 1969a) and Terra Amata (de Lumley 1969b) is stimulating in this regard, but too limited to warrant a discussion of such variables as group size, domestic patterning, and seasonal scheduling with any degree of confidence. In considering the example of Lazaret in particular, it is worth remembering that caves and rock shelters tend to shape the patterns of occupation by constricting the space within which domestic activities can be carried out. Here the freedom of separation of activities that characterizes an open site may be sacrificed in order to take advantage of the protection afforded by the restricted space of the shelter.

In conclusion, it may be useful to summarize some overall impressions of the Lower Paleolithic on the basis of our present evidence and to review several of the outstanding problems that can now be perceived. The overriding impression of the technological evidence in the archaeological record is one of almost unimaginable monotony. Perhaps the most overwhelming ex-

ample of this is the Acheulian of Olduvai Gorge, where for approximately a million years no significant innovation is discernable. In other areas, such as western Europe, some gradual trends which appear to represent refinements in man's ability to control the results of his techniques of stone flaking are evident. But even these innovations take place over hundreds of thousands of years; this means that we are talking about tens of thousands of generations of hominids maintaining patterns of technological traditions without discernable change. When, by contrast, we view the diverse succession of industries and proliferation of areally distinct patterns of the Upper Paleolithic, which may in its totality represent between 1200 and 1300 generations, the distinctive character of the Lower Paleolithic becomes evident. The evidence strongly suggests a more limited capacity for the control of variables upon which synthesis and innovation are based and suggests a qualitatively different kind of cultural activity from that familiar to us in the activities of *Homo sapiens sapiens*. There is thus good reason to refer to this Lower Paleolithic pattern as representing a *paleocultural* behavior which differed significantly from the cultural behavior of modern man. One aspect of this difference may have been the absence of the kind of linguistic communication that characterizes modern man. While this limitation has been suggested previously for Lower and Middle Pleistocene hominids it is notoriously difficult, if not impossible, to demonstrate anatomically; perhaps here our technological evidence is the best we will have on the behavior and abilities of these early men.

If we accept such behavioral differences for the Lower Paleolithic men, it follows that attempts to reconstruct their ways of life must, as Isaac has suggested (Isaac 1975), take into account the fact that their activities were not completely analogous to those of modern hunter-gatherers, but were distinct from those of any creatures we can presently observe. There is every likelihood that by the Middle Pleistocene, if not before, these hominids were the most intelligent and effective predators on the earth. Even without language they were surely more aware of the potentials of their environment and their fellows than any previous animal population. The adaptations that occurred in these tens of thousands of generations are part of the foundation that underlies modern man's behavioral and cognitive systems.

The Lower Paleolithic does see a transition from man's first use of deliberately fragmented pieces of stone to the manufacture of fully conceived implements whose final form is regularly patterned and in no way suggested by the shape or exterior texture of the stone from which they were made. This is certainly a significant step in conceptualization and foreshadows the more complex innovations of the Middle and Upper Paleolithic. It occurs, however, in the context of the very slow and gradual change that characterizes the whole of this period.

The problems that confront the prehistorian attempting to interpret the Lower Paleolithic are typical of those met by any young branch of science. The few scattered occupation sites that have been subjected to careful excavation are spread over immense distances of space and time. The remainder of our data are from early and less adequate excavations and materials naturally transported from their place of manufacture or use. We are continually attempting to extract any regularities from this slender evidence that we can relate to hypotheses about the activities of these long extinct hominids, beyond the forces that they applied to make their stone tools and the kinds of animal bones that they left as refuse in their camps. In order to see these regularities it is important that we develop a common language to discuss our evidence concerning tool manufacture. Agreement on a universally applicable descriptive vocabulary for the definition of artifact variability should be one of the strongest priorities for Lower Paleolithic research. Such a descriptive system is a necessary foundation for the comparative studies that will enable us to begin to generalize about this aspect of our evidence. It is very unfortunate that we have not yet reached agreement on this fundamental aspect of research. A second major problem area in Lower Paleolithic studies concerns the refinement of chronological relationships between sites and industries; until we are fully aware of the complexity of the Pleistocene record and develop techniques to link our archaeological evidence to an absolute time scale we will be unable to make more than the most general hypotheses concerning the changes occuring in early cultural development. Another area in need of clarification, and barely touched upon in this paper, is the relationship between fossil hominids and the Paleolithic industries. With every new find of *Homo erectus* and similar fossil men in the Middle Pleistocene (such as the recent discovery at Blizingsleben [Mania 1976]) the specter of "Pre-Sapiens," fostered by spuriously dated fossils such as Galley Hill and Piltdown, becomes less viable, and a gradual evolution paralleling the cultural record seems more likely. There is, however, still much work to be done to clarify this biological and cultural sequence.

Ultimately our aim is to provide a better understanding of the meaning of the variability and conservatism that we can observe in the paleocultural record of the Lower and Middle Pleistocene in terms of the behavior and development of the fossil men that preceded *Homo sapiens*. In order to do so we must continually reexamine the nature of our evidence and the assumptions that we are making in our interpretation of this record.

REFERENCES

Alimen, H. M. 1975. Les "isthmes" Hispano-Marocain et Siculo-Tunisien aux temps acheuléens. *Anthropologie* 79:399-436.

Biberson, P. 1964. Torralba et Ambrona. Notes sur deux stations acheuléens de chasseurs d'éléphants de la Vielle Castille. *Inst. Prehist. Arqueol. Barcelona Monogr.* 6:201-48.

Bordes, F. 1950. Principes d'une méthode d'étude des techniques de débitage et de la typologie du Paléolithique ancien et moyen. *Anthropologie* 54:19-34.

Bordes, F. 1961. Typologie du Paléolithique ancien et moyen. *Publ. Inst. Préhist. Univ. Bordeaux Mém.* 1, Vols. 1, 2.

Bordes, F. 1966. Acheulian cultures in Southwest France, in: *Studies in Prehistory* (D. Sen and A. K. Ghosh, Eds.), pp. 49-57. Calcutta.

Bordes, F. 1968. *The Old Stone Age.* McGraw-Hill, New York.

Bordes, F. 1971. Observations sur L'Acheuleen des grottes en Dordogne. *Munibe* 23:5-24.

Bordes, F., and Viguier, C. 1971. Sur la présence de galets taillés de type ancien dans un sol fossile à Puerto de Santa Maria au Nord-Est de la baie de Cadix (Espagne). *C. R. Acad. Sci. Paris Ser. D* 272:1747-1749.

Breuil, H. 1932. Les industries à éclats du Paléolithique ancien I—Le Clactonien. *Prehistoire* 1:125-190.

Breuil, H. 1939. Bone and antler industry of the Choukoutien *Sinanthropus* site. *Paleontol. Sin.* n.s. D, No. 6.

Butzer, K. W., and Isaac, G. Ll. 1975. Delimitation of the geologic time term "Middle Pleistocene," in: *After the Australopithecines: Stratigraphy, Ecology, and Culture Change in the Middle Pleistocene,* (K. W. Butzer and G. Ll. Isaac, Eds.), pp. 901-3. Mouton, The Hague.

Clark, G. 1969. *World Prehistory: A New Outline.* Cambridge University Press, Cambridge.

Clark, J. D. 1970. *The Prehistory of Africa.* Praeger, New York.

Clark, J. D., and Kleindienst, M. R. 1974. The Stone Age cultural sequence: Terminology, typology and raw material, in: *Kalambo Falls Prehistoric Site,* Vol. 2 (J. D. Clark, Ed.), pp. 71-106. Cambridge University Press, Cambridge.

Collins, D. 1969. Culture traditions and environment of early man. *Curr. Anthropol.* 10:267-316.

Coppens, Y., Howells, F. C., Isaac, G. Ll., and Leakey, R. E. F., Eds. 1976. *Earliest Man and Environments in the Lake Rudolf Basin.* University of Chicago Press, Chicago.

Cox, A. 1969. Geomagnetic reversals. *Science* 163:237-45.

Curtis, G. H., Drake, R. E., Cerling, T., and Hampel, J. H. 1975. Age of the KBS tuff in the Koobi Fora formation, East Rudolf, Kenya. *Nature* 258:395-98.

de Lumley, H. ed. 1969a. Une cabane acheuléenne dans la grotte du Lazaret (Nice). *Mémoires de la Société Préhistorique Française* 7.

de Lumley, H. 1969b. A Paleolithic camp at Nice. *Sci. Am.* 220 (5):42-50.

Doran, J. E., and Hodson, F. R. 1975. *Mathematics and Computers in Archaeology.* Edinburgh University Press, Edinburgh.

Emiliani, C., and Shackleton, N. J. 1974. The Brunhes epoch: Isotopic paleotemperatures and geochronology. *Science* 183:511-14.

Frenzel, B. 1969. Comment. *Curr. Anthropol.* 10:304-5.

Fridrich, J. 1976. The first industries from eastern and south-Eastern Central Europe. *Colloq. 8, 9e Congr. Int. Sci. Préhist. Protohist.,* Nice, pp. 8-23.

Frison, G. C. 1968. A functional analysis of certain chipped stone tools. *Am. Antiq.* 33:149-55.

Gould, R. A., Koster, D. A., and Sontz, A. H. 1971. The lithic assemblage of the Western Desert Aborigines of Australia. *Am. Antiq.* 36:149-69.

Graham, J. M. 1970. Discrimination of British Lower and Middle Paleolithic handaxe groups using canonical variates. *World Archaeol.* 1:321-37.

Harris, J. W. K., and Bishop, W. W. 1976. Sites and assemblages from the Early Pleistocene beds of Karari and Chesowanja. *Colloq. 5, 9e Congr. Int. Sci. Préhist. Protohist.,* Nice, pp. 70-117.

Hay, R. L. 1971. Geologic background of Beds I and II: stratigraphic summary, in: *Olduvai Gorge, Vol. 3: Excavations in Beds I and II 1960–1963* (M. D. Leakey, Ed.), pp 9-18. Cambridge University Press, Cambridge.

Hayes, J. D., Imbrie, J., and Shackleton, N. J. 1976. Variations in the Earth's orbit: Pacemaker of the Ice Ages. *Science* 194:1121-32.

Howell, F. C. 1966. Observations on the earlier phases of the European Lower Paleolithic. *Am. Anthropol.* 68:88-201.

Howell, F. C., Butzer, K. W., and Aguirre, E. 1962. Noticia preliminar sobre el emplazamiento acheulense de Torralba (Soria). *Excavaciones Arqueol. Esp.* 10:1-38.

Howell, F. C., and Clark, J. D. 1963. Acheulian hunter-gatherers of sub-Saharan Africa, in: *African Ecology and Human Evolution* (F. C. Howell and F. Bourlière, Eds.), pp. 458-533. Aldine, Chicago.

Isaac, G. Ll. 1975. Stratigraphy and cultural patterns in East Africa during the middle ranges of Pleistocene time, in: *After the Australopithecines: Stratigraphy, Ecology, and Cultural Change in the Middle Pleistocene* (K. W. Butzer and G. Ll. Issac, Eds.), pp. 495-542, Mouton, The Hague.

Isaac, G. Ll. 1976. The activities of early African hominids: A review of archaeological evidence from the time span two and a half to one million years ago, in: *Human Origins: Louis Leakey and the East African*

Evidence (G. Ll. Isaac and E. R. McCown, Eds.), pp. 483-514, Benjamin, Menlo Park, CA.

Isaac, G. Ll., and McCown, E. R. 1976. *Human Origins: Louis Leakey and the East African Evidence*. Benjamin, Menlo Park, CA.

Jelinek, A. J. 1976. Form, function, and style in lithic analysis, in: *Cultural Change and Continuity: Essays in Honor of James Bennett Griffin* (C. E. Cleland, Ed.), pp. 19-33. Academic, New York.

Kleindienst, M. R. 1961. Variability within the late Acheulian assemblage in Eastern Africa. *S. African Archaeol. Bull.* 16:35-52.

Kukla, G. J. 1975. Loess Stratigraphy of Central Europe, in: *After the Australopithecines: Stratigraphy, Ecology, and Culture Change in the Middle Pleistocene* (K. W. Butzer and G. Ll. Isaac, Eds.), pp. 99-188. Mouton, The Hague.

Laritchev, V. E. 1976. Discovery of hand-axes in China and the problem of local cultures of Lower Paleolith of East Asia. *Colloq. 7, 9e Congr. Int. Sci. Préhist. Protohist.,* Nice, pp. 154-78.

Leakey, L. S. B. 1951. *Olduvai Gorge*. Cambridge University Press, Cambridge.

Leakey, L. S. B., Evernden, J. F., and Curtis, G. H. 1961. Age of Bed I, Olduvai. *Nature* 191:478-79.

Leakey, M. D. 1971. *Olduvai Gorge, Vol 3: Excavations in Beds I and II, 1960–1963*. Cambridge University Press, Cambridge.

Leakey, M. D. 1975. Cultural patterns in the Olduvai sequence, in: *After the Australopithecines: Stratigraphy, Ecology, and Culture Changes in the Middle Pleistocene* (K. W. Butzer and G. Ll. Isaac, Eds.), pp. 477-93. Mouton, The Hague.

Leakey, R. E. F., and Walker, A. C. 1976. *Australopithecus, Homo erectus* and the single species hypothesis. *Nature* 261:572-74.

Malez, M. 1976. Excavation of the Vilafranchian Site Šandalja I near Pula (Yugoslavia). Colloq. 8, 9e *Congr. Int. Sci. Prehist, Protohist.,* Nice, pp. 104-133.

Mania, D. L. 1976. Altpaläolithischer Rastplatz mit Hominidenresten aus dem Mittelpleistozänen Travertin-Komplex von Bilzingsleben (DDR). *Colloq. 9, 9e Congr. Int. Sci. Prehist. Protohist.,* Nice, pp. 35-47.

Merrick, H. V. 1976. Recent archaeological research in the Plio-Pleistocene deposits of the Lower Omo, Southwestern Ethiopia, in: *Human Origins: Louis Leakey and the East African Evidence* (G. Ll. Isaac and E. R. McCown, Eds.), pp. 461-481. Benjamin, Menlo Park, CA.

Mortillet, G. de 1872. Classification des diverses périodes de l'Age de la Pierre. *C. R. 6e Congr. Int Anthropol. Archeol. Préhist.,* Bruxelles, pp. 432-444.

Movius, H. L. 1949. Lower Paleolithic archaeology in Southern Asia and the Far East, in: *Studies in Physical Anthropology, No. 1., Early Man in the Far East* (W. W. Howells, Ed.), pp. 17-81. Wistar Institute, Philadelphia.

Movius, H. L. 1950. A wooden spear of Third Interglacial age from Lower Saxony. *Southwest J. Anthropol.* 6:139-142.

Oakley, K. 1964. *Man the Tool Maker*. University of Chicago Press, Chicago.

Osborn, H. F. 1916. *Men of the Old Stone Age*. 2nd ed. Scribner's, New York.

Penck, A., and Brückner, E. 1909. *Die Alpen im Eiszeitalter*. Tauchnitz, Leipzig.

Radmilli, A. M. 1976. The first industries of Italy. *Colloq. 8, 9e Congr. Int. Sci. Préhist. Protohist.,* Nice, pp. 35-74.

Roe, D. A. 1968. British Lower and Middle Paleolithic handaxe groups. *Proc. Prehist. Soc.* 34:1-82.

Roe, D. A. 1970. Comments on the results obtained by M. J. Graham. *World Archaeol.* 1:338-342.

Shipman, P., and Phillips, J. E. 1976. On scavenging by hominids and other carnivores. *Curr. Anthropol.* 17:170-172.

Stekelis, M. 1960. The Paleolithic deposits of Jisr Banat Yaqub. *Bull. Res. Counc. Isr. Sect. G* 9:63-90.

Sutcliffe, A. J. 1970. Spotted hyaena: Crusher, gnawer, digester and collector of bones. *Nature* 227:1110-1113.

Thibault, C. 1976. Decouverte de Paléolithique Archaique dans le Nord-Est de l'Iran. *Résumé Commun. 9e Congr. Int. Sci. Préhist. Protohist.,* Nice, p. 117.

Walker, D., and Sieveking, A. 1962. The Paleolithic industry of Kota Tampan, Perak, Malaya. *Proc. Prehist. Soc.* 28:103-139.

Warren, S. H. 1922. The Mesvinian industry of Clacton-on-Sea, Essex. *Proc. Prehist. Soc. East Anglia* 3:597-602.

Warren, S. H. 1951. The Clactonian flint industry: A new interpretation. *Proc. Geol. Assoc.* 62:107-135.

White, J. P. 1968. Ston niap bilong tumbuna: The living Stone Age in New Guinea, in: *La Préhistoire: Problèmes et Tendances* (F. Bordes and D. de Sonneville-Bordes, Eds.), pp. 511-516. Centre Natl. Rech. Sci., Paris.

Wymer, J. J. 1968. *Lower Paleolithic Archaeology in Britain: As Represented by the Thames Valley*. Baker, London.

Wymer, J. J. 1982. *The Paleolithic Age*. St Martins Press, New York.

Part VI
Evolution of *Homo sapiens*

Parts VI and VII are concerned with the origin of our own species, *Homo sapiens*, and the relationships among various groups of fossil hominids during the Middle and Late Pleistocene. We have organized these chapters largely on a geographical rather than a chronological basis. Part VI contains articles discussing Middle and Late Pleistocene fossil hominid evolution worldwide as well as theoretical and molecular approaches. Part VII is restricted to the most extensively debated part of this problem, the relationship of Neandertals[1] from Europe and the Middle East to modern humans.

The diversity of Middle and Late Pleistocene hominids and their relationship to modern humans has been a topic of debate for many decades (see Chapters 49, 50). However, in recent years discussion of this topic has become an obsession that has yielded an endless series of conferences, books, and review papers (e.g. Smith and Spencer 1984; Lewin 1989; Mellars and Stringer 1989; Smith et al. 1989; Trinkaus 1989; Mellars 1990; Bräuer and Smith 1992). Surprisingly, for paleo-anthropology, this rash of analysis has neither been initiated by nor benefited from significant new fossil material that might lead to any resolution of the issues being debated (Tattersall 1991). Rather, the few new insights into the problem have largely come from molecular biology (Chapter 46; see also Lewin 1987; Cann 1988; Vigilant *et al.* 1991) and new dating for old sites (Schwarcz et al. 1988; Stringer *et al.* 1989; Grün and Stringer 1991). Most recent discussions have focused on two specific models for the origin of "anatomically modern *Homo sapiens*," the multiregional model (e.g., Chapters 44, 48, 60) which emphasizes morphological continuity between archaic and modern populations within separate regions of the world; and a monogenesis model (e.g., Chapters 45, 47, 52, 59; Stringer 1990) which emphasizes a single, probably African origin for "anatomically modern humans," followed by migration and replacement of other hominids throughout the world. As various reviewers have noted, the scenarios proposed are rarely as pure and divergent as these models would suggest. In addition, many solutions to the origin of "anatomically modern humans" fail to address the related problem of the origin of "archaic *Homo sapiens*," or more commonly, fail to distinguish clearly where they draw the boundaries for *Homo sapiens*.

Chapter 42, "Species Recognition in Human Paleontology" by Ian Tattersall, focuses on the basic question that must underly any attempt to resolve the phylogeny of later hominid evolution—how many species are represented in the fossil record? Most paleoanthropologists currently recognize three morphological groups within the species *Homo sapiens*: (1) "anatomically modern humans," (2) Neandertals, and (3) an "archaic" group, including fossils from Arago, Petralona, Bodo, Kabwe and Dali. Tattersall argues that the morphological differences between these groups are great enough that each should be considered a distinct species. Considering all of these diverse forms in a single species, he argues, obscures the diversity of human evolution during the Middle and Late Pleistocene and precludes the comparisons needed to understand the pattern of human evolution during that time. Conversely, any model that posits gene flow between these groups is, in effect, arguing for a single species.

Chapter 43, "Middle Pleistocene Hominid Variability and the Origin of Late Pleistocene Humans" by Christopher Stringer, reviews fossil hominids from the Middle Pleistocene of Europe with respect to four evolutionary models (see also Stringer 1990). He argues that the Middle Pleistocene of Europe shows an early record of "archaic *Homo sapiens*," preserving some primitive features of *Homo erectus*, that subsequently gave rise to primitive Neandertals. He argues that in Europe there is no known example of *Homo erectus* and no evidence of forms transitional to anatomically modern *Homo sapiens*. Rather he argues that modern humans originated elsewhere, probably Africa (see Chapters 45, 47).

In Chapter 44, "Regional Continuity in Australasian Pleistocene Hominid Evolution," Alan Thorne and Milford Wolpoff present evidence for a different pattern of morphological change in Southeast Asia and Australia. They argue that fossil hominids in this region have shown a cline of characteristic features from *Homo erectus* populations through anatomically modern humans, suggesting genetic continuity in this region during the last 700,000 years. They present a genetic model incorporating an equilibrium between low levels of gene flow from mainland Southeast Asia and low levels of local selection due to local conditions. They suggest that this model of regional

---

[1] Neandertals are the most well-known of the fossil hominids, due in part to their predominately European range and early discovery in 1829–1830. Because they have been studied since that early date there are long-held traditions associated with the usage of the term "Neandertal." In both Chapters 49 and 50, Howell and Vallois use the spelling "Neander*tal*" instead of the older spelling "Neander*thal*." In adopting this usage, which is explained in footnote 1 of Chapter 49, Howell and Vallois depart from more than a century of common usage among paleoanthropologists. Though linguistic correctness was on the side of the spelling "Neandertal", Howell (1957) later reverted to the more traditional *thal* spelling, which was also followed by the authors of Chapters 52, 53, 55, 58, and 60. In our introductions to Parts VI, VII and VIII, we follow the new orthography while maintaining whatever usage individual authors followed in their own chapters.

continuity characterized other Pleistocene populations of *Homo* as well (see Chapter 48, 53, 54, 60).

Chapter 45, "The 'Afro-European *sapiens* Hypothesis' and Hominid Evolution in East Asia During the Late Middle and Upper Pleistocene," by Günter Braüer, provides a detailed review of the theory that anatomically modern *Homo sapiens* originated in Africa, and subsequently migrated to other continents. He shows that in Africa there is continuity between archaic hominids and anatomically modern humans and that the latter group appears earlier on that continent than elsewhere. He then reviews the record of human evolution in East Asia. There he finds a considerable gap between archaic hominids and anatomically modern *Homo sapiens*, precluding a definitive answer to the question of whether anatomically modern humans orginated one or more times. He suggests, however, that a "hybridization *and* replacement" model appears to best agree with the facts.

Chapter 46, "Mitochondrial DNA and Human Evolution" by Rebecca Cann, Mark Stoneking, and Alan Wilson, reports genetic evidence of the origin of *Homo sapiens* that is one of the major technological developments in paleoanthropology (see Lewin 1987). From an examination of a worldwide sample of mitochondrial DNA, they find that the greatest diversity is among Africans, suggesting that the origin of the modern human gene pool was in Africa. Based on the genetic diversity among native peoples of New Guinea, Australia, and the New World—areas that humans colonized relatively recently—they calculate a rate at which mitochondrial DNA differences accumulate. This rate suggests that the last common ancestor of all humans lived between 90,000 and 180,000 years ago. More recent studies of mtDNA using a larger sampling of human populations have placed the age of the common ancestor of modern humans between 166,000 and 249,000 years (Vigilant *et al.* 1991). However, several reanalyses of this larger data set have shown that it does not, in fact, support an African origin of *Homo sapiens* to the exclusion of other hypotheses. Re-searchers are now questioning the ability of these data to provide any answers to this issue (Maddison 1991; Templeton 1992; Hedges *et al.* 1992). At present, the value of mtDNA data for understanding the origin of modern humans is very unclear and this approach is undergoing considerable revision. It now seems likely that the mitochondrial DNA evidence, which laid the groundwork for the African monogenesis model of antomically modern humans, may in itself prove insufficient to sustain this "revolution" (see Thorne and Wolpoff 1992).

Chapter 47, "Genetic and Fossil Evidence for the Origin of Modern Humans" by Chris Stringer and Peter Andrews, attempts to synthesize recent evidence on modern human origins. These authors generally support the single, African origin model for modern humans, but differ from other supporters of this view in seeing "anatomically modern humans" as a distinct species from other hominids often classified within *Homo sapiens* (see discussions by Delson 1988; Lewin 1988; Smith *et al.* 1989). Stringer and Andrews generate a series of predictions based on the different models of human evolution and find that both the genetic and the paleontological data are more compatible with the recent African model (but see Wolpoff *et al.* 1988; Chapter 48).

Chapter 48, "Multiregional Evolution: The Fossil Alternative to Eden" by Milford Wolpoff, is a recent (1989) reply to the preceding two chapters. Wolpoff evaluates both the genetic and the paleontological data for the origin of anatomically modern humans and more generally for the patterns of human evolution worldwide during the Middle and Upper Pleistocene. In particular he questions assumptions regarding gene flow that underly the mtDNA clock and reiterates the arguments of considerable morphological continuity between successively modern populations in many separate regions of the world. He corrects earlier mischaracterizations of the multiregional model and argues that this model, and not the single origin model, accords best with available genetic and fossil data.

REFERENCES

Braüer, G. and Smith, F. S., Eds. 1992. *Continuity or Replacement: Controversies in* Homo sapiens *Evolution*. Balkema, Rotterdam.

Cann, R. L. 1988. DNA and Human Origins. *Annu. Rev. Anthropol.* 17:127-143.

Delson, E. 1988. One source not many. *Nature* 332:206.

Grün, R. and Stringer, C. B. 1991. Electron spin resonance and the evolution of modern humans. *Archaeometry* 33:153-199.

Hedges, S. B., Kumar, S., and Stoneking, M. 1992. Human origins and analysis of mitochondrial DNA sequences. *Science* 255:737-739.

Howell, F. C. 1957. The evolutionary significance of variation and varieties of "Neanderthal" man. *Quart. Rev. Biol.* 32:330-343.

Lewin, R. 1987. The unmasking of mitochondrial Eve. *Science* 238:24-26.

Lewin, R. 1988. Modern humans under close scrutiny. *Science* 239:1240-1241.

Lewin, R. 1989. Species questions in modern human origins. *Science* 243:1666-1667.

Maddison, D. R. 1991. African origin of human mitochondrial DNA reexamined. *Syst. Zool.* 40:355-363.

Mellars, P. and Stringer, C. B., Eds. 1989. *The Human Revolution*. Princeton University Press, Princeton, New Jersey.

Mellars, P., Ed. 1990. *The Emergence of Modern Humans*. Cornell University Press, Ithaca, NY.

Schwarcz, H. P., Grün, R., Vandermeersch, B., Bar-Yosef, O., Vallades, H. and Tchernov, E. 1988. ESR dates for the hominid burial site of Qafzeh in Israel. *J. Hum. Evol.* 17:733-737.

Smith, F. H. and Spencer, F., Eds. 1984. *The Origins of Modern Humans: A World Survey of the Fossil Evidence*. Alan R. Liss, New York.

Smith, F. H., Falsetti, A. B., and Donnelly, S. M. 1989. Modern human origins. *Yrbk. Phys. Anthropol.* 32:35-68.

Stringer, C. B. Grün, R., Schwarcz, H. P. and Goldberg, P. 1989. ESR dates for the hominid burial site of Es Skhul in Israel. *Nature* 388:756-8.

Stringer, C. B. 1990. The emergence of modern humans. *Sci. Amer.* 263:98-104.

Tattersall, I. 1991. What was the human revolution? *J. Hum. Evol.* 20:77-83.

Tempelton, A. R. 1992. Human origins and analysis of mitochondrial DNA sequences. *Science* 255:737.

Thorne, A. G. and Wolpoff, M. H. 1992. The multiregional evolution of humans. *Sci. Amer.* 226(4):76-83.

Trinkaus, E., Ed. 1989. *The Emergence of Modern Humans: Biocultural Adaptations in the Later Pleistocene*. Cambridge University Press, Cambridge.

Vigilant, L., Stoneking, M., Harpending, H., Hawkes, K., and Wilson, A.C. 1991. African populations and the evolution of human mitochondrial DNA. *Science* 253:1503-1507.

Wolpoff, M. H., Spuhler, J. N., Smith, F. H., Radovcic, J., Pope, G., Frayer, D., Eckhardt, R., and Clark, G. 1988. Modern human origins. *Science* 241:772-773.

42

Species Recognition in Human Paleontology

I. Tattersall

INTRODUCTION

Over the past several years increasing attention has been paid to the search for patterns in the human fossil record (e.g., Cronin *et al.* 1981; Rightmire 1981; Eldredge and Tattersall 1982). The reliability of any attempt to recognize pattern, however, is constrained by the accuracy with which we are able to recognize species in that record; this is true whether one subscribes to the view that species are objective entities in time as well as in space, or, more traditionally, holds that the practical problem is to distinguish between separately evolving lineages within which species are ephemeral in time, if not in space. Irrespective of one's position on the nature of the evolutionary process, species or at any rate time-successive lineages of species, are the units with which one has to deal in trying to unravel the sequence of evolutionary events. The delineation of these units is thus of critical concern. My aim in this short essay is not to contribute to the debate over evolutionary mechanism, which will doubtless well outlive this century without my help. Rather it is, first, to focus attention upon the observation that whatever the exact nature of currently popular criteria of species recognition in paleoanthropology (and they are rarely if ever articulated), to judge by their results they are unrealistic; and, second, to point out some of the consequences of this for our interpretations of the later stages of human evolution.

In their seminal paper on Miocene hominoids, Simons and Pilbeam (1965) came about as close as any paleoanthropologist has yet to come to precision on the question of how one proceeds to sort assemblages of fossils into discrete groups: "In order to establish a valid species it should be necessary to show characters in the available fossil material which purport to be of the same magnitude as those which separate related living species" (p. 101). But although few have seen fit to quarrel with it, this sage advice has been honored almost exclusively in the breach, even by its authors themselves. For while Simons and Pilbeam specifically urged the evaluation of inter-species variation, recent paleoanthropological practice has been to focus attention on intra-species variation. The question is, in effect, most commonly rendered: "do the limits of variation we see in our fossils exceed the limits of variation we see in samples drawn from extant primate species?" Indeed, the years since Simons and Pilbeam wrote have seen a steady flow of theses that document the ranges of variation shown by numerous characters, mostly dental, in ape and human skeletal samples. Almost invariably, such studies have been aimed at establishing norms against which the variation seen in, say,

australopith samples may be evaluated. Hand in hand with this concern for variation has gone the triumph of the lumping ethic which, in laudably rejecting the typological thinking that bedeviled paleontology in the earlier years of this century, has in certain cases proceeded with an equal lack of realism to the opposite extreme.

It is not hard to see why intraspecies variation has proven so much more beguiling to paleoanthropologists than has inter-specific variation. For, doctrine of common sense though Simons and Pilbeam's exhortation appears to be, it offers no practical guide to the sorting-out of fossil assemblages. The reason for this is, of course, that there is no direct relationship, indeed no consistent relationship at all, between speciation and morphological change (e.g. Vrba 1980). On the one hand, speciation may take place in the absence of appreciable morphological divergence, while on the other considerable local differentiation may occur, particularly within geographically widespread species, without any rupture of the reproductive continuity that both binds and limits the species population. Thus, while few would disagree that there has been no more significant theoretical advance in systematics than the shift from the morphological to the biological concept of species, this change has opened the door to a host of practical problems when it comes to the actual interpretation of the fossil record. For quite apart from the considerable difficulty of translating magnitudes of variation from one species or species pair to another, it is also evident that such taxonomic decisions are critically affected by the choice of which living species—or pair of related species—is to be taken as arbiter of the variability permissible in a fossil assemblage recognized as species. There is no guarantee that the "closest living relative" (as it usually boils down to, whether or not this is determinable with any certainty) will be the most appropriate model to apply; for instance, a species occupying a limited relict distribution (one of the great apes, perhaps?) would almost certainly be an unreliable guide to the delineation of a widely-distributed related fossil species. Moreover, and much more importantly, almost invariably what is evaluated is *within-species* variation, which will be found to a greater or lesser extent in all anatomical systems. But what is important in distinguishing among species is *between-species* variation. Where species are closely related (and hence most likely to be confused in the fossil record), variation of this kind is likely to be restricted to a few characters only; the vast majority of anatomical characters will overlap substantially or totally.

Despite the lack of association between taxic and morphologic evolution, however, a certain amount of generalization from the living fauna is possible as a broad guide to systematic practice in analyzing the fossil record. For speciation rarely, if ever, involves quantum morphological leaps. If one surveys the primates as a whole, one finds that the morphological differences between closely related species (say species usually classified within the same genus or subgenus) are commonly small, and restricted to only one or a few characters. Especially where such species are very closely related, for instance where two species are descended from the same parental species, distinguishing features are often limited to soft tissue characteristics which do not preserve in the fossil record. And even in those cases where distinctions in certain hard-tissue characters are observable between closely related species, substantial or complete overlap would be expected in all others. Because of this it is easy for the paleontologist to confuse variations of the two kinds, especially when the time arrives for taxonomic judgement on small samples of fossils. The keener one's appreciation of the important fact of intra-species variability, firmly and justifiably fixed as the keystone of modern paleoanthropological systematics, the greater the danger of doing this becomes. Clearly, every species is variable, and this central reality cannot be ignored in comparing two fossils; for just as similarity in a given set of features does not guarantee that two forms belong to the same species, observed differences may not imply species distinction. Nevertheless, each species varies within limits, and it is hard to avoid the conclusion that under current taxonomic practice there is a distinct tendency to underestimate the abundance of species in the primate, and notably the hominid, fossil record.

This observation runs counter to Templeton's (1982) speculation that since mammals are more prone than other vertebrates to form polytypic species, the number of mammal species in the fossil record is likely to be overestimated. Templeton's argument, however, is based purely on presumed relative propensities of different population structures to promote rapid population divergence, hence polytypism, which he apparently equates with detectable morphological shifts. But as we have seen, it is unrealistic to make this equation, and morphology itself, certainly those aspects of it that preserve in the fossil record, tells a different story. Cranioskeletal differences between primate subspecies of the same species tend to be tiny, if observable at all. For example, differences on the order of those separating the various subspecies of *Propithecus diadema* would certainly be missed by a paleontologist with only teeth and bones to examine, especially if he had a keen sense of intra-population variation. Even the highly polytypic extant species *Homo sapiens* varies much less than one would infer from the variety of fossil morphs that has been crammed into it.

The tendency to underestimate low-level taxic diversity in the fossil record is, it must be said, infinitely preferable to the opposite fault, widespread in earlier days, of baptizing each new fossil specimen with its own name. But it may nonetheless subtly give rise to a destructive misconception. It may quite persuasively be argued that it is unimportant whether the species we recognize in the fossil record are "real" species or not. As long as those units we recognize as species are "natural," or monophyletic, does it really matter whether they consist of individual species or aggregates of closely related species?

Where there is no reasonable prospect of distinguishing such putative species on the basis of preserved materials there can, of course, be only one reasonable answer to the question. Nonetheless, where respect for intra-species variability leads to the inclusion within a single species of fossils representing more than one readily identifiable morph, it is absolutely crucial that we be totally confident that only a single species is in fact involved. This is no small matter. For while species are objective historical entities that we are obliged to confront, morphological varieties *within* species are acknowledged to be no more than epiphenomena, whose individual historical identity has not been established.

Species, reproductively isolated from the rest of the living world, acquire their discreteness as the result of an irreversible genetic and historical process. Subspecies, on the other hand, while distinguishable in some way and at some point, are in concept ephemera, unbounded by reproductive barriers; their unique identity may at least potentially be lost at any time in merging with other subspecies populations. Only with speciation, with the development of reproductive isolation does the identity of what began as subspecies become definitively established. Of course this does not necessarily mean that subspecies, as entities, do not demand study and explanation; they have origins and histories just as species do. But the fact remains that, to paleontologists in general, subspecies are epiphenomena which do not merit the attention paid to species: it is species, not subspecies, that are the units of evolution, or at least of evolutionary study. And indeed, to judge from the generally insignificant intertaxic diversity in hard parts exhibited at the lowest taxonomic levels in the modern primate fauna, the pursuit of subspecies in the fossil record is at best fraught with difficulty, and is more probably futile. This is why it is critical to avoid relegating distinct morphological variants observed in the fossil record to the status of subspecies—or their informal equivalent—without the best of reasons for doing so; for, as mere subspecies, even clearly identifiable morphs do not urgently demand analysis and explanation. Indeed, it might well be argued that it would be better for the comprehensiveness of our understanding of the human fossil record that, if err we must, we err (within reason!) on the side of recognizing too many rather than, as is the tendency, too few species units. After all, to hark back to an earlier comment, even a subspecies has a history worthy of investigation.

All this, of course, begs the problem of distinguishing separate morphs where differences are slight, while the nonconcordance of taxic with morphological change seems to eliminate any objective solution to the practical problem of species recognition. What I wish to emphasize here, however, is that where distinct morphs can readily be identified it would seem most productive to assume that they represent species unless there is compelling evidence to believe otherwise. To brush morphological diversity under the rug of an all-encompassing species is simply to blind oneself to the complex realities of phylogeny.

THE HUMAN FOSSIL RECORD

By 1950, at a time when the known hominid fossil record was vastly more limited than it is at present, the names of over a dozen genera, and many more species, were commonly encountered in the less than voluminous literature on fossil

Hominidae. In that year, however, a long overdue and highly influential paper by Ernst Mayr started the lumping bandwagon rolling with the declaration that: "the acceptance of the new concept of biologically defined polytypic species necessitates the upward revision of all other categories" (Mayr 1950, p. 110). Mayr spurned the idea of monotypic genera as leading to an "inequality of categories," and at that time he even argued for including *Australopithecus* in *Homo*, since "within this type there has been speciation resulting in *Homo sapiens*." Nonetheless, with infinitely clearer vision than those of his successors who raised the "single species hypothesis" to an article of faith, Mayr explicitly recognized not only that to arrive at this taxonomic conclusion required "a deliberate minimizing of the brain as a decisive taxonomic character," but also that the necessary assumption that "all of these forms, including *Australopithecus*, are essentially members of a single line of descent," was exceedingly fragile, for "Additional finds might easily disprove this" (pp. 110-111). Subsequent paleoanthropological discoveries have emphasized the wisdom of Mayr's caveat, but the three and a half decades following his salutory contribution have witnessed the ascendance of what has finally become a destructively minimalist approach to hominid systematics.

Today, happily, the realization has begun to dawn that a significant degree of taxonomic variety exists in the remoter stages of hominoid history, among the australopiths. The genus *Homo*, however, which following Mayr's exhortation has been expanded to embrace over two million years of time and a large array of distinct hominid morphs, is commonly viewed as containing only three species: *Homo habilis, H. erectus*, and *H. sapiens*. The first of these poses acute problems of definition and recognition, exacerbated by the fact that the only specimens in a motley collection that are truly distinctive morphologically are not associated with the name. The second has, in the years since Mayr wrote, expanded beyond its vague role as the "man of the middle Pleistocene" to include a diverse array of fossils that future scholars will surely find ample cause to subdivide—unless they can contrive to maintain the fiction of the "grade" to keep this diversity decently obscured. The interpretation of most human fossils subsequent to about 0.5 myr as belonging somehow to *Homo sapiens* is perhaps the most comprehensive smokescreen of all, and could only have been maintained by a zealous refusal to consider characters other than brain size. I have suggested elsewhere (Eldredge and Tattersall 1982) that the urge to include forms as diverse as Petralona, Steinheim, Neanderthal and you and me in the single species *Homo sapiens* must be sociological in origin—there is something vaguely disgraceful about discriminating against other large-brained hominids—and I do not wish to beat that horse further here; but the fact remains that the only rational explanation for the taxonomic corralling together of these widely differing fossils (for age will not do it, Wolpoff 1980, to the contrary) is the setting of an unconscious "cerebral Rubicon," perhaps at somewhere around 1200 ml. The fact that such a Rubicon, unconscious or otherwise, would exclude a good many members of the living species from *Homo sapiens* has gone unremarked. And while, if my surmise is correct, one can only applaud the generous liberal sentiment that leads to the inclusion in *Homo sapiens* of all hominids whose brain size falls comfortably within the modern range, one is equally obliged to point out that to conclude that no species differences exist within this array of hominids is to confuse the two kinds of morphological variation. The huge variation in normal brain size found among modern humans exemplifies within-species variation, and is largely or entirely irrelevant to the issue of taxic diversity. I have already suggested that closely-related primate species will show identical or substantially overlapping ranges of variation in almost all morphological features; and while it could, I suppose, be argued that both the lower-than-modern average brain size of the "archaic *Homo sapiens*" and higher-than-average brain size of the classic Neanderthals are features that could be used in demarcating both from *Homo sapiens*, what is much more important in weighing the question of how many hominid species we are faced with in the middle and late Pleistocene is the constellation of features in which both clearly differ from each other and from ourselves.

Even a relatively cursory survey of the spectrum of living primates is sufficient to reveal that modern *Homo sapiens*, by now numbering some four billion individuals and for long represented in virtually every inhabitable region of the earth, is a rather highly polytypic species. Nonetheless, like every other species, polytypic or otherwise, *Homo sapiens* is a cohesive biological entity which, while variable, is far from infinitely so. Regressing in time, we find that back to about 30-35 kyr ago more or less all human fossils fall into the morphological range bracketed by the living species. Some subspecies of *Homo sapiens* may well, of course, have emerged within that period only to become extinct, and thus it would be reasonable to expect to find, as indeed we do, the occasional *Homo sapiens* fossil that slightly exceeds this range in one character or another. If we look further back, however, we abruptly lose the ability to fit the human fossils we find into this frame of variation, with the exception of a few pieces that are either fragmentary or uncertainly dated. But although almost all human fossils prior to this time are very different in aspect from anything we see in our very variable living species, they are nonetheless regularly classified as *Homo sapiens*. With the proviso, to be sure, that they are "archaic," or otherwise different; but *Homo sapiens* nonetheless.

Rarely indeed, however, have paleontologists ever found it necessary to distinguish between "archaic" and "anatomically modern" types of the same species, and there seems scant justification for squeezing these distinct hominid morphs into a single species. In any group other than Hominidae the presence of several clearly recognizable morphs in the record of the middle to upper Pleistocene would suggest (indeed, demonstrate) the involvement of several species. Any mammalian paleontologist seeing morphological differences on the order of those separating modern humans from their various precursors, and the latter from each other, would have no difficulty in recognizing a number of separate species. And in this decision there is no obvious place for special pleading, even where it is our own closest relatives that are involved. It is not in the least surprising that various authors, for example Stringer *et al.* (1979), Wu (1981) and Rightmire (1983), have been able to discover derived features shared with their successors in such fossils as Kabwe, Ndutu, Petralona, Arago and Dali. This, however, is no argument for conspecificity when they also show differences of a magnitude that in any other primate family would be accepted without demur as demarcating separate species. Sisters there may be among these morphs; conspecifics, no.

It is not my intention here to go into detail on the morphological justifications for recognizing several separate species in the post-*Homo erectus* human fossil record. Indeed, even if this contribution were not cast as an essay rather than as a research report, this would be impractical for two interrelated reasons. In the first place, despite the existence of an extensive literature, discussion of the detailed morphological evidence for a multiplicity of human species over the past half-million years is difficult without extensive study of the actual fossil specimens involved. This is because studies undertaken to date have tended to focus on the continuities between, say, "archaic *H. sapiens*" and temporally contiguous species—*Homo erectus*, the Neanderthals, or "anatomically modern *Homo sapiens*"— and hence, presumably, largely on primitive characters. Most of the literature, indeed, though crammed with comparisons, is extraordinarily uninformative if one wishes to know if the character states being compared are primitive or derived, or how widely they are shared. Secondly, except very recently in the case of the Neanderthals, few attempts have been made to define distinctive later hominid groups as morphs, let alone as species, not only as a result of the search for continuity but also, one presumes, in consequence of their epiphenomenological status as intraspecific variants. One should note, however, that with the adoption by some paleoanthropologists of a more or less cladistic approach to the reconstruction of phylogeny, there have recently been some welcome positive moves. Thus Hublin (1978) listed a set of apomorphies of the skull rear among Neanderthals, and Day and Stringer (1982) proposed "working definitions" of the living species *Homo sapiens* and the Afro-Asian species *Homo erectus*. Most recently still, Stringer *et al.* (1984) have provided lists of "anatomical characters of modern *Homo sapiens*" (Table 1, p. 54) and "proposed Neandertal autapomorphies and common characteristics" (Table 2, p. 55), and Vandermeersch (1985) has also couched his discussion in these terms. Encouragingly, the contemplation of lists of this kind has led Stringer (1984a, 1985) to speculate on whether the name *Homo sapiens* might not best be reserved for humans of modern aspect, "extreme" as he felt the suggestion would appear. In any event, for the purposes of the present discussion it is sufficient to point out that several clearly different morphs of "*Homo sapiens*," each already considered sufficiently distinct to require an adjectival qualifier, are widely recognized in the fossil record, in addition to a considerable number of individual specimens whose status it has not generally been felt necessary to examine in detail given the umbrella existence of *Homo sapiens*.

To begin with, of course, there is "anatomically modern" *Homo sapiens*, with an impressive set of autapomorphies as listed by Day and Stringer (1982): cranium short but high; parietal arch long and high, narrow inferiorly and broad superiorly; frontal bone high; supraorbital torus not continuous, but divided into lateral and medial portions; occipital bone well curved, not angulated; mental eminence on mandible; gracile limb bones. Even as a preliminary approximation these characters reflect a morphology clearly distinct at the species level from that of any other hominid form. Although archaeological evidence does not strictly provide taxonomic characters, one might add that recognizing the distinctness of *Homo sapiens* in this restricted sense makes it much easier to understand the extraordinary behavioral advancements (see, for example, White 1982, and Klein 1985) that apparently accompanied the

appearance on earth of people of our own kind following a long period that witnessed relatively little technological or behavioral innovation.

As distinct as *Homo sapiens* is *Homo neanderthalensis*. "Definitions" of this group have traditionally amounted to descriptions, intermingling primitive and derived characters, but clarifications have recently begun to appear. Thus among the Neanderthal apomorphies identified by Hublin (1978) Stringer *et al.* (1984), and Vandermeersch (1985) are the following: lambdoid flattening and "bunning" of the occiput; the mid-saggital division of the occipital torus, with formation of a suprainiac fossa; the presence of an anterior mastoid tubercle and the conformation of the surrounding region as detailed by Vandermeersch (1985); the rounded ("en bombe") form of the cranium in posterior view; pronounced midfacial prognathism and its correlates, including a retreating zygomatic profile and retromolar spaces; nasal aperture capacious, with nasal bones projecting; relatively wide sphenoidal angle; extreme breadth of the anterior teeth. To listed postcranial characteristics such as the long and plate-like superior pubic ramus might be added pronounced radial curvature, flattening of the first carpometacarpal saddle joint, and phalangeal length proportions.

The longstanding dispute over whether the group of hominid fossils containing the Arago material should be classed as *Homo sapiens* or *Homo erectus* reflects the underlying reality that this form, most commonly referred to by Anglophone paleoanthropologists as "archaic *Homo sapiens*," actually belongs with neither species. Specimens such as those from Bodo, Kabwe, Petralona and Arago (*Homo heidelbergensis*, perhaps?) compose a variable morph (recognized in its having been named, however inappropriately) that is clearly demarcated at the species level from *Homo erectus*, from *Homo neanderthalensis*, and from *Homo sapiens*. Stringer (1985) has summarized several of its distinguishing characters in a Venn diagram which emphasizes the need for further analysis of the apomorphies of the group. One might point out, however, that except in the form of its supraorbital torus, this hominid species appears distinct also from that best represented by the Steinheim and possibly Swanscombe specimens (as Stringer, 1985, has also implied in commenting on characters of the rear of the cranium). Both Hublin (1982) and Vandermeersch (1985) have pointed to the presence in the Steinheim skull of a character interpretable as a suprainiac fossa, and have suggested that Steinheim represents a proto-Neanderthal; Stringer (1985) has, however, rejected this interpretation, while suggesting nonetheless that this form departs from the Neanderthals largely in plesiomorphous character states. Interestingly, most speculation on Steinheim's links with the Neanderthals has focused on the rear of the skull, while those who have discovered "Neanderthal-like" features in the Petralona-Arago group have pointed most convincingly to characters of the face (see Vandermeersch 1985).

This highly incomplete listing of characters, specimens and morphs is intended merely to be illustrative, and clearly a great deal of work remains to be done in sorting out the number of distinct morphs represented in the geographically scattered hominid fossil record of the Middle and Late Pleistocene. However, it does demonstrate that at least three or four (and quite probably more if the entire spectrum of material were considered) separate hominid groups can be distinguished among the "*Homo sapiens*" fossils of this time. Moreover, it strongly suggests that, when measured by the standards that apply to other primates the morphological differences between these groups amply justify species distinctions. If my operational criteria for species recognition appear somewhat informal this is necessarily the case, in consequence of the lack of correlation between speciation and degree of morphological change; but as I have already argued, morphological differences of the degree discussed invariably indicate among living forms that speciation has occurred.

Rightmire (1985) has similarly made the point that, if species are to be viewed as real in time as well as in space, it is necessary to recognize four species, *Homo erectus*, *Homo heidelbergensis*, *Homo neanderthalensis*, and *Homo sapiens*, in the middle to late Pleistocene human fossil record. He found this scheme wanting, however, in that many or all later Pleistocene hominids from Africa and China do not clearly fit into one or another of these species, and preferred Bonde's (1981) grouping of all as subspecies of *Homo sapiens*. But so to conclude is once again to use the device of an all-embracing *Homo sapiens* to obscure variability that actually exists, and requires analysis. If African and Chinese hominids of this period show apomorphies separating them from the essentially European scheme on which this division into species is based, it is certainly appropriate at least to enquire whether yet more species might be involved. Certainly the point is already conceded that more morphs are present than can be embraced by the European scheme, and these morphs require analysis and explanation of the kind they are most likely to be denied if they are dismissed as representatives of "*Homo sapiens*" in some undefined larger sense.

Recognizing a multiplicity of hominid species in the mid-to-late Pleistocene will, of course, go against the grain for many paleoanthropologists. After all, there is a beauty in linear simplicity that the aesthetes among us, in particular, would be reluctant to see vanish. Nonetheless, this systematic conclusion is hardly surprising when one considers the enormous climatic and sea-level fluctuations that marked the period. Without any doubt, and most especially in temperate latitudes, these fluctuations fragmented and recoalesced hominid populations, thereby providing ideal conditions for speciation and competition. The potential that existed during the middle and late Pleistocene for the local divergence of populations is even recognized in models such as that adopted by Wolpoff *et al.* (1984), who go on to posit longstanding continuities within regional human populations. However, if one accepts that different environments in different regions can produce morphological discontinuities between populations, then one must also accept that environmental change *in situ* can do the same. Perceived long-term morphological trends in local human populations over this period then become more difficult to defend, even when lavishly tricked out with genetic sophistry. Whatever reasonable model we accept of the pattern of evolution in the later part of the hominid fossil record, it is clear that not all of the hominid variants of the mid-to-late Pleistocene can have been ancestral to our own species, and that the origin of *Homo sapiens* is to be sought in a morph whose own origin was linked to a specific geographic region. Given the anatomical range already known among such morphs it is virtually certain that this population represented a distinct hominid species which coexisted, at least temporally, with others.

The discussion of the greater spectrum of middle to late Pleistocene human fossils, from sites worldwide, inevitably spills over into the problem of defining *Homo erectus*, recently ably discussed by Andrews (1984), Rightmire (e.g. 1984, 1985), Stringer (1984b), and Wood (1984). Stringer, in particular, makes the point that African and Asian *Homo erectus* can be assigned to a "grade" called *Homo erectus*, but not to a species of that name. However, like it or not, *Homo erectus* is a species name; "grades" are not recognized in the International Code of Zoological Nomenclature, and neither, in any objective sense, are they found in nature, Wolpoff *et al.* (1984) to the contrary notwithstanding. The "grade," indeed, is one of the most destructive canards that paleoanthropology has ever seen fit to inflict upon itself: a meaningless and undefined concept, apparently leaning heavily on brain size, that can be used to entomb all kinds of morphological loose ends and thus eliminate the need to examine them. As long as we apply standard systematic terminology to our fossil record, we should be clear about the meaning of the terms we use, and we should be wary of introducing others that serve only to obfuscate. The authors named above have elegantly shown that characters traditionally used to define *Homo erectus* include a mishmash of primitive and derived character states, and that the African and Asian forms are not distinguished by the same apomorphies. Moreover, Andrews makes the important point that comparisons of *Homo erectus* with other hominid species have been largely with *Homo sapiens* alone. Only when species have been adequately defined morphologically can appropriate comparisons be made, and the distribution of character states across species be used to generate phylogenetic hypotheses. Lumping diverse morphologies into "grades" kills this process before it can start.

In this note I have attempted to raise questions rather than to solve them, and above all to draw attention to the fact that by masking the significance of much observed morphological variation, inadequate concepts of species delineation have in the past impeded advancements in our understanding of hominid phylogeny. Although it appears difficult or even impossible to arrive at an objective, or universally applicable, solution to the problem of species recognition in the fossil record, cognizance of the general patterns of between-species morphological variation in the living biota will help us better to assess that record. That we do so is crucial, for we will make little useful progress in human evolutionary studies until we adopt more realistic working criteria of species recognition, and define those species we recognize in terms of derived, or at least of distinct, morphologies. As I have noted, this is so even under a gradualist model of evolution; for however one views the evolutionary process, paleoanthropology is a comparative science in which rational recognition is necessary of the units to be compared. Only when we have realistically defined the species we accept we will be able to broach the problem of the relationships between such species, whether linear or collateral, and then in turn proceed towards an understanding of larger-scale patterns in human evolution.

SUMMARY

The search for patterns in the human fossil record has been handicapped by the inadequacy of the criteria used to recognize species in that record. The fact that taxic and morphological change need not be associated directly means that there can be no objective means of sorting fossils into species. In general, however, closely related primate species show only minor morphological differences from one another, sometimes in parts of the anatomy that do not preserve in the fossil record. There is thus a tendency to underestimate species diversity in the fossil record; and while lumping may appear sophisticated because it is avowedly anti-typological, too much of a good thing has in the end become a liability to our interpretation of the substantial morphological diversity that exists in the human fossil record. Subspecific categories are regarded as epiphenomena that do not justify the attention accorded to species, so it is critical that where distinct morphs exist in the fossil record they are not relegated to subspecific status without good reason. Several morphs are distinguishable in the later part of the human fossil record that are distinct both from each other and from the living species *Homo sapiens*. These include *Homo neanderthalensis*, *Homo heidelbergensis*, and probably also *Homo steinheimensis*. The recognition of morphs in the later part of the human fossil record has been based largely on the assemblage of fossils from Europe, and many fossils from Asia and Africa do not fit the European scheme. Probably other species will prove identifiable from other areas of the world when the appropriate comparisons are made. The existence of a multiplicity of hominid species in the middle to late Pleistocene around the world would not be surprising in view of the great climatic and eustatic oscillations, doubtless involving the frequent fragmentation and recoalescence of human populations, that marked the period.

ACKNOWLEDGEMENTS

This article was improved by the comments of Eric Delson, Niles Eldredge, and three anonymous reviewers, none of whom necessarily agrees with anything it contains. I am indebted to the Richard Lounsbery Foundation for its generous support. This is Contribution no. 18 of the Lounsbery Laboratory of Biological Anthropology, American Museum of Natural History.

REFERENCES

Andrews, P. 1984. An alternative interpretation of characters used to define *Homo erectus*. *Cour. Forsch. Inst. Senckenberg* 69:167-175.

Bonde, N. 1981. Problems of species concepts in paleontology, in: *Concept. and Method in Palaeontology* (J. Martinelli, Ed.), pp. 19-34, University of Barcelona, Barcelona.

Cronin, J. E., Boaz, N. T., Stringer, C. B., and Rak, Y. 1981. Tempo and mode in hominid evolution. *Nature* 292:113-122.

Day, M. H., and Stringer, C. B. 1982. A reconsideration of the Omo Kibish remains and the *erectus-sapiens* transition. *1er Congr. Intern. Paléont. Hum.*, Vol. 2, pp. 814-846 (Prétirage). Nice, C.N.R.S.

Eldredge, N., and Tattersall, I. 1982. *The Myths of Human Evolution*. Columbia University Press, New York.

Hublin, J. J. 1978. Quelques caractères apomorphes du crane neandertalien et leur interprétation phylogénique. *C. R. Acad. Sci. Paris Ser. D* 287:923-926.

Hublin, J. J. 1982. Les anténéandertaliens: Présapiens ou prénéandertaliens? *Geobios*, Mém. Spéc. 6:345-357.

Klein, R. G. 1985. Breaking away. *Nat. Hist.* 94(1):4-7.

Mayr, E. 1950. Taxonomic categories in fossil hominids. *Cold Spring Harb. Symp. Quant. Biol.* 15:109-118.

Rightmire, G. P. 1981. Patterns in the evolution of *Homo erectus*. *Paleobiology* 8:241-246.

Rightmire, G. P. 1983. The Lake Ndutu cranium and early *Homo sapiens* in Africa. *Am. J. Phys. Anthrop.* 61:245-254.

Rightmire, G. P. 1984. Comparisons of *Homo erectus* from Africa and southeast Asia. *Cour. Forsch. Inst. Senckenberg* 69:83-98.

Rightmire, G. P. 1985. The tempo of change in the evolution of mid-Pleistocene *Homo*, in: *Ancestors: The Hard Evidence* (E. Delson, Ed.), pp. 255-264, Alan R. Liss, New York.

Simons, E. L., and Pilbeam, D. R. 1965. Preliminary revision of the Dryopithecinae (Pongidae, Anthropoidea). *Folia. Primat.* 3:81-152.

Stringer, C. 1984a. Human evolution and biological adaptation in the Pleistocene, in: *Hominid Evolution and Community Ecology* (R. Foley, Ed.), pp. 55-83, Academic Press, London.

Stringer, C. B. 1984b. The definition of *Homo erectus* and the existence of the species in Africa and Europe. *Cour. Forsch. Inst. Senckenberg* 69:131-143.

Stringer, C. B. 1985. Middle Pleistocene hominid variability and the origin of late Pleistocene humans, in: *Ancestors: The Hard Evidence* (E. Delson, Ed.), pp. 289-295, Alan R. Liss, New York.

Stringer, C. B., Howell, F. C., and Melentis, J. K. 1979. The significance of the fossil hominid skull from Petralona, Greece. *J. Arch. Sci.* 6:235-253.

Stringer, C. B., Hublin, J. J., and Vandermeersch, B. 1984. The origin of modern humans in western Europe, in: *The Origins of Modern Humans: A World Survey of the Fossil Evidence* (F.H. Smith and F. Spencer, Eds.), pp. 51-135, Alan R. Liss, New York.

Templeton, A. R. 1982. Genetic architectures of speciation, in: *Mechanisms of Speciation* (C. Barigozzi, Ed.), pp. 105-121, Alan R. Liss, New York.

Vandermeersch, B. 1985. The origin of the Neandertals, in: *Ancestors: The Hard Evidence* (E. Delson, Ed.), pp. 306-309, Alan R. Liss, New York.

Vrba, E. S. 1980. Evolution, species and fossils: How does life evolve? *S. Afr. J. Sci.* 76:61-84.

White, R. 1982. Rethinking the Middle/Upper Paleolithic transition. *Curr. Anthrop.* 23:169-192.

Wood, B. 1984. The origin of *Homo erectus*. *Cour. Forsch. Inst. Senckenberg* 69:99-111.

Wolpoff, M. H. 1980. *Paleoanthropology*. Knopf, New York.

Wolpoff, M. H., Wu, X., and Thorne, A. G. 1984. Modern *Homo sapiens* origins: A general theory of hominid evolution involving the fossil evidence from East Asia, in: *The Origins of Modern Humans: A World Survey of the Fossil Evidence* (F. H. Smith and F. Spencer, Eds.), pp. 411-483. Alan R. Liss, New York.

Wu, X. 1981. A well-preserved cranium of an archaic type of early *Homo sapiens* from Dali, China. *Sci. Sin.* 24:530-541.

43

Middle Pleistocene Hominid Variability and the Origin of Late Pleistocene Humans

C. B. Stringer

INTRODUCTION

The European Middle Pleistocene hominid record has received increasing attention in recent years as new fossils have been discovered and new dating techniques applied. The material has been reviewed in detail elsewhere (e.g., Oakley *et al.* 1971; Howells 1980; Wolpoff 1980a; Anonymous 1981; Cook *et al.* 1982), so only a brief introduction will be provided here, with detailed references to only the most relevant or recent discussions of the material.

Using a commonly accepted chronostratigraphic division of the Pleistocene (Butzer and Isaac 1975; Kukla 1978), the Middle Pleistocene spans the period between about 730,000 years (730 ky) and 128,000 years (128 ky) ago. Although there is archaeological evidence suggesting early human occupation, at least in southern Europe, the only known European fossil that might represent an Early Pleistocene hominid is the dubious cranial fragment from Venta Micena, Spain. Of the main hominid finds, the Mauer mandible, probably associated with a late "Cromerian" fauna like that of Mosbach, is likely to be the oldest, with a probable age in excess of 450 ky. Somewhat younger are finds dated within the "Mindel" faunal complex, such as Arago (Tautavel) and Vértesszöllös, perhaps ca. 400 ky. Hominids assigned to the Holsteinian/Hoxnian/Mindel-Riss complexes, such as Bilzingsleben, Swanscombe, Steinheim, and perhaps Montmaurin, may in fact derive from distinct stages covering a period of ca. 200 ky in the later Middle Pleistocene (Kukla 1978; Cook *et al.* 1982). Recent absolute dating of the Bilzingsleben site suggests the hominid fragments may be relatively early in this sequence. The well preserved Petralona cranium has been dated as Early Pleistocene by some workers (i.e., pre-Brunhes, >730 ky—Kurtén and Poulianos, 1981) or as late Middle Pleistocene by others (ca. 200ky—Hennig *et al.* 1982), but the actual age may lie between these extremes, perhaps approximating that of the morphologically comparable Arago 21 hominid (Stringer 1984). Similar dating problems now surround the Vértesszöllös hominids, since recent absolute age determinations of ca. 200 ky are considerably younger than had been expected from the associated fauna (Cook *et al.* 1982). A number of French hominid sites are assigned to the latest Middle Pleistocene ("Riss" complex), including material dated at less than 200 ky. These include Biache, La Chaise (Bourgeois-Delaunay and Suard), and Fontéchevade.

EVOLUTIONARY MODELS

Many evolutionary models have been proposed to explain variation in the European hominid record. Some of these can be summarised as follows.

a. Presapiens Model

This would require the existence of separate ancestors for Neanderthals and modern humans during the Middle Pleistocene (Vallois 1954). In this model, the Swanscombe and Steinheim hominids would lie on separate lineages ancestral to modern *H. sapiens* and Neanderthals, respectively.

b. Preneanderthal or Early Neanderthal Model

This model suggests that the divergence of modern humans and Neanderthals occurred in Europe or an adjoining area at the end of the Middle Pleistocene or early in the Late Pleistocene. In this model, the European Middle Pleistocene hominids would represent an undifferentiated stock of "archaic" *H. sapiens* or generalised Neanderthals showing the gradual establishment of distinctive modern or late Neanderthal characters (Breitinger 1957; Howell 1960; Le Gros Clark 1964).

c. *H. erectus—sapiens* Models

These suggest that the species *H. erectus* existed in the European Middle Pleistocene and evolved into, or was replaced by *H. sapiens*. (i) In a gradual evolutionary model of this type, chronological boundaries between the two species may be proposed (e.g., "end of Mindel" [Wolpoff 1980b] or 300 ky [Campbell 1972]). (ii) A further development of this model suggests that sexual dimorphism is perhaps the major component of variation in the Middle Pleistocene sample, such that specimens with a robust *erectus*-like cranial morphology are male individuals (e.g., Bilzingsleben, Petralona), while those with a more gracile morphology are females (e.g., Swanscombe, Steinheim) of the same lineage (Wolpoff 1980b).

Reprinted with permission from *Ancestors: The Hard Evidence*, edited by E. Delson, pp. 289–295, Alan R. Liss, Inc., New York. Copyright © 1985 by Alan R. Liss, Inc., New York.

(iii) Another variant of this model parallels the presapiens model except that two broadly contemporaneous groups are envisaged in the Middle Pleistocene, representing *H. erectus* in eastern Europe (Bilzingsleben, Vértesszöllös, Petralona) and *H. sapiens* in western Europe (e.g., Swanscombe, Steinheim). Further evolution in the latter group leads to premodern forms (e.g., Ehringsdorf) and preneanderthal forms (Vlcek 1978).

d. Primitive *sapiens*—Neanderthal Model

This model also suggests that there were two main groups in the European Middle Pleistocene. An earlier *erectus*-like group (e.g., Arago, Petralona, Bilzingsleben) gave way by replacement or, more probably, evolution to an early Neanderthal group (e.g., Swanscombe, Biache, and perhaps Steinheim and Pontnewydd in the later Middle Pleistocene (Stringer 1981; Cook *et al.* 1982; Hublin 1982).

TESTING THE MODELS

All of the above models require an adequate relative dating framework for the Middle Pleistocene hominids in order that they can be properly tested. Models a, c(ii), and c(iii) require the demonstration of the coexistence of two distinct species or morphologies, whereas the other models require a relative ordering of the relevant hominids. The dating problems of the European Middle Pleistocene record are still formidable, and even a relative ordering for the hominids cannot yet be established, let alone an absolute placement for each find (Cook *et al.* 1982). For this reason, most of the models cannot be fully tested, and the chronological classification systems of c(i) are not practicable (Stringer 1981). The specific fossils claimed as members of the presapiens lineage of model a (Swanscombe and Fontéchevade) have been interpreted more plausibly as early Neanderthals, although the Fontéchevade frontal fragment is still a problematic specimen (Hublin 1982; Stringer *et al.* 1984). Regarding model c(ii), I believe that the range in size, robusticity, and occipital morphology between specimens such as Petralona and Steinheim far exceeds that indicated for dimorphic *H. erectus* and Neanderthal samples (Stringer 1981, 1984), and therefore variation in the European Middle Pleistocene hominids must be predominantly attributed to population differences, rather than to sexual dimorphism (see Fig. 1). While this might appear to support model c(iii), there is no evidence as yet to demonstrate clearly that the two distinct morphologies ("*erectus*-like" and "*sapiens*-like") in fact coexisted in Europe. Another look at this problem is needed, since a similarly high degree of variation is also present in African hominids of this age (e.g., Bodo vs Ndutu).

My own preference would still be for model d, because the specimen that is most certainly dated to the earlier Middle Pleistocene (Mauer) does not, in my opinion, show any clear derived characters shared with either Neanderthals or modern humans. I am prepared to argue the same point for most of the Arago material (the Arago 2 mandible can be interpreted as Neanderthal-like, however) and the Vértesszöllös, Bilzingsleben, and Petralona fossils. Equally the specimens that are most certainly dated to the late Middle Pleistocene (Biache, Bourgeois-Delaunay, Suard) do show clear, derived Neanderthal characteristics, and I am prepared to argue the same point for the Swanscombe and Ehringsdorf fossils, with the possible

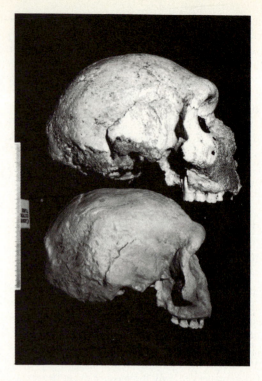

Figure l. *Right lateral view of Middle Pleistocene European hominid crania showing range of variation: Petralona (incompletely prepared) above, Steinheim (cast) below.*

addition of the Steinheim, Pontnewydd, and Atapuerca specimens.

CLASSIFICATION OF THE EUROPEAN HOMINIDS

Having stated my preference with regard to evolutionary models, it is necessary to discuss once again my reasons for questioning the existence of the taxon *H. erectus* in the known European record (I do not doubt its potential existence earlier in the European record). First, it is necessary to decide whether European specimens such as Mauer, Arago, Vértesszöllös, Bilzingsleben, and Petralona can be classified together, or whether they should be referred to more than one hominid group. There are obvious problems in comparing isolated mandibles or cranial fragments, which is why I have preferred to compare the fragmentary specimens to the more complete material from Arago and Petralona. Thus, an important preliminary question is to decide whether the Arago and Petralona fossils are similar enough to be classified together.

A new and skillfully produced composite reconstruction of the Arago 21/47 cranium has been studied and classified as *H. erectus,* while the Petralona specimen has been considered to be more Neanderthal-like (Vandermeersch 1985). The main distinctions appear to be in the narrower, flatter, frontal bone (and associated smaller endocranial volume), greater facial prognathism, and angular torus development of the Arago specimen, while the Petralona cranium appears to show more advanced or Neanderthal-like features in pneumatisation, morphology of the maxilla, nose and supraorbital torus, endocranial expansion, and reduced prognathism. As already indicated (Hemmer 1982; Stringer 1984) some of the supposed "*erectus*" characters of the Arago cranium could be attributed to distortion remaining in the reconstruction, and certainly differences in prognathism and nasal form between Arago 21 and Petralona could be reduced or virtually eliminated in an alternative reconstruction. The differences in pneumatisation, supraorbital torus form, and presence of an angular torus would remain, however, but it could be argued that in other respects (palate size and shape, dental size, overall cranial thickness) the Petralona specimen is the more archaic of the two. Certainly, it is unlikely that the missing Arago occipital bone could have been more archaic and less Neanderthal-like than that of the Petralona cranium (except, perhaps, if it resembled that of Bilzingsleben). For me, at least, the similarities between these specimens far outweigh their differences, and "advanced" characters they share resemble Late Pleistocene hominids but differ from those of Asian *H. erectus*. These "advanced" characters include endocranial morphology, increased mid-facial prognathism, lack of ectocranial buttressing, increased cranial height, distinctive parietal arch shape, and, perhaps, reduced total prognathism (Hemmer 1982; Holloway 1982; Stringer 1984).

If, therefore, the Arago and Petralona specimens can be regarded as representing the same hominid population, it is not difficult to extend this group by morphological similarities to include the Mauer mandible (Aguirre and de Lumley 1977) and the cranial and dental material from Bilzingsleben and Vértesszöllös, although in several respects the latter specimen does appear rather "advanced" (Wolpoff 1980b, 1982; Stringer 1980, 1981, 1984). Overall, the group is characterised by a cranial robusticity (e.g., in supraorbital and occipital torus development, bone thickness, muscularity) greater than in early or late Neanderthals or modern humans, and this can be interpreted as retained from an ancestral population that was even more *erectus*-like in morphology. However, the "advanced" features of the Petralona and Arago (and Vértesszöllös?) material assume a greater significance in my view than retained archaic characters that are more marked in the Bilzingsleben specimens (for which we lack facial, basicranial, temporal, or parietal parts that appear "advanced" in Petralona or Arago).

NEANDERTHAL CHARACTERS IN THE EARLY EUROPEAN HOMINIDS

Having attempted to establish the "archaic" *sapiens* character of these assumed earlier Middle Pleistocene specimens, it is still necessary to discuss whether synapomorphies with Neanderthals (or modern humans) also exist in them, as these would not be expected under model d unless a transitional population leading to Neanderthals was being sampled.

A number of Neanderthal autopomorphies have been proposed, and the relevant ones can be summarised as a high degree of mid-facial projection and associated anteriorly placed dentition, voluminous and projecting nasal opening, double arched and pneumatised supraorbital torus, cranial shape subpherical ("en bombe") in occipital view, large occipitomastoid crest relative to mastoid process, highly curved occipital plane, and double arched occipital torus with suprainiac fossa. Other features common in Neanderthals include the inflated and highly pneumatised maxillae, taurodont molars, H-O pattern of mandibular foramen, anterior mastoid tubercle, lambdoid flattening, and the high position of the auditory meatus relative to

the zygomatic process root (for further discussion see Stringer *et al.* 1984). The distribution of these and other features in Late Pleistocene hominids is graphically displayed in Figure 2.

Of the above list of Neanderthal characters, it is possible to identify an anteriorly placed dentition only in the Arago 2 mandible of the "archaic" European group, while midfacial prognathism in Arago 21 and Petralona, although marked, does not reach typical Neanderthal levels and is less developed than in Broken Hill 1 (Stringer 1984). Petralona certainly possesses a Neanderthal-like supraorbital torus and "inflated" maxilla, but with an even higher degree of pneumatisation. Given the morphology of Broken Hill 1 and Bodo 1, it may be that the level of pneumatisation and the maxillary form of Petralona were more widespread in the robust Middle Pleistocene hominids, and therefore they do not represent genuine synapomorphies with Neanderthals (but compare de Bonis and Melentis 1982). However, the supraorbital torus form is much more specifically Neanderthal-like. The nasal bones of Petralona are projecting, and the nasal opening is certainly absolutely large, yet when scaled against the overall size of the massive face, relative nasal size is similar to average modern values, unlike that of Bodo and most Neanderthals, where it remains distinctly larger. In the parietal and occipital region of Petralona there are no obvious Neanderthal characters, and this is also more generally true for the Arago, Bilzingsleben, and Vértesszöllös specimens, although the curved occipital plane of the latter fossil is certainly marked (Hublin 1982). Overall, then, it might be argued that an incipient Neanderthal morphology is present in the Petralona cranium, but most of the relevant characters can be matched in Middle Pleistocene specimens generally, and it is with these other fossils (probably including Broken Hill 1, Bodo, and perhaps Dali) that the principal allegiance of Petralona and the European "archaic" hominid group lies. This primitive group may be close to the common ancestor of Neanderthals and modern humans and could be classified as a primitive grade or subspecies of *H. sapiens* or as a distinct species (e.g., *H. heidelbergensis*).

Looking at the possible or probable late Middle Pleistocene European sample, it is evident that the Swanscombe fossil has a Neanderthal-like occipital torus and suprainiac fossa, and probably had a prominent occipitomastoid crest, while the Biache, Suard, and Bourgeois-Delaunay fossils show such features much more strongly, even to the extent of overall cranial shape in Biache. Mandibular material from the La Chaise sites also shows Neanderthal features, but it is only in the Pontnewydd upper molars that a significant level of taurodontism has yet been recognised. The Steinheim specimen is more problematic, since it is poorly preserved and distorted, yet a suprainiac fossa is present (Hublin 1982). However, for me, at least, this specimen sits less easily in the early Neanderthal group, since it apparently departs in a number of plesiomorphous retentions from the typical Neanderthal condition (e.g., in supraorbital form, cranial shape, basicranial morphology and flexion, lower level of midfacial prognathism, and occipitomastoid morphology).

CONCLUSIONS

Any evolutionary scheme to explain European Middle Pleistocene hominid variation at our present state of knowledge is likely to be an oversimplification. However, the most appropriate scheme has two main hominid groups. The "archaic" group resembles *H.*

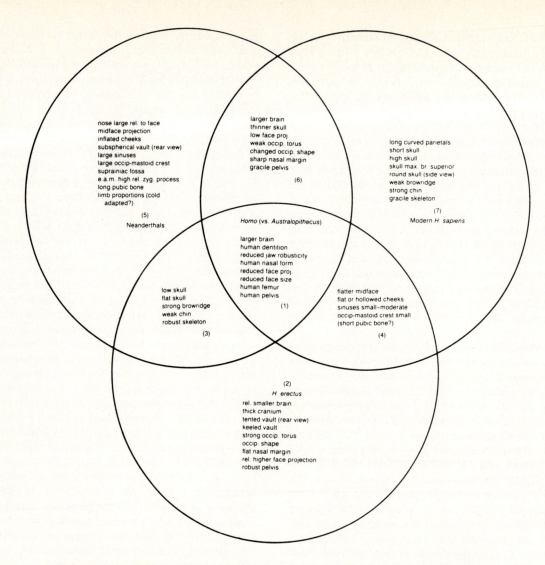

Figure 2. *Simplified Venn diagram showing characters typical of* H. erectus, *Neanderthals, and modern humans. Group 1 characters are synapomorphies for* Homo *generally. Group 3 can be interpreted as plesiomorphies retained in* H. erectus *and Neanderthals but lost in modern humans; group 4 as plesiomorphies retained in* H. erectus *and modern humans but lost in Neanderthals; group 6 as synapomorphies of Neanderthals and modern humans, or characters evolved in parallel. The "archaic" European hominids mainly show combinations of group 2, 3, or 4 characters. The late Middle Pleistocene hominids of Europe show more group 5 or 6 characters and may postdate the divergence of Neanderthals and modern humans.*

erectus in a number of respects and lacks significant autapomorphies found in either Neanderthals or modern humans. The second group contains late Middle Pleistocene hominids and does show synapomorphies with Neanderthals. It may have been derived from members of the other group by local evolution. The placement of individual specimens such as Petralona and Steinheim is difficult, and relative dating cannot yet demonstrate whether all members of the "archaic" group in fact predated all members of the Neanderthal-like group. Sexual dimorphism does appear to have contributed significantly to variation in the samples, but population differences are probably the primary source of variation.

Regarding the evolution of anatomically modern *H. sapiens*, the fact that Europe appears to record only the evolution of Neanderthal derived characters during the Middle and early Late Pleistocene suggests that modern humans evolved elsewhere. In western Europe,

the Saint-Césaire fossil at last provides clear evidence that some Neanderthals, at least, were simply too late and too specialised to have contributed to the evolution of modern hominids in the area. No genuinely transitional fossils displaying combinations of Neanderthal and modern derived characters have been found in Europe or southwest Asia, although it is true that in eastern Europe and southwest Asia less typical Neanderthal fossils are present. It is unclear whether their somewhat greater resemblance to modern humans is due to a greater retention of plesiomorphous characters, gene flow from contemporaneous anatomically modern populations, or to an *in situ* transition from a Neanderthal-like to a modern human morphology (Stringer *et al.* 1984).

It is only in Africa that fossils displaying a clear mosaic of non-modern and modern characteristics exist in the later Middle Pleistocene or early Late Pleistocene, and the presence of actual anatomically modern hominids in the early Late Pleistocene seems probable. Fossils such as Florisbad, Djebel Irhoud, and Omo-Kibish 2 do seem to represent the kind of morphological precursors of modern humans that are missing from the late Middle Pleistocene or early Late Pleistocene of Europe, and none could be described as Neanderthal-like in terms of synapomorphies. The evidence from the Klasies River Mouth, Border Cave, and Omo-Kibish 1 hominid fossils indicates an anatomically modern presence in southern and northeast Africa in the early Late Pleistocene. However, while the chronological position of the former fossils (KRM) is most secure, they are also the most fragmentary, and while the latter two sites provide unequivocal evidence of anatomically modern hominids, they are less certainly dated. Taken together, however, they may be used to place the origin of modern humans in Africa during the timespan of the Middle Stone Age.

Whether there was a single African centre of origin for modern humans, followed by a radiation to Asia and Europe later in the Late Pleistocene, or whether other non-European centres of origin existed is unclear. While the Zuttiyeh, Zhoukoudian, Hexian, and Ngandong fossils do not appear to this author to be transitional between archaic and modern humans, the relationships of the Dali specimen are less easy to determine, partly because of the lack of good data. The specimen may be part of the "archaic" Middle Pleistocene hominid group described earlier, lacking significant synapomorphies with either Neanderthals or modern humans. Alternatively, it might indeed represent a direct ancestor for modern humans in the area. Distinct local centres of origin for Australian populations may also be indicated by the high variability of Late Pleistocene samples. This may be a reflection of morphological changes acquired after the initial colonisation of Australia, of gene flow from more archaic populations in Southeast Asia, or a sign of derivation from ancestors already distinct from those of modern Africans and Europeans. Only a careful analysis of genuine local "clade" characters and their continuity through time can resolve this problem.

Finally, it is hoped that the wider, but careful, application of cladistic methods to the study of later Pleistocene hominid evolution will further clarify relationships. It should also lead to the replacement of the present wide use of subspecific categories based mainly on geographic or chronological criteria (Campbell 1972) by a more meaningful taxonomy based on morphological characters. This in turn may lead to the restriction of the specific name *H. sapiens* to the groups sharing the derived characters of modern humans. It would probably then be necessary on morphological grounds to return the Neanderthals to the status of a distinct species. Given some recent interpretations of the European evidence as recording the separate evolution of the Neanderthal lineage for some 300,000 years, followed by a brief period of coexistence of late Neanderthals and modern humans, this suggestion may not be as extreme as it sounds.

ACKNOWLEDGMENTS

I am most grateful to the American Museum of Natural History, and especially to its Director, Dr. T. D. Nicholson, and to Drs. I. Tattersall and E. Delson for the opportunity to take part in the enjoyable and stimulating events associated with the "Ancestors" symposium.

REFERENCES

Aguirre, E., and de Lumley, M. A. 1977. Fossil men from Atapuerca, Spain: Their bearing on human evolution in the Middle Pleistocene. *J. Hum. Evol.* 6:681-688.

Anonymous. 1981. *Les Premiers Habitants de L'Europe* (Exhibition Catalogue). Lab. Prehist. Musée de l'Homme, Paris.

Breitinger, E. 1957. Zur phyletischen evolution von *Homo sapiens*. *Anthropol. Anz.* 21:62-83

Butzer, K. W., and Isaac, G. L., Eds. 1975. *After the Australopithecines*. Mouton, The Hague.

Campbell, B. G. 1972. Conceptual progress in physical anthropology: Fossil man. *Ann. Rev. Anthropol.* 1:27-54.

Cook, J., Stringer, C. B., Currant, A. P., Schwarcz, H. P., and Wintle, A. G. 1982. A review of the chronology of the European Middle Pleistocene hominid record. *Yrbk. Phys. Anthropol.* 25:19-65.

de Bonis, L., and Melentis, J. 1982. L'Homme de Petralona: Comparaisons avec l'homme de Tautavel. *1er Congr. Internat. Paléont. Hum.*, pp. 847-874 (Prétirage). C.N.R.S., Nice.

Hemmer, H. 1982. Major factors in the evolution of hominid skull morphology. Biological correlates and the position of the Antenendertals. *1er Congr. Internat. Paléont. Hum.*, pp. 339-354 (Prétirage). C.N.R.S., Nice.

Henning, G. J., Herr, W., Weber, E., and Xirotiris, N. I. 1982. Petralona cave dating controversy. *Nature* 299:281-282.

Holloway, R. L. 1982. *Homo erectus* brain endocasts: Volumetric and morphological observations with some comments on the cerebral asymmetries. *1er Congr. Internat. Paléont. Hum.*, pp. 355-366 (Pretirage). C.N.R.S., Nice.

Howell, F. C. 1960. European and northwest African Middle Pleistocene hominids. *Curr. Anthrop.* 1:195-232.

Howells, W. W. 1980. *Homo erectus*—Who, when and where: A survey. *Yrbk. Phys. Anthropol.* 23:1-23.

Hublin, J. J. 1982. Les anténéandertaliens: Présapiens ou prénéandertaliens? *Geobios Mem. Spec.* 6:345-357.

Kukla, G., 1978. The classical European glacial stages: Correlation with deep-sea sediments. *Trans. Nebr. Acad. Sci.* 6:57-93.

Kurtén, B., and Poulianos, A. N. 1981. Fossil Carnivora of Petralona Cave (status 1980). *Anthropos* (Athens) 8:9-56.

Le Gros Clark, W. E. 1964. *The Fossil Evidence for Human Evolution*, 2nd ed. University of Chicago Press, Chicago.

Oakley, K. P., Campbell, B. G., and Molleson, T. I. 1971. *Catalogue of Fossil Hominids*, Vol. 2. *Europe*. British Museum (Natural History), London.

Stringer, B. B. 1980. The phylogenetic position of the Petralona cranium. *Anthropos* (Athens) 7:81-95.

Stringer, C. B. 1981. The dating of European Middle Pleistocene hominids and the existence of *Homo erectus* in Europe. *Anthropologie* (Brno) 19:3-14.

Stringer, C. B. 1984. Some further notes on the morphology and dating of the Petralona hominid. *J. Hum. Evol.* 12:731-742.

Stringer, C. B., Hublin, J. J., and Vandermeersch, B., 1984. The origin of anatomically modern humans in western Europe, in: *The Origin of Modern Humans* (F. H. Smith and F. Spencer, Eds.), pp. 51-136, Liss, New York.

Vallois, H. V. 1954. Neandertals and praesapiens. *J. R. Anthropol. Inst.* 84:111-130.

Vandermeersch, B. 1985. The origin of the Neandertals, in: *Ancestors: The Hard Evidence* (E. Delson, Ed.), pp. 306-309, Liss, New York.

Vlcek, E. 1978. A new discovery of *Homo erectus* in Central Europe. *J. Hum. Evol.* 7:239-251.

Wolpoff, M. H. 1980a. *Paleoanthropology*. Knopf, New York.

Wolpoff, M. H. 1980b. Cranial remains of Middle Pleistocene European hominids. *J. Hum. Evol.* 9:339-358.

Wolpoff, M. H. 1982. The Arago dental sample in the context of hominid dental evolution. *1er Congr. Internat. Paléont. Hum.*, pp. 389-410 (Prétirage). C.N.R.S., Nice.

44

Regional Continuity in Australasian Pleistocene Hominid Evolution

A. G. Thorne and M. H. Wolpoff

The notion that there is an evolutionary and morphological sequence embracing middle Pleistocene Indonesian hominids and late Pleistocene and Holocene Australians is of long standing (Weidenreich 1946; Coon 1963; Macintosh 1965; Howells 1973a; Sartono 1975; Jacob 1976). Despite the fragmentary nature of the Indonesian remains and the paucity and scattered nature of Australian Pleistocene and early Holocene skeletal materials, these and other authors have noted a series of general features that appear to link the two areas, although there have been a variety of opinions about the degree of relationship and its taxonomic significance.

The discovery of the Sangiran 17 *Homo erectus* cranium in 1969 (Sartono 1971, 1975; Jacob 1975) provides an opportunity to examine this relationship in detail, as this individual preserves not only an almost complete neurocranium but was the first *Homo erectus* specimen, Indonesian or otherwise, to retain the facial skeleton. Sangiran 17 stems from the lower part of the Kabuh formation in the Sangiran dome of central Java. Dates obtained from samples taken at the top or above the Kabuh beds suggest a minimum age of 500,000 years for the deposits, and determinations based on samples from within the Kabuh vary from 710,000 to 830,000 years (Jacob 1975). While accurate dating of these deposits remains unresolved, a date of approximately 750,000 years for Sangiran 17 seems reasonable at present (Ninkovich and Burckle 1978).

At the other end of the time-range, the recovery of a fairly large Australian sample of recent *Homo sapiens* specimens at Kow Swamp in northern Victoria, between 1967 and 1972 (Thorne 1969, 1971, 1976; Thorne and Macumber 1972) provides a new basis for establishing regional characteristics in Pleistocene Australians. The Kow Swamp series, the result of burials in lacustrine and aeolian sediments, spans the period between 9,500 and 14,000 years B. P. (Thorne 1976). Although adults, juveniles, and infants are represented in the remains, the most complete skeletons are the adult males KS1 and KS5. To this series the Cohuna cranium can be added, as this individual is part of the Kow Swamp population, both geographically and chronologically (Macumber and Thorne 1975).

While initial preparation and some reconstruction of the Sangiran 17 individual has allowed general observations of the cranium, backward and lateral displacement of the face against the cranial base has prevented an accurate assessment of its original form. The reconstruction of this individual and its comparison to the Kow Swamp and Holocene Australian cranial remains is the basis for this attempt to examine new evidence for regional continuity in Australasian hominids.

THE CRANIAL RECONSTRUCTIONS

Reconstructions of Kow Swamp 1 and 5 (A. G. T.) were based on assembly of face and vault as separate sections. Specimens were prepared following the procedures outlined in Partridge and Thorne (1963). For Kow Swamp 1, the complete subnasal and midline areas of the maxillae allowed accurate reconstruction of the palatal region; to this were added the frontal processes of the maxillae, both of which were virtually intact, particularly at their upper ends. The zygomatic bones were attached to the frontal bone using the 12-mm-long portions of the fronto-zygomatic sutures preserved on both sides. The maxillae were then placed in anatomical position, relative to the frontal and nasal bones, so as to place the preserved lower and medial edges of the zygomatic bones. In this position the nasomaxillary and frontomaxillary areas were correctly aligned. It should be noted that this cranium has undergone postmortem plastic deformation posteriorly. The distortion has resulted in twisting of the braincase relative to the frontofacial area, but this does not appear to affect significantly the reconstruction of the face, its attachment to the frontal bone, or the degree of prognathism.

For Kow Swamp 5 the maxillae are complete, as are the upper 10 mm of the nasal bones. The right zygomatic bone attaches directly to its maxillary neighbor along almost the total length of the zygomaxillary suture, but the bone is eroded along its upper margin so that only a small contact with the frontal bone is retained. The left zygomatic bone can be joined to the frontal along a substantial length of frontozygomatic suture, but it lacks a direct contact with the left maxillary bone. As both sides of the interorbital sutures are preserved, an accurate placement of the facial bones was achieved, which also positioned the right frontozygomatic contact correctly. It also correctly aligned the anteroinferior orbital margins of the left maxilla and the zygomatic bones.

As the interorbital and frontozygomatic areas of the Cohuna cranium are fully preserved, reconstruction of this individual (A. G. T.) presented no difficulties.

Reprinted with permission from *American Journal of Physical Anthropology*, Vol. 55, pp. 337–349. Copyright © 1981 by Alan R. Liss, Inc., New York.

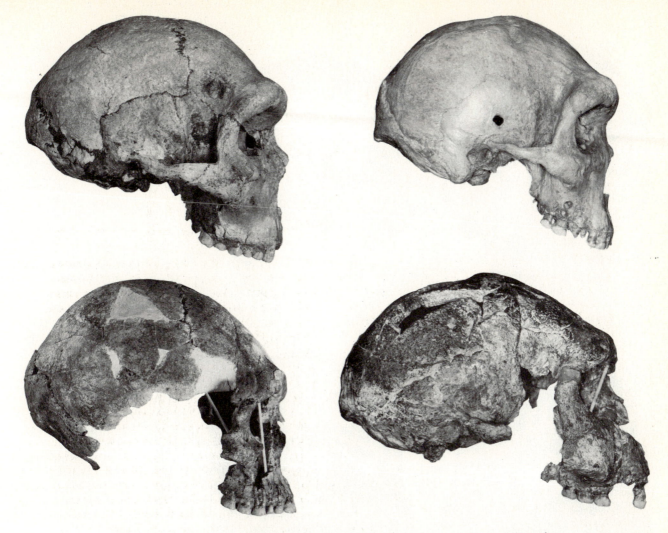

Figure 1. *Lateral view of four well-preserved males. Kow Swamp 1 (lower left) and Sangiran 17 (lower right) represent the Australoasian morphological clade, while Petralona (upper left) and Broken Hill (upper right) are the best preserved middle Pleistocene males from Europe and Africa. The specimens are not shown to the same scale.*

Reconstruction of the Sangiran 17 face (M. H. W.) utilized two bony contacts, the relative position of the right zygomatic and the zygomatic process of the frontal, and the orientation of the alveolar margin relative to the cranial base. The only contact between the lower face and the nasal region above it is along the left margin of the nose. When the bones were brought into an adjacent position, the inferior margin of the right orbit was found to be continuous, although a gap of several millimeters visible in Figure 2 was retained. Thus, the facial height cannot exceed that of the present reconstruction. After this contact was established, the entire face was swiveled and rotated at the broad contact line between the positions of nasion and glabella. The rotation aligned the palate midline with the midline of the vault. Swiveling was constrained by the alignment of the zygomatic process of the frontal and the frontal process of the zygomatic, although these do not contact in the present reconstruction because of missing bone on the superior end of the zygomatic. The face was oriented in the least prognathic position possible. Any further reduction of prognathism accomplished by additional swiveling at the broad nasal contact would (1) place the frontal process of the zygomatic markedly

posterior to the zygomatic process of the frontal on the right side (Fig. 1), (2) result in an unacceptably vertical angulation to the posterior portion of the curved alveolar margin, and (3) open up a wide crack along the nasal contact line. Conversely, a more prognathic orientation of the face was possible, but this would result in an even greater index of prognathism. Thus, in terms of the prognathism and the facial angle, the present reconstruction is conservative.

The symmetry visible in the reconstruction and the general condition of the vault suggests that Sangiran 17 did not undergo significant postmortem plastic deformation. The position of the face prior to reconstruction was the result of postmortem crushing, which brought the preserved parts of the right zygomatic and frontal bones into contact while opening a gap in the maxilla along the left margin of the nose.

COMPARATIVE ANALYSIS

The reconstructed Sangiran 17 cranium can be characterized as long, broad, and low (see Table 1), with a surprisingly short but broad and markedly prognathic face. The grade charac-

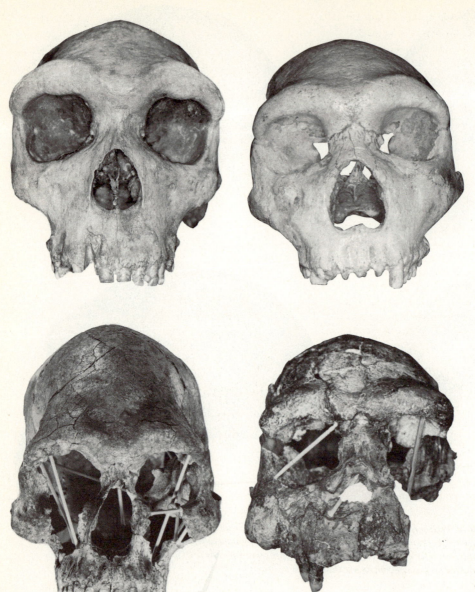

Figure 2. *Facial view of Kow Swamp 1 (lower left), Sangiran 17 (lower right), Broken Hill (upper left), and Petralona (upper right). The specimens are aligned in Frankfort horizontal, but are not shown to the same scale.*

teristics closely resemble other specimens regarded as *Homo erectus*, especially those Indonesian specimens associated with the Kabuh formation, but to a great degree the resemblances also involve variants from Choukoutien and East Africa (Turkana, and Olduvai). These grade similarities include vault proportions, continuity of the supraorbital torus across the midline, the presence of a broad continuous sulcus separating the torus from the frontal squama, marked postorbital constriction, the presence of a low and vertically thick nuchal torus extending to the lambdoidal suture, the presence of an angular torus (not in the earliest Africa specimens), marked depth of the orbits, facial prognathism, the position of maximum cranial breadth on the supramastoid crests, the superior medial slope of the parietals, the vertical separation of inion and endinion, the position of the tympanic crests adjacent to the anterior faces of the mastoid processes, the sagittal and transverse expansion of the nuchal plane, and the lack of a vertical edge at the posterior end of the temporal squama.

While there are some specific resemblances to what may be considered a broadly Asiatic regional group, particularly the pronounced vault thickening (see Table 4), resemblances to other Indonesian specimens are most marked. Trinil 2 and the Sangiran crania 2, 3, 10, 12, and 17 resemble each other (where comparable parts are preserved) in supraorbital projection and frontal flattening in the sagittal plane, the absence of any frontal boss, the sagittal profile of the vault, the low temporal squama (especially posteriorly), the presence of a sagittal torus extending onto the frontal bone, and frontal sinus development. On the other hand, dimensions of Sangiran 17 are much larger than those of the other Indonesian crania (except Sangiran 12, which approaches it in some measurements of cranial breadth), the zygoma are much larger than those of Sangiran 10, the supraorbitals are thicker and more projecting than in the comparable Indonesian crania, the vault is thicker, the mastoids are larger, and the nuchal torus is both thicker and vertically taller and preserves an inferiorally oriented triangular eminence at inion.

Because of the distinctions between Sangiran 17 and the above mentioned crania, a number of authors have suggested that this specimen is not the same taxon and instead is closely aligned with, if not actually the same as, the Ngandong sample (Jacob 1975; Sartono 1975). We do not believe this is the case and suggest that the similarities that do exist with Ngandong are mainly a consequence of size. The morphological differences between Sangiran 17 and the Ngandong sample (Weidenreich 1951) are paralleled by most of the Indonesian *Homo erectus* sample when compared with Ngandong. These differences that contrast with the Ngandong sample include the following characteristics of Sangiran 17: low posterior border of the temporal squama; angulation of the posterior portion of the foramen magnum relative to the nuchal plane (the are parallel in the Ngandong sample); the lack of either a distinct sulcus or an irregular depressed area (suprainiac fossa) above the nuchal torus, the presence of only a weak angular torus which at its most posterior position is still anterior to the lambdoidal suture; the lack of a distinct occipital boss on the midline of the occipital plane; the posterior displacement of the Glaserian fissure form the roof of the mandibular fossa (in the Ngandong specimens the fissure is at the most superior point on the roof); the fairly wide mandibular fossa (in the sagittal direction) with a sloping anterior face; the glabellar region of the supraorbital torus pronounced rather than depressed; the absence of a posteriorly elongated triangle at the lateral supraorbital corner formed by the convergence of the temporal line and the posterior supraorbital border.

In these and other details, the similarities of thee Sangiran 17 cranium are to the Indonesian *Homo erectus* sample. We take the differences between Sangiran 17 and this sample to reflect sexual dimorphism—it seems likely that Sangiran 17 is male, while Trinil 2 and Sangiran 2, 3, and 10 are female. Interestingly, the canine of Sangiran 17 lacks an anterior interproximal facet, although the posterior facet marking the premolar contact is well developed. Either the lateral incisor was not present or there was a precanine diastema. We view the second possibility as more likely and, indeed, this was a not uncommon condition in the earlier Putjangan-associated Sangiran canines. A precanine diastema is more likely in hominid males and its presence in Sangiran 17 supports the sexing diagnosis.

In sum, Sangiran 17 is characterized by grade features of *Homo erectus* and specifically resembles the Kabuh-associated Indonesian crania. At the same time, we find a number of specific features that suggest local or regional continuity with Pleistocene and recent populations of Australia. We believe that regional continuity spans the middle and upper Pleistocene and involves two species of the genus *Homo: Homo erectus* and *Homo sapiens.* For the moment we will describe this as a morphological clade within a lineage, and we wish to distinguish this usage of "clade" from the more general definition provided by Simpson (1961) and the more restricted application of Hennig (1966). We propose to use the concept of morphological clade to refer to a fossil sequence showing both continuity over time and differentiation from other contemporary morphological clade. We do not regard a morphological clade as a unique lineage, nor do we believe it necessary to imply a particular taxonomic status for it. The concept of a clade

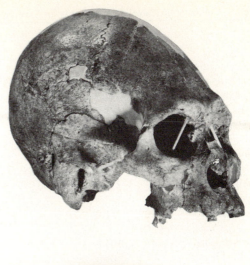

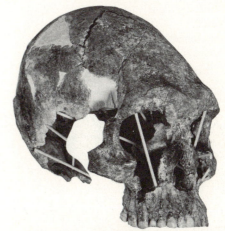

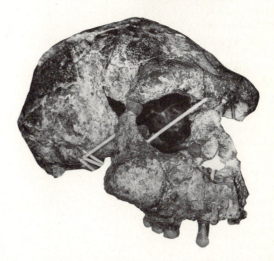

Figure 3. *Three Australasian males in three-quarter view: Sangiran 17 (below), Kow Swamp 1 (middle), and Kow Swamp 5 (above). The specimens are not shown to the same scale.*

is meant to apply to a monophyletic lineage. Our use of the morphological clade concept allows for the description of regional continuity in an evolving polytypic species without entering the poorly defined morass of subspecific taxonomy, which was never designed to describe a complex evolutionary situation.

Table 1. Comparative cranial measurements for Sangiran 17 and the best-preserved Kow Swamp males.

	Sangiran 17	Cohuna	Kow Swamp						
			1	3	5	9	14	15	20
Cranian length (maximum)	207.1	200.0	210.0		192.0		210.0		
Glabella–opisthion	159.1				142.4				
Cranial height	114.5	141.5							
Bregma–opisthion	132.5		159.0		158.0				
Glabella–lambda	190.0	196.0	200.4		189.7		205.5		
Maximum cranial breadth	160.8	134.0	135.3		139.0	138.0	144.0		
Biauricular breadth	149.1	128.0	122.3		117.0				
Bimandibular fossae	146.9	130.8	126.0		121.4				
Glabella–lambda arc	224.0	260.0	255.0		262.0		271.0		
Acr–chord index	117.9	132.7	127.2		138.1		131.9		
Basion–nasion	111.2	104.7							
Nasion–bregma	105.6	125.3	123.8		115.5				
Glabella–bregma	106.0	124.0	121.0		112.8		120.0		
Minimum frontal breadth	100.5	93.5	94.2	107.0	96.0	94.0	94.0	93.0	
Coronal breadth	118.6	105.4	106.2		115.6				
Outer biorbital breadth	122.8	115.5	119.7	123.8	110.8		107.2	123.0	
Glabella–bregma arc	112.0	130.0	125.0		118.0		130.0		
Arc–chord index	105.7	104.8	102.5		104.6		108.3		
Supraorbital projection from internal surface									
Lateral	31.0		24.5	20.9	20.5	26.5	18.2		26.0
Midorbit	29.5		20.0	13.6	14.8		12.3		20.0
Medial	28.5		24.0		15.7				22.0
Supraorbital thickness									
Lateral	13.8	8.8	8.5	9.9	9.3	9.8	8.7	11.1	10.0
Midorbit	16.8	8.0	16.0	5.8	9.2		12.2	17.6	7.7
Medial	19.2	18.6	21.5	19.8	16.9		15.8	19.3	19.6
Bregma–lambda	113.6	116.7	119.9		125.0	118.9	127.1		
Bregma–asterion	134.9	138.8	140.0		139.9	134.3	137.0		
Biparietal breadth	145.9	129.4	128.2		139.0	138.0	144.0		
Parietal mastoid angle breadth	144.7	129.4	121.5		126.6	138.0			
Lambda–opisthion	84.7		96.6		107.3				
Lambda–inion	60.0	62.7	63.9		74.2	62.7			
Opisthion–inion	52.5		49.2		40.1				
Occipital index	114.9		129.9		185.0				
Lambda–asterion	74.0	80.0	79.8		91.3	84.4			
Biasterioninc breadth	116.4	105.0	104.1		110.4	113.8			
Midline projection of auricular point to									
Prosthion	134.3	120.5	133.5		117.2				
Nasion	105.3	95.9	109.4		91.3				
Glabella	117.1	102.5	114.6		95.6		95.3		
Bregma	95.6	113.8	117.5		119.6		109.4		
Lambda	95.2	110.9	107.2		115.6		118.7		
Opisthocranion	93.5	106.1	101.4		108.9				
Inion	89.5		87.2		72.9				
Opisthion	40.9				49.1				

All data are in millimeters. Bimandibular fossae breadth was taken between the points on the lateral fossae surfaces at the highest points on the fossae. Minimum frontal breadth was taken between the temporal notches. Supraorbital thicknesses were measured in accordance with Weidenreich's (1943) description, except that the lateral breadth was measured in the immediate proximity of the frontozygomatic suture. Supraorbital projection from the internal surface, taken at the same positions, follows the technique described by Smith (1976). Parietal mastoid angle breadth was taken between the inferior posterior corners of the bone. This comparison emphasizes the greater height and narrower breadth of the Kow Swamp male crania. Differences can be noted in many of the measurements, although cranial length measures, minimum frontal breadth, the frontal index, (especially in contrast to the parietal index), medial supraorbital thickness, and projected measures from the auricular midline position to the face are similar. The generally greater similarities in facial measures supports our contention that in this region the face better reflects clade while the vault better reflects grade.

Continuity, of course, can be shown in any lineage. For this reason we wish to emphasize those elements of continuity which are either unique to or especially characteristic of this region. Continuity in features we do not discuss may well reflect the same clade relationship, but they cannot be used to establish the presence of a morphological clade. Moreover, in focusing on elements that do not seem to change significantly in Australasia, we do not wish to imply the absence of evolution for the period discussed. Our emphasis of morphological clade characteristics is not made in ignorance of the important changes in grade that separate Sangiran 17 from late Pleistocene Australians.

Evidence of local morphological continuity can be found in the vault and face. While we have observed that the facial region better expressed the clade relation (Table 1, 2), the flatness of the frontal in the sagittal plane, the posterior position of the minimum frontal breadth, the relatively horizontal orientation of the inferior supraorbital borders, the presence of a distinct prebregmatic eminence, the low position of the maximum parietal breadth (at or near the parietal mastoid angle), and other vault features are also suggestive.

The most striking clade features of the face are related to the maintenance of marked prognathism (Table 2). The gnathic index of Sangiran 17 is 121.9, an unusually high figure for any recent hominid [1]. Unfortunately, this index can only be determined for one of the Kow Swamp group males (Cohuna), because basion is not preserved on the other specimens (Table 2). Consequently, we have chosen to use two other means of comparing facial prognathism, (1) an auricular gnathic index calculated from the distances of prosthion and nasion from the auricular point projected into the sagittal plane, and (2) the angle at nasion formed by the nasion-prosthion line and the line from nasion to the sagittal projection of the auricular point.

The correlation of the auricular gnathic index with the gnathic index was found to be 0.536 in a sample of 25 male Australian Aborigines from the region near the town of Euston on the Murray River. This is significant at the 0.05% level. The gnathic index reaches its world wide maximum for living populations in Australians (Martin and Saller 1966) and populations showing significant Australoid admixture (Table 3). Thus, although the auricular gnathic index has not been calculated for a wide range of living populations, we feel confident in assuming that the Australian values are similarly maximum. In the Euston male sample, the mean for the auricular gnathic index is 119.5 (110.8-128.8), with a coefficient of variation of 3.6. All three indexes for the Kow Swamp group males (122.0, 125.7, and 128.4) are above this mean, although within the range, and the same applies to the Sangiran 17 value of 127.5.

An alternative approach to facial prognathism is via the facial angle at nasion. Once again, Australian populations or populations with significant Australoid admixture have the highest values for living groups for the nasion facial angle, calculated using basion (Table 3). When the nasion facial angle is calculated using the auricular point (allowing comparison with the Kow Swamp males), the three Kow Swamp specimens fall above the Euston male mean (86.4°) although within the range of 79.8-96.1°. These three values (90.7, 91.6, and 91.7°) are less than the Sangiran 17 angle of 97.3°. The angle calculated from the auricular point has a correlation of 0.729 with the angle calculated with basion.

Simply put, we suggest that marked facial prognathism is a regionally distinctive feature today, and that it has been maintained as such (with some reduction) for a considerable period of time.

There are a number of other facial features that reflect a clade relation. The Sangiran 17 zygomae are larger than any from the Kow Swamp group. Nonetheless, they share the presence of a marked ridge paralleling the course of the zygomaxillary suture. The ridge extends to the most anteroin-

Table 2. Comparative facial measurements for Sangiran 17 and the best preserved Kow Swamp males.

	Sangiran 17	Cohuna	Kow Swamp					
			1	3	5	9	14	15
Upper facial height	74.5	75.2		73.0				82.2
Alveolar height	24.8	26.7	22.6		21.8		23.9	26.2
Orbito–alveolar height	48.3	53.8	55.1	47.0	47.2	48.1	49.8	56.2
Bizygomatic breadth	156.0	140.5	143.5		140.0			
Midfacial breadth	124.0	111.2	104.5	116.0	115.7		100.0	104.0
Lateral facial length	90.4	75.7	81.1		77.9	76.0		
Zygomatic bone length along zygomaxillary suture	37.8	34.7	26.8		28.0		28.5	22.0
Nasal breadth	26.4	30.1	26.8		28.9		28.0	26.9
Nasal height	54.8	48.9	56.9		52.0			56.8
Nasal index	48.2	61.9	47.1		55.6			47.4
Gnathic index	121.9	106.1						
Auricular gnathic index	127.5	125.7	122.0		128.4			
Nasion–auricular/ nasion–prosthion angle	97.3°	90.7°	91.7°		91.6°			

Measurements are in millimeters and the angles are in degrees. Upper facial height was taken to the alveolar point, orbitoalveolar height was taken to the alveolar margin between M^2 and M^3, and the zm point used in midfacial breadth and zygomatic bone length was defined on the anterior inferior corner of the zygomatic process of the maxilla. The nasion angle represents the angle between the nasion-prosthion line and the line from nasion to the midline projection of the auricular point. It was calculated from measurements using the law of cosines. The metric similarities in this comparison are mainly in facial heights and nasal breadth.

Table 3. Measures of facial prognathism for males from living human populations.

Males from	Average gnathic index	Nasion angle (nasion–prosthion/nasion–basion)
Berg	95.1	65.6
Egypt	95.1	65.9
Norse	95.2	66.1
Zalayar	95.8	66.5
Arikara	95.9	66.0
Eskimo	96.8	67.5
Buriat	97.2	66.2
Mokapu	97.5	68.9
Peru	98.2	67.8
Bushmen	98.8	71.2
Andaman	99.2	70.3
Teita	100.2	71.3
Zulu	100.4	71.1
Dogon	101.4	72.1
Tasmanian	101.6	75.3
Euston (Upper Murray)	103.4	73.8
Swanport (Lower Murray)	103.5	74.8
Tolai (New Britain)	105.6	76.3

The gnathic index presented is the index of basion-prosthion by basion-nasion. The nasion angle, given in degrees, is formed by the nasion-prosthion line and nasion-basion line. The Euston male sample of 25 was measured by the authors. All other data are from Howells (1973b). Further information concerning the sample sizes and the details of the populations sampled can be found in this publication. By either measure, the four most prognathic populations are either Australian or have significant Australian admixture.

ferior lateral edge of the bone and marks the position of a sharp angle between the anterior and lateral surfaces. Because this angle has an inferolateral orientation, the faces combine transverse flattening and a triangular profile caused by the fact that the anteroinferior corner extends more laterally than either jugale or the superoanterior point on the zygotemporal suture. This feature, discussed as the eversion of the lower border of the malar bone by Larnach and Macintosh (1966, 1970) is very common in modern Australians.

Another facial character we consider important involves the zygomae; Sangiran 17 and the Kow Swamp group share a feature common in modern Australian Aborigines (Larnach and Macintosh 1966, 1970), the rounding of the inferolateral border of the orbit. In addition, the lower border of the nasal aperture lacks a distinct line dividing the nasal floor from the subnasal face of the maxillae, although in all cases the demarcation between these areas is clear. Also in the maxilla, continuity is shown in the marked expression of dental plane curvature, as seen in the lateral view. This is the maxillary counterpart to the curve of Spee, a normal characteristic in the mandibles of living Australians.

Finally, we contend that a morphological clade is reflected by the degree of facial and dental reduction. Indeed, reduction in the face and posterior dentition seems to have been characteristic of both this region and mainland Asia during the middle and upper Pleistocene, as evidenced by the facial remains from Choukoutien, Changyang, Dali, as well as Sangiran 10, 15 and 17. Just as is the case today, facial remains from middle Pleistocene Australasia were larger than their mainland contemporaries. In both regions, facial heights and posterior tooth sizes in the middle Pleistocene had already reduced to what might be thought of as the late upper Pleistocene (but not modern) condition. Thus, the Sangiran 17 facial heights fall within the

range of the Kow Swamp males (Table 2). Similarly, the dimensions of the Sangiran 17 teeth (C, P^3, M^{1-3}) fall almost exactly at the mean for the three Kow Swamp males (KS 1, KS 15, and Cohuna).

DISCUSSION

We recognize that many of these features found in Sangiran 17 can be found independently in other fossil crania of the genus *Homo*. Yet, in no other region can a specimen be found that combines so many features that seem unique or at least of high frequency in Pleistocene Australians. Considering the amount of time involved and the extent of evolutionary change, it is surprising that any elements of local continuity can be demonstrated. Regional morphological continuity need not be considered indicative of prolonged genetic isolation or the reflection of a "once pure Australoid race." Indeed, the grade differences between Sangiran 17 and the Kow Swamp group outweigh the similarities we regard as due to morphological clade, and by and large these differences reflect evolutionary trends that were worldwide.

The presence of a distinguishable morphological clade in this region is probably better interpreted as the result of clinal variation, with Australasia representing the end area of morphological clines that likely included all of continental Asia at one time. We believe that the persistence of long-standing clines is a more likely interpretation of the regional continuity recognized by Weidenreich (1946), Coon (1963), and others than the suggestion of a semi-isolated subspecies transcending the temporal boundaries of chronospecies. Moreover, a dynamic clinal model or regional differentiation eliminates the paradox of the static model with requires geneflow limitations which are strong enough to allow local continuity and continued differen-

Table 4. Comparison of variation in *Homo erectus* samples from East Africa Indonesia, and Choukoutien.

	East African			Indonesian			Choukoutien		
	$\bar{X}$	N	CV	$\bar{X}$	N	CV	$\bar{X}$	N	CV
Maximum cranial breadth	141.2	4	5.7	148.7	6	4.6	148.8	5	3.7
Biparietal breadth	131.3	4	13.3	135.1	8	6.4**	137.9	5	3.2**
Biasterionic breadth	111.6	5	12.4	114.0	8	7.1*	114.9	6	7.0*
Bregma-lambda	92.4	4	8.3	95.8	8	8.9	97.2	6	7.2
Lambda-inion	46.2	6	14.8	49.4	9	10.0	49.7	5	8.4
Temporal squama length	78.9	4	10.7	79.2	5	5.0*	70.4	5	6.5*
Supraorbital thickness (height) at midorbit	12.2	6	30.4	14.8	6	18.5	13.7	6	18.0
Supraorbital length at midorbit (after Weidenreich)	21.6	4	22.6	23.1	6	11.1*	18.8	6	11.0**
Parietal thickness at bregma	8.9	5	25.1	8.7	7	14.6*	9.0	6	17.5
Central parietal thickness	9.2	10	15.3	10.5	8	14.5	10.9	7	10.1
Breadth of M_1	12.2	8	8.0	12.5	11	7.3	11.7	16	6.7

All measurements are in millimeters. The comparisons utilize the coefficient of variation (CV). Where significance is indicated, it is between the variances, using an F test. While only some of the variance differences are significant, the pattern of greater variability in the East African sample for virtually every comparison tends to confirm our visual impressions.

*Variance difference significant at 0.10 compared with East African sample.

**Variance difference significant at 0.05 compared with East African sample.

tiation but at the same time are weak enough to allow the dissemination of widespread evolutionary changes throughout the inhabited world.

CENTER AND EDGE

Development of widespread long-lasting clinal differences involves two processes. First, the initial polytypic populations must be established. We propose that this event came as a consequence of the initial spread of hominids from Africa. Factors leading to the establishment of intraregional homogenity and interregional heterogeneity during this spread have been described in the "center and edge" hypothesis (Thorne 1981), whereby the morphological characteristics of polytypic species reveal "almost invariably that the degree of polymorphism decreases toward the border of the species, and that the peripheral populations are not infrequently monomorphic" (Mayr 1963). These processes are described as "homoselection" by Carson (1959). There are a variety of evolutionary factors leading to this pattern of polytypism. Geneflow through a population will tend to be greatest at the geographic center of the species range. This center is, by definition, the area of optimal conditions, and it is likely that a greater range of genotypes (and consequently of phenotypes) will be tolerated in groups from that area. Moreover, processes leading to the high level of variation found in central populations are facilitated by the tendency for these populations to be contiguous and to have relatively high population densities.

In the peripheral populations, or populations in ecologically marginal areas, events associated with both the initial habitation and the subsequent period of local adaptation help to develop the combination of pronounced differences between allopatric populations and relative homogeneity within them. During the initial habitation, reduced genetic and morphological variability can result from the founder and peninsula effects. Specific habitats encountered during these initial migrations to varying regions and the random aspects of drift help establish

genetic differences between the peripheral populations. While some of these may respond to habitat differences, the random nature of the latter ensures that other variations will not initially reflect differences in adaptation. As local adaptive responses develop, these initial genetic differences, diverse patterns of selection, and the action of drift in the regions with lower population densities help to retain, if not expand, the genetic variation initially established. Moreover, drift and reduced geneflow to the peripheral or ecologically marginal areas might help maintain relative homogeneity within these populations.

We believe that early *Homo erectus* is the first hominid form to migrate out of Africa. The available *Homo erectus* cranial materials appear to fit the model well, particularly if it is assumed that this species evolved in East Africa, or that at least the East African remains represent part of geographic center of the species range. While such an assumption is not universally accepted, thus far unequivocal antecedents of *Homo* are known only from Africa (Le Gros Clark 1964; Leakey and Walker 1976). We do not believe that "*Meganthropus*" either represents an australopithecine form (Robinson 1953, 1955) or that it is a valid genus or species (von Koenigswald, 1957a; Boaz and Howell 1977). Instead, we regard these remains, and the very similar molars from the Badong district and the Dragonbone cave of Jianshi district, Hupei province, South Chinca (Hsu, Wang, and Han 1975) as representing early *Homo erectus*. In contrast, the *Hemianthropus* remains (von Koenigswald 1957b) appear to represent a thick-enamelled Pongo-like primate rather than a hominid.

The available *Homo erectus* crania from East Africa (the "central" area) demonstrate high phenotypic variation. This material includes Olduvai hominids 9, 12 and the BMNH fragments EM 550 and 551, and Lake Turkana specimens KNM-ER-1466, 1805, 1808, 1821, 2598, 3733, and 3883. In contrast, the extensive series of Indonesian hominids, at one "edge" of the *Homo erectus* range, exhibit significantly reduced variability, holding sex constant. Regional homogeneity also characterizes the Choukoutien crania, in spite of the long timespan represented at the site. Our basis for these observations is largely visual. However, in an attempt to quantify them, we have chosen 10 cranial measurements and a dental dimension to both represent different vault regions and to maximize the sample sizes. In Table 4 we compare these for East African *Homo erectus*, the Indonesian *Homo erectus* sample, and Choukoutien. The coefficient of variation (CV) is greater for the East African sample in every case but one, and in this instance the CV for Indonesia is only slightly greater while the Choukoutien CV is less.

In Indonesia, a relatively homogeneous regional variant was maintained through a considerable time period as the distinguishing features of the Javan material can be perceived in remains from both the Putjangan and Kabuh formations at Trinil, Sangiran, and Sambungmachan.

LONGLASTING CLINAL EQUILIBRIUM

The second process underlying continued widespread clinal differences involves the maintenance of these regional differences over a timespan that may be as long as 750,000 years. We contend that the dynamic model of long-lasting morphological clines that results from a balance between geneflow and opposing selection (Hiorns and Harrison 1977), best accounts for the observed pattern. Indeed, the "center and edge" hypothesis provides a solution for one of the problems discussed by these authors by suggesting how marked genetic differences might be established over a continuous range before the leveling effect of geneflow resulted in their dispersion. Hiorns and Harrison (1977) show that numerous combinations of geneflow and opposing selection at low magnitudes can lead to a clinal equilibrium over a series of adjacent populations when the selection is uniform. In a more realistic approximation, varying magnitudes of selection would widen the range of combinations of these two forces over which such an equilibrium can be established. The initial presence of genetic variability may be factor resulting in differing magnitudes of selection, since there is an interdependence between selection and genetic polymorphism. Selection can only act on the genetic combinations present; different combinations can affect both the magnitude and conceivably even the direction of selection.

The model we propose is that differences in selection characterize the peripheral regions of the hominid range both because of local adaptive differences and because of genetic differences established during the period of initial habitation. In the absence of geneflow (i.e., geographic isolation), speciation would have been the ultimate result. In the absence of differences in selection, this early polytypism would have been lost. If it is a balance of these potentially opposing forces that maintains long-standing clines over the hominid range, as we suggest, our use of the concept "morphological clade" need not imply any special lineage relation for a specific region over the timespan involved (just as the water level may remain constant in an overflowing bathtub without the water at the surface of the tub remaining the same). The resulting appearance of morphological continuity in a region *simulates the appearance* of a longlasting subspecific taxon without necessarily being one in any meaningful genetic sense. Our description of longlasting regional continuity as a morphological clade within a lineage is by necessity a very different usage than the application of the clade concept tat higher taxonomic levels, wherein the lineage

itself is the clade. We propose that this is much more realistic means of dealing with regional continuity than the application of the race or subspecies concept, which would require the assumption of isolation and local genetic continuity as the main explanatory factors, and which would necessitate the application of subspecific categories across chronospecies boundaries.

For an example of how such a dynamic equilibrium might work, in the most peripheral regions of Australasia we hypothesize that food preparation techniques and marginal resources required a more powerful masticatory apparatus. Indeed, from the time of *Homo erectus* on, facial size and posterior tooth size have been larger at the Australasian periphery than at its center (Table 4). Technological advances in food preparation appeared in South China, and not in Australia. Thus, geneflow from the center to the more marginal areas of the periphery would be expected to carry the genetic basis for reduced masticatory structures resulting from new food preparation techniques, just as the innovations themselves might have spread. However, toward the periphery different conditions and opposing selection would be encountered. The consequence would be a clinal distribution of size and robustness in the masticatory structures across Australasia. While some changes might eventually characterize the periphery, by this time new technological developments would have led to further reduction at the center. We want to emphasize the idea that while the rate of geneflow would almost certainly have been low, the corresponding differences in selection between these hominid populations would have been small. It is the *balance* between these, and not their absolute magnitudes, that defines the gradient for the resulting clinal distribution.

Over the long periods of time involved, the result of this situation would be along-lasting cline in the size and robustness of the masticatory structures, stretching from South China to (eventualy) Australia. All across this cline, the masticatory structures would appear to reduce over time. Yet, relative differences would always remain and appear to support the interpretation of local genetic continuity because of the observed morphological continuity.

SUMMARY

In sum, we believe that the morphological data discussed here support the contention of a long-lasting cline at this margin of the hominid range, recognizable as an Australasian morphological clade. We hypothesize that initial differences between Australasian and other populations, as well as a degree of relative homogenity within the populations of this area, were established during the first habitation of the region by *Homo erectus*. Subsequent to this, a dynamic balance of geneflow and opposing selection, in both cases probably of very low magnitude, provided the basis for a long-standing clinical equilibrium involving a number of morphological features. The geneflow that was required to maintain this dynamic clinical equilibrium was a critical factor in the dissemination of evolutionary changes that characterized all populations of *Homo* during this timespan.

ACKNOWLEDGMENTS

We wish to express our sincere gratitude to G. H. R. von Koenigswald of the Natur-Museum und Forschung-Institut Senckenberg (Frankfort); T. Jacob of the Projek Penelitian

Paleoanthropologi National, Fakultas Kedokteran, Universitas Gadjah Mada (Jogjakarta); D. Kadar of the Museum Geologi (Bandung), Woo Ju-kang of the Institute for Vertebrate Paleontology and Paleoanthropology (Peking); M. D. Leakey and R. E. F. Leakey of the National Museums of Kenya (Nairobi); and B. A. Ogot, former director of The International Louis Leakey Memorial Institute for African Prehistory (Nairobi) for permission to study the hominid specimens in their care.

This research was supported by NSF Grant BNS 76-82729.

NOTES

[1] In australopithecine grade hominids, the index of prognathism is generally as high or even higher. Indexes for the known crania are 125.6 (STS 5), 126.8 (Chesowanja), 124.0 (SK 80/847), 122.8 (ER 406), 121.8 (OH 5), and 115.4 (ER 1813). In the only other complete *Homo erectus* cranium, the female specimen ER 3733, the index is 115.7. Moreover, Rightmire (1979) suggests that the OH 9 facial skeleton "occupied a position well forward of the braincase" because of the apparent anterior origin of the nasal septum.

REFERENCES

Boaz, N. T., and Howell, F. C. 1977. A gracile hominid cranium from Upper Member G of the Shungura Formation, Ethiopia. *Am. J. Phys. Anthrop.* 46:93-108.

Carson, H. L. 1959. Genetic conditions which promote or retard the formation of species. *Cold Spr. Harb. Symp. Quant. Biol.* 24:87-105.

Clark, W. E. Le Gros 1964. *The Fossil Evidence for Human Evolution.* 2nd ed. University of Chicago Press, Chicago and London.

Coon, C. S. 1963. *The Origin of Races.* Jonathon Cape, London.

Hennig, W. 1966. *Phylogenetic Systematics.* University of Illinois, Urbana.

Hiorns, R. W., and Harrison, G. A. 1977. The combined effects of selection and migration in human evolution. *Man* 12:438-445.

Hsu Chun-hua, Wang Ling-hong, and Han Kang-xin 1975. Australopithecine teeth associated with *Gigantopithecus. Vertebr. Palas.* 13:81-88.

Howells, W. W. 1973a. *The Pacific Islanders.* Weidenfeld and Nicolson, London.

Howells, W. W. 1973b. Cranial variation in man: A study of multivariate analysis of patterns of difference among recent human populations. *Papers of the Peabody Museum,* Vol. 67.

Jacob, T. 1975. Morphology and paleoecology of early man in Java, in: *Paleoanthropology, Morphology and Paleoecology* (R. H. Tuttle, Ed.), pp. 311-225. Mouton, The Hague.

Jacob, T. 1976. Early populations in the Indonesian region, in: *The Origin of the Australians* (R. L. Kirk and A. G. Thorne, Eds.), pp. 81-9. Aust. Inst. of Abor. Stud., Canberra.

von Koenigswald, G. H. R. 1957a. *Meganthropus* and the Australopithecinae. *Proc. 3rd Pan Afr. Congr. Preh.,* pp. 158-160.

von Koenigswald, G. H. R. 1957b. Remarks on *Gigantopithecus* and other hominid remains from Southern China. *Proc. Kon. Ned. Akad. Wet.* 60:153-159.

Larnach, S. L., and Macintosh, N. W. G. 1966. The Craniology of the Aborigines of Coastal New South Wales. *Oceania Monogr.* No. 13, Sydney.

Larnach, S. L., and Macintosh, N. W. G. 1970. The Craniology of the Aborigines of Queensland. *Oceania Monogr.* No. 15, Sydney.

Leakey, R. E. F., and Walker, A. C. 1976. *Australopithecus, Homo erectus* and the single species hypothesis. *Nature* (London) 261:572-574.

Macintosh, N. W. G. 1965. The physical aspect of man in Australia, in: *Aboriginal Man in Australia* (R. M. and C. H. Berndt, Eds.), pp. 29-70. Angus and Robertson, Sydney.

Macumber, P. G., and Thorne, A. R. 1975. The Cohuna cranium site—A re-appraisal. *Arch. Phys. Anthrop. Oceania* 10:67-72.

Martin, R., and Saller, K. 1956–1966. *Lehrbuch der Anthropologie.* Fischer, Stuttgart.

Mayr, E. 1963. *Animal Species and Evolution.* Harvard University Press, Cambridge, MA.

Ninkovich, D., and Burckle. L. H. 1978. Absolute age of the base of the hominid-bearing beds in Eastern Java. *Nature* (London) 275:306-308.

Partridge, J., and Thorne, A. 1963. A preliminary report on a collection of Marsupial fossils from Wellington Caves. *N. S. W. Syd. Univ. Speolog. Soc. J.* 6 (4):44-49.

Rightmire, G. P. 1979. Cranial remains of *Homo erectus* from Beds II and IV, Olduvai Gorge, Tanzania. *Am. J. Phys. Anthrop.* 51:99-116.

Robinson, J. T. 1953. *Meganthropus,* australopithecines and hominids. *Am. J. Phys. Anthrop.* 11:1-38.

Robinson, J. T. 1955. Further remarks on the relationship between *Meganthropus* and the australopithecines. *Am. J. Phys. Anthrop.* 13:429-445.

Sartono, S. 1971. Observations on a new skull of *Pithecanthropus erectus* (*Pithecanthropus* VIII) from Sangiran, Central Java. *Proc. Kon. L. Nederl. Akad. van Wetens., Amsterdam, ser. B.* 74:185-194.

Sartono, S. 1975. Implications arising from *Pithecanthropus* VIII, in: *Paleoanthropology, Morphology and Paleoecology* (R. H. Tuttle, Ed.), pp. 327-360. Mouton, The Hague.

Simpson, G. G. 1961. *Principles of Animal Taxonomy.* Columbia University, New York.

Smith, F. H. 1976. The Neandertal Remains from Krapina. A Descriptive Comparative Study. *The University of Tennessee Report of Investigations* No. 15, Knoxville.

Thorne, A. G. 1969. Preliminary Comments on the Kow Swamp skeleton. *Aust. Inst. Abor. Stud. Newsl.* 2:6-7.

Thorne, A. G. 1971. Mungo and Kow Swamp: Morphological variations in Pleistocene Australians. *Mankind* 8:85-89.

Thorne, A. G. 1976. Morphological variation in Pleistocene Australians, in: *The Origin of The Australians* (R. L. Kirk and A. G. Thorne, Eds.), pp. 95-112. Aust Inst. of Abor. Stud., Canberra.

Thorne, A. G. 1981. The centre and the edge: The significance of Australian hominids to African paleoanthropology, in: *Proceedings of the 8th Panafrican Congress of Prehistory and Quarternary Studies* (R. E. F. Leakey and B. A. Ogot, Eds.), pp. 180-181, T.I.L.L.M.I.A.P., Nairobi.

Thorne, A. G., and Macumber, P. G. 1972. Discoveries of late Pleistocene man at Kow Swamp, Australia. *Nature* (London) 238:316-319.

Weidenreich, F. 1943. The skull of *Sinanthropus pekinensis*: A comparative study of a primitive hominid skull. *Paleont. Sin.,* n. s. D, No. 10, pp. 1-484.

Weidenreich, F. 1946. *Apes, Giants and Man.* University of Chicago Press, Chicago and London.

Weidenreich, F. 1951. Morphology of Solo Man. *Anthrop. Papers Amer. Mus. Nat. Hist.* 43 (3).

45

The "Afro-European *sapiens*-Hypothesis" and Hominid Evolution in East Asia During the Late Middle and Upper Pleistocene

G. Bräuer

THE *SAPIENS* QUESTION

The last years have shown a rekindling of interest in the problems having to do with the *sapiens* question. This pertains to both the origin of archaic *Homo sapiens* as well as the evolution towards the anatomically modern subspecies, *Homo sapiens sapiens*. The primary reason behind this is the considerable increase in the number of hominid finds from the Old World; but criticism of the classic, mostly Eurocentric ideas has also grown.

On the basis of the Swanscombe and Steinheim hominids, it long appeared that the roots of anatomically modern *Homo sapiens* could be traced back in Europe as far as about 250,000 years B.P.; simultaneously, it was thought that Rhodesoid populations were spread throughout wide areas of Africa as recently as 30,000 years B.P. (Vallois 1949, 1954; Heberer 1950; Gieseler 1974). Coon (1962) once said: "If Africa was the cradle of mankind, it was only an indifferent kindergarten. Europe and Asia were our principal schools."

Today, this assumption enjoys little support. The Pre-*sapiens* hypothesis has become increasingly unlikely. There are no longer any real reasons to assume the existence of two parallel lines in Europe, one leading to the Neanderthals, and one, via Fontéchevade, to Cro-Magnon Man.

This is not the place for a detailed criticism of the Pre-*sapiens* hypothesis (cf. Bräuer 1981/83, 1984a, 1984b). At the present, the European hominids of the Middle and Upper Pleistocene can be best regarded as one line, characterized by a considerable variability, which led from the Ante-Neandertals, via the Pre-Neandertals (or early Neandertals), to the late Neandertals of the Würm (Howells 1978; De Lumley 1978; Hublin 1982).

Hence, the roots of the anatomically modern *Homo sapiens* of Europe must be found elsewhere. In this regard, the Near East has long been a focus for discussion (Howell 1951; Vandermeersch 1981). The results presently available, however, speak against anatomically modern man having originated in this area. There is thus a substantial morphological gap between the Neandertaloids of the Near East (Shanidar, Amud, Tabun) and the hominids from Qafzeh and Skhul, which are probably only

slightly younger (Farrand 1979; Jelinek 1982). The Qafzeh sample, moreover, encompasses already completely modern individuals; e.g. Qafzeh 9 (Vandermeersch 1981). Based upon facial morphology and the proportions of the extremities, Trinkaus (1981 a,b) provides some additional reasons arguing against a direct development of the Qafzeh/Skhul populations out of the Neandertaloids.

From the distribution of the Neanderthaloids, we know that there might have been gene flow to Northern Africa. Here, too, the populations which possessed Neandertaloid characteristics (e.g., Jebel Irhoud) were replaced during the Würm by anatomically modern populations (Dar-es-Soltan 5, the occipital from Témara), a fate shared with the Near Eastern Neandertals. Thus, for this western region, it is a valid question to ask whether anatomically modern *Homo sapiens* might not have originated in Africa.

Until the beginning of the 1970s, it was hardly possible to seriously consider such a likelihood. It was only with the drastic temporal expansion of the African Middle and Later Stone Age (Beaumont and Vogel 1972; Clark 1975, 1979, 1981; Deacon 1974) that a new period in the study of early *Homo sapiens* could begin. Moreover, there has been a considerable increase in the African Middle and Upper Pleistocene hominid material during the last years.

In the same way as our increased knowledge has led to the abandonment of the classical Pre-*sapiens* hypothesis, the traditional views about the Rhodesoids and the young age of the anatomically moderns from Africa have also fallen (Bräuer 1982a). The picture of the development of humans during the Middle and Upper Pleistocene in Africa has progressively come in need of revision, so that a reanalysis of all the collected hominid material has appeared ever more necessary.

During the past several years I have been able to carry out such a project and, based upon a comparative analysis of the hominid remains, to develop new ideas about the phylogenetic course during this time period.

Both the investigation and the findings of other authors concerning the European and Southwest Asian hominids (e.g. Stringer 1974, 1981; Vandermeersch 1978; Howells 1978; Wolpoff 1980a; Trinkaus 1981a) have led to a new phylogenetic hypothesis, which I named the "Afro-European *sapiens*-hypothesis," and first introduced at the "1er Congrés International de Paléontologie Humaine" in Nice in 1982 (Bräuer 1982b).

In the following sections, some of the main points of this hypothesis will be treated. More detailed presentations can be found in Bräuer (1983, 1984a).

THE AFRICAN HOMINIDS (500,000–30,000 YEARS B.P.)

An important element of any phylogenetic reconstruction is the dating of the hominids. Above the time span covered by the present C14-method, the datings become increasingly inaccurate. Yet in most cases various direct and indirect methods allow a more or less exact localization of the probable age of the hominid remains. Thus, many of the dates mentioned below should be considered as the most likely dates according to our present knowledge. Figure 1 presents an overview of the hominid sites.

According to the data currently available, Broken Hill and Hopefield most likely date from the middle to upper Middle Pleistocene (Klein 1973; Butzer 1979; Partridge 1982; Vrba 1982). The remains of several individuals from Klasies River Mouth and, probably, the hominids from Border Cave, belong

in the early Upper Pleistocene (Singer and Wymer 1982; De-Villiers 1976; Beaumont 1979, 1980). Recent investigations suggest that the Florisbad hominid could possess a similarly high or even greater age (Rightmire 1978; Beaumont *et al.* 1978; Butzer 1979; Partridge 1982).

The Bodo hominid dates from the Middle Pleistocene, probably from the middle to the upper part (Conroy *et al.* 1978; T. D. White, personal communication). A late Middle Pleistocene age appears more and more likely for the Eyasi hominids as Mehlman's (1984) recent work has indicated (cf. also Bräuer and Mehlman 1988). The Ndutu specimen also appears to date from the middle to upper Middle Pleistocene (M. Leakey and Hay 1982).

The hominids 1 and 2 recovered from the Omo Kibish Formation seem to date from the transition from the Middle to the Upper Pleistocene (Butzer *et al.* 1969; Day and Stringer 1982). Nitrogen and Uranium measurements (British Museum, N. H.) indicate that there are probably no substantial age differences between the two hominids, although they were found some 2.5 km apart (Leakey *et al.* 1969).

New U-series dates for Laetoli 18 indicate that this hominid also dates from the early Upper Pleistocene (Leakey and Hay 1982; Hay 1987). The long-known Singa skull might also possess an early Upper Pleistocene age, as based on new studies at Singa and Abu Hugar (Ziegert 1981). Finally, the

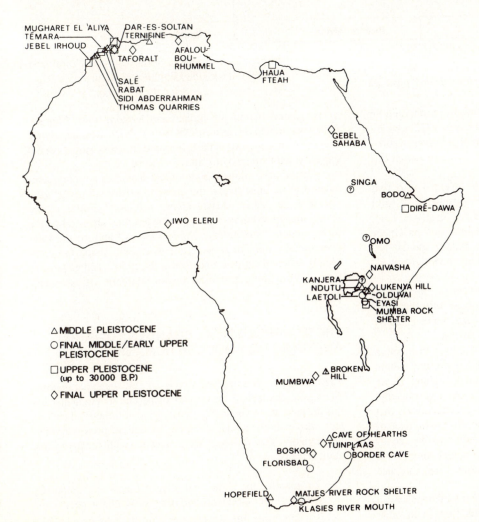

Figure 1. *Middle and Upper Pleistocene fossil hominid sites in Africa.*

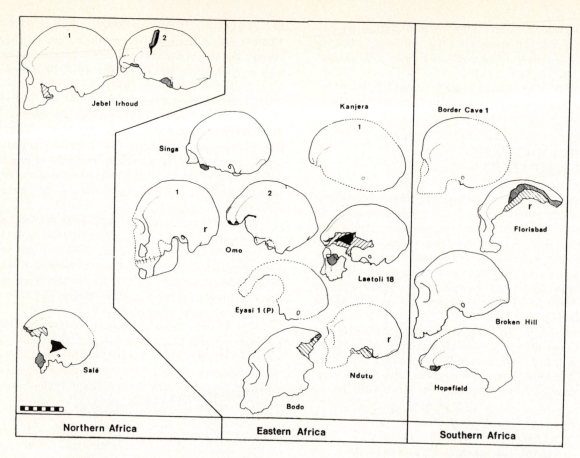

Figure 2. *The lateral views of the better preserved fossil hominids. The vertical ordering reflects their rough chronological positions.*

Kanjera remains most likely date from the early to the middle part of the Upper Pleistocene (L. S. B. Leakey 1972; Oakley 1974; R. Leakey 1981; Clark 1981). The probable ages of some other hominid remains from Eastern and Southern Africa can be taken from Figure 1.

The North African material can be divided into two chronological groups, a Middle Pleistocene group dating from between 500,000 and 200,000 years B.P. (Ternifine, Salé, Thomas Quarries, Sidi Abderrahman, Rabat), and an Upper Pleistocene group dating from between 60,000 and 30,000 years B.P. (Jebel Irhoud, Haua Fteah, Témara, Mugharet el' Aliya, Dar-es-Soltan 5).

While there is a considerable gap between the late Middle Pleistocene and the middle Upper Pleistocene with regard to Northern Africa, this important period is better represented by hominid remains in Eastern and Southern Africa.

Figure 2 shows the better preserved crania in a rough diachronic arrangement. The Rhodesoids, Bodo, and Ndutu indicate that robust populations of "early archaic *Homo sapiens*" (Kalb *et al.* 1982; Rightmire 1983) were spread from South Africa to at least as far as the Horn. It is also likely that there were connections to early archaic *Homo sapiens* of Europe, an assumption that is especially supported by the affinities between Bodo and Petralona. A principal components analysis based on facial measurements (Bräuer 1984a) has also underlined these similarities.

There follows—probably with some temporal distance—a number of morphologically heterogeneous finds with quite varying combinations of archaic and modern traits. This so-called heterogeneous group dates from the final Middle to early Upper Pleistocene. All of these hominids possess a great cranial capacity, with values lying above 1350 cc.

On the basis of the chronological sequence presently considered to be most likely, the question arises as to whether a spectrum of "early archaic *Homo sapiens*" similar to the Rhodesoid morphology can be considered as ancestral to the more modern "late archaic *Homo sapiens*" and, to the fully anatomically modern *Homo sapiens* as well. Using the completely different dating framework of the 1950's, and with fewer finds, Phillip Tobias proposed this for Southern Africa as early as 1956.

THE MORPHOLOGICAL CHANGES TOWARDS ANATOMICALLY MODERN HUMANS

The main aim of this investigation is to study the variability and diachronic changes of the cranial shape and its elements. For this purpose, up to about 100 metrical and non-metrical characters were examined, depending on the state of preservation of the remains. The variables were selected with regard to two main aspects:

1. To quantify the shape and size of the cranial bones by means of measurements and descriptive characters.

2. To determine the development of the phylogenetically

relevant superstructures by means of descriptive and, if possible, metrical characters.

In this section, the morphological changes from the archaic to the anatomically modern shape will be treated for some essential cranial regions. Distinct changes can be observed in the supraorbital region, the gracility or massivity of which primarily depends upon the masticating forces and the inclination of the frontal. The representatives of "early archaic *Homo sapiens*" (Bodo, Broken Hill 1, and Hopefield [see Plate 1]) exhibit strong affinities to one another in terms of the massive

tori. The torus is strongly developed, especially in the middle of the orbit, and slightly recessed in the region of the glabella. Towards the lateral processes, the torus generally becomes thinner. The tori of Eyasi and Ndutu are more gracile, but exhibit little lateral flattening. Due to the fragmentary states of preservation, however, their total shape cannot be diagnosed with certainty. It is quite probable that sexual dimorphism among archaic *Homo sapiens* is responsible for some of the observed variability.

The individuals of the heterogeneous group (Plate 1) reveal a considerable amount of variability, ranging from a supraorbi-

Plate 1. *The supraorbital regions of representatives of early archaic* Homo sapiens *and of the heterogeneous group (left: Bodo, Eyasi 1, Ndutu, Laetoli 18, Omo 1, Omo 2, Florisbad; right: Broken Hill 1, Hopefield, Petralona, Border Cave 1, Singa, Klasies River 16425, Kanjera 1); each side from top to bottom.*

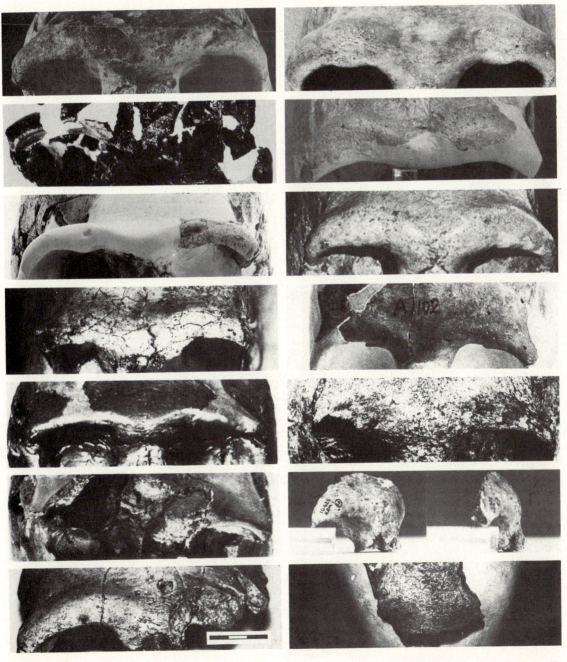

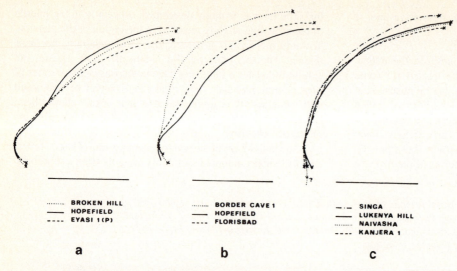

a　　　　　**b**　　　　　**c**

Figure 3. *The mid-sagittal curves of the frontals of some fossil hominids (orientated where possible to the Frankfurt Plane).*

tal torus running continuously above the orbits to the anatomically modern form. Laetoli 18 possesses the most torus-like shape. The strongly developed supraorbital region is interrupted in the glabella area; both parts exhibit little lateral flattening. In this aspect, the torus formation appears similar to that of Eyasi

1, but is considerably less projecting than those of the representatives of early archaic *Homo sapiens*.

The supraorbital region of Florisbad is also torus-like, although more gracile and less projecting than that of Laetoli. In spite of its plainly more modern overall frontal shape, Border

Figure 4. *A principal components analysis based upon frontal variables. PC I represents 46.5% and PC II 35.6% of the total variance. Variables: Glabella-bregma arc, glabella-bregma chord, glabella bregma subtense, glabela subtense fraction, frontal angle (FRA, but above the glabella-bregma chord), minimum frontal breadth. The comparative sample encompasses some 40 individuals, from various parts of Africa, dating to the final Upper Pleistocene (ca. 20,000-10,000 years B.P.) (see Bräuer 1984).*

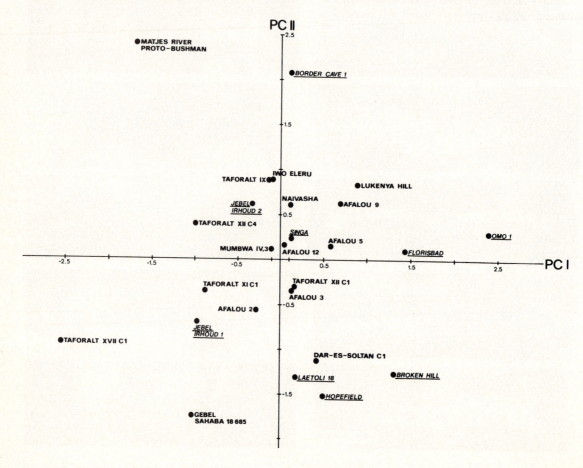

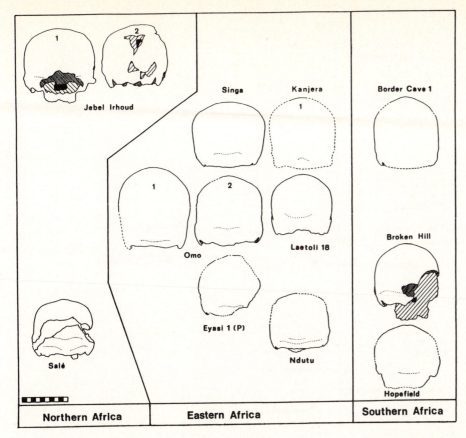

Northern Africa | **Eastern Africa** | **Southern Africa**

Figure 5. *The occipital views of the better preserved fossil hominids. The vertical ordering reflects their rough chronological positions.*

Cave 1 also shows certain reminiscences of a torus; it is not possible to clearly separate the arch and the trigone. The supraorbital margin is also strikingly broad and rounded in comparison th that of anatomically modern humans.

Omo 2's supraorbital region is more robust but also more similar to the modern type. In spite of its fragmentary nature, the prominent arch can be separated from the more flattened but robust supraorbital trigone. The supraorbital regions of the remaining hominids (Omo 1, Singa, Klasies River Mouth 16425), and Kanjera 1) fall within the anatomically modern range of variation. The same holds for Kanjera 3, which is not shown on Plate 1.

Another important characteristic of the heterogeneous group is the stronger transverse expansion of the frontal in the postorbital region as compared to early archaic *Homo sapiens*. Even hominids as robust as Omo 2, Laetoli 18, and Florisbad fall within the anatomically modern range of variation. In contrast, the representatives of early archaic *Homo sapiens* exhibit an obviously greater degree of postorbital constriction.

In their mid-sagittal frontal profiles (Fig. 3), the Rhodesoids strongly resemble one another. They exhibit a well developed glabella torus and a flattened curvature. Bodo (cf. Fig. 2) has a very similar shape. Florisbad's curvature reveals remarkable similarities to that of Hopefield, although the inclination of the frontal is somewhat greater with Florisbad when one tries to orientate it to the Frankfurt Plane. The affinities between Singa, Kanjera 1, and the two final Upper Pleistocene finds from Lukenya Hill and Naivasha are also remarkable.

In order to gain a more complex view of the affinities of the frontal morphology among the different hominids, a principal components analysis was carried out (Fig. 4). This analysis made use of 6 measurements of the frontal.

The first two principal components already account for more than 80% of the total variance. The first component may primarily represent a size factor, while the second reflects more the differences in the curvature of the frontal. Here, the spectrum reaches from the very flat frontals of Hopefield and Broken Hill 1 to the strongly rounded frontal of Border Cave 1.

Laetoli 18 clearly exhibits distinct affinities to the Rhodesoid frontal shape. The frontals of two final Upper Pleistocene individuals are also very flat (Dar-es-Soltan 1, Gebal Sahaba 18685). In spite of their great dimensions, the second component shows that Florisbad and Omo 1 show clear relationships to the spectrum of the anatomically modern specimens.

With regard to both components, Singa clearly falls among the Afalou individuals. Border Cave 1 exhibits remarkable relationships to the so called "Proto-Bushman" skull from the Matjes River Cave (South Africa), which has a very strangely curved frontal. This may perhaps show that Border Cave possessed Proto-Khoisanoid features, despite this early date (cf. Rightmire 1979).

Concerning the parietals (Fig. 5), the Rhodesoids and Ndutu do not exhibit the tent-like forms typical of *Homo erectus*. They rather have more strongly expanded parietals, which closely resemble the modern shape. The same holds for the occipital views of Laetoli 18 and Omo 1.

Omo 2 shows some slight upward convergence, but this trait can also be found with representatives of the Afalou sample (e.g., Afalou 2).

Fig. 6 shows the result of a Principal components analysis using sagittal and transversal dimensions of the parietals. On the left are the representatives of early archaic *Homo sapiens* and the heterogeneous group, on the right the anatomically

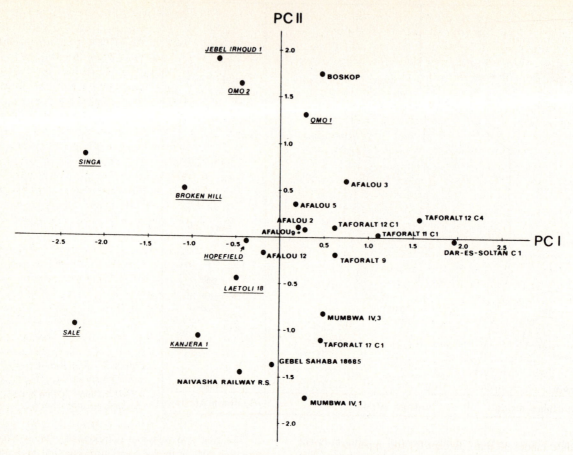

Figure 6. *A principal components analysis based upon parietal variables. PC I represents 61.7% and PC II 19.0% of the total variance. Variables: Maximum cranial breadth, parietal arc, parietal chord, parietal subtense, bregma subtense fraction, parietal angle (PAA).*

modern specimens which were used for comparison. The strong affinities between Hopefield and the anatomically modern spectrum are remarkable. Laetoli 18 also possesses a similar position. Kanjera 1 occupies an even more marginal position. The two Omo hominids exhibit certain affinities to one another. Singa and Salé differ greatly from all of the other individuals. With both of the hominids, it may be that pathological changes are at least partially responsible for this fact.

The occipitals of the hominids treated here show great variability, both in terms of the angulation between the nuchal and the squamal part and the border of the nuchal plane. The

Rhodesoids possess a distinct angulation (Fig. 7). Ndutu has a somewhat more rounded profile. With its chord-arc index of 75.0, it also lies below the examined final Upper Pleistocene finds (the lowest value is 79.0, the highest 87.0)

The torus development differs considerably among the Rhodesoids. The most marked torus—although not completely preserved medially–is probably that of Broken Hill 1. This prominent torus, which is curved slightly downwards, procedes to the occipitomastoid suture, where it merges into the mastoid crest. With Hopefield, however, the marked torus is limited to a medal part some 6 cm. long. The torus of Eyasi 1, which is

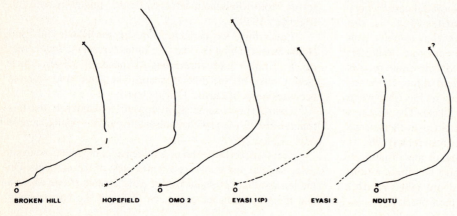

Figure 7. *A comparison of the mid-sagittal curves of the occipitals of some fossil hominids.*

only very slightly developed, is also restricted to the medial part of the occipital. Ndutu, finally, exhibits yet a differently expressed occipital torus. While this torus is again most strongly developed in the medial part, it is not characterized by a strong dorsal projection, but by a considerable height of about 1.6 cm. in the mid-sagittal plane.

The closest affinities to the Rhodesoid occipital form are exhibited by Omo 2. The opisthocranion coincides with the inion on the highly set torus. In profile, the supratoral and nuchal parts follow almost straight courses and from a clear angle with one another. The value of the chord-arc index is 72.0. Again we find that the thickening of the torus is essentially restricted to the medial portion. Among the remaining finds of the heterogeneous group from Eastern and Southern Africa, only Laetoli 18 has a distinct torus morphology. The occipital, which is fragmentary in the lower nuchal part, is not, however, angled, but rather flat and rounded, as with anatomically modern humans (Figs. 2, 5). The moderately developed torus is restricted to the central part and does not project dorsally.

With the remaining finds of the heterogeneous group, the development at the border of the nuchal plane—insofar as it is preserved—falls within the modern range of variation. The occipitals of these hominids are also not angulated. Based on its value for the chord-arc index (81.5), Omo 1 falls in the centre of the modern spectrum, while Kanjera 1 and Singa, with their relatively large arc-lengths, lie near the lower limit of the modern sample (see Bräuer 1984a).

The mastoid processes are also relatively long in the representatives of early archaic *Homo sapiens;* e.g. Broken Hill 1 and Ndutu (about 30 mm). Except for the apparently female hominid Laetoli 18, with a mastoid length of only 20.0 mm., the mastoid processes of the other representatives of the heterogeneous group fall within the modern range of variation. The same holds for the strongly developed processes of the two Omo hominids (Fig. 2).

The previous discussion of the morphology of the cranial vault has shown that a number of the representatives of the heterogeneous group exhibits individually very different mosaic-like combinations of archaic and modern features. The same holds for some other descriptive and metrical characteristics, as shown elsewhere (Bräuer, 1984a). Especially Omo 2, Laetoli 18, and Florisbad exhibit characteristics which may go back to early archaic *Homo sapiens.* Hence, there is little reason to doubt that these individuals come from populations which belong to the line from early archaic to anatomically modern *Homo sapiens.* As it is particularly these three hominids which hold a certain intermediate position with regard to morphology, they might, therefore, also be regarded as representatives of the "late archaic *Homo sapiens.*" Such an assignment to a more developed "grade" of archaic *Homo sapiens* does not, however, mean that the mosaic-like pattern could not have also been the result of mixing between populations of the still little known "late archaic *Homo sapiens*" and early anatomically modern humans.

Let us now turn to facial morphology. Here, the number of available remains is comparatively small. Nevertheless, it is still possible to make some important statements about both the representatives of early archaic *Homo sapiens* and the heterogeneous group. Bodo and Broken Hill 1 provide an example of the robust facial morphology of the male representatives of early archaic *Homo sapiens.* The upper facial

heights of these two hominids lie well above the variation shown by the final Upper Pleistocene sample. The subspinal part is longer with Broken Hill 1 than with Bodo. In the mid-facial region, however, Bodo is considerably broader. Bodo's zygomatic bones are situated more anteriorly while Broken Hill 1's are transversely arranged and located more posteriorly. Concerning the mid-facial width, Broken Hill 1 actually falls within the range of variation of the anatomically modern sample. The same holds for the nasal index. Both hominids lack a canine fossa, but Broken Hill 1 does exhibit a slight convexity in the region below the infraorbital foramen. A principal components analysis based on 8 facial measurements (Bräuer 1984a) has underscored the general morphological affinities between Bodo and Broken Hill 1.

With Ndutu, an apparently female representative of early archaic *Homo sapiens*, only parts of the maxilla have been preserved. The face may have been more gracile. The nasal width measures only 27 mm. The zygomatic process is strongly curved and laterally directed. The area around the infraorbital foramen might indicate a slight concavity in the middle face.

While these three hominids exhibit a considerable variability and differ strongly from the anatomically modern facial morphology, the existing mid-facial regions of the representatives of the heterogeneous group show quite close connections to the anatomically modern range of variation. However, Florisbad in connection with its broad frontal also possesses a great biorbital breadth, the value of which corresponds closely to that of Bodo. In contrast, the mid-facial region is much more gracile and features a distinct canine fossa (Plate 2).

Plate 2 also shows a combination of the left half of the maxilla of Laetoli 18 and the maxillary fragment of Broken Hill 2. Both hominids show striking affinities to one another in the development of the canine fossae. The zygomatic processes are directed transversely. In the subnasal part, Laetoli 18 exhibits a marked prognathism. Concerning Broken Hill 2, it is uncertain whether this hominid and hominid 1 (from the same site) date from a similar period (cf. Wells 1947). If they do, then they could provide evidence of a great degree of variability in the formation of the maxillary sinus, perhaps comparable to Arago 21 and Steinheim. The small maxillary or zygomatic fragments of Omo 1, Border Cave 1, Klasies River Mouth, and Kanjera 1 fall within the anatomically modern range of variation. Thus, the overall upper facial morphology places the heterogeneous group still closer to anatomically modern *Homo sapiens.*

Finally, the mandibular remains will also be briefly treated here (cf Bräuer 1984a). The following mandibular remains from Eastern and Southern Africa date to the final Middle or early Upper Pleistocene: Border Cave 2,3,5; Klasies River Mouth 41815, 13400, 21776, 14695, 16424; Omo 1; and the dental remains from Mumba Shelter. According to the studies by DeVilliers (1973, 1976), the Border Cave mandibles fall, metrically and non-metrically within the range of recent variation. Our studies were able to completely corroborate the anatomically modern morphology (Plate 3). Morphologically, the mandibular remains from the early MSA deposits at Klasies River Mouth appear somewhat more heterogeneous (Plate 3). Concerning the oldest (about 120,000 years B.P.), well-preserved mandible, No. 41815, there may be no doubts about its affiliation to a.m. *Homo sapiens* (cf, Singer and Wymer 1982). The chin region is well developed and has a prominent protuberantia mentalis. There is no planum alveolare. Metrically, the corpus

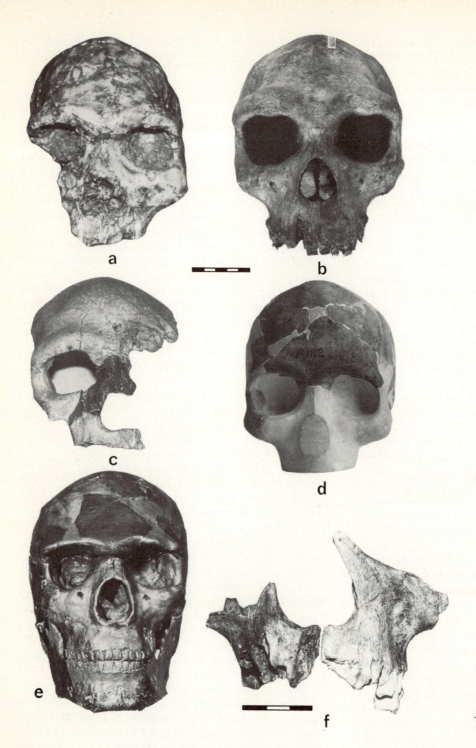

Plate 2. *a) Bodo; b) Broken Hill 1;*
c) Florisbad; d) Border Cave 1;
e) Omo 1 (photograph by M.H. Day);
f) left: Broken Hill 2; right: Laetoli 18
(photograph by C. B. Stringer).

falls within the anatomically modern spectrum of variation. Of the four remaining fragments which have been dated to between 120,000 and 95,000 years B.P., Nos. 21776 and 16424 can, with high probability, be regarded as anatomically modern (Singer and Wymer 1982; Bräuer 1984a). The body fragment of 21776 possesses a mentum osseum. While this body piece is relatively robustly built, No. 16424 exhibits an extreme gracility in both the body and the teeth (Plate 3). The body height at M1 is only about 20 mm. and thus lies below the observed range of the final Upper Pleistocene sample. The female mandible may be taken as an indication that there was considerable sexual dimorphism even among these early anatomically modern populations.

Measurements indicate that the body fragment no. 13400 falls within the range of anatomically modern variation, although it also exhibits some possibly archaic features (Plate 3). Despite a slight subalveolar depression, the mentum osseum is only weakly developed. If it is not assumed that this expression nevertheless belongs to the anatomically modern spectrum, then it could be possible that this individual might come from a population living during the transitional period from late archaic to anatomically modern *Homo sapiens*. It is also possible that the small symphyseal fragment no. 14695, which apparently featured a weakly developed chin, belongs to this spectrum as well.

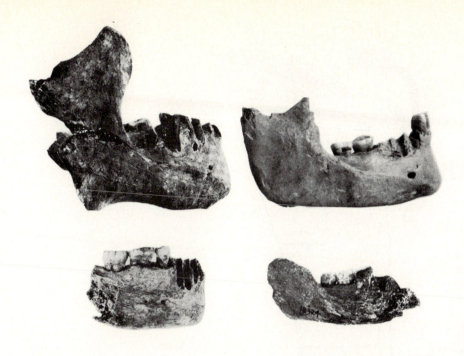

Plate 3. *a)-c) Klasies River 41815, 13400, 16424 (from Singer and Wymer 1982); d) Border Cave 5.*

Eastern Africa has yielded only a very few mandibular fragments dating from this period of time. Here, the fragments of Omo 1 are particularly worthy of mention (Fig. 2, Plate 2). These comprise most of the right ramus with the adjacent portion of the body and the chin region. Metrically, the ramus falls well within the Afalou spectrum. The same holds for the chin region, which possesses a well-developed trigonum mentale. There is no reason to question the anatomically modern morphology of this mandible.

As we can see from these examples from our comparative morphological analysis of vault and face, the spectrum of variation of the heterogeneous group is quite large. Practically all of the individuals exhibit distinct affinities to the cranial morphology of anatomically modern *Homo sapiens*. Although some hominids might be considered as late archaic *Homo sapiens* with regard to their more archaic features, and others as anatomically modern *Homo sapiens,* it is neither possible nor meaningful to see or look for direct lines of evolution within the heterogeneous group. The uncertainties concerning the dating of most of the hominids are too large for this. The morphological spectrum shown by the heterogeneous group can currently be best understood as the result of a network of mixtures between late archaic and early anatomically modern populations of *Homo sapiens.*

THE AFRO-EUROPEAN *SAPIENS*-HYPOTHESIS

The hominid material from Northern (especially North-Western) Africa, which has not been treated here in detail (see Bräuer 1984a), includes only a very few remains of the vault and upper face. Moreover, there is a considerable chronological gap between the Middle Pleistocene and the Upper Pleistocene specimens. The upshot is that there is no sufficient basis for connecting the changes that occurred here (found essentially in the mandibles) with the developments of the skull in Eastern and Southern Africa. Only further cranial finds from Northern

Africa can provide a better basis for evaluating all of the current, extremely hypothetical ideas on the kind of relations which existed between North and sub-Saharan Africa.

The middle to late Upper Pleistocene finds from Northern Africa, e.g., the Jebel Irhoud hominids, when considered in the light of the fossil finds from Eastern and Southern Africa, indicate that it is highly unlikely that a direct development to anatomically modern *Homo sapiens* took place in this northwestern part of Africa. For populations with Neandertaloid characteristics (e.g., Mugharet el' Aliya) were still living there some 30,000 years ago, while, much earlier, anatomically modern humans had already spread throughout sub-Saharan Africa. Thus, for Africa, the present hominid record makes it appear very probable that the development from archaic to anatomically modern *Homo sapiens* took place in Eastern and/or Southern Africa.

According to the dates which are currently the most probable, and on the basis of our numerous morphological and statistical studies of the African hominid material, we have undertaken a new reconstruction of the course evolution took in Africa. Yet the "Afro-European *sapiens*-hypothesis" (Bräuer, 1982a) was also developed with regard to the new findings of European and Southwest Asian hominids. This hypothesis relates the evolution on the two continents (Fig. 8).

The hypothesis can be summarized along three main points:

1. From parts of the early archaic *Homo sapiens*, represented by Bodo, Broken Hill 1, Ndutu and others, via late archaic forms, the early anatomically modern *Homo sapiens* evolved in Eastern and/or Southern Africa. This apparently took place during the late Middle Pleistocene.

2. Early anatomically modern *Homo sapiens*, represented by Omo 1, Singa, Klasies River, Border Cave, and other finds, may have already been widely spread throughout Africa in the early Upper Pleistocene.

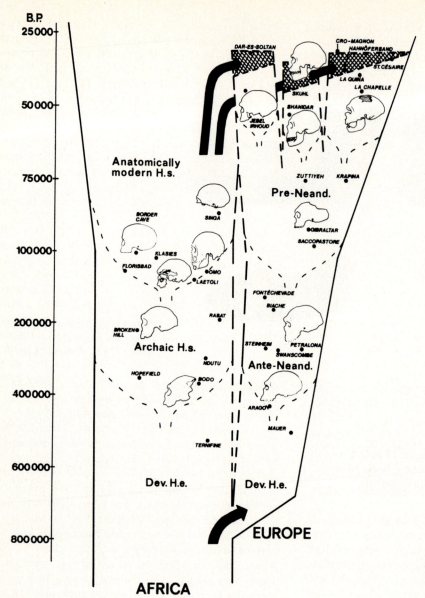

Figure 8. *The phylogenetic scheme of the "Afro-European sapiens-hypothesis."*

3. During the Würm glaciation, anatomically modern humans expanded farther into the North—apparently moving out of Eastern Africa. In both the Near East and Northern Africa, there followed an intermediate period of mixing, after which these forms caused the disappearance of the Neandertaloid populations which had been living there. During the next millennia—in what was probable a relatively slow process of hybridization and replacement—they also superseded the European Neandertals.

The phylogenetic line suggested by this hypothesis may be divided into two parts. The main part relates to Africa. Supported by relatively large number of finds, it indicates that anatomically modern humans had already developed in Africa at a time in which, in Europe, the developments which would eventually lead to the late, classic Neandertals had just begun.

If we do not hold to the assumption that Cro-Magnon man developed in Eastern Asia and expanded from there to Europe—a possibility which cannot be made to conform to the available hominid (see below)—then the second assumption of

the "Afro-European *sapiens* hypothesis" suggests that the anatomically modern humans of Europe ultimately came from Africa. Apart from this conclusion, which is based on the present fossil record and the chronological framework, there are also a number of other direct and indirect lines of evidence which either support this assumption or at least indicate that it is possible.

An important key fossil is Omo 1 (Plate 2). Although there are still some uncertainties as to the dating, this hominid is doubtlessly older than the anatomically modern *Homo sapiens* of the Near East or Europe. As shown above, Omo 1 exhibits strong morphological similarities to the Afalou type of North Africa, which basically represents a Cro-Magnoid type. Close morphological relationships between Omo 1 and the Cro-Magnoid representatives of the European Upper Paleolithic were also found by Day and Stringer (1982). It is a very improbable assumption that this modern morphotype arose twice—once some 100,000 years B.P. in Eastern Africa out of non-Neandertals, and again some 50,000 years later from Neandertals living in (perhaps) South West Asia.

Paleoclimatological findings indicate that population migrations, especially in Northern Africa, were not just possible during the early part of the Würm but were, in fact, likely because of frequent changes of arid and humid periods (Sarnthein, personal communication). Boaz *et al.* (1982) assume that the repeated increases in the desertification of the area and the eventuating shortages of resources probably resulted in population pressures among the hunter-gatherer populations living in parts of Western Asia and the area known today as the Sahara. This might have led to an expansion into the colder, but more productive steppe and tundra regions of Western Asia and Europe.

Today, it also seems clear that Cro-Magnon man can no longer be regarded as a morphotype related only to the Upper Paleolithic, but that his origin and early distribution took place during the Middle Paleolithic (Stringer 1982). Thus, the early anatomically modern humans of the Near East (e.g., Qafzeh) are linked with the Mousterian. In Europe, there are also indications of such an association (Staroselye).

Before this hypothesis was advanced, a number of specialists—usually referring to single finds—had pointed to the possibility that anatomically modern humans were present early in Africa and that they had spread from there to other continents. Such statements were made especially in connection with the revised dates for the Border Cave specimens (De Villiers 1973; Protsch 1975; Beaumont *et al.* 1978). Stringer (1974) considered the possibility of connections between Omo 1 and the anatomically modern Europeans. Such suppositions provided some of the impetus for our investigations of the African hominid material. Further studies are of course necessary to verify and elaborate the phylogenetic scheme proposed here. New hominid finds will be helpful in doing this.

THE CONNECTIONS TO EASTERN ASIA

If one considers the "Afro-European *sapiens*-hypothesis" to be a likely explanation for the more recent hominid evolution in the western part of the Old World, then a question arises: How can the developments which took place in Eastern Asia be reconciled with this hypothesis?

Two basic, contrary models are conceivable:

1. Anatomically modern *Homo sapiens* developed out of the East Asian *Homo erectus*, via archaic *Homo sapiens*; i.e., for the most part independently of the developments in Europe and Africa.

2. The comparatively early anatomically modern hominids in Africa could point to a basically monocentric transition from archaic to anatomically modern *Homo sapiens*. In this view, the East Asian archaic *Homo sapiens* was genetically replaced (like the *Homo sapiens neanderthalensis* in Europe and Western Asia) by anatomically modern populations whose origins ultimately lie in Africa.

There are numerous possible variants to these two basic models. For the first model, these variants have to do with the area in which anatomically modern *Homo sapiens* originated. Did he develop in the northern part; e.g., via *Homo sapiens daliensis*, or farther to the south, via *Homo sapiens soloensis*, or can we assume a parallel evolution in both parts of East Asia?

With the replacement model, the possible variants have to do with the extent of hybridization between the anatomically modern *Homo sapiens* coming from the West and the local, as yet unknown East Asian populations of archaic *Homo sapiens* which developed from the subspecies "*daliensis*" and "*soloensis*." On the one hand, it can be assumed that the anatomically modern *Homo sapiens* effected a nearly complete replacement of the local autochthonous populations; i.e., without any essential mixing. On the other hand, one can imagine that the gene pools of the different subspecies of *Homo sapiens* mixed more or less intensively, so that a certain regional morphological continuity can also be assumed. Thus, it is quite possible large proportions of local genes could have been preserved in several regions into the Holocene.

This second variant, which can be described as the "hybridization and replacement model" clearly demonstrates that it is nearly impossible to distinguish between this variant and the first model, which postulates local regional continuity when only isolated hominid finds are considered. Here we can see the difficulties associated with attempts to find out modes of evolution by analyzing the fossil hominids from a limited area. This is especially true when seeking proof of regional continuity.

After these more general considerations, let us turn briefly to the fossil record of Eastern Asia (Fig. 9). Among the representatives of archaic *Homo sapiens* from China, the hominids from Dali and Maba are of special importance. Both crania clearly differ from both anatomically modern *Homo sapiens* and *Homo erectus pekinensis*. The Dali hominid exhibits massively developed supraorbital tori—nearly comparable to those of Broken Hill 1—, a flat frontal with central sagittal keeling, and a generally robust cranial vault with an angulated occipital and a marked nuchal torus. The postorbital constriction, however, is slighter than that of the "*erectus*" specimens from Zhoukoudian; the parietals are also transversely more expanded (Wu 1981). The face is low and flat and exhibits a canine fossa.

This hominid, which was discovered in 1978, casts new light on the Maba cranium, which had long stood as an isolated find. This hominid, usually classified as Neandertaloid (e.g., Howells 1967) also exhibits specific affinities to the Dali cranium, which can by no means be considered as Neandertaloid (Wu and Wu 1982). In North and central East Asia, there are no more well-preserved cranial remains until the late Upper Pleistocene; these later finds are unequivocally anatomically modern. Hominid remains dated to the early and middle Upper Pleistocene, which would be helpful to the understanding of the connections between archaic and modern *Homo sapiens*, are extremely rare. They consist of isolated teeth from Dingcun (=Tingtsun), a small maxillary fragment found near Changyang, and some vault fragments from Xujiayao, some of which are infantile (Zhou *et al.* 1982). Thus, the present hominid record exhibits a considerable gap between archaic and anatomically modern *Homo sapiens*. When considering the questions of "local evolution" or "certain degrees of replacement," then any conclusions which may be reached can only be based upon the later, anatomically modern finds from the final Upper Pleistocene.

Well preserved crania from this time period come from the Upper Cave at Zhoukoudian as well as from Liujiang (=Liukiang) and Ziyang (=Tzeyang). Opinions differ as to the extent of Mongoloid features shown by these skulls (Coon 1962; Thoma 1964; Howells 1983). However, it is agreed that

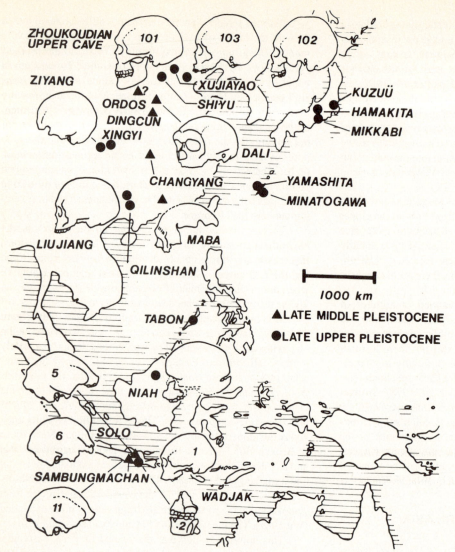

ZHOUKOUDIAN UPPER CAVE

101   103   102

ZIYANG

ORDOS
DINGCUN
XINGYI

XUJIAYAO
SHIYU

KUZUÜ
HAMAKITA
MIKKABI

DALI

CHANGYANG

YAMASHITA
MINATOGAWA

LIUJIANG

MABA

QILINSHAN

1000 km

TABON

▲ LATE MIDDLE PLEISTOCENE

● LATE UPPER PLEISTOCENE

5

NIAH

6   SOLO   1

SAMBUNGMACHAN

11

WADJAK

.2

Figure 9. *Late Middle and Upper Pleistocene fossil hominid sites in East Asia.*

these skulls differ in important characteristics from the living Mongoloids (Woo 1958; Schwidetzky 1979; Wolpoff 1980b).

The three crania from the Upper Cave, described in detail by Weidenreich (1939) and now dated absolutely to 10,500–18,300 years B.P., are considerably more robust than the skulls of living Mongoloids. The male skull no. 101 is flat and long, with a receding frontal, markedly developed superciliary arches, and low orbits. Several authors (e.g., Thoma 1964) have pointed to general affinities to the Cro-Magnon type. The Liujiang specimen exhibits a similarly robust morphology (Chang 1962), and even the female skull from Ziyang has well developed superciliary arches and prominent supramastoid crests. The recently described fossil calvaria from Huanglong County, which probably dates to the late Upper Pleistocene, has a high vault and a modern supraorbital region. However, there are also some affinities to a more archaic *Homo s. sapiens* (Wang 1983; Wang and Bräuer 1984). According to Suzuki (1981), the Japanese finds from Minatogawa also reveal similarities to this Chinese spectrum. Although some of these finds exhibit characteristics (e.g., the sagittal keeling, a certain degree of flatness of the middle face, shovel-shaped incisors, etc.) which could be interpreted as supporting an East Asian line (Wolpoff *et al.* 1984), these late Upper Pleistocene finds nevertheless differ

considerably in their overall appearance from the recent Mongoloids. These differences point towards a more undifferentiated, archaeomorphic type of anatomically modern *Homo sapiens*, a type which has morphological similarities to both early anatomically modern finds from western areas as well as to the Ainu. Even if one designates these East Asian specimens, which belong to the final Upper Pleistocene and some of them, perhaps, even to the early Holocene (Zhou *et al.* 1982), as Proto-Mongoloids (Woo 1959; Wu 1961), the possibility that a considerable portion of the gene pool is due to gene flow from the West or South-West, respectively, cannot be ruled out.

For South-East Asia, there is a similar large temporal gap between the Ngandong sample, which dates to the late Middle or early Upper Pleistocene (Jacob 1981; Sartono 1982), and the early anatomically modern finds. The oldest representative of these moderns may, perhaps, be the Niah skull. The ca. 40,000 years B.P. date for this find is, however, contested (Wolpoff 1980b). Brothwell (1960) found similarities between this juvenile female skull and the Australoids. The Wadjak hominids and the remains from Tabon probably also belong to this morphological spectrum (Jacob 1967). In its markedly developed supraorbital region and its frontal profile, the Tabon frontal appears to be quite similar to Upper Cave No. 101 (Wolpoff *et* al. 1984). The authors also point to general similarities between Wadjak 1 and Liujiang. These findings thus seem to point to a wide distribution of these early archaeomorphic populations of anatomically modern *Homo sapiens*. As Santa Luca (1980) has shown, there are considerable morphological differences between these moderns and the Ngandong specimens.

The sparse finds which fill the gap between the archaic and the anatomically modern *Homo sapiens* provide no definitive answer to the question as to whether anatomically modern humans developed monocentrically or polycentrically. The gaps are too large in both North and South Eastern Asia. Gene flow seems to be a plausible explanation for the morphological similarities between the early anatomically modern finds in the East and West of the Old World. Thus, the "hybridization and replacement model" appears to best agree with the facts, as it assumes that there were differentially mixed gene pools, moreover, it can also explain the presence of regional diachronic trends. Von Koenigswald (1982) considered it very unlikely that there was a direct line from Peking Man to the Mongoloid race. As he put it: "Wir dürfen aber annehmen, daß die großen Rassenkreise der heutigen Menschheit noch in wechselndem Ausmaß bestimmte Merkmalskomplexe zeigen, die bereits in früher Zeit geprägt worden sind" (1982:51).

ACKNOWLEDGMENTS

I would like to thank Dr. P. Andrews and Dr. J. Franzen for their invitation to present this paper at this Memorial Symposium in honor of the late G. H. R. Von Koenigswald, whose discussions with me about *sapiens* evolution proved valuable during my research. I an also grateful to the Werner Reimers—Stiftung, Bad Homburg, and the Stiftung Volkswagenwerk, Hanover, for supporting me.

I would like to thank Professor Phillip Tobias most sincerely for encouraging me, in 1977, to undertake this project; furthermore, for his indispensable support, especially during the initial phase of the investigations in Africa.

My sincere thanks go also to the persons who so kindly allowed me to study the hominid material under their care: C. K. Brain (Pretoria), Y. Coppens (Paris), M. H. Day (London). H. de Lumley (Paris), J. L. Heim (Paris), Q. B. Hendey (Cape Town), R. E. Leakey (Nairobi), C. Magori (Dar-es-Salaam), H. Oberholzer (Bloemfontein), C. B. Stringer (London), P. V. Tobias (Johannesburg), T. D. White (Berkeley).

This investigation would not have been possible without the continuous and generous support of the Deutsche Forschungsgemeinschaft, for which I am particularly grateful.

REFERENCES

Beaumont, P. B. 1979. Comment to: Rightmire, G. P. (1979). *Curr. Anthrop.* 20:26-27.

Beaumont, P. B. 1980. On the age of Border Cave Hominids 1-5. *Palaeont. Afr.* 23:21-33.

Beaumont, B. P., DeVilliers, H., and Vogel, J. C. 1978. Modern man in Sub–Saharan Africa prior to 49,0000 years B.P.: A review and evaluation, with particular reference to Border Cave. *S. Afr. J. Sci.* 74:409-419.

Beaumont, P. B., and Vogel, J. C. 1972. On a new radiocarbon chronology for Africa south of the Equator. *African Studies* 31:65-89, 155-182.

Boaz, N. T., Ninkovich, D., and Rossignol-Strick, M. 1982. Paleoclimatic setting for *Homo sapiens neanderthalensis*. *Naturwissenschaften* 69:29-33.

Bräuer, G. (1981–1983). Der Stirnbeinfund von Hahnöfersand—und einige Aspekte zur Neandertalerproblematik. *Hammaburg* 6:15-28.

Bräuer, G. 1982a. Current problems and research on the origin of *Homo sapiens* in Africa. *Humanbiol. Budapestinensis* 9:69-78.

Bräuer, G. 1982b. Early anatomically modern man in Africa and the replacement of the Mediterranean and European Neandertals. *Ier Congr. Intern. Paléont. Hum.*, p. 112 (Abstract). C.N.R.S., Nice.

Bräuer, G. 1983. Vom archaischen zum anatomisch modernen *Homo sapiens* in Afrika. *Habilitationsschrift*, Hamburg.

Bräuer, G. 1984a. A craniological approach to the origin of anatomically modern *Homo sapiens* in Africa and implications for the appearance of modern Europeans, in: *The Origins of Modern Humans* (F. H. Smith and F. Spencer, Eds.), pp. 327-410, Liss, New York.

Bräuer, G. 1984b. Prasapiens-Hypothese oder Afro-europäische Sapiens-Hypothese? *Z. Morph. Anthrop.* 75:1-25.

Bräuer, G., and Mehlman, M. J. 1988. Hominid molars from a Middle Stone Age level at Mumba Rock Shelter, Tanzania. *Am. J. Phys. Anthrop.* 75:69-76.

Brothwell, D. R. 1960. Upper Pleistocene human skull from Niah caves, Sarawak. *J. Sarawak Mus.* 9:323-349.

Butzer, K. W. 1979. Comment to: Rightmire, G. P. (1979). *Curr. Anthrop.* 20:28.

Butzer, K. W., Brown, F.H., and Thurber, D. L. 1969. Horizontal sediments of the Lower Omo Valley: Kibish Formation. *Quaternaria* 11:15-29.

Chang Kwangchi, 1962. New evidence on fossil man in China. *Science* 136:749-760.

Clark, J. D. 1975. Africa in prehistory: Peripheral or paramount? *Man* 10:175-198.

Clark, J. D. 1979. Radiocarbon dating and African archaeology, in: *Radiocarbon Dating* (R. Berger and H. E. Suess, Eds.), pp. 7-31, University of California Press, Berkeley.

Clark, J. D. 1981. Prehistory in southern Africa, in: *General History of Africa: I. Methodology and African Prehistory* (J. KI-Zebro, Ed.), pp. 487-529, UNESCO, Berkeley.

Conroy, G. C., Jolly, C. J., Cramer, D., and Kalb, J. E. 1978. Newly discovered fossil hominid skull from the Afar Depression, Ethiopia, *Nature* 276:67-70.

Coon, C. S. 1962. *The Origin of Races*. Knopf, New York.

Day, M. H., and Stringer, C. B. 1982. A reconsideration of the Omo Kibish remains and the *erectus-sapiens* transition. *Ier Congr. Internat. Paléont. Hum.*, pp. 814-846 (Prétirage). C.N.R.S., Nice.

Deacon, J. 1974. Patterning in the radiocarbon dates for the Wilton/Smithfield complex in Southern Africa. *S. Afr. Archaeol. Bull.* 29:3-18.

De Lumley, M. A. 1978. Les Anténéandertaliens, in: *Les Origines Humaines et les Epoques de l'Intelligence* (F. Bordes, Ed.), pp. 159-182, Masson, Paris.

De Villiers, H. 1973. Human skeletal remains from Border Cave, Ingwawuma District, KwaZulu, South Africa. *Ann. Transvaal Mus.* 28:229-256.

De Villiers, H. 1976. A second adult human mandible from Border Cave, Ingwawuma District, KwaZulu, South Africa. *S. Afr. J. Sci.* 72:212-215.

Farrand, W. R. 1979. Chronology and palaeoenvironment of Levantine prehistoric sites as seen from sediment studies. *J. Archeol. Sci.* 6:369-392.

Gieseler, W. 1974. Die Fossilgeschichte des Menschen, in: *Die Evolution der Organismen*, III (G. Herberer, Ed.), 171-517, G. Fischer, Stuttgart.

Hay, R. L. 1983. Origins of the Chinese people: Interpretations of the recent evidence, in: *The Origins of Chinese Civilization* (D. N. Keightly, Ed.), pp. 297-319, University of California Press, Berkeley.

Hay, R. L. 1987. Geology of the Laetoli area, in: *Laetoli: A Pliocene Site in Northern Tanzania*. Oxford University Press, Oxford.

Heberer, G. 1950. Das Präsapiens-Problem, in: *Moderne Biologie. Festschrift zum 60. Geburtstag von Hans Nachtsheim* (H. Gruneberg and W. Ulrich Eds.), pp. 131-162, Berlin.

Howell, F. C. 1951. The place of Neanderthal man in human evolution. *Am. J. Phys. Anthrop.* 9:379-416.

Howells, W. W. 1967. *Mankind in the Making.* Addison-Wesley, Garden City.

Howells, W. W. 1978. Position phyletique de l'homme de Neanderthal, in: *Les Origines Humaines et les Epoques de l'Intelligence* (F. Bordes, Ed.), pp. 217-237, Paris.

Howells, W. W. 1983. Origins of the Chinese people: Interpretations of the recent evidence, in: *The Origins of Chinese Civilization* (D. N. Keightly, Ed.), pp. 297-319. University of California Press, Berkeley.

Hublin, J. J. 1982. Les Anténéandertaliens: Présapiens ou Pré-Néandertaliens. *Géobios, mèm. spéc.* 6:345-357.

Jacob, T. 1967. *Some Problems Pertaining to the Racial History of the Indonesian Region.* Utrecht.

Jacob, T. 1981. Solo Man and Peking Man, in: *Homo Erectus. Papers in Honor of Davidson Black* (B. A. Sigmon and J. S. Cybulski, Eds.), 87-104, Toronto.

Jelinek, A. 1982. The Tabun Cave and Paleolithic man in the Levant. *Science* 216:1369-1375.

Kalb, J. E., Mebrate, A., Tebedge, S., Smart, C., Oswald, E. B., Cramer, D., Whitehead, P., Wood, C. B., Conroy, G. C., Adefris, T., Sperling, L., and Kana, B. 1982. Fossil mammals and artefacts from the Middle Awash Valley, Ethiopia. *Nature* 298:17-25.

Klein, R. G. 1973. Geological antiquity of Rhodesian Man. *Nature* 244:311-312.

von Koenigswald, G. H. R. (1982). Der Frühmensch tritt auf den Plan, in: *Kindlers Enzyklopädie "Der Mensch,"* Vol. 2 (H. Wendt and N. Loacker, Eds.), pp. 17-52, Zurich.

Leakey, L. S. B. 1972. *Homo sapiens* in the Middle Pleistocene and the evidence of *Homo sapiens'* evolution, in: *The Origin of Homo Sapiens* (F. Bordes, Ed.), pp. 25-29, Paris.

Leakey, M. D., and Hay, R. L. 1982. The chronological position of the fossil hominids of Tanzania. *1er Conr. Intern. Paléont. Hum.*, pp. 753-765, (Prétirage). C.N.R.S., Nice.

Leakey, R. E. F. 1981. African fossil man, in: *General History of Africa, I, Methodology and African Prehistory* (J. Ki-Zebro, Ed.), pp. 437-451, UNESCO, Berkeley.

Leakey, R. E. F., Butzer, K., and Day, M. H. 1969. Early *Homo sapiens* remains from the Omo River region of South-West Ethiopia. *Nature* 222:1132-1138.

Mehlman, M. J. 1984. Archaic *Homo sapiens* at Lake Eyasi, Tanzania: recent misinterpretations. *J. Hum. Evol.* 13:487-501.

Oakley, K. P. 1974. Revised dating of the Kanjera Hominids. *J. Hum. Evol.* 3:257-258.

Partridge, T. C. 1982. The chronological positions of the fossil hominids of southern Africa. *1er Congr. Intern. Paléont. Hum.*, pp. 617-675, (Prétirage). C.N.R.S., Nice.

Protsch, R. 1975. The absolute dating of Upper Pleistocene Sub-Saharan fossil hominids and their place in human evolution. *J. Hum. Evol.* 4:297-322.

Rightmire, G. P. 1978. Florisbad and human population succession in southern Africa. *Am. J. Phys. Anthrop.* 48:475-486.

Rightmire, G. P. 1979. Implications of Border Cave skeletal remains for Later Pleistocene human evolution. *Curr. Anthrop.* 20:23-35.

Rightmire, G. P. 1983. The Lake Ndutu cranium and early *Homo sapiens* in Africa. *Am. J. Phys. Anthrop.* 61:245-254.

Santa Luca, A. P. 1980. The Ngandong fossil hominids. *Yale Univ. Publ. in Anthrop.* 78:1-175. New Haven.

Sartono, S. 1982. Characteristics and chronology of early man in Java. *1er Congr. Intern. Paléont. Hum.*, pp. 491-541, (Prétirage). C.N.R.S., Nice.

Schwidetzky, I. 1979. *Rassen und Rassenbildung beim Menschen.* G. Fischer, Stuttgart.

Singer, R., and Wymer, J. J. 1982. *The Middle Stone Age at Klasies River Mouth in South Africa.* University of Chicago Press, Chicago.

Stringer, C. B. 1974. Population relationships of Later Pleistocene hominids: A multivariate study of available crania. *J. Arch. Sci.* 1:317-342.

Stringer, C. B. 1981. The dating of European Middle Pleistocene hominids and the existence of *Homo erectus* in Europe. *Anthropologie* (Brno) 19:3-14.

Stringer, C. B. 1982. Towards a solution to the Neandertal problem. *J. Hum. Evol.* 11:431-438.

Suzuki, H. 1981. Racial history of the Japanese, in: *Rassengeshichte der Menschheit, 8. Leiferung* (I. Schwidetzky, Ed.), pp. 7-69, München.

Thoma, A. 1964. Die Entstehung der Mongoliden. *Homo* 15:1-22.

Tobias, P. V. 1956. Evolution of the Bushmen. *Am. J. Phys. Anthrop.* 14:384

Trinkaus, E. 1981a Evolutionary continuity among archaic *Homo sapiens*, in: *The Transition from Lower to Middle Paleolithic and the Origin of Modern Man* (A. Ronen, Ed.), University of Haifa, Haifa.

Trinkaus, E. 1981b. Neandertal limb proportions and cold adaptation, in: *Aspects of Human Evolution* (C. B. Stringer, Ed.), pp. 187-224, London.

Vallois, H. V. 1949. The Fontéchevade fossil man. *Am. J. Phys. Anthrop.* 7:339-362.

Vallois, H. V. 1954. Neanderthals and Praesapiens. *J. Roy. Anthrop. Inst.* 84:111-130.

Vandermeersch, B. 1978. Le crâne pré-Würmien de Biache-Saint Vaast (Pas-de-Calais), in: *Les Origines Humaines et les Epoques de l'Intelligence* (F. Bordes, Ed.), pp. 153-157, Paris.

Vandermeersch, B. 1981. *Les hommes fossiles de Qafzeh (Israel).* CNRS, Paris.

Vrba, E. 1982. Biostratigraphy and chronology, based particularly on Bovidae, of southern hominid-associated assemblages: Makapansgat, Sterkfontein, Taung, Kromdraai, Swartkrans. *1er Congr. Intern. Paléont. Hum.*, pp. 707-752 (Prétirage). C.N.R.S. Nice.

Wang, L. 1983. On a fossil human calva unearthed from Huanglong County, Shaanxi Province. *Acta Anthropol. Sinica* 2:315-319.

Wang, L., and Bräuer, G. 1984. A multivariate comparison of the human calva from Huanglong County, Shaanxi Province. *Acta Anthropol. Sinica* 3:343-321.

Weidenreich, F. 1939. On the earliest representatives of modern mankind recovered on the soil of East Asia. *Peking Natural History Bull.* 13:161-174.

Wells, L. H. 1947. A note on the broken maxillary fragment from the Broken Hill cave. *J. Roy. Anthropol. Inst.* 77:11-12.

Wolpoff, M. H. 1980a. Cranial remains of Middle Pleistocene European hominids. *J. Hum. Evol.* 9:339-358.

Wolpoff, M. H. 1980b. *Paleoanthropology.* Knopf, New York.

Wolpoff, M. H., Wu Xinzhi, and Thorne, A. G. 1984. Modern *Homo sapiens* origins: A general theory of hominid evolution involving the fossil evidence from East Asia, in: *The Origins of Modern Humans* (F. H. Smith and F. Spencer, Eds.), pp. 411-483, Liss, New York.

Woo Jukang. 1958. Tzeyang Paleolithic man—earliest representative of modern man in China. *Am. J. Phys. Anthrop.* 16:459-471.

Woo Jukang. 1959. Human fossils found in Linjiang, Kwangsi, China. *Vertebr. Palasiat.* 3:109-118.

Wu Xinzhi. 1961. Study on the Upper Cave man of Choukoutien. *Vertebr. Palasiat.* 3:109-118.

Wu Xinzhi. 1981. A well-preserved cranium of an archaic type of early *Homo sapiens* from Dali, China. *Scientia Sinica* 24:530-541.

Wu Rukang and Wu Xinzhi. 1982. Comparison of Tautavel Man with *Homo erectus* and early *Homo sapiens* in China. *1er Congrès Intern. Paléont. Hum.*, pp. 605-616 (Prétirage). C.N.R.S., Nice.

Zhou Mingzhen, Li Yanxian, and Wang Linghong. 1982. Chronology of the Chinese fossil Hominids. *1er Congr. Intern. Paléont. Hum.*, pp. 593-604 (Prétirage). C.N.R.S., Nice.

Ziegert, H. 1981. Abu Hugar Palaeolithic Site (Blue Nile Province, Sudan). A preliminary report. *Paper on the UISPP Congr.*, Mexico.

46

Mitochondrial DNA and Human Evolution

R. L. Cann, M. Stoneking, and A. C. Wilson

Molecular biology is now a major source of quantitative and objective information about the evolutionary history of the human species. It has provided new insights into our genetic divergence from apes (Goodman 1963; Sarich and Wilson 1967; King and Wilson 1975; Ferris *et al.* 1981; Brown *et al.* 1982; Sibley and Ahlquist, 1984; Bianchi *et al.* 1985; O'Brien *et al.* 1985) and into the way in which humans are related to one another genetically (Cavalli-Sforza 1966, 1974; Nei 1985; Nei and Roychoudhury 1982; Constans *et al.* 1985; Wainscoat *et al.* 1986). Our picture of genetic evolution within the human species is clouded, however, because it is based mainly on comparisons of genes in the nucleus. Mutations accumulate slowly in nuclear genes. In addition, nuclear genes are inherited from both parents and mix in every generation. This mixing obscures the history of individuals and allows recombination to occur. Recombination makes it hard to trace the history of particular segments of DNA unless tightly linked sites within them are considered.

Our world-wide survey of mitochondrial DNA (mtDNA) adds to knowledge of the history of the human gene pool in three ways. First, mtDNA gives a magnified view of the diversity present in the human gene pool, because mutations accumulate in this DNA several times faster than in the nucleus (Wilson *et al.* 1985). Second, because mtDNA is inherited maternally and does not recombine (Olivo *et al.* 1983), it is a tool for relating individuals to one another. Third, there are about 10^{16} mtDNA molecules within a typical human and they are usually identical to one another (Brown 1980; Monnat and Loeb 1985; Monnat *et al.* 1985). Typical mammalian females consequently behave as haploids, owing to a bottleneck in the genetically effective size of the population of mtDNA molecules within each oocyte (Hauswirth and Laipis 1986). This maternal and haploid inheritance means that mtDNA is more sensitive than nuclear DNA to severe reductions in the number of individuals in a population of organisms (Wilson *et al.* 1985). A pair of breeding individuals can transmit only one type of mtDNA but carry four haploid sets of nuclear genes, all of which are transmissible to offspring. The fast evolution and peculiar mode of inheritance of mtDNA provide new perspectives on how, where and when the human gene pool arose and grew.

RESTRICTION MAPS

MtDNA was highly purified from 145 placentas and two cell lines, HeLa and GM 3043, derived from a Black American and an aboriginal South African (!Kung), respectively. Most placen-

tas (98) were obtained from U.S. hospitals, the remainder coming from Australia and New Guinea. In the sample, there were representatives of 5 geographic regions: 20 Africans (representing the sub-Saharan region), 34 Asians (originating from China, Vietnam, Laos, the Philippines, Indonesia and Tonga), 46 Caucasians (originating from Europe, North Africa, and the Middle East), 21 aboriginal Australians, and 26 aboriginal New Guineans. Only two of the 20 Africans in our sample, those bearing mtDNA types 1 and 81 (see below) were born in sub-Saharan Africa. The other 18 people in this sample are Black Americans, who bear many non-African nuclear genes probably contributed mainly by Caucasian males. Those males would not be expected to have introduced any mtDNA to the Black American population. Consistent with our view that most of these 18 people are a reliable source of African mtDNA, we found that 12 of them bear restriction site markers known (Johnson *et al.* 1983) to occur exclusively or predominantly in native sub-Saharan Africans (but not in Europeans, Asians or American Indians nor, indeed, in all such Africans). The mtDNA types in these 112 people are 2-7, 37-41, and 82 (see below). Methods used to purify mtDNA and more detailed ethnographic information on the first four groups are as described (Brown 1980; Cann 1982); the New Guineans are mainly from the Eastern Highlands of Papua New Guinea (Stoneking *et al.* 1986b).

Each purified mtDNA was subjected to high resolution mapping (Cann 1982; Stoneking *et al.* 1986b; Cann *et al.* 1984) with 12 restriction enzymes (*Hpa*I, *Ava*II, *Fnu*DII, *Hha*I, *Hpa*II, *Mbo*I, *Taq*I, *Rsa*I, *Hin*fI, *Hae*III, *Alu*I and *Dde*I). Restriction sites were mapped by comparing observed fragment patterns to those expected from the known human mtDNA sequence (Anderson *et al.* 1981). In this way, we identified 467 independent sites, of which 195 were polymorphic (that is, absent in at least one individual). An average of 370 restriction sites per individual were surveyed, representing about 9% of the 16,569 base-pair human mtDNA genome.

MAP COMPARISONS

The 147 mtDNAs mapped were divisible into 133 distinct types. Seven of these types were found in more than one individual; no individual contained more than one type. None of the seven shared types occurred in more than one of the five geographic regions. One type, for example, was found in two Australians. Among Caucasians, another type occurred three

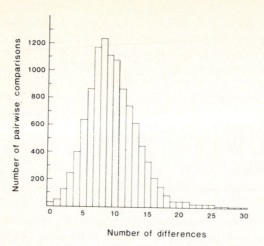

Figure 1. *Histogram showing the number of site differences between restriction maps of mtDNA for all possible pairs of 147 human beings.*

times and two more types occurred twice. In New Guinea, two additional types were found three times and the seventh case involved a type found in six individuals.

A histogram showing the number of restriction site differences between pairs of individuals is given in Figure 1; the average number of differences observed between any two humans is 9.5. The distribution is approximately normal, with an excess of pairwise comparisons involving large numbers of differences.

From the number of restriction site differences, we estimated the extent of nucleotide sequence divergence (Nei and Tajima 1983) for each pair of individuals. These estimates ranged from zero to 1.3 substitutions per 100 base pairs, with an average sequence divergence of 0.32%, which agrees with that of Brown (1980), who examined only 21 humans.

Table 1 gives three measures of sequence divergence within and between each of the five populations examined. These measures are related to one another by equation (1):

$$\delta = \delta_{xy} - 0.5(\delta_x + \delta_y)$$

where δ_x is the mean pairwise divergence (in percent) between individuals within a single population (X), δ_y is the corresponding value for another population (Y), δ_{xy} is the mean pairwise divergence between individuals belonging to two different populations (X and Y), and δ is a measure of the interpopulation divergence corrected for intrapopulation divergence. Africans as a group are more variable ($\delta_x = 0.47$) than other groups. Indeed, the variation within the African population is as great as that between Africans and any other group ($\delta_{xy} = 0.40$-0.45). The within-group variation of Asians ($\delta_x = 0.35$) is also comparable to that which exists between groups. For Australians, Caucasians, and New Guineans, who show nearly identical amounts of within-group variation ($\delta_x = 0.23$-0.25), the variation between groups slightly exceeds that within groups.

When the interpopulational distances (δ_{xy}) are corrected for intrapopulation variation (Table 1), they become very small ($\delta = 0.01$-0.06). The mean value of the corrected distance among populations ($\delta = 0.04$) is less than one-seventh of the mean distance between individuals within a population (0.30). Most of the mtDNA variation in the human species is therefore

Table 1. MtDNA divergence within and between 5 human populations.

	% Sequence divergence				
Population	1	2	3	4	5
1. African	0.47	0.04	0.04	0.05	0.06
2. Asian	0.45	0.35	0.01	0.02	0.04
3. Australian	0.40	0.31	0.25	0.03	0.04
4. Caucasian	0.40	0.31	0.27	0.23	0.05
5. New Guinean	0.42	0.34	0.29	0.29	0.25

The divergence is calculated by a published method (Nei and Tajima 1983). Values of the mean pairwise divergence between individuals within populations (δ_x) appear on the diagonal. Values below the diagonal (δ_{xy}) are the mean pairwise divergences between individuals belonging to two different populations, X and Y. Values above the diagonal (δ) are interpopulation divergences, corrected for variation within those populations with equation (1).

shared between populations. A more detailed analysis supports this view (Whittam *et al.* 1986).

FUNCTIONAL CONSTRAINTS

Figure 2 shows the sequence divergence (δ_x) calculated for each population across seven functionally distinct regions of the mtDNA genome. As has been found before (Cann *et al.* 1984; Whittam *et al.* 1986; Greenberg, *et al.* 1983), the most variable region is the displacement loop ($\overline{\delta}_x = 1.3$), the major noncoding portion of the mtDNA molecule, and the least variable region is the 16S ribosomal RNA gene ($\overline{\delta}_x = 0.2$). In general, Africans are the most diverse and Asians the next most, across all functional regions.

EVOLUTIONARY TREE

A tree relating the 133 types of human mtDNA and the reference sequence (Fig. 3) was built by the parsimony method. To interpret this tree, we make two assumptions, both of which have extensive empirical support: (1) a strictly maternal mode of mtDNA transmission (so that any variant appearing in a group of lineages must be due to a mutation occurring in the ancestral lineage and not recombination between maternal and paternal genomes) and (2) each individual is homogeneous for its multiple mtDNA genomes. We can therefore view the tree as a genealogy linking maternal lineages in modern human populations to a common ancestral female (bearing mtDNA type a).

Many trees of minimal or near-minimal length can be made from the data; all trees that we have examined share the following features with Figure 3: (1) two primary branches, one composed entirely of Africans, the other including all 5 of the populations studied; and (2) each population stems from multiple lineages connected to the tree at widely dispersed positions. Since submission of this manuscript, Horai *et al.* (1986) built a tree for our samples of African and Caucasian populations and their sample of a Japanese population by another method; their tree shares these two features.

Among the trees investigated was one consisting of five primary branches with each branch leading exclusively to one of the five populations. This tree, which we call the population-specific tree, requires 51 more point mutations than does the

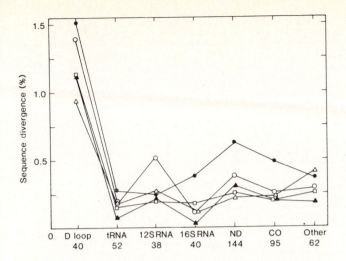

Figure 2. *Sequence divergence within 5 geographic areas for each of 7 functional regions in human mtDNA. Sequence divergence (δ_x) was estimated from comparisons of restriction maps [26]. Symbols for the 5 races are:* ●, *Africa;* ○, *Asia;* △, *Australia;* □, *Caucasian;* ▲, *New Guinea. Along the horizontal axis are the numbers of restriction sites in each functional region (D loop, transfer RNA genes, 12S and 16S ribosomal RNA genes, NADH dehydrogenase subunits 1-5, cytochrome oxidase subunits and other protein-coding regions).*

tree of minimum length in Figure 3. The minimum-length tree requires fewer changes at 22 of the 93 phylogenetically-informative restriction sites than does the population-specific tree, while the latter tree required fewer changes at four sites; both trees require the same number of changes at the remaining 67 sites. The minimum-length tree is thus favoured by a score of 22 to 4. The hypothesis that the two trees are equally compatible with the data is statistically rejected, since 22:4 is significantly different from the expected 13:13. The minimum-length tree is thus significantly more parsimonious than the population-specific tree.

AFRICAN ORIGIN

We infer from the tree of minimum length (Fig. 3) that Africa is a likely source of the human mitochondrial gene pool. This inference comes from the observation that one of the two primary branches leads exclusively to African mtDNAs (types 1-7, Fig. 3) while the seond primary branch also leads to African mtDNAs (types 37-41, 45, 46, 70, 72, 81, 82, 111 and 113). By postulating that the common ancestral mtDNA (type a in Fig. 3) was African, we minimize the number of intercontinental migrations needed to account for the geographic distribution of mtDNA types. It follows that b is a likely common ancestor of all non-African and many African mtDNAs (types 8-134 in Fig. 3).

MULTIPLE LINEAGES PER RACE

The second implication of the tree (Fig. 3)—that each non-African population has multiple origins—can be illustrated most simply with the New Guineans. Take, as an example, mtDNA type 49, a lineage whose nearest relative is not in New Guinea, but in Asia (type 50). Asian lineage 50 is closer

genealogically to this New Guinea lineage than to other Asian mtDNA lineages. Six other lineages lead exclusively to New Guinean mtDNAs, each originating at a different place in the tree (types 12, 13, 26-29, 65, 95 and 127-134 in Fig. 3). This small region of New Guinea (mainly the Eastern Highlands Province) thus seems to have been colonised by at least seven maternal lineages (Tables 2 and 3).

In the same way, we calculate the minimum numbers of female lineages that colonised Australia, Asia and Europe (Tables 2 and 3). Each estimate is based on the number of region-specific clusters in the tree (Fig. 3, Tables 2 and 3). These numbers, ranging from 15 to 36 (Tables 2 and 3), will probably rise as more types of human mtDNA are discovered.

TENTATIVE TIME SCALE

A time scale can be affixed to the tree in Figure 3 by assuming that mtDNA sequence divergence accumulates at a constant rate in humans. One way of estimating this rate is to consider the extent of differentiation within clusters specific to New Guinea (Table 2; see also Stoneking *et al.* 1986a,b), Australia (Stoneking *et al.* 1986a) and the New World (Wallace *et al.* 1985). People colonised these regions relatively recently: a minimum of 30,000 years ago for New Guinea (Jones 1979), 40,000 years ago for Australia (Wolpoff *et al.* 1984) and 12,000 years ago for the New World (Owen 1984). These times enable us to calculate that the mean rate of mtDNA divergence within humans lies between two and four percent per million years; a detailed account of this calculation appears elsewhere (Stoneking *et al.* 1986a). This rate is similar to previous estimates from animals as disparate as apes, monkeys, horses, rhinoceroses, mice, rats, birds and fishes (Wilson *et al.* 1985). We therefore consider the above estimate of 2%-4% to be reasonable for humans, although additional comparative work is needed to obtain a more exact calibration.

As Figure 3 shows, the common ancestral mtDNA (type a) links mtDNA types that have diverged by an average of nearly 0.57%. Assuming a rate of 2%-4% per million years, this implies that the common ancestor of all surviving mtDNA types existed 140,000-290,000 years ago. Similarly, ancestral types b-j may have existed 62,000-225,000 years ago (Table 3).

Table 2. Clusters of mtDNA types that are specific to one geographic region.

Geographic region	Number of region-specific clusters	Mean pairwise distance within clusters*	Average age of clusters†
Africa	1‡	0.36	90-180
Asia	27	0.21	53-105
Australia	15	0.17	43-85
Europe	36	0.09	23-45
New Guinea	7	0.11	28-55

* For clusters represented by two or more individuals (and calculated for individuals, not for mtDNA types) in Figure 3.

† Average age in thousands of years based on the assumption that mtDNA divergence occurs at the rate of 2-4% per million years (Wilson *et al.* 1985, Stoneking *et al.* 1986a).

‡ Assuming that Africa is the source, there is only African cluster.

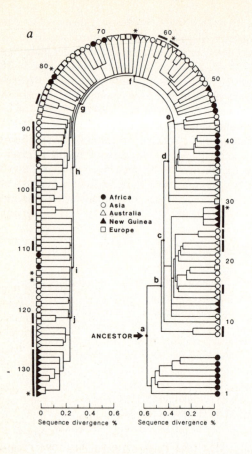

b

D LOOP: *8*j 2 5 8 9 23 81-83 85 86 118; *64*i *(16494)* 26 ; *134*l 3; *207*h 128-134; *255*l 39; *259*a 106; *340*j 112 **12S rRNA:** *663*e 43 48 53; *712*l 90; 740j 16-19; 748b 49; 1240a 7-9 37 110; *1403*a *(1448)* 11-18 20-29 34 49 50 55-57; 1463e 14; 1484e 2 4 5 8-11 14-17 19 23-25 30 32-35 41-43 45 52-58 61 107 110 120; *1536*f 31 **VAL tRNA:** 1610a 2 3 44 45 104; 1637c 47 102 108; 1667c 47 **16S rRNA:** 1715c 22 23 27 123; 1917a 70; 2208a 87; *2223*a *(2635)* 37; *2384*a *(2472)* 106; *2390*j 2 3 8 9 49 79 93; 2734a 18 22 54 73 101; 2758k 1-8; 2849k 112; 3123k 119 **ND 1:** 3315e 11; 3337k 94 118 133; *3391*e 41 105 122; 3537a 44; *3592*h 2-7 9 37-41; 3698f 130-132; *3842*e 44; 3849e 5 46; *3899*l 14 18 22 23 32 71 92 102 110 120; *3930*c 110; 3944 l 12; *4092*g 112 **MET tRNA:** 4411a 23 35 36 57; 4464k 129 **ND 2:** *4481*b *(10933)* 111 112; 4631a 2; *4643*k 87 100; *4732*k 115; *4769*a 110; *4793*e 76 85; 5176a 21 25 54-57; 5261e 118; 5269l 71; *5351*f 17-19 **TRP tRNA:** *5538*l 130; 5552c 10 **L. ORIGIN:** 5742l 15 44; *5754*l *(5755)* 81 **CO I:** 5978a 52; *5984*b/5983g 87; *5985*k/5983g 133 134; 5996a 87; 6022a 74; *6166*l *(6168)* 63; 6211g 37-41 82; 6260e 95; *6356*c 5 9; 6377c 68; *6409*l *(7854)* 68; *650*1i 78; *6610*g 12; *6699*b *(8719,8723)* 78; 6871g 18 19; *6915*k 5 49; 6931g 48; 6957e 44 45; 7025a 75-86 93 94 103-112; 7055a 3 6 7; *7241*k 72; 7335l 6 7 30 92 120; *7347*e 124 **SER tRNA:** 7461l 71; 7474a 121 **CO II:** *7617*l 55 73; 7750c 3-9 37 40 41 98; 7859j 120; *7970*g 10 24 71-74 77; 8074a 68; 8112i 1; 8150i 1 126 ; *8165*e 10; *8249* b *(8250)* /8250e 1 61 132 **LYS tRNA:** *8299*k 126 **ATP 8:** 8391e 31 120; 8515c 27 **ATP 6:** 8592j 21 23; 8783g 6 7; 8852f (8854, 8856) 109 110; 8994e60 61; *9009*a 15 16; 9053f 52 91-93 95-102 112; *9070*l 5-7; *9150*j 7 103 104 **CO III:** 9266e 28 49 67; 9294e 25; 9342e 27; 9380f 90; *9429*k 56 57; 9553e 37 117; *9714*e 98; 9746k 62; 9751l 48; *9859*g 86 **GLY tRNA:** 10028a 126 **ND 3:** *10066*l 45; *10084*l 45; 10352a 110; 10364e 96; *10394*c 1-29 39-45 49 50 84-89 94-100 111 120-123 **ARG tRNA:** *10413*a *(10536)* 16 46 56 85 98 **ND 4L:** *10644*k 19 20; 10689e 96; *10694*a 104; 10725e 22 46 96 **ND 4:** *10806*g 1-7 50 83 124; *10893*l 34; 11146c 61 110; *11161*i 6 7; *11329*e *(11690)* 2 4; *11350*a 15 37 110; *11806*a 65; 11922j 7; 12026h 124 **ND 5:** *12345*k *(12350,12528)* 88 127-134; 12406h 91-93; 12560a 19 52 93; *12795*j *(12798,12806,13374)* 40 90 98 99; *12810*k 5-7; 12925g 7; *12990*a *(13642)* 27; *13004*j *(13018,13182,13194)* 20; 13031g 1-6 9-16 18-23 26-35 37 39 40 42 43 45-64 82 83 92 93; 13051e 23 38-41; *13068*a 128; *13096*k 26; *13100*i 107; 13103g 7; 13208f 4 5 7 15 75 88; 13268g 65; 13367b 40 88 90 99; 13404l 8 9 79 ; *13635*l *(13641)* 39 115; 13702e 38-41; 14015a 14; *14050*l *(14366)* 125 **ND 6:** *14279*e 1; *14279*j 23; *14322*a 92; *14385*c 10; *14509*a 68 123-126; *14567*l 68; 14608c 5 **CYT b:** *14749*e 87; 14869j 86 126; 14956l 115; *15005*g 56 57; 15172e 10; *15195*j *(15221)* 64 100; 15250c 14-18 20 21 24 25 54 81 90 111; *15606*a 65 127-134; 15723g 43; *15790*j *(16373)* 82; 15883e 7 45 58 59 112 **THR tRNA:** .*15897*k 97 129; *15907*k 46; *15912*i 81; 15925i 15 81 90 **PRO tRNA:** 15996c/16000g 48 **D LOOP:** 16049k 15 22 46 74 81; 16065g 121 122; *16089*k 21; 16096k 119; 16125k 3 9 74 78 88-91 93 105 119 120 122; *16178*l 26-29; 16208k 11 15 51 52 55; *16217*l 95; *16246*g 46; *16254*a 127 132; 16303k 36 58 59 82 89-93 111 112 131 132; 16310k 1-3 5 6 8-14 20 26-31 58 73 78 82 94-97 99-102 120 125 126 133 134; *16389*g/16390b 11 35-41 82 89; *16398*e 5 11 34 37 66 118 119; *16490*g 10; 16517e 2 11-13 15-24 26-29 51-55 58 59 82 97 105-134.

Figure 3. *a, Genealogical tree for 134 types of human mtDNA (133 restriction maps plus reference sequence); b, comprehensive list of polymorphic restriction sites used. The tree accounts for the site differences observed between restriction maps of these mtDNAs with 398 mutations. No other order of branching tested is more parsimonious than this one. This order of branching was obtained (using the computer program PAUP, designed by Dr. David Swofford) by ignoring every site present in only one type of mtDNA or absent in only one type and confining attention to the remaining 93 polymorphic sites. The computer program produces an unrooted network, which we converted to a tree by placing the root (arrow) at the midpoint of the longest path connecting the two lineages (see Farris 1972). The numbers refer to mtDNA types, no. 1 being from the aboriginal South African (!Kung) cell line (GM 3043), no. 45 being from the HeLa cell line and no. 110 being the published human sequence (Anderson et al. 1981). Black bars, clusters of mtDNA types specific to a given geographic region; asterisks, mtDNA types found in more than 1 individual; type 134 was in six individuals, types 29, 65 and 80 each occurred thrice, and other types flagged with asterisks occurred twice. To place the nodes in the tree relative to the percent divergence scale, we took account of the differences observed at all 195 polymorphic sites. b, The numbering of sites is according to the published human sequence (Anderson et al. 1981), with 12 restriction enzymes indicated by the following single letter code: a, AluI; b, AvaII; c, DdeI; d, FnuDII; e, HaeIII; f, HhaI; g, HinfI; h, HpaI; i, HpaII; j, MboI; k, RsaI; l, TaqI. Italicized sites are present in the indicated mtDNA types and nonitalicized sites are absent in the indicated types; parentheses refer to alternative placements of inferred sites; sites separated by a slash are polymorphic for two different restriction enzymes caused by a single inferred nucleotide substitution; letters in bold face refer to noncoding regions and genes for transfer RNA, ribosomal RNA and proteins (ND, NADH dehydrogenase; CO, cytochrome oxidase; ATP, adenosine triphosphatase; CYT b, cytochrome b). For example, 8j indicates a MboI site beginning at nucleotide position 8 in the D loop that was not found in mtDNA type 1 but was present in type 2, etc. Note that since this site is not present in the reference sequence (type 110), the sequence beginning at position 8 is actually a semisite, differing from the MboI recognition sequence at one position (see Stoneking et al. 1986b for a detailed description of the method of mapping such inferred sites). Not all sites were scored in all individuals: 8j, 1484e and 7750c were not determined for types 1, 31, 59, 63, 68, and all of the New Guinea mtDNAs; mtDNAs 114 and 121 could not be typed with RsaI. The locations of some sites differ from those reported before (Stoneking et al. 1986b, Cann et al. 1984), as do the individuals in which some sites occur; these revisions are based on re-examination of previously-studied mtDNAs.*

Table 3. Ancestors, lineages and extents of divergence in the genealogical tree for 134 types of human mtDNA.

| Ancestor | Total | No. of descendent lineages or clusters specific to a region | | | | | % Divergence | Age *y |
		Africa	Asia	Australia	Europe	N. Guinea		
a	7	1	0	0	0	0	0.57	143-285
b	2	0	1	0	0	0	0.45	112-225
c	20	0	7	3	1	3	0.43	108-215
d	2	0	0	1	1	0	0.39	98-195
e	14	2	2	4	2	0	0.34	85-170
f	19	1	7	4	4	1	0.30	75-150
g	10	2	3	2	2	1	0.28	70-140
h	30	2	4	0	15	1	0.27	68-135
i	8	1	0	0	6	0	0.26	65-130
j	22	1	3	1	5	1	0.25	62-125
All	134	10	27	15	36	7	—	—

* Assuming that the mtDNA divergence rate is 2-4% per million years (Wilson *et al.* 1985; Stoneking *et al.* 1986a)

When did the migrations from Africa take place? The oldest of the clusters of mtDNA types to contain no African members stems from ancestor c and included types 11-29 (Fig. 3). The apparent age of this cluster (calculated in Table 3) is 90,000-180,000 years. Its founders may have left Africa at about that time. However, it is equally possible that the exodus occurred as recently as 23-105 thousand years ago (Table 2). The mtDNA results cannot tell us exactly when these migrations took place.

OTHER mtDNA STUDIES

Two previous studies of human mtDNA have included African individuals (Johnson *et al.* 1983; Greenberg *et al.* 1983); both support an African origin for the human mtDNA gene pool. Johnson *et al.* (1983) surveyed ~40 restriction sites in each of 200 mtDNAs from Africa, Asia, Europe and the New World, and found 35 mtDNA types. This much smaller number of mtDNA types probably reflects the inability of their methods to distinguish between mtDNAs that differ by less than 0.3% and may account for the greater clustering of mtDNA types by geographic origin that they observed. (By contrast, our methods distinguish between mtDNAs that differ by 0.03%.) Although Johnson *et al.* favoured an Asian origin, they too found that Africans possess the greatest amount of mtDNA variability and that a midpoint rooting of their tree leads to an African origin.

Greenberg *et al.* (1983) sequenced the large noncoding region, which includes the displacement loop (D loop), from four Caucasians and three Black Americans. A parsimony tree for these seven D loop sequences, rooted by the midpoint method, appears in Figure 4. This tree indicates (1) a high evolutionary rate for the D loop (at least five times faster than other mtDNA regions), (2) a greater diversity among Black American D loop sequences, and (3) that the common ancestor was African.

NUCLEAR DNA STUDIES

Estimates of genetic distance based on comparative studies of nuclear genes and their products differ in kind from mtDNA estimates. The latter are based on the actual number of mutational differences between mtDNA genomes, while the former rely on differences in the frequencies of molecular variants measured between and within populations. Gene frequencies can be in-

fluenced by recombination, genetic drift, selection, and migration, so the direct relationship found between time and mutational distance for mtDNA would not be expected for genetic distances based on nuclear DNA. But studies based on polymorphic blood groups, red cell enzymes, and serum proteins show that (1) differences between racial groups are smaller than those within such groups and (2) the largest gene frequency differences are between Africans and other populations, suggesting an African origin for the human nuclear gene pool (Nei and Roychoudhury 1982; Nei 1985; Mourant *et al.* 1978). More recent studies of restriction site polymorphisms in nuclear DNA (Wainscoat *et al.* 1986; Murray *et al.* 1984; Cooper & Schmidtke 1984; Cooper *et al.* 1985; Hill *et al.* 1985; Chapman *et al.* 1986; Chakravarti *et al.* 1984a, b) support these conclusions.

RELATION TO FOSSIL RECORD

Our tentative interpretation of the tree (Fig. 3) and the associated time scale (Table 3) fits with one view of the fossil record: that

Figure 4. *Genealogical tree relating the nucleotide sequences of D loops from seven human mtDNAs. This tree, which requires fewer mutations than any other branching order, was constructed by the PAUP computer program from the 900-bp sequences determined by Greenberg et al. (1983) and was rooted by the midpoint method. Symbols: ●, African origin (Black American); □, Caucasian.*

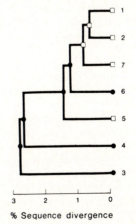

% Sequence divergence

the transformation of archaic to anatomically modern forms of *Homo sapiens* occurred first in Africa (Rightmire 1984, Bräuer 1984a, b), about 100,000-140,000 years ago, and that all present-day humans are descendants of that African population. Archaeologists have observed that blades were in common use in Africa 80-90 thousand years ago, long before they replaced flake tools in Asia or Europe (Isaac 1981, Clark 1981). But the agreement between our molecular view and the evidence from palaeoanthropology and archaeology should be treated cautiously for two reasons. First, there is much uncertainty about the ages of these remains. Second, our placement of the common ancestor of all human mtDNA diversity in Africa 140,000-280,000 years ago need not imply that the transformation to anatomically modern *Homo sapiens* occurred in Africa at this time. The mtDNA data tell us nothing of the contributions to this transformation by the genetic and cultural traits of males and females whose mtDNA became extinct.

An alternative view of human evolution rests on evidence that *Homo* has been present in Asia as well as in Africa for at least one million years (Pope 1983) and holds that the transformation of archaic to anatomically modern humans occurred in parallel in different parts of the Old World (Wolpoff *et al.* 1984; Coon 1962). This hypothesis leads us to expect genetic differences of great antiquity within widely separated parts of the modern pool of mtDNAs. It is hard to reconcile the mtDNA results with this hypothesis. The greatest divergences within clusters specific to non-African parts of the world correspond to times of only 90,000-180,000 years. This might imply that the early Asian *Homo* (such as Java man and Peking man) contributed no surviving mtDNA lineages to the gene pool of our species. Consistent with this implication are features, found recently in the skeletons of the ancient Asian forms, that make it unlikely that Asian *erectus* was ancestral to *Homo sapiens* (Stringer 1984; Andrews 1984a, b). Perhaps the non-African *erectus* population was replaced by *sapiens* migrants from Africa; incomplete fossils indicating the possible presence of early modern humans in western Asia at Zuttiyeh (75,000-150,000 years ago) and Qafzeh (50,000-70,000 years ago) might reflect these first migrations (Bräuer 1984b; Stringer *et al.* 1984).

If there was hybridization between the resident archaic forms in Asia and anatomically modern forms emerging from Africa, we should expect to find extremely divergent types of mtDNA in present-day Asians, more divergent than any mtDNA found in Africa. There is no evidence for these types of mtDNA among the Asians studied (Johnson *et al.* 1983; Horai *et al.* 1984; Bonne-Tamir *et al.* 1986; Horai and Matsunaga 1986). Although such archaic types of mtDNA could have been lost from the hybridizing population, the probability of mtDNA lineages becoming extinct in an expanding population is low (Avise *et al.* 1984). Thus we propose that *Homo erectus* in Asia was replaced without much mixing with the invading *Homo sapiens* from Africa.

CONCLUSIONS AND PROSPECTS

Studies of mtDNA suggest a view of how, where and when modern humans arose that fits with one interpretation of evidence from ancient human bones and tools. More extensive molecular comparisons are needed to improve our rooting of the mtDNA tree and the calibration of the rate of mtDNA divergence within the human species. This may provide a more reliable time scale for the spread of human populations and better estimates of the number of maternal lineages involved in founding the non-African populations.

It is also important to obtain more quantitative estimates of the overall extent of nuclear DNA diversity in both human and African ape populations. By comparing the nuclear and mitochondrial DNA diversities, it may be possible to find out whether a transient or prolonged bottleneck in population size accompanied the origin of our species (Wilson *et al.* 1985). Then a fuller interaction between palaeoanthropology, archaeology and molecular biology will allow a deeper analysis of how our species arose.

We thank the Foundation for Research into the Origin of Man, the National Science Foundation and the NIH for support. We also thank P. Andrews, K. Bhatia, F. C. Howell, W. W. Howells, R. L. Kirk, E. Mayr, E. M. Prager, V. M. Sarich, C. Stringer and T. White for discussion and help in obtaining placentas.

REFERENCES

Anderson, S. *et al.* 1981. Sequence and organization of the human mitochondrial genome. *Nature* 290:457-465.

Andrews, P. 1984a. An alternative interpretation of the characters used to define *Homo erectus*. *Courier Forsch. Inst. Senckenberg* 69:167-175.

Andrews, P. 1984b. The descent of man. *New Scient.* 102:24-26.

Avise, J. C., Neigel, J. E., and Arnold, J. 1984. Demographic influences on mitochondrial DNA lineage survivorship in animal populations. *J. Molec. Evol.* 20:99-105.

Bianchi, N. O., Bianchi, M. S., Cleaver, J. E., and Wolff, S. 1985. The pattern of restriction enzyme-induced banding in the chromosome of chimpanzee, gorilla, and orangutan and its evolutionary significance. *J. Molec. Evol.* 22:323-333.

Bonne-Tamir, B. *et al.* 1986. Human mitochondrial DNA types in two Israeli populations—a comparative study at the DNA level. *Am. J. Hum. Genet.* 38:341-351.

Bräuer, G. 1984a. The "Afro-European *sapiens*-hypothesis," and hominid evolution in East Asia during the late Middle and Upper Pleistocene. *Courier Forsch. Int. Senckenberg* 69:145-165.

Bräuer, G. 1984b. A craniological approach to the origin of anatomically modern *Homo sapiens* in Africa and implications for the appearance of modern Europeans, in: *Origins of Modern Humans: A World Survey of the Fossil Evidence* (F. H. Smith and F. Spencer, Eds.), pp. 327-410, Liss, New York.

Brown, W. M. 1980. Polymorphism in mitochondrial DNA of humans as revealed by restriction endonuclease analysis. *Proc. Natn. Acad. Sci. U.S.A.* 77:3605-3609.

Brown, W. M., Prager, E. M., Wang, A., and Wilson, A. C. 1982. Mitochondrial DNA sequences of primates: Tempo and mode of evolution. *J. Molec. Evol.* 18:225-239.

Cann, R. L. 1982. *The Evolution of Human Mitochondrial-DNA*. Ph.D. Thesis, University of California, Berkeley.

Cann, R. L., Brown, W. M., and Wilson, A. C. 1984. Polymorphic sites and the mechanism of evolution in human mitochondrial DNA. *Genetics* 106:479-499.

Cavalli-Sforza, L. L. 1966. Population structure and human evolution. *Proc. R. Soc. Lond.* B164:362-379.

Cavalli-Sforza, L. L. 1974. The genetics of human populations. *Sci. Am.* 231(3):81-89.

Chakravarti, A. *et al.* 1984a. Nonuniform recombination within the human B-Globin gene cluster. *Am. J. Hum. Genet.* 36:1239-1258.

Chakravarti, A. *et al.* 1984b. Patterns of polymorphism and linkage disequilibrium suggest independent origins of the human growth hormone gene cluster. *Proc. Natn. Acad. Sci. U.S.A.* 81:6085-6089.

Chapman, B. S., Vincent, K. A., and Wilson, A. C. 1986. Persistence or rapid generation of DNA length polymorphism at the B-globin locus of humans. *Genetics* 112:79-92.

Clark, J. D. 1981. Persistence or rapid generation of DNA length polymorphism at the Beta-globin locus of humans. *Proc. Br. Acad. Lond.* 67:163-192.

Constans, J. *et al.* 1985. Population distribution of the human Vitamin D binding protein: Anthropological considerations. *Am. J. Phys. Anthropol.* 68:107-122.

Coon, C. S. 1962. *The Origin of Races.* Knopf, New York.

Cooper, D. N., and Schmidtke, J. 1984. DNA restriction fragment length polymorphisms and heterozygosity in the human genome. *Hum. Genet.* 66:1-16.

Cooper, D. N. *et al.* 1985. An estimate of unique DNA sequence heterozygosity in the human genome. *Hum. Genet.* 69:201-205.

Farris, J. S. 1972. Estimating phylogenetic trees from distance matrices. *Am. Nat.* 106:645-668.

Ferris, S. D., Wilson, A. C., and Brown, W. M. 1981. Evolutionary tree for apes and humans based on cleavage maps of mitochondrial DNA *Proc. Natn. Acad. Sci. U.S.A.* 78:2432-2436.

Goodman, M. 1963. Serological analysis of the systematics of recent hominoids. *Hum. Biol.* 35:377-424.

Greenberg, B. D., Newbold, J. E., and Sugino, A. 1983. Intraspecific nucleotide sequence variability surrounding the origin of replication in human mitochondrial DNA. *Gene* 21:33-49.

Hauswirth, W. W., and Laipis, P. J. 1986. Transmission genetics of mammalian mitochondria: A molecular model and experimental evidence, in: *Achievements and Perspectives in Mitochondrial Research, Vol. 2 Biogenesis* (E. Quagliariello, E. C. Slater, F. Palmieri, C. Saccone, and A. M. Kroon, Eds.), pp. 49-60, Elsevier, New York.

Hill, A. V. S., Nicholls, R. D., Thein, S. L., and Higgs, D. R. 1985. Recombination with the human embryonic xi-globin locus: A common xi-xi chromosome produced by gene conversion of the psi xi gene. *Cell* 42:809-819.

Horai, S., and Matsunaga, E. 1986. Mitochondrial DNA polymorphism in Japanese. II. Analysis with restriction enzymes of four or five base pair recognition. *Hum. Genet.* 72:105-117.

Horai, S., Gojobori, T., and Matsunaga, E. 1984. Mitochondrial DNA polymorphism in Japanese. Analysis with restriction enzymes of base pair recognition. *Hum. Genet.* 68:324-332.

Horai, S., Gojobori, T., and Matsunaga, E. 1986. Distinct clustering of mitochondrial DNA types among Japanese, Caucasians and Negroes. *Jap. J. Genet.* 61:271-275.

Isaac, G. 1981. Emergence of human behavior patterns in archaeological tests of alternative models of early hominid behaviour: Excavation and experiments. *Phil. Trans. R. Soc. Lond.* B292:177-188.

Johnson, M. J. *et al.* 1983. Radiation of human mitochondrial DNA types analyzed by restriction endonuclease cleavage patterns. *J. Molec. Evol.* 19:255-271.

Jones, R. A. 1979. The fifth continent: Problems concerning the human colonization of Australia. *Ann. Rev. Anthropol.* 8:445-466.

King, M. C., and Wilson, A. C. 1975. Evolution at two levels in humans and chimpanzees. *Science* 188:107-116.

Monnat, R. J., and Loeb, L. A. 1985. Nucleotide sequence preservation of human mitochondrial DNA. *Proc. Natn. Acad. Sci. U.S.A.* 82:2895-2899.

Monnat, R. J., Maxwell, C. L., and Loeb, L. A. 1985. Nucleotide sequence preservation of human leukemia mitochondrial DNA. *Cancer Res.* 45:1809-1814.

Mourant, A. E. *et al.* 1978. *The Distribution of the Human Blood Groups and Other Polymorphism*, Oxford University Press, Oxford.

Murray, J. C. *et al.* 1984. Linkage disequilibrium and evolutionary relationships of DNA variants (restriction enzyme length polymorphisms) as the serum albumin locus. *Proc. Natn. Acad. Sci. U.S.A.* 81:3486-3490.

Nei, M. 1985. Human evolution at the molecular level, in: *Population Genetics and Molecular Evolution* (T. Ohta and K. Aoki, Eds.), pp. 41-64, Japan Sci. Soc. Press, Tokyo.

Nei, M., and Roychoudhury, A. K. 1982. Genetic relationship and evolution of human races. *Evol. Biol.* 14:1-59.

Nei, M., and Tajima, F. 1983. Maximum likelihood estimation of the number of nucleotide substitutions from restrictions sites data. *Genetics* 105:207-217.

O'Brien, S. J. *et al.* 1985. A molecular solution to the riddle of the giant panda's phylogeny. *Nature* 317:140-144.

Olivo, P. D., Van de Walle, M. J., Laipis, P. J., and Hauswirth, W. W. 1983. Nucleotide sequence evidence for rapid genotypic shifts in the bovine mitochondrial DNA D-loop. *Nature* 306:400-402.

Owen, R. C. 1984. The Americas: The case against an Ice-Age human population, in: *Origins of Modern Humans: A World Survey of the Fossil Evidence* (F. H. Smith and F. Spencer, Eds.), pp. 517-564, Liss, New York.

Pope, G. G. 1983. Evidence on the age of the Asian Hominidae. *Proc. Natn. Acad. Sci. U.S.A.* 80:4988-4992.

Rightmire, G. P. 1984. *Homo sapiens* in Sub-Saharan Africa, in: *Origins of Modern Humans: A World Survey of the Fossil Evidence* (F. H. Smith and F. Spencer, Eds.), pp. 295-326, Liss, New York.

Sarich, V. M., and Wilson, A. C. 1967. Immunological time scale for hominid evolution. *Science* 158:1200-1203.

Sibley, C. G., and Ahlquist, J. E. 1984. The phylogeny of the hominoid primates, as indicated by DNA-DNA hybridization. *J. Molec. Evol.* 20:2-15.

Stoneking, M., Bhatia, K., and Wilson, A. C. 1986a. Rate of sequence divergence estimated from restriction maps of mitochondrial DNAs from Papua New Guinea. *Cold Spring Harb. Symp. Quant. Biol.* 51:433-439.

Stoneking, M., Bhatia, K., and Wilson, A. C. 1986b. Mitochondrial-DNA variation in Eastern Highlanders of Papua New Guinea, in: *Genetic Variation and its Maintenance in Tropical Populations* (C. F. Roberts and G. Destefano, Eds.), pp. 87-100, Cambridge University Press, Cambridge.

Stringer, C. B. 1984. The definition of *Homo erectus* and the existence of the species in Africa and Europe. *Courier Forsch. Inst. Senckenberg* 69:131-143.

Stringer, C. B., Hublin, J. J., and Vandermeersch, B. 1984. The origin of anatomically modern humans in Western Europe, in: *Origins of Modern Humans: A World Survey of the Fossil Evidence* (F.H. Smith and F. Spencer, Eds.), pp. 51-136, Liss, New York.

Wainscoat, J. S. *et al.* 1986. Evolutionary relationships of human populations from an analysis of nuclear DNA polymorphisms. *Nature* 319:491-493.

Wallace, D. C., Garrison, K., and Knowler, W. C. 1985. Dramatic founder effects in Amerindian mitochondrial DNA. *Am. J. Phys. Anthropol.* 68:149-155.

Whittam, T. S., Clark, A. G., Stoneking, M., Cann, R. L., and Wilson, A. C. 1986. Allelic variation in human mitochondrial genes based on patterns of restriction site polymorphism. *Proc. Natn. Acad. Sci. U.S.A.* 83:9611-9615.

Wilson, A. C. *et al.* 1985. Mitochondrial DNA and two perspectives on evolutionary genetics. *Biol. J. Linn. Soc.* 26:375-400.

Wolpoff, M. H., Wu, X. Z., and Thorne, A. G. 1984. Modern *Homo sapiens* origins: A general theory of hominid evolution involving the fossil evidence from East Asia, in: *Origins of Modern Humans: A World Survey of the Fossil Evidence* (F. H. Smith and F. Spencer, Eds.), pp. 411-484, Liss, New York.

47

Genetic and Fossil Evidence for the Origin of Modern Humans

C. B. Stringer and P. Andrews

After a period of relative neglect, increasing attention is being given to the biological and behavioral changes that led to the evolution of *Homo sapiens*, the last major event in human evolution (Smith and Spencer 1984; Trinkaus 1989; Mellars and Stringer 1989; Gowlett 1987; Hublin 1987; Lewin 1987a, b). We examine two opposing models proposed to explain the origin of *Homo sapiens* and compare their compatibility with recent reviews of genetic (Andrews 1986) and paleontological (Stringer 1989a) data. These two models are not the only ones currently under discussion, but it is likely that one or other reflects the predominant mode of *Homo sapiens* evolution. Comparison of these two extreme models should allow the clearest tests for the models from existing data, tests which are not feasible for several other proposed models.

The two competing models for recent human evolution have been termed "regional continuity" (multiregional origins) and "Noah's Ark" (single origin) (Howells 1976). In the multiregional model (Thorne and Wolpoff 1981; Wolpoff *et al.* 1984; Wolpoff 1985, 1989), recent human variation is seen as the product of the early and middle Pleistocene radiation of *Homo erectus* from Africa. Thereafter, local differentiation led to the establishment of regional populations which successively evolved through a series of evolutionary grades to produce modern humans in different areas of the world. In contrast to Coon's version of this model in which the local lineages evolved independently (Coon 1962), the role of gene flow in maintaining grade similarities and preventing speciation is emphasized now, along with the development and persistence of regional features in morphology, particularly in peripheral areas (the "center and edge" corollary).

According to the multiregional model, some regional ("racial") features are considered to have preceded the appearance of the *Homo sapiens* morphology and to have been carried over from local *Homo erectus* ancestors. The exact manner of establishment of "modern" features in any area has depended on gene flow, local selection, and drift. The appearance of *Homo sapiens* was thus primarily the result of a continuation of long-term trends in human evolution, and it has occurred mainly through the re-sorting of the same genetic material under the action of selection, rather than by the evolution and radiation of novel genetic material and morphologies. Thus some advocates of this model have suggested that there have been no speciation events during the last 1.5 million years of human evolution and that

hominids usually referred to *Homo erectus* might instead be allocated to *Homo sapiens* (Wolpoff *et al.* 1984).

In contrast, the single origin model assumes that there was a relatively recent common ancestral population for *Homo sapiens* which already displayed most of the anatomical characters shared by living people. Proponents of this model have proposed Africa as the probable continent of origin of *Homo sapiens*, with an origin for the species during the early part of the late Pleistocene, followed by an initiation of African regional differentiation, subsequent radiation from Africa, and final establishment of modern regional characteristics outside Africa (Stringer 1989a; Bräuer 1984a, 1989). A single origin minimizes the amount of parallel evolution required to produce the widespread appearance of *Homo sapiens* characteristics (Stringer 1989a; Smith 1985). Cladistic versions of the model are based on the identification of a suite of derived features characterizing *Homo sapiens* and the recognition of these characters should be possible at an earlier date in the area of origin of the species (that is, Africa) than elsewhere (Stringer 1989a; Stringer *et al.* 1984).

In Table 1, predictions from the two models of *Homo sapiens* origins about geographic patterning, about the establishment of *Homo sapiens*, and about the role of selective and behavioral factors (the last of which we will not disccuss in detail here) are summarized. Throughout this article the use of the term *Homo sapiens* will be restricted to anatomically modern humans, following recent proposals (Stringer 1985; Tattersall 1986). A summary of suggested shared derived characteristics of *Homo sapiens* (Stringer *et al.* 1984) includes the following. (i) All living humans are characterized by a gracile skeleton compared with that of other species of the genus *Homo*, and this is reflected in features such as long bone shape and shaft thickness, depth or extent of muscle insertions, and the relative thin bone of the cranial walls and mandibular body: (ii) the cranium is voluminous (but no more so than in Neanderthals), and, like the brain it contains, is typically relatively short, high and domed; (iii) the supraorbital torus and external cranial buttressing are considerably reduced or absent; (iv) the dentition and supporting architecture are reduced in size; (v) perhaps related to these last differences, the face in *Homo sapiens* is orthognathous (tucked well under the anterior cranium); and (vi) a mental eminence is present on the mandible from a young age. Beyond such morphologically derived characters of *Homo*

Table 1. Theoretical predictions from models of *Homo sapiens* evolution.

Aspect	Multiregional evolution	Recent African evolution
1) Geographic patterning of human evolution	Continuity of pattern from middle Pleistocene to present	Continuity of pattern only from late Pleistocene appearance of *H. sapiens* to present
	Interpopulation differences are high, greatest between each peripheral area	Interpopulation differences relatively low, greatest between African and non-African populations
	Intrapopulation variation greatest at center of human range	Intrapopulation variation greatest in African population
2) Regional continuity and the establishment of *Homo sapiens*	Transitional fossils widespread	Transitional fossils restricted to Africa, population replacement elsewhere
	Modern regional characters of high antiquity at peripheries	Modern regional characters of low antiquity at peripheries (except Africa)
	No consistent temporal pattern of appearance of *Homo sapiens* characters between areas	Phased establishment of *Homo sapiens* suite of characters: (i) Africa, (ii) S.W. Asia, (iii) other areas
3) Selective and behavioral factors involved in the origin of *Homo sapiens*	Factors varied and widespread, perhaps related to technology; local behavioual continuity expected	Factors special and localized in Africa; behavioral discontinuities expected outside Africa

sapiens, there are also suggested novelties in ontogeny and in behavioral and ecological adaptations (Binford 1989; Trinkaus 1986; Foley 1989).

GEOGRAPHIC PATTERNING AND REGIONAL CONTINUITY

The patterns of regional genetic variation predicted by the two models are quite distinct. The multiregional model predicts that the same kinds of evolutionary changes occurred across the major continents, with local populations evolving gradually into *Homo sapiens*. This provided continuity of genes through time, whereas gene flow maintained continuity through time and space. However, local differences in drift, selection, and access to gene flow should have ensured that no universal patterns of *Homo sapiens* origins emerged. Restricted gene flow at the peripheries of the populated world allowed greater differentiation and stabilization of gene pools and morphology there, in comparison with central areas. Any central area might be expected to show most within-population variation, but the least differentiation, as a result of multidirectional gene flow. Each region should have displayed a distinctive, but essentially gradual, transition from local ancestral populations to modern humans, with a persistence of regional features. Transitional (mosaic) fossils should be common, with a wide geographic distribution, and no particular temporal restriction. However, multidirectional gene flow at the center of the species range should have allowed earlier establishment of combinations of *Homo sapiens* characters there than in any single peripheral region.

The model of a recent African origin, on the contrary, predicts different patterns of variation comparing African populations and those from elsewhere. Variation should be greatest within African populations (based on their earlier divergence, and assuming predominantly neutral genetic change), and they should be sharply distinguished in gene frequencies from non-African populations. Transitional fossils would not occur outside the African area of origin, and population replacement would represent the mode of establishment of *Homo sapiens* in

other areas. The earliest record of *Homo sapiens* fossils should occur in the continent of origin of the species (Africa), and the youngest records at the peripheries of the radiation. Population relationships in Europe, Asia, and Australasia would approximate those of the Holocene only in the later Pleistocene.

MODERN GENETIC DATA

The human species shows great morphological variation. However, in contrast to this, genetic variation between human populations is low overall. Genetic distances based on electrophoretic analyses of proteins are small in comparison with those found in other hominoids (King and Wilson 1975). There is also relatively little protein variation between human populations. As much as 84% of protein polymorphism in human populations results from variation among individuals within populations, a further 6% represents genetic divergence associated with nationality, and only 10% varies between human "racial" groups (Latter 1980). Thus differences between populations are small when compared with differences within populations.

Analyses of mitochondrial DNA (mtDNA) show similarly low variation between geographically distant human populations. The mean pairwise difference between human populations based on mapping of mtDNA by restriction nucleases is 0.3%. The nearest approach to this low figure in any other hominoid yet studied is for a single subspecies of gorilla, in which the mean mitochondrial sequence difference is about twice this figure, whereas the two subspecies of orangutan differ by as much as 5% [1], (see Ferris *et al.* 1981; Wilson *et al.* 1985). This remarkable difference in magnitude of population divergence in the globally distributed human species is an excellent illustration of the low level of geographic differentiation in *Homo sapiens*. Moreover, while each hominoid species has diverged into numerous mtDNA lineages (the two most divergent individuals differ by five sites in gorillas and 12 each in chimpanzees and orangutans), the two most divergent humans (again obtained from a large and globally distributed sample) differ by only two sites [1], (see also Ferris *et al.* 1981;

Wilson *et al.* 1985; Courtenay *et al.* 1988; Cann *et al.* 1987a; Stoneking and Cann 1989).

Sequencing of both mtDNA and nuclear DNA for human populations suggest that interpopulation divergences are relatively low in comparison with intrapopulation divergences (Cann *et al.* 1987a; Wainscoat *et al.* 1986). For mtDNA, percentage sequence divergence within sub-Saharan African populations is 0.47%; this compares with a range of divergence figures between African and other human populations of 0.40% to 0.45%. Interestingly, when the interpopulation distances are corrected for this intrapopulation variation they become very small, with a mean value of 0.04%, less than 15% of the mean within-population variation. Furthermore, there is little evidence that peripheral populations are always the most differentiated because samples from the peripheral areas of Europe, the Americas, and Australasia often appear similar to each other. Contrary to the multiregional model but consistent with the recent African origin model, when many different genetic data are examined, it is only the African periphery that consistently appears most differentiated from the others, and these populations, although not "central," are the most diverse.

The greater genetic diversity among sub-Saharan African populations may indicate a longer period of separation of populations within Africa [2], (Cann *et al.* 1987a; Wainscoat *et al.* 1986; Stoneking and Cann 1989) than elsewhere. Restriction mapping of mtDNA has shown that pairs of African populations are some 50% more genetically distinct from each other than are any other pairs of populations (Cann *et al.* 1987a; Stoneking and Cann 1989). If mtDNA changes are assumed to accumulate at a steady rate, genealogical trees constructed by minimizing genetic changes (through maximum parsimony analysis) distinguish two main branches. One leads exclusively to a number of African (or African origin) individuals, whereas the other leads to all other individuals of African or non-African origin. Dates for the branching points of the tree can be estimated from rates of mtDNA evolution in other organisms. This gives a date for the origin of the mtDNA of *Homo sapiens* at between 140,000 and 290,000 years ago, assuming constant rates of change at 2 to 4% per nucleotide site per million years. This rate has been claimed to be too high because it implies a human-African ape split at only 1.4 to 2.8 million years ago (Wolpoff 1989; Saitou and Omoto 1987), but this last calibration is erroneous (Cann *et al.* 1987b), and the rate appears reasonable when tested against archeological data on known colonization events (Stoneking *et al.* 1986). The initial mtDNA split was found between Africans and others, followed by progressively younger calibrated ages for specific Asian, Australian, New Guinea, and European mtDNA types, respectively (Cann *et al.* 1987a; Stoneking and Cann 1989; Stoneking *et al.* 1986).

However, by contrast, trees produced from the mtDNA genetic distances show a small but consistent African-New Guinea initial link where both groups have long branch lengths (Saitou and Omoto 1987), and the results of a smaller analysis of human mtDNA variation have been interpreted to show an Asian rather than African root (Johnson *et al.* 1983). Nevertheless, earlier surveys of a small sample of mtDNA showed Africans to possess both the highest mtDNA variability and the highest between-population variability of the displacement loop in a non-coding region of mtDNA (Greenberg *et al.* 1983). Moreover, the claim of an Asian mtDNA root has been challenged through a re-analysis of the data by midpoint rooting to

produce an African root instead (Stoneking and Cann 1989), and the use of mtDNA genetic distances to construct trees has been criticized (Cann *et al.* 1987b).

Expectations of a gradual and regular increase in human variation through time are based on the assumption that such variation is selectively neutral. Natural selection could either increase or decrease the rate of accumulation of variations in populations (Slatkin 1987). Any excess of variation maintained by selection could lead to an overestimate of time since the last common ancestor shared with other populations, while any selective removal of variation could affect conclusions about the presence of bottlenecks during evolution. However, predictions of allele frequencies based on the neutral model are largely consistent with the actual distributions for mtDNA (Whittam *et al.* 1986), so that for the human mtDNA system, at least, the assumption of neutrality does appear approximately valid. Departures from the neutral model that do occur can be explained by the effects of population expansion during the last 10,000 years.

Patterns of genetic differences in nuclear DNA are generally similar to those of mtDNA. In the beta-globin cluster, African populations share a haplotype not found in other populations, whereas the non-African populations share a limited number of haplotypes not present in Africans [3]. More recent work (Wainscoat *et al.* 1989) links a population of Canadian Indians to Eurasian populations, further extending the split between African and non-African populations, and a separate study, (Jenkins and Ramsay 1986) confirms the presence of the common African haplotype in Bantu-speaking South Africans (Wainscoat *et al.* 1986; Higgs *et al.* 1986). Moreover, there is a similar pattern of genetic diversity in the alphaglobin gene cluster (Wainscoat *et al.* 1989), with African populations showing striking similarities in frequencies of common polymorphisms. Eurasian populations are similar to each other (although Melanesians differ, perhaps through founder effect), but the separation of African and non-African patterns is again clear. These nuclear DNA patterns accord much better with the recent African origin model than with the multiregional model, as does research on Y-chromosome DNA, where an African root for modern human variation is most parsimonous (Lucotte 1989).

One line of genetic evidence that is more ambivalent in its implications is that of genetic distances, as we have already found in the case of mtDNA. Genetic distances calculated from blood groups show a close "caucasoid"-"mongoloid" relationship (as expected from the recent African origin model), but a smaller distance between "caucasoids" and "negroids" than between the latter and "mongoloids" (Nei and Roychoudhury 1982; Cavalli-Sforza and Bodmer 1971). This points to a closer African-European than African-Asian relationship. Protein analyses, however, show a consistent split between "negroids" and the other groups, in accordance with most results from mtDNA and nuclear DNA. There may be stronger selection on blood group types, and there is a less clear relationship between blood group phenotype and nucleotide sequence. Since the body of data from protein systems is also larger, the results from protein analyses are probably the most relevant here, and support the recent African origin model. These have been used to calibrate divergence times (again assuming selective neutrality and absence of gene flow) of about 110,000 years ago for the African–non-African split and about 41,000 years for the

European-Asian split (Nei and Roychoudhury 1982; Cavalli-Sforza and Bodmer 1971).

Regarding the role of gene flow, although this can prevent increasing genetic differentiation between adjacent populations [although not necessarily prevent speciation (Slatkin 1987)], it seems improbable that it could prevent increasing differentiation in a very widely distributed species over long periods of time. It has recently been calculated that for human populations with a density of 0.1 per square mile and a gene flow of 5% per generation (20 to 25 years), it might take 400,000 years for the spread of an advantageous gene from South Africa to China, and this does not take into account geographical, environmental, social, or possible specific barriers to gene flow [4], (Weiss 1984; Jones and Rouhani 1986; Rouhani 1989). This is strong evidence against the multiregional model, unless it is assumed that selection maintained a low genetic differentiation among populations or that there was an extraordinary (and quite unrealistic) level of gene flow.

PALEONTOLOGICAL DATA

In the middle Pleistocene, regional populations of early *Homo* are represented at fossil sites in Europe by early Neanderthals (for example, at Swanscombe in England, Biache in France, and Ehringsdorf in the German Democratic Republic) (Stringer *et al.* 1984; Blackwell and Schwarcz 1986), in the Far East by evolved *Homo erectus* (for example, at Zhoukoudian and Hexian in China) (Wolpoff *et al.* 1984), and in Indonesia by the poorly dated Ngandong (Java) material (Wolpoff *et al.* 1984; Santa Luca 1980). In southern Africa, specimens such as the skull from Broken Hill (Zambia) show similarities to other African fossils to the north (for example, at Bodo in Ethiopia), and to pre-Neanderthal or earliest Neanderthal material in Europe (for example, those from Arago, France, and Petralona, Greece) (Stringer *et al.* 1984; Rightmire 1984; Bräuer 1984b; Stringer 1984). As a result, indigenous features in southern African middle Pleistocene fossils are more difficult to identify (Rightmire 1989).

Comparing the patterns of variation in the fossil samples through time contradicts the expectations of the multiregional model because of marked changes in pattern and diversity. Prior to Neanderthal differentiation (>230,000 years ago), a basic west-east division of middle Pleistocene hominids can be recognized, as Asian late *Homo erectus* fossils are most distinct from those of Europe and Africa (Bräuer 1989; Santa Luca 1980; Stringer 1984). Such a pattern is not consistent with the multiregional model, since a closer relationship between Eurasian populations might be expected, either from assuming a common Eurasian *Homo erectus* founding population with continuing morphological clines, or from the projection of recent genetic relationships back to the middle Pleistocene.

Moreover, late middle to late Pleistocene fossils from China (for example, Yinkou and Dali) show a change from the middle Pleistocene pattern, through a greater resemblance to European and African middle Pleistocene hominids and a greater contrast with their supposed local ancestors (Wu Xinzhi and Wu Maolin 1985). Despite such contrasts, these same fossils are said to display transitional features between local *Homo erectus* and *Homo sapiens* populations, and have mainly been interpreted in terms of regional continuity (Wolpoff, *et al.*

1984; Wu Xinzhi and Wu Maolin 1985), although detailed comparative analyses of the best specimens have yet to be published. In addition, there are no very informative fossils known to derive from the critical time period (50,000 to 100,000 years ago) immediately preceding the local first appearance of *Homo sapiens*. For Australasia, there is a complete lack of fossil evidence from the early part of the late Pleistocene period (unless the Ngandong hominids date from that time). The only credible morphological intermediate between middle Pleistocene Indonesian hominids and late Pleistocene Australians (but not the Mungo and Keilor specimens) is the Willandra Lakes WLH-50 cranium (Wolpoff 1985, 1989; Habgood 1989), but this fossil is probably no older than the Mungo specimens and has not yet been well described. Furthermore, its thick cranial vault may reflect pathology rather than homology with that of *Homo erectus*.

The first appearance of *Homo sapiens* raises further problems for the multiregional model. Despite arguments to the contrary (Wolpoff 1985, 1989; Parkinton 1989), present evidence shows that Africa and the adjacent area of the Levant have the earliest known *Homo sapiens* fossils (Deacon 1989; Rightmire 1989; Bräuer 1989; Klein 1989; Valladas *et al.* 1988). Furthermore, Europe, the Far East, and Australasia appear to have a relatively late first known appearance of *Homo sapiens* compared with southwest Asia and Africa, and for Europe at least, a relatively late survival of other forms of *Homo*. There is a dramatic change of pattern at the appearance of *Homo sapiens*, with a reduction in skeletal variation compared with the greater diversity present in the middle and early part of the late Pleistocene (Fig. 1). Multivariate distance studies show relatively compact groupings for living and fossil *Homo sapiens*, compared with the greater differences found from and between earlier hominids (Howells 1970; Stringer 1974, 1978). The reasons for these apparent changes in pattern may be disputed, but since the multiregional model posits a consistent pattern for human population relationships through the middle and late Pleistocene, with a consequent maintenance or increase in levels of variation, such departures from the expected pattern need to be explained.

There is also an absence of evidence for morphological clines immediately prior to the global appearance of *Homo sapiens*. Neanderthals of Europe are present in western Asia and as far east as Uzbekistan (Trinkaus 1983), but there is little evidence of Neanderthal-derived characters in the Far East and Australasia (Wolpoff *et al.* 1984; Bräuer 1984a; Trinkaus 1986; Santa Luca 1980; Stringer 1984, 1978), nor in Africa (Bräuer 1984b, 1989; Smith 1985; Trinkaus 1983, 1986; Rightmire 1984, 1989; Stringer 1978). Neither, from the same sources, is there much morphological evidence of gene flow in reverse directions into Europe prior to the appearance of *Homo sapiens*. It is only with the emergence of *Homo sapiens* that "African" morphological characters (including primitive characters lost in the Neanderthal lineage, and derived characters which were already present in Africa) appear in Eurasia (Stringer 1978, 1989a; Stringer *et al.* 1984; Bräuer 1984b, 1989; Trinkaus 1983). As already indicated, this suggests there was a remarkable change in pattern at the appearance of *Homo sapiens*, when "modern" derived characters became distributed globally during a period of perhaps 60,000 years.

Although Europe and southwest Asia have the most complete fossil record for this period, there is an absence of Neander-

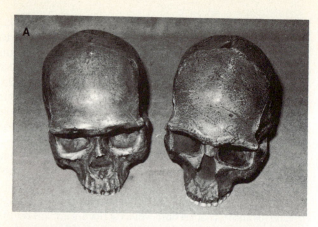

Figure 1. *Comparisons of late Pleistocene* Homo sapiens *crania from Czechoslovakia and China. (A) Casts of male crania from Predmostí (right) and Zhoukoudian Upper Cave. (B) Assumed female crania from Mladec (left) and Zhoukoudian Upper Cave. Under the multiregional model, the marked morphological and metrical similarities of these geographically distant crania are explained as the result of parallel evolution from distinct middle Pleistocene ancestors, together with gene flow. From the recent African origin model, the similarities are explained by descent from a common ancestral population that had originated in Africa during the early part of the late Pleistocene.*

thal-modern *Homo sapiens* transitional fossils in either area. Not only are such transitional forms lacking, but recent dating evidence suggests that true *Homo sapiens* was present in the Levant before Neanderthals, some 60,000 years prior to the last Neanderthals in western Europe (Stringer *et al.* 1984; Valladas *et al.* 1988). There is little or no continuity of genuine regional features, for the most distinctive and well-established characteristics of Neanderthals are poorly represented or absent in contemporaneous or immediately succeeding *Homo sapiens* fossils (Stringer 1978, 1989a; Stringer, *et al.* 1984; Bräuer 1984b; Trinkaus 1983, 1986; Gambier 1989), although there are undoubtedly shared primitive characters, such as relatively larger brows and teeth compared with modern Euopeans (Gambier 1989; Frayer 1984; Wolpoff 1989b; Smith *et al.* 1989), and homoplasies found elsewhere, such as protruding occipital regions (Arambourg *et al.* 1934; Ferembach 1962; Anderson 1968; Greene and Armelagos 1972; Trinkaus and LeMay 1982). The African record is sparser and covers a much greater area, yet "intermediate" fossils have been recognized from sites such as

Florisbad (South Africa), Ngaloba (Tanzania), Omo Kibish (Ethiopia), and Djebel Irhoud (Morocco). Here, at least, there is general agreement about regional continuity between earlier fossils and those of *Homo sapiens* (Stringer 1989a; Bräuer 1984a, b, 1989; Smith 1985; Trinkaus 1986; Rightmire 1984; Wolpoff 1980; Ferembach 1976).

As predicted by the recent African origin model, early *Homo sapiens* fossils from Africa and western Eurasia are morphologically rather similar, when due allowance is made for the fact that the earliest European *Homo sapiens* fossils (such as those from Cro Magnon, Stetten, and Mladec) are younger than those from southwest Asia (Qafzeh and Skhul) and Africa (Klasies, Omo-Kibish 1, Dar-es-Soltane 5, and perhaps Border Cave) (Stringer 1989a; Stringer *et al.* 1984; Bräuer 1984a; 1989; Ferembach 1976). Furthermore, late Pleistocene North African *Homo sapiens* fossils combine local regional features with those found in early *Homo sapiens* samples in Eurasia, showing that many supposed regional features in Europe, Asia, and Australia were at that time part of the normal range of variation in African *Homo sapiens* (Arambourg *et al.* 1934; Ferembach 1962; Anderson 1968; Greene and Armelagos 1972). Some of the east Asian and Australian early *Homo sapiens* fossils (such as the Liujiang, Upper Cave Zhoukoudian, Mungo, and Keilor specimens) are also more similar to those of western Eurasia than might be expected from the multiregional evolution model (Fig. 1) (Stringer 1989a; Bräuer 1984a, 1989; Howells 1983). However, other Australian fossil evidence poses serious problems for both models through its high level of cranial variation, which appears to be larger than that observed for any other comparable area or time span (Thorne and Wolpoff 1981; Wolpoff 1985, 1989; Wolpoff *et al.* 1984).

The high variation displayed in late Pleistocene and early Holocene samples in Australia would not be expected at a periphery of the human range under the multiregional model, nor in early *Homo sapiens* fossils outside Africa under the recent African origin model. Furthermore, some of the fossil samples display supposed features of regional continuity while others do not. Most of the features claimed to link the Willandra Lakes WLH-50 and Kow Swamp hominids with Indonesian *Homo erectus* clearly also occur in early *Homo* or *Homo sapiens* fossils from elsewhere (Habgood 1989; Groves 1989), and there are also losses of Indonesian-derived characters which must be accounted for under the multiregional model (Santa Luca 1980; Stringer 1984; Larnach and Macintosh 1974). But even if the claimed regional characteristics are disregarded as irrelevant to the establishment of an Indonesian *Homo erectus*-Australian *Homo sapiens* lineage, there is still a remarkable Pleistocene cranial variation to be explained, with some Australian early *Homo sapiens* fossils looking decidedly more "archaic" than their counterparts from elsewhere.

In order to account for such variation, some proponents of the multiregional model have argued that two separate founding populations must have colonized Australia (Wolpoff *et al.* 1984; Wolpoff 1985, 1989). A relatively gracile group (for example, Mungo and Keilor) originated in Asia, whereas the more robust population (for example, some of the Kow Swamp specimens and WLH-50) derived from Indonesian *Homo erectus*. However, genetic data give no indication of the heterogeneity that would be expected in modern Australasians from such a model [2], (Cann *et al.* 1987a; Wainscoat *et al.* 1986; Stoneking and Cann 1989; Stoneking *et al.* 1986; Johnson *et al.* 1983; Higgs 1986;

Nei and Roychoudhury 1982; Cavalli-Sforza and Bodmer 1971). Distinct regional features are claimed to exist in the two groups, but there are no suggested mechanisms for maintaining such a long-term coexistence of separate Australian populations.

From the recent African origin model, the first Australasian *Homo sapiens* should have been no more archaic than Eurasian early *Homo sapiens*. If the Niah Cave (Borneo) and Mungo and Keilor fossils can be taken as representative of the first *Homo sapiens* in the area, this is indeed true. However, if accurate dating can establish that more robust populations were also present at an early date, this would need to be explained. Perhaps Australia was a special case where local differentiation, cultural practices, or pathologies led in some cases to apparent evolutionary reversals (Stringer 1989a; Brown 1981, 1987). Alternatively, the initial radiation of *Homo sapiens* from Africa may have been by populations which retained primitive characters in features such as frontal bone form and cranial robusticity, but this would require some parallelism in the subsequent loss of such primitive characters in areas apart from Australia. A third option would be to argue for more than one founding population for Eurasian *Homo sapiens*, but this would be inconsistent with genetic data, as well as again introducing further homoplasy into the recent African origin model.

CONCLUDING REMARKS

Our review of recent genetic evidence on evolutionary processes in human evolution favors the model of a recent African origin for *Homo sapiens*. Several geneticists who previously favored a primary "Eurafrican"-Asian split in human populations now favor an African-Eurasian split instead (Cavalli-Sforza, *et al.* 1986), and many different genetic systems illustrate the distinctiveness and greater internal diversity of sub-Saharan African populations. Under the assumption of selective neutrality and regularity of change, this must indicate a greater age for African *Homo sapiens* evolution. There is some evidence of unexpectedly large differentiation in certain non-African populations, but such exceptions are uncommon and offer no particular support to the alternative model of multiregional evolution. Although precise calibration of events in human evolution from genetic data is still problematic, variation in mitochondrial and nuclear DNA indicates a recent origin for *Homo sapiens* and gives no support to an antiquity for peripheral human populations on the order of 750,000 years ago, as would be required for an area such as Australasia under the multiregional model.

Paleontological data in the middle Pleistocene do not match with the expectations of the multiregional model, nor with extrapolations of modern genetic data back into the past. Although the recent African origin model does not provide any particular predictions for middle Pleistocene data, growing evidence of an early appearance of *Homo sapiens* during the late Pleistocene in Africa and the Levant, coupled with a late persistence of Neanderthals in western Europe, provide excellent support for it. Evidence that *Homo sapiens* was present in the Levant before an appearance in more peripheral areas of Eurasia is also consistent with a dispersal event from Africa by way of southwest Asia. Arguments continue about the extent of gene flow between *Homo sapiens* and other forms of *Homo*, but it is possible that these will be settled from more genetic data rather than through the fossil record. This is particularly the case in the Far East and Australasia, where the sparse fossil record from the early part of the late Pleistocene prevents a resolution of arguments about local con-

tinuity, compounded by the confusing diversity of late Pleistocene Australasians. The fact that "colonization" events in Europe and Australasia can be calibrated at about the same antiquity from the genetic evidence might be taken to support either an early Pleistocene dispersal (multiregional model) or a late Pleistocene one (recent African origin). However, there is growing evidence for a recent replacement event in western Eurasia, and the considerable genetic similarities of European and Australasian populations in several recent studies also indicate a closer evolutionary relationship than would be expected through common ancestry and continuing gene flow over more than 500,000 years and 12,000 kilometers under Pleistocene conditions (Rouhani 1989).

Although we feel that an African origin for *Homo sapiens* is highly probable, the exact time, place and mode of origin of the species cannot yet be determined. The presence of *Homo sapiens* fossils in the early part of the late Pleistocene at both the southern tip of Africa (Deacon 1989; Rightmire 1989; Bräuer 1989; Klein 1989) and in the Levant (Valladas *et al.* 1988) means that a southern African origin as recent as 100,000 years ago is unlikely. The origin of the species must have been more ancient, and, as we have seen, plausible precursor populations are sampled at sites in northern, eastern, and southern Africa. Given the recently determined age of Qafzeh *Homo sapiens* fossils (Valladas *et al.* 1988), even the adjacent area of the Levant cannot be excluded as a possible source area for *Homo sapiens*. However, it appears that only the genetic divergence and diversity of sub-Saharan African populations now reflect an age appropriate for the species origin, presumably because areas of northern Africa and the Levant have been exposed to extensive subsequent gene flow from Eurasian populations, particularly in historic times.

In the next decade we will see important developments in the study of the origins of modern human variation. We can expect significant discoveries of fossil hominids to continue, and these are particularly required from the early late Pleistocene of the Far East and Australasia. Further study of the existing fossil and archeological records will provide new hypotheses about modern human origins that can be tested by future discoveries and the growing body of genetic data. New dating techniques may be developed that will help to calibrate events in human evolution more accurately, and radiocarbon accelerator dating should become a standard technique for directly dating the appearance of *Homo sapiens* in the fossil record of areas colonized during the last 50,000 years. Finally, we can expect a great deal of new genetic data, and much discussion on how best to analyze these and make them relevant to the subject of the origin of *Homo sapiens*. Improved communication between paleoanthropologists and geneticists should allow researchers in the latter field to make an increasingly important contribution to debate about our origins. As has proved to be the case in the study of hominid origins, paleoanthropologists who ignore the increasing wealth of genetic data on human population relationships will do so at their peril.

ACKNOWLEDGMENTS

We would like to acknowledge valuable discussions about the subject of this article with numerous colleagues over the last year, many of whose papers are cited in the references. We are especially grateful to J. S. Jones, A. C. Wilson, D. Pilbeam, and C. Groves for their comments on an earlier version of this article, and to three anonymous referees for their helpful comments.

NOTES

[1] Cleavage site differences are assumed to be the result of base substitution (Ferris *et al.* 1981; Wilson *et al.* 1985). The differences between the two orang subspecies are large compared with most subspecific comparisons. The populations on Borneo and Sumatra are completely allopatric, but they can and do interbreed in captivity and show considerable overlap in most morphological characters. Orang variation is discussed in more detail by J. Courtenay *et al.* (1988). Cann *et al.* (1987a) and Stoneking and Cann (1989) provide further corroboration, from larger samples, of the low mtDNA diversity of modern humans.

[2] A greater African diversity is indicated for protein and blood group loci, α and β globins, albumins, growth hormones, dihydrofolate reductase, and insulin.

[3] Wainscoat *et al.* (1986) rooted their phylogenetic tree by taking the greatest distance between populations studied, that is, between the African and non-African populations. See also Higgs *et al.* (1986).

[4] Evidence that gene flow can prevent an increase in genetic distance between populations was presented by, for example, Slatkin and Maruyama (1975).

REFERENCES

Anderson, J. 1968. Late Paleolithic skeletal remains from Nubia, in: *The Prehistory of Nubia* (F. Wendorf, Ed.), pp. 996-1040, Southern Methodist University Press, Dallas.

Andrews, P. 1986. Fossil evidence on human origins and dispersal. *Cold Spring Harbor Symp. Quant. Biol.* 51:419-428.

Arambourg, C., Boule, M., Vallois, H., and Verneau, R. 1934. Les grottes Paleolithiques des Beni Segoual (Algerie). *Arch. Inst. Paleont. Hum.* 13.

Binford, L. 1989. Isolating the transition to cultural adaptations: An organizational approach, in: *The Emergence of Modern Humans* (E. Trinkaus, Ed.), pp.18-41, Cambridge University Press, Cambridge.

Blackwell, B. and Schwarcz, H. 1986. U series analysis of the tower travertine of Ehringsdorf DDR. *Quat. Res.* 25:215-222.

Bräuer, G. 1984a. The "Afro-European *sapiens*-hypothesis," and hominid evolution in East Asia during the late Middle and Upple Pleistocene. *Cour. Forsch. Inst. Senckenberg* 69:145-165.

Bräuer, G. 1984b. A craniological approach to the origin of anatomically modern *Homo sapiens* in Africa and implications for the appearance of modern Europeans, in: *The Origin of Modern Humans: A World Survey of the Fossil Evidence* (F. H. Smith and F. Spencer, Eds.), pp. 327-410, Liss, New York.

Bräuer, G. 1989. The evolution of modern humans: A comparison of the African and non-African evidence, in: *The Human Revolution* (P. Mellars and C. Stringer, Eds.), pp. 123-154, Edinburgh University Press, Edinburgh.

Brown, P. 1981. Artificial cranial reformation, a component in the variation in Pleistocene Australian Aboriginal crania. *Archaeol. Oceania* 16:156-157.

Brown, P. 1987. Pleistocene homogeneity and Holocene size reduction: The Australian human skeletal evidence. *Archaeol. Oceania* 22:41-67.

Cann, R. L., Stoneking, M., Wilson, A. C. 1987a. Mitochondrial DNA and human evolution. *Nature (London)* 325:39-42.

Cann, R. L., Stoneking, M., Wilson, A. C. 1987b. Disputed African origins of human populations. *Nature (London)* 329:111.

Cavalli-Sforza, L. and Bodmer, W. 1971. *The Genetics of Human Populations*, Freeman, San Francisco.

Cavalli-Sforza, L. *et al.*, 1986. DNA markers and genetic variation in the human species. *Cold Spring Harbor Symp. Quant. Biol.* 51:411-417.

Coon, C. S. 1962. *The Origin of Races.* Knopf, New York.

Courtenay, J., Groves, C., and Andrews, P. 1988. Inter- or intra-island variation? An assessment of differences between Bornean and Sumatran Orang-utans, in: *Orang-Utan Biology* (J. Schwartz, Ed.), pp. 19-29, Plenum, New York.

Deacon, H. 1989. Late Pleistocene palaeoecology and archaeology in Southern Cape, South Africa, in: *The Human Revolution* (P. Mellars and C. Stringer, Eds.), pp. 547-564, Edinburgh University Press, Edinburgh.

Ferembach, D. 1962. *La Nécropole Épipaléolithique de Taforalt (Maroc Oriental)*, CNRS, Rabat.

Ferembach, D. 1976. *Bull Mem. Soc. Anthrop.* Paris 13 (no. 3), 183.

Ferris, S., Brown, W., Davidson, W., and Wilson, A. 1981. Extensive polymorphism in the mitochondrial DNA of apes. *Proc. Natl. Acad. Sci. U.S.A.* 78:6319-6325.

Foley, R. 1989. The ecological conditions of speciation: A comparative approach to the origins of anatomically-modern humans, in: *The Human Revolution* (P. Mellars and C. Stringer, Eds.), pp. 298-320, Edinburgh University Press, Edinburgh.

Frayer D. 1984. Biological cultural change in the European Late Pleistocene and early Holocene, in: *The Origin of Modern Humans: A World Survey of the Fossil Evidence* (F. H. Smith and F. Spencer, Eds.), pp. 211-250, Liss, New York.

Gambier, D. 1989. Fossil hominids from the early Upper Palaeolithic (Aurignacian) of France, in: *The Human Revolution* (P. Mellars and C. Stringer, Eds.), pp. 194-211, Edinburgh University Press, Edinburgh.

Gowlett, J. 1987. The coming of modern man. *Antiquity* 61:210-217.

Greene, D., and Armelagos, G. 1972. *The Wadi Halfu Mesolithic Population*, University of Massachusetts Press, Amherst.

Greenberg, B., Newbold, J., Sugino, A. 1983. Intrapecific nucleotide sequence variability surrounding the origins of replication in the human mitochondrial. *Gene* 221:33-49.

Groves, C. 1989. A regional approach to the problem of the origin of modern humans in Australasia, in: *The Human Revolution* (P. Mellars and C. Stringer, Eds.), pp. 274-285, Edinburgh University Press, Edinburgh.

Habgood, P. 1989. The Origin of anatomically modern humans in Australasia, in: *The Human Revolution* (P. Mellars and C. Stringer, Eds.), pp. 245-273, Edinburgh University Press, Edinburgh.

Higgs et al., 1986. Analysis of the human and globin gene cluster reveals highly informative genetic locus. *Proc. Natl. Acad. Sci. U.S.A.* 83:5165-5189.

Howells, W. W. 1970. Mount Carmel man: Morphological relationships. *Proc. VIIIth Int. Congr. Anthrop. Ethnol Sci.* 1:269-272.

Howells, W. 1976. Explaining modern man: Evolutionists *versus* migrationists. *J. Hum. Evol.* 5:477-495.

Howells, W. 1983. Origins of the Chinese people: Interpretations of recent evidence, in: *The Origins of Chinese Civilization* (D. Keightley, Ed.), pp. 297-319, University of California Press, Berkeley.

Hublin, J. J. 1987. Qui fut l'ancetre de l'*Homo sapiens*? *Pour la Science* 113:27-35.

Jenkins, T., and Ramsay, M. 1986. Beta-S and Beta-A-globin gene cluster haplotypes in southern African populations. *Abstr. 7th Int. Cong. Hum. Gen. Berlin* 2:462.

Johnson, M. *et al.*, 1983. Radiation of human mitochondrial DNA types analyzed by restriction endonuclease cleavage patterns. *J. Mol. Evol.* 19:255-271.

Jones, J. S., and Rouhani, S. 1986. Mankind's genetic bottle neck. *Nature (London)* 322:599-600.

King, M. C., and Wilson, A. C. 1975. Evolution at two levels in humans and chimpanzees. *Science* 188:107-116.

Klein, R. 1989. Biological and behavioural perspectives on modern human origins in southern Africa, in: *The Human Revolution* (P. Mellars and C. Stringer, Eds.), pp. 529-546, Edinburgh University Press, Edinburgh.

Larnach, S., and Macintosh, N. 1974. A comparative study of Solo and Australian aboriginal crania, in: *Grafton Eliot Smith: The Man and His*

Works (A. Elkin and N. Macintosh, Eds.), pp. 95-102, Sydney University Press, Sydney.

Latter, B. 1980. Genetic differences within and between populations of the major human subgroups. *Am. Nat.* 116:220-237.

Lewin, R. 1987a. Africa cradle of modern humans. *Science* 237:1292-1295.

Lewin, R. 1987b. The ummasking of mitochondrial Eve. *Science* 238:24-26.

Lucotte, G. 1989. Evidence for paternal ancestry of modern humans: Evidence from a Y–chromosome specific sequence polymorphic DNA probe, in: *The Human Revolution* (P. Mellars and C. Stringer, Eds.), pp. 39-46, Edinburgh University Press, Edinburgh.

Mellars, P. and Stringer, C., Eds. 1989. *The Human Revolution*. Edinburgh University Press, Edinburgh.

Nei, M. and Roychoudhury, A. 1982. Genetic relationship and evolution of human races. *Evol. Biol.* 14:1-59.

Parkington, J. 1990. A critique of the consensus view on the age of Howieson's Poort assemblages in South Africa, in: *The Emergence of Modern Humans: An Archaeological Perspective* (P. Mellars, Ed.), pp. 34-55, Edinburgh University Press, Edinburgh.

Rightmire, G. P. 1984. *Homo sapiens* in sub-Saharan Africa, in: *The Origins of Modern Humans: A World Survey of the Fossil Evidence* (F. H. Smith and F. Spencer, Eds.), pp. 295-325, Liss, New York.

Rightmire, G. P. 1989. Middle Stone Age humans from eastern and southern Africa, in: *The Human Revolution* (P. Mellars and C. Stringer, Eds.), pp. 109-122, Edinburgh University Press, Edinburgh.

Rouhani, S. 1989. Molecular genetics and the pattern of human evolution: Plausible and implausible models, in: *The Human Revolution* (P. Mellars and C. Stringer, Eds.), pp. 47-61, Edinburgh University Press, Edinburgh.

Saitou, N., and Omoto, K. 1987. Time and place of human origins from mtDNA data. *Nature (London)* 327:288.

Santa Luca, A. 1980. *The Ngandong Fossil Hominids*. Yale University Press, New Haven.

Slatkin, M. 1987. Gene flow and the geographical structure natural of natural populations. *Science* 236:787-792.

Slatkin, M., and Mauyama, T. 1975. Influence of gene flows on genetic distances. *Am. Nat.* 109:597-601.

Smith, F. H. and Spencer F., Eds. 1984. *The Origin of Modern Humans: A World Survey of the Fossil Evidence*, Liss, New York.

Smith, F. 1985. Continuity and change in the origin of modern *Homo sapiens*. *Z. Morph. Anthropol.* 75:197-222.

Smith, F. H., Simek, J. F., and Harrill, M. S. 1989. Geographic variation in supraorbital torus reduction during the later Pleistocene (*c.* 8000–15000 BC), in: *The Human Revolution*, (P. Mellars and C. Stringer, Eds.), pp. 172-193, Edinburgh University Press, Edinburgh.

Stoneking, M., Bhatia, K., and Wilson, A. 1986. Rate of sequence divergence estimated from restriction maps of mitochondrial DNAs from Papua, New Guinea. *Cold Spring Harbor Symp. Quant. Biol.* 51:433-439.

Stoneking M., and Cann, R. 1989. African origin of human mitochondrial DNA, in: *The Human Revolution* (P. Mellars and C. Stringer, Eds.), pp. 17-30, Edinburgh Unniversity Press, Edinburgh.

Stringer, C. 1974. Population relationships of Later Pleistocene hominids: A multivariate study of available crania. *J. Archaeol. Sci.* 1:317-342.

Stringer, C. 1978. Some problems in Middle and Upper Pleistocene hominid relationships, in: *Recent Advances in Primatology*, Volume 3, *Evolution* (D. Chivers and K. Joysey, Eds.), pp. 395-418, Academic Press, London.

Stringer, C. 1984. The definition of *Homo erectus* and the existence of the species in Africa and Europe. *Cour. Forsch. Inst. Senckenberg* 69:131-143.

Stringer, C. 1985. Middle Pleistocene hominid variability and origin of Late Pleistocene humans, in: *Ancestors: The Hard Evidence*, (E. Delson, Ed.), pp. 289-295, Liss, New York.

Stringer, C. 1989b. The origin of early modern humans: A comparison of the European and non-European evidence, in: *The Human Revolution* (P. Mellars and C. Stringer, Eds.), pp. 232-244, Edinburgh University Press, Edinburgh.

Stringer, C. 1989a. Documenting the origin of modern humans, in: *The Emergence of Modern Humans* (E. Trinkaus, Ed.), pp. 67-96, Cambridge University Press, Cambridge.

Stringer, C., Hublin, J. J., and Vandermeersch, B. 1984. The origin of anatomically modern humans in Western Europe, in: *The Origin of Modern Humans: A World Survey of the Fossil Evidence* (F. H. Smith and F. Spencer, Eds.), pp. 51-135, Liss, New York.

Tattersall, I. 1986. Species recognition in human paleontology. *J. Hum. Evol.* 15:165-175.

Thorne, A., and Wolpoff, M. 1981. Regional continuity in Australasian Pleistocene hominid evolution. *Am. J. Phys. Anthropol.* 55:337-349.

Trinkaus, E. 1983. *The Shanidar Neandertals*. Academic Press, New York.

Trinkaus, E. 1986. The Neandertals and modern human origins. *Annu. Rev. Anthropol.* 15:193-218.

Trinkaus, E., Ed. 1989. *The Emergence of Modern Humans*. Cambridge University Press, Cambridge.

Trinkaus, E., and LeMay, M. 1982. Occipital bunning among Later Pleistocene hominids. *Am. J. Phys. Anthrop.* 57:27-35.

Valladas, H., Reyss, J., Joron, J. L., Valladas, G., Bar-Yosef, O., and Vandermeersch, B. 1988. Thermolumenescene dating of Mousterian "Proto-Cro-Magnon" remains from Israel and the origin of modern man. *Nature (London)* 331:614-616.

Wainscoat, J. *et al.*, 1986. Evolutionary relationships of human populations from an analysis of nuclear DNA polymorphism. *Nature* 319:491-493.

Wainscoat, J., Hill, A. V. S., Thein, S. L., and Flint, J. 1989. Geographic distribution of alpha- and beta-globin gene cluster polymorphisms, in: *The Human Revolution* (P. Mellars and C. Stringer, Eds.), pp. 31-38, Edinburgh University Press, Edinburgh.

Weiss, K. 1984. On the numbers of the genus *Homo* who have ever lived and some of the evolutionary implications. *Hum. Biol.* 56:637-645.

Whittam, T. *et al.*, 1986. Allele variation in human mitochondrial genes based on patterns of restriction site polymorphism. *Proc. Natl. Acad. Sci. U.S.A.* 83:9611-9615.

Wilson, A. C. *et al.*, 1985. Mitochondrial DNA and two perspectives on evolutionary genetics *Biol J. Linn. Soc.* 26:375-400.

Wolpoff, M. 1980. *Paleoanthropology*. Knopf, New York.

Wolpoff, M. 1985. Human evolution at the peripheries: The pattern at the eastern edge, in: *Hominid Evolution: Past, Present and Future* (P. V. Tobias, Ed.), pp. 355-365, Liss, New York.

Wolpoff, M. 1989a. Multiregional evolution: The fossil alternative to Eden, in: *The Human Revolution* (P. Mellars and C. Stringer, Eds.), pp. 62-108, Edinburgh University Press, Edinburgh.

Wolpoff, M. 1989b. The place of the Neandertals in human evolution, in: *The Emergence of Modern Humans* (E. Trinkaus, Ed.), pp.97-141, Cambridge University Press, Cambridge.

Wolpoff, M., Wu Xin Zhi, and Thorne, A. 1984. Modern *Homo sapiens* origins. A general theory of hominid evolution involving the fossil evidence from East Asia, in: *The Origin of Modern Humans: A World Survey of the Fossil Evidence* (F. H. Smith and F. Spencer, Eds.), pp. 411-483, Liss, New York.

Wu Xin Zhi and Wu Maolin 1985. *Palaeoanthropology and Palaeolithic Archaeology in the People's Rupublic of China* (Wu Rukang and J. Olsen, Eds.), p. 91, Academic Press, Orlando.

48

Multiregional Evolution: The Fossil Alternative to Eden

M. H. Wolpoff

INTRODUCTION

In 1976 W. W. Howells reviewed the evidence concerning the origin or origins of modern populations, and used the description "Noah's Ark" hypothesis for one possible explanation—the contention that all living populations have a single recent origin from a source population that was already modern. In developing this hypothesis Howells proposed that once these modern populations appeared, they spread rapidly and replaced indigenous populations over the inhabited world. The "Noah's Ark" hypothesis is not a classic punctuational scheme; the modern populations may not be a different species according to Howells' interpretation, and the population divergence may not have been at the ecological *or* geographic periphery of the human range, as the punctuational model requires. Howells suggested "Noah's Ark" as one of several possibilities for the explanation of modern population origins, and was unsure as to which was correct.

In the past ten years, interpretations of new genetic evidence have been brought forward to modify the "Noah's Ark" hypothesis into a much more focused statement of a rapid punctuational event at the origin of modern *Homo sapiens*. The interpretations of several different lines of genetic evidence are said to combine to suggest that modern populations originated within the last 200,000 years, all descending from a common mother who lived in Africa and gave rise to a small population of a *new species* (cf. Stringer and Andrews 1988) with severely reduced genetic variability in their mitochondrian DNA (mtDNA). This explanation of the limited mdDNA variation is based on an assumption of recent common genetic ancestry (see reviews by Cann *et al.* 1987; Wainscoat 1987; and Jones 1986) and depends on the assertion that the descendant populations spread throughout the inhabited world and replaced the indigenous inhabitants without admixture, which is why they must be considered a new species. Therefore, combining as it does the contention of African origins, the descent from a single Eve (the mitochondrial mother common to all modern populations) and the subsequent spread of modern peoples 'out of Africa,' this interpretation of the genetic data might best be called the 'Garden of Eden' hypothesis.

The main elements of the Garden of Eden hypothesis are that modern humans *arose recently* from a small source popula-

tion, approximately 200,000 years ago in Africa, and that this population was a *new species*. It is contended that this new species split into two main branches in Africa and that one of these passed through a bottleneck of small population size in the process of emigration from Africa, and rapidly replaced indigenous human populations in other parts of the world without mixture.

Cann *et al* (1987: 35) claim that there is one interpretation of the human fossil record that fits the Garden of Eden hypothesis, and similar contentions have been offered by other geneticists. The purposes of this paper are threefold: to critically examine these interpretations of the genetic data, and their alternatives; to present and discuss evidence from the human fossil record which indicates that the palaeontological data *do not* fit the Garden of Eden hypothesis; and to indicate alternative interpretations of the fossil record in the context of multiregional evolution theory and in accordance with a different consistent set of interpretations of the genetic evidence. Human fossils are absolutely critical in the ongoing research on modern population origins. The human fossil record has the potential to provide a valid independent basis for attempting to refute the contention that all living populations have a single recent common origin as a new species.

THE GARDEN OF EDEN HYPOTHESIS

Invasion without Admixture

For the Garden of Eden interpretation of the mtDNA variation to be correct, the absence of admixture must necessarily characterize the relations between the invading populations and the indigenous natives they presumably replaced. This interpretation requires that these populations cannot have interbred at all, or the older mitochondrial lines would be found in living populations. Presumable when modern humans left their place of origin, this population must have been reproductively isolated from the indigenous natives they were replacing in order to account for the lack of mixture between Eve's mtDNA line and the more ancient mtDNA lineages that is claimed in the Garden of Eden interpretation (Gould 1987). Since successful human invaders would be expected to incorporate at least the females of the native populations into their societies, the inability to have fertile offspring is a critical assumption in this interpretation. Therefore, the Garden of Eden interpretation requires that these invaders are a different species. Further, the observation of what was taken to be a unique African mitochondrial lineage has been interpreted to show a lack of gene flow after the ancestors of modern populations left the continent (otherwise this lineage would not be unique to Africa). If true, this would mean that any subsequent world-wide evolutionary changes in the mtDNA must have happened in parallel, and it is unlikely that there were many of these. *It follows that according to the Garden of Eden hypothesis Eve was in a population that was either directly and uniquely ancestral to modern* Homo sapiens, *or itself was the earliest modern* Homo sapiens *population.*

The evidence said to support the hypothesis that the appearance of modern populations required the origin of a new species and its subsequent rapid geographic dispersal is not based on genetic data alone. It also incorporates evidence from the fossil record for ascertaining the details of 'who, what, when, where, and why' for the earliest modern humans (cf. Stringer and Andrews 1988). This is because if modern humans are a new species with a recent origin, both the time and the place of this origin can be discovered by finding the earliest modern specimens. It is just such evidence that Cann *et al.* (1987) cite in support of their contentions. In particular, data concerning the 'when' and 'where' are critical for this interpretation.

When and Where are the Earliest Moderns?

A good deal of effort has been expended in seeking the *earliest* remains of any fossils with the modern human form because according to the Garden of Eden hypothesis they will be discovered at the place of origin of all modern populations—*a presumption which assumes the hypothesis to be tested, namely that modern populations have a single migrational origin.* The 'when,' in other words determines the 'where' according to this hypothesis. Over the years, the candidate for the earliest modern human has changed considerably, and therefore so has the place of origin for modern *Homo sapiens.* Cautiously, in initially stating his 'Noah's Ark' hypothesis, Howells (1976) took no position as to where this source area might have been, but others have specifically suggested sub-Saharan Africa (Protsch 1975, 1978; Bräuer 1984a, 1984b; Stringer 1984a, 1984b, 1985, 1989; Wainscoat *et al.* 1986; Cann, Stoneking and Wilson 1987), the Levant (Vandermeersch 1970, 1981) or more generally (as the new Qafzeh dates suggest: Valladas *et al.* 1988) Western Asia (Howell 1951; Bodmer and Cavalli-Sforza 1976), China (Weckler 1957; Chang 1963; Macintosh and Larnach 1976; Denaro *et al.* 1981), Australia (Gribbin and Cherfas 1982), or even more unexpected places (Hogan 1977).

However, an important aspect of the Garden of Eden hypothesis is the specific evidence purported to reveal Africa as this place of origin. Some of this evidence is genetic (Wainscoat *et al.* 1986; Jones and Rouhani 1986a; Cann *et al.* 1987: but see Denaro *et al.* 1981; Johnson *et al.* 1983; Giles and Ambrose 1986). Morphological 'evidence' for an African origin relies on the presence of fossil human remains of modern *Homo sapiens* from this continent *with early dates* since there is no basis for the contention that there is anything plesiomorphic about the morphology of fossil or living Africans that would cause one to

believe that they specifically reflect the ancestral condition for all living populations on the basis of their morphology alone. Unfortunately, the question of which African fossils are earliest is confused by what seem to be endless problems involved in the accurate determinations of how long ago the individuals concerned died.

There are many potential African Eves, or at least many fossil remains that are possible members of Eve's immediate family (Rightmire 1981), or mitochondrial lineage (see below). These fossils are said to demonstrate an African origin of modern populations because they represent the earliest appearing populations to closely resemble modern humans from any region. Yet the dates for these Africans are riddled with problems. In fact, of the sub-Saharan sites in question—Klasies River Mount, Border Cave, and Omo Kibish—*not one single specimen thought to be an 'early modern' has a defensible radiometric date.*

In the case of Border Cave it is not even clear that most of the adult specimens have a provenience! Stringer (1989), who generally supports the interpretation of modern populations migrating out of Africa, expresses caution about the dates claimed for the Border Cave specimens because of the provenience issue and the possibility of burial from a more recent level for the infant and adult mandible (see also Klein 1989). As Rightmire, in his review of the situation at Border Cave, puts it (1979:26):

> With the except of a new adult mandible . . . all of the adult skeletal material was dug out of the cave by Horton and its original position in the deposits was not directly verified (p. 25) . . . The course of evolution outside of southern Africa cannot be determined from the evidence considered here.

As far as the Klasies River Mouth Cave specimens are concerned, the published dates are based on faunal correlations, attempts to relate the cave fauna to coastal faunas, and attempts to relate the coastal faunas to the oxygen-isotope-based sea-core chronology. These widely quoted 'dates' actually stand a good chance of being incorrect (Binford 1984, 1986) and the age of most of the specimens may be one half of what is generally assumed, and may correspond to the appearance of 'modern' populations in other regions. Moreover, it is important to consider exactly which specimens these dates are associated with. According to Stringer (1989) the more recent dates do not apply to three specimens: the mandible KRM 21776, the KRM 16425 frontal fragment, and a newly discovered maxilla. These three specimens are morphologically archaic. The frontal has a vertically thick although non-projecting, superciliary arch that is not unlike that of Florisbad in its central portion, lack of nasal root depression, and low nasal profile. The mandible is extraordinarily robust for a 'modern' find from any geographic region, let alone from Africa where gnathic reduction is early. It is *not* 'modern' by any reasonable set of morphological criteria. Stringer describes the maxilla as edentulous and very robust. In sum, because this *earlier* sample from the Klasies cave *is not modern,* the older dates reported from the base of the Klasies sequence are not obviously relevant to the problem of *modern* population origins.

The Omo radiometric dates have been continuously disputed ever since their first publication because radiocarbon determinations based on shells are notoriously inaccurate, and recent Uranium/Thorium dates are problematic. Various faunal and stratigraphic 'dates' have been suggested as replacements for the radiometric estimates (Day 1972; Stringer 1989) and according to these the age of the three fossil humans could range between 40,000 and 130,000 years. However, which of the various date estimates may be correct cannot be established, and the fact is that there is no particular reason to accept any of them as valid!

There is one other aspect of the allegedly earliest modern human specimens from these three sites that must be taken into account with regard to the validity of the Garden of Eden hypothesis. Specimens from these sites are fundamentally *African* in their morphological details (Rightmire 1979, 1984a; Wolpoff 1980; Bräuer 1984b). The basis of this claim is in the numerous comparisons I have had the opportunity to examine (for instance, see Wolpoff 1980); I make this statement knowingly, and in spite of Day and Stringer's (1982) multivariate assessment of their Omo I reconstruction. I do not believe this multivariate assessment is valid. While the Day and Stringer analysis concluded that of the living populations they chose for comparison, Omo I is most like the Norse sample (although the difference from other comparisons was not judged significant), unfortunately—while there are published data—neither living nor subfossil East Africans (cf. Robbins 1974, 1980) were included within the comparative samples.

The important fact is that even if we assume the 'early' sub-Saharan sites are dated correctly and that the specimens associated with the dates can validly be regarded as modern *Homo sapiens* (but see Wolpoff 1986), the fact is that these three sites preserve the remains of the earliest modern *Africans*, morphologically as well as geographically. If they truly represent the earliest modern populations from any region, they establish the presence of an African morphological complex in moderns prior to their leaving Africa, as is required by the Garden of Eden hypothesis. The Eve of the genes, of course, need not have been in a modern *Homo sapiens* population. Yet, even if pre-modern, the fossil specimens themselves suggest that the population she presumably lived in must eventually have evolved into the African version of modern humanity *before* expanding to replace other populations within Africa and beyond (Stringer and Andrews 1988). No matter how long ago Eve lived, the 'no admixture' requirement of the Garden of Eden hypothesis requires that the migration out of Africa was *by a new species, of morphologically-modern Africans*.

This, however, creates a contradiction. Throughout the history of attempts to find the origin of the *earliest* modern *Home sapiens* populations, in each place early modern remains are found their skeletal remains invariably have been recognized to exhibit the unique characteristics common to that region. Thus, for instance, in Australasia Niah and Mungo I closely resemble modern Australians; in China Liujiang specifically resembles modern south Chinese, and the similarities of the Zhoukoudian Upper Cave remains to modern North Asians are equally clear; and in Europe the Aurignacian Europeans such as the Mladec specimens uniquely resemble modern Europeans. However, according to the Garden of Eden hypothesis and following from the discussion above, the earliest modern Africans were already distinctly African in their morphology (see Bräuer 1984a, 1984b). Therefore, because it is claimed that the ancestors of these modern populations left Africa as a new species, according to the Garden of Eden

Hypothesis the characteristics of modern populations in each other region outside of Africa must have developed *in transit*, since by the time the populations arrived to presumably replace the indigenous inhabitants *they already were distinctly regional in morphology*.

Out of Africa: The Mitochondrial Connection

The most dramatic (and most highly publicized) statements of the Garden of Eden hypothesis are based on an analysis of mtDNA variation (Cann, Stoneking, and Wilson 1987). From the study of 147 people, these geneticists concluded that most human fossils dated earlier than the late Pleistocene have nothing to do with human evolution, because all living people have a common African origin and left Africa 100-200,000 years ago, as discussed above. The basis for this 'out of Africa' hypothesis, with its migration date, is the interpretation that the existing mitochondrial lineages reflect the consequences of a tree-like divergence network from a single common mother (or a few mothers with the same mitochondrial type: see Gould 1987) that lived at this time. An unavoidable implication is that all indigenous (presumably *Homo erectus*) populations that were not ancestral to this African Eve were replaced by the new species without admixture. Since this would presumably include some of the earlier African fossil hominids and surely all of the fossil hominids found outside of Africa dated earlier than 200,000 years ago, the classic text by the late Wilfred Le Gros Clark, *The Fossil Evidence for Human Evolution*, could, on revision, be shortened dramatically.

The main interpretations said to be 'explained' by the hypothesis of total replacement from the Garden of Eden are based on assessments of population relationships as determined from trees of genetic or morphological information which are interpreted to show a common recent origin for human populations (Edwards 1971; Cavalli-Sforza *et al.* 1964; Cavalli-Sforza and Edwards 1965; Nei and Roychoudhury 1982; Howells 1973; Guglielmino-Matessi *et al.* 1979; Jones 1981). These trees are used to show relationships based on shared features, and account for variation as the result of population splits and divergences from a common ancestor, with subsequent differences between the branches a consequence of random independent mutations.

However, there is a fundamental question as to whether trees based on genetics or morphology are actually useful for determining the relationships between human populations, let alone relevant to ascertaining the timing of their divergences (Weiss and Maruyama 1976; Morton and Lalouel 1973; Harpending 1974; Howells 1976). In fact, it has been suggested that branching analyses do not provide any insight into the reconstruction of population history (Livingstone 1973; Wolpoff, Wu, and Thorne 1984). This is because branching analysis necessarily assumes that population differences arose from a common ancestry through population splitting and continued isolation. For the analysis to be valid the branching must be recent (i.e. the bush must be shallow-rooted), the similarities on the branches must come from descent (i.e. must be shared with the stem population), and the branches can only be connected at their points of divergence (a prerequisite that is more likely to be valid when the branches are different species and not likely to be accurate when they are different populations within the same species). Unfortunately, just as a correlation analysis will provide a 'number' even when comparing apples to oranges, a branching analysis will provide branches to the form of the structure assumed to underlie population relationships whether or not these actually characterized population histories.

Interpretation of the branching pattern as clusters of relationships, and calibration of these associations in terms of evolutionary differences, assumes (1) that the differences are the consequence of constantly accumulating random mutations and drift, and (2) that gene flow did not occur. However, commonalities in selection may cause populations to appear more similar than their actual histories might suggest (Livingstone 1980, but see Cohan 1984). Even a small amount of gene flow between two populations will greatly reduce the observed magnitude of population differences and consequently minimize the time estimated to have passed since population splitting (Weiss and Maruyama 1976). Conversely, gene flow between one population in a recently-diverged sister pair and an "outside" population will make the population pair less closely related genetically. However, are they less closely related *phylo*genetically? They will certainly appear to have diverged from each other earlier than was actually the case (Weiss 1986).

The obvious historic fact is that there have been numerous invasions, and a marked rate of gene flow between human populations since the end of the Pleistocene. These have affected every human population on the planet. All populations, therefore, should appear genetically and morphologically to be more closely related than they might actually be, if the analysis of the populational relationships assumes a splitting model of populational divergences. Another Holocene phenomenon that affects modern genetic variability in unknown ways is the demographic instability of the past two millennia, with numerous population replacements, ubiquitous admixture, and dramatic population expansions.

There are some additional problems in the genetic analyses supporting the Garden of Eden hypothesis. Geneticists discussing the palaeontological data have gleefully reported on the lack of agreement among the palaeoanthropologists, when claiming that at least one set of palaeoanthropological interpretations fit their own data. It is therefore appropriate here to point out that the disarray among the geneticists over the interpretation of the mtDNA data provides the same opportunity for a palaeoanthropologist! One set of contradictory interpretations emerges from a consideration of what should have been a much less ambiguous determination than modern human population divergences—the separation of human and chimpanzee lineages. The problem spotlighted by this analysis involves the *rate* of mtDNA divergence in different lineages. The 2%-4% divergence rate for mtDNA assumed in the Cann *et al.* analyses give a 1.4-2.8 million year divergence estimate (that is, a 2.1 million year mean divergence date) for human and chimpanzee lines (Saitou and Omoto 1987). Using similar techniques, Hasegawa, Kishino and Yano (1985) earlier derived an estimate for the chimpanzee-human split of 2.7 ± 0.6 million years ago. In attempting to explain their surprising result, Hasegawa *et al.* admit there might be some problems in this estimated splitting time because of the earlier dates known for *Australopithecus afarensis*. Instead of regarding this species as a 'dental hominid,' as Sarich once described the australopithecines dated earlier than his divergence-date estimate, these authors propose that mtDNA passed across species boundaries between australopithecines and chimpanzee ancestors. This would ac-count for the 'too recent' divergence determined by their method, since one consequence of interspecies mtDNA transfer is to make the species appear less diverged than they actually were. Hasegawa *et al.* note (1985: 171):

> If interspecies transfer of mtDNA between proto-human and proto-chimpanzee did indeed occur, it is tempting to speculate in which direction the transfer occurred. The lesser intraspecies polymorphism of human mtDNA compared to that of chimpanzees . . . suggests that the transfer occurred from proto-chimpanzee into proto-human.

Therefore, because of the potential for inter*species* mtDNA transfer, the rate determination may be incorrect, and this estimate of the chimpanzee-human split time may be too recent. But what is the real rate? The rate that gives an estimated date of 2.1 million years for the chimpanzee-human divergence is associated with other inconsistent or too-recent split dates. For instance Cann *et al.* (1987: 33) determine their base substitution rate of 2%-4% per million years for modern population divergence from 'known' dates of migration that include 30,000 years ago for the peopling of New Guinea, 40,000 for Australia (a surprising difference since these were the same continent at this time), and 12,000 for the New World. These dates, at the low end of the ranges presented by Stoneking, Bhatia and Wilson (1986), are far too recent even by conservative estimates, perhaps by as much as 50 per cent of the real value. Therefore, in the Cann *et al.* study the mutation rate has been overestimated, just as it is overestimated in the determination of the chimpanzee-human divergence at 2.1 million years. The reason for the overestimation could be the same as for the chimpanzee-human split—i.e. gene flow between populations—but if so in this case the effort is quite likely to have been much greater since the gene flow was among populations within the same species (the error in the chimpanzee-human divergence estimate is by a factor of 2-3 times).

Perhaps an error of this magnitude is to be expected. Divergence rates calculated per base-pair per million years vary between 0.5% and 2.0% in primate studies by different researchers (reviewed by Honeycutt and Wheeler 1987). The *fastest* of these is used as the *slowest* rate in the discussions of divergence times by Hasegawa, Cann and their colleagues.

In fact, there is a convergence in the estimates of how 'too recent' these chimpanzee-human split-time determinations may be. Based on palaeontological data I believe there is a maximum divergence date estimate of no more than 8 million years, and a minimum estimate of no less than 5 million years. Other estimates of this divergence are also quite different. Independently, Nei (1985, 1987) derives an mtDNA divergence rate of 0.71%, *between 2.8 and 5.6 times slower than the estimates used by Cann and her colleagues*. This slower rate suggests divergence times much more in line with the palaeontological (as well as other) estimates. Thus, as calculated from this rate, the Nei estimate gives a chimpanzee-human divergence determination of 6.6 million years, a date that markedly contrasts with the other mtDNA estimates (Hasegawa *et al.* 1985; Brown *et al.* 1982) but conforms to the palaeontological data and is very similar to that determined from nuclear DNA hybridization data (6.3 million years as ascertained by Sibley and Ahlquist 1984).

The base substitution mutation rate of 0.71% per million years suggests a divergence time for modern populations of approximately 850,000 years. At so early a time this divergence would be among *Homo erectus* populations. Mixture with indigenous populations would not be an issue, since this would probably represent the first hominid migrations out of Africa. Therefore, it need not have been a speciation event, and in any case at this date—at the beginning of the Middle Pleistocene—it could not possibly represent the origin of *modern Homo sapiens*.

If this estimated rate is a reasonable alternative to the 2%-4% rate of mtDNA divergence used by Cann and her colleagues, and others, it dramatically effects the dates widely reported in newspapers, popular magazines (Gould 1987) and scientific journals (Cann *et al.* 1987; Stringer and Andrews 1988) for modern human populational divergences. *One wonders how much more of an underestimate is involved in the mtDNA calibration of population-splitting within* Homo sapiens *because of interpopulation mtDNA transfer?*

According to the assumptions required by the mtDNA analysis discussed above, there was no interpopulation transfer at all, since the expanding population was a different species (see Stoneking and Cann, 1989). If this was the case, the rate differences that are seen when comparing the slower rate calculated from the widely accepted 5-8 million year chimpanzee-human divergence with the faster rate suggesting recent modern population origins (i.e. Eve) are inexplicable. But if the Garden of Eden hypothesis is incorrect because modern populations are *not* a new species, admixture could explain the differences in calculated rates. Moreover, a reasonable alternative interpretation of the mtDNA data presented by Nei also indicates a much slower divergence rate, and is supported by the nuclear DNA hybridization data. This slower rate indicates an estimated divergence time for modern human populations that approximates the Early-Middle Pleistocene boundary, a time when an increasing number of recent estimates (reviewed by Wolpoff and Nkini 1985) suggest *Homo erectus* might have first left Africa. This 'revised' estimate of a divergence time based on the mitochondrial data also fits a divergence estimate based on independent evidence for other faunal migrations into Eurasia (Turner 1984).

The more ancient estimate of human populational divergences is also in accord with the multiregional evolution hypothesis (Wolpoff, Wu, and Thorne 1984) which proposes that human geographic variation dates to the initial emergence of *Homo erectus* from Africa. In fact, the only argument for not accepting the more ancient estimate for modern human populational divergences based on the slower rate of mtDNA evolution is that even at this age the time of divergence may be too recent for an accurate determination based on mtDNA analysis (Nei 1987; Honeycutt and Wheeler 1987). In sum, the slower (0.71% per base-pair per million years) mtDNA divergence rate determination is corroborated by other genetic data (nuclear DNA hybridization), and palaeontological data indicating a 5-8 million year chimpanzee-human divergence and a 0.75 to 1.0 million year date for the *Homo erectus* expansions out of Africa.

The contention that an actual divergence date can be determined from genetic data rests on two assumptions: that the main source of mtDNA lineage differences (i.e. variation) is mutations; and that the rate of mutation accumulation is constant (linear) for a finite period of time (presumably including the population divergences in question). But what direct evidence exists for rate constancy over this time? This 'evidence' may

not be as good as is generally supposed. A study of mtDNA variation in Amerindians (Wallace, Garrison, and Knowler 1985) revealed marked differences between Amerind tribes, important differences between the Amerindians and Asians, and the apparent retention of rare Asian variants in some of the Amerindian mtDNA lineages. Adhering to the assumption of a constant mutation rate, the authors account for these observations by presuming there were numerous founder events during the colonization of the New World, some of which established extremely rare Asian variants in Amerindian populations, *and that the living tribes studied each represent a separate migration from Asia some 20-40,000 BP.* In my view, a much more parsimonious explanation would be an inconsistent and erratic mutation rate for this period, or the presence of selection acting on the mtDNA—*a possibility that cannot be discounted* given independent data that suggests that there is significant selection against some mtDNA variants (Hale and Singh 1986; Saitou and Omoto 1987).

In all, the assumption of rate-consistency for mtDNA evolution in human populations over this time span is very problematic. In particular, it is far from clear that a date estimate for human populational divergences is even possible using the technique, especially if these divergences were recent. Because of the slow rate and stochastic nature of base-pair substitutions, it is far more likely that the calibration of recent events will engender significant error than the calibration of more ancient events. Thus, of the two determinations that potentially do not agree, the calibration of recent migrations (such as used in the rate determinations by Cann, Stoneking and their colleagues) is far more problematic than rate determinations based on the divergence of chimpanzee and human lineages.

Apart from differences in divergence rate estimates, there is some independent evidence to support the contention that population mixing has significantly altered the interpretation of mtDNA variation. Mixing is ubiquitous in the historic record of human population movements, regardless of how different the physical characteristics or cultural variations of the populations might be. The effects of mixing are to invalidate branching analysis, and to confuse both the clusters of relationships and their magnitudes based on mtDNA variation. Thus, for instance, in an analysis of the mtDNA-based genetic distances presented by Cann and her colleagues, the New Guineans seem to be most closely related to Africans and only distantly related to Australians on the resulting phylogenetic trees (Saitou and Omoto 1987). Yet, by virtually every other measure (including nuclear DNA analysis) New Guineans and Australians are the same people, only separated since the end of the Pleistocene. Clearly, mixing takes place in non-human populations as well. In fact, it is the analysis of mtDNA itself that provided evidence of significant hybridization between two deer species, white-tailed and mule deer (Carr *et al.* 1986). A study of two closely related mice species with ranges that overlap in southern Denmark showed that while the nuclear DNA of each species penetrates only a few kilometres into the range of the other, the mtDNA variants of one are widespread within the other throughout Scandinavia (Ferris *et al.* 1983). A tree analysis based on mtDNA for these two species would be totally misleading (Jones 1986).

Moreover, one can ask whether *any* rate for recent populational divergence can be accurately measured. In a recent paper on rate determination based on the peoplings of New Guinea,

Australia, and the Americas (Stoneking, Bhatia, and Wilson 1986) the potential sources of error presented (and discounted) include three that in reality contribute considerable uncertainty to the determination because they reflect assumptions that are almost certainly in part or even as a whole incorrect (these assumptions are discussed in Bryan (Ed.) 1986; Greenberg, Turner and Zegura 1986; Gruhn 1987; Kirk and Szathmary (Eds) 1985; Kirk and Thorne (Eds) 1976; Stewart 1974; Szathmary and Ossenberg 1978). Stoneking and his colleagues point out that the rate determination is based on the assumption that there were not multiple colonization events. However, the genetic, archaeological and linguistic evidence for multiple colonization events in the peopling of both greater Australia and the Americas is incontestable. A second assumption is that there was no appreciable back-migration from these areas. For North America, at least, this is unlikely to be correct. Finally, accurate colonization dates must be assumed. A review of the immense literature on this specific point suggests that the assumption of date accuracy is not supportable. My 25 years of reading the literature on this topic shows this assumption to be unrealistic, at best. A recent paper reviewing mtDNA variation concludes (Honeycutt and Wheeler 1987):

> The effectiveness of the molecular data to provide information on divergence times depends on a proper point of calibration as well as a demonstration that the molecules are evolving in a clock-like manner. When dealing with divergence times involving periods of less than one million years, the calibration must be accurate and errors small if meaningful estimates are desired. *Not only is there considerable disagreement as to the identification and date of key fossils, but the error or range of time estimates provided by both nuclear gene loci and mtDNA lead one to place little confidence in the dates* (my italics).

There are alternative interpretations of what the observed pattern of mtDNA variation reveals about evolutionary history. For instance, in a study of *Drosophila subobscura* (Latorre, Moya, and Ayala 1986), a species whose colonization of the New World involves known times and places of origin, an analysis of the mtDNA variation 'provides no clue of the precise geographic origin of the colonizers.' Nor, in fact, does it provide a realistic estimate for the age of the Eve of the flies. It is possible that this is because there was no Eve, and that there is a different explanation for the observed variation.

> Today's world population of *D. subobscura* consists of many millions of individuals. It might well be the case that, a few hundred thousand years hence, all *D. subobscura* flies have mtDNA as derived from morph I. That would not mean that the mtDNA of the descendants derives only from one *D. subobscura* currently living—morph I is found in 44% of the living population. More importantly, the individuals living in that remote generation would count among their ancestors not only those females from which they inherited their mitochondria, but also innumerable other females and males from which they inherited their nuclear hereditary material (Latorre, Moya, and Avise 1986: 8652-8653).

How could this be? It is clearly possible that differential lineage survivorship, rather than singular recent common ancestry for maternal lineages, is the cause of the limited mtDNA variation *Drosophila*, as well as *Homo* (Avise, Neigel, and Arnold 1984).

Probability models with stochastic survivorship assumptions show that virtually all existing mitochondrial lineages will become extinct, even in a stable population. With selection against some of the genome, and the variations in population sizes that almost certainly occurred, the process would be even more rapid. According to calculations by Avise *et al.*, a population *founded* by 15,000 *unrelated* females would have a 50 per cent chance of *appearing* to descend from a single female within 18,000 generations as a consequence of stochastic lineage extinctions in a stable population. After this time all of the *mitochondrial* lines would be traceable to a single female, although *contra* Gould (1987: 18), this much later population would have *multiple* nuclear DNA descent, possibly from most of the founders. There need not have been a mtDNA-nuclear DNA link through a 'killer' population spreading. It is interesting that 18,000 generations may represent perhaps as few as 300,000 years for humans, given the current estimates of a short lifespan for pre-modern humans (Trinkaus and Thompson 1987). This time-frame is similar to the Cann *et al.* estimate under a branching and replacement model. However, it is an overestimate if the likelihood of selection (Hale and Singh 1986; Whittam *et al.* 1986) and the virtual certainty that prehistoric human populations were much smaller (Weiss 1984) are taken into account. Therefore, a model of selection and differential lineage extinctions from an earlier population with equally limited mtDNA variation could account for today's limited DNA without recourse to assuming that there was a small original founding population of a new human species.

In a model much better fitting the fossil record, concordant with a number of interpretations of its evolutionary pattern (Weidenreich 1946; Wolpoff *et al.* 1984), female exchanges between indigenous populations of pre-modern humans, combined with a constant rate of stochastic lineage extinctions, may well have resulted in a homogeneous distribution of a few mtDNA lineages across widely spread human populations in the past (Saitou and Omoto 1987). This ancient distribution of genetic polymorphisms, perhaps itself the consequence of a previous long span of differential stochastic lineage extinctions, could have provided, by chance, a single surviving mtDNA line for descendant populations as the result of continued lineage extinctions. Therefore, the pattern of today may simply show random survivorship from what earlier was a single very common widespread mitochondrial lineage and would thereby not reflect a limited nuclear DNA source. A common origin for maternally-cloned cytoplasms can be completely independent of a common origin for nuclei, just as the descent of family names can be independent of genetic inheritance. The Late Pleistocene provides more than sufficient time to allow for the possibility that selection and stochastic lineage extinctions could account for the limited mtDNA variation reported by Cann *et al.* and others. If so, the dates estimated for population divergences from this variation, the discussions about a place of origin for 'Eve,' and the evidence for bottlenecks in human evolution (see below), are all without obvious meaning.

Bottlenecking: A Different Foundation for the Garden of Eden Hypothesis

The second source of a genetic argument for population replacement comes from recent discussions of bottlenecking. The idea that a bottleneck occurred during the foundation of *Homo sapiens* developed in part as a consequence of these same mtDNA studies (Brown 1980; Wilson *et al.* 1985). The bottleneck involved a period of small population size and is presumably marked in living populations by reduced genetic variability. The data supporting this interpretation derive in part from the low level of mtDNA variability reported within several human populations, and a nuclear DNA analysis for the beta-globin gene cluster (Wainscoat *et al.* 1986, 1989). The beta-globin data were interpreted to show a basic split between all African and non-African populations through a genetic distance analysis based on the 14 genotypes observed for this cluster. Moreover, the loss of what Wainscoat and his co-workers regard as the 'common' African genotype for this cluster in all non-African populations is regarded as evidence for genetic drift due to small population size (Wainscoat *et al.* 1986: 493) that presumably took place at the time that the populations split and *Homo sapiens* left Africa.

In a review article, Jones and Rouhani (1986a) bring together the mtDNA and beta-globin gene-cluster data to attempt an estimate of how small the bottleneck was. The size of the bottleneck is determined from the opportunity for drift and therefore is related to the length of time between leaving Africa and dispersing through the rest of the world. Jones and Rouhani provide us with an '*informed guess*' of 20,000 years. For the bottlenecked population (the ancestral group for all living non-African peoples) the estimated mean population size for a bottleneck of 20,000 years length is given as 600, or alternatively as 6 individuals for 200 years, or in the most blatantly stated Garden of Eden interpretation, a *single couple for 60 years.*

There are more difficulties with the bottlenecking argument than the biblical interpretation might suggest. Evidence now suggests that bottlenecks reduce fitness (Bryant, McCommas and Combs 1986)—hardly what one would expect in the population history of a new species that was so competitively superior to existing indigenous populations (of the old species) that it was able to rapidly replace them.

Moreover, the mtDNA bottleneck and the beta-globin bottleneck *cannot have been the same event.* The mtDNA bottleneck occurred during a speciation event and is used as evidence of modern *Homo sapiens* descending from Eve, or from a very small population. But if there was a split between a branch of the African and the non-African populations all of which remained within the same species, as the beta-globin evidence is taken to indicate, how could this split also be the *speciation event* required for the origin of modern populations by the Garden of Eden hypothesis? Therefore these events cannot be the same! The evidence for bottlenecking taken from the beta-globin analysis is often given as support for the recent African origin of modern humanity interpretation of mtDNA variation. This is incorrect. The two arguments contradict each other and therefore cannot both be valid, if in fact either is.

The beta-globin analysis also has its set of internal problems (Van Valen 1986). For instance, the divergence tree (and its calibration) is based on a genetic-distance analysis for ten populations in which three European populations (British, Cypriot and Italian) are analyzed separately while two African populations (one a mix of East and West Africans, and the other Nigerians from three tribes) are lumped together. This lumping makes the African data seem more distinct from the rest of the world than might actually be the case. The ancestral haplotype for the five sites studied in the beta-globin gene cluster is yet to

be identified, and therefore directionality of the changes cannot be determined (Honeycutt and Wheeler 1987). The African distinction is even more confused by Wainscoat *et al.*'s treatment of the discovery of what they regard as the unique African genotype for the beta-globin gene cluster *outside of Africa.* In fact, *both* of the African genotypes also appear in the Melanesian sample where, it is asserted, they are homoplasies. But there are no data presented to show that these have the 'independent non-African origin' claimed for them, and evidence in this case is absolutely critical because with both of the so-called 'unique' African genotypes found *outside* of Africa (and, suspiciously, in the same population), there is no longer any evidence for a bottleneck, let alone the basis for an estimate of when it might have occurred.

In sum, the bottlenecking interpretation of the beta-globin data is beset with a number of factual and interpretative difficulties, and contradicts the mtDNA interpretation discussed above, even though proponents of each of these tend to quote the other for support. There are similar citational circularities between the mtDNA analysis literature and the palaeoanthropological literature (Eckhardt 1987), in which geneticists quote the conclusions of papers written by palaeoanthropologists about the time of modern populational origins while in these papers the palaeoanthropologists quote the same geneticists for support. It is quite possible that *neither* interpretation of genetic data is correct. Perhaps the geneticists Jones and Rouhani were premature in claiming (1986a: 449): 'the main lesson to be learned from palaeontology is that evolution always takes place somewhere else.'

REGIONAL CONTINUITY

The Fossil Evidence

In spite of all the above considerations, if the interpretations of the genetic data suggesting there was a fairly recent single origin for modern human populations are considered correct, then this explanation must apply to all *populations.* There can be no continuity between archaic and modern populations except in sub-Saharan Africa, where ironically the morphological evidence for continuity between archaic and more modern populations is poorest (Thorne 1981; Thorne and Wolpoff 1981; Rightmire 1976, 1981, 1984b). The Garden of Eden hypothesis requires the conclusion that the archaeological and morphological evidence for continuity in Australasia (Weidenreich 1946; Thorne and Wolpoff 1981; Jelínek 1982), North Asia (Weidenreich 1943; Wolpoff, Wu, and Thorne 1984; Wolpoff 1985), North Africa (Ferembach 1979; Jelínek 1980, 1985), and Central Europe (Jelínek 1969, 1976, 1978, 1985; Smith 1982, 1984, 1985; Wolpoff 1982a) is incorrect. And indeed, some of those authors who support the interpretations of the genetic data discussed above recognize this and dismiss all these fossils (Cann *et al.* 1987; Gould 1987; Rightmire 1987; Stringer and Andrews 1988), although never with a discussion or refutation of the detailed morphological data presented by the fossil evidence which *supports* the regional evolution hypothesis.

However, because any convincing fossil evidence for morphological continuity outside of Africa refutes the Garden of Eden hypothesis (Eckhardt 1987), the fossil data especially at the peripheries provides the only potential refutation of the Garden of Eden hypothesis. At the same time, evidence of regional continuity at the peripheries would support the multi-regional evolution hypothesis (Wolpoff, Wu, and Thorne 1984; and see below) which is totally at odds with the Garden of Eden interpretation. Thus there can be either a Garden of Eden interpretation for modern population origins, or a substantial non-African fossil record of Early and Middle Pleistocene hominids showing morphological evidence of continuity with living populations, but not both.

Continuity and Admixture

In this context, it is important to re-emphasize that evidence for admixture is evidence *against* complete replacement of one population by another (cf. Bräuer 1980, 1981, 1982), and therefore is evidence against the Garden of Eden hypothesis. Historically, *complete* replacement of one human population by another is an 'accomplishment' *that has not ever been possible*, even for invading populations as technologically 'advanced' as the Europeans in Tasmania, since a large number of individuals showing admixture persist on that island. If in spite of the European technological advantage replacement was incomplete in Tasmania, how could complete replacement be expected to have characterized the interaction of two different groups of hunter/gatherer populations spread widely across Europe? Whatever the case for the extreme west of Europe, the fact is that apart from a very few exceptions (Protsch 1975; Stringer 1984a, 1989; Stringer and Andrews 1988), among the palaeoanthropologists even the most ardent believers of the replacement hypothesis do not contend that the replacement in Central Europe was without significant mixture.

For instance, while Bräuer argues that modern populations arose first in southern Africa, and over the past 50,000 years spread through the rest of the world (1984a, 1984b), he also interprets the morphology of the remains of early 'modern' Europeans such as the Hahnöfersand frontal *as the consequence of 'hybridization'* between the local Neanderthals and the invaders. One might add that the persistence of this morphology even into the Holocene (see Schwalbe 1904; Weinert 1951) could lend additional confirmation to this interpretation. Bräuer is led to this interpretation because of the obvious transitional characteristics of Hahnöfersand, and the fact that such characteristics are logically either the result of in situ change (an unacceptable hypothesis for Bräuer [1982], or of hybridization between the indigenous Neanderthals and the invading populations).

Invasion *with* hybridization, however, is no longer the Garden of Eden hypothesis as described here because this would mean the invading and indigenous populations were in the same species. It is for this reason that I find it curious to observe that both Cann and Stoneking, in various publications, each quote Bräuer's palaeoanthropological interpretations in support of the Garden of Eden Hypothesis when in fact if this interpretation was correct it would actually *invalidate* the hypothesis. Admixture between invading and indigenous populations would invalidate the interpretation of the genetic evidence discussed above because it would result in the introduction of more ancient mitochondrial lineages into the ancestry of modern populations. The observation of more ancient mitochondrial lineages could then be regarded as evidence for a much more ancient and not necessarily African origin for modern populations. *So ancient a history of population diver-gences would firmly establish that when humans left their place of origin, the ancestors of the indigenous populations around the inhabited world were not modern.* Moreover, admixture would confuse any attempt to ascertain a date for modern population origins from the mtDNA data.

The Pattern at the Eastern Edge

I believe that because the compelling evidence for regional continuity in East Asia is ancient, beginning with the earliest inhabitants, this evidence disproves the Garden of Eden hypothesis no matter what date is assumed for *modern* popula-tional origins. The regional interpretation of human evolution in East Asia is not new. The question of evolutionary continuity between archaic and modern populations outside of Africa was first approached by Weidenreich. By the end of the 1930s Weidenreich had accumulated first hand experience with the human fossil record of three regions. These were Europe (where he was trained and did his early work) North Asia (as the result of the rapidly accumulating Zhoukoudian finds from both the Lower and the Upper Cave); and Southeast Asia (as a conse-quence of communications and an exchange of casts with G. H. R. von Koenigswald, followed finally by an exchange of visits). Weidenreich was the only palaeoanthropologist of his time (and one of the very few of any time) with a detailed knowledge of three regions. As a scholar well educated in the morphological and evolutionary traditions of Central Europe, this put him in a unique position to appreciate the evidence for a world-wide pattern of human evolution. Weidenreich found such a pattern, and to explain it he developed his theory of polycentric evolu-tion.

According to Weidenreich's polycentric interpretation (1939, 1943) all fossil hominids belong to a single species, *Homo sapiens* (this original 'single species hypothesis' first appears clearly stated in his 1943 monograph). He contended that there was no single centre of evolution from which new hominid types appeared from time to time to replace older ones. Instead, according to his interpretation there were at least four centres of origin: Asia Minor, Eastern or Southern Africa, north China, and the Sunda islands (perhaps today better referred to as the Sunda subcontinent because of the extensive land areas exposed during the glaciations). He argued that no fossil group or type could be excluded from the ancestry of recent hominids, and that racial differences (which he regarded as 'minor details') were as old as human evolution.

Weidenreich's different geographic lines shared a common ancestry and evolved in the same direction. The crux of the problem he faced was in how to explain this. Here he failed. In the mid 1940s he proposed an explanation based on or-thogenesis (1947), just at the time when the foundations for the new evolutionary synthesis were being laid by Huxley, Mayr, Simpson, and others—a synthesis which denied any role for orthogenesis.

While the polycentric *interpretation* was widely dismissed when its orthogenic explanation failed, there remained his *ob-servations of continuity* which have never been refuted when accurately considered (despite the claims made by Stringer and Andrews [1988], based on highly selective quotations of Weidenreich's observations). Today the fossil records of these regions are much better than Weidenreich could have imagined. Within these two areas, the Weidenreich interpretations of human fossil remains have been taken up by local scholars, intimately acquainted with the palaeontological materials of their regions and particularly concerned with the origins of the populations that inhabit them now.

Australasia: the Southern End

From the Australasian perspective, links between the Sangiran *Homo erectus* specimens, the later hominids from Ngandong, and finally the recent inhabitants of Kow Swamp and Coobool Crossing in Australia have been recognized by most authors, although there are exceptions, such as Rightmire (1987) and Stringer and Andrews (1988: 1267) who deny that the resemblances show regional links and instead interpret them as reflecting 'apparent evolutionary reversals.' The case for specific ancestral-descendent relations between hominid samples more than a half million years apart has improved dramatically since Weidenreich (1943) first proposed it for Sundaland (Thorne and Wolpoff 1981; Sartono 1982). Sambungmachan (Jacob 1976) is an excellent intermediary between the Ngandong hominids and the Sangiran *Homo erectus* remains (*including* Sangiran 17 which, contrary to the claims of a number of authors, very clearly is a male *Homo erectus* specimen and not a male of a Ngandong-like population). While the Sambungmachan male is somewhat smaller than the Ngandong males, it resembles them in the development of an angular trigone at the lateral corner of the supraorbital torus, the reduction in basal pneumatization and the consequently higher position of the maximum cranial breadth, the flattening of the occipital plane of the occiput (and its vertical orientation), the doubled digastric sulci, and the tall, vertical posterior border of the temporal squama. Compared with the male *Homo erectus* fossils from the Kabuh levels, the Sambungmachan cranial capacity is larger, and the specimen is morphologically more similar to these remains than it is to the Ngandong hominids. Even without Sambungmachan, Weidenreich (1951) was able to link the Kabuh and Ngandong remains. With this specimen, the origin of the Ngandong hominids is firmly established.

Moreover the link between the Kabuh hominids and living Australians has long been evident even without consideration of the intermediate Ngandong sample. Recent discoveries further support this interpretation of evolutionary relationships in South Asia. A new reconstruction of Sangiran 17 (Thorne and Wolpoff 1981)—the most complete *Homo erectus* cranium and the only complete cranium of an adult male—allows comparisons of the face to be made in this region for the first time. This proved to be the anatomical area with the strongest evidence for regional continuity when the Sundaland and the latest Pleistocene and Holocene samples from Australia were compared.

From these comparisons, a number of regional (i.e. intraspecies clade) features were identified. Such features, of course, are not autapomorphic in the phylogenetic sense because they do not appear on genetically isolated lines. They are considered regional within the polytypic species because in combination they appear at higher frequencies in Australasia for much (or in some cases all) of human prehistory there, as compared with other regions of the world during equivalent time spans.

Features of the Sangiran 17 face, and of the other more fragmentary Sangiran faces, support the contention of a special relation between these and the living samples. Regional facial features include the marked ridge paralleling the zygomaxillary suture, the eversion of the lower border of the zygomatic, the rounding of the inferolateral orbital border, the lack of a distinct line dividing the nasal floor from the subnasal face of the maxilla, the curvature of the posterior alveolar plane of the maxilla that corresponds to the mandibular 'curve of Spee,' the posterior position of the minimum frontal breadth, the relatively horizontal orientation of the inferior border of the supraorbital torus, and the marked and dramatic nature of the supraorbital or superciliary expression. Moreover, Australasian faces fundamentally differ from the faces of other regions in their combination of dramatic size (holding sex constant), lateral orientation of the maxilla, and marked subnasal prognathism. It is clear that the inhabitants of this southern region have had their own distinct morphology throughout the entire time that East Asia has been inhabited (Thorne and Wolpoff 1981; Jacob 1981; Jelínek 1982; Wolpoff, Wu, and Thorne 1984).

At the same time there are equally firm links between the Ngandong hominids and the fossil and living Australians. Weidenreich (1943: 248-250) was able to relate the Ngandong specimens to the Australian Aborigines of today, seen in the virtual absence of an Australian fossil record. He thus argued for the interpretation of an unbroken line of descent from the earliest hominids of Sundaland. Weidenreich recognized evidence for continuity in the occasional appearance among Australian Aborigines of a morphological complex that included a well-developed supraorbital torus which combines a discontinuity at glabella with the lack of a supratoral sulcus, and a long, flat, receding forehead. Additional evidence was found in prelambdoidal depressions, sharp angulations between the occipital and nuchal planes, and short or even non-existent sphenoparietal articulations in the region of pterion. Weidenreich's contention was quantified through the implications of a study conducted by Larnach and Macintosh over a decade ago (1974). These authors compared a number of Australian and New Guinea crania with Europeans and Africans, scoring them for the 18 characters that Weidenreich (1951) claimed were unique for the Ngandong hominids. Six of these were absent in all modern samples, while 9 of the 12 other features were found to attain their highest frequencies in the Australian and New Guinea natives and thereby fit the definition of 'regional' as indicated above. These are as follows: the large rounded zygomatic trigone; absence of a supraorbital sulcus; suprameatal tegmen; transverse squamo-tympanic fissure; angling of the petrous to tympanic in the petro-tympanic axis; lambdoidal protuberance; marked ridge-shaped occipital torus; external occipital crest emerging from the occipital torus; marked supratoral sulcus on the occiput. The authors did not consider frontal flattening. If they had, this would emerge as a tenth Ngandong character found at its highest frequency in modern Australians.

Therefore, from the Australian perspective, an Indonesian link (in the words of Macintosh, 'the mark of Java') has long been recognized for the living aboriginal populations. The comparisons of the Ngandong fossils with the living Australian Aborigines are further borne out by Australian fossil remains uncovered since Weidenreich and Larnach and Macintosh published their observations. Beginning with the temporally earliest of these, the WLH 50 hominid from the Willandra Lakes of Australia is a *very* convincing morphological and temporal intermediary between the Ngandong specimens and the recent and modern aboriginals of the continent (cf. Stringer 1989, but interpreted differently in Stringer and Andrews 1988) because of its pattern of robust features, the thickness of its vault, the position of the maximum cranial breadth, the form of the supraorbitals and the region superior to them, and a number of additional distinct morphological features (Thorne 1984; Flood 1983). The specimen is not especially like Jebel Irhoud 2 or Ngaloba (*contra* Delson 1985), and the lack of any unique resemblance to African specimens, archaic or modern, bodes ill for the Garden of Eden hypothesis. WLH 50 is ignored in Rightmire's (1987) analysis of evolution in the region, an analysis which concludes that 'solid evidence for evolutionary continuity is in fact not readily compiled,' although he does not discuss most of the detailed evidence supporting the continuity interpretation in this region that has already been published for Australasia. This analysis is further flawed by a confusion of comparisons:

> Some of the traits said to link the Ngandong and Kow Swamp groups are either poorly expressed in the Sangiran fossils or differ explicitly . . . Indonesian *Homo erectus* displays many archaic features, whereas the Kow Swamp and Cohuna people are fully modern anatomically (Rightmire 1987).

The first point about links is irrelevant since the Sangiran folk are *earlier* than Ngandong and therefore would not necessarily be expected to have all of the special features shared by the Ngandong and sub-fossil Australian samples. With regard to the second point, about the differences between recent Australians and Indonesian *Homo erectus*, while the Kow Swamp sample is clearly distinguishable from living Australian aboriginal populations anatomically (Thorne and Wilson 1977), even if Kow Swamp and Coobool were exactly the same as the living populations it is unclear why a demonstration of evolution in the region over a span of more than half a million years disproves the regional continuity interpretation. Perhaps it is not surprising that what has come to be one popularly-quoted rebuttal (for instance quoted in both Stringer 1989 and Rightmire 1987) of the morphological evidence for regional continuity in Australasia is the paper by Kennedy (1984), which refutes claims of morphological continuity (if not identity) with *Homo erectus* for the postcranial remains of the subfossil Australians *that were never made!*

The Willandra Lakes 50 hominid is only the most recent addition to a substantial body of evidence linking hominid populations across the Pleistocene of the Sunda subcontinent. The Indonesian *erectus* connection is strengthened when the earlier discoveries of sub-fossil remains from Kow Swamp and Coobool Crossing are also taken into account, because so many of the evolutionary changes in Australia accelerated during the Holocene, after these populations lived. Because they were earlier, these late Upper Pleistocene/Holocene specimens retain a much higher frequency of features that are archaic in Sundaland than do the living populations of the continent, and thus reinforce the notion of morphological continuity.

In sum, if one firmly believed that modern populations had a single recent origin and replaced their predecessors throughout the world, the evidence discussed above would strongly suggest that Sundaland, if not greater Australia itself, comprised the region of origin. Not surprisingly, this has already been suggested (Gribbin and Cherfas 1982).

North China: The Opposite End

Of all those who would disagree with such a contention, the foremost would probably be among the scholars of the Institute for Vertebrate Palaeontology and Palaeoanthropology in Beijing (Wu and Zhang 1978; Wu and Lin 1985; Wu 1986). Since liberation there has been a continuous increase in the fossil record, with new discoveries of *Homo erectus* from Zhoukoudian, Lantian, Longgudong, and Hexian. New early (or archaic) *Homo sapiens* specimens include major remains from Dali, Maba, Yinnu Shan and Xujiayao, and a number of more fragmentary specimens. New individuals that are terminal Pleistocene or perhaps even Holocene in age include Chilinshan, Huanglong, Liujiang, Muchienchiao, Tzeyang, and a palate from south China found in a Hong Kong drugstore. Contrary to the assertions made by Stringer and Andrews (1988: 1266), these specimens confirm Weidenreich's interpretations, showing both morphological continuity within China and regional distinctions of the Chinese fossils from other areas with reasonably complete fossil records.

Working as he was in north China, Weidenreich (1939, 1943) was much more detailed in his discussions of morphological continuity for that region, in comparison with his rendering of the Australasian sequence. He described 12 features which he felt had particular importance in showing continuity between *Homo erectus* and the modern populations of north China. These were: mid-sagittal torus and parasagittal depression; metopic suture; Inca bones; 'Mongoloid' features of the cheek region; maxillary, ear and mandibular exostoses (the mandibular exostoses forming a mandibular torus); a high degree of platymerism in the femur; a strong deltoid tuberosity in the humerus; shovel-shaped upper lateral incisors; and the horizontal course of the nasofrontal and frontomaxillary sutures. While some of these, especially the postcranial features, are known to be generally characteristic of archaic populations everywhere, most of the others appear to be most frequent in combination in ancient and modern North Asians. Especially in combination, they characterize the region for a long period of time.

Over the decades since Weidenreich's death a number of additional observations have been added. Aigner (1976) pointed to: the profile contour of the nasal saddle and of the nasal roof; pronounced frontal orientation of the malar facies and the frontosphenoidal processes of the maxilla; and a rounded infraorbital margin, in line with the floor of the orbit. Wu (1981), in his description of the Dali cranium, was able to add a number of facial features which have great importance because the face seems to show more regional distinctions than does the cranial vault in north China, just as is the case in the Sundaland hominids (Thorne and Wolpoff 1981). Indeed, the Dali cranium (Wu 1981) and the morphologically similar, newly-discovered Yinnu Shan female (Wei 1984; Bunney 1984), have added much to an already very convincing case established by Weidenreich and elaborated upon the basis of more fragmentary remains recovered through the end of last decade (Wolpoff, Wu, and Thorne 1984). Besides facial flatness and the specific traits mentioned by Weidenreich and Aigner, we established additional regionally distinct features of these early *Homo sapiens* vaults which include the forehead profile (in particular the development of the frontal boss); the associated distinct angulation in the zygomatic process of the maxilla and anterior orientation of the frontal process of the zygomatic; lack of anterior facial projection and low degree of prognathism; rounded shape of the orbits; minimal nasal projection (the frontonasal and frontomaxillary sutures are virtually level); and a very low nasal profile. Other fragmentary remains of early *Homo sapiens*, especially those from Maba, Xujiayao, and Dingcun, also show these details when the appropriate parts are preserved. However, Dali and Yinnu Shan are clearly the centre-pieces of the continuity argument in North Asia. The combination of regional features in these specimens so clearly link them specifically with the more recent and modern populations of north China that it is unlikely future discoveries will refute this interpretation. *With regard to the Garden of Eden hypothesis, it is ominous that none of these earlier specimens possess features which resemble archaic or modern Africans* in anything other than grade features that characterize all hominids of the time period.

Among the remains representing the earliest modern populations, Liujiang from south China and the Upper Cave specimens from Zhoukoudian have a number of features that are characteristically regional (Woo 1959; Wu 1961; Wolpoff, Wu and Thorne 1984; Wu, and Wu 1985). They are very definitely *not* characteristically African, and therefore show an absence of any tendency for the earlier 'moderns' of the region to appear more African-like than the later populations (as would be expected according to the Garden of Eden hypothesis). Moreover, they are quite unlike other 'early modern' specimens such as Mladec, Pavlov, WLH 50 or Mungo 1. Wu argued strongly against Weidenreich's 'Eskimo, Chinese, Melanesoid' trichotomy for the Upper Cave crania, instead showing that they all fall within the expected range of variation for north China. The early *Homo sapiens* remains have been particularly important in providing firm evidence for a morphological link between the Late Pleistocene/early Holocene specimens and the Zhoukoudian *Homo erectus* sample—a link that was lacking in Weidenreich's time, hampering his interpretation (1939) of the Zhoukoudian Upper Cave specimens.

In sum, the basis for claiming regional continuity in China, especially northern China, is at least as good as in Sundaland for three stages of human evolution: *Homo erectus*; archaic *Homo sapiens*; and, the earliest modern *Homo sapiens*. Continuity, however, is generally not found in different character states of the same traits that are regional in Sundaland, and characterizations such as 'homoplasy' or 'regional pleisomorphy' cannot possibly apply in attempting to discount what any observer can see. The differences between features showing continuity in these two ends of the eastern periphery were recognized as long ago as in Weidenreich's time and have continued to be recognized by scholars familiar with the fossil remains from both areas (Jacob 1981; Wu and Zhang 1978; Wu and Wu 1982; Wolpoff, Wu, and Thorne 1984). It was this evidence that led to Coon's (1962) chapter headings 'Pithecanthropus and the Australoids' and 'Sinanthropus and the Mongoloids.'

The pattern of hominid evolution at the eastern periphery still appears much as Weidenreich described it. It involves a morphological gradient spread over the eastern periphery between north and south ends that are unique and distinguishable as far back into the past as the earliest evidence for habitation can be found, but also involves geographically and morphologically intermediate specimens that show there never was popula-

tional isolation. Because of the marked differences in the morphological features that show continuity at the north and south ends of the eastern periphery, *this pattern clearly discounts complete replacement as a valid explanation of Pleistocene hominid evolution.*

Instead, a great deal of continuous evolutionary change (from the earliest inhabitants of East Asia to the modern populations of the region) can be documented that involves *no* speciation events. This creates a problem for those who insist on a cladistic definition for *Homo sapiens* (Delson 1985; Tattersall 1986). This is because while a great magnitude of gradual change is documented in the region, at the southern periphery the pattern of change is so continuous that no boundary can be drawn between the archaic and the modern *Homo sapiens* populations (Wolpoff 1986).

Considerable magnitudes of change without a speciation event and subsequent replacements is hardly a prediction of the Garden of Eden hypothesis. Thus, without the evidence for a complete replacement interpretation in East Asia, it seems to me that the Garden of Eden hypothesis fails the test, and those who ignore this evidence of the fossils do so at their peril.

MULTIREGIONAL EVOLUTION THEORY

The multiregional evolution hypothesis (Wolpoff, Wu, and Thorne 1984) is a valid alternative to the Garden of Eden interpretation because it fits the data, especially in those places where the Garden of Eden hypothesis fails. It accounts for the appearance of modern populations throughout the hominid range without positing that they necessarily have a unique recent ancestry or represent the results of a recent speciation event. Specifically it proposes an evolutionary explanation for the observations of regional continuity at the northern and southern ends of East Asia, as discussed above, as well as elsewhere (Van Valen 1986). The observations which were contradictory in Weidenreich's explanatory scheme and were unconvincingly explained in Coon's, can be satisfactorily accounted for. This hypothesis does *not* account for modern populational origins by parallel evolution (Eckhardt 1987; *contra* Cann *et al.* 1987: 35; and Stringer and Andrews 1988), nor by simultaneous speciations in different parts of the world (*contra* Jones and Rouhani 1986b: 600). The parallelism interpretation of the regional continuity observations is as old as Howells' (1942) *mis*characterization of Weidenreich's 'trellis of human evolution' as a candelabra. The mischaracterization is as wrong now as it was then, and its continued restatement by supporters of the Garden of Eden hypothesis is misleading and counter-productive.

Fossil Hominids as a Polytypic Species

Explanations for the observation of regional continuity in long-lasting polytypic mammalian species do not abound in the palaeontological literature. This is because with only a very few exceptions (Freudenthal 1965; Martin 1970), fossil histories for polytypic species are virtually unknown. The hominids may prove to be an important exception to this (Van Valen 1966: 382):

> Our knowledge of the fossil history of non-human subspecies is almost negligible and *Homo* will probably furnish the first

well studied case of the evolution of several subspecies in geological time.

The absence of information about the evolutionary histories of polytypic species is probably not because geographic variation within fossil species was rare, but rather because the tendency has been to define polytypic species out of existence, and interpret regional variation to be at the species level because it fits the morphospecies or evolutionary species criteria of phylogenetics.

A good example of this can be found in a recent symposium on Middle Pleistocene human evolution attended by a number of cladistically-minded scholars who, among other things, dealt at length with variation in *Homo erectus* (see Andrews and Franzen 1984). There emerged a consensus that the considerable geographic variation recognized in this hominid reflects the 'fact' that the *Homo erectus* sample was actually comprised of more than one species (Andrews 1984), and that perhaps in none of its taxonomic guises was it ancestral to living populations. However, it might be well to heed Stringer's cautionary statement (1984b: 141):

> We must beware of the position of saying on cladistic grounds that *H. sapiens* did not evolve from *H. erectus* but from a different species showing similar characteristics that lived at the same time!

Tattersall (1986), following Andrews' phylogenetic conclusions and incorrectly quoting me, characterizes *Homo erectus* as a grade and not a taxon, in a paper explicitly claiming that there are not enough taxa named in the human fossil record. And the regional variation in *Homo erectus* has been treated in even odder ways (Van Vark 1983)! It is clear to me that variation formerly regarded as at the subspecies level cannot and will not be recognized in the fossil record when phylogenetic criteria are uncritically applied, no matter how problematic the consequences of applying these criteria may be. In a curious way, by confusing what is almost certainly subspecies variation with species variation, these publications show by counter-example that in closely related groups long-lasting geographic variation in the past can only be recognized when the interbreeding concept of biological species is used to help generate criteria for distinguishing fossil species. When, instead, it is the morphotypic definition that is applied to closely related fossils, the observed variability in the Middle Pleistocene hominids cannot be reasonably interpreted at the subspecies level, and Middle Pleistocene hominid variants are misidentified as different species although they show variation no greater than that which characterizes comparisons between the regions today.

Moreover, ironically, there are other views that suggest that the multiplication of palaeospecies which is urged upon us (Tattersall 1986) may be more than inappropriate or a misapplication of otherwise useful approaches. It may be biologically misleading and incorrect. For instance, according to Templeton (1982: 117):

> Different groups of organisms are subjected consistently to certain speciation modes because of their genetic, population-structural, and ecological attributes. For instance . . . there are very consistent differences in population structure between frogs and mammals such that mammals are much more likely to display higher degrees of population subdivision . . . this implies that mammals are more subject to rapid population divergence . . . (and) that mammals are more prone to form polytypic species. The result is that . . . the number of fossil mammalian species could actually be overestimated.

Indeed, commonplace as they are among the living taxa, polytypic species are mainly discussed in the evolutionary literature with regard to peripatric speciation. In most other contexts, the analysis of geographic variation is simplified with the panmictic assumption. The evidence of marked divergences within continuously distributed species (Endler 1977) argues against the peripatric model of speciation and therefore tends to be ignored (Barton and Charlesworth 1984). I believe the genesis of this situation is not so much in a conviction that polytypic species can only change through peripatric speciation, as in a lack of realization that polytypic species pose an evolutionary problem. While the alternative to gradualism— punctuated equilibrium—provides a potentially valid but different explanation for evolutionary change in a polytypic species, it cannot account for regional continuity in evolving populations across the 'boundary' created by speciation events.

Clinical Distributions of Regional Morphology

Multiregional evolution theory (Wolpoff, Wu, and Thorne 1984) attempts to explain there phenomena that characterize the Pleistocene evolution by the genus *Homo*: (1) the *initial* centre and edge contrast of a variable source population of early Middle Pleistocene African hominids, with a number of differing monomorphic peripheral populations (see Thorne 1981; Bryant, Coombs, and McCommas 1986; Goodnight 1987); (2) the *early appearance* of features which show evolutionary continuity (i.e. regional features) with modern populations at the peripheries, contrasted with the much later appearance of features showing regional continuity at the centre (Thorne and Wolpoff 1981); (3) the *maintenance* of these regional contrasts and the persistence of regional continuity through most of the Pleistocene (Thorne 1981) until the population explosions (and dramatic movements) of the Holocene. These three phenomena are related to the development and maintenance of long-lasting gradients throughout the hominid range, balancing gene flow against opposing selection and (especially at the peripheries) perhaps also against the effects of drift.

The observations of regional continuity reflect the results of processes that lead to the *maintenance* of distinctly regional variants for long periods of time, during which general evolutionary trends characterize the entire polytypic species (Van Valen 1986; Wolpoff, Wu, and Thorne 1984). This pattern of contrasting species-wide evolutionary trends and distinctly regional variations (especially for the peripheral populations of a polytypic species) is quite common (Mayr 1963, 1982). It is maintained through clines for multiple characters (Barton 1983), that can persist even in populations that have been in contact for very long periods of time (Clarke 1966; Endler 1977; White 1978).

Population differentiation is almost inevitable when species are widespread and subdivided (Wright 1943; Fisher 1950; Jain and Bradshaw 1966), a consequence of isolation by distance (Wright 1943). In the face of gene flow between and among such populations, the opposing selection may be at a very low level, or may even be replaced by drift in the maintenance of long-standing gradients (Barton and Charlesworth 1984). This is particularly likely when the contiguous populations along the gradients are small, as might be expected at the geographic or ecological peripheries of the range (Mayr 1982). The effects of drift are also maximized when populations are long lasting, providing the opportunity for fixations to occur (Slatkin 1987). Therefore the presence of clinal distributions is not necessarily a marker of corresponding selection differences over the range of the clines (Lande 1982). Moreover, clinal distributions involving small populations and a balance between gene flow and drift may be expected to produce (or maintain) more homogeneous populations at the geographic or ecological edge of the range of a polytypic species where population densities tend to be lower and the potential for drift is greater. The resulting morphological homogeneity at the peripheries provides the bases for the observations of regional continuities.

Gene Flow as a Source of New Alleles

Gene flow persists as the most *mis*understood aspect of multiregional theory. Gene flow plays several different roles in maintaining clines. Without gene flow, it is inevitable that there will be speciation. Thus, differential selection alone cannot maintain clines within a species for long spans of time and the very presence of long standing gradients for morphological features therefore indicates that gene flow was present, no matter what the form and magnitude that characterized it and whether or not there was also a gradient in selection.

Gene flow is commonly regarded as acting to spread new mutations among populations (Coon 1962; Ehrlich and Raven 1969) that may be promoted if they prove to be advantageous. Realistically, however, this probably represents only a small part of the creative role that gene flow normally plays in the evolutionary process (Slatkin 1987). In fact, a rather different assessment of the importance of new alleles in promoting morphological change follows from the implications of the extraordinary genetic similarity of humans and chimpanzees, recognized for more than a decade (King and Wilson 1975; Brown *et al.* 1982; Templeton 1983; Wilson *et al.* 1985). The contrast between the number of shared alleles and the divergent morphologies for these two living species has been interpreted in almost every possible way, but the most obvious is that *the notable morphological and behavioral differences between these two species are mainly a result of differing allele frequencies* (Lewontin 1974, 1984), and not of different alleles.

Studies of the nuclear DNA data from living humans have also revealed a surprising expression of genetic similarities among populations (Lewontin 1974, 1984; Nei and Roychoudhury 1982; Jones 1981). This similarity was also found in the mtDNA studies, and given a variety of interpretations (Cann, Brown, and Wilson 1982, 1984; Brown *et al.* 1982). But if these data mainly indicate that virtually all of the genetic differences between populations that have evolved over the course of human history are the result of frequency differences, *it follows that gene flow must primarily be regarded to function in changing frequencies of existing alleles, and not usually in introducing new ones.*

Therefore, gene flow cannot usually be expected to have a 'stimulating' effect on human evolution by introducing new alleles for selection to act on. Instead, the usual, perhaps invari-

able, effect of gene flow is *change in frequencies of existing alleles* affected by the balance between gene flow and local selection and/or drift. When this balance persists, the role of gene flow in any locale could be envisioned as mainly providing an unending source of recombinatorial possibilities (rather than a source of new alleles) which are then subjected to selection.

The Magnitude of Gene Flow

The magnitude of gene flow is a closely related issue. Problems here involve how much gene flow actually exists, and the effects of various magnitudes of gene flow under different conditions. Consideration of clines and the gradients between them as two-dimensional networks magnifies the potential effects of gene flow on equilibria, providing a greater role for gene flow at low magnitudes than workers such as Ehrlich and Raven (1969) allowed. However, when a gradient in selection exists, it has a predominating effect on the resulting cline's form (Livingstone 1973; Endler 1977; Barton 1983) almost independently of how great the magnitude of gene flow might be. Under these circumstances, the main effects of differences in the magnitude of gene flow are to change the steepness of the gradient across the clines, and in some cases to displace the geographic positions of equilibria frequencies. These effects are magnified when the discontinuous distribution of individuals who live in groups is also taken into account. For these reasons, and because clines can exist when there are selection gradients even in the absence of gene flow, in most cases clines will be maintained within a species regardless of the magnitude of gene flow. It follows that the degree of differentiation along a cline, the steepness of the gradient, and the form that the gradient takes are all somewhat independent of the magnitude of genetic interchange.

I conclude that clines will invariably form in a polytypic species, regardless of the levels of gene flow. The particular attributes of these clines will be dictated by all of the relevant variables, including the magnitude and direction of gene flow (and the degree to which it is reciprocal) and the intensity and distribution of local selection, but also the distribution of populations, population sizes and breeding structures, the effect on drift, and the pattern of initial genetic variation. *I reject the notions that selection or drift is likely to 'override' the influence of gene flow, or that gene flow is likely to 'swamp' the effects of selection.* The idea that gene flow magnitudes can be too small or too large makes no sense in terms of the balance model of clines. Variation in the evolutionary forces underlying clines can alter their form, but will not erase the clines themselves.

This point is important for understanding the effects of the magnitude of gene flow between populations. One argument is that the magnitude must be high to account for simultaneous speciation when there is polytypism (Jones and Rouhani 1986b), while there is a different contention suggesting that this magnitude is rather low (Ehrlich and Raven 1969; Endler 1977) that is based on the observation that the expected effects of higher magnitudes cannot be found. Neither extreme view, unfortunately, is based on actual measurements of gene flow, and in fact actual magnitudes of gene flow between living animal populations remain largely unknown (Slatkin 1987). While the gene flow reported between adjacent living human populations is usually anything but minuscule, it is possible that this magnitude may be lower in other species, or in human prehistory (as might be suggested by the emerging understanding of how different Pleistocene archaeological sequences in various regions actually were).

However, I believe that when considered over geologic time, the question of whether gene flow was of sufficient magnitude to account for the spread of morphological features without the populations themselves moving might be of less importance than it may seem. The potential importance of the magnitude of gene flow has been misunderstood because comparisons among human populations or between humans and the African apes show that the actual number of *new alleles* whose spread is to be accounted for during the evolution of *Homo* is surprisingly small, and therefore that it is changing allele frequencies and not new alleles that must be accounted for.

The Role of Gene Flow

A final point of interest concerning gene flow is its role in a polytypic species. This can be discussed on several different levels. It is clear that this role is complexly dependent on 'both the geographic distribution of the species and on the importance of other evolutionary forces' (Slatkin 1987: 787). Without gene flow, polytypic species will eventually speciate (Mayr 1963, 1982). However gene flow has importance far beyond preventing speciation. At various times it can act as both a constraining force and a creative force in the evolutionary process. Opposing the Ehrlich and Raven (1969) perspective of species as internally subdivided with little or no internal gene flow is the 'species-unifying' concept for the role of gene flow. In this perception the gene flow between populations is seen as supporting cohesion and stability within the species as a whole. However, a rather different problem arises from this concept—namely, how can gene flow both be responsible for maintaining stability in a homeostatic-like manner (small perturbations tend to be brought back to the mean) and at the same time be a mechanism of change?

One resolution to this potential contradiction is found in the precept that the genetic cohesion of species may not be maintained by gene flow alone. A rather different explanation for genetic cohesion is provided in the more recent discussions by Mayr (1982), Carson (1982), Lewontin (1984), and others. In these publications, the idea of co-adapted genetic systems representing the maximum fitness under balancing selection achieved by whole organisms has been envisioned as an internal restraint for change within a species, limiting how much a species can change without a complete reorganization of these genetic systems (Mayr's 'genetic revolution'). The co-adapted genetic system for a species is presumably not dependent on gene flow for its maintenance.

The problem I find with this concept is in the nature of normal subspecific or populational differences found within species. Such differences most often tend to reflect local adaptations. Consequently, the co-adapted genetic system model of species leads to a different contradiction. A single co-adapted genetic system is presumably established for an entire species because of the heterozygotic combinations promoted by balancing selection to maximize the fitness of individuals. Yet, at the same time the specific gene combinations in particular populations respond to local selection and change, often dramatically. To understand how this potential contradiction between co-adapted genetic systems at the species and subspecies (or

population) levels is avoided, we must distinguish factors that maintain species cohesion and stability, and factors that maintain the phenetic similarity of populations within species. These are not the same phenomena (Barton and Charlesworth 1984; Charlesworth 1983). *In fact, a special explanation for phenetic similarity beyond the normal effects of shared ancestry and gene flow is hardly required in the face of the extremely small number of genetic differences distinguishing populations enclosed within the protected gene pool of a biological species.*

If the phenetic similarity within biological species is a phenomenon distinct from the sources of its genetic cohesion, one can envision the stability and cohesion-maintaining mechanisms in a somewhat different manner. It is likely that in polytypic species, co-adapted genetic systems are not species-wide, but rather can be expected to differ from population to population. Indeed, such differences would magnify the isolation by distance phenomenon (Wright 1943). This model (Wolpoff, Wu, and Thorne 1984) resembles Wright's (1967, 1977, 1982) shifting balance theory, with morphologically distinct intraspecific groups reflecting different adaptive peaks maintained by stabilizing selection. The shifting balance model with its multiple adaptive peaks better fits what is known about polytypic species evolution in the absence of particular speciation events.

Gene flow is not so much the network that keeps the species whole, as it is the latticework that connects the populations of a polytypic species, represented by multiple adaptive peaks, through its participation in the support of clines and its contribution to the development of new recombinatorial possibilities. Therefore it can be suggested that the same mechanisms promoting stability and cohesion within a species can also provide for species-wide evolutionary changes; as the complex balances of gene flow and selection that produce clinal equilibria at the adaptive peaks vary, the clines change in response. Because the clines represent balances (albeit differing from area to area), evolutionary responses can be of much greater magnitude than the magnitude of changes in any of the equilibria-producing forces, just as a small shift in frequency can cause a great change in the interference pattern between two overlapping waves.

Evolutionary change in a species constituted as described here is neither directly related in magnitude to the amount of gene flow between populations, nor proportionately responsive to the magnitude of selection, nor directly limited by the inability to alter co-adapted genetic systems (if the distribution of these systems is the object of the clinal variation, as is likely since both unique genetic systems and the clines exist in polytypic species). One can envision the polytypic species as a *dynamic* system, externally bounded and protected by the limits to gene flow, and internally diversified by the evolutionary forces sustaining gradients between differentiated populations. The stability within such a species does not result in its stagnation.

Internal Diversification in *Homo*

With regard to the multiregional model of hominid evolution, it is particularly important to focus on the pattern of internal diversification. Clinal theory provides an explanatory basis for the maintenance of regional distinctions for populations at the periphery of the hominid range. Drift, due to small population effects, and differences in selection resulting from environmental variation as well as the existence of regionally distinct morphotypes, both characterized populations at the marginal or peripheral portions of the hominid range for long periods of time. The initially different gene pools of these populations were established during the process of first habitation (Thorne 1981). The pattern of regional variation was maintained throughout most of the Pleistocene by a balance between the local forces promoting homogeneity within populations and regional distinctions between them (selection, drift), and multidirectional gene flow which (*contra* Jones and Rouhani 1986b) for reasons discussed above need not have been particularly high (Slatkin 1987). As a consequence, a long-lasting dynamic system of morphological gradients came to characterize the multi-regional distribution of our polytypic lineage.

If this was the normal pattern guiding the evolution of the genus *Homo*, the conflict assumed to exist between gene flow and local selection that underlies so many interpretative disputes should not actually exist. All evolutionary changes affect a balance between these potentially opposing forces and must be accounted for by shifts in this balance (except in the extreme cases of latest Pleistocene and Holocene large-scale population movements for which the multiregional evolution model does not apply). It makes no sense to argue about whether gene flow or selection or drift 'predominated' to account for a specific local evolutionary sequence because the multiregional evolution model requires all of these, and focuses on the balance between them in its explanation of evolutionary change. In this clinal model, shifts in the magnitudes of the opposing forces change the gradient of the cline, and it is this changing gradient, viewed over time in a specific region, that provides the data to characterize regional evolutionary change. This is not an alternative to the gradualist model, as applied to a polytypic species, this *is* the gradualist model.

The evidence for regional continuity in two areas of the eastern periphery has been reviewed, and it is as good as probably could be expected given the nature of the fossil record. But what of the evidence for gene flow, an important element in the evolutionary model proposed to account for it? To some extent the presence of common major evolutionary trends constitutes a valid source of evidence for gene flow. At the north and south ends of the eastern periphery there are brain-size expansions, reductions in muscularity, in sexual dimorphism, and in anterior tooth size. These, and a number of additional common evolutionary trends, result in many of the features shared by the modern populations of these areas and could be taken as evidence of gene flow. This is especially the case given the lack of technological and other forms of adaptive similarities. However, this evidence is insufficient because the data which the hypothesis was created to explain can hardly also be taken as independent support of the hypothesis itself. Moreover, it is likely that there are also some common elements of selection promoting these changes across the human range, particularly in the rapid spread of ideas which may be unique to humanity.

There is a growing body of direct evidence for gene flow along the eastern end of the human range. For the Upper Pleistocene this evidence was first recognized by Weidenreich (1945) during his comparisons of the Wadjak remains with Australian fossils such as Keilor. He argued that these specimens are virtually identical, and my observations also support the notion that there is a marked degree of similarity between them in size, proportions, and facial breadth and flatness. Moreover, the south China specimen from Liujiang shares many, perhaps most, of these features (Wolpoff, Wu, and Thorne 1984). These and more fragmentary materials seem to provide a late-Pleistocene link between the Asian mainland, Sundaland, and greater Australia that indicates that there was persistent gene flow.

The evidence for gene flow begins much earlier, however. The Hexian *Homo erectus* cranium (Wu and Dong 1982, 1985) resembles the Zhoukoudian *erectus* remains in many details of the forehead profile as well as in the moderate frontal boss and the rounding of the superior orbital border. However, the weak expression of the supratoral sulcus on the frontal, the contrasting marked expression of the occipital's supratoral sulcus, the form of the basal pneumatization as seen in the posterior contour, the parietal angulation, and the expanded cranial breadths, all much more closely resemble the Indonesian hominids. Indeed, a case could be made that Hexian is a morphological as well as a geographical intermediary.

Yet it is interesting that to the west, the Narmada cranium (Lumley and Sonakia 1985) from Madhya Pradesh, Central India, closely resembles the later of the Chinese *Homo erectus* remains. Especially in the shape and configuration of the supraorbitals and the curvature of the frontal squama, its frontal is much like Hexian, while the round orbits resemble Maba. The temporal and occipital are similar to Zhoukoudian specimens (especially the H5 vault) in the form of the temporal squama, the expression and position of the angular torus, the curvature of the occipital in the sagittal plane, and the morphology of the nuchal torus. The much later Zuttiyeh frontofacial fragment, from even further west in Asia, also may reflect a strong East Asian influence in its morphology (Hublin 1976). Much like the Zhoukoudian hominids, its supraorbitals extend well anterior to the distinct frontal boss, creating a deep supratoral sulcus. Another resemblance lies in the very flat upper face and the anterior orientation of the orbital pillars, features shared with the later Skhul/Qafzeh samples from the Levant as well. Evidently, on the Asian mainland, the features first recognized in China predominate far to the west during the Middle and the earlier Upper Pleistocene, even though intermediate specimens may be found, especially along the southern portion of its eastern periphery. In its totality the Asian evidence supports the interpretation of long-standing clines with significant gene flow between the north and south end regions. Unlike the lack of contrast between East and West Asia, North and South Asia has populations which are distinct and were distinct in the past. There is a fossil record showing distinguishable origins for the modern populations that inhabit the regions today, in spite of the evidence for Pleistocene and Holocene gene flow.

These patterns of diversification and change in the hominids are complex. Yet, in them are to be found the origins of modern populations. The critical role played by gene flow contradicts and invalidates the interpretations of the mtDNA data that derive these modern populations from a single recent African Eve through a speciation event. Indeed, the multiregional hypothesis predicts that there will be no single origin for these populations that can be located on genetic or morphological grounds. In contrast, interpretations of the mtDNA data that are based on differential lineage extinctions are fully compatible with the multiregional hypothesis. Differential mtDNA lineage extinction only works as a valid explanation if the mtDNA variants were widespread to begin with, a consequence of gene flow.

SUMMARY

According to the 'Garden of Eden' hypothesis, all modern human populations have a single recent origin as a new species. *Homo sapiens* is said to have originated in Africa approximately 200,000 years ago, and within the next 100,000 years some of the populations (representing one of the two main mitochondrial lineages that developed in the new species) went through a period of very small population size and migrated out of Africa to replace the indigenous populations throughout the world, without mixing with them.

Evidence for an African origin is based on genetic and palaeontological inference. Neither of these bases are particularly strong. The genetic basis for claiming that Africa is the place of origin rests on the interpretation of the observation that there is more genetic diversity among African populations than among others. However, these genetic data can be interpreted in a different way. For instance, the trees of relationships developed from these data can be rooted on different continents, and the diversity arguments rest on as-yet unverified assumptions about which genetic variants are homologies and which are homoplasies. The palaeontological basis for claiming an African origin rests on the earlier dates claimed for modern *Homo sapiens* fossils in Africa than in other regions (which presupposes that there actually *was* a single unique place of origin for modern populations). However, the reality of the situation is that there are no firm dates for human fossils in the critical time span, and the early date for Qafzeh (if actually correct) is from *outside* the region (thousands of miles from where Eve's homeland is claimed to be) and applies to specimens described by Vandermeersch as 'Proto Cromagnoid'—hardly a reflection of perceived African resemblance (Valladas *et al.* 1988). In fact there are not even *equivocal* dates for the *African* specimens, so that it is far from clear that the earliest modern human populations first appeared there. Even without dates for the earliest modern humans, a different palaeontological problem arises from the claim that modern populations first evolved in Africa; the earliest modern human fossils from outside of Africa do not share any unique derived African features. Instead, in both North and South Asia, the earliest modern human fossil remains from each region show some of the unique features that characterized their predecessors in the same regions.

The genetic basis for the Garden of Eden hypothesis is most widely attributed to the interpretation of mtDNA variation. This interpretation rests on the reading of a genetic clock from the mitochondrial variation, which requires the assumptions that (1) the main source of mtDNA variation is mutations (selection and drift can be discounted); (2) the rate of mutations is constant everywhere, and mutation accumulation is linear with time; (3) the colonization events used in rate-determinations are accurately dated, singular, and unidirectional. It is unlikely that *any* of these assumptions are correct.

Moreover, rates of mtDNA evolution supporting the Garden of Eden hypothesis for modern populational origins are inconsistent with the mtDNA calibration of other more dramatic events, and inconsistent with the calibration of speciation events based on data from other genetic systems and from palaeontology. Using dates for the peopling of New Guinea, Australia, and the Americas, Cann and her colleagues determined a divergence rate of 2%-4% base substitutions per million years. It is the median rate in this range that is used in the estimate of 200,000 years for the divergence of modern human populations from their last common African source ancestor. However, when applied to other *species* divergences in the primate fossil record, this rate range gives a human-chimpanzee divergence date that averages only 2.7 million years ago by one estimate, and even less (2.1 million years ago) by another. Either date is clearly wrong, and is unambiguously disproved by the earlier presence of large samples of indisputable hominids in the fossil record, from Laetoli and Hadar.

Nei (1985, 1987) has shown that the length of time since these human migrations are supposed to have occurred is too short for the assumption of a consistent rate of base substitutions to apply. A combination of unknown earlier polymorphisms in the mtDNA, subsequent populational admixture (especially the effect of gene flow among recent populations), and the predominating effects of stochastic events over short periods of time, make it impossible to determine the time of the last common ancestor from a mitochondrial clock calibrated from recent migrations.

The average rate of base-pair substitutions is certainly much slower, perhaps only 0.71% per million years as Nei claims. This would give an estimate of the chimpanzee-human split at 6.6 million years, a date that closely approximates the estimate of 6.3 million years from nuclear DNA hybridization data, and that is also in conformity with estimates from the fossil record. *Estimates of modern populational divergence at 200,000 years based on a 2%-4% rate of base-pair substitutions per million years are therefore not likely to be correct.*

On the other hand, the 0.71% base-substitution-rate estimate indicates a divergence time for the ancestors of modern populations at about 850,000 years ago. At this date, near the beginning of the Middle Pleistocene, the appearance and spread of these populations out of Africa was probably not a speciation event; admixture with other populations is not an issue since there were probably no indigenous human populations to mix with. This date would suggest that *Homo erectus* was the first human species to be widely distributed around the world, and that the founders of many modern populations are to be identified in this species.

The mtDNA evidence said to support the Garden of Eden hypothesis requires that modern humans *be a new species*, reproductively isolated from all other populations that were contemporary with them at the time they originated. However, the bottlenecking evidence that is also said to support this hypothesis describes a population split *within a single species*. According to this interpretation the extra-African populations presumably underwent a period of small population size and substantial drift after they left Africa. This incident of bottlenecking could not have been the same as the speciation event because the descendant populations remain within the same species as the unbottlenecked (more variable) portion of *Homo sapiens* that remained in Africa. Therefore the bottleneck happened at a different, presumably later time. But if so, the bottleneck and not a recent time of origin could account for the lack of mtDNA diversity outside of Africa. *The fact is that these two sources of genetic data contradict rather than support each other.*

A rather different interpretation is much more likely for the small number of mtDNA lineages found among modern humans. The 'Eve' interpretation may be an artifact of tree analysis (which necessarily gives stems) and not an accurate reflection of population history. Population admixture, the migrations of recorded history, and the dramatic population expansions of the Holocene invalidates any tree analysis, even if populations actually diverged in a tree-like manner. The same pattern of mtDNA variation more probably reflects a history of stochastic differential mitochondrial lineage survivorship from numerous ancestors, especially if the small population sizes responsible for the bottlenecks described above actually characterized this portion of human evolution and if cytoplasmic variants were widespread because of gene flow. If so, a single mitochondrial line of cytoplasms would co-occur with populational descent from multiple nuclear DNA ancestors. Descent from a single Eve (or from a small population) would be an incorrect interpretation for the nuclear DNA evidence, which after all is the main focus of evolutionary studies. In terms of nuclear DNA descent, the idea of a single origin for the surviving lines would simply not apply.

Data from the human fossil record provide an independent basis for assessing the Garden of Eden hypothesis. This hypothesis suggests that the earliest dated specimens for modern *Homo sapiens* should be more similar to each other than are later ones, and that the later specimens should have more regional distinctions, as they would be more differentiated. The hypothesis also predicts that the earliest modern *Homo sapiens* from any region should have the most African characteristics of any sample in that region. *Fossil data do not conform to any of these predictions.* Instead, fossils from the peripheries of the human range show that the regional distinctions of today are as old as the earliest occupations of these regions. In fact, outside of Africa the regional distinctions precede the first appearance of modern *Homo sapiens* morphology. There definitely is no tendency for the earlier fossil specimens to diverge from a common morphological pattern (and certainly not from an African one). Moreover, in no region is modern *Homo sapiens* obviously distinct from earlier populations at a species level; indeed, in some places modern populations are not even particularly different from their Pleistocene predecessors at any taxonomic level.

A valid explanation of modern populational origins must account for two aspects of the human fossil record, recognized by Weidenreich a half century ago, both of which contradict the Garden of Eden hypothesis. These are the persistence of unique regional distinctions for long periods of time, even across species 'boundaries,' and the commonalities of human evolution during the Middle and Later Pleistocene in different regions. Because of these evolutionary patterns, the fossil data indicate that—especially at the peripheries—a replacement model for the origin of modern *Homo sapiens* populations cannot be sustained. Instead, the origins of modern populations in different regions seem to be rooted in the earlier archaic populations of the regions, in most cases without evidence of a speciation event. Perhaps the most telling aspect of these interpretations is that they are rooted most firmly in different and independent morphological observations in samples from the northern- and southern-most ends of the eastern (Asian)

periphery. There are different evolutionary patterns, based on complexes of different details and often of different character states for the same features, at the northern and southern ends of the eastern edge of the human range.

The Neanderthal problem of Europe, and the 'solutions' often accepted for it, might seem to support a replacement interpretation at the western margin of the human range. However, even if the European Neanderthals were replaced, it does not follow that the European situation necessarily supports the Garden of Eden hypothesis. This is because most workers, even those who generally believe that the Neanderthals were replaced by more modern populations, have come to accept the implications presented by intermediate-appearing specimens, suggesting that there was commonly hybridization between the Neanderthals and the invading populations. Hybridization, however, argues against the validity of the Garden of Eden hypothesis because it contradicts the necessary assumption that the immediate ancestor of modern populations was a new species.

The theory of multiregional evolution provides an alternative explanation for these patterns in the human fossil record. While the centre and edge hypothesis suggests how and why regional distinctions first appeared at the peripheries of the hominid range, regional continuity accounts for the persistence of these peripheral distinctions through the remainder of the Pleistocene. The pattern of central variability and regionally distinct peripheral monomorphisms was maintained by long-lasting gradients balancing gene usually from the centre toward the edges, against local selection and in some cases drift. This theory shares two things with the Garden of Eden hypothesis; it posits an African ancestry for all populations, and its validity relies on the widespread movements of genes. However, there are a number of notable differences between these hypotheses which allow one to determine whether data from various sources can refute one of them. In the multiregional perspective, all populations are potentially connected by gene flow, usually from the centre toward the edges, against local selection and imply the movement of people (when there were migratory movements they involved small groups and led to admixture with existing indigenous populations rather than replacement without mixture) and speciation as described by this hypothesis was gradual (and was not an 'event') once the hominids became a geographically-dispersed polytypic species. The multiregional pattern and the precept that local human populations were probably fairly small for most of the Pleistocene, provides the basis for the conclusion that differential mtDNA lineage survivorships and the dramatic population increases of historic times combine as the most likely explanation for the pattern of limited mtDNA variation seen in living populations. This would replace the alternative explanation of a shallow root (i.e. recent divergence) for a single tree that is part of the Garden of Eden hypothesis.

I believe that the fossil record clearly and unambiguously contradicts the Garden of Eden hypothesis. If this fossil evidence has been correctly interpreted, as I believe it has, the Garden of Eden hypothesis can be considered disproved on the evidence of the hominid fossils. Much can be said in support of the contention that the fossil record is not an irrelevant source of information about human evolution.

There is an additional basis for this seemingly strong claim, to be found in the other interpretations of the mtDNA data that have been advanced, and in the alternative calibration of rates of mtDNA change that results in date estimates in concordance with split-times ascertained from both the fossil record and from nuclear DNA hybridization studies. If there were early Middle Pleistocene population divergences from a common African ancestor for the predecessors of modern, regionally-distinct groups, this would also contradict the Garden of Eden hypothesis. At so early a date the newly-divergent populations (and their immediate common ancestor) could not possibly be modern *Homo sapiens*. Therefore, if science can be said to progress by discovering refutations, in my opinion the Garden of Eden hypothesis can be said to be refuted.

Finally, both Cann *et al.* (1987) and Gould (1987, 1988) have indicated that the Garden of Eden hypothesis should be regarded as an important justification for accepting the reality of 'the underlying unity of all humans.' This is because the recent common-ancestry interpretation is said to be a means of showing that all human beings are closely related. But the contrary is not true, and the opposing hypothesis about multi-regional human evolution does not support a different precept. In fact quite the opposite. The interpretation of human evolution as a persistent shifting pattern of population contacts and shared ideas may provide an even stronger biological basis for accepting the unity of all humanity. The spread of humankind and its differentiation into distinct geographic groups that persisted through long periods of time, with evidence of long-lasting contact and cooperation, in many ways is a more satisfying interpretation of human prehistory than a scientific rendering of the story of Cain, based on one population quickly, and completely, and most likely violently, replacing all others. This rendering of modern population dispersals is a story of 'making war and not love,' and if true its implications are not pleasant. Of course, that an alternative interpretation is more satisfying does not make it true, but if valid for factual reasons there is no reason not to be more satisfied! A factual basis for supporting the multiregional evolution interpretation is provided by the prehistoric record itself.

ACKNOWLEDGEMENTS

I am very grateful to Alan Mann, Chris Stringer, David W. Frayer, Con Childress, Rachel Caspari, Karen Rosenberg and Kathy Stoner for their indispensable help in editing this paper, and for aiding me in rethinking some of the precepts in it. I am deeply indebted to Alan Thorne and Wu Xinzhi, my co-workers in developing the multiregional evolution hypothesis, for permission to examine the fossil human remains in their care, and for allowing me to join them in the development of these ideas about the pattern of human evolution in the regions they know so well. For the courtesy, cooperation, and kindness extended during my visits to their institutions, I thank the late G. H. R. von Koenigswald of the Senckenberg Museum; T. Jacob of the Gadjah Mada University Medical School; D. Kadar of the Bandung Geological Museum; C. B. Stringer of the British Museum (Natural History); I. Tattersall of the American Museum of Natural History; and P. Brown of the Department of Prehistory, University of New England. The research upon which this paper is based was supported by NSF grants BNS 75-21756 and BNS 75-82729, and grants from the National Academy of Sciences Committee for Scholarly Exchange with the People's Republic of China.

REFERENCES

Aigner, J. S. 1976. Chinese Pleistocene cultural and hominid remains: A consideration of their significance in reconstructing the pattern of human bio-cultural development, in: *Le Paléolithique Inférieur et Moyen en Inde, en Asie Centrale, en Chine et dans le sud-est Asiatique* (A. K. Gosh, Ed.), pp. 65-90, CNRS, Paris.

Andrews, P. J. 1984. An alternative interpretation of the characters used to define *Homo erectus*, in: *The Early Evolution of Man, with Special Emphasis on Southeast Asia and Africa* (P. J. Andrews and J. L. Franzen, Eds.), *Courier Forschungsinstitut Senckenberg* 69:167-175.

Andrews, P. J., and Franzen, J. L., Eds. 1984. *The Early Evolution of Man, with Special Emphasis on Southeast Asia and Africa. Courier Forschungsinstitut Senckenberg* 69.

Avise, J. C., Neigel, J. E., and Arnold, J. 1984. Demographic influences on mitochondrial DNA lineage survivorship in animal populations. *Journal of Molecular Evolution* 20:99-105.

Barton, N. H. 1983. Multilocus clines. *Evolution* 37:454-471.

Barton, N. H., and Charlesworth, B. 1984. Genetic revolutions, founder effects and speciation. *Annual Review of Ecology and Systematics* 15:133-164.

Binford, L. R. 1984. *Faunal Remains From Klasies River Mouth.* Academic Press, New York.

Binford, L. R. 1986. Reply to Singer and Wymer: 'On Binford on Klasies River Mouth: Response of the excavators.' *Current Anthropology* 27:57-62.

Binford, S. R. 1968. Early Upper Pleistocene adaptations in the Levant. *American Anthropologist* 70:707-717.

Bodmer, W. F., and Cavalli-Sforza, L. L. 1976. *Genetics, Evolution and Man.* Freeman. San Francisco.

Bräuer, G. 1980. Die morphologischen affinitäten des Jungpleistozänen Stirnbeines aus dem Elbmündungsgebiet bei Hahnöfersand. *Zeitschrift fur Morphologie und Anthropologie* 71:1-42.

Bräuer, G. 1981. New evidence on the transitional period between Neanderthal and modern man. *Journal of Human Evolution* 10:467-474.

Bräuer, G. 1982. A comment on the controversy 'Allez Neanderthal.' *Journal of Human Evolution* 11:439-440.

Bräuer, G. 1984a. The 'Afro-European sapiens hypothesis' and hominid evolution in East Asia during the late Middle and Upper Pleistocene, in: *The Early Evolution of Man, with Special Emphasis on Southeast Asia and Africa* (P. J. Andrews and J. L. Franzen, Eds.), *Courier Forschungsinstitut Senckenberg* 69:145-165.

Bräuer, G. 1984b. A craniological approach to the origin of anatomically modern *Homo sapiens* in Africa and implications for the appearance of modern Europeans, in: *The Origins of Modern Humans: A World Survey of the Fossil Evidence* (F. H. Smith and F. Spencer, Eds.), pp. 327-410, Liss, New York.

Bräuer, G., and Leakey, R. E. 1986. The ES-11693 cranium from Eliye Springs, West Turkana, Kenya. *Journal of Human Evolution* 15:289-312.

Brown, W. M. 1980. Polymorphism in mitochondrial DNA of humans as revealed by restriction endonuclease analysis. *Proceedings of the National Academy of Sciences (USA)* 77:3605-3609.

Brown, W. M., Prager, E. M., Wang, A., and Wilson, A. C. 1982. Mitochondrial DNA sequences of primates: Tempo and mode of evolution. *Journal of Molecular Evolution* 18:225-239.

Bryan, A. L. (Ed.) 1986. *New Evidence for the Pleistocene Peopling of the Americas.* Centre for the Study of Early Man, University of Maine, Orono.

Bryant, E. H., Combs, L. M., and McCommas, S. A. 1986a. Morphometric differentiation among experimental lines of the housefly in relation to a bottleneck. *Genetics* 114:1213-1223.

Bryant, E. H., McCommas, S. A., and Combs, L. M. 1986. The effect of an experimental bottleneck on quantitative genetic variation in the housefly. *Genetics* 114:1191-1211.

Bunney, S. 1984. Chinese fossil could alter the course of evolution in Asia. *New Scientist* (11 September), p. 25.

Cann, R. L., Brown, W. M. and Wilson, A. C. 1982. Evolution of human mitochondrial DNA: A preliminary report, in: *Human Genetics: The Unfolding Genome* (B. Bonné-Tamir, P. Cohen and M. Goodman, Eds.), pp. 157-165, Liss, New York.

Cann, R. L., Brown, W. M., and Wilson, A. C. 1984. Polymorphic sites and mechanisms of evolution in human mitochondrial DNA. *Genetics* 106:479-499.

Cann, R. L., Stoneking, M., and Wilson, A. C. 1987. Mitochondrial DNA and human evolution. *Nature* 325:31-36.

Carr, S. M., Ballinger, S. W., Derr, J. N., Blankenship, L. H., and Bickham, J. W. 1986. Mitochondrial DNA analysis of hybridization between sympatric white-tailed deer and mule deer in west Texas. *Proceedings of the National Academy of Sciences (USA)* 83:9576-9580.

Carson, H. L. 1982. Speciation as a major reorganization of polygenic balances, in: *Mechanisms of Speciation* (C. Barigozzi, Ed.), pp. 411-433, Liss, New York.

Cavalli-Sforza, L. L., and Edwards, A. W. F. 1965. Analysis of human evolution, in: *Genetics Today: Proceedings of the XIth International Congress of Genetics* (S. J. Geerts, Ed.), pp. 923-933.

Cavalli-Sforza, L. L., Barrai, I., and Edwards, A. W. F. 1964. Analysis of human evolution under random genetic drift. *Cold Spring Harbor Symposium on Quantitative Biology* 29:9-20.

Chang, Kwangchi. 1963. *The Archeology of Ancient China*. Yale University Press, New Haven.

Charlesworth, B. 1983. Models of the evolution of some genetic systems. *Proceedings of the Royal Society of London* (Series B) 219:265-279.

Charlesworth, B., Lande, R., and Slatkin, M. 1982. A Neo-Darwinian commentary on macroevolution. *Evolution* 36:474-498.

Clark, W. E. LeGros 1964. *The Fossil Evidence for Human Evolution* (2nd edition). University of Chicago Press, Chicago.

Clark, B. C. 1966. The evolution of morph-ratio clines. *American Naturalist* 100:389-402.

Clark, B. C. 1975. The causes of biological diversity. *Scientific American* 233:50-60.

Clarke, R. J. 1985. A new reconstruction of the Florisbad cranium, with notes on the site, in: *Ancestors: The Hard Evidence* (E. Delson, Ed.), pp. 301-305, Liss, New York.

Cohan, F. M. 1984. Can uniform selection retard random genetic divergence between isolated conspecific populations? *Evolution* 38:495-504.

Coon, C. S. 1962. *The Origin of Races*. Knopf, New York.

Day, M. H. 1972. The Omo human skeletal remains, in: *The Origin of Homo Sapiens* (F. Bordes, Ed.), pp. 31-36, UNESCO, Paris.

Day, M. H., and Stringer, C. B. 1982. A reconsideration of the Omo Kibish remains and the *erectus-sapiens* transition, in: *L'Homo erectus et al Place de l'Homme de Tautavel Parmi les Hominides Fossiles*: Vol 2 (M. A. de Lumley, Ed.), pp. 814-846, Centre National de la Recherche Scientifique/Louis-Jean Scientific and Literary Publications, Nice.

Delson, E. 1985. Late Pleistocene human fossils and evolutionary relationships, in: *Ancestors: The Hard Evidence* (E. Delson, Ed.), pp. 296-300, Liss, New York.

Denaro, M., Blanc, H., Johnson, M. J., Chen, K. H., Wilmsen, E., and Cavalli-Sforza, L. L. 1981. Ethnic variation in Hpa 1 endonuclease cleavage patterns of human mitochondrial DNA. *Proceedings of the National Academy of Sciences (USA)* 78:5768-5772.

Eckhardt, R. B. 1987. Evolution east of Eden. *Nature* 326:749.

Edwards, A. W. F. 1971. Mathematical approaches to the study of human evolution, in: *Mathematics in the Archaeological and Historical Sciences* (R. Hodson, D. G. Kendall, and P. Tauto, Eds.), pp. 347-355, Edinburgh University Press, Edinburgh.

Ehrlich, P. R., and Raven, P. H. 1969. Differentiation of populations. *Science* 165:1228-1232.

Endler, J. A. 1973. Gene flow and population differentiation. *Science* 179:243-250.

Endler, J. A. 1977. *Geographic Variation, Speciation, and Clines*. Princeton University Press, Princeton.

Ferembach, D. 1979. L'émergence du genre *Homo* et de l'espèce *Homo sapiens*. Les faits. Les incertitudes. *Biométrie Humaine* 14:11-18.

Ferris, S. D., Sage, R. D., Huang, C. M., Nielsen, J. T., Ritte, U., and Wilson, A. C. 1983. Flow of mitochondrial DNA across a species boundary. *Proceedings of the National Academy of Sciences (USA)* 80:2290-2294.

Fisher, R. A. 1950. Gene frequencies in a cline determined by selection and diffusion. *Biometrics* 6:353-361.

Flood, J. 1983. *Archaeology of the Dreamtime*. Collins, Sydney.

Freudenthal, M. 1965. Betrachtungen über die Gattung *Cricetodon*. *Koninklijke Nederlandse Akademie Wetenschappen (Series B)* 68:293-305.

Giles, E., and Ambrose, S. H. 1986. Are we all out of Africa? *Nature* 322:21-22.

Goodnight, C. J. 1987. On the effect of founder events on epistatic variance. *Evolution* 41:80-91.

Gould, S. J. 1987. Bushes all the way down. *Natural History* (June): pp. 12-19.

Gould, S. J. 1988. A novel notion of Neanderthal. *Natural History* (June): pp. 16-21.

Greenberg, J. H., Turner, C. G., and Zegura, S. L. 1986. The settlement of the Americas: A comparison of the linguistic dental, and genetic evidence. *Current Anthropology* 27:477-497.

Gribbin, J., and Cherfas, J. 1982. *The Monkey Puzzle: Reshaping the Evolutionary Tree*. Bodley Head, London.

Gruhn, R. 1987. On the settlement of the Americas: South American evidence for an expanded time frame. *Current Anthropology* 28:363-365.

Guglielmino-Matessi, C. R., Gluckman, P., and Cavalli-Sforza, L. L. 1979. Climate and the evolution of skull metrics in man. *American Journal of Physical Anthropology* 50:549-564.

Hale, L. R., and Singh, R. S. 1986. Extensive variation and heteroplasmy in size of mitochondrial DNA among geographic populations of *Drosophila melanogaster*. *Proceedings of the National Academy of Sciences (USA)* 83:8813-8817.

Harpending, H. C. 1974. Genetic structure of small populations. *Annual Review of Anthropology* 3: 229-243.

Hasegawa, M., Kishino, H. and Yano, T. 1985. Dating of the human-ape splitting by a molecular clock of mitochondrial DNA. *Journal of Molecular Evolution* 22:160-174.

Hogan, J. P. 1977. *Inherit the Stars*. Ballantine, New York.

Honeycutt, R. L., and Wheeler, W. C. 1987. Mitochondrial DNA: Variation in humans and higher primates, in: *DNA Systematics: Human and Higher Primates* (S. K. Dutta and W. Winter, Eds.), CRC Press, Boca Raton.

Howell, F. C. 1951. The place of Neanderthal man in human evolution. *American Journal of Physical Anthropology* 9:379-416.

Howells, W. W. 1942. Fossil man and the origin of races. *American Anthropologist* 44:182-193.

Howells, W. W. 1973. *Cranial variation in man: A study by multivariate analysis of patterns of difference among recent human populations*. Papers of the Peabody Museum of Archaeology and Ethnology 67. pp. 1-259, Cambridge, MA.

Howells, W. W. 1976. Explaining modern man: Evolutionists versus migrationists. *Journal of Human Evolution* 5:477-496.

Hublin, J.-J. 1976. *L'homme de Galilée*. Mémoire de DEA de Paléontologie. Universite de Paris VI, Paris.

Jacob, T. 1976. Early populations in the Indonesian region, in: *The Origins of the Australians* (R. L. Kirk and A. G. Thorne, Eds.), pp. 81-93, Australian Institute of Aboriginal Studies, Canberra.

Jacob, T. 1981. Solo man and Peking man, in: *Homo erectus: Papers in Honor of Davidson Black* (B. A. Sigmon and J. S. Cybulski, Eds.), pp. 87-104, University of Toronto Press, Toronto.

Jain, S. K., and Bradshaw, A. D. 1966. Evolutionary divergence among adjacent plant populations. *Heredity* 21:407-441.

Jelínek, J. 1969. Neanderthal man and *Homo sapiens* in Central and Eastern Europe. *Current Anthropology* 10:475-503.

Jelínek, J. 1976. The *Homo sapiens neanderthalensis* and *Homo sapiens sapiens* relationship in Central Europe. *Anthropologie* (Brno) 14:79-81.

Jelínek, J. 1978. Comparison of mid-Pleistocene evolutionary process in Europe and in South-East Asia. *Proceedings of the Symposium on Natural Selection, Liblice*, pp. 251-267.

Jelínek, J. 1980. Variability and geography: Contribution to our knowledge of European and North African Middle Pleistocene hominids. *Anthropologie* (Brno) 18:109-114.

Jelínek, J. 1982. The East and Southeast Asian way of regional evolution. *Anthropologie* (Brno) 21:195-212.

Jelínek, J. 1985. The European, Near East and North African finds after *Australopithecus* and the principal consequences for the picture of human evolution, in: *Hominid Evolution: Past, Present and Future. Proceedings of the Taung Diamond Jubilee International Symposium* (P. V. Tobias, Ed.), pp. 341-354, Liss, New York.

Jepsen, G. L., Simpson, G. G., and Mayr, E., Eds. 1949. *Genetics, Paleontology and Evolution*, Princeton University Press, Princeton.

Johnson, M. J., Wallace, D. C., Ferris, S. D., Rattazzi, M. C., and Cavalli-Sforza, L. L. 1983. Radiation of human mitochondrial DNA types analyzed by restriction endonuclease cleavage patterns. *Journal of Molecular Evolution* 19:255-271.

Jones, J. S. 1981. How different are human races? *Nature* 293:188-190.

Jones, J. S. 1986. The origin of *Homo sapiens*: The genetic evidence, in: *Major Topics in Primate and Human Evolution* (B. Wood, L. Martin, and P. Andrews, Eds.), pp. 317-330, Cambridge University Press, Cambridge.

Jones, J. S., and Rouhani, S. 1986a. How small was the bottleneck? *Nature* 319:449-450.

Jones, J. S., and Rouhani, S. 1986b. Mankind's genetic bottleneck. *Nature* 322:599-600.

Kennedy, G. E. 1984. Are the Kow Swamp hominids 'archaic'? *American Journal of Physical Anthropology* 65:163-168.

Klein, R. 1989. Biological and behavioral perspectives on modern human origins, in: *The Human Revolution* (P. Mellars and C. Stringer, Eds.), pp. 529-564, Princeton University Press, Princeton.

King, M. C., and Wilson, A. C. 1975. Evolution at two levels in humans and chimpanzees. *Science* 188:107-116.

Kirk, R. L., and Szathmary, E. J. E., Eds. 1985. *Out of Asia. Journal of Pacific History.*

Kirk, R. L., and Thorne, A. G., Eds. 1976. *The Origin of the Australians*. Australian Institute of Aboriginal Studies, Canberra.

Lande, R. 1982. Rapid origin of sexual isolation and character divergence in a cline. *Evolution* 36:213-233.

Larnach, S. L., and Macintosh, N. W. G. 1974. A comparative study of Solo and Australian Aboriginal crania, in: *Grafton Elliot Smith: The Man and His Work* (A. P. Elkin and N. W. G. Macintosh, Eds.), pp. 95-102, Sydney University Press, Sydney.

Latorre, A., Mova, A., and Ayala, F. J. 1986. Evolution of mitochondrial DNA in *Drosophila subobscura*. *Proceedings of the National Academy of Sciences (USA)* 83:8649-8653.

Lewontin, R. C. 1974. *The Genetic Basis of Evolutionary Change*. Columbia University Press, New York.

Lewontin, R. C. 1984. *Human Diversity*. Freeman, San Francisco.

Livingstone, F. B. 1973. Gene frequency differences in human populations: Some problems of analysis and interpretation, in: *Methods and Theories of Anthropological Genetics* (M. H. Crawford and P. L. Workman, Eds.), pp. 39-67, University of New Mexico Press, Albuquerque.

Livingstone, F. B. 1980. Natural selection and random variation in human evolution, in: *Current Developments in Anthropological Genetics*. Vol 1: *Theory and Methods* (J. H. Mielke and M. H. Crawford, Eds.), pp. 87-110, Plenum Press, New York.

de Lumley, M.-A., and Sonakia, A. 1985. Première découverte d'un *Homo erectus* sur le Continent indien, à Hathnora, dans le Moyenne Vallée de la Narmada. *L'Anthropologie* 89:13-61.

Macintosh, N. W. G., and Larnach, S. L. 1976. Aboriginal affinities looked at in world context, in: *The Origin of the Australians* (R. L. Kirk and A. G. Thorne, Eds.), pp. 113-126, Australian Institute of Aboriginal Studies, Canberra.

Magori, C. C., and Day, M. H. 1983. Laetoli hominid 18: An early *Homo sapiens* skull. *Journal of Human Evolution* 12:747-753.

Martin, R. A. 1970. Line and grade in the extinct medium species of *Sigmodon*. *Science* 166:1504-1506.

Mayr, E. 1963. *Animal Species and Evolution*. Belknap, Cambridge, MA.

Mayr, E. 1982. Processes of speciation in animals, in: *Mechanisms of Speciation* (C. Barigozzi, Ed.), pp. 1-19, Liss, New York.

Morton, N. E., and Lalouel, J. 1973. Topology of kinship in Micronesia. *American Journal of Human Genetics* 25:422-432.

Nei, M. 1985. Human evolution at the molecular level, in: *Population Genetics and Molecular Evolution* (K. Aoki and T. Ohta, Eds.), pp. 41-64, Japan Science Society Press, Tokyo.

Nei, M. 1987. *Molecular Evolutionary Genetics*. Columbia University Press, New York.

Nei, M., and Roychoudhury, A. K. 1982. Genetic relationship and evolution of human races, in: *Evolutionary Biology* Vol. 14 (B. Wallace and G. T. Prace, Eds.), pp. 1-59, Plenum Press, New York.

Parsons, P. A. 1983. *The Evolutionary Biology of a Colonizing Species*. Cambridge University Press, Cambridge.

Protsch, R. 1975. The absolute dating of Upper Pleistocene sub-Saharan fossil hominids and their place in human evolution. *Journal of Human Evolution* 4:297-322.

Protsch, R. 1978. *Catalogue of Fossil Hominids of North America*. Fischer, New York.

Rightmire, G. P. 1976. Relationships of Middle and Upper Pleistocene hominids from sub-Saharan Africa. *Nature* 260:238-240.

Rightmire, G. P. 1978. Florisbad and human population succession in Southern Africa. *American Journal of Physical Anthropology* 48:475-486.

Rightmire, G. P. 1979. Implications of the Border Cave skeletal remains for later Pleistocene human evolution. *Current Anthropology* 20:23-35.

Rightmire, G. P. 1981. Later Pleistocene hominids of Eastern and Southern Africa. *Anthropologie* (Brno) 19:15-26.

Rightmire, G. P. 1984a. *Homo sapiens* in sub-Saharan Africa, in: *The Origins of Modern Humans: a World Survey of the Fossil Evidence* (F. H. Smith and F. Spencer, Eds.), pp. 295-325, Liss, New York.

Rightmire, G. P. 1984b. Comparisons of *Homo erectus* from Africa and Southeast Asia, in: *The Early Evolution of Man, with Special Emphasis on Southeast Asia and Africa* (P. J. Andrews and J. L. Franzen, Eds.), *Courier Forschungsinstitut Senckenberg* 69:83-98.

Rightmire, G. P. 1987. L'Evolution des premiers hominidés en Asie du Sud-Est. *L'Anthropologie* 91:455-465.

Robbins, L. H. 1972. Archaeology in the Turkana district, Kenya. *Science* 176:359-366.

Robbins, L. H. 1974. *The Lothagam Site*. Michigan State University Museum Anthropological Series 1(2).

Robbins, L. H. 1980. *Lopov: A Late Stone Age Fishing and Pastoral Settlement in the Lake Turkana Basin, Kenya*. Michigan State University Museum Anthropological Series 3(1).

Saitou, N., and Omoto, K. 1987. Time and place of human origins from mtDNA data. *Nature* 327:288.

Sartono, S. 1982. Characteristics and chronology of early men in Java, in: *L'Homo erectus et la Place de l'Homme de Tautavel Parmi les Hominides Fossiles*: Vol 2 (M. A. de Lumley, Ed.), pp. 491-541, Centre National de la Recherche Scientifique/Louis-Jean Scientific and Literary Publications, Nice.

Schwalbe, G. 1904. *Die Vorgeschichte des Menschen*. Friedrich, Braunschweig.

Sibley, C. G., and Ahlquist, J. E. 1984. The phylogeny of the hominoid primates, as indicated by DNA-DNA hybridization. *Journal of Molecular Evolution* 20:2-15.

Singer, R. 1958. The Rhodesian, Florisbad, and Saldanha skulls, in: *Hundert Fahre Neanderthaler* (G. H. R. von Koenigswald, Ed.), pp. 52-62, Bohlau, Koln.

Slatkin, M. 1987. Gene flow and the geographic structure of natural populations. *Science* 236:787-792.

Smith, F. H. 1982. Upper Pleistocene hominid evolution in South-Central Europe: A review of the evidence and analysis of trends. *Current Anthropology* 23:667-703.

Smith, F. H. 1984. Fossil hominids from the Upper Pleistocene of Central Europe and the origin of modern Europeans, in: *The Origins of Modern Humans: A World Survey of the Fossil Evidence* (F. H. Smith and F. Spencer, Eds.), pp. 137-209, Liss, New York.

Smith, F. H. 1985. Continuity and change in the origin of modern *Homo sapiens. Zeitschrift für Morphologie und Anthropologie* 75:197-222.

Stewart, T. D. 1974. Perspectives on some problems of early man common to America and Australia, in: *Grafton Elliot Smith: The Man and his Work* (A. P. Elkin and N. W. G. Macintosh, Eds.), pp. 114-135, Sydney University Press, Sydney.

Stoneking, M., Bhatia, K., and Wilson, A. C. 1986. Rate of sequence divergence estimated from restriction maps of mitochondrial DNAs from Papua New Guinea. *Cold Spring Harbor Symposia on Quantitative Biology* 51:433-439.

Stoneking, M. and Cann, R. 1989. African origin of human mitochondrial DNA, in: *The Human Revolution* (P. Mellars and C. Stringer, Eds.), 17-30, Princeton University Press, Princeton.

Stringer, C. B. 1984a. Human evolution and biological adaptation in the Pleistocene, in: *Hominid Evolution and Community Ecology: Prehistoric Human Adaptation in Biological Perspective* (R. Foley, Ed.), 55-83, Academic Press, London.

Stringer, C. B. 1984b. The definition of *Homo erectus* and the existence of the species in Africa and Europe, in: *The Early Evolution of Man, with Special Emphasis on Southeast Asia and Africa* (P. J. Andrews and J. L. Franzen, Eds.), *Courier Forschungsinstitut Senckenberg* 69:131-143.

Stringer, C. B. 1984c. The fate of the Neanderthals. *Natural History* (December), pp. 6-12.

Stringer, C. B. 1985. Middle Pleistocene hominid variability and the origin of Late Pleistocene humans, in: *Ancestors: The Hard Evidence* (E. Delson, Ed.), pp. 289-295, Liss, New York.

Stringer, C. B. 1989. Documenting the origin of modern humans, in: *Patterns and Processes in Later Pleistocene Human Emergence* (E. Trinkaus, Ed.), pp. 67-96, Cambridge University Press, Cambridge.

Stringer, C. B. and Andrews, P. 1988. Genetic and fossil evidence for the origin of modern humans. *Science.* 239:1263-1268.

Szathmary, E. J. E., and Ossenberg, N. S. 1978. Are the biological differences between North American Indians and Eskimos truly profound? *Current Anthropology* 19:673-701.

Tattersall, I. 1986. Species recognition in human palaeontology. *Journal of Human Evolution* 15:165-176.

Templeton, A. R. 1982. Genetic architectures of speciation, in: *Mechanisms of Speciation* (C. Barigozzi, Ed.), pp. 105-121, Liss, New York.

Templeton, A. R. 1983. Phylogenetic inference from restriction endonuclease cleavage site maps with particular reference to the evolution of humans and the apes. *Evolution* 37:221-244.

Thoma, A. 1985. *Eléments de Paléoanthropologie.* Institut Superieur d'Archeologie et d'Histoire de d'Art, Louvain-la-Neuve.

Thorne, A. G. 1981. The centre and the edge: The significance of Australian hominids to African palaeoanthropology, in: *Proceedings of the 8th Panafrican Congress of Prehistory and Quaternary Studies, Nairobi, September 1977* (R. E. Leakey and B. A. Ogot, Eds.), pp. 180-181, TILL MIAP, Nairobi.

Thorne, A. G. 1984. Australia's human origins: How many sources? *American Journal of Physical Anthropology* 63:227.

Thorne, A. G., and Wilson, S. R. 1977. Pleistocene and recent Australians: A multivariate comparison. *Journal of Human Evolution* 6:393-402.

Thorne, A. G., and Wolpoff, M. H. 1981. Regional continuity in Australasian Pleistocene hominid evolution. *American Journal of Physical Anthropology* 55:337-349.

Trinkaus, E., and Thompson, D. D. 1987. Femoral diaphyseal histomorphometric age determinations for the Shanidar 3,4,5, and 6 Neandertals and Neandertal longevity. *American Journal of Physical Anthropology* 72:123-129.

Turner, A. 1984. Hominids and fellow travellers: Human migration into high latitudes as part of a large mammal community, in: *Hominid Evolution and Community Ecology: Prehistoric Human Adaptation in Biological Perspective* (R. Foley, Ed.), pp. 193-217, Academic Press, London.

Valladas, H., Reyss, J. L., Joron, J. L., Valladas, G., Bar-Yosef, O., and Vandermeersch, B. 1988. Thermoluminescence dating of Mousterian 'Proto-Cro-Magnon' remains from Israel and the origin of modern man. *Nature* 331:614-616.

Van Valen, L. M. 1966. On discussing human races. *Perspectives in Biology and Medicine* 9:377-383.

Van Valen, L. M. 1986. Speciation and our own species. *Nature* 322:412.

Van Vark, G. N. 1983. Did our *Homo erectus* ancestors live in Eastern Asia? *Homo* 34:148-153.

Vandermeersch, B. 1970. Les origines de l'homme moderne. *Atomes* 25(272):5-12.

Vandermeersch, B. 1981. *Les Hommes Fossiles de Qafzeh (Israel).* Centre National de la Recherche Scientifique, Paris.

Wainscoat, J. 1987. Out of the Garden of Eden. *Nature* 325:13.

Wainscoat, J. S., Hill, A. V. S., Boyce, A. L., Flint, J., Hernandez, M., Thein, S. L., Old, J. M., Lynch, J. R., Falusi, A. G., Weatherall, D. J., and Clegg, J. B. 1986. Evolutionary relationships of human populations from an analysis of nuclear DNA polymorphisms. *Nature* 319:491-493.

Wainscoat, J. S. *et al.* 1989. Geographic distribuution of Alpha- and Beta-Globin gene cluster polymorphisms, in: *The Human Revolution* (P. Mellars and C. Stringer, Eds.), pp. 31-38, Princeton University Press, Princeton.

Wallace, D. C., Garrison, K., and Knowler, W. C. 1985. Dramatic founder effects in Amerindian Mitochondrial DNAs. *American Journal of Physical Anthropology* 68:149-155.

Weckler, J. E. 1957. Neanderthal man. *Scientific American* 197: 89-97.

Wei Liming. 1984. 200,000 year-old skeleton unearthed. *Beijing Review* 49 (December 3), p. 33.

Weidenreich, F. 1939. Six lectures on *Sinanthropus pekinensis* and related problems. *Bulletin of the Geological Society of China* 19:1-110.

Weidenreich, F. 1943. The skull of *Sinanthropus pekinensis:* A comparative study of a primitive hominid skull. *Palaeontologia Sinica* (n.s. D) 10 (whole series 127). Geological Survey of China, Beijing.

Weidenreich, F. 1945. The Keilor skull: A Wadjak skull from southeast Australia. *American Journal of Physical Anthropology* 3:21-33.

Weidenreich, F. 1946. *Apes, Giants and Man.* University of Chicago Press, Chicago.

Weidenreich, F. 1947. The trend of human evolution. *Evolution* 1: 221-236.

Weidenreich, F. 1951. Morphology of Solo man. *Anthropological Papers of the American Museum of Natural History* 43:205-290.

Weinert, H. 1951. *Stammesentwicklung des Menschheit.* Vieweg and Sohn, Braunschweig.

Weiss, K. M. 1984. On the number of members of the genus *Homo* who have ever lived, and some evolutionary implications. *Human Biology* 56:637-649.

Weiss, K. M. 1986. In search of times past: The roles of gene flow and invasion in the generation of human diversity, in: *Biological Aspects of Human Migration* (N. Mascie-Taylor and G. Lasker, Eds.), Cambridge University Press, London.

Weiss, K. M., and Maruyama, T. 1976. Archaeology, population genetics and studies of human racial ancestry. *American Journal of Physical Anthropology* 44:31-50.

White, M. J. D. 1978. *Models of Speciation.* Freeman, San Francisco.

Whittam, T. S., Clark, A. G., Stoneking, M., Cann, R., and Wilson, A. C. 1986. Allelic variation in human mitochondrial genes based on patterns of restriction site polymorphism. *Proceedings of the National Academy of Sciences (USA)* 83:9611-9615.

Wilson, A. C., Cann, R. L., Carr, S. M., George, M., Gyllensten, U. B., Helm-Bychowski, K. M., Higuchi, R. G., Palumbi, S. R., Prager, E. M., Sage, R. D., and Stoneking, M. 1985. Mitochondrial DNA and two perspectives in evolutionary genetics. *Biological Journal of the Linnean Society* (London) 26:375-400.

Wolpoff, M. H. 1980. *Paleoanthropology*. Knopf, New York.

Wolpoff, M. H. 1982a. Comment on F. H. Smith 'Upper Pleistocene hominid evolution in South-Central Europe.' *Current Anthropology* 23:693.

Wolpoff, M. H. 1982b. The Arago dental sample in the context of hominid dental evolution, in: *L'Homo erectus et la Place de l'Homme de Tautavel Parmi les Hominidés Fossiles:* Vol 1 (H. de Lumley, Ed.), pp. 389-410, Centre National de la Recherche Scientifique/Louis-Jean Scientific and Literary Publications, Nice.

Wolpoff, M. H. 1985. Human evolution at the peripheries: The pattern at the eastern edge, in: *Hominid Evolution: Past, Present and Future. Proceedings of the Taung Diamond Jubilee International Symposium* (P. V. Tobias, Ed.), pp. 355-365, Liss, New York.

Wolpoff, M. H. 1986. Describing anatomically modern *Homo sapiens*: A distinction without a definable difference, in: *Fossil Man: New Facts, New Ideas. Papers in Honor of Jan Jelínek's Life Anniversary* (V. V. Novotny and A. Miserová, Eds.), *Anthropos* (Brno) 23:41-53.

Wolpoff, M. and Nkini, A. 1985. Early and middle Pleistocene hominids from Asia and Africa, in: *Ancestors: The Hard Evidence* (E. Delson, Ed.), pp. 202-205, Liss, New York.

Wolpoff, M. H., Wu Xinzhi, and Thorne, A. G. 1984. Modern *Homo sapiens* origins: A general theory of hominid evolution involving the fossil evidence from East Asia, in: *The Origins of Modern Humans: A World Survey of the Fossil Evidence* (F. H. Smith and F. Spencer, Eds.), pp. 411-483, Liss, New York.

Woo Jukang (Wu Rukang) 1959. Human fossils found in Liujiang, Kwangsi, China. *Vertebrata PalAsiatica* 3:109-118.

Wright, S. 1931. Evolution in Mendelian populations. 16:97-159.

Wright, S. 1940. Breeding structure of populations in relation to speciation. *American Naturalist* 74:232-248.

Wright, S. 1943. Isolation by distance. *Genetics* 28:114-138.

Wright, S. 1967. 'Surfaces' of selective value. *Proceedings of the National Academy of Sciences (USA)* 58:165-172.

Wright, S. 1977. *Evolution and the Genetics of Populations.* Vol. 3: *Experimental Results and Evolutionary Deductions.* University of Chicago Press, Chicago.

Wright, S. 1982. Character change, speciation and higer taxa. *Evolution* 36:427-443.

Wu Rukang. 1986. Chinese human fossils and the origin of Mongoloid racial group, in: *Fossil Man: New Facts, New Ideas. Papers in Honor of Jan Jelínek's Life Anniversary* (V. V. Novotny and A. Miserová, Eds.), *Anthropos* (Brno) 23:151-155.

Wu Rukang, and Dong Xingren. 1982. Preliminary study of *Homo erectus* remains from Hexian, Anhui. *Acta Anthropologica Sinica* 1:2-13.

Wu Rukang, and Dong Xingren 1985. *Homo erectus* in China, in: *Paleoanthropology and Paleolithic Archaeology in the People's Republic of China* (Wu Rukang and J. W. Olsen, Eds.), pp. 79-89, Academic Press, New York.

Wu Rukang, and Lin Shenglong. 1985. Chinese paleoanthropology: Retrospect and prospect, in: *Paleoanthropology and Paleolithic Archaeology in the People's Republic of China* (Wu Rukang and J. W. Olsen, Eds.), pp. 1-27, Academic Press, New York.

Wu Rukang, and Wu Xinzhi. 1982. Comparison of Tautavel man with *Homo erectus* and early *Homo sapiens* in China, in: *L'Homo erectus et la Place de l'Homme de Tautavel Parmi les Hominidés Fossiles:* Vol. 2 (H. de Lumley, Ed.), pp. 605-616, Centre National de la Recherche Scientifique/Louis-Jean Scientific and Literary Publications, Nice.

Wu Xinzhi. 1961. Study on the Upper Cave man of Choukoutien. *Vertebrata PalAsiatica* 3:202-211.

Wu Xinzhi. 1981. A well-preserved cranium of an archaic type of early *Homo sapiens* from Dali, China. *Scientia Sinica* 24:530-541.

Wu Xinzhi and Wu Maolin. 1985. Early *Homo sapiens* in China, in: *Paleoanthropology and Paleolithic Archaeology in the People's Republic of China* (Wu Rukang and J. W. Olsen, Eds.), pp. 91-106, Academic Press, New York.

Wu Xinzhi, and Zhang Yinyun. 1978. Fossil man in China, in: *Symposium on the Origin of Man*, pp. 28-42, Science Press, Beijing.

Part VII
The Neandertal Question and the Emergence of Modern Humans

In contrast with the preceding part, which addressed the issue of the evolution of *Homo sapiens* and the origins of modern humans on a global scale, the chapters in this part have a more localized geographical and temporal focus.

For many decades, it has been clear that there were two types of fossil hominids in Europe and the Middle East during the last one hundred thousand years—Neandertals and Cro-Magnons or early modern humans. There are also two major lithic industries—the less sophisticated, Middle Paleolithic Mousterian industry and the more elaborate Upper Paleolithic, Aurignacian industry. The issues that remain a source of endless debate include:

1. The precise temporal relationships of these hominid types and lithic industries. Do all Neandertals precede anatomically modern *Homo sapiens* in time, and do all Middle Paleolithic technologies precede Upper Paleolithic industries? In the Middle East, both Neandertals and modern *Homo sapiens* were present, alternately if not synchronously, for approximately 60,000 years (Figure 1), with all evidence of Neandertal occupation disappearing at approximately 40,000 years ago. In Europe the record seems to span a shorter time with *Homo sapiens* succeeding Neandertals, as a rule (Figure 1). At present, the length of the temporal overlap, the nature of any genetic interchange, and the geographical or environmental patterning of the replacement of Neandertals by *Homo sapiens* remain unresolved (Stringer and Grün 1991; Grün and Stringer 1991).

2. The phylogenetic and biogeographical relationships of the hominids. Did Neandertals give rise to anatomically modern humans in Europe and/or the Middle East, or did anatomically modern humans originate elsewhere and replace Neandertals (driving them to extinction)? Or, was the scenario a more intermediate one in which anatomically modern humans originated elsewhere and replaced Neandertals, but with some degree of genetic interchange? These issues are discussed in chapters 45, 47, and 48 in the previous part and in chapters 50 through 54, and 58 as well as in many of the edited volumes referenced in the introduction to Part VI.

3. The relationship between the hominids and the lithic industries. Is the Mousterian uniquely associated with Neandertals and Upper Paleolithic industries with anatomically modern humans? Did the Aurignacian industry arise from the Mousterian or was it brought in from elsewhere? Was there any technological exchange? This is discussed in chapters 51, 52, and 55 (see also Mellars 1989; Klein 1992).

Chapter 49, "Pleistocene Glacial Ecology and the Evolution of 'Classic Neandertal' Man" by F. Clark Howell, attempts to relate the distribution of fossil hominids in the Middle and Upper Pleistocene of Europe to paleogeography and climatology. He argues that the Classic Neandertals of Western Europe were "isolated survivors of a formerly widespread 'Neandertaloid' group of people" occuring widely over Europe during the late Third Interglacial, and that those in the western part became "progressively isolated with the onset of arctic condi-

Figure 1. *Age estimates for* Homo sapiens, Homo neanderthalensis, *and Paleolithic technologies (from Stringer and Grün 1991).*

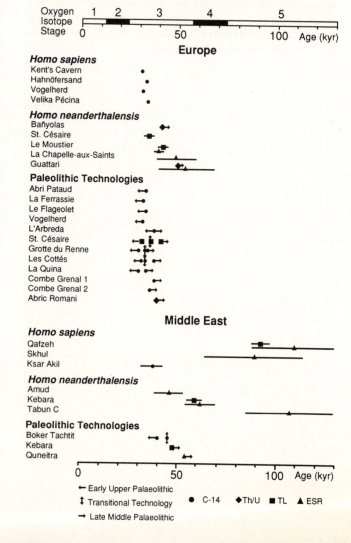

tions heralding the first advance of the Fourth glaciation," with many of their morphological characteristics being adaptations to a periglacial biotope. In discussing the fate of the Classic Neandertals, Howell leaves open the possibility that the Upper Paleolithic invaders (anatomically modern humans) who migrated into western Europe and replaced Neandertals could have coexisted with the latter for a brief period.

Chapter 50, "Neandertals and Presapiens" by Henri Vallois, is a classic paper advocating a non-Neandertal origin for modern *Homo sapiens*. Vallois' argument is based on two lines of evidence. The first, and stronger, is that the Neandertals from Western Europe are far too specialized in many anatomical features to lie in the ancestry of later human propulations. The second, and admittedly weaker, line of evidence, is that there are perhaps more suitable ancestors among the fossil hominids that preceded the Neandertals in Europe. He reviews various fossil hominids that had been proposed as modern human ancestors. While some of his assessments concerning particular fossils are not accepted today, his basic position is still very current (see Chapters 45, 47, 52, 58).

Chapter 51, "Early Upper Paleolithic Man and Late Middle Paleolithic Tools" by David S. Brose and Milford H. Wolpoff, argues that the transition from Neandertals in the Middle Paleolithic to modern *Homo sapiens* in the Upper Paleolithic is not an abrupt replacement. Rather they see gradual changes in both stone tool types and fossil hominid morphology throughout the Middle Paleolithic and between the late Middle Paleolithic and the early Upper Paleolithic. They thus argue that the appearance of modern *Homo sapiens* and Upper Paleolithic tools was a continuous change that took place independently in many parts of the world (see also Chapters 48 and 53). This issue is still far from resolved. Many authorities maintain that there is considerable archaeological evidence for a gradual transition in lithic industries from the Middle Paleolithic to Upper Paleolithic in many parts of both Europe and the Middle East (Clark and Lindly 1989). In contrast, other authors emphasize the striking differences between Middle Paleolithic and Upper Paleolithic industries and have argued for a more abrupt replacement of Middle Paleolithic by Upper Paleolithic industries (Klein 1992).

Chapter 52, "Neanderthals: Names, Hypotheses, and Scientific Method" by William W. Howells, is a direct rebuttal to the paper by Brose and Wolpoff. Howells argues that the arguments of Brose and Wolpoff are flawed in several respects. He suggests that comparing ranges of individual morphological features among all fossil hominids from a particular time period precludes the possibility of populational differences within any time or geographic region, and that examination of morphological features one by one obscures differences in shape or, as Le Gros Clark (1964) called it, "total morphological pattern." Finally, he argues that the problem of the origin of modern *Homo sapiens* is unlikely to be solved by a broad summation over the entire Old World, but by more careful examination of the transition in particular places. Only then will the global picture emerge.

Chapter 53, "Upper Pleistocene Hominid Evolution in South-Central Europe: A Review of the Evidence and Analysis of Trends" by Fred H. Smith, is one such regional study. Smith reviews the extraordinarily rich remains of Neandertals and modern *Homo sapiens* fossils from South Central Europe that have received far less attention than those from Western Europe. The Neandertal sample consists of an early group and a late group. He finds that many of the morphological changes between the early and the later Neandertals in this region are the same morphological trends that continue between the late Neandertals and early modern *Homo sapiens*. This is some of the strongest evidence of morphological continuity between populations of archaic hominids and succeeding modern *Homo sapiens*.

Chapter 54, "The Fate of the Neanderthals" by Erik Trinkaus and Fred H. Smith, provides a brief overview of the morphological similarities and differences between Neandertals, and what they tell us about the adaptive changes that took place during this transition. They first discuss the morphological differences in terms of their rate of change both before and after the transition (or replacement) between Neandertals and modern *Homo sapiens*. They find a mosaic pattern of change, with continuity of some features and abrupt change in others. They then discuss the behavioral significance of the morphological differences in reproduction, non-dietary tooth use, habitual activity levels, locomotor efficiency, and thermal adaptation. They find that the transition from Neandertals to anatomically modern *Homo sapiens* involved continuation of many long term trends, with the most striking changes probably related to technological innovations.

Chapter 55, "Mousterian, Chatelperronian, and Early Aurignacian in Western Europe: Continuity or Discontinuity" by Frank B. Harrold, examines the Chatelperronian industry of Spain. Previous authors have debated whether the Chatelperronian (found with Neandertals) provides evidence of a transition between the Mousterian industry and the early Aurignacian in Western Europe. Others have argued that the Chatelperronian is an Upper Paleolithic industry that replaced the Mousterian in this region. Harrold argues, however, that the Chatelperronian is neither an Upper Paleolithic industry nor a transitional industry. Rather, in Harrold's view it is a unique, local development of the Mousterian culture by Neandertals that is "probably due to diffusion and ultimately migration, of the Aurignacian and *Homo sapiens*....However, the biological and cultural details of this slow and doubtless complex process...still elude us" (p. 602). More than anything else, this paper emphasizes the fact that the archaeological evidence, even more than the skeletal evidence, concerning the replacement of Neandertals by modern *Homo sapiens* is complicated and beset with incongruities that seem to preclude any simple hypothesis (but see Klein 1992).

REFERENCES

Clark, G. A. and Lindly, J. W. 1989. The case for continuity: Observations on the biocultural transition in Europe and Western Asia, in: *The Human Revolution: Behavioral and Biological Perspectives on the Origins of Modern Humans* (P. Mellars and C. Stringer, Eds.), pp. 626-676, Princeton University Press, Princeton, NJ.

Grün, R. and Stringer, C. B. 1991. Electron spin resonance dating and the evolution of modern humans. *Archaeometry* 33:153-199.

Klein, R. G. 1992. The archeology of modern human origins. *Evolutionary Anthropology* 1:5-14.

Le Gros Clark, W. E. 1964. *The Fossil Evidence for Human Evolution*. 2nd Edition. University of Chicago Press, Chicago.

Mellars, P. 1989. Major issues in the emergence of modern humans. *Current Anthropol.* 30:349-385.

Stringer, C. B. and Grün, R. 1991. Time for the last Neanderthals. *Nature* 351:701-702.

49

Pleistocene Glacial Ecology and the Evolution of "Classic Neandertal" Man

F. C. Howell

Isolation is one of the most important factors leading to evolutionary change. In nature, a variety of isolating mechanisms are at work. One generally distinguishes between geographical and physiological isolation although a number of other subdivisions may be made (Mayr 1942; Dobzhansky 1951). In one way or another, isolation results in failure of forms of one group to interbreed with those of another, and thereby gives rise to discontinuous variation. So long as there is interbreeding between individuals of a population, or between population units (demes), hereditary differences between individuals or populations will be absorbed and the breeding isolate will be of heterogeneous composition. Thus, "the only way to preserve the differences between organisms is to prevent their interbreeding, to introduce isolation" (Dobzhansky 1941).

One of the most important barriers to gene flow between potentially interbreeding groups during the Pleistocene was that of climate. Simpson (1947) has noted the importance of climatic factors with regard to intercontinental expansion of mammals over a Bering Strait land-bridge during the Tertiary and Quaternary, since "the migration route clearly led through a cold area and filtered out all animals that could not survive in a more or less rigorous climate." On lower taxonomic levels, Mayr and Rand have presented some of the avifauna evidence, and Deevey has recently summarized much of the data bearing on plant and invertebrate distribution as affected by Pleistocene glaciation (Mayr 1942; Rand 1947; Deevey 1949).

Heretofore, there has been no attempt to examine human evolutionary data for possible evidence as to the influence of climatic factors on hominid distribution and development in the Pleistocene. The reasons for this are perhaps twofold: too few fossils and too much emphasis on morphological evidence with little attention to geography and climatology. Although a number of fossils have been assigned a phylogenetically collateral position, the basis for so doing has been almost exclusively the result of comparative morphological evidence alone. Since most workers in human paleontology are primarily anatomists, there has been little effort to view human evolution with regard to paleogeography and paleoclimatology. The necessity for such studies is obvious and the lack of them is greatly lamented.

In an attempt to clarify the relationships of one important and fairly numerous series of fossils, so-called "Neandertal" [1] man, I have suggested elsewhere (Howell 1951) that one group, designated "classic Neandertals," was most probably an iso-

lated descendant of an earlier and more widespread "Neandertal" type. The evidence previously discussed was primarily anatomical, and it is intended here to consider in greater detail the geochronological and paleoclimatological data bearing on the problem [2].

"CLASSIC NEANDERTAL" DISTRIBUTION, DATING, AND MORPHOLOGY

"Classic Neandertal" skeletal remains are restricted in distribution to western and southern Europe. The best preserved and most numerous specimens are from the departments of Charente (La Quina), Dordogne (Le Moustier, La Ferrassie), and Corréze (La Chapelle-aux-Saints) in southern France, an area well-known for its many discoveries of Cromagnon man. Other remains have been found as far north as Belgium (Engis, Spy) and near Dusseldorf, Germany (Neandertal). In southern Europe, remains are known from central Italy (Monte Circeo) and from the rock of Gibraltar (Forbes Quarry and Devil's Tower). Some of the specimens (Le Moustier, Neandertal, and the Forbes Quarry skull) lack stratigraphic information and cannot be dated but are assigned to the "classic Neandertal" group solely on the basis of morphology. For the other remains, there is good stratigraphic and faunal data available so that accurate dating is possible [3].

Hopwood surveyed the associated fauna of most of these fossils and Zeuner later reviewed both the faunal and stratigraphic evidence for dating these remains (Hopwood 1935; Zeuner 1940). What follows is both a summary of their work plus additional data drawn from the original literature.

On the basis of faunal evidence alone, it is possible to assign a number of the remains to the Upper Pleistocene (post-Third glacial) since the faunal content at this time is a distinctive one indicative of an arctic biotope. As Zeuner (1945) points out:

> The chief mark of the upper Pleistocene is the cold faunas of the three phases of the Last Glaciation. By this time, immigration and adaptive evolution had supplied a large number of species well fitted for the periglacial biotopes. Many, present in small numbers in earlier cold phases, now become abundant; arctic fox, varying hare, lemming and susliks (*Citellus*), caballine horses, woolly rhinoceros, reindeer, musk-ox, mammoth (*E. primigenius* s. str.).

Reprinted with permission from *Southwestern Journal of Anthropology*, Vol. 8, pp. 377–410. Copyright © 1952 by University of New Mexico, Albuquerque.

Table 1. Mammalian associations with "classic Neandertal" fossil men (modified after Hopwood 1935).

Fauna	Englis #2	Spy	Neandertal	La Chapelle	La Ferrassie	La Quina	Le Moustier	Monte Circeo	Gibraltar 1 (Forbes Quarry)	Gibraltar 2 (Devil's Tower)
Elephas primigenius (woolly mammoth)	+	+				+		sp.?		This fauna includes *Canis lupus*, *Hyaena crocuta*, *Sus scrofa*, *Cervus elaphus*, *Bos cf. primigenius*, *Equus caballus*; great auk, alpine and red-billed chough.
Rhinoceros tichorinus (woolly rhino)	+	+		+	+			sp.?		
Rangifer tarandus (barren-ground reindeer)	+	+	No associations known	+	+	+	No associations known		No associations known	
Cervus elaphus (red deer)	+	+			+			+		
Capra ibex (steinbok)	+			+				+		
Bos primigenius (urus)	+	+			+	+		+		
Bison priscus (bison)	+			+	+	+				
Sus scrofa (wild boar)	+				+					
Equus caballus (caballine horse)	+	+		+	+	+		+		
Ursus spelaeus (cave bear)	+	+				+		sp.?		
Canis lupus (wolf)	+			+	+	+				
Hyaena spelaea (cave hyaena)	+	+		+	+	+		sp.?		
Arctomys marmota (alpine marmot)				+	+					

This is Osborn's Third fauna containing arctic, tundra animals (Osborn 1910). It should be noted, however, that any one animal is not distinctive. For example, the Second fauna of the Pleistocene (Pohlig's *Elephas antiquus* stage), already contained the newly-arrived woolly mammoth (*E. primigenius*) which appears during the second maximum of the Third glacial (cf. Zeuner 1945) and apparently evolved from the earlier *E. trogontherii* characteristic of the Middle Pleistocene (Soergel 1912). Similarly, the woolly rhinoceros (*R. tichorhinus=antiquitatus*), "a steppe and tundra form which immigrated into Europe from the east," (Zeuner 1945) is also found in the glacial deposits of the Middle Pleistocene, but in association with *E. primigenius* is especially characteristic of the Upper Pleistocene. It is thus necessary to consider the associated fauna as a whole and not rely on any one species as a key, and also to examine the relative abundance of each species within the total faunal assemblage.

In the most northern deposits at Spy in Belgium (Fraipont and Lohest 1887)[4], the most abundant associated mammals are wooly rhino, caballine horse, reindeer, woolly mammoth, and cave hyena, with cattle less frequent. Farther south, in southern France, at La Chapelle and La Quina, reindeer remains seem to be most numerous with abundant remains of caballine horse, cattle and/or bison; there is scarce representation of either woolly rhino or mammoth in the presence of a few molar teeth (Bouyssonie and Bardon 1908; Boule 1911–13; Martin 1923). At La Ferrassie, the situation is similar but with primarily cattle or bison, some horse and deer, little reindeer, some boar, wolf, and fox (Capitan and Peyrony 1912; Perony 1934). This difference in faunal content (see Table 1 for the main faunal elements) is important because of the differing climatic conditions dependent upon proximity to the Scandinavian ice-sheet, a region of more continental climate and lower vegetation where large herbivores would be most numerous (see below).

On the shores of the Mediterranean, associated fauna is of less assistance because of persistence of temperate forms in the south during the time of the northern ice-sheets. At Monte Circeo, however, Blanc (1940, 1942) has convincingly demonstrated the age of the "classic Neandertal" skull found in the Grotta Guattari near Rome. From the presence of the gastropod *Strombus bubonius* in the lowest beach deposit, Blanc has shown that the deposit is of post-Tyrrhenian age (=later than Second interglacial) and that such a fauna indicates the late Monastirian (=Tyrrhenian II) shore line formed during the transgression sea-level of the Third interglacial. The grotto could thus have been occupied only during the post-Monasterian regression with sea-level lowering during the onset of the Last glaciation. The fauna associated with the human skull (and a mandible of another individual) is essentially of woodland type, including leopard, bear, caballine horse, and ibex. Blanc believes that this must coincide with the first stadial of the last glaciation because the "intense cold of Würm II should already have begun at the time when the grotto had been closed by the rock-fall" which sealed the cave until its recent opening by workmen. Zeuner points out that the latest date possible for the human skull was "the beginning of the second phase of the Last Glaciation when thermoclastic weathering could for the last time have produced the quantity of rock-waste which sealed the cave" (Zeuner 1950). It is interesting to note that a "middle layer" of the cave deposit (below the surface floor on which the skull rested) contained remains of *Hippopotamus (amphibius?)*, indicating a warmer climate prior to the human occupation period apparently coinciding with the onset of the post-Monasterian regression.

The Gibraltar child's skull from Devil's Tower is difficult to date (cf. Bate 1928; Zeuner 1940, 1945). Neither the mammals nor the mollusk fauna alone are especially indicative, although these plus the avifauna provide some evidence. The beach deposits (8.5 m) at the base of the rock-shelter suggest correlation with the "lowest level of the *Strombus*-sea, the Late Monasterian of the Mediterranean shores" (Zeuner 1945): the human occupation therefore postdates that time. The presence of the ibex suggests a woody vegetation but not necessarily a colder climate. The presence, however, of two birds (alpine chough and red-billed chough) found today in higher altitudes, plus the ibex, "lends support to the view that these beds were deposited during the incipient stage of the Last Glaciation, after the sea-level had begun to recede from the Late Monasterian level," and that the skull is therefore "contemporary with that from the Monte Circeo in Italy" (Zeuner 1945).

Thus far, the faunal data presented indicates that the "classic Neandertals" are found in Upper Pleistocene deposits indicating cold climatic conditions north of the Mediterranean (France and Belgium) and in the Mediterranean area a temperate wooded environment following the Late Monasterian regression and the onset of the Fourth glaciation. Stratigraphic data offers additional confirmation of this dating and makes it possible to assign the fossils to the first stadial of this glacial.

At Spy, the human skeletal remains rested on a weathered brown, sometimes, black clay, containing limestone pebbles (Fraipont and Lohest 1887), indicating temperate conditions (Zeuner 1940). The layer above and including the skeletons was a "yellow limey-clay," "presumably of loessic type" (Zeuner 1940), which would correlate with the Younger Loess I (Soergel 1919) of northern Europe, deposited during the last glaciation. This is apparently confirmed by the upper levels where there is a reddish, apparently weathered layer (interstadial), followed by a yellow clayey tufa representing the Younger Loess II. The top of this layer of fallen stone and brown clay equates with the "intense frost-weathering" during a cold period (which Zeuner also regards as the second advance of the Last glacial). This site offers almost conclusive evidence that the human remains were contemporary with the first stage of the Fourth glacial and not of earlier or later date.

In southern France, loess deposits are not found (Grahmann 1932), and it is necessary to seek other evidence of climatic alterations. The La Ferrassie rock-shelter offers an excellent stratigraphic sequence, although it has not as yet been carefully analyzed geologically. The basal layer is composed of small lime elements of reddish color which may represent weathering. The fauna here is predominantly horse, with less numerous cattle and deer, indicative of a temperate climate (Peyrony 1934). Almost at the surface, and near the base of the succeeding layer, are found reindeer teeth, indicating that the climate had become colder with the onset of the glacial stage which is fully present in the following layer containing the human skeletal remains. This is perhaps substantiated by a layer of yellowish limey sands apparently from disintegration of the walls and vault of the shelter (frost-weathering) interposed between the basal layer and the human skeletal remains. The brown earth layer containing the skeletons is indicative of a coniferous forest region, as is suggested by the fauna. The transition here from temperate to cooler conditions appears to indicate the onset of the Fourth glaciation. Reindeer become more abundant in the following layer, and as Zeuner points out, "this distinction is characteristic of the cold phase Würm I and Würm II. . . ." (Zeuner 1940)

Both at La Chapelle and La Quina there is stratigraphy but no data other than fauna which could make it possible to date the human remains accurately. The presence of an Upper Pleistocene cold fauna, plus the evidence from Spy and, more particularly, La Ferrassie, make it seem probable that here too it is a question of the first stage of the Fourth glacial.

The available evidence suggests that all "classic Neandertals," which can be dated, were *approximately* synchronous and

lived in western and southern Europe during the first stadial of the Last glaciation. These are the first known remains of a man in Europe living in a cold area during glacial times, all earlier hominids from Europe now known being associated with warm interglacial fauna and flora. Following the "classic Neandertals," however, are abundant remains of anatomically modern man found with cold faunas in western Europe during the later stadia of the Fourth glaciation.

It has been noted previously (cf. Howell 1951) that the "classic Neandertals" possessed a cranial morphology which can only be regarded as most peculiar and distinct. This was noticed in individual specimens by Morant, to mention but a few (Schwalbe 1901; Boule 1911-13; Martin 1923; Morant 1927). Both Weidenreich and Hooton defined the group primarily on the basis of morphology, with slightly different conclusions (Weidenreich 1928, 1940, 1943; Hooton 1946), but here the delineation of the group is based both on morphology and on chronology. Boule and Klaatsch also noted the distinctive features of the post-cranial skeleton (Boule 1911-13; Klaatsch 1901). The most striking anatomical features of the "classic Neandertals" may be briefly summarized as follows:

Long, low and wide cranial vaults; poorly flexed cranial bases; rather sharply angulated occipital bones with heavy occipital tori; horizontal orientation of the tympanic plate with heavy anterior and posterior portions; large facial skeletons; semicircular supraorbital tori with fused medial and lateral elements; shelving of maxillary bone into malar with no clear demarcation between these bones and lack of maxillary hollowing into a canine fossa; short massive vertebral column; cervical vertebrae with long spinous processes projecting perpendicularly to the vertebral column; cervical vertebrae with long spinous processes projecting perpendicularly to the vertebral body; reduced cervical and lumbar curvature; narrow, slightly arched sacrum set deeply between ilia; long and slender (but robust), considerably arched clavicles; scapulae with suleus ("Boule's fossa") on dorsal aspect of axillary border; robust, short humerus with massive head; pronounced curvature of the radius; marked development of olecranon process of ulna; pelvis with flattened ilia, great length relative to height; much bent femora with massive cylindrical shafts; strong, short tibiae with retroverted heads and supplementary malleolar facets; calcaneum with well-developed sustentaculum tali; forearm short in proportion to upper arm, and leg very short in relation to thigh.

The significance and origin of this interesting morphological pattern will be considered following a discussion of the climatic conditions in the "classic Neandertal" area and surrounding regions.

AN ISOLATING BARRIER: CLIMATE

Although the Fourth glacial age was apparently not as severe or as extensive as the previous glaciation, "in northern Europe, between latitudes 50 and 70, maritime air masses built up an ice-sheet that got its start in the Scandinavian mountains and gradually spread over an area of 1,650,000 square miles" (Flint 1947). The maximum extent southward of the first phase, represented in northern Europe by the Warthe drift (or the Brandenburg drift?) (Woldstedt 1942, 1950)[5], extends from the German North Sea coast towards the east through central Poland into western Russia. Although this was the ice-sheet margin, there was to the south, "a zone surrounding the ice-sheet, in which the cooling effect of the ice produced a frost climate" (Zeuner 1945) with severe *periglacial* conditions. This area, marked by dune building, loess deposition, mechanical weathering, ground-ice structures, solifluction, and stream terracing (Smith 1949), has received extensive study only during the last twenty-five years with the result that past climatic conditions are now fairly well understood.

Kessler pointed out some years ago that climate in the periglacial region was predominantly cold with northerly ice winds, considerable temperature fluctuation (but annual mean temperature not above -2°C) and with relatively low precipitation (Kessler 1926). He did not, however, attempt to delineate more completely climatic differences within the periglacial area. Zeuner delimited three main climatic zones: a northern tundra belt near the ice-sheet margin, a southern forest belt, and a central, broad loess-steppe between northern tundra and southern forest (Zeuner 1937). In the past few years, periglacial studies in Germany have made possible more detailed reconstructions of Pleistocene climatic zones during the Fourth glaciation (Poser 1947a,b; Büdel 1949).

For the reconstruction of climate at this time, it is important to recognize three main factors leading to the changes: depression of the snowline, lowering of temperature, and probably, increase of precipitation. Directions of prevailing winds would appear to have been the same as at present, although there was a major shift toward the equator of the zones as known today (Büdel 1949). Thus, the northern ice-sheet reached 55° N (present 77°), permafrost and tundra 45° N (present 69°), non-tropical forest 36° N (present 45°), Mediterranean vegetation 28° N (present 32°) (Büdel 1949). Compared to a postglacial vegetation map (Clark 1952), the differences are striking indeed.[6]

Through a study of periglacial features (ground ice wedges, block fields, and asymmetric valleys), Poser has reconstructed the permafrost boundary indicating the southern extent of perennially frozen soil (*tjaele*) (Poser 1947a, b). This line extended from Mount St. Michel eastward into the Seine-Marne area, curving southward to the western margin of the Alpine ice; east of the Alps, the boundary curved southward as far as the Serbian highlands and then continued eastward to the southern coast of the Black Sea. In western Europe, the polar forest boundary lay south of the permafrost line, extending eastward somewhat south of the Alps, then in the region of Agram turned northward through Moravia, the southern Carpathians, and north of the Black Sea. (Büdel extends this line much farther north in Russia along the eastern margin of the ice-sheet and coterminous with his 10.5° C July isotherm.) The crossing of permafrost boundary and polar forest boundary east of the Alps means an overlapping of forest growth on permanently frozen soil in eastern and southeastern Europe. (Poser points out that there are analogous conditions in Eurasia today.) With these boundaries demarcated, it is thus possible to work out climatic zones during the Last glaciation in Europe.

Poser distinguishes four major climatic zones (Fig. 1) (Poser 1948). Most extensive is a permafrost-tundra region extending in a broad band from the British Isles (linked to the continent at this time because of lowered sea-level) over central Europe into Russia. This can be further subdivided into three subzones: a western glacial-maritime, a central transitional glacial-maritime, and an eastern glacial continental. In this permafrost-tundra region, the July mean was below 10°C (about 3° to 6°) with a yearly mean below -2°C (permafrost climate ranging from -15° to -25°). Winters were cold and summers were cool, with maritime climate to the west and increasing continentality to the eastward. In central Europe, there was intense cold with heavy evaporation resulting in somewhat, but not extremely, dry climate. The central transitional zone had the most uncongenial climate, with heavy cloud formation in the brief summer months, high ground moisture, and snowfall; during the long winters, it was somewhat dry as a result of blowing and drifting snow over the light tundra vegetation. Poser regards loess deposition as taking place during the winter as a result of weathering and glaciofluval action at the margins and outwashed deposits of the ice-sheet. Klute points out, however, that this would occur primarily during the summer

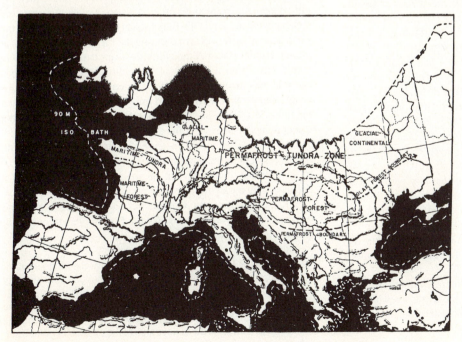

Figure 1. *Europe during the first advance of the Fourth glaciation. (Climatic zones after Poser 1947b; enlargement of continental land mass to 90 meter isobath after Klute 1951 and Pfannenstiel 1951; Scandinavian ice-sheet after Antevs 1929 and Woldstedt 1950; Alpine and Pyrenean mountain glaciation after Antevs 1929.)*

when the westerly winds would be able to pick up such weathered material (Klute 1949).

Both Penck and Zeuner, among others, regard loess deposition as taking place under somewhat arid or semi-arid conditions (Penck 1948; Zeuner 1945). However, as Flint points out, "it does not seem necessary to demand a semi-arid climate for the accumulation of the loess" since it does occur, though uncommonly, in fairly moist regions so long as there are abundant outwash sources from which the loess may be derived (Flint 1947). Thus, all that is required is that a region from which loess is picked up by winds "should have been largely free of vegetation instead of protected by it, as it is today" (Flint 1947). Such would have been true of the ice margins with their extensive outwash and drift deposits and supraglacial accumulations of debris. It should be noted, however, that the "rodent fauna of the European loess suggests both arctic tundra and steppe conditions" (Flint 1947; cf. Nehring 1890), so that the tundra climate may have been drier, but not necessarily so.

Zeuner has pointed out that in this subzone, "the middle European lowlands . . . were covered with a grass steppe with patches or stripes of woods in protected places along rivers and in the entries of the mountain valleys; (cf. Büdel 1949) . . . the German loess must have formed a biotope that offered fairly propitious conditions of life to a fauna of animals adapted to the cold of the winter," this being "confirmed by the numerous fossils found in the loess" (cf. Wernert 1928). Since the tundra regions were largely treeless with only shrub and ground vegetation, it would appear that an animal like the woolly mammoth and woolly rhino would adhere "to some region where he might obtain all the brush required, as he could on the extensive plains of both continents in summer, as well as among the small branchy trees at the edge of the forests in winter; the great length and complete curve of the tusks of these animals show that they were only fitted for traveling in such regions or in very open woods" (Bell 1898); such animals would thus have extreme difficulty in making their way through the more dense coniferous forests farther to the south. In light of the faunal contents at some of the sites in France, this is an important point.

The tundra zone nearest the northern ice-sheet was an area of dune sand, sandy loess, and outwash deposits, with vegetation restricted to patches and bolsters of ground foliage (Zeuner 1937). Except for the period of exposed vegetation during the brief summer, this area was probably to a large extent unoccupied by mammals during most of the year because of frozen surface snow forming a hard crust which made feeding extremely difficult. Farther southward, however, the loess-tundra zone was an area well-stocked periodically with Pleistocene mammals and offered rich hunting grounds for early man. In spring, with snow melting and additional solar heat, there was fairly heavy shrub and grass vegetation, although still cold. At this time, the area would have been a hunter's paradise with gathering of numbers of mammoth, rhino, reindeer, and horse. In autumn, however, with precipitation and falling temperature resulting in heavy snow cover, this area, too, would have become somewhat unfavorable and mammals would have moved into sheltered mountain valleys or farther south into the more heavily vegetated areas (cf. Soergel 1940).

In the more eastern area of the permafrost-tundra zone, the summers were warmer than central Europe with somewhat less cold winters. Büdel points out that in this eastern subzone (from the Dnieper to the Urals, and from the Caspian Sea far

northwards), there were trees of subarctic type (pine, birch, and willow) fairly widespread because of the milder summers but these were present as isolated clumps of trees rather than closed forests (Büdel 1949).

In southeastern Europe, with the overlapping of forest on permafrost soil, there was a continental permafrost-forest climate with larch, birch, and pine forests east of the Alps. Poser has calculated temperature ranges for this region and finds a winter mean of -12.7°C (January mean -14°) and summer mean of 8.7°C (July mean 10°) (Poser 1948).

In southwestern Europe there were two zones, the southernmost maritime forest climate (without permafrost) extending over the southern part of France, and north of this region a narrow zone of maritime-tundra climate (without permafrost) separating the maritime-forest zone of the southwest from the northern glacial-maritime province. The maritime-forest province had a yearly mean temperature between 5°C and 7°C (July mean 10° to 13°, January mean 0° to 3°). Closed forests were restricted apparently to the southern part of France (pine and birch), the more northern maritime-tundra zone having a light subarctic forest and shrub vegetation (Büdel 1949).

In the northern Mediterranean region, the present middle and north European subarctic vegetation prevailed, with pine, birch, larch, and willow, but lacking in warm plant species. South of the Pyrenees and Apennines, warm species of the present central European type were present (Büdel 1949). Büdel also notes that it must not have been very dry here during the summer—witness the perennial vegetation—and that this indicates rain-bearing westerlies during the summer months; differing, thus, from the present Mediterranean climate where the summer is almost rainless and most of the precipitation falls in the cooler seasons. There was apparently fairly heavy rainfall in the area along the Mediterranean coast including North Africa and the region of the Sahara, with the modern Mediterranean flora extending into Syria and Palestine (Picard 1937, 1938) and probably North Africa south of the Atlas mountains (Büdel 1949).

Although an understanding of the directions of prevailing winds and the areas of high and low pressure are extremely important in reconstructing past climatic conditions, there is rather meager evidence available. Büdel states that there was present the same general system of winds during the Pleistocene as there is at present (Büdel 1949). Although this was probably the case, there would have been a shifting of both climatic zones and winds towards the equator because of the extension of cold conditions away from the poles. This would bring "the 'polar front' between the polar east winds and the temperate west winds neared to the equator, and by increasing the temperature contrast between low and high latitudes would increase the storminess" and would further result in "a small but intense anti-cyclonic belt in about 20° to 25° latitude, a narrow belt of powerful trade winds, and a deepened equatorial trough of low pressure" (Brooks 1949).

Klute has recently worked out the pressure zones and directions of prevailing winds for the Fourth glacial maximum (Figs. 2 and 3) as follows:

In summer air currents seldom moved over the Mediterranean except for the current dVb. The low moved more strongly along dIV along the edge of the ice toward the northeast, bringing precipitation probably to the northern side of the ice-sheet. The winds were chiefly west winds, both on the front as well as on the reverse side of the cyclone or polar front.

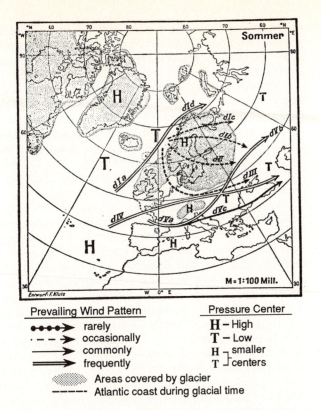

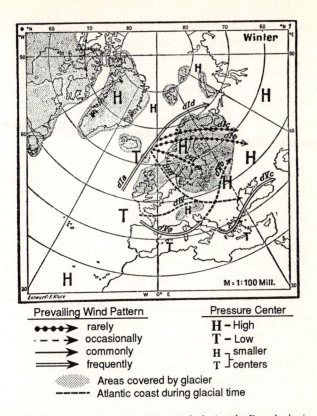

Figure 2. *Direction of prevailing winds during the Fourth glaciation—Summer (after Klute 1951).*

Figure 3. *Direction of prevailing winds during the Fourth glaciation—Winter (after Klute 1951).*

Since the pressure differences through the high pressure region on the Fennoscandian ice-sheet was greater than that of central Europe today, the winds were also stronger. The dry winds of the reverse portion of the front were likewise westerly winds, carrying loess and forming dunes. Currents dIa–d were also active during the summer.

In autumn, currents dIa–d were stronger and brought precipitation to the western portion of the ice-sheet. Current dId (as at present in winter) also passed northerly around the ice-sheet and invaded the continent, bringing precipitation to the northeast of the ice-sheet. The Mediterranean currents were active in autumn and influenced central Europe, from whence the westerly winds moved. Occasionally, however, the cyclone dIV moved into central Europe bringing snow. In winter, the cyclonic activity was reduced in central Europe, a high pressure area with still winds or with northwesterly to westerly winds prevailed, from the currents dVa–c. Also, at times, easterly winds came into the west from minima west of the British Isles. The ground was frozen deeply and covered with snow.

In spring, the high pressure descended over central Europe; current dIV gradually gaining ascendency, also dVa–c still active, plus dIa and now especially with its offshoots dIb–dId.

The pressure differences in terms of cyclonic activity was greater than at present and thus there were frequently stronger winds owing to the Fennoscandian and Alpine ice-sheets (Klute 1949, 1951) [7].

The prevailing climatic conditions in non-glacial areas most certainly had a marked effect on the distribution of the Neandertal food-gathers, and on the faunas and floras off which they lived. Severe weather conditions throughout most of the year in central Europe made this area uninviting and inhospitable for Neandertal man. Although there were undoubtedly movements of people from central and southern France

northward during the summer months in quest of game, these were probably only periodic and of limited duration. The maritime-forest climate of southwestern Europe obviously offered more suitable living conditions than that of the colder northern periglacial regions. Both the climatic factor and the presence of numerous caves and rock-shelters with streams nearby made southern France the place in which to live. The Italian and Iberian peninsulas likewise offered sheltered and genial surroundings for human habitation.

While it is most improbable that any movements of people were made through the central European corridor, there is a distinct possibility that such may have occurred north of the Adriatic Sea through northeast Italy to and from southeastern Europe. This is especially so since with sea-level lowering (probably about 90–100 meters), additional land would have become continental (cf. Blanc 1937; Pfannenstiel 1951). The subarctic forest present at the foot of the Alps, and extending eastward, probably sheltered a considerable fauna making for plentiful hunting, and thus have given cause for occupation and movement. The extent of such movement remains entirely unknown because of the postglacial marine transgression.

CULTURAL EVIDENCE FOR HUMAN DISTRIBUTION IN EUROPE IN THE FIRST STADIAL, FOURTH GLACIATION

It is necessary to examine the available archaeological evidence for further information of hominid distribution in central Europe during the first advance of the Fourth glaciation. In every instance in western Europe, the "classic Neandertals" have been found associated with so-called "Mousterian" flake implements. Yet there are a number of complications with regard to the concept of "Mousterian" as a distinct industry and there are major difficulties in terminology.

In France, there is one classification into "Mousterian" I, II, III, IV, beginning towards the end of Riss-Würm interglacial and persisting after the first advance of the Fourth glacial. There is also classification into lower, middle, and upper "Mousterian" rather like the foregoing. But to greatly complicate the picture, a number of other terms have been introduced to describe various assemblages of "Mousterian-like" artifacts. Some of these are: "Mousterian of Acheulean tradition," "Acheuleo-Mousterian," "Levalloiso-Mousterian," "Mikromousterian," "petit Mousterien," "Moustero-Tayacian," "typical Mousterian," "proto-Mousterian," and so on. Bordes has recently attempted to clarify this problem by analyzing statistically unselected tool assemblages in terms of the technological methods used in the production of flakes, and quantifying proportions of various flake and bifacial implements within a homogenous assemblage (Bordes 1950; Bordes and Bourgon 1951).

The "Mousterian" has been divided by Bordes into two main groups: "Mousterian" with bifaces and "Mousterian" with few, or without any, bifacial implements. Each group is further subdivided into "Levalloisian" or non-"Levalloisian" (prepared or unprepared striking platform) techniques, and additional categories are present in each subgroup. The characteristics of each group, subgroup and category can be expressed statistically in terms of the technology employed in manufacturing the implements, and the relative proportions present in the assemblage. This work has greatly clarified the "Mousterian" problem in terms of more exact delineation of assemblage content. It will be interesting to see the method applied to other assemblages from sites outside of France.

The problem of the "Micoquian" still remains and it should be noted that McBurney points out "that the whole conception of a Micoque stage as such rests on a distinctly flimsy and uncertain basis" (McBurney 1950). Here again a re-analysis of the older material is essential for a clarification of the relationships between unifacial and bifacial implements with emphasis on unselected assemblage content and geographical and chronological range.

McBurney (1950) has recently pointed out distinctions between the "Mousterian" of western Europe and that of the eastern and central portions of the continent. He finds a localized occurrence of the "cordiform hand-axe" between the Loire River and the Pyrenees, and in Brittany and Belgium (also possible in the west German plain). In central and eastern Europe, on the other hand, the "Mousterian" artifacts "virtually all show signs to a greater or less degree of that characteristic Middle Pleistocene device, faceted-platform flaking from miniature disc-shaped cores" with an absence of cordiform hand-axes. The geographical approach employed by McBurney, coupled with a careful analysis of assemblage content based on the technique developed by Bordes, promises to provide significant results on cultural distribution and human activities during this phase of the Pleistocene.

There was, of course, widespread occupation of maritime western Europe at this time, and the "Mousterian" is well-known in Italy, Spain, southwestern and central France, Belgium, and in parts of southern England. This more than covers the area from which "classic Neandertal" remains are known

although it should be noted that a large region extending to the south and east of the British Isles linked the latter with continental Europe and made available land which is today under water due to marine transgression following glacial retreat.

The archaeological situation in Germany is still considerably complicated (Zeuner 1950) [8]. Andree summarized the German evidence some years ago but was very uncritical, and many of the sites which he attributed to the first stadial of the Fourth glaciation are inadequately dated or dated not at all, either faunally or stratigraphically (Andree 1939). The only well-dated German sites from this time (Fig. 4) (cf. Zotz 1951) are summarized in the eleven points below:

In the northern Eifel mountains, just northeast of Luxembourg, "Micoquian" and "Mousterian" implements are known from the cave of Kartstein (1), dated as early Fourth glacial from a careful analysis of fauna, flora, and stratigraphy. To the south, in Würtemburg, two sites are known from the Lonetal in the Schwäbian Alps: both Vogelherd and Bocksteinschmiede (2) are well-stratified caves with early Fourth glacial "Micoquian" and "Mousterian" (the latter slightly later in both caves) in strata containing limestone fragments. In the northwest Swiss Juras near Neuenberg, the cave of Cotencher (3) contains a "Mousterian of Acheulean tradition" superimposed on a Third interglacial yellow clay layer, the former being then of pre-maximum Würm I. These sites are all within the western maritime zone and constitute the most eastward expansion of the early Fourth glacial inhabitants of western Europe. Both Sirgenstein and Schulerloch, caves in the Altmühltal, Fränkischen Juras, considerably to the east, containing a "Kleinmousterian" and a "Mousterian of Acheulean tradition" respectively, are post-maximum of the first Würm advance or are already interstadial.

Benet-Tygel notes in eastern Europe, "a distinct eastern area consisting of Poland, Russia, and the Ukraine, rather than an extension of the western province (Benet-Tygel 1944). Koslowski discusses a number of caves (4) in southern Poland, in the vicinity of Krakow, which are suggested as of early Fourth glacial date (Koslowski 1924). Both Mammuthöhle and Galoska contain a form of "Mousterian," whereas Okiennik and Ciemna contain "Micoquian" bifaces (althouth McBurney notes that if the implements from the former were found in Bavaria, they would be classed as "Mousterian"). As Zotz points out, both Galoska and Ciemna are poorly dated and may well be later than the first advance of Würm (Zotz 1951). Further north, Poland suffered extensive glaciation, and no human occupation is apparent. These sites are within the permafrost-tundra zone and one can rightfully suspect human occupation so far north during a glacial. None are well stratified nor were they properly excavated, so that there is still a question as to their correct chronological position.

Babor fails to mention "Mousterian" from Czechoslovakia at this time although Breuil claimed "Mousterian" implements associated with cold fauna from the Moravian sites of Sipka and Certovadirá (5).(Babor 1927; Breuil 1925). At one time Zotz listed these sites as "Uraurignacian" (as well as the two sites, Bachofenhöhle and Byciskala) (Zotz 1941). The latter two are poorly dated (cf. Zotz 1951) and their position remains uncertain although the industry is probably a form of "Mousterian." Although Sipka and Certovadirá may be early Fourth glacial, only the fauna offers evidence to suggest that this is the case. It is interesting to note that if so, the Sipka mandible fragment is more like that of anatomically modern man than it is "Neander-

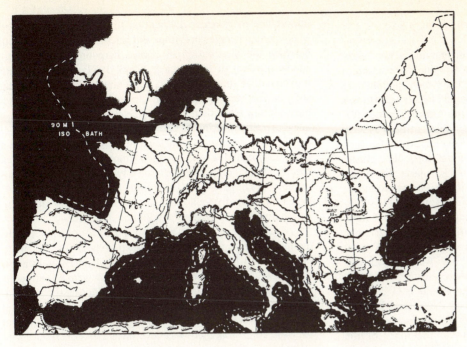

Figure 4. *Human occupation in the early Fourth Glacial of Europe. ("Classic Neandertal" skeletal remains: N—Neandertal, S—Spy, E—Engis, Q—La Quina, M—Le Moustier, F—La Ferrassie, C—La Chapelle, G—Gibraltar, MC—Monte Circeo. Numbers indicate archaeological evidence on human distribution; for key see discussion in the text.)*

taloid" (the same may be said of the Ochos mandible from Schwedentisch grotto). A number of "Mousterian" implements are reported from Predmost but the dating is uncertain (perhaps late Third interglacial) (Zotz and Freund 1951).

Although "Mousterian" cleavers have been reported associated with a cold Fourth glacial fauna from Gudenus cave near Krems (on the Danube), lower Austria, there is no certainty as to the dating. Zotz notes this as a "Micoquian" industry but points out lack of any evidence for dating the material since the fauna is mixed and stratigraphy lacking (Zotz 1951). No "Mousterian" or "Micoquian" implements are known from Switzerland at this time, since the area was heavily glaciated (Tschumi 1949).

To the southeast in Bulgaria, on the northern flank of the Balkan mountains, "Mousterian" flake implements are known from Bacho Kiro (6) and perhaps from Mirizlivka (7), near the Yugoslavian border (Garrod 1939). In Hungary, at Tata (near Budapest, right bank of the Danube), Breuil noted "upper Mousterian" artifacts in a loess layer with woolly mammoth and woolly rhino fauna (Breuil 1923); the lowest level of the Kiskevely cave contains similar implements which are perhaps contemporary (8). Brodar records no "Mousterian" artifacts from this time in Yugoslavia although the lack may be merely the result of the few caves excavated (Brodar 1938). Nicolaèscu-Plopsor, in his survey of the Roumanian Paleolithic, notes implements of a "Mousterian facies" with cold fauna at the site of Ripiceni (9), Moldavia and an "evolved Mousterian" in a cave at Baia-de-Fier in Oltenia (10) (Nicolaèscu-Plopsor 1935-36). The two caves of Fedri and Ohaba-Ponor in Transylvania (11) provide good faunal and stratigraphic evidence for dating the "Mousterian" implements found there.

There is far better representation of the earlier "warm Mousterian" through the central European region, as well as accurately dated remains of an "early Neandertal" type. Human remains of this type are known from Ehringsdorf, Thuringia, from Krapina, Croatia, probably from the Mussolini cave at Subalyuk, Hungary, and from Saccopastore, central Italy (Weidenreich 1928; Kramberger 1906; Mottl 1938; Blanc 1948). "Mousterian" artifacts are known from these sites as well as others in Switzerland (Drachenloch, Wildkirchli, Wildenmannisloch), and from a number of sites in western, central, and southern Germany (cf. Andree 1939; Zotz 1951).

It is necessary to note "the contrast between the maritime plain of western Europe and the much more broken topography forming the habitat of the suggested eastern variant of the Mousterian," with "discontinuous areas of plain separated by considerable mountain chains" (McBurney 1950). During a glaciation, the central European area of Germany would have been uncongenial and inhospitable; in the south, however, in valleys away from the Alpine ice, there would have been light forest cover to support a flora and fauna off which Neandertal man might have lived. The archaeological evidence indicates that there was human occupation in southwestern Germany, probably an extension of the western maritime zone. There is doubtful occupation in the southeastern region including lower Austria and probably Silesia. The central German area was unoccupied, from present evidence. The main eastern zone of occupation was undoubtedly the broad area south of the Carpathians and the eastern Alps, in the Danubian plain above the Balkans. Here under a permafrost climate supporting subarctic vegetation, there was an abundant fauna (and herbaceous flora) off which food gatherers might live, at times moving farther northward along river courses between the western Carpathians and the Austrian Alps. The physical remains of such people living here during the first stadial of the Fourth glaciation are thus far unknown (the Sipka mandibular fragment from Movavia may be from such a group) although it can be presumed that they more closely resembled the early Neandertals, and anatomically modern man, than they did the "classic Neandertals" of the western European maritime zone who were restricted to that westerly part of the continent and did not extend into central Germany or the more easterly regions.

CONCLUSIONS

The available human fossil material indicates that certain "early Neandertals" of Europe (Ehringsdorf, Krapina, Saccopastore) were most probably ancestral to the later, more peripherally western and southern "classic Neandertal" fossils (cf. Howell 1951). The restricted distribution of the "classic Neandertal" fossils and the discontinuity of archaeological artifacts as well, suggests that a considerable degree of isolation existed between human biotopes in western and eastern Europe. In a glacial period, the climatic severity of the central European area during much of the year would serve as an effective barrier to movements between the more western maritime zone and the southwestern subarctic forest zone. Although extensions of these areas into the wooded regions just north of the Alpine ice may very well have occurred, the frequency of contact between eastern gatherers moving westward, and western gatherers moving eastward, was undoubtedly low.

The extent of isolation for human groups is of course a cultural factor, and in attempting to weigh the cultural development of the prehistoric "classic Neandertals" one is on extremely shaky ground because of the incompleteness of the archaeological record. It is, however, probably safe to regard this group as primarily food-gatherers with limited emphasis on hunting, especially of the larger herbivores; the level of subsistence being not too different then from that of certain native North American groups in the northern Intermontane area between the Cascades and the Rocky Mountains. Steward (1938) has clearly shown the degree of adaptation of such groups as the Shoshoni to the rigorous intermontane environment and his general conclusions are probably applicable to the "classic Neandertals" as well, especially since the latter were considerably more culturally destitute, from all available evidence.

Specialized devices for hunting (like the atlatl or the bow and arrow) and clothing (other than simple robes of small mammal skins, perhaps) were most probably absent. Such groups were thus restricted to more genial climatic area where there were more abundant plants, berries, nuts, and small forest animals (with deer and occasional larger herbivorous forms) off which they might live, and in a habitat which offered protection from the weather. In fact, the evidence now at hand would probably tend to support the suggestion that man was for a long period a tropical or sub-tropical animal (cf. Bates 1952). Further, that prior to the advent of anatomically modern man and the rather elaborate cultural complexes which the artifactual record suggests for the Upper Paleolithic, he was most likely poorly prepared to cope with extreme climatic conditions such as occurred cyclically in the Eurasiatic continent during the Pleistocene.

It is necessary to emphasize the extreme difficulty of living in heavily snowed-in tundra areas without proper clothing and equipment. During the long winter months there is lack of game and vegetation in such an area. With the spring thaw, rivers become blocked with ice and the region becomes a true morass with streams overflowing their banks onto low areas. Travel is at such times nearly impossible. On the other hand, the periodic shifting of such animals as reindeer northward into barren-ground areas during summer is an important factor in the life of hunting peoples [9]. During the height of the summer, however, flies and other insects make such areas difficult to occupy even for animals like the caribou. Clark has recently brought out the importance of reindeer distribution to the area occupied by Magdalenian peoples in Europe and has shown the relationship between the distribution of barbed harpoon heads and the southern extent of the reindeer (Clark 1952). The northward movement of such animals in large numbers in early spring suggests that such people as the "classic Neandertals" may well have shifted from their own southerly wintering grounds in quest of game. The innate curiosity of the animals and the fact that females are heavy with fawn make killing at this time a fairly easy matter, even with such simple weapons as wooden spears. Other arctic animals probably also moved north for summer grazing, so that brief shifts in "classic Neandertal" bands undoubtedly took place as they did with the later reindeer-hunters of the Upper Paleolithic.

Broad areas of Europe and Asia during the glacial periods, though tolerable for specially adapted arctic birds and mammals, were ill-fitted for permanent human habitation. Regions such as western and southern Europe, which were a continuous part of the temperate-subtropical continent during the interglacial periods, became, during the glacial advances, peripheral refuge areas where, though climatic conditions may have not been too congenial, there was nevertheless loss of contact with other human groups because of the surrounding climatic barriers.

The effects of such a period of prolonged isolation (at least some *thousands* of years), because of the severe climatic barriers to continuous distribution and migratory movement, will be peculiar evolutionary developments as indicated by abundant neozoölogical evidence. Gene flow is restricted to interchange between the interbreeding groups within the limited habitat and no transference of genes (or relative none, which is the same thing) outside the biotope. Even within the habitat, gene interchange is limited to those groups contiguous with one another since most primitive food-gathering bands appear to have clearly defined occupation areas and only periodically join for purposes of communally gathering certain types of food or for carrying out religious or social activities (cf. Steward 1938). Even within the western and southern areas of "classic Neandertal" occupation, there were undoubtedly regional distinctions as a result of various physiographic factors, although it is impossible to recognize such and they must be inferred from ethnographic data from other food-gathering populations. Because of the intergroup relations, however, genes are transferred throughout the population of the biotope for the most part, so that the concept of "classic Neandertal" for the area is a valid one. Through the even distribution of the genes, all members of the isolate share common genes and gene complexes; there is thus a degree of homogeneity obtained, like that of inbreeding, which would be otherwise impossible it there were widespread transference over large areas between migratory groups.

In small populations, such as those found among living food-gatherers, it is possible for certain mutant genes, or combinations of genes, to survive and be maintained. In fact, "the smaller the effective population size, the greater are random variations in gene frequencies, and the less effective become weak selection pressures. In small populations, alleles favored by selection may be lost and the less favored ones may reach fixation" (Dobzhansky 1951). This phenomenon of genetic drift (Sewall Wright effect) may produce divergence which is non-adaptive (because of neutral genes); on the other hand, however, "although spread by drift and not by selection, [a mutant] may chance to improve the genotype and in fact be adaptive" (Carter 1951). Differentiation will also take place through recombination, or the rearrangement of genes present beforehand in the genotypes.

Actually so little is known of the significance of "racial" characteristics in living populations that any suggestions as to the adaptive or non-adaptive nature of "classic Neandertal" morphology can only be of uncertain validity at the present time. The morphology of this group is, to be sure, a distinctive and peculiar one, so that it is possible to recognize the group as a geographically localized racial entity, the result of prolonged isolation during the first stadial of the Fourth glaciation. The actual mechanism of this differentiation may have been drift. On the other hand, selection is likely to have played a part, perhaps a major one, since the environment was fairly demanding of groups at a low cultural level and the difficulties encountered in the food quest undoubtedly not only restricted population size but served effectively to allow only those individuals best suited and adapted to such a habitat to survive and procreate.

Birdsell has recently discussed what he regards as drift phenomena in certain aboriginal Australian tribes, especially with regard to blood groups (Birdsell 1950). Although drift has undoubtedly played an important role at times in the evolutionary history of man, at the food-gathering level selection is undoubtedly very important. Since, however, practically nothing is known of the adaptive nature of morphological traits in man, one is too easily led to the conclusion that certain phenomena may be the result of drift and such an explanation allowed to suffice. The writer is convinced that, at least in the structure of the "classic Neandertal" facial skeleton and cranial base, selective forces have been the major contributing evolutionary factor at work, genetic drift having been of minor or negligible import. Research now being carried on by N. C. Tappen on the structure of the face, and by the writer on the cranial base, promises to provide clarification of this important point.

The disappearance of "classic Neandertal" remains from the fossil record following the recession of the first phase of the Last glaciation remains a problem. It has been suggested that with glacial retreat, western Europe was occupied for the first time by blade-using, anatomically modern man, "classic Neandertal" forms having either previously become extinct or being extinguished by the newcomers. There is little evidence,

one way or the other, to settle the question at present. The archaeological record indicates, however, that the first western European blade-tool industry occurs during the first interstadial of the Fourth glacial and subsequent to this, abundant remains of anatomically modern type (including Combe Capelle, the Grimaldi "negroids," and many specimens of so-called Cromagnon man).

If one assumes, however, that in western Europe the "Mousterian" industry was a product of these "classic Neandertals" (and earlier Neandertaloid forms), then one is almost forced to the conclusion that in places, at least, Neandertals may well have persisted after the retreat of the first phase of the last glaciation. Zeuner notes the persisted of the "Mousterian" industry into the first interstadial of the Fourth glacial in parts of France, East Anglia, the Italo-French Riviera, and possibly the Pontine Marsh area of central Italy (western coast, south of Rome) (Zeuner 1950). Considerably more archaeological, as well as paleontological, evidence is needed before the reason for the disappearance can certainly be settled.

The evidence available at present indicates that the "classic Neandertals" were isolated survivors of a formerly widespread "Neandertaloid" group of people. Occurring widely over portions of southern Europe (Saccopastore), central Europe (Ehringsdorf) and southeastern Europe (Krapina) as well as in the Middle East (Tabun, Galilee, Skhul?, and Kafzeh) [10] during late Third interglacial time, those in the western periphery of Europe became progressively isolated with the onset of arctic conditions heralding the first advance of the Fourth glaciation. Through the action of selection, these forms became adapted to the periglacial biotope of western Europe. With the retreat of the first phase of this glacial, more genial climatic conditions were established in Europe and the western areas were open for occupation by anatomically modern man. Whether the "classic Neandertals" were already extinct at the time of this new peopling, or whether they were extinguished by, or hybridized with these invaders, remains a moot point at present.

The lack of "classic Neandertal" characters in these Upper Paleolithic invaders make hybridization doubtful, as does the fact that remains of the two peoples living together have never been found. On the other hand, "Mousterian" artifacts still occur in some places during early blade-tool times, and thus, "classic Neandertal" persistence in certain isolated refuge areas remains a distinct possibility.

NOTES

[1] Vallois (1952) has recently raised the problem of orthography with reference to the term "Neanderthal." The name was originally applied to the human remains found by Fuhlrott in 1856 in the valley of the Dussel, a tributary of the Rhine. This valley was linked with the poet Neander and thus the term "Neanderthal" (valley of Neander). Orthographic changes in German early in this century omitted the letter "h" following "t" in a number of words (thus, "th" changed to "t"; "Thal" to "Tal"). Writers in English and French have persisted in using the older orthography, but as Vallois notes, a standard usage should be adopted. Henceforth the term "Neandertal" will be used by the author.

[2] This work has been assisted by a grant from the Wenner-Gren Foundation for Anthropological Research.

[3] The fossils considered here include only those cases for which skulls and mandibles (and postcranial remains in some instances) are available. The La Naulette (Belgium) mandible and perhaps the child's

skull from Pech de l'Aze (Dordogne) are also of similar age. Many other specimens of a fragmentary nature cannot be adequately dated, i.e., Arcy-cur-Cure (Yonne), Gourdan (Haute-Garonne), Isturitz (Basses-Pyrenees), Malarnaud (Ariege), Montmaurin (Haute-Garonne), Banolas (Spain).

[4] I have been unable to find any data on the relative abundance of each species at Engis (Fraipont 1936).

[5] There is still disagreement as to the position of the Warthe drift, Woldstedt (cf. also Gams 1938) assigning it to the late Saale (Third) glacial, other workers (like Zeuner 1945) to the Last glaciation (cf. Flint 1947).

[6] Such as that found in Clark (1952).

[7] Translated from the German of Klute (1949); see also Klute (1951).

[8] Zeuner (1950) notes the lack of good evidence "in the formerly glaciated area of central Europe" where "the interval between Saale

(Third glacial) and Weichsel (Fourth glacial-second stadial) is still to be regarded as a chronological gap from the archaeological point of view." The recent summary by Zotz (1951) provides for the first time an excellent critical appraisal of the central European evidence.

[9]   Cf. Mowat's (1952) excellent treatment of the subject among the Inland Eskimo.

[10]   Data from such Near Eastern sites as 'Ksar Akil, Labanon (Ewing 1947; Wright 1951), Yabrud, Syria (Rust 1950), and Djebel Qafzeh

and Oumm Qatafa, Palestine (Neuville *et at.* 1951) suggests that revision of chronology is necessary with respect to the Mt. Carmel population (Garrod and Bate 1937). The writer regards the Tabun human remains as most probably early Würm, and those from Skhul as slightly later. This differs from my earlier statement (Howell 1951) but still does not affect the argument presented at that time on the phylogenetic position of those hominids.

REFERENCES

Andree, J. 1939. Die eiszeitliche Mensch in Deutschland und seine Kulturen, F. Enke, Stuttgart.

Antevs, E. 1929. Maps of the Pleistocene glaciations. *Bulletin, Geological Society of America* 40:631–720.

Babor, J. F. 1927. Das Palaolithikum in der Tchechoslowakei. *Die Eisheit* 4:79–80.

Bate, D. M. A. 1928. Excavation of a Mousterian rock-shelter at Devil's Tower, Gibraltar. The Animal remains. *Journal, Royal Anthropological Institute* 58:92–113.

Bates, M. 1952. *Where Winter Never Comes: A Study of Man and Nature in the Tropics*, Chas. Scribner's Sons, New York.

Bell, R. 1898. On the occurence of mammoth and mastodon remains around Hudson Bay. *Bulletin, Geological Society of America* 9:369–390.

Benet-Tygel, S. 1944. The Paleolithic period in Poland. *American Anthropologist* 46:292–316.

Birdsell, J. B. 1950. Some implications of the genetical concept of race in terms of spacial analysis. *Cold Spring Harbor Symposium on Quantitative Biology* 15:251–306, Cold Spring Harbor, New York.

Blanc, A. C. 1937. Low levels of the Mediterranean Sea during the Pleistocene glaciation. *Quarterly Journal, Geological Society of London* 93:621–651.

Blanc, A. C. 1940. Les grottes Paleolithiques et l'homme fossile du Mont Circe. *Revue Scientifique* 78:21–28.

Blanc, A. C. 1942. 1 Paleantropi di Saccopastore edel Circeo. *Quartär* 4:1–37.

Blanc, A. C. 1948. Notizie sui trovamenti e sul giacimento de Saccopastore e sulla posizione nel pleistocene laziale, in: *L'Uomo di Saccopastore, Paleontographica Italica* 42:3–23.

Bordes, F. 1950. L'evolution buissonnante des industries en Europe occidentale. Considérations théoriques sur le Paléolithique ancien et moyen. *L'Anthropologie*, series 4:393–420.

Bordes, F., and Bourgon 1951. Le complexe Moustérien: Mousterien, Levalloisien et Tayacien. *L'Anthropologie* 55:1–23.

Boule, M. 1911–13. L'homme fossile de la Chapelle-aux-Saints. *Annales de Paléontologie* 6:106–172, 7:21–192, 8:1–70.

Bouyssonie, A., Bouyssonie, J., and Bardon, L. 1908. Decouverte d'un squelette humain moustérien a la bouffia de la Chappelle-aux-Saints (Corrèze). *L'Anthropologie* 19:513–518.

Breuil, H. 1923. Notes de voyage paléolithique en central Europe. I. Les industries paleolithiques en Hongrie. *L'Anthropologie* 33:323–346.

Breuil, H. 1925. Notes de voyage paléolithique en central Europe. III. Les Cavernes de Moravie. *L'Anthropologie* 35:271–291.

Brodar, S. 1938. Das Paleolithikum in Jugoslavien. *Quartär*, 1:140–172.

Brooks, C. E. P. 1949. Climate Through the Ages. Review ed., McGraw Hill, New York.

Büdel, J. 1949. Die raumliche und zeitliche Gliederung des Eiszeitklimas. *Die Naturwissenschaften* 36:105–112, 133–139.

Capitan, L., and Peyrony, D. 1912. Station prehistorique de la Ferrassie. *Revue Anthropologie* 22:29–50, 76–99.

Carter, G. S. 1951. *Animal Evolution: A Study of Recent Views of its Causes*. Sidgwick and Jackson, Ltd., London.

Clark, J. G. D. 1952. *Prehistoric Europe, the Economic Basis*. Methuen, London.

Deevey, E. S. 1949. Biogeography of the Pleistocene. Part I: Europe and America. *Bulletin, Geological Society of America* 60:1315–1416.

Dobzhansky, T. 1941. *Genetics and the Origin of the Species*, 2nd ed., revised, Columbia University Press, New York.

Dobzhansky, T. 1951. *Genetics and the Origin of the Species*, 3rd ed., revised. Columbia University Press, New York.

Ewing, F. J. 1947. Preliminary note on the excavations at the Palaeolithic site of Ksar-Akil, Republic of Lebanon. *Antiquity* 21:186–196.

Flint, R. F. 1947. *Glacial Geology and the Pleistocene Epoch*. John Wiley and Sons, New York.

Fraipont, C. 1936. Les hommes fossiles d'Engis. *Memoirs, Archives de l'Institut de Paleontogoie Humaine* 16:1–52.

Fraipont, J., and Lohest, M. 1887. La race humaine de Neanderthal ou de Cannstadt en Belgique. *Archives de Biologie* 7:587-757.

Gams, H. 1938. Die bisherigen Ergebnisse der Mikrostatigraphie fur die Gliederung der letzten Eiszeit und de Jungpapaolithikums in Mittel- und Nordeuropa. *Quartär* 1:75–96.

Garrod, D. A. E. 1939. Excavations in the cave of Bacho Kiro, northeast Bulgaria [with sections of B. Howe and J. Gaul, fauna by R. Popov]. *Bulletin, American School of Prehistoric Research* 15:46–126.

Garrod, D. A. E., and Bate, D. M. 1937. *The Stone Age of Mt. Carmel. I: Excavations in the Wady el-Mughara*, Clarendon Press, Oxford.

Grahmann, R. 1932. Die Losz in Europa. *Mitteilungen der Gesellschaft fur Erdkunde zu Leipzig* 51:5–24.

Hooton, E. A. 1946. *Up from the Ape*. Rev. ed., Macmillan Co., New York.

Hopwood, A. T. 1935. Fossil elephants and man. *Proceedings, Geological Association*, London 46:46–60.

Howell, F. C. 1951. The place of Neanderthal Man in human evolution. *American Journal of Physical Anthropology*, n.s., 9:379–416.

Kessler, P. 1926. *Das eiszeitliche Klima und seine geologischen Wirkungen im nichtvereisten Gebiet*, Stuttgart.

Klaatsch, H. 1901. Das Gliedmassenskelett des Neanderthalmenschen. *Verhandlungen der Anatomischen Gesellschaft Kongress (Bonn), Erganzungsheft zum Anatomischen Anzeiger* 19:121–154.

Klute, F. 1949. Rekonstruction des Klimas letzten Eiszeit in Mitteleuropa aus Grund morphologischer und pflanzengeographischer Tatsache. *Geographische Rundschau* 1:81–89, 121–126.

Klute, F. 1951. Das klima Europas wahrend des maximums der Weichsel-Würm eiszeit und die Anderungen bis zur Jetztzeit. *Erdkunde* 5:273–283.

Koslowski, L. 1924. Die altere Steinzeit in Polen. *Die Eiszeit* 1:112–163.

Kramberger, J. G. 1906. *Der diluviale Mensch von Krapina in Kroatien*. Wiesbaden.

Mayr, E. 1942. *Systematics and the Origin of Species, from the Viewpoint of a Zoologist*, Columbia University Press, New York.

Martin, H. 1923. L'homme fossile de la Quina. *Archives de Morphologie Generale et Experimentale* 15:1–260. Librairie Octave Doin, Paris.

McBurney, C. M. B. 1950. The geographical study of the older Palaeolithic stages in Europe. *Proceedings, Prehistoric Society*, n.s., 16:163–183.

Morant, G. M. 1927. Studies of Paleolithic man. II: A biometric study of Neanderthaloid skulls and their relationships to modern racial types. *Annals of Eugenics* 2:318–381.

Mottl, M. 1938. Faunen und klima des Ungarischen Mousterien. *Verhandlungen der III Internationale Quartär-Konferenz, Vienna*, 1936, pp. 248–261.

Mowat, F. 1952. *People of the Deer*, Atlantic, Little Brown and Co., New York.

Nehring, A. 1890. *Uber Tundren und Steppen der Jetzt- und Vorzeit, mit besonderer Berucksichtigung ihrer Fauna*, F. Dummlers Verlag, Berlin.

Neuville, R. et al. 1951. Le Paleolithique et le Mesolithique du desert de Judee. *Archives de l'Institut de Paleontologie Humaine* 24:1–270, Paris.

Nicolaescu-Plopsor, C. S. 1935–36. Le Paleolithique en Roumanie. *Dacia: Recherches et decouvertes Archeologiques en Roumanie* 5–6:41–107, Bucharest.

Osborn, H. F. 1910. *The Age of Mammals in Europe, Asia, and North America*, Macmillan and Co., New York.

Penck, A. 1938. Die klima der Eiszeit. *Verhandlungen der III Internationale Quartar-Konferenz, Vienna*, 1936, pp. 83–96.

Peyrony, D. 1934. La Ferrassie. *Prehistoire* 3:1–92.

Pfannenstiel, M. 1951. Quartare Spiegelschwankungen des Mittelmeeres und der Schwarzen Meeres. *Vierteljahrsschrift der Natuforschenden Gesellschaft in Zurich*, 96(2):81–102.

Picard, L. 1937. Inferences on the problem of the Pleistocene climate of Palestine and Syria drawn from the flora, fauna and stratigraphy. *Proceedings, Prehistoric Society*, n.s., 3:58–70.

Picard, L. 1938. Uber fauna, flora und klima des Pleistozans Palastine-Syriens. *Verhandlungen der III Internationale Quartar-Konferenz, Vienna*, 1936, pp. 281–290.

Poser, H. 1947a. Dauerfrostboden und temperaturverhaltnisse wahrend der Würmeiszeit in nicht vereisten Mittel- und Weseuropa. *Die Naturwissenschaften* 34:10–18.

Poser, H. 1947b. Auftautiefe und frostzerrung im Bodens Mitteleuropa wahrend der Würmeiszeit. *Die Naturwissenschaften* 34:232–238, 262–267.

Poser, H. 1948. Boden- und Klimaverhaltnisse in Mitteleuropa wahrend der Würmeiszeit, *Erdkunde* 2:53–68.

Rand, A. L. 1947. Glaciation, an isolating factor in speciation. *Evolution* 2:314–321.

Rust, A. 1950. *Die Hohlenfunde von Jabrud*, Syrien, Neumunster.

Schwalbe, G. 1901. Der Neandertalschadel, *Bonner Jahrbucher* 106:1–72.

Simpson, G. G. 1947. Holarctic mammalian faunas and continental relationships during the Cenozoic. *Bulletin, Geological Society of America* 58:613–687.

Smith, H. T. U. 1949. Physical effects of Pleistocene climatic changes in non-glaciated Area: Eolian phenomena, frost action and stream terracing. *Bulletin, Geological Society of America* 60:1485–1516.

Soergel, W. 1912. *Elephas trogontherii* Pohl. und *Elephas antiquus* Falc., ihre Stammesgeschichte und ihre Bedeutung fur die Gliederung des Deutschen diluviums. *Palaeontographia* 60:1–114.

Soergel, W. 1919. Losse, *Eiszeiten und Palaothische kulturen; eine gliederung und altersbestimmung der Losse*, Gustav Fischer Verlag, Jena.

Soergel, W. 1940. Der klimacharakter des Mammuts. *Palaeontologische Zeitschrift* 22:29–55.

Steward, J. H. 1938. Basin-plateau aboriginal social-political groups. *Bulletin, Bureau of American Anthropology*, no. 120, pp. 1–346.

Tschumi, O. 1949. "Die steinzeitlichen Epochen," in *Urgeschichte der Schweiz*, 1:407–727, Verlag Huber und Co., Frauenfeld.

Vallois, H. 1952. Neanderthal-Neandertal? *L'Anthropologie* 55:557–558.

Weidenreich, F., ed. 1928. *Der Schadelfund von Weimer-Ehringsdorf: die Geologie der Dalktuffe von Weimer, die Morphologie des Schadels, die altsteinzeitliche Kultur des Ehringsdorfer Menschen*, Gustav Fischer Verlag, Jena. [Sections by F. Weidenreich, F. Wiegers, E. Schuster.]

Weidenreich, F., ed. 1940. Some problems dealing with ancient man. *American Anthropologist*, 42:375–383.

Weidenreich, F. ed. 1943. The "Neanderthal Man" and the ancestors of "*Homo sapiens.*" *American Anthropologist*, 45:39–48.

Wernert, P. 1928. La characterisation faunistique de loess ancien. *Comptes Rendue XIV Session, 1920 de Congres Geologique International*, Madrid, 1928, 4:1975–1987.

Woldstedt, P. 1942. Uber die Ausdehung der letzten Vereisung in Norddeutschland. *Berichte Reichsamtes fur Bodenforschugen*, Vienna, 1942; pp. 131–139.

Woldsted, p. 1950. *Norddeutschland und angrenzende Gebiete im Eiszeitalter*, K. F. Koehler Verlag, Stuttgard.

Wright, H. E., Jr. 1951. Geologic setting of Ksar-Akil, a Paleolithic site in Lebanon–Preliminary Report. *Journal of Near Eastern Studies* 10:115–119.

Zeuner, F. E. 1937. The climate of the countries adjoining the ice-sheet of the Pleistocene. *Proceedings, Geological Association, London* 48:379–395.

Zeuner, F. E. 1940. The age of Neanderthal Man, with notes on the Cotte de St. Brelade, Jersey, C. I. *Occasional Papers, No. 3, Institute of Archaeology, University of London*, pp. 1–20.

Zeuner, F. E. 1945. The Pleistocene period: Its climate, chronology and faunal successions, *The Ray Society*, vol. 130, London.

Zeuner, F. E. 1950. *Dating the Past: An Introduction to Geochronology*, 2nd ed., rev. and enlarged, Methuen and Co., Ltd. London.

Zotz, L. F. 1941. Eine Karte der Urgeschichtlichen Hohlenrastplatze Gross-Deutschlande. *Quartär* 3:132–155.

Zotz, L. F. 1951. *Altsteinzeitkuknde Mitteleuropas*, F. Enke Verlag, Stuttgart.

Zotz, L. F., and Freund, G. 1951. Die palaolithische und mesolithische Kulturentwicklung in Bohmen und Mahren. *Quartär* 5:7–40.

Illustration adapted from *Primate Adaptation and Evolution*, Academic Press, 1988.

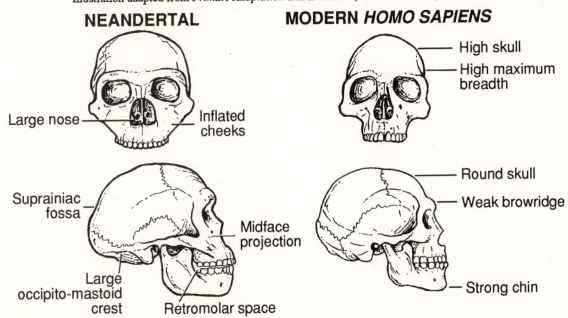

NEANDERTAL

Large nose — Inflated cheeks — Suprainiac fossa — Midface projection — Large occipito-mastoid crest — Retromolar space

MODERN *HOMO SAPIENS*

High skull — High maximum breadth — Round skull — Weak browridge — Strong chin

50

Neandertals and Praesapiens

H. V. Vallois

Thirty years ago, Professor René Verneau (1924) chose as the subject of his Huxley Memorial Lecture the study of two groups of Neandertal and of Grimaldi. A detailed comparison of their characters led him to the conclusion that Neandertal man was the ancestor of *Homo sapiens*, at the time of whose advent the first races to be formed were Negroid races which still retained many primitive Neandertal features; and that it was from these races that the yellow and the white races later became secondarily differentiated (Fig. 1A). Three years afterwards, and again in a Huxley Memorial Lecture, Dr. Ales Hrdlicka similarly asserted that *Homo sapiens* arose from the transformation of Neandertal man. Only, instead of considering the latter as a clearly delimited zoological group, he preferred to regard it as a "phase" of an evolutionary series leading progressively from *Pithecanthropus* to present-day man (Fig. 1B).

The object of these two Lectures—by eminent scientists, both of whom were repeatedly drawn to the problem of man's origin and had devoted important works to the study of human fossils—was the defense of a thesis long classic but opposed to a trend of opinion which had several times become apparent among anthropologists and had for a number of years been gaining fresh strength: Neandertal man, according to this trend, had not given rise to modern man. As a separate race, species, or, for some, even genus, he represented, in Boule's vivid phraseology, an archaic vanished group, a retarded form extin-

guished without issue. *Homo sapiens*, who was understood to appear in Europe during the Upper Palaeolithic, did not originate in the Neandertals who preceded him in the same regions. He was linked with another type-coeval with but independent of these Neandertals—whose ancestors had constituted a distinct phylum over a more or less protracted period. To this type, at first simply designated by the name of "primitive *sapiens*," there is now agreement in applying the term "Praesapiens" [1], without prejudice to its taxonomic or strict morphological significance but merely to denote probable phyletic affinities with present-day man. Since certain authors assert that this new idea is based on mistaken interpretations and that the theses skillfully defended by Verneau and Hrdlicka are still valid, it would seem of interest to review here the arguments in favour of the notion of Praesapiens and to try and trace the relationships that exist between the forms subsumed under the name of fossil man and the other human groups with which they could be connected. Such will be the object of this Huxley Memorial Lecture for 1954.

The reasons put forward to prove the existence of Praesapiens forms are of two orders: those, so to speak, of a negative kind which spring from the very great difficulty, indeed impossibility, of deriving *Homo sapiens*, as we see him appear in the Upper Palaeolithic, from the preceding Neandertals; and those of a positive kind, which depend on finds, contemporary with or even anterior to the age of Neandertal man, of human fossils closer to *Homo sapiens* than he was himself. Up to twenty or thirty years ago, considerations of the first order were obviously the only ones possible. From recent discoveries, however, those of the second order, which had long been inadequate, have assumed a special importance.

EVIDENCE OF THE NON-DERIVATION OF *HOMO SAPIENS* IN EUROPE FROM A NEANDERTAL FORM

From the beginnings of human palaeontology the idea that *Homo sapiens* was derived from *Homo neanderthalensis* [2] quickly impressed itself on the mind. It rested on some seductive arguments. In Europe, *Homo sapiens* appeared in the Upper Palaeolithic with the Aurignacian culture in the second phase of the Würmian period. Bearer of the Mousterian culture, *Homo neanderthalensis* preceded him on European soil, and the ever-increasing finds that have occurred at intervals since 1846, the

Figure 1. *The origin of* Homo sapiens. *(A), after Verneau (1924) and (B), after Hrdlicka (1927).*

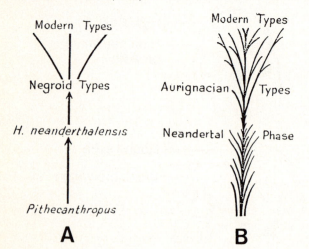

date of the discovery of the first Neandertal man at Gibraltar, have shown that he corresponded to the end of the Riss-Würm and the first phase of the Würmian period. More primitive from a cultural aspect, Neandertal man was thus chronologically anterior to *Homo sapiens*.

On the other hand, the study of his anatomical characters had not been long in showing that morphologically, too, he was the less advanced. Schwalbe (1901) in particular, as far as the skull was concerned, enumerated a whole series of features perceptibly intermediate between those of *Pithecanthropus* (and later on, it could be added, of *Sinanthropus* as well) and those of modern man; from the former to the latter, passing through Neandertal man, there were in fact noted: the gradual elevation of the calotte, the straightening of the forehead (with an increase in the size of the bregmatic and frontal angles and a forward shift of the bregma itself), the relative extension of the superior border of the parietal, the upward growth of the squamous part of the occipital and the gradual widening of the lambda angle. All these tendencies—to which such others as the steady disappearance of the supra-orbital and occipital tori, and the numerous modifications of the face, of the teeth, and of various parts of the post-cranial skeleton could easily be added—enabled a progressive series to be established which went from the anthropomorphous apes to *Pithecanthropus*, then from the latter to modern man, and into which Neandertal man seemed to be perfectly integrated.

It thus appeared that facts of a morphological order were added to those of an archaeological and chronological order so as to permit the conclusion that Neandertal man had directly produced *Homo sapiens*. It is not surprising, therefore, that several authors considered this supposition to be valid. Such was the opinion of Huxley. Busk and Karl Pearson in England, Dubois in the Netherlands, Houzé and Fraipont and Lohest in Belgium, de Quatre-fages and Hamy and Hervé and Mahoudeau in France, Kollmann in Switzerland, Stolyhwo in Poland, Gor-janovic-Kramberger in Yugoslavia, and finally Schwalbe in Germany and Guiseppe Sergi in Italy (in their earliest publications at least)—to mention only a few of the best-known names—all these scholars supported this conception. It is still upheld today. Hrdlicka devoted his 1927 Huxley Memorial Lecture to it, expanding the genealogical, archaeological, morphological, and physiological arguments that told in its favour. Composed with a complete knowledge of the subject and an acute critical sense, this work is certainly the most complete account of those written in favour of such a thesis. It is not without interest to observe, however, that, after having indicated that the resemblances between *Homo sapiens* and *Homo neanderthalensis* and the occurrence of transitional types could be accounted for on only three hypotheses, namely, common origin of the two groups in a single stock, intermixture, or the transformation of *Homo neanderthalensis* into *Homo sapiens*, Hrdlicka declared that he accepted the third and added: "This proposition is not yet capable of conclusive demonstration. There is not yet enough material to decide it one way or the other. But the thoroughly sifted indications appear to the speaker to favour this assumption" (Hrdlicka 1927, p. 273). The author considers, moreover, that Neandertal man shows too great a variability to be considered as a single species; it would be better to regard him as representing a "phase" of human evolution.

More recently, Weinert, in a series of volumes, has also described the evolution of the Hominidae as corresponding to a single line of descent in which a *Neandertaler-Stufe* preceded the *Sapiens-Stufe*. Now, while this German author in the first of his books (Weinert 1932) is still very categorical about the continuity between *Homo neanderthalensis* and *Homo sapiens* and cites as proof of it the existence of numerous transitional forms, in his most recent work (Weinert 1951) he makes certain reservations and observes that perhaps Western European *Homo sapiens* was not derived from the Neandertals of this region but from other Neandertals who had come from the east.

Himself another supporter of the passing of *Homo sapiens* through a Neandertal stage, up to his last work Weidenreich (1949) energetically defended this conception, but he, too, modified its original form in that he thought that the process had been brought about in a parallel fashion in the various continents by partially independent lines whose evolutionary rate could not have been everywhere the same. Quite recently, Sir Arthur Keith (1948), who had long been one of the most fervent supporters of the idea of the very considerable antiquity of *Homo sapiens*, announced that he now adhered to the thesis of his Neandertal origin. It is seen, then, that this view continues to be upheld by outstanding scientists in different countries. But the objections that have been advanced against it are very weighty ones.

I shall not emphasize those which depend on arguments of an archaeological kind. Much stress was laid a long time ago upon the differences between the Mousterian industry, which is that of Neandertal man, and the Aurignacian industry that succeeded it. In certain deposits the substitution of the one by the other can be observed in an unbroken sequence. At other times Aurignacian is seen to begin in a deposit, while in a neighboring and apparently contemporary one the Mousterian persists in a way which conveys the impression that the two types of industry, while remaining independent, have overlapped in time. Occasionally, however, transitional layers (of Abri Audi type) have occasionally been noticed, and the Lower Aurignacian of Châtelperronian tradition often yields Mousterian implements, so that the question of the exact relationship between the Mousterian and the Upper Palaeolithic is still debatable. Only facts of an anthropological order, then, will be considered here. From this point of view, the arguments which incline one to think that *Homo sapiens* is not derived from *Homo neanderthalensis* can be classed under two main heads: the morphological specialization of Neandertal man, and the manifest differences between the first Aurignacians and the last Neandertals.

Specialization of Neandertal Man

It was Boule (1911-13), in his classic monograph on the La Chapelle-aux-Saints man, who first drew attention to the fact that, if several characters of Neandertal man are intermediate between *Homo sapiens* and those of the Prehominians (*Pithecanthropus* and *Sinanthropus*), and even on occasion the anthropomorphs, a certain number of them could not be so classified: corresponding to specializations that were sometimes very well-marked, they place Neandertal man beyond the line of descent that led to *Homo sapiens*. No methodical enumeration of these characters ever seems to have been made. The following list brings together the most important of them.

A first group relates to the proportions of the limbs. The humero-radial index, which is very high among the anthropomorphs, 90 and above, falls to values of between 76 and 80 in Upper Palaeolithic man and in most of the dark-skinned races of the present day, and to values of between 71 and 74 among recent Europeans. Values above those of the Aurignacians would thus be expected to occur in Neandertal man; but his mean index is only 73.8, that is to say, the reduction of the forearm was quite as pronounced as it is among the majority of modern races.

No less characteristic is the femoro-tibial index: this ranges from 80 to 91 among the anthropomorphs, it is still 85.5 in Upper Palaeolithic man, and it falls to between 80 and 82 among present-day Europeans. But it is yet lower in Neandertal man, 76.6. This, even more than the previous index, indicates a shortening of the distal segment which could be called "ultra-human."

Other facts concern the actual form of the bones. The lateral border of the scapula in Neandertal man exhibits a very unusual structure which differs at the same time from that of the anthropomorphs and from that of *Homo sapiens*. One has here, as it were, a specialization, beyond the limits of both. The upper extremity of the ulna among the anthropomorphs is more or less flattened in a transverse direction, and the index that expresses this character, the index of platolenia, ranges from 83 to 86. In Upper Palaeolithic man, as in present-day Europeans, the mean fluctuates round 81, which means that the flattening is appreciably the same; at times, however, it is exaggerated and the index falls to 71. As regards the Neandertals, this index, on the contrary, rises, and its mean value for five bones examined is 101.4 (with individual variations of from 93 to 112), a figure which, as Boule (1912, p. 122) noted, is over twelve units above the highest mean, 89, recorded for *Homo sapiens*. By the rounded form of the superior extremity of the ulna, then, Neandertal man once more occupies a unique position.

Among the anthropomorphs, the height of the olecranon cap (the part of the olecranon above the horizontal plane passing through the base of this projection) is very slight. The index devised by Fischer (1906) to express this gives mean values that range from 0.8 to 1.4. It is a little higher among present-day Europeans, but the difference is slight, 1.7, with variations of from 1.0 to 3.7, and the same values are recorded for Upper Palaeolithic man. In Neandertal man the mean index rises to 4.7 (with a range of 4 to 6); one thus has yet again a feature lying beyond the limits of ape and modern man.

The lengthy study devoted by Fritz Sarasin (1931) to the skeleton of the hand enables attention to be drawn to a certain number of similar facts. These relate mainly to the length-breadth indices of the epiphyses (*Gelenkbreitenindices*) of the metacarpals and the proximal phalanx of the first three fingers, as determined by this author. In the case of the first metacarpal, for example, the indices for the chimpanzee and the gorilla are respectively 26.3 and 32.2, and for present-day man from 32.2 to 36.1; higher than all the preceding values, the mean index for three Neandertals is 38.2. The same is true of the proximal phalanx of the thumb: chimpanzee and gorilla, 35.1 and 48.5; modern man from 44.5 to 50.7; Neandertals 55.8. Unfortunately comparative material is lacking for Upper Palaeolithic man.

Other facts bear on the talus (astragalus): the height of this bone in the anthropomorphs, as among all monkeys and apes, is low in relation to its length. Measured according to the technique of Volkov (1903, pp. 682-5), the mean length-height index ranges from 46.5 to 54.8. It is slightly more in modern man, the means varying between 48.8 and 58.8. Among the Neandertals it reaches 61, that is to say, the relative height of the talus far exceeds that of the preceding two groups.

A number of other specializations are present in the skull. I shall not labour the fact that among the Neandertals the maximum cranial length is always very considerable, exceeding not only that of *Sinanthropus* and of *Pithecanthropus* but also the means of the most dolichocephalic representatives of *Homo sapiens*, recent and fossil. If Neandertal man were an intermediate form, there should have been at the time of his advent an elongation of the skull, and then, when he was transformed into *Homo sapiens*, a secondary reduction of it. More interesting, however, are various additional facts bearing on its structure.

Boule stressed at great length the absence of canine fossae in Neandertal man, since these occur in *Homo sapiens* as well as in at least two anthropomorphs, the gorilla and the orang. This anomalous situation as far as the Neandertal skull is concerned is still further accentuated by the fact that, as Weidenreich has shown, canine fossae exist in *Sinanthropus*. Even if account is taken of the fact that the occurrence of these fossae is doubtless only the counterpart of the ridging occasioned by the pronounced root of the canine tooth, it nevertheless remains true that here, too, the status of *Homo neanderthalensis* is not that of an intermediate form.

The nasal bones are very narrow in apes. They are larger in modern man, above all Europeans, and the index that compares their minimum and maximum breadths (Manouvrier's index of the breadth of the nasal bones) hardly exceeds 58 among the anthropomorphs and reaches, as a mean, a maximum of 62.7 in Europeans. This index rises to 66.6 in Neandertal man. From this fact and other features, such as the elongation of these bones or, again, the form of the inferior margin of the nasal cavities, Boule (1912, p. 31) concluded that "the nose of *Homo Neanderthalensis*, far from recalling by its morphology that of the apes, differs much more from it than that of present-day man" and that "his nasal region, instead of being ape-like, was, rather, *ultra-human*." It should, moreover, be added that in *Sinanthropus* at least one of these characters, the great breadth of the nasal bone, seems also present, in so far as it is an attribute of all primitive hominids and not only of the Neandertals.

Still further characters of the Neandertals can be regarded as specializations, for instance, the relative lowness of the temporal lines of the parietal, the more lateral alignment of the openings of the orbits, and the broad and low ascending ramus of the mandible with its short coronoid process, but the differences thus brought out are less clear-cut and are susceptible of other interpretations. I shall not, therefore, dwell on them. Kälin (1952) has recently pointed out that the direction of the spinous processes of the cervical vertebrae of Neandertal man indicates another specialization: among the Pongidae these processes are inclined dorsally. In *Homo sapiens* they are strongly inclined in a caudal direction. In Neandertal man only their proximal part is inclined caudally, the distal part being secondarily inclined in a cranial direction.

Perhaps it would also be as well to note the development of the occipital lobe of the brain, so far, at least, as endocranial casts reveal this: the degree to which it overlies the cerebellum is more pronounced in *Homo neanderthalensis* than in other hominids, living or fossil, as well as in the anthropomorphs [3]. In relation to the surface of the whole of the encephalon, the area of this lobe, which is 9% in modern man and 10.2% in apes, exceeds 12% in Neandertal man, but here, too, the data are inadequate.

A final character is certainly more important: the enlargement of the pulp-cavities of the molars called taurodontism. It is known that when Sir Arthur Keith (1913) drew attention for the first time to this feature, he considered it to be a specialization peculiar to the Neandertals and to them alone; its presence, he said, was sufficient to exclude such a fossil form from the line of descent of *Homo sapiens*. Later on it was established that the extreme degree of taurodontism observed by Keith in the material he studied did not occur among all Neandertals; on the other hand, various anthropologists, in particular Weidenreich (1937) and then Senyürek (1939), pointed out that some taurodontism could be seen among the primitive hominids and among monkeys and apes. This character, according to these authors, was consequently liable to be encountered in the whole line of human evolution. Nevertheless, it remains true that the accentuated taurodontism recorded for the majority of European Neandertals constitutes an exceptional exaggeration of this feature which is the opposite of the marked reduction usual in present-day man. Here *Homo sapiens* and *Homo neanderthalensis* have, in broad outline, followed separate evolutionary paths.

Lack of Morphological Continuity Between the European Neandertals and the First Aurignacians

The investigations of Schwalbe, Boule, and Henri Martin, confirmed by the very recent synthesis of Howell (1951), agree in showing that the Neandertals who lived in Europe during the first stage of the Würm glaciation constituted a markedly homogeneous assemblage exhibiting to the fullest degree the distinctive characters of their group. The Aurignacians who succeeded them are on the other hand unquestionably *Homo sapiens*. That so complete a morphological transformation could be produced in such a short space of time has always seemed practically impossible to the greater number of authorities and forms one of the most telling arguments against the idea of any genetical continuity between the two groups. Its force is particularly evident if the Neandertals are compared with the most ancient human remains from the Upper Palaeolithic so far recovered in Western Europe, those of the Combe-Capelle man and the Grimaldi "Negroids."

The Combe-Capelle skeleton was found, not at the classic site of this name, but in a nearby rock-shelter known as the "Roc de Combe-Capelle." It lay in the deepest part of a Lower Aurignacian deposit (Peyrony's Périgordian I) with a Châtelperronian industry. The relationships of this deposit with the Mousterian are borne out by the presence of implements recalling that industry. In the section they published of the shelter, Klaatsch and Hauser (1910), its discoverers, also noted the presence, immediately under an Aurignacian level and in direct contact with it, of a Mousterian level (Fig. 2). Peyrony (1943) denied the existence of such a level, but this author acknowledged never having seen the site until after it had been completely excavated. Even if he is correct, it still remains that the Combe-Capelle skeleton belonged to an altogether primitive Aurignacian, close in time to the Mousterian; could he not, perhaps, have even been contemporaneous with some of the late

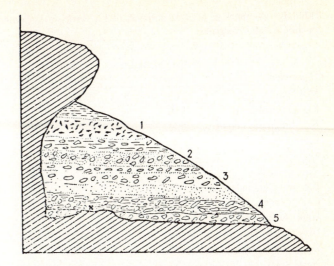

Figure 2. *Section of the Roc de Combe-Capelle shelter after Klaatsch and Hauser (1910). The position of the skeleton is marked by a cross. (1) Solutrian. (2) Upper Aurignacian. (3) Middle Aurignacian. (4) Lower Aurignacian. (5) Mousterian.*

Mousterian sites that seem to have prolonged their existence beyond Würm I?

The two Grimaldi skeletons that are termed "Negroid" come from the Grotte des Enfants and were found at a depth of 8.70 meters. Their relation to the Mousterian layer that forms the base of the deposits is near enough to them to be associated at first sight with it. A closer examination soon showed that a burial clearly associated with an Aurignacian industry was involved. Belonging to de Villeneuve's Layer I, this burial cut into the underlying Layer K, also Aurignacian; it did not penetrate into the Mousterian layer which lay directly beneath it (Boule 1906, Pl. XI). The two Grimaldi "Negroids" are thus incontestably Aurignacian, but they correspond to the first periods of this stage, and the slight thickness (0.75 meter) of the deposits that separate them from the Mousterian shows that at the moment of their death not much time would have passed since the Neandertals made their hearths on the underlying soil.

Table 1 compares the principal absolute measurements and indices of an extremely typical Neandertal man, La Ferrassie No. 1, with those of the Combe-Capelle man and the Grimaldi "Negroid" woman. The remains of the male subject from the last-named site have been excluded because of extreme distortion and also because the owner was not fully adult. The measurements of the La Ferrassie man and of the Grimaldi woman were taken by me on the original specimens, in the case of the Grimaldi woman after reconstruction of the distorted portions, so that in some instances they differ appreciably from those already published by Verneau (1906). The measurements of the Combe-Capelle man are those of Klaatsch and Hauser (1910), with the exception of the values indicated by reference marks, which are due to Saller (1925).

The table shows in a conclusive fashion the enormous difference between Mousterians and Lower Aurignacians. Among the last the skull is shorter and, above all, a lot less broad, and the height of the calotte very much greater; correspondingly, the cranial index is lower while the height indices, and in particular that of the calotte, are far higher; the forehead is upright and the glabellar angle considerably more

Table 1. Comparison of measurements of La Ferrassie I, Combe-Capelle, and female Grimaldi "Negroid."

Character	La Ferrassie I Male	Combe-Capelle Male	Grimaldi "Negroid" Female
Maximum length	209	198	191
Maximum breadth	158	130	130.5
Basi-bregmatic height	134	139	135
Calotte height [a]	86	104	107
Glabellar angle [b]	44°	58°	60°
Cranial index	75.5	65.7	68.3
Length-height index	64.1	70.2	70.6
Calotte index	42.1	54.4	60.1
Upper facial height	90	70 [c]	59.5
Bizygomatic breadth	149	130 ?	128
Upper facial index	60.4	53.9 [d]	46.4
Nasal index	54.6	52.0 [d]	52.1
Orbital index	76.6	70.0	72.4
Reconstructed stature [e]	160	166 ? [f]	159
Humero-radial index	74.3	79.2 [f]	80.1
Femoro-tibial index	77.5	88.8	83.9

[a] Above the glabello-inion line.

[b] Formed by the chords glabella-bregma and glabella-inion.

[c] Saller (1925, p. 199).

[d] Saller (1925, p. 201).

[e] Manouvrier's formulae.

[f] Saller (1925, p. 236).

open. The face is shorter and narrower, the upper facial index and the orbital index are smaller, and the humero-radial and femoro-tibial indices, as has been stated above, much larger. Corresponding to these numerical differences, there is, as one knows, an alteration in the structure of the head: the disappearance of the supra-orbital torus with the superciliary arches still marked in Combe-Capelle but quite unobtrusive in the Grimaldi individuals, an evident retreat of the massive face, scooping out of a canine fossa, considerable reduction in the size of the palatine vault and the teeth, etc.

It is pointless to dwell on these differences, which Klaatsch and Hauser have fully demonstrated for Combe-Capelle man and which emerge no less clearly from the study of the Grimaldi specimens. They are those which distinguish *Homo sapiens* from *Homo neanderthalensis* and are well known. But their great interest in this particular instance is that they already reveal themselves with perfect distinctiveness in the Upper Palaeolithic men who, by their stratigraphical position, would be the most liable to have retained Neandertal characters. Table I shows nothing of the kind. Figure 3 is no less categorical.

In his defense of the classic thesis, Hrdlicka attempted to minimize these facts. He stressed the selective influence that the glacial period exerted on the development of mankind; the more trying conditions of life and the increased want of food had entailed an intensification of physical and mental efforts which left only the fittest individuals to survive, namely, those which showed a trend towards *Homo sapiens*. But this demonstration is far from convincing. The discovery of the pre-Neandertals has in fact shown that, with the advent of the Würm, the Neandertals, far from evolving in the direction of *Homo sapiens*, became on the contrary more and more specialized in their own course. And one cannot see why climatic conditions which, with unbelievable speed, had completely transformed man during the Würm I-Würm II interstadial should have suddenly ceased to operate during the rest of the Würm when *Homo sapiens*, once emerged, has remained practically the same ever since!

Another argument, previously used by various anthropologist, was brought forward by Hrdlicka: the resurgence among the earliest members of *Homo sapiens* of types furnished with an appreciable supra-orbital torus recalling that of the Neandertals. For this purpose Hrdlicka referred to the Podkumok, Most (Brüx), Brno I, Predmost, Obercassel, Alcolea, and Jebel Fartas skulls, besides two Neolithic skulls from Warsaw and another from Belgium. Returning to the same argument, Weinert (1932) added to this list the Podbaba and the Kvalynsk skulls. Yet Boule (1913, p. 40) had already replied in advance to this line of argument by observing that none of the skulls appeared to possess an aggregate of Neandertal characters: at the very most they displayed "the fortuitous exaggeration of some of the morphological traits normally exaggerated in *Homo Neanderthalensis*." A further fact of which the importance must not be overlooked is that most of the remains mentioned by Hrdlicka and by Weinert are very far removed in time from Neandertal man. The skulls from Alcolea in the Province of Cordova in southern Spain are associated with a Neolithic or perhaps an Aeneolithic deposit. The Podkumok bones from the Caucasus are now recognized as being of Bronze Age date (Jegorow 1933). The Kvalynsk find was made on a surface of rolled pebbles of the bed of the Volga; it is impossible to date it stratigraphically

Figure 3. *Superposition of median sagittal sections of the La Chapelle-aux-Saints and Combe-Capelle crania. The specimens are oriented in the standard horizontal (porion-orbitale or ear-eye) plane. Because of the atypical position of the porion in the La Chapelle-aux-Saints cranium, the two orbitalia are superposed. The crosses correspond respectively to the nasion, the bregma, and the lambda.*

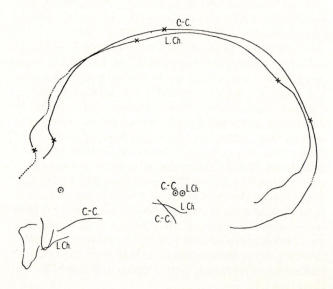

and its appearance is modern. The skull from Jebel Fartas (Department of Constantine, Algeria) is Neolithic. The Most skull, of long-disputed age, might, according to the latest investigations, be Tardenoisian. The only skulls in Hrdlicka's list which really date from the Upper Palaeolithic are those from Obercassel, which are Magdalenian, and Predmost and Brno I, which are Aurignacian. Now, detailed studies which were afterwards made of them have clearly shown that, even if their superciliary arches are pronounced, they are not at all of Neandertal type, so that the comparisons drawn are untenable.

Finally it has been urged that the complete and sudden extinction of an entire human stock was an extraordinary phenomenon of which no instance had so far been known: there was no reason why Neandertal man should be an exception to it. But neither has this remark any substance. It is indeed rather piquant to observe that those who have no difficulty in admitting that one human type could, within a few thousand years, be transformed into another, consider that the extinction of the first and the independent advent of the second could not have occurred in the same space of time. But the very fact of the rapid disappearance of a human group is far from being exceptional. The replacement of Indians in the United States by Europeans needed only a few centuries; that of the Tasmanians by other Europeans did not require even a hundred years, and during this same period the greater part of the Australians have also vanished.

It can be objected that the conditions in which the Whites replaced the natives were due to a very special circumstance, the overwhelming superiority of their civilization, but similar events had previously occurred almost everywhere without the intervention of Europeans: Polynesians superseded the Moriori in New Zealand, the Japanese replaced the Ainu over the greater part of their islands, the Bantu gradually drove out the Khoisan in South Africa, etc., all events which were completed within a few centuries and at the end of which the populations of certain regions had been, in an anthropological sense, totally altered. Certainly in the majority of cases intermixture took place between the ancient owners of the land and the newcomers in the same way as it could have occurred between Neandertals and Aurignacians, but these crossings were never such as to modify the hereditary potentialities of the invaders. Endowed with superior selective qualities, these last quickly ended by remaining the sole survivors, and the genes they could acquire by intermixture did not in practice alter their type. There is hardly any doubt that the same was true of the Aurignacian *vis-à-vis* the Neandertals. In North Africa during the Capsian was not an identical phenomenon also present: the advent of a Mediterranean type which very rapidly and from a few nearby islets completely overwhelmed the Ibero-Maurusian race of Mechta?

It is unnecessary to labour all these facts any further. They show plainly that, despite objections raised to the contrary, the thesis of the non-derivation of Upper Palaeolithic man from the Neandertals of Western Europe retains all its force. Our Aurignacians originate, then, in another line which, over a period of indefinite duration, developed parallel to Neandertal man; it is to this line that the name of Praesapiens is conventionally given. The necessity of its existence has already been implicitly recognized by many authors, since a great number of genealogical trees published over the past forty or so years represent Neandertal man as culminating in a phylum precociously detached from the main line and without issue. It is enough to mention the diagrams of Pilgrim (1915), Gregory (1920), Elliot

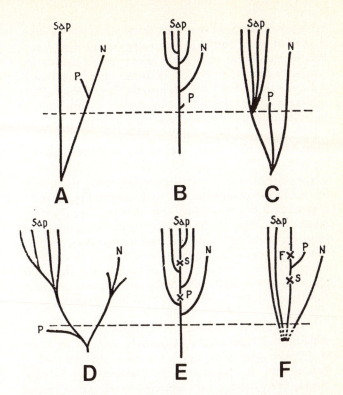

Figure 4. *Schematic representation of the genealogical trees of* Homo sapiens *and* Homo neanderthalensis *according to different authors: A. Pilgrim (1915), B. Elliot Smith (1924), C. Keith (1927), D. Osborn (1927), E. Hooton (1946), F. Kalin (1952). Sap = Homo sapiens, N = Homo neanderthalensis, P = Piltdown, S = Swanscombe, F = Fontéchevade. The broken line indicates the lower limit of the Pleistocene.*

Smith (1924), Osborn (1927), Keith (e.g. 1927) previous to 1948, Hooton (1946), etc. (Fig. 4). But as they were constructed, the majority of these trees had an essential defect: the position of the phylum of *Homo sapiens* before the Upper Palaeolithic was hypothetical. Only the negative arguments referred to above enabled his existence to be affirmed. The attempts made to give this a concrete form by placing human fossils in it have generally come to grief. Hrdlicka had already emphasized this lacuna, to which Weinert has on many occasions returned. Up to his death, Weidenreich also declared that the absence of a Praesapiens line was established by the fact that all the fossils which an attempt had been made to place in it had in reality a different significance. It is this important question which I am now going to examine.

EVIDENCE OF THE EXISTENCE OF PRAESAPIENS

On several occasions, and from the moment when the study of man's origin entered into its scientific phase, the existence of extremely ancient fossil human remains—and moreover of the same type as, or of a type near to, that of *Homo sapiens*—has been reported. Most of these remains were afterwards shown to be more recent than was at first believed. It was this consideration which to the minds of many anthropologists had brought Presapiens into disrepute. But some of them have an undoubted antiquity. Only others are doubtful. One can thus class the aggregate of the forms envisaged as such in three categories: remains of which neither the morphology nor the age—Upper Palaeolithic or still much more recent—really justifies any separation from other members of *Homo sapiens*; remains of debatable age and of which the antiquity in relation to *Homo sapiens* is possible but not certain; remains corresponding in fact to Praesapiens. I shall examine them in turn.

Remains Wrongly Considered as Those of Presapiens

About nine finds can be entered under this heading if only those are considered which at one time were supported by inferences that seemed genuine (Vallois and Movius 1952). They are restricted to France and Britain and, with one exception, come from alluvial deposits. Some have had only a fleeting celebrity. Others have been long regarded, especially by Keith, as irrefutable evidence of the antiquity of modern man. The lack of age, indeed the worthlessness, of this assemblage of remains is now beyond doubt. I shall not therefore dwell on them.

The Denise Remains. Found between 1884 and 1889 in the deposits of an extinct volcano in Haute-Loire, they have at different times been regarded as very old, and even of Pliocene date. But the deposits that contained them have obviously been overlaid and subjected to the phenomena of solifluxion. Then, again, the bones are fossilized. They cannot be taken into consideration.

The Moulin Quignon Jaw. Taken to Boucher de Perthes in 1863 by a workman who said he had founded it *in situ* in the Chellean layers of Abbeyville, this lower jaw, which an attempt has recently been made to vindicate, has absolutely no palaeontological value. Its low fluorine content (Oakley 1951) is conclusive in such a respect.

Clichy and Grenelle Skeletons. Included in the lands flooded by the Seine which have been subjected to constant changes up to quite recent time, these skeletons, which are practically unfossilized and which Rutot (1910) tried to trace back to the Chellean, are at the very most Neolithic. Although still occasionally regarded by some authors as corresponding to an ancient Palaeolithic type, any value has long ceased to be attributed to them in France.

The Foxhall Jaw. Found near Ipswich, Suffolk, in 1855 in the Red Crag, that is, of Lower Pleistocene date, it was at first assigned to this period and even to the Pliocene (Newton 1897). One of the reasons advanced in favour of its antiquity was its resemblance to the Moulin Quignon mandible, which would rather have been proof of the opposite! Very recently Eiseley (1943) again reported the presence in it of an archaic character, multiple foramina mentalia. But even on its discovery such experienced scientists as Huxley, Lyell, and Prestwich had doubts of its great age, and in spite of a subsequent attempt to establish this by Reid Moir (1924) it is not accepted today. It is sufficient to note that the mandible contains 8% of organic matter whereas the Red Crag fossils have only 6.5%. Moreover the specimen disappeared twenty years after its finding.

The Bury St. Edmunds Fragment. A portion of a calotte of modern type—found in 1882 at Westley, also in Suffolk, in a clay pocket of glacial age—has long been considered as of fairly early Pleistocene date because other similar pockets contain Acheulian implements. Sir Arthur Keith (1912) lent his authority to this opinion for some time. Recent investigations by Baden-Powell and Oakley (1953) by producing evidence of the very low fluorine content of this calotte have shown that its age was relatively late.

The Galley Hill Skeleton. Discovered in 1888 in gravels containing an Acheulian industry, the skeleton of remarkably modern appearance has given rise to very lively arguments. By demonstrating its very low fluorine content, Oakley and Montagu (1949) have given definite proof of its comparatively recent age.

The Ipswich Skeleton. Found in 1911 in a "redeposited boulder-clay" (Moir and Keith 1912) at Ipswich, Suffolk, it was first thought to be anterior to the Riss glaciation. Even its discoverer, Reid Moir, later recognized that it was at most of Upper Palaeolithic age.

The London Skull. This is in fact no more than a cranial fragment discovered in 1925 in one of the lower terraces of the Thames and has been assigned to the Middle Pleistocene. But this terrace is now relegated to the Würm, and here again the fluorine content (Oakley 1951) has shown that the skull is not old.

The Piltdown Skull. The arguments that have risen round the Piltdown remains are too recent and too close to the feelings for there to be any reason to dwell on this very celebrated find. The researches initiated by Weiner, Oakley and Le Gros Clark have, it seems definitively, shown the lack of age of the human remains and their fraudulent introduction into the site, at the same time as they established, and still more categorically, that the mandible belonged to an ape. No good grounds would exist for returning to these facts if they had not been utilized by some anthropologists as an argument against the existence of Praesapiens. Now if, at the time of its discovery, the so-called *Eoanthropus* had been considered as a precocious representative of modern man, it would have been quickly rejected from the phylum of the latter by the reason of the aberrant features of its mandible. Almost all the genealogical trees (Fig. 4) placed it on a side branch without descendants. Well before the sensational disclosures referred to (Weiner, Oakley, and Clark 1953; Weiner *et al.* 1955), the idea of Praesapiens had not for a long time relied on Piltdown man, whose exclusion from human fossils properly so called does not thus affect the essentials of the problem.

Remains of Doubtful Age

Apart from the African remains of Kanam and Kanjera, this category includes only two specimens, both from Italy, those of Olmo and of Quinzano.

The find at Olmo, in the province of Arezzo (Tuscany), consists essentially of a calotte found in 1863 at the bottom of a deep cutting, where it seemed to have been detached from a clay bed with *Elephas antiquus* and *Rhinoceros merckii* which also contained a Mousterian point. This fact assigns it if not to the Lower Pleistocene, as was first said, at least to the Riss-

Würm; but the circumstances of the discovery are unsatisfactory and doubt exists, which the very recent studies by Oakley, based on the skull's fluorine content, have been unable to clarify [4]. Nevertheless Olmo man, and with him the skeletons from Castenodolo, said to be Pliocene but whose recent age leaves no room for doubt, were long appealed to by the late Professor Giuseppe Sergi as a proof of the great antiquity of *Homo sapiens.*

The discovery at Quinzano, in the Province of Verona, consists of the squamous portion of an occipital bone also embedded in deposits of alluvial clay; whereas the workmen who found it, in 1938, attributed it to a level that corresponds at most to the Upper Palaeolithic, Battaglia (1948), on the grounds of its physical characters, was of the opinion that it came from underlying deposits of Riss-Würm age. As in the case of the Olmo skull, the fluorine analysis had not unfortunately been able to settle the question in a final way [5]. This uncertainty is the more regrettable because, while the Quinzano occipital is of general *Homo sapiens* type, it nevertheless displays certain peculiar features. On such a basis, Battaglia makes of it a *Protofanerantropus*, while Heberer (1950) does not venture to include it in the Praesapiens group.

The Real Praesapiens Forms

Only two finds, in Europe, can be accorded with adequate certainty to this group: Swanscombe man from Kent, discovered in 1935 in alluvial deposits containing an Acheulian industry and pre-Riss in age; and the Fontéchevade men from the Charente, discovered in 1947 in well-stratified cave deposits, in association with a Tayacian industry and dating from an early phase of the Riss-Würm. These remains are few enough, but it should not be forgotten that, for Europe at least, the discoveries of fossil man which are beyond all doubt previous to the Würm have always been extremely rare. Only five other finds, traditionally regarded as those of the predecessors of the Neandertals or as resembling them, can in fact be mentioned apart from the preceding: the Mauer jaw, from the Lower Pleistocene; the Steinheim cranium, belonging to the Riss or even possibly the Mindel-Riss; the Saccopastore and Weimar men and the Montmaurin mandible of Riss-Würm date—that is, all but a little more than double those of Praesapiens forms.

Few specimens unfortunately correspond to the last: a parietal and an occipital in the case of Swanscombe, a segment of the frontal (Subject No. 1) and an incomplete calotte (Subject No. 2) in that of Fontéchevade. We are quite ignorant of the face of the Praesapiens forms, as we are of their dentition and the remainder of their skeleton. These are serious gaps. At all events, the cranial characters can be adequately specified. The monographs of Le Gros Clark (1938) and of Morant (1938) on the Swanscombe skull and the paper I have published on the Fontéchevade men (Vallois 1949), itself a prelude to a more substantial memoir which has not yet appeared, set forth the essential points of these. The following diagnosis briefly summarizes them.

Skull very thick with a low vault, mesocranial and doubtless also chamaecranial and tapeinocranial. Biasterionic breadth both absolutely and relatively large. Forehead upright and completely lacking any torus. Parietal of *Homo sapiens* type but with very unobtrusive prominences. No parietal foramina and a primitive arrangement of the parieto-temporal articulation. Occipital little incurved vertically and without the characteristic "bun" of the Neandertals. Cranial capacity probably voluminous.

It is difficult to state precisely whether the foregoing characters are again met with in the Olmo skull, no full description of which has yet been published, but the Quinzano occipital shows two of the features to which attention was drawn above; great thickness of the bone and a large biasterionic breadth. Besides, in this specimen, as in the Swanscombe skull, the occipital is incurved vertically to a moderate degree and displays neither the torus nor the "bun," compressed from above downwards, which are characteristic of the Neandertal occiput. These resemblances, on which Battaglia has laid stress, speak in favour of the antiquity of the Italian specimen.

Comparison with Neandertals and Pre-Neandertals

One of the fundamental traits of Neandertal man, and a character which can be seen as clearly in the classic representations (for example in the La Chapelle-aux-Saints, La Ferrassie, and Monte Circeo men) as in the forms termed "transitional" and represented by the Neandertals of Palestine, is the presence of a supra-orbital torus. The pre-Neandertals, although less specialized in certain of their features, also have a torus and even more pronounced than in the Neandertals properly so called. The absence of this structure in Praesapiens forms is a difference of the first order which at once separates them from all the others mentioned. But is this torus really absent? The only specimen in which the corresponding region is preserved is the fragment of the Fontéchevade frontal known as F.I. Could not the lack of torus be attributed to the skull of a young person with its bony prominences still undeveloped?[6] On the other hand, several authors have repeatedly supposed that the Swanscombe occipital and parietal could have belonged to a skull identical with that of Steinheim, thus possessing, as it does, a very large torus. The same supposition has been put forward in regard to the Fontéchevade skull F. II. These objections have to be considered.

Furnished with a glabella and superciliary arches which are quite reduced, the F.I frontal has actually, for that very reason, an infantile appearance. But its thickness is at least as much as that of a modern adult frontal bone. Another adult character is the presence of a large frontal sinus, almost 3 cm. high. Now it is known that this sinus as much as in *Homo sapiens* as in *Homo neanderthalensis* (La Quina Child) is extremely reduced during infancy and starts to develop only with puberty at the same time as—if it occurs—the expansion of the glabella and the torus. F.I, then, is the skull of an adult: its absence of torus is not an infantile character but a specific or at least a racial one.

The Fontéchevade calotte F.II lacks the lower part of the frontal but, in the work I have mentioned (Vallois 1949), I have shown that it, too, could not have had a torus, the occurrence of which being incompatible with the position of the surviving portion of the frontal sinus. An additional argument is the absence of the post-orbital constriction characteristic of skulls possessing a torus. The comparison of the *norma verticalis* of F.II with that of a Neandertal man as with that of the pre-Neandertal of Steinheim typifies this aspect (Fig. 5).

The question of the Swanscombe skull is more difficult. While Le Gros Clark (1938) had dwelt on its great likeness to present-day skulls, Morant (1938) showed that for four metrical

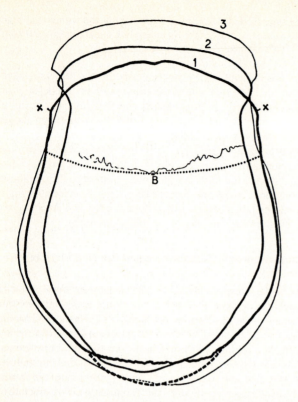

Figure 5. *Superposition of the* norma verticalis *of (1) Fontéchevade II, (2) Steinheim, (3) La Chapelle-aux-Saints. The three crania are centered on the bregma (B). The two crosses mark the limit of the intact lateral portion and the missing anterior portion of Fontéchevade II.*

characters—biasterionic breadth and three indices derived from this—its difference from these was more than three times the standard deviation of modern Europeans. These peculiarities, to which was added the great thickness of the skull, caused him to express the opinion that its anterior portion could also have been different from that of present-day man and to have been of the certainly later Steinheim type. This idea has been developed by Breitinger (1952), who declares that a skull as thick as that of Swanscombe ought necessarily to have a massive supra-orbital region. Sergio Sergi (1953) also considers that the architecture of Swanscombe—and particularly as it appears to him by his method of study of oblique planes—is so close to Neandertal man that the existence of a supra-orbital torus seems in his view probable.

The facts revealed by the Fontéchevade men do not favour the preceding arguments. The biasterionic breadth of F. II is, in fact, sensibly the same as that of Swanscombe, and the skull is as thick; yet a torus is lacking. The presence of the first two characters does not, then, inevitably entail that of the third, as Breitinger seems to think. A second instance of this lack of correlation is moreover provided by—whatever its age may be—the Piltdown cranium, of which the thickness and the biasterionic breadth exceed those of both the two specimens referred to, while the forehead certainly does not have a torus. Ashley Montagu (1951), by articulating the Wallbrook frontal bone, of modern type and probably recent date, with the Swanscombe parietal, obtained a plausible reconstruction. Without being conclusive, these facts indicate that the occurrence of a supra-orbital torus does not necessarily follow from

the structure of the surviving portions of Swanscombe as some would have it believed.

One last difference can still be considered: it is not so much to Neandertals proper, who are far later than they are, that an attempt has been made to assign the Praesapiens forms, but to the *pre*-Neandertals, particularly to that of Steinheim, which is the least removed from them in time and whose occiput has a certain resemblance to that of Swanscombe. Now the Steinheim skull is distinguished by its very small capacity, 1073 cc. according to Weinert (1936). The Swanscombe and Fontéchevade skulls, on the other hand, have a greater capacity which falls within the normal range of variation of *Homo sapiens*, 1325 cc. for Swanscombe, according to Morant (1938), and about 1460 cc. for F. II. The distinction is important.

Comparison with *Homo sapiens*

If the difference between Praesapiens and *Homo sapiens* are much less marked than those *vis-a-vis* the Neandertals, they none the less exist. I have said that Morant had already emphasized the significant increase in the biasterionic diameter of Swanscombe man and the changes in the related indices to which this gave rise. The same broadening recurs in Fontéchevade and is quite as fully pronounced. Still other differences can be pointed out. In Table 2 will be found a list of them which is a parallel of those which separate the Praesapiens forms from Neandertal man. It is not without interest to observe that some of these differences between Praesapiens forms and *Homo sapiens* turn out to bring the first nearer to the Neandertals; this is particularly so in the case of the increased biasterionic breadth, even more marked in certain Neandertals than in Swanscombe and Fontéchevade (Vallois 1949). This peculiarity, as Sergi (1953) has noted, reveals in all ancient forms a tendency to a development below and behind the cranial cavity. This would be a kind of survival of what occurs in the Prehominians (*Pithecanthropus* and *Sinanthropus*), where the greatest breadth of this cavity is situated close to the base.

The Significance of Praesapiens Forms

Two hypotheses have been put forward relating to Praesapiens forms. Struck by the similarities they displayed to the pre-Neandertals, Sergio Sergi (1953) considers it difficult to separate the two groups. Swanscombe and Fontéchevade were, as he puts it, "palaeoanthropiform Prophaneranthropi," while the pre-Neandertals for their part revealed, in the degree of flexion of their base and in the form of their occipital, "Phaneranthropic" characters. There thus existed, during pre-Würmian times, an assemblage of more or less intermingled types, in whom the features of the Neandertals and those of *Homo sapiens* forms were blended in varying proportions. It was from this complex that there were progressively differentiated, first the Neandertals, and later, perhaps from several sources, the existing members of *Homo sapiens*.

Alluring as this hypothesis may be, in that it rightly emphasizes the error of the old conception that reduced the whole of human evolution to three or four well-contrasted types arranged in a single continuous line, it still does not seem to correspond to the real facts. Nor does it take sufficient account of the differences that separate the pre-Neandertals and the Praesapiens forms. To unite in the same group Steinheim, with its powerful supra-orbital torus and small brain volume, and

Table 2. Comparison of morphological features of *Homo sapiens*, Praesapiens forms, and *Homo neanderthalensis*.

Character	H. sapiens (European)	Praesapiens Forms	H. neanderthalensis
Great thickness of vault	−	+	±
Frontal torus	−	−	+
Post-orbital constriction	−	−	+
Large biasterionic breadth	−	+	+
Platycephaly	−	±	+
"Bun"-shaped occipital	−	−	+
Superior parietal border > inferior	+	+	±
Absence of parietal foramina	−	+	+
Shortness of squamous suture	−	+	−

Fontéchevade, with its forehead bereft of a torus and its large brain volume, amounts to denying the value of morphological features. The Praesapiens forms of the Riss-Würm seem instead to constitute an independent stock. This second hypothesis, with which Heberer (1950) among others has fully identified himself, is certainly the more plausible as far as the facts are at present known.

Such a conception does not, however, imply that Praesapiens and pre-Neandertal forms have always been separated. To believe this would be to admit the existence of a polyphyleticism which all serious investigations contradict. There is no doubt that the two groups come from a common source. But at what time were they cut off from each other? Heberer suggests the very base of the Pleistocene, the Günz period, and immediately after the *Pithecanthropus-Sinanthropus* phylum had broken away. Kälin (1952) has rallied to the same idea (Fig. 4F). Breitinger (1952) who admits, as has been seen, that Swanscombe and Steinheim are identical, thinks that it is from these, during the Mindel-Riss, that there sprang on the one hand the Neandertals and on the other the Praesapiens forms, which he thus reduces to Fontéchevade man. Sergio Sergi (1953), who makes the pre-Neandertal and Praesapiens forms into two extremes of a single group, implies by this that the separation must have been still later, just before the Würm, and that it directly gave rise to the Neandertals and the different types of *Homo sapiens*.

All these hypotheses are of interest, but the palaeontological facts on which they depend are still so incomplete that it would certainly be premature to try to establish too-detailed phyletic connections from them. All that we are able to say at the moment is that while from the Steinheim to the Saccopastore skulls and then to the Neandertals properly so-called a line can be plotted which runs from the Riss period to that of the Würm, from the Swanscombe to the Fontéchevade skulls it is possible to plot in a parallel direction a line running from the Mindel-Riss to the Riss-Würm. Between the terminals of the base of these two lines, the Swanscombe skull on one side and the Steinheim skull on the other, the differences are marked. Their separation should thus be pushed back to a more distant epoch. To attempt to state the date of this precisely would be pure speculation: further discoveries must be awaited.

It is no easier at the moment to establish a link between European Praesapiens forms of the Riss-Würm and the representatives of *Homo sapiens* properly so-called, who appeared in our continent only at the second stage of the Würm glaciation. From a morphological point of view, it is scarcely debatable that the first were on the road that led to the second: the mutations necessitated by such a transformation are far less considerable than those which the Neandertals would have had to sustain, and the space of time which corresponds to the end of the Riss-Würm and the outset of the Würm could amply suffice for them. When the skeleton of the Praesapiens forms is better known, one will doubtless be able to establish that hardly more than differences of a racial order separate them from *Homo sapiens*, so that the name that is provisionally applied to them indicates at most a secondary taxonomic separation. From a stratigraphical point of view, however, an indeniable gap remains. Between the Riss-Würm Praesapiens forms and the first representatives of *Homo sapiens* in the Upper Palaeolithic, any records have so far failed to appear. Perhaps the few Praesapiens representatives of Western Europe were only the scattered emissaries of a stock whose main body was evolving elsewhere, and without doubt in Asia? Perhaps on the contrary they already constituted in our lands a relatively important group but one which had, towards the close of the last interglacial, completely yielded place to the Neandertals? The men of the Upper Paleolithic, descendants of these Praesapiens members, pressed back somewhere further east, must afterwards have taken final revenge on the Neandertals.

The future will make plain to us the worth of these hypotheses. One fact at all events seems now to be established: the European *Homo sapiens* is not derived from the Neandertal men who preceded him. His stock was for long distinct from, and, under the name of Praesapiens, had evolved in a parallel direction to, theirs. Long-debated, the Praesapiens forms are thus not a myth. They did exist. The few remains of them we possess are the tangible evidence of the great antiquity of the phylum that culminates in modern man.

NOTES

[1] It is difficult to specify the actual origin of this word. On several occasions since 1940 it has been used in private discussions or in the course of symposia (e.g. the 1947 Colloque international de Paléontologie at the Centre National de la Recherche Scientifique in Paris), but it seems that the first author to use it systematically may be Heberer (1950). Is it not, perhaps, only the modification, and a happy one from an etymological point of view, of the Graeco-Latin term *Proto-sapiens*, previously employed by Montandon (1940)? Battaglia (1948) is responsible for the synonym *Protofanerantropus*, which is the *Profanerantropus* of Sergio Sergi (1953).

[2] [The apparent inconsistency in dropping the *h* in "Neandertal"—without any doubt the better form, as the lecturer has indicated elsewhere (Vallois 1952)—and not in the trivial name of the species *Homo neanderthalensis* arises from the fact that the earlier German spelling, reformed in 1901, of *Tal* must be retained to accord with Article 19 of the International Code of Zoological Nomenclature. An English version of this reads: "The original orthography of a name is to be preserved unless an error of transcription, a *lapsus calami*, or a typogrphical error is evident" (Schenk and McMasters 1948, p. 37).—Ed.]

[3] It is appropriate to record, on the occasion of a lecture devoted to honouring his memory, that Thomas Henry Huxley (1863, p. 143) was the first to note that "notwithstanding the flattened condition of the occiput, the posterior central lobes" of the Neandertal skull "must have projected considerably beyond the cerebellum."

[4] For the source of this statement, see next note.

[5] Information kindly communicated by Dr. Kenneth P. Oakley.

[6] Personal communication from Dr. F. Clark Howell.

REFERENCES

Baden-Powell, D. F. W., and Oakley, K. P. 1953. Report on the re-investigation of the Westley (Bury St. Edmunds) Skull site. *Proc. Prehist. Soc., N.S.* 18:1–20.

Battaglia, R. 1948. Osso occipitale umano rinvenuto nel giacimento pleistocenio di Quinzano nel Commune di Verona. *Palaeontogr. ital.* 42:1–31.

Boule, M. 1911–13. L'Homme fossile de La Chapelle-aux-Saints. *Ann. Paléont.* 6:106–72, 7:21–192, 8:1–70.

Boule, M., and Vallois, H. V. 1952. Les Présapiens, in: *Les Hommes fossiles: Éléments de paléontologie humaine*, (4th ed.) pp. 178–201, Masson, Paris.

Boule, M. 1906. Géologie et paléontologie, in:*Les grottes de Grimaldi (Baoussé-Roussé)*, I (2), pp. 71–362, Imprimerie de Monaco Monaco.

Breitinger, E. 1952. Zur Morphologie und systematischen Stellung des Schädelfragmentes von Swanscombe. *Homo* 3:131–133.

Clark, W. E. Le Gros. 1938. General features of the Swanscombe skull bones. *J. R. Anthrop. Inst.* 68:58–60.

Eiseley, L. C. 1943. A neglected anatomical feature of the Foxhall jaw. *Trans. Kans. Acad. Sci.* 46:57–59.

Fischer, E. 1906. Die variationen an radius und ulna des Menschen. *Z. Morph. Anthrop.* 9:147–247.

Gregory, W. K. 1920–1. The origin and evolution of human dentition. *J. Dental Res.* 1:89–175, 215–73, 357–426, 607–717; 2:87–228.

Heberer, G. 1950. Das Präsapiens-problem, in: *Moderne Biologie, Festschrift zum 60. Geburtstag von Hans Nachtsheim* (H. Gruneberg and W. Ulrich, Eds.), pp. 131–162, Peters, Berlin.

Hooton, E. A. 1946. *Up from the Ape*, 2nd ed. Macmillan, New York.

Howell, F. C. 1951. The place of Neanderthal man in human evolution. *Am. J. Phys. Anthropol.* 9:379–416.

Hrdlicka, A. 1927. The Neanderthal phase of man (Huxley Memorial Lecture, 1927). *J. R. Anthrop. Inst.* 57:249–74.

Huxley, T. H. 1863. On some fossil remains of man, in: *Evidence as to Man's Place in Nature*, pp. 119–159, Williams and Norgate, London.

Jegorow, N. M. 1933. Zur frage über das alter des sogenannten Podkumok-Menschen. *Anthrop. Anz.* 10:223–225.

Kalin, J. 1952. Die ältesten Menschenreste und ihre Stammesgeschichtliche Deutung, in: *Historia Mundi* I, pp. 33–98, Francke, Bern.

Keith, A. 1912. On certain phases in the evolution of man: abstract of Hunterian lecture 1912. *Brit. Med. J.* 1:734–7, 788–90.

Keith, A. 1913. Problems relating to the teeth of the earlier forms of prehistoric man. *Proc. R. Soc. Med.*, Odont. Sec. 6:103–19.

Keith, Sir A. 1927. *Concerning Man's Origins*. Watts, London.

Keith, Sir A. 1948. *A New Theory of Human Evolution*. Watts, London.

Klaatsch, H., and Hauser O. 1910. *Homo aurignacensis hauseri*, ein paläolithischer Skelefund aus dem unteren Aurignacien der Station Combe-Capelle bei Montferrand (Perigord). *Prähist. Z.* 1:273–338.

Moir, J. R. 1924. The human jaw-bone found at Foxhall. *Am. J. Phys. Anthropol.* 7:409–16.

Moir, J. R., and Keith, A. 1912. An account of the discovery and characters of a human skeleton found beneath a stratum of chalky boulder clay near Ipswich. *J. R. Anthrop. Inst.* 42:345–79.

Montagu, M. F. A. 1951. The Wallbrook frontal bone. *Am. J. Phys. Anthropol.* 9:5–14.

Montandon, G. 1940. Nomenclature anthropologique. *Rev. Sci., Paris* 78:172–173.

Morant, G. M. 1938. The form of the Swanscombe skull. *J. R. Anthrop. Inst.* 68:67–97.

Newton, E. T. 1897. Palaeolithic man. *Proc. Geol. Assn., Lond.* 15:246.

Oakley, K. P. 1951. The fluorine-dating method. *Yearb. Phys. Anthrop.* 5:44–52.

Oakley, K. P., and Montague, M. F. A. 1949. A reconsideration of the Galley Hill skeleton. *Bull. Brit. Mus. (Nat. Hist.), Geol.* 1(2):27–46.

Osborn, H. F. 1927. Recent discoveries in human evolution. *Long Is. Med. J.* 21:3–7.

Peyrony, D. 1943. Combe-Capelle. *Bull. Soc. Préhist. Franc.* 40:243–57.

Pilgrim, G. E. 1915. New Siwalik primates and their bearing on the question of the evolution and the Anthropoidea. *Rec. Geol. Surv. India* 45:1–72.

Rutot, A. 1910. Revision stratigraphique des ossements humaines quaternaires de l'Europe. *Bull. Soc. Belg. Géol.* 24:123.

Saller, K. 1925. Die Cromagnonrasse und ihre Stellung zu anderen jungpaläolithischen Langschädelrassen. *Z. indukt. Abstamm. -u. VererbLehre* 39:191–247.

Sarasin, F. 1931. Die variationen im bau des Handskeletts verschiedener Menschenformen. *Z. Morph. Anthrop.* 30:252–316.

Schenk, E. T., and McMasters, J. H. 1948. *Procedure in Taxonomy*, 2nd ed. (rewritten in part by A. Myra Keen and Siemon William Muller), University Press, Stanford.

Schwalbe, G. 1901. Der Neanderthalschädel. *Bonn. Jb.* 106:1–72.

Senyürek, M. S. 1939. Pulp cavities of molars in primates. *Am. J. Phys. Anthropol.* 25:119–30.

Sergi, S. 1953. I profanerantropi de Swanscombe e di Fontéchevade. *R. C. Accad. Lincei* 14:601–608.

Smith, G. E. 1924. *The Evolution of Man: Essays*. Oxford University Press, London.

Vallois, H. V. 1949. The Fontéchevade fossil men. *Am. J. Phys. Anthropol.* 7:339–362.

Vallois, H. V. 1952. Néanderthal-Néandertal? *Anthropologie, Paris* 55:557–558.

Vallois, H. V., and Movius, H. L. Jr. 1952. Catalogue des hommes fossiles. *Proc. XIX Int. Geol. Congr.* (Algiers) 5:59–378.

Verneau, R. 1906. Anthropologie, in: *Les Grottes de Grimaldi (Baoussé-Roussé)*, II (1). Imprimerie de Monaco, Monaco.

Verneau, R. 1924. La race de Néanderthal et la race de Grimaldi; leur role dans l'humanité (Huxley Memorial Lecture, 1924). *J. R. Anthrop. Inst.* 54:211–230.

Volkov, T. 1903–4. Variations squelettiques du pied chez les races humaines. *Bull. Soc. Anthrop. Paris*, 5ᵉ ser. 4:632–708, 5:1–50, 5:201–331.

Weidenreich, F. 1937. The dentition of *Sinanthropus pekinensis*: A comparative odontography of the hominids, 2 Vols. *Palaeontol. Sin.* n.s. D, no. 1.

Weidenreich, F. 1943. The "Neanderthal man" and the ancestors of "*Homo sapiens*." *Amer. Anthrop.* 45:39–48.

Weidenreich, F. 1947. Facts and speculations concerning the origin of *Homo sapiens*. *Amer. Anthrop.* 49:187–203.

Weidenreich, F. 1949. Interpretations of the fossil material, in: *Early Man in the Far East. A symposium.* Stud. Phys. Anthrop. 1:149–58, Wistar, Philadelphia.

Weiner, J. S., Oakley, K. P., and Clark, W. E. Le Gros. 1953. The solution of the Piltdown problem. *Bull. Brit. Mus. (Nat. Hist.), Geol.* 2(3):139–46.

Weiner, J. S., Clark, W. E. Le Gros, Oakley, K. P., Claringbull, G. F., Hey, M. H., Edmunds, F. H., Bowie, S. H. U., Davidson, C. F., Fryd, C. F. M., Baynes-Cope, A. D., Werner, A. E. A., and Plesters, R. J. 1955. Further contributions to the solution of the Piltdown problem. *Bull. Brit. Mus. (Nat. Hist.), Geol.* 2(6):225–287.

Weinert, H. 1932. *Ursprung der Menscheit*, Enke, Stuttgart.

Weinert, H. 1936. Der urmenschädel von Steinheim. *Z. Morph. Anthrop.* 35:463–518.

Weinert, H. 1951. *Stammesentwicklung der Menscheit* Vieweg, Braunschweig.

51

Early Upper Paleolithic Man and Late Middle Paleolithic Tools

D. S. Brose and M. H. Wolpoff

The relationship of Neandertals to *Homo sapiens* has always been of great interest to anthropologists. This work seeks to examine one hypothesis concerning the origin of anatomically modern *H. sapiens*, and to test the implications of this hypothesis against the archaeological and palaeontological record.

By "Neandertals," we refer to all hominid specimens dated within the time span from the end of Riss to the appearance of anatomically modern *H. sapiens*. Applying the term in this way is not unique to this work. Numerous authors have referred to this set of specimens as "Neandertaloid," "Neanderthalian," "Paleoanthropinae," and so on. In fact, this usage is synonomous in content with the "Neandertal Peoples" referred to by Howell (1957:342 and Fig. 4). The specimens are identical, and include the often disputed remains from Fontechevade—again following Howell (1957 341–342). Grouping the specimens in this way can be justified on two grounds. First, there is a gap between this group and *H. erectus*. This gap is temporal, rather than morphological, and is probably the result of sampling accidents. Nevertheless, there are only a very few specimens spanning the time from the well-represented *H. erectus* populations at terminal Mindel to the beginning of Riss. With the discovery of additional specimens from this period, the temporal gap will close, as the morphological and archaeological gap has already done. Second, there is a general unity of grade among the specimens so referred. Neandertals evince crania expanded to modern size and posterior teeth reduced to modern size, along with anterior teeth and supporting facial architecture maintained in the very robust *H. erectus* condition (Brace 1967a, 1968; Wolpoff 1969, 1971). In most cases, this morphological pattern separates Neandertals from groups occupying the same areas before as well as after them.

We distinguish this usage from the more restricted term: "classic" Neandertals. The later refers only to the people who inhabited Western and Southern Europe from the beginning of Wurm to the appearance of anatomically modern *H. sapiens* (Howell 1952, 1957; Breitinger 1955; Howells 1967; Le Gros Clark 1964; Hooton 1947; and many others). Thus, an important distinction is maintained throughout this work. The total group referred to as Neandertal consists of two smaller and mutually exclusive groups: "classic," and "non-classic." The distinction is crucial to the case we make, because almost every statement made concerning Neandertal morphology, variation,

archaeology, and evolution will, when applicable, be shown to apply to both "classic" and "non-classic" groups. Following a technique used by Howells (1967:190, footnote), the two Neandertal subgroups are also explicitly defined by listing included specimens.

Evidence of hominid morphology, culture, and stratigraphy has been used to substantiate or reject any number of hypotheses concerned with the relationship of Neandertals to anatomically modern *H. sapiens*. One of the earliest hypotheses suggests the sudden replacement of Neandertals by a more modern taxon: anatomically modern *H. sapiens*. A close examination of the "sudden replacement" hypothesis indicates that the claim was established for tools, and not for hominids. For instance, as recently as 1966 Le Gros Clark stated:

> At the end of the Mousterian phase of paleolithic culture, the Neandertal inhabitants of Europe were abruptly replaced by people of completely modern European type. There is reason to suppose that this new population, the Aurignacians, having developed their distinctive culture elsewhere, probably in Asia, migrated into Europe and, with their superior social organization, quickly displaced Mousterian man and occupied his territory [1966:116-117].

ABSOLUTE DATES OF LATE NEANDERTALS AND EARLY ANATOMICALLY MODERN *HOMO SAPIENS*

In actuality, the extent of the hiatus measured between the radiocarbon dates of the youngest clearly defined Neandertal and the oldest clearly defined anatomically modern *H. sapiens* specimens is not known with any certainty. Radiocarbon dates for this period of human evolution are neither extensive (Brace 1964; Oakley 1966) nor exceptionally accurate (Butzer 1964). The faunal connections between levels at the same site, let alone between sites, are more often than not incorrect (Kurten 1968). For these reasons, only dates taken from the actual strata where hominid specimens have been found can be used. Even so, the methodology of many earlier investigators, and the possibility of burial, leave even this association of dates with specimens subject to doubt.

The youngest dates directly associated with Neandertals (A2 dates according to Oakley 1966:7) come from three sour-

Reprinted with permission from *American Anthropologist*, Vol. 73, pp. 1156-1194. Copyright © 1971 by American Anthropological Association.

ces: Haua Fteah Layer XXXIII (McBurney 1967) with mandibles I and II has a date of 40,000±500 BP; Tabun Layer C is dated at 40,900±1000 BP and Layer B at 39,700±800 BP (Oakley 1966); La Quina Level H1 is dated at 35,250±530 BP (Oakley 1966). There is some question concerning the validity of the La Quina date as representing a late Neandertal. The hominid from Level H1 at La Quina is #14. This subject is represented by the posterior-inferior section of a left parietal (Henri-Martin 1923:242). The individual represented was a juvenile, and the level has a "final Mousterian" industry. A fragment of this size and age cannot be clearly categorized as either Neandertal or anatomically modern *H. sapiens* (Piveteau 1967). Even if the association with the date is good, we do not know what type of hominid is thus dated.

The earliest dated specimens of anatomically modern *H. sapiens* come from the Pavlovian burials at Dolni Vestonice (25,820±180 BP) and Pavlov (26,620±260), according to Oakley (1966). An earlier date has been claimed for the Niah cave specimen (Harrison 1959). However, this specimen represents a burial (Harrison 1964:526), and the date does not even come from the level where the specimen was found but rather was taken in a "corresponding" area (Ibid.:526). Without further substantiation, the association of this crucial date with the specimen cannot be unequivocally accepted (see Fitting 1969:351).

With so few dates from this important period, it is difficult to draw well substantiated conclusions from the evidence available. It is interesting that even these few dates from widely scattered areas indicate Neandertals precede anatomically modern *H. sapiens*. In no instance do either relative stratigraphies or absolute dates indicate anatomically modern *H. sapiens* contemporary with or preceding Neandertals in any area as would have to be the case if the former evolved somewhere separately and then "suddenly replaced" Neandertals all over the world.

MIDDLE PALEOLITHIC INDUSTRIES

Not only do the hominids show a specific sequence and temporal separation, but industries do also. Classically, the Wurm I/II interstadial is said to separate Middle and Upper Paleolithic industries. Wurm I/II is here used in the most standard sense rather than as in the more restricted French terminology where this period is known as Wurm II/III. This general time period has been called Gottweiger (although the type site seems to be Eemian): Paudorf; Arcy; Laufen; Rixdorf; Stillfried B; Molga-Sheksna; Hengelo-Denekamp; Bryansk; Odderade; or Aurignacian interstadial. While Pleistocene sequences in Europe have not been completely worked out, and while stratigraphic correlations are still uncertain, we might quote from one of the most recent geological monographs to the effect that

> (of the last glaciation) the Middle Wurm which covers the time between 53,000 BP and 25,000 BP is the part of which not very much is known. While some authors assume the existence of the "Gottweig Interstadial" others deny the possibility of a *notable* interstadial (in central Europe). Certainly the Middle Wurm was not a continuous cold time without any temperature oscillation, but one has to suppose the existence of cooler and warmer periods and of corresponding advances and retreats of the ice sheets [Woldstedt:1967; italics added].

Most prehistoric archaeologists and quarternary geologists have found evidence for a warmer period of interstadial magnitude, during the Middle Wurm (Flint 1957:381-412, Alimen 1967:211, de Jong 1967:359, Bordes 1968:147, Kurten 1968:20ff, Bastin 1969:3-11, Vergnaud-Grazzini and Herman-Rosenberg 1969:279-92, Zubakov 1969:Table Z). While the exact dates of these warm periods are not precisely fixed all seem to have occurred some time after 38,000 BP and were concluded by the outset of extremely cold glacial conditions some time after 28,000 BP. It is this "interstadial" which we are using as a temporal horizon in this paper.

Wherever continuous archaeological sequences spanning this period are clear there seems to be no overlap or obviously rapid replacement, but rather a gradual transition from late Middle Paleolithic to early Upper Paleolithic industries. This can be seen in a number of ways. The relative frequencies of various types of stone tools which characterize the Middle and Upper Paleolithic do not display sudden or dramatic changes during the Wurm I to Wurm II period or its geographical equivalent.

Most of the tool types which are considered characteristic of the Upper Paleolithic are present (albeit in lower frequencies) in late Middle Paleolithic assemblages.

The evidence on which the validity of this statement rests is presented by geographic area in the body of this paper. Numerous examples of supposedly characteristic Upper Paleolithic tool types (described by excavators intimately acquainted with the material) are seen in what can only be regarded as Middle Paleolithic assemblages. One way of visualizing this evidence is simply to list the common Upper Paleolithic tool types (as described by DeSonneville-Bordes and Perrot 1953) and note the extensive and repeated occurrences in a Middle Paleolithic context (see Table I). The occurrences identified in Table I are based on both functional and morphological analogies.

In other words, the variation between these tool types occurring at Middle Paleolithic and Upper Paleolithic sites is no greater than the variation among the tool types at Upper Paleolithic sites alone. Purely stylistic variation in functionally similar chipped stone tools has only rarely been identified by Paleolithic archaeologists. There is, however, considerable variation among the various Middle Paleolithic assemblages in the morphology of what are regarded as functionally equivalent tools, just as there is variation among the same "type" of tool found in the numerous Upper Paleolithic industries. Indeed there is a surprising amount of variation within any Middle or Upper Paleolithic assemblage in terms of the morphology of any "functional" tool type (viz. Bordes 1969). The definition of Paleolithic tool types generally depends on their function, as inferred from their morphology, rather than on their method of production (Bordes 1969:1-4).

The gradual frequency changes between Middle and Upper Paleolithic industries demonstrated here are based on such tool type identifications, made by those workers personally familiar with the material; in addition, we have also attempted to document the gradual changes in production techniques, an important, but separate problem. If we were unwilling to classify morphologically and functionally similar tools as members of the same general category, we would face the reduction that follows when we recognize that every individual chipped-stone

Table I. Partial list of Upper Paleolithic tools (standard list) in Middle Paleolithic contexts.*

Number	Standard Type	Middle Paleolithic Occurrences
1.	Simple end scraper	La Quina; Arcy-sur-Cure; Šipka cave; Külna Cave; Haua Fteah; Ordos
2.	Atypical end scraper	Repolust Cave; Weimar; Skhul
3.	Double end scraper	Peche de l'Aze (lower layers)
4.	Ogival end scraper	Repolust cave; Skhul; Ordos
5.	End scraper on retouched blade or flake	Šipka Cave; Külna Cave; Haua Fteah
6.	End scraper on Aurignacian blade	La Chapelle-aux-Saints; Haua Fteah
7.	Fan shaped end scraper	Ordos; Kokkinopilos
8.	Scraper on flake	All sites
9.	Round or circular scraper	Arcy-sur-Cure; Šipka Cave; Weimar
10.	Thumbnail scraper	Peche de l'Aze
11.	Carinated scraper	La Chapelle-aux-Saints; Repolust Cave; Haua Fteah
12.	Atypical carinated scraper	La Chapelle-aux-Saints; Haua Fteah; Ordos
13.	Thick-nosed scraper	Krapina; Repolust Cave; Weimar; Haua Fteah; Quafzeh (E)
14.	Flat-nosed or shouldered scraper	
15.	Core scraper	Šipka Cave; Külna Cave; Weimar; Ordos
16.	Plane (rabot)	
17.	Scraper-graver	
18.	Scraper-truncated blade	El Wad (F)
19.	Graver-truncated blade	Skuhl; Ordos
20.	Borer-truncated blade	Šipka cave; Weimar; Peche de l'Aze II
21.	Borer-scraper	
22.	Borer-graver	
23.	Borer	Külna Cave; Šipka Cave; Weimar; El Wad; Ordos
24.	Atypical borer or beak	Arcy-sur-Cure; Ordos
25.	Multiple borer or beak	
26.	Micro-borer	Haua Fteah; Peche de l'Aze
27.	Straight dihedral graver	Arcy-sur-Cure; Krapina; Peche de l'Aze II
28.	Lopsided dihedral graver	Krapina
29.	Angle dihedral graver	Ordos
30.	Angle dihedral graver on broken blade or flake	Skhul; Abou-Sif
31.	Multiple dihedral graver	Peche de l'Aze II
32.	Busked graver	Quafzeh (E)
33.	Parrot-beak graver	Krapina; Weimar; Haua Fteah
34.	Graver on straight truncation	Arcy-sur-Cure
35.	Graver on oblique truncation	Repolust Cave; Ordos
36.	Graver on concave truncation	
37.	Graver on convex truncation	Krapina
38.	Transverse graver on lateral retouch	Tabun (B)
39.	Transverse graver on notch	
40.	Multiple graver on truncation	
41.	Mixed multiple graver	
42.	Noailles graver	
43.	Graver on core	Arcy-sur-Cure; Repolust Cave; Weimar; Ordos
44.	Flat graver	Kokkinopilos

tool is in some way different than every other chipped-stone tool in the world.

These considerations are readily apparent in the works of many authors with first hand knowledge of the technologies. For instance, Movius (1969:122) has noted for central France, the "Maginot Line" of the purported invasion, that:

> The Chatelperronian of the Grotte du Renne at Arcy-sur-Cure gives the impression of an assemblage which basically remains Middle Paleolithic on evidence of the majority of the flint tools, but is Upper Paleolithic in terms of the technology and style of the pieces.

The variations in relative frequency which do occur in the period from Wurm I to Wurm II seem no greater than differences between what Bordes has demonstrated (1955, 1961, 1968) to be several contemporaneous Mousterian facies in a single geographic area. The same situation seems also to exist in Eastern Europe (Klein 1969:262-264).

At the same time artifacts considered "typical" of the Middle Paleolithic continue with diminished frequency well into late Upper Paleolithic assemblages. Because of this fact industries or assemblages which can be considered "transitional" between Middle and Upper Paleolithic may or may not be segregated from the continuum, as the investigator's theoretical viewpoint dictates. This situation seems to occur in all areas of the Old World.

Throughout the following discussion of lithic assemblages problems of taxonomic nomenclature occur. In attempting to demonstrate the variability of these industries, the question constantly arises as to whether some particular manifestation should be properly considered Middle Paleolithic. Several solutions present themselves. First, all the assemblages discussed have been called Middle Paleolithic, or the equivalent, by the original investigators; an assignment which never has been seriously questioned. Second, these assemblages occur in a stratigraphic context indicating deposition no earlier than late Riss or Riss/Wurm, and no later than the end of those Middle Wurm "interstadial" oscillations which began about 38,000 BP.

Finally, most if not all of these lithic assemblages, although displaying great internal variability, display some degree of uniformity in terms of some proportion of the manufacturing techniques employed, or some of the tools produced. That is, typologically, as well as chronologically and *authoritatively*, the industries discussed herein may all be justifiably considered Middle Paleolithic.

Table I. (cont.)

Number	Standard Type	Middle Paleolithic Occurrences
45.	Audi knife	Abri Audi; La Quina; Regourdou
46.	Chatelperron point	Haua Fteah; Quafzeh; Ksar Akil; Peche de l'Aze
47.	Atypical Chatelperron point	Haua Fteah
48.	Gravette point	
49.	Atypical Gravette point	
50.	Micro gravette	Haua Fteah
51.	Vachoas point	
52.	Fort-Yves point	
53.	Humped pieces	All sites
54.	Flechette (dart)	Ksar Akil
55.	Tanged point	Krapina; Haua Fteah; Emireh; Quafzeh
56.	Atypical shouldered Perigoidean point	
57.	Shouldered piece	Haua Fteah
58.	Blade with continuous retouch	Arcy-sur-Cure; Abou-Sif; La Chapelle-aux-Saints; Peche de l'Aze; Kiik-koba; Molodova; Haua Fteah
59.	Blade with non-continuous retouch	Arcy-sur-Cure; Starosel'e; Molodova; Haua Fteah; Abou-Sif
60.	Piece with straight truncation	Krapina; Weimar; Ordos
61.	Piece with oblique truncation	Ordos
62.	Piece with concave truncation	Haua Fteah
63.	Piece with convex truncation	Haua Fteah; Ordos
64.	Piece with double truncation	
65.	Blade with continuous retouch on one edge	Nietoperzowa Cave; Molodova; Haua Fteah; Ordos; Quafzeh (E); Tabun
66.	Blade with continuous retouch on both edges	Starosel'e; Ksar Akil; Ordos; Peche de l'Aze
67.	Aurignacian blade	La Chapelle-aux-Saints; Kiik-koba; Tabun (B)
68.	Notched or strangled blade	Haua Fteah
69	Point with plane face (Solutrean)	Šipka Cave; Külna Cave; Lovas Cave; Krapina; Nietoperzowa Cave; Weimar; Salzgitter
70.	Laurel Leaf Point (Solutrean)	Lovas Cave; Krapina; Weimar; Salzgitter; Mauren Cave

*References by geographical area in text.

Western Europe

The common Middle Paleolithic industries of Western Europe are termed Mousterian. Bordes (1953, 1961) has clearly shown that this is not a homogeneous lithic assemblage but rather a number of facies each of which contains more or less the same types of tools but in quite different frequencies. The differences between these Mousterian facies are not chronological but rather seem to be functional (Binford and Binford 1966, 1969). In all of these assemblages numerous tool types occur which are generally considered characteristic of the early Upper Paleolithic (de Sonneville-Bordes 1963). In conjunction with Table I, it is significant that out of the standard list of sixty-two Lower and Middle Paleolithic tool types (Bordes 1953, 1955, 1961), over twenty-five percent (nos. 30-39, 42, 44, 52-54, 57, 63) are also characteristic of the Upper Paleolithic assemblages where they appear in relatively high frequency. Even in good Mousterian contexts these "Upper Paleolithic" end scrapers, burins, gravers, and backed blades may comprise a significant proportion of the tools. At Le Moustier they comprise twelve percent of the total lithic assemblage. At Pech-de-l'Aze (Level 4) they approach twenty percent of the total assemblage (Vandermeersch 1965). At La Chappelle-aux-Saints the industry is characterized as LaQuina Mousterian within which there existed a number of "Aurignacian" elements such as thin retouched blades, carinated end scrapers, and long, possibly pressure-flaked blades (Bardon and Bouyssonie 1908).

Bordes (1961:810) has noted that "in some Mousterian assemblages blades compromise up to forty percent of the debitage." In this quotation, Bordes did not specify the type of blades referred to. "Blade" is generally defined as any flake the length of which is greater than twice its width or as a long, thin, parallel-sided flake. Blades can be more precisely defined by their method of manufacture: either soft-hammer direct percussion, hard-hammer direct percussion, indirect percussion (punched), or pressure-flaked. Any of these may or may not have been struck from prepared cores of various types (Jelinek 1965). All of these production techniques have been employed with differing frequency in both Middle and Upper Paleolithic industries (Bordes 1968:242). No single archaeological assemblage regularly displays all of these techniques. While the presence of some sorts of blades, or tools made on the blades, is quite common at Upper Paleolithic sites, there are numerous Upper Paleolithic examples where functionally similar tools do not appear to have been produced by any particular "blade" techniques. Conversely, there are Middle Paleolithic sites which show the presence of blades produced by all of these techniques. If confusion is to be avoided, terms like "Mousterian Blades" and "Upper Paleolithic Blades" must be replaced by the well-defined descriptive terms based on methods of production or by detailed metric analyses of blade morphology.

Bone tools, long considered the *sine qua non* of the Upper Paleolithic also occur with some consistency at numerous Mousterian sites. In some cases these Middle Paleolithic bone tools appear morphologically and functionally indistinguishable from some Upper Paleolithic bone tool types (e.g., the bevel-base points from the Perigordian levels at Arcy-sur-Cure are identical to bevel-base bone points from the lower Middle Paleolithic layers [LeRoi-Gourhan 1961; Bordes 1968]; numerous other examples are cited in the Eastern Europe section). More important is the fact that no two Upper Paleolithic "cultures" or "traditions" have the same kinds of bone tools. Indeed the sequential stages of a single Upper Paleolithic "culture" are frequently defined by morphological changes in bone tools. Because of the stylistic dissimilarity of bone artifacts throughout the upper Paleolithic the traditional viewpoint had considered the presence of any type of well-made bone tool in any frequency as an indication of Upper Paleolithic affinity (Oakley 1962:27, 93-98, Burkitt 1963:79, Braidwood 1966:80). While Collie's statement (1928:50) that bone tools, as such, first appear in the Aurignacian, is not the latest word on the subject, it still appears reasonable to many. It is to this hypothesis we have addressed our arguments.

At Gibraltar Dorothy Garrod recovered two fragmentary bone artifacts either of which may have been points (1928:50, Fig. 6). Henri-Martin (1923:Figs.4, 8) noted the presence of a number of bone implements in the upper levels of La Quina. In England the Pin Hole cave contained a large number of ulnar bones awls and polished split bone points from both Middle Paleolithic and Aurignacian levels (Kitching 1963). At Arcy-sur-Cure LeRoi-Gourhan (1961:1-16) has excavated a "post-Mousterian" Mousterian level containing bevel-base bone points associated with a denticulate-looking Mousterian industry containing backed blades and burins. Movius (1969:112) has recently characterized the deposits from the Grotte du Renne at Arcy-sur-Cure as definitive evidence for the continuity between Mousterian and Chatelperronian.

In addition to the Chatelperronian at Arcy-sur-Cure, numerous other western European sites evince this transitional industry. A partial list of these sites includes Chatelperron, Combe Capelle, Les Cottes, La Ferrassie (E), Cueva Morin, Trou de la Chevre, Roc de Combe (Lot), Grotte d'Fees, and Reclau-Viver (de Sonneville-Bordes 1963; Freeman and Gonzalez-Echegaray 1970; Bordes 1968; Pradel 1966). As Bordes has recently observed, "it becomes more and more difficult to avoid the conclusion that this lower Perigordian is derived from a local development of an Acheulean-tradition Mousterian" (1968:148).

As early as 1956 Bordes noted the lack of any real hiatus between the Middle and Upper Paleolithic and stated that the Lower Perigordian represented a typologically traditional industry in western Europe. He also claimed that the hiatus between Mousterian and Aurignacian was less evident than imagined (1958:176-179). Indeed, Pradel's excavations at Les Cottes (Bordes 1968:150-153) and Le Fontenioux (Bordes, personal communication) seem to demonstrate the development of the Upper Perigordian from the Lower Perigordian, and Bordes has seen characteristic Aurignacian tool types in the La Quina Mousterian (1968:155-156) although he feels the centers of the Aurignacian development were not in southwestern France. More recently Movius (1969:117) has discussed this period and noted clear stylistic continuities between the Lower Perigordian and the Early Aurignacian.

Eastern Europe

The Middle Paleolithic industries of Eastern Europe cover a much larger geographical area than do those of Western Europe and correspondingly greater differences exist among them. Valoch (1968) has recently characterized a number of more-or-less chronological and regional varieties not all of which can be correlated with Bordes' Mousterian facies. The closest parallels seem to occur in south-central Europe (Valoch 1968) where the Middle Paleolithic industries approach the Denticulate and Charentian facies of France. At the Kulna cave (Level 7a) in Moravia (Jelinek 1969:479) there is an industry associated with a hominid jaw which seems to be like Mousterian of Acheulean Tradition B where "quartzite implements of the Mousterian type prevail, however, here and there were also found Acheulean implements as well as a few approaching the type of tools found in Upper Paleolithic cultures" (Jelinek 1966:701).

At the Sipka cave in Moravia, Maska reported an early Wurm industry with a high frequency of denticulate scrapers containing a large number of end scrapers, burins, and borers (Valoch 1968:356). The apparently contemporary Szletian industries of Hungary and circum-Carpathian central Europe contain a good proportion of true blades but many more flake tools, some showing the Levallois technique. Associated with these are "Upper Paleolithic" forms such as dorsally retouched end scrapers, carinated (Aurignacian) scrapers, simple burins and borers, and a large number of leaf-shaped points ranging from crude unifacial to fine bifacial retouch. At some Szletian sites (such as Lovas in Hungary) bone tools also occur (Valoch 1968:358). The latest of these manifestations seem to be stratigraphically dated to a moist cool period around 38,000 B.P. In this area the Lower Aurignacian (Gravettian) is similar to the early Aurignacian of France but contains up to twenty-five percent of Mousterian forms such as side-scrapers and points. The upper stages of these industries (dated to 31,840±250 B.P. at Willendorf II) are lithically quite similar but contain greater frequencies of split base and lozenge section bone points and awls (Valoch 1968:359).

As Jelinek noted (1969:484) the human burials at Predmosti are clearly E. Gravettian (e.g., red ocher burials, fired clay figures, mammoth ivory carving), but they are associated with "a stone industry in which numerous tools belong typologically to the traditions of the Mousterian, Acheulean, and even pebble tool cultures. This variability is reflected at the same time in the many Mousterian sites, both in Czechoslovakia and elsewhere in central and eastern Europe, that are regarded as atypical in containing indications of Upper Paleolithic blade tool types." From the Croatian site of Krapina, Gorjanovic-Kramberger (1913) has illustrated plano-convex bifacially flaked points (Plate V, Figs. 11-13), piercers (Plate VI, Figs. 6-8), graves (Plate IX, Figs. 1-7; Plate X, Figs. 1-5), natural and backed-blade knives (Plate X, Figs. 7-10), basally thinned bifacially worked points (Plate VIII, Figs. 4, 5) along with a large number of discs, scrapers and flake tools. The site also yielded several bone tools among which were two odd split-base bone points (Gorjanovic-Kramberger 1913; Plate XIII, Figs. 1, 2).

According to Wobst (1970:455) "a good case can be made for *in situ* evolution from Middle to Upper Paleolithic" in Slovakia. He reasons that the increased percentage of Upper Paleolithic tools in late Mousterian and the decreasing frequencies of Middle Paleolithic tools in the early Upper Paleolithic preclude the possibility of a "sudden immigration." The excellent evidence for a gradual change in activities, underlying the transition from Middle to Upper Paleolithic is based on the good preservation of interstadial open-air sites in numerous places.

Elsewhere in central Europe, the Repolust cave in Austria has a Middle Paleolithic industry which (on the basis of faunal evidence), may be as early as late Riss/Wurm. This industry is characterized by a high frequency of denticulates but also distinct end scrapers and oblique burins (Mottl 1951). From Thuringia in middle Germany there are several examples of a Middle Paleolithic industry containing Mousterian side scrapers and limaces, numerous unifacially and bifacially retouched points, end scrapers, burins, and borers (Behm-Blanke 1960). Valoch has noted that the Nietoperzowa cave in Galicia contained a Middle Paleolithic industry with leaf-shaped points mostly on blades which is as early as 38,000 BP (1968:358). In northern Germany at the site of Salzgitter-

Lebenstedt an industry characterized as Levalloisian Mousterian of Acheulean tradition contained bifacially retouched points, "Clactonian flakes," and a large number of bone and antler tools including "barbed" or split-base points. The site dates by radiocarbon to a slightly warmer period in early Wurm at 55,000 BP (Tode, *et al.* 1953).

In his summary of the Mousterian of European Russia, Klein (1969) has indicated both the sophistication of the cultural adaptations involved in the exploitation of this ecologically diverse area and the high degree of lithic variability which these Middle Paleolithic industries exhibit. Sites such as Starosel'e, Kiik-Koba and Molodova yield burins, end scrapers, and backed blades, although in low frequencies (Ibid.:261, Fig. 4). Klein also indicates the occurrence of some amount of worked bone in these Mousterian assemblages (Ibid.:264).

Within central and eastern Europe the Szletian is sometimes recognized as an example of an industry typologically transitional from Middle to Upper Paleolithic (Valoch 1968:358-359), but even in other traditions most of the tools characteristic of the Upper Paleolithic are clearly present in lower frequencies in the Middle Paleolithic.

North Africa

In north Africa, numerous sites have produced evidence for Middle Paleolithic Levalloiso-Mousterian industrial facies closely akin to those of France (McBurney 1960:129, 135; Bordes 1968:121-122). Many of these contain implements characteristic of the Aterian (equated with early Upper Paleolithic of Europe). The most thoroughly reported site in North Africa is the Haua Fteah of Cyrenacian Lybia. Here the levels deposited during early Wurm (Layers XXXV-XXIX) contain an industry typical of the local Levalloiso-Mousterian (called "evolved Hybrid-Mousterian," McBurney 1967:108-131). The succeeding levels are quite similar to this Levalloiso-Mousterian but include end scrapers on blades, several varieties of small retouched blades, flake awls, carinated scrapers, Chatelperron knives, and an "unexpectedly high lamellar element...approaching a true blade industry" (McBurney 1967:113). McBurney goes on to add "as a whole, this assemblage is characterized by a curious mixture of evolved Levalloiso-Mousterian elements (especially in the technique of primary flaking) and traits which are frankly Upper Paleolithic in their affinities" (1967:113). From the interface of Layers XXXIV/XXXIII two Neandertal mandibles were recovered and have been radiocarbon dated to 40,700±500 BP. Overlying these hominid remains are layers which seem to be rather normal Levalloiso-Mousterian (XXXII/XXXI), and above these, a series of layers (XXVII/XXXI) deposited at the end of early Wurm and containing again a number of assemblages with "Aterian" and "Upper Paleolithic" elements. The conclusion we reach, opposed to that given by McBurney, would clearly seem to be that in North Africa many of the late Levalloiso-Mousterian assemblages contain large numbers of tools characteristic of the local early Upper Paleolithic and of the later Emiran of the Near East (Garrod 1962).

The Near East

In the Levant, Perrot recognizes several "phyla" of Mousterian (1968:342), most of which are similar to the Levalloisian Mousterian facies of France but which have a relatively high frequency of blades, knives, gravers, and burins. Most common, however, is the Levalloiso-Mousterian (which is seen in the early Wurm equivalent in the Levant) which is characterized by a few denticulate tools (1968:346-349). The early Levalloiso-Mousterian levels at many interior sites in the Jordan River-Mount Carmel area shows clear affinities to the coastal sites such as Ras-el-kelb and Chekka where early Mousterian is correlated by beaches to the period just post-Riss/Wurm (Howell 1959:18-19; Perrot 1968:352-356). In the mountain wadi shelters these Mousterian deposits show industrial facies possibly reflecting functional differences (Howell 1959:19; Binford and Binford 1969). At Skhul the hominid remains from Level B were associated with a Levalloiso-Mousterian containing a few burins (Howell 1959:20). Similar assemblages occur mixed within the four meters of Mousterian deposits above Level L (with associated hominid remains) at Quafzeh (Howell 1959:13, 20-21). Perrot notes that it is difficult to determine just when the change from this Middle Paleolithic to the Upper Paleolithic occurs. Numerous sites yield transitional industrial assemblages throughout the area. At Quafzeh (Level E) and Ksar Akil above a number of good Levalloiso-Mousterian layers are levels which contain a large proportion of elongated Mousterian points and side scrapers but which also contain blade tools and "Chatelperron knives" associated with Levallois cores, Mousterian disc cores and prismatic blade cores (Perrot 1968:354-355). The "type-fossil" of this horizon (Garrod 1962) is the Emirah point. Both Bordes and Perrot feel these points are similar to the thinned Levalloisian points found as early as Level D at Shanidar in a late Levalloiso-Mousterian context (Perrot 1968; Bordes 1968). At any rate, it is clear that at sites such as Quafzeh (Level E), Ksar Akil, Tabun (Level B), Emirah, and El Wad (Level F) an evolved Levalloiso-Mousterian with thinned points, blade tools, prismatic cores, and backed knives exists.

Following these components are a number of levels with fewer of the "typical Mousterian" scrapers and points and with a higher frequency of gravers, retouched blades, and Chatelperron knives. The Emirah point is absent but burins (especially dihedral and busked burins), gravers on thick flakes, end-of-blade scrapers and carinated scrapers appear in great numbers "announcing the following 'Aurignacian' which has an even greater increase in retouched blades and points, burins, and gravers, and split-base bone points" (Perrot 1968:355). South of Shanidar in the Khorrambad valley the Kunji cave yields a Mousterian assemblage with Mousterian points and scrapers as well as blades but no evidence of Levalloisian technique (*senso stricto*). These levels are dated greater than 40,000 BP (Hole and Flannery 1968).

The earliest true Upper Paleolithic industrial assemblages (Neuville's stage III) occur at Quafzeh (Level D). Ksar Akil (Levels from seven to twelve meters with the twelve-meter level dating at 28,000 BP), Erg et Akmar (Levels E and F), Jabrud Shelter II (Levels 6 and 7), and Shanidar (Level C, dated at 29,000-26,000 BP). These clearly postdate transitional hominid populations. In the Near East it seems that the archaeological evidence, even when based only upon lithic assemblages, will not support any view of a rapid replacement of Middle by Upper Paleolithic either in terms of the morphological attributes of the tools themselves or their method of manufacture (cf. Binford 1968:707-708, 715). As Howell

(1959:40) concluded in an intensive review of the area, "The first recognized stage (1) of the Upper Paleolithic of Southwestern Asia had its roots in the local Mousterian (of Levallois facies)."

Asia

From Shanidar east the Middle Paleolithic is poorly understood (Ivanova 1969). At the site of Dara-i-kure a rock shelter in Afghanistan (Dupree, Lattman, and Davis 1970) Dupree (1969:492) describes a Middle Paleolithic assemblage with Levallois flakes, Mousterian points, large side scrapers, cleavers, flake hand axes, and tortoise cores, as well as flake blades and possible combination tools such as burin-points and burin-end-scrapers. At Teshik-Tash in Uzbekistan a rather generalized Mousterian is associated with an adolescent burial (Okladnikov et al. 1949), while at Kiik-Kova in the Crimea a Mousterian industry contained Levallois flakes, disc cores, and bone points (Mongait 1961:82). Mousterian assemblages have been found at numerous localities in China but are undated for the most part. A late site from the Ordos area which yielded several hominid cranial fragments contained an industry which was reanalyzed by the Bordes and is described by F. Bordes (1968:130) as a "Levallois-Technique Mousterian, with blades well represented (31%), 27% scrapers, 16.6% denticulates, 28% implements of Upper Paleolithic type (end-scrapers, burins, borers, occasional backed knives flakes and truncated blades) a few poor hand axes...discs, bladelets.... The impression given is in fact that of a very evolved Mousterian in the process of transition to an Upper Paleolithic stage. . . ."

Archaeological Summary

This brief review of the archaeological sequences clearly indicates several important facts. First and most evident, is the continuity which exists throughout the Old World between Middle and Upper Paleolithic industries.

Given the presence of local transitional industries throughout the Old World, indicated by the data discussed, the interpretation of "sudden replacement" *anywhere* in the Old World becomes both logically improbable and increasingly difficult to verify.

An Upper Paleolithic assemblage directly overlying a Middle Paleolithic assemblage is a common occurrence throughout the Old World, and indicates the relative chronological position of the two occupations. While the Middle Paleolithic is obviously not the same as the Upper Paleolithic, we have described numerous archaeological assemblages which can be considered typologically transitional between the two on a morphological-functional basis. We have also tried to indicate the artificiality of the traditional distinction between Middle and Upper Paleolithic archaeological assemblages, resting as it does upon arbitrary cut-off points in relative frequencies of particular types of stone tools present in both, or upon the purported presence or absence of worked bone tools.

In any area, demonstrating the total and rapid replacement of one tradition or archaeological complex by another requires that no transitional industries exist locally. We have found overwhelming evidence for local transitional industries everywhere Middle Paleolithic industries occur. While we have no doubt been guilty of overlooking numerous relevant publications, it is difficult to imagine what kinds of sources could be used to argue against the interpretation of gradual transition.

Finally, we would note that the Middle Paleolithic is characterized for the first time, by *significant* numbers of special purpose tools. Many of these—borers, gravers, burins, and numerous others—indicate that these functional types were not neglected until the Upper Paleolithic. In addition, a large number of characteristic types of bone tools so often diagnostic of the early Upper Paleolithic facies, have a clear prototype in the Middle Paleolithic.

THE ORIGIN OF ANATOMICALLY MODERN *HOMO SAPIENS*

Morphological evidence, too, indicates the continuity between Neandertals and anatomically modern *H. sapiens*. This continuity has been established for *all* Neandertal populations—even the "classic" Neandertals of glaciated Western Europe—by numerous authors in a series of publications spanning almost a century (Arambourg 1958; Brace 1962b, 1964, 1967c, 1968; Coon 1962; Fraipont and Lohest 1887; Gorjanovic-Kramberger 1906; Hrdlicka 1927, 1930; Jelinek 1969; Pouliancs 1969; Schwalbe 1901, 1914; Tobias 1964; Verneau 1924; Weidenreich 1940, 1947; Weinert 1925, 1936, 1944; Yakimov 1969). We propose that transitions in hominid morphology precede the established changes in hominid industries.

While Upper Paleolithic industries are always associated with anatomically modern *H. sapiens*, the converse is not necessarily true. Anatomically modern *H. sapiens* apparently arises from a Neandertal ancestor still associated with Middle Paleolithic industries. Thus, the earliest anatomically modern *H. sapiens* should be found with Middle Paleolithic cultural material. The earliest clearly dated specimens of anatomically modern *H. sapiens* are associated with an Upper Paleolithic industry, and not a particularly early one. However there are two lines of evidence indicating the *in situ* evolution of anatomically modern *H. sapiens* from Neandertal populations associated with Middle Paleolithic industries.

NEANDERTAL MORPHOLOGICAL VARIATION AND VARIABILITY

The first line of evidence stems from the variability within the Neandertal populations themselves. Neandertals, contrary to the opinion of many authors (Sergi 1958a; Coon 1962; Howell 1952, 1957; Breitinger 1955), had a high degree of both inter and intrapopulation variability (Brace 1962b). Witness the extent of difference among the so-called "classic" specimens from Le Moustier (Weinert 1925), La Ferrassie 1 (Hrdlicka 1930; Boule 1913), La Ferrassie 2 (Captain and Peyrony 1912a; Boule 1913; Heim 1968), and Monte Circeo (Sergi 1940), let alone among other Neandertals such as Mapa (Woo and Peng 1959), Broken Hill (Morant 1928), and Omo 2 (Leakey, Butzer, and Day 1969). Indeed, the normal variability within Neandertal populations is so great that almost every time more than one specimen is found at a single site, "hybridization" is the only explanation deemed sufficient by many to explain the extensive variation among the specimens. Such an explanation has been suggested for the material from Krapina (Gorjanovic-Kramberger 1910; Klaatsch 1923), Quafzeh (Thoma 1965:139), and Skhul (Hooton 1947:336-338; Weckler 1954:1014-1015;

Thoma 1958): three of the four Neandertal sites with the remains of more than ten individuals.

A brief perusal of the literature shows that at almost every site with more than one Neandertal specimen, whether "classic" Neandertals or "Neandertals" in the broader sense used here, an extensive amount of variation has been recognized by, among others, the authors who worked with the original material. In addition to those already discussed, skeletal variation which is at least as great as the variation found in small samples of extant populations, hominid or pongid, has been described at the following sites: La Ferrassie (Hrdlicka 1930; Brace 1962b; Captain and Peyrony 1909, 1912a, 1912b, 1921; Boule 1913; Piveteau 1969; Heim 1968), Ehringsdorf (Behm-Blancke 1960; Jelinek 1969; Virchow 1920; Weidenreich 1928; Kleinschmidt 1931), Spy (Morant 1927a; Fraipont and Lohest 1887; Brace 1968), Broken Hill (Wells 1947); Arcy-Sur-Cure (Leroi-Gourhan 1958); Solo (von Koenigswald 1958; Weidenreich 1951), Saccopastore (Howell 1960), Shanidar (Stewart 1958, 1961, 1963), Jebel Irhound (Ennouchi 1962, 1968, 1969), Subaluk (Kadic *et al.* 1933), and others.

The idea that "classic" Neandertals were particularly lacking in variability has implied, to many, that they were under the influence of extremely strong selection. In the words of Coon (1963:509), "They are in fact so homogenous that a strong selective agency must have been pruning off deviant individuals."

The evidence simply does not support this statement for either "classic" Neandertal specimens or all Neandertal specimens taken together. The coefficient of variation (CV), an index of the standard deviation divided by the mean, provides a convenient way of comparing variability between samples with different means. Coefficients of variation were calculated for the ten cranial measurements given in Table II. A number of samples were utilized in this comparison of Neandertals to chimpanzees, gorillas, and extant populations. The extant *H. sapiens* populations include Andamanese (Sullivan 1921), Australian aborigines (Morant 1927b), Negroes from both Congo and Gaboon areas (Benington 1911), prehistoric Naquada (Morant 1924), a sample from Harappa in India (Gupta, Dutta, and Basu 1962), Moriori (Thomson 1916), a sample from Egyptian dynasties XXVI through XXX (Pearson and Davin 1926), Lower Yukon River Eskimos (Hrdlicka 1942), and Carinthians (Shapiro 1929).

We have sorted the Neandertal sample into "classic" and "non-classic" groups in as conservative a manner as possible. That is, we have only identified as "classic" those specimens to which all other authors would agree on the basis of geographic associations, stratigraphic position, and skeletal morphology (see Howell 1952:378-379). Discovering extensive variability in this restricted sample becomes all-the-more important. Including a wider geographic or temporal range of specimens, or using individuals which workers in disagreement with our hypothesis would question, would increase the observed variation even further but at the same time cover up the meaning and importance of the variation—its range and its form—in the restricted "classic" Neandertal sample.

Measurements for the Solo sample, a "tropical" Neandertal group, were taken from publications by Weidenreich (1951) and von Koenigswald (1958). The site may be as old as the Eemian interglacial (Howell 1967:489). The "classic" Neandertals utilized in these calculations (following Howell 1967), include

Spy I and II (Morant 1927a; Fraiport and Lohest 1887), Gibraltar (Sollas 1908), La Quina 5 (Henri-Martin 1923), Le Moustier (Weinert 1925), Petralona (Kokkoros and Kannelis 1960; Poulianos 1966; Kannelis and Savas 1964), La Chapelle (Boule 1913; Morant 1927a), La Ferrassie 1 (Boule 1913; Coon 1963), Neandertal (Morant 1927a), and Monte Circeo (Sergi 1940). Other Neandertals, included with all of the above in the "total" sample, consist of both Wurm specimens from outside of Southern and Western Europe and pre-Wurm specimens from all areas. These are as follows: Broken Hill (Morant 1928), Saldahna (Singer 1954) Omo 2 (Leakey, Butzer, and Day 1969), Djebel Irhound 1 (Ennouchi 1962) and 2 (Ennouchi 1968), Galilee (Morant 1927a), Shanidar I (Stewart 1958), Sala (Vlcek 1965), Tabun 1 (McCown and Keith 1939), Saccopastore 1 (Sergi 1944) and 2 (Sergi 1948), Ehringsdorf H (Kleinschmidt 1931), Fontechavade 2 (Vallois 1958), Ganovce (Vlcek 1955), Krapina crania C and E (Gorjanovic-Kramberger 1906) as well as D (Schaefer 1964), Djebel Quafzeh 6 (Coon 1962; Boule and Vallois 1957), Amud (Suzuki 1965 and 1968), and Skhul 4, 5, 6, and 9 (McCown and Keith 1939). While additional comparisons could have been made with Steinheim (Weinert 1936; Howell 1960) and Swanscombe (Morant 1930), both the morphological position (Brace 1962b, 1964; Sergi 1958a; Stewart 1960; Weinert 1936) and the stratigraphic position (Howell 1960, 1967) of these specimens are clearly transitional between *H. erectus* and the Neandertals. The Upper Paleolithic sample was taken largely from Morant (1925, 1930), Matiegka (1938), Maska (1889), Werth (1928), Jelinek (1964) and von Bonin (1935).

Finally, the pongid samples were measured by Wolpoff. Specimens were obtained at the Field Museum in Chicago, the American Museum in New York, and from the Hamann-Todd collection at Case Western Reserve University and the Cleveland Museum of Natural Science. Length, breadth, and height measurements of the vault, disregarding crests and tori, were taken using techniques and measuring points suggested by Randall (1943-1944). In addition, nasion was defined on these primates according to Randall (1943-1944). These procedures were followed in order to make the pongid-hominid measurements as comparable as possible.

In six of the nine comparable measurements the "classic" Neandertals are either as variable or more variable than the total Neandertal sample, although the latter includes a far wider geographic area, and spans a greater time. Such extensive variation in a sample all authors recognize as "classic" renders "hybridization" explanations of "non-classic" Neandertal samples unnecessary. It denies support to the idea that "classic" Neandertals were under the influence of strong selective pressures which ultimately lead to their extinction. Finally, the extensive variation evinced by the "classic" sample specifically suggests climatic adaptation. This sample, spread across the climatic extremes of partially glaciated Europe, shows the greatest variation, and the greatest difference in variation compared with all Neandertals, in nasal breadth—a feature closely tied with respiratory adaptations to cold climates (Wolpoff 1968).

The "classic" Neandertals are more variable in most features than any extant group. The most similar sample of anatomically modern *H. sapiens* is, as one could well expect, the Upper Paleolithic Europeans (Schlaginhaufen 1946). Concomitantly, coefficients of variation for the latter sample and all

Table II. Mean (M) and Coefficient of Variation (CV) of Cranial Dimensions for Hominid Groups (mm) Discussed in this study.

Group		Cranial Capacity	Cranial Length	Cranial Breadth	Cranial Height	Nasion-basion	Upper Facial Height	Nasal Height	Nasal Breadth	Bizygomatic Breadth	Foramen Magnum Area
Solo Neandertals	(M)	1154	202	149	123	113					1383
	(CV)	7.3	4.8	3.6	3.9						
"Classic" Neandertals	(M)	1399	200	150	126	118	86	59	32.2	143	1374
	(CV)	10.4	2.9	4.7	5.4	6.7	8.2	8.9	11.6	6.6	
All Neandertals	(M)	1342	200	148	123	112	84	58	31.5	144	1223
	(CV)	12.6	4.2	4.4	5.4	6.6	9.2	7.7	8.5	6.3	12.8
Upper Paleolithic Europeans	(M)		191	140	134	102	68	50	26.0	135	1145
	(CV)		4.4	3.9	3.2	6.2	7.6	8.4	9.2	7.5	12.8
Andamanese	(M)	1199	163	134	127	92	59	45	22.9	122	880
	(CV)	8.8	4.2	3.2	4.0	4.0	6.8	6.9	6.8	4.7	
Australian Aborigines	(M)	1248	184	131	131	100	65	48	26.5	130	1026
	(CV)	8.2	3.6	3.7	4.0	4.2	6.3	6.3	7.4	4.7	10.7
Congo Negroes	(M)	1301	176	136	132	96	62	46	25.7	125	1056
	(CV)	9.4	3.5	4.5	3.6	4.7	8.2	6.4	7.9	5.5	11.1
Gaboon Negroes	(M)	1311	176	133	133	98	65	47	25.7	125	1021
	(CV)	10.3	3.5	3.6	4.5	4.2	9.0	6.8	8.3	4.9	12.2
Prehistoric Naqada	(M)	1326	181	133	132	97	67	48	24.6	121	1051
	(CV)	7.7	3.2	3.5	4.0	4.9	6.9	6.8	7.9	4.8	
Harappa	(M)	1340	181	133	130		65	48	25.0	125	
	(CV)	8.4	5.0	5.2	5.7		10.9	10.9	6.1	6.7	
Morioi	(M)	1376	183	141	134	104	74	56	25.0	133	1080
	(CV)	8.2	3.7	3.3	3.5	4.7	6.5	6.4	6.2	5.7	10.8
Egyptian dynasties XXVI–XXX	(M)	1386	182	138	132	100	69	51	24.0	127	1035
	(CV)	7.9	3.1	3.4	3.8	3.9	5.8	5.7	7.3	3.6	10.0
Lower Yukon River Eskimos	(M)	1435	178	140	135	102	77	52	23.5	135	
	(CV)	7.9	3.4	3.4	4.1	4.1	5.5	5.0	6.8	3.5	
Carinthians	(M)	1436	175	145	127	96	68	50	24.2	131	1140
	(CV)	7.7	4.0	3.8	4.3	4.3	6.9	6.0	7.7	3.9	10.9
Chimpanzees	(M)		132	101	87	95	82	54	24.7	123	693
	(CV)		6.7	6.7	6.2	9.3	13.1	10.6	17.3	12.3	11.3
Gorillas	(M)		159	109	101	121	109	80	32.4	158	996
	(CV)		12.2	11.7	11.5	13.7	15.4	16.6	17.4	14.7	14.9

Neandertals are almost identical. Variation in the fossil hominid samples is not, however, unusual for primates. Comparison with the two pongid samples evinces greater variation among the pongids. While high coefficients of variation for gorillas may result from the extensive sexual dimorphism, such an explanation cannot account for the nearly as high coefficient shown for chimpanzees. The same relation occurs for cranial capacities. The coefficient of variation for thirty Neandertals is 12.6. This compares favorably with the coefficient for 200 anatomically modern *H. sapiens* specimens of 11.7 (Ashton and Spence 1958) and of 14.1 for twelve specimens of *H. erectus* (Wolpoff 1969). Further, 144 chimpanzees have a cranial capacity coefficient of variation of 6.8, while the coefficient for 653 gorillas is 13.6 (Ashton and Spence 1958).

With one exception, the average dimensions for the "classic" Neandertals are almost identical with both those for the Solo sample and for the total sample. The exception is cranial base length or nasion-basion diameter. The significantly greater diameters for the "classic" specimens is a direct measure of the total facial prognathism separating nasal passages from brain which appears to be part of the Neandertal cold adaptation (Coon 1964). While all Neandertals have a longer cranial base that do any group of anatomically modern *H. sapiens* the "classic" sample dimensions are far greater yet.

Finally, Table II provides an excellent indication that the Upper Paleolithic Europeans are metrically transitional between succeeding Neandertal populations and extant Europeans.

After sorting out "classic" Neandertals on extremely conservative grounds, using among other things *morphological* criteria for specimens lacking adequate provenience such as Le Moustier, Neandertal, and Gibraltar, (Howell 1952:379), the same morphological criteria applied to all of the specimens available at this time indicate the largely arbitrary and anatomically unjustified basis of the initial sorting. Use of the *t* test evinces no significant differences between the "classic" and the "non-classic" samples for any of the measurements in Table II except nasion-basion; the only consistent differences occur in features reflecting climatic adaptation (Coon 1962). All of the differences between "classic" and "non-classic" groups discussed here, as well as differences discussed in the following sections, are far less than those which regularly occur among extant groups living side-by-side (see Hrdlicka 1928, 1942, DeVilliers 1958, Benington 1911, Larnach and Macintosh 1966). These extensive metric, variational, and morphologic similarities and the complete overlap of ranges occur between a group very restricted in time and space, thought by some to represent a genetic isolate and a much larger group representing a greater time span and occupying all of the Old World. If under these conditions the similarities do not indicate the phylogenic unity of the two groups, what further evidence could possibly be required to demonstrate this point?

The pattern of metric variation overlap is evinced by other morphological features presumably associated with the "classic" Neandertals. This is made particularly clear when one reviews the evidence underlying a compiled list of distinguishing "classic" Neandertal features such as that presented by Boule and Vallois (1957:251-2). The "simian" characters claimed for the vertebral column and limb bones will be ignored in the light of work by numerous authors demonstrating the completely modern anatomy of "classic" Neandertal post-

cranial skeletons (Schwalbe 1914; Patte 1955; Straus and Cave 1957). Extensive lists of presumably distinctive "classic" Neandertal cranial and facial features have been prepared by a number of authors (Howell 1951, 1952, 1957; Boule and Vallois 1957; Hooton 1947). We will show both that some "classic" specimens as well as some "non-classic" specimens have almost all of these features. On the other hand, many other specimens without these characteristics can be found in both groups. The latter fact is of greater potential importance, because no feature distinguishes all "non-classic" or all "classic" specimens from anatomically modern *H. sapiens*.

Conversely, all of the presumed "distinguishing characteristics" for anatomically modern *H. sapiens* occur, with regular frequency, in both "classic" and "non-classic" Neandertals. For instance, La Chapelle (Boule 1913), Ehringsdorf H (Kleinschmidt 1931), Cova Negra (de Lumley 1970), and Amud (Suzuki 1965, 1968) are large headed, while La Ferrassie 2 (Hrdlicka 1930; Heim 1968), Petralona (Kannelis and Savas 1964), Ganovce (Vlcek 1955), La Chaise (Krukoff 1970), Gibraltar (Sollas 1908), and Tabun (McCown and Keith 1939) are not. The forehead is high in Petralona (Jelinek 1969), La Ferrassie 1 (Coon 1962), Djebel Irhound 1 (Ennouchi 1962), Krapina E (Schaefer 1964) and Shanidar 1 (Stewart 1958), but is quite low in the Neandertal calvarium (Hrdlicka 1930), Broken Hill (Morant 1928), Saccopastore 1 (Sergi 1944), Krapina D (Gorjanovic-Kramberger 1906), and Tabun 1 (McCown and Keith 1939). Parietal bones of Krapina E (Schaefer 1964), Ehringsdorf H (Kleinschmidt 1931) and C (Behm-Blancke 1960), La Quina 5 (Henri-Martin 1923), and Saldanha (Singer 1954) are flat and evenly rounded, while Omo 2 (Leakey, Butzer, and Day 1969), Krapina K (Jelinek 1969), Broken Hill (Morant 1928), Ehringsdorf B and D (Behm-Blancke 1960), and Spy 2 (Hrdlicka 1930) have high, rooflike parietals with a pronounced boss. Heinz (1967) has shown that Neandertal parietal heights overlap extensively with those of anatomically modern *H. sapiens*. Thus, while La Ferrassie 1 (Boule 1913), Ganovce (Vlcek 1955), Fontechevade 2 (Vallois 1958), Saccopastore 1 (Sergi 1944), and Amud (Suzuki 1965, 1968) show rounded contours in norma occipitalis, Spy 2 (Hrdlicka 1930), Le Moustier (Weinert 1925), Ehringsdorf D (Behm-Blancke 1960), Broken Hill (Morant 1928), and Djebel Irhound 1 (Ennouchi 1962) have parallel sided contours.

The supraorbital torus is heavy with glabellar and lateral elements merged and the supraorbital sulcus obliterated in Mapa (Woo and Peng 1959), Broken Hill (Morant 1928), Neandertal (Boule 1913; Schwalbe 1914), Krapina D (Gorjanovic-Kramberger 1906), Galilee (Kurth 1965), Saccopastore 2 (Sergi 1948), Saldanha (Singer 1954), Mount Circeo (Sergi 1940), and Ehringsdorf H (Weidenreich 1928). It is lightly developed in Le Moustier (Weinert 1925), Gibraltar (Sollas 1908), Amud (Suzuki 1965, 1968), Krapina C (Gorjanovic-Kramberger 1906), Omo 2 (Leakey, Butzer, and Day 1969), and Djebel Irhound 2 (Ennouchi 1968). In addition, both Sala (Vlcek 1965) and Galilee (McCown and Keith 1939) have a sulcus separating glabellar and lateral portions. The occipital area is low, flattened, heavily muscled, and clearly displays the bunned condition in La Quina 5 (Henri-Martin 1923), Ganovce (Vlcek 1955), and the Spy crania (Hrdlicka 1930). Gibraltar (Sollas 1908) is bunned but lightly muscled. In other specimens, such as Broken Hill (Morant 1930), Amud (Suzuki 1965), Omo 2 (Leakey, Butzer, and Day 1969), and Djebel Irhound 2 (Ennouchi 1968), the bunning is not as apparent, although vertical compression of the occipital region is retained. Saldanha (Singer 1954) has a clear occipital torus but no bunning. Finally the occipital region of the cranium is not at all bunned, but rather is small and rounded with light muscle attachments in Le Moustier (Weinert 1925), Saccopastore 1 (Sergi 1944), Tabun 1 (McCown and Keith 1939), and Djebel Irhound 1 (Ennouchi 1962). The mastoid process is very small in La Quina 10 and 27 (Vallois 1969), Djebel Irhound 2 (Ennouchi 1968), Saccopastore 2 (Sergi 1948), Spy 1 and 2 (Hrdlicka 1930), Petralona (Poulianos 1966), and Broken Hill (Morant 1928). However, in Saccopastore 1 (Sergi 1944), Amud (Suzuki 1965, 1968), La Quina 5 (Henri-Martin 1923), Ehringsdorf H (Weidenreich 1928), and Djebel Irhound 1 (Ennouchi 1962) the process is quite large. According to data recently published by Vallois (1969:396 and Table 7) mastoid process size for La Chapelle and La Ferrassie 1 fit well within the range of variation for modern man. There is very little, if any, mid-facial prognathism in La Ferrassie 1 (Brace 1962b), Djebel Irhound 1 (Ennouchi 1962), and Broken Hill (Morant 1928), but a significant amount of prognathism in the nasal-maxillary region of Le Moustier (Weinert 1925), Petralona (Kokkoros and Kannelis 1960), and Tabun 1 (McCown and Keith 1939). The amount of mid-facial prognathism is sufficient to obliterate the canine fossa in most Neandertals. However, there is a definite canine fossa in Djebel Irhound 1 (Ennouchi 1962), Krapina C (Gorjanovic-Kramberger 1906), Kulna (Jelinek 1969), and to a lesser extent Broken Hill (Hrdlicka 1930).

The face is relatively long compared with the calvarium in Petralona (Kokkoros and Kannelis 1960; Kannelis and Savas 1964), Saccopastore 1 (Sergi 1944), and La Ferrassie 1 (Coon 1963), but it is significantly smaller in Le Moustier (Weinert 1925), Gibraltar (Sollas 1908), and Amud (Suzuki 1968). As with all of the other features, the claim of "large rounded orbits" is neither consistent within nor distinctive for the "classic" Neandertals. Orbit shape can be expressed in terms of the orbit index (height/breadth). For five "classic" Neandertals (Gibraltar, La Chapelle, La Ferrassie, Monte Circeo, and Le Moustier), the average index is 84, ranging from 75 to 100. Eight "non-classic" specimens average 85, and range from 76 to 100. As a size measure, the orbit areas of these two samples are, respectively, 1685 mm^2 and 1686 mm^2.

Shelving of the maxilla into the malar occurs in Saccopastore I (Sergi 1944), La Ferrassie (Boule 1913), and Shanidar I (Stewart 1958), but is completely absent (a 90 degree angle occurs) in Djebel Irhound I (Ennouchi 1962), Broken Hill (Morant 1928), and La Quina H5 (Henri-Martin 1923). With teeth, La Chapelle is intermediate.

There is a definite mental eminence in the mandibles of La Ferrassie 1 (Boule and Vallois 1957), La Quina 9 (Piveteau 1964), Monte Circeo 3 (Sergi 1958b), Tabun 2 (McCown and Keith 1939), Amud (Suzuki 1968), the Djebel Irhound juvenile (Ennouchi 1969), Shanidar 1 and 2 (Stewart 1958, 1961), and Sipka (Kadic et al. 1933). This region is receding in Arcy-sur-Cure 2 (Leroi-Gourhan 1958), Regardou (Piveteau 1964), Le Moustier (Weinert 1925), Tabun 1 (McCown and Keith 1939), La Quina 5 (Henri-Martin 1923), Ehringsdorf adult (Virchow 1920), Krapina H (Gorjanovic-Kramberger 1906) and Spy 1 (Hrdlicka 1930). The teeth have taurodont pulp cavities in the Krapina jaws (Gorjanovic-Kramberger 1907), Ochoz (Jelinek 1969), Spy 2 (Hrdlicka 1930), and Amud (Suzuki 1965). How-

ever, the pulp cavities are non-taurodont in the mandible from Abri Bourgeouis-Delaunay (Debenath and Piveteau 1969), Dire Dawa (Vallois 1951), and Tabun 2 (McCown and Keith 1939).

One could continue this demonstration indefinitely, but there seems little point in doing so. Two conclusions are apparent. First, the distinction long maintained between "classic" and "non-classic" Neandertals is without substantive basis. The few features which distinguish the group means (although not the individual specimens) show a tendency in the Western European Wurm group for heavier bunning in the occipital region and more extensive mid-facial prognathism. The trends do not have an elaborate basis, and are slight enough so that statistical significance usually cannot be verified. Second, it is quite apparent that Neandertals overlap with anatomically modern H. sapiens in almost every morphological feature, as well as almost every metric one.

The form, as well as the range, of variation within Neandertal populations clearly indicates their ancestral relationship to the succeeding populations of anatomically modern H. sapiens (Brace 1964) found occupying the same caves and hunting the same game at a later time (Hrdlicka 1927, 1930). Average Neandertal morphological and metric parameters are not always identical with those of modern man: Neandertals are not, after all, anatomically modern H. sapiens. On the other hand, there is extensive overlap between the range of almost every Neandertal characteristic and the range of the corresponding characteristic in modern man. It is not surprising that the group of anatomically modern H. sapiens represented in Table II showing the greatest metric similarity to the "classic" Neandertals are the Upper Paleolithic Europeans!

The close relationship of Neandertals and succeeding anatomically modern H. sapiens populations can be seen on an individual basis, in comparisons of La Ferrassie 1 with Predmost 3, let alone in the often discussed comparison of Skhul 5 with Predmost 3 (Brace 1967a, 1968). Predmost 3, the object of these comparisons, is gracile compared with some specimens associated with Upper Paleolithic industries such as Brux, Podkumok, and Brunn 1 (Weinert 1944:153-161). We believe that this similarity is the result of the in situ evolution of European Neandertals (see Jelinek 1969). In this respect, the hominids and the industries display the same relationship.

Finally, the clearly ancestral position of Neandertals is also evinced by the morphology, and postulated ontogeny, of Neandertal adolescents and children (Vlcek 1964; Fenart 1969; Carbonell 1965; Senyurek 1959; Piveteau, de Lumley, and Mme de Lumley 1963; Piveteau 1969; Thoma 1963). In a recent study of Neandertal characteristics in the ontogeny of anatomically modern H. sapiens Vlcek concludes "the development and presence of some morphological features typical for a Neandertal skeleton can be established on the skeleton of present man in his ontogenetic development" (1964:81).

These data suggest a re-examination of the conclusions based on Morant's metric analysis (1927a:374-375). First, Neandertals ("classic" or otherwise) are not "remarkably homogeneous." This conclusion is adequately demonstrated in Table II. If anything, they are remarkably variable. Second, the distinct hiatus reported between Neandertals and modern groups is no longer as distinct as first believed. While differences are demonstrable with modern population averages, numerous individuals overlap. In Europe, the Upper Paleolithic populations are clearly transitional (Jelinek 1969; Schwalbe

1906). Third, while no living group seems more closely related to Neandertals than any other, Upper Paleolithic Europeans are clearly transitional between European Neandertals and living European populations in both metric and morphological features. The final point is not only apparent in the distributions discussed here but has been convincingly demonstrated by Jelinek (1969), Maska (1889), Mateigka (1938), Jelinek, Palisek, and Valoch (1959), Brace (1964), Coon (1962), Schwalbe (1906), and others.

TRANSITIONAL SPECIMENS: THEIR IDENTIFICATION AND ARCHAEOLOGICAL ASSOCIATIONS

The second line of evidence indicating worldwide evolution of Neandertals into anatomically modern *H. sapiens* stems from the cultural associations of the truly transitional specimens.

Transitional specimens can best be seen in contrast to a general picture of the ways in which Neandertals differ from extant populations. While there is overlap in almost every feature, differences in averages can still be found.

Most distinctive Neandertal characteristics were maintained as the result of selection for *technological*, and sometimes also *climatic* adaptation. Indeed, it was the appearance of the greatest climatic extremes in sub-glacial Western Europe which resulted in both increased continent-wide variability and highest frequencies of characteristics associated with the so-called "classic" Neandertals.

Dental Adaptation

The most important features distinguishing Neandertal dentitions from those of extant modern groups are metric, rather than morphological (Dahlberg 1963). The major differences occur in the incisors and canines: the anterior teeth (Brace 1962a, 1964, 1968; Wolpoff 1970). The posterior dentition is not particularly distinctive. Table III shows the summed areas of the posterior teeth, mandibular and maxillary, for a number of hominid taxa and extant groups. The table was prepared by summing the individual averages for specimens in each group. Data for the fossil groups was taken from Wolpoff (1971), as were measurements for "Australoids," "Caucasoids," New Britain Islanders, and Dickson Mound Indians. The latter two were measured by

Table III. Summed Areas of Posterior Tooth Row For Maxilla and Mandible (mm^2).

	Maxilla	Mandible
Australopithecines	935	906
H. erectus	630	638
Neandertals	543	533
Anatomically modern *H. sapiens*	490	487
"Australoid"	581	539
New Britain	537	520
Dickson Mound Indian	495	495
Teso	483	482
"Caucasoid"	466	457
Japanese	449	449
Lapps	388	391

Wolpoff. The Japanese data was published by Miyabara (1916), Lapp data by Selmer-Olsen (1949), and Teso data by Barnes (1969). It is apparent that the Neandertal group average falls within the range of variation of extant group averages with respect to summed posterior areas.

The primary function of the anterior teeth is in gripping, holding, exerting torsion, and other manipulations. These uses have been established for extant groups (Campbell 1925, 1939; Van Reenen 1966; Brothwell 1959, 1963; Barnes 1969; Leigh 1928, 1937; Turner and Cadien 1969; Brace and Molnar 1967; Waugh 1937; Taylor 1963; Bailit, DeWitt, and Leigh 1968; Gessain 1959; Noble 1926). Other uses observed include such diverse functions as leather treating (Pedersen 1938), pulling (Noble 1926), fashioning thong, reed and thread (Dahlberg 1963), and straightening wooden shafts (Sollas 1908). Indications of similar, although more extensive, use of the anterior dentition is characteristic of Neandertals. For instance, Dahlberg (1963) shows extensive differential incisor wear for the right maxillary teeth of La Ferrassie 1. The right side is considerably more worn than the left resulting in an uneven and undulating occlusal plane. Brace (1962a:347-348) shows a similar pattern of wear in Shanidar 1, Ternifine 3 (an *H. erectus* specimen), and Krapina J. Wear of this nature clearly could not result from mastication alone (Brace and Molnar 1967).

The anterior teeth of Neandertals were apparently important tools in the manipulation of the environment. As such, they required robust roots and supporting structures. These features are characteristic of Neandertal jaws and faces. The anterior displacement and robustness of the maxilla in part causes the region in the vicinity of the canine fossa to become convex rather than concave, thus eliminating the fossa. In addition, these features are characteristic of *H. erectus* faces. These also exhibit robust anterior dentitions.

Tables IV and V give data for averaged individual mandibular (Table IV) and maxillary (Table V) anterior summed tooth lengths (L), breadths (B), and areas (L*B). Data for Illinois Indians and Sub-Saharan Africans have been published by Wolpoff (1971). In addition to average values, the ranges, sample sizes (N), and coefficients of variation (CV) are listed. Because of the presence of small sample sizes *t* tests were calculated to determine the significance of differences between *H. erectus* and Neandertals, as well as between Neandertals and anatomically modern *H. sapiens*. Comparing *H. erectus* with Neandertals at the five percent significance level, mandibular summed length is significantly greater in the former. All other dimensional comparisons for both jaws reveal no significant difference. On the one percent level *no* comparison of *H. erectus* with Neandertal reveals a significant difference. Comparing the Neandertals with anatomically modern *H. sapiens*, on the other hand, there is a significant difference at the five percent level for *every* dimension in both jaws. At the one percent level, the length comparisons for both jaws are not significant, but all other comparisons are. It appears that while the anterior dentitions of Neandertals and *H. erectus* are not statistically distinguishable for length, breadth, and area (for all intents and purposes), there is a very significant dimensional decrease for anatomically modern *H. sapiens*. The breadth, and subsequently area, decreases are slightly more significant. Therefore, the Middle Pleistocene anterior dentition is demonstrably larger than that of anatomically modern *H. sapiens*, with particular emphasis on increased breadth. The

Table IV. Averaged Mandibular Anterior Tooth Row Summed Lengths (L), Breadths (B), and Areas (L*B). N is the Sample Size and CV the Coefficient of Variation (mm).

	L(M-D)				B(B-L)				L*B			
	Mean	Range	N	CV	Mean	Range	N	CV	Mean	Range	N	CV
Australopithecines	20.3	17.2–23.0	14	7.8	23.0	20.0–26.5	13	8.6	160	129.6–197.1	13	13.3
H. erectus	21.1	18.2–23.8	12	7.6	23.8	21.4–27.8	12	7.5	170	145.6–201.8	12	10.0
Neandertals	20.0	17.5–22.8	31	6.7	24.3	21.4–28.0	29	6.8	166	130.3–200.8	29	9.9
Anatomically modern												
H. sapiens	19.2	14.2–22.4	180	7.8	20.4	14.5–25.0	170	7.8	133	82.0–178.0	167	12.9
"Australoid"	21.1	20.0–21.8	6	3.0	22.3	21.0–24.3	4	6.8	160	148.0–176.0	4	7.7
Sub-Saharan African	19.9	16.5–22.4	25	7.5	20.9	14.5–24.2	21	11.3	141	82.0–172.0	21	17.4
Illinois Indian	19.5	18.6–20.5	10	2.5	20.4	18.9–22.7	9	7.0	134	124.0–149.0	9	6.6
Dickson Mound Indian	19.4	17.4–22.2	85	5.2	20.0	17.1–23.0	84	6.6	132	101.0–158.0	84	9.7
New Britain	19.4	17.8–21.2	25	4.6	20.6	18.8–23.9	24	6.0	134	114.0–153.0	23	7.8
"Caucasoid"	17.4	14.2–21.3	28	11.4	21.0	18.4–25.0	25	7.8	124	94.0–178.0	25	18.3

Table V. Averaged Maxillary Anterior Tooth Row Summed Lengths (L), Breadths (B), and Areas (L*B). N is the Sample Size and CV the Coefficient of Variation (mm).

	L(M-D)				B(B-L)				L*B			
	Mean	Range	N	CV	Mean	Range	N	CV	Mean	Range	N	CV
Australopithecines	26.3	22.7–29.0	10	7.1	24.7	21.4–28.6	20	8.1	216	183.4–238.8	8	9.1
H. erectus	28.0	24.2–29.5	4	8.3	27.6	25.7–32.6	4	10.5	260	208.7–320.2	4	14.3
Neandertals	26.1	24.0–30.0	14	7.9	25.9	22.9–29.2	14	6.3	226	196.8–268.2	14	11.5
Anatomically modern												
H. sapiens	24.5	18.7–29.4	164	7.5	23.0	18.8–30.3	160	7.7	190	131.0–258.0	160	13.0
Sub-Saharan African	25.8	21.0–29.4	14	9.7	23.8	18.8–26.7	14	10.3	207	131.0–250.0	14	17.7
Dickson Mound Indian	24.9	21.9–27.6	85	4.8	22.7	19.1–25.7	85	5.4	190	140.0–227.0	85	8.9
New Britain	24.8	23.2–26.5	22	4.3	23.0	21.6–25.9	20	4.5	192	168.0–228.0	20	7.1
"Australoid"	24.4	21.8–26.9	8	8.0	25.2	19.8–30.3	8	15.2	208	145.0–258.0	8	20.1
Illinois Indian	24.2	20.9–25.2	8	5.9	22.4	20.0–23.8	8	5.5	182	146.0–195.0	8	9.0
"Caucasoid"	22.7	18.7–27.4	27	10.7	23.3	20.8–28.2	25	8.7	178	131.0–258.0	25	18.7

size difference has both statistical and morphological significance.

We feel that the large Neandertal anterior teeth are a specific adaptation to the type of extensive use implied by the pattern of anterior occlusion seen in Neandertal jaws, as well as the general muscularity evinced by Neandertal skeletal rugosity. This implication is substantiated by observation of tooth use in non-agricultural peoples. The increased breadth is an effective means of structural reinforcement. Indeed even slightly worn Neandertal incisors tend to be almost square.

Climatic Adaptation

Climate must also be considered in the analysis of Neandertal morphology, for the so-called "classic" Neandertals were clearly adapted to a cold climate (Coon 1962, 1964). The anterior displacement of the entire face from nasion downward, so characteristic of Western European Neandertals, is much reduced in specimens such as Broken Hill (Morant 1928), Djebel Irhound 1 (Ennouchi 1962), and others. This anterior displacement helps separate the nasal passage from the relatively low positioned brain (Coon 1962:533). Thus the brain is maximally separated from inspired cold air. The necessity of warming such inspired air accounts for the great breadth of the Neandertal nose (Wolpoff 1968). The resulting massive face is balanced with a relatively long and low cranium, with expanded nuchal area for muscle attachments. As a result, the Wurm adapted Neandertal crania have the highest incidence of bunning and greatest occipital breadths. The increased facial prognathism completely eliminates the canine fossa in this group, a feature which regularly appears in the "non-classic" Neandertals. The resulting total morphological pattern for the "classic" group is one of cold adaptation built upon the morphology of the Neandertal grade of evolutionary development. The postcranial morphology, particularly as reflected in limb to trunk proportions (Patte 1955; Vallois 1958), similarly displays a cold-adapted pattern.

This total morphological pattern includes the frontal sinus complex. While the form and size of the Neandertal frontal sinus is directly intermediate between that of *H. erectus* and that of anatomically modern *H. sapiens* (Vlcek 1967:188), the supraorbital torus is especially well developed in some of the Western European glacial Neandertals (Vlcek 1964). The size and form of this sinus is directly related to both the supraorbital torus and the extent of mid-facial prognathism. The intermediacy of the sinus form helps corroborate the hypothesis of direct Neandertal ancestry, while the excessive development of the sinus, and hence of mid-facial prognathism, in glacial adapted Neandertals substantiates the hypothesis of climatic selection.

Most Neandertal features are not too different from those of *H. erectus*. Neandertals differ from the latter mainly in the reduction of the posterior dentition and the expansion of the brain to modern size. Table 2 identifies many of the metric features characterizing the difference between Neandertal means and the means of extant groups. These data characterize Neandertal crania—"classic," "tropical" (Solo), and all referred specimens taken together, as long, low, and relatively broad. The great cranial length and nasion-basion diameter can be taken as an indication of the degree of total facial prognathism. The latter dimension is maximized in the Western European

Neandertals. While Neandertal nasal height is great, the breadth of Neandertal noses is almost one third again as large as the maximum for extant groups. Total facial size for the Neandertals is large. It is only partially approached by the Eskimo sample. With the exception of cranial capacity and cranial height the average Neandertal dimensions exceed those of all extant group averages. However, in cranial breadth, upper facial and nasal heights, and foramen magnum area the Neandertal sample is closely approached by some of the extant group averages. The specific pattern of the most significant differences results from a combination of climatic and dental adaptations. The general massiveness of Neandertal cranial dimensions and rugosity of muscle attachments attests to the major function of individual body strength in Neandertal pattern of life.

This complex of features is maintained by both climatic selection and selection maintaining the large anterior dentition. Neandertal populations maintain these characteristics at their highest frequencies in Europe where climatic selection is greatest. A large number of specimens come from outside of Europe. These retain features resulting from the massive anterior dentition and supporting structures, such as a long and low calvarium, large face, and so on. However, the additional effects of maxillary protrusion, nasal size, and other cold-weather adaptations, are not present. As a result, many of the features common to both dental and climatic adaptation appear in a less extreme form. Therefore a distinctive morphology resulting from the interaction of both climatic and dental adaptation is associated with the so-called "classic" Neandertals from Western Europe, forming an adaptive complex. Rather than indicating the isolation of Western European Neandertal populations from populations in other areas, this continuity emphasizes the presence of consistent gene flow.

The Transitional Specimens

A "transitional" Neandertal population can be defined with respect to these features. There are a number of specimens representing such transitional populations. The fact that they all are associated with Mousterian type industries constitutes the second line of evidence indicating the *in situ* evolution of Neandertals into anatomically modern *H. sapiens*.

The first specimen representing a transitional population comes from the Kulna cave in Czechoslovakia. The maxilla, described by Jelinek (1966, 1969) has a canine fossa indicating a decrease in anterior maxillary expansion. According to Jelinek (1966:701) other progressive features include the specific morphology of the canine and premolars, as well as the deep palate. These features are mixed with others more commonly distinctive of Neandertals. With PM^4 not fully in occlusion, the specimen can be aged at fourteen to fifteen. Even for an adult the lower facial height is unusualy large so that for an adolescent the very great size of the lower face is a Neandertal feature. Judging from the occlusal view (Jelinek 1969: Figure 4a), the anterior incisor sockets and the canine which is present indicate a great breadth for the anterior dentition. In addition, the maxilla has a prenasal fossa coupled with a very weakly developed anterior nasal spine.

The second transitional group comes from Arcy-sur-Cure in Western Europe. Here, along with the excellent sequence of industrial evolution from Middle to Upper Paleolithic (Movius

Table VI. Summed Breadths and Areas of Mandibular Incisors.

	Breadth				Area (mm²)			
	Mean	Range	N	CV	Mean	Range	N	CV
Neandertals								
Europeans	15.5	14.2–16.8	15	4.6	96.4	85.5–112.6	12	8.3
Skhul	14.2	13.2–15.7	4	7.8	83.9	71.9–107.7	4	19.3

1969), there is a corresponding sequence of hominid evolution (Leroi-Gourhan 1958). Hominids are found at almost every level, although most of the material recovered is dental. Teeth discovered in the highest Mousterian levels (12 to 15) are indistinguishable from those of anatomically modern *H. sapiens*. Some anterior teeth are represented (Ibid.: 113).

According to Jelinek (1969:477, 499), the Sipka mandible is dated in the Wurm I/II interstadial by both the geology and the fauna of the site. Because of this date and the association with a Mousterian industry (Maska 1882, 1886), one would expect the mandible to evince transitional characteristics, if the model proposed here is correct.

The dentition of the Sipka mandible suggests a transitional status (Vlcek 1969). Neandertals differ from anatomically modern *H. sapiens* in the size (breadth, area) of the anterior dentitions. Table VI gives anterior lower incisor breadth and area sums for fifteen European Neandertals. When an individual had both sides present, one was chosen at random. Four Skhul specimens are separately represented. The data for Sipka were published by Virchow (1882). References for most of the other specimens are given in another publication (Wolpoff 1971). The three Krapina mandibles (E, H, I) were measured by Dr. C. L. Brace; this data is used with his kind permission. While neither the summed breadths (15.0 mm) or the summed areas (87.2 mm²) of the Sipka incisors are the smallest in the European sample, they fall in the lower end of the range. Only two mandibles (the Subaluk adult and the Teshik-Tash adolescent) have a narrower summed incisor breadth, and only one (Regourdou) has a smaller summed area. Of greatest importance, *not one* European Neandertal has both smaller breadth *and* area sums. On the other hand, the Sipka values lie on the

upper end of the Skhul range, breadth and area only exceeded by Skhul 10. The transitional position of the Sipka dentition is clear.

No morphological characteristics of the mandible contradict the transitional interpretation (Jelinek 1969). The dimensions of the jaw, while robust, are not unusual for anatomically modern *H. sapiens* and can regularly be matched in extant populations (Ibid.:477)

A number of transitional specimens come from the Near East. While some of the Near Eastern Neandertals closely approach anatomically modern *H. sapiens* in their metric and non-metric morphology (Quafzeh 6, Skhul 5), others closely approach the "classic" Neandertals (Tabun, Shanidar I) save for the extremes of cold adaptation. Actually, there are excellent archaeological and anatomical reasons for considering all the specimens members of a late non-cold adapted Neandertal group, imperceptibly grading into anatomically modern *H. sapiens*.

Table VII presents measurements for the seven most complete Near Eastern Neandertal crania. All diameters from porion are projected in the median sagittal plane. Measurements for the Amud cranium were published by Suzuki (1965, 1968) or measured from the scaled photograph (1968:Fig. 3). The Shanidar I measurements were published by Stewart (1958), or measured from the several scaled photographs in that publication. The estimated cranial capacity, over 1700 cc. comes form Coon (1962:564). The three Skhul crania, and the Tabun cranium were measured by McCown and Keith (1939). Finally, measurements for Quafzeh 6 were taken from the scaled photograph published by Boule and Vallois (1957:Fig. 247) or from the photograph published by Coon (1962:Plate XXVIII),

Table VII. Cranial Measurements of the Seven Relatively Complete Near Eastern Neandertal Crania (mm).

	Amud	Shanidar 1	Skhul 9	Quafzeh 6	Skhul 4	Skhul 5	Tabun 1
Cranial Capacity (cc)	1800	1700	1587	1560	1554	1518	1271
Length	215	206	213	198	206	192	183
Breadth	155	157	145	146	148	143	141
Maximum Height							
Above Frankfort Plane	122	125	115	113	116	121	105
Porion–Prosthion	133	125		109	110	116	111
Nasion	116	111	109	102	109	95	100
Glabella	125	114	122	113	117	106	105
Lambda	115	116	111	104	104	108	100
Opistocranion	108	110	101	95	100	100	93
Inion	90	97	98	81	85	89	79
Upper Facial Height	91	88	74	73	79	73	79
Nasal Height		63	55	54	55	53	58
Calotte Height Above							
Glabella–Inion	94	103	87	102	99	100	85
Glabella–Lambda	63	66	53	55	64	68	47

scaled by computing the cranial length from the published cephalic index (73.7) and cranial breadth (146 mm).

Skhul cave at Mount Carmel is the origin of a large number of fossil hominids (McCown and Keith 1939) which taken together, represent a sample of a truly transitional group (Brace 1962b, 1964, 1967a; McCown and Keith 1939; Boule and Vallois 1957:376-378; Howell 1958). The morphological characteristics of these specimens are well known, so that repetition is not necessary. The direct association with a Levalloiso-Mousterian industry is unquestionable (Garrod and Bate 1937). As an individual specimen, Skhul 5 fits completely within the range of variation for anatomically modern *H. sapiens*.

At Djebel Quafzeh more than thirteen hominids have been recovered; although not one has been even partially described (Vandermeersch 1966, 1969b, 1970), the crania of one of the first six individuals has been pictured (Boule and Vallois 1957, Fig. 247; Coon 1962:Plate XXVIII). There has been a relatively great amount of reconstruction in the vault form , although the face is largely unreconstructed. The form, morphology, and shape of the cranial vault fit equally well within both Neandertal and anatomically modern *H. sapiens* ranges of variation. It is most similar to crania from Mount Carmel (Boule and Vallois 1957). The "Neandertalian" characteristics which it possesses, according to Boule and Vallois (1957:377), include a relatively broad nose and a very large palate. On the other hand, the index of upper facial height to cranial length—37, falls within the Skhul range (35-38, *n*=3) and far below the range of "classic" Neandertals (41-50, *n*=6). Similarly, the ratio is significantly smaller than the ratios for the three large-faced Near Eastern specimens: Amud (42), Shanidar I (43) and Tabun (43).

Table VII reveals a mixture of modern and archaic features in the metric dimensions and proportions. For instance, the distance from porion to glabella is greater than that of Skhul 5. However, the porion-prosthion measure is far less, while the porion-nasion measure is again greater. Quafzeh 6 shows the total facial prognathism common to Neandertals, rather than the alveolar prognathism evinced by Skhul 5. Another archaic feature of the specimen is a very low calvarium, as indicated by the small auricular height value. However, while they are of Neandertal proportion, the facial dimensions of the cranium are absolutely small: most distances from porion (excepting height) are best matched by Tabun 1, a far less transitional specimen with a much smaller cranial capacity. The calvarium is similar to many extant crania. Like Skhul 5 it bears some resemblances to crania of Australian aborigines. Comparison with a particularly rugged Australian aborigine cranium pictured by Larnach and Macintosh (1966: Plate I) is striking. The index of facial height to cranial length in this Australian aborigine specimen is 35. As we have already noted, the Quafzeh skeletons are unquestionably associated with a Levalloiso-Mousterian industry. Vandermeersch, who has recovered a number of the skeletons from the Quafzeh Mousterian levels, observes "les hommes de Quafzeh sont à ranger parmi les neanthropiens bien qu'ils soient associés à une industrie mousterienne" (1969a:17).

Another transitional specimen comes from the Amud cave (Suzuki 1965, 1968) associated with a Levalloiso-Mousterian industry (Binford 1968:709). The specimen combines a number of transitional characteristics (Vallois 1962) and is clearly related to other Near Eastern hominids from Skhul and Quafzeh on the one hand, but also to hominids from Shanidar. The

resemblance to Shanidar 1 (Stewart 1958) is marked. The anterior dentition, supraorbital torus, and upper third molars of this specimen are each relatively small. The mastoid process is well developed, the forehead high, and a mental eminence is present (Suzuki 1965). The calvarium is absolutely high. Maximum height above the Frankfort Horizontal, measured from the scaled photograph (Suzuki 1968) measures 122mm. This is higher than any "classic" Neandertal, but is exceeded by Shanidar 1. These, then, are features reminiscent of anatomically modern *H. sapiens*. On the other hand, the calvarium is extremely long (215mm) and broad (155mm); the face is long and broad with an upper facial height of 91mm. This is one of the largest Neandertal faces matched or exceeded only by Broken Hill, La Ferrassie I, and Petralona. The occipital contour of the skull is round, the occipital region is vertically compressed in a manner similar to that of Djebel Irhound 2, and the ratio of facial height to cranial length is relatively great (41), indicating a Neandertal sized and proportioned face. Measurements from porion to prosthion and porion to nasion (Table VII) indicate extensive mid-facial prognathism.

The remaining transitional specimens come from Africa. There, the recently discovered crania from the Kibish formation of the Omo basin evince a mixture of features found both in Neandertals and in anatomically modern *H. sapiens* (Leakey, Butzer, and Day 1969). No features occur which are not found in other Neandertals. However, the combinations are unique. The three skeletons have not been precisely dated. They are reported to come from Member I of the formation, although only some remains of Omo 1 were recovered *in situ*: Omo 2 and 3 were collected from the surface. A radiocarbon date of 37,000 BP was reported for an *Eutheria* bank in Member III, overlying Member I. The skeletal material is probably older, although some uncertainty stems from the fact that shell-based dates have a tendency to appear older than they actually are (Crane 1956). Corroborating dates from other sources would be useful. For the time being, the Omo skeletons appear to be roughly contemporary with European and Near Eastern Neandertals.

Table VIII gives metric data for the two better preserved Omo crania. For purposes of comparison the other reasonably complete African and Asian Neandertal crania are tabulated. The Omo measurements were taken from Day (Leakey, Butzer, and Day 1969), and measured from the photographs in this publication. The scale indicated for the photographs is at variance with the measurements published in the text. The text was assumed correct (Day, personal communication), and the photographs rescaled accordingly in order to obtain the data in Table VIII. Sources for most of the other material have been discussed. The "Africanthropus" calvarium was published by Weinert (1940).

Omo 1, like Skhul 5, would be identified as anatomically modern *H. sapiens* if found in another context. Modern features include the large mastoid process, high calvarium (the auricular height is 138mm and is the Neandertal maximum), rounded occipital region and low inion, and mandibular mental eminence. The breadth of the heavily worn upper canine, 8.1 mm, is at the low end of the Neandertal range of variation. Of 35 individuals, only Spy 1 and Skhul 1 are narrower. The length of 8.9 mm, on the other hand, is greater than that of twenty-five individuals, and is within 0.1 mm of an additional five. Following Day (Leakey, Butzer, and Day 1969:1142), the tooth is robust by modern standards. Other features falling within the Neandertal

Table VIII. Cranial Measurements of African and Asian Neandertal Crania (mm).

	Omo 1	Omo 2	African-thropus 1	Djebel Irhound 1	Djebel Irhound 2	Broken Hill	Saldanha	Solo 1	Solo 3	Solo 5	Solo 6	Solo 9	Solo 10	Solo 11
Cranial Capacity (cc)		1435		1400	1450	1280	1250	1200		1300	1175	1135	1055	1060
Length	210	215	191	198	197	209	200	196		220	192	201	203	200
Breadth	144	145	142	145	148	145	144	148		147	146	150	159	144
Maximum Height Above Frankfort Plane	138	118	98	113	108	106		108	107	116	108	115	117	111
Porion–Nasion	113	111		107	106	104		93		113	106		107	
Glabella	130	120	114	123	115	114		105	104	126	114	118	118	115
Lambda	121	113	90	96	94	103		104		107	99	97	105	104
Opistocranion	105	102	84	88	85	98		94		106	90	89	99	94
Inion	88	102	79	79	85	98		94	88	106	90	89	99	94
Calotte Height Above Glabella–Inion	105	90	75	81	84	85	90	84		81	78	78	80	80
Gabella–Lambda	66	57	55	63	68	55	60	58		56	55	52	48	51

range of variation include the heavy supraorbital torus coupled with the absence of a supraorbital sulcus (similar to "Africanthropus"), robust facial bones, low position of maximum cranial breadth, and great cranial length. In both metric and non-metric morphology, the cranium is extremely similar to Amud. Both share the heavy supraorbitals without a supraorbital sulcus, the mental eminence of the mandible, the rounded occipital contour and low inion position, the large mastoid process, and the evenly rounded lateral contour from glabella to inion. In dimensions the two are almost identical. They are clearly more similar to each other than either is to any other Neandertal cranium. This relation is even true of the relatively great distance from porion to glabella, characteristic only of these two crania. The only difference lies in the fact that the Amud cranium is about one centimeter lower and one centimeter broader.

Omo 2 differs from Omo 1 in a number of ways. Yet there is an apparent similarity between the two calvaria. They share a heavy supraorbital torus associated with a receding forehead and absence of a supraorbital sulcus. However, Omo 2 shows extensive and detailed similarities with Solo 5. Both are long and moderately high, with identical morphology of the supraorbital region as well as the region of inion. In both, inion and opistocranion are identical. The nuchal tori are massive, and the nuchal planes flat. Inion is somewhat higher in Solo 5: while the auricular heights are the same, height above the glabella-inion line is greater in Omo 2. Most dimensions of the two are nearly identical. Indeed, the resemblance of Solo 5 and Omo 2 is greater than to any other of the Solo calvaria.

Omo 1 clearly meets the criteria of a transitional specimen. It should not be surprising that in East Africa, in a sense geographically between Java and the Near East, two crania show detailed and extensive similarities with specimens from these other areas. The associated lithic materials (if any) have not been described.

In sum, where appropriate archaeological associations exist, unquestionable transitional populations are clearly associated with Middle Paleolithic industries in Eastern and Western Europe, Africa, and the Near East. The evolution of local populations associated with Middle Paleolithic industries is thus indicated.

AN ADAPTIVE MODEL

The hypothesis critically addressed by this work was recently summed by Howell (1969:xxi): "Beginning some 35,000 years ago new peoples with new ideas and new designs for living displaced and eventually replaced antecedent Neanderthal peoples and their Mousterian way of life."

To the contrary, we suggest that *in situ* transitions of both hominids and their industries took place throughout the Old World within the period of the last glaciation. These transitions did not occur at the same time. The evolution of anatomically modern *H. sapiens* clearly precedes that of Upper Paleolithic industries. Thus, the selective factors leading to the evolution of anatomically modern populations are not to be sought in the Upper Paleolithic. Rather, we must seek their origins in the Middle Paleolithic.

We must ask what factors throughout the Old World undergo significant change *within* the Middle Paleolithic, and, of course, what factors do not. There are several indications that

significant changes in human ecology do not occur at this time. The age distributions of "classic" Neandertals and an Upper Paleolithic sample, both published by Vallois (1961), are almost identical to each other and to the age distribution of Indians from Indian Knoll (Snow 1948). Similar adaptive effectiveness for groups spanning this time range is thus indicated (Birch 1948; Cole 1954; Cannon 1968). The extensive hunting of megafauna has already been demonstrated at numerous Acheulean sites (see Howell 1965; Hemmer 1965). The specialized and intensive hunting of particular species can be seen as early as locality 1 at Choukoutian (Howell 1964). These two hunting behaviors do not necessarily occur together, although they often do. The areas exploited by Acheulean hunter-gatherers included both ecologically homogeneous areas such as Ternifine (Arambourg 1963) and edge areas or ecotones such as Toralba (Butzer 1964:366-371). For these reasons, a recent suggestion concerning Neandertal evolution (Binford 1968) can be dismissed. It was suggested that the Neandertal exploitation of ecotones containing large game on a regular seasonal basis led to the formation of larger groups for more efficient exploitation. Clearly, such conditions were met long before the recent date Binford suggests. In any event, the formation of larger and more exogamous groups would slow, rather than hasten, the effects of selection, all other factors remaining equal (Wright 1938).

We see the major behavioral changes within the Middle Paleolithic in industrial factors. These do not relate to any single specific tool type, but rather to a general increase in the numbers of different types of tools. A single purpose tool is generally more effective for the purpose for which it was made than any general purpose tool. With respect to the action of selection upon hominid morphology, the major implication of changes from general to specific tools concerns the use of the jaws as a vice. The importance of this usage is indicated by the maintenance of large anterior teeth (actually increasing in breadth for *early* Neandertals) throughout the Lower and Middle Pleistocene, while the posterior dentition progressively reduces. To put a hole in a piece of wood with a knife requires more use of a vice than if one were using a drill. That is, the development of special purpose tools reduces selection for both *force* and *power* (force over time) in the anterior dentition through a combination of less strenuous use and use over shorter periods of time. Indeed, the reduction of the anterior dentition is part of a general trend reducing skeletal and muscular rugosity, replacing them with more efficient technology.

With the reduction of selection acting to maintain a large anterior dentition, and later the increasing efficiency of cultural adaptations to cold, there is a concomitant reduction of robustness and size of Neandertal anterior teeth, and ultimately of the supporting facial morphology. This reduction allows the redistribution of cranial mass in a more spherical array. Weidenreich was aware of this redistribution and of its importance in the evolution of anatomically modern *H. sapiens* from Neandertal ancestors, although he was unable to account for it by recourse to evolutionary principles (1940, 1941, 1945, 1947).

Evidence for a selective advantage to cranial mass distribution is considerable. Schultz (1942) was able to show that in both man and apes the weight of the head is always greater anterior to the occipital condyles that it is posterior to them. Because the occipital condyles act as a fulcrum about which the nuchal musculature works, the force which must be exerted by these muscles depends upon both the moment of inertia of the weight distribution in front of the condyles and the distance of the muscles behind the condyles. The counterbalancing effect of Neandertal bunning is not so much to bring additional weight behind the condyles, but is rather to lengthen the lever arm for the nuchal musculature as well as to provide a horizontal orientation of the nuchal plane, increasing its leverage. The changes furthest anterior to the condyles have the greatest effect upon the length and orientation of the nuchal lever arm. The anterior dentition, and its supporting facial architecture, are the most anterior features of the cranium. The reduction of this complex would, by necessity, result in selection acting to shorten the nuchal lever arm and make it more vertical. The resulting crania (anatomically modern *H. sapiens*) are shorter and narrower but higher, and thus maintain the same cranial capacities.

In this respect, Schultz's work (1942) was particularly important. His empirical determinations evince a surprisingly constant balance ratio for modern crania, associated with a consistant occipital condyle position. Apparently, the condi-

tions for balance in *H. sapiens* represent a selective optimum for erect hominids. A similar selective optimum, with longer anterior and posterior lever arms, was reached with Neandertals evincing larger faces and anterior dentitions.

Other studies of cranial balance yield much the same results (Schultz 1918; Fischer and Mollison 1923). The position of the occipital condyles is fairly constant, and the force exerted by the nuchal musculature in both static and dynamic functioning is sensitive to small mass changes maximally anterior to the condyles.

Therefore, the loss of the distinctive Neandertal cranial form is a direct consequence of selection relaxation for the anterior dentition and supporting facial architecture, and resulting change in selection action on the static and dynamic properties of the nuchal musculature. That succeeding cold-adapted populations did not develop mid-facial prognathism follows from the raised position of the calvarium relative to the nasal passages in anatomically modern *H. sapiens*.

We submit that these considerations are sufficient to account for the association of Early Upper Paleolithic man and Late Middle Paleolithic tools.

REFERENCES

Alimen, Marie-Henriette. 1967. The Quarternary of France, in: *The Quarternary*, Vol. 2 (Kalervo Rankama, Ed.), Interscience, New York.

Arambourg, C. 1958. Les stades évolutifs de l'humanité. *The Leech* 28:106-111.

Arambourg, C. 1963. Le gisement de ternifine. *Archives de L'Institute de Paleontologie Humaine* 32.

Ashton, E. H., and Spence, T. F. 1958. Age changes in the cranial capacity and foramen magnum of hominoids. *Proceedings of the Zoological Society of London* 130:169-181.

Bailit, H. L., Dewitt, S. J., and Leigh, R. A. 1968. The size and morphology of the Nasioi dentition. *American Journal of Physical Anthropology* 28:271-288.

Bardon, L. J., and Bouyssonie, A. 1908. Découverte d'un squelette humaine Moustérien à la Bouffia de la Chapelle-Aux-Saints. *L'Anthropology* 19:513-518.

Barnes, D. S. 1969. Tooth morphology and other aspects of the Teso dentition. *American Journal of Physical Anthropology* 30:183-194.

Bastin, B. 1969. Premiers résultats de l'Analyse pollinique des loess en Belgique. *Bulletin de l'Association pour l'Etude du Quarternaire* 1:3-12.

Behm-Blanke, G. 1960. Altsteinzeitliche rastplätze im traveringebiet Taubach, Weimar: Ehringsdorf. *Alt-Thüringen* 4:1-245.

Benington, R. C. 1911. A study of the Negro skull with special reference to the Congo and Gaboon crania. *Biometrika* 8:292-337.

Binford, S. 1968. Early Upper Pleistocene adaptations in the Levant. *American Anthropologist* 70:707-717.

Binford, L., and Binford, S. 1966. A preliminary analysis of functional variability in the Mousterian of Levallois facies. *American Anthropologist* 68:238-295.

Binford, L., and Binford, S. 1969. Stone tools and human behavior. *Scientific American* 220(4):70-84.

Birch, L. C. 1948. The intrinsic rate of natural increase of an insect population. *Journal of Animal Ecology* 17:15-26.

von Bonin. 1935. The Magdelenian skeleton from Cap-Blanc in the Field Museum of Natural History. *Illinois Medical and Dental Monographs* 1:1-76.

Bordes, F. 1953. Essai de classification des industries "Moustériennes." *Bulletin de la Société Préhistorique Française* 50:226-235.

Bordes, F. 1955. Le Paléolithique inférieur et moyen de Jabrud. *L'Anthropologie* 59:486-507.

Bordes, F. 1958. Le passage du Paleolithique moyen au superieur, in: *Hundert Jahre Neanderthaler* (G. H. R. von Konigswald, Ed.), pp. 175-181, Kemink en Zoon, Utrecht.

Bordes, F. 1961. Mousterian cultures in France. *Science* 134:803-810.

Bordes, F. 1968. *The Old Stone Age*. McGraw-Hill, New York.

Bordes, F. 1969. Reflections on typology and techniques in the Paleolithic. *Arctic Anthropology* 6:1-29.

Boule, M. 1913. *L'homme fossile de la Chapelle-aux-Saints*. Mason, Paris.

Boule, M., and Vallois, H. V. 1957. *Fossil Man*. Dryden, New York.

Brace, C. L. 1962a. Cultural factors in the evolution of the human dentition, in: *Culture and the Evolution of Man* (M. F. Ashley Montagu, Ed.), pp. 343-354, Oxford, New York.

Brace, C. L. 1962b. Refocusing on the Neanderthal problem. *American Anthropologist* 64:729-741.

Brace, C. L. 1964. The fate of the "classic" Neanderthals: A consideration of hominid catastrophism. *Current Anthropology* 5:3-43.

Brace, C. L. 1967a. *The Stages of Human Evolution*. Prentice Hall, Englewood Cliffs, N.J.

Brace, C. L. 1967b. Environment, tooth form, and size in the Pleistocene. *Journal of Dental Research* 46:809-816.

Brace, C. L. 1967c. More on the fate of the "classic" Neanderthals. *Current Anthropology* 7:204-214.

Brace, C. L. 1968. Neanderthal. *Natural History* 77:38-45.

Brace, C. L., and Molnar, S. 1967. Experimental studies in human tooth wear. *American Journal of Physical Anthropology* 27:213-222.

Braidwood, R. 1966. *Prehistoric Men*. Scott Foresman, New York.

Bretinger, E. 1955. Das schadelfragment von Swanscomb und das "Praesapiens" problem. *Mitteilunge der Anthropologischen Gesellschaft in Wien* 84/85:1-45.

Brothwell, D. R. 1959. Teeth in earlier human populations. *Proceedings of the Nutrition Society* 18:54-64.

Brothwell, D. R. 1963. The macroscopic dental pathology of some earlier human populations, in: *Dental Anthropology* (D. R. Brothwell, Ed.), pp. 271-288, Pergamon, New York.

Burkitt, M. 1963. *The Old Stone Age*. Atheneum, New York.

Butzer, K. W. 1964. *Environment and Archaeology*. Methuen, London.

Butzer, K. W., and Thurber, D. L. 1969. Some late Cenozoic sedimentary formations of the Lower Omo Basin. *Nature* 222:1138-1143.

Campbell, T. D. 1925. *Dentition and Palate of the Australian Aboriginal*. Hassell Press, Adelaide.

Campbell, T. D. 1939. Food, food values, and food habits of the Australian aborigines. *Australian Dental Journal* 43:1-15, 45-55, 73-87, 141-156, 177-198.

Cannon, K. D. 1968. *Homo neanderthalensis*: His Role in Human Evolution. Unpublished manuscript.

Captain, L., and Peyrony, D. 1909. Deux squelettles humains au milieu des foyers de l'epoque Mousterienne. *Revue de l'Ecole d'Anthropologie* 19:402-409.

Captain, L., and Peyrony, D. 1912a. Le station préhistorique de La Farrassie, Commune de Savignac-du-Bugue (Dordogne). *Revue Anthropologique* 22:29-50, 76-99.

Captain, L., and Peyrony, D. 1912b. Trois nouveaux squelettes humains fossiles. *Revue Anthropologique* 22:439-442.

Captain, L., and Peyrony, D. 1921. Decouverte d'un sixieme squelette Moustérien en La Ferrassie. *Revue Anthropologique* 31:382-388.

Carbonnell, V. M. 1965. The teeth of the Neandertal child from Gibraltar: A Re-evaluation. *American Journal of Physical Anthropology* 23:41-50.

Cole, L. C. 1954. The population consequences of life history phenomena. *Quarterly Review of Biology* 29:103-137.

Collie, G. 1928. The Aurignacians and their culture. *Logan Museum Bulletin 1*.

Coon, C. S. 1962. *The Origin of Races*. Knopf, New York.

Coon, C. S. 1964. Comment on: The fate of the "classic" Neanderthals: A consideration of hominid catastrophism, by Brace (1964). *Current Anthropology* 5:21-22.

Crane, H. R. 1956. University of Michigan radiocarbon dates I. *Science* 124:664.

Dahlberg, A. A. 1963. Dental evolution and culture. *Human Biology* 35:237-249.

Debenath, A., and Piveteau, J. 1969. Nouvelles découvertes de restes humains fossiles a La Chaise-de-Vouthon (Charente). Position Stratigraphique de Restes Humains de La Chaise (Abri Bourgeouis-Delaunay). *Comptes Rendue de L'Academie des Sciences*, Série D 269:24-28.

De Jong, J. 1967. The Quarternary of the Netherlands, in: *The Quarternary*, Vol. 2 (Kalervo Rankama, Ed.), Interscience, New York.

De Lumley, M. 1970. Le pariétal humain anténéandertalien de Cova Negra (Jativa, Espagne). *Comptes Rendus de L'Academie des Sciences*, Série D 270:39-41.

De Sonneville-Bordes, D. 1963. Upper Paleolithic cultures in Western Europe. *Science* 142:347-355.

De Sonneville-Bordes, D., and Perrot, J. 1953. Essai d'adaptation des méthodes statistiques au Paléolithique Superieur-Premiers resultas. *Bulletin de la Societe Préhistorique Français* No. 5-6.

De Villiers, H. 1958. *The Skull of the South African Negro*. Witwatersrand University, Johannesburg.

Dupree, L. 1969. Comment on: Neandertal man and *Homo sapiens* in central and eastern Europe. *Current Anthropology* 10:492.

Dupree, L., Lattman, L. J., and Davis, R. S. 1970. Ghar-i-mordeh Gusfand (Cave of the Dead Sheep): A new Mousterian locality in north Afghanistan. *Science* 167:1610-1612.

Ennouchi, E. 1962. Un Néandertalien: l'Homme der Jebel Irhound. *L'-Anthropologie* 66:279-299.

Ennouchi, E. 1968. Le deuxième crane de l'Homme d'Irhound. *Annales de Paléontologie Vertèbres* 54:117-128.

Ennouchi, E. 1969. Présence d'un enfant néanderthalien au Jebel Irhound. (Maroc). *Annales de Paléontologie Vertèbres* 55:251-265.

Fenart, M. R. 1969. Le crane de l'Enfant de l'Aze, etudié dans les axes vestibulaires d'orientation. *Comptes Rendu de L'Académie des Sciences*, Série D 268:2042-2045.

Fischer, E., and Mollison, T. 1923. *Kultur der Gegenwart*, part III. Teubner, Leipzig.

Fitting, J. E. 1969. Comment on: Early man in America, by A. L. Bryan. *Current Anthropology* 10:339-365.

Flint, R. F. 1957. *Glacial and Pleistocene Geology*. John Wiley and Sons, New York.

Fraipont, J., and Lohest, M. 1887. La race humaine de néanderthal ou de Canstadt en Belgique. *Archives de Biologie* 7:587-758.

Freeman, L. G., and Gonzalez Echegaray, J. 1970. Aurignacian structural features and burials at Cueva Morin (Santander, Spain). *Nature* 226:722-726.

Garrod, D. A. E. 1928. Excavations of a Mousterian rock shelter at Devil's Tower, Gibraltar. *Journal of the Royal Anthropological Institute* 58:33-56.

Garrod, D. A. E. 1962. An outline of Pleistocene prehistory in Palestine. *Quarternaria* 6:541-546.

Garrod, D. A. E., and Bate, D. M. A. 1937. *The Stone Age of Mount Carmel. Vol. 1: Excavations at the Wady el-Mughara*. Clarendon, Oxford.

Gessain, P. 1959. La dentition des Eskimo d'Angmassalik genetique croissance et Pathologie. Société d'Anthropologie de Paris, *Bulletin et Memoires*, Série 10:364-396.

Gorjanovic-Kramberger, D. 1906. *Der Diluviale Mensch von Krapina in Kroatien: ein Beitrag zur Palaoanthropologie*. Kriedel, Wiesbaden.

Gorjanovic-Kramberger, D. 1907. Die Kronen und Wurzeln der Mahlzähne des Homo Primigenius und ihre Genetische Bedeutung. *Anatomischer Anzeiger* 31:97-134.

Gorjanovic-Kramberger, D. 1910. *Homo aurignacensis* hauseri in Krapina? *Verhandlugen der Geologische Reichsanstalt* 14:312-317.

Gorjanovic-Kramberger, D. 1913. Zivot i kulture diluvijalonga covjeka iz Krapine u hrvatsko (Hominis Diluvialis e Krapina in Croatia Vita et Cultura). *Djela Jugoslavenske Akademije Znanosti i Umjetnosti* 23:1-54.

Gupta, P., Dutta, P. C., and Basu, A. 1962. Human remains from Harappa. *Anthropological Survey of India, Memoir* 9:3-186.

Harrison, T. 1959. Radio-Carbon dates from Niah. *Sarawak Museum Journal* 9:136-138.

Harrison, T. 1964. 50,000 Years of Stone Age culture in Borneo. *Annual Report of the Smithsonian Institution* 1964:521-530.

Heim, J-L. 1968. Les Restes Néandertaliens de La Ferrassie. Nouvelles données sur la stratigraphie et inventaire des squelettes. *Comptes Rendus de L'Académie des Sciences*, Série D 266:576-578.

Heinz, N. 1967. Evolution de la hauteur maximale du frontal, du pariétal, et du l'occipital Chez les hominides. *Annales de Paléontologie, Vertèbres* 53:50-75.

Hemmer, H. 1965. Die aussage der Saugetierfauna fur die okologie Pleistozaner Hominiden. *Homo: Zeitschrift fur die Vergleichende Forschung am Menschen* 16:95-109.

Henri-Martin, G. 1923. L'Homme fossile de La Quina. *Archives de Morphologie Générale et Experimentale* 15:1-253.

Hole, F., and Flannery, K. V. 1968. Prehistory of Southwestern Iran: A preliminary report. *Proceedings of the Prehistoric Society* 33:147-206.

Hooton, E. A. 1947. *Up from the Ape*. Macmillan, New York.

Howell, F. C. 1951. The place of the Neanderthal man in human evolution. *American Journal of Physical Anthropology* 9:379-416.

Howell, F. C. 1952. Pleistocene glacial ecology and the evolution of "classic Neandertal" man. *Southwest Journal of Anthropology* 8:377-410.

Howell, F. C. 1957. The evolutionary significance of variation and varieties of Neanderthal man. *Quarterly Review of Biology* 32:330-347.

Howell, F. C, 1958. Upper Pleistocene men of the southwest Asian Mousterian. In *Hundert Jahre Neanderthaler*. G. H. R. von Koenigswald, ed. pp. 185-198, Kemink in Zoon Utrecht.

Howell, F. C. 1959. Upper Pleistocene stratigraphy and early man in the Levant. *Proceedings of the American Philosophical Society* 103:1-65.

Howell, F. C. 1960. European and northwest African Middle Pleistocene hominids. *Current Anthropology* 1:195-232.

Howell, F. C. 1964. The hominization process, in: *Horizons of Anthropology* (Sol Tax, Ed.), pp. 49-59, Aldine, Chicago.

Howell, F. C. 1965. *Early Man*. Time, New York.

Howell, F. C. 1967. Recent advances in human evolutionary studies. *Quarterly Review of Biology* 42:471-513.

Howell, F. C. 1969. Foreword to *Man and Culture in the Late Pleistocene*, by R. H. Klein. pp. 21-26, Chandler, San Francisco.

Howells, W. W. 1967. *Mankind in the Making*. (Revised edition.) Doubleday, Garden City.

Hrdlicka, A. 1911. Human dentition and teeth from the evolutionary and racial standpoint. *Dominion Dental Journal* (Ontario) 21:1-15.

Hrdlicka, A. 1927. The Neanderthal phase of man. *Journal of the Royal Anthropological Institute* 57:249-274.

Hrdlicka, A. 1928. Catalog of human crania in the United States National Museum: Australians, Tasmanians, South African Bushmen, Hottentots, and Negroes. *Proceedings of the United States National Museum* 7:1-140.

Hrdlicka, A. 1930. The Skeletal Remains of Early Man. *Smithsonian Miscellaneous Collections* 83.

Hrdlicka, A. 1942. Catalog of human crania in the United States National Museum collections: Eskimo in general. *Proceedings of the United States National Museum* 91:169-429.

Ivanova, I. K. 1969. Etude Geologique des Gisemments Paléolithiques de L'U.R.S.S. *L'Anthropologie* 73:5-48.

Jelinek, A. 1965. Lithic technology conference, Les Eyzies, France. *American Antiquity* 31:277-278.

Jelinek, J. 1964. Betrachtungen über die Verwandschaft der Anthropologischen Funde Dolni Vestonice, Abri Pataud, und Markina Gora. *Zeitschrift für Morphologie und Anthropologie* 56:19-23.

Jelinek, J. 1966. Jaw of an intermediate type of Neandertal man from Czechoslovakia. *Nature* 212:701-702.

Jelinek, J. 1969. Neandertal man and *Homo sapiens* in central and eastern Europe. *Current Anthropology* 10:475-503.

Jelinek, J., Palisek, J., and Valoch, K. 1959. Der fossil mensch Brno II. *Anthropos* 9:17-22.

Kadic, O., Bartucz, L., Hillebrand, E., and Szabo, J. 1933. Preliminary report on the results of excavations in the Subalyuk Cave near Cserepfalu, Hungary. *International Geological Congress: Report of the XVI Session (United States)* 2:783-788.

Kannelis, A., and Savas. 1964. Kraniometriki meleti ton Homo neanderthalenis ton Petralonen epistimeniki. *Epetiris tis Physikomathematikis Sholos* 9:65-92.

Keith, A. 1915. *The Antiquity of Man*. Williams and Norgate, London.

Kitching, J. W. 1963. *Bone, Tooth, and Horn Tools of Paleolithic Man*. Manchester University, Manchester.

Klaatsch, H. 1923. *The Evolution and Progress of Mankind*. Stokes, New York.

Klein, R. G. 1969. Mousterian cultures in European Russia. *Science* 165:257-265.

Kleinschmidt, O. 1931. *Der Urmensch*. Quelle und Meyer, Leipzig.

Kokkoros, M. M., and Kannelis, A. 1960. Découverte d'un crane d'homme Paleolithique dans la Péninsule Chalcidique (Petralona). *L'-Anthropologie* 64:438-446.

Krukoff, S. 1970. L'occipital de La Chaise (Suard), caractères métriques, distances de forme et de format. *Comptes Rendus de L'Académie des Sciences*, Série D, 170:42-45.

Kurten B. 1968. *Pleistocene Mammals of Europe*. Aldine, Chicago.

Kurth, G. 1965. Die (Eu) Hominiden: Ein Jeweilsbild nach dem Kenntnisstand von 1964, in: *Menschliche Abstammtungslehre* (G. Heberer, Ed.), pp. 357-425, Fischer, Stuttgart.

Larnach, S. L., and Macintosh, N. W. G. 1966. The craniology of the aborigines of coastal New South Wales. *The Oceania Monographs* 13.

Leakey, R. E. F., Butzer, K. W., and Day, M. H. 1969. Early *Homo sapiens* remains from the Omo River region of south-west Ethiopia. *Nature* 222:1132-1138.

Le Gros Clark, W. E. 1964. *The Fossil Evidence for Human Evolution*. Revised edition. University of Chicago, Chicago.

Le Gros Clark, W. E. 1966. *History of the Primates*, Fifth edition. Phoenix, Chicago.

Leigh, R. W. 1928. Dental pathology of aboriginal California. *University of California Publications in American Archaeology and Ethnology* 23:399-440.

Leigh, R. W. 1937. Dental morphology and pathalogy of Pre-Spanish Peru. *American Journal of Physical Anthropology* 22:267-295.

Leroi-Gourhan, A. 1958. Etude des restes humains fossiles prouvenant des grottes d'Arcy-sur-Cure. *Annales de Paléontologie* 44:87-148.

Leroi-Gourhan, A. 1961. Les fouilles d'Archy-Sur-Cure (Yonne). *Gallia* 4:1-16.

McBurney, C. B. M. 1960. *The Stone Age of North Africa*. Penguin, New York.

McBurney, C. B. M. 1967. *The Haua Steah (Cyrenaica) and the Stone Age of the South-East Mediterranean*. Cambridge University, London.

McCown, T., and Keith, A. 1939. *The Stone Age of Mount Carmel. Vol. II: The Fossil Human Remains from the Levalloiso-Mousterian*. Clarendon, Oxford.

Maska, K. J. 1882. Über den diluvialen Menschen in Stramberg. *Mitteilungen der Anthropologischen Gesellschaft in Wien* 12:32-38.

Maska, K. J. 1886. Über den meschlichen Unterkeifers in der Sipkahahle. *Verhandlungen der Berliner Anthropologischen Gesellschaft* 18:341-344.

Maska, K. J. 1889. Die Lossfunde bei brunn un der diluviale Mensch. *Mitteilungen der Anthropologischen Gesellschaft in Wien* 19:46-64.

Matiegka, J. 1938. *Homo predmostensis*, fosilni clovek Z Predmosti No Morave. Czechoslovakian Academy of Science and Art Publication, Prague.

Miyabara, T. 1916. An anthropological study of the masticatory system in the Japanese. *Dental Cosmos* 16:739-749.

Mongait, A. L. 1961. *Archaeology in the USSR*. Pelican, New York.

Morant, G. M. 1924. A study of certain oriental series of crania including the Nepalese and Tibetan series in the British Museum (Natural History). *Biometrika* 16:1-105.

Morant, G. M. 1925. Studies of Paleolithic Man I. The Chancelade skull and its relations to the modern Eskimo skull. *Annals of Eugenics* 1:257-276.

Morant, G. M. 1927a. Studies of Paleolithic man II. A biometric study of Neanderthal skulls and their relationships to modern racial types. *Annals of Eugenics* 2:318-381.

Morant, G. M. 1927b. A study of the Australian and Tasmanian skulls, based on previously published measurements. *Biometrika* 19:417-440.

Morant, G. M. 1928. Studies of Paleolithic man III. The Rhodesian skull and its relationships to Neanderthal and modern types. *Annals of Eugenics* 3:277-336.

Morant, G. M. 1930. Studies of Paleolithic man IV. A biometric study of the Upper Paleolithic skulls of Europe and their relationships to earlier and later forms. *Annals of Eugenics* 4:109-214.

Mottl, M 1951. Die Repolusthole bei peggau und ihre eiszeitlichen Bewohner. *Archaeologia Austriaca* 8:1-78.

Movius, H. L. 1969. The Chatelperronian in French archaeology: The evidence of Arcy-sur-Cure. *Antiquity* 43:111-123.

Neuville, R. 1951. Le Paléolithique et la Mésolithique de desert de Judee. *Archives de l'Institute Paléontologie Humaine* 24:1-270.

Noble, H. E. 1926. The teeth of the Richmond River Blacks. *Australian Journal of Dentistry* 30:4-12.

Oakley, K. A. 1962. *Man the Tool-Maker*. University of Chicago Press, Chicago.

Oakley, K. A. 1966. *Frameworks for Dating Fossil Man*. Aldine, Chicago.

Okladnikov, A. P. *et al.* 1949. Teshik-Tash: Paleolithicheskii chelovek. Moscow: Trudy Nauchno-Issledovatelskogo Instituta Anthropologii.

Patte, E. 1955. *Les Néanderthaliens. Anatomie, Physiologie, Comparaisons*, Masson et Cie, Paris.

Pearson, K., and Davin, A. G. 1926. On the biometric constants of the human skull. *Biometrika* 16:328-363.

Pedersen, P. O. 1938. Investigation into the dental conditions of about 3000 ancient and modern Greenlanders. *Dental Record* 58:191-198.

Perrot, J. 1968. La préhistoire Paléstinienne. *Supplement au Dictionaire de la Bible* 8:286-446. Letouzey and Ane, Paris.

Pivetau, J., 1964. La grotte de Regourdou II. *Annales de Paléontologie Vertèbres* 50:23-62.

Pivetau, J. 1967. Un pariétal de la grotte du Lazaret (Alpes-maritimes). *Annales de Paléontologie Vertèbres* 53:166-199.

Pivetau, J. 1969. La paléontologie humaine en France. *Études Françaises sur Le Quarternaire*. INQUA, Paris.

Piveteau, E., De Lumley, H., and De Lumley, M. 1963. Découverte de restes Néanderthaliens dans la Grotte de L'Hortus. *Comptes Rendus de L'Academie des Sciences*, Serie D 256:40-44.

Poulianos, A. N. 1966. The place of the Petralonian man among the palaeoanthropoids. *Anthropos* 19:216-221.

Poulianos, A. N. 1969. Comment on Neandertal man and *Homo sapiens* in central and eastern Europe. *Current Anthropology* 10:496.

Pradel, L. 1966. Transition from Mousterian to Perigordian: Skeletal and industrial. *Current Anthropology* 7:33-50.

Randall, F. E. 1943-1944. The skeletal and dental development and variability of the gorilla. *Human Biology* 15:236-254, 307-337; 16:23-76.

Schaefer, U. 1964. *Homo neanderthalensis* (King) II. E-Schadel-fragment, frontale F-1, and torus-fragment 37.2 von Krapina. *Zeitschrift für Morphologie und Anthropologie* 54:260-271.

Schlaginhaufen, O. 1946. Über die Menschformen des jüngeren Palaolithikums in Europa. *Experientia* 2:303-306.

Schultz, A. H. 1918. Anthropologische untersuchungen an der schadelbasis. *Archiv für Anthropologie* 16:1-103.

Schultz, A. H. 1942. Conditions for balancing the head in primates. *American Journal of Physical Anthropology* 29:483-497.

Schwalbe, G. 1901. Der neanderthalschadel. *Bonner Jahrbuch* 106:1-72.

Schwalbe, G. 1906. *Studien zur Vorgeschichte des Menschen*. Schweizerbartsche, Stuttgart.

Schwalbe, G. 1914. Kritische Besprechung von Boule's Werk: "L'homme fossile de la Chapelle-aux-Saints." *Zeitschrift für Morphologie und Anthropologie* 16:527-610.

Selmer-Olsen, R. 1949. An odontometric study of the Norwegian Lapps, Skifter Det Norske Videnskaps-Akademi I (Oslo). *Mathematisk-Naturvidenkapelig Klasse* 65:1-168.

Senyurek, M. 1959. *A Study of the Deciduous Teeth of the Fossil Shanidar Infant*. Division of Paleoanthropology, University of Ankara, Publication No. 128.

Sergi, S. 1940. Der Neandertalschadel vom Monte Circeo. *Anthropologischer Anzeiger* 16:203-217.

Sergi, S. 1944. Craniometria e craniografia del primo paleanthropo di Saccopastore. *Richerche di Morfologia* 21:733-791.

Sergi, S. 1948. Il Cranio des seconco paleanthropo di Saccopastore. Craniografia e Craniometria. *Palaeontographia Italica* 42:4-164.

Sergi, S. 1958a. The Neanderthal palaeanthropi in Italy, in: *Ideas on Human Evolution* (W. W. Howells, Ed., 1962), pp. 500-506, Harvard University, Cambridge.

Sergi, S. 1958b. Die neandertalischen Palaeanthropen in Italien, in: *Hundert Jahre Neanderthaler* (G. H. R. von Koenigswald, Ed.), pp. 38-51, Kemink en Zoon, Utrecht.

Shapiro, H. L. 1929. Contributions to the craniology of central Europe 1: Crania from Greifenberg in Carinthia. *Anthropological Papers of the American Museum of Natural History* 31:1-120.

Singer, R. 1954. The Saldanha skull from Hopefield, South Africa. *American Journal of Physical Anthropology* 12:345-362.

Snow, C. E. 1948. Indian knoll skeletons of site OH 2, Ohio County, Kentucky. *University of Kentucky Reports in Anthropology* 4:371-554.

Sollas, W. J. 1908. On the cranial and facial characters of the Neanderthal race. *Philosophical Transactions of the Royal Society of London*, Series B 199:281-339.

Stewart, T. D. 1958. First views of the restored Shanidar I skull. *Sumer* 14:90-96.

Stewart, T. D. 1960. Indirect evidence of the primativeness of the Swanscombe skull. *American Journal of Physical Anthropology* 18:363.

Stewart, T. D. 1961. The skull of Shanidar II. *Sumer* 17:97-106.

Stewart, T. D. 1963. Shanidar skeletons IV and VI. *Sumer* 19:8-25.

Straus, W. L., Jr., and Cave, A. J. E. 1957. Pathology and the posture of Neanderthal man. *Quarterly Review of Biology* 32:348-363.

Sullivan, L. R. 1921. A few Adamanese skulls with comparative notes on Negrito craniometry. *Anthropological papers of the American Museum of Natural History* 23:175-200.

Suzuki, H. 1965. A paleoanthropic man from the Amud Cave, Israel. *Communications to the VII International Congress of Anthropological and Ethnological Sciences*, Moscow, pp. 1-8.

Suzuki, H. 1968. A paleoanthropic fossil man from Amud Cave, Israel. *Congres International de Sciences Anthropologiques et Ethnologiques* (Moscow, 1964) 3:305-316.

Taylor, R. M. S. 1934. Maori foods and methods of preparation. *New Zealand Dental Journal* 30, no. 147.

Taylor, R. M. S. 1963. Cause and effect of wear of teeth. *Acta Anatomica* 53:97-157.

Thoma, A. 1958. Metissage ou transformation? Essai sur les hommes fossiles de Palestine. *L'Anthropologie* 62:30-52.

Thoma, A. 1963. The dentition of the Subalyuk Neanderthal child. *Zeitschrift für Morphologie und Anthropologie* 54:127-150.

Thoma, A. 1965. The definition of the Neanderthals and the position of the fossil men of Palestine. *Yearbook of Physical Anthropology* 13:137-145.

Thompson, E. Y. 1916. A study of the crania of the Moriori or Aborigines, of the Chatam Island, now in the Museum of the Royal College of Surgeons. *Biometrika* 11:82-135.

Tobias, P. V. 1964. Comment on: The fate of the "classic" Neandertals: A consideration of hominid catastrophism. *Current Anthropology* 5:30-31.

Tode, A., Preul, F., and Kleinschmidt, A. 1953. Die Untersuchung der Palaolitischen Freilandstation von Salzgitter-Levenstedt. *Eiszeitalter und Gegenwart* 3:144-220.

Turner, C. G., and Cadien, J. D. 1969. Dental chipping in Aleuts, Eskimos, and Indians. *American Journal of Physical Anthropology* 31:303-310.

Vallois, H. V. 1951. La mandible humaine fossile de la grotte du porc-epic prés dire-dawa. *L'Anthropologie* 55:231-238.

Vallois, H. V. 1958. La grotte de Fontechevade: Anthropologie (deuxième partie). *Archives de l'Institut de Paleontologie Humaine, Mémoire* 29:5-156.

Vallois, H. V. 1961. The social life of early man: The evidence of skeletons, in: *The Social Life of Early Man* (S. L. Washburn, Ed.), pp. 214-235, Aldine, Chicago.

Vallois, H. V. 1962. Un nouveau Néanderthaloide en Palestine. *L'Anthropologie* 66:405-407.

Vallois, H. V. 1969. Le temporal Néandertalien H 27 de La Quina. *L'Anthropologie* 73:365-400.

Valoch, K. 1968. Evolution of the Paleolithic in central and eastern Europe. *Current Anthropology* 9:351-390.

Vandermeersch, B. 1965. Position stratigraphique et chronologie rélative des restes humains du Paléolithique Moyen du sud-ouest de la France. *Annales de Paléontologie Vertèbres* 51:69-126.

Vandermeerch, B. 1966. Nouvelles découvertes de restes humains dans les chouches Levalloiso-Moustériennes du gisement de Quafzeh (Israel) *Comptes Rendus de L'Academie des Sciences*, Serie D, 262:1434-1436.

Vandermeerch, B. 1969a. Quoted in: Rapport d'Activite 1968-1969. Centre National de la Recherche Scientifique. *Report on the Prehistoric and Protohistoric Civilizations of the Asiatic Near East*. D. Ferembach, Ed., No. 50.

Vandermeerch, B. 1969b. Les nouveaux squelettes Moustériennes découverte a'Qafzeh (Israel) et leur signification. *Comptes Rendus de L'Académie des Sciences*, Serie D 268:2562-2565.

Vandermeerch, B. 1970. Une sepulture Moustérienne avec offrandes découverte dans la grotte de Qafzeh. *Comptes Rendus de L'Académie des Sciences*, Serie D 270:298-301.

Van Reenen, J. F. 1966. Dental features of a low-caries primitive population. *Journal of Dental Research* 47:703-713.

Vergnaud-Grazzini, C., and Herman-Rosenberg, Y. 1969. Étude paléoclimatique d'une Carotte de mediterrance Orientale. *Révue de Géographie Physique et de Geologie Dynamique* 11:279-292.

Vernau, R. 1924. Le race de Néanderthal et la race de Grimaldi: Leurs roles dans l'humanite. *Journal of the Royal Anthropological Institute* 54:211-230.

Virchow, H. 1920. *Die Menschlichen Skelettreste aus dem Krampfeschen Bruch im Travertin von Ehringsdorf bei Weimar*. Fischer, Jena.

Virchow, R. 1882. Der Keifer aus Sipka-hühle und der Keifer la Naulete. *Zeitschrift für Ethnologie* 14:277-310.

Vlcek, E. 1955. The fossil man of Ganovce, Czechoslovakia. *Journal of the Royal Anthropological Institute* 85:163-171.

Vlcek, E. 1964. Einige in der Ontogenese des modernen Menschen untersuchte Neandertalmerkmale. *Zeitschrift für Morphologie und Anthropologie* 56:63-83.

Vlcek, E. 1965. Neuer fund eines neandertalers in der Tschechoslowakei. *Anthropologischer Anzeiger* 27:162-166.

Vlcek, E. 1967. Die sinus frontales bei Europaischen Neandertalern. *Anthropologischer Anzeiger* 30:166-169.

Vlcek, E. 1969. *Neandertaler der Tschechoslowakei*. Tschechoslowakischen Akademie die Wissenschaften, Prague.

Von Koenigswald, G. H. R. Ed. 1958. *Hundert Jahre Neanderthaler*. Kemink en Zoon, Utrecht.

Waugh, L. M. 1937. Influence of diet on the jaws and face of the American Eskimo. *Journal of the American Dental Association* 24:1640-1647.

Weckler, J. E. 1954. The relationships between Neandertal man and *Homo sapiens*. *American Anthropologist* 56:1003-1025.

Weidenreich, F. 1928. *Der Schadelfund von Weimar-Ehringsdorf*. Fischer, Jena.

Weidenreich, F. 1940. The "Neanderthal Man" and the ancestors of *Homo sapiens*. *American Anthropologist* 42:375-383.

Weidenreich, F. 1941. The brain and its role in the phylogenetic transformation of the human skull. *Transactions of the American Philosophical Society* 31:321-442.

Weidenreich, F. 1945. The brachycephalization of recent mankind. *Southwestern Journal of Anthropology* 1:1-54.

Weidenreich, F. 1947. Facts and speculations concerning the origin of *Homo sapiens*. *American Anthropologist* 49:187-203.

Weidenreich, F. 1951. Morphology of Solo Man. *Anthropological Papers of the American Museum of Natural History* 43(3):205-290.

Weinert, H. 1925. *Der Schädel des Eiszeitlichen Menschen von Le Moustier*. Springer, Berlin.

Weinert, H. 1936. Der Urmenschenshädel von Steinheim. *Zeitschrift für Morphologie und Anthropologie* 35:413-518.

Weinert, H. 1940. Africanthropus njarasensis. *Zeitschrift für Morphologie und Anthropologie* 38:252-308.

Weinert, H. 1944. *Ursprung der Menschenheit*. Enke, Stuttgart.

Wells, L. H. 1947. A note on the maxillary fragment from the Broken Hill Cave, in: *New Studies on Rhodesian Man* (J. D. Clark, K. P. Oakley, L. H. Wells, and J. A. C. McClelland), *Journal of the Royal Anthropological Institute* 77:7-32.

Werth, E. 1928. *Der Fossile Mensch*. Borntraeger, Berlin.

West, R. G. 1967. The Quarternary of the British Isles. In: *The Quarternary*, Vol. 2 (Kalervo Rankama, Ed.), Interscience, New York.

Wobst, R. 1970. Review of: Slovensko v starsej a strednej dobe kamannej, by J. Barta. Bratislava, Slovenska Akademia Vied, 1965. *American Anthropologist* 72:454-456.

Woldstedt, P. 1967. The quarternary of Germany, in: *The Quarternary*, Vol. 2 (Kalervo Rankama, Ed.), Interscience, New York.

Wolpoff, M. H. 1968. Climatic influence on the skeletal nasal aperture. *American Journal of Physical Anthropology* 29:405-424.

Wolpoff, M. H. 1969. Cranial capacity and taxonomy of Olduvai Hominid 7. *Nature* 223:182-183.

Wolpoff, M. H. 1971. Metric trends in hominid dental evolution. *Case Western Reserve University Studies in Anthropology* 2.

Woo, Ju-Kang, and Ru-Ce Peng. 1959. Human fossil skull of early Paleoanthropic stage found at Mapa, Shaoquan, Kwangtung Province. *Vertebrata Palasiatica* 3:176-182.

Wright, S. 1938. Size of population and breeding structure in relation to evolution. *Science* 87:430-431.

Yakimov, V. P. 1969. Comment on: Neandertal man and *Homo sapiens* in central and eastern Europe. *Current Anthropology* 10:498.

Zubakov, V. A. 1969. La chronologie des variations climatiques au cours du Pleistocene en Siberie Occidental. *Révue de Géographie Physique et de Géologie Dynamique* 11:315-324.

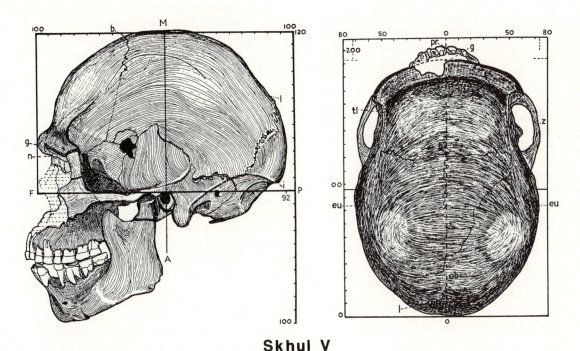

Skhul V

52

Neanderthals: Names, Hypotheses, and Scientific Method

W. W. Howells

These comments are stimulated by the Brose-Wolpoff article in the October, 1971, issue of the *American Anthropologist*. They are not directed primarily to specific matters of controversy; many such points have been dealt with by others in "Comments" accompanying Brace's 1964 article in *Current Anthropology*. Instead, I am concerned with some problems of applying scientific method in the field of paleoanthropology, especially the use of hypotheses and the need to inquire constantly into the population structure of late Pleistocene men.

The Brose-Wolpoff hypothesis (offered to refute that of a "sudden replacement" of the Neanderthals [1] by modern man) is as follows: Contrary to the common view, there did not take place a migration of anatomically modern *Homo sapiens* into the west, bringing Upper Paleolithic cultures and replacing Neanderthal populations and their Middle Paleolithic technologies. Instead, local "in situ transitions of both hominids and their industries took place throughout the Old World within the period of the last glaciation. These transitions did not occur at the same time." Rather, adaptive changes resulting from relaxation of selective factors (such as the prevailing use of the anterior teeth to supplement work with tools, and cold adaptation superimposed on this in Western Europe) led to the evolution of anatomically modern *Homo sapiens* in a Middle Paleolithic technology. On the biological side, this proposal is a descendant of the "Neanderthal stage" hypothesis, though the authors use the more judicious term of "grade."

They contribute various ideas and emphases, such as pointing out the too-ready tendency to judge the morphological form of a population from its archaeological associations, as has been done in the past to buttress the "sudden replacement" hypothesis in the case of Europe. However, just as this last hypothesis can be overdone and oversimplified, so I believe that of Brose and Wolpoff is too broad, as they develop it, to the point where it does more harm than good. It is these consequences I am considering; for, in the nonexperimental paleontological division of physical anthropology, we have had a hard time trying to reach scientific standards and methods, and we should do what we can to proceed carefully.

POPULATIONS VERSUS CATEGORIES

In general, using disciplined hypotheses, suitable in scope to the material dealt with, is important. Furthermore, hypotheses of interpretation rest not simply on the fossils, but also on the best possible inferences which can be drawn from vertebrate paleontology and from modern evolutionary theory in general. More is needed than a declaration of adherence to Darwinism and a recognition of the significance of mutation, selection and drift, when all this adds up simply to an acknowledgement that man, like other animals, has evolved over time [2]. For the impact of evolutionary theory on physical anthropology, the essential thing to appreciate is the additional aspect of population patterns: the basis and processes of interpopulation variation, subspeciation and speciation. This should by now be a banality, but can stand reiteration. Mayr (1959) has epitomized the general meaning of the Darwinian revolution as a shift from "typological" or "essentialist" thinking to "population" thinking. In anthropology the shift, and the related concepts, have more specific import for modern understandings; and Mayr in other writings (1963a, 1963b) has stressed the importance of the population viewpoint in human paleontology. F. C. Howell applied it in his important 1952 article. But in these terms I find the Brose-Wolpoff framework too broad and simple.

To begin with, their hypothesis involves the premise of a universal Neanderthal population in the Old World parental (at different times and places) to *all* populations *of* modern man. They define Neanderthals as "all hominid specimens dated within the time span from the end of the Riss to the appearance of anatomically modern *Homo sapiens*." This does not specify a biological taxon; it is purely a terminological definition (and is not unique to them, they note). It is not population thinking; it is conglomeration thinking. Its pernicious effect is the foreclosing, right here, of inquiry into just what populations *were* in existence in different localities of the period (Howell 1957), which is really the correct subject of inquiry into material known now and in the future. The authors distinguish two classes: "classic" Neanderthals of Europe (the conventional list [3], which are the result of cold adaptation of the face and body, added to a more general Neanderthal configuration, which is that of the "non-classics." This is their second category, which comprises all other specimens already implied, including Omo 2, Broken Hill and Saldanha in Africa, Mapa in China, and the Solo skulls as "tropical" Neanderthals in Java, along with all late Pleistocene North African and Near Eastern specimens.

As they say, quite correctly, they are not the first to use such categories. "Neanderthal," "Neanderthaloid," and "Neanderthalian" have been employed by various writers to cover the same spectrum of specimens. As Howell pointed out in 1957, without obvious success, this has been a serious source of confusion. Such writers have not been explicit as to what they mean by their usages, and have been content to allow the impression of a general kinship and/or morphological similarity over such a class without spelling out their ideas as to phylogeny or other problems which will have to be faced. If the Skhul group is called "Neanderthal," that seems to mean one thing—certainly to a reader to whose mind there come the European Neanderthals. If it is called "Neanderthaloid," which simply means Neanderthal-like, then what *is* being said? It is writers like Coon (1962), investigating a specific hypothesis of phylogeny, who avoid such usages, as well as those who, rightly or wrongly, propose distinguishing a Presapiens and a Preneanderthal pair of phyletic lines. Weidenreich (1943a) with his polyphyletic scheme, seemed to have it both ways, but by "Neanderthaloid" he specifically meant fossil hominids who approached *Homo sapiens* but were more advanced than *Pithecanthropus*, and he considered Broken Hill and Solo "well distinguished" from "typical Neanderthalians." Pilbeam (1972), noting the general confusion, thinks that many fossils previously called "Neanderthal," etc., would be better termed "primitive *Homo sapiens*" (in the broad sense of *sapiens*) or "archaic man." Certainly, I would recognize a group of "archaic *Homo sapiens*" which is not at all Neanderthal in the strict sense, but which shares a similar degree of archaism, and which does *not* include others often called "transitional," like Skhul, which come so close to modern man morphologically that "archaic modern" might be the descriptive term. "Archaic *Homo sapiens*" must be approximately what some would call a "Neanderthal phase"—and obviously such a grade had to be passed through by any imagined lineage, the maleficent thing being to label it "Neanderthal." It would be of benefit if the careless use of "Neanderthal" were scrupulously avoided (see below, in connection with the Solo population), rather than embraced as a basic premise for investigation as by Brose and Wolpoff. My point here is that these authors have gone beyond mere loose usage, and have created the formal idea of a homogeneous universal population of Neanderthals, lacking internal distinctions worth investigation, from which populations of modern man bubbled up, in complete independence, anywhere in the Old World. These are not their words, but that is how I understand them.

Addendum: I sent Wolpoff this article on its acceptance, and he and I have discussed it orally and by letter. He suggests some of my strictures come from misunderstanding. He and Brose did not mean to postulate a "homogeneous universal population of Neanderthals lacking internal distinctions" (my phrasing), nor intend that their use of a *t*-test was to legitimize putting all specimens into a single population; also, by "phylogenic unity" they meant to convey a segment of an evolving lineage composed of "Neanderthal" populations, all of which could interbreed. So we might agree on more than appears. In particular, though they use the words interchangeably, they meant "samples" rather than populations by such groups as their "classics" and others; Wolpoff does not even consider the Ngandong Solo sample as a proper "population." There is a real problem here of what to call assemblages of fossil specimens, some closely grouped archaeologically, others somewhat more scattered in space and time but

coherent morphologically, with none being provably real "populations." I may myself have used the word too broadly at points in this paper.

Wolpoff grants that their exposition might be deficient or inexplicit. I could quote them further to explain my understanding of them, but I would not like to misrepresent them: if I am shelling foxholes labeled Brose and Wolpoff which they are not actually occupying, I regret it. My critique is, of course, based on my reading of their article, which I meant to be a careful one, but my comments are addressed to the general approach implied by their hypothesis, i.e., the "Neanderthalizing" of Eem-Würm mankind, regardless of disclaimers in detail. I have therefore not modified my paper, and instead introduce Wolpoff's reservations here.

Wolpoff also tells me that the copious misspellings of names in the article were corrected in proof but editorially allowed to remain in printing. I had commented on these as unbecoming our national journal.

Let us return to the hypothesis and definition. From this primary departure there are various secondary results. One is such a paradox as the statement that Omo 1 "would be identified as anatomically modern *Homo sapiens* if found in another context." A second is that the very scope of their hypothesis and definition gives them more than they can deal with: they use evidence somewhat selectively, space preventing their testing the hypothesis by difficult ideas or evidence contra once they have presented arguments pro. Main difficulties, I believe, fall under the heads of methodology and of specific populations.

METHODOLOGY

The authors have conscripted all the varying known specimens or groups of post-Riss into a single "Neanderthal" population. They would legitimize this partly by the following demonstration. Coefficients of variation are found, in several measurements, for this total group and for the "classic" Neanderthals separately. On this basis, they find the latter to be much more variable than is generally assumed, and as variable as the total group. Then, by t-test, the classic and total groups are found not to differ significantly in measurements; and the means of the two groups are very close. All this is entirely correct. I reproduce their figures in Table I, substituting for those of their various modern populations single generalized figures of my own which I consider the best estimates available for the variation in real recent populations.

Unquestionably, variation in the "classics" is high—an interesting finding. (Possibly this is affected by the inclusion of Petralona; see [3].) Variation is clearly high for the total Neanderthals and the Upper Paleolithic group as well. This means to me that (apart from any influence of sex) none of these series can be looked on as true populations, so that the statistics are faulty. In such temporally and spatially heterogeneous agglomerations of large-headed Middle Paleolithic people, the means would naturally tend to converge, and internal variation would give such high standard deviations that t-tests would be unlikely to find significant differences anyhow. To use an absurd idea, if you measured all the animals in two zoos, you would find similar trends in means and t-tests. So it has not been shown that we have here anything like a single population of normal morphological variation, let alone one which could be called "Neanderthal" by any definition other than the authors'

Table 1. Cranial measurements

	"Classic" Neanderthals	All Neanderthals	Upper Paleolithic	Modern populations
Cranial length	2.9	4.2	4.5	3.2
Cranial breadth	4.7	4.4	3.9	3.6
Cranial height	5.4	5.4	3.2	3.7
Nasion-basion	6.7	6.6	6.2	3.9
Upper face height	8.2	9.2	7.6	5.9
Nasal height	8.9	7.7	8.4	5.3
Nasal breadth	11.6	8.5	9.2	6.9
Bizygomatic breadth	6.6	6.3	7.5	3.6

These coefficients are computed from means and standard deviations derived from seventeen modern (male) series (Howells 1973) carefully specified for time and locale so as to represent "true" populations as well as possible. The standard deviations are based on pooled within-group variances.

nonpopulational one. Nonetheless Brose and Wolpoff are satisfied as to the "phylogenic unity" of the whole lot: "What further evidence could possibly to required?" I would say that the answer is not statistics based on a pooled and mixed group of all specimens over a broad time zone, but a demonstration that actual populations within such a group really do not differ. This would be difficult here, in the nature of the material, but such tests should be made where possible; and, in any case, investigation should be ruled by the true population model. That, of course, is the meaning of "population thinking."

Put more abstractly, I would say that the authors fail to comprehend the need to seek distinctions in levels of variation, i.e., between individual variation within a population on one hand, and differences between populations on the other or, statistically, intrapopulation versus interpopulation variance. In fact, by implication, their approach rejects such distinctions: by demonstrating individual variation to be considerable for such a "population" as the western Neanderthals, it suggests that one scale of variation is sufficient to account for the world-wide variation in their "Neanderthal" supergroup, and thus, in addition, for the basis of transition anywhere between components of this group and anatomically modern *Homo sapiens*. Theoretically, this is a sizeable flaw.

To return to cases, after we note the inflated variability of the two defined Neanderthal "populations," another methodological query is in order as to the authors' satisfaction with the use of single measurements and traits for comparisons. They show, first, that there is extensive overlap between "Neanderthal" and modern populations in almost all individual morphological and metrical traits and, second, that the greatest metrical similarity (in individual measures) to the "classic" European Neanderthals is exhibited by the Upper Paleolithic Europeans. The last is taken to result from in situ evolution of the latter from the former. Now there is certainly a size effect involved in this second matter: skulls of Upper Paleolithic men were indeed larger than those of today. The flaw here is the comparison of a limited number of measurements separately, not of "total morphological pattern," the idea phrased by Le-Gros Clark. Aspects of such a pattern, I have attempted to show (1970), can be appreciated by multivariate analysis, so that shape and size can be dealt with separately. I was able to test the very same skulls spoken of by Brose and Wolpoff as showing the close relationship of Neanderthals and anatomically modern *Homo sapiens* (which expression of the authors will hereafter appear as a.m.H.s.), namely La Ferrassie 1, Predmost

3, and Skhul 5. On four of ten multiple discriminant functions based on a wide variety of modern populations, expressing definite patterns of shape rather than size or the effect of single measurements, the above relationship was flatly rejected. La Chapelle and La Ferrassie scored beyond the individual limits of any of seventeen modern populations (over eight hundred male skulls) including Australians and Norwegians. (Shanidar 1 was close to these two but not fully out of the modern range.) Skhul 5 was extreme on *one* of four functions, only. Predmost 3 was well within the distributions of the modern *mean* scores, let alone the ranges of the individuals, and, in two of four functions, was placed on the *other* side of the modern grand mean from the two Neanderthal individuals named. (This is no flash in the pan; the same things hold for several other prehistoric Europeans, such as Chancelade, Grimaldi, and some Mesolithic crania.) Predmost 3 takes these positions in spite of the skull's having some measurements of facial projection almost identical with Shanidar 1 (see Howells 1973).

This seems to me like a real test of the subhypothesis of European continuity, and it leads me, as far as Predmost 3 is concerned, to a conclusion opposite from Brose and Wolpoff, and thus to the belief that their hypothesis and method are incomplete. It would not be fair to accuse them of ignoring general aspects of morphology. They dwell appropriately on the essential forward displacement of the Neanderthal face, in connection with adaptation to cold and to industrial use of the anterior teeth—matters I am not discussing or objecting to here. Dealing with "overlap," however, their morphological examination does emerge as a recital of individual details, again seeming to display a lack of feeling for discrimination among actual Middle Paleolithic populations. I doubt that conscientious comparisons in the future will demonstrate a really transitional morphology between European Neanderthals and the living Europeans, though I may be wrong.

POPULATIONS

Certain Middle Paleolithic groups of the Near East and North Africa are treated as "transitional," including Skhul, Jebel Qafza and Jebel Ighoud (French "Irhoud," but appearing in the article as "Irhound"). Here again, the authors must operate from their own definition and hypothesis, which a priori make all these fossils Neanderthals. Although the samples are small, the three groups have distinguishing features and should be investigated as populations in their own right.

The Skhul people deserve a general reexamination, but provisionally I would agree (1970) with Brose and Wolpoff and with others that they are anatomically modern though archaic in morphology, and with a very few Neanderthal-like traits detectable irregularly in different individuals. The two Jebel Ighoud skulls are in the process of new preparation under Professor Piveteau. They are surely quite different from the Skhul population, with rather flattened vaults but, in the case of Ighoud 1, without the total facial projection characteristic of Eurasiatic Neanderthals. However, marked alveolar prognathism (contrasting with Qafza, see following) suggests large teeth, a supposition supported by the occlusal area of the first permanent molars in the juvenile mandible from the site (Ennouchi 1969), this being at the upper limit recorded for Neanderthal teeth. Altogether, therefore, the Jebel Ighoud skulls diverge in face and occiput from such Near Eastern Neanderthal skulls as Tabun, Shanidar, or Amud.

Particularly important are the now more numerous Qafza [4] remains. At least seven of thirteen or more individuals recovered can be safely assigned as burials in a small area in the shelter, at the same level (XVII of Vandermeersch, L of Neuville, the first excavator). The industry here is Mousterian "de débitage Levallois," of an early stage. While not yet dated radiometrically, it is suggested to belong to the early Würm by geological and sedimentological data according to Farrand (1972), who would broadly place the datable range of the Levalloiso-Mousterian of the region between 40,000 and "more than 52,000 B.P. with the onset of the last pluvial, at about 80,000 B.P., being the lower limit. There are thus indications that the Qafza population is early, and substantially earlier than Skhul, Tabun, or Ighoud.

The skeletons are still largely undescribed in publication (as Brose and Wolpoff point out), except for Qafza 6 (Vallois and Vandermeersch 1972) and a preliminary report by Vandermeersch (1972). Vandermeersch, noting the arbitrary character of existing definitions of "Neanderthal" and "modern," concludes, nonetheless, that the Qafza remains are much closer to the latter than the former. Citing specimens 6, 8, and 9 he finds the skull vault to be high, not very low, as Brose and Wolpoff estimate. Also, the "total facial prognathism common to the Neanderthals" attributed by them to No. 6 is entirely absent from that and other specimens, and the "museau facial" described by Boule for La Chapelle is, according to Vandermeersch, absolutely lacking. In fact, in Qafza 6 the distance from the auditory meatus to subspinale (taken by myself on the original), a good measure of subnasal prognathism, is just at the mean for modern man. (For details and comparisons of a number of fossils in this and related measurements, see Howells 1973)

Qafza orbits are apparently low and rectangular, and there is a canine fossa and a marked maxillary-malar angularity. Vault form is modern or virtually so. In No. 6 the supraorbital arcade is well developed but without the Neanderthal ("classic" sense) conformation, being especially marked in the medial third, weakening laterally and having no supratoral sulcus. Mandibular form is modern, with a well-developed chin, though teeth are large. My own brief inspection confirms all Vandermeersch's observations [5]. Furthermore, though I do not wish to anticipate what Dr. Vandermeersch may report in the future, it seems likely to me that No. 6, the one published in photographs, may turn out to have especially large brow ridges and teeth for the group as a whole. I noted another point on the older specimens (those recovered in the 1930s): the frontal sinuses appear to be ample, which contrasts markedly with the Skhul population. In Vandermeersch's opinion the Qafza people are "Homo sapiens" to the same degree as the early Upper Paleolithic men of Europe, specifically Predmost 3 (which in my view, above, is not "transitional").

The authors, of course, cannot be faulted for lack of good information on the Qafza remains, but only for a hypothesis which does not accommodate them appropriately. Their argument, in entire agreement with Vandermeersch and others, is the presence of a "transitional" (but in fact essentially a.m.H.s.)

population associated with a Mousterian culture as destroying the supposedly exclusive association of a.m.H.s. with Upper Paleolithic industries. The weak point is simply the subsuming of the now obviously important Qafza population in their omnium-gatherum of Neanderthal. What is the good of this? Qafza morphology is neither Neanderthal nor transitional in any presently visible sense, nor could it be called Neanderthal by Brace's (1964) definition as "the man of the Mousterian culture prior to the reduction in form and dimension of the Middle Pleistocene face." Instead of generalizing that the emergence of a.m.H.s. is a "late Middle Paleolithic local phenomenon," would it not be more productive to note the individuality of the three populations named, as something for intensive future attention, in the meanwhile asking why, in this important region south and east of Europe, such populations were apparently present together with, or alternating with, others of standard Neanderthal morphology for many thousands of years?

The Omo skulls of East Africa must be mentioned, although they cannot now be treated as a population, and in spite of my not wanting to take up too many matters in detail. I mention them because I believe the authors' observations concerning them to be colored by their hypothesis—another undesirable consequence of the hypothesis. I agree that Omo 1 is anatomically modern Homo sapiens and Day (1969) has described no feature of skull or skeleton inconsistent with this. I am at a loss to understand the assertion that the cranium is "extremely similar to Amud" in metric and nonmetric morphology. I also do not understand the statement that Omo 1 has no features not found in other Neanderthals, and that it "clearly meets the criteria of a transitional specimen." The specimen is large and robust, hence the likeness in metrical features, and the large brows; but the total morphological pattern cannot be seen as anything but a robustified a.m.H.s. Omo 2 is another matter (though, again, I agree as to the apparent similarity between the two skulls). Day also notes points of similarity to the Solo skulls; but I think the authors' remarks as to identity of morphology between Omo 2 and Solo 5 in supraorbital and inion regions are certainly overdone. The Omo skulls are treated as "transitional," like the other previously mentioned. From the population view, the question should be "transitional specifically from what?"

Of great importance is the Solo population which I feel has been strangely and unduly neglected. Weidenreich had virtually completed his anatomical description (1951) of the skulls before his death in 1948, but not his comparative study nor his conclusions. About three years ago, it being that time in a course, I followed up an impression and looked through a number of introductory texts and general books to see how Solo man had fared. The census was daunting. He seems to have been the victim of too little close reading of Weidenreich's monograph, and probably of plain lack of interest resulting from Weidenreich's not having written up his interpretations, which would have put Solo man into more general circulation. In some of the books I looked at, Solo appears either not at all or only in a list of Pleistocene hominids; in others, it gets a short description or some remarks which do not dwell at length on his significance. In the commonest case, however, Solo is simply referred to as an eastern Neanderthal, or perhaps merely shown on a map of "Neanderthal" finding sites [6]. Since Weidenreich's early discussion from casts (1943b), only a few students, notably Coon (1962), have attempted to use the Solo material on its own terms as a very fortunate discovery of supposedly late Pleistocene hominids, geographically remote from the Near East or Africa.

So Brose and Wolpoff are not alone in calling the Solo people tropical Neanderthals, as they are obliged to by their own definitions and hypothesis. On the other hand, they do give the Solo specimens a degree of special recognition and statistical treatment. Their Table II seems to demonstrate a relatively low variation in measurements, comparable to other single, normal populations and contrasting with the high variation found for their "Neanderthal" groupings. But this only underscores the need to compare Solo in detail with particular western hominids, as opposed to losing them in the crowd. It is true that metrical likenesses exist with "Neanderthals"; at the same time Coon (1962), using metrical features he took to be morphologically significant, found such differences from Neanderthal (s.s.) specimens that he put Solo on the *erectus* side of his *erectus-sapiens* grade line. And the Solo skulls have various features quite different from western Neanderthals. Large size, large supraorbitals and occipital markings, and a low vault do not mean identity of population. I have belabored this enough. As Pilbeam has said (1970), calling the Solo people tropical Neanderthals is like calling modern Javanese tropical Europeans.

In any case, an age estimate for the Solo skulls may have to be drastically increased, putting them out of consideration as "Neanderthals." Among other indications, the new (1973) Sambungmachan skull is apparently fully Solo-like but comes from the lowest levels of the Kabuh (Trinil) formations, i.e., Middle Pleistocene (Jacob 1975). This only affirms the affinity of Solo with *erectus*.

REGIONAL VERSUS ECUMENICAL DEVELOPMENT: SOUTHEAST ASIA AND SOUTHERN AFRICA

Let us return to the main question: the universality of the hypothesis, and its worth in this guise. Its elements again: local parallel evolution of populations of modern man, in a Middle Paleolithic context, from a Neanderthal population, "throughout the Old World." The adaptive factor: anterior tooth, and consequently facial, reduction as these teeth yielded their function as a vise, to hold objects, to more efficient external tools.

Now the Old World is a big place, incompletely known archaeologically. Let us look again at Southeast Asia. First, a less important point, the dismissal by the authors of the date for the Niah Cave deep skull. This was not a burial, as they assume, citing a secondary source; instead it was more likely a secondary deposition perhaps involving partial cremation, like the 25,000-year-old Lake Mungo remains in Australia (Bowler *et al.* 1972). It is not clear whether the skull was partly disarticulated; Brothwell (1960) feels it may have been intact when deposited, and if so, it was upside down, since the palate faced directly up (Solheim 1960). The upper face was missing and no mandibular fragments or lower teeth were found. Apparently, a few parts of long bones were present. All this was directly associated with the burnt material (some of which may have been human bone) which gave the 40,000 year date (information from Barbara Harrisson; see also Solheim 1960).

So the evidence is acceptable that anatomically modern *Homo sapiens* was present in Niah Cave by 40,000 years ago,

and had reached Australia by 30,000 B.C. at the latest (as shown by cultural remains, even though the Mungo cremation, which is decidedly a.m.H.s., is dated only to about 25,000 years ago within the occupation zone at the locality). Now the main point is that Southeast Asia, including New Guinea and Australia, exhibits nothing like a Middle Paleolithic giving way to an Upper Paleolithic. It is a totally different archaeological province. Southeast Asia and Indonesia had no "Acheulian"; early tools were pebble choppers and crude flaked tools made on primary flakes, apparently continuing through the Middle and Upper Pleistocene about to the level of the skull at Niah. At higher levels here, flakes are smaller, sometimes retouched. In Australia for many millennia tools are also limited to cores and flakes, simply retouched into scrapers and without variety in form, down to perhaps 5000 B.C. The most striking intrusion is edge-ground tools in North Australia at 20,000 B.C. and at Niah possibly by 15,000 years ago, and later still in New Guinea (on present knowledge). The situation in mainland Southeast Asia, though not brought up to date, is apparently similar, though with the commoner presence of the Hoabinhian unifacially flaked pebble.

Here we have met something quite unfamiliar to the archaeology of the west. As Golson (1971) and others have interpreted it, the late Pleistocene stone tools were a "maintenance tool kit"; the real "extractive" kit, shaped by the stone tools, consisted of wood, bamboo, and other perishable substances to a much greater extent than in the west. Only at about 5000 B.C. in Australia (Mulvaney 1969) did implements rather suddenly proliferate into a skillfully made variety of forms, including microliths, thus recalling the primary stone tools of the European Upper Paleolithic. So the whole industrial milieu of the region is different, whether we are looking for innovations and developments, or trying to use a formal framework like "Middle Paleolithic." Golson, in the lecture cited, particularly draws attention to the pall of misconception long cast over Southeast Asian prehistory by Eurocentric concepts and interpretations.

None of this means that history here did not follow a course something like that suggested by Brose and Wolpoff. But the point is that we are in an area and a tradition outside the range of their hypothesis, which should have been limited to a more useful compass.

Southern Africa, part of the Old World though outside the areas our authors actually attempt to cover, suggests other questions. Brose and Wolpoff do take notice of the Broken Hill and Saldanha crania—as Neanderthals, though the skulls are not like Neanderthals s.s. except in being massive in the brow, with Broken Hill also long in the face and large in teeth. The brows, and contained sinuses, are quite different in character, as is the vault form, if these things are diagnostic characters.

It is the chronological context which is becoming interesting. The Middle Stone Age of Southern Africa had in recent years been believed to begin about 35,000 B.C. and to run down to about 10,000 B.C. or later, and to be an equivalent of the European Upper Paleolithic, not simply for age but also for some contained technical ideas. Radiocarbon dates seemed generally in accord, though equivocal as to the early part of the range. However, new dates in stratigraphic series now suggest (Vogel and Beaumont 1972) that the Later Stone Age began about 35,000 B.C., not 10,000 B.C., while the Middle Stone Age was already in full development by 100,000 B.C. Vogel and

Beaumont see the MSA as beginning with a "Middle Paleolithic" aspect, but in later phases exhibiting innovations such as punch-struck blades and early "Upper Paleolithic" forms. The Earlier Stone Age (Acheulian) has also fallen back, out of conflict with the suggested change. Acheulian wood from Kalambo Falls, previously given dates (which should be regarded as minimum—see Isaac 1972) in the 50,000 to 60,000 year range, is estimated by amino acid racemization at 90,000 (J. L. Bada, personal communication); and Upper Acheulian has been dated at 260,000 (Isimila, uranium-thorium on bone; Howell *et al.* 1972) and 425,000 years (Olorgesailie, K/Ar; Isaac 1972).

Two groups of hominid fossils are involved in this. One is the "Rhodesian," perhaps including, along with Broken Hill and Saldanha, the Cave of Hearths mandible (Tobias 1971) and Eyasi. Broken Hill has heretofore been estimated (Oakley and Campbell 1967) at 40,000 years or less. Animal bone collagen from Saldanha has been dated by radiocarbon at 41,000 B.P. (Protsch 1973), while an estimate for Eyasi by amino acid racemization (*Ibid.*) on the human bone gave 38,000. However, the stone tools from the Cave of Hearths are Earlier Stone Age (Acheulian) and those from Saldanha have generally been placed in the late ESA or early MSA (but see Protsch), and those from Broken Hill as early MSA at latest. Klein (1973) finds geological evidence of MSA going back to the beginning of the Upper Pleistocene (i.e., the Eemian interglacial) in the form of tools on and in raised beaches of Eemian age on the South African coast; he also believes that the Broken Hill industry and fauna are much older than heretofore rated. And Bada *et al.* (1973) have tested two samples of Broken Hill hominid bone by aspartic acid racemization, getting results of over 100,000 years. Thus there is beginning to be hard evidence to support the radical down-dating of both the MSA and the Broken Hill find.

The second group of hominids consists of the several skulls or skeletons, all patently a.m.H.s. in character, which have been believed to have MSA associations, though all were retrieved some time ago, and reservations as to legitimacy of their antiquity must necessarily be weightier now with the suggested earlier dating of the MSA. Among them are the Border Cave infant and fragmentary adult, and the Fish Hoek skull, which from various evidence and dating methods Protsch (1973) has provisionally dated at around 60,000 and over 35,000 years, respectively. Fish Hoek is evidently a large (ancestral) Bushman (see, e.g., Howells 1973). Some of these supposedly MSA skulls have been dubbed "Australoid" because of pronounced brows and low vaults; but to call such slightly archaic-looking a.m.H.s. skulls "Australoid" is the equivalent of calling Solo, Broken Hill, and other such "Neanderthal." There is also the Florisbad skull which, though more archaic than those above, has a generally a.m.H.s. character (it escaped the Neanderthal net of Brose and Wolpoff). Physical context and several datings (including a/a racemization; Bada *et al.* [1973]) point to an age of not less than 38,000 years.

Altogether a situation has developed which would appear to remove Broken Hill as a contemporary of various less primitive (if slightly archaic) men of the MSA (as well as a contemporary of the classic Neanderthals, at least). Instead, a timespan would be opened up for evolution of man and culture as they appear later in the Middle Stone Age. Then, of course, there are the Omo skulls of East Africa. They have no usable cultural associations, and their strongest attestation of absolute age is the 37,000 year date from Member III of the Kibish Formation cited by Brose and Wolpoff. They are however, assigned to a much lower stratum, in Member I, near to an oyster shell bed in this member yielding a uranium-thorium date of 130,000. The method, on this material, is viewed with varying degrees of reserve as to reliability, but Isaac (1972) thinks the date is "very reasonable" in relation to the geology of the area. To be conservative we may agree with Brose and Wolpoff that the Omo individuals may be "roughly contemporary with European and Near Eastern Neanderthals."

The prevailing picture of southern Africa for the time corresponding to the late Eemian and early Würm of Europe has seemed a little odd: an Acheulian lingering on to 50,000 years ago, and a territory carrying a mélange of near-modern and near-*erectus* populations at the same time. If this can be dispensed with on new evidence, we would have instead a satisfying and hospitable hearth for an emergence of modern men at a moderate evolutionary pace. Now Brose and Wolpoff, in their broad hypothesis, have simply impressed Saldanha and Broken Hill into the Neanderthal brigade and do not consider history in southern Africa further. Like Southeast Asia, however, it lies outside their premises and definitions.

In other words, they appear to make no allowance for specificity of regional development and evolution. I would say they are half right. While it differs in essence, the African MSA has characteristics allowing it to be looked on as corresponding to the Middle Paleolithic of the north. If the new interpretation of events is correct as I have outlined it above, we have their main idea, of a.m.H.s. developing in a Middle Paleolithic context, borne out with a vengeance. Indeed the case is much better than for Europe. One does not have to defend what is generally agreed to be a sticky wicket: the evolution of "classic" Neanderthals into Upper Paleolithic Europeans in a space of less than 10,000 years.

THE NATURE OF POPULATION SUCCESSIONS

This brings us back to "sudden replacement." As the reverse side of their own hypothesis, Brose and Wolpoff tend to overstate, perhaps mainly by implication, the opposed notion of modern man arising somewhere and "suddenly" replacing Neanderthals all over the world. I think this idea has been applied by most writers only in relation to Europe and adjacent parts, and in fact its users have generally argued that a.m.H.s. did indeed appear in a Middle Paleolithic context. The replacement hypothesis is a valid one. Any admission of population thinking forces the view that, regardless of strong tendencies to parallelism, and continuous gene flow as well, a million years of evolution in *Homo* must have seen local divergence in morphology, in different major regions of the Old World, at every time level, as well as differential evolution in the regional populations. And this leads to the assumption that, especially with climatic swings, there must have been some migrations, leading to abrupt impacts on populations in the regions receiving them, be it by hybridizing, replacement or any combination of these. This is a regional situation: the original replacement by a.m.H.s. of his own antecedent population was by succession—normal evolution—and by present indications this could have taken place in or throughout the range from South Africa around the Near East and into Southeast Asia [7]. But this would be a major population in itself, not what is implied by "local phenomena"; this major population would, by migration into some places, have provided "sudden replacements."

Sudden replacement being just what Brose and Wolpoff would refute, we are getting back to the old controversy over the European Neanderthals. My present concern is not this but simply perspective and proportion. I may have been deceived semantically as to the Brose-Wolpoff hypothesis, in which case I have been making a mountain out of a molehill. But I do not think so. While, in fact they treat in detail only Europe, the Near East, and North Africa, they do specifically assert that continuity between Middle and Upper Paleolithic, homogeneity of their Neanderthal population base, and absence of "sudden replacement" all hold good throughout the Old World. Here we are back at the essential faults of the hypothesis: it is so broad and assertive that it fudges the distinctions it should be examining, and leads to a dubious method of morphological analysis and a mistaken view of population differences and their meaning.

Brose and Wolpoff show themselves to be scholars of energy and avidity. I would like to see them, and others in the field, carry their work and interpretations further, not by overfreighted hypotheses like the one discussed here, but by more limited ones to meet as much of a factual situation as can be seen in terms of morphology, stratigraphy, and dates (and of course of theory). For example, the Neanderthal problem

should be met by contracting it, not expanding it. Most writers have at least used some constrictions on it geographically or morphologically (e.g., recently Ferembach [1972] treats of a "nappe néandertalienne" which she attempts to delimit, pointing out what is involved in doing so).

It would surely help also if hypotheses could be stated in terms of their specific implications, and their testability: a given conclusion if such and such dates or morphological features can be sustained, etc. Also, they should not be framed so ambitiously that weak points cannot be considered, and contrary evidence considered in detail. Wolpoff himself (1971) has given as clear an example of this procedure as could be asked for, in a paper on the "single-species" hypothesis for australopithecines. In this way, workers could focus their ideas and information cooperatively and productively. It could lead to special tests or examinations of new points of existing material more systematically, as worthwhile problems were defined, and might give the curators of such material the opportunity to make such special reports, in place of the common situation in which the responsible person feels obliged either to make a preliminary summary description or to postpone things until he has time, if ever, for a major monograph on an important piece. But I feel that hypotheses like the present one are too unwieldly to do anything of the sort, tending to frustrate measured replies, and to cultivate polemics instead.

NOTES

[1]   For a discussion of the spelling of "Neanderthal," see Howells (1975).

[2]   E.g., S. Binford, 1972, in a generally thoughtful article by a leading theoretical archaeologist.

[3]   Spy I and II, Gibraltar, La Quina 5, Le Moustier, La Chapelle, La Ferrassie, Neanderthal, Monte Circeo. They also include Petralona, which is quite another matter. First writers on this important skull recognized it as an unequivocal Neanderthal but, although it has not been fully described or prepared, this is clearly unjustified. The skull lacks the characteristic Neanderthal facial protrusion as well as the transverse bulging above the ears; instead it has very great basal breath, a marked inward slope transversely above the ears, and a small degree of sagittal keeling. The occiput is sharply angled at the strongly developed occipital crest which forms the most posterior point of the skull (Kannellis and Sabbas 1964). This of course is characteristic of *Homo erectus* but not of Neanderthals (except the Spy skulls?), in which the well-known "bunning" of the occiput projects above and beyond the much more modest crest. The Petralona forehead is *not* high, as Brose and Wolpoff report it. Although the front teeth are missing, Poulianos (1967) says that they would form a straight line. Cranial capacity is given as 1220 cc (method?). Other estimates (Boev 1972) have been 1440 and 1384, but the former, at least, is based on the Lee-Pearson formulae, surely inappropriate for a skull of this shape and probable thickness.

Hemmer (1972) has reviewed much of this. Relating the 1220 capacity figure to other measures of size, he shows that Petralona falls on a regression line with crania of *Homo erectus* and the Solo skulls, which is descrete from and below the line describing Neanderthals. Also, as far as I can apply Coon's (1962) criteria of arc-chord indices of the vault, and brain-molar tooth index, the specimen falls in Coon's *erectus* ranges. Hemmer considers the skull best interpreted as an advanced form of early Middle Pleistocene *erectus*, a likely assessment. From photographs, some facets of its appearance, especially facial, suggest comparison with the recently found Java *erectus* (VIII; see Sartono 1971), admittedly a less advanced form.

Hemmer notes that still incomplete studies of the Petralona fauna make it very probably pre-Mindel. Sickenberg (1966) sees no indication of there having been more than one period of occupation of the cave (which was apparently sealed a very long time ago and found only recently by accident); the fauna, assigned to the Mosbach complex, lived in an interglacial climate and could be as late as the Mindel-Riss only if many forms represent survivals. Schütt (1971) has reviewed the Mosbach (and European generally) hyenas, using dental characters. She finds the spotted hyena which occurs at Petralona and Mosbach to be distinct from, and ancestral to, the later cave hyena, *Crocuta crocuta spelaea*, and assigns it to a new subspecies, *C. crocuta praespelaea*. The two sites, with Mauer, also share *Hyena perrieri*, which did not survive the Mindel, having been displaced by *Crocuta*. This appears to be the present most specific evidence of pre-Mindel date for Petralona or, at latest, the Mindel interstadial. (Schütt is not impressed by absence of *Crocuta* from Mauer as a sign of different age for the site, because of the paucity of all hyena remains at Mauer, the total being two teeth of *H. perrieri*.)

[4]   In various publications this also appears a Qafzeh or Kafzeh or Kafza. I am following Coon (1962:565) because of his knowledge of Arabic and transliterations thereof.

[5]   I have been allowed to see individuals 3 to 7 by the kindness of Professor Vallois, and the later finds by Professor Piveteau and Dr. Vandermeersch.

[6]   So pervasive is this fashion that a popular article of mine, published in 1972, was supplied editorially with just this kind of map, to my own dismay.

[7]   Diametrically opposed to the Brose-Wolpoff pangenetic view of recent man is the model implicit in studies of genetic distance among worldwide living populations using serological evidence, e.g., Edwards and Cavalli-Sforza (1965 and elsewhere). The distance measure is typically "minimum evolution" in a "random walk" configuration; that is, the measure of allelic change or gene substitution from accidental causes during and after dispersal of all populations from a common source. While the model is necessary in the

particular context, it is of course unrealistic as a hypothesis: it considers migration, drift, and mutation but neglects selection, and it takes no account of preexisting populations (and their genes) in regions occupied by the new diaspora. So, no matter how narrowly we might conceive the source of anatomically modern *Homo sapiens*, it can hardly have corresponded to this picture.

REFERENCES

Bada, J. L., Protsch R., and Schroeder R. A. 1973. The racemization reaction of isoleucine used as a paleotemperature indicator. *Nature* 241:394-395.

Binford, S. 1972. The significance of variability: A minority report, in: *The Origins of Homo sapiens* (F. Bordes, Ed.), pp. 199-210, Unesco, Paris.

Boev, P. 1972. *Die Rassentypen der Balkanhalbinsel und der Ostägäischen Inselwelt und deren Bedeutung für die Herkunft ihrer Bevölkerung*. Verlag der Bulgarischen Akademie der Wissenschaften, Sofia.

Bordes, F., Ed. 1972. *The Origins of Homo sapiens. Proceedings of the Paris Symposium*, 2-5 September, 1969 organized by Unesco in cooperation with the International Union for Quaternary Research (INQUA). Unesco, Paris.

Bowler, J. M., Thorne, A. G., and Polach, H. A. 1972. Pleistocene man in Australia: Age and significance of the Mungo skeleton. *Nature* 240:48-50.

Brace, C. L. 1964. The fate of the "classic" Neanderthals: A consideration of hominid catastrophism. *Current Anthropology* 5:3-46.

Brose, D. S., and Wolpoff, M. H. 1971. Early Upper Paleolithic man and Late Middle Paleolithic tools. *American Anthropologist* 73:1156-1194.

Brothwell, D. R. 1960. Upper Pleistocene human skull from Niah Cave, Sarawak. *Sarawak Museum Journal* 9:232-349.

Coon, D. C. 1962. *The Origin of Races*. Knopf, New York.

Day, M. H. 1969. Omo human skeletal remains. *Nature* 222:1135-1138.

Edwards, A. W. F., and Cavalli-Sforza, L. L. 1965. Analysis of human evolution. *Genetics Today: Proceedings, 11th International Congress of Genetics*, Vol. 3, pp. 923-933, The Hague.

Ennouchi, E. 1969. Présence d'un enfant Néandertalien au Jebel Irhoud (Maroc). *Annales de Paléontologie* 55:249-266.

Farrand, W. R. 1972. Geological correlation of prehistoric sites in the Levant, in: *The Origins of Homo sapiens* (F. Bordes, Ed.), pp. 225-235, Unesco, Paris.

Ferembach, D. 1972. L'Ancêtre de l'homme du Paléolithique supérieure était-il Néandertalien? in: *The Origins of Homo sapiens* (F. Bordes, Ed.), pp. 73-80, Unesco, Paris.

Golson, J. 1971. The remarkable history of Indo-Pacific man: Missing chapters from every world prehistory. *Fifth David Rivett Memorial Lecture*, CSIRO, Canberra.

Hemmer, H. 1972. Notes sur la position phylétique de l'homme de Petralona. *L'Anthropologie* 76:155-162.

Howell, F. C. 1952. Pleistocene glacial ecology and the evolution of "classic Neandertal" Man. *Southwestern Journal of Anthropology* 8:337-410.

Howell, F. C. 1957. The evolutionary significance of variation and varieties of "Neanderthal" man. *Quarterly Review of Biology* 32:330-343.

Howell, F. C., Cole, G. H., Kleindienst, M. R., Szabo, B. J., and Oakley, K. P. 1972. Uranium-series dating of bone from the Isimila prehistoric site, Tanzania. *Nature* 237:51-52.

Howells, W. W. 1970. Mount Carmel man: Morphological relationships. *Proceedings, 8th International Congress of Anthropological and Ethnological Sciences*. Vol. 1, pp. 269-272, Tokyo.

Howells, W. W. 1973. Cranial variation in man. A study by multivariate analysis of patterns of differences among recent human populations. *Peabody Museum Papers*, Vol. 67.

Howells, W. W. 1975. Neanderthal man: Facts and figures, in: *Paleoanthropology: Morphology and Paleoecology*, (R. H. Tuttle, Ed.), pp. 389-407, Mouton, The Hague.

Isaac, G. L. 1972. Chronology and the tempo of cultural change during the Pleistocene, in: *Calibration of Hominoid Evolution* (W. W. Bishop and J. A. Miller, Eds.), pp. 381-430, Scottish Academic Press, Edinburgh.

Jacob, T. 1975. Morphology and paleoecology of early man in Java, in: *Paleoanthropology: Morphology and Paleoecology*, (R. H. Tuttle, Ed.), pp. 311-326, Mouton, The Hague.

Kannelis, A., and Sabbas, A. 1964. Kraniometriki meleti ton *Homo neanderthalensis* ton Petralonon. *Kpistimonikis epetiridos tis Physicomathematikis Scholis* 9:65-91.

Klein, R. G. 1973. Geological antiquity of Rhodesian Man. *Nature* 244:311-312.

Mayr, E. 1959. Darwin and the evolutionary theory in biology, in: *Evolution and Anthropology: A Centennial Appraisal* (B. J. Meggers, Ed.), pp. 1-10, Anthropological Society of Washington.

Mayr, E. 1963a. *Animal Species and Evolution*. Belknap Press of Harvard University Press, Cambridge, MA.

Mayr, E. 1963b. The taxonomic evaluation of fossil hominids in: *Classification and Human Evolution* (S. L. Washburn, Ed.), pp. 332-346, Aldine, Chicago.

Mulvaney, D. J. 1969. *The Prehistory of Australia*. Praeger, New York.

Oakley, K. P., and Campbell, G. B. 1967 *Catalogue of Fossil Hominids. Part I: Africa*. British Museum (Natural History), London.

Pilbeam, D. 1970. *The Evolution of Man*. Thames and Hudson, London.

Pilbeam, D. 1972. *The Ascent of Man: An Introduction to Human Evolution*. Macmillan, New York.

Poulianos, A. 1967. The place of the Petralonian Man among palaeoanthropoi. *Anthropos* 11:216-221.

Protsch, R. R. R. 1973. *The Dating of Upper Pleistocene SubSaharan Fossil Hominids and Their Place in Human Evolution: The Morphological and Archaeological Implications*. Ph.D. Thesis, University of California, Los Angeles.

Sartono, S. 1971. Observations on a new skull of *Pithecanthropus erectus* (Pithecanthropus VIII) from Sangiran, Central Java. *Koninklijke Nederlandsche Akademie van Wetenschappen, Proceedings*, serie B, 74:185-194.

Schütt, G. 1971. Die Hyänen der Mosbacher Sande (Altpleistozän, Wiesbaden/Hessen) mit einem Beitrag zur Stammesgeschichte der Gattung *Crocuta*. *Mainzer Naturwissenschaftliches Archiv* 10:29-76.

Sickenberg, O. 1966. Die Wirbeltierfauna der Höhle bei Petralona (Griechenland). *Eiszeitalter und Gegenwart* 17:214-215.

Solheim, W. G. II 1960. The present status of the "Palaeolithic" in Borneo. *Asian Perspectives* II (2):93-90.

Tobias, P. V. 1971. Human skeletal remains from the Cave of Hearths, Makapansgat, Northern Transvaal. *American Journal of Physical Anthropology* 34:335-368.

Vallois, H. V., and Vandermeersch, B. 1972. Le crâne Moustérien de Qafzeh (*Homo* VI). Étude anthropologique. *L'Anthropologie* 76:71-96.

Vandermeersch, B. 1972. Récentes découvertes de squelettes humains à Qafzeh (Israël): Essai d'interpétation, in: *The Origins of Homo sapiens* (F. Bordes, Ed.), pp. 49-54, Unesco, Paris.

Vogel, J. C., and Beaumont, P. B. 1972. Revised radiocarbon chronology for the Stone Age in South Africa. *Nature* 237:50-51.

Weidenreich, F. 1943a. The "Neanderthal man" and the ancestors of *Homo sapiens*. *American Anthropologist* 45:39-48.

Weidenreich, F. 1943b. The skull of *Sinanthropus pekinensis*. *Palaeontologia Sinica*, New Ser. D, 10:1-292.

Weidenreich, F. 1951. Morphology of Solo Man. *Anthropological Papers, American Museum of Natural History* 43(3):205-290.

Wolpoff, M. H. 1971. Competitive exclusion among lower Pleistocene hominids: The single species hypothesis. *Man* 6:601-614.

53

Upper Pleistocene Hominid Evolution in South-Central Europe: A Review of the Evidence and Analysis of Trends

F. H. Smith

European Upper Pleistocene hominids are classified as either *Homo sapiens neanderthalensis* (archaic *H. sapiens*) or *H. sapiens sapiens* (modern *H. sapiens*). In the 126 years since the discovery of the Feldhofer Cave Neandertal specimen, numerous hypotheses have been formulated with regard to the phylogenetic relationship between these two taxa. (For discussions and analyses of the major ideas see Hrdlicka 1927; Howell 1952, 1957; Vallois 1954, 1958; Brace 1962, 1964: Brose and Wolpoff 1971; Howells 1973, 1976; Smith 1976b; Wolpoff 1980a; Spencer and Smith 1981). Although several of these hypotheses have been rendered untenable by accumulating data, there is still no universal agreement on the significance of the Neandertals for the ancestry of modern Europeans. At the present time the controversy centers on the extent to which gene flow into Europe contributed to the appearance of modern European *H. sapiens* (Howells 1976; Trinkaus and Howells 1979; Wolpoff 1980a; Spencer and Smith 1981). Some paleoanthropologists favor migration of modern *H. sapiens* into Europe (sometimes admitting the possibility of some assimilation of Neandertals) as the explanation for this phenomenon, while others favor substantial gene flow without extensive population movement. Still others (Brace 1979b; Brace and Montagu 1977; Wolpoff 1980a; Brose and Wolpoff 1971) argue for an indigenous transition from archaic to modern *H. sapiens*.

For a number of reasons, consideration of the relationship between Neandertals and modern *H. sapiens* in Europe has been based primarily on fossil material from Western Europe. Much less attention has been focused, at least by Western European and non-European anthropologists, on the Upper Pleistocene hominid remains from Central and Eastern Europe. To a certain extent this situation is understandable. In addition to the sociopolitical factors elucidated by Brace (1964; Brace and Montagu 1977), the fact that many Central or Eastern European specimens are described and many significant studies are published in languages and/or sources that are not generally accessible to many English- and French-oriented scientists cannot be overlooked. Perhaps more significant, however, is the apparent assumption (perhaps subconscious) of some scholars that Upper Pleistocene hominid evolution in other portions of Europe simply reflects what occurred in Western Europe and that there is no need to investigate closely the fossil hominid material from these areas independent of Western European specimens and evolutionary patterns. For example, relatively little attention is normally paid to Central European Neandertal remains such as Ochoz and Šipka, even though they were among the earliest discovered. The Krapina remains are rarely afforded the consideration they merit as the largest sample of Neandertal specimens known from a single locality and for the light they shed on questions of variation in European archaic *H. sapiens* populations. Furthermore, in most considerations of the early modern European *H. sapiens* sample, material from Western European sites such as Cro-Magnon and Grimaldi gets disproportionate attention, while that from sites such as Mladec and Brno is hardly mentioned. Also, the remains from Predmostí, which constitute the largest sample of early Upper Paleolithic- associated skeletons known, generally receive only cursory consideration. This neglect is especially unfortunate because of the strategic geographic position of Central (especially South-Central) Europe between Western Asia, viewed by most "migrationists" as the source for modern European *H. sapiens*, and the remainder of Europe. Any discussion of the transition to modern *H. sapiens* in Europe should carefully examine the Central European data.

One aim of this review is to attempt to rectify this situation to some extent by examining the Upper Pleistocene hominid remains from South-Central Europe on a site-by-site basis. A second aim is to describe the pattern of Upper Pleistocene hominid evolution in South-Central Europe and its relationship with and significance for that in other areas of Europe. Such a consideration should shed considerable light on the transition between *H. sapiens neanderthalensis* and *H. sapiens sapiens* not only in this region, but also in the continent as a whole [1].

GEOGRAPHICAL BACKGROUND

South-Central Europe is defined here as the Pannonian Basin and the drainage systems that extend into portions of the surrounding higher elevations. This region, schematically represented in Figure 1, includes most of Hungary, eastern Austria, western Rumania, northern Yugoslavia, and the southern portions of Moravia and Slovakia (Czechoslovakia). The highlands may be visualized as forming two partial crescents, one beginning with the Austrian Alps and extending south and east through Yugos-

Figure 1. *Schematic representation of South-Central Europe. Shaded areas represent elevations of greater than approximately 1,000 m. Areas enclosed by dotted lines are at elevations of greater than approximately 400 m. The general locations of the two most significant fossil hominid-producing regions are denoted by the letters A (Hrvatsko Zagorje, northern Yugoslavia) and B (Moravian karst and surrounding areas, Czechoslovakia).*

lavia, terminating in the Balkans, and the other stretching from the Transylvanian Alps through the Carpathians, Tatras, Sudetes, and Erz and the hilly regions of Bohemia. With some exceptions (e.g., the Alps), these highlands are not excessively high and are dissected by numerous river valleys; they are not impenetrable barriers, although some (particularly the southern group) are quite rugged [2]. Furthermore, to the northwest, the Bohemian highlands provide minimal separation between South-Central Europe and portions of Germany and Poland. Nevertheless, this region is one of the most distinctly defined geographic zones in Europe. Consequently, it is one of the best in which to investigate relatively localized "populational" changes in Upper Pleistocene fossil hominids.

South-Central Europe was an attractive and productive environment for Upper Pleistocene hunters. Even during cold phases, the plains were grassy steppe, not tundra (Frenzel 1965; see also Butzer 1971), supporting a large variety of herbivores (Thenius 1962). Archeological sites in the plains are mainly open-air, and many are characterized by extensive loess deposits (see Flint 1971). The lower highlands were characterized by woodlands interspersed with open grassland (Frenzel 1965, 1968). The majority of the sites in this zone, unlike those of the plains, are caves and rock-shelters. In certain regions, notably the Moravian karst, caves (or at least cave entrances) contain loess, which facilitates stratigraphic correlation between highlands and plains sites (Musil and Valoch 1966).

Most of the fossil hominid remains of South-Central Europe come from the karst and surrounding regions of Moravia and the semimountainous Hrvatsko Zagorje in northern Croatia (Yugoslavia). Sites in Moravia include Predmostí, Dolní Vestonice, Šipka, Külna, Mladec, and Brno; the sites of Krapina, Vindija, and Velika Pecina are located in the Hrvatsko Zagorje. Various other remains come from scattered locations including sites in Slovakia (Šala, Gánovce), Hungary (Subalyuk), Austria (Willendorf, Miesslingstal), and central Croatia (Veternica).

CHRONOLOGICAL FRAMEWORK

The chronological framework (Fig. 2) employed here is based on the division of the Würm outlined for the Moravian karst by Musil and Valoch (1966) and subsequently applied by Valoch (1968) to Central Europe in general. This framework has worked well in interpreting Upper Pleistocene stratigraphy in Moravia and agrees generally with chronological frameworks employed in other areas of Europe (Butzer 1971; Flint 1971), including the well-documented sequences in the Netherlands (Zagwijn 1974; Grootes 1978) and northwestern France (Woillard 1978; Woillard and Mook 1982). The one possibly significant difference is that in the latter two sequences the Hengelo dates consistently around 40,000 B.P. (Woillard and Mook 1982; Grootes 1978), while in the Musil-Valoch scheme the corresponding Podhradem dates to between 32,000 and

Figure 2. *Chronological subdivisions of the Upper Pleistocene in Central Europe (revised after Musil and Valoch 1966).*

	Upper Würm Stadial
	Upper Würm Interstadial (Stillfried B)
	Middle Würm Stadial
	Middle Würm Interstadial (Podhradem–Hengelo)
Würm Glacial	Lower Würm Stadial
	Early Würm Interstadial (Brørup)
	Early Würm Stadial II
	Early Würm Interstadial (Amersfoort)
	Early Würm Stadial I
Riss-Würm Interglacial	

40,000 B.P. The majority of the applicable Podhradem radio-carbon dates are around 40,000 B.P.; only a few are about 32,000 B.P. and there are essentially no dates in the mid-30,000-year range. It may be that the more recent dates are anomalous. If so, the Podhradem would be equivalent in age to the Hengelo.

Obviously, the Musil-Valoch framework can be applied to other areas of South-Central Europe only with considerable caution. Given the complexity of the Würm and the differences that can occur even between Würm deposit sequences from adjacent caves (Butzer 1971; Flint 1971; Zeuner 1959), it is unlikely that any scheme can be applied with great precision over so extensive a geographic region. Nevertheless, the Musil-Valoch scheme has been adequate as a framework in the Hrvatsko Zagorje (Wolpoff *et al.* 1981) and is consistent with available radiocarbon dates from other areas. Therefore, it appears to allow for at least rough chronological comparisons between the various subregions of South-Central Europe.

ARCHAEOLOGICAL BACKGROUND

The Upper Pleistocene fossil hominid specimens of South-Central Europe are associated with Middle and Upper Paleolithic assemblages. While a detailed discussion of the archaeological background is neither feasible nor appropriate here, certain aspects of the archaeological framework need to be considered. Recent detailed considerations of the Paleolithic in Central Europe may be found in Valoch (1968, 1972, 1976a), Kozlowski (1975), Ivanova (1979), Chmielewski (1972), Frayer (1978), Coles and Higgs (1969), and Hahn (1970, 1973, 1977).

As Valoch (1972:61) has pointed out, the Middle Paleolithic of Central Europe has never been subjected to the type of systematic, detailed analysis that has been accomplished for that of Western Europe. Consequently, it is exceedingly difficult to distinguish assemblages or facies within it. In fact, it is not clear what criteria should be employed in attempting to do so. Despite the difficulties, Valoch (1968, 1972) has identified four such facies: the Central European Typical Mousterian, spread throughout the region and comprised of two subfacies (Šipka Mousterian and Predmostí Mousterian); the Charentian, found in southern Germany but again extending into Moravia (Külna, upper assemblages [see Valoch 1970]) and Hungary (Érd); the Middle Paleolithic with leaf points, found primarily in southern Germany and Poland but again extending into Moravia (Külna middle assemblages); and the Tayacian, known from the sites of Külna (lower assemblage) and Gánovce. The Tayacian appears to be rather early, probably Riss-Würm interglacial (Valoch 1970), and exhibits some evidence of relationships with the later Predmostí Mousterian (Valoch 1972). The Charentian seems to be rather late. Some of the radio-carbon dates for Érd (Table 1) would place the Charentian from that site in the Podhradem interstadial. Stratigraphically, however, the Érd Charentian appears to fall in a colder period prior to the Podhradem (Gábori-Csánk 1968), and the radio carbon dates have been questioned (Gábori-Csánk 1970). The Central European Typical Mousterian (at least the Šipka type is found both at early Middle Paleolithic sites (Krapina) and at relatively late ones (Šipka).

Of the few radiocarbon dates available for the Middle Paleolithic in this region (Table 1), many only establish a minimum limit and are not particularly informative. The dates from Lebenstedt (North-Central Europe), Senftenberg, and Érd (e) all predate the Podhradem interstadial and are consistent with stratigraphic indications that most Middle Paleolithic assemblages predate it. On the other hand, there are a number of dates (Érd, Tokod, Tata) that are quite late for the Middle Paleolithic. All of these dates, however, have been called into question by Gábori-Csánk (1970) because they either do not fit with stratigraphic correlations in Hungary or are "too recent" for the Middle Paleolithic. Stratigraphic interpretations at Šipka place the late Middle Paleolithic assemblages in the Podhradem interstadial (Valoch 1965a).

The Szeletian and the Aurignacian represent the earliest Upper Paleolithic assemblages in South-Central Europe. Both radiocarbon dates (Table 1) and stratigraphic correlation (Valoch 1968, 1972, 1976a) indicate that the Szeletian is the older. Stratigraphic evidence suggests the Szeletian was present primarily during the Podhradem interstadial, while the Aurignacian extended from the end of the Podhradem into the Stillfried B (Valoch 1968). The Szeletian has a strong Middle Paleolithic component, and most archaeologists consider it to have evolved directly from some type of indigenous Middle Paleolithic (see Frayer 1978). The high frequency of foliate points in the Szeletian indicates a rather direct relationship with the "Middle Paleolithic with leaf point" tradition, but other aspects of Middle Paleolithic technology and artifact types are also retained and mixed with various elements more characteristic of Upper Paleolithic forms (Valoch 1968, 1972, 1976a; Chmielewski 1972). Earlier Szeletian assemblages tend to be more like the Middle Paleolithic than later ones. Finally, the Szeletian is generally found only in the eastern part of South-Central Europe (Rumania, Hungary, Moravia) and in parts of Poland and southern Germany (where it is known as Jerzmanowician and Praesolutrean respectively). Sites are known from mountain caves and open areas, with the former predominating (Valoch 1968).

Many elements characterizing the Szeletian continue into the Aurignacian of South-Central Europe (foliate points, Middle Paleolithic-type scrapers, etc.) albeit in much lower frequencies. Additionally the Aurignacian exhibits a greater frequency of typical Upper Paleolithic elements (various tools made from blades and bone tools) than the Szeletian and is more widespread. Split-based and Mladec-type bone points are characteristic (see Valoch 1968, Frayer 1978). Although Aurignacian radiocarbon dates tend to be more recent than Szeletian ones, some overlap exists (Table 1). The Szeletian may simply represent a functional component of the Aurignacian, oriented toward the exploitation of particular resources (see Frayer 1978). Most workers, however, view the two as separate cultural units (Valoch 1968, 1972, 1976a; Vértes 1955, 1961; Chmielewski 1972).

There is considerable disagreement about the origin of the Central and Eastern European Aurignacian. Although some archaeologists still look to the Near East (Kozlowski 1979), a number—notably Hahn (1970, 1973, 1977), Valoch (1972, 1976a), and Laplace (1958-61, 1970)—emphasize that its roots are evident in certain Central European Middle Paleolithic traditions. Furthermore, both Hahn and Valoch (also Bánesz 1963; Paunescu 1965) note that the frequency of Middle Paleolithic elements in the Aurignacian is significantly greater in the early phase than in later ones. Valoch (1967b) sees the development of Aurignacian from a Moravian Middle Paleolithic industry called the "Krumlovian." He believes that the Aurignacian developed rather early in Central and Eastern Europe, citing as evidence the early radiocaborn dates from

Table 1. Radiocarbon Dates for the Middle and Early Upper Paleolithic of Central Europe.

Site (Stratum)	Sample No.	Date k.y.a. B.P.	Source
Mousterian			
Senftenbert, Austria	GrN-1219	48,300±200	Movius (1960)
Veternica (i), Yugoslavia	GrN-4984	>43,300	Vogel and Waterbolk (1972)
*Lebenstedt, West Germany	GrN-1217	48,300±200	Movius (1960)
Tata (archaeological), Hungary	GrN-3023	33,330±900	Vogel and Waterbolk (1972)
Büdöspest, Hungary	GxO-198	>37,000	Gábori-Csánk (1970)
Tokod, Hungary	GxO-196	36,200	Gábori-Csánk (1970)
Érd (d), Hungary	GrN-4443	35,300±900	Vogel and Waterbolk (1972)
Érd (d), Hungary	GrN 4711	39,350±830	Vogel and Waterbolk (1972)
Érd (d), Hungary	GxO-200	>38,100	Gábori-Csánk (1970)
Érd (e), Hungary	GrN-4444	44,300±1,400	Vogel and Waterbolk (1972)
Crvena Stijera (Level 12), Yugoslavia	GrN-6083	40,770±900	Vogel and Waterbolk (1972)
Szeletian			
Szeleta (upper), Hungary	GrN-5130	32,620±4,400	Vogel and Waterbolk (1972)
Szeleta (lower), Hungary	GrN-6058	43,000±1,100	Vogel and Waterbolk (1972)
Szeleta (lower), Hungary	GxO-197	41,700	Gábori-Csánk (1970)
Brno-Bohunice, Czechoslovakia	GrN-6165	42,900+1,700−1,400	Mook in Valoch (1976a)
Brno-Bohunice, Czechoslovakia	GrN-6802	41,400+1,400−1,200	Mook in Valoch (1976a)
Brno-Bohunice, Czechoslovakia	Q-1044	40,173±1,200	Switsur in Valoch (1976a)
Certova pec, Czechoslovakia	GrN-2348	38,400+2,800−2,100	Valoch (1792)
*Nietoperzowa, Poland	GrN-2181	38,500±1240	Valoch (1972)
Aurignacian			
Willendorf II (4), Austria	GrN-1273	32,060±250	Vogel and Zagwijn (1967)
Willendorf II (1), Austria	GrN-1287	30,530±250	Vogel and Zagwijn (1967)
Willendorf II (5), Austria	H-246/231	32,300±3,000	Movius (1960)
Velika Pecina (i), Yugoslavia	GrN-4979	33,850±520	Vogel and Waterbolk (1972)
Velika Pecina (g), Yugoslavia	Z-189	31,168±1,400	Malez (1974)
Podhradem A, Czechoslovakia	GrN-1724	33,100±530	Vogel and Zagwijn (1967)
Podhradem A, Czechoslovakia	GrN-848	33,300±1,100	Vogel and Zagwijn (1967)
Peskö, Hungary	GrN-4950	35,200±670	Vogel and Waterbolk (1972)
Istállosko (lower), Hungary	GrN-4659	44,300±1,900	Vogel and Waterbolk (1972)
Istállosko (lower), Hungary	GrN-4658	39,700±900	Vogel and Waterbolk (1972)
Istállosko (upper), Hungary	GrN-1935	30,900±600	Gábori-Csánk (1970)
Vindija (Fd-Fd/d), Yugoslavia	Z-551	26,970±632	Srdoc et al (1979)
*Baco Kiro (6b/7), Bulgaria	GrN-7569	32,700±300	Kozlowski (1979)
*Baco Kiro (7/6a), Bulgaria	Ly-1102	29,150±950	Kozlowski (1979)
*Baco Kiro (11), Bulgaria[a]	GrN-7545	>43,000	Kozlowski (1979)
Samuilica Cave, Bulgaria[b]	GrN-5181	42,780±1,270	Vogel and Waterbolk (1972)
Early Gravettian or Pavlovian			
Dolní Vêstonice (lower), Czechoslovakia	GrN-2092	28,300±300	Vogel and Zagwijn (1967)
Dolní Vêstonice (lower), Czechoslovakia	GrN-2598	29,000±200	Vogel and Zagwijn (1967)
Dolní Vêstonice (upper), Czechoslovakia	GrN-1286	25,820±170	Vogel and Zagwijn (1967)
Pavlov (A), Czechoslovakia	GrN-1272	26,620±230	Vogel and Zagwijn (1967)
Pavlov (B), Czechoslovakia	GrN-1325	25,020±150	Vogel and Zagwijn (1967)
Velika Pecina (e), Yugoslavia	GrN-4980	26,590±300	Vogel and Waterbolk (1972)
Krems-Wachtberg, Austria	GrN-3011	27,400±300	Vogel and Zagwijn (1967)
Late Gravettian or Pavlovian			
Various		12,000-23,000	Movius (1960), Vogel and Waterbolk (1972), Gábori-Csánk (1970), Vogel and Zagwijn (1967)

*Near, not strictly within, the region defined for study.

[a]This component is described as Aurignacian-like by Kozlowski (1979) and called Bachokirien. On the basis of his analysis, it appears to be more suitably grouped with early Aurignacian than with any other early Upper Paleolithic culture.

[b]The industry associated with this date may not be early Aurignacian.

Istállöskő [3] and the various Podhradem-age early Aurignacian strata in Moravia.

The Eastern Gravettian (Pavlovian, in Moravia) follows, and appears to develop from, the Aurignacian in South-Central Europe. It consists almost entirely of tool types and technology characteristic of the Upper Paleolithic (Valoch 1968; Coles and Higgs 1969). Particularly interesting are the extensive and intricate bone and ivory industries, including both tools and art objects. Burials are also distinctive and include various accompaniments (e.g., Brno 2, Dolní Vestonice, Predmostí). The earliest Gravettian is found during the Middle Würm stadial, and the culture persists until ca. 12,000 years ago in some areas (Table 1; Frayer 1978; Valoch 1968; Gábori-Csánk 1970).

REMAINS OF *HOMO SAPIENS NEANDERTHALENSIS*

Krapina

A rock shelter on the Hušnjakovo Brdo, on the outskirts of the town of Krapina in the Hrvatsko Zagorje, Yugoslavia, was excavated by Gorjanovic-Kramberger between 1899 and 1905. It yielded an extensive array of faunal and archaelogical material and the largest series of Neandertal skeletal remains known from a single site. Gorjanovic-Kramberger spent virtually the rest of his life studying and publishing on the morphology of the fossil remains, the nature of the associated cultural remains, and their significance (Gorjanovic-Kramberger 1906, 1913a; see also bibliography in Smith 1976b). In recent years, a number of newer studies have provided additional information on and reinterpretation of the Krapina hominid remains (eg. Smith 1976b, 1978; Trinkaus 1978; Brace 1979b; Wolpoff 1979, 1980a; Alexeev 1979), site stratigraphy and chronology (Malez 1970a, 1978a) and fauna (Malez 1970b, 1978a).

The Krapina deposits are divisible into 13 stratigraphic units, the upper 9 containing cultural material and ranging from the Riss-Würm interglacial through through what appears to be the Lower Würm stadial (Malez 1970a, b, 1978a). While the stratigraphic positions of all the hominid specimens have not been determined from Gorjanovic-Kramberger's field notes (and some may never be), most are from Levels 3 and 4. These two levels have been collectively designated the "hominid zone" (Gorjanovic-Kramberger 1906) and are correlated with the end of the Riss-Würm interglacial [4]. A few specimens are known from levels stratigraphically more recent than the hominid zone (Smith 1976b; Malez 1978a), but all are from Mousterian levels (see Gorjanovic-Kramberger 1913; Malez 1970c). Although a few Upper Paleolithic-like elements are found in the upper strata, no evidence of Upper Paleolithic cultural units is present.

The Krapina hominid remains are fragmentary, at least in part because of cultural processes (Smith 1976b, c; Ullrich 1978). The sample for many elements is large enough, however, to allow considerably more consideration of Neandertal population variation than is possible of any other series from a single site in Europe or the Near East.

For the discussion of Central European Neandertals, the Krapina specimens provide the majority of the pertinent data available. Approximately 800 fragments make the sample, including almost 200 isolated teeth. On the basis of the dental remains, Wolpoff (1978, 1979) believes that around 80 individuals are represented.

The total morphological pattern of the Krapina hominids clearly places them within *H. sapiens neanderthalensis*, and there is no feature that would exclude any Krapina specimen from this taxon (Jelínek 1969; Smith 1976b, 1978; Trinkaus 1978; Wolpoff 1979). Since most specimens are from subadult individuals (Wolpoff 1979; Smith 1976b) some variation in the sample is unequivocally age-related. However, even adult specimens there is considerable variation. This is particularly true of anatomical regions represented by the largest samples—teeth, supraorbital tori, mastoid segments of temporals, and mandibles. Much of the non-age-related variation in these and other elements is probably explained by sexual dimorphism (Smith 1976b, 1980; Wolpoff 1980a; Zobeck 1980; Smith and Ranyard 1980).

Metrically, Krapina crania fall in the Neandertal range (often toward the small end) in every measurable feature (Gorjanovic-Kramberger 1906; Smith 1976b), and no morphological feature qualitatively differentiates Krapina and Western European Neandertal cranial forms (Smith 1976b, 1978; Wolpoff 1980a; Alexeev 1979; Jelínek 1969). Neurocranial specimens from Krapina exhibit long, broad, and relatively low vaults with receding foreheads and broad occiputs. Temporal bones are characterized by robust mandibular fossae and mastoid processes that project only slightly or not at all beyond the occipitomastoid crest of the cranial base. Faces are relatively large and robust with wide interorbital areas, pillar-like lateral orbital margins, and well-developed supraorbital tori (Fig. 3). Adult Krapina supraobital tori exhibit considerable variable in thickness and projection, but all form continuous ooseous bars over the orbits which are contiguous with the interorbital and lateral orbital regions in the characteristic Neandertal manner (Smith and Ranyard 1980). Frontal sinuses are large and restricted to the torus, a typically Neandertal feature. Nasal-root depressions and canine fossae are absent, indicating that Krapina nasal areas project anteriorly at the midsaggittal plane. This creates the "beaked face" morphology noted by Coon (1962) in "classic" Western European Neandertals. That the Krapina faces conform to this pattern is observable by visual inspection of the C cranium (Fig. 3) and is borne out by facial angles (Alexeev 1979). The two specimens at Krapina for which nasal breadths are measurable (Maxillae C and E) yield values approximately two standard deviations below the Western European Neandertal mean. While this might indicate that Krapina noses were narrower than Western European

Figure 3. *The Krapina C cranium.*

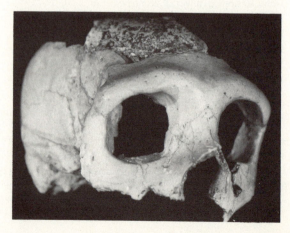

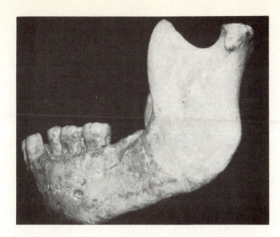

Figure 4. *The Krapina J mandible.*

Neandertal noses, it may also be simply a reflection of the subadult age (Wolpoff 1979:112) of both specimens.

Prognathism of the lower face is suggested by the presence of a retromolar space (a gap between the last molar and anterior edge of the ramus) in all mandibles preserving this area. The lower face is also characterized by broad and elongated alveoli (indicated by bicanine breadths and alveolar heights respectively). Mandibles lack both mental eminences and trigones, and their symphyses angle forward from the base to the the alveolus (Fig. 4). Thus all symphyseal angles (measured from the base margin) are greater than 90°, and the average is 99.6° (Wolpoff *et al.* 1981).

The anterior teeth in the Krapina sample are very large in both crown and root dimensions. In fact, no other Pleistocene sample has anterior teeth as large as Krapina's (Wolpoff 1979; Smith 1976b). That the Krapina teeth are larger than Western European Würm Neandertal anterior teeth (Table 2) is not surprising, since the majority of the Krapina teeth are probably earlier (Riss-Würm). Anterior tooth size appears to reach its peak in Riss-Würm Europe and decrease steadily from this point through the later Pleistocene (Brace 1979a; Wolpoff 1980a; Frayer 1978; Smith 1976b). Posterior teeth are also larger than in later European Upper Pleistocene hominids, but this simply continues a trend in dental reduction begun by hominids in the Lower Pleistocene. Molars exhibit extensive taurodontism.

The postcranial anatomy of the Krapina specimens is comparable to that of other Neandertals (in that it is characterized by general postcranial robusticity), although the predominance of subadult material in the Krapina sample gives the impression of less rugosity than is common in Western European Neandertals (Trinkaus 1978). Like other Neandertals, the Krapina people exhibit a complex of features in the pectoral girdle indicating a powerful, barrel-shaped upper thorax (Hrdlicka 1930; Smith 1976b, c; Wolpoff 1980a) and muscular hands (Musgrave 1970, 1977). One of the most distinctive features of the Neandertal postcranial is a dorsal axillary groove on the scapula (Steward 1962, 1964). This feature is rare in Upper Paleolithic hominids and virtually unknown in modern humans but present in 57.9% of Neandertals (Trinkaus 1977). At Krapina, 33.3% of adult scapulae exhibit this morphology, while 55.6% exhibit the Chancelade pattern [5] (Smith 1976b). Trinkaus (1977) notes that the Chancelade pattern characterizes 36.8% of the total Neandertal scapula sample. One Krapina scapula exhibits the only ventral sulcus known for a Neandertal. Trinkaus (1978) finds that the

lower postcranial elements at Krapina exhibit the same morphological pattern as those of other Neandertals and differ from those of modern humans only in average degree of robustness and in the presence of an elongated, thinned superior pubic ramus (see also Trinkaus 1976a; Smith 1976b). Stature estimates based on reconstructed adult long-bone lengths average 62.6 in. (*N*=5) for Krapina, compared with 63.3 in for Western European Neandertals (Smith 1976b).

Finally, it was noted in an earlier study (Smith 1976b) that the adult occipitals and parietals from Krapina indicated no lambdoidal flattening or occipital bunning and that this might constitute a difference between Krapina and Western Neandertals. After more analysis, it seems that the pertinent regions on the adult specimens at Krapina are too fragmentary to justify such a conclusion. The only specimen which preserves enough of the posterior neurocranium to allow an assessment of lambdoidal flattening and an occipital bunning is the juvenile B skull, and it clearly possesses both lambdoidal flattening and an occipital bun (see Smith 1976b:39 and Fig. 3).

In sum, the Krapina Neandertals are not qualitatively separable from the Western European Würm Neandertals on the basis of any morphological feature [6]. They do not, as a group, exhibit any feature or complex of features that justifies their being considered "progressive" in comparison with Western European specimens. Differences between the two samples, where documented, are quantitative only and derive largely from the fact that much of the Krapina sample represents subadults.

Gánovce

A largely complete travertine endocast (Fig. 5) of a hominid was recovered from the Hrádok travertine deposits near Gánovce in northern Slovakia in 1926. These deposits had been quarried since the 1880's; between the World Wars, Jaroslov Petrbok collected and reported on some of the paleontological remains they contained, among them an endocast that was recognized as hominid in 1937 and systematically analyzed by Vlcek (1953, 1955, 1969). When the significance of the find was recognized, an extensive, multidisciplinary investigation of the stratigraphy of the locality and its paleontological and archaeological remains was undertaken (Vlcek *et al.* 1958). This insvestigation established that the endocast belongs to a complex known as the younger travertine, dated to the Riss-Würm interglacial on the basis of its vertebrate faunal remains (especially the presence of *Elephas antiquus*) and its malacological and botanical material. Five Paleolithic horizons occur in the Hrádok travertine complex. The endocast is probably associated with Horizon 4, classified as "Mousterian," possibly a unique regional variant characterized by small tools (Vlcek 1969).

From the few adhering segments of the vault (portions of the left parietal, temporal, and occipital which are unseperable from the endocast itself) and the general shape of the endocast, an impression may be formed of the general shape of the cranium (Vlcek 1953, 1955, 1964a). It is long, quite low, and moderately broad, with its maximum breadth at the level of the midparietal area—a distincttive Neandertal feature (Wolpoff 1980a). In norma verticalis, the occiput appears rather projecting, and there is definite indication of lambdoidal flattening. Very probably the cranium possessed an occipital bun. Furthermore, details of the morphology and measurements of the endocast itself are all in the Neandertal range (Vlcek 1953,

Table 2. Buccolingual Dimensions (mm) of Teeth of Early Hominids from South-Central Europe.

	I^1	I^2	C	P^3	P^4	M^1	M^2	M^3
Maxilla								
Krapina								
$\overline{X}(\sigma)$	8.9(5.2)	8.6(5.8)	9.8(.73)	11.4(5.7)	10.8(.37)	12.3(.41)	12.4(1.02)	11.5(1.39)
Range	8.1–9.7	7.7–9.5	8.1–11.2	8.5–11.9	10.3–11.4	11.0–13.2	10.5–14.0	8.7–12.5
Vindija G₂								
$\overline{X}$	...	...	...	...	...	...	12.6(N=2)	...
Range	...	...	...	...	...	...	(11.8–13.0)	...
Külna	...	...	9.7	9.8	9.8	11.0	...	...
Vindija Aurignacian	8.3	8.4	10.6	...	...	...	...	...
Predmostí								
$\overline{X}(\sigma)$	7.5(.26)	6.9(.37)	8.6(.79)	9.5(.58)	9.7(.58)	12.2(.59)	12.3(.99)	12.2(1.13)
Range	7.1–7.9	6.4–7.3	7.8–9.8	8.7–10.6	8.9–10.8	11.4–13.0	11.1–13.7	10.8–13.1
Early Upper Paleolithic								
$\overline{X}(\sigma)$	7.5(2.8)	6.8(.52)	9.0(.91)	9.6(.59)	9.6(.75)	12.3(.73)	12.3(.95)	11.4(1.16)
Range	7.1–8.0	6.0–7.4	7.8–10.8	8.7–10.6	8.5–11.2	11.0–14.0	10.8–13.8	9.2–13.1
Mandible								
Krapina								
$\overline{X}(\sigma)$	7.7(.51)	8.3(.49)	9.4(.65)	9.1(.73)	9.7(.57)	11.4(.78)	11.7(.61)	10.8(.68)
Range	7.0–8.2	7.0–9.2	8.0–10.2	7.9–10.3	9.3–11.3	10.0–12.6	11.0–12.7	9.7–12.0
Ochoz[a]	7.7	8.0	9.7	9.6	9.3	11.1	11.6	11.7*
Subalyuk[a]	7.2	7.8	9.9	9.1*	9.0*	10.7	11.3	11.3
Vindija G₃								
$\overline{X}(\sigma)$	...	7.7	7.9	9.0	...	11.1(N=3)	11.7(N=2)	11.8(N=2)
Range	...	...	...	...	...	10.5–11.4	11.2–12.3	11.7–11.8
Šipka	7.0	7.0	...	8.0	8.0	...	...	...
Predmostí								
$\overline{X}(\sigma)$	6.2(.25)	6.7(.43)	8.8(.69)	8.4(.49)	8.5(.42)	10.9(.55)	10.8(.91)	10.7(1.03)
Range	5.9–6.5	6.0–7.0	8.0–9.8	7.8–9.0	8.0–9.1	10.0–111.8	10.0–12.0	9.9(11.9)
Early Upper Paleolithic								
$\overline{X}(\sigma)$	6.4(.44)	7.0(.60)	9.0(.67)	8.5(.54)	8.7(.58)	11.0(.61)	10.8(.80)	10.8(.96)
Range	5.9–7.1	6.0–8.5	7.9–10.0	7.8–9.3	8.0–10.0	10.0–12.0	9.8–12.0	9.3–12.4

Sources: Krapina, Smith (1976b); Vindija, Wolpoff et al. (1981); Predmostí, compiled from Matiegka (1934), and see Frayer (1978); Early Upper Paleolithic, Frayer (1978); all others from unpublished measurements by author.

[a]Value represents average of both sides of the individual except where marked with an asterisk.

1955, 1969). The low and flat frontal lobes, considered particularly primitive by Vlcek, may be due to subsequent corrosion (Jelínek 1969). Cranial capacity is estimated at 1,320 cc, only slightly below the Riss-Würm Neandertal average and above the average for female Neandertals (Smith 1976b). The Gánovce specimen, like other Neandertals, also exhibits less cranial kyphosis than is the case in modern humans.

During excavations in the Hrádok travertines in 1955, natural molds of a partial left fibula and a partial left radius were found (Vlcek 1955). Since the bones were apparently not well-preserved before they were molded, nothing significant can be determined about them (Vlcek 1969).

Ochoz

A hominid mandible was discovered by Rzehak in 1905 in Švédüv Stül Cave, near the village of Ochoz in the southern part of the Moravian karst region. Rzehak classified the specimen as a Neandertal, relating it most closely to the Krapina and Šipka remains. Kríz (1909) and Bayer (1925) argued that, since only Upper Paleolithic artifacts were found at the site, the specimen could not be a Neandertal. Kríz also claimned that it showed distant morphological similarities to the Predmostí hominids. Excavations between 1953 and 1955 (Klíma et al. 1962, Vlcek 1969) have provided a reasonably clear picture of the geological and cultural stratigraphic position of the mandible itself, but

Figure 5. *The Gánovce endocast, lateral view.*

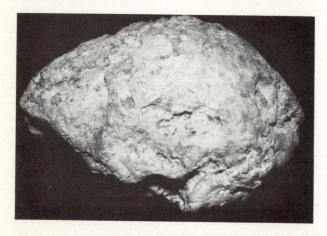

Klíma believes it comes from a late Mousterian level in the "brown earth complex." In 1964, two small human cranial vault fragments and a human molar were found in a layer corresponding to this "brown earth complex" (Vanura 1965). The fauna of this complex from both the 1953-55 (Musil in Klíma et al. 1962) and the 1964 excavations suggests a time span from the end of the Riss-Würm to the beginning of the Würm (Vlcek 1969:68).

The Ochoz mandible preserves the alveolar region and dentition. (Only the right M_3 is missing.) The rami and corpus base are missing, probably broken from the remaining portions by geological processes aftter deposition. Prognathism is indicated by the angled alveoloar plane and the certainty that a retromolar space was present. These and other features of the preserved portion of the mandible compare favorably with those of other Neandertals (Jelínek in Klíma et al. 1962; Jelínek 1969; Vlcek 1969). The dentition also conforms to the Neandertal pattern. The teeth are large, with all but one crown breadth (M_3) falling within a standard deviation of the corresponding Krapina means (Table 2). Only the values for C, P_3, and M_3 exceed the Krapina means. The anterior teeth, as in other Neandertals, are relatively expanded and quite heavily worn (Smith 1976d), and the molars are taurodont (Jelínek 1969). The 1964 tooth, a right M_3, morphologically and metrically indicates Neadertal affinities (Vlcek 1969). The two 1964 cranial fragments, portions of a parietal and temporal squama, are largely nondiagnostic (Vlcek 1969).

On the external face of the mandibular symphysis a gentle concavity begins just below the alveolar margin of the incisors and extends inferiorly to where the specimen is broken—a distance of some 25 mm (see Vlcek 1969: figs. 2,33, pl. 35). Rzehak (1905); Jelínek (1969 and in Klíma et al. 1962), and Vlcek (1969) all consider this to be incipient chin development, comparing it with Šipka and Tabun II. However, the lower portion of the mandibular symphysis is not present, so its morphology is unknown. Depressions below the incisors are associated with incipient mental eminence development in the Vindija and Šipka specimens, but their presence does not guarantee the presence of an incipient mental eminence. Both the J and H mandibles from Krapina, for example, have depressions comparable in development to those of the Ochoz, and neither shows the slightest trace of a mental eminence. In fact, the Ochoz remains would fit imperceptibly into the Krapina sample.

Subalyuk

In 1932, excavation of the Pleistocene deposits in Subalyuk Cave, on the southern slope of the Bükk Mountains overlooking the Hór Valley in northern Hungary, yielded the fragmentary remains of an adult and a child in association with Mousterian tools (Bartucz et al. 1940). Unlike many of the other South-Central European Upper Pleistocene sites, Subalyuk was apparently not excavated utilizing the best of methodologies, and consequently the stratigraphic positions of some of the finds are open to question. Four stratigraphic complexes comprised of 18 geological levels are identified in the 1940 monograph. The hominid remains are said to be contemporaneous and to come from the lower portion of Level 14 in Complex II (Bartucz et al. 1940). This complex contains "late Mousterian tools" and is supposed to coincide with the first Würm cold maximum (Lower Würm stadial). The earlier Complex I is said to correspond, on floral and faunal grounds, to the Tata loess beds, which in turn are estimated to represent the temperature phases of the Early Würm (Vértes 1964).

The Subalyuk adult is represented by a mandible (preserving the left corpus, with P_4 through M_3, the anterior portion of the left ramus, the symphysis with left C through right P_3, and the right molars) and a few postcranial elements, including a sacrum and a manubrium. The manubrium is ventrally concave, indicating a typically Neandertal "barrel-shaped" upper thorax (Coon 1962). Both manubrium and sacrum indicate a very small individual. The mandible, which does not necessarily represent the same individual as the postcranial specimens, exhibits a retromolar space, receding symphyseal contour, no mental eminence, and taurodont molars (Bartucz et al. 1940: pl. 4, 5). The symphysis and left corpus are high but relatively thin compared with those of most Neandertals, and the alveolar plane is shorter and more vertically oriented than in the Krapina and Ochoz mandibles. Tooth breadths for the Subalyuk adult (Szabò in Bartucz et al. 1940) fall within one standard deviation of the Krapina means, only the Subalyuk canine and third molars being larger (Table 2).

The Subalyuk child is represented by a neurocranium, most of both maxillae, most of the deciduous dentition, and a nasal bone. Odontometric and morphological features show it to be a Neandertal approximately three years of age (Thoma 1963). The maxillae exhibit no trace of canine fossae; the nose is broad (20 mm) for a young child, and the frontal process of the maxilla is also broad (Thoma 1963). Furthermore, the curvature of the nasal bone (see Bartucz et al. 1940: pl. 6; Jelínek 1969) is vertical or slightly concave for some distance inferior to nasion and then becomes sharply convex. This suggests a projection of the nose along the midsagittal plane, which fosters the beaked-face appearance of Neandertal crania. A projecting supraorbital torus is not developed, but, as in other Neandertal subadults (Smith and Raynard 1980), a distinct outline of a torus (in the form of a slight bulge) is observable (see Vlcek 1970). The neurocranium is long, relatively low, and broad compared with those of modern children of similar age (Thoma 1963). Biasterionic breadth is especially large, and there is a distinct indication of lambdoidal flattening and an incipient occipital bun. As in most other Neandertal children (Vlcek 1970; Smith 1976b), a metopic suture is present.

Vindija

Vindija, a large cave 50 km from Krapina, was first recognized as a Pleistocene-age locality in 1932, when Paleolithic artifacts and remains of Pleistocene animals were found there (Vukovic 1935; Brodar 1938). Since systematic excavations began in 1974, over 80 fragments of Pleistoccene human skeletal material, an extensive collection of Pleistocene fauna, and archaeological remains have been recovered (Malez 1975, 1978b, c; Malez et al. 1980). The stratified Pleistocene sediments provide an excellent sequence covering practically the entire Upper Pleistocene (Malez and Rukavina 1975, 1980; Wolpoff et al. 1981). Mousterian lithic material characterizes the Riss-Würm through Lower Würm levels and Aurignacian and Gravettian the Podhradem through Upper Würm levels. A radiocarbon date of 27,000 ± 600 years B.P. (Table 1) is associated with the Aurignacian (Malez 1978b).

The hominid remains from Vindija can be divided stratigraphically into three groups. The earliest and largest group comes from Level G_3 and is associated with a late Mousterian assemblage. This stratum is correlated with the Lower Würm stadial on the basis of stratigraphic, faunal, and cultural criteria (Malez et al. 1980; Wolpoff et al. 1981). The middle group comes partly from Level G_1, which probably represents the Podhradem interstadial. The only diagnostic artifact from this level is a split-based bone point, which is from the top of this layer and suggests that G_1 is Aurignacian. Also included with this group are three isolated teeth from the Aurignacian Level F_d. The latest group comes from Level D and is associated with a Gravettian industry.

The Vindija G_3 hominid sample consists of some 35 specimens. These remains are fragmentary, but various taxonomically relevant anatomical regions are well represented. An extensive descriptive and comparative study of these hominids (Wolpoff *et al.* 1981) has demonstrated that their total morphological pattern warrants their inclusion in the taxon *H. sapiens neanderthalensis*. This conclusion is based, in part, on the following criteria: the presence, in specimens preserving a supraorbital area (*N*=5), of supraorbital tori of Neandertal form (see also Smith and Ranyard 1980); frontal sinuses that are large and restricted to the torus proper (i.e., do not extend into the squama); the overall morphology and dimensions of the mandibles (*N*=4), including the presence of retromolar space (although the length of this gap is less than in the Krapina mandibles) (Fig. 6); the presence of a dorsal axillary groove on the single scapular fragment; the wide anterior alveolus of the maxilla (prosthion-to-postcanine distance); and various aspects of vault morphology (e.g., presence of suprainiac depressions and Breschet's sinuses).

Although unquestionably Neandertals, the Vindija hominids have certain features in which they approach the morphology of early South-Central European *H. sapiens sapiens* more than chronologically earlier Neandertals from the area (e.g., Krapina, Subalyuk). First, the supraorbital tori exhibit a distinct pattern of absolute and relative decrease in both thickness and projection in comparison with Krapina tori (Smith and Ranyard 1980 and Table 3). In addition, the relatively greater diminution in the midorbital region reflects an incipient tendency toward the division of the torus into medial and lateral portions (the arcus superciliaris and trigonum supraorbitale respectively). In size and form, the Vindija G_3 torus sample conforms to what one would expect of an intermediate between chronologically earlier Neandertals and early modern *H. sapiens sapiens* (Fig.7). Secondly, the symphyseal angles of all three specimens preserving this area are practically vertical (Vindija averages 87°, Krapina 99.6°, and Western European Neandertals 95°), and there is a slight mental eminence on two of the three (Fig. 6). Although these characteristics appear in some Western European Neandertal specimens, they are the exception rather than the rule. Thirdly, nasal breadths (estimated on the assumption of bilateral symmetry) are very small for the two maxillae preserved, more than three standard deviations *below* the Western European Neandertal mean (see Table 4). Both also have alveolar heights more than two and a half standard deviations below the Western European Neandertal mean. However, while certain dimensions of the lower face exhibit significant degrees of reduction compared with those of most other Neandertals, others (e.g., prosthion-to-postcanine distance) exceed the Neandertal average [7]. Fourthly, there is some indication of more vertical frontal squama than in other Neandertals (Fig. 8) Finally, there is no indication of lambdoidal flattening or occipital bunning. It must be noted, however, that the occipitals and posterior parietals are represented by only fragmentary specimens, making determination of the presence or absence of bunning and/or lambdoidal flattening rather tenuous.

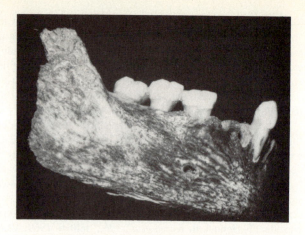

Figure 6. *The Vindija 206 mandible.*

The Vindija G_3 Neandertals as a group give clear indications of morphological change in the direction of what is characteristic for early modern *H. sapiens* in this region. This makes them one of the most interesting and significant Upper Pleistocene hominid samples yet recovered.

Külna

Külna Cave, some 45 km north of Brno, was first recognized as an important Paleolithic and paleontological site in 1880 by H. Wankel, and further excavations were conducted during the latter 19th and early 20th centuries by Martin Kríz and Jan Knies, who recovered a large series of Magdalenian and

Figure 7. *Browridge morphologies of Krapina (top; specimen Kr 28/37-9), Vindija (middle; specimen Vi 202), and Velika Pecina (bottom) in frontal, lateral, and inferior aspects. The dots marked by arrows on the inferior views denote the position of the frontal squama (after Smith and Ranyard 1980).*

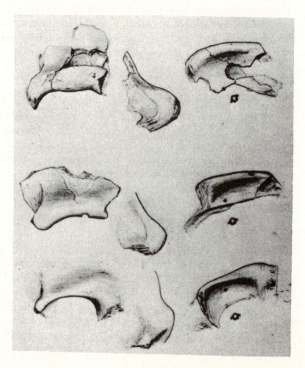

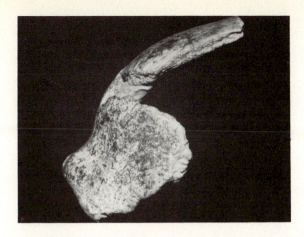

Figure 8. *The Vindija 261 frontal, lateral view.*

Mousterian artifacts (Valoch 1970). During World War II, the cave housed a munitions factory (Valoch 1967). In 1961, after reviewing its Middle Paleolithic industry, the Anthropos Institute of the Moravian Museum in Brno began a major project at Külna (Valoch 1968, 1970; Valoch *et al.* 1970). As a result of these excavations, Külna now provides one of the best stratigraphic sequences from the Riss-Würm interglacial to the end of the Lower Würm stadial in Europe (Valoch *et al.* 1970), as well as an excellent sequence of Middle Paleolithic components.

In 1965, a right maxillary fragment was found in situ in the Late Mousterian complex at Külna of the Lower Würm stadial (Jelínek 1966, Valoch 1967), between 40,000 and 50,000 B.P. (Jelínek 1980, 1981). The specimen is clearly *H. sapiens neanderthalensis* (Jelínek 1966, 1967a, 1969). Subsequently, a right parietal fragment and a few isolated teeth were recovered. The maxillary fragment is preserved from the midline to just behind M_1 with the canine, both premolars, and M_1 present. Jelínek ages the specimen at 14, which is a minimum estimate. The Külna maxilla has a narrow nose (based on reconstruction of nasal breadth assuming bilateral symmetry) compared with those of Western European Neandertals, but its alveolar height and prosthion-to-postcanine dimensions are at or above the Western European Neandertal means (Table 4). Compared with the roughly contemporaneous Vindija maxillae, it is much larger in all dimensions except prosthion-to-postcanine. The posterior teeth are narrower (each more than two standard deviations) than the appropriate Krapina means, but the canine is slightly broader (see Table 2). Also, there is a slight indication of a shallow canine fossa on the maxilla. The parietal exhibits curvature similar to that seen in Western European "classic" Neandertals and may represent the same individual as the maxilla (Jelínek 1980, 1981).

Šala

In 1961, a human frontal bone was found in gravel deposits of a sandbar in the Váh (Waag) River, near Šala in western Slovakia. Continued searching in the sandbar yielded remains of Pleistocene fauna, including a virtually complete steppe rhinoceros skull (*Dicerorhinus hemitoechus*), antler of the giant deer (*Megaceros giganteus*), and proboscidean remains. Subsequent fluorine tests support the contemporaneity of the fauna

and the hominid specimen, suggesting an Upper Pleistocene age for the Šala frontal (Vlcek 1968, 1969). The presence of the rhinoceros excludes the cold phases of the Early and Lower Würm, but an interstadial during these periods and the Riss-Würm are possibilities (Vlcek 1969). No cultural remains were recovered from the deposits.

The Šala frontal is complete, well-preserved, and adult (Vlcek 1964a, 1967a, 1968, 1969; Jelínek 1969). Over the lateral portion of the right orbit is a healed lesion. The frontal squama is rounded in sagittal curvature and appears to be relatively higher than those of some Western European and Krapina Neandertals (Vlcek 1969: 161-63). The interorbital area is broad and projected anteriorly, indicating absence of a nasal-root depression and presence of midfacial prognathism. The temporal lines are moderately developed. The most diagnostic and salient feature is the presence of a distinct supraorbital torus, which projects markedly. Projection dimensions are close to the corresponding Krapina means and larger than the Vindija means (Table 3). The injury to the supraorbital region has resulted in atrophy and thinning of the right lateral torus, but even excluding this the thicknesses of the torus are reduced and approach the Vindija means more closely than the Krapina means (Table 3). There is relatively greater midorbit thinning of the torus (on the nonpathological left side) than medially or laterally, and frontal sinuses are expansive and restricted to the torus.

Though the Šala frontal possesses some features which can be considered "transitional" or "progressive," its total morphological pattern is unquestionably Neandertal. Vlcek (1969) believes it to be related to the "transitional Neandertals" of the Near East (especially Zuttiyeh and Skhul V) because of its morphology and the reduction of the supraorbital torus. The specimen is considered female (Vlcek 1968, 1969; Jelínek 1969), which is reasonable because of its gracility and the gradual emergence of the torus from the squama in the glabellar area (see Smith 1980).

Šipka

One of the earliest Neandertal discoveries was made at Šipka Cave in the karst region near Stramberg, northeastern Moravia. In 1880, Maška recovered a symphyseal segment of a subadult mandible from a Mousterian level (Maška 1882). Since this discovery came at the height of arguments concerning the possible existence of a Neandertal phase of man, the Šipka jaw immediately became a subject of considerable interest. Those favoring the view that Neandertals represented a stage in human evolution (Maška, Wankel, Schaafhausen, Baume, de Quatrefages) argued that this was the mandible of an eight-to-ten-year-old Neandertal child. Virchow (1882) argued that it belonged to a modern adult with a pathological retention of incompletely developed, unerupted permanent teeth. Intense debate followed (see Jelínek 1965 and Vlcek 1969 for details), but, with the eventual demise of the pathological explanation of Neandertal morphology in general, Šipka was ultimately accepted as a Neandertal specimen (e.g., Hrdlicka 1930; Boule 1923; Vlcek 1958; Coon 1962; Boule and Vallois 1957).

Maška's excavations at Šipka were extensive and well done for their time. However, questions remained until 1950 regarding the division of the strata and the exact portion of the Upper Pleistocene represented in the Šipka sequence. In

Table 3. Browridge Dimensions (mm) in Early Hominids from South-Central Europe.

	Lateral	Projection Midorbit	Medial	Lateral	Thickness Midorbit	Medial
Krapina						
$\overline{X}(\sigma)$	24.3(1.38)	23.9(1.16)	20.3(2.27)	12.5(1.63)	10.7(1.81)	17.6(2.96)
Range	23.0–27.0	23.0–26.0	17.5–23.0	10.3–16.0	7.0–14.3	15.8–22.0
Vindija						
$\overline{X}(\sigma)$	22.1(1.78)	19.0(3.08)	...	10.6(0.51)	8.6(0.56)	...
Range	19.5–24.5	16.0–23.0	...	10.0–11.3	8.0–9.5	...
Šala[a]	25.0	22.5	20.0	11.0	7.1	15.0
Mladec 5[a]	23.0	19.0	17.5	10.1	7.7	23.7
Zlaty Kun[a]	22.0	19.0	16.0	8.4	5.8	16.7
Early Upper Paleolithic						
$\overline{X}(\sigma)$	20.3(2.58)	16.1(3.37)	13.0(3.01)	8.1(1.39)	5.4(1.72)	16.6(3.33)
Range	15.0–23.0	8.0–19.0	8.0–17.5	6.0–10.1	4.4–7.7	11.5–23.7

Source: Smith and Raynard (1980), revised.

[a]Values are averages of right and left sides of the specimen.

that year, F. Prošek excavated some sediments not removed by Maška, and sedimentation/petrographic analysis was undertaken by Kukla (in Valoch 1965a). The profiles of Maška and Prošek correspond closely (Valoch 1965a) and together provide a rather precise picture of the stratigraphic sequence at Šipka.

The most recent Würm-age strata contain Magdalenian artifacts and correspond to the first Late Würm oscillation. The oldest appear to be Lower Würm and contain extensive remains of the cave bear, *Ursus spelaeus* (Musil 1965a). The human mandible comes from Level 9 (Vlcek 1969: 55, 58) and is associated with fauna said by Musil (1965a) to be characteristic of Podhradem interstadial. The same conclusion is reached by Valoch (1965a: 17) on the basis of stratigraphic correlation. Also associated with the Šipka mandible is a lithic industry of essentially Mousterian character but containing slightly more than 14% of Upper Paleolithic elements (endscrapers, burins, and borers). Valoch, who analyzed this material using Bordes's French typological classification (Valoch 1965a), considers the industry a Šipka phase of the Central European Typical Mousterian (Valoch 1968) [8].

Unfortunately, there are a number of problems with the morphological assessment of the Šipka mandible. It consists of only the symphyseal region, the external (anterior) alveolus being largely missing or broken and distorted. Only the base of the symphysis remains intact externally. The internal (lingual) aspect of the symphysis, however, is completely preserved. Moreover, the specimen is a subadult (eight or nine years old, according to Vlcek 1969), and, as Jelínek (1965) notes, it is difficult to judge what adult morphology would have been. Finally, the original was destroyed in the fire at Mikulov Castle in 1945.

The breadths of the incisors, three of which are erupted and present, indicate some slight reduction compared with those of Krapina, Subalyuk, and Ochoz (Table 2). The Šipka values lie approximately one standard deviation below the corresponding Krapina means. Several teeth are preserved in their crypts on the right side (C, P_3, P_4), and these also appear small. All the teeth, however, are within the size range of both *H. sapiens neanderthalensis* and *H. sapiens sapiens* (Jelínek 1965, Smith 1976b), although the incisors are above the Predmostí range

(Matiegka 1934) and slightly above the Early Upper Paleolithic means reported by Frayer (1978).

Thickness and height of the Šipka symphysis are within one standard deviation below both the Vindija and Krapina (adult) means. On the ventral (lingual) aspect, the alveolar plane is not strongly angled, and the superior transverse torus is weakly developed. The external aspect of the symphysis appears somewhat receding (cf. Hrdlicka 1930), but there does seem to be some development of a subaveolar concavity below the incisor roots. Both Jelínek (1965, 1969) and Vlcek (1958, 1969) note that this contributes to the development of at least an incipient mental eminence, although they both see the alveolus projecting more anteriorly than the base of the mandible. Jelínek also finds the beginnings of a mental trigone. Finally, while it would probably be quite difficult to separate the Šipka mandible, on the basis of the morphology of the areas preserved, from an early *H. sapiens sapiens* sample, I concur with Jelínek (1965, 1969) and Vlcek (1969) that it is most reasonably considered late *H. sapiens neanderthalensis*.

Table 4. Maxillary Measurements (mm) in Early European Hominids.

	Alveolar Height	Nasal Breadth	Prosthion-to-Post-Canine
Krapina E	22.5	30.5*	25.2
Krapina F	24.2	...	...
Vindija 225	17.5	28.5*	27.3
Vindija 259	16.3	26.2*	24.3
Külna	29.9	30.0*	24.9
Western European Neandertal:			
$\overline{X}(\sigma)$	26.1(3.0)	33.3(1.5)	24.9(1.1)
Range	22.2–30.4	30.0–35.1	23.0–26.2
Early Upper Paleolithic			
$\overline{X}(\sigma)$	20.9(2.3)	27.4(1.7)	22.4(1.9)
Range	17.0–23.8	24.3–30.2	19.3–25.0

*These specimens preserve only one side of the nasal aperture, but each is preserved from the lateral margin to the midline (or beyond) along the inferior border. The breadth estimates given are determined with the assumption that nasal breadth is bilaterally symmetrical.

REMAINS OF *HOMO SAPIENS SAPIENS*

Mladec

The Mladec caves are located in the karst of northern Central Moravia, beside the village of Mladec (Lautsch). The main cave was discovered in 1828 and originally named the Furst-Johanns-Höhle. During the first systematic archaeological excavations in it (1881-82), hominid skeletal remains (Mladec 1, 2, and 3 and other fragments) and archaeological material were recovered (Szombathy 1925). From the information provided by Szombathy and a study of the stratigraphy of the remaining deposits in 1959-63 (by the Moravian Museum), it is known that these finds came from distinctive reddish-brown clayey sediments which constitute the fan of a talus cone formed by materials washed or thrown into the largest chimney of the main cave (Jelínek 1976). These deposits, which eventually closed off the chimney (Jelínek 1978), do not result from habitation of the cave. Similar depositional circumstances are common for caves in the Moravian karst (e.g. Zlaty Kun Cave [Prošek *et al.* 1952]). Later excavations in the same deposits of the main cave by Knies in 1903 provided more hominid remains (Mladec 4 and numerous smaller fragments) found with bone and lithic artifacts typical of the Aurignacian (Bayer 1922; Szombathy 1925). In addition, portions of a necklace consisting of drilled animal teeth were recovered (Szombathy 1925). Such items occur commonly in the Aurignacian and Pavlovian of Moravia (e.g., of Predmostí, Dolní Vestonice, Brno II). Of particular importance is the presence of numerous distinctive flat bone points (Mladec points), which are characteristic of early Aurignacian in this region (Jelínek 1978).

More human skeletal remains (Mladec 5 and 6 and other fragments) were discovered in 1904 during quarrying at a smaller cave adjacent to the main cave (Szombathy 1925). According to Jelínek (1976, 1978), descriptions of the deposits which contained the human remains in this second cave indicate that they may have accumulated in the same manner as in the main cave. The archaeological material accompanying the hominids in this second cave is identical to that associated with the hominids in the main cave, particularly in the presence of Mladec points. The two deposits and their hominids are, therefore, considered to be contemporaneous. The Mladec hominid-bearing deposits are correlated with the Podhradem interstadial (Jelínek 1969, 1976, 1978) [9] on the basis of their similarity to deposits in the Podhradem cave and the presence of early Aurignacian cultural material. The Mladec fauna indicates a "mildly cold" climate (Szombathy 1925).

The Mladec hominid remains are among the largest, oldest, and earliest-discovered Upper Paleolithic-associated skeletal samples in all of Europe. The material excavated by Szombathy in 1881 and 1882 is preserved at the Natural History Museum in Vienna (Mladec 1, 2, 3, and other fragments), and the Mladec 5 cranium is housed in the Moravian museum (Brno). From the postcranial sample preserved in Vienna and the descriptions provided by Szombathy of some of the fragments destroyed in the 1945 fire already mentioned, considerable variation in size and robusticity is evident. The two best-preserved femoral diaphyses in Vienna are slender but exhibit well-developed muscle markings. The two most complete humeral fragments are also slender but have more gracile muscle markings. Fragments of other arm bones, however, are obviously from larger and more robust individuals. Additionally, there are at least three in-nominate fragments from Mladec in Vienna, one of which is clearly female. Unfortunately, no pubic bones are preserved, and no axillary borders of scapulae are represented. Mladec femora are similar to later Upper Paleolithic femora and unlike those of Neandertals in their pronounced pilasters. The lengths of the better-preserved specimens indicate tall individuals.

The Mladec cranial sample also exhibits considerable variation due largely to sexual dimorphism. The total morphological patterns of these cranial specimens are consistent with their classification as *H. sapiens sapiens*, a conclusion supported by multivariate analyses. The latter place the Mladec crania in an Upper Paleolithic group differentiated from recent Europeans but more similar to them than to Neandertals (e.g., Morant 1930; Stringer 1974, 1978). At the same time, these crania exhibit features distinctly reminiscent of Neandertal cranial morphology.

The Mladec 1 cranium is well preserved, although only four teeth remain (M_1 and M_2 on both sides). Breadth dimensions for these teeth are slightly below the corresponding early Upper Paleolithic means reported by Frayer (1978). Upper facial height is moderate in comparison with that of other early Upper Paleolithic specimens, and facial breadth is small. Nasal breadth is moderate, and shallow canine fossae are present. There is a shallow nasal-root depression, and the mid-face does not project to the degree characteristic of European Neandertals (see Wolpoff 1980a: 312-13). Alveolar prognathism, however, is diminished to a lesser extent. The supraorbital region is divided into a superciliary arch and a supraorbital trigone (i.e., the modern European supraorbital morphology). Thicknesses of the supraorbitals consistently exceed the early South-Central European Upper Paleolithic mean (Smith and Ranyard 1980), but projection (though unmeasurable) appears less pronounced. On the basis of the relative size of the supraorbitals (compared with those of certain other Mladec specimens), small mastoids, and lack of marked development of other cranial superstructures (also compared with those of other Mladec specimens), Mladec 1 appears to be female.

The vault contour (see Szombathy 1925; Morant 1930) of Mladec 1 conforms to a dolichocranic modern *H. sapiens* pattern. In the lambdoidal area, however, there is distinct flattening associated with posterior projection of the occiput. The resulting structure is a type of occipital bun found rather commonly in Upper Paleolithic crania, particularly early Central European specimens. Because it differs from the Neandertal occipital bun in a number of ways, this structure is referred to here as an occipital hemi-bun. In Upper Paleolithic-associated crania, the area of lambdoidal flattening does not extend laterally to the degree observed in Neandertals. This difference is due to the expansion of certain aspects of the posterior parietal area. Viewed laterally (Fig. 9), the posterior parietal contour is more vaulted and curved than in Neandertals. Furthermore, the height of the planum nuchale (measured from inion to opisthion) is decreased and the plane less horizontally oriented. Inion is equally obvious in both groups, but in the Upper Paleolithic hominids it tends to project somewhat inferiorly from the remainder of the superior nuchal line. In the later group, this line is generally accompanied by a distinct demarcation, often in the form of a slight torus, between the nuchal and occipital planes. In Neandertals, these structures tend to run essentially in a straight line from inion in the direction of the lambdoidal suture (generally at the level of asterion). In the Upper

Paleolithic specimens, the structures incline slightly superiorly as they extend laterally from inion and tend to aproach the lambdoidal suture somewhat above the level of asterion.

The Mladec 2 calvarium has a rounder vault contour than Mladec 1 and lacks an occipital hemi-bun. The preserved part of the supraorbital area is identical to that of Mladec 1 except that it is less robust. This, along with its small mastoid processes, indicates that Mladec 2 is also female.

Mladec crania 4, 5, and 6 are much more robust than Mladec 1 and 2. Mladec 4 consists basically of the anterior half of a cranial vault; Mladec 5 is a virtually complete clavarium, lacking most of the base (and slightly distorted by the 1945 fire); and Mladec 6 preserves essentially the same areas as 5 except that the lateral supraorbital regions are missing. These three specimens are probably male and have long and relatively low vaults, lambdoidal flattening, occipital hemi-buns, expanded and robust nuchal areas, thick cranial vault bones, and massive supraorbitals. The supraorbital superstructures are basically modern (i.e., somewhat divided into superciliary arches and superorbital trigones) but, especially in Mladec 5 (Fig. 10), closely approach the condition of a Neandertal supraorbital torus (see Table 3), particularly that of late Neandertal tori in South-Central Europe (Smith and Raynard 1980; Wolpoff *et al.* 1981). Wolpoff (1980a:311) notes that the cranial contour of Mladec 5 is similar to that of La Chapelle-aux-Saints except for a slightly higher forehead and less projecting occiput. Stringer (1978), however, finds the contours of Mladec and other early Upper Paleolithic Central European crania more angular than Neandertal contours. Both Mladec 5 and 6 also have wide occipitals, and their maximum cranial widths are low on the parietals. Mladec 6 exhibits a nasal-root depression.

Two partial maxillae are also preserved in Vienna. Both have wide and shallow anterior palates, broad noses, and shallow canine fossae. One has anterior (C, I_2) and posterior (M_1, M_2) tooth breadths slightly above Frayer's (1978) early Upper Paleolithic means, while the other's posterior breadths (M_1, M_1, M_3) are slightly smaller than Frayer's means. All teeth exhibit extensive occlusal and interproximal attrition.

The Upper Paleolithic-associated hominids from Mladec are early, extremely robust members of *H. sapiens sapiens* that retain (especially in males) certain features reminiscent of their Neandertal ancestry: the form and dimensions of the supraorbital superstructures, the relative size of the nuchal plane, the

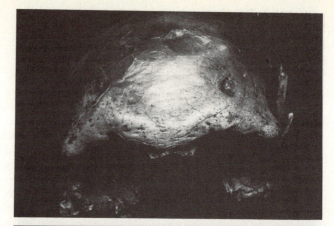

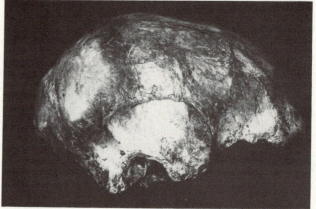

Figure 10. *The Mladec 5 male cranium, frontal and lateral views.*

presence of an occipital hemi-bun and lambdoidal flattening, and certain other aspects of facial morphology. These same features are also found in many other hominids associated with the Aurignacian and Gravettian in this portion of Europe.

Zlaty Kun (Koneprus)

At a cave in Zlaty Kun (Golden Horse) Hill in the Bohemian karst of Czechoslovakia, hominid specimens, Pleistocene fauna, and tools were found between 1950 and 1953 (Vlcek 1957a, 1967c). The deposits in the cave were a talus cone deposited through a chimney in the cave (Prošek *et al.* 1952), and the hominid-bearing deposits are from the early Middle Würm stadial (Vlcek 1951, 1957a, personal communication). Vlcek (1967c:268) describes the artifacts as an "Upper Paleolithic industry of Mousterian character," and there is a suggestion (Prošek *et al.* 1952) that the assemblage has affinities with the Szeletian.

The hominid specimens, Zlaty Kun 1 and 2 (Vlcek in Oakley *et al.* 1971), are actually portions of a single calvarium, lacking most of its base. Metrically, it resembles Mladec 1, but it is intermediate in robustness between Mladec 1 and 5. The Zlaty Kun calvarium exhibits a well-developed hemi-bun and a supraorbital area divided into a superciliary arch and a supraorbital trigone. Thickness and projection values for this specimen are among the largest for South-Central European early modern specimens (Smith and Ranyard 1980).

The face is represented by both zygomatics and a right maxilla. The zygomatics lack the columnar, pillar-like frontal processes characteristic of Neandertals. The maxilla has a nar-

Figure 9. *The Pavlov cranium, lateral view, exhibiting a well-developed occipital hemi-bun.*

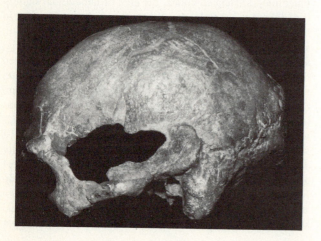

row nose and weakly developed canine fossa. The teeth (C through M2) are heavily worn. Their breadths fall consistently within one standard deviation below Frayer's (1978) early Upper Paleolithic means.

The Zlaty Kun mandible is robust and clearly of *H. sapiens sapiens* type. Its symphyseal angle is 81°, and a distinct mental eminence and mental trigone are present. Though both M3's were lost antemortem, there was clearly no retromolar space. The teeth (I2 through M2 on the left, C through M2 on the right) are heavily worn and smaller than Frayer's means. A few fragments of vertebrae and ribs are preserved but are non-diagnostic.

Vindija

Two stratigraphically separate samples of hominids are associated with Upper Paleolithic industries in Vindija Cave. From Level G$_1$ and F$_d$ comes a sample of seven specimens: three isolated teeth from F$_d$, portions of a left parietal and a right mandibular ramus/posterior corpus from G$_1$, and two isolated teeth also from G$_1$. Level F$_d$ contains Aurignacian cultural remains and is slightly younger than 27,000 B.P. (Wolpoff *et al.* 1981). Level G$_1$ yielded only one diagnostic artifact, a split-based bone point (from the top of the layer, slightly above the hominids), also indicating Aurignacian, and probably correlates with the Podhradem interstadial (Malez *et al.* 1980, Wolpoff *et al.* 1981).

The isolated teeth are closer in size (breadth) to the Krapina than to the early Upper Paleolithic sample (Table 2). Morphologically, they could be accommodated in either a late Neandertal or an early modern group (Wolpoff *et al.* 1981). The mandibular fragment is small and has a low ramus height compared with Neandertals (Wolpoff *et al.* 1981). There is a small retromolar space, and the mandibular foramen area is horizontal-oval in form. The parietal fragment is nondiagnostic. There is no significant difference between these Aurignacian-associated specimens from Vindija and the late Mousterian-associated material from Level G$_3$. This suggests that there is not necessarily a distinct morphological break in hominid forms corresponding to the Mousterian-early Upper Paleolithic dichotomy. Similar continuity has been noted in Western Europe (Lévêque and Vandermeersch 1980, 1981; ApSimon 1980). However, the Vindija sample is small, and only one specimen preserves diagnostic anatomical regions. More data are needed to establish the morphological affinities of the G$_1$ hominids.

The 34 hominid specimens from Level D are associated with a Gravettian industry (Malez *et al.* 1980). The morphology of these specimens conforms entirely to the total morphological pattern of *H. sapiens sapiens* and is consistent with their age. Cranial material is fragmentary and exhibits modern *H. sapiens* supraorbital morphology and cranial contours. The single mandible has a distinctive mental eminence and trigone, and the postcrania (mostly represented by femoral diaphyses) are modern.

Velika Pecina

Velika Pecina is a cave on the steep slopes of Ravna Gora in the Hrvatsko Zagorje (Yugoslavia). Investigation of the Pleistocene strata in the cave began soon after World War II, and systematic excavations were undertaken particularly in the early 1960s (Malez 1967, 1974). The deposits, 10 m thick, extend from possibly the late Riss-Würm through the end of the Würm and

have yielded an extensive sample of fauna and artifacts. Mousterian, Aurignacian, and Gravettian assemblages are present (Malez 1967, 1974), and several radio-carbon dates are associated with the latter two (Table 1).

The hominid specimen is from Stratum j, which correlates either with the late Podhradem interstadial or (most likely) with the basal Middle Würm stadial, consistent with an age of more than 34,000 years. (Stratum i, immediately above, has yielded a radiocarbon date of 33,850 ± 520 B.P. [Table 1].) The assemblage from Stratum j (see Malez 1967, 1974) probably represents an early phase of the Aurignacian. This is the earliest Upper Paleolithic hominid specimen in South-Central Europe associated this closely with a radiocarbon date. The specimen consists of the right half of an adult frontal bone (Smith 1976a; Malez 1978b, c). Morphologically, it falls clearly within the early *H. sapiens sapiens* group. This is particularly evident in the morphology of the supraorbital area. The dimensions of the supraorbital projections and the overall dimensions of the specimen are rather small (Smith 1976a; Smith and Ranyard 1980) and suggest a female.

Brno

In the immediate vicinity of the city of Brno, Moravia, three hominid specimens were recovered between 1885 and 1927. Brno 1 was discovered in 1885 at Cerveny Kopec (Red Hill) and consists of a calotte, a partial maxilla, and fragmentary postcranial elements (Makowsky 1888)[10]. No direct associations of this specimen with fauna or an archaeological assemblage were made at the time of excavation, but later excavations revealed a single cultural horizon at the site. The tools are Aurignacian-like, and Jelínek (personal communication) believes that the level dates to the later Podhradem interstadial. Morphologically, the calotte (lacking most of the occipital and nuchal planes) is relatively gracile. Suporaorbital development is similar to that of Velika Pecina except that it exhibits more projection. Vault contours are rounded. The maxilla has a deep palate, a narrow nose, moderate anterior alveolar height, and a shallow canine fossa. The teeth are moderate in size, with breadths below Frayer's (1978) early Upper Paleolithic means. Wear on the teeth is moderate to heavy.

Brno 2 was discovered accidentally in Francouzská ulice in the center of Brno in 1891. Subsequent excavation (Makowsky 1892) revealed that Brno 2 was a burial, covered with mammoth tusks and red ochre. The grave contained several disks of limestone, mammoth bones, and ivory, all with holes drilled in them, a stylized male figure of ivory 25 cm in height, and several hundred perforated *Dentalium* shells. All this suggests a Pavlovian cultural association for this specimen (Jelínek 1957, 1976; Valoch 1968). The specimen consists of a calvarium, a right zygomatic, a partial left mandible, a partial right maxilla, and a few fragmentary postcranial elements (Jelínek *et al.* 1959). The calvarium, exceeded only by Mladec 5 and 6 in size and robusticity, is unquestionably male and has very large mastoids, well-developed supramastoid ridges, a rugose nuchal plane, and a pronounced occipital hemi-bun. Cranial contours resemble those of the Mladec and Predmostí crania (Morant 1930, Stringer 1978). Supraorbitals are very well developed and second only to those of Mladec 5 in overall size and archaic appearance (Smith and Ranyard 1980). The zygomatic is modern in form in that the frontal process lacks the columnar morphology characteristic of Neandertals. The mandible exhibits a worn dentition and a mental eminence.

There was possibly a very small retromolar space. Brno 2 served as the basis for the so-called Brünn race (Makowsky 1892) or Brno type (Vlcek 1967b) of early *H. sapiens sapiens*.

Brno 3, an isolated burial covered with red ochre, was discovered in 1927 during the digging of a foundation in Zabovresky (Absolon 1929). No archaeological industry or faunal remains were associated with the specimen, but Jelínek (1960 and personal communication) feels it is probably Upper Paleolithic in age and roughly contemporary with Dolní Vestonice. A cranium and most of the postcranium were recovered but were destroyed by the 1945 fire. The cranium, described by Matiegka (1929), was smaller and much more gracile than Brno 2 and probably female. The supraorbital projections were weak and similar in size and form to those of Dolní Vestonice 3. The cranial contours were rounded, with little indication of lambdoidal flattening. The face was gracile, with a narrow nose and canine fossae.

Predmostí

The largest series of human remains from the Upper Paleolithic in Central Europe was recovered from the open-air site of Predmostí in northeastern Moravia. The first excavation of the Predmostí site was undertaken by J. Wankel in 1880, but finds were documented from the locality as early as 1571 (Matiegka 1934: 12). Wankel recovered the first hominid specimen, a right mandible (Predmostí 21) in 1884, lying under a mammoth femur. Maška began investigations here in 1882 and in 1894 discovered the communal grave in Chromecek's Garden (Matiegka 1934; Absolon and Klíma 1978), a 4 m X 2.5 m elliptical pit containing the remains of 18 individuals (Predmostí 1-18) of various ages and both sexes, most with their heads oriented to the north. The grave was covered with limestone slabs and mammoth bones (principally scapulae), a burial style characteristic of the Pavlovian in this region (Jelínek 1969). Two specimens (Predmostí 19 and 20) were found outside the grave by Maška but possibly belong with the hominids in it (Matiegka 1934). Further excavations by Maška, Kríz (in 1895), and Absolon (in 1928) yielded other hominid specimens. In all, some 29 individuals were recovered.

Of these, some are represented by only one or two skeletal elements and could be parts of other specimens. However, at least 20 individuals are definitely represented. If one accepts 29 individuals, they break down into the following age/sex categories (see Matiegka 1934): 15 subadults, ranging from a few months (e.g., Predmostí 11, 12, 13) to midteens (e.g., Predmostí 5, 7) in age; 6 adult males (Predmostí 1, 3, 9, 14, 18, 23); 2 to 4 adult females (Predmostí 4, 19?, 26?,); and 4 unsexed specimens. The Predmostí hominids were destroyed in 1945 at Mikulov Castle, although a few distorted fragments were recovered from the rubble. Fortunately, they had been carefully described in two monographs (Matiegka 1934, 1938) and other works (Absolon 1929, Morant 1930).

The excavations by Wankel, Maška, Kríz, and Absolon and also by Knies recovered a considerable amount of cultural material in addition to the hominid specimens (Zotz and Freund 1951, Absolon and Klíma 1978). The main cultural level yielded several thousand lithic artifacts, a rich bone and antler industry, and various art and decorative objects. The main cultural level is contemporary with the communal grave (Absolon and Klíma 1978) and is Pavlovian. Although numerous mammalian species were recovered from this component, the predominance of mam-

moth remains leaves little doubt that the mammoth was the primary prey of these hunters. Recent excavations by Klíma have provided radiocarbon dates for this level which conclusively establish that Predmostí is essentially the same age as Dolní Vestonice/Pavlov. Earlier cultural levels at Predmostí contain Aurignacian and Mousterian assemblages without hominid remains. A detailed discussion of the stratigraphy of the site, based on Absolon's excavations before World War II as well as recent work by Klíma, is to be found in Absolon and Klíma (1978).

The adult crania from Predmostí show morphological and metric variability, but no specimen has a total morphological pattern that would justify any classification other than *H. sapiens sapiens*. Cranial contours and overall shape conform to the early modern pattern (see Matiegka 1934; Morant 1930; Stringer 1974; Jelínek 1969), although certain specimens (e.g., Predmostí 3, 9, 18) have relatively low cranial vaults and/or foreheads. Predmostí 3 has its maximum width low on the temporals, indicating an exceptionally wide posterior cranial base. The vault morphology is quite robust, with strong indications of muscle attachments for both males and females. Predmostí males, however, exhibit much more pronounced supraorbital features and mastoid processes than females. Males show more pronounced development of an occipital hemi-bun (e.g., Predmostí 1, 3, 9) and a more robust nuchal plane. Female crania are characterized by hemi-buns (Predmostí 4, 10) smaller than those of the males. Interestingly, hemi-buns can already be seen in several of the subadult specimens at Predmostí (e.g., 2, 7). Metrically, the Predmostí males and females exhibit the same degree of sexual dimorphism as the specimens from Mladec, Brno, and Dolní Vestonice/Pavlov.

Predmostí supraorbitals are typical of those of early South-Central European Upper Paleolithic hominids (Smith and Ranyard 1980). They are thick and project markedly anteriorly but are clearly divided into superciliary arches and supraorbital trigones. Males such as Predmostí 3 and 18 exhibit the greatest degree of supraorbital development, but females possess the same morphological pattern (though reduced in size and robusticity).

Lower faces of the Predmostí hominids are robust but modern in form. Canine fossae are present, noses relatively narrow and high, distinct nasal-root depressions observable, and prognathism moderate (see Wolpoff 1980a: 313). Mandibles have mental eminences and trigones, although some are only weakly developed (Jelínek 1969). Moderate prognathism is further indicated by small retromolar spaces in certain mandibles (Predmostí 3, 1), while the ramus arises in the distal half of the third molar in others. Mean values for tooth breadths all fall very close to the corresponding means given by Frayer (1978) for the early Upper Paleolithic in Europe. The teeth, particularly the anteriors, are heavily worn.

Postcranial remains (Matiegka 1938) exhibit considerable variation. Interestingly, little of the variation results from sexual dimorphism. In fact, neither the European Neandertal nor the Upper Paleolithic sample is characterized by marked postcranial sexual dimorphism (Trinkaus 1980). Adult stature, according to Matiegka (1938: 68-69), averaged 66.5 or 64.8 in., depending on the techniques employed. Wolpoff (1980a: 341) computes averages of 64 and 61 in. respectively for male and female stature at Predmostí. Predmostí postcrania exhibit well-developed muscle markings and marked robustness. Joint surfaces are relatively reduced compared with those of Neandertals. Brachial and crural indices (Matiegka 1938: 70) show that the limbs of Predmostí hominids, like those of other Upper Paleolithic hominids, are relatively more elongated in their distal elements, unlike those of Neandertals (Trinkaus, personal communication). Pubicc morphology is modern. Trinkaus (1977) reports that all Predmostí scapulae preserving the axillary border exhibit the bisulcate or Chancelade pattern. However, Matiegka (1938: 35) describes Predmostí 14 (right and left) as exhibiting dorsal sulci (Neandertal pattern), and his illustrations (pl. 4) appear to support this.

In sum, the Predmostí hominids fit nicely into the population of early Upper Paleolithic hominids in this area of Central Europe. They are robust but clearly *H. sapiens sapiens*. Like many other hominid specimens associated with the Upper Paleolithic, they retain certain features reminiscent of Neandertal ancestry.

Dolní Vestonice/Pavlov

The mammoth-hunter occupation site of Dolní Vestonice (Unter Wisternitz), at the base of the Pavlovské Vrchy (Pavlovian Hills) in the Mikulov district of Moravia, was first excavated in 1924 (Absolon 1938). Discoveries of fossil mammoth remains are mentioned from this area as early as the 17th century, and stone tools were recovered from the site in the latter 19th century (Klíma 1963). On the basis of collections made at Dolní Vestonice in the early 1920's, J. Bayer concluded as early as 1924 that it was a very important Upper Paleolithic site. Excavations have been conducted at various times since under the direction of a number of scholars (Klíma 1963: 15-38)

The site is on a loess-covered terrace of the Dyje River and consists of the traces of several tentlike huts, a large accumulation of mammoth bones, and a large central fireplace. The largest "hut" measured some 9 X 15 m and contained numerous artifacts as well as five hearths. Smaller huts generally contained two hearths. Stone and bone tools, decorative items (various types of beads and pendants), and clay figurines were recovered (Klíma 1963). Of particular interest are a fired clay "Venus" (recovered from the central fireplace) and other "schematic" anthropomorphic figures. Several of the clay figurines were found in a hut located a few meters from the rest of the settlement. In this small (6 m in diameter) hut were a central oven and over 2,000 lumps of clay, some formed into the heads and bodies of animals (Klíma 1963). A small sculptured clay head (found in 1936) [Absolon 1938]) and a human face engraved on a small piece of mammoth ivory (discovered in 1948 [Klíma 1962, 1963]) exhibit asymmetry, with the features on the left side appearing to droop considerably (see Klíma 1963: 194). The two occupational phases identified are correlated with the early Upper Würm stadial and Stillfried B interstadial respectively (Klíma 1963: 52-53; Musil and Valoch 1966), and radiocarbon dates are available (Table 1). The stratigraphic and chronometric ages and cultural remains indicate that Dolní Vestonice belongs to the Pavlovian (Klíma 1963; Valoch 1968; Jelínek 1969, 1976).

Pavlov lies less than a kilometer from Dolní Vestonice and like it is an open site deposited in loess (Klíma 1955, 1959a, b). The archaeological remains closely resemble those from Dolní Vestonice and include animal and anthropomorphic figurines, decorative items, hut floors, and lithic and bone industries. The site corresponds to the early Upper Würm stadial (Klíma 1955) and has yielded two radiocarbon dates (Table 1).

The first hominid specimen was discovered at Dolní Vestonice in 1925, and ten specimens were recovered between 1925 and 1951 (see Vlcek in Oakley *et al.* 1971). The most complete specimen, Dolní Vestonice 3, was excavated in 1949 from a pit in the settlement covered by two mammoth scapulae (Klíma 1963). This specimen has been described in great detail by Jelínek (1954), but the other specimens are described only partially or not at all. Dolní Vestonice 1 and 2 are male and female calvaria (Absolon 1938, Maly 1939) of uncertain context. All but Dolní Vestonice 3, 9, and 10 (the latter two being isolated teeth) were discovered prior to 1934 and destroyed in 1945. At Pavlov, a male was recovered between 1954 and 1957 from a burial pit covered with mammoth scapula and other bones (Klíma 1959a). Fragmentary gnathic and dental remains of other individuals were recovered in 1967.

The Pavlov male is represented by a very robust cranial vault, parts of the face, and a partial postcranial specimen (Vlcek 1961a, b; Jelínek 1969, 1976). Cranial contours are clearly modern, and an occipital hemi-bun is present (see Fig.9). The supraorbitals are well-developed and, like those of several other specimens (e.g., Mladec 5, Brno 2), approach the condition seen in late South-Central European Neandertals (Smith and Ranyard 1980). While the preserved parts of the face are robust, the nose appears to have been narrow, and the zygomatic conforms to the modern pattern. The mandible is also robust but exhibits a distinct mental eminence and trigone. There is a small retromolar space. The teeth are heavily worn and tend to fall slightly above Frayer's (1978) means for early Uppper Paleolithic tooth breadths.

Dolní Vestonice 3 is a virtually complete skeleton, with the postcranium still *en bloc*. Jelínek (1954; see also 1969, 1976) has provided the definitive description of the specimen. It is a female *H. sapiens sapiens*, but certain archaic features (e.g., a small occipital hemi-bun) are observable. Supraorbitals are similar in form and extent of development to those of other early Upper Paleolithic females (e.g., Predmostí 4, Velika Pecina), and deformation is evident on the left side of the facial skeleton. This was perhaps caused by paralysis of the musculature in this region due to nerve damage and results in an asymmetrical face. The left side of the face would certainly have drooped, and effects of this condition (extreme arthritic deformation) are seen in the pathological nature of the left tempormandibular joint. The sculptured and engraved faces mentioned earlier show similar distortions and may be representations of the person whose remains are known as Dolní Vestonice 3 (Klíma 1962).

Others

Although no diagnostic hominid remains have been assocciated with the Szeletian, two mandibular molars from Silická Brezová (Vlcek 1967b) and one from Pálffy (both in Czecholslovakia) are suggested to be from Szeletian levels. Unfortunately, they yield no useful information. Other Upper Paleolithic specimens from this region were among the earliest such discoveries made. Some of these (e.g., Mladec, Predmostí, Brno 1 and 2) have already been discussed.

Upper Paleolithic hominid specimens were also recovered at Sv. Prokop (Czechoslovakia) in 1887 (Vlcek 1951), Balla (Hungary) in 1909 and 1911 (Bartucz *et al.* 1940), Pálffy (Czechoslovakia) in 1913, and Miesslingstal (Austria) in 1914 (Bayer 1927).

Two important Upper Paleolithic archaeological sites, Willendorf in Austria (Felgenhauer 1959) and Istállosko in Hungary (Vértes 1961), have yielded hominid specimens. The Istállosko specimen, dated at about 30,000 B.P., is the germ of a mandibular molar. From the Gravettian horizon (Level 9) of Willendorf comes a basal symphyseal fragment of a mandible and a femoral diaphysis. The former is characterized by a mental eminence, while the rather gracile femur exhibits a well-developed pilaster. Both would appear to be modern *H. sapiens*.

The cave of Veternica in the Medvednica (northwestern Croatia) has produced Upper Pleistocene remains (Malez 1965) including a hominid calvarium. It was formerly said to come from the Mousterian levels (Coon 1962; Škerlj 1958) and inferred to be contemporary with the Krapina Neandertals. Reinvestigation of the stratigraphy indicates that this specimen, which is dolichocranic but clearly *H. sapiens sapiens* (Smith 1976a, 1977), comes either from the Aurignacian levels (Malez 1978b, c) or from an even more recent stratum.

Additional Aurignacian-associated specimens include the facial skeleton from Svitávka in Czechoslovakia, which is very similar to Dolní Vestonice 3 and Brno 3 (Vlcek 1967c), and the Cioclovina calotte, which exhibits a slight occipital hemi-bun and is similar to the Predmostí crania (Necrasov and Cristescu 1965).

Finally, very fragmentary, undescribed hominid remains have been reported from Layer 11 at Baco Kiro in Bulgaria (Kozlowski 1979: 81). Their fragmentary condition may preclude accurate anatomical assessment, but Kozlowski reports that they are primitive modern *H. sapiens*. Since these remains are possibly associated with a date of >43,000 B.P., a detailed morphological study may establish them as the earliest chronometrically dated modern *H. sapiens* specimens from Europe.

EVOLUTIONARY PATTERNS

Neandertal remains from South-Central Europe can be divided into two temporal samples. The early sample consists of the remains from Krapina, Gánovce, Ochoz, and probably Subalyuk. The time span represented extends from the Riss-Würm through the Early Würm stadial. The late sample comprises the specimens from Vindija Level G₃ and Külna (Lower Würm stadial) and from Šipka (Podhradem). The Šala frontal fits best in the later group on morphological grounds, but it could date to an earlier part of the Upper Pleistocene.

The early Neandertals from this region exhibit as a group all the characteristic morphological features of *H. sapiens neanderthalensis*, and although many have often been considered more "progressive" or more "generalized" in their expression of Neandertal anatomical characteristics than Western European "classic" Neandertals there is no feature or complex of features that supports this. Where cranial, dental, and postcranial comparisons are possible, the early South-Central European Neandertals exhibit the same morphological pattern as their Western European contemporaries. For example, Western and early South-Central European Neandertal samples exhibit identical patterns of supraorbital torus and frontal sinus form, robust upper faces with wide interorbital and columnar lateral orbital margins, absence of canine fossae, inflated maxillary sinuses, buttressed zygomata, mastoid processes which generally do not project below the occipitomastoid crest, broad occipitals with robust nuchal planes, relatively low cranial vaults with receding foreheads, long and broad cranial vaults, high and broad anterior alveolar regions, mandibular symphyses which recede from alveolus to base, absence of mental eminences, presence of retromolar spaces, large and heavily

worn anterior teeth, and various diagnostic features of the postcranium (e.g., indications of robust and barrel-shaped thorax, elongated and thinned superior pubic rami, relative epiphyseal and articular surface expansion in long bones, and nonmodern scapular axillary border patterns).

The extent of similarity in certain other characteristics between Western and South-Central European Neandertals is more difficult to evaluate, usually because of the fragmentary condition of most of the remains in the later gorup. Lambdoidal flattening and occipital bunning are characteristic of Western European Neandertals but difficult to document in South-Central Europe because no adult specimen preserves an intact posterior cranial vault. Two juvenile specimens (Subalyuk and Krapina B) do preserve the pertinent area and exhibit at least incipient expression of both features. Furthermore, the contour of the Gánovce endocast also indicates the presence of both features. Midfacial prognathism, another characteristic feature of Western European Neandertals, is difficult to identify in South-Central Europe because no adult specimen preserves a complete face. However, the absence of a nasal-root depression and the midsagittal contour of the upper face in the most complete face, Krapina C, clearly denotes the presence of midfacial prognathism (see Fig. 3). The same features are also evident in Krapina E, and nasal-root depressions are absent in the other Krapina specimens that preserve the relevant areas. Furthermore, the contour of the Subalyuk juvenile nasal bone also indicates midfacial prognathism.

The only systematic difference which appears to exist between Western and early South-Central European Neandertals is one of average body size. The postcranial remains from Krapina and Subalyuk suggest that the South-Central European Neandertals were smaller than the Western European forms; however, this may be due to the apparent overabundance of subadult material represented in the Krapina sample.

The late Neandertal sample from South-Central Europe has basically the same morphological pattern as the early sample but exhibits a number of features in which it approaches the early modern *H. sapiens* condition to a consistently greater extent than the early group does. This fact, pointed out repeatedly by Central European scholars (e.g., Jelínek 1969; Vlcek 1958, 1964b, 1969) on the basis of the rather sparse material from Šipka, Külna, and Šala, has been confirmed by the discovery of the Vindija hominids. For example, the Vindija supraorbital tori exhibit both metric diminution (see Table 3) and certain morphological changes from the earlier Krapina (Smith and Ranyard 1980; Wolpoff *et al.* 1981), including an increase in midorbit reduction that can be considered an incipient stage in the emergence of distinct supraorbital trigone and superciliary arch segments. The Šala torus conforms to the Vindija pattern. Mandibular remains from Vindija exhibit (as a group) relatively vertical symphyses (all less than 90°), and two of the Vindija specimens, as well as Šipka, give indications of incipient mental eminences and trigones. The late group also shows reduction in certain significant facial characteristics. For example, the Külna and both Vindija maxillae exhibit narrow noses compared with the Western European sample. Furthermore, the Vindija specimens (but not Külna) have shallow palates and reduced alveolar heights (Table 4). Also, the Külna specimen and perhaps the Vindija ones possess shallow canine fossae. Several other indications of change in the direction of early modern *H. sapiens* are present but less certain because of inadequacies of the late Neandertal sample (e.g., fragmentation and/or unreliably small sample sizes). Both the Šala and certain

Vindija frontals appear to have had less receding frontal squama than the Krapina or Western European Neandertal samples (see Wolpoff *et al.* 1981, Vlcek 1969), and one Vindija specimen suggests that the extent of midfacial prognathism is less than in other European Neandertals (see Wolpoff *et al.* 1981 for details). Finally, there is some suggestion of size reduction in the anterior (but not so much in the posterior) dentition between early and late Neandertals in South-Central Europe (see Table 2).

The early modern *H. sapiens* (early Upper Paleolithic) sample from South-Central Europe exhibits several characteristics that indicate a close connection with late South-Central European Neandertals and suggest an intermediate position between Neandertals and later European modern hominid populations. For example, the supraorbital superstructures, although modern in form, are more salient and robust than in later *H. sapiens sapiens* populations. Furthermore, the division between the supraorbital trigone and superciliary arch is not always as distinct, and some specimens, such as Mladec 5 (Fig. 10), almost exhibit a supraorbital torus. It has been suggested (Smith and Ranyard 1980) that the supraorbital region in South-Central European hominids represents a morphological continuum from early Neandertals through late Neandertals to early modern *H. sapiens* (see Fig. 7 and Table 4). Also, hominids associated with the early Upper Paleolithic in Europe are intermediate in tooth size between Würm Neandertals and later Upper Paleolithic specimens (Frayer 1978; Smith 1976b), contributing to a distinct pattern of dental reduction traceable from Riss-Würm Neandertals through Mesolithic and Neolithic Europeans (Brace 1979a, Frayer 1978). Noses (especially at Mladec) tend to be only slightly narrower than those of late South-Central European Neandertals, and canine fossae are not extensively more excavated. Prognathism and facial robustness and rugosity are generally greater in early modern *H. sapiens* than in later European Upper Paleolithic populations. Occipital hemi-buns are common in the early Upper Paleolithic sample and much less frequent in later European populations.

Although these and other features indicate considerable morphological similarity between early Upper Paleolithic and late Neandertal specimens from South-Central Europe, the early Upper Paleolithic hominid total morphological pattern is clearly *H. sapiens sapiens*. No specimen, not even Mladec 5 or 6, possesses a complex of features that would warrant classification as Neandertal. Stringer (1974, 1978) has illustrated this by means of multivariate analysis of the pertinent material (see also Bräuer 1980; Trinkaus and Howells 1979). Multivariate evidence has reinforced the idea of a qualitative difference between Neandertal and early modern *H. sapiens* morphology, an idea which has its roots in earlier replacement concepts (Boule 1923). However, neither Stringer's nor Bräuer's analyses can include the late Neandertal remains from South-Central Europe, because of their fragmentary condition. If one assumes that overall vault and facial form had evolved in this group to the level suggested by the observable anatomical features, then the level of distinction between Neandertals and early modern *H. sapiens* indiccated by methodologies such as Stringer's and Bräuer's may not be nearly so marked.

Despite difference in overall craniofacial form, the high frequency with which Neandertal-reminiscent features are found in the early modern sample from South-Central Europe and the documented changes from early to late South-Central European Neandertal morphology in the direction of the early modern

pattern provide enough suggestion of a morphological continuum to require some explanation. There would appear to be three possible explanations [11]: (1) an in situ transition between Neandertals and modern humans in this area of Europe, without any significant outside influence; (2) a replacement of Neandertals by an influx of fully modern *H. sapiens* into Europe, with some assimilation of Neandertal genes into the invaders' gene pool; and (3) a transition brought about primarily as a result of gene flow, with "progressive" genes being introduced into Europe but no significant influx of modern people themselves.

Available evidence provides little support for the second possibility (Spencer and Smith 1981). In order for a fully modern *H. sapiens* group to have moved into Europe and replaced or hybridized with the indigenous Neandertals, modern *H. sapiens* would have had to be present in an adjacent region earlier than the appearance of modern Europeans. The area which is generally considered to be the source of modern Europeans is the Near East, and the hominid samples from Skhul and Qafzeh have been widely cited as evidence of the early emergence of essentially modern populations in this region (Vandermeersch 1981a). Recent archaeological and faunal information indicates, however, that the Skhul hominid sample is not contemporary with Tabun Level C, as was previously thought, but more recent (Jelínek 1982; see also Smith 1977). Tabun is now dated to approximately 50,000 B.P. (Jelínek 1982), and Skhul is estimated to be perhaps 10,000 years more recent (cf. Higgs 1961; Higgs and Brothwell 1961). The same analysis of Middle Paleolithic lithics in the Near East suggests that Qafzeh is roughly contemporary with Skhul (Jelínek 1982), and contemporaneity is also supported morphologically (Wolpoff 1980a). On the basis of his geological analysis, Farrand (1979) prefers an earlier age estimation for the Qafzeh hominids, but his data are also consistent with 30,000-40,000 B.P. age.

If a date of 35,000-40,000 B.P. is correct, the Skhul/Qafzeh hominids are not significantly earlier (if at all) that earliest modern *H. sapiens* in South-Central Europe and so cannot constitute a credible ancestral "population" for the latter group. However, should it be demonstrated that the Skhul/Qafzeh hominids are older than ca. 40,000 B.P., the replacement hypothesis (in some form) would be more difficult to reject.

Southern Africa has also been suggested as an area in which modern *H. sapiens* arose at a relatively early date. Remains of modern *H. sapiens* from Border Cave (South Africa) and the Omo-Kibish Formation (Ethiopia) are claimed to be in excess of 100,000 years old (Day 1969; Beaumont *et al.* 1978; Beaumont 1980; Rightmire 1979, 1981), and very fragmentary remains from Klasies River Mouth Cave 1 are more than 65,000 years old (Rightmire 1981). However, although the dating of all three sites appears sound, the contexts of the hominid remains at the first two are open to considerable question, and the Klasies specimens are so fragmentary that an accurate assessment of their morphology may not be possible (they have yet to be described in detail). Even if the ages for these specimens are accurate, their morphology is considerably different from that of early modern Europeans (see Wolpoff 1980a), making it unlikely that modern Europeans represent an actual migration from Southern Africa.

The present state of the art in paleoanthropology does not allow a definite choice between the other two possible explanations for the transition, because existing paleontological models are inadequate to deal effectively with gene flow (see Weiss and Maruyama 1976). It is impossible at this point to judge what effect gene flow (without major population replacement) may have had on the transition from Neandertals to modern *H. sapiens* in South-Central Europe. Certainly, there were no geographical barriers to populational contact between South-Central Europe and any adjacent region, and it is possible that gene flow played a major role. On the basis of existing data, however, there is no a priori reason that the transition in South-Central Europe need have been based on the influx of "progressive" alleles any more than the transitions in other regions were based on the influx of "progressive" alleles from South-Central Europe.

On the other hand, if the presence of modern *H. sapiens* is unequivocally established in Southern Africa at 60,000+ years and in Western Asia at 40,000+ years, a clinal pattern emerges relative to the earliest appearance of anatomically modern humans. This pattern is continued in Europe, with modern *H. sapiens* being earlier in Central than in Western Europe. Such a clinal pattern, if ultimately established, is much more likely to be the result of gene flow than of large-scale population movement and replacement because the observed regional differences in modern *H. sapiens* morphology and the existence of a morphological continuum in several areas are difficult to incorporate into a strict replacementist explanation. Whatever the importance of gene flow, the morphological continuum in Upper Pleistocene South-Central European hominids indicates some degree of genetic continuity between *H. sapiens neanderthalensis* and *H. sapiens sapiens* in this region of Europe, and on the basis of existing information the simplest and best explanation for this would seem to be that the transition was primarily the result of an indigenous process.

RELATIONSHIPS WITH OTHER AREAS OF EUROPE

North-Central Europe

Neandertal remains in North-Central Europe (Germany east of the Rhine and Poland) are know from the localities of Taubach and Ehringsdorf near Weimar, the Neander Valley near Düsseldorf, Salzgitter-Lebenstedt in Central Germany, and possibly Wildscheuer (see Knussman 1967). None of these specimens exhibit any such pattern of "progressive" features as is found in the late South-Central European sample, and morphologically all would appear to belong in the early South-Central and Western European category (see Wolpoff 1980a for discussions of the Ehringsdorf and Neander Valley material). However, none of these specimens are demonstrably late (i.e., Lower Würm stadial) in date. Ehringsdorf and Taubach are Riss-Würm in age, and Salzgitter-Lebenstedt dates to the Early Würm (Table 1). The others are undated.

Although North-Central Europe has yielded numerous Upper Paleolithic sites with hominid remains, most are rather late (see Oakley, Campbell, and Molleson 1971). Only the Aurignacian-associated remains from Stetten (Volgelherd Cave) (Gieseler 1937, 1941) and the recently discovered material from Paderborn (Henke and Protsch 1978) and Hahnöfersand (Bräuer 1980) seem to be early Upper Paleolithic specimens [12]. The Stetten calvaria and the Paderborn calvarium (the latter dated to ca. 26,000 B.P. by amino-acid racemization and 27,400 ± 600 B.P. by radiocarbon dating of residual bone collagen [see Henke and Protsch 1978]) are robust but certainly modern. They do not appear to exhibit strong indications of Neandertal-reminiscent

features. The various univariate, bivariate, and multivariate analyses of Henke and Protsch (1978) and Bräuer (1980) place Paderborn in *H. sapiens sapiens*.

Perhaps the most significant Upper Pleistocene specimen from this region is the frontal from Hahnöfersand (Bräuer 1980, 1981). It has no cultural associations and dates to 36,000 B.P. by amino-acid racemization and 36,000 ± 600 B.P. by radiocarbon (collagen). It exhibits well-developed superciliary arches, continuous over glabella. The arches appear to thin laterally, but it is difficult to determine to what extent because the lateral parts of both sides of the superorbitals are damaged. Bräuer (1980: 13-14) states that a division into superciliary arch and supraorbital trigone is visible on the right side, so that the specimen does not possesss a supraorbital torus in the classical sense. Also, the frontal sinus appears to extend slightly into the squama. Several of the bivariate and multivariate analyses of Hahnöfersand reported by Bräuer place it either with Neandertals or in an intermediate position between Neandertals and Upper Paleolithic hominids. Bräuer explains this combination of Neandertal and modern traits as the result of hybridization between Neandertals and early modern *H. sapiens* [13]. However, given the early date of the specimen and its morphology and geographic location, it can also be interpreted as an extension of the same early modern *H. sapiens* "population" which includes the Mladec, Brno, and Zlaty Kun remains in South-Central Europe and thus as a further indication of a transition between *H. sapiens neanderthalensis* and *H. sapiens sapiens* in Central Europe.

Western Europe

Western Europe has yielded an impressive array of Neandertal remains, generally referred to as "classic" Neandertals (see Howell 1952). The majority of these (e.g. La Chapelle-aux-Saints, La Ferrassie, La Quina, and Hortus) are correlated with Würm II [14] (Heim 1976a; de Lumley 1976; Vandermeersch 1976), between approximately 50,000 and 40,000 B.P. However, for various reasons, the placement of many of the specimens (particularly those found early in this century) in Würm II cannot be considered conclusive. Only a few Upper Pleistocene specimens seem to be pre-Würm II (see Wolpoff 1980a), and there appear to be very few systematic differences between the pre-Würm II and Würm II Neandertal samples in Western Europe. The morphological features which characterize the Western European Neandertals have been outlined, and further detail may be found in a number of recent discussions (e.g., Heim 1974, 1976b; Trinkaus and Howells 1979; Wolpoff 1980a).

Present evidence does not unequivocally indicate the presence of a late Neandertal *group* in Western Europe that exhibits a consistent overall pattern of change in the direction of modern *H. sapiens*. There is evidence of anterior dental reduction from the earlier to later Neandertal samples (Frayer 1978; Wolpoff 1980a), and reduction of Würm II anterior teeth is particularly evident at the late Würm II site of Hortus (de Lumley 1973, 1976), where the anterior teeth are consistently smaller than those of the rest of the Würm II sample. The only other indications of "progressive" features in the Würm II Western European sample are isolated occurrences of such traits as incipiently developed mental eminences on La Ferrassie 1 and Circeo 2 associated with what is otherwise "typically" Neandertal morphology.

The recent discovery of a Neandertal in a Châtelperronian context at Saint-Césaire in France (Lévêque and Vandermeersch 1980) deserves special attention. Although the preliminary considerations of the morphology of this specimen emphasize that it is virtually identical to earlier (Würm II) Neandertals (Lévêque and Vandermeersch 1980; ApSimon 1980; Vandermeerscch 1981b), my limited examination of it in Paris in 1979 left the impression of strong similarity to the Vindija Neandertals in the mandible and supraorbital torus. Others (Wolpoff, personal communication) have come to the same conclusion [15]. While more information is needed to be certain, the latest Neandertals in Western Europe (Saint-Césaire and possibly Hortus) indicate some morphological change in the direction of modern *H. sapiens*. However, if the age of the Saint-Césaire specimen is comparable to available radiocarbon dates for the Châtelperronian at other sites (e.g., Arcy-sur-Cure), 31,000 to 33,000 B.P., it is somewhat more recent than the late Neandertal group from South-Central Europe.

If the available dates are giving the correct temporal picture, it would also appear that Upper Paleolithic technology developed somewhat earlier in South-Central than in Western Europe. Combining this with the indication that the morphological transition between *H. sapiens neanderthalensis* and *H. sapiens sapiens* was under way in South-Central Europe before there is much evidence for it in Western Europe, it is possible that the transition in South-Central Europe served as a catalyst for events in Western Europe. However, a much better understanding of the exact chronological positions of many specimens (particularly many of the supposed Würm II Neandertals) and more data on the morphology and chronological position of the latest Western European Neandertals are necessary before the nature of the Neandertal–early modern relationship in Western Europe can be demonstrated.

Except for the Châtelperronian specimens, the earliest Western European Upper Paleolithic remains are Middle Aurignacian. Thus, a critical gap remains between the latest Neandertals and earliest moderns in Western Europe that complicates assessment of the relationship between them. The earliest *H. sapiens sapiens* specimens include the robust remains from Cro-Magnon and Grotte des Enfants (Billy 1976). However, this robustness, especially in the occipital region (often including hemi-buns), recall Neandertal morphology, as do other aspects of their morphology (see Wolpoff 1980a). The impression that little difference exists between these specimens and modern Europeans (e.g., Boule 1923; Boule and Vallois 1957) is far from the truth, as a significant amount of evolutionary change is documented from the early to late Upper Paleolithic samples in Western Europe (Billy 1976). Thus, the Western European early Upper Paleolithic material is intermediate in numerous features between Neandertals and later modern Europeans.

At the present time, Western Europe does not provide as convincing an indication of morphological continuity as South-Central Europe does. It is tempting (and perhaps more defensible) to hypothesize considerable extraneous effect on the Neandertal–early modern transition in Western Europe and to suggest that at least the immediate source area for this influence was South-Central Europe.

CONCLUSION

A distinct morphological continuum exists between *H. sapiens neanderthalensis* and *H. sapiens sapiens* in South-Central Europe. This is supported by the consistent pattern of change between early Neandertals (Krapina, Gánovce, Ochoz, Subalyuk) and late Neandertals (Vindija, Külna, Šipka, Šala?) in certain features, always in the direction of early modern *H. sapiens*, and the consistent presence of clearly Neandertal-reminiscent features in the earliest *H. sapiens sapiens* specimens. To what extent this continuum reflects the influence of gene flow from some adjacent region is difficult to assess because of the difficulty of identifying the effects of gene flow in a paleontological context. However, modern *H. sapiens* cannot conclusively be shown to occur any earlier in any of the regions adjacent to South-Central Europe, including the Near East, than in South-Central Europe itself. On the basis of the data available at present, there is no reason to believe that gene flow into this region from the Near East or anywhere else was any more responsible for the archaic-to-modern *H. sapiens* transition in South-Central Europe than gene flow from South Central Europe was for the same transition in the Near East or elsewhere. There is no convincing evidence, either archaeological or skeletal, to indicate a migration of fully evolved modern *H. sapiens* into South-Central Europe. In fact, both the Szeletian and Aurignacian, which represent the earliest Upper Paleolithic in the region, most likely have their roots in the Central European Middle Paleolithic. Until it can be disproven, the simplest and most logical hypothesis supportable on the basis of present knowledge is that the archaic-to-modern-*H.-sapiens* transition in South-Central Europe was indigenous. The nature of the relationship between this transition and the same transition in areas to the north and west in Europe is not clear. The rather sparse evidence from North-Central Europe seems to reflect the same morphological continuity, within the same chronological framework, as is documented for South-Central Europe. In Western Europe, the continuum is less distinct, but new discoveries appear to be closing the gap. Present chronological information suggests that the transition may occur somewhat later in Western Europe than in Central Europe. Although it is certainly a possibility, more data are necessary before suggesting that the origin of modern *H. sapiens* in Western Europe was the result of influence from South-Central Europe.

Finally, although some of the interpretations presented in this paper may not be convincing to all, there is no denying the critical importance of South-Central Europe and its Upper Pleistocene hominid sample to the question of the origin of modern Europeans and the "fate" of the Neandertals. Paleoanthropology has a long and distinguished tradition in this area of Europe, beginning with the work of Gorjanovic-Kramberger, Matiegka, Maška, Absolon, and others at sites like Krapina, Mladec, Ochoz and Šipka. Recent discoveries at new sites (e.g., Vindija, Külna, Velika Pecina) suggest that considerable information is yet to be recovered in South-Central Europe and that this region will continue to provide new insights into the nature and course of Upper Pleistocene hominid evolution.

NOTES

[1] I thank the following persons and institutions for permission to study material in their care and for various other forms of assistance: I.

Crnolatac and K. Sakac (Geological-Paleontological Museum, Zagreb), M. Malez (Institute for Paleontology and Quaternary Geology,

Yugoslav Acadamy of Sciences and Arts, Zagreb), J. Jelínek (Moravian Museum, Brno), M. Thurzo (National Museum, Bratislava), J. Szilvássy (Natural History Museum, Vienna), E. Vlcek (National Museum, Prague), J.-L. Heim (Museum of Man, Paris), B. Vandermeersch (University of Paris), E. Trinkaus and W. W. Howells (Harvard University, Cambridge), and C. Stringer (British Museum of Natural History, London), Sincere thanks for various forms of assistance are extended to J. Radovcic and D. Rukavina (Zagreb) and K. Valoch (Brno). Appreciation is also extended to Terry Faulkner and Maria O. Smith for their art and graphic work.

This research was supported by grants from the Wenner-Gren Foundation for Anthropological Research, the National Academy of Sciences, and the Faculty Research Fund of the University of Tennessee at Knoxville.

[2] During the Pleistocene, however, snow lines were considerably lower during cold periods (Butzer 1971), and other conditions would have made passage difficult at times for Paleolithic hunters.

[3] Early dates for an Aurignacian-like early Upper Paleolithic component at Baco Kiro in central Bulgaria (Kozlowski 1975, 1979) also support this contention and help offset some of the objections of Gábori-Csánk (1970) to the Istállosko dates.

[4] The faunal complex from the Riss-Würm levels at Krapina indicates a warm or moderate climate (Malez 1970b, 1978a). Above these levels is a 3-m-thick virtually sterile layer containing eight large blocks which have apparently fallen from the rock-shelter roof. Malez (1978a) interprets this layer as marking the beginning of the first Würm stadial. However, since the earliest phases of the Würm may have been mild (Butzer 1971; Zeuner 1959), it could represent the beginning of the first cold maximum of the Würm (Lower Würm stadial, in the scheme employed here), around 60,000 B.P. (Butzer 1971). This could mean that the hominid zone dates to a mild period after the Riss-Würm interglacial but prior to the Lower Würm stadial. Whether the hominid-zone specimens are considered late Riss-Würm or early Würm in age is not relevant to their relationships with other European fossil hominids investigated in this paper. Two radiocarbon dates have been obtained on bone from the Krapina deposits (Vogel and Waterbolk 1972). One, taken on Pleistocene rhinoceros, possibly from Level 1 or 2, is 3,200 ± 780 B.P. (GrN-4938) and is obviously unrealistic. The other, 30,700 ± 780 B.P. (GrN-4299), is of unkown stratigraphic context and consequently does not serve to anchor any part of the long Krapina sequence (Smith 1976b).

[5] See Trinkaus (1977), Smith (1976b) or Steward (1962, 1964) for further explanations of axillary border morphology.

[6] Wolpoff (1980a) has suggested that the juvenile A cranium may represent a transitional Neandertal-early modern specimen. He bases this suggestion on its stratigraphic position (it comes from Level 8 and is the only cranial vault known not to be derived from the hominid zone) and the fact that the vault is rather large for a Neandertal with so little browridge development. Though I do not object to this interpretation, I feel that we know so little about growth and development in Neandertals that this "disproportionate" relationship between browridge development and vault size may prove to be only an aspect of ontogenetic variability and not of phylogenetic significance.

[7] It might be argued that some of these features are simply related to small body size. This appears unlikely (see Wolpoff *et al.* 1981)

[8] This term was first suggested for this industry by Absolon (1933) on the basis of a typological analysis of the lithics. For him, however, it represented the "pre-Aurignacian." According to Vlcek (1969), Absolon subsequently claimed that Moravia was not occupied during the Mousterian and that the Šipka mandible was Upper Paleolithic.

[9] In 1922, the remains of five individuals (two adults and three children: Mladec 8, 9, 10) were discovered at the Mladec site. These remains were never studied scientifically and were destroyed in the fire of 1945. According to Jelínek (1976), these specimens were supposedly from a level older than the deposits containing the other hominids and were reported to resemble "Homo primigenius" (Neandertals). We shall never know, as not even a single picture or drawing of these specimens is known to exist.

[10] As Matiegka (1934: 83) points out, the numbering of the Brno crania is often confused. The Cerveny Kopec specimen is correctly Brno 1 and was so designated by Makowsky. The Francouzská ulice specimen is correctly Brno 2 but is often described as Brno 1 (see Morant 1930).

[11] These exclude the suggestion that a completely separate lineage existed contemporaneously with the Neandertals in Europe and ultimately resulted in *H. sapiens sapiens*. Although some French paleoanthropologists hold onto variations of this idea, there would appear to be little if any definitive evidence to support it.

[12] A specimen from Kelsterbach, near Frankfurt, is reported to date to ca. 32,000 B.P. (Henke and Protsch 1978) but is not yet described. Several of Bräuer's (1980) bivariate plots place it clearly in the *H. sapiens sapiens* group.

[13] This interpretation is based to some degree on the assumption that there were early modern *H. sapiens* populations in Germany (Paderborn, Kelsterbach) at the same time as classic Neandertals in Western Europe. Although many of the latter are dated to Würm II, there is little indication that they were contemporaneous with any modern *H. sapiens* population in either Western or Central Europe. However, should the Châtelperronian Neandertal from Saint-Césaire (Lévêque and Vandermeersch 1980, 1981; ApSimon 1980) prove to be ca. 33,000 years old, it would make the notion of contemporaneity between late Neandertals in Western Europe an early modern hominids in Central Europe more plausible and increase the attractiveness of Bräuer's hypothesis.

[14] This would be roughly equivalent to the Lower Würm stadial of Musil and Valoch (1966). It should be noted that specimens like Neander Valley are often included with classic Neandertals.

[15] The archaeological associations of Combe-Capelle and the Châtelperron calvarium are problematic, and neither should be considered of Châtelperronian age. With the exception of Saint-Césaire, this leaves only a few fragmentary specimens from Arcy-sur-Cure as definite Châtelperronian-associated remains. These specimens exhibit Neandertal affinities (Wolpoff 1980a).

REFERENCES

Absolon, K. 1929. New finds of fossil human skeletons in Moravia. *Anthropologie* (Prague) 7:79-89.

Absolon, K. 1933. O pravé podstate paleolitickych industrii ze Šipky a Certovy diry na Morave. *Anthropologie* (Prague) 11:253-72.

Absolon, K. 1938. *Vyzkum diluviální stanice lovcu mammutu v Dolních Vestonicích na Pavlovskych kopcich na Morave: Pracovní zpráva za druhy rok 1925.* Brno (German summary).

Absolon, K., and Klíma, A. 1978. *Predmostí: Ein Mammutjäger platz in Mähren.* Archeologicky Ústav CSAV v Brne, Brno.

Alexeev, V. P. 1979. Horizontal profile of the Neandertal crania from Krapina comparatively considered. *Collegium Anthropologicum* 3:7-13.

ApSimon, A. 1980. The last Neanderthal in France? *Nature* 287: 271-72.

Bánesz, L. 1963. Quelques considérations sur l'origine, la subdivision et l'extension de l'Aurignacien en Europa. *Slovenska Archeologia* 12:305-18.

Bartucz, L., Danucza, J., Hollendonner, F., Kadic, O., Mottl, M., Pataki, V., Palosi, E., Szabò, J., and Vendl, A. 1940. *Die Mussolini-Höhle (Subalyuk) bei Cserépfalu*. Geologica Hungarica, Series Paleontologica, 14.

Bayer, J. 1922. *Das Aurignac-Atler der Artefakte und menschlichen Skelettreste aus der Fürst-Johanns-Höhle bei Lautsch in Mähren*. Mitteilungen der Anthropologischen Gesellschaft in Wien 52.

Bayer, J. 1924. Eine Mammuthjägerstation im Löss bei Pollau in Südmähren. *Die Eiszeit* 1:81-88.

Bayer, K. 1925. Das jungpaläolithische Alter des Ochozkiefers. *Die Eiszeit* 2:35-40.

Bayer, K. 1927. Eine Station des Eiszeitjägers im Miesslingstal bei Spitz a. d. Donau in Niederösterreich. *Die Eiszeit* 4:91-94.

Beaumont, P. B. 1980. On the age of Border Cave hominids 1-5. *Paleontologica Africana* 23:21-33.

Beaumont, P. B., De Villiers, H., and Vogel, J. C. 1978. Modern man in sub-Saharan Africa prior to 49,000 years B.P.: A review and evaluation with particular reference to Border Cave. *South African Journal of Science* 74:409-19.

Billy, G. 1976. Les hommes du Paléolithique supérieur, in: *La Préhistoire Française*, Vol. 1 (H. de Lumley, Ed.), Centre National de la Recherche Scientifique, Paris.

Bischoff, J., and Rosenbauer, R. 1981. Uranium series dating of human skeletal remains from the Del Mar and Sunnyvale sites, California. *Science* 213:1003-5.

Boule, Marcellin. 1923. *Fossil Men*. Oliver and Boyd, Edinburgh.

Boule, M., and Vallois, H. V. 1957. *Fossil Men*. Dryden, New York.

Brace, C. L. 1962. Refocusing on the Neanderthal problem. *American Anthropologist* 64:729-41.

Brace, C. L. 1964. The fate of the "classic" Neanderthals: A consideration of hominid catastrophism. *Current Anthropology* 5:3-43.

Brace, C. L. 1967. *The Stages of Human Evolution*. Prentice Hall, Englewood Cliffs, N.J.

Brace, C. L. 1979a. Krapina "classic" Neanderthals and the evolution of the European face. *Journal of Human Evolution* 8:527-50.

Brace, C. L. 1979b. *The Stages of Human Evolution*. Prentice Hall, Englewood Cliffs, N.J.

Brace. C. L., and Montagu, A. 1977. *Human Evolution*. 2d edition. Macmillan, New York.

Bräuer, G. 1980. Die morphologischen Affinitäten des jungpleistozänen Stirnbeines aus dem Elbmündungsgebiet bei Hahnöfersand. *Zeitschrift für Morphologie und Anthropologie* 71:1-42.

Bräuer, G. 1981. New evidence on the transitional period between Neanderthal and modern man. *Journal of Human Evolution* 10:467-74.

Brodar, S. 1938. Das Palaolithikum in Jugoslawien. *Quartär* 1:140-72.

Brose, D. S., and Wolpoff, M. H. 1971. Early Upper Paleolithic man and late Middle Paleolithic tools. *American Anthropologist* 73:1156-94.

Butzer, K. 1971. *Environment and Archaeology*. Revised edition. Aldine, Chicago.

Cadien, J. 1972. Dental variation in man, in: *Perspectives on Human Evolution*, Vol. 1 (S. Washburn and P. Dolhinow, Eds.), Holt, Rinehart and Winston, New York.

Chmielewski, W. 1972. The continuity and discontinuity of the evolution of archaeological cultures in central and eastern Europe between the 55th and 25th millenaries B.C., in: *The Origin of Homo sapiens* (F. Bordes, Ed.), UNESCO, Paris.

Coles, J., and Higgs, E. 1969. *The Archaeology of Early Man*. Praeger, New York.

Coon, C. S. 1962. *The Origin of Races*. Knopf, New York.

Corruccini, R. 1975. Metrical analysis of Fontéchevade II. *American Journal of Physical Anthropology* 42:95-98.

Day, M. 1969. Omo human skeletal remains. *Nature* 222:1135-38.

De Lumley, J. 1973. *Anténéandertaliens et Néandertaliens du bassin mediterranéen occidental européen*. Etudes Quaternaires (Université de Provence), Mémoire 2.

De Lumley, J. 1976. Les Neandertaliens dans le Midi méditerranéen, in: *La Préhistorire Française*, Vol. 1 (H. de Lumley, Ed.), Centre Naccional de la Recherche Scientifique, Paris.

Farrand, W. R. 1979. Chronology and paleoenvironment of Levantine prehistoric sites as seen from sediment studies. *Journal of Archaeological Science* 6:369-92.

Felgenhauer, V. F. 1959. *Willendorf in der Wachau*. Mitteilungen der Prähistorischen Kommission, 8-9, Wien.

Flint, R. F. 1971. *Glacial and Quaternary Geology*. Wiley, New York.

Frayer, D. W. 1978. *Evolution of the Dentition in Upper Paleolithic and Mesolithic Europe*. University of Kansas Publications in Anthropology 10.

Frenzel, B. 1965. Über die offene Vegetation der letzten Eiszeit am Ostrande der Alpen. *Verhandlungen Zoologische-Botanische Gesellschaft in Wien* 103-4:110-43.

Frenzel, B. 1968. The Pleistocene Vegetation of northern Eurasia. *Science* 161:637-49.

Frenzel, B. 1973. *Climatic Fluctuations of the Ice Age*. Case Western Reserve University Press, Cleveland.

Gábori-Csánk, V. 1968. *La station du Paléolithique moyen d'Érd, Hongrie*. Monumenta Historica Budapestinensia 3.

Gábori-Csánk, V. 1970. C-14 dates of the Hungarian Paleolithic. *Acta Archaeologica Academiae Scientiarum Hungaricae* 22:1-11.

Gieseler, W. 1937. Bericht über die jungpaläolithischen Skelettreste von Stetten ob Lontal bei Ulm. *Verhandlungen der Deutschen Gesellschaft für Physiche Anthropologie* 8:41-48.

Gieseler, W. 1941. Die urgeschichtlichen Menschenfunde aus dem Lontal und ihre Bedeutung für die deutsche Urgeschichte. *Jahrbuch der Akademie der Wissenschaften Tübingen* 1:102-17.

Gorjanovic-Kramberger, D. 1906. *Der diluviale Mensch von Krapina in Kroatien: Ein Beitrag zur Paläoanthropologie*. Kriedel, Wiesbaden.

Gorjanovic-Kramberger, D. 1913. Zivot i kultura diluvijalnoga covjeka iz Krapine u Hrvatskoj. (German summary.) *Djela Jugoslavenske Akademije Znanosti i Umjetnosti* 23:1-54.

Gregory, W. 1922. *The Origin and Evolution of the Human Dentition*. Williams and Wilkins, Baltimore.

Grootes, P. M. 1978. Carbon-14 time scale extended: Comparison of chronologies. *Science* 201:11-15.

Hahn, J. 1970. Recherches sur l'Aurignacien en Europe centrale et orientale. *L'Anthropologie* 74:195-220.

Hahn, J. 1973. Das Aurignacien in Mittel- und Osteuropa. *Acta Praehistorica et Archaeologica* 3:77-107.

Hahn, J. 1977. *Aurignacien: Das altere Jungpaläolithikum in Mittel- und Osteuropa*. Fundamenta 9, series A.

Heim, J.-L. 1974. Les hommes fossiles de La Ferrasssie (Dordogne) et le problème de la définition des Neandertaliens classiques. *L'Anthropologie* 78:81-112, 321-77.

Heim, J.-L. 1976a. *Les Hommes Fossiles de La Ferrassie*, Vol. 1. Archives de l'Institut de Paléontologie Humaine Mémoire 35.

Heim, J.-L.1976b. Les Néandertaliens en Périgord, in: *La Préhistoire Française*, Vol. 1 (H. de Lumley, Ed.), Centre National de la Recherche Scientifique, Paris.

Henke, W., and Protsch, R. 1978. Die Paderborner Calvaria: Ein diluvialer *Homo sapiens*. *Anthropologischer Anzeiger* 36:85-108.

Higgs, E. 1961. Some Pleistocene faunas of the Mediterranean coastal areas. *Proceedings of the Prehistoric Society* 27:144-54.

Higgs, E., and Brothwell, D. 1961. North Africa and Mount Carmel: Recent developments. *Man* 61:138-39.

Howell, F. C. 1952. Pleistocene glacial ecology and the evolution of "classic Neandertal" man. *Southwestern Journal of Anthropology* 8:377-410.

Howell, F. C. 1957. The evolutionary significance of variation and varieties of "Neanderthal" man. *Quarterly Review of Biology* 32:330-47.

Howell, F. C. 1978. Hominidae, in: *Evolution of African Mammals* (V. J. Maglio and H. B. S. Cooke, Eds.), pp. 154-248. Harvard University Press, Cambridge, MA.

Howells, W. W. 1973. *Evolution of the Genus* Homo. Addison-Wesley, Reading.

Howells, W. W. 1976. Explaining modern man: Evolutionist *versus* migrationists. *Journal of Human Evolution* 5:577-96.

Hrdlicka, A. 1907. *Skeletal Remains Suggesting or Attributed to Early Man in North America*. Bureau of American Ethnology Bulletin 33.

Hrdlicka, A. 1927. The Neanderthal phase of man. *Journal of the Anthropological Institute* 57:249-74.

Hrdlicka, A. 1930. *The Skeletal Remains of Early Man*. Smithsonian Miscellaneous Collections 83.

Ivanova, S. 1979. Cultural differentiation in the Middle Paleolithic on the Balkan Peninsula, in: *Middle and Upper Paleolithic in Balkans* (J. Kozlowski, Ed.), Prace Archeologiczne 28.

Jelínek, A. 1982. The Tabun Cave and Paleolithic man in the Levant. *Science* 216:1369-75.

Jelínek, J. 1954. Nález fosilního cloveka Dolní Vestonice III. (English summary.) *Anthropozoikum* 3:37-91.

Jelínek, J. 1957. La nouvelle datation de la decouverte de l'homme fossile Brno II. *L'Anthropologie* 61:513-15.

Jelínek, J. 1960. The oldest finds of the primitive *Homo sapiens fossilis* and their chronology. *Proceedings of the VIth International Congress of Anthropological and Ethnological Sciences, Paris.*

Jelínek, J. 1965. Srovnávací studium sipecke celisti. (German summary.) *Anthropos* 17:135-79.

Jelínek, J. 1966. Jaw of an intermediate type of Neanderthal man from Czechoslovakia. *Nature* 212:701-2.

Jelínek, J. 1967a. Der Fund eines neandertales Kiefers (Külna I) aus der Külna-Höhle in Mähren. *Anthropologie* (Brno) 5:3-19.

Jelínek, J. 1967b. A new discovery of the jaw of an intermediate type of Neanderthal man in Czechoslovakia. *Anthropos* 19:148-49.

Jelínek, J. 1969. Neanderthal man and *Homo sapiens* in central and eastern Europe. *Current Anthropology* 10:475-503.

Jelínek, J. 1976. *The Homo sapiens neanderthalensis* and *Homo sapiens sapiens* relationship in central Europe. *Anthropologie* (Brno) 14:79-81.

Jelínek, J. 1978. *Earliest* Homo sapiens sapiens *from Central Europe (Mladec, Czechoslovakia)*. Paper presented at the Xth International Congress of Anthropological and Ethnological Sciences, Delhi, India.

Jelínek, J. 1980. Neanderthal remains in Külna Cave, Czechoslovakia, in: *Physical Anthropology of European Populations* (I. Schwidetzky, B. Chiarelli, and O. Necrasov, Eds.), Mouton, The Hague.

Jelínek, J. 1981. Neanderthal parietal bone from Külna Cave, Czechoslovakia. *Anthropologie* (Brno) 19:195-96.

Jelínek, J., Pelisek, J., and Valoch, K. 1959. Der fossile Mensch Brno II. *Anthropos* 9:5-30.

Klíma, B. 1955. Prinos nové stanice v Pavlove k probematice nejstarších zemedelskych nástroju. (German summary.) *Památky Archeologické* 46:7-29.

Klíma, B. 1959a. Zur Problematik des Aurignacien und Gravettien in Mittel-Europa. *Archeologia Austriaca* 26:35-51.

Klíma, B. 1959b. Objev paleolitického sidlište u Pavlova v roce 1956. *Archeologické Rozhledy* 11:305-16, 337-44.

Klíma, B. 1962. The first ground-plan of an upper Paleolithic loess settlement in middle Europe and its meanings, in: *Courses Toward Urban Life* (R. J. Braidwood and G.R. Willey, Eds.), Aldine, Chicago.

Klíma, B. 1963. *Dolní Vestonice: Vyzkum táboriště lovcu mamutu v letech 1947–1952*. (German summary.) Ceskoslovenská Akademie Ved, Prague.

Klíma, B., Musil, R., Pelíšek, J., and Jelínek, J. 1962. *Die Erforschung der Höhle Svéduv stul 1953–1955*. Anthropos 13.

Knussmann, R. 1967. Die mittelpaläolithischen menschlichen Knochenfragmente von der Wildscheuer bei Steeden (Oberlahnkreis). *Nassauische Annalen* 68:1-25.

Kozlowski, J. 1975. Badina nadd przejsciem od srodkowego do górnego paleolitu na Balkanach. (English summary.) *Przeglad Archeologiczny* 23:5-48.

Kozlowski, J. 1979. Le Bachokirien: La plus ancienne industrie du Páleolithique supérieur en Europa, in: *Middle and Upper Paleolithic in Balkans* (J. Kozlowski, Ed.), Prace Archeologiczne 28.

Kríz, M. 1909. Die Schwedentischgrotte bei Ochoz in Mähren und Rzehaks Bericht über Homo primigenius Wilseri. *Verhandlungen d. k. k. Reichsanstalt* 10:217-32.

Laplace, G. 1958–61. Recherches sur l' origine et l'evolution des complexes leptolithiques. *Quarternaria* 5:153-240.

Laplace, G. 1970. Le niveaux aurignaciens et l'hypothèse du synthétotype, in: *L'homme de Cro-Magnon* (G. Camps and G. Olivier, Eds.), Arts et Métiers Graphiques, Paris.

Lévêque, F., and Vandermeersch, B. 1980. Découverte de restes humains dans un niveau castelperronien à Saint-Césaire (Charente-Maritime). *Comptes Rendus de l'Academie des Sciences*, Series D, 191:187-89.

Lévêque, F., and Vandermeersch, B. 1981. Le néandertalien de Saint-Césaire. *La Recherche* 12:242-44.

Makowsky, A. 1888. Der Löss von Brünn und seine Einschlüsse an diluvialen Tieren und Menschen. *Verhandlungen des Naturforschungen Vereins in Brünn* 16:207-43.

Makowsky, A. 1892. Der diluviale Mensch im Löss von Brünn. *Mitteilungen der Anthropologischen Gesellschaft in Wien* 22:73-84.

Malez, M. 1965. Pecina Veternica u Medvednici. 1. Opci speleološki pregled. 2. Stratigrafija kvartarnih talozina. (German summary.) *Acta Geologica* 5:175-237.

Malez, M. 1967. Paleolit Velike Pecine na Ravnoj gori u sjeverozapadnoj Hrvatskoj. (German summary.) *Arheološki Radovi i Rasprave* 4/5:7-68.

Malez, M. 1970a. Novi pogledi na stratigrafiju krapinskog nalazista, in: *Krapina 1899–1969* (M. Malez, Ed.) (English and German summaries). Jugoslavenska Akademija Znanosti i Umjetnosti, Zagreb.

Malez, M. 1970b. Rezultati revizije pleistocenske faune iz Krapine, in: *Krapina 1899–1969* (M. Malez, Ed.) (English and German summaries). Jugoslavenska Akademija Znanosti i Umjetnosti, Zagreb.

Malez, M. 1970c. Paleolitska kultura Krapine u svjetlu novijih istrazivanja, in: *Krapina 1899–1969* (M. Malez, Ed.) (English and German summaries). Jugoslavenska Akademija Znanosti i Umjetnosti, Zagreb.

Malez, M. 1974. Noviji rezultati istrazivanja paleolitika u Velikoj Pecini, Veternici, i Šandalji. (German summary.) *Archeloški Radovi i Rasprave* 7:7-44.

Malez, M. 1975. Die Höhle Vindija: Eine neue Fundstelle fossiler Hominiden in Kroatien. *Bulletin Scientifique* (Yougoslavie), Section A, 20:5-6.

Malez, M. 1978a. Stratigrafski, paleofaunski, i paleolitski odnosi krapinokog nalazista, in: *Krapinski Pracovjek i Evolucija Hominida* (M. Malez, Ed.) (German summary). Jugoslavenska Akademija Znanosti i Umjetnosti, Zagreb.

Malez, M. 1978b. Populacije neandertalaca i neandertalcimi slicnih ljudi u Hrvatskoj, in: *Krapinski Pracovjek i Evolucija Hominida*. (M. Malez, Ed.) (German summary). Jugoslavenska Akademija Znanosti i Umjetnosti, Zagreb.

Malez, M. 1978c. Fossile Menschen aus Nordwestkroatien und ihre quartärgeologische, paläontologische und paläolithische Grundlage. *Collegium Anthropologicum* 2:29-41.

Malez, M., and Rukavina, D. 1975. Krioturbacijske pojave u gornjopleistocenskim naslagama pecine Vindije kod Donje Voce u sjeverozapadnoj Hrvatskoj. (German summary.) *Rad Jugoslavenska Akademije Znanosti i Umjetnosti* 371:245-65.

Malez, M., and Rukavina, D. 1980. Polozaj naslaga spilje Vindije u sustavu clanjenja Kvartara šireg prodrucja Alpa. *Rad Jugoslavenske Akademije Znanosti i Umjetnosti*.

Malez, M., Smith, F., Rukavina, D., and Radovcic, J. 1980. Upper Pleistocene fossil hominids from Vindija, Croatia, Yugoslavia. *Current Anthropology* 21:365-67.

Malez, M., and Vogel, J. C. 1970. Die Ergebnisse der Radio-karbonanalysen der Quartären Schichten der Velika Pecina in Nordwest-Kroatien. *Bulletin Scientifique* (Yougoslavie) 15:390-91.

Maly, J. 1939. Lebky fosilního cloveka z Dolních Vestonic. (German and French summaries.) *Anthropologie* (Prague) 17:171-92.

Martin, R., and Saller, K. 1956. *Lehrbuch der Anthropologie*. Fischer, Stuttgart.

Maška, K. 1882. Über den diluvialen Menschen in Stramberg. *Mitteilungen der Anthropologische Gesellschaft in Wien* 12:32-38.

Matiegka, J. 1929. The skull of the fossil man Brno III, and the cast of its interior. *Anthropologie* (Prague)7:90-107.

Matiegka, J. 1934. *Homo predmostensis: Fosiliní clovék z Predmostí na Moravé 1. Lebky.* (French summary.) Ceská Akademie Ved i Umení, Prague.

Matiegka, J. 1938. *Homo predmostensis: Fosiliní clovék z Predmostí na Moravé. 2. Ostatní cásti kostrové.* (French summary.) Ceská Akademie Ved i Umení, Prague.

Morant, G. M. 1930. Studies of Paleolithic man. 4. A biometric study of the Upper Paleolithic skulls of Europe and of their relationship to earlier and later types. *Annals of Eugenics* 4:109-99.

Movius, H. 1960. Radiocarbon dates and Upper Paleolithic archaeology in central and western Europe. *Current Anthropology* 1:355-91.

Musgrave, J. 1970. How dextrous was Neanderthal man? *Nature* 233:538-41.

Musgrave, J. 1977. The Neandertals from Krapina, northern Yugoslavia: An inventory of the handbones. *Zeitschrift für Morphologie und Anthropologie* 68:150-71.

Musil, R. 1965a. Zhodnoceni drívejších paleontologicych nálezu ze Šipky. (German summary.) *Anthropos* 17:127-34.

Musil, R. 1965b. Die Bärenhöhle Pod hradem: Die Entwicklung der Höhlenbären im letzten Glazial. *Anthropos* (Brno) 18:7-92.

Musil, R., and Valoch, K. 1966. Beitrag zur Gliederung des Würms in Mitteleuropa. *Eiszeitalter und Gegenwart* 17:131-38.

Necrasov, O., and Cristescu, M. 1965. Données anthropologiques sur les populations de l'age de la pierre en Roumanie. *Homo* 16:129-61.

Oakley, K., Campbell, B., and Molleson, T. 1971. *Catalogue of Fossil Hominids. Pt. 2: Europe.* British Museum (Natural History), London.

Paunescu, A. 1965. Sur la succession des habitats paléolithiques et postpaléolithiques de Ripiceni-Izvor. *Dacia* 9:5-32.

Prošek, R., Stárka, V., Hrdlicka, L., Hokr, Z., Lozek, V., and Dohnal, Z. 1952. Vyzkum jeskyne Zlatého Kone u Koneprus. *Ceskoslovensky Kras* 5:161-79.

Protsch, R. 1976. Comparison of absolute bone dates by radiocarbon and amino-acid dating on Upper Pleistocene hominids, in: *Datations Absolutes et Analyses Isotropiques en Préhistorie: Méthodes et Limites* (J. Labeyrie and C. Lalou, Ed.), CRNS, Paris.

Rightmire, G. P. 1978. Human skeletal remains from the southern Cape Province and their bearing on the Stone Age prehistory of South Africa. *Quaternary Research* 9:219-30.

Rightmire, G. P. 1979. Implications of the Border Cave skeletal remains for later Pleistocene human evolution. *Current Anthropology* 20:23-35.

Rightmire, G. P. 1981. Later Pleistocene hominids of eastern and southern Africa. *Anthropologie* (Brno): 19:15-26.

Rzehak, A. 1905. Der Unterkiefer von Ochoz: Ein Beitrag zur Kenntnis des altdiluvialen Menschen. *Verhandlungen des naturforschenden Vereines in Brunn* 44:91-114.

Sakura, H. 1970. Dentition of the Amud man, in: *The Amud Man and his Cave Site* (H. Suzuki and F. Takai, Eds.), University of Tokyo Press, Tokyo.

Schwarcz, H., and Skoflek, I. 1982. New dates for the Tata, Hungary, archaeological site. *Nature* 295:590-91.

Sergi, S. 1962. Morphological position of the 'Prophaneranthropi' (Swanscombe and Fontéchevade), in: *Ideas on Human Evolution* (W. W. Howells, Ed.), Harvard University Press, Cambridge, MA.

Škerlj, B. 1958. Were Neanderthalers the only inhabitants of Krapina? *Bulletin Scientifique* (Yougoslavie) 4:44.

Smith, F. H. 1976a. A fossil hominid frontal from Velika Pecina (Croatia) and a consideration of Upper Pleistocene hominids from Yugoslavia. *American Journal of Physical Anthropology* 44:127-34.

Smith, F. H. 1976b. *The Neandertal Remains from Krapina: A Descriptive and Comparative Study.* University of Tennessee Department of Anthropology Reports of Investigations 15.

Smith, F. H. 1976c. The Neandertal remains from Krapina, northern Yugos-

lavia: An inventory of the upper limb remains. *Zeitschrift für Morphologie und Anthropologie* 67:275-90.

Smith, F. H. 1976d. On anterior tooth wear at Krapina and Ochoz. *Current Anthropology* 17:167-68.

Smith, F. H. 1977. On the application of morphological "dating" to the hominid fossil record. *Journal of Anthropological Research* 33:302-16.

Smith, F. H. 1978. Some conclusions regarding the morphology and significance of the Krapina Neandertal remains, in: *Krapinski Pracovjek i Evolucija Hominida* (M. Malez, Ed.), Jugoslavenska Akademija Znanosti i Umjetnosti, Zagreb.

Smith, F. H. 1980. Sexual differences in European Neandertal crania with special reference to the Krapina remains. *Journal of Human Evolution* 9:359-75.

Smith, F. H., and Ranyard, G. C. 1980. Evolution of the supra-orbital region in Upper Pleistocene fossil hominids from South-Central Europe. *American Journal of Physical Anthropology* 53:589-609.

Spencer, F., and Smith, F. H. 1981. The significance of Aleš Hrdlicka's "Neanderthal phase of man": A historical and current assessment. *American Journal of Physical Anthropology* 56:435-59.

Srdoc, D., Sliepcevic, A., Obelic, B., and Horvatincic, N. 1979. Rudjer Boškovic Institute radiocarbon measurements V. *Radiocarbon* 21:131-37.

Steward, T. D. 1962. Neanderthal scapulae with special attention to the Shanidar Neanderthals from Iraq. *Anthropos* 57:779-800.

Steward, T. D. 1964. The scapula of the first recognized Neanderthal skeleton. *Bonner Jahrbuch* 164:1-14.

Stringer, C. B. 1974. Population relationships of later Pleistocene hominids: A multivariate study of available crania. *Journal of Archaeological Science* 1:317-42.

Stringer, C. B. 1978. Some problems in Middle and Upper Pleistocene hominid relationships, in: *Recent Advances in Primatology*, Vol.3 (D. Chivers and K. Joysey, Eds.), pp. 395-418, Academic Press, London.

Szombathy, J. 1925. Die diluvialen Menschenreste aus der Fürst-Johanns-Höhle bei Lautsch in Mähren. *Die Eiszeit* 2:1-34, 73-95.

Thenius, E. 1962. Die Grossäugetiere des Pleistozäns von Mitteleuropa. *Zeitschrift für Säugetierkunde* 27:65-83.

Thoma, A., 1963. The dentition of the Subalyuk Neandertal child. *Zeitschrift für Morphologie und Anthropologie* 54:127-50.

Trinkaus, E. 1976. The morphology of European and Southwest Asian Neandertal pubic bones. *American Journal of Physical Anthropology* 44:95-104.

Trinkaus, E. 1977. A functional interpretation of the axillary border of the Neandertal scapula. *Journal of Human Evolution.* 6:231-34.

Trinkaus, E. 1978. Functional implications of the Krapina Neandertal lower limb remains, in: *Krapinski Pracovjek i Evolucija Hominida* (M. Malez, Ed.), Jugoslavenska Academija Znanosti i Umjetnosti, Zagreb.

Trinkaus, E. 1980. Sexual differences in Neanderthal limb bones. *Journal of Human Evolution* 9:377-97.

Trinkaus, E., and Howells, W. W. 1979. The Neanderthals. *Scientific American* 241:118, 122-33.

Ullrich, H. 1978. Kannibalismus und Leichenzerstückelung bei Neandertaler von Krapina, in: *Krapinski Pracovjek i Evolucija Hominida* (M. Malez, Ed.), Jugoslavenska Akademija Znanosti i Umjetnosti, Zabreb.

Vallois, H. V. 1954. Neanderthals and presapiens. *Journal of the Royal Anthropological Institute* 84:111-30.

Vallois, H. V. 1958. *La Grotte de Fontéchevade II: Anthropologie.* Archives de l'Institut de Paleontologie Humaine, Mémoire 29.

Valoch, K. 1965a. Die Höhlen Šipka und Certova dira bei Štramberk in Mähren. *Anthropos* (Brno) 17:5-125.

Valoch, K. 1965b. Die altsteinzeitlichen Begebungen der Höhle Pod hradem. *Anthropos* (Brno) 18:93-106

Valoch, K. 1967. Die Steinindustrie von der Fundstelle des menschlichen Skelettrestes I aus der Höhle Külna bei Sloup (Mähren). *Anthropologie* (Brno) 5:21-32.

Valoch, K. 1968. Evolution of the Paleolithic in Central and Eastern Europe. *Current Anthropology* 9:351-90.

Valoch, K. 1970. Early Middle Paleolithic (Stratum 14) in the Külna cave near

Sloup in the Moravian karst (Czechoslovakia). *World Archaeology* 2:28-38.

Valoch, K. 1972. Rapports entre le Paléolithique moyen et la Paléolithique supérieur en Europe centrale, in: *The Origin of Homo Sapiens* (F. Bordes, Ed.), UNESCO, Paris.

Valoch, K. 1976a. Die altsteinzeitliche Fundstelle in Brno-Bohunice. *Studie Archeologického Ústavu Ceskoslovenské Akademie Véd v Brné* 4(1):3-120.

Valoch, K. 1976b. Neuemittelpaläolithische Industrien in Südmähren. *Anthropologie* (Brno) 14:55-64.

Valoch, K., Pelíšek, J., Musil, R., Kovanda, J., and Opravil, E. 1970. Die Erforschung der Külna-Höhle bei Sloup im Mahrischen Karst (Tschechoslowakei). *Quartär* 20:1-45.

Vandermeersch, B. 1976. Les Néandertaliens en Charente, in: *La Préhistoire Française*, Vol. 1 (H. de Lumley, Ed.), Centre National de la Recherche Scientifique, Paris.

Vandermeersch, B. 1981a. *Les Hommes Fossiles de Qafzeh (Israel)*. Centre National de la Recherche Scientifique, Paris.

Vandermeersch, B. 1981b. *A Neandertal Skeleton from a Châtelperronian Level at Saint-Césaire (France)*. Paper presented at the 50th annual meeting of the American Association of Physical Anthropologists, Detroit Mich.

Vanura, J. 1965. Prispevek k poznání jeskyne Svéduv stul v Moravském krasu. *Ceskoslovensky Kras* 15:59-63.

Vértes, L. 1955. Über einige Fragen des mitteleuropäischen Aurignacien. *Acta Archaeologica Academiae Scientiarum Hungaricae* 5:279-91.

Vértes, L. 1961. Das Verhältnis des Aurignacien zum Szeletien in der Istállósköer Höhle. *Germania* 39:295-98.

Vértes, L. Ed. 1964. *Tata, eine Mittelpäläolithische Travertin-Siedlung in Ungarn*. Archaeologica Hungarica n.s. 43.

Virchow, R. 1882. Der Kiefer aus der Schipka-Höhle und der Kiefer von La Naulette. *Zeitschrift für Ethnologie* 14:277-310.

Vlcek, E. 1951. Pleistocenní clovek z jeskyne Sv. Prokopa. (English summary.) *Anthropozoikum* 1:213-26.

Vlcek, E. 1953. Nález neandertálského cloveka na Slovensku. (English summary.) *Slovenská Archeologia* 1:5-132.

Vlcek, E. 1955. The fossil man of Gánovce, Czechoslovakia. *Journal of the Royal Anthropological Institute* 85:163-71.

Vlcek, E. 1956. Kalva pleistocénního cloveka z Podbaby (Praha XIX0) (English summary.) *Anthropozoikum* 5:191-217.

Vlcek, E. 1957a. Pleistocenní clovek z jeskyne na Zlatém Koni u Koneprus. (English summary.) *Anthropozoijum* 6:283-311.

Vlcek, E. 1957b. Lidsky zub pleistocenního Stári ze Silické Brezové. (German summary.) *Anthropozoikum* 6:397-405.

Vlcek, E. 1958. Die Reste des Neanderthalmenschen aus dem Gebiete der Tschecoslowakei, in: *Hundert Jahre Neanderthaler* (G. H. R. von Koenigswald, Ed.), Kemink en Zoon, Utrecht.

Vlcek, E. 1961a. Posustatky mladopleistocenního clovek z Pavlova (German summary.) *Památky Archeologické* 52:46-56.

Vlcek, E. 1961b. Nouvelles trouvailles de l'homme du Pléistocène récent de Pavlov (CSR). *Anthropos* 14:141-45.

Vlcek, E. 1964a. Neuer Fund eines Neandertalers in der Tschechoslowakei. *Anthropologischer Anzeiger* 27:162-66.

Vlcek, E. 1964b. Einige in der Ontogenese des modernen Menschen untersuchte Neandertalmerkmale. *Zeitschrift für Morphologie und Anthropologie* 56:63-83.

Vlcek, E. 1967a. Die Sinus frontales bei europäischen Neandertalern. *Anthropologischer Anzeiger* 30:166-89.

Vlcek, E. 1967b. Morphological relations of the fossil human types Brno and Cro-Magnon in the European late Pleistocene. *Folia Morphologica* 15:214-21.

Vlcek, E. 1967c. Der jungpleistozäne Menschenfund aus Svitávka in Mähren. *Anthropos* 19:262-70.

Vlcek, E. 1968. Nález pozustaku neandertálce v Šali na Slovensku. (English summary.) *Anthropozoikum* 17:105-44.

Vlcek, E. 1969. *Neandertaler der Tschechoslowakei*. Academia, Prague.

Vlcek, E. 1970. Étude comparative ontophylogénétique de l'enfant du Pech de l'Azé par rapport a d'autres enfants néandertaliens, in: *L'enfant du Pech de l'Azé*, pp. 149-78, Archives de l'Institut de Paléontologie Humaine, Mémoire 33.

Vlcek, E. 1971. Czechoslovakia, in: *Catalogue of Fossil Hominids*. Pt. 2: *Europe* (K. Oakley, B. Campbell, and T. Molleson, Eds.), British Museum (Natural History), London.

Vlcek, E., Prošek, F., Wolfe, J., Pelikan, J., Knéblová, V., Fejfar, O., and Lozek, V. 1958. *Zusammenfassender Bericht über den Fundort Gánovce und die Reste des Neanderthalers in der Zips* CSSR, Prague.

Vogel, J., and Waterbolk, H. 1972. Groningen radiocarbon dates X. *Radiocarbon* 14:6-110.

Vogel, J., and Zagwijn, W. 1967. Gronigen radiocarbon dates VI. *Radiocarbon* 9:63-106.

Vukovic, S. 1935. Istrazivanje prehistorijskog nalazista u spilji Vindiji kod Voće. *Spomenica Varazdinskog Muzeja 1925–1935*, pp. 73-80.

Weidenreich, F. 1937. The dentition of *Sinanthropus pekinensis*: A comparative odontography of the hominids. *Paleontologia Sinica*, new ser. D, no. 1.

Weidenreich, F. 1943. The "Neanderthal man" and the ancestors of *Homo sapiens*. *American Anthropologist* 45:39-48.

Weidenreich, F. 1947. Facts and speculations concerning the origin of *Homo sapiens*. *American Anthropologist* 49:187-203.

Weiss, K. M., and Maruyama, T. 1976. Archaeology, population genetics, and studies of human racial ancestry. *American Journal of Physical Anthropology* 44:31-49.

Woillard, G. M. 1978. Grand Pile peat bog: A continuous pollen record for the last 140,000 years. *Quaternary Research* 9:1-21.

Woillard, G. M., and Mook, M. G. 1982. Carbon-14 dates at Grand Pile: Correlation of land and sea chronologies. *Science* 215:159-61.

Wolpoff, M. H. 1978. The dental remains from Krapina, in: *Krapinski Pracovjek i Evolucija Hominida* (M. Malez, Ed.), Jugoslavenska Akademija Znanosti i Umjetnosti, Zagreb.

Wolpoff, M. H. 1979. The Krapina dental remains. *American Journal of Physical Anthropology* 50:67-114.

Wolpoff, M. H. 1980a. *Paleoanthropology*. Knopf, New York.

Wolpoff, M. H. 1980b. Cranial remains of Middle Pleistocene European hominids. *Journal of Human Evolution* 9:339-58.

Wolpoff, M. H. 1981. Allez Neanderthal. *Nature* 289:823.

Wolpoff, M., Smith, F., Malez, M., Radovcic, J., and Rukavina, D. 1981. Upper Pleistocene hominid remains from Vindija Cave, Croatia, Yugoslavia. *American Journal of Physical Anthropology* 54:499-545.

Zagwijn, W. H. 1974. Vegetation, climate, and radiocarbon datings in the late Pleistocene of the Netherlands. Part 2. Middle Weichselian. *Mededelingen Rijks Geologische Dienst*, n.s., 25:101-10.

Zeuner, F. 1959. *The Pleistocene Period*. Hutchinson, London.

Zobeck, T. S. 1980. *An Analysis of the Functional Significance and Sexual Dimorphism of the Neandertal Mastoid Process*. Ph.D. Thesis, University of Tennessee, Knoxville.

Zotz, F., and Freund, G. 1951. Die paläolithische und mesolithische Kulturentwicklung in Böhmen und Mähren. *Quartär* 5:7-40.

54

The Fate of the Neandertals

E. Trinkaus and F. H. Smith

INTRODUCTION: THE NEANDERTAL PROBLEM

Ever since it was recognized around the turn of the century that there was a group of archaic humans in Europe that immediately preceded the oldest anatomically modern humans and resembled the specimen unearthed in the Neander Valley in 1856, human paleontologists have been arguing about the phylogenetic relationship of the Neandertals to more recent humans (for recent reviews, see: Brace 1964; Mann and Trinkaus 1974; Trinkaus and Howells 1979; Wolpoff 1980a; Spencer and Smith 1981; Smith 1982; Stringer 1982; Trinkaus 1982a, 1983a; Spencer 1984). Originally, most paleoanthropologists saw the Neandertals as our natural predecessors, representing the more archaic stage through which humans must have passed. (Mortillet 1883; Schwalbe 1904; Sollas 1907; Keith 1911; Gorjanovic-Kramberger 1906). However, the discoveries of substantial Neandertal remains at several sites prior to 1910 and their subsequent analysis (esp. Boule 1911-1913) tipped the scales of opinion in the other direction and began the seemingly interminable argument as to how many, if any, of the Neandertals can be rightfully counted among our ancestors. The basic positions were established by the 1920s, with most paleoanthropologists perceiving the Neandertals as a side-branch in hominid evolution (e.g., Keith 1915; Osborn 1918; Boule 1921; Sollas 1924) and a persistent minority seeing them as the direct, local ancestors of subsequent human populations (Verneau 1924; Hrdlicka 1927; Weinert 1932). Our knowledge of this period of human evolution has increased markedly in recent years, and our models as to what might have happened and how to decipher the prehistoric record have improved in sophistication, but the basic argument regarding the "fate" of the Neandertals remains essentially the same [see comments in Smith (1982) and articles in Smith and Spencer (1984)].

THE NEANDERTALS

The Neandertals, although definable by lists of morphological characters that distinguish them from their geographic and temporal neighbors (e.g., Trinkaus 1983a; Stringer et al. 1984), are best considered a geographic subspecies (of H. sapiens) that occupied the northwestern Old World (Europe and western Asia north to 49° and east to 67°) from the end of the last interglacial to the middle of the last glacial. They represent the final group of archaic humans in the northwestern Old World and have their closest morphological affinities to preceding Middle Pleistocene humans from the same region, differing primarily in a slight reduction of robusticity (cranial and postcranial) and greater average brain size (Hublin 1978; Wolpoff 1980b; Cook et al. 1982; Trinkaus 1982b). The Neandertals differ from their African and perhaps East Asian contemporaries in their greater midfacial prognathism and the expression of certain masto-occipital traits. They contrast with their early anatomically modern human successors in a number of feature, which are discussed below.

PHYLOGENETIC ISSUES

Few paleontologists would argue that the morphological differences between the Neandertals and their early modern human successors were trivial, but there is considerable disagreement as to how significant they were. The primary issue remains whether the changes that took place in the middle of the last glacial in Europe and western Asia represent a *major* acceleration in the rate of Late Pleistocene human morphological evolution (and if so, what specific factors brought about this acceleration) or were merely a continuation of previously existing temporal trends with little or no change in the rate of alteration (for recent opinions see: Heim 1978; Howells 1978; Trinkaus and Howells 1979; Wolpoff 1980a; Smith 1982; Stringer 1982; Hublin 1983; Trinkaus 1983a; Stringer et al. 1984). A major acceleration in evolutionary tempo would require a marked shift in some combination of selective pressures, gene frequencies, and gene flow, and could be seen as the product of major population replacement. The second perspective would invoke only gradual changes in gene frequencies and associated selective pressures with no alteration of levels of gene flow. Since some continuities of form exist between Neandertals and modern H. sapiens in Europe and the Near East (Smith and Ranyard 1980; Wolpoff 1980a; Smith 1982, 1984; Trinkaus 1983a, 1984a), at least minimal genetic continuity must have occurred, and therefore, total population replacement need not be considered further, even if it occurred in some areas of the northwestern Old World.

One of the persistent problems in sorting out these issues is our inability to determine potential rates of morphological change. Many of the anatomical alterations around the time of this Late Pleistocene transition [1] can be partially accounted for by changes in environmental and biomechanical stress on the anatomy during development, without any change in genotype. However, the relative uniformity of most of the differentiating morphological patterns before and after the transition, and the appearance of most of the diagnostic postcranial and cranial features early in development (Vlcek 1970, 1973; Smith 1976; Hublin 1980; Tillier 1982; Heim 1982b; Trinkaus 1983a), argue that there was nonetheless a strong genetic component in the morphological differences. But were these genetic differences due to simple changes at a few loci that had systemic effects (through regulator genes, shifts in the timing and/or levels of endocrine secretion during development, secondary effects of shifts in relative rates of development of adjacent structures, and/or pleiotropy), or were they the products of multiple changes at a variety of loci, each affecting one paleontologically perceived portion of the anatomy? We favor the former explanation, but as is also the case with stress-induced versus genetically determined effects, a modest sample of bones is unlikely to be very informative in separating these different, complementary, and not necessarily mutually exclusive processes.

Even if one accepts a large genetic component in the morphological changes evident at the transition, there are a variety of population dynamics that could account for the presumed genetic shift. They could be due to 1) a shift in selective pressure, markedly changing the frequencies of genes within local gene pools; 2) an alteration of selection, shifting the balance between local stabilizing selection and a relatively constant rate of gene flow between neighboring groups (especially in a possible cul-de-sac like Europe); 3) a marked increase in gene flow into the region from neighboring populations; and/or 4) the in-migration of a substantial population from a neighboring region, with little genetic contribution to the subsequent population from the preceding Neandertals.

The decision as to which of these processes was dominant depends upon prior decisions as to the relative genetic versus stress-related components in the morphological changes (and their implications for potential ranks of changes) and observations as to how much time was available for the transition across the region occupied by Neandertals. The recent discovery of a Châtelperronian-associated Neandertal at Saint-Césaire (Lévêque and Vandermeersch 1981) reduces the available time for the transition in Western Europe to, at the most, a few thousand years (Stringer et al. 1984), but available dates for diagnostic human remains from further east in Europe (Smith 1982, 1984) and in western Asia (Trinkaus 1983a, 1984a) allow for considerable more time, upwards of 5,000-10,000 years (assuming that the Qafzeh specimens were contemporaneous with the Skhul sample at ca. 40,000 years BP (Jelínek 1982; Trinkaus 1983a); if they were markedly older [per Bar Yosef and Vandermeersch (1981) and Vandermeersch (1981)], there would be no time available in the Levant for such a morphological transition).

Interestingly, the time of the transition, indicated primarily by the earliest unequivocal dates for anatomically modern humans in each area, appears to have taken place first in the Near East (ca. 40,000 years BP) (Trinkaus 1984a), next in Eastern and Central Europe (ca. 35,000 years BP) (Smith 1984), and last in Western Europe (30-33,000 years BP) (Stringer et al. 1984). This indicates a sloping horizon, running from east to west through time, and suggests elevated gene flow into the

west with the new variants derived from more eastern populations. However, this pattern does not demonstrate to what extent the morphological changes were genetically based or give significant insight into the population dynamics in any one region of Europe or western Asia during the transition. Unfortunately, the earliest appearances of anatomically modern humans in Africa and East Asia are too poorly dated to indicate conclusively whether one or the other of those regions could have been a source for new genetic variation, although the possibility that the transition from archaic *H. sapiens* to modern humans occurred in excess of 50,000 years BP in subsaharan Africa (Beaumont et al. 1978; Singer and Wymer 1982) makes such an interpretation attractive.

MORPHOLOGICAL CHANGE AT THE TRANSITION

These speculations must come back, eventually, to a consideration of the paleontological record and the nature of change around this Late Pleistocene transition. It should be mentioned that all of the currently available evidence, cranial and postcranial, supports the conclusion that the Neandertals of the early last glacial evolved gradually out of Middle Pleistocene archaic *H. sapiens* during the last interglacial across Europe and western Asia (Hublin 1978; Wolpoff 1980a, b; Trinkaus 1982b, 1983a; Cook et al. 1982). The human morphological changes in the middle of the last glacial, between the Neandertals and early modern appearing humans, were significantly less gradual and more pervasive anatomically. The anatomical complexes for which the fossil record around this transition provides information can be divided into three groups: 1) those that exhibit no significant change, 2) those that underwent a morphological shift in which the ranges of variation on either side of the transition overlapped but the sample means changed markedly, and 3) those that demonstrate a discrete morphological change with little or no overlap between the two samples.

In considerations of morphological change, *all* anatomical complexes for which data are available should be evaluated, regardless of available sample size. There is a tendency for some complexes to be considered "more relevant" to paleontological interpretations, resulting usually in pronounced gnathocentrism. This approach assumes that the researcher knows *a priori* the roles of individual anatomical complexes in human adaptive evolution and can therefore make decisions as to relative importance. In actual practice, this is rarely the case.

A number of important human complexes changed little if at all during this Late Pleistocene transition, and it is primarily these that are responsible for the inclusion of the Neandertals in *H. sapiens*. They include brain size and cerebral sulcal morphology (Vlcek 1969; Kochetkova 1978; Holloway 1981; Trinkaus and LeMay 1982; Trinkaus 1983a), posture and locomotor anatomy indicative of fully efficient bipedalism (Straus and Cave 1957; Trinkaus 1975, 1983a), most upper limb articular morphology (Heim 1982a; Trinkaus 1983a) posterior dental dimensions and morphology (Brace 1979; Smith 1976; Trinkaus 1983a), deciduous dental dimensions (P. Smith 1978; Tillier 1979; Trinkaus 1983a), and average body mass (Trinkaus 1983a, 1984b).

Alterations in the second group of complexes were more ubiquitous. There was a shift in neurocranial shape to higher and more rounded cranial vaults, with an associated reduction in the size and frequency of occipital buns (Stringer 1978;

Smith 1983; Trinkaus and LeMay 1982). The frequency of mandibular foramina with the horizontal-oval morphology decreased (F. H. Smith 1978). Anterior teeth decreased in size, absolutely and relative to posterior teeth, and they became less frequently shovel-shaped (Patte 1959; Brace 1979; Smith 1983; Trinkaus 1983a). Deciduous teeth, especially molars, decreased in occlusal morphological complexity (P. Smith 1978). Thumb carpometacarpal articulations became universally double saddle-shaped, rather than frequently lacking a dorso-palmar concavity (Musgrave 1971; Vlcek 1975; Stoner and Trinkaus 1981; Trinkaus 1983a). There was an increase in mean stature (Trinkaus 1983a), and postcranial robusticity reduced markedly, especially in the Near East (Trinkaus 1983b, 1984a). This last is reflected in cervical vertebral spine thickness and length, rib thickness, upper limb muscular development, and lower limb diaphyseal proportions and cross-sectional areas; in some of these anatomical regions the change in robusticity was sufficiently pronounced to suggest that they should be included in the third category of pattern of change at the transition.

The third category includes several diverse regions. Midfacial prognathism reduced markedly; the reduction consisted primarily of a general facial shortening without any change in the position of the zygomatic region, and included, as secondary spatial and/or architectural effects, reduction in supraorbital torus thickness and projection (especially laterally), reduced nasal projection, increased zygomatic curvature and associated formation of canine fossae, reduction of retromolar spaces, more anterior positioning of mental foramina, and increased mental protuberance projection (Howells 1975; Stringer 1978; Smith and Ranyard 1980; Wolpoff *et al.* 1981; Smith 1983; Trinkaus 1983a, 1984a). There was a change in masto-occipital morphology and temporal (tympanic) configurations (Vallois 1969; Smith 1976; Hublin 1978; Santa Luca 1978; Trinkaus 1983a). Pubic morphology and dimensions shifted, producing less attenuated and shorter pubic bones, and hence smaller pelvic apertures (Trinkaus 1976, 1984b). Distal/proximal limb segment proportions shifted from the lower to the upper limits of modern human ranges of variation (Trinkaus 1981). Pollical and hallucial phalanges changed from being subequal in length to the distal one being shorter than its proximal phalanx (Musgrave 1971; Trinkaus 1983a, c). The final feature in this group may be meningeal vascular branching patterns, which became more complex in early modern humans (Saban 1977).

These various changes can also be sorted into 1) those that remained stable throughout the Late Pleistocene; 2) those that evidenced gradual change prior and subsequent to the transition, with no acceleration in the rate of change around the middle of the last glacial; 3) those that changed on either side of the transition but still accelerated their rates of change around the transition; and 4) those that exhibited relative stasis before and after the transition and changed markedly at the time of the transition.

The first are primarily those features that changed little if at all around the transition, namely brain size and sulcal morphology, deciduous dental dimensions, and body mass. The last did decrease slightly during the late last glacial (Frayer 1981) but changed little during the previous part of the Late Pleistocene.

The features that changed gradually throughout the Late Pleistocene, with little or no acceleration around the transition, are primarily those related to general mastication. These include posterior dental dimensions and reflections of general facial massiveness, such as the relative anterior positioning

and rugosity of masticatory muscle attachments, mandibular robusticity, and supraorbital torus thickness and projection. Interestingly, these are features that appear to have been reducing gradually during most of the Middle, as well as the Late Pleistocene.

The third group are primarily those related to paramasticatory use of the anterior dentition but include primarily those aspects relating to levels of stress generated by the activity, rather than patterns of tooth use. They comprise anterior dental dimensions, rates of anterior dental attrition, rugosity of the nuchal muscle attachments, and possibly meningeal vascular branching patterns.

The last group of features is more varied. In it are pubic bone morphology and relative breadth, limb segment proportions, mean stature, thumb phalangeal length proportions and carpo-metacarpal articular morphology, hallucial phalangeal length proportions, most aspects of postcranial robusticity, masto-occipital and tympanic morphology, total facial prognathism, and deciduous dental morphology.

It should be apparent from these lists that the changes in human morphology during the Late Pleistocene in the northwestern Old World were highly mosaic. They varied considerably in degree and constancy of rate of change, and therefore as many as possible should be taken into consideration when using them for formulating phylogenetic or adaptational scenarios.

PHYLOGENETIC IMPLICATIONS OF THE CHANGES

The evaluation of these and other observable morphological traits and their patterns of change through the Late Pleistocene for phylogenetic purposes is dependent upon the assumptions one brings to them. Their genetic and developmental determinants, as discussed above, should be evaluated, if that is possible. Perhaps more important—and more resolvable—are the criteria used to divide up the observed morphology into units of analysis.

For example, does one evaluate the entire dentition as a unit or divide it into anterior and posterior fields? Does one merely measure mid-facial prognathism or consider it to be a secondary reflection of relative positionings of the dentition and the primary masticatory muscles? Are pollical and hallucial phalangeal proportions reflections of manipulative versus locomotor demands or is one merely a pleiotropic effect of demands on the homologous structure in the other limbs? Do the changes in limb segment proportions indicate an improved ability to deal with thermal stress or more efficient long distance locomotion? And is it possible that the changes in neurocranial shape are secondary reflections of relative brain and cranial vault growth rates, determined by levels of perinatal stimulation of brain growth due to changing reproductive patterns, the last of which is best reflected in the pelvis? Or is it possible that shifts in the shape of the posterior cranium (including occipital bunning) relate to a change in the extent and orientation of the nuchal plane, which is in turn associated with the amount of paramasticatory use of the anterior dentition? These and other structurally related questions need to be answered before any attempts are made to identify plesiomorphic, apomorphic, or autapomorphic traits or engage in similar mental exercises. Otherwise, we will merely end up counting traits of uncertain functional and developmental correlation and unequal phylogenetic significance.

In addition, it should be recognized that the evolutionary fate of the Neandertals need not have been the same across the large geographical region occupied by the Neandertals during the early last glacial. In fact, the diversity of habitats and topographies, as well as accessibility to neighboring regions, suggests that patterns of gene flow and population dynamics varied considerably across this region.

The ultimate resolution of whether all, a few, or none of the Neandertals were ancestral to early anatomically modern humans in Europe and western Asia will be achieved when there is general agreement on how one should interpret the paleontological record and/or there is incontrovertible evidence of local contemporaniety of the two morphological patterns across the northwestern Old World. Neither of these conditions are currently met, and it is uncertain whether they will ever be. It may therefore be more profitable to set aside the ultimate phylogenetic question and concentrate efforts on functional evaluations of the discernible morphology and its patterns of change during the Late Pleistocene. Such a concentration of efforts may eventually hold the key to the phylogenetic question, since functional studies should ultimately allow us to evaluate whether, for example, supposed Neandertal autapomorphies were clearly functionally based and likely to change rapidly in response to specific behavioral shifts. We view this approach as the more profitable one in the long run, whether the ultimate goal is the resolution of either hominid phylogeny or the evolution of human adaptive patterns.

BEHAVIORAL IMPLICATIONS OF THE CHANGES

The human morphological changes during the Late Pleistocene indicate a series of behavioral shifts during this time period, most of which were concentrated around the Neandertal to anatomically modern human transition. The implied shifts in human adaptation are reflected in the contemporaneous archeological record.

It should be emphasized that it is possible to make behavioral interpretations irrespective of the actual phylogenetic relationships between the Neandertals and early modern humans. The morphological pattern of the Neandertals was replaced by that of modern humans, so that it is evident that the latter had selective advantages, in the context of a changing cultural adaptive system, vis-à-vis the former. The consistent differences between the two morphological patterns can therefore be investigated from a strictly functional perspective and, along with interpretations of the associated archeological record, provide insights into Late Pleistocene human adaptive evolution.

The changes in the masticatory apparatus during this period indicate a general reduction in force and repetitiveness of human chewing (Brace 1979, F. H. Smith 1978, 1983; Trinkaus 1983a). This is reflected in the posterior retreat of the masticatory muscles (which initially produced the mid-facial prognathism of the Neandertals), the reduction of mandibular robusticity and masticatory muscle attachment rugosity, and decreasing tooth size throughout the Late Pleistocene. This was associated with the extensive use of the anterior dentition by the Neandertals for paramasticatory purposes, which maintained their large anterior teeth and anteriorly placed dentitions (Ryan 1980; Smith 1983; Trinkaus 1983a). A marked reduction in

non-dietary anterior tooth use apparently occurred at the time of the transition to anatomically modern humans, which resulted in the associated reductions in anterior dental dimensions and rates of attrition and in total facial prognathism. The changes in the morphology of the nuchal region with the advent of modern appearing humans were probably related to the shift in the pattern of use of these muscles once they were no longer counteracting forces applied to the anterior dentition (Wolpoff 1980a; Smith 1983).

The shift in pubic morphology produced a decrease in pelvic aperture dimensions relative to adult body size, which indicates a shift from a gestation length close to the 11-12 months expected for humans of the brain and body size of Neandertals and early modern humans to the 9 months characteristic of modern humans (Trinkaus 1983b, 1984b). It is possible that the earlier exposure of the neonate to environmental stimuli, combined with the generally richer cultural environment of early modern humans, promoted an accelerated rate of brain growth relative to cranial vault ossification. This would produce more anterior and superior brain growth and hence higher and rounder adult neurocrania (Trinkaus and LeMay 1982; Trinkaus 1984a).

The marked decrease in postcranial massiveness evident across the transition indicates a shift from habitual use of elevated physical strength and high levels of activity among the Neandertals to a greater reliance on culturally based technology and planning to accomplish regular subsistence activities (Trinkaus 1983b). When combined with the increased stature, the lengthening of distal limb segments, and the narrowing of the pelvis, all of which would increase locomotor efficiency, it suggests that the early anatomically modern humans were better adapted to covering large distances and hence able to monitor more effectively and exploit more efficiently the available resources with less physical durability and strength. These changes were undoubtedly correlated with the shifts in thumb morphology, all of which indicate a decrease in use of the power grip and associated increased emphasis on the precision grip and fine manipulation (the hallucial phalangeal length shift was probably pleiotropically related to the more important pollical alterations) (Stoner and Trinkaus 1981; Trinkaus 1983c).

The shift in limb segment proportions also implies an increased adaptation to thermal stress, since the Neandertal pattern is indicative of cold stress in modern mammals and that of the early modern humans of warmer climates (Trinkaus 1981). Since both groups were subjected to similar climates, the shift implies a marked increase in heat generating and conserving abilities among early modern humans.

The morphological changes at the time of this Late Pleistocene transition therefore indicate a continuation of previous trends in the reduction of the masticatory apparatus associated with major changes in human reproduction, non-dietary tooth use, habitual activity levels, locomotor efficiency, and thermal adaptation. The contemporaneous archeological record largely confirms these interpretations. It indicates little change in food preparation techniques but a major increase in technology as reflected in artifact assemblages (lithic and osteological) (Sonneville-Bordes 1963; Klein 1973; Bordes 1981; White 1982; Harrold 1983; Marks and Volkman 1983). There are suggestions of a shift toward more efficient exploitation of animal resources and avoidance of carnivores (Binford 1982, 1984; Straus 1982; White 1982). These changes were accompanied by reflections of increased social complexity (larger, more complex, and more variable sites, elaboration of burials, emergence of style zones) (Harrold 1980; Klein 1973; Hietala 1983), major elaboration of information systems ("art") (Marshack 1972; Conkey 1983), and improved means of heat production and conservation (pit hearths, structures, sewn clothing) (Movius 1966; Klein 1973; Stordeur-Yedid 1979). All of these could have allowed the habitual birth of altricial infants, which in turn could have provided demographic and energetic advantages.

These adaptive shifts around the Late Pleistocene archaic to anatomically modern human transition undoubtedly involved complex biocultural feedbacks, with changes in each sphere permitting or promoting changes in the other. It is not possible to determine which sphere was the prime mover, but attempts to construct causal directions (e.g., Trinkaus 1983b) indicate that culture and biology were about equally important in setting the process in motion.

THE FATE OF THE NEANDERTALS

These considerations should make it evident that the available fossil record does not permit us to decide conclusively what the phylogenetic fate of the European and western Asian Neandertals might have been. However, comparative analyses of their functional morphology indicate that their fate was to provide a background for the evolutionary emergence of people behaviorally and anatomically similar to ourselves. It is ironic that it is through contrasts of early modern appearing humans to the much maligned Neandertals that we will have the means to understand the evolutionary processes responsible for the origins of anatomically modern humans.

ACKNOWLEDGMENTS

We would like to express our sincere appreciation to the many individuals in Europe, western Asia, and North America who have allowed us to examine fossil human remains in their care. This research has been supported by grants from the Wenner-Gren Foundation, the National Science Foundation, the National Academy of Sciences, the Alexander von-Humboldt Foundation, Harvard University, the University of Tennessee, and the University of New Mexico.

NOTES

[1] The period during which the morphological pattern of anatomically modern humans replaced that of archaic *H. sapiens* across the Old World will be referred to here as a "transition." The term "transition" is not intended to imply or deny the possibility of direct *in situ* evolution of populations from one group to another.

REFERENCES

Bar Yosef, O., and Vandermeersch, B. 1981. Notes concerning the possible age of the Mousterian layers in Qafzeh Cave, in: *Préhistoire du Levant* (P. Sanlaville and J. Cauvin, Eds.), pp. 281-285, Éditions du C.N.R.S., Paris.

Beaumont, P. B., Villiers, H. de, and Vogel, J. C. 1978. Modern man in sub-saharan Africa prior to 49,000 years B.P.: A review and evaluation with particular reference to Border Cave. *S. Afr. J. Sci.* 74:409-419.

Binford, L. R. 1982. Comment on: Rethinking the Middle/Upper Paleolithic transition. *Curr. Anthropol.* 23:177-181.

Binford, L. R. 1984. *Faunal Remains From Klasies River Mouth.* Academic Press, New York.

Bordes, F. 1981. Vingt-cing ans après: Le complexe moustérien revisité. *Bull. Soc. Préhist. Franç.* 78:77-87.

Boule, M. 1911–1913. L'homme fossile de La Chapelle-aux-Saints. *Ann. Paléontol.* 6:111-172; 7:21-56, 85-192; 8:1-70.

Boule, M. 1921. *Les Hommes Fossiles.* Masson, New York.

Brace, C. L. 1964. The fate of the "classic" Neanderthals: A consideration of hominid catastrophism. *Curr. Anthropol.* 5:3-43.

Brace, C. L. 1979. Krapina, "Classic" Neanderthals, and the evolution of the European face. *J. Hum. Evol.* 8:527-550.

Conkey, M. W. 1983. On the origins of Paleolithic art: A review and some critical thoughts, in: *The Mousterian Legacy: Human Biocultural Change in the Upper Pleistocene* (E. Trinkaus, Ed.), *Brit. Archaeol. Rep.* S164:201-227.

Cook, J., Stringer, C. B., Currant, A. P., Schwarcz, H. P., and Wintle, A. G. 1982. A review of the chronology of the European Middle Pleistocene hominid record. *Yrbk. Phys. Anthropol.* 25:19-65.

Frayer, D. W. 1981. Body size, weapon use, and natural selection in the European Upper Paleolithic and Mesolithic. *Am. Anthropol.* 83:57-73.

Gorjanovic-Kramberger. D. 1906. *Der diluviale Mensch von Krapina in Kroatien.* Kriedels Verlag, Wiesbaden.

Harrold, F. B. 1980. A comparative analysis of Eurasian Palaeolithic burials. *World Archaeol.* 12:195-211.

Harrold, F. B. 1983. The Châtelperronian and the Middle Upper Paleolithic transition, in: *The Mousterian Legacy: Human Biocultural Change in the Upper Pleistocene* (E. Trinkaus, Ed.), *Brit. Archeol. Rep.* S164:123-140.

Heim, J. L. 1978. Contribution du massif facial à la morphogenèse du crâne néanderthalien, in: *Les Origines Humaines et Epoques de l'Intelligence* (J. Piveteau, Ed.), pp.183-215, Masson, Paris.

Heim, J. L. 1982a. Les hommes fossiles de La Ferrassie II. *Arch. Inst. Paléontol. Hum.* 38:1-272.

Heim, J. L. 1982b. *Les Enfants Néandertaliens de La Ferrassie.* Masson, Paris.

Hietala, H. 1983. Boker Tachtit: Intralevel and interlevel spatial analysis, in: *Prehistory and Paleoenvironments in the Central Negev, Israel III* (A. E. Marks, Ed.), pp. 217-282, Southern Methodist University, Dallas.

Holloway, R. L. 1981. Volumetric and asymmetry determinations on recent hominid endocasts: Spy I and II, Djebel Irhoud I, and the Sale *Homo erectus* specimens, with some notes on Neandertal brain size. *Am. J. Phys. Anthropol.* 55:385-393.

Howells, W. W. 1975. Neanderthal man: Facts and figures, in: *Paleoanthropology: Morphology and Paleoecology* (R. H. Tuttle, Ed.), pp. 389-407, Mouton, The Hague.

Howells, W. W. 1978. Position phylétique de l'homme de Néanderthal, in: *Les Origines Humaines et les Epoques de l'Intelligence* (J. Piveteau, Ed.), pp 217-235, Masson, Paris.

Hrdlicka, A. 1927. The Neanderthal phase of man. *J. Roy. Anthropol. Inst.* 57:249-274.

Hublin, J. J. 1978. *Le Torus Occipital Transverse et les Structures Associées: Évolution dans le Genre Homo.* Thèse de Troisieme Cycle, Univ. de Paris.

Hublin, J. J. 1980. La Chaise Suard, Engis 2 et La Quina H 18: Développement de la morphologie occipitale externe chez l'enfant prénéandertalien et néandertalien. *C. R. Acad. Sci. Paris* 291D:669-672.

Hublin, J. J. 1983. Les origines de l'homme de type modern en Europe. *Pour la Science* 64:62-71.

Jelínek, A. J. 1982. The Tabun Cave and Paleolithic man in the Levant. *Science* 216:1369-1375.

Keith, A. 1911. *Ancient Types of Man*. Harper, London.

Keith, A. 1915. *The Antiquity of Man*. Williams and Norgate, London.

Klein, R. G. 1973. *Ice-Age Hunters of the Ukraine*. University of Chicago Press, Chicago.

Kochetkova, V. I. 1978. *Paleoneurology*. Winston and Sons, Washington.

Lévêque, F., and Vandermeersch, B. 1981. Le néandertalien de Saint-Césaire. *La Recherche* 12:242-244.

Mann, A. E., and Trinkaus, E. 1974. Neandertal and Neandertal-like fossils from the Upper Pleistocene. *Yrbk. Phys. Anthropol.* 17:169-193.

Marks, A. E., and Volkman, P. W. 1983. Changing core reduction strategies: A technological shift from the Middle to Upper Paleolithic in the southern Levant, in: *The Mousterian Legacy: Human Biocultural Change in the Upper Pleistocene* (E. Trinkaus, Ed.), *Brit. Archaeol. Rep.* S164:13-34.

Marshack, A. 1972. Cognitive aspects of Upper Paleolithic engraving. *Curr. Anthropol.* 13:445-477.

Mortillet, G. de 1883. *Le Préhistorique, orgine et antiquité de l'homme.* Reinwald, Paris.

Movius, H. L., Jr. 1966. The hearths of the Upper Périgordian and Aurignacian horizons at the Abri Pataud, Les Eyzies (Dordogne) and their possible significance. *Am. Anthropol.* 68:296-325.

Musgrave, J. H. 1971. How dextrous was Neanderthal man? *Nature* 233:538-541.

Osborn, H. F. 1918. *Men of the Old Stone Age*, 3rd ed. Scribners, New York.

Patte, E. 1959. La dentition des Néanderthaliens. *Ann. Paléontol.* 45:221-305.

Ryan, A. S. 1980. *Anterior Dental Microwear in Hominid Evolution: Comparisons With Humans and Nonhuman Primates.* Ph.D. Thesis, University of Michigan. University Microfilms, Ann Arbor.

Saban, R. 1977. Les impressions vasculaires pariétales endocrâniennes dans la lignée des Hominidés. *C.R. Acad. Sci. Paris* 284D:803-806.

Santa Luca, A. P. 1978. A re-examination of presumed Neandertal-like fossils. *J. Hum. Evol.* 7:619-636.

Schwalbe, G. 1904. *Die Vorgeschichte des Menschen.* Vieweg und Sohn, Braunschweig.

Singer, R., and Wymer, J. 1982. *The Middle Stone Age at Klasies River Mouth in South Africa.* University of Chicago Press, Chicago.

Smith, F. H. 1976. The Neandertal Remains from Krapina: A Descriptive and Comparative Study. *Univ. Tenn. Dept. Anthropol. Rep. Invest.* 15:1-359.

Smith, F. H. 1978. Evolutionary significance of the mandibular foramen area in Neandertals. *Am. J. Phys. Anthropol.* 48:523-532.

Smith, F. H. 1982. Upper Pleistocene hominid evolution in South-Central Europe: A review of the evidence and analysis of trends. *Curr. Anthropol.* 23:667-703.

Smith, F. H. 1983. A behavioral interpretation of changes in craniofacial morphology across the Archaic/Modern *Homo sapiens* transition, in: *The Mousterian Legacy: Human Biocultural Change in the Upper Pleistocene* (E. Trinkaus, Ed.), *Brit. Archaeol. Rep.* S164:141-164.

Smith, F. H. 1984. Fossil hominids from the Upper Pleistocene of Central Europe and the origin of modern Europeans, in: *The Origins of Modern Humans* (F. H. Smith and F. Spencer, Eds.), pp. 137-209, Liss, New York.

Smith, F. H., and Ranyard, G. C. 1980. Evolution of the supraorbital region in Upper Pleistocene fossil hominids from South-Central Europe. *Am. J. Phys. Anthropol.* 53:589-610.

Smith, F. H., and Spencer, F., Eds. 1984. *The Origins of Modern Humans.* Liss, New York.

Smith, P. 1978. Evolutionary changes in the deciduous dentition of Near Eastern Populations. *J. Hum. Evol.* 7:401-408.

Sollas, W. J. 1907. On the cranial and facial characters of the Neandertal race. *Phil. Trans. Roy. Soc. London*, ser. B 199:281-339.

Sollas, W. J. 1924. *Ancient Hunters*, 3rd ed. Macmillan, New York.

Sonneville-Bordes, D. de 1963. Upper Paleolithic cultures in western Europe. *Science* 142:347-360.

Spencer, F. 1984. The Neandertals and their evolutionary significance: A brief historical survey, in: *The Origins of Modern Humans* (F. H. Smith and F. Spencer, Eds.), pp. 1-49, Liss, New York.

Spencer, F., and Smith, F. H. 1981. The significance of Aleš Hrdlicka's "Neanderthal Phase of Man:" A historical and current assessment. *Am. J. Phys. Anthropol.* 56:435-459.

Stoner, B. P., and Trinkaus, E. 1981. Getting a grip on the Neandertals: Were they all thumbs? *Am. J. Phys. Anthropol.* 54:281-282 (Abstract).

Stordeur-Yedid, D. 1979. Les aiguilles à chas au Paléolithique. *Gallia Préhist. Suppl.* 11:1-215.

Straus, L. G. 1982. Carnivores and cave sites in Cantabrian Spain. *J. Anthropol. Res.* 38:75-96.

Straus, W. L., Jr., and Cave, A. J. E. 1957. Pathology and the posture of Neanderthal man. *Quart. Rev. Biol.* 32:348-363.

Stringer, C. B. 1978. Some problems in Middle and Upper Pleistocene hominid relationships, in: *Recent Advances in Primatology*, Vol. 3 (D. J. Chivers and K. A. Joysey, Eds.), pp. 395-418, Academic Press, London.

Stringer, C. B. 1982. Towards a solution to the Neanderthal problem. *J. Hum. Evol.* 11:431-438.

Stringer, C. B., Hublin, J. J., and Vandermeersch, B. 1984. The origin of anatomically modern humans in Western Europe, in: *The Origins of Modern Humans* (F. H. Smith and F. Spencer, Eds.), pp. 51-135, Liss, New York.

Tillier, A. M. 1979. La dentition de l'enfant moustérien Chateauneuf 2 découverte à l'Abri de Hauteroche (Charente). *L'Anthropol.* 83:417-438.

Tillier, A. M. 1982. Les enfants neanderthaliens de Devil's Tower (Gibraltar). *Z. Morphol. Anthropol.* 73:125-148.

Trinkaus, E. 1975. *A Functional Analysis of the Neandertal Foot.* Ph.D. Thesis, University of Pennsylvania. University Microfilms, Ann Arbor.

Trinkaus, E. 1976. The morphology of European and Southwest Asian Neandertal pubic bones. *Am. J. Phys. Anthropol.* 44:95-104.

Trinkaus, E. 1981. Neanderthal limb proportions and cold adaptation, in: *Aspects of Human Evolution* (C. B. Stringer, Ed.), pp. 187-224, Taylor and Francis, London.

Trinkaus, E. 1982a. A history of *Homo erectus* and *Homo sapiens* paleontology in America, in: *A History of American Physical Anthropology, 1930–1980* (F. Spencer, Ed.), pp. 261-280, Academic Press, New York.

Trinkaus, E. 1982b. Evolutionary continuity among archaic *Homo sapiens*, in: *The Transition from Lower to Middle Paleolithic and the Origin of Modern Man* (A. Ronen, Ed.), *Brit. Archaeol. Rep.* S151:301-314.

Trinkaus, E. 1983a. *The Shanidar Neandertals.* Academic Press, New York.

Trinkaus, E. 1983b. Neandertal postcrania and the adaptive shift to modern humans, in: *The Mousterian Legacy: Human Biocultural Change in the Upper Pleistocene* (E. Trinkaus, Ed.), *Brit. Archaeol. Rep.* S164:165-200.

Trinkaus, E. 1983c. Functional aspects of Neandertal pedal remains. *Foot Ankle* 3:377-390.

Trinkaus, E. 1984a. Western Asia, in: *The Origins of Modern Humans* (F. H. Smith and F. Spencer, Eds.), pp. 251-293, Liss, New York.

Trinkaus, E. 1984b. Neandertal pubic morphology and gestation length. *Curr. Anthropol.* 25:509-514.

Trinkaus, E., and Howells, W. W. 1979. The Neanderthals. *Sci. Amer.* 241(6):118-133.

Trinkaus, E. and LeMay, M. 1982. Occipital bunning among later Pleistocene hominids. *Am. J. Phys. Anthropol.* 57:27-35.

Vallois, H. V. 1969. Le temporal néandertalien H-27 de La Quina: Étude anthropologique. *L'Anthropol.* 73:365-400, 525-544.

Vandermeersch, B. 1981. *Les Hommes Fossiles de Qafzeh (Israël).* Éditions du C.N.R.S., Paris.

Verneau, R. 1924. La race de Neanderthal et la race de Grimaldi; leurs rôles dans l'humanité. *J. Roy. Anthropol. Inst.* 54:211-230.

Vlcek, E. 1969. *Neandertaler der Tschechoslowakei.* Tschoslowakische Akademie der Wissenschaften, Prague.

Vlcek, E. 1970. Étude comparative onto-phylogénétique de l'enfant du Pech-de-l'Azé par rapport à d'autres enfants néandertaliens. *Arch. Inst. Paleontol. Hum.* 33:149-178.

Vlcek, E. 1973. Postcranial skeleton of a Neandertal child from Kiik-Koba, U.S.S.R. *J. Hum. Evol.* 2:537-555.

Vlcek, E. 1975. Morphology of the first metacarpal of Neanderthal individuals from the Crimea. *Bull. Mem. Soc. Anthropol.* Paris, sér. 13 2:257-276.

Weinert, H. 1932. *Ursprung der Menschheit.* Enke, Stuttgart.

White, R. 1982. Rethinking the Middle/Upper Paleolithic transition. *Curr. Anthropol.* 23:169-192.

Wolpoff, M. H. 1980a. *Paleoanthropology.* Knopf, New York.

Wolpoff, M. H. 1980b. Cranial remains of Middle Pleistocene European hominids. *J. Hum. Evol.* 9:339-358.

Wolpoff, M. H., Smith, F. H., Malez, M., Radovcic, J., and Rukavina, D. 1981. Upper Pleistocene human remains from Vindija Cave, Croatia, Yugoslavia. *Am. J. Phys. Anthropol.* 54:499-545.

55

Mousterian, Châtelperronian and Early Aurignacian in Western Europe: Continuity or Discontinuity?

F. B. Harrold

INTRODUCTION

It is a commonplace in the study of Pleistocene prehistory that the contrasts between the Middle and Upper Paleolithic periods are both numerous and striking (e.g., Mellars 1973; White 1982). In brief, it is widely agreed that the Upper Paleolithic, when compared to the Mousterian, is characterized by (1) the adoption of blade technology for many or most stone tools; (2) lithic assemblages with more (and more complex) recognized tool types, whose formal variation in space and time is greater, and more clearly patterned; (3) the widespread use of bone, antler, and ivory artifacts shaped by complex new methods; (4) a proliferation of artifacts of apparent symbolic (often non-utilitarian) import, such as items of personal ornament, and both mobiliary and parietal art; (5) evidence for more sophisticated subsistence practices; and (6) indications of changed human settlement patterns and increased populations.

These changes in the archaeological record are generally interpreted as reflecting dramatic changes in human technology, subsistence, and social organization. Because this change in cultural remains roughly parallels the human fossil transition in Western Europe from Neanderthals (*Homo sapiens neanderthalensis*) to anatomically modern humans (*Homo sapiens sapiens*), it is possible that the archaeological record is monitoring not only changes in cultural systems, but changes in human cultural capacities. This possibility adds interest to our task of understanding this period, but also makes it even more complicated.

When the Mousterian is compared globally to the Upper Paleolithic, or especially, to a late manifestation like the Magdalenian (e.g., Straus 1983), these contrasts are among the most impressive to be seen in Pleistocene prehistory. When we focus attention on the times just before, during, and after the Middle-Upper Paleolithic transition, however, the differences are somewhat less salient. Furthermore, it is at this point that we face the

reality that our understanding of this transition in terms of Last Glacial human behavior and adaptations, and their relationship to the evolution of modern humanity, is still seriously incomplete.

This paper will be concerned with only certain aspects of the biological and behavioral changes concerning the origin of modern humans, and only in the corner of Europe with which I am most familiar. More specifically, it will examine continuities and discontinuities across the Middle-Upper Paleolithic transition and in the early Upper Paleolithic, in certain parts of France and Spain. There, the transition saw the Mousterian give way to the Châtelperronian industrial tradition and, essentially contemporaneously, the early Aurignacian.

Geographically, then, this study is restricted to a territory stretching from Cantabrian Spain through the western and central Pyrenees to include southwestern and much of central and north-central France. Topically, it is restricted to the continuity and change over time seen in the artifacts associated with these three culture-stratigraphic units. It will not deal with evidence relating to past subsistence-settlement systems or intrasite spatial analysis, which is treated elsewhere (see Chase 1989, Straus 1990). It will be more concerned with delineating patterning in the archaeological record than with detailed interpretations of it in terms of particular forms of social organization and subsistence.

This deliberately narrow focus precludes a comprehensive overview here of our understanding of the transitional period in the Châtelperronian geographical sphere. However, this understanding is in any event so limited that there is probably more to be gained by a relatively intensive examination of the patterning now apparent in this segment of the archaeological record. Such structure can then serve as part of the base for the focused future research which is so much needed before we can begin to explain the Middle-Upper Paleolithic transition in Western Europe.

CHÂTELPERRONIAN, MOUSTERIAN, AND EARLY AURIGNACIAN

Preliminary Considerations

Before treating the continuities and discontinuities among these traditions, some preliminary points should be made concerning all three.

The Mousterian (See Figures 1 and 2)

While the Mousterian is sometimes spoken of as an undifferentiated block, it is important to recognize its significant internal variability—not only in the form of the well-known Mousterian facies (whatever their nature may be), but also significant temporal and geographical variability. Temporally, for instance, there is the replacement of the Mousterian of Acheulean Tradition type A (MAT-A) in the Périgord by the MAT-B. Furthermore, there is the possibility on the basis of recent thermoluminescence dates from Le Moustier, of a greater temporal element to inter-facies variability than has previously been demonstrable (Mellars 1986). Spatially, one can point at the regional level to the absence of the MAT from Provence, or the "Vasconian" Mousterian with cleaver flakes, restricted to Spain and the Pyrenees. At a more local scale, there is almost

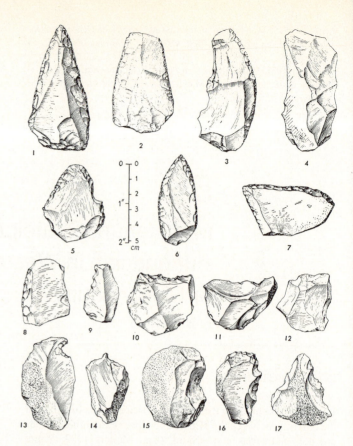

Figure 2. *More Mousterian stone tools: 1, 6, points; 2, 3, 8, sidescrapers; 4, Levallois flake; 5, endscraper on a flake; 7, transverse scraper; 9, 10, 16, 17, denticulates; 11-13, 15, notches; 14, borer. Adapted from Bordes (1961a).*

exclusive occurrence of the MAT in open-air contexts in the Périgord.

Nevertheless, the Mousterian in general shows far less artifactual variability over space and time than the Upper Paleolithic.

The Châtelperronian (See Figure 3)

Despite impressions to the contrary, due primarily to disturbed and mixed assemblages from La Ferrassie and Le Moustier, the Châtelperronian is a true early Upper Paleolithic industry (Harrold 1981, 1983, 1986; Farizy, 1990). Also known as the Castelperronian and Lower Périgordian, it is characterized by (in decreasing order of importance) Châtelperron knives, endscrapers, burins, truncated and retouched pieces, and such "Mousterian" types as sidescrapers, notches, and denticulates. High proportions of these tools are made on blades struck from prismatic cores.

The Early Aurignacian (See Figure 4)

There is some disorder in the time-space systematics of the other industry of the early Upper Paleolithic in France and Spain. A brief historical review might be in order:

Peyrony (1933) established the well-known sequence of five Aurignacian stages (I-V) primarily on the basis of the succession of bone point "fossil directors" found in his excava-

Figure 1. *Mousterian stone tools: 1, point; 2, sidescraper; 3, 9, endscraper; 4, 5, backed knives; 6, truncated flake; 7, denticulate; 8, double burin; 10, 11, borers; 12, 14, handaxes; 13, bladelet core. Adapted from Bordes (1961a).*

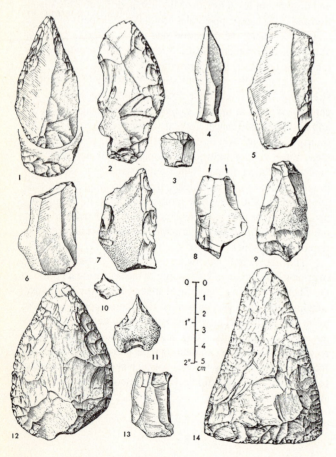

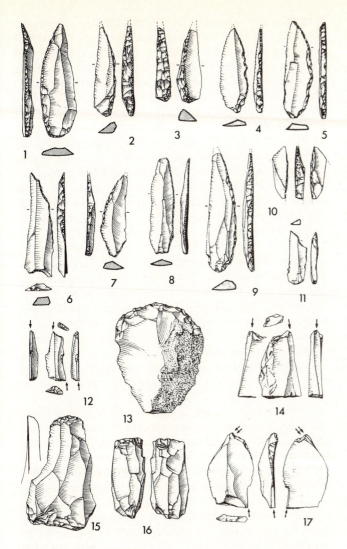

Figure 3. *Châtelperronian stone tools: 1-9, Châtelperron points; 10, broken Châtelperron point; 11, truncated blade; 12, burin; 13, endscraper on a flake; 14, 17, burins; 15, endscraper; 16, small blade core. Adapted from Bordes and Labrot (1967).*

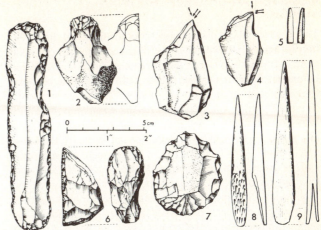

Figure 4. *Aurignacian stone and bone tools: 1, endcraper on an Aurignacian blade; 2, thick nosed scraper; 3, dihedral burin, 4, busked burin; 5, Dufour bladelet; 6, thick scraper; 7, denticulated scraper; 8, bone point with bevelled base; 9, split-base bone point. Adapted from Sonneville-Bordes (1963).*

tions at La Ferrassie, with split-base bone points identifying the Aurignacian I, and so on. But as the Aurignacian data base has expanded, the neat succession of stages has broken down—rather analogously to the putatively successive substages (a, b, c) of Peyrony's Périgordian V (Rigaud 1980), when fossil directors began to be found in the "wrong" stratigraphic sequence. The typological integrity of the Aurignacian industry is not in question, nor is the fact that it has some temporal patterning (classic Aurignacian I assemblages, for instance, seem reliably older than "evolved" ones).

That an earlier phase of the Aurignacian preceded the classic Aurignacian I with split-base bone points was suggested by Sonneville-Bordes (1960). She established that Peyrony's "Périgordian II" with Dufour bladelets at sites like La Ferrassie E', Dufour, and Chanlat, was actually Aurignacian in assemblage composition. Since it stratigraphically underlay the classic Aurignacian at La Ferrassie, it became an Aurignacian "0" (also variously called "Archaic Aurignacian," "Correzian" or "Proto-Aurignacian"). Since then,

various assemblages have been attributed to a phase of the Aurignacian which (a) preceded the Aurignacian I, and (b) differed typologically from it, lacking the characteristic bone points and perhaps other fossil directors (such as Aurignacian blades), and (in most formulations) containing small, semi-abruptly retouched "Dufour" bladelets. However, this typological unity, accepted previously by myself among others (e.g., Harrold 1983), is not apparent in all cases.

It no longer appears that a typologically coherent Archaic Aurignacian precedes the Aurignacian I throughout our geographical sphere of concern (e.g., Leroyer and Leroi-Gourhan 1983; Rigaud 1982:384-89,440-43; Sonneville-Bordes 1980b; Delporte and Mazière 1977; Bernaldo de Quiros 1980).

Some "Archaic" Aurignacian assemblages are fairly close to Sonneville-Bordes' original notion, and indeed antedate the Aurignacian I—as for example at sites in Languedoc (Bazile 1976) and, in our area, at El Pendo, Gatzarria, and still essentially unpublished assemblages at Saint-Césaire and Pataud. Others, however, are in overall typology quite close to Aurignacian I assemblages, except that they lack split-base bone points and/or contain Dufour bladelets (e.g., Chanlat and Dufour [Sonneville-Bordes 1960] or Le Piage [Champagne and Espitalié 1981]). Furthermore, assemblages of both sorts do not always antedate the Aurignacian I; they may be contemporaneous with it (e.g. Le Piage), or of unknown age (Dufour).

Thus an "Archaic Aurignacian" unified in space, time, and typology cannot clearly be distinguished. I will instead use the term "Early Aurignacian," in a strictly chronological sense. Early Aurignacian assemblages are those which are roughly contemporary in a given region with the Châtelperronian—that is, those assigned with reasonable certainty to the same chronostratigraphic periods as the Châtelperronian (see Table 1 and discussion below).

Two sets of relations will be examined—those between the Mousterian and Châtelperronian, and those between the Châtelperronian and Aurignacian:

MOUSTERIAN-CHÂTELPERRONIAN

There has long been disagreement over the nature of the transition between these two industries, which occurred some 37,000 to 35,000 years ago (see below for discussion of temporal and chronostratigraphic context). Three main views have been put forward:

(1) The Châtelperronian represents a tradition or culture intrusive into France and Spain, not derived from the local Mousterian. This view was more popular formerly than now (e.g., Breuil 1913; Peyrony 1933), though there are still some authors uneasy with assertions of Mousterian-Châtelperronian filiation (Ashton 1983). In support of this point of view, Mousterian-Châtelperronian *discontinuities* can be stressed—for example, the lack of well-documented "transitional" assemblages intermediate between the two, and the fact that the Châtelperronian is Upper Paleolithic in overall technology and typology.

(2) The Châtelperronian developed independently from the local Mousterian. This is the majority position among researchers (e.g., Laville, Rigaud, and Sackett 1980:267; Mellars 1973; Bahn 1983; Bricker 1976). François Bordes strongly supported this hypothesis; indeed, he saw the Châtelperronian as deriving specifically from one particular Mousterian facies, the Mousterian of Acheulean Tradition, or MAT (Bordes 1972a, 1972b). In this formulation, the relatively high occurrence in the MAT of blades and "Upper Paleolithic" types such as burins, backed knives, and endscrapers is seen as a harbinger of their elaboration during the Châtelperronian. In short, the theme of Mousterian-Châtelperronian *continuity* is stressed. Indeed, it has been suspected that such MAT-Châtelperronian industrial evolution may have been accompanied by Neanderthal-to-*Homo sapiens sapiens* biological evolution. Bordes (1968) has pointed out the lack of skeletal material associated with the MAT—with the implication that, for all we know, advanced or transitional Neanderthals may have made MAT assemblages. Elsewhere, a Denticulate-Châtelperronian link is inferred where all late Mousterian is Denticulate—at Arcy-sur-Cure (Girard 1980) and in Cantabria (Butzer 1986).

The question of the derivation of the Châtelperronian specifically from the MAT depends upon the much-debated issue of the nature of Mousterian facies variation. If facies represent cultural traditions associated with distinct human populations (e.g., Bordes 1973), then Bordes' hypothesis is at least possible; if they instead reflect different combinations of tool-making, tool-use, and discard behavior unrelated to ethnic identity (e.g., Binford 1973), and/or if they are in part artificial creations which partition continuous interassemblage variability (Freeman 1980), then Bordes' derivation is impossible. And if, as Mellars (1986) has argued, MAT is simply late Mousterian, then the Châtelperronian-MAT link means something quite different from what is usually envisioned. I shall not seek to settle that issue here, but will deal below with the question of Mousterian-Châtelperronian evolution.

A third possibility is intermediate between the first two:

3) The Châtelperronian represents a heavily acculturated derivation of the Mousterian. In this formulation there are important roles for *both* continuity and discontinuity. It was first cogently suggested by Klein (1973)[1] that the Châtelperronian resulted from a sort of bow wave effect, as cultural diffusion, and probably also population movement of anatomically modern humans, brought the Upper Paleolithic to western Europe in the form of the Aurignacian. This position has gained popularity in the wake of the the discovery (Lévêque and Vandermeersch 1980, 1981; Vandermeersch 1984) of Neanderthal remains in a Châtelperronian level at Saint-Césaire (e.g., Stringer, Hublin, and Vandermeersch 1984; Dibble 1983; Butzer 1986; Harrold 1983,1986).

Given the present amount and quality of data, and state of theory, concerning this issue, none of the above positions has won universal acceptance, or is susceptible of conclusive testing. However, we could suggest certain predictable consequences of each hypothesis, and compare them to the patterning currently visible in the archaeological record. This might suggest which (if any) scenario provides a "best fit" to such patterning, and suggest avenues for future research [2].

(1) For instance, if the first hypothesis presented above were true, we should expect to see an abrupt replacement of the Mousterian by the Châtelperronian, and strong technological and typological discontinuities in stone and other artifacts. "Transitional assemblages" intermediate in technology and typology between the two should not be found. We could not expect discontinuities to be absolute, since artifactual change in the Paleolithic was additive as well as substitutive (after all, chopping tools are found in the Upper Paleolithic); but the more dramatic such change is, the stronger our confidence in this hypothesis would be.

This hypothesis is not *necessarily* connected with human biological evolution. It is true nonetheless that strong morphological discontinuity between human remains associated with the Mousterian and those associated with the Châtelperronian would support it—for example, if Neanderthals making Mousterian artifacts were abruptly replaced by modern humans making Châtelperronian ones.

(2) If the Châtelperronian were autochthonously derived from the Mousterian, we should expect to see in the archaeological record a gradual enrichment of Mousterian assemblages in Upper Paleolithic technological and typological elements, culminating in the Châtelperronian. Transitional assemblages should be present; if the transformation lasted as long as several thousand years, a graded series of such assemblages should be available. The case for this hypothesis would be especially strengthened if such change occurred well before there were evidence of diffusion or incursion of the Upper Paleolithic from elsewhere.

In this case, the cultural and biological transformations of the mid-Last Glacial in the geographical area of our concern would be essentially localized phenomena, and presumably linked. This proposal would thus be supported by evidence for the gradual *in situ* evolution of local Neanderthals into *Homo sapiens sapiens*, rather than their replacement. Transitional or modern human remains should be associated with both the Mousterian and the Châtelperronian.

(3) If the third hypothesis were true, we should expect considerable Mousterian-Châtelperronian continuity in assemblage composition, but the relatively abrupt introduction of Upper Paleolithic elements at about the same time as the appearance of the other local manifestation of the Upper Paleolithic, the Aurignacian.

Furthermore, if the Châtelperronian represented a "bow wave," then any associated human remains should be those of

Neanderthals or of "hybrid" populations showing the effects of gene flow.

Unfortunately, these hypotheses are not currently definitively testable. We are unable satisfactorily to quantify and specify them, and their outcomes in the archaeological record may not always be mutually-exclusive. Just how much Mousterian-Châtelperronian continuity, how measured, is sufficient to support hypothesis (2) over hypothesis (3)? At what rate must artifactual change proceed to be judged as "abrupt?"

Especially vexing in this context is the crude temporal resolution of the dating methods available to us in this time range, radiocarbon dating and litho- and pollen-stratigraphic frameworks. Assemblages which could *appear* to us to be essentially synchronous might in fact be separated in true age by several centuries—and the crucial processes we are trying to elucidate could conceivably operate over just such a timespan. Nonetheless, I would argue that the process of pattern-seeking and hypothesis clarification is a useful one, especially in identifying those areas most in need of clarification and future research.

CHÂTELPERRONIAN-EARLY AURIGNACIAN

These two culture-stratigraphic units of the early Upper Paleolithic have long been recognized as distinctive and sequential. Even after Peyrony's (1933) schematization of the Périgordian (including the Châtelperronian) and Aurignacian as two parallel cultural traditions associated with two different races, they were perceived as mutually exclusive in any one region.

Since the 1960's, however, interstratification and other evidence (discussed below) have shown that the Châtelperronian and Aurignacian are at least partly contemporaneous. How do we interpret the phenomenon of two distinct but contemporary industries occupying the same geographical region?

(1) Here again, there is a clear majority opinion among prehistorians familiar with the region: that the Châtelperronian and Aurignacian indeed represent two distinct cultural traditions associated with different ethnic (and perhaps racial) groupings (e.g., Sonneville-Bordes 1960, 1980a; Laville, Rigaud and Sackett 1980:285; Howell 1984). According to this view, differences between the two sets of assemblages, especially in the mutually-exclusive occurrence of such fossil directors as Chatelperron knives, or Aurignacian blades, are too great to explain otherwise than as the result of different culturally-transmitted traditions of artifact manufacture.

(2) In an echo of the Bordes-Binford debate over the Mousterian, a minority opinion interprets Châtelperronian-Aurignacian differences as unrelated to sociocultural boundaries, but instead reflecting functionally differentiated sets of behavior at different sites, perhaps due to seasonal variations in behavior (S. Binford 1972; Ashton 1983).

Here again, we can propose that each hypothesis would entail different patterning in archaeological residues. In the case of the first, we would expect on close examination to see considerable discontinuity in artifact technology and typology, especially in terms of stylistically-distinct "fossil directors" characteristic of each industry [3]. We would not expect to find significant "contamination" of Châtelperronian assemblages with Aurignacian fossil directors, and *vice-versa*.

Associated human remains might or might not differ markedly between the industries.

In the case of the second hypothesis, we would expect just such contamination, as well as stylistic continuity between the two industries. Differences in assemblage content would be quantitative rather than qualitative, dependent on differing combinations of activities involving the making, use, modification, and discard of tools at different sites. Such interassemblage differences might even form a continuum, ranging from "pure Châtelperronian" assemblages with little Aurignacian content through a spectrum to "pure Aurignacian" ones. Skeletal remains associated with the two industries should necessarily represent the same human population.

Two caveats are appropriate here:

First, it is vital to emphasize that the classes of data considered here are only some of those relevant to these hypotheses. Information on faunas, settlement patterns, and the like would be absolutely necessary as well—particularly since advocates of hypothesis (2) have proposed that it is seasonal human movements and shifts in faunal exploitation which underlie Châtelperronian-Aurignacian interassemblage differences.

Second, as noted above for the Châtelperronian and Mousterian, we cannot yet neatly quantify the degrees of interassemblage variability which would confirm one explanation or the other. Again, however, the patterning found can be compared to our hypotheses for goodness-of-fit.

The rest of this paper will review the evidence for continuity and discontinuity—first temporal, then artifactual—among the three industries with which we are concerned.

TEMPORAL CONTINUITY

The evidence for temporal relationships among these industries falls into three categories: stratigraphic superposition, radiocarbon chronology and chronostratigraphic frameworks.

Stratigraphic Superposition

Stratigraphic relationships of Mousterian, Châtelperronian, and Aurignacian assemblages found at the same sites give, in aggregate, good indications of their relative ages.

At 24 sites [4], Châtelperronian assemblages have been found in at least minimally documented stratigraphic contexts. The following information is based on this sample.

Mousterian levels are known at 17 of these 24 sites. They are directly overlain by Châtelperronian levels at 16 of them (by "directly" I mean here that there is no other archaeological level between Mousterian and Châtelperronian levels; there may or may not be an interposed sterile stratigraphic unit). In one case (El Pendo), the Mousterian is directly overlain by an Aurignacian level. There are *no* cases of Mousterian atop either Châtelperronian or Aurignacian levels, or interstratified with them.

Aurignacian levels are documented at 19 of these sites. In 16 of them, the Aurignacian simply directly overlies one or more Châtelperronian levels. These overlying Aurignacian levels are variously characterized as Aurignacian 0, I, II, or "evolved" Aurignacian; some are well-dated, others are not.

In three cases, Châtelperronian-Aurignacian interstratification has been documented:

1. At Roc de Combe (Lot) (Bordes and Labrot 1967), an Aurignacian level (layer 9), lies sandwiched between two Châtelperronian ones layer (10 and 8), with an Aurignacian I level (layer 7) atop them all.

2. At nearby Le Piage (Lot) (Champagne and Espitalie 1981), a Châtelperronian level (F1) is underlain by three Aurignacian levels (K, J, G-I), and overlain by another (F).

3. And at El Pendo in Cantabria (González Echegaray, ed., 1980), two Aurignacian levels (VIIIb and VIIIa), one of them quite poor, lie under a scanty Châtelperronian level (VIII), and then an Aurignacian I level (VII).

Thus, Châtelperronian overlies Aurignacian in three cases, and underlies it in 19 (the 16 mentioned above, plus the three with interstratification). Interestingly, in no case does a classic Aurignacian I assemblage with split-base bone points underlie the Châtelperronian; the underlying Aurignacian at Roc de Combe is too scanty to characterize; at El Pendo, it is described as "archaic" ("Aurignacian 0"), and at Le Piage, it is like Aurignacian I, but lacks the split-base points, and in one case (K), has many Dufour bladelets.

The stratigraphic information strongly suggests that both the Aurignacian and the Châtelperronian postdate the Mousterian, and further that Aurignacian assemblages are *generally* more recent than Châtelperronian ones. It may be that fully-fledged classic Aurignacian I levels always postdate Châtelperronian ones.

Radiocarbon Chronology

The radiocarbon dates relevant to the Middle-Upper Paleolithic transition in our region of concern, listed in Table 1, are fewer than might be expected four decades after the development of the method. But the use of this method in European Paleolithic contexts developed slowly, and the period under scrutiny is so near its extreme range, that problems of contamination loom large (see Mellars *et al.* 1987).

In any event, the overall pattern visible in Table 1 is similar to that just noted. There is some overlap in the error ranges of dates among the three industries, but that between the two early Upper Paleolithic industries is far greater. The dates are consistent with a Mousterian-Châtelperronian-Aurignacian sequence, with the latter two clearly overlapping. Whether the Mousterian in this geographic sphere actually temporally overlaps with the early Upper Paleolithic is not yet clear on the basis of radiocarbon dates.

Table 1. Radiocarbon dates for Châtelperronian and other relevant contexts. Dates are excluded which are merely minima (e.g. >35,000) or dubious due to contamination or other causes, or without available documentation. Designations following site names indicate layer numbers. The dates are derived from the following sources: (1) Vogel and Waterbolk 1967; (2) Delibrias and Evin 1980; (3) Moure Romanillo and Garcia Soto 1983; (4) Vogel and Waterbolk 1963; (5) Stuckenrath 1978; (6) Delibrias 1984; (7) Mellars *et al.* 1987.

Provenience	Years BP	Sample Reference	Source
Mousterian (Youngest dates)			
La Rochette 7	36,000±500	GrN-6362	(1)
La Quina, Final Mousterian	35,250±530	GrN-2526	(1)
	34,100±700	GrN-4494	(1)
Les Cottés I	37,600±700	GrN-4421	(1)
Renne (Arcy) XXI	34,600±850	GrN-4217	(1)
Camiac	$35,100^{+2000}_{-1500}$	Ly-1104	(2)
Cueva Millan (Burgos, Spain) Ia	37,600±700	GrN-11021	(3)
Châtelperronian			
Renne (Arcy) VIII	33,500±400	GrN-1736	(4)
	33,860±250	GrN-1742	(4)
Les Cottés G	33,300±500	GrN-4333	(1)
Cueva Morín 10	36,950±6777	SI-951	(5)
Basal Aurignacian			
Abri Pataud 14	34,250±675	GrN-4507	(1)
	33,330±410	GrN-4720	(1)
	33,300±760	GrN-4610	(1)
Abri Pataud 12	33,000±500	GrN-4327	(1)
Early Aurignacian			
Cueva Morín 8a	28,435±556	SI-952	(6)
	28,155±757	SI-952A	(6)
	28,515±1324	SI-956	(6)
Aurignacian I			
Abri Pataud 11	32,600±550	GrN-4309	(1)
	32,000±800	GrN-4326	(1)
La Ferrassie K6	33,200±800	GrN-5751	(6)
La Quina, I	31,400±350	GrN-1493	(4)
Les Cottés I	30,800±500	GrN-4258	(1)
	31,000±320	GrN-4296	(1)
	31,200±410	GrN-4509	(1)
Cueva Morín 7	29,515±865	SS-955	(6)
	28,055±1535	SI-955A	(6)
Cueva Morín 7/6	32,415±901	SI-954	(6)
Other Aurignacian			
Le Flageolet XI	33,800±1800	OxA-598	(7)
La Ferrassie K4	31,300±300	GiF-4277	(6)
	28,000±1050	OxA-409	(7)

Chronostratigraphic Frameworks

As outlined in Table 2, pollen- and lithostratigraphic frameworks, especially those of Laville, Butzer, and Leroi-Gourhan, can be integrated with radiocarbon chronologies to produce a series of dated climatic periods to which many archaeological levels can be assigned, allowing for seriation of many sites which lack radiocarbon dates. The suggested correlations in Table 2 are tentative, but what is particularly noteworthy here is the broad convergence of results from

Table 2. Chronostratigraphic context of early Upper Palaeolithic industries in France and Cantabria.

Years BP (approx)	Climate	Phase Designations	Périgord Sites (After Laville 1975; Laville et al. 1980; Laville and Tuffreau 1984)	Other French Sites (after Leroyer & Leroi-Gourhan 1984 Lévêque & Misovsky 1983; Mazière & Raynal 1983; Laville 1976)	Cantabrian Sites (after Butzer 1981, 1986)
30,000	Temperate	Würm III, Phase III, Arcy Interstadial	*Aurignacian I, II, "evolué"*	*Aurignacial I, II, "evolué"*	Unit 33: *Aurignacian I* Morín VI, VII El Pendo VII La Flecha
31,500	Cold	Würm III, Phase II	*Aurignacian I & II:* La Ferrassie K4,5,6 Roc de Combe 7,6 (base) Le Piage F Caminade-Est G,F Pataud 12,11? Fonte-de-Gaume 3	*Châtelperronian:* Arcy (Renne) VIII *Aurignacian:* St. Césaire 5 Cottés E. inf.? (Aur. I) Gatzarria Cf (Aur. I) Grotte du Loup	Unit 32: *Aurignacian I* Morín VIII (Aur. "O") La Flecha (Aur. I)
33,000	Fluctuating Unstable	Würm III, Phase I	*Châtelperronian:* La Ferrassie L3A? Roc de Combe 10,8 Le Piage F1 La Chèvre 18-15 Font-de-Gaume 4-5 *Aurignacian:* Roc de Combe 7 (Aur. I),9 Le Piage G-I,J,K Pataud 14,13? LaChèvre 14 (Aur. I) Flageolet XI (?)	Arcy (Renne) IX Grotte du Loup 5,4 Les Cottés G Châtelperron B La Quina 4 Tambourets? Gatzarria Cj? Basté 3bm?' *Aurignacian:* St.-Césaire 6? Gatzarria Cj?	Unit 31: *Châtelperronian:* El Pendo VII *Aurignacian "O"* El Pendo VIIIa Morín IX Unit 30: *Chatelperronian:* Morín X *Aurignacian "O"* El Pendo VIIIb
34,500	Temperate	*Interstadial:* Würm II/III Cottés, Hengelo	? (Deposits typically removed by erosion) La Ferrassie L3b?	*Châtelperronian:* Arcy (Renne) X Grand-Roche Eg,En St.-Césaire 8,9	Unit 29: Mousterian: Morín XI (Denticulate)
37,000 to 40,000	Cold	End of Würm II Stadial (Laville); Unit 28 (Butzer)	Mousterian: MAT and Typical at Combe-Grenal MAT (?) at Pech de l'Azé I	Mousterian, including "Post-Mousterian" at Arcy-sur-Cure, Quina at Les Cottés?	Unit 28: Mousterian Morín XII (Denticulate) El Pendo VIIId (Denticulate)

Note: Grande-Roche Em, Ei, and La Côte III are assigned to Phase 1 and/or Phase 2 of Würm III.

different areas by workers in both palynology and geomorphology.

The patterning apparent in Table 2 is consonant with that derived from the data sources already mentioned; the Mousterian in any one area is succeeded by the Upper Paleolithic, with little or no temporal overlap, while the Aurignacian succeeds the Châtelperronian with a distinct overlap.

It is important to point out that the contemporaneity of assemblages assigned to the same units in Table 2 is very rough (within blocks of about 1500 years), but the best that can be done at present. A number of observations are worth noting:

1. The Mousterian apparently persisted in Cantabria later than elsewhere, into the "Würm II/III" (or Cottés/Hengelo)

Interstadial. However, as elsewhere, it is not known to have overlapped with the Châtelperronian there.

2. Several Châtelperronian levels are now dated to the Würm II/III Interstadial. With one possible exception [5], no Châtelperronian occurrences are yet reported from this interstadial from the Périgord, the richest Franco-Cantabrian prehistoric province; according to Laville, heavy erosion at the close of the interstadial typically destroyed whatever deposits may have accumulated during it.

3. In contrast, no Aurignacian occupations in our region of interest are known to date to the Würm II/III, although the Aurignacian is found at this time to the southeast in Languedoc (Leroyer and Leroi-Gourhan 1983).

4. Most Châtelperronian occupations date to the cool, fluctuating period identified by Laville as Phase I of the Würm III stadial. However, this industry persists in its northern periphery (at Arcy-sur-Cure) into the period equivalent to Laville's Phase II.

When these successive industrial replacements are considered from a geographical perspective, clear spatial-temporal patterning is apparent, as Leroyer and Leroi-Gourhan (1983) have suggested—despite the crudeness and shortcomings of our dating methods, and the small numbers of sites involved (see Figures 5-7).

At the end of the cold Würm II stadial, only Mousterian occupations are known in our area of interest. Then, during the succeeding interstadial (see Fig. 5), we find Mousterian on the periphery (Cantabria), Châtelperronian in the center and north (with uncertain developments in the Périgord)—and, just outside our sphere, archaic Aurignacian reported to the southeast in Languedoc. During the ensuing phase of fluctuating climate (see Fig. 6), numerous Châtelperronian levels are found throughout the sphere, while early Aurignacian occupations are found in its southern and central parts; overlapping distribution and interstratification of the two industries occur. Then, in the following cold phase (see Fig. 7), only Aurignacian levels are found, save for Châtelperronian in the northern periphery. Thereafter the Châtelperronian disappears, while the Aurignacian persists for several millennia.

In sum, various lines of evidence suggest that the Mousterian in our area of interest was replaced, to all appearan-

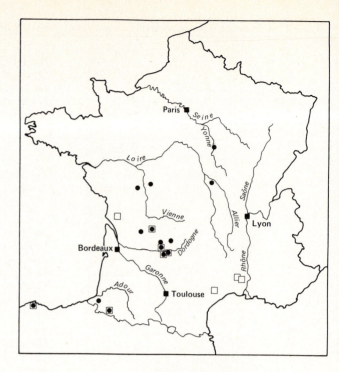

- ● Chatelperronian
- □ Aurignacian

Figure 6. *Distribution of dated Châtelperronian and Aurignacian sites during Laville's Würm III, Phase I.*

ces rather abruptly, by the Châtelperronian, which co-existed with the Aurignacian before giving way to it. Furthermore, spatial distribution of adequately dated sites suggests that the gradual replacement of the Châtelperronian by the Aurignacian was time-transgressive, from the south and east toward the north and west.

ARTIFACTUAL CONTINUITY AND DISCONTINUITY

Mousterian and Châtelperronian

We will here consider continuities and discontinuities between these artifacts associated with these industries, as found in my own examination of Châtelperronian and some Mousterian assemblages, and in the available literature. First, we will consider stone tools.

Lithic Artifacts

One striking Middle-Upper Paleolithic contrast is in respect to blank-production methods—i.e., the common occurrence of blades. Of course, ordinary flakes, and the discoid or irregular cores to produce them, continue to be found right through the Upper Paleolithic.

Strictly speaking, a blade is flake twice as long as it is wide, and one can produce a blade without necessarily trying—certainly without a specialized blade core. But Upper Paleolithic assemblages are generally characterized by numerous blades struck (though not necessarily punch-struck) from prismatic cores. The Châtelperronian is no exception in this wise; the 14 sizeable assemblages which I

Figure 5. *Distribution of dated Mousterian, Châtelperronian and Aurignacian sites during Würm II/III (= Hengelo/Cottés) Interstadial.*

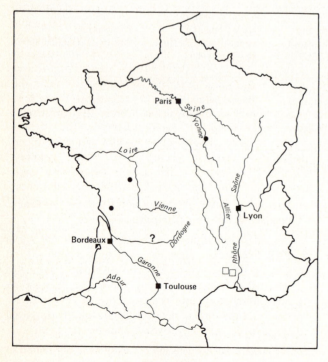

- ▲ Mousterian
- ● Chatelperronian
- □ Aurignacian

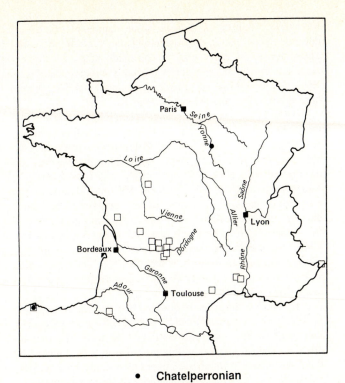

Chatelperronian
Aurignacian

Figure 7. *Distribution of dated Châtelperronian and Aurignacian sites during Laville's Würm III, Phase II.*

examined (see Table 3 for list) were characterized by a laminar or blade index, (I Lam), for retouched tools, ranging from 39.3 (i.e., 39.3% of tools were on blades) to 87.2, with a mean of 57.7; most of these blades had the parallel flake scar ridges characteristic of prismatic cores.

Unfortunately, systematic studies of Mousterian and Châtelperronian assemblages in terms of lithic reduction practices are quite rare. Exactly how many of these blades are produced from prismatic cores is not known, although it is my impression that such "true" blades are the rule in the Châtelperronian and very rare in the Mousterian.

Turning to the Mousterian, one finds that the laminar index is often unreported in assemblage descriptions. What data were available, though, show that blades, broadly defined, are indeed far less common than in the Upper Paleolithic. Data for 35 Mousterian assemblages from 11 sites [6] indicate a mean I Lam of 13.3, and a range from 0 to 35.5. This latter peak figure (at Goderville, *série mate*) is still lower than that of any Châtelperronian assemblage which I examined. And the Mousterian sample used here may be somewhat biased toward a high I Lam, in that collections are well-represented from two contexts unusually rich in blades—the loess deposits of the Paris basin (four assemblages), and the Grotte de l'Hyène and Grotte du Renne at Arcy-sur-Cure (eleven) assemblages [7]. Furthermore, in all these Mousterian cases, published illustrations of blades struck from Upper Paleolithic-style prismatic cores were quite rare.

It is also worth noting that these data provide no support for the notion that the *late* Mousterian tended toward higher blade production. Most of these Mousterian assemblages are not datable more precisely than as "Last Glacial;" but those

which are better dated (at Pech de l'Azé, Combe-Grenal, Le Moustier, Grotte du Renne, and El Pendo) show no temporal trend toward a higher laminar index. In the Pech de l'Azé, Arcy-sur-Cure, and El Pendo cases, superimposed series of assemblages likewise fail to exhibit such a trend.

Technologically, then, there is continuity in basic flake production methods between Mousterian and Châtelperronian, but also a notable discontinuity in the importance and regularity of blade production. Further work, however, is needed to clarify the nature of this technical contrast.

Châtelperronian-Mousterian lithic artifact comparisons can also be made in terms of the morphology of retouched tools—i.e., typologically. Two questions arise here. First, is the Châtelperronian in fact characterized by greater formal variability than the Mousterian? And second, is there a discernible trend in the late Mousterian toward more Châtelperronian-like typology?

In dealing with the first question, an immediately apparent problem is that direct interassemblage comparisons are difficult; different typologies are used to describe Middle Paleolithic (Bordes 1961b) and Upper Paleolithic (Sonneville-Bordes and Perrot 1954-55) assemblages [8].

A minor exception to this disjunction came about during my study of Châtelperronian assemblages some years ago (Harrold 1978), when I classified four Mousterian collections in the Upper Paleolithic typology. The four—Goderville *série mate* and *série lustrée*, and Pech de l'Azé levels B and 7—were chosen as assemblages which Bordes had described as evolved MAT (or in the case of Goderville *mate*, incipient Châtelperronian). It seemed that if any Mousterian collections should show typological continuity with the Châtelperronian, these should.

However, I found very little resemblance at all. The Mousterian assemblages did not fit well into the Sonneville-Bordes-Perrot system, exhibiting high proportions of "divers" (i.e., unclassifiable) tools. Furthermore, overall assemblage typological diversity was notably lower for these Mousterian assemblages than in the Châtelperronian. On the average, their tools fell into only 14 Upper Paleolithic types, versus a mean of 33.6 types for 14 Châtelperronian collections (see Table 3) [9]. The four Mousterian assemblages are of course too few to constitute a definitive sample, but this result is consistent with other sources of typological information.

A similar conclusion can be drawn within the confines of the Middle Paleolithic typology itself. Bordes' typological "Group III," includes the "Upper Paleolithic" types: endscrapers, burins, perforators, backed knives, and truncated pieces (types nos. 30-37 and 40). This group rarely exceeds 15% in Mousterian assemblages, even in the MAT, putatively ancestral to the Châtelperronian. For instance, the eight MAT assemblages from Pech de l'Azé I range in Group III percentage from 4.9 to 15.8. The great majority of these tools are made on typically Mousterian flakes, and while most would be recognized in the Upper Paleolithic typology, they would with very few exceptions be "atypical" examples.

I also typed 11 Châtelperronian assemblages in the Middle Paleolithic typology (those listed in Table 3, less La Chèvre 2 and 2a). Again, results were anomalous; these were unlike any Mousterian collections. Type lists were dominated by Bordes' Group III, which averaged 59.8% of all tools, and by unclassifiable pieces ("Divers").

Table 3. Assemblage diversity: number of Sonneville-Bordes/Perrot types represented.

	Mean No. of Types Represented	Range	Mean Assemblage Size
Mousterian [1] (4 assemblages)	14.0	10–21	121.5 tools
Châtelperronian [2] (14 assemblages)	33.6	23–42	281.8 tools [3]
Early Aurignacian [4] (13 assemblages)	42.1	32–54	617.6 tools

Notes:

1. Peche de l'Azé B and 7, Goderville *série mate* and *série lustrée*.

2. Roc de Combe 8, Le Piage F1, La Chèvre 1, 1a, 2, 2a, La Côte III, Grotte du Loup 4, 5, Basté 3bm, Tambourets (1973 excavation only), Cottés G, Châtelperron B, Morín 10. For bibliographic and other details see Harrold 1978, 1981, 1986.

3. When two large assemblages from the Grotte du Renne at Arcy-sur-Cure (Xb and Xc) are included (Farizy and Schmider 1985), this figure rises to 415.6. However, the number of types represented in these assemblages is unreported.

4. These are assemblages climatostratigraphically contemporary with the Châtelperronian, with typological information available: Le Piage K, J, G-I, F (Champagne and Espitalié 1981), La Chèvre 3 (Jude and Arambourou 1964), Caminade-Est G, F (Sonneville-Bordes 1970), Cottés E (Pradel 1961), La Ferrasie K6, K5, K4 (Delporte 1984), Morín 9 (González Echegaray and Freeman 1978), Pendo VIIIa (González Echegaray 1980).

Thus considerable overall typological discontinuity can be found between the Châtelperronian and Mousterian. But to go back to the second question raised above, is there evidence of change over time in the late Mousterian in a Châtelperronian direction?

One obstacle to a satisfactory answer to this question is the poor dating of many Mousterian assemblages. However, those in stratigraphically superimposed sequences, or which have been dated chronostratigraphically by Laville (1975), do not show such vectorial change. The latest Mousterian assemblages at Combe-Grenal, Pech de l'Azé I, and Le Moustier, for instance, are not particularly "evolved," while the four Mousterian assemblages mentioned above (examined because of their putatively evolved status) are all now known to date from the middle part of the Würm II stadial, not its end. Leroi-Gourhan and Leroi-Gourhan (1964) mention an evolved "Post-Mousterian" at the Grotte du Renne, underlying the Châtelperronian there. But this has been described in detail by Girard (1980) as "Denticulate Mousterian."

What about claimed "transitional" assemblages, those with characteristics intermediate between Mousterian and Châtelperronian which would demonstrate typological continuity? The classic, supposedly transitional assemblages (La Ferrassie E and Le Moustier K) are now known to be artificial mixtures.

Another assemblage needs to be mentioned, deriving from Delporte's re-excavation of La Ferrassie (Delporte 1984). The assemblage, from level L3b, has 200 retouched tools, and seems indeed to involve a mixture of Middle and Upper Paleolithic types and technology (Tuffreau 1984). However, it derives from a site where cryoturbation is known to have disturbed deposits dug by Peyrony. Several of the sidescrapers which I saw in a brief look at this assemblage carried Quina or demi-Quina retouch, like those from the underlying Charentian (Ferrassie)

Mousterian; this could indicate some degree of mixture of deposits. Nonetheless, this assemblage is clearly the best candidate yet for an industry of "transitional" status. Finally, excavations by Rigaud and Simek currently underway at Grotte XVI (Dordogne) may have located a transitional assemblage; here again, fuller details must be awaited.

The claim for vectorial change is sometimes extended into the Châtelperronian from the Mousterian; Châtelperronian assemblages with more Middle Paleolithic types such as sidescrapers and denticulates, or cruder handiwork, are described as early (only recently emerged from the Mousterian), while those with long, well-made blades and/or few sidescrapers are assumed to be "evolved." As I have detailed elsewhere, this assumption is not consistently upheld by available dating evidence (Harrold 1981: 32-35). At two multicomponent Châtelperronian sites (Grotte du Renne and Grande-Roche), for instance, the youngest Châtelperronian levels are the most "primitive" (or "regressive") in typological technological terms.

In sum, a picture of abrupt, rather than gradual and additive lithic change seems warranted by the available data. Of course, there *was* significant lithic continuity between the two industries. The Middle Paleolithic provided a technological and typological base to which the Upper Paleolithic added; and this base included the irregular appearance of forms which were to which were to become standardized and elaborated later on. But insofar as we can tell, the late Mousterian cannot be described as "evolving" in a Châtelperronian or Upper Paleolithic direction in our area of interest.

More geographically-circumscribed elements of continuity across the Middle-Upper Paleolithic transition have been pointed to; the continuing emphasis on notches and denticulates in Cantabria, for instance, and the persistence of small "pediform" sidescrapers at Arcy-sur-Cure (Leroi-Gourhan 1968). However, other explanations besides persistent, traditionally-transmitted craft norms are plausible here, including the demands of local raw material (which in both these cases is not very good). Detailed studies of these assemblages would be necessary to test competing explanations.

Bone Artifacts

We will consider here utilitarian items of antler and ivory as well as bone.

Bone was utilized and modified in the Mousterian, but usually without extensive shaping. Bones were broken, and sometimes flaked in a manner analogous to stone tools. Because the resultant items may be very difficult to distinguish from those gnawed by animals, there is strong disagreement over just how common this practice was (e.g., Binford 1982, 1983; Freeman 1983). Bone was also very occasionally shaped into recognizable forms such as punches and, rarely, "wands" or *baguettes* which resemble some of those encountered in Upper Paleolithic sites. Several sites, generally in Charente and Vienne, have yielded a number of such pieces (e.g., Debénath and Duport 1971; Pradel and Pradel 1954). However, Mousterian bone tools can broadly be characterized as unstandardized, and sporadic in occurrence.

In the Châtelperronian, by contrast, bone tools are far more numerous (cf. the discussion below of Châtelperronian and Aurignacian bonework, and Table 7). They make common use of Upper Paleolithic boneworking techniques, such as groove-and-splinter extraction, whittling, and polishing, and appear in the usual forms, including *poinçons*, points, *lissoirs*, and *baguettes*.

Overall, the Mousterian-Châtelperronian contrast is greater with regard to bone tools than for lithic ones. Perhaps because the bone artifact record is much less rich than the lithic one in both industries, no hint of a "transitional" bone tool assemblage is found.

Artifacts of Symbolic Significance

This class includes such categories as incised bone and stone, decorative items (e.g. pierced teeth), coloring materials, and figurative art. All seem to involve the imposition of arbitrary form on objects for non-utilitarian purposes.

First let us consider incised bones, i.e. those carrying incisions made by stone tools which are apparently not due to butchering, skinning, or tool manufacture. The term "apparently" should be emphasized here, for to my knowledge, we lack controlled experimental studies, of the sort profitably applied to Plio-Pleistocene African assemblages (e.g., Potts 1984), to determine reliably the agents and processes which produced marks on Middle and Upper Paleolithic bone.

However, careful observers have noted on both Middle and Upper Paleolithic bone examples of incisions without apparent utilitarian causes. Such marks are usually linear and grouped ("marques de chasse"), and most often short. They may be roughly parallel, or arranged in intersecting patterns, even in crude chevrons. Sometimes they are quite wide and deep. These marks occur occasionally in Mousterian sites, generally those which also furnish bone tools. Debénath and Duport (1971) report six such pieces from three sites in the Charente; several others are also known from L'Ermitage (Pradel and Pradel 1954), La Quina (Camps-Fabrer 1976), and La Ferrassie (Peyrony 1934).

Quite comparable items are found in the Châtelperronian, sometimes additionally carrying punctate and curvilinear marks. Incised stones, unreported from the Mousterian, are also known from the Grotte du Renne (Leroi-Gourhan 1976) and Grotte du Loup (White 1986:108) (see Table 8 and further discussion below regarding the Aurignacian).

Items of adornment, typically pierced or grooved for suspension, constitute a category whose existence in the Mousterian has not yet been established beyond a reasonable doubt (Mellars 1973; White 1982). The only reported examples are a pierced tooth and a pierced reindeer phalange from the early excavations at La Quina (Henri-Martin 1907-1910:130-139)), and perhaps the fragment of pierced bone from Pech de l'Azé II (Bordes 1969)—which may also be a utilitarian object.

Such artifacts are notably more common in the Châtelperronian, where four sites have yielded pierced or grooved teeth, two more, bone pendants, and another a piece of stalactite grooved for suspension (see Table 8).

Fragments of coloring materials—red and yellow ocher (iron oxide in various forms), and manganese—are not uncommon in the Mousterian (Wreschner 1980). They sometimes show scratches and polish from application to various surfaces (Bordes 1972b:92-95). These materials are very frequently found in the Châtelperronian, in at least 10 sites; and another (Roche-au-Loup, Yonne; Poplin 1986) has produced a fragment

of galena, which can be ground to produce a coloring material. From several sites, ocher is reported in prodigious quantities which deeply stain the sediments. At the Grotte du Renne, fire had been used to achieve color variations in the ocher, ranging from red to violet (Leroi-Gourhan 1976).

We might also mention that in both Mousterian and Châtelperronian sites, occasional "curios" are also found—fossils, pyrites, and concretions, apparently collected because of their unusual appearance.

No examples of figurative art are known from either Mousterian or Châtelperronian contexts.

Human Remains

In view of the impressive overall contrasts in complexity between Middle and Upper Paleolithic burials (Harrold 1980), a comparison of mortuary features between the Mousterian and Châtelperronian would be of great interest. Unfortunately, no burials are known from the Châtelperronian. The intentionally-buried anatomically-modern man from Combe-Capelle may or may not derive the Châtelperronian level there (Harrold 1978:252-58); and there is no published indication that the Neanderthal individual from Saint-Césaire represents a burial. The only other human remains known from Châtelperronian contexts are several teeth, large but undiagnostic, from the Grotte du Renne (Leroi-Gourhan 1959), and a sole undescribed tooth from Font-de-Gaume (Prat and Sonneville-Bordes 1969). However, available remains do indicate one strong element of continuity between the Mousterian and Châtelperronian; so far as we know, both are associated in our region of interest only with *Homo sapiens neanderthalensis*.

Conclusions

We can see important elements of continuity between the Mousterian and Châtelperronian. In stone tools, there is a common fund of flake production methods, and types such as sidescrapers and denticulates (and perhaps highly localized types) persist across the Middle-Upper Paleolithic transition. There is also the occurrence in both industries of simple bone tools, incised bones, coloring materials, and curios. Neither tradition is known to be associated with figurative art, and both are associated with Neanderthal man.

On the other hand, important discontinuities are apparent. Blade technology is important in the Châtelperronian, and numerous standardized Upper Paleolithic types such as Chatelperron points dominate its assemblages. New techniques and new tool forms also revolutionized bone-working, which was clearly more frequent in the Châtelperronian. Items of adornment, which had been extremely rare at best, became fairly common—and occasional traces of other "new" nonutilitarian behavior are found, such as incised stone plaques and burned ocher.

These discontinuities are notable, and they show no indication of having developed gradually in the late Mousterian. They appear, as far as we can now tell, abruptly in the archaeological record. Transitional assemblages remain elusive; the most economical explanation is that the transitional period was brief. To return to the three hypotheses concerning the Mousterian-Châtelperronian relationship put forward above, I would suggest that the third hypothesis best squares with the current evidence. Considering the important roles for both continuity and abrupt change which we have seen, as well as the early appearance of the Aurignacian in Languedoc and its gradual spread to the north and west, and the association of both Mousterian and Châtelperronian with Neanderthals, it seems most likely that the Châtelperronian represents an indigenous development of the Mousterian under the impact of diffusion and probably migration. For reasons given above this inference is tentative, but it represents a "best fit" to available evidence.

Châtelperronian and Aurignacian

In this section artifactual continuities and contrasts will be reviewed for these two early Upper Paleolithic industries in light of the hypotheses noted above concerning the nature of their relationship.

Lithic Artifacts

Let us first consider technological comparison. In terms of blank production technology, both industries are broadly characterized by blades, but more detailed information on, for example laminar indices of early Aurignacian assemblages, is difficult to obtain. As noted above for the Mousterian, this information is often not included in the literature. Laminar indices for four early Aurignacian collections were found: 39.7 for level Cbf (Aurignacian I?) at Gatzarria, and respectively, 35.3 and 48.1 for levels Cjn1 and Cjn2 ("Protoaurignacian") at the same site (Lévêque 1966); and 23.8 at El Pendo VIIIa (González Echegaray 1980). This sample is too small to be more than suggestive, but its mean index of 36.7 is actually lower than the Châtelperronian mean of 57.7.

Other indications of the importance of early Aurignacian blade technology are available from information from Sonneville-Bordes' (1960) synthesis of the Upper Paleolithic of the Périgord. In it are found percentages of blades, not among retouched tools, but among unretouched artifacts, for nine Aurignacian "0" or I assemblages [10]. It must be stressed that most of these assemblages are from old excavations and are not necessarily representative samples; furthermore, few are well-dated, either relative to the Châtelperronian, or absolutely. Thus they can be at most suggestive. Reported percentages of blades and bladelets among unretouched pieces ranged from 28.8 to 78.8, with a mean of 63.2, not far from the Châtelperronian mean of 57.7 for retouched tools.

Finally, data on cores are available for the same nine collections. Prismatic blade cores totalled between 0% and 56% of all cores in each collection (the mean is 29.8%). The comparable figures for nine Châtelperronian assemblages—from generally more recent excavations—is a range of 35.8% to 75% and a mean of 55.3%.

Not too much can be inferred from these various indicators, but there is so far no indication that early Aurignacian assemblages were more heavily laminar than Châtelperronian ones.

Another technological variable that should be considered here is an oft-noted characteristic of the Aurignacian, the distinctive scalar "Aurignacian" retouch. Since the occurrence of this retouch was incorporated into several type definitions in the Upper Paleolithic typology (e.g. no. 6, endscrapers on blades with Aurignacian retouch), details on differential occurrence of this mode of retouch will be found below in the discussion of typological differences. Suffice it to note here that such retouch is of variable frequency in Aurignacian assemblages, but almost utterly lacking in the Châtelperronian.

It is in regard to Aurignacian retouch that we will briefly discuss a question of direct Mousterian-Aurignacian comparison. This paper has not been organized in terms of such comparisons, because only rarely have the two industries been likened to each other. Each has been seen universally as having more points of comparison with the Châtelperronian than with the other. It has occasionally been suggested, though, that the similarity between Aurignacian retouch and Quina retouch could betoken an evolution of the Aurignacian from the Quina Mousterian, analogous to the putative evolution of the Châtelperronian from the MAT (e.g., Laville, Rigaud and Sackett 1980: 267).

However, this notion has never been seriously pursued. Aurignacian retouch is described by Sonneville-Bordes (1960:808) as "écailleuse," or scalar, with broad and overlapping flake scars. Bordes (1961b:8) characterized Quina retouch as "en écaille scalariforme," or scalar and scalariform (stair-step), noting that Quina scrapers are typically on thick flakes with the retouch giving a stair-step profile. However, scalariform retouch on thick pieces is not characteristic of Aurignacian retouch. Comparative study establishing a close degree of similarity between these two modes of retouch would be needed before Aurignacian-Quina connections can be entertained.

Turning to typological comparisons between the two industries, the comparative data base is richer here; Aurignacian assemblages described in the Sonneville-Bordes-Perrot system abound, and 14 Châtelperronian assemblages of adequate sample size (Harrold 1983) can be compared to them. The exact choice of Aurignacian assemblages, however, was a problem. Many, of course, are from old excavations, with serious questions concerning sample bias and stratigraphic integrity. Many others lack these problems, but are not either yet well-dated, or are known to postdate the Châtelperronian. I eventually chose 13 Early Aurignacian assemblages (listed in Table 3) with adequate credentials of provenience and sample size, which have been fitted into the chronostratigraphic framework outlined in Table 2, and found to be broadly contemporary with the local Châtelperronian. Those definitely postdating the Châtelperronian, such as those from Laville's Phase III or IV of Würm III, were excluded. This process reduced sample size, but had the advantage of eliminating Châtelperronian-Aurignacian contrasts which might be due to developments arising after the disappearance of the Châtelperronian.

Various measures of assemblage variability can be used to compare these two traditions. We may first look at assemblage diversity, as measured by numbers of tool types in each assemblage of retouched implements (Table 3). The Aurignacian assemblages have on the average 8.5 more tool types than the Châtelperronian ones (42.1 to 33.6); however, their mean assemblage size is also far greater. Given the positive relationship between assemblage size and diversity, is this difference a real one? If we consider only those eight Aurignacian assemblages with sizes in the same range as the Châtelperronian ones (89-583 tools), the mean number of types is reduced to 37.6, closer to the Châtelperronian mean, but still greater.

A summary measure of typological contrast between the two industries involves the typological groups devised by

Table 4. Summary statistics for Châtelperronian and Early Aurignacian assemblages. For details of the assemblages, see Table 3.

GA = Aurignacian Group (Sonneville-Bordes-Perrot Types 4, 6, 11–13, 32, 67, 68)
GP = Périgordian Group (Types 45–64, 85–87)
GM = "Mousterian Group" (Types 74, 75, 77) (after Harrold 1978)

		GA (%)	GP (%)	GM (%)
For 14 Châtelperronian Assemblages	Mean	2.6	31.8	20.6
	Range	(0–7.2)	(7.5–55.8)	(5.1–39.5)
For 13 Early Aurignacian Assemblages	Mean	19.8	3.8	12.0
	Range	(11.8–41.7)	(0.1–8.5)	(1.5–39.1)
For 13 *French* Châtelperronian Assemblages only	Mean	2.3	33.7	19.3
	Range	(0–7.2)	(14.5–55.8)	(5.1–39.5)
For 11 *French* Early Aurignacian Assemblages only	Mean	20.9	3.4	8.2
	Range	(13.4–41.7)	(0.1–8.0)	(1.5–19.0)

Sonneville-Bordes to total implements considered characteristic of each. The GA (*Groupe Aurignacien*) is an index totalling percentages of Aurignacian endscrapers and blades, keeled and nosed scrapers, and busked burins. The GP (*Groupe Périgordien*) includes primarily backed and truncated pieces, as well as some Upper Périgordian fossil directors which we may ignore here, since they are not found in the Châtelperronian. To this can be added a Mousterian group ("GM"; Harrold 1978), totalling the percentages of sidescrapers, notches and denticulates.

Table 4 shows that there is considerable variability in these indices within each industry, but that in the GA there are strong mean differences between Châtelperronian and Aurignacian, and no overlap at all; in the GP, very strong mean differences, and a bare overlap; and in the GM, moderate differences and a great overlap. Leaving aside the GM, then, the two groups differ notably in frequency in the two industries. Interestingly, if we temporarily remove the Cantabrian assemblages from consideration, Châtelperronian-Aurignacian contrasts become sharper (Table 4). In particular, there is no longer an overlap in the GP between them. The two industries are less clearly dif-

ferentiated from each other in Cantabria; this seems to be a general feature of the Upper Paleolithic in that region (Clark and Straus 1983; Butzer 1986).

Let us look in more detail at the individual fossil director types associated with each industry, and their occurrence in the Châtelperronian and Aurignacian. Table 5 displays the mean frequencies and ranges of Aurignacian fossil directors in both Aurignacian and Châtelperronian assemblages. Interestingly, most of these occur in rather modest frequencies in the Aurignacian, and some only occasionally (notably Font-Yves points). Just as interestingly, several of them, such as keeled scrapers, occur in some Châtelperronian collections, though never in great numbers. Aurignacian scrapers, however, are found in only one Châtelperronian assemblage, and Aurignacian blades, strangulated blades, and Font-Yves bladelets are never found. It is noteworthy that among the three types characterized by Aurignacian retouch (Nos. 6, 67, 68), exactly four examples of only one type are known from 14 Châtelperronian assemblages—and those are from a level (Le Piage F1) sandwiched between two Aurignacian levels. Given what is known about mixing of materials from different levels which can occur in sites (e.g., Villa 1982), one can agree with Sonneville-Bordes (1980a:117) that some characteristic Aurignacian tools with a particular retouch technique do *not* occur in the Châtelperronian.

Table 6 examines occurrences of types claimed as characteristic of the Châtelperronian. Truncated blades are fairly common in the Aurignacian, but Châtelperron points and backed blades are so rare that their occurrence may again be due to mixing. Furthermore, these are types characterized by a particular retouch technique, that of steep backing.

In opposition to Ashton's (1983) claim that Aurignacian-Châtelperronian typological differences are simply those of frequency variation, I agree with Rigaud (1982:381) that the very rare occurrence in one industry of characteristic types

Table 5. Aurignacian fossil directors in Early Upper Palaeolithic assemblages. (See Table 3 for list of assemblages.)

	13 Early Aurignacian Assemblages			14 Châtelperronian Assemblages		
	Mean Frequency	Range	Occurring in Assemblages	Mean Frequency	Range	Occurring in Assemblages
Endscrapers on Aurignacian blades (Sonneville-Bordes-Perrot Type 6)	3.0%	0.5–8.1%	13	0.2%	0–2.9%	1
Keeled scrapers (Type 11-12)	5.0%	1.4–11.6%	13	0.8%	0–2.2%	8
Nosed scrapers (Type 13-14)	7.4%	1.8–27.3%	13	1.6%	0–6.2%	6
Busked burins (Type 32)	0.6%	0–1.2%	11	0.1%	0–0.4%	2
Font-Yves points (Type 52)	0.2%	0–2.5%	1	0	0	0
Aurignacian blades (Type 67)	4.4%	0.4–17.9%	13	0	0	0
Strangulated blades (Type 68)	0.5%	0–2.4%	8	0	0	0
Dufour bladelets (Type 90)	2.6%	0–21.3%	8	0.3%	0–1.4%	4

Table 6. Occurrence of Châtelperronian fossil directors in Early Upper Palaeolithic assemblages. (See Table 3 for list of assemblages.)

	13 Early Aurignacian Assemblages			14 Châtelperronian Assemblages		
	Mean Frequency	Range	Occurring in Assemblages	Mean Frequency	Range	Occurring in Assemblages
Châtelperron Knives (Types 46-47)	0.2%	0–2.2%	3	18.4%	1.9–46.1%	14
Backed blades (Types 58-59)	0.7%	0–5.3%	4	5.3%	0–11.2%	13
Truncated blades (Types 60-64)	2.3%	0.5–5.1%	13	6.7%	2.1–15.4%	14

and retouch forms in the other is insufficient to infer typological continuity.

In sum, Aurignacian lithic assemblages seem to be larger, more typologically diverse, and poorer in "Mousterian types" than Châtelperronian ones. The two industries differ both in relative tool type frequencies, and in the absolute occurrence of a few key fossil directors.

Bone Artifacts

Utilitarian bone industries from Châtelperronian and Early Aurignacian assemblages are compared in Table 7. Information is less than complete, but the overall range and complexity of the two sets of bone assemblages seem quite comparable. It may be noted, however, that while 12 of our 13 Aurignacian assemblages (plus two others) report bone artifacts, only 6 of 14 Châtelperronian ones do—and that furthermore, bone points at least are clearly less numerous in the Châtelperronian (while split-base bone points are lacking entirely).

Despite this difference, none of the Aurignacian bone assemblages in Table 7 is really numerous, while the unquantified information available on the bone industry from the Grotte du Renne describes it as rich. Furthermore, the bone industries of the Aurignacian I and II are described generally as rather poor (e.g., Sonneville-Bordes 1980b:258-59; Rigaud 1982:384).

We do know of some Aurignacian I bone industries in the Périgord which were very abundant, notably at Abri Blanchard and Abri Cellier (Leroy-Prost 1975, 1979; Sonneville-Bordes 1960:98-100, 83-88), and La Ferrassie (Peyrony 1934). Blanchard and La Ferrassie, furthermore, contained examples of a tool type unknown in the Châtelperronian, the pierced baton. Unfortunately, though, dating of these assemblages is still imprecise, and the stratigraphic record of the first two is crude by later standards. Some Aurignacian I levels, at least, have yielded far richer bone assemblages than any Châtelperronian ones; but whether they were contemporary with the Châtelperronian is not yet known. In

any event, the Aurignacian bone industry on current evidence seems to have been somewhat more abundant.

Artifacts of Symbolic Significance

Table 8 compares the distributions of these objects in our two samples. There are problems with imprecise information from sites not yet fully published, but the overall impression is of comparable—and not terribly plentiful—amounts and types in the two industries.

Several points deserve mention in this respect. Pierced teeth are rather numerous in one Aurignacian level (Le Piage G-I); they are also said to be numerous at the Grotte du Renne, however. Also at the Grotte du Renne, Leroi-Gourhan (1967:77) has noted the continuity of a specific type of ornament, the ring-shaped bone pendant, reported from both Châtelperronian and Aurignacian levels there. The frequent and often heavy Châtelperronian use of ocher is reflected in the

Table 7. Early Upper Palaeolithic bone industries. The assemblages correspond with those listed in Table 33, with the addition of Roc de Combe 6 and 7. The sources are as in Table 3, plus Leroy-Prost 1979: 213-214, 365. X = present.

	Points	Poinçons	Lissoirs-Spatulas	Baguettes	Miscellaneous
Early Aurignacian					
Le Piage, K	6	7	1		1
Le Piage, J	6	1			
Le Piage, G-I	10	3		1	9
Le Piage, F	1				
Caminade-Est, G	1(?)				1
Caminade-Est, F	2				2
Cottés, E	3	1		1	X
Trou de la Chèvre, 3	X				
La Ferrassie, K6	X				
La Ferrassie, K5	1				X
La Ferrassie, K4	X	X			X
Roc de Combe, 7				1	
Roc de Combe, 6	7	2		2	
Morín, 9	1				
Châtelperronian					
La Chèvre, 1-2A	1				2
Roc de Combe, 8		4			2
Châtelperron, B		X	X		X
Cottés, G		X			
Grotte du Renne, 9, 10	X	X		X	X
Laussel	X		X		

Table 8. Symbolic/Decorative items in Early Upper Palaeolithic contexts. Sources as in Table 7, plus Poplin 1986; White 1986: 108; Dance 1975; Bouchud 1975. X = Present.

	Incised Bone	Incised Stone	Pendants	Pierced/ Grooved Teeth	Shells	Fossils	Colouring Materials
Early Aurignacian[1]							
Le Piage K				2			
Le Piage J				1			
Le Piage G-I	2			17		2	
Caminade-Est G							X
Caminade-Est F					1		X
Cottés E	3			≥3			X
La Ferrassie K6	1						
La Ferrassie K4	X			1			
Pataud, 14					X[3]		
Pataud, 12						1	
Pataud, 11				2			
Châtelperronian:							
La Chèvre, 1-2a						X	
Roc de Combe 8	2			1			X
Châtelperron B			2	2			X
Cottés G							X
Grotte du Renne, 9, 10	X	1	X	X		X	X
Grotte du Loup, 4, 5		1					X
Grande-Roche				X			
Gargas[2]					1		
Roche-au-Loup (Yonne)							X

[1] Among assemblages listed in Table 1.

[2] Association not certain.

[3] One is pierced for suspension.

table. Also noted is the absence from the table of any items from Cantabrian Spain, although the sample of levels there is small.

As with Table 7, though, Table 8 may reflect an incomplete picture for the Early Aurignacian. Once again, there are some relatively early Aurignacian levels which have yielded some very impressive artifacts in this class; but their exact temporal relationship to the Châtelperronian is unknown. Several sites (Blanchard, Cellier, Lartet) contained numerous bones with patterns of incisions and punctuations more complex than anything represented in Table 8 (Sonneville-Bordes 1960, 1972; Leroi-Gourhan 1967:300; White 1986:92-96, 1989). Some of these pieces have been interpreted as representing complex notational systems (Marshack 1972). A flute of bird bone from Blanchard may come from the Aurignacian I, and beads of stone, bone, and ivory are known from the Vallon des Roches in the Vézère Valley, where Blanchard and Castanet are located (Sonneville-Bordes 1972, pl. 56; White 1986:92-93).

Several examples of figurative art are also reported from Aurignacian I contexts: two sculpted bone pendants from Blanchard and Cellier (White 1986:94, 96), and engravings of apparent vulvas, on stone blocks from Cellier, Blanchard, and Abri du Poisson. There is even indirect evidence for parietal art, in the form of vault fragments bearing traces of paint and/or engraving incorporated into deposits at Castanet and La Ferrassie (Delluc and Delluc 1978).

These items of art and adornment are not on the lavish scale or in the sophisticated style of the Magdalenian, but are more numerous and elaborate than anything the Châtelperronian has to offer, and in the case of figurative art, involve a whole new universe of symbolic expression. Were they known to be contemporary with the Châtelperronian, they would demonstrate a more complex symbolic repertoire—perhaps even enhanced cultural capabilities—on the part of the makers of Aurignacian assemblages relative to their Châtelperronian contemporaries. Without more precise dating, however, it is also possible that these developments (though still impressively early) all postdate the Châtelperronian.

Human Remains

As noted above, the Châtelperronian is associated with Neanderthal remains. None of the Aurignacian assemblages examined here is associated with diagnostic human fossils. However, there is good reason for inferring the association of the Early Aurignacian with anatomically modern humans. First, the modern skeletons from the famous site of Cro-Magnon probably derived from a fairly early Aurignacian (?Aurignacian II) level (Movius 1969). Secondly, five other French sites have yielded modern skeletal remains which were *probably* associated with one stage or another of the Aurignacian (see Gambier, 1989). Finally, the "pseudomorph" burials from Cueva Morín (González Echegaray and Freeman 1978) were almost certainly of modern humans. They derived from levels postdating our Early Aurignacian level 9 at Morín, but which were typologically, like it, Aurignacian "0."

Conclusions

There is clearly considerable continuity or similarity between the material remains of the Aurignacian and Châtelperronian considered here—greater than that between the Mousterian and Châtelperronian. The two industries draw on the same basic repertoire of Upper Paleolithic artifact production techniques and morphologies—blades, endscrapers and burins, and Middle Paleolithic types like sidescrapers. Certain lithic types occur in both industries, but in different proportions. Whether there are subtle differences between the two industries (generally or locally) in the techniques for producing these common types remains to be investigated. Regarding both utilitarian bone artifacts, and those of decorative or artistic nature, the situation is ambiguous. Among contemporary assemblages from the two industries, the available inventories are comparable in both departments, though such artifacts are somewhat more frequent in the Aurignacian. However, the existence of much more numerous and elaborate examples of both these categories in poorly-dated Aurignacian contexts leaves open the possibility of a far more complex Aurignacian development of these aspects of material culture, with important implications for past human behavior and behavioral capacities.

In certain respects, clear artifactual discontinuity obtains between the two industries: in the differential occurrence of steep backing and Aurignacian retouch, and accordingly of several lithic fossil directors, as well as split-base bone points, the two industries are effectively mutually exclusive.

To return to the two hypotheses advanced concerning Châtelperronian-Aurignacian relations, there can be little doubt that the first one, of separate traditions of material culture, better fits the evidence currently available. This is partly because the second, "functional-variant" suggestion has never been developed in detail, and especially because evidence absolutely crucial to it—evidence relating to faunal exploitation, settlement patterns, and seasonality—is beyond the scope of this paper. However, even with these caveats in mind, the first hypothesis is stronger. Its provisional acceptance certainly entrains unanswered questions—for example, why would most Aurignacian technical practices have been borrowed in the Châtelperronian, but *not* Aurignacian retouch? But it better fits the mutually exclusive occurrence of certain fossil directors; the time-transgressive spread of the Aurignacian at the expense of the Châtelperronian (Figures 5-7); the probable association of the two industries with two different human populations; and the persistence of the Aurignacian thousands of years after the disappearance of the Châtelperronian.

CONCLUDING REMARKS

The two hypotheses favored here concerning the relations among Mousterian, Châtelperronian, and Aurignacian in the region of our concern combine to suggest a coherent sequence of events which, if not established beyond doubt, fits the available data. It should be stressed that this account is meant to apply to a restricted area of western Europe; as various papers in this volume make clear, very different developments seem to have taken place in other parts of the world (to the east, however, the Szeletian may provide a close analogy to the Châtelperronian).

I interpret the Châtelperronian as the handiwork of Neanderthals, developing rather rapidly from the local Mousterian. Its rise is probably due to diffusion and ultimately migration, of the Aurignacian and *Homo sapiens sapiens*, from points south and east of our area. Neanderthals thus seem to have been capable of producing much (if perhaps not all) of the range of Upper Paleolithic material culture. However, they seem also to have been at an adaptive disadvantage relative to modern humans, though maybe only a slight one (see Zubrow, 1989). Thus, over a period of 2-3,000 years, the Châtelperronian gradually lost ground to the Aurignacian, culminating in its disappearance (and, presumably, that of the Neanderthals) before 30,000 BP. The biological and cultural details of this slow and doubtless complex process—such as the extent of gene flow involved, or the nature of competing subsistence-settlement systems—still elude us entirely. If we seem to have a general picture of what happened and when, we still do not know *how*.

This paper has been as much an exercise in pointing out the limitations of the available data base as in interpreting it. It thus seems fitting that it should end in emphasizing, not the inferences to which current data seem to point, but rather, ways to improve that data base.

One way to improve it is to enlarge it in very traditional terms. The relatively few sites and assemblages analyzed in this paper, and the fewer still which are fully published, are an obvious handicap. For instance, the three arguably most important Châtelperronian sites (the Grotte du Renne at Arcy-sur-Cure, the rich multicomponent Grande-Roche, and Saint-Césaire) are only partly published.

Secondly, dating methods need to be more widely applied if we are to identify trends and processes with precision. More relevant stratigraphic units need to be integrated into chronostratigraphic frameworks, and radiocarbon-dated.

Third, systematic attention, of the sort exemplified by the papers by Chase (1989) and Straus (1990), needs to be paid to faunal, settlement, and subsistence data, which in turn must be integrated with the data sets discussed here.

Finally, relatively new methods which have been successfully applied elsewhere to relate artifactual variation to the behavior producing it should be brought to bear on the problems of the Middle-Upper Paleolithic transition in western Europe. These include microwear polish and other edge-damage assessment techniques; scanning electron microscope studies of modified bone; and detailed studies of lithic reduction sequences and patterns of artifact use, recycling and discard such as have been used by Dibble and others (e.g., Dibble 1984, 1987; McCartney 1985), primarily in southwest Asia.

Much of this suggested research could be performed using existing collections, without having to await a new generation of excavations, which unfortunately become slower and more expensive as they become more methodical and informative. It is thus within the realm of possibility for us, within the next decade, to improve notably the quality and quantity of our database concerning the Middle-Upper Paleolithic transition in the Châtelperronian sphere, and to begin formulating and testing hypotheses which will lead to a much-improved understanding of it.

ACKNOWLEDGEMENTS

I have profited in the preparation of this paper's final version from discussions with other participants at the Cambridge Symposium, especially Paul Mellars, Lawrence Straus, Catherine Farizy, Harold Dibble, Thomas Volman, Harvey Bricker, and

Jan Simek. Any shortcomings in the paper are, of course, my responsibility. I thank the American Council of Learned Societies and the L. S. B. Leakey Foundation for travel grants which allowed my participation at the Cambridge Symposium. I also thank Fay Self and Jane Nicol for their help with the tables, and Yafit Avizemal for drafting the figures.

NOTES

[1] It has been suggested (Howell 1964, Meiklejohn 1982) that the Châtelperronian was essentially a Mousterian industry with a few Upper Paleolithic blade tools added, perhaps due to acculturation. But it is now abundantly clear (Harrold 1981, 1983) that it is indeed an early Upper Paleolithic industry, typologically and technologically.

[2] These hypotheses are framed narrowly in terms of only those classes of evidence considered in this paper. Obviously, data regarding subsistence, settlement, and the like would be crucial in an overall consideration.

[3] Whether sylistic differences are conceived here in Sackett's (1982, 1986) terms, or Binford's (1972), I refer in this context to functionally more or less equivalent artifacts with distinctively different morphologies due to differences in traditionally-transmitted craft norms.

[4] The sites are: Roc de Combe, Le Piage, Trou de la Chèvre, La-Côte, Le Moustier, La Ferrassie, Laussel, Combe-Capelle, Font-de-Gaume, Grotte du Loup, La Quina, Pair-non-Pair, Basté, Belleroche, Gatzarria, Les Tambourets, Gargas, Les Cottés, La Grande-Roche de la Plématrie, Saint-Césaire, Châtelperron, Grotte du Renne (Arcy-sur-Cure), Cueva Morín, and El Pendo (for bibliographic information and details, see Harrold 1978, 1981, 1986).

[5] This is the possibly transitional assemblage from level L3b from the re-excavation of La Ferrassie (Laville and Tuffreau 1984; Tuffreau 1984).

[6] Goderville *série lustrée*, *série mate*, Houpeville *série claire* and Oissel (Bordes 1952); Pech de l'Azé I, c. 3,4,5,6,7,A,B, and C (Bordes 1954-55); Fontmaure, lower level, Le Moustier B and J, Combe-Grenal G, N, and X, La Ferrassie C (Bordes 1974); El Pendo XVI, XIV, XIII, XII-XI, and VIIId (Freeman 1980); Grotte de l'Hyène IVa, IVb1, IVb2, IVb3, IVb4, IVb5, and IVb6 (Girard 1978); Grotte du Renne XI, XII, XIII, XIV (Girard 1980).

[7] The impression of the Arcy assemblages' laminarity derived from the "*Indice Laminaire*" (I Lam) is probably exaggerated (Girard 1978, 1980). Girard calculated an "*Indice Laminaire restreint*" (I Lam r.), including only those pieces with length/width ratios classed as 3:1 and 4:1, but excluding those classed as 2:1 (pieces included in the I Lam). This new index ranges from 0 to 7.7 for the Arcy Mousterian assemblages, averaging 3.3, against the mean I Lam of 22.2.

[8] White (1982) has made this point, arguing further that Middle-Upper Paleolithic continuity may have been thus masked, because the two typologies are measuring different things (roughly, function versus style). However, the point can be made (and is supported by my attempts to type Mousterian assemblages in the Upper Paleolithic typology) that this dichotomy in typologies is due to the recognition, based on the extensive experience of Bordes and Sonneville-Bordes, that different sorts of variability obtain in Middle Paleolithic assemblages than in Upper Paleolithic ones.

[9] It is true that assemblage size is a factor here; the four Mousterian assemblages are smaller on average than the Châtelperronian ones (See Table 3), and there is a positive relationship between assemblage size and number of types represented. However, we can to some extent control for size by selecting only assemblages with between 100 and 200 tools. In that case, the two qualifying Mousterian collections contain 10 and 15 types, for an average of 12.5; the five Châtelperronian ones average 30 types. Thus the same relationship holds.

[10] Caminade-Ouest *inferieur*, Castanet I, Chanlat I and II, Les Cottés E, Dufour, La Ferrassie E, Abri Lartet, Abri du Poisson.

REFERENCES

Ashton, N. M. 1983. Spatial patterning in the Middle-Upper Palaeolithic transition. *World Archaeology* 15:224-235.

Bahn, P. G. 1983. *Pyrenean Prehistory: A Palaeoeconomic Survey of the French Sites.* Aris and Phillips, Warminster.

Bazile, F. 1976. Nouvelles données sur le Paléolithique supérieur ancien en Languedoc oriental. *Congrès Préhistorique de France* 20, Provence, 1974:24-28.

Bazile, F. 1984. Les industries du Paléolithique supérieur en Languedoc oriental. *L'Anthropologie* 88:77-88.

Bernaldo de Quiros, F. 1980. The early Upper Paleolithic in Cantabrian Spain, in: *L'Aurignacien et le Périgordien dans leur Cadre Ecologique* (L. Banesz and J. K. Kozlowski, Eds.), pp. 53-64, Institut Archéologique de l'Academie Slovaque des Sciences, Nitra.

Binford, L. R. 1972. Contemporary model building: Paradigms and the current state of Palaeolithic research, in: *Models in Archaeology* (D. L. Clarke, Ed.), pp. 109-166, Methuen, London.

Binford, L. R. 1973. Interassemblage variability—the Mousterian and the 'functional' argument, in: *The Explanation of Culture Change* (C. Renfrew, Ed.), pp. 227-254, Duckworth, London.

Binford, L. R. 1982. Comment on R. White: 'Rethinking the Middle/Upper Paleolithic transition.' *Current Anthropology* 23:177-181.

Binford, L. R. 1983. Reply to L. G. Freeman: 'More on the Mousterian: Flaked bone from Cueba Morín.' *Current Anthropology* 24:372-77.

Binford, S. R. 1972. The significance of variability: A minority report, in: *The Origin of Homo Sapiens* (F. Bordes, Ed.), pp. 207-210, UNESCO, Paris.

Bordes, F. 1952. Stratigraphie du Loess et évolution des industries Paléolithiques dans le ouest du Bassin de Paris. *L'Anthropologie* 56:1-39, 405-452.

Bordes, F. 1954–55. Les gisements du Pech de l'Azé. *L'Anthropologie* 58:401-432; 59:1-38.

Bordes, F. 1961a. Mousterian cultures in France. *Science* 134:803-810.

Bordes, F. 1961b. *Typologie du Paléolithique ancien et moyen.* Delmas, Bordeaux.

Bordes, F. 1968. La question périgordienne, in: *La Préhistoire: Problèmes et Tendances* (F. Bordes and D. de Sonneville-Bordes, Eds.), pp. 59-70, Centre National de la Recherche Scientifique, Paris.

Bordes, F. 1969. Os percé moustérien et os gravé acheuléen du Pech de l'Azé II. *Quaternaria* 11:1-6.

Bordes, F. 1972a. Du Paléolithique moyen au Paléolithique supérieur: continuité ou discontinuité? in: *The Origin of Homo Sapiens* (F. Bordes, Ed.), pp. 211-218, UNESCO, Paris.

Bordes, F. 1972b. *A Tale of Two Caves.* Harper and Row, New York.

Bordes, F. 1973. On the chronology and contemporaneity of different Palaeolithic cultures in France, in: *The Explanation of Culture Change* (A. C. Renfrew, Ed.), pp. 217-226, Duckworth, London.

Bordes, F. 1974. *Le Paléolithique en Europe.* Mimeographed course text, University of Bordeaux I.

Bordes, F., and Labrot, J. 1967. La stratigraphie du gisement de Roc de Combe et ses implications. *Bulletin de la Société Préhistorique Française* 64:15-28.

Breuil, H. 1913. Les subdivisions du Paléolithique supérieur et leur signification. *Congrès International d'Anthropologie et d'Archéologie Préhistorique*, Geneva, 1912:165-238.

Bricker, H. M. 1976. Upper Paleolithic archaeology. *Annual Review of Anthropology* 5:133-148.

Butzer, K. W. 1981. Cave sediments, Upper Pleistocene stratigraphy and Mousterian facies in Cantabrian Spain. *Journal of Archaeological Science* 8:133-184.

Butzer, K. W. 1986. Paleolithic adaptations and settlement in Cantabrian Spain, in: *Advances in World Archaeology*, Vol. 5 (F. Wendorf and A. Close, Eds.), pp. 201-252, Academic Press, New York.

Camps-Fabrer, H. 1976. Le travail de l'os, in: *La Préhistoire Française*: Vol. I (H. de Lumley, Ed.), pp. 717-722, Centre National de la Recherche Scientifique, Paris.

Chamgagne, F., and Espitalié, R. 1981. *Le Piage: Site Préhistorique du Lot*. Mémoires de la Société Préhistorique Française 15, Paris.

Chase, P. G. 1989. How different was Middle Palaeolithic subsistence?: A zooarchaeological perspective on the middle to upper Palaeolithic transition, in: *The Human Revolution* (P. Mellars and C. Stringer, Eds.), pp. 321-337, Princeton University Press, Princeton.

Clark, G. A., and Straus, L. G. 1983. Late Pleistocene hunter-gatherer adaptations in Cantabrian Spain, in: *Hunter-Gatherer Economy in Prehistory: a European Perspective* (G. Bailey, Ed.), pp. 131-148, Cambridge University Press, Cambridge.

Debénath, A., and Duport, L. 1971. Os travaillés et os utilisés de quelques gisements préhistoriques charentais. *Bulletins et Mémoires de la Société Historique et Archéologique de la Charente* 1971:189-202.

Delibrias, G. 1984. La datation par le carbone 14 des ossements de la Ferrassie, in: *Le Grand Abri de La Ferrassie: Fouilles 1968–1973* (H. Delporte, Ed.), Etudes Quaternaires, Université de Provence 7:105-107, Paris.

Delibrias, G., and Evin, J. 1980. Sommaire des datations 14C concernant la Préhistoire en France, II. *Bulletin de la Société Préhistorique Française* 77:215-244.

Delluc, B. and Delluc, G. 1978. Les manifestations graphiques aurignaciennes sur support rocheux des environs des Eyzies (Dordogne). *Gallia Préhistoire* 21:213-438.

Delporte, H. 1976. Le gisement de La Ferrassie, commune de Savignac-de-Miremont, in: *Livret-Guide à l'Excursion A₄ (Aquitaine-Charente)* (J.-P. Rigaud and B. Vandermeersch, Eds.), pp. 88-91, UISPP, 9th Congress, Nice.

Delporte, H., Ed. 1984. *Le Grand Abri de La Ferrassie: Fouilles 1968–1973*. Etudes Quaternaires, Université de Provence 7, Paris.

Delporte, H., and Mazière, G. 1977. L'Aurignacien de la Ferrassie: Observations préliminaires à la suite de fouilles récentes. *Bulletin de la Société Préhistorique Française* 74:343-361.

Dibble, H.L. 1983. Variability and change in the Middle Paleolithic of Western Europe and the Near East, in: *The Mousterian Legacy: Human Biocultural Change in the Upper Pleistocene* (E. Trinkaus, Ed.), Oxford: British Archaeological Reports International Series S164:53-72.

Dibble, H. L. 1984. Interpreting typological variation of Middle Paleolithic scrapers: function, style, and sequence of reduction. *Journal of Field Archaeology* 11:431-436.

Dibble, H. L. 1987. The interpretation of Middle Paleolithic scraper variability. *American Antiquity* 52:109-117.

Farizy, C. 1990. The transition from Middle to Upper Palaeolithic at Arcy-sur-Cure (Yonne, France): Technological, economic and social aspects, in: *The Emergence of Modern Humans: An Archaeological Perspective* (P. Mellars, Ed.), pp. 303-326, Cornell University Press, Ithaca, NY.

Farizy, C., and Schmider, B. 1985. Contribution à l'identification culturelle du Chatelperronien: les données de la couche X de la Grotte du Renne à Arcy-sur-Cure, in: *La Signification Culturelle des Industries Lithiques* (M. Otte, Ed.), Oxford: British Archaeological Reports International Series S239:149-169.

Freeman, L. G. 1980. Ocupaciones musterienses, in: *El Yacimiento de la Cueva de 'El Pendo'* (J. González Echegaray, Ed.), Madrid: Bibliotheca Praehistorica Hispana 17:29-74.

Freeman, L. G. 1983. More on the Mousterian: Flaked bone from Cueva Morín. *Current Anthropology* 24:366-372.

Gambier, D. 1989. Fossil hominids from the early Upper Palaeolithic (Aurignacian) of France, in: *The Human Revolution* (P. Mellars and C. Stringer, Eds.), pp. 194-211, Princeton University Press, Princeton.

Girard, C. 1978. *Les Industries Moustériennes de la Grotte de l'Hyène à Arcy-sur-Cure*. 11th Supplement to *Gallia Préhistoire*. Centre National de la Recherche Scientifique, Paris.

Girard, C. 1980. Les industries moustériannes de la Grotte du Renne à Arcy-sur-Cure (Yonne). *Gallia Préhistoire* 23:1-36.

González Echegaray, J. 1980. El Paleolítico superior, in: *El Yacimiento de la Cueva de 'El Pendo'* (J. González Echgaray, Ed.), Madrid: Bibliotheca Praehistorica Hispana 17:75-148.

González Echegaray, J., and Freeman, L. 1978. *Vida y Muerte en Cueva Morín*. Institucion Cultural de Cantabria, Paris.

Harrold, F. 1978. *A Study of the Châtelperronian*. Ph.D. Dissertation, University of Chicago.

Harrold, F. 1980. A comparative analysis of Eurasian Paleolithic burials. *World Archaeology* 12:195-211.

Harrold, F. 1981. New perspectives on the Châtelperronian. *Ampurias* 43:35-85.

Harrold, F. 1983. The Châtelperronian and the Middle-Upper Paleolithic transition, in: *The Mousterian Legacy: Human Biocultural Change in the Upper Pleistocene* (E. Trinkaus, Ed.), Oxford: British Archaeological Reports International Series S164:123-140.

Harrold, F. 1986. Une réévaluation du Chatelperronien. *Bulletin de la Société Préhistorique Ariège-Pyrenees* 41:151-169.

Henri-Martin, Dr. 1907–1910. *Recherches sur l'Evolution du Moustérien dans le Gisement de la Quina*, Vol. 1: *Industrie Osseuse*. Schleicher, Paris.

Howell, F. C. 1964. Comment. *Current Anthropology* 5:25-26.

Howell, F. C. 1984. Introduction, in: *The Origins of Modern Humans: A World Survey of the Fossil Evidence* (F. H. Smith and F. Spencer, Eds.), pp. xiii-xxii, Liss, New York.

Jude, P, and Arambourou, R. 1964. *Le Gisement de La Chèvre*. Magne, Périgueux.

Klein, R. G. 1973. *Ice-Age Hunters of the Ukraine*. University of Chicago Press, Chicago.

Laville, H. 1975. *Climatologie et Chronologie du Paléolithique en Périgord*. Etudes Quaternaires, Université de Provence 4, Paris.

Laville, H. 1976. Le remplissage de grottes et abris sous roche dans le Sud-Ouest, in: *La Préhistoire Française*: Vol. 1 (H. de Lumley, Ed.), pp. 150-270, Centre National de la Recherche Scientifique, Paris.

Laville, H., Rigaud, J.-P., and Sackett, J. 1980. *Rock Shelters of the Périgord*. Academic Press, New York.

Laville, H., and Tuffreau, A. 1984. Les dépôts du grand abri de La Ferrassie: Stratigraphie, signification climatique et chronologie, in: *Le Grand Abri de La Ferrassie: Fouilles 1968–1973* (H. Delporte, Ed.), Paris: Etudes Quaternaires, Université de Provence 7:25-50.

Leroi-Gourhan, A. 1959. Etudes des restes humains fossiles provenant des grottess d'Arcy-sur-Cure. *Annales de Paléontologie* 44:87-148.

Leroi-Gourhan, A. 1967. *Treasures of Prehistoric Art*. Abrams, New York.

Leroi-Gourhan, A. 1968. Le petit racloir chatelperronienne, in: *La Préhistoire: Problèmes et Tendances* (F. Bordes and D. de Sonneville-Bordes, Eds.), pp. 274-282, Centre National de la Recherche Scientifique, Paris.

Leroi-Gourhan, A. 1976. Les réligions de la préhistoire, in: *La Préhistoire Française*: Vol. 1 (H. de Lumley, Ed.), pp. 755-759, Centre National de la Recherche Scientifique, Paris.

Leroi-Gourhan, A., and Leroi-Gourhan, Arl. 1964. Chronologie des grottes d'Arcy-sur-Cure (Yonne). *Gallia Préhistoire* 7:1-64.

Leroi-Gourhan, Arl. 1984. La place du Néandertalien de St.-Césaire dans la chronologie Würmienne. *Bulletin de la Société Préhistorique Française* 81:196-198.

Leroi-Gourhan, Arl., and Renault-Miskovsky, J. 1977. La palynologie appliquée à l'archéologie: Méthodes, limites et résultats. *Bulletin de l'Association Française pour l'Etude du Quaternaire* 14 (Supplément): 35-49.

Leroy-Prost, C. 1975. L'industrie osseuse aurignacienne: Essai régional de classification: Poitou, Charentes, Périgord. *Gallia Préhistoire* 18:65-156.

Leroy-Prost, C. 1979. L'industrie osseuse aurignacienne: Essai régional de classification: Poitou, Charentes, Périgord. *Gallia Préhistoire* 22:205-370.

Leroyer, C., and Leroi-Gourhan, Arl. 1983. Problèmes de chronologie: Le castelperronien et l'aurignacien. *Bulletin de la Société Préhistorique Française* 80:41-44.

Lévêque, F. 1966. *La Grotte Gatzarria de Suhare, Basses Pyrénées.* Mémoire de Diplôme d'Etudes Supérieurs de Sciences Naturelles, Faculté de Sciences de Poitiers.

Lévêque, F., and Miskovsky, J.-C. 1983. Le Castelperronien dans son environnement géologique. *L'Anthropologie* 87:369-391.

Lévêque, F., and Vandermeersch, B. 1980. Découverte de restes humains dans un niveau castelperronien à Saint-Césaire (Charente-Maritime). *Comptes-Rendus de l'Academie des Sciences de Paris* (Série II) 291:187-189.

Lévêque, F., and Vandermeersch, B. 1981. Le Néandertalien de Saint-Césaire. *La Recherche* 12:242-244.

Marshack, A. 1972. *The Roots of Civilization.* McGraw-Hill, New York.

Mazière, G., and Raynal, J.-P. 1983. La grotte du Loup (Cosnac, Correze), nouveau gisement à Castelperronien et Aurignacien. *Comptes Rendus de l'Académie des Sciences de Paris* (Serie II) 296:1611-1614.

McCartney, P. 1985. Changes in behavioral organization during the Late Pleistocene: Preliminary evidence from chipped tools, in: *Status, Structure, and Stratification* (M. Thompson, M. T. Garcia and F. J. Kense, Eds.), pp. 269-275, University of Calgary Archaeological Association, Calgary.

Meiklejohn, C. 1982. Comment on R. White: 'Rethinking the Middle/Upper Paleolithic transition'. *Current Anthropology* 23:183-184.

Mellars, P. A. 1973. The character of the Middle-Upper Palaeolithic transition in south-west France, in: *The Explanation of Culture Change* (A. C. Renfrew, Ed.), pp. 255-276, Duckworth, London.

Mellars, P. A. 1986. A new chronology for the French Mousterian period. *Nature* 322:410-411.

Mellars, P. A., Bricker, H., Gowlett, J., and Hedges, R. 1987. Radiocarbon accelerator dating of French Upper Paleolithic sites. *Current Anthropology* 28:128-133.

Moure Romanillo, J. A., and Garcia Soto, E. 1983. Radiocarbon dating of the Mousterian at Cueva Millan (Hortigüela, Burgos, Spain). *Current Anthropology* 24:232-233.

Movius, H. L. 1969. The Abri de Cro-Magnon, Les Eyzies (Dordogne) and the probable age of the contained burials on the basis of the nearby Abri Pataud. *Anuario de Estudios Atlánticos* 15:323-344.

Peyrony, D. 1933. Les industries 'aurignaciennes' dans le bassin de la Vézère. *Bulletin de la Société Préhistorique Française* 30:543-559.

Peyrony, D. 1934. La Ferrassie. *Préhistoire* 3:1-92.

Poplin, F. 1986. Découverte et utilisation probable de galène dans le châtelperronien de Merry-sur-Yonne (Yonne). *Bulletin de la Société Préhistorique Française* 83:132.

Potts, R. 1984. Home bases and early hominids. *American Scientist* 72:338-347.

Pradel, L. 1961. La grotte des Cottés, commune de Saint-Pierre-de-Maillé (Vienne). *L'Anthropologie* 65:229-258.

Pradel, L., and Pradel, J. 1954. Le Moustérien évolué de l'Ermitage. *L'Anthropologie* 58:433-443.

Prat, F., and Sonneville-Bordes, D. de. 1969. Découvertes récentes de Paléolithique supérieur à la grotte de Font-de-Gaume (Dordogne). *Quaternaria* 11:115-131.

Rigaud, J.-P 1980. Données nouvelles sur l'Aurignacien et le Périgordien en Périgord, in: *L'Aurignacien et le Gravettien (Périgordien) dans leur Cadre Ecologique* (L. Banesz and J. Kozlowski, Eds.), pp. 213-241, Institut Archéologique de l'Academie Slovaque des Sciences, Nitra.

Rigaud, J.-P. 1982. *Le Paléolithique en Périgord: Les Données du Sud-Ouest Sarladais et leur Implications.* Doctoral Thesis, University of Bordeaux 1.

Sackett, J. R. 1982. Approaches to style in lithic archaeology. *Journal of Anthropological Archaeology* 1:59-112.

Sackett, J. R. 1986. Isochrestism and style: A clarification. *Journal of Anthropological Archaeology* 5:266-277.

Sonneville-Bordes, D. de. 1960. *Le Paléolithique Supérieur en Périgord.* Delmas, Bordeaux.

Sonneville-Bordes, D. de. 1963. Upper Paleolithic cultures in western Europe. *Science* 142:347-355.

Sonneville-Bordes, D. de. 1970. Les industries aurignaciennes de l'abri Caminade-Est, commune de la Canéda (Dordegne). *Quaternaria* 13:77-131.

Sonneville-Bordes, D. de. 1972. *La Préhistoire Moderne.* Pierre Fanlac, Périgueux.

Sonneville-Bordes, D. de. 1980a. Cultures et milieux d'*Homo sapiens sapiens* en Europe, in: *Les Processus d'Hominisation.* Paris: Centre National de la Recherche Scientifique 599:115-129.

Sonneville-Borde, D. de. 1980b. L'évolution des industries aurignaciennes, in: *L'Aurignacien et le Gravettien (Périgordien) dans leur Cadre Ecologique* (L. Banesz and J. K. Kozlowski, Eds.), pp. 255-273, Institut Archéologique de l'Academie Slovaque des Sciences, Nitra.

Sonneville-Bordes, D. de and Perrot, J. 1954-56. Lexique typologique du Paléolithique supérieur. *Bulletin de la Société Préhistorique Française* 51:327-335; 52:76-79; 53:408-412; 547-559.

Straus, L. G. 1983. From Mousterian to Magdalenian: Cultural evolution viewed from Vasco-Cantabrian Spain and Pyrenean France, in: *The Mousterian Legacy: Human Biocultural Evolution in the Upper Pleistocene* (E. Trinkaus, Ed.), Oxford: British Archaeological Reports International Series S164:73-112.

Straus, L. G. 1990. The early Upper Palaeolthic of Southwest Europe: Cro-Magnon adaptations in the Iberian peripheries, 40,000-20,000 BP, in: *The Emergence of Modern Humans: An Archaeological Perspective* (P. Mellars, Ed.), pp. 276-302, Cornell University Press, Ithaca, NY.

Stringer, C. B., Hublin, J. J., and Vandermeersch, B. 1984. The origin of anatomically modern humans in Western Europe, in: *The Origins of Modern Humans: a World Survey of the Fossil Evidence* (F. H. Smith and F. Spencer, Eds.), pp. 51-136, Liss, New York.

Stuckenrath, R. 1978. Dataciones de carbono-14, in: *Vida y Muerte en Cueva Morín* (J. González Echégaray and L. G. Freeman, Eds.), pp. 215, Institucion Cultural de Cantabria, Santander.

Tuffreau, A. 1984. Les industries moustériennes et castelperroniennes de la Ferrassie, in: *Le Grand Abri de la Ferrassie: Fouilles 1968-1973* (H. Delporte, Ed.), Paris: Etudes Quaternaires, Université de Provence 7:111-144.

Vandermeersch, B. 1984. A propos de la découverte du squelette néandertalien de Saint-Césaire. *Bulletins et Mémoires de la Société d'Anthropologie de Paris* (série 14) 1:191-196.

Villa, P. 1982. Conjoinable pieces and site formation processes. *American Antiquity* 47:276-290.

Vogel, J. C., and Waterbolk, H. T. 1963. Groningen radiocarbon dates IV. *Radiocarbon* 5:163-202.

Vogel, J. C., and Waterbolk, H. T. 1967. Groningen radiocarbon dates VII. *Radiocarbon* 9:1107-155.

White, R. 1982. Rethinking the Middle/Upper Paleolithic transition. *Current Anthropology* 23:169-192.

White, R. 1986. *Dark Caves, Bright Visions.* American Museum of Natural History, New York.

White, R. 1989. Production complexity and standardization in early Aurignacian bead and pendant manufacture: Evolutionary implications, in: *The Human Revolution* (P. Mellars and C. Stringer, Eds.), pp. 366-390, Princeton University Press, Princeton.

Wreschner, E. 1980. Red ocher and human evolution: A case for discussion. *Current Anthropology* 21:631-644.

Zubrow, E. 1989. The demographic modeling of Neanderthal extinction, in: *The Human Revolution* (P. Mellars and C. Stringer, Eds.), pp. 212-231, Princeton University Press, Princeton.

Part VIII

Concepts of Race and the Development of Modern Peoples

One of the most contentious and widely abused topics in human evolution is the concept of race and ethnic identity. In the past, studies of human variation, especially racial differences with respect to human evolution, have often been simplistic, unscientific, and clearly driven as much by social and nationalistic prejudices as by scientific inquiry (see Gould 1981). As discussed in Chapters 56 and 57, there were many problems with much of the early work on human racial differences including a common tendency to mix biological and cultural factors. Subsequently, efforts to classify human racial groups have been largely abandoned by most physical anthropologists with the realization that the number of groups that could be recognised, and the distribution of individual populations into these larger groups, varied considerably according to the particular traits being considered (see Chapter 58), and that most of the variation within *Homo sapiens* is within populations rather than between them.

Current research on human variation tends to focus in three major areas. First, there are efforts to use variation among modern populations to reconstruct broad patterns concerning the early evolution of *Homo sapiens*. Many of the articles in Parts VI and VII (including studies on mitochrondrial DNA) use patterns of modern human variation to understand the geographical distribution of various skeletal and genetic traits in human evolution, as does Chapter 58. Perhaps more successful are studies focusing on geographical patterns of variation in genetic and morphological features among extant populations that attempt to reconstruct the recent migration patterns and history of modern ethnic and language groups, such as in Chapter 59 (see also Sokal 1991). Finally there are numerous studies examining the selective importance of variation in modern human populations (e.g. Durham 1991) and the physiological mechanisms underlying these differences (e.g. Shea and Gomez 1988; Shea 1992). Although beyond the scope of this book, this work on evolution in action is some of the most exciting work in physical anthropology.

The first two chapters in this part (56 and 57) discuss the concept of race and human variation from social, philosophical, biological and educational perspectives, and arrive at the conclusion that its usefulness as a concept has passed. The next two chapters (58 and 59) discuss the development of modern peoples as regional populations, and include tree diagrams showing the relationships between all the living peoples of the world. The final chapter (Chapter 60) discusses the advent of symbolic behavior in Upper Paleolithic humans and demonstrates that this behavior is the culturally defining feature of anatomically modern *Homo sapiens* (people like ourselves).

Chapter 56, "The Study of Race" by Sherwood L. Washburn, was originally given as the presidential address at the annual meeting of the American Anthropological Association in 1962. Washburn, one of the great physical anthropologists of the mid-Twentieth Century, was also one of the field's best communicators. In this chapter he discusses "race" as a byproduct of human evolution; in Washburn's view, the races are the open parcels of variation within the human species, which in itself is a closed system. The processes of evolution, such as mutation, natural selection, migration, and genetic drift, are indeed responsible for the partitioning of humankind into a myriad of groups, but it is impossible to separate the genetic processes from the cultural systems that modified and channeled their development. Washburn points out that we are observing only the end product of human evolution; to understand the adaptive significance of any so-called "racial feature" today is a fruitless pursuit because the conditions under which a past feature evolved have long since vanished. Races did not evolve to fit the selective pressures of the modern world; they are the byproducts of past selective pressures and evolutionary events. From this perspective, race is a useful concept only when one is concerned with the genetic and morphological differences that were important in the past at the time of the origin of the races. Washburn also discusses the issue of race, culture, and IQ testing, and concludes that there is no basis for assuming that IQ tests actually *measure* intelligence across all cultures. Washburn closes his discussion by demonstrating that the races are relics of times and conditions that no longer exist on the earth.

In Chapter 57, "Redefining Race: The Potential Demise of a Concept in Physical Anthropology," Alice Littlefield, Leonard Lieberman and Larry Reynolds, take a unique approach to the study of race by surveying the application of the race concept in 58 textbooks of physical anthropology published in the United States between 1932 and 1979. They discovered that throughout the 1970's an increasing number of textbook authors challenged the concept of race as a valid means of describing human variation. At the end of the decade, only one-quarter of introductory physical anthropology textbooks continued to argue for the validity of the race concept. Littlefield, Lieberman and Reynolds argue that this dramatic shift was brought about by changes in the science of human variation itself, as well as by social and political factors in American society. Many of the arguments first raised by Washburn in 1962 (see Chapter 56) had become the established point of view by the end of the 1970's. Physical anthropologists had discovered that it was increasingly difficult: (1) to impose clear-cut boundaries between supposed geographical races, (2) to classify all existing populations into racial taxonomies, (3) to use clines or gradients of trait frequency to plot racial features across populations due to a lack of concordance when multiple traits were employed, and (4) to view racial taxonomies as anything more than a mere reflection of folk taxonomies.

In Chapter 58, "Explaining Modern Man: Evolutionists *versus* Migrationists," William Howells approaches the origin and differentiation of modern peoples from the perspective of two different data sets: serological or blood genetic traits *versus* craniological or anthropometric traits. Since all living humans belong to one polytypic species, Howells reasons that it should be possible to analyze the blood protein and craniological traits of geographic subsets of *Homo sapiens* to produce tree diagrams showing the relationships of all living peoples to one another and to the common ancestor of us all. Superimposed on this study of modern peoples is Howells' goal to resolve two conflicting hypotheses of the evolutionary origin of modern humans: the Neanderthal Phase Hypothesis and the Noah's Ark Hypothesis. These two hypotheses are same ones we encountered in Part VI and represent a mid-1970's view of the multiregional model of human origins *versus* the monogenesis model of human origins (for a more specific statement of these two models, compare Chapters 47 and 48). From the blood genetic data reviewed by Howells, there emerges a division between east and west among living peoples: Europeans and Africans cluster together, as opposed to Asians and Australo-Melanesians. On the other hand, the craniological data indicate the reverse: a north-south split appears, with an African and Australo-Melanesian pairing *versus* a European and Asian pairing. After a detailed discussion of both data sets, Howells concludes that the craniological, "morphometric" tree more likely represents divergence under the process of selection (see also Howells 1989), while the blood-protein "genetic" tree represents divergence by drift, but not at a constant or linear rate. Thus neither type of tree is equivalent to a phylogeny with a long time depth. On this basis Howells can support neither the Neanderthal Phase Hypothesis nor the Noah's Ark Hypothesis, and he goes on to argue that both hypotheses, in their strict applications, are probably faulty.

Chapter 59, "Reconstruction of Human Evolution: Bringing Together Genetic, Archaeological and Linguistic Data," by Luigi Cavalli-Sforza, Alberto Piazza, Paolo Menozzi and Joanna Mountain, is an attempt by a team of geneticists to link all major populations of the world in one large tree, based on analysis of 120 alleles from 42 populations. Genetic data, derived from blood group, protein, and enzyme polymorphisms, were analyzed using a new statistical technique, the bootstrap, a resampling method for obtaining standard errors that can be used to test the reproducibility of splits in a tree. The resulting genetic tree linked all 42 human populations, creating these patterns: (1) the first split separated African populations from nonAfricans; and (2) the second split within the non-African branch produced two clusters, (a) Northeurasians, linking Caucasoids (European, Middle Eastern and Indian) with East Asians, Arctic populations, and Amerindian populations, and (b) Southeast Asians linking insular and mainland Southeast Asian peoples with Pacific Islanders, New Guineans, and native Australians. Cavalli-Sforza *et al.* demonstrate that this genetic tree correlates with a recently proposed linguistic tree which groups the 5000 spoken languages of the world into 17 families, or phyla. Each of the linguistic phyla corresponds to only one of the six major genetic clusters defined in their tree (see Fig. 1 in Chapter 59). The authors also attempt to correlate archaeological data with their genetic–linguistic tree. They conclude their tree supports the monogenesis or "Eve Hypothesis" model of modern human origins (see Chapters 46 and 47).

Finally, in Chapter 60, "Symbolism and Modern Human Origins," by John Lindly and Geoffrey Clark, we leave behind the genetic and linguistic arguments used to recontruct trees of relatedness among modern human populations and return to the archaeological evidence for the origin of modern humans. Lindly and Clark investigate the development and elaboration of patterned symbolic behavior in the archaeological record. One feature that separates all living human populations from most of our fossil forbears is our ability to act symbolically (see Marshack 1989). In the archaeological record, the evidence for early symbolic behavior can be found in lithic assemblages, in burial data, in evidence for ritual behavior and in art. Lindly and Clark argue that prior to the beginning of the Upper Paleolithic (about 38,000 years ago) no hominids, whether they are anatomically modern humans, Neandertals, or archaic *Homo sapiens*, demonstrate significant symbolic behavior. However, the authors do not see the Middle-Upper Paleolithic transition as the key time period for the development of symbolic behavior in early humans. Rather, the key period is the tremendous elaboration of symbolic behavior that occurred in the late Upper Paleolithic, some 15,000 to 20,000 years ago. Lindly and Clark view this phenomenon as a worldwide multiregional "symbolic explosion" which they link to a multiregional model of biological and cultural continuity (but see Klein 1992).

REFERENCES

Durham, W. H. 1991. *Coevolution: Genes, Culture, and Human Diversity.* Stanford University Press, Stanford.

Gould, S. J. 1981. *The Mismeasure of Man.* W. H. Norton, New York.

Howells, W. W. 1989. Skull shapes and the map: Craniometric analyses in the dispersion of modern *Homo. Pap. Peabody Mus. Archaeol. Enthnol.* 79. Cambridge, MA.

Klein, R. G. 1992. The archaeology of modern human origins. *Evolutionary Anthropology* 1:5-14.

Marshack, A. 1989. Evolution of the human capacity: The symbolic evidence. *Yearbk. Phys. Anthropol.* 32:1-34.

Shea, B. and, Gomez, A. 1988. Tooth scaling and evolutionary dwarfism: An investigation of allometry in human pygmies. *Am. J. Phys. Anthropol.* 77:117-132.

Shea, B. 1992. A developmental perspective of size change and allometry in evolution. *Evolutionary Anthropology* 3: (in press).

Sokal, R. R. 1991. The continental population structure of Europe. *Annu. Rev. Anthropol.* 20:119-140.

56
The Study of Race

S. L. Washburn

The Executive Board of the American Anthropological Association has asked me to give my address on the subject of race, and, reluctantly and diffidently, I have agreed to do so. I am not a specialist on this subject. I have never done research on race, but I have taught it for a number of years.

Discussion of the races of man seems to generate endless emotion and confusion. I am under no illusion that this paper can do much to dispel the confusion; it may add to the emotion. The latest information available supports the traditional findings of anthropologists and other social scientists—that there is no scientific basis of any kind for racial discrimination. I think that the way this conclusion has been reached needs to be restated. The continuation of antiquated biological notions in anthropology and the oversimplification of facts weakens the anthropological position. We must realize that great changes have taken place in the study of race over the last 20 years and it is up to us to bring our profession into the forefront of the newer understandings, so that our statements will be authoritative and useful.

This paper will be concerned with three topics—the modern concept of race, the interpretation of racial differences, and the social significances of race. And, again, I have no illusion that these things can be treated briefly; I shall merely say a few things which are on my mind and which you may amplify by turning to the literature, and especially to Dobzhansky's (1962) book, *Mankind Evolving*. This book states the relations between culture and genetics in a way which is useful to social scientists. In my opinion it is a great book which puts the interrelations of biology and culture in proper perspective and avoids the oversimplifications which come from overemphasis on either one alone.

The races of man are the result of human evolution, of the evolution of our species. The races are open parts of the species, and the species is a closed system. If we look, then, upon long-term human evolution, our first problem must be the species and the things which have caused the evolution of all mankind, not the races, which are the results of local forces and which are minor in terms of the evolution of the whole species. (A contrary view has recently been expressed by Coon (1962) in *The Origin of Races*. I think that great antiquity of human races is supported neither by the fossil record nor by evolutionary theory.)

The evolution of races is due, according to modern genetics, to mutation, selection, migration, and genetic drift. It is easy to shift from this statement of genetic theory to complications of hemoglobin, blood groups or other technical information. But the point I want to stress is that the primary implication of genetics for anthropology is that it affirms the relation of culture and biology in a far firmer and more important way than ever in our history before. Selection is for reproductive success, and in man reproductive success is primarily determined by the social system and by culture. Effective behavior is the question, not something else.

Drift depends on the size of population, and population size, again, is dependent upon culture, not upon genetic factors as such. Obviously, migration depends on clothes, transportation, economy, and warfare and is reflected in the archeological record. Even mutation rates are now affected by technology.

Genetic theory forces the consideration of culture as the major factor in the evolution of man. It thus reaffirms the fundamental belief of anthropologists that we must study man both as a biological and as a social organism. This is no longer a question of something that might be desirable; it must be done if genetic theory is correct.

We have, then, on the one hand the history of genetic systems, and on the other hand the history of cultural systems, and, finally, the interrelation between these two. There is no evolution in the traditional anthropological sense. What Franz Boas referred to as evolution was orthogenesis—which receives no support from modern genetic theory. What the geneticist sees as evolution is far closer to what Boas called history than to what he called evolution, and some anthropologists are still fighting a nineteenth-century battle in their presentation of evolution. We have, then, the history of cultural systems, which you may call history; and the history of genetic systems, which you may call evolution if you want to, but if you use this word remember that it means selection, migration, drift—it is real history that you are talking about and not some mystic force which constrains mankind to evolve according to some orthogenetic principle.

There is, then, no possibility of studying human raciation, the process of race formation, without studying human culture. Archeology is as important in the study of the origin of races as is genetics; all we can do is reconstruct as best we can the long-term past, and this is going to be very difficult.

Now let me contrast this point of view with the one which has been common in much of anthropology. In the first place, anthropology's main subject, the subject of race, disregarded to

Delivered as the Presidential address at the Annual Meeting of the American Anthropological Association, November 16, 1962, in Chicago. Reprinted with permission from *American Anthropologist*, Vol. 65, pp. 521-531. Copyright © 1963 by American Anthropological Association.

an amazing degree the evolution of the human species. Anthropologists were so concerned with the subdivisions within our species and with minor detailed differences between small parts of the species that the physical anthropologists largely forgot that mankind is a species and that the important thing is the evolution of this whole group, not the minor differences between its parts.

If we look back to the time when I was educated, races were regarded as types. We were taught to go to a population and divide it into a series of types and to re-create history out of this artificial arrangement. Those of you who have read *Current Anthropology* will realize that this kind of anthropology is still alive, amazingly, and in full force in some countries; relics of it are still alive in our teaching today.

Genetics shows us that typology must be completely removed from our thinking if we are to progress. For example, let us take the case of the Bushmen. The Bushmen have been described as the result of a mixture between Negro and Mongoloid. Such a statement could only be put in the literature without any possible consideration of migration routes, of numbers of people, of cultures, of any way that such a mixing could actually take place. The fact is that the Bushmen had a substantial record in South Africa and in East Africa and there is no evidence that they ever were anywhere else except in these areas. In other words, they are a race which belongs exactly where they are.

If we are concerned with history let us consider, on the one hand, the ancestors of these Bushmen 15,000 years ago and the area available to them, to their way of life, and, on the other hand, the ancestors of Europeans at the same time in the area available to them, with their way of life. We will find that the area available to the Bushmen was at least twice that available to the Europeans. The Bushmen were living in a land of optimum game; the Europeans were living close to an ice sheet. There were perhaps from three to five times as many Bushmen ancestors as there were European ancestors only 15,000 years ago.

If one were to name a major race, or a primary race, the Bushmen have a far better claim in terms of the archeological record than the Europeans. During the time of glacial advance more than half of the Old World available to man for life was in Africa. The numbers and distributions that we think of as normal and the races whose last results we see today are relics of an earlier and far different time in human history.

There are no three primary races, no three major groups. The idea of three primary races stems from nineteenth-century typology; it is totally misleading to put the black-skinned people of the world together—to put the Australian in the same grouping with the inhabitants of Africa. And there are certainly at least three independent origins of the small, dark people, the Pygmies, and probably more than that. There is no single Pygmy race.

If we look to real history we will always find more than three races, because there are more than three major areas in which the raciation of our species was taking place.

If we attempt to preserve the notion of three races, we make pseudo-typological problems. Take for example, again, the problem of the aboriginal Australian. If we have only three races, either they must be put with the people of Africa, with which they have nothing in common, or they must be accounted for by mixture, and in books appearing even as late as 1950, a part of the aboriginal Australian population is described as

European, and listed with the Europeans, and the residue is listed with the Africans and left there.

The concept of race is fundamentally changed if we actually look for selection, migration, and study people as they are (who they are, where they are, how many they are); and the majority of anthropological textbooks need substantial revision along these lines.

Since races are open systems which are intergrading, the number of races will depend on the purpose of the classification. This is, I think, a tremendously important point. It is significant that as I was reviewing classifications in preparing this lecture, I found that almost none of them mentioned any purpose for which people were being classified. Race isn't very important biologically. If we are classifying races in order to understand human history, there aren't many human races, and there is very substantial agreement as to what they are. There are from six to nine races, and this difference in number is very largely a matter of definition. These races occupied the major separate geographical areas in the Old World.

If one has no purpose for classification, the number of races can be multiplied almost indefinitely, and it seems to me that the erratically varying number of races is a source of confusion to student, to layman, and to specialist. I think we should require people who propose a classification of races to state in the first place why they wish to divide the human species and to give in detail the important reasons for subdividing our whole species. If important reasons for such classification are given, I think you will find that the number of races is always exceedingly small.

If we consider these six or nine geographical races and the factors which produced them, I think the first thing we want to stress is migration.

All through human history, where we have any evidence of that history, people have migrated. In a recent issue of the *American Anthropologist* there is a suggestion that it took 400,000 years for a gene that mutated in China to reach Europe. We know, historically, that Alexander the Great went from Greece into Northern India. We know that Mongol tribes migrated from Asia into Europe. Only a person seeking to believe that the races are very separate could possibly believe such a figure as cited.

Migration has always been important in human history and there is no such thing as human populations which are completely separated from other human populations. And migration necessarily brings in new genes, necessarily reduces the differences between the races. For raciation to take place, then, there must be other factors operating which create difference. Under certain circumstances, in very small populations, differences may be created by genetic drift, or because the founders are for chance reasons very different from other members of the species.

However, the primary factor in the creation of racial differences in the long term is selection. This means that the origin of races must depend on adaptation and that the differences between the races which we see must in times past have been adaptive. I stress the question of time here, because it is perfectly logical to maintain that in time past a shovel-shaped incisor, for example, was more efficient than an incisor of other forms and that selection would have been for this, and at the same time to assert that today this dental difference is of absolutely no social importance. It is important to make this point because people generally take the view that something is always adaptive or never adaptive, and this is a fundamental oversimplification of the facts.

Adaptation is always within a given situation. There is no such thing as a gene which has a particular adaptive value; it has this value only under set circumstances. For example, the sickle-cell gene, if Allison and others are right, protects against malaria. This is adaptive if there is malaria, but if there is no malaria it is not adaptive. The adaptive value of the gene, then, is dependent on the state of medicine and has no absolute value. The same is true of the other characteristics associated with race.

I would like to go over some of the suggestions which have been made about the adaptive values of various structures in human beings, because I think these need to be looked at again.

I have stressed that the concept of race which comes from population genetics is compatible with what anthropologists have thought. I think that this concept represents great progress. But when I read the descriptions of the importance of adaptive characteristics, I am not sure that there has been any progress since the nineteenth century.

In this connection I should like to speak for a moment of the notion that the Mongoloids are a race which are adapted to live in the cold, that these are arctic-adapted people.

In the first place, in marked contrast to animals which are adapted to live in the arctic, large numbers of Mongoloids are living in the hot, moist tropics. Altogether unlike animal adaptation, then, the people who are supposed to be adapted to the cold aren't living under cold conditions, and I think we should stress this. For thousands of years the majority of this group have not been living under the conditions which are supposed to have produced them. They are presumed, as an arctic-adapted group following various laws, to have short extremities, flat noses, and to be stocky in build. They are, we might say, as stocky as the Scotch, as flat-nosed as the Norwegians, and as blonde as the Eskimos. Actually, there is no correlation, that is, none that has been well worked out, to support the notion that any of these racial groups is cold-adapted.

Let me say a few more words on this lack of correlation. If one follows the form of the nose, in Europe, as one moves north, narrow noses are correlated with cold climate; in Eastern Asia low noses are correlated with cold climate. In neither case is there the slightest evidence that the difference in the form of the nose has anything whatsoever to do with warming the air that comes into the face. Further, if we look at these differences expressed in this way, we see that they are posed in terms of nineteenth-century notions of what a face is all about.

Let us look at it differently. The nose is the center of a face. Most of a face is concerned with teeth, and bones, and muscles that have to do with chewing. The Mongoloid face is primarily the result of large masseter muscles and the bones from which these muscles arise (malar and gonial angles). This is a complex structural pattern related to the teeth, and a superficially very similar pattern may be seen in the Bushman, whose facial form can hardly be attributed to adaptation to cold.

The face of the Neanderthal man has recently been described also as cold-adapted, though it does not have the characteristics of the Mongoloid face. We are told that the blood supply to the Neanderthal face was greatly increased because the infraorbital foramen was large, bringing more blood to the front of the face. In actual fact, most of the blood to our face does not go through that artery. The artery that carries most of the blood to the face comes along to the outside, and even our

arteries are far too large to go through the mental or infraorbital foramen of Neanderthal man. This kind of statement, as well as the statement that the maxillary sinus warmed the air and that the function of a large orbit was to keep the eyes from freezing, seems to me an extraordinary retrogression to the worst kind of evolutionary speculation—speculation that antedates genetics and reveals a lack of any kind of reasonable understanding of the structure of the human face.

The point I wish to stress is that those who have spoken of the cold adaptation of the Mongoloid face and of the Neanderthal face do not know the structure of the human face. We have people writing about human faces who are anatomically illiterate. I am genetically illiterate; I do not know about the hemoglobins. I am not asserting that all of us should be required to be literate in all branches of physical anthropology. As Stanley Garn points out, the field has become complicated, but people who are writing about the structure of the human face should learn the elements of anatomy.

The adaptive value of skin color has been repeatedly claimed, but recently Blum (1961) has indicated that the situation is more complicated than it appeared. In the first place, he points out the melanin in the skin doesn't do what anthropologists have said it has done. The part of the skin which mainly stops ultraviolet light, the short-wave-length light, is a thickened *stratum corneum*, rather than melanin.

Again, the chimpanzee and the gorilla live in precisely the same climatic conditions in Uganda, but the gorilla has one of the blackest, most deeply pigmented skins of the primates and the chimpanzee has a very light skin. It simply is not true that skin color closely parallels climate. The point here is that racial classification tells us very little. The classification poses problems; it does not solve them.

In scientific method, as I see it, one looks at relevant data and when these data are laid out, as in, say, the classification of races, one may then find a correlation which is helpful. But after that, one has to do an experiment; one has to do something that shows that the correlation has validity. And it's no use continuing to correlate nose-form or skin color with climate. The crude correlations were made many years ago, and to advance the study of race requires new methods and more sophisticated analyses.

When I was a student, there were naive racial interpretations based on the metrical data. When these became unacceptable politically the same people used naive constitutional correlations to reach the same conclusions of social importance. Today we have naive concepts of adaptation, taking the place of the earlier interpretations, and a recrudescence of the racial thinking.

All along the line there have been valid problems in race, valid problems in constitution, and valid problems in adaptation. What I am protesting against strongly is the notion that one can simply take a factor, such as high cheekbone, think that it might be related to climate, and then jump to this conclusion without any kind of connecting link between the two elements—without any kind of experimental verification of the sort of material that is being dealt with. If we took really seriously this notion that a flat face with large maxillary sinuses, deep orbits and big brow ridges is cold-adapted, it is clear that the most cold-adapted animal in the primates is the gorilla.

Race, then, is a useful concept only if one is concerned with the kind of anatomical, genetic, and structural differences which were in time past important in the origin of races. Race in human thinking is a very minor concept. It is entirely worth while to have a small number of specialists, such as myself, who are concerned with the origin of gonial angles, the form of the nose, the origin of dental patterns, changes in blood-group frequencies, and so on. But this is a very minor, specialized kind of knowledge.

If classification is to have a purpose, we may look backward to the explanation of the differences between people—structural, anatomical, physiological differences—and then the concept of race is useful, but it is useful under no other circumstances, as far as I can see.

When the meaning of skin color and structure is fully understood, it will help us to understand the origin of races, but this is not the same thing as understanding the origin of our species. It will help in the understanding of why color was important in time long past, but it will have no meaning to modern technical society.

I turn now to a brief statement of the influence of culture upon race. Beginning with agriculture and continuing at an ever-increasing rate, human customs have been interposed between the organism and the environment. The increase of our species from perhaps as few as five million before agriculture to three billion today is the result of new technology, not of biological evolution. The conditions under which the races evolved are mainly gone, and there are new causes of mutation, new kinds of selection, and vast migration. Today the numbers and distribution of the peoples of the world are due primarily to culture. Some people think the new conditions are so different that it is better no longer to use the word race or the word evolution, but I personally think this confuses more than it clarifies.

All this does not mean that evolution has stopped, because the new conditions will change gene frequencies, but the conditions which produced the old races are gone. In this crowded world of civilization and science, the claim has been made repeatedly that one or another of the races is superior to the others. Obviously, this argument cannot be based on the past; because something was useful in times past and was selected for under conditions which are now gone, does not mean that it will be useful in the present or in the future.

The essential point at issue is whether the abilities of large populations are so different that their capacity to participate in modern technical culture is affected. Remember in the first place that no race has evolved to fit the selective pressures of the modern world. Technical civilization is new and the races are old. Remember also that all the species of *Homo* have been adapting to the human way of life for many thousands of years. Tools even antedate our genus, and our human biological adaptation is the result of culture. Man and his capacity for culture have evolved together, as Dr. Dobzhansky has pointed out. All men are adapted to learn language—any language; to perform skillful tasks—a fabulous variety of tasks; to cooperate; to enjoy art; to practice religion, philosophy, and science.

Our species only survives in culture, and, in a profound sense, we are the product of the new selection pressures that came with culture.

Infinitely more is known about the language and culture of all the groups of mankind than is known about the biology of racial differences. We know that the members of every racial group have learned a vast variety of languages and ways of life. The interaction of genes and custom over the millenia has produced a species whose populations can learn to live in an amazing variety of complex cultural ways.

Racism is based on a profound misunderstanding of culture, of learning, and of the biology of the human species. The study of cultures should give a profound respect for the biology of man's capacity to learn. Much of the earlier discussion of racial inferiority centered on the discussion of intelligence; or, to put the matter more accurately, usually on that small part of biological intelligence which is measured by the IQ. In the earlier days of intelligence testing, there was a widespread belief that the tests revealed something which was genetically fixed within a rather narrow range. The whole climate of opinion that fostered this point of view has changed. At that time animals were regarded as primarily instinctive in their behavior, and the genes were supposed to exert their effects in an almost mechanical way, regardless of the environment. All this intellectual climate has changed. Learning has proved to be far more important in the behavior of many animal species, and the action of the complexes of genes is now known to be affected by the environment, as is, to a great degree, the performance that results from them. For example, Harry Harlow has shown that monkeys learn to learn. Monkeys become test wise. They become skillful in the solution of tests—so monkeys in Dr. Harlow's laboratories are spoken of as naive or as experienced in the use of tests. To suppose that humans cannot learn to take tests is to suppose that humans are rather less intelligent than monkeys.

Krech et al. (1962) have shown that rats raised in an enriched environment are much more intelligent and efficient as maze-solvers than rats that have been given no opportunity to learn and to practice before the testing. To suppose that man would not learn through education to take tests more efficiently, is to suppose that our learning capacities are rather less than those of rats.

The human is born with less than a third of the adult brain capacity, and there is tremendous growth of the cortex after birth. There is possibly no mammalian species in which the environment has a longer and more direct effect on the central nervous system than man. We should expect, then, that test results are going to be more affected by the environment of man than in the case of any other animal. Deprivation studies of monkeys and chimpanzees and clinical investigations of man show that the lack of a normal interpersonal environment may be devastating to the developing individual.

Today one approaches the study of intelligence expecting to find that environment is important. This intellectual background is very different from that of the '20's. The general results on testing may be briefly summarized as follows:

> The average IQ of large groups is raised by education. I believe the most important data on this are the comparisons of the soldiers of Word War I and of World War II. More than 80 percent of the soldiers tested in World War II were above the mean of those tested in World War I. This means a wholesale massive improvement, judged by these tests, in the sons of the people who fought in World War I.

In the states where the least educational effort is made, the IQ is the lowest. In fact, as one looks at the review in Anastasi (1958), it is exceedingly difficult to see why anyone ever thought that the IQ measured innate intelligence, and not the genetic constitution as modified in the family, in the schools, and by the general intellectual environment.

I would suggest that if the intelligence quotients of Negroes and Whites in this country are compared, the same rules be used for these comparisons as would be used for comparisons of the data between two groups of Whites. This may not seem a very extreme thing to suggest, but if you look at the literature, you will find that when two groups of Whites differ in their IQ's, the explanation of the difference is immediately sought in schooling, environment, economic positions of parents, and so on, but that when Negroes and Whites differ in precisely the same way the difference is said to be genetic.

Let me give you but one example of this. Klineberg (1935) showed years ago in excellent studies that the mean test scores of many Northern Negro groups were higher than those of certain groups of Southern Whites. When these findings were published, it was immediately suggested that there had been a differential migration and the more intelligent Negroes had moved to the North. But the mean of Northern Whites test results is above that of Southern Whites. Are we to believe that the intelligent Whites also moved the North?

There is no way of telling what the IQ would be if equal opportunity were given to all racial and social groups. The group which is sociologically classified as Negro in the United States, about one-third of whose genes are of European origin, might well test ahead of the Whites. I am sometimes surprised to hear it stated that if Negroes were given an equal opportunity, their IQ would be the same as Whites'. If one looks at the degree of social discrimination against Negroes and their lack of education, and also takes into account the tremendous amount of overlapping between the observed IQ's of both, one can make an equally good case that, given a comparable chance to that of the White's, their IQ's would test out ahead. Of course, it would be absolutely unimportant in a democratic society if this were true, because the vast majority of individuals of both groups would be of comparable intelligence, whatever the mean of these intelligence tests would show.

We can generalize this point. All kinds of human performance—whether social, athletic, intellectual—are built on genetic and environmental elements. The level of all kinds of performance can be increased by improving the environmental situation so that every genetic constitution may be developed to its full capacity. Any kind of social discrimination against groups of people, whether these are races, castes, or classes, reduces the achievements of our species, mankind.

The cost of discrimination is reflected in the length of life. The Founding Fathers were wise to join life, liberty, and the pursuit of happiness, because these are intimately linked in the social and cultural system. Just as the restriction of social and economic opportunity reduces intelligence so it reduces length of life.

In 1900 the life expectancy of White males in the United States was 48 years, and in that same year the expectancy of a Negro male was 32 years; that is a difference of 50 per cent, or 16 years. By 1940 the difference had been reduced to ten years, and by 1958 to six. As the life expectancy of the Whites increased from 48 to 62 to 67 years, that of the Negroes increased from 32 to 52 to 61 years (see Dublin et al. 1949). They died of the same causes, but they died at different rates.

Discrimination, by denying equal social opportunity to the Negro, made his progress lag approximately 20 years behind that of the White. Somebody said to me, "Well, 61, 67, that's only six years." But it depends on whose six years it is. There are about 19 million people in this country sociologically classified as Negroes. If they die according to the death rate given above, approximately 100 million years of life will be lost owing to discrimination.

In 1958 the death rate for Negroes in the first year of life was 52 per thousand and for Whites 26. Thousands of Negro infants died unnecessarily. The social conscience is an extraordinary thing. A lynching stirs the whole community to action, yet only a single life is lost. Discrimination, through denying education, medical care, and economic progress, kills at a far higher rate. A ghetto of hatred kills more surely that a concentration camp, because it kills by accepted custom, and it kills every day in the year.

A few years ago in South Africa, the expectation of life for a Black man was 40 years, but it was 60 at the same time for a White man. At that same time a White woman could expect 25 more years of life than a Black woman. Among the Blacks the women lived longer than the men. People speak of the greater longevity of women, but this is only because of modern medicine. High birth rates, high infant mortality, high maternal mortality—these are the hallmarks of the history of mankind.

Of course there are biological differences between male and female, but whether a woman is allowed to vote, or the rate that she must die in childbirth, these are a matter of medical knowledge and of custom. Biological difference only expresses itself through the social system.

Who may live longer in the future—Whites or Negroes? There's no way of telling. Who may live longer in the future—males or females? There is no way of telling. These things are dependent of the progress in medical science and on the degree to which this progress is made available to all races and to both sexes.

When environment is important, the only way genetic difference may be determined is by equalizing the environment. If you believe in mankind, then you will want mankind to live on in an enriched environment. No one can tell what may be the ultimate length of life, but we do know that many people could live much longer if given a chance.

Whether we consider intelligence, or length of life, or happiness, the genetic potential of a population is only realized in a social system. It is that system which gives life or death to its members, and in so doing changes the gene frequencies. We know of no society which has begun to realize the genetic potential of its members. We are the primitives living by antiquated customs in the midst of scientific progress. Races are products of the past. They are relics of times and conditions which have long ceased to exist.

Racism is equally a relic supported by no phase of modern science. We may not know how to interpret the form of the Mongoloid face, or why Rh^o is of high incidence in Africa, but we do know the benefits of education and of economic progress. We know the price of discrimination is death, frustration, and hatred. We know that the roots of happiness lie in the biology of the whole species and that the potential of the species can only be realized in a culture, in a social system. It is knowledge and the social system which give life or take it away, and in so doing change the gene frequencies and continue the million-year-old interaction of culture and biology. Human biology finds its realization in a culturally determined way of life, and the infinite variety of genetic combinations can only express themselves efficiently in a free and open society.

REFERENCES

Anastasi, A. 1958. *Differential Psychology: Individual and Group Differences in Behavior*. The Macmillan Company, New York.

Blum, H. F. 1961. Does the melanin pigment of human skin have adaptive value? *The Quarterly Review of Biology* 36:50-63.

Coon, C. S. 1962. *The Origin of Races*. Knopf, New York.

Dobzhansky, T. 1962. *Mankind Evolving: The Evolution of the Human Species*. Yale University Press, New Haven and London.

Dublin, L. I., Lotka, A. J., and Spiegelman, M. 1949. *Length of Life: A Study of the Life Table* (Revised Edition). The Ronald Press Company, New York.

Klineberg, O. 1935. *Race Differences*. Harper & Brothers, New York and London.

Krech, D., Rosenzweig, M. R., and Bennett, E. L. 1962. Relations between brain chemistry and problem-solving among rats raised in enriched and impoverished environments. *Journal of Comparative and Physiological Psychology* 55:801-807.

ABO Blood Group Allele Distribution

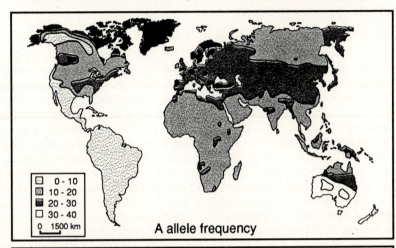

A allele frequency

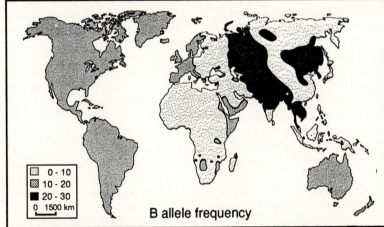

B allele frequency

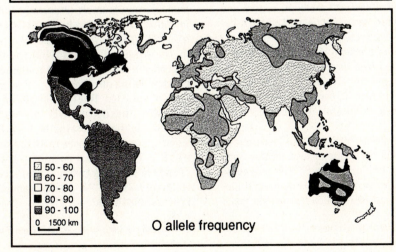

O allele frequency

57

Redefining Race: The Potential Demise of a Concept in Physical Anthropology

A. Littlefield, L. Lieberman, and L. Reynolds

If races do not have any biological coherence, why, then, were we all brought up to believe in them?

C. L. Brace and Ashley Montagu, *Human Evolution*

For many years the prevailing, almost monolithic view in physical anthropology was that the concept of race was a valid tool for the description and study of human variation. More recently, the race concept has been attacked as invalid because populations of humans separated by significant reproductive barriers and/or exhibiting concordant combinations of variable physical traits cannot be shown to exist. Its critics claim that the concept is not useful in research, obscures the understanding of human variation, and has harmful social consequences.

The earliest significant challenge to the race concept in American physical anthropology emerged in 1942 with the publication of Ashley Montagu's *Man's Most Dangerous Myth: The Fallacy of Race.* Montagu waged the battle almost single-handed until the 1960s, when several works critical of prevailing modes of racial analysis appeared. The diffusion of the new approach in textbooks of physical anthropology did not occur to any significant extent until after 1970, but by the end of the 1970s it had become the modal position.

This change is of interest for several reasons. First, physical anthropology textbooks reflect scientifically accepted opinion. Second, texts influence a number of publics, particularly teachers and students, whose opinions may be shaped as a result. Third, changes originating outside academia, particularly in the political arena, have an impact on the popularity and acceptance of scientific ideas, and textbook editors and publishers competing to capture and maintain markets are especially likely to be responsive to such influences.

Changes in the views of physical anthropologists on a matter as important as race invite us to examine influences that may operate to produce them. Explanations for change in our prevailing views about race lie partly in the discipline itself and partly in social and cultural changes occurring outside it.

Among scientists, the debate over race has occurred in three phases (Lieberman 1968). In the first phase, the key issue was whether races had one origin or several. The polygenic position carried with it the implication of inherent racial inequality. During the second phase, the explicit debate over racial equality replaced the monogenic-polygenic controversy. The 19th-century consensus favoring inequality was challenged early in the 20th century by a number of anthropologists, sociologists, and psychologists. Changing social conditions, as well as the influence of Franz Boas and his students at Columbia University, helped to shift the weight of scientific opinion toward the view that races are essentially equal in behavioral potential. During the third phase of the debate, a number of anthropologists began to question whether distinct races of *Homo sapiens* can be identified. Those who answered in the affirmative are referred to as splitters (e.g., Coon, Garn, and Birdsell 1950; Dobzhansky 1965). Those who answered in the negative and argued that race is not a scientifically useful concept are called lumpers (e.g., Montagu 1942, Livingstone 1962, Brace 1964a). As Lieberman and Reynolds (1978: 334) have put it,

> The issue is not whether there is factual proof of hereditary variations, but whether these variations are distributed in concordant patterns which correspond to the conception of races as identifiable populations. . . . The argument hinges on the significance of clines, or spatial gradations of gene frequencies. The splitters hold that these genetic gradations are intergradations between races. Lumpers believe that the gradations are not intergradations but are instead overlapping gradients which cross populations in such discordant patterns that identifiable boundaries cannot be established.

In the 1960s, there was active discussion of these issues in anthropology journals (especially *Current Anthropology*) and in collections of works by specialists (Montagu 1964, Mead *et al.* 1968). The revival of a theory of separate origins by Coon in *The Origin of Races* (1962) and the heated controversy it engendered also contributed to the reexamination of the race concept during these years.

In spite of lively discussion of the issues among specialists, the debate over the validity of the race concept was omitted from most textbooks prior to 1970. In the 1970s a discussion of the issues involved was usually included, and by 1975-79 the modal position was that of the lumpers. The change in textbook treatments of race has been dramatic and relatively swift. We shall examine this change and the processes involved in it [1].

Table 1. The race concept in physical anthropology textbooks, 1932–79

	Textbook Use of "Race" as Classified by Panel					
Period	Races Exist	Races Do not Exist	Author Is Non-committal	Race Not Mentioned	No Consensus	Total
1932–44	2	—	—	—	—	2
1945–49	2	1	—	—	—	3
1950–54	2	1	—	—	—	3
1955–59	1	—	—	—	—	1
1960–64	2	1	—	—	1	4
1965–69	4	—	—	2	1	7
1970–74	7	4	2	2	1	16
1975–79	5	10	2	1	4	22
Total	25	17	4	5	7	58

PROCEDURE

The 58 textbooks included in our study (see appendix) were selected according to the following criteria: each was (1) a comprehensive introductory textbook such as might be used for undergraduate survey courses in physical anthropology, (2) available in one volume devoted primarily to physical anthropology, and (3) not an anthology. Both original and subsequent editions of a text were included when copies were available. Only textbooks published in the United States were selected for inclusion [2].

A panel of university undergraduates, each working independently, was asked to read the sections of the textbooks dealing with human variation and to classify them into one of four possible categories in accordance with the authors' expressed views on race: (1) races exist (author uses the concept in describing human variation); (2) races do not exist (author rejects the race concept as invalid); (3) author seems contradictory or noncommittal (discusses the issues but comes to no clear conclusion); (4) race is not mentioned.

Each text was read by at least five students and its classification determined by the majority view of the panel members. In the seven cases where no majority emerged, the book was classified under "no consensus."[3] The results are summarized in Table 1.

FINDINGS

The Decline of Race

Of the books included in our study 20 were published between 1932 and 1969, and 13 of these expressed the prevailing outlook that races exist. Only 3 rejected the race concept; the race concept was not mentioned in 2, both published in the late 1960s, and in 2 cases the panel was unable to reach agreement on the text's classification. Clearly, physical anthropologists publishing textbooks during this period overwhelmingly accepted the race concept in the study of human variation. Furthermore, during this period a few key figures dominated the textbook field. E. A. Hooton and William Howells together produced 6 of the 13 splitting editions, while Ashley Montagu wrote all of the lumping texts. Indeed, these three authors were responsible for all but one of the texts published before 1960.

The picture changes dramatically after 1970. Of the 38 texts published in the 1970s, only 12 supported the race concept while 14 opposed it. The 14 texts written from the lumping perspective were written by ten different authors or sets of co-authors, indicating a wider support for that position. This shift became especially pronounced in 1975–79, when the view that races do not exist was expressed in 10 textbooks and became the modal position, with only 5 texts arguing that races are "real."

A further development of the 1970–79 period was the increasing number of texts (12) in which the author is noncommittal, does not mention race, or presents the issues in such a fashion that our panel was unable to reach a consensus. Where a text was classified as noncommittal, it usually meant that the author(s) presented both sides of the controversy over race but seemed to take no clear position. When these 12 are added to those that openly advocate the no-race position, they account for two-thirds of the texts produced during this period, indicating a dramatic decline in support for racial classification.

The decline of the race concept and the development of the no-race position in the 1970s is especially significant in that almost twice as many textbooks (38) were produced in that period as in the previous 38 years (20). A much larger group of anthropologists had become involved: the 38 books were written by 24 different authors or sets of co-authors. Presumably, they also reached a much larger audience of college students.

The Generation Gap?

The shift in textbook treatments of race which took place during the 1970s is impressive. When we classify textbook authors by the year in which they received their highest degree, as shown in Table 2, the decline in support for the race concept is even more dramatic. Only two authors who received their degrees after 1960 wrote texts classified as splitting (Downs and Bleibtreu, co-authors of two editions). While splitting texts continued to be published into the 1970s, they were overwhelmingly the products of an earlier generation of anthropologists.

Does this mean that racial analysis has been rejected by younger physical anthropologists in general? Available evidence does not support this conclusion. During the 1970s Lieberman and Reynolds studied the views on race of physical anthropologists in three institutional settings: graduate departments, four-year colleges, and two-year colleges. Little relationship was found between age and views on race, and in one subsample those in the 40–59-year age-group rejected the race concept more frequently than those of age 39 or less (Stark, Reynolds, and Lieberman 1979). These findings suggest that the changes in textbooks reflect more than changes in graduate training or the general scholarly climate in which younger physical anthropologists developed their ideas.

Table 2. Approach to "race" by year of author's highest degree

	Position on "Race" in Most Recent Edition		
Year of Degree	Splitter	Lumper	Other
Before 1960	9	3	2
1960 or after	2	9	5
Total	11	12	7

Anthropologists Who Switched

In seven cases, textbook authors changed their positions between earlier and later editions. In two cases (Birdsell, Kelso) the shifts represented a clear strengthening of the no-race position.

Birdsell changed from a splitter to a lumper. In the earlier edition he wrote (1951: 487, 508):

> *A race is an interbreeding population whose gene pool is different from all other populations.* . . . [B]asic adjacent breeding populations of man each constitute a unique race as was demonstrated for aboriginal Australia. . . . in many regions of the world today new races are in the process of being formed.

By 1975, however, his position had changed: "The use of the term race has been discontinued because it is scientifically undefinable and carries social implications that are harmful and disruptive" (1975: 505). His work in identifying gradients in gene frequencies (clines) among Australian Aborigines may have helped persuade him, as well as others, of the unscientific nature of racial classifications that place boundaries around populations (1975: 462).

In his 1970 edition, Kelso was very critical of the race concept, yet used it. After comparing typological, populational, and clinal approaches to the classification of human variation he concluded (p. 318):

> Why, then, is it that these descriptive geographic races are considered at all? Because, even with the above limitations, they continue to be useful. They identify trait clusters within contiguous geographic areas . . . and [provide] a basis for determining the effects that might be due to long-term geographical isolation.

By 1974, however, Kelso had also adopted the no-race position: "Clearly the concept of race is of negligible value in science. The racial approach is a deceptive strategy for collecting information on human variation, and the concept of race explains nothing at all" (1974: 309).

In another three cases (Barnouw, Haviland, the McKerns) the authors appeared to move away from an initial splitting position without explicitly taking a no-race position. The shift was clearest for the McKerns. While their 1969 text was classified as taking a "races exist" approach, the 1974 edition discusses clines and problems in the study of human variation without mentioning race.

In only two cases (Campbell, Lasker) did the authors' support for the race concept appear to strengthen, but little substantive change occurred in either case. The use of "subspecies" in Campbell's 1966 edition was replaced by the use of "race" in subsequent editions. In Lasker's case, all three editions approached the topic cautiously, although there was apparently somewhat greater willingness to use a carefully defined concept of race in the 1976 edition than in the earlier two.

Legitimation of Lumping

The debate over the existence of race gained momentum in the 1960s. Consideration of the issue in the pages of *Current Anthropology* in the early 1960s contributed to the legitimation of the no-race position, both because of the journal's international readership and because several widely respected scholars participated in the debate. Livingstone (1962) and Brace (1964a: 313-20) led the attack on the race concept, while Dobzhansky (1962: 280-81) and Coon, Garn, and Huxley (all 1964) defended it.

In 1966 a symposium on "Science and the Concept of Race" was held at the annual meetings of the American Association for the Advancement of Science, and a book by that title was published in 1968 (Mead *et al.*). Here again, noted scholars participated. Some called for the rejection of the race concept (Fried, Marshall, and Scott) or questioned its utility (Birch, Gordon, Glass), while others defended it (Dobzhansky, Baker, Mayr). Kelso (1974: 308) was led to comment, "What one finds within the book is one contradiction after another on even the most basic issues." Again, however, the result was to help legitimate the no-race position and give it broader circulation.

In addition, these discussions helped refocus attention on the concept of "cline" as both an approach to the measurement of human variation and a viable alternative to the race concept [4]. Clines may be defined as biological gradients in space. The distribution of a trait having been plotted, lines are drawn connecting the same frequencies, and what emerges is a pattern of curves rather like those on a weather map (Birdsell 1972: 423). Huxley (1938) originated the concept, but he did not propose it as an alternative to race. Those anthropologists who did not use the concept explicitly usually acknowledged that intergradations existed between "races." The distribution of frequencies of separate traits indicated, however, that gradients occurred not only between "races," but across their alleged geographic ranges, and in such a manner that the gradients of one trait did not accord with those of others. As new data on the distribution of genetic traits such as blood factors accumulated, and as computers facilitated the analysis of large quantities of information and the arrangement of the data in clinal patterns, many anthropologists came to the conclusion that no genuine racial boundaries could be identified.

The challenge to the race concept began to be reflected in physical anthropology textbooks in the late 1960s and early 1970s, but largely in a defensive way. While the splitters did not acknowledge the correctness of the critics' views, they did begin to discuss them and in so doing gave them grudging recognition:

> . . . some biologists and anthropologists have advocated the abandonment of the word *race* altogether. . . . We do not think such a drastic step is necessary. [Downs and Bleibtreu 1969: 137]

> The word represents a valid taxonomic category. . . . banning a word does not help solve the problems connected with its use. [Hulse 1971: 351]

> The "no-race" point of view, as it has been called, is a minority one at present in anthropological circles, but it has some able exponents. Later in this and the following chapter, we shall return to some of their contributions. Meanwhile, let us consider some attempts to account for the existence of racial differences. It seems undeniable, after all, that a blonde Swede, a Negro, and a Chinese look quite different from one another. How can we explain the development of such racial differentiation? [Barnouw 1971: 130]

Of course races exist! They exist today and they probably existed in the Pleistocene as well. Race is a perfectly useful and valid term, and I shall and do use it." [Buettner-Janusch 1973: 490]

By the end of the 1970s, however, the defense of the race concept was being phrased in a less defiant and more guarded way:

Since the distinctions among the races are not clear-cut, there are many ways of classifying the races. The classification that will follow is based on the main geographical races as they are most commonly recognized. In this discussion, we are using the term race purely in its biological sense to describe the biological nature of recognizably different human populations. The term carries no political implications or value judgments. [Campbell 1979: 438]

Lack of agreement about the adequacy of the traditional racial categories does not mean that we are not continuing to learn more; it means simply that we do not agree on how to describe what we know. . . . The wave proved to be a useful concept in dealing with some problems in physics; ether did not. The concept of race is still being tested. [Eckhardt 1979: 252]

As the decade closed, textbooks written by lumpers were asserting the following views:

Race is an arbitrary and unrealistic corner from which to look at human variability. [Weiss and Mann 1978: 508]

Concepts of race are so ambiguous and so much a product of cultural bias that race, as it is traditionally applied to humans, has no clear biological meaning. Thus, by using the term, one runs the risk of having it interpreted in ways that were not intended. No anthropologist would deny that race is an important way of organizing human variation in cultural terms. But these culturally defined categories cannot be translated into objective, clear biological categories. For this reason, physical anthropologists are abandoning the use of racial categories in studying human variation [Weitz 1979: 196]

The study of racial classifications is an activity that belongs to an era now ending. [Williams 1979: 87]

As the decade progressed, more and more physical anthropologists accepted the no-race position. Why did support for the race concept decline in American anthropology after 1960, and why did the textbook treatment of race change so dramatically in the 1970s?

INTERPRETATION

Anthropological views of race have been influenced by changes both in science itself and in its institutional relations to the larger society. The latter, we will argue, have been especially important in influencing textbook content.

Science as a Self-Correcting Activity

Because scientists subject their propositions to confirmation or disproof through empirical testing, science has the potential to be self-correcting. It is assumed that the gradual accumulation of evidence from empirical research will lead to the rejection of inaccurate conceptions and theories and the construction and refinement of better ones. From this point of view, it is clear that

anthropological conceptions of human variation have been altered by our expanding knowledge. The gathering of new kinds of data and, increasingly, the lack of concordance of the emerging trait distributions with the existing racial typologies have led investigators to turn away from those typologies altogether. It is tempting to view the race concept in anthropology as crumbling before this accumulation of new knowledge. Its demise, some might argue, was the result of the gradual diffusion into anthropology of advances in genetics, in biological science, and in computer technology. As science progresses, according to this view, it corrects itself.

While this process undoubtedly occurs to some degree, it does not explain why the race concept was so popular in anthropology in the first place or why it responded so slowly to criticism. It cannot be argued that alternative views were not available. Montagu cites various 19th-century writers who discussed the difficulty or lack of utility of prevailing racial classifications (Montagu 1965: 83-89). As early as the 1930s cogent criticisms of the concept were being offered by English scientists such as Hogben (1931) and Huxley and Haddon (1936). On this side of the Atlantic, however, the challenge to the race concept was ignored or even ridiculed by anthropologists until the 1960s.

The idea of race has not always been with us. Montagu (1965: 40) has described how the concept and accompanying racist ideology grew up together in the context of slavery and European imperialism. Race as an idea served not only to classify the human variety discovered by explorers and colonizers, but to justify the exploitation and dispossession of supposedly inferior peoples as Europeans extended their control over vast areas of the globe (Lieberman and Reynolds 1978: 333-34). Marshall's (1968: 157) examination of the racial typologies of earlier historical periods in America indicates that "both scientific and popular racial classifications reflect prevailing socio-political conditions."

In American anthropology, the no-race position did not gain currency until the 1960s, when the civil-rights struggle intensified at home and the United States became more and more involved in an unpopular colonial war. Scientifically valid criticisms of racial classifications and of the race concept itself were not entirely new, but they did not become widely accepted within anthropology until a more favorable political climate had developed.

Although anthropological views of race are responsive not only to developments within science, but also to those outside it, this process is far from a simple one. We are not arguing that anthropologists are simple weathervanes of public opinion. At times in our history we have managed to lead public opinion rather than to follow it. Boas's attacks on racist theories of differential intelligence or ability are one example.

While anthropologists are influenced by the larger socio-political milieu, this influence occurs within the context of particular institutions. For American anthropologists, the changing structure of higher education has been especially important. It is this context, we will argue, that explains the dramatic shift in textbook treatments of race that took place during the 1970s.

Anthropology and the Institutional Context

During the early years of American anthropology, Harvard and Columbia were the major institutions influencing anthropological views of race. Many of the early texts, both in physical anthropology and in general anthropology, were written by professors or graduates of these two institutions.

Harvard's influence on the race concept derived from the institution's prestige, E. A. Hooton's reputation, and the number of physical anthropologists who were trained there. Three of Hooton's students—Carleton Coon, Stanley Garn, and J. B. Birdsell—collaborated in the 1950 publication of *Races: A Study of the Problems of Race Formation in Man*. Although they rejected their mentor's approach to racial classification on the basis of nonadaptive traits, they did not challenge the race concept itself. These writers made a significant contribution, however, by recognizing that the characteristics of races could be mapped one at a time and correlations with environmental factors sought. With this approach, the clinal alternative to the race concept was but a step away. Of the three, however, only Birdsell was to take that step. Garn retained the race concept in *Human Races* (1961), as did Coon in *The Origin of Races* (1962). Of the textbook authors included in our study, other Harvard graduates who took splitting positions were Howells, Hulse, Lasker, and Bleibtreu.

It may be argued that the foundations for lumping were developed at Columbia during the period when Franz Boas chaired the department and led an earlier phase of the scientific debate over race—the debate over equality. While Boas did not reject the race concept itself, he led the attack on scientific racism and demanded proof of supposed racial differences in mentality or temperament.

In 1912, Boas published work demonstrating head shape changes in children of immigrants. This work weakened the older concept of the fixity of race and cast doubt on the utility of cranial morphology in racial classifications. He and his students also developed an alternative to scientific racism by explaining character as an outcome of institutions, history, and environment and by developing a relativistic approach to cultural differences. Boas also discussed the difficulties of racial classification (1928: 63):

> we have seen that from a purely biological point of view the concept of race unity breaks down. The multitude of genealogical lines, the diversity of individual and family types contained in each race is so great that no race can be considered as a unit. Furthermore, similarities between neighboring races . . . are so great that individuals cannot be assigned with certainty to one group or another.

Boas also stands out as a pioneer in recruiting women and minority students into anthropology. But while his students continued to chip away at scientific racism, Ashley Montagu was the first of them (and for quite some time the only one) to reject the race concept altogether (1942: 31-32):

> The process of averaging the characters of a given group, of knocking the individuals together, giving them a good stirring, and then serving the resulting omelette as a "race" is essentially the anthropological process of race-making. It may be good cooking but it is not science. . . . The omelette called race has no existence outside the statistical frying-pan in which it has been reduced by the heat of the anthropological imagination

Montagu lists Boas first among those who critically read the manuscript of *Man's Most Dangerous Myth*, from which we

have just quoted. Later however, he traced his views on race to sources in Europe such as Huxley and Haddon's *We Europeans* (1936) and Finot's *Race Prejudice* (1906). Whatever may have influenced Montagu, his views were definitely out of step with the prevailing outlook and were not taken seriously by most physical anthropologists until much later. Only one other Columbia graduate, Victor Barnouw, appears in our sample of textbook authors, and although his views on racial equality may reflect Boas's influence he did not reject the race concept itself.

During the 1940s and 1950s Montagu led the attack on race largely unaided. One reason for this seems to have been his lack of direct influence on younger physical anthropologists. As far as we have been able to determine, none of the other textbook authors in our sample studied with Montagu. Of perhaps greater importance, however, was the concentration of graduate training in anthropology during those years in a few elite institutions.

Before 1950, there were only 11 Ph.D.-granting departments of anthropology in the United States. By 1960, the number had increased to a mere 20 (Hurlbert 1976). Of these, 8 departments, all ranked among the discipline's most prestigious both by Cartter's reputational method (1966) and by Hurlbert's exchange method (1976), produced 24 of the 31 authors whose degrees we were able to identify. These departments were Arizona, California (Berkeley), Chicago, Columbia, Harvard, Michigan, Pennsylvania, and Yale. These figures are indicative of only one aspect of the elite nature of anthropology in the period before 1960. Not only was graduate training concentrated in a few institutions, but courses in anthropology were available to relatively few of America's undergraduates. Even today it is rarely represented in high-school curricula. Thus both the producers and the consumers of anthropological knowledge were concentrated in the nation's more prestigious institutions of learning and at levels of advanced study within those institutions. In spite of anthropology's commitment to the study of human diversity, its practitioners were quite homogeneous in terms of class origins and social background. Few women or individuals of minority background were represented in the profession, and even fewer specialized in physical anthropology. It is not surprising that physical anthropologists who received their training in this rarefied atmosphere adhered overwhelmingly to the splitting position.

The picture changed dramatically after 1960. By 1970 there were some 65 and by 1975 80 Ph.D.-granting departments of anthropology in the United States (Hurlbert 1976). As Rogge (1976) has pointed out, anthropology has been growing exponentially, with the number of departments doubling faster than the number of Ph.D.-granting departments. Including both graduate and undergraduate departments, by 1981 there were at least 337 departments of anthropology in the United States. A recent survey by the American Anthropological Association indicates that the 229 responding departments averaged 1,878 undergraduate enrollees and employed an average 9.8 faculty members. The 103 responding graduate departments had awarded 283 Ph.D.'s and 683 Master's degrees in the preceding year (American Anthropological Association 1981).

Anthropology has become a standard part of the curriculum in most undergraduate institutions and is frequently taught at two-year colleges as well. One major consequence of this expansion, which parallels that of higher education in general, was a phenomenal expansion in the numbers of anthropology students and in the textbook market. Another consequence was that people of more diverse social backgrounds gained entry to the profession. While representation of minorities is still limited (about 5% of faculty and 6% of graduate students), women now constitute 25% of full-time faculty members and 51% of graduate students (American Anthropological Association 1981).

In order to understand the changing treatment of the race concept in the textbooks we have examined, we must consider not only who produced them, but who consumed them. As already mentioned, most of our authors received their graduate training in elite institutions. We have little specific information on how the social backgrounds of those receiving their highest degrees after 1960 might differ from those trained earlier, but they are still overwhelmingly nonminority males. Indeed, there is only one woman in our sample. Changes in the class origins or other social characteristics of authors do not seem great enough to explain the changes we have reported in their textbooks.

A different picture emerges, however, if we consider the consumers of their texts. A large proportion of those currently teaching anthropology received their degrees from nonelite institutions in programs that did not exist 20 years ago. Also, those trained in nonelite institutions overwhelmingly find teaching positions in nonelite institutions as well (Hurlbert 1976).

Results of a separate study provide insight into the views on human variation of physical anthropologists in a variety of institutional settings. In 1973, 1975, and 1976, Lieberman and Reynolds surveyed three groups of physical anthropologists and received 374 usable responses: 66 from physical anthropologists in Ph.D.-granting departments, 136 from physical anthropologists in B.A.- and M.A.-granting departments, and 172 from persons teaching physical anthropology in two-year colleges. A no-race or lumping orientation was found among 47% of these respondents, but the proportions varied considerably by the type of institutional setting: 32% at Ph.D.-granting universities, 48% at B.A.- and M.A.-granting institutions, 53% at two-year colleges (Lieberman, Reynolds, and Kellum 1983).

These results not only indicate widespread support for the no-race position, but also show that the institutions with the largest numbers of undergraduate students are more frequently staffed by physical anthropology teachers who favor lumping. At the same time, it is clear that the splitting orientation still predominates among those who control professional training in physical anthropology, suggesting that the race concept may be perpetuated within the discipline for some time to come.

In addition to questions about their views on race, respondents in the above-mentioned study were asked several questions about their sociocultural backgrounds. Lieberman, Reynolds, and Kellum summarize the responses as follows:

> Briefly, our findings indicate that those who argue that races are real or that the concept is useful, tend to stem from backgrounds including one or more of the following: (1) First born, last, or only child, (2) male, (3) have all four grandparents born in the United States, (4) born of Catholic or conservative Protestant mother, and (5) born in the South or border states. Those who deny the existence of race tend to be characterized by at least one of the following: (1) intermediate

birth order, (2) female, (3) have all four grandparents born outside of the United States, Canada, North and West Europe, (4) born of a Jewish mother, or (5) born in the Third World.

These effects are intensified when those teaching in two-year colleges are eliminated from the analysis; the association of the lumping orientation with less-privileged characteristics and the splitting orientation with more-privileged characteristics is stronger among those teaching in four-year and graduate departments. This group is much more likely to have received specialized training in physical anthropology at the graduate level, and this suggests that such specialized training heightens rather than diminishes the influence of sociocultural characteristics on anthropologists' views of race.

A separate analysis of results for a sample of 131 physical anthropologists teaching in graduate and four-year departments also showed that the fathers of splitters tended to have more years of education and higher-ranking occupations than the fathers of lumpers, thereby providing additional evidence for the influence of sociocultural background on anthropologists' views of race (Stark, Reynolds, and Lieberman 1979).

We conclude, then, that the dramatic changes in the textbook treatments of race that took place in the 1970s reflect two important changes in the discipline: the movement of anthropology out of the elite institutions and into mass institutions and the entry into the profession of large numbers of people from less privileged sociocultural backgrounds. We further hypothesize that in those institutions which have the least-privileged students, the two-year colleges, the sociocultural characteristics of students have considerable impact on the views of teachers, since the background characteristics of the teachers in these institutions showed relatively little association with their orientation toward race.

There is an additional link in this explanatory scheme, about which we can only speculate: the role of the publishing industry. We do not know to what extent editors and publishers deliberately attempted to influence the approaches to race expressed in the textbooks included in our study. There is reason to believe, however, that publishers are more sensitive to the opinions of potential customers than are authors. In the late 1960s and the 1970s textbook publishers began to do systematic market research, sending lengthy questionnaires to faculty and soliciting their views on actual or potential textbook content. During the 1970s textbooks changed rather quickly in response to popular attitudes on certain subjects. For example, feminist concerns were reflected in the wholesale replacement of such expressions as "the study of man" and "the evolution of man" by gender-neutral phrasing. We suggest that the role of the publishing industry as a major mediating link between the producers (authors) and consumers (teachers and students) of physical anthropology textbooks is deserving of further study.

CONCLUSION

The race concept has been criticized in recent years for a number of reasons: it is difficult to draw clear-cut boundaries between the supposed geographic races; many populations cannot be classified in existing racial taxonomies; the clines or gradients in frequency that can be plotted for one trait do not accord with those plotted for others; scientific racial taxonomies are merely reflective of folk taxonomies.

Although the no-race view was rarely expressed in physical anthropology texts before 1970, it had become the most frequent view by 1975-79, with only one-quarter of the textbooks continuing to argue for the validity of the race concept. This rapid shift in textbook treatments of human variation cannot be explained solely in terms of the accumulation of new data and the self-correcting nature of empirical science. None of the criticisms of the race concept was entirely new. It may be asked why the elaboration of racial taxonomies has persisted as long as it has, in spite of their admitted imprecision.

Although the political milieu of the 1960s may have created an atmosphere of greater receptivity to criticisms of the race concept, we have argued that anthropology's changing institutional context has been of greater importance. It was during this same period that anthropology began to move out of the elite institutions and to become accessible to broad masses of college students from varied social backgrounds. At the same time, scholars of more diverse social origins gained entry into the profession. It was through this changing structure that the concerns of the larger society with race and racism began to influence the views of anthropologists.

It is our contention that the rapid expansion of anthropology and the changes in the characteristics of its practitioners have contributed to the decline of the race concept in physical anthropology textbooks. Although these texts are still most frequently written by graduates of elite institutions, they are directed toward a market that is largely made up of students attending nonelite institutions. Anthropologists who teach in such institutions, and whose social origins are relatively less privileged, tend to be more receptive to the no-race position than their colleagues in the elite institutions.

We are led to conclude that the rapid expansion of anthropology and of higher education in general during the 1960s and 1970s has played a key role in the increased incidence of the no-race view in physical anthropology texts. The logic of our argument, however, does not allow us to predict an early demise for racial classification and analysis in anthropology. For a variety of political and economic reasons, higher education in the United States is now contracting rather than expanding. Cuts in funding are making a college education less accessible to nonprivileged youth, those most likely to be receptive to a no-race viewpoint. In a highly competitive academic job market, holders of Ph.D.'s from nonelite institutions—whom we would expect to favor a no-race viewpoint—find fewer employment opportunities as teachers than Ph.D.-holders from elite institutions. In both academic and non-academic arenas, the civil-rights gains of the 1960s and 1970s are under attack. These trends suggest that the race concept may be with us for some time to come and may even experience a revival during the 1980s.

APPENDIX: TEXTBOOKS INCLUDED IN THE STUDY

The number in parentheses following each textbook indicates the classification given it by the majority of the panel: (1) races exist, (2) races do not exist, (3) author is noncommittal, (4) race is not mentioned, or (5) no consensus.

Adams, Fred T. 1968. *The Way to Modern Man: An Introduction to Human Evolution*. Teachers College Press, New York. (1)

Barnouw, Victor 1971. *An Introduction to Anthropology: Physical Anthropology and Archaeology*. Dorsey, Homewood, Ill. (1)

Barnouw, Victor 1975. 2d edition. (1)

Barnouw, Victor 1978. 3d edition. (5)

Bennett, Kenneth 1979. *Fundamentals of Biological Anthropology*. William C. Brown, Dubuque. (2)

Birdsell, Joseph B. 1972. *Human Evolution: An Introduction to the New Physical Anthropology*. Rand McNally, Chicago. (1)

Birdsell, Joseph B. 1975. 2d edition. (2)

Brace, C. L., and Montagu, M. F. Ashley. 1965. *Man's Evolution: An Introduction to Physical Anthropology*. Macmillan, New York. (5)

Brace, C. L., and Montagu, M. F. Ashley. 1977. 2d edition. *Human Evolution: An Introduction to Biological Anthropology*. Macmillan, New York. (5)

Buettner-Janusch, John 1966. *Origins of Man: Physical Anthropology*. Wiley, New York. (1)

Buettner-Janusch, John 1973. *Physical Anthropology: A Perspective*. Wiley, New York. (1)

Campbell, Bernard G. 1966. *Human Evolution: An Introduction to Man's Adaptations*. Aldine, Chicago. (4)

Campbell, Bernard G. 1974. 2d edition. (1)

Campbell, Bernard G. 1976. *Humankind Emerging*. Little, Brown, Boston. (1)

Campbell, Bernard G. 1979. 2d edition. (1)

Communications Research Machines, Inc. 1971. *Physical Anthropology Today*. CRM Books, Del Mar, Calif. (2)

Downs, James F., and Bleibtreu, Hermann K. 1969. *Human Variation: An Introduction to Physical Anthropology*. Glencoe, Beverly Hills. (1)

Downs, James F., and Bleibtreu, Hermann K 1972. Revised edition. (1)

Eckhardt, Robert B. 1979. *The Study of Human Evolution*. McGraw-Hill, New York. (5)

Haviland, William A. 1974. *Human Evolution and Prehistory*. Holt, Rinehart, and Winston, New York. (1)

Haviland, William A. 1979. 2d edition. (5)

Hooton, Earnest A. 1932. *Up from the Ape*. Macmillan, New York. (1)

Hooton, Earnest A. 1946. Revised edition. (1)

Howells, William W. 1944. *Mankind So Far*. Doubleday, Garden City. (1)

Howells, William W. 1947. 2d edition. (1)

Howells, William. W. 1952. 3d edition. (1)

Howells, William W. 1959. *Mankind in the Making*. Doubleday, Garden City. (1)

Hulse, Frederick S. 1963. *Human Species: An Introduction to Physical Anthropology*. Random House, New York. (1)

Hulse, Frederick S. 1971. 2d edition. (1)

Jolly, Clifford J., and Plog, Fred. 1976. *Physical Anthropology and Archaeology*. Knopf, New York. (2)

Jolly, Clifford J., and Plog, Fred. 1979. 2d edition. (2)

Kelso, A. J. 1970. *Physical Anthropology*. Lippincott, New York. (3)

Kelso, A. J. 1974. 2d edition. (2)

Kraus, Bertram S. 1964. *The Basis of Human Evolution*. Harper and Row, New York. (1)

La Barre, Weston 1954. *The Human Animal*. University of Chicago Press, Chicago. (1)

Lasker, Gabriel W. 1961. *The Evolution of Man: A Brief Introduction to Physical Anthropology*. Holt, New York. (5)

Lasker, Gabriel W. 1973. *Physical Anthropology*. Holt, New York. (5)

Lasker, Gabriel W. 1976. 2d edition. (1)

McKern, Thomas W., and McKern, Sharon. 1969. *Human Origins: An Introduction to Physical Anthropology*. Prentice Hall, Englewood Cliffs. (1)

McKern, Sharon, and McKern, Thomas W. 1974. *Living Prehistory: An Introduction to Physical Anthropology and Archaeology*. Cummings, Menlo Park, Calif. (4)

Montagu, Ashley. 1945. *An Introduction to Physical Anthropology*. Thomas, Springfield. (2)

Montagu, Ashley. 1951. 2d edition. (2)

Montagu, Ashley. 1960. 3d edition. (2)

Nelson, Harry, and Jurmain, Robert. 1979. *Introduction to Physical Anthropology*. West, St. Paul. (3)

Nickels, Martin K., Hunter, David E., and Whitten, Philip. 1979. *The Study of Physical Anthropology and Archaeology*. Harper and Row, New York. (2)

Pfeiffer, John E. 1969. *The Emergence of Man*. Harper and Row, New York. (4)

Pfeiffer, John E. 1972. 2d edition. (4)

Pfeiffer, John E. 1978. 3d edition. (4)

Poirier, Frank E. 1974. *In Search of Ourselves: An Introduction to Physical Anthropology*. Burgess, Minneapolis. (3)

Poirier, Frank E. 1977. 2d edition. (3)

Stein, Philip L., and Rowe, Bruce M. 1974. *Physical Anthropology*. McGraw-Hill, New York. (2)

Stein, Philip L., and Rowe, Bruce, M. 1978. 2d edition. (2)

Tullar, Richard M. 1977. *The Human Species: Its Nature, Evolution, and Ecology*. McGraw-Hill, New York. (1)

Weiss, Mark L., and Mann, Alan E. 1975. *Human Biology and Behavior: An Anthropological Perspective*. Little, Brown, Boston. (2)

Weiss, Mark L., and Mann, Alan E. 1978. 2d edition. (2)

Weitz, Charles A. 1979. *An Introduction to Physical Anthropology and Archaeology*. Prentice Hall, Englewood Cliffs. (2)

Williams, B. J. 1973. *Evolution and Human Origins: An Introduction to Physical Anthropology*. Harper and Row, New York. (2)

Williams, B. J. 1979. 2d edition. (2)

COMMENTS

Eliane S. Azevêdo, *Laboratorio de Genética Médica, Hospital Prof. Edgard Santos, Salvador, Bahia, Brazil*

Littlefield, Lieberman, and Reynolds employ a creative procedure that they call a "case study" to yield data leading to the unquestionable conclusion that the concept of race is being challenged among North American anthropologists. They do not limit themselves to presenting these results, but go on to reflect on their possible causes. However, anthropologists represent a small fraction of the entire U.S. academic world. What is the prevalent concept of race among those in medical school, in law school, and so on? What idea of race is in the minds of America's larger employers, of America's politicians, etc.? It would be a pity if the main contents of this paper did not reach the larger public through some serious newspaper or magazine. Those who read it in CA, even if they are lumpers, already know that it is impossible to divide mankind into distinct groups because man's biological variability is continuously distributed (Sunderland 1975). Any classification of race is arbitrary (Bodmer and Cavalli-Sforza 1976) and consequently depends more on the investigator's cultural inheritance than on scientific knowledge, for the simple reason that the demonstration of race is scientifically impossible (Young 1971). Thus the anthropologist's greatest responsibility to society today is to demonstrate the superficiality and unimportance of racial classifications at the biological level.

Kenneth L. Beals, *Department of Anthropology, Oregon State University, Corvallis, Oregon*

The authors have documented a decline in support of the race concept in introductory physical anthropology textbooks. There is no doubt that such a trend has been occurring. In a broader perspective, it can be considered part of the change in the emphasis of modern biology—less toward identification of taxonomic categories and more toward questions of process.

It might be mentioned that several authorities noted for racial taxonomies have also contributed to stimulating research in other directions. Two examples include the distribution maps of Biasutti, a standard of excellence in clinal depictions, and the emphasis on climatic adaptation in the cited works of Coon and Coon, Garn, and Birdsell. Duplicating or reorganizing the classifications already presented has little to offer toward the advancement of knowledge, and the process of doing so has had social stigma attached to it.

A stronger case for the decline can be made in terms of scientific inquiry. Probably, it would have gradually happened even without changes in social attitudes about race. I certainly concur, however, with the authors' premise that the social circumstances were a contributory factor. The culture area concept is in many ways parallel to the race concept. The former, however, remains alive and well as a method of organizing variation, while the latter may indeed find a textbook demise. Its general extinction is unlikely.

C. L. Brace, *Museum of Anthropology, University of Michigan, Ann Arbor, Michigan*

Littlefield, Lieberman, and Reynolds have concentrated on the impact on textbook contents of the nature of a recently expanding market and the background of the teachers who largely serve it. This is a refinement of Kuhn's (1962) consideration of how paradigm shifts occur in science, itself an improvement over the comment by Planck (1950: 33-34) that ideas change only when the generation that held them dies off individual by individual. The scenario they present deserves serious consideration, although, given the small sample, I wonder if their figures are statistically significant. At least they have made a thought-provoking addition to our understanding of the development of our field. There are, however, some missing pieces. For example, the authors begin with a question I posed in the revision of the text I wrote in collaboration with Montagu (Brace and Montague 1977), but they never examine the issue or suggest an answer.

It was this whole matter which led me to write the chapter "Race: The History of the Concept" for that second edition. I had intended to put such a chapter in the first edition (1965), as is evident in the organization of the book. Its absence was noted in one perceptive if relentlessly hostile review (Ehrich 1966). My original intention went unrealized when I found that the subject had not been explored systematically and I would have to work it up from scratch. This I attempted to do for Chapter 11 of our revision. I have since produced a documented development of it applied especially to the ethos of American physical anthropology (Brace 1982).

One thing Littlefield *et al.* clearly miss is the fact that the cessation of the conflict between the monogenists and the polygenists in the 19th century came about because the polygenists won. American polygenism, developed in sober fashion by Morton (1839, 1844, 1847) and applied in an unabashedly racist manner by Nott and Gliddon (1854, 1857; cf. critiques by Brace 1860, 1861, and Brace 1974), was adopted, strengthened with a commitment to Platonic essentialism, by

Broca as the core of the anthropology in his society and school in Paris (Broca 1859, 1860a, b; Pouchet 1864). Ripley (1899) reintroduced this to the English and American reading public as the distilled essence of continental sophistication. The allied victory in World War I, at bottom a Franco-German conflict, insured the high prestige of the realm of French ideas. These were granted a congenial reception, especially in the elitist institutions mentioned by Littlefield *et al*. In anthropology, this meant that the typological polygenism of the race concept continued with enhanced vigor.

Coon did not "revive" polygenism in 1962 as they claim, since in substance it had never really disappeared. The core of his work was simply the continuation of what Holton (1973, 1975) has called a "thema," although Coon himself was unaware of it. Keith, whose influence on Coon via Hooton was largely unacknowledged, had previously suggested precisely the same thing (Keith 1950: 631). Coon's earlier and more restricted rendition, *The Races of Europe* (1939), was done at the request of the publisher to update Ripley's work of the same name. The continuity of the polygenist paradigm is clearly apparent in all of this even though its roots in pre-Civil War America had been completely forgotten and its original name had been modified (cf. the "polyphyletism" of Vallois 1952) or dropped entirely.

That the race concept previously accepted without question in the popular and professional realms has a source that has not been discussed by Littlefield *et al*. should show that the elitism per se of the institutions they mention had nothing to do with the shaping of the views which flourished in their congenial milieux. Further, even if they are correct about the social context of the spread of the replacing paradigm, this does not explain the source of the view whose growth they discuss.

In this regard, it is indeed relevant to consider the "accumulation of new data and the self-correcting nature of empirical science." Hogben's (1931) and Huxley's (1938) earlier discussions were more abstract than concrete. What really forced the issue was the accumulation of data on genetically controlled traits. I well remember, as a graduate student at one of their "elite institutions" in the early 1950s, reading Birdsell's (1951) presentation of gene frequency data for a number of different traits in aboriginal Australia and being disturbed because these could not be made to fit into a framework of circumscribed "breeding populations," as it was then fashionable to do. Livingstone's subsequent accumulation and treatment of hemoglobin data from West Africa simply reaffirmed this (Livingstone 1958).

Meanwhile, the dramatic tussle between the adherents of the subspecies concept and the advocates of clinal views in the pages of *Systematic Zoology* gave the whole business a solid biological focus that was lacking in the earlier writings of Boas, Hogben, Huxley, and even Montagu (Wilson and Brown 1953; Brown and Wilson 1954; Mayr 1954; Smith and White 1956; Starrett 1958; and many others). The articulation by Livingstone (1962) and affirmation by myself (1964a, c) of the clinal view of the nature of human biological variation, then, was very much the product of new data presented in a context of critically reexamined biological theory.

One also has to realize that this was the time when what has been called the "synthetic theory of evolution" finally penetrated into anthropology. The anthropology which Keith and Hooton (and Hrdlicka also) copied from the earlier model developed by Broca was not grounded in evolutionary biology. Broca had been explicitly hostile to a Darwinian approach to evolution (Broca 1862), and Keith, and consequently Hooton, had rejected the assumptions of mechanism that underlie it (Brace 1981, 1982). The change in attitudes towards the concept of race, like the change in interpretations of the hominid fossil record (Brace 1964b; Spencer and Smith 1981), was part of the shift from the typological essentialism which characterized Broca's anthropology (and much of contemporary and subsequent French biology [Boesiger 1980; Ruse 1981]) to the stress on the dynamics of evolutionary mechanism that has dominated much of biological science since the 1930s. That the dynamics of the change were influenced by the emotion-laden social dimensions mentioned by Littlefield *et al*. cannot be denied, but aspects of basic science cannot be left out of the picture. One could make a good case that the very institutions they suggest were slow to accept the paradigm shift under discussion were also the places where the ethos of active research led to the demonstration of the scientific evidence for the validity of the nontraditional view.

I regret that they have used the terms "splitters" and "lumpers" to characterize the adherents to the two paradigms under consideration. These two terms have long been used to designate those who prefer more exclusive and more inclusive approaches to dealing with acceptable taxonomic categories. To use them in the present context is to guarantee that the differences between the groups they are attempting to deal with will be blurred. Calling them "categorizers" and "clinalists" would have been greatly preferable. In orthodox taxonomy, both lumpers and splitters accept the existence of population categories. Their only argument concerns where to draw the lines. Clines, however, "apply to characters, not to populations" (Rogers 1954: 126). In dealing with human variation, clinalists maintain that lines should not be drawn at all and that only when we trace the distribution and history of each trait separately in relation to the selective forces which control them can we really begin to understand the nature of human biological variation.

Stanley M. Garn, *Center for Human Growth and Development, University of Michigan, Ann Arbor, Michigan*

There are three reasons the term "race" appears less frequently in physical anthropology textbooks now, but none of these is the one imagined by Littlefield, Lieberman, and Reynolds.

The first reason is that the word "race" has been supplanted in part by "ethnic group" and in part by "population." ("Ethnic group" was introduced as an exact replacement for "race"; "population," of course, was borrowed from population genetics and is appropriately ambiguous.)

The second reason is that taxonomy has become of less interest and concern to physical anthropologists, as is true in the biological sciences in general. This decreased emphasis on taxonomy is evident in the texts and bears mentioning.

The third reason is that physical anthropologists have found many new directions of interest, such as bone biology, primate behavior, dental anthropology, demography, epidemiology, and human nutrition. These newer interests are reflected in contemporary texts and especially in the several journals that physical anthropologists support.

While it is true that there has been a great expansion in the number of doctoral degrees in physical anthropology awarded by state-supported institutions, it was never true that the private universities produced an academic "elite." The graduate students were largely impecunious; they tended to come from the state-supported schools, and so did the professors. Littlefield *et al.* should not confound the undergraduate students and the graduate students of such universities in their thinking.

The moral is that the history of a concept cannot be unravelled simply by setting undergraduate students to count words in textbooks. Even more to the point, it cannot be reconstructed by imagining what doctoral students were like in the depression, the war years, the years of the GI Bill, or the McCarthy Era.

P.-A. Gloor, *Ch. du Verger 2, CH-1008 Prilly/Lausanne, Switzerland*

This is an informative and useful contribution to the recent history of physical anthropology. The demise of the concept of race in Anglo-American studies is a reality. The concept is also on the decline, although to a lesser extent, in other parts of the world (see Schwidetzky 1974). In my opinion, this is an unfortunate trend, scientifically as well as psychologically.

The authors have carefully analyzed various factors: the impact of new scientific data, especially in genetics; the changing sociocultural characteristics of anthropologists; the fear that studying human races could be interpreted as condoning racism and imperialism.

To the first of these three factors another element might be added: the lack of discipline of anthropologists, who have been unwilling to obey the basic rule of zoological taxonomy opposing the use of synonyms. As a result, we have witnessed the emergence of fanciful "races" and of superfluous classification systems. The whole thing is thoroughly confusing for everyone. The traditional taxonomy has been accused of being pre-Mendelian; it has also been said that its most widely used parameters (height, cephalic index, eye color) have been affected by microevolutionary "secular" changes. In this context, the new developments of human genetics have given rise to doubts and reassessments; they have also fostered negative and defeatist attitudes (at least until the geneticists come up with a new geographical taxonomy for the variations in our species).

One solution for the problem of a high fever is to break the thermometer. Similarly, physical anthropology is in a crisis and for some the remedy is to eliminate the concept of race (at least from our vocabulary) altogether. Thus we have the following scenario: Palaeolithic "raciation" by natural selection; then the Neolithic, with its social selection and increased cross-breeding erasing the "raciation" process; then a unified humanity without distinct racial boundaries. But this is jumping to conclusions.

Turning to the second and third factors analyzed by the authors, it is indeed true that anthropologists have had to overcome many ethnocentrist and colonialist biases. For psychological reasons, we must repeat forcefully that the study of human races is *distinct* from fallacious applications which sometimes follow (Gloor 1980). Fear is a bad advisor. Replacing "race" with other words is an unnecessary measure; the suppression of a term leaves us with the facts of geographical variability. In my opinion, this attitude does

nothing to make things clearer and only helps feed racism instead of starving it.

Arthur R. Jensen, *Institute of Human Learning, University of California, Berkeley, California*

The substantive contents of textbooks used in the public schools, from the elementary through the high school level, are controlled to some degree by state legislatures and local school boards, usually on grounds having nothing to do with objective scientific considerations. To my knowledge, college textbooks do not suffer any such formally explicit and extrinsic constraints on their contents. At least in the case of science textbooks, then, one would expect the changes in the central theories and concepts seen in textbooks to be a result of advances in empirical knowledge which force revision of previous conceptions or of new theoretical formulations which provide a more satisfactory account of the existing knowledge or afford a more comprehensive integration with other fields of study.

Yet the emphasis by Littlefield, Lieberman, and Reynolds is not on factors such as these, but on such scientifically extrinsic influences as the social and family backgrounds of those who teach anthropology and the characteristics of the various college audiences that enroll in anthropology courses. It strikes me as surprising that Littlefield *et al.* seem to register no alarm at this state of affairs. Is such a reaction uncalled for when a field that presumably strives for the status of objective science is shown to allow one of its key concepts to be wafted about by the play of social and ideological forces on the political scene that are not at all intrinsically related to the scientific elements of the argument? If central concepts in physical anthropology can be pushed around by such nonscientific considerations as those described by Littlefield *et al.*, it would seem to be high time for those in the field to take stock of its status as objective science. I would say the same thing for my own field (psychology) and, indeed, for all of the behavioral and human sciences.

Concepts in science, even if we would wish it, cannot be importantly changed or permanently killed off by ideological edicts or by religious, political, or social attitudes. Scientific concepts change only through replacement by new ones which more clearly comprehend the objectively observable phenomena that gave rise to them, as oxidation replaced phlogiston in understanding the phenomena of combustion. The same kind of change could conceivably occur for the concept of race in our attempt to understand human variation, but so far there certainly seems to be little agreement that any such scientifically bona fide conceptual change has occurred in physical anthropology with respect to race.

Probably the vicissitudes of the race concept are largely attributable to the fact that the concept, albeit in a taxonomically unsophisticated form, extends far beyond the boundaries of its scientific utility in physical anthropology. "Race" as conceived in the prevailing "folk taxonomy" (as Littlefield *et al.* call it) has many educationally, socially, and economically important correlates, and it is most unlikely that such conspicuous covariation of race, as popularly perceived, and socially significant variables will be ignored, whatever anthropologists may say. I think that the proper response to this condition, by all behavioral and biological scientists, is to try to understand, by all of the objective scientific means available, the nature and causes of the observed covariation between racial taxonomies and socially significant forms of behavior.

Jack Kelso, *Department of Anthropology, University of Colorado, Boulder, Colorado*

As one who contributed 2 of the 58 volumes—one who preferred to switch rather than fight—I can only agree that there may be deep meaning in the shift from race to no race, but it did not seem that way at the time and it does not seem that way to me now.

Race is only one of many topics that has gone from extensive to minimal coverage in physical textbooks over the past few decades. Growth and development, anthropometry, somatology, somatotyping, and craniology come readily to mind as illustrations of subjects that share somewhat the same fate as race. In my view, these changes, together with those the authors discuss concerning race, are symptoms of a basic shift in the outlook of physical anthropologists (in this country) on the significance of human biological variability. I see the change in outlook as an expression of the impact of evolutionary theory, which hit the study of human variability with full force for the first time after World War II. The reason this may be difficult to see is that cause and effect are separated by nearly 100 years. But the racial approach to human variety was set firmly in place well before Darwin and Wallace, and it took a long time, especially in the case of human biology, for the evolutionary perspective to bring to light other ways of making sense out of the distributions of variability.

The "demise" of race seems to me not fundamentally different from the "demise" of culture area as an approach to understanding cultural variability. The culture area concept gave ground to other analytical strategies as essentially historical questions were replaced by questions of process and adaptation. Indeed, race is to biological variety as culture area is to cultural variety, and I wonder if Littlefield, Lieberman, and Reynolds regard the shift away from the latter as another instance of the "social management of knowledge."

There is still the question of timing. The authors could agree with my interpretation and continue to hold that the full force of the evolutionary blow struck when it did because physical anthropology instruction was extended from elite to mass institutions. Perhaps, but in retrospect it appears that the transformation of the field was well under way before the socialization of instruction began. As evidence of this I would cite the publications of Angel (1948), Boyd (1950), Demerec (1951), and Washburn (1951). These publications were signals of a basic change in outlook, and they came well before the subject matter began to move out of the institutions the authors regard as elite.

CA☆ treatment seems always to harden the differences brought to light between authors and commentators, but it also offers an opportunity for questions. I have two: (1) Do the authors see all of the many changes in the subject matter of physical textbooks (during roughly the same period as the treatment of race was changing) as caused by the spread from elite to mass institutions? and

(2) What evidence would they regard as contradictory to their interpretation?

Teresa Laska-Mierzejewska, *Academy of Physical Education, Marymoncka 34, Warsaw, Poland*

In my opinion, the rejection of the existence of races or the disappearance of the term in textbooks published since 1965 is indeed due to influences other than scientific evidence. This is apparent from the coincidence of the serious race conflicts in the United States beginning in the early 1960s with the increase in questioning of the scientific principle of dividing the human species into races. In Poland, the meaning of races in reference to human beings became devaluated in the years 1939-45 through Hitlerite racism. Instead we use the term "variety" in application to the three main varieties, white, black, and yellow. In English-American versions the terms Euro- and Afro-American have appeared. Terminology is, however, a marginal matter in the discussion of this issue.

It is true that physical anthropology is unable to offer a widely accepted definition of race and cannot indicate sharp boundaries between geographical races. Human races, however, do exist in the form of populations differing in the frequency of appearance of various genes in spite of the fact that they have for centuries inhabited the same territory, spoken the same language, and professed the same religion. The removal of the term "race" from textbooks cannot eliminate the centuries-old justification for the existence of races. The genetic factors distinguishing populations are often enhanced by environmental conditions that allow members of one race fully to take advantage of their genetic potential in body dimensions or intellectual features while members of another race may do so to a lesser degree. This causes differentiation between races that is sometimes associated with a value judgment. The existence in nature as a whole of abundant varieties of life does not justify this type of evaluation of groups of people any more than the valuing of one colour of the rainbow more highly than the others.

The denial of the existence of races is therefore a misunderstanding. With the use of only a few body measurements and their proportions and the application of Mahalanobis's distance method, I distinguished nearly 90% of white individuals from blacks in Cuba and demonstrated the hypothesis of a more masculine body build in both men and women of the black variety in comparison with whites (Laska-Mierzejewska 1982). More masculine body build creates a better chance of success in many competitive sports and is one of the most important reasons (besides the social) for the disproportionate representation of black athletes in many sports. Among 1,259 tested participants in the Mexican Olympics (Garay, Levine, and Carter 1974), the participation of black athletes was very high among sprinters, 400-meter runners, high jumpers, boxers, and basketball players. In swimming, diving, and water polo, however, black athletes were very sparsely represented. The thinner (on the whole) skinfolds of the black variety in comparison with the white may be the reason for the limited participation of blacks in water sports, since it may give the feeling of cold during long periods in the water.

The situation of race is similar in a way to that of the institution of marriage: some reject it, others admire it, and others are divorcing, but new marriages are continually being undertaken all over the world.

Frank B. Livingstone, *Department of Anthropology, University of Michigan, Ann Arbor, Michigan*

The enormous increase in our knowledge of human genetic variation in the last 20 years has led to considerable discussion and debate as to the explanation of this great amount of recently discovered genetic variation both within human populations and between them. However, one of the more striking findings of this new work is the relatively small amount of genetic variation that is explained by race. Lewontin (1972) estimated it to be only 6% of the total. These scientific advances and the great increase in the known gene frequencies for many loci in a vast number of human populations are obviously the most important reason for the success of the position that the concept of race has no utility for explaining human genetic variation. The authors, on the other hand, maintain that sociopolitical changes are the major cause of the increase in this position and dismiss the recent scientific advances. They do discuss science as a self-correcting activity, of which this change seems to be a good example, but they nevertheless by curious logic say that although this process undoubtedly occurs, it can't explain the previous popularity of the concept of race. However, for years race was just one of the generally accepted levels of the Linnaean taxonomy, but it happened to be the one most vulnerable to the new genetic data. Now genetic models of clinal variation and not racial classifications are proliferating because they can better explain the data. I emphasize this progress of science because my own experience seems to accord with it. My sociocultural characteristics fit better into the authors' splitter category, but my research on the sickle cell gene made me a lumper because the variation in this gene does not correlate with race at all, but instead demonstrates that natural selection is a more important factor determining human genetic variation than race or common ancestry.

When I first published on the nonexistence of human races Dobzhansky objected to this position since it "played into the hands of race bigots." More recent scientific advances have justified the no-race position even though, as Dobzhansky's comment shows, it first was thought to be socially unacceptable. More recent advances in ecological and evolutionary theory now seem to me to challenge the usual ideas about species. Just as genetic data conflicted with the usual concept of race, ecological data are now conflicting with the genetic definition of species, so that some human populations can be considered different species in that they coexist in the same ecosystem, occupy different ecological niches, have sufficient isolating mechanisms to prevent assimilation, and thus persist as distinct populations. In contrast to the no-race position, this concept conflicts with the dominant ethos of equality that pervades our society. It will be interesting to see if it will prevail.

Ashley Montagu, *Department of Anthropology, Princeton University, Princeton, New Jersey*

In commenting on this valuable paper I found myself writing a history of the manner in which I gradually became aware of the falsities of the anthropological concept of "race." This became a quite lengthy tract and seemed to me (unavoidably) self-referential, if not self-reverential. Perhaps at some future time I shall write a full account of my experiences, in a hostile world, as a critic of the idea of "race," but this is not the place.

A fascinating book remains to be written on the history of the idea of "race." There are literally thousands of works dealing with various aspects of the subject, so that the raw materials are already available. It awaits its Gibbon. Perhaps the authors may be persuaded to undertake the task. It would be very rewarding.

Steven Rose, *The Open University, Walton Hall, Milton Keynes, United Kingdom*

I find the data the authors offer interesting, but I don't fully accept their interpretation of their findings—that the change in treatment of human race amongst anthropologists is dependent largely on institutional factors. It seems to me that this interpretation ignores both changes in population biology made possible by new methods of genetic analysis (especially electrophoresis) that have substantially changed our understanding of the wealth of genetic diversity within populations and also the wider change in the social climate of the past decade and the mounting critiques of reductionism that this change has fostered.

Wenda R. Trevathan, *Department of Sociology, Anthropology, and Social Work, University of North Carolina at Charlotte, Charlotte, North Carolina*

I have no doubt that the sociocultural factors considered by the authors have had significant impact on the concept of race as it is taught in introductory physical anthropology classes. In particular, I think that their hypothesis about the influence of students on the views of their teachers can be taken a bit farther. I do not, however, think that it is necessarily the *views* of the teachers that are influenced by the students; rather, it is the ways of expressing those views.

I wonder, for example, if there is any systematic variation in lumpers and splitters according to the geographic location of the institution in which they are teaching. The results of the Lieberman, Reynolds, and Kellum study reviewed in this article suggest that the geographic origin of the teachers is important in producing splitter and lumper viewpoints, but I suggest that the geographic origin of their students may have even greater influence on the views expressed in the classroom.

I may be the exception rather than the rule, but I have found that my own expressed stand on race has shifted with changes in geographic location within the United States. I grew up in the South and attended a major and fairly elite Southern university in the second half of the 1960s. The term "race" had negative connotations for me, and I felt uncomfortable when racial taxonomies were discussed in my physical anthropology classes. At the time of graduation I believed that the concept of race had no validity in physical anthropology.

As a graduate student and teacher of physical anthropology in the Rocky Mountain West, I continued to treat races as though they did not exist; certainly human variation was discussed, but we did not use the word "race." I rarely heard the issue discussed among students, and attitudes toward races did not appear to vary between the Ph.D.-granting institution and the B.A. institutions with which I was associated.

A recent move back to the southern United States has

resulted in a fairly dramatic change, not in my views toward race, but in the ways in which I deal with it in the classroom. Racism is certainly not unique to the South, and it is not necessarily stronger there, but it appears to be more commonly expressed in various social settings and across all socioeconomic classes. Because of ignorance, misconceptions, and sociocultural background, Southern students in non-elite, B.A.-granting institutions such as the one with which I am currently associated are inherently more racist, at least overtly, than their counterparts elsewhere in the United States. (Unfortunately, as the article implies, the rest of the country may be growing ideologically more like Southerners rather than the other way around.) Race is a real concept to them, and for this reason it falls upon those of us who teach these students to deal with that issue. To sidestep race, treat it as though it did not exist as a valid or invalid concept in physical anthropology, is to take the ostrich approach at best, unethical at worst.

I am not prepared to tell others in my profession how to deal with the concept—whether to treat races as biological realities or simply as cultural constructs for dealing with human variation—but I feel strongly that the issue must be confronted in physical anthropology classes in the light of the resurgence of racism, conservatism, and cultural prejudices expected in this decade. Discussion of racial taxonomies, origins, and discrete characteristics seems to have little scientific validity today and can perhaps be abandoned or treated merely as an interesting stage in the history of physical anthropology. However, it remains incumbent upon teachers of physical anthropology to discuss in our introductory classes the cultural concept of race in the hope of broadening the minds and decreasing the unfounded prejudices of our students. Certainly no other discipline will do so if we do not.

Linda D. Wolfe, *Department of Anthropology, University of Florida, Gainesville, Florida*

The most important aspect of this paper is not the authors' finding on the issue of race. Rather, it is the evidence that culture has a significant impact on the research and attitudes of scientists who study human biology and behavior. Without an appreciation of this impact, future research will reflect only "the alteration of cultural contexts that influence it so strongly" (Gould 1981: 22). As Littlefield, Lieberman, and Reynolds suggest, it may be dangerous for scientists who study human biology and behavior to continue to believe that their professional attitudes and research are culture-free.

Although the central idea of their paper is praiseworthy, there are, I believe, two critical remarks to be made. First, I am concerned that they did not use coders unfamiliar with the hypothesis being tested and with the earlier papers of Lieberman and Reynolds. (They report that they used good students from their introductory courses.) Their paper begins with a quote from Brace and Montagu (1977) that seems to indicate a clear "races do not exist" position. However, in the appendix the Brace and Montagu text is coded "no panel majority emerged." No explanation is offered for this discrepancy.

Secondly, I believe that their categories are too broad. Some of the physical anthropologists who find usefulness in the concept of race define race as a breeding population and study such microevolutionary processes as genetic drift (e.g., Buettner-Janusch 1966). Other physical anthropologists who use the

race concept do so with the idea that a racial group has pre-historical/historical continuity. These physical anthropologists are, of course, interested in racial histories (e.g., Campbell 1979). On the other hand, some of those coded as holding the "races do not exist" position imply that races may well exist but we can learn the most about human variation by studying the clinal distribution of various traits (e.g., Bennett 1979). These physical anthropologists differ from the ones who really take the "races do not exist" position (e.g., Williams 1979).

For Westerners, a knowledge of origins provides an inherent explanation of the phenomenon under study. Thus knowledge of the origins of racial groupings provides an inherent explanation of human behavior and biology which can form the basis of an elitist ideology. Littlefield, Lieberman, and Reynolds would have had a stronger case if a relationship could have been shown between having attended an elite institution and holding the view that races exist because of a common origin.

REPLY

Alice Littlefield, Leonard Lieberman, and Larry T. Reynolds, *Central Michigan University, Mt Pleasant, Michigan*

Our article focuses on an observed change in physical anthropology textbooks, primarily during the period since World War II. We found that the only author of introductory texts rejecting the race concept before 1970 was Montagu but that a rapid shift toward the no-race position had taken place in textbooks by the end of the 1970s. We have attempted to explain this change. For a variety of reasons, we find the alternative explanations offered by our commentators to be insufficient.

We certainly agree with Garn that physical anthropologists have become less interested in taxonomy and more interested in other topics. From the point of view of a sociology of knowledge, however, this is no explanation at all for the phenomenon we observed. Why have they lost interest in racial taxonomies?

Beals, Brace, Kelso, and Livingstone agree with our assertion that support for the concept has declined in physical anthropology but argue that a better explanation is to be found in the internal development of science itself and the gradual accumulation of data. Obviously, developments within science contributed to the observed change. We referred to some of these, and our commentators have mentioned others. Yet some of the developments they cite raise questions as to the timing of the changes within physical anthropology. Kelso refers to the importance of evolutionary theory, which was not applied systematically to the study of human variability until after World War II. Why did it take nearly a century for the impact of evolutionary theory to be felt? Certainly Kelso would not argue that the organized opposition of established religion had no impact on the attitudes of the scientific community toward evolutionary theory.

We welcome the additional insights into the history of the race concept provided by Brace's comment and look forward to his forthcoming article on the subject. Nonetheless, we are puzzled by his argument that the race concept's detour through Broca's French school proves that the elitism of the institutions we mention "had nothing to do with the shaping of the views which flourished in their congenial milieux." Why were these institutions receptive to the ideas of Broca and Ripley rather than some other ideas? For a revealing discussion of the parallels between American folk and scientific racial taxonomies during the late 19th and early 20th centuries, we again draw attention to Marshall's (1968) enlightening article.

Brace rightly points to the importance of Wilson and Brown's (1953) article criticizing the subspecies concept on the basis of discordance of traits. Yet the debate provoked by this proposal in the pages of *Systematic Zoology* does not seem to have had much impact in physical anthropology until the early 1960s and took yet another decade to be reflected in textbooks. Given the basis laid in the even earlier works cited by Kelso and the persistent criticisms of Montagu, we find this delay a phenomenon which calls for explanation. Indeed, if cumulative scientific evidence were decisive, why would certain of our commentators continue to cling to the race concept?

Our article attempts to go beyond earlier general discussions of social and political influences on ideas about human variation by specifying some of the institutional and structural ways in which such influences are transmitted to anthropology and anthropologists. (Undoubtedly there are others, such as the decisions of public and private granting agencies about what kinds of research are to be funded.) Kelso asks what evidence we would regard as contrary to our interpretation. Quite simply, we think our interpretation could be falsified by quantitative data showing that anthropologists' views on human variation demonstrate no significant correlation with type of institutional affiliation, gender, minority-group membership, or other sociocultural characteristics, or that their views are related to these factors in ways other than those found in the study by Lieberman, Reynolds, and Kellum. Personal disavowals or anecdotes of the sort offered here by Garn, Kelso, and Livingstone do not constitute refutation.

The point is that the actors involved in scientific work are often unconscious of the sociocultural influences which affect them, especially when they have been steeped in the positivist faith that science is a neutral or objective activity, largely immune to "external" influences. The very assumption that certain influences are "internal" to science while others are "external" reifies a distinction which is not nearly so clear on closer examination. Scientists are members of the larger society and take its influences with them into the field, laboratory, and classroom. Wolfe suggests that it is important for scientists to develop a greater awareness of the sociocultural grounding of their professional attitudes and research. Trevathan's thoughtful comment about the development of her own views on race and the interests of her students is one example of such self-awareness.

We think the most telling criticism of our work is the one raised by Wolfe: the broad categories we used did not take account of the finer distinctions within each of the two camps—either among those who continue to use the term race or among those who reject it. Indeed, our commentators use the term in a variety of ways and exemplify the confusion which exists within anthropology as a whole. Although neither "population" nor "ethnic group" is the synonym for "race" that Garn asserts it to be, we agree that "population" is used ambiguously. Livingstone's suggested redefinition of "species" promises to add to the confusion.

Nonetheless, we think that our study reveals a growing rejection of the race concept however defined, and few of our commentators express regret over this state of affairs. Two exceptions are Jensen and Laska-Mierzejewska, who wish to continue the practice of categorizing individuals into "races" for the purpose of studying differential intellectual and athletic abilities. Critiques of Jensen's work are legion and too well-known to repeat here. We should like to point out, however, that both those who affirm and those who deny differential abilities between "blacks" and "whites" utilize racial categories the validity of which is not agreed upon among physical anthropologists. Certainly some of those who wish to preserve the race concept would nonetheless disagree with the anthropometric methods of classification utilized by Laska-Mierzejewska, methods which Kelso has consigned to the dustbin of our discipline's history along with somatotyping and craniology.

As for the hypothesis that racial characteristics account for differential athletic success, we wish to draw attention to a growing sociological literature which has criticized this view and offered alternative sociocultural explanations (e.g., Edwards 1972, 1973; Leonard 1980). With regard to swimming events in particular, lack of access to swimming pools and swimming coaches is likely more decisive than skinfolds, and this argument would apply not only to the United States, but to Cuba, where beaches were segregated until 1959.

We are not persuaded by Gloor's thermometer analogy that the study of races can be kept distinct from "the fallacious applications which sometimes follow." The thermometer measures a unidimensional variable and has long done so accurately enough to provide us with many proven practical applications. "Race" is a multidimensional concept which has failed to demonstrate practical applications of the same order as those provided by the study of single genetic traits. As in other scientific fields, the interaction of theory and practice cannot be ignored.

Some of the commentators raise methodological questions which merit a response. Wolfe is concerned that the student coders may have been aware of the hypothesis being tested. We found that students totally unacquainted with physical anthropology lacked the vocabulary recognition necessary to the coding task. The students we did use were not told what the hypothesis was, but their very exposure to physical anthropology courses in which the controversies over race were discussed may, we admit, have influenced their coding decisions. We can only reiterate the point made in note 3: coders tended to classify texts as taking the no-race position only when the authors stated their rejections very explicitly.

Brace raises the question of sampling. Since we included all the introductory-level, one-volume texts from the period 1932–79 that we could find, the books really do not constitute a sample, and the question of statistical significance does not arise. Some of the books suggested to us were not used because they did not meet the criteria, but we feel confident that we did not miss many that should have been included.

In closing, we should like to point to some patterns among the views expressed by our commentators, patterns which some of our readers may have noted. Our argument that physical anthropologists' views on race have been influenced by the changing institutional character of the discipline and the changing characteristics of its practitioners has been more sympathetically received by female and younger male commentators than by older male commentators. Our assertions about differences between elite and nonelite institutions have most criticized by those with degrees from elite institutions.

Two European commentators want to salvage the race concept, while the Americans seem to have few regrets about its passing. Azevêdo, our lone Third World commentator, is not only the most emphatic in pronouncing race's death sentence, but asks us to carry the message beyond our disciplinary boundaries. We suggest that at least some of these differences of viewpoint among our commentators reflect the different social realities that they have lived and continue to experience.

NOTES

[1] We are grateful to the authors of the many excellent textbooks analyzed in this paper.

[2] We realize that by excluding texts that combine physical and cultural anthropology in a single volume we are probably excluding some influential texts. We did this in order to be consistent, since physical and cultural anthropology now tend to be separate courses with separate textbooks. We do not feel that excluding these earlier general texts alters our results significantly, since the great majority of them approached the race concept from the splitting point of view.

[3] Panel members were asked to provide supporting quotations, including page numbers, for the classification assigned to each text. The completed coding sheets were examined for thoroughness and for the accuracy of the citations. All but one of the panel members had taken the introductory survey course in physical anthropology or were enrolled in the course at the time they worked on the project. These students were chosen in order to approximate most closely the circumstances in which the text would be interpreted by its intended audience. About half of the participating students were female, and all would be considered "white" in terms of American folk taxonomies. All had higher-than-average grades, a requirement we imposed to insure that the students' reading comprehension and attention to detail would be adequate to the task. In general, panel members tended to be conservative in their coding. That is, texts were not classified as taking a no-race position unless their authors were explicit about rejecting the race concept.

[4] Preliminary analysis of the concepts "cline" and "population" as used in introductory textbooks suggests that neither of these terms is simply a terminological substitute for the race concept. Although "population" can be used for taxonomic purposes with many of the same implications as "race," it is often simply a label for any aggregate of individuals. The cline concept does not lend itself as readily to taxonomic ends, although it has been employed by splitters as well as lumpers.

REFERENCES

American Anthropological Association. 1981. Enrollments rebounding, faculties shrinking. *Anthropology Newsletter* 22(8):1.

Angel, J. L. 1948. Physical anthropology in 1947: Time of transition. *Yearbook of Physical Anthropology* 3:1-10.

Barnouw, V. 1971. *An Introduction to Anthropology: Physical Anthropology and Archaeology.* Dorsey, Homewood, Ill.

Bennett, K. 1979. *Fundamentals of Biological Anthropology.* William C. Brown, Dubuque, Iowa.

Birdsell, J. B. 1951. Some implications of the genetical concept of race in spatial analysis. *Cold Spring Harbor Symposia on Quantitative Biology* 15:259-314.

Birdsell, J. B. 1972. *Human Evolution: An Introduction to the New Physical Anthropology.* Rand McNally, Chicago.

Birdsell, J. B. 1975. *Human Evolution: An Introduction to the New Physical Anthropology,* 2d edition. Rand McNally, Chicago.

Boas, F. 1912. Changes in bodily form of descendants of immigrants, in: *Race, Language, and Culture,* pp. 60-75. Macmillan, New York.

Boas, F. 1928. *Anthropology and Modern Life.* Norton, New York.

Bodmer, W. F., and Cavalli-Sforza, L. L. 1976. *Genetics, Evaluation, and Man.* Freeman, San Francisco.

Boesiger, E. 1980. Evolutionary biology in France at the time of the evolutionary syntheses, in: *The Evolutionary Synthesis* (E. Mayr and W. B. Provine, Eds.), pp. 309-21, Harvard University Press, Cambridge, MA.

Boyd, W. C. 1950. *Genetics and the Races of Man.* Heath, Boston.

Brace, C. L. 1860. Ethnological fallacies. *The Independent* 12, supplement.

Brace, C. L. 1861. Ethnological fallacies. *The Independent* 13:6.

Brace, C. L. 1964a. On the race concept. *Current Anthropology* 5:313-20.

Brace, C. L. 1964b. The fate of the "classic" Neanderthals: A consideration of hominid catastrophism. *Current Anthropology* 5:3-43.

Brace, C. L. 1964c. A nonracial approach towards the understanding of human diversity, in: *The Concept of Race* (A. Montagu, Ed.), pp. 103-52, Free Press of Glencoe, New York.

Brace, C. L. 1974. The "ethnology" of Josiah Clark Nott. *Bulletin of the New York Academy of Medicine* 50:509-28.

Brace, C. L. 1981. Tales of the phylogenetic woods: The evolution and significance of phylogenetic trees. *American Journal of Physical Anthropology* 56:411-29.

Brace, C. L. 1982. The roots of the race concept in American physical anthropology, in: *A History of American Physical Anthropology* (F. Spencer, Ed.), pp. 11-29, Academic Press, New York.

Brace, C. L., and Montagu, A. 1977. *Human Evolution: An Introduction to Biological Anthropology* 2d edition. Macmillan, New York.

Broca, P. 1859. Des phénomènes d'hybridité dans le genre humain. *Journal de la Physiologie de l'Homme et des Animaux* 2:601-25.

Broca, P. 1860a. Des phénomènes d'hybrideté dans le genre humaine. *Journal de la Physiologie de l'Homme et des Animaux* 3:392-439.

Broca, P. 1860b. *Recherches sur l'hybridité animal en général et sur l'hybridité humaine en particulier, considérées dans leurs rapports avec la question de la pluralité des espèces humaines.* J. Claye, Paris.

Broca, P. 1862. La linguistique et l'anthropologie. *Bulletin de la Société d'Anthropologie de Paris* 3:264-319.

Brown, W. L. Jr., and Wilson, E. O. 1954. The case against the trinomen. *Systematic Zoology* 3:174-76.

Buettner-Janusch, J. 1973. *Physical Anthropology: A Perspective.* Wiley, New York.

Campbell, B. G. 1979. *Humankind Emerging,* 2d edition. Little, Brown, Boston.

Cartter, A. M. 1966. *An Assessment of Quality in Graduate Education.* American Council on Education, Washington.

Coon, C. S. 1939. *The Races of Europe.* Macmillan, New York.

Coon, C. S. 1962. *The Origin of Races.* Knopf, New York.

Coon, C. S. 1964. Comment on: On the race concept, by C. L. Brace. *Current Anthropology* 5:314.

Coon, C. S., Garn, S. M., and Birdsell, J. B. 1950. *Races: A Study of the Problems of Race Formation in Man.* Thomas, Springfield, IL.

Demerec, M. 1951. Foreword. *Cold Spring Harbor Symposia on Quantitative Biology* 15:v-vi.

Dobzhansky, T. 1962. Comment on: On the non-existence of human races, by F. B. Livingstone. *Current Anthropology* 3:280-81.

Dobzhansky, T. 1965. *Mankind Evolving.* Yale University Press, New Haven.

Downs, J. G. and Bleibtreu, H. K. 1969. *Human Variation: An Introduction to Physical Anthropology.* Glencoe, Beverly Hills, CA.

Eckhardt, R. B. 1979. *The Study of Human Evolution.* McGraw-Hill, New York.

Edwards, H. 1972. The myth of the racially superior athlete. *Intellectual Digest* 2:58-60.

Edwards, H. 1973. *Sociology of Sport.* Dorsey, Homewood, Ill.

Ehrich, R. W. 1966. Review of: *Man's Evolution: An Introduction to Physical Anthropology,* by C. L. Brace and A. Montagu (New York: Macmillan, 1965). *Human Biology* 38:339-44.

Finot, J. 1906. *Race Prejudice.* Archibald Constable, London.

Garay, A. L., Levine, L., and Carter, J. E. L. 1974. *Genetic and Anthropological Studies of Olympic Athletes.* Academic Press, New York, London.

Garn, S. 1961. *Human Races.* Thomas, Springfield, IL.

Garn, S. 1964. Comment on: On the race concept, by C. L. Brace. *Current Anthropology* 5:316.

Gould, S. J. 1981. *The Mismeasure of Man.* Norton, New York.

Gloor, P.-A. 1980. A propos de la xénophobie et du racisme. *L'-Anthropologie* 84:583-601.

Hogben, L. 1931. The concept of the race, in: *Genetic Principles in Medicine and Social Science.* Williams and Norgate, London.

Holton, G. 1973. *Thematic Origins of Scientific Thought: Kepler to Einstein.* Harvard University Press, Cambridge, MA.

Holton, G. 1975. On the role of themata in scientific thought. *Science* 188:328-34.

Hulse, F. S. 1971. *The Human Species: An Introduction to Physical Anthropology,* 2d edition. Random House, New York.

Hurlbert, B. M. 1976. Status and exchange in the profession of anthropology. *American Anthropologist* 78:272-84.

Huxley, J. S. 1938. Clines: An auxiliary taxonomic principle. *Nature* 142:219-20.

Huxley, J. S. 1964. Comment on: On the race concept, by C. L. Brace. *Current Anthropology* 5:316-17.

Huxley, J. S., and Haddon, A. C. 1936. *We Europeans.* Harper, New York.

Keith, A. 1950. *An Autobiography.* Watts, London.

Kelso, A. J. 1970. *Physical Anthropology: An Introduction.* Lippincott, New York.

Kelso, A. J. 1974. *Physical Anthropology: An Introduction,* 2d edition. Lippincott, New York.

Kuhn, T. S. 1962. *The Structure of Scientific Revolutions.* University of Chicago Press, Chicago.

Lasker, G. W. 1961. *The Evolution of Man: A Brief Introduction to Physical Anthropology.* Holt, New York.

Lasker, G. W. 1973. *Physical Anthropology.* Holt, New York.

Lasker, G. W. 1976. *Physical Anthropology,* 2nd Ed. Holt, New York.

Laska-Mierzejewska, T. 1982. *Dymorfizm piciowy czlowieka odmiany bialej i czarnej z kuby* (Sexual dimorphism in humans of white and black varieties from Cuba). Akademia Wychowania Fizycznego, Warszawa.

Leonard, W. M., II. 1980. *A Sociological Perspective of Sport.* Burgess, Minneapolis.

Lewontin, R. C. 1972. The apportionment of human diversity. *Evolutionary Biology* 6:381-98.

Lieberman, L. 1968. The debate over race: A study in the sociology of knowledge. *Phylon* 29:127-41.

Lieberman, L, and Reynolds, L. T. 1978. The debate over race revisited: An empirical investigation. *Phylon* 39:333-43.

Lieberman, L., Reynolds, L. T., and Kellum, R. 1983. Institutional and sociocultural influences on the debate over race. *Catalyst* 15:45-63.

Livingstone, F. B. 1958. Anthropological implications of sickle cell gene distribution in West Africa. *American Anthropologist* 30:533-62.

Livingstone, F. B. 1962. On the non-existence of human races. *Current Anthropology* 3:279-81.

Marshall, G. A. 1968. Racial classifications: Popular and scientific, in: *Science and the Concept of Race* (M. Mead, T. Dobzhansky, E. Tobach, and R. E. Light, Eds.), pp. 132-48, Columbia University Press, New York.

Mayr, E. 1954. Notes on nomenclature and classification. *Systematic Zoology* 3:86-89.

McKern, T. W., and McKern, S. 1969. *Human Origins: An Introduction to Physical Anthropology.* Prentice Hall, Englewood Cliffs, N. J.

McKern, S., and McKern, T. W. 1974. *Living Prehistory: An Introduction to Physical Anthropology and Archaeology.* Cummings, Menlo Park, Calif.

Mead, M., Dobzhansky, T., Tobach, E., and Light, R. E., Eds. 1968. *Science and the Concept of Race.* Columbia University Press, New York.

Montagu, A. 1942. *Man's Most Dangerous Myth: The Fallacy of Race.* Columbia University Press, New York.

Montagu, A., Ed. 1964. *The Concept of Race.* Free Press, New York.

Montagu, A. 1965. *The Idea of Race.* University of Nebraska Press, Lincoln.

Morton, S. G. 1839. *Crania Americana.* J. Dobson, Philadelphia.

Morton, S. G. 1844. *Crania Aegyptiaca.* J. Penington, Philadelphia.

Morton, S. G. 1847. Hybridity in animals, considered in reference to the unity of the human species. *American Journal of Science,* 2d series, 3:39-50, 203-12.

Nott, J. C., and Gliddon, G. R. 1854. *Types of Mankind.* Lippincott, Grambo, Philadelphia.

Nott, J. C., and Gliddon, G. R. 1857. *Indigenous Races of the Earth.* Lippincott, Philadelphia.

Planck, M. 1950. *A Scientific Autobiography and Other Papers.* Williams and Norgate, London.

Pouchet, G. 1864. *De la pluralité des races humaines: Essai anthropologique,* 2d edition. Masson, Paris.

Ripley, W. Z. 1899. *The Races of Europe: A Sociological Study.* Macmillan, New York.

Rogers, J. S. 1954. Symposium: Subspecies and clines. Summary. *Systematic Zoology* 3:126, 133.

Rogge, A. E. 1976. A look at academic anthropology: Through a graph darkly. *American Anthropologist* 78:829-43.

Ruse, M. 1981. Review of: *The Evolutionary Synthesis,* E. Mayr and W. B. Provine, Eds. (Cambridge, MA.: Harvard University Press, 1980). *Science* 211:810-11.

Schwidetzky, I. 1974. *Grundlagen der Rassensystematik.* Zürich. [PAG]

Smith, H. N., and White, F. N. 1956. A case for the trinomen. *Systematic Zoology* 5:183-90.

Spencer, F., and Smith, F. H. 1981. The significance of Aleš Hrdlicka's "Neanderthal phase of man": A historical and current assessment. *American Journal of Physical Anthropology* 56:435-59.

Stark, J. A., Reynolds, L. T., and Lieberman, L. 1979. The social basis of conceptual diversity: A case study of the concept of "race" in physical anthropology. *Research in Sociology of Knowledge, Sciences and Art* 2:87-99.

Starrett, A. 1958. What *is* the subspecies problem? *Systematic Zoology* 7:111-155.

Sunderland, E. 1975. Biological components of the races of man, in: *Racial Variation in Man.* Blackwell, Oxford.

Vallois, H. V. 1952. Monophyletism and polyphyletism in man. *South African Journal of Science* 49:69-79.

Washburn, S. L. 1951. The new physical anthropology. *Transactions of the New York Academy of Sciences* 13:298-304.

Weiss, M. L., and Mann, A. E. 1978. *Human Biology and Behavior: An Anthropological Perspective,* 2d edition. Little, Brown, Boston.

Weitz, C. A. 1979. *An Introduction to Physical Anthropology and Archaeology.* Prentice Hall, Englewood Cliffs, N.J.

Williams, B. J. 1979. *Evolution and Human Origins: An Introduction to Physical Anthropology,* 2d edition. Harper and Row, New York.

Wilson, E. O., and Brown, W. L., Jr. 1953. The subspecies concept and its taxonomic application. *Systematic Zoology* 2:97-111.

Young, J. Z. 1971. *An Introduction to the Study of Man.* Clarendon, Oxford.

58

Explaining Modern Man: Evolutionists *Versus* Migrationists

W. W. Howells

INTRODUCTION

That part of human history covering the emergence of modern man and his regional differentiation continues to be surprisingly obscure. Locations of some elements of agreement or controversy, such as Neanderthal man, have long been clear, but the dimensions of the whole problem are far from obvious. The trees are familiar but the forest is not.

In fact, the present moment seems hospitable to a particularly wide span of hypotheses, rather than to progressive narrowing of possibilities, and that is the point of my paper. Such a divergence of premises and views is permitted by the poor state of the necessary fossil evidence; and it is this poor state of information, for a period so recent in hominid evolution, that is surprising. What do we really know? We have the whole panoply of human variation in the immediate present: skeletal and "racial" features noted and measured for two hundred years but not understood in terms of evolution; and "genetic" traits of protein polymorphisms, understood genetically but very little otherwise. Use of the information has been stultified by lack of mathematical methods of structuring the data, methods which have only recently appeared. All the rest of the evidence is palaeontological: hominid fossils of any period, but including few which clearly anticipate modern man, in both time and morphology. It is the paucity of these which surprises. Recent conscientious regional inventories (e.g. Jacob 1967; Aigner 1973; Rightmire 1974) demonstrate the sparseness.

Because of the very nature of the problem, the chronological period involved is unclear. It includes, of course, the time since the last Würm interstadial, about 35,000 years to use round numbers. From that point only anatomically modern *Homo sapiens* was present, as far as has ever been determined; and, as has often been noted, many of these remains are morphologically identifiable with later peoples of the appropriate regions, as in Europe, in South Africa (Fish Hoek), and in Indonesia/Australia (what I have called "Old Melanesia"— Howells 1973b). Also the degree of skeletal differentiation among these Late Pleistocene forms was already as great as that among their living descendants. Then there is a second class of remains, recognized as anatomically modern but not so clearly related to later local populations or major races, and having dates which are less satisfactory on the whole but which might in some cases be considerably earlier than 35,000 B.P.: Qafza

(Farrand 1972), Omo 1 (Butzer *et al.* 1969), Border Cave (Vogel and Beaumont 1972), Liukiang (Aigner 1973). Others are in addition somewhat archaic morphologically, though qualifying for the magic circle: e.g. Skhul, Florisbad. Some of these are almost certain to have overlapped temporally with the Neanderthals of western Europe but—if this is correct, an important point—not as far as is known with non-modern man elsewhere. The dating of the Broken Hill and Solo specimens, never very solid, now appears even less so (e.g. Klein 1973), with indications that Broken Hill, at least, may have been far earlier than previously estimated, so that the persuasion to seek close connection with recent racial groupings is removed.

Thus, if we begin at the present level in time we have, hanging down into the past, a tapestry picturing regional racial differentiation back into the late Pleistocene, exhibiting the same degree of difference already existing in those parts of the fabric extending so far, but also some dangling patches which do not show their real connections to that above. Then the whole shreds off completely, with the important exception of Europe where a special panel for the Neanderthals extends down to the beginning of Würm, where it becomes tattered and shredded in turn. That is to say, in spite of the many published phylogenetic graphs of man through the Middle and Upper Pleistocene, there are no reliable direct connections between recent man and known antecedent populations, whether classed as *Homo erectus* or as archaic *Homo sapiens* (e.g. Swanscombe, Steinheim).

In saying this I do not mean that there are no *prima facie* cases for continuity through these levels, as put forth by Weidenreich (1946) or Coon (1962), but only that the connections lack the objective support which it is possible to find (e.g. in multivariate analysis) between late Pleistocene and modern populations of a given area [1]. Obviously, modern man had ancestors. But there are no clear underpinnings for him, or for population differences, only a recognition of such differences existing as far back as 36,000 years at the least. We have nothing else by way of beginnings which is other than inferential. All that can be done now is to consider the nature of possible hypotheses, and of the evidence used.

HYPOTHESES

Ruling interpretations tend toward one of two polar positions: either there was a single local centre of origin for modern man

Reprinted with permission from *Journal of Human Evolution*, Vol. 5, pp. 477–495. Copyright © 1976 by Academic Press Limited, London.

with subsequent outward migration in all directions, or else there were many centres of origin and no dispersal (within the communal Old World). Naturally, these views base themselves on different materials and different judgements as to processes involved. My interest here lies not in elegance of data or analysis but in the actual contribution to solving the main problem.

The "Neanderthal Phase" hypothesis

This is the one proposing local evolution. Weidenreich (1946) introduced a version of it: *Homo* was distributed in much of the Old World before, or early in, the *erectus* stage; and major regional lineages led, in general independence, to modern principal races (though Weidenreich allowed for interregional gene flow, maintaining a single species pattern). Coon (1962, 1965) in major works elaborated this in greater detail, marshalling and organizing all the existing evidence of fossil hominids. He emphasized zonal distinctions and isolation: in five different geographic zones parallel evolution carried different subspecies of *Homo erectus* across the *Homo sapiens* threshold five separate times. I once (1959) dubbed this general view the "Candelabra" theory, to emphasize the essential branching near the base, but here I would borrow a term from Hrdlicka (1927) and call it the "Neanderthal Phase" hypothesis. I do so to recognize that we are dealing with a late phase only, the supposed ubiquitous emergence of strictly modern man from his immediate antecedents, and also to accord with what I believe to be the views of those advocating it, i.e. a general pre-modern stage to which "Neanderthal" is applied rather broadly by them.

This uniformist view has lately been best expressed by Brose and Wolpoff (1971; see also Howells 1974) Their attention is not addressed to regional differences or to ultimate racial or population distinctions. Instead they analyze, morphologically and metrically, all crania accepted as dating from the last interglacial and glacial phases. These exhibit, they hold, a general "Neandertal" character during the Middle Palaeolithic, and are not variable enough to be significantly subdivided; in the Upper Palaeolithic or its equivalents outside Europe, there has been an *in situ* transition in many different places to modern man, with such populations as that of the Upper Palaeolithic of Europe being transitional in turn to smaller-skulled modern Europeans. The probable agents of this evolutionary transition were mutation and selection, following a suggestion of Brace (1962). During the Middle Palaeolithic, stone tools everywhere became increasingly refined, culminating in the efficient flake blades and their derivatives of the Upper Palaeolithic. This removed a selective need for use of the anterior teeth in aiding the hands to hold various utensils or materials such as skin or wood, a relaxation which allowed the general observed diminution in size of the face and teeth.

Objections, general and detailed, can be made to this particular hypothesis, but they are not relevant here. The point is the nature of the explanation, which is evolutionary, involving adaptation and selection in the "progress." It is specifically anti-migration: Brose and Wolpoff are particularly concerned to refute the idea of "sudden replacement," e.g. of Neanderthals in western Europe by invaders of modern form. However, evolution and adaptation are not cited in relation to differentiation among populations or races, this not being the concern of Brose and Wolpoff. (Coon [1962, 1965] gave considerable

attention to adaptation, particularly climatic, in the modification of skeletal and soft parts; but the burden of his and Weidenreich's arguments was differentiation inherited from already differentiated ancestors.)

The "Noah's Ark" hypothesis

At the opposite pole is the view seeing outward migration, from a common source population which was already morphologically modern, as the explanation of recent man everywhere. In the Neanderthal Phase hypothesis there is no problem of locating a single geographical region of origin, since there was none; in the Noah's Ark hypothesis the region accepted is presently unknown. I do not use "Noah's Ark" in the derision, but only to label the pattern starkly: a single origin, outward migration of separate stirps, like the sons of Noah, and an empty world to occupy, with no significant threat of adulteration by other gene pools or even evaporating gene puddles.

This view is of particular interest at the moment because of the satisfyingly explicit and mathematically persuasive formulation given it by Cavalli-Sforza and various associates, above all Edwards, in a series of papers (see References). The following from Edwards (1971) appears to state the assumptions used by himself and Cavalli-Sforza rather explicitly:

> The Darwinian view of the evolution of man presents us with the hypothesis that all the races of man are descended from a common ancestor, and that the genetic differences which distinguish them have arisen by the accumulation of different genes, or of the same genes in different frequencies, through the influence of four agents. [These are mutation, selection, drift and migration, as usually defined] . . . the migration of man throughout the world has led to a "world trade" of genes.

> Our knowledge of the differences between the races of man . . . is very good . . . But our knowledge of how these differences arose, or even when . . . is very sketchy . . . It is not clear whether the present races of man all descend from a single race which existed 30,000 years ago or one which existed 100,000 years ago. Presumably, if we go back far enough we will encounter some group, ancestral to us all, which was sufficiently homogeneous to merit the title of a race, but we may have to travel very far indeed. I . . . wish . . . merely to point out that a fresh approach to the problem of the phylogeny of man, using data which is independent of that used so far, is most welcome

The evidence used is found in genetic traits of living populations. The model supposes a "random walk" or "Brownian motion" in all gene frequencies, in populations which separated at the beginning, or by later subdivision of primary strips; that is, change by random genetic drift, neglecting other agents of evolution. Various procedures are used to measure the amount of change from the parent, or the distance between two populations, typically using (a) angular transformations of the differences in all allele frequencies at all *loci* used between each pair of populations, (b) summing to give a single genetic distance figure, and (c) a "tree" of "minimum evolution" or similar criterion, using a scale of estimated average total gene substitution.

While genetic drift is not assumed to be exclusive as the agent of differentiation or gene change, it is a sufficient explanation: pitted against selection, "drift wins" (Cavalli-Sforza

1973). The adequacy of drift for small populations known to be recently related has been tested under good controls by Kidd and Cavalli-Sforza (1974). This is a fascinating study of blood antigens in Icelandic cattle and the Norwegian breeds from which they were derived about 1000 years ago. Available demographic (or, as they prefer, "bosographic"!) data include changing herd and population sizes, generation length and sex ratio, in addition to the known time of isolation (a millennium) of the Icelandic population. These data allow a prediction, using only the seven most suitable antigenic systems, of the effect of drift, or the amount of difference; and the close correspondence of the observed differences argues that no other explanation is necessary.

Cavalli-Sforza *et al.* have computed trees using up to 58 alleles, in a dozen or so blood systems, covering 10 to 15 selected world populations. Figure 1 shows the latest to be published (1974). In others, as in this, the apparent earliest, or a least basic, split is an east-west one, separating Europeans plus Africans from Monogloids/American Indians plus Australo-Melanesians. The pattern is a consistent one, across other runs using fewer genes and/or a number of added populations: other Africans are placed with the Pygmies and Bushmen; other American Indians, and also Polynesians, are joined with the main Asiatic branch. Africans and Australians are separated by the greatest total difference with Eskimos, in some runs but not in most, closest to Australians. Ainus are said (1974) to be indistinguishable from other Orientals, and likewise Lapps from other Europeans. In general, continental or major areal associations are consistent, and the whole can be grossly related, on a map, to geographical distances (Edwards and Cavalli-Sforza 1964, Figure 1)

This is a coherent and satisfying picture, and if it were the only evidence on the dispersal of modern man it might be taken at its face value. But it is not the only evidence, as we shall shortly see. And there is the problem of the model itself, which is obliged to be simple, not so much by defects as by constraints, which make it especially persuasive to accept drift as the only really effective agent. Such problems are recognized by Cavalli-Sforza, who is hardly a stranger to them. As to selection it is true that the effects cannot be expected to harmonize across various blood systems. Instead, they should diverge in direction within the summed effect, and end by imitating drift (Cavalli-Sforza and Edwards 1965, p. 933). In fact, Cavalli-Sforza (1965) has pointed out that the high world variance in the frequencies of some blood genes indicates that selective forces must have been at work in addition to drift; and Lewontin and Krakauer (1973), doing further testing of Cavalli-Sforza's values, agree (see also Workman 1968). There is, however, the possibility that total patterns of endemic disease might have differed in major regions, e.g. between east and west; and different diseases acting independently on different blood or serum systems might have produced the patterns of association and difference seen, as suggested by Hunt (1974).

The authors also recognize the differing importance (from selection?) of different loci in their contributions to distance, but perhaps not enough. Such African specialties as the Duffy

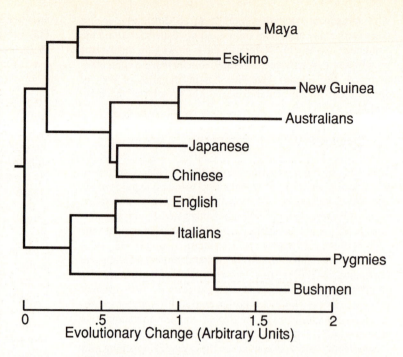

Figure 1. *Genetic evolutionary tree based on 58 alleles. The scale of change is proportional to the number of substitutions in this total number of genes. Redrawn from Cavalli-Sforza (1974) by permission.*

"silent" gene (generally rare elsewhere with exceptions such as Yemenite Jews), Hunter and Henshaw of the MNSs system, and Gm^{abc}, strike one intuitively as worth more weight than they get in the cumulated distances [2].

Cavalli-Sforza *et al.* also note the possible effects of gene flow and hybridization, though these are difficult to accommodate in the mathematical model, as are the effects of population sizes and changes therein; but none of these effects can be estimated. In fact, the goodness of control possible in the cattle study referred to above underlines the difficulties for human prehistory. This need not, however, vitiate the overall result of the genetic analysis [3].

GENETIC *VERSUS* ANTHROPOMETRIC TREES

More substantive queries arise from disagreements between these carefully developed blood "trees" and other projections. One of the latter is of course standard ideas of racial likenesses and differences, based on traditional descriptions and past attempts at classification. The blood trees actually do little violence to these; but disagreement is more marked when measured morphology is considered. Cavalli-Sforza's general point (e.g. 1974) is that external features have been "changed by natural selection to fit the environment to a far greater extent than the rest of our genes have," the rest being the single locus genes determining protein differences. So, he holds, the latter are the better measure of change and true mutual distance. At any rate, two quite different categories of evidence are to be recognized.

For specific comparison, Cavalli-Sforza has computed a tree from "anthropometric" characters, shown in Figure 2 (Cavalli-Sforza and Edwards 1965). This differs from the blood

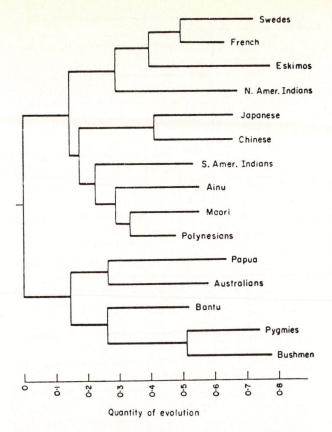

Figure 2. *"Anthropometric" tree computed from 26 traits, including height, weight, trunk and limb proportions, scapular index, indices of skull height and breadth, face nose and orbits, prognathism angle, skin colour, hair thickness, mouth width and ear length. From Cavalli-Sforza and Edwards (1965) by permission.*

trees in making Australo-Melanesians more similar to Africans, and Europeans to American Indians and other Mongoloids. While, as he correctly points out, these discrepancies indicate the way to future research, he concludes that the anthropometric characters are doubtless polygenic in background and subject to short-term environmental effects. His distinction, that "anthropological" characters are essentially controlled by selection while "genetic" characters are not, might seem gratuitous to some, but this is not necessarily so. Polygenic traits, by virtue of recombination and linkage, should be capable of relatively rapid, patterned response to selection-a long recognized point-while as we have seen, single-locus blood serum factors, apart from our ignorance of their fitness values, would appear to emulate drift, when differences are summarized.

There is a separate question. The anthropometric tree is apparently the only one attempted by Cavalli-Sforza, unlike his repeatedly revised and supplemented blood trees, and it leaves something to be desired as the best evidence. Cavalli-Sforza himself (Cavalli-Sforza and Bodmer 1971) considers it somewhat unsatisfactory. The populations involved are generalized ("North American Indians," "Bantu") rather than being specific in origin; and characters are taken from both living subjects and skeletons, embracing for example stature, mouth width, scapular index and skin colour. Thus they are hardly from the same samples. The data were culled from Martin's *Lehrbuch*, and a perusal of this does not make it obvious how they were selected. There would be other difficulties for a rigorous

analysis, such as the matter of standardization among different recorders, not a bugaboo of blood traits; but in this case the major problem is the way samples and characters were chosen.

I do not know of other attempts to make universal anthropometric "trees" from living subjects, but I can furnish them for crania, representing specific and carefully delimited populations, measured uniformly by myself. In various runs (Howells 1973a, 1976), Europeans, Africans, Australo-Melanesians and Mongoloids are all distinct. Australo-Melanesians tend to merge with Africans, but only at a high level; and analysis of the discrimination (Howells 1973a) shows clear cranial distinctions of the former, in elevation of the nasalia, heavy supraorbitals, and more prominent subnasal regions. They share with Africans only low faces and narrow skulls. Europeans are loosely linked with Mongoloids, especially American Indians, and with Polynesians. On the whole, these main pairings are opposite to those in blood trees. But Europeans (including dynastic Egyptians) are relatively undistinguished in cranial characters, as well as unstable in their relations to other main groups from run to run (see also Kidd 1973).

Figure 3 (from Howells 1976) is a multidimensional plot using scores on 10 simultaneous discriminant functions for 3 European, 3 African and 3 Australo-Melanesian male cranial series, showing that each is distinct from others in pattern. Figure 4 (ibid.), another such plot from a different analysis, shows the marked homogeneity among a total of 4 Japanese and Chinese series, and the divergence from these of 3 Australo-Melanesian series, and also of single Norwegian and Ainu series, which somewhat surprisingly are mutually rather close in this particular analysis (which is based primarily on Far Eastern, Pacific and American series, mostly not shown in Figure 4). In any case, the anthropometric tree of Cavalli-Sfor-

Figure 3. *Multidimensional plot of 9 cranial series (3 European, 3 African, 3 Southwest Pacific), using mean scores on 10 simultaneous discriminant functions, based on 70 cranial measurements (no indices) and angles. This kind of plot obviates the limits of two or three dimensions in graphing, by using a trigonometric function, which can accommodate as many terms as needed and gives values varying over the range of 2π. The method was suggested by Andrews (1972).*

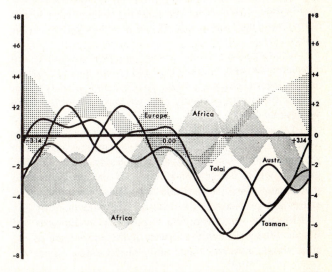

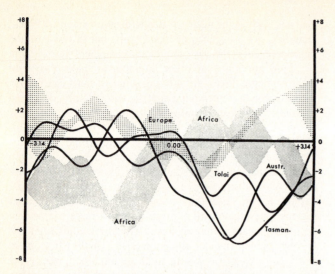

Figure 4. *Multidimensional plot of 5 Mongoloid cranial series and 3 Australo-Melanesian series, plus a Norwegian and an Ainu series. Based on 6 multiple discriminant functions.*

za, crude as it is, is not refuted, and in fact supported in its main features.

The best direct comparison of the two kinds of data comes from Kidd (1973) who has collaborated with Cavalli-Sforza on methods (e.g. 1971). Rather than displaying any of my own, I give in Figure 5 Kidd's cluster-analysis tree of 16 of my cranial populations, which shows a typical result (except for placing Egyptians with Andamanese and Africans in this run). Australo-Melanesians go with Africans at the first bifurcation, but break away at the second. The two European groups remain together with two American groups until the tenth bifurcation, in this run. For trees based on genetic data Kidd employs populations different from Cavalli-Sforza, cited above, and apparently more localized individually, though similarly widely distributed as to selection. I will not illustrate his results but the outline of relations is as in Figure 1; that is, Europeans with Pygmies and Bushmen, Australo-Melanesians with American Indians.

So, over all these attempts at analysis, blood genetic data suggest an east-west main split: Europeans and Africans *versus* Mongoloids and Australo-Melanesians. Morphological data suggest the reverse: a north-south split with opposite, though looser pairing African-Australoid *versus* European-Mongoloid. Kidd's study is addressed largely to statistical validity of this difference, and his testing leads him to conclude that the difference is real.

The foregoing sounds like coming down to a simple confrontation between morphological and genetic data as evidence for phylogeny. There are further qualifications, I believe, suggesting that we tread lightly until we know where the loose boards are.

We have already seen that real information as to possible selective forces is lacking. In fact, the various trees are without the benefit of the kind of ancillary input Kidd and Cavalli-Sforza were able to use on Norse cattle, and are rather simple in mathematical basis: a transformation of data into a Euclidean space, and a clustering by distance. They are more or less classifications (they were first so presented by Edwards and Cavalli-Sforza 1964) with estimates of distance introduced, the step which converts them into "phylogenies." The two

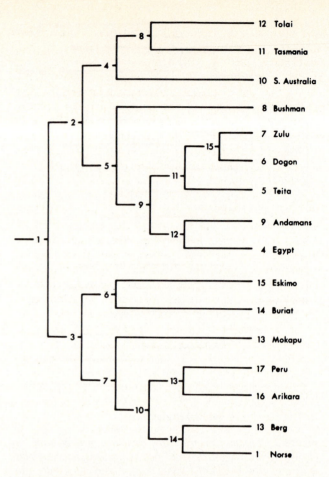

Figure 5. *Craniometric tree, a cluster analysis of 16 cranial series, proceeding by successive splits or bifurcations. The scale is arbitrary, but the numbers indicate the order of bifurcation from first to last. Redrawn from Kidd (1973) by permission.*

categories of data have their special advantages. The genetic trees do indeed go to the level of genes and DNA, the data being reliable and the gene frequencies lending themselves to comparable handling across the board. For morphological data on the other hand, though selection is actually an unknown factor, one can with the right treatment find the actual structures which create the "distances" among the populations in the tree.

THE ORIGIN OF DIFFERENTIATION

Acknowledging the above strictures, one can still ask whether differentiation by drift and/or selection, acting over 30 to 50 millennia, is a simple extension of what might be seen at the beginning of the process, and in this way judge the relative worths of phylogenetic trees. In other words, what can be said from divergences among populations known to have had a common ancestor in the more recent past?

Several studies, beginning with an early attempt by Sanghvi (1953), have allowed comparison of anthropometric and genetic data, some including distances based on language and geography as well, for sets of populations or villages clearly showing common ancestry or at least suggesting an original genetic community. Vocabulary has a drift of its own allowing estimates of relative time of separation of related linguistic groups; language also, in the typical "primitive" situation, demonstrates the fact of relatedness itself, or common origin, for such related dialects or languages. Geographic displacement, especially when measured in crude linear fashion, is of course far less satisfactory as a measure of change, or evolutionary distance. These studies have shown congruence, not divergence, between morphological and genetic trees, over periods of time which are not known certainly but which are within that of dispersal of the language groups involved, i.e. a few centuries or millennia.

Among recent studies of this sort are those on various numbers of villages of Yanomama Indians of Venezuela (Neel *et al.* 1974; Spielman 1973; Spielman *et al.* 1974), and on 19 villages of Bougainville in the Solomons by Friedlaender (1975), the latter making comparisons of all the kinds of data. For Bougainville the historical background must embrace 2000 to 3000 years, perhaps considerably more. Languages of the villages belong to one Austronesian and two Papuan families, so that there is primary and a secondary linguistic divergence to be inferred, suggesting also more than one settlement of the island. That is, within a general Melanesian population complex, there may have been a divergence among the communities now on Bougainville which did not take pace entirely on that island following a colonization by a single group. So, with some indications from prehistory as well (see Terrell, cited in Howells 1973b, Nash and Mitchell 1973), we have a time depth evidently of several millennia but involving a specifically Melanesian source or sources (New Guinea, the obvious source, was first settled over 25,000 years ago.)

Friedlaender finds good agreement between blood genetic and anthropometric patterns, i.e. at least as good a correspondence as each has with geographic distance among villages. (Dental and dermatoglyphic traits show considerably poorer agreement on this basis.) Language, geography and blood are all also similarly congruent. But language and anthropometry are in best agreement of all, at a level beyond that among the others named [4].

What does this last fact mean? On its face it suggests that anthropometry reflects history, and the course of drift, better than does blood. Naturally, there are special considerations here. Anthropometry gives the same main breakdown into three groups of villages as does language (blood does this only partially). Perhaps this represents two or three main immigrant language groups which were already differentiated physically. If so, we conclude that gene flow or local selection have not *reduced* morphological differences as much as they have blood differences; nor, contrariwise, has selection or drift *augmented* the (morphological) differentiation on Bougainville itself. An argument could therefore be made that local environmental selection has tended to homogenize blood differences *if* one does not ask why differences had already been greater among the immigrant groups, assuming the same effects of selection in rather similar localities westward in Melanesia, (But see Rhoads and Friedlander, below). In any case, the assumption that blood genetic differences are the truest reflection of regional history looks rather like a loose board.

There are other queries, as to rate of differentiation. The differences among groups, in the neodivergent population sets cited and others, are significant in degree. The process of differentiation evidently can be rapid at the start. Ward and Neel (1970), from data on villages of Makiritare and Yanomama Indians of Venezuela, have found mean inter-village genetic distances for the two tribes to be 85% and 92% respectively of

Indian intertribal distances, which in turn are about half of the mean distances among the major ethnic groups of Cavalli-Sforza *et al.* This seems to mean two things: first, that pooling villages to find intertribal differences masks intratribal variation, and second, that inter-village mean distances are not much below half the mean distance of worldwide differences. Yet the latter groups, the major racial populations of Cavalli-Sforza, would have been diverging anywhere from twenty to a hundred or more times as long as the Bougainville or Venezuelan villages. This is not surprising, of course: as Neel (1967) and Spielman (1973) have pointed out, and Giles *et al.* (1966) have found in practice, important differences arise at the very beginning because the village fissions are not random with respect to the gene pool, but tend to separate families and lineages, and thus the "drift" at this point does not correspond to the fluctuation between generations of one population. This is one more confounding element in estimating total times, or the significance of differences in the population variances of different genes with respect to both drift and selection.

Morphological traits (anthropometric or craniological), being based on polygenic traits, should be less subject to immediate marked differentiation, e.g. on village fission, because even in lineage separation the sampling of the total gene pool of the parent population will be broader than for the limited number of loci available for blood genetic analysis. This is not to say that micro-differentiation in morphology is inconsequential; we have seen above that it is highly significant.

There is one further qualification arising from all this local variation and microevolution. To use combined or generalized groupings rather than highly specific populations tends to gloss over the component of local variation and the processes responsible for it. On the other hand, in view of the amount of local difference, and the unknown factors behind it, to take a specific local population for use in worldwide comparisons also has hazards (Barnicot 1965). This is not to discredit the genetic trees cited herein, but only to point out that their primacy as evidence of the history of modern man is more questionable than the authors have assumed.

INTERMEDIATE DISTANCES

The above raises some questions as to the meaning of distances and differences between "tribes" or language groups, meaning agglomerations, made up of villages which are clearly closely related, which are in turn both separated and allied by ethnic criteria (such as related languages) which point to an ultimate relationship between the groupings. Rhoads and Friedlaender (1975) have treated both levels together, using 14 villages grouped by 4 Papuan languages in southern Bougainville. Blood and anthropometry agree in the results, which are that inter-language differences (contributions to total variance) clearly exist above the inter-village differences, their total degree of differentiation being about two to three times that among villages within language groups. They conclude that village and language boundaries both contribute to isolation, and thus to drift in both genetic and anthropometric traits. (They find a north-south cline in certain univariate anthropometric measurements, suggesting a possible external introduction at one end of the cline—or else an original difference in populations—apparently damped by the relatively very small amount of migration.)

Chai (1971), using aboriginal tribes of Formosa, which are mutually distant linguistically within the Austronesian stock and which have been isolated from one another probably for a least 3 or 4 millennia, found anthropometric and geographic distributions to correspond closely, as Friedlaender did with his Bougainville villages. Dermatoglyphic traits had a similar distribution with geography and anthropometrics, but Chai judged that the dermatoglyphic distances were smaller in an absolute sense. He assumes that dermatoglyphic traits are "genetic" in general nature, although the other authors cited found no strong correspondence between the distributions of dermatoglyphics and marker genes respectively. Chai suggests from this conclusion that anthropometric features are more affected by selection pressures, and are related to geography for this reason, while the dermatoglyphic net represents the original situation among the occupying tribes (without subsequent drift?). The same argument could be based on other studies cited above; however, Friedlaender's finding of the highest likeness between distances from anthropometry and language at the village level tends to refute it.

Hiernaux in an early (1956) but distinguished analysis of Bantu-speaking tribes of Kivu (Zaïre), Rwanda and Burundi, compared distances from anthropometry, blood (three systems, including Hb) and geography (measured by number of intervening tribal boundaries rather than simply over the ground). All three corresponded to a degree, with one another and with the known history of Bantu dispersion in East Africa; but anthropometry also reflected an axis of differences between upland savannah and lowland forest, so that there is an environmental effect which might reflect selection but might, for this axis, be largely the kind of phenotypic plastic response noted in migrant populations elsewhere.

Rightmire (1976) has made a "genetic-anthropometric" comparison using crania of six Bantu-speaking tribes in East and South Africa running from Rwanda to the Cape. Metric traits were subjected to discriminant analysis and multidimensional scaling to give generalized distances, while the "genetic" traits were 12 non-metric cranial variations similarly treated. The metric distances were in close agreement with language and known history, while the non-metric exhibited a "serious lack of correspondence" with the metric and did not agree substantially with the cultural evidence. This is interesting because of the generally (but not universally) held view that such discrete traits are indeed more "genetic" in nature than metric; they may be, but in Rightmire's case they do not give the appearance of divergence by drift suggested by language and craniometry. However, Laughlin and Jorgensen (1956) in an early study did find a correspondence in divergence of the two kinds of cranial trait in Greenland Eskimos, though this might correspond more to the village level than to the tribal. Zegura (1974), using 12 more widely distributed Eskimo cranial samples, reports finding a better agreement with linguistic distinctions for distances based on metric traits than on non-metric, as well as closer concordance between the sexes in the metric distances.

To return to the living, De Stefano (1973) using four Indian tribes of Nicaragua found no correspondence between blood and anthropometric distances. However the two kinds of data had been collected by different teams, and the biometric treatment, rather elementary, makes the result difficult to evaluate. Also, the languages belong to two different stocks, and the correspondence of genetics with both language and geography is very bad.

The above evidence is varied as to base and uneven in its indications. With other such material it suggests that inter-tribal or inter-language differences are extensions of within-tribal (village) differences, and that morphological (or cranial) divergences are more regular in their apparent agreement with linguistic or geographical separation over time, and may begin and proceed at a steadier pace. To these inter-village and intertribal levels then, the assumption of drift operating on morphology is more attractive than one of selection; the "genetic" data are too heterogeneous (and not really genetic) to allow much to be said except that they are hardly stronger indicators of past relationships than the anthropometric.

CRANIAL DIFFERENCES

Returning to world-wide ethnic differences, the craniometric evidence is a separate indicator. It does not agree, as we have seen, with the genetic data when shaped into trees (though more so, I would say, than does Cavalli-Sforza's anthropometric tree). If cranial features have been more strongly affected by selection than genetic traits, the effect is very ancient, which at once raises questions. For such specific cranial differences are at least 20 to 30 thousand years old, and were already as great as at present. This is not a typological assessment (though such would not disagree): Pleistocene crania from Europe, South Africa and Australia are clearly assignable as European, Bushman and Australoid by discriminant analysis (Howells 1973a) The only difference from modern crania, in some regions but not all, is one of size, not shape. This is not to say that the picture is uniform and complete: Omo and the confusing Palestinian fossils do not fall satisfactorily into place. But, on the simplified Noah's Ark model, one has to suppose that the original dispersal, the big bang, would have been much earlier than 30,000 years, unless the postulated but still mysterious differentiation of morphology by selection was very rapid. (I think any talk about "quantum evolution" would be irresponsible.) And if it was, then why has morphology remained so stable since? For early Australoids already inhabited contrasting environments at the same time (Indonesia and Australia), in the late Pleistocene. And there is the often noted failure of the American Indians to undergo substantial differentiation, cranially or externally, over perhaps 35 to 40 thousand years or more (see Bada et al. 1974).

Let us fill out the late Pleistocene situation a little further. In Europe, people of the Upper Palaeolithic ("Cro Magnons") simply appear, around the beginning of the Late Würm; If, as is required by the Noah's Ark hypothesis, they are actual invaders, their source and route are not known. The same obtains for greater Southeast Asia with slightly earlier dates: there are signs of Australo-Melanesian morphology up to 40,000 years ago in "Old Melanesia," comprising Australia-New Guinea, all of Indonesia including the Philippines, and part of the present mainland of Southwest Asia (see Howells 1973b). But this occupation cannot be extended outward (north and west) or downward in time, on current information.

For Africa, the evidence in this time range (beyond the Fish Hoek Bushman at perhaps 35,000) is too insubstantial to help, notwithstanding Rightmires' (1974) exacting review and evaluation. As to Mongoloids, the inference is that the basic populations, represented by American Indians and by various Asiatic aboriginals from the south up to pre-Yayoi Japanese, are early in origin (datable as no later than the emigration to

America, now suggested as verging on 50,000 B.P.—Bada *et al.* 1974). It has long been hypothesized, from distribution and appearance, that the specialized Mongoloids (Chinese, Koreans, Japanese, Northeast Siberians, Eskimos) emerged from the earlier matrix under selection by the cold of the last Würm maximum (see Coon, Garn and Birdsell 1950; although Steegmann 1970, failed to sustain the cold-engineering hypothesis by experiment). This phenomenon, or stage of differentiation, would presumably not be reflected in blood genetic trees if the blood traits changed only by drift.

CONFRONTATION OF HYPOTHESES

Let us return to comparison of the two extreme forms of hypothesis, treating them as stick men, for purposes of argument, without all their qualifications. That is, let us consider mainly their premises, since they are essentially ways of viewing the situation. They are, of course, irreconcilable. The Neanderthal Phase hypothesis is pro-evolutionary and anti-migration; the Noah's Ark hypothesis is the reverse. One of them has to be wrong.

The Neanderthal Phase view is pro-evolutionary in the traditional sense, taking selective forces and mutations as the tide which lifts the boats everywhere, in a progressive rise. Its anti-migration assumption necessarily ignores differentiation within one major stem as explaining modern variety. The assumption itself is also highly improbable. Pleistocene elephants, horses and other mammals were migrating and differentiating freely, at all time levels, often resulting in major "replacements," as von Koenigswald has shown (various papers) for Southeast Asia. It is now axiomatic that man, with his developing arsenal of culture, was less subject to a tendency to speciate (though certainly not free from it), but this does not mean he was no traveller. Evidence even exists for local Neanderthal movement (McBurney 1967; Butzer 1971); and the arrival of modern man in America and Australia were obviously energetic expansions, equivalent to those of horses or stegodonts. Other contemporary populations of modern men, not on the frontiers but hemmed in by neighbours, whether modern or archaic morphologically, would not have been restrained by gentlemanly feelings from contesting for space.

The Noah's Ark hypothesis is pro-migration, as long as migration is outward [5]. It allows for simple expansion but abhors collision and competition. It is anti-evolutionary in the general sense, at least when it rests on blood genetic materials; the model we have been reviewing at length above acknowledges only differentiation by chance events. In the currency of evolutionary writing, of course, the agents of genetic change are mutation, selection, migration (or hybridization) and drift. Edwards and Cavalli-Sforza explicitly recognize the first three but maintain they are unnecessary, and that unless they are disregarded the genetic model, in the scale used, is difficult to manage. I should repeat my understanding that the authors are by no means unaware or careless of these niceties, and are in fact authorities on them, but also that the notable feature of the model is its simplicity.

Therefore the two types of hypothesis are both faulty, as applied to the data, because both omit essential elements from their premises. One must be wrong in its conclusions, and from the data neither can be proved right. Can both be proved wrong? Unfortunately not, or else this would have happened already. Let us take a single well-known exhibit, the Skhul population of Palestine.

One school calls this "Neanderthal," though seeing it as a local, evolutionary transition from the Neanderthal to modern stage. The other view has been that the Skhul people were Neanderthal-modern hybrids, which would accord with the Noah's Ark view, in the sense that it would disprove the other hypothesis but not this one. But the case has not been settled either way.

There is an obvious intermediate hypothetical position, which uses all evolutionary agents, particularly the factor which both the others ignore: encounters between populations of modern man and of other forms, with consequent gene flow and population replacements, by absorption or elimination (the latter not meaning genocide, but rather pre-emption of resources by technical advantages and greater skills.) In other words, modern man did arise in one general region, as the progressive subspecies often named *Homo sapiens sapiens*, and owes his subsequent differentiation neither to pre-existing isolation and independent evolution (Neanderthal Phase proposition), nor to simple drift operating on populations separated by migration (Noah's Ark).

In concrete terms this view would resolve some of the apparent difficulties with the extreme views. It would allow for the known early cranial differences (as in part an effect of genes from pre-existing populations in the Old World,) together with the virtual absence of change since the late Würm, as in the Americas. Of course, explanation of genetic differences as due exclusively to drift would have to be given up. However, we have no more hard evidence for this view than for the other two, although it has been argued that Australoids exhibit influences or outright descent from the Solo people, and Europeans (or Central Siberians—see Thoma 1964) from the Neandertals. In any case, the situation points to the real importance of solving the Neandertal "problem." Only here, in the strictly defined Neanderthals of Europe and western Asia, have we a major body of skeletal evidence for non-modern man, clearly recognizable as representing mutually related populations of similar morphology, and falling in a time zone crucial for the problem. Since they were either the immediate source of modern man or were instead impinged upon by modern populations, only here have we, for the near future, a laboratory for the study of the actual nature and rate of change.

CONCLUSIONS

1. None of the above hypotheses has been fruitful for a phylogeny of recent man. We need hypotheses, but also ways of testing them; and material for this, as in other long-term phylogenies of animals, will have to be palaeontological.

2. It is quite likely that the genetic traits of modern populations have been diverging by drift, but not at a constant or linear rate of radiation, and not by drift alone.

3. It is quite likely that morphological features ("anthropometric" is a poor word) have diverged under selection, but to unknown and varying degrees; most cranial features have persisted largely unchanged over many millennia.

4. Accordingly, "trees" produced from Euclidean or other distances are not equivalent to long-term phylogenies. What holds for recently separated populations is probably not valid for major ethnic groups and vice versa [6].

5. Refinement of the same methods of analysis is nevertheless promising, both in detecting population affinities for

and among early skeletal specimens and groups, and in extending persuasive evidence from genetic materials of the present back in time (e.g. differentiating among polymorphisms as to responsiveness to selection etc.).

6. Paucity of fossils and infirmity of dates remains a central problem; the base for most attempts at reconstructing recent human history is weaker than we like to recognize.

NOTES

[1] Stringer (1974) finds that, in multivariate measures on crania, existing populations plus those of the Upper Paleolithic have a variation that is "extremely compact," in the relative sense, so much that D^2 differences among them are of a different order from those in fossil *Homo sapiens* (sensu lato) generally.

[2] Schanfield (1971) computed trees for Asiatic and Oceanic populations using different sets of systems. He found that the Gm system when present provided about 3/5 of the differentiating power of the whole set. In a more local investigation, of seven villages of Makaritari Indians, Ward and Neel (1970) produced quite different genetic trees by the Edwards-Cavalli-Sforza methods when different small sets of loci were entered. This also suggests a smoothing effect present in the use of major ethnic groups—see below.

[3] Cavalli-Sforza *et al.* are apparently only secondarily interested in the total time involved. For the earliest separation among major stocks (Caucasoid, Negroid, Mongoloid) he finds (1971) Negroid-Mongoloid separation as the first, on the basis of an estimate of *f*, the kinship coefficient (though this is followed by a separation of Caucasoids from Negroids, not from Mongoloids, as implied in the genetic trees). Calibrating this by an assumed date of 15,000 years for the emigration of American Indians, he gets a figure for the most ancient separation above (Negroids-Mongoloids) when drift is assumed to control the rate of change, of 35,000 to 40,000 years (1974). If this is corrected for more recent assessments of American Indian movements beginning at least 45,000 years ago, the Negroid-Mongoloid separation would go back to about 120,000 years in such estimates. (The use of a kinship coefficient may not be appropriate for such populations—see Harpending (1974).)

Nei and Roychoudhury (1974) have also estimated times since divergence using large numbers of protein and blood group *loci*, assembled from various sources for Mongoloids, Caucasoids and Negroids (the last two being mainly from U.S. Whites and Negroids respectively). Again Negroids appear the most divergent in net codon differences, leading to estimates of separation of 115 to 120 thousand

years ago from the other two. Mongoloids and Caucasoids separated 55,000 years ago according to these authors although, they point out, cross migration might have lowered the net difference here.

(Sir Ronald Fisher said, in a conversation Adelaide in 1961 a few months before his death, that he had always thought the Africans were the most distinct or earliest separated of main human groups. Unfortunately I did not question him on why he thought so.)

[4] Neel *et al.* (1974), Spielman (1973) and Spielman *et al.* (1974) have investigated most of these associations, by more exact methods, though in different reports and on varying numbers of Yanomama villages, 7 being a typical number. Language was found to correspond significantly with the genetic network, and to indicate a time depth of 1000 years. Anthropometry invariably corresponds most closely with geography (neither tested against language). Genetics corresponds well, though not as well as anthropometry; it corresponds with anthropometry only to the same degree as with geography. A dermatoglyphic network corresponds less well with all.

[5] In the present context, "migration" can be disastrously ambiguous. In the model, it has its public meaning, of displacement of populations leading to separation and to the isolation necessary for drift to be effective. In population genetics (and evolutionary theory generally) it signifies migration of *genes*, in a network of populations, i.e. hybridization, the antagonist of drift. (This is treated authoritatively and at length in Cavalli-Sforza and Bodmer 1971.)

[6] [See Harpending (1974) for a review of many matters dealt with herein, much more incisive than the present wandering discourse, and addressed more to methodology and theory. He concludes that studies of small populations have been successful for anthropological purposes, i.e. regional histories, but that they have not advanced knowledge of human evolution on the grand scale, or of the processes involved. In particular he doubts that drift, as exhibited among small populations, is of consequence over wide areas and long time periods; and that trees, on the same large scale but still within the species, can really be interpreted.]

REFERENCES

Aigner, J. S. 1973. Pleistocene archaeological remains from south China. *Asian Perspectives* 16:16-38.

Andrews, D. F. 1972. Plots of high-dimensional data. *Biometrics* 28:125-136.

Bada, J. L., Schroeder, R. A., and Carter, G. F. 1974. New evidence for the antiquity of man in North America deduced from aspartic acid racemization. *Science* 184:791-793.

Barnicote, N. A. 1965. Anthropology and population genetics, in: *Genetics Tools* (S. J. Geetrs, Ed.), Proceedings of the XIth International Congress of Genetics, 1963, vol. 3, pp. 953-963.

Brace, C. L. 1962. Cultural factors in the evolution of human dentition, in: *Culture and the Evolution of Man* (M. F. Ashley Montagu, Ed.), pp. 343-354. Oxford University Press, New York.

Brose, D. S. and Wolpoff, M. H. 1971. Early Upper Paleolithic man and late Middle Paleolithic tools. *American Anthropologist* 73:1156-1194.

Butzer, K. W. 1971. *Environment and Archaeology*, 2nd ed. Aldine-Atherton, Chicago.

Butzer, K. W., Brown, F. H., and Thurber, D. L. 1969. Horizontal sediments of the lower Omo valley: the Kibish formation. *Quarternaria* 11:15-29.

Cavalli-Sforza, L. L. 1965. Population structure and human evolution. *Proceedings of the Royal Society*, B164:362-379.

Cavalli-Sforza, L. L. 1967. Human populations, in: *Heritage from Mendel* (R. A. Brink, Ed.), pp. 309-331. University of Wisconsin Press, Madison.

Cavalli-Sforza, L. L. 1973. Analytic review: Some current problems of human population genetics. *American Journal of Human Genetics* 25:82-104.

Cavalli-Sforza, L. L. 1974. The genetics of human populations. *Scientific American* 231:81-89.

Cavalli-Sforza, L. L., Barria, I., and Edwards, A. W. F. 1964. Analysis of human evolution under random genetic drift. *Cold Spring Harbor Symposia on Quantitative Biology* 29:9-20.

Cavalli-Sforza, L. L., and Bodmer, W. F. 1971. *The Genetics of Human Populations*. W. H. Freeman, San Francisco.

Cavalli-Sforza, L. L., and Edwards, A. W. F. 1965. Analysis of human evolution, in: *Genetics Today* (S. J. Geerts, Ed.), Proceedings of the XIth International Congress of Genetics, 1963, vol. 3, pp 923-933.

Cavalli-Sforza, L. L., and Edwards, A. W. F. 1967. Phylogenetic analysis: Models and estimation procedures. *Evolution* 21: 550-570.

Chai, C. K. 1971. Analysis of palm dermatoglyphics in Taiwan indigenous populations. *American Journal of Physical Anthropology* 34:369-376.

Coon, C. S. 1962. *The Origin of Races*. Knopf, New York.

Coon, C. S. 1965. *The Living Races of Man*. Knopf, New York.

Coon, C. S., Garn, S. M., and Birdsell, J. B. 1950. *Races: A Study of the Problems of Race Formation in Man*. C. C. Thomas, Springfield, IL.

Edwards, A. W. F. 1971. Mathematical approaches to the study of human evolution, in: *Mathematics in the Archaeological and Historical Sciences* (F. R. Hodson, D. G. Kendall, and P. Tautu, Eds.), pp. 347-355. University Press, Edinburgh.

Edwards, A. W. F., and Cavalli-Sforza, L. L. 1964. Reconstruction of evolutionary trees. Phenetic and phylogenetic classification, in: *Systematics Association Publication No. 6* (F. Heywood and J. McNeill, Eds.), pp. 67-76.

Farrand. W. R. 1972. Geological correlation of prehistoric sites in the Levant, in: *The Origin of Homo sapiens* (F. Bordes, Ed.), pp. 227-235, Unesco, Paris.

Friedlaender, J. S. 1975. *Patterns of Human Variation: The Demography, Genetics, and Phenetics of Bougainville Islanders*. Harvard University Press, Cambridge, MA.

Giles, E., Walsh, R. J., and Bradley, M. A. 1966. Micro-evolution in New Guinea: The role of genetic drift. *Annals of the New York Academy of Sciences* 134:655-665.

Harpending, H. 1974. Genetic structures of small populations. *Annual Review of Anthropology*. 3:229-243.

Hiernaux, J. 1956. Analyse de la variation des caractères physiques humains en une région de l'Afrique centrale: Ruanda-Urundi et Kivu. *Annales du Musée Royal du Congo Belge*, série in 8°, *Anthropologie*, Vol. 3, 1-131.

Howells, W. W. 1959. *Mankind in the Making*. Doubleday, New York.

Howells, W. W. 1973a. Cranial variations in Man. A Study by Multivariate Analysis. *Peabody Museum Papers* 67:1-259.

Howells, W. W. 1973b. *The Pacific Islanders*. Weidenfeld and Nicholson, London; Scribners, New York.

Howells, W. W. 1974. Neanderthals: Names, hypotheses and scientific method. *American Anthropologist* 78:24-38.

Howells, W. W. 1976. The biological origin of the Australians: Multivariate analysis in the problem of Australian origins, in: *Origin of the Australians* (R. L. Kirk and A. G. Thorne, Eds.), Australian Institute of Aboriginal Studies, Canberra.

Hrdlicka, A. 1927. The Neanderthal phase of man. *Journal of the Royal Anthropological Institute* 17:249-269.

Hunt, E. E., Jr. 1974. Head shapes and human evolution. *Reviews in Anthropology* 1:285-291.

Jacob, T. 1967. *Some Problems Pertaining to the Racial History of the Indonesian Region. A study of human skeletal and dental remains from several prehistoric sites in Indonesia and Malaysia*. Drukkerij Neerlandia, Utrecht.

Kidd, K. K. 1973. Genetic approaches to human evolution. *Accademia Nazionale dei Lincei* 182:152-174.

Kidd, K. K., and Cavalli-Sforza, L. L. 1971. Number of characters examined and error in reconstruction of evolutionary trees, in: *Mathematics in the Archaeological and Historical Sciences* (F. R. Hodson, D. G. Kendall, and P. Tautu, Eds.), pp. 335-346, University Press, Edinburgh.

Kidd, K. K., and Cavalli-Sforza, L. L. 1974. The role of genetic drift in the differentiation of Icelandic and Norwegian cattle. *Evolution* 28: 381-395.

Klein, R. G. 1973. Geological antiquity of Rhodesian man. *Nature* 244:311-312.

Laughlin, W. S., and Jørgensen, J. B. 1956. Isolate variation in Greenlandic Eskimo crania. *Acta Genetica et Statistica Medica* 6:3-12.

Lewontin, R. C., and Krakauer, J. 1973. Distribution of gene frequency as a test of the theory of the selective neutrality of polymorphisms. *Genetics* 74:175-195.

McBurney, C. B. M. 1967. *The Hua Fteah (Cyrenaica) and the Stone Age of the South-east Mediterranean*. University Press, Cambridge.

Nash, J., and Mitchell, D. D. 1973. A note on some chipped stone objects from South Bougainville. *Journal of the Polynesian Society* 82: 209-212.

Neel, J. V. 1967. The genetic structure of primitive human populations. *Japanese Journal of Human Genetics* 12:1-16.

Neel, J. V., Rothhammer, F., and Lingoes, J. C. 1974. The genetic structure of a tribal population, the Yanomama Indians. X. Agreement between representations of village distances based on different sets of characteristics. *American Journal of Human Genetics* 26:281-303.

Nei, M., and Roychoudhury, A. K. 1974. Genic variation within and between the three major races of man: Caucasoids, Negroids, and Mongoloids. *American Journal of Human Genetics* 26:421-443.

Rightmire, G. P. 1974. The later Pleistocene and Recent Evolution of Man in Africa. *Module* 27:1-38. MSS Modular Publications, New York.

Rightmire, G. P. 1976. Metric *versus* discrete traits in African skulls, in: *The Measures of Man* (E. Giles and J. S. Friedlaender, Eds.), Peabody Museum, Cambridge, MA.

Rhoads, J. G., and Friedlaender, J. S. 1975. Language boundaries and biological differentiation on Bougainville: Multivariate analysis of variance. *Proceedings of the National Academy of Sciences* 72:2247-2250.

Sanghvi, L. D. 1953. Comparison of genetical and morphological methods for a study of biological differences. *American Journal of Physical Anthropology* 11:385-404.

Schanfield, M. S. 1971. *Population Studies on the Jm and Inv Antigens in Asia and Oceania*. Ph.D. Thesis, University of Michigan. University Microfilms, Ann Arbor.

Spielman, R. S. 1973. Differences among Yanomama Indian villages: Do the patterns of allele frequencies, anthropometrics and map locations correspond? *American Journal of Physical Anthropology* 39:461-479.

Spielman, R. S., Migliazza, E. C., and Neel, J. V. 1974. Regional linguistic and genetic differences among Yanomamo Indians. *Science* 184:637-644.

Steegman, A. T., Jr. 1970. Cold adaptation and the human face. *American Journal of Physical Anthropology* 32:243-250.

Stefano, G. F. de. 1973. A study of morphological and genetic distance among four Indian villages of Nicaragua. *Journal of Human Evolution* 2:231-240.

Stringer, C. B. 1974. Population relationships of later Pleistocene hominids: A multivariate study of available crania. *Journal of Archaeological Science* 1:317-342.

Thoma, A. 1964. Die Enstehung der Mongoloiden. *Homo* 15:1-22.

Vogel, J. C., and Beaumont, P. B. 1972. Revised radiocarbon chronology for the Stone Age in South Africa. *Nature* 237:50-51.

Ward, R. H., and Neel, J. V. 1970. Gene frequencies and microdifferentiation among the Makiritare Indians. IV. A comparison of a genetic network with ethnohistory and migration matrices; a new index of genetic isolation. *American Journal of Human Genetics* 22:538-561.

Weidenreich, F. 1946. *Apes, Giants, and Men*. University of Chicago Press, Chicago.

Workman, P. L. 1968. Gene flow and the search for natural selection in man. *Human Biology* 40:260-279.

Zegura, S. 1975. Taxonomic congruence in Eskimoid populations. *Amer. J. Phys. Anthro.* 43:271-284.

59

Reconstruction of Human Evolution: Bringing Together Genetic, Archaeological, and Linguistic Data

L. L. Cavalli-Sforza, A Piazza, P. Menozzi, and J. Mountain

The reconstruction of human phylogeny from contemporary genetic information was first attempted (Cavalli-Sforza and Edwards 1963, 1967a, 1967b; Edwards and Cavalli-Sforza 1964), by the use of gene frequencies of 20 alleles from five major blood-group systems known from 15 populations. The genetic information from all genes was cumulated by calculating a "genetic distance" between pairs of populations. Two independent methods developed for the purpose were used to reconstruct the phylogeny, with very similar results. One of them was based on independence of evolution in the branches resulting after every fission, and the other on maximum parsimony; neither, however, can define an origin (a "root") for the tree. When only information internal to the data set is used, it is necessary to assume constant evolutionary rates for setting a root. When this hypothesis was superimposed on constructed trees, the root separated African plus European populations on one side and the rest of the world on the other. The later addition of more genes (Kidd 1973), including *HLA* (Piazza *et al*. 1975), caused little change in the shape of the phylogenetic tree.

Many protein and enzyme polymorphisms were detected in the 1960s and 1970s by electrophoretic methods but were initially tested on few samples. By using only three populations (Africans, Europeans, and East Asians), Nei (1978) was able to consider many more genes. He concluded that blood groups and enzyme polymorphisms gave different results with respect to the location of the root, with blood groups still showing greater similarity between Africans and Europeans than between Europeans and East Asians, thus confirming earlier results on the position of the root. With enzymes and proteins, however, Europeans were closer to East Asians than to Africans. These markers carried more statistical weight than blood groups, so that the complete data located the root between Africa and Europe plus Asia. The conclusion remained unchanged on extension to other populations (Nei and Roychoudhury 1982), but the analysis did not include the rich set of *HLA* data.

Since that time, there have appeared results generated by DNA restriction analysis of mitochondrial DNA (Johnson *et al*. 1983; Cann *et al*. 1987), β-globin (Wainscoat *et al*. 1986), the Y chromosome (Lucotte and Ruffie 1987), and 44 nuclear gene markers (Cavalli-Sforza *et al*. 1986; Bowcock *et al*. 1987). With some contradiction, they tend to confirm the African/non-

African split, but they are affected by biological or statistical weaknesses that will be discussed in a separate paper in which we will also present new DNA-marker data. The classical marker data used here confirm this conclusion but are much more abundant, thus allowing us to study human evolution in greater detail and to test agreement with other sources of evolutionary information, both archaeological and linguistic.

EVOLUTIONARY ANALYSIS OF CLASSICAL GENETIC MARKERS

Materials and Methods

The literature data were collected in the course of preparation of an atlas of human variation. Selection of the present material was guided by the desire to study a representative sample of the world aboriginal populations, balancing the need to have as many genes as possible with the need to minimize the number of gaps in the gene × population matrix. Two genetic distances corresponding to different evolutionary models were used for comparing populations in pairs: (i) the most investigated one, a family (Reynolds *et al*. 1983) that also includes distances used in earlier papers (Cavalli-Sforza and Edwards 1963, 1967a, 1967b; Edwards and Cavalli-Sforza 1964; see also Nei 1987); and (ii) Nei's standard genetic distance (Nei 1987), always with correction for sample size. The two distances were highly correlated ($r = 0.86$) and the relation between them was of almost perfect proportionality except at short distances. We found it safe to use gene × population matrices that had gaps, provided these were not too frequent, by calculating distances between pairs of populations only for genes known in both of the populations being compared. Tests of this statement included comparison of results of principal components and tree analysis based on both an incomplete matrix and a complete subset of the same matrix, as well as extensive experiments of simulation of the effect of random gaps on principal component maps, which are highly related to the highest splits in the tree (Cavalli-Sforza and Piazza 1975). Gaps in the matrix used for the tree of Fig. 1 were 23.7%.

A recently introduced statistical technique, the bootstrap (Efron 1982), a resampling method for obtaining standard er-

Reprinted with permission from *Proceedings of the National Academy of Sciences U.S.A.*, Volume 85, pp. 6002–6006. Copyright © 1988 by PNAS.

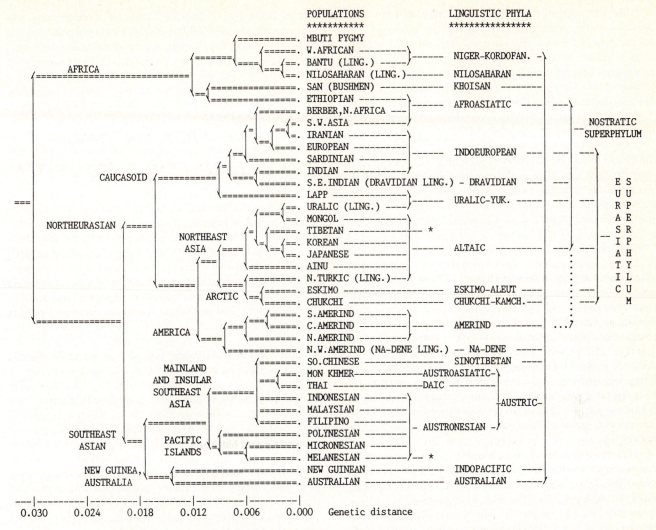

POPULATIONS / LINGUISTIC PHYLA tree diagram with genetic distance scale (0.030, 0.024, 0.018, 0.012, 0.006, 0.000 — Genetic distance).

Figure 1. *Comparison of genetic tree and linguistic phyla. See text for details. (Ling.) indicates populations pooled on the basis of linguistic classification. The tree was constructed by average linkage analysis of Nei's genetic distances. Distances were calculated based on 120 allele frequencies from the following systems: A1A2BO, MNS, RH, P, LU, K, FY, JK, DI, HP, TF, GC, LE, LP, PEPA, PEPB, PEPC, AG, HLAA (12 alleles), HLAB (17 alleles), PI, CP, ACP, PGD, PGM1, MDH, ADA, PTC, E1, SODA, GPT, PGK, C3, SE, ESD, GLO, KM, BF, LAD, E2, GM, and PG.*

rors that are difficult to estimate directly, proved very useful. According to this method, genes actually used are randomly sampled with replacement, generating a new matrix of genes × populations with the same number of genes as the original, but in which some genes are missing and others are repeated. The procedure is repeated a sufficient number of times ("bootstraps"), each time producing a new matrix. From each matrix a given statistic is calculated; its standard error is the standard deviation of the values taken by the statistic in the bootstrap samples. Felsenstein (1985) suggested using the bootstrap to test the reproducibility of the sequence of splits in the tree.

Tree of 42 World Populations

The tree shown in Figure 1 was generated by average linkage analysis (Sokal and Michener 1958) of 42 populations representing the world aborigines: 7 African, 5 American (natives),

5 Oceanian, 6 European, and the rest Asian including insular Southeast Asia. All values are average gene frequencies for all data found in the literature satisfying the criteria of being aboriginal, with little or no admixture, pooling populations geographically. When geographic pooling gave rise to potential heterogeneity, an ethnolinguistic criterion of classification was added. Six of the 42 groups were formed on the basis of linguistic affinity: Nilosaharan and Bantu in Africa; Samoyed and other Uralic language speakers living near the Ural mountains; Northwest Americans speaking northern and southern Na-Dene languages; North Turkic, i.e., Northeast Asian populations whose language belongs to this subgroup of the Altaic phylum; Southeast Indian, speaking Dravidian languages. The tree in Fig. 1 is slightly simplified with respect to the original one of 42 populations in that all Europeans that clustered compactly together (Basque, Dane, English, Greek, and Italian) were pooled to form one population. All analyses, however, were done on the full tree.

The first split in the tree separates Africans from non-Africans and is reproducible, given that in 84 out of 100 bootstrap trees the first split separated from all other populations a cluster containing at least the four "core" African populations (Pygmies, West Africans, Bantu, and Nilosaharan). In most of the 84 trees the African cluster also contains the other two sub-Saharan African populations (San and Ethiopians). When these two are not with the core Africans they tend to join the Caucasoid group.

The next bifurcation separates two major "superclusters," the first of which, Northeurasian, splits into (i) Caucasoids and then (ii) Northeast Asians plus Amerindians. The Northeast Asian cluster separates further into a small cluster of Arctic populations, including Eskimos, and a cluster including both East Asians and North Asians. Caucasoids form a fairly tight group consisting of 12 populations, 5 of which were pooled as "Europeans" in Fig. 1. Lapps leave the cluster in 32% of the bootstraps, joining Asian Arctic populations. Berbers and Dravidians leave the Caucasoid cluster 20% of the time and tend to join respectively the African and one of the two major East Asian clusters. The Northeast Asian cluster is also reasonably compact, 81% of trees having at least 4 of the 6 populations shown in the tree in Fig. 1; most often lost are Tibetans (25%), Uralic speakers (13%), and Ainu (12%). The Arctic Northeast Asian cluster (Chuckchi, Eskimo, and North Turkic) is not very tight but is still well recognizable on bootstrapping. Amerinds are the tightest cluster, as in 79% of bootstraps all 4 populations are together, with Northwest Amerindians (speaking Na-Dene languages) being most easily lost (21%).

The Southeast Asian supercluster splits into (i) Southeast Asians proper (mainland and insular), a fairly tight cluster of the six populations seen in the tree of Fig. 1; on bootstrapping, Filipinos are lost 29% of the time, Malaysians 23%, and Indonesians 7%; (ii) the Pacific islanders, a cluster of three populations, not tight but clearly recognizable; and (iii) New Guineans and Australians, which remain together more than 50% of the time.

The earlier splits are all statistically significant by tests that will be described elsewhere. Of special interest is the second bifurcation shown in Fig. 1, separating Northeurasians from Southeast Asians. This split occurs most often among the bootstraps, but two alternative partitions are also fairly frequent: one separates Caucasoids from all Asian, Oceanian, and Amerindian populations, and the second separates New Guinean and Australian populations from all other non-African populations. We shall see later that the second bifurcation given in the tree receives support from an independent source as well.

Constant Evolutionary Rates

The evolutionary model (Cavalli-Sforza and Edwards 1967a, 1967b) on which phylogenetic tree analysis is based postulates that populations undergo fissions repeatedly over the course of time, dividing into two subpopulations that continue evolving independently after splitting and that may later split again. For the root to be established by tree analysis without the help of external evidence, the evolutionary rate in the various branches must be constant. The method of "average linkage" (Sokal and Michener 1958), used to construct Fig. 1, is based on the validity of this hypothesis, which can be tested more explicitly

by the method of maximum likelihood. Unfortunately, this second method is virtually impossible with trees of 42 populations, but average linkage, which is computationally very rapid, give results close to those of maximum likelihood (Astolfi et al. 1981; citations in Nei 1987). We used two approaches for checking the constancy of rates: a test of internal consistency, by evaluation of the treeness (Cavalli-Sforza and Piazza 1975) with a procedure to be given in detail elsewhere, and a comparison with archaeological knowledge (next section). There are two major possible causes of deviation from constant evolutionary rate that may be avoided by appropriate selection and pooling of the samples.

(i) Populations that are or were of small size for long periods or that went through one or more severe demographic bottlenecks are affected by strong genetic drift and may show artificially long branches. We have therefore avoided as much as possible the use of individual populations, unless they were unique, and have pooled them with others of similar origin and used averages. A few unique, isolated populations, such as Mbuti pygmies, San, and Lapps, were in any case the averages of many samples.

(ii) Mixed populations have shorter branches. Shorter branches cannot be appreciated in an average linkage tree, in which all branches are forced to be of equal size, but they could be shown by methods such as two cited in the Introduction (Cavalli-Sforza and Edwards 1963, 1967a, 1967b; Edwards and Cavalli-Sforza 1964). By a simple extension of the algebra used for the model of admixture shown in Cavalli-Sforza and Piazza (1975), one can prove (as will be described elsewhere) that admixture between two branches of the tree, producing a third population, which then evolves independently from the two parental ones, has the following consequences: (a) the mixed population has a shorter branch; (b) the mixture attaches in the tree to the branch that has contributed the greater fraction; (c) the attachment takes place in a position that, in an average linkage tree, corresponds to an earlier time than that at which the admixture has taken place.

Bootstrapping, treeness tests, and independent methods of admixture analysis (Wijsman 1984) agreed in giving evidence (to be presented elsewhere) that, among other populations, San and Ethiopians are, respectively, old and young admixtures of a majority of Africans and a minority of Caucasoids; similarly, Lapps are admixtures of a majority of Caucasoids and a minority of North Asians.

CORRELATIONS WITH ARCHAEOLOGY

There has been in the last few years considerable interest in the dating of the earliest anatomically modern humans, *Homo sapiens sapiens*. There seems to have developed some consensus about the validity of dates of early modern humans from the Border Caves and the Klasies River Mouth, both in South Africa, now dated at more than 100 kyr (100,000 year ago), with a date of 125 kyr for Laetoli in Tanzania (Rightmire 1984) and 130 kyr for Omo I (Day and Stringer 1982). In the rest of the world, findings are very poorly dated; however, a recent analysis of modern human remains from the Qafzeh cave in Israel suggests the date of 92 ± 5 kyr (Valladas *et al.* 1988). This is about twice as old as the very approximate previous results.

If the current archaeological data are accepted at face value, the origin of modern humans was in Africa and the expansion to the rest of the world started there. Naturally, considering the paucity of samples and the uncertainties in their dating, one cannot exclude the possibility that new archaeological discoveries may alter this picture.

The timing of the steps in the expansion can be very useful for calibrating the process of genetic differentiation and testing the constancy of evolutionary rates in our tree. Dates used for this aim in Table 1 are as follows.

(i) A time ≥92 kyr for the split between African and non-African has been matched with the genetic differentiation due to the first split of the tree.

(ii) The first entry to Australia took place at least 40 kyr (Jones 1987), and the first settlement of New Guinea took place from Australia. We have matched this time with the node connecting Australia plus New Guinea with Southeast Asia (the third split in the tree).

(iii) The disappearance of Neanderthals and the first appearance of modern humans in southwestern Europe occurred 30-35 kyr, and somewhat earlier in Eastern Europe (Howell 1984), for which data are less satisfactory. A time of 35 kyr was matched with the separation of Caucasoids from Northeast Asia.

(iv) Two possible dates for the entry to America are 35 kyr and 15 kyr (Bray 1988; Fagan 1987). There seems to be more consensus for the second, late date, and in any case this is likely to have had greater demographic weight, given the relative number of sites. There is also uncertainty as to the best match in the genetic tree. Use of the fission between Northeast Asia and the Americas generates a genetic distance that is too large, if the tree has no direct descendants of the Northeast Asians who went to America. The fission between North Amerinds and Central plus South Amerinds generates a distance that is probably too small but that is at least uncomplicated by admixture with later arrivals to North America.

Table 1 shows the clusters defining the fissions listed above, the average genetic distances (G) between the clusters defining each fission, and the archaeological separation dates (T). If the evolutionary rates are constant, the G/T ratios should

be constant. Leaving aside the Americas, for which there is uncertainty, we see that there is satisfactory agreement between the three values that are more dependable, as shown by standard errors. The older fission used for America seems to accord with the older date, and the younger one with the younger date. At least one can say that the American data are not inconsistent with the conclusions from the other three dates, from which the average G/T of 0.40 ±0.05 was calculated. This is valid for long time intervals, for which there is the advantage that many distances are averaged and the distorting effects of admixture and drift are decreased and may even partially compensate for each other. For shorter intervals this G/T value should be used with caution.

CORRELATION WITH LINGUISTIC CLASSIFICATION

There are approximately 5000 languages spoken today, and in a recent taxonomic effort they have been classified in 17 families or phyla (Ruhlen 1987). The phyla of the languages spoken by the populations studied in the genetic tree are listed in Fig. 1. Of the 17 phyla proposed by Ruhlen (1987), only one, Caucasian, is missing for lack of adequate genetic data, but the limited genetic information available suggests that Caucasians are very similar to neighbors and would not generate anomalies if inserted into the tree. Inspection of Fig. 1 shows that every linguistic phylum corresponds to only one of six major genetic clusters defined by the tree. Exceptions are Mbuti Pygmies, who have lost their original language; Basques, who have kept their original language, which is an isolate (Ruhlen 1987); and Melanesians (starred in Fig. 1), who speak in part also Indopacific languages. More important exceptions are the following. (i) Ethiopians are classified genetically in the African cluster although they speak Afroasiatic languages, also spoken in North Africa and the Near East by people who are genetically Caucasoid. The evidence for genetic admixture of Ethiopians can explain the anomaly. (ii) Lapps associate linguistically with speakers of Uralic languages but genetically with Caucasoids and again have important genetic admixture. (iii) Tibetans (starred in Fig. 1) are associated genetically with the Northeast Asian cluster but linguistically with the Sinotibetan phylum, which is spoken in all of China. According to Chinese historians, the Tibetans originated from pastoral nomads of the steppes north of China; this origin explains their genetic association with the Northeast Asian cluster.

The correspondence between linguistic phyla and genetic clusters shows that they have similar origins, but phyla, being contained in the clusters, must have developed later. This suggests a time frame for their origin. Also of great interest are the "superfamilies" of languages recently proposed by some linguists. Greenberg (1987) has classified all the many preexisting phyla of American native languages into three, which are incorporated in the Ruhlen classification shown in Fig. 1: a superphylum including all languages of Central and South America and many of North America, a phylum (Na-Dene) of languages spoken in the Northwest, and the Eskimo-Aleut phylum. It is interesting that the Austric superfamily postulated by Ruhlen (1987) includes almost all of the Southeast Asian cluster, leaving out only the southern Chinese, who speak Sinotibetan languages.

Table 1. Comparison of genetic distances and archaeological time data

Clusters defining fission	Genetic distance (G)*	Time (T), kyr	G/T
African/non-African	29.7 ± 6.8	92	0.32 ± 0.07
Australian/S.E. Asian	18.4 ± 3.4	≥ 40	0.46 ± 0.09
Caucasoid/(N.E. Asian + Amerind)	16.6 ± 3.5	35	0.47 ± 0.10
N.E. Asian/Amerind	12.1 ± 1.8	15–35	0.81 ± 0.12 / -0.35 ± 0.05
N. Amerind/S. and C. Amerind	4.2 ± 1.0	15–35	0.28 ± 0.07 / –0.12 ± 0.03

*Nei's distances × 1000, with standard errors.

Two other superfamilies have been suggested and are indicated at the extreme right of Fig. 1: Nostratic and Eurasiatic. The first follows a proposal by Soviet linguists (summarized in Ruhlen 1987) and include six phyla that all belong to the Northeurasian major cluster; the sixth phylum, South Caucasian, is not given in Fig. 1 for reasons already discussed. The other superfamily, Eurasiatic, proposed by Greenberg and summarized by Ruhlen (1987), overlaps but does not coincide with Nostratic; it includes other phyla also belonging to the Northeurasian cluster. A link of Nostratic with Amerind (dotted vertical line in Fig. 1) was recently suggested by Shevoroshkin (1988). It is most striking that the union of Eurasiatic and Nostratic, with the Amerind extension, includes all, and only, the languages spoken in our major Northeurasian cluster, with the exception of Na-Dene, the origin of which is less clear. Greenberg (1988) noted that the apparent contradictions between his Eurasiatic superfamily and the Russians' Nostratic superfamily can be resolved by considering time levels of separation.

Languages evolve more rapidly than genes. They can also undergo rapid replacement, even if the new language is imposed by an invading minority, provided this minority has adequate political and military organization, as in the "elite dominance" model (Renfrew 1987). When this happens it may be difficult to find genetic traces of the invasion. Elites have developed only recently, however, rarely being older than 5000 years, and therefore episodes of rapid language replacement are relatively recent and often accounted for historically. In the more remote past, replacement was more rare, justifying the stability of the relation between linguistic phyla and genetic clusters.

THE PROCESS OF EXPANSION OF MODERN HUMANS

Reconstruction of human evolution can be truly satisfactory only if information from all relevant sources of acceptable reliability gives a coherent answer. The present data and analysis offer an attempt at a detailed joint approach. The tree of Fig. 1 may be wrong in details; it would be surprising if a tree of this size based on current information were completely correct. Any change in the archaeological, genetic, or linguistic conclusions will require adjustment. Current agreement remains nevertheless very encouraging.

The model we use (Cavalli-Sforza and Edwards 1963, 1967a, 1967b; Edwards and Cavalli-Sforza 1964) clearly assumes expansion of modern humans from a nuclear area and replacement of other local preexisting populations, a model that has found resistance in some anthropological circles. The major evidence cited against the replacement model comes from the continuity of some traits in fossil crania East Asia. This evidence has prompted Wolpoff *et al.* (1984) to suggest an alternative model, which they call "the theory of multiregional evolution," based on an almost continuous population network (Weiss and Maruyama 1976) and standard clinal theory. But the multiregional model cannot provide an explanation of the most important phenomenon, the rapid expansion of modern humans to the whole Earth. Its inability to do so derives from its assumption that genetic populations are at equilibrium, whereas a rapid expansion is a disruption of a former equilibrium.

Another hypothesis on which the model rests, the maintenance of potential interfertility among all living humans for very long periods, may be correct, but if interfertility can help to explain the local permanence of some traits, it does not help to understand the expansion of a new type.

First, one must explain the expansion. There are several examples of expansions, some easier to study because they took place in historic time (Cavalli-Sforza 1986). Archaeologists in the early 20th century postulated migrations in a facile way, often on the basis of inadequate evidence. Today they have reacted with a strongly antimigrationist stance, but they certainly do not deny all expansions; the important point is to find in every case whether there were conditions conducive to expansion and its maintenance (Renfrew 1987). The Neolithic expansions were due to the introduction of new technologies of food production, allowing a substantial increase in the carrying capacity of the land. The introduction of farming in West Asia was the stimulus and the support for the Neolithic expansion to Europe and most probably in other directions (Ammerman and Cavalli-Sforza 1984). The introduction of farming in the Sahel, in addition to the introduction of iron technology, stimulated and supported the Bantu expansion to central and southern Africa (Hiernaux 1974). Pastoral nomadism, coupled with new social structures and with new techniques of transportation and warfare, mostly using the horse, supported the expansions in which the steppe nomads have been major actors until very recently and for several millennia (Zvelebil 1980). A rapid expansion can be viewed as a punctuationist (Eldredge and Gould 1972) episode in evolution, and such events are likely to occur repeatedly in general and not only in human evolution.

Which stimuli determined, and which technologies helped, expansions of modern humans to the whole Earth? It seems very likely that an important role was played by a biological advantage that may have developed slowly over millions of years and undergone a final step only with the appearance of modern humans: a fully developed language. Isaac (1972) has indicated archaeological evidence in favor of this hypothesis. From a speculative point of view, it seems reasonable that more efficient communication can improve foraging and hunting techniques, favor stronger social ties, and facilitate the spread of information useful for migratory movements. It also makes it easier to understand the rapid disappearance of Neanderthals, if they were biologically provided with speech of more modest quality than modern humans. In our society, until 100-150 years ago, deaf-mute people had very little chance of reproducing because of strong adverse social selection (Fraser 1976). Even if interfertility was potentially complete and there was little or no impingement, Neanderthals must have been at a substantial disadvantage at both the between- and the within-population level.

ACKNOWLEDGEMENTS

We thank J. H. Greenberg, F. C. Howell, K. K. Kidd, M. Ruhlen, W. S.-Y. Wang, and A. C. Wilson for reading our manuscript and providing useful comments. This work was supported by National Institutes of Health Grant GM 20467.

REFERENCES

Ammerman, A. J., and Cavalli-Sforza, L. L. 1984. *The Neolithic Transition and the Genetics of Populations in Europe*, Princeton University Press, Princeton, NJ.

Astolfi, P., Kidd, K. K., and Cavalli-Sforza, L. L. 1981. A comparison of methods for reconstructing evolutionary trees. *Syst. Zool.* 30: 156-169.

Bowcock, A. M., Bucci, C., Hebert, J. M., Kidd, J. R., Kidd, K. K., Friedlaender, J. A., and Cavalli-Sforza, L. L. 1987. Study of 47 DNA markers in five populations from four continents. *Gene Geogr.* 1:47-64.

Bray, W. 1988. The palaeoindian debate. *Nature (London)* 332: 107.

Cann, R. L., Stoneking, M., and Wilson, A. C. 1987. Mitochondrial DNA and human evolution. *Nature (London)* 325: 31-36.

Cavalli-Sforza, L. L. 1986. Population structure, in: *Evolutionary Perspectives and the New Genetics* (H. Gershowitz, D. L. Ruchknagel, and R. E. Tashian, Eds.), pp. 13-30, Liss, New York.

Cavalli-Sforza, L. L., and Edwards, A. W. F. 1963. Analysis of human evolution, in: *Genetics Today* (S. J. Geerts, Ed.), *Proceedings of the 11th International Congress of Genetics, The Hague, The Netherlands*, No. 3, pp. 923-933, Pergamon, New York.

Cavalli-Sforza, L. L., and Edwards, A. W. F. 1967a. Phylogenetic analysis models and estimation procedures. *Am. J. Hum. Genet.* 19: 233-257.

Cavalli-Sforza, L. L., and Edwards, A. W. F. 1967b. Phylogenetic analysis: Models and estimation procedures. *Evolution* 21: 550-570.

Cavalli-Sforza, L. L., and Piazza, A. 1975. Analysis of evolution: Evolutionary rates, independence and treeness. *Theor. Popul. Biol.* 8:127-165.

Cavalli-Sforza, L. L., Kidd, J. R., Kidd, K. K., Bucci, C., Bowcock, A. M., Hewlett, B. S., and Friedlaender, J. S. 1986. DNA markers and genetic variation in the human species. *Cold Spring Harb. Symp. Quant. Biol.* 51:411-417.

Day, M. H., and Stringer, C. B. 1982. A reconsideration of the Omo Kibish remains and the *erectus-sapiens* transition. *Congres International de Paleontologie Humaine*, Vol. 2, pp. 814-846 (Pretirage). C.N.R.S., Nice.

Edwards, A. W. F. and Cavalli-Sforza, L. L. 1964. Reconstruction of evolutionary trees, in: *Phenetic and Phylogenetic Classification*, (U. H. Heywood and J. McNeill, Eds.), pp. 67-76, Systematics Assoc., Pub. No. 6, London.

Efron, B. 1982. *The Jackknife, the Bootstrap and Other Resampling Plans*. Soc. Industr. Appl. Math., Philadelphia.

Eldredge, N., and Gould, S. J. 1972. Punctuated equilibria: An alternative to phyletic gradualism, in: *Models in Paleobiology*, (T. J. M. Schopf, Ed.), pp. 82-115, Freeman, San Francisco.

Fagan, B. M. 1987. *The Great Journey: The Peopling of the Ancient Americas*. Thames and Hudson, London.

Felsenstein, J. 1985. Confidence limits on phylogenies: An approach using the bootstraps. *Evolution* 39:783-791.

Fraser, R. G. 1976. *The Causes of Profound Deafness in Childhood*. Johns Hopkins University Press, Baltimore.

Greenberg, J. H. 1987. *Language in the Americas*. Stanford University Press, Stanford, CA.

Greenberg, J. H. 1988. *Voprosy Jazykoznanija*. Moscow.

Hiernaux, J. 1974. *The People of Africa*. Scribner, New York.

Howell, F. C. 1984. Introduction, in: *The Origins of Modern Humans: A World Survey of the Fossil Evidence* (F. H. Smith and F. Spencer, Eds.), pp. 13-22, Liss, New York.

Isaac, G. 1972. Chronology and the tempo of cultural change during the Pleistocene, in: *Calibration of Hominid Evolution* (W. W. Bishop and J. A. Miller, Eds.), pp. 381-430, Scottish Academic Press, Edinburgh.

Johnson, M. J., Wallace, D. C., Ferris, S. D., Rattazzi, M. C., and Cavalli-Sforza, L. L. 1983. Radiation of human mitochondrial DNA types analyzed by restriction endonuclease cleavage patterns. *J. Mol. Evol.* 19:255-271.

Jones, R. 1987. Pleistocene life in the dead heart of Australia. *Nature (London)* 332:107.

Kidd, K. K. 1973. *L'Origine dell'Uomo*, Quaderno No. 182, Accad. Naz. Lincei, Rome.

Lucotte, G. and Ruffie, J. 1987. *Second Congress International Historical Demography*. Inst. Natl. Etudes Demographique, Paris.

Nei, M. 1978. The theory of genetic distance and evolution of human races. *Jpn. J. Hum. Genet.* 23:341-369.

Nei, M. and Roychoudhury, A. K. 1982. Genetic relationship and evolution of human races. *Evol. Bio.* 14:1-59.

Nei, M. 1987. *Molecular Evolutionary Genetics*, Columbia University Press, New York.

Piazza, A., Sgaramella-Zonta, L., Gluckman, P., and Cavalli-Sforza, L. L. 1975. The fifth histocompatability workshop gene frequency data: A phylogenetic analysis. *Tissue Antigens* 5:445-463.

Renfrew, C. 1987. *Archeology and Linguistics*. Cambridge University Press, Cambridge.

Reynolds, J., Weir, B. S., and Cockerham, C. C. 1983. Estimation of the coancestry coefficient; basis for a short-term genetic distance. *Genetics* 105:767-779.

Rightmire, G. P. 1984. *Homo sapiens* in Sub-Saharan Africa, in: *The Origins of Modern Humans: A World Survey of the Fossil Evidence* (F. H. Smith and F. Spencer, Eds.), pp. 295-325, Liss, New York.

Ruhlen, M. 1987. *A Guide to the World's Languages*, Vol. 1. Stanford University Press, Stanford, CA.

Shevoroshkin, V. 1988. *Methods in Inter-Phyletic Comparisons*, Wiesbaden, Germany.

Sokal, R. R., and Michener, C. D. 1958. A statistical method for evaluating systematic relationships. *Univ. Kans. Sci. Bull.* 28:1409-1438.

Valladas, H., Reyss, J. L., Joron, J. L., Valladas, G., Bar-Yosef, O., and Vandermeersch, B. 1988. Thermoluminescence dating of Mousterian 'Proto-Cro-Magnon' remains from Israel and the origin of modern man. *Nature (London)* 331:614-616.

Wainscoat, J. S., Hill, A. V. S., Boyce, A. L., Flint, J., Hernandez, M., Thein, S. L., Old, J. M., Lynch, J. R., Falusi, A. G., Weatherall, D. J., and Clegg, J. B. 1986. Evolutionary relationships of human populations from an analysis of nuclear DNA polymorphisms. *Nature (London)* 319:491-493.

Weiss, K. M., and Maruyama, T. 1976. Archeology, population genetics and studies of human racial ancestry. *Am. J. Phys. Anthropol.* 44:31-50.

Wijsman, E. M. 1984. Techniques for estimating genetic admixture and applications to the problem of the origin of the Kelanders and Ashkenazi Jews. *Hum. Genet.* 67:441-448.

Wolpoff, M. H., Wu, X., and Thorne, A. G. 1984. Modern *Homo sapiens* origins: A general theory of hominid evolution involving the fossil evidence from East Asia, in: *The Origins of Modern Humans: A World Survey of the Fossil Evidence* (F. H. Smith and F. Spencer, Eds.), pp. 411-483, Liss, New York.

Zvelebil, M. 1980. The rise of the nomads in central Asia, in: *The Cambridge Encyclopedia of Archeology*, (A. Sherratt, Ed.), pp. 252-256, Cambridge University Press, Cambridge.

60

Symbolism and Modern Human Origins

J. M. Lindly and G. A. Clark

Chase and Dibble (1987) have argued that there is little archaeological evidence for symbolism in the Middle Paleolithic of Eurasia and that this constitutes a significant cultural difference between the Middle and the Upper Paleolithic in this region. The behavioral system of Eurasian Middle Paleolithic hominids, labelled a "paleoculture" (after Jelinek 1977), is considered to have differed from "modern" systems in that it did not include regular, patterned symbolic behavior as part of the repertoire of human adaptation. This "paleocultural" system is contrasted with that of the Upper Paleolithic, considered en bloc and taken to exhibit a "fully modern" range of behaviors with evidence for numerous kinds of nonutilitarian, "symbolic" artifacts. The possible causes of the apparent difference in evidence for symbolism and the implications of Chase and Dibble's results for the current debate on modern human origins are not addressed, yet their conclusions bear on the nature and timing of the transition from archaic to morphologically modern humans and the question of the role of the Neanderthals in the biocultural evolution of the species (see, e.g., Gowlett 1987; Foley 1987a; Mellars 1988, 1989; Stringer 1988; Stringer and Andrews 1988; Feder and Park 1989; Gargett 1989; Bar-Yosef 1989b; Mellars and Stringer 1989; Otte 1988; Trinkaus 1989a).

We are concerned that Chase and Dibble's conclusions might be taken by anthropologists inclined to see marked discontinuity across the Middle/Upper Paleolithic transition as further "proof" of a major difference between these periods and, consequently, considerable evolutionary "distance" between archaic *Homo sapiens* and morphologically modern humans. From this perspective, absence of evidence for symbolic behavior in archaic *H. sapiens* would support the contention that archaic *H. sapiens* (including the Neanderthals) was an evolutionary dead end and was replaced throughout its range by humans of "modern" type with little or no genetic admixture (see, e.g., Bar-Yosef *et al.* 1986; Cann, Stoneking, and Wilson 1987; Valladas *et al.* 1988). While we think that this evolutionary scenario is extremely unlikely to be correct (either in a particular region or in general), the point is simply that there are clear-cut test implications of pattern in the evidence for and against symbolic behavior.

A pattern corresponding to the distinction between archaic *H. sapiens* and morphologically modern humans would support the argument that fully modern behavior did not evolve until and essentially coincided with the appearance of morphological moderns. If, in contrast, evidence for symbolic behavior crosscut the biological transition, it would support the model of multiregional, in situ evolution proposed by Brace (e.g., 1964, 1967, 1988a), Wolpoff (e.g., 1980, 1989; Wolpoff *et al.* 1988), and others (Clark and Lindly 1988, 1989a, b; Šimek and Snyder 1988; Šimek and Price 1990; Brooks 1988). As a practical matter it must be assumed in either case that human paleontologists can distinguish unambiguously among archaic *H. sapiens*, morphologically modern human, and Neanderthal populations, although we do not believe that they can actually do this (Clark 1988; Clark and Lindly 1988, 1989a, b). An additional entailment of replacement scenarios is that the biological and cultural transitions should have occurred over approximately the same time intervals in all regions, when in fact it appears that the biological transition took place much earlier than any discernible cultural transition in both the Near East and Europe. The evidence suggests that there is no major change in *adaptation* [2] until relatively late in the Upper Paleolithic in Europe, perhaps as much as 20,000 years after the biological transition to modern humans had taken place (Šimek and Snyder 1988; Šimek and Price 1990; Clark and Lindly 1989a; Straus 1977, 1990a; Straus and Heller 1988).

In order to examine the implications of Chase and Dibble's conclusions for the study of modern human origins, we consider archaeological evidence for symbolism from regions of the Old World in which the remains of morphologically modern humans occur long before the beginning of the Upper Paleolithic (or, in Africa, the Late Stone Age). The survey is exhaustive: these are the only sites in the world that have produced alleged morphologically modern human remains earlier than the Upper Paleolithic/Late Stone Age. If evidence for symbolic behavior can be correlated with hominid taxa, and if (as is widely assumed) "symbolism" has some adaptive significance, we should be able to detect differences between assemblages associated with archaic *H. sapiens* and those associated with pre-Upper Paleolithic moderns. To keep the results comparable, the archaeological evidence used to assess symbolic behavior is limited to the four classes of data examined by Chase and Dibble (1987:265): (1) lithic assemblages, (2) burial data, (3) evidence for ritual behavior other than that associated with burials, and (4) art [3].

Morphologically modern human skeletal remains dating to the Middle Paleolithic (or, in Africa, the Middle Stone Age) have been reported from Starosel'e (Alexeyev 1976; see also

A-M. Tillier, cited in Ronen 1982:315), Darra-i-kur (Angel 1972), Skhul (McCown and Keith 1939; Trinkaus 1982, 1984, 1986), and Qafzeh (Bar-Yosef and Vandermeersch 1981) in southwestern Asia; Dar-es-Soltane (Debénath 1975; Trinkaus 1986) and Temara (Ferembach 1976) in North Africa; and Klasies River Mouth (Singer and Wymer 1982; Rightmire 1984), Border Cave (Beaumont, de Villiers, and Vogel 1978; Butzer, Beaumont, and Vogel 1978), Mumba Rockshelter (Bräuer and Mehlman 1988), Laetoli (Rightmire 1984), Omo (Bräuer 1984; J.D. Clark 1988), Porc Epic (Bräuer 1984; J. D. Clark 1988), and Singa (Bräuer 1984; but cf. Stringer 1979) in Africa south of the Sahara. If the contexts surrounding these morphologically modern human remains have little or no evidence of symbolic behavior, it will be clear that no correlation of modern behavior with modern morphology can be proposed.

REVIEW OF THE EVIDENCE

Southwestern Asia

Four Middle Paleolithic sites in southwestern Asia have been reported to contain the remains of morphologically modern humans: Starosel'e (Soviet Crimea), Darra-i-kur (Afghanistan), Skhul, and Qafzeh (both in Israel).

Starosel'e Cave is located in a dry tributary valley of the Churuk-su River and was excavated by the Soviet prehistorian and anthropologist A. Formozov in 1952-56. Deposits at the site ranged in depth from 60 cm to 4 m. The skeletal remains consist of the partial skeleton of a child, the chin section of an adult mandible, and single fragments of radius and humerus, all considered directly associated with Mousterian artifacts. The infant skeleton, found at a depth of 70-90 cm, is classified as "modern" on the basis of a comparison with modern infant remains of similar age and a reconstruction of the dimensions of the skull as it would have appeared as an adult (Alexeyev 1976; see also A-M. Tillier, cited in Ronen 1982:315). The adult remains were found at approximately the same level as the infant, and the mandible fragment is considered "modern" in every sense of the word. None of the remains are judged to represent intentional burials (Klein 1965). The lithic assemblage is identified as Mousterian because of the presence of limaces, discoidal cores, bifacially flaked "Quina-type" sidescrapers, and simple, double, convergent, transverse, and déjeté sidescrapers made on flakes and is said to resemble Charentian industries of southwestern France (Klein 1965:63). Despite the recovery of more than 11,000 stone artifacts and some 60,000 unworked bone fragments (dominated by Equus), there is no indication of a stylistic component (by anyone's definition [see Sackett 1982; Binford 1989; Clark 1989b]) or of ritual paraphernalia or art.

At Darra-i-kur, a rock-shelter in western Badakhshan, the human remains consist of a right temporal fragment that is "modern in appearance" (Angel 1972). It is not considered to pertain to an intentional burial. The lithic assemblage is Mousterian, comprising more than 800 Levallois flakes and points, handaxes, sidescrapers, flake/blades, and debitage (Dupree and Davis 1972). The only object recovered that might, by a considerable stretch of the imagination, be considered symbolic is a fossil shark's tooth tentatively identified as "worked" (Dupree 1972:79). A so-called bone fabricator is reported to be worked on both ends, but it is not clear from the illustrations how it was "worked" and it is at least equally probable that it is a diaphysis fragment gnawed by carnivores. Since the excavation at Darra-i-kur predated the current concern with taphonomic processes, it is unlikely that the investigators would have distinguished between human and animal modification of bone except where the difference was fairly obvious. There is no art or unequivocal evidence of symbolic activity at this site.

Mugharet es-Skhul, on the Israeli coast, is the smallest of the Mt. Carmel caves investigated by Dorothy Garrod in the 1920s and 1930s. Skhul was also excavated by Theodore McCown in 1931. The human remains constitute one of the best samples in southwestern Asia (> 10 individuals and numerous fragments). Both classic and modern researchers consider them morphologically modern (McCown and Keith 1939; Trinkaus 1982, 1984, 1986). Many appear to have been purposefully buried, albeit for the most part without grave goods. Skhul 5 may have been interred with offerings; McCown (1937, p. 104) argues that a boar (Sus scrofa) mandible was clasped in its hands because "the left forearm rests upon the broken, hinder ends of the mandible" (p. 100; see his pl. 52[2], reproduced here as Fig. 1). Most of the ribs and vertebrae as well as part of the pelvis and most of the right leg are missing, however, and McCown notes some crushing of the lower part of the skeleton by "an ancient disturbance" and reports that "it was impossible to determine the exact limits of the grave" (p. 101). From this and the fact that Sus occurs throughout the Skhul deposits and is suggested to have been a dietary item (Bate 1937, p. 148) it seems reasonable to conclude that the boar mandible may have become spatially associated with the human remains through some process other than deliberate inclusion in a grave. The skeletal remains are associated with Middke Paleolithic artifacts recently classified as Phase 2/3 Mousterian and on these grounds argued to be "late" (ca. 40,000-50,000 years B.P.) (Jelinek 1982). Levantine Mousterian lithic assemblages have no clear stylistic component and appear instead to reflect variation in raw-material size and/or availability that constrains choice among reduction strategies (Clark and Lindly 1988, 1989a, b; Lindly and Clark 1987).

Qafzeh is an inland cave site located near the village of Nazareth in the lower Galilee. It was excavated by Neuville and Stekelis (1932-35) and by Vandermeersch and Bar-Yosef (1965-79, 1983-present). The cave contains both Middle and Upper Paleolithic deposits. The Qafzeh hominid remains are all morphologically modern humans and are similar morphologically to the remains found at Skhul (Vandermeersch 1981). Sixteen individuals have been recovered. One, Qafzeh II (an infant), is reported to have had associated grave goods; the antlers of a fallow deer (possibly Dama mesopotamica) are described as "held in the hand" of the child (Vandermeersch 1970). Dama mesopotamica is, however, an economic species that occurs in Level 22, with which Qafzeh II is associated (Bouchud 1974). While the remains of this species are not especially numerous, they nevertheless account for 20.4% of the faunal remains in Levels 18-22, and the possibility of a fortuitous association cannot be ruled out. Ochre is present throughout the deposits but not associated with the hominid remains (Vandermeersch 1969). There is no evidence of ritual behavior other than the equivocal burial data or of art.

The lithic industries of the Mousterian levels at Qafzeh have been classified as Tabun B/C or Levantine Mousterian

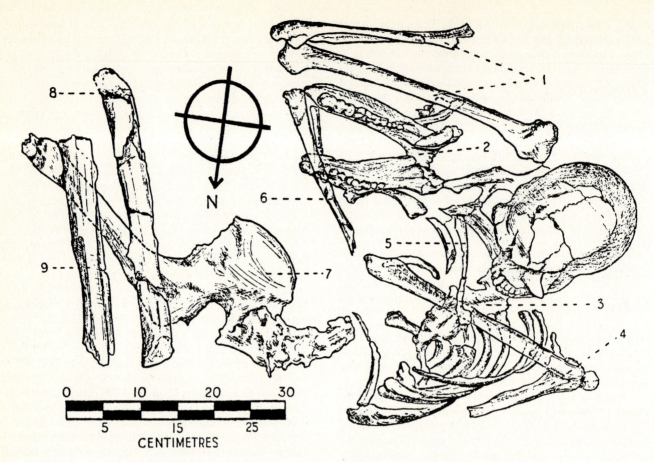

Figure 1. *Plan of the contracted burial of a tall male, Skhul 5. 1, right arm; 2, Sus scrofa mandible; 3, dorsal vertebrae; 4, left scapula and humerus; 5, left clavicle; 6, left radius; 7, right ilium; 8, left femur; 9, left tibia and fibula. (Reprinted from McCown 1937:pl. 52[2] by permission of the publisher.)*

Phase 2/3 and have until very recently been considered "late" (ca. 40,000-50,000 years B.P.) (Jelinek 1981, 1982). Jelinek's interpretation of the age of Qafzeh has been challenged by the recent evidence from geomorphology, the biostratigraphy of the microvertebrate faunas, and amino-acid racemization dates (Bar-Yosef and Vandermeersch 1981; Bar-Yosef 1989b). A series of thermoluminescence dates on burnt flint has yielded an average age of 92,000 +/- 5,000 years B.P. for the hominid-bearing deposits (Valladas *et al.* 1988), and a number of electron-spin-resonance determinations average 98,000 years B.P. (Schwarcz *et al.* 1988). If these dates are correct, the Qafzeh hominids are the earliest dated remains of morphologically modern humans in the world. It should be noted that the dates for the Qafzeh Mousterian levels are approximately the same age as is proposed for Tabun D/Phase I "early" Levantine Mousterian assemblage from Tabun, suggesting that the normative phase sequence currently used to organize Middle Paleolithic assemblages in a loose chronological order is in need of serious revision (see, e.g., Lindly and Clark 1987; Clark and Lindly 1988, 1989b).

North Africa

North Africa has also produced several sites with claimed early morphological modern human remains, in every case associated with Aterian lithic assemblages (J. D. Clark 1983, Ferring 1975).

Dar es-Soltane, a cave site on the coast of Morocco, has "lower" Aterian levels that have produced two partial human crania of essentially modern appearance (Debénath 1975; Trinkaus 1986). Single modern parietal and occipital fragments from the Grotte des Contrebandiers (Smugglers' Cave) at Témara are also associated with an Aterian assemblage (Ferembach 1976). There is no indication that these remains were buried intentionally. The Aterian is usually considered Middle Paleolithic. Although it has produced some radiocarbon dates younger than 30,000 years B.P., most Aterian assemblages are probably more than 40,000 years old (Ferring 1975; J. D. Clark 1982, 1983). Radiocarbon-dated Aterian assemblages range from 39,900 years B.P. in the Maghreb and 41,500-45,000 years B.P. (with enormous standard deviations) at the Haua Fteah (Cyrenaica) to 27,000 years B.P. in an upper level and 30,000 years B.P. in a lower one at Dar es-Soltane. Therefore, despite the assertion that the Dar es-Soltane Aterian in typologically "early," the site probably dates to the latest part of the Aterian sequence. There are no radiocarbon dates from Témara.

The Aterian "facies" of the North African Mousterian is composed primarily of Levallois debitage including blades with faceted platforms, sidescrapers, points, and endscrapers, but some assemblages include tanged pieces (pedunculates) and bifacial foliate points (Ferring 1975). Nothing in the published accounts of Aterian sites suggests the presence of symbolic behavior in the form of stylistic patterning in stone tool assemblages or of ritual or art (Ferring 1975).

Sub-Saharan Africa

Several Middle Stone Age sites in southern Africa contain what until the publication of the Qafzeh dates were considered the world's earliest morphologically modern human remains (Beaumont et al. 1978; Bräuer and Mehlman 1988; Grine and Klein 1985; Singer and Wymer 1982). There is some controversy about the age of these sites (Butzer 1982; Shackleton 1982), but there seems to be consensus that they all date prior to the limits of radiocarbon (Volman 1984).

Excavations in a series of caves and rock-shelters at the mouth of the Klasies River, on the east coast of the Republic of South Africa, have produced five partial mandibles, a maxilla, and various small craniofacial fragments, teeth, and postcranial bones considered to be those of morphologically modern humans (Singer and Wymer 1982; Rightmire 1984). None are thought to represent burials (Singer and Wymer 1982:147). The Middle Stone Age levels at these sites are primarily assigned to Stages 1-4 (including the lamellar Howieson's Poort industries), although there are also overlying Late Stone Age deposits (Singer and Wymer 1982). Some workers (e.g., Butzer 1982) have proposed a date for them as early as 120,000 years B.P. Middle Stone Age lithic assemblages from southern Africa consist mainly of flakes and flake/blades from well-prepared cores with retouched tool types such as points, denticulates, and sidescrapers. The Howieson's Poort is somewhat different from but an integral part of the Middle Stone Age. Instead of the "generic" Middle Stone Age flake tools, it contains an abundance of backed pieces (blade segments) and rather large but well-made geometrics, such as lunates (or crescents) and trapezoids (Volman 1984). The Howieson's Poort is seen by some as an "adaptive response" to environmental perturbation that included changes in mobility patterns and possibly the conservation of more distant and higher-quality raw-material sources (Mellars 1988, 1989; cf. Parkington 1990 for a more critical view), and from this perspective the technological changes it represents need not be considered matters of style.

Evidence for symbolism in the Middle Stone Age levels at Klasies River Mouth (and in all African Middle Stone Age sites) is extremely scarce. The lithic industries show no patterning that can be considered stylistic. The best-defined change is one in retouched tool forms that corresponds to the appearance of the Howieson's Poort industry in Layers 10-21 of Shelter 1A. Above Layer 10, there is a reappearance of the modal kind of Middle Stone Age assemblages. The African Middle Stone Age has been divided into stages according to debitage characteristics such as blank size and shape, percentage of faceted butts, and core types. The extremely questionable but time-honored practice of using retouched pieces in these classificatory schemata is hampered by extremely low tool frequencies (% in most cases) (Volman 1984:201). In many cases, it has proven difficult to separate Middle Stone Age stages from one another on the basis of characteristics of the lithic assemblages alone, and stratigraphic and paleoenvironmental information is often utilized. It is difficult to avoid the impression of an essential continuity and homogeneity in these African equivalents of the Middle Paleolithic. At present, the best single criterion for subdividing the African Middle Stone Age industries (including Howieson's Poort) appears to be changes in raw material linked, probably, to changes in the settlement-subsistence systems within which raw-material procurement was embedded (see Binford 1979).

There are four instances of worked bone from Klasies: two serrated rib fragments and one bone with thin, regular parallel grooves from a Middle Stone Age 2 level and a bone "point" from one of the Howieson's Poort levels. These very rare instances of worked bone correspond to Chase and Dibble's reports for the Eurasian Mousterian. Ochre was also found dispersed throughout the Middle Stone Age levels. Although there is no direct association of ochre with the hominid remains, some of the larger pieces show striations, faceting, and abraded surfaces suggesting use as a colorant. This evidence for symbolic behavior is, however, both equivocal and scarce, and there is no indication of a pattern in its occurrence.

Border Cave, on the Swaziland/Kwa-Zulu border in the Lebombo Range, has yielded a long Middle Stone Age sequence tentatively associated with skeletal material considered morphologically modern human (Beaumont, de Villiers, and Vogel 1978; Butzer, Beaumont, and Vogel 1978; Beaumont 1980). The hominid fossils consist of mandible and cranial fragments from three adult individuals, a relatively complete infant skeleton that is considered a burial, and postcranial remains of uncertain provenience recovered in uncontrolled digging for agricultural fertilizer at the site. One adult mandible and the infant burial were apparently found in situ (Rightmire 1984). The specimens associated with Middle Stone Age artifacts are all considered to be the remains of morphologically modern humans (Beaumont 1980).

Perhaps the best evidence for symbolic behavior from the site is the possible infant burial from the Middle Stone Age 2b level, with an associated perforated Conus shell that can only have come from the Straits of Madagascar, some 80 km distant. The Middle Stone Age 3 assemblage contains a notched rib fragment and seven spit-tusk "daggers," possibly from a warthog, that show signs of abrasion. It is not clear from the photographs (Beaumont, de Villiers, and Vogel 1978) whether the abrasion on the tusk fragments was produced by human agency (as Beaumont suggests) or, as seems more likely, by natural processes during the life of the animal. (Suid canines are typically broken and abraded in vivo, especially at the tip (Brain 1981)). As at Klasies River Mouth, hematite flecks are found throughout the levels, with some of the larger pieces showing wear facets, striae, and other signs of abrasion (Volman 1984).

Two additional sites in southern Africa are sometimes mentioned as having produced evidence for symbolic behavior. A Middle Stone Age level at Florisbad, in the Orange Free State, has produced a broken curved wooden implement with parallel markings on the end (Volman 1984). Since the famous hominid cranium from the Middle Stone Age deposits at this site has recently been reconstructed and is now considered archaic H. sapiens (Kuman and Clarke 1986), its co-occurence with a worked wooden object might be viewed as further support for the view that there is no link between symbolic behavior and modern morphology. Middle Stone Age 2b levels at Apollo II Cave in Namibia have yielded two notched bone fragments, and there are additional incised fragments of ostrich eggshell in the Howieson's Poort (Wendt 1976; Volman 1984), but there are no

Table 1. Evidence for Symbolic Behavior from Sites in the Old World Associated with Purported Pre-Upper Paleolithic Morphologically Modern Humans

Sites	Evidence	Source
Starosel'e	None	Klein (1965)
Darr-i-kur	Bone "fabricator" "Worked" (?) shark's tooth	Dupree (1972)
Skhul	Boar mandible associated with Skhul 5 burial	McCown (1937)
Qafzeh	Deer antler associated with Qafzeh II burial Ochre throughout deposit	Vandermeersch (1981)
Dar es-Soltane	None	Debénath (1975)
Témara	None	Ferembach (1976)
Klasies River Mouth	2 serrated rib fragments and a bone with thin regular parallel grooves in an MSA 2 level Bone "point" in a Howieson's Poort level Ochre with abrasions and facets dispersed througout MSA levels	Singer and Wymer (1982) Volman (1984)
Border Cave	*Conus* shell found with infant burial in an MSA 2b level Notched rib fragments and 7 split-tusk "daggers" in an MDS 3 level Hematite with wear facets	Veaumont et al. (1978) Volman (1984)
Mumba Rockshelter	None	Bräuer and Mehlman (1988)
Laetoli Hominid 18	None	J.D. Clark (1988)
Omo 1 & 3, Kibish Formation	None	J.D. Clark (1988)
Porc Epic	Hematite with wear facets	J.D. Clark (1988)
Singa	None	Stringer (1979)

hominid remains from this site to indicate who the makers of these artifacts might have been.

Mumba Rockshelter in Tanzania has produced three hominid molars from Middle Stone Age levels dated to ca. 130,000 years B.P. that supposedly fall within the range of variation seen in modern African populations and are consequently considered morphologically modern (Bräuer and Mehlman 1988). The Ngaloba Beds at Laetoli in Tanzania, dated by uranium series to 120,000 years B.P., have yielded an almost complete skull (Laetoli Hominid 18) with both "modern" (expansion of the vault, rounded occiput) and "archaic" (frontal flattening, supraorbital torus, thick cranial bones) features (Rightmire 1984). The fossil is associated with a Middle Stone Age assemblage that lacks a heavy-duty-tool component (J. D. Clark 1988). The Kibish Formation at Omo in Ethiopia has produced an incomplete calvarium with some associated postcranial bones (Omo 1), a second incomplete calvarium (Omo 2), and some fragmentary cranial bones (Omo 3) (Bräuer 1984; J. D. Clark 1988). Omo 1 was recovered from overbank deposits on the surface of Stratum e at the top of Member 1. It has morphologically modern human features and is associated with a small redeposited Middle Stone Age assemblage containing Levallois flakes. An age of ca. 130,000 years B.P. is suggested by a uranium-series date on shell from the sediments that produced the skull. Omo 2 was a surface find ca. 2.5 km away that could have come from the same geological horizon; interestingly, it has several *H. erectus* features that place it outside morphological modern humans and, indeed, archaic *H. sapiens*. If it is penecontemporaneous with Omo 1, a population of enormous morphological variability is indicated. Omo 3 comes from Member 3 and is probably somewhat (perhaps considerably) younger than the others. An age somewhere in the 100,000–40,000 years B.P. interval is suggested, since the finds lie outside the range of radiocarbon. In the Ethiopian Rift at Porc Epic, a robust mandible fragment associated with a Middle Stone Age assemblage was recovered

by Breuil in 1933. There is a minimum-age obsidian-hydration date of 60,000–70,000 years B.P. from artifacts in the brecciated cave earths from which the fossil was apparently extracted. Measurements and robusticity of the find indicate that it lies within the range of variation of modern humans, but it also has archaic features reminiscent of the Neanderthals (Bräuer 1984; J. D. Clark 1988). Finally, from Singa, on the Blue Nile in southeastern Sudan, a heavily mineralized skull with most of the face missing was found in 1924. It has recently been described both as archaic *H. sapiens* (Stringer 1979) and as "completely modern" (Bräuer 1984). There are no associated artifacts. Evidence for symbolic behavior is absent from all these East African morphologically modern human sites except for the occurrence of hematite with wear facets at Porc Epic (J. D. Clark 1988:299). In no case is the context of discovery primary and in most cases the skeletal remains have clearly been redeposited by geological agencies. The Middle Stone Age chipped-stone assemblages found with morphologically modern human fossils in this area are indistinguishable from those found with archaic *H. sapiens* fossils. In neither case are there examples of parietal or mobile art, ornaments, bone artifacts, or burials.

Concluding Remarks

The results of our survey (Table 1) suggest that, as Chase and Dibble have reported for archaic *H. sapiens*, the daily activities of pre-Upper Paleolithic morphologically modern humans had no archaeologically discernible symbolic component, at least in the regions we examined and quite probably in any region of the Old World that has produced an Upper Pleistocene archaeological record. Does this apparent "fact" render these morphologically modern humans significantly different from or less human than morphological moderns associated with Upper Paleolithic industries in Europe, who admittedly do exhibit symbolic behavior? Are they to be considered outside the evolutionary trajectory of modern humans? Clearly, the answer is no. Yet, on the basis of similar lack of evidence for behavior like that observed in the European Upper Paleolithic, Eurasian archaic *H. sapiens* has been considered different enough from morphologically modern humans to warrant rethinking of the biological and cultural relationships between these hominids (Bar-Yosef 1987, 1989b; Gargett 1989; Foley 1987a; Gowlett 1987; Mellars 1988, 1989; White 1982, 1989a; Clark and Lindly 1989a). Support for a hypothesis of no difference in this regard between archaic *H. sapiens* and morphologically modern humans of the Middle Paleolithic/Middle Stone Age calls into question the credibility of the replacement scenario for modern human origins and suggests that archaic *H. sapiens* cannot be relegated to an evolutionary backwater (see also Marshack 1988a, 1989).

That the pattern in the evidence for symbolic behavior is the same whether the hominids associated with Middle Paleolithic/Middle Stone Age archaeological assemblages are archaic *H. sapiens*, Neanderthals, or morphological modern implies that the taxonomic units themselves are unreliable (which we think very likely) and/or that the major shift in adaptation occurred late in the Upper Paleolithic/Late Stone Age and was largely unrelated to the perceived transition from the Middle to the Upper Paleolithic (see Chase 1986, 1989; Šimek and Price 1990; Šimek and Snyder 1988; Brooks 1988; Svoboda 1988, 1990; Geneste 1988; Böeda 1988; Straus 1990a; Straus and Heller 1988; Marshack 1988a, b, 1989; Clark and Lindly 1988, 1989a, b).

The latter conclusion is likely to be disputed by workers who argue from European data for a "symbolic explosion" at the beginning of the Upper Paleolithic (e.g., and esp., White 1982, 1989a, b). Though Europe, since it has not produced any early morphologically modern humans, is tangential to our major argument, we therefore wish to make our views on the European situation absolutely clear. We readily acknowledge an apparent latitudinal component to the archaeological evidence for symbolism that implies possible differences in social complexity between western Eurasia and the rest of the Old World at ca. 20,000-15,000 years B.P. To argue that the Middle/Upper Paleolithic transition at ca. 38,000-35,000 years B.P. is a major threshold in cultural evolution (cf. White 1982, 1989a, b) is, however, an over-simplification.

We are not suggesting that there is no evidence for symbolism in the early Upper Paleolithic of Europe (conventionally dated ca. 38,000-20,000 years B.P.). Indeed, Marshack (1988a, b, 1989) has demonstrated, through a series of exhaustive studies, that evidence for symbolic behavior, while rare and sporadic, extends well back into the *Middle* Paleolithic and, in aggregate, strongly supports the idea of behavioral continuity across the Middle/Upper Paleolithic transition (see also González Echegaray 1988). We do, however, seriously doubt that much of the early Upper Paleolithic evidence (i.e., ivory sculptures from Aurignacian sites in Germany; limestone engravings, ornaments from French Aurignacian sites; Aurignacian bone points; the Sungir and Dolní Vestonice burials; the Dolní Vestonice clay figurines; the Mladec ornaments; etc.) can be shown to date to the beginning of this period. Compared with the late Upper Paleolithic, the early Upper Paleolithic has relatively few radiometric dates, and in most cases "symbolic artifacts" are considered "early" only on the basis of allegedly time-sensitive "index-fossil" tool types and normative charac-

terizations of assemblage sequences—both notoriously unreliable as temporal indicators (Clark and Straus 1986, Straus 1987a, Straus and Heller 1988). It should be kept in mind that the conventional early Upper Paleolithic analytical units (Aurignacian, Perigordian, Uluzzian, Gravettian, Szeletian, etc.) span ca. 18,000-16,000 years and that aggregation of the evidence from any such unit may make change appear "explosive."

Again, while there is some unambiguous parietal and mobiliary art from the early Upper Paleolithic, when sites that have produced absolute determinations are examined the overwhelming majority of it postdates 20,000 years B.P. (Conkey 1983, 1987a,b, personal communication). This also applies to the worked bone and antler inventories and the burials (cf., e.g., White 1987, 1989a with Julien 1982, May 1986). All but 3 of the 74 relatively unambiguous Upper Paleolithic burials studied by May (1986) are not only from the late Upper Paleolithic (25,000-12,000 years B.P.) but from its latest phases. The recently discovered triple burial at Dolní Vestonice is radiocarbon-dated at 27,600 and 26,600 years B.P. (Bahn 1988). The Sungir burials are 20,000-25,000 years old (Fisher 1988). If one were to "scale" the incidence of art, bone/antler artifacts, and/or burials per unit time (e.g., number of items or occurrences per millennium), it would immediately become evident that, *contra* White (1987, 1989a), the "symbolic explosion" occurred not at the Middle/Upper Paleolithic transition but in the late Upper Paleolithic, at ca. 20,000-15,000 years B.P. The rate at which such evidence accumulates increases slowly during the early Upper Paleolithic, more rapidly during the late Upper Paleolithic, and even more rapidly in the Mesolithic and beyond (Clark and Neeley 1987).

Finally, abundant European archaeofaunal evidence shows few marked changes coincident with the local Middle/Upper Paleolithic boundaries, and those that are detectable can usually be attributed to climate (Straus 1977; Delpech 1983; Clark 1987). Since few would dispute that the character of faunal assemblages is a much more direct monitor of human adaptation than art, ornamentation, or mortuary practices, it is not unreasonable to conclude that here, too, is evidence for clinal, relatively gradual change, in some regions (e.g., northern Spain) accelerating sharply about 20,000 years ago (Clark and Straus 1983, 1986). In short, a model of regional continuity between Middle and Upper Paleolithic and between archaic and modern *H. sapiens* (see, e.g., Brace 1967, 1988; Wolpoff 1980, 1989) appears to be supported in Europe as well as elsewhere.

This is not to say that we or any of the other researchers cited in support of the continuity position consider the two transitions to have been simultaneous, but this is in fact a clear implication of the replacement scenario. In evolution, behavioral change always occurs well in advance of related morphological change. If some kind of relationship obtained between the emergence of morphologically modern humans and the Upper Paleolithic/Late Stone Age, the morphological changes that supposedly allow human paleontologists to distinguish between morphologically modern humans and archaic *H. sapiens* should have been preceded by many thousands of years by significant adaptive shifts. There is *no evidence whatsoever* for such adaptive shifts in Eurasia, Africa, or the Levant—although, admittedly, they would be exceedingly difficult to detect given the inadequacies of the time/space grid.

We irreverently conclude that the replacement scenario is

very likely a product of sampling bias and entrenched regional research traditions (Binford and Sabloff 1982). While no one disputes the European evidence for Upper Paleolithic symbolism, the case for the rest of the Old World is wholly dependent upon argument from negative evidence: areas outside of Europe are judged not to have been characterized by the same level of social complexity as Europe during the 25,000–10,000-years-B.P. interval because they have not produced comparable evidence of symbolism. Such areas are, of course, much less intensively investigated than Europe, and taphonomic and macroclimatic factors may have combined to erase any evidence of social complexity comparable to that of Europe. We do not imply, however, nor do we believe, that *rates* of Upper Pleistocene biocultural evolution were everywhere the same.

The question of symbolic behavior on either side of the archaic *H. sapiens*/morphologically-modern-human transition is one small part of the larger issue of the appearance of modern humans. In the absence of any evidence for differences in adaptation among archaic *H. sapiens*, Neanderthal, and early morphologically modern human populations—differences that would be expected if in fact these taxa were really distinct—the case for replacement of archaic *H. sapiens* by moderns rests solely upon the assertion that morphologically modern humans displaced archaic *H. sapiens* because they were more "advanced." We submit that the Old World Upper Pleistocene archaeological record exhibits none of the discontinuity implied by the replacement model and that it is incumbent upon its advocates to show how replacement could have occurred without leaving traces of disjunction in the typological and technological aspects of archaeological assemblages, in those aspects of the archaeofaunal record that monitor subsistence, and in the evidence from settlement-pattern studies (Clark and Lindly 1989a). In light of this continuity, acknowledged even by archaeologists who support biological replacement (e.g., Bar-Yosef and Meignen 1989), it seems more reasonable to suggest that the taxa employed by replacement systematics are defective and that archaeologists would be well advised not to take them at face value. A satisfactory explanation of the origins of modern humans must reconcile the archaeological and fossil evidence and the evidence from molecular biology. In our opinion, only a multiregional model of cultural and biological continuity can do so.

COMMENTS

O. Bar-Yosef, D. Lieberman, and J. Shea, *Department of Anthropology, Peabody Museum, Harvard University, Cambridge, Massachusetts*

Lindly and Clark have attempted to deal with the questions raised by the new thermoluminescence and electron-spin-resonance dated from Kebara, Qafzeh, and Skhul (Valladas *et al.* 1987, 1988; Schwarcz *et al.* 1988, 1989; Stringer *et al.* 1989). Until two years ago most scholars ignored the biostratigraphic evidence and the alternative palaeoclimatic interpretations for the Tabun sequence and other major cave sites, placing the Western Asian Neandertals (Amud, Kebara, Shanidar, Tabun) earlier than the early anatomically modern humans (Skhul, Qafzeh) to argue for local evolution of modern humans in Southwestern Asia (Bar-Yosef 1989b). The acceptance of the greater antiquity of the early anatomically modern

Homo sapiens from Qafzeh and Skhul has raised many interesting questions concerning human evolution in the Upper Pleistocene, especially questions of taxonomy, the relationship between archaeological assemblages and fossils, and the anthropological meaning of the transition from the Middle to the Upper Paleolithic—all of which are confused by Lindly and Clark.

They are correct in pointing out the paradoxical lack of any discernible behavioral differences in the archaeological record between early anatomically modern and archaic *H. sapiens.* We agree that there is evidence for significant differences of symbolic behavior between the archaeological records of the Middle and Upper Paleolithic and that symbolic expressions become much more prevalent and elaborate during the late glacial maximum/oxygen-isotope stage 2 (24,000–14,000 years ago). We strongly disagree, however, that the absence of archaeological evidence for different symbolic behaviors associated with archaic and modern *H. sapiens* during the Middle Paleolithic constitutes either support for the multiregional hypothesis or refutation of the single-origin hypothesis.

Lindly and Clark make a number of taxonomic and phylogenetic errors. Fossil taxa such as archaic and modern *H. sapiens* can only be defined on the basis of morphological criteria, some of which may imply behavioral differences (Mayr 1942). Although Lindly and Clark are justified in looking for different behaviors that are specific to these taxa (as predicted by the evolutionary principle of competitive exclusion), the absence of archaeological evidence for behavioral differences—particularly in connection with something as ephemeral as symbolism—is a poor basis on which to criticize taxonomy. Fossil species are defined not by their archaeological traces or by their presumed evolutionary relationships to modern humans but by the range of variation of their morphologies. Whether or not Neandertals and modern *H. sapiens* are different species is difficult to test and hence open to debate; however, to argue that there are no behavioral differences between these taxa (and hence that these taxa are incorrectly defined) ignores the large body of functional morphological data that clearly demonstrates otherwise (Trinkaus 1986).

Lindly and Clark incorrectly attempt to fit archaeological data (actually the absence of evidence for symbolic behavior) to the biological question of whether anatomically modern humans evolved in one region or in numerous regions. The evolutionary relationships between taxa such as archaic and modern *H. sapiens* can only be determined by analyzing their morphological characteristics (whether by cladistic and/or phenetic methods). For the Middle Paleolithic of the Levant, there is no close correspondence between hominid morphotypes and the lithic industries with which they are found. For example, hominids such as the Neandertal woman from Tabun layer C are associated with the same industry as the hominids from Qafzeh (layer 17-24). One can argue that the associations between burials and industries in Levantine caves are coincidental, but this argument ignores their repetitive nature. Lindly and Clark's argument concerning the purportedly "disturbed" Skhul and Qafzeh burials is at variance with photographic records and the illustration included in their article. (Perhaps they have confused McCown's reference to disturbance in the "lower part of the body," which clearly refers to the lower limbs of the Skhul 5 burial, with the stratigraphically "lower" portion of the thoracic region.) Again, it is true that fallow deer remains were uncovered at Qafzeh, but only as small fragments; the occurrence of the large antlers across the chest of the dead child can hardly be conceived as accidental. The mere observation that Mousterian burials are somewhat different from expectations based on Upper Paleolithic, Mesolithic, and Neolithic burials does not mean that these were unintentional or unaccompanied by offerings. This is why accurate, well-recorded field observations are essential (Villa 1989). Moreover, the nearly complete articulation of many of these skeletal remains at sites demonstrably frequented by hyenas is compelling evidence for their integrity (Trinkaus 1989).

Although the archaeological record can tell us little about the phylogeny of prehistoric hominids, behavioral inferences from archaeological residues can inform us about their coevolutionary relationships. There is no credible archaeological evidence for prolonged contact, interbreeding, or evolutionary continuity among Neandertals and early modern humans in the Levant, and current data suggest that they would have been ecologically incompatible. Lithic use-wear analysis (Shea 1989) indicates that tool functions were virtually identical in kind and in relative frequency among Levantine Mousterian sites located in the Mediterranean woodland phytogeographic zone. Moreover, the large-mammal components of the archaeofaunas from these sites are essentially the same (Tchernov 1988:219-222). Neandertals and early modern humans, it seems, utilized this part of the Levant in essentially the same way for a considerable period of time, which would likely have placed them in competition for the same set of plant and animal resources—a profound obstacle to prolonged coresidence. Not surprisingly, Neandertal and early modern human skeletal remains have not been found in the same strata of any Levantine site. Accordingly, the Levantine Mousterian archaeological record can most parsimoniously be modeled as documenting shifts in the occupation of what is today northern Israel by at least two distinct hominid taxa competing for approximately the same ecological niche. Indeed, a similar interpretation is possible for Late Pleistocene prehistory throughout western Eurasia.

Harold L. Dibble and Philip G. Chase, *Department of Anthropology/University Museum, University of Pennsylvania, Philadelphia, Pennsylvania*

The nature of Upper Pleistocene hominid behavioral and biological changes is the subject of considerable recent controversy. Three distinct issues, each entailing a quite different kind of evidence, are being debated simultaneously:

1. Whether the differences between archaic *Homo sapiens* and morphologically modern *H. sapiens* should be interpreted as inter- or intraspecific. Resolving this question depends principally on biological evidence, including functional anatomy and the growth and development of diagnostic skeletal features, and the geographic, environmental, and temporal distributions of hominid forms.

2. Whether there was a relatively recent replacement of populations in various parts of the Old World or whether each region exhibits local continuity of biological forms. Archaeological, chronological, paleoanthropological, and genetic data are all relevant here to show movements of and contacts between various populations.

3. The nature of the behavioral adaptation of Upper Pleistocene hominids. The most direct evidence for behavior is, of course, archaeological, though skeletal evidence may be important when the relationship between behavior and biology is well understood.

We concentrated on the last of these, reviewing the evidence that had been put forward by others for the presence of symbolic behavior in the Middle Paleolithic. Lindly and Clark expand on our review, with essentially identical results, but because they confuse the three issues they draw very different conclusions.

Lindly and Clark are clearly addressing the issues of taxonomy and replacement/continuity. In their introduction they state: "We are concerned that Chase and Dibble's conclusions might be taken . . . as further 'proof' of . . . considerable evolutionary 'distance' between archaic *Homo sapiens* and morphologically modern humans." This is a question of taxonomy. They go on to say that "absence of evidence for symbolic behavior in archaic *H. sapiens* would support the contention that archaic *H. sapiens* (including the Neanderthals) was an evolutionary dead end and was replaced throughout its range by humans of 'modern' type with little or no genetic admixture." This, of course, relates to the continuity issue.

If we consider the archaeological evidence for symboling as a behavioral issue divorced from taxonomy, we see nothing in Lindly and Clark's paper that would cause us to alter our position—in fact, the evidence they present concurs with ours. Nonetheless, they criticize our work, citing Conkey's objection that symbolic behavior might be manifest in more subtle ways than the presence or absence of art, style, and ritual activity. As we said (Chase and Dibble 1987:284), "It could be that most of the symbolic behavior of Middle Paleolithic hominids left no archaeological traces simply because Middle Paleolithic culture did not express symbolism in any archaeologically preservable form. If this is the case, then we as archaeologists will be in error because of the very nature of our data base. But it is an error that must be risked in order to avoid assuming that which we are trying to demonstrate." To argue that symbolism (or any other trait) *may* have existed in forms other than those that are available to us is not a very strong argument that it *did* exist.

A second criticism of our paper, again attributed to Conkey, is that it is "wholly dependent upon a distinction between culture . . . and paleoculture." Here it is clear that Lindly, Clark, and Conkey have missed the point of our study. We simply reviewed phenomena proposed by *others* as evidence of symbolism in the Middle Paleolithic. It turned out that much of the "evidence" was shaky because of taphonomic conditions, dubious dating, or inadequate documentation. Moreover, other claims of symbolism usually required the unwarranted assumptions of links with phenomena such as esthetics. When we used the word "paleoculture" we were simply acknowledging that the lack of evidence for symbolic behavior in the Middle Paleolithic was consistent with a difference in behavior between Upper Paleolithic and behavior from earlier periods (as was noted by Jelinek [1977], who coined the term) and that this difference did not appear to be due to lack of intelligence on the part of Middle Paleolithic hominids.

When Lindly and Clark review evidence for symbolism from Middle Paleolithic sites associated with anatomically modern human remains, they use essentially the same method we did. While we are encouraged that their findings agree with ours, we disagree with the conclusions they draw from them. Their argument is structured as follows: (1) Biological change and speciation result from changes in adaptation. (This premise is unstated.) (2) Symboling has adaptive significance. (3) "In evolution, behavioral change always occurs well in advance of related morphological changes"; therefore the development of symboling in hominids should precede biological change and speciation. (4) "The results of [this] survey suggest that, as Chase and Dibble have reported for archaic *H. sapiens* the daily activities of pre-Upper Paleolithic morphologically modern humans had no archaeologically discernible symbolic component." (5) The lack of evidence for symbolic behavior in both forms "implies that taxonomic units themselves are unreliable," and therefore they should be considered the same species. (6) If they are the same species, they have the same adaptation, and therefore "the assertion that morphologically modern humans displaced archaic *H. sapiens* because they were more 'advanced'" is untenable. We do not, of course, dispute the first two premises or the fourth. We must, however, take issue with the rest.

The chronological primacy of behavioral over biological change (the third point) provides the logic for their review of early modern *H. sapiens* sites. However, this is valid only if it can be shown that the behavioral change in question (the adoption of symbolic behavior) is the one responsible for changes in hominid morphology. If a different behavioral change underlies the morphological differences between archaic and modern *H. sapiens* then the timing of the first appearance of symbolic behavior in the archaeological record is irrelevant to the evaluation of these morphological differences. Generally speaking, the primary skeletal differences between archaic and modern *H. sapiens* relate to overall robustness and details of cranial morphology. We are not aware of any demonstration that symboling is related to these features. In fact, it seems that one of the points that Lindly and Clark want to make is that symboling cannot be linked to changes in biology—a conclusion that we would endorse. But if symbolic behavior and biology are not linked, then the presence or absence of symbolic behavior has no implications for the interpretation of taxonomic differences.

As we pointed out, "it is highly probable that Middle Paleolithic hominids had some capacity for symbolism" (1987:285). What we question is that the regular use of symbols was an integral part of their behavioral adaptation. Contrary to the characterization of this work by Lindly and Clark, Marshack (1988a, 1989) has not demonstrated habitual use of symbols in the Middle Paleolithic. What he has done is to argue for the Neanderthal *capacity* for symboling—a capacity more clearly suggested by the evidence from Saint-Césaire and Arcy-sur-Cure than by his analysis of isolated finds.

Thus, that there is no solid archaeological evidence for symbolism before the Upper Paleolithic, even at sites associated with modern *H. sapiens*, has no apparent bearing on the question of the biological differences between archaic and modern hominids. It just means that the appearance of this particular behavior and the development of this particular set of biological traits are neither causally nor temporally linked.

Nor does the absence of archaeological evidence for sym-

boling from sites associated with either form of pre-Upper Paleolithic hominid "imply that the taxonomic units themselves are unreliable" (point 5). It makes no sense to argue that the shared lack of any particular behavioral trait (especially one not linked to biology) in two populations implies that the forms are taxonomically the same. Frogs and humans share the absence of the ability to fly, but that does not make us one species. Even within the hominid line, no one would argue that australopithecines and modern *H. sapiens* from the Middle Paleolithic belong to the same species just because there is no archaeological evidence that either regularly used symbols.

In point 6, Lindly and Clark confuse the issues of behavior and taxonomy with the issue of replacement. It is true that different species often have different adaptations, at least if they overlap temporally and geographically. It does not follow, however, that there are no differences in adaptation within a species, especially one as plastic and as dependent on learned behavior as the human. One need only look at the difference in adaptation between traditional Australian peoples and modern inhabitants of Melbourne. Nor does it follow that one population cannot displace or genetically swamp another populaiton of the same species. There may have been a population movement into Europe, for example, whether or not modern *H. sapiens* is a species distinct from the Neanderthals. Such movements have virtually no taxonomic implications in the sense that replacement of one population by another cannot be taken as evidence of genetic distance. An obvious historical example is the colonization of the Caribbean, where the indigenous population was almost totally replaced by newcomers from first Europe and then Africa. In other words, an important implication of the "extrasomatic means of adaptation" characteristic of hominids is that significant changes in behavior need not be associated with changes in morphology.

There does appear to be good evidence for population replacement in Europe at the beginning of the Upper Paleolithic (Mellars 1989). Moreover, the coincidence of their replacement with the first good archaeological evidence of the habitual use of symbols is striking. Even if Conkey (as cited by Lindly and Clark) is right that symbolic behavior may have been too subtle for the archaeological record to monitor (an argument that is, *ipso facto*, difficult to support empirically), the common evidence of symboling in the archaeological record of even the early Upper Paleolithic of Europe implies a new and significantly different role for symbols in a new adaptation (see Gamble 1983, White 1985, and Whallon 1989 for ideas about what this may have involved). The temporal coincidence implies that it was this new adaptation that permitted the newcomers to replace or swamp the area's former inhabitants. The association of both Neanderthals and archaeological evidence for symboling with the Châtelperronian, on the one hand, and the absence of links between symboling and both modern and archaic *H. sapiens* elsewhere until considerably later, on the other, demonstrate that this new adaptation was purely behavioral in nature and neither the cause nor the result of biological change. Nor, as we have pointed out elsewhere (Chase and Dibble 1987), does replacement in Europe necessarily argue for replacement elsewhere in the world.

In sum, we hope that Lindly and Clark's findings will not be taken by anthropologists as "proof" that behavior did not change significantly during the early Upper Pleistocene or that there could not have been population movements during this time.

Clive Gamble, *Department of Archaeology, University of Southampton, Southhampton, England*

This paper is an ingenious exercise in moving the chronological goalposts in order to accommodate the argument for regional continuity between archaic *Homo sapiens* and anatomically modern humans. While the data that Lindly and Clark present come from throughout the Old World, the focus is strongly European, since it is here that the cultural, symbolic, and anatomical evidence most strongly favours the replacement model to which they are opposed. Their main point is that the European early Upper Paleolithic (ca. 40,000-20,000 B.P.) produces few data that can be interpreted as symbolic. Similarly, in sub-Saharan Africa modern skulls and mandibles predate the Late Stone Age/Upper Paleolithic "revolution" at 40,000 B.P. and are not associated with any symbolic objects. This situation contrasts with the creative explosion after 20,000 B.P. in Europe and 12,000 B.P. in southern Africa (Deacon 1990). This extra 20,000 years, they argue, is ample time for symbolically informed behavior to have developed, and as a result we do not have to posit rapid replacement to explain its appearance.

While welcoming Lindly and Clark's negative review of symbolic data from the Old World, I can see some problems. Not least among these, given the chronology just mentioned, is their contention that behavioral change always precedes anatomical change if, as they claim, the symbolic explosion after 20,000 B.P. is somehow more significant because of the volume of symbolic objects recovered after that time. Symbolism, once available, is not something that is either turned off and on or varies in intensity. For example, the colonization after 13,000 B.P. of the North European Plain and the entry of humans into North America are marked by very few if any symbolic artifacts. The world at the last glacial maximum (18,000 B.P.) has huge areas with no symbolic objects and a northern fringe with abundant art (Gamble and Soffer 1990; Wobst 1990). This does not mean that the populations settling the former areas for the first time or adapting to refuge conditions there had switched off their capacity for symbolism.

I am therefore surprised to see Lindly and Clark recognize, at a world scale, a "latitudinal component to the archaeological evidence for symbolism" but then ignore this component *within* Europe at different stages of the last glacial cycle. Nor can their argument be applied to the objects from the early Upper Paleolithic of Europe, especially now that the Aurignacian is getting older thanks to accelerator mass spectrometer dating (Mellars 1989). Consequently, it is unreasonable to dismiss such data as the southern German figurines, all dated to over 30,000 B.P., as unimportant because they are rare. As to the pieces from the Middle Paleolithic championed by Marshack, I follow Chase and Dibble (1987) and Davidson and Noble (1989) in considering their symbolic status improbable.

Moving the goalposts to make the pitch longer puts off answering the main problem, which supporters of regional continuity are often reluctant to address—the very rapid colonization by humans of the whole earth (Cavalli-Sforza *et al.* 1988:6005). This occurs not with the first modern skulls but in a pulse beginning 50,000-30,000 years ago with, for example, the colonization of Australia and Melanesia (Allen,

Gosden, and White 1989; Jones 1990) and continuing for 30,000 years. It seems likely that expansion on this scale required the "conscious production of meaning" (n. 3); Whallon (1989) has argued that it points to the development of efficient language and memory that increased the scale and intensity of interaction and resulted in humans' colonizing all the world's habitable zones. If this provided a context for selection and by proxy a chronology for modern human origins (irrespective, by the way, of the shapes of their skulls and stone tools), then we need be less concerned with negative evidence for symbolic artifacts. We can also avoid the problem of supposing different rates of biocultural change and social complexity in different regions of the world—a notion that is reminiscent of Coon's (1962) conclusion, from which for obvious reasons most supporters of regional continuity are keen to distance themselves, that some regional populations (no guesses which) crossed the line to humanity later than others.

What Lindly and Clark have not addressed is the fact that the massive extension of range, while not always associated with the evidence for symbolic artifacts they discuss, does *not* take place before such objects have appeared somewhere in the world. Current time scales indicate that this process is more readily explained by dispersion, which involved replacement in some parts of the Old World. A more adequate test for Lindly and Clark's model would therefore be the convincing documentation of Middle and Early Upper Pleistocene human presence in the Americas, Sahul, or any of the major environments of the Old World that remained deserted until after 50,000 years ago.

Robert H. Gargett, *Department of Anthropology, University of California, Berkeley, California*

Lindly and Clark find no unequivocal archaeological evidence for "symbolic behavior" in association with morphologically modern *Homo sapiens* in the Middle Paleolithic. They conclude that because neither Middle Paleolithic archaic *H. sapiens*, *H. sapiens neanderthalensis*, nor morphologically modern *H. sapiens* left evidence of ability to think symbolically, none can be ruled out as a potential ancestor of behaviorally modern humans. Exposing as specious the old equation of modern form with modern capacity does not, however, radically undermine the replacement hypothesis; it does force a reconsideration of the mode of replacement and of what constitutes good evidence of modern behavior.

Lindly and Clark present "evidence" for continuity across technological (i.e., Middle-to-Upper Paleolithic) and morphological (i.e., archaic-to-modern) "boundaries" that they contend should lay the replacement model to rest. Laid to rest, however, is any notion that the evidence they introduce can be used to refute the model of replacement of archaic *H. sapiens* by modern humans in Europe about 38,000 years ago. First, citing Marshack (e.g., 1988a), they assert that the human capacity for symbolic thought reaches back into the Middle Paleolithic; but Marshack's arguments are not universally accepted (see, for example, d'Errico 1989) and cannot in any case be taken as unequivocal evidence for the kind of cognitive abilities that characterize modern humans. They continue with the rather startling proposition that we should ignore the evidence of modern "symbolic behavior" from the early Upper Paleolithic and view the identical but more plentiful evidence from the late Upper Paleolithic as the "symbolic explosion" heralding the arrival of humans with modern abilities. One is left to infer that it is not the human ability to manifest "symbolic behavior" in sculpted antler and bone and painted and incised representations on stone of humans and animals but the ability to leave such artifacts around in quantity that makes modern humans modern. In producing an arbitrary quantitative distinction to demonstrate continuity, Lindly and Clark have masked a marked qualitative difference between the archaeological records of Europe before and after the appearance of modern humans.

Finally, they shift the discussion from evidence for "symbolic behavior" to "the character of faunal assemblages," on their account a much better "monitor of human adaptation" than traces of symbolic ability. They maintain that the changes in faunal composition visible across the technological and morphological boundary in Europe can be attributed to climatic changes and not to any adaptive differences between the two types of *H. sapiens*—that Neandertals and modern humans in Europe lived off the meat of just those animals available to them. They are right to point out that the faunal evidence may not be used to support the replacement model, but neither can it be used as a refutation. In order for the faunal evidence to serve as support for the continuity hypothesis, we would need to know, at a minimum, whether Neandertals acquired their food using cognitive abilities similar to those ascribed to behaviorally modern humans. Only then would it be possible to say with relative certainty that there is "evidence for clinal, relatively gradual change" in "human adaptation" until about 20,000 years ago. In sum, the argument for a multiregional model rests on equivocal "evidence" for continuity and on the unsuccessful attempt to use that evidence to refute the replacement hypothesis.

What, then, is the status of the two competing hypotheses for the emergence of modern humans, given early evidence (e.g., at Qafzeh about 90,000 years ago [Valladas *et al.* 1988]) for morphologically modern humans in the Middle Paleolithic? At Klasies River Mouth 40,000-50,000 years ago there is an arguably modern tool kit in association with morphologically modern humans (Singer and Wymer 1982, and see Mellars 1989), suggesting that some as yet unknown process of cognitive evolution had already taken place. This evidence comes to us from a time when Neandertals were still working stone with the technique that they had once shared with the morphologically modern form and that they had used without any real change for about 50,000 years. If we can take this as one line of evidence that what occurred in Africa did not happen in Europe (possibly because of geographical isolation), this should suggest that while a transition to modern behavior did not, after all, coincide with the emergence of modern skeletal morphology, *it did take place within the modern morphotype.*

The changes in question may have involved such uniquely human capacities as language and the (possibly) related ability to create archaeological traces of "symbolic behavior," as Davidson and Noble (1989) have persuasively argued. This could have profoundly affected two otherwise similar populations of protohumans by rendering them too different psychologically for mating to occur. Thus, while Neandertals and modern humans may have been potentially interfertile owing to their close phylogenetic relationship, they may have been behaviorally isolated—a potent mechanism of speciation that has not received much consideration in this debate. That

modern humans resemble morphologically modern populations of archaic *H. sapiens* more than they do Neandertals or other archaic forms may be viewed, quite plausibly, as the result of reproductive isolation and not of the willy-nilly gene exchange implied by the multiregional-origins scenario.

Lindly and Clark have given us a valuable summary of the archaeological record of Middle Paleolithic morphologically modern *H. sapiens*. The caution they display in making inferences of "symbolic behavior" from archaeological sediments is a position with which I am much in sympathy. Their arguments for continuity ultimately fail, however, to persuade me that the multiregional-origins hypothesis in any way accurately depicts recent human phylogeny.

Ken Jacobs, *Department d'anthropologie, Université de Montréal, Montréal, Quebec, Canada*

Lindly and Clark are to be congratulated for a thorough review of many less well-known Eurasian Upper Pleistocene hominid-bearing sites. They argue, with good cause, for the decoupling of the marked cultural discontinuity across the Middle/Upper Paleolithic transition from the putative biological discontinuity between "archaic *Homo sapiens*" and "morphologically modern humans." This suggested decoupling has been far too long in coming, and to have it so well presented and documented is helpful. However, several comments are called for:

The classic dichotomies of Middle versus Upper Paleolithic and archaic *Homo sapiens* (a euphemism for Neandertal or Neandertal-like) versus morphologically modern humans have hampered our efforts to understand the evolutionary processes involved in the "transition" between arbitrarily defined, and then reified, categories. We learn these categories, accept them, are beholden to them, and allow them to shape the trajectory of our research and discourse. Yet the underlying evolutionary dynamics are rarely addressed. For example, given the emphasis here on purposeful burial, it would have been interesting to see a discussion of why such burials, common in the "Middle Paleolithic," are virtually unknown in the "early Upper Paleolithic" yet become the rule in the "late Upper Paleolithic." The absence of sites in which "Upper Paleolithic" burials are found in sediments overlying sediments with "Middle Paleolithic" burials, which suggests different strategies and norms regarding site usage, would also seem pertinent to the themes discussed here.

Further, Lindly and Clark only briefly discuss the fact that major changes in symbolic behavior appear only at the beginning of the "late Upper Paleolithic," a time roughly corresponding to the last glacial maximum. This coincides nicely with the results of Soffer (1987), who has underlined the archaeological correlates of adaptive (including symbolic) strategies in an increasingly stressful environment. Similarly, I have shown (Jacobs 1985) that major human postcranial changes in sexual dimorphism and robusticity accelerate with the last glacial maximum. In the absence of an explicit model, one gets the impression that Lindly and Clark are suggesting that changes in the nature or intensity of symbolic behavior have little or no impact on human population biology. While their rejection of the classic Upper Pleistocene biocultural coupling is welcome, further and more informative investigation of the links between symbolic behavior and population biology is needed.

Paul Mellars, *Department of Archaeology, University of Cambridge, Cambridge, England*

Whilst I have a good deal of sympathy with many of Lindly and Clark's comments, I believe that their article reflects a number of persistent and recurrent confusions in discussions of the biological and cultural transition from archaic to modern humans. First, no one would disagree with them on the absence of a simple, one-to-one correlation between anatomically modern humans and characteristically Upper Palaeolithic culture (with its rich symbolic manifestation) throughout the world. The question is whether this is at all relevant to the issue of population continuity versus population replacement over the archaic/modern-human transition. As Lindly and Clark point out, there is absolutely no reason to assume that biological and cultural changes must have gone strictly hand-in-hand. A far more likely scenario is a pattern of "mosaic" evolution, in which behavioral changes in some cases preceded major biological changes and in other cases followed them. If this was the case, then there is no reason whatever to assume that either the initial emergence of anatomically modern populations in Africa or their subsequent postulated dispersal into more northern latitudes should have been connected in any simple or direct way with dramatic changes in the associated achaeological record, the lack of such correlations in no way "refutes" the hypotheses of either an initial emergence of anatomically modern humans in one particular area or their subsequent dispersal to other regions of the Old World.

Leaving aside these theoretical issues, Lindly and Clark skate lightly over a vast amount of evidence that over a large region of the Old World (i.e., Central and Western Europe—where the major debate has always centerd) there were in fact fundamental changes in human behavior that can be shown to correlate remarkably closely with an equally abrupt transition from anatomically archaic to anatomically modern forms. The whole character of "Aurignacian" culture (with which the earliest forms of fully anatomically modern humans seem invariably to be associated in this region [Howell 1984]) shows a dramatic contrast with earlier "Middle Palaeolithic" culture not only in the character of the lithic industries but in such features as complex personal ornaments, elaborately shaped bone, antler, and ivory artifacts, far-travelled marine shells, increased use of other "exotic" materials, and the earliest well-documented (and remarkably complex) art. The relatively sudden and abrupt appearance of these features over such a large area within such a short space of time (Mellars 1989:372-75; White 1989a; Bischoff *et al.* 1989; Cabrera Valdes and Bischoff 1989; Koztowski 1990) is far more consistent with the hypothesis of a major episode of population dispersal than with that of a gradual, in situ evolution of the local (and highly varied) Middle Palaeolithic industries within the same regions. Lindly and Clark also fail to mention the very late (and very typical) Neanderthal hominid from Saint-Césaire (western France), which is almost certainly contemporaneous with the earliest forms of anatomically modern humans in Western Europe and demonstrably much *later* than the appearance of these forms at sites in the Middle East. Nor do they mention the demonstrable 30,000-40,000 years' overlap between "modern" and "archaic" forms that has now been documented within the Middle Eastern sites (Valladas *et al.* 1988, Schwarcz *et al.* 1988).

A more general weakness in many recent discussions of the origins of modern humans is an apparent implicit equation between "advanced lithic technology" and "advanced culture." Even if many of the lithic industries associated with the earliest forms of anatomically modern hominids (e.g., in southern Africa and the Middle East) were relatively "simple" in technological terms, this may give little indication of other—potentially much more significant—aspects of culture, such as social organization, subsistence strategies, or language. Here again, Lindly and Clark downplay the available evidence. The fact remains that the boar's jaw and large deer antler associated with early (ca. 90,000-100,000 B.P.) anatomically modern hominids at Skhul and Qafzeh, respectively, are by far the most convincing examples of deliberate grave offerings yet recorded from pre-Upper Palaeolithic contexts in Eurasia. Similarly, the perforated *Conus* shell from Border Cave and the regularly notched bones from Klasies River Mouth, Apollo II, and other African Middle Stone Age sites provide much more convincing evidence for early "symbolic" artifacts than anything so far recorded from the Middle Palaeolithic/Neanderthal sites of Europe. And the character of the African Howieson's Poort industry is not simply "aberrant Middle Stone Age" but fully "Upper Palaeolithic" in almost every recognized technological and typological sense (Mellars 1988, 1989). It may well be, therefore, that the total "culture" associated with these early forms of anatomically modern humans in southern Africa was significantly more complex and advanced than anything so far documented from the contemporaneous Middle Palaeolithic/Neanderthal sites of Eurasia.

Finally, I have never really understood the argument that the significance of the symbolic and technological "explosion" at the start of the Upper Paleolithic is in some way diminished by the evidence of further increases in "cultural complexity" during the later stages of the Upper Palaeolithic sequence. I would see this as a natural and predictable outcome of progressive increases in population densities and other demographic and social pressures in some of the more ecologically favored areas, such as the Franco-Cantabrian region or the South Russian Plain (Mellars 1985, Soffer 1985b). To argue that this evidence for later Upper Palaeolithic cultural "intensification" rules out the significance of the far more radical innovations in behavior at the *start* of the Upper Palaeolithic would seem akin to dismissing the significance of the "Neolithic Revolution" on the grounds that things became even more complicated during the Bronze Age.

Anne Pike-Tay, *Department of Anthropology, New York University, New York, New York*

I consider two major aspects of Lindly and Clark's argument problematical. The first is their use of the concept of behavioral adaptation rather than culture. In my view, their definition of adaptation (n. 2) cannot encompass social and cultural change. Culture is not like any other "structure, physiological process, or behavioral pattern" that contributes to the reproductive "fitness" of a species, and its development cannot be monitored in the same manner. For modern humans, the habitual use of symbols through language defines the environment within a social and historical context. Changes in human adaptations involve not only the environmental stimuli but the group's response to them, grounded in its unique historical circumstances (see Bettinger 1980, Conkey 1987b).

Lindly and Clark's concept of behavioral adaptation directs the argument that negative evidence for symbolic behavior supports "a hypothesis of no difference" between archaic *Homo sapiens* and anatomically modern humans. I completely agree that "no correlation of modern behavior with modern morphology can be proposed." The former deals with social and cultural adaptations (including symbolic behavior), or what Conkey (1987b:65) has termed "human-human relationships," and the latter concerns biological adaptations. I disagree, however, with the assumption that the mechanisms that shape these two dimensions of human change and variability are the same.

Lindly and Clark also contend that the negative evidence for symbolic behavior on the part of the earliest moderns from the African continent challenges the replacement scenario. I find this troubling on two counts. First, the "out-of-Africa" model has never relied upon the premise that anatomically modern humans arrived in Europe fully equipped with symbolic behavior. Second, Lindly and Clark explicitly question (n. 3) the appropriateness of the categories that have been employed to monitor symbolic behavior, calling them "equivocal and inadequate," but they propose test implications for the replacement model based on these same classes of evidence.

The second problem in Lindly and Clark's argument lies in the assumption that the similarities and differences between Middle Paleolithic and early Upper Paleolithic subsistence adaptations have been adequately assessed. While the European archaeofaunal evidence may initially suggest few marked changes "co-incident with the local Middle/Upper Paleolithic boundaries," when we are able to go beyond the relative frequencies of prey species we begin to see differences suggestive of change through time. For example, studies such as that of Delpech and Rigaud (1974) on the systematic processing of bone and marrow provide insight into early Upper Paleolithic innovation that would have been otherwise overlooked. Interpretive frameworks recently developed for understanding the age profiles of Middle and Upper Paleolithic ungulate prey (esp. Stiner 1989a, b) allow us to consider planned, corporate involvement in prey acquisition in the Middle Paleolithic and early Upper Paleolithic (Pike-Tay 1990). For example, comparative study of strategies involved in seasonal red-deer hunting in the Gravettian and Final Magdalenian of southwestern France (Pike-Tay 1989) suggests that the success of the early Upper Paleolithic group of hunters may be attributed to cooperation rather than technology.

Testing for *seasonal* use of prey species in well-controlled archaeological contexts can now aid in monitoring changes in subsistence systems that might appear identical if only relative frequencies of species, anatomical parts represented, and age profiles were considered. In addition, indicators other than faunal assemblages, such as paleonutrition, must be considered in examining change in subsistence adaptations in the Middle and Upper Paleolithic. For example, Brennan's (1986) work with biological stress indicators (i.e., enamel hypoplasias and Harris lines) has demonstrated statistically significant differences between the Middle Paleolithic and the early Upper Paleolithic in southern France. Pending further analysis of this kind, it is perhaps premature to argue that the subsistence strategies of the Middle Paleolithic and the early Upper Paleolithic were identical or different.

Yuri Smirnov, *Institute of Archaeology, U.S.S.R. Academy of Sciences, Moscow, U.S.S.R.*

I cannot but agree with Lindly and Clark's major argument for a slow accumulation of traces of "symbolic" behavior and a "symbolic explosion" only at ca. 20,000 years B.P. Yet I think we should also bear in mind both the irregularity of historical development and the wide variety of its particular forms that are suggested by the irregular distribution of archaeological traces of such activities over time and space. Further, the time and space distribution of particular types of "symbolic" activities throughout the world from ancient to modern times testifies to the existence of certain zones of aggregation (centers) that contain the majority of sites producing material evidence of this or that kind of "symbolism." Thus, there are centers of primitive art (Formozov 1983) and centers of taphological activity (Smirnov 1989). In all probability, we can also speak of center of zoolatric cults, e.g., bear caves representing a bear cult. The existence of such centers does not, however, exclude the possibility that similar "symbolic" activities went on in other places, although those activities evidently took other forms undetectable by archaeological means (e.g., drawings on perishable materials, exposure rather than burial of dead bodies or the objects of zoolatric cults, etc.). There is good reason to believe that there were in fact no human societies that did not go in for some sort of "symbolism." Both the structural complexity of the human brain (Kochetkova 1973) and the evolution of the particular parts of the brain responsible for thinking and speech suggest the existence of various kinds of "symbolic" activity as far back as *Homo erectus*.

A few words about some archaeological evidence that Lindly and Clark have regrettably not taken into account: From Qafzeh we have evidence not simply of the burial of the dead but of more sophisticated forms of preburial treatment including ritual cannibalism (e.g., pathology of the occipital part of the Qafzeh 6 skull). Both the condition and the distribution of the skeletal remains in burials testify to the practice of mortuary decapitation (Qafzeh 6), defleshing (Skhul 1?), and reburial (Skhul 2?). They also indicate that there were two types of burial, of the whole body and of only parts of it (Skhul 2, 6?, Qafzeh 6, 10, 15), and there are grounds for belief that the Mousterians ritually substituted isolated teeth for the cranium or the mandible (Qafzeh 3) (Smirnov 1989:223). Finally, Lindly and Clark have omitted mention of two pieces of ochre found in association with the Qafzeh 8 burial (Vandermeersch 1969:2563). I think that the interred (?) bull's skull that partially interfered with the Skhul 9 burial can be considered further evidence of "symbolic" activity.

Lawrence Guy Straus, *Department of Anthropology, University of New Mexico, Albuquerque, New Mexico*

This is a useful article and one with whose perspective and conclusions I am in fundamental agreement. I have argued for a number of years that, at least in the specific case of Cantabrian Spain, cultural evolution in the second half of the Upper Pleistocene was overall gradual, cumulative, and mosaic in nature (e.g., Straus 1977, 1983, 1990a; Straus and Heller 1988). This is not to deny the apparently rather abrupt effect of human abandonment of northwestern Europe and the southward recession of the hominid range during the last glacial maximum on population densities and hence on subsistence strategies, social organization, and symbolic/ceremonial activity in the Franco-Cantabrian region after about 20,000 years ago (Straus 1990b, c), but such cases of relatively rapid change need to be identified and analyzed individually and in local context.

I continue to be surprised that archaeologists and human paleontologists can argue so intensely about notions, such as "*the* Middle-to-Upper Paleolithic transition" as if they were real and the true object (as opposed to prehistoric human adaptations) of paleoanthropological research. We have not yet escaped the unilineal evolutionism of our scientific ancestors. With each new reassignment of key fossils (e.g., Skhul, Qafzeh) or industries (e.g., Chatelperronian, Szeletian, Bohunician), the supposed "transition" is moved in time and redefined. We tend to jump on bandwagons, the current one being the punctuated-equilibrium paradigm. However, depending on one's time frame (long or short), the same phenomena may appear to be the results of either gradualistic or punctuated change. We continue to make the basic mistake of assuming that new forms of fossil hominids must be strictly correlated with new behaviors (and vice versa) in all or at least most domains of human activity (this despite the Skhul, Qafzeh, and Saint-Césaire discoveries). Lindly and Clark clearly show the error of this assumption in the supposedly critical realm of symbolic behavior (however that may be defined).

A few points may be added to their expose:

1. Many/most Upper Paleolithic human remains (even in the Late Paleolithic, even in France) lack clear grave goods; indeed, unequivocal burials are still rare, particularly in such regions as Vasco-Cantabria (Quechon 1976, Harrold 1980). Grave goods are variably present even at the same site even in the Late Upper Paleolithic; for example, in the Upper Magdalenian of Duruthy (southwestern France) the (unsexed) individual found in 1894 by Lartet and Chaplain-Duparc was associated with some 40 perforated and engraved lion and bear teeth, while the (female) individual found in 1961 by Arambourou (1978:28-29) lack "offerings."

2. Most rupestral and even mobile art in Vasco-Cantabria can be argued to be of Late Upper Paleolithic (Solutrean and Magdalenian) age; its appearance in this region may be linked to the specific density-dependent conditions of human settlement alluded to above (Straus 1982, 1987b).

3. There are of course some well-dated, early, unequivocal works of art (e.g., at Geissenklösterle in southwestern Germany, ca. 32,000 years b.p. [Hahn 1988], and at Apollo II in Namibia, ca. 27,500 years b.p. [Wendt 1976]), but their distribution is geographically spotty: some regions have "much" early art, other little or none. Not all of this variation can necessarily be explained by differential preservation.

It is futile to debate whether "the transition" or even one aspect of the transition (i.e., "symbolic behavior") took place universally at one time or another. These phenomena are regionally variable in timing and mosaic in nature. Although hominid distributions and adaptations worldwide did end up looking very different by the end of the Upper Pleistocene than they had at its beginning, this was the cumulative result of long-term, non-teleological, adaptive changes. Symbolism un-doubtedly does have adaptive value—in the context of certain physical, demographic, and social environments such as those of the resource-rich but relatively cold and crowded Franco-Cantabrian region.

It is ironic that, while the authors (correctly) imply that specific attribution of individual fossils to archaic or modern *Homo sapiens sapiens* is often tenuous, they seem to accept several very fragmentary or juvenile remains as definitely "modern." In addition, some of the supposed associations of "modern" fossils with Middle Paleolithic artifact assemblages are questionable (e.g., Border Cave, Starosel'e Cave). Finally, the relevant deposits at Skhul are now "dated" by electron spin resonance to ca. 90,000 B.P. (Stringer *et al.* 1989), but, being based on the same theoretical assumptions as thermoluminescence dating, this need not be taken as an independent check on the dates from Qafzeh (Valladas *et al.* 1988).

C. B. Stringer, *Department of Palaeontology, Natural History Museum, London, England*

The realization that the conventional archaeological division between Middle and Upper Palaeolithic recognized by most archaeologists does not neatly correspond with the distinction (whether subspecific or specific) between anatomically non-modern and modern skeletal morphologies recognized by virtually all palaeo-anthropologists should have been with us for a long time now. In this paper, Lindly and Clark use "symbolism" as their main criterion for recognizing "modern" behavior and conclude that a lack of symbolism prior to the Upper Palaeolithic therefore indicates a lack of "modern" behavior, thus (in their opinion) supporting a multiregional model of modern human origins. However, they do recognize a number of limitations in their archaeological arguments, and I will leave those to be dealt with by other commentators.

Before going on to deal with their arguments concerning the origins of modern humans, I would like to clarify a few points concerning the sites they discuss in their useful review. First, concerning the supposed "grave goods" with Skhul 5 and Qafzeh II: it is true that the species represented were common in the layers concerned outside the purported grave area, but it is also worth noting that the remains in question were well preserved, suggesting that they, like the skeletons, may have been protected by intentional burial. Regarding Skhul, there is further evidence to link the sample with the Qafzeh hominids from electron-spin-resonance age estimates (Stringer *et al.* 1989). The accuracy of the claim that the Qafzeh hominids represent "the earliest dated remains of morphologically modern humans in the world" depends on interpretations of a number of African hominid sites. Omo Kibish I (Day and Stringer 1991; Day, Twist, and Ward 1991), KNM-ER 3884 (Bräuer, Leakey, and Mbua 1992), and the Klasies MSA I sample (Grün, Shackleton, and Deacon 1990) may all be of comparable or greater age, and this would also apply to Laetoli hominid 18 and the Singa calvaria (Grün and Stringer 1991) if they are considered to be anatomically modern (for further evidence of an archaic morphology in Singa, see Stringer, Cornish, and Stuart-Macadam 1985). The dating of the Aterian hominids of North Africa also remains unclear, with some workers arguing for much greater ages (70,000 years) for Aterian assemblages (Wendorf *et al.* 1990). Finally, regarding Florisbad, it is likely that the hominid considerably predates the Middle Stone Age levels above Peat 2 (Clarke 1985).

The implication of Lindly and Clark's arguments is that if the archaeological evidence (which they claim supports a multiregional model) does fit with the palaeontological evidence, it must be the latter, specifically what they term "replacement systematics," that is at fault. Here they are not just taking on advocates of replacement models but attacking the view accepted by most workers that there are significant morphological differences (whether specific or subspecific) between anatomically non-modern and modern humans. As they recognize, acceptance of the latter view completely undermines their arguments, for given their assertion that "behavioral change always occurs well in advance of related morphological change," such behavioral changes should be observed in the Middle Paleolithic of Europe and Western Asia if the Neanderthal populations there were to transform themselves into anatomically modern ones. This brings me to a very important point stressed on numerous occasions by Trinkaus (e.g., 1986, 1989a, b; see also Stringer 1989), who can hardly be characterized as favoring overall replacement: if we *do* accept the reality of the appearance of a new, more gracile skeletal pattern with anatomically modern humans, and we also accept that such a pattern is a reflection of selection and adaptation for a habitual life-style, then there *must* have been significant behavioral differences between the Skhul-Qafzeh hominids and the Neanderthals, whatever the lithic remains are supposedly saying. Otherwise, why were the Neanderthals (and other archaic hominids throughout the Pleistocene) carrying around all that physiologically and nutritionally demanding muscle and bone?

Presumably, if the more comprehensive genetic analyses now being conducted (e.g., Vigilant *et al.* 1989, Long *et al.* 1990, Nei and Livshits 1989) also do not fit with Lindly and Clark's multiregional interpretations, these too must all be at fault. Although I agree that "a satisfactory explanation of the origins of modern humans must reconcile the archaeological and fossil evidence and the evidence from molecular biology," I think we are some way away from such a reconciliation, and I consider it unlikely to come from the view that nearly everyone else has got it wrong (see also Clark 1988; Clark and Lindly 1989). It *might* come, however, from a recognition that at the moment we are missing things that we need to achieve a resolution. Each area of research needs to recognize its own limitations, both in data and in interpretation.

Erik Trinkaus, *Department of Anthropology, University of New Mexico, Albuquerque, New Mexico*
The ongoing debate on the nature, the timing, and especially the constituent processes of what we call "the origins of modern humans" appears to be becoming increasingly polarized just at a time when new data, analyzes, and insights should be taking us away from the narrow, polemical, and nonproductive arguments formerly justifiable by major gaps in our paleoanthropological knowledge and understanding. This paper by Lindly and Clark appears to be another contribution to this polarization rather than to our understanding of what might have happened in the past.

The substance of their text requires little comment. It is difficult to make a convincing argument one way or the other concerning the "evidence" for symbolic behavior among Middle Paleolithic-associated early modern humans based on a mix of remains from some old excavations (Starosel'e, Skhul, Témara, Porc Epic, Singa), some recent carefully done excavations (Qafzeh, Klasies River Mouth, Mumba), mixed deposits (Darra-i-Kur), and surface finds (Laetoli-Ngaloba, Omo-Kibish), not all of which are sufficiently complete to be morphologically diagnostic as to their affinities with late archaic versus early modern humans (Darra-i-Kur, Témara, Porc Epic, Mumba) and some of which are better considered as late archaic humans (Laetoli-Ngaloba, Singa). Their argument is based on negative evidence when there is little possible confidence in the representativeness of the samples assessed.

More important, they seem to be particularly concerned to eliminate any hint of biological determinism, as in their statement "it will be clear that no correlation of modern behavior with modern morphology can be proposed." Yet they are perfectly content to use supposed evidence of behavioral continuity, including typo-technological data, archaeofaunal analyses, and settlement-pattern inferences (only the first of which have anything resembling a secure basis in current analyses of the archaeological record, and that only for select regions of the northwestern Old World), to argue that there must have been human biological (i.e., genetic) continuity. Isn't there a problem here? If we cannot use past human morphology to say anything about past human behavior (and I believe that in fact we can), then we should be more careful about using highly debatable archaeological inferences concerning "cultural" continuity to make inferences about human phylogeny.

Perhaps more concern with sorting out the actual behavioral processes during the general period related to the origins of modern humans, combining human paleontological and Paleolithic archaeological data and inferences, is in order. It is becoming increasingly apparent that it was a considerably more complex period of human evolution than many of us thought even a few years ago, and perhaps our efforts would be better spent focusing on the past rather than contributing to anthropologically generated controversies that tell us little about it.

Randall White, *Department of Anthropology, New York University, New York, New York*
I wish to restrict my comments to two subjects: (1) the out-of-Africa hypothesis as seen from the perspective of the European Paleolithic and (2) Early Upper Paleolithic evidence for symbol use. With respect to the first issue, I am in substantial agreement with Lindly and Clark. As for the second, I cannot imagine how we could be farther apart, either theoretically and factually.

It remains uncertain whether the out-of-Africa model of later hominid evolution will stand the test of time, although there is much reason to give it serious consideration. However, in many respects the Aurignacian is irrelevant to the question, since dates for the Near Eastern Aurignacian are substantially later than the earliest Aurignacian dates for Europe. Thus, the early Aurignacian must be viewed as a completely European phenomenon, with some later spill-over into the Levant. If modern humans came to Europe as the result of an out-of-Africa radiation, it was not with already developed Aurignacian culture in hand. Archaeological evidence for an out-of-Africa radiation, if it exists, must be sought in earlier European/Near Eastern similarities such as those between the little-known East European Bohunician (Svoboda 1990) and industries from

Boker Tachtit in Israel (Klein 1990; Marks 1983, 1990). The success of Upper Paleolithic culture in replacing the Mousterian is understandable, but we remain without any archaeological, biological, or behavioral explanation for a preceding movement out of Africa. The selective advantage of being an anatomically modern human is simply not self-evident.

Whether the out-of-Africa model proves to be a myth or a reality, I agree with Lindly and Clark that there is little if any pre-40,000-year-old symbolic evidence anywhere. But they imply that, if the out-of-Africa model were correct, there would be such evidence earlier in Africa. This is not a valid test implication unless one believes that symbolic behavior was necessarily a neurological/genetic correlate of the emergence of anatomically modern humans. The cultural developments of the Aurignacian, including the first known representational art and personal adornment, took place at least 50,000 years after the first anatomically modern humans appeared in Africa. Therefore, as I have previously emphasized (White 1982, 1985, 1989b), the developments across the Middle/Upper Paleolithic transition are not susceptible to neurological/biological explanations but may be understood solely in cultural evolutionary terms.

In a peculiar twist, Lindly and Clark go so far as to question the taxonomic distinction between morphologically modern humans and archaic modern humans on grounds that neither demonstrates symbolic behavior. In their sociobiological view of things, they have lost sight of the social and ideational dimensions of cultural evolution. Leslie White, who had no trouble reconciling a symbolic with an adaptional definition of culture, would have been surprised by the view that "the character of faunal assemblages is a much more direct monitor of human adaptation than art, ornamentation, or mortuary practices." In fact, the nature of faunal assemblages is directly linked to culture (no matter how defined) through ideas, beliefs, technology, and social organization. As I have recently emphasized (White 1989b:99), the first symbolic representation was at least as significant adaptively and evolutionarily as the first use of fire or stone tools. The consequences for innovation and change were profound. The Aurignacians and their Upper Paleolithic descendents were able to realize with increasing rapidity a wide range of social, technological, and ideational possibilities. In my view, much of this rapid evolutionary development, as is the case today, was due to the forming, manipulating, and sharing of images.

But Lindly and Clark dispute the very existence of *abundant* symbolic evidence in the Early Upper Paleolithic. Here, our disagreements are not ones of perspective but of fact. For the past four years, I have been struggling to understand the rich body of Aurignacian and Gravettian symbolic evidence, especially body ornaments, from Western, Central, and Eastern Europe. The quantity of material is staggering, and most of it carries adequate stratigraphic provenience, in some cases with radiocarbon dates. Lindly and Clark mistakenly state that for the early Upper Paleolithic symbolic artifacts are dates "only on the basis of allegedly time-sensitive 'index-fossil' tool types and normative characterizations of assemblage sequences." In my view, it is undeniable that the Aurignacian is a culture-stratigraphic entity with relatively well-defined chronological limits established by radiocarbon dates (see Mellars *et al.* 1987). Peyrony's classic Aurignacian sequence has been much amended, but his Aurignacian 1 , characterized by split-based

points, maintains its stratigraphic and chronological validity, with no radiocarbon dates placing it later than 30,000 b.p. and several placing it as early as 33,000-40,000 b.p. (see Cabrera Valdes and Bischoff 1989).

Some of the best-dated Aurignacian 1 levels are precisely those that have yielded the earliest known representational art, for example, the three-dimensional ivory animal figures from Geissenklösterle, dated to well before 30,000 b.p. (Hahn 1986, 1988), and a red-deer canine replicated in steatite from Castillo with accelerator dates (Straus 1989) of 37,000-39,900 b.p. Most Aurignacian 1 assemblages in which organic materials have been preserved have yielded personal ornaments and/or decorated objects, not to mention items of bone and antler technology. However, as in the Magdalenian, in which 90% of all the mobiliary art in Europe comes from a dozen or so sites, there are great intersite differences in quantity.

From the beginning to the end of the Aurignacian (at about 28,000 b.p.) in Europe, there are approximately 2,500 personal ornaments (see White 1989a, Lejeune 1987). Indeed, the number of basal Aurignacian beads, identical to those recovered from older excavations at several other sites, is growing rapidly with the meticulous recovery of dozens of these objects from Henri Delporte's ongoing excavations at Brassempouy. Aurignacian sites have yielded about 70 decorated, engraved, or painted slabs (Delluc and Delluc 1978), about 30 three-dimensional ivory carvings (Hahn 1971, 1972, 1975, 1983, 1986, 1988; White 1989b), at least one bone flute (Passemard 1944: pl. 7), and several thousand bone, antler, and ivory tools/projectiles (cf. Léroy-Prost 1975, Knecht 1990). Bone/antler/ivory implements made by complex grinding and polishing techniques (see White 1989a) are very abundant. For example, there were 70 split-based antler points in the Aurignacian 1 at Isturitz, 54 at Abri Castanet, and 114 at Abri Blanchard (H. Knecht, personal communication).

The number of such objects increases steadily in the succeeding Gravettian, with perhaps fewer bone and antler tools/weapons and hundreds more engravings and paintings. It is worth noting that there are more personal ornaments (ca. 12,000) from the 28,000-year-old (Hoffecker 1987, Bader 1978) Gravettian site of Sungir than exist in all French Magdalenian sites combined.

These observations clearly indicate that Lindly and Clark are unjustified in wishing to move the "symbolic explosion" forward to 20,000-15,000 b.p. While I have no doubt that there is an increase in representational art in the Magdalenian/Epigravettian, this change is quantitative. The appearance, in the Aurignacian, of substantial numbers of representational objects (after 2.5 million years in which they apparently did not exist) is a qualitative and revolutionary development with general evolutionary consequences (see White 1989a) at least as profound as those of such landmarks in cultural evolution as the emergence of food production.

Pre-Upper Paleolithic hominids, whether in Africa or Eurasia, collected interesting forms and colors but seldom if ever created such forms. One possible exception is the Bacho Kiro festoon (Marshack 1982). I share fully Chase and Dibble's (1987) skepticism and feel that Marshack (1988b) has overestimated the symbolic qualities of the very few well-provenienced "curiosities" while ignoring the severe provenience problems of others out of a firmly held belief in a gradualist versus punctuated view of symbolic evolution. In fact, however, these pre-Upper Paleolithic specimens contradict a gradualist perspective in lacking technical and formal redundancy through time and across space, attributes immediately visible from the outset of the European Upper Paleolithic.

REPLY

J. M. Lindly and G. A. Clark, *Arizona State University, Tempe, Arizona*

We thank those who have taken the trouble to address some of the implications of our paper for the issue of modern human origins. It would appear that the modern-human-origins debate is not for the faint of heart. Yet, although we disagree wholeheartedly with many comments, we think that a resolution of these problems will only come from such frank exchanges. It is unreasonable (*contra* Trinkaus) to expect everyone to agree about which data are "relevant" and what data "mean." Since data have no "meaning" (even existence) independent of the conceptual frameworks (or paradigms) that define and contextualize them, many of the differences of opinion expressed here are due to different conceptions of biological and cultural evolutionary models (or parts thereof).

Our objectives in this essay were considerably less ambitious than many commentators perceive them to be. If, for the sake of argument, one accepts the reality of the taxonomic infrastructure (i.e., the reality of archaic *Homo sapiens*, Neanderthal, and morphologically modern taxonomic units), one of the primary issues becomes the relative contributions of these different (or not so different) hominids to "the origins of us." Chase and Dibble (1987) argue for a significantly different adaptation in the Middle Paleolithic than that seen in the Upper Paleolithic of Eurasia, basing their case on an *absence* of evidence for symbolism in the Middle Paleolithic and its *presence* in the Upper Paleolithic. Their construal of pattern in the Middle Paleolithic is used to juxtapose this "paleocultural" system to a cultural system of "modern" form (i.e., the Upper Paleolithic) for the purpose of demonstrating the "nature" of the Middle Paleolithic adaptation. It seems clear, however, that this approach can only take us so far in the examination of this complex series of interrelated issues and problems.

What we tried to do was to turn the Chase and Dibble argument around and look instead for evidence of symbolic behavior in Middle Stone Age/Middle Paleolithic sites associated with the skeletal remains of pre-Upper Paleolithic morphologically modern humans. If there were significant differences in symbolic behavior between archaic *H. sapiens* and morphologically modern human populations of pre-Upper Paleolithic/pre-Late Stone Age date, one would expect them to be manifest in the comparisons made here. So far as we can tell, however, the pattern is *exactly the same* whether the hominids associated with Middle Paleolithic/Middle Stone Age archaeological assemblages are archaic *H. sapiens*, Neanderthals, or morphologically modern humans. This implies (1) that the taxonomic units themselves are suspect (which we think very likely) and (2) that the major quantitative shift in adaptation occurred relatively late and was largely unrelated to the perceived transition from the Middle to the Upper Paleolithic. The evidence for and against symbolism is only a small part of this complex equation, albeit one that, because of its ambiguity (conflicting conceptual and operational definitions), seems to have evoked strong feelings.

We simply do not believe that *any* version of the replacement scenario, *anywhere in the world*, can reconcile obvious inconsistencies in the biological and cultural records of Upper Pleistocene hominids. If one subscribes to the "out-of-Africa" hypothesis (Cann, Stoneking, and Wilson 1987, Stoneking and Cann 1989), the implication is that morphologically modern humans replace archaic *H. sapiens* (or Neanderthals) throughout their range with no admixture and therefore the two *must be different species*. If these two different species were living in the same region at the same time, given what we know about evolutionary ecology, *they must have had fundamentally different adaptations*. Our previous work suggests that in southwestern Asia, and probably in Europe, they did not (Clark and Lindly 1988; 1989a, b). An absence of symbolic evidence associated with both hominid "types" provides further, albeit circumstantial, evidence for a similar adaptation. We cannot comprehend how Mellars can argue that an "out-of-Africa" perspective, wherein anatomically modern populations migrate throughout the rest of the Old World, would not also be accompanied by discernible changes in the archaeological record. If there are no actual or conceivable empirical referents for such an event or process, then it can be no more than speculation. According to the competitive-exclusion principle (Mayr 1950), populations coming together in any region from different environments must show adaptive differences, especially if they were different but closely related species. The archaeological record would, therefore, reflect discontinuity wherever this replacement "event" or "process" occurred. Mellars (along with some other commentators) appears to regard the concept of migration as a plausible mechanism to explain his construal of pattern. We do not. With Trinkaus (1982) and Jelinek (1982), we consider migration to be a density-dependent phenomenon essentially confined to the latest protohistoric and historic periods (i.e., those periods when human population densities were locally high in some areas). We simply do not believe that the physical migration of peoples played a significant role in human macroevolution and are hard-pressed to come up with a single instance in which a more compelling alternative explanation is not possible (including the Aurignacian in Europe [see Straus 1989]).

It seems clear that many view symbolism as something modern humans "do" as a matter of course. Despite assertions by Dibble and Chase, Mellars, Stringer, and White that no one believes this anymore, we see plenty of evidence to the contrary (e.g., Gargett 1989, Smirnov 1989). We think that our survey indicates that symbolic behavior is not "species-specific" but situational in human adaptation. In other words, it solves an adaptive problem for humans that is probably related to information-processing requirements created by increased social complexity, population density, and/or subsistence uncertainty (Mithen 1988a, b). We would suggest to Gamble that symbolic objects do not occur during the colonization of the North European plain in the late Upper Paleolithic or in the initial colonization of the New World essentially because population densities were so low that there was no need for them. In other words, it would appear that symbolism of the kind that would leave unambiguous empirical referents conferred no particular adaptive advantage on these colonizing populations under conditions of low population density. We do *not* contend that symbolic behavior of other sorts did not occur—only that we cannot monitor it archaeologically. In our opinion, this is the major stumbling block to the study of symbolic behavior in the remote past; we simply do not know what aspects of the total repertoire of symbolic behavior are likely to leave traces in the archaeological record.

Our study concluded that evidence for "modern behavior" (*sensu* Chase and Dibble 1987) does not occur in the archaeological record until the Upper Paleolithic, regardless of the hominid associated with it. As this "modern behavior" is associated with a suite of adaptations present *after* 35,000 years B.P., it is logical to suppose that *before* this time a different suite of adaptations related to "nonmodern" behavior (however defined) must have existed. In these adaptations neither Neanderthals nor archaic *H. sapiens* nor morphologically modern humans appear to have utilized symbolism as part of their daily existence. As we see it, we are criticized for being interested in the variability of these Upper Pleistocene adaptations, what they might mean in terms of the archaeological record, and how they might be related to the various hominid taxa with which they are associated. While we admit to no great admiration for the present state of systematics in human paleontology, we are manifestly *not* using symbolism—a behavioral trait—to question the *identification* of fossil taxa (*contra* Bar-Yosef *et al.*, Dibble and Chase, Trinkaus, Stringer). We *are* using a behavioral trait in conjunction with other behavioral traits to examine whether human adaptations in western Eurasia during the Upper Pleistocene are similar or different in respect of the fossils with which they are associated. That Bar-Yosef et al. and Dibble and Chase take our statement about the "evolutionary distance" between Neandertals and moderns to mean "taxanomic distance" is troubling. Taxonomies do not evolve; individuals in a population do. By attempting to monitor one aspect of the adaptations of pre-Upper Paleolithic hominids in conjunction with what we already know about other aspects of these adaptations, we feel better able to assess similarities and differences in order to begin to understand the evolutionary relationship that might have obtained between the hominids themselves.

We think that archaeologists (and many paleoanthropologists) tend to take biological taxonomic units at face value. Doing so often constrains debate along the lines established by the taxonomic categories themselves. Although we would think it obvious, it is very important to emphasize that *taxonomic categories do not always correspond to biological categories* (Futuyma 1979:507). Most of this literature is concerned with the taxon "species." Biologists define species as "groups of actually or potentially interbreeding natural populations, which are reproductively isolated from other such groups" (Mayr 1942). Morphology by itself is *not* the only criterion for the identification of species (Futuyma 1979:190). Dependence on taxonomies created with reference to morphological traits in attempts to understand *evolutionary* relationships (as suggested by Bar-Yosef *et al.*, Dibble and Chase, Stringer, and Trinkaus) is precisely what is wrong with the cladistic approaches to taxonomy that are currently so popular in replacement systematics. Taxonomy is a means to an end, not an end in itself. That Trinkaus, who has consistently produced credible functional explanations for morphological features grounded in behavioral changes, should make this particular criticism is especially worrisome. Perhaps we are missing something here, but it seems entirely inconsistent with his functional morphological approach (an approach we regard as the most defen-

sible in a field littered with the wreckage of discredited empiricist systematics). We do not believe it is possible nor are we interested in trying to understand the dynamic evolutionary relationships of hominid species strictly in terms of sterile classification systems. To suggest that taxonomies are somehow "real" is reminiscent of the typological thinking in biological systematics pilloried by Mayr (1963) more than 25 years ago. We are also reminded of Maynard Smith's (1988:9) reference to essentialism, wherein species are identified because they are "obviously different from one another, and in possession of a common essence," rather than because they do not interbreed. Lest we be accused of being overly critical of paleoanthropology, we hasten to add that there are clear parallels in those Old World archaeological systematics that use retouched-stone-tool typologies as if they were somehow "real" or "meaningful" in their own right (or more meaningful than other categories of evidence) (Barton 1988; Clark and Lindly 1989c; Dibble 1987, 1988).

In order to identify species, one must first determine whether individuals could have interbred under natural conditions. Characteristics that prevent interbreeding are known as isolating mechanisms, and these can be morphological, physiological, environmental, and/or *behavioral* in nature. In evolutionary biology, behavioral criteria are perfectly acceptable for assisting in the identification of species by assessing the likelihood that interbreeding might have taken place between them. This is especially true of subspecies (such as *H. sapiens sapiens* and *H. sapiens neanderthalensis*)—a concept that most evolutionary biologists consider arbitrary (Futuyma 1979:205). Although in this essay we examine one particular aspect of behavior (symbolism), we have elsewhere examined others (Clark and Lindly 1988; 1989a, b). In our opinion, there is no compelling biological evidence that Neanderthals and modern humans could not have interbred and, given their nearly identical adaptations, much to suggest that they did.

Dibble and Chase in particular confuse the taxonomic and biological species concepts by contending that differentiation of species depends solely on biological evidence. In addition, they mistakenly claim that we suggest that symbolism *causes* the morphological differences between archaic and modern humans. This is related to a misconstrual of evolutionary process. Behavior need not promote speciation or enhance reproductive success to be important to the survival of a species. Symbolic behavior is contextual. It was probably a latent capacity in all later Upper Pleistocene hominids, "activated" when it was adaptively advantageous to do so. Granted, modern humans have a multitude of different adaptations and degrees to which evidence of symbolic behavior is reflected archaeologically. Yet there is no question that we comprise a single species morphologically, physiologically, and behaviorally. It is, moreover, quite an inferential leap to argue that two populations with nearly the same morphology and exactly the same adaptation are different species (i.e., *do not* interbreed) simply because they have been *classified* as such. That humans are extremely flexible in their behavior and variable in their morphology does not mean that we can ignore similarities and differences in adaptation if we hope to understand evolutionary relationships. In short, we think that the approach advocated by Dibble and Chase and by Bar-Yosef and his colleagues ignores the interplay that must exist between archaeological, morphological, and molecular evidence.

Stringer suggests that, if morphological differences between moderns and Neanderthals at Qafzeh, Skhul, and Kebara are an indication of different adaptations, there might be behavioral differences manifest in the skeleton and not reflected in the archaeological record (essentially the reverse of what we are arguing). This is an interesting idea but one that is difficult to test. The only kind of test that we would imagine to be widely convincing would be one based on significant differences in functional morphology, and Trinkaus, who has studied most of the western Asian material, does not detect any such differences. How much morphological variation is enough to suggest major differences in adaptation? Stringer seems to think that enough variation can already be documented between these two taxa to allow for the possibility of different adaptations. We disagree, but if he is correct archaeologists will have to reevaluate what our data and theories can really tell us about the past. We remain optimistic that the archaeological record is at least as informative about Upper Pleistocene hominid adaptation as is the morphology of the hominids themselves. The point, though, is that we really need both perspectives to address these evolutionary questions adequately.

Dibble and Chase, Mellars, and White, while emphatically agreeing that there is no discernible relationship between symbolism and fossil taxa, cannot help remarking on the apparent uniqueness and significance of symbolic objects associated with the Aurignacian of Europe. The "abrupt appearance" of the Aurignacian in Europe, allegedly bolstered recently by early (ca. 40,000 years B.P.) accelerator dates from L'Arbreda and El Castillo caves in Spain, can be interpreted in several ways (Bischoff *et al.* 1989, Cabrera Valdes and Bischoff 1989; cf. Straus 1989). Mellars suggests that the early dates could signify a rapid replacement of indigenous Neanderthals by a dispersing population of moderns. In our opinion, it is just as likely that the Aurignacian "represents a simultaneous technological development, largely the product of convergence" (Straus 1989:477). These dates, at the *far western end* of the Aurignacian geographical distribution, are as old as or older than early Aurignacian dates from eastern Europe (Svoboda and Simán 1989). The "facts" evidently do not "speak for themselves," and the Spanish dates could mean many things: (1) that the dates from eastern Europe are too young and older dates will eventually be found, (2) that the conventionally dated early Upper Paleolithic sites in western Europe are too young and will turn out to be a good deal older when the accelerator technique is more widely used, or (3) that Aurignacian technology developed in situ at different times in different places out of the local Middle Paleolithic technology (Straus 1989). We think that a good case can be made for multiregional continuity and in situ development, at variable rates, of Aurignacian technology in Europe. No human fossils are associated with the dated early Aurignacian levels at these sites, and if fossils with Neanderthal morphology are eventually found the replacement scenario will collapse like a house of cards. The same will be true if fossils of modern morphology are eventually discovered in a Chatelperronian context. White appears to support the possibility of an in situ European development of the Aurignacian, but we see no evidence to suggest the "ancestral" relationship he suggests between the European Aurignacian and the industries of Boker Tachtit in the Levant (Marks 1983, 1985; Marks and Volkman 1983), or the Bohunician of eastern and central Europe (Svoboda and Simán 1989). These industries are based on Levallois reduction strategies that are not usually seen in the European Aurignacian.

Gargett's assertion to the contrary, we never suggested that the evidence for early Upper Paleolithic symbolic behavior in Europe should be ignored. We only wished to point out that the "early" evidence is, for the most part, undated or dated in terms of *fossiles directeurs* that, *contra* White, are manifestly *not* an accurate means of arranging archaeological assemblages in a chronological sequence (Straus 1987, Straus and Heller 1988, Šimek and Snyder 1988). Although the numbers of objects "dated" to the early Upper Paleolithic are impressive, we remain unconvinced that most of them can be accurately placed in time. Those radiometrically dated show a pattern of relatively few early Aurignacian objects, with an increase in frequency in the later Aurignacian and Gravettian. This fact does not diminish the importance of these objects or their significance to the study of early Upper Paleolithic adaptations but only indicates that symbolic behavior became more important through time and that the trend continues unabated (in fact, accelerates) in the later Upper Paleolithic. It is clear that we do not know as much about the Aurignacian as we should and that dependence on differences in retouched-tool-type frequencies and undated "art" objects do not present a complete picture of the relationship of the Aurignacian to the Chatelperronian, the late Middle Paleolithic, or even the Gravettian.

We are pleased that Jacobs, Smirnov, and Straus support our argument for a significant adaptive shift at around 20,000 B.P. rather than at the beginning of the Upper Paleolithic. In addition, Jacobs's research on concurrent human morphological change during the late Upper Paleolithic complements the archaeological data in suggesting major adaptive change. Dibble and Chase claim that our construal of biocultural evolutionary patterns cannot be reconciled with a mosaic configuration. We emphatically disagree. Our viewpoint is entirely consistent with mosaic evolution—with the crossing of behavioral and biological "thresholds" (however defined) at different times in different regions (Clark 1989a, b). Differences in *rates* of change do not contradict and in fact are predicted by the multiregional-continuity model.

Bar-Yosef *et al.*, Mellars, and Stringer think that we undervalue the "grave goods" associated with the Skhul V and Qafzeh II burials, yet they are unable to explain why these "offerings" are any more significant than similar objects associated in similar ways with archaic *H. sapiens* that are dismissed as "utilitarian" and/or as inadvertently included in grave fills. We think that Gargett (1989) is correct in questioning the intentionality of Middle Paleolithic burials, many of them enshrined in the literature as if they were established "facts." In respect of Qafzeh and Skhul, however, we are questioning not the burials themselves but only the purported "grave goods." Finally, contrary to Bar-Yosef *et al.* it is crystal clear from McCown's comments and from his illustration (taken from a photograph) that Skhul V, while probably a grave, was in fact disturbed.

We welcome the comments of Smirnov, who represents a research tradition quite different from our own, He embraces a more eclectic view than ours (and most other commentators') in respect of what can be regarded as "symbolic" in the Upper

Pleistocene archaeological record (especially the evidence for ritual treatment of several of the Qafzeh and Skhul burials). Although we have not been able to evaluate these claims directly, we adopt a more conservative stance. Taphonomic research over the past decade has forced a much-needed reassessment of conventionally accepted evidence for cannibalism, ritual, burial, etc., and has provided a range of alternative interpretations as to what such evidence might "mean."

Straus's point regarding the scarcity of grave goods and unambiguous graves even in the Upper Paleolithic is well taken. Rather than accepting on faith the conclusions of earlier generations of prehistorians, we have an obligation to reanalyze grave contexts and possible associated objects on a case-by-case basis. We agree with Jacobs that the reasons behind apparent differences in the *frequency* of Middle and Upper Paleolithic burials need to be explored (see also Clark and Neeley 1987).

Gargett and Mellars contend that the Howieson's Poort industry found in the MSA sequence of South Africa is very "modern" in appearance, but we do not know what that means. If it is the presence of prismatic blades that makes a lithic industry "modern" in appearance, then there are numerous examples of "modern"-looking industries in the Middle Paleolithic of southwestern Asia and Europe, and industries lacking blades are found all over the world and throughout prehistory. Gargett's assertions about a correlation between modern behavior and morphology cannot be tested in default of adequate operational definitions of "modern" behavior and morphology.

We agree with Jacobs and Straus that the dichotomies utilized in the modern-human-origins debate (Middle vs. Upper Paleolithic, archaic vs. modern morphology) are too restrictive for the investigation of what was surely a dynamic process rather than a series of more or less discrete stages. We also share Jacobs's concern that the underlying evolutionary dynamics be examined and discussed. The biological and cultural transitions must be studied *as transitions*. En bloc comparisons between normative characterizations of the Middle and Upper Paleolithic or between archaic and modern *H. sapiens* cannot fail to throw differences into sharp relief, but they tell us nothing about process.

Trinkaus takes issue with our inclusion in the survey of certain fossils whose "early modern" status is debated. It should be clear, however, that one must depend on the published accounts of these finds. It is simply a fact that the taxonomic status of some of them is contested by reputable scholars. One of the things that struck us very forcefully is just how poor the fossil evidence really is for pre-Upper Paleolithic morphologically modern humans. It amounts to *almost nothing*, and it is characterized by the most inadequate time/space grid imaginable. The impression conveyed by general and popular accounts is that there is a lot of solid, unequivocal evidence for early moderns, but it just isn't so.

Pike-Tay, apparently making a distinction between cultural adaptation and biological adaptation, chastises us for emphasizing the latter. We readily admit to an "adaptationist" bias in respect of human social behavior (Binford 1962, 1964, 1965), mainly because "adaptation" has realistic empirical referents whereas many construals of "culture" do not. Obviously, much depends here on what is meant by "culture" and what is meant by "biology." We define adaptation as evolutionary biology does (see n. 2). Behavior can be viewed as the "dynamics of adaptation"—a strategy for survival and reproduction (Binford

1972:133; see also Maynard Smith 1978; Jochim 1981; Foley 1987b). Natural selection operates on the behavior, morphology, physiology, and biochemistry of an organism, through reproductive success, to minimize or solve problems posed by an organism's physical and social environment (Foley 1987b:61). Culture, in contrast, is so ambiguous a concept that it has defied any consensus definition for over a century (and is, therefore, analytically useless). At a minimum, Pike-Tay must tell us what she means by "cultural adaptation." In a backhanded way, though, she has put her finger on an important conceptual issue: can we in fact neatly separate biological and cultural components of adaptation, and, if so, what are the empirical referents of each?

In modern-human-origins research, one might be tempted to look for "cultural origins" in an effort to differentiate "culture" from "paleoculture," as Chase and Dibble (1987) have done. In our opinion, however, this is a dangerous tack because of the generally acknowledged mosaic character of cultural evolution. What aspects of behavior are to be considered exclusively "cultural"? How many such traits must a population exhibit before it can be said to be "cultural" rather than "paleocultural"? Even assuming that one could come up with unambiguous empirical referents for "culture" and "paleoculture" (which we regard as an impossibility), there is no parsimonious solution to this problem, since it is based on a false dichotomy. Behavior usually considered "cultural" can be found in a number of nonhominid primates (Foley 1987b). Some chimpanzees make, use, and transport tools and thereby exhibit displacement (a capacity to take future contingencies into account). Some (perhaps all) chimps have the capacity to symbol and can be taught to communicate through sign language. Lowly vervet monkeys have a communication system with vocalizations that are the functional equivalents of words in human speech (Foley 1987b:4). Many animals exhibit learned behavior to a greater or lesser degree and so can transmit (to a greater or lesser degree) adaptive behavior from one generation to the next. In short, we agree with Foley (1987b) that culture is not a useful concept in the study of human origins because the ambiguity of its empirical referents obscures our perceptions of the dynamic development and evolution of behavior in the archaeo/paleontological record.

We are astonished that Gargett, Pike-Tay, and White (in part) take issue with our contention that faunal remains are a comparatively direct monitor of adaptation and with our conclusion that subsistence patterns over the Middle/Upper Paleolithic transition in Europe demonstrate continuity (Clark 1987, Clark and Lindly 1989a, b). Admittedly, the data available to evaluate this proposition are somewhat inadequate (though better in Europe than anywhere else), but (*contra* Pike-Tay) we are not basing our conclusions on anything so simpleminded as species list (Chase 1986, Clark 1987, Straus 1986). Neither Gargett nor Pike-Tay presents data to contradict our findings. We, too, have read Stiner (1989a, b), and to us her results, from an analysis of age profiles across the late-Middle/early-Upper-Paleolithic transition in Italy, appear to suggest continuity between these periods. Subsistence organization is indeed difficult to understand, but we would remind Gargett that all we can do is to utilize the data in hand. While White's linkage of subsistence organization and culture is sometimes (although not always) demonstrable in ethnographic contexts, our inability to identify "cultures" unambiguously makes it impossible to link these aspects of adaptation archaeologically.

One might imagine that this last great hominid transition would be the best-understood of all, but, as the present controversy shows, there is as much diversity of opinion as ever. If we are ever going to understand the transition to modern humans, it must be studied *as a transition*. We can no longer afford to compartmentalize it into archaeology, paleoanthropology, and molecular-biology components. Preconceptions about biological evolution have important consequences for interpretations of the archaeological record (and vice versa), and archaeologists can ignore the findings of other disciplines only at their peril. The ancestors of modern humans represent a long-lasting adaptive phase immediately preceding us. To claim that they were extinguished without issue over most of their range without coming up with a plausible explanation of *why* and *how* does little to engender confidence in the explanatory potential of anthropological research designs.

NOTES

[1] We thank Margaret Conkey (University of California, Berkeley) for a critical evaluation of this manuscript and for sharing her thoughts about the nature of symbolism and its relationship to Paleolithic art and ritual behavior. J. Desmond Clark (University of California, Berkeley), Deborah Olszewski (University of Georgia), C. Michael Barton (Arizona State University), Philip Chase and Harold Dibble (University of Pennsylvania), Brian Hayden (Simon Fraser University), Alexander Marshack (Peabody Museum, Harvard University), and CA referees Bernard Wood, Herbert Ullrich, Paul Mellars, and Susan Pfeiffer also discussed, read, and/or commented upon earlier drafts. An anonymous referee made valuable comments as well. We have tried to incorporate suggestions whenever possible, reconcile different points of view, and clarify ambiguous statements, and doing so has noticeably improved the essay. However, all responsibility for errors of commission or omission remains ours.

[2] We define adaptation as evolutionary biology does: any structure, physiological process, or behavioral pattern that makes an organism more fit to survive and to reproduce (Wilson 1975:577). Behavior can be viewed as the dynamics of adaptation—a strategy for survival and reproduction (Binford 1972:133).

[3] Although we do not intend to develop the argument here, we consider Chase and Dibble's criteria for monitoring symbolic behavior equivocal and inadequate. No argument is presented to warrant their use as unambiguous indicators of the cognitive capacities of the hominids in question, nor are other potentially more informative monitors of symbolic behavior considered. To base a global evolutionary characterization on the limited archaeological evidence from a single region is increasingly problematic, especially in light of the allegedly "delayed" character of modernization events and processes in that small and well-studied region. Conkey (1987a, 1991) has pointed out that, if hominids were structuring their lives and activities in ways that we would recognize and understand as symbolic, this would probably be manifest in more subtle, contextual kinds of archaeological evidence than those examined by Chase and Dibble— in other words, that we should seek to develop more sophisticated ways of analyzing the archaeological record of symbolism than simply charting the presence or absence of "art," "style," or "ritual activity." While the point is well taken, the exceptionally coarse grain of the Old World Upper Pleistocene archaeological record makes these potentially more sensitive monitors of symbolic behavior exceedingly difficult to operationalize. Conkey has further pointed out (personal communication) that the Chase and Dibble essay is wholly dependent upon a distinction between culture (which seems to be equated with symbolism—the "conscious production of meaning") and paleoculture (consciousness apparently without symbolic behavior), but these terms are left undefined. Without a clear sense of what culture is, what symbolic behavior is, and what relationships might have obtained between them, it is difficult to put much faith in it.

REFERENCES

Alexeyev, V. P. 1976. Position of the Starosel'e find in the hominid system. *Journal of Human Evolution* 5:413-421.

Allen, J., Gosden, C., and White, J. P. 1989. Human Pleistocene adaptations in the tropical island Pacific: Recent evidence from New Ireland, a greater Australian outlier. *Antiquity* 63:548-561.

Angel, J. 1972. A Middle Paleolithic temporal bone from Darra-i-Kur, Afghanistan, in: *Prehistoric Research in Afghanistan (1959–1966)* (L. Dupree, Ed.). *Transactions of the American Philosophical Society* 62:54-56.

Arambourou, R. 1978. *Le gisement préhistorique de Duruthy a Sorde-l' Abbaye*. Mémoires de la Société Préhistorique Française 13.

Bader, O. N. 1978. *Sungir' verkhnepaleoliticheskaya stoyanka*. Nauka, Moscow.

Bahn, P. 1988. Triple Czech burial. *Nature* 332:302-303.

Barton, C. M. 1988. *Lithic Variability and Middle Paleolithic Behavior: New Evidence from the Iberian Peninsula*. British Archaeological Reports International Series 408.

Bar-Yosef, O. 1987. Pleistocene connections between Africa and southwest Asia: An archaeological perspective. *African Archaeological Review* 5:29-38.

Bar-Yosef, O. 1989a. Geochronology of the Levantine Middle Palaeolithic, in: *The Human Revolution: Behavioural and Biological Perspectives on the Origins of Modern Humans* (P. Mellars and C. Stringer Eds.), pp. 611-625, Edinburgh University Press, Edinburgh.

Bar-Yosef, O. 1989b. Upper Pleistocene human adaptation in south-west Asia, in: *The Emergence of Modern Humans: Biocultural Adaptation in the Later Pleistocene* (E. Trinkaus, Ed.), pp. 154-180, Cambridge University Press, Cambridge.

Bar-Yosef, O., and Meignen, L. 1989. *Levantine Mousterian Variability in the Light of New Dates from Qafzeh and Kebara Caves, Israel*. Paper presented at the 54th annual meeting of the Society for American Archaeology, Atlanta, Ga., April 5–9.

Bar-Yosef, O., and Vandermeersch, B. 1981. Notes concerning the possible age of the Mousterian layers in Qafzeh cave, in: *Préhistoire du Levant* (J. Cauvin and P. Sanlarville, Eds.) pp. 281-286. Colloque International CNRS 598.

Bar-Yosef, O., Vandermeersch, B., Arensburg, B., Goldberg, P., Laville, H., Meignen, L., Tchernov, E., and Tillier, A-M. 1986. New data on the origin of modern man in the Levant. *Current Anthropology* 27:63-64.

Bate, D. 1937. Paleontology: The fossil fauna of the Wadi El-Mughara caves, in: *The Stone Age of Mount Carmel*, Vol. 1 (D. Garrod and D. Bate, Eds.), pp. 139-227, Clarendon, Oxford.

Beaumont, P. 1980. On the age of Border Cave hominids 1-5. *Palaeontologia Africana* 23:21-33.

Beaumont, P., De Villiers, H., and Vogel, J. 1978. Modern man in sub-Saharan Africa prior to 49,000 B.P.: A review and evaluation with particular reference to Border Cave. *South African Journal of Science* 74:409-419.

Belfer-Cohen, A. 1988. The appearance of symbolic expression in the Upper Pleistocene of the Levant as compared to western Europe, in: *L'Homme de Neandertal*, vol. 5, *La Pensée* (O. Bar-Yosef, Ed.), pp. 25-29, ERAUL, Liège.

Bettinger, R. 1980. Explanatory predictive models of hunter-gatherer adaptation. *Advances in Archaeological Method and Theory* 3:189-255.

Binford, L. 1962. Archaeology as anthropology. *American Antiquity* 28:17-25.

Binford, L. 1964. A consideration of archaeological research design. *American Antiquity* 29:425-441.

Binford, L. 1965. Archaeological systematics and the study of culture process. *American Antiquity* 31:203-210.

Binford, L. 1972. Contemporary model building: Paradigms and the current state of Paleolithic research, in: *Models in Archaeology*, (D. L. Clarke, Ed.), pp. 109-166, Methuen, London.

Binford, L. 1979. Organization and formation processes: Looking at curated technologies. *Journal of Anthropological Research* 35:255-273.

Binford, L. 1989. Styles of style. *Journal of Anthropological Archaeology* 8(1):51-67.

Binford, L., and Sabloff, J. 1982. Paradigms, systematics, and archaeology. *Journal of Anthropological Research* 38:137-153.

Bischoff, J. L., Soler, N., Maroto, J., and Julià, R. 1989. Abrupt Mousterian/Aurignacian boundary at ca. 40 ka bp: Accelerator ^{14}C dates from L'Arbreda Cave (Catalunya, Spain). *Journal of Archaeological Science* 16(6):563-576.

Böeda, E. 1988. Le concept laminaire: Rupture et filiation avec le concept Levallois, in: *L'Homme de Neandertal*, Vol. 8, *La Mutation*. (M. Otte, Ed.), pp. 41-60, ERAUL, Liège.

Bouchud, J. 1974. Etude preliminaire de la faune provenant de la grotte du Djebel Qafzeh près de Nazareth (Israél). *Paleorient* 1:87-102.

Brace, C. L. 1964. The fate of the "classic" Neanderthals: A consideration of hominid catastrophism. *Current Anthropology* 5:3-43.

Brace, C. L. 1967. *The Stages of Human Evolution*. Prentice-Hall, Englewood Cliffs, N.J.

Brace, C. L. 1986. Modern human origins: Narrow focus or broad spectrum. *American Journal of Physical Anthropology* 69:180.

Brace, C. L. 1988a. *The Stages of Human Evolution: Human and Cultural Origins*. Prentice-Hall, Englewood Cliffs, N.J.

Brace, C. L. 1988b. Punctuationism, cladistics, and the legacy of medieval neo-Platonism. *Human Evolution* 3:121-138.

Brace, C. L., Bookstein, F., Smith, S., Hunt, K., and Holck, P. n.d. *Neanderthal to Modern Cranial Continuity: A Rear End View*. MS, Museum of Anthropology, University of Michigan, Ann Arbor, Mich.

Bräuer, G. 1984. A craniological approach to the origin of anatomically modern *Homo sapiens* in Africa and the implications for the appearance of modern humans, in: *The Origins of Modern Humans: A World Survey of the Fossil Evidence* (F. Smith and F. Spencer, Eds.), pp. 327-410, Liss, New York.

Bräuer, G., Leakey, R. E., and Mbua, E. 1992. A first report on the ER-3884 cranial remains from Ileret/East Turkana, Kenya, in: *Continuity or Replacement: Controversies in Homo Sapiens Evolution* (G. Bräuer and F. H. Smith, Eds.), pp. 111-119, Balkema, Rotterdam.

Bräuer, G., and Mehlman, M. 1988. Hominid molars from a Middle Stone Age level at the Mumba Rock Shelter, Tanzania. *American Journal of Physical Anthropology* 75:69-76.

Brain, C. 1981. *The Hunters or the Hunted? An Introduction to African Cave Taphonomy*. University of Chicago Press, Chicago.

Brennan, M. U. 1986. *Hypoplasias in the Middle and Upper Paleolithic*. Paper presented at the 85th annual meeting of the American Anthropological Association, Chicago, IL.

Brooks, A. 1988. *New Perspectives on Western European Prehistory*. Paper presented at the 53rd annual meeting of the Society for American Archaeology, Phoenix, Ariz., April 27–May 1.

Butzer, K. 1982. Geomorphology and sediment stratigraphy, in: *The Middle Stone Age at Klasies River Mouth in South Africa* (R. Singer and J. Wymer, Eds.), pp. 33-42, University of Chicago Press, Chicago.

Butzer, K., Beaumont, P., and Vogel, J. 1978. Lithostratigraphy of Border Cave, Kwazulu, South Africa: A Middle Stone Age sequence beginning c. 195,000 B.P. *Journal of Archaeological Science* 5:317-341.

Cabrera Valdes, V., and Bischoff, J. L. 1989. Accelerator ^{14}C ages for basal Aurignacian at El Castillo (Spain). *Journal of Archaeological Science* 16:577-584.

Cann, R., Stoneking, M., and Wilson, A. 1987. Mitochondrial DNA and human evolution. *Nature* 325:31-36.

Cavalli-Sforza, L. L., Piazza, A., Menozzi, P., and Mountain, J. 1988. Reconstruction of human evolution: Bringing together genetic, archaeological, and linguistic data. *Proceedings of the National Academy of Science, U.S.A.* 85:6002-6006.

Chase, P. 1986. *The Hunters of Combe Grenal*. British Archaeological Reports International Series 286.

Chase, P. 1989. How different was Middle Paleolithic subsistence? A zooarchaeological perspective on the Middle to Upper Paleolithic transition, in: *The Human Revolution: Behavioural and Biological Perspectives on the Origins of Modern Humans* (P. Mellars and C. Stringer, Eds.), pp. 321-327, Edinburgh University Press, Edinburgh.

Chase, P., and Dibble, H. 1987. Middle Paleolithic symbolism: A review of current evidence and interpretations. *Journal of Anthropological Archaeology* 6:263-296.

Clark, G. A. 1987. From the Mousterian to the Metal Ages: Long-term changes in the human diet of northern Spain, in: *The Pleistocene Old World: Regional Perspectives* (O. Soffer, Ed.), pp. 293-316, Plenum Press, New York.

Clark, G. A. 1988. Observations on the black skull (WT-17000, *A. boisei*): An archaeological assessment of systematics in human paleontology. *American Anthropologist* 90:357-371.

Clark, G. A. 1989a. Alternative models of Pleistocene biocultural evolution: A response to Foley. *Antiquity* 63:153-161.

Clark, G. A. 1989b. Romancing the stones: Biases, style, and lithics at La Riera, in: *Alternative Approaches to Lithic Analysis* (D. Henry and G. Odell, Eds.), pp. 27-50, Archaeological Papers of the American Anthropological Association 1.

Clark, G. A., and Lindly, J. M. 1988. The biocultural transition and the origin of modern humans in the Levant and western Asia. *Paleorient* 14:159-167.

Clark, G. A., and Lindly, J. M. 1989a. The case for continuity: Observations on the biocultural transition in Europe and western Asia, in: *The Human Revolution: Behavioural and Biological Perspectives on the Origins of Modern Humans* (P. Mellars and C. Stringer, Eds.), pp. 626-676, Edinburgh University Press, Edinburgh.

Clark, G. A., and Lindly, J. M. 1989b. Modern human origins in the Levant and western Asia: The fossil and archaeological evidence. *American Anthropologist* 91(4):962-985.

Clark, G. A., and Lindly, J. M. 1989c. Comment on: Grave shortcomings: The evidence for Neandertal burial, by Robert H. Gargett. *Current Anthropology* 30:178-179.

Clark, G. A., and Neeley, M. 1987. Social differentiation in European Mesolithic burial data, in: *Mesolithic Northwest Europe: Recent Trends* (P. Rowley-Conwy, M. Zvelebil, and H. P. Blankholm, Eds.), pp. 121-127, John R. Collis, Sheffield.

Clark, G. A., and Straus, L. G. 1983. Late Pleistocene hunter-gatherer adaptations in Cantabrian Spain, in: *Hunter-Gatherer Economy in Prehistory: A European Perspective* (G. Bailey, Ed.), pp. 131-148, Cambridge University Press, Cambridge.

Clark, G. A., and Straus, L. G. 1986. Synthesis and conclusions, Pt. 1: Upper Paleolithic and Mesolithic hunter-gatherer subsistence in northern Spain, in: *La Riera Cave: Stone Age Hunter-Gatherer Adaptations in Northern Spain* (L. Straus and G. Clark, Eds.), pp. 351-366, Arizona State University Anthropological Research Papers 36.

Clark, J. D. 1982. The cultures of the Middle Paleolithic/Middle Stone Age, in: *The Cambridge History of Africa: From Earliest Times to c. 500 B.C.* (J. D. Clark, Ed.), pp. 248-341, Cambridge University Press, Cambridge.

Clark, J. D. 1983. The significance of culture change in the early later Pleistocene in northern and southern Africa, in: *The Mousterian Legacy: Human Biocultural Change in the Upper Pleistocene*. (E.

Trinkaus, Ed.), pp. 1-12, British Archaeological Reports International Series 164.

Clark, J. D. 1988. The Middle Stone Age of East Africa and the beginnings of regional identity. *Journal of World Archaeology* 2:235-305.

Clarke, R. 1985. A new reconstruction of the Florisbad human cranium, with notes on the site, in: *Ancestors: The Hard Evidence* (E. Delson, Ed.), pp. 301-5, Liss, New York.

Conkey, R. 1987a. New approaches in the search for meaning? A review of research in "Paleolithic art." *Journal of Field Archaeology* 14:413-430.

Conkey, R. 1987b. Interpretive problems in hunter-gatherer regional studies, in: *The Pleistocene Old World* (O. Soffer, Ed.), pp. 63-77, Plenum Press, New York.

Conkey, M.W. 1983. On the origins of Paleolithic art: A review and some critical thoughts, in: *The Mousterian Legacy: Human Biocultural Change in the Upper Pleistocene* (E. Trinkaus, Ed.), pp. 201-227, British Archaeological Reports S164, Oxford, U.K.

Conkey, M. 1991. Magic, mythogram, and metaphors for modernity: The interpretation of Paleolithic art, in: *Handbook of Human Symbolic Evolution* (A. Lock and C. Peters, Eds.), Oxford University Press, Oxford.

Coon, C. 1962. *The Origin of Races*. Cape, London.

Davidson, I., and Noble, W. 1989. The archaeology of perception. *Current Anthropology* 30:125-155.

Day, M., and Stringer, C. 1991. Les restes crâniens d'Omo Kibish et leur classification à l'intérieur du genre *Homo*. *L'Anthropologie* 95:573-594.

Day, M., Twist, M., and Ward, S. 1991. Les vestiges post-crânien d'Omo I (Kibish). *L'Anthropologie* 95:595-610.

Deacon, J. 1990. Changes in the archaeological record in South Africa at 18,000 B.P. in: *The World at 18,000 B.P.*, Vol. 2, *Low Latitudes* (C. Gamble and O. Soffer, Eds.), pp. 170-88, Unwin Hyman, London.

Debénath, A. 1975. Découverte de restes humains probablement Aterien à Dar-es-Soltane (Maroc). *Comptes Rendus de l'Académie des Sciences de Paris*, Série D 281:875-876.

Delluc, B., and Delluc, G. 1978. Les manifestations graphiques aurignaciennes sur support rocheux des environs des Eyzies (Dordogne). *Gallia Préhistoire* 21:213-438.

Delpech, F. 1983. *Les faunes du Paleolithique supérieur dans le sud-ouest de la France*. Cahiers du Quaternaire 6.

Delpech, F., and Rigaud, J-Ph. 1974. Etude de al fragmentation et de la répartition des restes osseux dans un niveau d'habitation paléolithique, in: *L'industrie de L'os dans la Prehistoire* (H. Camps-Fabrer, Ed.), pp. 47-55, Université de Provence, Aix-en-Provence.

D'errico, F. 1989. Paleolithic lunar calendars: A case of wishful thinking? *Current Anthropology* 30:117-18.

Dibble, H. 1987. The interpretation of Middle Paleolithic scraper morphology. *American Antiquity* 52:109-117.

Dibble, H. 1988. Typological aspects of reduction and intensity of utilization of lithic resources in the French Mousterian, in: *Upper Pleistocene Prehistory of Western Eurasia* (H. Dibble and A. Montet-White, Eds.), pp. 181-196, University of Pennsylvania Press, Philadelphia.

Dupree, L. 1972. Tentative conclusions and tentative chronological charts, in: *Prehistoric Research in Afghanistan (1959–66)* (L. Dupree, Ed.). *Transactions of the American Philosophical Society* 62:74-82.

Dupree, L., and Davis, R. 1972. The lithic and bone specimens from Aq Kupruk and Darra-i-Kur, in: *Prehistoric Research in Afghanistan (1959–1966)* (L. Dupree, Ed.). *Transactions of the American Philosophical Society* 62:14-32.

Feder, K., and Park, M, 1989. *Human Antiquity*. Mayfield, Mountain View, CA.

Ferembach, D. 1976. Les restes humains ateriens de Témara (Campagne 1975). *Bulletin et Mémoires de la Société d'Anthropologie de Paris*, Série 13, 3:175-180.

Ferring, C. R. 1975. The Aterian in North African prehistory, in: *Problems in Prehistory: North Africa and the Levant* (F. Wendorf and A. Marks, Eds.), pp. 113-126, Southern Methodist University Press, Dallas.

Fisher, A. 1988. The more things change . . . . *Mosaic* 19(1):22-33.

Foley, R. 1987a. Hominid species and stone tool assemblages: How are they related? *Antiquity* 61:380-392.

Foley, R. 1987b. *Another Unique Species: Patterns in Human Evolutionary Ecology*. Longman, Essex.

Formozov, A. A. 1983. K probleme "ochagov pervobytnogo iskusstva" (Concerning the problem of "centers of primitive art"). *Sovetskaya Arkheologia*, no. 3, pp. 5-13.

Futuyma, D. J. 1979. *Evolutionary Biology*. Sinauer Associates, Sunderland.

Gamble, C. 1983. Culture and society in the Upper Palaeolithic of Europe, in: *Hunter-Gatherer Economy in Prehistory* (G. Bailey, Ed.), Cambridge University Press, Cambridge.

Gamble, C. 1986. *The Palaeolithic Settlement of Europe*. Cambridge University Press, Cambridge.

Gamble, C., and Soffer, O. 1990. Pleistocene polyphony: The diversity of human adaptations at the last glacial maximum, in: *The World at 18,000 B.P.*, Vol. 1, *High Latitudes* (O. Soffer and C. Gamble, Eds.), pp. 1-23, Unwin Hyman, London.

Gargett, R. 1989. Grave shortcomings: The evidence for Neandertal burial. *Current Anthropology* 30:157-177, 184-190.

Geneste, J-M 1988. Systémes d'approvisionnement en matiéres premiéres au Paléolithique moyen et au Paléolithique supérieur en Aquitaine, in: *L'homme de Néandertal*, Vol. 8, *La Mutation* (M. Otte, Ed.), pp. 61-70, ERAUL, Liège.

González Echegaray, J. 1988. Decorative patterns in the Mousterian of Cueva Morin, in: *L'homme de Néandertal*, vol. 5, *La Pensée*. (O. Bar-Yosef, Ed.), pp. 37-42, ERAUL, Liège.

Gowlett, J. 1987. The coming of modern man. *Antiquity* 61:210-219.

Grine, F., and Klein, R. 1985. Pleistocene and Holocene human remains from Equus Cave, South Africa. *Anthropology* 8:55-98.

Grün, R., and Stringer, C. 1991. Electron spin resonance dating and the evolution of modern humans. *Archaeometry* 33:153-199.

Grün, R., Shackleton, N., and Deacon, H. 1990. ESR dating of tooth enamel from Klasies River Mouth main site, South Africa. *Current Anthropology* 31(4):427-432.

Hahn, J. 1971. La statuette masculine de la grotte du Hohlensteinstadel (Württemberg). *L'Anthropologie* 75:233-244.

Hahn, J. 1972. Aurignacian signs, pendants, and art objects in Central and Eastern Europe. *World Archaeology* 3:252-266.

Hahn, J. 1975. *Der Vogelherd: Eine Wohnhohle der Altsteinzeit im Lonetal bei Stetten Gemeinde Niederstozingen Ldkr*. Heidenheim. Kulturdenkmale in Baden-Württemberg, Kleine Fuhrer, 16.

Hahn, J. 1983. Eiszeitliche Jager zwischen 35000 und 15000 vor heute, in: *Urgeschichte in Baden-Württemberg* (H.-J Müller-Beck, Ed.), pp. 273-330. Theiss, Stuttgart.

Hahn, J. 1986. *Kraft und Aggression*. Institut fur Urgeschichte, Tübingen.

Hahn, J. 1988. *Das Geissenklösterle I*. Theiss, Stuttgart.

Harrold, F. 1980. A comparative analysis of Eurasian Paleolithic burials. *World Archaeology* 12:195-211.

Hoffecker, J. 1987. Upper Pleistocene loess stratigraphy and Paleolithic site chronology on the Russian Plain. *Geoarchaeology* 2:259-284.

Howell, F. C. 1984. Introduction, in: *The Origins of Modern Humans: A World Survey of the Fossil Evidence* (F. H. Smith and F. Spencer, Eds.), pp. 13-22, Liss, New York.

Jacobs, K. 1985. Evolution in the postcranial skeleton of Late Glacial and early Postglacial European hominids. *Zeitschrift für Morphologie und Anthropologie* 75:307-326.

Jelinek, A. 1977. The Lower Paleolithic: Current evidence and interpretations. *Annual Review of Anthropology* 6:11-32.

Jelinek, A. 1981. The Middle Paleolithic in the southern Levant from the perspective of Tabun Cave, in: *Préhistoire du Levant* (J. Cauvin and P. Sanlaville, Eds.), pp. 265-280, Colloques International du CNRS 598.

Jelinek, A. 1982. The Middle Paleolithic in the southern Levant, with comments on the appearance of modern *Homo sapiens*, in: *The Transition from Lower to Middle Paleolithic and the Origins of Modern Humans* (A. Ronen, Ed.), pp. 57-101, British Archaeological Reports International Series 151.

Jochim, M. A. 1981. *Strategies of Survival*. Academic Press, New York.

Jones, R. 1990. From Kakadu to Kutikina: The southern continent at 18,000 years ago, in: *The World at 18,000 B.P.*, Vol. 2, *Low Latitudes* (C. Gamble and O. Soffer, Eds.), pp. 264-295, Unwin Hyman, London.

Julian, M. 1982. *Les Harpons Magdaleniens*. Gallia Préhistoire, 18th suppl.

Klein, M. 1965. The Middle Paleolithic of the Crimea. *Arctic Anthropology* 3:34-68.

Klein, S. 1990. Human cognitive changes at the Middle to Upper Palaeolithic transition: The evidence of Boker Tachtit, in: *The Emergence of Modern Humans: An Archaeological Perspective* (P. Mellars, Ed.), pp. 499-516, Cornell University Press, Cornell.

Knecht, H. 1990. Production and design of Aurignacian antler projectile technology, in: *Before Lascaux: Re-examining the early Upper Paleolithic* (H. Knecht, A. Pike-Tay, and R. White, Eds.), Telford Press, Caldwell, N.J.

Kochetkova, V. I. 1973. *Paleonevrologia* (Paleoneurology). Moscow: MGU.

Koztowski, J. K. 1990. A multi-aspectual approach to the origins of the Upper Palaeolithic in Europe, in: *The Emergence of Modern Humans: An Archaeological Perspective* (P. Mellars, Ed.), pp. 419-437, Cornell University Press, Cornell.

Kuman, K., and Clarke, R. J. 1986. Florisbad: New investigations at a Middle Stone Age hominid site in South Africa. *Geoarchaeology* 1:103-125.

Lejeune, M. 1987. *L'art mobilier paleolithique et mésolithique en Belgique*. Editions du Centre d'Etudes et de Documentation Archéologiques, Treignes.

Léroy-Prost, C. 1975. L'industrie osseuse de l'Aurignacien: Essai regional de classification, Poitou, Charente, Périgord. *Gallia Préhistoire* 18:65-156.

Lindly, J., and Clark, G. 1987. A preliminary lithic analysis of the Mousterian site of 'Ain Difla (WHS site 634) in the Wadi Ali, west-central Jordan. *Proceedings of the Prehistoric Society* 53:279-292.

Long, J., Chakravarti, A., Boehm, C., Antonarakis, S., and Kazazian, H. 1990. Phylogeny of human beta-globin haplotypes and its implications for recent human evolution. *American Journal of Physical Anthropology* 81(1):113-130.

McCown, T. 1937. Mugharet es-Skhul: Description and excavations, in: *The Stone Age of Mount Carmel*, Vol. 1 (D. Garrod and D. Bate, Eds.), pp. 91-107, Clarendon, Oxford.

McCown, T., and Keith, A. 1939. *The Stone Age of Mount Carmel*. Vol. 2. Clarendon, Oxford.

Marks, A. 1983. The Middle to Upper Paleolithic transition in the Levant. *Advances in World Archaeology* 2:51-98.

Marks, A. 1985. The Levantine Middle to Upper Paleolithic transition: The past and present, in: *Studi di paletnologia in onore di Salvatore M. Puglisi* (M. Liverani, M. Palmieri, and R. Peroni, Eds.), pp. 123 -136, Università di Roma, Rome.

Marks, A., and Volkman, P. 1983. Changing core reduction strategies: A technological shift from the Middle to the Upper Paleolithic in the southern Levant, in: *The Mousterian Legacy* (E. Trinkaus, Ed.), pp. 13-33, British Archaeological Reports International Series 164.

Marks, A. 1990. The Middle and Upper Paleolithic of the Near East and the Nile Valley: The problem of cultural transformations, in: *The Emergence of Modern Humans: An Archaeological Perspective* (P. Mellars, Ed.), pp. 56-80, Cornell University Press, Cornell.

Marshack, A. 1982. Non-utilitarian fragment of bone from the Middle Palaeolithic layer, in: *Excavation in the Bacho Kiro cave (Bulgaria): Final Report* (J. Kozlowski, Ed.), p. 117, Panstowowe Wydawnictwo Naukowe, Warsaw.

Marshack, A. 1988a. The Neanderthals and their human capacity for symbolic thought: Cognitive and problem-solving aspects of Mousterian symbol, in: *L'homme de Néandertal*, Vol. 5, *La Pensée* (O. Bar-Yosef, Ed.), pp. 57-92, ERAUL, Liège.

Marshack, A. 1988b. La pensée symbolique et l'art. *Dossiers Histoire et Archéologie* 124:80-90, 97, 98.

Marshack, A. 1989. Evolution of the human capacity: The symbolic evidence. *Yearbook of Physical Anthropology* 32:1-34.

May, F. 1986. *Les Sépultures Préhistoriques: Étude Critique*. Editions du CNRS, Paris.

Maynard Smith, J. 1978. Optimization theory in evolution. *Annual Review of Ecology and Systematics* 9:31-56.

Maynard Smith, J. 1988. *Games, Sex, and Evolution*. Harvester-Wheatsheaf, London.

Mayr, E. 1942. *Systematics and the Origin of Species*. Columbia University Press, New York.

Mayr, E. 1950. Taxonomic categories in fossil hominids. *Cold Spring Harbor Symposia on Quantitative Biology* 15:109-118.

Mayr, E. 1963. *Animal Species and Evolution*. Harvard University Press, Cambridge, MA.

Mellars, P. 1973. The character of the Middle-Upper Paleolithic transition in southwest France, in: *The Explanation of Culture Change* (C. Renfrew, Ed.), pp. 255-276. Duckworth, London.

Mellars, P. 1985. The ecological basis of social complexity in the Upper Paleolithic of southwestern France, in: *Prehistoric Hunter-Gatherers: The Emergence of Cultural Complexity* (T. D. Price and J. A. Brown, Eds.), pp. 271-297, Academic Press, Orlando.

Mellars, P. 1988. The origins and dispersal of modern humans. *Current Anthropology* 29:186-188.

Mellars, P. 1989. Major issues in the emergence of modern humans. *Current Anthropology* 30:349-385.

Mellars, P., Bricker, H. M., Gowlett, A. J., and Hedges, R. E. M. 1987. Radiocarbon accelerator dating of French Upper Paleolithic sites. *Current Anthropology* 28:128-133.

Mellars, P., and Stringer, C., Eds. 1989. *The Human Revolution: Behavioural and Biological Perspectives on the Origins of Modern Humans*. Edinburgh University Press, Edinburgh.

Mithen, S. 1988a. Looking and learning: Upper Paleolithic art and information gathering. *World Archaeology* 19:297-327.

Mithen, S. 1988b. To hunt or to paint: Animals and art in the Upper Paleolithic. *Man* 23:671-695.

Nei, M., and Livshits, G. 1989. Genetic relationships of Europeans, Asians, and Africans and the origins of modern *Homo sapiens*. *Human Heredity* 39:276-281.

Otte, M., Ed. 1988. *L'homme de Néandertal*, Vol. 8, *La Mutation*. ERAUL, Liège.

Parkington, J. 1990. A critique of the consensus view of the age of Howieson's Poort assemblages in South Africa, in: *The Emergence of Modern Humans: An Archaeological Perspective* (P. Mellars, Ed.), pp. 34-55, Cornell University Press, Cornell.

Passemard, E. 1944. La caverne d'Isturitz en Pays Basque. *Préhistoire* 9:1-84.

Pike-Tay, A. 1989. *Red Deer Hunting in the Upper Paleolithic of Southwest France: A Seasonality Study*. University Microfilms, Ann Arbor.

Pike-Tay, A. 1990. Hunting strategies in the Upper Perigordian: Organizational and technological perspectives, in: *Before Lascaux: Re-examining the early Upper Paleolithic* (H. Knecht, A. Pike-Tay, and R. White, Eds.), Telford Press, Caldwell, N.J.

Quechon, P. 1976. Les sépultures des hommes du Paléolithique supérieur, in *La Préhistoire Française* (H. de Lumley, Ed.), 1:728-733, CNRS, Paris.

Rightmire, G. P. 1984. *Homo sapiens* in sub-Saharan Africa, in: *The Origins of Modern Humans: A World Survey of the Fossil Evidence* (F. Smith and F. Spencer, Eds.), pp. 295-325, Liss, New York.

Ronen, A., Ed. 1982. *The Transition from Lower to Middle Paleolithic and the Origin of Modern Man*. British Archaeological Reports International Series 151.

Sackett, J. 1982. Approaches to style in lithic archaeology. *Journal of Anthropological Archaeology* 1:59-112.

Schwarcz, H., Grün, R., Vandermeersch, B., Bar-Yosef, O., Valladas, H., and Tchernov, E. 1988. ESR dates for the hominid burial site of Qafzeh in Israel. *Journal of Human Evolution* 17:733-737.

Schwarz, H. P., Buhay, W. M., Grün, R., Valladas, H., Tchernov, E.,

Bar-Yosef, O., and Vandermeersch, B. 1989. ESR dating of the Neanderthal site, Kebara Cave, Israel. *J. Archaeol. Sci.* 16:653-659.

Shackleton, N. 1982. Stratigraphy and chronology of the KRM deposits: Oxygen isotope evidence, in: *The Middle Stone Age at Klasies River Mouth in South Africa* (R. Singer and J. Wymer, Eds.), pp. 194-199, University of Chicago Press, Chicago.

Shea, J. 1989. A functional study of the lithic industries associated with hominid fossils in the Kebara and Qafzeh Caves, Israel, in: *The Human Revolution: Behavioural and Biological Perspectives on the Origins of Modern Humans* (P. Mellars and C. Stringer, Eds.), pp. 611-625, Edinburgh University Press, Edinburgh.

Šimek, J., and Snyder, L. 1988. Changing assemblage diversity in Perigord archaeofaunas, in: *Upper Pleistocene Prehistory of Western Eurasia* (H. Dibble and A. Montet-White, Eds.), pp. 321-332, University of Pennsylvania Press, Philadelphia.

Šimek, J., and Price, H. 1990. Chronological change in Perigord lithic assemblage diversity, in: *The Emergence of Modern Humans: An Archaeological Perspective* (P. Mellars, Ed.), pp. 243-261, Cornell University Press, Cornell.

Singer, R., and Wymer, J. 1982. *The Middle Stone Age at Klasies River Mouth in South Africa.* University of Chicago Press, Chicago.

Smirnov, Yu. A. 1989. Intentional human burial: Middle Paleolithic (Last Glaciation) beginnings. *Journal of World Prehistory* 3:199-233.

Soffer, O. 1985a. *The Upper Paleolithic of the Central Russian Plain.* Academic Press, New York.

Soffer, O. 1985b. Patterns of intensification as seen from the Upper Paleolithic of the Central Russian Plain, in: *Prehistoric Hunter-Gatherers: The Emergence of Cultural Complexity* (T. D. Price and J. A. Brown, Eds.), pp. 235-270, Academic Press, Orlando.

Soffer, O. 1987. Upper Paleolithic connubia, refugia, and the archaeological record from eastern Europe, in: *The Pleistocene Old World* (O. Soffer, Ed.), pp. 333-348, Plenum Press, New York.

Stiner, M. 1989a. *Mortality Patterns as Indicators of Upper Pleistocene Human Predator Niche: A Comparative Perspective.* Paper presented at the 54th annual meeting of the Society for American Archaeology, Atlanta, GA.

Stiner, M. 1989b. The use of mortality patterns in archaeological studies of human predatory adaptations. *Jour. Anthrop. Arch.* 9(4):305-351.

Stoneking, M., and Cann, R. 1989. African origin of human mitochondrial DNA, in: *The Human Revolution: Behavioural and Biological Perspectives on the Origins of Modern Humans* (P. Mellars and C. Stringer, Eds.), pp. 17-30, Edinburgh University Press, Edinburgh.

Straus, L. G. 1977. Of deerslayers and mountain men: Paleolithic faunal exploitation in Cantabrian Spain, in: *For Theory Building in Archaeology.* (L. Binford, Ed.), pp. 41-76, Academic Press, New York.

Straus, L. G. 1982. Observations of Upper Paleolithic art: Old problems and new directions. *Zephyrus* 34/35:71-80.

Straus, L. G. 1983. From Mousterian to Magdalenian: Cultural evolution reviewed from Vasco-Cantabrian Spain and Pyrenean France, in: *The Mousterian Legacy* (E. Trinkaus, Ed.), pp. 73-111, British Archaeological Reports International Series 164.

Straus, L. G. 1986. Late Würm adaptive systems in Cantabrian Spain: The case of eastern Asturias. *Journal of Anthropological Archaeology* 5:330-368.

Straus, L. G. 1987a. Paradigm lost: A personal view of the current state of Upper Paleolithic research. *Helinium* 27:157-171.

Straus, L. G. 1987b. The Paleolithic cave art of Vasco-Cantabrian Spain. *Oxford Journal of Archaeology* 6:149-163.

Straus, L. G. 1989. Age of the modern Europeans. *Nature* 342:476-477.

Straus, L. G. 1990a. The early Upper Paleolithic of southwestern Europe: Cro-Magnon adaptations in the Iberian peripheries, 40,000–20,000 BP, in: *The Emergence of Modern Humans: An Archaeological Perspective* (P. Mellars, Ed.), pp. 276-302, Cornell University Press, Cornell.

Straus, L. G. 1990b. The last glacial maximum in Cantabrian Spain: The Solutrean, in: *The World at 18000 B.P.*, Vol. 1 (C. Gamble and O. Soffer, Eds.), pp. 89-108, Unwin Hyman, London.

Straus, L. G. 1990c. Southwestern Europe at the last glacial maximum in: *The Pleistocene Perspective* (A. ApSimon and S. Joyce, Eds.), Unwin Hyman, London.

Straus, L., and Heller, C. 1988. Explorations of the twilight zone: The Early Upper Paleolithic of Vasco-Cantabrian Spain and Gascony, in: *The Early Upper Paleolithic: Evidence from Europe and the Near East* (J. Hoffecker and C. Wolf, Eds.), pp. 97-133, British Archaeological Reports International Series 437.

Stringer, C. 1979. A reevaluation of the fossil human calvaria from Singa, Sudan. *Bulletin of the British Museum of Natural History (Geology)* 32:77-93.

Stringer, C. 1988. The dates of Eden. *Nature* 331:565-566.

Stringer, C. 1989. Documenting the origin of modern humans, in *The Emergence of Modern Humans* (E. Trinkaus, Ed.), pp. 67-96, Cambridge University Press, Cambridge.

Stringer, C., and Andrews, P. 1988. Genetic and fossil evidence for the origins of modern humans. *Science* 239:1263-1268.

Stringer, C., Cornish, L., and Stuart-Macadam, P. 1985. Preparation and further study of the Singa skull from Sudan. *Bulletin of the British Museums of Natural History (Geology)* 38:347-358.

Stringer, C., Grün, R., Schwarcz, H., and Goldberg, P. 1989. ESR dates for the hominid burial site of Es-Skhul in Israel. *Nature* 338:756-758.

Svoboda, J. 1988. Early Upper Paleolithic industries in Moravia: A review of the recent evidence, in: *L'homme de Néandertal*, Vol. 8, *La Mutation* (M. Otte, Ed.), pp. 169-192, ERAUL, Liége.

Svoboda, J. 1990. The complex origin of the Upper Paleolithic in Czechoslovakia, in: *Before Lascaux: Re-examining the early Upper Paleolithic* (H. Knecht, A. Pike-Tay, and R. White, Eds.), Telford Press, Caldwell, N.J.

Svoboda, J., and Simán, K. 1989. The Middle-Upper Paleolithic transition in southeastern Central Europe (Czechoslovakia and Hungary). *Journal of World Prehistory* 3:283-322.

Tchernov, E. 1988. The biogeographical history of the southern Levant, in: *The Zoogeography of Israel* (Y. Yom-Tov and E. Tchernov, Eds.), pp. 159-251, Junk, Dordrecht.

Trinkaus, E. 1982. Evolutionary continuity among archaic Homo sapiens, in: *The Transition from Lower to Middle Paleolithic and the Origin of Modern Humans* (A. Ronen, Ed.), pp. 301-14, British Archaeological Reports International Series 151.

Trinkaus, E. 1984. Western Asia, in: *The Origins of Modern Humans: A World Survey of the Fossil Evidence* (F. Smith and F. Spencer, Eds.), pp. 251-294, Liss, New York.

Trinkaus, E. 1986. The Neanderthals and modern human origins. *Annual Review of Anthropology* 15:193-218.

Trinkaus, E. 1989. Comment on: Grave shortcomings: The evidence for Neandertal burial, by Robert H. Gargett. *Current Anthropology* 30:183-184.

Trinkaus, E., Ed. 1989a. *The Emergence of Modern Humans: Biocultural Adaptation in the Late Pleistocene.* Cambridge University Press, Cambridge.

Trinkaus, E. 1989b. The Upper Pleistocene transition, in: *The Emergence of Modern Humans: An Archaeological Perspective* (P. Mellars, Ed.), Cornell University Press, Cornell.

Valladas, H., Joron, J. L., Valladas, G., Arensburg, B., Bar-Yosef, O., Belfer-Cohen, A., Goldberg, P., Laville, H, Meignen, L., Rak, Y., Tchernov, E., Tillier, A. M., and Vandermeersch, B. 1987. Thermoluminescence dates for the Neanderthal burial site at Kebara in Israel. *Nature* 330:159-160.

Valladas, H., Reyss, J., Joron, J. L., Valladas, G., Bar-Yosef, O., and Vandermeersch, B. 1988. Thermoluminescence dating of Mousterian "Proto-Cro-Magnon" remains from Israel and the origins of modern humans. *Nature* 331:614-616.

Vandermeersch, B. 1969. Les nouveaux squelettes moustériens découverts à Qafzeh (Israël) et leur signification. *Comptes Rendus Hebdomadaires des Séances de l'Académie des Sciences* 268:2562-2565.

Vandermeersch, B. 1970. Une sépulture moustérienne avec offrandes découverte dans la grotte de Qafzeh. *Comptes Rendus Hebdomadaires des Séances de l'Académie des Sciences* 270:298-301.

Vandermeersch, B. 1981. *Les Hommes Fossiles de Qafzeh* (Israël). CNRS, Paris.

Vigilant, L., Pennington, R., Harpending, H., Kocher, T., and Wilson, A. 1989. Mitochondrial DNA sequences in single hairs from a southern African population. *Proceedings of the National Academy of Sciences*, U.S.A. 86:9350-9354.

Villa, P. 1989. On the evidence for Neandertal burial. *Current Anthropology* 30:324-326.

Volman, T. 1984. Early prehistory of southern Africa, in: *Southern African Prehistory and Paleoenvironments* (R. Klein, Ed.), pp. 169-220, Balkema, Rotterdam.

Wendorf, F., Close, A., Schild, R., Gautier, A., Schwarcz, H. P., Miller, G. H., Kowalski, K., Krolik, H., Bluszcz, A., Robins, D., and Grün, R. 1990. Le dernier interglaciaire au Sahara oriental. *L'Anthropologie* 94:361-391.

Wendt, W. 1976. "Art mobilier" from the Apollo II Cave, southwest Africa: Africa's oldest dated works of art. *South African Archaeological Bulletin* 31:5-11.

Whallon, R. 1989. Elements of cultural change in the Later Palaeolithic, in: *The Human Revolution: Behavioural and Biological Perspectives on the Origins of Modern Humans* (P. Mellars and C. Stringer, Eds.), pp. 433-454, Edinburgh University Press, Edinburgh.

White, R. 1982. Rethinking the Middle/Upper Paleolithic transition. *Current Anthropology* 23:169-192.

White, R. 1985. Some thoughts on social relationships and language in hominid evolution. *Journal of Personal and Social Relationships* 2(1):95-115.

White, R. 1989a. Production complexity and standardization in early Aurignacian bead and pendant manufacture: Evolutionary implications, in: *The Human Revolution: Behavioural and Biological Perspectives on the Origins of Modern Humans* (P. Mellars and C. Stringer, Eds.), pp. 366-390, Edinburgh University Press, Edinburgh.

White, R. 1989b. Visual thinking in the Ice Age. *Scientific American* 261(1): 92-99.

White, R. 1989c. Toward a contextual understanding of the earliest body ornaments, in: *The Emergence of Modern Humans Biocultural Adaptation in the Later Pleistocene* (E. Trinkaus, Ed.), pp. 211-231, Cambridge University Press, Cambridge.

Wilson, E. 1975. *Sociobiology: The New Synthesis*. Belknap, Cambridge.

Wobst, H. M. 1990. Minitime and megaspace in the Palaeolithic at 18K and otherwise, in: *The World at 18,000 B.P.*, Vol. 2, *Low Latitudes* (C. Gamble and O. Soffer, Eds.), pp. 322-334, Unwin Hyman, London.

Wolpoff, M. 1980. *Paleoanthropology*. Knopf, New York.

Wolpoff, M. 1989. Multiregional evolution: The fossil alternative to Eden, in: *The Human Revolution: Behavioural and Biological Perspectives on the Origins of Modern Humans* (P. Mellars and C. Stringer, Eds.), pp. 62-108, Edinburgh University Press, Edinburgh.

Wolpoff, M., Spuhler, J., Smith, F., Radovcic, J., Pope, G., Frayer, D., Eckhardt, R., and Clark, G. 1988. Modern human origins. *Science* 241:772-774.

Glossary

Abduction   the movement of a limb or part of a limb away from the midline of the body.

Absolute dating   the determination of the age, in years, of a fossil site, usually on the basis of the amount of change in radioactive elements in rocks.

Acheulian tradition   a stone tool technology containing large bifaces, often associated with *Homo erectus*.

Adaptation   the process whereby an organism changes in order to survive in its given environment; or, a specific new characteristic that enhances survival and/or reproductive success.

Adaptive radiation   a diverse array of related species with different morphological and ecological adaptations.

Adduction   the movement of a limb or part of a limb toward the midline of the body.

Allen's rule   a general physiological trend that mammals in cold climates tend to have shorter and bulkier limbs, allowing less loss of body heat while mammals in hot climates tend to have long, slender limbs, allowing greater loss of body heat; see also Bergman's rule.

Allometry   the relationship between the shape of an organism or its parts to size; also, the study of such relationships.

Amino acid   the basic unit of which proteins are composed. There are 20 different amino acids found in biological compounds.

Anagenesis   morphological change in a single species or lineage over time. Contrasts with cladogenesis.

Analogous features   morphological features with a similar function in two species but different construction. For example, the wings of a bird and those of a flying insect are an example of an analogous trait. See also convergent evolution.

Anatomically modern *Homo sapiens*   the extant modern form of *Homo* which characterizes all living populations as first appeared in the fossil record as early as 100,000 years ago.

Anthropometry   the measurement of the human body.

Antibody   substance that reacts to other substances invading the body (antigens).

Apomorph   a new morphological feature that has appeared in an evolving lineage that may signify a point of divergence.

Autapomorph   a new morphological feature confined to one group in an evolving lineage.

Arboreal   habitually living in trees.

Archaic *Homo sapiens*   an earlier variant of *Homo sapiens* (sometimes, but not always, including neandertals) that is more derived that *Homo erectus*, but lacks features characteristic of modern *Homo sapiens*.

Articulation   a joint between two or more bones.

Aurignacian   an early Upper Paleolithic tool industry of the Old World, dating from about 33,000 to 18,000 B.P., characterized by bone tools.

Australopithecine   general term for species in the genus *Australopithecus* or *Paranthropus*.

Australopithecus   genus of fossil hominid characterized by bipedal locomotion, small brain size, large face, and large teeth; found in Africa between 5 m.y.a. and 2 m.y.a. See also *Paranthropus*.

Aveolar prognathism   the forward projection of the portions of the jaws that bear teeth.

Basal metabolism   the energy requirements of an animal at rest.

Basalt   fine-grained extrusive igneous rock of dark color, low in silica. Basalt can be dated radiometrically.

Bergmann's rule   a physiological trend that among mammals of similar shape, the larger mammal loses heat less rapidly than the smaller mammal; and among mammals of similar size, the mammal with a linear shape will lose heat more rapidly than the mammal with a nonlinear shape; see also Allen's Rule.

Biface   a stone tool with both sides worked.

Biomass   the sum of the weights of the organisms in a particular area.

Biostratigraphy   sequential or temporal ordering of rocks based on the fossils they contain.

Bipedalism   mode of locomotion using only the hindlimbs.

Brachiation   a type of arboreal locomotion in which the animal moves below branches by grasping branches with alternating forelimbs.

Brachycephalic   broadheaded, having a Cephalic Index above 80.

Breccia   sedimentary rock composed of angular fragments of derived material embedded in a fine cement.

Brow ridge   the large ridge above the orbits formed by an anterior projection of the frontal bone.

Buccal   the cheek side of a tooth or tooth row.

Bunodont   teeth that possess low, rounded cusps.

Burin   an Upper Paleolithic chisel-like stone tool suitable for engraving bone, wood, horn or soft stone.

Calotte   the bones the cranial vault.

Calvarium   a skull without the bones of the face or mandible.

Canine diastema   the gap between the canine and first premolar or lateral incisor to accommodate the projecting canine from the opposing jaw; in the mandible, the diastema is between the canine and first premolar. On the maxilla, the diastema is between the lateral incisor and the canine.

Carabelli's cusp　an accessory cusp on the lingual surface of the crown of an upper molar tooth.

Carbon-14 dating　an absolute dating method based on the half-life of carbon-14. This method can be applied to organic remains up to a maximum age of about 50,000 years ago.

Carnivore　an animal that eats primarily the flesh of other animals; also often used to refer to the mammalian order Carnivora, which have tooth morphology adapted to this purpose.

Cephalic index　a measure of cranial shape, length of skull divided by the width of the skull.

Cerebrum　the area of the forebrain that consists of the outermost layer of brain cells; associated with memory, learning, and intelligence.

Character displacement　the tendency for enhanced character divergence in two closely related species occupying overlapping distributions, owing to the selective effects of competition.

Chignon　a protuberance of the occipital bone of the skull; characteristic of the Neandertals.

Chopper　a stone chipped at one end to create a sharp edge; typical tool of the Oldowan and other pebble-chopper industries.

Clade　a group composed of all the species descended from a single common ancestor; a monophyletic group.

Cladistics　phylogenetic systematics; a method of phylogeny reconstruction and classification in which organisms are grouped on the basis of shared derived traits (synapomorphies).

Cladogenesis　the formation of one or more new species from a common ancestor.

Cladogram　a branching tree diagram used to represent phyletic relationships among organisms.

Clinal variation　the variation of a trait characterized by gradual transitions occurring over geographical distance, as opposed to a sharp disjuncture.

Conspecific　belonging to the same species.

Continuous trait　a trait that is expressed over a range of values and is measured rather than counted; length of a femur is a continuous trait.

Convergent evolution　the independent evolution of similar morphological features from different ancestral conditions. For example, the wings of bats and birds or the tails of whales and fishes.

Coprolite　fossilized fecal remains.

Core　a stone that serves as a source of stone flakes capable of being used either unaltered or modified for specific functions.

Cranial capacity　the volume of the brain, usually determined by measuring the volume of the inside of the neurocranium.

Deciduous dentition　the "milk teeth" or the first set of teeth in the mammalian jaw. The deciduous dentition is replaced by the permanent dentition.

Deme　a physically distinguishable group of organisms inhabiting the same general area and forming an interbreeding population within species.

Dental eruption sequence　the order in which the different teeth erupt in the mouth.

Dental formula　a notation of the number of incisors, canines, premolars, and molars in the upper and lower dentition

of a species. For example, the adult human dental formula is 2.1.2.3.

Dental hypoplasias　defects in the enamel of teeth, usually resulting from stress, such as poor nutrition or infection.

Denticulate　a tool with tooth-like projections along its working edge.

Derived feature　a specialized characteristic that departs from the condition found in the ancestors of a species or group of species.

Diagnostic　the features of a group of organisms that are characteristic or distinguish that group.

Dietary hypothesis　a model first developed in the 1960s that posits two lineages with contrasting ecological adaptations of hominids during the Plio–Pleistocene—one group characterized by adaptation to a vegetarian diet, the other by adaptation to an omnivorous diet (and especially the development of a large brain).

DNA Hybridization　a method for establishing the biological distance between species based on the ability of strands of DNA from each species to bond to another.

Dolichocephalic　longheaded, having a Cephalic Index of less than 75.

Dorsal　toward the back side of the body; the opposite of ventral. The back of the hand and the "top" of the foot in humans are considered the dorsal side.

Ecological niche　the complex of features (such as diet, habitat, activity pattern) that characterizes the role a species occupies in the ecosystem.

Ecology　the study of the relationship between an organism and all aspects of its environment; or, all aspects of the environment of an organism that affect its way of life.

Electron spin resonance (ESR) dating　an absolute dating method usually applied to fossil teeth recovered from cave environments; the method measures the level of radioactive bombardment undergone by teeth by determining the number of electrons knocked off their shells which become trapped in crystals of apatite found in tooth enamel.

Endocast　an impression of the inside of the neurocranium which often preserves features of the surface of the brain.

Epiphyseal growth　the growth of bones characterized by the presence of an epiphyseal cartilage alongside the zone of hypertrophic growth; seen at the ends of the long bones and at the superior and inferior borders of the vertebrae.

Epiphysis　the ossification at the end of a mammalian long bone.

Ethnoarchaeology　the gathering of data on living populations to help reconstruct the past.

Extant　living organisms, as opposed to extinct organisms.

Extension　a movement that straightens or increases the angle between the bones of a limb joint; the opposite of flexion.

Faunal analysis　the examination of animal remains from archaeological sites.

Faunal correlation　the determination of the relative ages of different geological strata by comparing the fossils within them and assigning similar ages to strata with similar fossils; a method of relative dating.

Fission-track dating　an absolute dating method based on the number of tracks made across crystals in volcanic rock as uranium decays into lead.

Flexion   a movement indicating bending or a decreasing angle between the bones of a limb joint; the opposite of extension.

Flourine dating   a method of relative dating by measuring the amount of flourine in a specimen.

Folivore   an animal that feeds exclusively or primarily on leaves.

Foraging strategy   the behavioral adaptations of a species related to its acquisition of food items.

Foramen   an opening or hole in a bone.

Fossa   any depression on a bone, or tooth.

Founder effect   generic drift caused by the formation of a new population by a small number of individuals.

Frankfurt plane   a predefined plane in which skulls may be oriented for comparative purposes. Arranged horizontally, it passes through the lower orbital margin and forms a tangent to the upper margin of the external auditory meatus (ear).

Frugivore   an animal that feeds primarily on fruit.

Gallery forest   a forest along a river or stream.

Gene   a section of DNA that determines a given biological feature or function in an organism.

Gene flow   a mechanism for evolutionary change resulting from the movement of genes from one population to another.

Genetic drift   a mechanism for evolutionary change caused by the random fluctuations of gene frequencies from one generation to the next, or from any form of random sampling of a larger gene pool.

Genotype   the genetic make-up of an organism.

Gigantopithecus   a genus of fossil ape found in Asia, dating between 0.5 and 9 million years B.P.

Gracile   relatively slender or delicately built.

Grade   a level or stage of organization, or a group of organisms sharing a suite of features (either primitive or derived) that distinguishes them from more derived or more primitive animals but does not necessarily define a clade.

Gradistic classification   a classification in which organisms are grouped by the grade or level of organization rather than according to ancestry or phylogeny.

Graminivore   an animal that eats primarily grains; often used to describe an animal that eats seeds.

Growth allometry   the relationship between size and shape during the growth (or ontogeny) of an organism.

Holophyletic group   a taxonomic group of organisms which has a single common ancestor and includes all descendants of that ancestor.

Home bases   camp sites where members brought back food for sharing with other members of their group.

Home range   the area of land that is regularly used by a group of animals for a year or longer.

Hominid   a member of the family Hominidae.

Hominine   a member of sub-family Homininae.

Hominoid   a member of the zoological superfamily Hominoidea; includes apes and humans.

Homo   a genus of hominid characterized by a large brain with at least three recognized species *Homo erectus*, *Homo habilis*, and *Homo sapiens*.

Homologous   having the same developmental and evolutionary origin. The bones in the hands of primates and the wings of bats are homologous bones.

Hypodigm   the sample of all specimens attributed to a particular species.

Insertion   the attachment of a muscle or ligament farthest from the trunk or center of the body; the opposite of origin.

Intermembral index   a measure of the relative length of the forelimbs and hindlimbs of an animal: humerus plus radius length x 100 divided by femur plus tibia length.

Interspecific allometry   the relationship between size and shape among different species; for example, a comparison between humans and chimpanzees.

Interstitial wear   the wear between adjacent teeth, also called interdental wear.

k-selection   a reproductive pattern characterized by few offspring but extensive parental care.

Karstic caves   caves formed in limestone by the action of water; South African early hominids are found in Karst caves.

Knuckle-walking   a type of quadrupedal walking in which the upper body is supported on the dorsal surface of the middle phalanges of the hands, i.e. the knuckles. This form of locomotion is used by chimpanzees and gorillas.

Lambdoidal suture   the horizontal or transverse suture at the back of the top of the cranium where the parietal and occipital bones join.

Locomotion   movement from one place to another.

Loess   a fine-grained deposit of wind-blown material.

Lower Paleolithic   The Lower Older Stone Age. A general term used to refer collectively to the stone tool technologies of *Homo habilis* and *Homo erectus*.

Macroevolution   Large scale evolutionary change such as the origin of species and higher taxa.

Mandible   the jawbone.

Mastoid process   a prominence on the occipital bone behind the external auditory meatus on a human skull; in humans more pronounced in males than females.

Microevolution   Small scale evolutionary change such as that within populations and within species.

Middle Paleolithic   the Middle Old Stone Age, a term used to refer collectively to the Mousterian and Middle Stone Age industries.

Mitochondrial DNA   DNA that is found in the mitochondria of cells rather than the nucleus. Mitochondrial DNA (mtDNA) is inherited only through females.

Molecular clock   a technique for estimating the divergence times of two species based on biochemical differences between them.

Monogamy   a social system in which groups consist of a mated pair and their offspring.

Monophyletic group   a taxonomic group of organisms which has a single common ancestor.

Mosaic evolution   the concept that major evolutionary changes between taxa do not occur all together. For example the sequential appearance of bipedalism and later brain enlargement in human evolution is mosaic evolution.

Mousterian tradition   a stone tool technology characterized by the careful preparation of a stone core from which finished flakes can be removed; usually associated with Neandertals.

Multiregional evolution model   a model of the evolution of *Homo sapiens* that posits independent changes from archaic to modern forms in many different regions of the Old World (although not necessarily at the same time); contrasts with Out-of-Africa model.

Natural selection   a nonrandom differential preservation of genotypes from one generation to the next which leads to changes in the genetic structure of a population; the basis for adaptation.

Neandertal   a member of a regional population of archaic *Homo sapiens* characterized by very large brains, large brow ridges, large noses and robust limbs. They lived in the circumMediterranean area between roughly 30,000 to 125,000 years B.P.

Neoteny   the retention of juvenile characteristics into adulthood. The childlike rounded skull and large brain of adult humans are examples of neoteny.

Neurocranium   that part of a skull that houses the brain.

Nuchal   the area on the occipital bone at the nape of the neck.

Oldowan tradition   a stone tool culture characterized by simple tools made by removing several flakes from a stone. The flakes removed could also be used as cutting tools. Generally considered the earliest stone tools.

Ontogeny   the growth and development of an organism from conception to adulthood.

Orthognathous   no forward projection of either upper or lower jaw.

Osteodontokeratic culture   bone, tooth, and antler culture of australopithecines, hypothesized by Raymond Dart based on broken remains in South African cave sites.

Out-of-Africa model   a popular model of the evolution of *Homo sapiens* that posits a single, African origin for anatomically modern *Homo sapiens* and the replacement of other, archaic hominids in other regions of the Old World.

Paleoanthropology   the multidisciplinary approach to the study of human biocultural evolution. Includes physical anthropology, archeology, geology, ecology, and many other disciplines.

Paleomagnetism   the study of the magnetism of rocks that were formed in earlier time periods. More broadly, the study of pole reversals in the earth's magnetic fields during geological time.

Paleopathology   the study of disease in prehistoric species.

Palmar   referring to the palm side of the hand.

Palynology   the study of plants through the remains of their pollen grains.

Parallel evolution   independent evolution of similar (and homologous) morphological features in separate lineages.

Paraphyletic classification   a classification in which a taxonomic group contains some, but not all, of the members of a clade.

Parsimony   the principle that the theory that accounts for all of the known facts with the fewest assumptions is preferred.

Perigordian   an early Upper Paleolithic stone tool tradition that flourished in southwestern France and in Spain from about 33,000 to 18,000 B.P.

Phyletic classification   a classification in which taxonomic groups correspond to monophyletic groups.

Phyletic gradualism   a model of macroevolutionary change whereby evolutionary changes occur in small steps.

Phylogeny   the evolutionary or genealogical relationships among a group of organisms.

Pithecanthropus   the early name given to *Homo erectus* fossils from Java.

Plantar   referring to the sole of the foot.

Pleiotropic   a trait produced by an allele with multiple effects on the biological makeup of an organism.

Pneumatization   formation of the air spaces in skull bones, such as mastoid area, or nasal sinuses.

Polygyny   any type of social organization in which one male mates with more than one female.

Postcranial   the skeleton behind (below) the skull.

Postorbital constriction   the narrowness of the skull behind the eye orbits.

Potassium-argon dating   an absolute dating method based on the half-life of radioactive potassium (which decays into argon gas); can be used to date volcanic rock older than 100,000 years.

Primitive feature   a behavioral or morphological feature that is characteristic of a species and its ancestors; a pleisiomorphy.

Prognathism   prominence of the snout.

Pronation   rotation of the forearm so that the palm faces dorsally or downward; the reverse movement from supination.

Punctuated equilibrium   a model of macroevolutionary change which argues that most evolutionary change takes place in brief, relatively large changes that occur sporadically during long periods of little evolutionary change (called stasis); contrast with phyletic gradualism.

Quadrupedalism   locomotion that involves both forelimbs and hindlimbs.

Quadrumanous   four-handed; as in quadrumanous climbing, in which many suspensory primates use their feet in the same manner that they use their hands.

r-selection   a reproductive pattern characterized by large numbers of offspring and little parental care.

Ramus   the vertical part of the mandible, often called the ascending ramus.

Relative dating   a determination of whether a fossil or fossil site is younger or older than other fossils or sites, usually through study of the stratigraphic position or evolutionary relationships of the fauna; contrasts with absolute dating.

Reproductive strategy   an organism's complex of behavioral and physiological features concerned with reproduction; see k-selection, r-selection.

Reproductive success   the contribution of an individual to the gene pool of the next generation.

Rift Valley (Great Rift Valley)   a massive (1,200 mile long) geological feature in East Africa associated with mountain building, volcanoes, faulting, etc.

Sagittal crest   a bony ridge on the top of the neurocranium formed by the attachment of the temporalis muscles.

Savanna   a type of vegetation zone characterized by savanna(h) grasslands with scattered trees.

Secondary compounds   the poisons produced by plants which exist in leaves, flowers, etc., and deter animals from eating them.

Sectorial premolar   the compressed, single-cusped first lower premolar that occludes with the upper canine. Seen in great apes, many extinct hominoids and *Australopithecus afarensis*.

Sesamoid   a bone formed within a tendon.

Sexual dimorphism   any condition in which males and females of a species differ in some aspect of their nonreproductive anatomy such as body size or canine tooth size.

Shovel-shaped incisors   incisor teeth that are scooped out on their lingual surfaces.

Single-species hypothesis the theory that there has never been more than one hominid lineage at any time because all hominids are characterized by culture and thus all occupy the same ecological niche.

Sivapithecus a genus of fossil ape found in Asia, between 8 and 17 million years B.P. On the basis of cranial and dental remains, the Asian form *Sivapithecus* appears to be an ancestor of the modern day orangutan.

Soft percussion (soft hammer) a later Acheulean tool-making technique that used wood, bone, or antler instead of rock to chip flakes from the core.

Solutrean an Upper Paleolithic cultural tradition that flourished only from 18,000 to 15,000 B.P.; it is limited to southwestern France and Spain and distinguished by its laurel-leaf blades.

Speciation the appearance of new species.

Stasis little or no evolutionary change occurring over a long period of time; see also punctuated equilibrium.

Stratigraphy a branch of geology concerned with the sequence of stratified deposits and their correlation.

Supination the rotation of the forearm such that the palmar surface faces anteriorly or upward; the reverse movement from pronation.

Suspensory behavior locomotor and postural habits characterized by hanging or suspension of the body below or among branches rather than walking, running, or sitting on top of branches.

Suture a joint between two bones in which the bones interdigitate and are separated by fibrous tissue. The joints between most of the bones of the skull are sutures.

Sympatry overlap in the geographical range of two species or populations.

Synapomorphy a shared derived morphological feature shared between two or more groups in an evolving lineage that signifies their close and singular relationship.

Systematics the science of classifying organisms and the study of their genealogical relationships.

Taphonomy the study of the processes that affect the remains of organisms from the death (or before) of the organism through its fossilization and collection.

Taurodont teeth having enlarged pulp cavities.

Taxon (pl. taxa) the general term for a group of organisms within the Linnaean classification such as a species or a genus.

Taxonomy the science of describing, naming, and classifying organisms.

Terrestrial quadrupedalism four-limbed locomotion on the ground.

Thermoluminescene dating a method of dating archaeological material by the release of energy stored as electron displacements; the amount of energy released is proportional to the time elapsed since the formation of the material.

Tuff a consolidated deposit of volcanic ash often laid down in water; a tuff can be radiometrically dated.

Type specimen a single designated individual of an organism which serves as the basis for the original name and description of the species.

Upper Paleolithic the Upper Old Stone Age. A general term used to collectively refer to the stone tool technologies characterized by blades.

Valgus an angulation of the femur such that the knees are closer together than the hip joints; present in all hominids.

Ventral toward the belly side of an animal; the opposite of dorsal.

Woodland a vegetation type characterized by discontinuous stands of relatively short trees separated by grassland.